W9-BME-752

Boston MBTA

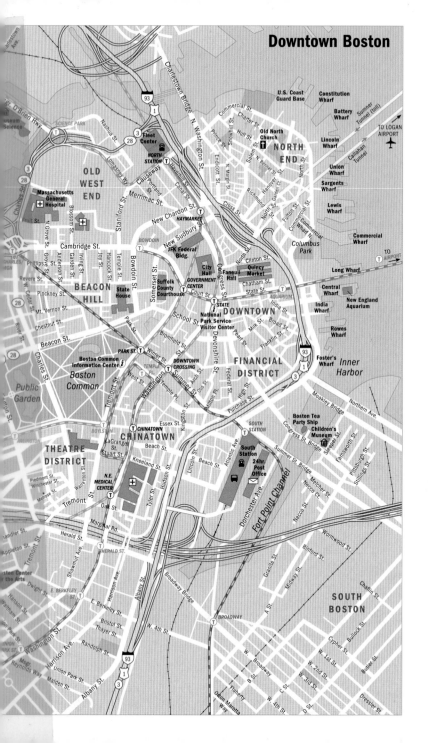

Downtown Boston

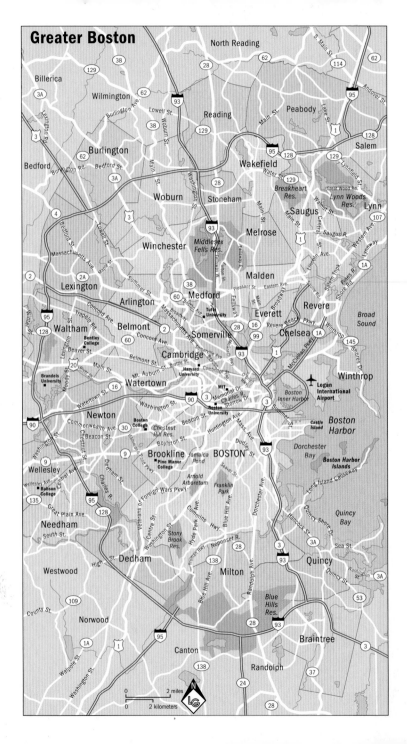

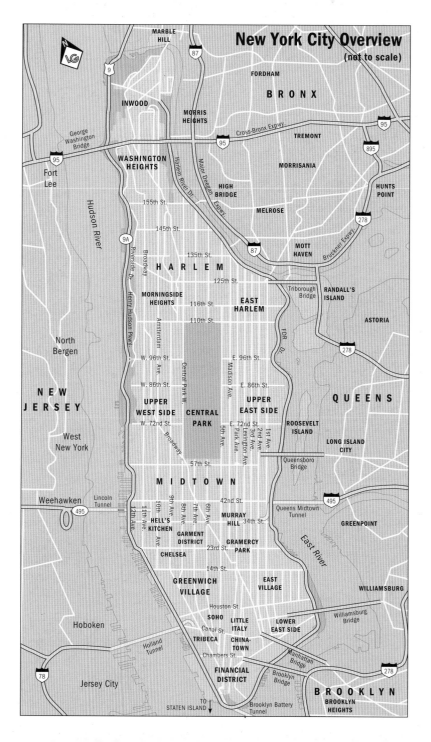

New York City Overview
(not to scale)

MARBLE HILL

FORDHAM

BRONX

INWOOD

MORRIS HEIGHTS

Cross-Bronx Expwy.

TREMONT

George Washington Bridge

WASHINGTON HEIGHTS

MORRISANIA

HUNTS POINT

Fort Lee

Hudson River

Harlem River Dr.

Major Deegan Expwy.

HIGH BRIDGE

MELROSE

155th St.

MOTT HAVEN

145th St.

Riverside Dr.

Broadway

135th St.

HARLEM

Triborough Bridge

RANDALL'S ISLAND

125th St.

Henry Hudson Pkwy.

MORNINGSIDE HEIGHTS

116th St.

EAST HARLEM

ASTORIA

North Bergen

110th St.

Amsterdam Ave.

W. 96th St.

E. 96th St.

FDR Dr.

W. 86th St.

E. 86th St.

NEW JERSEY

Central Park W.

Madison Ave.

UPPER WEST SIDE

CENTRAL PARK

UPPER EAST SIDE

West New York

W. 72nd St.

E. 72nd St.

2nd Ave.
3rd Ave.

ROOSEVELT ISLAND

Broadway

5th Ave.

Park Ave.
Lexington Ave.
1st Ave.

LONG ISLAND CITY

Queensboro Bridge

57th St.

MIDTOWN

Weehawken

Lincoln Tunnel

11th Ave.

10th Ave.
9th Ave.
8th Ave.
7th Ave.
6th Ave.

42nd St.

Queens Midtown Tunnel

East River

GREENPOINT

HELL'S KITCHEN

MURRAY HILL

34th St.

GARMENT DISTRICT

GRAMERCY PARK

Ave.

CHELSEA

23rd St.

14th St.

GREENWICH VILLAGE

EAST VILLAGE

WILLIAMSBURG

Houston St.

SOHO

LITTLE ITALY

LOWER EAST SIDE

Williamsburg Bridge

Hoboken

Canal St.

TRIBECA

CHINA-TOWN

Chambers St.

Manhattan Bridge

Holland Tunnel

FINANCIAL DISTRICT

Brooklyn Bridge

Jersey City

BROOKLYN

TO STATEN ISLAND

Brooklyn Battery Tunnel

BROOKLYN HEIGHTS

QUEENS

MTA New York City Subway

MTA Metropolitan Transportation Authority

with bus, railroad, and ferry connections

Key

- Local service only
- All trains stop (local and express service)
- Free subway transfer
- Free out-of-system subway transfer (excluding single-ride ticket)
- Normal service
- Additional express service
- Bus or AIRTRAIN to airport
- Accessible station

MTA New York City Transit

Subway in four boroughs, buses in five boroughs, and the MTA Staten Island Railway

The subway operates 24 hours a day, seven days a week, but not all lines operate at all times. For detailed information, consult Passenger Information Centers in stations or call our Travel Information Center (6am to 10pm) at 718-330-1234. Non-English-speaking customers call 718-330-4847. (7AM to 7PM)

visit www.mta.info

To show service more clearly, geography on this map has been modified.

© 2004 Metropolitan Transportation Authority
Design: Michael Hertz Associates, NYC.

May 2004

Part-time line extension

Part time service

Full-time service

Police
Station

Terminal

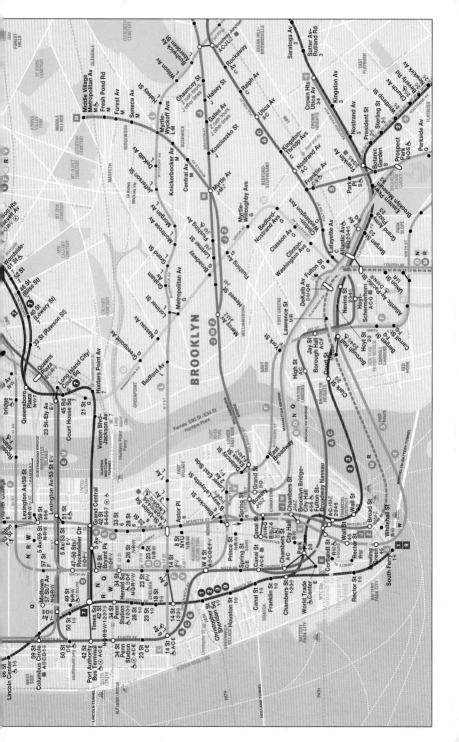

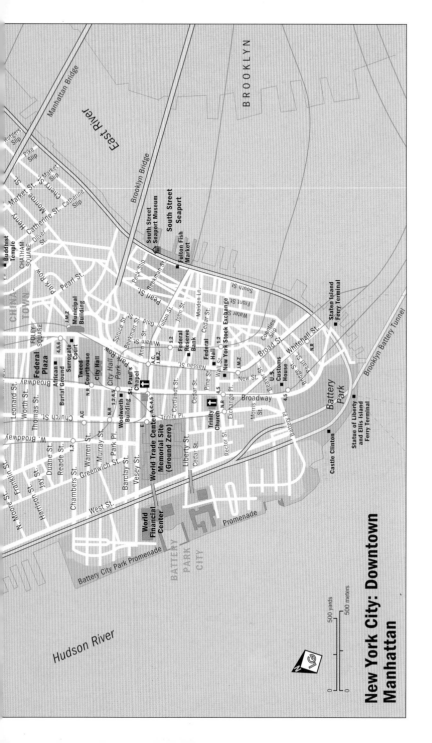

New York City: Downtown Manhattan

New York City: Midtown Manhattan

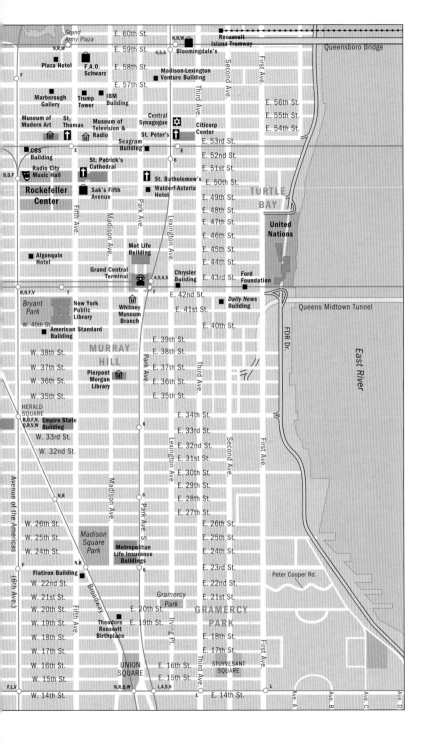

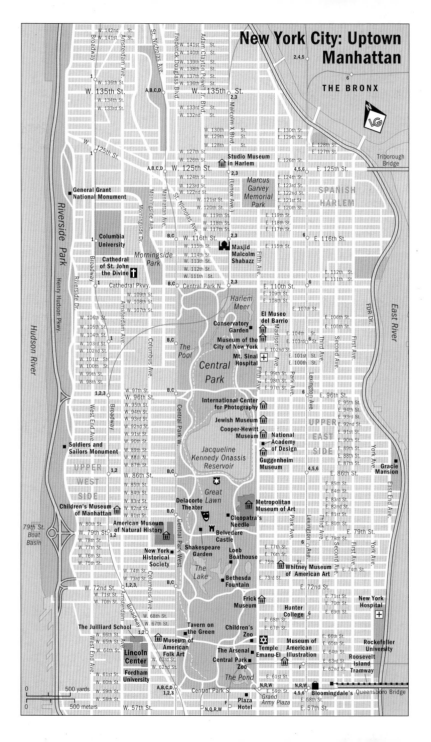

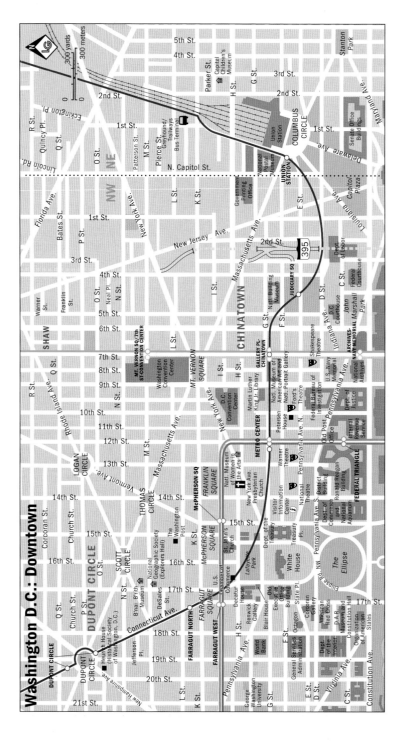
Washington D.C.: Downtown

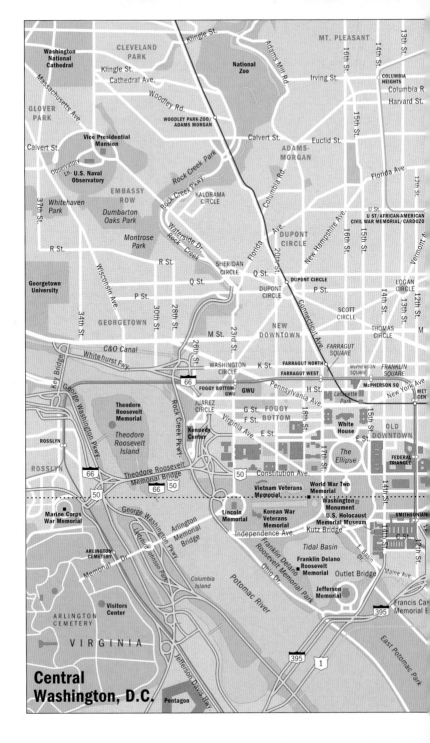

Central Washington, D.C.

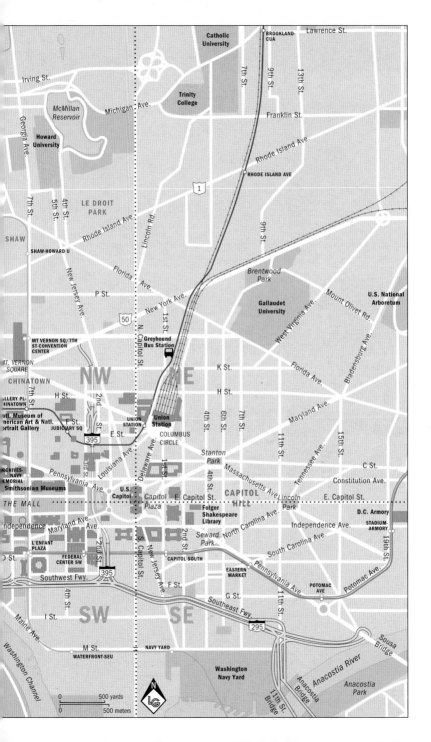

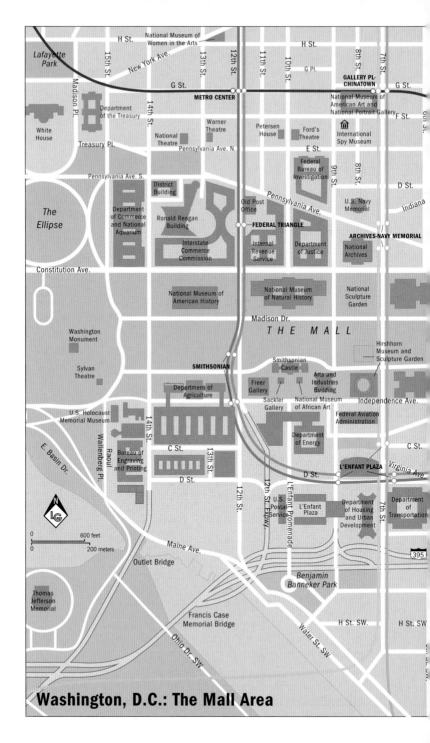

Washington, D.C.: The Mall Area

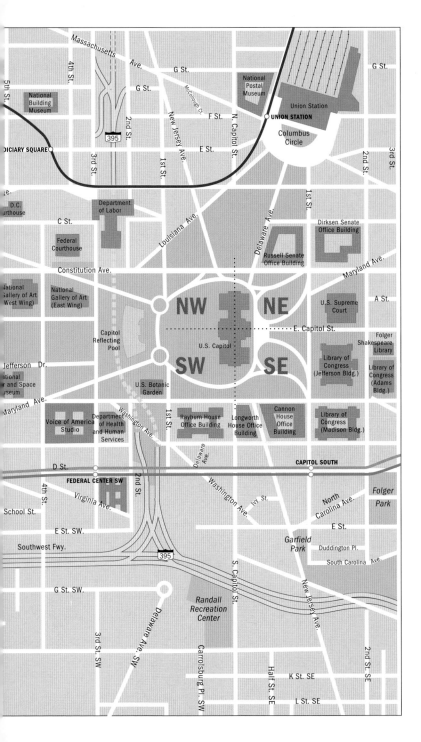

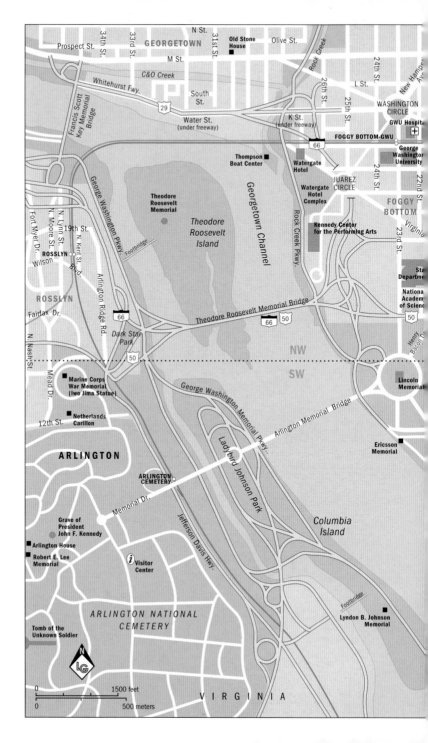

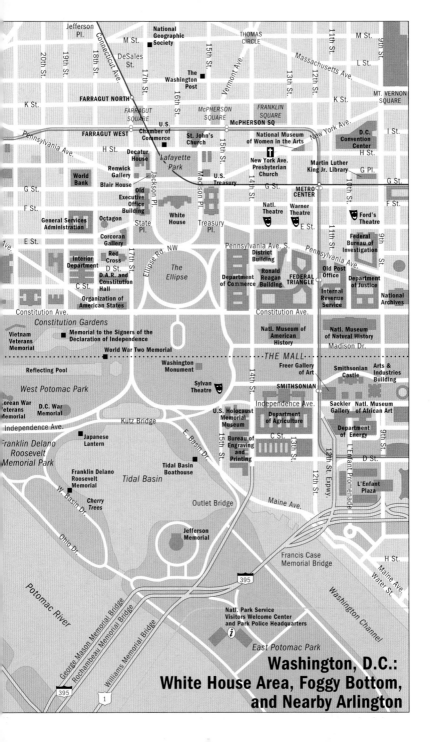

Washington, D.C.:
White House Area, Foggy Bottom,
and Nearby Arlington

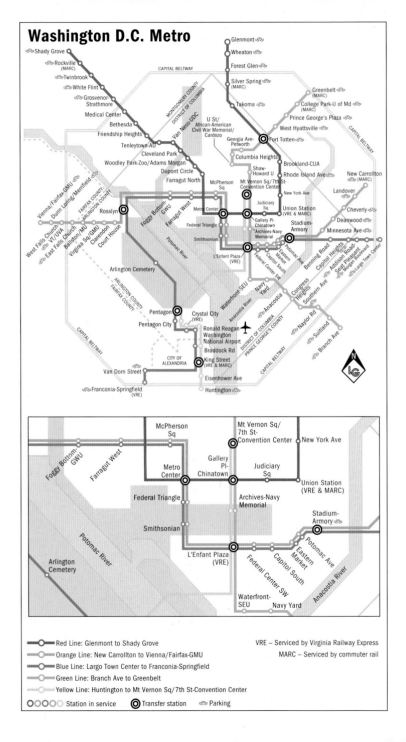

Washington D.C. Metro

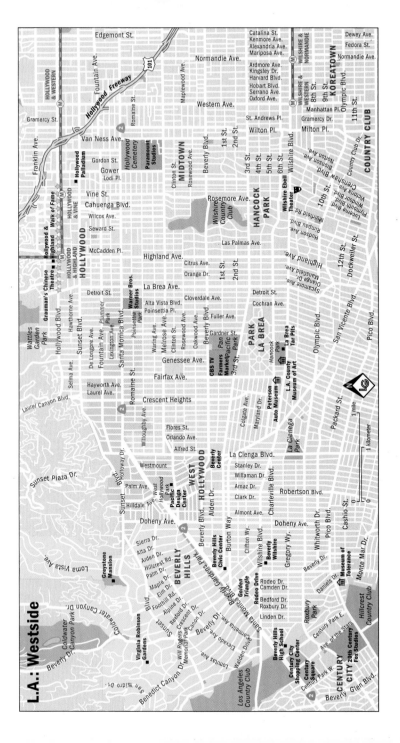

Metropolitan
Los Angeles

Metro Green Line
Metro Blue Line
Metro Red Line

2 miles
2 kilometers

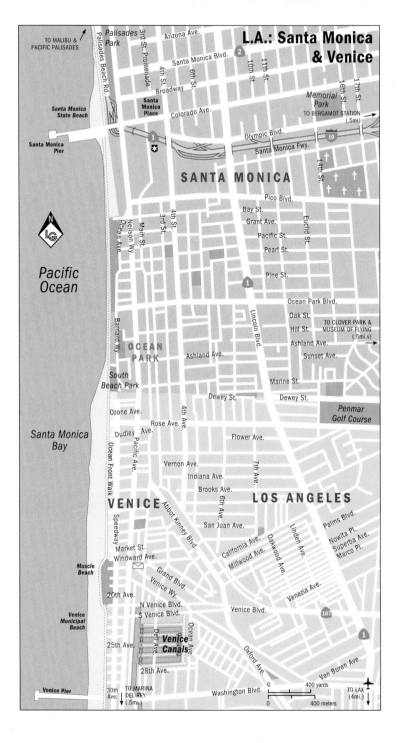

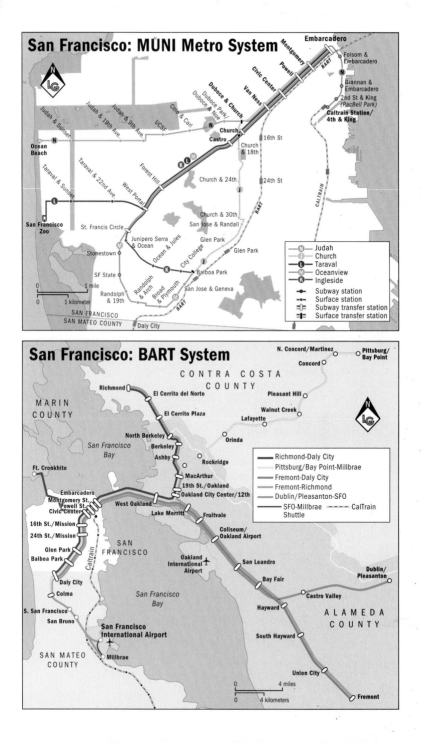

San Francisco: MUNI Metro System

Embarcadero
Folsom & Embarcadero
Montgomery
Powell
BART
Brannan & Embarcadero
Civic Center
2nd St & King (PacBell Park)
Van Ness
Caltrain Station/ 4th & King
Duboce & Church
Duboce Park/ Dubose & Noe
Judah & Sunset
Judah & 19th Ave.
Judah & 9th Ave.
Cole & Carl
UCSF
16th St
Church
Castro
Church & 18th
Ocean Beach
Taraval & 22nd Ave.
Taraval & Sunset
Forest Hill
Church & 24th
24th St
West Portal
L
Church & 30th
San Jose & Randall
CALTRAIN
San Francisco Zoo
St. Francis Circle
Junipero Serra & Ocean
Glen Park
Glen Park
Stonestown
M
Ocean & Jules
City College
J
SF State
K
Balboa Park
Randolph & Arch
Broad & Plymouth
San Jose & Geneva
0   1 mile
0   1 kilometer
Randolph & 19th
BART
SAN FRANCISCO
SAN MATEO COUNTY
Daly City

(N)	Judah
(J)	Church
(L)	Taraval
(M)	Oceanview
(K)	Ingleside
●	Subway station
●	Surface station
⊟	Subway transfer station
⊞	Surface transfer station

San Francisco: BART System

N. Concord/Martinez
Pittsburg/ Bay Point
Concord
CONTRA COSTA COUNTY
Richmond
El Cerrito del Norte
Pleasant Hill
MARIN COUNTY
El Cerrito Plaza
Walnut Creek
Lafayette
North Berkeley
San Francisco Bay
Berkeley
Orinda
Ashby
Rockridge
Ft. Cronkhite
MacArthur
19th St./Oakland
Embarcadero
Montgomery St.
Powell St.
Civic Center
West Oakland
Oakland City Center/12th
16th St./Mission
Lake Merritt
Fruitvale
24th St./Mission
Coliseum/ Oakland Airport
Glen Park
Balboa Park
SAN FRANCISCO
Oakland International Airport
San Leandro
Caltrain
Dublin/ Pleasanton
Daly City
Bay Fair
Colma
San Francisco Bay
Castro Valley
S. San Francisco
Hayward
ALAMEDA COUNTY
San Bruno
San Francisco International Airport
South Hayward
SAN MATEO COUNTY
Millbrae
Union City
0   4 miles
0   4 kilometers
Fremont

	Richmond-Daly City
	Pittsburg/Bay Point-Millbrae
	Fremont-Daly City
	Fremont-Richmond
	Dublin/Pleasanton-SFO
	SFO-Millbrae Shuttle
---	CalTrain

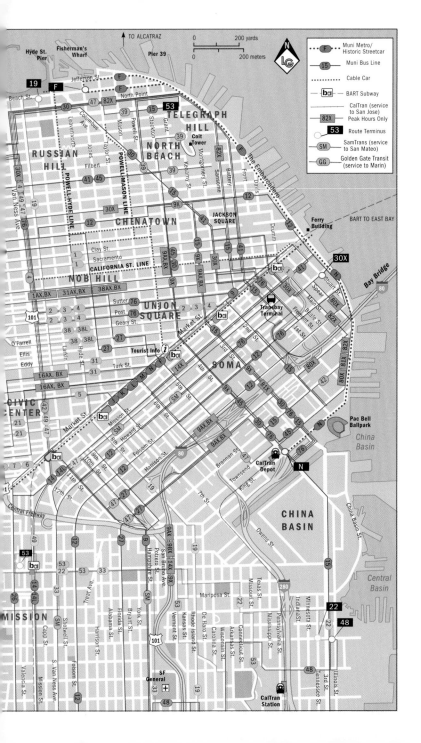

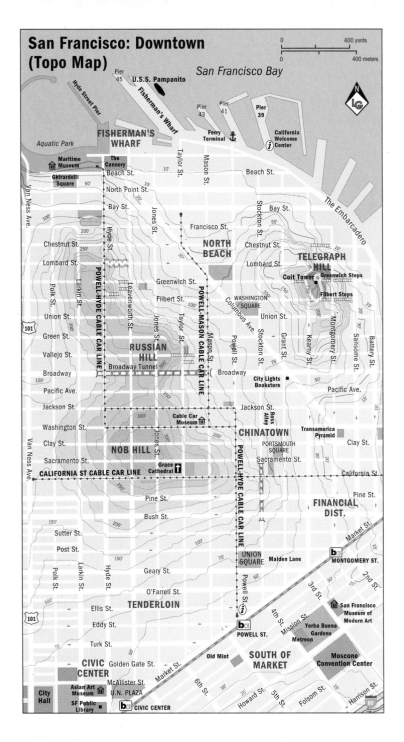

San Francisco: Downtown (Topo Map)

San Francisco Bay

0   400 yards
0   400 meters

N
LG

Pier 45   U.S.S. Pampanito
Fisherman's Wharf
Pier 43
Pier 41
Pier 39
Ferry Terminal
California Welcome Center

FISHERMAN'S WHARF
Aquatic Park
The Embarcadero

Hyde Street Pier
Maritime Museum
The Cannery
Ghirardelli Square
Beach St.   Beach St.
North Point St.
Bay St.   Bay St.
Francisco St.
NORTH BEACH
Chestnut St.   Chestnut St.
Lombard St.   Lombard St.

Van Ness Ave.

TELEGRAPH HILL
Coit Tower   Greenwich Steps
Filbert Steps

Hyde St.
Polk St.
Larkin St.
Leavenworth St.
Jones St.
Taylor St.
Mason St.
Stockton St.

Greenwich St.
Filbert St.
WASHINGTON SQUARE
Union St.   Union St.
Green St.
Vallejo St.
Broadway   Broadway Tunnel   Broadway
Pacific Ave.
Jackson St.   Jackson St.
Washington St.
Clay St.
Sacramento St.   Sacramento St.

RUSSIAN HILL

POWELL-HYDE CABLE CAR LINE
POWELL-MASON CABLE CAR LINE

Columbus Ave.
Powell St.
Stockton St.
Grant St.
Kearny St.
Montgomery St.
Sansome St.
Battery St.

City Lights Bookstore
Cable Car Museum
Pacific Ave.

CHINATOWN
Transamerica Pyramid
Ross Alley
PORTSMOUTH SQUARE
Clay St.

NOB HILL
Grace Cathedral
CALIFORNIA ST CABLE CAR LINE   California St.

101
Pine St.
Bush St.
Sutter St.
Post St.
Geary St.
O'Farrell St.
Ellis St.
Eddy St.
Turk St.

FINANCIAL DIST.

POWELL-HYDE CABLE CAR LINE

Market St.
MONTGOMERY ST.
2nd St.

UNION SQUARE   Maiden Lane

TENDERLOIN

San Francisco Museum of Modern Art
Yerba Buena Gardens
Metreon

3rd St.
4th St.
Mission St.
Powell St.

POWELL ST.

CIVIC CENTER
Golden Gate St.
McAllister St.
U.N. PLAZA
City Hall
Asian Art Museum
SF Public Library
CIVIC CENTER

Old Mint

SOUTH OF MARKET

Moscone Convention Center

Market St.
Howard St.
Folsom St.
Harrison St.
5th St.
6th St.

80

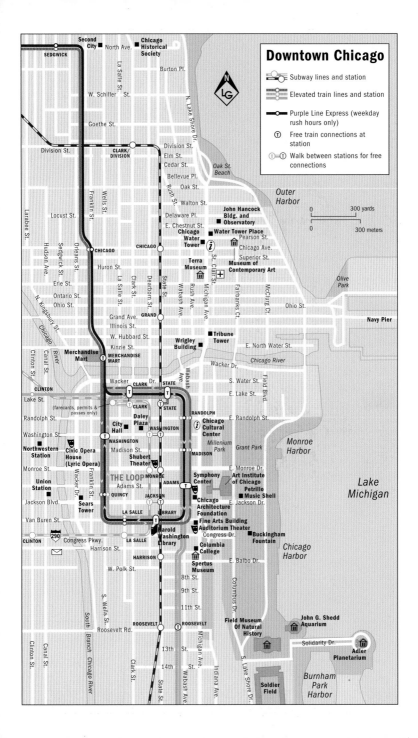

Downtown Chicago

- Subway lines and station
- Elevated train lines and station
- Purple Line Express (weekday rush hours only)
- ⓣ Free train connections at station
- ⓣ—ⓣ Walk between stations for free connections

Second City ■ North Ave. ■ Chicago Historical Society
SEDGWICK
La Salle St.
N. Lake Shore Dr.
Burton Pl.
W. Schiller St.
Goethe St.
Division St. CLARK/DIVISION Division St.
Franklin St.
Wells St.
Elm St.
Cedar St.
Oak St. Beach
Bellevue Pl.
Locust St.
Oak St.
Rush St.
Walton St.
Larabee St.
Delaware Pl. John Hancock Bldg. and Observatory
E. Chestnut St. Water Tower Place
Hudson Ave.
Sedgwick St.
Orleans St.
CHICAGO CHICAGO Chicago Water Tower Pearson St.
Outer Harbor
Chicago Ave.
Huron St.
Clark St.
La Salle St.
Dearborn St.
State St.
Wabash Ave.
Terra Museum Museum of Contemporary Art
Superior St.
Erie St.
Ontario St.
Ohio St.
N. Kingsbury St.
Rush St.
Michigan Ave.
St. Clair St.
Fairbanks Ct.
McClurg Ct.
Ohio St.
Olive Park
Chicago River
GRAND GRAND
Illinois St.
W. Hubbard St. Wrigley Building ■ Tribune Tower
Navy Pier
Kinzie St.
E. North Water St.
Canal St.
Clinton St.
Merchandise Mart ⓣ MERCHANDISE MART
Wacker Dr. Chicago River
Wacker CLARK Dr. STATE
Wabash Ave.
S. Water St.
Field Blvd.
CLINTON
Lake St.
(farecards, permits & passes only)
CLARK STATE E. Lake St.
Randolph St. Daley Plaza RANDOLPH Chicago Cultural Center E. Randolph St.
Washington St. City Hall WASHINGTON
Millenium Park Grant Park
Monroe Harbor
Northwestern Station Civic Opera House (Lyric Opera) WASHINGTON Madison St. Shubert Theater MADISON
Monroe St.
Union Station
Franklin St.
Wacker Dr.
THE LOOP MONROE Symphony Center Art Institute of Chicago
E. Monroe Dr.
Lake Michigan
Adams St. ADAMS
Jackson Blvd. Sears Tower QUINCY JACKSON Chicago Architecture Foundation Petrillo Music Shell
E. Jackson Dr.
LA SALLE LIBRARY
Van Buren St. Fine Arts Building Auditorium Theater
CLINTON ✉ 290 Congress Pkwy. LA SALLE Harold Washington Library Congress Dr. ■ Buckingham Fountain
Harrison St. Columbia College
Chicago Harbor
S. Wells St.
HARRISON
W. Polk St. Spertus Museum
8th St.
9th St.
Columbus Dr.
11th St.
Clinton St.
Canal St.
South Branch Chicago River
ROOSEVELT ROOSEVELT Field Museum Of Natural History John G. Shedd Aquarium
Roosevelt Rd.
Michigan Ave.
Solidarity Dr. Adler Planetarium
13th St.
14th St.
Clark St.
State St.
Wabash Ave.
Indiana Ave.
S. Lake Shore Dr.
Soldier Field
Burnham Park Harbor

0 — 300 yards
0 — 300 meters

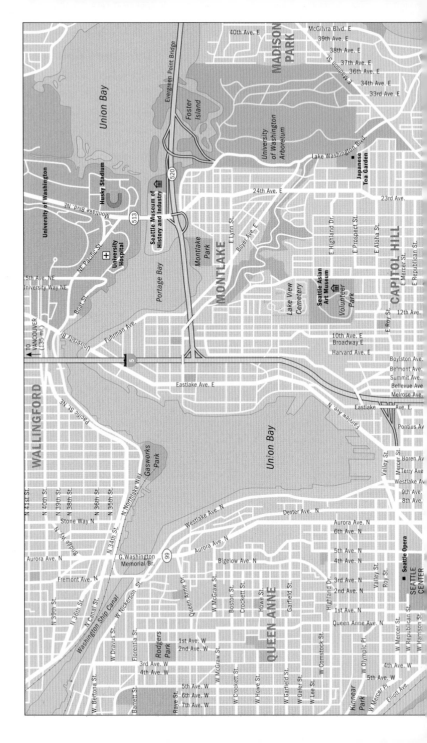

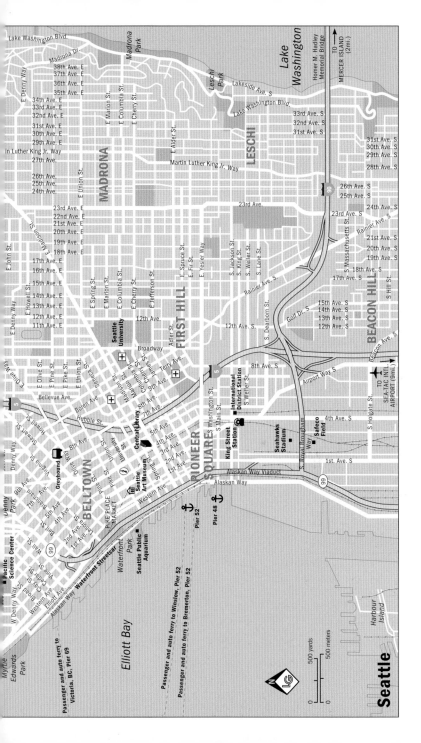

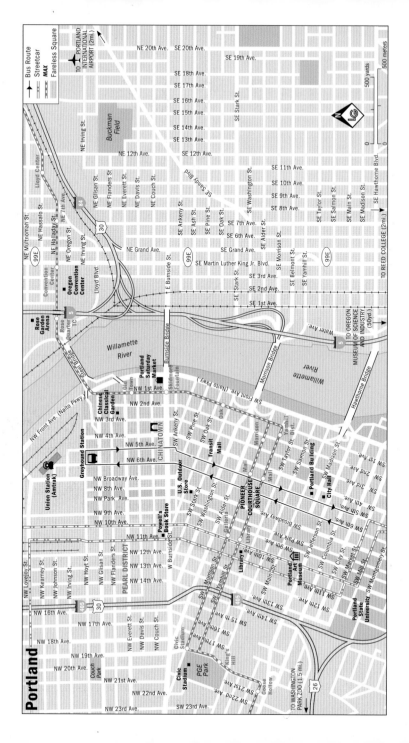

LET'S GO

■ PAGES PACKED WITH ESSENTIAL INFORMATION

"Value-packed, unbeatable, accurate, and comprehensive."

—*The Los Angeles Times*

"The guides are aimed not only at young budget travelers but at the independent traveler; a sort of streetwise cookbook for traveling alone."

—*The New York Times*

"Unbeatable; good sight-seeing advice; up-to-date info on restaurants, hotels, and inns; a commitment to money-saving travel; and a wry style that brightens nearly every page."

—*The Washington Post*

■ THE BEST TRAVEL BARGAINS IN YOUR BUDGET

"All the dirt, dirt cheap."

—*People*

"Let's Go follows the creed that you don't have to toss your life's savings to the wind to travel—unless you want to."

—*The Salt Lake Tribune*

■ REAL ADVICE FOR REAL EXPERIENCES

"The writers seem to have experienced every rooster-packed bus and lunar-surfaced mattress about which they write."

—*The New York Times*

"[Let's Go's] devoted updaters really walk the walk (and thumb the ride, and trek the trail). Learn how to fish, haggle, find work—anywhere."

—*Food & Wine*

"A world-wise traveling companion—always ready with friendly advice and helpful hints, all sprinkled with a bit of wit."

—*The Philadelphia Inquirer*

■ A GUIDE WITH A SPIRIT AND A SOCIAL CONSCIENCE

"Lighthearted and sophisticated, informative and fun to read. [Let's Go] helps the novice traveler navigate like a knowledgeable old hand."

—*Atlanta Journal-Constitution*

"The serious mission at the book's core reveals itself in exhortations to respect the culture and the environment—and, if possible, to visit as a volunteer, a student, or a teacher rather than a tourist."

—*San Francisco Chronicle*

LET'S GO PUBLICATIONS

TRAVEL GUIDES

Australia 8th edition
Austria & Switzerland 12th edition
Brazil 1st edition
Britain 2006
California 10th edition
Central America 9th edition
Chile 2nd edition
China 5th edition
Costa Rica 2nd edition
Eastern Europe 12th edition
Ecuador 1st edition
Egypt 2nd edition
Europe 2006
France 2006
Germany 12th edition
Greece 8th edition
Hawaii 3rd edition
India & Nepal 8th edition
Ireland 12th edition
Israel 4th edition
Italy 2006
Japan 1st edition
Mexico 21st edition
Middle East 4th edition
New Zealand 7th edition
Peru 1st edition
Puerto Rico 2nd edition
South Africa 5th edition
Southeast Asia 9th edition
Spain & Portugal 2006
Thailand 2nd edition
Turkey 5th edition
USA 23rd edition
Vietnam 1st edition
Western Europe 2006

ROADTRIP GUIDE

Roadtripping USA

ADVENTURE GUIDES

Alaska 1st edition
Pacific Northwest 1st edition
Southwest USA 3rd edition

CITY GUIDES

Amsterdam 4th edition
Barcelona 3rd edition
Boston 4th edition
London 15th edition
New York City 15th edition
Paris 13th edition
Rome 12th edition
San Francisco 4th edition
Washington, D.C. 13th edition

POCKET CITY GUIDES

Amsterdam
Berlin
Boston
Chicago
London
New York City
Paris
San Francisco
Venice
Washington, D.C.

LET'S GO
USA

MAYA SIMON EDITOR
MIA MORGENSTERN ASSOCIATE EDITOR
NATHAN ORION SIMMONS ASSOCIATE EDITOR
CAITLIN CLAIRE VINCENT ASSOCIATE EDITOR

RESEARCHER-WRITERS

REBECCA BARRON	**CATHERINE JAMPEL**
KATY BARTELMA	**MARCEL LAFLAMME**
KRISTIN BLAGG	**LINDSEY MORSE**
BEN COLLINS	**JOSH NEFF**
MATTHEW HARTZELL	**LAUREN SANCKEN**

JESSICA HUANG MAP EDITOR
ASHLEY EVA ISAACSON MANAGING EDITOR

ST. MARTIN'S PRESS ✿ NEW YORK

HELPING LET'S GO. If you want to share your discoveries, suggestions, or corrections, please drop us a line. We read every piece of correspondence, whether a postcard, a 10-page email, or a coconut. **Address mail to:**

> **Let's Go: USA**
> **67 Mount Auburn St.**
> **Cambridge, MA 02138**
> **USA**

Visit Let's Go at **http://www.letsgo.com,** or send email to:

> **feedback@letsgo.com**
> **Subject: "Let's Go: USA"**

In addition to the invaluable travel advice our readers share with us, many are kind enough to offer their services as researchers or editors. Unfortunately, our charter enables us to employ only currently enrolled Harvard students.

Maps by David Lindroth copyright © 2006 by St. Martin's Press.

Distributed outside the USA and Canada by Macmillan.

ISBN: 0-312-34897-5
EAN: 978-0-312-34897-7
Twenty-third Edition
10 9 8 7 6 5 4 3 2 1

Let's Go: USA is written by Let's Go Publications, 67 Mount Auburn St., Cambridge, MA 02138, USA.

Let's Go® and the LG logo are trademarks of Let's Go, Inc.
Printed in the USA.

HOW TO USE THIS BOOK

Every year, *Let's Go* sends dozens of researchers across the United States in search of the most authentic cuisine, the most bizarre Americana, and the best deals on the continent. This year's edition is revised, revamped, and ready to hit the road, complete with expanded national parks coverage, improved maps, and new daytrips. Here's what you'll find inside:

ORGANIZATION. This book will walk you (and probably ride with you) state by state through the US, starting on the East Coast and zigzagging from New England to the Pacific Northwest. Each chapter begins with a highlights box to help you pinpoint the best a region has to offer. New "Border Crossing" boxes make daytrips to Canada and Mexico even easier. To find the right region in a hurry, use the black tabs on the side of the book to guide you.

HELPFUL INFORMATION. The **Essentials** chapter (p. 9) is full of useful tips to help you plan a budget, navigate transportation, and pack just the right gear. **Life and Times** (p. 54) will get you up to speed with American history, food, and culture. The opportunities for study, work, and volunteerism in **Beyond Tourism** (p. 76) will alert you to exciting ways to make a difference during your travels.

PHONE CODES AND TELEPHONE NUMBERS. Phone numbers in text are preceded by the ☎ icon. The three-digit area code for each town appears opposite its name and is also denoted by the ☎ icon. Be prepared to dial the area code before the phone number—ten-digit dialing is now required in much of the US.

PRICE RANGES AND RANKINGS. Our researchers list establishments in order of value from best to worst. Our favorites are denoted by the *Let's Go* thumbs-up (🖐), our way of telling you that an establishment is too good to miss. Since the best value is not always the cheapest price, we have also incorporated a system of price ranges (p. xv). GLBT establishments are listed at the end of each section.

FEATURES. "The Local Story" tries to get at regional culture in a way that other coverage can't. You'll hear about an age-old rivalry between cheesesteak stands in Philadelphia, a haunted hotel in Arizona, and how a Montana smokejumper got his start. In keeping with our renewed focus on sustainable travel, "Giving Back" highlights service opportunities like maintaining the Appalachian Trail and volunteering with homeless teens in Chicago. We know you're traveling on a budget, so we've incorporated "The Big Splurge" to tell you when an extravagance is worth the sticker shock and "The Hidden Deal" to help your pennies go further.

SCHOLARLY ARTICLES. Two contributors with unique regional insight have written articles for *Let's Go: USA*. Bert Vaux's article on America's regional dialects will explain why some Americans say "soda" while others say "pop." A new "A Different Path" article chronicles author Glen Hanket's attempt to make America a little bit tidier.

A NOTE TO OUR READERS. The information for this book was gathered by *Let's Go* researchers from May through August of 2005. Each listing is based on one researcher's opinion, formed during his or her visit at a particular time. Those traveling at other times may have different experiences since prices, dates, hours, and conditions are always subject to change. You are urged to check the facts presented in this book beforehand to avoid inconvenience and surprises.

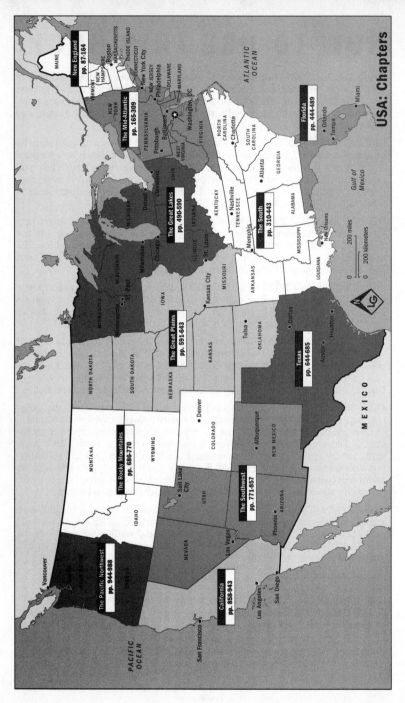

USA: Chapters

PACIFIC
OCEAN

ATLANTIC
OCEAN

Gulf of
Mexico

MEXICO

MAINE
VERMONT
NEW HAMPSHIRE
MASSACHUSETTS
RHODE ISLAND
CONNECTICUT
NEW YORK
NEW JERSEY
PENNSYLVANIA
DELAWARE
MARYLAND
WEST VIRGINIA
VIRGINIA
OHIO
MICHIGAN
WISCONSIN
MINNESOTA
NORTH DAKOTA
SOUTH DAKOTA
NEBRASKA
IOWA
ILLINOIS
INDIANA
KENTUCKY
TENNESSEE
NORTH CAROLINA
SOUTH CAROLINA
GEORGIA
ALABAMA
MISSISSIPPI
ARKANSAS
MISSOURI
KANSAS
OKLAHOMA
LOUISIANA
MONTANA
WYOMING
COLORADO
NEW MEXICO
UTAH
IDAHO
NEVADA
ARIZONA

Vancouver
Seattle
San Francisco
Los Angeles
San Diego
Las Vegas
Phoenix
Albuquerque
Salt Lake City
Denver
Austin
Houston
Dallas
Tulsa
Kansas City
St. Louis
St. Paul
Minneapolis
Milwaukee
Chicago
Detroit
Cleveland
Pittsburgh
Baltimore
Washington, DC
Philadelphia
New York City
Boston
Charlotte
Atlanta
Nashville
Memphis
New Orleans
Orlando
Tampa
Miami

0   200 miles
0   200 kilometers

CONTENTS

RESEARCHER-WRITERS

Rebecca Barron   *Florida, Georgia, and the Carolinas*

Rebecca's quiet determination and dedication made her the perfect person to battle the crowds of America's Southeast in high tourist season. Despite being swarmed by mosquitoes in the Everglades, turned away by bouncers in South Beach, and mobbed by oversized cartoon characters in Disney World, Rebecca kept on truckin', impressing everyone she encountered with her detective skills, outstanding writing, and serious sandal tan.

Katy Bartelma   *California and Nevada*

Not even a swarm of low-riders could stop this *Let's Go: USA 2005* vet from sending back elegant missives on the grit and glamour of the Golden State. Katy packed her no-nonsense attitude and trusty grey pants and hit the open road, enduring a Yosemite still snoy in June, minor language barriers in Tijuana, and oh-so-much driving. Crystal-clear writing and an eye for the unusual kept Katy's coverage as fresh as the hundreds of avocados she ate along the way.

Kristin Blagg   *New England*

A New England native, Kristin started her route in an exotic locale: her driveway. That doesn't mean her journey wasn't an adventure, though. Whether driving through the raging mudslides of upstate New York, hitting up 24hr. Wal-Marts, or traipsing through luxury hotels in rain-soaked research garb, Kristin made a habit of not letting anything get in the way of her research. Good thing, too, since her prose was always sharp, witty, and beautifully written.

Ben Collins   *The South*

With a perpetual smile on his face, Ben survived a press pass incident at space camp and a near-ruinous A/C failure near Hot-as-Hell, MS. When he wasn't licking his fingers for a post-barbecue snack, Ben was reevaluating his stance on Wal-Mart, shedding his Yankee demeanor, and producing polished copy and socially-conscious features. His only low point was celebrating his 21st birthday in a dry county, but don't worry—he made up for it in New Orleans.

Matthew Hartzell   *Texas, Oklahoma, and Kansas*

The former *Let's Go* map editor returned to the LG family to lend his infectious enthusiasm to our coverage of the Lone Star State. With stops in three states, Matt got around, but he always stayed loyal to his true love, the railroad. Matt's perseverance and unflinching attention to detail helped him sweet-talk Texan B&B owners, survive car trouble, eat his way through mounds of barbecue, and, of course, turn in tidy, thoughtful copy.

Catherine Jampel   *The Rockies*

A veteran of *Let's Go: USA 2005*, CJ made it her mission to uncover the best of the Rocky Mountains. Somewhere between crawling through cliff dwellings and chatting with cowboys, she found time to translate her love for the outdoors into thoughtful analyses of the Rockies' culture. CJ dedicated herself to eliminating sketch and improving our readers' travels, and in doing so, came up with a slew of new coverage. Look out, Montana—she'll be back.

Marcel LaFlamme
The Great Lakes

Armed with unshakeable enthusiasm, a silver Pontiac named Sylvia, and a temperamental laptop, this former associate editor (*Let's Go: Europe 2005*) took the Great Lakes by storm. When he wasn't exploring the vast wilderness of the Upper Peninsula or battling wizened librarians for Internet access, Marcel crafted masterful copy infused with witty one-liners and killer analogies. Embodying the voice and spirit of LG, Marcel made even fish boils sound good.

Lindsey Morse
The Great Plains

Lindsey left the frenetic pace of the city only to fall madly in love with the open sky, endless prairie, and the friendly folk she met along her route. A rowing superstar, she had the muscle to tackle wild thunderstorms, scorching Badlands heat, and any rogue bison that might cross her path. Lindsey was as thorough a researcher as they come and was always looking out for her readers, making her editors' job a delightfully easy one.

Josh Neff
The Pacific Northwest

Outwardly the most rugged of researchers, Josh's love for rock-climbing and road-tripping camouflaged a mild-mannered determination and a laid-back attitude that could calm even the most agitated editor. When he wasn't exploring the wilderness or writing meticulous descriptions, Josh impressed his editors with thoughtful social commentary. Even when the going got tough, Josh's dedication to the book and to our readers never faltered.

Lauren Sancken
The Southwest

Lauren trekked across the Southwest with unbounded energy, breaking hearts and happily sipping liquid caffeine as she went. Despite furnace-like temperatures and a hefty driving schedule, she found time to rappel into a slot canyon in Escalante, send postcards to her editors, and add important new sights to the book. Lauren's colorful prose and vivid descriptions always brought a breath of warm Southwestern air to the dim little office back in Cambridge.

REGIONAL RESEARCHER-WRITERS

Matthew Hudson — *New York City*
Mollie Kirk — *New Jersey and Delaware*
Arthur Koski-Karell — *Washington, D.C.*
Brian Kozlowski — *Philadelphia*
Joanna O'Leary — *Gettysburg and Lancaster County, PA*

CONTRIBUTING WRITERS

Professor Bert Vaux is a PhD in Linguistics and currently teaches at the University of Wisconsin-Milwaukee. He has written extensively on linguistics and dialects.
Glen Hanket is the author of *Underwear by the Roadside: Litterwalk Coast-to-Coast; WOW! What a Ride;* and numerous guides to cycling in Colorado.

ACKNOWLEDGMENTS

LET'S GO

TEAM USA THANKS: Our stellar RWs, without whom this book would be a pile of blank pages; Ashley, whose calm guidance and eagle-eyed edits made a daunting project feel possible; Jess, for the TLC our maps so badly needed; Rachel, for being a lovely (and tolerant) podmate; and Mariah, Juanes, Gerald Ford, CCGBs, the railroad, and the little girl at space camp. That's whack (in a good way).

MAYA THANKS: Mia, Nate, Caitlin: you kept me sane, made me laugh, and did one hell of a job. Ashley and Jess: thank you! The Slug Club and dinner party crew, who made LG more than just work. Julia, an outstanding roommate and my own #1 source of fun. VR, KD, BB, AN, for afterhours silliness. KAM & KJM, my BFFs. Mom, Dad, Lia: I love you oodles—thank you.

MIA THANKS: Caitlin, Nate, and Maya, for laughs and Mariah; Sam, for fun at 34K; no A/C, for character building; Mom, Dad, and Emma, for holding down the fort; my pals from the 'Ford, for lots of visits and love; Michael, for drives, Kimball's, and picnics.

NATHAN THANKS: Caitlin, Maya, and Mia for tardiness tolerance and great fun; CABS, CMS, and BLS for love and support; MLG, for lovin' me; MG for hot beats, Natetho for cleanliness, Ezay for lack thereof; Sliggitay, my alter ego; Spleezay, for keeping me up late; the Bay.

CAITLIN THANKS: Nate and Mia for constant hilarity, Maya for keeping us in line; West Virginia (a damn fine state); the sustaining powers of olive bread and pad see-ew; Mom, Dad, JBV, and my favorite Italian: FCN.

JESSICA THANKS: Team USA, for their fanatical edits but chill attitudes. The fine people of Mon., Wed., and Sun. night vball, consistently my excuse to leave early. Huang clan, yay!

Editor
Maya Simon
Associate Editors
Mia Morgenstern
Nathan Orion Simmons
Caitlin Claire Vincent
Managing Editor
Ashley Eva Isaacson
Map Editor
Jessica Huang
Typesetter
Ankur Ghosh

Publishing Director
Seth Robinson
Editor-in-Chief
Stuart J. Robinson
Production Manager
Alexandra Hoffer
Cartography Manager
Katherine J. Thompson
Editorial Managers
Rachel M. Burke, Ashley Eva Isaacson, Laura E. Martin
Financial Manager
Adrienne Taylor Gerken
Publicity Manager
Alexandra C. Stanek
Personnel Manager
Ella M. Steim
Production Associate
Ansel S. Witthaus
IT Director
Jeffrey Hoffman Yip
Director of E-Commerce
Michael Reckhow
Office Coordinator
Matthew Gibson

Director of Advertising Sales
Jillian N. London
Senior Advertising Associates
Jessica C.L. Chiu, Katya M. Golovchenko, Mohammed J. Herzallah
Advertising Graphic Designer
Emily E. Maston

President
Caleb J. Merkl
General Manager
Robert B. Rombauer
Assistant General Manager
Anne E. Chisholm

ABOUT LET'S GO

NOT YOUR PARENTS' TRAVEL GUIDE

At Let's Go, we see every trip as the chance of a lifetime. If your dream is to grab a machete and forge through the jungles of Brazil, we can take you there. If you'd rather bask in the Riviera sun at a beachside cafe, we'll set you a table. We write for readers who know that there's more to travel than sharing double deckers with tourists and who believe that travel can change both themselves and the world—whether they plan to spend six days in London or six months in Latin America. We'll show you just how far your money can go, and prove that the greatest limitation on your adventures is not your wallet, but your imagination.

BEYOND THE TOURIST EXPERIENCE

To help you gain a deeper connection with the places you travel, our fearless researchers scour the globe to give you the heads-up on both world-renowned and off-the-beaten-track attractions, sights, and destinations. They engage with the local culture, only to emerge with the freshest insights on everything from local festivals to regional cuisine. We've also opened our pages to respected writers and scholars to hear their takes on the countries and regions we cover, and asked travelers who have worked, studied, or volunteered abroad to contribute first-person accounts of their experiences. In addition, we increased our coverage of responsible travel and expanded each guide's Beyond Tourism chapter to share more ideas about how to give back while on the road.

FORTY-SIX YEARS OF WISDOM

Let's Go got its start in 1960, when a group of creative and well-traveled students compiled their experience and advice into a 20-page mimeographed pamphlet, which they gave to travelers on charter flights to Europe. Four and a half decades later, we've expanded to cover six continents and all kinds of travel—while retaining our founders' adventurous attitude toward the world. Laced with witty prose and total candor, our guides are still researched and written entirely by students on shoestring budgets, experienced travelers who know that train strikes, stolen luggage, food poisoning, and marriage proposals are all part of a day's work.

THE LET'S GO COMMUNITY

More than just a travel guide company, Let's Go is a community. Our small staff comes together because of our shared passion for travel and our desire to help other travelers see the world the way it was meant to be seen. We love it when our readers become part of the Let's Go community as well—when you travel, drop us a postcard (67 Mt. Auburn St., Cambridge, MA 02138, USA), send us an e-mail (feedback@letsgo.com), or post on our forum (http://www.letsgo.com/connect/forum) to tell us about your adventures and discoveries.

For more information, visit us online: www.letsgo.com.

①②③④⑤

PRICE RANGES>>USA

Our researchers list establishments in order of value from best to worst; our favorites are denoted by the Let's Go thumbs-up (🖐). Since the best value is not always the cheapest price, we have also incorporated a system of price ranges, based on a rough expectation of what you'll spend. For **accommodations,** we base our range on the cheapest price for which a single traveler can stay for one night. For **restaurants** and other dining establishments, we estimate the average price of an entree without beverages or appetizers. The table below tells you what you will *typically* find at the corresponding price range.

ACCOMMODATIONS	RANGE	WHAT YOU'RE *LIKELY* TO FIND
❶	under $30	Camping; most dorm rooms, such as HI or other hostels. Expect bunk beds and a communal bath; you may have to provide or rent linens.
❷	$30-50	Upper-end hostels or a small bed and breakfast. You may have a private bathroom, or a sink in your room.
❸	$51-70	A small room with a private bath. Should have decent amenities, such as phone and TV. Breakfast may be included in the price of a room.
❹	$71-100	A room of your own with a private bath. May have more amenities or be in a more touristed area.
❺	over $100	Large, posh hotels. If it doesn't have the perks you want, you've paid too much.
FOOD	RANGE	WHAT YOU'RE *LIKELY* TO FIND
❶	under $6	Mostly sandwich shops or greasy spoons. Don't worry about tucking your shirt in.
❷	$6-8	Sandwiches, appetizers at a bar, or low-priced entrees. May be sit-down or take-out.
❸	$9-12	Mid-priced entrees, possibly coming with soup or salad. Tip will bump you up a couple dollars, since you'll probably have a waiter or waitress.
❹	$13-16	A somewhat fancy restaurant or steakhouse. Either way, you'll have a special knife. Some restaurants may have a dress code; many will look down on t-shirts and jeans.
❺	over $16	Food with foreign names and a decent wine list. Slacks and dress shirts may be expected.

The United States

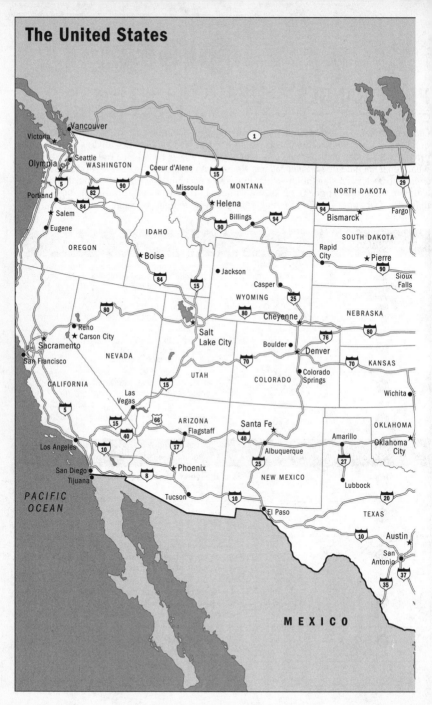

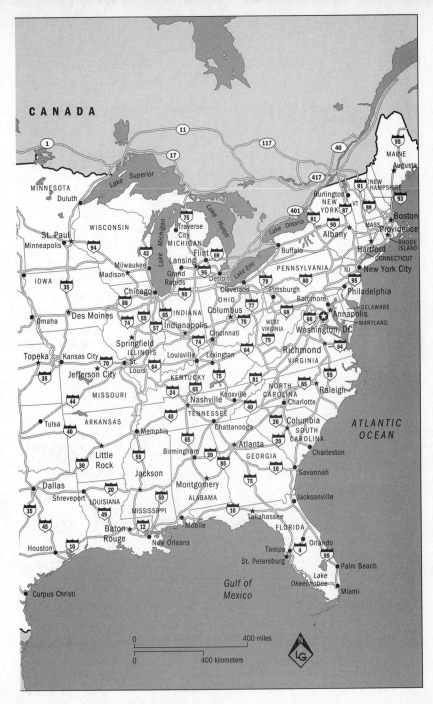

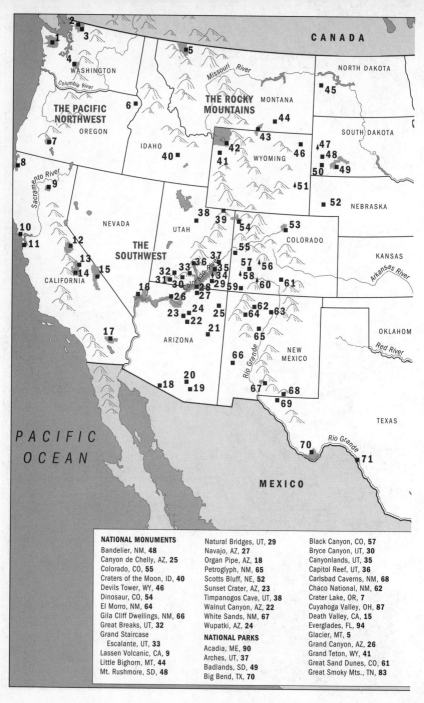

CANADA

NORTH DAKOTA

THE ROCKY
MOUNTAINS   MONTANA

Missouri River

THE PACIFIC
NORTHWEST

WASHINGTON

Columbia River

OREGON

IDAHO

SOUTH DAKOTA

WYOMING

Sacramento River

NEVADA

UTAH

THE
SOUTHWEST

NEBRASKA

CALIFORNIA

Colorado River

COLORADO

KANSAS

Arkansas River

ARIZONA

NEW
MEXICO

OKLAHOM

Red River

PACIFIC
OCEAN

Rio Grande

TEXAS

Rio Grande

MEXICO

USA National Park System: Highlights

MAINE

NEW ENGLAND

Lake Superior

VT

NEW HAMPSHIRE

NEW YORK

St. Lawrence River

MASS.

CONN.

RHODE ISLAND

Lake Huron

Lake Ontario

Hudson River

Lake Michigan

MICHIGAN

Lake Erie

THE MID ATLANTIC

PENNSYLVANIA

NEW JERSEY

DELAWARE

MARYLAND

MINNESOTA

WISCONSIN

Mississippi River

IOWA

THE GREAT PLAINS

Illinois River

THE GREAT LAKES

ILLINOIS

OHIO

INDIANA

WEST VIRGINIA

VIRGINIA

Ohio River

Missouri River

MISSOURI

KENTUCKY

NORTH CAROLINA

TENNESSEE

SOUTH CAROLINA

Arkansas River

Mississippi River

ARKANSAS

THE SOUTH

MISSISSIPPI

ALABAMA

GEORGIA

ATLANTIC OCEAN

LOUISIANA

FLORIDA

Gulf of Mexico

Lake Okeechobee

0   400 miles
0   400 kilometers

Guadalupe Mts., TX, **69**
Hot Springs, AR, **73**
Isle Royale, MI, **78**
Joshua Tree, CA, **17**
Kings Canyon, CA, **13**
Mammoth Cave, KY, **82**
Mesa Verde, CO, **59**
Mt. Rainier, WA, **4**
New River Gorge, WV, **84**
North Cascades, WA, **2**
Olympic, WA, **1**
Petrified Forest, AZ, **21**
Redwood, CA, **8**
Rocky Mt., CO, **53**
Saguaro, AZ, **19**

Saquero, AZ, **20**
Sequoia, CA, **14**
Shenandoah, VA, **85**
Theodore Roosevelt, ND, **45**
Voyageurs, MN, **76**
Wind Cave, SD, **50**
Yellowstone, WY, **42**
Yosemite, CA, **12**
Zion, UT, **31**

NATIONAL RECREATION AREAS
Amistad, TX, **71**
Bighorn Canyon, MT, **43**
Flaming Gorge, UT, **39**
Glen Canyon, UT, **28**
Golden Gate, CA, **11**

Hell's Canyon, OR, **6**
Lake Mead, NV, **16**
Ross Lake, WA, **3**

NATIONAL FORESTS
Allegheny, PA, **88**
Black Hills, SD, **47**
Chippewa, MN, **75**
Grand Mesa, CO, **56**
Manistee, MI, **81**
Manta-La Sal, UT, **34**
Medicine Bow, WY, **51**
Monongahela, WV, **86**
Ozark, AR, **74**
San Juan, CO, **60**
Uncompahgre, CO, **58**

White Mts., NH, **89**

NATIONAL LAKESHORES
Apostle Islands, WI, **77**
Pictured Rocks, MI, **79**
Sleeping Bear
    Dunes, MI, **80**

NATIONAL SEASHORES
Assateague, MD, **92**
Cape Cod, MA, **91**
Cape Hatteras, NC, **93**
Gulf Islands, FL, **95**
Padre Island, TX, **72**
Point Reyes, CA, **10**

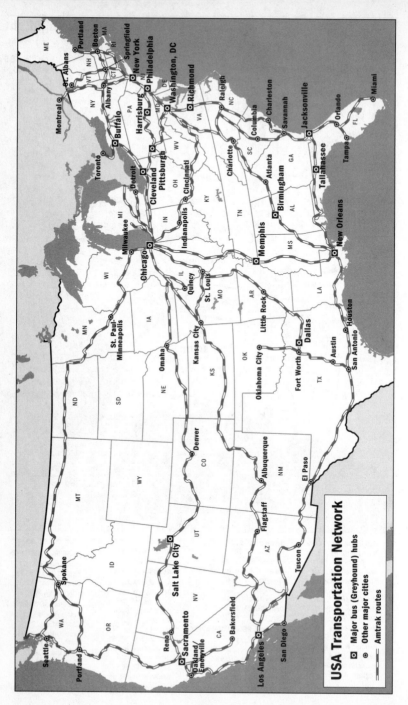

USA Transportation Network

⬚ Major bus (Greyhound) hubs
⊙ Other major cities
〰 Amtrak routes

DISCOVER THE UNITED STATES

The United States has its relics, of course: preserved colonial settlements on the Eastern seaboard, Spanish ruins in Florida, vestiges of native dwellings built and abandoned long before Christopher Columbus was even a twinkle in his mother's eye. Yet in the end, visitors to the US often come away struck by the sheer depth of the New World's infatuation with, well, newness. A nation of johnny-come-latelys, America cuts its teeth on stories of people and places reinventing themselves practically overnight. Movie stars become governors, sleepy cow towns become biotech meccas, and no one blinks at these madcap reversals because America is a country where looking forward trumps looking back time and time again.

Too often, it's the big cities of the United States that dominate the tourist imagination: the lights of New York, the monuments of Washington, D.C., the trolley cars of San Francisco. And perhaps these cities do give a glimpse of America in microcosm, whether it's the glamour of a gallery opening or the broken-window dreariness of a housing project. Still, seeing America's true colors means leaving the cities behind for a spell, and heading out to review the high-school marching band in some Alabama whistle-stop or to ponder the solemn immensity of Montana's Big Sky country. It's not that these two worlds are always so far apart; it's just that America is big and brash and bewildering enough that you'll need six or seven sides of the story to start wrapping your mind around the place. Relentlessly literal, exasperatingly impetuous, disarmingly provincial, America will sweep you off your feet and leave you yearning for another dose of its star-spangled energy.

USA FACTS AND FIGURES

POPULATION: 295,734,134.

LARGEST CITIES: New York City, Los Angeles, Chicago, Houston, Philadelphia.

MILES OF HIGHWAY: 3,980,688 (of which 2,577,693 mi. are paved).

MILES DRIVEN EACH YEAR: 1½ trillion (to the sun and back 7500 times).

COMMON PET NAMES: Patches, Misty, Buster, Princess, Bear, Sheba.

TVS PER HOUSE: 2.4.

WHEN TO GO

In general, the US tourist season consists of the summer months between Memorial Day and Labor Day (May 29-Sept. 4, 2006). National parks flood with visitors during the high season, but cities are less affected by seasonal variation. For regions where winter sports are popular or the winters are mild, as in the mountains and the southern US, the peak season is generally inverted (Dec.-Apr.).

10 4 2 6 1
7 8 5 3

TOP TEN LIST

SAVORY SPECIALTIES

1. Chicken 'n' waffles. The ultimate soul-food combination: warm waffles and crispy fried chicken. Ladle on the syrup in Atlanta, GA, or Los Angeles, CA.

2. Creole and Cajun. From chicken gumbo to shrimp étouffée, Louisiana serves a jambalaya of cultural cuisines.

3. Fish boils. Feast like a lumberjack on whitefish plucked from Lake Michigan and served straight out of a bubbling cauldron.

4. Texas barbecue. Clark's in Tioga, TX (p. 663), 1½hr. north of Dallas, has perfected the cowboy's craft of serving slow-cooked meat smothered in spicy sauce.

5. Philadelphia cheesesteak. Heavyweights Geno's and Pat's (p. 234) have been duking it out for nearly 50 years for the title of Philly cheesesteak champion.

6. Cuban. Miami, FL, simmers with *cocina cubana* so delicious, you'll want to make it your vice.

7. Saltwater taffy. Beloved by children (and despised by dentists), this East Coast shore treat is sweet, sticky, and delicious.

8. Cincinnati chili. Cincinnati chili distinguishes itself from its Texan analogue by its thinner consistency and unusual spices.

9. Deep-dish pizza. A Chicago, IL, classic, the double-thick crust comes piled high with toppings.

10. New Mexican chilies. Make like a native Southwesterner and add red or green chili sauce to eggs, enchiladas, and everything in between.

WHAT TO DO

Even this book's more than one thousand pages can't do justice to the vibrant, diverse offerings of the US. No two trips to the US are the same, and visitors who travel to several regions may feel like they've visited different countries. Nevertheless, there are a few common themes that should be a part of any thorough exploration.

MUST-SEE CITIES

No visitor should pass up the glitz and glamour of Los Angeles, the round-the-clock excitement of New York City, or the multicultural metropolis of Miami. Nonetheless, the curious traveler should also take time to explore the wealth of lesser-known American cities with their own regional flavor. Hidden between the twin giants of New York and Boston, compact and walkable **Providence, RI** (p. 152), beckons with a slower, more inviting pace. Standing guard as the gateway to the West, **St. Louis, MO** (p. 624), combines distinctive neighborhoods and eclectic dining with an energetic nightlife scene fueled by the world's biggest brewery, Anheuser-Busch. Travelers to **Charleston, SC** (p. 364), are rewarded with lush gardens, antebellum plantations, and Southern charm. No party animal should miss Mardi Gras in **New Orleans, LA** (p. 426), where the city's carefree attitude, rich musical tradition, and sumptuous Creole cookin' cast an enchanting spell. Arts and crafts enthusiasts flock to **Santa Fe, NM** (p. 836), where old adobe churches, gorgeous galleries, and authentic Southwestern cuisine share the streets with the ritzy shops and restaurants serving the city's wealthy second-homers. The bohemian metropolis of **Portland, OR** (p. 944), known as the microbrewery capital of North America, is worth seeing for its fantastic open-air market alone.

COLLEGE TOWNS

America's colleges, from sprawling state universities to tiny liberal arts academies, have engendered unique communities with youthful vitality and alternative spirit. **Ann Arbor, MI** (p. 515), is the epitome of an American college town, boasting an unparalleled bar scene and a mishmash of Midwest hipsters while still maintaining a relaxed, friendly atmosphere. The 50,000 students who run amuck in **Austin, TX** (p. 650), spurn stereotypes about the conservative Lone Star State, creating a liberal haven where collegiate energy and Southwestern grit thrive side by side. A bastion of hippie culture, **Boulder, CO** (p. 693), gives a new meaning to the Rocky Mountain high. The mountain hamlet of **Middlebury, VT** (p. 116), combines rural charm with a touch of youthful rowdiness. An increasingly diverse student community gives the Southern establishment a run for its money in **Charlottesville, VA** (p. 296), a gorgeous town known for its rolling hills and splendid architecture. **Missoula, MT** (p. 752), is one of the most fascinatingly cosmopolitan cities in the Prairie States. **Berkeley, CA** (p. 876), perhaps the most famous American college town, has become a city in its own right without sacrificing its collegiate charms.

AMERICANA

America boasts the biggest, smallest, and zaniest of almost everything. Kitschy roadside attractions dot the country's dusty roads, putting on public display a vast and truly baffling material culture. Out west in Polson, MT, the **Miracle of America Museum** (p. 756) enshrines reg'lar ol' American living. Evidence of American architectural ingenuity can be found at the **Corn Palace** in Mitchell, SD (p. 597); this gargantuan structure is rebuilt every year with a fresh crop. America also claims the largest **operational chainsaw** near Marquette, MI (p. 528), and the world's largest **folding pocketknife** in Natchitoches, LA (p. 431), neither of which can quite compete with the magnitude of **Carhenge**—a scale model of Stonehenge built from 36 old cars just north of Alliance, NE (p. 620). Bigger and brighter still are the lights of **Times Square** in New York (p. 182) and **the Strip** in Las Vegas, NV (p. 777). And no tour of American kitsch would be complete without a trip to the heart and soul of all Americana—Elvis's **Graceland** (p. 336).

BASEBALL STADIUMS

The Great American Pastime is enshrined in its ballparks, where baseball zealots cheer on their favorite teams. Nothing beats catching a game on a balmy summer evening. The oldest ballpark still in use is **Fenway Park** (p. 132) in Boston, MA, where the Red Sox have played since 1912. The Chicago Cubs make their home at **Wrigley Field** (p. 542), whose ivy-clad outfield fences are an enduring symbol of baseball's storied past. Known as the "House that Ruth Built," **Yankee Stadium** (p. 185) in the Bronx has more history than any other stadium and is still widely considered the greatest ballpark in America. On the West Coast, **Dodger Stadium** (p. 912) rivals its East Coast predecessors with breathtaking views of downtown Los Angeles and the promise of beautiful weather. But while many purists cling to these relics of baseball's heyday, a wave of modern stadiums has ushered in a new era, and today the competition among cities for the best ballpark often overshadows team rivalries. **Camden Yards** (p. 262) in Baltimore, MD, perfectly bridges the gap between old and new, combining brick architecture with the most modern amenities. Perhaps the most impressive new stadium is the Pittsburgh Pirates' **PNC Park** (p. 250), a classically styled ballpark that offers striking views of the Pittsburgh skyline and the chance to blast a homer into the Allegheny River. At **SBC Park** (p. 874), fans munch on gourmet concessions and cheer as their favorite sluggers launch dingers into the San Francisco Bay, while at **Mile High Stadium** (p. 692), Colorado fans decide which Rockies to gape at: the ones playing ball or the ones towering over the bleachers.

NATIONAL PARKS

From haunting red buttes to endless caves, the national parks of the United States protect some of the most phenomenal natural scenery in the world. While much of the land's beauty can be seen along the byways, the truly miraculous works of nature are cared for by the National Park Service. The easternmost park in the US, **Acadia National Park, ME** (p. 95), features unspoiled rocky beaches and dense pine forests. **Shenandoah National Park, VA** (p. 299), made its way into history as America's first land reclamation project, and today lures travelers with its mountain vistas. **Great Smoky Mountains National Park, TN** (p. 327), the largest national park east of the Mississippi, also contains the International Biosphere Reserve and World Heritage Site. Farther west lie America's larger, better-known parks. Arguably the most famous (and most crowded) of these is **Yellowstone National Park, WY** (p. 723), home to the geyser called Old Faithful. **Grand Canyon National Park, AZ** (p. 803), wows visitors with...well, the Grand Canyon, while **Yosemite National Park, CA** (p. 935), draws hordes of trekkers, trailers, and tourists with its steep mountains and stunning waterfalls. Smaller—but no less breathtaking—are the otherworldly hoodoos (pillar-like rock formations) of **Bryce Canyon National Park, UT** (p. 796), the varied and dramatic terrain of **Waterton-Glacier International Peace Park, MT** (p. 756), and the awe-inspiring mountains of **Grand Teton National Park, WY** (p. 734).

◪ LET'S GO PICKS

BEST SPOTS TO SHOW OFF YOUR BIRTHDAY SUIT: The dippin' is skinny at **Austin, TX's** Hippie Hollow (p. 657) and in the mineral-rich waters at **Ouray, CO's** Orvis Hot Springs (p. 718).

MOST UNAPPETIZING BEER NAMES: Montana's **Moose Drool** (p. 730), South Carolina's **Mullet** (p. 371), and Louisiana's **funkybuttjuice** (p. 426) definitely rank among the nation's finest name-impaired beverages.

BEST FAKES: Tour five continents in a day, from a miniature Eiffel Tower to New York City to the Egyptian pyramids, on The Strip in **Las Vegas, NV** (p. 777). Ogle a replica of Jerusalem at the Holy Land Experience in **Orlando, FL** (p. 453). See the Mississippi River in miniature at the Mud Island River Park in **Memphis, TN** (p. 338); only 3½hr. away, a model Parthenon perches in the "Athens of the South," **Nashville, TN** (p. 322).

BEST GATORS: Make friends with America's scariest reptiles in places like **Natchitoches, LA** (p. 431); the **Everglades, FL** (p. 472); **St. Augustine, FL** (p. 462); and **Myrtle Beach, SC** (p. 371).

BEST ALTERNATIVE TO A GLASS: Enjoy a "beer boot" at the Essen Haus in **Madison, WI** (p. 560).

BEST OPPORTUNITIES FOR MULTI-TASKING: At Soapbox, a "laundrolounge" in **Wilmington, NC,** you can party and do your laundry at the same time (p. 364). Lace up your bowling shoes and pray for a strike at the **Boone, NC** Bowling Center's weekly "Christian Cosmic Bowling" night (p. 356).

MOST LIKELY TO HAVE PIRATES: The *José Gasparilla's* crew of buccaneers invades **Tampa, FL** in the first week of February (p. 455). **Alexandria Bay, NY,** hosts an annual Pirate Week (p. 219), while an altogether different kind of pirates play ball at PNC Park in **Pittsburgh, PA** (p. 250).

BEST REENACTMENTS: Listen to Pilgrims narrate the tale of the Mayflower at Plimoth Plantation in **Plymouth, MA** (p. 139). At Saloon #10 in the gambling town of **Deadwood, SD,** the shooting of outlaw Wild Bill Hickok is reenacted several times a day (p. 605).

BEST PLACES TO CATCH SOME RAYS: Show off your tan among spring-breakers and NASCAR drivers in sunny **Daytona Beach, FL** (p. 458), or see and be seen on eclectic **Venice Beach, CA** (p. 903). To run with a different crowd, join the wild ponies in **Assateague, MD** (p. 266).

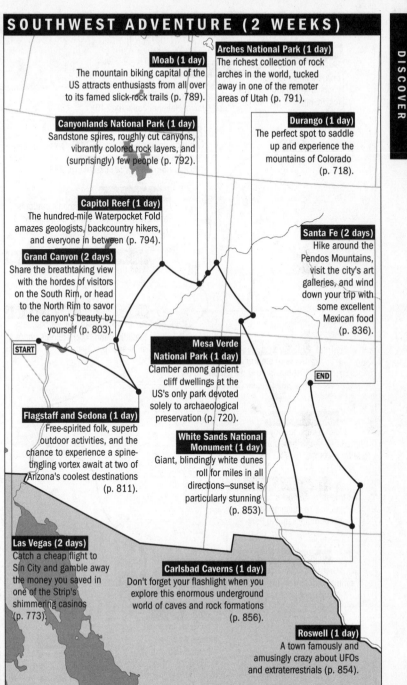

SOUTHWEST ADVENTURE (2 WEEKS)

Moab (1 day)
The mountain biking capital of the US attracts enthusiasts from all over to its famed slick-rock trails (p. 789).

Arches National Park (1 day)
The richest collection of rock arches in the world, tucked away in one of the remoter areas of Utah (p. 791).

Canyonlands National Park (1 day)
Sandstone spires, roughly cut canyons, vibrantly colored rock layers, and (surprisingly) few people (p. 792).

Durango (1 day)
The perfect spot to saddle up and experience the mountains of Colorado (p. 718).

Capitol Reef (1 day)
The hundred-mile Waterpocket Fold amazes geologists, backcountry hikers, and everyone in between (p. 794).

Santa Fe (2 days)
Hike around the Pendos Mountains, visit the city's art galleries, and wind down your trip with some excellent Mexican food (p. 836).

Grand Canyon (2 days)
Share the breathtaking view with the hordes of visitors on the South Rim, or head to the North Rim to savor the canyon's beauty by yourself (p. 803).

START

Mesa Verde National Park (1 day)
Clamber among ancient cliff dwellings at the US's only park devoted solely to archaeological preservation (p. 720).

END

Flagstaff and Sedona (1 day)
Free-spirited folk, superb outdoor activities, and the chance to experience a spine-tingling vortex await at two of Arizona's coolest destinations (p. 811).

White Sands National Monument (1 day)
Giant, blindingly white dunes roll for miles in all directions—sunset is particularly stunning (p. 853).

Las Vegas (2 days)
Catch a cheap flight to Sin City and gamble away the money you saved in one of the Strip's shimmering casinos (p. 773).

Carlsbad Caverns (1 day)
Don't forget your flashlight when you explore this enormous underground world of caves and rock formations (p. 856).

Roswell (1 day)
A town famously and amusingly crazy about UFOs and extraterrestrials (p. 854).

DISCOVER

ROCKY MOUNTAIN HIGH (3 WEEKS)

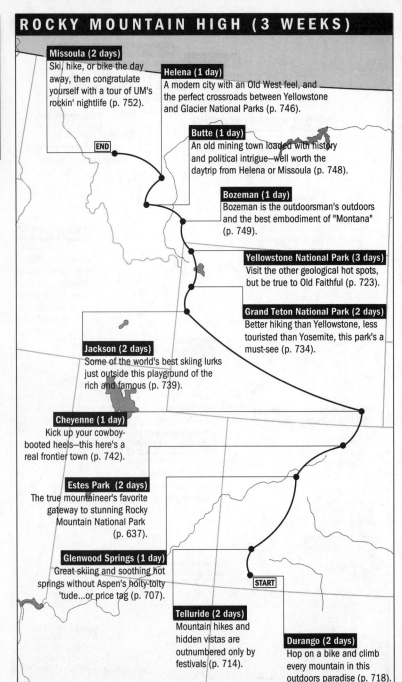

Missoula (2 days)
Ski, hike, or bike the day away, then congratulate yourself with a tour of UM's rockin' nightlife (p. 752).

Helena (1 day)
A modern city with an Old West feel, and the perfect crossroads between Yellowstone and Glacier National Parks (p. 746).

END

Butte (1 day)
An old mining town loaded with history and political intrigue—well worth the daytrip from Helena or Missoula (p. 748).

Bozeman (1 day)
Bozeman is the outdoorsman's outdoors and the best embodiment of "Montana" (p. 749).

Yellowstone National Park (3 days)
Visit the other geological hot spots, but be true to Old Faithful (p. 723).

Grand Teton National Park (2 days)
Better hiking than Yellowstone, less touristed than Yosemite, this park's a must-see (p. 734).

Jackson (2 days)
Some of the world's best skiing lurks just outside this playground of the rich and famous (p. 739).

Cheyenne (1 day)
Kick up your cowboy-booted heels—this here's a real frontier town (p. 742).

Estes Park (2 days)
The true mountaineer's favorite gateway to stunning Rocky Mountain National Park (p. 637).

Glenwood Springs (1 day)
Great skiing and soothing hot springs without Aspen's hoity-toity 'tude...or price tag (p. 707).

START

Telluride (2 days)
Mountain hikes and hidden vistas are outnumbered only by festivals (p. 714).

Durango (2 days)
Hop on a bike and climb every mountain in this outdoors paradise (p. 718).

BBQ NATION (2 WEEKS)

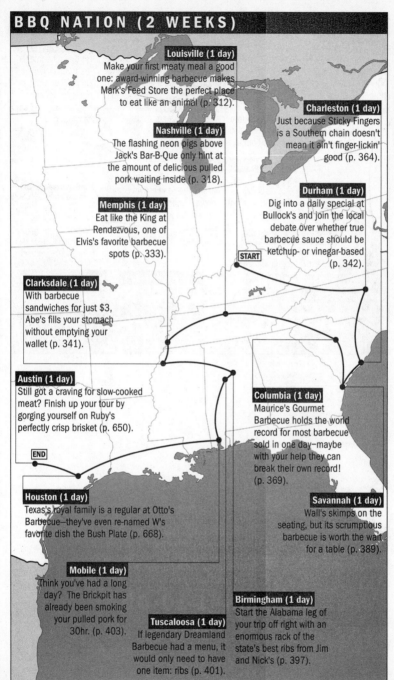

Louisville (1 day)
Make your first meaty meal a good one: award-winning barbecue makes Mark's Feed Store the perfect place to eat like an animal (p. 312).

Charleston (1 day)
Just because Sticky Fingers is a Southern chain doesn't mean it ain't finger-lickin' good (p. 364).

Nashville (1 day)
The flashing neon pigs above Jack's Bar-B-Que only hint at the amount of delicious pulled pork waiting inside (p. 318).

Durham (1 day)
Dig into a daily special at Bullock's and join the local debate over whether true barbecue sauce should be ketchup- or vinegar-based (p. 342).

Memphis (1 day)
Eat like the King at Rendezvous, one of Elvis's favorite barbecue spots (p. 333).

START

Clarksdale (1 day)
With barbecue sandwiches for just $3, Abe's fills your stomach without emptying your wallet (p. 341).

Austin (1 day)
Still got a craving for slow-cooked meat? Finish up your tour by gorging yourself on Ruby's perfectly crisp brisket (p. 650).

Columbia (1 day)
Maurice's Gourmet Barbecue holds the world record for most barbecue sold in one day—maybe with your help they can break their own record! (p. 369).

END

Houston (1 day)
Texas's royal family is a regular at Otto's Barbecue—they've even re-named W's favorite dish the Bush Plate (p. 668).

Savannah (1 day)
Wall's skimps on the seating, but its scrumptious barbecue is worth the wait for a table (p. 389).

Mobile (1 day)
Think you've had a long day? The Brickpit has already been smoking your pulled pork for 30hr. (p. 403).

Tuscaloosa (1 day)
If legendary Dreamland Barbecue had a menu, it would only need to have one item: ribs (p. 401).

Birmingham (1 day)
Start the Alabama leg of your trip off right with an enormous rack of the state's best ribs from Jim and Nick's (p. 397).

DISCOVER

MUSIC TO MY EARS (1 MONTH)

Portland (4 days)
There's nothing to be blue about during the remarkable Waterfront Blues Festival in early July (p. 944).

Detroit (3 days)
The rowdy Electronic Music Festival gets downtown thumping over Memorial Day weekend (p. 508).

Buffalo (3 days)
Hit the right note at the Buffalo Niagara Guitar Festival, the nation's first and largest all-guitar jam session (p. 207).

END

Chicago (4 days)
The Windy City winds up for summer with the Chicago Jazz Festival and then praises its lucky stars for the Chicago Gospel Festival, both in early June (p. 530).

START

Telluride (4 days)
Though it's staged miles from the Ozarks, June's Bluegrass Festival is an authentic, down-home treat (p. 714).

Newport (2 days)
Rub shoulders with... well, folks at the Newport Folk Festival in June (p. 155).

Oklahoma City (2 days)
The annual Charlie Christian Jazz Festival is guaranteed to toot your horn (p. 640).

Los Angeles (2 days)
Shout "olé" at the Mariachi USA Festival, the nation's largest celebration of its kind (p. 896).

Hot Springs (3 days)
Strike up the band—the Hot Springs Music Festival's classical sounds come to town in mid-June (p. 439).

Chattanooga (4 days)
Not just music, the nine-day Riverbend Festival also brings skydiving to the Tennessee River's banks (p. 330).

ESSENTIALS

PLANNING YOUR TRIP

ENTRANCE REQUIREMENTS

Passport (p. 10). Required of citizens of countries other than the US and Canada.

Visa (p. 11). Generally required of citizens of all countries other than the US and Canada, but requirement can be waived for residents of certain countries.

Inoculations (p. 21). None required.

Work Permit (p. 11). Required of all foreigners planning to work in the US.

EMBASSIES AND CONSULATES

US CONSULAR SERVICES ABROAD

Contact the nearest embassy or consulate to obtain info on the visas necessary to travel to the US. Listings of foreign embassies in the US and US embassies abroad can be found at www.embassyworld.com. The **US State Department** (http://travel.state.gov) provides a complete list of US embassy and consulate websites.

Australia: Moonah Pl., Yarralumla **(Canberra)**, ACT 2600 (☎61 02 6214 5600; http://usembassy-australia.state.gov). **Consulates:** 553 St. Kilda Rd., **Melbourne,** VIC 3004 (☎61 03 9526 5900; fax 9510 4646); 16 St. George's Terr., 13th fl., **Perth,** WA 6000 (☎61 08 9202 1224; fax 9231 9444); MLC Centre, Level 59, 19-29 Martin Pl., **Sydney,** NSW 2000 (☎61 02 9373 9200; fax 9373 9125).

Canada: 490 Sussex Dr., Ottawa, ON K1N 1G8 (☎1 613-238-5335; www.usembassycanada.gov). **Consulates:** 615 Macleod Tr. SE, Ste. 1050, **Calgary,** AB T2G 4T8 (☎1 403-266-8962; fax 264-6630); Ste. 904, Purdy's Wharf Tower II, 1969 Upper Water St., **Halifax,** NS B3J 3R7 (mailing address: P.O. Box 2130, CRO, Halifax, NS B3J 3B7; ☎1 902-429-2480; fax 423-6861); 1155 St. Alexandre St., **Montréal,** QC H3B 1Z1 (mailing address: P.O. Box 65, Station Desjardins, Montréal, QC H5B 1G1; ☎1 514-398-9695; fax 398-0973); 2 Place Terrasse Dufferin, B.P. 939, **Québec City,** QC G1R 4T9 (☎1 418-692-2095; fax 692-4640); 360 University Ave., **Toronto,** ON M5G 1S4 (☎1 416-595-1700; fax 595-0051); 1095 W. Pender 668-St., **Vancouver,** BC V6E 2M6 (☎1 604-685-4311; fax 685-5285); 201 Portage Ave., Ste. 860, **Winnepeg,** MB R3B 3K6 (☎1 204-940-1800; fax 940-1809).

Ireland: 42 Elgin Rd., Ballsbridge, Dublin 4 (☎353 01 668-8777; http://dublin.usembassy.gov).

New Zealand: 29 Fitzherbert Terr., Thorndon, **Wellington** (mailing address: P.O. Box 1190, Wellington, New Zealand; ☎644 462-600; www.usembassy.org.nz). **Consulate:** Citibank Building, 23 Customs St., 3rd fl., **Auckland** (mailing address: Private Bag 92022, Auckland, New Zealand; ☎649 303 2724, ext. 225, 226, or 250; fax 366 0870).

UK: 24 Grosvenor Sq., **London,** W1A 1AE, England (☎44 02074 999 000; www.usembassy.org.uk). **Consulates:** Danesfort House, 223 Stranmillis Rd., **Belfast,** N. Ireland BT9 5GR (☎44 02890 386 100; fax 681 301); 3 Regent Terr., **Edinburgh,** Scotland EH7 5BW (☎44 01315 568 315; fax 576 023).

CONSULAR SERVICES IN THE US

IN WASHINGTON, D.C.

Australia: 1601 Massachusetts Ave. NW, 20036 (☎202-797-3000; www.austemb.org).

Canada: 501 Pennsylvania Ave. NW, 20001 (☎202-682-1740; www.canadianembassy.org).

Ireland: 2234 Mass. Ave. NW, 20008 (☎202-462-3939; www.irelandemb.org).

New Zealand: 37 Observatory Circle NW, 20008 (☎202-328-4800; www.nzemb.org).

UK: 3100 Massachusetts Ave. NW, 20008 (☎202-588-7800; www.britainusa.com/consular/embassy).

TOURIST OFFICES

The US does not have a central tourism office; each state is responsible for its own tourist information. State tourist offices can be particularly helpful in guiding visitors to highlights of the region. Consult www.towd.com for the tourism websites of specific states.

DOCUMENTS AND FORMALITIES

PASSPORTS

REQUIREMENTS

All non-US and non-Canadian citizens need valid passports to enter the US and re-enter their home countries. Canadians can enter and leave the US with proof of citizenship and photo ID (a driver's license and birth certificate should suffice), but a Canadian passport is highly recommended. The US does not allow entrance if the holder's passport expires in under 6 months after the date of their departure; returning home with an expired passport is illegal and may result in a fine.

NEW PASSPORTS

Citizens of Australia, Canada, Ireland, New Zealand, the UK, and the US can apply for a passport at any passport office or at selected post offices and courts of law. Citizens of these countries may also download passport applications from the official website of their country's government or passport office. Any new passport or renewal applications must be filed well in advance of the departure date, though most passport offices offer rush services for a very steep fee. Note, however, that "rushed" passports still take up to two weeks to arrive. For more information, see the following websites: http://www.passports.gov.au (Australia); http://www.ppt.gc.ca (Canada); http://foreignaffairs.gov.ie (Ireland); http://www.passports.govt.nz (NZ); http://www.ukpa.gov.uk (UK); http://www.state.gov (US).

PASSPORT MAINTENANCE

Photocopy the page of your passport with your photo, as well as your visas, traveler's check serial numbers, and any other important documents. Carry one set of copies in a safe place, apart from the originals, and leave another set at home. Consulates also recommend that you carry an expired passport or an official copy of your birth certificate in a part of your baggage separate from other documents.

If you lose your passport, immediately notify the local police and the nearest embassy or consulate of your home government. To expedite its replacement, you must show ID and proof of citizenship; it also helps to know all information previously recorded in the passport. In some cases, a replacement may take weeks to process, and it may be valid only for a limited time. Any visas stamped in your old passport will be irretrievably lost.

VISAS, INVITATIONS, AND WORK PERMITS

VISAS

As of August 2005, citizens of certain non-English-speaking countries need a visa in addition to a valid passport for entrance into the US. Citizens of Canada do not need visas; citizens of Australia, Ireland, New Zealand, the UK, and most European countries can waive US visas through the **Visa Waiver Program (VWP).** Visitors qualify for VWP if they are traveling only for business or pleasure (*not* work or study), are staying for fewer than **90 days,** have proof of intent to leave (e.g., a return plane ticket), possess an I-94W form (an arrival/departure certificate issued upon arrival), are traveling on an approved air or sea carrier (most major carriers qualify—contact the carrier if you are in doubt), and have no visa ineligiblities (e.g., a criminal record). Visitors in the VWP must possess a **machine-readable passport** to be admitted to the US without a visa. See http://travel.state.gov or contact your local consulate for a list of countries participating in the VWP. For stays of longer than 90 days in the US, all travelers (except Canadians) must have a visa; travelers eligible to waive their visas and who wish to stay for more than 90 days must receive a visa before entering the US.

Each applicant for a visitor visa must pay a non-refundable fee of $100. In some cases, there may be a reciprocal issuance fee, depending on the applicant's nationality. This fee is refundable if your application is denied. How long you can stay in the US on a particular visit will be determined by a US official upon your arrival but is usually six months for tourism and business trips. Visas can be purchased at any US Consular office or at the Consular office with jurisdiction over an applicant's country. Expect an application to take anywhere from three days to four weeks or longer to process at different consulates.

Double-check entrance requirements at the nearest embassy or consulate of the US (listed under **US Consular Services Abroad,** on p. 9) for up-to-date info before departure. US citizens can also consult http://travel.state.gov.

Entering the US to study requires a special visa. For more information, see **Beyond Tourism** (p. 80).

WORK PERMITS

Admission as a visitor does not include the right to work, which is authorized only by a work permit, or Employment Authorization Document. To apply for a work permit, you must file an INS Form I-765 online or by mail to the US Citizenship and Immigration Services. There is a nonrefundable filing fee of $175. For more information on this process, visit the US Citizenship and Immigration Services website at http://uscis.gov.

IDENTIFICATION

When you travel, always carry at least two forms of identification on your person, including a photo ID; a passport and a driver's license or birth certificate is usually an adequate combination. Never carry all your IDs together; split them up in case of theft or loss, and keep photocopies of all of them in your luggage and at home.

STUDENT, TEACHER, AND YOUTH IDENTIFICATION

The **International Student Identity Card (ISIC),** the most widely accepted form of student ID, provides discounts on some sights, accommodations (20% or more off rooms in many chain hotels), food, and transportation (e.g., 5-15% off Alamo Car rentals); access to a 24hr. emergency helpline; and insurance benefits for US cardholders (see **Insurance,** p. 21). Applicants must be full-time secondary or post-secondary school students. Because of the proliferation of fake ISICs, some services (particularly airlines) require additional proof of student identity.

The **International Teacher Identity Card (ITIC)** offers teachers the same insurance coverage as the ISIC and similar but limited discounts. For travelers who are under 26 years old but are not students, the **International Youth Travel Card (IYTC)** also offers many of the same benefits as the ISIC.

Each of these identity cards costs $22 or equivalent. ISICs and ITICs are valid until the new year unless purchased between September and December, in which case they are valid until the beginning of the following new year. Thus, a card purchased in March 2006 will be valid until December 31, 2006, while a card purchased in November 2006 will be valid until December 31, 2007. IYTCs are valid for one year from the date of issue. To learn more about ISICs, ITICs, and IYTCs, see www.myisic.com. Many student travel agencies (p. 25) issue the cards; for a list of issuing agencies or more information, consult the **International Student Travel Confederation (ISTC)** website (www.istc.org).

The **International Student Exchange Card (ISE Card)** is a similar identification card available to students, faculty, and youths aged 12 to 26. The card provides discounts, medical benefits (covers up to $2,000 in medical expenses), access to a 24hr. emergency helpline, and the ability to purchase student airfares. An ISE Card costs $25; call ☎800-255-8000 for more info, or visit www.isecard.com.

CUSTOMS

Upon entering the US, you must declare certain items from abroad and pay a duty on the value of those articles if they exceed the allowance established by the US customs service. Note that goods and gifts purchased at **duty-free** shops abroad are not exempt from duty or sales tax; "duty-free" merely means that you need not pay a tax in the country of purchase. Duty-free allowances were abolished for travel between EU member states on June 30, 1999, but still exist for those arriving from outside the EU. Upon returning home, you must likewise declare all articles acquired abroad and pay a duty on the value of articles in excess of your home country's allowance. In order to expedite your return, make a list of any valuables brought from home and register them with customs before traveling abroad, and be sure to keep receipts for all goods acquired abroad.

MONEY

CURRENCY AND EXCHANGE

The currency chart below is based on August 2005 exchange rates between local currency and Australian dollars (AUS$), Canadian dollars (CDN$), European Union euros (EUR€), New Zealand dollars (NZ$), and British pounds (UK£). Check a large newspaper or the currency converter on websites like www.xe.com or www.bloomberg.com for up-to-date figures.

CURRENCY	
AUS$1= US$0.75	US$1= AUS$1.32
CDN$1= US$0.83	US$1= CDN$1.20
EUR€1= US$1.23	US$1= EUR€0.82
NZ$1= US$0.70	US$1= NZ$1.43
UK£1= US$1.80	US$1= UK£0.55

As a general rule, it's cheaper to convert money in the US than at home. While currency exchange will probably be available in your arrival airport, it's wise to bring enough foreign currency to last for the first 24 to 72 hours of your trip. When changing money abroad, try to go to banks that have no more than a 5% margin between buy and sell prices. Since you lose money with each transaction, **convert large sums** (unless the currency is depreciating rapidly), but **no more than you'll need.** If you use traveler's checks or bills, carry some in small denominations ($50 or less) for times when you are forced to exchange money at disadvantageous rates, but bring a range of denominations since charges may be levied per check cashed. Store your money in a variety of forms; ideally, at any given time you will be carrying some cash, some traveler's checks, and an ATM and/or credit card.

TRAVELER'S CHECKS

Traveler's checks are one of the safest and least troublesome means of carrying funds. American Express and Visa are the most-recognized brands. Many banks and agencies sell them for a small commission. Check issuers provide refunds if the checks are lost or stolen, and many provide additional services, such as toll-free refund hotlines abroad, emergency message services, and assistance with lost and stolen credit cards or passports. Traveler's checks are readily accepted in all regions of the US. Ask about toll-free refund hotlines and the location of refund centers when purchasing checks, and always carry emergency cash.

American Express: Checks available with commission at select banks, at all AmEx offices, and online (www.americanexpress.com; US residents only). American Express cardholders can also purchase checks by phone (☎800-721-9768). Checks available in Australian, British, Canadian, European, and Japanese currencies, among others. American Express also offers the Travelers Cheque Card, a prepaid reloadable card. Cheques for Two can be signed by either of two people traveling together. For purchase locations or more information, contact AmEx's service centers: in Australia ☎800 688 022, in New Zealand 423 74 409, in the UK 0800 587 6023, in the US and Canada 800-221-7282; elsewhere, call the US collect at 1-800-964-6665.

Travelex: Thomas Cook MasterCard and Interpayment Visa traveler's checks available. For information about Thomas Cook MasterCard in Canada and the US call ☎800-223-7373, in the UK 0800 622 101; elsewhere call the UK collect at +44 1733 318 950. For information about Interpayment Visa in the US and Canada call ☎800-732-1322, in the UK 0800 515 884; elsewhere call the UK collect at +44 1733 318 949. For more information, visit www.travelex.com.

Visa: Checks available (generally with commission) at banks worldwide. For the location of the nearest office, call the Visa Travelers Cheque Global Refund and Assistance Center: in the UK ☎0800 515 884, in the US 800-227-6811, elsewhere call the UK collect at +44 2079 378 091. Checks available in British, Canadian, European, Japanese, and US currencies, among others. Visa also offers TravelMoney, a prepaid debit card that can be reloaded online or by phone. For more information on Visa travel services, see http://usa.visa.com/personal/using_visa/travel_with_visa.html.

CREDIT, DEBIT, AND ATM CARDS

Where they are accepted, **credit cards** often offer superior exchange rates—up to 5% better than the retail rate used by banks and other currency exchange establishments. Credit cards may also offer services such as insurance or emergency help, and are sometimes required to reserve hotel rooms or rental cars. **MasterCard** and **Visa** are the most frequently accepted; **American Express** cards work at some ATMs and at AmEx offices and major airports.

The use of **ATM cards** is widespread in the US. Depending on the system that your home bank uses, you can most likely access your personal bank account while traveling. ATMs get the same wholesale exchange rate as credit cards, but there is often a limit on the amount of money you can withdraw per day (usually around $500). There is typically also a surcharge of $1-5 per withdrawal.

ESSENTIALS

Debit cards are as convenient as credit cards but have a more immediate impact on your funds. A debit card can be used wherever its associated credit card company (usually MasterCard or Visa) is accepted, yet the money is withdrawn directly from the holder's checking account. Debit cards often also function as ATM cards and can be used to withdraw cash from associated banks and ATMs throughout the US. Ask your local bank about obtaining one.

The two major international money networks are **MasterCard/Maestro/Cirrus** (for ATM locations ☎ 800-424-7787 or www.mastercard.com) and **Visa/PLUS** (for ATM locations ☎ 800-843-7587 or www.visa.com). Most ATMs charge a transaction fee that is paid to the bank that owns the ATM.

GETTING MONEY FROM HOME

If you run out of money while traveling, the easiest and cheapest solution is to have someone back home make a deposit to your bank account. If that is impossible, consider one of the following options.

WIRING MONEY

It is possible to arrange a **bank money transfer,** in which a bank at home wires money to a bank in the US. This is the cheapest way to transfer cash, but it's also the slowest, usually taking several days or more. Note that some banks may only release your funds in local currency, potentially sticking you with a poor exchange rate; inquire about this in advance. Money transfer services like **Western Union** are faster and more convenient than bank transfers—but also much pricier. Western Union has many locations worldwide. To find one, visit www.westernunion.com, or call in Australia ☎ 800 173 833, in Canada and the US 800-325-6000, or in the UK 0800 833 833. To wire money within the US using a credit card (Discover, MasterCard, Visa), call 800-225-5227. Money transfer services are also available to **American Express** cardholders and at selected **Thomas Cook** offices.

COSTS

The cost of your trip will vary considerably, depending on where you go, how you travel, and where you stay. The most significant expenses will probably be your round-trip (return) **airfare** to the US (see **Getting to the US: By Plane,** p. 24) and a **railpass** or **bus pass**. Be sure to factor in gas, which costs about $2.50 per gallon in the US as of August 2005. Before you go, spend some time calculating a reasonable daily **budget.**

STAYING ON A BUDGET

To give you a general idea, a bare-bones day in the US (camping or sleeping in hostels/guesthouses, buying food at supermarkets) costs about $40; a slightly more comfortable day (sleeping in hostels/guesthouses and the occasional budget hotel, eating one meal per day at a restaurant, going out at night) costs around $75; and for a luxurious day, the sky's the limit. Don't forget to factor in emergency reserve funds (at least $200) when planning how much money you'll need.

TIPS FOR SAVING MONEY

Some simpler ways include searching out opportunities for free entertainment, splitting accommodation and food costs with trustworthy fellow travelers, and buying food in supermarkets rather than eating out. Bring a **sleepsack** (see p. 17) to save on sheet charges in hostels, and do your **laundry** in the sink (unless you're explicitly prohibited from doing so). Museums often have certain days once a month or once a week when admission is free; plan accordingly. If you are eligible, consider getting an ISIC or an IYTC; many sights and museums offer reduced admission to students and youths. For getting around quickly, bikes are the most economical option. Renting a bike is cheaper than renting a moped or scooter.

Don't forget about walking, though; you can learn a lot about a city by seeing it on foot. Drinking at bars and clubs quickly becomes expensive. It's cheaper to buy alcohol at a supermarket and imbibe before going out. That said, there is no way to get around spending money. Though staying within your budget is important, don't do so at the expense of your health or a great travel experience.

TIPPING AND BARGAINING

In the US, it is customary to tip waitstaff and taxi drivers 15-20% (at your discretion). Tips are usually not included in restaurant bills unless you have a large party (generally six or more). At the airport and in hotels, porters expect $1-2 per bag tip to carry your bags—more if the bags are heavy. Bargaining is generally frowned upon and fruitless, except in open-air flea markets and farmers markets.

TAXES

State sales tax ranges 4-10% in the US, though some states have no sales tax, and many states do not tax grocery items, clothing, or prescription drugs. Many states and counties, especially in the South, charge a tax on hotel rooms; rates vary 3-18%. Sales tax is not usually included in the prices of listings in *Let's Go*.

PACKING

Pack lightly: Lay out only what you absolutely need, then take half the clothes and twice the money. The Travelite FAQ (www.travelite.org) is a good resource for tips on traveling light. The online **Universal Packing List** (http://upl.codeq.info) will generate a customized list of suggested items based on your trip length, the expected climate, your planned activities, and other factors. If you plan to do a lot of hiking, also consult **The Great Outdoors,** p. 42. Some frequent travelers keep a bag packed with all the essentials: passport, money belt, hat, socks, etc. Then, when they decide to leave, they know they haven't forgotten anything.

Luggage: If you plan to cover most of your itinerary by foot, a sturdy **frame backpack** is unbeatable. (For the basics to keep in mind when buying a pack, see p. 45.) Toting a **suitcase** or **trunk** is fine if you plan to live in one or two cities and explore from there, but not a great idea if you plan to move around frequently. In addition to your main piece of luggage, a **daypack** (a small backpack or courier bag) is useful.

Clothing: No matter when you're traveling, it's a good idea to bring a warm jacket or wool sweater, a rain jacket (Gore-Tex® is both waterproof and breathable),

TOP TEN WAYS TO SAVE IN THE US

A trip to the United States can be impossibly expensive—but it doesn't have to be. With a few small changes to your traveling routine, you can save lots more of your pennies for souvenirs.

1. Buy food and drinks at grocery stores or farmers markets instead of restaurants and bars.
2. If you'll be visiting two or more national parks, **invest in a National Parks Pass,** valid at any park in the US for a full year.
3. Take advantage of flyers and coupons in weekly papers that will allow you to bypass cover charges at clubs.
4. Buy a CityPass (www.citypass.com), which lets you skip the line at major tourist attractions in any of eight cities, and discounts admission up to 50%.
5. Snap up free Internet access in libraries and in tourist offices.
6. Use public transit or walk as much as possible.
7. Don't pay for entertainment: most US cities have frequent (and fun!) free festivals and concerts.
8. In major cities, make your base on the outskirts of town, where restaurants and accommodations tend to be cheaper.
9. Travel by train. The trip may take longer, but the savings (and views) will make it worthwhile.
10. If you have to fly, check out low-fare carriers. Southwest, JetBlue, and Independence Air all fly to smaller airports, which means cheaper tickets.

sturdy shoes or hiking boots, and thick socks. Flip-flops or waterproof sandals are must-haves for grubby hostel showers, and extra socks are always a good idea. You may also want one outfit for going out, and maybe a nicer pair of shoes. If you plan to visit religious or cultural sites, remember that you will need modest and respectful dress.

Sleepsack: Some hostels require that you either provide your own linen or rent sheets from them. Save cash by making your own sleepsack: fold a full-size sheet in half the long way, then sew it closed along the long side and one of the short sides.

Converters and Adapters: In the US, electricity is 120 volts AC, which is incompatible with the 220/240V appliances found in most other countries. Appliances from anywhere outside North America will need an adapter (which changes the shape of the plug, $5) and a converter (which changes the voltage, $10-30). Australians and New Zealanders (who use 230V at home) won't need a converter, but will need an adapter. For more on all things adaptable, check out http://kropla.com/electric.htm.

Toiletries: Toiletries are readily available in supermarkets and pharmacies, but it may be hard to find your preferred brand; bring extras. Contact lenses are likely to be expensive and difficult to find, so bring enough extra pairs and solution for your entire trip. Bring your glasses and a copy of your prescription in case you need emergency replacements.

First-Aid Kit: For a basic first-aid kit, pack bandages, a pain reliever, antibiotic cream, a thermometer, a multifunction pocketknife, tweezers, moleskin, decongestant, motion-sickness remedy, diarrhea or upset-stomach medication (Pepto Bismol® or Imodium®), an antihistamine, sunscreen, insect repellent, burn ointment, and an epinephrine kit (EpiPen®) in case of severe allergic reactions.

Film: Buying film and developing it in the US can be expensive (about $13 for a roll of 24 color exposures), so consider bringing along enough film for your entire trip and developing it at home. Less serious photographers may want to bring a disposable camera or two. Despite disclaimers, airport security X-rays can fog film, so buy a lead-lined pouch at a camera store or ask security to hand-inspect it. Always pack film in your carry-on luggage, since higher-intensity X-rays are used on checked luggage. If you don't want to bother with film, consider using a digital camera. Although it requires a steep initial investment, a digital camera means you never have to buy film again. Just be sure to bring along a large enough memory card and extra (or rechargeable) batteries. For more info on digital cameras, visit www.shortcourses.com/choosing/contents.htm.

Other Useful Items: For safety purposes, you should bring a **money belt** and a small **padlock.** Basic **outdoors equipment** (plastic water bottle, compass, waterproof matches, pocketknife, sunglasses, sunscreen, hat) may also prove useful. **Quick repairs** of torn garments can be done on the road with a needle and thread; also consider bringing electrical tape for patching tears. If you want to do laundry by hand, bring detergent, a small rubber ball to stop up the sink, and string for a makeshift clothes line. Other things you're liable to forget include: an umbrella, sealable **plastic bags** (for damp clothes, soap, food, shampoo, and other spillables), an **alarm clock,** safety pins, rubber bands, a flashlight, earplugs, garbage bags, and a small calculator. A **cell phone** can be a lifesaver (literally) on the road; see p. 34 for information on acquiring one that will work in the US.

Important Documents: Don't forget your passport, traveler's checks, ATM and/or credit cards, adequate ID, and photocopies of all of the aforementioned in case these documents are lost or stolen (see p. 10). Also check that you have any of the following that might apply to you: a hosteling membership card (see p. 36); driver's license (see p. 11); travel insurance forms (see p. 21); ISIC (see p. 11); and/or rail or bus pass (see p. 29).

ESSENTIALS

SAFETY AND HEALTH

GENERAL ADVICE

In any type of crisis situation, the most important thing to do is **stay calm.** Your country's embassy abroad (p. 10) is usually your best resource when things go wrong; registering with that embassy upon arrival in the country is often a good idea. The government offices listed in the **Travel Advisories** box (p. 19) can provide information on the services they offer their citizens in case of emergencies abroad.

LOCAL LAWS AND POLICE

DRIVING

If you are using a **car,** learn local driving signals and wear a seatbelt. You must obey all posted signs, including speed limit signs. If a police car sounds its siren behind you, slow down and pull over as soon as it is safe to do so. If an emergency vehicle approaches from either direction with its sirens on, slow down and pull over to the side of the road until the vehicle has passed and is several hundred feet away. The only exception to this law occurs if an emergency vehicle is approaching from the opposite direction on a divided highway; in this case, motorists on the side opposite the emergency vehicle need not pull over. Most localities require you to stop when school buses are picking up or dropping off passengers except, as above, when they are on the opposite side of a divided roadway.

Local police are often a good resource for help. If your car breaks down or you find yourself stranded, call or wait for local or state highway police to arrive.

DRUGS AND ALCOHOL

In the US, the drinking age is 21, and drinking restrictions are particularly strict. Younger travelers should expect to be asked to show government-issued identification when purchasing any alcoholic beverage. Drinking and driving is prohibited everywhere, not to mention dangerous. Open alcoholic beverage containers in your car will incur heavy fines; a failed sobriety test will mean fines, a suspended license, imprisonment, or all three. Most localities restrict where and when alcohol can be sold. Sales usually stop at a certain time at night and are often prohibited entirely on Sundays. Narcotics like marijuana, heroin, and cocaine are highly illegal in the US. If you carry prescription drugs while you travel, keep a copy of the prescription with you, especially at border crossings.

SPECIFIC CONCERNS

NATURAL DISASTERS

EARTHQUAKES. Earthquakes occur frequently in certain parts of the US, particularly California, but most are too small to be felt. If a strong earthquake does occur, it will last at most 1-2 minutes. Open a door to provide an escape route and protect yourself by moving underneath a sturdy doorway, table, or desk. If you are outside, move to an open area free from buildings, trees, and power lines.

TORNADOES AND HURRICANES. Tornadoes have been reported in every US state, though they are most common in the Great Plains during the spring and summer. If you are inside during a tornado, move to a basement or interior location away from windows. If you are outside, lie flat on the ground in a low place away from power lines. Hurricanes are most common on the Atlantic and Gulf of Mexico coasts. Often, these areas are evacuated in anticipation of particularly severe hurricanes. If you are not advised to evacuate, stay inside, away from windows.

LANDSLIDES/MUDSLIDES. Heavy rain, flooding, or snow runoff combined with hilly terrain can lead to landslides or mudslides, particularly on slopes where vegetation has been removed. This will most likely not be a concern in cities; however, if you are hiking after a heavy rainfall, be aware of the possibility of a slide. If you are caught in a mudslide or landslide, try to get out of its path and run to high ground or shelter. If escape is not possible, curl into a ball and protect your head.

FOREST FIRES. Dry spells are common in the western US, and 2005 marked the sixth consecutive year of drought for much of this area. In 2003, forest fires ravaged much of the eastern Cascades, as well as parts of California and Oregon. If you are hiking or camping and smell smoke, see flames, or hear fire, leave the area immediately. To prevent forest fires, always make sure campfires are completely extinguished; during high levels of fire danger, campfires will most likely be prohibited. Before you go hiking or camping, be sure to check with local authorities for the level of fire danger in the area.

TERRORISM
In light of the September 11, 2001 terrorist attacks, there is an elevated risk of further terrorist activities in the US. The threat of an attack is generally not specific or great enough to warrant avoiding certain places or modes of transportation. After the September 11 attacks, the Department of Homeland Security (DHS) was created to protect the US from further terrorist threats. Local and national news media often report changes in threat status, and travelers should be alert to these changes. The box on **travel advisories** (see below) lists offices to contact and webpages to visit to get the most updated list of your home country's government's advisories about travel.

PERSONAL SAFETY

EXPLORING AND TRAVELING
To avoid unwanted attention, try to blend in as much as possible. Respecting local customs (in many cases, dressing more conservatively than you would at home) may placate would-be hecklers. Familiarize yourself with your surroundings before setting out, and carry yourself with confidence. Check maps in shops and restaurants rather than on the street. If you are traveling alone, be sure someone at home knows your itinerary, and never admit that you're by yourself. When walking at night, stick to busy, well-lit streets and avoid dark alleyways. If you ever feel uncomfortable, leave the area as quickly and directly as you can.

There is no sure-fire way to avoid all the threatening situations you might encounter while traveling, but a good **self-defense course** will give you concrete

TRAVEL ADVISORIES. The following government offices provide travel information and advisories by telephone, by fax, or via the web:

Australian Department of Foreign Affairs and Trade: ☎1300 555 135; www.dfat.gov.au.

Canadian Department of Foreign Affairs and International Trade (DFAIT): ☎800-267-8376; www.dfait-maeci.gc.ca. Call for their free booklet, *Bon Voyage...But.*

New Zealand Ministry of Foreign Affairs: ☎044 398 000; www.mft.govt.nz/travel/index.html.

UK Foreign and Commonwealth Office: ☎02070 081 500; www.fco.gov.uk.

US Department of State: ☎202-647-5225; http://travel.state.gov. Visit the website for the booklet *A Safe Trip Abroad.*

ways to react to unwanted advances. **Impact, Prepare, and Model Mugging** can refer you to local self-defense courses in the US. Visit www.impactsafety.org (Impact), www.prepareinc.com (Prepare), or www.modelmugging.org (Model Mugging) for a list of nearby chapters. Impact workshops (2-4hr.) start at $50; full courses (20hr.) run $350-500.

If you are using a **car,** learn local driving signals and wear a seatbelt. Children under 40 lbs. should ride only in specially-designed carseats, available for a small fee from most car rental agencies ($7-10 per day); infants under 1 year or 20 lb. must ride in rear-facing carseats. All children under 12 must sit in the rear seat of the car. Study route maps before you hit the road, and if you plan on spending a lot of time driving, consider bringing spare parts. If your car breaks down, wait for the police to assist you. For long drives in desolate areas, invest in a cellular phone and a roadside assistance program (see p. 31). Park your vehicle in a garage or well-traveled area, and use a steering wheel locking device in larger cities. **Sleeping in your car** is one of the most dangerous (and often illegal) ways to get your rest. For info on the perils of **hitchhiking,** see p. 32.

POSSESSIONS AND VALUABLES

Never leave your belongings unattended; crime occurs in even the most demure-looking hostel or hotel. Bring your own padlock for hostel lockers, and don't ever store valuables in any locker. Be particularly careful on **buses** and **trains;** horror stories abound about determined thieves who wait for travelers to fall asleep. Carry your backpack in front of you where you can see it. When traveling with others, sleep in alternate shifts. When alone, use good judgment in selecting a train compartment: never stay in an empty one, and use a lock to secure your pack to the luggage rack. Try to sleep on top bunks with your luggage stored above you (if not in bed with you), and keep documents and valuables on your person.

There are a few steps you can take to minimize the financial risk associated with traveling. First, **bring as little with you as possible.** Second, buy a few combination **padlocks** to secure your belongings either in your pack or in a hostel or train station locker. Third, **carry as little cash as possible.** Keep your traveler's checks and ATM/credit cards in a **money belt**—not a "fanny pack"—along with your passport and ID cards. Fourth, **keep a small cash reserve separate from your primary stash.** This should be about $50 sewn into or stored in the depths of your pack, along with your traveler's check numbers and important photocopies.

In large cities **con artists** often work in groups that may include children. Beware of certain classics: sob stories that require money, rolls of bills "found" on the street, mustard spilled (or saliva spit) onto your shoulder to distract you while they snatch your bag. **Never let your passport and your bags out of your sight.** Beware of **pickpockets** in city crowds, especially on public transit. Also, be alert in public telephone booths: If you must say your calling card number, do so very quietly; if you punch it in, make sure no one can look over your shoulder.

If you will be traveling with electronic devices, such as a computer or a PDA, check whether your homeowner's insurance covers loss, theft, or damage when you travel. If not, you might consider purchasing a low-cost travel insurance policy. **Safeware** (☎800-800-1492; www.safeware.com) specializes in covering computers and charges $90 for 90-day comprehensive coverage up to $4000.

PRE-DEPARTURE HEALTH

In your **passport,** write the names of anyone you wish to be contacted in case of a medical emergency, and list any allergies or medical conditions. Matching a prescription to a foreign equivalent is not always safe or possible, so if you take prescription drugs, carry up-to-date, legible prescriptions or a statement from your doctor with the medication's trade name, manufacturer, chemical name, and dosage. While traveling, be sure to keep all medication with you in your carry-on luggage. For tips on packing a basic **first-aid kit** and other health essentials, see p. 17.

IMMUNIZATIONS AND PRECAUTIONS

Although no inoculations are required for US tourists, travelers over two years old should make sure that the following vaccines are up to date: MMR (for measles, mumps, and rubella); DTaP or Td (for diphtheria, tetanus, and pertussis); IPV (for polio); Hib (for *haemophilus* influenza B); and HepB (for Hepatitis B). For recommendations on immunizations and prophylaxis, consult the CDC (see below) in the US or the equivalent in your home country, and check with a doctor.

INSURANCE

Travel insurance covers four basic areas: medical/health problems, property loss, trip cancellation/interruption, and emergency evacuation. Though regular insurance policies may well extend to travel-related accidents, you may consider purchasing separate travel insurance if the cost of potential trip cancellation, interruption, or emergency medical evacuation is greater than you can absorb. Prices for travel insurance purchased separately generally run about $50 per week for full coverage, while trip cancellation/interruption may be purchased separately at a rate of $3-5 per day depending on length of stay.

Medical insurance (especially university policies) often covers costs incurred abroad; check with your provider. **Homeowners' insurance** (or your family's coverage) often covers theft during travel and loss of travel documents (passport, plane ticket, railpass, etc.) up to $500.

ISIC and **ITIC** (see p. 11) provide basic insurance benefits to US cardholders, including $100 per day of in-hospital sickness for up to 100 days and $10,000 of accident-related medical reimbursement (see www.isicus.com for details). Cardholders have access to a toll-free 24hr. helpline for medical, legal, and financial emergencies. **American Express** (☎800-338-1670) grants most cardholders automatic collision and theft car rental insurance on rentals made with the card.

USEFUL ORGANIZATIONS AND PUBLICATIONS

The US **Centers for Disease Control and Prevention** (**CDC;** ☎877-FYI-TRIP; www.cdc.gov/travel) maintains an international travelers' hotline and an informative website. Consult the appropriate government agency of your home country for consular information sheets on health, entry requirements, and other issues for various countries (see the listings in the box on **Travel Advisories,** p. 19). For quick information on health and other travel warnings, call the **Overseas Citizens Services** (M-F 8am-8pm ☎888-407-4747, from overseas 202-501-4444), or contact a passport agency, embassy, or consulate abroad. For information on medical evacuation services and travel insurance firms, see the US government's website at http://travel.state.gov/travel/abroad_health.html or the **British Foreign and Commonwealth Office** (www.fco.gov.uk). For general health info, contact the **American Red Cross** (☎800-564-1234; www.redcross.org).

STAYING HEALTHY

Common sense is the simplest prescription for good health while you travel. Drink lots of fluids to prevent dehydration and constipation, and wear sturdy, broken-in shoes and clean socks.

ONCE IN US

ENVIRONMENTAL HAZARDS

Heat exhaustion and dehydration: Heat exhaustion leads to nausea, heavy sweating, excessive thirst, headaches, and dizziness. Avoid it by drinking plenty of fluids, eating salty foods (e.g., crackers), abstaining from dehydrating beverages (e.g., alcohol and caffeinated beverages), and always wearing sunscreen. Continuous heat stress can eventually lead to heatstroke, characterized by a rising temperature, severe headache, delirium and cessation of sweating. Victims should be cooled off with wet towels and taken to a doctor. The southern US is particularly prone to heat waves, though travelers in all areas should be cautious during the summer and bring plenty of water on hiking or camping trips.

High Altitude: The Rocky, Sierra Nevada, and Cascades mountains in the western US are at particularly high altitudes. When visiting these locations, allow your body a couple of days to adjust to less oxygen before exerting yourself. Note that alcohol is more potent and UV rays are stronger at high elevations.

Hypothermia and frostbite: Travelers to the US during the winter months should be aware of the dangers of cold exposure. A rapid drop in body temperature is the clearest sign of overexposure to cold. Victims may shiver, feel exhausted, have poor coordination or slurred speech, hallucinate, or experience mental lethargy. *Do not let hypothermia victims fall asleep.* To avoid hypothermia, keep dry, wear warm, moisture-wicking layers (polyester, wool, silk), limit alcohol and caffeine intake, drink a lot of water, and eat plenty of carbohydrates. When the temperature is below freezing, watch out for frostbite, especially on ears, nose, hands, and feet. If skin turns white or purple, waxy, and cold, come out of the cold immediately and call for medical assistance. Do not rub the area. Drink warm, non-alcoholic, non-caffeinated fluids, and avoid gradually thawing the area until medical help arrives. To prevent frostbite, dress warmly, stay out of the wind, and apply skin moisturizer to any exposed body part.

Sunburn: Always wear sunscreen (SPF 30 is good) when spending excessive amounts of time outdoors. If you are planning on spending time near water, in the desert, or in the snow, you are at higher risk of getting burned, even through clouds. If you get sunburned, drink more fluids than usual and apply an aloe-based lotion. Severe sunburns can lead to sun poisoning, a condition that affects the entire body, causing fever, fatigue, and a blistering skin rash. Sun poisoning should always be treated by a doctor.

INSECT-BORNE DISEASES

Many diseases are transmitted by insects—mainly mosquitoes, fleas, ticks, and lice. Be aware of insects in wet or forested areas, especially while hiking and camping; wear long pants and long sleeves, tuck your pants into your socks, and use a mosquito net. Use insect repellents such as DEET and soak or spray your gear with permethrin (licensed in the US only for use on clothing). **Mosquitoes,** carriers of diseases including malaria, dengue fever, and yellow fever, can be particularly dangerous in wet, swampy, or wooded areas such as the southeastern US. **Ticks,** carriers of Lyme and other diseases, can be particularly dangerous in rural and forested regions, particularly the northeast, central north, and Pacific coast.

Lyme disease: A bacterial infection carried by ticks and marked by a circular bull's-eye rash of 2 in. or more. Later symptoms include fever, headache, fatigue, and aches and pains. Antibiotics are effective if administered early. Left untreated, Lyme disease can cause chronic joint pain, heart irregularities, and problems with the nervous system. If you find a tick attached to your skin, grasp its body with fine-tipped tweezers and steadily pull away from the skin. Do not try to remove ticks with petroleum jelly, nail polish remover, or a hot match. Cleanse the area with antiseptic. Removing a tick within

24hr. greatly reduces the chance of Lyme disease transmission. Tick bites usually occur in moist, shaded environments and wooded areas of the northeastern, central northern, and Pacific coastal regions and are most common during the late spring and summer months. If you are going to be hiking in these areas, wear long clothes and use DEET.

West Nile Virus: The West Nile Virus has been detected in all 48 continental states and is transmitted through the bite of an infected mosquito. Most victims do not have any symptoms, but some develop mild flu-like symptoms; less than 1% develop more severe symptoms including meningitis or encephalitis. Those at highest risk are the elderly and those with lowered immune systems, but people of all ages can develop a serious illness. To minimize the risk of infection, limit outdoor activity when mosquitoes are most active (dawn, dusk, and early evening), wear long clothes, and use DEET.

FOOD- AND WATER-BORNE DISEASES

In the US, city and suburban tap water is treated to be safe for drinking, though travelers should still exercise caution in remote rural areas or areas with untreated well water. Raw shellfish, unpasteurized milk, or dishes containing raw eggs may still present health risks. Watch out for food from markets or street vendors that may have been cooked in unhygienic conditions.

Backcountry hikers may purify their own water by bringing it to a rolling boil or treating it with **iodine tablets;** note, however, that some parasites such as giardia have exteriors that resist iodine treatment, so boiling is a more reliable treatment. Always wash your hands before eating or bring a quick-drying purifying liquid hand cleaner.

Gastroenteritis/Stomach Flu: Caused by a class of viruses called Noroviruses and spreads via contact with the body fluids of infected people, including exposure to contaminated foods, touching contaminated objects and then placing the hands in or near the mouth, and direct contact with infected persons. Symptoms appear within 48hr. of infection and include vomiting, nausea, chills, diarrhea, and abdominal cramping. Though the symptoms usually pass within a few days, the disease can be contagious for several weeks and a doctor should be consulted if any of these symptoms develop.

Giardiasis: Transmitted through parasites (microbes, tapeworms, etc. in contaminated water and food) and acquired by drinking untreated water from streams or lakes. Symptoms include diarrhea, abdominal cramps, bloating, fatigue, weight loss, and nausea. If untreated it can lead to severe dehydration. Giardiasis occurs worldwide.

OTHER INFECTIOUS DISEASES

Rabies: Transmitted through the saliva of infected animals; fatal if untreated. By the time symptoms (thirst and muscle spasms) appear, the disease is in its terminal stage. If you are bitten, wash the wound thoroughly, seek immediate medical care, and try to have the animal located. A rabies vaccine, which consists of 3 shots given over a 21-day period, is available and recommended for developing world travel, but is only semi-effective. Rabies is found all over the world, and is often transmitted through dogs, but travelers to backcountry and wooded areas should be wary of all wild animals.

HIV and AIDS: For detailed information on Acquired Immune Deficiency Syndrome (AIDS) in the US, call the US Centers for Disease Control's 24hr. hotline at ☎800-342-2437, or contact the Joint United Nations Programme on HIV/AIDS (UNAIDS), 20 ave. Appia, CH-1211 Geneva 27, Switzerland (☎+41 22 791 3666; fax 22 791 4187).

Sexually Transmitted Infections (STIs): Gonorrhea, chlamydia, genital warts, syphilis, herpes, and other STIs are easier to catch than HIV and can be just as deadly. **Hepatitis** B and C can also be transmitted sexually. Though condoms may protect you from some STIs, oral or even tactile contact can lead to transmission. If you think you may have contracted an STI, see a doctor immediately.

OTHER HEALTH CONCERNS

MEDICAL CARE ON THE ROAD

Medical care in the US is among the best in the world. In case of medical emergency, dial ☎911 from any phone and an operator will send out paramedics, a fire brigade, or the police as needed. Emergency care is available at any emergency room on a walk-in basis. If you do not have insurance, you will have to pay for medical care. Appointments are required for non-emergency medical services. If you are concerned about obtaining medical assistance while traveling, you may wish to employ special support services. The *MedPass* from **GlobalCare, Inc.**, 6875 Shiloh Rd. East, Alpharetta, GA 30005 (☎800-860-1111; www.globalcare.net), provides 24hr. international medical assistance, support, and medical evacuation resources. If your regular **insurance** policy does not cover travel abroad, you may wish to purchase additional coverage (see p. 21).

Those with medical conditions (such as diabetes, allergies to antibiotics, epilepsy, or heart conditions) may want to obtain a **MedicAlert** membership (first year $35, annually thereafter $20), which includes a stainless steel ID tag, among other benefits, like a 24hr. collect-call number. Contact the MedicAlert Foundation, 2323 Colorado Ave., Turlock, CA 95382, USA (☎888-633-4298, outside US ☎209-668-3333; www.medicalert.org).

WOMEN'S HEALTH

Women traveling in the backcountry are vulnerable to **urinary tract (including bladder and kidney) infections.** Over-the-counter medicines can sometimes alleviate symptoms, but if they persist, see a doctor. **Vaginal yeast infections** may flare up in hot and humid climates. Wearing loosely fitting trousers or a skirt and cotton underwear will help, as will over-the-counter remedies like Monostat or Gynelotrimin. **Tampons, pads,** and **contraceptive devices** are widely available in the US, but your favorite brand may not be stocked—bring extras of anything you can't live without. **Abortion** is legal in the US; for more information contact Planned Parenthood (☎800-230-7526; www.plannedparenthood.org).

GETTING TO THE US

BY PLANE

When it comes to airfare, a little effort can save you a bundle. If your plans are flexible enough to deal with the restrictions, courier fares are the cheapest. Tickets bought from consolidators and standby seating are also good deals, but last-minute specials, airfare wars, and charter flights often beat these fares. The key is to hunt around, be flexible, and ask persistently about discounts. Students, seniors, and those under 26 should never pay full price for a ticket.

AIRFARES

Airfares to the US peak during the summer, especially between June and September; holidays are also expensive. Generally, the cheapest times to travel are during the winter and during school sessions, but it depends on the high-season months of your destination. Midweek (M-Th morning) round-trip flights run $40-50 cheaper than weekend flights, but they are generally more crowded and less likely to permit frequent-flier upgrades. Not fixing a return date ("open return") or arriving in and departing from different cities ("open-jaw") can be pricier than round-trip flights. Patching one-way flights together is the most expensive way to travel. Flights between state capitals or regional hubs—New York, Los Angeles, Boston, Chicago, Washington, D.C.—will tend to be cheaper.

If the US is only one stop on a more extensive globe-hop, consider a round-the-world (RTW) ticket. Tickets usually include at least five stops and are valid for about a year; prices range US$1200-5000. Try **Northwest Airlines/KLM** (☎800-225-2525; www.nwa.com) or **Star Alliance,** a consortium of 16 airlines including United Airlines (www.staralliance.com).

Fares for round-trip flights to the US's East Coast from Western Europe cost $600-1200, $300-750 in the low season (Sept.-May); round-trip flights from Australia or New Zealand to the US's West Coast usually cost $900-$1600.

BUDGET AND STUDENT TRAVEL AGENCIES

While knowledgeable agents specializing in flights to the US can make your life easy and help you save, they may not spend the time to find you the lowest possible fare—they get paid on commission. Travelers holding **ISICs** and **IYTCs** (see p. 11) qualify for big discounts from student travel agencies. Most flights from budget agencies are on major airlines, but in peak season some may sell seats on less reliable chartered aircraft.

STA Travel, 5900 Wilshire Blvd., Ste. 900, Los Angeles, CA 90036, USA (24hr. reservations and info ☎800-781-4040; www.statravel.com). A student and youth travel organization with over 400 offices worldwide (check their website for a listing of all their offices), including US offices in Boston, Chicago, Los Angeles, New York, Seattle, San Francisco, and Washington, D.C. Ticket booking, travel insurance, railpasses, and more. Walk-in offices are located throughout Australia (☎1300 733 035), New Zealand (☎0508 782 872), and the UK (☎08701 600 599).

Travel CUTS (Canadian Universities Travel Services Limited), 187 College St., Toronto, ON M5T 1P7, Canada (☎800-592-2887; www.travelcuts.com). Offices across Canada and the US including Los Angeles, New York, Seattle, and San Francisco.

USIT, 19-21 Aston Quay, Dublin 2, Ireland (☎01 602 1904; www.usit.ie), Ireland's leading student/budget travel agency has 20 offices throughout Northern Ireland and the Republic of Ireland. Offers programs to work, study, and volunteer worldwide.

FLIGHT PLANNING ON THE INTERNET. The Internet may be the budget traveler's dream when it comes to finding and booking bargain fares, but the array of options can be overwhelming. Many airlines offer last-minute deals on the web. Check individual airlines' websites for more information. **STA** (www.sta-travel.com) and **StudentUniverse** (www.studentuniverse.com) provide quotes on student tickets, while **Orbitz** (www.orbitz.com), **Expedia** (www.expedia.com), and **Travelocity** (www.travelocity.com) offer full travel services. **Priceline** (www.priceline.com) lets you specify a price, and obligates you to buy any ticket that meets or beats it; **Hotwire** (www.hotwire.com) offers bargain fares, but won't reveal the airline or flight times until purchase. Other sites that compile deals include www.bestfares.com, www.flights.com, www.lowestfare.com, www.onetravel.com, and www.travelzoo.com. Increasingly, there are online tools available to help sift through multiple offers; **SideStep** (www.sidestep.com) and **Booking Buddy** (www.bookingbuddy.com) let you enter your trip information once and search multiple sites. An indispensable resource is the **Air Traveler's Handbook** (www.faqs.org/faqs/travel/air/handbook), a comprehensive listing of links to everything you need to know before you board a plane.

ESSENTIALS

COMMERCIAL AIRLINES

The commercial airlines' lowest regular offer is the **APEX** (Advance Purchase Excursion) fare, which provides confirmed reservations and allows "open-jaw" tickets. Generally, reservations must be made seven to 21 days ahead of departure, with seven- to 14-day minimum-stay and up to 90-day maximum-stay restrictions. These fares carry hefty cancellation and change penalties (fees rise in summer). Book peak-season APEX fares early. Use **Expedia** (www.expedia.com) or **Travelocity** (www.travelocity.com) to get an idea of the lowest published fares, then use the resources outlined here to try and beat those fares. Low-season fares should be appreciably cheaper than the **high-season** (mid-June to Aug.) ones listed here.

TRAVELING FROM THE UK AND IRELAND

Round-trip fares from the UK and Ireland to the eastern US range $200-750, with flights from London usually cheapest at $200-600. Standard commercial carriers like **American** (☎800-433-7300; www.aa.com), **United** (☎800-538-2929; www.ual.com), and **Northwest** (☎800-447-4747; www.nwa.com) will probably offer the most convenient flights, but they may not be the cheapest. Check **Lufthansa** (☎800-399-5838; http://cms.lufthansa.com), **British Airways** (☎800-247-9297; www.britishairways.com), **Air France** (☎800-237-2747; www.airfrance.us), and **Alitalia** (☎800-223-5730; www.alitaliausa.com) for cheap tickets from destinations in Europe to all over the US. Discount airlines such as **Icelandair** (☎800-223-5500; www.icelandair.com) may provide cheaper flights, though cheaper flights often mean fewer departure points.

TRAVELING FROM AUSTRALIA AND NEW ZEALAND

Check **Air New Zealand** (☎0800 737 000; www.airnz.co.nz), **Quantas Airways** (Australia ☎131 313, New Zealand 0800 101 500; www.qantas.com.au), and **Singapore Air** (Australia ☎131 011, New Zealand 0800 808 909; www.singaporeair.com) for cheap tickets from Australia and New Zealand to the US.

STANDBY FLIGHTS

Traveling standby requires considerable flexibility in arrival and departure dates and cities. Companies dealing in standby flights sell vouchers rather than tickets, along with the promise to get you to your destination (or near your destination) within a certain window of time (typically 1-5 days). You call in before your specific window of time to hear your flight options and the probability that you will be able to board each flight. You can then decide which flights you want to try to make, show up at the appropriate airport at the appropriate time, present your voucher, and board if space is available. Vouchers can usually be bought for both one-way and round-trip travel. You may receive a monetary refund only if every available flight within your date range is full; if you opt not to take an available (but perhaps less convenient) flight, you can only get credit toward future travel. Carefully read agreements with any company offering standby flights as tricky fine print can leave you in the lurch. To check on a company's service record in the US, contact the Better Business Bureau (☎703-276-0100; www.bbb.org).

TICKET CONSOLIDATORS

Ticket consolidators, or **"bucket shops,"** buy unsold tickets in bulk from commercial airlines and sell them at discounted rates. The best place to look is in the Sunday travel section of any major newspaper (such as *The New York Times*), where many bucket shops place tiny ads. Call quickly, as availability is typically extremely limited. Not all bucket shops are reliable, so insist on a receipt that

gives full details of restrictions, refunds, and tickets, and pay by credit card (in spite of the 2-5% fee) so you can stop payment if you never receive your tickets. For more info, see www.travel-library.com/air-travel/consolidators.html.

CHARTER FLIGHTS

Charters are flights a tour operator contracts with an airline to fly extra loads of passengers during peak season. Charter flights fly less frequently than major airlines, make refunds particularly difficult, and are almost always fully booked. Schedules and itineraries may also change or be cancelled at the last moment (as late as 48hr. before the trip, and without a full refund), and check-in, boarding, and baggage claim are often much slower. However, they can also be cheaper.

Discount clubs and fare brokers offer members savings on last-minute charter and tour deals. Study contracts closely; you don't want to end up with an unwanted overnight layover. **Travelers Advantage** (☎877-259-2691; www.travelersadvantage.com; $10 monthly fee includes discounts and cheap flight directories) specializes in tour and travel packages.

BORDER CROSSINGS

ENTERING THE US BY CAR

If you plan to drive to the US from either Canada or Mexico, you must enter the country through a staffed and open port of entry. Any other entry is illegal and can result in deportation or fines. It is always a bad idea to carry illegal drugs and substances over the border.

FROM CANADA

Crossing into the US from Canada is usually an easy process. However, it can be more difficult depending on who is crossing, what time of day or year it is, and the border guards themselves. There are many crossing points along the US-Canada border, most of which accept both commercial flow and traveler flow. Usually, there is a negligible delay in crossing the border into the US, but some points might be backed up for 10-20min. or more, depending on traffic and weather conditions. For required documents, see **Documents and Formalities,** p. 10. Although it is common to cross the border without incident or delay, it is also possible that border guards will want to check your vehicle or your documents. In an effort to decrease the risk of terrorism, both the US and Canada are tightening security measures and routinely performing more random checks during border crossings.

FROM MEXICO

As with the US-Canada border, there are many crossing points along the US-Mexico border. Mexican citizens entering the US are required to present both a passport and a non-immigrant visa upon entry. US citizens returning to the US from Mexico are technically not required to present a passport, but it is best to do so anyway to avoid delays. Travelers that are not citizens of the US or Mexico need the documentation required to enter the US via air in order to cross the overland border. Delays in crossing the US-Mexico border are generally short, but can be longer depending on traffic conditions. Customs and border patrol officials have the right to conduct random searches upon entry, and tightened security measures make these searches even more common.

GETTING AROUND THE US

BY PLANE

Basic round-trip fares within the US range roughly $80-500. Commercial carriers like American and United will probably offer the most convenient flights, but they may not be the cheapest. You will probably find flying one of the following "no-frills" airlines to be a better deal, if any of their limited departure points is convenient for you. Many of these airlines also offer one-way flights without the high fees imposed by some major airlines, and do not charge extra for travelers who are not staying over a Saturday night.

AirTran (☎800-247-8726; www.airtran.com). Cross-country and regional flights between 40+ US cities, including Atlanta, Boston, Los Angeles, Washington, D.C., and many small local or regional airports.

America West (☎800-327-7810; www.americawest.com). An extensive flight network serving the continental US, Alaska, Hawaii, Canada, and Mexico with destinations concentrated in the western US.

ATA (☎800-435-9282; www.ata.com). Serves over 45 cities in the continental US, Hawaii, Mexico, and the Caribbean.

Frontier (☎800-432-1359; www.frontierairlines.com). Serves an extensive network of cities and smaller airports in the continental US, Alaska, and Mexico.

Independence Air (☎800-359-3594; www.flyi.com). Budget airline servicing 44 destinations nationwide, mostly on the East Coast.

JetBlue (☎800-538-2583; www.jetblue.com). Serves 30+ locations in the US and Puerto Rico.

Song (☎800-359-7664; www.flysong.com). Delta's little sister airline flies a limited schedule within the US and to San Juan, Puerto Rico.

Southwest Airlines (☎800-435-9792; www.southwest.com). Serves 60+ locations within the US.

BY BUS

Buses generally offer the most frequent and complete service between the cities and towns of the US. Often, a bus is the only way to reach smaller locales without a car. In rural areas, however, bus lines tend to be sparse.

GREYHOUND

Greyhound (☎800-231-2222; www.greyhound.com) operates the most routes in the US. Schedule information is available at any Greyhound terminal or agency and on their web page.

Advance Purchase Fares: Reserving space far ahead of time ensures a lower fare, but expect smaller discounts June 5 to Sept. 15. Fares are often lower for 14-day, 7-day, or 3-day advance purchases. Call for up-to-date pricing or check their website.

Discounted Fares: Student Advantage cardholders (15% off); ages 62+ (5% off walk-up fares); military personnel and dependent family members (10% off); Veterans Advantage cardholders (15% off), children under 12 traveling with a full-fare adult (40% off).

Domestic Discovery Passes: US travelers can purchase a pass that allows unlimited travel within the continental US. Passes can be purchased on the Greyhound website. (7-60 days, US$249-689). Child, student, and senior discounts apply.

International Discovery Passes: For travelers from outside North America. Ameripass 4-60 days, US$179-639. Passes can be purchased on the Greyhound website. Child, student, and senior discounts apply.

BY TRAIN

Locomotion is still one of the least expensive (and most pleasant) ways to tour the US, but discounted air travel may be cheaper, and much faster, than train travel. As with airlines, you can save money by purchasing your tickets far in advance, so plan ahead and make reservations early. It is essential to travel light on trains, since many stations will not check luggage. **Amtrak** (☎800-872-7245; www.amtrak.com) provides the only nationwide rail service in the US; round-trip fares usually range $20-500, but check their website for special deals.

BY CAR

The US is most easily traversed by car, and once in the car, by highway. "I" (as in "I-90") refers to interstate highways, "U.S." (as in "U.S. 1") to US highways, and "Rte." (as in "Rte. 7") to state and local highways. There are often local alternatives to highways, which are worth investigating if you have extra time en route.

HOW TO NAVIGATE THE INTERSTATES

In the 1950s, President Dwight D. Eisenhower envisioned a well-organized **interstate highway system.** His dream has been realized: there is now a comprehensive, well-maintained, efficient means of traveling between major cities and between states. Luckily for travelers, the highways are named with an intuitive numbering system. Even-numbered interstates run east-west and odd ones run north-south, decreasing in number toward the south and the west. North-south routes begin on

ESSENTIALS

the West Coast with I-5 and end with I-95 on the East Coast. The southernmost east-west route is I-4 in Florida. The northernmost east-west route is I-94, stretching from Montana to Wisconsin. Three-digit numbers signify branches of other interstates (e.g., I-285 is a branch of I-85) that often skirt around large cities.

RENTING

Having a car will give you far better access to most places in the US. While some cities have excellent public transit, others have none, and it is often difficult to get from place to place without a car. Overall, driving is certainly your best option for seeing the US. The drawbacks of car rentals, however, include steep prices (a compact car rents for $25-45 per day) and high minimum ages for rentals (usually 25). Most branches rent to ages 21 to 24 with an additional fee. A few establishments will rent to those over 18, but it is rare and will almost certainly be accompanied by a hefty fee. When evaluating rental costs it is important to note that cheaper cars tend to be less reliable and harder to handle on difficult terrain. Less expensive 4WD vehicles in particular tend to be more top-heavy, and are more dangerous when navigating especially bumpy roads.

RENTAL AGENCIES

You can generally make reservations before you leave by calling major international offices in your home country. Occasionally, however, the price and availability of information they give isn't the same as what the local offices in your country will tell you. Try checking with both numbers to make sure you get the best price and accurate information. Local desk numbers are included in town listings; for home-country numbers, call your toll-free directory.

Car rental agencies fall into two categories: national companies with hundreds of branches, and local agencies that serve only one city or region. National chains usually allow you to pick up a car in one city and drop it off in another (for a hefty charge). **Alamo** (☎ 800-462-5266; www.alamo.com) rents to ages 21 to 24 with a clean driving record and major credit card for an increased rate. **Enterprise** (☎ 800-261-7331; www.enterprise.com) and **Dollar** (☎ 800-800-3665; www.dollar.com) rent to customers ages 21 to 24, while most, but not all, **Thrifty** (☎ 800-367-2277; www.thrifty.com) locations do likewise for varying surcharges. **Rent-A-Wreck** (☎ 800-944-7501; www.rent-a-wreck.com) specializes in supplying vehicles that are past their prime for lower prices; a bare-bones compact less than eight years old rents for around $30. There may be a charge for a **collision and damage waiver (CDW)**, which usually comes to about $12-15 per day. Major credit cards (including MasterCard and American Express) will sometimes cover the CDW if you use their card to rent a car; call your credit card company for specifics. Most agencies have frequent special rates—be sure to check online or ask the agent before renting.

COSTS

Rental car prices start at around $20-50 a day. Expect to pay more for larger cars and for 4WD. Many rental packages offer unlimited miles, although some do have mileage restrictions. Return the car with a full tank of gas to avoid high fuel charges. Be sure to ask whether the price includes **insurance** against theft and collision. If you are driving a conventional vehicle on an **unpaved road** in a rental car, you are almost never covered by insurance. Insurance plans almost always come with a **deductible.** This means you pay for all damages up to that sum, unless they are the fault of another vehicle. The deductible applies to collisions with other vehicles; collisions with non-vehicles, such as trees, will cost you even more.

AUTO TRANSPORT COMPANIES

These services match drivers with car owners who need cars moved from one city to another. Travelers give the company their desired destination and the company finds a car that needs to go there. Expenses include gas and tolls. Some companies insure their cars; with others, your security deposit covers any breakdowns or damage. You must be over 21, have a valid license, and agree to drive about 400 mi. per day on a fairly direct route. One popular transport company is **Auto Driveaway Co.**, 11 East Adams, Ste. 1402, Chicago, IL 60603 (☎ 800-346-2277; www.autodrive-away.com). Another option is **Across America Driveaway**, 10811 Washington Blvd. #302, Culver City, CA 90232 (☎ 800-677-6686; www.schultz-international.com).

DRIVING PERMITS AND CAR INSURANCE

INTERNATIONAL DRIVING PERMIT (IDP)

If you do not have a license issued by a US state or Canadian province or territory, you might want an **International Driving Permit (IDP)**—it is not required, but may help with police if your license is not written in English. Although the IDP does not require a driving test, you must carry your home license with your IDP at all times. Your IDP, valid for one year, must be issued in your own country before you depart. You must be over 18 to be eligible. An application for an IDP usually requires one or two photos, a current local license, an additional form of identification, and a fee. To apply, contact the national or local branch of your home country's automobile association. Be careful when purchasing an IDP online or anywhere other than your home automobile association. Many vendors sell permits of questionable legitimacy for higher prices.

CAR INSURANCE

Most credit cards cover standard insurance. If you rent, lease, or borrow a car, you may need to certify that you have liability insurance. If you do not have car insurance, most rental companies provide their own basic liability coverage for the duration of the rental.

ON THE ROAD

While driving, be sure to buckle up. ▧**Seatbelts** are required by law in most regions. The **speed limit** in the US varies considerably from region to region. Most urban highways have a 55-65 mph (89kph) limit, while rural routes range from 65 mph (104kph) to 75 mph (120kph). Heed the limit; not only does it save gas, but most local and state police forces make frequent use of radar to catch speed demons. Gasoline prices vary significantly. They are generally much cheaper on the East Coast than on the West, and small, independent stations often offer better prices than national chains. Expect to pay at least $3 per gallon (3.8 liters).

DANGERS

Road conditions vary considerably throughout the country. Some cities have excellent roads, while others have roads riddled with potholes. In rural areas, you may find dirt roads which are considerably slower than paved streets. Watch for signs warning about animal crossings; depending on the region, signs could caution drivers to look for ducks, longhorn, moose, or other animals. Another danger on the road is weather. Depending on the region, snow, ice, sleet, or rain can make driving particularly dangerous. Pay attention to road conditions in bad weather, especially at night, and slow down or pull over if it becomes unsafe to drive.

ESSENTIALS

DRIVING PRECAUTIONS. When traveling in the summer or in the desert, bring substantial amounts of **water** (at least 5L per person per day) for drinking and for the radiator. For long drives to unpopulated areas, register with police before beginning the trek, and again upon arrival at the destination. When traveling long distances, make sure tires are in good repair and have enough air, and get good maps. Since gas stations are harder to come by in rural areas, make sure you have enough gas to get to your destination, or that you know of a station on your route. A **compass** and a **car manual** can also be very useful. You should always carry a **spare tire**, a **jack, jumper cables, extra oil, flares, a flashlight,** and **heavy blankets** (in case your car breaks down at night or in the winter). If you don't know how to **change a tire,** learn before heading out, especially if you are planning on traveling in deserted areas. Blowouts on dirt roads are exceedingly common. If you do have a breakdown, **stay with your car;** if you wander off, there's less likelihood trackers will find you.

CAR ASSISTANCE

Most automobile clubs offer free towing, emergency roadside assistance, travel-related discounts, and random goodies. Travelers should strongly consider membership if planning an extended roadtrip.

American Automobile Association (AAA). Provides 24hr. emergency road service (☎800-222-4357) anywhere in the US. Free trip-planning services, maps, and guidebooks. Free towing and fee-free American Express Travelers Cheques from over 1000 offices across the country and online. Discounts on Hertz car rental (5-20%), Amtrak tickets (10%), and various motel chains and theme parks. Basic membership $48, Associate Membership $12. To sign up, call ☎800-564-6222 or go to www.aaa.com.

BY BICYCLE

U-shaped **Kryptonite** or **Citadel** locks ($30-60) carry insurance against theft for one or two years if your bike is registered with the police. **Bike Nashbar** (☎800-627-4227; www.nashbar.com) sells bike locks and accessories, ships throughout the US and Canada, and will beat any competitor's price. Their tech line (☎800-888-2710; open M-F 6am-8pm EST) fields maintenance questions. The **Adventure Cycling Association,** 150 E. Pine St., P.O. Box 8308, Missoula, MT 59802 (☎800-755-2453; www.adv-cycling.org), is a national, nonprofit organization that researches long-distance routes and organizes bike tours. Annual membership ($33) includes maps, member discounts, and a subscription to *Adventure Cyclist* magazine.

BY THUMB

Let's Go never recommends hitchhiking as a safe means of transportation, and none of the information presented here is intended to do so.

Let's Go strongly urges you to consider the risks before you choose to hitchhike. Hitching means entrusting your life to a stranger and risking assault, sexual harassment, theft, and unsafe driving. For women traveling alone (or even in pairs), hitching is just too dangerous. A man and a woman are a less dangerous combination; two men will have a harder time getting a lift, while three men will go nowhere. In the US, hitchhiking is actually illegal in many states. It is also fairly uncommon; not only is it dangerous to be picked up on the road, but it is unlikely that your hitchhiking attempts will be very successful.

KEEPING IN TOUCH

BY EMAIL AND INTERNET

Though in some places it's possible to forge a remote link with your home server, in most cases this is a much slower (and more expensive) way of checking email than taking advantage of free **web-based email accounts** (e.g., www.hotmail.com and www.yahoo.com). **Internet cafes** and the occasional free Internet terminal at a public library or university are listed in the **Practical Information** sections of major cities. Prices vary by location but are generally around $2-6 per half-hour. For lists of additional cybercafes, check www.netcafeguide.com or www.cybercafes.com.

Increasingly, travelers find that taking their **laptop computers** on the road with them can be a convenient option for staying connected. Laptop users can call an Internet service provider via a modem using long-distance phone cards specifically intended for such calls. They may also find Internet cafes that allow them to connect their laptops to the Internet. And most excitingly, travelers with wireless-enabled computers can take advantage of an increasing number of Internet "hotspots," where they can get online for free or for a small fee. Newer computers can detect these hotspots automatically; websites like www.jiwire.com, www.wi-fihotspotlist.com, www.locfinder.net, and www.wififreespot.com can help you find them. For information on **insuring your laptop** while traveling, see p. 20.

BY TELEPHONE

CALLING HOME FROM THE US

You can usually make **direct international calls** from pay phones, but if you don't have a phone card, you may need to drop your coins as quickly as your words. **Prepaid phone cards** are a relatively inexpensive means of calling abroad. Each one comes with a Personal Identification Number (PIN) and a toll-free access number. You call the access number and then follow the directions for dialing your PIN. To purchase prepaid phone cards, check online for the best rates; www.callingcards.com is a good place to start. Online providers generally send your access number and PIN via email, with no actual "card" involved. You can also call home with phone cards purchased in the US (see **Calling Within the US,** p. 34).

Another option is to purchase a **calling card,** linked to a major national telecommunications service in your home country. Calls are billed collect or to your account. Where available, there are often advantages to purchasing calling cards

---

PLACING INTERNATIONAL CALLS. To call the US from home or to call home from the US, dial:

1. The **international dialing prefix.** To call from **Australia,** dial 0011; **Canada** or the **US,** 011; **Ireland, New Zealand,** or the **UK,** 00.
2. The **country code** of the country you want to call. To call **Australia,** dial 61; **Canada** or the **US,** 1; **Ireland,** 353; **New Zealand,** 64; the **UK,** 44.
3. The **city/area code.** *Let's Go* lists the city/area codes for cities and towns in the US opposite the city or town name, next to a ☎. If the first digit is a zero (e.g., 020 for London), omit the zero when calling from abroad (e.g., dial 20 from the US to reach London).
4. The **local number.**

online, including better rates and immediate access to your account. To call home with a calling card, contact the operator for your service provider in the US by dialing the appropriate toll-free access number.

Placing a **collect call** through an international operator can be quite expensive, but may be necessary in case of an emergency. You can frequently call collect without even possessing a company's calling card just by calling its access number and following the instructions.

CALLING WITHIN THE US

The simplest way to call within the country is to use a coin-operated phone. **Prepaid phone cards** (available at newspaper kiosks and convenience stores), which carry a certain amount of phone time depending on the card's denomination, usually save time and money in the long run. Most prepaid telephone cards come with a PIN and a toll-free access number. Call the access number and follow the directions on the card to check your minutes. These cards can be used to make international as well as domestic calls. Phone rates typically tend to be highest in the morning, lower in the evening, and lowest on Sunday and late at night.

CELLULAR PHONES

While pay phones can be found in almost every city and town in the US, if you already own a cell phone you can avoid the hassle of scrounging up change or a phone card. Cell phone reception is clear and reliable throughout the country, though in remote areas or in the mountains, reception can be spotty; your provider may also slap on additional roaming fees of up to $1.25 per minute. Travelers who already use US cell phones may want to consider upgrading from local to national service plans to avoid long-distance and roaming charges. Call your service provider to check their coverage policies.

The international standard for cell phones is **Global System for Mobile Communication (GSM).** If you want to use a foreign cell phone in the US, you will be able to make and receive calls if your phone is **GSM-compatible.** The downside is that GSM-compatible phones will only get coverage in relatively populated areas and, even then, only if the phone is from North America or a **tri-band** phone. A tri-band phone

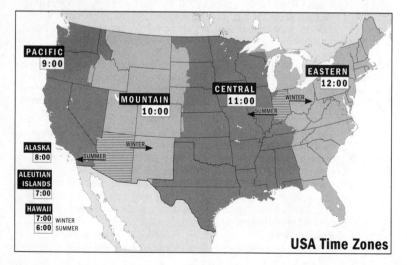

USA Time Zones

allows you to use both European frequencies as well as the North American frequency. You will also need a **SIM (Subscriber Identity Module) card,** a country-specific, thumbnail-sized chip that gives you a local phone number and plugs you into the local network. Many SIM cards are **prepaid,** meaning that they come with calling time included and you don't need to sign up for a monthly service plan. Incoming calls are frequently free. When you use up the prepaid time, you can buy additional cards or vouchers (usually available at convenience stores) to get more. For more information on GSM phones, check out www.telestial.com, www.roadpost.com, or www.planetomni.com. If your cell phone is not GSM-compatible, consider purchasing a cell phone with **prepaid minutes.** Verizon (www.verizonwireless.com) and T-mobile (www.tmobile.com) are well-known cellular providers that offer prepaid plans for a variety of budgets.

TIME DIFFERENCES

Because the US is divided into three different time zones, regions can vary between five and eight hours behind Greenwich Mean Time (GMT). New York, NY is five hours behind GMT, while Los Angeles, CA is eight hours behind. The majority of the US observes **Daylight Saving Time,** with the exception of Arizona (not including the Navajo Reservation) and the Eastern Time portion of Indiana. Clocks change for Daylight Saving at 2am local time.

BY MAIL

Sending a postcard within the US costs $0.23, while sending letters (up to 13 oz.) domestically costs $0.37 for the first ounce and $0.23 for each additional ounce.

SENDING MAIL HOME FROM THE US

Airmail is the best way to send mail home from the US; write "airmail" on the front of the envelope. **Aerogrammes,** printed sheets that fold into envelopes and travel via airmail, are available at most post offices. If regular airmail is too slow, **Federal Express (FedEx)** (☎ 800-247-4747) can get a letter from New York City to Sydney in two business days for a whopping $40. By **US Express Mail,** a letter will arrive within three to five days and will cost $17. **Surface mail** is by far the cheapest and slowest way to send mail. It takes one to two months to cross the Atlantic and one to three to cross the Pacific—good for heavy items you won't need for a while, such as souvenirs or other articles you've acquired along the way that are weighing down your pack. These are standard rates for mail from the US to:

Australia: Allow 4-7 days for regular airmail home. Postcards/aerogrammes cost $0.70. Letters up to 20g cost $1.70; packages up to 0.5kg $19 up to 2kg $33.

Canada: Allow 4-7 days for regular airmail home. Postcards/aerogrammes cost $0.70. Letters up to 20g cost $0.85; packages up to 0.5kg $13, up to 2kg $17.

Ireland: Allow 4-7 days for regular airmail home. Postcards/aerogrammes cost $0.70. Letters up to 20g cost $1.60; packages up to 0.5kg $16, up to 2kg $23.

New Zealand: Allow 4-7 days for regular airmail home. Postcards/aerogrammes cost $0.70. Letters up to 20g cost $1.70; packages up to 0.5kg $16, up to 2kg $30.

UK: Allow 4-7 days for regular airmail home. Postcards/aerogrammes cost $0.70. Letters up to 20g cost $1.60; packages up to 0.5kg $20, up to 2kg $32.

SENDING MAIL TO THE US

To ensure timely delivery of your mail, mark envelopes "airmail" or "par avion." In addition to the standard postage system whose rates are listed below, **Federal Express** (www.fedex.com; Australia ☎ 13 26 10, Canada 800-463-3339, Ireland 1800

535 800, New Zealand 0800 733 339, the UK 0800 123 800) handles express mail services from most countries to the US.

There are several ways to arrange pick-up of letters sent to you while you are abroad. Many hostels and hotels will agree to accept mail for guests; after confirming with your hotel or hostel that this is possible, have mail sent directly to your attention at the establishment's street address. Mail can also be sent via **General Delivery** (Poste Restante) to almost any city or town in the US with a post office, and it is very reliable. Address letters like so:

> Rip Van Winkle
> c/o General Delivery
> Post Office Street Address
> Phoenicia, NY 12464 USA

The mail will go to a special desk in the central post office, unless you specify a post office by street address or postal code. It's best to use the largest post office, since mail may be sent there regardless. It is usually safer and quicker, though more expensive, to send mail express or registered. Bring your passport (or other photo ID) for pick-up. *Let's Go* lists post offices and postal codes in the **Practical Information** section for each city and most towns.

ACCOMMODATIONS

HOSTELS

Many hostels are laid out dorm-style, often with large single-sex rooms and bunk beds, although private rooms that sleep two to four are becoming more common. They sometimes have kitchens and utensils for your use, bike or moped rentals, storage areas, transportation to airports, breakfast and other meals, laundry facilities, and Internet access. There can be drawbacks: some hostels close during certain daytime "lockout" hours, have a curfew, don't accept reservations, impose a maximum stay, or, less frequently, require that you do chores. In the US, a dorm bed in a hostel will average around $15-25 and a private room around $50-65.

> **A HOSTELER'S BILL OF RIGHTS.** There are certain standard features that we do not include in our hostel listings. Unless we state otherwise, you can expect that every hostel has no lockout, no curfew, a kitchen, free hot showers, some system of secure luggage storage, and no key deposit.

HOSTELLING INTERNATIONAL

Joining the youth hostel association in your own country automatically grants you membership privileges in **Hostelling International (HI),** a federation of national hosteling associations. Non-HI members may be allowed to stay in some hostels, but will have to pay extra to do so. HI hostels are scattered throughout the US, and are typically less expensive than private hostels. HI's umbrella organization's website (www.hihostels.com), which lists the web addresses and phone numbers of all national associations, can be a great place to begin researching hosteling in a specific region. Other comprehensive hosteling websites include www.hostelhandbook.com and www.hostels.com.

Most HI hostels also honor **guest memberships**—you'll get a blank card with space for six validation stamps. Each night you'll pay a nonmember supplement (one-sixth the membership fee) and earn one guest stamp; get six stamps and

ESSENTIALS

you're a member. A new membership benefit is the FreeNites program, which allows hostelers to gain points toward free rooms. Most student travel agencies (see p. 25) sell HI cards, as do all of the national hosteling organizations listed below. All prices listed below are valid for **one-year memberships**.

Australian Youth Hostels Association (AYHA), 422 Kent St., Sydney, NSW 200 (☎02 9261 1111; www.yha.com.au). AUS$52, under 18 AUS$19.

Hostelling International-Canada (HI-C), 205 Catherine St. #400, Ottawa, ON K2P 1C3 (☎613-237-7884; www.hihostels.ca). CDN$35, under 18 free.

An Óige (Irish Youth Hostel Association), 61 Mountjoy St., Dublin 7 (☎830 4555; www.irelandyha.org). EUR€20, under 18 EUR€10.

Hostelling International Northern Ireland (HINI), 22-32 Donegall Rd., Belfast BT12 5JN (☎02890 32 47 33; www.hini.org.uk). UK£13, under 18 UK£6.

Youth Hostels Association of New Zealand (YHANZ), Level 1, Moorhouse City, 166 Moorhouse Ave., P.O. Box 436, Christchurch (☎0800 278 299v (NZ only) or 03 379 9970; www.yha.org.nz). NZ$40, under 18 free.

Scottish Youth Hostels Association (SYHA), 7 Glebe Cres., Stirling FK8 2JA (☎01786 89 14 00; www.syha.org.uk). UK£6, under 17 £2.50.

Youth Hostels Association (England and Wales), Trevelyan House, Dimple Rd., Matlock, Derbyshire DE4 3YH (☎08707 708 868; www.yha.org.uk). UK£15.50, under 26 UK£10.

Hostelling International-USA, 8401 Colesville Rd., Ste. 600, Silver Spring, MD 20910 (☎301-495-1240; www.hiayh.org). $28, under 18 free.

> **BOOKING HOSTELS ONLINE.** One of the easiest ways to ensure you've got a bed for the night is by reserving online. Click to the **Hostelworld** booking engine through **www.letsgo.com,** and you'll have access to bargain accommodations from Alaska to Zion National Park with no added commission.

HOTELS

Budget hotel singles in the US cost about $45-70 per night, doubles $90-110. The cheapest options are usually at the generic chains common in most regions. You'll typically have a private bathroom and shower with hot water, although cheaper places may offer a shared bath. If you make reservations in writing, the hotel will send you a confirmation and may request payment for the first night. It is often easiest to make reservations over the phone with a credit card. Check out www.hotels.com and www.all-hotels.com for listings of hotels across the US.

OTHER TYPES OF ACCOMMODATIONS

YMCAS AND YWCAS

Young Men's Christian Association (YMCA) and **Young Women's Christian Association (YWCA)** lodgings are usually cheaper than a hotel but more expensive than a hostel. Not all locations offer lodging; those that do are often located in urban downtowns. Many YMCAs accept women and families; some will not lodge those under 18 without parental permission.

YMCA of the USA, 101 North Wacker Dr., Chicago, IL 60606 (☎888-333-9622 or 800-872-9622; www.ymca.net). Provides a listing of the nearly 1000 Ys across the US and Canada, as well as info on prices and services.

YWCA of the USA, 1015 18th St. NW, Ste. 1100, Washington, DC 20036 (☎202-467-0801 or 800-YWCA-US1; www.ywca.org). Provides a directory of YWCAs across the US.

World Alliance of YMCAs, 12 Clos Belmont, 1208 Geneva, Switzerland (☎+41 22 849 5100; www.ymca.int). Maintains listings of Ys worldwide.

BED AND BREAKFASTS (B&BS)

For a cozy alternative to impersonal hotels, B&Bs (private homes with rooms for travelers) range from the acceptable to the sublime. Rooms in B&Bs generally cost $70-90 for a single and $90-110 for a double in the US. Any number of websites provide listings for B&Bs; check out **Bed & Breakfast Inns Online** (www.bbonline.com), **InnFinder** (www.inncrawler.com), **InnSite** (www.innsite.com), **BedandBreakfast.com** (www.bedandbreakfast.com), **Pamela Lanier's Bed & Breakfast Guide Online** (www.lanierbb.com), or **BNBFinder.com** (www.bnbfinder.com).

UNIVERSITY DORMS

Many **colleges** and **universities** open their residence halls to travelers when school is not in session; some do so even during term-time. Getting a room may take a couple of phone calls and require advanced planning, but rates tend to be very low, and many dorms offer free local calls and Internet access. Some universities that host travelers include the University of Texas in Austin, TX (☎512-476-5678) and Ohio State University in Columbus, OH (☎512-476-5678). Most colleges and universities don't publicize their dorm vacancies, so get started by contacting individual schools in the regions you will be staying.

ESSENTIALS

HOME EXCHANGES AND HOSPITALITY CLUBS

Home exchange offers the traveler various types of homes (houses, apartments, condominiums, villas, even castles in some cases), plus the opportunity to live like a native and to cut down on accommodation fees. For more information, contact **HomeExchange.com**, P.O. Box 787, Hermosa Beach, CA 90254, USA (☎ 800-877-8723; www.homeexchange.com), or Intervac International Home Exchange (☎ 800-756-4663; www.intervac.com).

Hospitality clubs link their members with individuals or families abroad who are willing to host travelers for free or for a small fee to promote cultural exchange and good karma. In exchange, members usually must be willing to host travelers in their own homes; a small membership fee may also be required. **GlobalFreeloaders.com** (www.globalfreeloaders.com) and **The Hospitality Club** (www.hospitality-club.org) are good places to start. **Servas** (www.servas.org) is an established, more formal, peace-based organization, and requires a fee and an interview to join. An Internet search will find many similar organizations, some of which cater to special interests (e.g., women, GLBT travelers, or members of certain professions). As always, use common sense when planning to stay with or host someone you do not know well.

LONG-TERM ACCOMMODATIONS

Travelers planning to stay in the US for extended periods of time may find it most cost-effective to rent an **apartment.** Rent prices vary greatly between different regions and cities within the US: a basic one-bedroom (or studio) apartment in Boston, MA, will cost more than a studio in Des Moines, IA, but a studio in San Francisco, CA or New York City, NY will cost more than a studio in Boston. For most major cities in the US you should expect to pay at least $700-1500 per month. Besides the rent itself, prospective tenants usually are also required to front a security deposit (frequently one month's rent, which is returned after the lease is up) and the last month's rent. Aside from studio apartments, travelers can often find unoccupied bedrooms in multi-bedroom apartments. As long as you don't mind sharing a kitchen or bathroom with other tenants, this is often a cheaper and more convenient way of renting. A good online resource for finding apartment and housing rentals in the US is **www.craigslist.org,** which is free and posts daily listings for most major US cities. Other websites and services match potential roommates.

If you decide to rent a house or an apartment, make sure you have a written agreement or lease, and that you are clear on all of the specifications about your rental. Never sign an agreement that seems questionable and don't deal with landlords that you don't trust. A good way to avoid getting ripped off is to check with the housing department in the city or region in which you are renting for laws and regulations for tenants and landlords.

Another option for shorter stays (2-3 months) is **subletting,** which is popular and often easy in the summer months. Subletting involves making an agreement with the current tenants of a house or apartment to occupy their residence for a set amount of time. Sublets often come with furniture and are much more relaxed than formal lease agreements, which usually are set for a year. Before subletting, make sure that it is legal in your city or region, and make sure that the landlord of the property is aware of the sublet agreement.

Aside from renting an apartment or house, there are many other ways to find long-term housing during stays in the United States. Many hostels, motels, hotels, and YMCAs have long-term options for visitors who wish to stay more than a few nights. Also, homestays often provide a long-term option, whether for school, work, or some other arrangement. For accommodations not arranged through a university or organization, it is best to check newspapers or online lists (like www.craigslist.org) for lodging opportunities.

CAMPING

For those with the proper equipment, camping is one of the least expensive and most enjoyable ways to travel through the US. Camping opportunities are boundless, and many are accessible to inexperienced travelers. Generally, private campgrounds have sites for a small fee and offer safety and security. Well-equipped campsites (usually including prepared tent sites, toilets, and water) go for $10-25 per night in the US. **Backcountry camping,** which lacks all of the above amenities, is often free but can cost up to $20 at some national parks. Most campsites are first come, first served. For more information on outdoor activities in the US, see **The Great Outdoors,** below.

THE GREAT OUTDOORS

The **Great Outdoor Recreation Pages** (www.gorp.com) provides excellent general information for travelers planning on camping or spending time in the outdoors.

USEFUL RESOURCES

A variety of publishing companies offer hiking guidebooks to meet the educational needs of novice or expert. For information about camping, hiking, and biking, write or call the publishers listed below to receive a free catalog.

Family Campers and RVers, 4804 Transit Rd., Bldg. #2, Depew, NY 14043 (☎800-245-9755; www.fcrv.org). Membership ($25) includes *Camping Today* magazine.

Sierra Club Books, 85 Second St., 2nd fl., San Francisco, CA 94105 (☎415-977-5500; www.sierraclub.org). Publishes general resource books on hiking, camping, and backpacking, as well as specific guides on regions and cities in the US.

The Mountaineers Books, 1001 SW Klickitat Way, Ste. 201, Seattle, WA 98134 (☎206-223-6303; www.mountaineersbooks.org). Over 600 titles on hiking, biking, mountaineering, natural history, and conservation.

Wilderness Press, 1200 5th St., Berkeley, CA 94710 (☎800-443-7227 or 510-558-1666; www.wildernesspress.com). Carries over 100 hiking guides and maps for destinations across North America, focusing mainly on the western US.

Woodall Publications Corporation, 2575 Vista Del Mar Dr., Ventura, CA 93001 (☎877-680-6155; www.woodalls.com). Annually updates campground directories and has extensive national parks coverage.

NATIONAL PARKS

National Parks protect some of the most spectacular scenery in North America. Though their primary purpose is preservation, the parks also host recreational activities such as ranger talks, guided hikes, marked trails, skiing, and snowshoe expeditions. For info, contact the **National Park Service,** 1849 C St. NW, Washington, D.C. 20240 (☎202-208-6843; www.nps.gov).

Entrance fees vary. The larger and more popular parks charge a $4-20 entry fee for cars and sometimes a $2-7 fee for pedestrians and cyclists. The **National Parks Pass** ($50), available at park entrances, allows the passport-holder's party entry into all national parks for one year. National Parks Passes can also be purchased by writing to National Park Foundation, P.O. Box 34108, Washington, D.C. 20043 (send $50 plus $3.95 shipping and handling), online at www.nationalparks.org, or by calling ☎888-467-2757. For an additional $15, the Parks Service will affix a **Golden Eagle Passport** hologram to your card, which will allow you access to sites managed by the US Fish and Wildlife Service, the US Forest Service, and the Bureau of Land Management. US citizens or residents over 61 qualify for the **Golden Age Passport** ($10 one-time fee), which entitles the holder's party to free park entry, a 50% discount on camping, and 50% reductions on various recreational fees for the passport holder. Persons eligible for federal benefits on account of disabilities can enjoy the same privileges with the **Golden Access Passport** (free).

Most national parks have both backcountry and developed **camping.** Some welcome RVs, and a few offer grand lodges. At the more popular parks in the US, reservations are essential, available through MISTIX (☎800-365-2267; http://reservations.nps.gov) no more than five months in advance. Indoor accommodations should be reserved months in advance. Campgrounds often observe first come, first served policies; many fill up by late morning.

 LEAVE NO TRACE. *Let's Go* encourages travelers to embrace the "Leave No Trace" ethic, minimizing their impact on natural environments and protecting them for future generations. Trekkers and wilderness enthusiasts should set up camp on durable surfaces, use cookstoves instead of campfires, bury human waste away from water supplies, bag trash and carry it out with them, and respect wildlife and natural objects. For more detailed information, contact the **Leave No Trace Center for Outdoor Ethics,** P.O. Box 997, Boulder, CO 80306 (☎800-332-4100 or 303-442-8222; www.lnt.org).

NATIONAL FORESTS

Often less accessible and less crowded, **US National Forests** (www.fs.fed.us) are a purist's alternative to parks. While some have recreational facilities, most are equipped only for primitive camping—pit toilets and no water are the norm. When charged, entrance fees are $10-20, but camping is generally free or $3-4. Necessary wilderness permits for backpackers can be obtained at the US Forest Service field office in the area. *The Guide to Your National Forests* is available at all Forest Service branches, or call or write the main office (USDA Forest Service, Information Center, 1400 Independence Ave. SW, Washington, D.C. 20250; ☎202-205-8333). This booklet includes a list of all National Forest addresses; request maps and other info directly from the forest(s) you plan to visit. Reservations with varying fees are available for most forests, but are usually only needed during high season at popular sites. Call, up to one year in advance, the National Recreation Reservation Center (☎877-444-6777, international 518-885-3639; www.reserveusa.com).

WILDERNESS SAFETY

Staying **warm, dry,** and **well-hydrated** is key to a happy and safe wilderness experience. For any hike, prepare yourself for an emergency by packing a first-aid kit, a reflector, a whistle, high energy food, extra water, raingear, a hat, mittens, and extra socks. For warmth, wear wool or insulating synthetic materials designed for the outdoors. Cotton is a bad choice since it dries painfully slowly.

Check **weather forecasts** often and pay attention to the skies when hiking, as weather patterns can change suddenly. Always let someone—a friend, your hostel, a park ranger, or a local hiking organization—know when and where you are going. Know your physical limits and do not attempt a hike beyond your ability. See **Safety and Health,** p. 18, for information on outdoor medical concerns.

WILDLIFE

BEARS. The US is home to two species of bear, the brown bear (also called the grizzly bear) and the black bear. Grizzlies prefer semi-open spaces in mountainous areas, while black bears stick to forested regions. If you see a bear, calmly walk (don't run) in the other direction. The best way to avoid danger is to completely avoid the bear—bears will attack if they are surprised, threatened, or protecting their territory or cubs. Sing or talk loudly on the trail and hike in groups, if possible. If the black bear charges or attacks, the National Forest Service recommends that you stand your ground and fight back. For grizzly bears, the protocol for encounters is different. If you encounter a grizzly bear, the National Forest Service recommends that you play dead. Curl up in a ball facing downward, use your hands and arms to protect the back of your neck and face, and keep your pack on for added protection. Do not move or make noise until you are sure the bear has left the area. See the National Forest Service bear safety page at http://www.fs.fed.us/r1/wildlife/igbc/Safety/cwi/menu.htm for more information.

To avoid attracting bears, don't leave food or other scented items (trash, toiletries, the clothes that you cooked in) near your tent. Putting these objects into canisters is now mandatory in some national parks. **Bear-bagging,** hanging edibles and other good-smelling objects from a tree out of reach of hungry paws, is the best way to keep your toothpaste from becoming a condiment. Bears are also attracted to any **perfume,** as are bugs, so cologne, scented soap, deodorant, and hairspray should stay at home.

SNAKES. Poisonous snakes are hazards in many wilderness areas in the US and Canada and should be carefully avoided. The two most dangerous are coral snakes and rattlesnakes. Coral snakes reside in the Southwestern US and can be identified by black, yellow, and red bands. Rattlesnakes live in desert and marsh areas, and will shake the rattle at the end of their tail when threatened. Don't attempt to handle or kill a snake; if you see one, back away slowly. If you are bitten, clean the wound immediately, apply a pressure bandage, keep the wound below the heart to slow the flow of venom through the blood stream, and immobilize the limb. Do not attempt to suck the venom out with your mouth and do not ice the wound—studies have shown that cooling the wound makes it more difficult to extract the venom. Seek immediate medical attention for any snakebite that breaks the skin.

MOOSE. Mountain regions in the north are stomping grounds for moose. These big, antlered animals have been known to charge humans, so never feed or walk toward a moose. If a moose charges, get behind a tree immediately and raise your arms in the air with your fingers spread (but don't wave them) so that you appear larger. If the moose attacks you, curl up in the fetal position on the ground, cover your head with your arms, and stay still.

MOSQUITOES. While mosquitoes are certainly not as dangerous as bears or snakes, they can be a camper's main source of agony. Though these creatures start cropping up in spring, the peak season in the US runs June-August before tapering off at the approach of fall. Be especially careful around damp or swampy areas and at dawn and dusk. Mosquitoes can bite through thin fabric, so cover up as much as possible with thicker materials. 100% DEET is useful, but mosquitoes can be so ravenous that nothing short of a mosquito hood and netting really stops every jab.

CAMPING AND HIKING EQUIPMENT

WHAT TO BUY

Good camping equipment is both sturdy and light. North American suppliers tend to offer the most competitive prices.

Sleeping Bags: Most sleeping bags are rated by season; "summer" means 30-40°F (around 0°C) at night; "four-season" or "winter" often means below 0°F (-17°C). Bags are made of **down** (warm and light, but expensive, and miserable when wet) or of **synthetic** material (heavy, durable, and warm when wet). Prices range $50-250 for a summer synthetic to $200-300 for a good down winter bag. **Sleeping bag pads** include foam pads ($10-30), air mattresses ($15-50), and self-inflating mats ($30-120). Bring a **stuff sack** to store your bag and keep it dry.

Tents: The best tents are free-standing (with their own frames and suspension systems), set up quickly, and only require staking in high winds. Low-profile dome tents are the best all-around. Worthy 2-person tents start at $100, 4-person at $160. Make sure your tent has a rain fly and seal its seams with waterproofer. Other useful accessories include a **battery-operated lantern,** a plastic **groundcloth,** and a nylon **tarp.**

Backpacks: Internal-frame packs mold well to your back, keep a lower center of gravity, and flex adequately to allow you to hike difficult trails, while **external-frame packs** are more comfortable for long hikes over even terrain, as they carry weight higher and distribute it more evenly. Make sure your pack has a strong, padded hip-belt to transfer weight to your legs. There are models designed specifically for women. Any serious backpacking requires a pack of at least 4000 in^3 (16,000cc), plus 500 in^3 for sleeping bags in internal-frame packs. Sturdy backpacks cost anywhere from $125-420—your pack is an area where it doesn't pay to economize. On your hunt for the perfect pack, fill up prospective models with something heavy, strap it on correctly, and walk around the store to get a sense of how the model distributes weight. Either buy a **rain cover** ($10-20) or store all of your belongings in plastic bags inside your pack.

Boots: Be sure to wear hiking boots with good **ankle support.** They should fit snugly and comfortably over 1-2 pairs of **wool socks** and a pair of thin **liner socks.** Break in boots over several weeks before you go to spare yourself blisters.

Other Necessities: Synthetic layers, like those made of polypropylene or polyester, and a pile jacket will keep you warm even when wet. A **space blanket** ($5-15) will help you to retain body heat and doubles as a groundcloth. Plastic **water bottles** are vital; look for shatter- and leak-resistant models. Carry **water-purification tablets** for when you can't boil water. Although most campgrounds provide campfire sites, you may want to bring a small **metal grate** or **grill.** For those places that forbid fires or the gathering of firewood, you'll need a **camp stove** (the classic Coleman starts at $50) and a propane-filled **fuel bottle** to operate it. Also bring a **first-aid kit, pocketknife, insect repellent,** and **waterproof matches** or a **lighter.**

WHERE TO BUY IT

The online/mail-order companies listed below offer lower prices than many retail stores. A visit to a local camping or outdoors store will give you a good sense of the look and weight of certain items before you buy.

Campmor, 28 Parkway, P.O. Box 700, Upper Saddle River, NJ 07458, USA (☎800-525-4784; www.campmor.com).

Cotswold Outdoor, Unit 11 Kemble Business Park, Crudwell, Malmesbury Wiltshire, SN16 9SH, UK (☎08704 427 755; www.cotswoldoutdoor.com).

Discount Camping, 880 Main North Rd., Pooraka, South Australia 5095, Australia (☎08 8262 3399; www.discountcamping.com.au).

Eastern Mountain Sports (EMS), 1 Vose Farm Rd., Peterborough, NH 03458, USA (☎888-463-6367; www.ems.com).

Gear-Zone, 8 Burnet Rd., Sweetbriar Rd. Industrial Estate, Norwich, NR3 2BS, UK (☎1603 410 108; www.gear-zone.co.uk).

L.L. Bean, Freeport, ME 04033, USA (US and Canada ☎800-441-5713; UK 0800 891 297; www.llbean.com).

Mountain Designs, 443a Nudgee Rd., Hendra, Queensland 4011, Australia (☎07 3856 2344; www.mountaindesigns.com).

Recreational Equipment, Inc. (REI), Sumner, WA 98352, USA (US and Canada ☎800-426-4840, elsewhere 253-891-2500; www.rei.com).

CAMPERS AND RVS

Much to the chagrin of outdoors purists, the US is a haven for the corpulent homes-on-wheels known as **recreational vehicles (RVs).** Renting an RV costs more than tent camping or hosteling but less than staying in hotels while renting a car (see **Rental Cars,** p. 29). The convenience of bringing along your own bedroom, bathroom, and kitchen makes RVing an attractive option, especially for older travelers and families with children. Rates vary widely by region, season (July and August are the most expensive months), and type of RV. Rental prices for a standard RV are about $800 per week. **Cruise America,** 11 West Hampton Ave., Mesa, AZ 85210 (US ☎800-327-7799, elsewhere 480-464-7300; www.cruiseamerica.com), rents and sells RVs at 135 locations in the US and Canada.

ORGANIZED ADVENTURE TRIPS

Organized adventure tours offer another way of exploring the wild. Activities include hiking, biking, skiing, canoeing, kayaking, rafting, climbing, photo safaris, and archaeological digs. State or local tourism bureaus can often suggest parks, trails, and outfitters. Organizations that specialize in camping and outdoor equipment like REI and EMS (p. 46) also are good sources for info.

Specialty Travel Index, P.O. Box 458, San Anselmo, CA 94979 (US ☎888-624-4030, elsewhere 415-455-1643; fax 455-1648; www.specialtytravel.com).

TrekAmerica, P.O. Box 189, Rockaway, NJ 07866 (US ☎800-221-0596 or 973-983-1144, elsewhere +44 01295 256 777; www.trekamerica.com). Operates tours in the western US, including the Southwest, the Pacific Northwest, and California.

The National Outdoor Leadership School (NOLS), 284 Lincoln St., Lander, WY 82520 (☎800-710-6657; www.nols.edu). Offers educational wilderness trips all over the world, including many in the US. They also offer courses in wilderness medicine training and leave-no-trace ethics.

Outward Bound, 100 Mystery Point Rd., Garrison, NY 10524 (☎866-467-7651; www.outwardboundwilderness.com). Offers expeditionary courses in outdoor education throughout the US. Courses range from several days to over 40 days, and include special focuses, such as life and career renewal and trips for couples.

The Sierra Club, 85 2nd St., 2nd fl., San Francisco, CA 94105 (☎415-977-5522; www.sierraclub.org/outings), plans adventure outings at its branches throughout the US.

SPECIFIC CONCERNS

SUSTAINABLE TRAVEL

As the number of travelers on the road continues to rise, the detrimental effect they can have on natural environments becomes an increasing concern. With this in mind, *Let's Go* promotes the philosophy of **sustainable travel.** Through sensitivity to issues of ecology and sustainability, today's travelers can be a powerful force in preserving and restoring the places they visit.

Ecotourism, a rising trend in sustainable travel, focuses on the conservation of natural habitats and using them to build up the economy without exploitation or overdevelopment. Travelers can make a difference by doing advance research and by supporting organizations and establishments that pay attention to their impact on their natural surroundings and strive to be environmentally friendly. Consult www.planeta.com and www.earthfoot.org for info about ecotourism and links to related reading. For more information on ecotourism in the United States, see **Beyond Tourism,** p. 77.

RESPONSIBLE TRAVEL

The impact of tourist dollars on the destinations you visit should not be underestimated. The choices you make during your trip can have potent effects on local communities—for better or for worse. Travelers who care about the destinations and environments they explore should become aware of the social and cultural implications of the choices they make when they travel. Simple decisions such as buying local products instead of globally-available products and paying a fair price for the product or service can have a strong, positive effect on the community.

ESSENTIALS

ESSENTIALS

> **ECOTOURISM RESOURCES.** For more information on environmentally responsible tourism, contact one of the organizations below:
> **The Centre for Environmentally Responsible Tourism** (www.c-e-r-t.org).
> **Conservation International** (www.conservation.org).
> **Green Globe 21** (☎+61 2 6257 9102; www.greenglobe21.com/Travel-lers.aspx).
> **International Ecotourism Society,** 733 15th St. NW, Washington, D.C. 20005, USA (☎202-347-9203; www.ecotourism.org).
> **United Nations Environment Program** (**UNEP;** ☎+33 1 44 37 14 41; www.uneptie.org/pc/tourism).

Community-based tourism aims to channel tourist dollars into the local economy by emphasizing tours and cultural programs that are run by members of the host community and that often benefit disadvantaged groups. This type of tourism also benefits the tourists themselves, as these tours often take them beyond the traditional tours of the region. An excellent resource for general information on community-based travel is *The Good Alternative Travel Guide* (UK£10), a project of **Tourism Concern** (☎+44 020 7133 3330; www.tourismconcern.org.uk).

TRAVELING ALONE

There are many benefits to traveling alone, including independence and greater interaction with locals. On the other hand, any solo traveler is a more vulnerable target of harassment and street theft. As a lone traveler, try not to stand out as a tourist, look confident, and be especially careful in deserted or very crowded areas. Stay away from areas that are not well-lit. If questioned, never admit that you are traveling alone. Maintain regular contact with someone at home who knows your itinerary, and always research your destination before traveling. For more tips, pick up *Traveling Solo* by Eleanor Berman (Globe Pequot Press, US$18), visit www.travelaloneandloveit.com, or subscribe to **Connecting: Solo Travel Network,** 689 Park Rd., Unit 6, Gibsons, BC V0N 1V7, Canada (☎800-557-1757; www.cstn.org; membership US$30-55).

WOMEN TRAVELERS

Women exploring on their own inevitably face some additional safety concerns, but it's easy to be adventurous without taking undue risks. If you are concerned, consider staying in hostels that offer single rooms that lock from the inside or in religious organizations with rooms for women only. Stick to centrally located accommodations and avoid solitary late-night treks or metro rides.

Always carry extra money for a phone call, bus, or taxi. **Hitchhiking** is never safe for lone women, or even for two women traveling together. Look as if you know where you're going and approach older women or couples for directions if you're lost or uncomfortable.

Generally, the less you look like a tourist, the better off you'll be. Dress conservatively, especially in rural areas. Wearing a conspicuous **wedding band** sometimes helps to prevent unwanted overtures. Your best answer to verbal harassment is no answer at all; feigning deafness, sitting motionless, and staring straight ahead at nothing in particular will do a world of good that reactions usually don't achieve. The extremely persistent can sometimes be dissuaded by a firm, loud, and very public "Go away!" Don't hesitate to seek out a police officer or a passerby if you are being harassed. Call ☎**911** if you ever find yourself in an emergency situation. A self-defense course will both prepare you for a potential attack and raise your level of awareness of your surroundings (see **Self Defense**, p. 20). Also be sure you are aware of the health concerns that women face when traveling (see p. 24).

GLBT TRAVELERS

American cities are generally accepting of all sexualities, and thriving gay, lesbian, bisexual, and transgendered (GLBT) communities can be found in most cosmopolitan areas. Most college towns are GLBT-friendly as well. Still, homophobia is not uncommon, particularly in rural areas. To avoid unwanted attention in rural areas, refrain from public displays of affection. *Let's Go* includes local GLBT info lines and community centers when available.

To avoid hassles at airports and border crossings, transgendered travelers should make sure that all of their travel documents consistently report the same gender. Many countries (including Australia, Canada, Ireland, New Zealand, the UK, and the US) will amend the passports of post-operative transsexuals to reflect their true gender, although governments are generally less willing to amend documents for pre-operative transsexuals and other transgendered individuals.

Listed below are contact organizations, mail-order bookstores, and publishers that offer materials addressing some specific concerns. **Out and About** (www.planetout.com) offers a weekly newsletter and a comprehensive site addressing gay travel concerns. The online newspaper **365gay.com** also has a travel section (www.365gay.com/travel/travelchannel.htm).

> **FURTHER READING: GLBT.**
>
> *Spartacus 2004-2005: International Gay Guide.* Bruno Gmunder Verlag (US$33).
>
> *Damron Men's Travel Guide, Damron Road Atlas, Damron Accommodations Guide, Damron City Guide,* and *Damron Women's Traveller.* Damron Travel Guides (US$18-24). For info, call ☎800-462-6654 or visit www.damron.com.
>
> *Ferrari Guides' Gay Travel A to Z, Ferrari Guides' Men's Travel in Your Pocket, Ferrari Guides' Women's Travel in Your Pocket,* and *Ferrari Guides' Inn Places.* Ferrari Publications (US$16-20).
>
> *The Gay Vacation Guide: The Best Trips and How to Plan Them,* Mark Chesnut. Kensington Books (US$15).
>
> *Gayellow Pages USA/Canada,* Frances Green. Gayellow Pages (US$16). They also publish smaller regional editions. Visit Gayellow pages online at www.gayellowpages.com.

Gay's the Word, 66 Marchmont St., London WC1N 1AB, UK (☎+44 020 7278 7654; www.gaystheword.co.uk). The largest gay and lesbian bookshop in the UK, with both fiction and non-fiction titles. Mail-order service available.

Giovanni's Room, 1145 Pine St., Philadelphia, PA 19107 (☎215-923-2960; www.queerbooks.com). An international lesbian/feminist and gay bookstore with mail-order service (carries many of the publications listed below).

International Lesbian and Gay Association (ILGA), ☎+32 2 502 2471; www.ilga.org). Provides political information, such as homosexuality laws of individual countries.

TRAVELERS WITH DISABILITIES

Federal law dictates that all public buildings in the US should be wheelchair accessible, and laws governing building codes make disabled access more the norm than the exception. However, traveling with a disability still requires planning.

Those with disabilities should inform airlines and hotels of their disabilities when making reservations; some time may be needed to prepare accommodations. Call ahead to restaurants, museums, and other facilities to find out if they are handicapped accessible. Visiting rugged parks may be difficult or impossible if you have severe disabilities, but many parks do have handicapped-accessible trails.

In the US, both Amtrak and major airlines will accommodate disabled passengers if notified at least 72hr. in advance. Amtrak offers a 15% discount to physically disabled travelers (☎800-872-7245). Greyhound buses will provide a 50% discount for a companion if the ticket is purchased at least three days in advance. If you are without a fellow traveler, call Greyhound (☎800-752-4841, TDD 800-345-3109) at least two days before you plan to leave and they will make arrangements to assist you. For information on transportation availability in individual US cities, contact the local chapter of the **Easter Seal Society** (☎800-221-6827; www.easter-seals.org).

Certified **guide dogs** entering the US must have originated from or lived for six months in an area that is free from rabies (including Australia, Canada, Ireland, New Zealand, and the UK), or they must have unexpired vaccination certificates. For a list of rabies-free areas, see http://www.cdc.gov/travel/diseases/rabies.htm. In all areas in the US, guide dogs are legally allowed, free of charge, on public transit and in all "public establishments," including hotels, restaurants, and stores.

If you are planning to visit a national park or attraction in the US run by the National Park Service, obtain a free **Golden Access Passport,** which is available at all park entrances and from federal offices whose functions relate to land, forests, or wildlife. The passport entitles disabled travelers and their families to free park admission and provides a lifetime 50% discount on all campsite and parking fees.

USEFUL ORGANIZATIONS

Accessible Journeys, 35 West Sellers Ave., Ridley Park, PA 19078, USA (☎800-846-4537; www.disabilitytravel.com). Designs tours for wheelchair users and slow walkers. The site has tips and forums for all travelers.

The Guided Tour Inc., 7900 Old York Rd., Ste. 114B, Elkins Park, PA 19027 (☎800-783-5841; www.guidedtour.com). Organizes travel programs for persons with developmental and physical challenges in Canada and the US.

Mobility International USA (MIUSA), P.O. Box 10767, Eugene, OR 97440 (☎541-343-1284; www.miusa.org). Provides a variety of books and other publications containing information for travelers with disabilities.

Society for Accessible Travel and Hospitality (SATH), 347 Fifth Ave., Ste. 610, New York, NY 10016 (☎212-447-7284; www.sath.org). An advocacy group that publishes free online travel information and the travel magazine *OPEN WORLD* (annual subscription $13, free for members). Annual membership $45, students and seniors $30.

MINORITY TRAVELERS

The US is a multicultural nation, but general attitudes toward race relations in the US differ from region to region. Racial and ethnic minorities sometimes face blatant or subtle discrimination and/or harassment. Remain calm and report individuals to a supervisor and establishments to the **Better Business Bureau** for the region (www.bbb.org, or call the operator for local listings); contact the police in extreme situations. *Let's Go* always welcomes reader input regarding discriminating establishments. Be aware that racial tensions do exist, even in large, ostensibly progressive areas, and try to avoid confrontations.

In towns along the US-Mexican border, the **Border Patrol** for the US Immigration and Naturalization Service (INS) remains on a constant lookout for Mexican

ESSENTIALS

nationals who have crossed the border illegally. In border towns, they may pull over anyone who looks suspicious, search their vehicles for smuggled goods or people, and ask for identification.

FURTHER RESOURCES

United States Department of Justice (www.usdoj.gov/civilliberties.htm).

Go Girl! The Black Woman's Book of Travel and Adventure, Elaine Lee. Eighth Mountain Press ($18).

The African-American Travel Guide, Wayne Robinson. Hunter Publishing ($10).

DIETARY CONCERNS

Vegetarians should have an array of options in most parts of the country, especially along the veggie-friendly West Coast. *Let's Go* often indicates vegetarian options in restaurant listings; other places to look for vegetarian and vegan cuisine are local health food stores, as well as large natural food chains such as ⊠**Trader Joe's** and **Wild Oats.** Vegan options may be more difficult to find in smaller towns; be prepared to make your own meals. The travel section of the The Vegetarian Resource Group's website, at www.vrg.org/travel, has a comprehensive list of organizations and websites that are geared toward helping traveling vegetarians and vegans. For more information, visit your local bookstore or health food store, and consult *The Vegetarian Traveler: Where to Stay if You're Vegetarian, Vegan, or Environmentally Sensitive,* by Jed and Susan Civic (Larson Publications; $16), or *Vegetarian Restaurants & Natural Food Stores in the US: A Comprehensive*

Guide to Over 2500 Vegetarian Eateries, by John Howley (Torchlight Publications; $20). Vegetarians will also find numerous resources on the web; try www.vegdining.com, www.happycow.net, and www.vegetariansabroad.com.

Travelers who keep **kosher** should contact synagogues in larger cities for information on kosher restaurants. Your own synagogue or college Hillel should have access to lists of Jewish institutions across the nation. Search for kosher restaurants by state, city, or category at www.shamash.org/kosher. If you are strict in your observance, you may have to prepare your own food on the road. A good resource is the *Jewish Travel Guide*, edited by Michael Zaidner (Vallentine Mitchell; US$18). Travelers looking for **halal** restaurants may find www.zabihah.com a useful resource.

OTHER RESOURCES

Let's Go tries to cover all aspects of budget travel, but we can't put *everything* in our guides. Listed below are books and websites that can serve as jumping-off points for your own research.

USEFUL PUBLICATIONS

The Road Atlas United States 2005, Rand McNally ($20). For more info, visit www.Rand-McNally.com.

The Next Exit: The Most Complete Interstate Highway Guide Ever Printed, edited by Mark T. Watson ($13).

Colman National Forest Campground & Recreation Directory. Our Forests ($20).

American Ways: A Guide for Foreigners in the United States, Gary Althen, Amanda R. Doran, and Susan J. Szmania ($25).

Speak American: A Survival Guide to the Language and Culture of the USA, Dileri Dorunda Johnston ($8).

America Bizarro: A Guide to Freaky Festivals, Groovy Gatherings, Kooky Contests, and Other Strange Happenings Across the USA, Nelson Taylor ($15).

Eat Your Way Across the USA, Jane and Michael Stern ($15).

Hip Hotels USA, Herbert Ypma ($30).

WORLD WIDE WEB

Almost every aspect of budget travel is accessible via the web. In 10min. at the keyboard, you can make a hostel reservation, get advice on travel hotspots from other travelers, or find out how much a train from Denver to Detroit costs.

Listed here are some travel-related sites to start off your surfing; other relevant websites are listed throughout the book. Because website turnover is high, use search engines (such as www.google.com) to do some research of your own.

 WWW.LETSGO.COM *Let's Go's* website features a wealth of information and valuable advice at your fingertips. It offers excerpts from all our guides as well as monthly features on new hotspots in the most popular destinations. In addition to our online bookstore, we have great deals on everything from airfares to cell phones. Our resources section is full of information you'll need before you hit the road, and our forums are buzzing with advice from other travelers. Check back often to see constant updates, exciting new tips, and prize giveaways. See you soon!

THE ART OF TRAVEL

BootsnAll.com: www.bootsnall.com. Numerous resources for independent travelers, from planning your trip to reporting on it when you get back.

How to See the World: www.artoftravel.com. A compendium of great travel tips, from cheap flights to self defense to interacting with local culture.

Travel Intelligence: www.travelintelligence.net. A large collection of travel writing by distinguished travel writers.

Travel Library: www.travel-library.com. A fantastic set of links for general information and personal travelogues.

World Hum: www.worldhum.com. An independently produced collection of "travel dispatches from a shrinking planet."

INFORMATION ON THE USA

Atevo Travel: www.atevo.com/guides/destinations. Detailed introductions, travel tips, and suggested itineraries.

CIA World Factbook: www.odci.gov/cia/publications/factbook/index.html. Tons of vital statistics on the US's geography, government, economy, and people.

Geographia: www.geographia.com. Highlights, culture, and people of the US.

PlanetRider: www.planetrider.com. A subjective list of links to the "best" websites covering the culture and tourist attractions of the US.

World Travel Guide: www.travel-guides.com. Helpful practical info.

ESSENTIALS

LIFE AND TIMES

HISTORY

10,000 BC
The first Americans arrive in North America via the Bering Strait.

WATER UNDER THE BRIDGE. Archaeologists believe that the first inhabitants of the Americas crossed the Bering Sea from Siberia by a **land bridge** during the last Ice Age—about 12,000 years ago. Scientists have raised different theories to explain this migration, such as the pursuit of nomadic bison, a shift in living conditions in Asia, and simply a desire to explore. Whatever the reason, the Asiatic migrators gradually came to inhabit all corners of their new continent. The earliest Native American cultures were nomadic and flourished as they followed **megafauna** (giant mammals similar to today's horses, armadillos, and lions). Starting around AD 200, the ancestors of today's Pueblos fostered advanced civilizations; ruins are visible in the Anasazi Great Houses of **Chaco Canyon** (p. 850).

1499 AD
Nice name! Amerigo Vespucci explores the continents that will soon bear his name.

A BRAVE NEW WORLD. Though no one is certain, it is likely that the earliest Europeans to arrive in America did so accidentally, their ships blown off course by storms. Textbooks place the discovery of the Americas in 1492, when **Christopher Columbus,** an Italian explorer, found his voyage to the East blocked by Hispaniola in the Caribbean Sea. Thinking he had reached the Spice Islands of the East Indies, he dubbed the inhabitants "Indians." Columbus's arrival marked the beginning of European conquest, which, in addition to establishing what would become a permanent European presence in the New World, brought disease and death to Native Americans.

1584-1590
Hide and Seek: The colonists at Roanoke, off the coast of South Carolina, mysteriously disappear.

In the centuries after Columbus's voyage, Europeans rushed to the New World in search of gold and silver, prestige for themselves and their country, and in some cases, religious freedom. The Spanish expanded into the southern and southwestern regions of the US, while the French and Dutch created more modest empires to the north. The English settled the New World's east coast, and after a few failed attempts, established a successful colony at **Jamestown** (p. 293) in 1607. Their prosperity and growth hinged on an indigenous plant called tobacco, a product that gained instant popularity in England. In the years after 1620, the **Puritans,** religious separatists who had been persecuted by the Presbyterian majority in England, fled to present-day Massachusetts.

REVOLUTION AND INDEPENDENCE. In order to protect her holdings in the Americas from an impending French influence, Britain entered the **French and Indian War** in 1754 and fought a number of battles against the allied French and Native Americans. The British ultimately triumphed, but their victory increased the irrelevance of Britain's power in the Americas as the colonists no longer needed British protection from the

LIFE AND TIMES

French. Furthermore, the struggle more than doubled Britain's government expenditures and British leaders decided to shift responsibility onto the American colonists, who had previously been taxed lightly. The new taxes angered colonists, who rallied against "taxation without representation." Colonial committees created the **First Continental Congress,** which attempted to convince England of their rights. Tensions peaked in 1773 when patriots in Boston staged the **Boston Tea Party,** dumping over 10,000 pounds of tea into Boston Harbor to protest unfair tea taxation. This marked the beginning of violence between Great Britain and the colonies and led to the Second Continental Congress. This Congress prepared the colonies for the war, which officially began in 1775 after the battles of Lexington and Concord. In 1776, **Thomas Jefferson** drafted the **Declaration of Independence,** and **July 4th,** the date on which the declaration was adopted, remains America's most important non-religious national holiday. Fighting continued for the next eight years throughout the Eastern seaboard. In October 1781, outnumbered and surrounded by the colonial rebels, the British surrendered, ending the **Revolutionary War** and finally granting the colonists their own country.

THE CONSTITUTION, PROTECTOR OF FREEDOM. In 1787 the state legislatures of the original 13 states sent 55 delegates to draft what was to become the **Constitution.** The **Bill of Rights,** a set of 10 constitutional amendments which were passed shortly after the Constitution, has remained a cornerstone of the American political system. This document includes the rights to freedom of speech, freedom of the press, and freedom of religion. When the Constitution was ratified, **George Washington,** the former Commander-in-Chief of the Continental Army and a key participant in the Constitutional Convention, was unanimously elected the first President of the United States.

MANIFEST DESTINY. After Jefferson was elected third President of the US, he purchased the **Louisiana Territory** from Napoleon in 1803 for less than $0.03 an acre. This sprawling landmass stretched south from Montana to Louisiana and west from the Mississippi River to the Rocky Mountains. The next year, Jefferson sent **Meriwether Lewis** and **William Clark** to explore the territory and find a river route to the Pacific Ocean. Lewis and Clark never found a waterway linking the oceans, but they did chart the vast land west of the Mississippi. In the decades that followed, droves of people moved west along the grueling **Oregon Trail** in search of a new life. Over 40,000 prospectors traveled to California between 1848 and 1849 in a migration now known as the **Gold Rush.**

When the independent Republic of Texas (formerly part of Mexico) became a US state in 1845, President James Polk decided to expand further into Mexican territory. The tension that resulted from the Texas War of Independence against Mexico and Polk's designs on Mexico's territory led to the **Mexican-American War.** American soldiers successfully offered protection from Native Americans in exchange for surrender. Mexican troops were forced to capitulate when US troops invaded

1692
Toil and trouble: Witch trials terrorize Salem, MA.

1773
Costume party? Dressed as Mohawk Indians, colonists dump British tea into the harbor in the Boston Tea Party.

July 4, 1776
The Declaration of Independence, written by Thomas Jefferson, is signed by the Continental Congress.

1803
You bought what?! Thomas Jefferson purchases the Louisiana territory for $0.03 per acre. Lewis and Clark head west to explore America's new territory.

LIFE AND TIMES

LIFE AND TIMES

1838
The US government forces Cherokee Indians to leave their homes and march west on the Trail of Tears.

1848
Girl power: Elizabeth Cady Stanton, Lucretia Mott, and others give new meaning to women's rights at the Seneca Falls Convention.

1849
"Go-ald!" Gold Rush fever hits California and lures settlers west.

1860
Eleven southern states secede from the Union and form the Confederate States of America.

Mexico City. The treaty that ended the war in February 1848 granted the US nearly two-fifths of Mexico's territory, including New Mexico, California, Nevada, Utah, most of Arizona and Colorado, and parts of Wyoming, Kansas, and Oklahoma.

The **Homestead Act** of 1862 prompted the cultivation of the Great Plains by distributing government land to those who would farm and live on it. This large-scale settlement led to bloody battles with the Sioux, Hunkpapas, and Cheyenne Native American tribes who had long inhabited the Plains. From 1866 to 1891 conflicts with Native Americans raged, leading to the **Allotment Act** of 1891, which established Native American land reservations to end the fighting.

SLAVERY IN THE NEW WORLD. The first **Africans** were brought to America in 1619 on a Dutch slave ship that landed in Jamestown, VA. As the demand for cheap labor increased from the late 1500s into the 1600s, white settlers invaded Native American communities looking for slaves. Native Americans, however, suffered fatally from European diseases, so colonial America relied on African slaves to fill the gap. Thousands of Africans were forced across the Atlantic to be auctioned off in the US, a harrowing journey known as the **Middle Passage.** This lasted until 1808, when the slave trade was abolished. Slave ownership, however, continued until the mid-19th century.

Slavery exacerbated existing ideological differences between the North and the South. The South's economy was based on agriculture driven by slave labor, while the North was far more industrialized and technologically advanced. Because the federal government was designed to be relatively weak in order to prevent the "tyranny" of pre-Revolution days, each state could decide to allow or prohibit slavery independently. As the Northern states became more insistent that territories and new states should be kept free of slavery, the Southern states counteracted by citing the Revolutionary ideal of each state's right to self-determination. Northern abolitionists joined with free African-Americans to form the **Underground Railroad,** an escape route in which "conductors" secretly transported slaves into the free Northern states. Southern slave-owners often chased slaves down in an attempt to reclaim their "property," further fueling tensions between the North and South. It would take a fierce, bloody conflict to decide which region would prevail.

"A HOUSE DIVIDED": THE CIVIL WAR. Tensions between the North and South came to a head when **Abraham Lincoln,** an anti-slavery Congressman from Illinois, was elected President in 1860. In response, South Carolina, a hotbed of pro-slavery sentiment, seceded from the Union and was followed by 10 other Southern states. These rebellious states quickly united as the **Confederate States of America** under the presidency of Jefferson Davis. Lincoln, however, refused to accept the secession, setting the stage for war. On April 12, 1861, Southern troops fired on Fort Sumter in the harbor of Charleston, SC, and the **Civil War** began. For four years the country endured a savage, bloody conflict. Lincoln led the Union to eventual victory, but the price was high; the war claimed more American lives than any other conflict in US history. Lincoln was assassinated on April 14, 1865, by a Southern sympathizer named John Wilkes Booth.

RECONSTRUCTION, INVENTION, AND INDUSTRIALIZATION.
The period after the war brought reconstruction to the South and the Industrial Revolution to the North. The North's rapid industrialization rendered it a formidable contender in the world economy, while the South's agricultural economy began a slow decline. Injured and embittered by the war and dependent on an outdated agricultural tradition, Southerners struggled to readjust to new economic and social conditions. Meanwhile, the newly-freed blacks faced a difficult transition from plantation to free life. **Jim Crow** laws, imposed by white politicians, espoused a doctrine of segregation, impeded African-Americans' civil rights, and prohibited them from frequenting the same establishments and schools as whites. Even drinking fountains were classified according to race. Freedom from slavery, however, also meant new opportunities for African-Americans. Black colleges were founded, and a few prominent African-Americans were able to gain some political power. For many blacks, though, segregation, Jim Crow laws, and racial sentiments led only to share-cropping for white landowners, a livelihood not that different from slavery.

During the North's **"Gilded Age"** of the 1870s, captains of industry such as Cornelius Vanderbilt, Andrew Carnegie, and John D. Rockefeller built commercial empires and enormous personal fortunes amid an atmosphere of widespread corruption. But this massive wealth didn't make its way down to farmers, who toiled in a dying agricultural economy, facing low wages, violent strike break-ups, and unsafe working conditions. Even so, the fruits of the industrial age should not be overlooked. Major developments in transportation were a cornerstone of industrialization. Between 1850 and 1890, the number of miles of **railroad** tracks in the nation increased from around 9000 to over 200,000. The country became obsessed with aviation after the **Wright Brothers** flew the first **airplane** in 1903. **Thomas Edison** started the nation's first electricity generating station (in addition to inventing things like the **lightbulb** to utilize electricity), and Rockefeller began turning oil into the energy powerhouse it is today. In 1876, **Alexander Graham Bell** invented the **telephone,** forever changing communication.

THE WORLD MOVES: IMPERIALISM, IMMIGRATION, AND WWI.
The United States' victory in the **Spanish-American War** of 1898 seemed to validate its interventionist tendencies. Believing that the US should be a leader in world affairs, and continuing its tradition of **Manifest Destiny,** the nation acquired colonies in the Philippines, Puerto Rico, and Guam.

While the US displayed its proud face all over the globe, the late 19th and early 20th centuries brought a flood of new foreign faces to the nation. The flood of European **immigration** began in 1880, when nearly four million Italian immigrants fled the dismal economic climate of Italy to come to America. Between 1880 and 1900, the US population grew by 50 percent. New York's **Ellis Island** became the center for processing immi-

1862
President Abraham Lincoln issues his Emancipation Proclamation, ending slavery in the US.

LIFE AND TIMES

1865
Gen. Robert E. Lee of the Confederate Army surrenders to the Union, ending the Civil War.

1876
Say what? Alexander Graham Bell invents the first telephone.

1879
Seeing the light: Thomas Edison invents the ■ lightbulb after many failed attempts.

1896
First silent movie is shown in New York City. Popcorn sales skyrocket.

1903
Orville and Wilbur Wright make the first successful airplane flight.

1908
Henry Ford's $850 Model T zooms onto the market.

1917
The US enters WWI.

1927
Charles Lindbergh makes the first solo flight across the Atlantic Ocean.

grants. Near Ellis Island, the **Statue of Liberty** (p. 177), a gift from the people of France, greeted the shiploads of "tired, poor, huddled masses" yearning for freedom.

In 1901, **Teddy Roosevelt** took over the presidency following the assassination of William McKinley, and brought a youthful, progressive approach to the government. In response to the corrupt, monopolistic practices of big business, Roosevelt and his progressive **Bull Moose Party** promoted anti-trust reforms to regulate large companies. In foreign affairs, Roosevelt established the US as an international police power, and recommended that the nation "speak softly and carry a big stick." Meanwhile, a new breed of journalists, the "muckrakers," began writing articles like Upton Sinclair's *The Jungle*—a graphic exposé of the meatpacking industry—to try to unveil the corruption rampant in this industrial age.

After vowing to keep the US out of "Europe's War," President **Woodrow Wilson** entered **World War I.** US troops landed in Europe in 1917 and fought until Germany's defeat the next year. The expansion of US Armed Forces that was necessary to carry out the war meant that 6% of the labor force aged 15-44 was deployed, and at least a fifth of the nation's resources were devoted to the war. The war, and the US's sudden involvement, called for extensive production of military products. In fact, from an economic point of view, the money spent by the US on the war was completely offset by the increases in production that were necessary to fight it. Though the metal-consuming war jump-started America's industrial economy and established the US as a major international power, the war killed 10 million people, including 130,174 Americans. Ultimately, the human losses left Americans wary of future combat in Europe.

ROARING 20S, GREAT DEPRESSION, AND WWII. After the war, Americans returned their attention to the homefront, and entered a new age of affluence. Labor unrest and racial tension were blamed on communist influences, and during 1919 the US experienced a **"Red Scare,"** increased unease with the spread of communism. The same year, the perceived moral decline of America was addressed by the immensely unpopular **Prohibition** laws, which outlawed alcohol. In spite of these restrictions, America's fun-loving spirit thrived as Mafia-run ■"speakeasies" replaced neighborhood saloons and created a huge black market for bootleg liquor. The jazz scene raged, giving this era of music, leisure, and decadence the apt name **"The Jazz Age."**

During this period, women **suffragists** such as **Susan B. Anthony** mobilized for the right to vote, and put intense pressure on politicians at every level of the government. These efforts eventually met with success in 1920 with the passage of the 19th Amendment to the US Constitution, which extended suffrage to women.

The economic boom of the **"Roaring 20s"** was driven largely by overextended credit. The facade of economic stability crumbled on "Black Thursday," October 24, 1929, when the New York Stock Exchange crashed, initiating a period of financial collapse known as the **Great Depression.** In an urban, mechanized age, millions of workers (25-50% of the work force) were left unemployed and struggled to provide for their families. The United States, like the rest of the developed world, rebounded slowly, with poor economic conditions existing for almost a decade despite **New Deal** policies like the Social Security Act initiated by President **Franklin D. Roosevelt.**

In the aftermath of the Depression, Nazi Germany plowed through Europe, with America largely unaware of the extent of the horror due to cover-ups by the Nazi administration. The US entered **World War II** only after the Japanese attack on Pearl Harbor, HI on December 7, 1941. The war raged on two fronts, as the Allied powers fought both the Germans in Europe and the Japanese in the Pacific. The European front was resolved with the German surrender on May 8, 1945, less than a year after the immense **D-Day** invasion of continental Europe in June 1944. The war in the Pacific continued until August of 1945, when the US dropped two newly developed **nuclear bombs** on Japan, killing 80,000 civilians and demonstrating to the world the power of nuclear warfare. Defeating fascism in Europe and Asia established the US military as a permanent global force.

THE COLD WAR. Spared the wartime devastation faced by Europe and East Asia and empowered by nationalist pride, the US economy boomed after the war and secured the nation's status as the world's dominant economic and military power. The US population increased during this period, as jubilation over victory and a throng of males returning from war generated the **Baby Boomers.** While the 1950s are often nostalgically recalled as a time of prosperity and traditional values, the decade did have its share of international tumult and angst.

The ideological gulf between the world's two nuclear powers—the democratic, capitalist US and the totalitarian, communist Soviet Union—initiated the half-century **Cold War** between the two nations. Tension with the Soviet Union heightened as **President Harry Truman** installed a foreign policy of communist containment to prevent the spread of communism. Fear of communism led to American military involvement in Asia, where the Maoist revolution in China had created imitators in surrounding countries. From 1950 to 1953, the United States fought the **Korean War** on behalf of the South Koreans, who had been attacked by the communist North Korean government. The Soviet launch of Sputnik, the first artificial satellite, in 1957 rekindled fears that communist regimes were surpassing America in many ways. The **Cuban Missile Crisis** in 1962, during which **President John F. Kennedy** negotiated the removal of Soviet missiles from a Cuban base and narrowly avoided nuclear war, reinforced the perception that the United States had to protect the world from Soviet invasion.

Exploiting rising anti-communist feeling at home, the **House Un-American Activities Committee,** led by **Senator Joseph McCarthy,** conducted so-called witch-hunts delving into every aspect of American public life to root out communist sympathizers, with a special focus on Hollywood and the media as a whole. The power of McCarthy and the HUAC waned as the vast majority of accusations were proven to be unfounded.

1929
The New York Stock Exchange crashes, sparking a worldwide depression.

Dec. 7, 1941
The attack on Pearl Harbor pushes the US into WWII.

LIFE AND TIMES

1947
Play ball! Jackie Robinson joins the Dodgers, becoming the first African-American to play Major League Baseball.

1954
The Supreme Court decision in *Brown v. Board of Education* ends racial segregation in American schools.

1961
President John F. Kennedy establishes the Peace Corps to aid impoverished nations.

In 1963, Lee Harvey Oswald assassinated President Kennedy during a parade in Dallas, TX. The assassination of the young, charismatic President mirrored America's larger loss of innocence and optimism. Throughout the rest of the decade, cultural strife, stemming from the long-fought civil rights movement and the bloody, controversial Vietnam War, altered the nation's social fabric.

ALL YOU NEED IS LOVE...AND PROTEST. Driven by the dictates of the containment policy instituted after WWII, the United States became embroiled in Vietnamese politics, culminating in a large-scale deployment of combat troops in 1965 to protect the South Vietnamese state from the aggression of Ho Chi Minh's communist government to the north. The **Vietnam War** was seen as a test of America's credibility as a protector of nations struggling with communism, making retreat difficult even when it became apparent that the situation in Vietnam was more complex than originally expected and that victory was unlikely. Though most Americans supported the war at first, opposition grew as it dragged on and its moral premises were questioned. The first war "fought on television," Vietnam produced graphic images of war that had previously not been seen, and contributed to Americans' hopeless perception of the war. Members of the new hippie generation responded with shouts of "Make Love, Not War" at the 1969 **Woodstock** music festival. Increasing opposition by young people to the conflict catalyzed wrenching generational clashes that eventually climaxed in riots and subsequent violence at the **1968 Democratic National Convention** and the shooting of anti-war protestors by the National Guard at **Kent State** in 1970.

1969
Do the moonwalk: Neil Armstrong becomes ■ the **first man on the moon.**

The Vietnam War was not the only cause that captured the hearts and minds of idealistic young Americans. **Rosa Parks's** refusal to give up a bus seat in Montgomery, AL (p. 393) in 1955 sparked a period of feverish activity in the **civil rights movement,** in which African-Americans strove for recognition of equality. The struggle was characterized by countless demonstrations, marches, and sit-ins in the heart of a defiant and often violent South. Activists were drenched with fire hoses, arrested, and even killed by local mobs and policemen. The movement crested with a march on Washington, D.C. in 1963, where **Dr. Martin Luther King, Jr.** delivered his famous "I Have A Dream" speech, calling for non-violent racial integration. The tone of the civil rights movement changed as some blacks became fed up with peaceful moderation and turned to the more militant rhetoric of **Malcolm X,** who espoused separatist "Black Power." The **Black Panthers** used more aggressive tactics to assert the rights of African-Americans.

The second wave of the **women's movement** arose at this time as well. Sparked by Betty Friedan's book *The Feminine Mystique,* American women sought to erase the line between men's and women's roles in society, and demanded equal pay and access to male-dominated professions. Outside the **Miss America Pageant** in 1968, women crowned a sheep "Miss America" and exuberantly threw away their bras and high heels. The sexual revolution, fueled by the introduction of the birth control pill, heightened the debate over abortion. The 1973 Supreme Court decision in **Roe v. Wade** legalized abortion, but the battle between its opponents and advocates still divides the nation.

Despite civil rights legislation and anti-poverty measures passed under **President Lyndon B. Johnson's** Great Society agenda, the specter of the Vietnam War overshadowed his presidency. By the end of these tumultuous years, the nation had dropped seven million tons of bombs on Indochina—twice the amount used against America's WWII enemies—and victory was still out of reach. Under **President Richard Nixon,** America extracted the last of its troops from Vietnam.

In 1972, five burglars were caught breaking into the Democratic National Convention Headquarters in the **Watergate** apartments. Their attempt to bug the Democratic offices led to a broader scandal involving the President himself. Aided by the secret information of top FBI official Mark Felt (an anonymous source known until 2005 simply as "Deep Throat"), Washington Post reporters Carl Bernstein and Bob Woodward published a series of articles that exposed Nixon's links to the scandal and ultimately led to his resignation.

1974
The Watergate scandal causes President Richard Nixon to resign.

By the mid-1970s, America was firmly disillusioned with both the government and the idealistic counterculture of the previous decade. More frivolous activities, like dancing in platform shoes and powder blue suits under flashing lights—a phenomenon known as **disco**—became the mark of a generation that just wanted to have fun. Unfortunately, the international situation remained tenuous. The oil-rich Arab nations boycotted the US, causing an **energy crisis** that drove up gas prices, frustrated autophile Americans, and precipitated an economic recession.

THE 1980S. In 1980, **Ronald Reagan,** a politically conservative former California governor and actor, was elected to the White House. Reagan knew how to give the people what they needed: money. He cut government spending on public programs and lowered taxes. Though the decade's conservatives embraced certain social goals, the Reagan revolution was essentially economic. **Reaganomics** cut taxes for big corporations, reduced government spending, and attempted to limit inflation, initiating a "trickle-down" effect and spurring consumption. On the foreign policy front, the straight-talking, cowboy president negotiated the end of the Cold War.

1980
Stroke of genius? The Rubik's Cube becomes the hottest toy on the market.

THE 1990S: BILLS, BILLS, BILLS. The US remained an active force in the world through the early 1990s. **President George H.W. Bush** directed "Operation Desert Storm" in 1990 as a response to Iraq's invasion of neighboring Kuwait. The war freed Kuwait, but its popularity in the US was compromised by the economic recession that followed. In 1992, Americans elected young Democrat **Bill Clinton,** who promised a new era of government activism after years of laissez-faire rule.

1981
The first personal computers hit the market.

The Clinton administration found itself plagued with its own problems: a suspicious Arkansas real estate development called Whitewater, an alleged extramarital affair with Gennifer Flowers, and accusations of sexual harassment from Paula

1991
The US enters the Gulf War in the Middle East.

1997
"I'm the king of the world!" Tear-jerker *Titanic* becomes the highest grossing film of all time.

1998
Tripp-ing: A White House sex scandal involving President Bill Clinton and Monica Lewinsky shocks the public.

2001
Terrorists crash two airplanes into the World Trade Center towers of New York. City, killing thousands.

2003
President Bush calls for the invasion of Iraq.

Jones. Yet Clinton's public approval remained high, especially after the nation supported him in a struggle against Congressional Republicans whose attempts to balance the budget led to two government shutdowns between 1995 and 1996. Clinton was re-elected in 1996, but new scandal erupted in 1998 as reports of an inappropriate relationship between Clinton and White House intern **Monica Lewinsky** were plastered across the American media. Clinton initially denied the allegations, but later admitted that he lied, resulting in impeachment for perjury and obstruction of justice. The trial in the Senate ended with a vote for informal censure over conviction, and Clinton remained in office. Despite the scandal, in the 90s the United States saw its lowest unemployment and inflation rates in modern history, as well as in homeownership, decreased crime and welfare rolls, and the first balanced budget in years.

The 90s in America also saw the introduction of the **World Wide Web** in 1991, plus a vast increase in the use of **personal computers (PCs).** As the decade progressed, PCs became more prevalent and **email** jumped in popularity; by the turn of the century, 100 million Americans were using the Internet. The sudden demand for the Internet and the ripe market in the industry set the stage for the so-called **dot-com boom** of the 1990s. California's **Silicon Valley** played host to many of the startup Internet companies that enjoyed unbelievable success in the stock market. The dot-com bubble, however, was short-lived, and burst early on in the 21st century.

THE NEW ENEMY: TERROR. On **September 11th, 2001,** the most severe terrorist attack in US history occurred when four planes were hijacked by terrorists. The site of the most violent crash was the World Trade Center in New York City, where approximately 3000 lives were taken. Al-Qaeda, a militant terrorist group, claimed responsibility for the attacks. Since September 11th, **President George W. Bush** has waged a **War on Terrorism** designed to identify and capture terrorists, particularly those of Al-Qaeda. Immediately following the attacks on the US, patriotism was high, and Bush received sweeping support for the war that began with the US invasion of Afghanistan and the toppling of the ruling Taliban, who had supported Al-Qaeda terrorists. The War on Terrorism became more controversial at home when Attorney General John Ashcroft proposed (and Congress passed) measures like the **PATRIOT Act,** which were designed to protect the country from terrorists, but which many believed to endanger key civil liberties.

RECENT NEWS

President Bush declared war on Iraq in March 2003 to "disarm Iraq and free its people." The major fighting ended only three weeks after the American army entered Iraq, but forces remain, trying to restructure the government and stabilize the nation. The US has since transferred sovereignty to Iraq's governing body, and Iraq held its first democratic election in 2005.

With the highest voter turnout (nearly 60%) since the 1968 elections, the battle for the White House in 2004 was one for the ages. A heated campaign featured allegations from incumbent President Bush that Democratic challenger John Kerry's evolving positions on issues deemed him a "flip-flopper," and assertions from Kerry's side that Bush's wars on terrorism and Iraq had made the US less safe. Polls leading up to election day indicated a dead heat. In the end, Bush won reelection and earned 51% of the popular vote. While the media stressed the war in Iraq and the economy as the most important issues, polls showed that "moral values," an ambiguous category of issues like gay marriage and abortion, were a deciding factor. In addition to winning the presidency, Republicans increased their majority in Congress in 2004, ensuring conservative dominance and an uphill battle for the Left.

2003
Space shuttle Columbia explodes, prompting major changes in the US's space program.

2004
The Boston Red Sox win baseball's World Series for the first time in 86 years.

LIFE AND TIMES

PEOPLE

Considering that Native Americans make up less than 1 percent of the population, the US truly is a "country of immigrants." While the country's population is and always has been mostly white, waves of immigration of various ethnic groups at different points in history have changed US demographics. The US population is currently 76% white, 14% Hispanic and Latino, 12% African-American, and 4% Asian. Non-white populations are often concentrated in urban areas.

The **Establishment Clause** of the US Constitution states that the government and public institutions must remain neutral to religion. This "separation of church and state" ensures that Americans have the freedom to practice any religion they choose (or none at all) and still receive equal treatment from the government. Still, from the beginning religion has been a defining characteristic of the American consciousness, and some studies have concluded that 90% of Americans have some religious affiliation. Christianity dominates, as 76% of Americans identify themselves as Catholic, Protestant, Mormon, or another form of Christian. The so-called **Bible Belt** is composed of a number of Southern and Midwestern states where fervent Protestantism is a major part of the culture.

English is the official language of the US, and even those who speak another language often speak English as well. American dialects vary by region, but these differences are limited to individual words, phrases, or expressions (p. 585). In some regions of the country—particularly California, Texas, parts of the Southwest, and Miami—an influx of Spanish-speaking immigrants has made Spanish almost as common as English.

CULTURE

FOOD

While fast-food chains dot the country and trends like low-carb diets tailor the nation's eating habits, authentic American food is best found at the regional level. Local agricultural production, immigration patterns, and cultures have resulted in unique and delicious foods that far outshine the burger-and-fries stereotype of American cuisine.

NORTHEAST. America's English settlers landed in the Northeast and combined their staples of meats and vegetables with uniquely American foodstuffs like turkey, maple syrup, clams, lobster, cranberries, and corn. The results yielded such treasures as Boston brown bread, Indian pudding, New England clam chowder, and Maine boiled lobster. The shellfish in the Northeast is second to none.

SOUTH. Be prepared for some home cookin'. Fried chicken, biscuits, mashed potatoes, and collard greens are some highlights of Southeastern cuisine. Cheese grits or cornbread are a savory supplement to lunch and dinner dishes.

LOUISIANA. Chefs in New Orleans (p. 414) are among the best in the country, and creole and Cajun cooking tantalize the taste buds. Locals and tourists alike regard crawfish, fried catfish, jambalaya (rice cooked with ham, sausage, shrimp, and herbs), and gumbo (a soup with okra, meat, and vegetables) as delicacies. The faint of taste buds beware: Cajun and creole cooking bring in the heat.

TEXAS. From beef to pork to beef again, Texans like to throw it on the grill. Eat at any of the many barbecue joints and they'll tell you that the real secret is in the sauce. For those in the mood for something ethnic, enchiladas, burritos, nachos, and fajitas are scrumptious Tex-Mex options.

SOUTHWEST. Strongly influenced by Mexican cuisine, Southwestern grub relies on traditional Mexican ingredients like corn, flour, and chilies. Salsa made from tomatoes, chilies (especially New Mexico's famous hatch chilies), and *tomatillos* adds a spicy note to most dishes, including quesadillas, chilies rellenos, and tacos.

CALIFORNIA. California's trend-setting status extends beyond fashion and movies to fresh, natural foods. Home to acres of orange and avocado trees, California offers an array of organic produce in everything from smoothies to salads. Grapes also grow plentifully in the numerous vineyards that line the fields of Napa Valley (p. 882) and central California, the United States's prime wine country.

NORTHWEST. In close proximity to the arctic water frequented by halibut and salmon, many cities in the Pacific Northwest are known for superior seafood, which can be found in everything from chowder to tacos. If you're looking for a cold one to wash down your seafood, Portland, OR (p. 944) is the microbrewery capital of North America and has the beer to prove it.

CUSTOMS AND ETIQUETTE

TABLE MANNERS. In the US, good table manners means quiet eating. Loud chewing, talking with food in your mouth, or slurping is seen as rude, and burping is not seen as complimentary to the chef. Tipping etiquette generally requires a 10-15% tip at lunch and a 15-20% tip at dinner for servers at sit-down restaurants.

PUBLIC BEHAVIOR. Dress in the US tends to be more modest than in Europe. Toplessness, particularly by women, should be avoided. Many establishments will require a customer to wear a shirt and shoes. The most acceptable forms of public affection are hugging and holding hands; kissing in public will usually draw some glances. Although most cities are tolerant of homosexuality, gay or lesbian couples should be aware that they may receive unwanted attention for public displays of affection, especially in rural areas.

GESTURES. One of the most offensive gestures in the US is extending your middle finger at someone. Known as "giving the finger," this gesture is considered rude and obscene. A "thumbs up" gesture, though, is a sign of approval. It is also a widely recognized signal for hitchhiking, which *Let's Go* does not recommend.

THE ARTS

It did not take long for hearty American individualism to make its mark on the global canon, previously dominated by age-old European traditions. From the 19th-century Transcendentalist literature of New England to the unique musical stylings of bluegrass and jazz, America has established itself time and again as an innovator in the world of creative arts.

LITERATURE

THE FIRST FEW PAGES. The first best-seller printed in America, the *Bay Psalm Book*, was published in Cambridge, MA, in 1640. Reflecting the Puritanical culture of much of 17th- and 18th-century America, it was religious in nature. Very few enduring classics were created until the early 1800s, when artists began to explore the unique American experience in their writing. **James Fenimore Cooper's** *Last of the Mohicans* (1826), **Nathaniel Hawthorne's** *The Scarlet Letter* (1850), and **Herman Melville's** *Moby Dick* (1851)—among the first great American novels—all feature strong individualists navigating the raw American landscape. By the mid-19th century, the work of **New England Transcendentalists** like **Henry David Thoreau** *(Walden)* and **Ralph Waldo Emerson** *(Nature)* embodied a spirit of anti-materialism by focusing on self-reflection and a retreat into nature. **Walt Whitman** promoted a uniquely American style of poetry with his unorthodox verse expressing both his distaste for the conditions of the 19th century and his idealistic views about American democracy. Later in the century, **Mark Twain** became one of America's best-loved storytellers with his homespun tales out of Hannibal, MO. His novel *The Adventures of Huckleberry Finn* (1885) uses a young boy's journey to express social criticism and the human spirit.

Literature also provided 19th-century American women the opportunity both to express themselves and to comment critically on contemporary society. In 1852, **Harriet Beecher Stowe** published *Uncle Tom's Cabin*, an exposé of slavery that, according to some scholars, contributed to the outbreak of the Civil War. Poet **Emily Dickinson** secretly scribbled away in her native Amherst, MA home; her untitled and unpunctuated verses weren't discovered until after her death in 1886.

EARLY 20TH CENTURY EXPLORATIONS. Amidst the economic prosperity of the 1920s, a reflective, self-centered movement fomented in American literature in response to changing cultural values. **F. Scott Fitzgerald's** works *(The Great Gatsby)* portray restless individuals who are financially secure but unfulfilled by their conspicuous consumption. During this tumultuous time, many writers moved abroad in search of refuge; this **Lost Generation** included Fitzgerald, **Ernest Hemingway** *(The Old Man and the Sea)*, **T.S. Eliot** ("The Love Song of J. Alfred Prufrock"), **Ezra Pound,** and **e.e. cummings.** This group's sophisticated works conveyed an increasing disillusionment with the contemporary American experience. The **Harlem Renaissance,** a convergence of African-American artistic and political action in New York City, was spurred by the **Great Migration,** a large-scale African-American migration from the rural South to the urban North, and it fed off the excitement of the Jazz Age. **Langston Hughes** *(Montage of a Dream Deferred)*, **Nella Larsen** *(Quicksand)*, and **Zora Neale Hurston** *(Their Eyes Were Watching God)* brought an awareness about black talent and creativity to a broader audience as they struggled to define and express ideas about African-American identity and the black experience in America. The Harlem Renaissance also saw the rise of more radical black intellectualism led by **Marcus Garvey,** champion of the **Pan-African** movement, and **Alain Locke,** who wrote the essay "The New Negro."

LIFE AND TIMES

In the 1930s and 40s, as America struggled to recover from the Great Depression, the plight of decaying agricultural life and faltering industry of the Deep South and West began to infiltrate literature. **William Faulkner** *(The Sound and the Fury)* juxtaposed avant-garde stream-of-consciousness techniques with subjects rooted in the rot and decay of the rural South. Nobel Prize recipient **John Steinbeck** is best known for his 1939 novel *The Grapes of Wrath*, which depicts the condition of migrant laborers heading from the Great Plains to California in the wake of the Great Depression. The plays of **Tennessee Williams** *(A Streetcar Named Desire)* portray family dynamics within lower-class, uprooted Southern families. **Clifford Odets's** play *Waiting for Lefty (1935)*, detailing the plight of frustrated factory workers, was a grassroots hit, and audiences often joined with the actors in chanting the play's final lines, "Strike! Strike!" In his remarkable autobiography, *Black Boy* (1945), **Richard Wright** recounts growing up in the Jim Crow South.

POST-WAR MALAISE. In the conformist 1950s, literature provided an outlet for commentary on America's underlying social problems. **Ralph Ellison's** *Invisible Man*, published in 1952, confronted the division between white and black identities in America. In 1955, **Vladimir Nabokov**, a Russian émigré, redefined the style for a whole generation of writers with his controversial story about unconventional love, *Lolita*. **Gwendolyn Brooks,** the first black writer to win a Pulitzer Prize, published intense poetry highlighting social problems like abortion, gangs, and high school drop-outs. Members of the **Beat Generation,** led by cult heroes **Jack Kerouac** *(On the Road)* and **Allen Ginsberg** *(Howl)*, lived wildly and espoused a more free-thinking and laidback attitude. Playwright **Arthur Miller** delved into the American psyche with *Death of a Salesman* (1949), in which he explored the frailty of the American dream. He later wrote *The Crucible*, a play detailing the Salem witch-hunts, as a critique of Sen. McCarthy's communist "witch-hunts" (p. 59).

As Americans increasingly questioned society's conventions in the 1960s, writers began to explore more unorthodox material. **Anne Sexton** revealed the depths of her own mental breakdown, while **Sylvia Plath** paved the way for feminist authors, exposed her psychological deterioration, and hinted at her suicide in *The Bell Jar* (1963). The essays and stories of **James Baldwin** *(The Fire Next Time)* warned both white and black Americans about the self-destructive implications of racial hatred. **Flannery O'Connor** exposed the eerie, grotesque underbelly of the contemporary South in stories such as "A Good Man is Hard to Find" (1953).

The search for identity and the attempt to reconcile artistic and social agendas continued into the 1970s and 80s. **E.L. Doctorow's** *Ragtime* (1975) evokes vibrant images of a turn-of-the-century America, weaving together historical and fictional figures. **Toni Morrison** *(Beloved)* won the Nobel Prize for her visceral interpretations of the tension between gender, ethnic, and cultural identities. **Don DeLillo's** *White Noise* (1985) carries on the American absurdist tradition and, using both humor and uncanny insight, delves into America's obsession with mortality. Many stories have also focused on the fast pace and commercialism of modern society. In *American Psycho* (1991), **Bret Easton Ellis** exposes the conspicuous consumption of New York City in the 1980s, while the plays of **David Mamet** *(Glengarry Glen Ross)* are known for confronting the gritty underside of American business. Among more recent authors, the prolific **Philip Roth** *(American Pastoral)* continues to disassemble the American dream. **David Sedaris** *(Me Talk Pretty One Day)* draws raves for his hilarious, self-deprecating columns and essays about his childhood, family life, and his experience as an American living in France. Distressingly young **Jonathan Safran Foer's** newest novel, *Extremely Loud and Incredibly Close*, explores the post-9/11 world and a young person's place in it.

MUSIC

The United States has given birth to a plethora of musical genres, whose styles and songs have intermingled to produce the many distinct styles that can be heard today. **Scott Joplin** meshed African-American harmony and rhythm with classical European style to develop the first American piano form, ragtime. From this rich, upbeat, piano-banging dance music of the 19th century to the Deep South's mournful blues, early African-American music defined soul. The 1950s saw a new, "edgy" style of music arise from America's youth: rock 'n' roll. Soul and gospel music evolved into R&B, jazz, funk, and later, hip-hop, while rock exploded in the 60s and 70s into today's genre of "classic rock." Recent decades have ushered in the new styles of rap, metal, grunge alternative, and teeny-bopper pop.

SINGIN' THE BLUES. As with ragtime, black Southerners were primarily responsible for the blues, which was originally a blend of Northwest African slave calls and Native American song and verse forms. Blues songs were popularized by **W.C. Handy,** the legendary "father of the blues." His "St. Louis Blues" remains one of the most recorded songs ever. As Southern blacks migrated to industrial centers during the early 20th century, the blues, augmented by the contributions of women like **Mamie Smith, Billie Holiday,** and **Bessie Smith,** found an audience in the North. The blues heavily influenced the development of other popular American musical styles, most notably jazz and rock 'n' roll.

AND ALL THAT JAZZ. Ragtime, blues, and military brass combined in New Orleans in the early 20th century to create America's classical music, jazz. Its emphasis on improvisation and unique tonal and harmonic rules distinguished it from previous genres. The work of all-time jazz greats like **Louis Armstrong, Dizzy Gillespie,** and **Ella Fitzgerald** influenced the later work of classical composers; **Leonard Bernstein's** classical orchestrations and **George Gershwin's** theatrical style can both trace their roots and distinctly American sound to the jazz tradition. Early jazz also led to the era of big band music, during which the legendary **Duke Ellington** and the swing orchestra of **Glenn Miller** reigned supreme.

COUNTRY ROADS, TAKE ME HOME. Country music has its roots in the Appalachian Mountains, among a poor rural white population that put a new spin on ancestral European folk traditions. Sentimental, often spiritual lyrics were combined with simple melodies to create a characteristically honest American sound. The genre owes much of its attitude and sound to classic heroes: **Hank Williams** cultivated an air of tragic, honky-tonk mystique, while **Johnny Cash** left his mark with a brazen, devil-may-care honesty. Commercially, country didn't catch on until it was given a boost by radio and Nashville's famous 1930s program the **Grand Ole Opry.** Country artists like **Willie Nelson** and **Emmylou Harris** captured both Southern and Northern audiences. Recently, country artists like **Garth Brooks, Tim McGraw,** and **LeAnn Rimes,** as well as country-pop crossovers like the **Dixie Chicks** and **Faith Hill,** have combined to bring modern country into the mainstream limelight.

A related genre with a distinctly American style is folk. Folk music has often embraced political and social activism through its direct lyrics and honest spirit. **Woody Guthrie's** music touched upon issues of patriotism in the midst of the Great Depression ("This Land is Your Land"). Thanks to artists like **Bob Dylan** and **Joan Baez,** folk music popularly caught on in the 60s and spoke to social protesters across the nation. During this hippie generation, people used songs like "We Shall Overcome" and "Where Have all the Flowers Gone?" both to express their opinions about relevant issues and to unify their protests. Folk survives today in coffee shops and on street corners, and in folk musicians like **Dar Williams.**

PUT ANOTHER DIME IN THE JUKEBOX, BABY. No one can say exactly how rock 'n' roll was started, although it did grow out of African-American traditions of gospel and rhythm and blues. One thing is for certain, though: **Elvis Presley** was the first to be crowned "King." His rock kingdom of **Graceland** (p. 336) is a popular attraction for Memphis tourists. During the 50s and 60s rock 'n' roll's driving, danceable rhythms, rebellious attitude, and fascination with electric instruments dominated the popular music charts. Rock 'n' roll reflected the new post-WWII optimism and innocence throughout America, as teenagers looked for something more exciting and daring to express their style. The genre has produced most of America's more famous music icons—before Elvis, there were **Chuck Berry** and **Jerry Lee Lewis,** who ushered in a new era of poodle skirts and slicked-back hair. In the 60s and 70s, rock used bluegrass melodies, classic beats, and the wailing guitar solos made famous by **Jimi Hendrix** and **Led Zeppelin,** to create the new sub-genre of classic rock that lives on with artists like **Bruce Springsteen** and **Pink Floyd.**

MO' MUSIC. In 1961 Berry Gordy, Jr. started a little company in Detroit that revolutionized American music. **Motown** was an all-black record label that produced hit artists like **The Supremes, The Temptations, Marvin Gaye,** and **The Jackson Five,** which was **Michael Jackson's** first entry into the music world. Descended from gospel and the blues, the unmistakable "Motown sound" combined smooth lyrics with funky backing, sparking a new genre of soul music: R&B. Unlike previous African-American musical acts, Motown artists did not strive to integrate their sound into the white music world. Rather, Motown singers were the first African-American musicians to infuse their music with a socio-political message. Listeners changed **Martha and the Vandellas'** song "Dancing in the Street" from a party song into a theme song during civil rights riots in 1967 Detroit. **James Brown's** song "Say it Loud, I'm Black and I'm Proud" (1968) espoused black power and black pride. Today, R&B has drifted far from its roots and is often inseparable from hip-hop. Artists like **R. Kelly** and **Beyonce** have led R&B's charge toward hip-hop and the mainstream. R&B's links to Motown are now barely visible.

DISCO BALLS, HAIR BANDS, AND GANGSTA RAP. The 1970s will be forever remembered as the era of disco. Disco divas like **Gloria Gaynor** ("I Will Survive") and funk bands like **Parliament Funkadelic** dominated American nightlife and fostered a culture that celebrated dancing, drugs, and excess. The 1980s witnessed a rap revolution, spawned by East Coast stars **Public Enemy, Run-DMC,** and the **Beastie Boys.** The 80s also ushered in the popularity of "hair bands" like **Poison** and punk rockers like **The Ramones,** not to mention a little entertainer named **Madonna.** In the early 90s, grunge music escaped from the garage to the national spotlight largely because of Seattle's **Nirvana** and **Pearl Jam.** The West Coast birthed the "gangsta rap" movement (Dr. Dre, Snoop Dogg) in the 90s as well, sparking much debate over the promotion of violence and excessive misogyny in its lyrics. The early 90s legendary East Coast-West Coast feud between NYC's **Notorious B.I.G.** and L.A.'s **Tupac Shakur** split the rap community and only ended with both rappers' deaths six months apart in 1996-1997. Recently, **Eminem** exploded to international stardom with his provocative lyricism and outlandish persona, **50 Cent** stormed onto the scene as a tough-talking, big-selling bully, and **Jay-Z** cemented his place as B.I.G. and Shakur's successor.

DIRTY POP. Pop-Punk broke into the mainstream during the 90s with **Green Day's** rise to fame. With the help of artists like **Blink-182** and **Good Charlotte,** this toned-down and upbeat version of the heavy punk of the 80s has continued to be a major presence in young America's CD player. But the late 1990s and the millennium have been primarily dominated by a resurgence of bubblegum pop and dance tunes. Barely 16 years old when their first album was released, the **New Kids on the**

Block spearheaded the boy band phenomenon and the MTV generation of consumer teens has sustained the popularity of young superstars like **Britney Spears** and **Justin Timberlake.** MTV has blurred the lines between music, media, and culture with shows like *Newlyweds*, which features newlywed pop stars **Nick Lachey** and **Jessica Simpson,** who are shown both at home in daily life, and at work recording and performing. Although some purists criticize the genre for lacking real musical substance, pop's prominence on the Billboard charts indicates that young fans still love their pop stars. **Kelly Clarkson,** who was propelled to instant fame after winning the reality TV competition *American Idol*, exemplifies pop's stronghold on American media, culture, and music.

GREAT AMERICAN COMPOSERS. It may lag behind some European countries in famous composers per capita, but the US has had its fair share of musical heavyhitters. One of the earliest American composers was **William Billings,** a Boston-born composer of patriotic hymns such as *Chester* (1778). The 19th century played host to the "March King," **John Philip Sousa,** whose work includes the US's official march, *The Stars and Stripes Forever*, which is a favorite at 4th of July celebrations. **Charles Ives** was a businessman by day, yet still won the 1947 Pulitzer Prize for Music for his *Third Symphony.* **George Gershwin** *(Rhapsody in Blue)* made his mark as in the early 20th century before extending his talents to Broadway and Hollywood. He later teamed up with his brother, **Ira,** to write and compose classics like the operetta *Porgy and Bess.* Born in 1900, when the music world had not yet fully recognized Americans as great composers, **Aaron Copland** is considered by many to be the pioneer of American classical music. He is best known for concert *(Appalachian Spring)* and ballet *(Billy the Kid)* works, but also composed jazz and movie soundtracks. Perhaps the most influential classical composer of the 20th century, **Leonard Bernstein** is best known for his scores for Broadway musicals *West Side Story* and *On the Town.* He also played an important role in the increased popular acceptance of classical music. **Stephen Sondheim** learned his craft from a legend, **Oscar Hammerstein II,** and has since set the standard for Broadway musical composition. Winner of seven Tony Awards for his work on Broadway, Sondheim has also received acclaim for his big-screen compositions, and won the 1990 Academy Award for Best Original Song for *Sooner or Later.*

FILM

SILENT FILMS AND PRE-CODE TALKIES. Before sound was wedded to image in the first "talkie"—1927's *The Jazz Singer*—silent films ruled the screen. Silent films quickly went out of fashion once sound entered the picture, and **Hollywood,** CA quickly became the center of the movie business, owing to its sunny, filmfriendly climate, proximity to a variety of photogenic terrain, and previous preeminence as a theater center. By the 1920s, actors like **Charlie Chaplin, Buster Keaton,** and **Mary Pickford** were household names. Free from the control of domineering studios, these film artists brought a playful, exuberant, and innovative attitude to their work. Films such as *Sunrise* (1927) and *The Crowd* (1928), meanwhile, combined innovative cinematography and compelling stories that remain popular to this day. But early films often tapped into America's isolationist sentiments and grossly misportrayed or demonized foreign characters. When other countries protested, American filmmakers realized the monetary importance of audiences outside of America. Simultaneously, critics began wondering publicly about the moral value of movies. In an effort to keep foreign audiences and prevent what seemed like imminent federal regulation, filmmakers created the **Motion Pictures Producers and Distributors of America (MPPDA),** a self regulating board that would address the pertinent concerns internally.

CLASSIC ERA. The film industry's wild success soon gave rise to the expansion of the **studio system.** Giant production houses like **Paramount, MGM,** and **Warner** took up residence on the West Coast and turned movies into big business. American film's **golden age** took place during the height of the studio era, when Hollywood's four major studios standardized and dominated films. **Victor Fleming's** *Gone with the Wind* (1939), a Civil War epic, was the first large-scale movie extravaganza, redefining the bounds of cinematic scope. **Frank Capra,** who explored morality with films like *It's a Wonderful Life* (1946) and *Mr. Smith Goes to Washington* (1939), brought a conscience to entertainment. Michael Curtiz's *Casablanca* (1942), starring **Humphrey Bogart,** was a classic cinematic romance with a patriotic and politicized background. In 1941, **Orson Welles** unveiled his intricate masterpiece, *Citizen Kane,* a landmark work that revolutionized the potential of the medium. Fantasy, however, still sold tickets: **Walt Disney's** animated *Snow White* (1937) and Fleming's *The Wizard of Oz* (1939) kept producers well-fed.

PRETTY BOYS, MONSTERS, AND BOMBSHELLS. Heightened tensions with the Soviet Union and conflicts with communism abroad led to widespread communist witch-hunts at home. The film industry, under government pressure, took up the policy of blacklisting any artists with suspected, or even rumored, ties to communism. The resulting paranoia and dwindling box office returns brought about by competition with television eventually stimulated the production of a slew of movies that were sensational enough to draw crowds back to the theaters. Films such as *Invasion of the Body Snatchers* (1956) and *The Incredible Shrinking Man* (1957) used **science fiction** to grapple with cultural anxieties about communism and nuclear weapons, while larger than life **westerns** such as *High Noon* (1952) and *The Searchers* (1956) galloped across the screens. Meanwhile, **Alfred Hitchcock** *(Rear Window, North by Northwest)* and the ever-free-thinking **Orson Welles** *(The Lady from Shanghai)* created an entirely new cinematic genre: **film noir,** which lasted in its classic form until the 1960s.

The 1950s also saw the emergence of a cult of glamour surrounding the most luminous stars. Cloaked in glitz and scandal, sex symbols **Marilyn Monroe, James Dean** *(Rebel Without a Cause)*, **Elizabeth Taylor,** and **Rock Hudson** drew audiences to movies by name recognition alone. These stars, along with actors **Marlon Brando** *(A Streetcar Named Desire)* and **Audrey Hepburn** *(Breakfast at Tiffany's)*, brought their own mystique to the screen, and added to the art of the cinema.

SOCK IT TO ME. The 1960s and early 70s saw widespread social upheaval and tension between generations. Adapting to the demands of younger, more liberal audiences, studios enlisted directors influenced by the French New Wave as well as artists from other media to direct features, including Sidney Lumet, John Frankenheimer, and Robert Altman. With the studios more willing to take a gamble, and a new movie ratings board—the **Motion Picture Association of America (MPAA)**—to replace censorship, the work of a number of innovative filmmakers began to enter the mainstream. Stanley Kubrick's *Dr. Strangelove* (1964), *2001: A Space Odyssey* (1968), and *A Clockwork Orange* (1971) brought a literary importance to filmmaking. Dennis Hopper's *Easy Rider* (1969), a film about countercultural youth rebellion and the fruitlessness of the American dream, and the acclaimed documentary *Woodstock* (1970), established film as a viable medium for social criticism. Meanwhile, the first half of the 1970s flirted with the genre of **blaxploitation,** sensationalized portrayals of urban African-Americans, with films like *Shaft.*

Throughout the 1970s, experimentalism largely gave way to more polished treatment of equally serious issues. Film-schooled directors like Martin Scorsese *(Taxi Driver)*, Francis Ford Coppola *(The Godfather)*, and Michael Cimino *(The Deer Hunter)* brought technical skill to their exploration of the darker side of humanity. An influx of foreign filmmakers, like Milos Forman *(One Flew Over the Cuckoo's Nest)* and Roman Polański *(Chinatown),* introduced a new perspective to American film.

TAKING CARE OF BUSINESS. Driven by the mass global distribution of American cinema and the development of high-tech special effects, the late 1970s and 80s witnessed the rebirth of the **blockbuster. Steven Spielberg's** *Jaws* kicked off the trend in 1973 by piloting the now tried and true advertising methods of TV previews, movie merchandise, media stunts, and theme song publicity. Following his breakout success with *Jaws,* Spielberg produced *E.T.* (1982) and *Raiders of the Lost Ark* (1981). **George Lucas** followed the trend of creating widely appealing movies with impressive special effects with his *Star Wars* trilogy. Though such films were criticized for their reliance on effects, they almost single-handedly returned Hollywood to its former status as king.

Despite the increasing commercialism of Hollywood, quite a bit of highly imaginative work came out of the period, including Rob Reiner's *This is Spinal Tap* (1984), a hilarious send-up of popular music, and David Lynch's *Blue Velvet* (1986), a disturbing look at the primal terror beneath the tranquil surface of suburbia. The revival of the blockbuster continued into the new millennium, with such high-budget money-makers as the dinosaur thriller *Jurassic Park* (1993) and the decadent love-story *Titanic* (1997) drawing the largest crowds. Recently, a revolution in digital film technology has spawned such hits as *Shrek* and *Finding Nemo,* animated films with universal appeal.

INDIE FEVER. The recognition of independent, or **indie,** films—films that are either produced independently of any major studio or at least do not follow standard studio conventions—marks the most interesting turn for cinema in the last several years. Brothers **Joel and Ethan Coen** have created some of the most creative and original work of late, including the gruesome comedy *Fargo* (1996) and the hilarious, off-beat *The Big Lebowski* (1998). **Quentin Tarantino's** cool action *(Reservoir Dogs, Pulp Fiction),* **Paul Thomas Anderson's** emotionally charged and frequently sprawling storytelling style *(Boogie Nights, Magnolia),* and **Wes Anderson's** darkly quirky humor *(Rushmore, The Royal Tenenbaums)* have all injected new life into American cinema. Recently, however, films have been tackling heavier issues. **Michael Moore's** ultra-liberal documentaries *Bowling for Columbine* and *Fahrenheit 9/11,* and Mel Gibson's graphic and highly controversial film *The Passion of the Christ* are only a few examples. Documentaries have also gained in popularity recently, including Moore's queries into American culture and politics, **Morgan Spurlock's** fast-food exposé *Supersize Me* (2004), and **Jeffrey Blitz's** *Spellbound* (2004), which chronicles the dark side of spelling bees.

FINE ARTS

American art has often been dismissed as a pale reflection of European trends. Despite this stereotype, it has a rich history rooted in the country's expansion. Its raw and uncontrolled nature is reflected not only in the grandiose 19th-century landscape paintings that capture the beauty of the untamed West, but also in the unwieldy lines and shapes of American 20th-century abstract expressionism.

PAINTING. Portraiture flourished in colonial America. John Singleton Copley, Charles Willson Peale, and Gilbert Stuart rendered intimate likenesses of iconic revolutionary figures from Paul Revere to George Washington. In the first half of the 19th century, Thomas Cole and Asher B. Durand produced ambitious landscapes with didactic overtones. Cole was one of the earliest artists in the **Hudson River School,** a group of painters who combined expressive depictions of nature with ideas about the divine. Later, **Winslow Homer's** vibrant watercolors captured the wild side of nature in sweeping seascapes, while softer American Impressionists like Childe Hassam depicted the effects of light in New England city scenes. The turn of the 20th century saw an emphasis on Realism and the depiction of urban life; the group of painters known as the **Ash Can School,** led by Robert Henri, promoted "art for art's sake." By the 1940s, **Abstract Expressionism** had been reborn in the US. Country wide anxiety over international unrest and the threat of war bore heavily on the American psyche. In drip paintings and color field works, painters like **Jackson Pollock** and **Mark Rothko** reflected the ironic mix of swaggering confidence and frenetic insecurity that characterized Cold War America. Ushering in the age of **Pop Art, Roy Lichtenstein** and **Andy Warhol** used mass-produced, cartoonish images to satirize the icons of American popular culture. Art that enshrined the mundane blurred the boundaries between "high culture" and "mass culture," and became symbolic of the growing **postmodernist** movement. The 1980s art boom, stationed around private galleries in New York City and L.A., ushered in a decade of slick, idyllic paintings and the kitschy sculptures of **Jeff Koons.**

PHOTOGRAPHY. Beginning in the early 20th century, photography became the medium of choice for artists with a social conscience. **Jakob Riis** and **Lewis Hine** photographed the urban poor and child laborers, while **Walker Evans** and **Dorothea Lange** captured destitute farmers during the Great Depression. **Ansel Adams** used his photographs of rugged Western landscapes as tools in his quest for natural conservation in the 40s, 50s, and 60s. **Robert Frank's** snapshots caught the social transitions and tensions of 1960s America. In the 1970s, photography came into its own as back-to-basics 35mm photographs pushed the boundaries of defined art .

THE MEDIA

America is wired. Images, sounds, and stories from the television, radio, Internet, and magazines infiltrate every aspect of the American lifestyle. Fads have been popularized and fortunes have been made thanks solely to the power of mass media, but because of this intense power, constant debate rages over who should be held responsible for content. Despite controversy about policing the industry, American consumption of new media is continually growing.

TELEVISION. TV sets are found in 98% of US homes. Competition between the six national **networks** (ABC, CBS, Fox, NBC, UPN, and WB), cable television, and satellite TV has triggered exponential growth in TV culture. Network prime time (8-11 EST) often features America's most popular shows like the crime investigation drama *CSI* (CBS), the teen soap *The OC* (Fox), and recent sensation *Desperate Housewives* (ABC). One need not be bound to the networks, however, as **cable** provides special-interest channels that cover every subject from cooking to sports to science fiction. Meanwhile, **premium stations** air recently released movies along with regular programming; one favorite is HBO, which boasts the pleasingly offbeat *Curb Your Enthusiasm* and the mobster drama *The Sopranos*. Travelers will find that some hotel rooms come equipped with basic cable, while others offer premium stations or even pay-per-view channels.

Although **reality television** surged to what seemed to be its peak after *Survivor's* (CBS) popularity in the early 21st century, it has made a comeback with such ultra-popular shows as *American Idol* (Fox) and **Donald Trump's** *The Apprentice* (NBC). On *Idol*, one of the most-watched shows on television, contestants compete for a recording contract and instant fame, while Trump's contestants compete for the chance to work for "The Donald" himself. The modern father of reality television, *Survivor*, has slipped considerably in viewership since its early days, while Fox's ridiculous entrances into the genre like *The Swan*, on which women receive plastic surgery and then compete in a beauty pageant, have roused viewers' curiosity as well as turned some off to the genre entirely. Still, the cable station MTV seems to have gotten it right, as teenagers and young adults still spend hours glued to reality programs *The Real World* and *Road Rules*. Since the debut of *Beverly Hills 90210* in 1990, in fact, drama shows targeting teen audiences have skyrocketed. With beautiful young stars in even more beautiful clothing and beachside homes, *The OC* is the latest hit in the slew of teen dramas.

Special **comedy programs** also dominate much of TV-land. The long-running *Saturday Night Live* (NBC) is a perennial favorite and has helped launch the careers of comedians **Will Ferrell** and **Al Franken,** while late-night television is sustained by the comic stylings of talk-show hosts like David Letterman on *The Late Show* (CBS) and Conan O'Brien on *Late Night* (NBC). Daytime programming is less watched and fills the hours with tawdry **soap operas** and **talk shows.**

Television is the point of entry to **worldwide news** for most Americans. Twenty-four hour news coverage is available on cable stations such as **CNN, MSNBC,** and the **Fox News Channel.** Each major network presents local and national nightly news (usually at 5 and/or 11pm EST), while prime-time "newsmagazines" like *60 Minutes* (CBS), *Dateline* (NBC), and *20/20* (ABC) specialize in investigative reports and special-interest stories. **ESPN,** a cable channel, gives viewers "all sports, all the time" and has capitalized on America's sporting obsession with the ever-popular *SportsCenter*, the definitive sports news show. The **Public Broadcasting System (PBS)** is commercial-free and funded by viewer contributions, the federal government, and corporate grants. Its repertoire includes educational children's shows like *Sesame Street*—America's seminal childhood TV-watching experience—as well as nature programs, mystery shows, and British comedies.

PRINT. Despite the onset of more sophisticated technologies like TV and the Internet, Americans still cherish the feel of glossy pages and the smell of newsprint. Today, newsstands crowd city corners and transportation terminals throughout the country. Publications cover all areas of society, culture, and politics; whether it's for lounging away a Sunday afternoon at home or passing time in a doctor's waiting room, print media dominates the market.

Some of the most well-respected newspapers include *The New York Times* and *The Washington Post*, though every major city has at least one major paper. Women's magazines such as *Cosmopolitan* and men's magazines like *Maxim* feature articles and photos about sex and fashion. *The New Yorker* amuses its more intellectual subscribers with short stories and essays. Entertainment magazines like *People* and *US Weekly* chronicle celebrity gossip, while *Rolling Stone* focuses on music. Those interested in the stock market's ups and downs swear by *The Wall Street Journal* and *Forbes*. Sports buffs troll the pages of *Sports Illustrated*, the preeminent sports magazine. Ranging from trashy tabloids like the *National Enquirer* to the most influential and respected news organs, American print media is notably diverse and often subject to criticism for being too liberal, exploitative, or sensational, but remains generally accurate and accountable.

RADIO. Before television transformed American culture, the radio was the country's primary source of entertainment and news. Classic comedy programs like *The Jack Benny Show* and the crackly news coverage of **Edward R. Murrow** amused and informed Americans for decades. WDIA, an all black radio station in the late 1940s, disseminated ideas about religion and politics and was instrumental in uniting the African-American community in the years leading up to the civil rights movement. Even though the moving images and crisper sounds of television have reduced radio's earlier, widespread popularity, it remains a treasured medium in America's car-dependent culture. Radio is generally divided into AM and FM; talk radio comprises most of the low-frequency AM slots, and the high-powered FM stations feature most of the music. Each broadcaster owns a four-letter call-name, with "W" as the first letter for those east of the Mississippi River (as in WJMN), and "K" to the west (as in KPFA).

The more intellectually-minded listen to **National Public Radio (NPR).** Full of classical music and social pundits debating important issues, NPR disseminates information about everything from general news on *Morning Edition* to car repair on the irreverent but useful *Car Talk.* Supplying the country's regional needs, local stations give up-to-the-minute news reports and air a wide range of music from country western to the latest pop. College radio stations often play more alternative music to appeal to younger listeners.

SPORTS AND RECREATION

For Americans, sports are inseparable from commercialism and regional allegiances. Dressed in colorful jerseys and bloated with cheap beer, Americans fill stadiums or lounge at home to cheer on their local teams. The best athletes come from all over the world to compete in America's biggest sports—baseball, football, and basketball—providing for intense competition and thrilling entertainment.

BASEBALL. The slow-paced, tension-inducing game of baseball captures the hearts of dreaming Little League children and earns its place as America's national pastime. Baseball in the US centers on the **Major League Baseball (MLB)** season, lasting from spring training in early March until October. Every fall, the **World Series** matches the league's top two teams, and garners national attention.

(AMERICAN) FOOTBALL. Not for the weak, football combines the toughness of boxing with the athleticism of basketball. Nowhere is the commercialism of American sports more spectacularly displayed than in the **Super Bowl.** Every January, the **National Football League (NFL)** season ends in grandiose style with a championship featuring the league's two best teams and commercial campaigns costing millions of dollars. The game is especially dear to Middle America, where crazed fans applaud the padded warriors of the gridiron.

BASKETBALL. The professional basketball teams making up the **National Basketball Association (NBA)** hail from almost every major city. NBA players have come a long way since the first teams, who played with peach baskets and Converse All-Star sneakers. Today, professional basketball games are fast-paced, aerial shows. Women have gotten into the game with the **WNBA,** a young but exciting league.

ICE HOCKEY. The **National Hockey League (NHL),** comprised of both American and Canadian teams, features great ice hockey and some of the best fights in professional sports. As NHL teams vie for the **Stanley Cup,** the tension of competition often results in crowd-pleasing team brawls.

COLLEGE SPORTS. Sticking with their school allegiances, many Americans live and die by their college's sporting endeavors. College teams compete within regional conferences, creating fierce rivalries fueled by hordes of fanatical student supporters. Football draws the biggest crowds, and each January the National Champion is decided on a rotating basis at either the **Rose Bowl, Fiesta Bowl, Orange Bowl,** or **Sugar Bowl.** Enthusiasm for college hoops often surpasses that for the pros, and women's college basketball has become increasingly popular in recent years. Every spring, hoops fan-demonium reaches fever pitch during the NCAA tournament, fondly called **March Madness.** While more and more high-school players are skipping college to play professionally, the college courts are still a great place to see the NBA superstars of tomorrow.

OTHER SPORTS. Other sports claim smaller niches of the American spectatorship. Both golf and tennis have internationally publicized tournaments known as the **US Open.** Now America's largest spectator sport, **NASCAR auto racing** draws droves of fans to Daytona Beach, FL in February with the Daytona 500, but the heart of Middle America still beats the loudest at the Indianapolis 500, held on the Sunday before Memorial Day. The horse racing of the **Kentucky Derby** hones the betting strategies of seasoned gamblers and tries the tolerance of seasoned boozers. Amusingly named horses, filthy rich stable owners, and minute jockeys seek the coveted **Triple Crown,** which is composed of the Derby, the **Preakness,** and the **Belmont Stakes. Major League Soccer (MLS)** is an up-and-coming but not yet widely followed sport in the United States, but soccer continues to be promoted heavily as the US national team seeks to become a World Cup contender by 2010.

HOLIDAYS

2006 NATIONAL HOLIDAYS	
January 1	New Year's Day
January 16	Martin Luther King, Jr. Day
February 20	Presidents Day
May 29	Memorial Day
July 4	Independence Day
September 4	Labor Day
October 9	Columbus Day
November 11	Veterans Day
November 23	Thanksgiving
December 25	Christmas Day

LIFE AND TIMES

BEYOND TOURISM

A PHILOSOPHY FOR TRAVELERS

Let's Go believes that the connection between travelers and their destinations is an important one. We know that many travelers care passionately about the communities and environments they explore, but we also know that even conscientious tourists can inadvertently damage natural wonders and harm cultural environments. With this Beyond Tourism chapter, *Let's Go* hopes to promote a better understanding of the US and enhance your experience there. You'll also find Beyond Tourism information throughout the book in the form of special "Giving Back" sidebar features that highlight regional Beyond Tourism opportunities.

There are several options for those who seek to participate in Beyond Tourism activities. Opportunities for **volunteering** are plentiful, both with local and international organizations. **Studying** can also be instructive, whether through direct enrollment in a local university or in an independent research project. **Working** is a way both to immerse yourself in the local culture and to finance your travels.

As a **volunteer** in the US, you can participate in projects either on a short-term basis or as the main component of your trip. Opportunities for volunteerism, activism, and conservation abound, from cities to National Parks and everywhere in between. Spend several hours bringing food to the homeless (p. 79), several days building a house for a low-income family in the Mississippi Delta with Habitat for Humanity (p. 79), or several months mentoring a child through Big Brothers Big Sisters of America (p. 80). Later in this chapter, we recommend organizations that can help you find the opportunities that best suit your interests, whether you're looking to pitch in for a day or a year.

Studying at a college or language program, either by enrolling in a local university or through a study abroad program, allows for exploration of intellectual avenues while living as a "real" American student.

Many travelers also structure their trips by the **work** that they can do along the way—either odd jobs as they go, or full-time stints in cities where they plan to stay for some time. Regardless of whether you are looking for temporary work or something more permanent, a good place to start your search is the local newspaper, which is usually the best source of up-to-date job information. Internet search engines like **www.monster.com** are also helpful. Before signing on, be sure you have the correct visa and working papers (see **Visa Information,** p. 80).

BEYOND TOURISM HIGHLIGHTS

DISCOVER the natural beauty of the Southwest while volunteering at Utah's Canyonlands National Park (p. 78).

SPEAK OUT at the annual National Poetry Slam in Albuquerque, NM (p. 84).

IMMERSE yourself in architect Paolo Soleri's experimental community while working and learning about ecologically-friendly architecture (p. 84).

STUDY at one of America's private or public universities and experience the life of an American college student (p. 81).

Start your hunt for opportunities at ■**www.beyondtourism.com,** *Let's Go's* searchable online database of alternatives to tourism, where you can find exciting feature articles and helpful program listings divided by country, continent, and program type.

VOLUNTEERING

Volunteering can be one of the most fulfilling experiences you have in life, especially if you combine it with the thrill of traveling in a new place. The sheer size of the US guarantees that no matter where you are and what you're interested in, there will be a way for you to get involved. In urban areas, mentoring and literacy programs and organizations that work to combat hunger and homelessness offer an abundance of volunteer opportunities. Environmental conservation has become an increasingly popular activity for visitors to the country's many national and state parks. Search engines like **www.volunteermatch.org** can be a useful resource for finding local opportunities wherever you may be.

Most people who volunteer in the US do so on a short-term basis, at organizations that make use of drop-in or once-a-week volunteers. The best way to find opportunities that match your interests and schedule may be to check with local or national volunteer centers like the ones listed below. Social outreach work is generally the most common short-term volunteer activity—it can take as little as an afternoon to make a difference in a community.

Those looking for longer, more intensive volunteer opportunities usually go through a parent organization that takes care of logistical details and often provides a group environment and support system—for a fee. There are two main types of organizations—religious and non-sectarian—although there are rarely restrictions on participation for either.

ECOTOURISM AND CONSERVATION

A large number of ecotourism organizations have blossomed in the US, offering costly activities and tours developed to minimize environmental impact. More innovative programs arrange outings engineered to improve the environment and quality of life at the local level, while providing volunteers with the opportunity to research and experience the wilderness, and to build work skills. Meanwhile, conservation groups work to protect America's wilderness and wildlife.

American Society for the Prevention of Cruelty to Animals (ASPCA), 424 E. 92nd St., New York, NY 10128 (☎212-876-7700; www.aspca.org). Promotes the humane treatment of animals through awareness programs, public policy efforts, shelter support, and animal medical treatment. Look under "Find a Shelter" on their website to find a list of shelters needing volunteers, or apply to volunteer at the ASPCA's headquarters in New York City. The ASPCA is partnered with **www.petfinder.com,** which also has a database of shelters and rescue groups.

Backroads, 801 Cedar St. Berkeley, CA 94710 (☎510-527-1555; www.backroads.com). Week-long walking, biking, and multisport trips designed to minimize environmental impact by avoiding mechanized transport. Destinations include San Juan Islands, WA; the Gulf Coast; and northern New England. Most courses $1200-2000.

Earth Share, 7735 Old Georgetown Rd., Ste. 900, Bethesda, MD 20814 (☎800-875-3863 or 240-333-0300; www.earthshare.org). A network of national conservation organizations that offers links to short- and longer-term volunteer opportunities with community and state organizations in 19 states.

BEYOND TOURISM

↰ WHY PAY MONEY TO VOLUNTEER?

Many volunteers are surprised to learn that some organizations require large fees or "donations." While this may seem ridiculous at first glance, such fees often keep the organization afloat, in addition to covering administrative expenses and airfare, room, and board for the volunteers. (Other organizations must rely on private donations and government subsidies.) If you're concerned about how a program spends its fees, request an annual report or finance account. A reputable organization won't refuse to inform you of how volunteer money is spent. Pay-to-volunteer programs might be a good idea for young travelers who are looking for more support and structure (such as pre-arranged transportation and housing), or anyone who would rather not create a volunteer experience from scratch.

Earthwatch Institute, 3 Clock Tower Pl., Ste. 100, Box 75, Maynard, MA 01754 (☎800-776-0188 or 978-461-0081; www.earthwatch.org). Arranges 1- to 3-week programs to promote the conservation of natural resources and aid in field research. Under the supervision of leading scientists, volunteer teams perform tasks as far-ranging as tracking wildlife in Alaska's temperate rainforests to excavating prehistoric pueblos in the Southwest. Volunteers must be 16+. Expeditions generally cost $700-4000, depending on length and location.

Environmental Careers Organization, 30 Winter St., Boston, MA 02108 (☎617-426-4375; www.eco.org) Develop skills in communications, outreach, or as a field technician for organizations like the Bureau of Land Management, US Geological Survey, and the Environmental Protection Agency. 3-month to 2-year paid internships in 35 states and 3 US territories. Internships mostly available in summer but also during the year.

National Outdoor Leadership School (NOLS), 284 Lincoln St., Lander, WY 82520 (☎800-710-6657; www.nols.edu). NOLS designs 2- to 12-week wilderness expeditions that foster leadership abilities and valuable backcountry skills, such as backpacking, wilderness medicine, and caving. Age requirements vary by expedition. Most courses cost at least $100 per day.

Natural Resources Conservation Service, Attn: Conservation Communications Staff, P.O. Box 2890, Washington, D.C. 20013 (☎202-720-3210; www.nrcs.usda.gov). Volunteer on private farms and ranches, in classrooms, or in offices promoting conservation and improving wildlife habitats. Give tours and speeches, take photographs, or organize exhibits with wildlife specialists.

Orion Grassroots Network, 187 Main St., Great Barrington, MA 01230 (☎888-909-6568; www.oriononline.org). A network of 795 non-profit and community organizations that matches volunteers with paid and unpaid environmental internships.

Volunteers-in-Parks (National Park Service), 1849 C St. NW, Washington, D.C. 20240 (☎202-354-1800; www.nps.gov/volunteer). From the Great Smoky Mountains to Alaska's Glacier Bay, volunteers learn about park management, wildlife research, and environmental education by giving tours, monitoring wildlife, picking up trash, and planting trees in national parks. Applicants from abroad may receive free, reimbursed, or reduced-cost housing and food from the International Volunteers-in-Parks program.

World-Wide Opportunities on Organic Farms USA, P.O. Box 510, Felton, CA 95018 (☎831-425-3276; www.wwoofusa.org). Learn about organic farming and permaculture on one of over 200 host farms across the United States. Volunteers devote about 6hr. per day to farm work in exchange for accommodations and meals. Volunteers must be 18+ or accompanied by a legal guardian. Requested stay lengths vary from a weekend to 3 months. Membership $20; 2-person membership $30.

COMMUNITY OUTREACH

Communities in the United States face distinct and varied crises, such as hunger, homelessness, and lack of affordable health care. There are numerous opportunities to get involved in these communities and make a difference. Interested individuals can find short- and long-term volunteer opportunities through volunteer search engines, such as **www.volunteersolutions.org** and **www.networkforgood.org,** that help individuals locate organizations that fit their interests and locations.

America's Second Harvest, 35 E. Wacker Dr., #2000, Chicago, IL 60601 (☎800-771-2303 or 312-263-2303; www.2ndharvest.org). As the US's largest hunger organization, Second Harvest oversees more than 200 food banks throughout the country and feeds more than 23 million people each year. Sort and repackage salvaged food, prepare and serve food at a shelter, or tutor children.

Body Health Resources Corporation, 250 W. 57th St., New York, NY 10107 (www.thebody.com). "The Body" is an extensive, informative website about all things HIV/AIDS-related. Check out the "Helping and Getting Help" section of the website for a list of regional HIV/AIDS service organizations throughout the US that are in need of volunteers. The **United States Office of Minority Health's Resource Center,** P.O. Box 37337, Washington, D.C. 20013 (☎800-444-6472; www.omhrc.gov/OMHRC/index.htm), provides one of the most comprehensive lists of US state, federal, and other service organizations.

Habitat for Humanity International, 121 Habitat St., Americus, GA 31709 (☎229-924-6935, ext. 2551 or 2552; www.habitat.org). Volunteers build houses throughout the US (and in 100 other countries) to benefit low-income families. Projects take anywhere from 2 weeks to 3 years. Short-term program costs range $900-4000; check with local branches for free volunteer opportunities.

Meals on Wheels Association of America, 203 S. Union St., Alexandria, VA 22314 (☎703-548-5558; www.mowaa.org). Buy, prepare, and deliver meals to the elderly and the poor. Public awareness and research projects also available. Search the website for the region in which you would like to serve.

National Coalition for the Homeless, 1012 14th St. NW, #600, Washington, D.C. 20005 (☎202-737-6444; www.nationalhomeless.org/local/local.html). Maintains a website with listings of local homeless assistance programs and shelters, food banks, hospitals, and advocacy groups in every state.

National Hospice Foundation, 1700 Diagonal Rd., Ste. 625, Alexandria, VA 22314 (☎703-837-1500; www.hospiceinfo.org). Hospices offer emotional and spiritual support for those close to death, as well as counseling for their families. Search by name, state, or ZIP code to find a US hospice in need of volunteers.

SCI International Voluntary Service, 5505 Walnut Level Rd., Crozet, VA 22932 (☎206-350-6585; www.sci-ivs.org). Service Civil International organizes teams for 2- to 4-week work camps or 3- to 12-month volunteer postings on grassroots projects. Most camps also include opportunities to study social justice issues. Volunteers must be 16+. Fees run from $115, and include SCI-IVS membership, housing, and meals; additional fees for applicants who register through international affiliates.

LITERACY AND YOUTH OUTREACH

A quarter of American adults are not proficient in reading. Many experience difficulties because they did not finish high school, while others are immigrants or persons suffering from learning or vision disabilities. Educational and mentoring

BEYOND TOURISM

programs throughout the US also offer instruction and support to youth in need. These programs are most appropriate for volunteers who are willing to make a long-term commitment to working with their students.

America's Literacy Directory, (☎800-228-8813; www.literacydirectory.org/volunteer.asp). A service of the National Institute for Literacy, this online directory allows you to search for volunteer opportunities among more than 5000 literacy programs for adults and young adults.

Big Brothers Big Sisters of America, 230 N. 13th St., Philadelphia, PA 19107 (☎215-567-7000; www.bbbsa.org). This century-old organization provides mentorship, friendship, and support to hundreds of thousands of American kids. Paired "Bigs" and "Littles" work on homework together, participate in community service, or just hang out.

The National Mentoring Partnership, 1600 Duke St., Ste. 300, Alexandria, VA 22314 (☎703-224-2200; www.mentoring.org). Advocates the expansion of mentoring programs with the goal of serving the 17.6 million children in the US who could benefit from mentor relationships. Maintains a database of mentoring opportunities, including state and local mentoring partnerships, programs, and volunteer centers.

Proliteracy Worldwide, 1320 Jamesville Ave., Syracuse, NY 13210 (☎888-528-2224 or 315-422-9121; www.proliteracy.org). The world's largest adult volunteer literacy organization, with chapters in the US. Tutors teach basic literacy or English for Speakers of Other Languages (ESOL) to individuals and families.

STUDYING

Study-abroad programs range from basic language and culture courses to college-level classes, which can often be taken for credit. In order to choose a program that best fits your needs, research as much as you can before making your decision—determine costs and duration, as well as what kind of students participate in the program and what sort of accommodations are provided.

VISA INFORMATION

All foreign students must have a **visa** to study in the US. Travelers must also provide proof of intent to leave, like a return plane ticket or an I-94 card. Foreign students wanting to study in the US must apply for either an M-1 visa (non-academic or vocational studies) or an F-1 visa (for full-time students enrolled in a program to study or conduct research at an accredited US college or university). See www.unitedstatesvisas.gov/studying.html for further information. To get a visa or study permit, apply at a US embassy or consulate in your home country. If English is not your native language, you will probably want to take the Test of English as a Foreign Language (TOEFL), administered in many countries. The international students office at the institution you will be attending can give you specifics. Contact **TOEFL/TSE Publications,** P.O. Box 6151, Princeton, NJ, 08541 (☎877-863-3546, outside the US ☎609-771-7100; www.toefl.org). US **visa extensions** are sometimes attainable with a completed I-539 form; call the Bureau of Citizenship and Immigration Service's (BCIS) forms request line (☎800-870-3676) or get it online at www.immigration.gov/graphics/formsfee/forms/i-539.htm. See **http://travel.state.gov/visa** for more info. Security measures have made the visa application process more rigorous, and more lengthy. **Apply well in advance of your travel date.** The process may seem complex, but you must take the proper steps or risk deportation.

In programs that have large groups of students who speak the same language, there is a trade-off. You may feel more comfortable in the community, but you will not have the same opportunity to practice a foreign language or befriend other international students. For accommodations, dorm life provides a better opportunity to mingle with fellow students, but there is less of a chance to experience the local scene. If you live with a family, there is the potential to build lifelong friendships with natives and to experience day-to-day life in more depth, but conditions can vary greatly from family to family.

UNIVERSITIES

Most university-level study abroad programs in the US are conducted in English, with many offering classes for English learners and beginner- and lower-level language courses. Those relatively fluent in English may find it cheaper to enroll directly in a US university, though getting college credit may be more difficult. You can search **www.studyabroad.com** for various semester-abroad programs that meet your criteria, including your desired location and focus of study. The list below includes organizations that can help place students in university programs abroad, and those that have their own branch in the US.

In order to live the life of a real American college student, consider a visiting student program lasting either a semester or a full year. (Some institutions have trimesters, but most American universities have a fall semester Sept.-Dec. and a spring semester Jan.-May.) The best method is to contact colleges and universities in your home country to see what kind of exchanges they have with those in the US; college students can often receive credit for study abroad. A more complicated option for advanced English speakers is to enroll directly in an American institution. Each state maintains a public university system. The US also hosts a number of reputable private universities, as well as innumerable community, professional, and technical colleges. Tuition costs, however, are high in the US, and a full course of undergraduate study entails a four-year commitment.

LANGUAGE SCHOOLS

Language schools can be independent international or local organizations or divisions of foreign universities. They rarely offer college credit, but are a good alternative to university study if you desire greater focus on the language or a less rigorous courseload. These programs are also good for younger high school students who might not feel comfortable with older students in a university program.

American Language Programs, 56 Hobbs Brook Rd., Boston, MA 02493, USA (☎781-888-1515; www.alp-online.com). ALP runs programs in Arizona, California, Florida, New York, and Massachusetts that include homestays and intensive English training. $900-1080 per week (15-25hr.) for 1 person, $1600-1960 for 2 people.

Eurocentres, 1901 N. Fort Myer Dr., Ste. 800, Arlington, VA 22209 (☎703-243-7884; www.eurocentres.com) or in Europe, Head Office, Seestr. 247, CH-8038 Zurich, Switzerland (☎41 1 485 50 40; fax 481 61 24). Language programs for beginning to advanced students with homestays in the US.

Language Immersion Institute, JFT 214, State University of New York at New Paltz, 75 S. Manheim Blvd., New Paltz, NY 12561 (☎845-257-3500; www.newpaltz.edu/lii). 2-week summer language courses and some overseas courses in English. Program fees are around $1000 for a 2-week course, not including accommodations.

BEYOND TOURISM

Osako Sangyo University Los Angeles (OSULA) Education Center, 3921 Laurel Canyon Blvd., Studio City, CA 91604 (☎818-509-1484; www.osula.com). General or intensive English or Japanese classes in a residential college setting in suburban Los Angeles.

PROGRAMS IN THE ARTS

Those of a more creative persuasion can pursue artistic expression in the US—bohemian quarters of New York City and San Francisco, as well as the wide open spaces of the American interior, offer all types of artisic opportunities.

VISUAL AND PERFORMING ARTS

Chautauqua Institution, P.O. Box 28, Chautauqua, NY 14722 (☎800-836-ARTS/2782; www.chautauqua-inst.org). A National Historic Landmark that offers intensive summer programs in art, dance, music, and theater for talented students. Programs range from 2-7 weeks. Need- and talent-based scholarships available.

New York Foundation for the Arts, 155 Ave. of the Americas, 14th fl., New York, NY 10013 (☎212-366-6900; www.nyfa.org). From dance to music to visual arts, NYFA provides a national database of resources in the arts, including listings of current job and internship openings, and schedules for art events. The "For Artists" link on the website posts audition notices, calls for entry, and information about workshops.

National Association of Schools of Theatre, 11250 Roger Bacon Dr., Ste. 21, Reston, VA 20190 (☎703-437-0700; http://nast.arts-accredit.org). Supplies a list of accredited degree- and non-degree-granting institutions in the US that offer theater programs.

Santa Fe Art Institute, P.O. Box 24044, Santa Fe, NM 87502 (☎505-424-5050; www.sfai.org). A world-class artistic center, the Santa Fe Art Institute offers 1-week workshops ($900, including residency and tuition), and allows participants to learn from professional resident artists. Need-based scholarships are available.

Summer Theater, Box 727, Saxtons River, VT 05154 (www.summertheater.com). Each year, small local theaters throughout the country put out a series of dramatic productions, including musicals, comedy, drama, and opera. Tickets are affordable, and many young and talented actors get their first experiences on the stage. For audition and performance information, contact the individual summer theaters listed on the website.

FILM

Indiewire.com, 304 Hudson St., 6th fl., New York, NY 10013 (☎212-675-3908; www.indiewire.com). Explore the student and independent film scene in the US while you get the low-down on upcoming film festivals, lectures, and symposia. Classifieds list paid and unpaid positions for actors, crew, writers, and producers; you can also meet and find collaborators for your own projects.

New York Film Academy (NYFA), 100 E. 17th St., New York, NY 10003 (☎212-674-4300; www.nyfa.com). NYFA allows would-be actors, filmmakers, and screenwriters the chance to hone their skills on studio sets in several cities. Program lengths vary from 1 week to 1 year, and include classes in acting, screenwriting, digital imaging, filmmaking, comedy, and 3-D animation. Programs cost $1500-25,000.

University of Southern California School of Cinema-Television, Summer Program Enrollment, 850 W. 34th St., Los Angeles, CA 90089 (☎213-740-1742; www.uscsummerfilm.com). Boasting an alumni list that includes *Star Wars* mastermind George Lucas, screenwriter John Milius (*Apocalypse Now*), and producer Laura Ziskin (*Spiderman*), the world-renowned film school offers summer workshops with classes in writing, digital imaging, directing, and producing. University housing is available, as are classes for students who have already logged some hours (or years) in the industry. Students also have access to free seminars, workshops, and screenings.

WALK THIS WAY
Exploring America at a Slower Pace

I f you asked 100 people to describe a good way to discover America—to explore the heart of the country—you would likely get 100 different answers. Chances are, none of them would say, "Spending your honeymoon collecting discarded underwear from the highways across the land."

However, my wife and I did just that.

As we settled into our new marriage in the suburbs of Los Angeles, our lives felt out of touch. We dreamed of discovering small towns where no one feels a need to lock their doors, where stores have served 100+ years of customers and struggled to survive the invasion of Big Box Retail, and where communities keep local traditions alive as the country grows more generic. It's an America people rarely notice while flying at 35,000 feet. It's an America that defies detection as people race along the interstates at 75 mph. There's only one sure-fire way to find that country: give up your car.

My wife and I had both dreamed—independently—of taking a journey from coast to coast without a car. We needed a spark, and that spark came two months after our wedding. As we sat in another traffic jam on another crowded California freeway, I noticed a fresh pile of litter spread over the road shoulder. In that moment I blurted out, "If we're ever going to walk across the country, we should pick up litter while we're at it—do something productive."

Two years, 4100 mi., and four tons of litter later, we arrived on the other side of the country. In addition to the usual roadside junk, we picked up underwear in 22 of the 23 states we passed through—every one except Kansas. An old farmer there told us why. "We don't throw our underwear away here," he said. "We wear them until there's holes in it, then we use them for dustrags."

Connecting with people at every stop was one of the greatest benefits of touring under our own power. We now have friends scattered across the country, many of whom helped us experience traditions that grow scarcer each year. As we plodded along, we got to make maple syrup, milk cows, and herd sheep. We also got to escape the rat race. When your only deadline is making it to the next small town before the only cafe closes, the stress falls away from your life. Time loses its importance, and it hardly makes sense to wear a watch.

A true trip of discovery does carry a considerable cost. Though you save money on outrageous gas prices, you pay with the additional time needed to travel slowly. Unless you have friends or family driving alongside you, you also pay with a loss of comfort. That payment, though, can give you experiences and friendships that will enrich your life. Maybe you can't spare the time to walk across the country; you can achieve similar results, yet avoid much of the tedium, by taking a bike.

Be aware that adventure trips can become addictive. For me, the road beckoned again in 2002. This time I planned a coast-to-coast bike-ride, done in short segments spread over three years. Though biking interfered with bagging litter, the trash angle still permeated my journey. I arranged to begin most days speaking at a school, urging the kids to take care of this great land and encouraging them to seek out their own adventures.

As I learned, even clearing underwear off the highway makes the country a little more beautiful. Maybe while you discover America, you can make a difference in one corner of it.

Glen Hanket is an inveterate traveler and a lover of national parks. He is the author of Underwear by the Roadside: Litterwalk Coast-to-Coast, *the tale of his cross-country walk;* WOW! What a Ride, *which covers his bike ride across the US, along with other adventures; and over 20 guides on bicycling in Colorado.*

WRITING AND SPOKEN WORD

Poetry Slam Incorporated, 11462 East Ln., Whitmore Lake, MI 48189 (☎810-231-5435; www.poetryslam.com). All across the country, poets perform 3-5 minutes of their work in cafes and bars, and are judged by audience members on performance and writing ability. Poetry Slam Inc. compiles a massive list of these venues; most have at least 1 night a week devoted to slams or readings. Admission prices range from free to a small cover charge; you may have to sign up in advance to perform.

Poets and Writers, Inc., 72 Spring St., Ste. 301, New York, NY 10012 (☎212-226-3586; www.pw.org). Provides links to writing programs at universities in the US as well as an extensive list of conferences and residencies for writers.

Writer's Colonies allow writers to pursue writing projects without distraction. Residencies range from 1 week to several months; some programs include workshops and conferences. Costs generally cover room and board, though fellowships are occasionally available. A directory of several writer's colonies is available at www.poewar.com/articles/colonies.htm; for a more comprehensive listing of artist's retreats, try *Artist's Communities: A Directory of Residencies in the United States that Offer Time and Space for Creativity,* by Tricia Snell (Allworth Press 2000).

ARCHITECTURE AND DESIGN

Arcosanti, HC74, P.O. Box 4136, Mayer, AZ 86333 (☎928-632-7135; www.arcosanti.org). Founded by Frank Lloyd Wright's disciple Paolo Soleri (who still lives here), Acrosanti is a community 70 mi. north of Phoenix based on Soleri's theory of "arcology"—the symbiotic relationship between architecture and ecology. It hosts 1-week ($485) and 5-week ($1175) workshops in which participants help expand the settlement while learning about Soleri's project and developing their skills at construction and planning. An all-expenses-paid 3-month internship is available for those with some prior architectural background after they have completed the 5-week workshop.

Ecological Design Institute, P.O. Box 989, Sausalito, CA 94966 (☎415-332-5806; www.ecodesign.org). Integrating technology and nature into their vision of green design, EDI promotes education for sustainability, highlighting design projects along the West Coast that exemplify this principle. Their website has a list of institutions in the US that offer workshops and classes in ecologically friendly design and construction.

WORKING

As with volunteering, work opportunities tend to fall into two categories. Some travelers want long-term jobs that allow them to get to know another part of the world as a member of the community, while others seek out short-term jobs to finance the next leg of their travels. In the US, people who want to work long-term should consider exchange programs. Short-term work is most often found in service industries and agriculture.

For either type of work, local newspapers are the best places to start searching. Internet search engines like **www.monster.com** are also helpful. Note that working abroad often requires a special work visa; see the box below for more information.

LONG-TERM WORK

If you're planning on spending a substantial amount of time (more than three months) working in the US, search for a job well in advance. International placement agencies are often the easiest way to find employment abroad. **Internships** and seasonal jobs are a good way to transition into working abroad; although

VISA INFORMATION

All foreign visitors are required to have a **visa** if they intend to work in the US. In addition, travelers must provide proof of intent to leave, such as a return plane ticket or an I-94 card. A **work permit** (or "green card") is also required. Your employer must obtain this document, usually by demonstrating that you have skills that locals lack. Friends in the US can sometimes help expedite work permits or arrange work-for-accommodations exchanges. To **obtain visas and work permits,** contact a US embassy or consulate (see **Embassies and Consulates,** p. 9). Visa extensions in the US are sometimes attainable with a completed I-539 form; request forms from the Bureau of Citizenship and Immigration Service (☎800-870-3676; http://uscis.gov/graphics/formsfee/forms/index.htm). See **http://travel.state.gov/visa** for more information. Security measures have made the visa application process more rigorous, and therefore more lengthy. **Apply well in advance of your travel date.** The process may seem complex, but the alternative could be deportation.

interns are often unpaid or poorly paid, many say the experience is well worth it. Be wary of advertisements for companies claiming the ability to get you a job abroad for a fee—often the same listings are available online or in newspapers.

Alliances Abroad Group, Inc., 1221 S. Mopac Expwy., Ste. 250, Austin, TX 78746 (☎866-ABROAD; www.alliancesabroad.com). Organizes summer work in the service industry for university students ages 18-28.

British Universities North American Club (BUNAC), 16 Bowling Green Ln., London, EC1R OQH, UK (☎44 020 7251 3472, US 203-264-0901; www.bunac.com). Arranges short- and long-term job placements, visas, and work authorization in the US for individuals 18+. Work placement includes summer jobs, work training programs, and camp counselor positions. Some programs are open to non-students.

Camp America, 37a Queen's Gate, London, SW7 5HR, UK (☎44 020 7581 7373, US 203-399-5000; www.campamerica.co.uk). Summer camp jobs are popular in the US; most last about 9 weeks and can include time afterward for travel. Camp America places counselors in a variety of camps, including religious camps and camps for disadvantaged or special-needs children. Positions in service areas, such as kitchen or maintenance, are also available. **Camp Counselors USA,** 2330 Marinship Way, Ste. 250, Sausalito, CA 94965 (☎415-339-2728; www.ccusa.com) also places counselors, and has positions in specialty areas such as outdoor sports and the arts.

Council Exchanges, 3 Copley Pl., 2nd fl., Boston, MA 02116 (☎617-247-0350; www.councilexchanges.org). Charges a $300-475 fee for arranging working authorizations valid for 3-6 months. Extensive information about job opportunities in the US.

JOBS YOU ARRANGE

Looking beyond job placement programs may be the best way to find a job opportunity that fits your needs, skills, and time. However, most job service and search engines do not assist potential employees in acquiring visas or work permits, which you must have before applying for temporary work or internships. Keep in mind that individual employers may have specific policies with regard to non-US citizens, and allow for extra time to process applications. **About Jobs** has summer jobs, internships, and resort work in North America. (180 State Rd., Ste. 2U, Sagamore Beach, MA 02562. ☎508-888-6889; www.aboutjobs.com.) More listings of seasonal jobs are available from **Cool Works,** whose options include work at state parks, ski resorts, camps, ranches, and amusement parks. (P.O. Box 272, 511 Hwy. 89, Gardiner, MT 59030. ☎406-848-2380; www.coolworks.com.)

BEYOND TOURISM

AU PAIR WORK

Au pairs are typically women (though sometimes men), aged 18-27, who work as live-in nannies, caring for children and doing light housework in foreign countries in exchange for room, board, and a small stipend. Most former au pairs speak favorably of their experience. One perk of the job is that it allows you to really get to know the country without the high expenses of traveling. Drawbacks, however, often include mediocre pay and long hours. In the US, weekly salaries typically fall below $200, with at least 45hr. of work expected. Au pairs are expected to speak English and have at least 200hr. of childcare experience. Much of the au pair experience depends on the family with whom you are placed. A good starting point for those seeking employment is **Childcare International, Ltd.** (Trafalgar House, Greenville Pl., London NW7 3SA, UK. ☎+44 020 8906-3116; fax 8906-3461; www.child-int.co.uk.) A similar placement agency in the US is **InterExchange.** (161 Sixth Ave., New York, NY 10013. ☎212-924-0446; fax 924-0575; www.interexchange.org).

SHORT-TERM WORK

Traveling for long periods of time can get expensive; therefore, many travelers try their hand at odd jobs for a few weeks at a time to help finance another month or two of touring around. A popular option is to work several hours a day at a hostel in exchange for free or discounted room and/or board. Most often, these short-term jobs are found by word of mouth, or simply by talking to the owner of a hostel or restaurant. Due to the high turnover in the tourism industry, many places are eager for help, even if it is only temporary. *Let's Go* tries to list temporary jobs like these whenever possible; look in the practical information sections of larger cities. Help-wanted sections in local newspapers and on websites like **www.craigslist.com** are helpful resources for short-term jobs in popular destinations. It is illegal to take a paid job without a work permit or visa.

ADDITIONAL RESOURCES

Alternatives to the Peace Corps: A Directory of Third World and U.S. Volunteer Opportunities, by Jennifer S. Willsea. Food First Books, 2003 ($10).

Back Door Guide to Short-Term Job Adventures: Internships, Extraordinary Experiences, Seasonal Jobs, Volunteering, Working Abroad, by Michael Landes. Ten Speed Press, 2002 ($22).

Get Outside! A Guide to Volunteer Opportunities and Working Vacations in America's Great Outdoors, by American Hiking Society. Falcon, 2002 ($11).

Green Volunteers: The World Guide to Voluntary Work in Nature, by Ausenda and McCloskey. Universe, 2003 ($15).

Help America Read: A Handbook for Volunteers, by Fountas and Pinnell. Heinemann, 1997 ($17.50).

International Directory of Voluntary Work, by Whetter and Pybus. Peterson's Guides and Vacation Work, 2000 ($16).

International Job Finder: Where the Jobs Are Worldwide, by Daniel Lauber. Planning Communications, 2002 ($20).

Invest Yourself: The Catalogue of Volunteer Opportunities, published by the Commission on Voluntary Service and Action (☎646-486-2446).

Make a Difference: America's Guide to Volunteering and Community Service, by Arthur Blaustein. Jossey-Bass, 2003 ($13).

Taking Time Off, by Hall and Lieber. Princeton Review, 2003 ($13).

Volunteer Vacations: Short-term Adventures That Will Benefit You and Others, by Cutchins and Geissinger. Chicago Review Press, 2003 ($18).

NEW ENGLAND

New England considered itself a mecca for intellectuals and progressive politicians long before the States were United, and still does today. Scholars from every corner of the planet inundate New England's colleges and universities each fall, and town meetings still evoke the democratic spirit that inspired the American Revolution. While the region is heavy on historical landmarks that detail its break from "Old" England, New England's history didn't stop at Lexington and Concord, evident in its diversity and ever-evolving culture. Still,

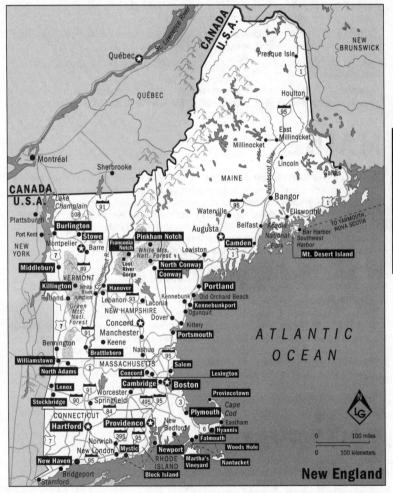

New England

some things never change: the region's unpredictable climate can be particularly disconcerting to unsuspecting tourists, but long-time locals are accustomed to the occasional May snowstorm or February heat wave. Today's visitors seek adventure in the rough edges that nearly ruined early settlers, flocking to the coastline to meander on pebbled beaches or heading to the slopes of the Green and White Mountains to ski, hike, and canoe. The perennial New England trademark is magnificent fall foliage, which fills northern roads in the gap between summer and ski season and transforms quiet towns into postcard-worthy bursts of brilliance.

HIGHLIGHTS OF NEW ENGLAND

CRACK the shell of a succulent Maine **lobster** in Bar Harbor (p. 94), which serves the freshest seafood around, and don't miss out on New England clam "chowda."

SPRAWL on the lawns of **Tanglewood** (p. 151) as classical music, performed by some of the world's most illustrious musicians, washes over you.

BUNDLE UP before you tackle the frigid and beautiful slopes that comprise the East Coast's best **skiing** and **snowboarding** (p. 98 or p. 109).

CRANE your neck to take in the stunning fall **foliage** as you drive along scenic highways in Franconia Notch (p. 103).

TRANSPLANT yourself to the days of revolutionary ferment and colonial austerity while walking the **Freedom Trail** (p. 127) or visiting **Plimoth Plantation** (p. 139).

MAINE

Ever since Leif Ericson and the Vikings set foot on the shores of Maine nearly a millennium ago, travelers have been captivated by the state's distinctive blend of sea salt and pine forest, schooners and logging trucks, and, more recently, workboots and polo shirts. Today, thousands pour into Maine each summer, swimming in the cool Atlantic waters and reveling in the towns and cities that line the coast. Journey inland, and you'll find a more rural side of Maine, where small towns and vast expanses of wilderness await the adventurous traveler.

◪ PRACTICAL INFORMATION

Capital: Augusta.

Visitor Info: Maine Tourism Information, 59 State House Station, Augusta 04333 (☎207-623-0363 or 888-624-6345; www.visitmaine.com). **Maine Information Center,** in Kittery, 3 mi. north of the Maine-New Hampshire bridge (☎207-439-1319; open daily July to early Oct. 8am-6pm, mid-Oct. to June 9am-5:30pm). **Bureau of Parks and Lands,** State House Station #22 (AMHI, Harlow Bldg.), Augusta 04333 (☎207-287-3821; www.state.me.us/doc/parks). **Maine Forest Service,** Department of Conservation, State House Station #22, Augusta 04333 (☎207-287-2791).

Postal Abbreviation: ME. **Sales Tax:** 5%.

MAINE COAST

Maine's 288 mi. Atlantic coastline, full of rocky inlets and promontories, makes for some of the most dramatic scenery in New England. The port towns are strung together by the two-lane U.S. 1, the region's only option for accessing most coastal spots north of Portland. Although driving your own vehicle is the best way to explore the coast, be prepared to take your time—traffic is often slow in summer, especially through towns and villages.

PORTLAND ☎ 207

Tucked between forested land and a wild sea, Portland is the largest port town in Maine. The city thrives as an urban center in an otherwise rural area, with a mixture of industry, arts, and well-preserved relics of colonial times. In summer, the streets fill with the exuberant sounds of parades and festivals. Meanwhile, laughter can be heard long into the night in the old port district, where pubs beckon the city's spirited youth to set aflame even the coldest night.

◼️🔃 ORIENTATION AND PRACTICAL INFORMATION.
Downtown is located in the middle of the peninsula along **Congress Street,** between State St. and Pearl St. A few blocks south, between Commercial and Middle St. on the waterfront, lies the **Old Port.** These two districts contain most of the city's sights and attractions. **I-295** (off I-95) forms the northwestern boundary of the city. **Amtrak,** 100 Thompson's Point Rd., on Connector Rd., off Congress St. (☎800-872-7245; www.thedowneaster.com; ticket office open M-F 5:30am-4:05pm, Sa-Su 5:30am-6:35pm), runs to Boston (2¾hr., 4 per day, $21). **Concord Trailways** (☎828-1151; office open daily 4:30am-9:30pm), in the same building, runs buses to Bangor (2½hr., 3 per day, $23) and Boston (2hr., 12 per day, $19). Metro buses run to and from the station (M-Sa every 20min., Su every hr.). **Greyhound/Vermont Transit,** 950 Congress St., on the western outskirts of town (☎772-6587; www.greyhound.com), runs to Bangor (2½-3½hr., 5 per day, $22-28) and Boston (2hr., 6 per day, $17-27). Use caution in this area at night. **Metro Bus** services downtown Portland. Routes run 5:30am-11:45pm; brochures are at the visitors center. (☎774-0351. $1, seniors with Medicare card $0.50, under 5 free.) **Visitor Info: Visitors Information Bureau,** 245 Commercial St., between Union and Cross St. (☎800-306-4193; www.gotoportland.com. Open M-F 8am-5pm, Sa 10am-3pm.) **Internet Access: Portland Public Library,** 5 Monument Sq. (☎871-1700. Open M, W, F 9am-6pm, Tu and Th noon-9pm, Sa 9am-5pm. Free with guest library card.) **Post Office:** 400 Congress St. (☎871-8464. Open M-F 8am-7pm, Sa 9am-1pm.) **Postal Code:** 04101. **Area Code:** 207.

🏠 ACCOMMODATIONS.
Portland has some inexpensive accommodations during the winter, but summer prices jump steeply, especially on weekends.

ON THE MENU

LOBSTER TALES

It's nearly impossible to travel the New England coast without trying its famous lobster, but eating the sea critter isn't so easy. To avoid the embarrassment of having to ask your waiter how to indulge in this local treat, you should heed the following advice.

Most lobsters come with a bowl and bib. Unless you're a seasoned lobster-eater, use the bib—it's far better than a shirt drenched in lobster juice. As a reward for your prudence, everyone in the restaurant will know what you're eating. Use the bowl to make room on your plate.

The edible meat is firm and creamy white and is delicious dipped in the melted butter provided. Tackle (literally) the claws first, breaking them off where they meet the body, then cracking the claw with a nutcracker to get at the meat. Don't forget the knuckles—the meat is some of the best. The tail is next. Twist it off the body, then break off the fins and get at the inside with your fork.

At this stage you'll probably find the tamale, an unappetizing mass of green guck in the body of the lobster. Some consider it a delicacy, others consider it gross. You can decide. If you're still hungry, try breaking off the small legs and sucking out the meat.

Still not feeling up to the task of lobster-eating? Try a "lazy lobster"—the dirty work is already done, and all you have to do is feast and enjoy.

Lodging in the smaller towns up and down the coast can be less expensive. Three miles from downtown, the **Budget Inn Motel ❸**, 634 Main St. off U.S. 1/Main St. in South Portland, offers clean rooms at reasonable prices. (☎773-5722. Rooms $55-75. AmEx/D/DC/MC/V.) Closer to downtown, **The Inn at St. John ❹**, 939 Congress St., may be surrounded by run-down buildings, but inside, guests are welcomed by elegant decor and old-fashioned hospitality. (☎773-6481 or 800-636-9127. Continental breakfast included. Bike storage, free local calls, and free parking. Rooms with private bath available. Singles or doubles in summer M-Th $70-135, F-Su $115-175; winter $55-100/$60-115. AmEx/D/DC/MC/V.) **Wassamki Springs ❶**, 56 Saco St., in Scarborough, is the closest campground to Portland. Take I-95 S to 22 W, Exit 46. RVs and tents cluster around a lake surrounded by sandy beaches. (☎839-4276. Free showers and flush toilets. Reserve 2 weeks in advance, especially July-Aug. Open May to mid-Oct. 2-person sites with water and electricity $34, with hookup $36; each additional person $5; lakefront sites $3 extra. MC/V.)

🞐 **FOOD.** Portland's harbor overflows with seafood, but non-aquatic and vegetarian fare are easy to find. The organic pizzas at the 🞐**Flatbread Company ❸**, 72 Commercial St., have creative names like "Punctuated Equilibrium" (with roasted red pepper and onion) and cost $8-14. (☎772-8777. Open in summer M-Th 11:30am-10pm, F-Sa 11am-10:30pm; winter M-Th 11:30am-9pm, F-Sa 11:30am-10pm. AmEx/MC/V.) **Federal Spice ❶**, 225 Federal St., just off Congress St., seasons all its wraps and soft tacos (all under $6) with fiery Caribbean, South American, and Asian ingredients. (☎774-6404. Open M-Sa 11am-9pm. V.) While the name may not sound appetizing, **Duck Fat ❷**, 43 Middle St., sells delicious specialty treats like *beignets* (doughnut-like pastries, $3.50), spiced duck broth ($5), and amazing french fries ($4.50) cooked in—what else?—duck fat. (☎774-8080. Open M-Sa 11am-9pm, Su noon-9pm. MC/V.) **Gilbert's Chowder House ❸**, 92 Commercial St., is the local favorite for seafood. A large bread bowl of chowder ($7-11) is a meal in itself. (☎871-5636. Entrees $10-21. Open June-Sept. M-Th and Su 11am-10pm, F-Sa 11am-11pm; Oct.-May call for hours. AmEx/D/MC/V.) The cavernous 🞐**Portland Public Market,** at Preble St. and Cumberland Ave., three blocks from Monument Sq., sells ethnic foods, seafood, and baked goods from over 20 small food vendors. (☎228-2000; www.portlandmarket.com. Open M-Sa 9am-7pm, Su 10am-5pm.)

🞐 **SIGHTS.** Offshore islands with secluded beaches are just a ferry ride from the city proper. **Casco Bay Lines,** on State Pier near the corner of Commercial and Franklin, runs daily to **Long Island** and **Peaks Island,** among a few others. (☎774-7871; www.cascobaylines.com. Long Island: operates M-Sa 5am-9:30pm, Su 7:45am-9:30pm. Round-trip $8, seniors and ages 5-9 $4. Peaks Island: operates M-Sa 5:45am-11:30pm, Su 7:45am-11:30pm. Round-trip $6, seniors and ages 5-9 $3.) Peaks Island has great biking and kayaking and holds a reggae concert every Monday in summer at Jones Landing. **Brad's Recycled Bike Shop,** 115 Island Ave., on Peaks Island, rents bikes. (☎766-5631. Open daily 10am-5pm. $5 per hr., $8.50 for 3hr., $12 per day.) Try **Two Lights State Park,** across the Casco Bay Bridge, accessed from State or York St., then south along Rte. 77 to Cape Elizabeth, for a spot to picnic or walk along the ocean. (☎799-5871; www.state.me.us/doc/parks. Day use $2.50.) A trip to the still-functioning **Portland Head Light** in **Fort Williams Park** is definitely worth the scenic detour. From Rte. 77 N turn right at the flashing signal onto Shore Rd. and proceed to the park. The **Portland Observatory,** 138 Congress St., the last maritime signal tower in the US, offers unrivaled views of the city and an excellent historical tour. (☎774-5561; www.portlandlandmarks.org. Open daily 10am-5pm; last tour 4:40pm. Admission and tour $5, ages 6-16 $3.) It takes about eight days to brew a batch of beer at the **Shipyard Brewing Co.,** 86 Newbury St., but it only takes 30min. to tour the brewery and try a free sample. (☎761-0807. Tours every 30min. in summer M-F 3-5pm, Sa-Su noon-5pm; winter W-F 3-5pm, Sa noon-5pm. Free.) The **Portland Museum of Art,** 7 Congress Sq., at the intersection of Congress, High, and Free St., holds a fascinating display of 19th-century American art. The museum includes the recently restored McLellan House, originally built in 1801, as well as a stunning collection of Winslow Homer paintings. (☎ 775-6148 or 800-639-4067; www.portlandmuseum.org. Open June to mid-Oct. M-W and Sa-Su 10am-5pm, Th-F 10am-9pm; mid-Oct. to May closed M. $8, students and seniors $6, ages 6-12 $2; F 5-9pm free. Wheelchair accessible.) The **Wadsworth-Longfellow House,** 489 Congress St., has been excellently restored and serves as a window into the life of the poet. (☎ 774-1822, ext. 208; www.mainehistory.org. Open June-Oct. M-Sa 10am-4pm, Su noon-4pm. $7, students and seniors $6, ages 5-17 $3. Price includes admission to a neighboring history museum. Tours every hr.)

🄳🄴 **ENTERTAINMENT AND NIGHTLIFE.** Signs for theatrical productions decorate Portland, and schedules are available at the visitors center (p. 89). The **Portland Symphony** presents concerts renowned throughout the Northeast. (☎ 842-0800. Performances at the Merrill Auditorium, 477 Congress St. Tickets through Porttix, online at www.porttix.com, or at 20 Myrtle St. Open M-Sa noon-6pm. Occasional 50% student discount.) Info on Portland's jazz, blues, and club scene is available in the *Portland Phoenix* and *FACE*, which are both free and widely distributed. During the last week of spring, the three-day **Old Port Festival** (☎ 772-6828) fills the blocks from Federal to Commercial St. with parades, music, and free public entertainment before the flood of summer tourists arrives. Throughout the summer, the **Weekday Music Series** (☎ 772-6828; www.portlandmaine.com) hosts bands in Post Office Sq. between Middle and Exchange St. The Old Port area, known as "the strip"—especially **Fore Street** between Union and Exchange St.—livens up after dark, as patrons from countless bars overflow into the cobblestone streets. **Brian Ború,** the red-painted building at 57 Center St., provides a mellow pub scene with top-notch nachos for $6. (☎ 780-1506. $2 pints with live Irish music Su 3-7pm. Open daily 11:30am-1am.) **Gritty MacDuff's,** 396 Fore St., brews beer (pints $2.50), serves hearty pub food ($7-13), and entertains locals with live music Saturday and Sunday nights. (☎ 772-2739. Open daily 11:30am-1am.) **Una Wine Bar & Lounge,** 505 Fore St., is hip and casual, mixing specialty martinis and serving wine by the taste, glass, or bottle. (☎ 828-0300. Tapas $3-15. Open daily 4:30pm-1am).

KENNEBUNKPORT   ☎ 207

Just 20 mi. south of Portland, Kennebunk and its coastal counterpart 8 mi. east, Kennebunkport, are popular hideaways for the wealthy—Kennebunkport grew famous as the summer home of former President George Bush—but their true charm lies in the little art galleries and bookstores that fill the town. For surfers, swimmers, and sunbathers, five public beaches are a short trip from town. Parking is $10 per day, $20 per week, and $50 for a season pass. Narrated **scenic cruises** aboard the *Deep Water II* offer glimpses of wildlife and historic sites along the coast. (☎ 967-5595. 1½hr. $15, seniors $12.50, ages 3-12 $7.50. Ticket booth on Ocean Ave. in front of The Landing Restaurant.) The 55 ft., gaff-rigged *Schooner Eleanor,* leaving from Arundel Wharf on Ocean Ave., provides a relaxed 2hr. yachting experience. (☎ 967-8809. $38. Call for reservations and times.) **Old Salt's Pantry ❶,** 5 Ocean Ave., serves breakfast and lunch. Be sure to sample one of the gigantic muffins for $1.50. (☎ 967-4966. Open daily 9:30am-5:30pm. MC/V.) For a quick lunch, **Aunt Marie's ❶,** 13 Ocean Ave., serves great burgers ($3.50) and amazing freshly squeezed lemonade. (☎ 967-0711. Hours vary. Cash only.) With river views, good brew, and live music, **Federal Jack's ❸,** 8 Western Ave., is the jack-of-all-trades for Kennebunkport dining. (☎ 967-4322. Live music F-Sa. Karaoke Th and

NEW ENGLAND

SLOW DOWN, YOU CRAZY CHILD. As you drive along the southern coast, be forewarned that speed traps are as common as clambakes in this area, and an out-of-state license plate is as good as a bulls-eye. When a sign carries the clause "strictly enforced," you can be sure that going 27 mph in a 25 mph zone will get you nailed faster than you can say "Kennebunkport."

Su. Open daily 11:30am-1am. AmEx/D/MC/V.) The **Kennebunk-Kennebunkport Chamber of Commerce,** 17 U.S. 9/Western Ave., in Kennebunkport, has a free area guide. (☎967-0857; www.visitthekennebunks.com. Open in summer M-F 11am-5pm.) The Chamber of Commerce also runs a hospitality center, 2 Union Center, next to Ben & Jerry's. (☎967-0857. Open M-F 10am-9pm, Sa 9am-9pm, Su 10am-8pm.)

NORTHERN MAINE COAST

Much like the coastal region south of Portland, the north boasts eye-catching cliffs, windswept ocean panoramas, and quintessential New England small towns. Here, where hiking boots give way to loafers, lodging and food isn't cheap. Still, passing through rewards even the budget traveler with the classic New England feel that sustains summer vacationers. U.S. 1 is the area's only thoroughfare, and it moves at a snail's pace for most of the summer.

CAMDEN   ☎207

In the summer, khaki-clad crowds mingle with the sea captains of Camden, 100 mi. north of Portland, docking their yachts alongside the tall-masted schooners in Penobscot Bay. If you don't have a private yacht, 2hr. **cruises** sail May-Oct. from the public landing, offering views of the many lighthouses and abundant wildlife. (Schooner Olad ☎236-2323; www.maineschooners.com. $27. Windjammer Surprise ☎236-4687; www.camdenmainesailing.com. $30.) The **Camden Hills State Park ❶,** 1¼ mi. north of town on U.S. 1, offers over 80 wooded sites, usually available for arrivals before 2pm. This secluded retreat also offers 25 mi. of trails and a popular auto road leading to a lookout from the top of Mt. Battie. (☎236-3109, reservations 800-332-1501 in ME only, 287-3824 out of state; www.campwithme.com. Free showers. Park information available at the office at the entrance to the campground, open 7am-10pm. Open mid-May to mid-Oct. Sites $20, ME residents $15; reservations $2 per day; day-use $3. MC/V.) The 🖼**Good Guest House ❸,** 50 Elm St., has two mammoth rooms with private bath in a cozy New England home at relatively low rates. (☎236-2139. Full breakfast. Double bed $65, king size $75. MC/V.) The **Birchwood Motel ❸,** in Lincolnville off U.S. 1, 3 mi. north of town, has clean, quiet rooms with A/C and cable TV, along with a beautiful outdoor porch. (☎236-4204; www.birchwoodmotel.com. Rooms $65-90. AmEx/D/MC/V.) **The Camden Deli ❷,** 37 Main St., stacks a variety of sandwiches at a good price. An outdoor deck overlooking the harbor and a full bar on the second floor with daily drink specials make this a versatile option. (☎236-8343. Open daily 7am-9pm. AmEx/D/MC/V.) **Cappy's Chowder House ❸,** 1 Main St., serves up seafood specialties (entrees $10-14) and homemade pies in its bakery. (☎236-2254. Open daily 11am-11pm; kitchen closes at 10pm. MC/V.) If you get sick of clams and lobster, **Zaddicks ❸,** 20 Washington St., serves Mexican and Italian dishes in a bright, casual dining room. (☎236-6540. Entrees $8-15. Open Tu-Su 5-10pm. Takeout available. MC/V.) Schooner crews crowd into **Gilbert's Publick House,** on Bay View Landing, for the cheap pub food, entertainment, and local brews. (☎236-4230. Open noon-12:45am.)

Maine Sports, on U.S. 1 in Rockport, just south of Camden, rents and sells a wide array of boats. (☎236-7120 or 800-722-0826. Open mid-June to Aug. daily 9am-8pm; Sept. to mid-June M-Sa 9am-6pm, Su 10am-5pm. Single kayaks $25-40 per day; doubles $30-50. Canoes $30 per day.) The **Maine State Ferry Service,** 5 mi. north of Camden in Lincolnville, floats to Islesboro Island, a quiet residential island. (☎800-491-4883. 20min.; 5-9 per day, last return trip 4:30pm; round-trip $5.25, with bike $10.25, car and driver $15.) The ferry also has an agency at 517A Main St., on U.S. 1 in Rockland, that runs to Vinalhaven and North Haven. (☎596-2202. Rates and schedules change with weather; call ahead.) The **Camden-Rockport Lincolnville Chamber of Commerce,** located just ashore from the public landing, has helpful information and an informative guide to the area. (☎236-4404 or 800-223-5459; www.camdenme.org. Open mid-May to mid-Oct. M-F 9am-5pm, Sa 10am-5pm, Su 10am-4pm; mid-Oct. to mid-May closed Su.)

MT. DESERT ISLAND ☎207

Roughly half of Mt. Desert Island is covered by Acadia National Park, which harbors some of the last protected marine, mountain, and forest environments on the New England coast. Sweetly scented air, icy waters, stunning vistas, and an abundance of wildlife, including the peregrine falcon, await the many tourists who frequent the island each summer. Bar Harbor, on the eastern side, is by far the most crowded and glitzy part of the island. Once a summer hamlet for the affluent, the town now welcomes a motley crowd of vacation-seekers.

ORIENTATION AND PRACTICAL INFORMATION. Mt. Desert Island is shaped roughly like a 16 mi. long and 13 mi. wide lobster claw. It promises not to hurt you, but keep an eye on your wallet. Rte. 3 reaches the island from the north and runs south to Bar Harbor, becoming Mount Desert St. and then Main St. **Mount Desert Street** and **Cottage Street** are the major areas for shops, restaurants, and bars in Bar Harbor. Continuing on Rte. 3, **Seal Harbor** rests on the southeast corner of the island. **Northeast Harbor** is just south on Rte. 198, near the cleft. Across Somes Sound on Rte. 102, **Southwest Harbor** is where fishing and shipbuilding thrive. Rte. 102 cuts through the western half of the island, while Rte. 3 circles the eastern half. **Bar Harbor Chamber of Commerce,** 93 Cottage St. (☎288-5103; open June-Oct. M-F 8am-5pm, Nov.-May M-F 8am-4pm), has an **info booth** at 1 Harbor Place, on the town pier. (Open mid-May to mid-Oct. daily 9am-5pm.) **Hotlines: Downeast Sexual Assault Helpline** (☎800-228-2470; operates 24hr.). **Internet Access: The Opera House,** 27 Cottage St. (☎288-3509. Open daily May-June 8am-11pm.; July-Oct. 7am-11pm. $2.50 first 15min., $0.10 each additional min.) **Post Office:** 55 Cottage St. (☎288-3122. Open M-F 8am-4:30pm, Sa 9am-noon.) **Postal Code:** 04609. **Area Code:** 207.

TRANSPORTATION. Greyhound (☎288-3211; www.greyhound.com) leaves Bar Harbor daily at 8:30am from the Villager Motel, 207 Main St., for Boston (7hr., $41) via Bangor (1½hr., $14). **Beal & Bunker** runs mail boat ferries (☎244-3575; open late June to early Sept. daily 8am-4:30pm; call for winter hours) from the Northeast Harbor town dock to Great Cranberry Island and Islesford (Little Cranberry Island). (15min.; 6 per day in summer; round-trip $14, under 12 $7, bicycles $5). **Bay Ferries (the Cat),** 121 Eden St., runs to Yarmouth, Nova Scotia. (☎888-249-7245; www.catferry.com. 3hr.; 1-2 per day; $58, children $25; cars $99, bikes $14. Reservations recommended. $5 fee for reservations.) The ticket shop and tourist information center are in Bar Harbor, at 4 Cottage St. (☎288-3395. Open daily 10am-9pm.) Free **Island Explorer** buses depart from Bar Harbor Green for the park and its campgrounds and run about every 30min. from each stop. A park pass is required to go through Acadia. *Acadia Weekly,* free and widely available in Bar Harbor, has schedules. **Acadia Bike & Canoe,** 48 Cottage St., in Bar Harbor, rents bikes and boats and leads kayak tours. (☎288-9605 or 800-526-8615. Bikes $15 per half-day, $20 per day. Kayak tours half-day $45, full day $69. Open May-Oct. daily 8am-6pm.)

NEW ENGLAND

ⅆ ACCOMMODATIONS. Though grand hotels recall the island's exclusive resort days, budget-friendly motels dot **Route 3** north of Bar Harbor. However, expect to pay $65-85 in peak season at most places. The newly renovated and sparkling clean ▧**Bar Harbor Youth Hostel ❶**, 321 Main St., accommodates 32 people in two dorm rooms, an annex dorm, and one private room that houses four people. A state-of-the-art kitchen, movie nights, lime-green walls, and magenta sheets add to this hostel's bright and perky charm, and the kind staff will help you navigate Bar Harbor with ease. (☎288-5587. Linen included. Check-in 5-8:30pm. Lockout 10am-5pm. Curfew 11pm. Open May-Nov. Dorms $25; private room $80. MC/V.) The **Harbor View Motel ❸**, 11 Ocean Way off Rte. 102 in Southwest Harbor, offers clean motel rooms and weekly-rental cottages overlooking the harbor. (☎244-5031 or 800-538-6463. Open May-Oct. Rooms $51-88. AmEx/D/MC/V.) Those looking for a roof over their heads will find that the simple **Robbins Motel ❷**, 4 mi. north of Bar Harbor on Rte. 3, offers the best deal in town. (☎288-4659; www.acadia.net/robbins. Reservations recommended. Doubles $56. D/MC/V.) Camping spots cover the island, especially on Rtes. 102 and 198 west of town. Most campgrounds charge $20-30 for a site. **White Birches Campground ❶**, on Seal Cove Rd. 1 mi. west of Rte. 102 in Southwest Harbor, has 60 wooded sites in a remote location ideal for hiking. (☎244-3797 or 800-716-0727. Showers, toilets, and pool. Coin-op laundry. Reservations recommended. Office open daily mid-May to mid-Oct. 8am-8pm. Sites for up to 4 people $21, with hookup $25; weekly $126/$150. Each additional person $4.)

ⅅ FOOD. Watch some flicks and munch on a few slices at ▧**Reel Pizza ❸**, 33 Kennebec Pl., at the end of Rodick off Main St. This movie theater/pizzeria shows two films every night for $6 and serves creative pizza pies like the "Godfather," topped with artichoke, garlic, tomato, and onion. Three rows of the theater are comfy couches and chairs. (☎288-3828. Pizzas $8-20. Open daily 5pm to end of last screening. MC/V.) **Beal's ❸**, off Main St. at the end of Clark Point Rd. in Southwest Harbor, sells lobsters live or boiled at superb prices on a bustling dock. Landlubbers can get turf food at a nearby stand. (☎244-3202 or 800-245-7178; www.bealslobster.com. Boiled lobster $9.50 per lb. Open daily May-Oct. 7am-8pm; Nov.-Apr. 7am-4pm. Seafood sold daily year-round 9am-5pm. AmEx/MC/V.) **Ben and Bill's Chocolate Emporium ❶**, 66 Main St., near Cottage St., boasts 64 flavors of homemade ice cream and gelato, including—no kidding—lobster. (☎288-3281. Fudge $14 per lb. Cones $4-6. Open mid-Feb. to Jan. daily 9am-11:30pm. MC/V.)

ⓖ SIGHTS. The staff at the **Mount Desert Oceanarium,** off Rte. 3 on the northeast edge of the island, are masters of the marine. The facility's museum and hatchery teaches everything that you need to know about lobsters with a museum and hatchery. Its sister oceanarium, at the end of Clark Pt. Rd. near Beal's in Southwest Harbor, has fascinating exhibits and a museum geared toward children. (☎244-7330. Open mid-May to mid-Oct. M-Sa 9am-5pm. Main oceanarium $10-12, ages 4-12 $7; Southwest Harbor $8/$6.) Just north of Bar Harbor, **Bar Island** is accessible at low tide, when receding waters reveal a gravel path accessed via Bridge St., off Rte. 3. (Tide times are published in *Acadia Weekly*.) At the end of Main St., pedestrians wander the **Shore Path** along the eastern edge of the harbor. The path offers the chance to explore the rocky coast's numerous tidal pools and boasts great views of nearby islands. For a relaxing and scenic drive, go north from Northeast Harbor on **Sargent Drive**, which runs along Somes Sound, the only fjord on the east coast. The four-masted schooner *Margaret Todd*, docked in front of the Bar Harbor Inn, dominates the view of the harbor and runs 2hr. tours of the islands. (☎288-4585 or 288-2373; www.downeastwindjammer.com. Tours depart 10am, 2pm, and sunset. Ticket office at 27 Main St. $30, under 12 $20.)

🔊 🎭 ENTERTAINMENT AND NIGHTLIFE. Most after-dinner pleasures on the island can be found in Bar Harbor's laid-back bars. **Geddy's Pub,** 19 Main St., provides a backdrop of brightly colored signs and lobster traps for the dancing frenzy that breaks out nightly during the summer months. (☎288-5077. Live music, mostly acoustic rock and folk, daily 7-10pm. No cover. Open Apr.-Oct. daily 11am-1am; winter hours vary. Pub-style entrees $10-26, served until 10pm. MC/V.) **Improv Acadia,** 15 Cottage St., is a Chicago-based comedy outfit that induces laughing fits and serves local treats like Bar Harbor Ales ($3.50) and ice cream. (☎288-2503. Tickets $12. Call for showtimes.) Locals adore the **Lompoc Cafe & Brew Pub,** 36 Rodick St., off Cottage St., which keeps the crowd content with Bar Harbor Real Ale ($4), a bocce court, and jazz, Celtic, and folk music. (☎288-9392. Open mic Th. Live music F-Sa nights. No cover. Open May-Oct. daily 11:30am-1am.)

ACADIA NATIONAL PARK　　　　☎207

The jagged, oceanside perimeter of Acadia National Park is lined with thick pine and birch forests and punctuated by dramatic rocks and secluded sandy shores. Park preservation efforts were aided by the philanthropy of millionaire John D. Rockefeller, Jr., who feared the island would be overrun by cars and funded 57 mi. of **carriage roads** accessible to hikers, mountain bikers, and, in the winter, skiers. For information regarding which trails are groomed for skiing, contact **The Friends of Acadia** (☎288-3340 or 800-625-0321). A carriage road ideal for biking is the **Eagle Lake Loop** (6½ mi.), accessible from Rte. 233 or the park loop road, which has gentle grades and a spectacular lake view. Weekly **park passes** cost $20. Seniors can purchase a $10 lifetime pass, which entitles them to half-price camping at the park campgrounds. The *Biking and Hiking Guide to the Carriage Roads* ($6), available at the visitors center, offers invaluable hiking information. **Wildwood Stables,** along Park Loop Rd. in Seal Harbor, takes tourists around the island via horse and carriage. (☎276-3622. 1hr. tour $16, ages 6-12 $8, under 5 $4.50. 2hr. tour $18-$22. Reservations recommended. Wheelchair accessible with advance notice.)

　　Peregrine falcons, the famed birds of Acadia, nest along the **Precipice Trail** (1½ mi.), on the western side of Mt. Champlain. The hike is quite strenuous and involves the use of iron ladders to ascend cliffs. When the trail is closed to accommodate the nesting falcons (June to late August), the birds may be viewed with telescopes provided by the park service daily 9am-noon in the trail parking lot. On the eastern half of the island, popular hikes include **Mt. Champlain/Bear Brook** (2½ mi. round-trip, moderate) and the strenuous **Beehive** (¾ mi. round-trip), both of which provide dramatic views of the Atlantic coastline. An easy ½ mi. amble along the **Bowl** trail from the summit of Mt. Champlain rewards hikers with a view of Sand Beach and Otter Point. To reach incredible vistas of both land and sea from the summit of **Cadillac Mountain** (1530 ft.), hike the **Cadillac Mountain North** (4½ mi.) or **South Ridge** (7½ mi.) trails or cruise up the paved **auto road** (accessed from the Park Loop Rd.). Early birds are among the first people in the US to see the sun rise. (Road open 1hr. before dawn to midnight.) About 4 mi. south of Bar Harbor on Rte. 3, **Park Loop Road** traces the granite shore of the island, making a 27 mi. circuit through the forests of Acadia. About 2-3hr. before high tide, strong waves loudly crash against a rock chasm at **Thunder Hole,** along the Otter Cliffs at the southwest side of the coast. Soft sand and refreshingly warm waters await at **Echo Lake,** along Rte. 102. **Sand Beach,** on the Park Loop along the island's eastern shore, is a beautiful spot sheltered by rocky cliffs, but the water is frigid, even in the summer.

　　Acadia National Park campgrounds include **Blackwoods ❶,** 5 mi. south of Bar Harbor on Rte. 3. Nestled within the thick birch forests of Acadia, Blackwoods is located in the heart of the park, and its 286 wooded sights are tightly packed in summer. (☎800-365-2267. Office open daily 8am-10pm. No hookups. Coin-operated showers

NEW ENGLAND

available at private facility located just outside of the campground. Reservations recommended. Sites mid-Mar. to Oct. $20; call for low-season rates. Park pass required for entry.) Along Park Loop Rd. (see below), **Jordan Pond House ❹** serves weary travelers tea and popovers ($8.25) under sweet-smelling white birch canopies. (☎276-3316. Lunch $10-20. Dinner $15-25. Open mid-May to late Oct. daily 11:30am-9pm; hours vary. Popovers served until 5:30pm. Reservations recommended. AmEx/MC/V.) **Acadia National Park Visitors Center,** 3 mi. north of Bar Harbor on Rte. 3, has a topographical map, a bookstore, and rangers ready to help. A basic 15min. video introducing the park is shown every 30min. (☎288-5262. Open daily mid-June to mid-Sept. 8am-6pm; mid-Apr. to mid-June and mid-Sept. to Oct. 8am-4:30pm.) The **Park Headquarters,** 3 mi. west of Bar Harbor on Rte. 233, provides visitor info during the low season. (☎288-3338. Open M-F 8am-4:30pm.) **Emergency: Acadia National Park Law Enforcement** (☎288-3369).

NEW HAMPSHIRE

There are two sides to New Hampshire: the rugged landscape and natural beauty of the White Mountains, and the tax-free outlets, tourist traps, and state liquor stores that line most highways. New Hampshire's inland towns often revolve around their "three seasons" resort destinations, catering to outdoorsmen in the summer, leafers in the colorful autumn, and skiers in the long winter season. The first colony to declare its independence from Great Britain, New Hampshire has retained its libertarian charm along with its motto, "Live Free or Die!"

🔢 PRACTICAL INFORMATION

Capital: Concord.

Visitor Info: Office of Travel and Tourism, 172 Pembroke Rd., P.O. Box 1856, Concord 03302 (☎271-2666 or 800-386-4664; www.visitnh.gov). **NH Parks and Recreation** (☎271-3556; www.nhparks.state.nh.us). The **Fish and Game Department,** 2 Hazen Dr., Concord 03301 (☎603-271-3421; www.wildlife.state.nh.us), provides info on regulations and licenses. **US Forest Service,** 719 N. Main St., Laconia 03246 (☎603-528-8721; www.fs.fed.us/r9/white). Open M-F 8am-4:30pm.

Postal Abbreviation: NH. **Sales Tax:** 8% on meals and lodgings. **Area Code:** 603.

PORTSMOUTH   ☎603

Though only 13 mi. of its perimeter touch the Atlantic Ocean, New Hampshire makes the most of its toehold on the water. Portsmouth, the colonial capital, boasts a rich history and a vibrant modernity. Colonial history is an integral part of Portsmouth, as most buildings date from the 18th century, but hip restaurants and artistic productions throughout the city reveal an affinity for present-day style.

🔢 TRANSPORTATION AND PRACTICAL INFORMATION. Just 57 mi. north of Boston, Portsmouth is situated at the junction of U.S. 1, 1A, and I-95. Cheap parking lots ($0.50-1 per hr.) are available downtown, but the town is best navigated by foot. **State Street/U.S. 1** and **Congress Street** are major roads that run northeast-southwest through town. **Market Street** runs southeast-northwest and is the central intersecting road. **Vermont Transit/Greyhound,** 22 Ladd St. (☎436-0163; www.greyhound.com; open 7am-6pm), inside Federal Tobacconists, heads to Boston (1¼hr., 3 per day, $16). Purchase tickets on-site. **Seacoast Trolley** (☎431-6975) is a scenic touring company that runs every hour in the summer from 11am-3pm, with 14 stops around Portsmouth. ($3 partial loop, $6 full loop with reboarding privileges.) **Taxi: Blue Star Taxi,** ☎436-2774. **Visitor Info: Greater Portsmouth Chamber of Commerce,** 500 Market St., outside downtown. (☎436-1118; www.portcity.org. Open M-F 8am-5pm, Sa-Su 10am-4pm.) The Chamber of Commerce **info kiosk** is in Market Sq. (Open May to mid-Oct. daily 10am-5pm.) **Hotlines: Violence and Rape Hotline,** ☎800-336-3795. **Medical Services: Portsmouth Regional,** 333 Borthwick Ave. (☎436-5110 or 800-991-4325). **Internet Access: Portsmouth Public Library,** 8 Islington St. (☎427-1540. Open M-Th 9am-9pm, F 9am-5:30pm, Sa 9am-5pm. Wireless Internet available. Free.) **Post Office:** 80 Daniel St. (☎800-275-8777. Open M-F 7:30am-5:30pm, Sa 8am-12:30pm.) **Postal Code:** 03801. **Area Code:** 603.

▟▐ ACCOMMODATIONS AND FOOD. Portsmouth is not exactly budget-friendly when it comes to hanging your hat; a common tactic to avoid steep prices is to take a short trip over the border to Maine, where accommodations are pleasant and more reasonably priced. **Camp Eaton ❷,** in York Harbor, ME, about 15 mi. north of Portsmouth off Rte. 1A, is mere steps from a beautiful New England beach. Immaculate bathrooms and well-kept, wooded sites make camping here a relative bargain. (☎207-363-3424. 2-person sites in summer $40; low season $25. Each additional person $6. MC/V.) The **Farmstead B&B ❹,** 999 Goodwin Rd., just east of the intersection with Rte. 236, in Eliot, ME, offers pristine rooms with views of the countryside only 10 mi. from downtown Portsmouth. (☎207-748-3145 or 207-439-5033; www.farmstead.qpg.com. Rooms $75. D/MC/V.)

Portsmouth offers a plethora of dining options, with establishments of every persuasion peppering Market St. **◙The Friendly Toast ❷,** 121 Congress St., a block and a half from Market Sq., is cluttered with the most ghastly artifacts the 1950s could produce: mannequins, pulp novels, formica what-nots, and stroke-inducingly bad art. Menu items like the "mission burrito" ($8) are nearly impossible to finish alone. (☎430-2154. Breakfast served all day. Entrees $6-8. Open M-Th and Su 7am-9pm, F-Sa 24hr. AmEx/D/MC/V.) With a giant golden stein above the entrance, **The Portsmouth Brewery ❷,** 56 Market St., offers great pub fare ($6-10) and some excellent brews. Their "Smutty Nose IPA" is ranked the #1 IPA in the US, and their "Old Brown Dog" is a local favorite. (☎431-1115. Open daily 11:30am-12:30am. AmEx/D/MC/V.) When you're sick of seafood, transport yourself down South at the **Muddy River Smokehouse ❸,** 21 Congress St. For the particularly ravenous, "The Squealer" includes a rack of pork ribs, a pound of pulled pork, half a smoked chicken, a pint of baked beans and mashed potatoes, and cornbread ($30). A downstairs club staves off food comas with live blues. (☎430-9582. Entrees $10-22. Open M-Th and Su 11am-9pm, F-Sa 11am-10:30pm. Blues club open Th-Sa. 21+. Cover and times vary. AmEx/D/MC/V.) Folks trail into the street for heavenly burgers and sandwiches at **Gilley's Lunchcart ❶,** 175 Fleet St. The Monday 11am-6pm "Dog Days" special offers $1.25 hotdogs. (☎431-6343. Fries $1.75. Burgers $2.25. Open M 11:30am-6pm, Tu-Su 11:30am-2:30am. Cash only.)

▣▐ SIGHTS AND ENTERTAINMENT. Modern Portsmouth sells itself with its colonial past. The prestigious **Strawbery Banke Museum,** on the corner of Marcy and Hancock St., encompasses several blocks of buildings and beautiful gardens, each restored to recreate the region as it evolved over time. Museum employees in period garb populate the various houses and shops. To find the museum, follow the signs that lead toward the harbor through a maze of shops. (☎433-1100; www.strawberybanke.org. Open May-Oct. M-Sa 10am-5pm, Su noon-5pm. $15, ages 7-17 $10; families $35. Tickets good for 2 consecutive days.) Across the street, **Prescott Park** hugs the bank of the Piscataqua River. A great place to picnic, these small, well-tended gardens offer an amazing view. For the naval enthusiast, try

NEW ENGLAND

climbing aboard through the hatches of the *USS Albacore*, 600 Market St., a research submarine built locally at the Portsmouth Naval Shipyard. (☎436-3680. Open May-Oct. daily 9:30am-5pm; winter hours vary. $5, ages 62+ or military with ID $3.50, ages 7-17 $2; families $10.) One of Portsmouth's oldest graveyards, **Old North Cemetery,** on Maplewood Ave., holds the burial sites of some of the city's most important skeletons, including signers of the Declaration of Independence and the US Constitution. The **Music Hall,** 28 Chestnut St., a 125-year-old theater, hosts shows in the summer, including movies, concerts, dances, and plays. (☎436-2400; www.themusichall.org. Box office open M-Sa noon-6pm or until 30min. after the show has started. Films $8; students, seniors, under 21, and military $6.)

NEW HAMPSHIRE SKI RESORTS ☎603

With sizeable mountains and abundant snow from November to April, New Hampshire is one of the East Coast's most popular skiing destinations. When the White Mountains thaw, each resort blossoms into its own sort of summer diversion. **Ski New Hampshire** (☎745-9396 or 800-937-5493; www.skinh.com), P.O. Box 10, Lincoln 03251, provides information and reservations for five resorts in the White Mountains. **Cranmore,** in North Conway (p. 105), offers 39 trails, 200+ skiable acres, and great shopping. Its **Children's Summer Camps** offer tennis, hiking, swimming, and more. (☎800-786-6754; www.cranmore.com. Lift operates in winter M-F 9am-4pm, Sa-Su 8:30am-4pm. Lift tickets $39, ages 13-18 $29, ages 6-12 and 65+ $19.) Located on U.S. 302 by North Conway, pricey **Attitash** has two mountains, 51 trails (evenly divided among beginner, intermediate, and expert), and 25 acres of glades. Biking, horseback riding, water slides, a climbing wall, trampolines, and an alpine slide keep summer visitors busy. (☎374-2368; www.attitash.com. Lift tickets in winter M-F and Su $49, Sa and holidays $55; ages 13-18 $39/$45, ages 6-12 and seniors $19/$25. Slide open in summer daily 10am-6pm. Single ride $13. Summer full-day value pack for all activities except golf and horseback riding $29, ages 2-7 $13.)

Just outside Pinkham Notch on Rte. 16, **Wildcat Mountain** features 47 trails (25% beginner, 45% intermediate, 30% expert) and mountainscape views from its 4062 ft. peak. (☎888-754-9453; www.skiwildcat.com. Lift tickets $55, ages 13-18 $42, ages 6-12 $25. Gondola rides late May to Oct. daily $10, ages 65+ $9, ages 6-12 $5.) Three miles east of Lincoln on Rte. 112, **Loon Mountain** has 43 ski trails, along with biking and horseback riding in warmer months. (☎745-8111; www.loonmtn.com. Lift tickets M-F $52, Sa-Su $59; ages 13-19 $42/$49; under 13 $32/37.) Just off I-93 in Franconia Notch State Park, **Cannon Mountain** has 42 trails (15% beginner, 50% intermediate, 35% expert) at slightly lower prices than other local resorts; on Tuesdays and Thursdays, a 2-person pass is just $40. Summer hiking, biking, canoeing, and swimming keep athletes in shape, while the Aerial Tramway (p. 104) whisks those with less energy up the mountain. (☎823-8800; www.cannonmt.com. Lift tickets M-F $34, Sa-Su $45; ages 13-17 $23/$37; seniors and children $23/$29.)

WHITE MOUNTAINS ☎603

Made up of 780,000 acres of mountainous forest, the White Mountains are a playground for outdoor enthusiasts. While many associate the area with powdery ski slopes, its warm-weather alternatives, such as hiking, camping, canoeing, kayaking, and fishing, make the White Mountains an attractive destination year-round.

▐ TRANSPORTATION. No matter which way you approach the White Mountains, the scenery will be breathtaking. **Concord Trailways** (☎228-3300 or 800-639-3317) runs from Boston to Conway (First Stop Market, W. Main St.; 2 per day, $27); and Franconia (Kelly's Foodtown, Exit 38 off I-93; 1 per day, $28). For hikers, the

AMC runs a **shuttle** between locations on the Appalachian Trail in the White Mountains. Consult AMC's *The Guide* for a map of routes and times or pick up a schedule at the AMC Pinkham Notch Visitors Center. (☎466-2727. Operates June to mid-Oct. daily 8am-4pm. Reservations highly recommended for all stops; required for some. $12, AMC members $10.)

ORIENTATION AND PRACTICAL INFORMATION.

The White Mountains can be daunting to an unfamiliar traveler, but are easily navigated with a good map and guide. The immense forest, spanning both New Hampshire and Maine, is bordered by a dozen or so towns and contains several commercial ski resorts. Many of the region's highlights can be found in three areas: **Pinkham Notch** (p. 102), northeast of the forest near Mt. Washington; the **Franconia Notch** area (p. 103), northwest of the National Forest; and **North Conway** (p. 105), to the southeast.

Any unattended vehicle parked on White Mountain National Forest land must have a **parking pass**, sold by the US Forest Service, the Appalachian Mountain Club, and the White Mountain Attraction Center; vehicles parked at national forest campground sites are an exception. (☎528-8721. $5 per week, $20 per year.) Purchase daily passes at any of the trailheads in the forest for $3. The **US Forest Service** operates four **ranger stations**, each of which provides free information on recreational opportunities, camping, and safety precautions in the White Mountains. **Pemigewasset/Ammonoosuc**, on Rte. 175 in Plymouth near Exit 25 of I-93, covers the southwest region of the forest. (☎869-2626. Open M-F 8am-4:30pm.) **Androscoggin**, 2½ mi. south of Gorham on Rte. 16, oversees the northern region. (☎466-2713. Open in summer daily 8am-5pm; in winter M-Sa 8am-4:30pm.) **Evans Notch**, 18 Mayville Rd., in Bethel, ME, covers the Maine section of the national forest. (☎207-824-2134. Open in summer daily 8am-4:30pm; winter Tu-Sa 8am-4:30pm.) **Saco**, 100 yd. west of the Rte. 16 junction on Hwy. 112 (Kancamagus Hwy.), oversees the southeast section of the forest. (☎447-5448. Open daily 8am-4:30pm.)

The **White Mountain Gateway and Visitors Center**, P.O. Box 10, N. Woodstock 03262, at Exit 32 off I-93, has info on mountain recreation. (☎745-8720. Open daily July-Sept. 8:30am-6pm; Apr.-July and Sept. to mid-Oct. 8:30am-5:30pm; mid-Oct. to Apr. 8:30am-5pm.) The **Appalachian Mountain Club (AMC)** is a nonprofit conservation and recreation organization that maintains 1400 mi. of trails in the northeastern US. They teach outdoor skills workshops, run environmental programs, and provide lodging at backcountry shelters, camps, and lodges. Members of the AMC

THE LOCAL STORY

MOOSE STOPPINGS

As you're driving through New Hampshire's White Mountains, it's wise to heed the constant warnings and keep an eye out for errant moose. These large and awkward creatures don't exactly have the wits to stay out of the road, and a collision can have deadly consequences. Yet to the surprise of unassuming, prudent drivers, there is another side to the moose story—the hundreds of tourists just waiting for the chance to see one. Moose mania is everywhere. Tour guides rattle off places where the antlered animals congregate. Local shops stock clothing and souvenirs branded with every imaginable pun on the creature ("nice rack" gets pretty old).

If you really must see a moose, there are certain steps you can take to improve your chances. Moose tend to emerge around sunrise and twilight, often near still bodies of water. The Kancamungus Scenic Highway and other isolated throughways provide the best odds for spotting a moose from the road. If your tracking skills aren't up to par and you really want to meet a moose, **Gorham Moose Tours** boasts a 93% success rate.

Gorham Moose Tours, on Rte. 16 in Gorham (☎877-986-6673). Tour departs daily June to mid-Aug. 6:30pm; mid-Aug. to mid-Sept. 6pm; mid-Sept. to mid-Oct. 5:30pm. $20, ages 5-12 $15, under age 4 $5.

receive discounts at their hiking destinations. Individual ($50) or family ($75) memberships may be purchased online (www.outdoors.org) or at the AMC's **Pinkham Notch Visitors Center,** 10 mi. north of Jackson on Rte. 16. As the base camp for Mt. Washington, the visitors center is the best source of info on weather and trail conditions, with maps, current weather reports, and a packroom, bathrooms, and showers for hikers. They handle lodging reservations and have comprehensive information on White Mountain trails, wilderness safety, and eco-friendly "Leave No Trace" backpacking. (AMC headquarters: ☎617-523-0636; www.outdoors.org. Visitors center: ☎466-2727. Open daily 6:30am-10pm.) **Area Code:** 603.

⌂ ACCOMMODATIONS. Outside the forest, numerous accommodations, from hostels to high-end resorts, lie within an hour's drive. For a guide to lodgings near the White Mountains, pick up the small *White Mountains Travel Guide*, free and available at any **info booth.** Other than ski resorts, most accommodations within the National Forest are operated by the AMC. The AMC operates **huts** along the White Mountains stretch of the Appalachian Trail, generally used by trail hikers to break up the vast distance of the trail. A free *AMC Huts and Lodges* brochure, available at the Pinkham Notch Visitors Center, has descriptions and locations. The huts only have co-ed bunkrooms, and some huts have no showers or electrical outlets. The **full-service ❸** huts provide a bunk, mattress, pillow, and three wool blankets, as well as breakfast and dinner. There are toilets, single-sex washrooms, and cold water. Bring sleeping gear and a flashlight. At the **self-service ❶** huts, guests must provide their own food, but have use of a kitchen stocked with cookware. Blankets are not provided—bring a warm sleeping bag. (☎466-2727; www.outdoors.org. No pets. No smoking or open flames. Huts open June to mid-Sept.; 6 huts open to mid-Oct.; 3 self-service huts open in winter. Full-service huts $85, under 15 $52; AMC members $77/$47. Some discounts for longer stays. Self-service huts $27, members $25. Reservations with AmEx/MC/V.) For car-accessible lodging, the AMC runs the **Joe Dodge Lodge ❸** (p. 103). The **Highland Center at Crawford Notch ❸,** off Rte. 302, is open year-round, with private and shared rooms and 16 bunks in the Shapleigh Bunkhouse. (☎466-2727. Dorms with breakfast and dinner $49, AMC members $43; doubles with breakfast and dinner $131/$109. Call for low-season rates. AmEx/MC/V.) The **White Mountains Hostel ❶** (p. 106) is also close by.

⌂ CAMPING. The US Forest Service maintains 23 designated **National Forest campgrounds ❶,** all of which are accessible by car. Four remain open in winter, although only one has plowed access. Some sites are first come, first served, but these can fill quickly. On weekends, arrive around check-out time (usually 10-11am) to snag a site. Bathrooms and firewood are usually available. (Reservations: ☎877-444-6777; www.reserveusa.com. Reservations accepted beginning Jan. 1 and must be made at least 1 week in advance. Sites $16-18; reservation fee $9, change/cancellation fee $10. Cars parked at campsite do not require a parking pass.) Camping is less expensive or free of charge at the many **backcountry campsites ❶,** which are only accessible via hiking trails. Regulations prohibit camping and fires above the treeline (approximately 4000 ft.); within 200 ft. of trails, certain bodies of water, and a few specific roads; or within ¼ mi. of huts, shelters, tent platforms, lakes, streams, trailheads, or roads. Rules are even stricter in the Great Gulf Wilderness around Mt. Washington—no wood or charcoal fires are allowed. Other areas have more special regulations; consult the US Forest Service's *Backcountry Camping Rules*, available for reference at any of the four regional ranger stations, for more info. A plethora of **private campgrounds ❶/❷,** the majority of which cater to RVs and families, surround the borders of the forest. A copy of *New Hampshire's Guide to Camping*, available at any highway rest stop or info booth in the state, provides a map, prices, and campgrounds' phone numbers.

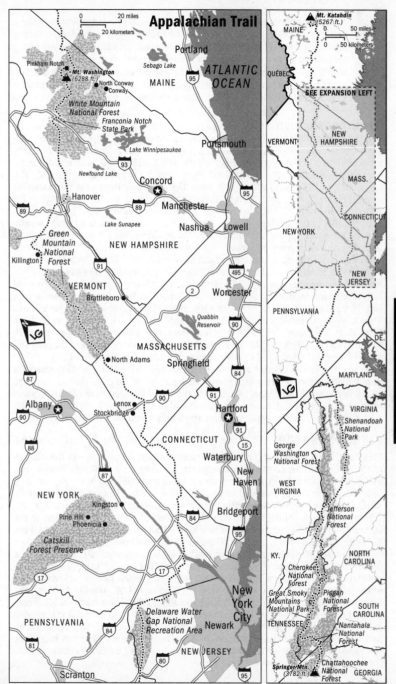

Appalachian Trail

New England

> No matter where you camp, **bears** are a threat. Stop by a ranger station or the AMC Visitors Center to pick up information on how to minimize the danger. Keep food hung high and well away from sleeping areas. Do not keep anything with the scent of food on it in or near your tent (clothes worn while cooking, for example). If you do encounter a bear, stay calm and back away slowly, being careful not to make direct eye contact. When hiking, make sufficient noise to alert bears to your presence, allowing them to move away from the trail.

🏃 OUTDOOR ACTIVITIES. If you are planning to do a significant amount of hiking, the invaluable *AMC White Mountain Guide* ($23; available in the AMC Visitor's Center and most bookstores) includes maps and descriptions of every mountain trail. A common formula for estimating hiking time is to allow 30min. for every horizontal mile and 1hr. for every 1000 ft. elevation gain. Weather and physical condition may affect this time. Because weather in the mountains is unpredictable, hikers should bring three layers of clothing in all seasons: one for wind, one for rain, and at least one for warmth—preferably wool or a synthetic material like polypropylene or fleece, not cotton. Black flies, ticks, and mosquitoes make insect repellent a must-have. Always bring more than enough water; dehydration can be a serious problem and hikes in the region are often more strenuous than anticipated. A high-calorie snack, like trail mix, is also a good idea.

Cycling is another popular way to tour the White Mountains. For help with planning, ask a ranger or consult *30 Bicycle Tours in New Hampshire* ($13; at local bookstores and outdoor equipment stores). **Great Glen Trails Outdoor Center,** across Rte. 16 from the Mt. Washington Auto Rd., rents bikes for use only on their trails. They also offer guided kayaking trips and, in the winter, ski rentals. (☎466-2333. Open daily 9am-5pm. Trail fee $7; included in rental. Bikes $20 for 2hr., under 18 $14; half-day $25/$20; full day $35/$25. Helmets $3 per day. Winter trail pass full day $15, ages 6-12 and 62+ $10; afternoon only $11/$7. Kayaking $60-150.)

To see the National Forest in a less strenuous way, drive along the ⬛**Kancamagus Scenic Highway (Route 12),** which connects the towns of Lincoln and Conway. The 35 mi. drive requires at least 1hr., though the many wooded outlooks are perfect for a picnic. Get gas at Lincoln, as no gas is available in the park, then head east on "the Kanc" to enjoy the scenic splendor stretching all the way to Conway.

PINKHAM NOTCH   ☎ 603

Pinkham Notch, New Hampshire's easternmost mountain pass, lies in the shadow of the tallest mountain in the northeastern US—the 6288 ft. **Mount Washington.** Pinkham's proximity to the peak makes it more crowded and less peaceful than neighboring areas, but secluded areas can be found not too far off the beaten path. AMC's **Pinkham Notch Visitors Center** lies between Gorham and Jackson on Rte. 16.

Stretching from behind the Pinkham Notch Visitors Center all the way up to the summit of Mt. Washington, **Tuckerman's Ravine Trail,** despite the deceiving 4¼ mi. distance, demands 4-5hr. of steep hiking each way. Authorities urge caution when climbing—Mt. Washington claims at least one life every year. Mt. Washington is one of the most dangerous mountains in the world because of its highly unpredictable weather, including wind speeds that frequently reach hurricane force. It has never been recorded to be warmer than 72°F on top of Mt. Washington, and the average temperature on the peak is a bone-chilling 27°F. The summit of Mt. Washington boasts the highest winds ever recorded (231 mph) and the peak is shrouded in fog 300 days of the year. In the right conditions, however, the trek offers excellent vistas and some of the best views in New England— on a clear day hikers are rewarded with a view of five states and Canada. A less daunting option for the steepest part of the ascent is the **Lion's Head Trail,** which diverges from the Tucker-man's Ravine Trail about 2 mi. into the hike. Because Tuckerman's Ravine is closed in winter due to the high frequency of avalanches, the Lion's Head Trail is the only option for those intrepid enough to make the hike in the snowy months.

Motorists can take the **Mt. Washington Auto Road,** a partially paved road that winds eight mi. to the summit. For most vehicles, the ascent is a minor test, but 1000 ft. drop-offs and an absence of guard rails will test even the most unshakable nerves. Drivers sturdy enough to reach the top receive bragging rights in the form of a free "This Car Climbed Mt. Washington" bumper sticker. The road begins three mi. north of the Pinkham Notch Visitors Center on Rte. 16. (☎466-3988. Road open daily June-Aug. 7:30am-6pm; May-June and Sept.-Oct. 8:30am-5pm. Road may close due to weather conditions. $18 per car and driver, free audio tour included; each additional passenger $7, ages 5-12 $4.) To enjoy the view without the drive (and to save your brakes from the long ride down), take a **stage tour,** across Rte. 16 from the Auto Road, where well-trained drivers escort you up the mountain. (☎466-2333. Open daily 8:30am-5pm. $24, seniors $22, ages 5-12 $11.)

Many of the region's lodging options are on or near Mt. Washington. Accessible by car, the **Joe Dodge Lodge ❸,** immediately behind the Pinkham Notch Visitors Center, pleases sleepy travelers with over 100 comfortable bunks. Those who don't fall asleep immediately can make use of seven family rooms, a small library, and a living room. (☎466-2727. Breakfast and dinner included. Reservations recommended. Check-in 2pm. Check-out 10:30am. $62, under 16 $39; AMC members $56/$36. Without meals $49/$26, AMC members $45/$24. Call for low-season rates. AmEx/MC/V.) About 2hr. up the Tuckerman Ravine Trail, **Hermit Lake Shelter ❶** has bathrooms but no showers, and sleeps up to 90 people on a first come, first served basis. Nightly passes are sold at the visitors center ($10). **Lakes of the Clouds Hut ❸,** 1½ mi. from Mt. Washington's summit, is one of AMC's most popular full-service huts. (Reservations ☎466-2727. See **Accommodations,** p. 100, for rates.)

FRANCONIA NOTCH AREA ☎603

Carved by glacial movements that began 400 million years ago, the granite peaks of Franconia Notch State Park are one of the most majestic spots in the White Mountains. Although one of the biggest attractions in the area, the famous rocky profile known as the "Old Man of the Mountain," collapsed in 2003, Franconia is still home to stunning waterfalls, woodlands, and natural rock formations.

▉▐ ORIENTATION AND PRACTICAL INFORMATION. Most of the area high-lights are accessible directly from I-93. The **Franconia Notch Chamber of Commerce,** on Main St. in Franconia, has maps and information on the region. (☎823-5516; www.franconianotch.org. Open mid-May to mid-Oct. Tu-Su 10am-5pm.) A note for those using old maps: the highway exit numbering system has recently changed. The old Exit 1 on the Franconia Notch Pkwy. corresponds to the new 34A, Exit 2 to 34B, and Exit 3 to 34C. **Area Code:** 603.

▌▐ ACCOMMODATIONS AND FOOD. Franconia Notch is a popular place for camping, but make sure to bring insect repellent if you plan to stay in the great outdoors. Nestled in the middle of the park, **Lafayette Place Campground ❶,** off I-93 S between Exits 34A and 34B, offers spacious campsites in an ideal location. (☎823-9513, reservations 271-3628; www.nhstateparks.org. Coin-operated showers, clean facilities, and a camp store. Reservations strongly recommended and must be made at least 3 days in advance for a $5 fee. Open mid-May to mid-Oct. 2-person sites $19-24; each additional adult $9.50-12, under 18 free. MC/V.) The scenic Pemi Trail passes through the campground; follow it toward the Flume (3½ mi.) and the Basin (2 mi.) to the south and toward Profile Lake and Cannon Mtn. (2½ mi.) to the north. A peaceful evening can be found at the **Fransted Family Campground ❶**, 3 mi. north of the Notch on Rte. 18. The expansive grounds contain over 100 well-tended sites, a small beach, volleyball, and an 18-hole miniature golf course. Facilities include showers, bathroom, and coin-operated laundry. (☎823-5675. Open May-Oct. Tent sites $22-29, with electricity and water $31, full hookup $29-33. MC/V.) Numerous cottages, private campgrounds, and motels cluster along the stretch of Rte. 3 between Woodstock and the entrance to Franconia Notch. For a quieter option, head north to the **Hillwinds Lodge ❸**, off Rte. 18 in Franconia, next to the scenic Gale River. In addition to clean rooms, guests enjoy the perks of nearby Franconia Inn, including free mountain bikes and an outdoor pool. (☎823-5551 or 1-800-473-5299. Rooms $55-75. AmEx/MC/V.)

▧**Polly's Pancake Parlor ❷**, on Rte. 117 in Sugar Hill, just 2 mi. from Exit 38 off I-93, is a homey restaurant with a dining room overlooking Mt. Washington. A stack of Polly's superb pancakes arrives with a tray of maple syrup, maple spread, and granulated maple sugar from the restaurant's own product line. (☎823-5575; www.pollyspancakeparlor.com. 6-pancake stack $6. Unlimited pancakes $12. Open mid-May to mid-Oct. daily 7am-3pm; Apr. and Nov. Sa-Su only. AmEx/D/DC/MC/V.) The endless menu at the **Woodstock Inn Brewery ❸**, on Rte. 3 in Woodstock, is sure to fuel your engine, with everything from not-so-standard sandwiches like the "Train Wreck" (roasted chicken, roast beef, and a big red Anaheim chili; $8), to pasta and seafood. (☎745-3951. Open daily 11:30am-10pm. AmEx/D/MC/V.)

◪ **SIGHTS.** Traveling north from Lincoln on I-93, ▧**The Flume,** Exit 34A on I-93, is a 2 mi. walk cutting through a spectacular granite gorge. An optional shuttle bus takes you to the highlights of the gorge and cuts the walk to half a mile. Although only 12-20 ft. apart, the moss-covered canyon walls are 70-90 ft. high. Take a leisurely stroll over centuries-old covered bridges and past the 35 ft. Avalanche Falls. Tickets can be purchased from the **Flume Visitors Center,** which provides area information and shows an excellent 15min. film acquainting visitors with the landscape and geological history of the area. (☎745-8391; www.flumegorge.com. Open daily May-June and Sept.-Oct. 9am-5pm; July-Aug. 9am-5:30pm. $8, ages 6-12 $5.) A 9 mi. paved **bike path** begins at the visitors center and parallels I-93 N through the park, providing easy access to attractions and sights along the way. To rent some wheels, head to 2 mi. north to **Franconia Sports Shop,** off Main St. in Franconia. (☎823-5241. Bike rental $7 per hr., half-day $15-19, full day $19-25. Open M-Sa 10am-6pm, Su 10am-4pm.) Between Exits 34A and 34B on I-93, visitors can find a well-marked turn-off for **The Basin.** A 5-10min. walk leads to a 20 ft. whirlpool that has been carved into the granite by a 15 ft. waterfall. (Wheelchair accessible.)

For years Franconia had been known as the home of the **Old Man of the Mountain,** but in May 2003, the granite profile fell from its perch. The viewing areas at Exit 34B on I-93 and between Exit 34A and 34B on I-93 are still open and provide a diagram and explanation of the Old Man's fall. A pleasant 10min. walk down the designated path from the parking lot at Exit 34B brings viewers to the banks of **Profile Lake,** which affords the best available view of the cliff where the Old Man used to rest. Also at Exit 34B, a small display of Old Man memorabilia and the history regarding his discovery and rise to popularity can be found at the **Old Man of the Mountain Museum.** (☎823-7722, ext. 717. Open daily mid-May to mid-Oct. 9:30am-5pm. Free.) The 80-passenger **Cannon Mountain Aerial Tramway,** Exit 34B, climbs over 2000 ft. in 7min. and carries visitors to the summit of the Cannon Cliff, a 1000 ft. sheer drop into the cleft between Mt. Lafayette and Cannon Mountain. (☎823-8800. Open daily mid-May to mid-Oct. 9am-5pm; mid-Dec. to mid-Apr. 9am-3:45pm. Trams run every 15min. Round-trip $10, ages 6-12 $6. One-way $8.) In winter, the tram takes skiers up the mountain (see **New Hampshire Ski**

Resorts, p. 98). Back at the base of the mountain, right next to the tramway station, sits the one-room **New England Ski Museum,** home to a variety of old ski equipment and an exhibit on Hannes Schnieder, who started the first ski school in America. (☎823-7177. Open mid-May to mid-Oct. and mid-Dec. to mid-Apr. daily 10am-5pm. Free.) While skiers enjoy Cannon Mtn. during the winter, on summer days, the life-guard-protected beach at **Echo Lake,** just off Exit 34C on I-93 at the base of Cannon Mtn., offers cool but often crowded waters. The lake is accessible until 10pm. (☎823-8800, ext. 784. Lifeguard on duty mid-June to early Sept. daily 10am-5pm. $3, ages 6-11 $1. Free when lifeguard isn't on duty. 7 RV sites with hook-up $29. Canoe or paddleboat rental ☎823-8800, ext. 783. $10 per hr. Last rental 4pm.)

🗺 **HIKING.** Franconia Notch provides excellent day-hikes and views; the **Hiking Information Center** adjacent to Lafayette Place Campground is the best source in the area for hiking suggestions and safety tips. (Open daily 8am-4pm.) In this area be prepared for severe weather, especially above 4000 ft. On the western rim, the **Lonesome Lake Trail** (2 mi.) winds from Lafayette Place Campground to **Lonesome Lake,** where the AMC operates its westernmost hut. The trails on the eastern rim boast an extensive network stretching into the wilderness of Franconia Notch. The **Greenleaf Trail** (2½ mi.), which starts at the aerial tramway parking lot, and the **Old Bridle Path** (3 mi.), beginning from Lafayette Place and known for its stellar views, are more ambitious. Both lead up to the AMC's **Greenleaf Hut,** near the summit of Mt. Lafayette overlooking Echo Lake. From Greenleaf, a 7½ mi. trek east along the **Old Bridle Path** and **Garfield Ridge** leads to the AMC's most remote hut, the **Galehead.** Mt. Garfield's summit is above the timberline, and storms intensify quickly. Ambitious hikers seek the **Falling Waters Trail,** accessed from Lafayette Place. With three waterfalls within 1½ mi. of the trailhead and a 1600 ft. elevation change, the trail is a strenuous hike. The well-maintained eastern rim trails are interconnected and can occupy trekkers for days; make sure to get adequate supplies before starting out.

LOST RIVER GORGE

Outside of Franconia Notch State Park, 🗺**Lost River Gorge,** located 6 mi. west of North Woodstock on Rte. 112, is a deep glacial gorge with a network of caves, massive boulders, complex rock formations, and beautiful waterfalls. The park also maintains a nature garden and a forestry center with information about the area. The walk through the gorge is less than 1 mi. along well-maintained suspended wooden walkways and bridges, but exploring the caves can easily take over an hour; each creatively named cavern (like the Lemon Squeezer) is open for exploration to those agile enough to wrench themselves through. (☎745-8031; www.findlostriver.com. Open daily July-Aug. 9am-6pm; mid-May to June and Sept. to mid-Oct. 9am-5pm. Last ticket sold 1hr. before closing. Solid walking shoes and active wear recommended. $11, ages 4-12 $7. Garden and forestry center free.)

NORTH CONWAY AND CONWAY ☎ 603

With its proximity to the White Mountains, the town of North Conway is one of New Hampshire's most popular vacation destinations. Rte. 16, the traffic-infested main road, houses the usual crop of outlet stores and a variety of smaller local shops. The town of Conway, 5 mi. south, has fewer touristy shops, but several excellent meal and lodging options. The **Mt. Washington Chamber of Commerce,** on Rte. 16 in North Conway, has info on area attractions. (☎800-367-3364; www.mtwashingtonvalley.com. Open June-Oct. M-F 9am-5pm, Sa-Su 10am-5pm. Call ahead for winter hours.) Numerous stores in the North Conway area rent outdoor equipment for the slopes, the water, and the roads. For ski goods in winter or bike and boat rentals during other seasons, **Joe Jones,** 2709 White Mtn. Hwy. at

GEORGIA TO MAINE, ONE STEP AT A TIME

While checking out the 2160 mi. Appalachian Trail (AT), *Let's Go* caught up with Anthony Bramante, who hiked the trail in 2002.

LG: What made you want to hike the AT?
A: I had been backpacking since I was three or four years old with my dad and my brother, and we'd always run into these scraggly-looking, smelly through-hikers, and they had some really cool stories, so I knew I'd love to through-hike the trail. So I decided to take the year off before college, and I did.

LG: Awesome. Did you through-hike alone?
A: Yup. I, and most people, through-hike alone—but you end up meeting such a diverse group of people from all different walks of life. Through-hiking the trail can be really great to form what we call trail families, where you and a bunch a hikers get to know each other real well, and never go more than a few days without seeing each other over months.

LG: So, what's a trail name?
A: A trail name is a kind of nickname that you're given, or that you give yourself, sometime towards the beginning of the hike, so it sticks with you throughout the entire time. And I would go months knowing someone very well—knowing about their family, their childhood, everything—but I

Mechanic St. in North Conway, has it all. (☎356-9411. Alpine skis, boots, and poles $20 per day, 2 days $36; cross-country equipment $15/$26; snowboards $25/$46. 4hr. bike rental $15, 8hr. $30. Canoes M-F $30, Sa-Su $35; kayaks $20/$25. Open July-Aug. daily 9am-8pm; Sept.-Nov. and Apr.-June M-Th and Su 10am-6pm, F-Sa 9am-6pm; Dec.-Mar. M-F 8:30am-6pm, Sa-Su 8:30am-8pm.) **Eastern Mountain Sports (EMS),** just north on White Mtn. Hwy. in the lobby of the Eastern Slope Inn, sells camping equipment and rents tents, sleeping bags, snowshoes, packs, and skis. The knowledgeable staff provides free first-hand info on climbing and hiking, and EMS also offers a summer climbing school. (☎356-5433. Tents $20 per day, each additional day $10. Sleeping bags $15/$5. Open June-Sept. M-Sa 8:30am-9pm, Su 8:30am-6pm; Oct.-May M-Th and Su 8:30am-6pm, F-Sa 8:30am-9pm.)

Located in the heart of Conway and maintained by friendly folk, the **White Mountains Hostel (HI) ❶,** 36 Washington St., off Rte. 16 at the intersection of Rte. 153, is meticulously clean and environmentally friendly. The hostel has 43 comfy bunks, a kitchen, wireless Internet, and a common room. (☎447-1001. Locker key deposit $10. Linen included. Towel $0.50. Laundry $3. Reception 7:30-10am and 5-10pm. Checkout 10am. Lockout 10am-noon. Dorms $23, members $20; private rooms $48. Reservations recommended during the summer and peak foliage season. MC/V.) Owned by Babe Ruth's son-in-law, the hostel at the beautiful **Cranmore Mt. Lodge ❶,** 859 Kearsarge Rd., in North Conway, has 22 bunks. The lodge is about two mi. from downtown, and has a living room, pool, jacuzzi, cable TV, refrigerator, wireless Internet, tennis courts, and a duck pond. A delicious full breakfast, included with each overnight stay, makes up for the tight bunkrooms and thin mattresses. Be sure to bring a warm blanket to ward off the nightly temperature drop in the basement rooms. (☎356-2044 or 800-356-3596. Linen and towel $3. Check-in 3-9pm. Check-out 11am. Reservations recommended. Dorms $25. MC/V.)

Dark wooden canoes and Adirondack decor mingle with sombreros on the bright pink and purple walls at ◨**Cafe Noche ❷,** 147 Main St. in Conway. On a menu filled with delicious Mexican dishes, the Montezuma Pie (Mexican lasagna; $8.50) comes highly recommended. (☎447-5050. Open daily 11:30am-9pm. AmEx/D/MC/V.) At **Delaney's ❷,** north of town along Rte. 16, hungry locals feast on sushi and excellent sandwiches like the "Cranmore Carver," with ham, turkey, and swiss smothered in peppercorn dressing and served on a honey loaf. (☎356-7776. Sandwiches $6-9. Live music W nights. Open daily 11:30am-11pm; bar open later. AmEx/D/

MC/V.) If the rugged wilderness has you longing for the culture of the city, the huge mugs of coffee ($1.60) at **The Met Coffee House ❶**, 2680 Main St. in North Conway, are sure to comfort you. Local artwork hangs above patrons munching on croissants and elaborate fruit tarts. (☎356-8278. Live music F nights. Internet access $3 per 15min., $8 per hr. Open daily 8am-10pm. MC/V.)

HANOVER   ☎603

Home to the beautiful campus of Dartmouth College, the quiet little town of Hanover comes alive when students flood the classrooms and streets, as well as the many trails, paths, and waterways that make the area ideal for those who love the outdoors. Full of muddy boots, ancient Ivy League streets, and classy bars, Hanover is an appealing blend of wild and sophisticated.

■✚✚ ORIENTATION AND PRACTICAL INFORMATION. Located along the Connecticut River near Vermont border, and along Rte. 10 and 120, Hanover is accessible from both I-91 and I-89. Nearby towns are **Lebanon** (5 mi. south on Rte. 120), **White River Junction** (4 mi. south on Rte. 10, encompassing the confluence of the White and Connecticut Rivers), and **Norwich** (1½ mi. northwest in Vermont). **Vermont Transit** (☎800-552-8737) runs buses from Hanover that stop in front of the Hanover Inn, 35 S. Main St. Buy tickets on the bus or from Garber Travel, 57 S. Main St. (☎643-2700). Buses go to Boston (3-4hr., 4-5 per day, $25) and Burlington (2½hr., 4-5 per day, $21-27). **Amtrak** (station information ☎295-7160; schedules and reservations 800-872-7245; www.amtrak.com), on Railroad Row off N. Main St. in White River Junction, rolls to Burlington (2hr., 1 per day, $19-27) and New York City (7½hr., 1 per day, $61-67). **The Hanover Chamber of Commerce,** 53. S. Main St., has area info. (☎643-3115; www.hanoverchamber.org. Open M-F 9am-4pm. Booth open daily June-Sept. 7:30am-5pm.) **Internet Access: Howe Library,** 13 E. South St. (☎643-4120. Open M-Th 10am-8pm, F 10am-6pm, Sa 10am-5pm; Sept.-May also Su 1-5pm. Free.) **Post Office:** 50 S. Main St. (☎643-4544. Open M-F 8:30am-5pm, Sa 8:30am-noon.) **Postal Code:** 03755. **Area Code:** 603.

▐▐ ACCOMMODATIONS AND FOOD. The **Sunset Motor Inn ❸** has simple rooms with soft beds. Just 2 mi. south of Hanover on Rte. 10, this small motel features river views and some of the area's most reasonably priced accommodations. (☎298-8721. A/C. Reservations recommended. $53-100 depending on season and room type. AmEx/D/MC/V.) Camping

would still only know them as High Octane or Night Frog. My trail name is Prudence, which was said to be an ironic nickname, as I'm very imprudent, and I would get lost or light my stove on fire—but not in the right way—and do lots of other things.

LG: And did you encounter any trail magic along the way?

A: Absolutely. Trail magic is when someone helps you out on the trail, whether when you're hitch-hiking and someone gives you a ride, or when someone invites you over to their house when you're in town and gives you a home-cooked meal. People will often hike out onto the trail with a bag of apples or oranges and pass them to hikers they see, and take their trash, or leave a cooler of drinks and candy bars at a trailhead.

LG: Cool! Do you have a favorite stretch of trail?

A: Um, New Hampshire was kinda my background, so I came into it for all the New Hampshire stuff, and really thought it was going to be...but the northern section of Maine, just after the New Hampshire border, for about that first hundred miles, where the Bigelowes and Sugarloaf and the Baldpate Mountains are, is just absolutely gorgeous. There was this one incredibly clear day, where from the summit of one of the mountains, I could see Mt. Katadin, Mt. Washington, and the Atlantic Ocean all at the same time. It was just absolutely mind-blowing.

FROM COW TO SPOON

Along Rte. 100 in Waterbury, VT. lies a little scoop of heaven for anyone with a sweet tooth: **Ben & Jerry's Ice Cream Factory.**

What began as two high school friends making ice cream in an old Burlington gas station has become an ice cream phenomenon. Today, people from across the country celebrate triumphs and nurse broken hearts with their favorite Ben & Jerry's flavor.

Closer to the company's local roots, visitors line up at the Waterbury factory for tours of the facility and a scoop of ice cream fresh off the conveyor belt. The tour starts with a short film about the company's history, then guests are taken to a viewing area to see the the making of the frozen treats below. The cherry on top is the tasting room, where the tour concludes with two delectable sample flavors.

A short walk from the factory lies the flavor graveyard, where short-lived concoctions like Miz Jelena's Sweet Potato Pie, Ethan Almond, and Holy Cannoli melt off into the sunset.

Sound good? The ambitious traveler might want to see if the factory has any openings—each employee gets three pints of ice cream to take home per day. Now that's a job with benefits!

Ben & Jerry's Ice Cream Factory, ☎ 882-3586. *Call for tour times. $3, seniors $2, under 12 free.*

with wooded sites, restrooms, pool access, two beaches on a lake, tennis courts, hiking, and hot showers are available at **Storr's Pond ❶**, 2 mi. north of Hanover off Rte. 10. (☎643-2134. Open May 15-Oct. 15. Reservations recommended. Sites for 1-4 people $20, each additional person $2; with electricity and water $25/$3. Cash only.) For a quick bite, try **Lou's ❶**, 30 S. Main St., which has been humming with the conversations of Dartmouth students and locals since 1947. The $1 crullers—choose from glazed, cinnamon sugar, chocolate frosted, or jelly-filled—are especially delicious. (☎643-3321. Most meals $5-7. Open M-F 6am-3pm, Sa-Su 7am-3pm. AmEx/MC/V.) For late-night munchies, travelers should head to **Everything But Anchovies ❷**, 5 Allen St. "E.B.A.'s" has an all-day buffet ($6) big enough to make it a perennial favorite of hungry Dartmouth athletes. Pizza, sandwiches ($7-8), and free wireless Internet add to the perks. (☎643-6135; www.ebas.com. Open M-F 9am-2am, Sa-Su 7am-2am. AmEx/MC/V.)

◙ **SIGHTS.** Virtually synonymous with Hanover is **Dartmouth,** the rural jewel in the Ivy League crown (☎646-1110; www.dartmouth.edu). The college offers tours starting from the admissions office in McNutt Hall on N. Main St. (☎646-2875. Open M-F 8am-4pm. Tours are free, times vary.) The **Hood Museum of Art,** on Wheelock St., houses collections that include African, Native American, ancient Asian, and contemporary art. (☎646-2808; www.hoodmuseum.dartmouth.edu. Open Tu and Th-Sa 10am-5pm, W 10am-9pm, Su noon-5pm. Free.) With the Appalachian Trail passing through town, Hanover is an ideal base for hiking. The **Dartmouth Outdoors Club,** in Robinson Hall on N. Main St., maintains hundreds of miles of trails, sells the *Dartmouth Outing Guide* ($15) as well as more detailed maps ($1-3), and is a good source of information about hiking in the area. A downstairs bulletin board provides lodging and food information for through-hikers. (M-F 8am-4pm ☎646-2428. Robinson Hall office ☎646-2429. Open M-Th and Su 2-6pm.)

▨ **NIGHTLIFE.** While crashing a Dartmouth party may be a option, a year-round supply of students ensure that the nightlife in Hanover is always in full swing. **Murphy's on the Green,** 11 S. Main St., is a preppy restaurant by day and a wild party by night. At 10pm, tables move aside for the throngs of students that crowd into the bar to enjoy dancing, drinks (pitchers $10), and music. (☎643-4075. Entrees $10-22. Open daily 11:30am-1am.) At **5 Olde Nugget Alley,** descend into a dimly lit, cozy basement bar with different specials each night of the week.

Cheers resound from the fans watching ESPN at the bar, while subdued conversation emanates from the secluded tables. (☎643-5081. W Buffalo wings $0.25. Open daily 11:30am-1am.)

VERMONT

In 1609, the explorer Samuel de Champlain dubbed the area "green mountain" in his native French, and the name Vermont stuck. Here, lush forests and crystal clear waterways share the land with roaming Holstein cattle. The Vermont of Champlain's time still exists in the Green Mountain National Forest, and rural charm can be found in the myriad villages tucked into hillsides and valleys. But the region has also taken on the world, drawing thousands to the natural beauty of its ski slopes and the trendy commercialism of its outlet stores and gift shops. A mix of these features can be seen in the state's cities, which boast a unique metropolitan atmosphere tinged with true Vermont sensibility and culture.

⁊ PRACTICAL INFORMATION

Capital: Montpelier.

Visitor Info: Vermont Information Center, 134 State St., Montpelier 05602 (☎802-828-3237; www.vermontvacation.com). Open daily 7:45am-8pm. **Department of Forests, Parks, and Recreation,** 103 S. Main St., Waterbury 05671 (☎802-241-3670). Open M-F 7:45am-4:30pm. **Vermont Snowline** (☎802-229-0531; www.skivermont.com) gives snow conditions Nov.-May. 24hr.

Postal Abbreviation: VT. **Sales Tax:** 5%, meals and lodgings 9%. **Area Code:** 802.

VERMONT SKI RESORTS   ☎802

> **:TIP:** **QUIET TIME.** Many ski towns in Vermont empty out when the snows melt, which can mean lower rates and less traffic for summer travelers. Be warned, however, that some restaurants and nightspots can close for months at a time in the low season, so it's best to call ahead to establishments on your itinerary.

Every winter, skiers pour into Vermont and onto the Northeast's finest slopes; in the summer and fall, these same inclines melt into the stomping grounds of hikers and mountain bikers. Towns surrounding each of the mountains make their livelihood on this annual avalanche, offering a range of tourist attractions. For information, contact **Ski Vermont,** 26 State St., P.O. Box 368, Montpelier 05601. (☎223-2439; www.skivermont.com. Open M-F 7:45am-5:30pm.) The Vermont Information Center (see **Practical Information,** above) also provides helpful info. Cheaper lift tickets can be found during low-season—before mid-December and after mid-March.

With three mountains, 78 trails, the highest vertical drop in Vermont, and the only triple-black-diamond run in the eastern US, **Smugglers' Notch,** just north of Stowe on Rte. 108, can satisfy even the most extreme adventure-seekers. The resort also offers great family programs. In summer, hiking and canoeing prevail. (☎644-8851 or 800-451-8752; www.smuggs.com. Lift tickets $56, ages 7-18 $40, ages 70+ free.) A beautiful but dangerous passage south through Smugglers' Notch along Rte. 108 leads to the **Stowe Mountain Resort.** Only minutes from the village of Stowe, the resort offers one-day lift tickets ($65, seniors and ages 6-12 $45) for 48 trails (16% beginner, 59% intermediate, 25% expert), and impressive summer facilities, including alpine slides (single ride $14, ages 6-12 $10) and a golf course and country club. (☎253-3000 or 800-253-4754; www.stowe.com. Attraction package: 3 alpine slide rides, 1 gondola ride, bungee, trampoline, climbing wall, $49; seniors and ages 6-12 $44.) West of Brattleboro on Rte. 100, in the town of West Dover, **Mount Snow** boasts 145 trails (22% beginner, 49% intermediate, 29% expert), 23 lifts, excellent snowmaking capabilities, and the first snowboard park in the Northeast. In summer, mountain bikers take advantage of the 45 mi. of trails. (☎800-245-7669; www.mountsnow.com. Open mid-Nov. to late Apr. M-F 9am-4pm, Sa-Su 8am-4pm; May to early Nov. daily 9am-4pm. Lift tickets M-F $59, Sa-Su $67; ages 13-19 $44/$46; under 13 and seniors $31/$33. Mountain biking $30 per day.) At the junction of U.S. 4 and Rte. 100 N, the mammoth **Killington Resort** is unrivaled as the largest of Vermont's frozen playgrounds. Maintaining a city of resort complexes at the base of its seven peaks and 200 trails, Killington hosts the East Coast's longest ski season (mid-Oct. to early June). The summer also keeps a fair pace in Killington (see below) with hiking, biking, and fishing, among other diversions. (☎800-621-6867; www.killington.com. Lift tickets $67, ages 13-18 $54, seniors and ages 6-12 $43.) Near the Canadian border in Vermont's Northeast Kingdom, **Jay Peak,** in Jay on Rte. 242, catches more snowfall than any other peak in New England. With excellent glade skiing, Jay Peak is an appealing option for thrill-seekers. (☎988-2611 or 800-451-4449; www.jaypeakresort.com. 76 trails; 40% expert. Lift tickets $56, half-day $42; ages 7-17 $42/$32.) Challenging visitors to "Ski it if you can," **Mad River Glen,** in Waitsfield, has loads of expert-level trails (only 15% with snowmaking), no snowboarding, and the last surviving single chair lift. (☎496-3551; www.madriverglen.com. Lift tickets $50, seniors and ages 6-12 $37.) Other resorts include **Stratton** (☎297-2200 or 800-787-2886; 90 trails, 16 lifts), on Rte. 30 N in Bondville, and **Sugarbush** (☎583-6100 or 800-537-8427; www.sugarbush.com; 2 mountains, 115 trails, 17 lifts), in Warren. Cross-country resorts include the **Trapp Family Lodge** (see Stowe, p. 117); **Mountain Meadows,** in Killington (☎775-7077; 90 mi. of trails); and **Woodstock** (☎457-1100; 40 mi. of trails).

KILLINGTON   ☎802

With 4241 ft. Mt. Killington rising overhead, the town of Killington is a shrine for those who worship chairlifts and snow. While winter brings out Killington's best, summer travelers will find numerous opportunities for hiking, biking, and more.

🖪🔁 TRANSPORTATION AND PRACTICAL INFORMATION. Vermont Transit (☎800-552-8737), in the Killington Deli on Rte. 4 at the intersection with Rte. 100 N, runs buses to White River Junction (1hr., departs 7am, $7.50-8.50). **The Bus** leaves from the Transit Station to shuttle visitors to over 15 stops around Rutland and Killington. (☎773-3244; www.thebus.com. Jan.-Mar. 12 per day 7:15am-11:15pm. Apr.-June and Sept.-Dec. 6 per day 7:15am-5:15pm; July-Aug. 10 per day, 7:15am-7:15pm. $2.) If you need more flexible wheels, **Gramp's Shuttle** (☎236-6600) will come to your aid. The **Killington Chamber of Commerce,** on U.S. 4, just west of Killington Rd., is the best source of area info. (☎773-4181 or 800-337-1928; www.killingtonchamber.com. Open M-F 9am-5pm; Dec.-Mar. also Sa 9am-5pm.) To gear up for the slopes, visit **The Basin Ski Shop,** 2886 Killington Rd., where the friendly staff will suit you up for a day in the mountains. (☎422-3234. Open late Oct. to May M-Th 8:15am-9pm, F 8:15am-midnight, Sa-Su 7:15am-9pm; May to late Oct. M and Th-Sa 10am-6pm, Tu-W and Su 10am-5pm. Ski, boot, and pole package $28 per day.) **Internet Access: Sherburne Memorial Library,** 2 mi. south of the intersection of Rtes. 4 and 100, on River Rd. (☎422-9765. Open M and F 10am-5:30pm, T and Th 1-5:30pm, W 10am-8pm, Sa 9am-1pm.) **Post Office:** 2046 Rte. 4, just west of the intersection with Killington Rd., attached to the Chamber of Commerce. (☎775-4247. Open M-F 8:30am-4:30pm, Sa 8:30am-noon.) **Postal Code:** 05751. **Area Code:** 802.

▐▐ ACCOMMODATIONS AND FOOD. Prices for lodging in the area are highly seasonal, lowest in the summer months and highest over holiday weekends at the peak of ski season. **Trailside Lodge ❸,** on Rte. 100 N 2½ mi. from the intersection with Rte. 4, is the best bargain in town. Peak-season perks include a full breakfast buffet, four-course family-style dinner, big-screen TV in the lounge, lift ticket discounts, hot tub and heated outdoor pool, and free bus tickets to the resort. Rates are directly proportional to group size, and each bunk-style room can accommodate up to 6 people. (☎ 422-3532 or 800-447-2209; www.trailsidelodge.com. Early and late season $35-50 per person. Mid-winter and holidays up to $70-85 per person. AmEx/MC/V.) In summer, camping at one of 27 sites or 21 lean-tos at the **Gifford Woods State Park ❶** is an inexpensive option with well-kept campsites. (May to mid-Oct. ☎ 775-5354, Jan.-May 888-409-7579. Hot showers $0.25 per 5 min. 4-person sites $14-16; lean-tos $21-23. Each additional person $4. MC/V.) Part diner and part gadget workshop, ⬛**Ppeppers ❸,** on Killington Rd. just below the Killington ski complex, attracts tourists and locals alike. Put in a request for their sizzling fajitas ($16) and famous fresh-squeezed orange juice ($3), then watch your oranges roll down the ramp to their squishing-machine fate. (☎ 422-3177. Open daily 9am-10pm. AmEx/MC/V.) A plow car that formerly kept the rail track clear of snow now houses **Casey's Caboose ❸,** 2½ mi. up Killington Rd. from Rte. 4., a restaurant and bar that gives away 40,000 lb. of free chicken wings every winter. Munch away on the raised deck or snuggle into a booth for salmon or prime rib for $16-22. (☎ 422-3795. Free wings daily 3-6pm. Open daily 3pm-midnight. AmEx/D/MC/V.) **Johnny Boy's Pancake House ❶,** 923 Killington Rd., is the place to start your morning with enormous breakfasts ($3.50-7.50) that will keep you energized all day. (☎ 422-4411. Open M and Th-F 8am-1pm, Sa-Su 7am-2pm.)

▐▐ OUTDOOR ACTIVITIES AND NIGHTLIFE. During the green season, the slopes and surrounding mountains turn into hiking and biking throughways. **Gifford Woods State Park** on Rte. 100, ¾ mi. from the intersection of Rte. 4 and Rte. 100 N, offers connecting trails to Vermont's major trails, the **Appalachian Trail (AT)** and the **Long Trail.** Trail information can be obtained at the park office. (☎ 775-5354. Park office open May to mid-Oct. M-Th and Su 9am-8:30pm, F-Sa 9am-9pm. Day-use fee $2.50, ages 4-13 $2. Fishing licenses available at the park office $15 per day, $41 per season.) The **Killington Resort Complex** also provides summer recreation options at Killington and Pico mountains. (☎ 422-3333. All-day adventure center pass $30, seniors and ages 6-12 $25; with mountain biking $40/$35. Mountain bike rentals 2hr. $30, under 12 $15; 4hr. $35/$17; full day $45/$22. Alpine slide $7, children $5.) Rent less expensive wheels at **First Stop,** south of the resort complex along Rte. 4. (☎ 422-9050. Open May-Sept. M and Th-Su 9am-6pm. Bikes $25 per day.) When the temperature drops, two of Vermont's best nightlife spots open up on Killington Rd. After Halloween, the **Wobbly Barn,** halfway up the Killington Rd., has dancing, live acts, and a free nacho bar. (☎ 422-6171; www.wobblybarn.com. Call for schedule.) Just past the Killington Shops at the Shack, **The Pickle Barrel,** whose past performers include Blues Traveler and Ziggy Marley, warms things up with happy hour events and late-night hubbub. (☎ 422-3035; www.picklebarrelnightclub.com. Info on tickets available online.) Free rides from the resort to the nightclub are provided by The Pickle Barrel (☎ 422-7433).

BURLINGTON ☎ 802

On the shore of Lake Champlain, Burlington's thriving downtown lures young and old to classy restaurants, independent bookstores, and excellent shopping. Along pedestrian-friendly Church St., the Birkenstocks of college students share the street with the worn sneakers of street performers and leather oxfords of office-

NEW ENGLAND

bound businessmen, but with the Adirondacks rising over the lake and the Green Mountains beckoning just beyond the city limits, even those who only don hiking boots have an excuse to venture to Burlington.

▤▨ TRANSPORTATION AND PRACTICAL INFORMATION. Two roads lead to Burlington, **Route 7** from Shelburne in the south, and **Route 2** connecting to I-89 from the east. Three miles east of Burlington, off Rte. 2, **Burlington International Airport** (☎ 863-2874) flies to a handful of major cities. **Chittenden County Transit Authority (CCTA)** runs U Mall/Airport shuttles to the airport. CCTA also serves the downtown area with unbeatable access and reliable service. Connections to Shelburne and other outlying areas also run frequently; catch buses downtown at the intersection of Cherry and Church St. (☎ 864-2282; www.cctaride.org. Buses operate at least every 30min. M-Sa 6:15am-10:10pm, depending on routes. $1.25; seniors, disabled, and ages 6-18 $0.60. Schedules available at the Chamber of Commerce.) **Amtrak,** 29 Railroad Ave., Essex Jct., 5 mi. east of Burlington on Rte. 15, runs to New York City (9hr., 1 per day, $62-68) and White River Junction (2hr., 1 per day, $19-27). (Station info ☎ 879-7298, schedules and pricing 800-872-7245; www.amtrak.com. Open 1hr. before and after departures.) **Vermont Transit,** 345 Pine St., runs buses to: Albany (4¾hr., 3 per day, $38); Boston (4¾hr., 4 per day, $45); Middlebury (1hr., 2 per day, $12); Montréal (2½hr., 5 per day, $26); White River Junction (2hr., 4 per day, $21). (☎ 864-6811 or 800-552-8737. Open daily 5:30am-9:30pm.) **Ski Rack,** 85 Main St., rents bikes and ski equipment. (☎ 658-3313 or 800-882-4530. Open M-F 10am-7pm, Sa 9am-6pm, Su 11am-5pm. Mountain bikes 1hr. $12, 4hr. $20, full day $25. Credit card required.) **Visitor Info: Lake Champlain Regional Chamber of Commerce,** 60 Main St., Rte. 100. (☎ 863-3489 or 877-686-5253; www.vermont.org. Open May to mid.-Oct. M-F 8am-5pm, Sa-Su 10am-5pm; mid-Oct. to Apr. M-F 8am-5pm.) **Internet Access: Fletcher Free Library,** 235 College St. (☎ 863-3403. Open M-Tu and Th-F 8:30am-6pm, W 8:30am-9pm, Sa 9am-5pm, Su noon-6pm. Free.) **Post Office:** 11 Elmwood Ave., at Pearl St. (☎ 863-6033. Open M-F 8am-5pm, Sa 8am-1pm.) **Postal Code:** 05401. **Area Code:** 802.

▟ ACCOMMODATIONS. The Chamber of Commerce has the complete rundown on area accommodations, which tend toward upscale lodgings. B&Bs can be found in the outlying suburbs. Reasonably priced hotels and guest houses line **Shelburne Road (Route 7),** south of downtown, and **Main Street (Route 2),** east of downtown. **▧Mrs. Farrell's Home Hostel (HI) ❶,** 27 Arlington Ct., 3 mi. north of downtown via North Ave. and Heineberg Rd., is a welcoming abode for the homesick traveler. Six beds are split between a clean, comfortable basement and a lovely "summer cottage." (☎ 865-3730, call for reservations 4-6pm. Check-in before 5pm. Bike rental $4 per day. Dorms first night stay $25; each additional night $20, members $17.50. Cottage $43, members $40.) If you're looking to drop some serious cash, look no further than the soft beds, five-star furnishings, and first-class service of the **Lang House ❺,** 360 Main St., only a 5-10min. walk from Church St. and downtown. With a view of Lake Champlain from the third floor rooms and a full gourmet breakfast, Lang House ensures a luxurious stay. (☎ 652-2500 or 877-919-9799; www.langhouse.com. Rooms with TV and A/C $135-225. AmEx/D/MC/V.) With low prices and sparkling clean rooms, the **G.G.T. Tibet Inn ❸,** 3 mi. south of Burlington on Rte.7, has refrigerators, A/C, outdoor pool, and a small library about the owner's native Tibet. (☎ 863-7110; www.ggttibetinn.com. Rooms $45-75. AmEx/MC/V.) The **North Beach Campsites ❶,** on Institute Rd., 1½ mi. north of town by North Ave., have 137 sites with access to a beach on Lake Champlain. Take Rte. 127 to North Ave., or the "North Ave." bus from the main terminal on Pine St. (☎ 862-0942 or 800-571-1198. Showers $0.25 per 5min. $5 parking fee for non-campers. Open May to mid-Oct. Sites $22, with water and electricity $28, full hookup

$30-31. AmEx/MC/V.) The beach is open to non-campers, rents canoes and kayaks, and is a stellar spot for picnics. (Beach open 24hr. for campers; beach parking closes at 9pm. Lifeguards on duty mid-June to Aug. 10am-5:30pm.) Boat rentals are available from **Umiak**. (☎253-2317. Canoes $18 per hr., kayaks $12-25 per hr. Open daily 10am-5pm.) See **Champlain Valley** (p. 115) for more camping options.

🍴 **FOOD.** With all the fantastic restaurants that crowd the Church Street Marketplace and its adjacent sidestreets, visitors could eat in this food lover's paradise for weeks without hitting the same place twice. A mostly vegetarian cafe, **Zabby and Elf's Stone Soup ❷**, 211 College St., offers a wide variety of stews, casseroles, rice, and customizable salads from the hot and cold bars ($6 per lb.), as well as sandwiches ($6-7) on freshly baked bread. (☎862-7616. Open M 7am-7pm, Tu-F 7am-9pm, Sa 9am-7pm. Cash or check only.) The college crowd heads to **Muddy Waters ❶**, 184 Main St., where large cups of coffee ($1.50), a selection of light fare (veggie chili $3.50), and a rustic, comfortable cafe area keep the conversation going for hours. (☎658-0466. Open M 7:30am-8:30pm, Tu-Sa 7:30am-midnight, Su 8:30am-10pm. Cash or check only.) At **Sweetwater's ❸**, 120 Church St., high ceilings and vast wall paintings dwarf those who come for the delicious French onion soup ($6) and wide variety of sandwiches ($7-10). When the warm weather rolls around, dine al fresco. (☎864-9800. Entrees $10-18. Live music F and Sa evenings. Open M-

Sa 11:30am-midnight, Su 11:30am-11pm. AmEx/D/DC/MC/V.) The **New England Culinary Institute (NECI) ❹**, 25 Church St., known around town for its superb food at very reasonable prices, is a proving ground for student chefs. (☎862-6324. Dinner entrees from $14. Open Tu-Th 11:30am-4pm and 5:30-10pm, F-Sa 11:30am-4pm and 5:30-10:30pm, Su 11am-3pm and 5:30-9pm; low season closes 30min.-1hr. earlier. AmEx/D/MC/V.)

■ **SIGHTS.** The ▓**Shelburne Museum,** 7 mi. south of Burlington on Rte. 7 S in Shelburne, houses one of the most impressive collections of Americana in the country. Visitors can see the enormous paddleboat Ticonderoga, a 1950s home, a 19th-century Vermont church, printing presses, a lighthouse, a covered bridge, and even a small collection of works by Degas, Monet and Cassatt. (☎985-3346; www.shelburnemuseum.org. Open mid-May to late Oct. daily 10am-5pm. $18, students $13, ages 6-18 $9; after 3pm $10/$10/$5; families $48.) Discover ecology, culture, and history at **ECHO**, 1 College St., a science center and lake aquarium near the water. The multitude of hands-on exhibits and interactive demos are fun for kids. (☎864-1848; www.echovermont.org. Open M-W and F-Su 10am-5pm, Th 10am-8pm. $9, students and seniors $8, ages 3-17 $6.) The **Ethan Allen Homestead** rests north of Burlington on Rte. 127 in the Winooski Valley Park. In the 1780s, Allen, his Green Mountain Boys, and Benedict Arnold forced the surrender of Fort Ticonderoga and helped establish the state of Vermont. Now, hourly tours visit the cabin and tell the story of the frontiersman. (☎865-4556; www.ethanallenhomestead.org. Open May-Oct. M-Sa 10am-4pm, Su 1-4pm; Nov.-Apr. Sa 10am-4pm. $5, seniors $4, ages 5-17 $3, families $15.)

Amateur historians love **South Willard Street,** where **Champlain College** occupies many of the Victorian houses that line the street. **City Hall Park,** downtown, and **Battery Street Park,** on Lake Champlain near the edge of downtown, are a wonderful escape to cool shade on hot summer days. For travelers who long to feel the wind in their sails, just north lies the **Lake Champlain Community Sailing Center,** 1 Lake St., where sailboat rentals ($25-$42 per hr.) and private instruction on the water ($45 per hr., $20 per hr. each additional person) are available. (☎864-2499; www.lccsc.org. Open M-F 9am-8pm, Sa-Su 10am-8pm. Lessons M-Th 5-8pm, Sa-Su 9am-noon.) The **Spirit of Ethan Allen III** runs a narrated, 500-passenger scenic cruise that departs from the boathouse at the bottom of College St. (☎862-8300; www.soea.com. 1½hr. cruises late May to mid-Oct. daily 10am, noon, 2, 4pm; 2½hr. sunset cruise 6:30pm. $12, ages 3-11 $6. Mid-June to Sept. sunset cruise $17/$13.)

▓▓ ▓ **FESTIVALS AND NIGHTLIFE.** With so many colleges in the area, Burlington's nightlife scene is always alive and kicking. A pedestrian haven, Church St. Marketplace nurtures offbeat puppeteers and musicians who entertain the crowds at all hours. Pick up a free *Seven Days* newspaper, available all over Burlington, to get the skinny on what's happening around town.

In the summer, the **Vermont Mozart Festival** brings Bach, Beethoven, and Mozart to local barns, farms, and meadows. (☎862-7352; www.vtmozart.com. Concerts late July to early Aug.) In mid-June, the **Discover Jazz Festival** features over 1000 musicians, with past performers including Ella Fitzgerald, Dizzy Gillespie, and Betty Carter. (☎863-7992; www.discoverjazz.com. Some performances are free but others are sold through the Flynn Theater Box Office.) The **Champlain Valley Folk Festival,** located about halfway between Burlington and Middlebury, enlivens summer days in early August. (☎877-850-0206; www.cvfest.org. Tickets $25-75.) The **Flynn Theater Box Office,** 153 Main St., handles sales for the Folk Festival and the Discover Jazz Festival. (☎652-4500; www.flynncenter.org. Open M-F 10am-5pm, Sa 11am-4pm.)

The birthplace of the band Phish, **Nectar's,** 188 Main St., still rocks with inexpensive food, including their legendary gravy fries ($3). The large stage and dance floor cater nightly to live tunes of all genres from bands both local and mainstream. (☎658-4771. Cover varies. Open M-Tu 11am-2:30am, W-F 6am-2:30am, Sa-Su 7am-2:30am.) One of Burlington's most popular night spots, **Red Square,** 136 Church St., rocks out to live music nightly. Bands play everything from funk to classic rock in the alley if the crowd gets large. (☎859-8909. Cover varies. Open daily 4pm-2am.) For a laid-back pint, try **Ri-Ra,** 123 Church St., a traditional Irish pub with deep booths and a quieter crowd. (☎860-9401. Beer $2.50-4.50. Irish music W 7pm. Live music Sa 10pm. Open M-Sa 11:30am-2am, Su 11:30am-1am.)

▓ DAYTRIP FROM BURLINGTON: CHAMPLAIN VALLEY. Stretching 100 mi. between Vermont's Green Mountains and New York's Adirondacks, **Lake Champlain** boasts plentiful opportunities for biking, hiking, and camping in the many well-kept state parks that dot the shorelines of the lake. Visitors can take a bridge or ferry across the lake to gain the best views of its silvery surface. The **Lake Champlain Ferry,** located on the dock at the bottom of King St., sails from Burlington to Port Kent, NY, and back. (☎864-9804; www.ferries.com. 1hr. each way. July-Aug. 11-13 per day 7:30am-7:30pm; mid-May to late June and Sept. to mid-Oct. 9 per day 8am-6:35pm. One-way $4, ages 6-12 $1.60; car and driver $14.75.) Throughout the day, service from Grand Isle, VT to Plattsburg, NY, and from Charlotte, VT, to Essex, NY, is also offered. (One-way $3, ages 6-12 $1; car and driver $8.25.) Campers can stock up on anything from fishing gear to local maple syrup at the **Hero's Welcome** complex, in North Hero off Rte. 2. The buildings house an eclectic array of food and goods at reasonable prices with a seating area overlooking Lake Champlain. (☎ 372-4161; www.heroswelcome.com. Open daily 6:30am-6pm.)

Fog drifts over the grasslands hiding the countless migratory birds that come to rest in the marsh of the **Missisquoi National Wildlife Refuge,** 2 mi. to the northwest of Swanton, VT on Rte. 78 at the northern end of the lake. The refuge provides extensive lands for hiking, bird watching, kayaking, and canoeing in warm weather, and cross-country skiing and snowshoeing in the winter. (☎868-4781. Office 5 mi. northwest of Swanton off Tabor Rd. Open M-F 8am-4:30pm. Refuge open dawn-dusk. Free.) **Mount Philo State Park ❶,** 15 mi. south of Burlington, off Rte. 7, offers pleasant, easy-to-moderate hiking and picnic facilities with an expansive view of deep forests, green pastures, and winding roads leading to a mountainous horizon. Camping is offered on seven sites and three lean-tos nestled on the side of the mountain. (☎425-2390. Open mid-May to mid-Oct. daily 10am-dusk. Entrance fee $2.50, ages 4-13 $2. 2-night min. stay. For 14-day advance reservations at any Vermont state park, call ☎888-409-7579. Sites $14; lean-tos $21.)

Also north of the lake, **Burton Island State Park ❶** is accessible only by private boats and a ferry which runs five times daily from Kill Kare State Park, 35 mi. north of Burlington and 3½ mi. southwest of U.S. 7 off of Town Rd., near St. Albans Bay. This secluded park provides a tranquil place to hike, swim, and picnic. (☎524-6353. Open late May to early Sept. daily 8am-8pm; call for schedule. Day use $2.50, ages 4-13 $2. Ferry service $3 each way. Bike rental $1. 4-night min. stay. 17 tent sites $16; 26 lean-tos $23. Each additional person $4. MC) Also along the Champlain Islands are myriad **biking trips** (☎597-4646; www.champlainbikeways.org), **state parks** available for day use (**Alburg Dunes** ☎796-4170; **Knight Point** ☎343-7236; **North Hero** ☎372-8727; **Knight Island** ☎524-6353; www.vtstateparks.com), and the **Lipizzan Stallions.** These horses, known for their grace and strength, perform four times weekly. (Located past the drawbridge between Grand Isle and North Hero on Rte. 2 W in Knight Point State Park. Champlain Islands Chamber of Commerce ☎372-8400 or 800-262-5226 for more information; www.champlainislands.com. Performances July-Aug. Th-F 6pm, Sa-Su 2:30pm. $17, seniors $14, ages 6-12 $10.)

NEW ENGLAND

MIDDLEBURY   ☎ 802

Built on the foundations of the countryside's ample marble supply, Middlebury
now thrives on the thick wallets of serenity-seeking tourists while maintaining an
atmosphere hip enough for the discriminating Middlebury College student. Middlebury's lush green hills and diverse residents create a blend of culture and history that makes this charming town stand out from the crowd.

⚏⚏ TRANSPORTATION AND PRACTICAL INFORMATION. Middlebury sits
along U.S. 7, 42 mi. south of Burlington. **Vermont Transit** stops at the Exxon station,
16 Court St., west of Main St. (☎388-9300. Station open daily 6am-10pm.) Buses
run to: Albany (4hr., 3 per day, $31); Boston (6hr., 3 per day, $48); Burlington (1hr.,
3 per day, $11); Rutland (1½hr., 3 per day, $8). **Addison County Transit Resources** provides free shuttle service in the immediate Middlebury vicinity, making stops
every hour at the town green, Marbleworks, Middlebury College, and along U.S. 7
S. (☎388-1946. Runs M-F 7am-8:30pm, Sa-Su 9am-5pm.) Exploring on foot is probably the easiest way around town, but for those who prefer wheels, the **Bike Center,** 74 Main St., rents bikes. (☎388-6666; www.bikecentermid.com. Open M-Th and
Sa 9:30am-5:30pm, F 9:30am-8pm; June-Sept. also Su 1-4pm. Bikes from $20 per
day.) The staff at the **Addison County Chamber of Commerce,** 2 Court St., provides
free area maps, bus schedules, and event information. (☎388-7951 or 800-733-8376;
www.midvermont.com. Open M-F 10:30am-5pm.) **Internet Access: Ilsley Public
Library,** 75 Main St. (☎388-4095. Open M, W, F 10am-6pm; Tu and Th 10am-8pm; Sa
10am-4pm. Free.) **Post Office:** 10 Main St. (☎388-2681. Open M-F 8am-5pm, Sa 8am-
12:30pm.) **Postal Code:** 05753. **Area Code:** 802.

⚏ ACCOMMODATIONS. Lodging with four walls and no mosquitoes isn't cheap
in Middlebury. The **Sugar House Motel ❸,** 202 Ethan Allen Hwy., 2 mi. north of
Middlebury on Rte. 7, has clean rooms with TV, refrigerator, microwave, and A/C,
as well as a pool. (☎388-2770 or 800-784-2746. Reservations recommended. Seasonal rates from $49-99. MC/V.) For those weary of small roadside motels, the **Mid-
dlebury B&B ❹,** 174 Washington St., has four comfortable rooms, soft beds, a
dedicated owner, and two Jack Russell terriers to make you feel right at home.
(☎388-4851. Rooms $75-125. Cash only.) **Branbury State Park ❶,** 7 mi. south on U.S.
7, then 4 mi. south on Rte. 53, stretches along Lake Dunmore, offering 45 spacious
sites and seven lean-tos on soft grassy fields shaded by a leafy canopy. (☎247-5925.
Hot showers $0.25 per 5min. Canoe rentals $7.50 per hr., $35 per day. Paddleboats
$5 per 30min. Open late May to mid-Oct. Sites $16-18; lean-tos $23-25.)

⚏⚏ FOOD AND NIGHTLIFE. Middlebury's restaurants cater chiefly to plump
wallets, but a student presence ensures the survival of less expensive options.
Noonie's Deli ❶, 137 Maple St., in the Marbleworks building just behind Main St.,
makes terrific sandwiches ($4-5) on thick slices of homemade bread in a sweet-as-
apple-pie cafe. (☎388-0014. Open M-F 8am-8pm, Sa 9am-8pm, Su 11am-7pm. Cash
or check only.) Turquoise and peach decor complements the larger-than-life
murals on the walls of **Amigos ❸,** 4 Merchants Row, which offers creative Mexican
dishes like the three enchilada Mexican Flag for $11. (☎388-3624. Lunch $6-8. Dinner $8-18. Open M-Sa 11:30am-9pm, Su 4-9pm; bar open daily until 10:30pm. AmEx/
D/MC/V.) **Mister Up's ❸,** a popular hangout on Bakery Ln., just off Main St., blends
a friendly pub atmosphere with outdoor, airy, cafe-style dining. Ample sandwiches
($6-7) are perfect with the nightly drink specials. (☎388-6724. Entrees $9-14. Open
M-Sa 11:30am-midnight, Su 11am-midnight. AmEx/DC/MC/V.) Night owls head to
Angela's Pub, 86 Main St. for live rock, the jukebox, or the cheers of a heated game
of pool. (☎388-6936. $1.50 Labatt pints Tu. DJ F. Live band Sa. 21+. No cover. Open

Tu-Th and Sa 8pm-2am, F 6pm-2am.) For a more mellow drinking atmosphere, laughter and the clinking of glasses harmonize with live jazz and rock at **Two Brothers,** 88 Main St. (☎388-0002. Beer $1.75-3.50. $1 off all pints and wine M, $1.50 Labatt pints Tu. No cover. Open M-F 11:30am-2am, Sa-Su 11am-2am.)

🞂 **SIGHTS.** Most of the town's cultural events are hosted by **Middlebury College;** the concert hall in the college **Arts Center,** just outside of town on S. Main St., has a terrific concert series. The **box office** has details on events sponsored by the college. (☎443-4168; www.middlebury.edu/cfa. Open Sept.-May M-F noon-5pm, also 1hr. before start of shows. Many events free, most $5-12.) Inside the Arts Center, the **Middlebury College Museum of Art** offers an intimate gallery filled with ancient art, sculpture, and innovative modern exhibits. (☎443-5007. Open Tu-F 10am-5pm, Sa-Su noon-5pm. Call for exact hours. Free.) Through the summer months, Middlebury's crack at an **International Film Festival** screens movies on Saturdays at 7 and 9:30pm in the Dana Auditorium. (☎443-5510; www.middlebury.edu/ls/film. Free.) **Tours** from the admissions office, in Emma Willard Hall on S. Main St., showcase the white marble houses and manicured fields of Middlebury's picturesque campus. (☎443-3000. Tours daily 10am and 2pm; Aug-Nov. also Sa 10am. Self-guided tour brochures are also available.) If you're too poor for a pint or just want some local flavor, trek ¾ mi. north of town to the **Otter Creek Brewery,** 793 Exchange St., for a free tour and samples of their award-winning copper ale. (☎800-473-0727. Tours daily 1, 3, 5pm. Shop open M-Sa 10am-6pm, Su 11am-4pm.) Fifteen miles east of the Middlebury College campus, the **Middlebury College Snow Bowl** entertains skiers in winter with 14 trails and three lifts. (☎388-4356; www.middlebury.edu/~snowbowl. Lift tickets M-F $28, Sa-Su $35; students and seniors $23/$28; preschool $7/$7.) The **Henry Sheldon Museum of Vermont History,** 1 Park St., offers a house full of artifacts collected by Henry Sheldon, who founded the museum in 1884. Wooden canes, furniture, silverware, and textiles paint a portrait of life in Addison County during the 19th century. (☎388-2117; www.henrysheldonmuseum.org. Open M-Sa 10am-5pm. Call ahead for winter hours. $5, seniors $4.50, students $4, ages 6-18 $3.)

The scenic outdoors surrounding Middlebury make for great hiking and paddling. Hiking and camping information for Green Mountain National Forest is provided by the **Middlebury Ranger Station,** 1077 Rte. 7 S. (☎388-4362. Open M-F 8am-4:30pm.) For paddling supplies, **Middlebury Mountaineer,** 5 Park St., can meet your needs and provide you with a license to hunt or fish. (☎388-1749; www.mmvt.com. One-person kayak full day $50, tandem $60, 50% discount each additional day. Licenses $15 per day, $41 season. Open M-Sa 10am-5:30pm, Su noon-3pm.) Exercise your mind at the **Robert Frost Interpretive Trail,** an easy 1 mi. trail starting from a parking lot 2 mi. east of Ripton on Rte. 125. Excerpts from the poet's works are mounted on plaques along the path in spots similar to ones that might have inspired the poems' creation. (☎388-4362. Free.)

STOWE

☎802

Stowe curls gracefully up the side of Mt. Mansfield, Vermont's highest peak at 4393 ft. A mecca for outdoor activities in all seasons, Stowe tries to offer the charm and character of an alpine ski village. The proliferation of Swiss chalets evokes the feeling of a charming Swiss village lost in the mountains of Vermont.

🞂🞂 **TRANSPORTATION AND PRACTICAL INFORMATION.** Stowe is 10 mi. north of I-89 off Exit 10, 27 mi. southwest of Burlington. The ski slopes lie along **Mountain Road (Route 108),** northwest of Stowe. **Vermont Transit** (☎244-7689 or 800-552-8737; open M-Sa 5am-9pm, Su 6am-8pm) comes only as close as **Depot Beverage,** 1 River Rd., in Waterbury, 11 mi. from Stowe, and runs to Boston (4hr., 1 per

NEW ENGLAND

day, \$53) and Burlington (30min., 1 per day, \$8-9). **Peg's Pick-up/Stowe Taxi** (☎253-9490 or 800-370-9490) will take you into Stowe for around \$25 plus \$5 for each additional passenger; call ahead. In winter, the **Stowe Trolley** runs up and down Mountain Rd. every 20-30min. (☎223-7287; www.stoweshuttle.org. Trolley runs in winter 7:30am-10pm. \$1, seniors and ages 17 and under \$0.50; weekly pass \$10, season pass \$20. July to mid-Oct. daily 1½hr. tours leave from town hall at 11am. \$2.) **Visitors Info: Stowe Area Association,** 51 Main St. (☎253-7321 or 800-247-8693; www.gostowe.com. Open June to mid-Oct. and mid-Dec. to Mar. M-Sa 9am-8pm, call for Su hours; mid-Oct. to mid-Dec. and Apr.-June M-F 9am-5pm.) Pick up the free *Stowe Scene* and the *Vacation Planner* for event and recreation info. **Internet Access: Stowe Free Library,** 90 Pond St. (☎253-6145. Open M, W, F 9:30am-5:30pm, Tu and Th 2-7pm, Sa 10am-3pm. Free.) **Post Office:** 105 Depot St., off Main St. (☎253-7521. Open M-F 8am-5pm, Sa 9am-noon.) **Postal Code:** 05672. **Area Code:** 802.

⌂ ACCOMMODATIONS. Foster's Place ❷, 4968 Mountain Rd., offers primarily long-term and group dorm rooms with a lounge, laundry, game room, outdoor pool, and hot tub/sauna in a recently renovated school building. (☎800-330-4880. Reservations recommended. Singles \$35-39, with private bath \$49-59; quads \$55. Call for seasonal rates. AmEx/D/MC/V.) A converted 19th-century farm house and adjacent motel, the **Riverside Inn ❸,** 1965 Mountain Rd., 2 mi. from town, offers good rates and great perks, such as free mountain bike loans, pool table, and fireplace in the lodge. (☎253-4217 or 800-966-4217. Rooms \$49-109. AmEx/MC/V.) **▓Smugglers' Notch State Park ❶,** 6443 Mountain Rd., 8 mi. west of Stowe, just past Foster's Place, has hot showers, tent sites, and lean-tos. Secluded sites, new facilities, and beautiful views of Mt. Mansfield make this an excellent camping option. (☎253-4014. Reservations recommended. Open late May to mid-Oct. 4-person sites \$14; lean-tos \$21. Each additional person \$4.)

▐▌▐ FOOD AND NIGHTLIFE. At the **▓Depot Street Malt Shoppe ❶,** 57 Depot St., sports pennants and vinyl records deck the walls, while rock 'n' roll favorites liven up the outdoor patio seating. The cost of a 1950s-style hot fudge sundae has been adjusted for inflation (\$4), but prices remain reasonable. (☎253-4269. Entrees \$5-8. Open M-Th and Su 11:30am-8pm, F-Sa 11:30am-9pm. AmEx/D/DC/MC/V.) Perfect for picnics, **Mac's Deli ❶,** located in Mac's Stowe Market, on S. Main St. ¼ mi. from the intersection of Rte. 100 and Rte. 108, has tasty sandwiches, subs, and wraps (\$4-6) made with any of the meats and cheeses in the market's deli selection. They also serve piping hot soups for \$2-3. (☎253-4576. No seating. Open M-Sa 7am-9pm, Su 7am-8pm. AmEx/MC/V.) **Gracie's Restaurant ❸,** on Mountain Rd. outside Stowe, will have you howling in delight with pooch-themed delights like "doggone good" burgers (\$9-10) and an on-site bakery. Don't forget to carry their "doggie bag" desserts. (☎253-8741. Open M-Th 11:30am-10pm, F-Su 11:30am-11pm. AmEx/D/MC/V.) Fans of little green men and all things not of this planet will enjoy **Pie in the Sky ❸,** 492 Mountain Rd. Their "Out of This World" pizzas include the "Blond Vermonter" with olive oil, Vermont cheddar, apples, and ham. (☎253-5100. Pizza \$8-17. Open daily 11:30am-10pm. MC/V.) For sports fans, the **Sunset Grille and Tap Room,** 140 Cottage Club Rd., off Mountain Rd., allows its guests to face off at the pool tables while they watch sporting events on more than 25 TVs. The adjacent restaurant offers an award-winning BBQ platter for \$14. (☎253-9281. Lunch \$5-10. Dinner \$10-20. Kitchen open daily 11:30am-midnight; bar open until 2am.) The weekday specials and six homemade microbrews served up in **The Shed,** 1859 Mountain Rd., make this brewery stand out. The space is divided into a restaurant and a tavern, so late-nighters can choose to share a quiet pint or a crazy one. (☎253-4364. Tu night \$2.50 pints. Open daily 11:30am-midnight.) Head to the **Rusty Nail,** 1 mi. from town center on Mountain Rd., to sample their full martini bar, dance to the tune of live music, or tap into one of the few sources of wireless Internet on the mountain. In the winter, the front patio becomes an ice bar that draws people from miles around. (☎253-6245. Live music or DJ Th-Sa 9pm-2am. 21+. Cover $5-15. Open daily 11:30am-2am; kitchen closes at 10pm.)

▨ SKIING. Stowe's ski offerings include the Stowe Mountain Resort (☎253-3000 or 800-253-4754) and Smugglers' Notch (☎644-8851 or 800-451-8752; see **Vermont Ski Resorts,** p. 109). Brush up on your skiing history at the **Vermont Ski Museum,** just south of the intersection of Mountain Rd. and Main St. in town. The small museum hosts a pseudo-chandelier of chairlifts, and is filled with skiing memorabilia. (☎253-9404. Open M and W-Su noon-5pm. Free, $3 suggested donation.) The hills are alive with cross-country skiing on 37 mi. of groomed trails and 25 mi. of backcountry trails on the softly undulating mountainsides surrounding **The Trapp Family Lodge,** 2 mi. off Mountain Rd., accessed from Luce Hill Rd. Budget traveler beware: prices for lodging climb to as much as $960 in the high season. However, inexpensive rentals and lessons coupled with the unparalleled serenity of backcountry skiing make this alpine winter wonderland a temptation hard to resist. (☎253-5719 or 800-826-7000; www.trappfamily.com. Trail fee $16, ski rentals $20, lessons $15-45 per hr. Ski school package includes all 3 for $40.) **AJ's Ski and Sports,** 350 Mountain Rd., rents ski equipment. (☎253-4593 or 800-226-6257. Skis, boots, and poles: downhill $26 per day, $50 for 2 days; cross-country $15/$28. Snowboard and boots $22 per day. Open in winter M-Th and Su 8am-8pm, F-Sa 8am-9pm.)

◉ ⚠ SIGHTS AND OUTDOOR ACTIVITIES. In summer, Stowe's frenetic pace drops off some, but it still burns with the energy of outdoor enthusiasts. **AJ's Ski and Sports** (see above) also rents bikes and kayaks in the summer. (Open in summer daily 9am-6pm. $18 half day, $27 full day; children $16/$24. Tandem kayak or canoe $42 per day.) Stowe's 5½ mi. asphalt **recreation path** runs parallel to Mountain Rd. (Rte.108) and begins behind the church on Main St. in Stowe, ascending toward Smugglers' Notch through peaceful meadows and thick forest glades. Perfect for biking, skating, and strolling in the summer, the path accommodates cross-country skiing and snowshoeing in the winter. A few miles past Smugglers' Notch on Mountain Rd. (Rte. 108), the road shrinks to one lane and winds past huge boulders and 1000 ft. high cliffs. Road closures through the pass are common in the winter, and strong caution should be observed if attempting any winter ascent. Stowe boasts several mountain streams, including the Winooski River, prime for fly-fishing. Seasoned and aspiring fly-fishers should head to the **Fly Rod Shop,** 2½ mi. south of Stowe on Rte. 100, to pick up the necessary fishing licenses ($15 per day, $30 per week, $41 per year; $20 per year for VT residents), rent fly rods and reels, and enroll in the free fly-fishing classes in the shop's pond. (☎253-7346 or 800-535-9763. Classes W 4-6pm, Sa 9-11am. Open Apr.-Oct. M-Sa 9am-6pm, Su 10am-4pm; Nov.-Mar. M-Sa 9am-5pm, Su 10am-4pm. Rods and reels $15 per day.) **Umiak,** on Rte. 100, ¾ mi. south of Stowe Center, rents kayaks and canoes in the summer. (☎253-2317. 2hr. river trip $30 per person, 4hr. trip $40 per person. Kayaks $25 after 1pm, $35 full day; canoes $35/$45. Open daily 9am-6pm.) Just 1¼ mi. north on Edson Rd., off Mountain Rd. north of Stowe, **Edson Hill Manor Stables** offers guided 1hr. horseback rides ($35) on the southeastern ridge of Smugglers' Notch through cool woodlands and green meadows. (☎253-8954 or 253-7371. Refreshments provided upon return. Call for tours and availability.) **Ziemke Glassblowing Studio,** 7 mi. south of Stowe along Rte. 100, allows free viewing of the entire glassblowing process—from a molten mass in the 2100°F furnace to finished vases, glasses, and candleholders. The wares being made are also for sale in the gallery. (☎244-6126. Open daily 10am-6pm.)

BRATTLEBORO ☎ 802

Hippie roots run deep in Brattleboro, VT, where bookstores, art galleries, and independent cafes compete with majestic scenery and outdoor adventure for attention. Bridging the divide between rural and urban sensibilities, Brattleboro's distinct mix of psychedelic progressivism and traditional values infuses the city with excitement. While downtown Brattleboro is always buzzing with activity, hiking and skiing in nearby parks provide a peaceful respite from the outside world.

⊞Ⱶ ORIENTATION AND PRACTICAL INFORMATION. Located along the southern part of the Vermont-New Hampshire border, Brattleboro is most easily reached by I-91 or Rt. 9. **Amtrak,** 10 Vernon St., (☎800-872-7245; www.amtrak.com; open M-F 9:30-11:30am and 3:30am-5:30pm, Sa-Su 11:30am-1:30pm and 3:30-5:30pm; no ticket office.) goes to New York City (6hr., 1 per day at 12:30pm, $52), and **Greyhound,** Jct. Rtes. 5 and 9, (☎254-6066; www.greyhound.com; open M-F 7:30am-4pm, Sa-Su 9:30am-noon and 2:15-3:15pm.) runs buses to Boston (3hr., 1 per day at 3:10pm, $30) and New York City (5½hr., 3 per day, $42). For visitor information, the **Brattleboro Chamber of Commerce,** 180 Main St., has hundreds of brochures on the area. (☎254-4565; www.brattleborochamber.org. Open M-F 9am-5pm, Sa 10am-2pm.) **Bike Rental: Brattleboro Bicycle Shop,** 165 Main St. (☎ 254-8644; www.bratbike.com. Full day $20, week $100. Open M-F 10am-6pm, Sa 10am-5pm, Su noon-4pm.) **Internet Access: Brooks Memorial Library,** 224 Main St. (☎254-5290; www.brooks.lib.vt.us. Open M-W 10am-9pm, Th-F 10am-6pm, Sa 10am-5pm in winter and 10am-1pm in summer. Wireless Internet available.) **Post Office:** 204 Main St. (☎275-8777. Open M-F 8am-5pm, Sa 9am-noon.) **Postal Code:** 05301. **Area Code:** 802.

Ⱶ◫ ACCOMMODATIONS AND FOOD. Latchis Hotel & Theater ❹, 50 Main St., is a prime location for lodging or movie-going in the heart of downtown Brattleboro. Comfortable rooms with A/C, cable TV, mini-fridge, and 1930s art deco decor make this hotel well worth the price. (☎254-6300; www.latchis.com. Rooms $75-150. AmEx/MC/V.) Follow South Main St. out of downtown to reach **Fort Dummer State Park ❶,** 517 Old Guilford Rd., which has 50 campsites and 10 lean-tos, as well as picnic areas and two hiking trails. (☎254-2610. Hot showers. Open mid-May to Labor Day. Sites $14. Lean-tos $21.) Along Rtes. 5 and 9, the luxurious **Colonial Motel and Spa ❹,** 889 Putney Road, boasts a tavern, indoor pool and spa, A/C, and cable TV, making any guest feel pampered. (☎257-7733; www.colonialmotel-spa.com. Rooms $60-120. AmEx/D/MC/V.) For caffeine and conversation, locals head to ⬛Mocha Joe's, 183 Main St., where the coffee is brewed with beans from around the world. Mexican hot chocolate ($2.25) is a specialty. (☎257-5637; www.mochajoes.com. Open M-Th 7am-8pm, F 7:30am-10pm, Sa 7:30am-10pm, Su 7:30am-7pm.) Sweeping river views and fresh dishes await at **Riverview Cafe and Bar ❹,** 36 Bridge St., where you can sample goat cheese cakes ($7.25) or Chicken Under a Brick ($17) while supporting local farms. (☎254-9841; www.riverview-cafe.com. Open M-Th 11am-8pm, F-Sa 11am-9pm, Su 11am-8pm. AmEx/D/MC/V.)

◧Ⱶ SIGHTS AND NIGHTLIFE. The **Brattleboro Museum & Art Center,** 10 Vernon St., is the artistic epicenter of the town. Housed in a former railway station, the museum has everything from rotating art exhibits to a children's activity room. (☎257-0124; www.brattleboromuseum.org. Open M and W-Su 11am-5pm. $4, seniors and students $2, under 6 free.) A map of Vermont's famous covered bridges, which can be seen throughout the state, is available at the Brattleboro Chamber of Commerce. The 125-year-old **Creamery Covered Bridge,** 0.3 mi. west on Rte. 9 from I-91, deserves a short visit for its simple beauty and idyllic setting. Grab drinks and great music at **Mole's Eye Cafe,** 4 High St., where you can enjoy simple entrees ($4-8), relax at the large bar, or indulge in the heavenly chocolate truffle cake. (☎257-0771; www.moleseyecafe.net. Open mic night Th. Open M-Th 4pm-midnight, F-Sa 11:30am-1pm. Food served until 9pm.)

MASSACHUSETTS

Massachusetts regards itself, with some justification, as the nation's intellectual center. Since the 1636 establishment of Cambridge's Harvard College, the oldest college in America, Massachusetts has been a breeding ground for academics and literati. The undisputed highlight of the state is Boston, the "Cradle of Liberty" and birthplace of the American Revolution, where colonial landmarks and cobble-stone streets coexist with hip eateries and crowded T stops. Beyond the hubbub of the Hub, Cape Cod's ample beaches and sea breezes fill the roads with sun-seeking tourists, while inland, the Berkshires draw those looking for art, inspiration, and stunning fall foliage in the area's bountiful golden hills.

PRACTICAL INFORMATION

Capital: Boston.

Visitor Info: Office of Travel and Tourism, 10 Park Plaza, Ste. 4510, Boston 02116 (☎617-973-8500 or 800-227-6277; www.massvacation.com). Free *Getaway Guide* available online or in person. Open M-F 9am-5pm.

Postal Abbreviation: MA. **Sales Tax:** 5%; no tax on clothing or pre-packaged food.

BOSTON   ☎617

Perhaps more than any other American city, Boston reveals the possibilities of the "melting pot." The Financial District's corporate sanctuaries are visible from the North End's winding streets. Aristocratic Beacon Hill is just across Boston Common from the nation's first Chinatown. The trendy South End abuts the less-gentri-fied neighborhoods of Roxbury and Dorchester. While Boston's famed Freedom Trail will expose you to some of the earliest history of the US, a walk through Bos-ton's neighborhoods lends a glimpse into a still-evolving metropolis. For more comprehensive coverage of the Boston area, see ▨*Let's Go: Boston.*

✈ INTERCITY TRANSPORTATION

Airport: Logan International (☎800-235-6426; www.massport.com/logan), 5 mi. northeast of downtown. T: Airport; a free shuttle connects all 5 terminals to the T stop. **Back Bay Coach** (☎888-222-5229; www.backbaycoach.com) runs door-to-door ser-vice to and from the airport (24hr. advanced reservation recommended). A **taxi** to downtown costs $15-20.

Trains: Amtrak (☎800-872-7245; www.amtrak.com) pulls into **South Station,** Summer St. at Atlantic Ave. T: South Station. Open 24hr. Trains run to **New York City** (3½-4½hr., 10 per day, $66-94), **Philadelphia** (5-6hr., 10 per day, $82-163), and **Washington, D.C.** (6½-8hr., 10 per day, $91-176).

Buses: Buses depart South Station, Summer St. at Atlantic Ave. T: South Station. **Bonanza Bus** (☎888-751-8800; www.bonanzabus.com) runs to **New York City** (4¾hr., 15 per day, $30) and **Providence** (1hr., 16 per day, $8-9).

Greyhound (☎800-231-2222; www.greyhound.com) runs to **New York City** (4½-6½hr., every 30min.-1hr., $35), **Philadelphia** (7-8½hr., every 1-2hr., $55),and **Washington, D.C.** (10-11hr., every 1-2hr., $66).

Peter Pan/Trailways (☎800-237-8747; www.peterpanbus.com) runs to **Albany** (4-4½hr., 2-3 per day, $37).

Plymouth & Brockton St. Railway (☎508-746-0378; www.p-b.com) goes to **Plymouth** (1hr., every 1-2hr., $11) and **Cape Cod,** including **Hyannis** (1½hr., 25 per day, $16) and **Provincetown** (3¼hr., 2 per day, $26).

Vermont Transit (☎800-552-8737; www.vermonttransit.com) goes north to: **Burlington** (5hr., 4 per day, $49) and **Montréal** (8hr., 5 per day, $61).

■ ORIENTATION

Boston, the capital of Massachusetts and the largest city in New England, is situated on a peninsula that juts into the Massachusetts Bay (bordered to the north and west by the **Charles River** and to the east by **Boston Harbor**). The city proper centers on the grassy **Boston Common;** the popular **Freedom Trail** (p. 127) begins here and links most of the city's major sights. The Trail heads east through crowded **Downtown** (still the same compact 3 sq. mi. settled in 1630), skirting the city's growing **Waterfront** district to the southeast. The Trail then veers north to the charming **North End,** Boston's "Little Italy," bounded by the **Fitzgerald Expressway (I-93),** before crossing the river to historic **Charlestown.**

Boston Common is sandwiched between aristocratic **Beacon Hill** to the north and **Chinatown** to the south. Much of Chinatown overlaps the nightlife-heavy **Theatre District** to the west. Just west of the Common, **Back Bay's** grand boulevards and brownstones surround beautiful Copley Sq., Newbury St.'s elegant shops, and Boylston St., a true bar-hopper's paradise. The **Massachusetts Turnpike (I-90)** separates Back Bay from the artsy and predominantly gay **South End,** which has a lion's share of the city's best restaurants. Farther west are **Kenmore Square** and **Fenway,** home to baseball's Red Sox, major museums, and the clubs of Lansdowne St. South of the Fenway is vibrant, gay-friendly **Jamaica Plain,** filled with green spaces and cheap restaurants.

■ LOCAL TRANSPORTATION

Public Transit: Massachusetts Bay Transportation Authority (☎222-5000; www.mbta.com). Known as the T, the subway has 5 colored lines—Red, Blue, Orange, Green, and Silver (Green splits into lettered lines B-E)—that radiate from Downtown. "Inbound" trains head toward T: Park St. or T: Downtown Crossing; "outbound" trains head away from those stops. All T stops have maps and schedules. Lines run daily 5:30am-12:30am; "Night Owl" buses runs F-Sa until 2:30am. Fare $1.25, ages 5-11 $0.60, seniors $0.35. **Visitor passes** for unlimited subway and bus use are good for 1 day ($7.50), 3 days ($18), or 7 days ($35). **MBTA Commuter Rail** trains run from T: **North Station** (Green/Orange) to **Concord** (Fitchburg line; $5), **Plymouth** (Plymouth/Kingston line; 1hr., $6), and **Salem** (Newburyport/Rockport line; 30min., $3.75).

Taxi: Boston Cab ☎262-2227. **Checker Taxi** ☎494-1500. **Town Taxi** ☎536-5000.

Car Rental: Dollar Rent-a-Car (☎634-0006 or 800-800-3665), at the airport. Open 24hr. Under-25 surcharge $30 per day. AAA discount 10%. Must be 21+ with major credit card. All other agencies have desks at the airport.

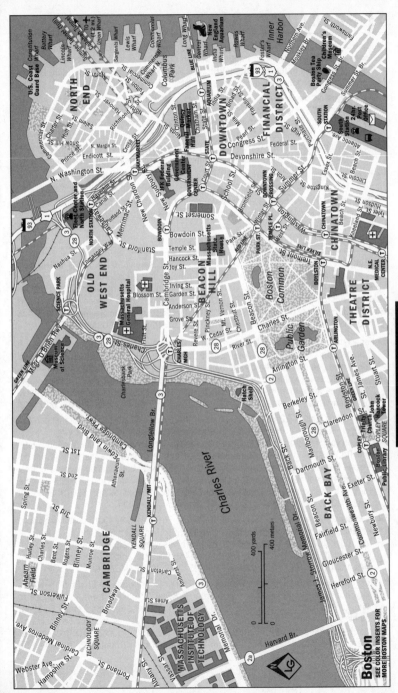

SEE COLOR INSERTS FOR MORE BOSTON MAPS

NEW ENGLAND

Boston

⚡ PRACTICAL INFORMATION

Visitor Info: Greater Boston Convention and Visitors Bureau (☎536-4100; www.bostonusa.com) has a booth at Boston Common, outside T: Park St. Open M-F 8:30am-5pm. Downtown's **National Historic Park Visitor Center**, 15 State St. (☎242-5642), has Freedom Trail info and tours. T: State. Open daily 9am-5pm.

Tours: Boston Duck Tours (☎267-3825; www.bostonducktours.com). Wacky conductors drive WWII amphibious vehicles past sights before splashing down in the Charles, offering cheesy commentary and quacking all the way. 1½hr. tours depart from the Prudential Ctr., T: Prudential, Apr.-Nov. daily every 30min.-1hr. 9am-1hr. before sunset. $25, students and seniors $22, ages 3-11 $16. Tickets sold online or at the Museum of Science, Faneuil Hall, and the Prudential Ctr. M-Sa 8:30am-8pm, Su 8:30am-6pm.

Hotlines: Rape Crisis Center, ☎492-7273. 24hr. **BGLT Help Line**, ☎267-9001. Operates M-F 6-11pm, Sa-Su 5-10pm.

Post Office: 25 Dorchester Ave. (☎800-275-8777), at T: South Station. Open M-F 6am-midnight, Sa 8am-7pm, Su noon-7pm. **Postal Code:** 02205. **Area Code:** 617.

⚡ ACCOMMODATIONS

Finding cheap accommodations in Boston is hard. Rates and bookings are highest in summer and during college-rush times in September, late May, and early June. Reservation services promise to find discounted rooms, even during sold-out periods. Try **Boston Reservations** (☎332-4199), **Central Reservation Service** (☎569-3800 or 800-332-3026; www.bostonhotels.net), or **Citywide Reservation Services** (☎267-7424 or 800-468-3593). Listed prices do not include Boston's 12.45% **room tax.**

▨ **Fenway Summer Hostel (HI)**, 575 Commonwealth Ave. (☎267-8599), in Fenway. T: Kenmore, lets out on Comm. Ave. Housed in a former luxury hotel, with 155 bright and airy 3-bed dorm rooms with private bath and A/C and a penthouse common room with a 360-degree view of Boston. Nightly events include free movie screenings and complimentary entrance to museums and dance clubs. Linen included. Laundry $1.50. Check-out 11am. Open June-Aug. Dorms $38, members $35; 3-bed room $90/87. MC/V. ❷

▨ **Oasis Guest House**, 22 Edgerly Rd. (☎267-2262; www.oasisgh.com), at Stoneholm St., in Back Bay. From T: Hynes/ICA, exit onto Massachusetts Ave. With the Virgin Megastore on your left, cross Boylston St., and turn right onto Haviland St.; the next left is Edgerly Rd. This rambling 16-room guest house is true to its name, serving as a calm respite from the hustle and bustle of the city. Continental breakfast daily 8-11am. Reservations recommended up to 2 months in advance. May to mid-Nov. singles $59; doubles with shared bath $69, with private bath $89. Mid-Nov. to Apr. $80/$90/$130. AmEx/MC/V. ❸

▨ **Newbury Guest House**, 261 Newbury St. (☎437-7666; www.newburyguesthouse.com), between Gloucester and Fairfield St. T: Hynes/ICA. This urban B&B offers 32 immaculate, bright, and tastefully decorated double rooms with private bath and digital cable. Breakfast daily 7:30-10:30am. Reception 24hr. Check-in 3pm. Check-out noon. Doubles Apr.-Oct. $125-170; Nov.-Mar. $99-125. AmEx/D/DC/MC/V. ❺

Boston International Youth Hostel (HI-AYH), 12 Hemenway St. (☎536-1027; www.bostonhostel.org), in Back Bay. From T: Hynes/ICA, walk down Massachusetts Ave., turn right onto Boylston St., then turn left onto Hemenway St. Central location, spotless bathrooms and quiet dorms. Same events and freebies as at the Fenway Summer Hostel (see above). Kitchen. Continental breakfast included. Free lockers and linen. Laundry facilities. Check-in noon. Check-out 11am. Dorms $35-38, members $32-35. AmEx/MC/V. ❷

Beantown Hostel, 222 Friend St., 3rd fl. (☎723-0800), in Downtown. Exit T: North Station onto Causeway St. and turn onto Friend St. Co-ed and single sex dorms (110 beds). Beantown curfew 1:45am; Irish Embassy (above a pub) has no curfew. Free lockers, linen, and kitchen use. Laundry facilities. Free buffet in summer Tu and Th 8pm. Check-out 10am. Dorms $25. Cash only. ❶

Greater Boston YMCA, 316 Huntington Ave. (☎927-8040). T: Symphony. An amazing location and access to world-class athletic facilities make the surprisingly hefty pricetag more tolerable. The long-term men-only residence is co-ed Sept. to mid-June with 2 floors of sterile, serviceable rooms with TV and shared bathrooms. 18+. Breakfast included. Reception 24hr. Check-out 11am. Key deposit $5. HI discount. Singles $46, with private bath $66; doubles $66; triples $81; quads $96. AmEx/D/MC/V. ❷

🗋 FOOD

Once a barren gastronomical wasteland whose only claim to fame was baked beans, Boston may not be a culinary paradise, but its cuisine has certainly become much more palatable. Trendy bistros, fusion restaurants, and a globetrotting array of ethnic eateries have taken their place alongside the long-standing "chowda" shacks, greasy-spoons, soul-food joints, and welcoming pubs.

DOWNTOWN

Downtown is the most heavily touristed part of Boston, so expect mediocre food, big crowds, and high prices. The best and most affordable food options are the interchangeable sandwich shops (sandwiches $5-7) found on almost every street corner and the more diverse food court inside **Quincy Market** (p. 128). Downtown is also near the fresh seafood shops lining Boston's **Waterfront** district.

Durgin Park, 340 Faneuil Hall Marketplace (☎227-2038). T: Government Ctr. Boston's most touristed restaurant, Durgin Park has been serving traditional New England dishes like fried seafood, Yankee pot roast, and Indian pudding since 1827. Entrees $7-30. Open M-Sa 11:30am-10pm, Su 11:30am-9pm. AmEx/D/MC/V. ❹

No Name, 17 Fish Pier St. W (☎338-7539), the next pier over from the World Trade Ctr. Take the free shuttle to the WTC from T: South Station. This waterfront eatery is one of Boston's best and cheapest seafood spots, serving fish fresh off the boat since 1917. Entrees $7-20. Open M-Sa 11am-10pm, Su 11am-9pm. Cash or check only. ❸

Legal Sea Foods, 255 State St. (☎227-3115), opposite the New England Aquarium, near T: Aquarium. Now a national chain, Legal Sea Foods remains Boston's finest seafood restaurant. Their clam chowder ($3.75-4.50) has been served at every Presidential Inauguration since 1981. Raw bar $8-9. Entrees $18-30. Open M-Th 11am-10pm, F-Sa 11am-11pm, Su noon-10pm. AmEx/D/DC/MC/V. ❺

NORTH END

Boston's Italian-American enclave is the place to go for authentic Italian fare, with over 100 restaurants packed into one sq. mi. Most establishments line **Hanover Street,** accessible from T: Haymarket. After dinner, try one of the countless *caffès*. For *cannoli* ($2-3) and other Italian sweets, join the lines at **Mike's Pastry,** 300 Hanover St., or **Modern Pastry,** 257 Hanover St.

Trattoria Il Panino, 11 Parmenter St. (☎720-1336), at Hanover St. A romantic North End *trattoria*—warm lighting, exposed brick, and intimate seating—with gigantic portions of classic fare. *Antipasti* $11-13. Entrees $10-17. Open M-Th and Su 11am-11pm, F-Sa 11am-midnight. AmEx/D/MC/V. ❹ Il Panino also runs the cheaper lunch counter **Il Panino Express,** down the street at 264 Hanover St. Calzones, 1 ft. subs, and salads $5-8. Open daily 11am-11pm. Cash only. ❷

Pizzeria Regina, 11½ Thacher St. (☎227-0765). With your back to Cross St., turn left off Hanover St. onto Prince St., then left again onto Thacher St. Since 1926, Regina's has served up the North End's best pizza, served piping hot and laden with toppings ranging from crushed garlic to sausage. 10" pizza $10, 16" $15-17. Beer $2.75. Open M-Th 11am-11:30pm, F-Sa 11am-midnight, Su noon-11pm. Cash only. ❶

L'Osteria, 104 Salem St. (☎723-7847). Turn left off Hanover St. onto Parmenter St., then right onto Salem St. A simple, reliable *trattoria* that serves all the robust Italian favorites found on Hanover St., but at lower prices. *Antipasti* $7-10. Entrees $13-17. Open M-Th and Su noon-10pm, F-Sa noon-11pm. AmEx/MC/V. ❸

CHINATOWN

Chinatown is *the* place for filling and cheap Asian food (not just Chinese) anytime. Stuck between the skyscrapers of the Financial District and the chaos of the Big Dig, the neighborhood is slightly grimy and run-down, but the prices are unbeatable, and most places stay open until 3-4am. T: Chinatown.

Shabu-Zen, 16 Tyler St. (☎292-8828; www.shabuzen.com), off Beach St. The signature do-it-yourself Japanese dish, *shabu-shabu*, is named for the swish-swish sound of dipping thinly sliced meat or veggies in your own pot of boiling broth. Entrees $10-19. Open M-W and Su 11:30am-11pm, Th-Sa 11:30am-midnight. AmEx/MC/V. ❸

Jumbo Seafood Restaurant, 579 Hudson St. (☎542-2823). Greet your dinner swimming in the tanks by the entrance at the best of Chinatown's Hong Kong-style seafood spots, with huge portions, a light touch, and a glowing velvet mural on the wall. Lunch specials $5-6. Dinner entrees $10-20. Open daily 11am-midnight. D/MC/V. ❸

Ginza, 16 Hudson St. (☎338-2261). Walk against traffic down Washington St., turn left onto Beach St., and turn right on Hudson St. Ginza's mouth-watering sushi doesn't come cheap ($3-10), but their full lineup of sake bombs will dull any pain your bill might inflict. Open M-Th 11:30am-2:30pm and 5-11pm, F 11:30am-2:30pm and 5pm-3:30am, Sa 11:30am-4pm and 4pm-3:30am, Su 11:30am-11pm. DC/MC/V. ❸

BACK BAY

The diverse eateries of Back Bay line elegant **Newbury Street,** accessible from T: Hynes/ICA or T: Back Bay. Though Newbury is known as Boston's expensive shopping district, affordable restaurants do exist.

▧ Parish Café, 361 Boylston St. (☎247-4777), near T: Arlington. Locals crowd tables and barstools to order sandwiches ($9-20) designed by the city's hottest chefs, who do marvelous things with chicken, portobello, lobster, brioche, and focaccia. Outdoor seating. Open M-Sa 11:30am-1am, Su noon-1am; bar open until 2am. AmEx/DC/MC/V. ❸

Island Hopper, 91 Massachusetts Ave. (☎266-1618), at Newbury St. Trendy yet casual, Island Hopper brings huge portions flavored with authentic Southeast Asian spices to this bright and spacious restaurant. Entrees $10-25. All-day special combos $8. Open M-Th 11:30am-11pm, F-Sa 11:30am-midnight, Su noon-11pm. AmEx/D/MC/V. ❸

Kashmir, 279 Newbury St. (☎536-1695), at Gloucester St. Marble floors and plush red seats create a setting as exotic as the subtle curries ($12-15) and vegetarian menu. Don't miss the *tandoori* specials. Entrees $15-25. All-you-can-eat buffet M-F (11:30am-3pm) $9, Sa-Su (noon-3pm) $12. Open daily 11:30am-11pm. AmEx/DC/MC/V. ❹

SOUTH END

The long waits and hefty bills here are worth it: the South End's upscale restaurants creatively meld flavors and techniques from around the world, creating amazing meals. Most eateries line **Tremont Street,** accessible from T: Back Bay.

▓ **Addis Red Sea,** 544 Tremont St. (☎426-8727). Curry- and veggie-heavy Ethiopian cuisine in an intimate setting. Entrees ($9-15) are served utensil-free, to be scooped up with spongy *injera* bread. Open M-F 5-11pm, Sa-Su noon-11pm. AmEx/D/MC/V. ❸

The Dish, 253 Shawmut Ave. (☎426-7866), at Milford St. Culinary and atmospheric perfection. Upscale decor meets a low-key clientele and eclectic comfort food, like Cajun-style meatloaf. Entrees $11-17. Open daily 5pm-midnight. AmEx/DC/MC/V. ❹

Flour, 1595 Washington St. (☎267-4300), at Rutland St. Near T: Prudential, Mass. Ave, or Back Bay. Chef/owner Joanne Chang bakes the most mouth-watering cakes, cookies, and pastries ($1-3) in the city. Gourmet sandwiches $6.50. Open M-Tu 7am-7pm, W-F 7am-9pm, Sa 8am-6pm, Su 9am-5pm. AmEx/D/MC/V. ❷

Laurel, 142 Berkeley St. (☎424-6711), on the corner of Columbus St. from T: Back Bay. Patrons enjoy artful culinary masterpieces ($10-20) like duck confit with sweet potatoes or shrimp and prosciutto ravioli. Open M-F 11:30am-2:30pm and 5:30-10pm, Sa 5:30-10pm, Su 11am-2:30pm. AmEx/D/DC/MC/V. ❸

JAMAICA PLAIN

Restaurants in "JP" are some of the best bargains in the city, with a wide variety of ethnic eateries—the Mexican offerings and vegetarian options are especially noteworthy. The action is, not surprisingly, centered on **Centre Street,** which runs parallel to the Orange Line (between T: Jackson Sq. and T: Forest Hills).

▓ **Bella Luna,** 405 Centre St. (☎524-6060). T: Jackson Square. Crispy gourmet pizza in a funky setting with hand-decorated plates, local art on the walls, and crayons at the tables for the inspired. Creative calzones and pizzas $5-18. To complete the celestial experience, check out **Milky Way Lounge & Lanes,** a bowling alley/karaoke bar downstairs. Open M-Th 11am-10pm, F-Sa 11am-11pm, Su noon-10pm. AmEx/MC/V. ❸

El Oriental de Cuba, 416 Centre St. (☎524-6464). Turn right out of T: Jackson Sq. A cheerful local hangout with a plantain- and meat-heavy menu. Don't miss the Cuban sandwiches or Puerto Rican *mofongo* (mashed garlicky plantains). Entrees $5-10. Tropical shakes $2. Open M-Th 8am-9pm, F-Sa 8am-10pm, Su 8am-8pm. AmEx/MC/V. ❷

Jake's Boss BBQ, 3492 Washington St. (☎983-3701). Turn right out of T: Green St., then right again onto Washington St. The first solo effort by Boston's most respected pitmaster, Kenton Jacobs (the "Jake" of the name), brings real down-home Texas smoked ribs and brisket to these cold northern reaches. Hefty sandwiches $5.50. "Boss dinners" with two sides $8.50-9.50. Open Tu-Su 11am-10pm. D/DC/MC/V. ❷

◎ SIGHTS

THE FREEDOM TRAIL

Passing the landmarks that put Boston on the map in colonial times, the 2½ mi. red-brick Freedom Trail is a great introduction to the city's history. Start at the **visitors center,** where the National Park Service offers free guided tours of the portion of the Trail from the Old South Meeting House to the Old North Church. (*15 State St., opposite Old State House. ☎ 242-5642; www.nps.gov/bost. Tours mid-June to Aug. daily 10, 11am, 2pm; mid-Apr. to mid-June M-F 2pm. Arrive 30min. before tour start time to get a required ticket. Limit 30 people per tour.*) You can also embark on the Freedom Trail from the **visitors center** on Boston Common, outside T: Park St.

BEACON HILL. The Trail first runs uphill to the **Robert Gould Shaw Memorial,** honoring the first black regiment of the Union Army in the American Civil War and their Bostonian leader. Opposite the memorial is the gold-domed **Massachusetts State House.** (*State House tours ☎727-3676. Open M-F 10am-3:30pm. 40min., tours depart every 20min.; self-guided tour pamphlet available at tourist desk. Free.*)

NEW ENGLAND

DOWNTOWN. Passing the **Park Street Church** (☎ 523-3383), the trail reaches the **Granary Burial Ground,** where John Hancock, Samuel Adams, Elizabeth Goose ("Mother Goose"), and Paul Revere rest. **Kings Chapel & Burying Ground** is America's oldest Anglican church; the latest inhabitants are Unitarian. The city's first cemetery, next door, is the final resting place of midnight rider William Dawes. *(58 Tremont St. Chapel ☎ 227-2155, Burying Ground 635-7389. Chapel open in summer daily 10am-4pm; Sept.-Nov. Th-Sa 10am-4pm; Nov.-Apr. Sa 10am-2pm. Suggested donation $1-3. Burying Ground open daily June-Oct. 8am-3pm; Nov.-May 9am-3pm. Free.)* The Charles Bulfinch-designed **Old City Hall** (☎ 523-8678), on School St., was built on the original site of the country's first public school, the Boston Latin School, which has since relocated to the Fenway. The **Old Corner Bookstore,** 1 School St., was once the city's intellectual and literary center. The **Old South Meeting House** was the site of the preliminary meeting that set the mood for the Boston Tea Party. *(310 Washington St. ☎ 482-6439; www.oldsouthmeetinghouse.org. Open daily Apr.-Oct. 9:30am-5pm; Nov.-Mar. 10am-4pm. $5, students and seniors $4, ages 6-18 $1.)* Formerly the seat of British government, the ◨**Old State House** is now a museum chronicling the history of Boston. *(206 Washington St. ☎ 720-1713. Open daily 9am-5pm. $5, students and seniors $4, ages 6-18 $1.)* The Trail passes a brick circle marking the site of the **Boston Massacre** en route to **Faneuil Hall** and **Quincy Market.** A former meeting hall and current mega-mall, the complex houses a food court and carts selling kitschy items. *(Faneuil Hall ☎ 523-1300. Open M-Sa 10am-9pm, Su noon-6pm.)*

NORTH END. Heading into the Italian-American North End, the Trail crawls through Big Dig rubble to the **Paul Revere House,** where a self-guided tour helps visitors navigate meticulously recreated 18th-century rooms. *(19 North Sq. ☎ 523-2338; www.paulreverehouse.org. Open mid-Apr. to Oct. daily 9:30am-5:15pm; Nov.-Dec. and early Apr. daily 9:30am-4:15pm; Jan.-Mar. Tu-Su 9:30am-4:15pm. $3, students and seniors $2.50, ages 5-17 $1, under 5 free.)* The **Old North Church** is where Robert Newman was instructed by Revere to hang lanterns—"one if by land, two if by sea"—warning patriots in Charlestown that the British were coming. The church still houses such Revolutionary relics as George Washington's wig and tea from the Boston Tea Party. *(193 Salem St. ☎ 523-6676. Open daily 9am-5pm. Suggested donation $3.)* **Copp's Hill Burying Ground,** up Hull St. from the church, is a final resting place for numerous colonial Bostonians and was a key vantage point in the Battle of Bunker Hill.

CHARLESTOWN. The Battle of Bunker Hill is the focus of much of the rest of the Trail, which heads across the Charles River to the **U.S.S. Constitution** (a.k.a. "Old Ironsides") and its companion museum. *(☎ 426-1812; www.ussconstitution.navy.mil. Ship open May-Oct. Tu-Su 10am-4pm; Nov-Apr. Th-Su 10am-4pm. Museum open daily May-Oct. 9am-6pm; Nov.-Apr. 10am-5pm. Free.)* The Trail winds through residential Charlestown toward the **Bunker Hill Monument,** which is actually on Breed's Hill—fitting given that the entire Battle of Bunker Hill was actually fought on Breed's Hill. A grand view awaits at the top of the obelisk's 294 steps. *(Monument Sq. Open daily 9am-5pm. Free.)* The Trail loops back to Boston from Monument Sq., passing **City Square,** settled in 1629 shortly after the Puritans' arrival in the Boston area.

DOWNTOWN

In 1634, Massachusetts Bay colonists designated **Boston Common** as a grazing ground for their cattle. Today, street vendors, runners, and tourists roam the green, and congregate near the **Frog Pond,** a wading pool in summer and ice-skating rink in winter. *(T: Park St.)* Across Charles St. from the Common is the lavish **Public Garden,** the nation's first botanical garden. Bronze versions of the title characters from the children's book *Make Way for Ducklings* point the way to the **Swan Boats,** graceful paddleboats that float around a willow-lined pond. *(☎ 522-1966;*

www.swanboats.com. $2.50, ages 2-15 $1 for a 15min. ride. Park open daily dawn-dusk. Boats open daily mid-Apr. to mid-June 10am-4pm; mid-June to Aug. 10am-5pm; Sept. M-F noon-4pm, Sa-Su 10am-4pm, weather permitting.) Steps from the Common is the pedestrian mall at **Downtown Crossing,** a shopping district centered around legendary **Filene's Basement,** a chaotic feeding frenzy for bargain hunters. *(426 Washington St. T: Downtown Crossing. ☎ 542-2011. Open M-F 9:30am-8pm, Sa 9am-8pm, Su 11am-7pm.)*

BEACON HILL

Looming over the Common is posh Beacon Hill, an exclusive residential neighborhood that was the first spot on the Shawmut Peninsula settled by Puritans. Antique shops, pricey cafes, and ritzy boutiques now line charming **Charles Street,** the neighborhood's main artery. For generations, the Hill was home to Boston's intellectual, political, and social elite, christened the "Boston Brahmins." For a taste of Brahmin life, visit the **Nichols House,** restored to its 19th-century state. *(55 Mt. Vernon St., off Charles St. T: Charles/MGH. ☎ 227-6993. Open May-Oct. Tu-Sa noon-5pm; Nov.-Dec. and Feb.-Apr. Th-Sa noon-5pm. $5, children under 12 free. Entrance by 30min. guided tour only, every 30min.; last tour 4pm.)* Quiet **Louisburg Square,** between Mt. Vernon and Pinckney St., was the birthplace of door-to-door Christmas caroling.

Boston was the first city in America to outlaw slavery, and many African-Americans moved to the Beacon Hill area after the Civil War. The **Black Heritage Trail** is a free 2hr. (1½ mi.) walk through Beacon Hill sights that were important during Boston's abolitionist era. The tour begins at the foot of Beacon Hill, near the Shaw Memorial (p. 127), and ends at the free **Museum of Afro-American History,** which contains a small collection of art and artifacts, a church, and an exhibit about Boston's relationship with slavery. *(46 Joy St. ☎ 725-0022; www.afroammuseum.org. Museum open June-Aug. daily 10am-4pm; Sept.-May M-Sa 10am-4pm. Heritage Trail tours June-Aug. daily 10am, noon, 2pm; Sept.-May by appointment. Both free.)* Also at the foot of the hill is the cheesy **Bull & Finch Pub,** 84 Beacon St., the inspiration for the bar in *Cheers*.

WATERFRONT

The Waterfront district refers to the wharves along Boston Harbor that stretch from South Station to the North End. The excellent ☒**New England Aquarium** features cavorting penguins, an animal infirmary, and briny beasts in a four-story tank. *(Central Wharf at T: Aquarium. ☎ 973-5200; www.neaq.org. Open July-Aug. M-Th 9am-6pm, F-Su 9am-7pm; Sept.-June M-F 9am-5pm, Sa-Su 9am-6pm. $16, students and seniors $14, ages 3-11 $9, under 3 free. IMAX $9.)* The Long Wharf, north of Central Wharf, is **Boston Harbor Cruises'** departure point. They lead history-minded sightseeing cruises and whale-watching excursions, and charter boats to the Harbor Islands. *(☎ 227-4321. Open late May to Sept. Cruises: Sightseeing 45min.-1½hr.; 3 per day; $18, students and seniors $16, under 12 $13. Whale-watching 3hr., $31/$28/$25. Reservations recommended.)*

BACK BAY

Back Bay was initially an uninhabitable tidal flat tucked into the "back" corner of the bay until the late 19th century. Today elegant Back Bay's stately brownstones and spacious, shady promenades are laid out in an easily navigable grid. Cross-streets are labeled alphabetically from Arlington to Hereford St. Running through Back Bay, fashionable **Newbury Street,** accessible from T: Hynes/ICA, is where Boston's trendiest strut their stuff and empty their wallets.

COPLEY SQUARE. Named for painter John Singleton Copley, Copley Sq. is popular with both lunching businessmen and busy Newbury St. tourists. The square is dominated by H.H. Richardson's Romanesque fantasy, **Trinity Church,** reflected in the 14 acres of glass used in I.M. Pei's stunning **John Hancock Tower,** now closed to the public. *(T: Copley. Church ☎ 536-0944. Open daily 8am-6pm. $4.)* Facing the church, the dramatic 🔳**Boston Public Library** is a museum in disguise; don't miss John Singer Sargent's recently restored *Triumph of Religion* murals or the hidden courtyard. (☎ 536-5400; www.bpl.org. Open M-Th 9am-9pm, F-Sa 9am-5pm; Oct.-May also Su 1-5pm. Free. Free Internet access. Free 1hr. art and architecture tours M 2:30pm, Tu and Th 6pm, F-Sa 11am; additional tour Oct.-May Su 2pm.) The 50th floor of the **Prudential Center** mall next door to Copley Sq. is home to the **Prudential Skywalk**, which offers a 360-degree view of Boston from a height of 700 ft. (T: Prudential. ☎ 859-0648. Skywalk open daily 10am-10pm. $7, seniors and children under 10 $4.)

CHRISTIAN SCIENCE PLAZA. Down Massachusetts Ave. from Newbury St., the 14-acre Christian Science Plaza is Boston's most underappreciated public space. This epic expanse of concrete, centered on a smooth reflecting pool, is home to the Byzantine-revival "Mother Church," a.k.a. **First Church of Christ, Scientist,** a Christian denomination of faith-based healing founded in Boston by Mary Baker Eddy. (T: Symphony. ☎ 450-2000. Open to public during services W noon and 7:30pm; July-Aug. Su 10am, Sept.-June Su 10am and 7pm. Doors open 30min. before each service.) The adjacent **Mary Baker Eddy Library,** another of Boston's library/museum hybrids, has exhibits on Mrs. Eddy's life and a surreal "Hall of Ideas," where holographic words bubble out of a fountain and crawl all over the floor and walls. Step inside the 🔳**Mapparium,** a three-story stained-glass globe depicts the world as it was in 1934 and details the changes that have occurred since then. The globe's perfect acoustics let you whisper in the ear of Pakistan and hear it in Suriname. (☎ 222-3711. Open Tu-W and Sa-Su 10am-5pm, Th-F 10am-9pm. $6; students, seniors, and children $4.)

JAMAICA PLAIN

Jamaica Plain offers everything quintessentially un-Bostonian: ample parking, good Mexican food, and Mother Nature. Although it's one of Boston's largest green spaces (over 265 acres), many Boston residents never make it to the lush **Arnold Arboretum,** which has flora and fauna from all over the world. A haven for bikers, joggers, and skaters, the Arboretum is the next-to-last link in Frederick Law Olmsted's Emerald Necklace, a ring of nine parks around Boston. (T: Forest Hills. ☎ 524-1718. Open daily dawn-dusk.) Near the Arboretum, **Jamaica Pond,** a glacier-made pond (Boston's largest), is a popular illicit skinny-dipping spot, and a great place for a quick sail. (T: Green St. Boathouse ☎ 522-6258. Sailboats and rowboats $10-15 per hr.) To conclude your JP junket, salute beer-guzzling patriots at the **Sam Adams Brewery.** At the end of the tour, the experts teach you how to "taste" beer. (30 Germania St. T: Stony Brook. ☎ 368-5080. Tours Th 2pm; F 2pm and 5:30pm; Sa noon, 1, and 2pm; additional tour May-Aug. W 1pm. Tastings 21+. Free.)

🏛 MUSEUMS

If you're planning on a Beantown museum binge, consider a **CityPass** (www.citypass.com), which covers admission to the JFK Library, MFA, the Museum of Science, Harvard's Museum of Natural History (p. 136), the Aquarium (p. 129), and the Prudential Center Skywalk (p. 129). Passes, available at museums or online, are valid for nine days. ($39, ages 3-11 $19.50.)

MUSEUM OF FINE ARTS. The exhaustive MFA showcases an international array of artwork from samurai armor to contemporary American art to medieval instruments. The ancient Egyptian and Nubian galleries (lots of mummies), Impressionist paintings (the largest collection outside France), and the colonial portrait gallery (includes the painting of George Washington found on the $1 bill) are a few highlights of the stunning collection. (465 Huntington Ave., in Fenway. T: Museum. ☎ 267-

9300; www.mfa.org. Open M-Tu 10am-4:45pm, W-F 10am-9:45pm (Th-F only West Wing open after 5pm), Sa-Su 10am-5:45pm. $15; students and seniors $13; ages 7-17 M-F $6.50, after 3pm free. W after 4pm and all day Sa-Su free, Th-F after 5pm $2 off.)

ISABELLA STEWART GARDNER MUSEUM. This astounding private collection remains exactly as eccentric Mrs. Gardner arranged it over a century ago—empty frames even remain where stolen paintings once hung. The Venetian-style palazzo architecture draws as much attention as the Old Masters, and the courtyard garden alone is worth the price of admission. Highlights include an original of Dante's *Divine Comedy* and Titian's *Europa*, considered the most important Italian Renaissance work in North America. (280 Fenway, in Fenway. T: Museum. ☎ 566-1401; www.gardnermuseum.org. Open Tu-Su 11am-5pm. M-F $10, Sa-Su $11; students $5; under 18 free. Individuals named "Isabella" always free with valid ID. Free guided tours Tu-F 2:30pm.)

JOHN F. KENNEDY LIBRARY AND MUSEUM. In a glass tower designed by I.M. Pei, this is a monument to Boston's favorite son, 35th US President John Francis Fitzgerald Kennedy. Exhibits trace JFK's career from the campaign trail to his assassination, as well as First Lady Jackie O. (At Columbia Point, just off I-93 in Dorchester, south of Boston. From T: JFK/UMass, take free shuttle #2 "JFK Library." Shuttle runs every 20min. daily 8am-5:30pm. ☎ 929-4500 or 877-616-4599; www.jfklibrary.org. Open daily 9am-5pm. $10, students and seniors $8, ages 13-17 $4, under 13 free. Wheelchair accessible.)

INSTITUTE OF CONTEMPORARY ART. Boston's bastion of the avant-garde, with installations from major contemporary artists beside lesser-known works. Thought-provoking exhibits rotate every 3-4 months. (955 Boylston St., in Back Bay. T: Hynes/ICA. ☎ 266-5152; www.icaboston.org. Open Tu-W and F noon-5pm, Th noon-9pm, Sa-Su 11am-5pm. $7, students and seniors $5, under 12 free. Th 5-9pm free.)

SPORTS MUSEUM OF NEW ENGLAND. The only way to understand Boston's fanatical sports obsession is to step inside it. Interactive exhibits each cover a different Boston sports franchise using archival footage, authentic gear, and reconstructions of lockers belonging to Boston's all-time greats. Don't miss the stuffed bruin (don't worry, it's an animal, not an ex-player) or Larry Bird's size 14 shoes. (Inside the TD Banknorth Garden, downtown. T: North Station. ☎ 624-1234. Open non-game days 11am-3pm. Hours vary on game days; call ahead. $6, seniors and ages 6-17 $4, under 6 free.)

MUSEUM OF SCIENCE. Boston's Museum of Science educates and entertains children of all ages with its countless interactive exhibits. The must-sees are the giant *Tyrannosaurus rex;* the wacky Theater of Electricity; and the Soundstair, stairs that sing out a tune when you step on them. A five-story OMNI Theater and various trippy laser shows are at the Hayden Planetarium. (Science Park. T: Science Park. ☎ 723-2500; www.mos.org. Open July-Aug. M-Th 9am-7pm, F 9am-9pm, Sept.-June M-Th and Sa-Su 9am-5pm, F 9am-9pm. $14, seniors $12, ages 3-11 $11. IMAX or laser show tickets $8.50/$7.50/$6.50.)

🎵 ENTERTAINMENT

The best publications for entertainment listings are the weekly *Boston Phoenix* (free from streetside boxes) and the *Boston Globe* Calendar section ($0.50, included with the Thursday *Boston Globe*). **Bostix** sells tickets to most major theater shows, and half-price, day-of-show tickets for select shows at locations in Faneuil Hall (p. 128) and Copley Sq. (p. 129). The website and booths post which shows are available for sale each day. (☎ 723-5181; www.artsboston.org. Tickets daily 11am. Cash only.)

THEATER

Boston's tiny two-block Theater District, near T: Boylston, west of Chinatown, was once the nation's premier pre-Broadway tryout area. Today it's a stop for touring Broadway and West End productions, not to mention a lively nightlife district. The **Charles Playhouse,** 74 Warrenton St., is home to the wacky whodunit *Shear Madness* and the dazzling performance art of *Blue Man Group.* (*Shear:* ☎426-5225; $34. *Blue Man:* ☎426-6912. $43-53. Box office open M-Tu 10am-6pm, W-Th 10am-7pm, F-Sa 10am-9pm, Su noon-6pm. Half-price student rush tickets often available from 10am on day of show. Volunteer to usher *Blue Man Group* and watch for free—call at least 5 days in advance.) The giant **Wang Center,** 265 Tremont St., hosts Broadway shows and other productions. (☎482-9393 or 800-447-7400; www.wangcenter.org. Box office open M-Sa 10am-6pm. $20-75; student discounts available for some shows.) For more avant-garde productions, check out the **Boston Center for the Arts,** 539 Tremont St. (☎426-5000), near T: Back Bay.

CLASSICAL MUSIC

Modeled on the world's most acoustically perfect music hall (the Gewandhaus in Leipzig, Germany), **Symphony Hall,** 301 Massachusetts Ave., T: Symphony, is home to both the **Boston Symphony Orchestra (BSO)** and its light-hearted sister the **Boston Pops.** Every 4th of July, the Pops gives a free evening concert at the **Hatch Shell,** near T: Charles/MGH, with patriotic music, fireworks, and Tchaikovsky's *1812 Overture*—with real cannons. (☎266-1200. Box office open daily 10am-6pm. BSO: season runs Sept.-Apr. $26-95; general seating at rehearsals W night and Th morning $12. Rush Tu and Th 5pm, F 9pm $8. Pops: season runs May-July. $20-250.)

SPORTS

While the sights along the Freedom Trail testify to Boston's Revolutionary roots, the city's true heart beats at the storied **Fenway Park;** the home-team Boston Red Sox finally won baseball's World Series in 2004 for the first time since 1918. The nation's oldest, smallest, and most expensive baseball park, Fenway is also home to the Green Monster (the left field wall) and one of only two manual scoreboards left in the major leagues (the other is at Chicago's Wrigley Field; p. 542). Get tickets from the **Ticket Office,** 4 Yawkey Way, T: Kenmore. (☎482-4769. Bleachers $12-20, grandstands $27-47, field boxes $44-70.) The **TD Banknorth Garden,** 50 Causeway St., T: North Station, formerly the FleetCenter, was built on the site of the legendary Boston Garden and hosts concerts and games for basketball's **Celtics** and hockey's **Bruins.** (☎624-1750. Box office open in summer M-F 10am-5pm; in season daily 10am-7pm. Celtics $10-140. Bruins $19-99.) At the newly-built **Gillette Stadium** in Foxborough, the 2003 and 2004 Super Bowl Champion **New England Patriots** grind it out on the gridiron from September to January (☎931-2222 or 800-494-7287; www.patriots.com). Raced every Patriot's Day (third M in Apr.), the **Boston Marathon** (www.bostonmarathon.org), the nation's oldest foot race and one of Boston's greatest sporting traditions, is a 26.2 mi. run that starts in Hopkinton, MA, in the west, passes over "Heartbreak Hill," and ends amid much hoopla at Copley Sq. The **Head of the Charles** (www.hocr.org), the world's largest crew regatta, has been drawing preppy throngs to the banks of the river every October since 1965.

■ NIGHTLIFE

Before you set out to paint the town red, there are a few things to keep in mind. Boston bars and clubs are notoriously strict about age requirements (usually 21+), so bring back-up ID. Puritanical zoning laws require that all nightlife shuts down by 2am. The T stops running at 1am, so bring extra cash for the taxi ride home.

DANCE CLUBS

Boston is a town for pubbers, not clubbers. The city's few clubs are on or near Kenmore Sq.'s **Lansdowne Street,** near T: Kenmore.

Avalon, 15 Lansdowne St. (☎262-2424). The flashy, trashy grand dame of Boston's club scene, and the closest Puritan Boston gets to Ibiza. World-class DJs, amazing light shows, gender-bending cage dancers, and throngs of hotties pack the giant dance floor. Th-F 19+, Sa-Su 21+. Cover $10-15. Open Th-Su 10pm-2am.

Pravda 116, 116 Boylston St. (☎482-7799), in the Theater District. T: Boylston. The caviar, red decor, long lines, and 116 brands of vodka may recall Mother Russia, but capitalism reigns supreme at commie-chic Pravda, the favored haunt of Boston's yuppified 20-somethings. Full house/Top 40 dance club and 2 bars (1 made of ice). 21+. Cover W $15, F-Sa $10. Bar open W-Sa 5pm-2am; club W and F-Sa 10pm-2am.

Sophia's, 1270 Boylston St. (☎351-7001). From T: Kenmore, walk down Brookline Ave., turn left onto Yawkey Way, then right onto Boylston St. Far from Lansdowne St. in distance and style, Sophia's is a fiery Latin dance club with 4 floors of Latin music from a mix of live bands and DJs. Trendy, international crowd. 21+. Cover $10; no cover before 9:30pm W-Th and Sa. Open Tu-Sa 6pm-2am.

Axis, 13 Lansdowne St. (☎262-2437). Smaller and less crowded than Avalon, but with a similar college crowd. Drag shows M, hosted by sassy 6 ft. diva Mizery. 19+. Cover M $7, Th $5, F $20, Sa $10. Open M and Th-Sa 10pm-2am. Tired of the dance floor? Chill upstairs in the chic lounge **ID.** 19+. Cover $15. Open Th-Sa 10pm-2am.

BARS AND PUBS

Boston's large student population means the city is filled with countless great bars and pubs. Most tourists stick to the various faux Irish pubs around **Downtown,** while the **Theater District** is the premier after-dark destination of the city's international elite. The shamelessly yuppie meat markets on Back Bay's **Boylston Street** are also popular.

Bukowski's Tavern, 50 Dalton St. (☎437-9999), in Back Bay off Boylston St., 1 block south of T: Hynes/ICA. Named for boozer poet Charles Bukowski, the casual ambience and 99+ bottles of beer on the wall is a welcome respite from Boylston St.'s trendy chic. Pints $3-20. 21+. No cover. Open M-Sa 11:30am-2am, Su noon-2am. Cash only.

Mantra/OmBar, 52 Temple Pl. (☎542-8111), Downtown. T: Temple Pl. Seductive. Scandalous. Incomprehensible. And that's just the bathroom, which has 1-way mirrored stalls and ice cubes in the urinals. A pricey Franco-Indian fusion restaurant by day, Mantra becomes OmBar by night, with a bar in the bank vault downstairs and a plush, smoke-free "hookah den" upstairs. Cocktails $9. Open M-Sa 5:30pm-2am.

Emily's/SW1, 48 Winter St. (☎423-3649), Downtown. T: Park St. Top 40 dance club that was catapulted to fame as the top hangout for the cast of MTV's *Real World: Boston.* Beer $4. Cover around $5. 21+. Open Tu-Th 5pm-midnight, F-Sa 5pm-2am.

Purple Shamrock, 1 Union St. (☎227-2060), Downtown. From T: Government Ctr., walk through City Hall Plaza to Congress St. Popular with professionals winding down after work and college kids preparing for a night on the town. If you're feeling decadent, try the sinfully sweet Chocolate Cake Martini ($8). Karaoke Tu starts 9-10pm. 21+ after 9pm. Cover Th-Sa $5. Open daily 11:30am-2am.

The Littlest Bar, 47 Province St. (☎523-9766), Downtown. T: Downtown Crossing. This local watering hole draws the curious hoping for a spot inside what is indeed actually the tiniest bar in Boston (just 16 ft. end to end). Pints $4. Open daily 8:30am-2:30am. Cash only.

LIVE MUSIC

Boston's live music scene is impressive—no surprise for the town that gave the world rockin' acts like Aerosmith and the Dropkick Murphys. The best acts often play across the river in **Cambridge** (p. 135). **Wally's Café,** 427 Massachusetts Ave., at Columbus Ave., is in the South End. Turn right out of T: Massachusetts Ave. or T: Symphony. Established in 1947, Wally's is Boston's longest-standing jazz joint, and has only improved with age. (☎424-1408. Live music daily 9pm-2am. 21+. No cover. Cash only.) **Paradise Rock Club,** 969 Commonwealth Ave., is visible from T: Pleasant St. This smoky, spacious venue has hosted rock acts including U2 and Soul Asylum. (☎562-8800. 18+. Cover $12-25. Call for schedule and hours.)

GLBT NIGHTLIFE

For up-to-date listings of gay and lesbian nightlife, pick up a free copy of the South End-based *Bay Windows*, a gay weekly available everywhere, or check the lengthy listings in the free *Boston Phoenix* and *Improper Bostonian*. The **South End's** bars and late-night restaurants, accessible from T: Back Bay, are all gay-friendly (sorry ladies, these are mostly spots for the boys). The sports bar **Fritz,** 26 Chandler St. (☎482-4428), and divey **The Eagle,** 520 Tremont St. (☎542-4494), are exclusively for gay men. Boston's other gay bar/clubs are the Theater District's **Vapor/Chaps,** 100 Warrenton St. (☎422-0862); **Jacques,** 79 Broadway (☎426-8902); and **Europa/Buzz,** 51 Stuart St. (☎267-8969), which also has evenings directed toward women. In Fenway is the all-encompassing **Ramrod,** 1254 Boylston St. (☎266-2986), a Leather & Levis spot that has spawned a non-fetish dance club known as **Machine.** Popular gay nights at straight clubs include Avalon's Sunday bash (p. 133)—preceded by the early evening "T-Dance" at Vapor—and sassy drag night at Axis on Monday (p. 133). Lesbians flock to **Jamaica Plain's** bookstores and cafes, many of which are queer-owned, and to lesbian-friendly **Midway Café,** 3496 Washington St. (☎524-9038), south of T: Green St.

⚠ OUTDOOR ACTIVITIES

For a major urban center, Boston has a number of outdoor opportunities, thanks largely to the **Emerald Necklace,** a string of nine parks ringing the city. Designed by Frederick Law Olmsted (1822-1903), who also created New York City's Central Park (p. 182) and San Francisco's Golden Gate Park (p. 860), the Necklace runs from Boston Common and the Public Garden along the Commonwealth Avenue Mall, the Back Bay Fens and Riverway, Jamaica Plain's Olmsted Park, Jamaica Pond, and Arnold Arboretum (p. 130), ending at far-flung Franklin Park.

The **Charles River** separates Boston from Cambridge. Though swimming in the unsettlingly grimy water is strongly discouraged, runners, bikers, and skaters crowd the **Charles River Esplanade** park, which runs along its banks. The Esplanade is home to the **Hatch Shell,** where Boston's renowned 4th of July festivities take place. Rent watercraft from **Charles River Canoe & Kayak,** beyond Eliot Bridge near T: Riverside. (☎965-5110. Canoes $13 per hr., $52 per day; kayaks $14/$56. Open Apr.-Oct. M-F 10am-sunset, Sa-Su 9am-sunset; Oct.-Mar. by appointment.)

Serious hikers should consider the **Harbor Islands National Park,** made up of the roughly 30 wooded islands floating in Boston Harbor. The most popular islands include Lovell's (with the islands' best beach) and Bumpkin (wildberry paradise). **Boston Harbor Cruises** runs ferries from Long Wharf at T: Aquarium to George's Island. (☎227-4321; www.bostonislands.com. Open May-Oct. daily 9am-sunset, hours vary by island. Ferries run daily July-Aug. on the hr. 9am-5pm, May-June and Sept.-Oct. 10am, 2, 4pm. Ferry ticket $10, seniors $7, children $6; includes free water taxis to five other islands from George's Island.)

▶ DAYTRIPS FROM BOSTON

CAMBRIDGE ☎617

Separated from Boston only by a small river, Cambridge (pop. 100,000), is often called Boston's "Left Bank" for its liberal politics and bohemian flair. The city has thrived as an intellectual hotbed since the colonial era, when it became the home of prestigious Harvard University, the nation's first college. The Massachusetts Institute of Technology (MIT), the country's foremost school for science and technology, moved here in the early 20th century. Cambridge's counterculture has died down since its 1960s heyday, but the city remains vibrant, with tons of bookstores and coffeeshops, a large student population, and great food and nightlife.

⬛️ ORIENTATION AND PRACTICAL INFORMATION. Cambridge is easily reached by public transit—it's just a 10min. T ride from downtown Boston. Cambridge's main artery, **Massachusetts Avenue ("Mass. Ave."),** runs parallel to the T's Red Line, which makes stops along the street. The **Kendall/MIT** stop is just across the river from Boston, near MIT's campus. The Red Line continues to: **Central Square,** a bar-hopper's paradise; **Harvard Square,** the city's chaotic heart; and largely residential **Porter Square.** Harvard Sq. sits at the intersection of Mass. Ave., Brattle St., JFK St., and Dunster St. The **Cambridge Office for Tourism** runs a booth outside T: Harvard with plenty of maps and info. (☎441-2884; www.cambridge-usa.org. Open M-Sa 9am-5pm, Su 10am-5pm. Hours may vary.) **Internet Access: Adrenaline Zone,** 40 Brattle St., in Harvard Sq. (☎876-1314. Open M-Th and Su 11am-11pm, F-Sa 11am-midnight. $5 per hr.) **Post Office:** 770 Mass. Ave. (☎876-0550), in Central Sq., and 125 Mt. Auburn St. (☎876-3883), in Harvard Sq. (Both open M-F 7:30am-6pm, Sa 7:30am-3pm.) **Postal Code:** 02138. **Area Code:** 617.

▢ FOOD. Cambridge is a United Nations of ethnic eateries, from Mexican to Tibetan. Most visitors stick to the spots in Harvard Sq. Indian restaurants come a dime-a-dozen in Cambridge, and most offer a budget-friendly all-you-can-eat lunch buffets ($7-9, served daily 11:30am-3pm). **Tanjore ❷,** 18 Eliot St., off JFK St., stands out from the crowd with its encyclopedic menu and range of regional specialties. (☎868-1900. Open daily 11am-3pm and 5-11pm. AmEx/D/MC/V.) **Punjabi Dhaba ❷,** 225 Hampshire St., in Inman Sq., gives it a run for its rupees, offering a cheap menu of spicy dishes. (☎547-8272. Veggie dishes $5; combos $8. Open daily noon-midnight. MC/V.) **Darwin's Limited ❷,** 148 Mt. Auburn St., is a 5min. walk from Harvard Sq. proper: exit the T onto Brattle St. and turn right at the Harvard Sq. Hotel onto Mt. Auburn St.; it's six blocks up on the left. The bohemian staff craft Boston's best gourmet sandwiches ($5.75-8), named after nearby streets. (☎354-5233. Open M-Sa 6:30am-9pm, Su 7am-9pm. V.) The recently-opened **Felipe's Taqueria,** 83 Mt. Auburn St., is quickly becoming a Harvard Sq. institution with its wicked cheap Mexican grub—filling chicken burritos, decadent *carnitas* quesadillas, and traditional tacos are served with fresh ingredients by a friendly staff. (☎354-9944. Open M-W and Su 10am-midnight, Th-Sa 11am-2am. Cash only.) For over 40 years, **Bartley's Burger Cottage ❸,** 1246 Mass Ave., has been serving some of the area's juiciest burgers, named after famous folk. Try the Ted Kennedy, a "plump liberal" burger. (☎354-6559. Burgers $5-12. Open M-Sa 11am-9pm. Cash only.) **Emma's Pizza ❷,** 40 Hampshire St., opposite the 1 Kendall Sq. complex, dishes up gourmet pizza with toppings like roasted sweet potatoes and rosemary chicken. (☎864-8534. 6-slice 12 in. pies $8; 8-slice 16 in. pies $11. Open M-W and Su 11am-10pm, Th-Sa 11am-11pm. AmEx/MC/V.) Everyone screams for ice cream at **Herrell's,** 15 Dunster St., off Mass. Ave., which offers every flavor imaginable, from

NEW ENGLAND

chocolate pudding to Twinkie, as well as a few you've never thought of—jalapeño anyone? (☎497-2179. Open in summer M-Th and Su noon-midnight, F-Sa noon-1am; in winter daily noon-midnight. Cash or check only.)

🔲 **SIGHTS.** Harvard Sq. is of course named after **Harvard University.** The student-led tours offered by **Harvard Events & Information,** Holyoke Ctr. Arcade (across Dunster St. from the T), are the best way to tour the university's dignified red-brick-and-ivy campus and learn about its history. (☎495-1573; www.harvard.edu. Open M-Sa 9am-5pm. Tours Sept.-mid-May M-F 10am and 2pm, Sa 2pm; June to mid-Aug. M-Sa 10, 11:15am, 2, and 3:15pm.) **Harvard Yard,** just off Mass Ave., is the heart of undergraduate life and the site of Commencement. The massive **Harry Elkins Widener Memorial Library,** in Harvard Yard, houses nearly 5 million of Harvard's 13.3 million books, making it the world's largest university library collection. Harvard's many museums are well worth a visit. The disorganized **Arthur M. Sackler Museum,** 485 Broadway, at Quincy St. just off Mass. Ave., has four floors of East Asian, pre-Columbian, Islamic, and Indian treasures. Across the street, the **Fogg Art Museum,** 32 Quincy St., offers a small survey of North American and European work from the Middle Ages to the early 20th century, with a strong Impressionist collection and several van Gogh portraits. Inside the Fogg, the excellent **Busch-Reisinger Museum** is dedicated to modern German work. (All 3 museums: ☎495-9400; www.artmuseums.harvard.edu. Open M-Sa 10am-5pm, Su 1-5pm. $5, students and seniors $4, under 18 free. W and Sa 10am-noon free.) Next door, the Le Corbusier-designed **Carpenter Center,** 24 Quincy St., displays the hottest contemporary art by both students and professionals. The **Harvard Film Archive (HFA),** in the basement of the Carpenter Center, has a great art-house film series. Schedules are posted outside the door. (Carpenter ☎495-3251. Open M-Sa 9am-11pm, Su noon-11pm. Galleries free. HFA ☎495-4700. $7, students and seniors $5.) The **Harvard Museum of Natural History,** 26 Oxford St., has exhibits on botany, zoology, and geology, including the famous **Glass Flowers**—over 3000 incredibly life-like, life-sized glass models of plants. (☎495-3045. Open daily 9am-5pm. $7.50, students and seniors $6, ages 3-18 $5. Su 9am-noon and Sept.-May W 3-5pm free.)

Kendall Sq. (T: Kendall/MIT) is home to the **Massachusetts Institute of Technology (MIT),** the world's leading institution dedicated to the study of science. Free campus tours begin at the **MIT Info Center,** 77 Mass. Ave., in Lobby 7/Small Dome building, and include visits to the Chapel and Kresge Auditorium, which touches the ground in only three places. (☎253-1000; www.mit.edu. Tours M-F 10am and 2pm.) The ◪**MIT Museum,** 265 Mass. Ave., features technological wonders in dazzling multimedia exhibitions. Highlights include a gallery of "hacks" (elaborate, if nerdy, pranks) and the world's largest hologram collection. (☎253-4444. Open Tu-F 10am-5pm, Sa-Su noon-5pm. $5; college students with ID, seniors, and ages 5-18 $2.)

🛇🎶 **ENTERTAINMENT AND NIGHTLIFE.** Some of the Boston area's best live music spots are in Central Sq., T: Central. **The Middle East,** 472-480 Mass. Ave. (☎864-3278), and **T.T. the Bear's Place,** 10 Brookline St. (☎492-2327), at Mass. Ave., feature live music every night from the nation's hottest indie rock and hip-hop acts. Harvard Sq.'s ◪**Club Passim,** 47 Palmer St., at Church St., off Mass. Ave., is a folk music legend: a 17-year-old Joan Baez premiered here, while Bob Dylan played between sets. Countless acoustic acts have hit this intimate venue before making it big. (☎492-5300. Shows 7-11:30pm. Open mic Tu 7pm. Cover $8-25.)

On weekend nights, **Harvard Square** is equal parts gathering place, music hall, and three-ring circus, with tourists, locals, students, and pierced suburban punks enjoying the varied street performers. Harvard Square abounds with bars, but Cambridge's best nightlife options are in **Central Square,** a bar-hopper's heaven. Most bars are open until 1am, with some staying open until 2am on the weekends.

The People's Republik, 878 Mass. Ave., keeps the proletariat happy with cheap beer and cheeky chalkboards enticing passersby to drop in for a drink with adages like "Drink beer—it's cheaper than gasoline." (☎ 491-6969. Beer $2-4; cocktails $4-4.50. No cover. 21+. Open M-W and Su noon-1am, Th-Sa noon-2am. Cash only.) The harem-like **Enormous Room,** 567 Mass. Ave., unmarked save an outline of a bull elephant on the window, is too seductive to resist. Amidst sultry arabesque lighting and floor pillows for lounging, a trendier-than-thou crowd jives to music from a hidden DJ. "Enormous plates" of appetizers ($14, vegetarian $12) include hummus, grape leaves, salmon skewers, and anything else that strikes the chef's fancy. (☎ 491-5550. Beer $4. Mixed drinks $6-9. Cover $3 after 10pm. 21+. Open M-F 5:30pm-1am, Sa-Su 7pm-1am. Cash only.) **ManRay,** 21 Brookline St., off Mass. Ave., rules the underground scene, with themed nights catering to various alternative crowds. The gay "Campus" night on Thursdays is popular. (☎ 864-0400. W goth/industrial, 18+. Th "Campus," 19+. 1st and 4th F of every month "Fetish," 19+; 3rd F fantasy, 21+. Sa retro New Wave, 19+. Dress code strictly enforced W and F. Cover up to $15. Open W 9pm-1am, Th-F 9pm-2am, Sa 10pm-2am.) A typical pub from the outside, **The Phoenix Landing,** 512 Mass. Ave., keeps a lively college crowd dancing with some of the area's best electric and downtempo grooves. (☎ 576-6260. 21+ except 19+ W. Cover $3-5. Open M-W and Su 11:30am-1am, Th-Sa 11:30am-2am.) **The Good Life,** 720 Mass. Ave., is a snazzy nightspot with a casual crowd and high-class atmosphere—jazz, plush booths, and 1950s-era cocktails. (☎ 868-8800. Drinks $5-7. Open M-W and Su 11:30am-1am, Th-Sa 11:30am-2am.)

LEXINGTON AND CONCORD ☎ 781 AND 978

"Stand your ground. Don't fire unless fired upon, but if they mean to have a war, let it begin here," said Captain John Parker to the colonial Minutemen on April 19, 1775. Although no one is certain who fired the "shot heard 'round the world," the American Revolution did indeed erupt in downtown Lexington. The site of the fracas lies in the center of town at **Battle Green,** where a Minuteman statue stands guard. Across the street, the **Buckman Tavern,** 1 Bedford St. (☎ 862-5598), housed the Minutemen on the eve of their decisive battle. The nearby **Hancock-Clarke House,** 36 Hancock St. (☎ 861-0928), and the **Munroe Tavern,** 1332 Mass. Ave. (☎ 862-1703), also played significant roles in the birth of the revolution. All three can be seen on a 30min. tour that runs continuously. (All open Apr.-Oct. M-Sa 10am-5pm, Su 1-5pm, but call ahead, as hours are subject to change. $5 per site, ages 6-16 $3; combo ticket for all 3 $12/$7.) The **Museum of Our National Heritage,** 33 Marrett Rd. (Rte. 2A), emphasizes a historical approach to understanding popular American life, especially at the time of the revolution. (☎ 861-6559; www.monh.org. Open M-Sa 10am-5pm, Su noon-5pm. Free.) The road from Boston to Lexington is a straight shot up Mass Ave. from Boston or Cambridge; the **Minuteman Trail** is an excellent bike trail to downtown Lexington (access off Mass Ave. in Arlington, or Alewife St. in Cambridge). MBTA bus #62/76 from T: Alewife runs to Lexington (20min., $0.90). A model and description of the Battle of Lexington adorns the **visitors center,** 1875 Mass. Ave., opposite Battle Green. (☎ 862-2480. Open Apr.-Nov. daily 9am-5pm; Dec.-Mar. M-Sa 10am-4pm.) **Area Code:** 781.

Nearby Concord was the site of the second conflict of the American Revolution, and is famous both for its military history and for its status as a 19th-century intellectual center. The period rooms at the **Concord Museum,** 200 Lexington Rd., on the Cambridge Turnpike, move through Concord's three centuries of history. Highlights include the original lamp from Paul Revere's midnight ride and Henry David Thoreau's bed desk and chair study (☎ 369-9609. Open June-Aug. daily 9am-5pm; Sept.-Dec. M-Sa 9am-5pm, Su noon-5pm; Jan.-Mar. M-Sa 11am-4pm, Su 1-4pm; Apr.-May M-Sa 9am-5pm, Su noon-5pm. $8, students and seniors $7, ages 5-18 $3.)

Down the road from the museum, the **Orchard House,** 399 Lexington Rd., was once home to the multi-talented Alcotts, whose daughter Louisa May wrote *Little Women.* (☎369-4118. Open Apr.-Oct. M-Sa 10am-4:30pm, Su 1-4:30pm; Nov.-Mar. M-F 11am-3pm, Sa 10am-4:30pm, Su 1-4:30pm. $8, students and seniors $7, ages 6-17 $5; families $20. By guided tour only.) Farther down the road lies **Wayside,** 455 Lexington Rd., the former residence of the Alcotts and Hawthornes. (☎369-6975. Open for tours June-Aug. Tu-Th 2 and 4pm, Sa-Su 11am, 1:30, 3, and 4:30pm. $4.) Today, Alcott, Hawthorne, Emerson, and Thoreau reside on "Author's Ridge" in the **Sleepy Hollow Cemetery** on Rte. 62, three blocks from the center of town.

The Battle of Concord, the second battle of the revolution, was fought at the **Old North Bridge.** From the parking lot, a 5min. walk brings visitors to the **North Bridge Visitors Center,** 174 Liberty St., to learn about the town's history, especially its involvement in the Revolutionary War. (☎369-6993. Open daily Apr.-Oct. 9am-5pm; Nov.-Mar. 9am-4pm.) The **Minuteman National Historical Park,** off Rte. 2A between Concord and Lexington, best explored along the adjacent 5mi. **Battle Road Trail,** includes an impressive **visitors center** that organizes battle reenactments and screens a multimedia presentation on the "Road to Revolution." (☎781-862-7753. Off Rte. 2A between Concord and Lexington. Open daily Oct.-Nov. 9am-4pm; reduced hours in winter.) Concord, north of Boston, is served by the Fitchburg commuter rail train ($5) that runs from T: North Station. **Area Code:** 978.

WALDEN POND   ☎978

In 1845, Thoreau retreated 1½ mi. south of Concord "to live deliberately, to front only the essential facts of life" (though the harsh essence was eased somewhat by his mother's home cooking; she lived within walking distance of his cabin). In 1845, he published his thoughts on his time here in *Walden*, one of the major works of the Transcendentalist movement. The **Walden Pond State Reservation,** 915 Walden St., off Rte. 126, draws picnickers, swimmers, and boaters. No camping, pets, or flotation devices allowed. (☎369-3254. Open daily 8am-dusk. Parking $5.)

SALEM   ☎978

Although Salem has more to offer than witch kitsch, its infamous past has spawned a Halloween-based tourist trade that culminates in the month-long **Haunted Happenings** festival in October (www.hauntedhappenings.org). The **Salem Witch Museum,** 19½ Washington Sq. N, gives a multimedia presentation detailing the history of the witch trials of 1692. It also has an exhibit on scapegoating throughout history. (☎744-1692. Open daily July-Aug. 10am-7pm, Sept.-June 10am-5pm; extended hours in Oct. $6.50, seniors $6, ages 6-14 $4.50.) Engraved stones commemorate the trials' 20 victims at the **Witch Trials Memorial,** off Charter St. next to the Old Burying Point Cemetery. The **Witch House,** 310½ Essex St., was owned by witch trial judge Jonathan Corwin and is the only remaining building in Salem with direct links to the trials. (☎744-0180. Open daily Mar. to early Nov. 10am-5pm; extended hours in Oct. $7, seniors $6, ages 6-14 $4. AAA discount $1.)

Escape the witch frenzy at the recently renovated and expanded ☒**Peabody Essex Museum,** on the corner of Essex and New Liberty St., itself worth the trip to Salem. The museum presents objects and art in their cultural contexts, including excellent exhibits of maritime, Asian export, and American decorative art. The museum's prize jewel is Yin Yu Tang, a Qing Dynasty merchant's house that was relocated piece by piece from China. (☎745-9500 or 866-745-1876; www.pem.org. Open daily 10am-5pm. $13, seniors $11, students $9, ages 16 and under free. Yin Yu Tang requires timed tickets, free with admission.) The **House of the Seven Gables,** 54 Turner St., became famous after the release of Nathaniel Hawthorne's gothic romance of the same name. (☎744-0991. Open daily July-Oct. 10am-7pm; Nov.-Dec. and mid-Jan. to June 10am-5pm. Closed early Jan. $11, seniors and AAA members $10, ages 5-12 $7.25. By 30min. guided tour only.)

The **Salem Maritime National Historic Site Visitors Center,** 2 New Liberty St., has free maps. (☎740-1650. Open daily 9am-5pm.) Salem, 15 mi. northeast of Boston, is accessible by the Newburyport/Rockport commuter rail train (30min., $3.75) from T: North Station, by MBTA bus #450 or 455 (45min., $3.45) from T: Wonderland, or by car from I-95 or U.S. 1 N to Rte. 128 and Rte. 114. **Area Code:** 978.

PLYMOUTH   ☎508

The Pilgrims' first step onto the New World was not actually at Plymouth—they stopped first at Provincetown (p. 142), then left because the soil was inadequate. **Plymouth Rock** is a small stone that has dubiously been identified as the rock on which the Pilgrims disembarked the second time. A symbol of liberty during the American Revolution, it has since moved three times before ending up beneath a portico on Water St., at the foot of North St. After several vandalizations and one dropping (in transit), it's cracked, and under "tight" security.

Three miles south of town off Rte. 3A, the historical theme park ▓**Plimoth Plantation** recreates the Pilgrims' early settlement. Costumed actors carry out their daily tasks in the **Pilgrim Village,** while **Hobbamock's Homesite** represents a Native American village of the same period. (☎746-1622. Open Mar.-Nov. daily 9am-5pm. $21, seniors $19, ages 6-12 $12.) Docked off Water St., the **Mayflower II** is a scale replica of the Pilgrims' vessel and is staffed by actors to recapture the atmosphere of the original ship. (Open Mar.-Nov. daily 9am-5pm. $8, seniors $7, ages 6-12 $6. Admission to both sights $24, students and seniors $21, ages 6-12 $14.)

Plymouth, 40 mi. southeast of Boston, is best explored by car; take Exit 6A from Rte. 3, off I-93. **Plymouth & Brockton Bus** (☎746-0378; www.p-b.com) runs from T: South Station to the Exit 5 Info Center. (45min.; $10, seniors $8). The Plymouth/Kingston commuter rail train goes from T: North Station to the Cordage Park Station (45min., 3-4 per day, $6). From the info center and Cordage Park Station, catch a local GATRA bus ($1, seniors and children $0.50) to Plymouth Center. The **Plymouth Visitors Center** is at 170 Water St. (☎747-7533 or 800-872-1620; www.visit-plymouth.com. Open M-F 8am-4pm.) **Area Code:** 508.

CAPE COD AND ISLANDS   ☎508

Writer Henry David Thoreau wrote in his book *Cape Cod:* "[the Cape] is wholly unknown to the fashionable world, and probably will never be agreeable to them." Hmmm. This thin strip of land, now one of New England's premier vacation destinations, draws droves of tourists with its charming towns and sun-drenched landscapes—everything from sandy beaches to cranberry bogs. Though parts of the Cape are famous for their frolicking blue-bloods and sky-high prices, it can be a choice for budget travelers, thanks in large part to abundant shoreline activities and excellent hostelling and camping options.

▓ ORIENTATION

Stretching out into the Atlantic Ocean south of Boston, Cape Cod resembles a flexed arm, with **Falmouth** and **Woods Hole** at its armpit, **Hyannis** at its tricep, **Chatham** at its elbow, the **National Seashore** tattooed on its forearm, and **Provincetown** at its clenched fist. The southern islands **Martha's Vineyard** (p. 144) and **Nantucket** (p. 147) are accessible by ferries from Woods Hole or Hyannis. **Upper Cape** refers to the suburbanized area closer to the mainland. Proceeding eastward away from the mainland and curving up along the Cape, you travel "down-Cape" through **Mid-Cape** (where two hostels are located, near **Eastham** and **Truro**) to the **Lower Cape** and the National Seashore. In the summer, "Cape traffic" is hellish: most vacationers drive out on Friday and return Sunday afternoon, so avoid traveling then.

Cycling is the best way to travel the Cape's terrain. The Cape has many trails, and the excellent *Cape Cod Bike Book* ($3), is available at most Cape bookstores. The 135 mi. **Boston-Cape Cod Bikeway** connects Boston to Provincetown, and scenic trails line either side of the **Cape Cod Canal** in the National Seashore and the 25 mi. **Cape Cod Rail Trail** from Dennis to Wellfleet. For discount coupons, pick up a free *Official 2006 Guide to Cape Cod* or *Cape Cod Best Read Guide*, available at most Cape info centers. **Area Code:** 508.

FALMOUTH AND WOODS HOLE ☎508

Coming from Boston, Falmouth and Woods Hole are the first true Cape towns daytrippers encounter. Unlike other places on the Cape, these towns sustain a decent-sized year-round population and have less of a touristy feel, since most people bypass them to drive farther up the Cape or catch the ferry to Nantucket or Martha's Vineyard. The beach reigns proudly as the main attraction, but on hot days, it's hard to find the sand in the sea of umbrellas. Check out **Chapoquoit**, south of Old Silver, on the western shore of North Falmouth to avoid the crowds and relax peacefully. **Falmouth Heights** on the southern shore of Falmouth, along Grand Ave., provides soft sands and great swimming. **Old Silver** and **Stoney** beaches are also popular. At the end of Water St., the **Woods Hole Science Aquarium** has two playful harbor seals outside and lots of local sealife swimming in indoor tanks. (☎495-2001. Open Tu-Sa 11am-4pm. Free.) Lodgings are plentiful and nearly identical. For diet-busting fried seafood ($5-12), check out the lively **Clam Shack ❷**, 227 Clinton Ave., an always-busy spot right on the water. (☎540-7758. Open late May to early Sept. daily 11:30am-7:45pm. Cash only.) Enjoy an enchanted evening at the **Firefly ❸**, 271 Main St., with wood-grilled pizza, a sleek bar, and frequent live entertainment. (☎548-7953. Entrees $8-20. Opens daily at 4:30pm, closes when patrons filter out. AmEx/D/MC/V.) After hours, don't miss **Captain Kidd,** 77 Water St., just after the drawbridge in Woods Hole. A local bar adorned with the wheels and props of old ships, local fishermen and tourists flock here for strong drinks and to watch boats motor by in the harbor. (☎548-8563. Open daily 11am-1am.) **Bonanza Bus** (☎888-751-8800; www.bonanzabus.com) goes from Falmouth Bus Station, on Depot St., to Boston (1½hr., 12 per day, $17). Buses also go from Logan Airport and South Station in Boston to Falmouth and on to the ferry in Woods Hole.

HYANNIS ☎508

Mostly a transportation hub (ferries to Nantucket depart from here) and industrial center, Hyannis offers less charm than the villages farther down the Cape. However, the town does boast a long Main St. lined with trendy stores, brewpubs, and motels. Hyannis's fame comes from its proximity to JFK's famous summer home in nearby Hyannisport, and its excellent beaches. **Kalmus Park Beach,** on Ocean St. in Hyannisport, is popular with windsurfers, while **Orrin Keyes Beach,** on Sea St., attracts more of a local crowd. **Veteran's Park Beach,** off Ocean St., is great for families. All have parking ($10), lifeguards, bath houses, snack bars, picnic areas, and wheelchair accessibility. The pride of the Hyannis industrial complex is the **Cape Cod Potato Chip Factory,** 100 Breeds Hill Rd. Tours trace the history and process of chip-making and visitors are rewarded with a free bag of delicious kettle-cooked chips. (☎775-3358. Tours M-F 9am-5pm. Free.) Hyannis is full of cookie-cutter motels and inns. The immense **Hyannis Inn Motel ❸**, 473 Main St., has spacious rooms with cable TV and mini-fridges, a sauna, and an indoor swimming pool.

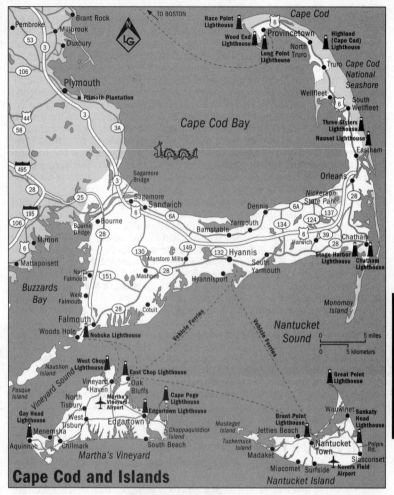

Cape Cod and Islands

(☎775-0255 or 800-922-8993. Open mid-Mar. to mid-Oct. Doubles $62-126. AmEx/D/ MC/V.) Upscale seafood restaurants line Main St., with entrees averaging $12-20. For inexpensive, delicious sandwiches ($4-6), head to **Box Lunch ❶**, 357 Main St., a Cape Cod chain that serves rolled sandwich combos in cute little boxes. (☎790-5855. Open M-F 9am-6pm, Sa 10am-10pm, Su 10am-5pm. Cash only.) **Plymouth & Brockton** (☎746-0378) buses run from Boston's South Station to the new Hyannis Transportation Center, off Main St. (1½hr.; M-F 24 per day, Sa-Su 17 per day; $16).

CAPE COD NATIONAL SEASHORE ☎508

As early as 1825, the Cape had suffered so much damage at the hands of mankind that the town of Truro required local residents to plant beach grass and keep their cows off the dunes. These conservation efforts culminated in 1961, when the National Park Service created the Cape Cod National Seashore. The seashore includes much of the Lower and Outer Cape, from Provincetown south to Chatham, and has six beaches: **Coast Guard** and **Nauset Light,** in Eastham; **Marconi,** in Wellfleet; **Head of the Meadow,** in Truro; and **Race Point** and **Herring Cove,** in Provincetown. **Parking** at the beaches is expensive (in summer Sa-Su and low-season holidays $10 per day). A $30 pass is the best deal, covering all areas in the park for an entire season. Among the best of the seashore's 11 self-guided **nature trails** are the **Great Island Trail** and the **Atlantic White Cedar Swamp Trail.** The moderately difficult Great Island Trail, in Wellfleet, traces an 8 mi. loop through pine forests and grassy marshes, rewarding trekkers with panoramic views of the bay and Provincetown. The most popular trail, the 1¼ mi. Atlantic White Cedar Swamp Trail, starts at Marconi Station in south Wellfleet and winds past swampy waters and under towering trees. There are also three bike trails: **Nauset Trail** (1½ mi.), **Head of the Meadow Trail** (2 mi.), and **Province Lands Trail** (5 mi.). Park rangers at the National Seashore's **Salt Pond Visitors Center,** at Salt Pond off Rte. 6 in Eastham, provide maps, schedules for guided tours, and additional information about the park. (☎255-3421. Open daily July-Aug. 9am-5pm; Sept.-June 9am-4:30pm.)

Camping in the National Seashore is illegal, but numerous private campgrounds are squeezed into the narrow space between Rte. 6 and the boundaries of the park. Two hostels on the seashore provide the most affordable accommodations on the Cape. With a beautiful private beach nearby and a spacious kitchen, ▨**Truro Hostel (HI)** ❶, 111 N. Pamet Rd., in Truro, is a genuine treasure for budget travelers. From Rte. 6, take the Pamet Rd. exit, which becomes N. Pamet Rd. (☎508-349-3889 or 888-901-2086. Free linen. Check-in 10am-10pm. Check-out 10am. Open late June to early Sept. Dorms $25-30, members $22-27. MC/V.) Eastham's **Mid-Cape Hostel (HI)** ❶, 75 Goody Hallet Dr., close to the bike path known as the **Cape Cod Rail Trail,** offers communal bungalow living in a woodsy location. From Rte. 6, take the Rock Harbor Exit at the Orleans Ctr. traffic circle, turn right onto Bridge Rd., then right again onto Goody Hallet Dr. By Plymouth & Brockton bus, ask the driver to let you off as close as possible, and call the hostel for the "shortcut" directions along bike paths. (☎255-2785 or 888-901-2085. Shared baths, kitchen, and barbecue facilities. 7-day max. stay. Open late May to mid-Sept. Dorms $23-27, members $20-24. MC/V.) **Plymouth & Brockton** (☎746-0378) runs buses from Boston's South Station through the towns on the seashore (2½ to 3 hr.), including Orleans ($22), Eastham ($23), and Truro ($25). To access the seashore by car, take Rte. 3 to Rte. 6 west, cross the Sagamore Bridge, and follow the signs.

PROVINCETOWN ☎508

The Pilgrims' first landing site in 1620, Provincetown was a key fishing and whaling center in the 1800s. In the early 20th century, the town's popularity soared with resident artists and writers like Norman Mailer, Tennessee Williams, and Edward Hopper. Today, Provincetown's tradition of open-mindedness has attracted a large gay community, making it a premier destination for gay vacationers, who fill the town to capacity in summer. Locals and visitors rock the town during the annual **Carnival Week** (August 13-19, 2006), which augments everything fun about P-town. Though far from inexpensive, Provincetown has better options for outdoor activities, dining, and nightlife than most of Cape Cod. It's easily accessible by public transit and just as easily navigated on foot.

◪▨ **ORIENTATION AND PRACTICAL INFORMATION. Commercial Street,** the town's main drag—home to countless art galleries, novelty shops, and trendy bars and eateries—runs along the harbor, centered on **MacMillian Wharf. Bradford Street,** the other main street, runs parallel to Commercial St. one block inland. Standish St. divides P-town into the **East End** and **West End.** Take the **Provincetown Shuttle**

(CCRTA) to outlying areas, including Herring Cove Beach and North Truro. Buy tickets on the bus or at the Chamber of Commerce. (☎800-352-7155. Operates late June to Aug. daily every hr. 7-9am, every 20min. 9am-12:30am. $1, seniors and ages 6-16 $0.50, under 6 free. Day pass $3; seniors, disabled, and children $1.50.) **Plymouth & Brockton** (☎746-0378) runs buses from Boston's South Station to Provincetown (3¼hr., $26). All but officially known as the "Fairy Ferry," **Boston Harbor Cruises** runs catamarans from Long Wharf, near T: Aquarium, in Boston. (☎617-227-4321 or 877-733-9425; www.bostonharborcruises.com. 1½hr.; $38, seniors $33.) **Bike Rental: Ptown Bikes,** 42 Bradford St. (☎487-8735; www.ptownbikes.com. $9 per 2 hr., $17 per day. Open daily 9am-6pm.) The **Provincetown Chamber of Commerce,** 307 Commercial St., is on MacMillian Wharf. (☎487-3424; www.ptownchamber.com. Open June-Sept. daily 9am-5pm; reduced hours in low season.) Head to the **Province Lands Visitors Center,** on Race Point Rd. off Rte. 6, for park info. (☎487-1256. Open May-Oct. daily 9am-5pm.) **Internet Access: Provincetown Public Library,** 330 Commercial St., has wireless Internet. (☎487-7094. Open M and F 10am-5pm, Tu and Th noon-8pm, W 10am-8pm, Sa 10am-2pm, Su 1-5pm.) **Post Office:** 219 Commercial St. (☎487-3580. Open M-F 8:30am-5pm, Sa 9am-noon.) **Postal Code:** 02657. **Area Code:** 508.

⌐ ACCOMMODATIONS. Provincetown teems with expensive lodging. **Dexter's Inn ❹,** 6 Conwell St., just off Bradford St., boasts hotel-quality rooms, plus a lush garden, expansive sundeck, and free parking. (☎487-1911. Mid-June to mid-Sept. 4-night min. stay. Singles and doubles mid-June to mid-Sept. $75-150, late May to mid-June and mid-Sept. to mid-Oct. $70-100, mid-Oct. to late May $50-70. AmEx/MC/V.) **Sunset Inn ❺,** 142 Bradford St., the inspiration for Edward Hopper's painting *Rooms for Tourists*, offers an excellent location, simple, well-kept rooms with shared bath, and a "clothing optional" sundeck. (☎487-9810 or 800-965-1801. Rooms June-Sept. $90-165; Apr.-May and Oct. $50-120. D/MC/V.) Though the Truro Hostel (p. 142) is infinitely better and just a few miles down the road, the only truly budget accommodation in P-town is **Outermost Hostel ❶,** 28 Winslow St., with 5 cramped cottages. (☎487-4378. Tiny kitchen for guest use. Linen $3. Key deposit $10. Reception 8-9:30am and 5:30-10pm. Open May to mid-Oct. Dorms $20. Cash only.) Excellent (and expensive) campgrounds border the dunes of the park. **Dunes Edge Campground ❶,** off Rte. 6, 1 mi. from Provincetown, has 100 wooded sites near the dunes. (☎487-9815. Reservations recommended 6 weeks in advance in summer. 2-person sites $28-32, each additional person up to 4 $12. Cash only.)

◖ FOOD. Sit-down meals in Provincetown are quite pricey. Fast-food joints line the Commercial St. extension (next to MacMillian Wharf) and farther west by the Aquarium Mall. Groceries are available at **Grand Union,** 28 Shankpainter Rd., in the West End. (☎487-4903. Open M-Sa 7am-11pm, Su 7am-10pm.) **Karoo Kafe ❷,** 338 Commercial St., is a self-described "fast food safari," serving up South African and Mediterranean favorites from falafel to tofu with peri-peri sauce. (☎487-6630. Most entrees $5-9. Open June to mid-Sept. M-F and Su 11am-8pm, Sa 11am-9pm; Mar.-May and Sept.-Nov. lunch hours only. D/MC/V.) Stop for some quick and delicious takeout at **Mojo's ❶,** 5 Ryder St., with a long list of surf and turf options that come at amazingly low prices. (☎487-3140. Open daily in summer 11am-11pm. Cash only.) **Tofu A Go-Go ❷,** 338 Commercial St., serves fresh vegetarian options on a balcony overlooking a sea of tourists. (☎487-6237. Entrees $5-12. Open June-Aug. M-Th 11am-4pm, F-Su 11am-9pm; call for hours Apr.-May and Sept.-Oct. Cash or traveler's check only.) **Café Edwidge ❸,** 333 Commercial St., serves American cuisine in a candlelit dining room adorned with local artwork. (☎487-4020. Breakfast $6-10. Dinner $8-22. Open late June to Aug. daily 8am-1pm and 6-10pm; mid-May to late June and Sept. to mid-Oct. Sa-Su 8am-1pm and 6-10pm. MC/V.)

NEW ENGLAND

◙ **SIGHTS.** The **Pilgrim Monument,** the tallest granite structure in the US at 253 ft., and the **Provincetown Museum,** on High Pole Hill just north of the center of town, commemorate the Pilgrims' first landing. Hike up to the top of the Italian Renaissance-style tower for stunning views of the Cape and the Atlantic. (☎487-1310. Open daily July-Aug. 9am-6:15pm; Apr.-June and Sept.-Nov. 9am-4:15pm. $7, students and seniors $5, ages 4-12 $3.50, under 4 free.) A large bas-relief **monument,** in the small park at Bradford St. and Ryder St. behind the town hall, depicts the signing of the Mayflower Compact on November 11, 1620, in Provincetown Harbor.

▨ **NIGHTLIFE.** Nightlife in P-town is almost completely gay- and lesbian-oriented. **Crown & Anchor,** 247 Commercial St., has a restaurant, two cabarets, the Wave video bar, and the techno-filled Paramount club, where the boys flock nightly. (☎487-1430. Beer $3.50-4.50. Mixed drinks $4-8. Sa "Summer Camp." 21+. Cover $10; no cover for Wave. Open in summer daily 11pm-1am; low season Sa-Su 11pm-1am.) Founded in 1798 by gay whalers, the **Atlantic House,** 6 Masonic Pl., just off Commercial St., still attracts its fair share of seamen with the low-key "little bar," the Leather & Levis "macho bar," and the "big room," where you, too, can be a dancing queen. (☎487-3821. Beer $3.50. Mixed drinks $4-10. 21+. Cover for dance club $10. Open daily 10pm-1am.) The major club for women is **Vixen,** 336 Commercial St., with a bar in front and a dance floor out back. (☎487-6424. Beer $3. Mixed drinks $5-8. 21+. Cover $5. Bar open daily noon-1am; club open daily 10pm-1am.)

▨ **OUTDOOR ACTIVITIES.** The National Seashore (2 mi. from town) stretches out from Race Point Rd. with beaches, forests, and sand dunes. At **Race Point Beach,** waves roll in from the Atlantic, while **Herring Cove Beach,** at the west end of town, shelters calmer waters. The **visitors center** offers free daily guided tours and activities during the summer. Directly across from Snail Rd. on Rte. 6, an unlikely path leads to a world of **sand dunes;** look for shacks where writers like Tennessee Williams, Norman Mailer, and John Dos Passos spent their days. At the west end of Commercial St., the 1¼ mi. **Breakwater Jetty** takes you to a secluded peninsula, with two working lighthouses and the remains of a Civil War fort.

Provincetown seafarers have traded harpoons for cameras, but they still enjoy whale-hunting—whale watches rank among P-town's most popular attractions. Most companies guarantee whale sightings. A 3hr. tour averages $18-20, but grab discount coupons at the Chamber of Commerce. **Boston Harbor Cruises Whale Watch** (☎617-227-4321 or 877-733-9425), **Dolphin Fleet** (☎349-1900 or 800-826-9300), and **Portuguese Princess** (☎487-2651 or 800-422-3188) all leave from MacMillian Wharf.

MARTHA'S VINEYARD ☎508

Martha's Vineyard is a favorite summertime escape, with New England's characteristic beaches, charm, and exorbitant prices. Since President Bill Clinton began summering here, "the Vineyard" has become one of the most popular vacation destinations for the region's socialites; in summer, the population swells from 15,000 to over 105,000. Savvy travelers might consider a weekend visit to the Vineyard in the spring or fall, when many private beaches are open and B&B prices plunge.

▨▨ **ORIENTATION AND PRACTICAL INFORMATION.** Six major towns and a smattering of smaller villages make up Martha's Vineyard. The rural towns of West Tisbury, Chilmark, and Aquinnah (Gay Head) take up the western side of the island, called **up-island** because sailors tack upwind to get to it. The three major **down-island** towns are Oak Bluffs, Edgartown, and Vineyard Haven (Tisbury). Only Oak Bluffs and Edgartown sell alcohol. Vineyard Haven has the main ferry port and the **Chamber of Commerce,** on Beach Rd., which has info on lodging, transportation, and island attractions. (☎693-0085. Open June-Oct. M-F 9am-5pm, Sa 10am-4pm, Su noon-4pm; Nov.-May M-F 9am-5pm, Sa 10am-2pm.)

The island is accessible by ferry or airplane only, but the latter is prohibitively expensive (flights begin at $130 each way). **Bonanza Bus** (☎888-751-8800; www.bonanzabus.com) runs from Boston's South Station to Woods Hole on Cape Cod (1½hr., $19), where the **Steamship Authority** (☎693-9130 on Martha's Vineyard, elsewhere 477-8600; www.steamshipauthority.com) sends 12-17 boats per day to Vineyard Haven (45min.; daily 7am-9:30pm; $6, ages 5-12 $3.50, cars $57, bikes $3) and Oak Bluffs (45min., May-Oct. daily 10:15am-5:45pm, same prices as Vineyard Haven). **Martha's Vineyard Regional Transit Authority (MVRTA)** runs summer shuttles between and within the six towns on the island. (☎693-9440. $1 per town; day pass $6.) Pick up a free schedule and map of all 15 routes at the ferry terminal, Chamber of Commerce, or info booths. **Bikes** are a scenic way to get around, but some parts of the island are outside of biking range. **Anderson's,** on Circuit Ave. in Oak Bluffs, has rentals. (☎693-9346. Bikes $15 per day, with maps and helmet included. Open daily July-Aug. 8am-6pm; Apr.-June and Sept.-Oct. 9am-5pm.) Taxi: **AdamCab,** ☎800-281-4462; **Atlantic Cab,** ☎877-477-8294. **Post Office:** 1 Lagoon Pond Rd., in Vineyard Haven. (☎693-2818. Open M-F 8:30am-5pm, Sa 9:30am-1pm.) **Postal Code:** 02568. **Area Code:** 508.

⚡**TIP**

THE WHEELS ON THE BUS. The bus system on Martha's Vineyard is easily the best way to navigate the island. The VTA schedule can be complicated, though, so it's a good idea to notify the driver of your intended destination, especially if you need to make a quick transfer. The drivers can often accommodate your requests, especially if the route isn't crowded.

▮ **ACCOMMODATIONS.** ◪**Martha's Vineyard Hostel (HI) ❶,** on Edgartown-West Tisbury Rd., has the 74 cheapest beds on the island and serves as a base camp for travelers on bikes looking to explore the less-crowded beaches and wildlife preserves up-island. From Vineyard Haven, take VTA bus #3 to West Tisbury and then bus #6 to the hostel. (☎693-2665 or 888-901-2087. Lockers $0.75. Linen included. Open Apr.-Oct. Dorms $23-27, members $20-24. MC/V.) A plethora of B&Bs line streets all over the island; **Nashua House ❹,** 30 Kennebec Ave., in Oak Bluffs, is cozy and convenient with 16 rooms (all with shared bath) in an old Victorian. From the ferry terminal, walk straight ahead along Lake Ave. and turn left onto Kennebec Ave. (☎693-0043. Singles and doubles $79-139; each additional person $20. AmEx/MC/V.) **Attleboro House ❹,** 42 Lake Ave., in Oak Bluffs, has a no-frills atmosphere in one of Oak Bluffs' famous gingerbread houses. (☎693-4346. Open June to mid-Sept. Doubles $95-115; each additional person $15. AmEx/D/MC/V.) Reserve months in advance for **Martha's Vineyard Family Campground ❷,** 556 Edgartown Rd., just outside of Vineyard Haven, which has sites with hot showers, laundromat, playground, and access to bike paths and bus routes. Call for directions and reservations. (☎693-3772; www.campmvfc.com. 2-person tent sites $40; RV sites $45. Each additional person up to 4 $10.)

▯ **FOOD.** Vineyard food is mostly overpriced, but cheap lunch places dot Vineyard Haven and Oak Bluffs. The island's tourists have made several excellent (but pricey) establishments very popular, including the **Black Dog** eateries (☎693-9223, tavern and two bakeries in Vineyard Haven), **Mad Martha's** ice cream parlor (☎693-5883, locations in Vineyard Haven, Oak Bluffs, and Edgartown), and **Murdick's Fudge,** which markets delicious homemade sweets (☎888-553-8343, locations in Vineyard Haven, Oak Bluffs, and Edgartown). Some of the Vineyard's best restaurants lie outside the main towns, often sporting great views and better deals. ◪**The**

Bite ❷, on Basin Rd. near the beach in Menemsha, features phenomenal service in a low-key setting, topped only by their decadent fried seafood and famous quahog chowder. (☎645-9239. Entrees $8-16. Open late May to early Oct. daily 11am-sunset. Cash only.) ⧉**Aquinnah Shop Restaurant ❺,** 27 Aquinnah Cir., in Aquinnah, serves excellent fishcakes ($14) and freshly brewed sun tea ($2) on a balcony atop the cliffs. The food here is rivaled only by the view. (☎645-3867. Entrees $18-30. Seafood $12-15. Open July-Aug. daily 8am-9pm; Apr.-June and Sept.-Oct. M-Th 8am-3pm, F-Su 8am-sunset. AmEx/D/MC/V.) Straight from the 1700s, **Newes From America ❷,** 23 Kelley St., in Edgartown, has a dedicated local following. (☎627-4397. Beer $4-5.50. Entrees $8-12. Open daily 11:30am-midnight. AmEx/DC/MC/V.) You'll be flying high at **Whosie's ❸,** next to the Katama Airfield near South Beach, where you can enjoy dishes like the Seatbelt Extender (3 eggs, meat, home fries, and pancakes; $9) as you watch private planes fly onto the grassy landing strip. (☎627-9018. Sandwiches $7-8.50. Breakfast $5-9. Open daily 7am-4pm. Cash only.)

◪ **SIGHTS.** Oak Bluffs, 3 mi. west of Vineyard Haven on Beach Rd., is the most youth-oriented of the Vineyard villages. A tour of **Trinity Park,** near the harbor, includes the elaborate, Victorian **Gingerbread Houses,** while the **Flying Horses Carousel,** in the center of town, is the oldest operating carousel in the nation. Snatch the brass ring and win a free ride. (☎693-9481. Open mid-May to Sept. daily 10am-10pm. $1.50.) **Chicama Vineyards,** a 1 mi. walk up a dirt road from the MVRTA #3 bus stop, in West Tisbury, has free tours and wine tastings. (☎693-0309. Open June-Oct. M-Sa 11am-5pm, Su 1-5pm; Nov.-Dec. M-Sa 1-4pm; Jan.-May Sa 1-4pm. Tours June-Oct. M-Sa noon, 2, 4pm; Su 2 and 4pm.) Martha's Vineyard has always been known for its shopping. The best shops are in **Vineyard Haven,** but with five locations, the famous **Black Dog** boutique can satisfy your tourist-trendy needs.

⚠ **OUTDOOR ACTIVITIES.** Exploring the Vineyard should involve more than pedaling around—hit the beach or trek down one of the great trails. **Felix Neck Wildlife Sanctuary,** on the Edgartown-Vineyard Haven road, offers five trails that meander through 350 acres and lead to the water. (☎627-4850. Office open June-Sept. M-Sa 8am-4pm, Su 10am-3pm; Oct.-May Tu-Sa 8am-4pm, Su 10am-4pm. Gate opens with office and closes around 7pm. $4, seniors and ages 3-12 $3.) **Menemsha Hills Reservation,** off North Rd. in the village of Menemsha, has 4 mi. of trails along the rocky Vineyard Sound Beach, leading to the island's second-highest point. **Cedar Creek Tree Neck,** off Indian Hill Rd. on the western shore, harbors 250 acres of headland with trails throughout, while **Long Point Park** in West Tisbury preserves 633 acres and a shore on the Tisbury Great Pond. The 20-acre ⧉**Polly Hill Arboretum,** 809 State Rd., in West Tisbury, boasts a complete collection of island plant species in a peaceful and remote setting. (☎693-9426. Open in summer M-Tu and Th-Su 7am-7pm; in low season dawn-dusk. Visitors center open in summer M-Tu and Th-Su 9:30am-4pm. Suggested donation $5.)

South Beach (Katama Beach), at the end of Katama Rd., 3 mi. south of Edgartown (shuttle from Edgartown $2), and **State Beach,** on Beach Rd. between Edgartown and Oak Bluffs, are free and open to the public. South Beach boasts sizeable surf but an occasionally nasty undertow. State Beach's warmer waters once set the stage for parts of *Jaws,* the granddaddy of beach horror films. For the island's best sunsets, stake out a spot at **Menemsha Town Beach** or ⧉**Aquinnah Beach (Moshup Beach),** New England's best clothing-optional spot. To access the private beach frequented by nude bathers, go to the beach's main entrance where signs say "no nudity," then walk down the beach toward the cliffs. The native Wampanoag used to save sailors shipwrecked on the **Gay Head Cliffs,** near Aquinnah. The 100,000-year-old precipice shines brilliantly and supports one of the island's five lighthouses. (☎645-2211. Lighthouse open F-Su 1½hr. before sunset to 30min. after sunset. $3, under 12 free.)

NANTUCKET ☎ 508

Nantucket has entered modern lore as Martha's Vineyard's conservative little sister. The spellbinding trance of the island's cobblestone streets, precious cottages, and gorgeous beaches is quickly broken when the price tag of such flavor is revealed. Nevertheless, a good hostel and a number of cheap sandwich shops make Nantucket a relatively affordable luxury.

█▲█ ORIENTATION AND PRACTICAL INFORMATION. As any fan of the TV show *Wings* (set in Nantucket's Tom Nevers Field airport) knows, flights are out-of-reach pricey, so take one of the ferries from Hyannis, on Cape Cod (both are near the bus station). **Hy-Line Cruises,** on Ocean St. Wharf (☎778-2600), runs to Nantucket's Straight Wharf on slow boats (2hr.; in summer 3 per day, low season 1-3 per day; $15, ages 5-12 $8, bikes $5) and fast boats (1hr., 5-6 per day, $35/$26/$5). The **Steamship Authority,** South St. Wharf (☎477-8600), goes to Steamboat Wharf on slow boats (2hr.; May-Oct. 6 per day, Nov.-Dec. 3 per day; $14, ages 5-12 $7.25, bikes $6) and fast boats (1hr., 5 per day 6am-7:20pm, $28/$21/$6).

Steamship Authority ferries dock at Steamboat Wharf, which becomes **Broad Street** inland. Turn left off Broad St. onto S. Water St. to reach **Main Street.** Hy-Line ferries dock at the base of this street. **Nantucket Regional Transit Authority** (☎228-7025; www.shuttlenantucket.com) has shuttles to destinations throughout the island. Buses to **Siasconset** and **Surfside** leave from Washington and Main St. (near the lamppost). Buses to **Miacomet** leave from Washington and Salem St., a block up from Straight Wharf; those to **Madaket** and **Jetties Beach** leave from Broad St., in front of the Peter Foulger Museum. (Buses run daily 7am-11:30pm; surfside bus every 40min. 10am-5:20pm. Fare $1-2, seniors half-price, under 6 free.) With most beaches close to town, bikes are the best way to see Nantucket. The cheapest rentals are at **Cook's Cycle,** 6 S. Beach St., right off Broad St. (☎228-0800. $20 per day. Open Apr.-Nov. daily 9am-5pm.) Get bus maps, island maps, brochures, and accommodation info at **Nantucket Visitor Services,** 25 Federal St., off Broad St. (☎228-0925. Open in summer daily 9am-6pm; in winter M-Sa 9am-5:30pm.)

▐ ACCOMMODATIONS. While lodging on Nantucket seems exclusively for the trust-fund set, creative visitors can stay on the island without digging too deep into their pockets. Note that camping on the island is illegal. Across the street from the beach, the **Nantucket Hostel (HI) ❶,** 31 Western Ave., a 3½ mi. bike ride from town at the end of the unlit Surfside Bike Path, is housed in a gorgeous 130-year-old lifesaving station with three large, clean dorm rooms. (☎228-0433 or 888-901-2084. Shuttle to hostel available during peak season daily 10am-6pm; $2. Full kitchen. Linen included. 7-day max. stay. Check-in 3-10pm. Lockout 11am-3pm. Open Apr.-Oct. Dorms $23-27, members $20-24. MC/V.) The **Nesbitt Inn ❹,** 21 Broad St., one block from the wharf, is the oldest and cheapest inn on Nantucket. It has small rooms and shared baths, but guests are treated to a fireplace, deck, continental breakfast, and beach towels. (☎228-0156. Reservations required. Open Mar.-Dec. Singles $85; doubles $95; quads $135. Mar.-Apr. and Oct.-Dec. $10 less. MC/V.) Most other accommodations on Nantucket are more expensive; the **Nantucket Accommodations Bureau** (☎228-9559) or **Nantucket & Martha's Vineyard Reservations** (☎800-649-5671) can help find deals, especially on last-minute accommodations.

▐ FOOD. If you want a sit-down meal on the island, be prepared to shell out $15-20 for an entree. The cheapest options are the takeout places on Steamboat Wharf. Get groceries at the **Grand Union,** off Straight Wharf. (☎228-9756. Open M-Sa 7am-10pm, Su 7am-7pm.) ▧**Something Natural ❶,** 50 Cliff Rd., a short walk north of town, serves still-warm cookies and amazing sandwiches on freshly baked

HAPPY TRAILS

While hikers, bikers, campers, and climbers all love spending time in the great outdoors, it's easy to overlook all the work that goes into making the outdoors so great. Ever wonder where all those trails, sites, and paths came from? Nature is good, but not *that* good. The manpower that makes nature safe and accessible is often provided by enthusiastic volunteers who have a passion for both service and the outdoors.

There are plenty of ways to join the ranks of these rugged do-gooders. The **Sierra Club** (☎415-977-5500; www.sierraclub.org) offers over 90 volunteer vacations in parks across the United States. You can spend a week on Maine's Monhegan Island, maintaining trails and removing the invasive Japanese barberry plant that threatens the island's native plants, or paddle your canoe through the Adirondacks, preserving portage trails and campsites. Trips usually last a week and cost between $100 and $500.

Similar trips are staged by the **American Hiking Society** (☎301-565-6704; www.americanhiking.org), which brings volunteers to Vermont's Green Mountains to repair bridges, or to New York's Allegheny State Park, where they level switchbacks while basking in the beauty of the Finger Lakes. These week-long excursions cost $95 for members, $120 for non-members.

bread—perfect for enjoying on the picnic tables out back. (☎228-0504. Full sandwiches $7-8; half sandwiches $4-5. Open May-Oct. M-Th 8am-6pm, F-Su 8am-6:30pm. Cash only.) **The Atlantic Café ❸**, 15 S. Water St., is nautical and nice, with friendly employees and American pub fare. (☎228-0570. Sandwiches $8-15. Entrees $13-22. Open daily May-Oct. 11:30am-1am; Nov.-Apr. 11:30am-midnight; kitchen closes at 10pm. MC/V.) For a gourmet meal that doesn't break the bank, **Even Keel Cafe ❸**, 40 Main St., serves grilled salmon salad ($15) and lobster risotto ($25) that are pure heaven. (☎228-1979. Open daily 7am-late. AmEx/D/MC/V.)

🪟 **SIGHTS.** The popular **Nantucket Whaling Museum**, 7 Broad St., displays the skeleton of a 40 ft. sperm whale, thousands of whaling tools, and a collection of intricate scrimshaw. A combination ticket grants access to four of Nantucket's oldest buildings, including the **Old Gaol** and a **Quaker meeting house.** (☎228-1894; www.nha.org. Open M-W and F-Sa 10am-5pm, Th 10am-9pm, Su noon-5pm. $15, ages 6-17 $8; combination ticket $18/$9.) For a panoramic view of the island, climb 92 stairs to the top of the **Congregational Church Tower,** 62 Centre St., off Broad St. The excellent views are rivaled only by the north vestry, an early 18th-century church attached to the more modern one. (☎228-0950. Open mid-June to Oct. M-Sa 10am-4pm; Apr. to mid-June F-Sa 10am-2pm. $2.50, ages 5-12 $0.50.)

🏖🎣 **BEACHES AND OUTDOOR ACTIVITIES.** Nantucket's silky public beaches are the island's highlight. The northern beaches (Children's, Jetties, and Dionis) edge much calmer seas than the southern beaches (Cisco, Surfside, Nobadeer). **Dionis** and **Jetties,** near town, are the most popular, with full facilities for daytrippers, while **Siasconset** and **Madaket** are more isolated. On the southern shore, **Miacomet** is the most peaceful, while the biggest waves are at **Nobadeer** and **Cisco,** which is the headquarters for the **Nantucket Island Surf School.** (☎560-1020; www.surfack.com. Rentals $40 per day, $25 per half-day. 1hr. private lesson $65; 2hr. group lesson $85.) **Nantucket Community Sailing,** at Jetties Beach, rents watercraft and gives sailing lessons. (For lessons ☎228-6600, for rentals 228-5358. Kayaks $15 per hr. Open mid-June to mid-Sept. daily 9am-5pm.) **Barry Thurston's,** 5 Salem St., at Candle St., left off Straight Wharf, rents rods and reels. (☎228-9595. Pole, reel, and three lures $20 per 24hr. Open Apr.-Dec. M-Sa 8am-6pm, Su 8am-5pm.) There are two popular **bike routes** on Nantucket. To reach them from Steamboat Wharf, turn right on N. Water St. and bear left on Cliff

Rd. to head for Madaket Beach (6¼ mi.). Many combine this with the **Sanford Farm Hike,** a single trail made up of several loops running through the brushy flatlands and gentle slopes of the old Sanford Farm, a preserved area at the heart of the island. A longer bike route runs to Siasconset (8¼ mi. of flat terrain) from Straight Wharf. Head up Main St. and turn left onto Orange St.; there are signs to the path after the traffic circle. To see more of the island, return from Siasconset Beach on the 10 mi. Polpis Road path. Look for maps of the bike routes at the visitors center and rental shops.

THE BERKSHIRES ☎413

A easy drive from Boston and New York City, the Berkshires are an attractive destination for a weekend getaway. Small towns sprinkled throughout the mountains offer homemade ice-cream, country stores, and scenic rural drives, as well as picturesque colleges and spas. Both modern and traditional, the Berkshires offer an amazing assortment of theater, music, contemporary art, and outdoor adventure.

✦ 🛈 ORIENTATION AND PRACTICAL INFORMATION

Comprising the western third of Massachusetts, the **Berkshire** region is bordered to the north by Rte. 2 (the Mohawk Trail) and Vermont, and to the south by Connecticut. From Williamstown, **Peter Pan/Bonanza Bus Lines** (☎888-751-8800; www.bonanzabus.com) runs buses to Boston via Pittsfield and Springfield. (4hr., 2 per day, $48). **Visitor Info: Berkshire Visitors Bureau,** 3 Hoosac St. in Adams. (☎743-4500 or 800-237-5747; www.berkshires.org. Open M-F 8:30am-5pm.) The **Pittsfield Visitor Center,** 121 South St. in Pittsfield, also provides information about the region. (☎395-0105. Open M-Sa 8:30am-5pm.) For info on hiking and camping at the 12 state parks in Berkshire County, stop by the **Region 5 Headquarters,** 740 South St., in Pittsfield. (☎442-8928. Open M-F 8am-5pm.) **Area Code:** 413.

NORTH ADAMS ☎413

Formerly a large industrial center, North Adams once had 100 trains passing through the Hoosac Tunnel each day. Over time, the factories metamorphosed into art studios and galleries—some of the best in New England—and today modern art stands where assembly lines and machinery once loomed. 🖾**Mass MoCA,** 1040 Mass MoCA Way, has galleries in 27 old factory buildings and is the largest center for contemporary visual and performing arts in the country. Pushing the envelope of modern art, the museum houses upside-down trees and large multimedia displays, as well as fascinating rotating exhibits. (☎662-2111; www.massmoca.org. Open July-Labor Day daily 10am-6pm; early Sept.-late June M and W-Su 11am-5pm. $10, students $8, ages 6-16 $4.) The **Contemporary Artists Center,** 189 Beaver St. (Rte. 8 N), contains an artists' studio and a stunning gallery inside an enormous brick factory. (☎663-9555; www.thecac.org. Open W-Sa 11am-5pm, Su noon-5pm. Free.) Celebrating the history of the Hoosac Tunnel, the **Western Gateway,** 115 State St., just after the Hadley Overpass off Rte. 8, is one of Massachusetts's five Heritage State Parks. The complex consists of a visitors center, a railroad museum, and a gallery, and hosts free outdoor concerts during the summer. (☎663-6312. Open daily 10am-5pm. Summer concerts Th 7pm. Donations accepted.) On Rte. 8, ½ mi. north of downtown, **Natural Bridge State Park** is home to a white marble bridge that spans a 60 ft. deep chasm. Navigate the labyrinth of stairs and stone leading to the bridge, or picnic on the grounds. (May-Oct. ☎663-6392, Nov.-Apr. ☎663-8469. Open late May-mid-Oct. daily 9am-5pm. Parking $2.)

Clarksburg State Park ❶, 1199 Middle Rd., a few miles north of town on Rte. 8, has 44 wooded campsites and nearly 350 acres of woods and water. (☎664-8345. No lifeguard on duty. Free showers. Reservations recommended on weekends. Sites $14, MA residents $12. Day use $5. D/MC/V.) Go to **Gideon's Luncheon and Nightery ❷,** 23 Eagle St., for live jazz and blues at the hippest place in town. Try the chef's "Soup of Yesterday" ($4), or just relax to the music. (☎664-0404. www.nightery.com. No cover. Open M 11:30am-2pm, Tu-W 11:30am-2pm and 5-9pm, Th 11:30am-2pm and 5pm-midnight, F-Sa 11:30am-2pm and 5pm-2am. AmEx/D/MC/V.) **Moulton's Pizzeria ❸,** 117 Main St., serves up crispy pizza with festive Italian flare. Try the Mayor, which is piled high with everything but anchovies. (☎663-3770. Medium pizzas $8-10. Delivery available. Open M-Th 11am-10pm, F-Sa 11am-midnight. MC/V.) Follow Rte. 2 east from Mass MoCa for the **North Adams Visitors Center,** on Union St. (Rte. 2/Rte. 8), which is operated by enthusiastic volunteers. (☎663-9204. Open June-Sept. daily 10am-4pm.)

WILLIAMSTOWN   ☎413

With a purple cow named "Ephs" (after college founder Ephraim Williams) as a mascot and a lively student population, **Williams College** injects youthful vitality into an otherwise quiet town. Maps of the campus are available from the admissions office, 33 Stetson Ct., in Bascom House. (☎597-2211; www.williams.edu. Open M-F 8:30am-4:30pm. Tours daily; call for times.) The **Williams College Museum of Art,** 15 Lawrence Hall Dr., #2, houses over 12,000 pieces ranging from medieval religious works to modern art. (☎597-2429; www.wcma.org. Open Tu-Sa 10am-5pm, Su 1-5pm. Free. Wheelchair accessible.) Half a mile down South St. from the traffic circle, the ▨**Clark Art Institute,** 225 South St., features impressive 19th-century works by artists like Renoir, Degas, and Cassat, as well as unique temporary exhibits. The 140-acre grounds encourage patrons to picnic in the gardens or stroll through the hillside pastures. Construction to expand the museum began in the fall of 2005, but the museum remains open to the public. (☎458-2303. Open July-Aug. daily 10am-5pm; Sept.-June Tu-Su 10am-5pm. Nov.-May free; June-Oct. $10, students with ID and under 18 free. Wheelchair accessible.) As the summer heats up, so do the stages at the **Williamstown Theater.** The Tony-award-winning ▨**Williamstown Theater Festival** hosts plays and musicals on two main stages and several secondary stages around town. (☎597-3399; www.wtfestival.org. Box office at 1000 Main St., open mid-June-late Aug. Tu-Sa 10am-8pm, Su 10am-4pm. Performances Tu-Su. Main Stage $20-52; Nikos Stage $33-35; F afternoon play readings $3.) The **Hopkins Memorial Forest** (☎597-2346) offers over 2500 acres of free hiking and cross-country skiing on 15 mi. of trails. Take Rte. 7 N (North St.), turn left on Bulkley St., and turn right onto NW Hill Rd. For bike, snowshoe, or cross-country ski rentals, check out **The Mountain Goat,** 130 Water St. (☎458-8445. Bike and ski rentals $25 per day, $35 for a weekend, $100 full week. Open M-W and F-Sa 10am-6pm, Th 10am-7pm, Su noon-5pm.) At 3,491 ft., **Mt. Greylock** is the tallest peak in Massachusetts and has more than 50 miles of trails, including the Appalachian Trail. At the top stands the **Veterans War Memorial Tower.**

Also at the summit of Mt. Greylock sits ▨**Bascom Lodge ❷,** which offers bunks, private rooms, and expansive mountain views. (☎743-1591; www.naturesclassroom.org. Accessible by Notch Rd., off Rt. 2, from the north and North Main St., off Rt. 7, from the south. Breakfast $8. Dinner $16. Bunks M-F $26, Sa-Su $36. Private rooms M-F $68-98. Parking $2. Reservations required for lodging and meals. AmEx/MC/V.) Affordable motels cluster along Rte. 2 east of town. The **Maple Terrace Motel ❹,** 555 Main St. (Rte. 2), is one of the nicest places in town, with beautiful gardens, bright rooms with cable TV, a heated outdoor pool, and continental breakfast. (☎458-9677; www.mapleterrace.com. Reservations strongly recommended. Rooms in summer $82-102; low-season $55-60. AmEx/D/DC/MC/V.) The comfortable **Chimney Mirror Motel ❸**, 295 Main St., is slightly cheaper, but rates on summer weekends jump significantly. Rooms are simple, clean, and have private baths and A/C. (☎458-5202; www.chimneymirror.com. Breakfast included. Rooms in summer M-Th and Su $52-78, F-Sa $99-120; low-season $50-68. Lower rates may be available upon request. Discounts for extended stays. D/DC/MC/V.) For a quick and easy meal, stroll to **Pappa Charlie's Deli ❶**, 28 Spring St., and sink your teeth into $5 celebrity-themed sandwiches such as the meaty "Columbo." (☎458-5969. Open M-Sa 8am-8pm, Su 8am-7pm. Cash only.) Serving gourmet ice cream ($2.95), incredible milkshakes ($3.50), and grilled burgers and hot dogs, **Lickety Split ❶**, 69 Spring St., is hopping in the early afternoon. (☎458-1818. Open Feb.-Nov. daily 11am-11pm, Dec.-Jan. M-Sa 11:30am-4pm. Cash only.) Get a taste of local student nightlife and great food at the **Purple Pub ❷**, 8 Bank St. Tasty dishes like the portobello and roast chicken sandwich ($6.75) and a variety of salads complement weekly drink specials. (☎458-3306; www.thepurplepub.com. M open mic night. Open daily 10am-1am. AmEx/MC/V.) The Williamstown Chamber of Commerce operates a **Visitors Information Booth** at the intersection of Rtes. 2 and 7 with info on events and a guide to lodging and dining. (☎485-9077; www.williamstownchamber.com. Open 24hr; staffed July-Aug. daily 10am-6pm; Sept. F-Su 10am-6pm.)

LENOX   ☎413

🏛**Tanglewood,** an enormous and scenic music center off Rte. 7, west of Lenox Village on West St. (Rte. 183), is one of the Berkshires' greatest treasures and the summer home of the **Boston Symphony Orchestra.** For an enchanting evening or a relaxing Sunday afternoon, lawn tickets and picnics are the way to go. Chamber concerts, many with young musicians training at Tanglewood over the summer, provide regular evening entertainment. The Boston Pops also gives summer concerts. For a rare treat, hear Tchaikovsky's 1812 Overture punctuated by cannon shots and fireworks at **Tanglewood on Parade,** held each year in late July. The summer comes to a close with a **jazz festival** at the end of August. (☎888-266-1200 for tickets and schedules; www.bso.org. Orchestral concerts late June-late Aug. F 8:30pm with 6pm prelude, Sa 8:30pm, Su 2:30pm; open rehearsals Sa 10:30am. Auditorium or "Music Shed" $19-96; lawn seats $16-23, under 12 free, students with valid ID half-price on F evenings.) Though best known for her works of fiction, **Edith Wharton** also dabbled in architecture, designing her own sparkling white mansion. Containing rooms decorated with classical stone sculptures and set above three acres of formal gardens and stables, **The Mount,** 2 Plunkett St., at the southern junction of Rte. 7 and 7A, offers tours and special events, including a summer lecture series on literature and architecture. (☎637-1899; www.edithwharton.org. Open late May-Nov. daily 9am-5pm. Tours M-F every hr., Sa-Su every 30min. 9:30am-3:30pm. $18, students with ID $9, under 12 free. Special events $18, with reservation $16.) Shakespeare's works never go out of style at **Shakespeare & Company,** 70 Kemble St. (Rte. 7A). Enjoy plays written by Berkshires authors at the **Founders' Theater.** Free matinees are also performed *al fresco* in the Rose Footprint, modeled after the Elizabethan Rose Playhouse. (☎637-3353; www.shakespeare.org. Box office open mid-Apr.-late Oct. daily 10am-2pm, or until performance begins. Founders Theater $10-50. Rose Footprint free. Call for showtimes.) At the base of Lenox Mountain, the **Pleasant Valley Wildlife Sanctuary** contains 1300 acres and 7 mi. of trails through forest, meadows, and wetlands. (☎637-0320; www.massaudubon.org. From Pittsfield, take Rte. 20 S to W. Dugway Rd. Follow W. Dugway 1½ mi. to the Nature Center. Open July-Sept. daily dawn-dusk. Nature Center open late Oct.-June M 9am-4pm, Tu-Sa 9am-5pm, Su 10am-4pm; July-late Oct. M and Su 10am-4pm, Tu-Sa 9am-5pm. No pets allowed. $4, ages 3-12 $3.)

NEW ENGLAND

Serving up breakfast, lunch, and the occasional psychic reading, **Carol's ❷**, 8 Franklin St., will satisfy any cravings for home cooking. With breakfast all day, you can try local celebrity James Taylor's favorite omelet or sample some of Carol's delicious pancakes. (☎637-8948. Pancakes from $4.95. Open daily 7am-4pm. Cash only.) Surf's up at **Betty's Pizza Shack ❷**, 26 Housatonic St., where pictures of Hawaiian waves lap at the walls and a surfboard hangs over the bar. Even the pizza is surf-themed: medium "short board" pizzas are $10-16 and large "long boards" are $13-20. (☎637-8171. Open M-F 10am-10pm, Sa 10am-midnight. Cash only.)

STOCKBRIDGE   ☎413

Stockbridge, like many other small towns in the Berkshires, glimmers with natural beauty and the afterglow of the Gilded Age. Enjoy some old-fashioned Americana at the ⬛**Norman Rockwell Museum,** 9 Glendale Rd. (Rte. 183), where you can visit the artist's studio and the largest single collection of his original works, including many *Saturday Evening Post* covers. Planned guest exhibits for early 2006 include illustrations from the book *Dinotopia*. (☎298-4100; www.nrm.org. Open May-Oct. daily 10am-5pm; Nov.-Apr. M-F 10am-4pm, Sa-Su 10am-5pm. $12, students $7, under 18 free. Audio tours available.) Just down the road lies **Chesterwood,** the home and studio of sculptor Daniel Chester French, best known for his sculpture at the Lincoln Memorial in Washington, D.C. (☎298-3579; www.chesterwood.org. Open May-Oct. daily 10am-5pm. Admission $10, under 18 $5, under 5 free, families $25.) Enjoy fresh fragrances and stunning flower arrangements at the 15-acre **Berkshire Botanical Gardens,** at the intersection of Rtes. 102 and 183. (☎298-3926; www.berkshirebotanical.org. Open May-Oct. daily 10am-5pm. $7, seniors and students $5, under 12 free.) Set in the rolling hills overlooking Stockbridge, **Naumkeag,** 5 Prospect Hill Rd., is the 44-room Choate family mansion surrounded by lavish gardens, a blue-roofed Chinese temple, and perfectly manicured trees. (☎298-3239; www.thetrustees.org. Open daily 10am-5pm, last tour at 4pm. Admission and tour $10, ages 3-12 $3. Admission to garden without tour $8/$3.)

RHODE ISLAND

Founded in 1636 by religious outcast Roger Williams, Rhode Island is the smallest state in the Union, but makes good use of its territory. Its winding coastline is smattered with seaside hamlets, while the scenic interior is criss-crossed with bike trails. Still, not everything in the state is tiny—Providence's cosmopolitan flair and the Gilded Age mansions of Newport are giants in their own right.

ⓘ PRACTICAL INFORMATION

Capital: Providence.

Visitor Info: Providence/Warwick Convention and Visitors Bureau: 1 W. Exchange St., in downtown Providence. (☎751-1177 or 800-233-1636; www.visitrhodeisland.com. Open M-Sa 9am-5pm.) **Division of Parks and Recreation,** 2321 Hartford Ave., Johnston 02919. (☎401-222-2632. Open M-F 8:30am-4pm.)

Postal Abbreviation: RI. Sales Tax: 7%.

PROVIDENCE   ☎401

Located at the mouth of the Seekonk River, Providence is undergoing a renaissance from the inside out. Artistic and collegiate flavor has brought trendy shops and restaurants to this compact city. Downtown rests at the base of two hills—one home to two world-class institutes of higher education, and the other to the State Capitol—allowing Providence to seamlessly blend the hustle and bustle of a busy capital city with the laid-back feel of a college town.

▌ TRANSPORTATION. T.F. Green Airport, south of the city at Exit 13 off I-95, is a Southwest Airlines hub. **Amtrak,** 100 Gaspee St., operates from a station southeast of the state capitol. (☎800-872-7245; www.amtrak.com. Open daily 5am-10:45pm; ticket booth open 5am-9:45pm. Wheelchair accessible.) Trains run to Boston (40min., 10 per day, $14) and New York City (3-4hr., 10 per day, $61-90). **Greyhound** has an info and ticket booth in Kennedy Center. (☎454-0790 or 800-231-2222; www.greyhound.com. Ticket window open 6:30am-8pm.) Buses run to Boston (1hr.; 7-8 per day; $7.50) and New York City (4-5hr.; 9-12 per day; $23). **Bonanza Bus,** 1 Bonanza Way, at Exit 25 off I-95 and at the RIPTA information booth in Kennedy Center (☎888-751-8800; www.bonanzabus.com; station open daily 4:30am-11pm, Kennedy Center ticket window daily 7am-6pm), has service to Boston (1hr., 18 per day, $8) and New York City (4-5hr., 7 per day, $33). **Rhode Island Public Transit Authority (RIPTA),** 265 Melrose St., runs an **info booth** at Kennedy Plaza that provides free bus maps. (☎781-9400; www.ripta.com. Terminal open 6am-8pm; ticket window M-F 7am-6pm, Sa 9am-noon and 1-5pm.) RIPTA's service includes Newport and a variety of other locations. (Schedules vary, buses run daily 5am-midnight. $1.50; day pass $6.) **Providence Link,** run by RIPTA, runs trolleys ($1.50) through the city with stops at major sights. **Yellow Cab** (☎941-1122) provides taxi service in the Providence metro area.

▌▐ ORIENTATION AND PRACTICAL INFORMATION. I-95 and the **Providence River** run north-south and split Providence into three sections. West of I-95 is **Federal Hill;** between I-95 and the Providence River is **Down City.** East of the river is **College Hill,** home to **Brown University** and **Rhode Island School of Design** (RISD, or Risdee). Walking or taking the Providence Link are the best ways to see the city during the day. **Visitor Info: Providence/Warwick Convention and Visitors Bureau,** 1 Sabin St., on the first floor of the convention center downtown. (☎751-1177 or 800-233-1636; www.goprovidence.com. Open M-Sa 9am-5pm.) The **Providence Preservation Society,** 21 Meeting St., at the foot of College Hill, has info on historic Providence and the *Guide to Providence Architecture* ($25), which traces 11 self-guided tours. (☎831-7440; www.ppsri.org. Open M-F 8:30am-5pm.) **Internet Access: Providence Public Library,** 225 Washington St. (☎455-8000. Open M noon-8pm, Tu-Th 10am-6pm, F-Sa 9am-5pm. Free.) **Post Office:** 2 Exchange Terr. (☎421-5214. Open M-F 8am-5pm.) **Postal Code:** 02903. **Area Code:** 401.

▌ ACCOMMODATIONS. Downtown motel rates make Providence an expensive overnight stay, and rooms fill up well in advance for graduation season in May and early June. Head 10 mi. south on I-95 to **Warwick** or **Cranston,** or northeast to **Seekonk, MA,** on Rte. 6, for cheaper motels. Catering largely to the university's international visitors, the stained-glass-windowed **International House of Rhode Island ❸,** 8 Stimson Ave., off Hope St. near the Brown campus, has three comfortable and unique rooms. Reservations are required and should be made far in advance. (☎421-7181. Laundry facilities, fridge, private bath, TVs, and shared kitchen. Reception June-July M-F 8:30am-4pm; Aug.-May M-F 9:30am-5pm. Singles $50, students $35; doubles $60/$45; $5 per night discount for stays of 5 nights or more. Monthly rate $550/$450. Cash only.) The **Knights Inn ❸,** 50 Mink St., on Rte. 6 1 mi. after entering Seekonk, has a kind staff and cushy rooms. (☎508-336-8050. Continental breakfast included. Singles $64-67; doubles $72-80; $6 per additional person.) The nearest campgrounds lie 30min. from town. **Colwell's Campground ❶,** in Coventry, has showers and hookups for 75 sites along the Flat River Reservoir, perfect for swimming or water-skiing. From Providence, take I-95 S to Exit 10, then go west 8½ mi. on Rte. 117 and look for Peckham Ln. on the right. (☎397-4614. Reservations recommended. Check-in 3-9pm. Sites $18, with hookup $20.)

🖺 FOOD. Providence provides excellent culinary options. **Atwells Avenue,** on Federal Hill just west of downtown, is Providence's "Little Italy"; **Thayer Street,** on College Hill to the east, is home to offbeat student hangouts and ethnic restaurants; and **Wickenden Street,** in the southeast corner of town, has inexpensive eateries. For cheap food downtown, the **Arcade,** the first indoor mall in America, has plenty of sandwich shops, as does its counterpart, the food court in the massive **Providence Place Mall. Geoff's Superlative Sandwiches ❶,** 163 Benefit St., in College Hill, attracts a diverse clientele with 85 creatively named sandwiches ($5-7), like the "Kevorkian," a sandwich that, with pastrami, bacon, and Frank's Hot Sauce, might facilitate your demise. Dive into the huge pickle barrel for a treat to complement your meal. (☎751-2248. Open M-F 8am-9pm, Sa-Su 9:30am-9pm. Cash only.) Specializing in Eggs Benedict (with five varieties; $5-8), **Julian's ❸,** 318 Broadway, near Federal Hill, is a funky sit-down eatery. (☎861-1770. Wraps and sandwiches $5-8. Dinner $11-22. Open M-F 9am-1am, Sa 9am-3pm and 5pm-1am, Su 9am-3pm and 6pm-1am. AmEx/D/MC/V.) A Federal Hill institution, **Angelo's Civita Farnese ❷,** 141 Atwells St., serves up Italian favorites family-style at reasonable prices. (☎621-8171. Entrees $3-12. Sandwiches $4-6. Open daily noon-6:30pm. Cash only.)

◎ SIGHTS. Take a jaunt down Benefit St. in College Hill, past the artsy RISD students, and stop by the 🗹**RISD Museum of Art,** 224 Benefit St. The museum's three floors of galleries have a collection of Native American, Egyptian, Indian, Impressionist, medieval, and Roman art, as well as a giant 12th-century Japanese Buddha. (☎454-6500; www.risd.edu/museum.cfm. Open Tu-Su 10am-5pm. $8, seniors $5, students $3, ages 5-18 $2. Free Su 10am-1pm, every 3rd Th 5-9pm, F noon-1:30pm, and last Sa of the month 11am-4pm.) Established in 1764, **Brown University** features 18th-century buildings, including the **Corliss-Brackett House,** 45 Prospect St., now the Office of Admission. (☎863-2378; www.brown.edu/admission. Open M-F 8am-4pm. Free campus tours M-F 9am-4pm.) The stunning marble dome of the **Rhode Island State Capitol** is visible from nearly every vantage point in the city. (☎222-3938; www.state.ri.us. Open M-F 8:30am-4:30pm. Free guided tours every hr. M-F 9am-noon. Tour guides on duty in the library until closing. Reservations recommended for groups. Self-guide booklets available in the library.) The **John Brown House Museum,** 52 Power St., is steeped in tranquil elegance. The 1hr. tour includes a brief video introducing the house built by John Brown himself in the late 18th century. Guides are well-versed in the house's exquisite architecture and the priceless antiques within. (☎273-7507. Open Tu-Sa 10am-5pm, Su noon-4pm. $7, students and seniors $5.50, ages 7-17 $3; families $18.) The factory that started the industrial revolution in America is preserved in Pawtucket at the **Slater Mill Historic Site,** 67 Roosevelt Ave., along the rushing waters of the Blackstone River. (☎725-8638; www.slatermill.org. Open June-Nov. Tu-Sa 10am-5pm, Su 1-5pm. Call for winter hours. Continuous tours, included in price of admission, last 1½hr. $8, seniors $7, ages 6-12 $6, under 6 free.) In addition to founding Rhode Island, Roger Williams founded the **First Baptist Church of America** in 1638. Its 1775 incarnation stands today at 75 N. Main St. (☎454-3418; www.fbcia.org. Guided tours available after the Su service. Self-guided tours during all other hours of operation. Open M-F 10am-noon and 1-4pm, Sa 10am-noon. Free.)

🖸🖭 ENTERTAINMENT AND NIGHTLIFE. For film, theater, and nightlife listings, read the "Weekend" section of the *Providence Journal* or pick up a free *Providence Phoenix.* On several evenings each summer, floating and stationary bonfires span the entire length of the downtown rivers during ☒**WaterFire,** a public art exhibition and festival. (☎272-3111; www.waterfire.org. Free.) The regionally acclaimed **Trinity Repertory Company,** 201 Washington St., typically offers $15 student rush tickets on the day of performances. (☎351-4242; www.trinity-rep.com for ticket info. Tickets $28-50.) The **Providence Performing Arts Center,** 220 Weybosset St., hosts a variety of high-end productions like concerts and Broadway musicals. (☎421-2787; www.ppacri.org. Box office open Sept.-May M-F 10am-6pm, Sa noon-5pm; May-Sept. M-Th 10am-3pm, or until curtain on show days. Tickets $30-68. Half-price tickets for students and seniors sometimes available 1hr. before weekday showtimes; call ahead.) The **Cable Car Cinema and Cafe,** 204 S. Main St., one block down from Benefit St., shows arthouse and foreign films in a small theater with comfy couches and refreshments. (☎272-3970. 2 shows per evening, times vary. $8, M-W students $6. Cafe open M-F 7:30am-11pm, Sa-Su 9am-11pm.)

Brownies, townies, and RISDs rock the night away at several hot spots throughout town. Something's going on every night at **AS220,** 115 Empire St., between Washington and Westminster St., a nonprofit, totally uncensored cafe/bar/gallery/performance space. (☎831-9327; www.as220.org for performance info. Cover usually around $6. Open M-F 3pm-1am, Sa-Su 7pm-1am.) **Trinity Brewhouse,** 186 Fountain St., behind Trinity Repertory Theatre, serves award-winning beer, as well as live blues on Wednesday nights. Diners and drinkers enjoy themselves under a "Last Supper" painting of musical greats from Beethoven to Lennon. (☎453-2337. Open M-Th 11:30am-1am, F 11:30am-2am, Sa noon-2am, Su noon-1am.) Local artists perform rock, jazz, and funk at the **Custom House Tavern,** 36 Weybosset St., in Down City, a tiny corner bar in the perpetual shadows of Providence's tallest towers. (☎751-3630. 21+. Open M-Th 11:30am-1am, F 11:30am-2am, Sa 8pm-2am, Su 8pm-1am.)

NEWPORT ☎401

Money has always found its way into Newport. Once a center of transatlantic shipping, the coastal town later became the summer escape for the elite of America's elite. Today, the awe-inspiringly opulent mansions of big-business tycoons still remain, but they are only a part of this high-priced tourist town—world-famous music festivals and the beautiful landscape are now the big draws.

■❼ **ORIENTATION AND PRACTICAL INFORMATION.** Parallel to the shore, **Thames Street** is home to the tourist strip and the wharves, while **Bellevue Avenue** contains many of Newport's mansions. The Newport/Pell bridge requires a $2 toll. **Bonanza Buses** (☎846-1820; www.bonanzabus.com) depart from the Gateway Center, as do **Rhode Island Public Transit Authority** (**RIPTA;** see **Transportation,** p. 153) buses. Parking at the Gateway Center is a cheap option ($2 per day with RIPTA receipt, 30min. free with visitors center validation). **Ten Speed Spokes,** 18 Elm St., rents bikes. (☎847-5609. Bikes $5 per hr., $25 per day. Credit card and photo ID required. Open M-F 10am-6pm, Sa 10am-5pm, Su noon-5pm.) A mecca of information, the **Newport County Convention and Visitors Bureau,** 23 America's Cup Ave., two blocks from Thames St., in the Newport Gateway Center, has floor-to-ceiling pictures and large maps. Be sure to ask at the information counter for visitor guides. (☎800-976-5122; www.gonewport.com. Open daily 9am-5pm.) **Internet Access: Public Library,** 300 Spring St. (☎849-8720. Open M 11am-8pm, Tu-Th 9am-8pm, F-Sa 9am-6pm. Wireless Internet available. Free.) **Post Office:** 320 Thames St. (☎847-2329. Open M-F 8:30am-5pm, Sa 9am-1pm.) **Postal Code:** 02840. **Area Code:** 401.

❮ **ACCOMMODATIONS.** Small and expensive lodging crowds Newport, but a new hostel proves that Newport's vacationers have changed since the days of railroads and steel monopolies. Many hotels and guest houses book solid two months in advance for summer weekends, especially during the popular festivals. A breakthrough for budget travelers, the newly opened ■**William Gyles Guesthouse ❷**, 16 Howard St., right in the heart of town, treats visitors to hostel accommodations, breakfast, an evening tour of Newport, and other goodies. (☎369-0243. Laundry $3. 3-night max. stay. Check-out 10am. Reservations recommended. Dorms in summer $20-29, during festivals $49; in winter $16. Inquire about student discounts. MC/V.) A few minutes from Newport's harborfront, the **Newport Gateway Hotel ❺**, 31 W. Main Rd., in Middletown, has cushiony and alluring doubles with A/C, minifridge, and cable TV. (☎847-2735. Breakfast included. M-Th and Su $65-99, F-Sa $159-195. AmEx/D/MC/V.) For less-expensive lodging, Rte. 114 (W. Main Rd.) and the adjacent Coddington Hwy. have a variety of vanilla chain motels about 4 mi. from Newport. **Fort Getty Recreation Area ❶**, on Fort Getty Rd. on Conanicut Island, provides 15 small tent sites in an open field with a great view of an old lighthouse. (☎423-7211. Free hot showers and beach access. Reservations recommended. Tent sites June-Oct. $20; RV sites $40. Cash only.)

🍴 **FOOD.** The vegetarian-friendly **Panini Grill ❶**, 186 Thames St., grills tasty sandwiches ($5-6) in a small and funky basement. (☎847-7784. Open M-Th and Su 11am-9:30pm, F-Sa 11am-2am. MC/V.) Choice mollusks are always the catch of the day at **Flo's Clam Shack ❸**, 4 Wave Ave., across from the east end of Easton Beach. This place is the perfect summer treat, but locals have already figured that out— be prepared for lines on hot evenings. (☎847-8141. Seafood platters with cole slaw and fries $8-14. Open in summer M-Th and Su 11am-9pm, F-Sa 11am-10pm; call for low-season hours. Cash only.) A Rhode Island staple, the **Newport Creamery ❷**, Bellevue Ave., across from the Tennis Hall of Fame, serves three meals and ice cream inside or at the takeout window. (☎846-6332. Locations throughout Rhode Island. Open 6:30am-11pm. AmEx/D/MC/V.) The **Franklin Spa ❶**, 229 Spring St., prepares breakfasts like the "Portuguese Sailor," with *chorizo* and eggs. (☎847-3540. Breakfasts $7-8. Open M-W 6am-2pm, Th-Sa 6am-3pm, Su 7am-1:30pm.)

📷 **SIGHTS.** George Noble Jones built the first "summer cottage" in Newport in 1839, anchoring the town's extravagant string of palatial summer estates. Most mansions lie south of downtown on Bellevue Ave. A self-guided walking tour or, in some mansions, a guided tour by the **Preservation Society of Newport**, 424 Bellevue Ave., gives you a chance to ogle the decadence. (☎847-1000; www.newportmansions.org. Open in summer daily 9am-5pm; in winter M-F 9am-5pm.) The five largest mansions are **The Elms,** 367 Bellevue Ave., **The Breakers,** 44 Ochre Point Ave., **Chateau-sur-Mer,** 474 Bellevue Ave., **Rosecliff,** 548 Bellevue Ave., and **Marble House,** 596 Bellevue Ave. Marble House is not to be missed. (☎847-1000. Mansions open M-F 10am-5pm. $10-15 per house, ages 6-17 $4. Combination tickets $22-32.)

Newport's gorgeous beaches are frequently as crowded as the streets. The most popular sandy spot is **Easton's Beach,** or First Beach, on Memorial Blvd. (☎848-6491. Parking late May to early Sept. M-F 10am-9pm $8, before 10am $6, Sa-Su $10.) Other beaches line Little Compton, Narragansett, and the shore between Watch Hill and Point Judith. Starting at Easton's Beach or Bellevue Ave., the ■**Cliff Walk** traverses Newport's eastern shore as a 3½ mi. walking/running trail (www.cliffwalk.com). Wildflowers and a rocky shoreline mark one side of the trail, while gorgeous mansions border the other. **Fort Adams State Park,** south of town on Ocean Dr., 2½ mi. from the visitors center, has showers, picnic areas, fishing piers, and a gorgeous view of downtown Newport alongside the largest coastal fort in America. (☎847-2400; www.fortadams.org. Park open daily dawn-dusk. Guided tours of fort every hr. 10am-4pm. Tours $8, ages 5-17 $5; families $20.) Near Fort Adams, **Ocean Drive** is a breathtaking car or bike ride along the coast.

Built in 1763, the **Touro Synagogue,** 85 Touro St., is the oldest synagogue in the US. The synagogue underwent renovation in 2005 and will reopen in 2006. (☎847-4794; www.tourosynagogue.org.) The **Tennis Hall of Fame,** 194 Bellevue Ave., is a white-and-green Victorian building that contains an in-depth look at the sport's history and a Wimbledon-esque grass court. (☎849-3990; www.tennisfame.com. Open daily 9:30am-5pm. $8, students and seniors $6, under 17 $4; families $20.)

◼◼ ENTERTAINMENT AND NIGHTLIFE. From June through August, Newport gives lovers of classical, folk, jazz, and film each a festival to call their own. Festival tickets sell out months in advance; look early if you want to attend. The **Newport Jazz Festival,** at Fort Adams State Park, is one of the oldest and best-known jazz festivals in the world. Also at Fort Adams State Park, folk singers entertain at the **Newport Folk Festival,** where former acts include Bob Dylan and Joan Baez. (Both festivals ☎847-3700; www.festivalproductions.net. Tickets $53-100 per day, under 12 $5.) The **Newport Music Festival** brings classical musicians from around the world for more than 60 concerts during two weeks in July. (☎846-1133, box office 849-0700; www.newportmusic.org. Box office at 850 Aquidneck Ave. in Middletown, open M-F 10am-6pm, Sa 10am-1pm. Tickets $35-45.) In June, the **Newport International Film Festival** screens films in the **Jane Pickens Theater** and the **Opera House Cinema.** (☎846-9100; www.newportfilmfestival.com.)

Even if you can't get to a festival, music fills the streets every night. Pubs and clubs line Thames St., but bring proper ID, as clubs are strict. The **Rhino Bar and Grille's Mamba Room,** 337 Thames St., is the place to dance the night away. (☎846-0707. 21+. Cover $5-20. Open W-Sa 9pm-1am.) **The Newport Blues Cafe,** 286 Thames St., hosts live music ranging from blues to rock to reggae. (☎841-5510. Live music nightly after 9:30pm. Business casual, no hats. Cover up to $15. Open in summer daily 6pm-1am; dinner until 10pm. Call for winter hours.) With three bars, a dockside location, and live music, **Christies,** 351 Thames St., keeps crowds coming back for more. (☎847-5400. Open in summer daily 11:30am-1am; call for winter hours.)

▣ DAYTRIP FROM NEWPORT: BLOCK ISLAND. A popular daytrip 20 mi. southwest of Newport, teardrop-shaped **Block Island** possesses an untamed natural beauty. All beaches are free, but many are a hike from the ferry stops; cycling is the best way to explore the island. **Aldo's Rentals,** on Chapel St. behind the Harborside Inn, rents bikes and other contraptions. (☎466-5018. Mountain bikes $7 per hr., $25 per day; mopeds $40/$85; kayaks $15 per hr., $35 per half-day; cars $90-155 per day. Open mid-May to mid-Oct. daily 8am-6pm. Coupons available at the visitors center.) A three-quarter mile hike along the shore to **North Light,** the granite lighthouse and maritime museum that rests on the northern tip of the island, is a pleasant excursion. (Open early July to early Sept. daily 10am-5pm. $2.) Don't miss the trail hidden behind the lighthouse that leads through the sand dunes to the northern coast. Follow the coast up to the very northern tip of the island, where a narrow pathway leads out into the Atlantic. Enjoy the most beautiful and secluded sands on the island, but do not swim here—currents are downright lethal.

The island does not permit camping; it's best to make it a daytrip unless you're willing to shell out at least $70, and probably much more, for a room in a guest house. Most moderately priced restaurants hover near the ferry dock in Old Harbor, but a few others are located in New Harbor, 1 mi. inland. **Rebecca's Seafood Restaurant ❶,** on Water St. across from the dock, serves up beach favorites in a small dining room and sunny patio. (☎466-5411. Seafood sandwiches $4-6. Open M-Th 7am-8pm, F-Su 7am-2am. Cash only.) Luscious sweets like thick slices of banana bread ($2.50-5) and iced coffee ($2-3) can be found alongside Internet terminals ($1 per 5min.) at **Juice 'n' Java ❶,** on Dodge St. (☎466-5220. Open daily 7am-midnight. Cash only.) If you reach Block Island with a hankering for pancakes and bacon, look no farther than **Ernie's Old Harbor Restaurant ❷**, on Water St. at Old Harbor. (☎466-2473. Open daily 6:30am-noon. MC/V.) The popular restaurant and bar at **Ballard's Inn** has live music most summer afternoons, which can be enjoyed for free on their public beach at the end of Water St.

The **Interstate Navigation Company** (☎783-4613 or 866-783-7340) provides **ferry service** to Block Island from State Pier at Point Judith, in Galilee. (1hr.; mid-June to early Sept. 8-9 per day; $9.45, seniors $9, ages 5-11 $4.75; car by reservation $39, driver and passengers must pay regular fare; bike $2.50); and Fort Adams State Park in Newport (2hr.; July-Aug. 1 per day; $9, seniors $8.50, ages 5-11 $4; bike $2.50). The **Block Island Express** (☎ 860-444-4624) runs a high-speed ferry from New London, CT (1hr.; mid-June to mid-Sept. 4-5 per day; $16.50, ages 2-11 $7.50; bike $10). The last ferry of the day usually leaves at 7pm, and schedules are available at any of the terminals. The **Block Island Chamber of Commerce** (☎466-2982 or 800-383-2474; www.blockislandchamber.com), located at the ferry dock in Old Harbor, provides maps and information on accommodations on the island. (Lockers and ATM in the visitors center next door. Open in summer daily 9am-5pm; low-season hours vary.) **Area Code:** 401.

CONNECTICUT

Connecticut is like a patchwork quilt; industrialized centers like Hartford and New Haven are interspersed with serene New England villages, a vast coastline, and woodland beauty. Home to Yale University and the nation's first law school, Connecticut has a rich intellectual history. But don't be fooled—the state that brought us the three-ring circus and the largest casino in the US knows how to party.

⏞ PRACTICAL INFORMATION

Capital: Hartford.

Visitor Info: Connecticut Vacation Center, 505 Hudson St., Hartford 06106 (☎800-282-6863; www.ctbound.org). Open M-F 8am-4:30pm.

Postal Abbreviation: CT. Sales Tax: 6%.

HARTFORD   ☎860

Hartford may be the world's insurance capital, but travelers will be more interested in the cool museums, historical sites, and lively theater scene. As Mark Twain—a revered resident of 17 years—boasted, "of all the beautiful towns it has been my fortune to see, this is the chief."

⏞ **PRACTICAL INFORMATION.** Hartford marks the intersection of the **Connecticut River, I-91,** and **I-84.** Union Place, between Church and Asylum St. along Spruce St., houses **Amtrak** (☎727-1778; www.amtrak.com; office open M-F 6am-7:30pm, Sa-Su 6:30am-7:30pm), which runs to New Haven (1hr., $13) and New York City (3hr., $41), and **Greyhound** (☎724-1397; www.greyhound.com; station open daily 5:45am-10pm), which goes to Boston (2hr., 12 per day, $23), New Haven (1½hr., 4-5 per day, $11), and New York City (2½-3hr., 17 per day, $24). **Connecticut Transit Information Center** is the round terminal at State and Market St. (☎525-9181; www.cttransit.com. Open M-F 7am-6pm, Sa 9am-3pm. Buses within the city $1.25, students $1, seniors $0.60. Day pass $3.25.) **Taxi: Yellow Cab,** ☎666-6666. **Visitor Info: Greater Hartford Welcome Center,** 45 Pratt St. (☎244-0253 or 800-793-4480;

www.hartford.com. Open M-F 9am-5pm.) The **Old State House,** 800 Main St., also provides tourist info. (☎522-6766. Open M-Sa 10am-4pm.) **Internet Access: Hartford Public Library,** 500 Main St. (☎695-6300. Wireless available. Open M-Th 10am-8pm, Sa 10am-5pm; Oct.-May also Su 1-5pm. Free.) **Post Office:** 80 State House Sq. (☎240-7553. Open M-F 8am-5pm.) **Postal Code:** 06103. **Area Code:** 860.

▐▌ ACCOMMODATIONS AND FOOD. The **Mark Twain Hostel (HI) ❶,** 131 Tremont St., has 42 bunks. It's not exactly squeaky clean, but the price is right. Head west on Farmington Ave., then turn right on Tremont St., or take the "Farmington Ave." bus west. (☎523-7255. Kitchen. Linen included. Laundry $2.50. Check-in 5-10pm. Check-out 10am. Dorms $24, members $20. Cash only.) Opposite Bushnell Park, the **YMCA ❶,** 160 Jewell St., provides accommodations. Use of the athletic facilities is included. (☎246-9622. Must be 18+ with ID and Social Security number. Key deposit $10. Check-in M-F 7:30am-10pm, Sa-Su 7:30am-2pm. Check-out 11am. No reservations. Singles $20, with private bath $25. D/MC/V.)

Eateries in downtown Hartford consist mainly of cheap lunch places and trendy restaurants. Corporate clock-punchers crowd around the food carts near the Old State House and fill the food court at State House Square in the middle of the day. **Black-Eyed Sally's BBQ & Blues ❷,** 350 Asylum St., serves down-home southern cooking. Enjoy jambalaya ($16) and decipher the thousands of signatures covering the walls. (☎278-7427; www.blackeyedsallys.com. Sandwiches $7-9. Half-rack of ribs $14. Live blues W-Sa nights. Cover F-Sa $5-10. Open M-Th 11:30am-10pm, F 11:30am-11pm, Sa 5-11pm; bar open late. AmEx/DC/MC/V.) Join the locals who crowd into **Max Bibo's ❶,** 208 Trumbull St., for ample sandwiches. (☎525-4035. Most sandwiches $4-7. Open M-F 6:30am-4pm, Sa-Su 10am-3pm. AmEx/MC/V.)

◙ SIGHTS. The ▓Wadsworth Athenaeum, 600 Main St., has collections of contemporary and Baroque art, including one of three Caravaggio paintings in the US. Rotating exhibitions, a breathtaking collection of Hudson River School landscapes, and a display of German and French porcelain round out an exceptional gallery. (☎278-2670. Open W-F 11am-5pm, Sa-Su 10am-5pm. $10, seniors $8, ages 13-18 and students with ID $5. Call ahead for tour and lecture info.) Designed by Charles Bulfinch in 1796, the gold-domed **Old State House,** 800 Main St., housed the state government until 1878. Now, historical actors take you into the chambers where Reverend Hooker delivered his revolutionary sermon in 1638 and the Amistad Trial began in 1839. On a lighter note, the museum of curiosities inside includes a crocodile, a tiger and a two-headed calf. (☎522-6766; www.ctosh.org. Open M-F 10am-4pm, Sa 11am-4pm. Free.) **Bushnell Park,** at Jewell St., has a 1914 **carousel,** complete with organ. (☎585-5411. Open May-Oct. Tu-Su 11am-5pm. $0.50 per ride.) The **Mark Twain House and Museum,** 351 Farmington Ave., presents entertaining tours of the intricately textured home where the author penned parts of *The Adventures of Huckleberry Finn* and *Tom Sawyer.* From the Old State House, take any "Farmington Ave." bus west. (☎247-0998. Open M-W and F-Su 9:30am-5:30pm, Th 9:30am-8pm; Jan.-Apr. closed Tu. Tours fill quickly; last tour 1hr. before closing. $14, seniors $13, students $12, ages 6-12 $10.) The **Harriet Beecher Stowe House,** 77 Forest St., adjacent to Twain's home, leads tours with information about the life and times of the *Uncle Tom's Cabin* author, whom Abraham Lincoln called "the little lady that started the big war." (☎522-9258; www.harrietbeecherstowe.org. Open June to mid-Oct. Tu-Sa 9:30am-4:30pm, Su noon-4:30pm; mid-Oct. to May closed M. $8, seniors $7, ages 6-16 $4.)

▐▌▐ ENTERTAINMENT AND NIGHTLIFE. The Tony Award-winning **Hartford Stage Company,** 50 Church St., stages productions of traditional masterpieces, American classics, and contemporary works. (☎527-5151; www.hartfordstage.org.

$20-60.) **TheaterWorks,** 233 Pearl St., is an off-Broadway-style theater that presents a variety of recent plays. (☎527-7838. www.theaterworkshartford.org. $35-55.) For more shows, head to **The Bushnell,** 166 Capitol Ave., home of Hartford's symphony, ballet, and opera companies, as well as a venue for Broadway hits, jazz, and family favorites. (☎987-5900; www.bushnell.org. Box office open M-Sa 10am-5pm, Su noon-4pm. Rush and student rate tickets sometimes available.)

Downtown is pretty empty on weeknights, but on weekends Hartford's nightlife is concentrated along Asylum St. and around the train station. Take advantage of the ultimate combination of food, nightlife, and entertainment at the **City Steam Brewery and BrewHaHa Comedy Club,** 942 Main St. Pool tables fill one room while red velvet couches line lounges complete with card tables and TVs. Nine brewing tanks hold home-brewed masterpieces like "Naughty Nurse" Pale Ale. Upstairs, the comedy club keeps guests in stitches. (☎525-1600. M $2 margaritas, M-F 10pm-midnight $3 martinis. Irish music W. Comedy shows Th 8pm, F 9pm, Sa 7 and 10pm. Live rock and blues F-Sa. Comedy cover $5-15. Kitchen open M-Th 11:30am-10:30pm, F-Sa 11:30am-midnight, Su 4-10pm; bar open M-Th until midnight, F-Sa until 1am, Su until 10pm.) With a loyal clientele, pool table, and weekday drink specials, **McKinnon's,** 114 Asylum St., is the best place to find cool brews and good times. (☎524-8174. Karaoke M. 21+. Cover varies. Open M-Th 11am-1am, F-Sa 11am-2am.) Across the street, the **Bar with No Name,** 115 Asylum St., is one of the most popular hangouts in the city. A different DJ each week pumps out loud beats for the sea of people in the center room while bartenders mix nightly drink specials. This is your classic weekend hot spot. (☎293-2344. Happy hour Th-Su 6-9pm with free food. 21+. Cover varies. Open Th-Su 6pm-2am.) If you want to ditch the raucous crowds, try **Tapas On Ann,** 126 Ann St., where great Greek food and tapas complement the full bar. (☎525-5988. Open M-Th 11am-1am, F 11am-2am, Sa 5pm-2am; kitchen closes M 9pm, Tu-Th 10pm, F-Sa 11pm.)

NEW HAVEN   ☎203

Despite a bad reputation that has proven hard to drop, New Haven is growing from the inside out. The center of the city is home to the solid stone foundations of Yale University, a shining academic light that continues to expand into the darker areas of the city's troubled past. Today, the "new" New Haven, especially the area immediately around Yale's campus, sustains a healthy assortment of ethnic restaurants, art galleries, divey pizza parlors, and coffee shops supported by both students and townies alike.

▇ ▞ ORIENTATION AND PRACTICAL INFORMATION. New Haven lies at the intersection of **I-95** and **I-91,** 40 mi. south of Hartford, and is laid out in nine squares surrounded by radial roads. Between Yale University and City Hall, the central square, called **The Green,** provides a pleasant place to sit and relax. At night, don't wander too far from the immediate downtown and campus areas; some of the surrounding sections can be very unsafe. **Amtrak,** at Union Station on Union Ave., Exit 1 off I-91 (☎773-6177; www.amtrak.com; ticket office open daily 6:30am-9:30pm), runs to: Boston (2½hr., 16 per day, $49); Mystic (1hr., 3-4 per day, $19); New York City (1½hr., 10 per day, $37); Washington, D.C. (5½hr., 10 per day, $84). Also at Union Station, **Greyhound** (☎772-2470; www.greyhound.com; ticket office open daily 7am-8pm) runs frequently to Boston (3½-5hr., 11 per day, $29), New York City (2½hr., 11 per day, $20), and Providence (2½hr., 11 per day, $21). The **New Haven Trolley Line** services the downtown area and Yale. (☎288-6282. Runs every 15min. M-Sa 11am-6pm. Free.) Taxi: **MetroTaxi,** ☎777-7777. **Internet Access: New Haven Public Library,** 133 Elm St. (☎946-8130. Open mid-Sept. to May M noon-

8pm, Tu-Th 10am-8pm, Sa 10am-5pm; June to mid-Sept. M-Th 10am-6pm, F 10am-5pm. Free with photo ID.) **Post Office:** 150 Court St., in the federal building. (☎752-3283. Open M-F 7:30am-5pm, Sa 8am-noon.) **Postal Code:** 06510. **Area Code:** 203.

⌐ ACCOMMODATIONS. Inexpensive lodgings are sparse; the hunt intensifies and prices jump around Yale Parents Weekend (mid-October) and Commencement (early June). Head 10 mi. south on I-95 to **Milford** for affordable motels. **Hotel Duncan ❸**, 1151 Chapel St., located in the heart of Yale's campus, exudes old-fashioned charm. Guests enjoy spacious rooms and the chance to ride in the oldest manually operated elevator in the state. (☎787-1273. Reservations recommended on weekends. Singles $44-50; doubles $60-70. AmEx/MC/V.) **Hammonasset Beach State Park ❶**, 20min. east of New Haven off I-95 N Exit 62 in Madison, has 558 sites just a few minutes from woods and a long sandy beach. (☎245-1817. Office open mid-May to Oct. daily 8am-10:30pm. Lifeguard on duty 8am-8pm. Free hot showers. Sites $15, $18 for walk-ins. Day use M-F $10, Sa-Su $14. Cash only.)

⌐ FOOD. For great, authentic Italian cuisine, work your way along Wooster St., in Little Italy, a 10min. walk east of downtown. Try to beat the lines at ▣**Frank Pepe's Pizzeria ❸**, 157 Wooster St., which claims to be the originator of the American pizza, originally known as "tomato pie," in the 1920s. The thin-crust pizza is served dripping with sauce and cheese and comes with an essential stack of napkins. (☎865-5762. Open M-Th 4-10pm, F-Sa 11:30am-11pm, Su 2:30-10pm. Cash only.) Next door, **Libby's ❶**, 139 Wooster St., has scrumtrilescent cannoli ($1.50-2.50) and gelato. (☎772-0380. Open M and W-Th 11:30am-10pm, F-Sa 11:30am-11pm, Su 11:30am-9pm. Cash only.) No condiments are allowed at **Louis' Lunch ❶**, 263 Crown St. Cooked in suspended grills, the beloved burgers ($4.50) go great with apple pie. (☎562-5507. Open Tu-W 11am-4pm, Th-Sa noon-2am. Cash only.)

◐ SIGHTS. The majority of the sights and museums in New Haven are located on or near the **Yale University** campus. Most of the campus buildings were designed in the English Gothic or Georgian Colonial styles, many of them with intricate moldings and a few with gargoyles. The **Yale Visitors Center**, 149 Elm St., faces the Green and is the starting point for **campus tours.** (☎432-2300; www.yale.edu. Open M-F 9am-4:45pm, Sa-Su 11am-4pm. Free 1hr. campus tours M-F 10:30am and 2pm, Sa-Su 1:30pm.) Bordered by Chapel, College, Grove, and High St., the charming Old Campus contains **Connecticut Hall,** which, raised in 1753, is the university's oldest remaining building. A block north, on the other side of Elm St., **Sterling Memorial Library,** 120 High St., is designed to resemble a monastery—even the telephone booths are shaped like confessionals. The design is not entirely without a sense of humor, though—carved stone brackets portray students sleeping, smoking, and lounging. (☎432-1852. Free Internet. Open Sept.-June M-Th and Su 8:30am-midnight, F 8:30am-10pm, Sa 10am-7pm; July-Aug. M-W and F 8:30am-5pm, Th 8:30am-10pm, Sa 10am-5pm.) Paneled with Vermont marble cut thin enough to be translucent, **Beinecke Rare Book and Manuscript Library,** 121 Wall St., is a massive modern structure containing more than 600,000 rare books and manuscripts, including one of the five Gutenberg Bibles in the US. Rotating exhibits allow visitors to see the collection. (☎436-1254. Open M-Th 8:30am-8pm, F 8:30am-5pm. Free.) Open since 1832, the **Yale University Art Gallery,** 1111 Chapel St., at York St., holds over 100,000 pieces, including an impressive array of classical Greek sculpture and works by Monet, Van Gogh, Matisse, and Picasso. (☎432-0600. Open Tu-W and F-Sa 10am-5pm, Th 10am-8pm, Su 1-6pm. Self-guided audio tours available. Free.) Just down the road, the **Yale Center for British Art**, 1080 Chapel St., holds the largest collection of British art outside the United Kingdom. (☎432-2800. Open Tu-Sa 10am-5pm, Su noon-5pm. Free.) The **Peabody Museum of Natural History,** 170 Whitney Ave., Exit 3 off I-91, houses Rudolph F. Zallinger's Pulitzer Prize-winning mural "Age of Reptiles" in a room populated with dinosaur skeletons. The museum also has a 100-million-year-old 8 ft. turtle and a mummy. (☎432-5050. Open M-Sa 10am-5pm, Su noon-5pm. $7, seniors $6, students and ages 3-15 $5.) Outside the campus area and accessed from East Rock Rd. northeast of the city, **East Rock Park** provides an excellent sunset view of New Haven and the Long Island Sound from an overlook 325 ft. above sea level. (☎782-4314. Open dawn-dusk.)

■■ **ENTERTAINMENT AND NIGHTLIFE.** New Haven was once the testing ground for Broadway-bound plays, and its theatrical tradition remains, fueled by student crowds. The **Yale Repertory Theatre,** 1120 Chapel St. (☎432-1234), performs a variety of classic and contemporary plays throughout the school year. Now more than 40 years old, the **Long Wharf Theatre,** 222 Sargant Dr. (☎787-4282), still serves as a springboard for new plays hoping to make the leap to Broadway. The **Shubert Performing Arts Center,** 247 College St. (☎562-5666 or 800-955-5566), is New Haven's entertainment centerpiece, offering musicals, dance, and opera.

■**Toad's Place,** 300 York St., has hosted Bob Dylan, the Rolling Stones, and George Clinton. Also a popular spot with students, Toad's throws dance parties Wednesday and Saturday nights during the school year. (☎562-5694, recorded info 624-8623. Box office open M-F 11am-6pm; buy tickets at the bar after 8pm. 21+. Cover $5-35 for shows; $5 for dance nights. Open M-Th and Su 8pm-1am, F-Sa 8pm-2am; closed when no show.) **Bar,** 254 Crown St., is a cool hangout with a pool table, lounge, dance floor/theater, five homemade beers brewing in tanks at the bar, and brick-oven pizza. Alternative Night ("Boom") every Tuesday attracts a large gay crowd. (☎495-8924. Live music 3-4 nights per week. Cover Tu $3, Sa $6. Open M-Tu and Su 4pm-1am, W-Th 11:30am-2:30pm and 4pm-1am, F-Sa 11:30am-2am.) If you didn't get enough Gothic flavor on the Yale tour, head to **Playwright,** 144 Temple St., where almost everything in the bar is imported from across the Atlantic. (☎752-0450. Live music F-Sa nights. Open M-Th and Su 11:30am-1am, F-Sa 11:30am-2am.)

MYSTIC AND THE CONNECTICUT COAST ☎860

When Herman Melville's white whale, Moby Dick, became a legend, Connecticut's coastal towns were busy seaports full of dark, musty inns and tattooed sailors. Today, vacationers and sailing enthusiasts still head to the coast seeking a whale of a good time. Along the Mystic River, **Mystic Seaport,** 1 mi. south on Rte. 27 from I-95 at Exit 90, offers a look at 18th-century whaling. In the recreated village, staff demonstrate historic life-saving techniques and help visitors navigate the decks of the museum's ships. (☎888-973-2767; www.mysticseaport.org. Open daily Apr.-Oct. 9am-5pm, F-Sa until 8pm; Nov.-Mar. 10am-4pm. $17, seniors and students $15, ages 6-12 $9. Tickets good for 2 days.) A few dollars more puts you on an authentic 1908 coal-fired steamboat for **Sabino Charters'** cruise along the Mystic River. (☎572-5351. 30min. trips every 30min. mid-May to early Oct. daily 10:30am-3:30pm. $5.50, ages 6-17 $4.50. 1½hr. cruise at 4:30pm $12/$10.) The **Mystic Aquarium and Institute for Exploration,** 55 Coogan Blvd., at Exit 90 off I-95, has a menagerie of seals, penguins, sharks, and white beluga whales. (☎572-5955; www.mysticaquarium.org. Open daily July to early Sept. 9am-6pm; early Sept. to June 9am-5pm. $19.75, seniors $19.25, ages 3-12 $14.25.) The **Denison Pequotsepos Nature Center,** 109 Pequotsepos Rd., 1½ mi. east of downtown, offers 8 mi. of trails through three diverse ecosystems. The nature center also has interactive exhibits like the awesome "after dark in the meadow." (☎536-1216; www.dpnc.org. Nature center open M-Sa 9am-5pm, Su 10am-4pm. Park open dawn-dusk. $6, seniors and under 12 $4.)

NEW ENGLAND

Budget lodgings are scarce in Mystic, though there are a few hotels at the intersection of Rte. 27 and I-95. The **Stonington Motel ❸**, 901 Stonington Rd., 5 mi. from Mystic on Rte. 1 N, has tidy rooms with A/C, cable TV, microwave, and mini-fridge. (☎599-2330. Rooms $55-80. AmEx/MC/V.) Close to Mystic, **Seaport Campground ❶**, on Rte. 184, 3 mi. north of Rte. 27 from Mystic, boasts a pool, mini-golf course, fishing pond, and live music on weekends. (☎536-4044. Open mid-Apr. to late Oct. Tent sites with water and electricity mid-May to mid-Sept. $34, Apr. to mid-May and mid-Sept. to late Oct. $26.50; RV sites $39/$32. Each additional adult $7, child $1.50. No arrivals after 11pm. D/MC/V.) Though Julia Roberts is no longer serving, **Mystic Pizza ❷**, 56 W. Main St., made famous by the film of the same name, still serves their heavenly pizza. (☎536-3700. Pizza $6-11. Open 11am-11pm. AmEx/D/MC/V.) For takeout that's almost gourmet, head to **Mystic Market East ❶**, 63 Williams St., which has terrific sandwiches ($5-7),like the Black Forest ham with French brie. (☎572-7992. Open M-Sa 7am-7pm, Su 7am-5pm. AmEx/D/MC/V.) A throwback to the days of sea captains and grog, ▨**Captain Daniel Packer Inne,** 32 Water St., serves the "Dark and Stormy," black rum with a splash of ginger beer. (☎536-3555. Live music begins at 10pm. Dining room open daily 11am-4pm and 5-10pm; bar open M-Th and Su until 1am, F-Sa until 2am.)

Amtrak (☎800-872-7245; www.amtrak.com; open daily 10am-4pm; no ticketing office), half a mile east of Mystic on Rte. 1, runs to Boston (1½hr., 3 per day, $30), New Haven (1hr., 3 per day, $19), and New York City (3hr., 4 per day, $49). The **Mystic Tourist and Information Center,** Bldg. 1D in Olde Mistick Village, at the corner of Rte. 27 and Coogan St., offers maps, discounted tickets to attractions, a 24hr. digital hotel board with listings of all vacancies, and a direct phone line to accommodations in the region. (☎536-1641; www.mysticinfo.com. Open mid-June to Sept. M-Sa 9:30am-6pm, Su 10am-5pm; Oct. to early June M-Sa 9am-5:30pm, Su 10am-5pm.) **Internet Access: Mystic and Noank Library,** 40 Library St., in Mystic. (☎536-7721. Open M-W 10am-9pm, Th-Sa 10am-5pm; mid-June to early Sept. closes Sa 1pm. $0.25 per 15min.) **Post Office:** 23 E. Main St. (☎536-8143. Open M-F 8am-5pm, Sa 8:30am-12:30pm.) **Postal Code:** 06355. **Area Code:** 860.

CONNECTICUT CASINOS

Foxwoods and Mohegan Sun, two tribally owned casinos in southeast Connecticut, bring sin to the suburbs. Although each has its own style, their shared propensity for decadence makes them both worth a traveler's while, especially if said traveler can afford to lose a few dollars. The 4.7 million sq. ft. **Foxwoods** (☎888-287-2369; www.foxwoods.com) contains a casino with 7400 slot machines, blackjack, craps, poker, and the other usual suspects, as well as three glitzy hotels, a spa, elaborate nightclubs and adult entertainment, a village for shopping, and fancy restaurants with food from all over the world. The 1450-seat **Fox Theatre** hosts live performances from boxing to pop music; past performers include Frank Sinatra, Bill Cosby, and the Dixie Chicks. (☎800-200-2882. Prices and performance times vary.) **Club BB King** is a place to dance the night away while leaving your wallet intact. (☎860-312-4361. 21+. Cover $5-15. Open Th 9pm-2am, F-Sa 9pm-2:30am.) While winning money on the casino floor is less than certain, paying handsomely for lodging in the casino is a sure thing. Lodging outside the casino is sparse—options for those who aren't cleaning up at the tables are the campgrounds that speckle the roadside along Rte. 2 west of the casino or the accommodations near Norwich, CT, roughly halfway between the two casinos. More than 10 bus companies run to Foxwoods from surrounding areas. **Greyhound** (☎800-229-9424; www.greyhound.com) provides service to Foxwoods from Boston (2-3hr., 9-10 per

day, $20-28) and New York City (3-5hr., 9-12 per day, $23). Driving is also convenient, with free parking at the resort. From I-95, take Exit 92 to Rte. 2 W, and from
I-84 take Exit 55 to Rte. 2 E. From Mohegan Sun, take Rte. 2A W to Rte 2 E. Once
on Rte. 2 follow the signs to the casino.

Mohegan Sun (☎ 888-226-7711) has two of the world's largest casinos: the Casino
of the Earth and the Casino of the Sky. While Foxwoods boasts classic casino
glamour, Mohegan Sun presents its services, entertainment, and shopping in tribal
packaging, with trees as pillars that change with the seasons and an enormous
waterfall. The **Mohegan Sun Arena** offers everything from sporting events to teeny-
bopper concerts in a vast 10,000-seat complex. (☎ 888-226-7711 ext. 27163. Show
times and prices vary.) With free parking and shuttles from each of the Mohegan
Sun's four lots, driving is the most convenient way to access the casino. From I-
395, take Exit 79A to Rte. 2A E. From Foxwoods, take Rte. 2 W to Rte. 2A E. Once
on Rte. 2A follow the signs to the casino. Bus lines also service the casino from
many points in the northeast. (Mohegan Sun bus hotline ☎ 888-770-0140.)

MID-ATLANTIC

From the Eastern seaboard of New York south through Virginia, the mid-Atlantic states claim many of the nation's major historical, political, and economic centers. This region has witnessed the rotation of US capitals: first Philadelphia, PA; then Princeton, NJ; Annapolis, MD; Trenton, NJ; New York, NY; and finally Washington, D.C. During the Civil War, the mid-Atlantic even housed the Confederate capital, Richmond, VA. Urban centers cover much of the land, but the great outdoors have survived. The Appalachian Trail meanders through the region, and New York's Adirondacks compose the largest national park in the lower 48 states.

HIGHLIGHTS OF THE MID-ATLANTIC

GAPE at the obelisk-like **Washington Monument** (p. 276), the glistening **Empire State Building** (p. 180), and the jagged crack in the **Liberty Bell** (p. 235).

ABSORB the majesty of world-class art at the **Metropolitan Museum of Art** (p. 187), the **Museum of Modern Art** (p. 188), and the **National Gallery of Art** (p. 277).

GIGGLE at the colonial costumes of reenactors in **Philadelphia** (p. 229), **Gettysburg** (p. 244), and **Williamsburg** (p. 291).

CATCH some rays during a break from **Atlantic City's** slot machines (p. 222), or spread your towel next to a starlet in the **Hamptons** (p. 197).

WHISTLE along with the heartstopping showtunes of a **Broadway** musical (p. 189).

NEW YORK

The Empire State offers a little bit of everything: the excitement of New York City, the grandeur of Niagara Falls, and the natural beauty of the Catskills and Adirondacks. While "The City that Never Sleeps" attracts cosmopolitan adventure-seekers, those grooving to a mellower tune head upstate. Here, surrounded by cool waterways and wooded mountainsides, you may find it difficult to remember that lattes and Prada even exist. Still, while the easy rolling cities of upstate New York are natural and sweet, there's nothing like the juicy tang of the Big Apple.

⚡ PRACTICAL INFORMATION

Capital: Albany.

Visitor Info: Division of Tourism, 1 Commerce Plaza, Albany 12245 (☎518-474-4116 or 800-225-5697; www.iloveny.state.ny.us). Operators available M-F 8:30am-4:45pm. **New York State Office of Parks and Recreation and Historic Preservation,** Empire State Plaza, Agency Bldg. 1, Albany 12238 (☎518-474-0456). Open M-F 9am-5pm.

Postal Abbreviation: NY. **Sales Tax:** 7-9%, depending on county.

MID-ATLANTIC

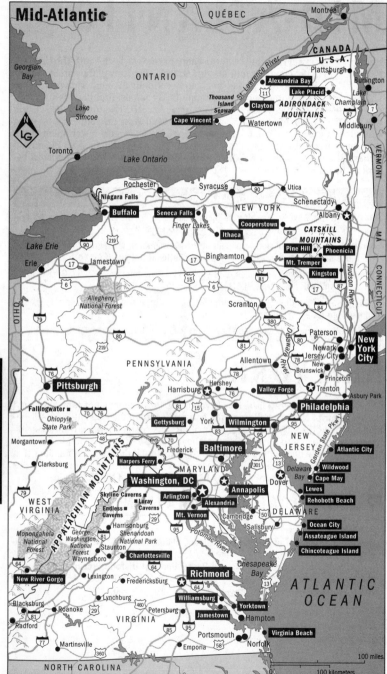

Mid-Atlantic

QUÉBEC

Montréal

CANADA
U.S.A.

ONTARIO

Georgian
Bay

Plattsburgh

Burlington

Alexandria Bay

St. Lawrence River

Lake Placid

Lake
Champlain

Thousand
Island
Seaway

Clayton

Watertown

ADIRONDACK
MOUNTAINS

Middlebury

Lake
Simcoe

Cape Vincent

87

7

VERMONT

Toronto

Lake Ontario

Rochester

Syracuse

Utica

90

Schenectady

MA

Niagara Falls

Buffalo

Seneca Falls

Finger Lakes

NEW YORK

Albany

Ithaca

Cooperstown

88

CATSKILL
MOUNTAINS

Lake Erie

90

219

Pine Hill

Phoenicia

Erie

6

Jamestown

Binghamton

Mt. Tremper

Kingston

17

15

81

17

87

Hudson River

CONNECTICUT

OHIO

79

Allegheny
National Forest

Scranton

84

380

Paterson

80

New
York
City

80

219

PENNSYLVANIA

Allentown

Newark
Jersey City

New
Brunswick

Princeton

76

Pittsburgh

78

Harrisburg

Hershey

Valley Forge

Trenton

Asbury Park

Fallingwater

70 76

Ohiopyle
State Park

81

15

76

Philadelphia

Gettysburg

York

Wilmington

95

NEW
JERSEY

Garden State Pkwy.

Atlantic City

Morgantown

48

Frederick

70

83

95

13

Delaware
Bay

Wildwood

Clarksburg

Harpers Ferry

Baltimore

Cape May

301

Lewes

79

Washington, DC

MARYLAND

Annapolis

Dover

Rehoboth Beach

WEST
VIRGINIA

Skyline Caverns

Arlington

Alexandria

Cambridge

50

DELAWARE

Ocean City

Endless
Caverns

Luray
Caverns

Mt. Vernon

Salisbury

Assateague Island

Monongahela
National
Forest

Harrisonburg

29

Potomac River

Chincoteague Island

George
Washington
National
Forest

Shenandoah
National Park

81

Chesapeake
Bay

New River Gorge

Staunton

Waynesboro

Charlottesville

64

ATLANTIC
OCEAN

APPALACHIAN MOUNTAINS

64

Lexington

Richmond

13

Fredericksburg

Blacksburg

Lynchburg

Williamsburg

Yorktown

81

Roanoke

29

460

Petersburg

Jamestown

Hampton

Radford

VIRGINIA

85

95

Portsmouth

Virginia Beach

77

Martinsville

360

Emporia

58

Norfolk

NORTH CAROLINA

100 miles

0

100 kilometers

MID-ATLANTIC

NEW YORK CITY   ☎212

The self-proclaimed "Capital of the World" puts its money where its mouth is. Eight million New Yorkers pack themselves into the city limits, and each one can tell you exactly why theirs is the greatest city on earth. This is the place where the legendary Yankees hold court, the lights of Broadway never dim, and every street corner promises a hot dog and a pretzel. Towering skyscrapers form the hub of American business by day, and the pounding beats of legendary clubs thump forth from neon-tinged shadows by night. When an act of terrorism destroyed the twin towers of the World Trade Center on September 11, 2001, New Yorkers were awakened to both horror and heroism. The city has moved on, but it hasn't forgotten. Though corporate skyscrapers and government buildings are heavily guarded, don't let security measures keep you from appreciating the ultimate big city. At any time of day or night, New York City's five boroughs teem with varied, thrilling action. For more info, check out ▨*Let's Go: New York City.*

▨ INTERCITY TRANSPORTATION

Airports: 4 airports serve the New York City metropolitan area.

John F. Kennedy Airport (JFK; ☎718-244-4444), at the end of the Van Wyck Expwy., in southern Queens. The airport is 15 mi. from midtown Manhattan, but the drive can take 1hr. JFK handles most international and many domestic flights. The AirTrain runs from JFK to 2 subway stops leading into the city. From Howard Beach Station, connect to the A subway train. From Jamaica Station, connect to E, J, or Z subway train. (Allow 1hr. for entire trip; AirTrain every 4-8min. 6am-11pm, every 12min. 11pm-6am; $5 plus subway fare on MetroCard. Taxi to Manhattan $45, plus tolls and tip.)

LaGuardia Airport (☎718-533-3400), off Exit 7 on the Grand Central Pkwy., in northern Queens. LaGuardia is 9 mi. from midtown Manhattan, a 25min. drive. Domestic flights. The MTA M60 bus connects to Manhattan subway lines 1 and 9 at 110th St./Broadway; A, B, C, D at 125th St./St. Nicholas Ave.; 2, 3 at 125th St./Lenox (Sixth) Ave.; 4, 5, 6 at 125th St./Lexington Ave. The Q33 bus goes to Jackson Heights/Roosevelt Ave. in Queens for 7, E, F, G, R, V; the Q48 bus goes to 74th St./Broadway in Queens for 7, E, F, G, R, V. (Allow at least 1½hr. for all routes. M60 runs daily 5am-1am, Q33 and Q48 24hr.; all buses $2.) Taxi to Manhattan $45, plus tolls and tip.

Newark Liberty International Airport (☎973-961-6000), off Exit 14 on I-95, 16 mi. west of Midtown in Newark, NJ. Domestic and international flights. Olympia Airport Express (☎973-964-6233) travels from the airport to Port Authority, Grand Central Terminal, and Penn Station (15-60min.); departs for Port Authority every 5-10min. 4:15am-11:45pm, departs for Penn Station 4am-11pm, departs for Grand Central every 20-30min. 4am-11pm; $12. Bus #107 by the New Jersey Transit Authority (☎973-762-5100) covers Newark, Newark International Airport (North Terminal), and Port Authority (25min., every 30-45min. 5:20am-1am, $3.60).

Islip Long Island MacArthur Airport (☎631-467-3210), 50 mi. from midtown Manhattan in Ronkonkoma, NY. Take the shuttle van service or the S57 bus to the Ronkonkoma train station. Shuttle ($5) departs from the baggage claim every 30min. 6am-10:30pm. Bus ($1.50) departs every hr., no service Su. From Ronkonkoma, the Long Island Rail Road (LIRR) runs trains into Penn Station (1½hr.; departs around every 30min. on-peak, every hr. off-peak, $6.50).

Trains: Grand Central Terminal, 42nd St. and Park Ave. (Subway: 4, 5, 6, 7, S to 42nd St./Grand Central), handles **Metro-North (☎800-638-7646)** commuter lines. **Amtrak** (☎800-872-7245; www.amtrak.com) runs out of **Penn Station,** 33rd St. and Eighth Ave. (Subway: 34th St./Penn Station/Seventh Ave.; 34th St./Penn Station/Eighth Ave.) To **Boston** (4-5hr., 10 per day, $69), **Philadelphia** (1½hr., 10 per day, $53), and **Washington, D.C.** (3-4hr., 10 per day, $80). The **Long Island Railroad (LIRR; ☎718-217-5477)** and **NJ Transit (☎973-762-5100)** commuter rails also run from Penn Station. At 33rd St. and Sixth Ave., **PATH (☎800-234-7284)** trains depart for New Jersey.

Buses: Greyhound (☎800-229-9424; www.greyhound.com) buses leave the **Port Authority Terminal,** 42nd St. and Eighth Ave. (☎564-8484. Subway: A, C, E to 42nd St./Port Authority.) To **Boston** (4-6hr., $35), **Philadelphia** (2-3hr., $21), and **Washington, D.C.** (4½hr., $35). Watch for con artists and pickpockets, especially at night.

MID-ATLANTIC

⚜ ORIENTATION

NYC is comprised of **five boroughs:** the Bronx, Brooklyn, Manhattan, Queens, and Staten Island. Flanked on the east by the East River (actually a strait) and on the west by the Hudson River, **Manhattan** is an island, measuring only 13 mi. long and 2½ mi. wide. **Queens** and **Brooklyn** are on the other side of the East River. **Staten Island,** southwest of Manhattan, is the most residential borough. North of Manhattan sits the **Bronx,** the only borough connected by land to the rest of the US.

BOROUGHS

MANHATTAN

Above 14th Street, Manhattan is an organized grid of avenues running north-south and streets east-west. Street numbers increase as you travel north. Avenues are slightly less predictable: some are numbered, while others are named. The numbers of the avenues increase as you go west. **Broadway** defies the pattern, cutting diagonally east across the island at 23rd St. **Central Park** and **Fifth Avenue** (south of 59th St., north of 110th St.) separate the city into the East Side and West Side. **Washington Heights** is located north of 155th St.; **Morningside Heights** (above 110th St. and below 125th St.) is sandwiched between **Harlem** (150s to 110th St.) and the **Upper West Side** (110th St. to 59th St., west of Central Park). The museum-heavy **Upper East Side** is across Central Park, above 59th St. on Fifth Ave. **Midtown** (59th St. to 42nd St.) includes Times Square and the Theater District. **Lower Midtown** (41st St. to 14th St.) includes **Herald Square, Chelsea,** and **Union Square.**

   Below 14th St., the city dissolves into a confusing tangle of old, narrow streets that aren't numbered south of Houston St. The bohemian **East Village** and **Alphabet City** are grid-like, with alphabetized avenues from Ave. A to Ave. D, east of First Ave. Intellectual **Greenwich Village,** to the west, is especially complicated west of Sixth Ave. Moving south, trendy **SoHo** (South of Houston St.) and **TriBeCa** (Triangle Below Canal St.) are just west of historically ethnic enclaves **Little Italy, Chinatown,** and the **Lower East Side.** The **Financial District/Wall Street area** at the tip of Manhattan, set over the original Dutch layout, is full of narrow, winding, one-way streets.

BROOKLYN

The **Brooklyn-Queens Expressway (BQE)** links to the **Belt Parkway,** and circumscribes Brooklyn. Ocean Pkwy., Ocean Ave., Coney Island Ave., and diagonal Flatbush Ave. run from the beaches of southern Brooklyn (**Coney Island** and **Brighton Beach**) to the heart of the borough in **Prospect Park.** The streets of western Brooklyn (including **Park Slope**) are aligned with the western shore and intersect central Brooklyn's main arteries at a 45-degree angle. In northern Brooklyn (including **Williamsburg, Greenpoint, Brooklyn Heights,** and **Downtown Brooklyn**), several avenues—Atlantic Ave., Eastern Pkwy., and Flushing Ave.—travel east into Queens.

QUEENS

The streets of Queens resemble neither the orderly grid of Upper Manhattan nor the haphazard angles of Greenwich Village. Streets generally run north-south and are numbered from west to east, from 1st St. in **Astoria** to 271st St. in **Glen Oaks.** Avenues run perpendicular to streets and are numbered from north to south, from Second Ave. to 165th Ave. The address of an establishment often tells you the closest cross-street (for example, the establishment at 45-07 32nd Ave. is near the intersection with 45th St.). Pick up the useful Queens Bus Map, free and available on most Queens buses.

THE BRONX

Major highways divide the Bronx. The **Major Deegan Expressway (I-87)** runs up the western border of the borough, right next to the Harlem River. The **Cross-Bronx Expressway (I-95)** runs across the borough, turning north on its eastern most edge. Up the center of the borough runs the **Bronx River Parkway.** Many avenues run north-south, including **Jerome Avenue** on the western side and **White Plains Road** and **Boston Road** to the east. East-west streets include **Tremont Avenue, Fordham Road,** and the **Pelham Parkway.**

STATEN ISLAND

Unlike the rest of the city, Staten Island is quite spread out. Pick up necessary maps of Staten Island's bus routes as well as other pamphlets at the **Chamber of Commerce,** 130 Bay St. (☎718-727-1900), left from the ferry station.

▐ LOCAL TRANSPORTATION

Public Transit: The **Metropolitan Transit Authority (MTA)** runs the city's subways, buses, and trains. The **subway** system is open 24hr; once inside, a passenger may transfer onto any other train without restrictions. Maps are available in any station. **Buses,** often slower than subways, stop roughly every 2 blocks and run throughout the city. Blue signposts announce bus numbers; glass-walled shelters display schedules and route maps. In the outer boroughs, some buses are run by independent contractors. Be sure to grab a borough bus map. **MetroCards** for subway and buses have a pre-set value (12 rides for the price of 10) and can make free bus and subway transfers within 2hr. The 1-day ($7), 7-day ($24), and 30-day ($76) "Unlimited Rides" MetroCards (as opposed to $2 "Pay-Per-Ride" cards) are good for tourists visiting many sights.

▐ PRACTICAL INFORMATION

Visitor Info: NYC & Company, 810 Seventh Ave. (☎212-484-1222; www.nycvisit.com). Open M-F 8:30am-6pm, Sa-Su 9am-5pm. Also in Grand Central and Penn Station.

GLBT Resources: Callen-Lorde Community Health Center, 356 W. 18th St. (☎212-271-7200), between Eighth and Ninth Ave. Open M 12:30-8pm, Tu and Th-F 9am-4:30pm, W 8:30am-1pm and 3-8pm. **Gay Men's Health Crisis-Geffen Clinic,** 119 W. 24th St. (☎212-807-6655), between Sixth and Seventh Ave. Walk-in counseling M-F 10am-6pm. Open M-F 11am-8pm. **Gay and Lesbian Switchboard,** ☎212-989-0999. Operates M-F 4pm-midnight, Sa noon-5pm.

Hotlines: AIDS Hotline, ☎800-825-5448. Operates daily 9am-9pm. **Crime Victims' Hotline,** ☎212-577-7777. **Sex Crimes Report Line,** ☎212-267-7273. Both 24hr.

Medical Services: Doctors Walk-in Clinic, 55 E. 34th St. (☎212-252-6001, ext. 2), between Park and Madison Ave. Open M-Th 8am-8pm, F 8am-7pm, Sa 9am-3pm, Su 9am-2pm. Last walk-in 1hr. before closing.

Post Office: General Post Office, 421 Eighth Ave. (☎212-330-3002), at W. 32nd St. Open 24hr. General Delivery at 390 Ninth Ave., at W. 30th St. **Postal Code: 10001.**

Area Codes: 212, 347, or 646 (Manhattan); 718 (other 4 boroughs); 917 (cell phones). All New York City calls made within and between all 5 area codes must be dialed using 10-digit dialing.

MID-ATLANTIC

Manhattan
SEE MAP KEY, p. 171

◯ SIGHTS

1 Columbia University
2 Cathedral of St. John the Divine
3 Guggenheim Museum
4 Metropolitan Museum of Art
5 American Museum of Natural History
6 Whitney Museum
7 Frick Collection
8 Lincoln Center for the Performing Arts
9 Columbus Circle
10 Carnegie Hall
11 Museum of Modern Art
12 Rockefeller Center
13 St. Patrick's Cathedral
14 Port Authority Bus Terminal
15 Times Square
16 New York Public Library
17 Grand Central Station
18 United Nations
19 General Post Office
20 Penn Station
21 Empire State Building
22 Union Square
23 Washington Square
24 World Trade Center Site
25 Battery Park

**SEE COLOR INSETS FOR MORE
NEW YORK CITY MAPS**

Manhattan
SEE MAP, p. 170

📍 ACCOMMODATIONS

Big Apple Hostel,	**1**	**B3**
Carlton Arms Hotel,	**2**	**C4**
Central Park Hostel,	**3**	**B1**
Chelsea International		
Hostel,	**4**	**B5**
Chelsea Star Hotel,	**5**	**B4**
Colonial House Inn,	**6**	**B5**
Gershwin Hotel,	**7**	**C4**
Hotel Stanford,	**8**	**C4**
Jazz on the Park,	**9**	**B1**
Larchmont Hotel,	**10**	**C5**
New York International		
Hostel (HI),	**11**	**B1**

🍴 FOOD

@SQC,	**12**	**B2**
Becco,	**13**	**B3**
Big Nick's Burger Joint		
and Pizza Joint,	**14**	**B2**
Chinatown Ice-Cream		
Factory,	**15**	**C6**
Doyers Vietnamese		
Restaurant,	**16**	**C6**

Frank,	**17**	**C5**
Fried Dumpling,	**18**	**C6**
Gray's Papaya,	**19**	**B2**
Il Vegabondo,	**20**	**C3**
Island Burgers and		
Shakes,	**21**	**B3**
Joe's Shanghai,	**22**	**C6**
Kangsuh Korean		
Restaurant,	**23**	**C4**
Katz's Delicatessen,	**24**	**D6**
Kossar's Bialys,	**25**	**D6**
La Mela,	**26**	**C6**
Lips,	**27**	**B5**
Lombardi's Coal		
Oven Pizza,	**28**	**C6**
Mottsu,	**29**	**C6**
Moustache,	**30**	**B5**
Payard,	**31**	**C2**
Pop Burger,	**32**	**B5**
Rice,	**33**	**C6**
Say Cheese!,	**34**	**B4**
Second Avenue		
Delicatessen,	**35**	**C5**
Vermicelli,	**36**	**C2**
Zabar's,	**37**	**B2**

🍸 NIGHTLIFE: BARS

The Big Easy,	**38**	**C1**
Blind Tiger Alehouse,	**39**	**B5**
B'Lo,	**40**	**B5**
Circa Tabac,	**41**	**C6**
Coral Room,	**42**	**B4**
d.b.a.,	**43**	**B5**
Dive 75,	**44**	**B2**
Dorrian's Red Hand,	**45**	**C2**
The Evelyn Lounge,	**46**	**B2**
Joe's Pub,	**47**	**C6**
Local 138,	**48**	**D6**
Lotus Lounge,	**49**	**D6**
Milady's,	**50**	**C6**
The White Horse		
Tavern,	**51**	**B5**

🕺 NIGHTLIFE: DANCE CLUBS

Eugene,	**52**	**C4**
Filter 14,	**53**	**D5**
Go,	**54**	**B5**

🏳️‍🌈 NIGHTLIFE: GLBT

Boiler Room,	**55**	**C5**
g,	**56**	**B5**
Henrietta Hudson,	**57**	**B5**
SBNY,	**58**	**C5**
Stonewall Bar,	**59**	**B5**

🏛 ACCOMMODATIONS

Accommodations are very expensive, with a capital "V" (as in "very," not "expensive"). Travelers can expect a basic dorm bed in a hostel to run around $35, with private rooms running at rates closer to $50. Hotel singles start around $60, with the upper-limit being determined by the highest number you can think of, times three.

HOSTELS

🏨 **Central Park Hostel,** 19 W. 103rd St. (☎212-678-0491; www.centralparkhostel.com), between Manhattan Ave. and Central Park W. Subway: 103rd St./Central Park W. 5-story walk-up brownstone with a nice lounge and spotless guest rooms, all with A/C. Lobby has hand-painted murals and funky tiled floor. Internet access $2 per 20min. Lockers available. Linen and towels included. Key deposit $2. 13-night max. stay. Reservations recommended. Dorms $26-35; private doubles $75-129. Cash only. ❶

🏨 **New York International Hostel (HI),** 891 Amsterdam Ave. (☎212-932-2300; www.hinewyork.org), at 103rd St. Subway: 103 St./Broadway; 103rd St./Central Park W. Housed in a landmark building, this is the largest youth hostel in the US, with 624 beds available for its steady stream of guests. Tight security, spotless bathrooms, and A/C. Kitchens, dining rooms, TV lounges, and garden. Internet access $2 per 20min. Linen and towels included. 14-night max. stay, extendable to 20 nights upon request. Check-in after 4pm. Check-out 11am. Credit card reservations required. May-Oct. 10- to 12-bed dorms $33, members $30; 6- to 8-bed dorms $35/$32; 4-bed dorms $38/$35. Nov.-Apr. dorms $2 less. Several family rooms with queen bed and 2 bunks available. Groups of 10 or more people should ask about private rooms. AmEx/MC/V. ❶

Big Apple Hostel, 119 W. 45th St. (☎212-302-2603; www.bigapplehostel.com), between Sixth and Seventh Ave. Subway: 42nd St./Times Sq. Clean, carpeted rooms (co-ed and single-sex), kitchen, deck with grill, common rooms, and laundry facilities. No elevator. Reception 24hr. Internet access $1 per 8min. Safe ($0.25) at reception. 21-day max. stay. Check-in and check-out 11am. Aug.-Sept. reservations only accepted on website or by fax. 4-bed dorms $35-47; private singles and doubles $92-127. MC/V. ❸

Chelsea International Hostel, 251 W. 20th St. (☎212-647-0010; www.chelseahostel.com), between Seventh and Eighth Ave. Subway: 23rd St./Seventh Ave.; 23rd St./Eighth Ave. Popular destination for European escape artists. Enclosed courtyard, kitchens, laundry, and TV rooms. Internet access $1 per 8min. Key deposit $10. Passport required. Check-in 1pm. Check-out 1pm. Reservations recommended 1-3 months in advance. 4- and 6-person dorms $28; private rooms $70. AmEx/D/MC/V. ❶

Jazz on the Park, 36 W. 106th St./Duke Ellington Blvd. (☎212-932-1600), between Manhattan Ave. and Central Park W. Subway: 103rd St./Central Park W. Brightly colored hostel with fun decor and 255 beds. A/C and lockers. Live jazz in the lounge on weekends. Internet access $1 per 9min. Breakfast, linen, and towels included. Laundry. Check-in and check-out 11am. Reservations essential June-Oct. 10- to 12-bed dorms $27; 6- to 8-bed dorms $29; 4-bed dorms $32; private rooms $75-130. MC/V. ❶

HOTELS AND GUEST HOUSES

▦ **Carlton Arms Hotel,** 160 E. 25th St. (☎212-679-0680; www.carltonarms.com), between Third and Lexington Ave. Subway: 23rd St. The insignia shield for this brutally hip hotel sports the Latin phrase for "There's no mint on your pillow." What it lacks in mints, TV, and phones, it makes up for in wild decor. 54 spacious rooms, all with A/C and sink, some with private bath. Check-in noon. Check-out 11:30am. Reserve for summer 1 month ahead. Rooms $70, with bath $85. Student discount around $10. MC/V. ❸

▦ **Gershwin Hotel,** 7 E. 27th St. (☎212-545-8000; www.gershwinhotel.com), between Madison and Fifth Ave. Subway: 28th St./Broadway; 28th St./Park Ave. S. The hotel's red facade is ornamented with stunning glass. Warhol in the lobby. Private rooms with bath, cable TV, A/C, and phone. Wireless Internet $10 per day, $35 per week. Reception 24hr. Check-in 3pm. Check-out 11am. 6- to 10-bed dorms $40-45; economy rooms $99; standard $109-249; suites available. AmEx/MC/V. ❸

Hotel Stanford, 43 W. 32nd St. (☎212-563-1500 or 800-365-1114; www.hotelstanford.com), between Fifth Ave. and Broadway. Subway: 34th St./Herald Sq. This Herald Sq. hotel's lobby has sparkling lights, a marble floor, and a front desk with great service. Impeccable rooms with A/C, bath, cable TV, phone, hair dryer, safe, and fridge. Breakfast included. Wireless Internet $10 per 24hr. Check-in 3pm. Check-out noon. Reservations recommended. Singles $99-130; doubles $184-254. AmEx/MC/V. ❺

Larchmont Hotel, 27 W. 11th St. (☎212-989-9333; www.larchmonthotel.com), between Fifth and Sixth Ave. Subway: 14th St./Union Sq. Spacious, clean, quiet rooms in a whitewashed brownstone. Rooms come with A/C, closet, desk, TV, wash basin, and continental breakfast. Shared bath. Check-in 3pm. Check-out noon. Reserve 4-6 weeks ahead. Singles $75-105; doubles $99-125; queens $119-135. AmEx/MC/V. ❹

Crystal's Castle Bed & Breakfast, 119 W. 119th St. (☎212-865-5522; www.crystalscastlebandb.com), between Lenox (Sixth) Ave. and Adam Clayton Powell Blvd. Subway: 116th St. or 125th St./Lenox (Sixth) Ave. Family-owned, century-old brownstone. All rooms have private bath and TV, one has A/C. Continental breakfast included. Check-in 10pm. Check-out 1pm. Reserve at least 1 month in advance. 25% deposit. 1-week cancellation notice required. Singles $76; doubles $98. All rooms $456 per week. 5-night discount 20%. Low-season (May-Sept. and Dec. to mid-Jan.) discount. MC/V. ❹

Chelsea Star Hotel, 300 W. 30th St. (☎212-244-7827 or 212-877-827-6969; www.starhotelny.com), at Eighth Ave. Subway: 34th St./Penn Station/Eighth Ave. Madonna reportedly lived here as a struggling artist. Stay in 1 of the 16 themed rooms, or choose a normal "luxe" room. Clean and coveted. All rooms with shared bath (20 rooms, 4 per bath) and A/C. Safe deposit box $5. 14-night max. stay. Reception 24hr. Check-in 1pm. Check-out 11am. Reserve at least 1 month ahead. Dorms $40-45; singles $95-99; doubles $109-119; quads $139; queens $179-199. AmEx/D/MC/V. ❸

Colonial House Inn, 318 W. 22nd St. (☎212-243-9669 or 800-689-3779; www.colonialhouseinn.com), between Eighth and Ninth Ave. Subway: 23rd St. Very comfortable B&B in a classy Chelsea brownstone. All rooms have A/C, cable TV, and phones; some have baths and fireplaces. "Clothing optional" sun deck. Internet access $0.20 per min. Reception 24hr. Check-in 2pm. Check-out noon. Double-bed "economy" room $85-104; queens $104-130, with private bath and fridge $135-150. Call or check the website for the 15% reduced rate Jan. to mid-Mar. MC/V. ❹

◻ FOOD

Nobody needs to go hungry in New York. If you are one of those lucky few with a rumbly in your tumbly and a charge card in your wallet, the city can be your succulent oyster of culinary delight.

CHINATOWN

▨ **Doyers Vietnamese Restaurant,** 11-13 Doyers St. (☎212-693-0725), between Bowery and Pell St. Follow the steps downstairs. Doyers (formerly known as Vietnam) has great Vietnamese cuisine, served quickly by the friendly staff. Appetizers are delicious and often unusual—try the shrimp paste grilled on sugar cane ($6.25). Also excellent are the hot pot soups ($17, serves 4-6), stuffed with simmering meat, vegetables, and seafood. Serves beer. Open daily 11am-9:30pm. AmEx. ❷

▨ **Joe's Shanghai,** 9 Pell St. (☎212-233-8888), between Bowery and Mott St. Also at 13621 37th Ave., in Flushing, Queens. From fried turnip cakes ($3.25) to crispy whole yellowfish ($14), this branch of the Queens legend serves tasty Shanghai specialties. Delicious *xiao long bao* (crab meat and pork dumplings in savory soup; $7). Be prepared for communal tables, long lines on weekends, and prices slightly above a typical Chinatown restaurant. Open daily 11am-11pm. Cash only. ❸

Chinatown Ice-Cream Factory, 65 Bayard St. (☎212-608-4170; www.chinatownicecreamfactory.com), at Elizabeth St. Unbeatable homemade ice cream in exotic flavors like lychee, ginger, red bean, and green tea. 1 scoop $3, 2 $5, 3 $6. Crowded, but the line moves quickly. Open M-Th 11am-11pm, F-Su 11am-11:30pm. ❶

Fried Dumpling, 106 Mosco St. (☎212-693-1060), between Mulberry and Mott St. For half the price of a subway ride ($1), get 5 dumplings or 4 pork buns. Only other items are soy milk ($1) and hot-and-sour soup ($1). Open daily 10am-6pm. Cash only. ❶

LITTLE ITALY AND NOLITA

▨ **Lombardi's Coal Oven Pizza,** 32 Spring St. (☎212-941-7994), between Mott and Mulberry St. Lombardi's credits itself with creating the NY-style thin-crust, coal-oven pizza. Their large pie ($15.50) feeds 2. Toppings $3 for 1, $5 for 2, $6 for 3. Reservations accepted for groups of 6 or more. Try to visit on off-peak hours: the line is invariably out the door. Open M-Th 11:30am-11pm, F-Sa 11:30am-midnight, Su 11:30am-10pm. Cash only. ❸

■ **Rice,** 227 Mott St. (☎212-226-5775; www.riceny.com), between Prince and Spring St. Basics—basmati, brown, sticky, Japanese, and Thai black—are all here. So are exotic species like Bhutanese red and green rice. Sauces range from mango chutney to aleppo yogurt ($1). Ratatouille, coconut curry, or chicken satay are among other enticing toppings ($7-10). Open daily noon-midnight. Cash only. ❷

La Mela, 167 Mulberry St. (☎212-431-9493), between Broome and Grand St. Raucous dining, chummy staff. Generous portions served family-style. 4-course dinners $32 per person, 3-course $22; min. 2 people. 1.5L house wine $28. Huge dessert concoction (ice cream, cake, coconut, glazed bananas) $7 per person. Pasta $7-10. Family-style only after 6pm. Open M-Th and Su noon-2am, F-Sa noon-3am. AmEx/MC/V. ❷

Mottsu, 285 Mott St. (☎212-343-8017), between E. Houston and Spring St. One of Nolita's few sushi spots. Tuna roll $6. Eel-avocado roll $6.50. Open M-Th 12:30-3pm and 5:30-10:30pm, F 12:30-3pm and 5-11:30pm, Sa 5-11:30pm, Su 5-10pm. ❸

LOWER EAST SIDE

Katz's Delicatessen, 205 E. Houston St. (☎212-254-2246, between Orchard and Ludlow St. Subway: Lower East Side/Second Ave. An LES institution since 1888. Orgasmic food (as Meg Ryan confirmed in *When Harry Met Sally*); you pay extra for Katz's fame. Knishes and franks $3. Reuben, knoblewurst, and corned beef sandwiches around $10. Open M-Tu and Su 8am-10pm, W-Th 8am-11pm, F-Sa 8am-3am. ❸

Kossar's Bialys, 367 Grand St. (☎212-473-4810), between Essex and Norfolk St. Subway: Delancey St. New York City's best bialy emporium. What's a bialy? Find out here. You can get 2 onion bialys for a buck, or 13 for $6. Bagels also served. Open all night Sa. Open M-Th 6am-8pm, F 6am-5pm, Sa 9pm to Su 8pm. ❶

GREENWICH VILLAGE

Lips, 2 Bank St. (☎212-675-7710; www.lipsnyc.com), at Greenwich Ave. Subway: 14th St./Eighth Ave.; 14th St./Seventh Ave. Italian-Continental cuisine and impromptu "performances" from a high-heeled staff in a room decked out with lips. Try the RuPaul (grilled chicken with mashed potatoes and spinach; $15). Entrees $14-22. Reservations recommended. Open M-Th 5:30-midnight, F-Sa 5:30pm-1:30am, Su 5:30pm-11pm; Su brunch 11:30am-4pm. ❹

Moustache, 90 Bedford St. (☎212-229-2220), between Barrow and Grove St. Subway: Christopher St. Sumptuous Middle-Eastern fare served on copper tabletops. Inhale the enticing smell of fresh pita. Try the succulent leg of lambwich ($8). Lentil soup $4. Salads $4.50-10. Falafel sandwich $6. Open daily noon-11pm. ❷

EAST VILLAGE

■ **Second Avenue Delicatessen,** 156 Second Ave. (☎212-677-0606), at 10th St. Subway: Astor Pl. The definitive New York deli. The Lebewohl family has proudly maintained this strictly kosher joint since 1954. The chopped liver ($8.75), *kasha varnishkes* ($6.25), and mushroom barley ($4.25) are among the best in the city, but you can't go wrong with a classic pastrami or corned beef sandwich (on rye, of course; $8-11). Challah french toast $11. Open M-Sa 10am-8:30pm, Su 11am-7pm. ❸

Frank, 88 Second Ave. (☎212-420-1232), between E. Fifth and Sixth St. Subway: Astor Pl. At this Italian bistro, the menu, like the restaurant, is happily cramped—there's often a wait. Try the roasted rosemary chicken with mashed potatoes, gravy, olives and slow cooked tomatoes ($12), the *prosciutto di parma* sandwich ($8), or Uncle Tony's gnocchi ($10). Delivery available. Open M-Th 10:30am-4pm and 5pm-1am, F-Sa 10:30am-4pm and 5pm-2am, Su 10:30am-midnight. Cash only. ❸

CHELSEA

■ **Kangsuh Korean Restaurant,** 1250 Broadway (☎212-564-6845), on 32nd St. between Fifth and Sixth Ave. Subway: Herald Sq. Homestyle Korean cooking served family-style with efficient service in a clean, 2-story restaurant. The delectable *hwe dup bap* (spicy sashimi salad with rice; $17) and the stellar *kalbi* barbecue ($21) draw hordes of hungry Koreans. Entrees $10-18. Open 24hr. ❹

Pop Burger, 58-60 Ninth Ave. (☎212-414-8686), between 14th and 15th St. Subway: 14th St./Seventh Ave; 14th St. The fast-food front counter and wait-service back lounge cater to both those who pop "mini" burgers (2 for $5) and those who eat filet mignon ($25). The food is acclaimed, and the decor stainless enough to be a little out of this world. Chocolate, strawberry, and vanilla shakes $3.75. Beer $5. Open daily 11am-1am. Lounge open M-Tu and Su 5pm-2am, W-Sa 5pm-4am. ❸

THEATER DISTRICT

■ **Becco,** 355 W 46th St. (☎212-397-7597; www.becconyc.com), between Eighth and Ninth Ave. Great Italian food for a moderate splurge. 70 wines priced at $20 per bottle. $17 prix-fixe lunch (dinner $22) gets you a gourmet antipasto platter or caesar salad, plus unlimited servings of the 3 pastas of the day. Dinner $16 food min. per person, lunch $14. Try the mesclun salad with Tuscan beans and ripe tomatoes, tossed with an aged Chianti vinaigrette ($6), or the grilled Atlantic salmon with poached potatoes, green beans, and grain mustard ($23). Open daily noon-3pm and 5pm-midnight. ❹

Island Burgers and Shakes, 766 Ninth Ave. (☎212-307-7934; http://island.citysearch.com), between 51st and 52nd St. Burgers so good that Island sells more than 150 lb. of meat per day. More than 50 burgers ($5-8) on the menu; you can also craft your own. Sadly, no fries. Open daily noon-10:30pm, F until 11pm. Cash only. ❷

Say Cheese!, 649 Ninth Ave. (☎212-265-8840), between 45th and 46th St. This tiny soup-and-sandwich joint specializes in any and all permutations of grilled cheese ($4.25-7.50). The Chokes on Tuna (tuna fish plus artichokes, fresh oregano, roasted garlic, and American cheese on pizza bianca; $7) is a must. Open M-F noon-9pm, Sa-Su 10am-9pm. ❷

UPPER EAST SIDE

■ **Payard,** 1032 Lexington Ave. (☎212-717-5252; www.payard.com), between 73rd and 74th St. Subway: 77th St. With prices as rich as the pastries (which is saying something), this decadent Parisian-style patisserie/bistro serves some of the most sinful desserts ($5.25-7) in town. Try "The Louvre," a concoction of chocolate and hazelnut mousse with a twist of hazelnut *dacquiose* ($6). Gourmet sandwiches and savory tarts $12-14. Try the potato *tourte* ($13), with goat's milk brie, mushrooms, caramelized onions, and walnuts. Open M-Th noon-10:30pm, F-Sa noon-11pm. ❹

Il Vagabondo, 351 E. 62nd St. (☎212-832-9221), between First and Second Ave. Subway: 59th St. An Upper East Side staple since 1971. You won't find many tourists here, but the regulars have been flocking to this Italian spot for decades. Don't miss the veal shank *osso bucco* ($21). Lunch entrees $8-29, dinner $18-39. Open daily noon-11pm. ❺

Vermicelli, 1492 Second Ave. (☎212-288-8868), between 77th and 78th St. Subway: 77th St. Vietnamese spring rolls with warm vermicelli, coriander, and roasted peanuts $8. Their $6 box lunches are a popular eat-on-the-go option, served with vegetables, soup, salad, and steamed rice. Try the spicy lemongrass chicken with peppers. Open daily 11:30am-10:45pm. ❷

UPPER WEST SIDE

🏮 **Big Nick's Burger Joint and Pizza Joint,** 2175 Broadway (☎212-362-9238 or 724-2010), at 77th St. Subway: 79th St. Telephone-book-like menu (27 pages thick!). Burgers and pizza are obvious choices, but you can also get all-day breakfast and vegan and vegetarian options. Wrestle with a plate-sized burger ($5-7.50), a full homestyle Italian dinner ($9-15), or crispy sweet potato fries ($2.75). Free delivery. Open 24hr. Second location 70 W. 71st St. (☎212-799-4444), at Columbus Ave. ❷

🏮 **Zabar's,** 2245 Broadway (☎212-787-2000), between 80th and 81st St. Subway: 179th St. All the imported delicacies you need for a 4-star meal at home. In a pinch, arrive with a toothpick and make a meal of the legendary free samples. On weekend mornings, masses of hungry New Yorkers stand in line for bagels and coffee. Open M-F 8am-7:30pm, Sa 8am-8pm, Su 9am-6pm; cafe open M-Sa 7:30am-7pm, Su 8am-6pm. ❸

Gray's Papaya, 2090 Broadway (☎212-799-0243), at 72nd St. Subway: 72nd St. A local, but landmark, chain. Lively takeout with amazing deals on hot dogs. The "recession special" is 2 franks and 1 fruit drink (banana daiquiri, pineapple, piña colada, papaya) for $2.75. Also at 539 Eighth Ave. and 402 Sixth Ave. Open 24hr. ❶

@SQC, 270 Columbus Ave. (☎212-579-0100), between 72nd and 73rd St. Subway: 72nd St. Plush pillows, white candles, and large orange-tinted windows set the scene for American food with French and Asian influences. If your wallet doesn't feel up to dinner here (average entree $20-26), breakfast is the perfect way to bask in the glow. Excellent pastries (apple-cinnamon brioche $2.50). Open M-Th 8am-11pm, F 8am-midnight, Sa 9am-midnight, Su 9am-11pm. ❹

HARLEM AND MORNINGSIDE HEIGHTS

🏮 **Amir's Falafel,** 2911A Broadway (☎212-749-7500), between 113th and 114th St. Subway: 110th St.; 116th St. Small and simple, with Middle Eastern staples like shwarma and *baba ghanouj*. Substantial vegetarian options (platters $5.50). Falafel $3.50. Open daily 11am-11pm. Free delivery within Morningside Heights. Cash only. ❶

🏮 **Amy Ruth's,** 113 W. 116th St. (☎212-280-8779; www.amyruthsrestaurant.com), between Adam Clayton Powell Blvd. and Lenox (Sixth) Ave. Subway: 116th St. Named in honor of the owner's grandmother, this intimate restaurant serves cuisine straight from a southern kitchen. Try the "Rev. Calvin O. Butts III" (chicken wings and waffles; $7.50) or the "Foxy Brown" (pan-seared jumbo shrimp; $17). Open M-Th 7:30am-11pm, F 7:30am to Su 11pm. Free delivery. ❸

Hispaniola, 839 W 181st St. (☎212-740-5222; www.hispaniolarestaurant.com), at Cabrini Blvd. Subway: 181st St./Ft. Washington Ave. Delectable Dominican-Asian fusion cuisine. Innovative sushi includes tempura coconut shrimp pineapple rolls ($10) and tilapia asparagus mesclun rolls ($10). The $14 "conto boxes" come with coconut shrimp and salad, plus grilled salmon, miso butterfish, fried chicken, or steak. Happy hour M-F 4-8pm. Open M-Sa 11am-4pm and 5:30pm-midnight; bar open until 2am. ❹

BROOKLYN

🏮 **Planet Thailand,** 115 Berry St. (☎718-599-5758), between N. 7th and 8th St. Subway: Bedford Ave. High-ceilinged space that's too trendy for a sign. Expansive menu includes Thai beef and chicken curries ($8), *pad thai* ($7), hibachi table fare ($9-16), and Japanese items (sushi dinner $11). If you go on a weekend night, be prepared for a wait: Planet Thailand takes no reservations, and people from across the city flock here. DJ nightly 9pm. Open M-Th and Su 11:30am-1am, F-Sa 11:30am-2am. Cash only. ❸

DuMont Restaurant, 432 Union Ave. (☎718-486-7717), at Devoe St. Subway: Lorimer St. Excellent service, a solid wine list, and garden dining in warm weather. Feels like a French speakeasy—if France had ever endured prohibition. A mere handful of plates remain on the menu day to day, of which the burger and the DuMac and Cheese (both $8) are signature pieces. Specials, like the pancetta-wrapped monkfish ($16), use only the freshest ingredients. Brunch Sa-Su. Open daily 11am-3pm and 6-11pm. ❹

Jacques Torres Chocolate, 66 Water St. (☎718-875-9772), between Dock and Main St. Subway: High St.; York St. Watch chefs make chocolate-covered almonds ($5 per ¼ lb.), chocolate croissants ($1.50), and chocolate bars ($4). Truffles take center stage, coming in varieties such as fresh-squeezed lemon, cappuccino, and Love Potion #9 ($0.80). Hot chocolate $2.50. Mocha cappuccino $3. Open M-Sa 9am-7pm. ❶

QUEENS

▨ **Flushing Noodle,** 135-42 Roosevelt Ave. (☎718-353-1166). Subway: Flushing/Main St. One of Flushing's finest Chinese noodle shops. Try the spare ribs ($8) and noodles ($4-5). Lunch specials ($5; 11am-3:30pm) give you 37 entree choices. Limited seating, and it's always packed. Takeout available. Open daily 9am-10pm. ❶

Zygos Taverna, 22-55 31st St. (☎718-728-7070). Subway: Broadway. Greek restaurant serves thinly sliced leg of lamb with lemon potatoes ($11), grilled baby octopus ($10), and *moussaka* ($10). Spreads ($4.50) are served with hot pita bread. Open daily 11am-midnight. Free delivery in Astoria, $10 min. ❷

Bohemian Hall and Beer Garden, 29-19 24th Ave. (☎718-274-4925; www.bohemian-hall.com). Subway: 30th Ave. Operated by the Bohemian Citizens' Benevolent Society, this Czech restaurant and 900-seat outdoor beer garden is packed every night. Enjoy Bohemian staples like fried cheese with french fries ($8) and crunchy pork schnitzel ($10.50). Open M-F 5pm-3am, Sa-Su noon-3am. ❸

◎ SIGHTS

THE STATUE OF LIBERTY AND ELLIS ISLAND

The Statue of Liberty, long a symbol of hope for immigrants, stands at the entrance to New York Harbor. In 1886, the French government presented Frederic-Auguste Bartholdi's sculpture to the US as a sign of goodwill. The statue's crown and torch were closed in September 2001; views are limited to the 150-ft. concrete pedestal. Ellis Island, accessible by the same ferry, was the processing point for millions of immigrants from 1897 to 1938. The museum chronicles immigrant life in the New World. (*Subway: 4, 5 to Bowling Green; R, W to Whitehall St.; 1, 9 to South Ferry. ☎212-363-3200; www.nps.gov/stli. Ferries leave for Liberty Island from the piers at Battery Park every 30min. M-F 9:15am-3:30pm, Sa-Su 9am-4pm. Ferry information ☎212-269-5755; www.statueof-libertyferry.com. Tickets for ferry with access to Liberty Island and Ellis Island $11.50, seniors $9.50, ages 4-12 $4.50, under 4 free.*)

FINANCIAL DISTRICT AND CIVIC CENTER

The southern tip of Manhattan is a financial powerhouse. The physical proof is in the skyline: the Wall St. area, less than ½ mi. long, has one of the highest concentrations of skyscrapers in the world. Crooked streets retain the city's original Dutch layout; lower Manhattan was the first part of the island to be settled. (*Subway: 1, 9 to Wall St./William St.; 4, 5 to Bowling Green, Wall St./Broadway; N, R, W to Rector St., Whitehall St.; 1, 2, 4, 5, A, C, J, M, Z to Fulton St./Broadway/Nassau St.; J, M, Z to Broad St.*)

FINANCIAL DISTRICT. Once the northern border of the New Amsterdam settlement, Wall St. is named for the wall built in 1653 to shield the Dutch colony from British invasion. By the early 19th century, the area was the financial capital of the US. On the southwest corner of Wall and Broad St. stands the **New York Stock Exchange.** This 1903 temple to capitalism sees billions of dollars change hands daily. The exchange, founded in 1792 at 68 Wall St., is now off-limits to tourists. Around the corner, at the end of Wall St., stands the seemingly ancient **Trinity Church,** with its delicately crafted steeple. *(74 Trinity Place. ☎ 212-602-0800.)* Peter Minuit purchased Manhattan for the equivalent of $24 at **Bowling Green,** at the intersection of Battery Pl., Broadway, and Whitehall St. The Beaux Arts **US Custom House** overlooks the park. *(1 Bowling Green St.)*

WORLD TRADE CENTER MEMORIAL SITE (GROUND ZERO). The site where the World Trade Center once stood is a sobering one. The poignancy of the vast empty landscape can only really be understood in person. Plans have finally been solidified for the new **Freedom Tower,** which, when completed in 2008, will be the world's tallest building, at 2000 ft. On August 2, 2004, construction began on a 945-ft.-tall skyscraper, which will also open in 2008. The site will also hold a subway terminal and memorials to the victims of the 9/11 attacks.

CIVIC CENTER. The city's center of government is located north of its financial district. The New York City mayor's office is in **City Hall;** around it are courthouses, civic buildings, and federal buildings. The building's interior is closed indefinitely to the public. *(Broadway at Murray St., off Park Row.)* The **Woolworth Building,** a 1913 Neo-Gothic skyscraper and "Cathedral of Commerce" built for $15.5 million to house F.W. Woolworth's five-and-dime store empire, looms south of City Hall. *(233 Broadway, between Barclay St. and Park Pl. Closed to the public.)* A block and a half south on Broadway lies **St. Paul's Chapel,** Manhattan's oldest public building in continuous use. George Washington prayed here on his inauguration day. *(Between Vesey and Fulton St. ☎ 212-602-0747. Open M-F 9am-3pm, Su 7am-3pm. Su mass 8am.)*

SOUTH STREET SEAPORT. The shipping industry thrived at the South Street Seaport for most of the 19th century, when New York City was the most important port city in the US. During the 20th century, bars, brothels, and crime flourished. Now a 12-block "museum without walls," the seaport displays old schooners, sailboats, and houses. *(Between FDR Dr. and Water St., and between Beekman and John St. Subway: 2, 3, 4, 5, A, C, J, M, Z to Fulton St./Broadway/Nassau St. Visitors center: 12 Fulton St. ☎ 212-748-8600; www.southstseaport.org. Open daily 10am-5pm. Admission to ships, shops, and tours $8; students and seniors $6; under 12 free. Walking around the museum is free.)* The **Fulton Fish Market,** the largest fresh-fish market in the country, is on South St., on the other side of the overpass. *(☎ 212-748-8786. Market opens at 4am. Market tours May-Oct. 1st and 3rd W of each month, 6am. $12. Reservations required, call 1 week in advance.)*

CHINATOWN AND LITTLE ITALY

Mott and **Pell Street,** unofficial centers of Chinatown, brim with restaurants and commercial activity. Chinese-style baby jackets, bamboo hats, and miniature Buddhas crowd the storefronts. **Canal Street** offers tons of low-priced, creatively labeled merchandise (those are *not* Rolexes). **Mulberry Street** remains the heart of Little Italy, which has been largely taken over by Chinatown in recent decades. *(Subway: A, C, E to Canal St./Sixth Ave.; J, M, Z to Canal St./Centre St.; N, Q, R, W to Canal St./Broadway; 6 to Canal St./Lafayette St.; F to E Broadway; B, D, F, V to Broadway/Lafayette St.)*

LOWER EAST SIDE

The Lower East Side was once the most densely settled area in New York City. The Irish came in the mid-1800s, Eastern Europeans in the 50 years preceding WWI, African-Americans and Puerto Ricans post-WWII, and Latin Americans and Asians in the 1980s and 90s. Main thoroughfares like E. Broadway reflect the area's multicultural roots. Orchard St., a historic shopping area that fills up on Sundays, still has traces of the Jewish ghetto. *(Subway: F, V to Lower East Side/Second Ave.; F to E Broadway; F, J, M, Z to Delancey St./Essex St.)* **The Lower East Side Visitors Center** is a source of maps and brochures, and also organizes a free area shopping tour. *(261 Broome St., between Orchard and Allen St. ☎ 212-226-9010. Open daily 10am-4pm.)* At the **Lower East Side Tenement Museum**, tours lead through three meticulously restored apartments of immigrant families. *(90 Orchard St. ☎ 212-431-0233. Call for info on tours of tenements and neighborhood. $12, students and seniors $10.)* The **Eldridge Street Synagogue** *(12 Eldridge St. ☎ 212-219-0888)* and **Congregation Anshe Chesed** *(172-176 Norfolk St., at Stanton St. ☎ 212-865-0600)* are two splendid old synagogues.

SOHO AND TRIBECA

The architecture in the area **South of Houston**—with Canal St. on the south, Broadway on the west, and Crosby St. on the east—is American Industrial, notable for its cast-iron facades. SoHo is filled with artists and galleries (see **Galleries,** p. 222), chic boutiques, and expensive shopping. *(Subway: C, E to Spring St./Ave. of the Americas (Sixth Ave.); 6 to Spring St./Lafayette St.; N, R, W to Prince St.; 1, 9 to W Houston St.; B, D, F, V to Broadway/Lafayette St.)* TriBeCa, or **Triangle Below Canal Street,** contains trendy lofts, restaurants, bars, and galleries—without the upscale airs. Admire the cast-iron edifices lining White St., Thomas St., and Broadway, the Federal-style buildings on Harrison St., and the shops, galleries, and bars on Church and Reade St. *(Subway: 1, 9 to Canal St./Varick St.; A, C, E to Canal St./Ave. of the Americas (Sixth Ave.); 1, 9 to Franklin St.; 1, 2, 3, 9 to Chambers St./W Broadway; A, C to Chambers St./Church St.)*

GREENWICH VILLAGE

Greenwich Village has layered grime, activism, and artistry atop a tangle of wandering streets. The area was once covered in farms and hills. In the mid-19th century, it developed into a high-society playground that fostered literary creativity. Henry James captured the Village's spirit in his 1880 novel, *Washington Square*. The last 40 years have brought the Beat movement, the gay community around Christopher St., and the punk scene. Gentrification in the 1980s and 90s made the Village a fashionable settlement for wealthier New Yorkers with more spunk than their uptown counterparts. *(Subway: W 4th St.; 14th St./Eighth Ave.; 14th St./Seventh Ave.; 14th St./Ave. of the Americas (Sixth Ave.); Eighth Ave., Ave. of the Americas (Sixth Ave.); 14th St./Union Sq.; Houston St., Christopher St.; 8th St./NYU; Sixth Ave., Eighth Ave.; Bleecker St.)*

WASHINGTON SQUARE. Washington Square Park has a rich history. On the north side of the park is **The Row,** a stretch of 1830s brick residences that were once populated by writers, dandies, and professionals. At the north end of the park stands the **Washing-**

ton Memorial Arch, built in 1889 to commemorate the centennial of George Washington's inauguration. **New York University,** the country's largest private university, has some of the Village's least appealing contemporary architecture. On the park's southeast side, where Washington Sq. S meets LaGuardia Pl., NYU's **Loeb Student Center** sports pieces of scrap metal representing birds in flight.

WEST VILLAGE. The area of Greenwich Village west of 6th Ave. boasts eclectic summer street life and excellent nightlife. A visible gay community thrives around **Sheridan Square,** at the intersection of Seventh Ave., W. 4th St., and Christopher St. The 1969 Stonewall Riot, arguably the beginning of the modern gay rights movement, started here. The neighborhood is a magnet for literary pilgrimages. **Chumley's,** a former speakeasy, was a hangout for such authors as Ernest Hemingway and John Dos Passos. *(86 Bedford St., between Grove and Barrow St. ☎212-675-4449. Open M-F 4pm for drinks, 5pm for dinner, Sa-Su noon for brunch, 5pm for dinner.)* Off 10th St. and Sixth Ave., you'll see an iron gate and street sign marking **Patchin Place.** Theodore Dreiser, e. e. cummings, and Djuna Barnes lived in the 145-year-old buildings that line this path. The Village's narrowest building, **75½ Bedford Street,** only 9½ ft. in width, housed writer Edna St. Vincent Millay in the 1920s, when she founded the nearby **Cherry Lane Theater,** 38 Commerce St. Actors Lionel Barrymore and Cary Grant also appreciated the cramped quarters.

EAST VILLAGE

The East Village—north of Houston St., east of Broadway, and south of 14th St.—was carved out of the Bowery and the Lower East Side in the early 1960s, when artists and writers moved here to escape high rents in Greenwich Village. Today the East Village's wide-ranging population includes punks, hippies, ravers, rastas, guppies, goths, and beatniks. **St. Mark's Place** is full of tiny ethnic eateries, street-level shops, sidewalk vendors, and tattoo shops. Simmering with street life, **Astor Place,** at the intersection of Lafayette, E. 8th St., and Fourth Ave., is distinguished by a large black cube balanced on its corner. The tensions of gentrification have forged the East Village into one of the city's most politicized neighborhoods. *(Subway: 6 to Astor Pl., Bleecker St.; L to First Ave., Third Ave.; F, V to Lower East Side/Second Ave.)*

LOWER MIDTOWN

UNION SQUARE. At the intersection of Fourth Ave. and Broadway, Union Square and the surrounding area sizzled with high society before the Civil War. Today, the park hosts the **Union Square Greenmarket,** a pleasant farmers market. *(Between Broadway and Park Ave. S, between 14th and 17th St. Subway: 4, 5, 6, L, N, Q, R, W to 14th St./Union Sq. Greenmarket open M, W, F-Sa 8am-6pm.)* Originally named the Fuller Building, the photogenic **Flatiron Building** was nicknamed after its dramatic wedge shape, imposed by the intersection of Broadway, Fifth Ave., 22nd St., and 23rd St.

CHELSEA. Home to fashionable clubs, bars, and restaurants, Chelsea (west of Fifth Ave., between 14th and 30th St.) boasts a large GLBT community, a growing artsy-yuppie population, and **art galleries** (p. 188) fleeing high SoHo rents. *(Subway: 1, 2, 3, 9 to 14th St./Seventh Ave.; A, C, E, L to 14th St./Eighth Ave.; C, E to 23rd St./Eighth Ave.; 1, 9 to 23rd St., 28th St./Seventh Ave.)* **Hotel Chelsea,** between Seventh and Eighth Ave., has pampered such artists as Sid Vicious of the Sex Pistols. Countless writers have sought inspiration here, including Vladimir Nabokov and Dylan Thomas. *(222 W. 23rd St., between Seventh and Eighth Ave. ☎212-243-3700.)*

HERALD SQUARE AREA. Herald Square is located between 34th and 35th St., between Broadway and Sixth Ave. The area is a center for shopping. *(Subway: B, D, F, N, Q, R, V, W to 34th St./Herald Sq.)* The **Empire State Building,** now the city's tallest building, dominates postcards, movies, and the city's skyline. The limestone-and-granite structure stretches 1454 ft. into the sky, and its 73 elevators run through 2 mi. of shafts. The nighttime view from the top is spectacular. *(350 Fifth Ave., at 34th St. Observatory:* ☎ *212-736-3100. Open daily 9:30am-midnight; last elevator up at 11:30pm. $12, seniors $11, under 12 $7. Skyride:* ☎ *212-279-9777. Open daily 10am-10pm. $16, ages 12-17 $15, seniors and ages 4-11 $13.)* East on 34th St. stands **Macy's.** This Goliath of department stores sponsors the **Macy's Thanksgiving Day Parade,** a NYC tradition buoyed by 10-story Snoopys, marching bands, and floats. *(Between 7th Ave. and Broadway, in Herald Sq.)* The **Garment District,** surrounding Macy's but selling cheaper clothing, purportedly contained the world's highest concentration of apparel workers during the 1930s. *(Between Broadway and Eighth Ave.)*

MIDTOWN

East of Eighth Ave., from about 42nd St. to 59th St., lie Midtown's mammoth office buildings, posh hotels, and high-brow stores. *(Subway: 4, 5, 6, 7, S to 42nd St./Grand Central; B, D, F, V to 42nd St./Ave. of the Americas (Sixth Ave.); 7 to Fifth Ave./42nd St.; E, V to Fifth Ave./53rd St.; N, R, W to Fifth Ave./59th St.; 1, 2, 3, 7, 9, N, Q, R, S, W to 42nd St./Times Square; A, C, E to 42nd St./Port Authority; 7, B, D, F, V to 42nd St./Bryant Park.)*

FIFTH AVENUE. A monumental research library in the style of a classical temple, the main branch of the **New York Public Library,** between 40th and 42nd St., contains the world's seventh-largest research library and an immense reading room. *(42nd St. and Fifth Ave.* ☎ *212-869-8089.)* Behind the library, **Bryant Park** features free summertime cultural events, like classic film screenings and live comedy. *(*☎ *212-484-1222 for events schedule. Open daily 7am-9pm.)* Designed by James Renwick, the twin spires of **St. Patrick's Cathedral** stretch 330 ft. into the air, making it the largest Catholic cathedral in the US. *(51st St.* ☎ *212-753-2261.)* The **Plaza Hotel,** on 59th St., at the southeast corner of Central Park, was constructed in 1907 at an astronomical cost. Its 18-story, 800-room French Renaissance interior flaunts five marble staircases, ludicrously named suites, and a two-story Grand Ballroom.

ROCKEFELLER CENTER. The main entrance to Rockefeller Center is on Fifth Ave. between 49th and 50th St. **The Channel Gardens,** so named because they sit between the **Maison Française** on the left and the **British Empire Building** on the right, usher pedestrians toward **Tower Plaza.** This sunken space, topped by the gold-leafed statue of Prometheus, is surrounded by the flags of over 100 countries. During spring and summer an **ice-skating rink** lies dormant beneath an overpriced cafe. The rink, which is better for people-watching than for skating, reopens in winter in time for the **annual Christmas tree lighting,** one of New York City's greatest traditions. **Tours of Rockefeller Center** are available through NBC. *(Departs every hr. from the GE Building. M-Sa 10am-5pm, Su 10am-4pm. No children under 6. $10, ages 6-16 $8.)*

Behind Tower Plaza is the **General Electric Building,** a 70-story skyscraper. **NBC,** which makes its home here, offers an hour-long tour that traces the history of the network, from its first radio broadcast in 1926, through the heyday of TV programming in the 1950s and 60s, to today's sitcoms. The tour leads visitors through six studios, including the infamous 8H studio, now the home of *Saturday Night Live. (Departs every 15min. from the NBC Experience Store in the GE Building. M-Sa 8:30am-5:30pm, Su 9:30am-4:30pm. No children under 6. $18, seniors and ages 6-16 $15.)* A block north is **Radio City Music Hall.** Narrowly escaping demolition in 1979, this Art Deco landmark received a complete interior restoration shortly thereafter. Radio City's main attraction is the Rockettes, a high-stepping, long-legged troupe of dancers. Tours of the Music Hall take visitors through The Great Stage and various rehearsal halls. *(50th St. at Sixth Ave.* ☎ *212-247-4777. Departs every 30min. daily 11am-3pm. $17, seniors $14, under 12 $10.)*

MID-ATLANTIC

PARK AVENUE. A luxurious boulevard with greenery running down its center, **Park Avenue,** between 45th and 59th St., is lined with office buildings and hotels. Completed in 1913, the **Grand Central Terminal** has a richly classical main facade on 42nd St., topped by a beautiful sculpture of Mercury, Roman god of transportation. An info booth sits in the middle of the commuter-filled Concourse. *(Between 42nd and 45th St.)* Several blocks uptown is the *crème de la crème* of Park Avenue hotels, the **Waldorf-Astoria.** *(Between 49th and 50th St.)* The **Seagram Building,** Ludwig Mies Van der Rohe's dark, gracious modern monument, stands a few blocks uptown. *(375 Park Ave., between 52nd and 53rd St.)*

UNITED NATIONS AREA. The **United Nations,** a "center for harmonizing the actions of nations" founded in 1945 in the aftermath of WWII, is located in international territory along what would be First Ave. The UN complex consists of the Secretariat Building (the skyscraper), the General Assembly Building, the Hammarskjöld Library, and the Conference Building. The only way into the General Assembly Building is by guided tour. *(First Ave., between 42nd and 48th St. ☎ 212-963-4475. 1hr. tours depart from the UN visitors' entrance at First Ave. and 46th St. Held every 15min. in 20 languages. Mar.-Dec. M-F 9:15am-4:45pm, Sa-Su 9:30am-4:45pm; Jan.-Feb. M-F only. $11, ages 62+ $8, students $7, ages 5-14 $6.)* At the **Chrysler Building,** a spire influenced by radiator grille design tops this Art Deco palace. *(On 42nd St. and Lexington Ave.)*

TIMES SQUARE AND THE THEATER DISTRICT. Times Square, at the intersection of 42nd St., Seventh Ave., and Broadway, once gave New York City its reputation for strip clubs and filth. Today, the smut has been replaced by 30 ft. tall billboards, Disney musicals, and nearly 40 million tourists per year. For info on rush ticketing or anything else, stop by the **Times Square Visitors Center,** 1560 Broadway, at W. 46th St. *(☎ 212-869-1890; www.timesquarebid.com. Open daily 8am-8pm.)*

57TH STREET AND CENTRAL PARK SOUTH. Luxury hotels, including the **Essex House,** the **St. Moritz,** and the **Plaza,** overlook Central Park from their perch on Central Park S, between Fifth and Eighth Ave., where 59th St. should be. Amid 57th St.'s galleries and stores, New York City's musical center is **Carnegie Hall** (p. 192). A $60 million restoration has returned the 1891 building to its earlier splendor. *(881 Seventh Ave., at W. 57th St. ☎ 212-247-7800; www.carnegiehall.org. Tours M-F 11:30am, 2, 3pm. 1hr. Purchase tickets at box office on tour days. $6, students and seniors $5, under 12 $3.)*

CENTRAL PARK

> Central Park is fairly safe during the day, but less so at night. Don't be afraid to go to events in the Park at night, but take large paths and go with someone. Do not wander the darker paths at night, especially if you are a woman. In an **emergency,** use one of the call-boxes located throughout the park. **24hr. Police Line** ☎ 570-4820.

Central Park was founded in the mid-19th century when wealthy New Yorkers advocated the creation of a park in the style of the public grounds of Europe. Frederick Law Olmsted and Calvert Vaux designed the park in 1858; their Greensward plan took 15 years and 20,000 workers to implement. Expansive fields like the **Sheep Meadow,** from 66th to 69th St., and the **Great Lawn,** from 80th to 85th St., complement developed spaces such as the **Mall,** between 66th and 71st St., the **Shakespeare Garden,** at 80th St., and the **Imagine Mosaic,** commemorating the music of John Lennon, on the western side of the park at 72nd St. Don't miss free summer shows at **Central Park Summerstage** and **Shakespeare in Central Park.** (Free park maps at Belvedere Castle, located mid-park at 79th St.; the Charles A. Dana Discovery Center, at 110th St. near 5th Ave.; the North Meadow Recreation Center, mid-park at 97th St.; and the Dairy, mid-park near 65th St.)

UPPER EAST SIDE

Since the late 19th and early 20th centuries, when some of New York City's wealthiest citizens built elaborate mansions along **Fifth Avenue,** the Upper East Side has been home to the city's richest residents. Today, some of these mansions have been turned into museums, such as the Frick Collection and the Cooper-Hewitt Museum. They are just two of the world-famous museums that line **Museum Mile,** from 82nd to 104th St. on Fifth Ave. (p. 186). **Park Avenue** from 59th to 96th St. is lined with dignified apartment buildings. Lexington and Third Ave. are commercial, but as you go east, the neighborhood becomes more and more residential. *(Subway: N, R, W to Fifth Ave./59th St.; 4, 5, 6, N, R, W to 59th St./Lexington Ave.; F to Lexington Ave./63rd St.; 6 to 68th St., 77th St., 96th St.; 4, 5, 6 to 86th St./Lexington Ave.)*

UPPER WEST SIDE

While Central Park W and Riverside Dr. flank the Upper West Side with residential quietude, Columbus Ave., Amsterdam Ave., and Broadway buzz with action. Organic fruit and progressive politics dominate the area between 59th and 110th St., west of Central Park. *(Subway: 1, 9, A, B, C, D to 59th St./Columbus Circle; 1, 9 to 66th St., 79th St., 86th St./Broadway; 1, 2, 3, 9 to 72nd St./Broadway; B, C to 72nd St., 81st St., 86th St., 96th St./Central Park W; 1, 2, 3, 9 to 96th St./Broadway.)*

LINCOLN CENTER. Broadway intersects Columbus Ave. at **Lincoln Center,** the cultural hub of the city (p. 191). The airy architecture recalls the public plazas of Rome and Venice, but the center's performance spaces for opera, ballet, and classical music take center stage. *(Between 62nd and 66th St.)*

MORNINGSIDE HEIGHTS. Above 110th St. and below 125th St., between Amsterdam Ave. and the Hudson River, **Morningside Heights** centers around **Columbia University's** urban campus. *(Subway: 1 to Cathedral Pkwy. (110th St.), 116th St./Columbia University, 125th St./Broadway.)* The centerpiece of the campus is the majestic Roman Classical **Low Library,** which looms over College Walk, the school's central promenade. *(Morningside Dr. and Broadway, from 114th to 120th St.)* The still-unfinished cathedral of **St. John the Divine,** under construction since 1892, is the largest in the world. It features altars and bays dedicated both to the sufferings of Christ and to the experiences of immigrants, victims of genocide, and AIDS patients. *(Amsterdam Ave., between 110th and 113th St. Subway: 1 to Cathedral Pkwy. (110th St.)/Broadway. ☎ 212-316-7540, tours 932-7347; www.stjohndivine.org. Open daily 7am-6pm. Tours Tu-Sa 11am, Su 1pm. $5, students and seniors $4. Parish box office ☎ 212-662-2133.)* **Riverside Church,** near Columbia, has an observation deck in its tower and an amazing view, as well as the world's largest carillon (74 bells), a gift of John D. Rockefeller, Jr. *(490 Riverside Dr., at 120th St. Subway: 1 to 116th St./Columbia University. ☎ 212-870-6792; www.theriversidechurch.org. Open M-F 9am-4:30pm. Tours Su 12:30pm, after services, and upon request. Free.)* **Grant's Tomb,** a huge presidential grave commemorating the Union Civil War general, lies at 122nd St. and Riverside Dr. *(Open daily 9am-5pm. Free.)*

HARLEM

Manhattan's largest neighborhood extends from 110th S. to the 150s, between the Hudson and East Rivers. Harlem began its transformation into a black neighborhood between 1910 and 1920. The 1920s brought prosperity and the artistic Harlem Renaissance; Civil Rights and radical Black Power activism came in the 1960s. Today, thanks to community activism and economic boom in recent decades, Harlem is thriving. *(Subway: 6 to 103rd St., Central Park N (110th St.), 116th St./Lexington Ave.; 4, 5, 6 to 125th St./Lexington Ave.; 2, 3 to Central Park N (110th St.), 116th St., 125th St., 135th St./Lenox (Sixth) Ave.; 3 to 145th St./Lenox (Sixth) Ave., 148th St.; B, C to Cathedral Pkwy. (110th St.), 116th St., 135th St. at Central Park W; A, B, C, D to 125th St./Central Park W, 145th St./St. Nicholas Ave.; 1, 9 to 125th St., 137th St., 145th St./Broadway.)*

MID-ATLANTIC

SUGAR HILL. African-Americans with "sugar" (a.k.a. money) moved here in the 1920s and 30s. Musical legends Duke Ellington and W.C. Handy lived in the neighborhood, while leaders W.E.B. DuBois and Thurgood Marshall inhabited 409 Edgecombe Ave. Some of the city's most notable gangsters operated here. The area is also the birthplace of Sugarhill Records, the rap label that created the Sugarhill Gang. Their 1979 *Rapper's Delight* became the first hip-hop song to enter the Top 40. Today, skyrocketing real estate prices in Manhattan have made Sugar Hill's beautiful brownstones prized possessions once more. *(143rd to 155th St., between St. Nicholas and Edgecombe Ave. Subway: A, B, C, D to 145th St./St. Nicholas Ave.)*

WASHINGTON HEIGHTS. North of 155th St., **Washington Heights** affords a taste of urban life with an ethnic flavor. Eat a Greek dinner, buy Armenian pastries and vegetables from a South African, and discuss the Talmud with a **Yeshiva University** student. Fort Tryon Park is home to **The Cloisters,** a museum specializing in medieval art. *(Subway: C to 155th St./St. Nicholas Ave., 163rd St.; 1, A, C to 168th St./Broadway; A to 175th St., 181st St., 190th St.; 1, 9 to 181st St./St. Nicholas Ave., 191st St.)*

BROOKLYN

Part of NYC since 1898, Brooklyn is now the most populous borough. In the coverage below, neighborhoods are arranged from north to south.

WILLIAMSBURG AND GREENPOINT. Home to a growing number of artists, Williamsburg's galleries match its artsy population (see **Galleries,** p. 188). **Greenpoint,** bounded by Java St. to the north, Meserole St. to the south, and Franklin St. to the west, is Brooklyn's northernmost border and home to a large Polish population. The birthplace of Mae West and the Union's Civil War ironclad the *USS Monitor*, Greenpoint features charming Italianate and Greek revival houses built during the 1850s shipbuilding boom. *(Subway: L to Bedford Ave.; G to Nassau Ave.)*

FULTON LANDING. Fulton Landing is reminiscent of the days when the ferry—not the subway or the car—was the primary means of transportation between Brooklyn and Manhattan. Completed in 1883, the nearby ■**Brooklyn Bridge**—spanning the gap between lower Manhattan and Brooklyn—is the product of elegant calculation, careful design, and human exertion. A walk across the bridge at sunrise or sunset is one of the most exhilarating strolls New York City has to offer. *(From Brooklyn: entrance at the end of Adams St., at Tillary St. Subway: A, C to High St./Cadman Plaza E. From Manhattan: entrance at Park Row. Subway: 4, 5, 6, J, M, Z to Brooklyn Bridge/City Hall.)*

DOWNTOWN. Brooklyn Heights, a well-preserved 19th-century residential area, sprang up with the development of steamboat transportation between Brooklyn and Manhattan in 1814. Rows of posh Greek Revival and Italianate houses in this area essentially created New York City's first suburb. **Montague Street,** the main drag, has the stores, cafes, and mid-priced restaurants of a cute college town. **Downtown** is the location of Brooklyn's **Civic Center** and holds several grand municipal buildings. *(Subway: 2, 3, 4, 5, M, R to Court St./Borough Hall.)*

PROSPECT PARK. Park Slope is a residential neighborhood with charming brownstones. Neighboring **Prospect Park,** the borough's answer to Central Park, has a zoo, an ice-skating rink, and a children's museum. Frederick Law Olmsted and Calvert Vaux designed the park in the mid-1800s. In the 1890s, the 80 ft. high **Memorial Arch** was built in Grand Army Plaza to commemorate the Union's Civil War victory. *(Bounded by Prospect Park W, Flatbush Ave., Ocean Ave., Parkside Ave., and Prospect Park SW. Subway: 2, 3 to Grand Army Plaza; F to 15 St./Prospect Park; B, Q, S to Prospect Park.)*

BROOKLYN BOTANIC GARDEN. Adjacent to the park, this 52-acre fairyland features the **Fragrance Garden for the Blind** (with mint, lemon, violet, and other appetizing aromas) and the more formal **Cranford Rose Garden.** *(1000 Washington Ave.; entrances also on Eastern Pkwy. and on Flatbush Ave. Subway: S to Botanic Garden; B, Q, S to Prospect Park; 2, 3 to Eastern Pkwy./Brooklyn Museum. ☎ 718-623-7000, events hotline 623-7333; www.bbg.org. Open Apr.-Sept. Tu-F 8am-6pm, Sa-Su 10am-6pm; Oct.-Mar. Tu-F 8am-4:30pm, Sa-Su 10am-4:30pm. $5, students with ID and seniors $3, under 16 free, groups free. Free Tu and Sa 10am-noon; seniors also free F.)*

CONEY ISLAND. Once an elite resort (until the subway made it accessible to the masses), **Coney Island** is now a rickety slice of Americana. The **Cyclone,** 834 Surf Ave., built in 1927, was once the most terrifying roller coaster in the world. Meet sharks and other beasties at the **New York Aquarium.** *(At Surf and W. 8th St. Subway: F, Q to W 8th St./NY Aquarium. ☎ 718-265-3474; www.nyaquarium.com. Open May-Oct. M-F 10am-6pm, Sa-Su and holidays 10am-7pm; Nov.-Apr. daily 10am-4:30pm. $11, seniors and ages 2-12 $7. No bikes, in-line skates, or pets allowed. Wheelchair accessible.)*

QUEENS

ASTORIA AND LONG ISLAND CITY. In the northwest corner of Queens lies Astoria, where Greek-, Italian-, and Spanish-speaking communities mingle amid lively shopping districts and cultural attractions. Long Island City is just south, across the river from the Upper East Side. The **Isamu Noguchi Garden Museum** and the **Museum for African Art** have temporarily relocated to Long Island City. *(Astoria is in the northwestern corner of Queens, across the river from Manhattan. Long Island City is southwest of Astoria, and can be reached by walking south on 21st or 31st St. Subway: All N, W stops between 36th Ave. and Astoria Ditmars Blvd. G, R, V to 36th St. or Steinway St.)*

SOCRATES SCULPTURE PARK. Led by sculptor Mark di Suvero, artists transformed this former landfill into an artistic exhibition space with 35 stunning dayglo and rusted metal abstractions. *(At the end of Broadway, across the Vernon Blvd. intersection. Subway: N, W to Broadway. ☎ 718-956-1819; www.socratessculpturepark.org. Park offices located across from Broadway entrance. Open daily 10am-dusk. Free.)*

FLUSHING AND FLUSHING MEADOWS PARK. Flushing boasts colonial neighborhood landmarks, a bustling downtown, and a huge Asian immigrant population. Nearby **Flushing Meadows-Corona Park** was the site of the 1939 and 1964 World's Fair, and now holds **Shea Stadium** (home of the Mets), the **USTA National Tennis Center** (where the US Open is played), and the simple yet interesting **New York Hall of Science.** *(47-01 111th St., at 48th Ave. Subway: 7 to 111th St. ☎ 718-699-0005; www.nyhallsci.org. Open July-Aug. Tu-Su 9:30am-5pm; Sept.-June Tu-W 9:30am-2pm, Th-Su 9:30am-5pm. $11; seniors, students, and ages 5-17 $8; ages 2-4 $3; under 2 free. Free Sept.-June and F 2-5pm.)* The **Unisphere,** a 380-ton steel globe in front of the New York City Building, is the retro-futuristic structure featured in the 1997 movie *Men In Black*. *(Subway: 7 to Flushing/Main St; 7 to 111th St. or Willets Point.)*

THE BRONX

The relentless stream of immigration, once Italian and Irish but now mostly Hispanic and Russian, has created vibrant ethnic neighborhoods (including a Little Italy that puts its Manhattan counterpart to shame).

YANKEE STADIUM. In 1923, Babe Ruth's success as a hitter inspired the construction of the Yankees' own ballpark. Inside the 11½-acre park (the field itself measures only 3½ acres), monuments honor Yankee greats like Lou Gehrig, Joe

MID-ATLANTIC

DiMaggio, and the Bambino himself. *(E. 161st St., at River Ave. Subway: 4, B, D to 161st St./Yankee Stadium.* ☎ *718-293-6000; www.yankees.com. 1hr. tours start at noon. In summer $14, students and seniors $7; in winter $12/$6.)*

THE BRONX ZOO. The hugely popular **Bronx Zoo/Wildlife Conservation Park** houses over 4000 animals. Soar on the **Skyfari** aerial tramway ($2) between Wild Asia and the **Children's Zoo,** or ride a camel. *(Subway: 2, 5 to West Farms Sq./E. Tremont Ave. Follow Boston Rd. for 3 blocks until the Bronx Park S gate. Bus: Bx9, Bx12, Bx19, Bx22, and Q44 pass various entrances to the zoo.* ☎ *718-367-1010; www.bronxzoo.com. Open daily M-F 10am-5pm, Sa-Su 10am-5:30pm. Parts of the zoo closed Nov.-Apr. $11, seniors and ages 2-12 $8; W free.)*

NEW YORK BOTANICAL GARDEN. Located adjacent to the zoo, the city's most extensive botanical garden (250 acres) includes a 40-acre **hemlock forest,** kept in its natural state. Although it costs an extra few dollars to enter, the different ecosystems in the gorgeous domed greenhouse **Conservatory** are worth a visit. *(Bronx River Pkwy. Exit 7W and Fordham Rd. Subway: 4 to Bedford Park Blvd./Lehman College; B, D to Bedford Park Blvd. Walk 8 blocks east or take the Bx26 bus. Bus: Bx19 or Bx26. Train: Metro-North Harlem line goes from Grand Central Terminal to Botanical Garden station.* ☎ *718-817-8700; www.nybg.org. Open Apr.-Oct. Tu-Su 10am-6pm; Nov.-Mar. Tu-Su 10am-5pm. $13, seniors $11, students $11, children 2-12 $5. Call for tours.)*

BELMONT. Arthur Ave. is the center of this uptown **Little Italy,** which is home to wonderful homestyle southern Italian cooking. To get a concentrated sense of the area, stop into **Arthur Avenue Retail Market,** 2334 Arthur Ave., between 186th and Crescent St. The recent Kosovar influx has put Kosovar flags in the fronts of many stores and eateries. *(Centering on Arthur Ave. and E. 187th St., near the Southern Blvd. entrance to the Bronx Zoo. Subway: B, D to Fordham Rd./Grand Concourse. Walk 11 blocks east or take Bx12 to Arthur Ave. and head south.)*

STATEN ISLAND

Staten Island has a lot to offer, but tourism is often limited. Its parks are vast and lush, and there are beaches, historical sites, and gardens to explore. The **Staten Island Ferry** is itself a sight not to be missed; it offers the best and cheapest (free) tour of NY's harbor. *(Leaves from South Ferry in Manhattan; Subway: N, R to Whitehall St.; 1, 9 to South Ferry.)* The 19th-century **Snug Harbor Cultural Center** houses the **Newhouse Center for Contemporary Art,** a small gallery with a summer sculpture show, and the **Staten Island Botanical Gardens.** *(1000 Richmond Terr. Bus S40.* ☎ *718-448-2500. 90min walking tours Apr.-Nov. Sa 11:15am and 1:30pm, Su 2pm, starting at the visitors center, $10. Botanical Garden:* ☎ *718-273-8200. Open daily dawn-dusk.)*

🏛 MUSEUMS

Whether you're looking to examine medieval armor, T. Rex fossils, or abstract color field paintings, New York City has a museum for you. For listings of current and upcoming exhibits, consult *The New Yorker, New York* magazine, and Friday's *New York Times* "Weekend" section. Beware: most museums are closed on Mondays and packed elbow-tight on weekends. Many request a "donation" in place of an admission fee—don't be embarrassed to give as little as a dollar.

UPPER WEST SIDE

■**AMERICAN MUSEUM OF NATURAL HISTORY.** The American Museum of Natural History is one of the world's largest museums devoted to science. The main draw is the 4th-floor dinosaur halls, which display real fossils in 85% of the exhibits (most museums use fossil casts). Perhaps the most impressive part of the museum is the sparkling Hayden Planetarium in the Rose Center for Earth and Space. *(Central Park W, between 77th and 81st St. Subway: 81st St. ☎ 212-769-5100. Open daily 10am-5:45pm; Rose Center also open F until 8:45pm. Suggested donation $14, students and seniors $10.50, children $8. Wheelchair accessible.)*

NEW-YORK HISTORICAL SOCIETY. Founded in 1804, this is New York City's oldest continuously operating museum. The Neoclassical building houses a library and museum, with exhibits on subjects ranging from slavery to early New York restaurant menus. *(2 W. 77th St., at Central Park W. Subway: 79th St.; 72nd St/Central Park W/ 81st St. ☎ 212-873-3400; www.nyhistory.org. Open Tu-Su 10am-6pm. $10, students and seniors $5, children free. Wheelchair accessible.)*

UPPER EAST SIDE

■**METROPOLITAN MUSEUM OF ART.** The largest in the Western Hemisphere, the Met's art collection boasts over 2 million works spanning 5000 years. Highlights are the Egyptian holdings (including the reconstructed Temple of Dendur), the European paintings collection, and extensive exhibits of American art. The Costume Institute houses over 75,000 costumes and accessories from the 17th century to the present. *(1000 Fifth Ave., at 82nd St. Subway: 86th St./ Lexington Ave. ☎ 212-535-7710, concerts and lectures 570-3949, wheelchair info 535-7710. Open Tu-Th and Su 9:30am-5:15pm, F-Sa 9:30am-8:45pm. Suggested donation $15, seniors $10, students $7.)*

■**GUGGENHEIM MUSEUM.** The Guggenheim's most famous exhibit is the building itself, an inverted white, multi-ridged shell designed by Frank Lloyd Wright and hailed as a modern masterpiece. Interdependent gallery spaces make up a spiral design. The large collection of modern and postmodern paintings includes significant works in Cubism, Surrealism, American Minimalism, and Abstract Expressionism. *(1071 Fifth Ave., at 89th St. Subway: 86th St./Lexington Ave. ☎ 212-423-3500. Open M-W and Sa-Su 10am-5:45pm, F 10am-8pm. $15, students and seniors $10, under 12 free.)*

FRICK COLLECTION. Henry Clay Frick left his house and art collection to the city, and the museum retains the elegance of his chateau. The Living Hall displays 17th-century furniture, Persian rugs, Holbein portraits, and paintings by El Greco, Rembrandt, Velázquez, and Titian. The courtyard is inhabited by elegant statues surrounding the garden pool and fountain. *(1 E. 70th St., at Fifth Ave. Subway: 68th St. ☎ 212-288-0700. Open Tu-Sa 10am-6pm, Su 1-6pm. $12, seniors $8, students $5. Children under 10 not allowed, under 16 must be accompanied by an adult. Wheelchair accessible.)*

MUSEUM OF THE CITY OF NEW YORK. This fascinating museum details the history of the Big Apple, from the construction of the Empire State Building to the history of Broadway theater. Cultural history of all varieties is on parade here—don't miss the various model ships, NYC paintings, hot pants, and Yankees World Series trophies—if you can stomach the sight of them. *(1220 Fifth Ave., at 103rd St. Subway: 103rd St. ☎ 212-534-1672. Open Tu-Su 10am-5pm. Suggested donation $7; students, seniors, and children $5.)*

THE JEWISH MUSEUM. The gallery's permanent collection details the Jewish experience throughout history using ancient Biblical artifacts and ceremonial objects, as well as contemporary masterpieces by Marc Chagall, Frank Stella, and George Segal. *(1109 Fifth Ave., at 92nd St. Subway: 96th St. ☎ 212-423-3200. Open M-W and Su 11am-5:45pm, Th 11am-9pm, F 11am-3pm. $10, students and seniors $7.50, members and under 12 free. Th 5-9pm pay-what-you-wish.)*

WHITNEY MUSEUM OF AMERICAN ART. The museum with a historical mandate to champion the works of living American artists has assembled the largest collection of 20th- and 21st-century American art in the world, including Jasper Johns's

Three Flags and Frank Stella's *Brooklyn Bridge*. *(945 Madison Ave., at 75th St. Subway: 77th St. ☎212-570-3676. Open W-Th and Sa-Su 11am-6pm, F 1-9pm. $12, students and seniors $9.50, under 12 free. F 6-9pm pay-what-you-wish.)*

MIDTOWN

■ **MUSEUM OF MODERN ART.** The reopening of MoMA was *the* cultural event in New York in 2005. The new space, nearly twice the size of the old, was conceived by Japanese architect Yoshio Taniguchi and cost a staggering $858 million. The results are nearly as impressive as the museum's collections of 19th- and 20th-century art, including Matisse's *The Dance*, van Gogh's *Starry Night*, and Warhol's signature *Marilyn Monroe*. *(11 W. 53rd St., between Fifth and Sixth Ave. Subway: Fifth Ave./53rd St.; Fifth Ave./59th St. ☎212-708-9400. Open M 10:30am-5:30pm, W-Th 10:30am-5:30pm, F 10:30am-8pm, Sa-Su 10:30am-5:30pm. $20, seniors $16, students $12.)*

MUSEUM OF TELEVISION AND RADIO. More archive than museum, this shrine to modern media contains over 100,000 easily accessible TV and radio programs. Unique film screenings focus on social, historical, or artistic topics and can't be seen anywhere else. *(25 W. 52nd St., between Fifth and Sixth Ave. Subway: 47th-50th St.-Rockefeller Center/Sixth Ave.; Fifth Ave./53rd St. ☎212-621-6600. Open Tu-W and F-Su noon-6pm, Th noon-8pm. Suggested donation $10, students and seniors $8, under 13 $5.)*

BROOKLYN

■ **BROOKLYN MUSEUM OF ART (BMA).** If it weren't for the Met, the BMA would be NYC's most magnificent museum. Oceanic and New World art collections reside on the 1st fl.; ancient Greek, Roman, Middle Eastern, and Egyptian galleries are on the 3rd fl. *(200 Eastern Pkwy., at Washington Ave. Subway: Eastern Pkwy./Brooklyn Museum. ☎718-638-5000. Open W-F 10am-5pm, Sa-Su 11am-6pm; 1st Sa of each month open until 11pm. $8, students and seniors $4, under 12 free. 1st Sa of each month free.)*

▣ GALLERIES

New York City's galleries provide a riveting—and free—introduction to the contemporary art world. To get started, pick up a free copy of *The Gallery Guide* at any major museum or gallery. Most galleries are open Tuesday to Saturday, from 10 or 11am to 5 or 6pm. Galleries are usually only open on weekend afternoons in the summer, and many are closed from late July to early September.

Artists Space, 38 Greene St. 3rd fl. (☎212-226-3970; www.artistsspace.org), at Grand St. Subway: 1, 9 to Canal St./Varick St.; A, C, E to Canal St./Ave. of the Americas (Sixth Ave.). Nonprofit gallery founded in 1972. Champions work by emerging and unaffiliated artists. Often used for multiple small exhibits. Presents works in all media, but the focus is on works in architecture and design. The Irving Sandler Artists File, containing slides and digitized images of works by more than 3000 unaffiliated artists, is open to critics, curators, and the public by appointment (F-Sa). Open Tu-Sa 11am-6pm. Closed Aug.

The Drawing Center, 35 Wooster St. (☎212-219-2166; www.drawingcenter.org), between Grand and Broome St. Subway: 1, 9 to Canal St./Varick St.; A, C, E to Canal St./Ave. of the Americas (Sixth Ave.). Specializing in original works on paper, this nonprofit space sets up high-quality, rotating exhibits. Open Tu-F 10am-6pm, Sa 11am-6pm. Closed Aug. Suggested donation $3. More space at the **Drawing Room,** 40 Wooster St.

525 W. 22nd St., between 10th and 11th Ave. Houses a handful of excellent, petite galleries of contemporary art, including the **303 Gallery** (☎212-255-1121; www.303gallery.com), **D'Amelio Terras** (☎212-352-9460; www.damelioterras.com), and the **DCA Gallery** (☎212-255-5511; www.dcagallery.com). Call for hours.

NEW YORK CITY ■ 189

529 W. 20th St., between 10th and 11th Ave. This 11-fl. colossus boasts over 20 contemporary art galleries, including the **I-20 Gallery** (☎212-645-1100; www.I-20.com), the **ACA Galleries** (☎212-206-8080; www.acagalleries.com), and the famed **Dorfman Projects** (☎212-352-2272; www.dorfman-projects.com). Call for hours.

Leo Castelli, 59 E. 79th St. (☎212-249-4470; www.castelligallery.com), between Park and Madison Ave. Subway: 6 to 77th St. Founded in 1957 by Leo Castelli, a highly influential art dealer known for showcasing the early efforts of Frank Stella and Andy Warhol. A selection of both established and up-and-coming artists is on display. Open mid-Aug. to late June Tu-Sa 10am-6pm; late June to mid-Aug. Tu-F 11am-5pm. Occasionally closed; call ahead.

🎵 ENTERTAINMENT

Publications with noteworthy entertainment and nightlife sections are the *Village Voice, New York* magazine, and the Sunday edition of the *New York Times. The New Yorker* has the most comprehensive theater survey.

THEATER

Broadway tickets usually start from $50. **TKTS,** Duffy Square, at 47th St. and Broadway, sells tickets for many Broadway and some larger off-Broadway shows at a 25-50% discount on the day of the performance. The lines begin to form an hour or so before the booths open, but they move fairly quickly. More tickets become available as showtime approaches, so you may find fewer possibilities if you go too early. (☎768-1818. Tickets sold M-Sa 3-8pm for evening performances, W and Sa 10am-2pm for matinees, Su 11am-7pm for matinees and evening performances.) Reserve full-price tickets over the phone and pay by credit card using **Tele-Charge** (☎239-6200 or 800-432-7250) for Broadway shows; **Ticket Central** (☎279-4200) for off-Broadway shows; and **Ticketmaster** (☎307-4100 or 800-755-4000) for all types of shows. All three services have a per-ticket service charge, so ask before purchasing. You can avoid these fees if you buy your tickets directly from the theater box office.

Shakespeare in the Park (☎539-8750) is a New York City summer tradition. From June through August, two plays are presented at the **Delacorte Theater** in Central Park, near the 81st St. entrance on the Upper West Side, just north of the main road. Tickets are free, but lines form extremely early.

THE LOCAL STORY

LULLABY OF BROADWAY

Few things make theater-lovers' hearts palpitate like the word "Broadway." More than just a slanty, inscrutable thoroughfare, the "Great White Way" is the home of "legit" (live) theater in the United States. The basic breakdown is between "tuners" (musicals, generally comedies) and "straight-plays" (no singing or dancing, alas), though the "one-hander" (solo shows that usually feature a single, well-known performer like Billy Crystal or Whoopi Goldberg) has become increasingly common in recent years.

A show "bows" (plays its first performance) long before "opening night" (the final performance before reviews run in the newspapers, always accompanied by a large party), but "previews" (pre-opening performances where the show is still being finished) generally aren't any cheaper. A show's "scribe" (playwright) is considered to be its primary artistic force, but the "helmer" (stage director) can just as easily lay claim to that title.

The $100 "ducats" (tickets) purchased by "auds" (audiences) go toward recouping the show's "capitalization" (the cost of mounting the show, frequently over $10 million for big musicals). "Tonys" (Antoinette M. Perry Awards) can help fuel successful shows, but the peculiar alchemy of luck, glitz, and talent that makes up a hit is all part of the magic of Broadway.

EXPERIMENTAL/PERFORMANCE SPACES

◪**The Kitchen,** 512 W. 19th St., between 10th and 11th Ave., is a world-renowned arts showcase in an unassuming Meatpacking District location. The space features experimental and avant-garde film and video, as well as concerts, dance performances, art exhibits, public lectures, and poetry readings. (Subway: 23rd St./ Eighth Ave. ☎212-255-5793; www.thekitchen.org. Box office open Tu-Sa 2-6pm.) The **Knitting Factory,** 74 Leonard St., between Broadway and Church St., is a multi-level performance space featuring several shows nightly, ranging from avant-garde and indie rock to jazz and hip-hop. (Subway: Franklin St. ☎212-219-3006; www.knittingfactory.com. Cover $5-25. Tickets are available for purchase on the Internet, phone, or at the box office. Box office open for walk-up sales M-Sa 10am-2am, Su 2pm-2am. Bar open 6pm-4am.)

JAZZ JOINTS

The **JVC Jazz Festival** puts on all-star performances from June to July. Many events are outdoors and free. Check the newspaper or call ☎212-501-1390. Annual festivals sponsored by major corporations draw local talent and industry giants. The concerts take place throughout the city (some free), but center at TriBeCa's **Knitting Factory** (see above). **Smoke,** 2751 Broadway, between 105th and 106th St, may no longer be a den of fumes, but the fantastic music keeps it smokin'. A sultry cocktail lounge jumps with jazz every night, and, although slightly congested, the intimate space swells with music. Surprise guests have included jazz legends like Dr. Lonnie Smith, George Benson, and Ronnie Cuber; the regular lineup includes John Farnsworth, Larry Willis, and Steve Wilson. (Subway: 103rd St./Broadway. ☎212-864-6662; www.smokejazz.com. Retro happy hour daily 5-8pm; mixed drinks $3, other drinks $2 off. $10 drink min. per person per set. Sets usually at 9, 11pm, 12:30am. Tu and Th jam sessions 6-8:30pm. Jazz vocalist series Su 6-8:30pm. 21+. F-Sa cover $16-20. Open daily 5pm-4am.) **Detour,** 349 E. 13th St., between First and Second Ave., is a critically acclaimed club with nightly jazz and no cover—a perfect combo. It would be the local hole-in-the-wall if it weren't for the impressively packed calendar. (Subway: First Ave. ☎212-533-6212; www.jazzatdetour.com. 2-drink min. Mixed drinks $6. Bottled beer $5-6. Wine $6-8. Happy hour daily 4-7pm, $3 drinks. 21+. Open M-Tu and Su 4pm-2am, W-Sa 4pm-4am.) The **Cotton Club,** 656 W. 125th St., on the corner of Riverside Dr., has been around since 1923 and seen jazz greats like Lena Horne, Ethel Waters, and Calloway. (Subway: 125th St./Broadway. ☎212-663-7980 or 800-640-7980; www.cottonclub-newyork.com. M evening swing/big band. Buffet dinner and jazz show Th-Sa evenings. M and Th-Sa evenings 21+; call for age restrictions at other events. Su brunch and gospel shows $25; dinner jazz shows $32. Call 2 weeks in advance for reservations and schedule.)

ROCK, POP, PUNK, FUNK

New York City has a long history of producing bands on the vanguard of popular music and performance. **Music festivals** provide the opportunity to see tons of bands at a (relatively) low price. The **CMJ Music Marathon** (☎877-633-7848) runs for four nights in late October or early November, including over 400 bands and workshops on the alternative music scene. **The Digital Club Festival** (☎677-3530), a newly reconfigured indie-fest, visits New York City in late July. The **Macintosh New York Music Festival** presents over 350 bands over a week-long period in July.

◪**SOBs (Sounds of Brazil),** 204 Varick St., at W. Houston St., is a dinner-dance club that has some of NYC's best live music and hip-hop's best talents, including recent acts Talib Kweli, Blackalicious, and the Black Eyed Peas. Brazilian food goes well with the sounds: try lobster empanadas ($10), calypso chicken ($18), or crab cakes ($22). Monday nights feature a 1hr. Latin dance class ($5) at 7pm; Latin bands play at 9pm. Friday nights feature emerging artists; the late-night French-Caribbean dance party ($15-30) starts at midnight. (Subway: Houston St. ☎212-243-4940; www.sobs.com. Sa samba 6:30pm-4am $20. Box office, next door at 200 Varick St., open M-F 11am-6pm, Sa noon-6pm. Usually 21+, sometimes 18+. Opens M-Sa at 6:30pm.) ◼Southpaw, 125 Fifth Ave., between Sterling and St. John's Pl., is a former 99-cent store that now hosts DJs, local musicians, and plenty of well-known talent. The past two years have seen performances from Ben Lee, the late Elliot Smith, and members of Wu-Tang Clan. (Brooklyn. Subway: Union St.; Seventh Ave.; Bergen St. ☎718-230-0236; www.spsounds.com. Most shows 18+. Cover $7-20. Doors usually open around 8pm.) ◼Mercury Lounge, 217 E. Houston St., between Essex and Ludlow St., is a converted gravestone parlor—there's a tombstone in the bar's counter top—that attracts an amazing range of big-name acts to its fairly small-time room. The alterna-rocker and singer-songwriter are frequent performers: past standouts include spoken-word artist Maggie Estep, Morphine, and Mary Lou Lord. (Subway: Delancey St. ☎212-260-4700; www.mercuryloungenyc.com. 21+. Cover varies. Box office open M-Sa noon-7pm.)

OPERA AND DANCE

You can do it all at ◼Lincoln Center, the world's largest cultural complex, where many of the city's best opera, dance, and performance groups set up shop. (Between 62nd and 66th St. and Columbus and Amsterdam Ave. ☎212-875-5456. Subway: 66th St.) Check *The New York Times* listings. The **Metropolitan Opera Company's** premier outfit performs on a Lincoln Center stage as big as a football field. You can stand in the orchestra for $16 or all the way back in the Family Circle for $12. (☎212-362-6000; www.metopera.org. Season Sept.-May M-Sa. Box office open M-Sa 10am-8pm, Su noon-6pm. Upper balcony around $65.) The **New York City Opera** has also come into its own. "City" has a split season (Sept.-Nov. and Mar.-Apr.) and keeps its ticket prices low. (☎212-870-5630; www.nycopera.com. Box office open M 10am-7:30pm, Tu-Sa 10am-8:30pm, Su 11:30am-7:30pm. Tickets $12-105; $15 student rush tickets the morning of the performance: ☎212-870-5630.) **Dicapo Opera Theatre,** 184 E. 76th St., between Third and Lexington Ave., is a small company that garners standing ovations after every performance. (☎212-288-9438; www.dicapo.com. Subway: 23rd St./Broadway. Tickets around $50.)

   The **New York State Theater** in Lincoln Center is home to the late George Balanchine's ◼New York City Ballet. Tickets for the *Nutcracker* in December sell out almost immediately. (☎212-870-5570; www.nycballet.com. Season Nov.-Mar. Tickets $16-88. Student rush tickets $12; ☎212-870-7766.) The **American Ballet Theatre** dances at the Metropolitan Opera House. (☎212-477-3030, box office 362-6000; www.abt.org. Tickets $20-90.) **City Center,** 131 W. 55th St. (☎212-581-1212; www.citycenter.org), has the city's best dance, from modern to ballet, including the ◼Alvin Alley American Dance Theater. De La Guarda (think disco in a rainforest with an air show overhead) performs at 20 Union Sq. E. (☎212-239-6200. Standing-room only. $65; some $20 tickets sold 2hr. before show. Box office open Tu-Th 1-8:15pm, F 1-10:30pm, Sa 1-10pm, Su 1-7:15pm.) Other dance venues include **Dance Theater Workshop,** 219 W. 19th St. (☎212-924-0077; www.dtw.org), between Seventh and Eighth Ave.; **Joyce Theater,** 175 Eighth Ave. (☎212-242-0800; www.joyce.org), between 18th and 19th St.; and **Thalia Spanish Theater,** 41-17 Greenpoint Ave. (☎718-729-3880), between 41st and 42nd St. in Queens.

CLASSICAL MUSIC

Lincoln Center has the most selection in its halls. The **Great Performers Series** packs the Avery Fisher and Alice Tully Halls and the Walter Reade Theater from October until May (see above for contact info; tickets from $20). **Avery Fisher Hall** presents the annual **Mostly Mozart Festival.** Show up early; there are usually recitals 1hr. before the main concert that are free to ticket holders. (☎212-875-5766. July-Aug. Tickets $25-70.) The **New York Philharmonic** begins its regular season in mid-September. Students and seniors can sometimes get $10 tickets the day of; call ahead. (☎212-875-5656. Tickets $20-80.) For a few weeks in late June, the Philharmonic holds **free concerts** (☎212-875-5709) on the Great Lawn in Central Park, at Prospect Park in Brooklyn, at Van Cortlandt Park in the Bronx, and elsewhere. Free outdoor events at Lincoln Center (☎212-875-5928) occur all summer.

Carnegie Hall, on Seventh Ave., at 57th St., sometimes offers rush tickets (☎212-247-7800. Box office M-Sa 11am-6pm, Su noon-6pm. Tickets $20-80.) A good, cheap way to absorb New York City musical culture is to visit a music school. Except for opera and ballet productions ($5-12), concerts are usually free and frequent. The best options are the **Juilliard School of Music,** Lincoln Center (☎769-7406), the **Mannes College of Music,** 150 W. 85th St. (☎212-580-0210), and the **Manhattan School of Music,** 120 Claremont Ave. (☎212-749-2802).

SPORTS

Most cities are content to have one major-league team in each big-time sport. New York City has two baseball teams, two hockey teams, NBA and WNBA basketball teams, two football teams...and one lonely soccer squad. The beloved **Mets** bat at **Shea Stadium** in Queens. (Subway: Willets Point-Shea Stadium. ☎718-507-6387. $13-30.) The **Yankees** play ball at **Yankee Stadium** in the Bronx. (Subway: 161st St. ☎718-293-4300. $8-65.) Both the **Giants** and the **Jets** play football across the river at **Giants Stadium** in East Rutherford, NJ (☎201-507-8900; tickets from $25), and the **New York/New Jersey Metrostars** play soccer in the same venue. The **Knickerbockers** (that's the **Knicks** to you), as well as the WNBA's **Liberty,** play basketball at **Madison Square Garden** (☎212-465-5800; from $22 and $8, respectively), where the **Rangers** also play hockey (from $25). The **Islanders** hit the ice at the **Nassau Veterans Memorial Coliseum** in Uniondale. (☎516-794-9300. Tickets $27-70.) New York City also hosts a number of other world-class events. Get tickets three months in advance for the prestigious **US Open,** held in late August and early September at the USTA Tennis Center in Flushing Meadows, Queens. (☎888-673-6849. $33-69.) On the first Sunday in November, two million spectators witness the 30,000 runners of the **New York City Marathon.** The race begins on the Verrazano Bridge and ends at Central Park's Tavern on the Green (☎212-860-4455).

⚑ NIGHTLIFE

Whether you prefer a Chelsea nightclub or Harlem jazz, a smoky Brooklyn bar or a Lower East Side be-seen-ery, New York has it all. A number of publications print daily, weekly, and monthly nightlife calenders; try the *Village Voice, New York* magazine, and *The New York Times* (particularly the Sunday edition).

BARS

LOWER EAST SIDE

🞑 **Local 138,** 138 Ludlow St. (212-477-0280), between Stanton and Rivington St. Subway: Delancey/Essex St. Neighborhood bar with nary a decoration: just tables, bar, and booths. Lay low and grab a beer ($5), watch a game on TV, or make friends with the locals. Happy hour daily 4-9pm with $3 drafts. Open daily 4pm-4am.

Lotus Lounge, 35 Clinton St. (☎212-253-1144), at Stanton St. Subway: Delancey St./Essex St. A lovely, low-key cafe by day; an even lovelier, lantern-lit bar by night. Bookshelves line the back wall. Live DJ nightly, starting around 10pm. Happy hour daily 4-8pm with $2 Buds, $3 drafts. Open M-Sa 8am-4am, Su 8am-2am.

SOHO AND TRIBECA

■ **Circa Tabac,** 32 Watts St. (☎212-941-1781), between Sixth Ave. and Thompson St. Subway: Spring St./Ave. of the Americas (Sixth Ave.). Claims to be the world's first, and perhaps only, cigarette lounge. The bar has remained a smoker's haven despite Bloomberg's ban, thanks to the same law that protects cigar lounges. 180 kinds of cigarettes ($9-25), plus beer ($5-6) and mixed drinks ($8-12). Open daily 5pm-4am.

Milady's, 160 Prince St. (☎212-226-9069), at Thompson St. Subway: Spring St./Ave. of the Americas (Sixth Ave.). Down-to-earth staff matches no-frills atmosphere. Beer bottles ($3.50), drafts ($3.50-5), and SoHo's only pool table ($1 per game). All drinks under $7. Veggie burgers $7. Grilled strip steak $8.50. Open daily 11am-4am; kitchen open M-Th 11am-midnight, F-Sa 11am-1am, Su 11am-11pm.

GREENWICH VILLAGE

■ **Blind Tiger Alehouse,** 518 Hudson St. (☎212-675-3848; www.blindtigeralehouse.com), at 10th St. Subway: Christopher St. Neighborhood pub that draws a diverse group of regulars for an amazing selection of microbrews (pints $5) and tasty freebies. M 6pm free hot dogs steamed in Brooklyn Beer, W 6pm free gourmet cheese tasting, Sa-Su noon free bagels and cream cheese. Happy hour M-F noon-8pm, $1 off pints and $3.50 mixed drinks. Open M-F noon-4am, Sa-Su 1pm-4am.

The White Horse Tavern, 567 Hudson St. (☎212-243-9260), at W. 11th St. Subway: Christopher St. Boisterous students playing drinking games, plus locals who reminisce about the tavern's $0.20 beers. Poet Dylan Thomas drank himself to death here. Expansive pub interior with a great jukebox. Outdoor patio. Beer $4-5. Open daily 6pm-4am,

EAST VILLAGE

■ **d.b.a.,** 41 First Ave. (☎212-475-5097), between E. 2nd and 3rd St. Subway: Lower East Side/Second Ave. For your inner alcohol connoisseur. With 19 premium beers on tap ($5-6), well over 100 bottled imports and microbrews, 50 bourbons, 130 single-malt whiskeys ($5-8), and 45 different tequilas, this friendly space lives up to its motto, "drink good stuff." Outdoor beer garden open until 10pm; space heaters keep it toasty on cold nights. Happy hour 5-7pm; $4 drinks. Open daily 1pm-4am.

Joe's Pub, 425 Lafayette St. (☎212-539-8777; www.joespub.com), between Astor Pl. and E. 4th St. Subway: Astor Pl. Located at the Joseph Papp Public Theater. Norwegian acid-folk, classical chamber music, and dance contests are common. 2-3 bands perform each night; set times around 7, 9, and/or 11pm. Late-night DJs spin hip-hop, rock, and 80s hits for the large, dancing crowd. Open daily 6pm-4am.

CHELSEA AND UNION SQUARE

Coral Room, 512 W 29th St. (☎212-244-1965), between 10th and 11th Ave. Subway: 34th St./Penn Station. Coral walls plus big fish tank equals aquarium kitsch. A "mermaid" swims in the 9000-gallon aquarium behind the bar (on Su, it's a "merman"). Tiny VIP section has portholes through which you can (literally and figuratively) look down on the dancing crowd below. Fun crowd and excellent DJs. Surprisingly little hassle at the door. Cover $10-20. Open daily 10pm-4am.

B'Lo, 230 W. 19th St. (☎212-675-3848), between Seventh and Eighth Ave. Subway: 18th St. This sexy club attracts Manhattanites to its cave-like lounge. Low ceilings, stone columns, and 40-ft. bar. Lines form around midnight, but the bouncers are fair. Just make sure you know how to pronounce it: "Be-low." DJs spin pop, hip-hop, and house beats. Drinks $8. Those who'd like to sit might choose table service, buying a bottle for $150-1500. Cover $10-20. Open F-Sa 10pm-4am.

UPPER EAST SIDE

The Big Easy, 1768 Second Ave. (☎212-348-0879), at 92nd St. Subway: 96th St. Perfect for those who miss college, with 3 beer pong tables in back. A good spot for cheap, strong drinks before a long NYC night. Bud $2 11pm-midnight. Open daily 5pm-4am.

Dorrian's Red Hand, 1616 Second Ave. (☎212-772-6600), at 84th St. Subway: 86th St. The preppy hot spot all the others aspire to be. The still-in-college, recently graduated, and young moneyed come to this Irish pub to meet, mingle, and down some drinks ($5-8). The likely meeting place of many a *New York Times* wedding section couple. Open M-Th and Su 11:30am-1am, F-Sa 11:30am-2am.

UPPER WEST SIDE

Dive 75, 101 W. 75th St. (☎212-501-9283), between Columbus and Amsterdam St. Subway: 72nd St. All the joys of your favorite dive without the unusable bathroom. Locals lounge on couches, soaking in pop-rock tunes from the jukebox. A stack of board games sits in the corner. Free wings M in football season. Palm readings Th. Happy hour 5-7pm; Buds $2.50, well drinks $4. Open daily M-Th 5pm-4am, F 2pm-4am, Sa-Su noon-4am.

The Evelyn Lounge, 380 Columbus Ave. (☎212-724-2363), at 78th St. Subway: 81st St. Lively upscale bar complete with brick, vintage sofas, and fireplaces. Popular with the after-work and late-night set. The lounge downstairs is open on weekends, with 5 more rooms and 2 additional bars. DJs spin dance and hip-hop. Cultured locals sip martinis ($9-10) and beer ($5-6). Open M-Th and Su 5pm-2:30am, F-Sa 5pm-4am; lounge Th-Sa 8pm-4am.

BROOKLYN

Galapagos, 70 N. 6th St. (☎718-782-5188; www.galapagosartspace.com), between Kent and Wythe St., in Williamsburg. Subway: Bedford Ave. Once a mayonnaise factory, and now one of the hipper cultural spots in the city. Sleek decor, complete with enormous reflecting pool. Su 7pm *Ocularis*, an avant-garde and experimental film screening ($7), M 9:30pm bawdy burlesque show (free). Tu-W live rock bands ($6-7), F "floating burlesque" 10pm-1am ($5). More live bands throughout the week ($5-8). DJs every Tu-Sa, start late (usually after 11pm; no cover). Happy hour M-Sa 6-8pm. Check website for event calendar. Open M-Th and Su 6:30pm-2am, F-Sa 6pm-4:30am.

The Gate, 321 Fifth Ave. (☎718-768-4329), corner of Third St. Subway: Union St. A few short years ago, Park Slope was a nightlife wasteland, but The Gate's welcoming atmosphere and 24 beers on tap ($4-5) paved the way for a Fifth Ave. renaissance. Large patio fills when the weather is warm. Happy hour M-Th 4-8pm, F 3-7pm, $1 off drafts and well drinks. Open M-Th 4pm-4am, F 3pm-4am, Sa-Su 1pm-4am.

Pete's Candy Store, 709 Lorimer St. (☎718-302-3770; www.petescandystore.com), between Frost and Richardson St. Subway: Lorimer St. This soda-shop-turned-bar includes a "make-out" hallway and a small performance room in the back. A local crowd comes for live local music nightly at 9pm. Tu Bingo and W Quizz-Off (both 7-9pm) are extremely popular. M night spelling bee. During the summer, stop by the barbecues (Sa-Su 5-9pm, $5) in the backyard for burgers, hot dogs, and salads. Pomegranate margarita $8, other cocktails $6-8. Open M-Tu and Su 5pm-2am, W-Sa 5pm-4am.

Union Pool, 484 Union Ave. (☎718-609-0484), off Skillman Ave. Subway: Bedford Ave. The expanded backyard has a fountain, butterfly chairs, picnic tables, and restored 50s Ford pickups. The bar, an old pool supply depot, hosts whimsical events, from circus performances to local film festivals. Frequent barbecues. DJ every night at 10pm. Beer $4-5. Cocktails $6-7. Occasional live music, usually 9pm. Happy hour daily 5-8pm, Yuengling $2, Bud and shot of Jim Beam $6. Photobooth $3. Open daily 5pm-4am.

DANCE CLUBS

Club scenes are about carefree crowds, unlimited fun, and huge pocketbook damage. It can pay to call ahead to put your name on the guest list. Come after 11pm; the real party starts around 1 or 2am. A few after-hours clubs keep at it until 5-6am. All clubs listed are 21+ unless otherwise noted.

Eugene, 27 W. 24th St. (☎212-462-0999), between Fifth and Sixth Ave. Subway: 23rd St./Seventh Ave.; 6 to 23rd St./Park Ave. S; F, V to 23rd St./Ave. of the Americas (Sixth Ave.); N, R 23rd St./Broadway. Vegas-casino atmosphere with an Atlantic City crowd. Doubles as an expensive restaurant by day. Party heats up when the DJ arrives, around 11pm. Plenty of dimly lit nooks for private moments with bridge-and-tunnel crowd. Drinks $9-12. Dress to impress. Cover W $15-20, Th-Sa $20. Open W-Sa 9pm-4am.

Filter 14, 432 W. 14th St. (☎212-366-5680), at Washington St. Subway: 14th St./Eighth Ave.; 1, 2, 3 to 14th St./Seventh Ave. Small club that leaves both decor and pretense behind: everyone here is all about the music. W electro/break beat, F house, Sa hip-hop/pop/rock. Intimate, no-frills club that still packs the dance floor. Funky Meatpacking District crowd. Cover $5-10. Open W-Sa 10pm-4am.

Go, 73 Eighth Ave. (☎212-463-0000), between W. 13th and 14th St. Subway: 14th St./Seventh Ave.; A, C, E, L to 14th St./Eighth Ave. Small club with beautiful people. The entirely white decor makes a perfect canvas for the "light DJ" to change the club's color scheme depending on his mood. Cover $20. Open Th-Su 10pm-4am.

GLBT NIGHTLIFE

Gay nightlife in New York City is centered in **Chelsea,** especially along Eighth Ave. in the 20s, and in the **West Village,** on Christopher St.

Boiler Room, 86 E. 4th St. (☎212-254-7536), between First and Second Ave. Subway: Lower East Side/Second Ave. Popular locale caters to alternative types, NYU students, and refugees from the Chelsea scene. Predominantly gay men, but a mixed crowd, especially on weekends. Jukebox and pool table. Beer $4. Happy hour daily 4-8pm and 10pm-4am, 2-for-1 draft and domestic beers. Open daily 4pm-4am.

g, 223 W 19th St. (☎212-929-1085), between Seventh and Eighth Ave. Subway: 18th St./Seventh Ave. Glitzy, popular bar shaped like an oval racetrack—perhaps an appropriate choice, given the pumped-up Chelsea men who speed around this circuit to the sound of DJ-ed house. Fortunately, the famous frozen cosmos ($7) satisfy the thirst of those logging their miles. Drinks $6-8. Open daily 4pm-4am.

Henrietta Hudson, 438 Hudson St. (☎212-924-3347; www.henriettahudsons.com), between Morton and Barrow St. Subway: Christopher St. Young, clean-cut lesbian crowd. Transitions from after-work hangout to weekend late-night hot spot. Pool table and 2nd bar in quiet back room. Also gay male- and straight-friendly. Happy hour M-F 5-7pm, $3 beer. Busiest Th-Sa. M old school, Tu requests, W karaoke, Th world, F house, Sa pop, Su Latin. Cover Sa-Su $7-10. Open M-F 4pm-4am, Sa 1pm-4am, Su 3pm-4am.

SBNY, 50 W. 17th St. (☎212-691-0073; www.splashbar.com), between Fifth and Sixth Ave. Subway: 18th St./Seventh Ave.; 23rd St./Ave. of the Americas (Sixth Ave.). One of the most popular gay mega-bars, the renovated **S**plash **B**ar **N**ew **Y**ork (formerly known simply as Splash) is a huge 2-fl. complex. A crowded scene, with industrial decor, a dance floor, and high-energy house music. Beer $5.50. Cocktails $6-7.50. Happy hour with 2-for-1 drinks M-Th 4-9pm, F-Sa 4-8pm. 21+ usually, 18+ occasionally. Cover M-W $5 after 11pm, Th $10, F $20. Open M-Th and Su 4pm-4am, F-Sa 4pm-5am.

Stonewall Bar, 53 Christopher St. (☎212-463-0950), at Seventh Ave. S. Subway: Christopher St. Legendary bar of the 1969 Stonewall Riots. Join the diverse crowd in the former Stonewall Inn to toast the brave drag queens who fought back. Enter the Su night male amateur strip contest "Meatpacking," and win $200. 3 bars in 1. M hip-hop, W and Sa Latin. Happy hour M-F 3-9pm, 2-for-1 drinks; Sa-Su $4 cosmos, $3 Bud Lights. Free hors d'oeuvres nightly. M, W, Sa-Su cover $6. Open daily 3pm-4am.

LONG ISLAND ☎631

Long Island, a sprawling suburbia stretching 120 mi. east of Manhattan, is both a home to over 2.7 million New Yorkers (excluding those who live in Queens and Brooklyn) and a sleepy summertime resort for wealthy Manhattanites. It is, not surprisingly, expensive and difficult to navigate without a car.

◪ **PRACTICAL INFORMATION. Long Island Railroad (LIRR)** services the island from Penn Station in Manhattan (34th St. at Seventh Ave.; Subway: 1, 2, 3 to 34th St./Penn Station/Seventh Ave.; A, C, E to 34th St./Penn Station/Eighth Ave.) and stops in Jamaica, Queens (Subway: E, J, Z), before proceeding to "points east." (☎718-217-5477. Fares vary daily and by zone.) To reach **Fire Island,** take the LIRR to Sayville, Bayshore, or Patchogue. The **Sayville Ferry** serves Cherry Grove, the Pines, and Sailor's Haven. (☎589-0810. Round-trip $13, under 12 $6.50.) The **Bay Shore Ferry** sails to Fair Harbor, Ocean Beach, Ocean Bay Park, Saltaire, and Kismet. (☎516-665-3600. Round-trip $12, under 12 $5.50.) The **Patchogue Ferry** shuttles to Davis Park and Watch Hill. (☎516-475-1665. Round-trip $11, under 12 $4.25.) The Hamptons are accessible by LIRR or by car. Take the Long Island Expwy. to Exit 70, go south to Rte. 27 (Sunset Hwy. or Montauk Hwy.), and head east to Montauk (approx. 50 mi. on Rte. 27). **Long Island Convention and Visitors Bureau** has four locations throughout the island. Call ☎951-2423 or 877-386-6654 for locations and hours. **Area Code:** 631 and 516. In listings, 631 unless otherwise noted.

FIRE ISLAND

Tranquil towns dot Fire Island, and the state protects most Fire Island areas by declaring them either state parks or federal "wilderness areas." This lack of infrastructure ensures both peace and inconvenience; visitors must often take water taxis to travel between towns. Fire Island's 17 summer communities have forged distinct niches—middle-class residential clusters, openly gay communities, and havens for vacationing Hollywood stars. Two prominent Fire Island resort hamlets, **Cherry Grove** and **Fire Island Pines** (called **"the Pines"**), host largely gay communities—and parties that rage late into the night. Crowded "streets," or wooden pathways, border spectacular beaches. Weekdays provide an opportunity to enjoy the island in a low-key setting, Thursdays and Sundays offer an ideal balance of sanity and scene, and Fridays and Saturdays see mounting crowds and prices.

Gay nightlife on Fire Island has an established rhythm that may be confusing to newcomers. Since neither Cherry Grove nor the Pines is very big, it's best just to ask around. More commercial than the Pines, the roadless Grove is lined with narrow, raised boardwalks leading to the small, uniformly shingled houses overflowing with men. Lesbian couples make up the majority of the town's population. A night in Cherry Grove usually begins at the **Ice Palace,** attached to the **Cherry Grove Beach Hotel,** where you can disco until dawn. (☎597-6600. Open daily July-Aug. noon-4am; Sept.-June noon-10pm). Most go to the Pines for late-night partying;

you can catch a water taxi from the docks at Cherry Grove, or walk 10min. up the beach. Houses here are spacious and often stunningly modern. Unfortunately, the Pines' active nighttime scene has a bit of a secret club feel to it—you need to be in the know or somehow be able to look like you are. **Tea Dance** (a.k.a. "Low Tea," 5-8pm) takes place inside and around the Yacht Club bar/club beside the Botel Hotel (☎597-6500). Move on to disco **High Tea** at 8pm in the **Pavilion** (☎597-6131), the premier disco in Cherry Grove, but make sure you have somewhere to disappear to during "disco naptime" (after 10pm). You can unabashedly dance until dawn at the **Island Club and Bistro** (☎597-6001), better known as the Sip-and-Twirl. The Pavilion becomes hot again late-night on weekends, including Sundays during the summer.

THE HAMPTONS AND MONTAUK

West Hampton, Southampton, Bridgehampton, and East Hampton make up the entity known as **the Hamptons,** where the upper crust of society roams the sidewalks before heading to the beach for the afternoon. Prices are high here; try going to **Montauk,** at the eastern tip of Long Island, for slightly cheaper accommodations. While lodging anywhere on the South Fork requires some research and often reservations, clean rooms can be had at **Tipperary Inn ❺**, 432 West Lake Ln., accessible via the S-94 bus to Montauk Dock. The inn provides A/C, TV, phone, and fridge. (☎668-2010. Rooms for 2-6 people in summer $125-160; low season $75-95.)

Many beaches in the Hamptons require a permit to park, but anyone can walk on for free. Sights include the **Montauk Point Lighthouse and Museum,** off Rte. 27 at the far eastern tip of the island, which was built in 1796 by special order of President George Washington. (☎668-2544. Open June-Sept. M-F and Su 10:30am-6pm, Sa 10:30am-7:30pm; call for low-season info. $6, seniors $5, under 12 $3.) Whaling buffs shouldn't miss the **Sag Harbor Whaling Museum,** at the corner of Main and Garden St. in Sag Harbor. (☎725-0770. Open May-Sept. M-Sa 10am-5pm, Su 1-5pm. $3, seniors $2, ages 6-13 $1. Tours by appointment $2.)

THE CATSKILLS   ☎845

According to legend, the Catskills cradled Rip Van Winkle during his century-long repose. The mountain region is still ideal for quiet solitude, despite the infamous Woodstock rock festival of 1969 that hit the small town of Bethel like a twister. Today, the region's best attractions are its miles of pristine hiking and skiing trails and the crystal-clear fishing streams of the Catskill Forest Preserve. Small mountain villages are home to art galleries and shops permeated with local flavor.

▨ PRACTICAL INFORMATION. Traveling from **I-87,** follow **Rte. 28 W** from Exit 19 to reach the many small villages in the area. **Rte. 212** from Exit 20 or the **Rte. 23-23A loop**—termed the "Rip Van Winkle Trail"—from Exit 21, are also easy ways to explore the region. **Adirondack/Pine Hill Trailways** provides excellent service throughout the Catskills. The main stop is in **Kingston,** 400 Washington Ave., on the corner of N. Front St. (☎331-0744 or 800-858-8555. Ticket office open daily 5:45am-11:00pm.) **Buses** run to New York City (2hr., 10-15 per day, $21). Other stops in the area include Delhi, Hunter, Pine Hill, and Woodstock; each connects with Albany, Cooperstown, New York City, and Utica. Two stationary **tourist cabooses,** one at the traffic circle in Kingston and one on Rte. 209 in Ellenville, dispense info, including the extremely useful *Ulster County: Catskills Region Travel Guide.* (Open May-Oct. daily 9am-5pm, but hours vary depending on volunteer availability.) Further information on the region can be obtained from the Catskills regional office of the **NY Department of Environmental Conservation** (☎256-3009; www.dec.state.ny.us). **Area Code:** 845, unless otherwise noted.

CATSKILL FOREST PRESERVE

The nearly 300,000-acre Catskill Forest Preserve contains many small towns and outdoor adventure opportunities. Ranger stations distribute free permits for **back-country camping ❶**, which are required for stays over three days or groups of ten or more. Hiking trails are generally well maintained, though less-used paths sometimes fall into disrepair. Lean-tos are also maintained, but can become crowded. For more info, call the **Department of Environmental Conservation** (☎256-3000; open M-F 8:30am-4:45pm) or ask a ranger at one of the state campgrounds in the region. Most campgrounds sit at trailheads that mark great day-long jaunts. Reservations are vital in summer, especially on weekends. Required permits for **fishing** (out-of-state residents $15 per day, $25 per week) are available in sporting goods stores and at many campgrounds. **Ski season** runs from November to April, with slopes on numerous mountainsides along Rte. 28 and Rte. 23A.

KINGSTON

Kingston, NY, was founded by the Dutch in the mid-1600s as the first capital city of New York state. Although much quieter now that the state government has changed locales, Kingston still teems with vibrant colonial history. The rough stone **Senate House**, 296 Fair St., was the home of merchant Abraham Van Gaasbeek and was used as a meeting place for the rebel colonists' State Senate. Today the house is filled with antique artifacts and rich history. A nearby museum chronicles art and life in colonial New York. (☎338-2786. Open mid-Apr. to Oct. M and W-Sa 10am-5pm, Su 11am-5pm. Tours every 30min. $4, seniors $3, under 12 $1.) For bells and whistles, stop by the **Volunteer Fireman's Hall and Museum**, 265 Fair St., an 1857 fire station that is full of firefighting memorabilia and even has a working antique fire alarm system. (☎331-0866. Open Apr.-Oct. W-F 11am-3pm, Sa 10am-4pm. Donations accepted.) The **Stockade District**, an area bounded by Washington Ave. to the west and Clinton Ave. to the east, was originally surrounded by 14 ft. high wooden walls for protection from the Esopus Indians, but now is the commercial and historical center of town. Built in 1774, the site of New York's first two-year college is now home to **El Rodeo ❶**, 35 Crown St., where delicious quesadillas and fajitas have replaced exams and books. (☎340-9895. Entrees $5-10. Opens M-F at 11am, Sa at noon, Su at 3pm; closes when crowds filter out.) For baked goods with artistic flair, locals head to **Bread Alone ❶**, 34 Main St., where artisan breads ($1-5) and panini ($6.25) anchor the menu and delight the taste buds. (☎339-1295. Open M-Sa 7am-6pm, Su 9am-3pm.)

MT. TREMPER

▧**The Kaleidostore,** in Emerson Place on Rte. 28, brings art to new levels with the world's largest kaleidoscope. With its 60 ft. mirrors, the best way to view it is to lie in the middle of the floor as music and color wash over you. (☎688-5800. Open Th-Su 10am-6pm, but call ahead. $7, seniors $5, under 12 free.) The **Kenneth L. Wilson Campground ❶** has 76 sites nestled in a tranquil forest. The lake allows for canoeing, kayaking, and paddleboating. From Rte. 28, exit onto Rte. 212, then make a hard right onto Wittenburg Rd./County Rte. 40 and follow it 5 mi. to the campground. (☎679-7020. Canoes and 2-person kayaks $15 per 4hr. Paddleboats $5 per hr. Showers $0.25 per 6min. Reception 8am-9pm. Weekend reservations recommended. Sites $17. Registration fee $2.75. Day use $4 per car, $1 on foot or bike.)

PHOENICIA

Phoenicia is a small town in the heart of the Catskills. **Esopus Creek,** to the west, has great trout fishing, and **The Town Tinker,** 10 Bridge St., rents inner tubes for river-riding on the ripples and rapids. (☎688-5553; www.towntinker.com. Inner tubes $10 per day, with seat $12. Driver's license or $15-75 deposit required. "Tube taxi" transportation $5 per trip on either the railroad (see below) or a bus. Life jackets required $3. Wet suits $15. Package with seated tube, life jacket, and single transport $20; package with wetsuit $30. Wet suits not necessary on hot summer days. Open mid-May to Sept. daily 9am-6pm; last rental 3:30-4pm.) A more relaxing alternative is the 100-year-old **Catskill Mountain Railroad,** which follows Esopus Creek for three scenic miles from Bridge St. to Mt. Pleasant along antique tracks. (☎688-7400; www.catskillmtrailroad.com. Two routes run Sa-Su and holidays, 1 per hr. May-early Sept. 11am-5pm, Oct. noon-4pm. Shuttle $5 one-way, $8 round-trip, ages 4-11 $5; "round-trip scenic route" $12/$8.) A 12 mi. round-trip hike to the 4180 ft. summit of **Slide Mountain** rewards hikers with 360° views of New Jersey, Pennsylvania, and the Hudson Highlands; begin at Woodland Valley Campground (see below). Nestled in the woods, the **Zen Mountain Monastery,** off Rte. 40 north of Rte. 28, houses 35-40 Buddhists who live and work together while receiving Zen training. (☎688-2228. Phone lines open Tu 2-5pm, W-Sa 8:30am-5pm. Closed to the public except during meditation training sessions W 7pm and Su 8:45am. Free, but $5 suggested donation on Su, when lunch is provided.)

Surrounded by mountains, the **Cobblestone Motel ❸,** within walking distance from Phoenicia on Rte. 214, has friendly managers, an outdoor pool, and clean, quiet rooms with refrigerators. (☎688-7871. Queen $56; queen and single $61; 2 doubles or queens with futon and kitchen $75-95; cottages with kitchen $109-129.) With 72 sites, the secluded **Woodland Valley Campground ❶,** on Woodland Valley Rd. off High St., 7 mi. southeast of Phoenicia, has a stream, showers ($0.25 per 6min.), and access to day hikes to Giant Ledge or Wittenberg Mountain. (☎688-7647. Reception daily 8am-9pm. Open late May-early Oct. Sites $15. Registration fee $2.75.) Customers line up outside of **Sweet Sue's ❶,** on Main St., to take a stab at finishing thick french toast and stacks of enormous 9 in. pancakes. (☎688-7852. Entrees $7-9. Open M and W-Su 7am-3pm.) With a menu longer than Main St., **Brio's ❷,** 68 Main St., keeps local customers happy with everything from omelets ($5-7) to burritos ($7-9) in a diner flickering with the light of the wood-fired pizza oven. Their southern-fried chicken ($10) is pure heaven. (☎688-5370. Takeout available. Open M-Th and Su 7am-10pm, F-Sa 7am-11pm.)

PINE HILL

The small town of Pine Hill sits near **Belleayre Mountain,** which offers hiking trails and **"Sky Rides"** on a chairlift to the summit during the summer, as well as downhill and cross-country ski slopes when the snow starts to fall. (☎254-5600 or 800-942-6904. Lift tickets M-F $35, Sa-Su $42; ages 13-22 and 62+ $30/$34. Equipment rental $25. Sky Ride $8, ages 13-17 and seniors $5; open mid-June to mid-Oct. Sa-Su 10am-6pm.) **Belleayre Music Festival,** held at the Belleayre Mt. ski resort, hosts a series of classical, jazz, country, opera, and folk concerts in a tent pavilion during July and August. Past performers include musical legends Ray Charles and Ritchie Havens. (☎800-942-6904; www.belleayremusic.org. Lawn tickets $15, some concerts free.) The **Belleayre Beach at Pine Hills,** ½ mi. south of Pine Hills on Rte. 28, provides warm-weather recreation, including swimming, hiking, volleyball, and a playground. (☎800-942-6904. Open late May to mid-June Sa-Su 10am-6pm, mid-June-Sept. M-F 10am-6pm, Sa-Su 10am-7:30pm. Beach has lifeguards while park is open. $6 per car, $1 per person on foot.) For info on the mountain and beach, visit www.belleayre.com. Next to Belleayre Mt., **Evergreen ❹,** 1625 Main St. in Fleishmanns, 2 mi. north of Pine Hill, is a fully organic B&B housed above an organic restaurant, art gallery, and nightclub. (☎254-5392. Live music Sa-Su. Rooms $75-105.) Under a colorful mural of a tequila-guzzling gaucho, **El Rey ❷,** 297 Main St., serves steaming fajitas ($7-11) and huge burritos ($6-7.50) with fresh homemade salsas, all to the tune of mariachi music. (☎254-6027. Entrees $5-11. Open summer M, W-F noon-9:30pm, Sa-Su 8:30am-10:00pm, winter M-Th 4-9:30pm, F-Su noon-9:30pm.)

ALBANY   ☎ 518

Albany, the capital of New York State and the oldest continuous European settlement in the original 13 colonies, calls itself "the most livable city in America." Albany has the intensity expected of the capital of one of America's most influential states, but outside the government offices, upstate New York's tranquility endures. On weekdays, downtown shops and restaurants thrive on the purses of politicians, while weekend nightlife erupts outside the government center.

⬛⬛ ORIENTATION AND PRACTICAL INFORMATION. Amtrak, 525 East St.
(☎462-5710; www.amtrak.com; station and ticket booth open daily 4:30am-midnight), across the Hudson from downtown, has service to Buffalo (5hr., 4 per day, $50-60) and New York City (2½hr., 8-9 per day, $43-50). **Greyhound,** 34 Hamilton St. (☎436-9651 or 800-231-2222; www.greyhound.com; station open 24hr., ticket window open daily noon-11:30pm), runs buses to Buffalo (6½hr., 7-8 per day, $56) and New York City (3hr., 15 per day, $34). Be careful here at night. From the same station, **Adirondack Trailways** (☎800-776-7548; www.trailwaysny.com) goes to Kingston (1hr., 7 per day, $11) and Lake Placid (4hr., 1 per day, $29). The **Capital District Transportation Authority (CDTA;** ☎482-8822; www.cdta.org) runs buses in Albany, Schenectady, and Troy (all fares $1, day pass $3). Get schedules and shuttle routes at the Amtrak and bus stations and visitors center. The **Albany Visitors Center,** 25 Quackenbush Sq., at Clinton Ave. and Broadway, runs trolley and horse-drawn carriage tours of downtown and has self-guided walking tours. (☎434-0405; www.albany.org. Open M-F 9am-4pm, Sa-Su 10am-4pm. Carriage tours Aug.-Sept. Th 10am. Trolley tours W and F-Sa 11am. July-Aug. arrive 20min. early for a film about the city. Tours $10, seniors $5.) **Internet Access: Albany Public Library,** 161 Washington Ave. (☎427-4300. Open June-Sept. M-Th 9am-9pm, F 9am-6pm, Sa 9am-5pm; Sept.-June also open Su 1-5pm.) **Post Office:** Capitol Plz., near State St. (☎462-4635. Open M-F 9am-4:45pm.) **Postal Code:** 12224. **Area Code:** 518.

⬛ ACCOMMODATIONS. Five gorgeous rooms at the **Pine Haven Bed & Breakfast** ❹, 531 Western Ave., at Madison Ave., make this ornate Victorian house a haven indeed. (☎482-1574; www.pinehavenbedandbreakfast.com. Cable TV, wireless Internet, A/C, parking. Reservations required. Rooms $69-114.) **Red Carpet Inn** ❸, 500 Northern Blvd., between downtown and the airport, has decent rooms with A/C and cable TV. Take Exit 6 from I-90 and turn onto Northern Blvd. (☎462-5562. Rooms $54-60.) **Thompson's Lake State Park** ❶, 18 mi. southwest of Albany, is the closest campground, with 140 wooded sites within walking distance of the lake's sandy beach. Take Madison Ave./Rte. 20 north to Rte. 85. Follow Rte. 85 out of Albany, turn right on Rte. 157, and look for signs. (☎872-1674. Free hot showers. Sites $13. Registration fee $2.75. Row boats $5 per hr., $20 per day. Paddle boats $4 per 30min. Lifeguard on duty June-Sept. M-F 10am-6pm, Sa-Su 10am-7pm.)

⬛⬛ FOOD AND NIGHTLIFE. **Lark Street** is full of ethnic eats and coffeeshops with a young, college-town atmosphere, while **N. Pearl St.** and **S. Pearl Street** are dotted with traditional American eateries. The lunch carts that set up shop along State St. near the State Capitol around lunchtime are always good for a cheap meal. In the city proper, the best dining option involves doing time with a "TNT" wrap, stuffed with Buffalo chicken and jalapeños, a large pile of nachos, and some Al Capone Amber Ale at the **Big House Brewing Company** ❷, 90 N. Pearl St., at Sheridan St. (☎445-2739. www.bighouseonline.com. Entrees $5-8. Pints $2. Happy hour 4-7pm. Live bands F. Kitchen open Tu-W 4-9pm, Th-Sa 4-10:30pm. Bar open Tu-W until 1am, Th-Sa until 3am.) Beneath frescoes of the sea and windows capped with terra cotta, **A Taste of Greece** ❷, 193 Lark St., serves excellent lamb and vegetarian

dishes. Classic gyros and Greek salads ($6-8), are part of a menu is filled with authentic Greek specialties. (☎426-9000. Entrees $7-10. Open M-Th 11am-9pm, F 11am-10pm, Sa 2-10pm.) The two-floor **Bomber's Burrito Bar ❶**, 258 Lark St., offers food, a lounge, pool tables, and the longest happy hour in New York (pints $2 11am-8pm). Twelve-inch burritos and mountainous nachos share the menu with barbecue tofu fries and witty catchphrases like "we know how to roll a fatty." (☎463-9639. Burritos $6. Open daily 11am-1am. Delivery 11am-2pm.) Head to the **Bayou Cafe ❸**, 79 N. Pearl St., for tangy Cajun food and a wild southern setting. With no set closing time (establishments can serve until 3am on weekends), live rock and blues play long into the night Thursday through Saturday. (☎462-9033; www.bayoucafe.com. Entrees $8-16. Open M-F at 11:30am, Sa at 4:30pm.) **De Johns Restaurant and Pub ❹**, 288 Lark St., is an award-winning spot for candlelit dinners and excellent service. Smoked chicken carbonara and pecan-encrusted trout topped with sherry are specialties. (☎465-5275; www.dejohns.com. Sandwiches $8-10. Entrees $15-18. Open M-Th 4-11pm, F 4pm-midnight, Sa-Su 11am-midnight.)

🎭🎵 **SIGHTS AND ENTERTAINMENT.** Albany's sights are centered on the **Rockefeller Empire State Plaza,** between State and Madison St., a modernist Stonehenge made of 900,000 cubic yards of concrete and 232,000 tons of steel. The plaza houses state offices, a bus terminal, a post office, a food court, several war memorials, and the largest outdoor display of modern art in the country, set in and around two large reflecting pools. The **Plaza Information Center,** in the north concourse, is the departure spot for **Plaza Tours,** which visit the buildings, memorials, and certain works of art. (Information center ☎474-2418, tours ☎473-7521. Open M-F 8:30am-5pm. Tours M-F 11am and 1pm. Free.) The huge flying saucer at one end of the Plaza is the **Empire Center for the Performing Arts,** also known as "The Egg," a venue for professional theater, dance, and concerts. (☎473-1845. Box office open June-Sept. M-F 10am-4pm; Sept.-May M-F 10am-5pm, Sa 11am-2pm. Tickets $8-40.) Across the street, the huge █ **New York State Museum** has exhibits on the state's history, people, and wildlife. Both kids and adults will delight in the museum's working carousel, built in 1895. One wing is dedicated to the memory of the World Trade Center, housing large portions of the buildings, crushed FDNY trucks, and the famous American flag recovered from under the wreckage. This powerful exhibit is not to be missed. (☎474-5877. Open daily 9:30am-5pm. Donations accepted.) Between the museum and The Egg, an elevator ride up the 42 floors of the **Corning Tower** provides a 60 mi. view on clear days. (☎474-2418. Open daily 10am-2:30pm. Photo ID required. Free.) Since 1899, the magnificent **New York State Capitol,** adjacent to the plaza, has provided New York politicians with luxury quarters amid a tempest of political activity. Tours leave from the Plaza Information Center. (☎474-2418. Tours M-F 10am, noon, 2, 3pm; Sa-Su 11am, 1, 3pm. No backpacks allowed. Free.) The **Capitol Repertory Theatre,** 111 N. Pearl St., stages some of Albany's best plays in a modern theater adorned with scarlet chairs. (☎445-7469. Box office open M 10am-5pm, T-Th 10am-7:30pm, F 10am-8pm, Sa 10am-8:30pm, Su noon-4pm. $31-39.) Reminiscent of majestic movie theatres of yore, the **Palace Theatre,** 19 Clinton Ave., presents concerts, plays, musicals, and comedy. (☎465-3334. Box office open M-F 10am-6pm; Sept.-June also Sa 10am-2pm. Tickets $15-60.)

Bounded by State St. and Madison Ave. north of downtown, **Washington Park** has tulip gardens, tennis courts, and plenty of room to sprawl. The **Park Playhouse** stages free musical theater in a pastoral setting from July to mid-August. (☎434-2035; www.parkplayhouse.com.) **Alive at Five** hosts free concerts on Thursdays 5-8pm at the **Tricentennial Plaza,** across from Bank of America on Broadway, or in the amphitheater in the **Hudson Riverfront Park.** (☎434-2032. Open June-July. More info at visitors center.) The annual **Tulip Festival** (☎434-2032), held in early May in Washington Park, celebrates the town's Dutch heritage and the blooming of over

MID-ATLANTIC

100,000 tulips with food, song, dance, crafts, and a Tulip Queen crowning. Call the **Albany Alive Line** (☎434-1217) or visit www.albanyevents.org for info. The **Mohawk-Hudson Bikeway** (☎386-2225) passes along old railroad grades and canal towpaths, weaving through the capital area and along the Hudson River. The **Down Tube Cycle Shop,** 466 Madison Ave., has rentals. (☎434-1711. Full day $25, 2 days $35. Open Apr.-Sept. M-F 11am-7pm, Sa 10am-5pm; Sept.-Apr. M-F 10am-6pm.)

COOPERSTOWN ☎845

In the early 19th century, four cloth bases were placed in a diamond on the Cooperstown green, and an American legend was born—baseball. Set on a hill overlooking Otsego Lake, Cooperstown pays homage to the history and legends of the sport. Each year, half a million make the pilgrimage to the town's pristine streets, wearing their favorite team uniforms and requisite baseball caps. But small Cooperstown is more than just a baseball town. Wander farther afield and you'll find hiking, farmers markets, and art galleries in "America's most perfect village."

■▪ **ORIENTATION AND PRACTICAL INFORMATION.** Cooperstown is accessible from **I-90** and **I-88** via **Route 28.** Only four blocks by five blocks, the town is centered around **Main Street (Route 31),** which is chock full of baseball shops and restaurants. Street parking is rare in Cooperstown; park in the free lots just outside of town on Maple St. off Glen Ave. (Rte. 28), Rte. 28 south of town, or adjacent to the Fenimore Art Museum—it's an easy walk to Main St. **Trolleys** leave from the lots every 20min., dropping riders off at major stops in town, including the **Hall of Fame,** the **Farmer's** and **Fenimore Museums, Doubleday Field,** the Pine Hill Trailways stop, and the **Chamber of Commerce.** (Trolleys run late June to early Sept. daily 8:30am-9pm; early June to mid-June and mid-Sept. to mid-Oct. Sa-Su 8:30am-6pm. All-day pass $2, children $1.) **Pine Hill Trailways** (☎547-2519 or 800-858-8555; open M-F 8am-5:30pm, Sa 9am-noon), picks up visitors at AAA Tri-County Motor Club at the corner of Elm St. and Chestnut St., and goes to Kingston (3½hr., 2 per day, $23) and New York City (5½hr., 2 per day, $45). **Cooperstown Area Chamber of Commerce and Visitor Information Center,** 31 Chestnut St., on Rte. 28 near Main St., provides maps and information on lodging and attractions. (☎547-9983; www.cooperstown-chamber.org. Open daily June-Sept. 9am-7pm; Oct.-May 9am-5pm.) **Internet Access: Village Library of Cooperstown,** 22 Main St. (☎547-8344. Open M-Tu and Th-F 9am-5pm, W 9am-8pm, Sa 10am-2pm.) **Post Office:** 40 Main St. (☎547-2311. Open M-F 8:30am-5pm, Sa 8:30am-noon.) **Postal Code:** 13326. **Area Code:** 607.

▪ **ACCOMMODATIONS.** Lodgers can really strike out during peak season, between late June and mid-September. It's cheapest to camp, or to travel in the low season, when many motels and guest houses slash rates by $20-50. The **Mohican Motel ❹,** 90 Chestnut St., a 10min. walk from the Hall of Fame, offers well-kept rooms, cable TV, and A/C. (☎547-5101. 2- to 6-person rooms late June to early Sept. M-F and Su $86-138, Sa $131-183; Apr. to late June and early Sept. to late Oct. M-F and Su $55-81, Sa $75-101.) The beautiful pines and lakeside view of **Glimmerglass State Park ❶,** 8 mi. north of Cooperstown on Rte. 31, on the north shore of Lake Otsego, make it an ideal camping location, with 43 campsites, including four wheelchair-accessible sites. The park offers hiking and biking; in the summer, visitors can swim, fish, and boat in the lake's cool water. (☎547-8662. Park open 8am-dark. Free hot showers. Dumping station; no hookups. Beach opens at 11am. Lifeguard on duty 11am-7pm. Sites $13. Registration fee $2.75. Day use $7 per vehicle.) **Cooperstown Beaver Valley Campground ❶** has wooded sites, cabins, a pool, recreation area, small pond, and, naturally, a well-maintained baseball diamond. Drive south of town 5 mi. on Rte. 28 and follow the signs. (☎293-7324 or 800-726-7314. Showers $0.25 per 6min. Sites $28-32, with hookup $37; cabins without indoor plumbing or linens $63-68, with plumbing $150.)

◘ FOOD. The popular **Doubleday Cafe ❶**, 93 Main St., serves meals amidst eye-catching memorabilia while TVs show baseball games taking place around the country. (☎547-5468. Omelets $2-4. Hot sandwiches $3-9. Kitchen open June-Sept. M-Th and Su 7am-10pm, F-Sa 7am-11pm; Oct.-May M-Th and Su 7am-9pm, F-Sa 7am-10pm; bar closes after kitchen.) For elegant dishes, **Hoffman Lane Bistro ❸**, 2 Hoffman Ln., off Main St. across from the Hall of Fame, has airy rooms and out-door seating along a quiet side street. (☎547-7055. Entrees $13-20. Kitchen open daily 5-10pm; bar open M-Th and Su until 1am, F-Sa until 2am.) Follow your nose to **Schneider's Bakery ❶**, 157 Main St., and your taste buds will thank you. A Coo-perstown institution, this bakery has been serving their $0.55 "old-fashioneds"—homemade doughnuts—since 1887. (☎547-9631. Open M-Sa 6:30am-5:30pm.) The restaurant at **Tunnicliff Inn ❸**, 36 Pioneer St., just off Main St., serves local Old Slug-ger Ale and huge "smothered steak" sandwiches. (☎547-9611. Entrees $7-17. Open M-Th and Su 11am-4pm and 5-9pm; F-Sa 11am-4pm and 5-10pm.)

◙ SIGHTS. With almost 400,000 visitors per year, the ⬛**National Baseball Hall of Fame and Museum,** on Main St., is an enormous, glowing monument to America's national pastime. Containing more than 35,000 pieces of memorabilia, the museum is a haven for baseball fans, with baseballs from every "no-hitter" in his-tory and a collection of World Series rings. Exhibits include the multimedia pre-sentation "The Baseball Experience," the history of African-Americans and women in baseball, and of course, the luminous Hall of Fame itself, where plaques commemorate the best players the sport has ever seen. (☎547-7200 or 888-425-5633; www.baseballhalloffame.org. Open daily Apr.-Oct. 9am-9pm; Nov.-Mar. 9am-5pm. $14.50, seniors $9.50, ages 7-12 $5.) The biggest event of the year, drawing over 20,000 visitors, is the annual **Hall of Fame Induction Weekend,** when new mem-bers of the Hall of Fame are inducted with appropriate pomp and circumstance. On the last weekend in July, the ceremonies are held at the **Clark Sports Center** on Susquehanna Ave., a 10min. walk from the Hall. The event is free and open to the public. The annual **Hall of Fame Game** between two rotating Major League teams is played every June on the intimate Doubleday Field. Contact the Hall of Fame for tickets and info on these two events and reserve accommodations far in advance.

Overlooking a refined lawn and Lake Otsego, the **Fenimore Art Museum,** on Lake Rd./Rte. 80, one mile from Main St., houses a collection of American folk art, Hud-son River School paintings, and an impressive array of Native American art. One highlight is the Browere busts—true-to-life sculptures of American greats like John Adams and the Marquis De Lafayette. (☎547-1400 or 888-547-1450; www.fen-imoreartmuseum.org. Open June-Oct. daily 10am-5pm; Apr.-May and Nov.-Dec. Tu-Su 10am-4pm. $11, seniors $9.50, ages 7-12 $5.) Go back in time to an 1845 farming village at the **Farmer's Museum,** complete with blacksmiths, musicians, dis-plays about farming, and the unmistakable aroma of farm animals. (☎888-547-1450; www.farmersmuseum.org. Open June-Oct. daily 10am-5pm; Apr.-May by tour only Tu-F 10:30am and noon. $9, seniors $8, students with ID $5, ages 7-12 $4. Combo ticket for Hall of Fame, Fenimore Museum, and Farmer's Museum $29, children $12.) Eight miles north of Cooperstown on Lake Rd./Rte. 80, the **Glimmer-glass Opera** stages summer performances of contemporary and little-known works as well as new takes on favorite operas. (☎547-2255; www.glimmerglass.org. Box office at 18 Chestnut St. in Cooperstown open June-Aug. M-Sa 9am-6pm; Dec.-May M-F 10am-5pm. Tickets M-Th $35-97, F-Su $63-110.)

MID-ATLANTIC

ITHACA AND THE FINGER LAKES ☎607

According to Iroquois legend, the Great Spirit laid his hand upon the earth to bless it, and the impression of his fingers resulted in the Finger Lakes: Canandaigua, Cayuga, Seneca, and eight others. From the shores of the lakes rise steep rolling hills and breathtaking gorges; millennia of rainfall and snowmelt have carved more than a thousand waterfalls into the stratified rock. Cornell University and Ithaca College overlook downtown Ithaca, where the bookstores and cafes of a classic college town line the streets. Beyond the city lies a more potent treasure—the region's rich vineyards, where the fruits of the land fill many a visitor's glass.

■ ▼ ORIENTATION AND PRACTICAL INFORMATION. Downtown Ithaca centers around **Ithaca Commons,** a pedestrian area lined with shops and restaurants. A steep uphill walk leads to Cornell's campus. Adjacent to Cornell's campus and overflowing with students, the **Collegetown** area is packed with hole-in-the-wall bars, cheap ethnic restaurants, and family-run diners. **Ithaca Bus Terminal,** 710 W. State St., at the intersection of Rte. 13 (☎272-7930), houses **ShortLine** (☎277-8800; www.shortlinebus.com), with service to New York City (5hr., 8 per day, $43), and **Greyhound** (☎800-231-2222; www.greyhound.com; open 6:30am-6pm), with service to Buffalo (3½hr., 3 per day, $31), New York City (5hr., 3 per day, $44), and Philadelphia (8hr., 3 per day, $57). Although Ithaca sits close to the base of Cayuga Lake, **Tompkins Consolidated Area Transit (T-CAT;** ☎277-7433) is the only way to get there without a car. Buses stop at Ithaca Commons; westbound buses also stop on Seneca St. and eastbound buses stop on Green St. (Buses run daily; times vary by route. $1.50-3, ages 6-17 and seniors $0.75-1.50. Schedules available from the visitors center.) The **Ithaca/Tompkins County Convention and Visitors Bureau,** 904 E. Shore Dr., has maps and the free (and invaluable) *Ithaca Gorges & Waterfalls* guide to outdoor recreation. (☎272-1313 or 800-284-8422. Open mid-May to early Sept. M-F 9am-5pm, Sa 10am-5pm, Su 10am-4pm; mid-Sept. to early May M-F 9am-5pm.) Info is also available at the **Clinton House,** 116 N. Cayuga St. (Open M-F 10am-5:30pm, Sa 10am-2pm and 3-5pm.) **Internet Access: Tompkins County Public Library,** 101 E. Green St. (☎272-4557. Open July-Aug. M-Th 10am-8:15pm, F-Sa 10am-5pm; Sept.-June also Su 1-5pm.) **Post Office:** 213 N. Tioga St., at E. Buffalo. (☎800-275-8777. Open M-F 8:30am-5pm, Sa 8:30am-noon.) **Postal Code:** 14850. **Area Code:** 607.

▼ ACCOMMODATIONS. Budget accommodations are surprisingly abundant in Ithaca. There is beautiful camping during the summer months, and reasonably priced B&Bs are a great option during the winter. The motels lining the many roads to the city are affordable any time of year. The **Sweet Dreams B&B ❸,** 228 Wood St., rests a few blocks south of downtown and is accessible from Albany St. With only two guest rooms, this cozy B&B ensures friendly interaction with the kind owners. (☎272-7727. Reservations required. Rooms $75-85.) A "way cool family-friendly earthy groovy place," the **Turtle Dreams B&B ❸,** 418 Lafayette Road, lives up to its motto with negotiable group rates, ample organic breakfasts, and a lovely setting in the Finger Lakes countryside. From Ithaca, take Rte. 366 west to Church St. in McLean. The B&B is 2½ mi. down the road on the right. (☎838-3492. www.dreamingturtles.com. Rooms with private bath M-F $60, Sa-Su $65. Shared bath $50/$55.) Just outside Cornell, the **Embassy Motel ❸,** 1083 Dryden Rd. on Rte. 366, has the cheapest rates in town and clean, simple rooms with A/C and cable. (☎272-3721. Rooms $45-85.) Featuring a waterfall that plummets 215 ft. (more than the Niagara Falls drop), **Taughannock Falls State Park ❶,** eight miles north on Rte. 89, offers woodland camping, access to the shores of Cayuga Lake, and Saturday evening concerts in July and August. (☎387-6739. Free hot showers. Sites $13, with electricity M-Th $19, F-Su $22. Cabins for 4 people $40 per night, $160 per

week. Registration fee $2.75. Day use $7.) A huge, foaming waterfall dominates the entrance to the campsite at **Buttermilk Falls ❶**, on Rte. 13 south of Ithaca. The closest park to Ithaca, Buttermilk has 60 small sites in a birch forest, and miles of trails trace Buttermilk Creek through the woods and across idyllic bridges. (☎273-5761. Free showers. Sites $13. Registration fee $2.75. Day use $7.)

❏ FOOD. ▧Wegmans ❶, 500 S. Meadow St., is food paradise for the budget traveler. Food by the pound is available at a wok bar, wing bar, cheese bar, or pizza bar ($5-7 per lb.); the deli sells mammoth 14 in. subs ($7); the candy section holds over 50 tubes of sweets stretching to the ceiling; and the produce section offers every fruit and vegetable imaginable at near-wholesale prices. (☎277-5800. Open 24hr.) Restaurants in Ithaca are focused around Ithaca Commons and Collegetown. With a new menu every day, jazz and folk music on the weekends, and ethnically themed nights on Sundays, **Moosewood Restaurant ❷**, 215 N. Cayuga, at Seneca St. in the Dewitt Mall, features a completely vegetarian selection of fresh and creative dishes. (☎273-9610. Dinner $10-16. Open Sept.-May M-Th 11:30am-3pm and 5:30-8:30pm, F-Sa 11:30am-3pm and 5:30-9pm, Su 5:30-8:30pm; June-Oct. M-Th 11:30am-3pm and 5:30-9pm, F-Sa 11:30am-3pm and 6-9:30pm, Su 5:30-8:30pm.) Choose from a daily menu of appetizer-size tapas ($2-8) at **Just a Taste ❸**, 116 N. Aurora St. Wine flights ($6-11) and rich desserts ($2-5) are perfect for the outdoor patio during the summer. (☎277-9463. Open M-Th 11:30am-3:30pm and 5:30-10pm, F 11:30am-3:30pm and 5:30-11pm, Sa 10:30am-2:30pm and 5:30-11pm, Su 10:30am-2:30pm and 5:30-10pm.) At **Gino's NY Pizzeria ❶**, 106 N. Aurora St., a 16 oz. soda and the two largest slices of pizza you will ever consume ($3) could keep you going all the way to New York City. (☎277-2777. Open M-Th and Su 10:30am-10pm, F-Sa 10:30am-2am.) For a quick bite, **Jimmy John's ❶**, 122 N. Aurora St., serves up fast and fresh 8 in. subs ($4) for the traveler on the go. (☎645-0075. Open daily 11am-3am.)

◙ SIGHTS. Cornell University, the youngest of the Ivy League schools, sits on a steep hill in Ithaca between two tremendous gorges. Accessed by a steep flight of steps across University Ave. from the Johnson Art Museum, the suspension bridge above Fall Creek provides a heart-pounding walk above one gorge, while the **College Avenue Stone Arch Bridge** above Cascadilla Creek has a brilliant sunset view. The **Information and Referral Center,** in the 2nd floor lobby of Day Hall on East Ave., has info on campus sights and activities and offers **campus tours** that showcase the harmonious blend of architectural styles and landscaping that make Cornell one of the most beautiful campuses in the country. (☎254-4636. Open M-F 8am-5pm; phone also staffed Sa 8am-5pm. Tours Apr.-Nov. M-F 9, 11am, 1, and 3pm; Sa 9, 10:30am, 1pm; Su 1pm. Dec.-Mar. daily 1pm.) The funky, box-like cement edifice rising from the top of the hill houses Cornell's **Herbert F. Johnson Museum of Art,** at the corner of University Ave. and Central Ave. The museum holds a small but impressive collection of works by Giacometti, Matisse, O'Keeffe, Picasso, and Degas, as well as an equally impressive 5th floor Asian art exhibit and rooftop sculpture garden. (☎255-6464. Open Tu-Su 10am-5pm. Free.) Part museum and part paleontology lab, the **Museum of the Earth,** north along Rte. 98, gives visitors a look back into the natural history of the Finger Lakes. (☎273-6623; www.museumoftheearth.org. $8, seniors and students $5, ages 3-17 $3.) The extensive **botanical gardens** and **arboretum** that compose the **Cornell Plantations** lie serenely in the northeast corner of campus. Visitors can ramble through the Slim Jim Woods, drive to Grossman Pond, or take a short hike to a lookout point with a view of campus and the surrounding area. (☎255-3020. Open daily dawn-dusk. Free.) Parking permits ($1) are required at the art museum and gift shop (M-F 9am-4pm) and are available at the small booths at each entrance to campus.

MID-ATLANTIC

Information on hiking the numerous and beautiful trails in the region can be found in the *Passport to the Trails of Tompkins County* ($1), available at the Ithaca visitors center. A community gathering place on weekends, the **Ithaca Farmers Market,** 3rd St. off Rte. 13, has much more than produce under its eaves: vendors also bring ethnic food, cider tastings, and hand-crafted furniture to the market. (☎273-7109. Open Apr.-Dec. Sa 9am-3pm; May-Oct. also Su 9am-3pm, June-Aug. Tu 3-7pm.) The fertile soil and cool climate of the Finger Lakes region has made it the heart of New York's wine industry. Designated **wine trails** provide opportunities for wine tasting and vineyard touring—the fall harvest is the best time to visit. (For more information, contact the Visitors Bureau, p. 204.) The trail closest to Ithaca, the **Cayuga Trail** (☎800-684-5217; www.cayugawinetrail.com) contains 15 vineyards, 11 of which are located along Rte. 89 between Seneca Falls and Ithaca. Other wineries are on the **Seneca Lake Trail** (☎877-536-2717; www.senecalakewine.com), with 25 wineries encircling the lake on Rte. 414 (east side) and Rte. 14 (west side). The **Keuka Trail** (☎800-440-4898; www.keukawinetrail.com), with nine wineries along Rte. 54 and 76, is also easily accessible from Ithaca. Some wineries offer free picnic facilities and tours. All give free tastings; some require the purchase of a glass for a nominal charge.

■■ **ENTERTAINMENT AND NIGHTLIFE.** Befitting its Ivy League roots, Cornell offers excellent theater productions year-round. The **Hangar Theatre,** 2 mi. from downtown at the Rte. 89 N. Treman Marina entrance, stages musicals and plays. **"The Wedge,"** an experimental theater in the same building, gives free performances before and after the mainstage show. (☎273-8588; www.hangartheatre.org. Shows Tu-Th and Su 7:30pm, F-Sa 8pm; matinees Sa 3pm, and some Su 2pm. $12-31. Call ahead for Wedge showtimes.) The intimate 73-seat **Kitchen Theatre,** 116 N. Cayuga, is always cooking up something new, hosting everything from one-man shows to full plays. After the main performance, "Kitchen Sink" shows—experimental and cutting-edge theater—are often performed. (☎272-0403. $16-20. Students $12. Kitchen Sink shows $5, $4 with ticket to main show.) In the same building, the **Ticket Center at Clinton House** sells tickets to events at the Hangar Theatre, the Kitchen Theatre, and many local college theater events. (☎273-4497 or 800-284-8422. Open M-Sa 10am-5:30pm.) The free and widely available *Ithaca Times* has complete listings of entertainment options.

A romantic path along the **Cascadilla Creek** gorge starts near the Stone Arch Bridge on College Ave. Nearby Collegetown, centered on College Ave., harbors favorite student hangouts. **Stella's,** 403 College Ave., has the dual personality of most college students—there is a cafe on one side where intellectuals linger over offerings like the Velvet Hammer (two shots of expresso, steamed milk, and raspberry; $4) and a funky jazz bar where patrons down hip drinks and forget what they learned in class. (☎277-1490. No cover. Free wireless Internet. Food served daily 11am-midnight; cafe open in summer daily 7am-1:30am. Jazz bar open daily 11am-1am.) Named after a local serial killer, **Rulloff's,** 411 College Ave., has a large bar in a dimly-lit pub overflowing with college students. At 5:30pm, during happy hour, and at half past midnight, the bartender spins the "wheel of fortune" to pick the night's drink special, while $6 pitchers keep the college crowd happy. (☎272-6067; www.rulloffs.com. 21+. Open M-Sa 11:30am-1am, Su 10am-1am.) With plush red and purple curtains and masks on the walls, it's Mardi Gras all year long at **Maxie's Supper Club,** 635 W. State St. Between the Shrimp and Grits ($11), Cajun Bloody Mary ($6), and live music on Sunday nights, you'll swear you're in New Orleans. (☎272-4136; www.maxies.com. Raw bar and "mini-plates" $8-16. Entrees $14-24. Raw bar open daily 4pm-midnight, half-price 4-6pm; kitchen open M-Th and Su 5pm-midnight, F-Sa 5pm-1am; bar open daily 4pm-1am. Su brunch 11am-3pm.) For passage to a world of weirdness, head to the **Rongovian Embassy to the**

USA ("The Rongo"), on Rte. 96 in Trumansburg, 10 mi. north of Ithaca, for Mexican
and Cajun food (entrees under $11), an eclectic array of local music, and an atmo-
sphere well worth the drive. (☎387-3334; www.rongo.com. Beer $2.50-3.75. Live
music some nights. Cover $5 or less. Open Tu-F 4pm-1am, Sa-Su noon-1am.)

SENECA FALLS   ☎315

In 1848, the town of Seneca Falls hosted the first Women's Rights Convention and
thus claimed an eternal place for itself in American history books. An essential
first stop is the **Seneca Falls Heritage Area Visitor's Center,** 115 Fall St. (☎568-2703;
www.senecafallsheritage.com. Open M-Sa 10am-4pm, Su noon-4pm.) ◼**Women's
Rights National Park,** 136 Fall St., sits next to the frame of the Wesleyan Chapel,
where the Women's Rights Convention was held. It's an excellent spot to contem-
plate the convention's powerful Declaration of Sentiments, immortalized on the
outdoor memorial. The **Elizabeth Cady Stanton Home** and the **McClintock House,** both
part of the park, are nearby. (☎568-2991; www.nps.gov/wori. Open daily 9am-5pm,
but call ahead as hours vary seasonally. $3, under 17 free.) Documenting the lives
of more than 100 great American women, the **National Women's Hall of Fame,** 76 Fall
St., allows you to nominate your own favorite heroine. (☎568-8060; www.great-
women.org. Open May-Sept. M-Sa 10am-4pm; Oct.-Apr. W-Sa 11am-4pm. $3,
seniors and students $1.50; families $7.)

   The best deal in town for lodging is the **Starlite Motel ❸,** on Rtes. 5 and 20 west
of Seneca Falls, where the rooms have kitchenettes, HBO, and A/C. (☎568-6149.
Rooms in summer $55-75; in low season $40-75.) South of Seneca Falls on Rte. 89,
Cayuga Lake State Campgrounds ❶ offers more than 250 campsites and a prime
beach location. (☎568-5163. Sites $13, with electricity $19. Registration fee $2.75.
Day use $7 per vehicle.) With deep red booths and a slick retro decor, **Downtown
Deli ❶,** 53 Fall St., serves large sandwiches and wraps. In summer, they fire up the
grill on the deck overlooking the canal. (☎568-9943; www.downtowndelis.com.
Subs $4. Open M-F 7:30am-9pm, Sa 9am-9pm, Su 9am-5pm.) A classic bar and res-
taurant with a family-friendly feel, **Tavern on the Flats ❸,** 6 Ovid St. off Fall St.,
offers barbecue, live music on Friday and Saturday nights after 10pm, and the best
canal view in town. (☎568-2910. Sandwiches $4-10. Open Tu-Th 11am-1am, F-Sa
11am-2am, Su noon-9pm; kitchen open until 9pm.)

BUFFALO   ☎716

Combining a vibrant cultural scene with rough-around-the-edges charm, Buffalo is
a city of synergy. The city is an architectural delight, filled with everything from
Gothic church spires to the angular simplicity of homes designed by Frank Lloyd
Wright. Here, classic cafes and budget-friendly diners share the streets with hip
clubs and professional theater companies. From the downtown skyline to funky
Elmwood Village, Buffalo balances small-town warmth with big-city culture.

◼ **TRANSPORTATION. Buffalo Niagara International Airport,** 4200 Genesee St.,
Cheektowaga (☎630-6000; www.buffaloairport.com), 10 mi. east of downtown off
Hwy. 33. Take the MetroLink Airport-Downtown Express (#204) from the **Transportation Center,** 181 Ellicott St., at N. Division St. **Airport Taxi Service** (☎633-8294 or
800-551-9369; www.buffaloairporttaxi.com) offers shuttles to downtown for $15.
Call or reserve online. **Amtrak,** 75 Exchange St. (☎856-2075; www.amtrak.com;
office open M-F 6am-3:30pm), at Washington St., runs to New York City (8½hr., 3
per day, $63) and Toronto (4½hr., 1 per day, $26). **Greyhound,** in the Buffalo Metropolitan Transportation Center (☎855-7531 or 800-454-2487; www.greyhound.com;
station open 24hr.), sends buses to Boston (11½hr., 12 per day, $56); New York

City (8½hr., 13 per day, $72); Niagara Falls, ON (1hr., 7 per day, $4); and Toronto, ON (2½hr., 12 per day, $16). The **Niagara Frontier Transit Authority (NFTA)** offers bus and rail service in the city (☎855-300; www.nfta.com; $1.50-2.25; seniors, children, and disabled $0.65-0.95), with additional buses to Niagara Falls, NY, and free rides on the above-ground Main St. Metro Rail. **Taxi: Cheektowaga Taxi** (☎822-1738).

⑦ PRACTICAL INFORMATION. Visitor Info: Visitor Center, 617 Main St., in the Theater District. (☎852-2356 or 800-283-3256; www.visitbuffaloniagara.com. Open M-F 9am-5pm.) **GLBT Resources: Pride Buffalo, Inc.,** 266 Elmwood Ave., Ste. 207 (☎879-0999; www.pridebuffalo.org); **PFLAG,** P.O. Box 617 (☎883-0384; www.pflag-buffalo-niagara.org). **Police:** ☎855-2222 (non-emergency). **Suicide, Rape, Crisis, and Emergency Mental Health Hotline:** ☎834-3131. Operates 24hr. **Medical Services:** Buffalo General Hospital, 100 High St. (☎859-5600). Take the Metro Rail to the Allen-Hospital stop, go up Main St. and turn right on High St. **Internet Access: Buffalo and Erie County Public Library,** 1 Lafayette Sq. at Washington St., offers Internet access with $1 temporary library membership. (☎858-8900. Open M-Sa 8:30am-6pm.) **Post Office:** 701 Washington St. (☎856-4603. Open M-F 8:30am-5:30pm, Sa 8:30am-1pm.) **Postal Code:** 14203. **Area Code:** 716.

🏠🍴 ACCOMMODATIONS AND FOOD. Budget lodgings are a rarity in Buffalo, but chain motels can be found near the airport and off I-90, 8-10 mi. northeast of downtown. Set in the heart of downtown, **⬛Hostel Buffalo (HI) ❶,** 667 Main St., has cheery common rooms, a kitchen, and a genial staff. The hostel also has free linen, laundry facilities, and Internet access. (☎852-5222; www.hostelbuffalo.com. Reception 24hr. with reservation; otherwise 9-11am, July-Aug. also 4-11pm; Sept.-June 5-10pm. Check-out 10am. Reservations recommended in summer. Dorms $23, members $20; private rooms $50-$65; $10 per additional adult and $5 per additional child. Wheelchair accessible.) The **Lenox Hotel & Suites ❸,** 140 North St., at Delaware Ave., has old-fashioned, functional rooms only 5min. from Allentown/Elmwood Village nightlife. Take bus #11, 20, or 25 to North St.(☎884-1700; www.lenoxhotelandsuites.com. Cable TV, A/C, coin laundry, free parking, kitchens available. Singles from $59; suites $69-119.)

Elmwood Village, up Elmwood Ave. between Virginia Ave. and Forest Ave., is full of funky boutiques, coffee shops, and ethnic restaurants. Despite its imposing statue, **Gabriel's Gate ❷,** 145 Allen St., is a friendly, rustic bar and eatery reminiscent of a saloon. Enjoy the famous "Richmond Ave." burger ($5) or the portobello sandwich ($6) from the comfy shaded patio. (☎886-0602. Open M-W and Su 11:30am-midnight, Th 11:30am-1am, F-Sa 11:30am-2am.) At **Emerson Commons ❶,** 70 W. Chippewa St., high school culinary students serve cheap, hot breakfasts and lunches. (☎851-3018. Breakfast $2-5. Lunch sandwiches $6. Open school days 7:30-10:15am and 11:15am-1:30pm.) Skip Starbucks and head to **Spot Coffee,** 227 Delaware Ave., where you can get anything from a plain cup o' joe to specialty espresso drinks and iced blended shakes. A funky side room features mismatched furniture and local musicians on Wednesday and Sunday evenings. (☎856-2739. Coffee drinks $2-4. Open M-Th 6am-11pm, F 6am-midnight, Sa 7am-midnight, Su 7am-11pm. Kitchen closes 2hr. before cafe.)

🎵 NIGHTLIFE. Downtown, bars and clubs are concentrated on **Chippewa Street** and **Franklin Street,** but live music can be found throughout the city. From Thursday to Saturday bars are open until 4am, and thousands of Western New Yorkers are out all night. Pick up a copy of *Artvoice* (www.artvoice.com) for event listings in Buffalo. Music is burned into the walls at **Nietzsche's,** 248 Allen St., where Ani DiFranco and the 10,000 Maniacs got their big breaks. (☎886-8539; www.nietzsches.com. Beer on tap from $2.50. Live rock, reggae, blues, or jazz every night. Open mic night M. 21+; call ahead for special 18+ nights. Open daily noon-4am.) **D'Arcy McGee's Irish Pub and Sky Bar,** 257 Franklin St., is an authentic Irish pub on the first floor, a nightclub on the second, and Buffalo's only open-air rooftop lounge on top. Patrons can ride a glass elevator up to the sky bar to relax above the bustling scene below. (☎853-3600. Entrees $10-14. Pints of Guinness $4. 21+. Sky bar cover $3-4 after 10pm. Open daily 11am-4am, weather permitting.) **Club Marcella,** 622 Main St., is a gay nightclub, but clubbers of all persuasions party on its two dance floors. (☎847-6850; www.marcellashowclub.com. Drag shows W, F, Su. Th and Sa hip-hop. 18+. Cover usually $3, but varies. Open W-Su 9pm-4am.)

◎ 🎵 **SIGHTS AND ENTERTAINMENT.** The **Albright-Knox Art Gallery,** 1285 Elmwood Ave., houses an internationally recognized collection of over 6000 modern pieces, including works by Picasso and Rothko. (☎882-8700; www.albright-knox.org. Take bus #20. Open W-Su 10am-5pm, F 10am-10pm. $10, seniors and students $8, 12 and under free; F 3-10pm free.) Next to the gallery, **Delaware Park,** the center of Buffalo's park system, was designed by legendary landscape architect Frederick Law Olmsted. Frank Lloyd Wright also designed several important houses in the area. Architecture buffs can take a 2hr. self-guided **walking tour** of historic downtown Buffalo; pick up the free guide *Walk Buffalo* at the tourist office. For a great view of Buffalo, head to **Buffalo City Hall,** 65 Niagara Sq., take the elevator to the 25th floor, and walk up three more flights for a spectacular panoramic view from the outdoor observation deck. (☎851-5891. Open M-F 9am-4pm. Free.) **Shea's Performing Arts Center,** 646 Main St. (☎847-1400), features Broadway musicals in an elegant opera house, while the **Irish Classical Theatre Company,** 625 Main St. (☎853-4282), performs the works of Gaelic playwrights in a three-row theater-in-the-round. The **Studio Arena Theatre,** 710 Main St. (☎856-8025), is a nationally-recognized company that produces a wide variety of plays. The Allentown Village Society organizes the **Allentown Art Festival,** a two-day celebration of local artists, craftsmen, and musicians. (☎881-4269; www.allentownartfestival.com. June 10-11, 2006.) The **Buffalo Niagara Guitar Festival** (☎845-7156; www.guitarfestival.org) is America's first and largest all-guitar music festival, featuring such luminaries as Bo Diddley. From September to January, **Ralph Wilson Stadium,** in Orchard Park, hosts the NFL's **Buffalo Bills** (☎648-1800; www.buffalobills.com), while the NHL's **Sabres** (☎855-4444, ext. 82; www.sabres.com) play at the **HSBC Arena,** 1 Seymour H. Knox III Plaza, from September to April.

NIAGARA FALLS ☎716

Niagara Falls, one of the seven natural wonders of the world, is flat-out spectacular. The giant falls are best viewed from the Canadian side of the Niagara River, where the natural grandeur is complemented by well-developed tourist attractions, nightlife, and a thriving honeymoon industry. Meanwhile, on the American side, a giant resort-casino built on Seneca tribal land promises to revitalize the area. Although the area around the falls teems with commercialized gimmicks, the real draw is the magnificence of the falls—something not to be missed.

 BORDER CROSSING. Traveling between the US and Canada is generally an easy process, but security is still taken very seriously. Crossing can be as simple as a wave of the passport or as time-consuming as a full search of your car. To keep things moving along, make sure to have all necessary documents handy. It is illegal to cross the border anywhere except an open crossing station. See **Essentials,** p. 10, for more details on documents and procedures.

▣ TRANSPORTATION

Trains: In Canada, **VIA Rail Canada,** 4267 Bridge St. (☎888-842-7245). Take the Niagara Falls Shuttle (see **Public Transit,** below) from downtown. Runs to **New York City** (10hr.; 11:30am; M-Th and Sa CDN$86, F and Su CDN$102) and **Toronto** (2hr.; daily 5:45am, M-F 6:45am, Sa-Su 7:40am; CDN$31, with ISIC CDN$22). Open M-F 6am-8pm, Sa-Su 7am-8pm. In the US, **Amtrak,** at 27th and Lockport St. (☎285-4224; www.amtrak.com), 1 block east of Hyde Park Blvd., runs to **New York City** (9hr.; M-Th and Sa $63, F and Su $75) and **Toronto** (3hr.; M-Th and Sa $23, F and Su $30). Taxis meet each incoming train ($7-10 to downtown), or wait for bus #52 (runs daily 7am-4:30pm). Open daily 7:30am-5:30pm.

Buses: In Canada, the **bus terminal,** 4267 Bridge St. (☎357-2133; www.greyhound.com), across from the train station, sends **Greyhound** buses to **Toronto** (2hr., 23 per day, CDN$23). Open daily 7am-10:30pm. **The Magic Bus** (☎877-856-6610; www.magicbuscompany.com) runs between Hostelling International hostels at Niagara Falls and Toronto. (Tu, Th, Sa-Su 5pm; CDN$20.) In the US, **Niagara Falls Bus Terminal,** at 4th and Niagara St. (☎282-1331), sells **Greyhound** tickets for direct service to **New York City** (8hr., 1 per day, $72). Open M-F 9am-4pm, Sa-Su 9am-noon. To get a bus in Buffalo, take bus #40 "Grand Island" from the Niagara Falls bus terminal to the **Buffalo Transportation Center,** 181 Ellicott St. (1hr., 19 per day, $2.25).

Public Transit: On the Canadian side, the **Niagara Falls Shuttle** (☎356-1179) runs between the bus and train stations, downtown, and other touristy areas. (June 20-Aug. 31 every 30min. 8:45am-2am. All-day pass CDN$6.) **Niagara Frontier Metro Transit System** (☎285-2002; www.nfta.com) provides local city transit in the US ($1.50). **ITA Buffalo Shuttle** (☎800-551-9369) has service from the Niagara Falls info center and major hotels to Buffalo Niagara International Airport ($50).

Taxi: In Canada, **Niagara Falls Taxi,** ☎905-357-4000. In the US, **Blue United Cab,** ☎285-9331. Travelers should beware of taxi drivers who charge full fare for each rider.

Bike Rental: In Canada, **Leisure Trails,** 4362 Leader Ln. (☎905-371-9888), near the Niagara Whirlpool. $5 per hr., $20 per day, including lock and helmet. Open daily 9am-6pm, but later drop-offs can be arranged. In the US, **Bikes & Hikes,** 526 Niagara St. (☎278-0047; www.bikesandhikes.com). 2hr. rental with helmet, lock, and map $12.

✦ ▣ ORIENTATION AND PRACTICAL INFORMATION

Niagara Falls spans the US-Canadian border (addresses given here are in New York, unless noted). Take **U.S. 190** to the Robert Moses Pkwy., which leads directly to the Falls and downtown. On the **Canadian** side, most attractions are scattered along **Niagara Parkway (River Road),** and the main entertainment and shopping district is **Clifton Hill** between Victoria Ave. and River Rd. On the **American** side, **Niagara Street** is the main east-west artery, ending at the **Rainbow Bridge,** which crosses to Canada (pedestrian crossings $0.50, cars $2.50; tolls only charged going into Canada). North-south streets are numbered, increasing toward the east. Budget motels line **Route 62 (Niagara Falls Boulevard)** outside of town. Many businesses in the Niagara area accept both American and Canadian currency.

Visitor Info: Niagara Falls Tourism, 5515 Stanley Ave., in Canada (☎800-563-2557 or 905-356-6061; www.discoverniagara.com), has information about the Canadian side. Open M-F 8am-6pm, Sa 10am-6pm, Su 10am-4pm. In the US, the **Orin Lehman Visitors Center** (☎278-1796) is in front of the Falls' observation deck; the entrance is marked by a garden. Open daily 7am-10:15pm.

Hotlines: Sexual Assault Crisis Line, ☎905-682-4584.

Medical Services: In Canada, **Greater Niagara General Hospital,** 5546 Portage Rd. (☎905-358-0171). In the US, **Niagara Falls Memorial Medical Center,** 621 10th St. (☎278-4000; www.nfmmc.org).

Internet Access: In Canada, **Niagara Falls Public Library,** 4848 Victoria Ave. (☎905-356-8080), offers free Internet access. Open M-Th 9am-9pm, F-Sa 9am-5:30pm. In the US, **Niagara Falls Public Library,** 1425 Main St. (☎286-4894; www.niagarafallspubli-clib.org), also has free access. Open M-W 9am-9pm, Th-F 9am-5pm.

Post Office: In Canada, 4500 Queen Ave. (☎1-800-267-1177). Open M-F 8am-5pm. In the US, 615 Main St. (☎285-7561). Open M-F 8:30am-5pm, Sa 8:30am-2pm. **Postal Code:** L2E 2L0 (ON). 14302 (NY). **Area Code:** 905 (ON). 716 (NY). In text, 716 unless otherwise noted.

█ ACCOMMODATIONS

Many newlyweds spend their honeymoons by the awesome beauty of the Falls. In Canada, cheap motels (from CDN$35) advertising free wedding certificates line **Lundy's Lane,** while many moderately priced B&Bs overlook the gorge on **River Road** between the Rainbow Bridge and the Whirlpool Bridge.

Hostelling International Niagara Falls (HI), 4549 Cataract Ave., Niagara Falls, ON (☎905-357-0770 or 888-749-0058). Just off Bridge St., about 2 blocks from the bus station and VIA Rail. The inside of this hostel is brightly painted with earth-friendly messages. Daily social activities, Fair Trade coffee, and an organic garden. Internet access CDN$1 per 15min. Lockers CDN$2. Linen CDN$2 (free with ISIC). Laundry and kitchen facilities. Key deposit CDN$5. Reception 24hr. in summer, 8am-midnight in winter. Check-out 11am. Quiet hours 11pm-7am. Reservations recommended May-Nov. Dorms CDN$23, members CDN$19; singles $59/$50. ❶

Backpacker's International Hostel, 4219 Huron St., Niagara Falls, ON, at Zimmerman Ave. (☎905-357-4266 or 800-891-7022; www.backpackers.ca), a 5min. walk from the bus station. Take Bridge St. to Zimmerman Ave.; the hostel is a few blocks to the right. In a beautiful home with clean dorms, lovely private rooms, and yummy breakfasts. Bike rentals CDN$15 per day. Free Internet access. Breakfast, linens, and parking included. Reception 24hr. with reservation. Dorms CDN$20; singles $50; doubles $65. ❶

Bampfield Hall Bed & Breakfast, 4671 Zimmerman Ave., Niagara Falls, ON (☎905-353-8522 or 877-353-8522; www.niagaraniagara.com). Located right off the Niagara River Pkwy., this beautiful, newly restored B&B offers well-decorated and comfortable rooms at fairly reasonable rates. Includes an antique hat museum on premises. No smoking. Reservations required. Rooms CDN$80-115; low season from CDN$65. 10% cash discount. ❸

◘ FOOD

Niagara Cumpir ❶, 4941 Victoria Ave., ON, serves a young clientele affordable Mediterranean and American fare on two spacious patios. Falafel is CDN$3.75, and a whole pizza with any or all toppings is only CDN$12. (☎905-356-9900. Open M-Th 11am-11pm, F-Sa 11am-3am, Su 11am-9pm.) The oldest restaurant in town, **Simon's Restaurant ❷,** 4116 Bridge St., ON, just one block from the HI hostel, is more than a hundred years old. Huge breakfasts (CDN $6) and classic cheeseburgers (CDN $3) at historic prices prove why this diner is still a local favorite. (☎905-356-5310. Open M-Sa 5:30am-7pm, Su 5:30am-2pm.) For a touristy location without the touristy prices, head to **Spicy Olive ❸,** 5026 Center St., ON. The hip atmosphere and live music on weekends set this place a step above the other restaurants in the surrounding area. (☎905-371-2323. Entrees CDN $12-20. Open daily noon-2am.)

⚙ SIGHTS

In Canada, walk the ▧promenade from Clifton Hill to Table Rock Point for spectacular views of Bridal Veil Falls and Horseshoe Falls. Both sides of the border provide plenty of additional attractions. In Canada, the **casinos** and entertainment industry keep tourists occupied, while the American side enjoys a full calendar of historical and cultural festivals (☎ 800-338-7890; www.niagara-usa.com).

CANADIAN SIDE. On the Canadian side, **Queen Victoria Park** provides the best view of **Horseshoe Falls.** Starting 1hr. after sunset, the Falls are illuminated for 3hr. every night, and a fireworks display lights up the sky every Friday and Sunday at 10pm from May 16 to September 1. Parking close to the park is expensive (CDN$12), but farther down Niagara Pkwy., across from the Greenhouse, parking is CDN$3 per hr. **People Movers** buses tourists through the 30km area on the Canadian side of the Falls, stopping at attractions along the way. Fare includes rides on the incline railway to nearby casinos. (☎ 877-642-7275. Mid-June to early Sept. daily 9am-11pm; low-season hours vary. CDN$7.50, children 6-12 CDN$4.50.) Bikers, in-line skaters, and walkers enjoy the 32km **Niagara River Recreation Trail,** which runs from Fort Erie to Fort George and passes historical sights dating back to the War of 1812. Far above the crowds and excitement, **Skylon Tower** has the highest view of the Falls at 520 ft. above ground and 775 ft. above the base of the falls. On a clear day, you can see all the way to Toronto. The tower's **Observation Deck** also offers incredible views. (5200 Robinson St. ☎ 905-356-2651. Open June-Oct. M-F 8am-11pm, Sa-Su 8am-midnight; Nov.-May daily 9am-11pm. CDN$11.50, seniors CDN$9.50, children 6-12 CDN$6; families CDN$27.) The **Adventure Pass** includes entrance to the **Maid of the Mist** boat tour; **Journey Behind the Falls,** a tour behind Horseshoe Falls; **White Water Walk,** a long boardwalk next to the Niagara River Rapids; the **Butterfly Conservatory,** on the grounds of the world-famous Niagara Parks Botanical Gardens; CDN$2 discounts for the **Spanish Aero Car,** an aerial cable ride over the rapids' whirlpool waters; and all-day transportation on the People Movers. (Adventure Pass: CDN$38, children CDN$24. www.niagaraparks.com has details and sells passes online. Maid of the Mist: ☎ 905-357-7393. www.maidofthemist.com. Open in summer daily 9:45am-5:45pm. Trips every 15min. CDN$13, children CDN$8. Journey Behind the Falls: ☎ 905-354-1551. Open in summer daily 9am-7:30pm. CDN$10/CDN$6. White Water Walk: ☎ 905-374-1221. Open in summer daily 9am-5pm. CDN$8/CDN$5. Guided tours available. Butterfly Conservatory: ☎ 905-358-0025. Open in summer daily 9am-7:30pm, call for updated times. CDN$10/CDN$6. Aero Car: ☎ 905-354-8983. CDN$11/CDN$7. Open in summer daily 9am-6:45pm.)

In contrast to the natural wonder of the falls, attractions of a different sort exist on **Clifton Hill,** in the form of fun-houses, wax museums, arcades, and thrill rides. A popular destination, **Ripley's Believe It or Not Museum** displays wax wonders and a selection of medieval torture devices. (4960 Clifton Hill. ☎ 905-356-2238. Open in summer daily 9am-2am; low-season hours vary. CDN$13, seniors CDN$10, children CDN$6.)

AMERICAN SIDE. For over 150 years, the **Maid of the Mist** boat tour has entertained visitors with the awe-inspiring (and wet) views from the feet of both falls. (☎ 284-8897. Open Apr.-Oct. daily 10am-6pm. Tours in summer every 15min. $11.50, ages 6-12 $6.75, $1 for entrance to observation deck only.) The **Cave of the Winds Tour** hands out souvenir (read: ineffective) yellow raincoats and sandals for a drenching hike to the base of the Bridal Veil Falls, including an optional walk to Hurricane Deck where gale-force waves slam down from above. (☎ 278-1730. Open May to mid-Oct.; hours vary depending on season and weather conditions. Trips leave every 15min. Must be at least 42 in. tall. $8, ages 6-12 $7.) The **Master Pass,** available at the park's visitors center, covers admission to the Maid of the Mist; the Cave of the Winds Tour; the **Discovery Geological Museum,** in Prospect Park, which has gorge trail hikes and an elevator ride that simulates the geological history of the Falls; the **Aquarium of Niagara,** which houses the endangered Peruvian Penguin; and the **Niagara Scenic Trolley,** a tram-guided tour of the park and the best transportation between the sights on the American side. *(Master Pass: $27.50, ages 6-12 $19.25. Geological Museum: ☎278-1780. Film every 30min. Open June-Aug. daily 9am-7pm; Sept.-May 9am-5pm. $5, children $3. Aquarium: 701 Whirlpool St., across from the Geological Museum. ☎285-3575; www.aquariumofniagara.org. Open daily 9am-5pm. $7.50, children and seniors $5.50. Trolley: ☎278-1730. Open May-Aug. M-Th and Su 9am-9pm, F-Sa 9am-10pm. Runs every 10-20min. $2, ages 6-12 $1.)* The **Niagara Power Project,** 4 mi. north on Robert Moses Pkwy., features hands-on exhibits and videos on energy, hydropower, and local history. *(5777 Lewiston Rd. ☎286-6661. Open daily 9am-5pm. Call ahead to arrange a guided tour. Free.)* Eight miles north in Lewiston, NY, at the foot of 4th St., the 150-acre state **Artpark** focuses on visual and performing arts, offering opera, musicals, pops concerts, and rock shows. *(☎800-659-7275. Shows May-Aug.; call for schedule. Box office open M-F 10am-4pm, later on event days. Shows at 8pm. Tickets $15-40.)* Nestled between Niagara River and Lake Ontario, **Old Fort Niagara** was built for French troops in 1726 and was the site of battles during the French and Indian War and the American Revolution. *(Follow Robert Moses Pkwy. north from Niagara Falls. ☎745-7611. www.oldfortniagara.org. Open June-Aug. daily 9am-8pm; low-season hours vary. $8.50, seniors $6, ages 6-12 $5.)*

NORTHERN NEW YORK

THE ADIRONDACKS   ☎518

The largest state park in the US, Adirondacks State Park encompasses six million acres of cloud-topped mountains, glittering lakes, and knotted pine trees. Thousands of miles of trails carve through the mountainous terrain, leading to scenic vistas and isolated streams. In the green valleys between the peaks, small towns fit snugly between surrounding lakes and forests. The immense dimensions of the park allow the Adirondacks to be one of the few places in the Northeast where hikers can still spend days without seeing another soul, providing solitude for the world-weary traveler. Of the six million acres in the Adirondacks State Park, 40% are open to the public and provide a slew of outdoor activities. Fourteen **scenic byways** offer passage to even the most remote villages and waterways carry kayakers, canoers, and whitewater rafters through breathtaking gorges and forests.

🛈 PRACTICAL INFORMATION

Adirondacks Trailways (☎800-858-8555) services the region. From Albany, buses set out for Lake Placid and Lake George. From the Lake George bus stop at Lake George Hardware, 35 Montcalm St., buses go to Albany (4 per day, $14), Lake Placid (1-2 per day, $20), and New York City (4-5 per day, $49). The **Adirondack Mountain Club (ADK)** is the best source of info on outdoor activities in the region. Two excellent booklets available free of charge through the ADK are the *Adirondacks Waterways* and the *Adirondack Great Walks and Day Hikes* guides, which detail hundreds of hikes and paddles of all difficulty levels throughout the park. Offices are located at 814 Goggins Rd., in Lake George (☎668-4447; www.adk.org; open M-Sa 8:30am-5pm), and at Adirondack Loj Rd., in Lake Placid. (☎523-3441. Phone lines operate M-Th and Sa-Su 8am-8pm, F 8am-10pm.) The Lake Placid ADK, also known as the **High Peaks Information Center,** 3 mi. east of Lake Placid then 5 mi. down Adirondack Loj Rd. in the Loj itself, is the area's best resource for weather conditions, trail closures, and backcountry info. The center has washrooms (showers $0.25 per min.) and sells basic outdoor equipment, trail snacks, and a variety of helpful guides to the mountains for $11-25, including the ADK guides specific to each region of the mountains ($20). The center also runs an education program center that provides training in outdoor skills via 1- to 3-day excursions or lecture sessions. Classes include canoeing, rock climbing, and wilderness medicine. (☎523-3441. Classes $35-265, including all food and equipment. Open May-Oct. M-Th and Su 8am-5pm, F-Sa 8am-8pm; Oct.-May daily 8am-5pm. Hours often increase with seasonal traffic. Parking $9.) **Area Code:** 518.

LAKE TUPPER/BLUE MOUNTAIN LAKE

The western part of the Adirondacks, where small lakes and hamlets speckle the pine-filled forests, is perfect for a relaxing mountain getaway. The 21 exhibits at the ◾Adirondack Museum, off Rte. 30 in Blue Mountain Lake, showcase the history, culture, and lifestyles of the Adirondacks through the ages. The collection of 25 boats and the complete, richly decorated railcar are among the more impressive exhibits. (☎352-7311; www.adkmuseum.org. Open late May to mid-Oct. daily 10am-5pm. $14; seniors $13; students, military, and ages 13-17 $7; under 13 free.) In late June, Tupper hosts the **Tin Man Triathlon,** a 1¼ mi. swim, 56 mi. bike ride, and 13 mi. run through town. (Tupper Lake Chamber of Commerce: 60 Park St. ☎359-3328 or 888-887-5253. Open daily 9am-5pm.) There are many lodging options throughout the western Adirondacks, especially along Rtes. 3 and 30. Two miles east of Tupper Lake, **Northwood Cabins ❸,** 92 Tupper-Sara Hwy., rents nine cabins with cable TV and heat; some have kitchenettes and fireplaces. The soft beds and friendly owner offer a welcome alternative to the damp floor of the Adirondack forest. (☎359-9606 or 800-727-5756. Open mid-May to mid-Oct. Cabins $42-68.) The **White Birch Cafe ❷,** 6 Demars Blvd., in Tupper Lake, serves good, fresh food at reasonable prices. (☎359-8044. Sandwiches $4-6. Open M and W-Su 11am-8pm; other hours vary.) At the intersection of Rtes. 30 and 28 in Long Lake, **Hoss's General Store** provides camping supplies and groceries for visitors looking to hit the trails. (☎624-2451. Open daily July-Aug. 9am-10pm; Sept.-June 9am-5pm.) Hoss's also houses a bakery and an **Internet** cafe. (☎624-6466. Internet access $5 per 15min., including complimentary beverage. Open daily 10am-6pm.) The **Adirondack Park Visitor Interpretive Center,** just west of Newcomb on Rte. 28 N, is a great place to get park information and potentially spot moose, bears, minx, and otters. (☎582-2000. Visitors center open daily 9am-5pm; trails open dawn-dusk. Free.)

AUSABLE CHASM/TICONDEROGA

At the eastern end of the park, hikers revel in the above-treeline views of the High Peaks region and the beauty of nearby Lake Champlain. The ADK runs two lodges near Lake Placid. The ◾Adirondack Loj ❷, at the end of Adirondack Loj Rd., off Rte. 73, lures hikers looking for a place to rest their sore feet. Heated by an imposing fieldstone fireplace in the winter, the cozy den, decorated with skis and a moose trophy, is the perfect place to warm up after exploring the wilderness trails on skis or snowshoes. In summer, guests swim, fish, and canoe on Heart Lake, located 100 ft. from the lodge's doorstep. (☎523-3441. Breakfast included. Lunch $5.50. Dinner $14. Reservations highly recommended. Bunks $34-45; private rooms $110; lean-tos $26; campsites $23; canvas cabin $32; 4-person wood cabins $100; 16-person $320. Snowshoe rentals $10 per day; cross-country ski rentals $20 per day. Canoe or kayak rental 8am-8pm; $5 per hr., guests $3.) ADK's second lodge, the **John's Brook Lodge ❷,** offers the outdoor-savvy a more secluded and rustic atmosphere. From Lake Placid, follow Rte. 73 for 15 mi. through Keene to Keene Valley, turn right at the Ausable Inn, and drive 5 mi. to the parking lot at the end of the dirt road (parking $5). Reaching the lodge requires a 3½ mi. hike over the rolling hills and through the damp woods of the Adirondacks. Though the basic comforts of linens and showers are not available, three complimentary meals await the weary hiker. John's Brook is no secret, however, and beds fill completely on weekends. (Call the Adirondack Loj for reservations, ☎ 523-3441. Blankets provided. July to mid-Oct. bunks $42-45.) Twelve miles south of Plattsburgh on Rte. 9 lies one of the state's most beautiful campgrounds, **Ausable Point ❶.** Dotted with wildflowers and situated on the banks of Lake Champlain with a sandy beach, the park is ideal for camping or as a daytrip for boating or fishing. (☎ 561-7080. Make reservations far in advance for prime waterfront sites during weekends and holidays. Office open 8am-9pm. Registration fee $3. Sites $17, with electricity $20. Day use $6 per car. Lifeguard on duty June to late Aug. M-F 10am-7pm, Sa-Su 10am-8pm.) **Backcountry camping** rules have recently changed in sections of the eastern half of the High Peaks region, where self-issued permits are required. In designated areas camping is prohibited except at prescribed sites; campfires are banned within the entire section. Furthermore, a recent increase in bear activity has prompted rangers to make the use of bear canisters for food mandatory. Areas affected by these changes are identified on the new maps sold by the ADK and can be viewed or purchased at the High Peaks Information Center ($8). Otherwise, camping is free anywhere on public land in the backcountry as long as it is at least 150 ft. away from a trail, road, water source, or campground, and below 3500 ft. in altitude. Inquire about the locations of free trailside shelters before planning a hike in the forest. Contact the **Department of Environmental Conservation** (☎ 402-9428) for more info on backwoods camping. When you get sick of s'mores, join the locals at **Burleigh's Luncheonette ❶,** where you can munch on sandwiches ($3-5) and hearty breakfasts ($2.50-4) amidst 1950's decor. (☎ 585-6262. Open M-Sa 7am-4pm.) A number of the trails that wind their way through the highest peaks begin at the Adirondack Loj at the end of Adirondack Loj Rd. 3 mi. east of town along Rte. 73. **Algonquin Peak,** an 8 mi. round-trip hike, has a total rise in elevation of nearly 3,000 ft., but yields a spectacular, above-treeline view. **Mount Marcy,** a 7½ mi. hike to the state's highest peak (5344 ft.), is a daytrip that promises to test even the most avid hiker, finishing with a 360° aerial view of Adirondack Park and a commanding view of Lake Placid to the northwest. **Mount Jo,** a steep 2 mi. round-trip journey, provides views of the surrounding peaks and Heart Lake in the valley below.

Stroll down **Ausable Chasm,** a gorge cut deep into the earth by the roaring Ausable River, 12 mi. south of Plattsburgh on Rte. 9. The chasm includes numerous waterfalls and is surrounded by Adirondack forest seemingly untouched by civilization. At the conclusion of the walk, the relatively calm water provides the opportunity to raft through a labyrinth of age-old rock formations. (☎ 800-537-1211; www.ausablechasm.com. Open mid-May to late June daily 9:30am-4pm; late June to Sept. M-Th and Su 9:30am-5pm, F-Sa 9:30am-6:30pm. Entrance to the walkway $16, seniors and ages 12-19 $14, ages 5-11 $9. Entrance and raft trip $24/$22/$17.) Farther south along the shores of Lake Champlain, one mile east of the town of Ticonderoga, lies ◪**Fort Ticonderoga.** From atop the towering walls of the fortress, poised menacingly over the cascading hillsides below, bronze cannons stand guard over the ancient waterways that held the "key to the continent" during the wars for control of the colonies. Fully restored, the fortress houses a museum full of historical weapons and artifacts, provides daily historical talks and musket demonstrations, and stages reenactments of historical battles, occasionally with as many as 1000 actors. (☎ 585-2821; www.fort-ticonderoga.org. Open May to late Oct. daily 9am-5pm. $12, seniors $11, ages 7-12 $6.) Experienced rock climbers and those who want to break into the sport should consult the experienced staff at **The Mountaineer,** in Keene Valley, between I-87 and Lake Placid on Rte. 73. The Mountaineer reels in all types of alpine enthusiasts with the **Adirondack International Mountainfest,** a weekend of clinics and classes for all manner of mountain sport. (☎ 576-2281. Open in summer M and F-Su 8am-7pm, Tu-Th 9am-6pm; low season M-F 9am-5:30pm, Sa 8am-5:30pm, Su 9am-5:30pm. Snowshoes $15 per day, ice-climbing boots and crampons $20, rock shoes $12. Mountainfest is held in Jan. on Martin Luther King Day weekend.)

LAKE PLACID   ☎518

Tucked away among the High Peaks Mountains, Lake Placid lives and breathes winter sports but still maintains a lively summer schedule full of outdoors events. Host to the Olympic Winter Games in both 1932 and 1980, this modest city has still managed to maintain a small-town ambience while basking in Olympic glory. World-class athletes train year-round in the town's extensive facilities, lending an international flavor that distinguishes Lake Placid from its Adirondack neighbors.

🔖🎫 ORIENTATION AND PRACTICAL INFORMATION. Lake Placid sits at the intersection of Rtes. 86 and 73 in the northeastern quarter of Adirondack Park. Rte. 73 runs north and connects with Rte. 86 south of the Olympic Skating Center, becoming Main St. as it runs north through the town. Downtown Lake Placid is located on Main St. along the shores of Lake Placid. **Adirondack Trailways** (☎800-776-7548) stops at Lake Placid IGA, 6137 Sentinel Road, and has extensive service in the area. Destinations include the Albany airport ($27), Lake George ($15), and New York City ($63). (Open M-Sa 8am-7pm, Su 9am-5pm.) The **Placid Xpress** shuttle travels through town every 15-20min. with stops at the various parking areas, including free municipal lots. (☎523-2585. Route maps, including low-season routes, available at the visitors center. Runs July-Sept. 8am-10pm; low-season hours vary. Free.) The Lake Placid that exists today is a product of its rich Olympic past. The **Olympic Regional Development Authority**, 2634 Main St., inside the Olympic Center, operates the sports facilities. (☎523-1655 or 800-462-6236; www.orda.org. Open M-F 8:30am-5pm.) Also in the Olympic Center is the **Lake Placid-Essex County Visitors Bureau**, which provides information about food, lodging, weather, and attractions in the area. (☎523-2445; www.lakeplacid.com. Open M-F 8am-5pm, Sa-Su 9am-4pm; closed Su in the spring and fall.) **Internet Access: Lake Placid Public Library**, 2417 Main St. (☎523-3200. Open M-Th 10am-5:30pm, F 10am-7pm, Sa 10am-4pm. No email.) The visitors center has limited Internet service. (15min. limit when others are waiting.) **Post Office:** 2591 Main St. (☎523-3071. Open M-F 8:30am-5pm, Sa 8am-noon.) **Postal Code:** 12946. **Area Code:** 518.

🎫 ACCOMMODATIONS. If you avoid the resorts on the west end of town, both lodgings and food are reasonable in Lake Placid. Many inexpensive motels line Rtes. 86 and 73 just east of town. The visitors center can also provide suggestions. Just half a mile south of downtown on Rte. 73, the 25 comfortable bunks at the **◪High Peaks Hostel ❶** will make any traveler feel at home. The complimentary homemade breakfasts, well-equipped kitchens, free linens and towels, and friendly owners make this an excellent lodging option. (☎523-4951. Lockout 10am-4pm. Bunks $20; private rooms $48-60.) The **Jackrabbit Inn and Hostel ❶**, 3½ mi. east of town on Rte. 73, also offers affordable rooms and bunks in a bunkhouse with a large social lounge and a kitchen. Linens, towels, and use of tennis court are included. (☎523-0123 or 800-584-7006. Bunks $20; private rooms $48-85.) Two state park campgrounds, some of the nicest in the area, are within 10 mi. of Lake Placid. **Meadowbrook State Park ❶**, 5 mi. west of town on Rte. 86 in Ray Brook, has relatively secluded, wooded campsites and provides easy access to several trailheads. (☎891-4351. Hot showers. Sites $11 plus $3 registration fee. Day use $4 per car, $1 walk-in.) **Wilmington Notch State Campground ❶**, about 9 mi. east of Lake

Placid on Rte. 86, also has shady, if somewhat more crowded, sites close to all of the trailheads and ski slopes of Whiteface Mountain. (☎946-7172. Hot showers. Open May to mid-Oct. Registration 8am-9pm. Sites $13. Day use $4 per car.)

◗◖ **FOOD AND NIGHTLIFE.** Lake Placid Village, concentrated primarily along Main St., has a number of reasonably priced dining establishments. The lunch buffet in the Terrace Dining Room at the **Hilton Hotel ❷**, 1 Mirror Lake Dr., serves all-you-can-eat sandwiches, soups, salads, and a hot entree for only $8 with a view overlooking the lake. (☎523-4411. Buffet daily noon-2pm.) Bright orange walls, local artwork, and the biggest muffins you'll ever see ($2) greet patrons at **Soulshine Bagels ❶**, 2526 Main St. In addition to a vegetarian-friendly menu, this cafe boasts some genuine local flavor. (☎523-9772. Open daily 6:30am-5pm, summer until 9pm.) **The Black Bear Restaurant ❸**, 2573 Main St., dishes out meals hot off the grill as well as a few vegetarian and vegan options. Large wraps ($7-10) and sandwiches ($9) served with delicious homemade potato chips keep locals and visitors happy. (☎523-9886. Free wireless Internet. Open daily 6:30am-4pm, with later hours in the summer.) On the shore of Mirror Lake, **The Cottage ❷**, 5 Mirror Lake Dr., creates sandwiches and salads (all under $9) that, along with the view, can be enjoyed on the outside deck. (☎523-9845. Kitchen open daily 11:30am-10pm; bar open until midnight or 1am, depending on the crowd.) A local favorite, the **Lake Placid Pub and Brewery ❸**, 14 Mirror Lake Dr., off the east end of Main St., features dishes like Bangers and Mash (English sausage in local Ubu Ale with red potatoes; $9), and drink specials like Two-for Tuesdays, where you can get two pints for the price of one after 6pm. (☎523-3813. Entrees $10-17. Open daily 11:30am-3am; kitchen closes at 11pm.) One of Lake Placid's few late-night hot spots, **Wise Guys**, 3 School St., east of the Olympic Center, has both a sports bar and a dance club. DJs and occasional live rock fill the air in the spacious bar, and on Fridays draft beers cost $1.05. (☎523-4446. M-F no cover, Sa-Su up to $3. Bar open M-F 3pm-3am, Sa-Su noon-3am; club open Th-Sa 9pm-3am.)

◙ **SIGHTS.** The **Olympic Center**, in downtown Lake Placid, houses the 1932 and 1980 hockey arenas, as well as the petite, memorabilia-stuffed **Winter Olympic Museum.** Packed with ice skates, bobsleds, and medals, the museum is a walk through decades of Olympic glory. (☎523-1655, ext. 226; www.orda.org. Open daily 10am-5pm. $4, seniors $3, ages 7-12 $2. **Public skating:** ☎523-1655. Open year-round M-F 8-9:30pm; call ahead for weekend hours. $5, children and seniors $4; skate rental $3.) During the summer, purchase tickets to watch ski jumpers and aerial freestylists practice for upcoming competitions by sailing down astroturf-covered ramps onto astroturf-covered hillsides or into a swimming pool in the **Olympic Jumping Complex,** just east of town on Rte. 73. Travelers can take a chairlift and an elevator to the top of the ramp for a look down. (☎523-2202. Open Dec.-Sept. daily 9am-4pm; call ahead for hours in April and May. $6, with chairlift $9; seniors and children $6.) About 5 mi. east of town on Rte. 73, the **Verizon Sports Complex** at **Mount Van Hoevenberg** offers bobsled rides down the actual 1980 Olympic track. Reaching speeds of 50 mph around gut-wrenching curves, the bobsleds run on ice during the winter ($40) and wheels during the summer ($30). If rocketing down the side of the mountain at high speeds isn't for you, narrated bus tours drive more slowly up and down the mountain for a view of the tracks. (☎523-4436. Open W-Su 10am-12:30pm and 1:30-4pm. Winter bobsled runs Dec.-Mar.; summer June-Nov. Must be at least 48 in. tall; under 18 must have parent present. Bus tours 9am-4pm. $5, seniors and ages 7-12 $4.) Whip yourself into shape Olympian-style at the cross-country skiing venue. Cross-country skiing and biathlon courses are available to the public in the winter, and mountain biking trails are uncovered in the summertime. Cross-country ski and bike rentals are available inside the com-

MID-ATLANTIC

plex. (☎523-2811. Open for skiing daily 9am-4:30pm; last rental 4pm. $14 per day trail fee, seniors and students $12, ages 70+ free. Equipment rental $16, under 18 $12. Open for biking mid-June to early Sept. daily 10am-5pm; early Sept. to early Oct. Sa-Su 10am-5pm. Bikes $10-50 per day; trail fee—not included in rental—$6 per day, $10 per 2 days; helmet required and included with bike rental, $3 per day.) For those planning to take in all or most of Lake Placid's Olympic attractions, the **Olympic Sites Passport** is the best bargain. For $25 per person, the pass includes entrance to the Olympic Jumping Complex (including chairlift and elevator ride), the bus tour of the bobsledding complex, a $5 coupon toward a bobsled ride on Mt. Van Hoevenberg, admission to the Winter Sports Museum, the **Scenic Gondola Ride** to the top of Little Whiteface, and access to the **Veterans Memorial Highway** that climbs Whiteface Mountain. Purchase the passport at any Olympic venue or at the **Olympic Center Box Office** in Lake Placid (☎523-3330).

After touring the Olympic venues, get outfitted for your own sporting adventures at **High Peaks Cyclery,** 2733 Main St. Renting and selling all manner of bicycles, climbing gear, camping equipment, skis, snowshoes, and much more, the experts there can make sure you are prepared for any outing. If you aren't ready to head out alone, inquire about the guide services offered. (☎523-3764. Open M-Sa 9am-6pm, Su 10am-5pm. Bikes $25-50 per day. Tents $15-20 per day. Cross-country skis $20-35 per day. Snowshoes $15 per day.) To climb to the 4867 ft. summit of Whiteface Mountain without breaking a sweat, drive your car up the ▓**Veterans Memorial Highway,** 11 mi. east of Lake Placid on Rte. 86. Waiting at the summit is a castle in the clouds, perched on 250 ft. of solid granite that must be ascended via an elevator or a spectacular ridge trail. (☎946-7175. Open July-Sept. daily 8:30am-5pm; mid-May to July and Sept. to mid-Oct. daily 9am-4pm, longer if weather permits. Car or motorcycle and driver $9; $4 per passenger.) Eight miles east of town on Rte. 86, 700 ft. of waterfalls cascade down through the small, picturesque **High Falls Gorge.** Winter admission comes with ice cleats for steady footing and hot chocolate to warm chilled bones. (☎946-2278; ww.highfallsgorge.com. Open July-Aug. 9am-5:30pm, Sept.-June 9am-5pm, last admission 30min. before close. In summer $10, ages 4-12 $6; call for winter rates.)

Lost in the intensity of the Olympic legacy, visitors to Lake Placid often forget the unparalleled peace that the lake offers to serenity-seekers. Departing from the Lake Placid Marina on the west end of town, **tour boat cruises** quietly glide around the 16 mi. perimeter of the lake in long, sleek, turn-of-the-century boats, providing glimpses of the stately homes that line the shores and illuminating the history of the area. (☎523-9704. Cruises depart mid-May to late June M-F 10:30am and 2:30pm; Sa-Su 10:30am, 2:30, 4pm. Late June to Sept. daily 10:30am, 1, 2:30, 4pm. Sept to mid-Oct. daily 10:30am, 1:30, 3pm. Arrive at least 15min. early. $8, seniors $7, children $5.50.) **Mirror Lake Boat Rentals,** 1 Main St., rents boats. (☎524-7890. Open May to mid-Oct. 10am-dark. $20 per hr. for paddleboats, canoes, and hydrobikes; $40 per hr. for sailboats and electric cruisers.) For a cool dip in the waters, head to the **Mirror Lake Public Beach** on Parkside Dr. (☎523-3109. Lifeguards on duty late June to Sept. 9am-7pm, weather permitting. Free.)

Athletics and natural beauty embody the spirit of Lake Placid, but no trip to upstate New York can be complete without a sampling of its famous vineyards. Selections of the award-winning wine produced by Finger Lakes-based **Swedish Hill Winery** are available 1 mi. east of downtown on Rte. 73. After sampling there, bring your glass with you to complete your tasting tour with another eight tastes at the **Goose Watch Winery,** 2527 Main St. in the Alpine Mall, for an additional $0.01. (☎523-1955. Open M-Th 10am-6pm, F-Sa 10am-9pm, Su noon-6pm. 8 tastes and a wine glass $3.) Nearby Saranac Lake hosts a 10-day, no-holds-barred **carnival** in early February, for which an ice palace is created. (Saranac Lake Chamber of Commerce: 39 Main St. ☎891-1990; www.saranaclake.com.)

THOUSAND ISLAND SEAWAY ☎ 315

Spanning 100 mi. from the mouth of Lake Ontario to the first of the locks on the St. Lawrence River, the Thousand Island region of the St. Lawrence Seaway forms a natural US-Canadian border. Surveys conducted by the US and Canadian governments determined that there are 1,864 islands in the seaway, with an island defined as at least one square foot of land above water year-round with at least two trees growing on it. Many islands, however, are developed with private residences, lighthouses, and towering 19th-century castles. The Thousand Island region is also a fisherman's paradise and a mecca for vacationers, with an incredible array of festivals during the long days of the short summer months.

▨▨ ORIENTATION AND PRACTICAL INFORMATION. The Thousand Island region hugs the St. Lawrence River and is less than 2hr. from Syracuse by way of **I-81 North.** From southwest to northeast, **Cape Vincent, Clayton,** and **Alexandria Bay** ("Alex Bay" to locals) are the main towns in the area. Cape Vincent, the smallest of the three, maintains a rich French heritage along the shores of Lake Ontario. Clayton, the most peaceful of the three seaside hamlets, boasts museums and galleries. Alex Bay is alive with countless riverside bars, clubs, and restaurants and hosts "themed" weeks throughout the summer, such as "Pirate Week" in August, when pirate ships and scalawags take control of the town. For Wellesley Island, Alexandria Bay, and the eastern 500 islands, stay on I-81 until you reach Rte. 12 E. For Clayton and points west, take Exit 47 and follow Rte. 12 to Rte. 12 E. **Greyhound,** 540 State St., in Watertown, runs to Albany (6hr., 2 per day, $43), New York City (8hr., 2 per day, $51-57), and Syracuse (1¾hr., 2 per day, $13-15). (☎ 788-8110 or 800-231-2222; www.greyhound.com. Open M-F 9am-1pm, 3-4pm, and 6:10-6:30pm; Sa-Su only at departure times.) **Thousand Islands Bus Lines** (☎ 287-2790) departs from the same station M-F at 1pm for Alexandria Bay ($5.60) and Clayton ($3.55). Return trips leave Clayton from Gray's Florist, 234 James St. (departs daily 8:45am), and Alexandria Bay from the Dockside Cafe, 17 Market St. (departs daily 8:30am). The **Clayton Chamber of Commerce,** 517 Riverside Dr., hands out the free and helpful *Clayton Vacation Guide* and *Thousand Islands Seaway Region Travel Guide.* (☎ 686-3771; www.1000islands-clayton.com. Open mid-June to mid-Sept. daily 9am-5pm; mid-Sept. to mid-June M-F 9am-5pm.) The **Alexandria Bay Chamber of Commerce,** 7 Market St., is just off James St. and offers the *Alexandria Bay Vacation Guide* to aid your travel in the area. (☎ 482-9531; www.alexbay.org. Open May-Sept. M-F 8am-4:30pm, Sa 10am-4:30pm.) The **Cape Vincent Chamber of Commerce,** 175 James St., by the ferry landing, welcomes visitors and distributes the *Cape Vincent Vacation Guide.* (☎ 654-2481; www.capevincent.org. Open May-Oct. Tu-Sa 9am-5pm; late May to early Sept. also M and Su 10am-4pm.) **Internet Access:** In Clayton, **Hawn Memorial Library,** 220 John St. (☎ 686-3762. Open M and Th-F 10am-5pm, Tu-W 10am-8pm, Sa 9am-noon.) In Alexandria Bay, **Macsherry Library,** 112 Walton St. (☎ 482-2241. Open M-Th 9am-noon, 1-5pm, 7-9pm; F-Sa 9am-noon and 1-5pm.) In Cape Vincent, **Cape Vincent Community Library,** 157 N. Real, at Gouvello St. (☎ 654-2132. Open Tu and Th 9am-8pm, F-Sa 9am-1pm.) **Clayton Post Office:** 236 John St. (☎ 686-3311. Open M-F 9am-4:30pm, Sa 9am-noon.) **Postal Code:** 13624. **Alexandria Bay Post Office:** 13 Bethune St. (☎ 482-9521. Open M-F 8:30am-

▨TIP▨ SAIL AWAY. The boundary between the US and Canada in the Thousand Island Seaway is complex and can be tricky for boaters who wish to explore the islands on both sides of the border. In foreign waters, a vessel doesn't have to pass through customs as long as it's in motion. Back on dry land, customs procedures usually take place at small booths on the dock.

5pm, Sa 9am-noon.) **Postal Code:** 13607. **Cape Vincent Post Office:** 362 Broadway St., across from the village green. (☎654-2424. Open M-F 8am-1pm and 2-4:30pm, Sa 9:30-11:30am.) **Postal Code:** 13618. **Area Code:** 315.

⌐ ACCOMMODATIONS. Near Cape Vincent, where Lake Ontario meets the St. Lawrence, **◪Tibbett's Point Lighthouse Hostel (HI) ❶**, 33439 County Rte. 6, is a friendly beacon for the weary traveler. Take Rte. 12 E into town, turn left on Broadway, and follow the river until the road ends. (☎654-3450. Full kitchen with microwave. Linen included. Check-in 5-10pm. Check-out 7-9am. Reservations strongly recommended on weekends July-Aug. Open mid-May to late Oct. Dorms $17, members $14. Cash only.) The **Bridgeview Motel ❷**, 42823 Rte. 12 between Alex Bay and Clayton, offers clean, no-frills rooms with air conditioning and TVs for reasonable rates. (☎482-4906. Open May to mid-Oct. Rooms $39-59.)

There are numerous state and private campgrounds in the area, especially along Rte. 12 E. Sites, however, are usually close together and fill up well in advance on weekends. **◪Wellesley Island ❶**, across the toll bridge ($2) on I-81 N before Canada, boasts 2600 acres of marshes and woodland for hiking and cross-country skiing. The beach in the park hosts swimmers in the summer and ice fishers in the winter. (☎482-2722. 438 sites plus cabins. Waterfront sites B19-23 or B1-8 are incredible, but require reservations far in advance. Hot showers and nature center. Sites $13-19, with electricity $19; full hookup $25. Registration fee $2.75. Cabins with 4 beds, refrigerator, stove, microwave, and picnic table $40-51. Day use $7 per car. Boat rentals $15 per day for rowboats and canoes, $60 per day plus gas for 16 ft. motor boats. Lifeguard on duty mid-June to early Sept. daily 11am-8pm, weather permitting.) The less crowded **Burnham Point State Park ❶**, on Rte. 12 E, 4½ mi. east of Cape Vincent and 11 mi. west of Clayton, has a wonderful view of the water and two picnic areas among the 50 sites, but lacks a beach. (☎654-2324. Hot showers. Open late May to early Sept. daily 7am-9:30pm. Sites $13-19, with electricity $19-23. Registration $2.75. Boat dockage $6 per day. Day use $6 per car. Wheelchair accessible.) Reservations for all state parks can be made for $9 at www.reserveamerica.com or by calling ☎800-456-2267.

◪◪ FOOD AND NIGHTLIFE. The Thousand Island Seaway hosts diverse food options, and the nightlife of Alex Bay ranges from comfortable seaside decks to wild bars that fill the night air with music and laughter. The most popular destination for cheap eats in Alex Bay is **Poor John's ❶**, off James St. at the main intersection downtown, where locals line up for double-stacked burgers ($2.50) and ice cream cones. (☎408-2502. Open daily 11am-10pm; no hot food after 7pm.) A floating restaurant, **Captain's Table ❸** in Alex Bay, offers the best view in the Thousand Islands, provided you don't get seasick. The parking lot is reached by turning left at Uncle Sam Tours, then following the road. While the main level serves expensive entrees ($11-32), savvy travelers head upstairs for an ample lounge menu (sandwiches $7-8) and a beautiful balcony. (☎482-7777. Open daily 7am-9:30pm.) Nowhere is the relaxed atmosphere of Clayton more apparent than at the **St. Lawrence Gallery Cafe ❷**, off Riverside Dr. downtown. Try a reuben made with authentic Thousand Island dressing ($7) or a blueberry fruit tea ($3) amid the craftwork of local artisans. (☎794-0871. Open May-Oct. daily 9am-3pm.) **Aubrey's Inn ❷**, 126 S. James St. in Cape Vincent, serves ample homestyle meals at delightfully low prices in a nautically themed dining room complete with a mural of the Tibbett's Point Lighthouse. (☎654-3754. Breakfast $1.50-6. Most entrees $7-9. Open daily 7am-9pm.) Nightlife in the Thousand Islands region is located in the heart of Alexandria Bay. Numerous bars and clubs line the docks of the seaway and most offer live music and drink specials, but the liveliest place is **Skiffs,** at the corner of James St. and Market St. A wide variety of live music and nightly drink specials like "Dollar Labatt Wednesdays" cause flocks of tourists and locals of all ages to pack this bar nightly. (☎482-7543. Open M-Th 1pm-2am, F-Su noon-2am.)

☉ EXPLORING THE SEAWAY. Clayton and Cape Vincent tend to be quieter and less expensive, while Alex Bay is busier and more touristy. Popular activities include scenic tours of the waterways and ferry rides. With fact-packed live narrations, **Uncle Sam Boat Tours,** 47 James St., in Alexandria Bay, delivers good views of the islands and their plush estates, including the famous **Boldt Castle** on Heart Island. (☎482-2611 or 800-253-9229. Tours leave daily from Alex Bay May to late Oct. $7-35, ages 4-12 $4.50-25; prices vary with type and duration of tour. Boldt Castle: $7, ages 4-12 $3. Reserve in advance for lunch or dinner cruises.) In Alexandria Bay, **Empire Boat Lines,** 4 Church St., sends out smaller boats able to navigate very close to the islands, and provides scenic tours, tours to Boldt Castle, and regular service to **Singer Castle,** packed full of secret rooms and passageways. (☎482-8687 or 888-449-2539. Tours $13-30, ages 7-14 $10-24. Singer Castle $10, ages 6-12 $5.) **Ferries** run from Cape Vincent to **Wolfe Island,** a quaint island with a strawberry farm and golf course, and a stepping stone to the shops and restaurants of Kingston in Canada. (☎783-0638. Ferries depart from the Cape Vincent Ferry Dock along Club St. and run May to mid-Oct., 10 per day. Tickets may be purchased on the ferry. $2 per person, $10 per car, $2 per bicycle. Picture ID required.)

For many, fishing trips and charters are the preferred way to explore the islands and waterways. **Fishing licenses** are available at the **Town Clerk's Office,** 405 Riverside Dr., in Clayton. (☎686-3512. Open M-F 9am-noon and 1-4pm. Licenses $15 per day, $25 per week, $40 per season.) Many bait shops and sporting goods stores stay open longer hours and sell licenses to fishermen. Tell the tale of the big one that got away with **1000 Islands Fishing Charters,** 335 Riverside Dr., inside the 1000 Islands Inn in Clayton. Offering both drift fishing trips with larger groups of people and private charters, 1000 Islands can accommodate your preferences. (☎686-2381 or 877-544-4241. Trips July to late Aug. Reservations required. 4hr. "Drift Trip" $45 per person, tackle and bait included. 7½hr. private charter $75-160 per person, depending upon the number of people in the group. Tackle included.) Check out **Hunt's Dive Shop,** 40782 Rte. 12 between Alex Bay and Clayton, for an underwater peek at one or more of the many wrecks that line the floor of the seaway. (☎686-1070. $65 per person, min. 2 people. Equipment rentals $50 per person. Must have certification. Open May-Sept. daily 9am-5:30pm.)

LOCAL LEGEND

LONELY HEARTS

With elegant towers, manicured lawns, and formidable spires, Boldt Castle dominates the seaway outside Alexandria Bay. The castle, however, is hardly a relic from some forgotten age in history. In 1900, George C. Boldt, the millionaire proprietor of the Waldorf Astoria Hotel, purchased Hart Island and set about creating a monumental valentine for his wife, Louise. He renamed the territory Heart Island, and began constructing a decadent, six-story, 120-room mansion. Sparing no expense, Boldt took care to ensure that hearts were inscribed in the stonework, the railings, and even the surrounding gardens.

Four years into the massive project, Louise Boldt died suddenly, and an urgent telegram was sent to the island ordering all work on the house to cease at once. Heartsick, George Boldt never returned.

But the story doesn't end there. Since Louise's death, rumors have been circulating that she had a secret lover, or that she fled to Europe and faked her death in an attempt to escape her husband. Whatever the truth may be, there is no doubt that recent efforts to finally finish the castle have made many locals uneasy. Perhaps the true charm of the castle is not its majestic presence, but rather the air of mystery that lingers in its midst.

The **Antique Boat Museum,** 750 Mary St., in Clayton, houses practically every make and model of boat ever built. Admission includes free rentals on a variety of skiffs. On Wednesdays in summer, the museum offers free sailing classes and sailboat usage to increase boating awareness. (☎686-4104. Open mid-May to mid-Oct. daily 9am-5pm. $8, seniors $7, students and ages 6-17 $4, under 5 free. Call for info on sailing classes.) **French Creek Marina,** 250 Wahl St. (☎686-3621), off Strawberry Ln. just south of the junction of Rtes. 12 and 12 E, rents 14 ft. fishing boats ($50 per day), launches boats ($5), and provides overnight docking ($20).

NEW JERSEY

It's difficult to appreciate the wealth and variety of destinations in the Garden State the way many travelers see the state: cruising the New Jersey Turnpike on the way to somewhere else. From antiquing to gambling to reenactments of George Washington crossing the Delaware River, New Jersey bursts with all manner of history and activity. One of New Jersey's best-kept secrets is its 127 miles of white-sand beaches. Between the dazzle of Atlantic City's casinos and the tranquility of Cape May's "diamond" sand, the Jersey shore is one of the Mid-Atlantic's prime vacation spots.

❼ PRACTICAL INFORMATION

Capital: Trenton.

Visitor Info: State Division of Tourism, P.O. Box 820, Trenton 08625 (☎609-777-0885; www.visitnj.org). **State Bird:** The mosquito.

Postal Abbreviation: NJ. **Sales Tax:** 6%; no tax on clothing. **Tolls:** Keep a fistful of change handy; New Jersey's tunnels, bridges, and turnpikes are littered with toll booths.

ATLANTIC CITY   ☎609

For 70 years, board game enthusiasts have been wheeling and dealing with Atlantic City geography, famously depicted on the Monopoly game board. Meanwhile, the opulence of the original Boardwalk and Park Place faded into neglect and then into mega-dollar tackiness. During a 1970s refurbishment effort, giant casino-resorts were built over the rubble of the old boardwalk, sacrificing the city's old-time charm in hopes of attracting tourist dollars with glitz and glamour. The reincarnation failed to turn Atlantic City into a second Las Vegas, leaving poverty and crime lurking around the fringes of the modern downtown. Yet there is still plenty to enjoy here: gambling, tanning, games, and rides make Atlantic City an exhilarating destination.

▐ TRANSPORTATION

Atlantic City sits about 30 mi. north of the southern tip of the New Jersey shoreline. It is accessible by car via the **Garden State Parkway** and the **Atlantic City Expressway,** and easily reached by train or bus from Philadelphia or New York City.

Airport: Atlantic City International (☎645-7895 or 800-892-0354; www.acairport.com), 20min. west of Atlantic City in Egg Harbor.

MID-ATLANTIC

Buses: Greyhound, 1995 Atlantic Ave. (☎345-6617; www.greyhound.com). Buses travel to **New York Port Authority** (2½hr., every 30min., from $23) every 30min. and to **Philadelphia** (1½hr., $10) and most major casinos several times per day. **New Jersey Transit** (☎800-772-2222; www.nj.com/njtransit), on Atlantic Ave. between Michigan and Ohio St., has service to **New York City** (2½hr., 1 per hr., $25 round-trip).

Taxi: Atlantic City Airport Taxi (☎383-1457). **Egg Harbor Atlantic City Taxi Alliance** (☎457-0624). $27 flat rate from airport to Atlantic City, $8 maximum within the city.

Alternative Forms of Transportation: On the boardwalk, plentiful **Rolling Chair Rides** (☎347-7148) will take 2-3 passengers a maximum of 26 blocks. The **Atlantic City Jitney** (☎344-8642) minibuses serve the entire city ($1.50).

Free Parking: Meterless parking is available in some residential areas. Try Oriental Ave. at New Jersey Ave. for free 3hr. parking within walking distance of the Boardwalk, but be careful at night: this area is relatively isolated.

■ ? ORIENTATION AND PRACTICAL INFORMATION

Attractions cluster on and around the **Boardwalk,** which runs east-west along the Atlantic Ocean. Running parallel to the Boardwalk, **Pacific** and **Atlantic Avenue** offer cheap restaurants, hotels, and convenience stores. Getting around on foot is easy on the Boardwalk. **Parking lots** nearby run $3-7. Atlantic Ave. can be dangerous after dark, and any street farther out can be dangerous even by day.

Visitor Info: Atlantic Expressway Visitors Center, 1 mi. after the Pleasantville Toll Plaza (☎449-7130). Offers pamphlets, brochures, and help with free parking. Open daily 9am-5pm. The **Atlantic City Convention Center and Visitors Bureau,** 2314 Pacific Ave. (☎888-228-4748; www.atlanticcitynj.com), is near the Boardwalk. Open daily 9am-5pm. On the Boardwalk, try the **Visitor Info Center** at Mississippi St. (☎888-228-4748). Open late May-early Sept. M-W 9:30am-5:30pm, Th-Su 9:30am-8pm; mid-Sept.-mid-May daily 9:30am-5:30pm.

Medical Services: Atlantic City Medical Center, 1925 Pacific Ave. (☎344-4081).

Hotlines: Rape and Abuse Hotline (☎522-6489). **Gambling Abuse** (☎588-5515). Both 24hr.

Post Office: 1701 Pacific Ave. (☎345-4212), at Illinois Ave. Open M-F 8:30am-6pm, Sa 8:30am-12:30pm. **Postal Code:** 08401. **Area Code:** 609.

▌ ACCOMMODATIONS

Lodging prices in Atlantic City have skyrocketed in recent years. Less expensive motels cluster around the Black Horse Pike about 1 mi. from downtown. For accommodations closer to the beach, particularly for summer and holiday weekends, reservations made several months in advance are essential.

Inn of the Irish Pub, 164 St. James Pl. (☎344-9063; www.theirishpub.com), between New York and Tennessee Ave. Just off the boardwalk, the inn specializes in simple, comfortable rooms cooled by ocean breezes. Entertainment nightly in downstairs bar. Key deposit $5. One-time service fee $2. Singles with shared bath M-F $25, Sa-Su $30; doubles with shared bath $40/$45, with private shower and twin beds $55/$80. Must be 21+. AmEx/D/MC/V. ❸

Golden East Motel, 169 S. Kentucky Ave. (☎344-7001). A block from the ocean, this recently-renovated motel offers clean rooms with cable TV, A/C, and private balconies. Singles with king-sized bed M-F from $55, Sa-Su from $99. AmEx/D/MC/V. ❸

Red Carpet Motel, 1630 Albany Ave. (☎348-3171), a mile from the boardwalk, off the Black Horse Pike on the way into town. Comfortable, basic rooms for low prices. Cable TV, restaurant. Doubles $39-59; quads $55-79. Prices for quads jump to $130 on summer weekends. The area is isolated, so be careful at night. ❸

Shady Pines Campground, 443 S. 6th Ave. (☎652-1516), in Absecon, 6 mi. from Atlantic City. Take Exit 12 from the Expwy. or Exit 40 from the Garden State Pkwy. This leafy, 140-site campground sports a pool, playground, laundry, firewood service, and new showers and restrooms. Quiet hours 10pm-7am. Call ahead for summer weekend reservations. Open Mar.-Oct. Sites with full hookup $37. MC/V. ❷

FOOD

Along the Boardwalk, shore favorites like hot dogs, pizza, and funnel cake compete with all-you-can-eat buffets for the business of hungry beachgoers. Bored by Boardwalk fare? More diverse options can be found farther west, in town.

Inn of the Irish Pub, 164 St. James Pl. (☎345-9613; www.theirishpub.com), serves filling British and Irish classics. The "Poor Richard" lunch special (11:30am-2pm; $2) includes a sandwich and cup of soup. Sandwiches $5. All-you-can-eat Su brunch $7. Dinner specials $6. Domestic drafts $1. Open 24hr. Cash only. ❶

White House Sub Shop, 2301 Arctic Ave. (☎345-8599), at Mississippi Ave. According to local legend, Frank Sinatra had these immense subs (even the half-size sandwiches are nearly a foot in length) flown to him while he was on tour. Pictures of White House Sub-lovers Joe DiMaggio, Wayne Newton, and Mr. T adorn the walls. Half sandwiches $5-7, whole $9-14. Open M-F 7am-9pm, Sa-Su 7am-9:30pm. Cash only. ❷

Tony's Baltimore Grille, 2800 Atlantic Ave. (☎345-5766), at Iowa Ave. Personal jukeboxes add to the old-time atmosphere, while the $3-8 pizzas are hard to resist. Open daily 11am-3am. Bar open 24hr. Cash only. ❷

New Melaka, 28 S. Tennessee Ave. (☎344-8928). Boasting the only Malaysian food in town, New Melaka also serves traditional Chinese dishes to hungry locals. Vegetarian options available. Most entrees $8-15. Open daily 11:30am-1am. AmEx/MC/V. ❸

CASINOS, BOARDWALK, AND BEACHES

All casinos on the Boardwalk fall within a dice toss of one another. The farthest south is the elegant **Hilton** (☎347-7111 or 800-257-8677; www.hiltonac.com), on the boardwalk between Providence and Boston Ave., and the farthest north is the gaudy **Showboat,** 801 Boardwalk (☎343-4000 or 800-342-7724; www.harrahs.com/our_casinos/sac), at Delaware Ave. Donald Trump's glittering **Trump Taj Mahal,** 1000 Boardwalk (☎449-1000; www.trumptaj.com), at Virginia Ave., is an Atlantic City landmark and too glitzy to be missed. In true Monopoly form, Trump owns two other hotel-casinos in the city: the recently remodeled **Trump Plaza,** at Mississippi and Boardwalk (☎441-6000 or 800-677-7378; www.trumpplaza.com), lures in classy types looking for an elegant stay, while the **Trump Marina's** motto—"Play hard, live wild"—appeals to a younger, more scantily dressed crowd on Huron Blvd. (☎441-2000; www.trumpmarina.com), at the Marina. In summer, energetic partiers "rock the dock" at Trump Castle's indoor/outdoor bar and restaurant, **The Deck** (☎877-477-4697). **Caesar's Boardwalk Resort and Casino,** 2100 Pacific Ave. (☎348-4411 or 800-433-0104; www.caesarsatlanticcity.com), at Arkansas Ave, is the classic choice for those looking to toss the dice. The flashy **Sands** (☎441-4000 or 800-227-2637; www.acsands.com), at Indiana Ave., markets itself to serious gamblers as "the players' place." The two newest casinos are **The Borgata** (☎317-1000 or 866-692-6742; www.theborgata.com), a scintillating golden beacon in the

Marina district, near the Trump Marina Hotel Casino and Harrah's, and **Resorts Atlantic City** (☎ 344-6000 or 800-336-6378; www.resortsac.com), next to the Taj Mahal. Resorts Atlantic City offers scandalous-sounding "rendezvous rooms" in addition to its regular hotel and casino operations. All are open 24hr.

The Boardwalk's many arcades and carnival games test a different kind of luck. The historic **Steel Pier** (☎ 345-4893 or 866-386-6659; www.steelpier.com), at Virginia Ave. across from the Trump Taj Mahal, juts into the coastal waters with a Ferris wheel that spins riders over the Atlantic. (Open M-F 3pm-midnight, Sa-Su noon-1am. Rides $25 for 35 tickets, W-Th $35 all-day unlimited pass.) **Go-karts** and **paintball** are popular among more active thrill-seekers, who crowd around **Central Pier Arcade & Speedway**, at the Boardwalk and Tennessee Ave., near St. James Pl. (☎ 345-5219), waiting for their turn at the wheel. For something a little sandier, step off the boardwalk and onto **Atlantic City Beach.** (Open daily 6am-10pm. Free.)

CAPE MAY ☎ 609

At the southern extreme of New Jersey's coastline, Cape May is the oldest seashore resort in the US. Though the town's history goes back to the mid-1700s when Philadelphians would come to the shore for recreation and relaxation, Cape May is best known for the Victorian-era houses and hotels that give the resort its nickname, Gingerbread Town. Architecture isn't Cape May's only claim to fame; the town is also known for its fine dining, bird-watching, and sparkling white beaches.

█ ▐ ORIENTATION AND PRACTICAL INFORMATION. At the tip of a peninsula which pokes out into the Delaware Bay, Cape May is easily accessible by car or bus. Start digging for loose change as you follow the tollbooth-laden **Garden State Parkway** as far south as it goes (most tolls $0.35). Watch for signs to Cape May until Lafayette St., which leads directly into town. Alternatively, take the slower, scenic **Ocean Drive** (Rte. 9) 40 mi. south along the shore from Atlantic City. **NJ Transit** (☎ 800-772-2222) makes a stop at the bus depot on the corner of Lafayette and Ocean St. and runs to: Atlantic City (2hr., hourly, $3.20); New York City (5hr., 4 per day, $30); Philadelphia (2½hr., 18 per day, $15). From the D.C. area, the 1¾hr. **Cape May-Lewes Ferry** presents a pleasant and more direct alternative to the potentially-laborious 3-4hr. drive north to New Jersey. (☎ 800-643-3779; www.capemaylewesferry.com. Office open daily 8:30am-4:30pm. 8 per day. Reservations required; call at least 24hr. in advance. Check-in 30min. prior to

WAWA WORLD

From central New Jersey south to Virginia, the convenience store chain Wawa (named for the Leni Lenape tribe's word for the Canadian goose) has pushed other national chains to the margins. From the outside, the stores do not look especially remarkable, and the unwitting out-of-towner might easily overlook the heavenly options awaiting within. Besides the usual sodas and cigarettes, Wawa sells its own brand of salads and cut fruits and vegetables—perfect for diners on the go. What really makes locals line up, however, is the near-limitless variety of made-to-order sandwiches and wraps. Around lunchtime there's usually a crowd near the sandwich order touchscreens, a sure-fire guarantee that your tuna salad hasn't been sitting behind the counter for the past week. While the yum factor grabs diners, the prices keep them coming back for more. A 6-in. hoagie (that's local-speak for "sub") costs under $4, and sandwiches cost even less.

With thousands of locations across the region, a satisfying and inexpensive snack is never far away. Most stores are open 24hr., so late-night cravings need not go unfulfilled. To find the nearest location, check the store locator on their website, www.wawa.com. If you're in the Mid-Atlantic, odds are good that there's a Wawa just down the road.

departure. Passenger cars Apr.-Oct. $25; Nov.-Dec. $20. Motorcyclists $22/$17. Bicyclists $8/$6.) **Cape May Seashore Lines** runs three old-fashioned trains per day to attractions along the 26 mi. stretch to Tuckahoe. (☎884-2675; www.seashorelines.com. One-way $5; round-trip $8, ages 2-12 $5.) Bike the beach with the help of **Shields's Bike Rentals,** 11 Gurney Ave. (☎898-1818. Open daily 7am-7pm. $4 per hr., $9 per day; surreys $15/$30.) Other services include: **Welcome Center,** 609 Lafayette St. (☎884-9562; open daily 8:30am-4:30pm); **Chamber of Commerce,** 513 Washington St. Mall (☎884-5508; www.capemaychamber.com; open M-F 9am-5pm, Sa-Su 10am-6pm); **Washington Street Mall Information Booth,** at Ocean St. (☎800-275-4278; www.capemaymac.org; open in summer daily 9:15am-4pm and 6-9pm; call for low-season hours); **Internet Access: Cape May City Library** (☎884-9568; www.capemay.county.lib.nj.us; open M, W, F 9am-5pm; Tu and Th 9am-5pm and 7pm-9pm; Sa 9am-4pm; free); **Post Office:** 700 Washington St., at Franklin St. (☎884-3578; open M-F 9am-5pm; Sa 8:30am-12:30pm). **Postal Code:** 08204. **Area Code:** 609.

▌ ACCOMMODATIONS. Sleeping does not come cheaply in Cape May. Luxurious hotels and Victorian B&Bs along the beach run $85-250 per night. Farther from the shore, prices drop. Although the **Hotel Clinton ❷,** 202 Perry St. at S. Lafayette St., may lack stately suites and A/C, the Italian family-owned establishment offers 16 breezy rooms, the most affordable rates in town, and very charismatic proprietors. (☎884-3993. Open mid-June to Sept. Reservations recommended. Singles with shared bath M-F $35, Sa-Su $40; doubles with shared bath $45/$50. Cash or traveler's checks only.) Next door, the **Parris Inn ❸,** 204 Perry St., rents a variety of spacious, comfortable rooms and apartments, most with private bath, A/C, and TV. (☎884-6363. Open mid-Apr. to Dec. High-season singles $40-$85, doubles $45-$115; low-season doubles $35-65.) Antique furniture fills the air-conditioned rooms at **Poor Richard's Inn ❹,** 17 Jackson St., an elegant option less than a block from the beach. (☎884-3536; www.poorrichardsinn.com. Check-in 1-10pm. Check-out 10:30am. Continental breakfast included. Memorial Day-Oct. doubles $75-120, with private bath $120-165; low season $65-110/$110-150.) Campgrounds line U.S. 9 just north of Cape May. In a prime seashore location, **Cape Island Campground ❷,** 709 Rte. 9, is connected to Cape May by Seashore Lines (p. 225). The campground features mini-golf, two pools, a playground, a store, and laundry facilities. (☎884-5777 or 800-437-7443; www.capeisland.com. Sites with water and electricity $27-40; with sewage, cable, and lamp post $32-46. MC/V.)

▐▌ FOOD AND NIGHTLIFE. Along **Beach Avenue,** generic burger joints and posh beachside restaurants tempt Cape May's sun-lovers. For those hunting for fudge and saltwater taffy, the **Washington Street Mall** supports several popular food stores and eateries. Start the morning off right with a gourmet breakfast on the porch of the **Mad Batter ❸,** 19 Jackson St. at the Carroll Villa Hotel. Try the blueberry blintz crepes with warm syrup ($7.50) or the orange and almond french toast for $6. (☎884-5970; www.madbatter.com. Dinner entrees $12-20. Open daily 8am-10pm.) A meal in the smoky interior of **Ugly Mug ❹,** 426 Washington St. Mall, is well worth the risk of suffocation. For some fresh air, inhale that New England cup o' chowder ($3) on the patio. (☎884-3459. Dinner entrees $16-25. Open M-Sa 11am-2am, Su noon-2am. Hot food served until 11pm. MC/V.) Check your email beachside at the ▨**Magic Brain Cybercafe,** 31 Perry St., a spotless Internet cafe with an amicable staff and a variety of pastries and espresso drinks. (☎884-8188; www.magicbraincybercafe.com. Internet access $4 per 15min., $7 per 30min., $12 per hr. Open daily 8am-6pm. Cash only.) The rock scene collects around **Carney's,** 429 Beach Ave., with nightly entertainment in the summer beginning at 10pm. (☎884-4424. Tu karaoke. Su jams 4-9pm. 21+ after 10pm. Cover $5. Open daily 11:30am-2am. Kitchen closes at 10pm.) A chic crowd congregates at **Cabana's,** at the corner of Decatur St. and Beach Ave. across from the beach. You'll have to find a lot of sand dollars if you want to try the sesame crusted tuna with wasabi in this classy setting, but there is no cover for the nightly blues or jazz. (☎ 884-4800; www.caban-asonthebeach.com. Entrees $17-25. Open daily 11:30am-1:30am. Dinner served until 10pm. Happy hour daily 4-7pm. 21+ after 10pm. AmEx/D/DC/MC/V.)

◪ **HITTING THE BEACH.** Cape May's sands actually sparkle, studded with the famous Cape May "diamonds" (actually quartz pebbles). A **beach tag** is required for beachgoers over age 11 from late May to early September 10am-5pm. Tags are available from roaming vendors on any beach access ramp or from the **Beach Tag Office,** 714 Beach Ave. (☎ 884-9522. Open daily 10am-5pm. Day passes $4, 3-day $9, week pass $13, season pass $25.) For a bit of exercise and a spectacular view, ascend the 199 steps to the beacon of the 1859 **Cape May Lighthouse** in **Cape May Point State Park,** west of town at the end of the point. (Lighthouse ☎ 884-8656, visitors center 884-2159; www.capemaymac.org. Park open daily 8am-dusk. Free. Lighthouse open daily 10am-4pm with extended summer hours. Call ahead for more information.) The behemoth bunker next to the lighthouse is a WWII gun emplacement, once used to scan the shore for German U-boats. In summer, several shuttles run the 5 mi. from the bus depot on Lafayette St. to the lighthouse ($5, ages 3-12 $4). Three trails start at the Lighthouse Visitors Center: the red (½ mi., wheelchair accessible), yellow (1¼ mi., moderate and flat), and blue trails (2 mi., moderate and flat, last leg takes hikers along the oceanfront back to the start) boast excellent bird-watching and clearly marked paths through marsh and oceanside dunes. Bicyclists or serious hikers may want to consider taking the 40 mi. section of the New Jersey Coastal Heritage Trail from Cape May to Ocean City. The trail passes the Hereford Inlet Lighthouse, the Wetlands Institute, and Corson's Inlet State Park. Glimpse more than 300 types of feathered vacationers at the **Cape May Bird Observatory,** 701 E. Lake Dr., on Cape May Point. Bird maps, field trips, and workshops are available, along with advice about where to go for the best birdwatching. (☎ 884-2736; www.njaudubon.org/Centers/CMBO. Open daily 9am-4:30pm.) For a look at some larger creatures, **Cape May Whale Watch and Research Center** offers 2-3hr. tours. (☎ 898-0055 or 888-531-0055; www.capemaywhale-watch.com. Trips run Apr.-Dec. $23-30, ages 7-12 $12-18. One child age 6 and under free with each paid adult.) **South End Surf Shop,** 311 Beach Ave., rents boards to budding surfers. (☎ 898-0988. Open Apr.-Sept. daily 9am-10pm. Surfboard $20 per day, or $35 per 2 days.) If you want to venture a little farther, **Miss Chris Marina,** on the corner of 3rd St. and Wilson Dr., rents **kayaks.** (☎ 884-3351. Open daily 6am-7pm. Single kayak $20 per hr.; double kayak $30 per hr.)

THE WILDWOODS ☎ 609

The Wildwoods—Wildwood, North Wildwood, and Wildwood Crest—occupy a barrier island just north of Cape May along New Jersey's southern coast. A quieter alternative to Atlantic City's crowds, the Wildwoods are home to many miles of pristine, guarded **beaches.** (Department of Recreation ☎ 522-5837. Beach open June-Sept. daily 10am-5:30pm.) If bobbing in the ocean doesn't suit your tastes, boat rentals from **Lake View Dock,** at Park Blvd. and Sunset Lake, can get you out on the water without getting soaked. (☎ 522-0471. Paddleboat $25 per hr. Powerboat $80 per hr. Single kayak $20 per hr. Jet ski $50 per 30min.) Back on land, **Morey's Piers,** on the boardwalk between 25th Ave. and Spencer Ave., will entertain the entire family with roller coasters, carnival games, and waterslides. (☎ 522-3900. Rides and games $50 for 35 tickets.) Throughout Wildwood Crest, rows of restored doo-wop style motels take kitsch to a glorious extreme with bright colors, classic neon signs, and names like "The Astronaut" and "Waikiki," Wildwood's motels recall the best of the rock 'n' roll-happy 1950s. In summer, the **Doo-Wop Preservation League,** 3201 Pacific Ave., leads tours of the architectural landmarks around town. (☎884-5404. Tours daily June-Aug. 7:45pm. $8, children $4.)

The recently renovated ▓**Caribbean Motel ❸,** 5600 Ocean Ave. in Wildwood Crest, one of the most distinctive of Wildwood's many historic motels, offers architectural interest at comparatively reasonable rates. (☎522-8292; www.caribbeanmotel.com. Doubles June-Aug. M-Th and Su $50-120, F-Sa $79-120; May and Sept.-Oct. $45-65/$59-110. AmEx/D/MC/V.) On the mainland, **Acorn Campgrounds ❷,** 419 Rte. 47 S. in nearby Green Creek, ensures its visitors remain happy campers with its selection of swimming pools, modern bathhouses, weekend movies, and free Wi-Fi. (☎886-7119; www.acorncampground.com. Sites with full hookup $35-40 per day, $210-240 per week. MC/V.) Shore treats like hot dogs and taffy abound along the 2 mi. stretch of boardwalk, while slightly fancier restaurants have sprung up on New Jersey Ave. and Atlantic Ave. in Wildwood and around Pacific Ave. in Wildwood Crest.

If you're famished from a day on the sands of Wildwood, head to **Boardwalk Bar & Grill ❷,** 3500 Atlantic Ave., and try tackling the 1 lb. Kahuna Burger ($9)—finishing it gets your picture in their Hall of Fame. (☎522-2431; www.boardwalkbarandgrill.com.) **Russo's Restaurant & Bar ❹,** 4415 Park Blvd., cooks up satisfying Italian specialties and seafood entrees. (☎522-7038. Entrees $12-20. Bar open daily 7am-3am. Dinner served daily 5-10pm.) There's no better relief from Wildwood's summer sun than a sundae enjoyed in one of the Cadillac-shaped booths at 50s-themed **Cool Scoops Ice Cream Parlour ❶,** 1111 New Jersey Ave. (☎729-2665; www.coolscoops.com).

Wildwood is best reached via the **Garden State Parkway** or the slower, scenic **Rte. 9.** From the west, take the **Atlantic City Expressway,** then follow the Parkway south. **NJ Transit** (☎800-772-2222; www.nj.com/njtransit) runs buses from the Wildwood Bus Terminal, 4510 Washington Ave., daily to Cape May, Atlantic City, and Philadelphia with connections to New York City. Within Wildwood, the **Five Mile Beach Electric Trolleys** (☎884-5230; www.gatrolley.com) make a loop through the city with routes to neighboring towns ($1-2). The **Greater Wildwood Chamber of Commerce,** 3306 Pacific Ave., has helpful brochures about local attractions and events. (☎729-4000; www.gwcoc.com. Open M-F 9am-5pm.) **Internet Access: Wildwood Crest Public Library,** 6301 Ocean Ave. (☎522-0564. Opens daily at 9am. Closing times vary seasonally; call for hours.) **Post Office:** 3311 Atlantic Ave. (☎800-275-8777. Open M-F 7am-5:30pm, Sa 9am-2pm.) **Postal Code:** 08260. **Area Code:** 609.

PENNSYLVANIA

Established as a colony to protect Quakers from persecution, the state of Pennsylvania has since that time been central to the American fight for religious and political freedom. In 1776, it served as the birthplace of the Declaration of Independence. In 1976, Philadelphia groomed its historic shrines for the nation's bicentennial, and today its many colonial monuments serve as the centerpiece of the city's ambitious renewal. Pittsburgh, the steel city with a raw image, was once dirty enough to fool streetlights into burning during the day, but has lately begun a cultural renaissance of sorts. Removed from the noise of its urban areas, central Pennsylvania's landscape has retained much of the rustic beauty discovered by colonists centuries ago, from the farms of Lancaster County to the gorges of the Allegheny Plateau.

🛈 PRACTICAL INFORMATION

Capital: Harrisburg.

Visitor Info: Pennsylvania Travel and Tourism, 400 North St., Harrisburg 17120, 4th fl. (☎717-787-5453 or 800-237-4363; www.experiencepa.com). Open daily 8am-5pm. **Bureau of State Parks,** Rachel Carson State Office Bldg., 400 Market St., Harrisburg 17108 (☎888-727-2757; www.dcnr.state.pa.us/stateparks). Open M-Sa 7am-5pm.

Postal Abbreviation: PA. **Sales Tax:** 6% (7% in Philadelphia and Pittsburgh).

PHILADELPHIA   ☎215

With his band of Quakers, William Penn founded the City of Brotherly Love in 1682. But it was Ben, not Penn, who laid the foundation for the metropolis it is today. Benjamin Franklin, the ingenious American ambassador, inventor, and womanizer, almost single-handedly built Philadelphia into an American colonial capital; his name is ever-present in the city's museums and landmarks. Sightseers will eat up Philly's historic attractions, world-class museums, and architectural accomplishments along with the famous cheesesteaks and endless culinary choices within the city's ethnic neighborhoods.

✈ INTERCITY TRANSPORTATION

Airport: Philadelphia International (☎800-745-4283 or 937-6937; www.phl.org), 8 mi. southwest of Center City on I-76. **SEPTA Regional Rail - Airport Line R1** (☎580-7800; www.septa.org) runs from the airport to the 30th St. station daily every 30min. 5am-12:09am. (Tickets $5.50). A taxi to downtown is a flat rate of $25. Most auto rental companies and hotels offer free shuttles.

Trains: Amtrak, 30th St. Station (☎800-872-7245; www.amtrak.com), at Market St. in University City. Station open 24hr. To: **Baltimore** (1-2hr., M-F 10 per day, $47); **Boston** (5-6hr., 10 per day, $87); **New York City** (1½-2hr., 10 per day, $53); **Pittsburgh** (7½hr., 2 per day, $40); **Washington, D.C.** (1½-2hr., 10 per day, $50). Ticket office open M-F 5:10am-10:30pm, Sa-Su 6:10am-10:30pm.

Buses: Greyhound, 1001 Filbert St. (☎800-231-2222; www.greyhound.com), at 10th St. downtown. To: **Atlantic City** (1-1½hr., 18 per day, $14); **Baltimore** (3hr., 7 per day, $21); **Boston** (7hr., 16 per day, $55); **New York City** (2-3hr., 24 per day, $21); **Pittsburgh** (6-7hr., 7 per day, $41); **Washington, D.C.** (3hr., 10 per day, $22). Station open 24hr. **New Jersey Transit** (☎569-3752 or 800-772-3606; ticket window open daily 5:45am-9:30pm) in the same station, runs to **Atlantic City** (1½hr., every 30min., $12) and points on the New Jersey shore.

🧭 ORIENTATION

Penn planned his city as a logical, easily accessible grid, though the prevalence of one-way streets can cause a migraine behind the wheel. Whether you are walking or driving, the maps and arrows pointing to major destinations that are posted on every downtown street corner are lifesavers. The north-south streets ascend numerically from the **Delaware River,** flowing from **Penn's Landing** and **Independence Hall** on the east side to the **Schuylkill River** (SKOO-kill) on the west. The first street is **Front;** others follow consecutively from 2nd to 69th across the Schuylkill. Moving outward from the downtown area known as **Center City** along Rte. 676, poorer areas lie to the south and northeast, and more affluent neighborhoods are in the northwest. The intersection of **Broad (14th)** and **Market Street** is the focal point of Center City, marked by ornate City Hall. Street addresses often refer to alleys not pictured on standard maps of the city. The **SEPTA transportation map,** available free from the tourist office, is probably the most complete map of the city.

Driving around town is not difficult, but finding a place to park your car and then paying for it can be a nightmare. If you are extremely lucky or patient, you may be able to find curbside metered parking. Otherwise, parking in most lots near the historic sites is about $13 per day or $3-4 per half hour. If you are willing to get up early, most lots run an "early bird special," charging only $8-10—as long as you park before 9 or 10am and leave before 6pm. Meterless 2hr. parking spaces are sometimes available in the Washington Sq. district or on the cobblestones of Dock St. In Chinatown, you can park in the lot on Arch St. between 9th and 10th St. for only $8. There is also parking directly behind the Philadelphia Art Museum for $5-8, though it is far from downtown. A final option is to park outside the city, ride the train into Philly, and then walk, bike, or take a bus to major downtown destinations (see **Local Transportation,** below) Public transit can be unsafe after dark.

The **Historic District** stretches from Front St. to 6th St. and from Race St. to South St. The **Washington Square District** runs from 6th St. to Broad St. and Vine St. to South St. The northern half of the historic district is also referred to as **Old City,** while the southern half is also called **Society Hill.** The affluent **Rittenhouse Square District** lies to the west of **Society Hill,** between Walnut and Pine St. **Chinatown** comprises the blocks around the intersection of 10th and Arch St., while the **Museum District,** in the northwest quadrant of the city, is centered around the Benjamin Franklin Pkwy. Across the Schuylkill River to the west, **University City** includes the sprawling campuses of the **University of Pennsylvania** and **Drexel University.**

▐ LOCAL TRANSPORTATION

Public Transit: Southeastern Pennsylvania Transportation Authority (SEPTA), 1234 Market St. (☎580-7800). Extensive bus and rail service to the suburbs. Buses serve the 5-county area. Most operate 5am-2am, some 24hr. There are 2 major subway routes: the blue, east-west **Market Street line** (including 30th St. Station and the historic area) and the orange, north-south **Broad Street line** (including the stadium complex in south Philadelphia). The subway is unsafe after dark; buses are often safer. Pick up a free SEPTA system map at any subway stop. $2, transfers $0.60. Unlimited all-day pass for both $5.50, weekly pass $19, monthly pass $70. The subway closes around midnight, when **all-night shuttle** service begins, stopping at the major subway stops about every 10-15min. until morning.

Tours: In the tourist area, **Phlash** buses provide non-narrative transport between 19 of the major downtown sights. (☎923-8522; www.phillyphlash.com. Mar.-Nov. daily 10am-6pm. $1, day pass $4). The trollies of **Philadelphia Sightseeing Tours** have knowledgeable drivers and guides and the longest tours in the city. (☎925-8687; www.phillytour.com. Apr.-Nov. 9:30am-6pm. $23, ages 6-12 $5; second day $6/$3). For excellent narration while the wind runs through your hair, try the open-air double-decker buses of the **Big Bus Company.** (☎866-324-4287; www.bigbustours.com. Runs daily 9am-6pm. $27, seniors $22, ages 4-12 $10.) Finally, the kazoo-blowing amphibious vehicles of **Ride the Ducks** stop at 10 city locations before cruising the river. (☎227-3825; www.phillyducks.com. Runs daily 10am-7pm. $23, ages 3-12 $13.)

Taxi: Yellow Cab, ☎333-3333 **City Cab,** ☎492-6500.

Car Rental: Alamo, ☎492-3960 or 800-327-9633.

Bike Rental: Frankenstein Bike Works, 1529 Spruce St. (☎893-0415). Open May-Sept. M-Sa 11am-6:30pm, Su noon-4pm. Bikes $8 per hr., $25 per day. Tough to spot the shop, but look for stairs going underground.

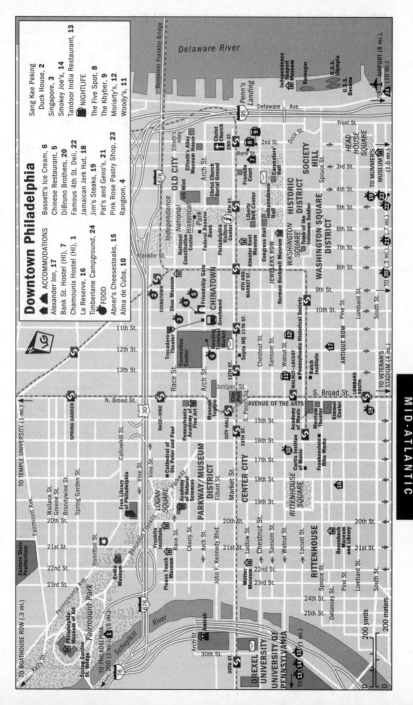

Downtown Philadelphia

▲ ACCOMMODATIONS
Alexander Inn, 17
Bank St. Hostel (HI), 7
Chamounix Hostel (HI), 1
La Reserve, 16
Timberlane Campground, 24

● FOOD
Abner's Cheesesteaks, 15
Alma de Cuba, 10
Bassett's Ice Cream, 6
Chinese Restaurant, 5
DiBruno Brothers, 20
Famous 4th St. Deli, 22
Jamaican Jerk Hut, 18
Jim's Steaks, 19
Pat's and Geno's, 21
Pink Rose Pastry Shop, 23
Rangoon, 4
Sang Kee Peking Duck House, 2
Singapore, 3
Smokey Joe's, 14
Tandoor India Restaurant, 13

☾ NIGHTLIFE
The Five Spot, 8
The Khyber, 9
Moriarty's, 12
Woody's, 11

MID-ATLANTIC

🔁 PRACTICAL INFORMATION

Visitor Info: The Independence Visitor Center (☎925-6100 or 800-537-7676; www.independencevisitorcenter.com) at the intersection of 6th and Market St., has brochures and event schedules as well as desks for the city and National Park Service. Open daily 8:30am-5pm, but often unstaffed in summer 5-7pm.

GLBT Resources: Gay and Lesbian Peer Counseling Services, ☎732-8255. Operates M-F 6-9pm. **William Way Lesbian, Gay, and Bisexual Community Center** (☎732-2220; www.waygay.org), 1315 Spruce St., has info about GLBT events and activities. Open M-F 11:30am-10pm, Sa 11:30am-7pm, Su 10:30am-7pm.

Hotlines: Suicide and Crisis Intervention, ☎686-4420. **Youth Crisis Line,** ☎787-0633. **Women Against Abuse,** ☎386-7777. All operate 24hr.

Internet Access: The *Free Library of Philadelphia* (p. 238) offers free Internet access with ID. Open M-W 9am-9pm, Th-Sa 9am-5pm. The **Ben Franklin Parkway, Independence Visitors Center,** and **Reading Terminal Market** all have free wireless Internet.

Post Office: 1234 Market St. (☎800-275-8767), downtown. Open daily 8:30am-5:30pm. **Postal Code:** 19104. **Area Code:** 215.

🔁 ACCOMMODATIONS

Inexpensive lodging in Philadelphia is uncommon, but with advance arrangements, its possible to get rooms close to Center City for around $60. The motels near the airport at Exit 9A on I-95 sacrifice location for affordable rates. **Bed and Breakfast Connections/Bed and Breakfast of Philadelphia,** in Devon, PA, books rooms in Philadelphia and southeastern Pennsylvania. (☎610-687-3565; www.bnb-philadelphia.com. Open M-F 9am-5pm. Reserve at least a week in advance; one-time registration fee $10. Singles $60-90; doubles $75-250.)

🔲 **Chamounix Mansion International Youth Hostel (HI),** 3250 Chamounix Dr. (☎878-3676 or 800-379-0017; www.philahostel.org). Take bus #38 from lower Market St. to Ford and Cranston Rd.; from Ford Rd., turn left on Chamounix Dr. An energetic staff maintains the lavish Chamounix hostel with 80 beds. Kitchen, piano, bikes, and free parking. Internet access $1 per 5min. Linen $2. Laundry $2. Check-in 8-11am and 4:30pm-midnight. Lockout 11am-4:30pm. Curfew midnight. Dorms $18, members $15. MC/V. ❶

Bank Street Hostel (HI), 32 S. Bank St. (☎922-0222 or 800-392-4678; www.bankstreethostel.com). From the bus station, walk down Market St.; it's in an alleyway between 2nd and 3rd St. 70 beds, A/C, TV, pool table, and kitchen. Movies nightly 9pm. Laundry $3. Internet access $1 per 4min. Linen $3. Lockout 10:30am-4:30pm. Curfew 2:30am. Dorms $23, members $20. Cash only. ❶

La Reserve (Bed and Breakfast Center City), 1804 Pine St. (☎735-1137; www.centercitybed.com). Take I-676 to the 23rd St. exit and bear right. After 10 blocks, turn left onto Pine St. A stately house with a Steinway in the entryway and 8 guest rooms with 19th-century decor. Full breakfast and A/C. Doubles in summer $89-159; in winter $79-129. Student discount 10-20%. MC/V. ❹

Alexander Inn, 12th and Spruce St. (☎923-3535 or 877-253-9466; www.alexanderinn.com). Spacious rooms with wireless Internet access, cable TV, A/C, hot breakfast, access to a fitness room, and just about everything else you could imagine. Popular with the professional set. Rooms $99-159. MC/V. ❺

Timberlane Campground, 117 Timberlane Rd. (☎856-423-6677; www.timberlane-campground.com), 15 mi. from Center City, across the Delaware River in Clarksboro, NJ. Take U.S. 295 S to the first turnoff for Exit 18A, follow the campground signs for ½ mi., and turn right on Friendship Rd. Timberlane is 1 block down on the right. Hot showers, toilets, fishing pond, pool, and batting cages. Reservations recommended. Sites $28, with hookup $30. ❶

☐ FOOD

Street vendors are major players in Philly's cuisine scene, hawking cheesesteaks, hoagies, cashews, and soft pretzels on every corner. Ethnic eateries gather in several areas: **South Street,** between Front and 7th St., **18th Street,** around Sansom St., and **2nd Street,** between Chestnut and Market St. The nation's third-largest **Chinatown** is bounded by 11th, 8th, Arch, and Vine St., and has reasonable restaurants, bakeries, and markets, all worth a lunchtime wander.

The immense **Italian Market** spans the storefronts, sidewalks, and stalls around 9th St. below Christian St. Make yourself a gourmet Mediterranean picnic from the thousands of meats, cheeses, and olives available at **DiBruno Brothers,** 930 S. 9th St. (☎888-322-4337; http://dibruno.com. Open M 9am-5pm, Tu-Sa 8am-6pm, Su 8am-2pm. AmEx/MC/V.) Philadelphia's original farmers market (since 1893), the **Reading Terminal Market,** at 12th and Arch St. across from the Pennsylvania Convention Center, is the largest indoor market in the US. A food court on steroids, the market has everything from traditional Amish meat mongers to trendy Asian-fusion stalls. Most places have seating for the jumbled lunchtime crowd of cops, moms, and suits. (☎922-2317; www.readingterminalmarket.org. Open M-Sa 8am-6pm; Amish merchants W 8am-3pm, Th-Sa 8am-5pm.)

HISTORIC DISTRICT

Famous 4th Street Delicatessen, 700 S. 4th St. (☎922-3274 or 888-922-3535), at Bainbridge St. This deli rivals New York City's finest. A landmark since 1923, it has earned a cult following for its hot corned beef sandwiches ($9.50), classic Reubens ($10), and borscht ($5). Open M-Sa 7:30am-6pm, Su 7:30am-4pm. AmEx/MC/V. ❷

Jim's Steaks, 400 South St. (☎928-1911; www.jimsteaks.com), at 4th St. Customers flock to this Philly classic at all hours for authentic hoagies ($6), cheesesteaks ($6), and takeout beer. Right up there with Geno's and Pat's. Open M-Th 10am-1am, F-Sa 10am-3am, Su noon-10pm. Cash only. ❶

Pink Rose Pastry Shop, 630 S. 4th St. (☎592-0565; www.pinkrosepastry.com), at Bainbridge St. across from the deli. Friendly students serve homemade delicacies at tables graced with freshly cut flowers and grandmotherly decorations. The sour cream apple pie ($5.25) is unbelievable. Open M-Th 8am-10:30pm, F 8am-11pm, Sa 9:30am-11pm, Su 9am-10:30pm. AmEx/MC/V. ❶

CHINATOWN

▨ **Chinese Restaurant,** 104 N. 10th St. (☎928-0261). It doesn't get more authentic than this dirt-cheap little restaurant, crowded with locals. Unless you are fluent in Chinese, plan to point at the menu (they are in the process of translating one). Open M-Th and Sa-Su 9am-8pm. Cash only. ❶

Singapore, 1006 Race St. (☎922-3288), between 10th and 11th St. The health-conscious flock here for kosher-vegetarian roast "pork" with black bean sauce ($7) or the tofu pot with assorted vegetables ($7). The $7.50 lunch specials come with soup, a spring roll, and rice. Open daily 11am-11pm. AmEx/D/MC/V. ❷

Sang Kee Peking Duck House, 238 N. 9th St. (☎925-7532), near Arch St. Locals pack in for the extensive menu. Duck requires lengthy preparation, but they serves so much of it you are always just minutes from the delectable fowl (half $16.50, whole $24.50). Entrees $6-10. Open M-Th and Su 11am-11pm, F-Sa 11am-midnight. Cash only. ❸

MID-ATLANTIC

A BEEFY RIVALRY

In a town known for its cheesesteaks and, not surprisingly, for its staggering obesity rates, every Philadelphian has a favorite corner shop to loudly champion whenever the subject of cheesesteaks arises. Even after Mayor Street created a city-wide "Health and Fitness Czar" (shortly after Philly surpassed Houston in 2000 as "fattest city" in a *Men's Health* survey), cheesesteak consumption remained astronomical. Philadelphia is bursting with shops serving up the caloric concoctions, but none is more famous than **Pat's King of Steaks** (☎468-1546; www.patskingofsteaks.com), unless it's his cross-street rival, the larger, more neon **Geno's Steaks** (☎389-0659; www.genosteaks.com).

Pat Olivieri founded his cheesesteak shop on a corner in 1930, amidst rumors that he invented the famous sandwich. Some 36 years later, Joe Vento, foiled by a pre-existing store called "Joe's," was inspired by some alleyway graffiti to name his shop, and later his son, Geno. The flashier Geno's boasts fans like Justin Timberlake and Jessica Simpson, while the more sedate Pat's has hosted Steve Case and Larry King. Tourists can sample either side of the controversy (or both) for $6.25 per steak daily at 9th St. and Passyunk Ave.—just be prepared to order quickly, or get roundly cursed by the hungry crowd in line behind you.

Rangoon, 112 N. 9th St. (☎829-8939), between Cherry and Arch St. Plastic decor belies the spicy scents of Burmese cooking wafting outside. The *Let Thoke* ($6.50), a noodle dish with shrimp, has earned this place its fantastic reputation. Lunch specials $5.50. Open M-Th and Su 11:30am-9pm, F-Sa 11:30am-10pm. MC/V. ❸

CENTER CITY

Alma de Cuba, 1623 Walnut St. (☎988-1799; www.almadecubarestaurant.com), near Rittenhouse Sq. Trendy spot for hot Latin food. Try the *sancocho de pollo* soup ($7), made with coconut-chicken broth. Free tapas and discounted drinks during happy hour (M-F 5-7pm). Live Cuban jazz W 9pm-midnight. Entrees from $21. Open M-Th 5-11pm, F-Sa 5pm-midnight, Su 5-10pm. MC/V. ❹

Jamaican Jerk Hut, 1436 South St. (☎545-8644), near Broad St. While chefs jerk Negril garlic shrimp ($16) to perfection, Bob Marley tunes blast on the backyard veranda. BYOB, but be prepared to pay a $2 corking fee on your bottle of wine or 6-pack. Live music F-Sa 7pm; cover $2. Entrees $9-18. Open Tu-Th 11am-10pm, F-Sa 11am-11pm, Su 5-10pm. Cash only. ❹

Bassett's Ice Cream (☎925-4315), in Reading Terminal Market at 12th and Arch St. Established in 1861, Bassett's is the oldest ice-creamery in the state, and some say the best in the nation. Originals like pumpkin ice cream may be throwbacks to the olden days, but modern concoctions—moose tracks, mocha chip, and rum raisin—also await. 2 scoops $2.75, 3 scoops $3.50. Open M-F 9am-6pm, Sa 8am-6pm. Cash only. ❶

UNIVERSITY CITY

☒ **Tandoor India Restaurant,** 106 S. 40th St. (☎222-7122), between Chestnut and Walnut St. Every campus may have a good, cheap Indian restaurant, but this is one of the best. Vegetarians come for the *bhindi* (spicy okra; $8). Lunch buffet daily 11:30am-3:30pm ($7); dinner buffet daily 4-10pm ($10). Student discount on buffets 20%. Open daily 11:30am-10:30pm. AmEx/D/MC/V. ❷

Smokey Joe's, 208 S. 40th St. (☎222-0770), between Locust and Walnut St. Hearty meals at student-friendly prices. Burgers $6. Open daily 11am-2am. AmEx/D/MC/V. ❷

Abner's Cheesesteaks, 3813 Chestnut St. (☎662-0100), at 38th St. This bright, spacious, and cleaner-than-average joint is a local favorite. Cheesesteak $5.20. Open M-Th and Su 11am-midnight, F-Sa 11am-3am. AmEx/D/DC/MC/V. ❷

◎ SIGHTS

INDEPENDENCE MALL

REVOLUTIONARY SIGHTS. The **Independence National Historical Park**, bounded by Market, Walnut, 2nd, and 7th St., contains dozens of historical buildings. The National Park Service map, available at the visitors center, marks sundry minor historical houses that often provide a more illuminating stop than the major buildings. At night, the patriotic **Lights of Liberty Show** illuminates the park. A 1hr., half-mile guided walking tour with an elaborate audio program narrates the events of the Revolution while the $12 million laser light show projects five-story-tall film sequences onto historic buildings. *(Park: ☎965-7676 or 800-537-7676; www.independencevisitorcenter.com. Open daily June-Aug. 8:30am-5:30pm; Sept.-May 9am-5pm. Free. Light Show: PECO Energy Liberty Center, at the corner of 6th and Chestnut St. ☎542-3789 or 877-462-1775; www.lightsofliberty.org. Shows May-Aug. Tu-Sa, Sept.-Oct. Th-Sa; all shows begin at dusk. $17.76, seniors and students $16, ages 6-12 $12. Parking available on 6th St. between Arch and Market St., under the visitors center.)* Directly across from the visitors center is a new security building that visitors must pass through to get to the Liberty Bell, Independence Hall, and Congress Hall. No tickets are required to go through the security building. While freedom still rings at the new **Liberty Bell Center,** the Liberty Bell unfortunately does not (it cracked the first time it was rung). The petite bell inside the center is also visible through a glass wall from Chestnut Street. *(On Market St., between 5th and 6th St. ☎597-8974. Open daily 9am-5pm. Free.)* One of the most significant sites in American history, **Independence Hall** is also one of Philadelphia's most popular attractions. After Jefferson drafted the Declaration of Independence, the delegates signed the document here in 1776, then reconvened in 1787 to ink their names onto the US Constitution. Today, knowledgeable park rangers take visitors on a brief but informative tour through the nation's first capitol building. *(Between 5th and 6th St. on Chestnut St. Open daily 9am-5pm. Tickets, distributed at the visitors center, are required for admittance to the free guided tours that leave every 15min.)* The US Congress assembled in nearby **Congress Hall** from 1790 to 1800, when Philadelphia was the nation's first capital. While soaking up the history, rest in the plush Senate chairs. *(At Chestnut and 6th St. Open daily 9am-5pm.)*

The First Continental Congress, predecessor of the US Congress, united against the British in 1774 in **Carpenters' Hall.** Now a mini-museum heralding the carpenters responsible for Old City Hall and the Pennsylvania State House, the hall also houses the oldest continuously operating trade guild in America, founded in 1724. The hall is located in a fenced green area that also contains a military museum, the nation's second bank, and several historical homes worth a look. *(320 Chestnut St. ☎925-0167; www.carpentershall.org. Open Mar.-Dec. Tu-Su 10am-4pm; Jan.-Feb. W-Su 10am-4pm. Free.)* Behind the visitors center, the **National Constitution Center** provides visitors with a multimedia introduction to the Constitution and a variety of exhibits that give a more in-depth look at its history. *(525 Arch St., in Independence National Historical Park. ☎409-6600 or 866-917-1787; www.constitutioncenter.org. 17min. multimedia presentation prior to entrance to exhibits; last show 4:10pm. Open M-F and Su 9:30am-5pm, Sa 9:30am-6pm. $9; seniors, students, and under 12 $7.)*

OTHER SIGHTS. The rest of the park preserves residential and commercial buildings of the Revolutionary era. On the northern edge of the mall, a white molding delineates the size and location of Ben Franklin's home in ◪**Franklin Court.** The original abode was razed by the statesman's heirs in 1812 in order to erect an apartment complex. The site contains a museum of Franklin's inventions and personal possessions, a 20min. movie, a replica of Franklin's printing office with a working 18th-century printing press, and a post office. This post office was the first in the nation. *(318 Market St., between 3rd and 4th St. ☎597-8974. Open in summer daily 9am-5pm; call for winter hours. Free.)* On a more somber note, a statue of George Washington presides over the **Tomb of the Unknown Soldier,** in Washington Sq., where an eternal flame commemorates the fallen heroes of the Revolutionary War.

Located next to Independence Park is the **Federal Reserve Bank of Philadelphia,** which exhibits money from the 13 original colonies and even a $100,000 bill featuring President Woodrow Wilson. *(Federal Reserve: 100 N. 6th St., between Arch and Race St. ☎574-6257; www.phil.frb.org. Open M-F 9:30am-4:30pm; June-Aug. also Sa-Su 10am-4pm. Free.)* Philadelphia's official history museum, the **Atwater Kent Museum,** has a wide range of rare Pennsylvania artifacts, including the wampum belt given to William Penn by the Lenni Lenape at Shakamaxon in 1682 and a giant floor map of Philadelphia. *(16 S. 7th St. ☎685-4830; www.philadelphiahistory.org. Open M and W-Su 10am-5pm. $5, seniors and ages 13-17 $3, under 12 free.)*

OUTSIDE INDEPENDENCE MALL

COLONIAL MADNESS. A penniless Ben Franklin arrived in Philadelphia in 1723 and strolled by the rowhouses that line the narrow **Elfreth's Alley,** near 2nd and Arch St. The oldest continuously inhabited street in America now houses a museum that provides a glimpse into the daily lives of Philadelphians throughout the years. *(Museum: 124 Elfreth's Alley. ☎574-0560; www.elfrethsalley.org. Open Mar.-Nov. M-Sa 10am-5pm, Su noon-5pm; Dec.-Feb. Th-Sa 10am-5pm, Su noon-5pm. 20min. tours; last tour 4:40pm. $3, ages 6-18 $1.)* Several blocks away, the **Betsy Ross House** is a child-oriented museum honoring America's most beloved seamstress and her masterpiece, the American flag. *(239 Arch St. ☎686-1252; www.betsyrosshouse.org. Open Apr.-Sept. daily 10am-5pm; Oct.-Mar. Tu-Su 10am-5pm. $3, children and students $2. Audio tour $5.)*

OTHER SIGHTS. For those who like to get off on the right foot, the Temple University School of Podiatric Medicine contains the **Shoe Museum.** The collection of 900 pairs features footwear from the famous feet of Reggie Jackson, Lady Bird Johnson, Julius Erving, Nancy Reagan, and others. Recent additions to the collection include Ella Fitzgerald's gold boots and a pair of 6-inch-tall, blue satin platform sandals worn by Sally Struthers on the popular television show *All in the Family. (8th and Race St., 6th fl. ☎625-5243. Tours W and F 9am-1pm. Free but by appointment only.)* The powder-blue **Benjamin Franklin Bridge,** the longest suspension bridge in the world when it opened in 1926, off Race and 5th St., connects Philadelphia to New Jersey, and provides an expansive view of the city.

SOCIETY HILL AND THE WATERFRONT

Society Hill proper begins on Walnut St., between Front and 7th St., east of Independence Mall, and is filled with townhouses over 200 years old and cobblestone walks illuminated by electric "gaslights." Move eastward through Society Hill and you will eventually hit the Delaware River. The restaurants along the commercialized waterfront are great places to watch ships go by during the day or see the back-lit Philadelphia skyline at sunset.

HISTORICAL SIGHTS. Historic **Head House Square,** at 2nd and Pine St., is America's oldest firehouse and marketplace, and now contains restaurants and boutiques. Bargain hunters can test their haggling skills at an outdoor arts and crafts fair. *(☎790-0782. Open June-Aug. Sa noon-11pm, Su noon-6pm. Free workshops Su 1-3pm.)* Each January, sequin- and feather-clad participants join in a rowdy New Year's Day Mummer's Parade, which began in celebration of the masked festival actors known as "mummers." South of Head House Sq., the **Mummer's Museum** swells with glamorous old costumes. *(1100 S. 2nd St., at Washington Ave. ☎336-3050; www.riv-*

erfrontmummers.com. Free string band concerts Tu 8pm. Open May-Sept. Tu 9:30am-9:30pm, W-Sa 9:30am-4:30pm, Su noon-4:30pm; July-Aug. closed Su; Oct.-Apr. Tu-Sa 9:30am-4:30pm, Su noon-4:30pm. $3.50; students, seniors, and under 12 $2.50.)

ON THE WATERFRONT. A looming neon sign at the easternmost end of Market St. welcomes visitors to **Penn's Landing.** There are free concerts throughout the year, and the walk from the Market St. entrance over the footbridge to South St. is a gorgeous night trek. *(☎629-3257; www.pennslandingcorp.com. Major bands Apr.-Oct. Th 8pm. Children's theater Su 10am-noon.)* Philadelphian shipbuilding, cargo, and immigration unfold at the **Independence Seaport Museum** at Penn's Landing. Kids can get their sea legs at the "Boats Float" exhibit. Near the museum a host of old ships bobs at the dock, including the *USS Olympia*, the oldest steel warship still afloat, and the *USS Becuna*, a WWII submarine. *(☎925-5439; www.phillyseaport.org. Open daily 10am-5pm. Museum and ships $9, seniors $8, children $6.)*

CENTER CITY

As the financial and commercial hub of Philly, Center City barely has enough room to accommodate the professionals who cram into the area bounded by 12th, 23rd, Vine, and Pine St. Rife with activity during the day, the region retires early at night.

ART AND ARCHITECTURE. The country's first school and art museum, the **Pennsylvania Academy of Fine Art** has permanent displays of works by Winslow Homer and Mary Cassatt, while current students show their theses and accomplished alumni get their own exhibits each May. A new building across the street displays more than 250 paintings in 15 gallery rooms. *(118 N. Broad St., at Cherry St. ☎972-7600; www.pafa.org. Open Tu-Sa 10am-5pm, Su 11am-5pm. Tours 45-60min.; M-F at 11:30am and 12:30pm, Sa-Su at noon and 1pm. $7, students and seniors $6, ages 5-18 $5.)* Presiding over Center City, the granite-and-marble **City Hall** took 30 years to build. Until 1908, it reigned as the tallest building in the US, aided by the 37 ft. statue of William Penn bedecked in hat and stockings at its summit. A law prohibited building anything higher than Penn's hat in Philadelphia until entrepreneurs overturned it in the mid-1980s. *(At Broad and Market St. ☎686-2840. Open M-F 9:30am-4:30pm. Tower-only tour every 15min. daily 9:15am-4:15pm, 5 people max. per tour; reservations recommended. Free.)* The **Masonic Temple** is a commanding building that contains a research library, a cache of period art, and breathtaking architecture. The short tours give a glance at the secretive history of the Masons in America. *(1 N. Broad St. ☎988-1900; www.pagrandlodge.org. Entry by tour only. Tours Tu-Th 11am, 2, 3pm; Sat 10, 11am. Suggested donation $3.)*

RITTENHOUSE SQUARE

In the early 20th century, architect Paul Phillipe Cert overhauled the Rittenhouse Sq. District, leaving his mark on the ritzy, brick-laden neighborhood southeast of Center City. This part of town cradles the musical and dramatic pulse of the city, housing several performing arts centers.

RITTENHOUSE MUSEUMS. For the best results, completely digest lunch before viewing the bizarre and often gory medical abnormalities displayed at the highly intriguing **⬚Mütter Museum.** Among the potentially unsettling fascinations are a wall of skulls and a collection of preserved body parts of famous people, including John Marshall's bladder stones and a cancerous section of John Wilkes Booth's neck. The museum also contains a Level 4 biohazard suit, a medicinal herb garden, and a bizarre gift shop. *(19 S. 22nd St. ☎563-3737, ext. 211. Open daily 10am-5pm. $10; seniors, students, and ages 6-18 $7.)* Just south of the square, the non-descript exterior of the **⬚Rosenbach Museum and Library** hides an enormous, must-see collection of rare books and manuscripts, from a handwritten copy of James Joyce's

Ulysses to Lewis Carroll's copy of *Alice in Wonderland* with original sketches. *(2010 Delancey St. ☎ 732-1600; www.rosenbach.org. Open Tu and Th-Su 10am-5pm, W 10am-8pm. Exhibition and tour $8, students and seniors $5.)*

PARKWAY/MUSEUM DISTRICT

Nicknamed "America's Champs-Elysées," the **Benjamin Franklin Parkway** sports a colorful international flag row in downtown Philly. **Logan Circle,** one of the city's five original town squares, was the site of public executions until 1823 but now delights the children who frolic in its **Swann Memorial Fountain.** Designed by Alexander Calder, the fountain represents the Wissahickon Creek, the Schuylkill River, and the Delaware River, the three bodies of water that surround the city.

SCIENCE. A modern assemblage of everything scientific, the highly interactive ◪**Franklin Institute** would make the old inventor proud. The complex includes three floors of exhibits dedicated to the laws of science, an IMAX theater, a flight simulator used by the Navy, and free shows on everything from dissecting a cow's eye to putting on a spacesuit. The newly installed "skybike" allows kids and adults to pedal across a tightrope suspended nearly four stories high. *(At 20th St. and Ben Franklin Pkwy. ☎ 448-1200; www.fi.edu. Open daily 9:30am-5pm, F-Sa IMAX open until 9pm. $13.75, seniors and ages 4-11 $11. IMAX Theater ☎ 448-1111; $9; $5 with a museum entry. Skybike $2.)* Part of the Institute, the **Fels Planetarium** takes visitors on daily tours of the stars and stages MTV2's SonicVision hourly from 9pm-midnight on weekends. *(222 N. 20th St. One show included free in Franklin Institute ticket. $8, seniors and ages 4-11 $5.)* Across from the Institute, the **Academy of Natural Sciences** allows budding archaeologists to try their hand at digging up dinosaur fossils. *(1900 Ben Franklin Pkwy., at 19th St. ☎ 299-1000; www.acnatsci.org. Open M-F 10am-4:30pm, Sa-Su 10am-5pm. $10, seniors and military $8.25, ages 3-12 $8. AAA discount $1. Wheelchair accessible.)*

ART. Sylvester Stallone may have etched the sight of the ◪**Philadelphia Museum of Art** into the minds of movie buffs everywhere when he bolted up its stately front stairs in *Rocky* (1976), but it is the artwork within that has earned the museum its fine reputation. The world-class collection includes famous works such as Van Gogh's *Sunflowers,* Cezanne's *Large Bathers,* and Toulouse-Lautrec's *At the Moulin Rouge.* The museum also contains a Japanese Tea House and extensive Asian, Egyptian, and American art collections. *(Ben Franklin Pkwy. and 26th St. ☎ 763-8100; www.philamuseum.org. Open Tu-Su 10am-5pm, F 10am-8:45. Tours daily 10am-3pm. Live jazz, wine, and appetizers F 5:45pm-8:15pm. $12; students, seniors, and ages 13-18 $8; 12 and under free. Su free.)* A casting of *The Gates of Hell* outside the **Rodin Museum** guards the most extensive collection of the prolific sculptor's works this side of the Seine. One of the five original castings of *The Thinker* (1880) marks the museum entrance from afar. *(Ben Franklin Pkwy. and 22nd St. ☎ 763-8100; www.rodinmuseum.org. Open Tu-Su 10am-5pm. 1hr. guided audio tour available for $5 in the gift shop. Free guided tour Tu and Th 11am, Su 1pm. Suggested donation $3.)*

BOOKS AND INMATES. The **Free Library of Philadelphia** has earned a stellar reputation for its orchestral music and rare book collection, one of the largest in the nation. Philadelphia art students frequently seek inspiration within the classical architecture of the building. *(At 20th and Vine St. ☎ 686-5322; www.library.phila.gov. Open M-W 9am-9pm, Th-Sa 9am-5pm. Tour of rare books M-F 11am. Free.)* In a reversal of convention, guests line up to get into prison at the castle-like **Eastern State Penitentiary,** once a ground-breaking institution for criminal rehabilitation. Tours twist through the smoldering dimness Al Capone once called home, and guides recount fascinating stories of daring inmates and their attempted escapes. The award-winning Halloween Haunted House (late September to November) is not for the faint of heart.

(2124 Fairmount Ave. at 22nd St. ☎ 236-3300; www.easternstate.org. Open W-Su 10am-5pm. Entry includes guided tours every hr. Last entry 4pm. $9, students and seniors $7, ages 7-12 $4, under 7 not permitted.)

UNIVERSITY CITY

In West Philly, across the Schuylkill from Center City, the **University of Pennsylvania** and **Drexel University** make up University City (U-City), a neighborhood comprised almost entirely of students. The Penn campus, a thriving assemblage of green lawns and red brick quadrangles, contrasts sharply with the dilapidated buildings surrounding it. Ritzy shops and cafes spice up 36th St., while a statue of the omnipresent Benjamin Franklin greets visitors at the campus entrance on 34th and Walnut St. Much of the area surrounding University City is unsafe at night.

U-CITY SIGHTS. The **University Museum of Archaeology and Anthropology** journeys through three floors of the world's major cultures under a beautiful stone and glass rotunda. *(At 33rd and Spruce St. ☎ 898-4001; www.upenn.edu/museum. Open Tu-Sa 10am-4:30pm, Su 1-5pm. $8, students and seniors $5.)* In 1965, Andy Warhol had his first one-man show at the cutting-edge **Institute of Contemporary Art.** Today, the ICA features works by some of the newest big names on the art scene. *(118 S. 36th at Sansom St. ☎ 898-7108; www.icaphila.org. Open W-F noon-8pm, Sa-Su 11am-5pm. $6; students, seniors, and artists $3. Su 11am-1pm free.)* North of the university area, the **Philadelphia Zoo,** the oldest zoo in the country, houses more than 2000 animals, including lowland gorillas, bearded pigs, and giant anteaters. The endangered animals exhibit provides a glimpse of some extremely rare species. If you'd rather get a bird's-eye view, take a ride on the Zooballoon and rise 400 ft. above the giraffes and zebras below. *(3260 South St. at 34th and Girard St. ☎ 243-1100; www.philadelphiazoo.org. Open daily Feb.-Nov. 9:30am-5pm; Dec.-Jan. 9:30am-4pm. $17, seniors and ages 2-11 $13. Zooballoon open Apr.-Oct. $12. Parking $8.)*

♫ ENTERTAINMENT

The non-profit **Kimmel Center for the Performing Arts,** 260 S. Broad St., dominates the performing arts scene in Philadelphia, the home of eight resident performing companies and the manager of multiple theaters in the city. The **Philadelphia Orchestra** performs in the Center's Verizon Hall from September to May while **Philadance,** a contemporary dance company, and the **Philadelphia Chamber Music Society** reside in the smaller Perelman Hall. The Center's **Academy of Music,** at Broad and Locust St., was modeled after Milan's La Scala and is the nation's oldest, continuously-running opera house. The Academy hosts the **Opera Company of Philadelphia** and the six annual productions of the **Pennsylvania Ballet.** The outdoor **Mann Music Center,** at 52nd St. and Parkside Ave., in Fairmount Park, hosts big name entertainers like Tony Bennett, Willie Nelson, and the Gipsy Kings, as well as a variety of jazz and rock concerts. (For all performances, contact Kimmel Center: ☎ 790-5800 or 893-1999; www.kimmelcenter.org. Box office open daily 10am-6pm and until performances begin. Schedule and ticket prices vary by show and venue.)

The 120-year-old and still independent **Trocadero,** 1003 Arch St. at 10th St., is the oldest operating Victorian theater in the nation and hosts both local and big-name rock bands. (☎ 922-5483; www.thetroc.com. Box office open M-F 11:30am-6pm, Sa 11:30am-5pm.) The **Robin Hood Dell East,** on Ridge Ave. near 33rd St. in Fairmount Park, brings in top names in pop, jazz, and gospel in July and August. In September, theatrical entertainment graces the stage. (☎ 685-9560. Box office open M-F 10am-5pm, Sa-Su 10am-showtime.) The students of the world-renowned **Curtis Institute of Music,** 1726 Locust St., give free concerts. (☎ 893-5252; www.curtis.edu. Mid-Oct. to Apr. M, W, F 8pm.) **Merriam Theater,** 250 S. Broad St. in Center City, stages performances ranging from student works to Broadway hits. Katharine Hepburn, Laurence Olivier, and Sammy Davis, Jr. have all graced this stage. (☎732-5446; www.broadwayacrossamerica.com. Box office open M-Sa 10am-5:30pm.) The Old City, from Chestnut to Vine and Front to 4th St., comes alive for the **First Friday** celebration, when streets fill with live music and 40 art galleries, museums, and restaurants open their doors to entice visitors with free food and sparkling wine. (☎800-555-5191; www.oldcity.org. Oct.-June, first F of each month 5-9pm.)

Philly gets physical with plenty of sports venues—four professional teams play a short ride away on the Broad St. subway line. Baseball's **Phillies** (☎463-1000; www.phillies.com) step up to the plate at **Citizens Bank Park,** 1 Citizens Bank Way, just off Pattison Ave. between 11th and Darien St. Football's **Eagles** (☎463-5500; www.philadelphiaeagles.com) take the field at **Lincoln Financial Field,** at Broad St. and Pattison Ave. Across the street, fans fill the **Wachovia Center** (☎336-3600; box office open M-F 9am-6pm, Sa 10am-4pm) for the NBA's **76ers** (☎339-7676; www.sixers.com) and the NHL's **Flyers** (☎755-9700; www.philadelphiaflyers.com). Baseball and hockey tickets start at $10; football and basketball run $15-50. Since the venues are in close proximity, expect parking difficulty on game nights.

🎵 NIGHTLIFE

Check the Friday *Philadelphia Inquirer* for entertainment listings. The free Thursday *City Paper* and the Wednesday *Philadelphia Weekly* have listings of city events. Gay and lesbian weeklies *Au Courant* (free) and *PGN* ($0.75) list events throughout the Delaware Valley. Many pubs line **2nd Street** near Chestnut St., close to the Bank St. Hostel, catering to a young, bar-hopping crowd. Continuing south to Society Hill, an older crowd fills dozens of more expensive bars and cafes. **Delaware Avenue,** or **Columbus Boulevard,** running along Penn's Landing, has recently become a trendy hot spot full of nightclubs and dance clubs that attract droves of yuppies and students. Most bars and clubs that cater to a gay clientele congregate along **Camac, South 12th,** and **South 13th Street.**

The Khyber, 56 S. 2nd St. (☎238-5888; www.thekhyber.com). A speakeasy during the days of Prohibition, the Khyber now legally gathers a young crowd to listen to a range of punk, metal, and hip-hop music. The ornate wooden bar was shipped over from England in 1876. Vegetarian sandwiches $3. Happy hour M-F 5-8pm. Live music daily 10pm. 21+. Cover $8. Open M-F noon-2am, Sa-Su 1pm-2am. Cash only.

The Five Spot, 5 S. Bank St. (☎574-0070), off Market St. between 2nd and 3rd St. A large club with 5 themed lounges, 4 bars, and several dance floors. Most weekends find indie-rock bands playing on the top floor. DJ spins modern, rap, and R&B F-Sa. Dress to impress: no sneakers or shorts. 21+. Cover $5-20. Open daily 9pm-2am.

Moriarty's, 1116 Walnut St. (☎627-7676; www.moriartysrestaurant.com), near 11th St. and the Forest Theater. This Irish pub draws a sizeable crowd late into the night with a quiet, comfortable bar scene and surprisingly good Mexican food. Over 28 beers on tap. Daily drink specials. Open daily 11am-2am; kitchen closes 1am.

Woody's, 202 S. 13th St. (☎545-1893; www.woodysbar.com), at Walnut St. An outgoing gay crowd frequents this lively club. Most nights, patrons are a happy mix of ages, genders, and sexual orientations. Happy hour daily 5-7pm. Karaoke M. Open for meals daily noon-3:30pm and 4-11pm; bar open daily 11am-2am.

🏞 OUTDOOR ACTIVITIES

Philly's finest outdoor opportunities can be found in the resplendent **Fairmount Park** (www.phila.gov/fairpark; open dawn-dusk). Ten times the size of New York City's Central Park, Fairmount is covered with bike trails and picnic areas, offering city-weary vacationers the adventure of the great outdoors and views of the Schuylkill River. The Andorra Natural Area inside the park is a 210-acre preserve of native plants and includes an environmental education center on the banks of Wissahickon Creek. **Mountain biking** is very popular in the Wissahickon and Pennypacker Valleys north of Philadelphia, where both flat and more challenging trails are available. (☎683-0200. Permit required to bike trails, but rarely enforced. $20 per yr.) The premier location for wildlife observation in the Philadelphia area is the **John Heinz National Wildlife Refuge,** just off I-95 near the south end of Philadelphia in Tinicum. This 205-acre freshwater tidal marsh is home to hundreds of bird species, including migrants from both tropical and northern climes.

The abandoned **Waterworks,** Greek-style ruins by the waterfall immediately behind the Museum of Art, were built between 1819 and 1822. Free 90min. tours of the Waterworks' romantic architecture and technology begin on Aquarium Dr., behind the museum. (☎685-4935; www.fairmountwaterworks.org. Open Sa-Su 1-3:30pm.) Farther down the river, Philly's place in the rowing world is evidenced by a line of crew clubs forming the historic **Boathouse Row.** The Museum of Art hosts the Schuylkill Stroll, a $6 guided tour of Boathouse Row (F 6-7:30pm), Su 1-2:30pm, as well as trolley tours to some of the mansions in Fairmount Park (☎763-8100 for mansion tour schedules). The area near Boathouse Row is also Philly's most popular in-line skating spot, and joggers seeking the refreshing river breeze crowd the local paths. In the northern arm of Fairmount Park, trails follow the secluded Wissahickon Creek for 5 mi., as the concrete city fades into a distant memory. The **Japanese House and Garden,** off Montgomery Dr. near Belmont Ave., is designed in the style of a 17th-century *shoin;* the authentic garden defines tranquility. (☎878-5097; www.shofuso.com. Open May-Oct. Tu-F 10am-4pm, Sa-Su 11am-5pm; call for winter hours. Ask about the tour. $4; students, ages 6-17, and 55+ $3.) The park and the surrounding neighborhoods are not safe at night.

⬛ DAYTRIP FROM PHILADELPHIA

VALLEY FORGE

Valley Forge lies 40min. from Philadelphia by car. To get to the visitors center, take I-76 west from Philadelphia for about 12 mi. until Exit 327 (old Exit 25) and make a right at the bottom of the ramp. SEPTA runs buses from Philadelphia to the visitors center daily; catch #125 in front of the Sheraton Hotel at 16th and JFK ($3.50). Valley Forge is open daily 9am-10pm; entrance is free.

In 1777-78 it was the frigid winter, not the British military, that almost crushed the Continental Army. When George Washington selected Valley Forge as the winter camp for his 12,000 troops after a defeat at Germantown in October, he could not have predicted the fate that would befall his soldiers. Three arduous months of starvation, bitter cold, and disease nearly halved his forces. It was not until Baron Friedrich von Steuben arrived with reinforcements and supplies on February 23, 1778, that recovery seemed possible. Reinvigorated, the Continental Army left Valley Forge on June 19, 1778 to win the Battle of Monmouth.

The hills that once tormented the frost-bitten soldiers now constitute the **Valley Forge National Historical Park.** The **visitors center,** 1400 Outer Line Dr., features a small museum and a 20min. film. (☎610-783-1099; www.nps.gov/vafo. Open daily in summer 9am-6pm; in winter 9am-5pm.) Visitors can explore the park by car, foot, bus, bicycle, or even horse, but no in-line skates or skateboards are allowed. The 10 mi. self-guided **auto tour** (tape $10, CD $12), begins at the visitors center. If you prefer live narration and question time, the quarter-mile **walking tour,** led by a knowledgeable park ranger and culminating in an antique musket demonstration, also leaves from the visitors center (in summer daily 10:50am, 12:30, 1:50pm; in winter Sa-Su 10:50am and 1:50pm. Free). The 1½hr. **bus tour** allows visitors to explore sites in air-conditioned comfort. (In summer M and Th-Su. $16, ages 13-16 $11, under 12 $7.50.) All tours pass Washington's headquarters, reconstructed soldier huts and fortifications, and the Grand Parade Ground where the Continental Army drilled. The park has three picnic areas but no camping. Joggers can take a trip down a fairly flat, paved 6 mi. trail through deer-populated forests. Near the park, shoppers delight in the **King of Prussia Mall,** the largest retail mall in the nation and conveniently located in a region that exempts clothing from sales tax. Follow signs from I-76 or use SEPTA bus #125.

LANCASTER COUNTY ☎717

Lancaster County is known as the heart of Pennsylvania Dutch Country, but its residents, the Pennsylvania Dutch, aren't actually Dutch. When in the 1700s Amish and Mennonite settlers migrated to the area in search of religious freedom and introduced themselves as "Deutsch," English settlers mistook the German word for "Dutch." Lancaster is still home to the largest Old Order Amish population in the US, a group that strives to maintain its simple lifestyle in the face of modernity.

⊞◪ ORIENTATION AND PRACTICAL INFORMATION. Lancaster County covers an area almost the size of Rhode Island. Driving in from Philadelphia and other cities to the east is easiest on **Route 30 W;** from southern destinations, take **Route 83 N** to **Route 30 E.** County seat **Lancaster City,** in the heart of Dutch country, has red brick rowhouses huddled around historic **Penn Square.** The rural areas are mostly accessible by car (or horse and buggy), but it is easy to see the tourist sites with a bike or to walk the mile or two between public transit drop-offs. To sample the Amish and Mennonite traditions, stick to the towns along Rte. 340, such as **Bird-in-Hand** and the unfortunately named **Intercourse.** Because the area is heavily Mennonite, most businesses and all major attractions are closed on Sundays. **Amtrak,** 53 McGovern Ave. in Lancaster City (☎291-5080; www.amtrak.com; ticket office open M-F 5:30am-9pm, Sa-Su 7am-8:45pm), runs to Philadelphia (1½hr., 8-10 per day, $13) and Pittsburgh (6½hr., 2 per day, $37). **Capitol Trailways** (☎397-4861; open daily 8am-10pm), in the same location, runs buses to Philadelphia (3hr., 3 per day, $17) and Pittsburgh (6hr., 3 per day, $55). **Red Rose Transit,** 45 Erick Rd., has bus service within Lancaster City and to Bird-in-Hand, Paradise, Park City, and other areas in the surrounding countryside. (☎397-4246. Buses run daily approximately 5am-6pm. $1.15-$2.25.) The **Pennsylvania Dutch Visitors Bureau,** 501 Greenfield Rd., on the east side of Lancaster City off Rte. 30, shows an excellent video and dispenses info on the region, including maps and walking tours. (☎299-8901 or 800-723-8824; www.padutchcountry.com. Open M-Sa 8:30am-5pm, Su 9am-5pm.) **Post Office:** 1400 Harrisburg Pike. (☎396-6925 or 800-275-8777. Open M-F 7:30am-7pm, Sa 9am-2pm.) **Postal Code:** 17604. **Area Code:** 717.

▛ ACCOMMODATIONS. Hundreds of hotels, campgrounds, and B&Bs cluster in this area, as do several working farms with guest houses. The lodging guide published by the visitors center is an essential resource for wading through all the options. If you are considering staying in a B&B, call the **Authentic Bed and Breakfasts of Lancaster County Association** (☎800-552-2632; www.authenticbandb.com).

 DON'T SHOOT. Tempted as you may be to point your camera at those oh-so-quaint Amish folk, please refrain out of respect for their culture. Most Amish and Mennonite orders consider photographs to be sacrilegious graven images, and take offense at rapacious tourist paparazzi.

The amicable staff at the **Mennonite Information Center** (see **Sights**, p. 243) can put you in touch with Mennonite-run guest houses. For an affordable stay in a conveniently located working farm home, the **Verdant View Farm Bed and Breakfast ❸**, 429 Strasburg Rd., in Paradise, is the place to go. The farmhouse has five bedrooms, all with A/C and three with private baths, plus a visitors cottage with a full kitchen. Guests interested in the "Mennonite experience" can milk cows, feed calves, crawl through hay tunnels, and attend church service with their hosts. (☎ 687-7353 or 888-321-8119; www.verdantview.com. Check-in 2-5pm. Doubles $62-77. AmEx/MC/V.) Six miles east of Lancaster lies the **Amish Country Motel ❸**, 3013 Old Philadelphia Pike, where the price of a room includes a 2hr. bus tour of the area. (☎ 768-8396. Closed Dec.-Mar. Doubles $54-90. AmEx/D/MC/V.) For the B&B experience on a budget, look to the **Blue Ball B&B ❸**, 1075 Main St., in Blue Ball, east of Lancaster City on Rte. 23. This cozy guesthouse provides A/C, cable TV, private bath, and a full breakfast, all at $20 less than its competitors. (☎ 800-720-9827; www.blueballbandb.com. Singles and doubles $70-80.) The quiet wilderness of **Beacon Hill Camping ❶**, Rte. 772 W, half a mile from Rte. 340, makes it a perfect place to spend a night in one of 50 level sites. (☎ 768-8775. Check-in 1pm. Sites $24, with full hookup $29. Cabins $50. 7th night free. D/MC/V.)

❏ **FOOD.** Amish food, German in derivation and generous in portion, is characterized by a heavy emphasis on potatoes and vegetables. Palatable alternatives to high-priced "family-style" restaurants are the **farmers markets** and produce stands that dot the roadway. The **Central Market,** in downtown Lancaster City at the northwest corner of Penn Sq., next to the Heritage Center Museum, has been doing business since the 1730s. Nowadays, simply dressed Pennsylvania Dutch pour into the city to sell affordable fresh fruit, bologna, seasonings, and homemade desserts like shoofly pie. (☎ 291-4739. Open Tu and F 6am-4pm, Sa 6am-2pm.) Tourists who keep kosher can find items to fit their diet at **Central Pennsylvania's Kosher Mart,** 2249 Lincoln Hwy. E, Lancaster City. To be treated like the VIP that you are, head to **The Pressroom ❷**, 26 W. King St., in Lancaster City. Deep leather booths give this lunch and dinner spot a club-like feel, while the sandwiches ($6-8), named after cartoon characters, lighten the mood. Try one of the pizzas or grill items ($8-11), which remain economical choices even at dinner. (☎ 399-5400; www.thepressroomrestaurant.com. Lunch daily 11:30am-3pm. Dinner Tu-Th 5-9:30pm, F-Sa 5-10:30pm, Su 5-9pm.) If you have a hankering for something a little more historic, the **Revere Tavern ❸**, 3063 Lincoln Hwy., in Paradise, has a legacy of excellent service that dates back to its construction in 1740. Seven working fireplaces give the dining room a cozy feel in the winter. Lunch options here include croissant sandwiches ($5-10), snapper turtle soup ($4), and a deli buffet. (☎ 687-8601. Dinner entrees $11-30. Open M 5-10pm, Tu-Sa 11am-2pm and 5-10pm, Su 4-9pm.) At the **Amish Barn ❸**, 3029 Old Philadelphia Pike, in Bird-in-Hand, quilts for sale hang on the walls surrounding tables where patrons devour Amish specialties after frolicking in the on-site petting zoo. Though hardly an authentic family restaurant, it's perfect for big groups. (☎ 768-8886. Entrees around $10. Open June-Aug. M-Sa 7:30am-9pm; in spring and fall M-Sa 8am-8pm; call for winter hours.)

◧ **SIGHTS.** From April to October every year, quilt and art fanatics flock to Amish country to see the **People's Place Quilt Museum,** 3510 Old Philadelphia Pike. (☎ 800-828-8218; www.ppquiltmuseum.com. Open Apr.-Oct. M-Sa 9am-5pm.) The Mennonites believe in outreach and have established the **Mennonite Information Center,** 2209 Millstream Rd., off Rte. 30 east of Lancaster, to help tourists distinguish between the Amish and Mennonite faiths. Kind hostesses guide guests through the Biblical Tabernacle. (☎ 299-0954; www.mennoniteinfoctr.com. 2hr. private tours available.) To explore the Amish countryside by car, try winding through the fields off U.S. 340, near Bird-in-Hand. Cyclists can capture the unostentatious spirit on the **Lancaster County Heritage Bike Tour,** a reasonably flat 46 mi. route past covered bridges and historic sites maintained by the visitors center. A visit to Lancaster is not complete without using the preferred mode of local transportation, the horse and buggy. ■**Ed's Buggy Rides,** 253 Hartman Bridge Rd., on Rte. 896, 1½ mi. south of U.S. 30 W in Strasburg, offers 30min. and 1hr. tours that bump through scenic backwoods, covered bridges, and working farms. (☎687-0360; www.edsbuggy-rides.com. Open daily 9am-5pm. 30min. rides $8, under 11 $4. 1hr. rides $12/$6.) **Amish Country Tours** leads 1½hr. trips that include visits to one-room schoolhouses, Amish cottage industries, cheery farmland vistas, and roadside produce and craft stands. (☎768-8400. Tours given Apr.-Oct. M-Sa 10:30am and 2pm, Su 11:30am; Nov. daily 11:30am; Dec.-Mar. Sa-Su 11:30am. $25, ages 4-12 $10.) Old country crafts, food, and even a mock hanging can be found from late June to early July at the **Pennsylvania Dutch Folk Life and Fun Festival,** in Kutztown, which offers an unusual combination of polka bands, pot pies, and petting zoos. (☎888-674-6463; www.kutztownfestival.com. $10 per day, seniors $9, under 12 free.)

GETTYSBURG   ☎717

In the sweltering heat of July 1-3, 1863, perhaps the most memorable period of the Civil War, Union and Confederate forces clashed spectacularly at Gettysburg. The Union forces ultimately prevailed, though the victory cost over 50,000 casualties. President Lincoln arrived in Gettysburg four months later to dedicate the Gettysburg National Cemetery, where 979 unidentified Union soldiers still rest alongside hundreds of other marked graves. Today, the National Soldier's Monument towers where Lincoln once delivered his legendary Gettysburg Address. Sights here are heavily historical; each year thousands of visitors from north and south of the Mason-Dixon line visit to retrace the movements of Generals Meade and Lee.

⊓ PRACTICAL INFORMATION. Inaccessible by Greyhound or Amtrak, Gettysburg is in south-central Pennsylvania, about 30 mi. south of Harrisburg and a straight shot along U.S. 15. The **Gettysburg Convention and Visitors Bureau,** 102 Carlisle St., has maps and brochures. (☎800-337-5015; www.gettysburgcvb.com. Open daily 8:30am-5pm.) **Post Office:** 115 Buford Ave. (☎337-3781 or 800-275-8777. Open M-F 8am-4:30pm, Sa 9am-noon.) **Postal Code:** 17325. **Area Code:** 717.

⌐ ACCOMMODATIONS. Follow Rte. 34 N to Rte. 233 to reach the closest hostel, ■**Ironmasters Mansion Hostel (HI) ❶,** 1212 Pine Grove Rd., 20 mi. from Gettysburg, within Pine Grove Furnace State Park. Large and luxurious, the building holds 46 beds in a tranquil area. Spacious porches, an ornate dining room, and a decadent jacuzzi make this hostel seem more like a resort. (☎486-7575. Kitchen, laundry, volleyball, ping-pong. Internet access $3 per 15min. Linen $2. Reception 7:30-9:30am and 5-10pm. Reservations recommended year-round, required in Jan. Dorms $18, members $15.) Many motels line Steinwehr Rd. near the battlefield, but finding summer rates below $100 is difficult in the downtown area. For those willing to sacrifice proximity to attractions, the **Red Carpet Inn ❸,** 2450 Emmitsburg Rd., 4 mi. south of Military Park, has a pool and comfortable rooms with A/C. (☎334-1345 or 800-336-1345. Singles and doubles Apr.-Nov. $70; Dec.-Mar. $52. AAA discount $10.) **The Brickhouse Inn ❺,** 452 Baltimore St., downtown, offers 10 mid-to-upscale B&B rooms in a three-story Victorian house. (☎338-9337 or 800-864-3464; www.brickhouseinn.com. Gracious hosts, breakfast, and parking included. Check-in 3:30-8pm. Check-out 11am. Rooms $90-155 in summer, less in winter; check website for specials.) **Artillery Ridge ❶,** 610 Taneytown Rd., 1 mi. south of the Military Park Visitors Center, maintains over 200 campsites with access to hot showers, stables, laundry, a pool, and a pond. (☎334-1288; www.artilleryridge.com. Open Apr.-Oct. daily; Nov. Sa-Su. Sites $22, with partial hookup $30, with full hookup $33. Each additional person $4, children $2.)

❒ FOOD. In addition to the scenic beauty of its battlefields, Gettysburg features a downtown area full of small shops and lively restaurants. Hefty rations prevail in the town's square and just beyond the battlefield entrance. Vegetarians would do well to seek out the sizable salads on most tavern menus since there aren't many other options. Local nightlife takes the form of saloons that cluster around the central square. In Gettysburg's first building (circa 1776), now the ▧**Dobbin House Tavern ❸,** 89 Steinwehr Ave., patrons can create their own grilled burger ($6-7) and view an Underground Railroad shelter. For finer dining, the tavern also serves elegant entrees for $18-28. (☎334-2100; www.dobbinhouse.com. Salads $6. Sandwiches $8. Open daily 11:30am-9pm.) **Kilwins ❶,** 37 Steinwehr Ave., takes guests to celestial heights with classic flavors of ice cream ($3-4). The peanut fudge ($15 per lb., free ½ lb. with 1 lb. purchase) is as addictive as it is pricey. (☎337-2252. Open M-Th and Su 11am-10pm, F-Sa 11am-midnight.) Plain but bountiful, **General Pickett's Buffet ❷,** 571 Steinwehr Ave., serves fresh, homestyle dishes like roasted chicken, green beans, and mac 'n' cheese in a Civil War-themed dining room. (☎334-7580. Lunch buffet $6. Dinner buffet $10. AmEx/MC/V.)

◱ SIGHTS. A sensible starting point is the **National Military Park Visitors Information Center,** 97 Taneytown Rd., which distributes free maps for an 18 mi. self-guided driving tour. Ranger walks are also available by reservation. (☎334-1124, ext. 431, ranger walk reservations 877-438-8929; www.nps.gov/gett. Visitors center open daily June-Aug. 8am-6pm; Sept.-May 8am-5pm. Park open daily 6am-10pm. Free.) An electronic map inside the visitors center uses lights to show the course of the Battle of Gettysburg. ($4, seniors $3, under 15 $2.) Be prepared to spend some extra cash for an in-depth look at the historic grounds. The visitors center bookstore carries a variety of **audio driving tours.** (Tape $11-12, CD $13-18. Most 2hr.) For a personalized experience, one of the ▧**licensed battlefield guides** will squeeze into the family car to guide visitors through the monuments, narrating and answering questions. (☎334-1124, ext. 470; www.gettysburgtourguides.com. 2hr. tours 8am-close. 1-6 people $40, 7-15 people $60, 16-49 people $90. Arrive by 9am to ensure a time slot or pay a surcharge to reserve in advance. Cash or traveler's check only.) The chilling sights and sounds of battle surround the audience at the **Cyclorama Center,** next to the visitors center. The center shows "Gettysburg 1863" (20min., begins 5min. after the hr.), "The American Civil War" (10min., 35min. after the hr.), and a 20min. light show (every 30min.) around a 9500 sq. ft. mural of the battle. The "cyclorama" itself is an 1824 oil painting of Pickett's Charge that is 26 ft. high and 356 ft. in circumference. (☎334-1124, ext. 422. Open daily 9am-5pm. $3, seniors $2.50, ages 6-16 $2. Last show 4:30pm. Cash or traveler's check only.) Bus tours to the **Eisenhower House and Farm** include a 20min. house tour and self-guided tour of the grounds. (Departures every 30min. 9am-4pm. $7, ages 13-16 $4, ages 6-12 $3.) Artillery Ridge Campgrounds (see **Accommodations,** above) conducts **horseback tours.** (1hr. horseback tour $33, 2hr. horseback and history tour $58. No one under age 8 or over 240 lb.) Adjacent to the campground office is a meticulously detailed diorama of the Gettysburg battle, along with other exhibits ($4.50, seniors and children $3.50). **Historic Tours** trundles visitors around the battlefield in double-decker buses. (☎334-8000; www.gettysburg.com. 2½hr. tours $17, AAA and AARP members $16, children $11.)

The ▧**Shriver House,** 309 Baltimore St., a museum dedicated to the civilian experience of the Civil War, features energetic tour guides in period costume. A house tour covers daily 19th-century life as revealed in the diary entries from a

MID-ATLANTIC

wartime inhabitant of the house. The tour also showcases relics discovered under the floorboards of the house's attic. (☎337-2800; www.shriverhouse.com. Open Apr.-Nov. M-Sa 10am-5pm, Su noon-5pm; Dec. and Feb.-Mar. Sa-Su noon-5pm. $7, seniors $6.50, ages 6-12 $4.50.) Based on the chilling tales told by author Mark Nesbitt, a former park ranger and inhabitant of a haunted Gettysburg house, candlelit **Ghosts of Gettysburg,** 271 Baltimore St., reawakens the war's dead. Three different tours, covering different parts of the town and their resident ghosts, run each night. (☎337-0445; www.ghostsofgettysburg.com. Tours Mar.-Nov. 8, 8:15, 9, 9:45pm; call for low-season times. Reservations recommended. $6-6.50, under 8 free.) Don't miss the living history programs or the disturbingly lifelike multimedia presentations on display at the **American Civil War Museum,** 297 Steinwehr Ave., across from the Military Park entrance. (☎334-6245; www.e-gettysburg.com. Open Mar.-Dec. daily 9am-8:15pm; Jan.-Feb. weekends and holidays only. $5.50, ages 13-17 $3.50, ages 6-12 $2.50, under 6 free. Cash or traveler's check only.)

PITTSBURGH ☎412

While other Rust Belt cities staggered and stumbled after the steel industry fell flat, Pittsburgh dusted itself off and transformed into a center for higher education, health care, and robotics. The city has not had an easy time emerging from the shadow of better-touristed Philadelphia, but has cultivated a heady music scene, tightly knit ethnic neighborhoods, and an affordable housing market. Streets plunge up and down steep embankments that have prompted some to dub Pittsburgh "a poor man's San Francisco," but abundant riches are in store for the traveler who veers off the beaten path to explore the city's charms.

▉ TRANSPORTATION

Airport: Pittsburgh International (☎472-3525; www.pitairport.com), 15 mi. west of downtown, encircled by I-279 and Rte. 60. The Port Authority's **28x Airport Flyer** bus serves downtown and Oakland. Runs daily every 20min. 5:45am-midnight. $2.25. **Airline Transportation Company** (☎472-3180 or 800-991-9890) runs downtown M-F every 30min. 7am-11:40pm, reduced service Sa. $17. Taxi to downtown $30.

Trains: Amtrak, 1100 Liberty Ave. (☎471-6170; www.amtrak.com), at Grant St. on the northern edge of downtown, near Greyhound and the post office. Be careful in this area at night. Station open 24hr. To **Chicago** (9½hr., daily at 11:45pm, $48-74), **New York City** (11hr., 3 per day, $54-80), and **Philadelphia** (8-10hr., 2 per day, $40-51).

Buses: Greyhound, 55 11th St. (☎392-6513; www.greyhound.com), at Liberty Ave. Open 24hr. To **Chicago** (10-13hr., 7 per day, $39-52), **Cleveland** (2½-4hr., 8 per day, $25), and **Philadelphia** (6-8hr., 8 per day, $29-42).

Public Transit: Port Authority of Allegheny County (☎442-2000; www.ridegold.com). Within downtown, subway free and bus free until 7pm. Beyond downtown, bus and light rail $1.75; transfers $0.50; weekly pass $17. Ages 6-11 half-price.

Taxi: Yellow Cab, ☎321-8100.

▉▉ ORIENTATION AND PRACTICAL INFORMATION

Pittsburgh's downtown, the **Golden Triangle,** is shaped by two rivers—the **Allegheny** to the north and the **Monongahela** to the south—which flow together to form a third river, the **Ohio.** Streets in the Triangle that run parallel to the Monongahela are numbered one through seven. The **University of Pittsburgh** and **Carnegie Mellon University** lie east of the Triangle in Oakland. Be careful in the area north of PNC

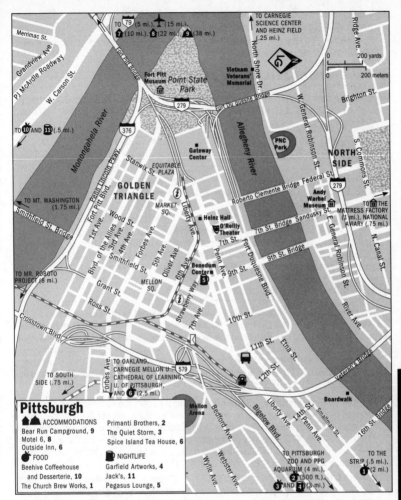

Pittsburgh

🔼🔼 ACCOMMODATIONS
Bear Run Campground, **9**
Motel 6, **8**
Outside Inn, **6**

🍴 FOOD
Beehive Coffeehouse
and Desserterie, **10**
The Church Brew Works, **1**

Primanti Brothers, **2**
The Quiet Storm, **3**
Spice Island Tea House, **6**

🎷 NIGHTLIFE
Garfield Artworks, **4**
Jack's, **11**
Pegasus Lounge, **5**

Park. The city's streets and 40-odd bridges are notoriously difficult to navigate; don't venture into one of Pittsburgh's many dense neighborhoods without getting directions first. The **Wayfinder system** helps tourists and locals alike navigate the city's often confusing streets. The 1500 color-coded signs point the way to major points of interest, business areas, and universities.

Visitor Info: Pittsburgh Convention and Visitors Bureau, 425 6th Ave., 30th fl. (☎281-7711 or 800-359-0758; www.visitpittsburgh.com). Open M-F 8:30am-5:30pm. There are 2 **visitors centers,** 1 downtown on Liberty Ave. (open M-F 9am-5pm, Sa 9am-3pm) and 1 at the airport (open M-Sa 10am-5pm).

Hotlines: Hate Crime Hotline, ☎820-0111. **Rape Action Hotline,** ☎866-363-7273. Both operate 24hr. **Gay & Lesbian Community Center,** ☎422-0114. Operates M-F 6:30-9:30pm, Sa 3-6pm.

Internet Access: Carnegie Library of Pittsburgh, 4400 Forbes Ave. (☎622-3114). Open M-Th 10am-8pm, F-Sa 10am-5:30pm, Su 1-5pm.

Post Office: 700 Grant St. (☎642-2984). Open M-F 7am-6pm, Sa 7am-2:30pm. **Postal Code:** 15219. **Area Code:** 412.

ACCOMMODATIONS

Dealing a major blow to budget travelers, the sole hostel closed in 2004. Those in search of a cheap bed should try along U.S. 60 near the airport or I-79 at Exit 60A.

Motel 6, 211 Beecham Dr. (☎922-9400), off I-79 at Exit 60A. Basic rooms with TV and A/C. Singles $30; doubles $36. Each additional person $3. AmEx/DC/MC/V. ❷

Outside Inn, 980 Rte. 228 (☎724-776-0626 or 800-947-2783; www.outsideinn-npa.com), 20min. north of downtown; from I-79 take the Cranberry/Mars exit. This B&B features wine tasting and beautiful gardens. Internet access, fridge, patio, hot tub. Singles $65, with breakfast $75; doubles $95. Discounts for longer stays. AmEx/MC/V. ❹

Bear Run Campground, 184 Badger Hill Rd. (☎724-368-3564 or 888-737-2605), in Portersville, 40min. north of Pittsburgh. From I-79 N, take PA-488 Exit 96, turn right, then turn left on Badger Hill Rd. Next to Morain State Park, the 60-acre Bear Run campground has fishing, hiking, and other outdoor activities. Check-in 4pm. 2-person sites $25, with water and electricity $29, full hookup $30. 4-person cabins with $30 security deposit from $69. Each additional person $4. AmEx/MC/V. ❶

FOOD

Aside from the pizza joints and bars downtown, **Oakland** is the best place to find a good, inexpensive meal. Collegiate watering holes and cafes pack **Forbes Avenue** around the University of Pittsburgh, while colorful eateries and shops line **Walnut Street** in Shadyside and **East Carson Street** in the South Side. The **Strip District** on Penn Ave. between 16th and 22nd St. (north of downtown along the Allegheny) bustles with Italian, Greek, and Asian cuisine. The Saturday morning **farmers market** sells an abundance of fresh produce and fish.

▨ **The Church Brew Works,** 3525 Liberty Ave. (☎688-8200). The hand-finished pews and stained-glass windows are right where the diocese left them, but copper and steel brewing equipment have replaced the altar in this church-cum-brewpub. The menu's fussier entrees run over $20, but brick-oven pizzas are a good bet at $13-15. Pints $4. Open M-Th 11:30am-midnight, F-Sa 11:30am-1am, Su noon-10pm; kitchen closes M-Th 9:30pm, F-Sa 11pm, Su 9pm. AmEx/D/MC/V. ❹

▨ **Beehive Coffeehouse and Desserterie,** 1327 E. Carson St. (☎488-4483), on the South Side. With a disco ball, clouds painted on the ceiling, and a lime-green study room crackling with wireless, Beehive could have been transplanted to Pittsburgh directly from Amsterdam. Art students doodle in their sketchbooks and devour sandwiches, while waifish grungeboys sip *yerba mate* ($2) and hum abstractedly under their breath. Open M-Th and Su 8am-1am, F-Sa 8am-2am. MC/V. ❶

Spice Island Tea House, 253 Atwood St. (☎687-8821), in Oakland. Votive candles and warm earth-tones set the tone for deep plates of curry ($8-9) and fried rice ($7). A large pot of after-dinner darjeeling ($3.75) can be a great way to draw out an early-evening date. Open M-Th 11:30am-9pm, F-Sa 11:30am-10pm. ❷

Primanti Brothers, 46 18th St. (☎263-2142), in the Strip District. Designed for truckers with big appetites and no time for side orders, the cheese steaks ($5) are piled high with cole slaw, tomato, and french fries. Add on a bowl of Pittsburgh-style chili ($2.75), and wash it all down with an Iron City beer for the true 'Burgh experience. Open 24hr. 4 other locations in the city. Cash only. ❶

The Quiet Storm, 5430 Penn Ave. (☎661-9355). From the mismatched armchairs to the retro pinball machine in back, this vegetarian cafe keeps East End hipsters happy with options like the Maelstrom Quesadilla ($6), served with chickpeas, mushrooms, spinach, and a glob of herbed *tzatziki*. Live music F-Sa 8pm. Su brunch 10am-2pm. Open M-Th and Su 7am-11pm, F-Sa 7am-1am. Cash only. ❷

⊙ SIGHTS

GOLDEN TRIANGLE. The **Golden Triangle** is home to **Point State Park** and its famous 200 ft. fountain. Near the park entrance, the **Fort Pitt Museum** is constructed in the shape of the battlements that once guarded the rivers. *(☎281-9284; www.fortpittmuseum.com. $5, seniors $4, ages 6-17 $2. Open W-Su 9am-5pm.)* The **Monongahela** and **Duquesne Inclines,** in the South Side, hoist visitors up for a sweeping view of the Pittsburgh skyline. *(Inclines operate M-Sa 5:30am-12:45am, Su 7am-12:45am. $1.75.)*

CARNEGIE. Industrialist Andrew Carnegie's rise to wealth involved ruthless business practices on par with the other robber barons of America's Gilded Age. After Carnegie sold his empire to New York financiers in 1901, however, he built a legacy for himself as a philanthropist by endowing museums, libraries, and universities. The beloved dinosaur collection at the **Carnegie Museum of Natural History** will spend the next two years in New Jersey for restoration, but the neighboring **Carnegie Museum of Art** picks up the slack with a major exhibit on artists and animals in the industrial era set to open spring 2006. *(4400 Forbes Ave. ☎622-3131; www.carnegiemuseums.org. Open Tu-Sa 10am-5pm, Su noon-5pm; July-Aug. also M 10am-5pm. $10, seniors $7, students and ages 3-18 $6.)* Up on the North Shore, the **Carnegie Science Center,** next to Heinz Field, sends visitors into the bowels of a WWII submarine and gives them aerodynamic foam wings to test a wind tunnel. The SportsWorks annex features a 25 ft. climbing wall and a chance to sprint against a digitally projected Jackie Joyner-Kersee. *(1 Allegheny Ave. ☎237-3400; www.carnegiesciencecenter.org. Open M-F and Su 10am-5pm, Sa 10am-7pm. $14, seniors and ages 3-18 $10; Omnimax $8/$6.)*

FLORA AND FAUNA. Just south of the Carnegie museums, the **Phipps Conservatory and Botanical Gardens** has plants from around the world and allows visitors to walk amidst live butterflies. *(1 Schenley Park. ☎622-6914; www.phipps.conservatory.org. Open Tu-Th and Sa-Su 9am-5pm, F 9am-9pm. $7.50, seniors $6.50, students $5.50, ages 2-12 $4.50. Tours Tu-Sa 11am and 1pm, Su 1pm.)* Northeast of downtown, the **Pittsburgh Zoo & PPG Aquarium** leads visitors through Asian forests and African savannahs, while sharks and stingrays dart around Pennsylvania's only public aquarium. *(1 Wild Pl. ☎665-3640 or 800-474-4966; www.pittsburghzoo.com. Open daily late May to Aug. 10am-6pm; Sept.-May 9am-4pm. Apr.-Nov. $9, seniors $8, ages 2-13 $7; Dec.-Mar. $7, seniors and ages 2-13 $6. Parking $3.50.)* Back on the North Side, the **National Aviary** is home to more than 600 exotic and endangered birds. *(Allegheny West Commons. ☎323-7235; www.aviary.org. Open daily 9am-5pm. $6, seniors $5, ages 2-12 $4.)*

OTHER SIGHTS. The ◙**Andy Warhol Museum,** on the North Side, is the world's largest museum dedicated to a single artist. Seven floors of the Pittsburgh native's artwork include his familiar soup cans, oxidation sculptures of urine on metal, and an installation called "Silver Clouds," where visitors can play among floating metallic pillows. *(117 Sandusky St. ☎237-8300; www.warhol.org. Open Tu-Th and Sa-Su 10am-5pm, F 10am-10pm. $10, seniors $7, students and ages 3-18 $6. Admission half-price F 5-10pm.)* Deeper into the North Side, ◙**The Mattress Factory** has dedicated itself to site-specific installation art daring artists to engage with the parameters of a converted warehouse space in creating new pieces. Check the website for directions. Be careful in the surrounding area. *(500 Sampsonia Way, between Brighton and Federal St. ☎231-3169; www.mattress.org. Open Tu-F 10am-5pm, Sa 10am-7pm, Su 1-5pm. $8, students* *and seniors $5, under 12 free. Half-price on Th.)* The soaring Gothic spires of the **Cathedral of Learning** have become symbols of the **University of Pittsburgh,** featuring 26 "nationality classrooms" decorated by artisans from the city's many ethnic traditions. The stark arches of the Armenian room and the baroque grandeur of the Austrian room are among the most striking. Remarkably, Chancellor John Gabbett Bowman relied on 90,000 $0.10 contributions from the city's schoolchildren to finance the Cathedral's construction. *(☎ 624-6000; www.pitt.edu/~natrooms. Audio tours Sa 9:30am-2:30pm, Su 11am-2:30pm; May-Aug. also M-F 9am-2:30pm. $3, seniors $2, ages 8-18 $0.50.)* In Penn Hills, an eastern suburb of Pittsburgh sits the elaborately carved **Sri Venkateswara (S.V.) Temple,** modeled after a 7th-century temple in the Andhra Pradesh in India; it has become a major pilgrimage site for American Hindus. Non-Hindus can see the Great Hall and observe prayer services. *(1230 S. McCully Dr. ☎ 373-3380; www.svtemple.org. Open M-Th and Sa-Su 9am-7:30pm.)*

🎵 🎭 ENTERTAINMENT AND NIGHTLIFE

The weekly *City Paper* provides a recommended "Short List" and a comprehensive "Big List" of entertainment options. The three conductors of the acclaimed **Pittsburgh Symphony Orchestra** take their bows at **Heinz Hall,** 600 Penn Ave. *(☎ 392-4900; www.pittsburghsymphony.org. Box office open M-F 9am-8pm, Sa noon-4pm. Tickets $19-73; student rush 2hr. before performance $14.)* The **Pittsburgh Public Theater** performs at the **O'Reilly Theater,** 621 Penn Ave. *(☎ 316-1600; www.ppt.org. Box office open daily 10am-5:30pm, or until curtain Tu-Su. Tickets $30-76, students and under 26 $12.50.)* Musicals, ballets, and operas light up the stage at the **Benedum Center,** 719 Liberty Ave. *(☎ 456-6666; www.pgharts.org. Matinees $14-40, evening shows $20-60. Half-price student tickets to select shows are available 1hr. before curtain.)* **Pittsburgh Filmmakers,** 477 Melwood Ave., screens indie and foreign films at three theaters around Pittsburgh, and sponsors the **Three Rivers Film Festival** each November. *(☎ 681-5449; www.pghfilmmakers.org. Most films $6.)*

On the North Shore, **PNC Park,** 115 Federal St., will host baseball's 2006 All-Star Game, even though the **Pirates** *(☎ 321-2827; tickets $9-35)* fielded just one All-Star player in 2005. The **Steelers** *(☎ 323-1200)* storm the gridiron down the road at **Heinz Stadium,** but it's nearly impossible to score tickets. The NHL's **Penguins** *(☎ 800-642-7367; tickets $16-106)* rock the ice at **Mellon Arena.**

East Carson Street, on the South Side, is jammed with revelers throughout the week, while the galleries and performance spaces along the **Penn Corridor** echo with the city's best underground music. The **Station Square** complex, across the Smithfield St. Bridge, is another option for boisterous clubs and music venues.

🖼 **Garfield Artworks,** 4931 Penn Ave. *(☎ 361-2262; www.garfieldartworks.com),* displays work by local artists in one of Pittsburgh's hippest music venues for alt-country, folk, and indie rock. With no liquor license, it's the music and the sense of community that keep scenesters coming back. Cover $5-7. Most shows start at 8pm. Call for schedule.

Mr. Roboto Project, 722 Wood St. *(☎ 247-9639; www.therobotoproject.org),* in Wilkinsburg. Founded in 1999 as a cooperatively run music venue and magazine library, this unpretentious storefront has become a node of Pittsburgh's punk and hardcore scene with September's all-vegan Punks' Picnic and as many as 20 shows per month. Cover $5-7. Most shows start at 7pm. Call for schedule.

Jack's, 1117 E. Carson St. *(☎ 431-3644),* at S. 12th St., in the South Side. This rowdy, neon-splashed Pittsburgh institution keeps its doors open 365 days a year; an unpretentious, back-slapping climate makes Jack's an obligatory stop on South Side pub crawls. M hot dogs $0.25. W wings $0.15. Open M-Sa 7am-2am, Su 11am-2am.

Pegasus Lounge, 818 Liberty Ave. (☎281-2131), downtown, features a sweaty, jam-packed dance floor thronged by young gay men and their admirers. W drag shows. 21+, Tu and Th-F 18+. Open Tu-Sa 9pm-2am.

⬛ DAYTRIPS FROM PITTSBURGH

OHIOPYLE STATE PARK. Masses come each year to raft Ohiopyle's 8 mi. of class III and IV rapids, a two hr. drive south of Pittsburgh. Some of the best whitewater rafting in the East, the rapids take about 4-5hr. to conquer. For novices, class I and II rapids ease rafts down sections of the river. Four outfitters front Rte. 381 in "downtown" Ohiopyle: **White Water Adventurers** (☎800-992-7238; www.wwaraft.com), **Wilderness Voyageurs Outfitters** (☎800-272-4141; wilderness-voyageurs.com), **Laurel Highlands River Tours** (☎800-472-3846), and **Ohiopyle Trading Post** (☎888-644-6795). Trip prices on the Youghiogheny River ("The Yough," pronounced YOCK, to locals) vary depending on the season, day of the week, length of trip, and difficulty ($20-145). Prices for rentals are more stable. (Rafts about $17-25 per person; canoes $25-50; single kayaks about $25-35.) In order to float anything without a guide, you need a **launch permit** from the park office. (☎724-329-8592. M-F free, Sa-Su $2.50. $3 shuttle fee. Call at least 2 weeks in advance for Sa permits. Rental companies provide free permits.) Ohiopyle also offers biking, fishing, rock climbing, and camping opportunities. (Bikes from $3-5 per hr., full-day guided tour $15-25.) The **visitors center,** off Rte. 381 on Sheridan St., has information on the park and surrounding areas. (☎724-329-1127, 888-727-2757 for camping reservations. Visitors center open May-Oct. daily 10am-4:30pm; Nov.-Apr. M-F 8am-4pm. Primitive sites $12-17, full hookup $2 extra; cottages $27-36.)

FALLINGWATER AND KENTUCK KNOB. Fallingwater, 8 mi. north of Ohiopyle on Rte. 381, is a masterpiece by the king of modern architecture, Frank Lloyd Wright. Designed in 1935, the house exemplifies Wright's concept of organic architecture, incorporating original boulders into its structure and striking a perfect symbiosis with its surroundings. The house appears as though it will cascade over the waterfall it sits on, and the water's gentle roar can be heard in every room. (☎724-329-8501; www.paconserve.org. Open mid-Mar. to Nov. Tu-Su 10am-4pm; also some weekends in Dec. and the first 2 weekends in Mar. 10am-3pm. Reservations required. Access to grounds $6. Tours M-F $13, ages 6-18 $8; Sa-Su $15/$10. In-depth tours $50. Children under 6 must be left in child care, $3 per hr.) For a more intimate and quaint Frank Lloyd Wright home, head to the nearby **Kentuck Knob,** on Kentuck Rd., 6 mi. north of U.S. 40, where a guided tour examines the rustic house, the grounds, and greenhouse. (☎724-329-1640; www.kentuckknob.com. Open May-Aug. M-F and Su 9am-4pm, Sa 9am-6pm; daily Mar.-Apr. and Sept.-Dec. 9am-4pm; Jan.-Feb. 11am-3pm. Call for reservations. Tours M-F $12, under 18 $10; Sa-Su $15/$12. In-depth tours $50.)

DELAWARE

Tiny Delaware is a sanctuary of beaches, B&Bs, and tax-free shopping in a region dominated by the sprawling cities of New York, Philadelphia, and Washington, D.C. Though Delaware was first explored by Henry Hudson in 1609, it was not until 1664 that it was officially claimed as one of England's 13 colonies in the New World. In 1787, Delaware proudly became the first state to ratify the US Constitution. The more recent history of Delaware centers around the wealthy DuPont clan, whose gunpowder mills evolved into one of the world's biggest chemical

MID-ATLANTIC

companies. Today, Delaware's laid-back mix of city and shore attracts visitors in search of a break from the Mid-Atlantic's hustle and bustle, while its favorable tax laws offer local businesses a different kind of break.

⁊ PRACTICAL INFORMATION

Capital: Dover.

Visitor Info: Delaware State Visitors Center, 406 Federal St., Dover 19901 (☎302-739-4266; www.destatemuseums.org/vc). Open M-Sa 8am-4:30pm, Su 1:30-4:30pm.

Postal Abbreviation: DE. **Sales Tax:** 8% on accommodations only.

WILMINGTON/BRANDYWINE VALLEY ☎302

In 1683, a Swedish ship, the *Kalmar Nyckel*, sailed from Europe to the banks of what was then called the "South River," leaving its passengers to successfully establish the colony of New Sweden. These days, the city of Wilmington might as well be named DuPontville, because from the grand Hotel DuPont downtown to the DuPont mills along the Brandywine River and the DuPont estates out in the valley, there's no escaping the name. Today, the DuPont estates and the rich colonial history draw visitors to Wilmington and the Brandywine Valley.

◼◼ ⁊ ORIENTATION AND PRACTICAL INFORMATION. Wilmington is situated in northern Delaware, directly across the Delaware Memorial Bridge from New Jersey. **I-95** connects Wilmington to Philadelphia 29 mi. to the north and Baltimore 76 mi. to the southwest. Downtown Wilmington is set up on a grid of one-way streets. Numbered streets run east-west starting from the south, while named streets run north-south. The two major roads leading into the downtown are **Martin Luther King, Jr. Boulevard (Route 48)** and **Delaware Avenue (Route 52),** which also runs out of town, toward the DuPont estates. Exercise caution in the area between the restored riverfront and downtown and in the non-riverfront areas south of 8th St. Parking is free at riverfront attractions and curbside on weekends and after 6pm on weekdays. Otherwise, lots charging $5-8 per day can be found through the **Wilmington Parking Authority** (☎655-4442). **Airport: Philadelphia International Airport** (☎215-937-6937; www.phl.org) is 20 mi. north of Wilmington on I-95. **Amtrak,** 100 S. French St., runs trains to Boston (5-6½hr., 10 per day, $84) and Washington, D.C. (1½hr; $46). Use caution in this area at night. (☎800-872-7245; www.amtrak.com. Open M-F 5:45am-9:30pm, Sa 6am-8:45pm, Su 6am-9:30pm.) **Greyhound,** 101 N. French St. (☎655-6111; www.greyhound.com), in the Wilmington Transport Center, runs to Boston (9-12hr.; $75), New York (4hr.; $40), and Washington, D.C. (4-6hr.; $22). **DART** runs buses in the Wilmington area: #7 criss-crosses downtown M-F 8am-4pm, and #32 runs between riverfront attractions and downtown (M-F 7am-7pm, Sa 7:45am-7:30pm). (☎800-652-3277; www.dartfirststate.com. $1.15; all-day pass $2.40. Bus #32 $0.25 per ride.) **Taxi: Yellow Cab,** ☎658-4340. **Greater Wilmington Convention and Visitors Bureau,** 100 W. 10th St., Ste. 20, at Orange St. (☎652-4088 or 800-489-6664; www.visitwilmingtonde.com. Open M-F 9am-5pm.) **Internet Access: Wilmington Public Library,** at the corner of 10th and Market St. (☎571-7400. Open M-Th 9am-8pm, F-Sa 9am-5pm.) **Post Office:** 1101 N. King St. at 11th St. (☎800-276-8767. Open M-F 7am-5:30pm, Sa 9am-2pm.) **Postal Code:** 19801. **Area Code:** 302.

⁊ ACCOMMODATIONS. Wilmington's hotels cater to businesspeople, so rates tend to be far lower on weekends than during the week. Upscale chains and the city's landmark **Hotel DuPont** can be found on **King Street** downtown. Otherwise, look to **Newark, DE**, just south on I-95, for budget chain motels. The best value in Wilmington is the **McIntosh Inn ❸**, 300 Rocky Run Pkwy., at the Concord Pike (Rte. 202), which includes continental breakfast, an exercise room, and a 24hr. convenience center, in addition to spacious rooms. (☎479-7900 or 800-444-2775. Doubles M-Th and Su from $95, F-Sa from $68.) B&Bs in the Brandywine Valley range from pricey to very pricey. For those willing to splurge, the elegant and relaxing **Faunbrook B&B ❺**, 699 W. Rosedale Ave., in West Chester, PA, 20min. north of Wilmington on Rte. 100, is a perfect base from which to explore the Brandywine River Valley. Faunbrook's Italian-style estate, complete with a vast mahogany porch, boasts seven guest rooms with private baths and two acres of gardens. (☎610-436-5788; www.faunbrook.com. No smoking. 3-course candlelight breakfast included. Check-in 3-9pm. Check-out 11am. Rooms $105-140.) Though there is no camping in the immediate Wilmington vicinity, **Lums Pond State Park ❶**, 1068 Howell School Rd., 30 mi. south of the city, offers a retreat from the urban grind. Drive south on I-95 to Exit 1A (Middleton), onto Rte. 896 S, then follow it 6 mi. until you cross Rte. 40. Turn left onto Howell Rd. at the third light after Rte. 40. Campers have access to showers, flush toilets, bicycle and horseback-riding trails, fishing, and rowboat and canoe rentals. (Reservations ☎368-6989 or 877-987-2757; www.destateparks.com. 4-person tent sites $21; each additional person $2. Rowboats $6 per hr., $30 per day; canoes $5/$25.)

◻ FOOD. Authentic Indian cuisine is hard to come by, even in big cities, but the **Panghat Indian Restaurant ❷**, 301 W. 4th St., at Tantall St., is loyal to its origins. From the chicken *makhani* (chicken with mild tomato sauce and butter cooked in a traditional clay oven; $11) to the vegetarian specialty *navratan korma* (nine vegetables with nuts in a mildly spiced yogurt sauce; $9) this restaurant is sure to please. (☎658-6276. $6 lunch buffet daily 11:30am-2:30pm; dinner daily 5-9:30pm. AmEx/D/MC/V.) Be cautious in the neighborhood after dark. For simple diner fare, head to the **Sterling Grill ❶**, 919 Orange St. This local breakfast and lunch favorite in the center of town serves short stacks of pancakes for $2 and waffles for $3; add an order of "scrapple," a regional meat medley, for only $1.10. (☎652-3575. 9 in. subs $4. Open M-F 5:30am-3pm, Sa 7:30am-1pm.) The **Iron Hill Brewery ❹**, 710 S. Madison St., serves Asian fusion cuisine beside a stunning view of the Brandywine River. (☎472-2739; www.ironhillbrewery.com. Entrees $14-20. Open M-Sa 11:30am-1am, Su 11am-1am. AmEx/D/MC/V.)

◪ SIGHTS. The DuPont estates are among the most popular tourist attractions in the area. Closest to downtown Wilmington, the **Hagley Museum**, 1 Brandywine Blvd., emphasizes the home and work life of the DuPonts, with tours of the original family home and black powder works. Mechanical minds will love the enormous stone mills, water turbines, steam engines, and powder testers. Take I-95 north to Exit 5B (Newport), follow Rte. 141 north for 7 mi., and after crossing Rte. 100 look for the Hagley entrance on the left. (☎658-2400; www.hagley.lib.de.us. Open mid-Mar. to Dec. daily 9:30am-4:30pm; Jan. to mid-Mar. Sa-Su 9:30am-4:30pm with one tour at 1:30pm M-F. $11, seniors $9, children ages 6-14 $4.) Botany enthusiasts should not miss the **Winterthur Estate and Gardens**, on Rte. 52, 6 mi. northwest of Wilmington. Samuel DuPont used specific combinations of flowers to create harmony of both color and design. The mansion's interior and furnishings are so extensive that several differently themed guided tours are required to cover it all. (☎888-4600 or 800-448-3883; www.winterthur.org. Open Tu-Su 10am-5pm, last tickets sold at 3:45pm. Guided tours leave frequently; call ahead for info about particular tours. Garden tram operates Mar.-Dec. 2-day pass includes one guided tour, unlimited tram rides, and access to the galleries and special exhibitions; $20, students and seniors $18, ages 2-11 $10. Wheelchair accessible.) The farthest DuPont estate from Wilmington is the **Longwood Gardens,** over 1050 acres of woodlands, meadows, and (surprise!) gardens. Nature-lovers will delight in Longwood's fountains, topiaries, wild and hothouse flowers, Italian-style lakes, and open-air theaters. Take Rte. 52 northwest 12 mi. from Wilmington, just over the Pennsylvania state line, then turn west onto Rte. 1 and follow it to Kennett Sq. (☎610-388-1000 or 800-737-5500; www.longwoodgardens.org. Open daily Apr.-Oct. 9am-6pm; Nov.-Mar. 9am-5pm. Hours extended to 10pm on Tu, Th, and Sa evenings in summer. Mid-Jan. to Mar. M and W-Su $12, Tu $8; Apr.-Nov. $14/$10; Dec.-Jan. daily $15. Under 20 $6, under 15 $2, under 6 free. Wheelchair accessible.) On Rte. 1, just east of Longwood Gardens in Chadds Ford, PA, the ▨**Brandywine River Museum** displays an extensive collection of the works of N.C., Andrew, and Jaime Wyeth in a restored mill house. From Wilmington, take Rte. 52 N to Rte. 1 and follow it east approximately 3½ mi. (☎610-388-2700; www.brandywinemuseum.org. Open daily 9:30am-4:30pm. $8; seniors, students, and ages 6-12 $5.)

The story of the first Swedish settlers in Delaware is retold daily at **Fort Christiana Park** and the **Kalmar Nyckel Shipyard,** 1124 E. 7th St. (☎429-7447 or ☎888-783-7245; www.kalnyck.org. Tours on Sa in summer; call for hours. $5, students $4, ages 12 and under $3. Pirate-themed trips to Lewes Sa in summer; call for hours. $40, students $30, ages 12 and under $12.) At the **Old Swedes Church and Hendrickson House Museum,** 606 Church St., just west of the shipyard, visitors can tour a Swedish farmhouse and church built in the 1690s, as well as the Hendrickson's collection of colonial artifacts. (☎652-5629; www.oldswedes.org. Tours W-Sa 10am-4pm. $2.) The **Delaware History Museum,** 504 Market St. Mall, is home to the interactive exhibit "Distinctively Delaware" and covers over 400 years of history, beginning with the region's Native American inhabitants. (☎656-0637; www.hsd.org. Open M-F noon-4pm, Sa 10am-4pm. $4, seniors $3, ages 2-18 $2.)

▨▨ **ENTERTAINMENT AND NIGHTLIFE.** Music, theater, and dance venues cluster in the downtown area, particularly on **Market Street.** The **Grand Opera House,** 818 N. Market St. (☎652-5577), home to OperaDelaware, also presents Broadway-bound shows for much less than the cost of tickets in a larger city. Meanwhile, a rowdier crowd gathers at college bars and clubs in the **Trolley Square** area on the northwest side of town, centered around Delaware Ave. For cocktails in a calmer setting, try the restaurant-bars along the **Riverfront.** Though it rubs shoulders with the waterfront's stateliest restaurants, **Kahunaville** is strictly for the brave of heart. Young crowds flock to this entertainment mega-complex for the slamming rock, heavy drinking, and an arcade room. Themed nights are common. (☎571-8402; www.kahunaville.com. Live music F-Sa after 11pm, DJ Th and Su. No hats, sleeveless shirts, or work boots. 21+ after 10pm. Cover $7 after 8pm. Open M-Sa 11:30am-1am, Su 11:30am-10pm. Reduced menu M-Th after 10pm.) The **4W5 Cafe,** 4 W 5th St., serves up simple, cheap breakfast and lunch dishes for less than $5 before reopening in the early evening for live music and jam sessions, usually with no cover. (☎661-0100. Kitchen open daily 7am-3pm. Live music nightly 6:30pm. Call for performance schedule.) **Baxter's,** 2006 Pennsylvania Ave., at Union St., draws a mixed, gay-friendly crowd to its upscale lounge. (☎654-9858; www.baxtersclub.com. $1 off drinks during happy hour M-F 4-7pm. 21+ if not dining. Open M-F 4pm-2am, Sa 5pm-2am, Su 6pm-2am.)

LEWES   ☎302

While the Swedes were settling the Brandywine Valley, the Dutch gained a foothold in America with Lewes (LEW-iss). Today, year-rounders populate the town's Victorian homes and in the summer savvy tourists come for the beautiful beach. Secluded among scrub pines 1 mi. east of Lewes on the Atlantic Ocean is the 4000-

acre **Cape Henlopen State Park,** where kids frolic in the waves under the watchful eyes of lifeguards. The park is also home to sparkling dunes, a 2 mi. paved trail, and a WWII observation tower. (☎645-8983; www.destateparks.com. Open daily 8am-sunset. $5 per car; bikes and pedestrians free.) Bike rentals are free at the **Seaside Nature Center,** just inside the entrance to the park. (☎645-6852; www.destateparks.com. Open daily July-Aug. 9am-5pm; Sept.-June 9am-4pm. Bikes and helmets available 9am-4pm; 2hr. limit. Bikes must be used within park boundaries.) The **Zwaanendael Museum,** 102 Kings Hwy., is filled with relics of maritime history. (☎645-1148; www.destatemuseums.org/zwa. Open Tu-Sa 10am-4:30pm, Su 1:30-4:30pm. Free.) For a hands-on experience, tour the **Overfalls Lightship,** located on the Lewes & Rehoboth Canal north of the Savannah Rd. bridge. Built in 1938 as a floating lighthouse, it retired to Lewes after suffering structural damage in a storm off the Massachusetts coast. (☎645-4733; www.overfalls.org. Guided tours late May to early Sept. F-Sa 11am-4pm, Su 1-4pm. $2, students $1.) Tours of Lewes's 12 historic homes begin at the **Historical Society,** 110 Shipcarpenter St. (☎645-7670. Open June-Aug. M-F 10am-4pm, Sa 10am-1pm. $6.)

Summer weekend stays in Lewes are expensive. For lodging close to the beach, try the very clean **Vesuvio Motel ❹,** 105 Savannah Rd. (☎645-2224. A/C, cable TV. May-Sept. singles $75-95; doubles $90-125. Low season $45-65/$55-85.) The **Captain's Quarters Motel ❸,** 406 Savannah Rd., has similar rates and simple rooms a bit farther from the water. (☎644-2003. A/C, cable TV. Rooms in summer M-Th and Su $85, F-Sa $100.) To camp at **Cape Henlopen State Park ❶,** take Rte. 1 to Cape Henlopen Dr.; signs mark the park on the left. A short walk from the beach, the park also has fishing, birdwatching, and nature programs. (☎645-2103, reservations 877-987-2757; www.destateparks.com. Hot showers, flush toilets. Open Mar.-Nov. 4-person sites $26, with water faucet $28. Additional persons $2.) Restaurants in Lewes cluster primarily on 2nd St. Once a sea captain's house, **The Buttery ❹,** at 2nd and Savannah St., serves delicious nouveau French cuisine in an elegant Victorian house. (☎645-7755. Open daily 11am-2:30pm and 5pm-late; Su brunch 10:30am-2:30pm.) **Kings Homemade Ice Cream Shop ❶,** 201 2nd St., is a local favorite. (☎645-9425. 1 scoop $2.50, 2 scoops $3.50. Open May-Oct. daily 11am-11pm.)

Lewes is best reached by car; from points north, Rte. 1 S runs directly to Savannah Rd., which bisects the town. From the west, travel east on Rte. 404, then take Rte. 9 E from the junction in Georgetown to Rte. 1; continue south to Savannah Rd. **Delaware Resort Transit** shuttles run from the ferry terminal through Lewes to Rehoboth and Dewey Beach. (☎800-553-3278; www.beachbus.com. Every 30min. late May to early Sept. daily 7am-2am. $1, seniors and disabled $0.40; day pass $2. Park and ride for free all day $7.) **Taxi: Seaport Taxis** ☎645-6800. The **Fisher-Martin House Information Center,** 120 Kings Hwy., next to the Zwaanendael Museum, offers tourist info, including walking tour maps. (☎645-8073 or 877-465-3937; www.leweschamber.com. Open M-F 10am-4pm, Sa 9am-3pm, Su 10am-2pm.) **Internet Access: Lewes Public Library,** 111 Adams St. (☎645-2733; www.leweslibrary.org. Open M-Th 10am-8pm, F 10am-5pm, Sa 10am-2pm.) **Post Office:** 116 Front St. (☎644-1948. Open M-F 8:30am-5pm, Sa 8am-noon.) **Postal Code:** 19958. **Area Code:** 302.

REHOBOTH BEACH   ☎302

Rehoboth Beach lies between Lewes and Ocean City, both geographically and culturally. While Lewes tends to be quiet and family-oriented and Ocean City attracts rowdy high-schoolers, Rehoboth manages to balance its discount-boardwalk fun with serene, historic B&Bs. The massive outlet mall on Rte. 1 on the way into town floods Rehoboth with bargain hunters eager to snag tax-free Delaware deals all year long. On summer weekends, the beach is a zoo, packed end to end with vacationing families and the town's burgeoning gay population.

MID-ATLANTIC

⚞ ⑦ ORIENTATION AND PRACTICAL INFORMATION. To reach Rehoboth, take **Route 1B** to **Rehoboth Avenue** and follow it to the water. Parking near the beach is a rare commodity—rather than worry constantly about the pesky meter monitors, drop your friends and family off at the beach with your gear and find a parking spot off the main drag. **Greyhound/Trailways,** 801 Rehoboth Ave. (☎227-1080 or 800-454-2487; www.greyhound.com), runs buses to Boston (11hr., $49), Philadelphia (4hr., $29), and Washington D.C. (3½ hr., $29). The 1¾hr. **ferry** to Cape May is the best option for island-hopping. (☎800-643-3779; www.capemaylewesferry.com. Office open daily 8:30am-4:30pm. 8 per day. Reservations required; call at least 24hr. in advance. Check-in 30min. prior to departure. Passenger cars Apr.-Oct. $25, Nov.-Dec. $20; motorcyclists $22/$17; bicyclists $8/$6.) The **Rehoboth Beach Chamber of Commerce,** 501 Rehoboth Ave., around the traffic circle next to an imitation lighthouse, provides info on area attractions, dining, and accommodations. (☎227-2233 or 800-441-1329; www.beach-fun.com. Open M-F 9am-5pm, Sa-Su 9am-1pm.) **Internet Access: Rehoboth Beach Public Library,** 226 Rehoboth Ave. (☎227-8044. Open M and F 10am-5pm, Tu and Th noon-8pm, W 10am-8pm, Sa 10am-3pm). **Post Office:** 179 Rehoboth Ave., at 2nd St. (☎227-8406. Open M-F 9am-5pm, Sa 8:30am-12:30pm.) **Postal Code:** 19971. **Area Code:** 302.

⚞ ⚞ ACCOMMODATIONS AND FOOD. Inexpensive lodging in Rehoboth disappears as the summer season reaches its peak. Unless you want to spend over $100 (or, more likely, over $200), forget staying on the boardwalk. The comfortable **Abbey Inn ❸,** 31 Maryland Ave., is just a block from Rehoboth Ave. (☎227-7023. 2-night min. stay. Reception open late May-early Sept. Singles and doubles with shared bath from $48; triples and quads from $61. 15% more on weekends.) The Kandler family owns and operates the **Pirate's Cove Motel ❹,** 625 Rehoboth Ave., and prides itself on the clean rooms. (☎227-2844; www.rehobothbeach.com/piratescove. A/C, cable TV. Rooms $75-130, with peak rates in July. AmEx/D/MC/V.) Just off of Rehoboth Ave., three long blocks from the beach, the **High Seas Motel ❹,** 12 Christian St., provides cable TV, a microwave, and a mini-fridge in each simple, comfortable room. (☎227-2022. Summer M-Th and Su $30-90, F-Sa $80-150; low-season $30-90. 2-night min. stay June-Aug. AmEx/D/MC/V.) **Big Oaks Family Campground ❶,** 1 mi. off Rte. 1 on Rte. 270, has laundry, a pool, a general store, and a bus to the beach. (☎645-6838. Tent sites $34, RV sites $42.)

Rehoboth is known for its high-quality beach cuisine, but a lot of it comes at resort prices. At the charming **Back Porch Cafe ❹,** 59 Rehoboth Ave., just blocks from the beach, you can enjoy a healthy gourmet lunch on the open-air patio. (☎227-3674. Open daily 11am-3pm and 6-10pm. Su brunch 11am-3pm.) At **Cafe Papillon ❷,** 42 Rehoboth Ave., in the Penny Lane Mall, French cooks serve fresh crepes, croissants, and sandwiches. (☎227-7568. Crepes $3. Sandwiches $5-8. Open June-Aug. M-Sa 8am-11pm. Call for hours in May and Sept.) **Royal Treat ❷,** 4 Wilmington Ave., flips pancakes and bacon for just $5.90; omelets are around $8. (☎227-6277. Open daily June-Aug. 8-11:30am. Ice cream served 1-11:30pm.)

⚞ NIGHTLIFE. Rehoboth partygoers head out early to maximize their time before 1am last calls. **The Summer House Saloon,** 228 Rehoboth Ave., across from City Hall, is a favorite flirtation spot for college-aged singles. (☎227-3895; www.summerhousesaloon.com. Half-price daiquiris Su 4-8pm. Half-price burgers M. Live blues-rock 9:30pm-1:30am Th. Live DJ 9pm-1am F. Open May-Sept. M and Sa-Su 4pm-1am, Tu-F 5pm-1am. AmEx/D/MC/V.) Look for live music on weekends at **Dogfish Head Brewings & Eats,** 320 Rehoboth Ave. Try one of their 13 award-winning homemade microbrews, or get a five-beer sampler tray for $5. (☎226-2739; www.dogfish.com. Happy hour M-F 4-6pm, with $2 rum and gin drinks. Live music

F-Sa 10pm-1am. Open May-Aug. M-Th 4-11pm, F 4pm-1am, Sa noon-1am, Su noon-11pm; Sept.-Apr. M and Th 4pm-midnight, F 4pm-1am, Sa noon-1am, Su noon-11pm.) **The Frog Pond,** on the corner of 1st St. and Rehoboth Ave., is known for serving the best Buffalo wings and quesadillas in town. (☎227-2234. Happy hour M-F 4-7pm. Live music F-Sa. Karaoke Th. Open M-Sa 11am-1am.) **Cloud 9,** 234 Rehoboth Ave., serves haute cuisine and cocktails for haute prices. (☎226-1999; www.cloud9restaurant.com. Happy hour M and Th-Su 4-7pm. DJ F-Su. Open Apr.-Oct. daily 4pm-1am; Nov.-Mar. M and Th-Su 4pm-1am.)

MARYLAND

Once upon a time, folks on Maryland's rural eastern shore trapped crabs, raised tobacco, and ruled the state. Meanwhile, across the bay in Baltimore, workers loaded ships and ran factories. Then the federal government expanded, industry shrank, and Maryland had a new focal point: the Baltimore-Washington Pkwy. As a result, suburbs grew, Baltimore was revitalized, and the Old Line State gained a new, liberal urbanity. Still, even as D.C.'s generic suburbs swell and Baltimore revels in its immensity, Annapolis—the state capital—remains a small town of sailors.

🔢 PRACTICAL INFORMATION

Capital: Annapolis.

Visitor Info: Office of Tourism, 217 E. Redwood St., 9th fl., Baltimore 21202 (☎866-639-3526; www.mdisfun.org).

Postal Abbreviation: MD. **Sales Tax:** 5%.

BALTIMORE   ☎410

Nicknamed "Charm City" for its mix of small-town hospitality and big-city flair, Baltimore impresses visitors with its lively restaurant and bar scene, first-class museums, and devotion to history. The pulse of the city lies beyond its star attraction, the glimmering Inner Harbor, in Baltimore's overstuffed markets, coffee shops, and diverse citizenry. The city's Southern heritage is evident in Roland Park, where friendly neighbors greet you from front porches in a "Bawlmer" accent. Though it would be unwise to head into Baltimore expecting to find only the shining touristy sights, gentrification and restoration efforts have succeeded in returning the Inner Harbor, Fells Point, Camden Yards, and Canton to their former glory, complete with attractive, walkable streets.

◧ TRANSPORTATION

Airport: Baltimore-Washington International (**BWI;** ☎859-7111; www.bwiairport.com), on I-195 off the Baltimore-Washington Pkwy. (I-295), about 10 mi. south of the city. Take MTA bus #17 to the Nursery Rd. light rail station. Airport **shuttles** to hotels (☎703-416-6661 or 800-258-3826; www.supershuttle.com) run daily every 30min. 5:45am-11:30pm. $11 to downtown Baltimore. Shuttles leave for D.C. daily every hr. 5:45am-11:30pm ($26-34). **Amtrak** trains from BWI run to Baltimore ($14) and D.C. ($14). **MARC** commuter trains run M-F to Baltimore ($3.25) and D.C. ($5).

Trains: Penn Station, 1500 N. Charles St., at Mt. Royal Ave. Easily accessible by bus #3 or 11 from Charles Station downtown. **Amtrak** (www.amtrak.com) trains run every 30min.-1hr. to **New York City** (2½-3hr., 10 per day, $76), **Philadelphia** (1hr., 10 per day, $47), and **Washington, D.C.** (45min., 10 per day, $17). On weekdays, **MARC commuter rail** (☎539-5000) connects to D.C.'s Union Station from Penn Station (with stops at BWI) or **Camden Station**, at Howard and Camden St. Ticket office open daily 5:30am-9:30pm; self-serve ticketing kiosks available 24hr.

Buses: Greyhound (☎800-231-2222; www.greyhound.com) has 2 locations: downtown at 2110 Haines St. (☎752-7682); and at 5625 O'Donnell St. (☎633-6389), 3 mi. east of downtown, at Exit 57 off I-95, just north of the toll tunnel. To **New York City** ($38), **Philadelphia** ($20), and **Washington, D.C.** ($11).

Public Transit: Mass Transit Administration (MTA), 300 W. Lexington St. (☎866-743-3682, schedule info M-F 6am-7pm 539-5000; www.mtamaryland.com), near N. Howard St. Bus, Metro, and light rail service to most major sights in the city. Some buses run 24hr. Metro runs M-F 5am-midnight, Sa 6am-midnight. Light rail runs M-F 6am-11pm, Sa 8am-11pm, Su 11am-7pm. $1.60, students $1.10, seniors and disabled $0.55; higher on light rail to outer suburbs. Day pass $3.50.

Water Taxi: Harbor Boating, 1732 Thames St. (☎563-3901 or 800-658-8947; www.thewatertaxi.com). Main stop in the Inner Harbor; other stops at harbor museums and restaurants, Harborplace, Fells Point, Little Italy. Runs Apr.-Oct. every 15min.; Nov.-Mar. every 40min. Service May-Aug. M-Th 10am-11pm, F-Sa 10am-midnight, Su 10am-9pm; Apr. and Sept.-Oct. M-Th 11am-8pm, F 11am-midnight, Sa 10am-midnight, Su 10am-8pm; Nov.-Mar. daily 11am-6pm. Day pass $6, ages 10 and under $3.

Taxi: American Cab, ☎636-8300. **Arrow Cab,** ☎261-0000.

⚡🛈 ORIENTATION AND PRACTICAL INFORMATION

Baltimore lies 35 mi. north of D.C. and about 150 mi. west of the Atlantic Ocean. From D.C., take the **Baltimore-Washington Parkway. Exit 53** from **Route 395** leads right into the **Inner Harbor;** without traffic, the trip takes less than an hour. **Baltimore Street** (east-west) and **Charles Street** (north-south) divide the city. The **Inner Harbor,** at Pratt and Charles St., is home to historic ships and attractions. **Little Italy,** served by city buses #7 and 10, sits on the bay a few blocks east of the Inner Harbor, past the Jones Falls Expressway. A short walk to the southeast brings you to bar-happy **Fells Point,** also served by city bus #10. Be careful: Moving north or east from Fells Point, away from the waterfront, will lead you into dangerous neighborhoods. The museum-laden **Mount Vernon** neighborhood, served by city buses #3 and 11, occupies **North Charles Street,** north of Baltimore St., around **Monument Street** and **Centre Avenue.** Old-fashioned **Federal Hill,** accessed by city buses #1 and 64, contains Fort McHenry. Use caution in Federal Hill and areas to the south. The **Camden Yards** baseball stadium and M&T Bank Stadium lie across I-395 from Federal Hill. Venturing more than a few blocks north of Camden Yards will place you in the historic, but dangerous, West Side.

Visitor Info: Baltimore Area Visitors Center, 401 Light St. (☎877-225-8466; www.baltimore.org). Provides maps, brochures, and the free *Quickguide*. Open daily 9am-6pm.

Hotlines: Suicide Line, ☎531-6677. **Sexual Assault and Domestic Violence,** ☎828-6390. Both 24hr. **Gay and Lesbian Line,** ☎837-8888. Operates daily 7pm-midnight.

Internet Access: Enoch Pratt Free Library, 400 Cathedral St. (☎396-5430; www.pratt.lib.md.us). Open M-W 11am-7pm, Th 10am-5:30pm, F-Sa 10am-5pm; Oct.-May also Su 1-5pm. Free.

Post Office: 900 E. Fayette St. (☎347-4202). Open M-F 7:30am-10pm, Sa 8:30am-5pm. **Postal Code:** 21233. **Area Code:** 410.

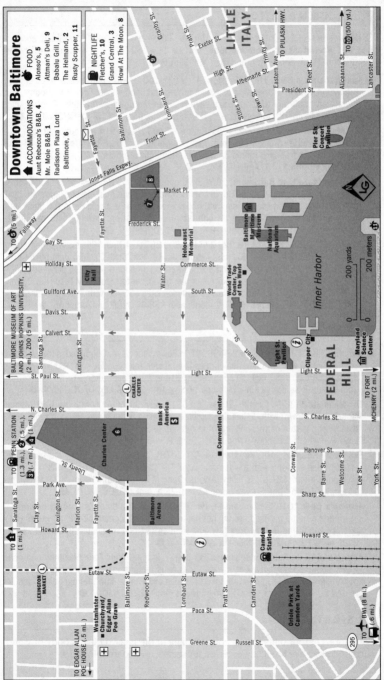

Downtown Baltimore

ACCOMMODATIONS
Aunt Rebecca's B&B, 4
Mr. Mole B&B, 1
Radisson Plaza Lord
Baltimore, 6

● FOOD
Alonso's, 5
Attman's Deli, 9
Babalu Grill, 7
The Helmand, 2
Rusty Scupper, 11

● NIGHTLIFE
Fletcher's, 10
Grand Central, 3
Howl At The Moon, 8

LITTLE ITALY

TO PULASKI HWY.
TO (500 yd.)

Granby St.
Pratt St.
Exeter St.
High St.
Albemarle St.
Stiles St.
Fawn St.
Trinity St.
Eastern Ave.
Fleet St.
President St.
Aliceanna St.
Lancaster St.

Lombard St.
Baltimore St.
Front St.
Fayette St.
Gay St.
Holiday St.
Guilford Ave.
Davis St.
Calvert St.
St. Paul St.

Saratoga St.
Charles St.
Liberty St.
Park Ave.
Marion St.
Fayette St.
Clay St.
Howard St.
Lexington St.

Jones Falls Expwy.
Falsway

TO (5 mi.)

Market Pl.
Frederick St.
Holocaust Memorial
Commerce St.
Water St.
South St.

City Hall

Pier Six Concert Pavilion

Baltimore Maritime Museum
National Aquarium

Inner Harbor

World Trade Center, Top of the World

Light St. Pavilion
Clipper City

Maryland Science Center

FEDERAL HILL

0   200 yards
0   200 meters

Light St.
S. Charles St.
Conway St.
Hanover St.
Barre St.
Welcome St.
Lee St.
York St.
Sharp St.
Howard St.

Convention Center

Charles Center

CHARLES CENTER

Bank of America

Baltimore Arena

N. Charles St.

BALTIMORE MUSEUM OF ART AND JOHNS HOPKINS UNIVERSITY, (2 mi.), ZOO (5 mi.)

TO PENN STATION (1.3 mi.), (7 mi.), (5 mi.), (1 mi.)

Lexington St.
Eutaw St.

LEXINGTON MARKET

Westminster Churchyard/ Edgar Allan Poe Grave

TO EDGAR ALLAN POE HOUSE (.5 mi.)

TO (1 mi.)

Camden Station

Oriole Park at Camden Yards

Eutaw St.
Lombard St.
Paca St.
Camden St.
Pratt St.
Greene St.
Russell St.
Redwood St.

Howard St.

295

TO BWI (8 mi.), (.6 mi.)

TO FORT McHENRY (2 mi.)

MID-ATLANTIC

⌐ ACCOMMODATIONS

Expensive hotels dominate the Inner Harbor. To reserve bed and breakfasts, contact **Bed and Breakfast Accommodations, Ltd.** (☎413-582-9888; www.bedandbreak-fastdc.com. From $65 per night. Open M-F 9am-5pm.)

▣ **Aunt Rebecca's B&B,** 106 E. Preston St. (☎625-1007; www.auntrebeccasbnb.com), in the Mount Vernon district. Full of gilded mirrors and chandeliers. Only 3 bedrooms, but if you can book one of them you'll save big over the downtown hotels. Free parking. Queen bedroom with full breakfast $100; additional person $15. AmEx/D/MC/V. ❺

Mr. Mole Bed and Breakfast, 1601 Bolton St. (☎728-1179; www.mrmolebb.com), in the Bolton Hill district on the northwest edge of town. This B&B offers suites for the same price as standard rooms downtown. Phone, private bath, A/C, and Dutch breakfast. Suites from $149. AmEx/D/MC/V. ❺

Radisson Plaza Lord Baltimore, 20 W. Baltimore St. (☎539-8400; www.radisson.com), between Hanover and Charles St., in the Inner Harbor. A national historic landmark built in 1928 with a Renaissance-inspired lobby. The location—6 blocks from the Inner Harbor—and historic flavor prove an unbeatable combination. Parking $25 per night. Rooms from $149. AAA discount 10%. AmEx/D/DC/MC/V. ❺

Capitol KOA, 768 Cecil Ave. (☎923-2771 or 800-562-0248), in Millersville, 20min. from Baltimore. Take I-97 south 8½ mi. to Exit 10A (Benfield Blvd. E). Turn right at the KOA sign. Mostly RVs, some cabins, and a small wooded area for tents. Pool, playground, toilets, showers. Free shuttle to MARC commuter train Odenton Station M-F; to New Carrollton Metro Sa-Su. Open Mar. 25-Nov. 1. 2-person sites $33-41; with water and electricity $38-48; with full hookup $43-57. 1-room cabin $58-69. Additional adult $5. ❷

⌐ FOOD

▣ **Babalu Grill,** 32 Market Pl. (☎234-9898), in Power Plant Live. Cuban sides like rice and beans ($3) go well with creative entrees like lobster and coconut rice ($31). Turns into a hot salsa club F-Sa nights ($5 cover 10-11pm, $10 cover after 11pm). Open Tu-Th 5pm-10pm, F-Sa 5pm-11pm; club open F-Sa 11pm-2am. AmEx/D/DC/MC/V. ❹

The Helmand, 806 N. Charles St. (☎752-0311; www.helmand.com). The best Afghan restaurant in town, with dishes like *kabuli* (rice baked with chunks of lamb tenderloin, raisins, and glazed carrots). Plenty of vegetarian options and enough desserts to satisfy any sweet tooth. Open M-Th and Su 5-10pm, F-Sa 5-11pm. AmEx/D/MC/V. ❷

The Rusty Scupper, 402 Key Hwy. (☎727-3678), in the Inner Harbor, is a landmark, serving fresh seafood with a waterfront view. The "waterman's po' boy," with oysters or popcorn shrimp ($9-10), is justly famous. Open M-Th 11:30am-10pm, F-Sa 11:30am-11pm, Su 10am-9pm. Su jazz brunch 11am-2pm. AmEx/D/DC/MC/V. ❹

Attman's Deli, 1019 E. Lombard St. (☎563-2666), on Baltimore's "corned beef row," has made a name for itself serving hot pastrami ($6) and corned beef sandwiches ($6) just like you'd find in New York City. The Reuben ($7.50) was voted Baltimore's best. Open M-Sa 8am-6:30pm, Su 8am-5pm. MC/V. ❷

Alonso's, 415 W. Cold Spring Ln. (☎235-3433), in the Roland Park neighborhood near Johns Hopkins University, Exit 9A from I-83 N, is famous for 1 lb. burgers ($12). The portobello panini ($8) and crab cake sandwich ($14) are more manageable. Open M-Th and Su 11am-11pm, F-Sa 11am-midnight. AmEx/D/DC/MC/V. ❸

⌐ SIGHTS

Baltimore's harbor ends with a colorful bang in the **Inner Harbor,** a body of water surrounded by five blocks of eateries, museums, and boardable ships.

■ THE NATIONAL AQUARIUM. The **National Aquarium** is one of the US's best places to ogle and learn about sealife. Though a visit to the outdoor sea pool to watch slap-happy seals play is free to the general public, it is worth the time and money to venture inside. The eerie **Wings in the Water** exhibit showcases 50 species of stingrays in an immense backlit pool. In the steamy **Tropical Rainforest**, piranhas, parrots, and a pair of two-toed sloths peer through the dense foliage in a 157 ft. glass pyramid. At the **Marine Mammal Pavilion,** dolphins perform every hour on the half-hour. *(Pier 3, 501 E. Pratt St. in the Inner Harbor. ☎576-3800; www.aqua.org. Open July-Aug. M-Th and Su 9am-6pm, F-Sa 9am-8pm; Mar.-June and Sept.-Oct. M-Th and Sa-Su 9am-5pm, F 9am-8pm; Nov.-Feb. M-Th and Sa-Su 10am-5pm, F 10am-8pm. Last entrance 1½hr. before close. $18, ages 60+ $17, ages 3-11 $11, under 3 free. Tickets are sold for a particular entrance time on busy summer days and can be purchased in advance online.)*

BALTIMORE MARITIME MUSEUM. Several ships grace the harbor by the aquarium, most of which belong to the Baltimore Maritime Museum. Visitors may clamber through the interior of the **USS Torsk,** the intricately-painted submarine that sank the last WWII Japanese combat ship, or board one of the survivors of the Pearl Harbor attack, the Coast Guard cutter **Roger B. Taney,** and ascend the **octagonal lighthouse** on Pier 5. For these historic sites and more, purchase the **Seaport Day Pass,** which grants access to the **Maritime Museum,** the **Museum of Industry,** Baltimore's **World Trade Center,** and the **USS Constellation,** the last all-sail warship built by the US Navy. Water taxi service to and from attractions is included. *(Piers 3 and 5. ☎396-3453; http://baltomaritimemuseum.org. In the summer the Taney is open daily 10am-5:30pm, the Chesapeake lightboat 10am-6pm, the Torsk 10am-8:30pm. All boats open in spring and fall M-Th and Su 10am-5pm, F-Sa 10am-6pm; in winter F-Su 10am-5pm. Boats stay open 1hr. later than ticket stand. $7, seniors $6, ages 5-13 $4. Seaport Day Pass $16/$14/$9.)*

MARYLAND SCIENCE CENTER. From the prehistoric to the futuristic, the **Maryland Science Center** is a kid- and adult-friendly museum that explores how science touches our daily lives and our imaginations. The Hubble Space Telescope Visitors Center and the new traveling exhibit about Jane Goodall and the chimps of Gombe, Tanzania are fascinating, and children will love the dinosaur dig exhibit. *(601 Light St. ☎685-5225; www.marylandsciencecenter.org. Open in summer M-W and Su 10am-6pm, Th-Sa 10am-8pm; in low season Tu-F 10am-5pm, Sa 10am-6pm, Su noon-5pm. $14.50, with admission to traveling exhibits $20, with IMAX movie $18.50; ages 60+ $13.50/$19/$17.50; ages 3-12 $10/$14/$13.)*

WALTERS ART MUSEUM. Spanning 50 centuries, the **Walters Art Museum** houses one of the largest private art collections in the world. The museum's pride and joy is its ancient art collection, featuring sculpture, jewelry, and metalwork from Egypt, Greece, and Rome. Byzantine, Romanesque, and Gothic art are also on display. At the **Hackerman House,** a mansion attached to the Walters, rooms filled with dark wooden furniture, patterned rugs, and plush velvet curtains display Asian and South Asian art. *(600 N. Charles St. Take bus #3 or 11. ☎547-9000; www.thewalters.org. Open W-Su 10am-5pm. $10, seniors $8, ages 18-25 $6, 18 and under $2. Admission to permanent collection free Sa 10am-1pm and first Th of every month. Audio tour $2.)*

EDGAR ALLAN POE HOUSE. Horror pioneer Edgar Allan Poe was born in 1809 in what is now a preserved historical landmark. In between doses of opium, Poe penned famous stories such as *The Tell-Tale Heart* and *The Pit and the Pendulum,* as well as macabre poems like *The Raven* and *Annabel Lee.* The house exhibits on the former owner, impeccably maintained by a staff eager to regale visitors with all sorts of Poe stories. Steer clear of this neighborhood at night. *(203 N. Amity St., near Saratoga St. Take bus #15 or 23. From Lexington Market, walk on N. Lexington St. away from downtown and turn right on Amity St. It is the 2nd house on the right. ☎396-7932. Open Aug.-Dec. W-Sa noon-3:45pm. $3, under 13 and active military free.)*

MID-ATLANTIC

JOHNS HOPKINS UNIVERSITY. Approximately 3 mi. north of the harbor, prestigious **Johns Hopkins University (JHU)** spreads out from 33rd St. Johns Hopkins was the very first research university in the country and remains a world leader in developments in the research and study of medicine, public health, and engineering. The campus was originally the Homewood estate of Charles Carroll, Jr., the son of the longest-lived signer of the Declaration of Independence. Free 1hr. campus tours begin at the **Office of Admissions** in Garland Hall. *(JHU: 3400 N. Charles St. Take bus #3 or 11. ☎516-8171; http://apply.jhu.edu/visit/guidedtours.html. Tours Sept.-May M-F 10am and 1pm, Sa by reservation; call for summer hours.)* One mile north of the main campus, **Evergreen House** is an exercise in excess—the bathroom of this elegant mansion is plated in 23-carat gold. Purchased in 1878 by railroad tycoon John W. Garret, the ornate house, along with its collections of fine porcelain, rare artwork, and Tiffany silver, was bequeathed to JHU in 1942. *(Evergreen House: 4545 N. Charles St. ☎516-0341; www.jhu.edu/~evrgreen/evergreen.html. Take bus #11. Open Tu-F 11am-4pm, Sa-Su noon-4pm. Tours every hr.; last tour 1hr. before close. $6, seniors $5, students and children $3.)*

🎵 ENTERTAINMENT

Much of Baltimore's finest entertainment can be enjoyed free of charge. At Harborplace, street performers delight tourists with magic acts and juggling during the day. The **Baltimore Museum of Art** offers jazz concerts on summer Saturdays at 7pm (May-Sept.) in its sculpture garden. (☎396-6314; www.artbma.org. $20.) The **Pier 6 Concert Pavilion** presents concerts from May to October, ranging from classical to R&B. (☎625-3100; www.piersixpavilion.com. Tickets $15-50. Pier Pass to 4 concerts $100.) Never thought you were the type to go to the orchestra? The **Baltimore Symphony Orchestra** is out to change your mind. The orchestra plays at **Meyerhoff Symphony Hall,** 1212 Cathedral St., from September to May and during the month-long Summerfest. The real secret is the venue's college nights: the $10 student tickets include a reception with complimentary food and $1 beers. (☎783-8000; www.baltimoresymphony.org. Box office open M-F 10am-6pm, Sa-Su noon-5pm, and 1hr. before performances. Tickets $15-52. Discounts available 1hr. before concerts.)

The Lyric Opera House, 140 W. Mt. Royal Ave., near Maryland Ave., hosts the **Baltimore Opera Company** from October to May. (☎727-6000; www.baltimoreopera.com. Box office, down the road, open M-F 10am-4:30pm. Tickets $37-130.) The **Theater Project,** 45 W. Preston St., near Maryland St., experiments with theater, poetry, music, and dance. (☎752-8558; www.theatreproject.org. Box office open 1hr. before shows; call to reserve tickets. Shows Th-Sa 8pm, Su 3pm. $16, seniors and students $11, visiting productions more.) The **Arena Players,** the longest continually-running African-American theater company in the country, performs comedies, drama, and musicals. (801 McCulloh St., at Martin Luther King, Jr. Blvd. ☎728-6500. Box office open M-F 11am-2pm, Sa 10am-8pm, Su noon-4pm. Tickets from $15.) From June through October, the **Showcase of Nations Ethnic Festivals** celebrate Baltimore's numerous ethnic neighborhoods with food, music, vendors, and special ceremonies. A different culture is featured each week. Call the Baltimore Area Visitors Center for info (p. 258).

The beloved **Baltimore Orioles** play baseball at **Camden Yards,** situated just a few blocks from the Inner Harbor at the corner of Russell and Camden St. (Box office ☎685-9800, M-Sa 9am-5pm, Su noon-5pm. Tickets $9-55.) The NFL's **Ravens** play in **M&T Bank Stadium,** which is right next to Camden Yards. (☎261-7283; www.baltimoreravens.com.)

NIGHTLIFE

Nightlife in **Mount Vernon** is reminiscent of *Cheers*, with neighborhood bars that know their middle-aged patrons by name, while the loud music and sweaty dance floors of **Fells Point** and **Power Plant Live** cater to a college and twentysomething crowd. Be prepared for the 1:30am last call. If you make it through the dozens of bars in Fells Point, head to **Canton** for a similar scene.

Howl At The Moon, 22 Market Pl. (☎783-5111; www.howlatthemoon.com), in Power Plant Live. An amusing dueling-piano bar where the crowd runs the show, with frequent sing- (or "howl-") alongs. Crowd ranges from just-barely-adults to could-be-your-parents. More relaxed than the testosterone-fueled bars of Fells Point. Happy hour F 5-8pm with half-price drinks and free buffet. Beer $3.50-5. Cocktails $4.50-8. Cover Th $5 after 9pm, F-Sa $8 after 8pm. Open W-Th 7pm-2am, F 5pm-2am, Sa 5:30pm-2am.

Grand Central, 1001-1003 N. Charles St. (☎752-7133; www.centralstationpub.com), at Eager St. Chill under chandeliers from the set of *A Few Good Men* and *Batman* or play some pool with a mixed gay/straight crowd. Happy hour daily 4-8pm with $1 off beer. $2 Skyy vodka drinks Su. The disco club next door is the spot for bumping and grinding W-Su 9pm-2am. Cover for dance club $6. Open daily 4pm-2am.

Fletcher's, 701 S. Bond St. (☎558-1889; www.fletchersbar.com), brings in live bands on the weekend to entertain its barflies, most often featuring rock, rap, and blues acts. Happy hour M-Th 4:30-6:30pm and all day Su. Beer from $2.50. Cover $5-13. Doors open at 7, 8, or 9pm depending on the show. Closing time daily 2am.

ANNAPOLIS ☎410

Annapolis became the capital of Maryland in 1694, and in 1783 enjoyed a stint as capital of the US. Since then, the city has lived a dual life of residential port town and naval garrison. The historic waterfront district retains its 18th-century appeal despite the presence of ritzy boutiques. Crew-cut "middies" ("midshipmen," a nickname for Naval Academy students) do sailors proud at the pubs while shaggier students from St. John's (the country's third oldest college) chill at the coffeeshops, all amid middle-age couples ogling the US's highest concentration of historical homes.

ORIENTATION AND PRACTICAL INFORMATION. Annapolis lies 30 mi. east of D.C. and 30 mi. south of Baltimore. The city extends south and east from two landmarks: **Church Circle** and **State Circle. School Street,** in a blatantly unconstitutional move, connects Church and State. **East Street** runs from the State House to the Naval Academy. **Main Street,** where food and entertainment venues abound, starts at Church Cir. and ends at the docks. Downtown Annapolis is compact and easily walkable, but finding a cheap parking space can be tricky. If a convenient metered spot doesn't come your way, parking at the visitors center ($1 per hr., $8 max. weekdays, $4 max. weekends) is the best bet. There is also free weekend parking in State Lots A and B, at the corner of Rowe Blvd. and Calvert St. **Greyhound** (☎800-231-2222; www.greyhound.com) buses stop at the Mass Transit Administration bus stop, 308 Cinquapin Rd., and run to Baltimore (30min., 3 per day, $10), Philadelphia (4-5hr., 3 per day, $24), and Washington, D.C. (1-2hr., 3 per day, $14). Tickets (cash only) are available from the bus driver. The **Annapolis Department of Public Transportation** operates a web of buses connecting the historic district with the rest of town. (☎263-7964. Buses run M-Sa 5:30am-10am, Su 8am-7pm. $0.75, seniors and disabled $0.35.) **Taxi: Annapolis Cab Co.,** ☎268-0022. **Checker Cab,** ☎268-3737. **Car Rental: Budget,** 2001 West St. (☎266-5030). **Visitor Info: Annapolis and Anne**

Arundel County Conference and Visitors Bureau, 26 West St., has free maps and brochures. (☎280-0445; www.visit-annapolis.org. Open daily 9am-5pm.) **Post Office:** 1 Church Cir. (☎263-9292. Open M-F 9am-5pm.) **Postal Code:** 21401. **Area Code:** 410.

⌂ ACCOMMODATIONS. The heart of Annapolis favors elegant and pricey B&Bs over cheap motels. Rooms should be reserved in advance, especially for weekends, spring graduations, and the summer. The **Annapolis Bed and Breakfast Association** (www.annapolisbandb.com) is a good place to start your search. The **Historic Inns of Annapolis ❺,** 58 State Circle, three properties that ring the state capitol, sometimes offer their beautifully appointed rooms for bargain rates. (☎263-2641; www.annapolisinns.com. Breakfast included. Rooms $110-200. AmEx/D/DC/MC/V.) The **Scotlaur Inn ❺,** 165 Main St., sits atop Chick & Ruth's Delly. Ten guest rooms with queen, double, or twin beds, A/C, TV, and private bath grace this homey "bed & bagel." (☎268-5665; www.scotlaurinn.com. Check-in 2pm. Check-out 11am. Rooms $100-145. MC/V.) Similar prices but less character can be found a few miles outside of town at the local **Days Inn ❹,** 2451 Riva Rd., where clean, well-lit rooms come with cable TV and A/C. (☎800-329-7466. Continental breakfast included. Doubles $100; additional person $7. AmEx/D/MC/V.)

◻ FOOD. Most restaurants cluster around **City Dock,** an area packed with people in the summer. Find cheap eats at the **Market House** food court, at the center of City Dock, where a hearty meal costs less than $6. A Swedish coffeehouse with an Idaho twist, **Potato Valley Cafe ❷,** 47 State Cir., across from the State House, specializes in giant oven-roasted potatoes stuffed with fillings ($5-7). Toppings range from standard sour cream to exotic curry dressing with pineapple. (☎267-0902. Open M-F 10am-5pm, Sa 11:30am-5pm. MC/V.) Of course, Main St. wouldn't be complete without a lovable deli. The staff at **Chick and Ruth's Delly ❷,** 165 Main St., serves up over 40 specialty sandwiches ($3.50-7), along with a bewildering array of salads, desserts, and all-day breakfasts. (☎269-6737; www.chickandruths.com. Dinner platters $5-10. Open M-Th and Su 6:30am-11:30pm, F-Sa 6:30am-12:30am Cash only.) Locals flock to **Carrol's Creek Bar & Cafe ❷,** 410 Severn Ave., in the Annapolis City Marina Complex, for home-cooked food and cheap drinks along the waterfront. Texas barbecued shrimp ($10) and Maryland crab soup ($6.50) are favorites. Happy hour (M-F 5-7pm) features half-price appetizers. (☎263-8102; www.carrolscreek.com. Open M-Sa 11:30am-4pm and 5-10pm; Su $19 all-you-can-eat brunch 10am-1:30pm, dinner 3-9pm. AMEx/D/MC/V.)

◎ SIGHTS. In many senses the **US Naval Academy,** 52 King George St., is the soul of Annapolis. The legendary military school turns harried, short-haired "plebes" (first-year students) into Naval-officer "middies" (midshipmen) through rigorous drilling and physical and emotional obstacles. President Jimmy Carter and billionaire H. Ross Perot are among the Academy's celebrity alumni. Once at the Academy, the first stop should be the **Leftwich Visitors Center,** in the Halsey Field House, which doubles as a food court and hockey rink. (☎263-6933; www.navyonline.com. Open Mar.-Dec. 9am-5pm, Jan.-Feb. 9am-4pm.) Guided walking tours take visitors through historic Bancroft Hall, the chapel's crypt, a dorm room, and the athletic facilities, where the middies test their seafaring prowess on land. **King Hall,** the world's largest dining facility, is a madhouse at lunchtime, when the entire student populace assumes "Brigade Meal Formation" and is served in under 20 frenzied minutes. On Saturdays in the summer, alumni weddings take place in the Academy's chapel (open M-Sa 9am-4pm, Su 1-4pm). Underneath the chapel is the final resting place of **John Paul Jones,** father of the United States Navy, who uttered the famous words, "I have not yet begun to fight!" as he rammed his sinking ship into an attacking British vessel. (75min. campus tours July-Aug. M-Sa

9:30am-3pm, Su 12:30-3pm; Apr.-June and Sept.-Nov. M-F 10am-3pm, Sa 9:30am-3pm, Su 12:30-3pm; Dec.-Mar. M-Sa 10am-2:30pm, Su 12:30-2:30pm. $7.50, seniors $6.50, students $5.50.)

The historic **Hammond-Harwood House,** 19 Maryland Ave., an elegant 1774 building designed by colonial architect William Buckland, retains period decor right down to the candlesticks. The **William Paca House,** 186 Prince George St., was the first Georgian-style home built in Annapolis, and has two acres of lush vegetation. Paca, an early governor of Maryland, was one of the original signers of the Declaration of Independence. Both houses feature exhibits on life in the late 1700s, stocked with artifacts from archaeological digs on the grounds. (Hammond-Harwood: ☎263-5553; www.hammondharwoodhouse.org. Open Apr.-Oct. W-Su noon-5pm; Nov.-Mar. F-Sa noon-4pm. 40min. tours every hr.; last tour 1hr. before close. $6, students $5.50, under 12 $3. William Paca House: ☎990-4538 or 800-603-4020; www.annapolis.org. Open Mar.-Dec. M-Sa 10am-5pm, Su noon-5pm. Tours every 30min. Garden or house $5, seniors and AAA $4, ages 6-17 $3; garden and house $8/$7/$5. Uniformed armed service personnel and ages 5 and under free.)

Built between 1772 and 1779, the Corinthian-columned **State House,** in the center of State Circle, is the oldest functioning capitol building in the nation. It was the US capitol building from 1783 to 1784; the Treaty of Paris was signed here on January 14, 1784. Visitors can explore the historical exhibits and silver collection, or watch the state legislature bicker (politely, of course) in two exquisite marble halls. Cordial guides clad in colonial garb gladly field questions. (☎974-3400. Open M-F 9am-5pm, Sa-Su 10am-4pm; grounds 6am-11pm. Tours daily 11am and 3pm. Legislature in session mid-Jan. to mid-Apr. Free.)

🎭🎵 **ENTERTAINMENT AND NIGHTLIFE.** Locals and tourists generally engage in one of two activities in Annapolis: wandering along City Dock or schmoozing 'n' boozing at the city's various upscale pubs. The bars and taverns that line downtown Annapolis draw crowds every night. If you want more culture than drink can provide, check out **The Colonial Players, Inc.,** 108 East St., for performances of innovative and often unknown plays. (☎268-7373; www.cplayers.com. Shows Th-Sa 8pm, Su 2:30 and 7:30pm. $15, students $10.) In the summer, the **Annapolis Summer Garden Theater,** 143 Compromise St., presents musical "theater under the stars" on a terraced lawn overlooking an open courtyard theater. (☎268-9212; www.summergarden.com. Th-Su at 8:30pm. Lawn seats $12.) The **Naval Academy Band** performs on City Dock every Tuesday night at 7:30pm. (☎293-0263; www.usna.edu/usnaband. Free.)

As close as you can get to the water without falling in, **Pusser's Landing,** 80 Compromise St., facing City Dock, is located on a working pier. (☎626-0004; www.pussers.com. Beer $2-4. Kitchen open M-Th and Su 7am-11pm, F-Sa 7am-midnight; bar open daily until 2am.) Midshipmen and tourists alike enjoy 135 different ales, lagers, and stouts at **Ram's Head Tavern,** 33 West St. Happy hour (M-F 4-7pm) includes $2 drafts and free tacos. There is free live music on the patio many evenings; for bigger-name bands, a dinner and show combination ticket gets you a 10% discount on your meal and a free drink. (☎268-4545. Happy hour with $2 drafts daily midnight-1am. Open daily 10am-2am.) Locals and officers pack in under the two-story ficus tree that grows through **Irish McGarvey's,** 8 Market Space. Two bars in the establishment serve Aviator Lager, the manliest-sounding beer in town (10 oz. draft $3.50, pint $5.50), but not much else. Summer parties on Tuesday nights invite patrons to don tropical attire and enjoy frozen Zombies ($4) with their red beans and rice ($6). Happy hour (M and W 10pm-2am) features buffalo wings for $3-10, 32 oz. drafts for $3, and 10 oz. mugs for $1. (☎263-5700. Th 6pm-1am house beer $1.50. Open M-Sa 11:30am-2am, Su 10am-2am.)

ASSATEAGUE AND CHINCOTEAGUE   ☎757

Local legend has it that wild mustangs first came to Assateague Island by swimming ashore from a sinking Spanish galleon. A more likely theory is that miserly colonial farmers put their horses out to graze on Assateague to avoid mainland taxes. Whatever their origins, the famous horses, called ponies because of their slightly stunted growth, now roam free across the unspoiled beaches and forests of the island, and, on the last Wednesday and Thursday in July, swim from Assateague to Chincoteague during Pony Penning.

■■🚩 **ORIENTATION AND PRACTICAL INFORMATION.** Telling the two islands apart, especially since their names are sometimes used interchangeably, can often leave visitors bewildered. **Assateague Island** is the longer barrier island facing the ocean, while the resort-y **Chincoteague Island** is nestled between Assateague and mainland Eastern Shore. Maryland and Virginia share Assateague Island, and **Chincoteague Wildlife Refuge** is actually on Assateague. Due to Assateague's lack of civilization, most resources are located on Chincoteague. The best way to get to Chincoteague is by car; the best way to explore it is by bike. From D.C., take Rte. 50 E to Salisbury, MD, then take Rte. 13 S and turn left onto Rte. 175 E. **Visitor Info: Chincoteague Chamber of Commerce,** 6733 Maddox Blvd. (☎336-6161; www.chincoteaguechamber.com. Open M-Sa 9am-4:30pm, Memorial Day-Labor Day also Su 12:30-5pm.) **Internet Access: Vacation Internet Cafe,** 4407 Deep Hole Rd. (☎336-3616; www.vacationinternetcafe.com. $3 per 15min., $10 per hr. Free Wi-FI access with $3 food purchase. Open M-Sa 9am-6pm.) **Post Office:** 4144 Main St. (☎336-2934. Open M-F 8am-4:30pm, Sa 8am-noon.) **Postal Code:** 23336. **Area Code:** 757.

🚩🏠 **ACCOMMODATIONS AND FOOD.** Unless you're planning to snuggle up with the ponies and graze on grass, the only accommodations and food are located on Chincoteague. The **Blue Heron Inn ❸,** 7020 Maddox Blvd., has clean, spacious rooms with A/C, phones, refrigerators, cable TV, a pool, and boat/camper parking. (☎336-1900 or 800-615-6343; www.chincoteague.com/blueheron. Room rates peak at $139 during the Pony Penning. June-Aug. weekdays $74-99; weekends $84-99; Sept.-May $49-90/$59-90. AmEx/D/MC/V.) For rooms with breathtaking views and access to pools and an exercise room, head to the waterfront **Island Motor Inn Resort ❺,** 4391 Main St. (☎336-3141; www.islandmotorinn.com. Check-in 4pm. Check-out 11am. Rooms June-Sept. $105-175; Mar.-May $82-150; Dec.-Feb. $68-140. Low season senior discount 10%. AmEx/D/MC/V.) The sprawling **Maddox Family Campground ❶,** 6742 Maddox Blvd., across from the visitors center, has 550 campsites, a pool, laundry, and hot showers. (☎336-3111. For full hookup, reserve 3 months in advance. Sites with water and electricity $33, full hookup $36.)

AJ's on the Creek ❹, 6585 Maddox Blvd., specializes in steaks and grilled fish in a dining room decked out in lace and mahogany. (☎336-5888. Lunch entrees $4-10. Dinner entrees $15-25. Open in summer M-Sa 11:30am-9:30pm, lounge open until 1am. AmEx/D/MC/V.) **Not Just Salads ❶,** 6349 Maddox Blvd., has an all-you-can-eat-salad bar ($6.50), but, as the name suggests, also serves sandwiches, burgers, and subs. (☎336-7333. Open daily 10am-9pm. MC/V.) Treat yourself to towering ice cream cones and inventive sundaes at **Mister Whippy ❶,** 6201 Maddox St. (☎336-5122. Cone $1.50. Open daily 11am-10:30pm. Cash only.)

🔲 **SIGHTS.** The ◼Chincoteague National Wildlife Refuge stretches across the Virginia side of Assateague Island. Avid bird-watchers come to see rare species like snowy egrets and black-crowned night herons. The **Pony Penning,** held the last consecutive Wednesday and Thursday in July (after the month-long Chincoteague Volunteer Firefighter's Carnival), brings thousands of tourists to Assateague. During slack tide, firemen herd the ponies together and swim them from Assateague to Chincoteague Island, where the fire department auctions off the foals the following day. The remaining horses swim back to Assateague to mate, providing next year's crop. Head to the **visitors center,** located just inside the refuge, to learn about biking, hiking, walking, and bird and nature tours. Guided wildlife bus tours are also available. (☎336-3696. $12, ages 62+ $10, ages 2-12 $5. Memorial Day-Labor Day daily 10am, 1, 4pm; Labor Day-Memorial Day 1 per day.) Trails include the 3 mi. **Wildlife Loop,** which circles a fresh-water impoundment (open 3pm-dusk for cars, all day for pedestrians and bicyclists), the forested 1½ mi. **Woodland Trail** (cars not permitted), and the quarter-mile **Lighthouse Trail,** which runs to the historic Assateague Lighthouse (pedestrians only). Park rangers request that visitors maintain a safe distance from the wild ponies and resist the urge to feed them; if fed by guests, the ponies could become dependent on humans for survival. (8231 Beach Rd. ☎336-6122; http://chinco.fws.gov. Absolutely no pets permitted. Park open daily May-Sept. 5am-10pm; Apr. and Oct. 6am-8pm; Nov.-Mar. 6am-6pm. Visitors center open daily Memorial Day-Labor Day 9am-5pm; Labor Day-Memorial Day 9am-4pm. 7-day pass $10 per car.) The **Oyster & Maritime Museum** is a non-profit museum that tells the story of the island's history and oystering and seafood industry. Don't miss the 1865 First Order Fresnel lens from the Assateague Lighthouse, one of only 21 in the US. Retired in 1961, its light could be seen from 23 mi. away. (7125 Maddox Blvd. ☎336-6117. Open May-Sept. M-Sa 10am-5pm, Su noon-4pm. Free.) The **Chincoteague Pony Centre** offers pony rides and showcases veterans of the pony swim. (6417 Carriage Dr. ☎336-2776; www.chincoteague.com/ponycentre. Heading north on Main St., turn right onto Church St., left onto Chicken City Rd., and right onto Carriage Dr. Open in summer M-Sa 9am-10pm. Pony rides M-Sa 9am-1pm and 3:30-6pm. Rides $5.)

OCEAN CITY ☎410

Ocean City is a lot like a kiddie pool—it's shallow and plastic, but can be a lot of fun if you're the right age or in just the right mood. This 10 mi. strip of prime Atlantic beach packs endless bars, all-you-can-eat buffets, boardwalks, mini-golf courses, flashing neon lights, and sun-seeking tourists into a thin region between the ocean on the east and the Montego, Assawoman, Isle of Wight, and Sinepuxent bays to the west. The siren call of senior week beckons droves of recent high school and college graduates to alcohol and hormone-driven fun, turning O.C. into a city-wide block party in late May and June. During July and August, the city caters more to families and professional singles looking for fun in the sun.

■◪ **ORIENTATION AND PRACTICAL INFORMATION.** Driving is the least painful mode of transportation to reach the ocean resort, though beach traffic can make getting to O.C. a headache no matter how you plan to do it. From the north, simply follow Rte. 1, which becomes **Coastal Highway (Philadelphia Avenue).** From the west, Rte. 50 also leads directly to Ocean City. From points south, take Rte. 113 to Rte. 50 and follow that to town. At most points, Philadelphia Ave. is the only major road running north-south. Numbered streets run east-west, linking the ocean to the bay. Most hotels are in the lower-numbered streets to the south, toward the ocean; most clubs and bars are uptown toward the bay. **Greyhound/Trailways** (☎289-9307; www.greyhound.com; open daily 10am-1:30pm), at 2nd St. and Philadelphia Ave., sends buses to Baltimore (3¾hr., 2 per day, $33) and Washington, D.C. (4½-5½hr., 3 per day, $43). In town, **public buses** (☎723-1607) run the length of the strip and are the best way to get around town 24hr. a day ($2 per day for unlimited rides). The **Ocean City Visitors Bureau,** 4001 Coastal Hwy., at 40th St. in the Convention Center, gives out coupons and brochures for local establishments. (☎723-8610 or

800-626-2326; www.ococean.com. M-F 8am-5pm, Sa-Su 9am-5pm.) **E-Point Internet Cafe,** 1513 Philadelphia Ave., in the 15th St. Shopping Center complex, offers Internet access. (☎289-9844. $4 per 30min., $7 per hr. Open daily 10am-2am. Cash only.) **Post Office:** 7101 Coastal Hwy. (☎524-4978. Open M-F 9am-5pm, Sa 9am-noon.) **Postal Code:** 21842. **Area Codes:** 410, 443. In text, 410 unless otherwise noted.

⌐ ACCOMMODATIONS. Reservations are essential in the summer, or you won't find a room at any price within 30 mi. of the beach. Weekend prices are about $20-25 higher than weekday prices, but many guest houses and motels offer weekly rates at a discount. The **Atlantic House Bed and Breakfast ❺,** 501 N. Baltimore Ave., half a block from the ocean and the boardwalk, provides a full breakfast buffet and a wholesome change of pace from the Ocean City motel trend. (☎289-2333; www.atlantichouse.com. Complimentary beach chairs, umbrellas, and towels. A/C, cable TV, hot tub, parking. Closed Oct.-Mar. May-Aug. rooms with shared bath $85-150, with private bath $115-195. D/MC/V.) The only in-town camping option is **Ocean City Travel Park ❸,** 105 70th St., only 1½ blocks from the ocean. It's expensive for a campground, but still the cheapest lodging in town. (☎524-7601; www.occamping.com. Laundry, showers, toilets. Tent sites late May to Sept. weekdays $39, weekends $52, holidays $62. Small RVs $49/$59/$69. Large RVs $59/$69/$79. Apr. to mid-May $27-49; Oct.-Nov. $25-35.)

▢ FOOD. Ocean City's cuisine oscillates between linen-napkin gourmet and cheap, grease-laden buffet. Ice cream, funnel cakes, and sno-ball stands beckon from the boardwalk, but most sit-down eateries are just off the beach. ▨**Brass Balls Saloon & Bad Ass Cafe ❶,** on the Boardwalk between 11th and 12th St., is known for its $1.25 Jell-O shots (after 10pm) and its motto: "Drink Hearty, Eat Healthy." Specials like the $5.25 Oreo waffles and the $7 pizzas seem to defy the latter imperative, though college crowds can't get enough of the "drink hearty" part. (☎289-0069. Open Mar.-Oct. M-F 8:30am-2am, Sa-Su 8am-2am. AmEx/D/MC/V.) With fresh catches and a friendly atmosphere, **The Embers ❺,** 2305 Philadelphia Ave., boasts the biggest seafood buffet in town. All the clams, oysters, Alaskan crab legs, prime rib, steak, sides, and dessert you can eat are $27. (☎289-3322 or 888-436-2377; www.embers.com. Open daily 2pm-9:30pm. AmEx/D/MC/V.) **Reflections ❹,** 6600 Coastal Hwy., at 67th St., on the ground floor of the Holiday Inn, offers tableside cooking and fine dining, Las Vegas-style. (☎524-5252. Early Bird dinner entrees $10-19 if seated by 6pm; regular entrees $20-48. Open daily 5-10pm.)

▤▥ ENTERTAINMENT AND NIGHTLIFE. Ocean City's star attraction is its beautiful beach. The wide stretch of surf and sand runs the entire 10 mi. worth of town and can be accessed by taking a left onto any of the numerous side streets off Philadelphia and Baltimore Ave. The breaking waves know no time constraints, but the beach is technically only open daily 6am-10pm. When the sun goes down, professional party-goers will be impressed by **Seacrets,** on 49th St., in the bay, a virtual entertainment mecca and amusement park for adults. This oasis features 17 bars, including two floating on the bay. Wander from bar to bar or listen to live bands while floating on personal rafts. A magnificent sunset view ushers in early revelers for cocktails in the raft pool. (☎524-4900; www.seacrets.com. 21+. Cover Th $5 after 9pm, F-Sa $5 at 5pm and goes up $1 each hr. until 10pm. Open daily 11am-2am.) The elder statesman of the bayside clubs, **Fager's Island,** 60th St., in the bay, has hordes walking the plank to its island location. Live rock, R&B, jazz, and reggae play nightly to accompany the 100+ beers, and the *1812 Overture* booms every sunset. (☎524-5500; www.fagers.com. Dress code: no jerseys, caps, cutoffs, sleeveless shirts, or sagging, baggy, or oversized pants. 21+ after 8pm. Cover after 9pm $5. Open daily 11am-2am.) **The Party Block,** 17th St. and Coastal

Hwy., charges one cover for three different clubs: Rush Club plays hip-hop and techno, the Paddock has modern rock, and the dance party at the Big Kahuna grooves to 80s music. (☎289-6331; www.partyblock.com. $1.75 Budweiser long-necks. 21+. Cover $5-10 after 10pm. Open daily 8:30pm-2am.) If you're under 21 but want to party like you're older, check out the nightly dancing and occasional foam parties at **Club H2O**, at Worcester and the Boardwalk. (☎289-7102; www.partyblock.com. Cover $10 before 8:30pm, $20 after. Open daily 8pm-12:45am.)

WASHINGTON, D.C.

Visitors to the nation's capital often think they've seen it all after a tour of the White House and the Lincoln Memorial. But locals and savvy travelers know that D.C. is a thriving international metropolis and one of the most affordable cities in the country. Pierre L'Enfant's diamond-shaped dream now encompasses a bewildering array of world-class cultural and culinary delights, including the avant-garde galleries of Dupont Circle, the glittering mosaic of Adams Morgan nightlife, and the colonial chic of Georgetown. Now far more than just the world's most powerful city, D.C. has hit the big-time, with Broadway shows at the Kennedy Center, the latest bands jamming on the "New U" St. corridor, and (finally!) major-league baseball in front of positively giddy fans at RFK Stadium. For expanded coverage of the D.C. area, check out ■*Let's Go: Washington, D.C.*

■ INTERCITY TRANSPORTATION

Airports: Ronald Reagan National Airport (☎703-417-8000; www.mwaa.com/national). Metro: National Airport. If you're flying to D.C. from within the US, this airport is your best bet: it's on the Metro and close to the city. Taxi from downtown $12-15. The **SuperShuttle** bus (☎800-258-3826; www.supershuttle.com) runs between National and the city (about $10 per person). **Dulles International Airport** (☎703-572-2700; www.mwaa.com/dulles) is 25min. farther from the city. Taxis to downtown start at $45-50. The **Washington Flyer Coach Service** (☎888-927-4359; www.washfly.com) departs from Dulles every 30min. M-F 5:45am-10:15pm, Sa-Su 7:45am-10:15pm; from Metro: West Falls Church M-F 6:15am-10:45pm, Sa-Su 8:15am-10:45pm ($8; discounts for groups of 3 or more, seniors, and international students). Travel between Dulles and metro area takes approx. 30min. The **SuperShuttle** bus also runs from Dulles to downtown daily ($22, $10 each additional person).

Trains: Amtrak operates from Union Station, 50 Massachusetts Ave. NE (☎484-7540; www.amtrak.com). 12 trains per day to: **Baltimore** (30-45min., $17); **Boston** (7¾hr., $96); **New York City** (3¼hr., $80); **Philadelphia** (2hr., $51). Maryland's commuter rail, **MARC** (☎866-743-3682), runs from Union Station to **Baltimore** ($7) and the suburbs.

■ ORIENTATION

D.C. stretches in the four cardinal directions. The **Potomac River** forms the jagged southwest border, its waters flowing between the District and Arlington, VA. **North Capitol, East Capitol,** and **South Capitol Street** slice the city into four quadrants: NW, NE, SE, and SW. The **Mall** stretches west of the Capitol. The suffixes of the quadrants distinguish otherwise identical addresses in Washington's grid (e.g. 800 G St. NW and 800 G St. NE). Streets that run east-west are labeled alphabetically in relation to North Capitol St./South Capitol St., which runs through the Capitol. There is no J St. After W St., east-west streets take on two-syllable names, then three-syllable names, then the names of trees and flowers, all in roughly alphabetical order. Streets running north-south are numbered up to 52nd St. NW and 63rd St. NE. Addresses on lettered streets indicate the number of the cross street. For instance, 1100 D St. SE is on the corner of D and 11th. While navigation on foot is relatively easy, both drivers and pedestrians should be aware of possible road blocks and detour routes set up by city officials to protect the security of political buildings.

Major roads include **Pennsylvania Avenue, Connecticut Avenue, Wisconsin Avenue, 16th Street NW, K Street NW, Massachusetts Avenue, New York Avenue,** and **North Capitol Street.** D.C. is ringed by the **Capital Beltway** (**I-495**—except where it's part of I-95). The Beltway is bisected by **U.S. 1** and meets **I-395** from Virginia. The **Baltimore-Washington Parkway** connects Washington, D.C., to Baltimore, MD. **I-595** trickles off the Capital Beltway toward Annapolis, MD, and **I-66** heads west into Virginia.

NEIGHBORHOODS

Postcard-perfect, **Capitol Hill** symbolizes the democratic ideal, with the Capitol, Supreme Court, and Library of Congress all facing each other. Extending west from the Capitol building is the grassy pedestrian **Mall,** punctuated by the Washington Monument and World War II Memorial before it ends at the Lincoln Memorial. The Mall is flanked by the Smithsonian museums and the National Gallery of Art. Cherry trees ring the Jefferson Memorial and the Potomac River Tidal Basin, just south and directly across the Mall from the **White House,** which is north of the Mall at 1600 Pennsylvania Ave. The State Department, Kennedy Center, and the infamous Watergate Complex make up **Foggy Bottom,** on the west side of the city. The **Federal Triangle** area is home to a growing commercial and banking district. It's a wonderful (corporate) life along the glass-walled blocks of **Farragut,** where government agencies, lobbying firms, and lawyers feather their nests.

There's more to D.C. than politics, though. **Adams Morgan,** in the northwest, is a hub of nightlife and good food. In **Chinatown,** authentic Chinese restaurants bump up against the vast MCI Center and its ring of sports bars. Though its cobblestone back streets are home to Washington's power elite, picturesque **Georgetown** pairs its high-end shops with enough nightlife to keep any college student entertained. **Dupont Circle,** the city's cultural nexus, has developed a powerful trinity of good food, trendy clubs, and cutting-edge art galleries. At night, travelers should avoid walking through the circle itself. Another nighttime hot spot is the **U District,** a historically African-American area with clubs that blast trance and techno until the sun rises. Be careful in this area at night. **Upper Northwest,** an upper-class residential neighborhood, is home to American University and the National Zoo.

▐ LOCAL TRANSPORTATION

Public Transit: Washington Metropolitan Area Transit Authority (☎637-7000; www.wmata.com) operates the city's public transit. The subway, called the **"Metro,"** runs M-Th 5am-midnight, F 5am-3am, Sa 7am-3am, Su 7am-midnight. $1.35-3.90; day pass $6.50. The **Fast Pass** ($30) allows 7 days of unlimited travel. The **Metrobus** system serves Georgetown, downtown, and the suburbs. $1.25. Free bus transfers are available on the upper platforms of most subway stations.The **DC Circulator** (☎962-1423; www.dccirculator.com), is a cross-town bus that loops from Georgetown to Union Station and from the MCI Center to the SW Waterfront. Runs daily 7am-9pm. $1.

Taxi: Yellow Cab, ☎544-1212.

Car Rental: Union Station, 50 Massachusetts Ave., boasts several major rental agencies, including **Hertz Rent-a-Car** (☎842-0819; www.hertz.com) and **Budget** (☎800-527-0700; www.budget.com). Both open M-F 8am-6pm, Sa-Su 10am-6pm.

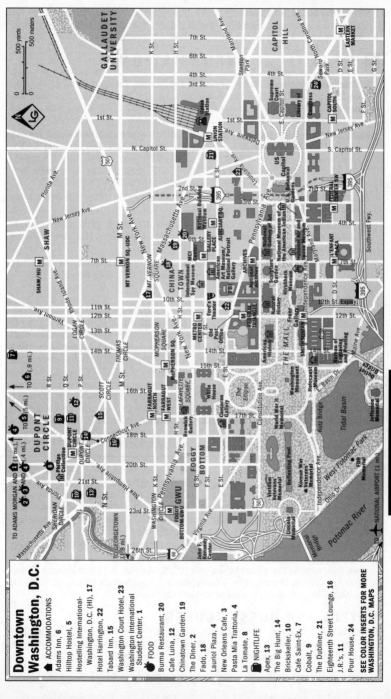

MID-ATLANTIC

Downtown Washington, D.C.

▲ ACCOMMODATIONS
Adams Inn, 6
Hilltop Hostel, 5
Hosteling International-
Washington, D.C. (HI), 17
Hotel Harrington, 22
Tabard Inn, 15
Washington Court Hotel, 23
Washington International
Student Center, 1

🍴 FOOD
Burma Restaurant, 20
Cafe Luna, 12
Chinatown Garden, 19
The Diner, 2
Fado, 18
Lauriol Plaza, 4
New Orleans Cafe, 3
Pasta Mia Trattoria, 4
La Tomate, 8

🍷 NIGHTLIFE
Apex, 13
The Big Hunt, 14
Brickskeller, 10
Cafe Saint-Ex, 7
Cobalt, 9
The Dubliner, 21
Eighteenth Street Lounge, 16
J.R.'s, 11
Pour House, 24

SEE COLOR INSERTS FOR MORE
WASHINGTON, D.C. MAPS

Bicycle Rental: Better Bikes (☎293-2080; www.betterbikesinc.com). 10-speed bikes $25 per day, $95 per week; mountain bikes $38/$185; hybrids $48/$215. Helmet, map, backpack, locks, and breakdown service included. $25 deposit. Open 24hr.

⚑ PRACTICAL INFORMATION

Visitor Info: Washington, D.C. Convention and Tourism Corporation, 1212 New York Ave. NW, Ste. 600 (☎789-7000; www.washington.org). Open M-F 9am-5pm. **D.C. Visitor Info Center,** in the Reagan International Trade Center, 1300 Pennsylvania Ave. NW (☎866-324-7386; www.dcvisit.com). Open M-F 8:30am-5:30pm, Sa 9am-4pm.

Hotlines: Rape Crisis Center, ☎333-7273. 24hr. **Gay and Lesbian National Hotline,** ☎888-843-4564. Operates M-F 4pm-midnight, Sa noon-5pm. **Traveler's Aid Society** (www.travelersaid.org) at Union Station (☎371-1937; open M-Sa 9:30am-5:30pm, Su 12:30-5:30pm), National Airport (☎703-417-3972; open M-F 9am-9pm, Sa-Su 9am-6pm), and Dulles Airport (☎703-572-8296; open M-F 8am-9pm, Sa-Su 8am-7pm).

Medical Services: Georgetown University Medical Center, 3800 Reservoir Rd. NW (☎444-2000; www.gumc.georgetown.edu).

Internet Access: The Cyberstop Cafe, 1513 17th St. NW (☎234-2470), near P St. Open M-F 7am-midnight, Sa-Su 8am-midnight. $7 per 30min., $9 per hr. Free wireless Internet with purchase from cafe.

Post Office: Martin Luther King, Jr. Station, 1400 L St., in the lobby (☎523-2001). Open M-F 8am-5:30pm, Sa 8am-2pm. **Postal Code:** 20005. **Area Code:** 202.

⚑ ACCOMMODATIONS

You might think that inexpensive lodgings in Washington, D.C. would be harder to come by than straight-talking politicians, but the sheer size of the city and its massive volume of tourist traffic support a few hostels and several relatively inexpensive B&Bs. Like other major cities in the US, D.C. charges a hefty hotel tax (14.5%).

HOSTELS

⚑ Hostelling International-Washington D.C. (HI), 1009 11th St. NW (☎737-2333; www.hiwashingtondc.org), 3 blocks north of Metro: Metro Center. Use caution in this area after dark. In the heart of D.C., 5 blocks from the White House. 250 beds and oodles of activities. Internet access $1 per 5min. Reception 24hr. Check-in 2pm-1am; call ahead if arriving later. Check-out 11am. Reservations recommended. Dorms $32-35, members $29-32. Singles $72/$69; doubles $82/$79. Wheelchair accessible. MC/V. ❷

Hilltop Hostel, 300 Carroll St. NW (☎291-9591), on the border of D.C. and Takoma Park, close to Metro: Takoma. Hostelers can come and go as they please, smoke and drink in certain areas, or fire up a grill in the backyard. A/C in some rooms. Free Internet access. Satellite TV, kitchen, and coin-op laundry. Linen included. 18+. 7-night max. stay. Reception 8am-midnight. Reservations recommended. Co-ed dorms $20. Private rooms with shared bath $42. Cash or traveler's check only. ❶

Washington International Student Center, 2451 18th St. NW (☎800-567-4150; www.washingtondchostel.com), in the middle of Adams Morgan. An incredible location, next door to some of the most fun nightlife D.C. has to offer. Breakfast included. Reception 8am-11pm. Towel service, kitchen, lockers, free Internet access, cable TV. No smoking. Co-ed dorms $25. Cash or traveler's check only. ❶

HOTELS AND GUEST HOUSES

⚑ Adams Inn, 1744 Lanier Pl. NW (☎745-3600 or 800-578-6807; www.adamsinn.com), 2 blocks north of the center of Adams Morgan. 25 rooms with A/C, tasteful furnishings, and private sinks (some with private bath). Complimentary continental breakfast and snacks. Cable TV in common area, free Internet access, and laundry facilities. Limited parking $10 per night. 2-night min. stay if staying Sa night. Reception M-Sa 8am-9pm, Su 1-9pm. Check-in 3-9pm. Check-out noon. Singles $80, with private bath $90; each additional person $10. AmEx/D/DC/MC/V. ❹

Tabard Inn, 1739 N St. NW (☎785-1277; www.tabardinn.com), between 17th and 18th St. 40 rooms in 3 townhouses done up with rich tapestry and hardwood floors. A/C, phone, wireless Internet, and data port (but no TV). Patio, bar, and lounges. Continental breakfast and passes to the YMCA included. Reception 24hr. Singles $98-128, with private bath $143-203; each additional person $15. AmEx/D/DC/MC/V. ❺

Hotel Harrington, 11th and E St. NW (☎628-8140). Metro: Metro Center or Federal Triangle. Simply furnished rooms with cable TV and A/C in a great location. Parking $10 per day. Double room with queen bed $89-99, two double beds $109, king bed $139-159. $10 off if you call ahead from the airport, train, or bus station; 10% off on stays of 5+ days. Student and AAA discount 10%. AmEx/D/DC/MC/V. ❹

Washington Court Hotel, 525 New Jersey Ave. NW (☎628-21000 or 800-321-3010; www.washingtoncourthotel.com). Metro: Union Station. A 5min. walk from the Capitol. Caters primarily to government contractors and their expense accounts, but has reasonable rates given its superb location and appealing amenities. Rooms come with marble bath, cable TV, A/C, and high-speed Internet. 2 double beds or king-sized bed $102, deluxe rooms $117. AAA discount 10%. AmEx/D/DC/MC/V. ❺

◪ FOOD

How do you feast like a senator on an intern's budget? Savvy natives go grubbing at happy hours, since bars often have free appetizer platters to bait early evening clients (see **Nightlife,** p. 283). For budget eateries, **Adams Morgan** and **Dupont Circle** are home to the *crème de la crème* of ethnic cuisine. Suburban **Bethesda, MD** (Metro: Bethesda), features over 100 restaurants within a four-block radius.

ADAMS MORGAN

▨ **New Orleans Cafe,** 2412 18th St. NW (☎234-0420). With Dixieland rattling the speakers, murals of jazz bands, and an owner who epitomizes Southern hospitality, this popular cafe rewards its customers with great jambalaya, Cajun linguine ($8-15), and gumbo ($4-8). Open Tu-F 11am-9:30pm, Sa-Su 10am-10pm. ❸

The Diner, 2453 18th St. NW (☎232-8800). The Diner's hours and quintessential American food earn it rave reviews from local college kids and other late-night revelers. Omelets $6-8. Pancakes $5. Burgers $6-8. Vegetarian options available. Open 24hr. ❷

Pasta Mia Trattoria, 1790 Columbia Rd. NW (☎328-9114), near 18th St. When the moon's in the sky like a big pizza pie, huge bowls of steaming pasta are *amore*. Pasta Mia is an aging but perennial favorite, serving generous helpings of Italian classics ($10-13) with a reasonable wine list ($16-30). The tortellini in a tomato-cream sauce is delicious. No reservations accepted. Open M-Sa 6:30-10pm. ❸

CHINATOWN

▨ **Burma Restaurant,** upstairs at 740 6th St. NW (☎638-1280), between G and H St. Burmese curries, unique spices, and a plethora of garnishes. Try the green tea salad ($7), followed by the squid sautéed in garlic, ginger, and scallions ($8). Vegetarians will enjoy the papaya and tofu salads ($6). Open M-F 11am-3pm and 6-10pm, Sa-Su 6-10pm. ❷

Chinatown Garden, 618 H St. NW (☎737-8887). Features an extensive 2-part menu—half Americanized fare, half authentic dishes. Try the lunch special ($6.50-7) if you're on a budget, or the sea cucumbers with stewed shrimp roe ($25) if you're feeling frisky. Lunch $6-8. Dinner $9-13. Open M-Th and Su 11am-11pm, F-Sa 11am-midnight. ❷

MID-ATLANTIC

Fado, 808 7th St. NW (☎789-0066). This old-world Irish restaurant has little trace of sports bar generics despite its location, right across the street from the MCI Center. Traditional fare (corned beef and cabbage; $16) and an all-day Irish breakfast ($14) are served alongside pub favorites like fish and chips ($9). Happy hour daily 4-7pm entails plenty of cheap finger food ($2). Open daily 11:30am-2am. ❸

DUPONT CIRCLE

▨ **Lauriol Plaza,** 1835 18th St. NW (☎387-0035), at T St., between Dupont Circle and Adams Morgan. Lauriol occupies half the block, with a rowdy roof deck and 3 magnificent floors of Mexican dining. Large entrees ($10-17), appetizers like fried plantains and guacamole ($4-7), and excellent margaritas ($5.50, pitchers $24). Free parking. No reservations accepted, and the wait grows exponentially, so arrive early. Su brunch 11:30am-3pm. Open M-Th and Su 11:30am-11pm, F-Sa 11:30am-midnight. ❹

La Tomate, 1701 Connecticut Ave. NW (☎667-5505), at R St. This Dupont Circle mainstay features attentive service, a creative menu, and some of the best outdoor seating in the entire city. Pastas ($13-18) include the delectable *farfalle prosciutto e funghi* (bowtie pasta with prosciutto, mushrooms, and cream; $15). Entrees $15-27. Reservations recommended. Open M-Th 11:30am-11pm, F-Sa 11:30am-11:30pm, Su 11:30am-10pm. ❹

Cafe Luna, 1633 P St. NW (☎387-4005), near 17th St. A popular basement restaurant serving a mix of Italian, vegetarian, and low-fat fare. Breakfast ($2-5) served all day. Huge sandwiches ($4-6) satisfy almost any appetite. W and Su half-price pizzas (otherwise $5-7). Brunch Sa-Su 10am-3pm. Open M-Th 8am-11:30pm, F 8am-1am, Sa 10am-1:30am, Su 10am-11:30pm. ❶

GEORGETOWN

▨ **Clyde's of Georgetown,** 3236 M St. NW (☎333-9180), between Potomac St. and Wisconsin Ave. Join the crowds of preppy students and professor-types at Clyde's for delicious sandwiches ($7-12), salads ($12-14), seafood ($13-17), and pasta ($13-15). Open M-Th 11:30am-2am, F 11:30am-3am, Sa 10am-3am, Su 9am-2am. ❹

Red Ginger, 1564 Wisconsin Ave. NW (☎965-7009), serves flavorful Caribbean food, like curried oxtail stew ($15) and adobo-spiced duck with quinoa pumpkin salad ($21). Complimentary champagne tops off the weekend brunch (Sa-Su 11:30am-5pm). Open Tu-Th and Su 11:30am-10pm, F-Sa 11:30am-11pm. ❹

Moby Dick House of Kabob, 1070 31st St. NW (☎333-4400). A local favorite, the huge, cheap portions of Greek food at this ramshackle hole-in-the-wall will leave you feeling like a whale beached and gone to heaven. Get salads ($4), gyros ($6), or combo meals ($8) to go, and enjoy on a quiet bench by the C&O canal, just around the corner. Open M-Th 10am-11pm, F-Sa 11am-4am, Su noon-10pm. ❶

Patisserie Poupon, 1645 Wisconsin Ave. NW (☎342-3248), near Q St. Start the day with a buttery brioche, pear danish, or croissant ($1.30-2.25). Sandwiches and salads $4-7. Open Tu-Sa 8am-6:30pm, Su 8am-4pm. ❶

UPPER NORTHWEST

▨ **2 Amys Neapolitan Pizzeria,** 3715 Macomb St. NW (☎885-5700), near Wisconsin Ave. Superb, fresh-from-the-oven pizzas ($8-13) in a pastel yellow and orange dining area. The "Narcia" pizza (tomato, salami, roasted peppers, mozzarella, and garlic; $13) is excellent. Many locals consider this Washington's best pizza—expect a wait at dinnertime. Open Tu-Sa 11am-11pm, Su noon-10pm. ❸

Yanni's, 3500 Connecticut Ave. NW (☎362-8871). Find home-style Greek cooking in this airy restaurant, adorned with classical statues and murals of Greek gods. Try charbroiled octopus, crunchy on the outside and delicately tender within, served with rice and vegetables ($13). Entrees $6-17 (vegetarian options $9-12). Strong Greek coffee ($2.50) goes well with the baklava ($4.50). Open daily 11:30am-11pm. ❸

Max's Best Ice Cream, 2416 Wisconsin Ave. NW (☎333-3111), just south of Calvert St. Known in D.C. as the premier purveyor of homemade ice cream, Max himself dishes out old favorites and exotic flavors. The only hard part is picking between lychee, lemon cream, and Heath bar. Single scoop $3. Open M-Sa noon-midnight, Su noon-10pm. ❶

Mama Maria and Enzio's, 2313 Wisconsin Ave. NW (☎965-1337), near Calvert St. Amazing southern Italian cuisine with a casual, family atmosphere and exceptionally warm service. Shrimp in lemon sauce ($16) is worth the price. Pizzas $9-12. Calzones $7. Cannoli $5. Lunch $7-11. Open M-F 11:30am-10pm, Sa 5-10pm, Su 5-9pm. ❸

◉ 🏛 SIGHTS AND MUSEUMS

CAPITOL HILL

THE CAPITOL. The ▉US Capitol impresses visitors with a grandeur uncommon even among the city's other historical buildings and memorials. From the time of nineteenth-century frontiersman Andrew Jackson to the present, it has been the site of the presidential inauguration. The East Front entrance, facing the Supreme Court, brings visitors into the 180 ft. high rotunda, where soldiers slept during the Civil War. From the lower-level crypt, visitors can climb to the second floor for a view of the House or Senate visitors chambers. Though much of the real political action takes place behind the scenes, visitors can get gallery passes to view the legislature at work—just don't be disappointed if all that's going on is a roll call vote. Americans may obtain gallery passes from the office of their representative or senator in the House or Senate office buildings near the Capitol; foreigners can get one-day passes by presenting identification at the appointments desks in the crypt. *(Metro: Capitol South or Union Station. ☎225-6827; www.aoc.gov. Generally open M-Sa 9am-4:30pm. Access by 30min. guided tour only. Free, but tickets are required. Same-day tickets available at the Garfield Circle kiosk on the West Front, across from the Botanic Gardens. Kiosk is open from 9am until all tickets are distributed; get there about 45-60min. before opening to guarantee a ticket.)* The real business of Congress, however, is conducted in **committee hearings.** Most are open to the public; check the *Washington Post*'s "Today in Congress" box for times and locations. If you can find a senator to chaperone you, you can take a ride on the free **Capitol subway** (the "Capitol Choo-Choo"), which shuttles between the basement of the Capitol and the House and Senate office buildings; a buzzer and flashing light signal an imminent vote.

SUPREME COURT. In 1935, the **Supreme Court** justices decided it was time to take the nation's separation of powers literally and moved from their makeshift offices in the Capitol into a new Greek Revival courthouse across the street. Oral arguments are open to the public; show up early to get a seat. *(1 1st St. Metro: Capitol South or Union Station. ☎479-3221; www.supremecourtus.gov. In session Oct.-June M-W 10am-noon and open 1-3pm for 2 weeks every month; courtroom open when Justices are on vacation. The "3min. line" shuffles visitors through standing gallery of the courtroom for a glimpse. Court open M-F 9am-4:30pm. Seating before 8:30am. Free.)*

LIBRARY OF CONGRESS. With over 126 million objects stored on 532 mi. of shelves (including a copy of *Old King Cole* written on a grain of rice), the ▉**Library of Congress** is the largest library in the world. The collection was torched by the British in 1814 and then restarted using Thomas Jefferson's personal stocks. These

SECRET SYMBOLS

No need to confine your conspiracy theories to the CIA or FBI—an initiated eye can spot the influence of Freemasonry practically everywhere you look in D.C. This secret society pervaded the Revolutionary generation—52 of the original 55 signatories of the Declaration of Independence were Masons. Capitol architect Benjamin Latrobe, White House architect James Hoban, Washington Monument architect Robert Mills: all Masons. The George Washington Masonic Memorial features a large mural depicting the man himself laying the cornerstone of the Capitol in full Masonic regalia.

The very shape of the city reflects the tenets of Freemasonry, which treasures symbols like the builder's square. Look at the original plan for Washington, D.C., which used to encompass Arlington, VA, and a square is exactly what you get. Members seek to "turn to the light," so perhaps it's no mistake that the statue of Freedom atop the Capitol faces due east, towards the rising sun. Freemasons were also taken with Egyptian symbolism, traces of which can be seen in many of the city's memorials, including one tall, central monument in particular.

Interested in exploring these symbols? The **George Washington National Masonic Memorial** now gives free tours that explore the famous Freemason's life. Call ☎ 703-683-2007 for info.

days, it's open to anyone of college age or older with a legitimate research purpose. A tour of the facilities is also available; exhibits change frequently and range from collections of Pulitzer Prize-winning political cartoons to texts documenting the Supreme Court decisions that ended racial segregation in public schools. The **Jefferson Building's** green copper dome and gold-leafed flame top a spectacular reading room. *(1st St. SE. Metro: Capitol South. ☎ 707-5000; www.loc.gov. Great Hall open M-Sa 10am-5:30pm. Tours M-F 10:30, 11:30am, 1:30, 2:30, and 3:30pm; Sa 10:30, 11:30am, 1:30, and 2:30pm. Visitors center and galleries open daily 10am-5pm. Free.)*

MONUMENTS

■ **WASHINGTON MONUMENT.** With a $9.4 million restoration project completed in 1999, this shrine to America's very first president is incredible. Once nicknamed the "the Beef Depot monument" after the cattle that grazed in the surrounding area here during the Civil War, the Washington Monument was built with rock from multiple quarries, which explains the stones' multiple colors. The beautiful **Reflecting Pool** mirrors Washington's obelisk. *(Metro: Smithsonian. ☎ 426-6841; www.nps.gov/wamo/homt.htm. Open daily 9am-5pm. Tours every 30min. 9am-4:30pm. Admission to the monument by timed ticket. Free if obtained on day of visit; arrive early. $1.50 if reserved in advance.)*

■ **VIETNAM VETERANS MEMORIAL.** Maya Lin, who designed the Vietnam Veterans Memorial, received a "B" when she submitted her memorial concept for a grade as a Yale senior. She went on to beat her professor in the public memorial design competition. In her words, the monument is "a rift in the earth—a long, polished black stone wall, emerging from and receding into the earth." The wall contains the names of the 58,235 Americans who died in Vietnam, indexed in books at both ends. *(Constitution Ave. at 22nd St. NW. Metro: Smithsonian or Foggy Bottom-GWU. ☎ 634-1568; www.nps.gov/vive. Open 24hr. Free.)*

■ **LINCOLN MEMORIAL.** The Lincoln Memorial, at the west end of the Mall, recalls the rectangular grandeur of Athens's Parthenon, complete with 36 Doric columns. It was from these steps that Martin Luther King, Jr. gave his famous "I Have a Dream" speech during the 1963 March on Washington, D.C. Inside, a seated Lincoln presides over the admiring visitors. Though you may find Lincoln's lap inviting, climbing on the 19 ft. president is a federal offense; a camera will catch you if the rangers don't do it first. *(Metro: Smithsonian or Foggy Bottom-GWU. ☎ 426-6841; www.nps.gov/linc. Open 24hr. Free.)*

JEFFERSON MEMORIAL. A 19 ft. hollow bronze statue of Thomas Jefferson stands in this open-air rotunda, encircled by massive Ionic columns and overlooking the Tidal Basin. Quotes from the Declaration of Independence, the Virginia Statute of Religious Freedom, and *Notes on Virginia* adorn the walls. *(A long walk from Metro: L'Enfant Plaza or Smithsonian. ☎ 426-6841; www.nps.gov/thje. Open 24hr. Free.)*

KOREAN WAR MEMORIAL. The 19 colossal polished-steel statues of the Korean War Memorial trudge up a hill, rifles in hand, expressions of weariness and fear frozen upon their faces. The statues are accompanied by a black granite wall with over 2000 sandblasted photographic images from this war, in which 54,246 Americans lost their lives. *(At the west end of the Mall, near Lincoln. Metro: Smithsonian. ☎ 426-6841; www.nps.gov/kwvm. Open daily 8am-midnight. Free.)*

FRANKLIN DELANO ROOSEVELT MEMORIAL. Occupying a broad stretch of West Potomac Park, the FDR Memorial deviates from the presidential tributes nearby, replacing their marble statuary with serene sculpted gardens, cascading fountains, and thematic alcoves. Four "rooms" each represent a phase of FDR's lengthy presidency. Whether or not to display the disabled Roosevelt in his wheelchair was hotly debated; as a compromise, Roosevelt is shown seated, as in a famous picture of him taken at Yalta. *(A long walk from Metro: Smithsonian, but a short walk from the Jefferson or Lincoln Memorials. ☎ 426-6841; www.nps.gov/fdrm. Open daily 8am-midnight. Free.)*

NATIONAL WWII MEMORIAL. Its prominence of place on the Mall may have been a subject of local controversy, but this newest monument makes clear how impossible it is to understate the impact of World War II on modern American history. This immense neo-classical plaza is part tribute to the 16 million Americans who served in the armed forces during WWII, including the more than 400,000 soldiers who died, and part triumphal arch, with an archway symbolizing each of the major theaters of battle, 56 granite pillars to represent the contribution of each of the US's states and territories, and a shimmering rainbow pool. *(Metro: Smithsonian or Foggy Bottom-GWU. ☎ 426-6841; www.nps.gov/nwwm. Open 24hr. Free.)*

THE MALL

The Smithsonian Institution's museums on the Mall constitute the world's largest museum complex. The **Smithsonian Castle,** on the south side of the Mall, has an introduction to and info on all of the Smithsonian buildings. (Metro: Smithsonian or Federal Triangle. ☎ 357-2700; www.si.edu. Castle open daily 8:30am-5:30pm.)

■ **NATIONAL AIR AND SPACE MUSEUM.** This is the world's most popular museum, with 7.5 million visitors each year. Record-breaking airplanes and space vehicles hang from the ceilings. Exhibits include the Wright brothers' original biplane, which hangs in the entrance gallery, the walk-through Skylab space station, the Apollo XI command module, and a DC-7. *(On the south side of the Mall. Metro: Smithsonian or Federal Triangle. ☎ 357-2700; www.nasm.si.edu.)*

■ **NATIONAL GALLERY OF ART.** The National Gallery is not a part of the Smithsonian, but is considered a close cousin because of its prime Mall-front location. The West Building, the gallery's original home, contains masterpieces by Leonardo da Vinci, El Greco, Rembrandt, Vermeer, and Monet. The East Building is devoted to 20th-century art, from Magritte and Matisse to Man Ray and Miró. Don't miss the whimsical sculpture garden behind the West Building. *(Metro: Smithsonian or Federal Triangle. ☎ 737-4215; www.nga.gov. Open M-Sa 10am-5pm, Su 11am-6pm.)*

HIRSHHORN MUSEUM AND SCULPTURE GARDEN. The Hirshhorn is D.C.'s best collection of modern, postmodern, and post-post-modern works from around the world. The slide-carousel-shaped building has outraged traditionalists since 1966.

Each floor consists of two concentric circles: an outer ring of paintings and an inner corridor of sculptures. *(On the south side of the Mall, west of Air and Space. Metro: Smithsonian.* ☎ *633-4674; http://hirshhorn.si.edu. Open daily 10am-5:30pm. Free.)*

FREER GALLERY OF ART. The Freer's collection is an intriguing jumble of American and Asian art. The permanent American collection, as dictated by Charles L. Freer himself, focuses on works by James McNeill Whistler. The rotating Asian collections have pieces from 2500 BC through the present. *(On the south side of the Mall, just west of the Hirshhorn. Metro: Smithsonian or Federal Triangle.* ☎ *357-4880; www.asia.si.edu. Open daily 10am-5:30pm. Free.)*

NATIONAL MUSEUM OF AMERICAN HISTORY (NMAH). The NMAH's plexiglass-encased clutter of old goods have earned it the nickname "the nation's attic." When the Smithsonian Institution inherits quirky pop culture artifacts, like Dorothy's slippers from *The Wizard of Oz*, they end up here. The Hands On History Room contains a working telegraph and an interactive introduction to the Cherokee language. *(On the north side of the mall. Metro: Smithsonian or Federal Triangle.* ☎ *357-2700; http://americanhistory.si.edu. Open daily 10am-5:30pm. Free.)*

NATIONAL MUSEUM OF NATURAL HISTORY (NMNH). The NMNH contains three floors of rocks, animals, gift shops, and displays selected from the museum's 124 million possessions. The Hope Diamond and dinosaur skeletons are major attractions. The Behring Hall of Mammals presents stuffed and fossilized mammals in recreations of their natural habitats. The museum is rightly proud of its new IMAX & Jazz Cafe, where you can enjoy a live performance and then take in the latest nature/action film. *(Metro: Smithsonian or Federal Triangle.* ☎ *633-1000; www.mnh.si.edu. Open daily 10am-5:30pm. Free. IMAX & Jazz shows F 6-10pm; cover $10.)*

OTHER MUSEUMS. Built in 1987, the **National Museum of African Art** and the **Arthur M. Sackler Gallery** hide their treasures underground, below the four-acre **Enid A. Haupt Garden.** The Museum of African Art displays artifacts from sub-Saharan Africa, such as masks, ceremonial figures, and musical instruments. *(Metro: Smithsonian or Federal Triangle.* ☎ *633-4600; www.nmafa.si.edu. Open daily 10am-5:30pm. Free.)* The Sackler Gallery showcases an extensive collection of illuminated manuscripts, Chinese and Japanese paintings, jade miniatures, and friezes from Egypt, Phoenicia, and Sumeria. *(Metro: Smithsonian or Federal Triangle.* ☎ *633-4880; www.asia.si.edu. Open daily 10am-5:30pm. Free.)* The Smithsonian's newest addition to the Mall is the sweeping **National Museum of the American Indian.** Created through ongoing collaboration with existing American Indian tribes, the exhibits focus on contemporary interpretation and performance to retell the stories of Native American peoples from the Inca to the Inuit. *(Metro: Smithsonian or Federal Triangle.* ☎ *633-1000; www.nmai.si.edu. Open daily 10am-5:30pm. Free.)*

SOUTH OF THE MALL

■**HOLOCAUST MEMORIAL MUSEUM.** Opened in 1993, the privately-funded Holocaust Memorial Museum examines the atrocities of the Holocaust. Special exhibitions, which can be viewed without passes, include the **Wall of Remembrance,** a touching collection of tiles painted by American schoolchildren in memory of the 1.5 million children killed during the Holocaust, the Wexner Learning Center, and an orientation film *(every 30min. 10:15am-4:15pm).* The permanent gallery is divided into three chronologically organized floors. *(14th St. between C St. and Independence Ave. SW. Metro: Smithsonian.* ☎ *488-0400; www.ushmm.org. Open daily 10am-5:30pm. Free. Not recommended for children under 11; kids can tour the exhibition "Daniel's Story," an account of Nazi occupation told from a child's perspective. Arrive early to ensure tickets.)*

BUREAU OF ENGRAVING AND PRINTING. The buck starts here, at the Bureau of Engraving and Printing, the largest producer of currency, stamps, and security documents in the world. Guided tours of the presses that print $696 million in money and stamps each day are available. *(At 14th and C St. SW. Metro: Smithsonian. ☎874-2330 or 866-874-2330; www.moneyfactory.com. Mar.-Sept. ticket booth opens M-F at 8am to distribute free tickets for same-day tours 9am-2pm. Arrive early to obtain tickets, most are gone by 9am. Oct.-Feb. no tickets required. Tours 10am-2pm.)*

FEDERAL TRIANGLE

■ **NATIONAL ARCHIVES.** Visitors line up at the National Archives to view the original Declaration of Independence, US Constitution, and Bill of Rights as they make their daily appearance from the recesses of a nuclear-bomb-proof vault. This building houses 16 million pictures and posters, 18 million maps, and billions of pages of text—about 2-5% of the documents the government produces each year. *(8th St. and Constitution Ave. NW. Metro: Archives-Navy Memorial. ☎501-5000; www.nara.gov. Open daily Apr. to early Sept. 10am-9pm; early Sept. to Mar. 10am-5:30pm. Free.)*

INTERNATIONAL SPY MUSEUM. Visitors navigating the flash-bang movie set-like backdrops may wonder whether this is an amusement park about to blow its museum cover, but the Spy Museum is legitimately overloaded with fascinating facts and artifacts from centuries of espionage, doing justice to the city with the world's highest concentration of spies. *(800 F St. NW, at 9th St. Metro: Gallery Place-Chinatown. ☎393-7798; www.spymuseum.org. Open daily Apr.-Aug. 9am-8pm; Aug.-Oct. 10am-8pm; Oct.-Mar. 10am-6pm. Last admission 2hr. before closing. Tickets with timed admission $14, seniors and military $13, children $11, under 5 free. Long lines late in the day yield entry times that may be more than 1hr. after ticket purchase.)*

FEDERAL BUREAU OF INVESTIGATION. The **J. Edgar Hoover Building** closed to visitors in 2002 for extensive renovations. Tours are expected to resume sometime in late 2005; call for details. *(935 Pennsylvania Ave. NW. ☎324-3447; www.fbi.gov.)*

FORD'S THEATER. John Wilkes Booth shot President Abraham Lincoln during a performance at the preserved Ford's Theater. Nonetheless, every president since 1868 has taken his chances and seen a play at here at least once a year. Of course, they sit front row center to avoid the unlucky box. Park rangers describe the events with animated gusto during a 15min. talk. *(511 10th St. NW. Metro: Metro Center. ☎426-6924; www.nps.gov/foth. Open daily 9am-5pm. Free. Talks in the theater at 9:15, 10:15, 11:15am, 2:15, 3:15, 4:15pm. Shows: www.fordstheatre.org. Sept.-May. Nighttime shows Tu-Su 7:30pm, $25-42; matinees M-F noon, $30-36; Sa-Su 2:30pm, $35-48.)*

OLD POST OFFICE. A refuge from D.C.'s summer heat, this classical masterpiece of arched windows, conical turrets, and a clock tower actually holds an expansive food court and shopping pavilion. If you can't make it up to the Washington Monument, the Old Post Office's soaring tower has the second-best view of the city. *(Pennsylvania Ave. and 12th St. NW. Metro: Federal Triangle. ☎289-4224; www.oldpostofficedc.com. Tower open mid-Apr. to mid-Sept. M-Sa 9am-7:45pm, Su 10am-5:45pm; low season M-F 9am-4:45pm, Sa-Su 10am-5:45pm. Shops open M-Sa 10am-7pm, Su noon-6pm. Free.)*

NATIONAL MUSEUM OF WOMEN IN THE ARTS. In a former Masonic Temple, the National Museum of Women in the Arts showcases works by the likes of Mary Cassatt, Georgia O'Keeffe, and Frida Kahlo. This museum is the only one in the world dedicated solely to the celebration of achievements of women in the visual, performing, and literary arts, and is comprised of over 3000 pieces dating from the 16th century to the present. *(1250 New York Ave. NW. Metro: Metro Center. ☎783-5000; www.nmwa.org. Open M-Sa 10am-5pm, Su noon-5pm. $8, ages 60+ and students $6, ages 18 and under free. 1st Su and W of each month free.)*

WHITE HOUSE AND FOGGY BOTTOM

■ **WHITE HOUSE.** With its simple columns and expansive lawns, the White House seems a compromise between patrician lavishness and democratic simplicity. Thomas Jefferson proposed a design for the building, but his entry lost to that of amateur architect James Hoban. Today the President's staff works in the West Wing, while the First Lady's cohorts occupy the East Wing. Staff who cannot fit in the White House work in the nearby **Old Executive Office Building.** The President's official office is the **Oval Office,** site of many televised speeches. *(1600 Pennsylvania Ave. NW. ☎456-7041; www.whitehouse.gov. Tours of the White House can be arranged only by calling your congressional representative more than 1 month in advance. Phone numbers for representatives available at www.house.gov. All tours free.)*

LAFAYETTE PARK. Historic homes surround Lafayette Park north of the White House and include the Smithsonian-owned **Renwick Gallery Craft Museum,** which has some remarkable 1980s sculptures. *(17th St. and Pennsylvania Ave. NW. Metro: Farragut North, Farragut West, or McPherson Sq. ☎633-2850; www.nmaa.si.edu. Open daily 10am-5:30pm. Free.)* The nearby neo-classical **Corcoran Gallery** boasts an expansive collection ranging from colonial to contemporary American art. *(17th St. between E St. and New York Ave. NW. ☎639-1700; www.corcoran.org. Open M, W, F-Su 10am-5pm, Th 10am-9pm. Free tours daily noon, Th 7:30pm, Sa-Su 2:30pm. $6.75, seniors $4.75, students $3; families $12. Free all day M and Th 5-9pm.)* The **Octagon House,** designed by Capitol architect William Thornton, was home to President and Mrs. Madison after the White House was burned down by British soldiers during the War of 1812. Today it is a restored example of Federalist architecture and allegedly houses several ghosts. *(Open Tu-Su 10am-4pm. $5, seniors and students $3.)*

KENNEDY CENTER. Completed in the late 1960s, the **John F. Kennedy Center for the Performing Arts** is a monument to the assassinated president, boasting four major stages, a film theater, three breathtaking halls replete with sumptuous red carpets and crystal chandeliers, and a roof deck with stunning views of the Potomac and the D.C. skyline. *(25th St. and New Hampshire Ave. NW. Metro: Foggy Bottom-GWU. ☎467-4600 or 800-444-1324; www.kennedy-center.org. Open daily 10am-midnight. Free tours leave from the level A gift shop M-F 10am-5pm, Sa-Su 10am-1pm; call ☎416-8340.)* Across the street is "Tricky Dick" Nixon's **Watergate Complex.**

GEORGETOWN

■ **DUMBARTON OAKS ESTATE.** Home to several acres of some of the most beautiful gardens in Washington, Dumbarton Oaks was the site of the 1944 Dumbarton Oaks Conference, which helped form the United Nations charter. The estate is now a museum with an impressive collection of Byzantine and pre-Columbian art. *(1703 32nd St. NW, between R and S St. ☎339-6401, tour info 339-6409; www.doaks.org. Mansion: Open Tu-Su 2-5pm. Suggested donation $1. Gardens: Open daily mid-Mar. to Oct. 2-6pm. $6, seniors and children $4; also Nov. to mid-Mar. 2-5pm, free.)*

GEORGETOWN UNIVERSITY. Archbishop John Carroll oversaw construction in 1788, and Georgetown University opened the following year, becoming the nation's first Catholic institution for higher learning. Today the original neo-gothic spires overlook a bustling campus, with several stores, cafes, and sporting venues open to the public. *(37th and O St. ☎687-3600; www.georgetown.edu. Campus tours M-Sa mornings through the admissions office; call for details.)*

UPPER NORTHWEST

■ **WASHINGTON NATIONAL CATHEDRAL.** Since the Cathedral's construction in 1909, religious leaders from Rev. Martin Luther King, Jr. to the Dalai Lama have preached from its pulpit. The solemnity of the vast gothic nave is lightened by fanciful stained glass and sculpture, including a Darth Vader gargoyle near the ceiling. The Pilgrim Observation Gallery reveals D.C. from the city's highest vantage point. *(Massachusetts and Wisconsin Ave. NW. From Metro: Tenleytown, take a 30-series bus toward Georgetown, or walk up Cathedral Ave. from Metro: Woodley Park-Zoo. ☎ 537-6200; www.nationalcathedral.org. Open mid-May to early Sept. M-F 10am-5:30pm, Sa 10am-4pm, Su 8am-6:30pm; early Sept. to mid-May M-F 10am-5:30pm. Su mass 8, 9, 11am. Organ demonstration 12:45pm. Tours M-F 10am-11:30am and 12:45-4pm, Sa 10-11:30am and 12:45-3:15pm, Su 12:45-2:30pm. Suggested donation $3, seniors $2, children $1. Behind-the-scenes tours July-Feb. M-F at 10:30am and 1:30pm, $10.)*

NATIONAL ZOO. Founded in 1889 and designed by Frederick Law Olmsted, who also designed New York City's Central Park (p. 182), the National Zoo is one of D.C.'s least crowded sights. Tigers, elephants, and gorillas (oh my!) await. The zoo's giant pandas are perpetual Washington celebrities; their cub is expected to begin receiving visitors in 2006. The zoo also features two roaming endangered golden lion tamarin monkeys who wander the grounds freely. *(3001 Connecticut Ave. Metro: Woodley Park-Zoo. ☎ 673-4800; www.si.edu/natzoo. Grounds open daily Apr.-Oct. 6am-8pm; Nov.-Mar. 6am-6pm. Zoo buildings open daily Apr.-Oct. 10am-6pm, Nov.-Mar. 10am-4:30pm. Free.)*

DUPONT CIRCLE

■ **PHILLIPS COLLECTION.** Situated in a stately mansion, the Phillips was the nation's first museum of modern art and still turns heads with its variety of Impressionist and Post-Impressionist masters. Visitors gape at Renoir's masterpiece, *Luncheon of the Boating Party*, and works by Delacroix, Miró, and Turner. *(1600 21st St., at Q St. NW. ☎ 387-2151; www.phillipscollection.org. Open Tu-W and F-Sa 10am-5pm, Th 10am-8:30pm; in summer also Su noon-5pm. Tu-F permanent collection free; Sa $8, students and seniors $6, 18 and under free. Audio tours free with admission.)*

ART GALLERY DISTRICT. A triangle of creativity, the **Art Gallery District** contains over two dozen galleries displaying everything from contemporary photographs to tribal crafts. They hold a joint open house on the first Friday of each month (6-8pm) with complimentary drinks at each venue. *(Bounded by Connecticut Ave., Florida Ave., and Q St. www.artgalleriesdc.com lists any changes to open house schedule.)*

EMBASSY ROW. The stretch of Massachusetts Ave. between Dupont Circle and Observatory Circle is also called **Embassy Row.** Before the 1930s, socialites lived along the avenue in extravagant edifices; diplomats later found the mansions perfect for their purposes (and sky-high budgets). At the northern end of Embassy Row, flags line the entrance to the **Islamic Center.** Inside the brilliant white mosque, stunning designs stretch to the tips of spired ceilings. *(2551 Massachusetts Ave. NW. ☎ 332-8343. No shorts allowed; women must cover their heads, arms, and legs. Open daily 10am-5pm; prayers 5 times daily.)*

🎵 ENTERTAINMENT

MUSIC

The D.C. punk scene is, or at least was, one of the nation's finest, but performers of all kinds call on the city. Check the *Weekend* section in the Friday edition of the Washington Post for details on upcoming concerts, shows, and other events. The bigger, more mainstream events take place at the sports arenas: **RFK Stadium,** 2400 E. Capitol St., in the summer (box office ☎608-1119; open M-F noon-5pm), and the **MCI Center,** 601 F St., year-round (box office ☎628-3200; open daily 10am-5:30pm). In its 73rd season, the ▓**National Symphony Orchestra** continues to delight D.C., primarily in the Kennedy Center's concert hall (☎467-4600 or 800-444-1324; www.kennedy-center.org/nso). D.C. also has a diverse and thriving jazz and blues scene, with venues perfect for any budget. The **Kennedy Center** (p. 280) and **Smithsonian Museums** (p. 277) often sponsor free shows, especially in the summer.

THEATER AND DANCE

Arena Stage, 6th St. and Maine Ave. SW, is often called the best regional theater company in America due to its innovative take on classics and frequent successes with new works. (☎488-3300; www.arenastage.org. Metro: Waterfront. Box office open M-Sa 10am-8pm, Su noon-8pm. Tickets $45-66. Discounts for students, seniors, and the disabled. A limited number of half-price tickets usually available 1½hr. before start of show.) The ▓**Kennedy Center,** at 25th St. and New Hampshire Ave., presents various ballet, opera, and dramatic productions. (☎416-8000, for rush tickets info 467-4600; www.kennedy-center.org. Tickets $10-75.) The **Shakespeare Theatre** at the Lansburgh, 450 7th St. NW, at Pennsylvania Ave., puts on lively performances. The company's 2006 schedule includes *Don Juan* (Jan. 24-Mar. 19), *The Persians* (Apr. 4-May 21), and *Love's Labor's Lost* (June 6-July 30). Each summer the theater puts on the "Free for All," a no-charge production of a Shakespearean work, usually one of the comedies. (Metro: Archives-Navy Memorial. ☎547-1122 or 877-487-8849; www.shakespearetheatre.org. Tickets $23-68; during preview week $13-59. Discounts for students and seniors. $10 standing-room tickets available 1hr. before sold-out performances.) To further satisfy any Shakespearean craving, head to the stately **Folger Theater,** 201 E. Capitol St. SE. The theater is a reproduction of the Bard's Globe in London, and a small museum is adjacent to the performance space. In 2006, you'll find *Measure for Measure* (Jan. 9-Feb. 26) and *The Game of Love and Chance* (Apr. 7-May 14). Students receive 20-25% discounts on most regular tickets and 50% rush discounts 1hr. prior to showtime. Seniors, teachers, and military personnel receive 15-20% discounts on most regular tickets. (☎544-7077; www.folger.edu. Box office open M-F 10am-5pm in person, M-Sa noon-4pm by phone.) In the **14th Street Theater District,** tiny repertory companies explore and experiment with new shows; check *CityPaper* for listings. ▓**The Source Theatre,** 1835 14th St. NW, between S and T St., is dedicated to the local community of artists. (Metro: U St.-Cardozo. ☎462-1073; www.sourcetheatre.com.) The famous ▓**Woolly Mammoth Theater Company** offers pay-what-you-can and under-25 performances of contemporary works. (Metro: Gallery Place-Chinatown. ☎393-3939; www.woollymammoth.net.)

SPORTS

The 20,000-seat **MCI Center,** 601 F St. NW, in Chinatown, is D.C.'s premiere sports arena. (☎628-3200. Metro: Gallery Pl.-Chinatown. Open daily 10am-5:30pm.) Having finally earned some respect for their astounding 2005 season, the **Wizards** are no longer the laughingstock of the NBA. (☎661-5065; www.washingtonwizards.com. Tickets $7-120.) The WNBA's **Mystics** play from May to September. (www.wnba.com/mystics. Tickets $8-60.) The **Capitals** are back with the rest of the NHL for the 2006 season, running October-April. (☎661-5065; www.washingtoncaps.com. Tickets $10-100.) Washington's most successful and least known pro sports team is soccer's **D.C. United,** with a strong local fan base and several MLS championship titles. (☎587-5000; http://dcunited.mlsnet.com. Tickets $16-$40.) Washington's current heroes are the **Nationals,** who round the bases in **RFK Stadium.** (http://washington.nationals.mlb.com. Tickets $5-65.) Will Washington, D.C.

always remain a football town? Their beloved, if politically incorrect, **Redskins** still draw faithful to **Fed-Ex Field**, Raljon Dr., in Raljon, MD. (☎301-276-6050; www.redskins.com. Season runs Sept.-Dec. Tickets $40-200.)

◤ NIGHTLIFE

BARS AND CLUBS

Talk about a double life: D.C. denizens who crawl through red tape by day paint the town red by night. If you find yourself taking Jell-O body shots off a beautiful stranger at an all-you-can-drink-fest, don't say we didn't warn you. If you ache for a pint of amber ale, swing by the Irish pub-laden **Capitol Hill.** Hit up **Georgetown** for youthful prepsters in upscale bars. **Dupont Circle** is home to glam GLBT nightlife, while **Adams Morgan** hosts an international crowd. To party with rock stars, head to the hopping **U District.** For more tips, try www.dcnites.com.

DUPONT AND U DISTRICT

▨ **Brickskeller,** 1523 22nd St. NW (☎293-1885). The largest selection of beer in the world, with 1072 different bottled brews to choose from ($3.25-19). With so many options, expect to get laughed at if you order a Miller Lite. Try a "beer-tail," a mixed drink made with beer ($3.25-6.50). Monthly beer tastings Sept.-May. Open M-Th 11:30am-2am, F 11:30am-3am, Sa 6pm-3am, Su 6pm-2am; kitchen closes 1hr. earlier.

Eighteenth Street Lounge, 1212 18th St. NW (☎466-3922; www.eslmusic.com/lounge). For the last decade, ESL has set the bar for the D.C. lounge scene with its top-shelf DJs, most of whom are signed to ESL's independent record label. Jazz bands often chill out the top floor while DJs work it downstairs, spinning house, hip-hop, and dance. Cover generally $10-20, no cover Tu. Ladies often free after midnight. Open Tu-W 9:30pm-2am, Th 5:30pm-2am, F 5:30pm-3am, Sa 9:30pm-3am.

Cafe Saint-Ex, 1847 14th St. NW (☎265-7839; www.saint-ex.com), at T St. The vintage aviation-themed bar, named after Antoine de Saint-Exupery, aviator and author of *The Little Prince,* attracts a mixed crowd of alt-hippies and legal yuppies. It anchors an increasingly lively row of funky nightspots along 14th St. Upstairs bar and patio cafe. Downstairs Gate 54 lounge. Beer $3-6, rail drinks $6. Happy hour daily 5:30-7pm offers $3 drinks. 21+ after 10:30pm. No cover. Open M-F 5pm-2am, Sa-Su 11am-2am.

The Big Hunt, 1345 Connecticut Ave. NW (☎785-2333). The steam isn't a prop at this jungle-themed 3-floor bar, where the casual khaki-and-flip-flops crowd

IN RECENT NEWS

NATIONAL TREASURE

Like in any good baseball yarn, the protagonists of this particular love story seemed to have stepped out of a Greek play. Here, a still-grieving city abandoned by major-league baseball over 30 years ago. There, an orphan team; luckless and unloved. And then, joy. Finally brought together in 2005, Washington and its Nationals began the process of writing a summer classic. Having finished last in their division for more seasons than any Quebecois cared to count, the Montreal Expos made the move to RFK Stadium with no owner, a 74-year old manager (baseball legend Frank Robinson), and the lowest payroll in the league. Yet by May, this scrappy, no-name team was sitting atop the NL East. Cautious pride on the part of Washingtonians soon turned into full-blown adoration, with the city awash in red and blue Nats caps.

Whether or not the Nats soar to the top of their league, one thing is certain: D.C. area residents can finally enjoy a cool summer evening of Cracker Jacks and cracking bats in their own city. Say what you will about the heat, the traffic, the politics, and the difficulty of hitting a home run in this 1960s-era ballpark; all of a sudden the nation's capital is a little bit more like America again.

Washington Nationals play home games at RFK Stadium Mar.-Oct. See http://washington.nationals.mlb.com for schedule. $7-65.

hunts for potential mates. Notorious pickup joint for college kids and Hill workers pretending they're still in college. 24 brews on tap ($3.75-5). Solid pub fare, plus surprisingly delicious Guinness ice cream. Pool table. Happy hour M-F 4-7:30pm. 21+. No cover. Open M-Th 4pm-2am, F-Sa 4pm-3am, Su 11am-midnight.

ADAMS MORGAN

■ **Madam's Organ,** 2461 18th St. NW (☎667-5370; www.madamsorgan.com), near Columbia Rd. A 3-floor blues bar with an intimate rooftop patio serving soul food. Live band plays nightly on first floor to an international crowd. Pool tables. 2-for-1 drinks during happy hour (M-F 5-8pm), and redheads always drink Rolling Rock for half-price. Drafts $3.75-5.75; mixed drinks $4.75-6.75. Pitchers $14. 21+. Cover M-Th and Su $2-4, F-Sa $5-7. Open M-Th and Su 5pm-2am, F-Sa 5pm-3am.

Millie & Al's, 2440 18th St. NW (☎387-8131). This jukebox bar draws a party-hungry, polo-shirt-wearing crew. Think pitchers, not martinis. Cheap pizza, fries, subs, and $1 Jell-O shots. Nightly specials 4-7pm. DJs play rock and hip-hop F-Sa. Draft beer $2-3.50; bottles $3-4.25. 21+. No cover. Open M-Th 4pm-2am, F-Sa 4pm-3am.

Larry's Lounge, 1840 18th St. NW (☎483-1483), at the southern end of Adams Morgan. Glam in a 1960s sort of way, this funky bar may be a long walk from the Metro, but its Singapore Slings ($6.50) make the trip here worth it. Happy hour daily 4-8pm. Open daily 4pm-2am.

CAPITOL HILL

■ **The Dubliner,** 520 N. Capitol St. NW (☎737-3773). Metro: Union Station. A subdued crowd enjoys Guinness and the house brew, Auld Dubliner Amber Ale ($5 a pint), in what many consider to be D.C.'s most authentic Irish pub. A large patio turns lounge-style for celebrators as the night ticks on. Live Irish music nightly around 9pm. Open M-Th and Su 7am-2am, F-Sa 7am-3am; kitchen closes at 1am.

Pour House, 319 Pennsylvania Ave. SE (☎546-1001; www.politiki-dc.com). Metro: Capitol South. 3 levels: German biergarten atmosphere downstairs, martini bar upstairs (Tu-Sa), and a typical sports bar in between that stays packed with Hill staffers all week long. Nightly drink specials and a free buffet M-Th and Su 4pm-1:30am. Happy hour M-F 5:30-8pm. Open M-Th 4pm-1:30am, F 3pm-2:30am, Sa-Su 10am-2:30am.

GLBT NIGHTLIFE

The *Washington Blade* is the best source for gay news and club listings; published every Friday, it's available in virtually every storefront in Dupont Circle. *Metro Weekly,* a gay and lesbian Washington-area magazine, is another good reference for weekend entertainment and nightlife.

■ **J.R.'s,** 1519 17th St. NW (☎328-0090), at Church St. D.C.'s busiest gay bar for good reasons: hot bartenders, fun events like bachelor auctions, and great drink deals. Packed every night with hordes of "guppies" (gay urban professionals). Happy hour (M-W 5-8pm) brings $3 mini-pitchers, $2 rail drinks and domestic beers, and $1 sodas; the famous Power Hour follows (8-9pm), during which everything is half-price. Open M-Th 4pm-2am, F-Sa 12:30pm-3am, Su noon-2am.

■ **Cobalt,** 1639 R St. NW (☎462-6569), at 17th St. No sign marks this hot spot; look for the blue light and bouncer. Shirtless bartenders serve drinks ($4.75-5.75) to a preppy gay male and straight female crowd. Tu 70s and 80s night. No cover M-W or Su. Cover Th $8 for open bar, F after 11pm and all night Sa $5. Open Tu-Th 10pm-2am, F-Sa 10pm-3am, Su 8:30pm-2am. Downstairs, **30°** is a relaxed lounge with half-price martinis during happy hour (M-F 5-8pm). 21+. Open M-Th and Su 5pm-2am, F-Sa 5pm-3am.

Apex, 1415 22nd St. NW (☎296-0505), near P St. Formerly known as Badlands, this 2-story dance complex is one of Dupont Circle's old standbys. DJs attract a young crowd with a mix of house, trance, and Top 40. "Liquid Ladies" night Sa, with $7 cover and $3 Long Island iced teas, draws a sizeable crowd of lesbians. College night Th, $5 cover (free with student ID), $3 mixed drinks. Cover F before 10pm $8, after 10pm $10; drag karaoke starts 11pm. 18+. Open Th-Sa 9pm-4am.

⊡ DAYTRIPS FROM D.C.

ARLINGTON, VA

The 612-acre **Arlington National Cemetery** holds the graves of over 260,000 service-men and women, including veterans of every American war from the Revolution-ary War to the present. A simple walking tour can begin at the **Tomb of the Unknowns,** which honors unidentified servicemen who died fighting for the US. It is guarded by soldiers from the Army's Third Infantry, who execute a perfect chang-ing of the guard (Apr.-Sept. every 30min. 8am-6pm; Oct.-Mar. every hr. 8am-4pm). A 10min. walk directly north of the Tomb are the **Kennedy gravesites.** Here lie the remains of President John F. Kennedy, his brother Robert F. Kennedy, and his wife Jacqueline Kennedy Onassis. It is said that shortly before that fateful day in November, JFK visited this hillside spot and was so enchanted by the view that he declared "I could stay here forever"; now the Eternal Flame flickers above his sim-ple memorial stone. A brief walk up the hill from the Kennedy gravesites toward the distinctive orange columns of **Arlington House** is a memorial to **Pierre L'Enfant,** whose grave overlooks the city he designed. The classical edifice crowning the hill, Arlington House (open daily 9:30am-4:30pm) was once the home of Confeder-ate general Robert E. Lee, who was originally offered command of the Union Army by President Lincoln. Torn between his country and his state, Lee decided he could not bear arms against his fellow Virginians and left for Richmond. The Union Army occupied Arlington House shortly thereafter and, to ensure that Lee never returned, began burying their war dead on the property. Lee's home, now a museum of antebellum life, provides one of the best views of D.C.

Farther down the hill among the plain headstones lies General of the Armies **John J. "Blackjack" Pershing,** commander of US forces during WWI, who asked to be buried among his men. Arlington also holds the bodies of Arctic explorers **Robert E. Peary** and **Richard Byrd,** legendary politician **William Jennings Bryan,** and heavy-weight champion **Joe Louis.** Each year on Memorial Day, a small American flag is placed on each of the cemetery's gravesites; the President lays a wreath at the Tomb of the Unknowns and makes a speech commemorating the day. The **Women in Military Service for America Memorial** fits into its somber surroundings with a cir-cular stone wall and reflecting pool. A memorial for the victims of the September 11th attacks and a memorial dedicated to the crew of the space shuttle *Columbia* were recently added. (Metro: Arlington Cemetery. ☎703-607-8000; www.arlington-cemetery.org. Open daily Apr.-Sept. 8am-7pm; Oct.-May 8am-5pm. Free. Parking $1.25 per hr. for first 3hr., $2 per hr. thereafter.)

Exit the cemetery through Weitzel Gate and walk north for 20min. to get to the **Iwo Jima Memorial,** based on Joe Rosenthal's Pulitzer Prize-winning photo of Marines straining to raise the US flag on Mt. Suribachi. **The Pentagon,** south of the Arlington National Cemetery, is the world's largest building, with 17½ mi. of hall-ways, 7754 windows, 131 stairways, and four postal codes of its own. The wall that took the impact of the hijacked airplane on September 11, 2001, has been com-pletely restored. Tours of the Pentagon are currently suspended due to security concerns; the Tour Office (☎703-695-3324) has information about the future of Pentagon tours. Just down S. Hayes St. from the Pentagon is the **Drug Enforcement**

Administration, which operates a fascinating museum on the history of illegal drugs in America. Changing exhibits have focused on topics such as drugs' effects on their users and how the agents operate on land, in the air, and on the sea. (Metro: Pentagon City. ☎307-3463; www.deamuseum.org. Open Tu-F 10am-4pm. Free.)

ALEXANDRIA, VA

Alexandria was once the young nation's sixth-busiest port, but it didn't become a tourist attraction until the 1980s, when city residents backed away from proposed high-rises and decided to revitalize Old Town. Capitalizing on original 18th-century architecture and the legacy of historical all-stars like George Washington and Robert E. Lee, the town re-cobbled the streets, re-bricked the sidewalks, installed gardens, restored over 1000 original facades, and invited tall ships and hip shops. As a result, **Old Town Alexandria** is now packed with tourists. (Metro: King Street; 10min. drive from downtown over Roosevelt Bridge and south on George Washington Parkway.) Sights cluster along Washington and King St. Looming over western Alexandria, the lofty **George Washington Masonic National Memorial,** 101 Callahan Dr., is an imposing testament to the strength of Masonry and the legacy of Washington, the only person to have been a Masonic chartermaster and US president at the same time. (☎703-683-2007; www.gwmemorial.org.) Formerly a hotbed of political, business, and social life, the restored **Gadsby's Tavern,** 134 N. Royal St., takes you back to ye good olde days of hospitality, when as many as four hotel guests slept in one bed. Adams, Jefferson, Madison, and Lafayette all quaffed here. (☎703-838-4242; www.gadsbystavern.org. Open Apr.-Oct. M and Su 1-5pm, Tu-Sa 10am-5pm; Nov.-Mar. W-Sa 11am-4pm, Su 1-4pm. Last 30min. tour 15min. prior to closing. $4, students 11-17 $2, ages 10 and under free.) The **Ramsay House Visitors Center,** 221 King St., offers free maps. The house, a 1724 building shipped upriver from Dumfries, VA, was the home of Scottish merchant and Lord Mayor William Ramsay. (☎703-838-4200; www.alexandriacity.com. Open daily 9am-5pm.)

MOUNT VERNON

George Washington's fabulous **Mount Vernon** estate is easily accessible in Fairfax County, VA. Enthusiastic curators have turned the estate into a living 1760s experience. Visitors can tour Washington's bedroom and tomb and watch demonstrations on the estate's fields, where slaves once grew corn, wheat, and tobacco. The rocking chairs on mansion's immense veranda are perfect for enjoying the breezes off the Potomac River below. The estate maintains 30-40% of Washington's original furnishings, all of which are on display. To get there, take the Fairfax Connector 101 bus from the Huntington Metro stop, or take the George Washington Pkwy. south, which becomes Washington St. in Alexandria, to the entrance. The fit and adventurous can bike the scenic, 20 mi. Mt. Vernon trail. (☎703-780-2000 or 800-429-1520; www.mountvernon.org. Open daily Apr.-Aug. 8am-5pm; Mar. and Sept.-Oct. 9am-5pm; Nov.-Feb. 9am-4pm. $11, seniors $10.50, ages 6-11 $5, under 6 free.)

VIRGINIA

Many of America's formative experiences took place in Virginia—the English settlement of North America, the boom in the slave trade, the definitive establishment of American independence, and much of the Civil War. The powerful antebellum imagery proffered by the state's many historical sites can be overwhelming, especially since today's cosmopolitan Virginia is a far cry from its colonial origins. Travel down the state's eastern shore to indulge your historical nostalgia, and if you seek solitude and rejuvenation, head west to explore towering Appalachian forests and fascinating underground caverns.

🔋 PRACTICAL INFORMATION

Capital: Richmond.

Visitor Info: Virginia Division of Tourism (motto: "Virginia is for lovers"), 901 E. Byrd St., Richmond 23219 (☎800-847-4882; www.virginia.org). Open M-F 8:30am-5pm. **Department of Conservation and Recreation,** 203 Governor St., Ste. 213, Richmond 23219 (☎804-786-1712; www.dcr.state.va.us). Open M-F 8am-5pm.

Postal Abbreviation: VA. **Sales Tax:** 5%.

RICHMOND   ☎804

Virginia's capital city has a survivor's history of conflicts, disasters, and triumphs. Richmond was officially chartered in 1742, but William Mayo's handiwork was burned to the ground in 1781 in a British attack led by American traitor Benedict Arnold. The city was rebuilt and went on to become the capital of the ill-fated Confederate States of America during the Civil War. However, this tenacious town held on after the South's loss in the war, and by 1946 Richmond's economy and industrial strength outpaced every other US city.

📧 TRANSPORTATION

Trains: Amtrak, 7519 Staple Mills Rd. (☎800-872-7245; www.amtrak.com). To: **Baltimore** (3-4hr., 8 per day, $47-55); **Virginia Beach** (3½hr., 2 per day, $30-33); **Washington, D.C.** (2¼hr., 8per day, $31-40); **Williamsburg** (1¼hr., 2 per day, $19). Station open 24hr. Taxi to downtown $17-18.

Buses: Greyhound, 2910 N. Blvd. (☎254-5910 or 800-231-2222; www.greyhound.com), 2 blocks from downtown. To: **Baltimore** (3-5hr., 19 per day, $23-25); **Charlottesville** (1¼hr., 4 per day, $18); **New York City** (7-8hr., 22 per day, $55-59); **Norfolk** (2½hr., 6 per day, $18-20); **Philadelphia** (6-8hr., 10 per day, $42-45); **Washington, D.C.** (2½hr., 14 per day, $19-21); **Williamsburg** (1hr., 5 per day, $10).

Public Transit: Greater Richmond Transit Co., 101 S. Davis Ave. (☎358-4782). Get maps in the basement of City Hall (900 E. Broad St.), the 6th St. Marketplace Station, and the Yellow Pages. Most buses leave from stops on Broad St. downtown. Bus #24 goes to the Greyhound station. $1.25; transfers $0.15. Supersaver tickets $10 for 10.

Taxi: Veterans Cab, ☎275-5542.

🔋🔋 ORIENTATION AND PRACTICAL INFORMATION

Broad Street is the city's central artery, and its cross streets are numbered from west to east. Most parallel streets to Broad St., including **Main Street** and **Cary Street,** run one-way. Both **I-95,** going north to Washington, D.C., and **I-295** encircle the urban section of the city—the former to the east and north, the latter to the south and west. On the southeast edge of the city, **Shockoe Slip** and **Shockoe Bottom** overflow with partiers at night. Farther east, on the edge of town, the **Court End** and **Church Hill** districts comprise the city's historic center. **Jackson Ward** to the north, bounded by Belvedere, Leigh, Broad, and 5th St., recently underwent major construction to revamp its City Center and revitalize the surrounding community—it is still wise to use caution in this area at night. The **Fan** is bounded by the Boulevard, I-195, the walk of statues along **Monument Avenue,** and **Virginia Commonwealth University.** The Fan has a notoriously dangerous reputation, but has become more gentrified in recent years. The pleasant bistros and boutiques of **Carytown,** west of the Fan on Cary St., and the tightly knit working community of **Oregon Hill** add texture to the cityscape. Be careful in Oregon Hill at night.

Visitor Info: Richmond Metropolitan Visitor's Bureau, 405 N. 3rd St. (☎783-7450; www.richmondva.org), in the Richmond Convention Center. Tours, maps, and discounted lodging. Open daily Memorial Day-Labor Day 9am-6pm; low season 9am-5pm.

Hotlines: Rape Crisis, ☎643-0888. 24hr. **AIDS/HIV,** ☎800-533-4148. Operates M-F 8am-5pm.

Internet Access: Richmond Public Library, 101 E. Franklin St. (☎646-4867). Open M-W 9am-9pm, Th-F 9am-6pm, Sa 10am-5pm. Free with photo ID.

Post Office: 1801 Brook Rd. (☎775-6304). Open M-F 7am-6pm, Sa 9am-2pm. **Postal Code:** 23232. **Area Code:** 804.

▐ ACCOMMODATIONS

▨ **Be My Guest Bed and Breakfast,** 2926 Kensington Ave. (☎358-9901). Located in the heart of Richmond, Be My Guest is truly a hidden deal: neither a sign nor a Yellow Pages listing marks it. Pleasing decor, full breakfast, and friendly owners make this B&B worth the hunt. Rooms $70-135. Cash only. ❹

Travelodge, 5221 Brook Rd. (☎266-7603 or 800-637-3297). Take I-95 to Exit 81, bear right at the first light, and make a left on Brook Rd. This brand-new location offers continental breakfast, free parking, an outdoor pool, cable TV, and microfridges. Singles and doubles $49 on weekdays, $59 on weekends. AmEx/D/MC/V. ❸

Pocahontas State Park, 10301 State Park Rd. (☎796-4255 or 800-933-7275; www.dcr.state.va.us). Take I-95 south to Rte. 288 (Exit 67); go 5 mi., connect to Rte. 10, exit on Ironbridge Rd. east, and turn right on Beach Rd.; the park is 4 mi. down on the right. Showers, biking, boating, picnic areas, and the second-largest pool in Virginia. Rent a canoe, rowboat, kayak, or paddleboat (rowboats, paddleboats, canoes $6 per hr.; kayaks $8-10). Sites with water and electricity $24. MC/V. ❶

◖ FOOD

Strawberry Street Cafe and Market, 421 and 415 Strawberry St. (cafe ☎353-6860, market 353-4100; www.strawberrystreetcafe.com), offers an unlimited salad bar ($8), a brunch bar ($10; available Sa-Su until 3pm), and an array of American classics ($7-14) in a pleasant setting. Open M-Th 11am-2:30pm and 5-10:30pm, F 11am-2:30pm and 5pm-midnight, Sa 11am-midnight, Su 10am-10:30pm. AmEx/MC/V. ❸

Bottoms Up, 1700 Dock St. (☎644-4400), at 17th and Cary St. Bottoms Up is perfect for post-nightclub pizza cravings, with a creative assortment of toppings for your pie. Create your own, or go with the Chesapeake (with spicy crabmeat). Slice $4.25-7. Pies $10-21.50. Open M-Tu and Su 11am-10pm, W-Th 11am-11pm, F-Sa 11am-2am. AmEx/D/MC/V. ❷

Zuppa, 104 N. 18th St. (☎249-8831), in Shockoe Bottom. Freshly baked bread, a daily selection of soups, and just-about-gourmet salads, sandwiches, and appetizers make Zuppa's the place to go for a quick and tasty meal. Sandwiches $6. Soup $2-5. Open Tu-Th 11am-10pm, F 11am-2am, Sa 5pm-3am. AmEx/D/MC/V. ❶

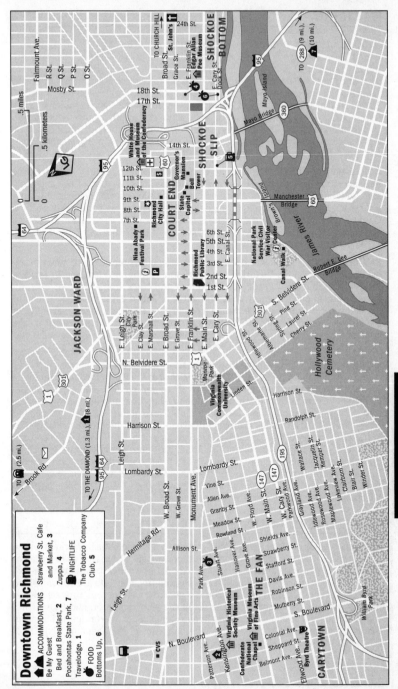

MID-ATLANTIC

Downtown Richmond

⬤ **ACCOMMODATIONS**
Be My Guest Bed and Breakfast, **2**
Pocahontas State Park, **7**
Travelodge, **1**

⬤ **FOOD**
Bottoms Up, **6**
Strawberry St. Cafe and Market, **3**
Zuppa, **4**

🎵 **NIGHTLIFE**
The Tobacco Company Club, **5**

◉ SIGHTS

AROUND ST. JOHN'S CHURCH. St. John's Church is the site of Patrick Henry's famed "Give me liberty or give me death" speech. In the summer, orators re-create the 1775 speech on Sundays at 2pm. The church still serves as an active house of worship. *(2401 E. Broad St. ☎648-5015; www.historicstjohnschurch.org. 25min. tours M-Sa 10am-3:30pm, Su 1-3:30pm. Services Su 8:30 and 11am. Admission $5, ages 62+ $4, ages 7-18 $3.)* Nearby is the **Edgar Allan Poe Museum,** in Richmond's oldest standing house (circa 1737), where visitors try evermore to unravel the author's mysterious death. Poe memorabilia and first editions of his works fill the museum. *(1914 E. Main St. ☎648-5523; www.poemuseum.org. Open Tu-Sa 10am-5pm, Su 11am-5pm. Tours every hr., last tour 4pm. $6; students, seniors, and AAA $5; under 9 free.)*

CONFEDERATE SOUTH. Explore the historical relevance of the Civil War at the **Museum of the Confederacy.** The poignant painting "Last Meeting of Lee and Jackson" and the collection of military medical artifacts are especially intriguing. Next door, friendly guides run tours through the **White House of the Confederacy.** *(1201 E. Clay St. ☎649-1861; www.moc.org. Museum open M-Sa 10am-5pm, Su noon-5pm. White House guided tours every 30min-1hr. Tickets to White House $7, ages 62+ $6, ages 7-18 $4. Museum $7/$6/$3. Combination tickets $10/$9/$5.)*

FAN DISTRICT. This old-world section of Richmond is home to the country's largest and best-preserved Victorian neighborhood. Stroll down **Monument Avenue,** a boulevard lined with graceful old houses and towering statues of Virginia heroes—Richmond's memory lane. The statue of **Robert E. Lee** faces south toward his beloved Dixie; **Stonewall Jackson** faces north so that the general can scowl at the Yankees for all eternity. The statue of African-American tennis hero **Arthur Ashe** created a storm of controversy when it was added to the end of the avenue that had previously featured only Civil War generals.

MUSEUM ROW. The ▧**Virginia Historical Society** maintains an impressive collection in an even more impressive building. Marvel at the elegant classical architecture before moving on through the extensive "Story of Virginia" exhibit, tracing the history of Virginians from pre-history to the present. The museum's showcase feature is a series of murals known as the "Four Seasons of the Confederacy," painted by the French artist Charles Hoffbauer between 1914 and 1921. *(428 N. Blvd. ☎358-4901; www.vahistorical.org. Open M-Sa 10am-5pm, Su 1-5pm. $5, seniors $4, students and children $3.)* The **Virginia Museum of Fine Arts** is the South's largest art museum, and houses a collection by some of the world's most renowned painters—Monet, Renoir, Picasso, and Warhol—as well as ancient treasures from Rome, Egypt, and Asia. *(200 N. Blvd. ☎340-1400; www.vmfa.state.va.us. Open W-Su 11am-5pm. Suggested donation $5; admission for special exhibitions varies.)*

🎵 🎭 ENTERTAINMENT AND NIGHTLIFE

At the marvelous old **Byrd Theatre,** 2908 W. Cary St., movie buffs buy tickets for the latest movies from a tuxedoed agent. On Saturdays, guests are treated to midnight shows and a Wurlitzer organ concert. *(☎353-9911; www.byrdtheatre.com. Shows $2; Sa midnight movie $3.)* **Friday Cheers** presents free concerts at Brown's Island on Friday evenings during the summer. Check at the visitors center for schedules. *Style Weekly,* a free magazine available at the visitors center, and *Punchline,* found in most hangouts, list concert lineups and events. Cheer on the **Richmond Braves,** Richmond's AAA minor-league baseball team, at The Diamond, Exit 78 off I-95. *(☎359-4444; www.rbraves.com. Tickets $3-9.)*

Student-driven nightlife enlivens **Shockoe Slip** and the **Fan**. After dark, **Shockoe Bottom** turns into college-party central, with bars pumping bass-heavy music. Be cautious in the Bottom's alleys after dark. At **The Tobacco Company Club,** 1201 E. Cary St., in the Tobacco Company Restaurant, an older crowd—with some young'uns who try to act old—drinks martinis, smokes cigars, and revels in the comfort of Southern living. (☎ 782-9555; www.thetobaccocompany.com. Live music at restaurant Tu-Sa 9pm. No bikini contests here—or tennis shoes, jeans, or boots. 21+. Happy hour M-F 4:30-7pm. Cover $3. Open Th-Sa 8pm-2am.)

WILLIAMSBURG   ☎ 757

With every part of the reconstructed town screaming 1770s, Colonial Williamsburg is a living snapshot of American life on the eve of the Revolutionary War. The historical re-creation extends right down to the fife-and-drum corps that periodically marches down the town's streets. If Williamsburg alone doesn't satiate your colonial nostalgia, check out the nearby towns of Jamestown and Yorktown, which are the respective locations of the first permanent British settlement in what would become the United States of America and the most decisive battle of the American Revolutionary War.

TRANSPORTATION

Airport: Newport News and Williamsburg International Airport (☎ 877-0221; www.nnwairport.com), 20min. away in Newport News. Take state road 199 W to I-64 S. The only shuttle service serving the airport is the **Williamsburg Limousine Service** (☎ 877-0279). $26 to Newport News; $65 to Norfolk.

Trains: Amtrak (☎ 800-872-7245 or 229-8750; www.amtrak.com), 468 N. Boundary St. To: **Baltimore** (5-6hr., 2 per day, $52); **New York City** (7-9hr., 2 per day, $91); **Philadelphia** (6-7hr., 2 per day, $69); **Richmond** (1¼hr., 2 per day, $19).

Buses: Greyhound (☎ 800-231-2222 or 229-1460; www.greyhound.com), 468 N. Boundary St. To: **Baltimore** (5½-7hr., 7 per day, $45-48); **Norfolk** (1-2hr., 5 per day, $12-14); **Richmond** (1hr., 6 per day, $9-10); **Virginia Beach** (2½hr., 3 per day, $16-18); **Washington, D.C.** (4-6hr., 6 per day, $30-32). Ticket office open M-F 8am-noon and 1-5pm, Sa 8am-noon and 1-2pm.

Public Transit: Williamsburg Area Transport (WAT); (☎ 259-4093; www.williamsburgtransport.com). Bus service along Rte. 60 and to all major Williamsburg destinations. 8 lines operate May-Sept. M-Sa 6am-10pm; Sept.-May M-Sa 6am-8pm. $1.25, seniors and disabled $0.50; all-day pass $1.50. Transfer $0.25.

Taxi: Yellow Cab, ☎ 722-1111.

ORIENTATION AND PRACTICAL INFORMATION

Williamsburg lies 53 mi. southeast of Richmond. The beautiful **Colonial Parkway** connects the three towns in the historic triangle—Williamsburg, Jamestown, and Yorktown. Take the Colonial Pkwy. exit off I-64 to reach Colonial Williamsburg.

Visitor Info: Williamsburg Area Convention and Visitors Bureau, 421 N. Boundary St., provides information about area attractions. (☎ 253-0192 or 800-368-6511; www.visitwilliamsburg.com), a half-mile northwest of the Transportation Center. Open M-F 8:30am-5pm. **Colonial Williamsburg Visitors Center,** 100 Visitors Center Dr. (☎ 800-447-8679 or 229-1000; www.colonialwilliamsburg.com), 1 mi. northeast of the Transportation Center. Open daily 8:45am-5:30pm; winter hours vary.

Post Office: 425 N. Boundary St. (☎800-275-8777). Open M-F 8am-5pm, Sa 9am-2pm. **Postal Code:** 23185. **Area Code:** 757.

ACCOMMODATIONS

Williamsburg is teeming with classy hotels and unique B&Bs. Budget chains cluster around the junctions of Rte. 5, 31, 60, 132, and 162. The 1 mi. walk into the colonial area might be strenuous during the scorching summers, but if you can't get a room in town, this may be your best bet.

Bryant Guest House, 702 College Terr. (☎229-3320). From Scotland Rd., turn right on Richmond Rd., then left on Dillard St. 4 rooms with private baths, TV, and limited kitchen in a brick home. Singles $40; doubles $50; 5-person suite $75. Cash or traveler's check only. ❷

Tioga Motel, 906 Richmond Rd. (☎229-4531 or 800-527-5370), just east of the colonial area, has 26 ground-floor rooms with A/C, refrigerator, and TV, as well as a pool. Rooms $45-50. AmEx/D/MC/V. ❸

Econolodge, 1900 Richmond Rd. (☎229-6600). Some of the lowest prices in town and a central location. Wheelchair-accessible rooms available. Outdoor pool and continental breakfast. Doubles M-F $65, Sa-Su $75. AmEx/D/MC/V. ❸

FOOD

The Old Chickahominy House, 1211 Jamestown Rd. (☎229-4689), 1½ mi. from Williamsburg's historic district. The Complete Luncheon has Virginia ham, hot biscuits, fruit salad, homemade pie, and iced tea or coffee ($7.25). 2 pancakes $5. Open M-F 8:30-10:30am and 11:30am-2:30pm, Sa-Su 8:30-10am and 11:45am-2pm. MC/V. ❷

Chowning's Tavern, Duke of Gloucester St. (☎229-2141 or 800-828-3767). Quasi-authentic British pub fare. After 9pm, peanuts are at stake as patrons roll the dice against their servers. Costumed waiters sing 18th-century ditties and challenge guests to card games and sing-alongs over light meals ($3.50-5.50). Sandwiches $5-14. Cover $3, no cover for dinner guests. Open daily 11am-9pm. AmEx/D/MC/V. ❷

Berret's, 199 S. Boundary St. (☎253-1847), located at Merchant's Sq., combines 2 restaurants in 1. The more casual **Tap House Grill** serves upscale sandwich plates like the chicken pecan apple salad sandwich ($8-12) and seafood entrees ($14-19). **Berret's Restaurant and Bar** features mouth-watering (albeit pricey) dishes such as the chilled shrimp in puff pastry with herbed goat cheese appetizer ($8.50). Live music in summer Su 6:30-9:30pm. Tap House open daily 5-10pm. Restaurant and Bar open daily 11:30am-3:30pm and 5:30-10pm. AmEx/D/MC/V. ❸/❺

SIGHTS

COLONIAL WILLIAMSBURG. Every day is a historical reenactment at Colonial Williamsburg. In the summer, ask the pedestrians in 18th-century apparel what's on their minds and you'll enjoy an informed discussion of the issues of 1776. The year 1774 is reenacted in the spring, 1775 in the fall, and 1773 in the winter. Armed with enthusiastic actors and meticulously restored buildings, the site prides itself on its authenticity. Immersing yourself in the colonists' world doesn't require a ticket: visitors can walk the streets, interact with the locals, and use the restrooms without ever opening their wallets. However, to enter any building, with or without an actor inside, or to attend any of the performances, you'll have to pay for a ticket. The weekly *Visitor's Companion* newsletter lists free events, evening programs, and complete hours. (☎ 229-1000; www.colonialwilliamsburg.org. Visitors center open daily 8:45am-5:30pm. Most sights open 9am-5pm. Day pass $34, ages 6-17 $15; 2 consecutive days and admission to Governor's Palace $48/$24.)

COLLEGE OF WILLIAM AND MARY. Spreading west from the corner of Richmond and Jamestown Rd., the College of William and Mary, founded in 1693, is the second-oldest college in the United States (after Harvard University in Massachusetts, p. 135) and has educated luminaries such as Presidents Jefferson, Monroe, and Tyler. The Wren Building is the oldest academic building in continuous use in America, and still hosts classes today. The Office of Admissions, in Blow Hall, leads free tours throughout the year. (☎ 221-4223; www.wm.edu. Tours M-F 10am and 2:30pm, also Sa 10am.)

▶ DAYTRIPS FROM WILLIAMSBURG

JAMESTOWN AND YORKTOWN

The Historic Triangle brims with US history. Less crowded than the Colonial Williamsburg tourist empire, Jamestown and Yorktown show visitors where it all really began. The **Colonial National Park** preserves American colonial and revolutionary history with branches in both Jamestown and Yorktown. Southwest of Williamsburg on Rte. 31, in the Jamestown branch, you'll see the remains of the first permanent English settlement in America (1607) and exhibits on colonial life. The visitors center presents a film emphasizing the courage of America's first settlers, a 35min. walking tour (10:15am and 2:45pm; free with admission), and a 45min. audio tape tour ($2) for the Island Loop Route. Southeast of Williamsburg on the Colonial Pkwy., Yorktown recreates the last battle of the Revolutionary War with an engaging film and an electric map. The visitors center rents cassettes and players ($2) for the battlefield's 3- or 5-mi. car routes. (☎ 229-1733; www.nps.gov/colo. Open daily 9am-5pm. Visitors centers close 30min. before park. Jamestown $8, Yorktown $5, under 17 free; both parks $10. Passes good for 7 days.)

On Rte. 31, near the Jamestown branch of Colonial National Park, the **Jamestown Settlement** has a museum with changing exhibits, a reconstruction of James Fort, a Native American village, and full-scale replicas of the three ships that brought the original settlers to Jamestown in 1607. Children will enjoy the educational riverfront "discovery area." (☎ 253-4838 or 888-593-4682. Open daily June 15-Aug. 15 9am-6pm; Aug. 16-June 14 9am-5pm. $12, ages 6-12 $6. Combination ticket including Yorktown Victory Center $17, ages 6-12 $8.25, under 6 free.)

The 1781 American and French triumph over British forces in the final battle of the Revolutionary War is celebrated daily at the **Yorktown Victory Center.** The center features two recreated areas—a Continental Army camp and a traditional 1780s farm—where reenactors interpret history. Admission to the center also includes informative exhibits and a 30min. film about the Yorktown battle. (☎ 253-4838 or 888-593-4682; www.historyisfun.org. Visitors center open daily 9am-4:30pm. $8.25, ages 6-12 $4, under 6 free.)

VIRGINIA BEACH ☎ 757

This boardwalk-centered town overflows with the all-you-can-eat buffets, age-old motels, and cheap discount stores that are the hallmarks of seemingly every beach town in America. So load up on saltwater taffy, homemade fudge, and tacky t-shirts, because the best part of a Virginia Beach vacation is not getting wrapped up in the stuffiness that can plague more pretentious resort towns.

MID-ATLANTIC

▐ TRANSPORTATION

Trains: Amtrak (☎800-872-7245 or 245-3589; www.amtrak.com). The nearest train station, at 9304 Warwick Blvd. in Newport News, runs 45min. bus service to and from the corner of 19th and Pacific St. Station open 7am-8pm. From Newport News to: **Baltimore** (6hr., 2 per day, $60-65); **New York City** (9½hr., 1 per day, $91); **Philadelphia** (7½hr., 1 per day, $69-74); **Richmond** (1½hr., 2 per day, $24); **Washington, D.C.** (4hr., 1 per day, $47-54); **Williamsburg** (20min., 1 per day, $19).

Buses: Greyhound, 1017 Laskin Rd. (☎800-231-2222 or 422-2998; www.greyhound.com). Open M-Sa 7-11am and 12:30-7pm. Half-mile from oceanfront area. To **Richmond** (3½-6hr., 5 per day, $18), **Washington, D.C.** (6-11hr., 5 per day, $30), and **Williamsburg** (2½-5hr., 5 per day, $16).

Public Transit: Virginia Beach Transit/Trolley Information Center (☎222-6036; www.vbwave.com), Atlantic Ave. and 24th St. Info on area transportation and tours, including trolleys, buses, and ferries. Trolleys transport riders to most major points in Virginia Beach. The Atlantic Ave. Trolley runs from Rudee Inlet to 42nd St. Open May-Sept. daily 8am-2am. $1, seniors and disabled $0.50, under 38 in. free; all-day passes $3, 3-day $5, 5-day $8. Other trolleys run along the boardwalk, the North Seashore, and to Lynnhaven Mall.

Taxi: Beach Yellow Cab, ☎460-0605. **Beach Taxi,** ☎486-6585.

Bike Rental: RK's Surf Shop has a bike stand at 10th St. and Atlantic Ave, which rents bikes for $4 per hr. or $16 per day. Open June-Sept. daily 8am-11pm. Bikes must be returned 2hr. before closing.

✷❷ ORIENTATION AND PRACTICAL INFORMATION

In Virginia Beach, east-west streets are numbered and the north-south avenues, parallel to the beach, are named. **Atlantic Avenue** is next to the beach and home to many of the town's hotels and shops. **Pacific Avenue** is the next street over and the major thoroughfare. **Arctic, Baltic,** and **Mediterranean Avenue** are farther inland.

Visitor Info: Virginia Beach Visitors Center, 2100 Parks Ave. (☎800-822-3224 or 491-7866; www.vbfun.com), at 22nd St. Info on budget accommodations and area sights. Open daily June-Aug. 9am-8pm; Sept.-May 9am-5pm.

Internet Access: Virginia Beach Public Library, 4100 Virginia Beach Blvd. (☎431-3001). Open M-Th 10am-9pm, F-Sa 10am-5pm; Oct.-May also Su 1-5pm. Free.

Post Office: 501 Viking Dr. (☎340-0981). Open M-F 7:30am-6pm, Sa 10am-2pm. **Postal Code:** 23452. **Area Code:** 757.

▐ ACCOMMODATIONS

Virginia Beach has two kinds of lodging: high-rise hotels along the boardwalk and motor courts one block off the boardwalk. The ocean-view high-rises don't come cheap; in summer the cheapest rooms go for $150. Most motels run $70-100, and are still convenient to the beach and the boardwalk's social scene.

▨ **Angie's Guest Cottage, Bed and Breakfast, and HI Hostel (HI),** 302 24th St. (☎428-4690; www.angiescottage.com). Barbara "Angie" Yates and her staff welcome international guests with coveted parking passes and advice about the beach. 34 beds. No A/C. Kitchen, lockers, and beach mats available. Linen $2. Reservations recommended. Open Apr.-Sept. Check-in 9:30am-9pm. Check-out 10am. Dorms $20, members $17; low season $17/$13. Singles $38, doubles $60; low season $32/$48. MC/V. ❶

The Castle Motel, 2700 Pacific Ave. (☎425-9330). 1 block from the beach. Spacious rooms have cable TV and 2 full beds. Check-out 11am. 21+. Open May-Oct. Rooms in summer from $59; in winter M-Th and Su $79-99, F-Sa $129-159. AmEx/D/MC/V. ❹

First Landings, 2500 Shore Dr. (☎ 225-3867 or 800-933-7275; www.dcr.state.va.us/parks/1stland), about 8 mi. north of town on Rte. 60, has 2-bedroom cabins and camp-sites amidst the beauty of the Virginia coastline. Reservations are required for camp-sites; call up to 11 months ahead for cabins. Cabins are close to picnic areas, a private swimming area on a sprawling beach, a bathhouse, and boat launching areas. Campsites have hot showers and grills. Cabins June-Aug. $68-108; Apr.-May and Sept.-Nov. $51-65. Sites $22, with water and electricity $28. ❹/❶

False Cape State Park (☎800-933-7275 or 225-3867). Exit I-64 on Indian River Rd. E, drive 13 mi. and turn left on Newbridge Rd., right on Sandbridge Rd., and right on Sand-piper Rd. to parking at Little Island City Park. 4 primitive campsites at False Cape, with drinking water and pit toilets, are worth the 6-9 mi. hike to their secluded locations. Reservations required. Campsites $9. Parking in summer M-F $3, Sa-Su $4. ❶

◖ FOOD

Tropical Smoothie Cafe, 211 25th St. (☎422-3970; www.tropicalsmoothie.com). Silky smoothies ($3-5), healthy wraps ($5), and fresh salads ($4-5) served in a sleek, mod-ern setting near the oceanfront. Open daily 9am-11pm. AmEx/MC/V. ❶

Cuisine and Co., 3004 Pacific Ave. (☎428-6700; www.cuisineandcompany.com). Gour-met sandwiches to go. Specialties include the California grilled chicken with avocado ($7.50) and the turkey with cranberry mayonnaise ($7.20). Open early Sept. to late May M-Sa 9am-7pm, Su 9am-6pm. AmEx/D/MC/V. ❶

Guadalajara, 200 21st St. (433-0140; www.guadalajaravb.com). This authentic Mexican restaurant is a hot post-beach spot for cooling down with a margarita ($5.50, jumbo $9). Burritos $6.75. Crabmeat quesadillas $8. Open M-Th 5pm-1am, F-Su noon-1:30am. AmEx/D/DC/MC/V. ❷

◉ SIGHTS

BACK BAY NATIONAL WILDLIFE REFUGE. The islands, dunes, forests, marshes, ponds, and beaches that fill this national refuge are a sanctuary for an array of endangered species and other wildlife. Visitors camping, hiking, or fishing in the park can gawk at nesting bald eagles, white-tailed deer, ospreys, egrets, and other wildlife on a tram tour departing daily from Little Island City Park, up the road. *(Take General Booth Blvd. to Princess Anne Dr.; turn left, then turn left on Sandbridge Rd. and continue 6 mi. Turn right on Sandpiper Rd., which leads directly to the visitors center.* ☎721-2412; http://backbay.fws.gov. Visitors center open M-F 8am-4pm, Sa-Su 9am-4pm. Closed Sa Nov.-Mar. $5 per car, $2 per family on foot or bike. Tram daily Apr.-Oct. 9am, returns 12:45pm. ☎426-3643; www.bbrf.org. $8, seniors and under 12 $6.)

FALSE CAPE STATE PARK. The origin of the title "False Cape" comes from the 17th century, when ships trying to reach Cape Henry, the landing site of America's first English settlers, would mistakenly touch shore in the present-day state park. The Back Bay National Wildlife Refuge's tram stops at False Cape State Park, where walkers trek 1 mi. to the beach. If you miss the tram, prepare for an adven-turous 4 mi. hike or canoe ride, as foot and water are the only ways to get where you want to go. *(*☎225-3867 or 800-933-7275; www.dcr.state.va.us/parks.)* **Kayak Nature Tours** offers kayak excursions to these areas. *(*☎480-1999 or 888-669-8368 for tours. 2½hr. sunset or sunrise tours $40, half-day $50, full day $80.)

VIRGINIA MARINE SCIENCE MUSEUM. One mile south of the downtown board-walk on Pacific Ave. (which becomes General Booth Blvd.), the Virginia Marine Science Museum contains Virginia's largest aquarium and is home to hundreds of species of fish, including sharks and stingrays. The mammoth museum also houses a six-story IMAX theater and offers excursion trips for dolphin observation in summer and whale-watching in winter. (*717 General Booth Blvd.* ☎*425-3474; www.vmsm.com. Open daily Memorial Day-Labor Day 9am-7pm; Labor Day-Memorial Day 9am-5pm. $12, ages 62+ $11, ages 3-11 $8. IMAX tickets $7.50/$6.75/$6.50. Combined museum and IMAX admission $17/$16/$13.)*

◪ NIGHTLIFE

Mahi Mah's, 615 Atlantic Ave. (☎437-8030; www.mahimahs.com), at 7th St. inside the Ramada Hotel. This nightlife hot spot hosts live rock performances that lure onlookers into its slick interior. Sushi, tiki parties, and a well-dressed crowd. Music nightly 7-11pm. Open daily 7am-1:30am; kitchen closes 11pm.

Chicho's, 2112 Atlantic Ave. (☎422-6011), on "The Block" of college bars clustered between 21st and 22nd St. One of the hottest spots. Gooey pizza ($2.25-3.25), tropical drinks ($5-7), and live rock 'n' roll M. 21+ after 10pm. Open May-Sept. M-F 6pm-2am, Sa 3pm-2am, Su noon-2am; Oct.-Apr. M-Th 6-10pm, F-Su noon-2am.

Harpoon Larry's, 216 24th St. (☎422-6000; www.harpoonlarryskillerseafood.com), at Pacific Ave., serves tasty fish in an everyone-knows-your-name atmosphere. M $0.35 oysters. W $0.25 jalapeño poppers. F $10.95 prime rib and crab legs. Happy hour (M-F 4-7pm) with $1 domestic drafts and $2 rail drinks. Open daily May-Sept. noon-2am; Sept.-May usually 4pm-2am, but call ahead.

CHARLOTTESVILLE   ☎434

Thomas Jefferson, colonial Renaissance man and the primary author of the Declaration of Independence, built his dream house, Monticello, high atop his "little mountain" just southeast of the town Charlottesville. Around his personal paradise, Jefferson endeavored to create the ideal community. In an effort to breed intellect and keep himself busy, Jefferson created the University of Virginia (UVA), which now lends Charlottesville a blend of college town vibrance and old-fashioned southern charm.

◪ TRANSPORTATION

Airport: Charlottesville-Albemarle Airport (☎973-8342; www.gocho.com), 8 mi. north of Charlottesville, 1 mi. west of Rte. 29 on Airport Rd.

Trains: Amtrak, 810 W. Main St. (☎296-4559 or 800-872-7245; www.amtrak.com). To **New Orleans** (23hr., 1 per day, $205) and **Washington, D.C.** (3hr., 1 per day, $24-30). Ticket office open daily 6am-9pm.

Bus: Greyhound/Trailways, 310 W. Main St. (☎295-5131 or 800-231-2222; www.greyhound.com). To **Baltimore** (5hr., 3 per day, $40), **Richmond** (1¼hr., 3 per day, $16), and **Washington, D.C.** (3¼hr., 2 per day, from $21).

Public Transit: Charlottesville Transit Service (☎296-7433). Bus service within city limits M-Sa 6:30am-midnight. $0.75, seniors and disabled $0.35, under 6 free. All-day pass $2. Free trolley service between UVA and downtown area runs daily 6am-midnight.

Taxi: Carter's Airport Taxi, ☎981-0170. **AAA Cab Co.,** ☎975-5555.

MID-ATLANTIC

ORIENTATION AND PRACTICAL INFORMATION

Charlottesville's streets are numbered from east to west, using compass directions; 5th St. NW is 10 blocks from (and parallel to) 5th St. NE. There are two downtowns: **The Corner,** on the west side across from the university, is home to student delis and coffee shops. **Historic downtown** is about a mile east, centered on a pedestrian mall on E. Main Street. The two are connected by the east-west **University Avenue,** which starts as Ivy Rd. and becomes Main St.

Visitor Info: Chamber of Commerce, 415 E. Market St. (☎295-3141), at 5th St. Maps, guides, and info about lodging and local events. Open M-F 9am-5pm. **Charlottesville-Albemarle County Convention and Visitors Bureau** (☎977-1783 or 877-286-1102; www.charlottesvilletourism.org), off I-64 on Rte. 20. Open daily 8:30am-5:30pm.

Hotlines: Region 10 Community Services, ☎972-1800. **Sexual Assault Crisis Center,** ☎977-7273. Both 24hr. **Mental Health,** ☎977-4673. Operates M-F 9am-5pm.

Internet Access: Jefferson Madison Regional Library, 201 E. Market St. (☎979-7151). Open M-Th 9am-9pm, F-Sa 9am-5pm; Sept.-May also Su 1-5pm. Free.

Post Office: 513 E. Main St. (☎963-2661). Open M-F 8:30am-5pm, Sa 10am-1pm. **Postal Code: 22902. Area Code:** 434.

ACCOMMODATIONS

The Budget Inn, 140 Emmet St. (☎800-293-5144; www.budgetinn-charlottesville.com), is the closest motel to the university. 36 large rooms with sunlight, cable TV, and wireless Internet. Rooms Apr.-Sept. $45-75; Oct. $60-90; Nov.-Mar. $40-70. Each additional person $5. AAA discount. AmEx/D/MC/V. ❸

English Inn of Charlottesville, 2000 Morten Dr. (☎800-786-5400), has standard rooms with full breakfast, Internet, A/C, cable TV, a pool, airport shuttle, and access to a local health club. Rooms $60-90. AAA and AARP discount. AmEx/D/MC/V. ❸

Charlottesville KOA Kampground, 3825 Red Hill Rd./Rte. 708 (☎296-9881 or 800-562-1743; ww.charlottesvillekoa.com), 9 mi. south of downtown. Take Rte. 20 S to Rte. 708. Shady campsites with bathrooms and a pool. Sites $22, with water and electricity $26, full hookup $28. Cabins $40-52. Each additional person $5. MC/V. ❶

FOOD

littlejohn's, 1427 University Ave. (☎977-0588). This deli is as overstuffed as its sandwiches at lunch, and in the wee hours of the morning, barflies trickle in to kick back and relax with the Easy Rider (baked ham, mozzarella, and cole slaw; $3.75). Beer $2-3. 3-egg omelets $3.50. Breakfast 5-11am. Open 24hr. MC/V. ❶

Blue Light Grill and Raw Bar, 120 E. Main St. (☎295-1223; www.bluelightgrill.com), on the Mall. Ideal for seafood lovers, this grill has a modern atmosphere with sparse decor, red walls, and high ceilings. The citrus-crusted monkfish ($17) is excellent. Dinner entrees $12-20. Open daily 4:30pm-2am. AmEx/D/MC/V. ❹

Jabberwocky, 1517 University Ave. (☎984-4973). Looks more like a trendy bar than a local pizza joint, but make no mistake. Entrees $8-10. Sandwiches $5-6. Large pizzas from $10. Open M-W and Su 11am-10pm, Th-Sa 11am-11pm. AmEx/D/MC/V. ❷

Chaps, 223 E. Main St. (☎977-4139). A favorite for homemade ice cream and cheap grub with a diner-that's-been-here-forever feel. Burgers and sandwiches $3.50-7. Open M-Th 8am-10pm, F-Sa 8am-11pm, Su 11am-9pm. Cash only. ❶

MID-ATLANTIC

TRUCKIN' ALONG. Gas prices can differ wildly between states, and it's easy to pay too much at gas stations on unfamiliar highways. Along interstates throughout the US, truck stops such as Pilot Travel Centers have consistently low prices for gasoline, plus cheap coffee to perk you up behind the wheel.

◉ SIGHTS

UNIVERSITY OF VIRGINIA (UVA). Most activity on the grounds of the **University of Virginia** clusters around the fraternity-lined **Rugby Road** and the ▨**Lawn,** a terraced green carpet that is one of the prettiest spots in American academia. Professors live in the Lawn's pavilions, each of which was designed in a different architectural style and includes a view of Monticello. *(☎ 924-7969. Free tours meet at Rotunda entrance facing the Lawn. Tours mid-Jan. to mid-Dec. daily 10, 11am, 2, 3, 4pm; no tours early to mid-May. Free.)*

HISTORIC MANSIONS. Jefferson oversaw every stage of the development of his beloved homestead at ▨**Monticello,** which reflects the personality of its brilliant creator. The house is a quasi-Palladian jewel filled with fascinating 18th-century innovations, such as a fireplace dumbwaiter and a mechanical manuscript copier. *(1184 Monticello Loop. ☎ 984-9844; www.monticello.org. Open daily Mar.-Oct. 8am-5pm; Nov.-Feb. 9am-4:30pm. $14, ages 6-11 $6. 30min. tour included with admission.)* **Ash Lawn-Highland** was the 535-acre plantation home of President James Monroe. Though less majestic than Monticello, the estate provides a glimpse of family life in the early 19th century. *(1000 James Monroe Pkwy. Off Rte. 792, 2½ mi. east of Monticello. ☎ 293-9539; www.ashlawnhighland.org. Open daily Apr.-Oct. 9am-6pm; Nov.-Mar. 11am-5pm. Tours $9, seniors and AAA $8, ages 6-11 $5.)* The partially reconstructed **Michie Tavern** has an operating grist mill and a general store. Lagers and ales are served alongside a southern buffet lunch. *(Just west of Monticello on Thomas Jefferson Pkwy. ☎ 977-1234; www.michietavern.com. Open daily 9am-5pm; last tour 4:20pm. Tours $8, seniors and AAA $7, ages 6-11 $3. Buffet lunch $14.50, ages 12-15 $10, ages 6-11 $7.25, ages 5 and under free.)* Twenty-seven miles north of Charlottesville on Rte. 20, James Madison's **Montpelier** once supported his slaves and tobacco crops. *(11407 Constitution Hwy./Rte. 20. ☎ 540-672-2728; www.montpelier.org. Open Apr.-Oct. 9:30am-5:30pm, Nov.-Mar. 9:30am-4:30pm. $11, seniors and AAA $10, ages 6-14 $6. Audio tours available.)*

◉ NIGHTLIFE

Buddhist Biker Bar and Grille, 20 Elliewood Ave. (☎971-9181). UVA students and local twentysomethings flock to this bar for its huge lawn and drink specials. Try the spinach dip ($4) or pork dumplings ($5). Beer $2.50-4. M $1 beer. W $2 cocktails. Live music Tu-W. Open M-Sa 3:30pm-2am.

Baja Bean, 1327 W. Main St. (☎293-4507). Cheap burritos, tamales, and chimichangas go for $5-8 in this festively decorated Mexican bar and restaurant. Beer $2-3.50. M open mic night. Tu $2 Corona. Happy hour M-F 3-7pm. Open daily 11am-2am; kitchen closes at midnight.

Orbit, 102 14th St. NW (☎984-5707). A hot bar and restaurant combo with a *2001: A Space Odyssey* theme downstairs. 8 pool tables and another bar upstairs. Happy hour daily 5-9pm. Th $3 drafts all night. Occasional live acoustic music Su. Open daily 5pm-2am; kitchen closes at 1am.

SHENANDOAH NATIONAL PARK ☎540

When Shenandoah National Park was purchased by the state of Virginia in 1926, it was a 280-acre tract of over-logged and over-hunted land. A 1936 decree from Franklin Roosevelt made Shenandoah America's first great nature reclamation project. The park now spans 10,600 acres and contains more plant species than all of Europe. In the same day, visitors can explore mineral-encrusted caves and pay homage to Civil War battlefields.

DRIVING SKYLINE DRIVE. When planning your trip through Shenandoah National Park, give yourself plenty of extra time for driving to and from your destinations. The speed limit in the park is only 35 mph, and tourists love to pull on and off the road to see the sights. You can still make the most of your drive, though, since plenty of wildlife and scenery is visible from the roads.

■ ⁊ ORIENTATION AND PRACTICAL INFORMATION

The park runs nearly 105 mi. along the famous **Skyline Drive,** which extends from Front Royal in the north to Rockfish Gap in the south before evolving into the **Blue Ridge Parkway.** Skyline Drive remains open year-round except during bad weather, and from dusk to dawn on some nights in hunting season. Mile markers are measured north to south and denote the location of trails and stops. Three major highways divide the park into sections: the **North Section** runs from Rte. 340 to Rte. 211; the **Central Section** from Rte. 211 to Rte. 33; and the **South Section** from Rte. 33 to I-64. A park pass is required to enter the park and is valid for seven days. (Entrance fee $10 per vehicle; $5 per hiker, biker, or bus passenger; disabled persons free.) Most facilities close in winter; call ahead. **Greyhound** (☎800-231-2222; www.greyhound.com), on the corner of Arch Ave. and W. Main St. in Waynesboro near the park's southern entrance, sends and receives one bus a day from Charlottesville (30min., $9.50-10.50), Richmond (2hr., $28-30), and Washington, D.C. (5hr., $40-43). No bus or train serves Front Royal, near the park's northern entrance.

The **Dickey Ridge Visitors Center,** at Mi. 4.6, and the **Byrd Visitors Center,** at Mi. 51, answer questions and maintain small exhibits about the park. The park rangers conduct informative presentations on local wildlife, guide short walks among the flora, and wax romantic during outdoor, lantern-lit evening discussions. Pick up a free *Shenandoah Overlook,* available at park entrances and visitors centers, for a complete listing of programs. (Dickey Ridge: ☎635-3566. Byrd: ☎999-3283. For both, visit www.nps.gov/shen for camp and park info and www.visitshenandoah.com for info and reservations. Both open Apr.-Oct. daily 8:30am-5pm; July-Sept. also F-Sa until 6pm.) For emergencies, call ☎800-732-0911. **Area Code:** 540.

⌐ ACCOMMODATIONS

The Appalachian Trail Conference's **Bears Den Hostel ❶,** 18393 Blue Ridge Mountain Rd., 35 mi. north of Shenandoah on Rte. 601, sleeps 20 travelers in two dorms. There are also private cabins for families or groups and a third bunk room for Appalachian Trail hikers. An in-house convenience store, kitchen, sleepsacks, and laundry ($2) are available. Take Rte. I-81 to Rte. 7 E and follow it for 17 mi. to Blue Ridge Mountain Rd.; turn right and drive a half-mile until you see a gate and a sign for the Bears Den on your right. (☎554-8708. 5-day max. stay. Reception 8-9am and 5-10pm. Check-out 9:30am. Curfew and quiet hours from 10pm. Camping $6 per person. Dorms $18; private double $50. MC/V.) The park maintains two lodges—essentially motels with rustic rooms. **Skyland Resort ❹,** Mi. 42 on Skyline Dr., offers wood-furnished cabins and more upscale motel rooms. (☎743-5108 or 800-999-4714. Open Apr.-Nov. Cabins $62-117; lodge rooms $85-135. Wheelchair-accessible rooms available. AmEx/D/DC/MC/V.) **Big Meadows Lodge ❹**, Mi. 51, has very similar services, with a "historic" (read: no phones or TV) lodge and cabins. (☎743-5108 or 800-999-4714. Open late Apr. to early Nov. Cabins $85-99; lodge rooms $67-130. AmEx/D/DC/MC/V.) Dining is available at both of the two lodges. **Lewis Mountain Cabins ❸**, Mi. 57, also owned by the park service, operates cabins with private baths and outdoor grill areas, as well as spartan "tent cabins." (☎743-5108 or 800-999-4714. Open May-Oct. Tent cabins $25; cabins $71-80. AmEx/D/DC/MC/V.)

🏕 CAMPING

The park service (☎800-365-2267; www.reservations.nps.gov; open 10am-10pm) maintains four major campgrounds. The northernmost, **Mathews Arm ❶**, Mi. 22 (179 sites; $16), is convenient to nearby **Elkwallow**, Mi. 24, which has a gas station, eatery, and gift shop. The popular **Big Meadows ❶**, Mi. 51 (sites $19), boasts secluded sites close to a visitors center, major trailheads, and several waterfalls. **Lewis Mountain ❶**, Mi. 58 (sites $16), is more private. Closest to the southern entrance, **Loft Mountain ❶**, Mi. 80 (sites $16), has shaded sites. The latter three have stores, showers, and laundry. All but Lewis Mountain have dump stations; none have hookups. Only Big Meadows accepts reservations. All campgrounds have a 14-day max. stay, allow pets, and are open from spring through October.

A 101 mi. section of the **Appalachian Trail (AT)** runs the length of the park. Twelve three-sided shelters are strewn at 8-10 mi. intervals along the AT. Unwritten trail etiquette usually reserves the cabins for those hiking long stretches of the trail. **Backcountry camping** is free, but you must obtain a permit at park entrances, visitors centers, or ranger stations. Camping without a permit or above 2800 ft. is illegal and unsafe. The **Potomac Appalachian Trail Club (PATC) ❶**, 118 Park St. SE, a volunteer organization, maintains six cabins in backcountry areas of the park that sleep 8-12 people each. Bring lanterns and food; the primitive cabins contain only bunk beds, blankets, and stoves. Pit toilets and spring water are nearby. (☎703-242-0693; www.patc.net. 1 group member must be 21+. Headquarters open M-W 7-9pm, Th noon-2pm and 7-9pm, F noon-2pm. Reservations required. M-W and Su $18 per group, Th-Sa $28. MC/V.) Trail maps and the PATC guide can be obtained at the visitors centers. The PATC also puts out topographical maps ($6).

🏃 OUTDOOR ACTIVITIES

HIKING
The trails off Skyline Dr. are heavily used and generally safe for cautious day-hikers with maps, appropriate footwear, and water. The middle section of the park, from **Thorton Gap**, Mi. 32, to **South River**, Mi. 63, bursts with photo opportunities and stellar views, although it also tends to be crowded with tourists. Rangers can recommend hikes of appropriate length and difficulty level for any visitor.

> **Whiteoak Canyon Trail** (Mi. 42.6; 4½ mi., 4hr. round-trip) is a strenuous hike that opens up on the 2nd-highest waterfall in the park (86 ft.), rewarding those who ascend the 1040 ft. elevation with views of the Limberlost hemlocks.
>
> **Limberlost Trail** (Mi. 43; 1¼ mi., 1hr. round-trip) is the easiest and only wheelchair-accessible trail in the park. From the trailhead (½ mi. from Skyland Lodge), Limberlost plunges into forest, weaves through orchards, and passes over a footbridge. No pets.

Old Rag Mountain Trail (Mi. 45; 8¾ mi., 6-8hr. round-trip) starts outside the park. From U.S. 211, turn right on Rte. 522, then right on Rte. 231. The trail scrambles up 3291 ft. to triumphant views of the valley below. Be careful of slippery rocks in damp weather and bring plenty of food and water. Strategically placed ladders ease the steep ascent.

Corbin Cabin Cutoff Trail (Mi. 37.8; 4 mi., 2½ hr. round-trip) is popular among history buffs. The trail leads down into a hollow, where an old cabin has been preserved so that hikers can see how the area's settlers lived. The ascent back up is fairly strenuous.

OTHER ACTIVITIES

There are two other ways to explore Shenandoah: by boat and by beast. **Downriver Canoe Company** in Bentonville offers canoe, kayak, raft, and tube trips. From Skyline Dr. Mi. 20, follow U.S. 211 W for 8 mi., then take U.S. 340 N 14 mi. to Bentonville; turn left on Rte. 613 and go 1 mi. The store is on the right. (☎ 635-5526 or 800-338-1963; www.downriver.com. Open M-F 9am-6pm, Sa-Su 7am-7pm.) Guided **horseback rides** are available at the Skyland Lodge, Mi. 42. (☎ 999-2210; www.visit-shenandoah.com. Riders must be at least 4 ft. 10 in. Open Apr.-Nov. 1hr. ride $23-25. 1-day advance reservation required.)

DAYTRIPS FROM SHENANDOAH

LURAY CAVERNS. Though the billboards that appear every 10 mi. along the highway scream tourist trap, the **Luray Caverns** defy all expectations. Take Exit 264 from U.S. 81 onto U.S. 211 E; many signposts point out the caverns from there. The 1hr. guided tours feature a variety of formations; be sure not to miss the reflecting pool, which creates such a convincing optical illusion that you can't even tell the water is there. The equally unforgettable cathedral room houses the world's largest natural musical instrument: a 37-mallet organ created from the caverns' own stalactites. It took Leeland W. Sprinkle, a Virginia organist, three years and over 3000 trials of different cave formations to finish his masterpiece in 1957; since that time the room has hosted hundreds of underground weddings. Bring a sweater for the cool caverns, and your patience along with it—the caverns can get extremely busy in the summer. A ticket into the caverns will also get you into the on-site vintage automobile museum, which displays over 140 vehicles, including an 1892 Mercedes-Benz and a Conestoga wagon. (☎ 743-6551; www.luraycaverns.com. Open mid-June to early Sept. daily 9am-7pm; Apr. to mid-June and Sept.-Oct. daily 9am-6pm; Nov. to Mar. M-F 9am-4pm, Sa-Su 9am-5pm. Adults $19, seniors $16, ages 6-12 $9. Wheelchair accessible.)

ENDLESS CAVERNS. Discovered in 1879, the **Endless Caverns** are considered "endless" because they encompass over 5 mi. of mapped cave passages with no visible end. Take Exit 257 or 264 from U.S. 81 and continue to the intersection of U.S. 11 and U.S. 211 in New Market. Follow the signs from here to 1800 Endless Caverns Rd. Bring a jacket and sturdy shoes. (☎ 896-2283; www.endlesscaverns.com. Open daily mid-Mar. to mid-June 9am-5pm; mid-June to early Sept. 9am-6pm; early Sept.-Oct. 9am-5pm; Nov. to mid-Mar. 9am-4pm. $14, ages 4-12 $6, under 4 free.)

SKYLINE CAVERNS. Smaller than Endless and Luray Caverns, Skyline Caverns, on U.S. 340, 1 mi. from the junction of Rte. 340 and Skyline Dr., are famous for their collection of orchid-like anthodites. These rare crystal formations, which only grow 1 in. every 7000 years, have formed a garden of white rock spikes. Tour stops include the Capitol Dome, the Wishing Well, Cathedral Hall, and Rainbow Falls, which pours 37 ft. from one of the three cavern streams. (☎ 635-4545 or 800-296-4545; www.skylinecaverns.com. Open June-Aug. daily 9am-6pm; Sept.-May M-F 9am-5pm, Sa-Su 9am-6pm. $14; seniors, AAA, and military $12; ages 7-13 $7; ages 6 and under free.)

MID-ATLANTIC

WEST VIRGINIA

With 80% of the state cloaked in untamed forests, commercial expansion and economic prosperity once seemed a distant dream for West Virginia. When the state's coal reserves began to run out, government officials decided to capitalize on the area's raging rivers and wooded wilderness. Today, thousands of tourists forge paths into West Virginia's breathtaking landscape, and thousands more settle for good. Park officials and state planners now face the challenging task of trying to accommodate the new human residents without encroaching too much upon the animals that already call West Virginia home.

⁊ PRACTICAL INFORMATION

Capital: Charleston.

Visitor Info: Department of Tourism, 90 MacCorkle Ave. SW, South Charleston 25305; P.O. Box 30312 (☎800-225-5982; www.callwva.com). **US Forest Service,** 200 Sycamore St., Elkins 26241 (☎304-636-1800; www.fs.fed.us/r9/mnf). Open M-F 8am-4:45pm.

Postal Abbreviation: WV. **Sales Tax:** 6%.

HARPERS FERRY ☎304

Harpers Ferry, on the Shenandoah and Potomac Rivers, earned its fame when a band of abolitionists led by John Brown raided the US armory there in 1859. Although Brown was captured and executed, the raid brought the clash over slavery even more momentum. The town of Harpers Ferry also became a major theater of conflict, changing hands eight times during the Civil War. Today, Harpers Ferry's guests are more mild-mannered, ranging from outdoors enthusiasts to field trippers looking for a taste of American history.

◢⁊ ORIENTATION AND PRACTICAL INFORMATION. Harpers Ferry is on West Virginia's eastern panhandle, less than a 10min. drive south to Virginia or north to Maryland. **Amtrak** (☎800-535-6406; www.amtrak.com; no ticketing office), on Potomac St. on the eastern side of the historic district, runs to Washington, D.C. (1¾hr., 1 per day, $12). At the same depot you'll find the **Maryland Rail Commuter (MARC;** ☎866-743-3682; www.mtamaryland.com), which offers cheaper, more frequent service to Washington, D.C. (M-F 2 per day, $9). **Pan Tran,** also at the train station, sends buses to Charles Town for $1.50 per person. (☎263-0876; www.pantran.com. Buses run M-F 6am-7pm, reduced hours Sa.) **The Outfitter,** 180 High St. (☎888-535-2087; www.theoutfitteratharpersferry.com), about halfway along the Appalachian Trail, sells outdoor equipment. **Visitor Info: Jefferson County Convention and Visitors Bureau,** on Shoreline Dr. just off Rte. 340 in Harpers Ferry (☎535-2627; www.hello-wv.com). The **Cavalier Heights Visitors Center** is inside the Harpers Ferry National Historic Park entrance, off Rte. 340. (☎535-6298; www.nps.gov/hafe. Open daily 8am-5pm.) The Cavalier Heights Visitors Center is the closest **public parking** to the historic district. The **Historic Town Area Visitor Information Center,** at the end of Shenandoah St., has free tour info. (☎535-6029; www.nps.gov/hafe. Open daily 8am-5pm.) **Internet Access: Bolivar and Harpers Ferry Public Library,** 151 Polk St. (☎535-2301. Open M-Tu and F-Sa 10am-5:30pm, W-Th

10am-8pm. Free.) **Post Office:** 1010 Washington St., at the corner of Washington and Franklin St. (☎535-2479. Open M-F 8am-4pm, Sa 9am-noon.) **Postal Code:** 25425. **Area Code:** 304.

ACCOMMODATIONS. Ragged hikers are welcome at the social █Harpers Ferry Hostel (HI) ❶, 19123 Sandy Hook Rd., at Keep Tryst Rd. off Rte. 340 in Knoxville, MD. This renovated auction house has a backyard trail to Potomac overlooks, a library, Internet access, kitchen, and shuttle pickup from the Greyhound station in Frederick, MD. (☎301-834-7652; www.harpersferryhostel.org. Laundry $2. Check-in 6-10pm. Check-out 7-9am. 5-night max. stay. Open mid-Mar. to mid-Nov. Dorms $20, members $17. Camping $9; includes use of kitchen and bathrooms. D/MC/V.) The **Hillside Motel** ❷, 19105 Keep Tryst Rd., 3 mi. from town in Knoxville, MD, has clean rooms and a fairly convenient location. (☎301-834-8144. In summer singles $40, doubles $50; in winter $30/$40. AmEx/D/V.) Those who like to rough it can camp along the **C&O Canal** ❶, where free primitive sites lie 5 mi. apart all along the canal's 180 mi. length. Camping is first come, first served. **Greenbrier State Park** ❶, on Rte. 40 E off Rte. 66, has 165 campsites and a lakeside recreation area. (☎301-791-4767; http://reservations.dnr.state.md.us. Reservations are recommended. Open Apr.-Oct. Sites $25, with electricity $30. MC/V.)

FOOD AND NIGHTLIFE. Chain restaurants welcome fast-food fanatics along Rte. 340. Nearby Charles Town's █La Mezzaluna Cafe ❸, Somerset Village Ste. B3, off Rte. 340 S, serves delicious Italian favorites. (☎728-0700. Pasta $9-15. Open Tu-Th 11am-3pm and 4-9pm, F-Sa 11am-3pm and 4-10pm, Su 2:30-9pm. AmEx/D/MC/V.) Across the street from the Hillside Motel, the **Cindy Dee Restaurant** ❶, 19112 Keep Tryst Rd., in Knoxville, MD, is usually full of people clamoring for fried chicken (from $5.75) and delicious apple dumplings. (☎301-695-8181. Open daily 6am-11pm. AmEx/D/MC/V.) Harpers Ferry's historic area around High St. and Potomac St. caters to the lunch crowd and empties out during dinner hours when most tourists have left. One exception is the **Armory Pub** ❸, 109 Potomac St., which gives pub fare a twist with fresh fish ($12) and chargrilled burgers ($6) and has live music on weekend nights. (☎535-2469. Open daily 11am-10:30pm. MC/V.) A tiny college town, **Shepherdstown**, 11 mi. north of Harpers Ferry, is a veritable culinary oasis in these quiet parts. Take Rte. 340 S for 2 mi. to Rte. 230 N, or bike

IN RECENT NEWS

GUMMING AROUND

Though jokes about toothless hillbillies mock Appalachia's populace to no end, some may not be that far off. The central Appalachian states lead the US in toothlessness rates, and West Virginia holds the title of most toothless state. Forty-three percent of its residents have lost six or more teeth because of decay or gum disease, according to the Centers for Disease Control.

The severe tooth decay and gum disease in Appalachia stems from an abundance of sugary foods, cigarettes, chewing tobacco, and a lack of fluoridated water, but cultural attitudes toward dental health do little to ameliorate the problem. Many residents of mountain communities have the mistaken idea that tooth loss is a normal part of growing old, despite the fact that medical advances are making it almost an archaic malady in other parts of the country.

But not everybody sees Appalachian toothlessness as a joke. Dentists are starting to bring free dental care to the poorest parts of Appalachia, and charitable organizations have opened free clinics or hosted dental-care events in Wal-Mart parking lots. Volunteers are trying to reach children and people who cannot afford dental care but make too much money to qualify for Medicaid. Perhaps with time, concerted volunteer efforts will be able to alter the fate of the gap-toothed smile.

13 mi. along the C&O towpath. Caffeine addicts flock to **Lost Dog,** 134 E. German St., which brews 30 different blends of coffee and over 50 kinds of tea. (☎876-0871. Open M-Th and Su 6:30am-6pm, F-Sa 6:30am-7pm. AmEx/D/MC/V.) Amid the colonial architecture of E. German St., the **Mecklinburg Inn,** 128 E. German St., provides rock 'n' roll and Rolling Rock ($2.50) on open mic nights every Tuesday from 9pm to midnight. (☎876-2126. Happy hour M-F 4:30-6:30pm. 21+. Open M-Th 3pm-12:30am, F 3pm-1:30am, Sa 1pm-2am, Su 1pm-12:30am.)

◙ **SIGHTS.** The **Harpers Ferry National Historic Park** is composed of several museums. Entrance to the museums, parking, and shuttle rides from the parking lot to the historic area are all included with admission. (☎535-6298. Open daily 8am-5pm. Shuttles every 10min., last pickup 5:45pm. 3-day admission $6 per car; $4 per pedestrian, bike, or motorcycle.) Parking in historic Lower Town is nearly nonexistent; unless you snag one of the pricey spots in the lot at the end of Shenandoah St., it's necessary to park at the visitors center and board the free shuttles to town or walk about 20min. The bus stops at **Shenandoah Street,** where a barrage of replica 19th-century shops greets visitors. The **Harpers Ferry Industrial Museum,** on Shenandoah St., describes the methods used to harness the powers of the Shenandoah and Potomac rivers and details the town's status as the endpoint of the nation's first successful rail line. The unsung stories of Harpers Ferry captivate visitors at **Black Voices,** on the corner of High and Shenandoah St., where visitors can listen to audio clips from actors reading the memoirs of fettered and freed slaves expressing their opinions on John Brown and his raid. Next door on High St., the plight of Harpers Ferry's slaves is further elaborated upon in the **Civil War Museum.** A dauntingly steep staircase hewn into the hillside off High St. follows the **Appalachian Trail** to **Upper Harpers Ferry,** which has fewer sights but is laced with interesting historical tales. Allow 45min. to ascend past **Harpers House,** the restored home of town founder Robert Harper, and to explore the insides of **St. Peter's Church,** where a pastor flew the Union Jack during the Civil War to protect the church. Just a few steps uphill from St. Peter's lie the ruins of **St. John's Episcopal Church,** used as a hospital and barracks during the Civil War.

⚠ **OUTDOOR ACTIVITIES.** After digesting the town's historical sights, many choose to soak up the outdoors. The park's visitors center has trail maps. The moderately difficult **Maryland Heights Trail,** across the railroad bridge in the Lower Town of Harpers Ferry, wanders 4 mi. through the Blue Ridge Mountains and includes glimpses of crumbling Civil War-era forts. The strenuous 7½ mi. **Loudon Heights Trail** starts in the Lower Town off the Appalachian Trail and leads to Civil War trenches and scenic overlooks. The moderate 2½ mi. **Camp Hill Trail** passes by the Harper Cemetery. Civil War era battlefields and infantry trenches dominate the **Bolivar Heights Trail,** which starts at the northern end of Whitman Ave.

The **Chesapeake & Ohio Canal** towpath, off the end of Shenandoah St. and over the railroad bridge, serves as a lasting reminder of the town's industrial roots and is the point of departure for a 180 mi. bike ride to Washington, D.C. It's possible to ride the whole towpath in one day, but only by getting on the trail at or before daybreak. The **Appalachian Trail Conference** (see **Orientation and Practical Information,** p. 303), 799 Washington St., at Jackson St., offers catalogs with deals on hiking books and trail info. (☎535-6331; www.appalachiantrail.org. Open M-F 9am-5pm; May-Oct. also Sa-Su 9am-4pm. Membership $30, seniors and students $25.) **River & Trail Outfitters,** 604 Valley Rd., 2 mi. from Harpers Ferry off Rte. 340 in Knoxville, MD, rents canoes, kayaks, inner tubes, and rafts. They also organize everything from scenic daytrips to wild overnights, all on the Shenandoah River. (☎301-695-5177 or 888-446-7529; www.rivertrail.com. Raft trips $50-60, ages 16 and under $45-50.

Canoes $60 per day. Tubing $22 per day.) At **Butt's Tubes,** on Rte. 671 off Rte. 340, adventurers and loungers can float down the river for minimal cost. (☎888-434-9911 or 800-836-9911; www.buttstubes.com. Open M-F 10am-3pm, last pickup from the river at 5pm; Sa-Su 10am-4pm, last pickup 6pm. $13-25.) **Elk Mountain Trails,** 921 Hoffmaster Rd., off Sandy Hook Rd., leads horseback riding trips in the area. (☎301-834-8882; www.elkmountaintrails.com. Rides $21-125.)

MONONGAHELA NATIONAL FOREST   ☎304

Monongahela National Forest sprawls across the eastern portion of West Virginia and is home to nine endangered species, limestone caverns, and hordes of weekend canoers, fly-fishermen, cavers, and skiers. The **Cranberry Mountain Nature Center,** near the Highland Scenic Hwy. at the junction of Rte. 150 and Rte. 39/55, has excellent wildlife exhibits and provides maps of local hiking trails. (☎653-4826 or 653-8564; www.fs.fed.us/r9/mnf. Open Apr.-Nov. daily 9am-4:30pm.) They also conduct free weekend tours of the **Cranberry Glades.** (30min.-1hr. tours June-Aug. Sa-Su 2pm.) Wrapping around the glades is the **Cow Pasture Trail** (6 mi.), which passes a WWII German prison camp. Two popular hikes are **Big Beechy Trail** (6½ mi.; the trailhead is next to a parking lot at the Highland Scenic Hwy. and Rte. 461 junction) and the awesome **Falls of Hills Creek Trail** (1½ mi.), off Rte. 39/55 south of the Nature Center, with three waterfalls ranging in height from 25 to 63 ft. A small concrete pathway leads to a cascade of wooden steps down to the falls—good knees are a must. The **Highland Scenic Highway (Route 150)** stretches 43 mi. from Richwood to U.S. 219, 7 mi. north of Marlinton, and affords gorgeous views. This is particularly true for the section of **Route 39** from Marlinton to Goshen, VA, which passes by swimming sites on the Maury River which are signposted from the highway. Tempting as it is to gaze at the forest's splendor, driving on the winding and often foggy roads can be treacherous.

Those with several days to spend might choose to hike, bike, or ski part of the **Greenbrier River Trail** (75 mi., 1-degree grade), which runs from Cass to North Caldwell; the trailhead is on Rte. 38 off U.S. 60 in North Caldwell. Lined with access points and campgrounds, the trail offers easily hikeable and bikeable terrain and, in the late summer, a chance to witness monarch butterfly migration. Downhill delights abound on the 54 ski trails at the **Snowshoe Resort,** accessible from Rte. 66 between Rte. 219 and Rte. 28. (☎572-1000 or 877-441-4386; www.snowshoemtn.com. Open Dec.-Mar. daily 8:30am-10pm. M-F lift tickets $49, students and seniors $40, children $34; Sa-Su $63/$58/$45. Ski rental $24-28, children $16-20.) When the snow melts, mountain bikers move in for the summer; the **Mountain Adventure Center** at Snowshoe offers bike rentals, tours, and lift passes. (☎877-441-4386; snowshoemtn.com. Bikes from $25 for half-day, $35-125 full day. Trail access passes $10 per day, with access to the lift and mountain bike park $20 per day.)

Travel north to ◼**Cass Scenic Railroad State Park,** off Rte. 28/92, for novel train rides on the remaining 11 mi. of the once-burgeoning 3000 mi. lumber railroad lines of West Virginia. Ascend to 4842 ft. on the oldest steam engine locomotive in continual use in the US, which offers specialty trips and overnight stays on Cheat Mountain. (☎456-4300 or 800-225-5982; www.cassrailroad.com. Trains run Memorial Day-Oct., call for schedules. $13-19, ages 5-12 $8-12.) Science and physics lovers will appreciate the **National Radio Astronomy Observatory,** off Rte. 28/92, which houses **The Robert C. Byrd Green Bank Telescope,** the largest fully steerable telescope in the world. Not only is this where the Search for Extra-Terrestrial Intelligence (The SETI Project) started, it is also the largest moveable structure on land. Free tours take you to the base of the looming 17 million lb. telescope. (☎456-2150; www.gb.nrao.edu. Tours late May to early Sept. every hr. daily 9am-6pm; early Sept. to Oct. W-Su 9am-6pm; Nov. to late May W-Su 11am, 1, 3pm.)

MID-ATLANTIC

Each of Monongahela's six districts has a campground and recreation area, with ranger stations off Rte. 39 east of Marlinton and in the towns of Bartow and Poto-mack. Established sites are $8; backcountry camping is free, though you must register at the Cranberry Mountain Nature Center. **Cranberry Campground ❶**, in the Gauley district, 13 mi. from Ridgewood on Forest Rd. 76, has hiking trails through cranberry bogs and campsites. (☎846-2695. Sites $8.) **Watoga State Park ❶**, in Marlinton, has maps and a lake. (☎799-4087; www.watoga.com. Sites $15, with electricity $19. AmEx/D/MC/V.) If you don't feel like roughing it, travel up a driveway flanked by a profusion of wildflowers to the 🏠**Morning Glory Inn ❹**, 1½ mi. north of Slatyfork on Rte. 219. This B&B offers gargantuan rooms with cathedral-like ceilings, whirlpool tubs, and a sprawling porch. (☎572-5000 or 866-572-5700; www.morninggloryinn.com. Check-in 4-9pm. Check-out 11am. Doubles $80-100; Jan.-Mar. $100-155. AmEx/D/MC/V.) Five miles farther from the slopes, the **Jerico B&B ❸**, on Rte. 219 in Marlinton just south of the junction with Rte. 39, has pre-Civil War themed cabins in addition to bedrooms in the main house. (☎799-6241; www.jericobb.com. Rooms $50-$85. Cabins $85-185. AmEx/D/MC/V.) **The Restaurant at Elk River ❹**, on Rte. 219 in Slatyfork, has a steak- and seafood-based menu with similar prices but a less touristy feel than the posh resort restaurants. The rainbow trout is a specialty. (☎572-3771. Open Th-Su 5-9pm. AmEx/D/MC/V.) The **Route 66 Sub Shop ❶**, on Rte. 66 at the base of Snowshoe, serves salads, pizzas, and wraps that will fill you up without breaking the bank. (☎572-1200. Breakfast all day. Subs $4-6. Open M-F 7am-9pm, Sa-Su 7am-10pm. AmEx/D/MC/V.)

Amtrak, 315 W. Main St., across from the Greenbrier Resort, is in White Sulphur Springs at the forest's southern tip. (☎800-872-7245; www.amtrak.com. No ticket office.) Trains run W ($42), F ($33), and Su ($42) to Washington, D.C. **Greyhound** (☎800-231-2222; www.greyhound.com) will drop passengers with a Charleston ticket off along Rte. 60 but does not run from the forest. The forest **Supervisor's Office,** 200 Sycamore St., in Elkins, distributes a list of campsites and fees, as well as fishing and hunting info. (☎636-1800. Open M-F 8am-4:30pm.) **Area Code:** 304.

NEW RIVER GORGE ☎304

The New River Gorge is a testament to the raw beauty and power of nature. One of the oldest rivers in the world, the New River has carved a narrow gorge through the Appalachian Mountains, creating precipitous valley walls that tower 1000 ft. above the white waters. These steep slopes remained untouched until 1873, when industrialists drained the region to uncover coal and timber. With the coal mines now defunct, the New River Gorge has become a sanctuary for outdoors enthusiasts with rafters cruising its rapids and climbers ascending its cliffs.

🚗🗺 ORIENTATION AND PRACTICAL INFORMATION. Amtrak, on Rte. 41 N in Prince and Hinton, runs through the heart of the gorge. (☎800-872-7245 or 253-6651; www.amtrak.com. Prince open W, F, Su 9:30am-9pm. Hinton open W, F, Su 11am-1pm and 4:30-6:30pm.) **Greyhound** stops at 105 3rd St. in Beckley. (☎800-231-2222 or 253-8333; www.greyhound.com. Open M-Sa 7am-5pm, Su 7-10am and 2-5pm.) Buses go to Charleston (1hr., 3 per day, $20), Charlottesville (7hr., 2 per day, $59), and Philadelphia (6hr., 3 per day, $96). The park operates four visitors centers, each of which has info on hiking trails and the area's history. Off Rte. 19 just north of Fayetteville and the New River Gorge Bridge, 🏠**Canyon Rim** provides the best view in the entire park. (☎574-2115. Open daily 9am-5pm.) If you're heading to New River Gorge from the south, **Sandstone,** on Rte. 64 east of Beckley, is a good place to start. The gorgeous building is eco-friendly and features a scale model of the New River and its tributaries in colored stone, as well as a room full of hands-on exhibits. (☎466-0417. Open daily 9am-5pm.) **Grandview,** on Rte. 9 near

Beckley, attracts visitors in May when the rhododendrons are in bloom. (☎ 763-3715. Open May-Sept. daily noon-5pm.) **Thurmond,** on Rte. 25 off I-19, has access to hiking trails down in the river valley. (☎ 465-8550. Open May-Sept. daily 10am-5pm.) Signs on Rte. 19 labeled "Rafting and Recreation Information" lead to the **New River Convention and Visitors Bureau,** 310 Oyler Ave., in Oak Hill, which has extensive information on rafting outfitters, area attractions, and the various Bridge Day festivities. (☎ 465-5617; www.newrivercvb.com. Open daily 9am-5pm.) **Area Code:** 304.

ᴦ ACCOMMODATIONS. A slew of budget motels can be found off **I-77** in Beckley ($45-60). The **Green Banks Motel ❷,** 505 S. Eisenhower Dr., in Beckley, is a basic motel with rooms that are clean and affordable and come with microwaves and refrigerators. (☎ 253-3355. HBO. Singles $45; doubles $50. AmEx/D/MC/V.) **Babcock State Park ❶,** on Rte. 41 south of U.S. 60, 15 mi. west of Rainelle, has shaded campsites, a bath house, laundry facilities, and 28 cabins, including two deluxe cabins with kitchen and A/C. Activities include swimming, horseback riding, and tennis. (☎ 438-3004 or 800-225-5982. No alcohol. Sites $15, with electricity $18; cabins $49-110. Cash only, unless booking by phone.) Many raft companies operate private campgrounds that offer both lodging and package rafting-lodging-dining deals. **ACE Adventure Center ❶,** at the end of Minden Rd. in Oak Hill, offers rafting, recreation, and lodging options. From Rte. 19, take the Oak Hill Main St. exit eastbound and turn left onto Minden Rd. (☎ 800-787-3982; www.aceraft.com. Tent sites $10 per person; RV sites $29; cabin tents $39 for 1-2 guests; bunkhouses for groups of 6 or more $16 per adult, $13 per child under 17. AmEx/D/MC/V.) **North American River Runners (NARR) ❶,** on Hwy. 60, has rafting, kayaking, bath houses, and a cafe. Lodging options include primitive camping, four-person cabin tents, and 24-person bunkhouses. (☎ 800-950-2585; www.narr.com. No outlets or linens. Sites $10 per person; cabin tents $70-80; bunk houses $15 per person. AmEx/D/MC/V.)

ᑕ FOOD. The **Western Pancake House ❶,** on Whitewater Dr. off Rte. 19, just south of Fayetteville, serves country cooking all day. Whether it's a stack of pancakes ($4.50) or a hot turkey dinner plate ($6), this is the best deal in town. (☎ 564-1240. Open 24hr. MC/V.) The **Sedona Grill ❸,** on Rte. 16, just north of the Appalachian Dr. exit from Rte. 19, offers upscale New American cuisine. Lunch wraps and sandwiches ($6-8) are reasonable, while delicious entrees like barbecued pork ($14-18) and the more exotic shrimp

FREE FALLIN'

Billed as the "Super Bowl of BASE Jumping," Bridge Day (p. 308) attracts hundreds of brave souls to New River Gorge every year. On the third Saturday of October, some of the craziest BASE jumpers (skydivers that jump from Buildings, Antennas, Spans, and Earth) in the world leap off the New River Gorge bridge with only a parachute to slow their descent into the churning waters of the New River, 876 ft. below.

The New River Gorge Bridge is closed to traffic on Bridge Day and becomes the epicenter for a weekend-long party with food, live music, theater, and even a classic car show. Spectators watch as hundreds of BASE jumpers perform somersaults and stunts, compete for the most accurate landing, or just splash down into the frigid river below. Festivalgoers can also ride down the "high line," rigged from the beams beneath the bridge's roadway and descending a spine-tickling 600 ft. to the floor of the gorge.

Bridge Day spectators often witness over 1000 bridge jumps. But in case you are tempted to do a solo Superman show, take note that at any time during the year other than 9am-3pm on Bridge Day, jumping from the bridge is illegal. Remember to heed the rules, or a jump into the river might just land you in jail.

Bridge Day will be held on Oct. 21, 2006. For more information, visit www.officialbridgeday.com.

and apple curry ($15) are a bit pricier. (☎574-3411. Open M-Tu and Th 4-9pm; F-Sa 11:30am-10pm; Su 11:30am-9pm. AmEx/D/MC/V.) If only barbecue can satisfy your post-rafting hunger, try **Dirty Eddie's Rib Pit ❹**, at 310 Keller St. near the northern Fayetteville exit off Rte. 19. Racks of ribs start at $12; prime rib is $16. (☎574-4822. Open daily 4-10pm. AmEx/D/MC/V.)

◙ SIGHTS. In 1973, the breathtaking ▧**New River Gorge Bridge** was completed, becoming the second-highest bridge in the US. Best seen on foot, the bridge towers 876 ft. above New River and claims the world's largest single steel arch span. The Canyon Rim Visitors Center offers a decent vista, but for an unobstructed view, descend the zig-zag wooden stairs to the lower level lookout. On **Bridge Day,** the third Saturday in October, thousands of extreme sports enthusiasts leap off the bridge by bungee or parachute as on-lookers enjoy the festival's food and crafts. (☎800-927-0263; www.wvbridgeday.com. Oct. 21, 2006.) In Beckley, retired coal miners lead 35min. tours down a mine shaft at the **Beckley Exhibition Coal Mine,** on Ewart Ave. (Exit 44 from I-77) at New River Park. See how coal mines operated while riding in a coal car through 150 ft. of underground passages. The tunnels are chilly; bring a jacket. (☎256-1747. Open Apr.-Oct. daily 10am-6pm, Nov.-Mar. Tu-Sa 10am-5pm; last tour leaves 30min. before close. $15, seniors $13, ages 4-12 $10.)

⚙ OUTDOOR ACTIVITIES. The **New River Gorge National River** runs north from Hinton to Fayetteville, falling over 750 ft. in 50 mi. In order to conserve its magnificent natural and historic value, the New River Gorge has been protected by the National Park Service since 1958. Rafting companies offer trips on the Upper (gentler) and Lower (wilder) New River, as well as the Gauley River, 15 mi. north of New River National Park. The **West Virginia Division of Tourism** (☎800-225-5982; www.callwva.com), will connect you to outfitters on both rivers.

Though the renowned rapids draw the most tourists, leisurely hiking allows visitors time to take in the scenery. The most rewarding trails are the strenuous **Kaymoor Trail** (2 mi.) and the easy **Thurmond-Minden Trail** (6½ mi. round-trip, only 3 mi. round-trip to main overlook). Kaymoor starts at the bridge on Fayette Station Rd., near Canyon Rim Visitors Center, and runs past the abandoned coal-processing ovens of Kaymoor, a coal-mining community that shut down in 1962. Thurmond-Minden is fairly flat and has vistas overlooking the New River and Dunloup Creek, but is not clearly marked in some areas. To get to the trailhead, exit Rte. 19 at Main St. in Oak Hill. Turn left onto Main St. if coming from the south, right if from the north, then make a left on Minden Rd. Continue for 2 mi. and take a right across a small bridge. The trail is distinguished from the other paths in the vicinity by the gate that blocks vehicles from entering. Hikers of all levels can take advantage of the gorge's spectacular rock-climbing opportunities with **New River Mountain Guides,** at Wiseman and Court St. in downtown Fayetteville. (☎574-3872 or 800-732-5462; www.newriverclimbing.com. Half-day trips with climbing and rapelling start at $95, full-day trips at $200.) Experienced climbers can climb the challenging **Endless Wall,** which runs southeast along the New River and has great river views from a height of 1000 ft. The wall is accessible from a 2½ mi. trail off Lansing-Edmond Rd. (Rte. 5) north of the Canyon Rim Visitors Center along Rte. 19.

Horseback-riding trips are another way to explore the gorge. ▧**New River Trail Rides,** in Oak Hill, leads 2hr. rides, sunset trips, and overnight adventures year-round from their stables off Wonderland Rd. From E. Main St., turn on Gatewood Rd. eastbound, then right on Wonderland Rd. (☎465-4819 or 888-742-3982; www.ridewva.com. 2½hr. rides from $42. Scenic Overlook Ride departs 9:30am, 1, 3:30pm. Sunset rides are $45 and depart June-Aug. 6:30pm, May and Sept. 5:30pm, Mar.-Apr. and Oct. 5pm.) For a more mechanical mode of transport, bike tours, rentals, and repairs are available at **New River Bike and Touring,** 103 Keller Ave., off the Fayetteville historic district exit on Rte. 19. (☎574-2453; www.newriverbike.com. Open daily 9am-6pm. Bike rentals $35 half-day, $60 full day; bike tours $70 half-day, $110 full day.) **ACE Adventure Center,** on Minden Rd. in the town of Oak Hill, also provides rentals and tours. (☎888-223-7238; www.bikewv.com. Bike rentals $29-35 half-day, $39-45 full day; tours $54-65.)

THE SOUTH

The American consciousness has become much more homogeneous since the 1860s, but differences, though not as dramatic, persist between North and South. Outside the area's commercial capitals, Southerners continue to live slower-paced lives than their northern countrymen. Nevertheless, the South's legacy of racial tension is still an ugly blemish on its history; the effects of slavery have not yet been completely washed away, and the Civil Rights movement is too recent a development to be comfortably relegated to textbooks.

At the same time, the South's racial differences have inspired many aspects of American culture for which the country is known the world over, from great literature to nearly *all* music native to the country: gospel, blues, jazz, country, R&B, and rock 'n' roll all claim the South as their birthplace. The South's distinctive architecture, cuisine, and language are all products of its Spanish, French, and Native American influences throughout the years. Landscapes are equally varied—the region is filled with mountains, beaches, and of course, the bayou. The traveler here should forget facile stereotypes and discover a part of the world that is overlooked and underestimated. In the South you'll find Bible factories and booze distilleries, rural backcountry and raging cities, traditional comfort food and finger lickin' good barbecue, and some of the best entertainment the US has to offer.

HIGHLIGHTS OF THE SOUTH

GNAW on juicy ribs at local joints like **Dreamland Barbecue** (p. 401) and wash them down with some old-fashioned Southern sweet tea.

GYRATE like Elvis at **Graceland** (p. 336), kick up your heels to zydeco in **New Orleans** (p. 425), or wallow in your sorrows in **Memphis** (p. 339), where blues is king.

FANCY yourself a Southern Belle as you tour **historic plantations** like the ones in Charleston, SC (p. 367), that capture the grandeur of the Old South.

REMEMBER the Civil Rights Movement at **The Martin Luther King Center** (p. 379) in Atlanta, GA and the **Birmingham Civil Rights Institute** (p. 399) in Birmingham, AL.

KENTUCKY

Legendary for the duels, feuds, and stubborn spirit of its earlier inhabitants (such as the infamous Daniel Boone), Kentucky invites travelers to kick back, take a shot of the legendary local bourbon, and relax amid rolling hills and the sound of bluegrass. The state also boasts an extensive network of caves, including the longest known cave in the world. Today, the spirit of Kentucky can be boiled down to one pastime: going fast. The state is home to the signature American sports car, the Corvette, and to the world's premier horse race, the Kentucky Derby. Louisville tends to ignore its vibrant cultural scene and active nightlife at Derby time, and Lexington devotes much of its farmland to breeding champion racehorses.

In August 2005, Category Five Hurricane Katrina struck the Gulf Coast of the United States, devastating cities and killing thousands in the states of Alabama, Louisiana, and Mississippi. While progress has been made, much of the South is still trying to recover from the emotional and physical impact of the disaster.

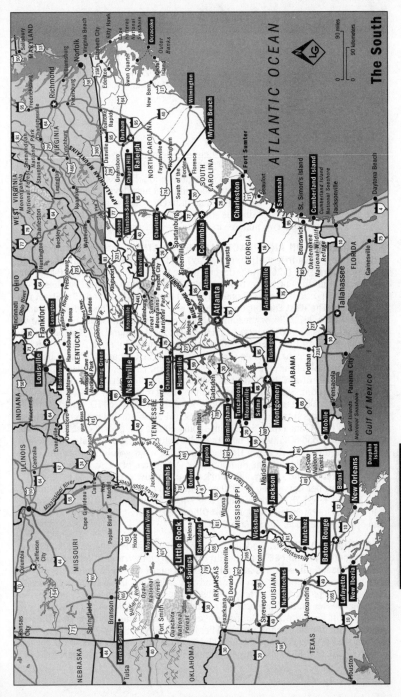

The South

⑦ PRACTICAL INFORMATION

Capital: Frankfort.

Visitor Info: Kentucky Dept. of Tourism, Capital Plaza Tower, 500 Mero St., Ste. 2200, Frankfort 40601 (☎502-564-4930 or 800-225-8747; www.kentuckytourism.com). **Kentucky State Parks,** Capital Plaza Tower, 500 Mero St., Ste. 1100, Frankfort 40601 (☎800-255-7275; www.parks.ky.gov).

Postal Abbreviation: KY. **Sales Tax:** 6%.

LOUISVILLE   ☎502

When the familiar gremlins of white flight and deindustrialization caught up with Louisville (say "LOO-uh-vuhl") in the 1950s, Kentucky's largest city spent a decade or two adrift before setting its sights on revitalization. Residents can't quite agree on what a revitalized Louisville should look like, yet new development determined to "keep Louisville weird" has achieved an unlikely synergy that has to be experienced firsthand. The biggest draw is still the Kentucky Derby. The horse race that some call "the greatest two minutes in sports" will return to town on May 6, 2006.

■⑦ ORIENTATION AND PRACTICAL INFORMATION. Interstates through the city include **I-65** (north-south expressway), **I-71,** and **I-64.** The easily accessible **Watterson Expressway (I-264)** rings the city, while the **Gene Snyder Freeway (I-265)** circles farther out. In central downtown, **Main Street** and **Market Street** run east-west in opposite directions (both are one-way), and **Preston Highway** and **19th Street** run north-south. The **West End,** beyond 20th St., is a rough area. The **Louisville International Airport** (☎367-4636; www.louintlairport.com) is 15min. south of downtown on I-65; take bus #2 into the city. A taxi to downtown is around $16. **Greyhound,** 720 W. Muhammad Ali Blvd. (☎561-2805; www.greyhound.com; open 24hr.), between 7th and 8th St., runs to: Chicago (6hr., 9 per day, $47); Cincinnati (2hr., 8 per day, $20); Indianapolis (2hr., 9 per day, $21); Lexington (2-4hr., 4 per day, $20). The **Transit Authority River City (TARC)** bus system serves the metro area. (☎585-1234; www.ridetarc.com. Schedules vary by route; buses run as early as 4:30am until as late as 11:30pm. $1, ages 6-17 and seniors 65+ $0.50 with TARC ID; transfers free.) Two trolley routes service Main St./Market St. (M-F 6:45am-6:30pm, Sa 10am-6pm) and 4th St. (M-F 7am-11pm, Sa 9:30am-10pm). Riding the trolley costs $0.25. **Taxi: Cardinal Cab,** ☎636-5511. **Visitor Info: Louisville Visitor Information Center,** 320 Jefferson Ave., in the Hyatt Regency Hotel. (☎584-2121; www.gotolouisville.com. Open M-F 10am-5pm, Sa 11am-4pm, Su noon-4pm; Oct.-Mar. closed Su.) **Internet Access: Louisville Free Public Library,** 301 York St., downtown. (☎574-1611. Photo ID required. 1hr. per day. Open M-Th 9am-9pm, F-Sa 9am-5pm, Su 1-5pm.) **Hotlines: Rape Hotline,** ☎581-7273. **Crisis Center,** ☎589-4313. Both operate 24hr. **GLBT Hotline,** ☎454-7613. Operates daily 6-10pm. **Post Office:** 835 S. 7th St. (☎584-6045. Open M-F 8am-5pm.) **Postal Code:** 40203. **Area Code:** 502.

⑦ ACCOMMODATIONS. Lodging in downtown Louisville is plentiful, but pricey. Budget motels are on **I-65** near the airport or across the river in **Jeffersonville, IN. Newburg Road,** 6 mi. south, is also a budget haven. Derby Week lodging is expensive; make reservations up to a year in advance. Starting around January, the visitors center helps travelers arrange rooms for the event. The cheapest beds are the foam mattresses on the basement of the **Emily Boone Guest House and Hostel ❶,** 102 Pope St., off Franklin Ave. Boone houses up to three backpackers at a time in exchange for 20min. of chores around her house and yard. Expect to get cozy with her long-haired dog, Violet, who also sleeps in the basement. (☎585-3430. No linens provided. Bed $10. Cash only.) For more in the way of comfort, **Super 8 ❸,** 101

Central Ave., near Churchill Downs and the University of Louisville, has clean rooms and a stellar location. (☎635-0799. Laundry. Breakfast and airport shuttle included. Singles $65; doubles $75. AmEx/D/MC/V.) **Louisville Metro KOA ❶**, 900 Marriott Dr., across the river in Indiana, has campsites 10min. from town. (☎812-282-4474. Make reservations well in advance. 2-person sites $24-27, with hookup $32. Each additional person $4, under 18 $2.50. 2-person cabins $42-45.)

❏ FOOD. Good budget food is hard to find downtown. **Bardstown Road** is lined with cafes, budget eateries, and global cuisine, while **Frankfort Road** is rapidly catching up. Downtown, **Fourth Street Live!**, at Broadway and 4th St., has various lunch options. The mannequin legs jutting out of the day-glow walls at ▧ **Lynn's Paradise Cafe ❸**, 984 Barret Ave., give an inkling of what it would be like to live in a surrealist painting where breakfast is served all day. Try the pancakes filled with cinnamon granola ($6.75) or dinner platters like fried catfish with mustard-shallot sauce ($10), available after 11am. (☎583-3447. Open M-F 7am-10pm, Sa-Su 8am-10pm. AmEx/MC/V.) **Mark's Feed Store ❸**, 1514 Bardstown Rd., serves award-winning barbecue in a dining room decorated with checkered tablecloths and metal animal feed ads. (☎458-1570. Sandwiches $6-8. Baby-back ribs $12. M free dessert after 4pm. Tu kids eat free. Open M-Th and Su 11am-10pm, F-Sa 11am-11pm. Call for other locations. D/MC/V.) You can look after both your health and your karma at **Zen Garden ❷**, 2240 Frankfort Ave., a quiet vegetarian restaurant that donates all of its profits to hungry children in Vietnam. (☎895-9114. Noodle dishes $6.50-9.50. Open M-Th 11am-10pm, F-Sa 11am-11pm. AmEx/D/MC/V.) Gourmet pastry chef Debbie Richter frequently pokes her nose out of the kitchen to mingle with customers at **Sweet Surrender ❶**, 1416 Bardstown Rd., where huge slices of caramel pound cake and chocolate ganache torte ($4.95) almost qualify as meals by themselves. (☎458-6363. Open Tu-Th 9am-6pm, F-Sa 9am-11pm. D/MC/V.)

◪ SIGHTS. The record stores, cafes, boutiques, and antique shops on the **Highlands** strip can easily fill an afternoon with shopping or browsing. The strip runs along Baxter Ave. and Bardstown Rd. between Broadway and Trevilian Way. (Take buses #17 or 23.) Down by the University of Louisville campus, the **Speed Art Museum**, 2035 S. 3rd St., shows off a treasure trove of European paintings. As the largest art museum in Kentucky, the Speed also draws major temporary exhibitions; summer 2006 will bring a retrospective of African-American artist Sam Gilliam's work. (☎634-2700; www.speedmuseum.org. Open Tu-W and F 10:30am-4pm, Th 10:30am-8pm, Sa 10:30am-5pm, Su noon-5pm. Free; special exhibitions $5-10.) J.F. Hillerich & Son started out manufacturing butter churns in the 1870s, but the enormous baseball bat leaning up against the **Louisville Slugger Factory and Museum**, 800 W. Main St., belongs to the company's more lucrative product line. The museum traces the history of the Slugger, while a factory tour leads visitors through sawdust and past lengths of wood that have been earmarked for specific major-leaguers. At the tour's end, visitors receive a miniature bat of their own. (☎588-7228; www.sluggermuseum.org. Open Apr.-Nov. M-Sa 9am-5pm, Su noon-5pm; Dec.-Mar. closed Su; last tours 4pm. $8, seniors $7, ages 6-12 $4.) The **American Printing House for the Blind**, 1839 Frankfort Ave., has a small but fascinating museum on the development of Braille and other technologies for aiding the blind. The facility is the world's largest publishing house dedicated to the visually impaired. (☎895-2405; www.aph.org. Open M-F 8:30am-4:30pm, Sa 10am-3pm. 1hr. tours M-Th 10am and 2pm. Free. Wheelchair accessible.)

▰▰ ENTERTAINMENT AND NIGHTLIFE. Two free weeklies, *Leo* and *Velocity*, are available throughout the city and spotlight current happenings. Broadway shows, comedy acts, and big-name music performers take the stage at the lavishly

THE SOUTH

decorated **Louisville Palace,** 625 S. 4th Ave. (☎583-4555. Tickets $20-100. Box office open M-F 9am-5pm.) The well-respected **Actors Theatre,** 316 W. Main St., raises the curtain on a season of comedy, drama, and March's **Humana Festival of New American Plays.** (☎584-1205; www.actorstheatre.org. Box office open M 10-5:30pm, Tu-W 10am-8pm, Th-F 10am-8:30pm, Sa 10am-9pm, Su 1-8pm. $15 student and senior rush tickets available 15min. before curtain.) On the **"First Friday"** of every month, more than a dozen of Louisville's downtown galleries treat visitors to special openings and refreshments until 9pm. Trolleys provide free transportation between galleries 5-11pm. The **Kentucky Shakespeare Festival,** at the amphitheater in Central Park in Old Louisville, struts upon the stage from late June to July. (☎637-4933; www.kyshakes.org. Performances 8pm. Free.) Quirky **Lebowski Fest** draws fans of the 1998 Coen brothers comedy *The Big Lebowski* for a summer weekend of bowling, live music, and opportunities to quote obscure dialogue to like-minded "Achievers." (☎583-9290; www.lebowskifest.com. Tickets $15-25.)

Clubs cluster on Baxter Ave. near Broadway. **Phoenix Hill Tavern,** 644 Baxter Ave., cranks out blues and rock with live bands and DJs on three stages. (☎589-4957; www.phoenixhill.com. Beer from $3. W college night, beer from $0.75. F ladies night. "Phriday Phever" happy hour 5-8pm. 21+. Cover $2-5. Open W and Sa 8pm-4am, Th 8pm-3am, F 5pm-4am.) Downtown nightlife centers on multiple-venue clubs. Get four clubs for the price of one at **O'Malley's Corner**—and a karaoke bar to boot. If you don't dig country-western or disco, just migrate to the hip-hop or Top 40 rooms. (133 W. Liberty St., entrance at the corner of Jefferson and 2nd. ☎589-3866; www.omalleyscorner.com. F line dancing lessons 7:30-9pm and ladies' night all-male review 8-11pm. W 18+, Th-Sa 21+. Cover $3-5, includes all bars. Open W-Th 8pm-4am, F-Sa 7pm-4am.) **The Connection,** 120 S. Floyd St., is the crown jewel of Kentucky's gay nightlife, with six amazing venues under one roof. Multiple bars, a showroom for drag performances, and a vast dance floor draw capacity crowds as the week wears on. (☎585-5752. Happy hour daily 5-10pm. 21+. Cover $3-5, includes all bars. Open M-Tu 5pm-2am, W-Su 5pm-4am; dance floor open W-Su.)

▶ DAYTRIPS FROM LOUISVILLE

BARDSTOWN. Kentucky's second-oldest city, 17 mi. east on Rte. 245 from I-65 Exit 112, charms visitors with its historic downtown district. The real attractions, however, are the bourbon distilleries outside of town. Bardstown, once home to 29 distilleries, is still proudly known as the "Bourbon Capital of the World." It all started in 1791, when Kentucky Baptist Reverend Elijah Craig left a fire unattended while heating oak boards to make a barrel for his aging whiskey. The boards were scorched, but Rev. Craig carried on, and bourbon was born in that charred oak barrel. Today, 90% of America's native bourbon still hails from Kentucky, and 60% of that is distilled in Nelson and Bullitt Counties.

Jim Beam's American Outpost, 15 mi. west of Bardstown in Clermont, off Rte. 245, treats visitors to samples of the world's best-selling bourbon (M-Sa), lemonade, coffee, and bourbon candies. Peek into a warehouse that holds thousands of the 53-gallon barrels of aging bourbon stored at the distillery, check out an authentic moonshine still and Jeremiah Beam's historic home, or watch a video about the company's 200-year history. (☎502-543-9877. Open M-Sa 9am-4:30pm, Su 1-4pm. Free.) Visitors can take a factory tour at **Maker's Mark Distillery,** 19 mi. southeast of Bardstown on Rte. 52 E in Loretto. Any day but Sunday, buy a bottle of bourbon and hand-dip it yourself in the label's trademark red wax. (☎865-2099; www.makersmark.com. Tours every hr. M-Sa 10:30am-3:30pm, and Mar.-Dec. also Su 1:30-3:30pm. Gift shop open M-Sa 10am-4:30pm, Mar.-Dec. also Su 1-4:30pm.) Bardstown also hosts the **Kentucky Bourbon Festival** every September, with several days of tours, events, and bourbon-drinking (☎800-638-4877; www.kybourbonfestival.com). **Bardstown-Nelson County Tourism Office,** 1 Court Sq., is in the courthouse. (☎502-348-9545; www.visitbardstown.com. Open in summer M-F 8am-6pm, Sa 9am-6pm, Su 11am-3:30pm; call for winter hours.)

MAMMOTH CAVE NATIONAL PARK. Plummeting sinkholes and narrow crawl-spaces burrow their way through the limestone underneath **Mammoth Cave National Park,** 80 mi. south of Louisville in central Kentucky. From I-65, turn off at Exit 48 (Park City) or Exit 53 (Cave City) and follow signs to the visitors center. With over 365 mi. of mapped caves, Mammoth Cave comprises the world's longest network of cavern corridors—over three times longer than any other known cave system. Tours depart from the visitors center. (☎758-2328 or 800-967-2283; www.nps.gov/maca. Open daily 8am-7pm; low season 8:45am-5pm. Call for tour schedule.) The **Frozen Niagara Tour** (¾ mi., 2hr.) provides a good introduction to the cave's geology ($11, ages 6-12 $8), while the **Violet City Lantern Tour** (3 mi., 3hr.) shuns electricity in favor of some old-fashioned spelunking ($15/$11); reservations for the lantern tour should be made in advance. Bring a jacket, even in summer, as temperatures underground hover around 54°F year round. Above ground, the 52,000-acre park has walking, biking, and horseback riding trails, plus fishing and canoeing. Camping with bathhouses, a camp store, and laundry is available at the pleasant **Headquarters Campground ❶,** near the visitors center. (☎758-2424. RVs allowed, but sites have no hookups. Showers $2. Open Mar.-Nov. Sites $16.) Free **backcountry camping** permits can also be obtained at the visitors center, and motel rooms start at $35 on the outskirts of nearby Cave City.

LEXINGTON   ☎859

Home to the first institution of higher learning west of the Alleghenies, Lexington has more than two centuries of experience as a college town. These days, the basketball wizardry of the University of Kentucky plays second fiddle only to the thoroughbred horses that are groomed for the Kentucky Derby on farms outside the city. Lexington is Kentucky's second-largest city, yet the pedestrian-friendly downtown lends the place a relaxed, down-home feel.

▐ TRANSPORTATION

Airport: Blue Grass Airport, 4000 Terminal Dr. (☎425-3114; www.bluegrassairport.com), off Man O' War Blvd. about 6 mi. west of downtown. Ritzy downtown hotels run shuttles, but there is no public transit. Taxi to downtown about $15.

Buses: Greyhound, 477 New Circle Rd. NW (☎299-0428). Open M-F 7:30am-midnight, Sa-Su 7:30am-7pm. To **Cincinnati** (1½hr., 4 per day, $20), **Knoxville** (3½hr., 5 per day, $46),and **Louisville** (2-5hr., 4 per day, $20).

Public Transit: LexTran (☎253-4636; www.lextran.com). Buses leave from the Transit Center, 220 E. Vine St., on a long block between Limestone and Rose St. Office open M-F 6am-6pm, Sa 8am-noon. Serves the university and city outskirts. Most routes run 5am-9pm. $1, ages 5-18 $0.80, seniors and disabled $0.50; transfers free.

Taxi: Lexington Yellow Cab, ☎231-8294.

▐ ▐ ORIENTATION AND PRACTICAL INFORMATION

I-64 and **I-75** pass Lexington to the northeast. **New Circle Road (Route 4, U.S. 60 bypass, U.S. 421 bypass,** and **U.S. 25 bypass)** loops around the city, intersecting with many roads that connect the downtown district to the surrounding towns. **High,**

Vine and **Main Street,** running east-west, and **Limestone** and **Broadway Street,** running north-south, are the major routes through downtown. Beware of the curving one-way streets downtown and near the **University of Kentucky (UK)** to the south.

> **Visitor Info: Lexington Convention and Visitors Bureau,** 301 E. Vine St. (☎233-7299 or 800-845-3959; www.visitlex.com), at Rose St. Open in summer M-F 8:30am-5pm, Sa 10am-5pm, Su noon-5pm; low season closed Su.
>
> **Hotlines: Crisis Intervention,** ☎253-2737 or 800-928-8000. **Rape Crisis,** ☎253-2511 or 800-656-4673. Both 24hr.
>
> **Medical Services: Saint Joseph East Hospital,** 150 N. Eagle Creek Dr. (☎967-5000).
>
> **Internet Access: Lexington Public Library,** 140 E. Main St. (☎231-5500), at Limestone St. 1hr. slots. Open M-Th 9am-9pm, F-Sa 9am-5pm, Su 1-5pm.
>
> **Post Office:** 210 E. High St. (☎254-6156). Open M-F 8am-5pm. **Postal Code:** 40507. **Area Code:** 859.

ACCOMMODATIONS

Three-star hotels and antique-heavy B&Bs offer little in the way of affordable lodgings downtown. The cheapest rooms are outside the city on New Circle Rd. or near I-75 at Winchester Rd. and Newtown Pike.

> **Motel 6,** 2260 Elkhorn Rd. (☎293-1431), off I-75 at Exit 110, 3½mi. west of downtown. Young families and weekend revelers can make it a noisy place to stay, although you'll sleep easier knowing that you're getting the lowest rates around. Pool, A/C, cable TV. Singles M-Th and Su $38, F-Sa $46; each additional person $6. AmEx/D/DC/MC/V. ❷
>
> **Extended Stay America,** 2750 Gribbin Dr. (☎266-4800 or 800-398-7829; www.ext-stay.com). From New Circle Rd., take Exit 15, and follow Richmond Rd.; turn right onto Patchen Dr. and left onto Gribbin Dr. Spacious rooms include fully equipped kitchenettes, cable TV with HBO, and free local calls. Pool and on-site laundry facilities. Studio with queen bed $60. For stays 1 week or longer $37. AmEx/D/MC/V. ❸
>
> **Kentucky Horse Park Campground,** 4089 Ironworks Pkwy. (☎259-4257 or 800-370-6416, ext. 257; www.kyhorsepark.com), 10 mi. north of downtown off I-75 at Exit 120. Well-manicured campsites with bath houses, Internet access, laundry, playground, basketball/volleyball/tennis courts, and swimming pool. Apr.-Oct. tent sites $15; with hookup $25. Nov.-Mar. $13/$19. ❶

FOOD

On the east end of downtown, cafes and sandwich shops cluster around **South Broadway** and the onetime slave market of **Cheapside.** Funkier student haunts line **High Street,** on the southern edge of the UK campus. The **Lexington Farmers Market** sells fresh produce, breads, and cheeses in summer. The stalls at **200 South Broadway** open at 7am on Tuesdays and Thursdays, while the **300 Southland Drive** vendors start hawking their wares at 11am on Sundays.

> ▨ **Alfalfa Restaurant,** 141 E. Main St. (☎253-0014; www.alfalfarestaurant.com). Certainly praiseworthy for its exposed-brick dining room and live music. But it's the food that puts this downtown mainstay in a league of its own. Vegetarian entrees $12-16. Live music F-Sa 8-10pm. Open M-Tu 11am-2pm, W-Th 11am-2pm and 5:30-10pm, F 11am-2pm and 5:30-11pm, Sa 9am-2pm and 5:30-11pm, Su 9am-2pm. MC/V. ❸
>
> **Ramsey's,** 496 E. High St. (☎259-2708), dishes up generous portions of meatloaf and country-fried steak. Play it safe with a side of mashed potatoes or expand your horizons with fried green tomatoes. Home to the $9.95 dinner platter. 2-for-1 mixed drinks 4-7pm. Open Su-Tu 11am-11pm, W-Sa 11am-1am. AmEx/MC/V. ❷

Common Grounds Coffee House, 343 E. High St. (☎233-9761), serves towering slices of delicious cake for $4. You'll need an espresso drink to snap out of your blissful cake-induced lethargy. Free wireless Internet. Live music F-Sa 9pm. Open M-Th 7am-midnight, F 7am-1am, Sa 8am-1am, Su 9am-midnight. D/MC/V.

👁 SIGHTS

THINGS EQUESTRIAN. A visit to one of the private horse farms in the Lexington area is the best way to get an insider's perspective on life beyond the Derby; the visitors center distributes a list of farms that welcome visitors. Farms rarely charge an up-front fee, but plan to tip the groom $5-10. **Kentucky Horse Park** is a more touristy alternative to individual visits, with live horse shows, horse-drawn tours of the grounds, and two small museums that trace the role of the horse in history. On Sunday afternoons in summer, thrifty enthusiasts can watch polo matches for only the cost of parking. *(4089 Ironworks Pkwy., off Exit 120 from I-75. ☎233-4303 or 800-678-8813; www.kyhorsepark.com. Open mid-Mar. to Oct. daily 9am-5pm; Nov. to mid-Mar. W-Su 9am-5pm. Mid-Mar. to Oct. $14, ages 7-12 $7; Nov. to mid-Mar. $9/$6; horse shows, museums, and 15min. horse-drawn tours included. 45min. horseback rides additional $15; ages 7+ only. Pony rides $4; ages 12 and under only. Parking $3.)*

The *Lexington-Herald-Leader* has described the **Keeneland Race Track,** west of the city off U.S. 60, as the "closest thing to a non-religious cathedral" for its ivy-covered grandstand and procession of maple trees along the main drive. Every April, the final prep race for the Kentucky Derby is run on the original dirt track. Numerous other races take place during April and October, while a new synthetic training track means that visitors can watch morning workouts year-round. A sparkling new library houses historical photographs, while the Track Kitchen offers breakfast for $3.75 and the chance to chat up a jockey or horse owner. *(4201 Versailles Rd., across U.S. 60 from the airport. ☎254-3412 or 800-456-3412; www.keeneland.com. Races Apr. and Oct.; general admission $3. Workouts free and open to the public; dirt track workouts mid-Mar. to Nov. 6-10am, training track year-round 6-11am. Library open M-F 8:30am-4:30pm. Track Kitchen open daily 5:30-11am.)*

UNIVERSITY OF KENTUCKY. When local residents profess to "bleed blue" for the Wildcats and the entire metropolitan area changes its area code to spell out "UKY" on the keypad, it should come as no surprise that the state's largest university plays a prominent role in the cultural life of Lexington. The **University of Kentucky Art Museum,** 116 Singletary Center, at Rose St. and Euclid Ave., has an eclectic collection that ranges from 19th-century portraits and landscapes to splashy Abstract Expressionist canvases. *(☎257-5716; www.uky.edu/artmuseum. Admission to permanent collection free. Exhibitions $5-10, students free. Open Tu-Th and Sa-Su noon-5pm, F noon-8pm.)* On the other side of campus, the **University of Kentucky Arboretum and State Botanical Garden,** 500 Alumni Dr., offers a two-mile "Walk Across Kentucky" with plants from each of the state's seven regional landscapes. *(☎257-6955; www.uky.edu/arboretum. Open daily dawn-dusk. Visitors center open M-F 8:30am-4:30pm. Free.)*

HISTORIC HOMES. The austere Federal-style homes in South Hill and their stately Greek Revival neighbors in Gratz Park give visitors an inkling of Lexington's rich architectural heritage. Four historic homes in and around the city are open to the public for tours, and the visitors center sells an invaluable combo pass for just $10. **The Hunt-Morgan House,** 201 N. Mill St., was home to slippery Confederate General John Hunt Morgan, who was said to have steered his horse up the front steps and out the back door with Union troops in hot pursuit. *(☎233-3290; www.bluegrasstrust.org/hunt-morgan. Guided tours only, 15min. past the hr. Open mid-Mar. to mid-Dec. W-F 1-5pm, Sa 10am-4pm, Su 1-5pm. $7, students $4.)* A few blocks to the south, the **Mary Todd Lincoln House,** 578 W. Main St., was the childhood home of the misunderstood presidential widow. (☎ 233-9999; www.mtlhouse.org. Open mid-Mar to Nov. M-Sa 10am-4pm. $7, ages 6-12 $4.) West of downtown, in Ashland, **The Henry Clay Estate,** 120 Sycamore Rd., features an 18-room mansion with the original furnishings of the Southern orator's family. (☎ 266-8581; www.henryclay.org. Guided tours on the hr. Open Feb.-Dec. M-Sa 10am-4pm, Su 11am-4pm; Nov.-Mar. closed M.)

◎ NIGHTLIFE

The pages of *Ace Weekly* and *Nougat* are full of ideas for evening entertainment; both are free and available throughout the city. The "Weekender" section of Friday's *Herald-Leader* ($0.50) is also a valuable resource.

◙ **Woodsongs Old-Time Radio Hour,** 214 E. Main St. (☎ 252-8888; www.woodsongs.com), at the Kentucky Theatre. This nationally syndicated radio program tapes live bluegrass and folk music on Monday nights. Mountain music at its best. Tapings 6:45pm. Reservations required. $5.

The Dame, 156 W. Main St. (☎ 226-9005; www.dameky.com). For live rock and punk shows, look no further. Pale girls in vintage sundresses and skinny boys with mod haircuts abound. 21+. Cover $3-10. Shows M-Sa; doors open 8-9pm.

The Bar, 224 E. Main St. (☎ 255-1551; www.thebarcomplex.com). Draws a gay and lesbian crowd with a neon-soaked dance floor, mod art in the lounge, and lively weekend drag shows. Th and Sa are *the* nights to go. Happy hour M-Sa 4-7pm. DJs Th-Sa 11pm-2:30am. 21+. Cover F-Sa $5 after 8pm. Open M-W 4pm-1am, Th-Sa 4pm-2:30am.

TENNESSEE

Though Tennessee's land ranges from the Great Smokies to the flat banks of the Mississippi River in the west, the Volunteer State has one unifying theme: music. From the twang of eastern bluegrass and the woes of Nashville country to the gut-wrenching blues of Memphis and the roots of rock 'n' roll at Graceland, music is the soul of the state. Other elements of the state seem to cancel each other out—Tennessee distills Jack Daniel's Tennessee whiskey while simultaneously producing the largest number of Bibles in the US—but both the boozin' and the proselytizin', and just about anything else you can think of, can be found in the music.

◪ PRACTICAL INFORMATION

Capital: Nashville.

Visitor Info: Tennessee Department of Tourist Development, 320 6th Ave. N, 5th fl., Nashville 37243 (☎ 615-741-2159 or 800-462-8366 for a free guide; www.tnvacation.com). Open M-F 8am-4:30pm. **Tennessee State Parks Information,** 401 Church St., Nashville 37243 (☎ 800-421-6683; www.tnstateparks.com). Open M-F 8am-4:30pm.

Postal Abbreviation: TN. **Sales Tax:** 9.25% (13.25% for accommodations).

NASHVILLE ☎ 615

Nashville is often called "nouveau dixie", with much of its wealth being poured into gaudy, glitzy entertainment. Nashville also bears a number of other unusual nicknames. Known as "the Athens of the South," the city is home to an array of

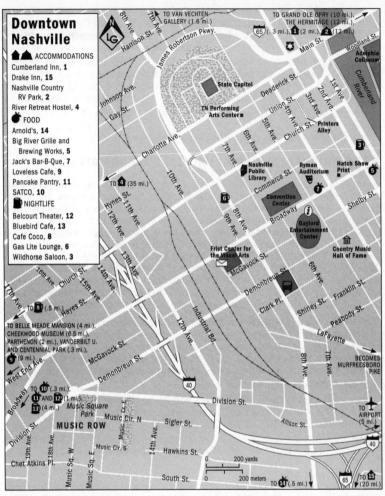

Downtown Nashville

▲▲ ACCOMMODATIONS
Cumberland Inn, 1
Drake Inn, 15
Nashville Country
    RV Park, 2
River Retreat Hostel, 4

🍎 FOOD
Arnold's, 14
Big River Grille and
    Brewing Works, 5
Jack's Bar-B-Que, 7
Loveless Cafe, 9
Pancake Pantry, 11
SATCO, 10

🎵 NIGHTLIFE
Belcourt Theater, 12
Bluebird Cafe, 13
Cafe Coco, 8
Gas Lite Lounge, 6
Wildhorse Saloon, 3

Greek architecture. The area has also been called the "buckle of the Bible belt," a reference to its Southern Baptists. But Nashville's most popular moniker by far is "Music City USA," and for good reason: this town has long been the banjo-pickin', foot-stompin' capital of country music. No matter which Nashville you visit, you're sure to have a rollicking good time, with music and beer flowing around the clock.

⌐ TRANSPORTATION

Airport: Nashville International Airport, 1 Terminal Dr. (☎275-2098, information center 275-1675; www.flynashville.com), 8 mi. south of downtown. From downtown, take I-40 E and turn off at Exit 216A. **Gray Line Tours** runs a **shuttle** (☎275-1180) to major downtown hotels daily 6am-11pm. $12, round-trip $18. Taxi to downtown about $20.

THE SOUTH

Buses: Greyhound, 200 8th Ave. S (☎255-3556; www.greyhound.com), at Demonbreun St., downtown. Borders a rough area, but station is well-lit. Open 24hr. To: **Birmingham** (4hr., 6 per day, $32); **Chattanooga** (2½hr., 6 per day, $23); **Knoxville** (3½hr., 5 per day, $30); **Louisville** (3½hr., 15 per day, $30); **Memphis** (4hr., 6 per day, $36).

Public Transit: Metropolitan Transit Authority (MTA; ☎862-5950; www.nashvillemta.org). Buses operate on limited routes. Times vary route to route, but none run M-F before 5:30am or after 11:15pm. Sa last bus from downtown 10:15pm, Su last bus from downtown 9:15pm and only hourly service. $1.10, under 19 $0.60, ages 65+ and disabled $0.55, under 4 free; transfers $0.10; express fare $1.50. All-day pass $3.25, under 19 $2. Weekly pass $15, under 19 $9.

Taxi: Nashville/Allied Cab, ☎242-7070. **Music City Taxi,** ☎742-3030.

■❷ ORIENTATION AND PRACTICAL INFORMATION

Nashville's roads are fickle, often interrupted by curving parkways and one-way streets. Names change without warning. **Broadway,** the main east-west thoroughfare, runs through downtown, then veers left after passing over I-40; **West End Avenue** continues straight ahead. Broadway joins **21st Avenue** after a few blocks, passing through **Vanderbilt University.** Downtown, numbered avenues run north-south, parallel to the Cumberland River and divided by Broadway into north and south. The curve of **James Robertson Parkway** encloses the north end, becoming **Main Street** on the other side of the river (later **Gallatin Pike**) and turning into **8th Avenue** downtown. The area south of Broadway between 2nd and 7th Ave. can be unsafe at night. Metered street parking is free after 12:30pm on Saturdays and all day Sundays; spots are prized possessions at night, and lot parking costs $10.

Visitor Info: Nashville Visitor Information Center, 501 Broadway (☎259-4747; www.nash-villecvb.com), in the Gaylord Entertainment Center, off I-65N/I-40 at Exit 209A; from the exit ramp, follow Broadway eastbound towards downtown. Open M-Sa 8:30am-5:30pm, Su 10am-5pm, and on event days until the event starts. Attraction ticket packages, coupon book, walking tour guide, and info on events is distributed for free.

Hotlines: Crisis Line, ☎244-7444. 24hr.

Internet Access: Nashville Public Library, 615 Church St. (☎862-5800), between 6th and 7th Ave. Register at the desk for a guest user card for 30min. free access. Open M-Th 9am-8pm, F 9am-6pm, Sa 9am-5pm, Su 2-5pm.

Post Office: 901 Broadway (☎256-3088), in the same building as the Frist Center for the Visual Arts. Open M-F 8:30am-5pm. **Postal Code:** 37203. **Area Code:** 615.

▮ ACCOMMODATIONS

Rooms in downtown Nashville can be expensive, especially in summer. The visitors center offers several deals on motel rooms, and budget motels are plentiful around **West Trinity Lane** and **Brick Church Pike,** off I-65 at Exit 87. There are cheap hotels around **Dickerson Road** and **Murfreesboro,** and near downtown, motels huddle on **Interstate Drive** over the Woodland St. Bridge.

Drake Inn, 420 Murfreesboro Rd. (☎256-7770). Great location and small, clean, comfortable rooms. Fridge, hair dryer, and country music-influenced murals. Laundry and a pool. Singles M-Th and Su $37.50, F-Sa $42; doubles $42/$45. AmEx/D/MC/V. ❸

River Retreat Hostel, 1227 Bloom Landing Road., in Charlotte. (☎789-5157; directions and online booking at www.hostels.com). It may be a 1hr. drive from the city, but this hostel feels more like a home, with ample breakfasts and friendly owners. Book well in advance. Pickup from airport or bus station $10. Shuttle to Nashville $5. Dorms $18; private single $20. Student discount 10%. Cash or check only. ❶

THE SOUTH

Nashville Country RV Park, 1200 Louisville Hwy. (☎859-0348), 12 mi. north of downtown off I-65 at Exit 98. Significantly cheaper than the campgrounds surrounding Opryland USA, with shaded sites, showers, laundry, a pool, an exercise room, and free wireless Internet. Sites $16, with water and electricity $17.25. AmEx/D/MC/V. ❶

Cumberland Inn, 150 W. Trinity Ln. (☎226-1600 or 800-704-1028). From downtown on I-65N, take Exit 87 and turn right at the bottom of the ramp even though it says "East Trinity Lane"; the Inn is on the right. The rates are among Nashville's lowest, but you get what you pay for. A/C, HBO, laundry. Singles $30; doubles $33. AmEx/D/MC/V. ❷

◪ FOOD

In Nashville, the initials of the Grand Ole Opry grace even the local candy: **goo-goo clusters** (peanuts, pecans, chocolate, caramel, and marshmallow) are sold in specialty shops throughout the city. Nashville's other finger-lickin' traditions, barbecue and fried chicken, are no less sinful. Restaurants catering to collegiate tastes and budgets cram **21st Avenue, West End Avenue,** and **Elliston Place,** near Vanderbilt.

▨ **Loveless Cafe,** 8400 Rte. 100, at the end of the Natchez Trace Pkwy. (☎646-9700; www.lovelesscafe.com). Follow West End Ave. to where it becomes Harding Pike/Rt. 100. A Nashville tradition since 1951, with the best fried chicken, country breakfast, and made-from-scratch biscuits with fresh preserves you'll ever taste. Breakfast all day. Open daily 7am-9pm. AmEx/D/MC/V. ❸

Arnold's, 605 8th Ave. S (☎256-4455). The best meat-and-3-vegetable special for miles around is only $7. Open M-F 10:30am-3pm. MC/V. ❷

SATCO (San Antonio Taco Company), 416 21st Ave. S (☎327-4322), near Vanderbilt. Not gourmet, but crazy cheap. Fajitas $1.50-2. Tacos $1.50. Beer from $2.25. Open in summer M-W and Su 11am-midnight, Th-Sa 11am-1am; in winter M-W and Su 11am-11pm, Th-Sa 11am-midnight. AmEx/D/MC/V. ❶

Pancake Pantry, 1796 21st Ave. (☎383-9333), serves stacks of delicious pancakes, from traditional buttermilk to orange-walnut or apricot-lemon ($6.65). Other breakfast and lunch items also available. Open M-F 6am-3pm, Sa-Su 6am-4pm. MC/V. ❶

Jack's Bar-B-Que, 416A Broadway (☎254-5715; www.jacksbarbque.com), is a bit of a legend, both for the flashing neon-winged pigs above the door and for its succulent, tender pork. Sandwiches $3-5. Plates $8-12. Open in spring and summer M-Th 10:30am-8pm, F-Sa 10:30am-10pm, Su noon-6pm; in winter Th 10:30am-8pm, F-Sa 10:30am-10pm. Also at 334 W. Trinity Ln. (☎228-9888). AmEx/D/MC/V. ❷

Big River Grille and Brewing Works, 111 Broadway (☎251-4677), is a microbrewery in the heart of downtown. Their rotating choice of specialty beers and selection of salads come as a relief to vegetarians and those in need of a fried-free night, but don't worry—you can still get ribs ($18). Open M-Th 11am-11pm, F-Sa 11am-midnight, Su 11am-10pm; bar open 1hr. later. AmEx/D/MC/V. ❸

◉ SIGHTS

COUNTRY LOVIN'. Country music drives this city. The first stop for any traveler—country fan or not—should be the state-of-the-art ▨ **Country Music Hall of Fame,** where visitors can view live performances or design their own CDs. Wander through the well-crafted displays on the history of country, listen to samples from greats like Johnny Cash and Patsy Cline, and watch videos of performances and interviews with modern artists. An extra $8 will upgrade tickets to include a guided tour of RCA's **Studio B,** where over 1000 American Top 10 hits have been recorded. A Grayline shuttle runs between the two venues. *(222 5th Ave. S. ☎416-*

THE SOUTH

2001; www.countrymusichalloffame.com. Open daily 9am-5pm. $17, seniors and students $15, ages 6-17 $9, under 6 free. AAA discount $1. Audio tours and combination passes with Ryman Auditorium available.) Two-step over to the **Ryman Auditorium,** where the legendary **Grand Ole Opry** radio show was recorded for more than 30 years. The Opry eventually moved to a bigger studio to accommodate the growing crowd of fans, but the Ryman continues to host fantastic shows. View a short video outlining the history of the building, peruse display cases of costumes and photos, and even climb on stage. *(116 5th Ave. N. ☎889-3060; www.ryman.com. Open daily 9am-4pm. $8.50, ages 4-11 $4.25. Backstage tour $11.75. Times and prices for shows vary.)* The primary country venue in the nation is the 🎵 **Grand Ole Opry House.** Visitors can enjoy musical performances, tour the backstage areas, or visit the free museum detailing the Opry's history. Upcoming weekend shows are listed in *The Tennessean* and online. *(2804 Opryland Dr. Exit 11 off Hwy. 155, accessible from both I-40 and I-65. ☎871-6779; www.opry.com. Museum open daily 10am-5pm. Free. Tours M-Sa 10am, noon, 2, 3pm; no 3pm tour on show days. $11.50, ages 4-11 $5. Shows F 7:30, Sa 6:30 and 9:30pm, sometimes Tu 7pm. Tickets $28-45, available at ☎800-871-6779, online, or through Ticketmaster. Wheelchair accessible.)*

MUSEUMS AND MORE. Right in the heart of downtown, the **Frist Center for the Visual Arts** inspires both young and old with an interesting array of rotating exhibits and a hands-on learning center that allows visitors to paint, draw, and make prints. *(919 Broadway. ☎244-3340; www.fristcenter.org. Open M-W and F-Sa 10am-5:30pm, Th 10am-8pm, Su 1-5pm. $8.50, students with ID $7.50, military and ages 65+ $6.50, 18 and under free. Wheelchair accessible.) (316 Broadway. ☎256-2805. Open M-F 9am-5pm, Sa 10am-5pm. Free.)* **Fisk University's Carl Van Vechten Gallery** consists of a portion of the private collection of Alfred Steiglitz, donated by his widow Georgia O'Keeffe. The gallery is tiny, but the fascinating Steiglitz photographs hanging among works by Picasso, Cézanne, and Renoir should not be missed. *(At Jackson St. and D.B. Todd Blvd., off Jefferson St. ☎329-8720. Open during the school year Tu-F 10am-5pm, Sa-Su 1-5pm; in summer Tu-F 10am-5pm. Donations appreciated.)*

Across West End Ave. from Vanderbilt, the pleasant **Centennial Park** stretches between 25th and 28th Ave. A visit to the park will reveal why Nashville is known as the "Athens of the South": a full-scale replica of the Greek **Parthenon** sits on top of a low hill. Built as a temporary exhibit for the Tennessee Centennial in 1897, the Parthenon was so popular that it was maintained and finally rebuilt with permanent materials in the 1920s. Out-of-place as the structure may be, it is nonetheless impressive—especially the 42 ft. golden statue of Athena inside. In its first floor gallery, the building contains the **Cowan Collection of American Paintings,** a selection of 19th- and early 20th-century American art. *(☎862-8431; www.parthenon.org. Open Tu-Sa 9am-4:30pm; in summer also Su 12:30pm-4:30pm. $4, ages 4-17 and 62+ $2.50. Wheelchair accessible.)* At the **Capitol,** a stately Greek Revival building on Charlotte Ave. north of downtown, visitors can tour the Governor's Reception Room, the legislative chambers, the former Tennessee Supreme Court, and the grounds, including the tomb of President James K. Polk. *(On Charlotte Ave. between 6th and 7th Ave. ☎741-0830. Photo ID required. Open M-F 8am-4pm. Tours every hr. M-F 9-11am and 1-3pm; self-guided tours also available. Free. Wheelchair accessible.)*

CHEEKWOOD MUSEUM AND BELLE MEADE MANSION. For a break from the bustle of downtown, head to the **Cheekwood Botanical Garden and Museum of Art.** The well-kept gardens, complete with a woodland sculpture trail, are a peaceful spot for a stroll. The museum features American and contemporary sculpture and paintings and a collection of English and American decorative arts. *(1200 Forrest Park Dr., off Page Rd., between Rte. 100 and Belle Meade Blvd. 8 mi. southwest of town. ☎356-8000; www.cheekwood.org. Audio tours available for museum. Open Tu-Sa 9:30am-4:30pm, Su 11am-4:30pm. $10, seniors $8, students and ages 6-17 $5; families $30. Half-price after 3pm.)*

The nearby **Belle Meade Plantation** was once one of the nation's most famed thoroughbred nurseries. The lavish 1853 mansion has hosted seven US presidents, including the 380 lb. William Howard Taft, who allegedly spent some time lodged in the mansion's bathtub. Today, visitors can explore the house and grounds, including a collection of antique carriages. *(5025 Harding Rd. ☎ 356-0501 or 800-270-3991. Open M-Sa 9am-5pm, Su 11am-5pm. 2 guided tours per hr.; first tour 30min. after opening, last tour 4pm. $11, seniors $9, ages 6-12 $5. AAA discount. 1st fl. and grounds wheelchair accessible.)*

THE HERMITAGE. The **Hermitage**, the graceful manor of the seventh president of the United States, Andrew Jackson, holds an impressive array of its original furnishings. Admission includes a 15min. film about Jackson's life, access to the house and grounds, and a visit to the nearby **Tulip Grove Mansion** and **Hermitage Church.** *(4580 Rachel's Ln. Exit 221 off I-40 E, continue 4 mi. on Old Hickory Blvd; entrance is on the right. ☎ 889-2941; www.thehermitage.com. Open daily 9am-5pm; in summer grounds open until 6pm. Last tickets sold at 4pm. Guided tour included in admission. $12, ages 13-18 and 62+ $11, ages 6-12 $5; families $34. AAA discount. Partially wheelchair accessible.)*

🎵 ENTERTAINMENT

The hordes of visitors that swoop down upon Nashville have turned the **Grand Ole Opry** (see above) into a grand ole American institution. However, there are many other great forms of entertainment in the capital city as well. The **Tennessee Performing Arts Center,** 505 Deaderick St. at 6th Ave. N, hosts the Nashville Symphony, opera, ballet, Broadway shows, and other theater productions. (☎ 255-2787; www.tpac.org. Tickets $15-75. Wheelchair accessible.) The **Dancin' in the District Music Festival** runs from mid-June to mid-September every year in Riverfront Park and features three live bands every Thursday evening. Past performers have included Better than Ezra, Cake, and Blondie. (☎ 800-594-8499; www.dancininthedistrict.com. Gates open at 5:30pm. Tickets $5 in advance, $8 at the gate.) Listings for the area's music and events fill the free *Nashville Scene* and *Rage*, available at most establishments.

Two professional franchises dominate the Nashville sports scene. The NFL's **Tennessee Titans** play at **Adelphia Coliseum,** 460 Great Circle Rd., just across the river from downtown. (☎ 565-4200; www.titansonline.com. Open M-F 8:30am-5pm. Tickets $12-52.) The NHL's **Nashville Predators** face off at the **Gaylord Entertainment Center,** 501 Broadway. (☎ 770-2040. Open M-F 10am-5:30pm. Tickets $10-85.)

THE BEST LEGISLATURE MONEY CAN BUY

Even in the US, the world's longest-lived modern democracy, money from the coffers of certain lobbyists has a way of "greasing the wheels" of the country's political system. But as the FBI discovered in a June 2005 undercover bribery sting, corrupt politicians seldom do their homework, or even know where bribes are coming from.

During 2004 and 2005, the FBI set up a fake company, E-Cycle, and offered bribes to politicians to introduce and promote a bill in the Tennessee legislature that undercover agents posing as lobbyists for the "corporation" claimed would help the company receive state contracts.

After the FBI pumped nearly $10,000 through E-Cycle lobbyists to Tennessee legislators in exchange for their support of the bill, they had assembled over 2000 hours of secret recordings. This incriminating evidence was enough to indict a bipartisan slate of four state senators and one state representative.

With trial dates set for November 2005, Tennessee citizens are already clamoring for reform in response to this embarrassing episode. But a Tennessee appeals court added a bizarre twist to the ongoing "Tennessee Waltz" saga in July 2005, ruling that each of the indicted legislators would still be eligible for their state pensions upon retirement.

🎧 NIGHTLIFE

Nashville has a vivacious nightlife scene fueled by country music; if you are into line dancing, you're good to go. Other, smaller scenes, such as hip-hop spots and gay clubs, are a little more out of the way. Downtown, country nightlife centers on Broadway and 2nd Ave. Parking can be difficult in summer, especially when something is going on at the Gaylord Entertainment Center. Near Vanderbilt, **Elliston Place** hops with college-oriented music venues, and **Hillsboro Village**, on 21st Ave. at Belcourt Ave., attracts a young crowd to its late-night bars and coffee shops. For info on GLBT nightlife in Nashville and Knoxville, check out the monthly *Out and About* or the weekly *Xenogeny*, available at some venues downtown.

■ **Bluebird Cafe,** 4104 Hillsboro Pkwy. (☎383-1461; www.bluebirdcafe.com), near the mall at Green Hills. From 21st Ave., it's on the left after you cross Richard Jones Rd. This famous bird sings original country and acoustic every night. Country stars Garth Brooks and Kathy Mattea started their careers here. $7 per person food and drink min. if sitting at a table. Cover for shows usually $4-10; no cover Su. Open M-Sa 5:30pm-close, Su 6pm-close. Early show 6:30pm. Reservations recommended Tu-Sa.

 THE EARLY 'BIRD. The Bluebird Cafe hosts some of Nashville's most talented songwriters each week. Although their late show at 9:30pm has a cover charge and sells out quickly, their early show, at 6:30pm, is a good way to hear some great music in a relaxed, coffeehouse-style atmosphere with no cover.

Wildhorse Saloon, 120 2nd Ave. N (☎902-8200; www.wildhorsesaloon.com). Bring your boots and hat and two-step 'til dawn in this country dance hall. It's loud and brash, but ain't that country? Dance lessons M-F 7-9pm, Sa-Su 6-9pm. Live music Tu-Sa. Cover after 7pm M-Th and Su $4, F-Sa $6. Open M-Th and Su 11am-1am, F-Sa 11am-3am.

Cafe Coco, 210 Louise Ave. (321-2626; www.cafecoco.com), off Elliston Pl. A coffeehouse/bar/sandwich shop popular with the college set. At night, the patio and bar heat up with live music. Happy hour daily 7-11am and 3-6pm with $1 coffee and $2 domestic beers. Cover usually $5 for live music. Free wireless Internet. Open 24hr.

Belcourt Theater, 2102 Belcourt Ave. (☎383-9180; www.belcourt.org), at 21st St. in Hillsboro Village. Once a silent movie theater, the Belcourt now profits from the marketing miracle of blockbusters and booze. Indie and classic films with beer and wine to make your entertainment experience that much better. Tickets $7.75, matinees $5.25. Call or check online for showtimes and events.

Gas Lite Lounge, 167½ 8th Ave. N (☎254-1278), between Church and Commerce. 2 doors down from the world headquarters of the Baptist Church, this self-styled "Gay Cheers" bar is a casual local hangout. Plenty of pool ($0.50 per game), piano playing, and even board games during the afternoon. Upstairs balcony ideal for people-watching. Straight-friendly. Karaoke Th and Sa. Open M-Sa 4:30pm-3am, Su 3pm-3am.

KNOXVILLE ☎865

Knoxville was settled after the Revolutionary War and later named for George Washington's Secretary of War, Henry Knox. It was once the capital of the "Territory South of the River Ohio," part of which became the state of Tennessee. Shaded by the stunning Great Smoky Mountains and hemmed in by vast lakes created by the Tennessee Valley Authority, Knoxville is a friendly, easily-navigated city that is home to the 26,000 students of the University of Tennessee (UT). Though less glitzy and touristy than Nashville, Knoxville features a lively college town atmosphere and a vibrant bluegrass and country music scene.

⚒️🏠 ORIENTATION AND PRACTICAL INFORMATION. Downtown Knoxville stretches north from the Tennessee River, bordered by **Henley Street** and **World's Fair Park** to the west and **Clay Street** to the east. The **McGhee Tyson Airport** (☎342-3000; www.flyknoxville.com) is on Hwy. 129, 10 mi. south of downtown and just past the intersection of Hwy. 129 and I-140. **Greyhound,** 100 E. Magnolia Ave. (☎524-0369 or ☎800-231-2222; www.greyhound.com; open 24hr.), at Central St., sends buses to: Chattanooga (2hr., 4 per day, $16-17.50), Lexington (4hr., 5 per day, $42-45), and Nashville (3-3½hr., 7 per day, $28-31). Be cautious in this area and don't walk alone here at night. Public **KAT buses** cover the city. (☎637-3000 or 525-1525; www.katbus.com. Weekdays 6:15am-7:15pm, reduced service on Saturdays. Call for availability. Night Rider and Sunday Rider routes run M-F 8:45pm-midnight, Sa 6:45pm-midnight, Su 10:15am-6:30pm. $1, ages 18 and under or 65+ $0.50, 4 and under free. Transfers $0.20.) Four free **trolley** lines run throughout the city: Blue (M-F 6am-6pm) runs to the Coliseum, Blount Mansion, and the Women's Basketball Hall of Fame; Orange (M-F 7am-6pm) heads downtown and westward to World's Fair Park and the UT campus; Green (M-F 7am-6pm) travels between the Fort Sanders neighborhood and UT; the Late Line (Aug.-May F-Sa 8pm-3:30am) serves UT, the Cumberland Avenue Strip, Market Square, and the Old City. Trolley and bus schedules are available at the visitors center downtown.

The **visitors center** at 301 S. Gay St. downtown has a coffeehouse with musical performances weekdays at noon. (☎523-7263 or 800-727-8045; www.knoxville.org. Open M-F 7:30am-6pm, Sa 9am-5pm, Su noon-4pm.) **Hotlines: Sexual Assault Crisis Center** (☎522-7273. 24hr.) **Internet Access:** Lawson McGhee Public Library, 500 W. Church Ave. (☎215-8700. 1hr. free Internet access with guest card. Open M-Th 9am-8:30pm, F 9am-5:30pm, Sa noon-5pm, Su 1-5pm.) **Post Office:** 501 W. Main Ave. (☎522-1070. Open M-F 7:30am-5:30pm.) **Postal Code:** 37902. **Area Code:** 865.

🏠 ACCOMMODATIONS. Several mid-range motels can be found off of **I-75** and **I-40** west of downtown and **I-75** north of downtown. The **Knoxville Hostel ❶,** 404 E. 4th Ave., is just a 10min. walk from the restaurants and clubs of the Old City. The hostel has a kitchen and common room, plus free Internet access and breakfast. Be cautious around this neighborhood at night and don't walk around here alone. Call ahead to arrange for pick-up from the Greyhound station. (☎546-8090. Beds $15. Shuttle service to Gatlinburg $7.60, students $6.45, hostel guests $6. Laundry $1.75. Reception usually daily 8am-noon and 1-6pm. Cash or check only.) The clean, basic rooms at **Scottish Inns ❷,** 201 Callahan Rd., at Exit 110 off I-75, are farther from downtown. Odd-numbered rooms face away from I-75 and are quieter than even-numbered rooms. (☎689-7777. Continental breakfast included. Outdoor pool. A/C. HBO. Internet access. Singles M-Th and Su $37, F-Sa $44; doubles $43/$49. AAA and AARP discount $2. D/MC/V.) **Volunteer Park Family Campground ❶,** 9514 Diggs Gap Rd., at Exit 117 off I-75, is 12 mi. from the city and has a pool, basketball court, coin-operated laundry, convenience store, and live bluegrass and country music during the summer. (☎938-6600 or 800-238-9644; www.volpark.com. Music Tu and F 7-10:30pm in summer. Tent sites $18, with water and electricity $20. Rates are for two adults and two children, additional person $3.)

🍴 FOOD. Market Square, a shaded plaza with restaurants and fountains east of World's Fair Park, bustles during the day and slows down at night. The other center for dining, browsing, and carousing, the **Old City,** spreads north up Central and Jackson St. and is usually hopping until at least 2am. Part of Cumberland Ave. along campus proper, **The Strip** is lined with student hangouts, bars, and restaurants. **The Tomato Head ❶,** 12 Market Sq., prepares gourmet pizzas (slices $1.40-4.90) and sandwiches ($4.50-7), with a variety of creative vegetarian options.

THE SOUTH

(☎637-4067. Open M 11am-3pm, Tu-Th 11am-10pm, F-Sa 11am-11pm, Su 10am-9pm. AmEx/MC/V.) **Chandler's ❶**, 3101 Magnolia Ave., serves up authentic Tennessee barbecue. Their $4.35 special includes meat, bread, and vegetables. Though the specialty is ribs, Chandler's also has vegetarian dishes. (☎595-0212. Open M-Th 11am-7:30pm, F 11am-8:30pm, Sa noon-8:30pm, Su noon-6pm. MC/V.)

◧ **SIGHTS.** The ▓**Women's Basketball Hall of Fame,** 700 Hall of Fame Dr., traces the history of amateur and professional women's basketball and inducts new members at a ceremony each June. Visitors can watch a video called "Hoop Full of Hope," sit in on simulated locker room pep-talks by famous coaches, and show off their skills on the indoor court. (☎633-9000; www.wbhof.com. Open M-Sa 10am-7pm, Su 1-6pm. $8, seniors and ages 6-15 $6. AAA discount $2. Wheelchair accessible.) Across the street, the **James White Fort,** 205 E. Hill Ave., preserves portions of the original stockade built in 1786 by Knoxville's founder. Guided tours describe the lives of the first white settlers in the area. (☎525-6514. Open Mar. to mid-Dec. M-Sa 9:30am-5pm; Jan.-Feb. M-F 10am-4pm. 1hr. tours every 30 min. 9:30am-3:30pm. Admission by tour only. $5, seniors and AAA $4.50, ages 5-12 $2.) The **Museum of Appalachia,** 16 mi. north of Knoxville at Exit 122 off I-75 in Norris, showcases 300 years of Appalachia's cultural history. The museum consists of old buildings relocated from the surrounding countryside, including barns, a blacksmith's shop, a smokehouse, and the cabin where Mark Twain's family lived. Live mountain music is played daily from 9:30am to 4:30pm. Also at the museum is the annual **Tennessee Fall Homecoming Festival,** which is held the second full weekend in October and draws musicians, writers, craftspeople, and huge crowds. (☎494-7680; www.museumofappalachia.com. Open daily June-Aug. 8am-8pm; Sept.-May 8am-dusk. $13, seniors and AAA $10, ages 6-12 $5, families $30; higher during festival.) **World's Fair Park,** west of downtown, underwent major reconstruction that expanded the convention center and added a vast green swath stretching toward the river. (Open daily dawn-dusk.) The **Knoxville Museum of Art,** 1050 World's Fair Park Dr., houses fascinating rotating exhibits and a small but dynamic permanent collection of modern and postmodern art. The museum hosts "Alive after Five" on Fridays, with live music, food, and drinks. (☎525-6101; www.knoxart.org. Open Tu-W noon-8pm, Th-F noon-9pm, Sa-Su 11am-5pm. $5, ages 17 and under free. Alive after Five typically bi-monthly F in spring and summer, 5:30-8pm. $6. Wheelchair accessible.)

♫▐ **ENTERTAINMENT AND NIGHTLIFE.** Knoxville is a great place for sports fans; UT's **football** (in the Neyland Stadium) and **women's basketball** (in the Thompson Bowling Arena) consistently rank among the top teams in the nation. (☎656-1200; www.utsports.com. Football tickets $38-45. Basketball $8-14.) Smokies Park, 20 mi. east of downtown on I-40, Exit 407, is home to the Tennessee Smokies, a AA minor league baseball team that plays over 60 home games from April to September each year. Most games start at 7:15pm. (☎286-2300; www.smokiesbaseball.com. Tickets $5-9.) **Sundown in the City,** a free concert series held in Market Sq., draws big-name rock and blues bands on Thursday nights in summer. (☎523-2665; www.sundowninthecity.com. Apr.-July Th 6-10pm.) The annual **Dogwood Arts Festival** brings crafts, food, a parade, and biking competition to Market Sq. every April. (www.dogwoodarts.com. Apr. 5-23, 2006. Free.)

The Old City is the center of Knoxville's nightlife; the Strip and Market Sq. also host a number of popular bars. For goings-on around town, pick up a free copy of *Metro Pulse* (www.metropulse.com). The hip **Blue Cats,** 125 E. Jackson St., is a cool venue in a gritty district that draws big rock, blues, and country acts. (☎544-4300; www.bluecatslive.com. 18+. Beer from $2.75. Cover varies. Doors usually open at 9pm.) On Saturday nights, the club hosts **Fiction,** Knoxville's hottest dance party. (☎329-0039; www.fictionfx.com. 18+. Cover $3-5. Open Sa 10pm-3am.) **Pres-**

ervation Pub, 28 Market Sq., is a happening, friendly bar with great beer ($3.50) and fun quotes adorning the walls. (☎524-2224; www.preservationpub.com. Live music nightly. Happy hour daily 5-7:30pm. 21+ after 10pm. Open M-F 3pm-2:30am, Sa-Su noon-2:30am.) **Kurt's,** 4928 Homburg Dr. in the Homburg Place mini-mall, is a relaxed, friendly gay bar west of the city. Take the Kingston Pike from downtown and Homburg Dr. will be on your left. (☎558-5720. 21+. Happy hour W-Su 6-8pm. Open M-Tu 9pm-3am, W-Su 6pm-3am.)

GREAT SMOKY MOUNTAINS ☎865

As the largest wilderness area in the eastern US, Great Smoky Mountains National Park encompasses over 500,000 acres of gray-green Appalachian peaks bounded by the misty North Carolina and Tennessee valleys. Described by the Cherokee as "shaconage," or "blue, like smoke," the mountains are populated by black bears, wild hogs, and turkeys, along with more than 1500 species of flowering plants. Spring sets the mountains ablaze with wildflowers; in June and July, rhododendrons bloom. By mid-October, the mountains are a vibrant quilt of autumnal color.

ORIENTATION AND PRACTICAL INFORMATION

The **Newfound Gap Road (U.S. 441)** is the only road connecting the Tennessee and North Carolina sides of the park. On the Tennessee side, **Gatlinburg** and **Pigeon Forge** lie just outside of the park; both are overwhelmingly touristy, especially in summer. **Townsend,** to the west near Cades Cove, is less crowded. In North Carolina, the town of **Cherokee** lies near the park entrance on U.S. 441. **Bryson City,** near the Deep Creek campground, is quieter. The free *Smokies Guide* details the park's tours, lectures, activities, and changing natural surroundings.

Visitors Centers: Sugarlands (☎436-1291), on Newfound Gap Rd. 2 mi. south of Gatlinburg, next to the park's headquarters, shows a video that introduces the Smokies. There is also an interesting and comprehensive exhibit on regional plants and animals. Open daily June-Aug. 8am-7pm; Apr.-May and Sept.-Oct. 8am-6pm; Mar. and Nov. 8am-5pm; Dec.-Feb. 8am-4:30pm. On the North Carolina side of the park, **Oconaluftee** (☎828-497-1900), on U.S. 441 about 2 mi. north of Cherokee, shares its grounds with an outdoor **Mountain Farm Museum** made up of historic buildings relocated from throughout the park in the 1950s. Open daily 8am-dusk; low-season hours vary. Free.

Hotlines: Park Info Line (☎436-1200; www.nps.gov/grsm; operates daily 8am-4:30pm). **Park Headquarters** (☎436-1294). **Area Code:** 865; 828 in Cherokee and Bryson City, NC. In text, 865 unless otherwise noted.

Post Office: 130 Slope Street, Bryson City, NC. (☎828-488-3481.) Open M-F 8:30am-5pm, Sa 10am-noon. **Postal Code:** 28713.

ACCOMMODATIONS

The chain **motels** lining Rte. 441 and Rte. 321 decrease in price with increasing distance from the park. Small motels cluster in both Cherokee and Gatlinburg but there are few "budget" options. Rooms are at least $40 and prices soar on weekends and during the summer and fall. The best value is to camp in the park if campsites are available or to stay in hostel-style accommodations a little farther out.

Nantahala Outdoor Center (NOC), 13077 U.S. 19 W (☎888-662-2199), 13 mi. southwest of Bryson City. Beckons with cheap beds and 3 restaurants. Also arranges beginner-friendly whitewater rafting on the nearby river. Hot showers. Kitchen. Laundry facilities. Call ahead. Bunks in simple "basecamp" cabins $15. ●

THE SOUTH

Folkestone Inn, 101 Folkestone Rd. (☎828-488-2730 or 888-812-3385; www.folke-stone.com). From Rte. 19 southbound in Bryson City, turn right onto Everett St. and follow signs for Deep Creek Campground. Rooms with a gorgeous mountain backdrop, most with deck or balcony. Children must be 10 or older. 2-night min. stay on weekends May-Oct. Check-in 3-7pm. Check-out 11am. Call ahead. Singles $82-142; doubles $88-148. Each extra person $20. AmEx/D/MC/V. ❹

Landmark Inn North, 680 Winfield Dunn Pkwy. (Rte. 441/66; ☎865-429-7797 or 800-429-7798; www.landmarkinnthesmokies.com), in Sevierville off Rte. 441 in front of Kroger's. 15 mi. from the park entrance with standard rooms and reasonable rates. Singles M-Th and Su $29-39, F-Sa $39-49; doubles $33-43/$45-55. AmEx/D/MC/V. ❷

CAMPING

Ten **campgrounds** ❶ lie scattered throughout the park, each with tent sites, limited trailer space, water, and bathrooms with flush toilets. There are no showers or hookups. **Smokemont, Elkmont,** and **Cades Cove,** the largest and most popular campgrounds, accept reservations from mid-May to late October. (Sites $17-20 during reservation period; $14 rest of the year.) The other campgrounds are first come, first served; the visitors centers have info about availability. (Sites $12-14.) In summer, reserve spots as early as your travel plans allow. (☎800-365-2267, park code GRE; http://reservations.nps.gov. Open daily 10am-10pm.) Cades Cove and Smokemont are open year-round, while the other campgrounds open between March and May and close in October or November. **Backcountry camping** is permitted at many of the park's 100 primitive backcountry sites, but requires reservations as well as a permit that can be obtained for free at ranger stations and visitors centers. (☎436-1231. Office open daily 8am-6pm.)

FOOD

Although there are a variety of restaurants in and around the park, a cheaper option is to pack food into the park. **The Village General Store,** 9400 Hwy. 19 W, opposite Nantahala Village Lodge, is a good place to stock up on camping supplies and food if you're entering the park from the South. If entering the park from the North, the **Kroger's** supermarket behind the Landmark Inn on Rte. 441 in Sevierville is accessible and affordable.

Pizza by the River, on Hwy. 19, 1½ mi. past Nantahala Outdoor Ctr., 14½ mi. southwest of Bryson City. This roadside stand with outdoor decks overlooking the Nantahala is a local favorite. If coming by river, look for the Italian pizza flag or the skull and crossbones on your right as you go downstream. Slices $2.50-3. 12 in. pies $10. Sandwiches $5-7. Open Apr. to mid-Oct. M-Th and Su 11am-10pm, F-Sa 7am-10pm. ❷

Pear Tree Cafe, Rt. 441 in downtown Gatlinburg (☎430-8082), at the intersection of Rtes. 441 and 321. A taste of gourmet at reasonable prices. Off-the-beaten-path specialties include fried green tomatoes ($6.50) and chilled pear and mint soup ($5). Sandwiches ($7-9) range from fried catfish to ham and brie with apple slices, and come with great sweet potato fries. Internet access $3. Open M-Th and Su noon-8pm, F-Sa noon-9pm, low-season hours vary. D/MC/V. ❷

Smokin' Joe's Bar-B-Que, 8303 Rte. 73 (☎448-3212), in Townsend 1 mi. outside the park entrance. Authentic Tennessee cookin' is the order of business here. Succulent, slow-cooked meats and homemade side dishes smoke the competition. Dinners ($7-12) come with meat, 2 sides, and bread—enjoy one on the porch next to the river. Sandwiches $2.50-4.50. Beer from $2.50. Open May-Nov. M-Th and Su 11am-9pm, F-Sa 11am-10pm; low-season hours vary. D/MC/V. ❷

⚡ OUTDOOR ACTIVITIES

HIKING

Over 900 mi. of hiking trails and 170 mi. of road meander through the park. Trail maps and a guide to area day-hikes are also available at the visitors centers ($1 each; the $5 "starter pack" has all the maps you need for day hiking, fishing, auto touring, and camping). The Great Smokies are known for phenomenal **waterfalls,** and many of the park's most popular hikes culminate in stunning vistas or fantastic views of the surrounding mountains. Less-crowded areas include **Cosby** and **Cataloochee,** both on the eastern edge of the park. Wherever you go, bring water and don't feed the bears. **Rainbow Falls** (5½ mi., 4hr. round-trip), accessible from Cherokee Orchard Rd., is the park's most popular hike, a moderate to strenuous hike that reveals the Smokies' highest single-plunge waterfall. About 4 mi. west of Sugarlands Visitors Center on Little River Rd., **Laurel Falls** (2½ mi., 2hr. round-trip) is one of the easier (and more crowded) hikes on the Tennessee side of the park, following a paved trail through a series of cascades before reaching the 60 ft. falls. Accessible from the Maddron Bald trailhead east of Gatlinburg, **Albright Grove Loop** (6½ mi., 4hr. round-trip via Maddron Bald Trail), is less crowded and goes through one of the last remaining stands of old-growth forest in the park, passing by some gigantic ancient maple trees. **Ramsay Cascades** (8 mi., 5hr. round-trip) is a strenuous hike leading to cascades that fall 100 ft. down the mountainside. The trailhead is in the Greenbrier area—from Gatlinburg, the park entrance is 6 mi. east on Hwy. 321. **Clingman's Dome** (1 mi., ½hr. round-trip), off Clingman's Dome Road, ascends a steep, paved path to a viewing tower atop the highest vantage point in the park, which offers fantastic views of sunrise and sunset. **Chimney Tops** (4 mi., 2hr. round-trip) is a steep scramble leading up to two 4755 ft. rock spires. **Newfound Gap** offers handicapped-accessible views from Newfound Gap Road.

BIKING

Biking is permitted along most roads within the park, with the exception of the Roaring Fork Motor Nature Trail. The best opportunities for cyclists are at the **Foothills Parkway, Cades Cove,** and **Cataloochee.** On Wednesday and Saturday mornings from May to September, the 11 mi. Cades Cove Loop is closed to car traffic to allow bicyclists full use of the road from dawn to 10am. While the Smokies have no mountain biking trails, a few gravel trails in the park, including the **Gatlinburg Trail,** the **Oconaluftee River Trail,** and **Deep Creek** (lower section) allow bicycles. Another option is neighboring **Tsali Recreation Area,** where there are four mountain biking loops available for a small fee. Contact the Cheoah Ranger in the **Nantahala National Forest** for more information. (☎828-479-6431. Open M-F 8am-5pm.) Bike rental is available at **Cades Cove Campground Store.** (☎448-9034. $4 per hr., $20 per day. Open June to mid-Aug. daily 9am-7pm; late Aug. M-F 9am-5pm, Sa-Su 9am-7pm; Apr.-May and Sept.-Oct. daily 9am-5pm, no rental after 2:30pm. W and Sa bike rental begins 7am. Closed-toe shoes required.)

FISHING

Forty species of fish swim in the park's rivers and streams. The Smokies permit fishing in open waters year-round from 30min. before dawn to 30min. after sunset. Anglers over 12 (over 15 in North Carolina) must possess a valid Tennessee or North Carolina **fishing license.** (3-day passes for ages 16+ $16.50, year-long licenses for ages 13-15 $9, ages 12 and under free.) The park does not sell licenses; check with local chambers of commerce, sports shops, and hardware stores to purchase. Visitors centers have a free leaflet and map detailing fishing regulations.

RIDING

Over 500 mi. of the park's trails are open to horses. For travelers with horses, five drive-in **horse camps** provide facilities within the park: **Cades Cove, Big Creek, Cataloochee, Round Bottom,** and **Tow String.** (☎800-362-2267; http://reservations.nps.gov for reservations. Reservations required. $20-25 per night. Open mid-Mar. to Oct.) There are also four **riding stables** offering guided rides on scenic trails. (Cades Cove Riding Stable: ☎448-6286; open mid-Mar. to Nov. **Smokemont Riding Stable:** ☎828-497-2373; open mid-Apr. to Thanksgiving. **Smoky Mountain Riding Stable:** ☎436-5634; open mid-Mar. to Oct. **Sugarlands Horseback Riding Stable:** ☎430-5020; open mid-May to Nov. All $20 per hr. Age and weight restrictions vary.)

AUTO TOURS

The park offers a number of auto tours. The **Cades Cove Loop, Newfound Gap Road,** and **Roaring Fork** tours are favorites, and can get crowded in summer and on weekends. Pamphlets and maps are available in the visitors centers ($1 each). The **Cataloochee** tour ($0.50) goes through the area where elk have been reintroduced.

WHITEWATER RAFTING

South of Bryson City, NC, Rte. 19 winds past a number of whitewater rafting outfitters on the Nantahala River. The **Nantahala Outdoor Center (NOC),** 13077 U.S. 19 W (☎888-662-2199), 13 mi. southwest of Bryson City, is the largest and most comprehensive of these, offering guided and unguided rafting trips in 4-, 6-, and 8-person rafts as well as 1- and 2-person "duck-boats." (Guide-assisted rafting trips for beginners offered M-F $33 per person, Sa-Su $37 per person. Guide and rental rates vary depending on season, type of raft, and length of rental. Call for details.)

CHEROKEE RESERVATION

The Cherokee Indian Reservation, on the southeast border of the National Park, has a number of attractions, including a 24hr. dry casino in the town of Cherokee itself. For a look at the history and traditions of the Cherokee people, visit the **Museum of the Cherokee Indian,** at Drama Rd. and Tsali Blvd./U.S. 441. (☎828-497-3481; www.cherokeemuseum.org. Open daily June-Aug. 9am-8pm; Sept.-May 9am-5pm. $9, ages 6-13 $6.) From May to October, the reservation offers tours of the **Oconaluftee Indian Village,** 276 Drama Rd., a recreated mid-18th-century Cherokee village. Tours educate visitors about Cherokee crafts, political organization, and village life. Tours leave every 10min. and last 1-1½hr. (☎828-497-2315; www.oconalufteevillage.com. Open mid-May to late Oct. daily 9am-5:30pm. $13, ages 6-13 $6. Wheelchair accessible.) **"Unto these Hills,"** an outdoor drama, chronicles the story of the Cherokee people from the first European arrival to the Trail of Tears. Follow signs from Rte. 441. (☎828-497-2111; www.untothesehills.com. Box office on U.S. 441, downtown Cherokee. Shows early June-late Aug. daily 8:30pm, pre-show singing 7:45pm. $16, ages 6-13 $8. All reserved seats $18.) For lighter entertainment, roll the dice at **Harrah's Cherokee Casino,** 777 Casino Dr. off Hwy. 19 N. More than 2800 games, three restaurants, and an entertainment pavilion keep visitors entertained into the night. (☎800-427-7247 or 828-497-7777; www.harrahs.com. 21+. Open 24hr.) The **Cherokee Visitors Center,** 498 Tsali Blvd./Rte. 441, provides information; follow the signs. (☎800-438-1601 or 828-497-9195; www.cherokee-nc.com. Open mid-June-late Aug. 8:15am-7pm; low-season hours vary.)

CHATTANOOGA ☎423

Chattanooga, once famous for being home to the legendary "Chattanooga Choo-Choo," has recently made great strides towards modernization. Although its history as a transportation hub still flavors the city, Chattanooga is a bustling family destination, complete with a new "21st Century Waterfront," the result of a renovation project that has forever changed the face of the city. Now, Chattanooga's plot on the shores of the Tennessee River is adorned with fountains, greenery, and newly expanded cultural attractions that complement the city's old charm.

⛝ 🗺 ORIENTATION AND PRACTICAL INFORMATION. Chattanooga straddles the Tennessee/Georgia border at the junction of I-24, I-59, and I-75. Downtown, **Lookout Mountain** and the **Bluff View Art District** comprise the city's most popular areas. The **Chattanooga Metropolitan Airport** lies about 5 mi. east of the city. From downtown, take I-24 E to I-75 N, Exit 4, and follow signs to the airport. (☎855-2200; www.chattairport.com.) **Greyhound,** 960 Airport Rd. (☎892-1277; www.greyhound.com; open daily 6:30am-9:30pm) sends buses to Atlanta (2hr., 5 per day, $21-23), Knoxville (2hr., 3 per day, $16-17.50), and Nashville (3hr., 5 per day, $21-23). **Chattanooga Area Transportation Authority (CARTA)** operates a free downtown electric shuttle service with stops on every block between the aquarium and the Holiday Inn. (☎629-1473; www.carta-bus.org. Shuttles run every 5min. M-F 6am-9:30pm, Sa 9am-9:30pm, Su 9am-8:30pm. Wheelchair accessible.) **Visitors Info: Visitors center,** 2 Broad St., next to the aquarium. (☎800-322-3344; www.chattanoogafun.com. Discounted attraction tickets and free city maps. Open daily 8:30am-5:30pm.) **Internet Access: Public Library,** 1001 Broad St., at 10th St. (☎757-5310. Open M-Th 9am-9pm, F-Sa 9am-6pm, Su 2-6pm. Free.) **Post Office:** 900 Georgia Ave., between Martin Luther King Blvd. and 10th St. (☎267-1609. Open M-F 8am-4:30pm.) **Postal Code:** 37402. **Area Code:** 423.

⛏ ACCOMMODATIONS. Chain hotels congregate east of the city on I-24/I-75. **King's Lodge ❷,** 2400 West Side Dr., Exit 181A off I-24 E or Exit 181 off I-24 W, has inexpensive, clean rooms and a nice view of the city. (☎698-8944 or 800-251-7702. A/C, cable TV, HBO, pool. Doubles M-Th and Su $40, F-Sa $45. AmEx/D/MC/V.) The **Stadium Inn ❸,** 100 W. 21st St., Exit 178B off I-24, has clean, standard rooms in a convenient downtown location. (☎265-3151. A/C, cable TV, HBO, pool, and continental breakfast. Rooms from $59; low-season from $49. AAA and AARP discount 10%. AmEx/D/MC/V.) **Best Holiday Trav-L-Park ❶,** 1709 Mack Smith Rd., occupies a Civil War battlefield. From Chattanooga, take I-24 E to I-75 S and turn off at Exit 1. Turn right at the top of the ramp, then left at the 2nd light. (☎706-891-9766 or 800-693-2877; www.chattacamp.com. Bathrooms, showers, laundry, wireless Internet, and a pool. Sites with 30-amp hookup $26; 50-amp $28; cabins $40; without electricity $19. AARP discount 10%.) Exceptional hospitality, afternoon tea, and a hearty breakfast make the **Chanticleer Inn ❺,** 1300 Mockingbird Ln., down the street from Rock City, worth the splurge. (☎706-820-2002; www.stayatchanticleer.com. Internet access, A/C, cable TV, pool. Rooms $110-195. AAA discount. AmEx/D/MC/V.)

▢ FOOD. In the Bluff View Art District, ▧**Rembrandt's Coffee House ❶,** 204 High St., offers gourmet sandwiches and salads at reasonable prices. The lovely brick patio is the perfect spot to relax and sample the incredible pastries (under $4) or sip some coffee. (☎265-5033. Sandwiches and salads $3-6. Open M-Th 7am-10pm, F 7am-11:30pm, Sa 8am-11:30pm, Su 8am-10pm. AmEx/D/MC/V.) **Tomato Tango's Cafe ❶,** 18 West 8th St., is a small Italian eatery in the business district with great pasta and panini. (☎355-2937. Entrees $5-8. Open M-F 9am-9pm, Sa 11am-4pm. AmEx/MC/V.) **The Pickle Barrel ❶,** 1012 Market St., serves satisfying sandwiches ($4.25-6.25) and daily gourmet specials. Sit downstairs or on the open-air deck upstairs. (☎266-1103. Upstairs bar 21+ after 9pm. Open M-Sa 11:30am-3am, Su noon-3am. AmEx/D/MC/V.) **Jack's Alley** is lined with places to eat, including **Sticky**

Fingers ❸, 420 Broad St., the best place in town for ribs ($13). The $7 Sunday brunch has an all-you-can-eat buffet. (☎265-7427; www.stickyfingersonline.com. Open M-Th 11am-10pm, F-Su 11am-11pm. AmEx/D/MC/V.)

◙ SIGHTS. Downtown Chattanooga, a small area between 10th St. and the river, is crammed with attractions, shops, and restaurants. The ◙**Tennessee Aquarium**, 1 Broad St., on Ross's Landing, is home to the largest freshwater tank in the world as well as the newly opened "Ocean Journey" exhibit featuring sharks and other ocean life. The aquarium entertains visitors with an IMAX screen, mesmerizing seahorses, and some hideously ugly fish. (☎800-262-0695; www.tnaqua.org. Open daily 10am-6pm, with extended hours in summer. $18, ages 3-12 $9.50; IMAX theater $8/$5.50; aquarium and IMAX combo pass $22/$12.50. Behind-the-scenes tour daily 3-4:45pm $7, with purchase of aquarium admission $5. Tour ages 10+ only.) **The Passage**, on Market St. next to the aquarium, is a new memorial to the Trail of Tears which celebrates the art, culture, and history of the Cherokee Native Americans. The memorial exits into **Riverfront Park**, which has great views of the Tennessee River. The **International Towing and Recovery Hall of Fame and Museum**, 3315 S. Broad St., chronicles the creation and life of the tow truck. Even if you're not interested in trucks, this museum is worth seeing as a testament to human ingenuity. (☎267-3132; www.internationaltowingmuseum.org. Open M-Sa 9am-5pm, Su 11am-5pm. $8, ages 6-18 and 55+ $7, under 6 free. AAA discount.)

The **Bluff View Art District** (www.bluffviewartdistrict.com) is a neighborhood of upscale shops and cafes, anchored by the ◙**Hunter Museum of American Art**, 10 Bluff View Ave. From downtown, take 4th St. to High St. and turn left. Exhibits include contemporary art and classical American paintings. (☎267-0968; www.huntermuseum.org. Open M-Tu and F 10am-5pm, Th 10am-9pm, W and Su noon-5pm. $7, seniors $6, children $3.50, under 5 free. AAA discount. Special events and classes Th 6-9pm. Wheelchair accessible.) Across the street, the **Houston Museum**, 201 High St., is the life work of Anna Houston, an eccentric who lived in a barn she built herself. She left her belongings, including music boxes and an amazing glass collection, to a committee that started a museum on the river banks. To see the exhibits, visitors must join a 45min. tour. (☎267-7176; www.thehoustonmuseum.com. Open M-F 9:30am-4pm, Sa 11am-5pm. $7, ages 4-12 $3.50, under 4 free.)

One of the most popular destinations in Chattanooga is **Lookout Mountain.** Take S. Broad St. and follow the signs. Billed as "America's most amazing mile," the **Incline Railway** is the world's steepest passenger railway, chugging visitors up an insane 72.7% grade to an observation deck. The deck is accessible by car, allowing you to take in the incredible views for free. (☎821-4224; www.carta-bus.org. Open M-F 9am-5:30pm, Sa-Su 9am-6:40pm. One-way $9, round-trip $10; ages 3-12 $4.50/$5.) The nature trail at **Rock City Gardens** combines scenic lookouts and narrow rock passages with singing and dancing elves and strategically placed shops. (☎706-820-2531 or 800-854-0675; www.seerockcity.com. Open daily Jan.-May 8:30am-5pm, June-Aug. 8:30am-8pm, Sept. to mid-Nov. 8:30am-6pm. Open mid-Nov. to Dec. until 4pm and evenings 6-9pm for the "Enchanted Garden of Lights." $13, ages 3-12 $7.) One thousand feet inside the mountain, the **Ruby Falls** cavern formations and an impressive 145 ft. waterfall—complete with colored lights and sound effects—add pizzazz to a day of sightseeing, but be prepared to endure long waits and narrow passageways crowded with tourists. (☎821-2544; www.rubyfalls.com. Open daily 8am-8pm. 1hr. tour $13, ages 3-12 $6.) **Combo passes** ($33, ages 3-12 $16.50) for Incline Railway, Rock City, and Ruby Falls are available.

◙ ◙ ENTERTAINMENT AND NIGHTLIFE. For entertainment listings, check the "Weekend" section of the Friday *Chattanooga Times Free Press* or *The Pulse* and *Enigma*, two weekly alternative papers. Most nightlife options are downtown, especially in the area surrounding **Jack's Alley,** from Broad St. to Market St., between 4th and 5th St. There are several bars off the commercialized alley; **Taco Mac's,** 423 Market St., has the best selection of beers with over 50 on tap. (☎267-8226. Outdoor seating available. Beer from $2.85. Happy hour M-F 4-7pm. Open M-F 11am-3am, Sa-Su 11:30am-3am.) Nearby, the **Big River Grille and Brewing Works,** 222 Broad St., offers six original beers, plus seasonal ales and lagers. (☎267-2739. Pints $3.25. Happy hour M-F 4-7pm. Pool tables. Live local music Th-Sa. Open M-Th and Su 11am-1am, F-Sa 11am-2am; kitchen closes at 11pm M-Th and Su, midnight F-Sa.) **Rhythm and Brews,** 221 Market St., is the town's best live music venue. (☎267-4644; www.rhythm-brews.com. 21+. Cover $5-20. Usually open W-Sa 8pm-late; music starts around 9:45pm.) **Alan Gold's,** 1100 McCallie Ave., just over the bridge from Central on National, is a popular gay venue that boasts two bars, a dance floor, lounge areas, and balconies. (☎629-8080. Tu-Sa drag shows 12:30am. Cover F-Sa $5. Happy hour 4:30-10pm. Open daily 4:30pm-3am.) **Big Chill Grill,** on Market St. next to Taco Mac's, is a lively bar downtown. (☎267-2435. 21+. Tu night karaoke. Happy hour 2-8pm. Open M-Sa 2pm-3am, Su 5pm-2am.)

The **Chattanooga Lookouts,** a minor league baseball team for the Reds, play at Bell-South Park, at 2nd and Chestnut St. (☎267-2208. Tickets $4-8, seniors and under 12 $2.) For nine nights in June, the riverfront shuts down for live rock, country, blues, jazz, and reggae during the **Riverbend Festival.** (☎756-2211; www.riverbendfestival.com. Tickets $35, $26 in advance.) The mountains surrounding Chattanooga also offer opportunities for whitewater rafting; ask for info at the visitors center.

MEMPHIS   ☎901

Music is the pulse of Memphis and the reason why most visitors visit the city. Still, all the blues, funk, soul, country, and rock is deeply entwined with the history of civil rights and social change in the United States. White farmers brought country music, black workers brought the blues, and their synthesis resulted in a melting pot of contemporary musical styles. Black and white musicians were also playing together and thus challenging the segregation laws of the time. Today, most visitors make the Memphis pilgrimage to see Graceland, the former home of Elvis Presley and one of the most deliciously tacky spots in the US. There's plenty to do after you've paid your respects to "The King"; unusual museums, fantastic ribs, and live music are just some of the reasons you might want to stay a few days.

▆ TRANSPORTATION

Airport: Memphis International, 2491 Winchester Rd. (☎922-8000; www.mscaa.com), south of the southern loop of I-240. Taxi to the city around $25—negotiate in advance.

Trains: Amtrak, 545 S. Main St. (☎526-0052; www.amtrak.com), at G.E. Patterson Ave., on the southern edge of downtown. This area can be unsafe. Main St. trolley runs to the station. Ticket office open daily 6:30am-11pm. To **Chicago** (10½hr., 1 per day, $155), **Jackson** (4½hr., 1 per day, $46), and **New Orleans** (8½hr., 1 per day, $68).

Buses: Greyhound, 203 Union Ave. (☎523-9253; www.greyhound.com), at 3rd St. downtown. The area can be unsafe at night. Open 24hr. To **Chattanooga** (7-10hr., 4 per day, $41), **Jackson** (4-6hr., 6 per day, $35), and **Nashville** (4hr., 13 per day, $32).

Public Transit: Memphis Area Transit Authority, or MATA (☎274-6282; www.matatransit.com), corner of Auction Ave. and Main St. Bus routes cover most suburbs but run infrequently (every 30min. at best). Major routes run on Front, 2nd, and 3rd St. Buses run M-F beginning between 4:30 and 6am and stopping between 7 and 11pm, depending on the route. Sa-Su service less frequent. $1.40, transfers $0.10. Refurbished 19th-

THE SOUTH

century **trolley cars** cruise Main St. and the Riverfront, operating M-F 6am-midnight, Sa 9:30am-1am, Su 9am-6pm. $1, seniors $0.50, under 5 free. Exact change required. 1-day pass $3.50, 3-day pass $8.

Museum Shuttles: Sun Studio and Graceland both offer free shuttle service between attractions. The **Elvis Express,** operated by Graceland, runs between Graceland and Beale St. The **Sun Studio shuttle** transports travelers between Graceland, Sun Studio, and the Rock 'n' Soul museum, departing from Graceland on the hr., from Sun Studio at 15min. past the hr., and from the Rock 'n' Soul Museum on the half-hour daily 10am-6pm. Call attractions for further info. (☎800-441-6249; www.sunstudio.com.)

Taxi: City Wide, ☎722-8294. **Yellow Cab,** ☎577-7700.

◼◼ ORIENTATION AND PRACTICAL INFORMATION

Downtown, named avenues run east-west, and numbered ones run north-south. **Madison Avenue** divides north and south addresses. Two main thoroughfares, **Poplar** and **Union Avenue,** are east-west; **2nd** and **3rd Street** are the major north-south routes downtown. **I-240** and **I-55** encircle the city. **Riverside Drive** takes you to U.S. 61, which becomes **Elvis Presley Boulevard** and leads south straight to Graceland. **Midtown,** east of downtown, is home to a funky music scene and gay venues and is a break from the tourist attractions (and tourist traps) of **Beale Street.**

Visitor Info: Tennessee Welcome Center, 119 Riverside Dr. (☎543-6757; www.memphistravel.com), at Jefferson St. Open daily 7am-9pm; building closes 11pm.

Hotlines: Crisis Line, ☎274-7477. **Gay/Lesbian Switchboard,** ☎278-4297. Both 24hr.

Internet Access: Cossitt Branch Library, 33 S. Front St. (☎526-1712), downtown at Monroe. Open M-F 10am-5pm. Farther away, the **Main Library** is at 3030 Poplar Ave. (☎415-2700). Open M-Th 9am-9pm, F-Sa 9am-6pm, Su 1-5pm. Both free.

Post Offices: 1 N. Front St. (☎576-2037). Open M-F 8:30am-5pm, Sa 9am-1pm. **Postal Code:** 38103. Also at 555 S. 3rd St. (☎521-2559). Open M-F 8:30am-5pm. **Postal Code:** 38101. **Area Code:** 901.

◼ ACCOMMODATIONS

A few downtown motels have prices in the budget range; more budget lodgings are available near Graceland at **Elvis Presley Boulevard** and **Brooks Road.** Coupons from the visitors center are good for substantial discounts at many chain hotels, particularly midweek, but call ahead to confirm room availability. For the celebrations of Elvis's historic birth (Jan. 8) and death (Aug. 16), as well as for the Memphis in May festival, book rooms six months to one year in advance.

American Inn, 3265 Elvis Presley Blvd. (☎345-8444), Exit 5B off I-55, close to Graceland. Despite its shabby exterior, you can't help falling in love with the large, comfy rooms and the Elvis-themed mural in the lobby. Cable TV, A/C, pool, and continental breakfast. Singles $30; doubles $46. AmEx/D/MC/V. ❷

Super 8, 340 W. Illinois St. (☎948-9005), Exit 12C off I-55, is closer to downtown. Rooms are basic but clean and include refrigerator, microwave, and safe. Even-numbered rooms are quieter—they face away from I-55. Pool, continental breakfast, laundry. $3 shuttle to downtown. Rooms M-Th and Su $40-50, F-Sa $50-60. AmEx/D/MC/V. ❸

Homestead Studio Suites Hotel, 6500 Poplar Ave. (☎767-5522). Though about 16 mi. from downtown, these impeccable rooms come with full kitchen, high-speed Internet, and access to laundry facilities—just like your own apartment. The surrounding area also offers plenty of dining options. Rooms $70-90. Weekly rates $55-65 per night. AAA and AARP discount. AmEx/D/MC/V. ❸

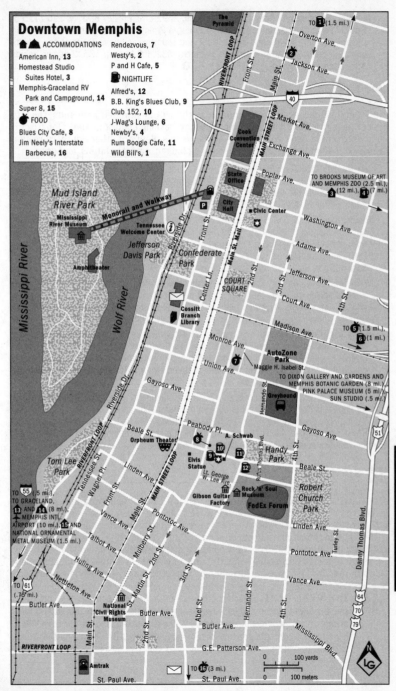

Downtown Memphis

🏠🏕 ACCOMMODATIONS

American Inn, **13**
Homestead Studio
 Suites Hotel, **3**
Memphis-Graceland RV
 Park and Campground, **14**
Super 8, **15**

🍎 FOOD

Blues City Cafe, **8**
Jim Neely's Interstate
 Barbecue, **16**

Rendezvous, **7**
Westy's, **2**
P and H Cafe, **5**

🍸 NIGHTLIFE

Alfred's, **12**
B.B. King's Blues Club, **9**
Club 152, **10**
J-Wag's Lounge, **6**
Newby's, **4**
Rum Boogie Cafe, **11**
Wild Bill's, **1**

THE SOUTH

Memphis-Graceland RV Park and Campground, 3691 Elvis Presley Blvd. (☎396-7125 or 866-571-9236), beside the Heartbreak Hotel, a 2min. walk from Graceland. Very little privacy, but the location is great. Pool and laundry facilities. Reservations recommended. Sites $22, with water and electricity $32, full hookup $35. 2-person cabins $35, each additional person $5. D/MC/V. ❶

🍴 FOOD

In Memphis, barbecue is as common as rhinestone-studded jumpsuits; the city even hosts the **World Championship Barbecue Cooking Contest** in May. Don't fret if gnawing on ribs isn't your thing—Memphis has plenty of other Southern restaurants with down-home favorites like fried chicken, catfish, chitlins, and grits.

Jim Neely's Interstate Barbecue, 2265 S. Third St. (☎775-2304), off I-55 at Exit 7. Great barbecue, plain and simple. The chopped pork Bar-B-Q sandwich ($4.75) is excellent, as is the rib dinner (full rack of ribs; $8.50). Open M-Th 11am-11pm, F-Sa 11am-midnight. AmEx/D/MC/V. ❷

Rendezvous, 52 S. 2nd St. (☎523-2746; www.hogsfly.com). The entrance is around back on Maggie H. Isabel St., in the alley opposite the Peabody Hotel. A Memphis legend, serving charcoal-broiled ribs (half rack $14, full rack $17), cheese and sausages ($8), and sandwiches ($6-7); look for the long line. Open Tu-Th 4:30-10:30pm, F 11am-11pm, Sa 11:30am-11pm. AmEx/D/MC/V. ❸

Westy's, 346 N. Main St. (☎543-3278), at Jackson Ave., downtown on the trolley line. Westy's serves delicious tamales, stuffed potatoes, and creole dishes (all $6-11) in a relaxed atmosphere. Over 270 beers available. Sandwiches on home-baked bread $6-8. Happy hour daily 4-7pm. Pool tables. Open daily 10:45am-3am. AmEx/D/MC/V. ❷

Blues City Cafe, 138 Beale St. (☎526-3637; www.bluescitycafe.com). Chef Bonnie Mack serves tamales (six for $6) and huge ribs (half rack $14). Prices may be inflated due to the cafe's Beale St. location, but the chili and three tamale combo ($5) is a cheap and tasty complement to Beale St. beer. Open M-Th and Su 11am-3am, F-Sa 11am-5am. AmEx/D/MC/V. ❷

P and H Cafe, 1532 Madison Ave. (☎726-0906; www.pandhcafe.com). The initials stand for Poor and Hungry; this "beer joint of your dreams" still grills food for wallet-watchers. During Elvis Week in Aug., P and H hosts the "Dead Elvis Ball," with impersonators and live bands. Burgers $5.50. Live music M. Trivia night Tu. Featured artist W. Poker night Th. Local singers Sa. Open M-F 11am-3am, Sa 5pm-3am. AmEx/D/MC/V. ❷

👁 SIGHTS

GRACELAND. The best strategy for visiting Elvis Presley's home is to know what you want to get out of it before you go, since it's easy to be overwhelmed by the crowds once you're there. Crowds are lightest in the mornings before 10am. The **Graceland Mansion** itself can be seen in about 1½-2hr.; it takes a whole morning or afternoon to visit the array of secondary shops, museums, and restaurants. The crush of tourists swarms in a delightful orgy of gaudiness around the tackiest mansion in the US. The faux-fur furnishings, mirrored ceilings, green shag-carpeted

THE REAL DEAL. Graceland now offers a **VIP Tour** package that lets you skip the lines to get in and includes a souvenir "backstage" pass. But at $55 for all ages, it's a lot of money spent for very little time saved: once inside, even VIPs have to wait behind hordes of visitors moving through The King's palace. You might as well just pick and choose the sights you want to see. —Ben Collins

walls, ostrich-feather pillows, and yellow-and-orange decor of Elvis's 1974 renovations are not easily forgotten. A blinding sheen of hundreds of gold and platinum records illuminates the **Trophy Building**, where exhibits detail Elvis's stint in the army and his more than 30 movie roles. The King is buried in the adjacent **Meditation Gardens**. *(3763 Elvis Presley Blvd. Take I-55 S to Exit 5B or bus #43 "Elvis Presley." ☎ 332-3322 or 800-238-2000; www.elvis.com contains info on Graceland as well as all peripheral attractions. Ticket office open Mar.-Nov. M-Sa 9am-5pm, Su 10am-4pm; Dec.-Feb. M and W-Su 10am-4pm. Attractions remain open 2hr. after ticket office closes. Mansion closed Tu. Graceland Mansion tour including audio headset $22, students and ages 62+ $20, children ages 7-12 $7. Parking $5, RVs $10. Trophy Building and Meditation Gardens are fully wheelchair accessible; mansion only partially accessible. AAA discount $1-2.)*

MORE ELVIS. If you love him tender, love him true, visit the peripheral Elvis attractions across the street from the mansion. **Walk a Mile in My Shoes**, a free 20min. film screened every 30min., traces Elvis's career from the early (slim) years through the later (fat) ones. The **Elvis Presley Automobile Museum** houses a fleet of Elvis-mobiles, including pink and purple Cadillacs and motorized toys aplenty. *($8, students and ages 62+ $7.20, ages 7-12 $4. Wheelchair accessible.)* Visitors to **Elvis's Custom Jets** can walk through the King's private plane, the *Lisa Marie*, complete with a blue suede bed and gold-plated seatbelts, and peek into the tiny *Hound Dog II* Jetstar. *($7, seniors $6.30, children $3.50.)* The **Sincerely Elvis** exhibit offers a glimpse into Elvis's private side, displaying his wedding announcements, a collection of Lisa Marie's toys, and items from his wild wardrobe, as well as memorabilia and heaps of fan letters. *($6, seniors $5.40, children $3. Wheelchair accessible.)* The **Platinum Tour Package** discounts admission to the mansion and attractions. *($28, students and seniors $25.20, ages 7-12 $13. AAA discount $3.)*

MUSIC: THE MEMPHIS HEARTBEAT. Memphis's musical roots run deep into the fertile cultural soil of the Mississippi delta region. During the early- and mid-1900s, Memphis's musical scene blended jazz, soul and folk traditions to create a new and unique blues sound. Downtown Memphis's historic **Beale Street** saw the invention of the blues and the soul hits of the Stax label. At the must-see ⬛**Rock 'n' Soul Museum**, the numerous artifacts on display include celebrity stage costumes and B.B. King's famous guitar, Lucille. Best of all, the audio tour contains 100 complete songs. The museum also provides an account of rock 'n' roll's origins, from the cotton fields to the coming together of black and white

ALL SHOOK UP

Elvis Presley's Graceland mansion receives thousands of visitors every day of the year. During Memphis's annual celebration of "Elvis Week" in August, diehard Elvis fans join rhinestone-clad impersonators for a week of commemoration and revelry. Elvis Week events range in tone from light-hearted to somber and include Elvis film festivals, impersonator contests, Elvis karaoke, and even Elvis bingo. The week reaches its climax with a candlelight vigil from sundown on August 15th at Graceland until the morning of August 16th, the date of Elvis's death.

Fans who attend Elvis Week emphasize his significance as a successful challenger to the cultural and racial barriers of 1950s America. Though Elvis's music and live performances may seem tame by today's standards, his gyrating pelvis caused such a scandal that the *Ed Sullivan Show* would only film him from the waist-up when he performed on television. As historian Michael Bertrand argues in *Race, Rock and Elvis*, Elvis's music blended black and white musical traditions into a new sound with crossracial appeal that helped to break down cultural segregation among American youth.

As you don your sequins to get "all shook up" for Elvis Week, keep in mind that the Elvis fan empire may have changed the course of American history.

music. *(On Third St. across from the Gibson Guitar factory. 1 block south of Beale St. ☎ 205-2533; www.memphisrocknsoul.org. Open daily 10am-7pm. $9, ages 5-17 $6; audio tour included. Wheelchair accessible.)* For rock 'n' roll fans, no visit to Memphis is complete without a visit to ⍟**Sun Studio**, where rock 'n' roll was conceived. In this legendary one-room recording studio, Elvis was discovered, Johnny Cash walked the line, and Jerry Lee Lewis was consumed by great balls of fire. Tours go through a small museum area and proceed to the studio itself, where visitors listen to the recording sessions that earned the studio its fame. *(706 Union Ave. ☎ 800-441-6249; www.sunstudio.com. Open daily 10am-6pm. 35min. tours every hr. on the half-hour. $9.50, under 12 free. AAA discount.)* Long before Sam Phillips and Sun Studio produced Elvis and Jerry Lee Lewis, the **Gibson Guitar Factory,** across the street from the Rock 'n' Soul Museum, was lovingly crafting guitars. Even these days, the factory only produces about 35 instruments each day. Tours detail the various stages of the guitar-making process; visit during the week to see the craftsmen at work. *(145 Lt. George W. Lee Ave. ☎ 543-0800, ext. 101; www.gibsonmemphis.com. 35-45min. tours run M-W and Su noon, 1 and 2pm, Th-Sa every hr. 11am-2pm. $10. Must be 12 or older.)*

UNIQUE MUSEUMS. On April 4, 1968, Dr. Martin Luther King, Jr. was assassinated at the **Lorraine Motel** in Memphis. Today, the powerful ⍟**National Civil Rights Museum** occupies the original building. Relive the courageous struggle of the Civil Rights movement through photographs, videos, and interviews in this moving exhibit, which ends in Dr. King's motel room. The main exhibition's presentation of the Civil Rights movement of the 1960s is comprehensive, engaging, and among the best of the South's many similar museums. Even so, the museum's annex across the street devotes an entire floor to the assassination of Dr. King and the investigation and trial of James Earl Ray, which some may find excessive. *(450 Mulberry St. ☎ 521-9699; www.civilrightsmuseum.org. Open June-Aug. M and W-Sa 9am-6pm, Su 1-6pm; Sept.-May M and W-Sa 9am-5pm, Su 1-5pm. $12, students and ages 55+ $10, ages 4-17 $8.50. Free M after 3pm. 1hr. audio tours $2; children's version available. AAA and military discounts.)* South of downtown, the ⍟**National Ornamental Metal Museum,** the only institution of its kind in the US, displays fine metalwork from international artists. Get a better idea of the artistic process at the working blacksmith shop behind the museum, and check out the front gate as you walk in. *(374 Metal Museum Dr. Exit 12C from I-55. ☎ 774-6380; www.metalmuseum.org. Open Tu-Sa 10am-5pm, Su noon-5pm. $4, ages 62+ $3, ages 5-18 $2. AAA discount $1.)* A general store, antique museum, and clothing shop rolled into one, **A. Schwab** has stood on Beale St. since 1876. Used clothing treasures abound for the bargain-hunter. *(163 Beale St. ☎ 523-9782. Open M-Sa 9am-5pm.)*

OVERTON PARK. The **Brooks Museum of Art,** in the southwest corner of Overton Park, east of downtown, showcases a diverse collection of paintings and decorative art and features visiting exhibits. On the first Wednesday of each month, the museum hosts a celebration (6-9pm, $5) with food, films, live music, and drinks. *(1934 Poplar Ave. ☎ 544-6200; www.brooksmuseum.org. Open Tu-F 10am-4pm, Sa 10am-5pm, Su 11:30am-5pm. $6, ages 65+ $5, students and ages 7-17 $2. W usually free. AAA discount 50%. Audio tour $3/$2/$2. Wheelchair accessible.)* Also in the park, the small but impressive **Memphis Zoo** is one of four places in the US where you can see giant pandas. Kids will enjoy the sea lion show (daily 10:30am and 2:30pm) and taking a spin on the carousel. *(2000 Prentis Pl. ☎ 276-9453; www.memphiszoo.org. Open daily Mar.-Oct. 9am-6pm; Nov.-Feb. daily 9am-5pm; last admission 1hr. before close. $13, ages 60+ $12, ages 2-11 $8. Parking $3. Tram tour $1. Wheelchair accessible.)*

MUD ISLAND RIVER PARK. A quick walk or monorail ride over the Mississippi to **Mud Island** allows you to stroll and splash along the **River Walk,** a scale model of the Mississippi River the length of five city blocks that's sure to impress anyone interested in maps. Free tours of the River Walk run several times daily. The **Mississippi River Museum** on the island charts the history and culture of the river over the past 10,000 years with videos, musical recordings, and life-sized replicas of steamboats and ironclads. *(Monorail leaves from 125 N. Front St. every 10min., round-trip $2; pedestrian bridge free. ☎576-7241 or 800-507-6507; www.mudisland.com. Park open June-Aug. daily 10am-8pm; Mar.-May and Sept.-Oct. Tu-Su 10am-5pm. Last admission 1hr. before close. 3-5 tours daily. Museum $8, ages 62+ $6, ages 5-12 $5. Wheelchair accessible. Monorail free with museum admission.)* Visitors can paddle around on the Mississippi or pedal through the streets of downtown Memphis. *(1hr. kayak rental $15 for 1 person, for 2 people $20; 1hr. canoe for 2 people $20. Bike rental $10 per 2 hr.)* The newest feature is the **Sleep Out on the Mississippi,** held the second Friday of each month in summer. Though it may sound like a form of political protest, it's actually a camping trip under the stars with dinner, music, kayaks, and breakfast provided. *(Reserve in advance. Reservations ☎576-7241 or 800-507-6507. $40.)*

PARKS AND GARDENS. The 96-acre **Memphis Botanic Garden,** with 22 distinct gardens, is the perfect place for a stroll. Relish the fantastic 57-variety rose garden, the sensory garden, or the peaceful Japanese garden. *(750 Cherry Rd., in Audubon Park off Park Ave. ☎685-1566; www.memphisbotanicgarden.com. Open daily 9am-6pm. $5, ages 62+ $4, ages 3-12 $3, under 2 free. Wheelchair accessible.)* Across Park Ave., the **Dixon Gallery and Gardens** flaunts an impeccable garden with an impressive range of sculptures and a collection of European art with work by Renoir, Degas, and Monet. *(4339 Park Ave. ☎761-2409 or 761-5250; www.dixon.org. Open Tu-F 10am-4pm, Sa 10am-5pm, Su 1-5pm. $5, ages 60+ $4, students and children free. Audio tours $3.)*

🎵 🎭 ENTERTAINMENT AND NIGHTLIFE

W.C. Handy's 1917 "Beale St. Blues" claims that "you'll find that business never closes 'til somebody gets killed." Today's visitors are more likely to encounter the Hard Rock Cafe and all the mega-commercialism that comes with it than the rough-and-tumble juke joints of old. Despite all the change, the strip between 2nd and 4th St. is still the place to go for live music. On Friday nights, a $15 wristband lets you into any club on the strip, except Alfred's. You must show ID to get into Beale St. at night; police officers card at entrances to the pedestrian area. The free *Memphis Flyer* and the "Playbook" section of the Friday *Memphis Commercial Appeal* can tell you what's goin' down in town.

THE LOCAL STORY

CONTROVERSIAL COMMEMORATION

Most visitors to Memphis's Civil Rights Museum wouldn't think twice about the educational value of its exhibits, but the debate over how best to preserve the memory of Dr. Martin Luther King, Jr. for future generations remains unresolved. Jacqueline Smith has camped out across the street from the Civil Rights Museum for over 17 years in protest of a museum that she argues has betrayed Dr. King's vision. Suggesting that the museum has turned the site of Dr. King's assassination into a sensationalized tourist trap, Smith criticizes the museum's new exhibit on the assassination of Dr. King. Why spend millions commemorating King's death, Smith argues, when the poverty and *de facto* racial segregation he fought against are still present in Memphis, even in the neighborhood surrounding the museum?

The Civil Rights Museum's powerful exhibits provide at least one compelling answer to Smith's criticisms—only by learning about past struggles against racial injustice can we understand how to face the problems of the present. Regardless of your opinions on the issue, don't miss the opportunity to engage with this issue yourself—Ms. Smith and the museum both plan on sticking around for a while.

Learn more about Ms. Smith's protest at www.fulfillthedream.net.

BEALE STREET BLUES

Beale St. is a great place to enjoy a quiet beer, but come the weekend, people are cartwheeling down the street. While some bars are frequented by a spring-break crowd, older (and pricier) standbys feature the music that made Beale St. famous.

Rum Boogie Cafe, 182 Beale St. (☎528-0150). One of the first clubs on Beale St., Rum Boogie still rocks with homegrown blues and a friendly ambience. Check out the celebrity guitars hanging from the ceiling. Live music M-Th and Su 8pm, F-Sa 9pm. Happy hour M-F 5-7pm. 21+ M-Th and Su after 9pm, F-Sa after 8pm. Cover M-Th and Su after 8pm $3, F-Sa after 9:30pm $5. Open M-Th and Su 11am-12:30am, F-Sa 11am-2am.

B.B. King's Blues Club, 143 Beale St. (☎524-5464; www.bbkingsclub.com). The live blues makes this place popular with locals, visitors, and celebrities. Drinks are expensive, even for Beale St. B.B. himself occasionally plays a show, though tickets can reach $200 and typically sell out. Entrees $11-19. Music starts at 6pm, house band starts at 8:30pm. Cover $5-7. Open M-Th and Su noon-1:30am, F-Sa 11am-3am.

Club 152, 152 Beale St. (☎544-7011). One of the most popular clubs on Beale, offering 3 floors of dancing and drinks. Live music acts range from blues to techno; on weekends DJs spin upstairs. Check out the "mood elevator," a wildly painted elevator that takes you to hip-hop (F 2nd fl.), techno (Sa 3rd fl.), and beyond. Beer from $3.50. 21+. Cover Th $5, F $5-8, Sa $5-10. Open M-Th and Su 11am-2am, F-Sa 11am-5am.

Alfred's, 197 Beale St. (☎525-3711; www.alfreds-on-beale.com), is a favorite with locals for its karaoke, live music, and DJs spinning into the wee hours. Outdoor patio. 21+ after 10pm. Live music nightly 6-10pm. Cover some Th and most F-Sa $5. $15 wristbands are not accepted here. Open M-Th and Su 11am-3am, F-Sa 11am-5am.

NIGHTLIFE OFF BEALE STREET

For a collegiate climate, try the **Highland Street** strip near **Memphis State University.** The city's gay bars are in **Midtown;** take the Main St. trolley down Madison to the end of the line by J-Wag's and progress from there. This area can be unsafe after dark. Ask any bar to call you a cab. For info on gay clubs and happenings, *Triangle Journal News* can be found in any gay venue.

Newby's, 539 S. Highland St. (☎452-8408; www.newbysmemphis.com), is a dark, lively college bar with pool tables, comfy red booths, and an outdoor patio. Live bands play everything from rock to reggae almost every night beginning at 10pm. Beer from $3. Happy hour daily 3-10pm. 21+. Cover usually $3-5. Open daily 3pm-3am.

Wild Bill's, 1580 Vollintine Ave. (☎726-5473), a neighborhood restaurant and music joint, lies off the beaten track and contrasts with the touristed places downtown. Live music F-Sa 11pm, Su 10pm. Cover F-Su $5. Open M-Th 10am-11pm, F-Su 10am-3am.

J-Wag's Lounge, 1268 Madison (☎725-1909), is a relaxed gay- and straight-friendly bar with pool, darts, and several drink specials, including $1.75 long-necks during happy hour daily 10am-7pm. Drag shows F-Sa 3am. Cover F-Sa midnight-4am $3. Open 24hr.

ENTERTAINMENT

The majestic **Orpheum Theatre,** 203 S. Main St., hosts Broadway shows and big-name performers. On Fridays during the summer, the grand old theater shows classic movies with an organ prelude and a cartoon. (☎525-3000; www.orpheum-memphis.com. Box office open M-F 9am-5pm and before shows. Movies 7:15pm; $6, seniors and under 12 $5. Concerts and shows $15-55; $3 booking fee except on day of show.) Just as things are really beginning to heat up in the South, the legendary **Memphis in May** celebration hits the city, continuing throughout the month with concerts, art exhibits, food contests, and sporting events. (☎525-4611; www.memphisinmay.org.) One such event is the **Beale Street Music Festival,** featuring some of the biggest names from a range of musical genres. There's also the **World Championship Barbecue Cooking Contest** and the **Sunset Symphony,** a concert near the river given by the Memphis Symphony Orchestra.

◤ DAYTRIP FROM MEMPHIS

THE MISSISSIPPI DELTA

The Mississippi Delta begins south of Memphis and encompasses parts of Mississippi, Tennessee, and Arkansas. From Memphis, take U.S. 61 south.

South of Memphis lie the swamps and flatlands of the Mississippi Delta region, where cotton was king and the blues—a blend of African tribal songs, gospel, and work chants—was born. Here, cotton fields are juxtaposed with glittering casinos, a testament to the changing times. The helpful staff of the **Tunica Visitor Center** on U.S. 61 S, just across the Mississippi border, provides maps of the region. (☎ 662-363-3800 or 888-488-6422; www.tunicamiss.com. Open M-F 8:30am-5pm, Sa 10am-5pm, Su 1-5pm.) Tunica is a major center for gambling and casinos, several of which constitute a resort area along the Mississippi shore.

Playwright Tennessee Williams was raised in **Clarksdale, MS,** 70 mi. south of Memphis in the heart of the Delta, and many of his writings are based on his experiences growing up in the area. Housed in an old train depot, the **Delta Blues Museum,** 1 Blues Alley, off 3rd St. at the intersection of John Lee Hooker Ln., displays regional artwork, photographs, and rare Delta artifacts, including harmonicas owned by Sonny Boy Williamson and a guitar fashioned by ZZ Top from a log cabin Muddy Waters once lived in. (☎ 662-627-6820; www.deltabluesmuseum.org. Call to inquire about special events and exhibits. Open Mar.-Oct. M-Sa 9am-5pm; Nov.-Feb. M-Sa 10am-5pm. $7, seniors and ages 6-12 $5.) Take a minute to walk over to ▧**Ground Zero ❶,** 0 Blues Alley, for a plate lunch complete with beverage, cornbread, and dessert for $7. The vegetables, including okra, turnip greens, and purple peas, are excellent. From Wednesday through Saturday, stay late for local tunes. (☎ 662-621-9009; www.groundzerobluesclub.com. Lunch special 11am-2pm. Open M-Tu 11am-midnight, W 11am-midnight, Th 11am-11pm, F-Sa 11am-midnight. MC/V.) For some of the area's best barbecue, try **Abe's ❷,** 616 State St., where a pulled pork sandwich is only $3.25, and ribs cost $12. (☎ 662-624-9947. Open M-Th 10am-9pm, F-Sa 10am-10pm, Su 11am-2pm. Cash only.) The newly renovated **Uptown Motor Inn ❸,** 305 E. 2nd St., is a basic, comfortable motel close to downtown Clarksdale. Check out the vintage "Teletype Mileage Calculator" in the lobby. (☎ 662-627-3251. Rooms $33-40. AmEx/D/MC/V.) From Clarksdale, **Greyhound,** 1604 State St. (☎ 662-627-7893; www.greyhound.com; open M-Sa 7am-5:30pm and 9-9:30pm, Su 4:30-5:15pm and 9-9:30pm), runs buses to Memphis (1½hr., 2 per day, $18.50), New Orleans (11hr., 2 per day, $69), and other destinations.

On U.S. 49, across the river in Arkansas, lies **Helena,** the site of a major defeat for the Confederate army on July 4, 1863. Every year on Columbus Day weekend in October, the town attracts thousands to its **King Biscuit Blues Festival,** the largest free blues festival in the South (870-338-8798; www.kingbiscuitfest.org).

NORTH CAROLINA

Fields of tobacco, pastel sunsets, and rocking chairs on porches—these generalizations about North Carolina aren't far from the truth, but visitors rarely just sit around drinking sweet tea. Outdoorsy types revel in the awesome landscapes of the western mountains, while the central Piedmont region combines the sophistication of the North with the South's slower pace and is filled with cultural activities and historical sights. There's no denying the marked diversity of the state; North Carolina is home to gorgeous beaches, some of the nation's top universities, and the country's second-largest financial center. One thing can be said for the whole of the "Tarheel State": natural beauty and Southern hospitality are the rule.

🛂 PRACTICAL INFORMATION

Capital: Raleigh.

Visitor Info: Dept. of Commerce, Travel, and Tourism, 301 N. Wilmington St., Raleigh 27601 (☎919-733-8372 or 800-847-4862; www.visitnc.com). **Division of Parks and Recreation,** 512 N. Salisbury St., Archdale Building 7th fl., Room 732 (☎919-733-4181).

Postal Abbreviation: NC. **Sales Tax:** 7%.

THE TRIANGLE   ☎919

Clustered in the northern Piedmont region, the Triangle is comprised of Raleigh, Durham, and Chapel Hill. In the 1950s, the three towns were united by the creation of the spectacularly successful Research Triangle Park, a research hub responsible for inventions as inspiring as the AIDS drug AZT and as down-to-earth as Astroturf. **Raleigh,** the state capital and home to North Carolina State University (NC State), is a historic town with recently revamped tourist attractions. **Durham,** formerly a major tobacco producer, now supports medical research projects devoted to finding cancer cures and is the site of Duke University. The University of North Carolina (UNC), chartered in 1789 as the nation's first state university, is located down the road in **Chapel Hill.** College culture infuses all three cities with a hot music scene, popular bars, and unconventional stores.

⬅ TRANSPORTATION

Airport: Raleigh-Durham International (☎840-2123; www.rdu.com), 10 mi. southeast of Durham and 10 mi. northwest of Raleigh, between U.S. 70 and I-40 on Aviation Blvd. From Durham, take Exit 284B from I-40 E or Exit 292 from U.S. 70 E. From Raleigh, take Exit 285 from I-40 W or Exit 292 from U.S. 70 W. A **taxi** to downtown Raleigh or Durham costs about $30; to Chapel Hill costs about $35. Triangle Transit Authority has shuttle service from RDU to surrounding areas; see **Public Transit,** below.

Trains: Amtrak (www.amtrak.com) has stations in Raleigh and Durham. Raleigh: 320 W. Cabarrus St. (☎833-7594), 4 blocks west of the Civic Ctr. Open daily 5:30am-9:30pm. To: **Durham** (30min., 2 per day, $4-7); **New York City** (13hr., 1 per day, $87-145); **Richmond** (4hr., 1 per day, $24-52); **Washington, D.C.** (6hr., 1 per day, $37-81). Durham: 400 W. Chapel Hill St. (☎956-7932). Open daily 7am-9pm. To **Raleigh** (30min., 2 per day, $4-7).

Buses: Greyhound (www.greyhound.com) has stations in both Raleigh and Durham. Raleigh: 314 W. Jones St. (☎834-8275). Open 24hr. To **Chapel Hill** (1¼hr., 3 per day, $10.50-12), **Charleston** (7-8hr., 2 per day, $52-56), and **Durham** (40min., 9 per day, $6-7). Durham: 820 W. Morgan St. (☎687-4800), 2 blocks off Chapel Hill St. downtown, just around the corner from Duke's East Campus. Open daily 7:30am-10pm. To **Chapel Hill** (25min., 4 per day, $7) and **Washington, D.C.** (6hr., 5 per day, $45-48).

Public Transit: Triangle Transit Authority (☎549-9999; www.ridetta.org). Buses run throughout the Triangle M-F 6am-10pm, Sa 7am-6:30pm. $2. **Capital Area Transit,** Raleigh (☎828-7228). Buses run throughout the city M-Sa 5am-10:30pm. $0.75;

transfers free. **Durham Area Transit Authority (DATA),** Durham (☎683-3282; www.ci.durham.nc.us/departments/works/data.cfm). Most routes start downtown at 521 Morgan St. Operates daily; hours vary by route and day. $1, seniors and ages 12 and under free, disabled $0.50; transfers free. There is a **free shuttle** between Duke's East and West campus (☎684-2218). **Chapel Hill Transit,** Chapel Hill (☎968-2769; www.townofchapelhill.org/transit). Buses run M-F 6am-7pm, Sa-Su 7am-6pm. Free.

Taxi: Cardinal Cab, ☎828-3228. Serves all 3 cities.

¿ PRACTICAL INFORMATION

Visitor Info: All 3 of the cities' visitors centers provide brochures, guides to the cities, maps, and helpful advice. **Capital Area Visitor Center,** 301 N. Blount St. in Raleigh (☎834-5900 or 800-849-8499; www.visitraleigh.com). Open M-F 8:30am-5pm. **Durham Convention and Visitors Bureau,** 101 E. Morgan St. (☎687-0288 or 800-446-8604; www.durham-nc.com). Open M-F 8:30am-5pm, Sa 10am-2pm. **Chapel Hill Orange County Visitors Bureau,** 501 W. Franklin St., near Carrboro (☎968-2060 or 888-968-2060; www.chocvb.org). Open M-F 8:30am-5pm, Sa 10am-2pm.

Hotlines: Mental Health and Detox Crisis, ☎683-8628. 24hr.

Internet Access: The public libraries in all three cities provide 1hr. free Internet access. Bring identification for a visitor's library card. **North Regional Library,** 200 Horizon Dr. in Raleigh (☎870-4000). Take Exit 8 from the Rte. 440 beltline, head north on Six Forks Rd., then turn left on Horizon Dr. Open M-F 9am-9pm, Sa 10am-5pm, Su 1-5pm. **Durham County Public Library,** 300 N. Roxboro St. in Durham (☎560-0100), near the visitors center. Open M-Th 9am-9pm, F 9am-6pm, Sa 9:30am-6pm, Su 2-6pm; June-July closed Su. **Chapel Hill Public Library,** 100 Library Dr. in Chapel Hill (☎968-2777). From UNC, go down Franklin St. toward Durham. Turn left on Estes Dr. and it's on your right. Open M-Th 10am-9pm, F 10am-6pm, Sa 9am-6pm, Su 1-8pm.

Post Office: Raleigh: 311 New Bern Ave. (☎832-1604). Open M-F 8am-5:30pm, Sa 8am-noon. **Postal Code:** 27611. **Durham:** 323 E. Chapel Hill St. (☎683-1976). Open M-F 8:30am-5pm. **Postal Code:** 27701. **Chapel Hill:** 125 S. Estes St. (☎929-9892). Open M-F 8:30am-5:30pm, Sa 8:30am-noon. **Postal Code:** 27514. **Area Code:** 919.

⌂ ACCOMMODATIONS

Budget lodging in Raleigh surrounds the major exits to the Rte. 440 beltline, especially at **Glenwood Avenue, Forest Road,** and **Capital Boulevard.** In Durham, economy motels line **I-85,** especially between Exits 173 and 175, north of Duke. Mid-range motels can be found at the intersection of **I-40** and **U.S. 15/501** in Chapel Hill.

Homestead Suites, 4810 Bluestone Dr. (☎510-8551; www.homesteadhotels.com), off Glenwood Ave. in Raleigh. New, comfortable rooms with full kitchens, A/C, cable TV, and free local calls. Free access to local gym. Internet access available for a fee. Laundry facilities available. Queen $56; 2 queen beds or king with pull-out couch $66; for stays of a week or longer $36/$46. AmEx/D/DC/MC/V. ❷

Best Value Carolina Duke Inn, 2517 Guess Rd. (☎286-0771 or 800-438-1158), off I-85 at Exit 175 in Durham, has clean rooms, coin laundry facilities, pool, A/C, and cable TV. Free local calls and continental breakfast. Doubles have fridge and microwave. DATA bus access across the street; free shuttle to RDU. Wheelchair accessible. Singles $43; doubles $50; family rooms $60. AAA and AARP discount 10%. AmEx/D/MC/V. ❷

Hampton Inn, 1740 U.S. 15/501 (☎968-3000; www.hamptoninn.com/hi/chapelhill), 1 mi. south of I-40 Exit 270 near Chapel Hill. Continental breakfast, pool, wireless Internet, and complimentary access to nearby health club. Singles usually $79; doubles $89. Rates highest in summer. AmEx/D/DC/MC/V. ❹

Falls Lake State Recreation Area, 13304 Creedmoor Rd. (☎676-1027; www.ils.unc.edu/parkproject/visit/fala/home.html), about 10 mi. north of Raleigh off Rte. 98, 1 mi. north of N.C. 50. Falls Lake has 4 campgrounds. The main campground, **Holly Point,** is adjacent to the lake and has both open lakefront sites and secluded shady sites, showers, boat ramps, 2 swimming beaches, and a dump station. Max. stay 14 days within a 30-day period. Gates close May-Aug. 9pm; Apr. and Sept. 8pm; Mar. and Oct. 7pm; Nov.-Feb. 6pm. Reservations required for stays of more than 7 days. Walk-in sites and non-electric sites $15, ages 62+ $10. Electric sites $20/$14. Day fee $5 per car, seniors $3. Cash only. ●

🏠 FOOD

The area's universities have spawned a swath of affordable eateries; Raleigh's **Hillsborough Street** and **Capital Boulevard,** Durham's **9th Street,** and Chapel Hill's **Franklin Street** cater to a college (read: budget-oriented) crowd. In Raleigh, travelers can find good dining options in **City Market's** shops, cafes, and bars a few blocks from the capitol. In Durham, **Brightleaf Square,** a mile east of 9th St. on Main St., has renovated warehouses that hold galleries, shops, and quality restaurants.

RALEIGH

The Rockford, 320½ Glenwood Ave. (☎821-9020), near Hillsborough St. A trendy 2nd fl. restaurant that serves delightful, inexpensive food. A popular choice is the ABC sandwich (apple, bacon, and cheddar on french toast; $6.75). Entrees $7 or less. Beer from $1.50. Open M-W 11:30am-2pm and 6-10pm, Th-Sa 11:30am-2pm and 6-10:30pm, Su 6-10pm; bar open M-W and Su until midnight, Th-Sa until 2am. AmEx/MC/V. ●

Irregardless Cafe, 901 W. Morgan St. (☎833-8898; www.irregardless.com), after Morgan splits off of Hillsborough St. International gourmet food that favors seafood, vegetarian, and vegan dishes. Entrees $14-21. Lunch $6-10. Live jazz, acoustic, or bluegrass most nights. Dancing 9:30-11pm Sa. Open for lunch Tu-F 11:30am-2:30pm; for dinner Tu-Th 5:30-9:30pm, F-Sa 5:30-10pm. Su brunch 10am-2pm. D/DC/MC/V. ❸

Roly Poly Sandwiches, 137 E. Hargett St. (☎834-1135; www.rolypoly.com), downtown. Serves 50 different imaginative wraps. Vegetarians will enjoy the "Nut and Honey," while those looking for a grilled wrap should try the "Peachtree Melt" (baked ham, melted brie and swiss, peach and pepper relish served with dill horseradish). Half wraps $3.25-4. Full wraps $5.25-7. Open M-F 10am-4pm, Sa 11am-3pm. AmEx/D/MC/V. ●

Marrakesh Cafe, 2500 Hillsborough St. (☎341-1167), across from NC State, is North Carolina's 1st hookah bar, offering Morrocan-influenced wraps and sandwiches ($4-5.50), salads ($3-4), and other goodies. Hookah $6. Flavors include strawberry, mint, and melon. Open M-W 9am-1am, Th-Sa 9am-3am, Su 10am-10pm. MC/V. ●

DURHAM

🔲 **The Mad Hatter's Cafe and Bake Shop,** 1802 W. Main St. (☎286-1987; www.madhattersbakeshop.com), 1 block from 9th St. A wide selection of delectable dishes including pizza, Asian noodles, and wraps. The modern restaurant has an outdoor patio and uses local, organic produce. Pizza, soups, and wraps $7-8. Cookies $1.50-2.25. Occasional live music. Open M-Th 7am-9pm, F-Sa 7am-11pm, Su 8am-4pm. AmEx/V. ❷

Pao Lim Asian Bistro and Bar, 2505 Chapel Hill Blvd. (☎419-1771), just off the 15/501 Business Rte., serves exceptional Asian cuisine, blending Chinese, Indian, and other flavors. Dinner entrees from $8. Lunch specials $5.50-9. Open M-Th 11:30am-9:30pm, F 11:30am-10pm, Sa noon-10pm, Su noon-9:30pm. AmEx/D/DC/MC/V. ❷

Francesca's, 706 9th St. (☎286-4177), serves only beverages and desserts, but their focus pays. Sample the homemade gelato for just $2.50. Drinks from $1.25. Desserts $1.75-4.50. Open M-Th 11am-11pm, F-Sa 11am-midnight, Su 11am-10pm. MC/V. ●

CHAPEL HILL

Mama Dip's Kitchen, 408 W. Rosemary St. (☎942-5837). This soul food restaurant feels more like a comfy back-porch picnic. From the sweet potato waffles to the fried okra to the chicken and dumplings, Mama Dip's serves some of the best regional delicacies around. Most entrees $6-9. Open M-Sa 8am-10pm. MC/V. ❷

Foster's Market, 750 Airport Rd. (☎967-3663; www.fostersmarket.com). Turn off Franklin St. onto Columbia St., which becomes Airport Rd. This upscale market-restaurant serves pizza and sandwiches like the Jammin' Turkey Breast (with 7-pepper jelly, herb cream cheese, onions, and lettuce on sourdough; $6.50) as well as a variety of other gourmet food. Pizzas $8.50-9. Open daily 7:30am-9pm. Also in Durham, 2694 Chapel Hill Blvd. (☎489-3944). Open daily 7:30am-8pm. AmEx/D/MC/V. ❷

Cosmic Cantina, 128 E. Franklin St. (☎960-3955), in the Franklin Centre shopping complex. Great for authentic and quick Mexican. Entrees $1-6.50. Margaritas $3. Open M-W and Su 11am-3am, Th-Sa 11am-4am. Also in Durham, 1920 Perry St. (☎286-1875), at the end of the 9th St. shops. Open daily 11am-4am. AmEx/D/MC/V. ❶

Jack Sprat Cafe, 161 E. Franklin St. (☎933-3575), whips up salads and hot and cold sandwiches ($5-7) as well as coffee and desserts in a pleasant, laid-back environment. Order the "Salad Sampler" ($8) and try 3 different selections. Open M-Th 8am-9pm, F-Sa 8am-10pm, Su 8am-5pm. D/MC/V. ❷

🄖 SIGHTS

RALEIGH

MUSEUMS. Downtown Raleigh offers a number of free attractions. Across from the capitol building in the center of downtown Raleigh are two first-rate museums. The **Museum of Natural Sciences** has four floors full of exhibits that both adults and children will enjoy. Highlights include a 15 ft. giant ground sloth unearthed near Wilmington, and "Willo," a rare dinosaur fossil with an iron concretion within the ribcage—possibly a fossil of the creature's heart. *(11 W. Jones St. ☎733-7450 or 877-462-8724; www.naturalsciences.org. Open M-Sa 9am-5pm, Su noon-5pm. Free. Audio tours $2.)* Just down the block, the **North Carolina Museum of History** looks back at North Carolina history through an exhibit on the Civil War, the N.C. Sports Hall of Fame, and a variety of temporary exhibits. Past exhibits include "Women of Our Time" and "Pioneers of Aviation," a collection of artifacts from North Carolina inventors, daredevils, and military aces. Program and tour info is available on the website. *(5 E. Edenton St. ☎715-0200; www.ncmuseumofhistory.org. Open Tu-Sa 8am-5pm, Su noon-5pm. Free.)*

ARTSPACE. This collection of 46 artists' studios in three exhibition galleries features work by regional, national, and international artists. Watch masters create art of all types, from watercolor and oil paintings to 3-D fabric arts. Call ahead or check online for guided tours and special events. *(201 E. Davie St. ☎821-2787; www.artspacenc.org. Open Tu-Sa 10am-6pm, 1st F of each month 10am-10pm. Studio hours vary. Free.)*

OAKWOOD. Stretching east from the visitors center, **Historic Oakwood** is a Victorian neighborhood featuring some of Raleigh's most notable architecture, with attractive homes constructed in the late 19th and early 20th centuries. This neighborhood and the adjacent **Oakwood Cemetery** provide a pleasant escape from the bustle of the city center. *(Historic Oakwood is bordered by Franklin, Watauga, Linden, Jones, and Person St. Free walking tour guides available at the visitors center in the lobby of the North Carolina Museum of History. Cemetery entrance at 701 Oakwood Ave. ☎832-6077. Open daily 8am-6pm; office closes at 4pm. Free maps available in the cemetery office.)*

THE SOUTH

DURHAM

DUKE UNIVERSITY. The Duke family's principal legacy, Duke University, is divided into East and West Campus. The majestic, neo-Gothic **Duke Chapel,** completed in the early 1930s, looms grandly at the center of West Campus. Over a million pieces of glass were used to make the 77 stained glass windows depicting hundreds of figures from the Bible and Southern history. (☎ 684-2572. Open daily June-Aug. 8am-8pm; Sept.-May 8am-5pm. Free. Self-guided tour available.) Nearby on Anderson St., the gorgeous **Sarah P. Duke Gardens** has over 55 acres divided into three segments: the Bloomington garden of native plants, the Culberson Asiatic arboretum, and the Terraces. (☎ 684-3698. Open daily 8am-dusk. Free. 1½hr. guided tours available by appointment; donations appreciated. 45min. trolley rides $25.)

MUSEUM OF LIFE AND SCIENCE. At the other end of Durham, the Museum of Life and Science is a must-see for families with children. Visitors can romp through the musical playground, pet barn animals, ride a train through the Nature Park, and explore hands-on exhibits about everything from bubbles to outer space. In the **Magic Wings Butterfly House,** almost 1000 butterflies flutter among tropical plants. (433 Murray Ave., off N. Duke St. ☎ 220-5429; www.ncmls.org. Open M-Sa 10am-5pm, Su noon-5pm. $8.50, ages 65+ $7.50, children 3-12 $6, under 3 free. Train $2.)

DUKE HOMESTEAD. Visitors can explore the original farm, home, and factories where Washington Duke first planted and processed the tobacco that would become the key to the city's prosperity. Duke's sons founded the American Tobacco Company, which dominated the industry for decades, putting Durham on the map and generating enough profits to found the university. The free historic tour includes an early factory, a curing barn, and a packhouse, as well as the restored home. The adjoining **Tobacco Museum** explains the history of the tobacco industry and displays fascinating old cigarette advertisements. (2828 Duke Homestead Rd., off Guess Rd. ☎ 477-5498. Open Tu-Sa 10am-4pm. Homestead tours depart 15min. after the hr. and last 45min. Free.)

OTHER SIGHTS. The 1988 movie *Bull Durham* was filmed in **Durham Athletic Park,** the **Durham Bulls'** ballpark, 409 Blackwell St. The AAA farm team for the Tampa Bay Devil Rays plays here, minus Kevin Costner, who starred as a minor league baseball player in the film. (Take "Durham Bulls Stadium" Exit off I-40. ☎ 687-6500, tickets 956-2855; www.durhambulls.com. Games Apr.-Sept. Tickets $5-8.) Travelers visiting the area during June and July should not miss a modern dance performance showcasing the likes of the Paul Taylor Dance Company at the **American Dance Festival,** hosted annually at Duke. (☎ 684-6402; www.americandancefestival.org. Tickets $12-40.)

CHAPEL HILL

UNIVERSITY OF NORTH CAROLINA. Chapel Hill and neighboring Carrboro are inseparable from the beautiful **University of North Carolina at Chapel Hill** campus. (Tour info ☎ 962-1630 or www.unc.edu. Tours M, W, F 1:30pm. Brochures and maps available in the lobby of the Morehead Planetarium.) The **Dean Dome** hosts sporting events and concerts. (Tickets ☎ 834-4000; www.ticketmaster.com.) Until 1975, NASA astronauts trained at UNC's **Morehead Planetarium;** of the 12 astronauts who have walked on the moon, 11 worked here. Today, Morehead gives live sky shows and presentations in the 68 ft. domed Star Theater, and houses small exhibits on outer space. (250 E. Franklin St. ☎ 962-1236; www.moreheadplanetarium.org. Open mid-June to mid-Aug. M and Su 12:30-5pm, Tu-W 10am-5pm, Th-Sa 10am-5pm and 6:30-9pm. Call for low-season hours and showtimes. Shows $5; students, seniors, and children $4. Exhibits free.) For more info about campus attractions, including the Ackland Art Museum and the North Carolina Botanical Garden, visit the **Campus Visitors Center** in Morehead Planetarium.

THE SOUTH

♪ 🎦 ENTERTAINMENT AND NIGHTLIFE

Pick up a free copy of the weekly *Spectator* and *Independent* magazines, available at many restaurants and bookstores, for listings of Triangle events. Info on happenings in Raleigh can be found at www.raleighnow.com. Chapel Hill offers the best nightlife in the Triangle. Popular bars line Franklin St., and several live music clubs are clustered where Franklin St. becomes Main St. in the neighboring town of Carrboro. **Cat's Cradle,** 300 E. Main St. in Carrboro, hosts local and national acts ranging from hip-hop to country. (☎967-9053; www.catscradle.com. Cover $5-15. Doors open 7:30-9pm and shows usually begin 8-10pm.) **Local 506,** 506 W. Franklin St., focuses on indie rock. (☎942-5506; www.local506.com. 18+. Cover around $5. Open daily 2pm-2am. Shows start around 10pm.)

Nightlife options are also plentiful in Raleigh; the area around Glenwood by Hillsborough St. is home to a number of popular, trendy bars. **Mitch's Tavern,** 2426 Hillsborough St., a second-floor bar across from N.C. State, is a favorite among students and locals for a late-night brew. The dark, smoky charm of the tavern's interior led the producers of *Bull Durham* to select this as the set for two scenes. (☎821-7771; www.mitchs.com. Pints $2.25-3.50. Pitchers $8-13. Open M and Su 11:30am-midnight, Tu-Sa 11:30am-2am.) **Rum Runners,** 208 E. Martin St., a boisterous bar with a tropical flair, hosts interactive "dueling piano" shows where two pianists face off. (☎755-6436; www.rumrunnersusa.com. Open W 8pm-2am, Th 9pm-2am, F-Sa 7pm-2am, Su 9:30pm-2am.) For dancing, head to **Five Star,** 511 W. Hargett St., in downtown Raleigh. This popular Chinese restaurant becomes a nightclub at around 10:30pm. (☎833-3311. Live DJs Th-Sa 10pm. F-Sa 21+ after 10:30pm. Cover after 10:30pm F $5 women, $10 men; Sa $5. Open nightly 5:30pm-2am. Dinner menu served all night long.) **Legends,** 330 W. Hargett St., is gay- and transgendered-friendly. (☎831-8888; www.legends-club.com. Cabaret night Tu. Women's night W. "Dark waves" gothic night Th. Drag show Su 11:30pm and 12:45am. Cover $2-8, under 21 up to $12. Open nightly 9pm-3am, later on F-Sa.) In Durham, **George's Garage,** 737 9th St., serves great sushi and drinks into the wee hours. (☎286-4131. Jazz jam sessions M. DJ F-Sa. Salsa lessons every other Sa. Bar open M-Th and Su 4pm until at least 12:30am, F-Sa 4pm-2am.)

WINSTON-SALEM ☎336

Winston-Salem was, as its name suggests, originally two different towns. Salem was founded in 1766 by the Moravians, a Protestant sect from what is the present-day Czech Republic. One of America's most successful utopian communities, Salem was bolstered by religious fervor, dedication to education, and the production of crafts. Winston, meanwhile, rose to prominence as a center of tobacco production, home to the famous tobacco mogul R.J. Reynolds. When the two towns merged in 1913, a dynamic, bustling city was born. Today, the skyline of Winston-Salem testifies to the towns' continued prominence. Visitors can experience the history of the two towns when they visit Old Town Salem or the Reynolda House.

🚆 **PRACTICAL INFORMATION. Piedmont Triad International Airport** (☎721-0088; www.ptia.org), at Exit 210 off I-40, 9 mi. west of the intersection of I-85 and I-40, is the closest commercial airport. **Amtrak Connector** buses run from 100 W. 5th St. to the Amtrak station at 2603 Oakland Ave. in Greensboro. (☎800-872-7245; www.amtrak.com. Departs daily 8am. Return trips available at night.) **Greyhound,** 250 Greyhound Ct., is downtown at Exit 110A off Rte. 52N. (☎724-1429; www.greyhound.com. Open daily 8am-1am.) **Winston-Salem Transit Authority** has its main depot at 100 W. 5th St. between Liberty and Trade St. (☎727-2000. Buses operate

M-F 5:30am-11:30pm, Sa 6am-6:30pm. $1; transfers free.) **Winston-Salem Visitor Center,** 200 Brookstown Ave., has brochures and maps. (☎728-4200 or 866-728-4200; www.visitwinstonsalem.com. Open daily 8:30am-5pm.) **Internet Access: Public Library,** 660 W. 5th St., at Spring St. (☎727-2264. Open M-W 9am-9pm, Th-F 9am-6pm, Sa 9am-5pm, Su 1-5pm; June-Aug. closed Su. Free.) **Post Office:** 1500 Patterson Ave. (☎721-6070. Open M-F 8:30am-5pm.) **Postal Code:** 27101. **Area Code:** 336.

▐ ACCOMMODATIONS. There are scores of motels that are perfect for the budget traveler on the way into town at Exit 184 off I-40. On the northern side of the city, budget motels center around Rte. 52, just past Patterson Ave. Most rooms run $39-69, and many hotels off the I-40 Business Route run $59 specials on weekend nights. The **Microtel Inn ❸,** on Hanes Mall Blvd. between I-40 and the Silas Creek Pkwy., is a great value with free local and long distance calls, cable TV, data ports, and a pool. (☎659-1994 or 888-771-7171. Singles $52; doubles $55-65. AmEx/D/DC/MC/V.) The **Innkeeper ❸,** 2113 Peters Creek Pkwy., is close to downtown and offers large rooms along with a pool, A/C, cable TV, and continental breakfast. (☎721-0062. Rooms from $41. AAA and AARP discount. AmEx/D/DC/MC/V.) **Motel 6 ❷,** 3810 Patterson Ave., has some of the least expensive lodging available in the city. Though a bit far from downtown, the clean rooms are a good deal, with A/C, HBO, data ports, a pool, and laundry facilities. (☎661-1588. Singles $36-38; doubles $42-44; additional adults $3. AARP discount 10%. AmEx/D/DC/MC/V.) **Summit Street Inns ❺,** 434 Summit St., at W. 5th St. a few blocks from downtown, is a two-house B&B that will reward those in the mood for a splurge. The luxurious rooms are outfitted with jacuzzis, stereos, TVs, bathrobes, and refrigerators stocked with free goodies, plus amaretto french toast is brought to your door in the morning. (☎777-1887 or 800-301-1887; www.bbinn.com. Exercise room and pool table. Doubles M-Th and Su $119-169, F-Sa $139-189. One room without jacuzzi for 1-2 people M-Th and Su $79-89, F-Sa $89-99. All rooms non smoking. AmEx/D/MC/V.)

▐ FOOD. The **West End Cafe ❷,** 926 W. 4th St., is a laid-back local favorite that makes every kind of sandwich under the sun. Patrons line up for the curry chicken salad sandwich ($5.75), the Frosted Flakes-crusted brie over raspberry puree ($9), and other creative dishes. (☎723-4774. Salads $5.25-9. Burgers $5.25-6.75. Dinner entrees $10-22. Open M-F 11am-10pm, Sa noon-10pm. AmEx/D/MC/V.) Winston-Salem is the birthplace of national doughnut company Krispy Kreme, and no visit to the city would be complete without stopping by the **Krispy Kreme Shop ❶,** 259 S. Stratford Rd., where you can watch the famous doughnuts being made fresh on-site. (☎724-2484. Doughnuts $0.69-0.89. Open M-Th and Su 6am-11pm, F-Sa 6am-midnight; drive-thru open M-Sa 6am-midnight, Su 6am-11pm. AmEx/D/MC/V.) In the heart of the Old Salem Village, the romantic **Old Salem Tavern ❸,** 736 Main St., tickles the fancy and the taste buds with dishes served by waiters in traditional Moravian garb. Lunch entrees range from quiche to Southern-style catfish. Dinner includes selections such as salmon corn cakes, pork schnitzel, and duck. (☎748-8585; www.oldsalemtavern.com. Lunch and dinner entrees $6.75-22.50. Open for lunch M-F 11:30am-2pm, Sa 11:30am-2:30pm, Su 11am-2pm except Su during January; dinner M-Th 5-9pm, F-Sa 5-9:30pm. Reservations recommended. AmEx/MC/V.) For a change of scenery, head to the swanky **6th and Vine ❸,** 209 W. 6th St., which offers salads ($6-8), panini ($7.50-9), and a rotating selection of entrees ($17-22). Various types of live music play Tu-Th and sometimes Sa. (☎725-5577; www.6thandvine.com. Open Tu-Sa 11am-late, Su 11am-2am. AmEx/D/MC/V.)

◙ SIGHTS. Old Salem Village takes visitors back in time to a restored Moravian village, outlining its fascinating history and traditions. The area stretches south from downtown and includes a visitors center, museums exhibiting Moravian life, and a multitude of traditional Moravian homes and buildings, including shoemaker and gunsmith shops. Tickets include admission to all of the museums and build-ings. (☎888-653-7253; www.oldsalem.org. Visitors center open Tu-Sa 8:30am-5:30pm, Su 12:30-5:30pm. Most attractions open Tu-Sa 9am-5pm, Su 1-5pm. Tickets $21-22, ages 6-16 $10. AAA discount $3; look for other coupons on the website. Tickets can also be purchased at the Boys School, located at the intersection of Main and Academy St., or at the Horton Museum Center, 924 S. Main St.) Old Salem's **Frank L. Horton Museum Center** features a number of museums, the most extensive of which is the **Museum of Early Southern Decorative Art (MESDA).** The MESDA showcases furnishings from around the Southeast, representing the period from 1690-1820. Not only are the rooms set up entirely "ropes free," to rec-reate the full feel of Southern homes, but all of the furnishings are original, right down to the bricks in the fireplace. (Open M-Sa 9:30am-3:30pm, Su 1:30-3:30pm. 1hr. guided tours every 30min., free with admission to Old Salem Village; advance appointment required at the ticketing desk or visitors center.) The **Toy Museum,** in the same building, displays toys spanning 1700 years. Don't be fooled by its name—this museum is geared toward adults and older children. All of the toys are delicate antiques housed in glass cases.

Winston-Salem's other premier attraction is the **Reynolda House,** 2250 Reynolda Rd., one of the South's most famous houses. The Reynolda was once home to tobacco tycoon R.J. Reynolds and his visionary wife, Katherine, credited with making the household completely self-sufficient and creating a working "village" on the grounds. Today, the Reynolda is affiliated with Wake Forest University and houses a collection of American art from colonial times to the present. (☎758-5150 or 888-663-1149; www.reynoldahouse.org. Open Tu-Sa 9:30am-4:30pm, Su 1:30-4:30pm; no admittance after 4pm. $10, seniors $9, AAA $8.50, students and chil-dren free. Wheelchair accessible.) The manor's primary allure is the two- acre gar-den that surrounds it. The **Reynolda Garden,** created for the enjoyment of the public as well as the Reynolds family, remains one of the most beautiful spots in Winston-Salem. (☎758-5593. Open daily dawn-dusk. Free.)

🎭 **ENTERTAINMENT.** Look for listings of local events in the free weekly newspa-per *Go Triad* or in *Relish,* the Thursday entertainment supplement to the *Win-ston-Salem Journal.* On weekends from May to August, the city hosts three live music performance series of varying genres in the downtown area: **Alive After Five** every Thursday evening (Corpening Plaza, 100 W. 2nd St.), **Fourth Street Jazz and Blues** every Friday evening (W. 4th St.), and **Summer on Trade** every Saturday evening (6th and Trade St.). Check out www.winstonsalemevents.com for more info. You'll find quality live rock, roots, and reggae music at **Ziggy's,** 433 Baity St., off University Pkwy. near the Coliseum. (☎748-1064; www.ziggyrock.com. Beer from $2. Cover $5-25. Open Tu-Su 8pm-2am; live music starts around 9pm.) Musi-cians also rock out at **The Garage,** 110 W. 7th St., at Trade St. Call ahead or check online for the acts of the night, since featured bands play New Grass, pop punk, and everything in between. (☎777-1127; www.the-garage.ws. Beer from $2. Cover $5-15, $2 extra if under 21. Open Th-Sa, sometimes also W. Showtimes vary.)

CHARLOTTE ☎704

Named in the mid-1700s after the wife of England's King George III, Charlotte is still referred to as the "Queen City." Settlers flooded the region in the nation's first gold rush, around the turn of the 18th century, after a boy discovered a 17 lb. gold nugget near Charlotte. Shortly thereafter, the first branch of the US Mint was established here in 1837. Now the biggest city in the Carolinas, Charlotte has expanded both outward and upward. For visitors, the city offers top-notch muse-ums, ritzy clubs, and a wide variety of professional sports.

⚒ ⁊ ORIENTATION AND PRACTICAL INFORMATION. The nucleus of Charlotte, the busy uptown area, has numbered streets laid out perpendicular to named streets in a simple grid pattern. **Tryon Street,** running north-south, is the major crossroad. **I-77** crosses the city north-south, providing access to uptown, while **I-85** runs southwest-northeast, connecting the uptown to the UNC campus. Uptown is also accessible from **I-277,** which circles the city, and is called the **John Belk Freeway** to the south of uptown and the **Brookshire Freeway** to the north. **Charlotte-Douglas International Airport,** about 7 mi. west of the city at 5501 Josh Birmingham Pkwy. (☎359-4910; www.charlotteairport.com), accessible from the Billy Graham Pkwy. (Rte. 521), is a hub for US Airways. **Amtrak,** 1914 N. Tryon St. (☎376-4416; www.amtrak.com; open 24hr.), sends trains once daily to Atlanta (5hr., $52) and New Orleans (17hr., $116) and twice daily to New York City (12hr., $157), Raleigh (4hr., $21), and Washington D.C. (9hr., $94-117). **Greyhound,** 601 W. Trade St. (☎375-3332; www.greyhound.com; open 24hr.), sends buses to Charleston, WV (7hr., 3 per day, $72-77), Columbia, SC (2hr., 4 per day, $17-18.50), and Richmond, VA (5-9hr., 11 per day, $55-59). The **Charlotte Area Transit System (CATS)** operates local buses; the central terminal is at 310 E. Trade St. (☎336-7433; www.ridetransit.org. Most buses operate M-Sa 5:30am-1:30am, Su 6:30am-1:30am. $1.10, $1.55 for express service in outlying areas; most transfers free, local to express transfers $0.45.) Uptown, CATS runs **Gold Rush,** free shuttles that resemble cable cars. A **visitors center** is located at 330 S. Tryon St. (☎800-231-4636; www.visitcharlotte.com. Open 9am-12:30pm and 1:30-4:30pm.) **Hotlines: Rape Crisis,** ☎375-9900. **Suicide Line,** ☎358-2800. Both 24hr. **Gay/Lesbian Hotline,** ☎535-6277. Operates M-Th and Su 6:30-9:30pm. **Internet Access: Public Library of Charlotte and Mecklenburg County,** 310 N. Tryon St., in uptown. (☎336-2572. 2hr. free Internet access per day. Open M-Th 9am-9pm, F-Sa 9am-6pm, Su 1-6pm.) **Post Office:** 201 N. McDowell St. (☎704-333-2542. Open M-F 7:30am-6pm, Sa 10am-1pm.) **Postal Code:** 28204. **Area Code:** 704.

⚒ ⁊ ACCOMMODATIONS AND FOOD. There are several clusters of budget motels in the Charlotte area: on Independence Blvd. off the John Belk Freeway; off I-85 at Sugar Creek Rd. (Exit 41); off I-85 at Exit 33 near the airport; and off I-77 at Clanton St. (Exit 7). The **Continental Inn ❷,** 1100 W. Sugar Creek Rd., Exit 41 off I-85, has immaculate and inviting rooms. (☎597-8100. A/C, cable TV with free HBO, and continental breakfast. Rooms $42-49. AAA and AARP discount 10%. AmEx/D/MC/V.) **Homestead Studio Suites Hotel ❸,** 710 Yorkmont Rd., near the airport, provides clean, spacious rooms with full kitchenettes and wireless Internet connections ($4 activation fee) as well as coin-operated laundry facilities and free access to a local Bally's health club. (☎676-0083; www.extendedstayhotels.com. 24hr. reception. Rooms from $66; rates drop to $38 for stays of a week or longer. AAA and AARP discount 10%. AmEx/D/DC/MC/V.) The **McDowell Nature Preserve ❶,** 15222 York Rd., offers RV, rent-a-tent, and primitive campsites in a shady, tranquil environment. RV and rent-a-tent sites have water and electricity; rent-a-tent sites include a 9x12 tent and two cots. (Go south on Tryon St. until it becomes York Rd. ☎583-1284; www.parkandrec.com. Open Mar.-Nov. daily 7am-sunset; Dec.-Feb. F-Su 7am-sunset. Rent-a-tent sites $38. RV sites $18. Primitive sites $9.)

Two areas outside of uptown offer attractive dining options at reasonable prices. **North Davidson ("NoDa"),** around 36th St., is home to a small artistic community inhabiting a set of historic buildings. South of the city center, the **Dilworth** neighborhood, along East and South Blvd., is lined with restaurants serving everything from authentic ethnic meals to pizza and pub fare. For eccentric, tasty cuisine, the hip **Cosmos Cafe ❸,** 300 N. College St., at E. 6th St., has a versatile menu ranging from tapas and *mezes* ($6-9.50) to sushi and wood-fired pizzas ($8.75-10). The restaurant becomes a popular yuppie bar around 10:30pm; swing by Wednesday nights for superb gourmet martinis at half price. (☎372-3553; www.cosmoscafe.com. 2-for-1 tapas M-Sa 5-7pm. Latin night with free salsa lessons Th. Open M-F 11am-2am, Sa 5pm-2am. AmEx/D/DC/MC/V.) **Thomas Street Tavern ❷**, 1218 Thomas Ave. Follow E. 10th St. out of uptown; after E. 10th becomes Central Ave., turn right on Thomas Ave. The Tavern is a local favorite with pool tables, an extensive beer menu, and food that ranges from pub fare to gourmet. Try the "Thomas Street Tuna Steak" ($8.75), served on a croissant with citrus aioli. (☎376-1622. Grill items $4-9. Sandwiches $5-7. Pizzas $6-8. Open M-Sa 11am-2am, Su noon-2am. MC/V.) Find scrumptious organic food at **Talley's Green Grocery ❶**, 1408-C E. Blvd. in Dilworth, an upscale market behind the Outback Steakhouse. Cafe Verde, in the back of the store, offers excellent sandwiches and prepared dishes. (☎334-9200; www.talleys.com. Sandwiches $6-7, served until 2pm. Open M-Sa 9am-9pm, Su 10am-7pm. AmEx/D/MC/V.) The friendly **Smelly Cat Coffeehouse ❶**, 514 E. 36th St., in NoDa, serves delectable coffee drinks ($1.50-4) as well as a selection of pastries. Add a sugar rush to your caffeine high with the "Muddy Kitten" ($4), a combination of ice cream, chocolate, and espresso. (☎374-9656. Ice cream $1.75. Cinnamon rolls $2.25. Live music some weekends. Open M-Tu 7am-8pm, W-Th 7am-10pm, F 7am-midnight, Sa 8am-midnight, Su 9am-5pm. D/MC/V.)

◙ **SIGHTS.** Charlotte has a number of museums, most of which are located in the uptown area, that give visitors an insider's perspective on the region. The ▨**Levine Museum of the New South**, 200 E. 7th St., is a fantastic new museum that explores the history of the Charlotte and Carolina Piedmont area. From a working cotton gin to a re-creation of a soda fountain that was occupied during the civil rights sit-ins, the Levine shows how the "New South" has developed from the end of the Civil War to the present. (☎333-1887. Open Tu-Sa 10am-5pm, Su noon-5pm. $6; students, seniors, and ages 6-18 $5; under 6 free.) Admission will grant you access to both the **Mint Museum of Craft and Design**, 220 N. Tryon St., in uptown, and the **Mint Museum of Art**, 2730 Randolph Rd., about 2½ mi. to the southeast. The Museum of Craft and Design features contemporary work in glass, wood, metal, and fiber. Even the chandelier in the lobby is an impressive work of craftsmanship, and previous exhibits have highlighted such topics as goldsmithing and quilting. The Museum of Art focuses on more traditional painting and ceramics and displays pieces from local students. The building that now houses the art museum once functioned as Charlotte's mint; visitors can peruse coins produced here. (Both museums ☎337-2000; www.mintmuseum.org. Craft and Design Museum open Tu-Sa 10am-5pm, Su noon-5pm; Museum of Art open Tu 10am-10pm, W-Sa 10am-5pm, Su noon-5pm. $6, college students and ages 62+ $5, ages 6-17 $3. Free admission to Craft and Design Museum Tu 10am-2pm. Museum of Art free Tu 5-10pm.)

◪◩ **ENTERTAINMENT AND NIGHTLIFE.** In addition to its arena football, NHL, NFL, NBA, WNBA, and AAA baseball teams, Charlotte is also home to the fastest-growing sport in national popularity—stock car racing. The **Lowe's Motor Speedway**, Exit 49 off I-85, hosts several major NASCAR events each year. (Tickets and schedule information ☎800-455-3267; www.gospeedway.com.) The latest expansion team to enter the NBA, the **Charlotte Bobcats**, is owned by Black Entertainment Television founder Robert Johnson. In 2005, their first season, the Bobcats' own Emeka Okafor was named NBA Rookie of the Year. The Bobcats and Charlotte's WNBA team, the **Sting**, shoot hoops in the brand-new Charlotte Arena, 333 E. Trade St. (Tickets ☎800-495-2295; www.newcharlottearena.com. Call or check website for box office hours.) Football fans can catch an NFL game when the **Carolina Panthers** play in Bank of America Stadium, 800 S. Mint St. (Tickets ☎522-6500; www.carolinapanthers.com. Tickets $45-70. Stadium tours $4, ages 55+ $3, ages 5-15 $2.) Ten miles south, the Charlotte **Knights** play AAA minor league baseball at Knights Castle, off I-77 S at Exit 88. (Tickets ☎364-6637; www.charlotteknights.com. Box office open M-F 10am-5pm and 10am until game time on game days. Tickets $6-10.)

To check out nightlife, arts, and entertainment listings, grab a free copy of *Creative Loafing* in one of Charlotte's shops or restaurants, visit www.charlotte.creativeloafing.com, or look over the E&T section of the *Charlotte Observer*. Many of Charlotte's hippest clubs can be found uptown, especially on College St. from 5th to 7th St. For live rock bands, pool, and foosball, head to **Amos's Southend,** 1423 S. Tryon St. Live acts are often cover bands of rock's greats, from Led Zeppelin and Pink Floyd to Guns N' Roses and Journey. (☎377-6874; www.amossouthend.com. Call for showtimes, cover, and age restrictions.) **The Evening Muse,** 3227 N. Davidson St., in NoDa, is a laidback venue for a wide variety of musical acts, from acoustic and jazz to rock. (☎376-3737; www.theeveningmuse.com. Cover around $5. Open Tu-Sa 6pm-midnight.) Have a good laugh at **The Comedy Zone,** 516 N. College St. (☎348-4242; www.thecomedyzone.net. 18+. Call for prices and showtimes.)

CAROLINA MOUNTAINS

The sharp ridges and rolling slopes of the southern Appalachian range create some of the most spectacular scenery in the Southeast. Scholars, ski bums, farmers, and artists all find reasons to call this gorgeous region home. The aptly named High Country stretches from Boone in the north to Asheville in the south. The 469 mi. Blue Ridge Parkway, cuts through the mountaintops and connects Virginia's Shenandoah National Park in the north to Tennessee's Great Smoky Mountains National Park in the south. Views from many of the Parkway's scenic overlooks are staggering, particularly on days when mist shrouds the tree-carpeted peaks.

ASHEVILLE   ☎828

Hazy blue mountains, deep valleys, and spectacular waterfalls form the impressive backdrop of this small, friendly city. Once a popular retreat for the well-to-do, Asheville hosted enough Carnegies, Vanderbilts, and Mellons to fill a 1920s edition of *Who's Who on the Atlantic Seaboard*. The population today leans toward dreadlocks, batik, and vegetarianism, providing funky nightlife and festivals all year. The urban feel extends to Asheville's downtown, where boutiques and polished office buildings look like they belong in Manhattan rather than Appalachia.

◪ PRACTICAL INFORMATION. The **Asheville Regional Airport** is at Exit 9 off I-26, 15 mi. south of the city. (☎684-2226; www.flyavl.com.) **Greyhound,** 2 Tunnel Rd. (☎253-8451; www.greyhound.com; open daily 8am-9pm), 2 mi. east of downtown near the Beaucatcher Tunnel, sends buses to Charlotte (2½-3½hr., 5 per day, $23-31), Knoxville (2-2½hr., 7 per day, $27-29), and Raleigh (8-11hr., 5 per day, $39-61). The **Asheville Transit System** handles bus service within city limits. Pick up a copy of bus schedules and routes from the visitors center or visit the **Asheville Transit Center,** 49 Coxe Ave., by the post office. (☎253-5691. Hours vary by route, all M-Sa between 6am and 7pm. $0.75, short trips in downtown area free. Discounts for seniors, disabled, and multi-fare tickets; transfers $0.10.) The **Chamber of Commerce and Visitor Center,** 151 Haywood St., Exit 4C off I-240, on the northwest end of downtown, dispenses a wealth of knowledge about activities and accommodations, as well as a free downtown-area map. (☎258-6101 or 800-257-1300; www.exploreasheville.com. Open M-F 8:30am-5:30pm, Sa-Su 9am-5pm.) **Internet Access: Pack Memorial Library,** 67 Haywood St. (☎255-5203. $2. Max. 55min. per day.

Open M-Th 10am-8pm, F 10am-6pm, Sa 10am-5pm; Sept.-May also Su 2-5pm.) **Post Office:** 33 Coxe Ave., off Patton Ave. (☎271-6429. Open M-F 7:30am-5:30pm, Sa 9am-1pm.) **Postal Code:** 28802. **Area Code:** 828.

ⓘ ACCOMMODATIONS. Two fabulous new hostels in Asheville have made staying the night here much more budget-friendly. ▨**Bon Paul and Sharky's Hostel ❶**, 816 Haywood Rd., features a number of amenities, including a common room with a huge TV and a DVD collection, outdoor hot tub, foosball table, communal kitchen, free lockers, linens, and wireless Internet, off-street parking, bicycles for biking downtown, and free bus station and airport pickup. (☎350-9929; www.bonpaulandsharkys.com. Reception daily 9am-noon and 4:30-10:30pm. Check-in 24hr. Dorms $20, $17 if staying for 3 nights or if 3 people are staying together; private room $50; camping on grounds $8 per person. Max. stay 21 days. Cash only.) The funky, new-age **Arthaus Hostel ❶**, 16 Ravenscroft Rd., is located downtown and offers brightly painted, spotless rooms, a communal kitchen, laundry ($5), and wireless Internet. (☎225-3278. Linens included. Call to arrange check-in. Restricted access noon-4pm. Dorms $20; private rooms $50-65. MC/V.) The **Log Cabin Motor Court ❸**, 330 Weaverville Hwy., 5 mi. north of downtown, provides immaculate, inviting cabins with HBO, wireless Internet, and laundry. Some also have fireplaces, kitchenettes, and A/C. (☎645-6546. Reception 10am-8pm. Cabins with one bedroom and bath $50, with kitchenette $70; 2 bedrooms and bath $100-110. AAA and military discount 10%. D/MC/V.) **Days Inn ❸**, 201 Tunnel Rd., has huge rooms with A/C, cable, microwaves, refrigerators, and coffeemakers, as well as a pool and full breakfast. (☎252-4000. Singles $59-79; doubles $75-119. AAA and AARP discount. AmEx/D/DC/MC/V.) **Powhatan Lake Campground ❶**, 375 Wesley Branch Rd., 12 mi. southwest of Asheville off Rte. 191, is in the **Pisgah National Forest** and has wooded sites on a trout lake open for swimming and fishing. Sites fill fast in summer; call for reservations. (☎670-5627, 877-444-6777 for reservations. Some sites have hookups; hot showers and dump station available. Open Apr.-Oct. Gates close 10pm. Sites $17-20.)

ⓒ FOOD. Downtown Asheville is packed with excellent places to eat. At the ▨**Laughing Seed Cafe ❸**, 40 Wall St., the international lineup of vegetarian dishes tastes even better when served on the sunny patio; try the "Curried Eggplant Napoleon." (☎252-3445. Entrees $9-15. Sandwiches $6-8.50. Dinner specialties $10.50-15. Open M-Th 11:30am-9pm, F-Sa 11:30am-10pm, Su 10am-9pm. AmEx/D/DC/MC/V.) Nearby, the **Tupelo Honey Cafe ❷**, 12 College St., prepares Southern home cookin' with organic ingredients and an innovative twist. (☎255-4404. Entrees $6-15. Sandwiches $5-8. Open Tu-Th 9am-3pm and 5:30-10pm, F-Sa 9am-3pm and 5:30-midnight, Su 9am-3pm. AmEx/MC/V.) The quirky, laid-back **Beanstreets ❶**, 3 Broadway St., serves coffee ($1-4), sandwiches ($3.50-6), and omelets ($3-5) on cheerfully mismatched tables. (☎255-8180. Open mic Th 9-11:30pm. Live music most F 9pm. Open M-W 7:30am-6pm, Th-F 7:30am-midnight, Sa 9am-midnight, Su 9am-10pm. Cash or check only.) The downtown area is also home to the colorful **Anntony's Caribbean Cafe ❷**, 1 Page Ave. Ste. 129, in the Historic Grove Arcade Building. Before enjoying Jamaican chicken, beef empanadas, or the roast pork sandwich, start with plantain chips and salsa. (☎255-9620. Entrees $4-10. Restaurant open M-Th 11:30am-9pm, F-Sa 11:30am-10pm, Su noon-4pm. Coffee bar opens M-Sa 7:30am. AmEx/D/DC/MC/V.)

◉ SIGHTS. George Vanderbilt's palatial **Biltmore Estate**, 1 Approach Rd., just north of I-40, was constructed in the 1890s and is the largest private home in America. A self-guided tour of the house and grounds can take all day; try to arrive early. Entrance fee includes complimentary wine tastings at the on-site winery. (☎225-

1333 or 800-543-2961; www.biltmore.com. Estate open daily Jan.-Mar. 9am-4pm; Apr.-Dec. 8:30am-5pm. Winery open daily Jan.-Mar. noon-6pm; Apr.-Dec. 11am-7pm. $39, ages 6-16 $19.50, ages 5 and under free. Audio tour $7. Behind the Scenes tours (North and South Wings) $15. Carriage rides $35. Trail rides $50. Wheelchair accessible.) If Biltmore is a bit more than your wallet can handle, enjoy the free **Botanical Gardens,** 151 W. T. Weaver Blvd., which contains plants native to the Carolina Mountains. The best time to visit is when the wildflowers are blooming, from April to mid-May. (☎252-5190; www.ashevillebotanicalgardens.org. Open daily dawn-dusk.) The **Thomas Wolfe Memorial,** 52 N. Market St., between Woodfin and Walnut St., celebrates one of the early 20th century's most influential American authors with a museum and a re-creation of his "old Kentucky home." (☎253-8304; www.wolfememorial.com. Open Apr.-Oct. Tu-Sa 9am-5pm, Su 1-5pm; Nov.-Mar. Tu-Sa 10am-4pm, Su 1-4pm. 30min. tours every hr. on the half-hr. $1, students $0.50.) The **Asheville Art Museum,** 2 S. Pack Sq., displays 20th-century American artwork. The most prominent ongoing exhibit is "Vantage Points: Perspectives on American Art 1960-1980." (☎253-3227; www.ashevilleart.org. Open Tu-Th and Sa 10am-5pm, F 10am-8pm, Su 1-5pm. $6; students, seniors, and ages 4-15 $5. Wheelchair accessible.) Twenty-five miles southeast of Asheville on U.S. 64/74A, the scenic setting for *Last of the Mohicans* rises up almost ½ mi. in **Chimney Rock Park.** After driving to the base of the Chimney, take the 26-story elevator to the top or walk up for a 75 mi. view. Savor your time on the mountaintop with one of the five hikes that range in length from ½ to 1½ miles, some leading to breathtaking waterfalls. (☎625-9611 or 800-277-9611; www.chimneyrockpark.com. Ticket office open daily Apr.-Oct. 8:30am-5:30pm; Nov.-Mar. 8:30am-4:30pm. Park open 1½hr. after office closes. $14, ages 6-15 $6.)

🎬🎭 ENTERTAINMENT AND NIGHTLIFE. The popular **Asheville Pizza and Brewing Company,** 675 Merrimon Ave., shows second-run movies for $2 and serves pizza ($10.50-11.50 for 12") and home-brewed beer. (☎254-1281. Th all pints $2.50. Open daily 11am-midnight.) Indie and arthouse flicks play at the **Fine Arts Theatre,** 36 Biltmore Ave. (☎232-1536; www.fineartstheatre.com. $7.50, seniors and matinees $5.50. Ticket sales begin 30min. before showtimes. Box office opens at 12:30pm.) **Shakespeare in Montford Park,** at the Hazel Robinson Amphitheater, produces one play each summer. (☎254-4540; www.montfordparkplayers.org. Performances July F-Su 7:30pm. Free.) The downtown area, especially the southeast end around the intersection of Broadway and College St., is a haven for music, munchies, and movies. **Jack of the Wood,** 95 Patton Ave., heats up at night with live celtic, bluegrass, and old-time mountain music. While you enjoy the soundtrack, fill up with traditional pub fare. (☎252-5445. Local beer $3.50. Trivia night M 8pm. 21+ after 9pm. Cover F-Sa $5-7. Open M-F 4pm-2am, Sa noon-2am, Su 3pm-2am.) The free weekly paper *Mountain Xpress* and *Community Connections*, a free gay publication, have arts, events, and dining listings.

BOONE ☎828

Nestled among the breathtaking mountains of the High Country, Boone has a laid-back feel. Home to Appalachian State University, the small city is heavily populated with students but also attracts skiers, nature lovers, and everyone in between. Thrift shops and used book stores abound, and the bright colors of tie-dye and vegetarian cuisine are everywhere you turn.

🛈 PRACTICAL INFORMATION. Boone AppalCart, 274 Winklers Creek Rd., provides **local bus** service. (☎264-2278. Hours vary. $0.50.) **Visitor Info: Boone Area Chamber of Commerce,** 208 Howard St. (☎800-852-9506; www.boonechamber.com. Open M-F 9am-5pm.) The **North Carolina High Country Host Visitor Center,** 1700

Blowing Rock Rd./U.S. 321, has regional info. (☎800-438-7500; www.mountain-sofnc.com. Open M-Sa 9am-5pm, Su 9am-3pm.) **Internet Access: Watauga County Public Library,** 140 Queen St., at N. Depot St. (☎264-8784. Open M-Th 9am-7pm, F-Sa 9am-5pm.) **Post Office:** 1544 Blowing Rock Rd. (☎264-3813. Open M-F 8:30am-5pm, Sa 8:30am-noon.) **Postal Code:** 28607. **Area Code:** 828.

⚏⚏ ACCOMMODATIONS AND FOOD. The neighboring community of Blowing Rock offers plenty of pricey inns. In Boone, the **Hidden Valley Motel ❸,** 8725 Hwy. 105 S, is located in the stunning Foscoe Valley, reasonably close to downtown, and offers large, well-decorated rooms. (☎963-4372. A/C, cable. Singles $50-75; doubles $55-85. D/MC/V.) Along the Parkway near Boone, the **Julian Price Campground ❶,** Mi. 297, has spectacular tent and RV sites. Sites around Loop A are on a lake. (☎963-5911. Flush toilets and water; no hookups or showers. Open May-Oct. Sites $14. Cash or check only.) King St. offers great little restaurants, most with a healthy, earthy feel. The small, hip **▧Black Cat ❶,** 127 S. Depot St. off King St., makes humongous and tasty burritos; vegetarian options are cooked on a separate grill. Bluegrass musicians perform some weeknights during the school year, while other acts play on weekends. (☎263-9511. Burritos, quesadillas, and nachos from $4. Margaritas $3.50. Open M-Th and Su 11:30am-9pm, F-Sa 11:30am-10pm. MC/V.) Vegetarians have plenty of options, but none combines quality with low prices as well as **Angelica's ❷,** 506 W. King St., which prepares tasty sandwiches, vegetarian sushi, and smoothies. (☎265-0809. Entrees $6-10. Smoothies $4. Open M-Th and Su 11am-9pm, F-Sa 11am-10pm. AmEx/MC/V.) For less healthy but equally filling fare, head to **Mel's Diner ❶,** 1286 Hwy. 105 S, which serves burgers, sandwiches, and breakfast atop a pink counter. (☎265-1344. Burgers and sandwiches $5.50-8. Breakfast $3-7. Open M-Th 7am-midnight, F-Sa 24hr. AmEx/D/MC/V.)

◙ SIGHTS. ▧Grandfather Mountain, near the intersection of U.S. 221 and the Blue Ridge Parkway (Mi. 305), is a great sight for families and wildlife enthusiasts. The habitat walk features bald eagles, black bears, mountain lions, and other animals, while a nature museum, suspension bridge, and a series of hikes round out the park. (☎800-468-7325; www.grandfather.com. Open daily June-Aug. 8am-7pm; Mar.-May and Sept.-Nov. 8am-6pm; Dec.-Feb. 8am-5pm. $14, seniors $12, ages 4-12 $6, under 4 free. Ticket sales stop 1hr. before closing. Wheelchair accessible.) Hiking or camping on Grandfather Mtn. requires a permit ($6), available at the park entrance or at several area stores, including the historic **Mast General Store,** 630 W. King St., downtown. (☎262-0000. Open M-Sa 10am-6pm, Su noon-6pm. Cash or check only.) The free *Grandfather Mountain Trail Map and Backcountry Guide,* available anywhere permits are sold, details area hikes. The carless can take the **Boone AppalCart** (p. 354) up to the mountain. Near Boone, **Wilson Creek** offers waterfalls, swimming holes, and trails. **Linville Gorge** is perfect for backcountry camping and rock climbing. For more info, call the ranger's office (☎737-0833).

Didn't think you could ski this far south? Think again. Boone is conveniently located near three ski resorts. **Sugar Mountain,** off Hwy. 184 in Banner Elk (☎898-4521 or 800-784-2768; www.skisugar.com; weekend lift tickets $53, ages 4-11 $39, under 4 and 70+ free), and **Ski Beech,** 1007 Beech Mtn. Pkwy. also off Hwy. 184 (☎800-438-2093; www.skibeech.com; weekend lift tickets $50, ages 5-12 and 60-69 $37, under 5 and 70+ free), are the largest resorts. The Appalcart runs a free winter shuttle from Boone to Sugar Mountain. Call ☎800-962-2322 for info about daily ski conditions.

ASU's **Appalachian Cultural Museum,** on University Hall Dr. off Blowing Rock Rd. (U.S. 321), strives to preserve the rich cultural traditions of the region with exhibits on crafts, storytelling, moonshine, and even NASCAR. (☎262-3117. Open Tu-Sa 10am-5pm, Su 1-5pm. $4, seniors $3.50, ages 10-18 $2. Wheelchair accessible.)

THE SOUTH

🔊🎦 **ENTERTAINMENT AND NIGHTLIFE.** In the town of Todd, 11 mi. north of Boone at the edge of Ashe County, the **Todd General Store** hosts live mountain music concerts on Friday nights and Saturday afternoons during the summer. From downtown Boone, take U.S. 421 S and turn left on Hwy. 194; continue 11 mi. and make a right onto Todd Railroad Grade Rd. It's on the left after half a mile. (☎336-877-1067. Most events free, some concerts up to $10. Times vary; call for schedule.) For a cold beer or a game of pool, head to **Murphy's Pub,** 747 W. King St. (☎264-5117. Beer from $1.50. Live music ranging from hip-hop to bluegrass usually Th-Sa. 21+. Cover $3-5. Open daily 11am-2am.) For a little culture with your drink, check out the **Boone Saloon,** 489 W. King St., which has billiards, modern art decor, and live music of all varieties during the week. (☎264-1811. Beer from $1.50. 21+ after 10pm. Open M-Sa 11:30am-2am, Su 6pm-2am, sometimes closes earlier.) The **Boone Bowling Center,** 261 Boone Heights Dr., has a variety of special deals. The third Friday of every month is Christian cosmic night (10pm-midnight; $17.75 including shoes). The other Fridays are glow bowling (8pm-11pm; $3.25 per game), while Saturdays are cosmic night (11pm-2am; $4.50 per game). Daytime bowling on weekdays is less flashy, but cheaper. (☎264-3166; www.boonebowling.com. Open M-F 10am-11pm, Sa 10am-2am, Su 2-10pm. M-F before 5pm $2.75 per game, seniors and under 10 $2; after 5pm $3/$2.50; Sa-Su $3.75. Shoe rental $2.50.)

NORTH CAROLINA COAST

Lined with islands that shield inlanders from Atlantic squalls, the Carolina Coast has a history as stormy as the hurricanes that pummel its beaches. England's first attempt to colonize North America ended in 1590 with the peculiar disappearance of the Roanoke settlement, now known as the "Lost Colony." Later, the coast earned the title "Graveyard of the Atlantic"—over 1000 ships have foundered on the Outer Banks' southern shores, leaving hundreds of wrecks for scuba exploration. The winds that sank ships lifted the world's first flight in 1903, with some assistance from the Wright brothers. Flying now forms the basis of much of the area's recreational activities such as hang-gliding, parasailing, kiteboarding, and good ol' kite-flying. Those not interested in taking to the sky can take advantage of the abundance of natural sea life by fishing, crabbing, or aquarium hopping.

OUTER BANKS   ☎252

Locals claim that the legendary pirate Blackbeard once roamed the waters off the Outer Banks; some think that his treasures still lie beneath the beaches. But whether or not you dig up Blackbeard's loot, you'll find other gems on these islands, from historic lighthouses to gorgeous sand dunes. On the northern half of Bodie Island, the three contiguous towns of **Kitty Hawk, Kill Devil Hills,** and **Nags Head** are heavily trafficked, commercial, and filled with restaurants, mini-golf courses, and souvenir super-stores. However, follow Rte. 12 south to Hatteras Island to find largely undeveloped, pristine beaches, thanks to the protection of the National Park Service. **Ocracoke Island,** the southernmost of the islands, retains a sense of community despite its growing popularity.

📠 **TRANSPORATION**

Ferries: Free ferries run between **Hatteras** and **Ocracoke** (40min., daily 5am-midnight; no reservations accepted). Lines to board and disembark from the ferry may take 10min., so a one-way ferry trip may take up to 1hr. Toll ferries run between **Ocracoke** and **Cedar Island,** east of New Bern on Rte. 12, which becomes U.S. 70 (2¼hr.; pedestrians $1, bicycles $3, motorcycles $10, cars $15). Toll ferries also travel between Ocracoke and **Swan Quarter,** on U.S. 264 (2½hr., same prices as Cedar Island). Call ahead for schedules and reservations: for ferries from Ocracoke ☎800-345-1665, from Cedar Island ☎800-856-0343, from Swan Quarter ☎800-773-1094. General info and reservations at ☎800-293-3779; www.ncferry.org.

Taxi: Beach Cab (☎441-2500), for Nags Head. **Coastal Cab** (☎449-8787), Bodie Island. **Island Hopper Shuttle** (☎995-6771), Cape Hatteras.

Bike Rental: Ocean Atlantic Rental (☎441-7823), in Nags Head. Adult bikes $10 per day, $35 per week. Open daily 9am-9pm.

✈ ORIENTATION

The Outer Banks consist of four narrow islands strung along the northern half of the North Carolina coast. The northernmost, **Bodie Island,** is joined to the mainland by the **Wright Memorial Bridge,** which allows U.S. 158 to cross the Currituck Sound and run the length of the island. For most of Bodie Island, Rte. 12 (known as the Beach Road and the Virginia Dare Trail) and U.S. 158 (called the Bypass and the Croatan Hwy.) run parallel to each other. **Roanoke Island** lies between the southern end of Bodie and the mainland and provides the only other point of entry via car. U.S. 64 runs from the mainland to **Manteo** on Roanoke over the Virginia Dare Bridge and then to Bodie just south of Nags Head over the Washington Baum Bridge. From the **Whalebone Junction,** where U.S. 158 ends and U.S. 64 runs into Rte. 12, the **Cape Hatteras National Seashore** stretches south for 70 mi. across the southern end of Bodie Island and almost all of Hatteras Island. Rte. 12 is the only major road running north-south through the Cape Hatteras National Seashore and connects Bodie to Hatteras Island via another bridge. Southernmost **Ocracoke Island** is linked by ferry to Hatteras Island to the north and mainland towns to the south. Ocracoke Island is almost all park land and has only one town, Ocracoke Village. Directions to locations on Bodie Island and Hatteras Island are usually given in terms of miles from the Wright Memorial Bridge. There is no public transit on the Outer Banks. Hectic traffic calls for extra caution and travel time.

✂ PRACTICAL INFORMATION

Visitor Info: Outer Banks Welcome Center on Roanoke Island, 1 Visitors Center Cir., (☎877-629-4386; www.outerbanks.org), at the base of the bridge to the mainland in Manteo. Info for all the islands except Ocracoke. Open daily June-Aug. 9am-6pm; Sept.-May 9am-5:30pm; info by phone M-F 8am-5:30pm, Sa-Su 10am-4pm. **Aycock Brown Welcome Center** (☎261-4644; www.outerbanks.com/dare/brown.htm), Mi. 1.5 on U.S. 158 in Kitty Hawk, has maps and tons of brochures. Open daily 9am-6pm. **Cape Hatteras National Seashore Information Centers: Bodie Island** (☎441-5711), on Rte. 12 between Mi. 22 and 23 at the north entrance to the National Seashore at Whalebone Junction. Open daily June-Aug. 9am-6pm; Sept.-May 9am-5pm. **Hatteras Island Visitor Center** (☎995-4474), on Rte. 12 at the Cape Hatteras Lighthouse. Open daily high season 9am-6pm; low season 9am-5pm. **Ocracoke Island Visitor Center** (☎928-4531), next to the ferry terminal at the south end of the island. Open daily June-Aug. 9am-6pm; Sept.-May 9am-5pm. Park info online at www.nps.gov/caha.

Internet Access: Free in the **Dare County Libraries.** On Bodie Island, **Kill Devil Hills Branch,** 400 Mustian St. (☎441-4331), 1 block west of U.S. 158, behind the post office. Open M and Th-F 9am-5:30pm, Tu-W 10am-7pm, Sa 10am-4pm. On Roanoke, **Manteo Branch** on Rte. 64 at Burnside St. (☎473-2372). Open M and Th 10am-7pm,

Tu and F 8:30am-5:30pm, W 10am-5:30pm, Sa 10am-4pm. **Hatteras Branch** (☎986-2385), on Hwy. 12 in the Community Building. Open Tu and Th-F 9:30am-5:30pm, W 1-7pm, Sa 9:30am-12:30pm.

Post Office: 3841 N. Croatan Hwy./Rte. 158 (☎261-2211), in Kitty Hawk. Open M-F 9am-4:30pm, Sa 10am-noon. **Postal Code:** 27949. **Area Code:** 252.

ACCOMMODATIONS AND FOOD

Most motels line **Route 12** on crowded Bodie Island. More privacy awaits farther south; Ocracoke is the most secluded. Rates everywhere are highest from June through August, especially on weekends. Although inter-season rates are good for April, May, September, and October, April can be rainy, October cold, and September hurricane-ridden. For a good deal without sacrificing pleasant weather, schedule for May. No matter when you visit, make reservations far in advance.

CAMPING

While sleeping on public beaches is punishable by fines and oceanview hotel rooms cost an arm and a leg, you can nod off to the sounds of the surf if you camp in one of the National Park Service's four oceanside **campgrounds ❶**. Each of the campgrounds is located on the Cape Hatteras National Seashore and has water, restrooms, picnic tables, grills, and cold-water showers. The northernmost site is **Oregon Inlet,** near the southern tip of Bodie Island and thus best-suited for excursions into town. The next two sites, **Cape Point** and **Frisco,** both lie near the elbow of Hatteras Island, close to the lighthouse. Cape Point's flat terrain tends to flood in wet weather, while a number of Frisco's campsites are perched atop dunes, allowing for unobstructed views of the Atlantic. Farthest south, **Ocracoke** is located on Ocracoke Island, 3 mi. north of Ocracoke Village. Soil in the campgrounds is sandy, so rangers recommend bringing longer-than-usual stakes for tents. There are no shade trees in the campgrounds. (☎473-2111. All sites $20. RVs allowed, no hookups available. Cape Point open late-May to early-Sept.; all others open late-Mar. to mid-Oct. Reservations may be made only for Ocracoke Campground (☎800-365-2267); all others first come, first served.)

BODIE ISLAND

Outer Banks International Hostel (HI) ❶, 1004 W. Kitty Hawk Rd., is the best deal in the northern islands. This friendly, bustling hostel has 60 beds, two kitchens, a common room, A/C, volleyball, shuffleboard, and laundry. Late risers, beware: peacocks live on the premises and begin screeching at sunrise. (☎261-2294; www.outerbankshostel.com. Linens $2.50. Reception 8am-9pm. Dorms $20, members $17; private rooms $49-55 for 1-2 people and $17-20 for each additional person. **Camping** on the grounds $20 for 1-2 adults June-Aug., $17 Sept.-May; each additional person $5 June-Aug., $4 Sept.-May; tent rental $6. Children under 12 half-price; children under 5 free. AmEx/MC/V.) One alternative to the pricey beachside options is **Cavalier Motel ❹,** 601 Beach Rd., near Mi. 8.5. This motor court comes with most of the amenities of a large hotel at a fraction of the price: refrigerators, microwaves, free local calls, cable TV, A/C, pool, hot tub, children's play area, and volleyball court. (☎441-5585; www.thecavaliermotel.com. Room with twin and double bed June-Aug. $88, Apr.-May and Sept. $57, Oct.-Mar. $34-39; ocean view and 2 double beds $139/$93/$53-58; with full bath and kitchenette $168/$103/$59-64. Multiple-bedroom cottages available. D/MC/V.) A cheaper option on Beach Rd. (though non-oceanside) is the **Ebb Tide Motel ❸,** Mi. 10 on Beach Rd., which offers moderately-sized rooms with refrigerator, microwave, cable TV, and A/C, as well as a pool and restaurant. (☎441-4913. Room with double bed June-Aug. $63, Sept.-May $39; 2 double beds $45/74; prices go up on weekends. MC/V.)

The oceanfront deck at **Quagmires ❸**, Mi. 7.5 on Beach Rd., is a popular spot to grab a drink or to enjoy fresh seafood and Mexican specialties like the crab enchilada ($14). The house specialty is the Bushwacker ($6.50), a huge, creamy mixed drink containing almost every alcohol known to man. (☎441-9188. Entrees $10-18. Beer from $1.50. Open daily 11:30am-2am. D/MC/V.) **Tortuga's Lie ❸**, Mi. 11 on Beach Rd. in Nags Head, serves Caribbean-influenced seafood, sandwiches, pasta, and grill items in a casual setting. The Pork Antonio ($14) is a spicy option rubbed with jerk seasoning and topped with habanero yellow currant glaze. (☎441-7299. Sandwiches and burgers $4-8. Dinner entrees $13-17. Sushi night W after 10pm. Open daily 11:30am-10:30pm. No reservations. AmEx/D/MC/V.) Pacific Rim fare reigns at **Mama Kwan's Tiki Bar and Grill ❸**, Mi. 8.5 on U.S. 158, where Asian flair enhances local dishes in a faux thatch hut. Try the popular "Jawaiian Spiced Chicken Breasts" ($15), a fusion of Hawaiian and Jamaican flavors drizzled with butter-rum sauce. (☎441-7889. Sandwiches $7-9. Open M-Sa 11:30am-2am, Su noon-2am. AmEx/D/MC/V.) With "no grits, no glory" as their motto, **Grits Grill ❷**, Mi. 14 on U.S. 158 in the Outer Banks Mall, serves the Southern specialty with breakfast items ($3.50-9), sandwiches ($3-7.50), and fresh Krispy Kreme Donuts in a 50s-style diner setting. (☎449-2888. Open daily 6am-3pm.)

OCRACOKE ISLAND

Hatteras Island is almost exclusively parkland, so there are few lodging options other than pitching a tent at one of the area's many campgrounds. In Ocracoke, accommodations and restaurants cluster on the southern tip in Ocracoke Village. For pleasant, wood-paneled rooms at some of Ocracoke's lowest prices, head to **Blackbeard's Lodge ❹**, 111 Back Rd. Turn right off Rte. 12 before the boat filled with seashells. The swing and rocking chairs on the front porch are perfect for relaxing and people-watching. (☎928-3421, reservations 800-892-5314; www.blackbeardslodge.com. Game room, A/C, cable TV, and heated pool. Double beds $85, lower in winter. D/MC/V.) **Edwards of Ocracoke ❸**, at Old Beach and Sand Dollar Rd., offers bright, elegantly furnished rooms for reasonable prices. (☎928-4801; www.edwardsofocracoke.com. A/C, cable TV, laundry. 2-person bungalow $68, higher on weekends. AmEx/D/MC/V.) The spic-and-span rooms at the **Sand Dollar Motel ❹**, 70 Sand Dollar Rd. in Ocracoke, have a nautical allure. (☎928-5571. Open Apr.-late Nov. Breakfast included. Refrigerators, microwaves, A/C, cable TV, and pool. Queen bed $80; 2 double beds $85; winter rates vary. AmEx/D/MC/V.)

PONY OVERBOARD!

To the unsuspecting passerby, the **Pony Pasture** (p. 361) on Rte. 12 in Ocracoke may seem like just another horse farm. In fact, the 30 or so ponies in the pasture have a rich, if mysterious, history unique to the island of Ocracoke.

Some attribute the origin of the ponies to English explorers who arrived in the 16th century. Others claim shipwrecked Spanish sailors tossed the ponies overboard to lighten their load. Either way, the creatures are indubitably distinct from their equine counterparts: the ponies have 5 lumbar vertebrae (horses have 6), 17 ribs (18), and a unique shape, posture, and color.

As the wild pony population increased over the years, the animals became an increasing nuisance to the people of Ocracoke, raiding gardens and consuming dune vegetation. Until the 1950s, locals staged "pony pennings" every 4th of July, during which the herd was corralled, and selected ponies were sold in order to limit their numbers. In 1957, with the paving of Rte. 12, car-pony accidents became a serious problem. When Cape Hatteras gained National Seashore status, the National Park Service believed that the herd was a threat to the natural ecosystem and wanted to remove it. Residents protested, and the NPS agreed to keep some of the ponies penned on the island, allowing the mystery of the Ocracoke ponies to live on.

Seafood lovers will feel right at home at **Jolly Roger ❷,** on Rte. 12 by the harbor in Ocracoke, for laid-back waterfront dining. Inhale the ocean breeze while indulging in local fresh fish specials and sandwiches. (☎928-3703. Beer from $2.50 a pint or $7.50 a pitcher. Open mid-Mar. to mid-Nov. daily 11am-10pm. AmEx/D/MC/V.) For a caffeine jolt, head to **Ocracoke Coffee Co. ❶,** on Back Rd., which serves up coffee, pastries, and bagels with homemade cream cheese on an outdoor patio. (☎928-7473; www.ocracokecoffee.com. Bagel with cream cheese $2.75. Open May-Sept. M-Sa 7am-8pm, Su 7am-5pm; call for winter hours. AmEx/D/MC/V.)

🔘 SIGHTS

The **Wright Brothers National Memorial,** Mi. 8 on U.S. 158, marks the spot where Orville and Wilbur Wright soared in history's first powered flight. Exhibits in the visitors center and First Flight Pavilion document aerospace technology from the first airplane to the first moon landing. (☎441-7430; www.nps.gov/wrbr. Open daily June-Aug. 9am-6pm; Sept.-May 9am-5pm. $3, under 16 free.) At the nearby **Jockey's Ridge State Park,** Mi. 12 on U.S. 158, **Kitty Hawk Kites** (☎441-4124 or 877-359-8447; www.kittyhawk.com) trains aspiring hang-gliding pilots. Beginner lessons last 3hr. and include five solo flights (from $89). Those preferring ground level excitement can slide down Jockey Ridge's dunes, the tallest on the East Coast, comprised of some 30 million tons of sand. (Park ☎441-7132. Open daily in summer 8am-9pm; low season closes between 6 and 8pm. Free.)

Roanoke Island is a concentration of historic and cultural attractions. The **Fort Raleigh National Historic Site,** 1409 National Park Rd., just off U.S. 64, marks the spot where the British first attempted to settle in the New World. Settlers occupied this area beginning in 1585, but a lack of supplies and tensions with local tribes forced their return to England. A second colony, established in 1587, disappeared without explanation around 1590. Today, visitors can see artifacts from the settlement and attend talks by park interpreters at the Lindsay Warren Visitor Center. (☎473-5772; www.nps.gov/fora. Open daily in summer 9am-6pm; low season 9am-5pm.) During the summer, actors perform **The Lost Colony,** a musical version of the settlers' story, in a theater overlooking the sound near the Fort Raleigh site. (☎473-3414 or 866-468-7630; www.thelostcolony.org. Shows June-Aug. M-Sa 8:30pm. $16, ages 62+ $15, 11 and under $8.)

Just down U.S. 64, the child-friendly **Roanoke Island Festival Park** contains a spectacle of museum exhibits, costumed reenactments, outdoor activities, and historical replicas reflecting 400 years of Outer Banks history. (☎475-1500; www.roanokeisland.com. Park and museum open daily June-Aug. 10am-7pm; Apr.-May and Sept.-Oct. 10am-6pm; mid-Feb.-Mar. and Nov.-Dec. 10am-5pm. Two-day tickets $8, ages 6-17 $5, 5 and under free. Drama, dance, and music performances in the park's outdoor pavilion at 8pm Tu-Sa in July.) Nearby, in the romantic **Elizabethan Gardens,** visitors can wander among fountains, antique statues, and beds of seasonal flowers. (☎473-3234; www.elizabethangardens.org. Open June-Aug. M-Sa 9am-8pm, Su 9am-7pm; low-season hours vary. $6, ages 62+ $5, ages 6-18 $2, under 5 free. Wheelchair accessible.)

SCENIC DRIVE: CAPE HATTERAS NATIONAL SEASHORE

The Cape Hatteras National Seashore actually offers two shores for the price of one: as you drive the 70 mi. of Rte. 12 running between Whalebone Junction and Ocracoke Village, you can see the Atlantic Ocean to the east and the Pamlico Sound to the west. Traffic may force you to crawl along at 30 mph if you drive south from Hatteras to Ocracoke in the summer, but the leisurely pace is perfect for appreciating the unobstructed bi-coastal view.

Route 12 is a paved two-lane road and the main artery of the park, running from the northern entrance of the park at Nags Head on Bodie Island to the southern tail in the town of Ocracoke Village. A free 40min. ferry shuttles cars from Hatteras to the northern end of Ocracoke Island (see **Transportation**, p. 356). Total transport time from Whalebone to Ocracoke is about 2½hr.

All of the park's major attractions are accessible and clearly marked from Rte. 12. The chief of these are the Outer Banks' three lighthouses on Bodie, Hatteras, and Ocracoke Islands. The tallest brick lighthouse in North America is the 196 ft. **Cape Hatteras Lighthouse**, built in 1870. Due to beach erosion, the lighthouse was relocated in 1999. To scale the tower for an impressive view, take one of the self-guided tours. (Tickets sold 8am-20min. before closing. Open daily Apr. 9am-5pm; June-Aug. 9am-6pm; Sept. 9am-5pm. Adults $6; children under 12, disabled, and ages 62+ $3.) Duck into the **visitors center** to see a section of the original lens, an inspiring feat of early engineering. (☎995-4474. Open daily in summer 9am-6pm; low season 9am-5pm.) Another set of attractions along Rte. 12 reminds visitors that lighthouses have value apart from being picturesque—several shipwrecks can be seen from the shore. Turn off Rte. 12 at Coquina Beach to see the wreck of the *Laura A. Barnes*, which was grounded in 1921. Visibility varies. For a schedule of the various ranger programs covering natural history that run daily at the visitors centers at each lighthouse, pick up the free paper *In The Park*.

The **Pea Island National Wildlife Refuge** on the northern tip of Hatteras Island boasts over 365 species of birds, including endangered peregrine falcons. The **Charles Kuralt Nature Trail,** next to the visitors center, affords trekkers a chance to glimpse blackbirds, pelicans, loggerhead turtles, and Carolina salt marsh snakes. The ½ mi. **North Pond Wildlife Trail,** also beginning at the visitors center, is wheelchair accessible. (Visitors center ☎987-2394; www.peaisland.fws.gov. Usually open daily 9am-5pm. Beaches in the refuge are open only during daylight.) Farther south, the **Pony Pasture,** on Rte. 12 in Ocracoke, is the stomping ground for a herd of semi-wild horses, said to be the descendants of horses left there by shipwrecked explorers in the 16th or 17th century.

WILMINGTON   ☎910

Situated on the Carolina coast at the mouth of the Cape Fear River and only a few miles from the beaches of the Atlantic, Wilmington has long been an important center for shipping and trade. Home to the

HITTING THE BEACH

Figuring that there was no better place to try flying than in the Wright Brothers' old haunt, I signed up for a beginner's hang gliding lesson with Kitty Hawk Kites in Jockey's Ridge State Park (p. 360). The giant dunes would surely soften the impact if I crashed. As I signed a waiver holding just me responsible in the event of an accident, I hoped I was right.

After a brief lesson in hang-gliding maneuvers, I suited up for the fun part. Strapping on my less-than-fashionable harness and helmet and removing my shoes, I trekked out to the dunes with the rest of the class.

When we reached the beach, bad news greeted us: hang-gliders require about 20 mph of wind, and the wind that day was a measly 2 mph. After calculating that I would need to run 18 mph, I realized I was going nowhere. Students were given the options of getting a partial refund, taking a "wind check," or staying put until the park closed, hoping the wind would pick up. I chose the latter and despite watching one student nose-dive, made a run for it. Strapped into the glider, I sprinted down the dune, my heart racing with anticipation and visions of high-flying grandeur. I lifted off and was actually airborne for a moment, before crashing onto the beach. Most of the "gliding" I did was in the sand.

—*Rebecca Barron*

largest film production facility east of L.A., the city is sometimes referred to as "Wilmywood" and "Hollywood East." Over 400 feature films and TV projects have been shot along the picturesque Cape Fear coast since 1983, including the hit TV series *Dawson's Creek*. Even if you don't glimpse a celebrity, the historic downtown area has plenty to offer, from historic memorials and excellent restaurants to picturesque views of the waterfront.

⁊ PRACTICAL INFORMATION. Wilmington International Airport, 1740 Airport Blvd., off 23rd St., 2 mi. north of Market St. and the downtown area. (☎341-4333; www.flyilm.com.) **Greyhound,** 201 Harnett St. (☎762-6073; www.greyhound.com; open daily 8:30-10am, 1-4:45pm, and 8:15-9:15pm), between 3rd and Front St., about a mile north of downtown, departs to Charlotte (9hr., 1 per day, $29-47) and Raleigh (6hr., 1 per day, $31-33.50). The **Wilmington Transit Authority** (☎343-0106; www.wavetransit.com) runs **local buses** (buses run M-F 6am-9:30pm, Sa 8am-9:30pm, Su 9:30am-6pm; $0.75; ages 65+, disabled, and students $0.35) and a **free trolley** that travels along Front St. between Ann and Hanover St. (runs M-F 7:30am-9:30pm, Sa 11am-9:30pm). A **river taxi** ferries passengers across the river between downtown Market St. and the *USS North Carolina*, aboard the *J. N. Maffitt*. (☎343-1611 or 800-676-0162. Runs June-Aug. daily 10am-5pm. 15min., round-trip $3. Riverboat sightseeing cruises lasting 45min. also available at 11am and 3pm; $10, ages 2-12 $5.) Taxi: **Port City Taxi** (☎762-1165). **Visitor Info: Visitors Center,** 24 N. 3rd St., at the corner of 3rd and Princess. (☎341-4030 or 800-222-4757; www.cape-fear.nc.us. Open M-F 8:30am-5pm, Sa 9am-4pm, Su 1-4pm.) The visitors center also runs an **information kiosk** at the foot of Market St. by the waterfront. (Open daily June-Aug. 9:30am-5pm; Apr.-May and Sept.-Oct. 9am-4:30pm.) **Internet Access: New Hanover County Library,** 201 Chestnut St., at 3rd St., one block from the visitors center. (☎798-6302. Open M-W 9am-8pm, Th-Sa 9am-5pm, Su 1-5pm. Free. Internet access limited to 1hr.) **Post Office:** 152 N. Front St., at Chestnut St. (☎313-3293. Open M-F 9am-5pm, Sa 9am-noon.) **Postal Code:** 28401. **Area Code:** 910.

┌ ACCOMMODATIONS. Wilmington's best lodging comes in the form of B&Bs; most are conveniently located in the historic downtown area. Though rooms usually cost $100-200 per night, the unique rooms, convenient location, and riverfront views make Wilmington's B&Bs worth the extra cash. Be sure to reserve far in advance, especially during the summer. The **Dragonfly Inn ❺,** 1914 Market St., differs from antiques-and-lace B&Bs with its earthy, holistic approach to hospitality, complete with all-natural bath products and aromatherapy. (☎762-7025; www.dragonflyinn.com. Internet access, off-street parking. Doubles from $89. AmEx/D/MC/V.) For less expensive lodging, nearly every budget chain can be found on Market St. between College Rd. and 23rd St. Weekend rates often run $10-20 higher than weekday prices. The **Greentree Inn ❷,** 5025 Market St., has large green rooms with A/C and cable TV. (☎799-6001; www.greentreenc.com. Pool, continental breakfast. June-Aug. M-Th and Su from $45, F-Sa from $64; in winter $36/$46. AmEx/D/DC/MC/V.) **Travel Inn ❷,** 4401 Market St., a single-floor motor court, provides basic rooms with tiny showers for some of the lowest rates around. (☎763-8217. Pool, cable TV with free HBO, A/C. Rooms in summer M-F $50, Sa-Su $70; lower in winter. AAA and AARP discount 10%. AmEx/D/DC/MC/V.) The **Carolina Beach State Park ❶,** about 18 mi. south of Wilmington on U.S. 421, offers spacious, wooded campsites as well as hiking, picnic areas, and a marina. (☎458-8206. Restrooms, hot showers, laundry facilities, water, and grills. No RV hookups. Open year-round. Sites $15.)

⌂ FOOD. Quality restaurants are plentiful in historic downtown Wilmington. **▦Rim Wang ❷,** 128 S. Front St., offers authentic Thai cuisine, with options that will please both those looking for something spicy and those with less daring palates.

Lunch specials range from traditional *pad thai* to chicken *massaman* and include a bowl of zesty coconut soup. (☎ 763-5552. Lunch specials $9. Most noodle, rice, stir-fry, and curry dishes $11. Open M-Th 11am-3pm and 5-10pm, F 11:30am-3pm and 5-11pm, Sa 11:30am-11pm, Su 3-10pm. AmEx/D/MC/V.) **Nikki's ❶**, 16 S. Front St., is a downtown bistro where the atmosphere is casual, the waitresses dreadlocked, and the vegetarian fare delectable; sample the "Avocado on Wheat" ($6.25) for a healthful treat. (☎ 772-9151. Sandwiches $4.25-7. Wraps $5.25-6.50. Sushi from $3.50 for 8 pieces. Open M-Th 11am-4pm and 5:30-10pm; F-Sa 11am-4pm and 5:30-11pm; Su noon-4pm and 5:30-9pm. MC/V.) Head over to kid-friendly **McDaniel Farms Creamery and Restaurant ❶**, 614 S. College Rd., for some home cookin'. Housed in a barn complete with a silo, McDaniel Farms whips up homemade ice cream in addition to sandwiches, burgers, and other entrees. (☎ 793-9994; www.mcdanielfarms.com. Entrees $5-15. Open M-Th 11am-11pm, F-Sa 11am-midnight. Free wireless Internet. AmEx/MC/V.)

◙ SIGHTS. No visit to historic Wilmington would be complete without an afternoon spent winding down at the relaxing **Wrightsville Beach.** From Market St. downtown, take Eastwood Rd. to the bridge leading over Wrightsville Sound to the beach. Fifteen miles down Rte. 421, **Carolina Beach** has a charming boardwalk and a state park where the carnivorous Venus fly trap plant flourishes. Five miles farther on Rte. 421 is **Kure Beach,** a state recreation area. The **Fort Fisher Aquarium** in Kure Beach draws visitors from all over the country to see three habitat exhibits: freshwater, coastal marsh, and open ocean. Don't miss the freshwater alligators or the quarter-million gallon Cape Fear Shoals tank, full of eels, sharks, coral reefs, and a variety of fish. (☎ 458-8257; www.ncaquariums.com. Open daily 9am-5pm. $7, ages 62+ and active military $6, ages 6-17 $5, under 6 free.)

For Wilmington's glamorous side, **Screen Gems Studios,** 1223 N. 23rd St., near the airport, is the largest movie and TV production facility east of Hollywood. Guided 1hr. studio tours provide a fascinating behind-the-scenes glimpse of the industry. (☎ 343-3500; www.screengemsstudios.com. Tours June-Aug. Sa-Su noon and 2pm; Sept.-May Sa noon. $12, seniors $8, children under 12 $5.) Art aficionados shouldn't miss the **Louise Wells Cameron Art Museum,** 3201 S. 17th St., at the intersection of Independence Blvd., which displays the work of American masters, including a collection of works by Mary Cassatt and the work of North Carolinian artists from the 18th to 21st centuries. (☎ 395-5999; www.cameronartmuseum.com. Open Tu-Sa 10am-5pm, Su 10:30am-4pm. $7, ages 6-18 $2, ages 5 and under and active military free, families $15.)

The military-minded can take a self-guided tour of the massive **Battleship North Carolina,** moored in the Cape Fear River across from downtown, at the junction of Hwys. 17, 74, 76, and 421. This sturdy warship and its crew of 2339 participated in every major naval offensive in the Pacific during WWII. Highlights of the ship include the bridge, soldiers' quarters, and galley. (☎ 251-5797; www.battleshipnc.com. Open daily mid-May to mid-Sept. 8am-8pm; mid-Sept. to mid-May 8am-5pm. Ticket sales end 1hr. before closing. $9, ages 65+ and military $8, ages 6-11 $4.50, 5 and under free.) For a change of pace, take in a jazz or folk concert at the **Airlie Gardens,** 300 Airlie Rd., just off Oleander Dr., or stroll through the **New Hanover County Arboretum,** 6206 Oleander Dr., which includes a Japanese garden with a teahouse. (Airlie Gardens: ☎ 798-7700; www.airliegardens.org. Open Tu-Su 9am-5pm. $5, children under 10 and ages 65+ $3. Concerts Apr.-Oct. 1st and 3rd F 6-8pm, free with admission. Arboretum: ☎ 452-6393. Open daily dawn-dusk. Free.)

◪◧ ENTERTAINMENT AND NIGHTLIFE. For local entertainment info, pick up a free copy of *Encore* or *The Outrider,* weekly newspapers with event listings that are available in most hotels and cafes. Wilmington's historic **Thalian Hall,** 310

Chestnut St., offers a wide range of entertainment, including theater, dance, music, and comedy acts. Tours of the hall showcase its history, from the design created by famous architect John Trimble to the famous guests—including Buffalo Bill Cody and John Philip Sousa—hosted during its nearly 150 years of continuous use. (Box office ☎343-3664 or 800-523-2820; www.thalianhall.com. Box office open M-F noon-6pm, Sa 2-6pm. Tour info ☎343-3660. Tours by appointment $6.)

Downtown Wilmington is jumping on Friday and Saturday nights; most bars and clubs cluster around Front St. The **Reel Cafe,** 100 S. Front St., offers three big-screen TVs, a rooftop bar, a dance floor, and live music on the courtyard patio. (☎251-1832; www.thereelcafe.net. Dress code strictly enforced. 18+ after 11pm. Cover F-Sa $5, Sa ladies free. Open daily 11am-2am. Rooftop bar open Th-Su, dance floor F-Sa.) Arcade junkies will delight in **Blue Post,** 15 S. Water St., by Dock St., at the back corner of the parking lot, which offers pool tables, classic video games, pinball, air hockey, over 60 kinds of beer, and a young, casual crowd. (☎343-1141. Beer from $2.50. 21+. Open M-F 3pm-2am, Sa-Su 2pm-2am.)

Are your socks dirty? Spend an evening at **Soapbox,** 255 N. Front St., a "Laundro-Lounge" where you can do your laundry as you booze. (No, we aren't kidding.) Downstairs, you'll find foosball, pool, occasional live music, a bar, and plenty of washers and dryers. Upstairs you'll find a more conventional nightclub with another bar and a stage for live music, which is played almost every night and ranges from hip-hop and reggae to jazz and good old rock 'n' roll. (☎251-8500; www.soapboxlaundrolounge.com. Cover downstairs $3, upstairs $5-15, more for under 21. Open daily noon-2am.) For a change of pace, head to **Lula's,** 138 Orange St., off S. Front St., a charming pub popular with Wilmingtonians of all ages. (☎763-0070. Tu $2 pint night. Open daily 7pm-2am.)

SOUTH CAROLINA

To some, South Carolina's pride in the Palmetto State may seem extreme. Inspired by the state flag, the palmetto tree logo decorates hats, bottles and bumper stickers across the area. This pride is justified, though, in the unrivaled beaches of the Grand Strand and the stately elegance of Charleston. Columbia, though less well known, offers an impressive artistic and cultural experience without the smog and traffic that plague other cities of the New South. Tamed for tourists and merchandising, the Confederate legacy of this first state to secede from the Union is groomed as a cash cow. Beyond the commercialized strips, however, South Carolina retains its old-style grace and charm—not to mention its rebellious spirit.

▓ PRACTICAL INFORMATION

Capital: Columbia.

Visitor Info: Department of Parks, Recreation, and Tourism, 1205 Pendleton St., Rm. 110, Columbia 29201 (☎803-734-1700; www.discoversouthcarolina.com). **South Carolina Forestry Commission,** 5500 Broad River Rd., Columbia 29212 (☎803-896-8800).

Postal Abbreviation: SC. **Sales Tax:** 5-7%.

CHARLESTON ☎843

Built on rice and cotton, Charleston's antebellum plantation system yielded vast riches that are now visible in its numerous museums, historic homes, and ornate architecture. Three hundred years worth of cultural capital flows like the natives' long, distinctive drawl. Several of the South's most renowned plantations dot the city, while two venerable educational institutions, the **College of Charleston** and **The**

Downtown Charleston

🏕️ **ACCOMMODATIONS**
1837 Bed and Breakfast, **7**
Bed, No Breakfast, **6**
Campground at James Island County Park, **2**
Charleston's Not So Hostel, **3**
Motel 6, **1**

🍴 **FOOD**
Gaulart & Maliclet, **12**
Hyman's Seafood Company, **10**
Jestine's Kitchen, **8**
Sticky Fingers, **9**

🍸 **NIGHTLIFE**
Coast, **5**
Meritage, **11**
Music Farm, **4**

Citadel, add a youthful vitality. Horse-drawn carriages, cobblestone streets, pre-Civil War homes, beautiful beaches, and some of the best restaurants in the Southeast explain why Charleston often tops the list of the nation's best destinations.

TRANSPORTATION

Trains: Amtrak, 4565 Gaynor Ave. (☎ 744-8264; www.amtrak.com), 8 mi. west of downtown. Open daily 6pm-midnight. Runs to **Richmond** (7hr., 2 per day, $92-120), **Savannah** (1¾hr., 2 per day, $17-20), and **Washington, D.C.** (9½hr., 2 per day, $122-158).

Buses: Greyhound, 3610 Dorchester Rd. (☎ 744-4247; www.greyhound.com), in N. Charleston. Avoid this area at night. Open daily 8:30am-9:30pm. Runs to **Charlotte** (4½-5hr., 2 per day, $43-46), **Myrtle Beach** (2½hr., 1 per day, $26-28), and **Savannah** (2½hr., 2 per day, $26-28). CARTA's "Upper Dorchester" bus serves this area.

Public Transit: CARTA, 36 John St. (☎ 724-7420), runs area buses and the **Downtown Area Shuttle (DASH),** trolleys that circle downtown. $1.25, seniors $0.60, disabled $0.35; 1-day pass $4, 3-day $9. Runs daily 6am-11pm. Visitors center has schedules.

Taxi: Yellow Cab, ☎ 577-6565.

Bike Rental: The Bicycle Shoppe, 280 Meeting St. (☎ 722-8168), between George and Society St. Open M-F 9am-7pm, Sa 9am-6pm, Su 1-5pm. $5 per hr., $20 per day.

■ 🔁 ORIENTATION AND PRACTICAL INFORMATION

Old Charleston lies at the southernmost point of the mile-wide peninsula below **Calhoun Street.** The major north-south routes through the city are **Meeting, King,** and **East Bay Streets.** The area north of the visitors center is run-down and uninviting. **Savannah Highway (U.S. 17)** cuts across the peninsula going south to Savannah and north across two towering bridges to Mt. Pleasant and Myrtle Beach. There are plenty of metered parking spaces and plenty of police officers giving tickets.

Visitor Info: Charleston Visitors Center, 375 Meeting St. (☎853-8000 or 800-868-8118; www.charlestoncvb.com), across from Charleston Museum. Open daily Apr.-Oct. 8:30am-5:30pm; Nov.-Mar. 8:30am-5pm.

Hotlines: Crisis Line, ☎744-4357. **People Against Rape,** ☎745-0144 or 800-241-7273. Both 24hr.

Medical Services: Charleston Memorial Hospital, 326 Calhoun St. (☎792-2300).

Internet Access: Charleston County Public Library, 68 Calhoun St. (☎805-6801). Open M-Th 9am-9pm, F-Sa 9am-6pm, Su 2-5pm. Free; 1 hr. limit.

Post Office: 83 Broad St. (☎577-0690). Open M-F 9am-5pm. **Postal Code:** 29402. **Area Code:** 843.

🛏 ACCOMMODATIONS

Luckily for budget travelers, Charleston has a great hostel; motel rooms in historic downtown Charleston are quite expensive. If you have the bucks, opt for the charming B&Bs. Cheap motels are just outside the city, around Exits 209-211 on I-26 W in N. Charleston, or across the Ashley River on U.S. 17 S in Mt. Pleasant.

Charleston's Not So Hostel, 156 Spring St. (☎722-8383; www.notsohostel.com). Friendly, clean, and comfortable, with dorms, private rooms, and a camping platform. Internet, make-your-own waffle breakfast, and off-street parking included. Laundry facilities available. Dorms $15-19; private rooms $30-38; camping $10. AmEx/D/MC/V. ❶

Bed, No Breakfast, 16 Halsey St. (☎723-4450). A simple, charming option, this 2-room inn offers a cozy and affordable stay in the historic heart of the city. Shared bathroom. Reservations recommended. Rooms $75-95. Cash or check only. ❸

1837 Bed and Breakfast, 126 Wentworth St. (☎723-7166 or 877-723-1837; www.1837bb.com), in a wealthy cotton planter's former home. Walking distance to downtown. Each of the 9 rooms is beautifully furnished, with A/C and microfridge. Reservations recommended. Rooms $79-175. AmEx/D/MC/V. ❹

Motel 6, 2058 Savannah Hwy. (☎556-5144), 5 mi. south of town. Be sure to call ahead and reserve one of these clean rooms; the popular chain motel is often booked solid for days. Cable TV. A/C. Free local calls. Pool. Rooms M-Th and Su $47-53, F-Sa $57-63; each additional person $3. AARP discount 10%. AmEx/D/DC/MC/V. ❸

Campground at James Island County Park (☎795-4386 or 800-743-7275). Take U.S. 17 S to Rte. 171 to Hwy 700 and follow the signs. 125 spacious sites, each with picnic table, bicycle trails, and a small water park. Bike and boat rental. Primitive sites $16, tent sites $26, hookup $28. Max. stay 7/14/21 days. Seniors discount 10%. ❶

🍴 FOOD

Most restaurants cater to big-spending tourists, but there are plenty of budget-friendly opportunities to sample the Southern cooking, barbecue, and fresh seafood that have made the Low Country famous.

Jestine's Kitchen, 251 Meeting St. (☎ 722-7224). Serving up some of the best southern food in Charleston, Jestine's has become a local favorite with its daily Southern blue plate specials ($7-10) and "blue collar special" (peanut butter and banana sandwich; $3). Open Tu-Th 11am-9:30pm, F-Sa 11am-10pm, Su 11am-9pm. MC/V. ❷

Sticky Fingers, 235 Meeting St. (☎ 853-7427). Rightly voted the best barbecue in town, Sticky Fingers is a Charleston legend for its mouth-watering ribs ($14-20), prepared 5 different ways. Open daily 11am-10pm. AmEx/D/DC/MC/V. ❸

Gaulart & Maliclet, 98 Broad St. (☎ 577-9797). Known colloquially as "G & M," "Fast & French," and "Pig & Chicken," this gem of a cafe serves inexpensive, delectable, French-inspired fare, from escargot ($8 for 6) to blue cheese fondue ($13). Open M 8am-4pm, Tu-Th 8am-10pm, F-Sa 8am-10:30pm. AmEx/D/MC/V. ❷

Hyman's Seafood Company, 215 Meeting St. (☎ 723-6000). Since 1890, this casual restaurant has offered 15-25 different kinds of fresh fish daily ($8-15), served in any of 8 styles. Try the po' boy sandwich with your choice of oyster, calamari, crab, or scallops ($8-11). No reservations; expect long waits. Open daily 11am-11pm. AmEx/D/DC/MC/V. ❸

🅖 SIGHTS

Charleston's ancient homes, historical monuments, churches, galleries, and gardens can be seen by foot, car, bus, boat, horse-drawn carriage, or on one of the nine ghost tours. **City Market,** 188 Meeting St., stays abuzz in a newly restored 19th-century building. (Open daily 9am-5pm.) **Liberty Square,** at the end of Calhoun St., is home to the aquarium and the fantastic Fort Sumter Visitors Center.

PLANTATIONS AND GARDENS. The best value is to be had at **Drayton Hall,** a 265-year-old plantation that has survived both the Revolutionary and Civil Wars, as well as numerous earthquakes and hurricanes. Entrance includes a guided tour of the stately plantation house. Afterwards, stroll along the scenic marsh or bring a picnic lunch to enjoy on tables under moss-draped oak trees. *(On Rte. 61, 9 mi. northwest of downtown. ☎ 769-2600; www.draytonhall.org. Open daily Mar.-Oct. 9:30am-5:30pm, entrance gates close at 4pm; Nov.-Feb. 9:30am-4:30pm, gates close at 3pm. $12, ages 12-18 $8, 6-11 $6. Grounds only $5. AAA discount. Wheelchair accessible.)* The 300-year-old **Magnolia Plantation and Gardens** is by far the most majestic of Charleston's plantations and the oldest major public garden in the country. Visitors can enjoy the staggering wealth of the

GRITS GALORE

Every April, the population of St. George, SC swells to about 20 times its normal size as tens of thousands of people from all over the world descend on this small town (pop. 2100) to celebrate the annual World Grits Festival.

In 1985, the manager of a local supermarket was placing an order with the broker of a large grits company when the broker remarked that his company sure shipped a lot of grits to St. George, given its small size. Subsequent research revealed that St. George residents ate more grits per capita than anywhere else in the world. They considered themselves grits-eating champions. To celebrate, they held the first-ever grits festival.

Now, the three-day festival includes a multitude of grits-themed events, such as grits eating contests, grits grinding, and the popular Roll in Grits contest, in which contestants are weighed before and after diving into a huge pool of grits and win by amassing the most "grits weight." Roll in Grits strategies include wearing clothing with lots of pockets, and showing up to the event with unbelievably long hair. Whether you love the dish or have never even tried it, the festival is the perfect opportunity to dive in and soak up some grits.

The 2006 World Grits Festival is scheduled for April 7-9, 2006. For more information, visit www.worldgritsfestival.com.

Drayton family by exploring their 50 acres of gorgeous gardens. Other attractions include a hedge maze, bike and canoe rental, swamp, and bird sanctuary. *(On Rte. 61, 10 mi. out of town off U.S. 17. ☎571-1266 or 800-367-3517; www.magnoliaplantation.com. Open Mar.-Oct. daily 8am-dusk, ticket sales end at 5:30pm; call for winter hours. Gardens and grounds ticket $14, seniors $13, ages 6-12 $8. After purchase of ticket, additional prices as follows: house tour $7 per person, under 6 not allowed; swamp $7/$6/$5; nature train $7/$7/$5; nature boat tour $7/$7/$5.)* Farther away from Charleston, **Cypress Gardens** lets visitors paddle their own boats out onto the eerie, gator-filled swamps. *(3030 Cypress Gardens Rd. Off Rte. 52. ☎553-0515; www.cypressgardens.org. Open daily 9am-5pm. $10, seniors $9, ages 6-12 $3.)*

CHARLESTON MUSEUM AND HISTORIC HOMES. The **Charleston Museum** and its **Historic Homes** make up the nation's oldest museum and are a great way to become acquainted with the city's historical offerings. The museum boasts outstanding exhibits on the Revolutionary and Civil Wars and a thorough look into the history of the Low Country. Across the street, the **Joseph Manigault House** reflects the lifestyle of a wealthy, rice-planting family and the African-American slaves who lived there. Farther downtown, the **Heyward-Washington House** was home to Thomas Heyward, Jr., a signer of the Declaration of Independence. It was rented to George Washington during his 1791 trip through the South. *(Museum: 360 Meeting St. ☎722-2996; www.charlestonmuseum.org. Open M-Sa 9am-5pm, Su 1-5pm. Joseph Manigault House: 350 Meeting St. ☎723-2926. Heyward-Washington House: 87 Church St. ☎722-0354. Both houses open M-Sa 10am-5pm, Su 1-5pm. Museum $10, 1 house $9, 2 sights $16, 3 sights $21. Wheelchair accessible.)* For more historic home tours, try the **Nathaniel Russell House** or **Aiken Rhett House.** The Nathaniel Russel House's graceful interior demonstrates the luxurious lifestyle of its former inhabitants. The audio tour of the Aiken Rhett House is heavily focused on the slave quarters. *(Nathaniel Russell House: 51 Meeting St. ☎724-8481. Aiken Rhett House: 48 Elizabeth St. ☎723-1159. Houses open M-Sa 10am-5pm, Su 2-5pm. Each house $10, both for $16.)*

PATRIOT'S POINT AND FORT SUMTER. Climb aboard four Naval vessels, including a submarine and a giant aircraft carrier, at **Patriot's Point Naval and Maritime Museum,** the world's largest naval museum. *(40 Patriots Point Rd. Across the Cooper River in Mt. Pleasant. ☎884-2727; www.patriotspoint.org. Open daily 9am-6:30pm, ticket sales end at 5pm. $14, seniors and military $12, ages 6-11 $7.)* From Patriot's Point in Mt. Pleasant, **Spirit Line Cruises** leads boat excursions to the National Historic Site where Confederate soldiers bombarded Union forces in April 1861, turning years of escalating tension into open war. There is a dock at Liberty Square next to the South Carolina Aquarium in Charleston. *(Tours: ☎881-7337. Fort Sumter: ☎883-3123; www.spiritlinecruises.com. 2¼hr. tour. 1-3 tours per day. $13, seniors $12, ages 6-11 $6.50.)*

BEACHES. Folly Beach is popular with Citadel, College of Charleston, and University of South Carolina students. *(Over the James Bridge and U.S. 171, about 20 mi. southeast of Charleston. ☎588-2426.)* The more expansive **Isle of Palms** extends for miles toward the less-crowded **Sullivan's Island.** *(Isle of Palms: Across the Cooper Bridge, drive 10 mi. down Hwy. 17 N, turn right onto the Isle of Palms Connector. ☎886-3863.)*

LIBERTY SQUARE. Two of Charleston's finest sights are located in Liberty Square. The ▓**Charleston Aquarium** has quickly become the city's greatest attraction. Although a bit overpriced, its exhibits showcase aquatic life from the region's swamps, marshes, and oceans. Stare down the fishies at the 330,000-gallon Great Ocean Tank, which boasts the nation's tallest viewing window. *(At the end of Calhoun St. on the Cooper River, overlooking the harbor. ☎720-1990; www.scaquarium.org. Open Apr. to mid-Aug. M-Sa 9am-6pm, Su noon-6pm, last ticket sold at 5pm; mid-Aug. to Mar. M-Sa 9am-5pm, Su noon-5pm, last ticket sold at 4pm. $15, seniors $13, ages 3-11 $8. Wheelchair accessible.)*

Next door, the **Fort Sumter Visitor and Education Center** has a fascinating exhibit on the cultural, economical, and political differences between the North and South prior to the Civil War. *(340 Concord St. ☎577-0242. Open daily 8:30am-5pm. Free.)*

BULL ISLAND. To get away from human civilization, take a ferry to Bull Island, a 5000-acre island off the coast of Charleston. Boats are often greeted by dolphins swimming in some of the cleanest water on the planet. Once on the island there are 16 mi. of hiking trails populated by 278 different species of birds. *(☎881-4582. ½hr. ferries depart from Moore's Landing, off Seewee Rd., 16 mi. north of Charleston off U.S. 17. Departs Mar.-Nov. Tu and Th-Sa 9am, 12:30pm; returns Tu and Th-Sa noon, 4pm. Departs Dec.-Feb. Sa 10am; returns 3pm. Round-trip $30, under 12 $15.)*

🎵 🎸 ENTERTAINMENT AND NIGHTLIFE

The density of bars and clubs downtown, combined with the abundance of twentysomethings attending Charleston's colleges, give Charleston a lively nightlife scene. Free copies of *City Paper*, in stores and restaurants, list concerts and other events. Big-name bands take center stage at **Music Farm,** 32 Ann St. (☎853-3276. Call for schedule and ticket prices.) Charleston's trendiest flock to **Coast,** 39-D John St. With its high ceilings and tropical decor, after a few drinks you'll swear you're on the beach. The largest crowds are on Sunday nights, when all bottles of wine are half-price until 8pm, and tacos are $3. (☎722-8838. Live jazz Th. DJ Su. Bar open daily 5pm-late; dinner served M-Th and Su 5:30-10pm, F-Sa 5:30-11pm.) **Meritage,** 235 E. Bay St., is popular for its late-night scene. Tasty tapas ($4-9) and a wide selection of brews keep the party going strong. (☎723-8181. Open daily 5pm-2am; food served until 1am. Live music Tu-Th.) The city explodes with music, theater, dance, and opera, as well as literature and visual arts when Charleston hosts the annual **Spoleto Festival USA,** the nation's most comprehensive arts festival. Founded in 1977, it is the counterpart to the Festival of Two Worlds in Spoleto, Italy. (☎722-2764; www.spoletousa.org. May 26-June 11, 2006. $10-125.)

COLUMBIA ☎803

Much ado is made over Columbia's Civil War heritage, and understandably so, as Old South nostalgia brings in big tourist dollars. Despite this nostalgia, more antebellum buildings have been lost to developers in the last century than were burned by Sherman and his rowdy troops. Still, the town is the heart of the nation's "rebel" child, and a defiant spirit imbues Columbia's bars, businesses, and citizens. Southern pride and passion are perpetuated at the **University of South Carolina (USC),** with its sprawling green spaces and fascinating museums.

📧 🎫 ORIENTATION AND PRACTICAL INFORMATION. The city is laid out in a square, bordered by Huger and Harden St. running north-south and Blossom and Calhoun St. east-west. **Assembly Street** is the main drag, running north-south through the city, and **Gervais Street** is its east-west equivalent. The Congaree River marks the city's western edge. The Beltline offers little for tourists and, for safety purposes, is best avoided. **Columbia Metropolitan Airport,** 3000 Aviation Way (☎822-5000; www.columbiaairport.com), is in West Columbia. A **taxi** to downtown costs about $15-17. **Amtrak,** 850 Pulaski St. (☎252-8246; www.amtrak.com; open daily 10pm-5:30am), sends one train per day to Miami (16½hr., $98), Savannah (2½hr., $22), and Washington, D.C. (11hr., $103). **Greyhound,** 2015 Gervais St. (☎256-6465; www.greyhound.com), at Harden St., sends buses to Atlanta (3½-6hr., 7 per day, $47-50), Charleston (2½hr., 2 per day, $28-30), and Charlotte (2hr., 3-4 per day, $17-19). **Central Midlands Regional Transit Authority** runs buses and trolleys throughout

Columbia. (☎255-7100; www.gocmrta.com. Runs M-F 5:30am-midnight, Sa 6am-midnight, Su 7:30am-10pm; call for schedules. $1, seniors and disabled $0.50. Transfers free.) **Taxi: Capital City Cab** ☎233-8294. **Visitor Info: Columbia Metropolitan Convention and Visitors Bureau,** 1501 Lincoln St., has maps and info. (☎545-0000; www.columbiacvb.com. Open M-F 9am-5pm, Sa 10am-4pm.) For info on USC, visit the **University of South Carolina Visitors Center,** 816 Bull St. (☎777-0169 or 800-922-9755. Open M-F 8:30am-5pm, Sa 11am-3pm. Free parking.) **Medical Services: Palmetto Richland Memorial Hospital,** 5 Richland Medical Park. (☎434-7000.) **Internet Access: Richland County Public Library,** 1431 Assembly St. (☎799-9084. 1hr. free per day. Open M-Th 9am-9pm, F-Sa 9am-6pm, Su 2-6pm.) **Post Office:** 1601 Assembly St. (☎733-4643. Open M-F 7:30am-6pm.) **Postal Code:** 29201. **Area Code:** 803.

⌐ ACCOMMODATIONS. Generally, the cheapest digs lie farthest from the city center. A short drive from downtown, the **Masters Inn ❷,** 613 Knox Abbott Dr., has great rates and offers spacious, modern rooms with free local calls, microwaves, mini-fridges, a pool, and cable TV. Take Blossom St. across the Congaree River, where it becomes Knox Abbott Dr. (☎796-4300. Rooms $36-48. AmEx/D/DC/MC/V.) If the Masters Inn is full, a good alternative is the nearby **Riverside Inn ❷,** 111 Knox Abbott Dr., which provides large, well-furnished rooms with free local calls, a coffee maker, cable, A/C, a pool, and continental breakfast. (☎939-4688. Singles $55; doubles $60. AAA and AARP discount 10%. AmEx/D/DC/MC/V.) Inexpensive motels also line the three interstates (I-26, I-77, and I-20) that circle the city. Rooms at the **Knights Inn ❷,** 1987 Airport Blvd., Exit 113 off I-26, have refrigerators, microwaves, cable TV, A/C, free local calls, and pool access; some have kitchenettes. (☎794-0222. Singles and doubles M-Th and Su $38, F-Sa $42. Senior discount 10%. AmEx/D/DC/MC/V.) The 1400 acres of **Sesquicentennial State Park ❶** include swimming and fishing, a nature center, hiking trails, and 84 wooded campsites with electricity and water. Public transit does not serve the park; take I-20 to Two Notch Rd./U.S. 1, Exit 17, and head 3 mi. northeast. (☎788-2706. Open daily Apr.-Oct. 7am-9pm; Nov.-Mar. 8am-6pm. Campsites M-Th and Su $16, F-Sa $18. Entrance ages 16+ $2, ages 65+ $1.25. D/MC/V.)

◘ FOOD. It's little wonder that **Maurice's Gourmet Barbecue ❶,** 800 Elmwood Ave. and 10 other SC locations, holds the world record for "most BBQ sold in one day." Maurice's cash "pig" is his exquisite, mustard-based sauce, which smothers the $5.50 Big Joe pork barbecue sandwich. (☎256-4377. Open M-Th 10am-9pm, F-Sa 10am-10pm. AmEx/D/DC/MC/V.) Gamecocks past and present give highest marks to **Groucho's ❷,** 611 Harden St., where the famous "dipper" sandwiches (from $6) have been delighting patrons for over 60 years. (☎799-5708. Open M-Sa 11am-4pm. AmEx/MC/V.) Charge over to the upscale **Rhino Room ❹,** 807 Gervais St., for some of the best food in town; try the Fettuccini Gervais (chicken, bacon, red onions, and spinach in a white wine cream sauce; $15). Patrons often glimpse politicians on their lunch or dinner breaks. (☎931-0700. Lunch Tu-F 11:30am-2pm. Dinner May-July M-Sa 5:30pm-1am; Aug.-Apr. M-Sa 5:30-11pm. AmEx/D/MC/V.) The popular, funky **Hunter Gatherer ❸,** 900 Main St., offers a variety of tasty sandwiches, pizzas, and entrees, in addition to home-brewed beer. (☎748-0540. Sandwiches and pizzas $6-10. Entrees $10-16. Beer $3.50. Open Tu-Sa 4-11pm; bar open until midnight. Jazz night Th. AmEx/D/MC/V.)

◙ SIGHTS. Bronze stars mark the impact of Sherman's cannonballs on the **Statehouse,** 1100 Gervais St., an Italian Renaissance high-rise. Home to South Carolina's governmental proceedings, it also holds the state's two most prized symbols—the Senate Sword and a British mace, both of which reflect the rebellious reputation of Carolinians. Survey the surrounding grounds, which have monuments and sculptures scattered throughout lush and tranquil gardens. (☎734-2430. Open M-F 9am-5pm, Sa 10am-5pm; 1st Su each month 1-5pm. Free tours available. Wheelchair accessible.) Across Sumter St. from the Statehouse is the central green of the USC campus—the **Horseshoe.** Here, students play frisbee, sunbathe, study, and nap beneath a canopy of trees. At the head of the green, **McKissick Museum,** 816 Bull St., explores the folklore of South Carolina and the Southeast through history, art, and science. (☎777-7251; www.cla.sc.edu/mcks. Open M-F 8:30am-5pm, Sa 11am-3pm. Free.) The **South Carolina Confederate Relic Room and Museum,** 301 Gervais St., traces South Carolina's military history and contains an exhaustive collection of Civil War artifacts and displays. (☎737-8095; www.state.sc.us/crr. Open Tu-Sa 10am-5pm. $3, under 21 free. Wheelchair accessible.) Two 19th-century mansions, the **Robert Mills Historic House and Park** and the **Hampton-Preston Mansion,** 1616 and 1615 Blanding St., two blocks east of Bull St., compete as examples of antebellum opulence and are both survivors of Sherman's Civil War rampage. Both have been lovingly restored with period fineries. For a broader experience of 19th-century life, stop by the **Manns-Simons Cottage,** 1403 Richland St., once owned by a freed slave, and the **Woodrow Wilson Boyhood Home,** 1705 Hampton St. (☎252-1770; www.historiccolumbia.org. Tours every hr. Tu-Sa 10am-3pm, Su 1-4pm. Tours $5; students, ages 65+, military, and AAA $4; ages 6-17 $3; under 6 free. Combo tickets with tours of all 4 houses $18/$14/$10. Buy all tickets at Mills House Museum Shop.) One of the top 10 zoos in the country, **Riverbanks Zoo and Garden,** on I-126 at Greystone Blvd., northwest of downtown, recreates natural habitats that house over 2000 species. After ogling the adorable koalas and wallabies at the Koala Knockabout, check out the zoo's newest addition—hyenas. (☎779-8717; www.riverbanks.org. Open mid-Apr. to mid-Oct. M-F 9am-4:45pm, Sa-Su 9am-5:45pm; mid-Oct. to mid-Apr. M-F 9am-4pm, Sa-Su 9am-5pm. $8.75, students $7.50, ages 62+ $7.25, ages 3-12 $6.25.)

🎵 **NIGHTLIFE.** Columbia's nightlife centers around the collegiate **Five Points District,** at Harden and Devine St., and the slightly more mature **Vista** area, on Gervais St. before the Congaree River. The weekly publication *Free Times* gives details on Columbia's club and nightlife scene. *In Unison* is a weekly paper listing gay-friendly nightspots. In the Vista, the **Art Bar,** 1211 Park St., attracts a funky crowd to match its ambience. Glow paint, Christmas lights, 1950s bar stools, and a troop of life-sized plastic robots are complemented by an eclectic music line-up. (☎929-0198. Open M-F 8pm-late, Sa-Su 8pm-2am.) The oldest bar in Columbia, **Group Therapy,** 2107 Greene St., helps locals drown their sorrows the old-fashioned way; try the Mullet (warm Jack Daniel's with a touch of Budweiser; $8.50) and you'll never need to see a shrink again. (☎256-1203. Open daily 4:30pm-late.) Across the street, and a bit more uplifting, is **Billy's,** 749 Saluda Ave. A suave local crowd shoots pool, smokes stogies, and downs drinks in this dark den. (☎758-0700. Open M-F 5pm-late, Sa 5pm-2am, Su 9pm-2am.) A popular late-night spot, **Bar None,** 620 Harden St., features shuffleboard. (☎254-3354. Open M-F 3pm-6am, Sa-Su noon-2am.)

MYRTLE BEACH AND THE GRAND STRAND ☎843

Each summer, millions of Harley-riding, RV-driving Southerners make Myrtle Beach the second-most-popular summer tourist destination in the country. During spring break and early June, Myrtle Beach is jammed with students looking for a good time. The rest of the year, families, golfers, and shoppers partake in the unapologetic tackiness of the town's themed restaurants, amusement parks, and shops. The pace slows significantly on the rest of the 60 mi. Grand Strand. South of Myrtle Beach, Murrell's Inlet is the place to go for good seafood, Pawley's Island is lined with beach cottages and beautiful private homes, and Georgetown showcases white-pillared 18th-century-style rice and indigo plantation homes.

THE SOUTH

■ 🔁 **ORIENTATION AND PRACTICAL INFORMATION.** Most attractions are on **Kings Highway (Route 17),** which splits into a business route and a bypass 4 mi. south of Myrtle Beach. **Ocean Boulevard** runs along the ocean, flanked on either side by cheap pastel motels. Avenue numbers repeat after reaching 1st Ave. in the middle of town; note whether the Ave. is "north" or "south." Take care not to confuse north **Myrtle Beach** with the town **North Myrtle Beach,** which has an almost identical street layout. **Route 501** runs west toward Conway, **I-95,** and the factory outlet stores. Unless otherwise stated, addresses on the Grand Strand are for Myrtle Beach. **Greyhound,** 511 7th Ave. N (☎ 448-2471; www.greyhound.com; open M-F 10am-1pm and 3:30pm-6:45pm, Sa-Su 10am-1pm and 4pm-6:45pm), runs buses once daily to: Atlanta (10hr., $58); Charleston (3hr., $28); Columbia (4½hr., $38.50); New York City (17hr., $95); Washington D.C. (12hr., $70). **The Waccamaw Regional Transportation Authority (WRTA),** 1418 3rd Ave., provides minimal busing; pick up a copy of schedules and routes from the Chamber of Commerce or from area businesses. (☎ 488-0865. Runs daily 5am-2am. Local fares $0.75-2.) WRTA also operates the **Ocean Boulevard Lymo,** which shuttles tourists up and down the main drag. (☎ 488-0865. Runs daily 8am-2am. $2 each way.) Rent bikes at **The Bike Shoppe,** 715 Broadway, at Main St. (☎ 448-5335. Beach cruisers $5 per half-day, $10 per day; mountain bikes $8/$15. Open M-F 8am-6pm, Sa 8am-5pm.) **Visitor Info: Myrtle Beach Chamber of Commerce,** 1200 N. Oak St., parallel to Kings Hwy., at 12th Ave. N. (☎ 626-7444; www.myrtlebeachinfo.com. Open M-F 8:30am-5pm, Sa-Su 9am-5pm.) **Medical Services: Grand Strand Regional Medical Center,** 809 82nd Pkwy. (☎ 692-1000). **Internet Access: Chapin Memorial Library,** 400 14th Ave. N. (☎ 918-1275. 2hr. limit per day. Visitors must purchase an $8 library card to use the Internet. Open M and W 9am-6pm, Tu and Th 9am-8pm, F-Sa 9am-5pm; in summer Sa 9am-1pm.) **Post Office:** 505 N. Kings Hwy., at 5th Ave. N. (☎ 626-9533. Open M-F 8:30am-5pm, Sa 9am-1pm.) **Postal Code:** 29577. **Area Code:** 843.

🔆 **ACCOMMODATIONS.** Hundreds of motels line Ocean Blvd., with those on the ocean side fetching higher prices than those across the street. Cheap motels also dot Rte. 17. From October to March, prices plummet as low as $20-30 a night for the luxurious hotels right on the beach. Call the **Myrtle Beach Lodging Reservation Service,** 1551 21st Ave. N., #20, for free help with reservations. (☎ 626-9970 or 800-626-7477. Open M-F 8:30am-5pm.) Across the street from the ocean, the family-owned **Sea Banks Motor Inn ❷,** 2200 S. Ocean Blvd., has immaculate rooms with mini-fridges, cable TV, laundry, and pool and beach access. (☎ 448-2434 or 800-523-0603; www.seabanks.com. Mid-Mar. to mid-Sept. singles $34-48; doubles $43-78. Mid-Sept. to mid-Mar. $22-28/$26-33. MC/V.) The **Hurl Rock Motel ❷,** 2010 S. Ocean Blvd., has big, clean rooms with access to a pool and hot tub. (☎ 626-3531 or 888-487-5762; www.hurlrockmotel.com. 25+; couples 21+. High-season singles $37-47; doubles $54-64. Low season $29/$37. AmEx/D/MC/V.) The **Coral Sands Motel ❷,** 301 N. Ocean Blvd., is close to the Pavilion and Family Kingdom amusement parks and has small rooms with cable TV, A/C, fridges, and microwaves. (☎ 448-3584 or 800-248-9779. Singles $40; doubles $50. Winter rates $25/$35. AARP discount 5% in summer. D/MC/V.) **Huntington Beach State Park Campground ❶,** 3 mi. south of Murrell's Inlet on U.S. 17, is located in a diverse environment including lagoons, salt marshes, and a beach; campsites are situated around a mostly open field as well as in a more wooded area. (☎ 237-4440, reservations 866-3455-7275. Open daily Apr.-Oct. 6am-10pm; Nov.-Mar. 6am-6pm. Tent sites Apr.-Oct. $20, water and electricity $25, full hookup $28. Nov.-Mar. $15/$20/$22. Day-use $4.)

🍽 **FOOD.** The Grand Strand offers hungry motorists over 1800 restaurants serving every type of food in every imaginable setting. Massive family-style all-you-can-eat joints beckon from beneath the glow of each traffic light. **Route 17** offers countless steakhouses, seafood buffets, and fast-food joints. Seafood, however, is best on **Murrell's Inlet**. With license plates adorning the walls and discarded peanut shells crunching underfoot, the **River City Cafe ❶**, 404 21st Ave. N., celebrates a brand of American informality bordering on delinquency. Peruse the patrons' signatures on tables and walls as you polish off a burger ($3-6) or knock back a $2 beer. (☎448-1990. Open daily 11am-10pm. D/MC/V.) While most of the restaurants in the Broadway at the Beach entertainment complex (see below) seem to sacrifice quality for elaborate decor, **Amici's ❸**, in the "Caribbean Village" section, serves delightful stuffed shells ($10) and calzones ($7) that will make you forget the screaming children and blaring lights outside. (☎444-0006. Open daily 11am-10:30pm. D/MC/V.) Take a break from Ocean Dr. at **Dagwood's Deli ❷**, 400 11th Ave. N., where beach bums and businessmen come together to enjoy a "Shag" (ham, turkey, and swiss cheese; $8), reminiscent of the monster sandwiches from the comic strip. (☎448-0100. Sandwiches $5-8. Open M-Sa 11am-6pm.) If you're looking for country cookin' on the beach, **Caroline's Cafe ❷**, 1709 N. Ocean Blvd., has all-you-can-eat breakfast and lunch buffets with stewed apples, fried bacon, and other South Carolinian fare. (☎626-5926. Open daily 6am-2pm. MC/V.)

◻◼ SIGHTS AND NIGHTLIFE. The boulevard and the beach are both "the strand," where fashionable teens strut their stuff, low-riders cruise the streets, and beachgoers showcase their sunburns. Never pay full price for any attraction in Myrtle Beach; pick up a copy of the *Monster Coupon Book, Sunny Day Guide, Myrtle Beach Guide,* or *Strand Magazine* at any tourist info center or hotel.

The colossal **Broadway at the Beach**, Rte. 17 Bypass and 21st Ave. N. (☎444-3200 or 800-386-4662), is a sprawling 350-acre complex designed to entertain with shops and theaters, a waterpark, mini-golf, 20 restaurants, nightclubs, and other attractions. In Broadway's **Ripley's Aquarium**, guests roam through a 330 ft. underwater tunnel and gaze upward at the ferocious sharks and terrifying piranha swimming above. (☎916-0888 or 800-734-8888; www.ripleysaquarium.com. Open daily 9am-11pm. $17, ages 5-11 $10, ages 2-4 $4. Wheelchair accessible.) The reptile capital of the world is ◩**Alligator Adventure**, 4604 Rte. 17 in North Myrtle Beach at Barefoot Landing, where fans are mesmerized by the exotic collection of snakes, lizards, and frogs and the hourly gator feedings. Don't miss the park's 20 ft., 2000 lb. resident, Utan—the world's largest captive croc. (☎361-0789; www.alligatoradventure.com. Open daily June-Aug. 9am-11pm; call for low-season hours. $15, seniors $13, ages 4-12 $10. Wheelchair accessible.)

The **NASCAR Speedpark**, across from Broadway at the Beach at 1820 N. 21st St., provides seven tracks of varying difficulty levels, catering to the need for speed. (☎918-8725. Open daily 10am-11pm. Unlimited rides $25, under 13 $15.) The 9100-acre **Brookgreen Gardens**, 1931 Brookgreen Dr., off Rte. 17 opposite Huntington Beach State Park, south of Murrell's Inlet, provides a respite from the touristy tackiness that dominates Myrtle Beach. Over 500 American sculptures are scattered beneath massive oaks. Guided tours of the gardens and wildlife trail are offered in addition to summer drama, music, and food programs. (☎235-6000; www.brookgreen.org. Open mid-June to mid-Aug. M-Tu and Sa-Su 9:30am-5pm, W-F 9:30am-9pm; mid-Aug. to mid-June daily 9:30am-5pm. 7-day pass $12, seniors and ages 13-18 $10, 12 and under free. Wheelchair accessible.)

For a night on the town, the New Orleans-style nightclub district **Celebrity Square**, at Broadway at the Beach, facilitates stepping out with 10 nightclubs, ranging from classic rock to Latin. Elsewhere, **2001**, 920 Lake Arrowhead Rd. off Rte. 17 just south of North Myrtle Beach, brings party-goers two clubs under one roof. (☎449-9434. 21+. Cover varies. Open daily 8pm-2am.) The **Freaky Tiki** caters to wild college crowds. (☎445-2582; www.freakytiki.com. 18+. Cover $10, ladies free 8-10pm. Open M-F 8pm-3am, Sa-Su 8pm-2am.)

GEORGIA

Georgia has many faces; the rural southern region contrasts starkly with the sprawling commercialism of the north. Atlanta packs the punch of a booming metropolis, while Savannah fosters a distinctively antebellum atmosphere and collegiate Athens breeds "big" bands. Perhaps nowhere are the state's contrasting natures as evident as at Cumberland Island, where deserted beaches and marshes lie just hundreds of yards from the ruins of Gilded Age mansions. In this state of contradictions, only one thing remains constant: enduring Southern hospitality.

■ PRACTICAL INFORMATION

Capital: Atlanta.

Visitor Info: Georgia Department of Economic Development, Tourism Division, 75 5th St. Ste. 1200 Technology Sq., Atlanta 30308 (☎404-962-4000 or 800-847-4842; www.georgia.org). **Department of Natural Resources,** 2 Martin Luther King, Jr. Dr. SE, Ste. 1252 East Tower, Atlanta 30334 (☎404-656-3500).

Postal Abbreviation: GA. **Sales Tax:** 4-7%, depending on county.

ATLANTA   ☎404

An increasingly popular destination for recent college grads wary of fast-paced cities, Atlanta is cosmopolitan with a smile. Northerners, Californians, the third-largest gay population in the US, and a host of ethnic groups have diversified this unofficial capital of the South, modifying its distinctly Dixie feel. An economic powerhouse, Atlanta houses 400 of the Fortune 500 companies, including the headquarters of Coca-Cola, UPS, and CNN. Nineteen colleges, including Georgia Tech, Morehouse College, Spelman College, and Emory University, also call "Hotlanta" home. The city is equally blessed with hidden gems; touring Atlanta's streets reveals an endless number of delightful restaurants and beautiful old houses.

■ INTERCITY TRANSPORTATION

Airport: Hartsfield International Airport (☎209-1700; www.atlanta-airport.com), off I-85 south of the city. MARTA (see **Public Transit,** p. 376) goes downtown, with rides departing from the Airport Station (15min., every 8min. daily 5am-1am, $1.75).

Atlanta Airport Shuttle (☎524-3400) runs vans from the airport to over 100 locations in the metropolitan area and outlying areas (every 15min. daily 7am-midnight, shuttle to downtown $16). Taxi to downtown $20.

Trains: Amtrak, 1688 Peachtree St. NW (☎800-872-7245; www.amtrak.com), 3 mi. north of downtown at I-85, or 1 mi. north of Ponce de Leon on Peachtree St. Take bus #23 from MARTA: Arts Center. Open daily 7:30am-10pm. Trains go to **New Orleans** (11½hr., 1 per day, $50) and **New York City** (18hr., 1-3 per day, $162-203).

Buses: Greyhound, 232 Forsyth St. SW (☎584-1728; www.greyhound.com), across from MARTA: Garnett. Open 24hr. To **New York City** (19-23hr., 14 per day, $95-99), **Savannah** (5hr., 6 per day, $39-45), and **Washington, D.C.** (14-19hr., 14 per day, $79).

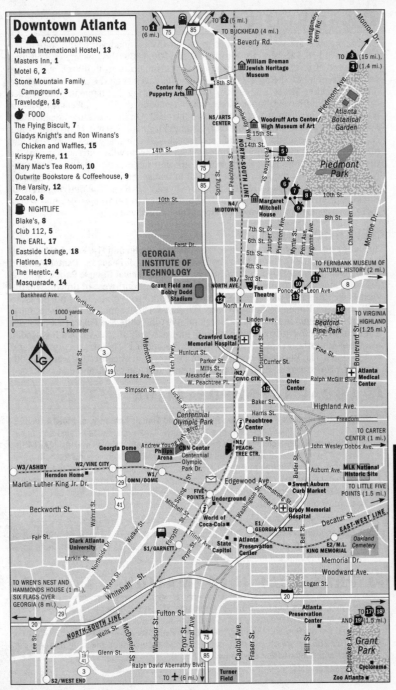

Downtown Atlanta

🏠 🏠 ACCOMMODATIONS
Atlanta International Hostel, **13**
Masters Inn, **1**
Motel 6, **2**
Stone Mountain Family
  Campground, **3**
Travelodge, **16**

🍴 FOOD
The Flying Biscuit, **7**
Gladys Knight's and Ron Winans's
  Chicken and Waffles, **15**
Krispy Kreme, **11**
Mary Mac's Tea Room, **10**
Outwrite Bookstore & Coffeehouse, **9**
The Varsity, **12**
Zocalo, **6**

🍸 NIGHTLIFE
Blake's, **8**
Club 112, **5**
The EARL, **17**
Eastside Lounge, **18**
Flatiron, **19**
The Heretic, **4**
Masquerade, **14**

TO ■1 (6 mi.)
TO ■2 (5 mi.)
TO BUCKHEAD (4 mi.)
Beverly Rd.

Montgomery Ferry Rd.
Monroe Dr.

TO ■3 (15 mi.),
■4 (1.4 mi.)

William Breman
Jewish Heritage
Museum

Center for
Puppetry Arts
18th St.

Piedmont Ave.

Atlanta
Botanical
Garden

N5/ARTS
CENTER

Woodruff Arts Center/
High Museum of Art
15th St.

Piedmont
Park

14th St.
14th St.
12th St.
■5

W. Peachtree St.
Peachtree St.
NORTH SOUTH LINE

10th St.
■6
■7
■8
■9

Spring St.

N4/
MIDTOWN
Margaret
Mitchell
House
10th St.

8th St.

Charles Allen Dr.

Monroe Dr.

10th St.

Juniper St.
Piedmont Ave.
Myrtle St.
Penn Ave.
Argonne Ave.

GEORGIA
INSTITUTE OF
TECHNOLOGY

Ferst Dr.

7th St.
6th St.
5th St.
4th St.
3rd St.
N3/
NORTH AVE.
Fox
Theatre
Ponce de Leon Ave.
■10
■13
■11
TO FERNBANK MUSEUM OF
NATURAL HISTORY (2 mi.)
■8

Grant Field and
Bobby Dodd
Stadium
■12
North Ave.

Linden Ave.
■15

Bedford
Pine Park

■14
TO VIRGINIA
HIGHLAND
(1.25 mi.)

Bankhead Ave.
Northside Dr.

0   1000 yards
0   1 kilometer

N
LG

Vine St.
■3
■19
Marietta St.
Tech Pkwy.
Luckie St.

Crawford Long
Memorial Hospital
Hunicut St.
Parker St.
Mills St.
Alexander St.
W. Peachtree Pl.

N2/
CIVIC CTR.

Courtland St.
Currier St.
Pine St.

Boulevard St.

Ralph McGill Blvd.
Atlanta
Medical
Center

Jones Ave.
Simpson St.

Baker St.
■16
Civic
Center

Highland Ave.

Harris St.
Centennial
Olympic Park

Peachtree
Center
Freedom

TO CARTER
CENTER (1 mi.)
John Wesley Dobbs Ave.

Georgia Dome
Andrew Young Intl. Blvd.
Philips
Arena
CNN Center
Centennial
Olympic
Park Dr.

Ellis St.
N1/
PEACH-
TREE CTR.

Butler St.

Auburn Ave.
MLK National
Historic Site

W3/ASHBY
W2/VINE CITY
Herndon Home
Martin Luther King Jr. Dr.

W1/
OMNI/DOME
29

Edgewood Ave.
Sweet Auburn
Curb Market

TO LITTLE FIVE
POINTS (1.5 mi.)

Beckworth St.

Spring St.
Mitchell St.
FIVE
POINTS
Underground
World of
Coca-Cola

Armstrong St.
Gilmer St.
Washington St.
Grady Memorial
Hospital

Decatur St.
EAST-WEST LINE

Oakland
Cemetery

Fair St.

Clark Atlanta
University
Larkin St.

Walker St.
Walnut St.
Northside Dr.
41

S1/GARNETT
Forsyth St.
Trinity Ave.
Pryor St.
State
Capitol
Atlanta
Preservation
Center
E1/
GEORGIA STATE

Bell St.

E2/M.L.
KING MEMORIAL

Memorial Dr.
Woodward Ave.

TO WREN'S NEST AND
HAMMONDS HOUSE (1 mi.),
SIX FLAGS OVER
GEORGIA (8 mi.)

20
29

Peters St.
Whitehall St.
Windsor St.
Pryor St.
Central Ave.

Capitol Ave.
Fraser St.
Logan St.

Hill St.

Cherokee Ave.

Grant
Park

NORTH-SOUTH LINE

Fulton St.

75
85

Atlanta
Preservation
Center
TO ■17 ■18
AND ■19 (1.5 mi.)

Lee St.
19
41
Wells St.
McDaniel St.
Glenn St.
S2/WEST END
Ralph David Abernathy Blvd.
TO ✈ (6 mi.)
Turner
Field
20

Cyclorama
Zoo Atlanta

✈ ORIENTATION

Atlanta sprawls across ten counties in the northwest quadrant of the state at the junctures of **I-75, I-85** (the city "thruway"), and **I-20. I-285** (the "perimeter") circumscribes the city. Maneuvering around Atlanta's main thoroughfares, which are arranged much like the spokes of a wheel, challenges even the most experienced native. **Peachtree Street** (one of over 100 streets bearing that name in Atlanta), is a major north-south road; **Spring Street,** which runs only south, and **Piedmont Avenue,** which runs only north, are parallel to Peachtree St. On the eastern edge, **Moreland Avenue** traverses the length of the city, through Virginia Highland, Little Five Points (L5P), and East Atlanta. **Ponce de Leon Avenue** is the primary east-west road and takes travelers to most major destinations (or intersects with a street that can). To the south of "Ponce" runs **North Avenue,** another major east-west thoroughfare. Navigating Atlanta requires a full arsenal of transportation strategies. Midtown and downtown attractions are best explored using MARTA. The outlying areas of Buckhead, Virginia Highlands, and L5P are easiest to get to by car; once you're there, the restaurant- and bar-lined streets encourage walking.

NEIGHBORHOODS

Sprouting out of downtown Atlanta, the **Peachtree Center** and **Five Points MARTA** stations deliver hordes of tourists to shopping and dining at **Peachtree Center Mall** and **Underground Atlanta.** Downtown is also home to **Centennial Olympic Park** as well as Atlanta's major sports and concert venues. Directly southwest of downtown, the **West End** is the city's oldest historic quarter. From Five Points, head northeast to **Midtown,** from Ponce de Leon Ave. to 17th St., for museums and **Piedmont Park.** East of Five Points at Euclid and Moreland Ave., the **Little Five Points (L5P)** district is a local haven for artists and youth subculture. North of L5P, **Virginia Highland,** a trendy neighborhood east of Midtown and Piedmont Park, attracts yuppies and college kids. The **Buckhead** area, north of Midtown on Peachtree St., greets both Atlanta's professionals and its rappers, housing designer shops and dance clubs.

☰ LOCAL TRANSPORTATION

Public Transportation: Metropolitan Atlanta Rapid Transit Authority, or **MARTA** (☎848-4711; trains run daily 5am-1am, bus hours vary). Clean, uncrowded trains and buses provide hassle-free transportation to Atlanta's major attractions, making MARTA the "SMARTA" way to get around downtown. A $1.75 MARTA token is good for both trains and buses, as well as free transfers between either. Exact change or a token from a station machine needed. Unlimited weekly pass $13. Pick up a system map at the **MARTA Ride Store** (at Five Points Station downtown), or at the airport, Lindbergh, or Lenox stations. Most trains, rail stations, and buses are wheelchair accessible.

Taxi: Atlanta Yellow Cab, ☎521-0200. **Checker Cab,** ☎351-3179.

Car Rental: Atlanta Rent-a-Car, 3185 Camp Creek Pkwy., (☎763-1110). 2½ mi. east of the airport, just inside I-285. 3 other locations in the area. 21+ with major credit card. $27 per day, $0.24 per mi. over 100 mi.

⑦ PRACTICAL INFORMATION

Visitor Info: Visitors Center, 65 Upper Alabama St., on the upper level of Underground Atlanta. MARTA: Five Points. Open M-Sa 10am-6pm, Su noon-6pm. The **Atlanta Convention and Visitors Bureau,** 233 Peachtree St. NE, Peachtree Center #100 (☎521-6600 or 800-285-2682; www.atlanta.net), is geared toward convention planning but operates an automated **information service** (☎222-6688).

> **!** While recent efforts to beef up police presence in high-risk areas of the city are having an effect, travelers—especially women—should exercise caution in the area south of Freedom Pkwy. and especially the West End. Additionally, be aware that panhandlers throughout the city can be quite verbally aggressive.

GLBT Resources: Gay Yellow Pages (☎892-6454; www.atlantagaypages.com).

Hotlines: Rape Crisis Counseling, ☎616-4861. 24hr.

Medical Services: Piedmont Hospital, 1968 Peachtree Rd. NW (☎605-5000).

Internet Access: Central Library, 1 Margaret Mitchell Sq. (☎730-1700). Open M-Th 9am-9pm, F-Sa 9am-6pm, Su 2-6pm. Free.

Post Office: Phoenix Station (☎524-2960), at the corner of Forsyth and Marietta St., 1 block from MARTA: Five Points. Open M-F 9am-5pm. **Postal Code:** 30303. **Area Code:** 404 inside the I-285 perimeter, 770 outside. In text, 404 unless otherwise noted.

꙰ ACCOMMODATIONS

▧ **Atlanta International Hostel,** 223 Ponce de Leon Ave. (☎875-9449 or 800-473-9449; www.hostel-atlanta.com), in Midtown. From MARTA: North Ave., exit onto Ponce de Leon and walk 3½ blocks east to Myrtle St., or take bus #2. Look for the "Woodruff Inn: Bed and Breakfast" sign. This family-owned establishment has immaculate dorms in a home with TV, pool table, and kitchen. Internet $1 per 10min. Free lockers. No sleeping bags allowed. Towels $1. Dorms $21; private rooms $39-58. AmEx/D/DC/MC/V. ❶

Masters Inn, 2682 Windy Hill Rd. (☎770-951-2005), Exit 260 off I-75 in Marietta. Standard, clean rooms. Cable TV, A/C. Singles from $36; doubles $40. AmEx/D/DC/MC/V. ❷

The Highland Inn, 644 N. Highland Ave. NE (☎874-5756; www.thehighlandinn.com). Built in 1927 and renovated for the 1996 Olympics, this hotel has over 80 uniquely decorated rooms with A/C, cable TV, and mini-fridges. Continental breakfast. Reception 24hr. Rooms $70-106. AAA and AARP discount 10%. AmEx/MC/V. ❸

Travelodge, 311 Courtland St. NE (☎659-4545; www.atlantatravelodge.com), in the heart of downtown Atlanta. Clean rooms in a central location. A/C, cable TV, pool, continental breakfast. Free parking and a friendly desk staff. Rates vary in summer; call ahead for reservations. Singles $80, doubles $90. AmEx/D/DC/MC/V. ❸

Motel 6, 2820 Chamblee Tucker Rd. (☎770-458-6626), Exit 94 off I-85 in Doraville. Spacious, tidy rooms. Free local calls, cable TV, and A/C. Singles $46, doubles $50. Be cautious in this area, especially if you are traveling alone. AmEx/D/MC/V. ❷

Stone Mountain Family Campground (☎770-498-5710), on U.S. 78. Far from the commotion of the city, this campground has stunning sites, bike rentals, and a free laser show. Wireless Internet access available for a fee. Max. stay 2 weeks. Sites $22-29. Full hookup $32-49. Entrance fee $8 per car. AmEx/D/MC/V. ❶

ꙩ FOOD

From Vietnamese to Italian, fried to fricasseed, Atlanta cooks options for any craving, but "soul food" nourishes the city. Head to "Chicken and Waffles" restaurants for the uncommon and terrific combination. A depot for soul food's raw materials since 1923, the **Sweet Auburn Curb Market,** 209 Edgewood Ave., has an eye-popping assortment of goodies, from cow's feet to oxtails. (☎659-1665. Open M-Th 8am-6pm, F-Sa 8am-7pm.) For sweet treats, you can't beat the Atlanta-based **Krispy Kreme Doughnuts,** whose glazed delights ($0.79-0.89) are a Southern institution. The factory store, 295 Ponce de Leon Ave. NE (☎876-7307), continuously bakes their wares. (Open M-Th and Su 5:30am-midnight, F-Sa 24hr.; drive-through 24hr.)

THE SOUTH

BUCKHEAD

Fellini's Pizza, 2809 Peachtree Rd. NE (☎266-0082). 3 watchful gargoyles and an angel welcome customers into this pizzeria, the flagship of 5 Atlanta locations, complete with a spacious deck and mouth-watering pizza. If Hotlanta has become too warm, enjoy your slice (from $1.65) or pie ($10.50-19) inside, where classic rock is combined with a romantic atmosphere. Open M-Sa 11am-2am, Su noon-midnight. MC/V. ❶

The Shipfeifer, 1814 Peachtree Rd. (☎875-1106). The Shipfeifer serves up fresh Mediterranean and vegetarian food at reasonable prices. Entrees $8.25-10. Wraps $5-7. Quesadillas and burritos $4.50-6.50. Open M-Th and Su 11am-10pm, F 11am-10:30pm, Sa 11am-11pm. AmEx/D/MC/V. ❷

MIDTOWN

▨ **Gladys Knight's and Ron Winans's Chicken and Waffles,** 529 Peachtree St. (☎874-9393). MARTA: North Ave. Situated on the southern border of Midtown, this upscale but reasonably priced joint screams "soul" with incredible dishes like the Midnight Train (4 southern-fried chicken wings and a waffle; $8.75). Among the side dishes are collard greens, cinnamon raisin toast, and corn muffins. Open M-Th 11am-11pm, F-Sa 11am-4am, Su 11am-8pm. AmEx/D/DC/MC/V. ❷

Eats, 600 Ponce de Leon Ave. (☎888-9149). Quickly whips up terrific pasta, meat, and vegetables for amazingly low prices. Meat and vegetable plates $3.50-7. Pasta from $3.75. Takeout available. Open daily 11am-10pm. Cash only. ❶

The Varsity, 61 North Ave. NW (☎881-1706), at Spring St. MARTA: North Ave. Established in 1928, The Varsity claims to be the world's largest drive-in restaurant. Subject of a landmark Supreme Court ruling in the 1960s abolishing racial segregation in restaurants, The Varsity has since delighted patrons with cheap and delicious hamburgers ($1.10), classic Coke floats ($2.30), and famous onion rings ($1.50). Open M-Th and Su 10am-11:30pm, F-Sa 10am-12:30am. Cash only. ❶

Mary Mac's Tea Room, 224 Ponce de Leon Ave. (☎876-1800), at Myrtle. MARTA: North Ave. Whether you're sipping the house specialty tea ($1.25) or enjoying the baked turkey, you'll appreciate the stellar service, charming tea rooms, and elegant dining hall. Entrees ($8.75-9.75) come with 2 side dishes. Open daily 11am-9pm. AmEx/MC/V. ❸

10TH STREET

The Flying Biscuit, 1001 Piedmont Ave. (☎874-8887). Packed with loyal patrons, mostly professionals and families, the Flying Biscuit serves breakfast feasts. Enjoy the Flying Biscuit Breakfast ($6.50) and the signature Delio (double espresso mochaccino; $3.59). Open M-Th and Su 7am-10pm, F-Sa 7am-10:30pm. AmEx/MC/V. ❷

Outwrite Bookstore and Coffeehouse, 991 Piedmont Ave. (☎607-0082). Rainbow beach balls grace the windows at this unique gay-friendly establishment. A relaxed and stylish air with remarkably friendly service. Try the espresso specialty drink "Shot in the Dark" ($2). Open daily 10am-11pm. AmEx/D/MC/V. ❶

Zocalo, 187 10th St. (☎249-7576). Woven baskets, tequila advertisements, and cool patio seating, just like in Zihuatanejo. Some of the best margaritas in Atlanta and all the Mexican favorites. *Chiles rellenos* $10.50. Taquitos $9. Open M-Th 11am-11pm, F-Sa 11am-12am, Su 10am-10pm. AmEx/D/MC/V. ❸

VIRGINIA HIGHLAND

Doc Chey's, 1424 N. Highland Ave. (☎888-0777), serves heaping mounds of noodles at super prices. This pan-Asian restaurant is ultra-popular among young Atlanta locals. Try the delicious Chinese lo mein ($6) or the Marco Polo (shrimp, vegetables, and udon noodles in a zesty Thai sauce; $8), one of Doc's originals. Open M-Th and Su 11:30am-10pm, F-Sa 11:30am-11pm. AmEx/D/DC/MC/V. ❷

Everybody's, 1040 N. Highland Ave. (☎873-4545). Receives high accolades for selling Atlanta's best pizza. Inventive pizza salads with a colossal mound of greens and chicken on a pizza bed $12.50. Pizza sandwiches $8.50-9.50. Open M-Th 11:30am-11pm, F-Sa 11:30am-1am, Su noon-10:30pm. AmEx/D/DC/MC/V. ❸

Highland Tap, 1026 N. Highland Ave. (☎875-3673). Home of the best steaks in the Highlands; springing for the gorgonzola crust ($2.50) is well worth it. Happening bar scene on weekends. Steaks $12-28. Burgers $8.50. Lunch Tu-F 11:30am-3pm. Dinner M-Th and Su 5pm-midnight, F-Sa 5pm-1am. Brunch Sa-Su 11am-3pm. Bar open M-Sa 11:30am-3am, Su 12:30am-2am. AmEx/D/DC/MC/V. ❸

◉ SIGHTS

SWEET AUBURN DISTRICT

MARTIN LUTHER KING, JR. The most moving sights in the city run along Auburn Ave. in Sweet Auburn. The Reverend Martin Luther King, Jr.'s birthplace, church, and grave are all part of the 23-acre ■**Martin Luther King, Jr. National Historic Site.** The visitors center houses poignant displays of photographs, videos, and quotations oriented around King's life and the African-American struggle for civil rights. *(450 Auburn Ave. NE. MARTA: King Memorial. ☎331-5190; www.nps.gov/malu. Open daily June-Aug. 9am-6pm; Sept.-May 9am-5pm. Free.)* The center also gives tours of the Birth Home of MLK. *(501 Auburn Ave. Tours every 30min. June-Aug.; every hr. Sept.-May. Arrive early; reservations not accepted.)* Across the street from the visitors center stands **Ebenezer Baptist Church,** where King gave his first sermon at age 17 and co-pastored with his father from 1960 to 1968. *(407 Auburn Ave. ☎688-7263. Open June-Aug. M-Sa 9am-6pm, Su 1-6pm; Sept.-May M-Sa 9am-5pm, Su 1-5pm.)* Next door at the **Martin Luther King, Jr. Center for Nonviolent Social Exchange** lies a beautiful blue reflecting pool with an island on which King has been laid to rest in a white marble tomb. The center's Freedom Hall contains a collection of King's personal articles (including his Nobel Peace Prize medal), an overview of his role model, Gandhi, and an exhibit on Rosa Parks. *(449 Auburn Ave. NE. ☎526-8920. Open daily June-Aug. 9am-6pm; Sept.-May 9am-5pm. Free.)* In the surrounding area, plaques describing the architecture and past residents of this historic neighborhood line the streets.

DOWNTOWN VICINITY

WALKING TOURS. From March to November, the **Atlanta Preservation Center** offers walking tours of seven popular areas, including Druid Hills, the setting of the film *Driving Miss Daisy.* Other popular tour destinations include Inman Park, Atlanta's first trolley suburb, and Historic Downtown. *(327 St. Paul Ave. NE. ☎876-2041; www.preserveatlanta.com. $7, ages 60+ $6. Call ahead for wheelchair-accessible tours.)*

GRANT PARK CYCLORAMA. The world's largest painting (42 ft. tall and 358 ft. in circumference) is in Grant Park, directly south of Oakland Cemetery and Cherokee Ave. The 117-year-old Cyclorama takes visitors back in time, revolving them on a huge platform in the middle of the "1864 Battle of Atlanta." *(800 Cherokee Ave. SE. Take bus #97 from Five Points. MARTA: King Memorial. ☎624-1071. Open daily 8:50am-4:30pm. $6, seniors and students $5. Wheelchair accessible.)*

ZOO ATLANTA. Lions and tigers and...panda bears? This is one of only four zoos in the nation to exhibit rare giant pandas; when coupled with the East African lion and Sumatran tiger exhibits, the Atlanta Zoo will certainly provoke an "Oh my!" *(800 Cherokee Ave. SE. Take bus #97 from Five Points. ☎624-5600; www.zooatlanta.org. Open Apr.-Oct. M-F 9:30am-4:30pm, Sa-Su 9:30am-5:30pm; Nov.-Mar. daily 9:30am-4:30pm. $17, seniors $13, ages 3-11 $12. Wheelchair accessible.)*

THE SOUTH

STATE CAPITOL. On the corner of Washington and Mitchell St. is the **Georgia State Capitol Building,** a classical structure built in 1889 with Georgia's own natural resources: Cherokee marble, Georgian oak, and gold mined in Lumpkin County. Exhibits on the 4th floor detail Georgia's often tumultuous history. (☎ 463-4536; www.sos.state.ga.us. Call for tour availability. Open M-F 8am-5pm. Free.)

WORLD OF COCA-COLA (WOCC). Two blocks from the capitol, the World of Coca-Cola educates tourists on the rise of "the real thing" from its humble beginnings in Atlanta to its position of world domination. Uncap the secrets of Coke as you walk through two floors of Coca-Cola history and memorabilia, complete with a "soda jerk" demonstration and TVs that loop old Coca-Cola advertisements. The psychological barrage is so intense that even those with the strongest of willpowers will soon be craving a Coke. Luckily, visitors get to sample 46 flavors of Coke from around the world at the tour's end, from the long-lost Tab to Mozambique's "Krest." (55 Martin Luther King, Jr. Dr. MARTA: Five Points. ☎ 676-5151; www.woccatlanta.com. Open June-Aug. M-Sa 9am-6pm, Su 11am-5pm; Sept.-May M-Sa 9am-5pm, Su noon-5pm. $9, seniors $8, ages 4-11 $5, under 4 free. Wheelchair accessible.)

UNDERGROUND ATLANTA. Adjacent to the WOCC, this former railroad underpass is now a subterranean mall with over 120 restaurants, shops, and nightspots. Once a hot spot for alternative music, the underground now resembles a carnival-like labyrinth of marketing and merchandise. (Descend at the entrance beside the Five Points subway station. ☎ 523-2311. Shops open June-Sept. M-Sa 10am-9:30pm, Su 11am-7pm; Oct.-May M-Sa 10am-9pm, Su noon-6pm. Bars and restaurants close later.)

CNN. Overlooking beautiful Centennial Park is the global headquarters of the **Cable News Network (CNN).** Check out the 45min. studio tour, which reveals "the story behind the news." Sit inside a replica control room, learn the secrets of teleprompter magic, and peer into the renowned CNN newsroom. (At Centennial Olympic Park Dr. and Marietta St. MARTA: Omni/Dome/GWCC Station at W1. ☎ 827-2300; www.cnn.com/studiotour. Tours every 20min. daily 9am-5pm. $10, seniors $8, ages 4-12 $7. Wheelchair-accessible tours with 24hr. notice.)

OLYMPIC PARK. Amidst the commerce and concrete of bustling downtown Atlanta, you can find serenity at the **Centennial Olympic Park,** a 21-acre state park that is both a public recreation area and a lasting monument to the 1996 Olympic Games. Eight enormous torches and an array of flags (each representing a nation that has hosted one of the modern Olympic Games) surround the park's central feature, the **Fountain of Rings,** which enthralls (and soaks) children and adults alike. Check out one of the 20min. fountain shows (daily 12:30, 3:30, 6:30, 9pm) in which the water dances to symphonic melodies and dazzling lights. (265 Park Ave. West NW. MARTA: Peachtree Center. ☎ 222-7275; www.centennialpark.com. Park open daily 7am-11pm. Wheelchair accessible.)

CARTER PRESIDENTIAL CENTER. Just north of L5P, a charming garden and a circle of state flags surrounding the American flag welcome visitors to this museum, which relates the works, achievements, and events of Jimmy Carter's life and presidency. Attached to the museum, the **Jimmy Carter Library** serves as a depository for historic materials from the Carter Administration. (441 Freedom Pkwy. Take bus #16 to Cleburne Ave. ☎ 865-7101; www.jimmycarterlibrary.org. Museum open M-Sa 9am-4:45pm, Su noon-4:45pm; grounds open daily 6am-9pm. $7; students, seniors, and military $5; under 16 free. Wheelchair accessible.)

WEST END

AFRICAN-AMERICAN HISTORY. Dating from 1835, the West End is Atlanta's oldest neighborhood. A tour of the historic **Wren's Nest** offers a number of twists on the typical "historic home" tour. Home to author Joel Chandler Harris, who popularized the African folktale trickster Br'er Rabbit, the Wren's Nest offers a glimpse into middle-class life as it was at the beginning of the 20th century. *(1050 R.D. Abernathy Blvd. Take bus #71 from West End Station/S2. ☎ 753-7735. Open Tu-Sa 10am-2:30pm. Tours every hr. on the ½hr. $8, seniors and ages 13-19 $6, ages 4-12 $5. Wheelchair accessible.)* The **Hammonds House,** the home-turned-gallery of Dr. Otis Hammonds, a renowned African-American physician and art lover, displays unique contemporary and historic works in Georgia's only collection dedicated entirely to African-American and Haitian art. *(503 Peeples St. SW. ☎ 752-8730; www.hammondshouse.org. Open Tu-F 10am-6pm, Sa-Su 1-5pm. $4, children, students, and seniors $2. Wheelchair accessible.)* Born a slave, Alonzo F. Herndon founded Atlanta Life Insurance Co., eventually becoming Atlanta's wealthiest African-American in the early 1900s. A Beaux-Arts Classical mansion, the **Herndon Home** was built in 1910; today it is dedicated to the legacy of Herndon's philanthropy. *(587 University Pl. NW. Take bus #3 from Five Points station to the corner of Martin Luther King, Jr. Dr. and Maple, walk 1 block west, turn right on Walnut, and walk 1 block. ☎ 581-9813; www.herndonhome.org. Tours by appointment. $5, students $3. Wheelchair accessible.)*

MIDTOWN

WOODRUFF ARTS CENTER. Cultural connoisseurs, the **Woodruff Arts Center (WAC)** is your place. To the west of Piedmont Park, Richard Meier's award-winning buildings of glass, steel, and white porcelain are rivaled only by the treasures they contain. Within the WAC, the **High Museum of Art** features a rotation of incredible temporary exhibits; past exhibits have included the works of Pablo Picasso, Edgar Degas, Edward Hopper, and Ansel Adams. *(1280 Peachtree St. NE. MARTA: Arts Center; exit at Lombardy Way. WAC: ☎ 733-4200. High Museum of Art: ☎ 733-4400; www.high.org. Open Tu-Su 10am-5pm. $10, students with ID and seniors $8, ages 6-17 $6.)*

MARGARET MITCHELL HOUSE. Located between the 10th St. district and Midtown is the apartment where Mitchell wrote her Pulitzer Prize-winning novel, *Gone with the Wind.* Tour the house, and view her typewriter and autographed copies of the book. Across the street, the **Gone with the Wind Movie Museum** has memorabilia such as the door to Tara Plantation and the portrait of Scarlett at which Clark Gable hurled a cocktail onscreen—complete with stain. *(990 Peachtree St., at 10th St., adjacent to MARTA: Midtown. ☎ 249-7015; www.gwtw.org. Open daily 9:30am-5pm. 1hr. tours every hr. $12, students and seniors $9, ages 6-17 $5.)*

WILLIAM BREMAN JEWISH HERITAGE MUSEUM. The largest Jewish museum in the Southeast features a powerful Holocaust exhibit and a gallery tracing the history of Atlanta's Jewish community from 1845 to the present. *(1440 Spring St. NW. From MARTA: N5/Arts Center, walk 3 blocks north to 18th St. and Spring St. ☎ 873-1661; www.thebreman.org. Open M-Th 10am-5pm, F 10am-3pm, Su 1-5pm. $10, seniors $6, students $4, ages 3-6 $2, under 3 free. Wheelchair accessible.)*

CENTER FOR PUPPETRY ARTS. The complexity and sophistication of "puppeteering" will surprise and interest even those who haven't watched "The Muppet Show" in years. As it happens, the highlight of the tour is the Jim Henson exhibit, which showcases some of the puppet-master's most famous creations. *(1404 Spring St. NW, at 18th St. ☎ 873-3391; www.puppet.org. Open Tu-Sa 9am-5pm, Su 11am-5pm. $8, students and seniors $7, under 18 $6. Wheelchair accessible.)*

FERNBANK MUSEUM OF NATURAL HISTORY. Sporting outstanding dinosaur and sea-life exhibits, an IMAX theater, and interactive discovery centers, the Fernbank is one of the best science museums in the South. *(767 Clifton Rd. NE. Off Ponce de Leon Ave.; take bus #2 from North Ave. or Avondale Station. ☎ 929-6300; www.fernbank.edu/museum. Open M-Sa 10am-5pm, Su noon-5pm. Museum $12, students and* *seniors $11, ages 3-12 $10; IMAX film $10/$9/$8; both attractions $17/$15/$13. Wheelchair accessible.)* The adjacent **R.L. Staton Rose Garden** is free for all visitors and blossoms from spring until December. *(Corner of Ponce de Leon Ave. and Clifton Rd.)*

BUCKHEAD

A drive through **Buckhead,** north of Midtown and Piedmont Park, off Peachtree St. near W. Paces Ferry Rd., reveals Atlanta's Beverly Hills. The majority of these gaudy mansions were built by Coca-Cola bigwigs; the architectural style of this area has been aptly dubbed "Rococo-cola." The main drag along Peachtree Dr. is slowly turning from a hip yuppie hangout to that of a younger, and often unruly, crowd. The area, however, remains conducive to wining and dining and is strung with dance clubs and restaurants frequented by Atlanta's twentysomethings.

BUCKHEAD ATTRACTIONS. One of the most exquisite residences in the Southeast, the Greek Revival **Governor's Mansion** has elaborate gardens and one of the finest collections of furniture from the Federal Period. *(391 W. Paces Ferry Rd. ☎ 261-1776. Tours Tu-Th 10-11:30am. Free.)* In the same neighborhood, the **Atlanta History Center** traces Atlanta's development from a rural area to an international cityscape. Its Civil War Gallery spotlights the stories of both Confederate and Union soldiers, while the Folklife Gallery details Southern culture from grits to banjos. Also on the grounds are exquisite mansions from the early 20th century, including the **Swan House,** a lavish Anglo-Palladian Revival home built in 1928, and the **Tullie Smith Farm,** an 1845 Yeoman farmhouse. Abutting the homes, 33 acres of trails and gardens are perfect for an afternoon stroll. *(130 W. Paces Ferry Rd. NW. ☎ 814-4000; www.atlantahistorycenter.com. Open M-Sa 10am-5:30pm, Su noon-5:30pm. $12, students and seniors $10, ages 4-12 $7; house tours free with museum admission. Wheelchair accessible.)*

🎦 ENTERTAINMENT

For hassle-free fun, buy a MARTA pass (see **Local Transportation,** p. 376) and pick up the city's free publications on music and events. *Creative Loafing,* the *Hudspeth Report,* and "Leisure" in the Friday edition of the *Atlanta Journal and Constitution* contain the latest info and are available in most coffee shops and on street corners. Check for free summer concerts in Atlanta's parks.

The **Woodruff Arts Center** (see **Midtown,** p. 378) houses the Atlanta Symphony, the Alliance Theater Company, the Atlanta College of Art, and the High Museum of Art. **Atlantix,** 65 Upper Alabama St. and 3393 Peachtree Rd. NE at Lenox Sq., MARTA: Five Points, offers same-day, half-price rush tickets to dance, theater, music, and other attractions (walk-up service only). Full price advance tickets are available online. *(☎ 678-318-1400; www.atlantaperforms.com. Open Tu-Sa 11am-6pm, Su noon-4pm.)* The **Philips Arena,** 1 Philips Dr. *(☎ 878-3000),* hosts concerts, the **Atlanta Hawks** NBA team, and the **Atlanta Thrashers** NHL team. The pride and joy of Atlanta, the National League's **Atlanta Braves,** play at **Turner Field.** *(755 Hank Aaron Dr., MARTA: Georgia State, or take Braves Shuttle from Five Points. ☎ 522-7630; Ticketmaster 800-326-4000. Tickets $1-53.)* 1hr. tours of Turner Field include views of the diamond from the $200,000 skyboxes. *(☎ 614-2311. Open non-game days M-Sa 9am-3pm, Su 1-3pm; evening-game days M-Sa 9am-noon; no tours on afternoon or Su game days. $10, 13 and under $5.)* See the **Atlanta Falcons** play football at the **Georgia Dome,** MARTA: OMNI/Dome/World Congress Center, the world's largest cable-supported dome. *(☎ 223-8687. Open daily 10am-3pm. Tours available Tu-Sa on the hr., except during events; call ahead. $6, students and seniors $4.)*

Six Flags Over Georgia, 275 Riverside Pkwy., at I-20 W, is one of the largest amusement parks in the nation. Take bus #201 "Six Flags" from Hamilton Homes. Check out the 54 mph "Georgia Scorcher" roller coaster and the "Superman" roller

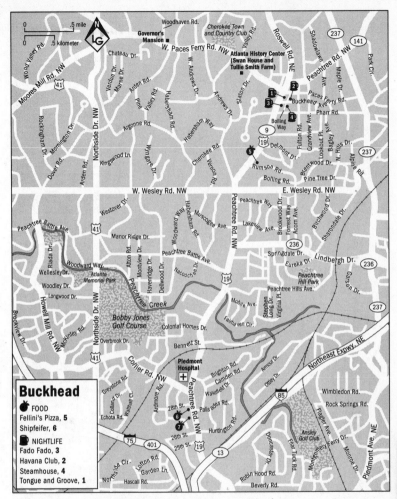

Buckhead

🍎 FOOD
Fellini's Pizza, **5**
Shipfeifer, **6**

🎵 NIGHTLIFE
Fado Fado, **3**
Havana Club, **2**
Steamhouse, **4**
Tongue and Groove, **1**

coaster, with a pretzel-shaped inverted loop. (☎770-948-9290. Open mid-June to July M-F 10am-9pm, Sa 10am-10pm; low-season hours vary, so call ahead. $44, seniors and under 4 ft. $27. Parking $10-12.)

🎵 NIGHTLIFE

Atlanta's rich nightlife lacks a clear focal point. Fortunately, however, it also lacks limits; young people can be found partying until the wee hours and beyond. Scores of bars and clubs along Peachtree Rd. and Buckhead Ave. in **Buckhead** cater to a younger crowd. Pricier **Midtown** greets the glitzy and the glamorous. Alternative **L5P** plays host to bikers and goths, while **Virginia Highland** and up-and-coming **East Atlanta** feature an eclectic mix.

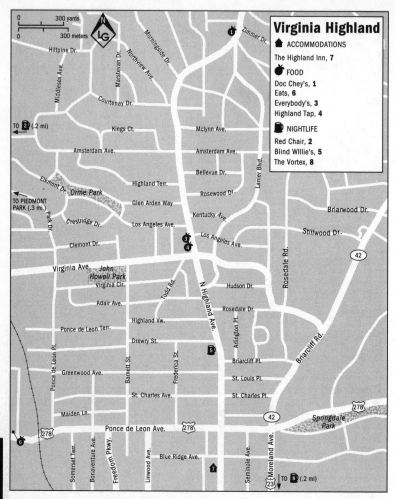

Virginia Highland

🏠 ACCOMMODATIONS

The Highland Inn, **7**

🍴 FOOD

Doc Chey's, **1**
Eats, **6**
Everybody's, **3**
Highland Tap, **4**

🍺 NIGHTLIFE

Red Chair, **2**
Blind Willie's, **5**
The Vortex, **8**

BARS AND PUBS

Blind Willie's, 828 N. Highland Ave. NE (☎873-2583). Blind Willie's is the quintessential blues club: the brick-lined interior is dark and cramped, and the bar serves mostly beer ($3-4) to its loyal patrons. Despite its hole-in-the wall appearance, Blind Willie's is an Atlanta legend. Live blues, zydeco, and folk music start around 9:30pm. Cover $3-10. Open M-Th and Su 8pm-2am, F 8pm-3am, Sa 8pm-2:30am.

The Vortex, 438 Moreland Ave. (☎688-1828), in L5P. An incredible restaurant that also doubles as an even cooler bar, The Vortex is the spot for serious eaters and drinkers alike. With mammoth burgers named "Coronary Bypass" ($8) and "Italian Stallion" ($7.45), you'll need a drink to make it through the night. Open M-W and Su 11am-midnight, Th-Sa 11am-3am.

Masquerade, 695 North Ave. NE (☎577-8178, concert info 577-2007), occupies an original turn-of-the-century mill. The bar has 3 levels: "heaven," with live music from touring bands; "purgatory," a more laid-back pub and pool house; and "hell," a dance club with everything from techno to 1940s big band jazz. An outside space provides dancing under the stars, while the 4000-seat amphitheater caters to metal and punk tastes. Cover from $3. Call for showtimes.

Eastside Lounge, 485 Flat Shoals Ave. SE (☎522-7841). If the streets of East Atlanta seem empty, it's because everyone is packed into this suave hideout. Couches near the bar and tables in the small upstairs offer rest for the weary, but be prepared to stand with the rest of the trendsetters. DJ spins F-Sa. Open M-Sa 9pm-3am.

Flatiron, 520 Flat Shoals Ave. (☎688-8864). Set on the corner of Glenwood and Flat Shoals, this L5P hot spot is a favorite with locals who are tired of the bohemian scene and in the mood for punk-laced rock and roll. Beer $3-4. Open M-Th 11:30am-2am, F-Sa 11:30am-3am, Su 12:30pm-2am.

The EARL, 488 Flat Shoals Ave. (☎522-3950), has live music most nights ranging from hip-hop to alternative country and serves award-winning burgers ($6.50-8.50) and onion rings ($3.25). Open M 5pm-3am, Tu-Sa 11:30am-3am, Su noon-midnight.

Steamhouse, 3041 Bolling Way (☎233-7980). For those who like raw oysters ($8 for a dozen on the half shell) with their beer, Steamhouse has plenty of both. A great place on lazy hot summer evenings, the party often spills out onto the patio. Beer $3.50. Open M-Sa 11:30am-2am, Su 11:30am-midnight.

Fado Fado, 3035 Peachtree Rd. NE (☎841-0066). The interior of this bar was imported from Ireland—right down to the wood of the bar itself. *The* yuppie hang-out in Buckhead. The boxty (rolled Irish pancake; $13-14) complements a Guinness nicely. Open M-Sa 11:30am-3am, Su 11:30am-midnight.

DANCE CLUBS

🎵 **Tongue and Groove,** 3055 Peachtree Rd. NE (☎261-2325; www.tongueandgrooveon-line.com). The club that is taking Atlanta by storm, Tongue and Groove has received praise from both the media and locals. Whether you decide to kick back at one of the 2 gorgeous bars or shake it on the dance floor, you're sure to have fun. Cover around $10. Open W-Sa 10pm-3am. Dress code strictly enforced.

Havana Club, 247 Buckhead Ave. (☎869-8484). Latin hot spot with a mature crowd. M night hip-hop. Live music F-Sa. Cover $10 for men after 11pm. Open M-Sa 8pm-3am.

Club 112, 1055 Peachtree St. NE (☎670-7277). A premier hip-hop club with a dark, cavernous interior. Cover $20; ladies free F before midnight, Sa before 11pm. Open Th 10pm-3am, F-Sa 9pm-3am.

GLBT NIGHTLIFE

Atlanta is the gay capital of the south, which makes **Midtown** the mecca of southern gay culture. In Atlanta, straight and gay often party together since some of the city's best all-around joints are rainbow-colored. For information on gay nightlife and events, check out the free *Southern Voice* newspaper, available everywhere.

Blake's, 227 10th St. (☎892-5786). Midtown males flock to this friendly bar, where see-and-be-seen is a way of life. A prime location in gay-friendly Midtown and just steps from Piedmont Park, this popular bar is also a destination for the young lesbian crowd. "Drag Races" M nights. Open M-Sa 2pm-2:30am, Su 2pm-midnight.

Red Chair, 550-C Amsterdam Ave. (☎870-0532), in Midtown. A *tapas*-style menu and 6 huge video screens playing VH-1 jams have quickly vaulted Red Chair to the top of Midtown's gay scene. 21+ after 9pm, Th 18+ until 11pm. Open W 6:30pm-midnight, Th-Sa 6:30pm-3am, Su 11:30am-3pm and 6:30pm-midnight.

THE SOUTH

The Heretic, 2069 Cheshire Bridge Road NE (☎325-3061), a little outside of the center of Midtown. Many guys head here in search of Mr. Right—or at least Mr. Right Now. If the action on the smoky dance floor gets a little too hot for you, cool off on the outdoor patio. 21+. Cover F-Sa $4. Open M-Sa 10:30am-3am, Su 12:30pm-midnight.

⚠ OUTDOOR ACTIVITIES

In the heart of Midtown, **Piedmont Park** is a hotbed of fun, free activities. Look for the **Dogwood Festival** (www.dogwood.org), an art festival in the spring, and the **Jazz Festival** (www.atlantafestivals.com) in May. In June, the park celebrates the **Gay Pride Festival** (www.atlantapride.org), and on July 4th, Atlanta draws 55,000 people to the world's largest 10K race, the Peachtree Road Race. Every summer Turner Broadcasting and HBO present **"Screen on the Green,"** a series of free films shown once a week in the meadow behind the visitors center. The **Atlanta Botanical Garden** occupies the northern end of the park and provides refuge from the hustle and bustle of everyday life. Stroll through 15 acres of landscaped gardens, a hardwood forest with trails, and an interactive children's garden focusing on health and wellness. The Garden is also home to the Storza Woods and the **Dorothy Chapman Fuqua Conservatory,** which houses some of the world's rarest plant species. (1345 Piedmont Ave. NE. Take bus #36 or MARTA: Arts Center; on Su, bus #27 from MARTA: Five Points. ☎876-5859; www.atlantabotanicalgarden.org. Open Apr.-Sept. Tu-Su 9am-7pm; Oct.-Mar. Tu-Su 9am-5pm. $12, seniors $9, students $7; Tu $2 off.)

Sixteen miles east of the city on U.S. 78, one of Georgia's top natural attractions, **Stone Mountain Park,** provides a respite from the city with beautiful scenery and the remarkable **Confederate Memorial.** Carved into the world's largest mass of granite, the 825 ft. "Mt. Rushmore of the South" profiles Jefferson Davis, Robert E. Lee, and Stonewall Jackson. On summer nights, be sure to check out the dazzling laser show that illuminates the side of the mountain. (Take bus #120 "Stone Mountain" from MARTA: Avondale. ☎770-498-5600 or 800-317-2006; www.stonemountainpark.com. Park open daily 6am-midnight. Attractions open daily in summer 10am-8pm; low season 10am-5pm. Entrance $8 per car, $7 per attraction. All day pass $20, ages 3-11 $17. Free laser show daily 9:30pm.)

ATHENS ☎706

In the grand Southern tradition of naming college towns after great classical cultural centers, Athens is perhaps the most successful at living up to its namesake. Still, the only Greeks around here live in the University of Georgia's (UGA) fraternities and sororities, and the city is better known for its production of rock stars than philosophers or mathematicians—the university and surrounding bars have spawned hundreds of popular bands, including R.E.M. and the B-52s. Strolling around the beautiful campus and downtown, it's easy to see why the nearly 34,000 students who live in Athens choose to spend their college years here.

■⚠ **ORIENTATION AND PRACTICAL INFORMATION.** Situated 70 mi. northeast of Atlanta, Athens can be reached from I-85 via U.S. 316, which runs into U.S. 29. Although the **Athens-Ben Epps Airport** is located in Athens (1010 Ben Epps Dr. ☎549-5783), it's easier to fly into Atlanta and take the **AAA Airport Express** shuttle (☎800-354-7874) to various points in and around Athens ($35). **Southeastern Stages,** 220 W. Broad St., runs buses to Atlanta and Augusta. (☎549-2255. Call for schedules and prices. Open M-F 7:15am-8pm, Sa-Su 7:15am-2:30pm and 7-8pm.) The **Athens Transit System** runs buses throughout Athens. (☎613-3430. Buses M-F 6:15am-7:15pm, Sa 7:30am-7pm; call for schedules. $1.25, ages 6-18 $1, seniors $0.60; transfers free.) UGA's **Campus Transit System** runs everywhere on campus and to some stops downtown. (☎369-6220. Buses run daily 7am-12:45am. Free.) **Taxi: Alfa Taxi,** ☎583-8882. Two blocks north of the UGA campus is the **Athens Welcome Center,** 280 E. Dougherty St., in the Church-Waddel-Brumby House. (☎353-1820. Open mid-Apr. to mid-Oct. M-Sa 10am-6pm, Su noon-6pm; mid-Oct. to mid-Apr. M-Sa 10am-5pm, Su noon-5pm.) The **UGA Visitors Center,** at the intersection of College Station and River Rd. on campus, provides info on UGA attractions. (☎542-0842. Open M-F 8am-5pm, Sa 9am-5pm, Su 1-5pm.) **Hotlines: Sexual Assault Crisis Line,** ☎353-1912. **Community Connection,** ☎353-1313. **Medical Services: Athens Regional Medical Center,** 1199 Prince Ave. (☎549-9977.) **Post Office:** 115 E. Hancock Ave. (☎354-8066. Open M-F 8am-5pm.) **Postal Code:** 30601. **Area Code:** 706.

⌂ ACCOMMODATIONS. Accommodations are usually reasonably priced, but rates rise during football weekends. For a luxurious stay, check out **The Foundry Park Inn ❺,** 295 E. Dougherty St. at Thomas St., in one of Athens's oldest historic sites. Thoughtfully decorated rooms and suites with cable TV, A/C, microwaves, minifridges, coffeemakers, and down bedding. (☎549-7020; www.foundryparkinn.com. Rooms from $99. AmEx/D/DC/MC/V.) The **Perimeter Inn ❷,** 3791 Atlanta Hwy., 5 mi. from downtown, is a comfortable, independently-owned motel with Spanish flair. (☎548-3000. Cable, A/C, continental breakfast. Singles $45; doubles $53. AmEx/D/DC/MC/V.) **Watson Mill Bridge State Park ❶,** 650 Watson Mill Rd., 21 mi. east of Athens, is the best place in the area to camp, with horse and hiking trails, canoe and boat rentals, and plenty of fishing. (☎783-5349 or 800-864-7275. Park open daily 8am-10pm; office 8am-5pm. Sites $15-17, with water and electricity $17-19; secluded primitive sites $20. AmEx/D/MC/V.) For camping closer to the city, try **Sandy Creek Park ❶,** 400 Bob Holman Rd., 4 mi. north of Athens Hwy. 441 N, 3 mi. outside of the loop. (☎613-3631. Park open in summer Tu-Su 7am-9pm; call for low-season hours. Primitive sites $10.)

◗ FOOD. The **Last Resort Grill ❸,** 174 and 184 W. Clayton St., at the corner of Hull St., is an eclectic restaurant with a gourmet atmosphere and reasonable prices. You may never again see a fried green tomato sandwich ($4.75) presented so elegantly, and the desserts are widely considered the best in Athens. (☎549-0810. Lunch $4-8. Dinner $8-15. Open M-Th and Su 11am-3pm and 5-10pm, F-Sa 11am-3pm and 5-11pm; bar until 2am. AmEx/D/MC/V.) **The Grit ❷,** 199 Prince Ave., stands for the Greatest Restaurant in Town, and it certainly comes close. Serving a wide array of tempting and exclusively vegetarian food ranging from stir-fry ($6) to samosas ($6), the Grit is sure to please even meat-lovers. (☎543-6592. Sandwiches $5-6. Entrees $4-7. Open M-F 11am-10pm, Sa-Su 10am-3pm and 5-10pm. MC/V.) R.E.M. fans who wonder what "automatic for the people" means should ask Dexter Weaver, the owner of **Weaver D's Fine Foods ❶,** 1016 E. Broad St., to whom the phrase originally belongs. Located in a small roadside house, Weaver D's offers a true taste of Athens, with pork chop sandwiches ($4.25) and soul-food lunches ($4-9). R.E.M. repaid Weaver for the use of his phrase as their 1992 album title by inviting him to the Grammy Awards. (☎353-7797. Open M-Sa 11am-6pm. AmEx/D/DC/MC/V.) **The Grill ❷,** 171 College St., is Athens's version of the all-night burger-and-malt joint. In addition to the standard hamburger platter ($6.25) and luscious malts ($3.50), the Grill has a mean vegetarian side. (☎543-4770. Open 24hr. AmEx/D/MC/V.) For the best baked goods in town, head to **Big City Bread ❶,** 393 N. Finley St., which serves amazing biscuits and sandwiches on home-baked bread. (☎543-1187. Sandwiches $6-8. Open M-Sa 7am-6pm, Su 7am-3pm. AmEx/MC/V.)

◙ SIGHTS. The **University of Georgia,** chartered in 1785 as the first land-grant college in the US, is the very reason Athens exists, and it also tops Athens's list of tourist attractions. The campus **visitors center,** at the corner of College Station and

River Rd. in south campus, has self-guided tours, maps, and helpful answers. (☎542-0842. Open M-F 8am-5pm, Sa 9am-5pm, Su 1-5pm.) The campus begins downtown on Broad St., where the Arch guards the official entrance to the institution. **Sanford Stadium** is the home turf of UGA's "Dawgs," the white English bulldogs that serve as the school's mascot. **Butts-Mehre Heritage Hall,** on the corner of Pinecrest Dr. and Rutherford St., houses the school's athletic offices and the Heritage Museum, which celebrates UGA athletes and, more importantly, white English bulldogs. (☎542-9036. Open M-F 8am-5pm.) The **Georgia Museum of Art,** 90 Carlton St., in the Performing and Visual Arts Complex off East Campus Dr., is an impressive state-funded collection of over 7000 works of art. (☎542-4662. Open Tu and Th-Sa 10am-5pm, W 10am-9pm, Su 1-5pm. Suggested donation $1.)

Beyond the university, Athens boasts a wealth of historic sites, homes, and artifacts chronicling the town's rich history. The many lush gardens and arboretums encourage long walks and picnics. Maps and tours of the city's historic areas and green spaces are available at the Athens Welcome Center (see **Practical Information,** p. 386), the oldest residence in town. The **US Navy Supply Corps School and Museum,** 1425 Prince Ave., was originally a teacher's college, then a Carnegie library, and is now one of only 11 official US Navy Museums. Exhibits of ship models, uniforms, and all manner of Navy flotsam are on display. (☎354-7349. Open M-F 9am-5:15pm. Visitors must call ahead. Free.) The city's most elaborate garden, the **State Botanical Garden of Georgia,** 2450 S. Milledge Ave., houses trails, a tropical conservatory, and a day chapel. (☎542-1244. Open daily Apr.-Sept. 8am-8pm, Oct.-Mar. 8am-6pm; visitors center open Tu-Sa 9am-4:30pm, Su 11:30am-4:30pm. Free.)

If you hesitate to bequeath your property to undeserving offspring, consider making your favorite plant an heir. Professor William H. Jackson set the legal precedent when he willed to a beloved oak tree all the land within 8 ft. of its trunk. Today, **The Tree That Owns Itself** flourishes at the intersection of Finley and Dearing St., south of Broad St. downtown. By far Athens's best Civil War relic, the nearby **Double-Barreled Cannon** was a great idea that failed spectacularly. On the grounds of City Hall, at Washington and College St., the two barrels are still ominously pointed north.

🎭🎵 **ENTERTAINMENT AND NIGHTLIFE.** Athens has cradled hundreds of fledging bands in all genres of music over the years. R.E.M. is arguably Athens's most well-known homegrown band, but those plugged into the music world will know that most musicians show up in Athens at one point or another to play in a true-blue music mecca. In late June, **Athfest** takes over the town. (☎548-1973. 1 day $10, entire festival $15.) Take a look at Athens's free weekly newspaper, *Flagpole Magazine,* available everywhere downtown, to find out which bands are in town. As soon as you're within spitting distance of Athens, tune in to **WUOG 90.5,** one of the nation's last bastions of real college radio. The students who run the station play tons of local music and liven it up with unscripted, unplanned, and occasionally incoherent commentary. R.E.M. got its start at **The 40 Watt Club,** 285 W. Washington St. Conceived in 1979 as a raucous Halloween party lit by a single 40-watt bulb, the club has had numerous incarnations and locations, but currently kicks with live music most nights. (☎549-7871. Cover $5-15. Open daily 10pm-2am.) Downtown, bars line the streets between Lumpkin and Thomas St., and you're sure to find a bar that fits your style, though the **Flicker Theater and Bar,** 263 W. Washington St. (☎546-0039), **The Globe,** 199 N. Lumpkin St. (☎353-4721), and the **Manhattan Cafe,** 337 N. Hull St. (☎369-9767), are current hot spots. If you're looking for something beyond music and booze, Athens lives up to its name intellectually. **Jittery Joe's,** 1210 S. Milledge Ave., offers a classy coffeeshop atmosphere. (☎208-1979. Open M-F 6:30am-midnight, Sa 6:30am-1am, Su 7:30am-midnight.) **The Morton Theatre,** 195 W. Washington St., was built in 1910 as a vaudeville theater and was entirely owned and operated by African-Americans. Today it is a fully restored, high-tech performing arts center home to all sorts of theater and music. (☎613-3771; www.mortontheatre.com. Call for schedules and ticket prices.)

ANDERSONVILLE ☎229

Fifty-five miles south of Macon and 10 mi. northeast of Americus on Rte. 49, the **Andersonville National Historic Site** preserves the location where 45,000 Union soldiers were confined in a primitive prison pen without food, water, or shelter in 1864 near the end of the Civil War. Nearly 13,000 men died horrible deaths within the camp's wooden walls due to the barbaric conditions and severe overcrowding—at one point more than 32,000 men were confined in a space intended to hold 10,000. On the grounds, the excellent **National Prisoner of War Museum** memorializes the experiences of American POWs with artifacts, interactive video testimonials, recordings, photographs, and journals. The museum is extraordinarily sobering as you pass actual rations that kept men alive for days, view myriad portrayals of horrible suffering and amazing strength, and finally exit into a small memorial in the sunlight. Also on the grounds, the **Andersonville National Cemetery** is a fitting place to end the visit. (☎924-0343; www.nps.gov/ande. Park open daily 8am-5pm; museum 8:30am-5pm. Special talks daily 11am and 2pm. Audio driving tours $1.) Directly across Rte. 49 from the park exit is the tiny town of Andersonville. The **Welcome Center**, 114 Church St., doubles as a little museum stuffed with bric-a-brac. Up the street a quarter mile on the left, the **Andersonville Restaurant ❶** serves a country buffet lunch for $6.25 ($8.25 on Su) with a side of chatty conversation for free. (☎928-8480. Open M-Th 11am-2pm, F 11am-2pm and 5-9pm (fish night), Su noon-3pm. Cash or check only.)

SAVANNAH ☎912

In February 1733, General James Oglethorpe and his band of 120 vagabonds founded the city of Savannah and the state of Georgia. General Sherman later spared the city during his rampage through the South. Some say he found Savannah too pretty to burn, presenting it instead to President Lincoln as a Christmas gift. Today, anyone who sees Savannah's stately trees and Federalist and English Regency houses interwoven with spring blossoms will agree with Sherman.

■▶ **ORIENTATION AND PRACTICAL INFORMATION.** Savannah rests on the coast of Georgia at the mouth of the **Savannah River,** which runs north of the city along the border with South Carolina. The city stretches south from bluffs overlooking the river. The restored 2½ sq. mi. **downtown historic district,** bordered by East Broad St., Martin Luther King Jr. Blvd., Gwinnett St., and the river, is best explored on foot. A parking pass ($8), available at the visitors center (p. 389), allows 2-day unlimited use of all metered parking, city lots, and garages. **Savannah/ Hilton Head International Airport,** 400 Airways Ave. (☎964-0514; www.savannahairport.com), at Exit 104 off I-95, serves coastal Georgia and the Low Country of South Carolina. **Amtrak,** 2611 Seaboard Coastline Dr., chugs to Charleston (1½hr., 1 per day, $17-22). (☎234-2611; www.amtrak.com. Open daily 4:30pm-midnight.) **Greyhound,** 610 W. Oglethorpe Ave. (☎232-2135; www.greyhound.com; open 24hr), at Fahm St., sends buses to Atlanta (5hr., 7 per day, $39-42), Charleston (2½hr., 2 per day, $26-28), and Jacksonville (2-3hr., 13 per day, $25-27). **Chatham Area Transit (CAT),** 124 Bull St. (☎233-5767), in the Chatham County Court House, runs buses and a free shuttle through the historic area. (Open daily 7am-11pm. Shuttle operates M-Sa 7am-7pm, Su 9:40am-4:20pm. $1, seniors $0.50; no transfers. Weekly pass available at 124 Bull St.; $12.) **Hotline: Rape Hotline,** ☎233-7273. Operates 24hr. **Taxi: Yellow Cab,** ☎236-1133. The **Savannah Visitors Center,** 301 Martin Luther King Jr.

Blvd., at Liberty St., is housed in a former train station. (☎944-0455; www.savannahgeorgia.com. Open M-F 8:30am-5pm, Sa-Su 9am-5pm.) **Medical Services: Georgia Regional Hospital,** 1915 Eisenhower Dr. (☎356-2045.) **Internet Access: Public Library,** 2002 Bull St. (☎652-3600. Open M-Th 9am-9pm, F-Sa 9am-6pm, Su 2-6pm. Wireless Internet available.) **Post Office:** 2 N. Fahm St., at Bay St. (☎800-275-8777. Open M-F 7am-6pm, Sa 9am-3pm.) **Postal Code:** 31402. **Area Code:** 912.

⌂ ACCOMMODATIONS. Downtown motels cluster near the historic area, visitors center, and Greyhound station. Venture into the Historic District for a number of very fine B&Bs. For those with cars, **Ogeechee Road (U.S. 17)** has several budget options. **Savannah Pension ❶,** 304 E. Hall St., only minutes from some of Savannah's greatest sights, is the best budget accommodation in the historic district, featuring bright, clean rooms with A/C. (☎236-7744. Reservations required. Rooms from $45. Cash only.) **The President's Quarters ❺,** 225 E. President St., and its adjoining inns (The Guest House and 17Hundred90) offer it all. Rooms in all three buildings seamlessly combine the classic (antique furnishings) with the modern (high-speed Internet access). If staying with a group, the ground floor in 17Hundred90, with a sitting room and a courtyard with 8-foot walls, allows you to feel like a member of Savannah high society, if only for a night. (☎233-1600 or 800-233-1776; www.presidentsquarters.com. Breakfast and daily tea included. Reservations recommended. Ask for daily "walk-in" specials. Rooms $125-225. AmEx/D/MC/V.) **EconoLodge ❹,** 512 W. Oglethorpe St., has spacious, clean rooms with A/C, cable TV, free local calls, coffeemakers, and continental breakfast. While the rates are no bargain, they're tough to beat in the historic district. (☎233-9251 or 800-221-2222. Rooms M-Th and Su $90, F-Sa $110. AAA and AARP discount 10%. AmEx/D/DC/MC/V.) **Skidaway Island State Park ❶** is 6 mi. southeast of downtown off Diamond Causeway; take Liberty St. east until it becomes Wheaton St., turn right on Waters Ave., and follow the signs for the park. (☎598-2300 or 800-864-7275. Restrooms, hot showers, electricity, and water. Open daily 7am-10pm. Check-in before 10pm. Sites $24, with hookup $26.)

◖ FOOD. Wall's BBQ ❶, 515 E. York Ln., in an alley running from Houston to Price St., parallel to York St. and Oglethorpe Ave., serves mouth-watering barbecue in an honest-to-goodness hole-in-the-wall location. Don't plan on devouring your delicious barbecue sandwich or ribs ($5-11) here; most locals relish their incredible meal in one of the neighboring public squares. (☎232-9754. Baked deviled crabs $3.25. Open Th-Sa 11am-9pm. Cash only.) **Mrs. Wilkes Boarding House ❸,** 107 W. Jones St., is a Southern institution where friendly strangers gather around large tables for homestyle atmosphere and soul food. Fried chicken, butter beans, and superb biscuits are favorites. (☎232-5997. All-you-can-eat $13. Open M-F 11am-2pm. Cash only.) **Clary's Cafe ❶,** 404 Abercorn St., has been serving some of Savannah's best breakfasts since 1903 and was the setting of many scenes in the film *Midnight in the Garden of Good and Evil*. Weekend brunch features $5 malted waffles. (☎233-0402. Open M-Th 7am-4pm, F 7am-5pm, Sa 8am-5pm, Su 8am-4pm. AmEx/D/DC/MC/V.) The **Crystal Beer Parlor ❷,** 301 W. Jones St. at Jefferson St., serves up some of the best burgers and seafood. Try the CBP Crab Stew ($5) or the Crystal Cornbread ($1), staple dishes of this 72-year-old restaurant. (☎443-9200. Burgers and sandwiches $7-9. Open M-Th 11am-10pm, kitchen closes at 9:30pm; F-Sa 11am-midnight, kitchen closes at 11pm. Happy hour M-F 4-6pm. Live jazz F 7:30-10:30pm. AmEx/D/DC/MC/V.)

◧ ◪ SIGHTS AND ENTERTAINMENT. Most of Savannah's 21 squares contain some distinctive centerpiece. Elegant antebellum houses and drooping vine-wound trees often cluster around the squares, adding to the classic Southern aura.

> **SO SWEET.** A cold drink may sound refreshing on a hot Southern afternoon, but only Yanks order "iced tea." To blend in, ask for "sweet tea" instead, but beware: the drink is pre-sweetened and can range in sugariness from barely noticeable to practically gag-inducing. If you'd rather sweeten your tea yourself, order an "unsweet tea" and stir in as much (or as little) sugar as you'd like.

Bus, van, and horse carriage **tours** leave from the visitors center and City Market, but walking can be more rewarding. Two of Savannah's best-known historic homes are the **Davenport House,** 324 E. State St., on Columbia Sq., and the **Owens-Thomas House,** 124 Abercom St., one block away on Oglethorpe Sq. Built in 1820, the Davenport House is nearly exactly as Isaiah Davenport left it in the mid-19th century, complete with the original furniture, cantilevered staircase, and exemplary woodwork. The Owens-Thomas House is similar, but the carriage house, containing artifacts and relating stories about slave life, is free. (Davenport: ☎236-8097; www.davenportsavga.com. Open M-Sa 10am-4pm, Su 1-4pm. $7, ages 7-18 $3.50. Owens-Thomas: ☎233-9743. Open M noon-5pm, Tu-Sa 10am-5pm, Su 1-5pm; last tour 4:30pm. $8, seniors $7, students $4, ages 6-12 $2.) The **Green Meldrim House,** 14 W. Macon St., on Madison Sq., is a Gothic Revival mansion that served as General Sherman's Savannah headquarters following his famed "march to the sea." It was from this house that Sherman wrote the famous telegram to President Lincoln, giving him the city as a gift. (☎233-3845. Open Tu and Th-F 10am-4pm, Sa 10am-1pm. Tours every 30min. $5, students $3.)

Savannah's four forts once protected the city's port from Spanish, British, and other invaders. The most intriguing, **Fort Pulaski National Monument,** 15 mi. east of Savannah on U.S. 80 E and Rte. 26, marks the Civil War battle where Union forces first used rifled cannons to decimate the Confederate opposition. (☎786-5787. Partially wheelchair accessible. Open daily 9am-5pm. $3, under 16 free.)

Special events in Savannah include the annual **NOGS Tour of the Hidden Gardens** of Historic Savannah (☎961-4805), April 21-22 in 2006, when private walled gardens are opened to the public, who can partake in a special Southern teatime. Green is the theme of the **St. Patrick's Day Celebration on the River,** a multi-day, beer- and fun-filled party that packs the streets and warms celebrants up for the annual **St. Patrick's Day Parade,** the second-largest in the US. (Celebration: ☎234-0295. Parade: ☎233-4804. Mar. 17, 2006. Begins 10:15am.) **First Saturday on the River** (☎234-0295) brings arts, crafts, entertainment, and food to historic River St. each month. The free paper *Connect Savannah,* found in restaurants and stores, has the latest in news and entertainment.

■ **NIGHTLIFE.** The waterfront area running along Savannah's **River Street** brims with endless oceanfront dining opportunities, street performers, and a friendly pub ambience. While you're allowed to freely walk the streets with one drink in hand, better not have two or the police will peg you with a $150 ticket. The **Warehouse,** 18 E. River St., boasts the "coldest and cheapest beer in town." (☎234-6003. Happy hour M-F 2:30-7pm. Open M-Th and Su 11am-2am, F-Sa 11am-3am.) At **Kevin Barry's Irish Pub,** 117 W. River St., the Guinness flows, and the entire bar jigs with live Irish folk music. (☎233-9626. Music daily 8:30pm. Cover $2. Open M-F 2pm-3am, Sa 11:30am-3am, Su 12:30pm-2am.) Students eat, drink, and shop at **City Market,** the largest historic district in the US. (Jefferson at W. St. Julian St.) For the best alternative scene and a gay-friendly atmosphere, check out **Club One,** 1 Jefferson St. near Bay St., where Lady Chablis, a character featured in *Midnight in the Garden of Good and Evil,* performs regularly. (☎232-0200. Cover $3-10. Open M-Sa 5pm-3am, Su 5pm-2am.)

CUMBERLAND ISLAND   ☎912

The prized jewel of Georgia's National Seashore, Cumberland Island was once a playground for the wealthy robber barons of the Gilded Age. Wild horses now outnumber the few remaining private homes, loggerhead turtles lay their eggs on the island's beaches, and maritime forests slowly reclaim the ruins of enormous mansions. The **Ice House Museum,** at Dungeness Dock, displays historical artifacts from the island. (No phone. Restrooms. Open daily 8am-4pm.) Off the main road about ½ mi. south of Dungeness Dock lie the ruins of **Dungeness,** the abandoned winter home of Thomas Carnegie. **Plum Orchard,** the ruins of a Georgian-Revival home built for Carnegie's son and his wife in 1898, is accessible by a short hike from the main road about 7 mi. north of Sea Camp Dock or by bi-monthly ferry from the dock. (Ferries 2nd and 4th Su of each month, departing Sea Camp Dock at 12:45pm and returning at 4:15pm. $6. Free ranger presentation 1:30pm.) The northern and central portions of the island are pine and hardwood forest, while the western side is a tidal marsh, excellent for birdwatching. The ranger-led **Dungeness Trail** runs from Dungeness Dock to the beach passing the Carnegie mansion's spooky ruins along the way. The more adventurous can catch the **Parallel Trail** at Sea Camp Beach and follow it 5½ mi. through shady oak groves and palmetto stands to the Hickory Hill campsite, where a number of other trails converge for further exploration. Since most visitors head straight for the trails, sun-lovers can have the beautiful white sand beaches practically to themselves.

If you wish to spend the night on the island, come prepared—aside from water, all provisions must be carried in and out. The only developed campground, **Sea Camp Beach ❶,** is a 15min. walk from the Sea Camp dock and has restrooms, cold showers, and drinking water. Sites are under a canopy of beautifully gnarled oaks and just steps from the beach ($4 per person). A slightly longer trek rewards hardy campers with **backcountry camping ❶,** magnificent in its isolation and scenery. Each of the four camping areas—**Stafford Beach, Hickory Hill, Yankee Paradise,** and **Brickhill Bluff**—has a well, but the water should be treated before drinking. Campfires are not permitted in the backcountry, so bring a cook stove. (☎882-4335 or 888-817-3421. All camping requires a reservation and a permit that can be obtained at the ranger station at Sea Camp Dock. Backcountry sites $2 per person.) For those less inclined to the outdoors, St. Mary's has plenty of overnight options. The **Riverview Hotel ❷,** 105 Osborne St., is located across the street from the ferry docks. (☎882-3242. Continental breakfast included. Singles from $45; doubles from $55. AmEx/D/DC/MC/V.) The **Cumberland Kings Bay Lodges ❷,** 603 Sand Bar Dr. at Charlie Smith Sr. Hwy./U.S. 40 Spur, is 10min. from the dock and offers mini-suites with kitchenettes, a pool, and continental breakfast. (☎882-8900. Singles $44; doubles $48.) As there is no food on the island, either bring your own or stuff yourself silly before you board the ferry. There are numerous restaurants near the ferry dock, though the **Riverside Cafe ❷,** 106 St. Mary's St., is one of the better choices, offering an extensive selection of tasty breakfast dishes, sandwiches, burgers, and entrees for reasonable prices. (☎882-3466. Entrees $1.25-17. Open M 7:30am-2pm, Tu-Su 7:30am-9pm. D/MC/V.)

Cumberland Island, Georgia's southernmost coastal island, is 17½ mi. long and nearly 3 mi. wide. The vast majority of the land is owned and operated by the National Parks Service. The **Cumberland Queen,** a ferry operated by the National Parks Service from St. Mary's, GA (Exit #3 off I-95), is the only transportation to the island and leaves from the dock at St. Mary's St. and Osborne Rd., arriving at **Dungeness Dock** and **Sea Camp Dock,** about a mile north of Dungeness Dock. Reservations are strongly recommended. (☎882-4335 or 877-860-6787. $15, ages 65+ $12, ages 12 and under $10. No pets, bicycles, kayaks, or cars. Departs St. Mary's Mar.-Nov. daily 9 and 11:45am; Dec.-Feb. M and Th-Su 9 and 11:45am. Departs Dungeness Dock and Sea Camp Dock on Cumberland Island Mar.-Nov. daily 10:15am and 4:45pm; Dec.-Feb. M and Th-Su 10:15am and 4:45pm; also Mar.-Sept. W-Sa 2:45pm.) The **Cumberland Island National Seashore Visitors Center,** 113 St. Mary's St., is located next to the dock in St. Mary's. (☎888-817-3421; www.nps.gov/cuis. Open daily 8:15am-4:30pm.) On the island, the **Sea Camp Ranger Station,** at Sea Camp Dock, has restrooms, water, exhibits on the island's natural history, and information on trails. (Open daily 8am-4:30pm.) **Area Code:** 912.

ALABAMA

Forty years later, the "Heart of Dixie" is still haunted by its controversial role in the Civil Rights movement of the 1960s, when Governor George Wallace fought a vicious campaign opposing integration. Today, the state has made efforts to broaden its image and has constructed a series of important monuments and homages to the tumult of the Civil Rights movement. While the state's rich colonial past, Native American heritage, and legacy of immigration are on full display, Alabama "the beautiful" offers unique cuisine, nationally acclaimed gardens, and frequent festivals that constantly create an alternative image for the state.

◪ PRACTICAL INFORMATION

Capital: Montgomery.

Visitor Info: Alabama Bureau of Tourism and Travel, 401 Adams Ave., Ste. 126, Montgomery 36104 (☎334-242-4169 or 800-252-2262; www.touralabama.org). Open M-F 8am-5pm. **Division of Parks,** 64 N. Union St., Montgomery 36104 (☎800-252-7275). Open M-F 8am-5pm.

Postal Abbreviation: AL. **Sales Tax:** usually 10%, varies by county.

MONTGOMERY   ☎334

Montgomery's numerous monuments and historical sites commemorate its turbulent past as the first capital of the Confederacy and the birthplace of America's Civil Rights movement. Montgomery's role in the movement began in 1955 with the arrest of Rosa Parks, a black seamstress and activist who refused to give up her seat to a white man on a city bus. The success of the ensuing bus boycott, organized by local minister Dr. Martin Luther King, Jr., encouraged nationwide reform. Montgomery's marketing now relies on its prominent past, proclaiming itself "courageous, visionary, rebellious."

■◪ **ORIENTATION AND PRACTICAL INFORMATION.** Downtown follows a grid pattern. Major east-west routes are **Madison Avenue** downtown and **Vaughn Road** south of **I-65;** main north-south roads are **Perry Street** and **Decatur Street,** which becomes Norman Bridge Rd. farther south. **Dexter Avenue** is Montgomery's main street, running east-west up an imposing hill to the capitol. West of downtown, **I-65** runs north-south and intersects **I-85,** which forms downtown's southern border. A ring road, varyingly called East, South, West, and North Blvd., encircles both downtown and the outlying neighborhoods. **Greyhound,** 950 W. South Blvd. (☎286-0658 or 800-231-2222 for reservations; www.greyhound.com; open 24hr.), at Exit 168 on I-65 and a right onto South Blvd., runs to: Atlanta (3-4hr., 10 per day, $31); Birmingham (2hr., 5 per day, $20); Mobile (3-4hr., 8 per day, $34); Selma (1hr., 5 per day, $20); Tuskegee (45min., 7 per day, $20). **Montgomery Area Transit System**

(MATS) runs local buses. (Operates M-Sa 6am-6pm. "Fixed route" bus $1.) The **Lightning Route Trolley** arrives every 25min. at well-marked stops near downtown attractions. Take the Gold route for the State Capitol and Civil Rights Monument and the Green route for the Rosa Parks Museum and the Old Town Museum. (Operates M-Sa 9am-5:40pm. $0.25 per stop, seniors and disabled with MAP card $0.10. Day pass $1; seniors, children, and disabled $0.50.) **Taxi: New Deal Cab, ☎** 262-4747. A **visitors center,** 300 Water St., in Union Station, has a short video about the city and free maps. (☎ 262-0013; www.visitingmontgomery.com. Open M-Sa 8am-5pm, Su noon-4pm.) **Hotlines: Council Against Rape, ☎** 286-5987 or 800-656-HOPE. Operates 24hr. **Internet Access: Montgomery City-County Public Library,** 245 High St., between McDonough and Lawrence St. (☎ 584-7144. Open M-Th 9am-9pm, F-Sa 9am-6pm, Su 1-6pm. Free.) **Post Office:** 135 Catoma St. (☎ 263-4974. Open M-F 9am-5pm.) **Postal Code:** 36104. **Area Code:** 334.

⌂ ACCOMMODATIONS. For those with a car, South Blvd., Exit 168 off I-65, overflows with inexpensive lodging options, while most exits off I-85 lead to standard, more expensive chains. Beware: the cheapest of the cheap can be fairly seedy. If you're looking to stay close to the historic downtown, the **Red Bluff Cottage ➍**, 551 Clay St., is a B&B worth the price tag. Gorgeous rooms, full baths, free Internet, TV, bathrobes, and flowers add to the cottage's allure. (☎ 264-0056 or 888-551-2529; www.redbluffcottage.com. Rooms $99-195. AmEx/D/MC/V.) For a more affordable bed, travelers should check out the **Comfort Inn ➌**, 1035 W. South Blvd., Exit 168 off of I-65 S, which has exceptionally clean rooms, continental breakfast, A/C, mini-fridges, microwaves, free local calls, a pool, wireless Internet, and cable TV. (☎ 281-5090. Singles $53-59; doubles $62-69. AAA and AARP discounts. AmEx/D/DC/MC/V.) **Inn South ➋**, Exit 168 off I-65 at South Blvd., has reasonably clean and spacious rooms for very cheap rates as well as free local calls, wireless Internet, breakfast, and cable TV with HBO. (☎ 288-7999 or 800-642-0890. Singles $35; doubles $40. AmEx/D/MC/V.) The site of a 1763 French stronghold, **Fort Toulouse Jackson Park ➊**, 12 mi. north of Montgomery on Ft. Toulouse Rd., off U.S. 231, has 39 sites with water and electricity under hanging Spanish moss in beautiful woods. (☎ 567-3002. Reception daily 8am-5pm. In spring and fall, reservations are recommended 2 weeks in advance. Tent sites $11; RV hookups $14, ages 62+ $11.)

❏ FOOD. In a tiny pink house filled with lovely paintings and posters, **⬛Martha's Place ➊**, 458 Sayre St., is a Southern family affair. Fried chicken, pork chops, collard greens, and black-eyed peas are all included in Martha's gigantic, authentic soul food lunch. Don't miss the pound cake and sweet tea. (☎ 263-9135. Traditional lunch $5.50. 4-vegetable plate $4. Open M-F 11am-3pm. AmEx/MC/V.) **⬛Farmers Market Cafe ➋**, 315 N. McDonough St., is a Montgomery institution, founded in 1958 and open ever since. Grab breakfast or lunch canteen-style; a two-course meat and vegetable lunch will set you back $7.60. Montgomery's politicians eat here, as do farmers and builders on their way to or from work. (☎ 262-1970. Open M-F 5:30am-2pm. AmEx/D/MC/V.) The oldest restaurant in town, **Chris's Hot Dogs ➊**, 138 Dexter Ave., has been making hot dogs ($1.70) like nobody else since 1917. A stone's throw away from the State House, Chris's draws in the politicos for hamburgers ($1.70), grilled cheese ($1.70) and other authentic diner fare. "Freedom Fries" are only $1.40. (☎ 265-6850. Open M-Th and Sa 10am-7pm, F 10am-8pm. Cash only.) **Arirang ➌**, 1633 Eastern Blvd., in the mall across from Lowe's and Best Buy, serves very good Korean specialties. Grilled meat you cook yourself on a hotplate runs $13-15, while other meat and vegetarian dishes range $9-13. (☎ 215-3251. Open daily 11am-10pm. AmEx/D/MC/V.)

◉ SIGHTS. The **State Capitol,** at Bainbridge St. and Dexter Ave., is an imposing Greek Revival structure sporting marble floors, cantilevered staircases, and neat echo chambers. On the front steps, a bronze star commemorates the spot where

Jefferson Davis took the oath of office as president of the Confederacy. (☎242-3935. Open M-Sa 9am-5pm. Self-guided tours available. Free.) Only a few feet away is the 112-year-old **King Memorial Baptist Church,** 454 Dexter Ave., where Martin Luther King, Jr. was pastor for six years. (☎263-3970. Open Tu-Sa 10am-4pm. Admission $3, children $2. Cash only.) Maya Lin, the architect who designed the Vietnam Veterans Memorial in Washington, D.C. (p. 276), also designed Montgomery's newest sight, the ⬛**Civil Rights Memorial,** 400 Washington Ave., in front of the Southern Poverty Law Center. A circular black granite table over which water continuously flows pays tribute to activists who died fighting for civil rights. (Open 24hr. Free. Wheelchair accessible.) The **Alabama Department of Archives and History,** 624 Washington Ave., not only houses important state documents, but is also a museum. Come here to explore Civil War and Civil Rights history or, for younger visitors, to interact with the past in the "Hands-On Gallery." Visit the second-floor exhibit of Spider Martin's "Selma to Montgomery: A March for the Right to Vote" photography exhibit. Twenty-two of Martin's images—from Bloody Sunday to the 54 mi. march from Selma to Montgomery—are housed here. (☎242-4365. Museum open M-F and 1st Sa of every month 8:30am-4:30pm. Free. Wheelchair accessible.) The **Rosa Parks Library and Museum,** 252 Montgomery St., was dedicated 45 years after Rosa Parks refused to give up her bus seat on December 1, 1955. The museum uses video, artifacts, audio, and an actual 1955 Montgomery bus to recreate that fateful day and the subsequent events that influenced the nation. (☎241-8661. Open M-F 9am-5pm, Sa 9am-3pm; last entry 1hr. before close. $5.50, under 12 $3.50.)

Old Alabama Town, 301 Columbus St., at Hull St., reconstructs 19th-century Alabama with over 40 period buildings, including a pioneer homestead, an 1892 grocery, and an early African-American church. Allow at least 2hr. to wander around the grounds and use the audio tour at your own pace; if you only want to visit a few blocks rather than the whole museum, you can get a reduced entrance fee. (☎240-4500. Tickets sold M-Sa 8am-2pm; grounds open until 4pm. $8, seniors $7.20, ages 6-18 $4.) The **Hank Williams Museum,** 118 Commerce St., across from the Montgomery Civic Center, features the Montgomery native's outfits, memorabilia, and even the '52 Cadillac in which the songwriter died at the young age of 29. (☎262-3600. Open M-Sa 9am-6pm, Su 1-4pm. $8, under 12 $3. AAA discount $1.) A modest exterior hides the quirky **F. Scott and Zelda Fitzgerald Museum,** 919 Felder Ave., off Carter Hill Rd. at Dunbar. The curator will be happy to show you photographs, Zelda's paintings, Scott's original manuscripts, and evidence of the couple's stormy marriage. (☎264-4222. Open W-F 10am-2pm, Sa-Su 1-5pm. Free.) The **Montgomery Museum of Fine Arts,** 1 Museum Dr., part of the Blount Cultural Park (see below), houses a collection of 19th- and 20th-century American paintings including works by southern painters like Georgia O'Keeffe and Edward Hopper. (☎244-5700. Open Tu-W and F-Sa 10am-5pm, Th 10am-9pm, Su noon-5pm. Free, but donations appreciated.)

🔊🎭 **ENTERTAINMENT AND NIGHTLIFE.** The nationally acclaimed **Alabama Shakespeare Festival,** considered by many to be Montgomery's leading attraction, is staged at the **Carolyn Blount Theater** on the grounds of the 300-acre private estate, **Wynton M. Blount Cultural Park;** from Exit 6 off I-85, follow Eastern Blvd. south and turn left on Woodmeere Blvd.; the park will be on your right. The theater also hosts a mix of contemporary and Shakespearean plays year-round on its two stages. (☎271-5353 or 800-841-4273; www.asf.net. Box office open M-Sa 10am-6pm, Su noon-4pm; performance nights until 9pm. Orchestra $35, balcony $19; 25 and under $15. Senior citizen discount 10%.) For regional music, head to Montgomery's **1048 Bar,** 1104 E. Fairview Ave., to enjoy a beer and listen to the best acts in town. It's jazz and blues every night 10pm-2:30am, and the house jazz band plays every Sunday 5:30-9pm. (☎834-1048. Domestics $2.75, imports $3.75-5. Maker's Mark on the rocks $5.25. 21+. $3 cover most nights. Open M-F and Su 4pm-3am, Sa 4pm-

2am.) **Gator's,** 5040 Vaughn Rd., at Vaughn Plaza, blasts delta, acoustic, blues, and rock in its cafe and nightclub. (☎274-0330. Live music Tu-Sa usually 8pm-late. Kitchen open M-W 11am-2pm and 4-9pm, Th-Sa 4-10pm, Su 11am-2pm.) **Kokopelli's,** 281 Vaughn Plaza in the Vaughn Pike Shopping Mall, is an inexpensive sports bar that attracts a twenty-something crowd and has live music Wednesday through Saturday from 10:30pm. (☎213-0707. 21+. Open M-F 5pm-late, Sa-Su 6pm-late.) Montgomery's only independent movie theater, the **Capri Theater,** 1045 E. Fairview, shows arthouse films nightly. (☎262-4858. Tickets $6.50, children $2.) The **Nova Theater,** in the Stratford Square mall, plays first-run movies. (☎279-5800; www.novacinemas.com. Tickets $3.75.) The Thursday *Montgomery Advertiser* ($0.50), *The Buzz,* and *King Kudzu* (both free) list more entertainment options.

◗ DAYTRIP FROM MONTGOMERY: TUSKEGEE.

After Reconstruction, "emancipated" blacks in the South remained segregated and disenfranchised. **Booker T. Washington,** a former slave, believed that blacks could best improve their situation through hard work and learning a trade, and the curriculum of the college he founded reflected that philosophy. "What we need we will ourselves create," Washington asserted, a claim made concrete by the fact that virtually the entire school was made through student labor. Today, a more academically oriented **Tuskegee University** (☎727-8347 for free tours by the Park Service) fills 160 buildings on 5000 acres, while the buildings of Washington's original institute comprise a national historical site. On campus, the **George Washington Carver Museum** has exhibits and films on its namesake and Booker T. Washington, and on the history of Tuskegee University. Artist, teacher, scientist, and head of the Tuskegee Agricultural Dept., Carver improved the daily lives of Macon County's poor by discovering hundreds of practical uses for common, inexpensive products like the peanut. (☎727-3200. Open daily 9am-4:30pm. Free.) Across the street from the campus lies **The Oaks,** a restoration of Washington's home. (30min. tours daily; call for schedule.) Grab a wholesome and hearty meal in the **Kellogg Conference Center ❷** on campus. The lunch buffet is $8.75, and Sunday brunch is $11. (☎727-3000. Open for lunch M-Sa 11am-2pm, Su 11am-3pm. Open for dinner M-Th 5:30-8:30pm. F-Sa 5:30-9pm. AmEx/DC/MC/V.) To get to Tuskegee, take I-85 toward Atlanta, get off at Exit 32, and follow the signs. **Greyhound,** 205 E. MLK, Jr. Blvd./Hwy. 80 (☎727-1290; www.greyhound.com; open M-F 8:30am-5pm, Sa 8:30am-2pm), runs to and from Montgomery (45min., 7 per day, $11). **Area Code:** 334.

SELMA ☎334

Selma, perhaps more than any other place in Alabama, is haunted by the past. The small Southern town was shaped by two momentous events that took place 100 years apart. As a stronghold for the Confederate armies, its fall in 1865 marked a decisive victory for the North. A century later, Selma gained notoriety during the Voting Rights movement. In the Selma of 1964, state-imposed restrictions gave only 1% of eligible blacks the right to vote. In 1965, Civil Rights activists organized an ill-fated march on the state capitol that was quashed by troops using night sticks, cattle prods, and tear gas. Their spirits battered but not destroyed, the marchers kept trying. A third attempt resulted in the 54 mi. trek from Selma to Montgomery that Dr. King declared the "greatest march ever made on a state capitol in the South." Five months later, Congress passed the Voting Rights Act, prohibiting states from using prerequisites to disqualify voters on the basis of color.

Today, these events are remembered in the museums and sights around town. Selma has the largest historical district in Alabama and calls itself home to one of America's most unique festivals, the **Tale Tellin' Festival.** Storytellers and yarn-spinners from across the South converge on Selma during the second Friday and Saturday in October. (☎800-457-3562; www.taletellin.com. $10, children $5.) The **National Voting Rights Museum and Institute,** 1012 Water Ave., houses memorabilia relating to the Voting Rights Act of 1965 and continues to disseminate information about voting rights and responsibilities. (☎418-0800. Open Tu-F 9am-5pm, Sa 10am-3pm. $6; seniors, students, and children $4.) The **Brown Chapel AME Church and King Monument,** 410 Martin Luther King, Jr. St., served as the headquarters for many Civil Rights meetings during the movement and was the starting point for the march to Montgomery. (☎874-7897. Call for hours and tours.) South of Water Ave., at the end of Broad St., you can walk over the famous **Edmund Pettus Bridge,** where the march left Selma on its way to Montgomery. **The Old Depot Museum,** 4 Martin Luther King, Jr. St., explores the history of Selma with artifacts of past and present, some dating back to the area's original inhabitants, the Cherokee and Creek Indians. Check out the photography collection by the 19th-century Alabama native Mary Morgan Keipp. (☎874-2197. Open M-Sa 10am-4pm, Su by appointment. $4, seniors $3, students 19-25 $2, ages 6-18 $1, children under 6 free.) The **Vaughan Smitherman Museum,** 109 Union Street, is housed in a mansion that was a hospital for Confederate soldiers. The museum recounts Selma's history and is worth visiting in conjunction with the Voting Rights Museum for two starkly contrasting perspectives on Selma's history. (☎874-2174. Open Tu-Sa 9am-4pm. $3.)

For lodging options, **Budget Inn ❷,** 601 Highland Ave. (Hwy. 80 W), opposite McDonald's, is the best of the budget motels along Highland Ave., with basic, clean rooms and a pleasant staff. (☎872-3451. Cable TV, free local calls, pool, fridge, and microwave. Singles $41; doubles $49. AmEx/D/MC/V.) ◪**Strong's ❷,** 118 Washington St. off Broad St, offers superb soul food prepared from scratch and is worth the wait. Really fresh chicken (boxes $4.50-5.75), fish ($4.50-6.25), and a choice of 15 vegetable side orders ($1.30) make for a wholesome and filling meal. (☎875-8800. Open M-F 10am-7pm, Sa 10am-6pm. Cash only.)

Downtown Selma is bordered by **Jeff Davis Avenue** to the north and the **Alabama River** to the south. **U.S. 80,** which becomes **Broad Street,** runs straight through town. **Greyhound,** 434 Broad St. (☎874-4503; www.greyhound.com; open daily 7am-10pm), runs to Atlanta (4½-6hr., 5 per day, $38), Dallas (12-13½hr., 4 per day, $102), and Montgomery (1hr., 5 per day, $15). **Visitors Center:** 2207 Broad St. (☎875-7485. Open daily 8am-8pm.) **Internet Access: Selma/Dallas County Public Library,** 1103 Selma Ave., 2nd fl. (☎874-1727. Open M-Sa 9am-5pm. Free Internet access with library card.) **Post Office:** 1301 Alabama Ave. (☎874-4678. Open M-F 8am-4:30pm, Sa 8am-noon.) **Postal Code:** 36703. **Area Code:** 334.

BIRMINGHAM ☎205

For many people, Birmingham is reminiscent of the struggle for black civil rights in the 1960s. Leaders like Martin Luther King, Jr. and Fred Shuttleworth faced some of their toughest fights in what was labeled "Bombingham" after dozens of bombs rocked the city in the early 1960s. Alabama's largest city has made strides to come to terms with its past, evident in many of its excellent museums, especially the Civil Rights Museum and its efforts to build a substantial medical research community in recent years. The city's past looms large, however, in today's residential segregation and the downtown sites in the old black neighborhoods where many of the worst racial crimes took place.

▮ TRANSPORTATION

Airport: Birmingham International Airport (☎595-0533; www.flybirmingham.com), Exit 129 off I-20.

Trains: Amtrak, 1819 Morris Ave. (☎324-3033 for station information or 800-872-7245 for ticket purchases; www.amtrak.com), south of 1st Ave. N at 19th St. Open daily 9am-5pm. 1 train per day to **Atlanta** (4hr., $20-49) and **New Orleans** (7hr., $23-57). Use caution in this area, especially at night.

Buses: Greyhound, 618 19th St. N. (☎252-7190; www.greyhound.com). Open 24hr. To: **Atlanta** (3hr., 7 per day, $28); **Mobile** (6hr., 5 per day, $48); **Montgomery** (2hr., 5 per day, $21.50); **Nashville** (3½-5½hr., 6 per day, $32).

Public Transit: Metropolitan Area Express (MAX) and **Downtown Area Rapid Transit (DART)** (☎521-0101; www.bjcta.org). MAX: most routes M-F 6am-8pm. $1, students $0.60; transfers $0.25. DART trolley runs to downtown tourist destinations. Most routes every 10min. M-Th 10am-5pm, F-Sa 10am-midnight, Su 10am-9pm. Free.

Taxi: Yellow Cab ☎252-1131.

ORIENTATION AND PRACTICAL INFORMATION

While most of the city is pancake-flat, the southeastern edge climbs up suddenly into the bluffs, and the streets curl, wind, and become both very beautiful and very confusing. Downtown Birmingham is organized in a grid with numbered avenues running east-west and numbered streets running north-south. **Richard Arrington, Jr. Boulevard** is the one exception, running along what should have been called 21st St. Downtown is divided by railroad tracks running east-west through the center of the city—thus avenues and streets are designated "N" or "S." Avenue numbers decrease as they near the railroad tracks (with 1st Ave. N and S running alongside them), while street numbers increase from 11th St. at the western edge of downtown to 26th St. at the east. **Five Points South,** the center of nightlife, is at the intersection of 20th St. S and 11th Ave. S, while the **University of Alabama-Birmingham** is northwest of Five Points South, between 6th and 10th Ave. along University Blvd.

Visitor Info: Greater Birmingham Convention and Visitors Center, 2200 9th Ave. N, 1st fl. (☎458-8000; www.birminghamal.org), has helpful staff and useful maps of the city. Open M-F 8:30am-5pm. **Birmingham Fun Line** (☎458-8000) has weekly information on upcoming events.

Hotlines: Crisis Center, ☎323-7777. **Rape Response,** ☎323-7273. Both 24hr.

Internet Access: Birmingham Public Library, 2100 Park Pl. (☎226-3600), at the corner of Richard Arrington, Jr. Blvd. near the visitors center. Tell them you're from out-of-town to get a sign-on code for a library computer or log on to their wireless network. Open M-Tu 9am-8pm, W-Sa 9am-6pm, Su 2-6pm.

Post Office: 351 24th St. N (☎521-7990). Open M-F 7am-8pm. **Postal Code:** 35203. **Area Code:** 205.

ACCOMMODATIONS

Relatively cheap hotels and motels dot the greater Birmingham area along the various interstates. The closer to downtown, the more expensive the room.

The Hospitality Inn, 2127 7th Ave. S (☎322-0691), 4 blocks north of Five Points South near the university, is a good value and boasts a convenient location. Rooms with 2 twin beds $44.50; 2 double beds $49.50. Wheelchair accessible. AmEx/D/MC/V. ❷

Delux Inn and Suites/Motel Birmingham, 7905 Crestwood Blvd. (☎956-4440). Take Exit 132B from I-20 E. Turn right at Montevallo Rd. and left on Crestwood Blvd. Comfortable rooms, A/C, cable TV, patios, continental breakfast, and a pool. One of the better deals for its price. Rooms for 1-2 people M-Th $50, F-Su $53. AmEx/D/MC/V. ❸

Oak Mountain State Park Campground (☎620-2527 or 800-252-7275), 15 mi. south of the city off I-65 in Pelham at Exit 246. 10,000 acres of horseback riding, golfing, and hiking, and an 85-acre lake with a beach and fishing. Campground has bathrooms, showers, and laundry. Park open 7am-8pm. 2-night min. stay required for reservations. Sites $10.75; with water and electricity $15, full hookup $17. ❶

◐ FOOD

An old streetcar suburb near the University of Alabama-Birmingham, Five Points South, at the intersection of 20th St. S and 11th Ave. S, is the best place to find great restaurants with reasonable prices.

▨ **Bahama Wings and Soul Food,** 321 17th St. N (☎324-9464), downtown. A hole-in-the-wall that's so local, you'll be the only diner who doesn't live 2 doors down. *The* place for tasty and cheap wings, with 2 pieces served with a slice of toast and fries for $1.75. Flavors range from Spicy Jerk to Bahama Breeze. BBQ plates $5.75-7.25. Catfish dinner $7.75. Open M-Th 11am-7pm, F 11am-11pm, Sa 10am-11pm. ❷

Jim and Nick's, 1908 11th Ave. S (☎320-1060), in Five Points South. Jim and Nick's began as a roadside barbecue joint over 50 years ago and has grown into a casual restaurant. The ribs are excellent (half-rack $14, full-rack $18). Open M-Th and Su 10:30am-9pm, F-Sa 10:30am-10pm. AmEx/D/MC/V. ❸

Bogue's, 3028 Clairmont Ave. (☎254-9780), follow University Ave. east until it turns into Clairmont. Established in 1936, Bogue's is a Birmingham institution known for its breakfasts and sweet rolls. Breakfast platters $4.75-6.75. Lunch specials with choice of two vegetables and sweet rolls $6.45. Open M-Sa 6am-2pm. AmEx/MC/V. ❷

Fish Market Restaurant, 622 22nd St. S (☎322-3330), at the corner of 22nd St. and 6th Avenue S. Birmingham's oldest seafood wholesaler doubles as a no-frills joint with cheap catches. Snapper and flounder are very popular, but the adventurous go for the frog legs. Entrees $6-9. Open M-Th 10am-9pm, F-Sa 10am-10pm. AmEx/D/MC/V. ❷

◉ SIGHTS

CIVIL RIGHTS. Birmingham's commemoration of the civil rights struggles of the 1950s and 1960s centers around the **Birmingham Civil Rights District,** nine blocks dedicated to the battles and bombings that took place there. **Kelly Ingram Park** was the site of numerous protests, and commemorative statues and sculptures now grace the green lawns. (At 5th and 6th Ave. N between 16th and 17th St. Open daily 6am-10pm. Audio tours available at Civil Rights Institute Tu-Sa 10am-3pm. Tours $5.) The **Sixteenth Street Baptist Church** served as the focal point of Birmingham's Civil Rights movement. Four young black girls were killed here on September 15, 1963, when white segregationists bombed the building, spurring protests in the nearby park. A small exhibit in the church's basement chronicles its past. (1530 6th Ave. N. ☎251-9402. Open Tu-F 10am-4pm, Sa by appointment. Admission $3.) Across the street from the church, the fascinating ▨**Birmingham Civil Rights Institute** traces the nation's Civil Rights struggle through the lens of Alabama's segregation battle. Displays and documentary footage balance the imaginative exhibits and disturbing artifacts from the Jim Crow era, like the burnt-out shell of a torched Greyhound bus and the Birmingham Segregation Ordinances. (520 16th St. N. ☎328-9696 or 866-328-9696; www.bcri.org. Audio walking tours of neighboring Kelly Ingram Park $5 with ID deposit. Open Tu-Sa 10am-5pm, Su 1-5pm. $9, seniors $5, students $4, under 18 free; Su free.)

4TH AVENUE. In the heart of the old historic black neighborhood, now known as the **4th Avenue District,** sits the ▨**Alabama Jazz Hall of Fame.** Jazz greats from Erskine Hawkins to the magnificent Ella Fitzgerald each get a small display on their life work. There are free concerts on Sundays 1-3pm and 2-4pm. *(1631 4th Ave. N, in the Carver Theater 1 block south of Kelly Ingram Park. ☎254-2731. Open Tu-Sa 10am-5pm, Su 1-5pm. Admission $2, guided tours $3. AmEx/D/MC/V.)* Two blocks away, the **Birmingham Museum of Art** is the largest municipal art museum in the South, containing over 18,000 works and a sculpture garden. The gallery also houses the Hanson Library, which features the largest collection of Wedgewood china outside the UK. *(2000 8th Ave. N. ☎254-2565. Self-guided audio tour available. Open Tu-Sa 10am-5pm, Su noon-3pm. Donations appreciated.)* Alabama's sports greats, from Willie "The Say Hey Kid" Mays to runner Carl Lewis, are immortalized in the **Alabama Sports Hall of Fame.** *(2150 Civic Center Blvd., at the corner of 22nd St. N. ☎323-6665. Open M-Sa 9am-5pm, Su 1-5pm. $5, seniors $4, students $3, under 6 free. AAA $1 discount. AmEx/MC/V.)*

SMELTING. Birmingham remembers its days as the "Pittsburgh of the South" at the **Sloss Furnaces National Historic Landmark.** Although the blast furnaces closed 20 years ago, they are the only preserved example of 20th-century iron smelting in the world. Plays and concerts are held in a renovated furnace shed by the stacks. *(20 32nd St. N, adjacent to the 1st Ave. N overpass off 32nd St. downtown. ☎324-1911; www.slossfurnaces.com. Open Tu-Sa 10am-4pm, Su noon-4pm. Tours Sa-Su 1, 2, 3pm. Free.)* For more insight into the city's history, head to **Vulcan,** 1701 Valley View Dr., the largest statue ever made in the US and the largest cast-iron statue in the world. Vulcan, the Roman god of metallurgy, was sculpted by Italian artist Giuseppe Moretti to represent Alabama at the 1904 St. Louis World's Fair and rises to a staggering height of 180 ft. on top of a hill to the south of the city. From the top you get a 360-degree view of the region, but you can also get a great view of Birmingham from the base for free. If you do go up the tower, the first thing you'll see as you emerge from the elevator is Vulcan's huge iron butt. Don't worry, the view gets better. *(Go south on 20th St. S and follow the signs. ☎933-1409; www.vulcanpark.org. Open M-Sa 10am-6pm, Su 1-6pm. Open until 10pm some nights for great nighttime views. $6, seniors $5, ages 5-12 $4, under 5 $3. Wheelchair accessible.)*

OTHER SIGHTS. For a break from the heavy-duty ironworks, revel in the marvelously manicured grounds of the **Birmingham Botanical Gardens.** Spectacular floral displays, an elegant Japanese garden, and an enormous greenhouse occupy a 67-acre site. You can arrange a tour if you want expert commentary on the garden's flora and fauna. *(2612 Lane Park Rd., off U.S. 31. ☎414-3900. Garden Center open daily 8am-5pm; gardens open from dawn to dusk. Free.)* If you prefer cogs and grease to petals and pollen, the **Mercedes-Benz U.S. International Visitors Center** is a 24,000 sq. ft. museum that spares no technological expense to celebrate the history of all things Mercedes. Currently undergoing a major expansion, the center will be closed until mid-2006. *(I-20/59 off Exit 89 on Mercedes Dr. at Vance St. ☎507-2253 or 888-286-8762.)*

🎵 🎭 ENTERTAINMENT AND NIGHTLIFE

Opened in 1927, the **Historic Alabama Theater,** 1817 3rd Ave. N, is booked 300 nights of the year with films, concerts, and live performances. Their organ, the "Mighty Wurlitzer," entertains the audience before each show. *(☎251-0418. Open M-F 9am-4pm. Order tickets at the box office 1hr. prior to show. Showtimes generally 7pm, Su 2pm. Organ plays 15min. before the official show time. Free.)* Mid-June *means* everything from country to gospel to big-name rock groups at **City Stages.** The three-day festival, held on multiple stages in downtown's blocked-off streets, is the year's biggest event and includes food, crafts, and children's activities. *(☎251-1272 or 800-277-1700; www.citystages.org. 1-day pass $25, 3-day weekend pass $40.)*

Nightlife centers around **Five Points South,** at 20th St. S and 11th Ave. S. The hippest people jam at **The Nick,** 2514 10th Ave. S, at the corner of 26th St. Locals call it "the place." *(☎252-3831. Live rock music most nights. Cover $5-6 for local bands,*

$10-15 for big names; M usually free. Happy hour M-F 3-9pm. Open M-F 3pm-late, Sa-Su 8pm-6am.) **The Garage,** 2304 10th Terrace S, is a very cool bar tucked out of sight down 23rd St. A former architecture studio turned antique store, all the materials are still there—customers just drink around the statues, tools, and artwork. Try a Jubel German beer in the weed-covered courtyard, or munch on a simple sandwich among the nymphs and Greek art. (☎322-3220. Open daily 11am-3am.)

TUSCALOOSA AND MOUNDVILLE   ☎205

Moundville is one of the best preserved and most important indigenous sites in North America. The Mississipian people made this one of their most important settlements, and from AD 1000 to 1500 their fortified city of 3000 people was the prehistoric metropolis of the South. The settlement thrived thanks to rich soil, ample water, and a long growing season. Its dirt mounds were constructed over a 300-year span, and their orderly arrangement suggests some kind of master plan that is still not fully understood. Tuscaloosa, the nearest city, is 13 mi. north of Moundville on Hwy. 69 and 60 mi. southwest of Birmingham along I-59/20. **Moundville Archaeological Park** is well worth the effort of getting there. You can drive around the earthen mounds and climb the highest one, which, at 60 ft., is thought to be the original chief ceremonial mound and provides a great view of the lesser mounds. The park provides an informative video. (☎371-2234 for tours. $4; seniors, students, and children $2; under 5 free.) Inside the park, the **Jones Archaeological Museum** displays exhibits and artifacts from the mounds, and a model Indian village features reenactments of the daily life of the Mississipian people. Every year during the first full week of October, the **Moundville Native American Festival** is held on the grounds and celebrates Native American dances, crafts, and storytelling. (☎371-2234. Open M-F 9am-4pm, Sa 9am-5pm.)

In Tuscaloosa, home to the University of Alabama, take a trip on the Black Warrior River aboard the paddle ship **Bama Belle,** 1 Greensboro Ave. (☎339-1108; www.bamabelle.com). Sunset cruises with live entertainment set sail Tuesdays at 6:30pm and "Something to Do" cruises are on Sundays at 3pm. (Both 1½hr.; $8, seniors $7, ages 2-12 $5). The ship also offers dinner cruises on Fridays (1½hr., $40; reservations required). The **Tuscaloosa Visitors Center** (☎391-9200; open M-F 8:30am-5pm, Sa 10am-2pm) is housed in the basement of the **Jemison-Van de Graf House,** 1305 Greensboro Ave., one of the finest examples of Italianate architecture in the South. The 1862 mansion is open to visitors; inquire at the visitors center.

Accommodations in Tuscaloosa cluster along McFarland Blvd./Hwy 82 near the University of 'bama. **Masters' Inventory ❺,** 3600 McFarland Blvd. E, has clean, standard rooms, some with refrigerator and microwave, and continental breakfast. (☎556-2010. Singles $40; doubles $45. AAA discount. AmEx/D/MC/V.) **La Quinta Inn ❸,** 4122 McFarland Blvd. E, is a comfortable motel with a pool and good breakfast. (☎349-3270. Room with 2 beds $60-70. AAA discount. D/MC/V.) **Camping ❶** is available in Moundville itself in a quiet, wooded setting among the mounds and under the stars. The 30 sites come with hot showers, electricity, and some with sewage connection for RVs. (☎371-2572. Registration at the Jones Museum daily 9am-5pm. Tent and RV sites $10.) In Tuscaloosa, ◩**Dreamland Barbecue ❸,** 5535 15th Ave. E., is pure barbecue heaven. From McFarland Blvd. E, turn onto Jug Factory and look for the sign. There's no menu to complicate things here—just choose from a plate of three ribs for $6, six for $9.50, or a full slab for $18. (☎758-8135. Open M-Th 10am-9pm, F-Sa 10am-10pm, Su 11am-9pm. AmEx/MC/V.) The **Super China Buffet ❷,** 4127 McFarland Blvd. E, around the corner from Foodworld, offers a huge selection of Chinese food, made-to-order stir-fry, and sushi. (☎752-8998. Dinner buffet $8. Lunch buffet M-Sa $5.25, Su $6.50. Open M-Th and Su 11am-10pm, F-Sa 11am-11pm. AmEx/MC/V.) In Moundville, **Miss Melissa's Cafe ❶,** 384 Market St., resembles a small school cafeteria—but the cooking you get here is the real deal. There's an all-you-can-eat breakfast ($5) and a canteen-style lunch with meat and three vegetables for $5.70. (☎371-9045. Open M-Sa 6am-2pm. Cash or check only.)

In Tuscaloosa, **Greyhound**, at 2520 Stillman Blvd. (☎758-6651; www.greyhound.com; open M-F 7:30am-6pm, Sa 7:30am-5pm, Su 7:30-9am and 1:30-5pm), runs to: Birmingham (1hr., 7 per day, $12); Jackson (3-8hr., 6 per day, $22); Memphis (7-10hr., 5 per day, $47). **Postal Code:** 35405. **Area Code:** 205.

HUNTSVILLE   ☎256

Huntsville, 80 mi. north of Birmingham, was the first English-speaking settlement in Alabama and the location of the state's Constitutional Convention in 1819. Far more momentous, however, was the 1950 decision to locate the nation's rocket program here. Initially proposed by Wernher von Braun, the program has endowed the city with a museum, visitors center, and Space Camp, as well as one of NASA's ten national research facilities. A 363 ft. replica of a Saturn V rocket at the **US Space and Rocket Center,** Exit 15 off I-565, is visible for miles around, and the center features space-flight simulators, an IMAX theater, and decommissioned rockets, missiles, and spacecraft, including the original Apollo 16 capsule. (☎837-3400. Open daily 9am-5pm. Last admission 4pm; allow 3hr. for museum and film. $19, ages 3-12 $13.) **Huntsville Botanical Garden,** 4747 Bob Wallace Ave., provides welcome relief from dull strip malls. Designed for kids' entertainment as well as adults' appreciation, the garden has bonsai trees, inviting water features, a new butterfly house, an aquatic garden, and a 110-year-old dogwood tree. (☎830-4447; www.hsvbg.org. Open Memorial Day-Labor Day M-Sa 9am-8pm, Su 1-8pm; winter M-Sa 9am-5pm, Su 1-5pm. $8, seniors $6, ages 3-18 $3.) The **Huntsville Stars,** a AA affiliate of the Milwaukee Brewers, round the bases at Joe Davis Stadium from April to September. (☎882-2562; www.huntsvillestars.com. Tickets $5-8.)

Miles of budget motels and chain restaurants are located on **University Drive,** northwest of downtown, and also at the exits near the airport. To peruse possible lodgings, get off I-565 at Exit 19 and head northwest to University Dr. For discount lodging vouchers, pick up a copy of *Alabama Travel Coupons* at the visitors center. **Knight's Inn ❷,** 4404 University Dr., has 60 rooms with refrigerator, wireless Internet, and microwave in a two-story complex. (☎864-0388. Free local and long-distance calls and continental breakfast. Rooms $43-57. AmEx/D/MC/V.) The **Red Carpet Motel ❷,** 3200 University Dr., has rooms that are clean, if a bit dark, with a pool. From I-565, exit Jordan Ln. N and take a right on University Dr. (☎539-8448. Check-out 11am. Singles $35-37; doubles $42. AmEx/D/DC/MC/V.) For a bite to eat, the **Wild Rose Cafe ❷,** 121 N. Side Sq., is easy to find in the main square, opposite the courthouse. A traditional lunch counter, it serves quality meat-and-three (vegetables, that is) platters for $6. There are at least 17 vegetables to choose from each day and desserts from $1.25. (☎539-3658. Open M-F 7-9:30am and 11am-2:00pm. AmEx/D/MC/V.) **Judge Crater's ❶,** in the basement at 110 South Side Ave., is a themed sandwich joint by day and a bar by night. (☎534-6116. Lunch combos $5.25-6. Happy hour 4-7pm. Open M-F 11am-2am, Sa 5pm-2am. AmEx/D/DC/MC/V.) **Papou's ❷,** 110 South Side Ave. above Judge Crater's, features Greek cuisine, as well as daily lunch specials. (☎534-5553. Entrees $6-8. Open M-Tu 11am-2pm, W-F 11am-2pm and 5-9pm, Sa 5-9pm. AmEx/D/MC/V.)

Greyhound, 601 Monroe St. (☎534-1681; www.greyhound.com; open daily 7:30am-11:45pm), runs buses to Birmingham (2½-7hr., 5 per day, $21), Memphis (7½-8½hr., 3 per day, $77), and Nashville (2hr., 4 per day, $20). A **tourist shuttle** runs between downtown, museums, points on University Dr., and the Space and Rocket Center. The trolley can also make hotel pickup stops by reservation. (1 per hr. M-F 6:40am-6:40pm, Sa 8:40am-7:10pm. $1, all-day pass $2. Wheelchair accessible.)

Huntsville Shuttle runs 11 routes infrequently; the tourist loop is one. (☎532-7433 for schedule. Runs M-F 6am-6pm. $1; students, seniors, and children under 7 $0.50; transfers free.) **Visitor Info,** 500 Church St., has a very helpful and talkative staff who can provide a variety of local and state maps. (☎551-2230 or 800-772-2348; www.huntsville.org. Open M-Sa 8am-5pm, Su noon-5pm.) **Area Code:** 256.

MOBILE   ☎251

Although Bob Dylan lamented being stuck here, Mobile (MO-beel) has had plenty of fans in its time—French, Spanish, English, Sovereign Alabama, Confederate, and American flags have each flown over the city since its founding in 1702. This historical diversity is revealed in both the population and local architecture; ante-bellum mansions, Italianate dwellings, Spanish and French forts, and Victorian homes line the city's azalea-edged streets. The site of the country's very first Mardi Gras, Mobile still hosts a three-week-long Fat Tuesday celebration without the hordes that plague its Cajun counterpart, giving the city the feel of a more untour-isted New Orleans.

▣ ▢ ORIENTATION AND PRACTICAL INFORMATION. The downtown district borders the Mobile River. **Dauphin Street,** which is one-way downtown, and **Govern-ment Boulevard (U.S. 90),** which becomes **Government Street** downtown, are the major east-west routes. **Airport Boulevard, Springhill Avenue,** and **Old Shell Road** are secondary east-west roads. **Royal Street** and **Broad Street** are major north-south byways. **Water Street** runs along the river downtown, becoming the **I-10 causeway.** A road variously called **I-65 East/West Access Road, Frontage Road,** and the **Beltline** lies west of down-town. **Amtrak,** 11 Government St. (☎800-872-7245; www.amtrak.com), next to the convention center, uses an unstaffed "station" where passengers can be dropped off or picked up with advance notice; Mobile is on the Jacksonville-New Orleans line. **Greyhound,** 2545 Government Blvd. (☎478-9793 or 478-6089; www.greyhound.com; open 24hr.), at Pinehill St. west of downtown, goes to: Atlanta (6-9hr., 10 per day, $50); Birmingham (5hr., 4 per day, $40); Montgomery (3hr., 7 per day, $32); New Orleans (3hr., 7 per day, $30). **Metro Transit** provides local transportation. (☎344-5656. Runs every hr. M-F 6am-6pm, reduced service Sa-Su. $1. Transfers $0.10.) **Moda!** runs free **trolleys** to most sights downtown, including the visitors center. The loop route takes about 15min.; trolleys stop at each location every 10min. (☎344-6600; www.mainstreetmobile.org. Operates M-F 7am-6pm.) **Taxi: Yellow Cab,** ☎476-7711. **Visitor Info: Fort Condé Info Center,** 150 S. Royal St. off I-10 at Exit 26A, in a reconstructed French fort near Government St. Ask for their great self-guided walking tour of historic houses. (☎208-7304. Open daily 8am-5pm.) **Post Office:** 168 Bay Shore Ave. (☎478-5639. Open M-F 9am-4:30pm.) **Postal Code:** 36607. **Area Code:** 251.

▟ ACCOMMODATIONS. Few budget lodging options exist in historic Mobile. In lieu of expensive chains, try the **Malaga Inn ❹,** 359 Church St., at Claiborne, in front of the Civic Center, where local charm comes in a pink-stucco package. Occupying two 1862 townhouses, the hotel has a delightful central courtyard and gorgeous rooms with private bath and cable TV. (☎438-4701; www.mala-gainn.com. Continental breakfast. Rooms $79-99. AmEx/D/MC/V.) Roughly 7 mi. from downtown, a slew of affordable motels lines I-65 on Beltline, from Spring Hill Rd. to Government Blvd., and U.S. 90. **Olsson's Motel ❷,** 4137 Government Blvd. (U.S. 90 W), Exit 1 off I-65, has quirky perks like recliners and four-poster beds. (☎661-5331. Fridge, free local calls. Singles $39; doubles $45. AmEx/D/MC/V.) **Mobile's I-10 Kampground ❶,** 6430 Theodore Dawes Rd., 7½ mi. west on I-10, south off Exit 13, is a quiet spot in a forest with shady sites, a pool, and a less-than-clean bathhouse. (☎653-9816 or 800-272-1263. Pool and laundry facilities. Sites with water and electricity $15, with hookup $20-24. Each additional person $1. MC/V.)

🖪🖪 **FOOD AND NIGHTLIFE.** Mobile's Gulf location means fresh seafood and Southern cookin'. 🔳**Wintzell's Oyster House ❸**, 605 Dauphin St., is a long-time local favorite; oysters are served "fried, stewed, or nude." (☎432-4605. Entrees $8-14. Lunch special $8. $0.25 raw oysters, $1 drafts at happy hour M-F 4-7pm. Open M-Th and Su 11am-10pm, F-Sa 11am-11pm. AmEx/MC/V.) To taste some of the simple American goodness that Mobilians have been enjoying since 1924, head to the **Dew Drop Inn ❶**, 1808 Old Shell Rd., Mobile's oldest restaurant, for a hamburger ($2.25), hot dog ($2.25), or seafood ($6-10). Mull over your options as you sip Coke from a classic green bottle. (☎473-7872. Open Tu-F 10am-8pm, Sa 10am-3pm. AmEx/D/MC/V.) For delicious barbecue, follow the cloud of wood smoke to **Dreamland ❷**, 3314 Old Shell Rd. The famous ribs, cooked over an open fire in the large dining room, will stick to yours. Don't expect much flora with your fauna, though; the only vegetarian option is the house salad. (☎479-9898. Half-slab $10. Half-chicken $6.50. Open M-Sa 10am-10pm, Su 11am-9pm. MC/V.) The **Brick Pit ❷**, 5456 Old Shell Rd., is dedicated to "serious barbecue"—their pulled pork is smoked for 30hr. (☎343-0001. Half-slab $9. Pulled pork sandwich $5.50. Open Tu-Th 11am-8:30pm, F-Sa 11am-9:30pm. MC/V.)

Downtown Mobile's late-night scene is a bit one-dimensional—pool is the name of the game. The **Lower Dauphin Street Entertainment District** is a fancy name for the downtown block of bars, each of which has pool tables, youngish locals, and drinks for under $5. Most places close around 2 or 3am. If you're tired of the downtown scene head to the **Bubble Lounge,** 5546 Old Shell Rd., where you can sip a top-shelf martini ($7) and enjoy the funky, dimly-lit atmosphere. (☎341-5556. 21+. Open M-F 5pm-2am, Sa 6pm-2am, Su 8pm-2am.) Seize the day at **Carpe Diem,** 4072 Old Shell Rd., just slightly west of I-65. Because this locally-adored coffeehouse has its own roaster, the grounds used to make your coffee are never more than two weeks old. (☎304-0448. Tea and coffee from $1.30. Specialty mudslides from $2. Open M-Sa 6am-11pm, Su 7am-10pm. MC/V.) Check the free weekly *Lagniappe* in boxes around town for other entertainment options.

🖸 **SIGHTS.** Mobile's attractions are scattered inland, around downtown, and near the bay. The **Museum of Mobile,** 111 S. Royal St., celebrates and documents Mobilian history in all its glory. Exhibits cover "The Founding of Mobile," the fate of the slave ship *Clotilda,* and the private collections of prominent Mobile families. (☎208-7569. Open M-Sa 9am-5pm, Su 1-5pm. $5, seniors $4, students $3; families $20.) The **MuseuBienville Square,** at the intersection of Dauphin and Conception St., is the locals' main hangout. Eight separate historic districts, all well-marked, display the city's varied architectural and cultural influences. The **Church Street East Historic District** showcases Federal, Greek Revival, and Victorian architecture, and several spectacular houses have been converted into museums. In the **DeTonti Historical District,** north of downtown, brick townhouses with ornate wrought-iron balconies surround the restored **Richards-DAR House Museum,** 256 North Joachim St. (☎208-7320. Open M-F 11am-3:30pm, Sa 10am-4pm, Su 1-4pm. Tours $5, children $2. Free tea and cookies.) Adjacent to the Historic DeTonti District, the **African-American Archives and Museum,** 564 Dr. Martin Luther King, Jr. Ave., is housed in what was the first African-American library. The museum has portraits, biographies, books, carvings, and other artifacts that represent the lives of numerous African-Americans from the Mobile area and elsewhere. (☎433-8511. Open Tu-Sa 10am-4pm. Free admission and parking; donations appreciated.) **Oakleigh Historical Complex,** 350 Oakleigh Pl., 2½ blocks south of Government St. at George St., contains the grandiose **Oakleigh House Museum,** the working-class **Cox-Deasy Cottage Museum,** and the **Mardi Gras Cottage Museum** with a 19th- and 20th-century art collection. The houses portray the lives of various classes of Mobilians in the 1800s. (☎432-1281; www.historicmobile.org. Open M-Sa 9am-3pm. Tours every 30min., last tour 2:30pm. $5, seniors and AAA $4, ages 6-11 $3.)

The **Bragg-Mitchell Mansion,** 1906 Springhill Ave., is Mobile's grandest antebellum home. The mansion has seven large bedrooms and was completed in Greek-Italianate style. (☎471-6364. Open for 30-45min. tours Tu-F 10am-3:30pm. $5, seniors and AAA $4.50, children $3.) The *USS Alabama,* moored 2½ mi. east of town at Battleship Park (accessible from I-10 and Government St.'s Bankhead Tunnel), earned nine stars from battles fought in WWII. Open passageways let landlubbers explore the ship's depths. The park is also home to the submarine *USS Drum* and a collection of airplanes. (☎433-2703; www.ussalabama.com. Open Apr.-Sept. daily 8am-6pm. $10, seniors $9, ages 6-11 $5. Simulated ride $4. Coupon available at Fort Condé Visitors Center. AAA discount $2. Parking $2.) **Bellingrath Gardens,** 12401 Bellingrath Gardens Rd., Exit 15A off I-10, has lush roses, oriental gardens, and a bayou boardwalk in a 900-acre setting. Admission includes a 1-2hr. tour of the gardens. Visitors can also tour the Bellingrath mansion or take a river cruise on the Southern Belle. (☎800-247-8420. Open daily 8am-dusk; ticket office closes 5pm. Gardens $9; gardens and home $16.50; gardens, home and river cruise $25; ages 5-11 $5.25/$10.50/$15.75. MC/V.) Early spring is the time to be in Mobile. Beginning at the visitors center, azaleas bloom in a 27 ft. pink line marking the twisting **Azalea Trail.** In February, Mobile's **Mardi Gras,** the precursor to New Orleans's debauchery, erupts with parades, costumes, an Out-of-Towners ball, and the crowning of the Mardi Gras King and Queen. Check out the free *Mobile Traveler* and *Mobile Bay Monthly,* available at Fort Condé Visitors Center, for details.

🔀 DAYTRIP FROM MOBILE: DAUPHIN ISLAND. First settled by French colonists, Dauphin Island was named after the heir of King Louis XIV of France and became the capital of France's vast Louisiana Territory in 1718. Dauphin Island's public beaches are free and accessible from Bienville Blvd. east of downtown; follow the signs once you cross the bridge to the island. The **Dauphin Island Audubon Sanctuary,** off Bienville Ave. eastbound, has walking trails and boardwalks that traverse its 164 acres of dunes, maritime pine forest, and freshwater lakes. (☎861-5524. More info available at the visitors center. Free.) Dauphin Island is home to **Fort Gaines,** 109 Bienville Blvd., a pentagonal, cannon-studded stronghold that was captured by the Union navy in the battle of Mobile Bay during the Civil War. (☎861-6992. Open daily 9am-6pm. $5, ages 5-12 $3, 4 and under free.) **Dauphin Island Estuarium,** the public aquarium of the Dauphin Island sea lab, presents exhibits on the many ecosystems of coastal Alabama. (☎861-7500. Open Mar.-Aug. M-Sa 9am-6pm, Su noon-6pm; Sept.-Feb. M-Sa 9am-5pm, Su 1pm-5pm. $6, seniors $5, ages 5-18 $3.) The **Cow and Bean ❷,** 200 LeMoyne Blvd., serves breakfast, lunch, and dinner, along with a tempting selection of ice cream. (☎861-2277. Breakfast $3.30-5.50. Sandwiches $6.50-8.50. Open M-Sa 6am-10pm, Su 6am-8pm. MC/V.) Island lodging is expensive, but the **Dauphin Island Campground ❶,** 109 Bienville Blvd. E, has full RV hookups and tent sites in a shady campground next to the Audubon Sanctuary. (☎861-2742. $15 per night, with hookup $34. Rates lower Aug.-Apr. MC/V.) For more information about Dauphin Island, the **Dauphin Island Visitor Center** on Bienville Blvd. west of downtown has lodging and attractions info. (☎861-5524. Open W-Sa 10am-2pm.) To get to Dauphin Island from Mobile, take Exit 17 off I-10 onto Rte. 193 southbound. The island is a 30min. drive from downtown Mobile. The **Mobile Bay Ferry** operates between Dauphin Island and Fort Morgan. (☎540-7787; www.mobilebayferry.com. 30min.; runs daily from 8am, last ferry 7:15pm from Ft. Morgan. $5; autos $14, extra passengers $4 each.) **Area Code:** 251.

MISSISSIPPI

The pervasive legacy of cotton, slavery, racial strife, and economic ruin are still visible in Mississippi. Cotton is now machine harvested and mention of slavery is confined to museums, but racial tension persists. In spite of, or perhaps because of, this complex past, Mississippi also had its share of triumphs. You can get a taste of the disparate traditions that make up this past at Biloxi, home of the Confederacy's only president, and Tupelo, birthplace of Elvis Presley. Mississippi produced several renowned authors, including William Faulkner, Eudora Welty, and Tennessee Williams. Mississippi is notably the American home of the blues. The Crossroads State yielded Robert Johnson, Bessie Smith, W.C. Handy, Muddy Waters, and B.B. King, whose riffs spread upriver and throughout the world.

⁊ PRACTICAL INFORMATION

Capital: Jackson.

Visitor Info: Division of Tourism, P.O. Box 1705, Ocean Springs 39566 (☎800-927-6378; www.visitmississippi.org). **Department of Parks,** P.O. Box 451, Jackson 39205 (☎800-467-2757).

Postal Abbreviation: MS. **Sales Tax:** 8%. **Hotel Tax:** 10%.

JACKSON   ☎ 601

As Mississippi's political and cultural capital, Jackson boasts impressive museums, sights, and a cultured perspective. It is one of only four cities in the world to host the International Ballet Competition, held at the Thalia Mara Center every four years. North Jackson's lush homes and country clubs epitomize wealthy Southern living, while refreshing reservoirs and forests invite outdoor exploration in nearby state parks. Just don't arrive on a Sunday—true to its deep Southern roots, Jackson is always closed for a day of rest.

⁊ **PRACTICAL INFORMATION.** West of I-55 and north of I-20, downtown is bordered on the north by **High Street,** on the south by **South Street,** and on the west by **Lamar Street.** North-south **State Street** bisects the city. **Jackson International Airport,** 100 International Dr. (☎939-5631; www.jmaa.com), is east of downtown off I-20. **Amtrak,** 300 W. Capitol St. in Union Station (☎355-6350; www.amtrak.com; open daily 10:15am-5:45pm), runs to Memphis (4½hr., 7 per week, $33) and New Orleans (4hr., 7 per week, $21). **Greyhound,** also in Union Station (☎353-6342; www.greyhound.com; open 24hr.), goes to Memphis (5hr., 1 per day, $30-32), Montgomery (5hr., 7 per day, $50-53), and New Orleans (4½hr., 4 per day, $27-29). **Jackson Transit System (JATRAN)** offers limited public transit. Find maps at bus stops and JATRAN headquarters, 1025 Terry Rd. (☎948-3840. Open M-F 8am-6pm. Runs from Union Station M-F 5:30am-6:30pm every 30min.; Sa 7am-6pm every hr. $1, transfers free.) **Taxi: City Cab,** ☎355-8319. **Visitor Info: Jackson Convention and Visitors Bureau,** 921 N. President St., downtown. (☎960-1891 or 800-354-7695; www.visitjackson.com. Open M-F 8am-5pm.) **Internet Access: Jackson Library,** 300 State St. (☎968-5801. Open M-Th 9am-5pm, F 9am-6pm, Su 1-5pm. Free.) **Post Office:** 401 E. South St. (☎351-7096. Open M-F 7am-6pm, Sa 8am-noon.) **Postal Code:** 39205. **Area Code:** 601.

⛫ **ACCOMMODATIONS.** Standard mid-range chains crowd **I-20** and **I-55. Parkside Inn ❷,** 3720 I-55 N, at Exit 98B off the access road, is a cheap, clean motel with a pool, cable TV, and free local calls. (☎982-1122. Some rooms with microwave and fridge. Singles $32; doubles $42. AmEx/D/MC/V.) The more expensive but extremely comfortable **Cabot Lodge ❹**, 120 Dyess Rd., in Ridgeland, has cocktails, an extensive breakfast, and a pool, plus free Internet access. (☎957-0757 or 800-342-2268; www.cabotlodgejacksonnorth.com. Singles $84; doubles $89. AmEx/D/MC/V.) For camping, head to **Timberlake Campgrounds ❶**. Take I-55 N to Lakeland East (Exit 98B), turn left after 6 mi. onto Old Fannin Rd., and go 4 mi.; it's inside the Barnett Reservoir. (☎992-9100. Office open daily 8am-11pm. Tent sites with water and electricity $15, full hookup $20. MC/V.)

◖ FOOD. Delicious and deliciously cheap, the ▨**Big Apple Inn ❶**, 4487 N. State St., serves up tasty biscuit sandwiches with your choice of sausage, hamburger or pig's ear for $0.90. Six hot tamales go for $4. (☎934-3704. Open M-Sa 10am-9pm. MC/V.) **Two Sisters ❸**, 707 N. Congress St., around the corner from George St., offers another Southern smorgasbord in a delightful, creaky-staired home. Eat all you want for $9.50; salad bar and dessert are included. (☎353-1180. Open M-F and Su 11am-2pm. AmEx/D/MC/V.) **Mayflower ❷**, 123 W. Capitol St., has been serving diner fare and fresh seafood since 1935. A scene from the movie *Ghosts of Mississippi* was shot here in the cafe. (☎355-4122. Blue-plate lunch specials $6. Seafood dinners $11-16. Open M-F 11am-10pm, Sa 4:30-10pm. AmEx/D/MC/V.)

◙ SIGHTS. The ▨**International Museum of Muslim Cultures (IMMC)**, 117 E. Pascagoula St., was created initially as a temporary satellite to an exhibit at the Mississippi Museum of Art, but became permanent in response to overwhelming community enthusiasm. The museum has extraordinary exhibits on world mosques and the Muslim diaspora. (☎960-0440; www.muslimmuseum.org. Open M-Th 9:30am-5pm, F 9:30am-12:30pm. $7; seniors $5; students, children, and disabled $4.) The **New State Capitol**, 400 High St., between West and President St., completed in 1903, has recently been restored to preserve its Beaux Arts grandeur. Don't miss a ride on the antique elevator when you visit the galleries of the House and Senate chambers. (☎359-3114. Self-guided tours M-F 8am-5pm. Free.) The **Mississippi Museum of Art (MMA)**, 201 E. Pascagoula St., at Lamar St., amazes visitors with galleries displaying over 3100 works of art, from regional and local artists to rotating national and international exhibits. (☎960-1515; www.msmuseumart.org. Open M-Sa 10am-5pm, Su noon-5pm. $5, seniors $4, students $3, ages 6-17 $2.) Adjacent to the MMA, the **Russell C. Davis Planetarium**, 201 E. Pascagoula St., presents movies and astronomy shows with music and lasers. (☎960-1550. Shows daily; call ahead. Movies $5.50, seniors and under 12 $4; planetarium shows $4.50/$3.) Tour the sumptuous Pumpkin Bedroom and Gold Bedroom in the grandiose **Governor's Mansion**, 300 E. Capitol St., one of only two inhabited governor's mansions in the US. (☎359-6421. Tours every 30min. Tu-F 9:30-11am. Free.) The **Old Capitol Museum**, at Capitol and State St., houses Mississippi's old House and Senate chambers and a small collection of exhibits on the state's history. (☎359-6920. Open M-F 8am-5pm, Sa 9:30am-4:30pm, Su 12:30-4:30pm. Free.)

◪ NIGHTLIFE. To get the scoop on all the goings-on in Jackson, pick up the *Clarion-Ledger* on Thursday for a list of weekend events. Two other free publications with events listings are the *Planet Weekly* and *Jackson Free Press* (the city's alternative magazine), available around town. **930 Blues Cafe**, 930 N. Congress St., has live blues every night at 8:30pm in a restored 1901 house. National and regional bands play Fridays and Saturdays. (☎948-3344. Open M-Sa 5:30-late. Cover W-Th $5, F-Sa $10.) **Hal & Mal's Restaurant and Brew Bar**, 200 S. Commerce St., near the corner of State and Pascagoula, has live music in a huge, old, relic-strewn warehouse. Acts range from bluegrass on Wednesdays to jazz on Thursdays and country on Fridays. (☎948-0888. Gumbo $6. Cover F-Sa under $5. Restau-

THE SOUTH

rant open M 11am-3pm, Tu-F 11am-11pm, Sa 5-11pm; bar Tu-Th until midnight, F-Sa until 2am.) **The Joint and the Galaxy**, 206 W. Capital St., attracts a young twenty-something crowd with live alt-rock bands. (☎944-0123. Cover $5 for 21+, under 21 $7. Bar serves beer only. Open Th-Sa 9pm-late.)

VICKSBURG   ☎ 601

President Lincoln, referring to Vicksburg, said the Civil War would "never be brought to a close until that key is in our pocket." After a 47-day siege, the Confederacy surrendered to Ulysses S. Grant's army on July 4, 1863. Memorials and combat site markers riddle the grassy 1700-acre **Vicksburg National Military Park,** giving the grounds a sacred air. The park sits on the eastern and northern edges of the city. The **visitors center** is on Clay St., about half a mile west of I-20 Exit 4B. Driving along the 16 mi. path, there are three options: taking a self-guided tour with a free map available at the entrance, using an informative audio tour, or hiring a guide to narrate the sights. (☎636-0583; www.nps.gov/vick. Park center open daily 8am-5pm. Grounds open daily in summer 7am-7pm; in winter 7am-5pm. $8 per car. Tape $6.50, CD $11, live guide $30. Driving tour 1-3hr.) In the park, the **USS Cairo Museum** contains artifacts salvaged from the sunken and saved battleship. (☎636-2199. Usually open daily Apr.-Oct. 9:30am-6pm; Nov.-Mar. 8:30am-5pm. Free with park admission.) During the 1863 siege of Vicksburg, Confederate troops used the cupola at the **Old Courthouse Museum,** 1008 Cherry St., as a signal station and held Union prisoners in the courtroom. The restored building now houses Jefferson Davis memorabilia. (☎636-0741; www.oldcourthouse.org. Open Apr.-Sept. M-Sa 8:30am-5pm, Su 1:30-5pm; Oct.-Mar. M-Sa 8:30am-4:30pm, Su 1:30-5pm. $5, seniors $4.50, children $3.)

Vicksburg also has attractions not related to the war; most are along the river on **Washington Street.** One half of the ▧**Corner Drug Store,** 1123 Washington St., is a fully operating modern pharmacy. The other half is an elaborate 1800s drug store museum, complete with archaic drugs like cocaine, arsenic, opium, and "haschissh." Old implements adorn the walls and moonshine jugs sit in the corner. (☎363-2756. Open M-Sa 8am-6pm, Su 9-11am. Free.) Grab an ice cream cone at the **Biedenharn Museum of Coca-Cola Memorabilia,** 1107 Washington St. In the 1900 soda fountain you can learn all about the bottling of "the ideal brain tonic." (☎638-6514. Open M-Sa 9am-5pm, Su 1:30-4:30pm. $2.75, ages 6-12 $1.75. AAA discount $1.)

The **Battlefield Inn ❸,** 4137 I-20 N/Frontage Rd., is built on part of the actual battlefield—complete with cannons—right next to the National Military Park. (☎800-359-9363. Breakfast included. Pool, laundry, mini-golf. Singles $65; doubles $75. AmEx/D/MC/V.) The well-worn but adequate rooms at the **Beechwood Motel ❶,** 4449 E. Clay St., have cable TV, and some have microwave and fridge. (☎636-2271. Singles $33; doubles $37. AmEx/D/MC/V.) Close to the military park is **Battlefield Kampground ❶,** 4407 I-20/Frontage Rd., off Exit 4B. (☎636-2025. Pool and laundry. Free shuttle to casinos. Tent sites with water and electricity $12, full hookup $20. Motel rooms $40.) At ▧**Walnut Hills ❸,** 1214 Adams St., just north of Clay St., noon is "dinnertime." First-rate all-you-can-eat round-table dinners of catfish, ribs, okra, snap peas, biscuits, iced tea, and dessert cost $12. The individual "blue plate special" comes with meat, three vegetables, iced tea, and dessert for $7.50. (☎638-4910. Round-table dinners M-F and Su 11am-2pm. Open M-F 11am-8:30pm, Su 11am-2pm. D/MC/V.) At the **Tree House Cafe ❸,** 1837 Cherry St., you can play pinball or race miniature slot cars while you eat. Entrees can get quite pricey, but sandwiches and po' boys ($7-8) are reasonable. (☎638-7561. Open M-F 11am-2pm and 5pm-10pm, Sa 11am-11pm. AmEx/D/MC/V.)

A car is necessary in Vicksburg. The bus station, the visitors center, downtown, and the far end of the sprawling military park mark the city's extremes; no public transit runs between them. **Greyhound,** 1295 S. Frontage Rd. (☎638-8389;

www.greyhound.com; open daily 7am-8:30pm), goes to Jackson (1hr., 4 per day, $12). The **Tourist Information Center,** on Clay St., across from the military park entrance west off I-20, has a helpful city map and coupons. (☎636-9421 or 800-221-3536; www.visitvicksburg.com. Open in summer daily 8am-5:30pm; in winter M-F 8am-5pm, Sa-Su 8am-4pm.) **Post Office:** 3415 Pemberton Blvd., off U.S. 61 S. (☎636-1022. Open M-F 8:30am-5pm, Sa 9am-noon.) **Postal Code:** 39180. **Area Code:** 601.

OXFORD   ☎662

When westward explorers first came to this site in northern Mississippi, they decided to name it "Oxford" in hopes of getting the state government to open a university here. The plan worked brilliantly, eventually landing Oxford the **University of Mississippi (Ole Miss).** Today, the lively college-town atmosphere is an even greater attraction than Oxford's old-fashioned architecture and rich history.

■■ 🎁 **ORIENTATION AND PRACTICAL INFORMATION.** Oxford is 30 mi. east of **I-55** on **Rte. 6** (Exit 243), 55 mi. south of Memphis and 140 mi. north of Jackson. The main east-west roads are **Jackson Avenue** and **University Avenue,** while **Lamar Boulevard** runs north-south. The center of town is **Courthouse Square,** at the intersection of Jackson Ave. and Lamar St., bordered by Van Buren Ave. The **Oxford Tourism Info Center,** 107 Courthouse Sq., in the back of the City Hall, offers free audio walking tours and info on the city's famous author, William Faulkner. (☎234-4680 or 800-758-9177. Open M-F 8am-5pm. The Skipwith Cottage, next door, replaces the info center at City Hall on weekends and is open Sa 10am-4pm, Su 1-4pm.) **Greyhound,** 715 Hwy. 35 N (☎563-3046; www.greyhound.com), operates out of Batesville, a 20min. drive from Oxford. **Internet Access: Public Library,** 401 Bramlett Blvd., at Jackson Ave. (☎234-5751. Open M-Th 10am-8pm, F-Sa 10am-5:30pm, Su 2-5pm. Free.) **Post Office:** 401 McElroy Dr. (☎234-5615. Open M-F 9am-5pm, Sa 9:30am-12:30pm.) **Postal Code:** 38655. **Area Code:** 662.

🎁 **ACCOMMODATIONS.** Lodging is easy to find in Oxford—unless you're in town during the Ole Miss football season. Look for rooms at the best independently owned budget hotel, **Johnson's Motor Inn ❷,** 2305 W. Jackson Ave., west of town off Hwy. 6, 3 mi. from Courthouse Sq. and only 1½ mi. from campus. It sports spacious rooms with microwaves, fridges, and cable TV. (☎234-3611. Singles $35; doubles $40. AmEx/D/MC/V.) The **Ole Miss Inn ❷,** 1517 E. University Ave., is within walking distance of downtown and has clean, basic rooms. (☎234-2424. Singles $35; doubles $45. AmEx/D/MC/V.) **Wall Doxey State Park ❶,** 23 mi. north of town on Rte. 7, has scenic campsites along an expansive lake. (☎252-4231 or 800-467-2757. Sites with water and electricity $9; RV sites with dump stations $13. Cabins $52-58 per night. 3-night min. stay for cabins. Entrance fee $2 per car.)

🎁🎁 **FOOD AND ENTERTAINMENT. Courthouse Square,** at Jackson Ave. and Lamar Blvd., is the center of it all. 🎁**Square Books ❶,** 160 Courthouse Sq. is one of the best independent bookstores in the nation. The owner also happens to be the city's mayor. Expand your belly while opening your mind—coffee drinks and pastries are just $1-2. (☎236-2262. Open M-Th 9am-9pm, F-Sa 9am-10pm, Su 10am-6pm. AmEx/D/MC/V.) Lunchtime at nearby **Ajax Diner ❷,** 118 Courthouse Sq., means excellent meat-and-vegetable platters ($8) accompanied by jalapeño cornbread. (☎232-8880. Dinner entrees $9-11. Open M-Sa 11:30am-10pm. AmEx/D/MC/V.) The **Bottletree Bakery ❷,** 923 Van Buren Ave., serves large deli sandwiches ($7-8) and fresh pastries in a relaxed atmosphere with brightly painted walls and recycled furniture. (☎236-5000. Open Tu-F 7am-4pm, Sa 9am-4pm, Su 9am-2pm. MC/V.) At night, live music rolls from **Proud Larry's ❸,** 211 S. Lamar Blvd., where hand-tossed pizzas are served piping hot. Elvis Costello played here last year. (☎236-0050. Pizzas $8-10. Music F-Sa 10pm-1am, also some weeknights 10pm-midnight. Cover $5-7. Kitchen open M-Sa 11am-10pm, Su 11:30am-2:30pm. AmEx/D/MC/V.) Four student-friendly bars lie on Jackson Ave., just west of Courthouse Sq. Of these, **Jubilee,** 1002 West Jackson Ave., is the most reliably cool, with a variety of bar food (wraps and sandwiches $7-8) and live music most Tuesdays. (☎236-3757. Kitchen open daily 11am-10pm; bar open M-Th and Su until midnight, F-Sa until 1am.) For local entertainment listings, check the free weekly *Oxford Town.*

◢ **SIGHTS.** William Faulkner remains the South's favorite son, and his home, **Rowan Oak,** just south of downtown on Old Taylor Rd., off S. Lamar Blvd., is Oxford's biggest attraction. Entranced by the home's history (it once belonged to a Confederate general), Faulkner bought the place in 1930 and named the property after the Rowan tree, a symbol of peace and security. The plot outline of his 1954 novel *A Fable* is etched in pencil on the walls of the study. (☎234-3284. Mansion open for self-guided tours Tu-Sa 10am-4pm, Su 1-4pm. Grounds open sunrise to sunset. Suggested donation $5.) Aside from Faulkner, Oxford's sights are all affiliated with another symbol of Southern intellectualism—Ole Miss. The town's covered sidewalks and tall cedar trees make it a fitting home for the **Center for the Study of Southern Culture,** a university department in the old Barnard Observatory. The center hosts the ever-popular annual **Faulkner & Yoknapatawpha Conference** during the last full week of July. Other conferences and festivals sponsored by the center include the **Oxford Conference on the Book,** in April, which celebrates a different author each year, and the **Southern Foodways Symposium,** which brings people together in late October to discuss weighty academic subjects like barbecue and other Southern food traditions. (☎915-5993; www.olemiss.edu/depts/south. Center open M-F 8am-5pm. Free.) Oxford also hosts a **film festival** during the third week in June (☎236-6429; www.oxfordfilmfest.com). The **Civil Rights Memorial,** next to the library, is scheduled to open in 2006 and will "commemorate equality in education" on the Ole Miss campus. Blues fans love the **Ole Miss Blues Archive,** on the 2nd floor of the main library on University Circle, which has one of the largest collections of blues memorabilia in the world. (☎915-7753. Open M-F 8am-5pm. Free.)

TUPELO   ☎ 662

This former industrial town was the birthplace of Elvis Presley and now milks that fact for all it's worth. Tupelo is 1½hr. east of Oxford along Hwy. 6; a prettier drive, however, is along Rte. 30 through the **Holly Springs National Forest** and Rte. 78 from New Albany. The **Elvis Presley Birthplace,** 306 Elvis Presley Blvd., is definitely worth a visit (something that can't be said of the peripheral sights), especially if you've never been to Graceland. There's also an **Elvis Presley Museum** and the **Memorial Chapel** for meditation, alongside features like a fountain, a statue of 13-year-old Elvis, and a walking tour that explores his life. You can even take an Elvis driving tour and visit places he frequented as a kid. (☎841-1245; www.elvispresleybirthplace.com. Open M-Sa 9am-5pm, Su 1-5pm; May-Sept. open M-Sa until 5:30pm. Birthplace $2.50, children $1.50. Museum $6/$3. Combination ticket $7/$3.50.) Antique car fanatics will be in heaven at the **Tupelo Automobile Museum,** 1 Otis Blvd., off E. Main St., which includes hot rides like a gull-wing DeLorean and a customized Corvette. (☎842-4242; www.tupeloauto.com. Open Tu-Su 10am-6pm. $10, seniors and AAA $8, children $5.) Tupelo is also home to the headquarters of the **Natchez Trace Parkway** (see **Natchez,** p. 412), a beautiful, if slow, drive from Natchez, MS, to Nashville, TN. The parkway follows old Native American routes and is free of commercial traffic and advertising. Civil War buffs may want to visit the **Tupelo National Battlefield** (☎305-7417), on W. Main St., where the last Civil War battle in Mississippi was fought, as well as **Brice's Crossroads,** on Rte. 45 north of town, the site of a major Confederate victory (☎365-3969; www.bricescrossroads.com). The Trace's **Visitors Center,** 2680 Natchez Trace Pkwy., near the Rte. 78/45 junction, includes information on early settlers, nature, and history along the route. (☎680-4025 or 800-305-7417; www.nps.gov/natr. Open daily 8am-5pm.)

Accommodations are concentrated around the intersection of McCullough Blvd. and Gloster St. **Economy Inn ❷,** 708 N. Gloster St., is a great value with clean, spacious rooms close to downtown. (☎842-1213. Microwaves, fridges, free wireless Internet. Singles $27; doubles $32. AmEx/D/MC/V.) **Commodore Motel ❷,** 1800 E. Main St., east of downtown, is located close to Elvis's birthplace and provides basic rooms. (☎842-9074. Rooms $30-40. Cash only.) Six miles south of the city, **Tombigbee State Park ❶,** 264 Cabin Dr., has primitive campsites overlooking Lake Lee, and slightly less attractive developed campsites with water, electricity, and showers. (☎842-7669. Entrance fee $2. Reception 8am-5pm; park gates close at 10pm. Primitive sites $10; developed sites $16. Cabins $41-68; 2- to 3-night min. stay. MC/V.) Grab a bite at Elvis's old haunt, **Johnnie's Drive-In ❶,** 908 E. Main St., where a barbecue burger and shake will only run you $5. (☎842-6748. Open M-Sa 6am-9pm, closed Su because they've "gone to church." Cash only.) **Romie's ❶,** 804 W. Jackson St., is a local favorite for lunch with their $6 meat and three vegetable special. (☎842-8986. Open M-F and Su 11am-2pm. AmEx/D/MC/V.)

Greyhound, 201 Commerce St. (☎842-4557 or 800-231-2222; www.greyhound.com; open M-F 8am-5pm, Sa-Su 9am-noon), sends buses to Jackson (6-12hr., 4 per day, $43), Memphis (2½hr., 4 per day, $28), and Nashville (6-9hr., 2 per day, $51-55). **Taxi: A-1 Taxi Cab** (☎842-5262) and **Tupelo Cab Company** (☎842-1133). The **Convention and Visitors Bureau** is at 399 E. Main St. and has a guidebook with lots of useful coupons. (☎841-6521. Open M-Th 9am-8pm, F-Sa 9am-5pm.) **Internet Access: Lee County Library,** 219 N. Madison St., at the corner of Jefferson and Madison. (☎841-9013. Open M-F 9am-8pm, Sa 9am-5pm.) **Post Office:** 500 W. Main St. (☎841-1286. Open M-F 8:30am-5pm.) **Postal Code:** 33804. **Area Code:** 662.

BILOXI   ☎228

When the French arrived in 1699, Biloxi was made capital of French Louisiana. Though modern Biloxi rings with the sound of slot machines, the remains of that municipal grandeur are visible in the town's antebellum homes, such as **Beauvoir,** 2244 Gulf Beach Rd., the home of Confederate President Jefferson Davis. The fascinating estate gives insight into both the man and the Confederate cause. The self-guided tour (allow 1½hr.) begins with a 15min. film, then meanders through the home and grounds, including the **Presidential Library** (unrecognized by the federal government), a museum, and the **Tomb of the Unknown Confederate Soldier.** (☎388-9074 or 800-570-3818. Open daily 9am-5pm, last admission 4:30pm. $7.50, seniors and AAA $6.75, students and children $4.50.) A self-guided historical **walking tour** of Biloxi's buildings, free at the visitors center (allow 1-2hr.), sheds light onto the influences that pervade local architecture. The tour ends at the **Ohr-O'Keefe Museum of Art,** 136 Ohr St., which boasts the largest collection of George Ohr's work in the US, along with three galleries of contemporary art, including an exhibit of artistic responses to the September 11th terrorist attacks. Frank Gehry is working on a new building for the museum, due to open in July 2006. (☎374-5547. Open M-F 9am-5pm, in summer until 6pm. $6, seniors $5, students and children free. Cash only.) From nearby Gulfport, 15 mi. west of Biloxi, catch a ferry to the idyllic **Ship Island,** which played a major role in US colonial and Civil War history. (☎864-1014 or 866-466-7386; www.msshipisland.com. Boat times vary; call ahead to check. $20, seniors $18, ages 3-10 $10.) **Spanish Trail Books,** 781 Vieux Marche (Howard Ave.), has an excellent selection of new and used books for those seeking a literary escape from Biloxi's slot machines and neon lights. (☎435-1144. Open M-F 11am-5pm.)

Accommodations are expensive during peak season (July-Aug.), and rates can vary wildly; cheaper rooms are easier to find midweek. Look for a lodging coupon book at the visitors center (below) for additional savings. **Jubilee Inn ❷**, 1678 Beach Blvd., is across from the beach and near the casinos, with rooms as low as $49 during the week. (☎432-1984 or 888-765-1984. Continental breakfast. Free local calls and pool. Rooms M-Th and Su $49-69, F-Sa $79-109. AmEx/D/DC/MC/V.) With comfortable, large rooms, **Gulf Beach Resort ❸**, 2428 Beach Blvd., is farther from downtown but very convenient for Beauvoir and quieter beaches. (☎385-5555 or 800-323-9164; www.gulfbeachresort.com. Weekdays $60-80, weekends $75-90. AmEx/D/MC/V.) For cheap camping options, ask at the visitors center about the National Seashore protected area to the east of town. **Java Joe's ❶**, 834 Vieux Marche (Howard Ave.), serves breakfast and lunch to diners lounging on cozy sofas in the back. (☎435-9990. Coffee $1-2. Sandwiches $4-6. Open M-W 8am-5pm, Th-F 8am-8pm. MC/V.) Good values and family-size portions are staples at **Ole Biloxi Schooner's Restaurant ❹**, 159 E Howard Ave. Sandwiches are $6-8, and overflowing platters go for $15-17. (☎374-8071. Open M 7am-8:30pm, T-Th 7am-9pm, F 7am-10pm, Sa 7am-9:30pm. MC/V.) **McElroy's Harbor House ❸**, across from McDonald's at 695 Beach Blvd., is the place to go for seafood. (☎435-5001. Appetizers $6-7. Seafood entrees $7-20. Open daily 7am-10pm. AmEx/D/DC/MC/V.) **Kim Long ❸**, 832 Division St., has reasonably authentic Vietnamese food. (☎435-0507. Dinner entrees $8-12. Open daily 8am-8pm. Cash only.) Biloxi's **casinos,** anchored offshore, are a staple of nighttime excitement and are usually open 24hr. You can often get into casinos and enjoy the shows for free; pick up a copy of *Jackpot* for the latest on casino offers. For a tamer evening, take a **schooner cruise** on a replica ship and sail between the beaches and the gulf islands. (☎435-6320. 2½hr. trip. Call for times. $20, ages 3-12 $10.) Boats depart from the Small Craft Harbor, on Hwy. 90 E. **Just Us Lounge,** 906 Division St., at Calliavet, is a friendly gay venue, with cheap beer and free drag shows most nights. (☎374-1007. Open 24hr.)

Biloxi is 1hr. west of Mobile and 2hr. east of New Orleans. **Greyhound,** 166 Main St., rolls to Mobile (1hr., 6 per day, $17), New Orleans (2hr., 3 per day, $21), and Pensacola (3hr., 4 per day, $31) from its downtown station. (☎436-4335; www.greyhound.com. Open daily 8:30am-8:30pm.) **Historical tours** of the city depart from the lighthouse on Hwy. 90. (☎374-8687 or 866-411-8687. 90min. Reservations recommended. Tours M-Sa 9:30, 11am, 1, 2:30pm. $13, seniors and AAA $12, ages 5-12 $5.) A **city bus** roams up and down Beach Blvd. every 30min. (☎896-8080; www.coasttransit.com. Runs 5am-10pm. $1, ages 5-14 $0.75, seniors $0.50; day pass $5.) **Visitors Center:** 710 Beach Blvd., by Main St. (☎374-3105 or 800-245-6943. Open M-F 8am-4:30pm, Sa-Su 9am-4pm.) **Taxi:** Livery Cab, ☎863-1175. **Internet Access: Biloxi Library,** 139 Lameuse St., near the visitors center. (☎374-0330. Open M-Th 9am-8pm, F-Sa 9am-5pm. Free.) **Post Office:** 135 Main St. (☎374-0345. Open M-F 8:30am-5pm, Sa 10am-noon.) **Postal Code:** 39530. **Area Code:** 228.

NATCHEZ   ☎601

Natchez lies on the east bank of the Mississippi River, about 1½hr. south of Vicksburg. It's also the start of the **Natchez Trace Parkway,** the National Park road that follows the original Natchez, Chickasaw, and Choctaw Indian trading route (p. 410). Visitors flock to the historic antebellum homes and the **Spring Pilgrimage** (Mar. 11-Apr. 15, 2006), when over 30 historic houses open their doors, guides lead tours in period dress, and various musical performances are held around town. During the **Fall Pilgrimage,** held from late October to early November, Natchez celebrates its homes and gardens with music and historically-themed events.

The historic downtown area, full of antique and specialty shops, is bordered by U.S. 84 to the south, Madison St. to the north, Martin Luther King, Jr. St. to the east, and the Mississippi River to the west. The **Museum of African-American History**

and Culture, 301 Main St., downtown, recounts African-Americans' struggles to secure economic and political equality. (☎445-0728. Open Tu-Sa 1-4:30pm.) Farther from town, two antebellum homes stand out from the crowd. **Longwood,** 140 Lower Woodville Rd., was built circa 1860 and has a beautiful cupola on top of its Greek-style tower. (☎442-5193. Open daily 9am-4:30pm. Tours every 30min. $8, children $4.) **Melrose,** 1 Melrose-Montebello Pkwy., was built about 20 years earlier and has four imposing Greco-Roman columns and an ornate balcony. (☎446-5790. Open daily 8:30am-5pm. 45min. tours leave every hr. $8, children and seniors $4.) The **Grand Village of the Natchez Indians,** 400 Jefferson Davis Blvd., has a museum with small displays on the daily life of the Natchez. (☎446-6502. Open M-Sa 9am-5pm, Su 1:30-5pm. Free.) About 20min. west of Natchez over the Louisiana border, the **Frogmore Plantation,** 11054 U.S. 84, provides an opportunity to reflect on slavery and life in the 1800s. (☎318-757-2453; www.frogmoreplantation.com. Open Mar. to mid-Nov. M-F 9am-3pm, last tour 2pm; Sa 10am-2pm, last tour 1:30pm. June-Aug. closed Sa. $10, ages 6-18 $5, under 5 free.)

Scottish Inn ❷, 40 Sgt. Prentiss Dr., has basic rooms, a pool, and continental breakfast. (☎442-9141. Singles $30; doubles $35. MC/V.) Listed on the National Register of Historic Places, the **Eola Hotel ❹,** 110 N. Pearl St., is a comfortable downtown splurge with riverside rooms and sunset views. The **visitors center coupon** (valid May-Aug.) cuts rates by more than half. (☎445-6000. Doubles weekdays $116, weekends $163. MC/V.) Campers should head for **Natchez State Park ❶,** 230B Wickcliff Rd., off Hwy. 61 N. Tent and RV sites are located near a lake; the ranger will come around to check you in, so settle in anytime. (☎442-2658. Showers. Sites $13-15. MC/V.) For good Southern cookin' try **Cock of the Walk ❸,** 200 N. Broadway, which serves fried catfish ($11) and steaks ($18) with all the trimmings. (☎446-8920. Open daily 5-8pm; lunch hours vary. AmEx/D/MC/V.) **Pig Out Inn ❷,** 116 South Canal St., has counter service and great barbecue. (☎442-8050. Barbecue sandwiches $4.50. Open M-Sa 11am-9pm. AmEx/D/MC/V.) Grab a dozen signature tamales ($6.50) and a "nock-u-naked" margarita ($4.50) at **Fat Mama's Tamales ❷,** 500 S. Canal St. (☎442-4548; www.fatmamastamales.com. Beer $2-2.50. Open M-Th 11am-9pm, F-Sa 11am-10pm, Su noon-7pm. Cash only.)

Greyhound, 103 Lower Woodville Rd. (☎445-5291; www.greyhound.com; open M-Sa 7:15am-5:30pm, Su 9am-12:30pm and 3:30-5:30pm), travels to Jackson (3hr., 1 per day, $28-32) and New Orleans (5hr., 1 per day, $39-44). The **Natchez Convention and Vistors Bureau,** 640 S. Canal St., clearly marked from Hwy. 61, provides information on the area. (☎446-6345; www.natchez.ms.us. Open M-Sa 8:30am-5pm, Su 9am-4pm.) The visitors center also sells tickets for a 50min. trolley tour of downtown ($15, ages 12 and under $7.50), which focuses on the antebellum homes and churches, or a 40min. horse-drawn carriage tour ($10). **Internet Access: Judge George W. Armstrong Library,** 220 S. Commerce St., has six computers. (☎445-8862. Open M-Th 9am-6pm, F 9am-5pm, Sa 9am-1pm.) **Post Office:** 214 N. Canal St. (☎800-275-8777. Open M-F 8:30am-5pm.) **Postal Code:** 39120. **Area Code:** 601.

LOUISIANA

After exploring the Mississippi River Valley in 1682, Frenchman René-Robert Cavalier proclaimed the land "Louisiane" in honor of Louis XIV. The name has endured three centuries, though French ownership of the region has not. The territory was tossed between France, England, and Spain before Thomas Jefferson and the US snagged it in the Louisiana Purchase of 1803. Nine years later, a smaller, redefined Louisiana was admitted to the Union. Each successive government lured a new mix of settlers to the bayous: Spaniards from the Canary Islands,

French Acadians from Nova Scotia, Americans from the East, and free blacks from the West Indies. Louisiana's multinational history, Creole culture, Catholic governmental structure (under which counties are called "parishes"), and Napoleonic legal system are unlike anything found in the other 49 states. Here the swamps seep into the towns, French words slide into local speech, and a certain *joie de vivre* is evident in bars and music venues that never close.

⚡ PRACTICAL INFORMATION

Capital: Baton Rouge.

Visitor Info: Office of Tourism, P.O. Box 94291, Baton Rouge 70804 (☎225-342-8100 or 800-261-9144; www.louisianatravel.com). Open M-F 8am-4:30pm.

Office of State Parks, P.O. Box 44426, Baton Rouge 70804 (☎888-677-1400; www.lastateparks.com). Open M-F 8am-4:30pm.

Postal Abbreviation: LA. **Sales Tax:** 8%.

NEW ORLEANS ☎504

First explored by the French, la Nouvelle Orléans was ceded secretly to the Spanish government in 1762; the citizens of the town didn't find out about the change until 1766. Spain returned the city to France just in time for the fledgling United States to grab it in 1803. Centuries of cultural cross-pollination in the city have resulted in a heady cultural mélange of Spanish courtyards, Victorian verandas, Cajun jambalaya, and French *beignets*, to name but a few unique hallmarks of New Orleans. The city's nickname, "The Big Easy," reflects the carefree attitude characteristic of this fun-loving place where food and music are the two ruling passions—come late February, there's no escaping the month-long celebration of Mardi Gras, the peak of the city's already festive mood.

> In August 2005, Hurricane Katrina laid waste to coastal areas in the states of Alabama, Louisiana, and Mississippi. Low-lying New Orleans was further devastated when the levees that normally hold back the waters of Lake Ponchartrain burst, flooding 80% of the city. Mass evacuations left hundreds of thousands of Gulf Coast residents stranded in neighboring states. As of press time, the full extent of damage and loss of life is unknown, as is the date by which these areas will again be viable tourist destinations. Travelers should call ahead to avoid surprises.

⚔ INTERCITY TRANSPORTATION

Airport: Louis Armstrong New Orleans International Airport, 900 Airline Dr. (☎464-0831), 15 mi. west of the city. Cab fare to the Quarter is set at $28 for 1-2 people; $12 each additional person. An **airport shuttle** runs to and from downtown hotels. (☎522-3500; www.airportshuttleneworleans.com. $13.) The **Louisiana Transit Company,** 118 David Dr. (☎818-1077), travels from the airport to Elk St. downtown M-Sa 5:10am-7pm. Buses run every 23min. and every 10-15min. during peak times in the afternoon and evening. After 7pm, buses go to Tulane Ave. and Carollton Ave. (mid-city) until 11:30pm. Station open M-F 8am-4pm. $1.60; exact change needed. Pick-up on the upper level of the airport, near the exit ramp, outside Delta Airlines area.

St. Charles Streetcar

Lake Pontchartrain

Lakeshore Dr.

Pontchartr ain Park

LAKE VISTA

West End Park

Lake Pontchartrain Causeway

Robert E. Lee Blvd.

University of New Orleans

Canal Blvd.

Paris Ave.

Franklin Ave.

TO 1 (.5 mi.)

WEST END

W. Esplanade Ave.

City Park

Wisner Blvd.

Bayou St. John

Elysian Fields Ave.

Bombabel Ave.

Oaklawn Dr.

Pontchartrain Blvd.

Lake Ave.

Harrison Ave.

GENTILLY

Gentilly Blvd.

90

10

Veterans Memorial Blvd.

S. Causeway Blvd.

10

Dillard University

Storyland and Botanical Garden

610

St. Bernard Ave.

TO 2 (18 mi.)

Metairie Cemetery

City Park Ave.

New Orleans Museum of Art

Almonaster Ave.

Florida Ave.

TO AIRPORT (5 mi.)

OLD METAIRIE

Metairie Rd.

Longue Vue House and Gardens

Canal St.

Carrollton Ave.

Esplanade Ave.

Orleans Ave.

N. Claiborne Ave.

St. Claude Ave.

Airline Dr.

Earhart Expwy.

61

TREME

Ursuline Ave.

FAUBOURG MARIGNY

3139

Earhart Blvd.

Xavier University

MID-CITY

Jefferson Davis Pkwy.

Broad St.

Tulane Ave.

Bienville St.

FRENCH QUARTER

Jefferson Hwy.

River Rd.

90

Carrollton Ave.

Broadway

10

Poydras

Jackson Square

SEE "DOWNTOWN NEW ORLEANS," p. 419

ALGIERS POINT

Patterson Rd.

Gov. Huey P. Long Bridge

River Rd.

Loyola University

Sophie Newcomb University

Fountainbleau

S. Claiborne Ave.

Napoleon Ave.

90

Washington Ave.

Louisiana Ave.

Lafayette Square

Franklin Ave.

Gen. Meyer Ave.

BUS 90

18

Old Spanish Trail

UPTOWN

Tulane University

5

St. Charles Ave.

Jackson Ave.

Crescent City Connection Toll Bridge

90

WESTWEGO

Audubon Park

Audubon Zoo

Jefferson Ave.

Prytania St.

Magazine St.

Tchoupitoulas St.

9

GARDEN DISTRICT

10

6

7

8

New Orleans

Mississippi River

Ath St.

18

▲▲ ACCOMMODATIONS

Columns, 9

India House, 4

Jude Travel Park and Guest House, 1

Marquette House New Orleans International Hostel (HI-AYH), 6

St. Bernard State Park, 2

St. Charles Guest House, 7

🍎 FOOD

Dunbar's, 5

Juan's Flying Burrito, 8

🎵 NIGHTLIFE

Mid City Lanes

Rock 'n' Bowl, 3

Tipitina's, 10

18 BUS

90

0   1 mile

0   1 kilometer

Trains: Amtrak, 1001 Loyola Ave. (☎800-872-7245; www.amtrak.com), in the Union Passenger Terminal, a 10min. walk to Canal St. via Elk St. Station. Open daily 6am-10pm. Ticket office open M, W, F-Sa 6:15am-8:30pm; Tu, Th, Su 6:15am-11pm. To **Atlanta** (12hr., 7 per week, $50-97), **Houston** (9hr., 3 per week, $45-80), and **Jackson** (5hr., 7 per week, $19-38).

Buses: Greyhound, 1001 Loyola Ave. (☎524-7571 or 800-231-2222; www.greyhound.com), in the Union Passenger Terminal. Station open 24hr.; tickets sold 5:15am-1:30am. To **Atlanta** (10-14hr., 9 per day, $67), **Austin** (12-15hr., 5 per day, $91), and **Baton Rouge** (1½-2hr., 7 per day, $13).

✠ ORIENTATION

The majority of New Orleans's attractions crowd around the city center. The city's main streets follow the curve of the **Mississippi River,** hence the nickname "the Crescent City." Directions from locals reflect watery influences—"lakeside" means north, referring to **Lake Pontchartrain,** and "riverside" means south. Uptown lies west, upriver; downtown is downriver. The city is concentrated on the Missis-

> **! SAFETY IN NEW ORLEANS.** Travelers should be aware of New Orleans's capacity for quick change—safe and decidedly unsafe areas are often separated by a block or less, and usually safe areas can become dangerous in a heartbeat. The tenement areas directly north of the French Quarter and northwest of Lee Circle pose particular threats to personal safety; after dark, do not linger in the area of the bus station—head into the French Quarter and do not venture northwest. At night also avoid Tremé and the area immediately north of Carondelet in the Garden District. Stick to busy, well-lit roads, never walk alone after dark, and downplay the tourist image.

sippi's east bank, but **"The East"** refers only to the easternmost part of the city. On-street **parking** in New Orleans is abundant. Many streets throughout the city have meters, which are free on weekdays after 6pm, on weekends, and on holidays.

NEIGHBORHOODS

Tourists flock to the **French Quarter (Vieux Carré)**, bounded by the Mississippi River, **Canal Street, Rampart Street,** and **Esplanade Avenue.** Streets in the Quarter follow a grid pattern. Just northeast, or "downtown/downriver," of the Quarter across Esplanade Ave. is **Faubourg Marigny,** a residential neighborhood full of trendy nightclubs, bars, and cafes. Northwest of the Quarter across Rampart St., the little-publicized African-American neighborhood of **Tremé** has a storied history, but has been ruined somewhat by the encroaching construction of a highway overpass and the housing projects lining its Canal St. border. Uptown, the residential **Garden District,** bordered by **Saint Charles Avenue** to the north and **Magazine Street** to the south, is distinguished by its elegant homes. The scenic **Saint Charles Streetcar route** picks up passengers at Canal St. and Carondelet St., passes through parts of the **Central Business District** ("CBD" or "downtown"), the Garden District via St. Charles Ave., and the **Uptown** and **Carrollton** neighborhoods along **South Carollton Avenue** and past **Tulane** and **Loyola Universities.** Less populated regions of the city, like **Algiers Point,** are on the **West Bank** across the river. For a guide to the city's neighborhoods, pick up *Historic Neighborhoods of New Orleans* at the Jackson Sq. visitors center.

⊏ LOCAL TRANSPORTATION

Public Transit: Regional Transit Authority (RTA), 6700 Plaza Dr. (☎248-3900). Open M-F 5am-11pm. Most buses pass Canal St., at the edge of the French Quarter. Major buses and streetcars run 24hr. but are notoriously irregular after midnight; expect to wait up to 45min. for late-night buses and streetcars. Most buses and streetcars $1.25 in exact change; seniors and disabled passengers $0.40; transfers $0.25. Express buses $1.50. 1-day pass $5, 3-day pass $12; passes sold at major hotels in the Canal St. area and on streetcars. Office has bus schedules and maps.

Taxi: United Cabs, ☎522-9771. **Checker Yellow Cabs,** ☎943-2411.

⊿ PRACTICAL INFORMATION

Visitor Info: Metropolitan Convention and Visitors Bureau, 529 St. Ann St. (☎568-5661; www.neworleanscvb.com), by Jackson Sq. in the French Quarter. Beware of private visitors centers in the Quarter that give less than impartial information, pushing their own services first—the Jackson Sq. center is the only official center in the French Quarter. It is understaffed and often overcrowded but very helpful; grab a good map or a series of walking tour guides. Open daily 9am-5pm.

Hotlines: Cope Line, general crisis help, ☎523-2673. **Domestic Violence Hotline,** ☎486-0377. Both 24hr.

Medical Services: Charity Hospital, 1532 Tulane Ave., and **LSU Medical Center,** 433 Bolivar St. (both hospitals ☎903-3000).

Internet Access: New Orleans Public Library, 219 Loyola Ave. (☎529-7323), 1½ blocks west of Canal St. Open M-Th 10am-6pm, F-Sa 10am-5pm. If they know you're from out of town, it's $3 per hr. **Carrolton Station** and **d.b.a.** both have free wireless Internet—see nightlife listings below for hours.

Post Office: 701 Loyola Ave. (☎589-1775), near the bus station. Open M-F 7am-8pm, Sa 8am-5pm, Su noon-5pm. **Postal Code:** 70113. **Area Code:** 504.

ⓕ ACCOMMODATIONS

Finding inexpensive yet decent rooms in the **French Quarter** can be as difficult as staying sober during Mardi Gras. Luckily, other parts of the city compensate for the absence of cheap lodging downtown. Several hostels cater to the young and almost penniless, as do guest houses near the **Garden District.** Accommodations for Mardi Gras and the Jazz Festival get booked up to a year in advance. During peak times, proprietors will rent out any extra space, so be sure you know what you're paying for. However, rates tend to sink in the low season (June to early Sept.) when business is slow, and negotiation can pay off. As for campers, there are oodles of campsites to discover, but even those get pricey during Mardi Gras. The *Louisiana Official Tour Guide,* available at the Jackson Sq. Visitors Center, has the most comprehensive, unbiased campsite listings available.

▨ **India House,** 124 S. Lopez St. (☎821-1904), at Canal St. between N. Broad and Jefferson Davis. What this bohemian haunt lacks in tidiness it makes up for in character. Murals and pictures of past guests fight for space on the walls. Communal eating (and, on busier nights, sleeping) and a backyard patio with pool. Canal St. streetcar provides easy access to French Quarter and downtown (15min. ride). Internet access $2 per 30min. Kitchen, turtle pond out back, A/C, and lounge areas. Key deposit $5. Coin laundry $1.50. Reception 24hr. Dorms $17; long-term guests may be able to help with housekeeping duties for discounted lodging. Private rooms $40-45. MC/V. ❶

▨ **St. Charles Guest House,** 1748 Prytania St. (☎523-6556; www.stcharlesguesthouse.com). In the Garden District, one of New Orleans's most spectacular neighborhoods, a 5min. walk from the St. Charles streetcar. Clean rooms, a large, leafy courtyard, pool, and continental breakfast. Large, antique signs hang haphazardly in the hallway, and the friendly staff lives out back. Small, single "backpacker" rooms $30-35, with A/C and private bath $55. Rooms with 1 queen-sized bed or 2 twins $55-95, during Jazz Fest and Mardi Gras $100-150. AmEx/MC/V. ❷

Marquette House New Orleans International Hostel, 2249 Carondelet St. (☎523-3014), in the Garden District, near the St. Charles streetcar route. A very quiet hosteling experience and a pretty safe bet due to its no-alcohol policy, cleanliness, and mandatory quiet hours (midnight-7am). Large, semi-rustic private rooms also available. 200 beds. A/C, kitchen (no stove), and study rooms. Linen $2, towel $0.50. Key deposit $5. Dorms $20, weekly $99; 2-person private rooms weekdays $53, weekends $60, each additional person $10. Wheelchair accessible. MC/V. ❷

Columns, 3811 St. Charles Ave. (☎899-9308). Known for its easy-going elegance and classic comfort, this is one of New Orleans's treasures. Gorgeous, oak-paneled lounge and a picturesque front porch right across from the streetcar make this splurge worth the price. Full Southern breakfast. If your pockets aren't deep enough to sleep here, stop by to sip a cocktail on the porch swing. Rooms $125-190. AmEx/MC/V. ❺

Lamothe House Hotel, 622 Esplanade Ave. (☎947-1161 or 800-367-5858), is an imposing 1839 pink townhouse across the street from the French Quarter. 20 rooms featuring antique furniture, cable TV, A/C, and full bath. Continental breakfast is served in the house's decadent dining room, and the large pool is an ideal place to enjoy the complimentary afternoon sherry. Rooms May-Sept. and Dec. weekdays $69, weekends $99; Mardi Gras and holidays $150-170; call for low-season rates. AmEx/D/MC/V. ❸

CAMPING

Jude Travel Park and Guest House, 7400 Chef Menteur Hwy./U.S. 90 (☎241-0632 or 800-523-2196), just east of the eastern junction of I-10 and U.S. 90, Exit 240B. From downtown New Orleans, take the #55 bus to the corner of Gentilly Blvd. and Elysian Fields and transfer to the #98 bus, which drives past the front gate of the Travel Park. Pool and hot tub, showers, laundry, and 24hr. security. 46 tent/RV sites for 2 people $26, each additional person $4. Rooms in 5-room guest house $50-$75 per night. ❶

St. Bernard State Park, 501 St. Bernard Pkwy. (☎682-2101), 18 mi. southeast of New Orleans; take I-10 Exit 246A, turn left onto Rte. 46, travel for 7 mi., then turn right on Rte. 39 S for 1 mi. 51 sites with water and electricity, as well as swimming pools and walking trails. Office open daily 7am-9pm. Sites $12. ❶

🗗 FOOD

If the eats in the Quarter prove too trendy, touristy, or tough on the budget, there are plenty of other options, most notably on **Magazine Street** and in the Tulane area, both of which are accessible via the St. Charles Streetcar.

FRENCH QUARTER

🖼 **Coop's Place,** 1109 Decatur St. (☎525-9053), near the corner of Ursuline Ave., has some of the Quarter's best Southern cooking. The gumbo ($4.35) is thick and spicy, the beer-battered alligator bits ($9) have won awards, and the jambalaya ($6.50-9) is unbeatable. Open M-Th and Su 11am-3am, F-Sa 11am-4am. AmEx/D/MC/V. ❷

🖼 **Napoleon House,** 500 Chartres St. (☎504-9572), at the corner of St. Louis St. A classy joint with a courtyard and a candlelit dining room with portraits of General Bonaparte, Napoleon's is known for cocktails like the Pimm's Cup ($5) and a menu of New Orleans favorites. Po' boys $6. Beer $3-4. Open daily 11am-1am or later. Cash only. ❷

🖼 **Cafe du Monde,** French Market, across Decatur St. from Jackson Sq. (☎525-4544). Centrally-located in the heart of the Quarter, Cafe du Monde is the place to go for a *beignet* ($1.60), the fried, puffed-up doughnut that is a French Quarter tradition. Enjoy with a *cafe au lait* ($1.59). Open 24hr. MC/V. ❶

Johnny's Po' Boys, 511 St. Louis St. (☎524-8129), near the corner of Decatur St. This French Quarter institution, with 40 varieties of the famous sandwich, has been the place to grab a po' boy ($4-7.50) since 1950. Creole fare is also on the menu. Gumbo $5. Open M-F 8am-4:30pm, Sa-Su 9am-4pm. MC/V. ❷

Clover Grill, 900 Bourbon St. (☎598-1010). Greasy and delicious burgers grilled under an American-made hubcap (makes 'em cook faster), as well as breakfast available all day. The only place in New Orleans where bacon comes with a side of sexual innuendo—"You can beat our prices, but you can't beat our meat." Burgers from $4.50. Breakfast $3-7. Sandwiches $5-8. Open 24hr. MC/V. ❶

Acme Oyster House, 724 Iberville St. (☎522-5973). At the bar, patrons slurp fresh oysters (6 for $4, 12 for $7) shucked before their eyes by Hollywood, the senior shucker. Typically crammed full of tourists, Acme is at least partly responsible for Bourbon St. debauchery—their motto is "Eat Louisiana oysters, love longer." Open M-Th and Su 11am-10pm, F-Sa 11am-11pm. AmEx/D/DC/MC/V. ❷

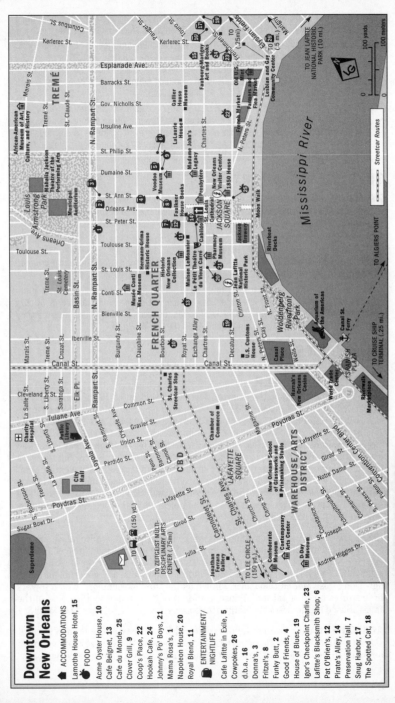

THE SOUTH

Downtown New Orleans

▲ ACCOMMODATIONS
Lamothe House Hotel, **15**

🍴 FOOD
Acme Oyster House, **10**
Cafe Beignet, **13**
Cafe du Monde, **25**
Clover Grill, **9**
Coop's Place, **22**
Hookah Cafe, **24**
Johnny's Po' Boys, **21**
Mama Rosa's, **1**
Napoleon House, **20**
Royal Blend, **11**

🎭 ENTERTAINMENT/
NIGHTLIFE
Cafe Lafitte in Exile, **5**
Cowpokes, **26**
d.b.a., **16**
Donna's, **3**
Fritzel's, **8**
Funky Butt, **2**
Good Friends, **4**
House of Blues, **19**
Igor's Checkpoint Charlie, **23**
Lafitte's Blacksmith Shop, **6**
Pat O'Brien's, **12**
Pirate's Alley, **7**
Preservation Hall, **7**
Snug Harbor, **17**
The Spotted Cat, **18**

Cafe Beignet, 334B Royal St. (☎524-5530). Stop in for *beignets* ($1.50), coffee, and a relaxing atmosphere—rare in New Orleans. Open daily 7am-5pm. MC/V. ❶

Royal Blend, 621 Royal St. (☎523-2716). The quiet courtyard provides an escape from the hustle of Royal St. and the chain coffee stores in the Quarter. Over 20 hot and iced coffees available, as well as teas and fresh-baked treats. Sandwiches, quiches, and salads $5-6. Pastries $1-2. Internet cafe in an adjoining room across the courtyard; $3 per 15min. Open M-Th and Su 9am-8pm, F-Sa 9am-10pm. AmEx/D/MC/V. ❶

Mama Rosa's, 616 N. Rampart St. (☎523-5546). Locals adore this Italian *ristorante*. Across from Louis Armstrong Park and near some of the city's best sounds (see **Donna's** and **Funky Butt,** p. 426), Mama Rosa serves excellent pizza alongside its "outrageous muffuletta" (meats, cheeses, and olive salad on Italian bread; $7). 14 in. cheese pie $9. Open M and Su 11am-11pm, Tu-W 11am-9:30pm, Th-Sa 11am-midnight. D/MC/V. ❷

OUTSIDE THE QUARTER

🌮 **Juan's Flying Burrito,** 2018 Magazine St. (☎569-0000), makes the best burritos on the planet. Get the "gutter punk" burrito ($6.50), a meal the size of your head, and wash it down with Mexican beer ($2.50). Open M-Sa 11am-11pm, Su noon-10pm. MC/V. ❶

Dunbar's, 4927 Freret St. (☎899-0734), at the corner of Robert St. Take St. Charles Ave. west to Upperline St., turn right on Upperline, and then left onto Freret. Residents call it the best place to get mama-just-cooked-it soul food. Seafood and barbecue plates $11-13. Po' boys $5-9. Open M-Sa 7am-9pm. AmEx/D/MC/V. ❸

Hookah Cafe, 500 Frenchmen St. (943-1101). Indian food in a friendly and fun atmosphere. The samosas ($5) are excellent. The elegant dining room has plenty of cozy nooks in which to enjoy over 20 flavored hookah tobaccos ($11-20). Live music nightly around 10pm. Open daily 5:30pm-2am. AmEx/D/DC/MC/V. ❸

◎ SIGHTS

FRENCH QUARTER

Allow at least a full day in the Quarter. The oldest section of the city is famous for its ornate wrought-iron balconies—French, Spanish, and uniquely New Orleans architecture—and raucous atmosphere. Known as the **Vieux Carré** (vyuh ca-RAY), the historic district of New Orleans encompasses dusty used bookstores, voodoo shops, museums, art galleries, bars, and tourist traps. **Bourbon Street** is packed with touristy bars, strip clubs, and pan-handlers disguised as clowns, but there's a distinct change as you leave the trashy straight end and cross the "Lavender Line" into the more sophisticated gay end, where there's less neon and you can hear yourself speak. **Decatur Street** has mellow cafes and bars, and if you're searching for some bona fide New Orleans tunes, head northeast of the Quarter to **Frenchmen Street,** a block of bars preferred by locals.

ROYAL STREET. A streetcar named "Desire" once rolled down Royal St., one of the French Quarter's most aesthetically pleasing avenues. Pick up the free *French Quarter Self-Guided Walking Tour* from the visitors center on St. Ann St. to begin an informed jaunt past Louisiana's oldest commercial and government buildings. Don't miss **Maison LeMonnier,** known as the "first skyscraper," which towers three stories high, or **LaLaurie House,** rumored to be haunted by the souls of the slaves abused by the LaLaurie family. *(LeMonnier: 640 Royal St. LaLaurie: 1140 Royal St.)*

JACKSON SQUARE. During the day, much of the activity in the French Quarter centers around Jackson Sq., a park dedicated to Gen. Andrew Jackson, victor of the Battle of New Orleans. The square swarms with artists, mimes, musicians, psychics, magicians, and con artists. Bargain down a horse-drawn tour of the Quarter to $10; wait on the Decatur St. side. The oldest Catholic cathedral in the US, **Saint Louis Cathedral,** though inconspicuous from the outside, has gorgeous murals inside. Open since 1718, the cathedral still holds daily services. *(615 Père Antoine Alley. ☎ 525-9585; www.stlouiscathedral.org. Open M, W, F-Su 7am-5pm; Tu and Th 7am-6pm. Tours every 15-20min. Free.)* Behind the cathedral lies **Cathedral Garden,** also known as Saint Anthony's Garden, bordered by Pirate's Alley and Père Antoine's Alley. Legend has it that Pirate's Alley was the site of covert meetings between pirate Jean Lafitte and Andrew Jackson as they conspired to plan the Battle of New Orleans. In reality, the alley wasn't even built until 16 years later. Pirate's Alley is also home to **Faulkner House Books,** where the late American author William Faulkner wrote his first novel, *Soldier's Pay.* The small bookshop is a treasure trove of Faulkner's essays and books, alongside an extensive catalogue of other Southern writers. *(624 Pirate's Alley. ☎ 524-2940. Open daily 10am-6pm.)*

FRENCH MARKET. The historic French Market takes up several city blocks east of Jackson Sq., toward the water along N. Peters St. and Decatur St. *(☎ 522-2621. Shops open daily 9am-8pm.)* The market begins at the famous **Café du Monde** and for the first few blocks is a strip mall of touristy shops in a historical building. By Gov. Nicholls St., it becomes the outdoor **Farmers Market,** which never closes and has been selling "most anything that grows" since 1791. Beyond the Farmers Market is the **Flea Market,** where vendors sell everything from feather boas to woodcarvings. The Jackson Sq. Visitor Center has free maps. *(Flea Market open daily 8:30am-5pm.)*

OTHER SIGHTS. The **Jean Lafitte National Historical Park and Preserve Visitors Center** conducts free walking tours through the Quarter. *(419 Decatur St. ☎ 589-2636. 1½hr. tour daily 9:30am. Come early; only the first 25 people are taken; tickets are given out starting at 9am. Other programs on New Orleans culture and history begin at 11:30am. Office open daily 9am-5pm.)* Just south of Decatur St. along the Riverfront streetcar line, the **Moon Walk** has great views of the Mighty Mississippi. Be extremely careful in this area at night. At the southwest corner of the Quarter, the **Aquarium of the Americas** houses an amazing collection of sea life and birds. Among the 500 species are endangered sea turtles and extremely rare white alligators. Come face to face with sharks as you walk through a 30 ft. acrylic-and-glass tunnel. *(1 Canal St. ☎ 581-4629. Open daily May-Aug. 9:30am-7pm; Sept.-Apr. 9:30am-6pm. $16,*

ON THE MENU

NOSHING IN N'AWLINS

With a lingo all its own, dining in New Orleans can be more than a little confusing without a guide to the most popular local cuisine.

Beignet: A "French-style" donut, the beignet is a deep-fried blob of dough that is typically smothered in powdered sugar. Cafe du Monde's are oddly-shaped, Cafe Beignet's are round, and both versions are delicious.

Gumbo: Louisiana's signature soup, New Orleans's seafood gumbo starts with a *roux* broth with regional spices, is usually thickened with okra, and can include crab, shrimp, or crawfish. Coop's Cafe makes a good one.

Muffuletta: Invented in 1906 by Salvatore Lupo, the owner of the Central Grocery on Decatur St., the muffuletta sandwiches ham, salami, provolone cheese, and olive relish between slices of round muffuletta bread. These can get messy to eat, but are worth the extra napkins. Try one at Central Grocery or Mama Rosa's.

Po' boy: A New Orleansian pronunciation of "poor boy," this is basically New Orleans's version of the grinder, hoagie, submarine or hero sandwich. The name originates from the Great Depression of the 1930's, when oyster po' boys were the cheapest meal you could buy in the city. Served on french bread, today's po' boy may feature oysters, catfish, shrimp, or more traditional lunchmeats.

seniors $10, ages 2-12 $9.50.) From a dock near the aquarium, the steamboat **Natchez** breezes down the Mississippi on 2hr. cruises with live jazz and narration on riverside sights. *(☎586-8777 or 800-233-2628. Departs 11:30am, 2:30, 7pm. Morning and afternoon cruises $19, with lunch $26. Evening cruises $32, with live jazz band and buffet dinner $54. AmEx/D/MC/V.)* The **Zoo Cruise** plies the river between the aquarium and the Audubon Zoo. *(Departs from the aquarium at 10am, 1, 2, 4pm and from the zoo at 11am, 1, 3, 5pm. $17, with zoo entry $23, with aquarium entry $26, with zoo and aquarium entry $38.)*

OUTSIDE THE QUARTER

WATERFRONT. For an up-close view of the Mississippi River and a unique New Orleans district, take the free **Canal Street Ferry** to Algiers Point. The Algiers of old was home to many of New Orleans's African-Americans and was the birthplace of several of the city's famous jazz musicians. Once called "The Brooklyn of the South," it is now a quiet, beautiful neighborhood to explore by foot. Stop at the **Dry Dock Cafe,** just off the ferry landing, to pick up a free map of the area. At night, the ferry's outdoor observation deck affords a panoramic view of the city's sights. *(Departs daily every 30min. 5:45am-midnight from the end of Canal St. Free for pedestrians. Cars $1. For further information contact the Mississippi Bridge Authority ☎376-8100.)* The **Riverwalk,** a multimillion-dollar conglomeration of overpriced shops overlooking the port, stretches along the Mississippi. *(☎522-1555. Open M-Sa 10am-9pm, Su 11am-7pm.)* Dispose of your spare change at **Harrah's New Orleans Casino,** at Canal St. and the river, where an endless Mardi Gras of slot machines suck down depressingly endless buckets of quarters. *(☎800-427-7247. 21+. Open 24hr.)*

CEMETERIES. New Orleans's high water table makes it impossible to get a coffin to stay six feet under without floating away periodically. Because of this inconvenience, NOLA's cemeteries are crowded with above-ground tombs that range from the plain to the extravagant. Cemeteries are free and open most weekdays from 9am-4pm. **Lafayette Cemetery #1** is one block south of the Washington Ave. stop on the St. Charles Streetcar. The most extravagant tombs can be found at the sprawling **Metairie Cemetery** at the northern end of the Canal St. streetcar. Cemeteries can be dangerous; use caution and go with a group. Shadowing the numerous guided tours is a way to stay safe. Do not go to the cemeteries at night.

WAREHOUSE/ARTS DISTRICT. Relatively new to the downtown area, the **Warehouse/Arts District,** centered roughly at the intersection of Julia and Camp St., contains several revitalized warehouse buildings turned contemporary art galleries and many of the city's museums. The galleries feature free exhibition openings the first Saturday of every month. On **White Linen Night,** the first Saturday in August, thousands attend the galleries in their fanciest white finery. *(Arts District info: www.neworleansartsdistrictassociation.com.)* In an old brick building with a modern glass-and-chrome facade, the **Contemporary Arts Center** mounts exhibits ranging from puzzling to cryptic. The large complex feels like a refuge for all the artists escaping the tourists. *(900 Camp St. ☎528-3805; www.cacno.org. Internet access free with any purchase in the cafe. Open Tu-Su 11am-5pm. Exhibits $5, students and seniors $3, under 12 free. Th free. Galleries rotate frequently; call ahead for details.)* In the rear studio of the **New Orleans School of Glassworks and Printmaking Studio,** observe students and instructors transform blobs of molten glass into vases and sculptures. *(727 Magazine St. ☎529-7277. Open in summer M-F 10:30am-5pm; in winter M-Sa 10am-6pm. Free. Glassblowing usually runs from Sept.-May; call ahead during the summer to see if any glasswork is taking place.)* The **Jonathan Ferrara Gallery** hosts local artists and the annual "No Dead Artists: A Juried Exhibition of New Orleans Art Today" every April. Ferrara was nationally recognized for his involvement in "Guns in the Hands of Artists," a 1996 program in which people turned in guns to be made into works of art. *(841 Carondelet St. ☎ 522-5471. Open Tu-Sa noon-6pm. Free.)* Just west of the Warehouse District, the **Zeitgeist Multi-Disciplinary Arts Center** offers films, theatrical and musical performances, and art exhibitions. Alternative, experimental, and provocative, the center states their mission as, "Something for and against everyone!" *(1724 Oretha Castle Haley Blvd., 4 blocks north of St. Charles Ave., going uptown on O'Keefe. Do not go into this area after dark. ☎ 525-2767 or 525-6246. Open Tu-Sa 10:30am-5pm.)* A few blocks west on St. Charles Ave., in **Lee Circle,** a bronze statue of Gen. Robert E. Lee faces north, continuing to stare down the Yankees.

■ **SAINT CHARLES STREETCAR.** Much of the Crescent City's fame derives from the **Vieux Carré,** but areas uptown have their fair share of beauty and action. The **Saint Charles Streetcar** still runs west of the French Quarter, passing some of the city's finest buildings, including the 19th-century homes along **Saint Charles Avenue.** *Gone With the Wind* fans will recognize the whitewashed bricks and elegant doorway of the house on the far right corner of Arabella St.—it's a replica of Tara. But frankly, my dear, it's not open to the public. For more views of fancy living, get off the streetcar in the **Garden District,** an opulent neighborhood around Jackson and Louisiana Ave. For a great introduction to these neighborhoods, buy a $5 streetcar day-pass from any streetcar driver and hop on and off the St. Charles line as much as you want.

CITY PARK. Brimming with golf courses, ponds, statues, Greek Revival gazebos, softball fields, a stadium, and **Storyland** (a theme park for kids), City Park is a huge green wonderland of non-alcoholic activities. Storyland is the kind of kids' entertainment parents long for, with an antique carousel and fishing from paddle boats in the 11 mi. of lagoons. The **New Orleans Botanical Garden** is home to over 2000 varieties of plants and many great Art Deco sculptures. *(1 Palm Dr., at the northern end of Esplanade Ave. www.neworleanscitypark.com. Maps at Jackson Sq. Visitors Center.)*

HISTORIC HOMES AND PLANTATIONS

Across from downtown New Orleans, **River Road** curves along the Mississippi River and accesses several preserved 19th-century plantations. *Great River Road Plantation Parade: A River of Riches*, available at the New Orleans or Baton Rouge visitors centers, contains a good map and descriptions of the houses. Pick carefully, since a tour of all the privately owned plantations is expensive, and some are a 45-60min. drive from downtown New Orleans.

LAURA: A CREOLE PLANTATION. ■**Laura,** unlike the others on the riverbank, was owned and operated by slave-owning Creoles who lived a different life from that of white antebellum planters. A 45min. drive from downtown New Orleans, Laura is also the only plantation near New Orleans that has preserved slave quarters. Br'er Rabbit hopped into his first briar patch here, the site of the first recorded "Compair Lapin" West African stories. Laura presents a valuable and unique look at plantation life in the South. *(2247 Hwy. 18/River Rd., at the intersection of Rte. 20 in Vacherie. Take Exit 194 off I-10, then take Rte. 641 S and follow signs. ☎ 225-265-7690 or 888-799-7690. 1hr. tours based on the "memories" of the old plantation home daily 9:30am-4pm. Max. 20min. wait. $10, ages 6-17 $5. AAA discount $1. Cash only.)*

LONGUE VUE HOUSE AND GARDENS. Called the "Great Showplace of New Orleans," **Longue Vue** epitomizes the grand Southern estate with lavish furnishings, opulent decor, and sculpted gardens inspired by the Spanish Alhambra. A 10min. drive from downtown New Orleans, this plantation is much closer to the city than similar estates. *(7 Bamboo Rd., off Metairie Rd. ☎ 488-5488. 35min. guided tours depart every hr. M-Sa 10am-4:30pm, Su 1-5pm. Self-guided tours available in 6 languages. $10, seniors $9, students $5, under 5 free. AAA discount $1.)*

NOTTOWAY PLANTATION. The largest plantation home in the South, **Nottoway** is often called the "White Castle of Louisiana." A 64-room mansion with 22 columns, a large ballroom, and a three-story stairway, it was the first choice for the filming of *Gone with the Wind*, but the owners wouldn't allow it. *(30970 Hwy. Rte. 405., between Bayou Goula and White Castle, 18 mi. south of Baton Rouge on the southern bank of the Mississippi. 1hr. from New Orleans. ☎ 225-545-2730 or 888-323-8314. Open daily 9am-5pm. Lunch served daily 11am-3pm. Admission and 1hr. tour $10, under 12 $4, under 5 free.)*

OAK ALLEY PLANTATION. The name **Oak Alley** refers to the magnificent lawn-alley bordered by 28 oaks that correspond to the 28 columns surrounding the bright pink Greek Revival house. You can take a picture of the gorgeous oak-bordered driveway framing the house for free from across Rte. 18 and save the price of admission. *(3645 Rte. 18., between St. James and Vacherie St. 5min. west of Laura plantation, 50min. from downtown New Orleans. ☎ 800-442-5539. Tours daily every 30min. Mar.-Oct. 9am-5:30pm; Nov.-Feb. 9am-5pm. $10, ages 13-18 $5, ages 6-12 $3.)*

HISTORIC HOMES DOWNTOWN. Located in the French Quarter and built in 1831, **Hermann-Grima Historic House** exemplifies urban elegance with guillotine windows, a fan-lit entrance, and parterre beds. On Thursdays from October to May, volunteers demonstrate period cooking in an 1830s Creole kitchen. *(820 St. Louis St. ☎ 525-5661. Tours every hr. in the morning, every 30min. in the afternoon. M-F 10am-4pm; last tour 3:30pm. $6, seniors and ages 8-18 $5.)* Nearby, the **Gallier House Museum** is another example of antebellum architecture. James Gallier, Jr., the city's most famous architect, lived here in the 1860s. *(1118-1132 Royal St. ☎ 525-5661. Open M-Sa 10am-4pm; last tour 3:30pm. $6; students, seniors, and ages 8-18 $5; under 8 free.)*

🏛 MUSEUMS

■ **NEW ORLEANS PHARMACY MUSEUM.** This enthralling look into medical history is housed in an apothecary shop built by America's first licensed pharmacist in 1823. Among the exhibits are 19th-century "miracle drugs" like cocaine and opium, voodoo powders, a collection of old spectacles, and live leeches. *(514 Chartres St., between St. Louis and Toulouse St. ☎ 565-8027. Open Tu-Su 10am-4:30pm. $5, students and seniors $4, under 5 free. AAA discount $1.)*

■ **NATIONAL D-DAY MUSEUM.** The D-Day Museum, founded by historian Stephen Ambrose and dedicated in 2000 by Tom Hanks and Stephen Spielberg, has a refreshingly engaging study of WWII, confronting the lesser-known, gruesome Pacific battles and issues of race and propaganda. The museum is truly remarkable for its unbiased scrutiny. *(945 Magazine St., at Andrew Higgins Dr. in the Historic Warehouse District. ☎ 527-6012. Open daily 9am-5pm. $14; students, seniors, and military $8; under 12 $6; military in uniform and under 5 free. AAA discount $2.)*

■ **AFRICAN-AMERICAN MUSEUM OF ART, CULTURE, AND HISTORY.** In an 1829 Creole-style villa rescued from blight in 1991, this museum displays a variety of changing and permanent exhibits showcasing African-American artists, along with important historical themes. Slightly off the beaten path, the collection reveals a different New Orleans from the showy one of the French Quarter. *(1418 Gov. Nicholls St., 4 blocks north of Rampart St. in Tremé. ☎ 587-0024. Open M-F 10am-5pm, Sa 10am-2pm. $6, seniors $4, ages 4-17 $3.)*

NEW ORLEANS MUSEUM OF ART (NOMA). This museum houses art from North and South America, a magnificent glass collection, opulent works by the jeweler Fabergé, a strong collection of French paintings, and impressive African and Japanese cultural collections. The inspiring new sculpture garden sprawls over acres of walkways. *(In City Park, at the City Park/Metairie exit off I-10. ☎ 488-2631; www.noma.org. Open Tu-Su 10am-5pm. $8, seniors $7, ages 3-17 $4. Call for tickets to special exhibits.)*

LOUISIANA STATE MUSEUM. The "State Museum" really encompasses 8 separate museums, 6 of which are in New Orleans. *(For all museums: ☎ 800-568-6968; http://lsm.crt.state.la.us.)* The **Cabildo** presents the history of Louisiana and houses Napoleon's death mask. *(701 Chartres St.)* The **Arsenal** recounts the history of the Mississippi River and New Orleans as a port city. *(615 St. Peter, enter through the Cabildo.)* The **Presbytère** features an interactive exhibit about Mardi Gras. *(751 Chartres St.)* The **1850 House** is—you guessed it—a recreated house from the 1850s. *(523 St. Ann St., on Jackson Sq.)* **Madame John's Legacy** showcases Creole architecture as well as contemporary self-taught Louisiana artists. *(632 Dumaine St.)* The **Old US Mint** focuses not only on currency, but on the history of jazz in an exhibit that includes Satchmo's first horn. *(400 Esplanade. All museums open Tu-Su 9am-5pm. Old US Mint, Cabildo, Presbytère: $5; students, seniors, and active military $4. 1850 House, Mme. John's Legacy: $3/$2. Under 12 free for all museums. 20% discount on tickets to 2 or more museums.)*

THE VOODOO MUSEUM. Learn why dusty shops in the Quarter sell *gris-gris* and alligator parts. A priest or a priestess will do a reading or a ritual for $30, or visitors can just walk through the rooms full of artifacts for the entrance fee. *(724 Dumaine St., in the Quarter. ☎ 680-0127. Open daily 10am-6pm. $7; students, seniors, and military $5.50; high school students $4.50; ages 12 and under $3.50.)*

MUSÉE CONTI WAX MUSEUM. Thirty-one tableaux of wax figures make for a great mix of the historically important, sensationally infamous, and just plain kitschy history of New Orleans. *(917 Conti St., between Burgundy and Dauphine St. ☎ 525-2605 or 800-233-5405. Open M-Sa 10am-5:30pm. $6.75, seniors $6.25, under 17 $5.75.)*

♫ ENTERTAINMENT

THEATER AND MUSIC

Le Petit Théâtre du Vieux Carré, 616 St. Peter St., is the oldest continuously operating community theater in the US. The 1789 building replicates the early 18th-century abode of Joseph de Pontalba, Louisiana's last Spanish governor. About five musicals and plays go up each year, as well as three fun productions in the "Children's Corner." *(☎ 522-9958; www.lepetittheatre.com. Box office open Tu-Sa 10:30am-5:30pm, Su noon-showtime. Plays $21, musicals $26. Shows Th-Su 8pm; weekly matinee Su 2pm.)* Born at the turn of the century in **Armstrong Park,** traditional New Orleans jazz still wails nightly at the tiny, historic **Preservation Hall,** 726 St. Peter St. With only two small ceiling fans trying to move the air around, the joint heats up in more ways than one. *(Daytime ☎ 522-2841 or 800-785-5772, after 8pm 523-8939; www.preservationhall.com. No food or drink allowed. Cover $5. Doors open at 8pm; music 8:15pm-midnight.)* Keep your ears open for **Cajun** and **zydeco** bands, which use accordions, washboards, triangles, and drums to perform hot dance tunes and saccharine waltzes. Anyone who thinks couple-dancing went out in the 50s should try a *fais-do-do*, a traditional dance that got its name from the custom parents had of putting their children to sleep before dancing the night away *(Fais-do-do* is Cajun baby talk for "to make sleep"). **Uptown** tends to play host to authentic Cajun dance halls and popular university hangouts, while the **Marigny** is home to New Orleans's alternative/local music scene. Check out *Off Beat*, free in many local restaurants; *Where Y'At*, another free entertainment weekly; or the Friday *Times-Picayune* to find out who's playing where.

FESTIVALS

New Orleans's **Mardi Gras** celebration is the biggest party of the year, a world-renowned, epic bout of lascivious debauchery that fills the three weeks leading up to Ash Wednesday—the beginning of Lent and a time of penance and deprivation in the Catholic tradition. Mardi Gras, which literally means "Fat Tuesday," is an all-out hedonistic pleasure-fest before 40 days of purity—and tourists pour in by the plane-full (flights into the city and hotel rooms fill up months in advance). In 2006, Mardi Gras falls on February 28th, and the biggest parades and the bulk of the partying will take place the two weeks prior to that. The ever-expanding **New Orleans Jazz and Heritage Festival** attracts 7000 musicians from around the country to the city's fairgrounds. The likes of Aretha Franklin, Bob Dylan, and Wynton Marsalis have graced this festival. Music plays simultaneously on 12 stages in the midst of a food and crafts festival; the biggest names perform at evening riverboat concerts. (☎522-4786; www.nojazzfest.com. Apr. 28-May 7, 2006.)

▟ NIGHTLIFE

BARS

FRENCH QUARTER

▨ **Funky Butt,** 714 N. Rampart St. (☎558-0872), is an awesome hideout to hear live jazz and marvel at the wonder of the *derrière*. Walk in to face a gigantic, languorous nude painting and hear the strains of a live band 5 ft. from the door. Fats Domino's hat hangs above the bar. Stay to sip a funkybuttjuice ($6) and sit with a select group in the tiny space alongside the band. Beers $3-4. House band plays from 7:30-9:30pm. Sets most nights 10pm and midnight. Cover $5-10. Open daily 7pm-2am.

▨ **Lafitte's Blacksmith Shop,** 941 Bourbon St. (☎522-9377), at Phillip St. Appropriately, one of New Orleans's oldest standing structures is a bar, one of the oldest bars in the US. Named for the scheming hero of the Battle of New Orleans, it offers shaded relief from the elements of the city and a dimly lit hiding place for celebrities. Beer $4-5. Live piano 8pm-late. Open daily 10 or 11am to 4 or 5am.

Donna's, 800 N. Rampart St. (☎596-6914). As one fan says, this is "the place where you can sit and watch New Orleans roll by." On the edge of the French Quarter, with good barbecue, music, and a relaxed ambience. Open M, W and F-Su 8:30pm-1:30am.

Fritzel's, 733 Bourbon St. (☎561-0432), between Orleans and St. Ann, was opened over 30 years ago by a German proprietor who wanted to give musicians of all abilities the chance to play. It hosts some of the best traditional and Dixie band jazz in the Quarter every night. Although drinks are pricey (most beers $5-6), there's no cover. Open daily 1pm-2am, with entertainment from 8 or 9pm.

Pat O'Brien's, 718 St. Peter St. (☎525-4823 or 800-597-4823). Housed in the first Spanish theater in the US, Pat O'Brien's is one of the most famous bars in the French Quarter, bursting with rosy-cheeked patrons who carouse in the courtyard. Home of the

 THE REAL DEAL. Wandering around Bourbon St. with a beer and watching the mayhem unfold can be fun for a night, but the bars elsewhere in the French Quarter, uptown in the Garden District, and along Frenchman St. usually have better music and cheaper drinks. If you still can't tear yourself away from the Bourbon St. scene, keep your wallet happy by patronizing the drink stands along the sidewalk—their $3-4 24 oz. beers are a much better bargain than the $5 bottles of Bud in most of the street's bars and clubs. —Ben Collins

original Hurricane, a fruit punch-flavored cocktail. If you're feeling sentimental, purchase your first in a souvenir glass ($9, without glass $6.50). Open M-Th 11am-4am, F-Su 10am-5am.

Pirate's Alley, 622 Pirate's Alley (☎524-9332), down the alley on your left when facing the St. Louis Cathedral. Its location on a side street, compounded by the plain wooden walls and awnings, make this bar feel like a safe haven in what can be a sensory-overload city. Beers $3-8. Absinthe $8. Open daily noon-close.

OUTSIDE THE QUARTER

■ **The Spotted Cat,** 623 Frenchmen St. (☎943-3887), is what you might have imagined most New Orleans bars would be like: cheap beer ($2-4), a place to sit and chill, and passion-filled trumpets, voices, and piano solos that pour out the front door onto the sidewalk. The wooden walls and floors make for excellent acoustics. "Early" band 6:30pm, "late" band 10pm. Domestic beers $2 during happy hour. Live music until 2am most nights. No cover. 1-drink min. Open M-F 2pm to 2 or 3am, Sa-Su from noon to 4 or 5am.

d.b.a., 618 Frenchmen St. (☎942-3731), next to Snug Harbor. Popular, wood-paneled bar with free wireless Internet and a wide selection of beers on tap ($3-7). A twentysomething kind of place. Live music most nights at 10pm. No cover. 1-drink min. Open M-F 4pm-4am, Sa-Su 4pm-5am.

Snug Harbor, 626 Frenchmen St. (☎949-0696), near Decatur St. Regulars include big names in jazz like Charmaine Neville and Ellis Marsalis. Cover is sometimes steep ($10-25), but the music, played in the beautiful, intimate cypress "jazz room," is incredible. Shows nightly 9, 11pm. All ages. Restaurant open M-Th and Su 5-11pm, F-Sa 5pm-midnight; bar until 1am. The kitchen closes early some nights; call ahead to find out if they are serving. Advance ticket purchase recommended, especially for weekend events.

Igor's Checkpoint Charlie, 501 Esplanade (☎949-7012), is a combination bar, laundromat, and restaurant that feels like a cozy neighborhood coffeeshop or a wild nightclub, depending on where you're standing. You can drink while you wash your clothes ($1.50 per load), listen to a poetry slam over jazz, buy a used book, or have a greasy burger while shooting a game of pool. Beer $3-4, pitchers $7.50. Burgers $5-7. Live music nightly, usually starting around 8pm. No cover. Open 24hr. **Igor's Lounge,** 2133 St. Charles Ave. in the Garden District (☎522-2145), has a similar vibe and is known for its Bloody Marys ($4.50). Also open 24hr.

DANCE CLUBS

■ **Tipitina's,** 501 Napoleon Ave. (☎895-8477). The best local bands and some big national names—like the Neville Brothers and Harry Connick, Jr.—play so close you can almost touch them. Beer $2-5. Cajun *fais-do-dos* (p. 425) Su 5-9pm. 18+. Cover $7-10, higher for national acts. Music usually W-Su 9pm-3am; call for times and prices.

House of Blues, 225 Decatur St. (☎529-2624), in the French Quarter. A sprawling complex with a large music/dance hall (capacity over 1000) and a balcony and bar overlooking the action. Check out the gospel brunch on Su ($35; 90min. performances at 9:30 and 11:25am). Concerts nightly 9:15pm. 18+. Tickets $12-50. Restaurant open M-Th and Su 11am-10pm, F-Sa 11am-11pm.

Mid City Lanes Rock 'n' Bowl, 4133 S. Carrollton Ave. (☎482-3133), in the mini-mall at Tulane Ave. Since 1941, this place has attracted multi-tasking partiers to its rockin' lanes. The "home of Rock 'n' Bowl" is a bowling alley by day and traditional dance club by night (you can bowl at night, too). Drinks $1.75-3.50. Lanes $15 per hr. plus $1 for shoes. Live music Tu-W 8:30pm, F-Sa 10pm; local zydeco Th 9:30pm. 18+ at night when the bar gets hopping. Cover $5-10. Open daily noon to around 1 or 2am.

▼ GLBT ACTIVITIES

New Orleans has a long history of sexual diversity, touching on all strands of society, but it never really met with public approval. In spite of the private clubs and mixed bars that have existed for hundreds of years, only today does the city have an open and vibrant gay scene less exclusive than many other urban gay scenes. Many straight people visit gay venues because the drinks are cheaper and stronger. Someone is also keeping track of gay history in New Orleans: Robert Batson, "history laureate," leads the ▓**Gay Heritage Tour**—a walking tour through the French Quarter—leaving from Alternatives, 909 Bourbon St. It lasts 2½hr. and is perhaps the best possible introduction to New Orleans for anyone, gay or straight. (☎945-6789. W 4pm and Sa 1pm. $20 per person. Reservations required.)

You'll find the majority of gay establishments toward the northeast end of Bourbon St. ("downriver"), and along St. Ann St., known to some as the **"Lavender Line."** A good point of reference is where St. Ann and Bourbon St. cross—**Oz** is to the river side and **Bourbon Pub** is to the lake side. These are the two biggest gay danceclubs and principal gay institutions in the city. To find the real lowdown of gay nightlife, get a copy of *The Whiz Magazine*, a locally produced guide; there's always a copy on top of the radiator in Cafe Lafitte in Exile. *Ambush* is a more impersonal, mass-produced gay entertainment mag that can be found at many French Quarter businesses. **Faubourg-Marigny Art and Books,** 600 Frenchmen St., on the corner of Frenchmen St. and Chartres St. in Marigny, has books, photos, and art on GLBT New Orleans. (☎947-3700. Open daily noon-7pm.) For info and tailored entertainment and community fact sheets, go to the **Lesbian and Gay Community Center of New Orleans,** 2114 Decatur St., in Marigny. (☎945-1103. Open M-F 2-8pm, Sa 11am-6pm. Report hate crimes to ☎943-4325.)

GLBT NIGHTLIFE

Cafe Lafitte in Exile, 901 Bourbon St. (☎522-8397). Exiled from Laffite's Blacksmith Shop in 1953 when Lafitte's came under new management, the ousted gay patrons trooped up the street to found the oldest gay bar in America. On the opening night, surrounded by patrons dressed as their favorite exile, Cafe Lafitte in Exile lit an "eternal flame" (it still burns today) that aptly represents the soul of the gay community in New Orleans. Today, though Cafe Lafitte has video screens, occasional live music, pageants, and shows, it's still the same old neighborhood gathering place at heart. Open 24hr.

Good Friends, 740 Dauphine St. (☎566-7191). This is a gay "Cheers" episode. A cozy, friendly neighborhood bar full of locals happy to welcome in a refugee from Bourbon St. Despite the occasional pool tournament, drink specials, and "hot buns" contest, usually things are pretty calm. Don't miss Su afternoon sing-alongs. Open 24hr.

Cowpokes, 2240 St. Claude Ave. (☎947-0505), 1 block off Elysian Fields in Marigny. Line dancing, lube wrestling on W, 10-gallon hats, and spurs can be as wholesome as you want to make them. Both cowgirls and pardners are welcome. Tu country line dancing lessons at 8pm, free. Happy hour daily 4-9pm. Open M-Th and Su 4pm-1am, F-Sa 4pm-2am. Cowpokes also has a great **theater** that does 4 productions per year (for info ☎947-0505; www.dramano.org). Take a cab here, as the area can be unsafe at night.

▲ OUTDOOR ACTIVITIES

The St. Charles Streetcar eventually makes its way to **Audubon Park,** near **Tulane University.** Audubon contains lagoons, statues, stables, and the award-winning ▓**Audubon Zoo,** 6500 Magazine St., where white alligators swim in a recreated Louisiana swamp. Tigers, elephants, rhinos, and sea lions, among others, are grouped into exhibit areas that highlight historical and natural regions of the globe, while peacocks roam the walkways freely. There is a free museum shuttle between the streetcar stop and zoo entrance every 15min. (☎581-4629. Zoo open in summer M-F 9:30am-5pm, Sa-Su 9:30am-6pm. $12, seniors $9, ages 2-12 $7. Combination zoo/aquarium tickets $22/$18/$14. AAA discount.) The **New Orleans Zephyrs,** a AAA affiliate of Major League Baseball's Washington Nationals, play home games from April to August at Zephyr Field, on Airline Dr. west of Transcontinental Dr. (☎734-5155; www.zephyrsbaseball.com. Tickets $7-9.50, children and seniors $6-8.50.)

One of the most unique sights in the New Orleans area, the coastal wetlands along Lake Salvador make up a segment of the **Jean Lafitte National Historical Park** called the ◼**Barataria Preserve,** 7400 Barataria Blvd. South of New Orleans; take Business 90 to Rte. 45 southbound, turn left onto Lafitte Parkway and follow signs to the preserve. (☎589-2330. Daily park-sponsored foot tour through the swamp 11am. Ranger-led canoe trips Mar.-May Sa 9:30am. Free maps and trail guides for ¼-2 mi. walks. Open daily 7am-5pm; extended summer hours. **Visitors center** open daily 9am-5pm. Free.) Many commercial boat tours operate in the park. Tours typically travel by airboat and involve feeding alligators. Prices vary and many have discounts in the *Sizzlin' Summer* coupon book available at the New Orleans Visitor Center next to Jackson Park. Ask how many people fit into each tour boat; boats vary from small airboats to large pontoon cruisers. **Cypress Swamp Tours** will pick you up from your hotel. (☎581-4501 or 800-633-0503. 2hr. tours 9:30, 11:30am, 1:30pm. $22, with hotel pick up $39; ages 6-12 $12/$22. Call for reservations.)

BATON ROUGE ☎225

Once the site of a tall cypress tree marking the boundary between rival Native American tribes, Baton Rouge ("red stick") has blossomed into Louisiana's second-largest city. Though the city's meat-and-potatoes flavor contrasts with the sauciness of New Orleans, fiery state politics have shaped this town—it was once home to governor, senator, and demagogue Huey "Kingfish" Long—and **Louisiana State University (LSU)** adds an element of youth vigor and rabid Tigertown loyalty.

◼◼ **ORIENTATION AND PRACTICAL INFORMATION.** From east to west, the three main streets in Baton Rouge are **N. Foster Drive, N. Acadian Throughway,** and **22nd Street.** Beginning in the north, Florida Blvd. and Government St. run perpendicular to these. Though public transportation is useful for getting around downtown, driving is the best way to see the rest of the city. Close to downtown, **Greyhound,** 1253 Florida Blvd. (☎383-3811 or 800-231-2222; www.greyhound.com; open 24hr.), at 12th St., sends buses to Lafayette (1hr., 8 per day, $15) and New Orleans (2hr., 6 per day, $17). Use caution in this area at night. **Capitol Transportation** (☎389-8282) runs buses throughout downtown every 30min. 7:15am-7:30pm. ($1.25, seniors and children $0.90.) **Taxi: ABC Transit,** ☎355-3133. **Visitor Info: State Capitol Visitors Center,** on the first floor of the state capitol, has maps and brochures for area attractions. (☎342-7317. Open daily 8am-4:30pm.) The more corporate **Baton Rouge Convention and Visitors Bureau** is at 730 North Blvd. (☎383-1825; www.visitbatonrouge.com. Open M-F 8am-5pm.) **Internet Access: State Library of Louisiana,** 701 N. 4th St., is a beautiful library with free, fast Internet access. (☎342-4915. Open M-F 8am-5pm.) On weekends, access is available at **East Baton Rouge Parish Library,** 7711 Goodwood Blvd. (☎231-3740. Open M-Th 8am-10pm, F-Sa 8am-6pm, Su 2-10pm. Free.) **Post Office:** 750 Florida St., off River Rd. (☎381-0325. Open M-F 7:30am-5pm, Sa 8am-12:30pm.) **Postal Code:** 70821. **Area Code:** 225.

◼ **ACCOMMODATIONS.** Downtown rooms are pricey, especially during midweek when state capitol business is underway. The university area, however, is home to several motels. For the budget-savvy, **Deluxe Inn ❷,** 10245 Airline Drive, south off I-12 at Exit 2, has clean rooms with refrigerators, microwaves, free wireless Internet, pool, and continental breakfast. (☎291-8152. Rooms $38. AmEx/D/MC/V.) The **Highland Inn ❸**, 2605 S. Range Ave., at Exit 10 off I-12 in Denham Springs, is 15min. from downtown. (☎667-7177. Cable TV, continental breakfast, free local calls, and pool. Singles $45-55; doubles $49-59. AmEx/D/MC/V.) **KOA Kampground ❶**, 7628 Vincent Rd., 1 mi. off I-12 at the Denham Springs exit, keeps 110 great sites, clean facilities, hot showers, and a pool. (☎664-7281 or 800-562-5673. Sites $19, full RV hookup $30, 50 amp $32. Cabins $40. MC/V.)

❑❑ **FOOD AND NIGHTLIFE.** Downtown, sandwich shops and cafes line 3rd St.; the **casinos** boast some of the city's best cuisine. For simple, small-town fare, check out the **Frostop ❶**, 402 Government St., downtown, with a giant, gracefully aging root beer can out front. Burgers with "freedom fries" and a drink go for $5.50, but po' boy sandwiches ($4.50-6) and seafood platters ($8-10) are also popular. (☎344-1179. Floats and shakes $2-4. Open M-F 10am-7pm, Sa noon-7pm.) Head to LSU at the intersection of Highland Rd. and Chimes St., off I-10, for cheap chow, bars, and smoothie shops. **Chelsea's Cafe ❷**, 148 W. State Street, serves vegetarian-friendly meals. The grilled cheese and vegetables on focaccia bread ($7) is superb. (☎387-3679. Live music Th-Sa. Open M-F 11am-10pm, Sa noon-10pm; bar open until 2am. AmEx/MC/V.) At **The Chimes ❸**, 3357 Highland Rd., at Chimes St., you can sample a beer from almost every country; Chimes stocks 120 brews with 30 on tap. Start with Louisiana alligator (fried or blackened, with Dijon mustard sauce) for $8, then dig into some crawfish *étouffée* for $9. (☎383-1754. Entrees $10-15. Open M-Sa 11am-2am, Su 11am-11:45pm. AmEx/D/MC/V.) Next door is **Varsity**, 5535 Highland Rd., which has hosted big names like Tori Amos and They Might Be Giants. (☎383-7018. Beer $2.50-4. Cover $10-$45, depending on band. Usually open 8pm-2am; hours vary.) Thirsty LSU students flock to **Tigertown,** a collection of nearly identical bars along Bob Pettit Blvd. west of Nicholson Drive, for live music and drinks. For nightlife listings, pick up a copy of *Reveille*, LSU's free bi-weekly paper (published daily during school time), at Louie's cafe.

◪ **SIGHTS.** In a move reminiscent of Ramses II, Huey Long ordered the construction of the ◪**Louisiana State Capitol,** referred to as "the new capitol"—a somewhat startling skyscraper completed over a mere 14 months in 1931 and 1932. "The house that Huey built," was meant to raise Louisiana's prestige and pave Long's path to the presidency. Ironically, Long was assassinated inside it three years later; a display marks the spot of the shooting. The **observation deck,** on the 27th floor, provides a panoramic view of the surrounding area. (☎342-5914. Open daily 8:30am-4:00pm. Free.) The **Old State Capitol,** 100 North Blvd., resembles a cathedral with a fantastic cast-iron spiral staircase and domed stained glass. Inside, interactive political displays urge voter responsibility alongside exhibits about the "Kingfish" and Louisiana's tumultuous (and often corrupt) political history. (☎800-488-2968. Open Tu-Sa 10am-4pm, Su noon-4pm. $4, seniors $3, students $2.) The **Old Governor's Mansion,** 502 North Blvd., may look familiar—Huey Long insisted that his governor's residence resemble his dream dwelling, the White House. Inside, peruse many of Long's personal belongings, including a book he wrote, somewhat prematurely, called *My First Days in the White House.* (☎387-2464. Open Tu-F 10am-4pm; hours may vary. Last tour 3pm. $6, seniors $5, students $4.)

The **Louisiana Art and Science Museum (LASM),** 100 S. River Rd., is a strange combination of art gallery and hands-on science museum that recently opened a state-of-the-art planetarium. (☎344-5272; www.lasm.org. Open Tu-F 10am-4pm, Sa 10am-5pm, Su 1-5pm. Planetarium open until 8pm on Sa. Admission to galleries and planetarium $8; students, seniors, and children $7. First Su of every month free admission to galleries and discounted admission to planetarium.) At the **USS**

Kidd and Nautical Center, 305 S. River Rd., at Government St., you can check out the destroyer *Kidd,* which was hit directly by a kamikaze during its career and has been restored to its WWII glory. (☎342-1942. Open daily 9am-5pm. $7, students $6, ages 6-12 $4, under 5 free.) The ◼LSU Rural Life Museum, 4560 Essen Ln., just off I-10 at Exit 160, depicts the life of 19th-century Creoles and working-class Louisianans through their original furnished shops, cabins, and storage houses. Next door, explore the lakes, paths, and flowers of the **Windrush Gardens.** The semi-formal gardens contain native plants used during the time period. (☎765-2437. Both open daily 8:30am-5pm. Joint admission $7, seniors $6, ages 5-11 $5, under 5 free.)

NATCHITOCHES   ☎318

Don't say it how it's spelled. Pronounced "NAK-ah-tish," the oldest city in Louisiana was founded in 1714 by the French as an outpost to guard against the Spanish. The town was named after the original Native American inhabitants of the region. With its strategic location along the banks of the Red River, Natchitoches should have become a major port city; a big logjam, however, changed the course of the city's history, redirecting the river and leaving the town high and dry, with only a 36 mi.-long lake running along historic downtown. Today, it makes for a romantic setting as you stroll along the manicured lakefront park.

◼◪ **ORIENTATION AND PRACTICAL INFORMATION.** Downtown Natchitoches is tiny. **Highway 6** enters town from the west off I-49 and becomes **Front Street,** the main drag, where it follows the **Cane River,** running north until it becomes Hwy. 6 again. **Second Street** runs parallel to Front St., and the town stems across the lake from those two streets. Historic homes populate downtown, while plantations lie 7 to 18 mi. south, off **Route 1 S.** The plantations and Rte. 1 follow the Cane River. **Greyhound,** 331 Cane River Shopping Center (☎352-8341; www.greyhound.com; open M-F 8am-4:30pm, Sa 8am-noon), sends buses to Dallas (6hr., 3 per day, $56), Houston (8-10hr., 4 per day, $61), and New Orleans (6-8hr., 3 per day, $51). Maps and accommodations info are available at the **Natchitoches Convention and Visitors Bureau,** 781 Front St. (☎352-8072 or 800-259-1714; www.natchitoches.net. Open M-F 8am-6pm, Sa 9am-5pm, Su 10am-4pm.) **Internet Access: Natchitoches Public Library,** 450 2nd St. (☎357-3280. Open M-F 9am-6pm, Sa 9am-5pm. Free.) **Post Office:** 240 Saint Denis St. (☎352-0378. Open M-F 8am-4:30pm, Sa 9-11am.) **Postal Code:** 71457. **Area Code:** 318.

◪ **ACCOMMODATIONS.** Natchitoches isn't a cheap town. As the "B&B Capital" of Louisiana, the city abounds with cozy rooms in historic homes, but during the annual **Christmas Festival of Lights** (see p. 433), held the first weekend in December, room rates can triple, and reservations are needed months in advance. Get an authentic taste of Natchitoches at the elegant and reasonably priced ◼Chaplin House Bed and Breakfast ❸, 434 2nd St. The well-traveled proprietors of this exquisitely restored and decorated 1892 home boast a wealth of local knowledge. (☎352-2324. Gay friendly. Continental breakfast, including fresh home-baked muffins. Singles $55; doubles $85. MC/V.) One of the best deals is the **Fleur de Lis Bed and Breakfast ❹,** 336 2nd St., near the southern end of town, an adorable, gingerbready Victorian with a whimsical pastel exterior and quirky flavor all its own. (☎352-6621 or 800-489-6621. Rooms $70-90; higher during Festival of Lights in December. AmEx/MC/V.) West of town, you'll find the well-furnished **Microtel Inn ❸,** 5335 Rte. 6 W at University Pkwy. (☎214-0700 or 888-771-7171. A/C, cable TV, fridges, pool access, wireless Internet, free long distance, and continental breakfast. Doubles weeknights $58, weekends $68. AAA discount 10%. AmEx/D/MC/V.) Farther out, the 600,000-acre **Kisatchie National Forest** offers basic camping with trails and sce-

THE SOUTH

> Though many places in Louisiana have fixed opening times, closing times are often up for negotiation. If people are having a good time, businesses will often stay open into the wee hours or not close at all. If it's slow, however, owners may decide to close up early and go home. Keep in mind that when the hours of an establishment just say "open till," they mean "open till we feel like closing."

nic overlooks. The park is about 25 mi. south of the Rte. 6 Ranger Station near Natchitoches. Many of its sites, though equipped with bathhouses, are primitive. The **Kisatchie Ranger District ❶**, 106 Rte. 6 W, a quarter-mile past the Microtel Inn, has maps and park conditions and provides help finding the well-hidden, primitive sites. (☎352-2568. Office open M-F 7am-4pm. No bathrooms. Sites $3.)

FOOD AND NIGHTLIFE. ◙Lasyone's ❷, 622 2nd St., is the place to go for down-home cooking. Their specialty is meat pie ($3), and travelers can get an eyeful of the 5 ft. meat pie model in the window before enjoying one of more manageable dimensions. (☎352-3353. Lunch specials $6. Open M-Sa 7am-till, usually after 6pm. MC/V.) **Mama's Oyster House ❷**, 606 Front St., is a downtown institution, cooking up lunch gumbo for $9 a bowl and oyster po' boys for $7. For dinner, fried crawfish ($12) complements live jazz and rock on the first and third Friday of each month. (☎356-7874. Open M-Sa 11am-10pm. MC/V.) Next door to Mama's is, of course, **Papa's ❶**, 604 Front St., with Natchitoches meat pies for $7 and po' boys and burgers for $6-7. (☎356-5850. Open M-Sa 11am-10pm.) One of the few establishments in Natchitoches open late is the **Pioneer Pub**, 812 Washington St., opposite the visitors center. Its neon lighting and musty old-world charm work surprisingly well. Skip the mediocre food and have a beer ($2-3) instead. (☎352-4884. Live music Sa 9pm. Open daily 11am-2am, or until the crowd leaves. MC/V.)

SIGHTS AND ENTERTAINMENT. Much of Natchitoches's charm lies on the Cane River Lake along **Front Street,** where coffeeshops, casual restaurants, and antique stores fill the storefronts of historical buildings that date back to the mid-19th century. To see Natchitoches's landmarks—including many of the sites where *Steel Magnolias* was filmed—from the comfort of a large, green trolley, take a 1hr. ride with the **Natchitoches Transit Company,** 100 Rue Beau Port, next to the visitors center. (☎356-8687. Call for departure times. $8, seniors $7, ages 3-12 $5.) Many of the most popular tourist destinations are in the **Cane River National Heritage Area,** the plantation-dotted countryside around Natchitoches. The visitors center has information about all the plantations and a free tourist guide, *Cane River Heritage Area,* which lists points of interest in the area. The **Fort St. Jean Baptiste State Historic Site,** 155 Rue Jefferson, provides a glimpse of daily life in Nachitoches's original French outpost, founded in 1714. The 15min. video and full-scale replica of the Fort explain the history of French and Indian settlement in the area. (☎357-3101. Open daily 9am-5pm. $2, children and seniors free.)

To see a zoo's worth of bayou wildlife, drive out to **Alligator Park,** 8 mi. north of Natchitoches off Rte. 1 N (look for the school bus in the shape of a gator off Rte. 1). Originally a conservation project, the park now entertains visitors with regular feeding shows every 30min., a snake house, an aviary, and an exhibit on nutria, swamp rats the size of small dogs. (☎354-0001 or 877-354-7001. Open mid-Apr. to mid-Aug. daily 10am-6pm; mid-Aug. to early October Sa-Su 10am-6pm. Alligators hibernate when it's cold, so plan accordingly. $7, children $5. Seniors and AAA discount 10%.) A string of plantation homes lines the Cane River, south of downtown along Rte. 1. The **Melrose Plantation,** 14 mi. south on Rte. 1, then left on Rte. 493, is unique in origin—its female founder was an ex-slave. The African House, one of the outbuildings, is the oldest example of Congo-like architecture in North Amer-

THE SOUTH

ica. An engaging, but long (1½-2hr.) tour leaves daily at noon. Don't miss the gorgeous ▨paintings by folk artist Clementine Hunter upstairs. (☎379-0055. Open daily noon-4pm. $7, ages 13-17 $4, ages 6-12 $3.)

While Natchitoches may not see a white Christmas, she'll most definitely see a bright one. The town's residents spend months putting up some 300,000 Christmas bulbs, only to be greeted in turn by 150,000 camera-toting tourists flocking like moths to the **City of Lights** display, held during the **Christmas Festival of Lights.** After a barge parade down the river on Friday, the month-long exhibition peaks the first Saturday in December when a carnival-like atmosphere fills the town. (☎800-259-1714; www.christmasfestival.com.) From April to November, all can enjoy the **Cane River Green Market,** a wonderful farmers market on the banks of the Cane River downtown. It's big on organic produce, locally grown fruit, and recycling initiatives. (☎352-2746. Open Apr.-Nov. Sa 9am-1pm; June-July also Tu 4-8pm.)

ACADIANA

Throughout the early 18th century, the English government in Nova Scotia became increasingly jealous of the prosperity of French settlers (Acadians) and deeply offended by their refusal to kneel before the British Crown. During the war with France in 1755, the British rounded up the Acadians and deported them by the shipload in what came to be called *le grand dérangement*, or "the Great Upheaval." The "Cajuns" (as they are known today) of St. Martin, Lafayette, New Iberia, and St. Mary parishes are descendants of these settlers. In the 1920s, Louisiana passed laws forcing Acadian schools to teach in English. Later, during the oil boom of the 1970s and 80s, oil executives and developers envisioned the Acadian center of Lafayette as the Houston of Louisiana and threatened to flood the area with mass culture. Even so, the proud people of southern Louisiana have resisted such homogenization, and in fact, the state is officially bilingual.

LAFAYETTE ☎337

The center of Acadiana, Lafayette is ripe with soul-moving zydeco, the sweet flavor of boiled crawfish, and the splendor of the magnificent Atchafalaya Basin. Get beyond the highway's chains and into downtown on Jefferson St., and there is no question that Cajuns rule the roost. Dance floors heat up every night of the week, and many locals continue to answer their phones with a proud *bonjour*.

▰ ▰ **ORIENTATION AND PRACTICAL INFORMATION.** Lafayette stands at a crossroads. **I-10** leads east to New Orleans and west to Lake Charles, **U.S. 90** heads south to New Iberia and the Atchafalaya Basin, and **I-49** heads north to Alexandria and Shreveport. Most of the city is west of the **Evangeline Throughway (I-49/U.S. 90),** which runs north-south. **Johnston Boulevard** intersects Evangeline Thwy. and is the main street through town. **Jefferson Street** runs north-south through central downtown and is full of fun places to eat and drink. **Amtrak,** 133 E. Grant St. (☎800-872-7245; www.amtrak.com), is where the "Sunset" comes three times per week en route to Houston (5½hr., $36), New Orleans (4hr., $21), and San Antonio (11hr., $55). Next door, **Greyhound** (☎235-1541; www.greyhound.com; open 24hr.) runs to Baton Rouge (1hr., 6 per day, $13.50) and New Orleans (3-5hr., 5 per day, $21). **Public Transit:** The **Lafayette Bus System,** 100 Lee Ave., is centered at Lee and Garfield St. (☎291-8570; www.lafayettelinc.net for schedules. Operates approximately every 30min. M-Sa 6:30am-6:30pm; some routes until 11:30pm. $0.75, ages 5-12 $0.50, seniors and disabled $0.35.) **Taxi: Yellow/Checker Cab Inc.,** ☎234-2111. **Visitor Info: Lafayette Parish Convention and Visitors Commission,** 1400 N. Evangeline Thwy.

THE SOUTH

(☎232-3808; www.lafayettetravel.com. Open M-F 8:30am-5pm, Sa-Su 9am-5pm.) **Medical Services: Lafayette General Medical Center,** 1214 Coolidge Ave. (☎289-7991). **Internet Access: Lafayette Public Library,** 301 W. Congress St. (☎261-5787. Open M-Th 9am-9pm, F 9am-6pm, Sa 9am-5pm, Su 1-5pm. Free.) **Post Office:** 1105 Moss St. (☎269-7111. Open M-F 8am-4:30pm.) **Postal Code:** 70501. **Area Code:** 337.

⌂ ACCOMMODATIONS. A comfortable and friendly lodging experience awaits at ⬛Blue Moon Guest House ❶, 215 E. Convent St. As you enter, check out the walkway paved with (fake) doubloons and the local art showcased on the surrounding walls. A large air-conditioned dorm and comfy private rooms are accompanied by a spacious common area, a deck out back, and a "saloon" where bands whoop it up Wednesday through Saturday. Guests get free concert access and a complimentary drink at the bar, as well as Internet access ($3 per day) and use of the kitchen and laundry room. (☎877-766-2583; www.bluemoonhostel.com. Dorms $18; private rooms $40-80. AmEx/MC/V.) Inexpensive hotels line the Evangeline Thwy. **Travel Host Inn South ❷,** 1314 N. Evangeline Thwy., rents large, clean rooms with cable TV, microwaves, refrigerators, continental breakfast, and an outdoor pool. (☎233-2090. Singles $33; doubles $40. AmEx/D/MC/V.) Close to the center of Lafayette, **Acadiana Park Campground ❶,** 1201 E. Alexander, off Louisiana Ave., has 75 sites near tennis courts and a soccer field. (☎291-8388. Office open M-Th and Sa-Su 8am-5pm, F 8am-8pm. Campsites with water and electricity $18. Cash only.) The lakeside but more commercial **KOA Lafayette ❶,** 5 mi. west of town off I-10 at Exit 97, has over 200 sites, a store, mini-golf, and two pools. (☎235-2739. Reception M-Th and Su 7:30am-8pm, F-Sa 7:30am-9pm. 2-person tent sites with water and electricity $22; additional person $3. Reservations recommended. MC/V.)

🍴 FOOD. It's not hard to find reasonably priced Cajun and Creole cuisine in Lafayette, a city that prides itself on food. Of course, music is also a priority, and can be found live in most of those same restaurants at night. Since 1927, ⬛Dwyer's Cafe ❶, 323 Jefferson St., a diner with stained glass and murals on the walls, has been the best place in town to get breakfast and lunch. They serve a bang-up breakfast (grits, eggs, ham, biscuits, juice, and coffee) for $4. At lunch, locals saunter in from the heat to eat a plate lunch (different every day; $7) of gigantic proportions. (☎235-9364. Open M and Su 6am-2pm, Tu-Sa 6am-2pm and 5:30pm-late. AmEx/D/MC/V.) Down Jefferson St. from Dwyer's, ⬛Borden's ❶, 1103 Jefferson St., has great malts ($2.50-4.25), sundaes ($2.50-3.50), and huge banana splits ($4). Established in 1940, the joint gets jumping on Sundays after church as patrons indulge in the heavenly strawberry cheesecake ice cream. (☎235-9291. Open Tu-Th 1-8pm, F-Sa noon-9pm, Su noon-8pm. Cash or check only.) **Chris's Po' Boys ❷,** 631 Jefferson St., offers seafood platters ($8-12) and—you guessed it—po' boys for $5-8. (☎234-1696. Live Cajun music F night in the spring and fall. Open M-F 11am-8pm. AmEx/MC/V.) For great alternative cuisine on the cheap check out the **Cedar Deli ❶,** 1115 Jefferson St., across the parking lot from Blue Moon Guest House. For 25 years, Syrian owner Nabil Loli has been serving up muffulettas, gyros, halloumi, and falafel. (☎233-5460. Open M-F 9am-5pm, Sa 9am-4pm. Cash only.) Save room for ice cream at **The Filling Station ❷,** 900 Jefferson St. Occupying the shell of an old gas station, the restaurant also serves gigantic burritos and burgers ($4.75-7.25) and, from March to May, shrimp and crawfish ($8). Their full bar will fill your tank nicely, and you can rock out to live music on Thursdays and Fridays. (☎291-9625. Beer $2.75-4. Kitchen open M-F 11am-9pm, Sa 5pm-9pm; bar open until people empty out. AmEx/D/MC/V.)

◉ SIGHTS. Driving through south-central Louisiana means driving over America's largest swamp, the **Atchafalaya Basin.** It's a unique environment consisting of hundreds of miles of shallow waterways inhabited by alligators, wildcats, and residential and migratory birds. The **Atchafalaya Freeway** (I-10 between Lafayette and Baton Rouge) crosses 32 mi. of swamp and cypress trees. For swamp tours, **McGee's Landing**, 1337 Henderson Rd., sends four 1½hr. **boat tours** into the basin each day. (☎228-2384. Tours daily 10am, 1, 3, 5pm. Spring and fall sunset tours by reservation. $15, seniors $12, under 12 $8, under 2 free.) The ✎**Acadian Cultural Center**, 501 Fisher Rd. (take Johnston St. to Surrey, then follow the signs), is a unit of the **Jean Lafitte National Historical Park and Preserve**, which runs throughout the delta region of Louisiana. The Acadian Center has a dramatic 40min. documentary chronicling the arrival of the Acadians in Louisiana, as well as a 16min. film on conservation efforts in the Atchafalaya swamp and terrific bilingual exhibits on Cajun history and culture. (☎232-0789. Open daily 8am-5pm. Shows every hr. 9am-4pm. Free.) Next door to the cultural center, you can take a self-guided tour of a "living museum" that recreates the Acadian settlement of **Vermilionville**, 300 Fisher Rd., with Acadian music, crafts, food, actors in costume, and dancing on the Bayou Vermilion banks. (☎233-4077 or 800-992-2968. Live bands Su 1-4pm. Cajun cooking demos daily 10:30am, 12:30, 1:30pm. Open Tu-Su 10am-4pm. Last admission 3pm. $8, seniors $6.50, ages 6-18 $5. AAA discount $1.) **Acadian Village**, 200 Greenleaf Rd., is similar and features authentic 19th-century Cajun homes with an array of artifacts and period displays. While at the village, see the collection of 19th-century medical paraphernalia at the **Doctor's House**. (☎981-2489 or 800-962-9133. Both open daily 10am-4pm. $7, seniors $6, ages 6-14 $4. AAA discount $1. Bluegrass concerts in summer; call Lafayette visitors center for info. Tickets $10.)

Closer to downtown, the University of Louisiana's recently-opened **University Art Museum**, 710 E. St. Mary Blvd., houses temporary and permanent exhibits of sculpture, photography, and paintings in a gorgeous glass building. (☎482-5326; www.louisiana.edu/UAM. Open Tu-Sa 10am-5pm. $5, seniors $4, students $3.) The **Cathedral of Saint John the Evangelist**, 515 Cathedral St., is worth a peek for its stunning 19th-century ecclesiastical architecture. (☎232-1322. Open daily 6am-6pm. Free.) Skip the church museum and check out the nearby **Saint John's Cathedral Oak**, 914 St. John St., which shades an entire lawn with spidery branches reaching from a trunk 19 ft. in circumference. Astronomy buffs may want to check out the **Lafayette Natural History Museum and Planetarium**, 433 Jefferson St., which has planetarium shows and a variety of rotating exhibits like one on Chinese astronomy. (☎291-5544. Open M-F 9am-5pm, Sa 10am-6pm, Su 1-6pm. $5, seniors $3, children $2.)

🎭🎶 **ENTERTAINMENT AND NIGHTLIFE.** While in Lafayette, be sure to take advantage of the many local festivals and music performances, starting with **Downtown Alive!**, a 12-week annual concert series held at the 700 block of Jefferson St., playing everything from New Wave to Cajun and zydeco. (☎291-5566. Apr.-June and Sept.-Nov. F 6-8:30pm.) The **Festival International de Louisiane** is the largest free outdoor francophone festival in the US, and transforms Lafayette into a gigantic, French-speaking fairground for one wild weekend in April. Book a hotel or campground well in advance; rates will likely be twice as high as normal. (☎232-8086; www.festivalinternational.com. Apr. 26-30, 2006.) The **Festivals Acadiens** began with the idea of educating Acadiana youth about their Cajun culture. It now attracts some of the state's best Cajun and zydeco musicians and has tons of other cultural and culinary events. (☎232-3737; www.festivalsacadiens.com. Sept. 15-17, 2006.) The **Breaux Bridge Crawfish Festival** in nearby Breaux Bridge, 10 mi. east on I-10 at Exit 109, stages crawfish races, live music, dance contests, cook-offs, and a crawfish-eating contest. (☎332-6655; www.bbcrawfest.com. May 5-6, 2006.)

Local college students frequent the numerous bars and dance clubs along Jefferson St. downtown. Some bars have live music on Fridays or Saturdays; pick up a free copy of the *Independent* for listings. To find the best zydeco in town, check out *The Times*, free at restaurants and gas stations. Most clubs and bars have

THE SOUTH

cover charges around $5-10 when they feel like it or depending on bands playing that night. On Sunday afternoons, the place to be is **Angelle's Whiskey River Landing,** 1365 Henderson Levee Rd., in Breaux Bridge, where live Cajun music has people dancing on the very lip of the levee looking out over the swamp. On weekends you'll see boatmen pulling ashore right outside and coming in to join the party—it sometimes feels like the whole floor could collapse into the swamp with all the stamping. (☎228-8567. Live music Su 4-8pm.) **Hamilton's Zydeco Club,** 1808 Verot School Rd., is one of the best places in Louisiana to cut loose at night, since live Cajun bands make for some wild dancing. (☎991-0783. Open sporadically; call or drive by to see the marquee for upcoming events and times.) **Grant Street Dance Hall,** 113 Grant St., features bands playing everything from zydeco to metal. (☎237-8513. 18+. Cover usually $5-10, up to $50 depending on the act. Open on show days, usually F and Sa nights; call ahead.)

NEW IBERIA   ☎337

New Iberia is off the beaten track, and though it is only 20 mi. south of Lafayette, you might feel as though you've traveled farther. Home to the Tabasco Sauce factory, the town calls itself "too hot to pass up." New Iberia is also a great place from which to explore the Atchafalaya Swamp. Once the home of a silent film star famous for his role as the sleepy fairy-tale character, the **Rip Van Winkle House,** 5505 Rip Van Winkle Rd., sits atop Jefferson Island, a gigantic subterranean salt dome that fell in 1980, causing the island to collapse into the swamp. The house has an amazing 15min. video with footage of the collapse, as well as expansive gardens. Tours of the house and gardens leave every hour. (☎359-8525; www.ripvanwinkle-gardens.com. Open daily 9am-5pm. $10, children and seniors $8, under 8 free.) **Shadows on the Teche,** downtown at 316 E. Main St., is a beautiful plantation house surrounded by gardens overlooking the Bayou Teche. Take a 1hr. guided tour of the plantation or a self-guided tour of the gardens. (☎369-6446. Open M-Sa 9am-4:30pm, Su noon-4:30pm. $7, seniors and AAA $6.25, ages 6-11 $4, under 6 free.)

Seven miles south of New Iberia lies **Avery Island.** It costs $1 to cross the bridge, but on the other side you will find the **Tabasco Sauce factory,** where pepper plants, soon to be made into the famous sauce, are grown. The factory offers a bizarre 8min. film that doubles as a commercial for Tabasco's new sauces, followed by a brief guided tour of Tabasco's bottling plant. The plant operates Monday through Thursday. (☎800-634-9599; www.tabasco.com. Open daily 9am-4pm. Free.) Next door on Avery Island is the **Jungle Gardens and Bird City.** This 250-acre park originates from the son of the sauce founder Edmund McIlhenney, a keen naturalist who established the preserve to save the snowy egret from extinction. Today, you can enjoy the forest and swamps and, if you are lucky, spot alligators, armadillos, and deer in addition to the beautiful azaleas and bamboo. (☎369-6243. Open daily 9am-5pm. $6.25, ages 6-12 $4.50, under 6 free.) A 20min. drive to the east (50min. from Lafayette) takes you to the **Marshfield Boat Landing,** where you can take an airboat tour over the swamp to see the flora and fauna up close. Reserve in advance as the seats fill up quickly. To get there, take Hwy. 86 to Loreauville and Marshfield Rd. to the landing, or pick up a map from the visitors center. (Reservations ☎229-4457. Open Tu-Sa 8am-5pm, Su 8am-noon. 1hr. tour $20.)

In a quiet part of town near the bayou, the affordable **Teche Motel ❷,** 1829 E. Main St., has air-conditioned wooden cabins that can sleep two people. (☎369-3756. Cabins $40. Cash or traveler's checks only.) **Freez-O ❶,** 1215 Center St., has chili dogs ($2.50), burgers ($3) and seafood platters ($8-13). Don't be scared off by the lunchtime crowds; it's worth the wait. (☎369-9391. Open M-Sa 10am-9pm. Cash only.) You can grab a wonderful po' boy at **Bon Creole Lunch Counter ❶,** 1409 St. Peter St. From outside it looks like a New Age mural, but inside it's a very traditional meat, biscuits, and gravy style canteen. Burgers cost $3-5, while phenomenal "overstuffed" sandwiches go for $4-8. (☎367-6181. Open M-Sa 11am-9pm, Su 11am-2pm. AmEx/D/MC/V.) Try the **farmers market ❶**, at Bouilgny Plaza on Main St., for great home cooking. Fresh produce is turned into all sorts of wholesome, unpretentious meals in the $5-7 range. (☎369-2330. Open Tu 4-7pm, Sa 7-10:30am.)

Visitor Info: Iberia Parish Convention and Visitors Bureau, 2513 Hwy. 14, offers maps, free Internet access, and mini Tabasco sauce bottles. (☎365-1540; www.iberiatravel.com. Open daily 9am-5pm.) **Post Office:** 817 E. Dale St. (☎275-8777. Open M-F 8am-5pm, Sa 8:30am-noon.) **Postal Code:** 70560. **Area Code:** 337.

ARKANSAS

Encompassing the Ozark and Ouachita mountains, the clear waters of Hot Springs, and miles of lush pine forests, the "Natural State" lives up to its nickname. Arkansas can be divided into distinct geographies: the mountainous northwest is home to the University of Arkansas at Fayetteville and gave birth to Wal-Mart, and the flat plains of the southeast are poorer and support cotton and rice farming. The bluesy Mississippi Delta region seeps into east Arkansas, while Hot Springs National Park is an easy daytrip from the capital.

⚡ PRACTICAL INFORMATION

Capital: Little Rock.

Visitor Info: Arkansas Department of Parks and Tourism, 1 Capitol Mall, Little Rock 72201 (☎501-682-7777 or 800-628-8725; www.arkansas.com). Open daily in summer 8am-6pm; low season 8am-5pm.

Postal Abbreviation: AR. **Sales Tax:** 6%.

LITTLE ROCK   ☎501

Located squarely in the middle of the state along the Arkansas River, Little Rock became a major trading city in the 19th century, when a small rock served as an important landmark for boats pushing their way upstream. Though this "little rock" is still visible today, it doesn't loom as large as the historical landmark of Central High School, where, in 1957, Governor Orval Faubus and local white segregationists violently resisted nine black students who entered the school under the protection of the National Guard. Today, this and other historical events are remembered in the many museums in the downtown area. The most recent attraction is the new Clinton Presidential Library, which overlooks the Arkansas River.

⚡ **PRACTICAL INFORMATION.** Little Rock is at the intersection of **I-40** and **I-30,** 140 mi. west of Memphis. Downtown, numbered streets run east-west, while named streets run north-south. The four major thoroughfares are **I-630, Cantrell Road, University Avenue,** and **Rodney Parham Road.** Near the river, Markham is 1st St. and Capitol is 5th St. The east side of Markham St. is now President Clinton Ave. and moves through the lively **Riverwalk** district. North Little Rock is linked to downtown Little Rock by three bridges spanning the Arkansas river.

Amtrak, 1400 W. Markham St. (☎372-6841; www.amtrak.com; open daily 11pm-7:45am), at Victory St., runs from Union Station Sq.; take bus #1 or 8. Trains run to Dallas (6½hr., 1 per day, $60), Malvern, AR (1hr., 1 per day, $10), and St. Louis (7hr., 1 per day, $53). **Greyhound,** 118 E. Washington St. (☎372-3007; www.greyhound.com; open 24hr.), is in North Little Rock; take bus #7 or 18. Buses run to Memphis (2½hr., 8 per day, $26), New Orleans (12½hr., 4 per day, $78), and St. Louis (8½hr., 1 per day, $52). **Central Arkansas Transit (CAT)** operates an extensive and tourist-friendly bus system through downtown and the surrounding towns. Catch CAT buses and get detailed route info at the **River Cities Travel Center,** 310 E. Capitol St. (☎375-1163. Buses run M-Sa every 30-40min. 6am-6pm, some routes until 10pm; Su 9am-4pm. $1.10, seniors $0.55; transfers $0.10.) CAT also runs two **trolley** routes. The South trolley route runs east-west along Clinton Ave. and 2nd St., while the North trolley route runs north-south along Main St. from Clinton Ave. across the river to 7th St. in North Little Rock. (☎375-1163. $0.50, seniors $0.25. M-W 11am-10pm, Th-Sa 11am-midnight, Su 11am-5pm.) **Visitor Info: Little Rock Visitor Information Center,** 615 E. Capitol Ave., in the newly renovated Curran Hall. Take the 6th or 9th St. exit off I-30 and follow the signs. (☎370-3290 or 877-220-2568; www.littlerock.com. Open M-Sa 8:30am-5pm, Su 1-5pm.) **Internet Access: Main Library,** 100 Rock St., near River Market. (☎918-3000. Open M-Th 9am-8pm, F-Sa 9am-6pm, Su 1-5pm. Free.) **Post Office:** 600 E. Capitol Ave. (☎375-5155. Open M-F 7am-5:30pm.) **Postal Code:** 72701. **Area Code:** 501.

⌂ ACCOMMODATIONS. Budget motels are dense around I-30 southwest of town and at the intersection of I-30 and I-40 in North Little Rock. Exit 130 off I-30 has a cluster of discount hotels lining the access road. The **Cimarron Motel ❷,** 10200 I-30, off Exit 130 on the westbound access road, has clean, standard rooms with fridge and microwave and a pool. (☎565-1171. Singles $32; doubles $37. AmEx/MC/V.) **Maumell Park ❶,** 9009 Pinnacle Valley Rd., on the Arkansas River, has 129 sites near the beautiful Pinnacle Mountain State Park. From I-430, take Rte. 10 (Exit 9) west 2½ mi., turn right on Pinnacle Valley Rd., continue for 2 mi., and look for the sign. (☎868-9477 or 753-0086. Office open daily 10am-10pm. Sites with 30 amp hookup $18, 50 amp hookup $20.) The historic **Capital Hotel ❺,** 111 W. Markham St., at Louisiana St., is by far the most lavish accommodation in Little Rock. Lauded by the Clintons for its beauty and stellar dining, the hotel is a local mainstay. (☎800-766-7666. Full buffet breakfast included. Singles M-F $129, Sa-Su from $108; doubles $120-150. AmEx/D/MC/V.)

❏ FOOD. The city has revamped the downtown area starting with **River Market,** 400 President Clinton Ave. The downtown lunch crowd heads here for a wide selection of food shops, coffee stands, delis, and an outdoor **farmers market.** (☎375-2552. Market Hall open M-Sa 7am-6pm; many shops only open for lunch. Farmers market open May-Oct. Tu and Sa 7am-3pm.) Near Market Hall, ▨**The Flying Fish ❷,** 511 President Clinton Ave., has quickly become downtown's most popular hangout for its unpretentious atmosphere and walls covered with photos of fish caught by patrons. Hungry diners clamor for catfish baskets (2 fillets $5.79), oyster and catfish po' boy sandwiches ($6.59), and on-tap brews. (☎375-3474. Open daily 11am-10pm. MC/V.) Just past the Hillcrest area, **Pizza D'Action ❶,** 2919 W. Markham St., boasts some of the tastiest pizza and most eclectic crowds in the area, along with live music most nights. (☎666-5403. Large pies $11-15. Burgers and sandwiches $4. Open M-F 3pm-1am, Sa-Su 11am-1am. AmEx/D/MC/V.) Chef Nate Townsend cooks up fantastic feasts at **Grampa's Catfish House ❷,** 1218 Mission Rd., in North Little Rock, off Rte. 176 N. In addition to the popular catfish dinners ($8-10), you can try the chicken-fried steak, oysters, and scallops. (☎758-4654. Open Tu-Sa 4:30-9:30pm, Su 4:30-9pm. AmEx/D/MC/V.)

◪ SIGHTS. Tourists can visit **"Le Petite Roche,"** the actual "little rock" of Little Rock, at Riverfront Park at the north end of Rock St. From underneath the railroad bridge at the north end of Louisiana St., look straight down. Look carefully; the rock is part of the embankment (it's that small), and it's been covered in graffiti since its plaque was stolen. The ◪**Clinton Presidential Library**, 1200 E. President Clinton Ave., is an architecturally distinctive glass building hailed by admirers as a metaphor for Clinton's "Bridge to the 21st Century." Highlights include Clinton's presidential limo, replicas of the Oval Office and Cabinet Room, and a presentation on White House humor. (☎370-8000; www.clintonpresidentialcenter.com. Open M-Sa 9am-5pm, Su 1-5pm. $7, students and seniors $5, ages 6-17 $3.) The aftermath of Little Rock's Civil Rights struggle is manifest at the corner of Daisy L. Gatson Bates Dr. (formerly 14th St.) and Park St., where **Central High School** remains a fully functional school. It's therefore closed to visitors, but a ◪**visitors center,** 2125 Daisy L. Gatson Bates Dr., in a restored gas station across the street, contains an excellent exhibit on the "Little Rock Nine." (☎374-1957; www.nps.gov/chsc. Open M-Sa 9am-4:30pm, Su 1-4:30pm. Free.) The **Arkansas Art Center**, 501 E. 9th St., is a huge complex with out-of-the-ordinary landscapes and still lifes; one of the most prominent sculptures, *Heavy Dog Kiss*, depicts a huge human head kissing a huge dog head. (☎372-4000; www.arkarts.com. Open Tu-Sa 10am-5pm, Su 11am-5pm. Free, suggested donation $5.) When the legislature is not in session, visitors can explore the **State Capitol,** at the west end of Capitol St. (☎682-5080. Open M-F 7am-5pm, Sa-Su 10am-5pm.) In the middle of downtown, the **Historic Arkansas Museum,** 200 E. 3rd St., recreates life in 19th-century Little Rock using period actors who show off old-time tricks of frontier living. (☎324-9351; www.arkansashistory.com. Open M-Sa 9am-5pm, Su 1-5pm. $2.50, seniors $1.50, under 18 $1.) Just a 15min. drive to the west of the city is **Pinnacle Mountain State Park**, 11901 Pinnacle Valley Rd., in Roland. The interpretive trails and the **Arkansas Arboretum** provide information on the area's flora. (☎868-5806; www.arkansasstateparks.com. Call for hours.)

◪ **NIGHTLIFE. Vino's,** 923 W. 7th St., at Chester St., is Little Rock's original microbrewery-nightclub with a clientele ranging from lunchtime's corporate businessmen to midnight's younger set. (☎375-8466. Pizza slices $1.15. Live rock music Th-Sa. 18+ at night. Cover $5-10. Open M-W 11am-10pm, Th 11am-11pm, F 11am-midnight, Sa 11:30am-midnight, Su 1-9pm.) **Sticky Fingerz,** 107 S. Commerce St. across President Clinton Ave. from the River Market, serves its signature chicken fingers ($5.50) with a side of alt-rock. (☎372-7707; www.stickyfingerz.com. Open daily 11am-2pm and 4:30pm-late.) **The Underground Pub,** 500 President Clinton Ave., offers British fare. Enjoy music, darts, pool, and football (British style) on big-screen TVs. (☎707-2537. Happy hour daily 4-7pm. Open M-W 11am-midnight, Th-F 11am-2am, Sa 11am-1am.) **Weekend Theater,** on W. 7th St. across from Vino's, stages Off-Broadway theater productions. (☎374-3761. Call for showtimes.)

HOT SPRINGS   ☎501

Since the region was settled in 1807, visitors have flocked to Hot Springs seeking health and relaxation in its steamy waters. Today, the springs manifest themselves in fountains and water outlets around the town of Hot Springs, most of which are very hot (143°F and 62°C)—consider yourself warned. The main drag of Hot Springs, known as **Bathhouse Row,** is lined with spas and baths. A former bathhouse, **Fordyce House Visitors Center,** 369 Central Ave., is home to the Hot Springs National Park Visitor Center, which has free, self-guided tours of the restored Fordyce Bathhouse and ranger-guided tours of Bathhouse Row. (☎624-2701. Open June to mid-Aug. M-Th and Su 9am-6pm, F-Sa 9am-7pm; mid-Aug. to May daily 9am-5pm. Guided tours in summer daily 10am and 2:30pm.) The **Buckstaff House,** three houses up the road, is the only bathhouse continuously active since 1912. Visitors can rejuvenate with mineral baths ($20), Swedish massages ($23), manicures, pedicures, and facials. (509 Central Ave. ☎623-2308; www.buckstaff-baths.com. Open M-Sa 7-11:45am and 1:30-3pm, Su 8am-1pm; Dec.-Feb. closed Sa

MODERN EMPIRE

Although Wal-Mart is currently the largest private employer in America with revenues rivaling the economies of small nations, it traces its humble beginnings back to Bentonville, a tiny town that once blended into the unassuming landscape of northwestern Arkansas. It was here that Sam Walton opened his first Walton's 5 and 10 over 50 years ago. Walton's business has since grown into a corporate fixture whose motto, "Always Low Prices," has seeped into popular culture and revolutionized how (and for how much) Americans shop. Though Walton died in 1992, according to Forbes Magazine his commercial visions have left his heirs with a collective fortune of over $90 billion.

Bentonville is now home to Wal-Mart global headquarters and the Wal-Mart visitor center. The nerve center for Wal-Mart's nationwide distribution network, the town has recently sought to expand its airport to accommodate its ever-growing population of Wal-Mart's corporate management officers. Although Bentonville's prairie charm may not be able to match the California chic of Silicon Valley, with over twenty new Wal-Marts opening each month, Wal-Mart is unlikely to go the way of the 1990s dot-com bubble anytime soon. In fact, it just might be Middle America's next and even greatest corporate enterprise.

afternoons and Su.) The **hot springs** themselves are in town along Central Ave., and drinking the water is actually encouraged by the National Park. On a clear day at the **Hot Springs Mountain Tower**, 401 Hot Springs Mountain Dr., you can see 70 mi. in every direction. From the end of Bathhouse Row, turn right down Fountain St., then continue up Hot Springs Dr. (☎ 623-6035; www.hotsprings.org. Open daily 9am-9pm. $6, seniors $5, ages 5-11 $3.) **Walking trails** of all levels crisscross Hot Springs Mountain. Trail maps are available at Fordyce House and the Visitors Center, both on Central Ave. During the first two weeks of June, the **Hot Springs Music Festival** brings thousands to the town for classical music concerts. (☎ 623-4763; www.hotmusic.org. June 5-18, 2006.)

Heavy tourism has pushed lodging prices sky-high in Hot Springs. One of the best values in town is the **Happy Hollow Motel ❷**, 231 Fountain Ave., on the edge of the park. Built in the late 1940s, it has a funky aluminum patio and clean rooms in a quiet location. (☎ 321-2230; www.happyhollowmotel.com. Fridge, microwave, VCR, and free wireless Internet. Singles from $42; doubles from $46. D/MC/V.) Just outside of town, the **Alpine Inn ❷**, 741 Park Ave., has spacious themed rooms with refrigerators and a pool. (☎ 624-9164; www.alpine-inn-hot-springs.com. Singles $35-42; doubles $40-48. AmEx/D/MC/V.) **McClard's ❸**, 505 Albert Pike Rd., an old Clinton hangout, has served fabulous Southern fare in large portions for over 75 years. The tamales (2 for $8.35) are delectable and the selection of ribs is mouth-watering. (☎ 624-9586; www.mcclards.com. Open Tu-Sa 11am-8pm. Cash only.) For a fast, cheap meal, **King Kone Drive-In ❶**, 1505 Malvern Ave., is an original burger joint with burgers ($2-3), ice cream, and pickle juice slushies. (☎ 321-9766. Open M-Sa 9am-10pm. Cash or check only.) **Granny's Kitchen ❷**, 361 Central Ave., right across from bathhouse row, has standard Southern plate lunches ($6-7) and dinners ($7-9), as well as a selection of sandwiches and breakfast specials. (☎ 624-6183. Open M-Th and Su 7am-7pm, F-Sa 7am-8pm. D/MC/V.) To occupy Hot Springs's steamy evenings, the amazing **Poet's Loft**, 514B Central Ave., is a groovy hangout with a variety of poetry readings, music recitals, and jam sessions. (☎ 627-4224; www.poetsloft.com. Open W and F-Sa 5-10pm.) **100 Exchange Jazz Lounge**, 100 Exchange Pl., has live jazz Wednesdays, blues on Thursday, and dance music on Saturdays. (☎ 624-9463 or 623-3663. 21+. Open W-F 4pm-3am, Sa noon-2am.)

One hour southwest of Little Rock, Hot Springs is easy to reach. Most of the town's noteworthy buildings, plus the National Park headquarters, are along **Central Avenue. The Convention and Visitors Bureau,** 134

Convention Blvd. (☎321-2277; open M-F 8am-5pm) and the downtown **visitors center,** 629 Central Ave. (open daily 9am-8pm), both have tourist info. **Greyhound,** 229 W. Grand St. (☎623-5574; www.greyhound.com; open daily 8am-noon and 4-7pm), runs to Atlanta (12hr., 1 per day, $120), Little Rock (1hr., 2 per day, $14), and Memphis (4hr., 2 per day, $40). Wireless **Internet** is available at the cyber cafe in the visitors bureau. (Open M-F 9am-5pm. Free.) **Post Office:** 100 Reserve St., in the Federal Building. (☎623-8217. Open M-F 8am-4:30pm, Sa 9am-noon.) **Postal Code:** 71901. **Area Code:** 501.

OZARKS

The mountains that encompass the northwest region of Arkansas are accessible from the capital and provide a convenient escape with good roads, good food, and comforting green scenery. Up until the last few decades, the region was isolated, but a booming tourist industry and an influx of retirees has helped the Ozarks grow in recent years. Mountain View and Eureka Springs are two of the most popular towns to visit, although they can get very busy during the summer months.

EUREKA SPRINGS   ☎479

Achieving an intoxicatingly high quaintness-to-square-footage ratio, Eureka Springs, near the intersection of Hwy. 62 and Rte. 23 in northwest Arkansas, peddles its patent charm, natural scenery, and slow pace to travelers. The site of the first Native American and white settlements in Eureka Springs, the **Blue Spring Heritage Center,** at the end of Eureka Springs Garden Road off Hwy. 62, has 33 acres of gardens, trails, and azure spring waters. (☎253-9244; www.bluespringheritage.com. Open daily March 15-Thanksgiving 9am-6pm. $7.25, ages 10-17 $4, under 10 free. AAA discount $1.) **Turpentine Creek Wildlife Refuge,** on Hwy. 23 7 mi. south of Eureka Springs, is home to over 100 lions, tigers, and leopards rescued from around the US. The best time to see the cats is at their 6pm feeding time; otherwise they'll probably be dozing. (☎253-5841; www.tigers.tc. Open daily 9am-7pm. Hourly tours daily 11am-5pm. $15; military, seniors, and under 12 $10.) If you're driving from Little Rock, take a detour to the ▧**Dickson Street Bookshop,** 325 W. Dickson St. in downtown Fayetteville, an hour west of Eureka Springs. Behind a humble storefront, a seemingly endless maze of shelves overflows with used books ranging from bargain paperbacks to out-of-print collector's items. (☎442-8182. Open M-Sa 10am-9pm, Su 1-6pm.)

Eureka's most famous tourist attraction is **The Great Passion Play,** 935 Passion Play Rd., off Hwy. 62, and the Bible-inspired sights that surround it. Hundreds of actors depict the final days of Christ on an elaborate outdoor set. The dialogue is pre-recorded, but at least it's not in Aramaic. (☎253-9200 or 800-882-7529; www.greatpassionplay.com. Tickets $23, ages 6-11 $10. Shows May-Aug. M-Tu and Th-Sa 8:30pm; Sept.-Oct. M-Tu and Th-Sa 7:30pm.) The **Bible Museum** has over 6000 copies of the Good Book in 600 languages, and the **Sacred Arts Center** features works inspired by Christ. Both are located on the grounds of the Passion Play and are open from 10am-8pm on days that it is running. Admission is included in the ticket price. Nearby, visitors marvel at the seven-story **Christ of the Ozarks** statue.

Lodging prices fluctuate greatly with the ebb and flow of tourists; peak season is from late September to early October. The visitors center is a good place to find deals on lodging, numerous budget motels line Hwy. 62 east of Eureka Springs. **The Trails Inn ❷,** 2060 E. Van Buren/Hwy. 62, is one of the better motels on Hwy. 62, with clean rooms, breakfast, and a pool. (☎253-9390 or 800-962-4691; www.thetrailsinn.com. Singles and doubles M-Th and Su $39-45, F-Sa $54-59. AmEx/D/MC/V.) The **Rose Garden Inn ❷,** on Hwy. 62 east of downtown, is a good value with surprisingly comfortable rooms. (☎253-9335. Rooms on weekdays $34-39; on weekends $42-45. AmEx/D/MC/V.) Campers head to **Kettle Campgrounds and Cabins ❶**, 4119 E. Van Buren St./Hwy. 62, which offers tent and RV sites as well as a pool, laundry, and showers. (☎253-9100 or 800-899-2267. Primitive sites $13, with water and electricity $17, with full hookup $21; cabins $40. Cash or check only.)

Hwy. 62 offers plenty of all-you-can-eat dinner buffets packed with Southern food staples at reasonable prices. The subterranean **Mud St. Cafe ❷**, 22G S. Main St., serves breakfast ($3-7), sandwiches, burgers, and delicious desserts. Local artwork funkifies the classic timber and stained-glass saloon decor, and the menu provides plenty of tantalizing vegetarian options. (☎253-6732. Open Feb.-Dec. M-Tu and Th-Su 8am-3pm. AmEx/MC/V.) For dinner, **Ermilio's ❸**, 26 White St., lets patrons mix and match a variety of pastas and homemade sauces ($9-11) in a casual dining room. (☎253-8806. Open daily 5-9pm. Closed mid-Feb to mid-Mar. MC/V.) At **Bubba's BBQ ❷**, 166 W. Van Buren St., barbecue sandwiches ($3.50-6) are topped with cole slaw in the traditional Southern fashion. Heaping dinner plates run $8.25-10. (☎253-7706. Open M-Sa 11am-9pm. Cash or check only.) The **Pine Mountain Jamboree**, 2075 E. Van Buren St., and **Ozark Mountain Hoedown**, 3140 E. Van Buren St., have live country variety shows, with bluegrass, gospel, and country music and comedy routines. (Pine Mountain: ☎253-9156. Shows Mar.-Dec. M and W-Su 7:30. $17.50, children $6.50. AmEx/D/MC/V. Ozark Mountain: ☎253-7725. Shows nightly at 8pm, with pre-show bluegrass at 7:30pm. Tickets $18.50, children $10.50.) Wash down that wholesome feeling with a cold one at **Chelsea's Corner**, 10 Mountain St., off Center St. (☎253-8231. Live music weekends. 21+. Cover $5. Open M-Th noon-10pm, F-Sa noon-midnight, Su 4-8pm.)

Downtown is hilly but walkable; park at free lots on Rte. 23 N south of the railroad or on Hwy. 62 W. **Trolleys** run to every destination around town. (☎253-9572; www.eurekatrolley.org. Operates May-Oct. M-Th and Su 9am-5pm, F-Sa 9am-6pm; Mar.-Apr. and Nov. daily 9am-5pm; Dec.-Feb. limited service F-Sa 10am-4pm. Day pass $4, children $1.) The **Eureka Springs Chamber of Commerce Visitors Center** is on Hwy. 62 W, two blocks west of Hwy. 23 N. (☎253-8737; www.eurekaspringschamber.com. Open daily 9am-5pm.) **Post Office:** 101 Spring St. (☎253-9850. Open M-F 8:15am-4:15pm, Sa 10am-noon.) **Postal Code:** 72632. **Area Code:** 479.

MOUNTAIN VIEW   ☎870

Mountain View is located 123 mi. north of Little Rock, the closest big city. The self-proclaimed "folk music capital of the world" has plenty of music to offer, starting with the free outdoor music on central **Courthouse Square**. Locals bring along deck chairs or sit on the grass to listen or even join in. Other venues offer music at a price. The **Jimmy Driftwood Barn**, 2 mi. north of town past the junction of Hwy. 5/9/14 N, is a performance space created by Jimmy Driftwood, known as the "Bard of the Ozarks" and most famous for his song "The Battle of New Orleans." Although Jimmy died in 1998, you can still hear folk music there year-round. (☎269-4578. Shows F and Su 7pm. Gospel concerts 2nd Sa of each month 7pm. Donations encouraged.) **Cash's White River Hoedown**, 507 Sylamore Ave., at the junction of Hwy. 5/9/14 N just north of town, has a family-geared comedy and music show. (☎800-759-6474. Apr.-Aug. Th-Sa comedy warm-up 7:30pm, show 8pm; Aug.-Oct. Th-Sa comedy warm-up 7pm, show 7:30pm; Nov.-Dec. shows Sa only, warm up 7pm. $15, under 16 free.) **Brickshy's Backstreet Theater**, on Jefferson St. behind White River Furniture, rotates four bands: Harmony, The Leatherwoods, The River Rat Band, and Homemade Jam. (☎269-6200. Shows Apr.-Aug. M and Th-Sa at 8pm; Sept.-Nov. M and Th-Sa 7:30pm. Tickets $12, children 12 and under free; available after 5pm.) The **Mountain View Gospel Opry** performs on Thursdays and Saturdays at 7pm in the Folklore Society building, on Franklin St. just off the square. In the nearby **Ozark National Forest,** the spectacular **Blanchard Springs Caverns** offer fascinating underground tours. From downtown Mountain View, take Hwy. 5/9/14 N to 14 W. There are three levels of caverns; two are accessible to the public. The Dripstone Trail tour takes visitors through the highlights. The area also has hiking trails, a mountain-bike trail, and a shooting range. (☎757-2211 or 888-757-2246. Tours $10, children $5, under 5 free.)

Angler's White River Inn ❸, at the junction of Hwy. 5/9/14, provides motel-style accommodations with a fabulous deck overlooking the river. (☎585-2226 or 800-794-2226; www.anglerswhiteriver.com. Singles M-Th and Su $49, F-Sa $54; doubles $54/$59. MC/V.) **Mountain View Motel ❷,** 2 blocks east of Court House Square on Main St., has small but clean rooms decorated like your grandmother's guest room. (☎269-3209. Singles $30. Cash or check only.) The cheapest place to stay is at one of the **Ozark National Forest Campgrounds ❶,** near the Blanchard Springs Caverns, 15 mi. northwest of Mountain View. The campsites are first come, first served, with toilets, showers, and plenty of local fishing, swimming, and hiking trails. (☎269-3228. Sites $10 per night.) Just north of town on Rte. 14, the **Sylamore Creek Campground ❶** has cabins as well as campsites, with clean bathrooms and hot showers. (☎585-2326 or 877-475-4223; www.sylamorecreek.com. Sites $10, with electricity $15. 2-person cabins $65-90, $5 each additional person. MC/V.) One block west of Court House Sq., ▧**Woods Pharmacy and Soda Fountain ❶,** 301 W. Main St., recreates an old-fashioned soda fountain with "phosphate" sodas that come with your choice of flavored syrup ($1.45). A fully functional pharmacy, Woods also serves ice cream sodas and sandwiches. (269-8304. Open M-Sa 8am-5pm. MC/V.) At **Jo Jo's Catfish Wharf ❷,** 6 mi. north of town on Hwy. 5 N, chow down on classic Arkansas catfish in a no-nonsense setting by the river. (☎585-2121. Open M-Th and Su 11am-8pm, F-Sa 11am-9pm. AmEx/D/MC/V.)

Getting to Mountain View is virtually impossible without a car; the town is not accessible by bus and there is no public transit within the town. Your best bet is to drive up from Little Rock. **Visitor Info: Chamber of Commerce and Tourist Information Center,** 199 Peabody St. (☎269-8068; www.yourplaceinthemountains.com. Open M-F 9am-5pm, Sa 10am-3pm.) **Post Office:** 802 Sylamore Ave. (☎269-3520. Open M-F 8:30am-4:30pm.) **Postal Code:** 72560. **Area Code:** 870.

THE SOUTH

FLORIDA

Ponce de León landed in Florida in 1513, looking for the elusive Fountain of Youth. Although the multitudes who flock to Florida today aren't seeking fountains, many find their youth restored in the Sunshine State, whether they're dazzled by the spectacle of Disney World or bronzed by the sun on the state's seductive beaches. Droves of senior citizens also migrate to Florida—jokingly referred to as heaven's waiting room—where the sun-warmed air is just as therapeutic as de León's fabled magical elixir. Florida's recent population boom has strained the state's natural resources; commercial strips and tremendous development have turned pristine beaches into tourist traps. Still, it is possible to find a deserted spot on the peninsula on which to plop down with a paperback and dig your toes into the sand.

HIGHLIGHTS OF FLORIDA

WALTZ around Walt's magical collection of amusements at **Disney World** (p. 448).

SOAK up the rays and the cocktails at the beaches and nightclubs of **Miami** (p. 464).

HOP aboard a cruise through the swamps and islands of the **Everglades** (p. 472).

DIG into a slice of the famous **Key Lime Pie** in the Florida Keys (p. 474).

PRACTICAL INFORMATION

Capital: Tallahassee.

Visitor Info: Florida Division of Tourism, 126 W. Van Buren St., Tallahassee 32301 (☎888-735-2872; www.flausa.com). **Division of Recreation and Parks,** 3900 Commonwealth Blvd., #536, Tallahassee 32399 (☎850-488-9872).

Postal Abbreviation: FL. **Sales Tax:** 6%. **Accommodations Tax:** 11%.

CENTRAL FLORIDA

ORLANDO ☎407

When Walt Disney was flying over the small towns of Central Florida in search of a place to put his Florida operation, he marveled at the endless lakes and streams that dominate the Orlando area. Amidst this beautiful setting, he foresaw a world full of thrill-packed amusement rides and life-sized, cartoonish figures. While Orlando is older than Disney World, most of the city's resources are dedicated to supporting the tourism industry that is the lifeblood of the economy. Theme parks, hotels, diners, and other kitschy treats line every major street; even downtown Orlando, 20 mi. from Disney, overflows with tourist attractions.

TRANSPORTATION

Airport: Orlando International, 1 Airport Blvd. (☎825-2001; www.orlandoairports.net). From the airport take Rte. 436 N, exit to Rte. 528 W/Bee Line Expwy., then head east on I-4 for downtown, and west on I-4 to the attractions, including Disney and Universal. LYNX buses #42 and 51 make the trip to International Drive and downtown for $1.50.

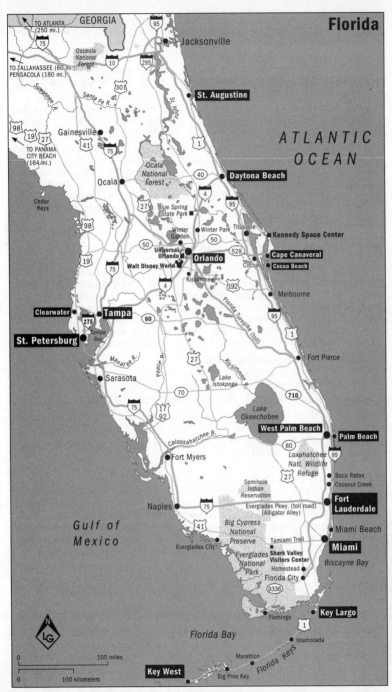

Florida

TO ATLANTA
(250 mi.)

GEORGIA

95

Jacksonville

Osceola
National
Forest

10

295

75

TO TALLAHASSEE (60 mi.),
PENSACOLA (180 mi.)

301

St. Augustine

Santa Fe R.

Suwannee R.

St. Johns R.

1

ATLANTIC
OCEAN

98

19

27

Gainesville

41

75

TO PANAMA
CITY BEACH
(164 mi.)

Cedar
Keys

Ocala
National
Forest

40

Daytona Beach

27

Ocala

4

95

Blue Spring
State Park

Winter Park

Titusville

Kennedy Space Center

98

50

Winter
Garden

50

528

Universal
Orlando

Orlando

Cape Canaveral

19

Walt Disney World

Cocoa

Cocoa Beach

75

Kissimmee

4

192

Melbourne

Clearwater

275

Tampa

60

Florida Turnpike (toll)

95

1

St. Petersburg

Tampa
Bay

Manatee R.

Peace R.

Kissimmee R.

Fort Pierce

Sarasota

75

17
92

70

Lake
Istokpoga

710

Lake
Okeechobee

Caloosahatchee R.

27

West Palm Beach

Palm Beach

Fort Myers

80

95

*Loxahatchee
Natl. Wildlife
Refuge*

Boca Raton

27

Coconut Creek

Gulf of
Mexico

Naples

75

Seminole
Indian
Reservation

Everglades Pkwy. (toll road)
(Alligator Alley)

41

**Fort
Lauderdale**

Big Cypress
National
Preserve

Tamiami Trail

Miami Beach

Everglades City

Everglades
National
Park

Shark Valley
Visitors Center

Miami

Homestead

Biscayne Bay

Florida City

9336

Flamingo

Key Largo

N

L G

Florida Bay

1

Islamorada

0   100 miles

Marathon

0   100 kilometers

Key West

Florida Keys

Big Pine Key

Mears Motor Shuttle (☎423-5566; www.mearstransportation.com) has booths at the airport for transportation to most hotels (about $25 round trip). No shuttle reservations are necessary from the airport; for return, call 1 day in advance.

Trains: Amtrak, 1400 Sligh Blvd. (☎843-7611; www.amtrak.com), 3 blocks east of I-4. Take S. Orange Ave., head west on Columbia, then take a right on Sligh. Station open daily 7:30am-9:30pm. To: **Jacksonville** (3hr., 2 per day, $19-24); **Kissimmee** (20min., 2 per day, $5-7); **Miami** (6-8hr., 1-2 per day, $30); **Tampa** (2hr., 2 per day, $8).

Buses: Greyhound, 555 N. John Young Pkwy. (☎292-3440; www.greyhound.com), just south of W. Colonial Dr. (Rte. 50). Open 24hr. To **Jacksonville** (2½-4hr., 10 per day, $30-32) and **Kissimmee** (40min., 5 per day, $8.50-9.50).

Public Transit: LYNX, 455 N. Garland Ave. (☎841-2279; www.golynx.com). Downtown terminal 5 blocks north of Central St., 1 block west of Orange Ave., and 1 block east of I-4. Buses operate daily 4:30am-2am, hours vary with route. $1.50, seniors 0.75; transfers free. Weekly pass $12. Look for signposts with a colored paw. Serves the airport, downtown, and all major parks. The **Lynx Lymmo** is a free downtown transportation service with 11 stations and 8 stops scattered along and around Magnolia Ave.

Taxi: Yellow Cab, ☎699-9999.

■✦❷ ORIENTATION AND PRACTICAL INFORMATION

Orlando lies at the center of hundreds of lakes, toll highways, and amusement parks. **Orange Blossom Trail (Route 17/92 and 441)** runs north-south and **Colonial Drive (Route 50)** east-west. The **Bee Line Expressway (Route 528)** and the **East-West Expressway (Route 408)** exact several tolls for their convenience. The major artery is **I-4,** which actually runs north-south through the center of town, despite being labeled an east-west highway. The parks—**Disney World, Universal Orlando,** and **Sea World**—await 15-20 mi. southwest of downtown; **Winter Park** is 3-4 mi. northeast.

Visitor Info: Orlando Official Visitor Center, 8723 International Dr., Ste. 101 (☎363-5872; www.orlandoinfo.com), southwest of downtown; take bus #8. Free "Magic Card" offers discounts at sights, restaurants, and hotels. Open daily 8am-7pm. Tickets sold 8am-6pm.

Hotlines: Sexual Assault Hotline, ☎497-6701. **Crisis Hotline,** ☎843-4357.

Internet Access: Orlando Public Library, 101 E. Central Blvd. (☎835-7323). Open M-Th 9am-9pm, F-Sa 9am-6pm, Su 1-6pm. Internet access $10 for 7-day unlimited use.

Post Office: 46 E. Robinson St. (☎425-6464), downtown. Open M-F 7am-5pm. **Postal Code:** 32801. **Area Code:** 407.

▐ ACCOMMODATIONS

With over 120,000 hotel rooms, Orlando has options for all wallet sizes. Prices rise as you approach Disney. **Irlo Bronson Memorial Highway (U.S. 192)** runs from Disney World to downtown Kissimmee and has cheap motels. **International Drive (I-Drive),** a north-south road that parallels the interstate, is the center of Orlando's lodging world. Many accommodations have free transportation to Universal and Disney.

The Courtyard at Lake Lucerne, 211 N. Lucerne Circle E (☎648-5188 or 800-444-5289), 30min. from Disney. From I-4, take Exit 82C on to Anderson St., right on Delaney Ave., and right on N. Lucerne Circle. This beautiful B&B offers lavish rooms in 4 houses (of which Wellborn is the best deal). Complimentary wine upon arrival and a nightly cocktail hour. TV and phone. Rooms $89-250. AmEx/D/DC/MC/V. ❺

Disney's All-Star Resorts (☎939-5000), in Disney World, cater to vacationing families looking for full Disney immersion. From I-4, take Exit 64B and follow the signs to Blizzard Beach—the resorts are just behind it. Disney's All-Star Movie, Music, and Sports

Resorts, the "value resorts," are a great deal for large groups. Each of the hotels has 2 pools, a food court, a pool bar, and laundry facilities. Get info and tickets at the Guest Services Desk to avoid long lines at park gates. Free parking and Disney transportation. A/C, phone, and TV. Rooms $88-99; under 18 free with adult. AmEx/D/DC/MC/V. ❹

Palm Lakefront Resort & Hostel, 4840 W. Irlo Bronson Hwy./U.S. 192 (☎396-1759), features simple dorm-style rooms, private rooms, and a common kitchen. Only 5 mi. from Disney with easy bus access, the hostel is a great crash pad for serious park hoppers. Free Internet access. Dorms $16; private rooms $40. MC/V. ❶

Gator Motel, 4576 W. Irlo Bronson Hwy./U.S. 192 (☎396-0127), has bright, clean rooms, A/C, cable TV, a pool, and close proximity to Disney. Continental breakfast included. Rooms $27, additional person $8. AmEx/D/DC/MC/V. ❷

◖ FOOD

Most eating in the Orlando area is either fine dining or done on-the-run. Prices are exorbitant inside theme parks; pack food if you have space. Cheap buffets line International Dr., U.S. 192, and Orange Blossom Trail.

Viet Garden, 1237 E. Colonial Dr. (☎896-4154), near Mills Ave. Nestled in a strip of international restaurants, this little gem serves delectable Vietnamese and Thai cuisine. Savor the array of garnished rice platters, featuring pork, chicken, beef, and quail ($6-8). Open M-Th and Su 10am-9pm, F-Sa 10am-10pm. AmEx/D/MC/V. ❶

Tijuana Flats, 50 E. Central Blvd. (☎839-0007). Colossal burritos like the "megajuana" ($7) will satisfy any appetite, while the taquitos ($6) are a meal of more manageable proportions. Open M-Th 11am-10pm, F-Sa 11am-10:30pm, Su 11am-9pm. MC/V. ❶

Couscous Moroccan Restaurant, 8255 International Dr. (☎363-7052), in the Goodings shopping plaza, offers scrumptious, authentic Moroccan dishes like lamb tagine with prunes (lamb served with dried prunes cooked in a honey cinnamon syrup; $14). While you await your feast, try the mint tea ($1.50) and ask the owner/chef to tell you about his native land. Open daily 11am-11pm. AmEx/D/DC/MC/V. ❸

Beefy King, 424 N. Bumby Ave. (☎894-2241), off E. Colonial Dr. Voted "Best Beefy Experience" by *Florida Magazine*, this family eatery has been pleasing residents for 30 years with its fantastic sandwiches ($3-5), served at an old-fashioned lunch counter. Open M-F 10am-3pm, Sa 11am-3pm, drive-through open M-F 10am-5:30pm. MC/V. ❶

♫ ◖ ENTERTAINMENT AND NIGHTLIFE

The best options for one-stop partying are Disney's **Pleasure Island** or Universal's **CityWalk** (p. 453), but downtown is also a lively scene. Check listings in the Calendar in Friday's *Orlando Sentinel* or the free *Orlando Weekly*. Cheap bars line **North Orange Avenue.** For tourist-oriented attractions, head to the bright lights of **International Drive,** where mini-golf, Ripley's Believe It or Not, the world's largest McDonald's, and Wonderworks (a science funhouse in an upside-down building) await.

▧ SAK Comedy Lab, 380 W. Amelia St. (☎648-0001), at Hughey Ave. downtown. With its trademark family-friendly humor, SAK manages to produce top-notch hilarity that all audiences can enjoy. Shows Tu-W 9pm, Th 8pm, F-Sa 8 and 10pm. Tickets $13.

Tabu, 46 N. Orange Ave. (☎648-8363), downtown, is a South Beach-style haven for twentysomethings. Tu and Th college night, with all-you-can-drink included in the cover. Stylish dress. Usually 18+. Cover $12. Open Tu-Sa 10pm-3am.

Back Booth, 37 W. Pine St. (☎999-2570), downtown, keeps the crowds coming with a loaded concert schedule and 27 beers on tap. Bands range from jazzy funk to ska punk. Cover $5-10. Shows usually 9 or 10pm; call for schedule.

Waitiki, 26 Wall St. (☎481-1199), downtown, hosts live reggae W-Th 10pm and live bands F-Sa 9-10pm in an upscale tiki hut. On F-Sa 10pm, the street shuts down, outdoor stages go up, and $5 gets you into all 8 bars on the block. Open daily 11am-2am.

WALT DISNEY WORLD   ☎407

Disney World is the Rome of central Florida: all roads lead to it. Its name is more apt than one might imagine, as Disney indeed creates a "world" of its own, even hosting a full marathon run entirely on its grounds. Within this Never-Neverland, theme parks, resorts, theaters, restaurants, and nightclubs all come together as the embodiment of fun. The only setback is that magical amusement comes at a price—everything in Walt Disney's world costs almost three times as much as it does in the real world. Every attraction here is a marketing machine, and all rides end in their very own gift shop. In the end, though, the Disney empire leaves no one bored.

> **ℜD** **THE REAL DEAL.** Though the FASTPASS option numbs some of the pain induced by Disney theme park crowds, it only takes the relief so far. Getting a FASTPASS for a particular ride may prevent you from being able to obtain another pass for a set amount of time (sometimes upward of an hour). If you're looking to avoid long lines, arrive in the evening, or ditch Disney altogether until the quieter (and cooler) low-season months. —Rebecca Barron

🛈 PRACTICAL INFORMATION

Disney dominates **Lake Buena Vista,** 20 mi. west of Orlando via I-4. (☎824-4321 or 939-4636; www.disneyworld.com.) Ticketing options are vast and complex, and the best way to acquaint yourself with them is to visit the Disney World website (www.disney.com). The one-day base ticket ($59.75, ages 3-9 $48) admits visitors to one of the parks, allowing them to leave and return later in the day. A better value, the **Park-Hopper Pass** buys admission to all four parks for a flat rate of $35, plus the cost of a one- or multiple-day base ticket. The **Park-Hopper Plus** includes a set number of days of admission to the four parks plus a specified number of visits to other Disney attractions for a flat rate of $45 plus the cost of a one- or multiple-day Park-Hopper Pass. The Hopper passes need not be used on consecutive days, but must be used within 14 days of the first use unless the **No Expiration** option is added (from $10).

Disney provides free transportation between attractions. Attractions that charge separate admissions include **Typhoon Lagoon** ($34, ages 3-9 $28), **Blizzard Beach** ($34/$28), **Disney's Wide World of Sports** complex ($10/$8), and **Pleasure Island** ($21, 18+ unless with adult). For descriptions, see **Other Disney Attractions** (p. 451). Never pay full fare for a Disney park; official Tourist Info Centers sell Park Hopper passes for about $10-15 less.

Disney World opens its gates 365 days a year, but hours fluctuate by season. Expect the parks to open at 9am and close between 7 and 11pm, but call beforehand—the schedule is set only a month in advance. Prepare for crowds (and afternoon thunderstorms) in summer, but the enormously crowded peak times are Christmas, Thanksgiving, and the month around Easter. The parks are least crowded in January and October. The free **FASTPASS** option at all of the theme parks allows you to bypass long lines on popular rides.Simply insert your park entrance ticket into a FASTPASS station, and you will receive a ticket telling you when to return, usually 30min. to 2hr. later.

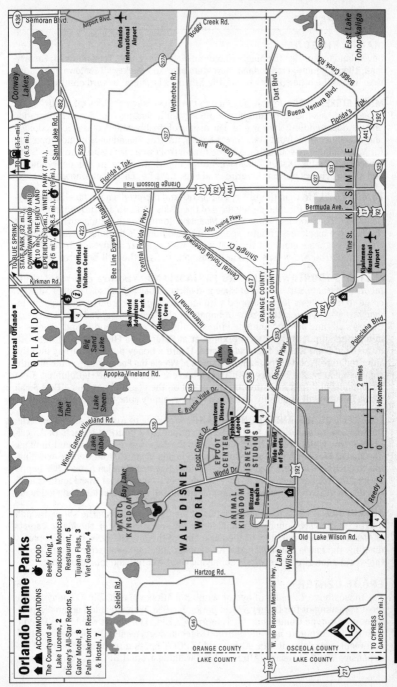

Semoran Blvd.

Airport Blvd.

Orlando International Airport

Boggy Creek Rd.

East Lake Tohopekaliga

Conway Lakes

Wetherbee Rd.

Dart Blvd.

Buena Ventura Blvd.

Florida's Tpk.

KISSIMMEE

Sand Lake Rd.

Orange Ave.

Bermuda Ave.

Orange Blossom Trail

Florida's Tpk.

John Young Pkwy.

Vine St.

Kissimmee Municipal Airport

TO BLUE SPRING STATE PARK (32 mi.), DOWNTOWN ORLANDO AND THE HOLY LAND EXPERIENCE (3 mi.), WINTER PARK (7 mi.),

Bee Line Expwy. (Toll Road)

Central Florida Pkwy.

Central Florida Greenway

Shingle Cr.

Kirkman Rd.

Orlando Official Visitors Center

Sea World Adventure Park

Discovery Cove

International Dr.

ORANGE COUNTY

OSCEOLA COUNTY

Poinciana Blvd.

Universal Orlando

ORLANDO

Big Sand Lake

Lake Bryan

Osceola Pkwy.

Apopka-Vineland Rd.

Reedy Cr.

Lake Tibet

Lake Sheen

Lake Mabel

Winter Garden-Vineland Rd.

E. Buena Vista Dr.

Downtown Disney

Typhoon Lagoon

WALT DISNEY WORLD

MAGIC KINGDOM

Bay Lake

Epcot Center Dr.

EPCOT CENTER

World Dr.

DISNEY-MGM STUDIOS

Wide World of Sports

ANIMAL KINGDOM

Blizzard Beach

Old Lake Wilson Rd.

Lake Wilson

Hartzog Rd.

Seidel Rd.

W. Irlo Bronson Memorial Hwy.

TO CYPRESS GARDENS (20 mi.)

ORANGE COUNTY

OSCEOLA COUNTY

LAKE COUNTY

LAKE COUNTY

0   2 miles

0   2 kilometers

FLORIDA

Orlando Theme Parks

ACCOMMODATIONS

The Courtyard at Lake Lucerne, **2**
Disney's All-Star Resorts, **6**
Gator Motel, **8**
Palm Lakefront Resort & Hostel, **7**

FOOD

Beefy King, **1**
Couscous Moroccan Restaurant, **5**
Tijuana Flats, **3**
Viet Garden, **4**

🔎 THE PARKS

MAGIC KINGDOM

Seven lands comprise the Magic Kingdom: **Main Street, USA; Tomorrowland; Fantasyland; Liberty Square; Frontierland; Adventureland;** and **Mickey's Toontown Fair.** More than any of the other Disney parks, the Kingdom is geared toward children.

MAIN STREET, USA. As the entrance to the "Most Magical Place on Earth," Main Street captures the spirit and bustle of early 20th-century America, with parades and vendors peddling their wares. The aroma of freshly baked, overpriced cookies and cakes beckons from **Main Street Bakery,** and the **Emporium** is a one-stop shop for Magic Kingdom souvenirs. A horse-drawn trolley carries visitors up Main St. to **Cinderella's Castle,** Disney World's centerpiece, where there are frequent dancing and singing shows by your favorite (and least favorite) Disney characters.

TOMORROWLAND. In the 1990s, Tomorrowland received a neon facelift that skyrocketed it out of the space-race days of the 1960s and into a futuristic intergalactic nation. The indoor coaster **Space Mountain** dominates the landscape, providing thrills in the blackness of outer space. An added bonus is the long corridor with A/C in which guests can beat the heat while waiting. **Buzz Lightyear's Space Ranger Spin** equips *Toy Story* fans with laser cannons to fight the Evil Emperor Zurg.

MICKEY'S TOONTOWN FAIR AND FANTASYLAND. Visitors can meet their favorite characters at the **Hall of Fame** and **Mickey's Country House.** To meet Mickey, come to the **Judge's Tent** equipped with an autograph book and a camera, but be ready to wait in line with dozens of impatient children. **Fantasyland** brings some of Disney's all-time favorite animated films to life. Soar above London and Neverland in a pirate ship sprinkled with pixie dust at **Peter Pan's Flight,** then dance with dwarves at **Snow White's Scary Adventures.** Board a honey pot and journey into the Hundred Acre Wood at **The Many Adventures of Winnie the Pooh,** where you will withstand a blustery day, bounce with Tigger, and encounter bizarre Heffalumps. Meet mechanical children from around the world on the classic boat ride **"It's a Small World,"** which will fiendishly engrave its happy, happy song into your brain.

LIBERTY SQUARE AND FRONTIERLAND. Welcome to Americana, Disney-style. Liberty Square introduces visitors to educational and political aspects of American history, while Frontierland showcases the America of cowboys and Indians. The **Hall of Presidents** is a fun exhibit on US heads of state, from George Washington to George W. Bush. Next door, the spooky **Haunted Mansion** houses 999 happy ghouls. In Frontierland, take a lazy raft ride over to **Tom Sawyer Island** and explore, or take on the two thrill rides—**Splash Mountain** and **Big Thunder Mountain Railroad.**

ADVENTURELAND. The classic **Pirates of the Caribbean** steals the show, though don't expect to see Johnny Depp hidden in the shadows. Fly on the **Magic Carpets of Aladdin** for an aerial view of the park. One of the original rides from the park's opening, the **Jungle Cruise** provides a tongue-in-cheek take on exploration, touring the world's amazing rivers while supplying good wet fun and lots of bad puns.

EPCOT CENTER

For those above 12 years of age or without a Mickey fetish, EPCOT may be the most appealing of the Disney World parks. In 1966, Walt dreamed up an "Experimental Prototype Community Of Tomorrow" (EPCOT), which would evolve constantly to incorporate new ideas from US technology, eventually becoming a self-sufficient, futuristic utopia. At present, EPCOT splits into **Future World** and the expansive **World Showcase.** After a day of walking around EPCOT, you'll see why some joke that the acronym actually stands for "Every Person Comes Out Tired." The trademark 180 ft. high geosphere (or "golf ball") at the entrance to Future World houses the **Spaceship Earth** attraction, in which visitors board a "time machine" for a tour through the evolution of communications. **Body Wars** takes visitors on a tour of the human body using a simulator. At nearby **Test Track,** riders experience life in the fast lane on one of Disney's fastest and longest rides.

In the **World Showcase,** architectural styles, monuments, and typical food and crafts represent 11 countries from around the world, while people in traditional dress perform various forms of cultural entertainment. **Maelstrom** is an amusing and thrilling boat ride through Norway, complete with Vikings and trolls. Every night at 9pm, EPCOT presents a magnificent mega-show called **IllumiNations** with music, dancing fountains, laser lights, fireballs, and fireworks. The World Showcase also specializes in regional cuisine—each "country" offers both a sit-down restaurant and a more reasonably priced cafeteria-style option. The all-you-can-eat meat, seafood, and salad buffet ($20) at **Restaurant Akershus ❹,** in the Norway Pavilion, is actually a Disney dining bargain. Those with an affinity for brew can create their own around-the-world tour, sampling a beer from each country. Though drinking a Corona in Mexico and a Casablanca in Morocco is truly magical, at $4-7 a beer, doing so will demolish both your sobriety and your budget.

DISNEY-MGM STUDIOS

Disney-MGM Studios creates a living movie set, built around stunt shows and mini-theatricals. Restaurants resemble their Hollywood counterparts, and movie characters stroll the grounds signing autographs. The **Studios Backlot Tour** takes visitors on a behind-the-scenes tour into the magic of movie making. **The Twilight Zone Tower of Terror** drops guests 13 stories in a runaway elevator. The thrilling, twisting, "limo" ride **Rock 'n' Roller Coaster** will take you from 0 to 60 mph in less than three seconds while Aerosmith blasts in your ears; it's also the only Disney ride to take you upside down. Based on the hit TV game show, **Who Wants to Be a Millionaire? Play It!** replicates the real show, save affable host Regis Philbin. The **Indiana Jones Epic Stunt Spectacular** shows off some of the greatest scenes from the trilogy in live action. If screeching, synchronized cars are your thing, check out the new **"Lights, Motors, Action" Extreme Stunt Show** and learn what goes into creating complex vehicle stunts. **The Magic of Disney Animation,** a tour that introduces you to actual Disney animators, explains how Disney animated films are created and offers a sneak peak at the sketches of upcoming Disney flicks.

DISNEY'S ANIMAL KINGDOM

If plastic characters are getting to be too much, the Animal Kingdom is a dose of reality, in a carefully managed Disney presentation, of course. **Kilimanjaro Safaris** depart for the Harambe preserve, where elephants, hippos, giraffes, and other creatures of the African savannah roam. A **Maharajah Jungle Trek** drops riders among tigers, tapirs, and bats, and the **Kali River Rapids** is a whitewater adventure exposing the threats facing our planet. Like any Disney park, shows and rides make up a large part of Animal Kingdom (the park's catchphrase is NAHTAZU: "not a zoo"). **DINOSAUR,** the best ride in the park, puts travelers in the middle of the early Cretaceous. Another 3-D spectacular, **It's Tough to be a Bug!,** put on by the cast of the animated flick *A Bug's Life,* is sure to entertain all ages and species.

OTHER DISNEY ATTRACTIONS

Besides the four main parks, Disney offers several other draws with different themes and separate admissions. **Blizzard Beach** is a water park built on the premise of a melting mountain. Ride a ski lift to the fastest water-slide in the world and plummet down the 120 ft. descent. **Typhoon Lagoon,** a 50-acre water park, cen-

FLORIDA

ters on the nation's largest wave pool and its 7 ft. waves. In addition to eight water slides, the lagoon has an inner-tubing creek and a saltwater coral reef stocked with tropical fish and harmless sharks. Water parks fill up early on hot days; late arrivals may be turned away. With venues for over 30 sports, **Disney's Wide World of Sports** complex is a hub of athletic activity. Catch the Atlanta Braves in spring training and the Tampa Bay Buccaneers during pre-season camp. The larger-than-life **Downtown Disney** is a neon conglomeration of theme restaurants, nightlife, and shopping encompassing the **Marketplace, Pleasure Island,** and the **West Side. Pleasure Island** is hedonistic Disney with an attitude. Party and drink the night away at eight nightclubs, from comedy to jazz to 80s pop. **Mannequins,** with a spinning dance floor and stunning strobes, trumps any South Beach club in terms of venue, though perhaps not coolness of clientele. (18+ unless accompanied by parent. Cover $21. Open daily 7pm-2am.) In the Marketplace at the **LEGO Imagination Center,** take a photo with large LEGO sculptures or create your own. In the West Side, **Cirque Du Soleil** presents *La Nouba,* a blend of circus acrobatics and theater with a price higher than the tightropes. ($59-87, ages 3-9 $44-65.) Next door, the high-tech games of **Disney Quest** guarantee a "virtually" exciting time ($34, ages 3-9 $28).

LIFE BEYOND DISNEY   ☎ 407

Believe it or not, it exists. In fact, many visitors will tell you that Universal's **Islands of Adventure** is Orlando's best park. Further, Disney has such a domination that the other parks band together in competition with Mickey: "FlexTickets" combine admission prices to various parks at a discount, though their prices can fluctuate. A four-park ticket ($185, ages 3-9 $151) covers Sea World, both Universal Studios parks, and Wet 'n' Wild, and allows 14 days of fun with free transportation. The five-park ticket ($225/$190; 14 days) adds Tampa's Busch Gardens (p. 455). Universal City Travel (☎ 800-224-3838) sells tickets.

👁 THE PARKS

UNIVERSAL ORLANDO

Swap Mickey and Goofy for Spider-Man and Shrek, and you get a theme park less annoying to mature crowds. Universal has movie-themed rides that thrill, spin, and make you squeal. With two parks (**Universal Studios Florida** and **Islands of Adventure**), three resort hotels, and an entertainment complex called **CityWalk,** Universal stands toe-to-toe with the "other park." *(I-4 Exit 74B or 75A. ☎ 363-8000. Open daily 9am, closing times vary. CityWalk open until 2am. 2-park pass $70/$60. CityWalk is ungated and free; club, dinner, and movie packages available. Parking $9, free after 6pm.)*

UNIVERSAL STUDIOS FLORIDA. The first park to "ride the movies" showcases a mix of rides and behind-the-scenes extravaganzas. Live the fairy tale courtesy of "OgreVision" at **Shrek 4-D,** the park's best attraction. **Back to the Future...The Ride,** a staple of any Universal visit, utilizes seven-story OmniMax screens and spectacular special effects. **Men in Black: Alien Attack** puts you through agent training as you navigate your way through an alien-infested city armed with your own blaster gun.

ISLANDS OF ADVENTURE. This park encompasses 110 acres of technologically advanced rides and typically has short waits. Five islands portray different themes, ranging from cartoons to Jurassic Park. **The Amazing Adventures of Spider-Man** is the park's crown jewel. A fast-moving car whizzes around a 3-D video system as you and Peter Parker find the stolen Statue of Liberty. The most amusing island is **Seuss Landing,** home of the **Green Eggs & Ham Cafe ❷** (green eggs and hamwich $5.60). **The Cat in the Hat** turns the classic tale into a ride on a wild couch that loops its way through the story. If that's too tame, the **Dueling Dragons** is the world's first inverted, dueling roller coaster.

CITYWALK. CityWalk greets the eager tourist upon entering Universal Studios. A unique mix of restaurants, bars, clubs, and a cineplex makes it an appealing alternative to Pleasure Island. **The NASCAR Cafe, Jimmy Buffet's Margaritaville,** and **Emeril's** are a few of the pricey theme restaurants that line the main street. Clubs on the walk include **Bob Marley's** and **The Groove.** Packages make it possible to enjoy a meal, a movie, and partying at an affordable price. *(All-club access $10, with a movie $14. Meal and a movie or meal and club access $20.)*

SEA WORLD

One of the largest marine parks in the US, **Sea World Adventure Park** makes a splash with shows, rides, and exhibits. In recent years, it has worked to transform itself into a full-fledged park emphasizing the marvels and mysteries of sea creatures. Eels, barracudas, sharks, and other beasties lick their chops in **Shark Encounter,** the world's largest collection of dangerous sea creatures. **The Shamu Adventure** thrills with aquatic acrobatics smartly executed by a family of orcas and their trainers. Whale belly flops send waves of salt water into the cheering "soak zone." The park's first thrill ride, **Journey to Atlantis,** gets rave reviews, as does **Kraken,** a floorless roller coaster billed as the highest, fastest, and longest in Orlando. In summer, stick around until 10pm for **Mystify,** a fireworks spectacular. *(12 mi. southwest of Orlando off I-4 at Rte. 528/Bee Line Expwy. Take bus #8.* ☎*351-3600. Open daily 9am-7pm; extended hours in summer. $60, ages 3-9 $48. Parking $8.)* Orlando's newest destination is the adjacent **Discovery Cove.** Swim with dolphins, snorkel among tropical fish, and frolic in an aviary with more than 200 birds. *(*☎*877-434-7268; www.discovery-cove.com. Open daily 9am-5:30pm. $129-409. Reservations required.)*

OTHER SIGHTS

THE HOLY LAND EXPERIENCE. Step back in time at this small, controversial, proselytizing park billed as a "living biblical museum." Take in the architecture and sights of ancient Jerusalem and watch costumed performers reenact biblical scenes. The Scriptorium is a one-of-a-kind museum displaying Bible-related artifacts. *(4655 Vineland Rd. I-4 Exit 78.* ☎*367-2065. Open M-F 10am-5pm, Sa 9 10am-6pm, Su noon-6pm, with extended seasonal hours. $30, ages 6-12 $20, ages 5 and under free.)*

CYPRESS GARDENS. Cypress Gardens's botanical gardens feature over 8000 varieties of plants and flowers amidst winding walkways and boat rides. Despite the pretty flowers, the water-ski shows attract the biggest crowds and the loudest applause. *(Southwest of Orlando in Winter Haven. Take I-4 SW to Rte. 27 S, then Rte. 540 W.* ☎*863-324-2111. Open daily 10am-6pm, with extended summer hours. $39, ages 6-12 $32.)*

TAMPA   ☎813

Even with beautiful weather and ideal beaches, Tampa has avoided the plastic pink flamingos that plague its Atlantic Coast counterparts. While Busch Gardens is Tampa's primary tourist attraction, the rest of the city provides less-commercial fun. Ybor City (EE-bor), Tampa's Cuban district, is a hotbed of energy and activity where sun-bleached tourists can find many of Tampa's best restaurants and bars.

■ ⋈ ORIENTATION AND PRACTICAL INFORMATION. Tampa wraps around Hillsborough Bay and sprawls northward. **Nebraska Avenue** and **Dale Mabry Road** parallel **I-275** as the main north-south routes; **Kennedy Boulevard, Columbus Street,**

FLORIDA

and **Busch Boulevard** go east-west. With some exceptions, numbered streets go north-south and numbered avenues run east-west. **Ybor City** is bounded roughly by Nuccio Pkwy., 22nd St., Palm Ave., and 5th Ave. Be careful outside these boundaries; the surrounding area can be dangerous. **Tampa International Airport** (☎870-8770; www.tampaairport.com) is 5 mi. west of downtown, Exit 39 off I-275. HART-line bus #30 runs between the airport and downtown. **Amtrak**, 601 Nebraska Ave. (☎221-7600; www.amtrak.com; open daily 9am-6pm), at the end of Zack St. two blocks north of Kennedy St., runs to Miami (5½hr., 1 per day, $39). **Greyhound,** 610 Polk St. (☎229-2174; www.greyhound; open 24hr.), sends buses to Atlanta (11-14hr., 5 per day, $69-74), Miami (7-10hr., 11 per day, $38-41), and Orlando (2hr., 8 per day, $19-21). **Hillsborough Area Regional Transit (HARTline)** provides public transit in the Tampa area. Buses #8 and 46 run to Ybor City from downtown. (☎254-4278. $1.30, seniors and ages 5-17 $0.65; exact change required.) HARTline also operates Tampa's **Streetcar System** (☎254-4278; www.tecolinestreetcar.org; $1.50), which runs from Ybor City to downtown Tampa. **Visitor Info: Tampa Bay Convention and Visitors Bureau,** 400 N. Tampa St., Ste. 2800. (☎223-1111 or 800-448-2672; www.visittampabay.com. Open M-F 8:30am-5pm.) **Tampa Bay Visitor Information Center,** 615 Channelside Dr. (☎223-2752 or 800-448-2672. Open M-Sa 9:30am-5:30pm, Su 11am-5pm.) **Hotlines: Crisis Hotline,** ☎234-1234. **Internet Access: John F. Germany Public Library,** 900 N. Ashley Dr., downtown. (☎273-3652. Open M-Th 9am-9pm, F 9am-6pm, Sa 9am-5pm, Su 10am-6pm. Free.) **Post Office:** 401 S. Florida Ave. (☎223-4332. Open M-F 8:30am-4:30pm.) **Postal Code:** 33601. **Area Code:** 813.

⌂ ACCOMMODATIONS. The only hosteling option in Tampa is **Gram's Place ❶,** 3109 N. Ola Dr., Exit 46B off I-275 N. What the "train" dorm lacks in spaciousness it makes up for in quirkiness, and you're sure to bunk alongside some interesting folks. (☎221-0596. Dorms M-Th and Su $22.50, F-Sa $25; private rooms from $45. AmEx/MC/V.) Chain hotels and motels hug I-275 and can be found at most exits. Motels are particularly abundant along bustling Busch Blvd. **Motel 6 ❸,** 333 E. Fowler Ave., Exit 51 off I-275 and 4 mi. from Busch Gardens in northwest Tampa, has cheap rooms with cable TV. (☎932-4948. Singles $39-45; doubles $42-48. AmEx/D/DC/MC/V.) **Villager Lodge ❷,** 3110 W. Hillsborough Ave., conveniently located 5 mi. from the airport at Exit 30 off I-275, has 33 small rooms with A/C, cable TV, and pool access. (☎876-8673. Singles around $50; doubles around $65. AmEx/D/DC/MC/V.) With spacious, comfy rooms, the classy **Baymont Inn ❹,** 9202 N. 30th St., is a great alternative to motels. (☎930-6900 or 877-229-6668. A/C, cable TV, Internet access, and continental breakfast. Rooms $69-99. AmEx/D/DC/MC/V.)

◻ FOOD. Ybor City's 7th Ave. is lined with a number of fun and funky eateries, many of which stay open late to satiate post-clubbing cravings. Mostly a dinner spot, the swanky **Bernini ❹,** 1702 E. 7th Ave., whips up piping hot pizzas ($10-15), savory pasta dishes ($15-21), and the house favorite, crispy duck ($24). Hungry customers enjoy their meals under photos and replicas of the eponymous sculptor's works. (☎248-0099. Open M-Th 11:30am-10pm, F 11:30am-11pm, Sa 4-11pm, Su 5-10pm. AmEx/D/DC/MC/V.) Buried in North Tampa lies the legendary **Skipper's Smokehouse ❷,** 910 Skipper Rd., off Nebraska Ave., a backcountry eatery whose thatched hut restaurant is complemented by an adjacent oyster bar (21+) and the popular backyard "Skipper Dome," which hosts live music nightly. (☎971-0666. Happy hour Tu-F 4-8pm. Open Tu 11am-10pm, W-F 11am-11pm, Sa noon-11pm, Su 1-10pm. AmEx/MC/V.) The king of buffets, **Sweet Tomatoes ❷,** 1902 N. Dale Mabry Hwy., greets diners with an extensive salad bar, delectable soups, freshly baked goods, three types of pasta, a sundae bar, and fresh fruit. A meal here won't put too much of a dent in your wallet, either: lunch is a mere $7.29, and dinner goes for $9. (☎874-6566. Open M-Th and Su 11am-9pm, F-Sa 11am-10pm. AmEx/D/DC/MC/V.)

⑥ SIGHTS. Tampa blossomed through Ybor City, a planned community once known as the cigar capital of the world. Early 20th-century stogie manufacturer Vincent Martínez Ybor employed a host of immigrants, and the city soon displayed the influence of intermingled Cuban, Italian, and German heritages. The **Ybor City State Museum,** 1818 9th Ave., details the rise and fall of the tobacco empire and its workers. Exhibits include a detailed look at 19th- and early 20th-century Ybor life, while a display is dedicated to the art of hand-rolled cigars, complete with a viewing of a cigar roller at work. (☎247-6323; www.ybormuseum.org. Open daily 9am-5pm. $3, under 6 free. Neighborhood walking tours Sa 10:30am, $6.)

The **Florida Aquarium,** 701 Channelside Dr., invites you to get up close and personal with fish from Florida's lagoons. Head into the wetlands exhibit to gape at gators, turtles, and fighting river otters, and then check out the coral reef, where menacing sharks and enigmatic jellyfish haunt the waters. Wild dolphins of the gulf stage a meet 'n' greet on **Dolphin Quest Eco-Tours** in Tampa Bay. (☎273-4000; www.flaqarium.org. Open daily 9:30am-5pm. $18, seniors $15, ages 3-11 $12. 1½hr. Eco-Tours M-F 2pm, Sa-Su 2, 4pm. $19/ $18/$14. Combo tickets available.) Built in 1891, Henry B. Plant's Tampa Bay Hotel was once considered the most luxurious resort in all the South. A wing of the lavish hotel is open today as the **Henry B. Plant Museum,** 401 W. Kennedy Blvd. View restored bedrooms, card rooms, and authentic artifacts from the opulent mansion, complete with Edison carbonfilament lighting and classical music. (☎254-1891; www.plantmuseum.com. Open Tu-Sa 10am-4pm, Su noon-4pm. Suggested donation $5.)

Anheuser-Busch's addition to Florida's theme parks, **Busch Gardens,** 3605 E. Bougainvillea Ave., is the most prized weapon in the arsenal of Tampa tourism. Thrill-seekers head for roller coasters Kumba, Montu, and Gwazi, while others watch animals roam, fly, slither, and swim through the African-themed zoo areas. The "Edge of Africa" safari experience is among the park's most popular attractions. (☎987-5082 or 888-800-5447; www.buschgardens.com. Hours vary, usually open daily 9:30am-7:30pm. $56, ages 3-9 $46. Parking $7.)

🎵🎭 ENTERTAINMENT AND NIGHTLIFE. Brief yourself on city entertainment with the free *Tampa Weekend* or *Weekly Planet*, in local restaurants and bars and on street corners. Gay travelers should check out the free *Stonewall*. Every year during the last week of January, the **José Gasparilla,** a 165 ft., fully rigged pirate ship loaded with "buccaneers," invades Hillsborough Bay, kicking off a month of

GUAVAWEEN

Every year during the last week of October, more than 100,000 people flock to Tampa to participate in one of the nation's biggest and baddest street parties. Held in the notoriously festive neighborhood of Ybor City, Guavaween is a Halloween celebration infused with Latin spice and southern soul.

In the 19th century, Tampa residents tried to cultivate a guava industry on the Gulf Coast, and, though the effort was largely unsuccessful, guavas became synonymous with the region. Columnist Steve Otto noted that if New York City was the "Big Apple," then Tampa could be called the "Big Guava." The analogy stuck, and for the last 20 years, "Mama Guava" has kicked off the Guavaween bash by leading the legendary "Mama Guava Stumble Parade" through the streets of Ybor. The festival has tons of concerts and costume contests, and winners take home prizes of up to $2000. Guavaween has recently toned down some of its wild antics and now appeals to both partiers and families, entertaining children during the day with a scavenger hunt. Still, don't be fooled—sin and skin prevail when the sun goes down, as revelers party early into the morning in search of a trick or a treat. The countdown to the next Guavaween has already begun.

For more information on Guavaween, call ☎ 248-0721 or visit www.cc-events.org/gw.

pirate-themed parades and festivals (www.gasparillapiratefest.com). Thousands pack Ybor City on the last Saturday in October for **Guavaween** (☎248-0721), a Latin-style Halloween celebration. With over 35 clubs and bars, Ybor City is brimming with energetic nightlife. Most nighttime hangouts are on bustling 7th Ave., though fun can be found on 8th Ave. and 9th Ave. as well. Use caution when walking down side streets. During the week, many restaurants close at 8pm, and clubs don't open until 10pm. 7th Ave. is closed to vehicular traffic at night, making bar-hopping very easy. For those first drinks, try **Adobe Gilas,** 1600 E. 8th Ave., a great place to warm up before hitting the more pounding club scene. (☎241-8588. Open M-Sa 11am-3am, Su 1pm-3am.) **Coyote Ugly Saloon,** 1722 E. 7th Ave., is the hottest club on the Ybor strip. Taking its cue from the movie *Coyote Ugly,* the rowdy bar serves mostly single liquor shots with complimentary bar dancing and body licking. Their motto? "You will get drunk, you will get ugly." (☎228-8459. Happy hour daily 5-7pm. 21+. Open daily 5pm-3am.) **Green Iguana Bar & Grill,** 1708 E. 7th Ave., serves cheap, tasty food by day and turns into a multi-level clubbing extravaganza at night, with $1 drinks on Wednesdays. (☎248-9555. Open daily 11am-3am; kitchen closes at midnight.) **The Castle,** 2004 N. 16th St., at 9th Ave., caters to a bohemian crowd but is open to all who want to cross the metaphorical moat. (☎247-7547. 80s night M. 18+. Cover $3-7. Open M and F-Su 9:30pm-3am.)

ST. PETERSBURG AND CLEARWATER ☎727

Across the bay, 22 mi. southwest of Tampa, St. Petersburg is home to a relaxed beach community of retirees and young singles. The town basks in soft white beaches, emerald water, and about 361 days of perfect sunshine each and every year. The St. Petersburg-to-Clearwater stretch caters to beach bums and city strollers alike. While the outdoor scenery draws crowds, indoor activities are equally captivating—museum exhibits on Salvador Dalí and John F. Kennedy rival even the sunset.

■ ▶ **ORIENTATION AND PRACTICAL INFORMATION.** In St. Petersburg, **Central Avenue** parallels numbered avenues, running east-west in the downtown area. **34th Street (U.S. 19), I-275,** and **4th Street** are major north-south thoroughfares. The beaches line a strip of barrier islands on the west side of town facing the Gulf of Mexico. Several causeways, including the **Clearwater Memorial Causeway (Route 60),** lead to the beaches from St. Petersburg. Clearwater sits at the far north of the strip. **Gulf Boulevard** runs down the coastline, through Belleair Shores, Indian Rocks Beach, Indian Shores, Redington Shores, Madeira Beach, Treasure Island, and St. Pete Beach.

Greyhound, 180 9th St. N, at 2nd Ave. N in St. Petersburg (☎898-1496; www.greyhound.com; open daily 4:30am-11:30pm), runs to Clearwater (30min., 5 per day, $9.50-10.50) and Orlando (3-4½hr., 6 per day, $19-21). The Clearwater station is at 2811 Gulf-to-Bay Blvd. (☎796-7315. Open M-Sa 6am-9pm, Su 6am-noon and 1:30-9pm.) **Pinellas Suncoast Transit Authority (PSTA)** handles public transit; most routes depart from Williams Park at 1st Ave. N and 3rd St. N. (☎530-9911. $1.25, students $0.75, seniors $0.60. Day pass $3.) To reach Tampa, take bus #100X from the Gateway Mall ($1.50). A **beach trolley** runs up and down the shore. (Daily every 20-30min. 5am-10pm, $1.25. Day pass $3.) Jump on the **Looper Trolley** ($0.25), which runs a 30min. tour of downtown St. Pete (☎821-5166). Taxi: **Yellow Cab,** ☎799-2222. **Visitor Info: St. Petersburg Area Chamber of Commerce,** 100 2nd Ave. N. (☎821-4069; www.stpete.com. Open M-F 8:30am-7pm, Sa 9am-7pm, Su noon-6pm.) **The Pier Information Center,** 800 2nd Ave. NE, is also in St. Petersburg. (☎821-6443. Open M-Th 10am-9pm, F-Sa 10am-10pm, Su 11am-7pm.) **Hotlines: Rape Crisis,** ☎530-7233. **Medical Services: Bayfront Medical Center,** 701 6th St. S. (☎823-1234.) **Internet Access:**

St. Petersburg Main Library, 3745 9th Ave. N. (☎ 893-7724. Open M-Th 9am-9pm, F-Sa 9am-6pm, Su 10am-6pm. Free.) **Post Office:** 3135 1st Ave. N, at 31st St. (☎ 322-6696. Open M-F 8am-6pm, Sa 8am-2:30pm.) **Postal Code:** 33701. **Area Code:** 727.

ⓕ ACCOMMODATIONS. Many cheap motels line **4th Street N** and **U.S. 19** in St. Pete. To avoid the worst neighborhoods, stay on the north end of 4th St. and the south end of U.S. 19. In Clearwater, several inexpensive motels cluster along **Gulf Boulevard.** Tucked snugly away on the sandy Clearwater shore, the **Clearwater Beach International Hostel (HI) ❶,** 606 Bay Esplanade Ave., off Mandalay Ave. at the Sands Motel in Clearwater Beach, is the ultimate beach pad, with spacious, well-furnished rooms and a friendly staff. Bikes and kayaks are available for cruising the beaches. (☎ 443-1211. Internet access $5 per hr. Linen and key deposit $5. Reception 9am-noon and 5-9pm. Dorms $15, members $14; private rooms $36-59. MC/V.) In St. Petersburg, the **Landmark Motel ❷,** 1930 4th St. N, has bright rooms nestled among tropical plants. (☎ 895-1629. A/C and cable TV. Singles from $46; doubles from $60. AmEx/D/MC/V.) ▧**Fort De Soto County Park ❶,** 3500 Pinellas Bayway S, composed of five islands, has perhaps the best camping in all of Florida. Though its namesake, Fort De Soto, is available for exploration, you may never want to leave your beautiful campsite. (☎ 582-2267; www.pinellascounty.org/park. Showers, electricity, and laundry. Front gate locked 9pm. Curfew 10pm. Sites $28.)

ⓒ FOOD. St. Petersburg's cheap, health-conscious restaurants cater to retirees and generally close by 8 or 9pm. **Dockside Dave's ❷,** 13203 Gulf Blvd. S, in Madeira Beach, is one of the best-kept secrets on the islands. The half-pound grouper sandwich (market price, around $9) is simply sublime. (☎ 392-9399. Open M-Sa 11am-10pm, Su noon-10pm. MC/V.) Locals rave about **Tangelo's Grille ❷,** 226 1st Ave. N, a superb Cuban restaurant. Their imported *mole negro* sauce accents the grilled chicken sandwich ($6) nicely. (☎ 894-1695. Open M 11am- 4pm, Tu-Th 11am-8pm, F-Sa 11am-9pm. MC/V.) Also in St. Pete is the **Fourth Street Shrimp Store ❷,** 1006 4th St. N, a purveyor of all things shrimp. (☎ 822-0325. Chipotle shrimp salad $7. Open M and Su 11am-8:30pm, Tu-Sa 11am-9pm. MC/V.) After a day of relaxing under the Clearwater sun, make your way over to **Frenchy's Cafe ❸,** 41 Baymont St., and cool off with a salted margarita ($2.50). Have a seat at one of the picnic tables for the boiled shrimp ($13), which comes dusted with secret seasonings. (☎ 446-3607. Open M-Th 11:30am-11pm, F-Sa 11:30am-midnight, Su noon-11pm. AmEx/MC/V.)

ⓢ SIGHTS. Grab *See St. Pete* or the *St. Petersburg Official Visitor's Guide* for the lowdown on area events, discounts, and useful maps. Downtown St. Pete is cluttered with museums and galleries, including the ▧**Florida International Museum,** 244 2nd Ave. N. The "Cuban Missile Crisis: When the Cold War Got Hot" exhibit allows visitors to relive the Cold War era of the 1960s, recounting day-by-day the Cuban Missile Crisis. "John F. Kennedy: The Exhibition" provides a look at JFK's personal and political life. (☎ 822-3693 or 800-777-9882; www.floridamuseum.org. Open Tu-Sa 10am-5pm, Su noon-5pm; ticket office closes 4pm. $10, seniors and AAA $8, students $5. Wheelchair accessible.) The highlight of St. Petersburg is the ▧**Salvador Dalí Museum,** 1000 3rd St. S, the largest private collection of the surrealist's work in the world. The South's most-visited museum houses 95 of Dalí's oil paintings and provides guided tours offering fascinating glimpses into the enigmatic artist's life and works. (☎ 823-3767 or 800-442-3254; www.salvadordalimuseum.org. Open Sept.-May M-W and F-Sa 9:30am-5:30pm, Th 9:30am-8pm, Su noon-5:30pm; June-Aug. F 9:30am-8pm. $14, seniors $12, students $9. Free tours daily. Wheelchair accessible.) The **Florida Holocaust Museum,** 55 5th St. S, traces Jewish life and anti-Semitism from early Europe to the present. (☎ 820-0100 or 800-960-7448; www.flholocaustmuseum.org. Open M-F 10am-5pm, Sa-Su noon-5pm; last admission 4pm. $8, students and seniors $7, ages 6-18 $4.)

FLORIDA

The museum exhibits may impress you with their thorough and informative displays, but for a scene a little more characteristic of gulf coast Florida, hit the beaches. The nicest beach in the area may be **Pass-a-Grille Beach,** but its parking meters eat quarters by the bucketful. Check out **Clearwater Beach,** at the northern end of the Gulf Blvd. strand, where mainstream beach culture finds a fantastic white-sand setting. The **Sunsets at Pier 60** festival brings arts and entertainment to Clearwater Beach, but it's the sunsets that draw the crowds. (☎449-1036; www.sunsetsatpier60.com. Festival daily 2hr. before sundown until 2hr. after.)

◪ **NIGHTLIFE.** St. Pete caters to those who want to end the night by 9 or 10pm; most visitors looking for nightlife head either to Tampa or to the beach. However, if you're staying in St. Pete and are in the mood for a concert, don't overlook **Jannus Landing,** 15 2nd St. N, which hosts local and big-name bands. The courtyard accommodates 1500 and the bar keeps listeners in good spirits. (☎896-1244. Call for tickets.) For a more consistent scene infused with youthful energy, Clearwater's hotels, restaurants, and parks often host free concerts. Free copies of *Weekly Planet* or *Tampa Tonight/Pinellas Tonight* can be found at local restaurants and bars, though an evening stroll through the blocks surrounding the rotary should turn up the night's hottest spot. The younger crowd likes to make a dash for the mainland and party at **Liquid Blue,** 22 N. Ft. Harrison Ave., Clearwater's premier techno nightspot. (☎446-4000. 18+. Open Tu-Sa 9:30pm-2am.)

ATLANTIC COAST

DAYTONA BEACH   ☎386

When locals first started auto-racing on the hard-packed shores of Daytona Beach more than 60 years ago, they combined two aspects of life that would come to define the town's entire mentality: speed and sand. Daytona played an essential role in the founding of the **National Association of Stock Car Auto Racing (NASCAR)** in 1947, and the mammoth Daytona International Speedway still hosts several big races each year. Though races no longer occur on the sand, 23 mi. of Atlantic beaches still pump the lifeblood of the community.

▚ **ORIENTATION.** Daytona Beach lies 53 mi. northeast of Orlando and 90 mi. south of Jacksonville. **I-95** parallels the coast and the barrier island. **Atlantic Avenue (Route A1A)** is the main drag along the shore, and a scenic drive up A1A goes to St. Augustine and Jacksonville. **International Speedway Boulevard (U.S. 92)** runs east-west from the ocean, through downtown and to the racetrack and airport. Daytona Beach is a collection of smaller towns; many street numbers are not consecutive and navigation can be difficult. To avoid the gridlock on the beach, arrive early (8am) and leave early (around 3pm). Visitors must pay $5 to drive onto the beach, and police strictly enforce the 10 mph speed limit. Free parking is plentiful during most of the year but sparse during spring break, **Speedweek, Bike Week, Biketoberfest,** and the **Pepsi 400.** See p. 460 for festival dates.

▐ **PRACTICAL INFORMATION. Amtrak,** 2491 Old New York Ave. (☎734-2322; www.amtrak.com; open daily 6am-10pm), in DeLand, 24 mi. west on Rte. 92, runs to Miami (7-9½hr., 2 per day, $38-50). **Greyhound,** 138 S. Ridgewood Ave. (☎255-7076; www.greyhound.com; open daily 7:30am-10:30pm), 4 mi. west of the beach, runs to Jacksonville (2hr., 6 per day, $16-18) and Orlando (1½hr., 7 per day, $10-11). **Volusia County Transit Co. (VOTRAN),** 950 Big Tree Rd., operates local buses and a trolley that covers Rte. A1A between Granada Blvd. and Dunlawton Ave. All buses have bike racks. (☎761-7700. Regular service M-Sa 6am-7pm, Su 6am-6pm. Night service on select routes. Trolley M-Sa noon-midnight. $1, seniors and ages 6-17 $0.50. Free maps available at hotels.) **Taxi: Yellow Cab,** ☎255-5555. **Visitor Info: Daytona Beach Area Convention and Visitors Bureau,** 126 E. Orange Ave., on City Island. (☎255-0415 or 800-544-0415; www.daytonabeachcvb.org. Open M-F 9am-5pm.) **Hotline: Rape Crisis Line,** ☎258-7273. 24hr. **Medical Services: Halifax Medical Center,** 303 N. Clyde Morris Blvd. (☎254-4000). **Internet Access: Volusia County Library Center,** 105 E. Magnolia Ave. (☎257-6036. Open M-Th 9am-7pm, F 9am-5pm, Sa 9am-3pm, Su 1-5pm. 1hr. limit.) **Post Office:** 220 N. Beach St. (☎258-9352. Open M-F 8:30am-5pm, Sa 10am-noon.) **Postal Code:** 32115. **Area Code:** 386.

⌂ ACCOMMODATIONS. Almost all of Daytona's lodgings front **Atlantic Avenue (Route A1A),** either on the beach or across the street; those off the beach offer the best deals. Spring break and race events drive prices upward of $150 a night even at budget places, but low-season rates are more reasonable. Many of the motels facing the beach cost $70 for a low-season single; on the other side of the street it's $35-40. The **Camellia Motel ❷,** 1055 N. Atlantic Ave. (Rte. A1A), across the street from the beach, has cozy, bright rooms, free local calls, cable TV, and A/C. (☎252-9963. Singles from $40; doubles from $50. Rates drop to $30 for stays of a week or longer. MC/V.) For a change in budget motel scenery, try the **Travelers Inn ❷,** 735 N. Atlantic Ave. Each of the 22 rooms has a different theme—find the force in the *Star Wars* room or rock out in the Jimi Hendrix room or the Beatles room. (☎253-3501 or 800-417-6466. Singles from $45; doubles from $55; each additional person $10. Kitchen additional $10. AmEx/D/MC/V.) For a more typical experience, head to the **Daytona Shore Inn ❷,** 805 N. Atlantic Ave., which has small but clean rooms with cable TV and A/C. (☎253-1441. Singles from $35; doubles from $45. MC/V.) The gay-friendly **Streamline Hotel ❷,** 140 S. Atlantic, has some of the cheapest rooms in town. The top floor is a sky-roof bar with an expansive view of the beach. (☎258-6937. No reservations. Singles from $33; $6 per additional person. 3-night special $69, $99 during special events. MC/V.) **Tomoka State Park ❶,** 2099 N. Beach St., 8 mi. north of Daytona in Ormond Beach, has 100 campsites under a tropical canopy. Enjoy salt-water fishing, nature trails, and a sculpture museum. (☎676-4050, reservations 800-326-3521. Open daily 8am-dusk. Sites $22.50. $3 per vehicle, $4 with more than 1 occupant. Pedestrians and bicyclists $1.)

⬦ FOOD. One of the most famous seafood restaurants in the area is **Aunt Catfish's ❸,** 4009 Halifax Dr., at Dunlawton Ave. on the mainland side of the Port Orange Bridge. Order any seafood, and you're in for a treat, though the lobster and crab receive the most praise. (☎767-4768. Entrees $9-15. Salad buffet $9. Open M-Sa 11am-9 or 10pm, Su 9am-9 or 10pm. AmEx/D/MC/V.) At **Maria Bonita ❷,** 1784 S. Ridgewood Ave., the food is authentic and delicious, the service fast and friendly, and the portions generous. It is heralded for its Mexican food, but the Cuban specials take the prize; the *pechuga de pollo a la plancha* (grilled chicken breast; $12) is a fiesta for your mouth. (☎767-9512. Open M-Th 11:30am-9pm, F 11:30am-10pm, Sa noon-10pm, Su noon-9pm. 2-for-1 *mojitos* Th after 4pm. AmEx/D/DC/MC/V.) The **Dancing Avocado Kitchen ❶,** 110 S. Beach St., is a delicious alternative to the Daytona seafood-and-grill scene, serving fantastic breakfasts. Enjoy the "Dancer" Avocado Melt (avocado, onions, cheddar jack cheese, sprouts and tomato on multigrain bread; $6.25) or the signature symphony salad ($5.50) in this endearing organic eatery. (☎947-2022. Open M-Sa 8am-4pm. AmEx/D/DC/MC/V.) Though a little out of the way, **Boondocks ❷,** 3948 Adventure Marina in Wilbur by the Sea, an entirely outdoor restaurant overlooking the Halifax River, serves excellent burgers, sandwiches, and a variety of seafood and meat entrees. (☎760-9001. Take Atlantic Ave. south and turn right onto Mallard Ave. Sandwiches and burgers $3-7. Entrees $9-20. Open daily 11am-10pm. MC/V.)

🏁 **START YOUR ENGINES.** The center of the racing world, the **Daytona International Speedway** hosts NASCAR's biggest race, the Daytona 500 (Feb. 19, 2006). **Speedweek** (Feb. 4-19, 2006) precedes the legendary race, while the **Pepsi 400** (for those who think young) heats up the track on July 1, 2006. (NASCAR tickets ☎253-7223.) Next door, **Daytona USA**, 1801 W. International Speedway Blvd., is a must-see for any NASCAR fan, though the admission price will seem ridiculous if you're not. This interactive experience includes a new simulation ride, an IMAX film on NASCAR, and a fun teaching program on NASCAR commentating. The breathtaking **Speedway Tour** is a unique chance to see the garages, grandstands, and famous 31-degree banked turns up close. (☎947-6800. Open daily 9am-7pm. $22, seniors $19, ages 6-12 $16. Tours every 30min. daily 9:30am-5:30pm, $7.50.) The **Richard Petty Driving Experience** puts fans in a stock car for a ride-along at 150 mph. (☎800-237-3889. 16+. $143.) **Bike Week** draws biker mamas for various motorcycle duels, and **Biketoberfest** brings them back for more. (Bikeweek: Mar. 3-12, 2006; www.bikeweek.com. Biketoberfest: Oct. 19-22, 2006; www.biketoberfest.com.)

🎵 **NIGHTLIFE.** When spring break hits Daytona, all manner of concerts, hotel-sponsored bashes, and other events answer the call of party-hungry students. News about these events travels fastest by word of mouth, but the *Calendar of Events* and *SEE Daytona Beach* make good starting points. On mellow nights, head to the boardwalk to play volleyball or shake your groove thing at the **Oceanfront Bandshell,** an open-air amphitheater made of *coquina* (a mixture of crushed seashells and concrete). Dance clubs line Seabreeze Blvd. just west of N. Atlantic Ave. **Razzle's,** 611 Seabreeze Blvd., caters to the traditionally scandalous spring break crowd with its high-energy dance floors, flashy light shows, and nightly drink specials. (☎257-6236. Cover varies. Open daily 8pm-3am.) **Ocean Deck,** 127 S. Ocean Ave., stands out among the clubs with its live music on the beach and nightly drink specials. Chow down on the "shipwreck" (shrimp, crab, oysters, and clams; $19) and boogie down to reggae, jazz, calypso, or rock. (☎253-5224; www.oceandeck.com. Music nightly 9:30pm-2:30am. 21+ after 9pm. Open daily 11am-3am; kitchen until 2am.)

COCOA BEACH AND CAPE CANAVERAL   ☎321

During the Cold War, Cape Canaveral and the surrounding "Space Coast" were the base of operations for major space explorations, from the Apollo moon landings to the current International Space Station effort. Even the local area code (3, 2, 1... liftoff!) reflects the space obsession. The towns of Cocoa Beach and nearby Melbourne are home to Florida's best waves; surfers head to ⊠**Ron Jon Surf Shop,** 4151 N. Atlantic Ave., for two floors of boards, shirts, shorts, and sunscreen. (☎799-8888. Open 24hr.) All of **NASA's** shuttles take off from the **Kennedy Space Center (KSC),** 18 mi. north of Cocoa Beach on Rte. 3; by car via Rte. 405 E off I-95, or Rte. 528 E from the Bee Line Expwy. From Cocoa Beach, take Rte. A1A to Rte. 528, then follow Rte. 3 N. The renovated **Kennedy Space Center Visitors Complex** has two 3-D IMAX theaters, a Rocket Garden, and exhibits on current space exploration. Standard admission ($30, children $20) will let you into the Visitors Complex; "Maximum Access" includes the Astronaut Hall of Fame and simulators ($37/$27). **NASA Up Close** tours the shuttle launch pads and gets into the International Space Station Center; the tour **Cape Canaveral: Then and Now** guides visitors through Amer-

ica's first launch sites from the 1960s, the Air Force Space & Missile Museum, and the Cape Canaveral Lighthouse (tours $22/$16). A closely guarded secret is that after 3:45pm (and sometimes earlier) the price for museum admission drops to $10. Check NASA's **launch schedule**—you may have a chance to watch space shuttles thunder off into the blue yonder. (☎449-4444; www.kennedyspacecenter.com. Open daily 9am-5:30pm; extended hours in summer.) Nearby, the **Merritt Island National Wildlife Refuge** teems with sea turtles, manatees, wild hogs, otters, and over 300 bird species. Take Exit 80 off I-95 and go east on Garden St. to Rte. 402. (☎861-0667. Open daily dawn-dusk. Visitors center open Apr.-Oct. M-F 8am-4:30pm, Sa 9am-5pm; Nov.-Mar. M-F 8am-4:30pm, Sa-Su 9am-5pm. Closed 4 days before and day of NASA launches.) On the northeastern shore, ◼**Canaveral National Seashore** is an undeveloped beach with gorgeous dunes. Take Rte. 406 E off U.S. 1 in Titusville. (☎267-1110. Open daily Apr.-Oct. 6am-8pm; Nov.-Mar 6am-6pm. Closed 3 days before and day of NASA launches. Cars $5, pedestrians and bicyclists $3.)

Around summer launch dates, tourists pack the area and hotel prices soar into the stratosphere. The **Dixie Motel ❷,** 301 Forrest Ave., has clean rooms, huge windows, A/C, cable TV, and a pool. (☎632-1600. Laundry. 21+. Rooms $50. AmEx/ MC/V.) Year after year, loyal patrons return to the lovely **Luna Sea Motel ❷,** 3185 N. Atlantic Ave., to bask in the sun by the pool and at the nearby beach. (☎783-0500 or 800-586-2732. Cable TV, A/C, microwave, fridge, and continental breakfast. Rooms from $59. AAA and AARP discount 10%. Military discount 15%. AmEx/D/ DC/MC/V.) Partying teenagers and vacationing families flock to the **Cocoa Beach Comfort Inn ❸,** 3901 N. Atlantic Ave., which has giant rooms with A/C, cable TV, free Internet, and, in some rooms, a wet bar. (☎783-2221. Pool and whirlpool. 18+. Rooms Nov.-Apr. from $100; May-Oct. from $110. AAA and AARP discount 10%. AmEx/D/DC/MC/V.) You can pitch your tent at the small **Jetty Park Campgrounds ❶,** 400 E. Jetty Rd., at the northern tip of Cape Canaveral. (☎783-7111. Jan.-Apr. sites $24, with water and electricity $28, with full hookup $31; May-Dec. $18/$22/$24.) Bikini contests, live music, karaoke, drink specials, and tasty seafood make **Coconut's on the Beach ❸,** 2 Minutemen Cswy. at Rte. A1A, a popular hangout for locals. (☎784-1422. Entrees $7-22. Open daily 11am-2am. D/DC/MC/V.) For a Chinese fix, **Bamboo Panda ❷,** 3680 N. Atlantic Ave., has tasty dishes that are well under $10. (☎783-5312. Open M-Th and Su 11am-9:30pm, F-Sa 11am-10:30pm. D/MC/V.) New York-style pizza can be found at **Bizzarro ❶,** 4 Rivercrest Dr., off Rte. A1A in Indialantic. (☎724-4799. Slices $2. Open M-Th 11am-9pm, F-Sa 11am-11pm, Su noon-9pm. Cash only.)

The Space Coast, 50 mi. east of Orlando, consists of mainland towns Cocoa and Rockledge, oceanfront Cocoa Beach and Cape Canaveral, and Merritt Island. **Greyhound,** 1220 S. Washington Ave. (☎267-8760; www.greyhound.com; open M-Sa 6am-2am, Su 7am-midnight), in Titusville, 15 mi. north of Cocoa, runs buses to Daytona Beach (3-5hr., 3 per day, $13-15) and Orlando (1hr., 3 per day, $3-15). **Space Coast Area Transit (SCAT)** has North Beach and South Beach routes and stops at every town in Brevard County. (☎633-1878. Operates M-F 8am-9:30pm, Sa-Su service on some routes. $1; students, seniors, and disabled $0.50; transfers free.) **Visitor Info: Cocoa Beach Chamber of Commerce,** 400 Fortenberry Rd., on Merritt Island. (☎459-2200; www.cocoabeachchamber.com or www.visitcocoa-beach.com. Open M-F 9am-5pm.) **Space Coast Office of Tourism,** 2725 Judge Fran Jamieson Way, in Viera. (☎637-5483 or 877-572-3224. Open M-F 8am-5pm.) **Medical Services: Cape Canaveral Hospital,** 701 W. Cocoa Beach Cswy. (☎799-7111). **Internet Access: Cocoa Beach Public Library,** 550 N. Brevard Ave. (☎868-1104. Open M-W 9am-9pm, Th 9am-6pm, F-Sa 9am-5pm, Su 1-5pm. Free.) **Post Office:** 500 N. Brevard Ave., in Cocoa Beach. (☎783-2544. Open M-F 9am-5pm, Sa 9am-noon.) **Postal Code:** 32931. **Area Code:** 321.

FLORIDA

ST. AUGUSTINE   ☎ 904

Spanish adventurer Pedro Menéndez de Áviles founded St. Augustine in 1565, making it the first European colony in North America and the oldest continuous settlement in the US. Thanks to preservation efforts and a desire to trap as many tourist dollars as possible, much of St. Augustine's Spanish flavor remains. This city's pride lies in its provincial cobblestone streets, *coquina* walls, and antique shops rather than in its token beaches. With a little effort the tourist traps can be avoided and the charm, history, and lively nights of St. Augustine can be yours.

✦ 🏄 ORIENTATION AND PRACTICAL INFORMATION

Most of St. Augustine's sights lie within a 10-15min. walk from the hostel, motels, and bus station, which is convenient since narrow streets and frequent one-ways make driving unpleasant. The city's major east-west routes, **King Street** and **Cathedral Place,** run through downtown and become the **Bridge of Lions** that leads to the beaches. **San Marco Avenue** and **Avenida Menéndez** run north-south. **Castillo Drive** grows out of San Marco Ave. near the center of town. **Saint George Street,** a charming north-south pedestrian-only route, contains most of the shops and many of the sights in town. **Greyhound,** 1711 Dobbs Rd. (☎829-6401; www.greyhound.com. Open daily 7:30am-8:30pm.), about 2 mi. outside of downtown, runs to Daytona Beach (1hr., 4 per day, $15-17) and Jacksonville (1hr., 2 per day, $9-10). If the station is closed, drivers accept cash. **Sightseeing Trains,** 170 San Marco Ave., shuttles travelers on a 20-stop trolley that hits all the major attractions. (☎829-6545 or 800-226-6545. Runs every 15-20min. 8:30am-5pm. $18, ages 6-12 $5. Ticket good for 3 consecutive days.) **Taxi: Ancient City Taxi,** ☎824-8161. **Visitor Info: St. Augustine Visitor Information Center,** 10 Castillo Dr., at San Marco Ave. From the bus station, walk three blocks north on Riberia St., then turn right on Orange St. (☎825-1000. Open daily 8:30am-5:30pm. 2-day parking $6.) **Post Office:** 99 King St. (☎825-0628. Open M-F 8:30am-5pm, Sa 9am-1pm.) **Postal Code:** 32084. **Area Code:** 904.

🏠 ACCOMMODATIONS

▨ **Pirate Haus Inn and Hostel,** 32 Treasury St. (☎808-1999), just off Saint George St. From Rte. 16 E, go south on U.S. 1, make a left on King St. and then left on Charlotte St.; parking is available in the metered lot behind the inn. Hands-down the best place to stay, with spacious dorms, beautiful private rooms, and a great location. Free lockers. Internet access ($1 per 15min.), A/C, laundry service ($4 per load). Key and linen deposit $5. Reception 8-10am and 5-10pm; no lockout for registered guests. Dorms $18; private rooms M-Th and Su $55, F-Sa $65. Under 13 free. MC/V. ❶

Casablanca Inn, 24 Avenida Menéndez (☎829-0928), in historic downtown, stands out among St. Augustine's many B&Bs. Feast on a 2-course gourmet breakfast and unwind on the porch with rocking chairs and a spectacular view of the river. Large rooms boast cable TV, pleasant artwork, and fireplaces. Rooms $99-319. AmEx/D/MC/V. ❺

Seabreeze Motel, 208 Anastasia Blvd. (☎829-8122), has clean rooms with refrigerators and pool access. A/C, cable TV, kitchenette, and free local calls. Singles M-Th and Su $40, F-Sa $59, holidays and special events $69; doubles $50/$59/$79. D/MC/V. ❷

Anastasia State Recreation Area, (☎461-2033), on Rte. A1A, 4 mi. south of the historic district. From town, cross the Bridge of Lions and turn left just past the small alligator farm. Small but shady and secluded campsites. Nearby opportunities for great windsurfing, fishing, swimming, and hiking. Office open daily 8am-dusk. Reservations a must (☎800-326-3521). Sites with water and electricity $25. Vehicle entrance $3-5, pedestrians $1. ❶

📷🍴 FOOD AND NIGHTLIFE

The bustle of daytime tourists and the abundance of budget eateries make lunch in St. Augustine's historic district a delight, especially in the cafes and bars of **Saint George Street**. The **Bunnery Bakery and Cafe ❶**, 121 Saint George St., is a bakery-diner combo popular with the vacationing crowd. The Bunnery has hearty breakfasts ($2-6) and delectable panini sandwiches ($4-7) at lunch. (☎829-6166. Open daily 8am-6pm. Cash only.) Worth the short drive, the **Manatee Cafe ❶**, 525 S. R. 16 #106, is a delightful little eatery that serves organic, vegetarian fare. Try the Tofu Cajun Style ($6.50) or the whole grain waffles for $6. (☎826-0210. Open M-Sa 8am-4pm, Su 8am-3pm. AmEx/MC/V.) You'll get more barbecue than you can handle at **Scarlett O'Hara's ❷**, 70 Hypolita St., at Cordova St. Patrons will never go hungry again after discovering the burgers ($7.50) and full slabs of ribs ($15) dished up in this slat-board house. Live music, usually rock or acoustic, entertains each night. (☎824-6535. Happy hour M-F 4-7pm. Open M-Sa 11am-12:30am, Su 11am-midnight. AmEx/D/MC/V.) **Pizzalley's ❶**, 117 Saint George St., is the best pizza place in the historic district. Scarf down a piping hot slice ($2.35) or a tremendous sub ($7) in this small but worthwhile eatery. (☎825-2627. Open daily 11am-9pm. MC/V.)

Many of St. Augustine's bars are on Rte. A1A S and Saint George St. *Folio Weekly*, free and available throughout the city, has event listings. Local string musicians play on the two stages at the **Milltop**, 19½ Saint George St., a tiny but illustrious bar above an old water mill in the restored district. (☎829-2329. Music daily 1pm-close. Cover varies. Open M-Sa 11am-1am, Su 11am-10pm.) Sample your choice of 24 drafts at the **Oasis Deck and Restaurant**, 4000 Rte. A1A S at Ocean Trace Rd., a family restaurant by day, romping party by night. (☎471-3424. Gator tail $7. Seafood sandwiches $6-8. Happy hour 4-7pm. Live music nightly. Open daily 6am-11pm.) Throw a few back with Flagler College students at their campus watering hole, the **St. George Tavern**, 116 Saint George St. (☎824-4204. Happy hour with $2.25 beers M-Th 4-8pm, F 4pm-1am. Open daily 11am-1am.) If you're looking for late-night grub to accompany your booze, head to **A1A Ale Works**, 1 King St., which brews its own beer and serves food late into the night. (☎829-2977. Open daily 11am-1am. Happy hour M-F 4-7pm. Live music Th-Sa.) Dinner and a movie *and* a beer? You betcha, and all at once at **Pot Belly's**, 36 Granada St. Screening just-out-of-theaters movies, this combination pub, deli, and cinema serves a range of sandwiches ($2.50-5), junk food (from $2.25), and brews (pitchers $7.50) to the in-house tables. (☎829-3101. Movie tickets $5. Call for showtimes. Cash only.)

👁 SIGHTS

SPANISH HERITAGE. The oldest masonry fortress in the continental US, **Castillo de San Marcos National Monument** has 14 ft.-thick *coquina* walls. The fort, originally built by the Spanish in 1627, is shaped like a four-pointed star complete with drawbridge and moat. It contains a museum, a large courtyard, a jail, a chapel, and the original cannon brought overseas from Spain. *(1 Castillo Dr., off San Marco Ave. ☎829-6506. Open daily 8:45am-5:15pm, last admission 4:45pm. $6, under 16 free.)* The **La Leche Shrine and Mission of Nombre de Dios** is the birthplace of American Catholicism. The first mass in the US was held here over 400 years ago. A huge steel cross marks the city's religious roots, and the shaded lawns make for peaceful strolls. *(27 Ocean St., off San Marco Ave. ☎824-2809. Open M-F 8am-5pm, Sa 9am-5pm, Su 9:30am-5pm. Mass M-F 8:30am, Sa 6pm, Su 8am. Donation suggested.)*

HISTORICAL SIGHTS. Not surprisingly, the longest continuous settlement in the US holds some of the nation's oldest artifacts. The **González-Álvarez House** is the oldest house listed on the National Registry of Historic Places. Built in the 17th cen-

FLORIDA

tury, the tiny house now serves as a tourist haven, with exhibits on the area's Spanish, British, and American heritage. *(14 Saint Francis St. ☎824-2872. Open daily 9am-5pm, last admission 4:30pm. $8, seniors $7, students $5, families $16. Partially wheelchair accessible.)* For the best view of the city and the water, climb the 219 stairs of the **St. Augustine Lighthouse and Museum,** one of only six lighthouses in the state open to the public. Tour the 19th-century tower and keeper's house to learn about marine archaeological studies in the surrounding waters. *(81 Lighthouse Ave., off Rte. A1A across from the Alligator Farm. ☎829-0745. Open daily 9am-6pm. Tower, grounds, and house $7.50, seniors $6.50, ages 7-11 $5. House and grounds $5/$4/$3.)* For a view of American history through a shotgun's barrel, check out the **Museum of Weapons and Early American History.** For over 18 years the owner-curator of the museum has collected early American artifacts. *(81-C King St. www.museumofweapons.com. Open daily 9:30am-5pm.)* In the **Colonial Spanish Quarter,** period craftsmen, soldiers, and housewives go about their business in this charming recreation of an 18th-century colonial Spanish town. Lucky for us, 18th-century Spanish colonists were apparently bilingual. *(53 Saint George St. ☎825-6830. Open daily 9am-5:30pm. $6.50, seniors, military, and college students $5.50, children $4, families $13.)*

RESTORATIONS. Flagler College is a small liberal arts institution in the restored Spanish Renaissance-style **Ponce de León Hotel.** Built by railroad and Standard Oil tycoon Henry Flagler in 1888, the hotel was the playground for America's social elite. Celebrity heavyweights like John Rockefeller and Will Rogers once strolled through the gorgeous interior. *(74 King St. ☎823-3378; www.flagler.edu. Tours mid-May to mid-Aug. daily on the hr. 10am-3pm. $6, under 12 $1. Wheelchair accessible.)* The **Memorial Presbyterian Church,** a beautiful model of St. Mark's Cathedral in Venice, was also built by Flagler, but these Tiffany windows are fake. The workmanship is so fine, though, that no one would guess that the church only took 361 days to finish. *(36 Sevilla St. ☎829-6451. Open M-Sa 9am-4pm, Su 12:30-4pm. Services Su 8:30 and 11am. Free.)* In 1947, Chicago publisher and art lover Otto Lightner converted the Alcazar Hotel into the **Lightner Museum,** which now holds an impressive collection of cut, blown, and burnished glass, along with old clothing and oddities. Today, the museum's eccentricity is its strongest feature, as it houses everything from a shrunken head to nuns' and monks' beer steins. *(75 King St. ☎824-2874; www.lightner-museum.org. Open daily 9am-5pm. Live 18th-century music daily 11am and 2pm. $8, military $6, students and ages 12-18 $2. Wheelchair accessible.)*

JUST FOR FUN. Across the Bridge of Lions, the ■**St. Augustine Alligator Farm** allows visitors to get personal with the gators. The park, delighting visitors since 1893, is the only place in the world where all 23 known crocodilian species live. *(On Rte. A1A S. ☎824-3337. Open daily 9am-6pm. Presentations every hr. Feeding daily at noon and 3pm. $18, ages 5-11 $10. AAA, military, and senior discount.)*

SOUTH FLORIDA

MIAMI ☎305

No longer purely a vacation spot for "snowbirds" (wealthy East Coasters escaping harsh winters), Miami's heart pulses to a beat all its own, fueled by the largest Cuban population this side of Havana. Appearance rules in this city, and nowhere is this clearer than on the shores of South Beach, where visual delights include Art Deco hotels and tanned beach bodies. South Beach is also host to a nightclub scene that attracts some of the world's most beautiful (and famous) people. But it's not all bikinis—Miami is the entry point for one of America's great natural habitats, the Everglades, as well as the gateway to the Florida Keys and the Caribbean.

Miami

TO ORLANDO (240 mi.)

TO FT. LAUDERDALE (27 mi.), WEST PALM BEACH (55 mi.)
Miami Gdns. Dr.

NW 37th Ave.
NW 27th Ave.
NW 57th Ave.
NW 47th Ave.

Florida Tpk.

860

Palmetto Expwy.
826

NE 167th St.

NE 163rd St.

Ocean Blvd.

OPA-LOCKA

Opa-Locka Airport
955

NORTH MIAMI BEACH

NE 6th Ave.

826

Oleta River State Recreation Area

Biscayne Blvd.

817
Tri-Rail

NW 138th St.

TO 75

Gratigny Pkwy. (toll)
NW 135th St.

NE 135th St.

NORTH MIAMI

NE 125th St.

922 Broad Causeway (toll)

A1A

Amelia Earhart Park

Perim Ave.
Red Rd.

NW 42nd Ave.
NW 37th Ave.
NW 27th Ave.

924

NW 119th St. (Gratigny Rd.)

NW 7th Ave.

915 Museum of Contemporary Art

INDIAN CREEK VILLAGE

Collins Ave.

W. 49th St.
932

NW 103rd St.

HIALEAH

9

W. 4th Ave.

Hialeah Race Track

Metrorail
27

NW 95th St.

95

MIAMI SHORES

934 JFK Causeway

Normandy Dr.
71st St.

Alton Rd.
Pine Tree Dr.

E. 25th St.

Tri-Rail

NW 79th St. 934

LITTLE HAITI

934

E. 9th St.

MLK Blvd.

NW 62nd St.

441

Biscayne Bay

MIAMI BEACH

Hialeah Dr.
944

NW 54th St.

LIBERTY CITY

N. Miami Ave.
NW 1st Ave.
NE 2nd Ave.

Mt. Sinai Medical Center

MIAMI SPRINGS

Airport Expwy. (toll)

112

Julia Tuttle Causeway

41st St. (Arthur Godfrey Rd.)

195

27

NW 36th St.

Metrorail

NW 12th Ave.

1

A1A

Miami International Airport

NW 27th St.

NW 20th St.

Jackson Memorial Hospital

836

Dolphin Expwy. (toll)

395

American Airlines Arena

Venetian Causeway (toll)

Parrot Jungle Island

Lincoln Rd.

Collins Ave.
Meridian Ave.
Ocean Dr.

WEST MIAMI

959

W. Flagler St.

Versailles

968

NW 7th St.

Orange Bowl

LITTLE HAVANA

41 SW 8th St. (Calle Ocho)

GOVERNMENT CENTER

Bayside

MacArthur Causeway

Port Blvd.

5th St.

SEE "SOUTH BEACH," p. 469

Tamiami Trail

9

933

BRICKELL

95

DOWNTOWN MIAMI

Port of Miami

Fisher Island

CORAL GABLES

Miami Children's Hospital

Coral Way

972 SW 24th St.

Venetian Pool

SW 42nd Ave. (Le Jeune Rd.)
Douglas Rd.
SW 17th Ave.

VIZCAYA

Vizcaya Museum and Gardens

Rickenbacker Causeway (toll)

Virginia Key

953

Coco-Walk

Metrorail

S. Dixie Hwy.
S. Bayshore Dr.

Bird Rd.

Miami Museum of Science and Planetarium

Miami Seaquarium

University of Miami

1

COCONUT GROVE

Ingraham

Crandon Park

SOUTH MIAMI

TO KEY LARGO (60 mi.)
KEY WEST (164 mi.)
EVERGLADES NATIONAL PARK (40 mi.)

Old Cutler Rd.
Red Rd.

Matheson Hammock Park

■ Fairchild Tropical Garden

Biscayne Bay

ATLANTIC OCEAN

Crandon Park Blvd.
Harbor Dr.

KEY BISCAYNE

Bill Baggs Cape Florida State Park

0   2 miles

0   2 km

N

LG

FLORIDA

MIAMI FOR POCKET CHANGE. With a little know-how, travelers can enjoy Miami's glamour without breaking the bank. Before holing up at the hip **Clay Hotel and International Hostel** (p. 467), savor a deliciously cheap meal at the **Flamingo Cafe** (p. 468). On Fridays from 6-9pm, the **Wolfosonian Museum** (p. 470) has free admission. If you prefer beautiful people to beautiful paintings, the price of an espresso will buy you hours of people-watching pleasure at **Ocean Drive's** trendy cafes (p. 469). Of course, die-hard sun-worshippers know that Miami's public **beaches** (p. 469) can always be enjoyed gratis.

▐ TRANSPORTATION

Airport: Miami International (☎876-7000; www.miami-airport.com), at Le Jeune Rd. and NW 36th St., 7 mi. northwest of downtown. Bus #7 runs downtown. From downtown, take bus "C" or "K" to South Beach. Taxi to Miami Beach $28 flat rate.

Trains: Amtrak, 8303 NW 37th Ave. (☎835-1223; www.amtrak.com), near the Northside Metrorail station. Bus "L" goes to Lincoln Rd. Mall in South Beach. Open daily 8:15am-7:30pm. To: **Charleston** (13hr., 1 per day, $99-129); **Orlando** (5-7hr., 2 per day, $39); **Tampa** (5hr., 1 per day, $39); **Washington, D.C.** (23-27hr., 2 per day, $167).

Buses: Greyhound, 4111 NW 27th St. (☎871-1810; www.greyhound.com). Open 24hr. To: **Atlanta** (15-17hr., 8 per day, $95-101); **Fort Lauderdale** (1hr., 20 per day, $6); **Key West** (5hr., 3 per day, $35-38); **Orlando** (5½-11hr., 13 per day, $33-36).

Public Transit: Metro Dade Transportation (☎770-3131; info M-F 6am-10pm, Sa-Su 9am-5pm). **Metrobus** lines converge downtown, where most long trips transfer. Over 100 routes, but the major lettered bus routes A, C, D, G, H, J, K, L, R, S, and T serve Miami Beach. Runs M-F 4am-2:30am. $1.50, transfers $0.50; students, seniors, and disabled $0.75/$0.25. Call for weekend schedule. Exact change only. **Metrorail** serves downtown's major business and cultural areas. Rail runs daily 5am-midnight. $1.50, rail-to-bus transfers $0.50. The **Metromover** loop downtown is linked to the Metrorail stations. Runs daily 5am-midnight. It glows at night, and is also free. **Tri-Rail** (☎800-874-7245) connects Miami, Fort Lauderdale, and West Palm Beach. Trains run M-F 4am-10pm, Sa 7am-11pm, Su 7am-9pm. $2-10; children, students, seniors, and disabled with Tri-Rail ID 50% discount. The **Electrowave** (☎843-9283) sends shuttles along Washington Ave. from S. Pointe to 17th St. Pick up a brochure or just hop on in South Beach. $0.25.

Taxi: Metro, ☎888-8888. **Central Cab,** ☎532-5555.

Bike Rental: Miami Beach Bicycle Center, 601 5th St. (☎531-4161), at the corner of Washington Ave. Open M-Sa 10am-7pm, Su 10am-5pm. $8 per hr., $20 per day, $70 per week. Credit card or $200 cash deposit required.

✴ ORIENTATION

Three highways crisscross the Miami area. **I-95,** the most direct north-south route, merges into **U.S. 1 (Dixie Highway)** just south of downtown. U.S. 1 runs to the Everglades entrance at Florida City and then continues as the Overseas Hwy. to Key West. **Route 836 (Dolphin Expressway),** a major east-west artery through town, connects I-95 to **Florida's Turnpike,** passing the airport in between.

When looking for addresses, pay attention to the systematic street layout; it's easy to confuse addresses in North Miami Beach, West Miami, Miami Beach, and Miami (all different places). Streets in Miami run east-west, avenues north-south; both are numbered. Miami divides into NE, NW, SE, and SW quadrants; the dividing lines downtown are **Flagler Street** (east-west) and **Miami Avenue** (north-south). Some numbered roads also have names; be sure to get a map that lists both.

Several causeways connect Miami to **Miami Beach.** The most useful is **MacArthur Causeway,** which becomes 5th St. Numbered streets run east-west across the island, increasing as you go north. In South Beach, **Collins Avenue (A1A)** is the main north-south drag, parallel to the club-filled **Washington Avenue** and the beachfront **Ocean Drive.** The commercial district sits between 6th and 23rd St. One-way streets, traffic jams, and limited parking make driving around **South Beach (SoBe)** frustrating. Tie on your most stylish sneakers and enjoy the small island at your leisure—it only takes about 20min. to walk up Collins Ave. from 6th to 16th St.

Back in Miami, the life of **Little Havana** is on **Calle Ocho**—between SW 12th and SW 27th Ave.; take bus #8, 11, 17, or 37. **Coconut Grove,** south of Little Havana, centers on the shopping and entertainment district on **Grand Avenue** and **Virginia Street. Coral Gables,** an upscale residential area, rests around the intersection of **Coral Way (SW 24th Street)** and **Le Jeune Road,** also known as **SW 42nd Avenue.** Though public transit is reliable and safe, a car can be useful to get around the city.

🛈 PRACTICAL INFORMATION

Visitor Info: Miami Beach Visitors Center, 1920 Meridian Ave. (☎672-1270; www.miami-beachchamber.com). Open M-F 9am-6pm, Sa-Su 10am-4pm. **Coconut Grove Chamber of Commerce,** 2820 McFarlane Rd. (☎444-7270). Open M-F 9am-5pm. **Greater Miami Convention and Visitors Bureau,** 701 Brickell Ave. (☎539-3000; www.miamiand-beaches.com), 27th fl. of Bank of America Bldg., downtown. Open M-F 8:30am-5pm.

Hotline: Crisis Line, ☎358-4357. 24hr.

Medical Services: Mt. Sinai Medical Center, 4300 Alton Rd., in Miami Beach (☎674-2121). **Rape Treatment Center and Hotline,** 1611 NW 12th Ave. (☎585-7273), at Jackson Memorial Hospital. Open 24hr.

Internet Access: Miami Public Library, 101 W. Flagler St. (☎375-2665), across from the Museum of Art. Open M-W and F-Sa 9am-6pm, Th 9am-9pm; Oct.-May also Su 1-5pm. 1hr. free. There are a number of cheap Internet options in SoBe around Washington Ave. and 15th, including **Kafka's Cafe,** 1464 Washington Ave. (☎673-9669), in Miami Beach. Open daily 8am-midnight. $3 per hr., noon-8pm $6 per hr.

Post Office: Downtown: 500 NW 2nd Ave. (☎371-7099). Open M-F 8am-5pm, Sa 9am-1:30pm. Miami Beach: 1300 Washington Ave. (☎672-2447). Open M-F 8am-5pm, Sa 8:30am-2pm. **Postal Code:** 33101; Miami Beach 33119. **Area Code:** 305.

⌂ ACCOMMODATIONS

Cheap rooms abound in South Beach. Hostels in Miami Beach are the cheapest option for solo travelers. If young and bohemian isn't your thing, cruise down Collins Ave. to the funky, hot-pink Art Deco hotels. Get a discount when you stay more than two nights in one of the trendy **South Beach Group Hotels,** including Whitelaw, Mercury, Shelly, Chelsea, Chesterfield, and Lily. High season for Miami Beach runs late December through mid-March; during low season, hotel clerks are often quick to bargain. The Miami Beach Visitors Center (see **Practical Information,** above) can get you the cheapest rates. Camping is not allowed on Miami Beach.

HOSTELS

🏚 **The Clay Hotel and International Hostel (HI),** 1438 Washington Ave. (☎534-2988 or 800-379-2529), located on the pedestrian-only Española Way; take bus "C" from downtown. This Mediterranean-style building is home to the best hostel in SoBe and hosts an international crowd. Kitchen, laundry facilities, and A/C. Dorms come with phone and fridge; some have TV. Internet access $0.10 per min. Lockers $1 per day. Linen/key deposit $10. 4- to 8-bed dorms $20, members $18; private rooms $53-105. MC/V. ❶

FLORIDA

The Tropics Hotel/Hostel, 1550 Collins Ave. (☎531-0361), across the street from the beach. From the airport, take bus "J" to 41st St., transfer to bus "C" to Lincoln Rd., walk 1 block south on Collins, and it's next to the parking garage. This quiet refuge from the SoBe scene offers large, comfy rooms with A/C, pool access, and an outdoor kitchen. Lockers at front desk. Free linen. Laundry $1. Internet access $1 per min. Key deposit $10. Dorms $19; singles and doubles $44-88. ISIC discount for dorms. MC/V. ●

Miami Beach International Travelers Hostel (9th St. Hostel), 236 9th St. (☎534-0268 or 800-978-6787), at Washington Ave. From the airport, take bus "J" to 41st and Indian Creek, then transfer to bus "C" or "K." Right in the heart of SoBe's club scene. Common room with TV and movie library. Laundry $1. Internet access $5 per hr. Dorms with A/C and bath $19, members $17; singles from $49; doubles from $59. MC/V. ●

HOTELS

▧ **Kent Hotel,** 1131 Collins Ave. (☎604-5068; www.thekenthotel.com). The Kent's tagline, "savvy affordability," is right on the mark. With lavender rooms and a dramatic lobby, vibrant colors energize this hotel. Great location, free continental breakfast and Internet access, TV, and A/C. Rooms Oct.-Apr. $145; May-Sept. $130. AmEx/D/DC/MC/V. ●

Whitelaw Hotel, 808 Collins Ave. (☎398-7000). From 7-8pm, bright white leather and chrome greet party people lured into the hotel's lobby by complimentary cocktails. Down comforters, continental breakfast, TV, A/C, fridge, free Internet access (wireless $15 per day), free airport shuttle, and VIP passes to SoBe clubs. Doubles Oct.-Mar. $175-200; Apr.-Sept. $95-110. AmEx/DC/MC/V. ●

Chesterfield Hotel, 855 Collins Ave. (☎531-5831). Deep house music pumps through this uber-chic retreat. Great location and a helpful staff. Continental breakfast, TV, A/C, Internet access ($15 per day), free airport shuttle, bar, cafe, and free VIP passes to area clubs. Doubles Dec.-Mar. $195; Apr.-Nov. from $90. AmEx/MC/V. ●

Hotel Shelley, 844 Collins Ave. (☎531-3341). With marble bathrooms and bright white bedspreads, the Shelley offers luxury with a slightly less hefty price tag. Continental breakfast, TV, A/C, fridge, complimentary cocktails, VIP passes to nearby clubs, and free airport shuttle. Rooms around $90. AmEx/DC/MC/V. ●

🍴 FOOD

Food in Miami is incredibly diverse. Four-star restaurants owned by celebrities and celebrity chefs are as prevalent as local sandwich counters known for their affordability. The South Beach strip along Ocean Dr. has regulars like **TGI Friday's** and **Johnny Rockets,** favorites like **China Grill** and **News Cafe,** and pseudo-clubs like **Mango.** Head at least one block inland to find more wallet-pleasing prices.

▧ **Opa,** 36 Ocean Dr. (☎673-6730). At 7pm every night, while you're enjoying a filling Greek *souvlaki* ($6) or the oak-grilled pork loin ($11), the music strikes up and the manager tosses hundreds of napkins in the air while Greek belly dancers gyrate on table tops. Open daily from 4pm until the *ouzo* runs out. AmEx/D/MC/V. ●

▧ **Flamingo Cafe,** 1454 Washington Ave. (☎673-4302), near the Clay Hostel in Miami Beach. Overwhelming amounts of delicious food for staggeringly low prices. Breakfast plate with eggs, toast, and meat $2.80. Beef tacos and salad $3. *Frijoles con queso* $3. Lunch specials $5-7. Open M-Sa 6:30am-9:30pm. AmEx/D/MC/V. ●

Versailles, 3555 SW 8th St. (☎444-0240), in Little Havana. Miami-Cuban to the core. Sit in the company of power-brokers as you enjoy classic Cuban dishes like the deliciously salty *ropa vieja* with a side of fried sweet plantains ($9). Open M-Th 8am-2am, F 8am-3:30am, Sa 8am-4:30am, Su 9am-2am. AmEx/D/DC/MC/V. ●

Taystee Bakery, 1450 Washington Ave. (☎538-4793). A haven for anyone with a South American sweet tooth, Taystee has a large selection of super-cheap baked goods, including no salt/no sugar selections and Latin favorites. Guava pastries $0.85. *Empanadas* $1.50. *Pan cubano* sandwiches $4. Open daily 6am-10pm. MC/V. ❶

Pizza Rustica, 863 Washington Ave. (☎674-8244). This popular eatery, along with its 2 other Miami locations, serves up some of the best pizza in South Florida. Try the spinach and blue cheese, the NY steak, or any of the creative specials. Slices $3-4. Whole pizzas $7.50-15.50. Open daily 11am-6am. Cash only. ❶

Fairwind Island Bar & Tropical Grill, 1000 Collins Ave. (☎538-9351), across from the Essex House. One of the best-kept secrets in South Beach, Fairwind creates masterful seafood dishes at low prices. Try the wasabi crusted salmon ($16) or the seafood pasta ($11). Happy hour daily 4-7pm. Open daily 7am-1am. AmEx/DC/MC/V. ❸

News Cafe, 800 Ocean Dr. (☎538-6397). Though the food is outstanding, you're really paying for one of the best people-watching locations on Ocean Dr. Go in the evening just for dessert (chocolate fondue for two $13) and gaze upon the stylish hardbodies strolling by. Open 24hr. AmEx/D/DC/MC/V. ❸

👁 SIGHTS

SOUTH BEACH. South Beach is the reason to come to Miami. The liberal atmosphere, hot bodies, Art Deco design, and excellent sand make the 17 blocks between 6th and 23rd St. seem like their own little world. **Ocean Drive** is where Miami's hottest come to see and be seen. Bars and cafes cram this tiny strip of land, which is part fashion show, part raging party. The **Art Deco Welcome Cen-**

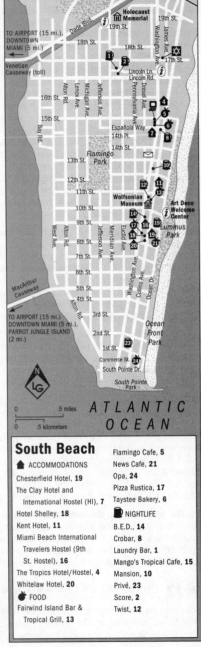

South Beach

🏠 ACCOMMODATIONS

Chesterfield Hotel, **19**

The Clay Hotel and
   International Hostel (HI), **7**

Hotel Shelley, **18**

Kent Hotel, **11**

Miami Beach International
   Travelers Hostel (9th
   St. Hostel), **16**

The Tropics Hotel/Hostel, **4**

Whitelaw Hotel, **20**

🍴 FOOD

Fairwind Island Bar &
   Tropical Grill, **13**

Flamingo Cafe, **5**

News Cafe, **21**

Opa, **24**

Pizza Rustica, **17**

Taystee Bakery, **6**

🍸 NIGHTLIFE

B.E.D., **14**

Crobar, **8**

Laundry Bar, **1**

Mango's Tropical Cafe, **15**

Mansion, **10**

Privé, **23**

Score, **2**

Twist, **12**

ter dispenses free maps and advice, features a free museum, and hosts walking tours. (*1001 Ocean Dr.* ☎ *531-3484; www.mdpl.org. Open M-Sa 9am-7pm, Su 9am-6pm. 90min. walking tours W and F-Su 10:30am, Th 6:30pm. $20, students and seniors $15.*) Hidden in the heart of South Beach is the fantastic ◼**Wolfsonian Museum.** The museum's collection of modern art and design projects far outstrips its floor space, so call or check the website for current exhibition info. (*1001 Washington Ave.* ☎ *531-1001; www.wolfsonian.org. Open Th-F 11am-9pm, Sa-Su noon-6pm; in winter also M-Tu 11am-6pm. Tours Th-F 6pm. $7, students and seniors $5. Free F 6-9pm. Wheelchair accessible.*) The **Holocaust Memorial** commemorates the 6 million Jews who fell victim to genocide in WWII. Marvel at the 42 ft. bronze arm protruding from the ground, the base of which is supported by dozens of sculpted human figures struggling to escape persecution. (*1933-45 Meridian Ave.* ☎ *538-1663. Open daily 9am-9pm. Free. Wheelchair accessible.*) Since 1936, visitors to **Parrot Jungle Island** have walked among free-flying parrots, strutting flamingos, and swinging orangutans. Also on site are the Parrot Bowl amphitheater, the Serpentarium, the clay cliffs of Manu Encounter, and the Treetop Ballroom. (*1111 Parrot Jungle Tr. From downtown, take the MacArthur Cswy. east toward South Beach. Parrot Jungle Tr. is the first exit after the bridge.* ☎ *258-6453; www.parrotjungle.com. Open daily 10am-6pm. $25; seniors, military, and students $23; ages 3-10 $20. Parking $6.*)

COCONUT GROVE. A stroll through lazy **Coconut Grove** uncovers an unlikely combination of haute boutiques and tourist traps. People-watching abounds at the open-air mall, **CocoWalk,** along Grand Ave. On the bayfront between the Grove and downtown stands the ◼**Vizcaya Museum and Gardens.** The 70-room Italianate villa has been the scene of many a rap video shoot. The villa is as bling-bling as it comes, but even a stroll through the garden is magnificent. (*3251 S. Miami Ave., Exit 1A off I-95.* ☎ *250-9133; www.vizcayamuseum.com. Open daily 9:30am-5pm; last entry 4:30pm. $12, ages 6-12 $5. ISIC discount $1. Partially wheelchair accessible.*)

BAYSIDE. On the waterfront downtown, Miami's sleek **Bayside** shopping center hops nightly with street performers. Stores and restaurants cater mostly to cruise ship guests and tourists, though a tour through the center and its surrounding statues makes it a worthwhile trip. (*From Miami Beach, take bus "F" or "C."* ☎ *577-3344. Open M-Th 10am-10pm, F-Sa 10am-11pm, Su 11am-9pm; restaurants and bars stay open later.*)

CORAL GABLES. In addition to the **University of Miami,** scenic **Coral Gables,** 7 mi. south of downtown, boasts one of the most beautiful planned communities in the region. Nearby, the family-friendly **Venetian Pool,** built in 1923, draws visitors to its 800,000 gallon oasis. Waterfalls and Spanish architecture dress up this swimming hole, which is always crowded on hot summer weekends. (*2701 De Soto Blvd. From U.S. 1, head north of Granada Blvd.* ☎ *460-5356; www.venetianpool.com. Open Apr.-May Tu-F 11am-5:30pm, Sa-Su 10am-4:30pm; June-Aug. M-F 11am-7:30pm, Sa-Su 10am-4:30pm; Sept.-Oct. Tu-F 11am-5:30pm, Sa-Su 10am-4:30pm; Nov.-Mar. Tu-Su 10am-4:30pm. Apr.-Oct. $9.50, ages 3-12 $5.25; Nov.-Mar. $6.25/$3.25. Partially wheelchair accessible.*)

NORTH MIAMI. The **Museum of Contemporary Art (MOCA)** is known for its often eccentric exhibits and displays. Having played host to Versace dresses and steel drummers alike, MOCA supports uncommon means of artistic expression. (*770 NE 125th St.; Exit 10A off I-95.* ☎ *893-6211; www.mocanomi.org. Open Tu-Sa 11am-5pm, Su noon-5pm; last F of the month also 7-10pm. $5, students and seniors $3. Wheelchair accessible.*)

🎵📷 ENTERTAINMENT AND NIGHTLIFE

For news on Miami entertainment, check out the "Living Today," "Lively Arts," and "Weekend" sections of the *Miami Herald.* Weekly *Oceandrive, New Times, Street,* and *Sun Post* list local happenings. *TWN* and *Miamigo,* free gay papers, are available along Ocean Dr. Music is a big part of Miami life, whether its grinding techno in a SoBe nightclub, a street performance on **Calle Ocho** in little Havana, or the nightly performances at **CoCoWalk**. Spring and summer are festival season, which opens with **Carnaval Miami**, the nation's largest Hispanic festival, filling 23 blocks of Calle Ocho in early March with the world's longest conga line.

Nightlife in the Art Deco district of South Miami Beach starts late (after midnight) and continues until well after sunrise. Gawk at models, stars, and beach bunnies while eating at one of Ocean Drive's open cafes or bars, then head down to **Washington Avenue**, between 6th and 18th St., for some serious fun. Miami Beach's club scene is transient; what's there one week may not be there the next. Clubs themselves change character depending on the night, so check beforehand or you may be in for a surprise. Many clubs don't demand covers until after midnight, and often the $20+ door charge includes an open bar. However, even a willingness to pay a steep cover is no guarantee of admission. Difficult doormen can prove impossible after 1am, so it is to your advantage to show up early. Stunningly beautiful or scantily clad women generally have the easiest time. Most clubs have dress codes and everyone dresses to the nines, even on so-called "casual" nights. If discos aren't your thing, check out one of the frat-boy party bars along the beach.

◼ **Mansion,** 1235 Washington Ave. (☎532-1525; www.mansionmiami.com). An assault on all the senses, the richly decorated Mansion sets the standard among SoBe clubs. The VIP section is littered with celebrities sipping Cristal. By midnight lines are around the corner, so arrive early. 21+. Cover around $20. Open Tu-Su 11pm-5am.

Crobar, 1445 Washington Ave. (☎531-8225). No longer the clear winner among Washington Ave.'s super-clubs, Crobar is still no slouch. The packed dance floor oozes with trendiness. 21+. Cover around $20-25. Open M and Th-Su 10pm-5am.

Mango's Tropical Cafe, 900 Ocean Dr. (☎673-4422). The noise you hear while walking up Ocean Dr. is coming from here. Order a "Surfer on Acid" (Jagermeister, peach schnapps, and pineapple juice) and stay for a set of live music, concluded with a bartop dance by waitresses and waiters. The atmosphere here is party, be it 2pm or 2am. No cover during the day, $10-20 at night. Open daily 11am-5am.

Privé, 136 Collins Ave. (☎531-5535). SoBe's best hip-hop party. If you forgot your white linen Armani suit, you'll have a bit more luck at the door here than at some of the other clubs. The Betty Ford party on Th is legendary. Cover $20. Open 10pm-5am.

B.E.D., 929 Washington Ave. (☎532-9070). The acronym stands for Beverage, Entertainment, and Dining, but yes, they do have beds. Patrons lounge on the king-sized variety as they enjoy dinner, drinks, and the atmosphere of silky seduction that oozes from every corner of this SoBe favorite. No cover. Open W-Sa 8pm-5am.

GLBT NIGHTLIFE

South Beach's vibrant gay scene takes to the street at night in search of the new "it club." Gay and mixed clubs in the area have bragging rights as the most trendy, amorphous hot spots, attracting a large crowd of both gay and straight partiers.

Twist, 1057 Washington Ave. (☎538-9478). A popular club with an outdoor lounge, dance floor, and 7 bars. Happy hour 1-9pm. 21+. Cover varies. Open daily 1pm-5am.

Laundry Bar, 721 N. Lincoln Ln. (☎531-7700). Men and women alike flock to the unusual Laundry Bar, where the chic and friendly clientele sips cocktails to the beat of DJ-spun house music and the hum of real laundry machines. A great place for an early drink before dinner or clubbing. 21+ starting at 10pm. No cover. Open 7am-5am.

Score, 727 Lincoln Rd. Mall (☎535-1111). Plenty of style and attitude. Men frequent this multi-bar hot spot with a packed dance floor. Tu is the night to be here. 21+. Cover Tu and F-Sa $5-10. Open daily M-Sa 3pm-5am, Su 3pm-2am.

EVERGLADES NATIONAL PARK ☎ 305/239

Encompassing the entire tip of Florida and spearing into Florida Bay, Everglades National Park spans 1.5 million acres, making it the second-largest national park and of one of the world's most unique and fragile ecosystems. Vast prairies of sawgrass range through broad expanses of shallow water, creating the famed "river of grass," while tangled mazes of mangrove swamps wind up the western coast. To the south, delicate coral reefs lie below the shimmering blue waters of the bay. A host of species, many of which can be found nowhere else in the world, inhabits these lands and waters: American alligators, dolphins, and sea turtles, as well as the endangered Florida panther, Florida manatee, and American crocodile. Unfortunately, the mosquito is the most prevalent Everglades species.

AT A GLANCE

AREA: 1,508,508 acres.

CLIMATE: Subtropical grassland.

HIGHLIGHTS: Be terrified by the denizens of the Everglades Alligator Farm, be amazed by the flora and fauna of Anhinga Trail, and sleep it off at the spectacular Everglades International Hostel.

CAMPING: Reservations can be made in person, at least 1 day in advance, at the Flamingo or Gulf Coast visitors centers. $14. $10 permit plus $2 per person for backcountry camping; free in summer.

FEES: $10 per car, $5 per pedestrian or bike, good for 7 days.

ORIENTATION AND PRACTICAL INFORMATION

The **Ernest Coe Visitors Center,** 40001 Rte. 9366, is at the park's main entrance, just inside the eastern edge of the Everglades. (☎242-7700; www.nps.gov/ever. Open daily 9am-5pm. Hours may be reduced June-Sept.; call ahead.) Rte. 9366 cuts 40 mi. through the park to the **Flamingo Visitors Center** (☎239-695-2945; open daily mid-Nov. to Apr. 8am-5pm; hours vary in summer.) At the northern end of the park off U.S. 41, the **Shark Valley Visitors Center** has access to a 15 mi. loop through a swamp by foot, bike, or tram. Shark Valley is an ideal site for those who want a taste of the freshwater ecosystem but aren't inclined to venture too deep into the park. (☎221-8776. Open daily 9am-5pm.) The **Gulf Coast Visitors Center,** 815 Copeland Ave. S, in Everglades City in the northwestern end of the park, provides access to the western coastline and the vast river network throughout the park. (☎239-695-3311. Open daily Nov.-Apr. 8am-4:30pm, May-Sept. 9am-4:30pm.) The **entrance fee** is $10 per car, $5 per pedestrian or bike at the Ernest Coe and Shark Valley entrances. Your receipt gets you into the park for the next seven days. The Gulf Coast entrance is free. For info on lodgings, check out the **Tropical Everglades Visitors Association,** on U.S. 1 in Florida City. (☎245-9180 or 800-388-9669; www.tropicaleverglades.com. Open M-Sa 9am-5pm, Su 10am-2pm.) **Emergency: Park Headquarters,** ☎247-7272. **Area Codes:** 305 and 239; in text, 305 unless otherwise specified.

ACCOMMODATIONS AND FOOD

Outside the eastern entrance to the park, **Florida City** offers cheap motels along U.S. 1, but the ◪**Everglades International Hostel (HI) ❶,** 20 SW 2nd Ave., off Rte. 9336 (Palm Dr.), is a far better option. After venturing into the Everglades on one of the guided tours ($50), hang out with fellow travelers in the hostel's gazebo, gardens, or kitchen, which has a big-screen TV and free video collection. This amazing hostel is also a fantastic base for daytrips to the Keys. (☎248-1122 or 800-372-3874; www.evergladeshostel.com. Free Internet access. Laundry $1. Linen $2. Bike rental $10. Canoe rental $20. Dorms $17, with A/C $18; members $13/$14. Private rooms $36/$38, members $33/$35. MC/V.) The only option for lodging inside the park, **Flamingo Lodge ❸**, 1 Flamingo Lodge Hwy., has large rooms with A/C, TV, and a great view of Florida Bay. Two-room cottages with full kitchens are also available. (☎239-695-3101 or 800-600-3813; www.flamingolodge.com. Reservations recommended. Mid-Dec. to Mar. rooms $95, cottages $135; May-Oct. $65/$89; Apr. and Nov. to mid-Dec. $79/$99. AmEx/D/DC/MC/V.) In the park, both **Long Pine** and **Flamingo Campgrounds ❶** offer developed camping. Flamingo is a sun-bleached campground offering beautiful vistas of the bay, while Long Pine provides a bit more shade. (☎800-365-2267. Reservations required Nov.-Apr. Sites in winter $14; in summer free.) There are dozens of **backcountry camping ❶** options in the park, though many are accessible only by boat (see **boating**, p. 474). Required **permits** are available on a first come, first served basis at the Flamingo and Gulf Coast visitors centers. (Applications can be made in person up to 24hr. in advance. Permit Dec.-Apr. $10 plus $2 per person, good for 14 days; mid-Apr. to mid-Nov. free.)

Across the street from the hostel, **Rosita's ❶**, 199 Palm Dr., has fabulous Mexican food. *Huevos rancheros* ($4.75) can get you ready for a long day of exploring the park. Come back to relax with *chiles rellenos* or enchiladas. (☎246-3114. Open daily 8:30am-9pm. AmEx/MC/V.) The pinnacle of Homestead eateries, the vegan-friendly **Main St. Cafe ❷**, 128 N. Krome Ave., serves great sandwiches and wraps ($7) in a hip coffee bar-style restaurant that doubles as a concert venue on the weekends. (☎245-7575. Open mic Th 8-midnight. Live folk, blues, country, or rock F-Sa 8pm-midnight. Open Tu-W 11am-4pm, Th-Sa 11am-midnight. AmEx/D/DC/MC/V.) Just 3 blocks from the hostel, **Farmers' Market Restaurant ❸**, 300 N. Krome Ave., urges you to enjoy hearty portions of oh-so-fresh produce. (☎242-0008. Breakfast $4.50-9. Lunch $6-11. Dinner $9-15.50. Open daily 5:30am-9pm. MC/V.) **Tippy's ❶**, on U.S. 41 west of the Shark Valley Visitors Center, is a combination grocery store/bait shop that also serves absolutely scrumptious chocolate cake. (☎559-6080. Cake $1.35 per slice. Open daily 8am-11pm. Cash only.)

◤◢ OUTDOOR ACTIVITIES

The park is swamped with fishing, hiking, canoeing, biking, and wildlife-watching opportunities. Forget swimming within the park, though—alligators, sharks, and barracuda patrol the waters. However, if you're hot for some water sports, the nearby Biscayne National Park is there to satisfy (see **Swimming**, p. 474). From November through April, the park sponsors amphitheater programs, canoe trips, and ranger-guided Slough Slogs (swamp tours).

HIKING

The Everglades offers hikes suited for both skilled adventurers and novices who wish to stay within sight of their cars. Even for short hikes, it is advisable to pick up a copy of the *Wilderness Trip Planner*, which provides info on trails and conditions. The wheelchair-accessible **Anhinga Trail** yields a good time with minimal commitment. Those willing to brave the half-mile stroll down the boardwalk are guaranteed up-close encounters with alligators, birds, and turtles. Low water from December to March makes for a higher concentration of wildlife, though the walk is a must any time of year. Take the turnoff for the Royal Palms Visitors Center, 4 mi. inside the park from the main entrance. The **Pa-hay-okee Overlook,** 13 mi. from the main entrance off Rte. 9336, rewards visitors with a stunning view of the park after a quarter-mile boardwalk stroll. For a more difficult trail, try the Long Pine Key (6 mi. from the main entrance), where the **Long Pine Key Trail** ventures through 10 mi. of slash pine forests. Another arduous hike is the **Mahogany Hammock Trail**

(20 mi. from the main entrance, wheelchair accessible). The trail is made up of incredible routes through freshwater prairie and pineland, but mosquitoes have the run of the land in the summer, making it most enjoyable in the winter.

BOATING

To experience the Everglades, start paddling. The 99 mi. **Wilderness Waterway** winds its way from the northwest entrance to the Flamingo station in the south. **Camping ❶** spots include chickees (elevated wooden platforms above swamps), beaches, and groundsites. (Permit required. In winter $10 plus $2 per person; in summer free.) **Everglades National Park Boat Tours,** at the **Gulf Coast Visitors Center,** rents canoes ($25) and is the best option for guided boat tours. The **Ten Thousand Island Cruise** ($21, ages 5-12 $11) is a 1½hr. tour through the Everglades' tiny islands. Expect to see bald eagles, dolphins, and manatees. The **Mangrove Wilderness Cruise** ($35/$17.50) is a 1¼hr. cruise through the inland swamps that brings its you face-to-face with alligators. (☎239-695-2591. Tours 9am; call for schedules.) For those who would rather be on their own, **Hell's Bay Canoe Trail,** about 29 mi. from the entrance, is the premier spot for canoeing. For more information on navigating the park's waterways, consult the rangers at the **Flamingo Visitor Center.**

BIKING

While the Everglades mostly caters to those with walking sticks and canoe paddles, it does boast some excellent biking opportunities. The best route is at the **Shark Valley Visitors Center,** where a 15 mi. loop awaits the adventurous. The trail peaks at an incredible observation tower that offers great views of the park. (Bike rental daily 8:30am-3pm. $5.75 per hr., including helmet.) For the less athletic, tram tours through the Shark Valley area are 2hr. round-trip and are worth the time and money. (Runs daily Dec.-Apr. every hr. 9am-4pm; May-Nov. 9:30, 11am, 1, 3pm. $13.25, under 12 $8. Reservations recommended. Wheelchair accessible.)

SWIMMING

It can be easy to overlook the nearby **Biscayne National Park,** as 95% of it is aquatic. Just 15min. from the Everglades Hostel, Biscayne features amazing diving and snorkeling and remote camping on Boca Chita and Elliott Key, accessible only by boat. (Visitors center: 9700 SW 328th St. ☎230-7275. For info on the snorkel cruise and the Keys ferry, call ☎230-1100.) For a lazy swim in a heavenly (and gator-free) lagoon, stop by the **Homestead Bayfront Park,** south of the Biscayne Visitors Center.

GARDENS AND GATORS

For a truly bizarre experience, head up U.S. 1 to **Coral Castle,** 28655 S. Dixie Hwy., in Homestead. After his fiancée changed her mind the day before the wedding, Latvian immigrant Ed Leedskalnin spent the next 20 years constructing an homage to his lost love. The heartbroken bachelor turned hundreds of tons of dense coral rock into a garden of odd sculptures. (☎248-6345; www.coralcastle.com. Guided tours daily. Open daily 7am-8pm. $9.75, seniors $6.50, ages 7-12 $5. Wheelchair accessible.) View gators, crocs, and snakes at the **Everglades Alligator Farm,** 40351 SW 192 Ave., 4 mi. south of Palm Dr. Though touristy, this is the place to see thousands of gators, from little hatchlings clambering for a bit of sunlight to 18-footers clambering for a bit (or bite) of you. (☎247-2628 or 800-644-9711; www.everglades.com. Open daily 9am-6pm. Feedings at noon and 3pm. Alligator shows free with admission 11am, 2, 5pm. $17, ages 4-11 $10. Wheelchair accessible.)

KEY LARGO   ☎305

Over half a century ago, Hollywood stars Humphrey Bogart and Lauren Bacall immortalized the name "Key Largo" in their hit movie of the same name. Quick-thinking locals of Rock Harbor, where some of the scenes were shot, soon changed the name of their town to Key Largo to attract tourists. It worked—Key Largo is now the gateway to the rest of the enchanting Florida Keys. Though laid-back in attitude, the Keys can be hard on the budget, especially during winter high season. Key Largo can be a bit cheaper than the more westward Keys and is renowned for its natural beauty, coral reefs, and great fishing. Pennekamp State Park was the country's first underwater park, and divers of all abilities flock to the isle for the chance to glimpse at the reef ecosystem and the numerous shipwrecks.

■✚⚡ **ORIENTATION AND PRACTICAL INFORMATION.** The **Overseas Highway (U.S. 1)** bridges the divide between the Keys and the southern tip of Florida, stitching the islands together. Mile markers section the highway and replace street addresses. **Biking** along U.S. 1 is treacherous due to fast cars and narrow shoulders; instead of riding, bring your bike on the bus. Spirits flow freely in the Keys, and drunk driving has recently become a problem—stay alert when on the roads. **Greyhound,** Mi. 99.6 (800-231-2222; www.greyhound.com), runs to Key West (3hr., 3 per day, $28-30) and Miami (1¾hr., 3 per day, $15-17). Most bus drivers will stop at mile markers along the road, though you must do all in your power to catch their attention. Tiny Greyhound signs along the highway indicate bus stops (usually hotels), where you can buy tickets or call the **info line** on the red phones provided. **Taxi: Mom's Taxi,** ☎852-6000. **Visitor Info: Key Largo Chamber of Commerce/Florida Keys Visitors Center,** 106000 U.S. 1, Mi. 106 (☎451-1414 or 800-822-1088; www.key-largo.org. Open daily 9am-6pm.) **Medical Services: Mariners Hospital,** Mi. 91.5 (☎434-4000). **Post Office:** 100100 U.S. 1, Mi. 100. (☎451-3155. Open M-F 8am-4:30pm, Sa 10am-1pm.) **Postal Code:** 33037. **Area Code:** 305.

⚡ **ACCOMMODATIONS.** Ed and Ellen's Lodgings ❸, 103365 U.S. 1, Mi. 103.4 (on Snapper Ave.), has large rooms with cable TV, A/C, and kitchenettes. Ed, the entertaining owner, is helpful with everything from restaurant suggestions to diving and snorkeling reservations. (☎451-9949 or 888-333-5536. Doubles $59-79; low season $49-59; each additional person $10. Rates increase on weekends, holidays, and during lobster season. MC/V.) The waterside **Hungry Pelican ❸,** Mi. 99.5, boasts an explosion of bougainvillea vines, tropical birds in the trees, and cozy rooms with double beds, fridges, and cable TV. (☎451-3576. Free use of paddleboats, canoes, and kayaks. Continental breakfast included. Rooms $60-170; each additional person $10. AmEx/D/MC/V.) The **Bay Cove Motel ❹,** 99446 Overseas Hwy., Mi. 99.5, borders a small beach on the bay side of the island. Rooms have cable TV, A/C, toasters, coffeemakers, microwaves (upon request), and mini-fridges. (☎451-1686. Rooms $75-200, depending on season. MC/V.) The **Sea Trail Motel ❷,** Mi. 98.6, offers an inexpensive (for Key Largo), no-frills place to stay. Rooms are clean and comfortable, and each has a refrigerator, A/C, and cable TV. (☎852-8001. Rooms $45-55. Cash only.) Reservations are strongly recommended for the popular **John Pennekamp Coral Reef State Park Campground ❶** (see **Sights,** p. 476). The 47 sites have water, electricity, picnic tables, and grills, and are well-located, making them worth the effort required to obtain reservations. Most sites (90%) are available for reservation online; the other 10% are set aside for walk-ins on a first come, first served basis. (☎451-1202; www.reserveamerica.com. Bathrooms and showers. No pets allowed. 14-day max. stay. Park open 8am-sunset. Sites $32. AmEx/D/MC/V.)

⚡ **FOOD.** Seafood restaurants of varying price, quality, and specialty litter Overseas Hwy. The neighboring Islamorada boasts one of the best seafood restaurants in all the Keys. The **Islamorada Fish Company ❸,** Mi. 81.5, offers an incredible array of seafood sandwiches ($7-13) and entrees ($17-20), which patrons enjoy under the sunset. For dessert, try the legendary Key Lime Pie. (☎664-9271 or 800-258-2559. Open daily 11am-9pm, sometimes later. AmEx/D/MC/V.) For a scrumptious breakfast, head to **The Hideout Restaurant ❶,** concealed on the ocean side of Mi. 103.5 at the end of Transylvania Ave. Plate-size pancakes (2 for $3) and not-soon-forgotten French toast ($4) make this the affordable meal you can't afford to miss. Stop by this hidden treasure on Friday nights for an all-you-can-eat fish fest—complete with hush puppies, beans, conch fritters, and free Bud Light—for a paltry $10. (☎451-0128. Open daily 7am-2pm, F also 5-9pm. Cash only.) Tucked away on a quiet residential street, **Calypso's ❷,** 1 Seagate Blvd., at Ocean Bay Dr. near Mi. 99.5, offers delectable Buffalo shrimp and dolphin fish sandwiches that each go for $8. (☎451-0600. Open M and W-Th 11:30am-10pm, F-Sa 11:30am-11pm, Su noon-10pm. Cash only.) **Mrs. Mac's Kitchen ❷,** Mi. 99.4 on the bay side, cooks up overwhelming hamburgers ($4.50) and famous steak sandwiches ($5-6) for eager patrons. (☎451-3722. Open M-Sa 7am-9:30pm. AmEx/D/DC/MC/V.)

◪ **SIGHTS.** Key Largo is the self-proclaimed "Dive Capital of the World," and many diving instructors offer their services via highway billboards. The best place to go is **John Pennekamp Coral Reef State Park,** Mi. 102.5. The park extends 3 mi. into the Atlantic Ocean, safeguarding a part of the coral reef that runs the length of the Keys. (☎451-1202; www.pennecamppark.com. Vehicle with 1 occupant $3.50, 2 occupants $6; each additional person $0.50. Pedestrians or bicycles $1.50.) Stop by the park's **visitors center** for free maps, boat and snorkeling tour info, and films on the park. To see the reefs, visitors must bring or rent their own boat, or hop on a charter. (☎451-9570, reservations 451-6325. Open daily 8am-5pm. 18 ft. motor boat $135 per 4hr. Canoes $12 per hr. Deposit required.) **Scuba trips** leave from the dive shop. (☎451-6322. 9:30am and 1:30pm. 2-tank dive $45 per person. Deposit required.) A **snorkeling tour** also allows you to enjoy the underwater quiet. (☎451-6300. 2½hr. total, 1½hr. water time. Tours 9am, noon, 3pm. $29, under 18 $24; equipment $6. Deposit required.) **Glass Bottom Boat Tours** provides a crystal clear view of the reefs without wetting your feet. (☎451-6300. 2½hr. tours 9:15am, 12:15, 3pm. $22, under 12 $15.) Head to any of the local marinas to charter a spot on a **fishing boat.** To avoid paying a commission, hang out on the docks and ask one of the friendly captains yourself. At Mi. 100 on the ocean side, the **Holiday Inn** also runs a plethora of scuba, snorkel, and boat trips. The best-known is the **Key Largo Princess,** which leads 2hr. glass bottom boat tours. (☎451-4655. $25.) Aside from its active dock, the hotel has become a tourist destination, as it houses the **African Queen,** the original boat on which Humphrey Bogart and Katherine Hepburn sailed in the movie of the same title.

KEY WEST   ☎305

The small "last island" of the Florida Keys, Key West has always drawn a cast of colorful characters to its shores, ever since its days of pirates and smugglers. Henry Flagler, Ernest Hemingway, Tennessee Williams, Truman Capote, and Jimmy Buffett have all called the quasi-independent "Conch Republic" home. Today thousands of tourists hop on the Overseas Hwy. to glimpse the past, visit hundreds of bars, and kick back under the sun. The crowd is as diverse as Key West's past: families take a week to splash in the water, twentysomethings come to party and work, and a swinging gay population finds a haven of gay-only clubs and resorts. Key West is as far south as you can get in the continental US. This is the end of the road—enjoy it.

▐ **TRANSPORTATION**

Buses: Greyhound, 3535 S. Roosevelt Blvd. (☎296-9072; www.greyhound.com), at the airport. Open daily 8am-6pm. To **Miami** (4½hr., 3 per day, $35-37.50).

Public Transit: Key West Port and Transit Authority (☎292-8247). 6 routes service Key West. $1, students with ID $0.50.

Taxi: Keys Taxi, ☎296-6666.

Bike Rental: Keys Moped & Scooters, 523 Truman Ave. (☎294-0399). Open daily 9am-6pm. Bikes $8 per day. Single scooter $30 per day, double scooter $55 per day.

☀️🚹 ORIENTATION AND PRACTICAL INFORMATION

Key West lies at the end of **Overseas Highway (U.S. 1)**, 155 mi. southwest of Miami (3-3½hr.). The island is divided into two sections. The eastern part, known as **New Town,** harbors tract houses, chain motels, shopping malls, and the airport. Beautiful old conch houses fill **Old Town,** west of White St. **Duval Street** is the main north-south thoroughfare in Old Town; **U.S. 1 (Truman Avenue)** is a major east-west route. A car is the easiest way to get to Key West, though driving in town is neither easy nor necessary. Do not park overnight on the bridges.

Visitor Info: Key West Welcome Center, 3840 N. Roosevelt Blvd. (☎296-4444 or 800-284-4482), just north of the intersection of U.S. 1 and Roosevelt Blvd., is a private reservation service. Open M-Sa 9am-7:30pm, Su 9am-6pm. **Key West Chamber of Commerce,** 402 Wall St. (☎294-2587 or 800-527-8539; www.keywestchamber.org), in old Mallory Sq. Open M-F 8:30am-6:30pm, Sa-Su 9am-6pm.

GLBT Resources: The Key West Business Guild Gay and Lesbian Information Center, 513 Truman Ave. (☎294-4603). Helps find gay guest houses. Open daily 9am-5pm.

Hotlines: Help Line, ☎296-4357. 24hr.

Internet Access: Sarah Jean's, 500 Truman Ave. #7 (☎294-9118). $10 per hr. Open daily 9am-8pm.

Post Office: 400 Whitehead St. (☎294-9539), west of Duval St. at Eaton St. Open M-F 8:30am-5pm, Sa 9:30am-noon. **Postal Code:** 33040. **Area Code:** 305.

🛏️ ACCOMMODATIONS

Key West is packed year-round, especially from January to March; reserve rooms far in advance. **Pride Week** (www.pridefestkeywest.com), in June, is generally a busy time of the year. In Old Town, the multi-colored 19th-century houses capture the flavor of the Keys. B&Bs dominate, and "reasonably priced" still means over $50. Some of the guest houses in Old Town are exclusively for gay men.

Key West Youth Hostel and Sea Shell Motel, 718 South St. (☎296-5719). The cheapest option in town, with simple rooms and a good location. Dorms $31, members $28; motel rooms $95-115, low season $75-95. MC/V. ❶

Casablanca Hotel, 900-904 Duval St. (☎296-0815), in the center of the main drag. This stately B&B once played host to Humphrey Bogart. Pool, A/C, cable TV. Reserve early during Fantasy Fest. Rooms Dec.-May $125-450; June-Nov. $99-295. AmEx/MC/V. ❺

Caribbean House, 226 Petronia St. (☎296-1600 or 800-543-4518), has festive Caribbean-influenced rooms with A/C, cable TV, fridge, and comfy double beds. Continental breakfast included. Rooms in winter $80-90; in summer $60-70. MC/V. ❸

Boyd's Campground, 6401 Maloney Ave. (☎294-1465), sprawls over 12 oceanside acres and provides modern facilities. Heading south, take a left off U.S. 1 onto Macdonald Ave., which becomes Maloney. 2-person sites in summer $50, water and electricity $65, full hookup $75; in winter $60/$75/$95; each additional person $10. Waterfront sites additional $10-15. MC/V. ❸

🍴 FOOD

Expensive and trendy restaurants line festive **Duval Street.** Side streets offer lower prices and fewer crowds, but many visitors appear to skip the chow and jump straight to the bars.

Blue Heaven, 729 Thomas St. (☎296-8666). Feast upon the town's best cuisine in a lovely outdoor setting. Healthy breakfasts with fresh banana bread ($4-11), Caribbean or Mexican lunches ($7-12), and heavenly dinners ($11.50-34). Open mid-Oct. to Aug. daily 8am-2pm and 6:30-10pm. AmEx/D/MC/V. ❸

El Siboney, 900 Catherine St. (☎296-4184). Breaking with the Key West tradition of overpriced food, this Cuban establishment serves heaping mounds of beans, rice, and meat—all for around $10. Open M-Sa 11am-9:30pm. Cash only. ❷

The Cafe, 509 Southard St. (☎296-5515). Ideal for vegetarians and vegans. Serves up a wide variety of tempting dishes, from Szechuan stir fry ($9.25) to barbecued tofu ($7.75), plus better prices than anywhere else in all of Old Town. Open M-Sa 11am-10pm. MC/V. ❷

👁 SIGHTS

ON LAND. Because of limited parking, traversing Key West by bike or moped is more convenient and comfortable than driving. For those who rather take a tram, the **Conch Tour Train** is a fun but pricey 1½hr. narrated ride through Old Town. *(Leaves from Mallory Sq. ☎294-5161. Runs daily July-Aug. 9am-5:30pm, Sept.-June 9am-4:30pm. $25, ages 4-12 $12.)* **Old Town Trolley** runs a similar narrated tour, but you can get on and off throughout the day at 10 stops. *(☎296-6688. Tours daily 9am-5:30pm. Full tour 1½hr. $25, ages 4-12 $12.)* No one can leave Key West without a visit to the ✪**Ernest Hemingway Home,** where "Papa" wrote *For Whom the Bell Tolls* and *The Snows of Kilimanjaro.* Take a tour with hilarious guides who relate Hemingway and Key West history, then traipse through on your own among 50 descendants of Hemingway's cat, half of which have extra toes. *(907 Whitehead St. ☎294-1136; www.hemingwayhome.com. Open daily 9am-5pm. $11, ages 6-12 $6. Partially wheelchair accessible.)* Tucked into the affluent Truman Annex Gated Community, the **Harry S. Truman Little White House Museum** provides an insightful look into the life of President Truman and his idyllic getaway in Key West. *(111 Front St. ☎294-9911; www.trumanlittlewhitehouse.com. Open daily 9am-5pm, last tour at 4:30pm. $11, children $5; includes tour. Partially wheelchair accessible.)* In addition to its serene garden, the **Audubon House**

shelters fine antiques and a collection of original engravings by naturalist John James Audubon. *(205 Whitehead St. ☎294-2116; www.audubonhouse.com. Open daily 9:30am-4:30pm. $10, seniors $9, students $6.50, ages 6-12 $5. Wheelchair accessible.)*

MARITIME MUSEUMS. The ▓Mel Fisher Maritime Heritage Society Museum brings to life the amazing discovery and salvaging of the Spanish galleon *Atocha*, which sank off the Keys in the 17th century with millions of dollars in gold and silver. The museum also has an entire floor dedicated to the study of the slave trade. *(200 Greene St. ☎294-2633; www.melfisher.org. Open daily 9:30am-5pm. $11, students $9.50, ages 6-12 $6.)* The **Key West Shipwreck Historeum Museum,** located in Mallory Sq., boasts the remains of the *Isaac Allerton*, the 594-ton ship that sank in 1856. Live demonstrations give a glimpse into the lives of classic adventurers by surveying artifacts and the original cargo that the *Allerton* was carrying. The museum's 65 ft. Lookout Tower offers a great view of the island. *(1 Whitehead St. ☎292-8990; www.shipwreckhistoreum.com. $9, ages 4-12 $5. Open daily 9:45am-5pm.)* On Whitehead St. is the 92 ft. **Key West Lighthouse and Museum.** Climb the 88 steps to the top to be rewarded with the best view in town. *(938 Whitehead St. ☎294-0012. Open daily 9:30am-4:30pm. $8, seniors and AAA $7, students $4. Partially wheelchair accessible.)*

ON WATER. The **glass-bottomed boat** *Pride of Key West* cruises to the reefs and back. *(☎296-6293. 2hr. cruises daily noon, 2, 4pm; sunset cruise 6pm. $30, sunset cruise $35; ages 5-12 $15.)* Down Whitehead St., past the Hemingway House, you'll come to the southernmost point in the continental US, at the fittingly named **Southernmost Beach.** A colorful, buoy-like monument marks the spot: "90 miles to Cuba." Beachgoers take part in the daily tradition of watching the sun go down. At the **Mallory Square Dock,** street entertainers and kitsch-hawkers work the crowd, while boats parade in revue during the daily **Sunset Celebration.**

◪ NIGHTLIFE

The free *Island News*, found in local restaurants and bars, lists dining spots, music, and clubs. Nightlife in Key West, centered around upper **Duval Street,** revs up at 11pm and winds down in the wee daylight hours. Key West nightlife reaches its annual high in the third week of October during **Fantasy Fest** (☎296-1817; www.fantasyfest.net), when decadent floats filled with drag queens, pirates, and wild locals take over Duval St.

▓ **The Green Parrot,** 601 Whitehead St. (☎294-6133). Though a little ways from the main drag, this neighborhood hangout has enough of a reputation to have warranted a nod from *Playboy* as Key West's best. Open daily 11am-4am.

Capt. Tony's Saloon, 428 Greene St. (☎294-1838), the oldest bar in Key West and allegedly Tennessee Williams's preferred watering hole, this saloon has been serving since the 1930s. Live music nightly. Open M-Sa 10am-2am, Su noon-2am.

Rick's, 202 Duval St. (☎296-4890). An unabashed meat market, Rick's boasts well-placed body shots and the occasional mullet. Happy hour, with $2 longneck Buds, daily 3-6pm. W-Th all-you-can-drink $10. Open M-Sa 11am-4am, Su noon-4am.

Sloppy Joe's, 201 Duval St. (☎294-5717). For the best party you'll most likely forget, stop by Hemingway's favorite hangout and be blown away by the house specialty, the Hurricane (Bacardi Light, Meyers rum, fruit juices, and a Bacardi 151 float; $7). 21+ after 9pm. Open M-Sa 9am-4am, Su noon-4am.

GLBT NIGHTLIFE

Known for its wild, outspoken gay community, Key West hosts more than a dozen fabulous drag lounges, night clubs, and private bars for the gay man's enjoyment. Most clubs also welcome straight couples and lesbians, but check with the bouncer first before entering. Most gay clubs in town line Duval St., just south of Fleming Ave. Check out *Celebrate!* for extensive coverage of the Key West gay and lesbian community.

Aqua, 711 Duval St. (☎294-0555), has become the hottest drag club in Key West. You're likely to see many wide-eyed tourists checking out the singing beauties, the Aquanettes. Happy hour daily 3-8pm. Open M-Th and Su 3pm-2am, F-Sa 3pm-4am.

KWEST MEN, 705 Duval St. (☎292-8500), is a scandalous dance club where boys in G-strings gyrate on the dance floor. Amateur strip night Sa. 21+. Open daily 4pm-4am.

The Bourbon Street Pub, 724 Duval St. (☎294-9354; www.bourbonstreetpub.com). Lacking the jock-strap-clad waiters common at the other bars, this is a more traditional bar, though antics can still get wild. Drag shows daily 9 and 11pm. Open M-Sa 11am-4am, Su noon-4am. Its sister club, **801 Bourbon,** 801 Duval St. (☎294-9354), is also very popular. Open M-Sa 11am-4am, Su noon-4am.

FORT LAUDERDALE ☎954

During the past two decades, Fort Lauderdale has transformed from a beer-stained spring break mecca to the largest yachting center in North America. City streets and highways may be fine for the commoner's transportation needs, but Fort Lauderdale adds another option: canals. Intricate waterways connect ritzy homes with the intracoastal river and even mere mortals can cruise the canals via the WaterTaxi, an on-the-water bus system. "The Venice of America" also boasts 23 mi. of beach where spring break mayhem still reigns supreme, making Fort "Liquordale" fun even for those who can't afford a yacht.

▐ TRANSPORTATION

Airport: Fort Lauderdale/Hollywood International, 320 Terminal Dr. (☎359-6100; www.broward.org/airport/), 3½ mi. south of downtown on U.S. 1. Or take I-595 E from I-95 to Exit 12B. Buses to and from the airport go through Broward Country Transit Central Terminal (☎367-8400). Take bus #1 to and from the airport.

Trains: Amtrak, 200 SW 21st Terr. (☎587-6692; www.amtrak.com), just west of I-95, ¼ mi. south of Broward Blvd. Take bus #22 from downtown. Open daily 9am-7:15pm. To **Orlando** (4½-6½hr., 2 per day, $28). **Tri-Rail** (☎800-874-7245) connects West Palm Beach, Fort Lauderdale, and Miami. Trains run M-F 4am-10pm, Sa 7am-11pm, Su 7am-9pm. Schedules available at airport, motels, or Tri-Rail stops. $2-10; children, disabled, students, and seniors with Tri-Rail ID 50% discount.

Buses: Greyhound, 515 NE 3rd St. (☎764-6551; www.greyhound.com), 3 blocks north of Broward Blvd. downtown. Be careful in this area, especially at night. Open 24hr. To **Daytona Beach** (7-11hr., 6-7 per day, $35-37.50), **Miami** (1hr., 20 per day, $5.50), and **Orlando** (4½-5½hr., 13 per day, $33-35.50).

Public Transit: Broward County Transit (BCT) (☎357-8400). Central Terminal at NW 1st Ave. and Broward Blvd. downtown. Buses #11 and 36 run north-south on A1A through the beaches. Operates daily 6am-11pm. $1; seniors, under 18, and disabled $0.50. 1-day pass $2.50, 7-day $9, 10-ride pass $8. Schedules available at hotels, libraries, and the central terminal. **City Cruiser** (☎761-3543) loops through downtown and between Sunrise Blvd. and Las Olas Blvd. Runs every 30min. F-Sa 6pm-1am. Free.

Taxi: Yellow Cab, ☎777-7777. **Public Service Taxi,** ☎587-9090.

Bike Rental: Big Wheels Cycles, 5429 N. Federal Hwy. (☎493-5277). Open M-F 10am-7pm, Sa 10am-5pm. A variety of bicycles $20 per day, $50 per week; racing bikes $30/$100. Credit card deposit required.

✈ ORIENTATION

North-south **I-95** connects West Palm Beach, Fort Lauderdale, and Miami. **Rte. 84/ I-75 (Alligator Alley)** slithers 100 mi. west from Fort Lauderdale across the Everglades to Florida's Gulf Coast. Florida's Turnpike runs parallel to I-95. Fort Lauderdale is bigger than it looks, extending westward from its 23 mi. of beach to encompass nearly 450 sq. mi. Streets and boulevards run east-west and avenues run north-south, and all are labeled NW, NE, SW, or SE. The two major roads in Fort Lauderdale are **Broward Boulevard,** running east-west, and **Andrews Avenue,** running north-south. The brick-and-mortar downtown centers around **U.S. 1 (Federal Highway)** and **Las Olas Boulevard,** about 2 mi. west of the oceanfront. Between downtown and the waterfront, yachts fill the ritzy inlets of the **Intracoastal Waterway. The Strip** (a.k.a. Rte. A1A, Fort Lauderdale Beach Blvd., 17th St. Causeway, Ocean Blvd., or Seabreeze Blvd.) runs 4 mi. along the beach between Oakland Park Blvd. to the north and Las Olas Blvd. to the south.

🔃 PRACTICAL INFORMATION

Visitor Info: Greater Fort Lauderdale Convention and Visitors Bureau, 100 E. Broward Blvd. Ste. 200 (☎765-4466, 800-227-8669 for travel directions and hotel info 9am-9pm; www.sunny.org), has the useful *Superior Small Lodgings,* a comprehensive list of low-priced hotels. Open M-F 8:30am-5pm. **Chamber of Commerce,** 512 NE 3rd Ave. (☎462-6000), 5 blocks north of Broward Blvd., just north of 5th St. Open M-F 8am-5pm.

Hotlines: First Call for Help, ☎537-0211. **Sexual Assault and Treatment Center,** ☎761-7273. Both 24hr.

Medical Services: Fort Lauderdale Hospital, 1601 E. Las Olas Blvd., at SE 16th Ave. (☎463-4321).

Internet Access: Broward County Library, 100 S. Andrews Ave. (☎357-7444). Open M-Th 9am-9pm, F-Sa 9am-5pm, Su noon-5:30pm. Free with ID.

Post Office: 1900 W. Oakland Park Blvd. (☎765-5720). Open M-F 7:30am-7pm, Sa 8:30am-2pm. **Postal Code:** 33310. **Area Code:** 954.

🏠 ACCOMMODATIONS

Thank decades of spring breakers for the abundance of beachfront hotels. It's easy to find a room at any time of the year, depending on how much you are willing to pay. Motels north of the strip and a block west of Rte. A1A are the cheapest. High season runs from mid-February to early April and many hotels offer low-season deals for under $50. The **Greater Fort Lauderdale Lodging and Hospitality Association,** 1412 E. Broward Blvd. (☎462-5663), provides a free directory of area hotels. The *Fort Lauderdale News* and the *Miami Herald* occasionally print listings by local residents who rent rooms to tourists in spring.

Fort Lauderdale Beach Hostel, 2115 N. Ocean Blvd./Rte. A1A (☎567-7275), between Sunrise and Oakland Park Blvd. Take bus #11 from the central terminal. Mingle in the tropical courtyard, TV-equipped common room, and well-stocked kitchen. A/C, grill, and local phone calls. Breakfast included. Free lockers. Linen deposit $10. Free Internet access. Call ahead for free daytime pickup. Reservations suggested Dec.-June. Dorms $18; private rooms $43 for one person, $50 for two people. MC/V. ❶

Floyd's Hostel/Crew House, 445 SE 16th St. (☎462-0631). From downtown take bus #1 or 40 and get off at 17th St. Call ahead for free pickup in the Fort Lauderdale area. A homey hostel catering to international travelers and boat crews. Free Internet access, cable TV, lockers, linen, and laundry. Check-in until midnight. Passport or US driver's license required. 4-bed dorms $20, $130 per week; private rooms $40. MC/V. ❶

Bridge II Hostel, 506 SE 16th St. (☎522-6350). From downtown take bus #1 or 40 and get off at 17th St. Across the street from Floyd's and also home to both backpackers and boat crews. Spacious dorms, free Wi-Fi, kitchens, cable TV, free local calls, and pool. Dorms $20-25, $135-140 per week; private rooms $33-35/$150-160. D/MC/V. ●

Tropic-Cay Beach Hotel, 529 N. Ft. Lauderdale Beach Blvd./Rte. A1A (☎564-5900 or 800-463-2333), directly across from the beach; take bus #11 or 44. Right across from the beach. Outdoor patio bar and central pool. Kitchens available. During spring break 18+ with advance reservations and ID. Key deposit $10. Doubles June-Nov. $79-99, Dec.-May $109-139. $10 per extra person. AmEx/D/DC/MC/V. ●

🍴 FOOD

Though clubs along the strip offer massive quantities of free happy hour grub—wieners, chips, and hors d'oeuvres come on surfboard-sized platters—most bars have hefty cover charges (from $5) and drink minimums (from $3).

The Floridian, 1410 E. Las Olas Blvd. (☎463-4041), is a local favorite, serving up heaping portions of french toast ($6), cheeseburgers ($5.75), and veggie burger platters ($7.50). The milkshakes ($4) are to-die-for. Open 24hr. AmEx. ●

Jaxson's, 128 S. Federal Hwy. (☎923-4445), in Dania Beach. Scrumptious scoops of homemade ice cream. Try the Kitchen Sink and see just how much ice cream your stomach can handle ($10 per person). Open M-Th 11:30am-11pm, F-Sa 11:30am-midnight, Su noon-11pm. AmEx/D/MC/V. ●

Argie Grill, 300 SW 1st St. Suite 105 (☎463-2686), offers 19 varieties of *empanadas* like the spinach and portobello ($3.20), in addition to sandwiches, pizza, salads, and burgers. Open M-Th and Su 11am-10pm, F-Sa 11am-4:30am. MC/V. ●

Tokyo Bowl, 1720 S. Federal Hwy. (☎524-8200). Think McDonald's meets sushi, with higher-quality fare. The best deal is the teriyaki chicken bowl ($4), though the all-you-can-eat sushi ($13) is also fantastic. Delivery available. Open M-Th 11am-11:30pm, F 11am-midnight, Sa 11:30am-midnight, Su noon-11:30pm. AmEx/DC/MC/V. ●

👁 SIGHTS

Most visitors flock to Fort Lauderdale to lounge on the sunny beaches. When floating in the crystal-clear waves of the Atlantic, it's easy to forget the city's other notable attractions. Cruising down the palm-lined shore of Beachfront Ave. (Rte. A1A), biking through a nature preserve, or boating through the winding intracoastal canals reveals the less sandy side of Fort Lauderdale.

ON THE BEACH. Spring break lasts 365 days a year on Fort Lauderdale Beach, and after a Corona or two in any of the big bars along Rte. A1A, you'll swear you're in Cancún. If extreme inebriation isn't your thing, have no fear; the beach area offers plenty of booze-free activities. For a family-friendly overview of Fort Lauderdale, take a tour aboard the **Jungle Queen.** The captain's commentary acquaints you with the changing scenery as you cruise up the New River. *(801 Seabreeze Blvd. At the Bahía Mar Yacht Center, on Rte. A1A, 3 blocks south of Las Olas Blvd. ☎462-5596; www.junglequeen.com. 3½-4hr. tours daily 10am, 2, 7pm. $14, ages 2-10 $10; 7pm tour $32/ $17.50, dinner included.)* If you'd like to hit the water in more active style, **Water Sports Unlimited** has water sport rentals and trips. Sail the ocean or enjoy its serene blue water from above on a parasailing trip. Wave runners are also available. *(301 Seabreeze Blvd./Rte. A1A. ☎467-1316. Open daily 9am-5pm. Boat rental $95 for 2hr. Parasailing trips $65.)* For a different kind of high-seas adventure, doggy-paddle over to the **International Swimming Hall of Fame and Museum** for exhibits on the sport and its greatest athletes. *(1 Hall of Fame Dr., 1 block south of Las Olas Blvd. on Rte. A1A. ☎462-*

Fort Lauderdale

♠ ACCOMMODATIONS
Bridge II Hostel, **9**
Floyd's Hostel/Crew House, **8**
Fort Lauderdale Beach
    Hostel, **1**
Tropic-Cay Beach Hotel, **12**
✦ FOOD
Argie Grill , **6**
The Floridian, **7**
Jaxson's, **11**
Tokyo Bowl, **10**

◼ NIGHTLIFE
Dicey O'Riley's Irish Pub, **3**
Elbo Room, **13**
Ramrod, **2**
Tarpon Bend, **4**
The Voodoo Lounge, **5**

6536; www.ishof.org. Open M-F 9am-7pm, Sa-Su 9am-5pm. $3; students, seniors, and military $1. Wheelchair accessible.) Get lost in an oasis of subtropical trees and animals in the middle of urban Fort Lauderdale at **Hugh Taylor Birch State Park.** Bike, jog, canoe, or drive among mangroves and royal palms, or relax in the freshwater lagoon area with herons, gophers, tortoises, and marsh rabbits. (3109 E. Sunrise Blvd., west off Rte. A1A. ☎ 564-4521. Open daily 8am-dusk. $4 per vehicle, $1 per person. Canoes $5.30 per hr.)

IN TOWN. The **Riverwalk** provides a shaded stroll along the banks of the New River, which cuts through downtown. Beginning at U.S. 1, the brick-lined, oak-shaded path meanders along the river, passing numerous sights and enormous mega-yachts. (☎ 468-1541; www.goriverwalk.com.) First along the route is Fort Lauderdale's **Museum of Art,** 1 E. Las Olas Blvd., home to an extensive collection of American painter William Glacken's work and remarkable temporary exhibits, which have included everything from Surrealism to photojournalism. (☎ 525-5500; www.moafl.org. Open daily 11am-7pm, Th until 9pm. $6, seniors $5, students $3. Wheelchair accessible.) The next stop is the **Las Olas Waterfront,** the latest on-the-beach mall, boasting a bevy of clubs, restaurants, and bars. (2 SW 2nd St.) Two hundred yards farther, the Riverwalk cuts through **Old Town,** a district loaded with bars and cheap eateries. The **Water Taxi** offers a relaxing way to beat the rush-hour traffic. The friendly captains will drop you off anywhere along the Intracoastal

FLORIDA

Waterway of New River. Alternatively, ride through the entire route for an intimate viewing of the colossal houses along the canal. *(651 Seabreeze Blvd./Rte. A1A.* ☎*467-6677; www.watertaxi.com. Open 10am-11:30pm. $4, seniors and under 18 $2; 1-day unlimited pass $5, 3-day pass $10.)* A bit farther from downtown are a number of attractions. Anointed by Guinness as the "fastest game in the world," jai alai still remains mostly unknown to Americans outside the state of Florida. Take a break from the beach heat and watch a match at **Dania Jai-Alai,** which sports one of the largest *frontons* (courts) in the state. *(301 E. Dania Beach Blvd. Off U.S. 1, 10min. south of Fort Lauderdale.* ☎*927-2841. Games Tu and Sa noon and 7pm, W-F 7pm, Su 1pm. General admission $1.50.)* Cast your line at the **International Game Fishing Association's Fishing Hall of Fame and Museum,** where a gallery of odd fish, the inside scoop on fishing spots, and an interactive reel exercise amaze even the most determined non-fisherman. Check out the wooden replicas of world-record catches adorning the museum's ceiling and the film *Journeys* in the big-screen theater. *(300 Gulf Stream Way. Off I-95 at Griffin Rd., Exit 23.* ☎*922-4212; www.igfa.org. Open daily 10am-6pm. $6, seniors and ages 3-16 $5. IGFA members free. Wheelchair accessible.)*

◼ NIGHTLIFE

Locals will tell you that the real nightlife action is in **Old Town.** On 2nd St. near the **Riverwalk** district, the 100 yards of Old Town are packed with raucous bars, steamy clubs, cheap eats, and a stylish crowd. More expensive and geared toward spring breakers, the **Strip** houses several popular nightspots across from the beach.

▩ **Tarpon Bend,** 200 SW 2nd St. (☎523-3233). Always the busiest place on the block. Starched shirts from the office converge with flirty black tube tops around the icy beer tubs of "the Bends." Bottled beer $3-4.50. Happy hour daily 4-7pm, F until 9pm. Live music M-Sa. Ladies drink free W until 11pm. Open daily 11:30am-1am.

Dicey O'Riley's Irish Pub, 217 SW 2nd St. (☎522-1908). This establishment has undergone beautiful renovations to its interior, which on F nights is packed. Happy hour pints (domestic $2, imported $3), a free buffet on F afternoons, live music W-Sa 10pm-2am, and cheap, delicious fare (shepherd's pie $8). Open M-F 5pm-4am, Sa-Su 4pm-4am.

Elbo Room, 207 S. Atlantic Blvd. (☎463-4615), on prime real estate at the corner of Rte. A1A and Las Olas Blvd. The booming sidewalk bar, chock full of scantily clad beach beauties, is one of the most visible and packed scenes on the Strip. Live local rock music nightly. Beer from $3. Open M-Th 11am-2am, F-Sa 11am-3am, Su noon-2am.

The Voodoo Lounge, 111 SW 2nd Ave. (☎522-0733). This upscale club offers a more refined approach to fun. Drag shows Su. Ladies night W. T-Dance Su 5-11pm. 21+. Cover F-Sa $10. Open W and F-Sa 10pm-4am, Su 5pm-4am.

Ramrod, 1508 NE 4th Ave. (☎763-8219; www.ramrodbar.com). Gay club with nightly happy hour 3-9pm. Cover varies. Open M-Th and Su 3pm-2am, F-Sa 3pm-3am.

PALM BEACH/WEST PALM BEACH ☎561

Nowhere else in Florida is the line between the "haves" and the "have-nots" as visible as at the intracoastal waterway dividing the aristocratic vacationers of Palm Beach Island from the blue-collar residents of West Palm Beach. Five-star resorts and guarded mansions reign over the "Gold Coast" island, while auto repair shops and fast-food restaurants characterize the mainland. Budget travel may be difficult here, but the region still offers some unique museums and stunning houses.

◼◪ **ORIENTATION AND PRACTICAL INFORMATION.** Palm Beach is approximately 60 mi. north of Miami and 150 mi. southeast of Orlando. **I-95** runs north-south through West Palm Beach, continuing south to Fort Lauderdale and Miami.

The more scenic coastal highway, **A1A,** also travels north-south, crossing Lake Worth at the Flagler Memorial Bridge to Palm Beach. Large highways cut through urban areas and residential neighborhoods; finding your way around can be a bit confusing. Stick to the major roads like north-south **Highway 1** (which turns into S. Dixie Hwy.), A1A, east-west **Palm Beach Lakes Boulevard,** and **Belvedere Road.** The heart of downtown West Palm Beach is **Clematis Street,** across from the Flagler Memorial Bridge, which offers both affordable restaurants and wild nightclubs.

Palm Beach International Airport (☎ 471-7420; www.pbia.org), 1000 Turnage Blvd. at Belvedere and Australian Ave., between Exits 68 and 69 on I-95 N, is 2½ mi. east of downtown West Palm Beach. The Tri-Rail (see below) stops at the airport, as does bus #44 from the downtown West Palm Beach Quadrille station. **Amtrak,** 201 S. Tamarind Ave. (☎ 832-6169; www.amtrak.com; open daily 10:15am-6:15pm), east of I-95 in the downtown West Palm Beach Quadrille runs to Charleston (12hr., 1 per day, $72-94) and Orlando (3½-5½ hr., 2 per day, $23). **Greyhound** leaves from the same station (☎ 833-8534; www.greyhound.com; open daily 7am-11:30pm) for Miami (2hr., 14 per day, $9) and Orlando (4hr., 12 per day, $31-33.50). **Public Transit: Palm Tran,** 3201 Electronics Way, has 32 routes from North Palm Beach Gardens to Boca Raton, with #41 and 42 traveling through the Palm Beach area. The major hub is at the intersection of Quadrille Blvd. and Clematis St. in downtown West Palm Beach. Schedules are available on all buses, at the main office, or at any public library. (☎ 841-4200 or 877-870-9489. $1.25; seniors, under 21, and disabled $0.60; 1-day pass $3/$2.) **Tri-Rail** connects West Palm Beach to Fort Lauderdale and Miami and leaves from the train station on Tamarind. (☎ 800-874-7245. Hours vary by route, generally M-F 4am-10pm, Sa 7am-11pm, Su 7am-9pm. $2-10; students, seniors, and disabled half-price; under 4 free.) **Taxi: Yellow Cab,** ☎ 689-2222. **Visitor Info: Palm Beach County Convention and Visitors Bureau,** 1555 Palm Beach Lakes Blvd. (☎ 471-3995; www.palmbeachfl.com. Open M-F 8:30am-5:30pm.) **Medical Services: Columbia Hospital,** 2201 45th St. (☎ 842-6141). **Hotlines: Center for Information and Crisis Services,** ☎ 383-1111. **Internet Access: Clematis St. News Stand,** 206 Clematis St. (☎ 832-2302. Open M-W and Su 7:30am-10pm, Th-Sa 7:30am-midnight. $4 per ½hr.) **Post Office:** 640 Clematis St., in West Palm Beach. (☎ 833-0929. Open M-F 8:30am-5pm.) **Postal Code:** 33401. **Area Code:** 561.

ⓕ ACCOMMODATIONS. Extravagant resorts and hotels are arguably the most notable attraction lining the Gold Coast. While the idea of mingling with royalty might sound like a fairy tale come true, the words "budget" and "hostel" will only receive blank stares from receptionists. Many reasonably priced B&Bs are booked far in advance; reserve a room long before you arrive. West Palm Beach is the best bet for an affordable room near the action, but the absolute cheapest options are the chain hotels near I-95. **Hotel Biba ❹,** 320 Belvedere Rd., in West Palm Beach, accessible by bus #44, is fun, funky, and eclectic. Rooms are painted in shagadelic tones, and beautiful bodies lounge on the pool deck. Wednesday nights feature deep house music, with a cool scene that burns until 2am. (☎ 832-0094. Continental breakfast included. Rooms mid-Nov. to mid-Apr. $170-200; mid-Apr. to mid-Nov. $109-129. AmEx/DC/MC/V.) Built in 1922 by a former Palm Beach mayor and elegantly restored in 1990, **Hibiscus House Bed & Breakfast ❹,** 501 30th St., in West Palm Beach at the corner of Spruce St. west of Flagler Dr., is affordable without sacrificing luxury. Sleep in one of nine antique-decorated bedrooms and wake up to a two-course gourmet breakfast. Rooms have terraces, TVs, phones, and A/C. (☎ 863-5633 or 800-203-4927. Rooms Dec.-Apr. $100-190; May-Nov. $95-150. AmEx/ D/MC/V.) Perhaps the cheapest option around, **Motel 6 ❸,** 1310 W. Lantana Rd., exit 61 off I-95, has tidy rooms with A/C and cable TV. (☎ 585-5833. Singles $46-50; doubles $52-56; $3 per additional person. AmEx/D/DC/MC/V.)

🄲🄵 FOOD AND NIGHTLIFE. Clematis St. in downtown West Palm Beach offers a lively option for travelers on the cheap, and a Wednesday to Saturday nightlife scene that rivals any college town. Voted "Best Burger" and "People's Choice" in a recent cook-off, **O'Shea's Irish Pub and Restaurant ❷**, 531½ Clematis St., at Rosemary St., will modify any dish to fit vegetarian needs. Locals and those nostalgic for Dublin flock here for the live music W-Sa, usually Irish rock or folk, and for Mrs. O'Shea's $10 savory chicken pie. (☎833-3865. Open M-Tu and Su 11am-10pm, W-Th 11am-midnight, F-Sa 11am-1am. Bar open M-Th and Su until 3am, F-Sa until 4am. AmEx/D/MC/V.) **Sushi Jo ❷**, 319 Belvedere Rd. #12, stays open on Wednesday until 2am when parties wind down. The Bahama Roll (spicy conch with scallions; $8) is for the adventurous. (☎868-7893. Open M-Sa 11:30am-2pm and 5-11pm, W until 2am, Su 5-11pm. AmEx/MC/V.) **Paradise Bar and Grill ❷**, 300 Clematis St., serves Caribbean-influenced dishes like pulled pork ($7) and coconut shrimp ($9). Paradise also boasts over 70 different beers and live music Thursday through Saturday. (☎296-2337. Happy hour M-F 4-7pm. Open M-W and Su 11:30am-11pm, Th-Sa 11:30am-3am. AmEx/D/DC/MC/V.)

Known for exclusive dinner parties and black-tie galas, nightlife on Palm Beach is an invitation-only affair. You won't find a "local bar" anywhere in the ritzy downtown area. You will, however, find **Sprinkles Ice Cream & Sandwich Shop ❶**, 279 Royal Poinciana Way, the best bargain for a hungry stomach. (☎659-1140. Homemade ice cream $3.25. French bread pizza $7. Open M-Th and Su 10am-10pm, F-Sa 10am-11pm. AmEx/D/MC/V.)

🄶 SIGHTS. The prize of blue-collar West Palm Beach is **▦Ragtops,** 2119 S. Dixie Hwy., as fine a collection of Americana as you'll find. It just so happens that all the items have four wheels and some muscle under the hood. Once a Cadillac dealership, the five show floors are now home to over 70 beautiful classic cars, and should you fall in love with one, you need not leave broken-hearted—most of the cars are for sale. (☎655-2836; www.ragtopsmotorcars.com. Open M-Sa 10am-5pm. $5, seniors $4, ages 12 and under $3. Wheelchair accessible.) The **Norton Museum of Art,** 1451 S. Olive Ave., is well known for its well-chosen collection of European, American, contemporary, and Chinese art. Stop by the central garden, which features its own fountain of youth. (☎832-5196; www.norton.org. Open May-Sept. Tu-Sa 10am-5pm, Su 1-5pm; Nov.-Apr. M-Sa 10am-5pm, Su 1-5pm. $8, ages 13-21 $3, under 13 free. Tours daily 2-3pm; lectures Nov.-Apr. M-F 12:30-1pm. Free. Wheelchair accessible.)

In early spring, catch the training seasons of the **Florida Marlins** and **St. Louis Cardinals** at **Roger Dean Stadium,** 4751 Main St. in Jupiter, 14 mi. north of West Palm Beach. (☎775-1818. Call for schedules.) In Palm Beach, walking around can be one of the most enjoyable (and affordable) activities. Known as the "Rodeo Drive of the South," **Worth Avenue,** between S. Ocean Blvd. and Cocoanut Row, outfits Palm Beach's rich and famous in the threads of fashion heavyweights. Walk or drive along **Ocean Boulevard** to gawk at the spectacular, enormous mansions owned by celebrities and millionaires. One particularly remarkable complex is **The Breakers,** 1 S. County Rd., a sizable Italian Renaissance resort. Even if you can't afford the bare-minimum $285 price tag for a night of luxury, you can still live vicariously and stroll the grounds of the resort or take a guided tour. (☎655-6611 or 888-273-2537. Tour W 2pm. $15 for non-guests.) Of course, a trip to Palm Beach County is incomplete without relaxing on one of its picturesque beaches. Although you'll see few residents swimming (they all go to country clubs or their own private beaches), the sand is beautiful and the water serene. Good options on Palm Beach include the popular **Mid-town Beach,** 400 S. Ocean Blvd., and **Phipps Ocean Park,** 2145 S. Ocean Blvd. (☎585-9203).

FLORIDA

NORTH FLORIDA

PANAMA CITY BEACH   ☎ 850

Panama City Beach, a 27 mi. strip along the Gulf of Mexico, is the place for everything touristy, beachy, and kitschy. Regardless of whether you're in college, the
"PCB" experience is the essence of spring break. There is no pretense or high culture here—just miles of parties and loud, thumping bass.

⚑ PRACTICAL INFORMATION. After crossing Hathaway Bridge from the east,
Thomas Drive and **Front Beach Road** (marked as Alt. U.S. 98) fork off from U.S. 98
and run along the gulf. This becomes the **"Miracle Strip,"** the main drag of PCB.
Though there is no ticket office, **Greyhound,** 917 Harrison Ave. (☎785-6111;
www.greyhound.com), stops at the junction of U.S. 98 and 79 and rolls on toward
Atlanta (8-10hr., 4 per day, $49-52) and Orlando (8-11hr., 6 per day, $65-70). **Bay
Town Trolley,** 1021 Massalina Dr., shuttles along the beach. (☎769-0557. M-F 6am-
5:30pm. $1, students and seniors $0.50. Transfers $0.25. Day pass $3.) **Panama City
Beach Convention and Visitors Bureau,** 17001 Panama City Beach Pkwy., has info and
a free **Internet** kiosk. (☎233-6503 or 800-722-3224; www.thebeachloversbeach.com.
Open daily 8am-5pm.) **Post Office:** 420 Churchwell Dr. (☎236-0589. Open M-F
8:30am-5pm, Sa 9am-12:30pm.) **Postal Code:** 32407. **Area Code:** 850.

⚐ ACCOMMODATIONS. Depending on the time of year, lodging rates range
from outrageous to extremely outrageous. Your best bet is to camp on the beach at
◪**Saint Andrews State Recreation Area ❶,** 4607 State Park Ln., at the east end of Thomas Dr. All 176 sites are near the water, with full hookups and showers, bathrooms, and laundry facilities. Be sure to ask for the passcode to the front gate if
you plan on getting back to your campsite after the gate locks at 8pm. (☎233-5140,
reservations 800-326-3521. Reserve far in advance. Sites with hookup for up to 8
people and 2 cars $24. AmEx/D/MC/V.) **Sugar Sands ❸,** 20723 Front Beach Rd., at
the west end of the strip, has well-appointed rooms with kitchenettes in a resort-
like atmosphere with a pool, hot tub, and deck directly on the beach. (☎234-8802
or 800-367-9921; www.sugarsands.com. 4-person rooms in spring and summer $85-
150, in fall and winter $45-90. Min. stays during high season; call ahead for details.
Aug. 8-Sept. 1 35% off; Apr. 4-May 22 25% off. AmEx/D/MC/V.) **The Plaza Motel ❸,**
12830 Front Beach Road, in the middle of the strip, has standard rooms, a pool,
and is across the street from the beach. (☎233-0028. High-season singles M-Th and
Su $66, F-Sa $77; doubles $88/$99. Call for low-season rates. AmEx/D/MC/V.)

◖◗ FOOD AND NIGHTLIFE. Buffets stuff the Strip and Thomas Dr. "Early
bird" specials (usually 4-6pm) get you the same food at about half the price.
Scampy's ❸, 4933 Thomas Dr., is a notable exception to the strip's often low-qual-
ity food, offering delicious seafood in a smaller, less harried atmosphere than the
mega-troughs. (☎235-4209. Lunch specials $4-8. Dinner entrees $11-20. Open M-Th
and Su 11am-10pm, F-Sa 11am-11pm. AmEx/D/MC/V.) A refreshing alternative to
options along the beach, **Andy's Flour Power Bakery and Cafe ❷,** 3123 Thomas Ave.,
has fresh-baked pastries, omelets, and deli sandwiches. (☎230-0014. Sandwiches
$7-8. Open M-Sa 7am-2pm. AmEx/D/MC/V.) At night, many of the restaurants on
the Strip turn into bars and clubs, and most have live bands. Cool off at **Sharky's ❷,**
15201 Front Beach Rd., with a Hurricane or a Sharkbite specialty drink ($6.50).
More adventurous spirits will savor the signature "shark bites" (fried shark cubes;
$7). Live music on the beach deck most nights tends toward country and 80s.

FLORIDA

(☎235-2420. Entrees $15-21. Sandwiches $10-11. Kitchen open daily 11:30am-11pm; club open until 2am. AmEx/D/MC/V.) The back patio at **Harpoon Harry's,** 12627 Front Beach Rd., overlooks the beach. (☎234-6060. Frozen drinks $8. Lunch $6-8. Open daily 11am-2am. AmEx/D/MC/V.) The largest club in the US (capacity 8000), **Club LaVela,** 8813 Thomas Dr., has eight clubs and 48 bar stations under one roof. Live bands play every night. Wet t-shirt, bikini, and male hardbody contests fill the weekends and every night during Spring Break. (☎234-3866. 18+. Cover $5-10 weekdays, $10-15 weekends. Open daily 10am-4am. AmEx/D/MC/V.)

■ **SIGHTS.** Over 1000 acres of gators, nature trails, and the cleanest and most secluded beaches in the city make up the **Saint Andrews State Recreation Area.** (Open daily 8am-8pm. $4 per car; free if you're camping in the park.) The park also runs a catamaran boat shuttle to **Shell Island,** a state-run nature preserve with kayak and snorkel rentals. Shuttles leave from the park at the east end of Thomas Dr. (☎233-0504; www.shellislandshuttle.com. Shuttles daily every 30min. 9am-5pm. $11.50 round-trip, children $5.50; snorkel and ferry packages $19/$13.) **The Glass Bottom Boat** takes visitors on a dolphin-watching excursion and sails to Shell Island from **Treasure Island Marina,** 3605 Thomas Dr. (☎234-8944. 3hr. trips M-F 9am, 1, 4:30pm; Sa 1, 4:30pm; Su 4:30pm. Reservations required. $18, seniors $17, under 12 $11.) For the Glass Bottom Boat and the Shell Island rentals, look for the $3 coupon available at the visitors center. The **Sea Dragon,** 5325 N. Lagoon Rd., takes swashbucklers on Pirate Cruises. (☎234-7400. 2hr. cruises; call for times. $17, seniors $15, ages 3-14 $15, under 2 $5. AmEx/D/MC/V.) **Gulf World Marine Park,** 15412 Front Beach Rd., has shows that feature dolphins, sea lions, and parrots, as well as exhibits on coastal creatures. Take it a step further and swim with dolphins or learn how to be a trainer. (☎234-5271; www.gulfworldmarinepark.com. Open daily 9am-7:30pm, last admission 4:30pm. $22, ages 5-11 $15.50.)

PENSACOLA   ☎850

A military population and conservative reputation have characterized Pensacola since before the Civil War, when three forts on the shores of Pensacola guarded its ports. Though one of the forts, Fort Pickens, remains, most visitors are drawn to the **Gulf Island National Seashore's** sugar-white beaches and secluded, emerald waters. The **National Museum of US Naval Aviation** in the Naval Air Station at Exit 2 off I-10, is the home of the Blue Angels US Air Force Display Team and has over 130 planes, a flight simulator ride, and an IMAX theater. (☎452-3604. 5 mi. southwest from downtown. Open daily 9am-5pm. 1½hr. tours daily 9:30, 11am, 1, 2:30pm. Films 9am-4pm. Admission free; flight simulator $4.50; films $6. AmEx/D/MC/V.) At the **Naval Live Oaks Area,** 1801 Gulf Breeze Pkwy., paths meander through a forest that John Quincy Adams established as the US's first and only naval tree reservation. (☎934-2600. Open daily 8am-5:30pm. Free.) The Pensacola Beach Bridge leads to **Santa Rosa Island** for some of the best beaches ($1 toll); the island's coast feels cleaner, gets more waves, and is less crowded than the inland beaches. ■**Fort Pickens,** where Apache leader Geronimo was imprisoned in the late 1800s, commands the western part of Santa Rosa. Visitors can explore the ruins and sunbathe on the secluded seashore. (☎934-2600. The fort was hit hard by a hurricane in 2004 but is set to reopen in 2006. Call for info.)

Pensacola experienced extensive hurricane damage in 2004, when many of the inexpensive hotels on the beach were damaged or destroyed. **Paradise Inn ❹,** 21 Via De Luna, offers rooms and villas with a private beach, pool, and cable TV. (☎800-301-5925; www.paradiseinn-pb.com. High-season rooms $125-300; low season $70.) Cheaper options lie north of downtown at the exits of I-10 and I-110, a 15min. drive from the beach. Clean and well-furnished, the **Harbor Inn ❷,** 200 N.

Palafox St., is close to downtown and budget-friendly. (☎432-3441. Continental breakfast, A/C, TV. Key deposit $5. Singles M-Th and Su $40, F-Sa $50; doubles $50/ $60.) Also near downtown, ⚑Jerry's ❶, 2815 E. Cervantes, has been serving fabulous diner fare since 1939. (☎433-9910. Burgers $1.75. Sandwiches $2-4.50. Pitchers of beer $5. Open M-F 10am-10pm, Sa 7am-10pm. Cash only.) Tre Fratelli ❸, 304 Alcaniz St., a Sicilian restaurant and pizzeria, makes fantastic pasta sauces. (☎438-3663. Pasta $9-15. Pizza $10-18. Open M-Sa 11am-3pm and 5-10pm. AmEx/D/MC/ V.) All are welcome at the End of the Line Coffee Shop, 610 E. Wright St., which serves fair trade coffee ($1.50) and a mean slice of quiche ($6). It also doubles as an Internet cafe ($0.10 per min.) and features punk music and poetry readings; call for details. (☎429-0336. Open M-Sa 11am-10pm, Su 11am-8pm.) Captain Fun, 235 East Garden St., is a standard sports bar populated with pool enthusiasts and college students. (☎439-6404. 21+. DJs most nights. Open M-Sa 3pm-3am. MC/V.)

The city itself lies next to Pensacola Bay. Palafox Street, which becomes one-way near the bay, and I-110 are the main north-south roads. The Pensacola Beach Road leads to Santa Rosa Island and Pensacola Beach, while Gulf Breeze Parkway trails along the coast. Amtrak, 980 E. Heinburg St. (☎433-4966 or 800-872-7245; www.amtrak.com; open M-F 12am-8pm), runs to New Orleans (7hr., 3 per week, $30-65) and Orlando (13hr., 3 per week, $50-108). Greyhound, 505 W. Burgess Rd. (☎476-4800; www.greyhound.com; open daily 4:15am-11pm), goes to Atlanta (8-12hr., 4 per day, $51), New Orleans (4-7hr., 4 per day, $44), and Orlando (10-11hr., 5 per day, $63). In summer, two free Tiki Trolley shuttles run along the beach. (☎932-1500. F 6pm-midnight, Sa noon-midnight.) Pensacola Convention and Visitors Bureau, 1401 E. Gregory St., has coupons for expensive lodgings. (☎800-874-1234; www.visitpensacola.com. Open M-F 8am-5pm, Sa 9am-4pm, Su 11am-4pm.) Post Office: 101 S. Palafox St. (☎439-0169. Open M-F 8:30am-5pm.) Postal Code: 32501. Area Code: 850.

FLORIDA

GREAT LAKES

Though the region's alternative name—the Midwest—evokes a bland image of cornfields and small-town, white-picket-fence America, the states that hug the five Great Lakes encompass a variety of personalities. The world's largest freshwater lake, Lake Superior, and its unpopulated, scenic coast cradle some of the most stunning natural features in the region—from the dense forests in northern Wisconsin to the waterfalls of the Upper Peninsula in Michigan. Meanwhile, the Lake Michigan coast hosts sand dunes, swimming, sailing, and deep-water fishing. Minneapolis and St. Paul form a bona fide coastal metropolis, while Chicago dazzles with a stunning skyline, incredible culinary offerings, and world-class museums.

HIGHLIGHTS OF THE GREAT LAKES

DEVOUR deep-dish **pizza** in Chicago (p. 534), traditional **pasties** in Michigan's Upper Peninsula (p. 525), and the feast-like results of a Door County **fish boil** (p. 561).

SIMPLIFY your life among the Amish in Ohio's **Hardin County** (p. 498).

GROOVE to the music at the **Motown Historical Museum** (p. 512) and the **Rock and Roll Hall of Fame** (p. 494).

DON your stovepipe hat and iconic facial hair for the brand-new **Abraham Lincoln Presidential Library and Museum** (p. 548).

PRESS your nose against the glass of the fish tanks and watch penguins pummel each other at the **Shedd Aquarium** (p. 544).

OHIO

America's eyes were trained on Ohio on Nov. 2 2004, as George W. Bush squeaked past John Kerry to pick up the state's 20 electoral votes and a second term in the White House. Ohio's inscrutable political climate reflects the diversity of the state's population; unionized machinists in Cleveland, farmers in the western plains, and coal miners on the Allegheny Plateau will not always see eye to eye. Even so, Midwestern friendliness and a practical view of the world make natives of Ohio the perfect candidates to welcome visitors into the Great Lakes region.

🛈 PRACTICAL INFORMATION

Capital: Columbus.

Visitor Info: State Office of Travel and Tourism, 77 S. High St., 29th fl., Columbus 43215 (☎614-466-8844; www.ohiotourism.com). Open M-F 8am-5pm. **Ohio Tourism Line,** ☎800-282-5393.

Postal Abbreviation: OH. **Sales Tax:** 6%.

CLEVELAND   ☎216

Ohio Congressman Louis Stokes once observed that "the Cuyahoga will live in infamy as the only river that was ever declared a fire hazard." The industrial ooze that once lapped up on the shores of Cleveland is now gone, and Cleveland has

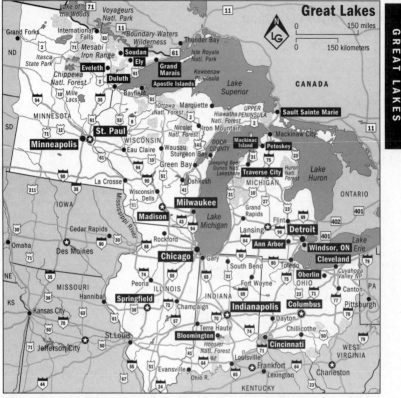

Great Lakes

made valiant efforts to spruce up its civic center. Yet, the city is still struggling to reinvent itself. Hip coffee shops and music venues abound on the eastern and western edges of Cleveland, and residents are hopeful that these enclaves will become increasingly integrated with the museums and playhouses downtown.

⌐ TRANSPORTATION

Airport: Cleveland Hopkins International (☎265-6030; www.clevelandairport.com), 13 mi. southwest of downtown. RTA line #66X "Red Line" to Terminal Tower. Taking a taxi downtown takes roughly 22min. and costs $20.

Trains: Amtrak, 200 Cleveland Memorial Shoreway (☎696-5115; www.amtrak.com), across from the Browns Stadium. Open daily 9:30pm-1pm. To **Chicago** (7hr., 2 per day, $41-64) and **Pittsburgh** (3½hr., 1 per day, $19-30).

Buses: Greyhound, 1465 Chester Ave. (☎781-0520; www.greyhound.com), at E. 14th St., 7 blocks from Terminal Tower. Open 24hr. To: **Chicago** (7-8hr., 6 per day, $39-44); **Cincinnati** (5hr., 8 per day, $29-35); **Columbus** (2½hr., 8 per day, $19); **New York City** (9-14hr., 8 per day, $49-62); **Pittsburgh** (2½-4hr., 8 per day, $23).

Public Transit: Regional Transit Authority (RTA), 1240 W. 6th St. (☎621-9500; www.rideRTA.com). Open M-F 7am-6pm. Bus lines, connecting with Rapid Transit trains, travel from downtown to most of the metropolitan area. Service daily 5am-midnight; call for info on "owl" service (after midnight). Train $1.50. Bus $1.25, express $1.50, down-

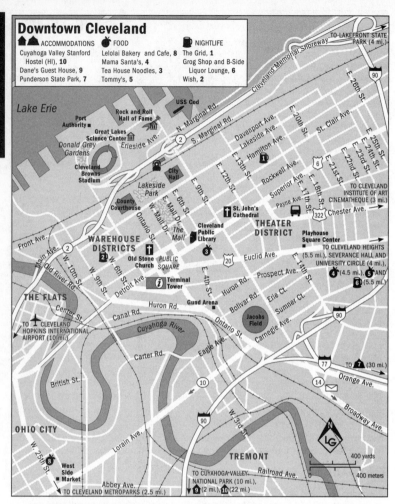

Downtown Cleveland

▲▲ ACCOMMODATIONS
Cuyahoga Valley Stanford
   Hostel (HI), **10**
Dane's Guest House, **9**
Punderson State Park, **7**

🍺 FOOD
Lelolai Bakery and Cafe, **8**
Mama Santa's, **4**
Tea House Noodles, **3**
Tommy's, **5**

🌙 NIGHTLIFE
The Grid, **1**
Grog Shop and B-Side
   Liquor Lounge, **6**
Wish, **2**

town loop $0.75. 1-day pass $3, seniors and children $1. Travelers can park for free at one of the many park-and-rides and take the train to Terminal Square for $1.50. The **Waterfront Line** runs along the Lake Erie waterfront and serves the Science Center and Rock and Roll Hall of Fame.

   Taxi: Ace Cab, ☎ 361-4700. **Americab,** ☎ 881-1111.

⚡🛈 ORIENTATION AND PRACTICAL INFORMATION

Terminal Tower, in **Public Square,** at the intersection of Detroit Ave. and Ontario St., forms the center of downtown and splits the city into east and west. Many street numbers correspond to the distance of the street from Terminal Tower; e.g., E. 18th St. is 18 blocks east of the Tower. To reach Public Sq. from **I-90** or **I-71,** take the Ontario St./Broadway exit. From **I-77,** take the 9th St. exit to Euclid Ave., which runs into Public Sq. The residential stretch of the East Side between 30th and 80th should be avoided, even during the daytime, and travelers should be cautious downtown at night. **Coventry Road,** in Cleveland Heights, and Ohio City, to the southwest, are the happening spots for food and nightlife.

Visitor Info: Cleveland Convention and Visitors Bureau, 50 Public Sq. (☎621-7981; www.travelcleveland.com), on the ground floor of Terminal Tower. Open M-F 9:30am-4:30pm, Sa-Su 11am-4pm.

Hotline: Rape Crisis Line, ☎619-6192. Operates 24hr.

Internet Access: Cleveland Public Library, 525 Superior Ave. (☎623-2800), allows 1hr. slots at its terminals. Open M-Sa 9am-6pm, Su 1-5pm; closed Su in summer.

Post Office: 2400 Orange Ave. (☎443-4494, after 5pm 443-4096.) Open M-F 7am-8pm, Sa 8am-4pm. **Postal Code:** 44101. **Area Code:** 216; 440 or 330 in suburbs. In text, 216 unless otherwise noted.

ACCOMMODATIONS

With hotel taxes (not included in the prices listed below) as high as 14.5%, cheap lodging is hard to find in Cleveland. Those with cars might consider staying in the suburbs or near the airport, where prices tend to be lower. Most accommodations will not rent to those under 21.

Cuyahoga Valley Stanford Hostel (HI), 6093 Stanford Rd. (☎330-467-8711), in Peninsula, 22 mi. south of Cleveland in the Cuyahoga Valley National Park. Housed in a 19th-century farmhouse, this idyllic hostel offers cozy dorms and nightly cricket serenades. Lockout 9am-5pm. Curfew 10pm, but arrangements can be made for later arrivals. Reservations recommended. Dorms $17, under 18 with guardian half price. Cash only. ●

Danes Guest House, 2189 West Blvd. (☎961-9444). Follow I-90 west of downtown to the West Blvd. exit. 2 rooms in a 1920s colonial revival house are a particularly good deal for travelers in groups. Homemade breakfast included. Room with double bed $65, room with queen bed $75, both rooms $110. $10 off for 2+ nights. Cash only. ●

Punderson State Park, 11755 Kinsman Rd. (☎440-564-1195), off Exit 29 on I-271, 45min. east of downtown. Once a vacation spot for wealthy Clevelanders, the park now has 196 campsites and 26 2-bedroom cottages, plus trails and a golf course. Campsites $22, cottages from $120. AmEx/D/MC/V. ●

FOOD

Colorful cafes grace **Coventry Road,** in **Cleveland Heights** between Mayfield Rd. and Euclid Heights Blvd. The sounds of Italian crooners fill the sidewalks of **Little Italy,** around **Mayfield Road.** Over 100 vendors hawk fresh produce, meat, and cheese at the Old-World-style **West Side Market,** 1979 W. 25th St., at Lorain Ave. (☎781-3663; www.westsidemarket.com. Open M and W 7am-4pm, F-Sa 7am-6pm.)

Tommy's, 1824 Coventry Rd. (☎321-7757), in Cleveland Heights. This bright, spacious cafe stays busy throughout the day serving vegetarian fare like falafel ($4.50-7) and a tempeh Reuben ($6.79), although meat-eaters get in on the action with juicy burgers ($3.50-6). Open M-Th 7:30am-10pm, F-Sa 7:30am-11pm, Su 9am-10pm. MC/V. ●

Lelolai Bakery and Cafe, 1889 W. 25th St. (☎771-9956), in Ohio City. Revered for its velvety flan ($2) and sandwiches slathered with garlic mayonnaise ($5.50), this Hispanic bakery also offers buttery breakfast pastries ($1.50) that are perfect with a steaming cup of *café con leche.* Open M-W 8am-5pm, Th-Sa 8am-6pm. D/MC/V. ●

Mamma Santa's, 12305 Mayfield Rd. (☎231-9567), in little Italy, serves fresh pasta (from $6) and pizza (from $5.50) at half the prices of neighboring trattorias. Open M-Th 11am-11pm, F-Sa 11am-11:30pm; closed most of Aug. MC/V. ❷

Tea House Noodles, 1900 E. 6th St. (☎623-9131), downtown, earns rave reviews from the white-collar lunch crowd for its bowls of rice noodles ($6) and fresh-squeezed juices ($2-4). Open M-F 10:30am-3:30pm. AmEx/D/MC/V. ❶

👁 SIGHTS

DOWNTOWN. A spit of land jutting out into Lake Erie became the focal point of downtown revitalization with I.M. Pei's 📷**Rock and Roll Hall of Fame.** The permanent collection traces a chronology of rock music, narrated through artifacts ranging from a Jimi Hendrix guitar to a Madonna bustier. *(1 Key Plaza. ☎781-7625; www.rockhall.com. Open M-Tu and Th-Su 10am-5:30pm, W 10am-9pm; June-Aug. Sa until 9pm. $20, students $18, seniors $14, ages 9-11 $11, under 9 free.)* Next door, the **Great Lakes Science Center** trots out high-tech toys like infrared cameras and a solar car to create interactive exhibits that are fun for all ages. *(601 Erieside Ave. ☎694-2000; www.greatscience.com. Open daily 9:30am-5:30pm. Science Center or OMNIMAX $9, seniors $8, ages 3-17 $7; both $13/$11/$9. Parking for Hall of Fame and Science Center $7.50.)*

THE WILD SIDE. Nearly 20,000 acres of undeveloped land comprise the **Cleveland Metroparks,** perfect for biking, horseback riding, and hiking; the trail along the northern edge of Big Creek Reservation's Lake Isaac is a great place to listen for songbirds. The **Cleveland Metroparks Zoo,** 5 mi. south of Cleveland on I-71 at the Fulton Rd. exit, offers a more manicured look at Mother Nature, from the nation's largest primate collection to the Australian Adventure walk. *(☎661-6500; www.clem-etzoo.com. Open daily 10am-5pm. $9, children 2-11 $4, under 2 free.)*

UNIVERSITY CIRCLE. A compound of museums, parks, and academic buildings forms a kind of second downtown on the eastern edge of Cleveland. Regrettably, the **Cleveland Museum of Art** will close its doors for nine months in January 2006, as it embarks on the first stage of a renovation project. Art-starved visitors will have to wait until October 2006 for the museum's next major exhibition, which will focus on the painters of modernity. *(11150 East Blvd. ☎421-7340; www.clevelandart.org.)* In the meantime, the **Cleveland Museum of Natural History** showcases a menagerie of animals preserved by taxidermists, while live river otters and great horned owls populate the Wildlife Center outside. *(1 Wade Oval Dr. ☎231-4600 or 800-317-9155; www.cmnh.org. Open M-Tu and Th-Sa 10am-5pm, W 10am-10pm, Su noon-5pm. $7; students, seniors, and ages 7-18 $5; ages 3-6 $4.)* The **Cleveland Botanical Garden's** Eleanor Armstrong Smith Glasshouse recreates a Costa Rican cloud forest and the spiny desert of Madagascar, while outdoor herb and rose gardens offer an ideal place to stroll. *(11030 East Blvd. ☎721-1600; www.cbgarden.org. Open Apr.-Oct. M-Sa 10am-5pm, Su noon-5pm; Nov.-Mar. closed M. $7.50, ages 3-12 $3.)* On the far side of the Botanical Garden, Frank Gehry's **Peter B. Lewis Building** houses the Weatherhead School of Management at Case Western Reserve. The undulating, metallic armature of the building echoes Gehry's iconic Guggenheim Museum in Bilbao. *(10900 Euclid Ave. 30min. tours offered Sa-Su 1-3:30pm. Reserve in advance at www.weatherhead.cwru.edu/tour. Free.)*

🎵 📷 ENTERTAINMENT AND NIGHTLIFE

Football reigns supreme in Cleveland, where the **Browns** grind it out on the gridiron at the **Cleveland Browns Stadium,** north of Lakeside Ave. between W. 3rd St. and E. 9th St. (☎241-5555. Tickets from $25.) Baseball's **Indians** round the bases at **Jacobs Field,** 2401 Ontario St. (☎420-4487. Tickets from $10.) The NBA's **Cavaliers** take the court at **Gund Arena,** 1 Center Ct. (☎420-2000. Tickets from $10.)

The **Cleveland Orchestra** can be heard at **Severance Hall,** 11001 Euclid Ave. (☎231-1111; www.clevelandorch.com. Box office open June-Aug. M-F 9am-5pm; Sept.-May M-F 9am-6pm, Sa 10am-6pm. Tickets from $25; $10-15 student tickets available for select performances. Call for info.) **Playhouse Square Center,** on Euclid Ave., 10min. east of Terminal Tower, includes the **Palace, State,** and **Allen Theaters,** as well as two smaller venues. The **State Theater,** 1519 Euclid Ave., hosts the **Cleveland Opera** (☎575-0903; www.clevelandopera.org. Box office open daily 11am-6pm.) The **Cleveland Institute of Art Cinematheque,** 11141 East Blvd., screens classic and foreign films. (☎421-7450; www.cia.edu/cinematheque. Shows W-Su. $8.)

A few pubs and music venues stay open at major hotels downtown. The **Warehouse District** features upscale clubs, while edgier crowds favor nightspots along **Coventry Road** in Cleveland Heights or along **W. 25th Street** in Ohio City. For more info on clubs and concerts, pick up a free copy of *Scene* or the *Free Times.* The *Gay People's Chronicle* and *OUTlines* can be found at libraries and bookstores.

▨ **Grog Shop,** 2785 Euclid Heights Blvd. (☎321-5588; www.grogshop.gs), at Coventry Rd., in Cleveland Heights, is a mainstay of Cleveland's punk, indie rock, and hip-hop scenes. Cover $8-12, under 21 $2 extra. Open daily 9pm-2am. Downstairs, the **B-Side Liquor Lounge** mixes martinis (from $7) for an eclectic crowd splayed on sleek leather couches. Open M-Th and Su 8pm-2:30am, F-Sa 7pm-2:30am.

Wish, 621 Johnson Ct. (☎902-9474), just off W. 6th St. in the Warehouse District. While this shadowy, 3-floor complex has lost some of its gothic edge, it's a still-funky dance club that isn't afraid to work The Smiths into the evening's playlist. No cover. Open Th and Su 10pm-2:30am, F-Sa 9pm-2:30am.

The Grid, 1437 St. Clair Ave. (☎623-0113), attracts a predominantly gay crowd with 3 bars and strategic views of the dance floor. Lesbian night W. Male strippers Th. Cover Sa $7, under 21 $10. Open daily 9pm-2:30am; dance floor open F-Sa until 3:30am.

▨ DAYTRIPS FROM CLEVELAND

CUYAHOGA VALLEY NATIONAL PARK

From Cleveland, take I-77 south to Rockside Rd., take a left after the exit, continue to Canal Rd., and make a right into the park.

Just 10 mi. south of Cleveland lies the northern edge of the scenic **Cuyahoga Valley National Park.** The park's lifeline is the **Cuyahoga River,** which winds 30 mi. through dense forests and open farmland, passing stables, aqueducts, and mills along the way. The best way to see the park is to hike or bike its long trails. The **Ohio & Erie Canal Towpath Trail** runs through shaded forests and past the numerous locks used during the canal's heyday, when it served as a vital link between Cleveland and the Ohio River. The park's **visitors center,** 7104 Canal Rd., has maps and information on the canal. (☎524-1497 or 800-445-9667; www.nps.gov/cuva. Open daily 10am-4pm.)

OBERLIN

From Cleveland, drive 30min. west on I-90 to Exit 140, then follow Rte. 53 for 6mi. into Oberlin's downtown area.

Two young missionaries from the East Coast founded the Oberlin Collegiate Institute in 1833. Their commitment to coeducation and racial integration left its imprint on the small town of Oberlin; three years before the Civil War broke out, local abolitionists swarmed the nearby village of Wellington to rescue a fugitive slave who was being returned to captivity. Progressive politics are still alive and well in Oberlin, as Birkenstocked students from **Oberlin College** pad around South Main St. and dream of a free Tibet. The college's **Conservatory of Music** is one of the best in the nation, and free recitals are open to the public year-round. (☎440-775-8044; www.oberlin.edu/con.) The **Allen Memorial Art Museum,** 87 N. Main St., features a strong collection of 17th-century Dutch and Flemish canvases, although its modern holdings are also vast. (☎440-775-8665; www.oberlin.edu/allenart. Open Tu-Sa 10am-5pm, Su 1-5pm. Free.) Town-gown relations are at their rosiest during the **Big Parade,** held on the first Saturday in May, while mid-June's **Juneteenth** celebration commemorates the signing of the Emancipation Proclamation in 1865. Grilled sandwiches ($4.50-6) and salads ($5-7) are daytime staples at **The Feve ❶,** 30 S. Main St., and the upstairs bar gets lively during the school year with $3 drafts. (☎440-774-1978. Restaurant open June-Aug. M-F 11am-10pm, Sa 10am-10pm, Su 10am-2:30pm; Sept.-May M-F 11am-midnight, Sa-Su 9:30am-midnight. Bar open June-Aug. M-Sa 5pm-1am, Su 9pm-1am; Sept.-May daily 5pm-2:30am. AmEx/MC/V.) **MindFair Books,** 13 W. College St., delights bookworms, and the upstairs annex hosts live jazz and spoken-word on Friday nights during the school year. (☎440-774-6463. Open M-W and Sa 9am-6pm, Th-F 9am-8pm, Su noon-5pm.)

CEDAR POINT AMUSEMENT PARK

Cedar Point, off U.S. 6 in Sandusky, is 65 mi. west of Cleveland. (☎419-627-2350 or 800-237-8386; www.cedarpoint.com. Laser light shows in summer nightly at 10pm. Open daily July to mid-Aug. 10am-11pm; June 10am-10pm; May 10am-8pm; Sept.-Oct. hours vary. Parking $8. $45, ages 3 and older and less than 4 ft. $25.)

Consistently ranked the "best amusement park in the world" by *Amusement Today,* 🏅**Cedar Point Amusement Park,** off U.S. 6, 65 mi. west of Cleveland in Sandusky, earns its superlatives. Many of the world's highest and fastest roller coasters reside here. The towering **Top Thrill Dragster** takes the cake in both categories, launching thrill-seekers 420 ft. before plummeting down at 120 mph, while the brand new **maXair** spins riders until their inner ears beg for mercy.

COLUMBUS   ☎614

Less a single, coherent metropolis than a collection of freeway exits, Columbus pulled past Cleveland in 1990 to take its place as Ohio's most populous city. White-collar workers hit the freeways at 5pm and make for the inner-ring suburbs, while immigrants and young artists keep parts of downtown aglow after dark. Though no one would call mild-mannered Columbus "edgy" and keep a straight face, the capital's museums and galleries are well worth a day or two of exploration.

■🔁 **ORIENTATION AND PRACTICAL INFORMATION.** Columbus is laid out in a simple grid. **High Street,** running north-south, and **Broad Street,** running east-west, are the main thoroughfares, dividing the city into quadrants. Most of the city's activity is centered around **High Street,** which heads north from downtown to the galleries and coffee shops of the **Short North.** It continues up through the campus of **Ohio State University (OSU).** South of downtown, the **German Village** and **Brewery District** recall the Old World with narrow streets and traditional crafts.

    Port Columbus International Airport, 4600 International Gateway (☎239-4000; www.port-columbus.com), is 8 mi. east of downtown. A taxi to downtown is about $18. **Greyhound,** 111 E. Town St. (☎228-2266; www.greyhound.com), offers service to Chicago (7-12hr., 5-7 per day, $39-52), Cincinnati (2-3½hr., 9-11 per day, $17), and Cleveland (2-4½hr., 8 per day, $19). The **Central Ohio Transit Authority (COTA),** 60 E. Broad St., runs local buses until 11pm or midnight, depending on the route. (☎228-1776; www.cota.com. $1.25, express $1.75; transfers $0.10.) **Taxi: Yellow Cab,** ☎444-4444. **Visitor Info: Experience Columbus** maintains an administrative office downtown at 90 N. High St., and a **visitors center** on the 1st floor of the Easton Town Mall, just north of the airport on I-270. (☎221-6623 or 800-345-2657;

www.experiencecolumbus.com. Visitors center open M-Sa 10am-9pm, Su noon-6pm; administrative office open M-F 8am-5pm.) **Internet Access: Columbus Metropolitan Library**, 96 S. Grant St. (☎645-2275. Photo ID required. 1hr. per day. Open M-Th 9am-9pm, F-Sa 9am-6pm, Su 1-5pm.) **Post Office:** 850 Twin Rivers Dr. (☎469-4226. Open M-F 8am-7pm, Sa 8am-2pm.) **Postal Code:** 43216. **Area Code:** 614.

🏠🍴 **ACCOMMODATIONS AND FOOD.** A city ordinance prevents hotels from renting to visitors under age 21. Budget options can be found at almost any exit off I-270. In the summer, **OSU ❷** offers clean dorm rooms near High St.'s bars and restaurants. (☎292-9725. Linens included. Open mid-June to mid-Aug. Singles $25; doubles $40. MC/V.) Northwest of downtown, the **Westerville Inn Bed and Breakfast ❸**, 5 S. West St., maintains three homey rooms in an 1854 cottage. Take I-270 to Exit 27; take Cleveland Ave. north, turn right on W. Main St., then right on West St. (☎882-3910. Rooms $65-105. D/MC/V.) The **German Village Inn ❸**, 920 S. High St., has large rooms with cable TV and A/C. (☎443-6506. Singles M-Th and Su $45, F-Sa $48; doubles $54/$59; each additional person $5. AmEx/D/DC/MC/V.) For great budget eats, don't miss the **North Market,** 59 Spruce St., in the Short North Arts District, which is packed with food vendors selling everything from falafel to chocolate. (☎463-9664. Meals around $5. Open Tu-F 9am-7pm, Sa 8am-5pm, Su noon-5pm.) 🍴**Katzinger's Delicatessen ❸**, 475 S. 3rd St., charges a whopping $11.25 for its incredible half-pound Reuben. But with Black Angus corned beef shipped down from Detroit and Bill Clinton's personal approval, Katzinger's can't be beat for sandwiches ($9-12) or Sunday morning bagels and lox. (☎228-3354. Open M-F 8:30am-8:30pm, Sa-Su 9am-8:30pm. AmEx/MC/V.) Magdiale Wolmark, the chef and owner of **Dragonfly ❹**, 247 King Ave., received one of the Aspen Center's 2005 Platinum Carrot awards for his inspired Asian-influenced vegetarian cuisine. (☎298-9981. Entrees $16-20. Open Tu-Th 5-10pm, F-Sa 5-11pm; Sa brunch 11:30am-3pm. AmEx/D/MC/V.) **Nancy's Home Cooking ❶**, 3133 N. High St., offers diner-style counter service to regulars who swear by the $1 pancakes. (☎265-9012. Open M-Th 6am-2pm and 4-7pm, F 6am-2pm, Sa-Su 6am-noon. Cash only.)

📷 **SIGHTS.** OSU's newly renovated **Wexner Center for the Arts**, 1871 N. High St., now sports a 5-story "permanent scaffold," an aesthetic of unfinished construction that matches its commitment to avant-garde visual art and performance. (☎292-0330; www.wexarts.org. Call for hours. Galleries free. Films $6, students and seniors $4, under 12 $2.) The **Columbus Museum of Art,** 480 E. Broad St., has an unusually strong permanent collection of early modern canvases, from European luminaries like Matisse and Klee to lesser-known Americans like George Bellows. (☎221-6801; www.columbusmuseum.org. Open Tu-W and F-Su 10am-5:30pm, Th 10am-8:30pm. $6; students, seniors, and ages 6-18 $4. Parking $3. Wheelchair accessible.) Down the street in Franklinton, the superb **Center of Science and Industry (COSI),** 333 W. Broad St., is part museum and part theme park, ruffling feathers with giant propellers in the Gadgets exhibit and sending kids out on a high-wire unicycle. (☎228-2674; www.cosi.org. Open W-Sa 10am-5pm, Su noon-6pm. $12, seniors $10, ages 2-12 $7. Extreme Screen movie admission $6. Combo $17/$15/$12. Wheelchair accessible.) Back by the Museum of Art, James Thurber's childhood home, the **Thurber House,** 77 Jefferson Ave., off E. Broad St., is a shrine to the beloved writer-illustrator and a literary center with monthly readings. (☎464-1032. Open daily noon-4pm. Free. Guided tours Su $2.50, students and seniors $2.)

South of downtown, the **German Village** neighborhood appeals to pedestrians with brick streets, slate roofs, and ivy-covered mansions. Rescued from the wrecking-ball version of urban renewal in the 1960s, German Village combines young professionals and families into a community-minded clan of neighbors. The **Ger-**

man Village Society Meeting Haus, 588 S. 3rd St., provides visitors with info and arranges late June's annual *Haus und Garten* tour. (☎221-8888; www.germanvillage.com. Tour $15. Open M-F 9am-4pm, Sa 10am-2pm; shorter hours in winter.)

🎭🎵 **ENTERTAINMENT AND NIGHTLIFE.** Alternative weeklies *Columbus Alive* and *The Other Paper* run a list of entertainment options and are available throughout the city. The **Ohio State Buckeyes** play football in historic **Ohio Stadium.** It's not easy to score tickets, but call the Athletic Ticket Office (☎292-2624; open M-F 7:30am-4:30pm) for more info. Major League Soccer's **Columbus Crew** (☎447-2739; tickets $16-35) hit the field at **Crew Stadium,** while the NHL's **Blue Jackets** (☎246-3350; tickets $17-93) play at **Nationwide Arena.** In early August, the **Ohio State Fair** rolls into town, as it has for more than 150 years, with livestock competitions, rides, and concerts. (☎888-646-3976; www.ohiostatefair.com. Take Exit 111 off I-71 to 17th Ave. $8, seniors and ages 5-12 $7. Ride wristbands $18. Parking $5.)

Columbus's nightlife scene is driven by rock 'n' roll, and it's hard to find a bar that doesn't have live music on the weekend. Big national acts stop at the **Newport,** 1722 N. High St. (☎294-1659; www.newportmusichall.com. Tickets $5-40.) To see alternative bands before they hit the big time, head to **Little Brothers,** 1100 N. High St. (☎421-2025. 18+. Cover $5-20. Most shows at 9 or 10pm.) As Ohio State's iconic college bar, the **Varsity Club,** 278 W. Lane Ave., at the upper edge of North Campus near the intersection of High St., is the favorite haunt of students and alums. (☎299-6269. Draft beer $2, pitchers $6.50. Open daily 11am-2am; opens at 9am for home football games.) Gay and lesbian partygoers spend their weekends at **Axis,** 775 N. High St., where the third Friday of every month brings a "steam" party with showers dropping down from the ceiling. (☎291-4008. 18+. Cover $3-6. Open F-Sa 10pm-2:30am, sometimes Su for drag shows or other special performances.)

▶ **DAYTRIPS FROM COLUMBUS**

HARDIN COUNTY
Most visits start in the county seat of Kenton; from Columbus, take I-270 N to Exit 17B, and then Rte. 33 W to Marysville. Pick up Rte. 31 N, and follow the scenic two-lane road 30 mi. north into Kenton.

The winding country roads and serene fields of undiscovered Hardin County offer budget travelers a chance to see small-town Ohio at its best. The **Sullivan-Johnson Museum,** 223 N. Main St., showcases local history in a lovely Victorian mansion. Keep an eye out for the ghost at the top of the staircase. (☎419-673-7147; www.hardinmuseums.org. Open M-F 1-4pm. Free.) Just down the street, the **Hardin County Convention and Visitors Bureau,** 128 N. Main St., arranges outdoor excursions and directs visitors to the Amish farms southeast of Kenton. (☎888-642-7346; www.tourhardin.com. Open M, W, F 9am-5pm.) Roughly 130 Amish families live in the area east of Rte. 31 and south of Rte. 309; look for the simple white signs along the road to see what products a family has to offer. The Hardin County Amish have managed to avoid the commercialism that has overtaken other Amish communities in Ohio. Leave your camera in the car—it's considered rude to take pictures—and be sure to respect the families' privacy, especially on Sundays. The front porch of **Pfeiffer Station General Store ❶,** at the intersection of Rtes. 144 and 265, is a great place to savor a dish of homemade ice cream ($1.75) and watch the horse-drawn buggies on their way back from the fields. (☎419-674-4103. Open M-Sa 8am-7pm, Su noon-5pm. Cash only.)

HOPEWELL CULTURE PARK
The park, at 16062 Rte. 104, is open daily dawn-dusk; entrance fee is $5 per car.

One hour south of Columbus, the area around Chillicothe (CHILL-ih-CAW-thee) features several Native American cultural sights. the **Hopewell Culture National Historical Park** swells with 23 Hopewell burial mounds spread over 13 acres. A small museum offers theories on the mounds and historical background on the 2000-year-old Hopewell culture. (☎774-1125; www.nps.gov/hocu. Visitors center open daily 8:30am-5pm; June-Aug. until 6pm.) Between mid-June and late August, the outdoor **Sugarloaf Mountain Amphitheater,** in Chillicothe off Rte. 23, presents a reenactment of the life of the Shawnee leader, Tecumseh. (☎775-0700; www.tecumsehdrama.com. Shows M-Sa 8pm. Tickets M-Th $16, under 10 $8; F-Sa $18/$9.)

CINCINNATI ☎513

Founded in 1788 as a frontier outpost, Cincinnati soon emerged as a vital gateway between the South and the West. Industry thrived as trade routes passed through the city, and a profusion of meat-packing plants earned Cincinnati the nickname "Porkopolis"—slightly less flattering than the title coined by Longfellow, "Queen City of the West." Recently, an aggressive downtown development plan and a burgeoning art scene have put Cincinnati on the map as a fun-loving hub of activity.

▐ TRANSPORTATION

Airport: Cincinnati/Northern Kentucky International (☎859-767-3151; www.cvgairport.com), in Kentucky, 13 mi. south of Cincinnati and accessible by I-71, I-74, and I-75. **Airport Executive Shuttle** whisks new arrivals into downtown Cincinnati. (☎859-261-8601. Reserve 24hr. in advance. $15.) The **Transit Authority of Northern Kentucky,** or **TANK,** sends the #2X Airport Express to and from downtown daily 5am-midnight. (☎859-331-8265; www.tankbus.org. $1.25.)

Trains: Amtrak, 1301 Western Ave. (☎651-3337; www.amtrak.com), in Union Terminal. Open Tu-Su 11pm-6:30am. To **Chicago** (8½hr., 1 per day, $34-42) and **Indianapolis** (3½hr., 1 per day, $17-22). Be cautious in the area to the north of the train station, especially along Liberty St.

Buses: Greyhound, 1005 Gilbert Ave. (☎352-6012; www.greyhound.com), 1 block east of the intersection of E. Court and Broadway. Open 24hr. To **Cleveland** (5hr., 5-8 per day, $35), **Columbus** (2hr., 5-8 per day, $17), and **Louisville** (2hr., 5-8 per day, $20).

Public Transit: Cincinnati Metro and **TANK,** both in the bus stop in the Mercantile Center, 121 E. 5th St. (☎621-9450; www.sorta.com). Open M-F 6:30am-6pm. Most buses run down 5th and Main St. $1; zone 2 $1.50; transfers $0.25; $2 extra to suburbs.

Taxi: Yellow Cab, ☎241-2100.

▣ ▐ ORIENTATION AND PRACTICAL INFORMATION

The downtown business district is an easy grid centered around **Fountain Square,** at **5th** and **Vine Street.** Numbered cross streets are designated E. or W. by their relation to Vine St. **Downtown** is bounded by E. Central Pkwy. on the north, Broadway on the east, 3rd on the south, and Central Ave. on the west. The **University of Cincinnati** spreads out from the Clifton area north of the city. To the south, the **Great American Ballpark,** the **Serpentine Wall,** and the **Riverwalk** border the Ohio River. Be careful outside of the downtown area at night, especially north of E. Central Pkwy.

Visitor Info: Cincinnati USA Visitor Center at Fifth Third Center, 511 Walnut St. (☎621-6994; www.cincinnatiusa.com), offers a wealth of brochures and discounted tickets to sights. Free Internet access. Open M-Sa 10am-5pm, Su noon-5pm; Jan.-Mar. closed Su.

Hotlines: Rape Crisis Center, ☎872-9259. **Gay/Lesbian Community Switchboard,** ☎591-0200. Both 24hr.

Internet Access: Cincinnati Public Library, 800 Vine St. (☎369-6900). Unlimited 90min. slots. Open M-W 9am-9pm, Th-Sa 9am-6pm, Su 1-5pm.

Post Office: 525 Vine St. (☎684-5667. Open M-F 8am-5pm.) **Postal Code:** 45202. **Area Codes:** 513; Kentucky suburbs 859. In text, 513 unless otherwise noted.

▌ ACCOMMODATIONS

Cheap hotels are scarce in downtown Cincinnati. About 30 miles north, in **Sharonville,** budget motels lie along **Chester Road.** Twelve miles south of the city, inexpensive accommodations line I-75 in **Florence, KY.** Closer to downtown, the motels at **Central Parkway** and **Hopple Street** offer good, mid-priced lodging.

Xavier University, 17 University Dr., Brockman Hall, (☎745-3203; www.xavier.edu/reslife). Take I-71 N to Exit 5, turn right on Dana St. and then right again on Ledgewood Ave. Rock-bottom weekly rates for dorm rooms are affordable even for 2 or 3 nights. Common bathrooms, kitchen, and laundry. Reserve 1 week in advance. Open mid-May to early Aug. Shared double $65 per week; private single $95 per week. D/MC/V. ❸

Ross Bed and Breakfast, 88 Silverwood Circle (☎671-2645). Take I-75 N to I-275 W, and take Exit 42B to Kemper Ave. An affable couple rents out 2 rooms with a private bath in their home. Reservations recommended. Rooms $45-54. Cash only. ❸

Knights Inn-Cincinnati/South, 8048 Dream St. (☎859-371-9711), in Florence, just off I-75 at Exit 180, has standard motel rooms, cable TV, A/C, and outdoor pool. 21+. Doubles M-Th and Su $39, F-Sa $49. AmEx/D/MC/V. ❷

Stonelick State Park, 2895 Lake Dr. (☎625-6593, reservations 866-644-6727), 35 mi. east of the city, outside the I-275 loop. 114 campsites at the edge of a lake with boating, fishing, and swimming. Sites $16, with electricity $20; lakeside $22. ❶

▐ FOOD

Cincinnati's greatest culinary innovation is its chili, which consists of noodles, meat, cheese, onions, kidney beans, and a distinctive secret ingredient (some say chocolate). The city has also given rise to a number of noteworthy fast-food chains. Fine restaurants can be found in the **Mount Adams** area, while more moderately priced chains are common at **Newport on the Levee** and **Covington Landing** just across the river.

Skyline Chili, 643 Vine St. (☎241-2020; www.skylinechili.com), at 7th St., with locations all over Cincinnati, dishes up the best beans in town. The ambience may smack of a Wendy's off the New Jersey Turnpike, but Skyline's curiously sweet, meaty sauce is one of the first things transplanted Cincy natives say that they miss. 5-way chili from $3.69. Open M-F 11am-8pm, Sa noon-4pm. AmEx/D/MC/V. ❶

Graeter's, 41 E. 4th St. (☎381-0653), between Walnut and Vine St. downtown, with 14 other locations. A Cincy institution since 1870, Graeter's uses a time-intensive "French pot" process to make ice cream 2 gallons at a time. Oprah Winfrey is a devoted fan. Single-dip cone $2. Open M-F 7am-6pm, Sa 7am-3pm. AmEx/D/MC/V. ❶

Myra's Dionysus, 121 Calhoun Ave. (☎961-1578), on the edge of the University of Cincinnati. This tiny vegetarian cafe has 25 soups on rotation. The *gado gado* ($6.50) packs a punch. Open M-Th 11am-10pm, F-Sa 11am-11pm, Su 5-10pm. MC/V. ❶

Izzy's, 800 Elm St. (☎721-4241), serves the local lunch crowd famously thick Reubens ($7) and corned beef sandwiches ($6), garnished with a dense potato pancake. Open M-F 8am-8pm, Sa 10am-5pm. AmEx/MC/V. ❷

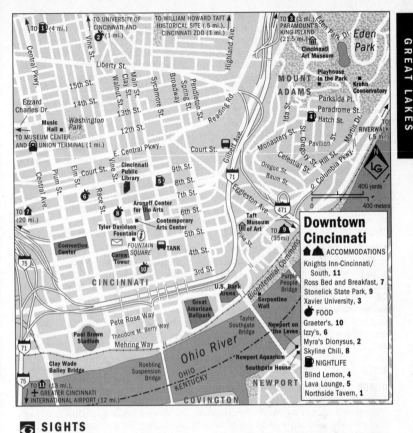

Downtown Cincinnati

▲▲ ACCOMMODATIONS

Knights Inn-Cincinnati/
   South, 11
Ross Bed and Breakfast, 7
Stonelick State Park, 9
Xavier University, 3

🍴 FOOD

Graeter's, 10
Izzy's, 6
Myra's Dionysus, 2
Skyline Chili, 8

◼ NIGHTLIFE

Blind Lemon, 4
Lava Lounge, 5
Northside Tavern, 1

👁 SIGHTS

DOWNTOWN. Downtown Cincinnati centers around the **Tyler Davidson Fountain,** at 5th and Vine St., a towering bronze masterpiece from the 19th century. Around **Fountain Square,** business complexes and shops are connected by a series of skywalks. The 49th-floor observation deck atop **Carew Tower,** Cincinnati's tallest building, provides a ranging view of the riverfront. *(441 Vine St. ☎579-9735. Open M-Th 9:30am-5:30pm, F-Sa 9:30am-9pm, Su 11am-5pm. $2, ages 5-11 $1.)* Just to the east, the ▨**Contemporary Arts Center** has been called "the most important American building to be completed since the end of the Cold War." Baghdad-born architect Zaha Hadid is the first woman ever to win the prestigious Pritzker Prize, and her airy, angular design houses six floors of avant-garde art. The photography of Taryn Simon and the "fantasy coffins" of Paa Joe will be featured during the spring of 2006. *(44 E. 6th St. ☎345-8420; www.contemporaryartscenter.org. Open M 10am-9pm, W-F 10am-6pm, Sa-Su 11am-6pm. $7.50, seniors $6.50, students $5.50, ages 3-13 $4.50. M 5-9pm free.)* At the eastern edge of downtown, the **Taft Museum of Art** contains a modest collection of Old Masters and Chinese ceramics in a mansion dating to 1820. *(316 Pike St. ☎241-0343; www.taftmuseum.org. Open Tu-W and F 11am-5pm, Th 11am-8pm, Sa 10am-5pm, Su noon-5pm. $7, seniors and students $5, under 18 free. W Free.)*

EDEN PARK. Flowering trees and a sea of daffodils mark the arrival of spring in Eden Park, although skating on Mirror Lake ensures that Cincinnati's own Garden of Eden remains charming even in winter. Just be sure to steer clear of the Tree of Knowledge, or trouble may ensue. *(Northeast of downtown and Mt. Adams. Take bus #49 to Eden Park Dr. Open daily 6am-10pm.)* The impressive **Cincinnati Art Museum,** inside the park, greets visitors with a serpentine chandelier designed by glassblower Dale Chihuly. Highlights of the collection include Impressionist landscapes from both sides of the Atlantic and the Cincinnati Wing with period furniture and portraits of native son Frank Duveneck. *(953 Eden Park Dr. ☎721-5204; www.cincinnatiartmuseum.org. Open Tu and Th-Su 11am-5pm, W 11am-9pm. Tours Tu-F 1pm; Sa 1, 2pm; Su 1, 2, 3pm. Free. Admission to some temporary exhibitions $6-8.)* The nearby **Krohn Conservatory** teems with palm trees, orchids, and tropical plants, while May and early June bring a cloud of butterflies to the conservatory's Show Room. *(950 Eden Park Dr. ☎421-5707; www.cinci-parks.org. Open daily 10am-5pm. Suggested donation $5, under 17 $2. Butterfly show $6/$3.)* To encounter some more sizeable wildlife, head to the **Cincinnati Zoo,** where you can rub elbows with rare Sumatran rhinos and duck into the domed Vanishing Giants building for a glimpse of an Asian elephant. *(3400 Vine St. ☎281-4700; www.cincinnatizoo.org. Open June-Aug. M-F and Su 9am-6pm, Sa 9am-8:30pm; check website for low-season schedule. $13, seniors $11, ages 2-12 $8. Parking $6.50.)*

MUSEUM CENTER. Built in 1933 as part of a West End renaissance, the enormous Art Deco **Union Terminal** fell into disrepair in the 1970s, and then reopened in 1990 with three major museums. The **Cincinnati History Museum** takes visitors back to Cincy's past as a garrison town of the Early Republic and the cultural mecca of the Civil War era. A giant mastodon skeleton welcomes visitors into the **Museum of Natural History and Science,** where explorers can uncover the secrets of the Ice Age and descend into a cave's damp depths to see bats. Kids are in control at the **Cinergy Children's Museum,** where they can clamber through a giant playscape or try to generate hydropower in the WaterWorks area. *(1301 Western Ave. ☎287-7000; www.cincymuseum.org. Open M-Sa 10am-5pm, Su 11am-6pm. Admission to 1 museum $7.25, ages 3-12 $5.25; 2 attractions $10.25/$7.25; 3 attractions $13.25/$9.25. Parking $4.50.)*

OTHER SIGHTS. Just across the river in Kentucky, the spectacular ◪**Newport Aquarium** routes visitors through glass tunnels where tiger sharks swim six inches from their heads. Tiny American alligators are about as cute as carnivorous reptiles get, while the aquarium's beautiful Jellyfish Gallery features glass chandeliers and gilded frames. *(Located at Newport on the Levee. ☎859-261-7444; www.newportaquarium.com. Open in summer M-F and Su 9am-7pm, Sa 9am-9pm; in winter daily 10am-6pm. $18, seniors $16, children 3-12 $11.)* One mile from downtown, the **William Howard Taft National Historic Site** was the childhood home of the portly US President and Supreme Court Justice. *(2038 Auburn Ave. ☎684-3262; www.nps.gov/wiho. 30min. tours daily 8am-4pm. Free.)*

♫ ENTERTAINMENT

The free newspapers *City Beat, CinWeekly,* and *Downtowner* list happenings around town. Cincinnati's **Playhouse in the Park,** 962 Mt. Adams Cir., won a 2004 Tony award for best regional theater in the US with its dramas, comedies, and musicals inside Eden Park. *(☎421-3888; www.cincyplay.com. Performances mid-Sept. to June Tu-Su. $34-48. Senior and student rush tickets 2hr. before show $15.)* The **Music Hall,** 1241 Elm St. *(☎621-2787),* hosts the **Cincinnati Symphony Orchestra** and the **Cincinnati Pops Orchestra** from September through May. *(☎381-3300. $17-77; student tickets for Th-Su performances $10-12.)* The **Cincinnati Opera** sings in the Hall's Springer Auditorium. *(☎241-2742; www.cincinnatiopera.org. $26-130.)* A summer series of classical concerts and operas takes place at the **Riverbend Music**

Center, 6295 Kellogg Ave., on the banks of the Ohio River. The **Cincinnati Ballet** (☎621-5219; www.wguc.org/cincinnatiballet) performs at the **Aronoff Center for the Arts,** 650 Walnut St., which also hosts the **Broadway in Cincinnati** series. (☎241-7469. Ballet performances late Sept. to mid-May $18-47. Broadway Sept.-June $25-65.) Early June kicks off the edgy, mixed-media productions of the ☒**Cincinnati Fringe Festival** (☎391-9385; www.cincyfringe.com), while September brings almost 300 bands to town for the **MidPoint Music Festival** (☎877-572-8690; www.mpmf.com).

Northeast of the city, off I-71 at Exit 24, **Paramount's King Island** cages **The Beast,** the world's longest wooden roller coaster, while the new **Italian Job** puts thrillseekers behind the wheel for a car chase full of special effects. (☎573-5800 or 800-288-0808; www.pki.com. Open late May to late Aug. M-Th and Su 10am-10pm, F-Sa 10am-midnight; call for low-season hours. $35, seniors and ages 3-6 $27. Parking $9.) Major League baseball's **Reds** (☎381-7337; tickets $5-60) take the field at the **Great American Ball Park,** 100 Main St., and football's long-suffering **Bengals** (☎621-8383; tickets $49-60) play at **Paul Brown Stadium** five blocks west.

▌ NIGHTLIFE

Overlooking downtown from the east, the winding streets of **Mount Adams** have spawned some offbeat bars and music venues, creating a relaxed environment removed from the bustling city below. On the Kentucky side of the river, a more commercialized nightlife scene has emerged in **Newport.**

Northside Tavern, 4153 Hamilton Ave. (☎542-3603), in the Northside. Pool tables and a jukebox set the tone inside this favorite hangout for twentysomethings. Drafts $3-4. Live music daily 10pm. 21+. Open M-F 5pm-2:30am, Sa-Su 8pm-2:30am.

Lava Lounge, 835 Main St. (☎333-0889). Patterned after the hipster mecca of the same name in Chicago's Ukrainian Village, Lava is packed with impeccably dressed partygoers on the weekend. 21+. Cover $5-10. Open F-Sa 10pm-4am, Su 10pm-2:30am.

Blind Lemon, 936 Hatch St. (☎241-3885), at St. Gregory St. Live blues and rock fill the cavernous tavern where Jimmy Buffett got started. During the colder months, bonfires light up the outdoor courtyard Th-Sa. Drafts $2. Live music daily 8:30pm. 21+. Open M-Tu 5:30pm-1am, W-F 5pm-2am, Sa-Su 3pm-2:30am.

INDIANA

The cornfields of southern Indiana's Appalachian foothills give way to expansive plains in the industrialized north, where Gary's smokestacks spew black clouds over the waters of Lake Michigan and urban travel hubs string along the interstates. Despite its official motto—"The Crossroads of America"—Indiana is a modest, slow-paced state, where farms roll on and on, big cities are a rarity, and countless Hoosier school kids grow up dreaming of becoming the next Larry Bird.

▌ PRACTICAL INFORMATION

Capital: Indianapolis.

Visitor Info: Indiana Division of Tourism, 1 N. Capitol Ave., #700, Indianapolis 46204 (☎317-232-8860; www.state.in.us/tourism). **Division of State Parks,** 402 W. Washington St., #W-298, Indianapolis 46204 (☎317-232-4124; www.in.gov/dnr/parklake).

State Bird: Larry. **Postal Abbreviation:** IN. **Sales Tax:** 5%.

Time Zone: Indiana will adopt Daylight Savings Time in the summer of 2006; this will mark the first time that the entire state has ever turned its clocks forward. As of 2005, 82 out of Indiana's 92 counties observe Eastern Standard Time, while 10 counties in the western corners of the state observe Central Standard Time. A definitive decision on whether the state should go Eastern, Central, or split down the middle is expected from the U.S. Department of Transportation by April 2006.

INDIANAPOLIS   ☎ 317

After years of being known by such epithets as "Napville" and "India No Place," Indiana's sprawling state capital resolved to build a cultural infrastructure that would outlast the seasonal boom of the Indianapolis 500. Superb museums and a diverse music scene promptly rose to the occasion. Bands of poverty still separate the sparkling downtown from outlying neighborhoods, but on the whole, Indianapolis pulses with the energy of a city on the move.

■ ⁊ **ORIENTATION AND PRACTICAL INFORMATION.** The city is laid out in concentric circles, with a dense central cluster of skyscrapers and low-lying outskirts. The very center of Indianapolis is just south of **Monument Circle,** at the intersection of **Washington Street (U.S. 40)** and **Meridian Street.** Washington St. divides the city north-south; Meridian St. divides it east-west. **I-465** circles the city and provides access to downtown. **I-70** cuts through the city east-west. Meter parking is abundant along the edge of the downtown area.

Indianapolis International Airport (☎ 487-7243; www.indianapolisairport.com) is located 7 mi. southwest of downtown off I-465, Exit 11B; take bus #8 "Washington St." Taxi to downtown costs around $17. **Amtrak,** 350 S. Illinois St. (☎ 263-0550; www.amtrak.com; open daily 11pm-2:30pm), runs to Chicago (5hr., 1 per day, $16-32) and Cincinnati (3hr., 1 per day, $17-22). **Greyhound,** inside the same terminal (☎ 267-3076; www.greyhound.com; open 24hr.), sends buses to Chicago (3-4hr., 9-11 per day, $31-34), Cincinnati (2-5hr., 7 per day, $20), and Detroit (7-11hr., 5-6 per day, $40). **Indygo,** 209 N. Delaware St., runs routes throughout the city, as well as shuttles to special events. (☎ 635-3344; www.indygo.net. $1.25, under 6 free.) **Taxi: Yellow Cab,** ☎ 487-7777. **Visitor Info: The Artsgarden Cultural Concierge,** on the first floor of Circle Centre Mall, gives out info on arts events and the Cultural Districts Guide. (☎ 624-2563; www.indyarts.org. Open M-Sa 10am-9pm, Su noon-6pm.) **Post Office:** 125 W. South St., across from Amtrak. (☎ 464-6874. Open M-F 7am-5:30pm.) **Postal Code:** 46206. **Area Code:** 317.

⌐ **ACCOMMODATIONS.** Budget motels line the I-465 beltway, 5 mi. from downtown. Make reservations a year in advance for the Indy 500, which drives rates up drastically in May. The friendly ▩**Indy Hostel ❶,** 4903 Winthrop Ave., three blocks from N. College Ave., has quickly carved out a niche for itself with summer interns in the city. Short-term guests also find the convivial common spaces, well-stocked kitchen, and open-door atmosphere refreshing. (☎ 727-1696; www.indyhostel.us. Free Internet access. Laundry $1. Dorms M-Th and Su $22, F-Sa $25; private room $45. MC/V.) Closer to downtown, the **Renaissance Tower Historic Inn ❹,** 230 E. 9th St., offers suites with cable TV, A/C, and stately canopy beds. (☎ 261-1652 or 800-676-7786. Reception desk open M-F 8am-7pm, Sa-Su 10am-5pm; call ahead for late arrivals. Rooms $75 per night, $431 per week. AmEx/DC/MC/V.) **Motel 6 ❷,** 6330 Debonair Ln., at Exit 16A off I-465, may be the middle ground between hostel prices and hotel comfort; expect pleasant rooms with A/C and cable TV. (☎ 293-3220. Singles $35; doubles $40. AmEx/D/MC/V.) The **Indiana State Fairgrounds Campgrounds ❶,** 1202 E. 38th St., bus #4 or 39 from downtown, has 170 sod-and-gravel sites packed with RVs. (☎ 927-7500. Sites with hookup $19.)

■ **FOOD.** Ethnic food stands, vegetable markets, and knick-knack vendors fill the spacious **City Market,** 222 E. Market St. Meals start around $5. (☎634-9266. Open M-F 6am-6pm, Sa 8am-4pm.) Massachusetts Ave. houses some of the liveliest restaurants and bars in the city; in the summer, diners crowd outdoor patios. **Bazbeaux Pizza ❸,** 334 Massachusetts Ave. (☎636-7662) and 832 E. Westfield Blvd. (☎255-5711), is the go-to spot for a casual date and a legendary slice of thin crust. Stay basic with the margherita pizza ($10), or try the intoxicating Tchoupitoulas ($11.50) and brave the one-two punch of Cajun shrimp and andouille sausage. (Both locations open M-Th and Su 11am-10pm, F-Sa 11am-11pm. AmEx/D/MC/V.) **The Abbey ❷,** 825 Pennsylvania Ave., cultivates a celestial vibe with cloud-painted ceilings, church-style lanterns, and an array of vegetarian sandwiches that puts most other coffeeshops to shame. (☎269-8426. Free wireless Internet. Open M-Th 7am-midnight, F 7am-1am, Sa 8am-1am, Su 8am-midnight. MC/V.) **Yat's ❷,** 5463 N. College Ave. and 659 Massachusetts Ave., serves Cajun and Creole fare at jaw-droppingly low prices. The long line is a drawback, but chunky succotash and a rotating menu of spicy stews (all $5.50) make a splash just the same. (☎253-8817. Open M-Th 11am-9pm, F-Sa 11am-10pm, Su 11am-7pm. Cash only.)

■ **SIGHTS.** The attractions in and around White River State Park, bordered by West St. and W. Washington St., form an axis of activity that has anchored the city's downtown revitalization efforts. At the eastern edge of the park, the **Eiteljorg Museum of American Indians and Western Art,** 500 W. Washington St., put the finishing touches on a $40 million expansion project in June 2005. The new wing includes a gallery of provocative pieces by contemporary Native American artists, rounding out the museum's collection of tribal crafts and paintings of frontier life. (☎636-9378; www.eiteljorg.org. Open M-Sa 10am-5pm, Su noon-5pm; Oct.-Apr. closed M. Tours daily 1pm. $7, seniors $6, students and ages 5-17 $4. Wheelchair accessible.) The **Indiana State Museum,** 650 W. Washington St., has a fascinating collection of artifacts that create evocative portraits of life in the 19th and 20th centuries; look for the bottles of patent medicine and the 1887 barber's chair. (☎232-1637; www.indianamuseum.org. Open M-Sa 9am-5pm, Su 11am-5pm. $7, ages 60+ $6.50, ages 3-12 $4. IMAX $8.75/$7.50/$6. Combo $12.50/$11/$8. Wheelchair accessible.)

No sports fan should miss the **NCAA Hall of Champions,** 700 W. Washington St., which pays homage to the best in American college sports. Experience the passion of the Final Four in the March Madness Theater and try your hand at hitting a clutch shot in the 1930s-style gymnasium. (☎916-4255; www.ncaahallofchampions.org. Open M-Sa 10am-5pm, Su noon-5pm. $3, students $2, under 5 free.) A majestic stained-glass dome graces the marbled interior of the **State House,** 200 W. Washington St. (☎233-5293. Open M-F 8am-4pm. 3-5 1hr. guided tours per day. Call ahead. Free.) Animal lovers should check out the seemingly cageless **Indianapolis Zoo,** 1200 W. Washington St. Adjacent to the zoo, frolic with butterflies amidst exotic flora at **White River Gardens.** (☎630-2001; www.indyzoo.com. Open June-Aug. M-Th 9am-5pm, F-Su 9am-6pm; Sept.-Oct. M-Th 9am-4pm, F-Su 9am-5pm. Zoo $11.50, ages 2-12 and 62+ $7; gardens $7/$6; combo $12.50/$8. Parking $5.)

Although it is almost 4 mi. north of downtown, the ◪**Indianapolis Museum of Art,** 4000 Michigan Rd., rewards those who make the trek with its galleries and stunning formal gardens. The African art collection reopens in 2006. The StarStudio gives kids a crack at edgy, interactive installation work. (☎923-1331; www.imaart.org. Open Tu-W and F-Su 10am-5pm, Th 10am-9pm. $7, seniors $5, college students and under 12 free. Free Th.) Young people are foremost on the agenda of the **Indianapolis Children's Museum,** 3000 N. Meridian St., where the mood-lit fossils of the museum's signature Dinosphere exhibit open up on an art studio and a simulated archaeological dig. (☎334-3322; www.childrensmuseum.org. Open Mar.-Aug. daily 10am-5pm; Sept.-Feb. Tu-Su 10am-5pm. $12, ages 60+ $11, ages 2-17 $7.)

DAYS OF THUNDER. America's passion for fast cars reaches fever pitch during the **500 Festival** (☎927-3378; www.500festival.com), an entire month of parades and hoopla leading up to race day at the **Indianapolis Motor Speedway,** 4790 W. 16th St., off I-465 at the Speedway exit. (Take bus #25.) The festivities begin with time trials in mid-May and culminate with the "Gentlemen, start your engines" of the **Indianapolis 500** the Sunday before Memorial Day. During quieter times, buses full of tourists drive around the 2½ mi. track at slightly tamer speeds. (☎492-6784; www.indy500.com. Track tours daily 9am-4:40pm. $3, ages 6-15 $1.) The **Speedway Museum,** at the south end of the infield, houses the Indy **Hall of Fame** and a collection of cars that have tested their mettle on the storied track over the years. (Open daily 9am-5pm. $3, ages 6-15 $1.) Tickets for the race usually sell out within a week after the previous year's race. After the smoke clears from the racetrack, more than 400 bands pull into town for July's **Midwest Music Summit.** (☎459-8634; www.midwestmusicsummit.com. 3-day pass $25.) August 2005 marked the inaugural celebration of the **Indianapolis Fringe Theatre Festival,** featuring experimental plays in four venues around the city. (☎822-4386; www.indyfringe.com. Tickets $10 per show.) October brings the feel-good flicks of the **Heartland Film Festival.** (☎464-9405; www.heartlandfilmfestival.org. Tickets $7 per film.)

ENTERTAINMENT AND NIGHTLIFE. The **Madame Walker Theatre Centre,** 617 Indiana Ave., used to be the headquarters of African-American entrepreneur Madame C.J. Walker's beauty enterprise. Today the national historic landmark hosts arts programs, including the bi-weekly **Jazz on the Avenue.** (☎236-2099; www.walkertheatre.com. Tours M-F 9am-3:30pm. Jazz every other F 6-10pm. $10.) The **Indianapolis Symphony Orchestra** performs in the **Hilbert Circle Theater** on Monument Circle. (☎639-4300; www.indyorch.org. Box office open M-F 9am-5pm, Sa 10am-2pm.) The shining star of the city's theater scene is the **Indiana Repertory Theatre,** 140 W. Washington St. (☎635-5252; www.indianarep.com. Box office open M-F noon-6pm, or until 30min. before showtime. Tickets from $19.) Basketball fans watch the **Pacers** from November to April at **Conseco Fieldhouse,** 125 S. Pennsylvania St. (☎917-2500. Tickets $10-96.) The WNBA's **Indiana Fever** take over in the summer months. (☎239-5151. Tickets $10-75.) The NFL's **Colts** toss the pigskin at the **RCA Dome,** 100 S. Capital Ave. (☎239-5151. Tickets $15-65.)

Adjacent to the campus of Butler University, the **Broad Ripple** area, 6 mi. north of downtown at College Ave. and 62nd St., is the best area for nightlife. **The Jazz Kitchen,** 5377 N. College Ave., draws intimate trios and swinging big bands alike. (☎253-4900; www.thejazzkitchen.com. Latin dance party Th 9pm. 21+. Cover $7-10; $15-20 for national acts. No cover M. Open M-Sa 5pm-midnight; sets usually begin at 9pm and 11pm.) **The Vogue,** 6259 N. College Ave., hosts national acts in a restored movie house and transforms itself into the city's favorite megaclub after hours. Expect to wait in a line that stretches halfway down the block. (☎255-2828; www.thevogue.ws. Shows 8pm. 21+. Cover $3-5; ladies free F before 11:30pm. Open W and F-Sa 10pm-3am.) **Radio Radio,** 1119 Prospect St., 2 mi. southeast of downtown off Virginia Ave., lures PBR-sipping hipsters down to Fountain Square with its parade of indie bands. (☎955-0995; www.futureshock.net. 21+. Cover $3-5. Shows F-Sa 10pm.) Back downtown, the **Slippery Noodle,** 372 S. Meridian St., is the oldest bar in Indiana, as well as one of the country's best venues for live blues. (☎631-6974. 21+. Cover Th-Sa $5. Open M-Sa 11am-3am, Su 4pm-12:30am.)

BLOOMINGTON
☎812

While the rolling hills of Monroe County are home to tiny communities, they also open up on the cosmopolitan college town of Bloomington. Indiana University (IU) drums up a rowdy fan base for Big Ten basketball games, while scruffy kids skateboard by ethnic restaurants and students chalk "not my government" on the sidewalk. With the shores of Monroe Lake just 10 mi. to the south, Bloomington is within striking distance of natural resources that rival its heady cultural life.

At the eastern end of Kirkwood Ave., the **Sample Gates** mark the entrance to the IU campus. Veer to the left past the red-roofed Student Building and cut across **Dunn Meadow,** where students have been known to stage protests and erect shanty-towns. Several blocks further east, I.M. Pei's angular, sunlit **Art Museum,** 1133 E. 7th St., counts Stuart Davis' bold *Swing Landscape* as a cornerstone of its collection. (☎855-5445; www.indiana.edu/~iuam. Open Tu-Sa 10am-5pm, Su noon-5pm. Free.) Nearby, the **Mathers Museum of World Cultures,** 416 N. Indiana Ave., near E. 8th St., has just unveiled a new permanent exhibit comparing and contrasting the Bloom-ington of the 1960s to the Hausa tribe of central Africa. (☎855-6873; www.indi-ana.edu/~mathers. Open Tu-F 9am-4:30pm, Sa-Su 1-4:30pm. Free.) South of town, the **Tibetan Cultural Center,** 3655 Snoddy Rd., recently came within days of foreclo-sure, but a new board of directors promises to keep the compound's sacred stupas and interfaith temple open for years to come. (☎334-7046; www.tibetancc.com. Grounds open daily 10am-5pm. Center open Su noon-3pm.)

Inexpensive rooms crowd the intersection of Rte. 46 and North Walnut St. **Motel 6 ❷,** 1800 North Walnut St., has basic rooms just north of downtown. (☎332-0820. A/C. Cable. Singles M-Th and Su $36, F-Sa $46; doubles $42/$52. AmEx/D/MC/V.) Usually, rooms at the **Scholars Inn Bed & Breakfast ❹,** 801 N. College Ave., go for over $100, but on weekdays the comfortable beds drop in price. (☎332-1892. Gour-met breakfast included. Check-in 4-6pm. Rooms from $79. AmEx/MC/V.) **Payne-town "Peyton" State Recreation Area ❶,** 10 mi. southeast of downtown on Rte. 446, has open campsites on Lake Monroe with access to trails, a beach, boat rentals, and a fishing dock. (☎837-9546. Primitive sites M-W and Su $13, Th-Sa $16; with electricity $19/$23. Vehicle registration $5, IN residents $4. Rent boats from Lake Monroe Boat Rental. ☎837-9909; www.lakemonroeboatrental. Kayaks and canoes $9 per hr., $25 per 8hr. with $50 deposit; fishing boats $75 per 8hr., $90 per day, with $100 deposit.) **Anyetsang's Little Tibet ❷,** 415 E. 4th St., offers an authentic menu of Tibetan dumplings and Thai curries (both $10), and hosts IU's Students for a Free Tibet on weekday nights. (☎331-0122. Open M and W-Su 11am-10pm. MC/V.) The brightly colored picnic tables out on the deck of the Kenwood Manor Building point the way into **Laughing Planet Cafe ❶,** 322 E. Kirkwood Ave. Burritos bulging with beans and brown rice ($4.75) can get messy, but a tabletop guide recalls that it is "a violation of Natural Law" to eat a burrito with a fork. (☎323-2233. Open daily 11am-9pm. MC/V.) Downstairs, **Soma Coffee House ❶** makes Fair Trade coffee and smoothies. (☎331-2770. Free wireless Internet. Smoothies $3-4. Open June-Aug. M-Sa 7am-10pm, Su 8am-10pm; Sept.-May. open until 11pm. MC/V.) **The Cinemat,** 123 S. Walnut St., screens foreign and independent films at bar-gain-basement prices. (☎333-4700; www.thecinemat.com. $4, matinees $3.) **Nick's English Hut,** 423 E. Kirkwood Ave., looks like a quaint Yorkshire cottage on the out-side, and crowds of IU students squeeze into its booths during term-time. (☎332-4040. Pints from $2.25. 21+ after 8pm. Open M-Sa 11am-2am, Su noon-midnight.)

The city of Bloomington lies south of Indianapolis on Rte. 37. **North Walnut Street** and **College Avenue** are the main north-south thoroughfares. The town centers on **Courthouse Square. Bloomington Transit** sends buses on through town and the IU campus. Service is infrequent. (☎336-7433; www.bloomingtontransit.com. $0.75, seniors and ages 5-17 $0.35.) The campus also has a shuttle bus service ($0.75). The **visitors center,** 2855 N. Walnut St., offers free local calls and a helpful staff. (☎334-8900 or 800-800-0037; www.visitbloomington.com. Open Apr.-Oct. M-F 8:30am-5pm, Sa 9am-4pm; Nov.-Mar. M-F 8:30am-5pm, Sa 10am-3pm. Brochure area open 24hr.)

MICHIGAN

Pressing up against four of the Great Lakes, two peninsulas present visitors with two distinct Michigans. The sparsely populated Upper Peninsula hangs over Lake Michigan, containing moose, wolves, and the stunning waterfalls of the Hiawatha National Forest. Campers and hikers have recently discovered the U.P., and the resplendent forests now entertain backpackers and families alike. In the Lower Peninsula, beach bums hang out in the many quaint communities along the western coast of the state, sunning and boating along some of Michigan's 3000 mi. of coastline. Those craving an urban environment head to Ann Arbor, the intellectual center of the state, or to industrial Detroit for world-class museums.

◪ PRACTICAL INFORMATION

Capital: Lansing.

Visitor Info: Travel Michigan, 300 N. Washington Sq., Lansing 48909 (☎800-644-2489; www.michigan.org). **Department of Parks and Recreation,** Information Services Ctr., P.O. Box 30257, Lansing 48909 (☎517-373-9900). State parks require a motor vehicle permit ($6 per day, $24 per year). Call ☎800-447-2757 for reservations.

Postal Abbreviation: MI. **Sales Tax:** 6%.

DETROIT   ☎313

Heavyweight champ Joe Louis is one of Detroit's best-known native sons and a fitting icon for the city; Detroit resembles an aging slugger, caught up on the ropes in the seventh round but determined to stay standing until the final bell. Violent race riots in the 1960s spawned a massive exodus to the suburbs, while the decline of the auto industry in the late 1970s chiseled away the city's industrial base and left behind a weary, crumbling shell of Motown's glory days. Detroit continues to shrink with each succeeding census, and yet the stalwarts who have stayed behind love their city with an almost cultish ferocity. With Super Bowl XL set to kick off in February and a generation of young DJs reinventing the Detroit sound, this plucky boomtown is not about to go down without a fight.

▐ TRANSPORTATION

Airport: Detroit Metropolitan (☎734-247-7678; www.metroairport com), 20 mi. southwest of downtown, off I-94 at Merriman Rd. in Romulus. **Metro Cabs** (☎800-745-5191) offers taxi service to downtown for $39.

Trains: Amtrak, 11 W. Baltimore St. (☎873-3442; www.amtrak.com). Open daily 7am-3pm and 3:45-11pm. To **Chicago** (5½hr., 3 per day, $25) and **New York** (16hr., 1 per day, $66). **VIA Rail,** 298 Walker Rd., Windsor, ON (☎888-842-7245; www.viarail.ca) runs to **Toronto** (4hr., 4 per day, CDN$88) and other Canadian destinations.

Buses: Greyhound, 1001 Howard St. (☎961-8011; www.greyhound.com). Station open 24hr.; ticket office open daily 5:30am-11:30pm. Be cautious in this area at night. To **Ann Arbor** (1½hr., 4 per day, $8), **Chicago** (5½-7½hr., 7 per day, $31), and **Cleveland** (3½-4½hr., 10 per day, $24).

Public Transit: Detroit Department of Transportation (DOT), 1301 E. Warren Ave. (☎933-1300; www.ci.detroit.mi.us/ddot). Serves downtown, with limited service to the suburbs. Many buses stop service at midnight. $1.50, some short routes $0.50; transfers $0.25. An elevated tramway, **People Mover,** 1420 Washington Blvd. (☎962-7245;

www.thepeoplemover.com), circles the Central Business District on a 2¾ mi. loop; worth a ride just for the view of the riverfront and downtown. Runs M-Th 7am-11pm, F 7am-midnight, Sa 9am-midnight, Su noon-8pm. $0.50. **Suburban Mobility Authority for Regional Transportation (SMART),** 660 Woodward Ave. (☎866-962-5515; www.smart-bus.org), runs bus service to the suburbs 4am-midnight. $1.50, transfers $0.25.

☀🛈 ORIENTATION AND PRACTICAL INFORMATION

Detroit lies on the Detroit River, which connects Lake Erie and Lake St. Clair. Across the river to the south, the town of **Windsor, ON,** can be reached by a tunnel just west of the Renaissance Center (toll $3.50), or by the Ambassador Bridge ($2.75). Those planning to make the crossing should expect delays because of heightened security. American citizens need to have a passport or copy of their birth certificate, not just a driver's license. Detroit can be a dangerous town, but it is generally safe during the day; expect to be approached by panhandlers, and avoid walking alone at night. Office buildings and sports venues dominate the downtown, while up-and-coming neighborhoods like **Corktown** open out to the west. Driving is the best way to get around town.

Detroit's streets form a grid. The numbered Mile Roads run east-west and measure the distance away from downtown. **Eight Mile Road** is the city's northern boundary and the beginning of the suburbs. **Woodward Avenue/Route 1** is the city's main north-south artery and divides both Detroit into "east side" and "west side." **Gratiot Avenue** flares out northeast from downtown, while **Grand River Avenue** shoots west. Both I-94 and I-75 pass through downtown. Streets tend to end suddenly and reappear several blocks later; for a particularly helpful map, check *Visit Detroit,* available at the Visitors Bureau.

Visitor Info: Convention and Visitors Bureau, 211 W. Fort St., 10th fl. (☎202-1800 or 800-338-7648; www.visitdetroit.com). Open M-F 9am-5pm.

GLBT Resources: Triangle Foundation of Detroit, ☎537-3323. **Affirmations,** 195 W. 9 Mile Rd. (☎248-398-7105; www.goaffirmations.org), in Ferndale, has a large library.

Hotlines: Crisis Hotline, ☎224-7000. **Rape Counseling Center,** ☎224-4487. Both 24hr.

Internet Access: The David Adamany Undergraduate Library at Wayne State University, 5155 Gullen Mall, offers free **Internet** access in 1hr. slots. Photo ID required. Open May-Aug. M-Th 8am-11pm, F 8am-6pm, Sa 9am-5pm, Su 11am-7pm; Sept.-Apr. M-Th 8am-11pm, F 8am-9pm, Sa 9am-9pm, Su 11am-11pm.

Post Office: 1401 W. Fort St. (☎226-8304). Open 24hr. **Postal Code:** 48233. **Area Codes:** 313 (Detroit); 810, 248, and 734 (suburbs). In text, 313 unless noted.

▐ ACCOMMODATIONS

Staying in downtown Detroit often leaves travelers with the choice of high-end hotels or questionable dives. There are a few options along **East Jefferson Avenue,** but it may be easier to find chain motels in the northern suburbs or across the border in **Windsor.** *Visit Detroit* lists accommodations and prices by area.

▨ **University of Windsor,** 750 Sunset Ave. (☎519-973-7041), in Windsor, rents palatial, hotel-style dorm rooms. Refrigerators, A/C, free Internet access, and continental breakfast. Open early May to late Aug. Parking CDN$5 per day. Hostel bed CDN$29; single in a two-bedroom suite CDN$39; two-bedroom suite CDN$79. AmEx/MC/V. ❷

Shorecrest Motor Inn, 1316 E. Jefferson Ave. (☎568-3000 or 800-992-9616), located 3 blocks east of the Renaissance Center. Rooms with A/C and fridge. Key deposit $20. Reservations recommended. 21+. Singles $69; doubles $89. AmEx/D/DC/MC/V. ❸

Motel 6, 8300 Chicago Rd. (☎586-826-9300), in Warren, 20min. northeast of downtown. Take I-696 to the Van Dyke Rd. exit, and then turn right on Chicago. Comfy rooms near the restaurants of Royal Oak. Singles $43; doubles $49. AmEx/D/MC/V. ❷

Pontiac Lake Recreation Area, 7800 Gale Rd. (☎248-666-1020), in Waterford, 45min. northwest of downtown. Take I-75 to Rte. 59 W, turn right on Williams Lake northbound and left onto Gale Rd. 176 wooded sites with electricity and showers. Vehicle permit $6 per day for Michigan residents, non-residents $8; $24/$29 per year. Sites $16. ❶

🍴 FOOD

Gourmet restaurants may have cast their lot with the northern suburbs, but city-dwellers continue to dine in the city's ethnic neighborhoods. At the **Greektown** People Mover stop, Greek restaurants line one block of Monroe St., east of Beaubien St. Joseph Campau Ave., in **Hamtramck** (Ham-TRAM-eck), is the center for Polish fare, while **Mexican Town,** 3 mi. west of downtown, brims with affordable restaurants and markets. The **Eastern Market,** at Gratiot Ave. and Russell St., is a 43-acre bonanza of open-air produce and farm-fresh meat; almost 50,000 people turn up on Saturdays to gather ingredients. (☎567-2400. Open Sa 7am-5pm.)

🏅 **Oslo,** 1456 Woodward Ave. (☎963-0300). Owner Brook Campbell dropped out of architecture school to design this downtown lounge and sushi bar, where recessed wood paneling puts space-age acoustics next to DJs who spin Th-Sa nights. Open Tu-Th 5:30-10:30pm, F-Sa 5:30pm-midnight; lounge open F-Sa until 2am. AmEx/D/MC/V. ❸

Cass Cafe, 4620 Cass Ave. (☎831-4100). Voted "best place to take friends from New York" back in 2003, Cass Cafe has understated white walls, skylights, and a lentil-walnut burger ($6) that will satisfy the appetite of any carnivore. Live DJ Su. Open M-Sa 11am-2am, Su 5pm-midnight. Entrees $8-10. AmEx/D/MC/V. ❷

Cyprus Taverna, 579 Monroe St. (☎961-1550), serves *moussaka* ($10) and other Greek specialties in the heart of Greektown. If you're tired of the flaming cheese routine, try *haloumi,* a fried Cypriot cheese served warm ($6). Lunch specials from $5.25. Dinner $10-13. Open M-Th and Su 11am-2am, F-Sa 11am-4am. AmEx/D/MC/V. ❸

American Coney Island, 114 W. Lafayette St. (☎961-7758). A Detroit landmark for 88 years with beefy and crisp Coney dogs ($2.35). Open 24hr. Cash only. ❶

Xochimilco, 3409 Bagley St. (☎843-0179), draws huge crowds with delicious enchiladas and burritos ($5-8). The dim lighting may force you to squint a bit, but muraled walls, great service, and warm chips with salsa make Xochimilco (so-she-MO-ko) exceptional. Open daily 11am-2am. AmEx/DC/MC/V. ❷

👁 SIGHTS

The freeways and housing projects that divide up downtown Detroit mean that public space can be hard to come by. Both civic leaders and local artists have worked to carve out new areas for people to congregate, even as they respect the institutions that have anchored the community for decades. **John K. King Used and Rare Books,** 901 W. Lafayette St., is one of these institutions, a resolutely uncomputerized warehouse for books ranging from $3 paperbacks to a $6500 Hemingway first edition. Friendly staff use walkie-talkies to help guide customers through the cavernous building. (☎961-0622. Open M-Sa 9:30am-5:30pm.)

CAMPUS MARTIUS PARK. The same firm that gave the Bellagio casino in Las Vegas its famous fountains designed the centerpiece of Detroit's newest public space. The park borrows its name from an 18th-century military drill ground and has already emerged as a center for activity with its shaded gardens and outdoor skating rink that opens during the winter months. (*800 Woodward Ave., between Fort and Michigan Ave. Open M-Th 7am-10pm, F 7am-11pm, Sa 9am-11pm, Su 9am-8pm.*)

GREAT LAKES

Downtown Detroit

🏠🏠 ACCOMMODATIONS
Motel 6, **1**
Pontiac Lake Recreation Area, **2**
Shorecrest Motor Inn, **10**
University of Windsor, **11**

🍎 FOOD
American Coney Island, **7**
Cass Cafe, **3**
Cyprus Taverna, **8**
Oslo, **6**
Tunnel Bar-B-Q, **13**
Xochimilco, **5**

🍺 NIGHTLIFE
Phog, **12**
Saint Andrews Hall, **9**
Town Pump Tavern, **4**

DETROIT ZOO. Exotic animals like tigers and red pandas roam the grounds of the **Detroit Zoological Park.** The National Amphibian Conservation Center allows visitors to get up close and personal with enormous salamanders, while the Arctic Ring of Life exhibit showcases polar bears and a trek through the tundra. *(8450 W. Ten Mile Rd., just off the Woodward exit of Rte. 696 in Royal Oak. ☎ 248-398-0900; www.detroit-zoo.org. Open July-Aug. M-Tu and Th-Su 10am-5pm, W 10am-8pm; April-June and Sept.-Oct. daily 10am-5pm; Nov.-Mar. W-Su 10am-4pm. $11, seniors $9, ages 2-12 $7. Parking $5.)*

ONE HELL OF A PREP SCHOOL. Founded by Detroit philanthropists in 1922, the **Cranbrook Schools** give more than 1600 students a world-class education in the posh suburb of Bloomfield Hills, 15 mi. north of Detroit. Public gardens and a house designed by Eliel Saarinen are well worth a look, and the **Cranbrook Institute of Science,** 39221 N. Woodward Ave., will please the entire family. The new Bat Zone area houses bats, sloths, and other creatures that go bump in the night. *(☎ 248-645-3209 or 877-462-7262; www.cranbrook.edu. Open M-Th and Sa-Su 10am-5pm, F 10am-10pm. $7, seniors and ages 2-12 $5. Planetarium shows $3, under age 2 $1. Bat Zone free with general admission. Hourly shows cost an extra $3/$1.)*

THE HEIDELBERG PROJECT. Drawing on the imagery of painters like Dubuffet and Basquiat, Tyree Guyton has spent the better part of two decades transforming a row of crack houses and abandoned lots on Detroit's Near East Side into installation art. Rows of vacuum cleaners line up in waist-high weeds like a formation of soldiers, while hundreds of stuffed animals hang from the sides of a building around the corner. The **Charles H. Wright Museum of African-American History** is planning a Heidelberg Retrospective in 2006 for the 20th anniversary of the Project's creation. *(Heidelberg St., between Ellery and Mt. Elliott; pick up Gratiot Ave. downtown and follow it north for 1 mi. ☎ 267-1622; www.heidelberg.org. Free.)*

🏛 MUSEUMS

🎵**MOTOWN HISTORICAL MUSEUM.** Entrepreneur and producer Berry Gordy founded Motown Records with an $800 loan from his family and built it up into a recording empire that would leave a permanent impression on American music. Knowledgeable tour guides lead visitors past the hat and gloves donned by Michael Jackson in his "Thriller" video, before descending to the legendary Studio A where Stevie Wonder and Diana Ross laid down their first soulful tracks. *(2648 W. Grand Blvd. ☎ 875-2264; www.motownmuseum.org. Open Tu-Sa 10am-6pm. $8, under 13 $5.)*

HENRY FORD MUSEUM. The astonishing eight acres of exhibit space in the Henry Ford Museum includes iconic artifacts like the bus where Rosa Parks stood her ground and the convertible in which JFK breathed his last breath. In addition to chronicling the history of transportation in America, the museum takes snapshots of popular culture through the 20th century; sit for a few minutes to play with a vintage Mr. Potato Head. Next door, the Greenfield Village outdoor museum is an overly precious tribute to Americana, while the new and impressive Ford Rouge Factory Tour brings visitors out on a catwalk over the F-150 assembly line. *(20900 Oakwood Blvd., off I-94 in Dearborn. Take SMART bus #200 or 250. Museum open daily 9:30am-5pm; factory open daily 9:30am-2:30pm, tours every 30min. Museum and factory tour each $14, seniors $13, ages 5-12 $10. Combination pass including museum, village, and factory tour $26/$24/$20.)*

DETROIT INSTITUTE OF ARTS. The most recent reports indicate that major renovations to Detroit's Museum of Fine Art are slated to drag on until late 2007. For the moment, handpicked selections from the permanent collection hold the fort, along with the signature Diego Rivera mural depicting scenes from Detroit's industrial history. *(5200 Woodward Ave. ☎ 833-7900; www.dia.org. Open W-Th 10am-4pm, F 10am-9pm, Sa-Su 10am-5pm; first F of each month 11am-9pm. Suggested donation $4.)*

MUSEUM OF AFRICAN AMERICAN HISTORY. The MAAH features a core exhibit entitled "And Still We Rise" that follows the African Diaspora from a marketplace in Benin to a reconstructed 1960s lounge from Detroit's East Side. *(315 E. Warren Ave. ☎ 494-5800; www.maah-detroit.org. Open Tu-Sa 9:30am-5pm, Su 1-5pm. Reception with free hors d'oeuvres F 6pm. $8, seniors and ages 3-12 $5.)*

THE NEW DETROIT SCIENCE CENTER. Interactive exhibits that manage to be both educational and fun. Write a concerto on the stringless laser harp, or take in the mammoth space exhibition co-presented by NASA through mid-May 2006. *(5020 John R St. ☎ 577-8400; www.detroitsciencecenter.org. Open mid-June to early Sept. M-F 9am-5pm, Sa-Su 10:30am-6pm; mid-Sept. to early June M-F 9am-3pm, Sa-Su 10:30am-6pm. $7, seniors and ages 2-12 $6; IMAX additional $4.)*

DETROIT HISTORICAL MUSEUM. The Detroit Historical Museum explores the region's transformation from "frontiers to factories"—visitors can tour a streetscape of old town Detroit and gawk at a working piece of the Cadillac assembly line. *(5401 Woodward Ave. ☎ 833-1805; www.detroithistorical.org. Open W-F 9:30am-5pm, Sa 10am-5pm, Su 11am-5pm. $5, college students $3.50, seniors and children 5-18 $3.)*

 ENTERTAINMENT

The brassy anthems of The Supremes and the surly guitar riffs of The White Stripes may define Detroit's sonic palette in the popular imagination, but the **Detroit Symphony Orchestra** sticks to a more traditional repertoire with concerts at **Orchestra Hall,** 3711 Woodward Ave., at Parsons St. (☎ 576-5100, box office 576-5111; www.detroitsymphony.com. Open M-F 10am-6pm. Tickets $15-105. Half-price student and senior rush tickets 1½hr. prior to show.) The **Theater District,** on either side of Woodward Ave. at Grand Circus Park, is anchored by the historic **Fox Theatre,** 2211 Woodward Ave., which draws nationally recognized musicians and entertainers. (☎ 983-6611. Box office open M-F 10am-6pm. $25-100.) The **State Theatre,** 2115 Woodward Ave. (☎ 961-5450; www.statetheatredetroit.com), hosts smaller concerts, while the acclaimed **Detroit Repertory Theatre,** 13103 Woodrow Wilson Ave., shakes things up with a deep-seated commitment to race-transcendent casting. (☎ 868-1347; www.detroitreptheatre.com. Shows Th-F 8:30pm, Sa 3 and 8:30pm, Su 2 and 7:30pm. General admission $17.)

Detroit is a big sports town. During the dog days of summer, baseball's **Tigers** round the bases in the newly built **Comerica Park,** 2100 Woodward Ave.

GIVING BACK

A SHADY OPERATION

Once known as the "Paris of the Midwest" for its gracious, tree-lined avenues, Detroit lost ground as a garden city after the catastrophic fire of 1805, the rapid industrialization in the late 19th century, and an outbreak of Dutch elm disease around 1950. By 1989, the city was losing four trees for every new one being planted. A nonprofit organization called the Greening of Detroit then stepped in with the intention of preserving and restoring the urban forest, using environmental education and advocacy alongside direct planting initiatives. The group planted its 40,000th tree in 2004 and has announced plans to build an urban farm and fruit orchard in southwestern Detroit over the next five years.

The Greening of Detroit holds community tree plantings every Saturday morning during the spring and fall and sometimes on weekdays. They also sponsor as many as six paid internships each year for undergraduates with an interest in environmental studies. Clearly a few clusters of hackberry trees won't be enough to overcome Detroit's reputation as a post-industrial eyesore. But the folks at the Greening of Detroit are convinced that encouraging residents to engage with the landscape around them is a step in the right direction.

For more information, contact the **Greening of Detroit** *(☎ 237-8733; www.greeningofdetroit.com).*

(☎471-2255. $5-60.) Football's **Lions** hit the gridiron next door at **Ford Field,** 2000 Brush St. (☎262-2003. $40.) Inside the **Joe Louis Arena,** 600 Civic Center Dr., the 2002 Stanley Cup champion **Red Wings** play hockey. (☎396-7575. $20-40.) Thirty minutes north of Detroit in Auburn Hills, basketball's **Pistons** play at **The Palace at Auburn Hills,** 2 Championship Dr. (☎248-377-0100. $10-80.)

❋ ♟ FESTIVALS AND NIGHTLIFE

Hart Plaza, a sprawling green space on the banks of the Detroit River, is the epicenter of Detroit's open-air festivals. ▧**Fuse-in** draws electronic music enthusiasts from around the country for a futuristic Memorial Day weekend full of skittering jungle beats. (☎758-0833; www.fuse-indetroit.com. Day pass $10, 3-day pass $25.) Hart Plaza plays host to the four-day **Ford Detroit International Jazz Festival** (☎963-2366; www.detroitjazzfest.com), although new stages were added in 2005 to reach even more of the city. Late June's **International Freedom Festival** (☎923-7400) celebrates the friendship between the US and Canada, and the continent's largest fireworks display erupts over the Detroit River with 10,000 colorful explosions. Steer clear of the crowds at Hart Plaza, and head out to Belle Isle for an equally spectacular view. More than a million visitors arrive for the **African World Festival** (☎494-5860; third weekend in August), even as the **Michigan State Fair** (☎369-8250), at Eight Mile Rd. and Woodward Ave., celebrates 101 years of bake-offs, and 500-pound pumpkins for two weeks during the heart of August.

Metro Detroit's trendiest lounges and nightclubs tend to be out in the northern suburbs, and Ferndale has cultivated a lasting reputation for GLBT nightlife. Still, the downtown area has its own hot spots; check the *7daysindetroit* section of the free weekly *Real Detroit* for listings. Alternative fans should check out **Saint Andrews Hall,** 431 E. Congress St., Detroit's mainstay for national acts along the lines of Le Tigre and Teenage Fanclub. **Shelter,** the more intimate venue downstairs, gives local acts the spotlight, while the entire building lights up every Friday with the **Three Floors** dance party. (☎961-8961; www.standrewshall.com. Most shows 18+; Three Floors 21+. Advance tickets through Ticketmaster $10-20.) The State Theater (see **Entertainment,** p. 513) is the place to be Saturday night for the glittery **Altered State** party. (☎961-5451; www.alteredstateclub.com. 18+. Cover starts at $5. Sa 10pm-2am.) If all you want is a good pint, try the **Town Pump Tavern,** 100 W. Montcalm St., behind the State Theater. Good beer abounds at this watering hole, which is cloaked in ivy and features a mock study with comfy leather chairs. (☎961-1929. Live music Th and Sa-Su. Drafts $3-5. Open daily 11am-2am; bar fare served until 10pm.) Across the river, Windsor (see below) has its own bevy of nightlife options.

▶ DAYTRIP FROM DETROIT

WINDSOR, ONTARIO   ☎519

Though Windsor may not quite live up to its utopian portrayal in Michael Moore's documentary "Bowling for Columbine," Canada's southernmost city does offer a respite from the gritty streets of Detroit. Riverfront parks and sidewalk cafes give the City of Roses a leisurely European feel, while a string of auto plants employs workers outside of the tourist economy. Windsor made a name for itself in the 1800s as a terminus of the Underground Railroad, although today it is underage refugees from Detroit's 21+ bar scene who cross the river for a night of freedom.

Cupped between Riverside Dr. and the Detroit River, the **Odette Sculpture Garden** stretches east from the Ambassador Bridge and includes standout pieces like Edwina Sandys's *Eve's Apple* and Ted Bieler's *Tower Song*. (☎253-2300; www.windsorsculpturepark.com. Open daily dawn-dusk. Free.) At the eastern edge of the park, the **Art Gallery of Windsor,** 401 Riverside Dr. W, boasts a strong permanent collection of Canadian painters and rounds it out with exhibitions from around the world. (☎977-0013; www.artgalleryofwindsor.com. Open W noon-5pm, Th-F noon-8pm, Sa-Su 11am-5pm. CDN\$2.) **Point Pelee National Park of Canada,** 407 Monarch Ln., Leamington, ON, 45 mi. southeast of Windsor, houses more endangered species of plants and animals than any other Canadian national park. Birdwatchers flock to the park in May, while monarch butterfly enthusiasts make the trip in September. (☎322-2365. Open daily Apr. and June-Oct. 6am-9:30pm; May 5am-9:30pm; Nov.-Mar. 7am-6:30pm. CDN\$6, seniors CDN\$5, students CDN\$3; families CDN\$15. Guided birdwatching tours in May W-Su CDN\$10.)

Inexpensive Chinese and Vietnamese restaurants are plentiful along Wyndotte Ave. as it approaches the University of Windsor. Just across from the tunnel exit, **Tunnel Bar-B-Q ❸,** 58 Park St. E, has been serving up finger-lickin' barbecue ribs for more than 40 years. You can't go wrong with an order of the half-strip rib dinner (CDN\$14)—unless you forget to ask for extra napkins. (☎258-3663. Open M-Th and Su 8am-2am, F-Sa 8am-4am. AmEx/D/MC/V.) Sidewalk dining is the name of the game along Ouellette (OH-let) Ave., downtown, where flush-faced American minors stumble in and out of sweaty pubs doling out \$2 shots. Indie rock shows and local microbrews (CDN\$5.50) cultivate a very different vibe at ▩**phog,** 157 University Ave. W, where hipsters recline on a battered-chic leather couch rescued from the curb. (☎253-1605; www.phoglounge.com. Live music Th-Sa; check website for other shows in summer. Cover CDN\$3-5. Open daily 4pm-2am.) **Casino Windsor,** 377 Riverside Dr., offers three floors of gambling and draws gamers from across the river who have told themselves that they are losing less money because of the exchange rate. (☎800-991-7777; www.casinowindsor.com. 19+. Open 24hr.)

Canada's national rail service, **VIA Rail,** 298 Walker Rd. (☎888-842-7245; www.viarail.ca; ticket window open M-Sa 5:10am-9pm), provides service to Toronto (4hr.; 4 per day; CDN\$88, ISIC discount 35%). **Transit Windsor,** 3700 N. Service Rd. E, sends buses throughout the city. (☎944-4111. CDN\$2.35, seniors CDN\$1.60.) **Taxi: Veteran's Cab,** ☎256-2621. **Visitor Info: Convention and Visitors Bureau of Windsor, Essex County, and Pelee Island,** 333 Riverside Dr. W, #103. (☎255-6530 or 800-265-3633; www.visitwindsor.com. Open M-F 8:30am-4:30pm.) The **Ontario Travel Center,** 110 Park St., offers maps, currency exchange, and a knowledgeable staff. (☎973-1338 or 800-668-2746; www.ontariotravel.net. Open daily June-Aug. 8am-8pm; Sept.-May 8:30am-5pm.) **Post Office:** City Centre, corner of Park St. and Ouellette Ave. (☎253-1252. Open M-F 8am-5pm.) **Postal Code:** N9A 4K0. **Area Code:** 519.

ANN ARBOR ☎734

Ann Arbor's namesakes, Ann Rumsey and Ann Allen—the wives of two of the area's early pioneers—supposedly enjoyed sitting under grape arbors. Now known to locals as "A2," the town has managed to prosper without losing its relaxed charm, despite being tucked between several major industrial hubs. Meanwhile, the huge and well-respected University of Michigan adds a hip collage of young, liberal Middle Americans. Ann Arbor is the prototype for a great college town, and is well worth a visit for anyone traveling in the area.

⚡🄷 ORIENTATION AND PRACTICAL INFORMATION. Ann Arbor's streets lie in a grid, but watch out for the slant of Packard St. and Detroit St. **Main Street** divides the town east-west, and **Huron Street** cuts it north-south. The central campus of the **University of Michigan (U of M)** lies east of Main St. and south of E. Huron, a 5min. walk from downtown. In spite of plentiful meter parking, authorities ticket ruthlessly, and one-way streets and frequent dead-ends can make driving stressful. Luckily, downtown Ann Arbor is walkable, and a car is generally unnecessary.

Amtrak, 325 Depot St. (☎994-4906; www.amtrak.com; ticket window open daily 7:15am-11:30pm), runs to Chicago (4½hr., 3 per day, $25-43) and Detroit (1hr., 3 per day, $10-13). **Greyhound,** 116 W. Huron St. (☎662-5511; www.greyhound.com; open M-F 8am-6pm, Sa-Su 8am-3pm), sends buses to Chicago (5-7hr., 4 per day, $31), Detroit (1½hr., 3 per day, $7), and Grand Rapids (4-5hr., 2 per day, $21). **Ann Arbor Transportation Authority (AATA),** 331 S. 4th Ave., provides public transit in Ann Arbor and neighboring Ypsilanti. (☎996-0400; www.theride.org. Station open M-F 7:30am-9:30pm, Sa noon-6:15pm. Buses run M-F 6:45am-11:30pm, Sa-Su 7:30am-7pm. $1, ages 6-18 $0.50; seniors can obtain card for $0.25-0.50 fares.) AATA's **Nightride** provides door-to-door transportation within city limits. (☎528-5432 to reserve; call at least 1hr. in advance. Runs M-F 11:30pm-6am, Sa-Su 7pm-7:30am. $3.) **Checker Sedan** runs between Ann Arbor and the Detroit Metro Airport. (☎800-351-5466. $48. Reserve in advance.) **Visitor Info: Ann Arbor Convention and Visitors Bureau,** 120 W. Huron St., at Ashley. (☎995-7281 or 800-888-9487; www.annarbor.org. Open M-F 8:30am-5pm.) **Hotlines: Sexual Assault Crisis Line,** ☎483-7273. **Psychiatric Emergency Services,** ☎936-5900. (Both 24hr.) **Internet Access: Ann Arbor District Library,** 343 S. 5th Ave. (☎324-4200. Open M 10am-9pm, Tu-F 9am-9pm, Sa 9am-6pm, Su noon-6pm. Free with ID.) **Post Office:** 2075 W. Stadium Blvd. (☎662-0223. Open M-F 8am-6pm, Sa 10am-2pm.) **Postal Code:** 48103. **Area Code:** 734.

🄵 ACCOMMODATIONS. Rooms in Ann Arbor don't come cheap; keep an eye out for discount chains on the southern edge of town or in Ypsilanti, 5 mi. southeast along I-94. Frederika the Hungarian watch-cat keeps an eye on guests at ▧**The Eighth Street Trekkers Lodge ❸,** 120 8th St., where innkeeper Heather O'Neal sells Nepalese crafts out of her garage and plans excursions into the Himalayas. (☎369-3107. Breakfast included. Double $65; singles may be available for $50. Reserve in advance. Cash only.) Should you have a falling out with Frederika, there's always good ol' **Motel 6 ❸,** 3764 S. State St., with cable TV, A/C, and a pool just 10min. from downtown. (☎665-9900. Singles M-Th and Su $47, F-Sa $50; doubles $52/$59. AmEx/D/MC/V.) Seven **campgrounds ❶** lie within a 20 mi. radius of Ann Arbor, including the **Pinckney Recreation Area,** 8555 Silver Hill, in Pinckney, and the **Waterloo Recreation Area,** 16345 McClure Rd., in Chelsea. (Pinckney ☎426-4913. Waterloo ☎475-8307. Primitive sites $10, with water and electricity $22. Vehicle permit $6 per day for Michigan residents, $8 for non-residents; $24/$29 per year.)

🄲 FOOD. Where there are students, there are cheap eats. The cheapest cram the sidewalks of **State** and **South University Street,** while more upscale establishments line **Main Street.** ▧**Zingerman's Deli ❸,** 422 Detroit St., is an Ann Arbor institution deservedly famous for its gourmet breads, cheeses, and deli sandwiches ($8-12). Expect a line out the door during the lunchtime rush. Try **Zingerman's Next Door ❶** for baked goods and homemade gelato. (☎663-3354. Open daily 7am-10pm. AmEx/D/MC/V.) **Krazy Jim's Blimpy Burger ❶,** 551 S. Division St., near campus, caters to the college crowd with gorgeously greasy "cheaper than food" burgers, from a single patty all the way up to the monstrous half-pound "Quint." (☎663-4590. Burgers $2-4.50. Open M-Sa 11am-10pm, Su noon-8pm. Cash only.) For something less likely to induce cardiac arrest, hit up **Seva ❸,** 314 E. Liberty St., for vegetarian entrees like spinach lasagna and North African couscous. (☎662-1111. Entrees $10-14.

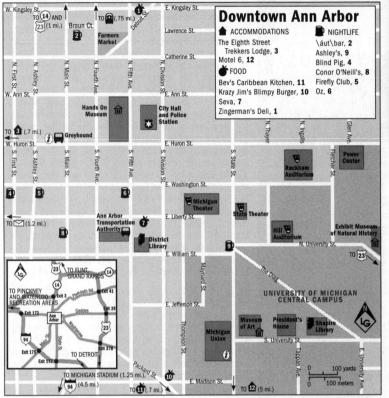

Downtown Ann Arbor

🛏 ACCOMMODATIONS

The Eighth Street
  Trekkers Lodge, 3
Motel 6, 12

🍴 FOOD

Bev's Caribbean Kitchen, 11
Krazy Jim's Blimpy Burger, 10
Seva, 7
Zingerman's Deli, 1

🍸 NIGHTLIFE

\áut\bar, 2
Ashley's, 9
Blind Pig, 4
Conor O'Neill's, 8
Firefly Club, 5
Oz, 6

Open M-Th 11am-9pm, F-Sa 11am-10pm, Su 10am-9pm. AmEx/D/DC/MC/V.) Perch on one of five stools at the counter of **Bev's Caribbean Kitchen ❷**, 1232 Packard Rd., for curried goat ($8.75) with a side of Jamaican philosophy from the staff. (☎741-5252. Jerk sandwiches $4.50. Open Tu-Sa 11:30am-9pm. AmEx/D/MC/V.)

🎭🎵 **SIGHTS AND ENTERTAINMENT.** Not surprisingly, the University of Michigan is the driving force behind Ann Arbor's rich cultural life. The **University of Michigan Museum of Art (UMMA),** 525 S. State St., houses one of the foremost university art collections in the country, although the exhibition hall will close its doors in July 2006 for a major renovation. (☎764-0395; www.umma.mich.edu. Open Tu-W and F-Sa 10am-5pm, Th 10am-9pm, Su noon-5pm. Free.) A pair of enormous mastodon skeletons guards the second floor of the **University of Michigan Exhibit Museum of Natural History,** 1109 Geddes Ave., flanked by a saber-tooth tiger and the skull of a T. rex. The anthropology exhibits on the fourth floor are a bit spotty, but weekend shows at the planetarium bring the stars that much closer. (☎764-0478; www.exhibits.lsa.umich/edu. Open M-Sa 9am-5pm, Su noon-5pm. Museum free; planetarium $3.75.) Security won't escort you to the door for touching displays at the **Ann Arbor Hands-On Museum,** 220 E. Ann St., which has four floors of exhibits designed to be tugged, twisted, and turned. (☎995-5439; www.aahom.org. Open M-Sa 10am-5pm, Su noon-5pm. $7.50; students, seniors, and ages 2-17 $6.) The stalls

RADIO DAYS

Music is a must when I am on the road. I can't separate the memory of my drive across northern Wisconsin from the brittle ballads of Iron & Wine, and I don't know how I would have weathered that Upper Peninsula morning of post-graduation angst without the constipated braying of Alanis's *Jagged Little Pill.* An iPod can be a Let's Go researcher's best friend, and yet after a while even my favorite albums start to sound stale. I can edify myself with NPR for an hour or two, but after that, it's new music that I'm craving. Meanwhile, commercial radio is serving up its usual flavorless gruel, and I have another hundred miles to drive.

Ann Arbor offered me three days' respite from this quandary, courtesy of the university's student-run radio station, WCBN-FM 88.3. WCBN traces its history to the Campus Broadcasting Network established by students in 1952, bouncing from AM to FM in the following years and eventually ending up "all the way to the left" of the dial. Instead of carving up its music library into rigid genres, WCBN encouraged DJs to mix and match tracks from different artistic traditions in order to keep listeners on their toes. And yes, it can be jarring to hear a frenetic cut from Japanese punk rockers Zeni Geva hot on the heels of a Burt Bacharach schmaltzfest. But it's also exciting, and worth a listen as you cruise through town.

—Marcel LaFlamme

in front of the historic **Kerrytown Shops** play host to a vibrant **farmers market,** 315 Detroit St. (☎994-3276. Open May-Dec. W and Sa 7am-3pm; Jan.-Apr. Sa 8am-3pm.) Paintings and pottery take over the market space on Sundays, when local artists display their creations at the **Artisans Market.** (Open May-Dec. Su 11am-4pm.) It's nearly impossible to get tickets for a **Wolverine football game** at U of M's 115,000 capacity stadium, but fans can give it a shot by calling the athletics office (☎764-0247). After the students depart for the summer, the **Ann Arbor Summer Festival** (☎647-2278; www.annarborsummerfestival.org) draws local crowds from mid-June to early July for dance and musical performances at the **Power Center.** Thrifty festivalgoers tend to prefer **Top of the Park,** a nightly series of free movies and concerts that was held for years on top of a Fletcher St. parking garage. Check the summer festival website for the 2006 location. Late July draws thousands for the **Ann Arbor Street Art Fair** (☎994-5260; www.artfair.org), while the **University Musical Society** sponsors classical concerts from September to April. (☎764-2538 or 800-221-1229; www.ums.org. Balcony seats from $10.)

▣ **NIGHTLIFE.** Free in restaurants and music stores, the monthly *Current* has detailed nightlife listings, although Detroit's *Metro Times* and the monthly *Ann Arbor Paper* are also good resources. For GLBT info, pick up a copy of the Detroit-based *Between the Lines.* For gritty rock 'n' roll shows and a cool indie vibe, nobody upstages the **Blind Pig,** 208 S. 1st St. (☎996-8555; www.blindpigmusic.com. Shows Tu-Sa 9:30pm. 18+. Cover $5-10, under 21 $3 extra. Open daily 3pm-2am.) The **Firefly Club,** 207 S. Ashley St., offers an intimate setting for jazz, ranging from traditional big band to modern avant-garde. (☎665-9090; www.fireflyclub.com. Latin jazz every Th. 21+. Cover $5-10. Open M, W-Th, and Su 7pm-2am, F-Sa 8pm-2am.) You're definitely not in Kansas anymore at **Oz,** 210 S. 5th Ave., a Middle Eastern lounge where revelers nestle into armchairs and smoke hookahs ($10-15) or roust themselves for a stint on the dance floor. Martinis start at $2 when the doors open, and increase in price by $1 every hour as the night goes on. (☎222-4770; www.ozannarbor.com. DJ Tu-Su. Belly dancer F 12:30am. Cover varies. Open Tu-Th 8pm-2am, F-Sa 8pm-4am, Su 6pm-midnight.) There are Irish bars, and then there are bars that like to think that they're Irish bars. **Conor O'Neill's,** 318 S. Main St., is solidly in the first camp; a mixed crowd of locals and students bang their pint glasses on the tables in time with the freedom ballads being yowled at the microphone. (☎665-2968. Open daily 11:30am-2am; breakfast served Sa-Su 8am-2pm.

Kitchen closes M-Th and Su 11pm, F-Sa midnight.) **\áut\ bar,** 315 Braun Ct., near
the intersection of Catherine St. and 4th Ave., is a straight-friendly gay bar catering
to twinkly college boys and a laid-back older crowd. (☎994-3677. Open daily 4pm-
2am. Su brunch 10am-3pm.) They take their beer seriously at **Ashley's,** 338 S. State
St., with an encyclopedic menu of the 70 brews on tap. Try a sampler set of perfumed Belgian ales for $10. (☎996-9191; www.ashleys.com. Pints $4.50-6. Open M-
Sa 11:30-2am, Su noon-midnight.)

LAKE MICHIGAN SHORE

The freighters that once powered the rise of Chicago still steam along the coast of
Lake Michigan, but these days they are greatly outnumbered by pleasure boats
cruising along the coast. Valleys of sand beckon sunbathers, while hikers trek
through the virgin forests of Michigan's state parks. When autumn comes, the
weather forbids swimming, but inland, festivals celebrate local fruits and blossoms, from cherries in July to apples in September. Snow covers much of the
coast in winter, drawing snowmobiling, skiing, and ice-skating enthusiasts. The
coastline stretches 350 mi. north from the Indiana border to the Mackinac Bridge;
its southern end is a scant two hours from downtown Chicago.

▨ PRACTICAL INFORMATION

Many of the region's attractions lie in the small coastal towns that cluster around
Grand Traverse Bay in the north. **Traverse City,** at the southern tip of the bay, is the
famous "Cherry Capital of the World." The main north-south route along the coast
is **U.S. 31.** Numerous green "Lake Michigan Circle Tour" signs lead closer to the
shoreline, providing an excellent view. Coastal accommodations can be expensive; head inland for cheaper lodging. Determined travelers can occasionally find a
good deal lakeside, and numerous camping options exist in the summer months.
Based in Grand Rapids, the **West Michigan Tourist Association,** 3665 28th St. SE, Ste.
B, hands out info on the area. (☎616-245-2217 or 800-442-2084; www.wmta.org.
Open M-F 8:30am-5pm.) **Area Codes:** 616 and 231.

CENTRAL MICHIGAN SHORE

SLEEPING BEAR DUNES   ☎231

The Sleeping Bear Dunes lie along the western shores of the Leelanau Peninsula,
20 mi. west of Traverse City on Rte. 72. **Sleeping Bear Dunes National Lakeshore**
encompasses 25 mi. of shoreline in Leelenau and Benzie Counties, as well as both
the Manitou Islands, located a few miles off the mainland coast. Access to both
mainland and offshore areas of the Lakeshore is administered by the National
Park Service, and visitors hoping to do anything more than drive along the county
roads must pay an entrance fee at the **National Parks Service Visitors Center,** 9922
Front St., in Empire. (☎326-5134. Vehicles $10, pedestrians or bikers $5. Fee
includes 7-day admission. Open daily June-Aug. 8am-6pm; Sept.-May 8am-4pm.)

Near the historic Fishtown shops at the end of River St., **Manitou Island Transit,** in
Leland, makes daily trips to slightly less rugged South Manitou from June to
August. The ferry schedule makes South Manitou an ideal destination for day hik-
ers, dropping visitors off at 11:30am and whisking them back to Leland at 4:30pm.
Visitors who set foot on North Manitou should take note—the ferry returns to
Leland immediately after dropping off passengers at 11am, and hikers are cut off
from the modern world until the next morning. The ferries will not run during bad

weather, so campers on either island should bring at least 2 extra days of supplies. (☎256-9061. Check-in 9:15am. Trips to North Manitou 3-5 times per week in June, daily July-Aug. Call ahead for May and Sept.-Nov. schedule. Round-trip $25, ages 11 and under $14. Reservations recommended.) Hardcore backpackers looking for an adventure can **camp** on both islands with the purchase of a **camping permit** ($5) from the Manitou Island Transit office, though there is an entrance fee ($10 per 7 days; available at the visitors center). The Manitou Islands do not allow wheeled vehicles, including cars and bikes.

Back on the mainland, hikers can make an exhausting 3 mi. trip up the side of a sand dune and down to the waters of Lake Michigan. The **Dune Climb** starts 5 mi. north of Empire on Rte. 109; the full route takes roughly 3hr. to complete, and hikers should bring plenty of drinking water. Visitors up for a more leisurely day at the beach should turn off Rte. 22 just before it crosses the Platte River, and follow Lake Michigan Rd. all the way to the end. The waters of Lake Michigan are often quite cold until August, but the Platte River flows into the lake at **Platte River Point** and creates warmer conditions in early summer. After toweling off, drivers can inch their way along the 7 mi. **Pierce Stocking Scenic Drive**, off Rte. 109 just north of Empire. The best-known outlook presents a sweeping view from the top of a sand cliff 450 ft. above the surface of Lake Michigan. The drive stays open from late April to early November, weather permitting. As night falls on the dunes, the silver screen lights up at **Cherry Bowl Drive-in Theatre**, 9812 Honor Hwy., in Honor. Heading south on Rte. 22, take a left onto Rte. 708 and drive 5 mi. until you see the signs. (☎325-3413; www.cherrybowldrivein.com. Open June-Aug. Movies start at dusk. $7.50, under 12 free.) **Riverside Canoes,** on Rte. 22 at Platte River Bridge, organizes 2½hr. canoe and kayak excursions, as well as relaxed tubing trips. (☎325-5622; www.canoemichigan.com. Open May to early Oct. daily 8am-10pm. Inner tubes $7 per hr. Kayak trips from $24. Canoe trips from $33.)

The Sleeping Bear Dunes are home to four different **campgrounds. Platte River ❶**, just off of Rte. 22, 10 mi. south of Empire, is the most luxurious, with showers and electrical hookups. (☎325-5881 or 800-365-2267. $16, with electricity $21). **D.H. Day ❶**, 1 mi. west of Glen Arbor on Rte. 109, offers drinking water and flush toilets. (☎334-4634. $12.) Two backcountry campsites, **Whitepine ❶** and **Valley View ❶**, have fire rings and vault toilets; reservations are not accepted, but permits can be purchased for $5 at Platte River or D.H. Day. Whitepine is popular for its proximity to the water.

TRAVERSE CITY   ☎231

Bearing a certain resemblance to the Ann Arbor of 20 years ago, Traverse City is quickly emerging as a hip town and a magnet for young people from around the state. Bikes are a very popular way to explore the surrounding area, and abandoned railroad beds have been reclaimed as the **Traverse Area Recreation and Transportation (TART)** trail that extends 19 mi. northwest of Traverse City to Suttons Bay. The demanding **Vasa Pathway** draws mountain bikers to the hills of Pere Marquette State Forest, while the **Cherry Capital Cycling Club** leads Monday evening excursions up into scenic Old Mission Peninsula, northeast of town. **McLain Cycle and Fitness,** 750 E. 8th St., rents road bikes and mountain bikes. (☎941-7161. Open in summer M-F 9am-6pm, Sa 9am-5pm, Su 11am-4pm; low season closed Su. All bikes $10 per 2hr. Road bikes $20 per day, mountain bikes $30 per day.)

With half of America's cherries produced in the region around Traverse City, the **National Cherry Festival** (☎800-968-3380; www.cherryfestival.org), held during the first full week of July, has every right to be a massive wingding. Eight nights of live music and daily events ranging from a pit-spitting tournament to a fireworks display ensure that festivalgoers will get a chance to see Traverse City with all of its flags flying. In early to mid-July, many orchards near Traverse City let visitors pick their own cherries, including **Elzer Farms**, 9 mi. north of Traverse City on Rte. 37. (☎223-9292. Open May-Sept. M-Sa 9am-6pm, Su 9am-4pm. $3 per quart. Pies $10.) Sophisticated fruit connoisseurs can also indulge their taste buds at one of the area's many well-respected wineries.

East Front St. (U.S. 31) is lined with motels, and during the summer rates generally start at $50. **Northwestern Michigan College ❷**, 1701 E. Front St., West and East Halls, offers spartan dorm rooms with unyielding mattresses, and is most cost-effective for travelers in bigger groups. Guests have access to laundry, a common room, and outdoor athletic facilities. (☎995-1400. Open June-Aug. Single beds $40; 2-bed suites $70; 4-bed suites $60. Reserve several weeks in advance. D/MC/V.) For those who prefer to commune with nature, **Traverse City State Park ❶**, 1132 U.S. 31 N, 2 mi. east of town, has 324 wooded sites crowded along U.S. 31, adjacent to the beach. (☎922-5270 or 800-447-2757. Toilet and shower facilities. Sites with hookup $23; cabins $45. Vehicle permit fee $6 per day for Michigan residents, $8 for non-residents; $24/$29 per year.) Downtown, Front St. offers a range of appealing food options. Start off the day with breakfast at **The Omelette Shoppe ❷**, 124 Cass St., where local art hangs on the walls and a dozen fluffy omelets come in under $7. (☎946-0912. Open M-F 6:30am-3pm, Sa-Su 7:30am-3pm. Another location at 1209 E. Front St., ☎946-0590, in the Campus Plaza complex. Open M-Sa 7am-3pm, Su 10am-3pm. AmEx/D/MC/V.) Polish off a mid-afternoon snack at **Grand Traverse Pie Company ❶**, 525 W. Front St., where Old Mission cherry pie sells by the slice ($2.75) and by the pan. (☎922-7437; www.gtpie.com. Open M-Sa 9am-6pm. AmEx/D/MC/V.) If you're looking for a spot to bring a date for dinner, **Poppycock's ❸**, 128 E. Front St., offers pasta ($12) and multi-ethnic vegetarian entrees ($13-14) in a bistro setting that manages to be both convivial and elegant. From Thursday to Saturday, the restaurant dims the lights and brings in live jazz. (☎941-7632. Open in summer M-W 11am-10pm, Th-Sa 11am-midnight, Su noon-9pm; low season M-W 11am-9pm, Th-Sa 11am-midnight. MC/V.) After hours, head down to **Union Street Station**, 117 S. Union St., where an artsy twentysomething crowd grooves to live music and $3 drafts. (☎941-1930. Live music Tu and Th-Sa 10pm. No cover Tu or Th; $5 F-Sa. Open M-Sa 11am-2am, Su noon-2am.) For an alternative to the bar scene, stop by the recently opened **InsideOut Gallery,** 229 Garland St., where TC's alternative set congregates for live music and rotating exhibitions of pop art. (☎929-3254; www.insideoutgallery.com. Open M-Th 11am-6pm, F-Sa 11am-8pm, Su noon-5pm. Free.) For more entertainment info, pick up the excellent weekly *Northern Express* at corner kiosks in the city, or seek out the sporadically published *Thirdeye* for a more radical take on life in Traverse City.

Indian Trails, 3233 Cass Rd. (☎946-5180 or 800-231-2222), runs buses to Grand Rapids (3½hr., 1 per day, $23) and destinations in the Upper Peninsula via St. Ignace (3hr., 1 per day, $19). The **Bay Area Transportation Authority (BATA)** runs five regular bus routes around Traverse City with a service called the **Cherriot.** They also pick up passengers given 24hr. notice. (☎941-2324. Open daily 6am-6pm. Cherriot routes $1, seniors and under 12 $0.50. Pick-up service $2/$1.) The **Traverse City Convention and Visitors Bureau,** at Union St. and Grandview Parkway, maintains a massive binder with info on each week's events. (☎947-1120 or 800-872-8377; www.mytraversecity.com. Open M-Sa 9am-6pm, Su 11am-3pm.) **Internet Access:** the **Traverse City District Library,** 610 Woodmere Ave., doles out free Internet in 1hr. slots. (☎932-8580. Open M-Th 9am-9pm, F-Sa 9am-6pm, Su noon-5pm.) **Post Office:** 202 S. Union St. (☎946-2418. Open M-F 8am-5pm.) **Postal Code:** 49684.

GREAT LAKES

NORTHERN MICHIGAN SHORE

STRAITS OF MACKINAC   ☎231

First things first, Mackinac is pronounced "MACK-i-naw," so curb the urge to rhyme your syllables by saying "MACK-i-nack." The **Mackinac Bridge** ("Mighty Mac") soars over the intersection of Lake Michigan and Lake Huron, connecting **Mackinaw City** to St. Ignace in the Upper Peninsula. Measuring 950 ft. longer than the Golden Gate Bridge, the 5 mi. span is the third-longest suspension bridge in the world. A local tradition that is not to be missed is the annual **Labor Day Bridge Walk,** where Michigan's governor leads thousands north across the bridge to St. Ignace. Chain motels and tacky gift shops dominate the town, although the **Mackinac State Historic Parks** are well worth a look. Just west of the Mackinac Bridge's southern landfall, **Colonial Michilimackinac** reconstructs a fort built in 1715 by French fur traders and recently unearthed by a tireless team of archaeologists. (☎436-4100; www.mackinacparks.com. Open daily early May to mid-Oct. 9am-5pm; mid-June to mid-Aug. until 6pm. $9.50, ages 6-17 $6, under 6 free.) A 5min. walk away, the **Old Mackinac Point Lighthouse** opened in 2005 as a restoration project in progress. Warped wood and cracked plaster walls give the visitor a sense of the work that remains to be done, although the four-story climb to the tower already offers a sweeping view of the surrounding straits. (Open daily mid-May to mid-Oct. 9am-4pm, mid-June to mid-Aug. until 6pm. Closed-toe shoes required to climb the tower. $6, ages 6-17 $3.50, under 6 free.) **Fort Mackinac** (on Mackinac Island, see below) and **Historic Mill Creek,** a complex with a water-powered sawmill and nature trails 3 mi. south of Mackinaw City, round out the list of Mackinac State Historic Parks. (Mill Creek open daily early May to late Sept. 9am-4pm; mid-June to mid-Aug. until 6pm. $7.50, ages 6-17 $4.50, under 6 free.) A Mackinac Combination ticket buys seven days of unlimited admission to all four sights. ($25, ages 6-17 $15.50. Available at all 4 sights.)

Lakeshore accommodation options abound on Rte. 23, south of the city. The best lodging deals in the area lie across the Mackinac Bridge on the **I-75 Business Loop** in St. Ignace. Five minutes from the docks, the **Harbor Light Motel ❷,** 1449 State St. on I-75, rents basic rooms with cable TV, A/C, and refrigerators. A volleyball net and the occasional bonfire on the beach make this a good bet for travelers. (☎906-643-9439. In summer singles $38; doubles $45; low season $30/$35. D/MC/V.) For an outdoor escape, campers can crash at one of the 600 sites of **Mackinac Mill Creek Campground ❶,** 3 mi. south of town on Rte. 23. The grounds provide beach access and biking trails. (☎436-5584; www.campmackinaw.com. Internet access, public showers, and heated pool. Sites $22, with full hookup $28. Cabins in summer from $55; low season from $35. Free shuttle to island ferry. AmEx/D/MC/V.) Their recipe for the Upper Peninsula's favorite meat pie may trace its way back to Cornwall, but **Mackinaw Pastie & Cookie Co. ❶,** 117 W. Jamet St., two blocks south of Colonial Michilimackinac, actually recruits summer workers from overseas in the spirit of cultural exchange. Ask the help at the counter which country they call home. (☎231-436-8202; www.mackinawpastie.com. Pasties $5-7. Open daily 8:30am-11pm. Other location at 516 S. Huron. AmEx/D/MC/V.)

The **Michigan Welcome Center,** on Nicolet St. off I-75 at Exit 338, has maps and brochures about area attractions. (☎436-5566. Open daily mid-June to Aug. 8am-7pm; Sept. to mid-June 9am-5pm. Free reservation service.)

MACKINAC ISLAND   ☎231

Mackinac Island, a 16min. ferry ride from the mainland, has been a destination for summer vacationers since the 1870s. Railroad barons lined the south-facing bluffs with elegant Victorian homes and, by banning automobiles from the island in 1896, tried to guarantee that Mackinac would retain its genteel, unhurried atmosphere for years to come. The slew of shops pressing **Mackinac fudge** (½ lb. $6) on day-trippers proves that the early inhabitants weren't entirely successful, although there are still quiet corners of the island to explore. Walk off the ferry landing, cross the garish strip that is Main St., and never look back.

Commanding a lofty view of the island's southern harbor, **Fort Mackinac** was a hotly contested piece of military architecture during the War of 1812. Today cannon firings, carefully restored buildings, and the sounds of fife and drum lure a steady stream of visitors up to the bluffs. (☎436-4100; www.mackinacparks.com. Open daily May to mid-Oct. 9:30am-4:30pm, June-Aug. until 7:30pm. $9.50, ages 6-17 $6, under 6 free.) During June, July, and August, tickets to the fort also include access to a number of historic buildings on Market St. (open daily 11am-6pm) as well as Mission Church, near the southeastern corner of the island (open daily noon-4pm). Travelers willing to don a three-cornered hat should inquire into weeklong **volunteer opportunities** at the fort, which include free housing on the island. Call for details. **Mackinac Island Carriage Tours,** Main St., sends horse-drawn buggies on a 2hr. trot around the southern half of the island veering as far east as the Arch Rock formation before circling back to showcase the sumptuous grounds of the Grand Hotel. Keep an eye out for weepy devotees of the 1980 Christopher Reeve film *Somewhere in Time*, which was set at the hotel. (☎906-847-3307; www.mict.com. Tours daily early May to mid-Oct. 9am-3pm; July-Aug. until 5pm. $18, ages 5-12 $8.) For those who would rather take the reins themselves, **Jack's Livery Stable,** 331 Mahoney Ave., off of Cadotte Ave., rents saddle horses and buggies. (☎847-3391. Saddle horses $30 per hr. 2-person horse and buggy $48 per hr.; 4-person $60 per hr. Open daily May-Oct. 8am-5pm; June-Aug. until 6pm.) Bicycles are the best way to see the island's beaches and forests. Rental shops line Main St. by the ferry docks and generally offer identical rates ($4 per hr., $25 per day). Encompassing 80% of the island, **Mackinac Island State Park** features a circular 8¼ mi. shoreline road that takes about an hour by bike and two by foot.

Hotel rates on the island generally reach into the stratosphere, but ▨McNally Cottage ❹, on Main St., offers a haven for thrifty travelers. Situated in the heart of downtown, this B&B has been owned and operated by the same family every summer since its construction in the 1880s. (☎847-3565; www.mcnallycottage.net. Shared baths. Single room with twin bed $50; double beds $65-70. Call well in advance for reservations. Cash only.) Take your cue from the locals and "shop across" in Mackinaw City for food; everything is more expensive on the island, whether you buy it in a restaurant or a convenience store. **Marquette Park,** just below Fort Mackinac, is a good spot for a picnic; otherwise, carry your food up shady, flower-lined Cupid's Pathway behind the fort and grab a cold can of beer ($2) at **Harrisonville General Store ❶,** on Hoban Ave. This outpost is the spot where year-round residents stop for groceries and gossip during the low season. (Open daily May-Sept. 10am-8pm; Nov.-Apr. noon-5:30pm. Cash only.) If you're just not the picnicking type, stop by **3 Brothers Sarducci Pizzeria ❶,** on Main St., for an over-sized slice of Sicilian-style pizza ($3.95) and a song on the jukebox. (☎847-3880. Open daily in summer 11am-8pm; low season 11am-5pm. Cash only.)

Transportation to the island via ferry is quick and pleasant, if egregiously over-priced. Three ferry lines, **Shepler's** (☎800-828-6157), **Arnold Transit Co.** (☎800-542-8528), and **Star** (☎800-638-9892), leave Mackinaw City (in summer every 30min. M-Th and Su 8am-10pm, F-Sa 8am-11pm) and St. Ignace, though service from St. Ignace is slightly less frequent. (Round-trip $18, ages 5-12 $9, bikes and strollers $6.50. All lines charge identical rates.) The **Mackinac Island Tourism Bureau,** on Main St., has a free visitors guide. (☎800-454-5227; www.mackinacisland.org. Open May-Oct. M-W and Su 9am-5pm, Th-Sa 9am-9pm; Nov.-Apr. daily 9am-5pm.)

SCENIC DRIVE: NORTHERN MICHIGAN SHORE

Heading north from Traverse City, the northern shore of Lake Michigan skirts cherry orchards, monied resort towns, and broadleaf forests before meeting up with Lake Huron at the Straits of Mackinac. U.S. 31 follows the shoreline for some 65 mi. north of Traverse City, while Rte. 119 picks up the route at Petoskey and terminates in Cross Village. Drivers should expect to be both careful and patient on the 27 mi. stretch of Rte. 119 between Harbor Springs and Cross Village. Known as the Tunnel of Trees, this stretch of road is very narrow and twists through many sharp curves, keeping speeds down around 30 mph and giving drivers plenty of time to enjoy glimpses of the lake through the branches.

From Traverse City, U.S. 31 winds its way east along the southern shore of Grand Traverse Bay, and then passes through miles of cherry orchards just south of tiny **Acme.** For a more leisurely look at the orchards, turn right on Elk Lake Rd. as you pull into the town of **Elk Rapids,** 10 mi. north of Acme. Follow the road over the county line as far as Williamsburg, and then double back to the main road. Just north of Elk Rapids, U.S. 31 threads its way across a narrow spit of land between Grand Traverse Bay to the west and Elk and Torch Lakes to the east; in Eastport, at the tip of Torch Lake, **Barnes County Park** beckons to swimmers and sunbathers with a quiet, sandy beach. The town of **Charlevoix** (SHAR-le-voy) is the next major stop along U.S. 31, and while the community once inspired Ernest Hemingway to pen his series of Nick Adams stories, today yachting and upscale shopping leaves little of interest for budget travelers. However, affordable accommodations can be found south of town. The west-facing rooms at **Courtside Motel ❷,** 1526 Bridge St., get warm in the afternoon, but A/C and in-room fridges manage to cool things down. (☎547-0505. In summer singles $40-50, doubles $55-65; low season $35/$45. AmEx/D/MC/V.) Campers who don't mind going without showers and electricity can take one of 81 rustic sites on the shores of Lake Michigan at **Fisherman's Island State Park ❶,** on Bells Bay Rd., 5 mi. south of Charlevoix on U.S. 31. The park offers 5 mi. of undeveloped shoreline, and the bell-like whistle of the endangered piping plover can sometimes be heard near the water. (☎547-6641 or 800-447-2757. Sites $10. Vehicle permit required. Michigan residents $6, nonresidents $8. MC/V.)

Charlevoix also serves as the gateway to **Beaver Island,** the most remote inhabited island in the Great Lakes and a paradise of loon-dotted shores and apple groves. **Ferries** depart from the dock located at 103 Bridge St. in Charlevoix. (☎547-2311 or 888-446-4095; www.bibco.com. 2hr; 1-4 per day. Round-trip $38, ages 5-12 $19; bikes $16.) The **Beaver Island Chamber of Commerce** is just north of the ferry dock and has info about campgrounds. (☎448-2505; www.beaverisland.org. Open in summer M-F 8am-4pm, Sa 10:30am-2:30pm; low season M-F 8am-noon.)

You can circle back to Charlevoix for a good night's rest, but in the meantime continue north for 16 mi. as far as **Petoskey,** a resort town that has developed into a hub for galleries and traditional crafts. **Crooked Tree Arts Center,** 461 E. Mitchell St., has led the way with rotating collections of visual art and music classes, as well as theater and dance performances. Look for a juried exhibition of northwestern Michigan landscape paintings in July and August 2006. (☎347-4337; www.crookedtree.org. Galleries open M-F 9am-5pm, Sa 10am-4pm; in summer also Su noon-4pm. Free admission to galleries. Call for student discounts on selected performances.) In the heart of Petoskey's quaint **Gaslight District,** an arch-shaped mosaic of colorful coffee cups marks the entrance to the **Roast & Toast Cafe ❶,** 309 E. Lake St. A young, funky staff serves up fresh sandwiches ($5-6) and coffee that's roasted on-site; bring your grub out to the patio on a sunny day. (☎347-7767. Open mic Su 6-8pm. Open in summer daily 7am-9pm; low season M-Th 7am-7pm, F-Su 7am-8pm. AmEx/D/MC/V.) Friday and Saturday nights, young people head out on the town to **The Upstairs Club,** 434 E. Mitchell St. (☎347-2739. Cover $5.

21+. Open F-Sa 10:30pm-1:30am.) Sunday nights during summertime mean taking in a set by the Jelly Roll Blues Band at the **Legs Inn**, on the left as Rte. 119 pulls into Cross Village. (☎526-2281; www.legsinn.com. Cover $5. Check website for live music on other nights. Open mid-May to mid-Oct. M-Sa noon-9pm, Su noon-1am.) Early July also brings the earthy-crunchy ▧**Blissfest Music Festival** to the northern Michigan shore, as three days of folk music unfolds just east of Cross Village on an old farmstead. (☎348-7047; www.blissfest.org. 1-day ticket $30-35, weekend pass $67. Rustic camping $17 per night.) If these plans fall through, then there's no better way to finish a day on the Lake Michigan shore than watching the sunset from the gazebo at **Sunset Park Scenic Overlook,** just off Rte. 31 in Petoskey.

UPPER PENINSULA

Overlooked by natives and first-time visitors alike, Michigan's Upper Peninsula (U.P.) has vast stretches of unspoiled land and a low cost of living that makes it a must-see region for budget travelers. With only 20,000 people in **Marquette**, the peninsula's largest town, a folksy, homespun approach to life tends to prevail; locals joke that they can always spot tourists because they're the only ones who tuck their purses under their arms when they go up to the salad bar. Sophistication may not be the U.P.'s strong suit, but the opportunities for world-class hiking, kayaking, and snowshoeing more than make up for the spotty cell phone reception.

The U.P.'s state parks give beginners plenty of opportunities for day hikes, while seasoned trailblazers make their way across Michigan's section of the **North Country Trail,** a scenic trail extending from New York to North Dakota. The **North Country Trail Association,** 229 E. Main Street, Lowell 49331 (☎866-445-3628; www.northcountrytrail.org), provides details on the path. At its best, Michigan's fall foliage can rival New England's vivid colors, making autumn an appealing time to hike the U.P. In the winter, cross-country skiers and snowmobilers replace hikers as layers of snow blanket the trails. After the ice thaws, dozens of pristine rivers beckon canoers. Those who heed the call of the water should contact the **Michigan Association of Paddlesport Providers,** 801 S. Garfield Ave., Traverse City 49686 (☎231-947-3345; www.michigancanoe.com), for canoeing tips.

Lodging is fairly inexpensive throughout the U.P., and outside the major tourist spots motel rooms start at around $30. The peninsula is littered with **campgrounds.** (Reservations at National Forest sites: ☎877-

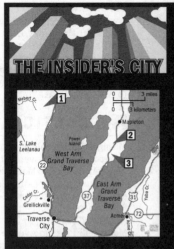

THE INSIDER'S CITY

WATCH YOUR BACK, NAPA

France. California. Traverse City? Michigan resort towns are not usually named among the world's great wine producers, but a handful of wineries are quietly bottling a revolution in the hills to increasing acclaim—and we're not just talking about blue ribbons at the county fair.

1 **L. Mawby,** 4519 S. Elm Valley Rd., south of Sutton's Bay, makes only sparkling wines, including a vintage known simply as Sex. (☎271-3522; www.lmawby.com.)

2 **Chateau Grand Traverse,** 12239 Center Rd., makes a mean Dry Johannisberg Riesling ($10). Free tastings and tours. (☎223-7355; www.cgtwines.com.)

3 **Peninsula Cellars,** 11480 Center Rd., off Rte. 37 north of Traverse City, offers free tastings in an 1895 schoolhouse. Don't miss the world-class Gewurztraminer, $15. (☎933-9787; www.peninsulacellars.com.)

444-6777; www.reserveusa.com. Reservations at state parks: ☎800-447-2757; www.michigan.gov/dnr.) Bring extra blankets, as temperatures in these parts can drop to 50°F or lower, even in July. Keep in mind that the counties of the U.P. that border Wisconsin are on Central Time, while the northern counties are on Eastern Time. And be sure to save room for a **pastie** (PASS-tee) during your stay; the meat pie was imported by Cornish miners during the 19th century. Tourists tend to drown the concoction in brown gravy, but ask for a bottle of ketchup if you want to pass for a local.

⁊ PRACTICAL INFORMATION

Michigan Travel Centers surround the Upper Peninsula at its six main entry points: **Ironwood,** 801 W. Cloverland Dr. (☎932-3330; open daily June-Aug. 8am-7pm; Sept.-May 8am-4pm); **Iron Mountain,** 618 S. Stephenson Ave. (☎774-4201; open daily June-Aug. 7am-5pm; Sept.-May 8am-4pm); **Marquette,** 2201 U.S. 41 S (☎249-9066; open daily June-Aug. 8am-7pm; Sept.-May 9am-5pm); **Menominee,** 1343 10th Ave. (☎863-6496; open daily 8am-4pm); **Saint Ignace,** on I-75 N north of the Mackinac Bridge (☎643-6979; open daily June-Aug. 8am-7pm; Sept.-May 9am-5pm); and **Sault Sainte Marie,** 843 Portage Ave. (☎632-8242; open daily 9am-7pm). The **Upper Peninsula Travel and Recreation Association** (☎800-562-7134; www.uptravel.com; info line staffed M-F 8am-4:30pm) publishes the invaluable *Upper Peninsula Travel Planner.* For additional help planning a trip in the area, write or call the **USDA Forest Service** in the Hiawatha National Forest, 2727 N. Lincoln Rd., Escanaba 49829 (☎786-4062). **Area Code:** 906.

SAULT SAINTE MARIE   ☎906

The shipping industry has long been the hallmark of gritty Sault ("Soo") Ste. Marie, although an emerging tourist industry is gussying up the pedestrian-friendly downtown. St. Mary's River, the only waterway linking Lake Superior to the other Great Lakes, drops 21 vertical feet over one mile here, and Ojibwe traders were once forced to carry their canoes and skirt the rocky rapids on land. In 1853, entrepreneurs built the first modern canal between the lakes, and today more than 11,000 vessels make their way through the three locks each year. This volume of commercial traffic has also brought Sault Ste. Marie under the scrutiny of the Department of Homeland Security. Don't mistake a certain wariness to answer questions about the locks for unfriendliness on the part of locals; it's mostly 9/11 talking.

There are a number of ways to watch ships passing through the locks. **Soo Locks Park,** which faces E. Portage Ave., gives visitors a good view of the 1000 ft. freighters that make their way through the southernmost MacArthur lock. As many as 15 ships pass through within a 24hr. period. (☎253-9101. Park open 8am-midnight. Visitors center open May-Nov. daily 8am-8pm.) On **Engineers' Day,** the last Friday in June, the public can venture behind the fence that normally cordons off the locks and see the passing ships up close. For travelers with other plans in late June, a 2hr. **Soo Locks Boat Tour** leaves from both 515 and 1157 E. Portage Ave., and explains the mechanics of the locks' operation even as it gets lifted up to the level of the lake. (☎632-6301 or 800-432-6301; www.soolocks.com. Tours leave every hr. July-Aug., at least 3 per day mid-May to June and Sept. to mid-Oct. $18.50, ages 4-12 $8.50, under 4 free. Call ahead for specific dock.) Diehard history buffs might take time to ascend the **Tower of History,** 326 E. Portage Ave., but even incorrigible landlubbers should be sure to visit the ⌧**Museum Ship Valley Camp,** on the waterfront, at the end of Johnston St. They'll be free to wander the decks of a 1917 steam-powered freighter, peering into the tiny quarters of the ship's crew and surveying the mangled lifeboats that washed ashore after the sinking of the *Edmund Fitzgerald*. (☎632-3658. Open mid-May to June and mid-Aug. to Sept. 10am-6pm; July to mid-Aug. 10am-7pm; early Oct. 10am-5pm. $9, ages 6-16 $4.50, under 6 free.)

Chain **motels** line the I-75 Business Spur, and the most reasonable rates can be found closer to the downtown. Locals head to **Penny's Kitchen ❶**, 112 W. Spruce St., for fresh sandwiches ($5-7) and thick slices of warm raspberry pie ($3.25). Three computers against the back wall provide free Internet access for customers. (☎632-1232. Open M-F 7am-6pm, Sa 8am-5pm. AmEx/D/MC/V.) A string of **bars** on E. Portage Ave. gets lively during the school year, when students from **Lake Superior State University** trot downhill for dance and drink.

MIDDLE OF THE PENINSULA ☎906

The West Unit of the **Hiawatha National Forest** runs like a thick green stripe down the middle of the peninsula, offering hiking and cross-country skiing opportunities all the way from the Superior to the Michigan lakeshores. The **visitors center,** at the junction of Rte. 28 and County Rte. H-58 in **Munising,** serves as the primary gateway to the forest and helps administer over a dozen rustic **campsites ❶,** south of town on County Rte. 13. (☎387-3700, or 877-444-6777 for reservations at all National Forest Service sites. Open mid-May to mid-Oct. daily 8am-6pm; mid-Oct. to mid-May M-Sa 9am-4:30pm. Pit toilets, fire rings, and well water. Campsites open mid-May to Sept. Sites $12.) The Munising visitors center also administers the remarkable **Pictured Rocks National Lakeshore,** where Lake Superior's waters—saturated with copper, manganese, and iron oxide—paint the sandstone cliffs with multicolored bands. Prices are steep, but the **Pictured Rocks Boat Cruise,** at the city dock in Munising, does give the best view of the cliffs. (☎387-2379; www.picturedrocks.com. Tours leave daily July to mid-Aug. every hr. 9am-5pm; June and mid-Aug. to mid-Oct. 3-5 per day. 3hr. tour $29, ages 6-13 $12, under 6 free.)

Four miles east of Munising on County Rte. 58, Miner's Castle Rd. leads up to the **Miner's Castle Overlook,** affording the best view of the cliffs accessible from the road. Miner's Castle Rd. also has the trailhead to **Miner's Falls,** a 60 ft. cascade accessible by a 10min. hike down a gravel trail lined with sugar maples and yellow birch. More intrepid hikers can ogle the colorful cliffs along Lake Superior via the 9 mi. **Chapel Basin loop.** The route takes approximately 5hr. to complete, and the trailhead can be found at the end of unpaved Chapel Rd., off of County Rte. 58 in Melstrand. Rte. 58 is paved as far east as Melstrand, but then reverts to "primitive" conditions until the **Log Slide Overlook,** west of Grand Marais. The unpaved sections of bumpy gravel road can be an adventure, but they can also be a precursor to a front-end alignment; conditions are best after the road is graded in the spring. For a quicker and less jarring route from Munising to Grand Marais, go east on Rte. 28, then north on Rte. 77. The white sands of **Twelvemile Beach** are most easily accessed from the Grand Marais end of Rte. 58, and self-registered rustic **campsites ❶** go for $12. (Pit toilets, well water. Open May-Oct. Cash only.)

For those campers looking to venture farther off the beaten path, **backcountry camping permits ❶** are available from the Munising visitors center (see above) or the **Grand Sable Visitors Center,** 3 mi. west of Grand Marais on Rte. 58. (☎494-2660. Open mid-May to early Oct. daily 9am-5pm. $4 per person per night, plus $15 reservation fee per group.) Inexpensive motels are plentiful in Newberry, 1hr. east of Munising on Rte. 28 and 30min. south of **Tahquamenon Falls State Park** (say "phenomenon", and then substitute in the right consonants). The ruddy waters of the Upper Falls take their color from tannin leached out of tree roots, and the waterfall is one of the largest east of the Mississippi River. Hike the 4 mi. down to the burbling Lower Falls, where the observation deck at the end of the boardwalk gets you close enough to feel the spray on your face. (☎492-3415. Open daily May-Oct.

BRING BACK THE LIGHTS

Ladders, rubble, and empty coffee cups litter the rooms, while gaping holes in the stage wall mark the spots where two theater organs were once installed. In June 2005, the Soo Theatre did not much resemble the elegant performance space that opened in 1930. Yet echoes of its former grandeur still resounded in the spooky stillness, and with $100,000 from the state of Michigan's Cool Cities Project, the Soo is poised to emerge from the ashes as a center for the arts and an icon of civic revitalization on the Upper Peninsula.

The Cool Cities Project, the brainchild of Governor Jennifer Granholm, is an investment in slowing the flight of young "knowledge workers" out of Michigan. In June of 2004, Granholm doled out catalyst grants to 17 communities across Michigan, and the Soo Theatre Project suddenly found itself with an infusion of cash and some high-profile recognition of the work at hand. Volunteers appeared out of the woodwork. A local attorney even swam 30 miles to raise more funds for the project. "This shouldn't be possible," admitted Dianna George, president of the Theatre Project. Yet with music and dance studios scheduled to open in the fall of 2005 and renovations continuing into the new year, Sault Ste. Marie's quest to "bring back the lights" is only a few miracles away from success.

8am-10pm; Nov.-Apr. 8am-4:30pm. Vehicle permit required. Permits $6 per day for Michigan residents, $8 for non-residents; $24/$29 per year.)

KEWEENAW PENINSULA   ☎906

Arching its way north into Lake Superior, the Keweenaw (KEE-wa-naw) Peninsula is possibly the wildest quadrant of the U.P. The copper mine and mill industries once put a chicken in every family's pot, but when labor unrest and new technologies started to erode the bottom line, Big Copper up and left. A tourist economy has started to emerge, but thus far, the peninsula's geographical isolation has conspired to leave it largely undiscovered.

The **Porcupine Mountain Wilderness State Park ❶**, affectionately known as "The Porkies," hugs Lake Superior at the base of the peninsula, 18 mi. west of **Ontonagon** on Rte. 107. (☎800-447-2757; www.michigan.gov/dnr. Backcountry sites and outpost sites with outhouses $10; with toilets, showers, and electricity at Union Bay $21. Call the park directly at ☎885-5275 for 2- to 8-person cabins, $55. Lakeside cabins come with rowboats for use within the park; reserve well in advance.) The **visitors center** on S. Boundary Rd. near the junction of Rte. 107, provides required vehicle permits good for all Michigan state parks. (☎885-5208. Open mid-May to mid-Oct. daily 10am-8pm. Permits $6 per day for Michigan residents, $8 for non-residents; $24/$29 per year.) Eight miles inside the park on Rte. 107, the **Lake of the Clouds** scenic overlook opens up on a stunning mountain lake nestled in the Big Carp River valley. Although **Summit Peak,** off S. Boundary Rd., is the highest point in the park, the northwest view from the observation tower is not worth the ascent unless the autumn foliage is out. Instead, continue 13 mi. further to the end of S. Boundary Rd. and pay a visit to the three roaring waterfalls at **Presque Isle.** Casual hikers can pick up the 4 mi. **Union Spring Trail** just south of the visitors center, while more experienced hikers can make a 12 mi. loop through old growth forest on the **Big Carp River, Correction Line,** and **North Mirror Lake Trails.**

The college towns of **Houghton** and **Hancock** link the Porkies to the rest of the peninsula. During the month of January, the campus of Houghton's Michigan Technological University is taken over by the construction of 40 ft. **snow sculptures,** which are judged during the festivities of early February's **Winter Carnival.** Houghton and Hancock are also home to an enclave of fiercely proud Finns, and locals head to **Suomi ❶,** 54 Huron St. in downtown Houghton, for *pannukakku* ($4), a thick breakfast custard served with raspberry jam and sweet toast. (☎482-3220. Entrees $4-8. Open M-F 6am-6pm, Sa 6am-4pm, Su 7am-2pm. Cash only.) Farther north, in Calumet, a yellowing 1906 mural overlooks the antique wooden bar at **Michigan House Cafe & Brewpub ❸**, 300 6th St., five blocks off of Rte. 41. Sink your teeth into a charbroiled Black Angus burger ($7.45), and wash it down with a mug of in-house Red Jacket stout ($3.50), the most northerly brew in the state of Michigan. (☎337-1910. Entrees $7-12. Occasional live music F-Sa; call for schedule. Open M-Tu and Th-Sa 11:30am-10pm, Su noon-9pm. AmEx/D/MC/V.) Eight miles south of Calumet on Rte. 203, **McLain State Park ❶** offers campsites in close proximity to a 2 mi. agate beach and a small lighthouse at the end of a pebbly sandbar. (Reservations ☎482-0278 or 800-447-2757. 103 sites with electricity $22; cabins $45-65. 17 walk-in sites. Vehicle permit required.) To the east in Lake Linden, the **Houghton County Historical Museum** pieces together artifacts from the copper boom and gives visitors a ride on a restored steam locomotive. (☎296-4121. Open June-Sept. M-Sa 10am-4:30pm, Su noon-4pm. $8, seniors and students $5, under 12 free.) One of the river dredges used by the Quincy Mining Company is still visible from Rte. 26 as it passes through Hubble. Today **Quincy Mine Hoist and Underground Mine,** just north of Hancock on Rte. 41, offers 2hr. tours that descend deep into the old mine shafts. (☎482-3101; www.quincymine.com. Open mid-June to early Sept. M-Sa 8:30am-7pm, Su 12:30-7pm; mid-May to mid-June and early Sept. to late Oct. M-Sa 9:30am-5pm, Su 12:30-5:30pm. Tours $12.50, ages 6-12 $7.50, under 6 free.)

Rte. 41 is the most direct route to the northern tip of the peninsula, although drivers and bikers can take Rte. 26, off Rte. 41, to wind their way through lakeside villages and desolate ghost towns where copper miners once toiled. Rising over 1300 ft. above sea level, the breathtaking **Brockway Mountain Drive** (6 mi.), between Eagle Harbor and Copper Harbor, presents a panoramic view of the pine-covered peaks and sloping valleys of the Upper Peninsula. In **Copper Harbor,** the northernmost town in the entire state of Michigan, the **Keweenaw Adventure Company,** 155 Gratiot St., provides kayaks and mountain bikes to those who wish to explore the wild side of Keweenaw. (☎289-4303. 2½hr. kayak intro $29. Bike rentals $30 per half-day, $40 per day.)

ILLINOIS

At first glance, Illinois seems like a state with dual personalities. In the northern part of the state, Chicago gleams as a Midwestern metropolis with top-notch museums, stunning architecture, and suburban sprawl stretching all the way into two neighboring states. Once removed from suburbia, a second Illinois—the "Land of Lincoln"—reaches outward with endless miles of corn fields and small towns. In its politics and its culture, Illinois is a compromise between these contrasting landscapes and can claim a mix of urban chic and rural values as perhaps no other state can.

⁊ PRACTICAL INFORMATION

Capital: Springfield.

Visitor Info: Chicago Cultural Center, 77 E. Randolph St., Chicago 60607. (☎800-226-6632; www.enjoyillinois.com.) **Springfield Convention and Visitors Bureau,** 109 N. 7th St. (☎800-545-7300; www.visit-springfieldillinois.com. Open M-F 8:30am-5pm.)

Postal Abbreviation: IL. **Sales Tax:** 6.25-9.25%, depending on the city.

CHICAGO
☎312

Students in Hyde Park can ponder philosophy and floor traders at the Board of Exchange can make electronic millions, but at the end of the day, Chicago places its trust in what is tangible and solid. Its heroes are builders and magnates; its version of the American Dream raises a glass to anyone who can get ahead in this clamorous boomtown. Long a city of immigrants and underdogs, Chicago knows how to rub elbows with sophistication and then hop the wheezing, clanking El for the long ride home.

▐ INTERCITY TRANSPORTATION

Airports: O'Hare International (☎773-686-3700; www.ohare.com), off I-90. Although O'Hare is only 18 mi. away, the drive from downtown can take up to 2hr., depending on traffic. The Blue Line **Rapid Train** runs between the Airport El station and downtown (40-60min.; M-F 5am-8pm, Sa-Su 5am-11pm; $1.75). **Midway Airport** (☎773-839-2500), on the western edge of the South Side, often offers cheaper flights. To get downtown, take the El Orange Line from the Midway stop. **Airport Express** (☎888-284-3826; www.airportexpress.com) connects to downtown hotels from O'Hare (45-60min., daily every 10-15min. 4am-11:30pm, $24) and Midway (30-45min., daily every 15min. 4am-10:30pm, $19).

Trains: Amtrak, Union Station, 225 S. Canal St. (☎655-2101; www.amtrak.com), at Adams St. just west of the Loop. Amtrak's nationwide hub. From O'Hare, take the El to Clinton (1hr.) and then walk 2 blocks north on Clinton. A number of CTA buses also make stops at the station, including buses #1, 60, 125, 126, 151, and 156. Station open daily 5:30am-10:30pm; tickets sold daily 7:30am-8:30pm. To: **Detroit** (6½hr., 3 per day, $23-32); **Milwaukee** (1½hr., 7 per day, $20); **New York City** (18-24hr., 4-5 per day, $83-110); **St. Louis** (5½hr., 3 per day, $21-28).

Buses: Greyhound, 630 W. Harrison St. (☎408-5980; www.greyhound.com), at Jefferson and Desplaines Ave. Take the El to Linton, or buses #60, 125, 156, or 157 to the terminal. Station open 24hr.; tickets sold 5am-2am. To **Detroit** (7hr., 6 per day, $30-33), **Indianapolis** (3½-4½hr., 11 per day, $31), and **Milwaukee** (2hr., 11 per day, $13). **Van Galder** in Union Station (☎608-752-5407 or 800-747-0994; www.vangalder-bus.com) runs to **Madison** (3-4hr., 4 per day, $22).

✈ ORIENTATION

Chicago dominates the entire northeastern corner of Illinois, running along 29 mi. of the southwest Lake Michigan shorefront. Almost all roads lead to Chicago; the city sits at the center of a web of interstates, rail lines, and airplane routes, so most cross-country traffic swings through the city. A good map is essential for navigating Chicago; pick up a free one at the tourist office or any CTA station.

The flat, sprawling city's grids usually make sense. Navigation is pretty straightforward, whether by car or by public transit. At the city's center is the **Loop** (p. 540), Chicago's downtown business district and the public transit system's hub. The block numbering system starts from the intersection of State and Madison, increasing by about 800 per mi. The Loop is bounded loosely by the Chicago River to the north and west, Wabash Ave. to the east, and Congress Pkwy. to the south. Directions in *Let's Go* are usually from downtown. South of the Loop, east-west street numbers increase toward the south. Many ethnic neighborhoods lie in this area (see **Neighborhoods,** p. 532), but travelers should avoid the struggling South Side. Most of the city's best spots for food and nightlife jam into the first few miles north of the Loop. Beware the 45 mph speed limit on **Lake Shore Drive,** a scenic freeway hugging Lake Michigan that offers express north-south connections.

GREAT LAKES

Chicago

🏠 ACCOMMODATIONS
International House, **7**
Chicago International
  Hostel, **1**

🍎 FOOD
Ann Sather, **4**
Army & Lou's, **8**
Dixie Kitchen &
  Bait Shop, **6**
Kopi, A Traveler's Cafe, **3**
Sunshine Cafe, **2**

🎷 NIGHTLIFE
The Green Mill, **5**

0	2 miles
0	2 kilometers

> It is a good idea to stay within the boundaries of tourist maps. Aside from small pockets such as Hyde Park and the University of Chicago, areas south of the loop and west of the little ethnic enclaves are mostly industrial or residential and pose a safety threat to the unwary tourist. **Cabrini Green** (bounded by W. Armitage Ave. on the north, W. Chicago Ave. on the south, Sedgwick St. on the east, and Halsted St. on the west) was once the site of an infamously dangerous public housing development and sits within tourist map borders. The neighborhood is now part of a city experiment in mixed-income housing and is surrounded by redeveloped areas, but travelers should still be cautious.

To avoid driving and parking in the city, daytrippers can leave their cars in one of the suburban park-and-ride lots ($1.50-1.75 per day); call CTA (p. 532) for info. Parking downtown costs around $8-15 per day. Check out the lots west of the South Loop and across the canal from the **Sears Tower** (p. 540) for the best deals.

NEIGHBORHOODS

The diverse array of communities that composes the Windy City justifies its title as a "city of neighborhoods." North of the Loop, LaSalle Dr. loosely defines the west edge of the posh **Near North** area; here, most activity is centered along the **Magnificent Mile** of Michigan Ave. between the Chicago River and Oak St. A trendy restaurant and nightlife district, **River North** lines N. Clark St., just north of the Loop and west of Michigan Ave. The primarily residential **Gold Coast** shimmers on N. Lake Shore Dr. between Oak St. and North Ave. The **Bucktown/Wicker Park** area, at the intersection of North, Damen, and Milwaukee Ave., is the place to be for artsy, cutting-edge cafes and nightlife. **Lincoln Park** revolves around the junction of N. Clark St., Lincoln Ave., and Halsted St. To the north, near the 3000 block of N. Clark St. and N. Halsted St., sits **Lakeview**, a gay-friendly area teeming with food and nightlife that becomes **Wrigleyville** in the 4000 block. **Andersonville**, 5 mi. farther up N. Clark St. north of Foster Ave., is the center of the Swedish community, though immigrants from Asia and the Middle East have recently settled here.

The near south and west sides are filled with other vibrant ethnic districts. While much of the German community has scattered, the beer halls and restaurants in the 3000 and 4000 blocks of N. Lincoln Ave. keep local German culture alive. The former residents of **Greektown** have also moved, but S. Halsted St. still houses authentic Greek restaurants. This area is bustling and generally safe until the restaurants close, at which point tourists wisely clear out. Although nearby **Little Italy** has fallen prey to the encroachments of the **University of Illinois at Chicago (UIC)**, good dining options remain. Jewish and Indian enclaves center on Devon Ave., from Western Ave. to the Chicago River. The **Pilsen** neighborhood, around 18th St., offers a glimpse of Mexico and a developing art community. Chicago's Polish population is the largest of any city outside of Warsaw; those seeking Polish cuisine should go to N. Milwaukee Ave. between blocks 2800 and 3100.

⊟ LOCAL TRANSPORTATION

Public Transit: The **Chicago Transit Authority (CTA),** 350 N. Wells (☎836-7000 or 888-968-7282; www.transitchicago.com), on the 7th fl. of the **Mart,** runs efficient trains, subways, and buses. The **elevated rapid transit train system,** called the **El,** encircles the Loop. The El operates 24hr., but check ahead for schedules, as late-night service is infrequent. Some buses do not run all night; call the CTA for schedules and routes. Many routes are "express," and different routes may run along the same track. Helpful CTA maps are available at many stations and at the Chicago Visitor Information Center.

Train and bus fare $1.75; express routes $2. Transfers ($0.25) allow for up to 2 more rides on different routes during the following 2hr. Buy **transit cards** (min. $1.75) for fares and transfers at all CTA stations, on the Internet, and at some museums. CTA also offers a variety of consecutive-day passes for tourists, available at airports and Amtrak stations ($5-18, depending on length of pass). On Sa from early May to late Oct., a **Loop Tour Train** departs on a free 40min. elevated tour of the downtown area (tickets must be picked up at the **Chicago Cultural Center;** see p. 533. Tours start at 11:35am, 12:15, 12:55, 1:35pm).

Commuter Rail: METRA, 547 W. Jackson St. (M-F ☎322-6777, Sa-Su ☎836-7000; www.metrarail.com), distributes free maps and schedules for its extensive commuter rail network of 11 rail lines and 4 downtown stations. Open M-F 8am-5pm. Fare $2-7, depending on distance.

Suburban Bus: PACE (☎836-7000; www.pacebus.com) runs the suburban bus system. Many free or cheap shuttle services run throughout the Loop.

Taxi: Yellow Cab, ☎829-4222. **Flash Cab,** ☎773-561-4444.

Car Rental: Dollar Rent-a-Car (☎800-800-3665; www.dollar.com), at O'Hare and Midway. Must be 21 with major credit card to rent; under-25 surcharge $18 per day.

🛈 PRACTICAL INFORMATION

Visitor Info: The Chicago Cultural Center, 77 E. Randolph St., at Michigan Ave., houses a **visitor information center** with all manner of essential maps and brochures. Take a peek at the building's free galleries before heading out into the city. Open M-F 10am-6pm, Sa 10am-5pm, Su 11am-5pm. **Water Works Visitors Center,** 163 E. Pearson St. at Michigan Ave., is located in the Water Tower Pumping Station. Open daily 7:30am-7pm. **Visitor hotline,** ☎877-244-2246; operates 24hr.

GLBT Resources: Gay and Lesbian Hotline, ☎773-929-4357. Operates M-W, F, Su 6-10pm. For current info on events and nightlife, pick up the *Windy City Times* or *Gay Chicago* at Lakeview's **Unabridged Books,** 3251 N. Broadway (☎773-883-9119).

Medical Services: Northwestern Memorial Hospital, 251 E. Huron St. (☎926-2000), near Michigan Ave.; **emergency division** at 250 E. Erie St. (☎926-5188). Open 24hr.

Internet Access: Free at the **Chicago Public Library.** Main branch at 400 S. State St. (☎747-4300), at Congress. Check for other locations at www.chicagopubliclibrary.org. Open M-Th 9am-7pm, F-Sa 9am-5pm, Su 1-5pm.

Post Office: 433 W. Harrison St. (☎983-8183 or 800-275-8777), at the Chicago River. Open 24hr. **Postal Code:** 60607. **Area Code:** 312 (downtown) or 773 (elsewhere in Chicago); 708, 630, or 847 (outside the city limits). In text, 312 unless noted.

🛏 ACCOMMODATIONS

Find cheap beds at one of Chicago's many hostels or in the moderately priced motels on **Lincoln Avenue** in Lincoln Park. **At Home Inn Chicago** (☎800-375-7084) offers a reservation and referral service for many downtown B&Bs. Most have a two-night minimum stay, and rooms average $120. Travelers should be aware of Chicago's 15% tax on most accommodation rates.

Arlington House, 616 W. Arlington Pl. (☎773-929-5380; www.arlingtonhouse.com). Take the El Red or Blue to Fullerton, walk 3 blocks east on Fullerton, then turn left on Orchard and right on Arlington. Located on a quiet residential street in tony Lincoln Park, this tidy hostel may be Chicago's best answer to the question of location versus price. Free Internet. Kitchen, TV room, laundry. Linen and deposit $10. Dorms $25; doubles with shared bath $54, with private bath $68. MC/V. ❶

GREAT LAKES

Chicago International Hostel, 6318 North Winthrop Ave. (☎773-262-1011; www.chicagointernationalhostel.com), just south of the Loyola University campus. Take the El Red to Granville, turn right out of the station, and then left on Winthrop. Out of the way? You bet. But with low prices, a friendly staff, and common areas packed with thrift-store gewgaws, this place is well worth the trek. Internet $3.50 per hr. Laundry and kitchen. Lockout 11am-2pm. Check-out 9:30am. Dorms $21; doubles $46-69. Reservations a must for private rooms. MC/V. ❶

Hostelling International—Chicago (HI), 24 E. Congress Pkwy. (☎360-0300; www.hichicago.org), off Wabash Ave. in the South Loop. Disorganized and somewhat worn around the edges, this megahostel's central location may be its greatest asset. Loop attractions are just a few stops away on the El, and organized activities draw guests out into the city. Internet access $0.25 per min. Laundry and kitchen. Check-out 11am. Reservations recommended. Dorms $38, members $35. MC/V. ❷

Ohio House Motel, 600 N. LaSalle St. (☎943-6000), at Ohio St. This 2-story inn looks out of place among its skyscraping neighbors, but it puts guests within easy walking distance of Near North and Loop attractions. Free parking. TV, A/C, and private baths. Reservations recommended. Queen or 2 twin beds $85; 2 doubles $115. AmEx/MC/V. ❹

Cass Hotel, 640 N. Wabash Ave. (☎787-4030 or 800-227-7850; www.casshotel.com), just north of the Loop. Take the El to Chicago. Reasonable rates, a convenient location near the Magnificent Mile, and $2 breakfasts at the coffeeshop make this hotel a favorite of the budget-conscious. Small but clean rooms with TV, A/C, and private bath. Coin laundry. Key deposit $5 if paying cash. Parking $20 per day. Reservations recommended. Rooms from $69; check website for lowest rates. Wheelchair accessible. ❹

International House, 1414 E. 59th St. (☎773-753-2270), in Hyde Park, off Lake Shore Dr. Take the Illinois Central Railroad from the Michigan Ave. station (20min.) or METRA South Shore Line to 59th St. and walk ½ block west. On the grounds of the University of Chicago; avoid walking off-campus at night. This hostel closed for renovations in May 2005, but will reopen early in 2006. Call for details. ❸

◪ FOOD

Chicago's many culinary delights, from pizza to po' boy sandwiches, are among its main attractions. One of the best guides to city dining is the monthly *Chicago* magazine, which includes an extensive restaurant section, indexed by price, cuisine, and quality. It can be found at tourist offices and newsstands everywhere.

PIZZA

No trip to Chicago is complete without indulging in a deep-dish pizza or two. Over the years, several deep-dish empires have competed to conquer the Windy City. Most pizzerias will allow customers to pre-order while they wait in the line for a table, leaving just enough time to debate over whose pizza really is the best.

Giordano's, 730 N. Rush St. (☎951-0747), is the home of the famous stuffed crust. An absurdly overfilled pizza, with heaps of cheese and a tangy tomato sauce, runs upwards of $12. The "not less famous" thin crust pie (from $8) is also satisfying. Open M-Th and Su 11am-11:30pm, F-Sa 11am-12:30am. Call for other locations throughout the city. AmEx/D/DC/MC/V. ❸

Lou Malnati's, 439 N. Wells St. (☎828-9800), at Hubbard. After running a string of pizzerias in the northern suburbs, Lou brought his deep-dish pizza and his love for sports memorabilia to River North in 1986. Individual pies start at $4.75 and take 30min. to prepare, although you can pre-order while waiting out the inevitable line. Open M-Th 11am-11pm, F-Sa 11am-midnight, Su noon-10pm. ❷

Downtown Chicago

🏠 ACCOMMODATIONS

Cass Hotel, **2**
Hostelling International–
  Chicago (HI), **15**
Ohio House Motel, **4**

🍎 FOOD

Al's Italian Beef, **3**
Artopolis, **13**
Billy Goat's Tavern, **9**
Frontera Grill, **8**

Giordano's, **1**
Gold Coast Dogs, **10**
Heaven on Seven–
  Lou Malnati's, **7**
Lou Mitchell's, **14**
The Parthenon, **12**
Pizzeria Uno, **5**

🌙 NIGHTLIFE

Funky Buddha
  Lounge, **6**

Pizzeria Uno, 29 E. Ohio St. (☎321-1000), at Wabash. Uno's may have dropped "pizzeria" from the name of their national franchises, but the low-ceilinged Chicago original isn't about to run from the P-word. Individual pies (from $5) take 45min. to prepare, and are well worth the wait. Open M-F 11:30am-1am, Sa 11:30am-2am, Su 11:30am-11:30pm. AmEx/D/DC/MC/V. ❷

THE LOOP

As Chicago's historic business district, the Loop once teemed with elegant steakhouses and all-American diners. Today, dime-a-dozen fast-food chains dominate the culinary landscape, although there are a handful of notable exceptions.

☒ **Lou Mitchell's,** 565 W. Jackson Blvd. (☎939-3111), 2 blocks west of the Sears Tower. Situated at the jumping-off point of historic Route 66, this old-school diner has been stuffing faithful customers for more than 80 years. Start the day with "meltaway pancakes" that take up the whole plate ($6) or hearty omelets served simmering in the skillet ($8-9). Open M-Sa 5:30am-3pm, Su 7am-3pm. Cash only. ❷

Heaven on Seven, 111 N. Wabash Ave. (☎263-6443), Garland Bldg. Mardi Gras beads festoon shelves of hot sauce at this folksy Louisiana-style eatery. Weekday lunch lines run out the door as workers queue for jambalaya ($10), but visit Sa for a quieter vibe and sweet potato pie ($3.50). Open M-F 8:30am-5pm, Sa 10am-3pm. Also at 600 N. Michigan Ave. (☎280-7774) and 3478 N. Clark St. (☎773-477-7818). Cash only. ❸

Gold Coast Dogs, 159 N. Wabash Ave. (☎527-1222), between Randolph and Lake St. This Chicago-based chain is favored by locals for serving up hot dogs Second City style: on a poppy-seed bun, topped with hot peppers, tomato, celery salt, and a long pickle spear. "Magnificent Dog" $2.50. Open daily 10am-8pm. Cash only. ❶

RIVER NORTH

River North houses some of the trendiest eateries in town, as well as Chicago's famous pizzerias (see **Pizza,** p. 534).

☒ **Billy Goat's Tavern,** 430 N. Michigan Ave. (☎222-1525). The service may be curt, but there are few better places to watch a Cubs game than at this hard-boiled tavern. Order a "cheezeborger" ($2.85) at the counter, and check your latte at the door. Open M-F 6am-2am, Sa 10am-3am, Su 10am-2am. Cash only. ❶

Frontera Grill, 445 N. Clark St. (☎661-1434), between Illinois and Hubbard St. Take the El Red Line to Grand. When locals are willing to wait 90min. for a table, you know that something good must be cooking. Frontera is widely acclaimed for its delicate, sophisticated approach to Mexican cuisine, which uses the freshest seasonal ingredients in the superb entrees ($15-20). Lunch Tu-F 11:30am-2:30pm, Sa 10:30am-2:30pm. Dinner Tu 5:20-10pm, W-Th 5-10pm, F-Sa 5-11pm. AmEx/D/DC/MC/V. ❹

Al's Italian Beef, 169 W. Ontario (☎943-3222), at Wells. Featuring layers of beef on top of a huge sausage, an Italian beef sandwich ($4.29) is a Chicago institution guaranteed to expand your waistline. Open M-Th 10am-midnight, F-Sa 10am-3am, Su 11am-10pm. AmEx/D/DC/MC/V. ❶

SOUL FOOD

Head to the **South Side** for good, cheap ribs, fried chicken, and collard greens. Be very careful south of the Loop, though, especially after dark. **Wicker Park,** to the north, is another option for satisfying soul food.

The Smoke Daddy, 1804 W. Division St. (☎773-772-6656; www.thesmokedaddy.com), north of the Loop in Wicker Park. Pulled pork sandwiches ($7) and finger-lickin' rib platters ($9.50-20) definitely merit the neon "WOW" sign that dangles out front. Live blues and jazz M-W and Su 8:30pm, Th-Sa 9:30pm. Open M-W and Su 11:30am-midnight, Th-Sa 11:30am-1am. AmEx/MC/V. ❷

Northside

▲ ACCOMMODATIONS
Arlington House, **10**

🍖 FOOD
Bourgeois Pig, **11**
Cafe Ba-Ba-Reeba!, **12**
Cozy Noodles
  & Rice, **5**
Mia Francesca, **6**
Penny's Noodle Shop, **3**

🍸 NIGHTLIFE
Berlin, **2**
B.L.U.E.S., **9**
Hydrate, **4**
Kingston Mines, **8**
Smart Bar, **7**
Tiny Lounge, **1**

Dixie Kitchen & Bait Shop, 5225A S. Harper St. (☎ 773-363-4943). Take bus #6 to 51st and Lake Park, walk 2 blocks south, and cut through the parking lot on your right. You'll see this local hot spot at the back. Feast on an oyster po' boy sandwich smeared with New Orleans remoulade ($8.25), and wash it down with dark Dixie Voodoo beer ($3.75). Open M-Th and Su 11am-10pm, F-Sa 11am-11pm. AmEx/D/DC/MC/V. ❷

Army & Lou's, 422 E. 75th St. (☎ 773-483-3100), on the South Side. Take bus #3 to 75th. Founded in 1945, this upscale southern eatery was a favorite of Harold Washington, Chicago's 1st black mayor. Fried chicken and 2 sides $8.95. Open M and W-Su 9am-9:45pm. AmEx/D/DC/MC/V. ❷

GREEKTOWN

The Parthenon, 314 S. Halsted St. (☎ 726-2407). The grande dame of Chicago's Greek restaurants continues to impress. Waiters prepare flaming, brandy-soaked cheese ($5) at tableside, while the combination plate ($12.50) gives guests a taste of grape leaves, moussaka, and roast lamb. Open daily 11am-midnight. AmEx/MC/V. ❸

Artopolis, 306 S. Halsted St. (☎ 559-9000). After dinner, loosen your belt a notch and then duck into this "bakery, cafe, and agora" for dessert. Play it safe with baklava ($1.95), or branch out with the mango yogurt mousse ($2.50). Open M-Th 9am-midnight, F-Sa 9am-1am, Su 10am-midnight. AmEx/MC/V. ❷

LINCOLN PARK

Penny's Noodle Shop, 950 W. Diversey Ave. (☎773-281-8448), at Sheffield Ave. One of the best budget options in town, Penny's presents generous portions of Asian noodles (all under $6) in a bright, inviting setting. Open M-Th and Su 11am-10pm, F-Sa 11am-10:30pm. Call for additional locations. MC/V. ❷

Cafe Ba-Ba-Reeba!, 2024 N. Halsted St. (☎773-935-5000), just north of Armitage. With a bustling interior behind its colorful facade, Ba-Ba-Reeba pleases an upbeat crowd with unbeatable *tapas* ($4-8) and hearty Spanish *paellas* ($10-15). During the summer, sip *sangria* ($5) on the outdoor terrace. Lunch Sa-Su noon-5pm. Dinner M-Th and Su 5-10pm, F-Sa 5pm-midnight. Reservations recommended. AmEx/D/DC/MC/V. ❸

Bourgeois Pig, 748 W. Fullerton Ave. (☎883-5282). A neighborhood institution, complete with creaky hardwood floors and well-worn Oriental rugs. Sink your teeth into a Great Gatsby sandwich on herbed focaccia ($6.75), or settle down with a cup of rousingly dark Pig Blend ($2). Open M-F 6:30am-11pm, Sa-Su 8am-11pm. AmEx/MC/V. ❶

BUCKTOWN AND WICKER PARK

Alliance Bakery & Cafe, 1736 W. Division St. (☎773-278-0366). When the owners of an 80-year-old Polish bakery scrape together the cash to buy the adjacent storefront, you might expect them to use it for storing cake flour. In Wicker Park, however, they convert the space into a luminous coffeehouse where twentysomethings type away at their laptops. Espresso drinks $2.50-4. Open M-Sa 6am-9pm, Su 7am-9pm. AmEx/MC/V. ❶

Mod, 1520 N. Damen Ave. (☎773-252-1500). From the candy-orange foyer to the playful, futuristic decor, Mod comes across as gourmet with a twist of hip. The menu is more than up to the task, using locally grown produce as the building blocks for inventive, Mediterranean-influenced fare. A great place to keep in mind if you're willing to splurge. Appetizers $7-9. Entrees $18-20. AmEx/DC/V. ❺

Handlebar, 2311 W. North Ave. (☎773-384-9546). Launched in 2003 by a local brewer who loved bicycling, Handlebar features bar stools made out of the recycled rims of bicycle wheels, as well as a list of imported beers ($4-6) that goes on seemingly forever. Dive into a dish of West African groundnut stew ($7.75), or swing by for brunch on the weekend. Open M-Th 4pm-midnight, F 4pm-1am, Sa 10pm-1am, Su 10am-11pm. AmEx/D/DC/MC/V. ❷

WRIGLEYVILLE

Cozy Noodles & Rice, 3456 N. Sheffield Ave. (☎773-327-0100). The curries ($5.95) and rice noodles ($5.50) are tasty and inexpensive, but it's the playful ambience and attentive waitstaff that lift Cozy head and shoulders above other Thai spots in the area. Open M-Th and Su 11am-10pm, F-Sa 11am-10:30pm. AmEx/D/MC/V. ❷

Mia Francesca, 3311 N. Clark St. (☎773-281-3310), is a stylish urban trattoria decorated with black-and-white photographs of rural Italy. An ideal spot for a date. Entrees $11-19. Pizzas $8. Open M-Th 5-10pm, F 5-11pm, Sa 11:30am-2pm and 5-11pm, Su 11:30am-2pm and 5-10pm. Reservations recommended. AmEx/D/DC/MC/V. ❹

ANDERSONVILLE

Kopi, A Traveler's Cafe, 5317 N. Clark St. (☎773-989-5674). Take the El Red to Berwyn and walk 10min. down Berwyn Ave. to Clark. Named after the Indonesian word for coffee, Kopi caters to locals and visitors alike with an extensive travel library. Nestle into the pillows by the window, where nose-ringed moms sip hearty miso soup ($3) and soothing mango jet tea ($4). Open M-Th 8am-11pm, F-Sa 8am-midnight, Su 10am-11pm. D/MC/V. ❶

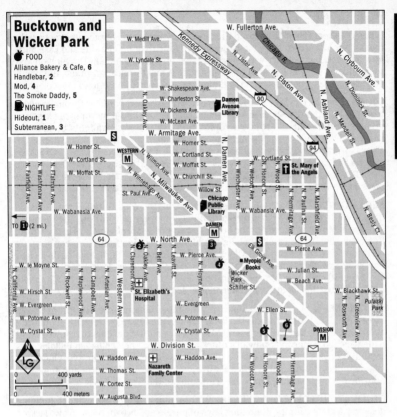

Bucktown and Wicker Park

🍎 FOOD
Alliance Bakery & Cafe, **6**
Handlebar, **2**
Mod, **4**
The Smoke Daddy, **5**

🎵 NIGHTLIFE
Hideout, **1**
Subterranean, **3**

Sunshine Cafe, 5449 N. Clark St. (☎773-334-6214). Locals swear by this restaurant's cheap Japanese fare. Fill up on generous portions of udon noodles ($6.75), or cool down with a serving of soba noodles topped with seaweed ($6.75). Open Tu-Su noon-9pm. D/MC/V. ❷

Ann Sather, 5207 N. Clark St. (☎773-271-6677). Rustic murals adorn the walls of this popular Swedish-American eatery, known for the gooey cinnamon rolls that accompany its dishes. Swedish pancakes with lingonberries ($5.45) are available all day, or try pairing a burger ($8-10) with a side of pickled herring. Open M and W-F 7am-2:30pm, Sa-Su 7am-4pm. AmEx/D/DC/MC/V. ❷

⊙ SIGHTS

Only a fraction of Chicago's eclectic sights are revealed by tourist brochures, bus tours, and strolls through the downtown area. Sights range from well-publicized museums to undiscovered back streets, from beaches and parks to towering sky-scrapers. To see it all requires some off-the-beaten-path exploration.

THE LOOP

When the **Great Fire of 1871** razed Chicago's downtown, the burgeoning metropolis had an opportunity to start anew. Bounded by the river on one side and **Lake Michigan** on the other, the city was forced to build up rather than out. Drawing on new technologies including steel-frame construction and the elevator brake, the Windy City assembled a daring skyline regarded today as one of America's most elegant.

TOURS. Visitors can take a crash course on columns and cornices through **walking tours** organized by the **Chicago Architecture Foundation.** Two-hour tours of skyscrapers and architecture start at the foundation's gift shop. Highlights include the stained glass windows of the Marquette Building, the Art Deco flourishes of the Board of Trade, and the revolutionary aesthetics of Mies van der Rohe. *(224 S. Michigan Ave.* ☎ *922-3432, ext. 240; www.architecture.org. Historic Skyscrapers May-Oct. M-Tu and Th-Su 10am and 3pm, W 10am; Nov.-Apr. daily 10am. Modern Skyscrapers daily 1pm. $12, students and seniors $9. Both tours $20/$15. Call for tours in French, German, or Italian.)*

SEARS TOWER. A few blocks west on Jackson, the 1454 ft. tall Sears Tower is undoubtedly Chicago's most recognizable landmark. Early in 1997, the Petronas Towers in Malaysia edged out the Sears Tower as the tallest buildings in the world; however, the Tower can still claim the highest occupied floor. The ear-popping elevator ride to the 103rd fl. Skydeck earns visitors a view of four states on a clear day. *(233 S. Wacker Dr.; enter on Jackson.* ☎ *875-9696; www.the-skydeck.com. Open daily May-Sept. 10am-10pm; Oct.-Apr. 10am-8pm. $12, seniors $10, children $8.50. Expect waits of at least 1hr., or try visiting after 4pm for shorter lines.)*

STATE STREET. State and Madison St., the most famous intersection of "State Street, that great street," forms the focal point of the Chicago street grid. Louis Sullivan's signature **Carson Pirie Scott** store is adorned with exquisite ironwork and wide Chicago windows. Sullivan's other masterpiece, the **Auditorium Building,** sits several blocks south at the corner of Congress St. and Michigan Ave. Once Chicago's tallest building, it typifies Sullivan's obsession with form and function, housing a hotel and an opera house with some of the world's finest acoustics.

OTHER ARCHITECTURAL WONDERS. Burnham and Root's **Monadnock Building** deserves a glance for its alternating bays of purple and brown rock. *(53 W. Jackson Blvd.)* Just to the southeast, the **Sony Fine Arts Theatre** screens current arthouse and foreign films in the grandeur of the **Fine Arts Building.** *(410 S. Michigan Ave.* ☎ *427-7602. Open M-Th. $8.25; students $6; seniors, children, and matinees $5.)* The $144 million **Harold Washington Library Center** is a researcher's dream, as well as a postmodern architectural delight. *(400 S. State St.* ☎ *747-4300. Open M-Th 9am-7pm, F-Sa 9am-5pm, Su 1-5pm.)* On the north side of the Loop, at Clark and Randolph, the glass **State of Illinois Building** offers an elevator ride to the top that gives a thrilling (and free) view of a sloping atrium, circular floors, and hundreds of employees.

SCULPTURE. In addition to its architectural masterpieces, Chicago is decorated with a fantastic collection of outdoor sculpture. The Chicago Cultural Center (p. 533) sells the *Loop Sculpture Guide* for $4. The piece known simply as "The Picasso," at the foot of the **Daley Center Plaza,** was the first monumental modern statue to be placed in the Loop, eventually becoming an unofficial symbol of the city. *(Intersection of Washington and Dearborn St.)* Directly across Washington St. rests Surrealist Joan Miró's *Chicago,* the artist's gift to the city. *(69 W. Washington St.)* Two blocks north on Clark St., Jean Dubuffet's *Monument with Standing Beast* stands guard in front of the State of Illinois Building (see above). Three blocks south on Dearborn at Adams, Alexander Calder's *Flamingo,* a stark red structure, stands in front of the Federal Center Plaza. Calder's other Chicago masterpiece, *The Universe,* swirls in the lobby of the Sears Tower.

NEAR NORTH

MAGNIFICENT MILE. Chicago counts Paris as one of its sister cities, and the Magnificent Mile must be the Windy City's answer to the Champs-Elysées. Expensive shopping on the order of Tiffany's and Cartier lines the stretch of N. Michigan Ave. between the Chicago River and Oak St. Up as far as Pearson Ave., the squat **Chicago Water Tower** and **Pumping Station** stand out among the orgy of consumption. Built in 1869, these two buildings were the only ones in the area to survive the Great Chicago Fire. The Pumping Station houses a visitors center (p. 533), and the Water Tower has a free gallery dedicated to exhibitions of photography. *(Gallery open M-Sa 10am-6:30pm, Su 10am-5pm.)* One block north, the **John Hancock Building's** exoskeleton of black steel girders and glass casts a stunning figure on the skyline. *(Observation deck open daily 9am-11pm. Adults $9.75, seniors $7.50, ages 5-12 $6.)*

TRIBUNE TOWER. Critics of the Tribune Tower, a skyscraper built in 1925, dubbed it the "Cathedral of Commerce" for its marriage of Gothic religious architecture and base American money-grubbing. *The Chicago Tribune* still publishes the largest newspaper in town from the upper floors of this tower, although a museum paying tribute to the First Amendment will open at street level in spring of 2006. *(435 N. Michigan Ave. For museum info, check www.mccormickmuseum.org.)*

NAVY PIER. With a concert pavilion, dining options, nightspots, sightseeing boats, a spectacular Ferris wheel, a crystal garden with palm trees, and an IMAX theater, the mile-long pier is like Las Vegas, Mardi Gras, and the State Fair rolled into one. Now *that's* America. From here, explorers can rent bicycles to navigate the Windy City's streets or book a seat on a boat tour taking in Chicago's skyline. *(600 E. Grand Ave. Take the El Red Line to Grand/State and transfer to a free pier trolley bus. Bike rental open daily Apr.-May 9am-7pm; June-Aug. 8am-10pm; Sept.-Oct. 9am-7pm. $8.75 per hr., $34 per day. Boat tours at 2 pier locations daily June-Aug. 10am-11pm; May and Sept. 11am-5pm. 30min. cruises $10, seniors $9, under 12 $5.)*

OLD TOWN. The bells of the pre-fire **Saint Michael's Church** ring one mile north of the Magnificent Mile in **Old Town,** a neighborhood settled by German immigrants and later transformed into a hub for the Chicago counterculture. Long since gentrified, Old Town still maintains ties to its past through the annual **Old Town Art Fair** and through performances at

GIVING BACK

TAKING IT TO THE STREETS

In June 2005, the *Chicago Tribune* reported that there were an estimated 26,000 homeless young people in Illinois, half of whom were on the streets of Chicago. Yet with only 212 shelter beds in the state to accommodate this population, stopgap measures are essential for providing at-risk kids with even the most basic care. One organization that has stepped up to the task is **The Night Ministry,** a nondenominational, nonprofit social service agency that works with the homeless and other groups who have "fallen through the cracks" in Chicago. The Ministry runs a 16-bed youth shelter and sends a Health Outreach Bus out into targeted neighborhoods six nights a week.

There are a variety of opportunities for service through the Night Ministry. On the first Saturday of each month, volunteers gather to pack hygiene kits and meals for those in need. Visitors who are in Chicago long enough to attend a series of training sessions might consider leading an activity for residents at the youth shelter or serving on the Hospitality Crew of an outreach bus. Internship opportunities may also be available in fields from social work to public policy.

Visit The Night Ministry on the Web at www.thenightministry.org. For more information, contact the volunteer coordinator at ☎ 773-784-9000, ext. 216.

the **Old Town School of Folk Music,** 4544 N. Lincoln Ave. *(Take the El Purple or Brown to Armitage or Sedgwick. The Old Town Art Fair takes place in early June. Check www.oldtown-school.org for info about performances at the School of Music.)*

NORTH SIDE

LINCOLN PARK. Bounded by Armitage Ave. to the south and Diversey Ave. to the north, swanky Lincoln Park caters to young professionals and (increasingly) to families. Proximity to greenspace keeps property values high, while cafes and nightspots draw in visitors from other parts of the city.

LAKEVIEW. North of Diversey Pkwy. on N. Clark St., the streets of Lincoln Park become increasingly diverse as they melt into Lakeview around the 3000 block. Shopping plazas alternate with tiny markets and vintage clothing stores in this onetime summer getaway for Chicago's upper crust, while apartment towers and hotels spring up between aging two-story houses. North of Belmont St., N. Halsted also serves as the *axis mundi* of Boystown, one of the city's most visible gay communities. Leather bars are still around, but nightlife in Boystown increasingly caters to gay and straight partygoers alike.

WRIGLEYVILLE. Around the 4000 block of N. Clark, Lakeview shifts into **Wrigleyville.** Even though the **Cubs** (p. 546) haven't won a World Series since 1908, Wrigleyville residents remain fiercely loyal to their hometown team. Tiny, ivy-covered **Wrigley Field** is the North Side's most famous institution, and tours of the historic park are available during summer weekends when the Cubs are away. *(1060 W. Addison St., just east of the junction of Waveland Ave. and N. Clark St. Take bus #22 "Clark" or #152 "Addison." ☎ 773-404-2827. Tours $15.)*

NEAR WEST SIDE

Old St. Patrick's Church remains a symbol of the area's Irish roots, although waves of immigrants from southern and eastern Europe, as well as African-Americans from the American South, arrived into the 1950s. The area is still negotiating tensions between new development and affordable housing for longtime residents.

JANE ADDAMS HULL-HOUSE MUSEUM. The Corinthian mansion of real estate magnate Charles Hull became the epicenter of the American settlement house movement, under the stewardship of activists Jane Addams and Ellen Gates Starr. Today, the museum commemorates Addams's and Starr's work in immigrant communities of the early 20th century and occasionally sponsors public lectures on issues in present-day immigration. *(800 S. Halsted St. Take the El Blue Line to UIC-Halsted. ☎ 413-5353; www.uic.edu/jaddams/hull. Open Tu-F 10am-4pm, Su noon-4pm. Free.)*

SOUTH OF THE LOOP

HYDE PARK AND THE UNIVERSITY OF CHICAGO. Seven miles south of the Loop along the lake, the scenic campus of the ivy-clad **University of Chicago** dominates the **Hyde Park** neighborhood. The university's efforts at revitalizing the area have resulted in a community of scholars and a lively campus life amidst the degenerating neighborhoods surrounding it. University police patrol the area bounded by 51st St. to the north, Lakeshore Dr. to the east, 61st St. to the south, and Cottage Grove to the west—but don't test these boundaries, even during the day. Lakeside Burnham Park, east of campus, is fairly safe during the day, but not at night. The impressive **Oriental Institute, Museum of Science and Industry** (see **Museums,** p. 543), and **DuSable Museum of African-American History** are all in or near Hyde Park. On the first weekend in May, the **Festival of the Arts** *(http://fota.uchicago.edu)* showcases the diverse cultural offerings of the area. *(From the Loop, take bus #6 "Jefferson Express" or the METRA Electric Line from the Randolph St. Station south to 59th St.)*

ROBIE HOUSE. On campus, Frank Lloyd Wright's famous **Robie House,** designed to resemble a hanging flower basket, is the seminal example of his Prairie-style house. Now in the midst of a 10-year restoration project to return Robie House to its original 1910 state, the house will remain open to visitors during the renovation. *(5757 S. Woodlawn, at the corner of 58th St. ☎ 773-834-1847. Tours M-F 11am, 1, 3pm, Sa-Su every 20 min. 11am-3:30pm. $12, seniors and ages 7-18 $10. Not wheelchair accessible.)*

WEST OF THE LOOP

OAK PARK. Gunning for the title of the most fantastic suburb in the US, Oak Park sprouts off Harlem St. *(10 mi. west of downtown, I-290 W to Harlem St.)* Frank Lloyd Wright endowed the downtown area with 25 of his spectacular homes and buildings, all of which dot the Oak Park Historic District. His one-time home and workplace, the ⬛**Frank Lloyd Wright House and Studio,** offers an unbeatable look at his interior and exterior stylings. *(951 Chicago Ave. ☎ 708-848-1976; www.wrightplus.org. Bookshop open daily 10am-5pm. 45min. tours of the house M-F 11am, 1, 3pm; Sa-Su every 20min. 11am-3:30pm. 1hr. self-guided tours of Wright's other Oak Park homes, with a map and audio cassette, available daily 10am-3:30pm. Guided tours Mar.-Nov. Sa-Su every hr. 11am-4pm; Dec.-Feb. Sa-Su every hr. noon-2pm. $12, seniors and under 18 $10; combination interior/exterior tour tickets $20/$16. Limited wheelchair access.)* Visitors should also stop by the former home of Ernest Hemingway. Throughout the year, fans flock to the **Ernest Hemingway Birthplace and Museum** to take part in the many events honoring an architect of the modern American novel. The museum features rare photos of Hemingway, his letters, and other memorabilia. *(Birthplace: 339 N. Oak Ave. Museum: 200 N. Oak Park Ave. ☎ 708-848-2222. House and museum open Th-F and Su 1-5pm, Sa 10am-5pm. Combined ticket $7, seniors and under 18 $5.50.)* Swing by the **visitors center** for maps, guidebooks, tours, and local history. *(1118 Westgate. ☎ 708-524-7800; www.visitoakpark.com.)*

🏛 MUSEUMS

Chicago's museums range from some of the largest collections in the world to one-room galleries. The first five listings (known as the **Big Five**) provide a diverse array of exhibits, while a handful of smaller collections target specific interests. Lake Shore Dr. has been diverted around Grant Park, linking the Field Museum, Adler, and Shedd. This compound, known as **Museum Campus,** offers a free shuttle between museums. Visitors who plan on seeing the Big Five, plus the Hancock Observatory, can save money by purchasing a **CityPass** that grants admission to the sights and provides discount coupons for food and shopping. *($49.50, ages 3-11 $39; available at each attraction and good for 9 days.)* All museums are wheelchair accessible unless otherwise noted.

⬛**ART INSTITUTE OF CHICAGO.** It's easy to feel overwhelmed in this expansive museum, with a collection spanning 4 millennia of art from around the world. Make sure to see Chagall's stunning *America Windows*—the artist's blue-stained glass tribute to the country's bicentennial—between visits to Wood's *American Gothic*, Hopper's *Nighthawks*, and Monet's *Haystacks*. *(111 S. Michigan Ave., at Adams St. in Grant Park. Take the El Green, Brown, Purple, or Orange Line to Adams. ☎ 443-3600; www.artic.edu/aic. Open M-W and F 10:30am-4:30pm, Th 10:30am-8pm, Sa-Su 10am-5pm. $12, students and children $7, under 6 free. Tu free.)*

GREAT LAKES

SHEDD AQUARIUM. The Shedd, the world's largest indoor aquarium, has 650 species of fish and marine life. The Oceanarium features beluga whales, dolphins, and penguins in a giant pool that appears to flow into Lake Michigan. Explore the coral formations of the Wild Reef, or say hi to piranhas in the steamy Amazon Rising exhibit. (*1200 S. Lake Shore Dr., in Grant Park. Take the El Red to Roosevelt, then bus #12 or the museum trolley away from the Loop. ☎939-2438; www.sheddaquarium.org. Open June-Aug. M-W and F-Su 9am-6pm, Th 9am-10pm (Oceanarium closes at 8pm); Sept.-May M-F 9am-5pm, Sa-Su 9am-6pm. All-access pass $23, seniors and ages 3-11 $16.*)

FIELD MUSEUM OF NATURAL HISTORY. Sue, the Field Museum of Natural History's mascot and the largest Tyrannosaurus rex skeleton ever unearthed, has been lonely for the past 2 years. But she'll perk up in March 2006, when the museum reopens its permanent exhibit of dinosaur bones and launches a major archaeological exhibit on King Tut. Meanwhile, tribal masks, mummies, and the Hall of Jade are keeping visitors happy. (*1400 S. Lake Shore Dr., on the Museum Campus in Grant Park. ☎922-9410; www.fieldmuseum.org. Open daily 9am-5pm; last admission at 4pm. Free tours M-F 11am and 2pm, Sa-Su 11am and 1pm. $17, students and seniors $14, ages 3-11 $8, under 3 free.*)

MUSEUM OF CONTEMPORARY ART. The white-and-chrome immensity of this cutting-edge museum provides an ideal backdrop for the ambitious rotating exhibitions within. Silkscreen paintings by Andy Warhol take center stage in March 2006; Catherine Opie's photographs of Chicago will be the focus of the summer. Check the website for info on First Fridays, a hip cocktail hour held monthly at the museum. (*220 E. Chicago Ave., 1 block east of Michigan Ave. Take the El Red to Chicago, and then walk 4 blocks east on E. Chicago. ☎280-2660; www.mcachicago.org. Open Tu 10am-8pm, W-Su 10am-5pm. $10, students and seniors $6, under 12 free. Tu 5-8pm free.*)

MUSEUM OF SCIENCE AND INDUSTRY. Earmark the better part of a day for reaching and then exploring this glittering megaplex of a museum. The crown jewel of its collection is the German U-boat captured by the U.S. Navy in 1944; tours of the interior are $5, but the exhibit is free. Other highlights include the *Apollo 8* command module and a full-sized replica of an Illinois coal mine. (*5700 S. Lake Shore Dr., at 57th St. in Hyde Park. Take buses #2, 6, or 10 south from the Loop; #10 runs in summer daily, rest of the year Sa-Su and holidays. ☎773-684-1414; www.msichicago.org. Open June-Aug. M-Sa 9:30am-5:30pm, Su 11am-5:30pm; Sept.-May M-Sa 9:30am-4pm, Su 11am-4pm. Admission $9, seniors $7.50, ages 3-11 $5. Parking $12.*)

ADLER PLANETARIUM. Traditional and digital sky shows bring you face to face with the awesome glory of the cosmos. Look for a "Stars of the Pharaohs" sky show starting in March 2006, in conjunction with the Field Museum's King Tut exhibit. (*1300 S. Lake Shore Dr., on the Museum Campus in Grant Park. ☎922-7827; www.adlerplanetarium.org. Open daily 9:30am-4:30pm. Admission and choice of sky show $13, seniors $12, ages 4-17 $11. Digital sky shows $5 extra.*)

SPERTUS MUSEUM. A moving Holocaust Memorial is the only permanent exhibit at this small museum on Jewish art and history. (*618 S. Michigan Ave., near Harrison St. ☎322-1700; www.spertus.edu/museum. Open Mar.-Dec. M-W and Su 10am-5pm, Th 10am-7pm, F 10am-3pm; Jan.-Feb. Th 10am-5pm. ARTiFACT center for kids open M-Th and Su 1-4:30pm, F 1-3pm. $5; students, seniors, and children $3. F free.*)

CHICAGO HISTORICAL SOCIETY. Currently undergoing renovations, the Society will reopen in Sept. 2006 with brand-new galleries and programming in place. In the meantime, check the website for info on 2005-2006 walking tours, lectures, and film screenings. (*1601 Clark St., in Lincoln Park. ☎642-4600; www.chicagohs.org.*)

♫ ENTERTAINMENT

The free weeklies *Chicago Reader* and *New City*, available in many bars, record stores, and restaurants, list the latest events. The *Reader* reviews all major shows with times and ticket prices. *Chicago* magazine includes theater reviews alongside exhaustive club, music, dance, and opera listings. *The Chicago Tribune* includes an entertainment section every Friday. *Gay Chicago* provides info on social activities as well as other news for the area's gay community.

THEATER

One of the foremost theater centers of North America, Chicago's more than 150 theaters feature everything from blockbuster musicals to off-color parodies. Downtown, the recently formed Theater District centers around State St. and Randolph, and includes the larger venues in the city. Smaller theaters are scattered throughout Chicago. Most tickets are expensive. Half-price tickets are sold on the day of performance at **Hot Tix Booths**, 78 W. Randolph (open Tu-F 8:30am-6pm, Sa 10am-6pm, Su noon-5pm), and 163 E. Pearson in the Water Works Visitors Center (☎977-1755. Open Tu-Sa 10am-6pm, Su noon-5pm). Purchases must be made in person. **Ticketmaster** (☎559-1212) supplies tickets for many theaters; ask about discounts at all Chicago shows. The "Off-Loop" theaters on the North Side put on original productions, with tickets usually under $18.

▨ **Steppenwolf Theater,** 1650 N. Halsted St. (☎335-1888; www.steppenwolf.org). Where Gary Sinise and John Malkovich got their start and still stop by. Tickets $10-60, rush tickets available. Box office open M-Sa 11am-5pm, Su 11am-7:30pm.

Goodman Theatre, 170 N. Dearborn (☎443-3800; www.goodman-theatre.org), presents consistently solid original works. Tickets around $40-60; half-price after 6pm or after noon for matinees; $12 for students after 6pm or after noon for matinees. Box office open M-F 10am-5pm; 10am-8pm show nights, usually W-Su.

Bailiwick Repertory, 1229 W. Belmont Ave. (☎773-883-1090; www.bailiwick.org), in the Theatre Bldg. A mainstage and experimental studio space. Tickets from $10. Box office open M-W 10am-6pm, Th-Su noon-showtime.

COMEDY

Chicago boasts a plethora of comedy clubs. The most famous, ▨**Second City,** 1616 N. Wells St. (☎337-3992; www.secondcity.com), at North Ave., spoofs Chicago life and politics. Alums include Bill Murray, Chris Farley, and John Belushi. Most nights a free improv session follows the show. At next-door **Second City Etc.,** 1608 N. Wells St. (☎642-8189), up-and-coming comics offer more laughs. (Tickets $10-19. Shows for Second City Tu-Th 8:30pm, F-Sa 8 and 11pm, Su 8pm, touring company M at 8:30pm; free improv sessions M-Th 10:30pm, Sa 1am, Su 10pm. Second City Etc. shows Th 8:30pm, F-Sa 8 and 11pm, Su 8pm. Box office opens M-Sa 10:30am, Su noon. Reservations recommended for weekend shows.) Watch improv actors compete at **Comedy Sportz,** 2851 N. Halsted. Two teams of comedians create sketches based on audience suggestions. (☎773-549-8080. Tickets $17. Shows Th 8pm, F-Sa 8 and 10:30pm.)

DANCE, CLASSICAL MUSIC, AND OPERA

Ballet, comedy, live theater, and musicals are performed at **Auditorium Theatre,** 50 E. Congress Pkwy. (☎922-2110; www.auditoriumtheatre.org. Box office open M-F noon-6pm.) From October through May, the sounds of the **Chicago Symphony Orchestra** resonate throughout **Symphony Center,** 220 S. Michigan Ave. (☎294-3000; www.cso.org). **Ballet Chicago,** 218 S. Wabash Ave., 3rd fl., pirouettes throughout theaters in Chicago. (☎251-8838; www.balletchicago.org. Tickets $12-45.) The acclaimed **Lyric Opera of Chicago** performs from September through March at the **Civic Opera House,** 20 N. Wacker Dr. (☎332-2244; www.lyricopera.org.) The **Grant Park Music Festival** (☎742-4763; www.grantparkmusicfestival.com) affords a taste of classical music for free. From mid-June through late August, the acclaimed **Grant Park Symphony Orchestra** plays a few free evening concerts per week at the new **Jay Pritzker Pavilion** in **Millennium Park.**

FESTIVALS

The city celebrates summer on a grand scale. The **Taste of Chicago** festival cooks for eight days in late June and early July. Seventy restaurants set up booths with endless samples in Grant Park, where crowds chomp to the blast of big-name bands. The Taste's fireworks are the city's biggest. (Free entry; food tickets $0.50 each.) In mid-June, the **Blues Festival** and the **Chicago Gospel Festival** celebrate Chi-town's soul, and locals gets a taste of Nashville during the **Country Music Festival** at the end of the month. The **¡Viva Chicago!** Latin music festival steams up in late August, while the **Chicago Jazz Festival** scats over Labor Day weekend. All festivals center at the Grant Park Petrillo Music Shell. For more information on these events, contact the Mayor's Office's **Special Events Hotline** (☎744-3370; www.ci.chi.il.us/SpecialEvents/Festivals.htm).

The **Ravinia Festival,** in the northern suburb of Highland Park, runs from late June to early September. During the festival's 14-week season, the Chicago Symphony Orchestra, ballet troupes, folk and jazz musicians, and comedians perform. On certain nights, the orchestra allows students free lawn admission with student ID. (☎847-266-5100; www.ravinia.org. Shows 8pm, occasionally 11am, 4:30, and 7pm—call ahead. The festival runs 1½hr. every night. Round-trip on the METRA costs about $7. Charter buses $12. Lawn seats $10-15, other $20-75.)

SPORTS

The National League's **Cubs** step up to bat at **Wrigley Field,** 1060 W. Addison St., at N. Clark St., one of the few ballparks in America to retain the early grace and intimate feel of the game. (☎773-404-2827; www.cubs.com. $6-50.) The **White Sox,** Chicago's American League team, swing on the South Side at new **Comiskey Park,** 333 W. 35th St. (☎866-769-4263. $12-45.) The **Bears** of the NFL play at the newly renovated **Soldier Field,** 425 E. McFetridge Dr. (☎847-617-2327; www.chicago-bears.com. $45-315.) The **Bulls** have won three NBA championships at the **United Center,** 1901 W. Madison, just west of the Loop. (☎455-4000; www.nba.com/bulls. $30-450.) Hockey's **Blackhawks** skate onto United Center ice when the Bulls aren't hooping it up. (☎455-4500; www.chicagblackhawks.com. $25-100.) **Sports Information** (☎976-1313) has up-to-the-minute info on local events.

▉ NIGHTLIFE

"Sweet home Chicago" takes pride in the innumerable blues performers who have played here over the years. Jazz, folk, reggae, and punk clubs throb all over the **North Side.** The **Bucktown/Wicker Park** area stays open late with various bars and clubs. Aspiring pickup artists swing over to **Rush Street** and **Division Street.** Full of bars, cafes, and bistros, **Lincoln Park** is frequented by singles and young couples, both gay and straight. The bustling center of gay culture is between 3000 and 4500 **North Halsted Street.** Many of the more colorful clubs and bars line this area. For more upscale raving and discoing, there are plenty of clubs near **River North,** in Riverwest, and on Fulton St.

LIVE MUSIC

▨ **Hideout,** 1354 W. Wabansia Ave. (☎773-227-4433; www.hideoutchicago.com). Take the El Red to North and Clybourn, then take bus #72 to Elston. Walk 2 blocks up Elston, in a group if possible, and then turn right on Wabansia. Tucked away in a municipal truck parking lot, this bar and performance space lures hipsters with indie rock shows and families with a late Sept. block party. Cover Tu-F $5-10. Open M 7:30pm-2am, Tu-F 4pm-2am, Sa 7:30pm-3am.

The Green Mill, 4802 N. Broadway Ave. (☎773-878-5552; www.greenmilljazz.com). Take the El Red to Lawrence. Once a Prohibition-era speakeasy favored by Al Capone, the Green Mill has phased out gangsters and gun-runners in favor of elegant live jazz. Patrons keep their voices low during sets, but things get lively again late in the evening, especially during the cover-free jam sessions after weekend headliners wrap up. Cover $3-12. Open M-Th 9pm-4am, F 9pm-4am, Sa 8pm-5am, Su 7pm-4am.

Kingston Mines, 2548 N. Halsted St. (☎773-477-4646; www.kingstonmines.com). Mick Jagger and Led Zeppelin have been known to drop in for a jam session at this venerable club, which has dueling blues acts alternating on 2 stages. Live blues M-F and Su starting at 9:30pm, Sa 8pm. College students with ID free M-W and Su. 21+. Cover M-Th and Su $12-15, F-Sa $15 or more. Open M-Th and Su 8pm-4am, F-Sa 8pm-5am.

Subterranean, 2011 W. North Ave. (☎773-278-6600; www.subt.net), in Wicker Park. Take the El Blue to Damen. Sink into a green leather couch in the downstairs lounge of this funky hangout, or else clamber upstairs to take in live music in the opulent, recently renovated ballroom. Hip-hop open mic Tu. Cover for shows $8-10. Open M 7pm-2am, Tu-F 6pm-2am, Sa 7pm-3am, Su 8pm-2pm.

B.L.U.E.S., 2519 N. Halsted St. (☎773-528-1012; www.chicagobluesbar.com). Smaller and more intimate than nearby Kingston Mines, B.L.U.E.S. focuses on local blues acts and packs in patrons elbow-to-elbow on weekends. Live music every night 9:30pm-close. Dual cover for Kingston Mines and B.L.U.E.S. on Su. 21+. Cover $7-10. Open M-F and Su 8pm-2am, Sa 8pm-3am.

BARS AND CLUBS

▨ **Tiny Lounge,** 1814 W. Addison St. (☎773-296-9620). Take the El Brown to Addison. With abstract art on the wall and smooth funk on the stereo, Tiny Lounge is the last word in understated elegance. Bartender-owner Colleen will pour you the smoothest chocolate martini ($10) you've ever had. Live music W. Open M-F 5pm-2am, Sa 5pm-3am, Su 7pm-2am.

Hydrate, 3458 N. Halsted St. (☎773-575-5244), in Lakeview. Cool off with a frozen cocktail ($6) after grooving on this trendy gay bar's red-hot dance floor. Cover M and Th $3, F-Sa $5-10. Open M-F 8pm-4am, Sa 6pm-5am, Su 6pm-4am.

Smart Bar, 3730 N. Clark St. (☎773-549-4140; www.smartbarchicago.com). Resident DJ spins punk, techno, hip-hop, and house. Swing by after 2am to rub elbows with "industry" types. 21+. Cover $3-10. Open M-F and Su 10pm-4am, Sa 10pm-5am.

Funky Buddha Lounge, 728 W. Grand Ave. (☎666-1695; www.funkybuddha.com). Take the El Blue to Chicago. Trendy, eclectic dance club where hip-hop and funk blend with leopard and velvet decor. W and Su soul. Cover for women $10, for men $20. Free before 10pm. Open M-W 10pm-2am, Th-F 9pm-2am, Sa 9pm-3am, Su 6pm-2am.

Berlin, 954 W. Belmont Ave. (☎773-348-4975; www.berlinchicago.com). Take the El Red or Brown Line to Belmont. Anything goes at Berlin, long a mainstay of Chicago's nightlife scene. Crowds pulsate to house/dance music as go-go girls and go-go boys rock out on stages. 21+. Cover Th $3, F-Sa $5. Open M and Su 8pm-4am, Tu-F 5pm-4am, Sa 5pm-5am.

⚠ OUTDOOR ACTIVITIES

A string of lakefront parks fill the area between Chicago proper and Lake Michigan. On sunny afternoons dog walkers, in-line skaters, and skateboarders storm the shore. Close to downtown, the two major parks are Lincoln and Grant. **⚄Lincoln Park** extends across 5 mi. of lakefront on the north side with winding paths, groves of trees, and asymmetrical open spaces. The **Lincoln Park Zoo** features some of humankind's distant cousins in its new Great Apes exhibit. (☎742-2000; www.lpzoo.com. Open in summer M-F 10am-5pm, Sa-Su 10am-6:30pm; low season daily 10am-4:30pm. Free.) Next door, the **Lincoln Park Conservatory** provides a glass palace of plants from varied ecosystems. (☎742-7736. Open daily 9am-5pm. Free.)

Grant Park, covering 14 lakefront blocks east of Michigan Ave., follows the 19th-century French park style: symmetrical and ordered with corners, a fountain, and wide promenades. The Grant Park Concert Society hosts free summer concerts in the **Petrillo Music Shell,** 520 S. Michigan Ave. (☎742-4763). Colored lights illuminate **Buckingham Fountain** from 9 to 11pm. On the north side, Lake Michigan lures swimmers and sunbathers to **Lincoln Park Beach** and **Oak Street Beach.** Beware, though: the rock ledges are restricted areas, and swimming from them is illegal. Although the beaches are patrolled 9am-9:30pm, they can be unsafe after dark. The **Chicago Parks District** (☎742-7529) has more info.

The **⚄Indiana Dunes State Park** and **National Lakeshore** lie 45min. southeast of Chicago on I-90, but a world away. The State Park's gorgeous dune beaches on Lake Michigan harbor trail through dunes, woods, and marshes. Info about the State Park is available at the park's office, 1600 N. 25 E in Chesterton, IN (☎219-926-1952). Obtain Lakeshore details at their **visitors center,** 1100 N. Mineral Springs Rd., in Porter, IN (☎219-926-7561).

SPRINGFIELD   ☎217

"The town that Lincoln loved" was a hotbed of political activity during the years leading up to the Civil War, and half a century later, the capital of Illinois became the birthplace of the NAACP. Today, Springfield pays tribute to the legacy of the Great Emancipator, even as fiercely political lo-fi radio stations remind listeners that America is still in the process of desegregating. The crown jewel of Springfield's Lincoln sights is the brand-new **⚄Abraham Lincoln Presidential Library and Museum,** 112 N. 6th St., which welcomed more than 200,000 visitors in its first three months of operation. The library is geared toward scholarly research, but the superb museum tells the story of Lincoln's life through realistic recreations and iconic artifacts like the president's stovepipe hat. (☎558-8844; www.alplm.org. Open M-Tu and Th-Su 9am-5pm, W 9am-8:30pm; last admission M-Tu and Th-Su 4pm, W 7pm. $7.50, seniors and students $5.50, ages 5-15 $3.50, under 5 free.) On the other side of Springfield's sleepy downtown, the **Lincoln Home Visitors Center,** 426 S. 7th St., distributes free tickets for tours of the **Lincoln Home,** at 8th and Jackson St., where Abraham and Mary Todd Lincoln raised their sons during the 1840s and 50s. (☎492-4241. Open daily 8:30am-5pm. 20min. tours every 5-10min., starting at the front of the house. Arrive early in summer.) Lincoln served as a legislator in the **Old State Capitol,** where he gave his prophetic "House Divided" speech in 1858. (☎785-9363. Open Tu-Sa Mar.-Oct. 9am-5pm; Nov.-Feb. 9am-4pm. 30min. tours every 10-20min. Last tour 1hr. before closing. Suggested donation $2.) The fallen president's final resting place is marked by the imposing **Lincoln Tomb,** 1500 Monument Ave., inside Oak Ridge Cemetery. (☎782-2717. Open daily Mar.-Oct. 9am-5pm; Nov.-Feb. 9am-4pm.) Should you start to overdose on Honest Abe, the **Dana-Thomas House,** 301 E. Lawrence Ave., was one of Frank Lloyd Wright's early experiments in the Prairie Style and still features the original fixtures. (☎782-6776. Open W-Su 9am-4pm. 1hr. tours every 15-20min. Suggested donation $3, under 18 $1.)

Chain motels line I-55 south of downtown, and the cheapest rooms are at **Motel 6 ❷**, 6011 S. 6th St. (☎529-1633. A/C, cable TV, and pool. Singles M-Th and Su $36, F-Sa $46; doubles $43/$53. AmEx/D/DC/MC/V.) **Trout Lily Cafe ❶**, 218 S. 6th St., offers sandwiches ($4.25-5.50), quiche ($4.25), and espresso drinks ($2-4). Stop by on weekdays between noon and 1pm for an hour of acoustic music. (☎391-0101. Open M-F 7am-4:30pm, Sa 9am-3pm. MC/V.) **Cozy Drive-In ❶**, 2935 S. 6th St., is a landmark on historic Rte. 66 and the birthplace of the "Cozy Dog," or corndog ($1.65). Today, it's a family-owned diner devoted to roadside memorabilia and deep-fried food. (☎525-1992. Burger $1.70. Open M-Sa 8am-8pm. Cash only.) For live music, look no further than the **Underground City Tavern,** 700 E. Adams St., beneath the Hilton Springfield. Americana and country-rock bands take the stage during the week, while early July's Rooftop Roots Fest draws big names like blues guitarist Corey Harris. (☎789-1530. Shows 10pm. 21+. Cover $5-10.)

Amtrak (☎753-2013; www.amtrak.com; station open daily 6am-9pm), at 3rd and Washington St., near downtown, runs trains to Chicago (3½hr., 4 per day, $17-48) and St. Louis (2hr., 5 per day, $12-34). **Greyhound,** 2351 S. Dirksen Pkwy., (☎544-8466; www.greyhound.com; depot open M-F 9am-noon and 2-7pm, Sa-Su 9am-noon and 2-4pm), sends buses to Chicago (4-6hr., 6 per day, $37), Indianapolis (4-9hr., 2 per day, $46), and St. Louis (2hr., 4 per day, $19). **Taxi: Lincoln Yellow Cab,** ☎522-7766. **Visitor Info: Springfield Convention and Visitors Bureau,** 109 N. 7th St., provides visitors with parking passes. (☎789-2360 or 800-545-7300; www.visit-springfieldillinois.com. Open M-F 8am-5pm.) **Internet Access: Lincoln Library,** 326 S. 7th St. (☎753-4900. 30min. slots, up to 2hr. per day. Open June-Aug. M-Th 9am-9pm, F 9am-6pm, Sa 9am-5pm; Sept.-May also open Su noon-5pm.) **Post Office:** 411 E. Monroe St. (☎753-3432. Open M-F 7:30am-5pm.) **Postal Code:** 62701. **Area Code:** 217.

WISCONSIN

Hospitality is served up with every beer and every piece of Wisconsin cheddar sold in the Great Lakes's most wholesome party state. A wide variety of wily creatures make themselves at home in the thick woods of Wisconsin's extensive park system, while the state's favorite animal—the cow—grazes near highways. Along the shoreline, fishermen haul in fresh perch, and on rolling hills, farmers grow barley for beer. Visitors to "America's Dairyland" encounter cheese-filled country stores en route to the ocean-like vistas of Door County and the ethnic *fêtes* (not to mention other, less-refined beer bashes) of Madison and Milwaukee.

ⓘ PRACTICAL INFORMATION

Capital: Madison.

Visitor Info: Department of Tourism, 201 W. Washington Ave., P.O. Box 8690, Madison 53708 (☎608-266-2161 or 800-432-8747; www.tourism.state.wi.us).

Postal Abbreviation: WI. **Sales Tax:** 5%.

MILWAUKEE   ☎414

Home to beer and countless festivals, Milwaukee is a city with a reputation for *Gemütlichkeit* (hospitality). Ethnic communities throw rollicking, city-wide parties each summer weekend, from the traditional Oktoberfest to the Asian Moon festival. When the weather turns cold, the city celebrates with the International Arts Festival Milwaukee, during which galleries and museums extend their hours.

Milwaukee's countless bars and taverns fuel the revelry with as much beer as anyone could ever need. In addition to merrymaking, the city boasts top-notch museums, German-inspired architecture, and a long expanse of scenic lakeshore.

▐ TRANSPORTATION

Airport: General Mitchell International Airport, 5300 S. Howell Ave. (☎747-5300; www.mitchellairport.com). Take bus #80 from 6th St. downtown (30min.; $1.75), or try out Amtrak's new Hiawatha service from the downtown train station (11min., 6-7 per day, $6). **Airport Connection,** ☎769-2444 or 800-236-5450. 24hr. pickup from most downtown hotels. $11, round-trip $20. Reservations required.

Trains: Amtrak, 433 W. St. Paul Ave. (☎271-9037; www.amtrak.com), downtown. Use caution in the area at night. To **Chicago** (1½hr., 6-7 per day, $20) and **St. Paul** (6½hr., 1 per day, $42-93). Tickets sold daily 5:30am-9pm; station open daily 5:30am-10pm.

Buses: Greyhound, 606 N. James Lovell St. (☎272-2156; www.greyhound.com), off W. Michigan St., 3 blocks from the train station. To **Chicago** (2-3hr., 11 per day, $13) and **Minneapolis** (7hr., 6 per day, $52). Station open 24hr.; tickets sold daily 6am-7:15pm. **Coach USA Milwaukee** (☎262-542-8861), in the same terminal, covers southeastern Wisconsin. **Badger Bus,** 635 N. James Lovell St. (☎276-7490; www.badgerbus.com), across the street, burrows to **Madison** (1½hr., 6 per day, $15). Open M-Sa 6:30am-8pm, Su 9:30am-8pm. Be cautious near these stations at night.

Public Transit: Milwaukee County Transit System, 1942 N. 17th St. (☎344-6711; www.ridemcts.com). Efficient metro area service. Most lines run daily 5am-12:30am. $1.75, seniors and children $0.85; weekly pass $13. Fare includes transfer that can be used for 1hr. after 1st ride. Free maps at the library or at Grand Avenue Mall. Call for schedules. The **Trolley** (☎344-6711) runs in a loop through downtown. All-day ride $12, seniors and children $1. Runs late May to early Sept. W-Th 11am-10pm, F-Sa 11am-midnight, Su 11am-6pm.

Taxi: Veteran, ☎220-5000. **Yellow Cab Co-op,** ☎271-1800.

▟ ▟ ORIENTATION AND PRACTICAL INFORMATION

Most of Milwaukee's action is downtown, which lies between **Lake Michigan** and **10th Street.** Address numbers increase north and south from **Wisconsin Avenue,** the center of east-west travel. North-south streets west of the Milwaukee River are numbered, increasing toward the west. The **interstate system** forms a loop around Milwaukee: **I-43 S** runs to Beloit, **I-43 N** runs to Green Bay, **I-94 E** is a straight shot to Chicago, **I-94 W** goes to Madison and then Minneapolis/St. Paul, **I-794** cuts through the heart of downtown Milwaukee, and **I-894** connects with the airport.

Visitor Info: Greater Milwaukee Convention and Visitors Bureau, 400 W. Wisconsin Ave. (☎908-6205 or 800-554-1448; www.milwaukee.org), in the Midwest Airlines Center lobby. Open M-F 9am-1pm and 2-5pm; in summer also Sa 9am-2pm, Su 11am-3pm.

Hotlines: Crisis Intervention, ☎257-7222. **Women's Center Hotline,** ☎933-2722. Both operate 24hr.

Internet Access: ▧**Node Coffee Shop,** 1504 E. North Ave (☎431-9278). Workstations $4 per hr., wireless access $2 per hr. Open 24hr. **Milwaukee Public Library,** 814 W. Wisconsin Ave. (☎286-3000). Open M-Th 9am-8:30pm, F-Sa 9am-5:30pm; Oct.-Apr. also Su 1-5pm. $2 per week; limit 2hr. per day.

Post Office: 345 W. St. Paul Ave. (☎270-2308), east of the Amtrak station at 4th Ave. Open M-F 7:30am-8pm. **Postal Code:** 53201. **Area Code:** 414.

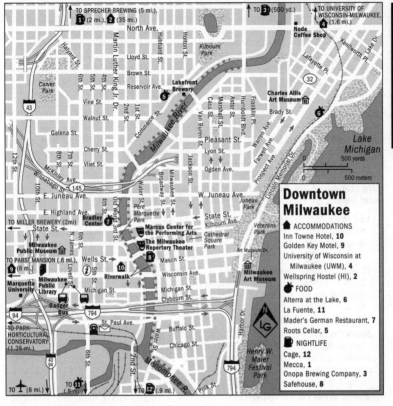

Downtown Milwaukee

⌂ ACCOMMODATIONS
Inn Towne Hotel, **10**
Golden Key Motel, **9**
University of Wisconsin at
    Milwaukee (UWM), **4**
Wellspring Hostel (HI), **2**

🍎 FOOD
Alterra at the Lake, **6**
La Fuente, **11**
Mader's German Restaurant, **7**
Roots Cellar, **5**

🍸 NIGHTLIFE
Cage, **12**
Mecca, **1**
Onopa Brewing Company, **3**
Safehouse, **8**

🔦 ACCOMMODATIONS

The rates at the hotels located along Wisconsin Ave. downtown are almost uniformly expensive, but thankfully motels with much more reasonable rates are just a short ride away in the northern and western suburbs, as well as down by the main airport.

Wellspring Hostel (HI), 4382 Hickory Rd. (☎262-675-6755), in Newburg. Take I-43 N to Exit 96, and then follow Rte. 33 W 10 mi. into Newburg. Bear right onto Main St. and take a sharp right onto Hickory Rd. This homey 10-bed hostel shares the grounds of a rambling organic farm and garden school. It's only 45min. to downtown Milwaukee, but the city feels like it's a world away. Linens included. Office open daily 8am-9pm. Dorms $21, members $18. MC/V. ❶

University of Wisconsin at Milwaukee (UWM), Sandburg Hall, 3400 N. Maryland Ave. (☎229-4065 or 299-6123). Take bus #30 north one stop past Hartford Ave. Spotless dorm-style suites close to East Side restaurants and bars. Linens provided. Laundry facilities and free local calls. Parking M-Sa $8.50 per day, Su free. 24hr. advance reservations required. Open June to early Aug. Singles with shared bath $36, with A/C $49; doubles $45/$70. Cash only. ❷

GREAT LAKES

Golden Key Motel, 3600 S. 108th St. (☎543-5300), in Greenfield. Take I-894 to Exit 3, then turn right on W. Beloit Rd. Proceed for ½ mi. and turn right on S. 108th. With a pool and high-speed Internet, this basic motel packs in more than its fair share of amenities. Singles $45-50; doubles $60. AAA discount 10%. AmEx/D/MC/V. ❸

Inn Towne Hotel, 710 N. Old World Third St. (☎877-484-6835), downtown. This centrally located Best Western offers comfortable rooms along with exercise facilities, cable TV, and A/C. Proximity to Water St. provides endless food and nightlife options. Parking $10 per day. Singles from $64; doubles $69. AmEx/D/MC/V. ❹

FOOD

From *Bratwurst* to *Bier*, Milwaukee is best known for its German traditions. Downtown restaurants tend to favor traditional menus heavy on the meat and potatoes, although the **Friday Night Fish Fry** cuts through the veneer of formality with a table-bending feast (polka band optional). Inexpensive Polish and Mexican fare crop up on the **South Side,** while **Bradley Street** and the **Water Street Entertainment District** are each a nexus for trendy, upscale dining.

La Fuente, 625 S. 5th St. (☎271-8595), in the South Side. Locals flock here for authentic Mexican food and Milwaukee's best margaritas. Murals, mariachi music, and an expansive patio add to the laid-back atmosphere. 3 tacos $6.65. 3 enchiladas $8.75. Open M-Th and Su 10am-11pm, F-Sa 10am-midnight. AmEx/D/DC/MC/V. ❷

Mader's German Restaurant, 1037 N. Old World Third St. (☎271-3377). Founded in 1902 and known for serving the likes of Cary Grant and Ronald Reagan. Traditional German fare against a backdrop of dark wood and stained glass. Entrees $8.50-14. Open M-Th 11:30am-9pm, F-Sa 11:30am-10pm, Su 11am-9pm. Reservations recommended. AmEx/D/DC/MC/V. ❸

Roots Cellar, 1818 N. Hubbard St. (☎374-8480). While entrees at the Roots Restaurant upstairs can easily top $25, the more casual Cellar offers the same refined ambience and a light, summery menu at a much lower price. Try a pita pocket with green onion hummus ($7) or the blackened salmon salad ($11). Open M-Sa 10am-2pm and 5-9pm, Su 11am-2pm. AmEx/D/DC/MC/V. ❸

Alterra at the Lake, 1701 N. Lincoln Memorial Dr. (☎223-4551), brews freshly-roasted coffee and prepares inventive sandwiches ($6-7). Lines snake out the door on weekends, but the ample seating inside and out usually accommodates everyone. Open M-F 6:30am-10pm, Sa-Su 7am-10pm. Kitchen closes M-Th and Su 9pm. AmEx/MC/V. ❶

SIGHTS

BREWERIES. Although many of Milwaukee's breweries have relocated, beer is still a tried-and-true staple. The **Miller Brewery,** a corporate giant well-known to American college students for low-end beers like "the Beast," offers a free 1hr. tour with a three-screen video presentation and a sample at the end. *(4000 W. State St. ☎931-2337; www.millerbrewing.com. Under 18 must be accompanied by an adult. ID required. Open M-Sa 10am-5:30pm; 2 tours per hr., last tour 3:30pm.)* Of course, breweries needn't be huge to be successful, and workers at the **Lakefront Brewery** joke that the volume of beer they sell each year is roughly the same amount Anheuser-Busch spills on the floor in one shift. Tours are informal, even raucous, and the souvenir pint glasses given to visitors don't stay empty for long. *(1872 N. Commerce St. ☎372-8800; www.lakefrontbrewery.com. Tours year-round F 3, 6, 7pm; Sa 1, 2, 3pm; in summer also M-Th 2, 3pm. $5, non-beer drinkers $3. 21+ unless accompanied by legal guardian.)* For a taste of a few other microbreweries, take a 3hr. **Riverwalk Boat Tour.** The "Brew City Queen" travels to the Lakefront Brewery, the Milwaukee Ale House, and the Rock

Bottom Brewery for guided tours and samples. *(☎ 283-9999; www.cafevecchio.com/riverwalkboat. Tours in summer Sa-Su; 3 per day, each starting from one of the 3 breweries. $20.)* One of the state's most renowned microbreweries, **Sprecher Brewing** is the champion of Old World brewing techniques. The 1hr. tour, which includes a visit to an old lager cellar and the Rathskellar museum of beer memorabilia, is followed by four beer samples. *(701 W. Glendale, 5 mi. north on I-43, then east on Port Washington St. ☎ 964-2739; www.sprecherbrewery.com. Tours F 4pm, Sa 1, 2, 3pm, Su 1:30 and 2:30pm; June-Aug. additional tours M-Th 4pm. $3, under 21 $1. Reservations required; call ahead to confirm tour times.)*

MUSEUMS. Without question, the pride and joy of Milwaukee's public art space is the lakeside ◨**Milwaukee Art Museum,** with its dramatic white pavilion and enormous sunscreen designed by Santiago Calatrava. The art on the walls is just as impressive, ranging from paintings from the European Renaissance to a significant collection of Haitian folk art. Feature exhibitions for 2006 include installations by Bruce Nauman in February and March, plus comic strips and books by leading American illustrators from May to mid-August. *(700 N. Art Museum Dr., on the lakefront downtown. ☎ 224-3200; www.mam.org. Free audio tour available. Open M-W and F-Su. 10am-8pm. $8, seniors $6, students $4, under 12 free. Feature exhibitions $2-4 extra.)* Beleaguered by a budgetary crisis over the past two years, the **Milwaukee Public Museum** is doing what it can to preserve the luster of signature exhibits like the Rainforest and the Streets of Old Milwaukee. The neighboring Discovery World still offers hands-on activities for kids. *(800 W. Wells St., at N. 8th St. ☎ 278-2700; www.mpm.edu. Open daily 9am-5pm. $8, seniors $7, children $5.50, under 2 free; Discovery World $7/$6/$4.75; combo tickets $13/$11.50/$9.25. Parking available. Wheelchair accessible.)* The **Charles Allis Art Museum,** an almost perfectly preserved 1911 mansion, combines period art and furnishings with rotating exhibitions of contemporary Wisconsin artists. *(1801 N. Prospect Ave. at E. Royal Pl., 1 block north of Brady. Take bus #15 or 30. ☎ 278-8295; www.cavtmuseums.org. Open W 1-5pm and 7-9pm, Th-Su 1-5pm. $5, students and seniors $3, children free. Classic movie screenings every other W at 7:30pm.)* The 1892 **Pabst Mansion** came within weeks of being turned into a Holiday Inn parking lot, but it was swooped up by a group of civic-minded benefactors and today stands as a monument to the extravagance of Milwaukee's beer barons. *(2000 W. Wisconsin Ave. ☎ 931-0808; www.pabstmansion.com. Open M-Sa 10am-4pm, Su noon-4pm. Mandatory tours leave on the hr.; last tour leaves at 3pm. $8, students and seniors $7, ages 6-17 $4. Prices go up by $1 around Christmas.)*

THE HIDDEN DEAL

HAVIN' A BALL

With tickets to see the Milwaukee Brewers starting at just $10, there's no need to travel any farther than Miller Park for a dose of America's pastime. Yet minor league baseball has an allure all its own. It has a laid-back charm that comes hand-in-hand with hokey promotions between innings, kids wandering around while parents socialize, and speculation that one of the players snagging fly balls might be called up to the majors for a date with destiny. Budget-friendly ticket prices are just icing on the cake.

The Beloit Snappers play in the Class A Midwest League, and they square off against rivals like their in-state nemesis, the Wisconsin Timber Rattlers. Their home turf, Pohlman Field, holds 3500 fans, and the shaded bleacher seats in the center sections are always coveted. Sunburnt dads bring radar guns to the game to clock the speed of pitches as they streak toward home plate, and a large snapping turtle mascot (call him Snappy) appears at regular intervals to rev up the crowd. Whether or not the Beloit players are teetering on the brink of big-league glory, they play a snappy game of small-town ball.

*The **Beloit Snappers** (☎ 362-2272; www.beloitsnappers.com) at Pohlman Field. From Milwaukee, take I-43 south into Beloit, and turn right on Cranston Rd; the field is 1½ mi. farther on the right. $5.50, ages 5-14 $4.50.*

PARKS. With almost 15,000 acres of parks in Milwaukee County, you won't need to go far to get some grass under your feet. Lake, Back Bay, and Veterans Parks are all popular spots by Lake Michigan. Farther afield, the **Boerner Botanical Gardens** cultivate gorgeous blossoms and host open-air concerts on Thursday nights. *(9400 Boerner Dr. in Hales Corner, Exit I-894 at S. 92nd St. ☎525-5601. Open May-Sept. daily 8am-sunset. $4, seniors $3, ages 6-17 $2.)* The **Mitchell Park Horticultural Conservatory,** otherwise known as "The Domes," has recently fallen on hard times, although the seven-story conical glass greenhouses are still in place, waiting to be restored to their former splendor. *(524 S. Layton Ave., at 27th St. Take bus #10 west to 27th St., then #27 south to Layton. ☎649-9830. Open daily 9am-5pm. $5, ages 5-17 $3.50, under 5 free.)*

OTHER SIGHTS. A road warrior's nirvana, locally headquartered **Harley-Davidson** gives 1hr. tours of its engine plant that will enthrall any aficionado. *(11700 W. Capitol Dr. in Wauwatosa. ☎343-7850. Tours at regular intervals M-F 9:30am-1pm; call ahead for details and plan to arrive early. Reservations required for groups larger than 10. Closed-toe shoes must be worn. No children under 12. Photo ID required for over 18.)* Olympic hopefuls in figure skating and speed skating train at the **Pettit National Ice Center,** but daily open skates ensure that even beginners get ice time. *(500 S. 84th St., at I-94, 10min. west of downtown. ☎266-0100; www.thepettit.com. Open skate daily 7-9pm; check website for other times. $6, seniors and children $5. Skate rental $2.50.)*

🎵 ENTERTAINMENT

Summer brings free entertainment to Milwaukee, like the popular **Cathedral Park Jazz** series (☎271-1416), Thursdays at 6:30pm in Cathedral Square Park, at N. Jackson St. between Wells and Kilbourn St. In Père Marquette Park, at 3rd and Kilbourn St., **River Flicks** (☎276-6696) screens free movies at dusk Fridays in August. **Cathedral Park Jazz** (☎271-1416) jams for free in Cathedral Square Park. The **Marcus Center for the Performing Arts,** 929 N. Water St., also hosts a series of free concerts at the Peck Pavilion. (☎273-7121; www.marcuscenter.org. Concerts Tu noon and 7:30pm.) The music moves indoors during the winter with the **Milwaukee Symphony Orchestra,** the **Milwaukee Ballet,** and the **Florentine Opera Company.** (☎273-7206. Symphony tickets from $15, ballet and opera tickets from $10. Ballet and symphony offer $10 student rush tickets; opera student rush tickets $15. Box office open M-F 11:30am-9pm, Sa-Su noon-9pm.) From September through May the **Milwaukee Repertory Theater,** 108 E. Wells St., opens its three stages, presenting a mix of innovative shows and classics. (☎224-9490; www.milwaukeerep.com. $8.50-49; students and seniors $2 discount, as well as half-price rush 30min. before shows. Box office open M-Sa 10am-6pm, Su noon-6pm.)

Baseball's **Brewers** step up to bat at **Miller Park,** at the interchange of I-94 and Rte. 41. (☎902-4000 or 800-933-7890; www.milwaukeebrewers.com. Seats $10. Tours daily Apr.-Sept. 10:30am, noon, 1:30, 3pm; no tours on days with games. $6, seniors and under 14 $3.) Fresh off their #1 pick in the 2005 draft, the NBA's **Bucks** shoot hoops at the **Bradley Center,** 1001 N. 4th St. (☎227-0500. Tickets from $10.)

🎉 FESTIVALS

With street fairs lined up for every single weekend during the summer months, it's not hard to see why Milwaukee calls itself "the city of festivals." ⚑**Summerfest** is the mother of them all, drawing more than a million visitors during 11 days of big-name music, roasted corn, and overpriced beer. (☎273-2680 or 800-273-3378; www.summerfest.com. Late June to early July. Tickets $12, seniors and ages 3-10 $3; 3-day pass $30.) In early August, the **Wisconsin State Fair** rolls into the fairgrounds, next to the Pettit National Ice Center, with live music, rides, cream puffs, fireworks, and an aquatic pig race. (☎266-7000 or 800-884-3247; www.wsfp.state.wi.us. $8, seniors $6, ages 7-11 $3.) Smaller, but still popular, ethnic festivals are held in the **Henry W. Maier Festival Park,** on the lakefront of the Historic Third Ward. Among the most popular are: **Asian Moon** (☎483-8530; www.asianmoon.org) and **Polish Fest** (☎529-2140; www.polishfest.org), both in mid-June; **Festa Italiana** (☎223-2808; www.festaitaliana.com) in mid-July; **Bastille Days** (☎271-1416; http://bastille.easttown.com) around July 14; and **German Fest** (☎464-9444; www.germanfest.com) in late July. (The Milwaukee County Transit System runs shuttles directly to the festivals. Call ☎344-6711 for more information. Most festivals $8-10, under 12 free; some free plus price of food.)

▐ NIGHTLIFE

Milwaukee never lacks something to do after sundown. The downtown business district becomes desolate at night, but the area along **Water Street** between Juneau and Highland Ave. hosts breweries and Irish pubs frequented by a staunchly local clintele. The college crowd heads toward the intersection of **North Avenue** and **North Farwell Street,** near the UWM campus. Running east-west between Farwell St. and the Milwaukee River, **Brady Street** tends to have more upscale lounges, while **South 2nd Street** hosts Latin dancing and most of the city's gay nightlife.

▧ **Safehouse,** 779 N. Front St. (☎271-2007; www.safe-house.com), across from the Pabst Theater downtown. An enigmatic sign that reads "International Exports, Ltd." welcomes guests to this bizarre world of spy hideouts and secret passwords. Teeming with atmosphere and intrigue, Safehouse prides itself on an "Ultimate Martini" that's propelled through a maze of pneumatic tubes before being served without so much as a hint of vermouth. Mixed drinks $5-6. Cover $1-5. Open M 11:30am-1:30am, Tu-Th 11:30am-2am, F-Sa 11:30am-2:30am, Su 4pm-midnight.

Onopa Brewing Company, 735 E. Center St. (☎264-3630; www.onopabrewery.com). The dim lighting completes the vibe of understated hipness that prevails at this RiverWest hangout. Live music ranging from country to electroclash packs the premises even fuller on weekend nights. Shows F-Sa, sometimes other nights. Cover for shows $5-10. Open M-Th 4pm-2am, F 4pm-2:30am, Sa noon-2:30am, Su noon-2am.

Cage, 801 S. 2nd Ave. (☎383-8330; www.cagenightclub.com). A two-decade veteran of Milwaukee's nightlife, Cage draws a primarily gay crowd with 5 bars, a massive dance floor and a cage suspended from the ceiling. Weekday nights can be quiet, but Saturdays always crackle with energy. Drag show F. Cover F-Sa $6. Open M-Th and Su 9pm-2am, F-Sa 9pm-2:30am.

Mecca, 3811 W. Hampton Ave. (☎462-474-3811). From downtown, take I-43 north to Exit 77b, and follow W. Hampton Ave. 1 mi. to the corner of 38th St. Deep into Milwaukee's West Side, Mecca spins hip-hop and R&B on weekend nights. On Sundays, the bar becomes the epicenter of the city's spoken word community, and gifted poets spit rhymes by the glow of an antique lamp. Cover $3-5. Spoken word Su 9pm. Open M 9pm-midnight, Tu-Th and Su 8pm-midnight, F-Sa 9pm-2am.

MADISON ☎608

Locals in Madison refer to their downtown as "the Isthmus." For those who have forgotten their geography, that's a narrow strip of land that connects two larger landmasses. It is a dramatic place to build a city and places the Capitol and the **University of Wisconsin-Madison** in very close quarters. The coupling results in an active, lively community with a strong sense of history and civic-mindedness seen in its museums, outdoor activities, restaurants, and arts. Madison's distinct flavor is a fine blend of mature stateliness and youthful vigor.

GREAT LAKES

⊏ TRANSPORTATION

Airport: Dane County Regional Airport (MSN), 4000 International Ln. (☎246-3380; www.co.dane.wi.us/airport), 5 mi. northeast of downtown. Take U.S. 151 (E. Washington Ave.) to U.S. 51N (Stoughton St.). Taxis to downtown run $12-16. Bus to downtown: Metro #24 to North Transfer Point, then #2 or 4 to Capital Square (M-F only).

Buses: Greyhound, 2 S. Bedford St. at W. Washington Ave. (☎257-3050; www.greyhound.com), goes to **Chicago** (3-4hr., 6 per day, $28.50) and **Minneapolis** (5-6hr., 4 per day, $49). **Badger Bus** (☎255-6771; www.badgerbus.com), at the same address, runs to **Milwaukee** (1½hr., 6-8 per day, $15). Open daily 8:30am-8:45pm.

Public Transit: Madison Metro Transit System, 1101 E. Washington Ave. (☎266-4466; www.ci.madison.wi.us/metro), serves downtown and campus. $1.50, 1-day pass $3. 10-ride card $10. Open M-F 6:15am-6pm, Sa 6am-4:30pm, Su 12:30pm-4:30pm.

Taxi: Union Cab *(☎242-2000;* www.unioncab.com). Wheelchair-accessible cabs available. Meter, $2.50 base fare. To airport from downtown $12-15. **Badger Cab** (☎256-5566; www.badgercab.com). Fares by zone.

✦? ORIENTATION AND PRACTICAL INFORMATION

Madison's main attractions are centered around the Capitol and the University of Wisconsin-Madison. **State Street,** which is reserved for pedestrians, bikers, and buses, connects the two and is the city's hub for eclectic food, shops, and nightlife. **Lake Monona** to the southeast and **Lake Mendota** to the northwest lap at Madison's shores. The northeast and southwest ends of the isthmus are joined by **Washington Avenue (U.S. 151),** the city's main thoroughfare, which, along with Regent St., divides streets into north and south. Wisconsin Ave. and Martin Luther King, Jr. Blvd. split streets into east and west. **I-90** and **I-94** skirt the city to the west. I-94 E goes to Milwaukee, then Chicago; I-94 W goes to Minneapolis/St. Paul; I-90 E goes directly to Chicago through Rockford, IL; I-90 W goes to Albert Lea, MN.

Visitor Info: Greater Madison Convention and Visitors Bureau, 615 E. Washington Ave. (☎255-2537 or 800-373-6376; www.visitmadison.com). Open M-F 8am-5pm. The Bureau also has a booth at the Dane County Airport near baggage claim.

Internet Access: Madison Public Library, 201 W. Mifflin St. (☎266-6300; www.madisonpubliclibrary.org). Open M-W 8:30am-9pm, Th-F 8:30am-6pm, Sa 9am-5pm; Oct.-Apr. also open Su 1-5pm. Ask at reference desk for code for wireless service.

Post Office: 215 Martin Luther King, Jr. Blvd., Ste. 101 (☎250-6487). Open M-F 8am-5pm, Sa 9am-noon. **Postal Code:** 53703. **Area Code:** 608.

⌂ ACCOMMODATIONS

Motels stretch along E. Washington Ave. (U.S. 151) just west of its intersection with I-90, with rooms starting at $40-60. From the Capitol, bus routes #6 and 7 drive the 5 mi. between the Washington Ave. motels and downtown. Prices get steeper downtown, starting around $60-80.

Hostelling International—Madison (HI), 141 S. Butler St. (☎441-0144; www.madisonhostel.org), at King St. A good bet for budget travelers. No-shoe policy helps keep rooms clean and comfortable. Free Internet access, kitchen, and coin laundry. Reception in summer M-Th and Su 8am-9pm, F-Sa until 10pm; in winter daily 8-11am and 5-9pm. Dorms $21, members $17; private rooms $44/$41. MC/V. ❶

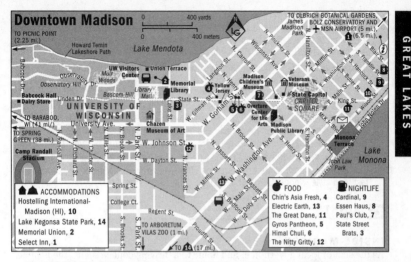

Downtown Madison

TO PICNIC POINT (2.25 mi.)

TO OLBRICH BOTANICAL GARDENS, James Madison Park, BOLZ CONSERVATORY AND MSN AIRPORT (5 mi.), (6.5 mi.)

400 yards / 400 meters

Lake Mendota

Howard Temin / Lakeshore Path

UW Visitors Center ■ Union Terrace

Observatory Hill Dr.

Muir Woods

Memorial Library

Babcock Hall • Dairy Store

Linden Dr.

Bascom Hill

Library Mall

State St.

UNIVERSITY OF WISCONSIN

University Ave.

Chazen Museum of Art

Madison Children's Museum

Veterans Museum

Yellow Jersey

State Capitol CAPITOL SQUARE

Overture Center for the Arts

Madison Public Library

Monona Terrace

Lake Monona

John Law Park

TO BARABOO, WI (41 mi.)

TO SPRING GREEN (38 mi.)

Camp Randall Stadium

W. Johnson St.

W. Dayton St.

Spring St.

College Ct.

Regent St.

TO ARBORETUM, VILAS ZOO (1 mi.)

TO ⑭ (17 mi.)

▲▲ ACCOMMODATIONS
Hostelling International-
Madison (HI), **10**
Lake Kegonsa State Park, **14**
Memorial Union, **2**
Select Inn, **1**

🍎 FOOD
Chin's Asia Fresh, **4**
Electric Earth, **13**
The Great Dane, **11**
Gyros Pantheon, **5**
Himal Chuli, **6**
The Nitty Gritty, **12**

🍸 NIGHTLIFE
Cardinal, **9**
Essen Haus, **8**
Paul's Club, **7**
State Street
Brats, **3**

Memorial Union, 800 Langdon St. (☎262-1583), on the UW campus. Spacious rooms with excellent lake and city views. Cable TV, A/C, and free parking. Call ahead; the 6 rooms fill—especially on football weekends—up to a year in advance. No-frills college cafeterias dole out quick and cheap meals for $5-8. Doubles from $58. Check-in 2pm, check-out 11am, at the UW Visitors Center. MC/V. ❸

Select Inn, 4845 Hayes Rd. (☎249-1815; www.selectinn.com), west of the junction of I-94 and U.S. 151. Large rooms with refrigerators, cable TV, A/C, hot tub, and laundry. Free wireless Internet. Continental breakfast included or 10% off at Perkins next door. Singles from $46; doubles from $51; suites $54-99. AmEx/D/MC/V. ❸

Lake Kegonsa State Park, 2405 Door Creek Rd. (☎873-9695, 888-947-2757 for reservations; www.wiparks.net), south on I-90 to Stoughton (Exit 147). Pleasant single, family, and group sites near the beach. Showers and flush toilets. Parking $10 per day. Office open 8am-11pm; park open 6am-11pm; campground open May-Oct. Sites M-F $10, WI residents $8; Sa-Su $12/$10. Electricity additional $5. ❶

🍴 FOOD

Delicious and eclectic restaurants pepper Madison, spicing up the university and capitol areas. **State Street** hosts a variety of cheap places, including chains and Madison originals; at the Library Mall on its west end, vendors peddle international delicacies, including Thai, Indonesian, and East African treats.

The Great Dane, 123 E. Doty St. (☎284-0000; www.greatdanepub.com), at King St., near the Capitol. This popular brew pub serves hearty sandwiches, burgers, and other pub favorites along with a host of hand-crafted beers. Outdoor garden patio in summer. Entrees $6-19. Open M-Th and Su 11am-2am, F-Sa 11am-2:30am. AmEx/D/MC/V. ❷

Himal Chuli, 318 State St. (☎251-9225). This family-owned Newar eatery welcomes patrons with the aroma of spices. With Nepalese specialties such as *daal* (bean soup) and *momo* (steamed dumplings), the menu is vegetarian- and carnivore-friendly. Entrees $6-12. Open M-Sa 11:30am-9pm, Su noon-9pm. Cash only. ❸

The Nitty Gritty, 223 N. Frances St. (☎251-2521; www.nittygrittybirthdaybar.com), at Johnston St. For your fill of beer and burgers, head to the Nitty Gritty, which celebrates a gazillion birthdays each day with balloons and free beer (for the birthday person only). Pub fare $5-10. Open M-Sa 11am-late, Su noon-midnight. AmEx/D/MC/V. ❷

Electric Earth, 546 W. Washington Ave. (☎255-2310), across from the bus station. Smoothies ($4) and sandwiches ($5-7) are made with fresh and organic ingredients at this funky cafe. Vegetarian- and vegan-friendly. Free wireless Internet. Open M-F 7am-midnight, Sa-Su 8am-midnight; May-Sept. closes daily at 10pm. AmEx/D/MC/V. ❶

Gyros Pantheon, 316 State St. (251-6311), next door to Himal Chuli. The first Greek restaurant in Madison, this place is tasty and popular. Gyros and souvlaki $5. Roof garden and street seating. Public phone and ATM inside. Open daily 11am-3am. D/MC/V. ❶

Chin's Asia Fresh, 422 State St. (661-0177; www.chins.com), near W. Gorham St. Chin's serves up all kinds of Asian food—Thai, Vietnamese, Chinese, and Japanese—fast-food style. Noodle bowls $5.50. Open daily 11am-9pm. AmEx/D/MC/V. ❶

👁 SIGHTS

INSIDE MADISON

As the seat of local government and home to a thriving college scene, the isthmus has an eclectic mix of sights. The **State Capitol,** at the center of downtown, boasts beautiful ceiling frescoes, mosaics, and an observation deck. (☎266-0382; www.doa.state.wi.us/dbps/capitol. Open M-F 8am-6pm, Sa-Su 8am-4pm. Free tours every hr. from the ground floor info desk M-F 9am-noon and 1-4pm, Sa 9-11am and 1-3pm, Su 1-3pm.) Facing the Capitol is the **Veterans Museum,** 30 W. Mifflin St., which traces US military history from the Civil War to the Persian Gulf War with a focus on Wisconsin-born soldiers. (☎267-1799; http://museum.dva.state.wi.us. Open Mar.-Sept. M-Sa 9am-4:30pm; Apr.-Sept. also Su noon-4pm. Audio tours $2. Free.) Between the Capitol and Lake Monona lies the **Monona Terrace Community and Convention Center,** 1 John Nolen Dr., an adaption of a design by Frank Lloyd Wright. The rooftop gardens offer beautiful views and a performance space. (☎261-4000; www.mononaterrace.com. Open daily 8am-5pm. 1hr. guided tours available daily 1pm. Tours $3.)

Every Wednesday and Saturday morning from late April to early November, visitors swarm the capitol grounds for the **Dane County Farmers Market,** where farmers, food vendors, and artisans sell fresh-picked crops and other local treats. (☎455-1999; www.dcfm.org. Open Apr.-Nov. W 8:30am-2pm, Sa 6am-2pm.) The **University of Wisconsin-Madison (UW)** has several noteworthy museums. One of the state's most acclaimed art museums, the recently renamed **Chazen Museum of Art** (formerly Elvehjem) boasts an astounding collection of ancient Greek vases in addition to American and European art. (800 University Ave. ☎263-2246; www.chazen.wisc.edu. Open Tu-F 9am-5pm, Sa-Su 11am-5pm. Tours of permanent galleries Th 12:30pm, of temporary galleries Su 2pm. Audio tours $1. Free.) In the mornings before 10:30am, visitors can watch their favorite ice cream flavors being made at UW's own **Babcock Hall Dairy Store,** 1605 Linden Dr., at Babcock Dr. (☎262-3045; www.wisc.edu/foodsci/store. Store open M-F 9:30am-5:30pm, Sa 10am-1:30pm.) Also part of UW, the outdoor **Olbrich Botanical Gardens** and indoor **Bolz Conservatory,** 3330 Atwood Ave., showcase changing plant exhibits, from butterfly-attracting flora to the exquisite Thai Pavilion, constructed out of teak and adorned in gold leaf. Take E. Washington Ave., turn right on Fair Oaks Ave., then left on Atwood Ave. (☎246-4550; www.olbrich.org. Gardens open daily Apr.-Sept. 8am-8pm; Oct.-Mar. 9am-4pm. Free. Conservatory open M-Sa 10am-4pm, Su 10am-5pm. $1, under 5 free; free W and Sa 10am-noon.)

Hikers and botanists alike will enjoy trekking the 20 mi. of trails among the 1260 acres of the **University Arboretum,** 1207 Seminole Hwy. Enter at McCaffery Dr. (☎263-7888. Grounds open daily 7am-10pm. Visitors center open Sept.-May M-F 9:30am-4pm, Sa-Su 12:30-4pm; June-Aug. M-F 9:30am-4pm, Sa-Su 11am-3pm.) For more info, visit the **UW Visitors Center,** 716 Langdon St., inside the Memorial Union (☎263-2400). Next door to the Arboretum, stop by the **Henry Vilas Park Zoo,** 702 S. Randall Ave., a small zoo with more than its share of interesting animals. (☎266-4732; www.vilaszoo.org. Open daily; grounds 9:30am-5pm, buildings 10am-4pm. Free.) For those with children under 8, the **Madison Children's Museum,** 100 State St., will provide educational entertainment for the entire family with its interactive displays. (☎256-644; www.madisonchildrensmuseum.org. Open Tu-F 9am-4pm, Sa 9am-5pm, Su noon-5pm, last M of each month 1-5pm; Memorial Day-Labor Day also M 9am-4pm. $4, seniors $3, 1st Su of each month free.)

OUTSIDE MADISON

Some of Madison's most unique sights are daytrips from the city proper. Forty miles from Madison near Spring Green, Frank Lloyd Wright's famed **Taliesin** home and neighboring buildings hug the hills that inspired his organic architecture. Five tours ($15-75) examine various aspects of the estate. The Hillside and Walking Tours are the most affordable. Take U.S. 14W to Rte. 23 and County C. (☎877-588-7900; www.taliesinpreservation.org. Open May-Oct. daily 9am-6pm. Call for tour schedules.) Next door, the **American Players Theatre** puts on satires, Shakespeare, and other plays in an outdoor theater. (☎588-2361; www.playinthewoods.org. Shows June-early Oct. Tickets $29-48.) Nine miles south of Taliesin, the **House on the Rock,** 5754 Rte. 23, is an unparalleled multilevel house built into a chimney of rock and stocked with a kitschy collection of bizarre trinkets and artifacts. Home to the world's largest carousel—of its 269 animals, not one is a horse—the house is interesting but perhaps not worth the steep admission price. (☎935-3639; www.thehouseontherock.com. Open daily July-Aug. 9am-7pm; June and late Aug. to early Sept. 9am-6pm; mid-Mar. to May and Sept. to early Nov. 9am-5pm. $19.50, ages 5-12 $10.50, ages 4 and under free. MC/V.)

In Baraboo, 40 mi. northwest of Madison on U.S. 12, the **Circus World Museum,** 550 Water St., once the winter home of the world-famous Ringling Brothers Circus, pays homage to circus history with a full lineup of big-top shows and other events. (☎356-8000 or 888-693-1500; www.circusworldmuseum.com. Open in summer daily 9am-6pm; for low-season check website. Big-top shows 11:30am and 3:30pm. $15, seniors $13, ages 5-11 $8. AmEx/D/MC/V.) Garbage never looked as cool as at Tom Every's **Forevertron,** the world's largest scrap metal sculpture. The sculpture is just outside Baraboo, next to Paul's Surplus. (☎644-1450; www.drevermor.com. Open M-Sa 10am-5pm, Su noon-5pm. Free.) Seven miles north of Baraboo, the **International Crane Foundation,** on Shady Lane Rd., is worth a visit for birdlovers. (☎356-9462; www.savingcranes.org. Open Apr. 15-Oct. 31 daily 9am-5pm. Tours at 10am, 1, 3pm. Adults $8.50, ages 62+ $7, ages 5-11 $4. MC/V.)

🎭 ENTERTAINMENT

Twenty thousand music-lovers flood Capitol Sq. for six Wednesday nights in June and July when the **Wisconsin Chamber Orchestra** performs free **Concerts on the Square.** (☎257-0638; www.wcoconcerts.com. Concerts at 7pm.) Leading out from the Capitol, State Street exudes a lively college atmosphere, sporting many offbeat clothing stores and record shops, as well as a host of bars and restaurants. Slated to open in 2006, the **Overture Center for the Arts,** 201 State St., will present theater, music, visual art, and dance. (☎258-4177 for tickets and info; www.overture-center.com. Ticket office open M-F 11am-5:30pm, Sa 11am-2pm. Call for tour info.

FROM BREAKER TO BUILDER

Born in Madison, WI, in 1938, Tom Every, fondly known as Dr. Evermor by Wisconsin locals, fell in love with old-fashioned machinery at a young age and found inspiration in the work of Thomas Edison and Nikola Tesla.

After he entered the business of industrial wrecking and salvaging, he began collecting metal pieces from his different sites. In 1984, Every started transforming his collection of parts into wholes. His masterpiece, the 400-ton sculpture Forevertron, is the largest sculpture of its kind in the world. Pieced together from scraps of iron, steel, brass, and bronze, as well as from objects like the decontamination chamber from an Apollo space mission, the rocketship likeness is a feat both of artistic design and sheer determination.

Dr. Evermor does have other creations—smaller sculptures of birds, insects, mammals, and instruments—though none is as startling as Forevertron. While his work might be seen as junk art or kitsch by some, the scrap artisan, now in his late 60s, continues to build and have a vision for his art. Dr. Evermor's passion for industrial history is evident in Forevertron, which, in addition to being an impressive and mind-boggling structure, pays true homage to the ability to make something out of "nothing."

Tours $4, seniors and students $3.) Overture Hall is home to the **Madison Symphony Orchestra** and a huge concert organ, installed in 2004. (☎257-3734; www.madisonsymphony.org. Season runs late Aug.-May. Tickets $16-68.) The **Madison Museum of Contemporary Art** (formerly the Art Center) will open in April 2006. (☎257-0158; www.madisonartcenter.org.) The **Madison Repertory Theatre** will also have a new home at the Overture Center in the Playhouse, opening February 2006, where classic and contemporary works will be performed. (☎256-0029; www.madisonrep.org. Showtimes vary. Tickets $36-44.) Students and locals pass their days on the signature chairs of UW's gorgeous **Union Terrace** on Lake Mendota. (800 Langdon St. ☎265-3000.) The terrace is home to free weekend concerts year-round, which take place on the lakeshore in the summer and move indoors in the winter.

■ NIGHTLIFE

Fueled by the 40,000-plus students who pack an aptly labeled party school, Madison's nightlife scene is active, with crowded bars scattered throughout the isthmus, particularly along **State Street** and **U.S. 151.**

Essen Haus, 514 E. Wilson St. (☎255-4674; www.essen-haus.com), at S. Blair St. A lively German bar known for its infamous "beer boot" (from $15) and hearty fun. On the menu, traditional German fare rubs shoulders with American cuisine. Incredible beer selection from $1.50. Open Tu-Sa 3pm-close, Su 3-11pm. Kitchen closes at 10pm.

Cardinal, 418 E. Wilson St. (☎251-0080; www.cardinalbar.com). A benchmark of Madison's gay scene, Cardinal also attracts straight clubbers who come for its wide array of themed dance nights, from goth industrial and electronic underground to Latin jazz and 80s hits. Cover usually $5. Open Tu-Th and Su 8pm-2am, F-Sa 8pm-2:30am.

State Street Brats, 603 State St. (☎255-5544; www.statestreetbrats.com). Head to "Brats" for a healthy dose of collegiate debauchery and some serious sports. Long list of Wisconsin microbrews. Brats and burgers $3-8. Open daily 11am-2am.

Paul's Club, 212 State St. (☎257-5250). Mingle under the branches of the faux-oak tree that adorns the bar at Paul's Club, a laid-back lounge that offers a quieter alternative to the many bars with louder, younger crowds. Enticing leather couches provide a great place to chat. Open M-Th 4pm-2am, F 4pm-2:30am, Sa noon-2:30am, Su 5pm-2am.

◤ OUTDOOR ACTIVITIES

Madison's many parks and lakeshores offer endless recreational activities. There are 10 gorgeous public **beaches** along the two lakes for swimming or strolling (☎266-4711 for info). Back on dry land, **bicycling** is possibly the best way to explore the city and surrounding parklands. Madison is, in fact, the bike capital of the Midwest, with more bikes than cars traversing the landscape. **Budget Bicycle Center,** 1230 Regent St., rents all types of two-wheeled transportation. (☎251-8413. Bikes $10 per day, $30 per week; tandems $15-30 per day. Open M-F 9am-9pm, summer also Sa 9am-7pm and Su 11am-7pm.) For mountain bike rentals, **Yellow Jersey,** 419 State St., is your best bet. (☎257-4737; www.yellowjersey.org. Bikes $9.50 per day, $38.50 per 4 days; tandem $25 per day. Open M and Th 10am-8pm, Tu-W and F 10am-6pm, Su noon-5pm.) Hikers and picnickers can enjoy great views of the college at **Picnic Point** on Lake Mendota, a bit of a hike off University Bay Dr. For other city parks, the **Parks Department,** 215 Martin Luther King, Jr. Blvd., Ste. 120, in the Madison Municipal Building, can help with specific park info. (☎266-4711. Office open M-F 8am-4:15pm; parks open daily 4am-dusk. Admission free.) Canoes for use on Lake Mendota and equipment for croquet, volleyball, and horseshoes is available through **Outdoor Rentals** in the Memorial Union boathouse. (☎262-7351. Canoe rental $8.25 per hr., $24.70 per day. Call for other rates and hours.) At nearby Lake Wingra, the **Wingra Canoe and Sailing Center,** 824 Knickerbocker Pl., rents canoes, kayaks, and other boats. (☎233-5332; www.wingraboats.com. $30 per day. Open May-Oct. daily 9am-dusk.)

DOOR COUNTY ☎920

Jutting out like a thumb from the Wisconsin mainland, the Door Peninsula is not quite the undiscovered coastal getaway that it once was. Sleepy fishing villages now hawk trinkets and fudge to tourists, while "the boat people" plan chamber music festivals in their picturesque tumbledown cottages. The world may have gotten wise to Door County, but the undeveloped beauty of the eastern shore and the grassy stillness of the peninsula's county roads still testify to an earlier time.

■◢ **ORIENTATION AND PRACTICAL INFORMATION.** Door County begins in earnest at **Sturgeon Bay,** where Rte. 42 and 57 converge and then split again. Rte. 57 hugs the eastern coast; Rte. 42 runs up the west. The peninsula's east coast contains sleepy villages and lakeside parks, while the western side tends to be more expensive and touristy. From south to north along Rte. 42, **Egg Harbor, Fish Creek, Ephraim, Sister Bay,** and **Ellison Bay** are the largest towns. Public transit only comes as close as **Green Bay,** 50 mi. southwest of Sturgeon Bay, where **Greyhound** has a station at 800 Cedar St. (☎432-4883; www.greyhound.com. Tickets sold M-F 7:30am-5pm, Sa-Su 10:30am-4:30pm.) Buses run to Madison (5-8hr., 4 per day, $25) and Milwaukee (2-3hr., 4 per day, $23). Reserve tickets at least a day in advance. All of the major settlements have their own visitors centers, but the **Door County Chamber of Commerce,** on Rte. 42/57 entering Sturgeon Bay, serves as a kind of clearinghouse for information about the county. (☎743-4456 or 800-527-3529; www.doorcounty.com. Open Apr.-Oct. M-F 8:30am-5pm, Sa-Su 10am-4pm; Nov.-Mar. M-F 8:30am-4:30pm.) **Internet Access: Door County Library,** 104 S. 4th Ave., in Sturgeon Bay. (Open M-Th 9am-9pm, F 9am-6pm, Sa 9am-5pm. Free.) **Post Office:** 359 Louisiana St., at 4th St. in Sturgeon Bay. (☎800-275-8777. Open M-F 8:30am-5pm, Sa 9:30am-noon.) **Postal Code:** 54235. **Area Code:** 920.

ACCOMMODATIONS. Rooms in Door County during July and August are uniformly expensive; plan a visit for May or September to take advantage of low-season rates. Two of the best options for budget travelers are in the north-central part of the peninsula. **Century Farm Motel ❸,** 10068 Rte. 57, 3 mi. south of Sister Bay on Rte. 57, rents cozy two-room cottages hand-built in the 1920s. The motel, situated on a chicken farm and family homestead, is rare for its refusal to hike prices as the summer progresses. (☎854-4069. A/C, TV, and fridge. Open mid-May to mid-Oct. One-bedroom cabin $45, two bedrooms $65. Cash only.) Two miles to the north, **Patio Motel ❸,** 200 Orchard Dr., just off of Rte. 57, offers a more traditional motel experience, although its rates are some of the lowest in the upper half of the peninsula. (☎854-1978. Open May to late Oct. D/MC/V.) Down in the Sturgeon Bay area, budget travelers would do well to check out **Chal-A-Motel,** 3910 Rte. 42/57. It's a 30min. northerly drive to the other villages on the peninsula, but year-round accommodations at reasonable prices may make the commute worthwhile. (☎743-6788. Doubles July-Oct. $64; Nov.-June $44. MC/V.)

CAMPING. Without question, the most economical way to spend a summer night in Door County is under the stars. The area's **state parks ❶** are an appealing choice for backpackers with tents. (Reservations for all parks ☎888-947-2757; www.wiparks.net. M-Th and Su $13, WI residents $11; F-Sa $15/$13.) All state parks require a **motor vehicle permit** ($3 per hr.; $10/$5 per day; $30/$20 per yr.), which can be purchased by mail or at the park. **Peninsula State Park,** just past Fish Creek on Rte. 42, is far and away the most popular, and reservations can be made up to 11 months in advance. (☎868-3258. 469 sites with showers and toilets; 25 reserved for walk-ins. $3 extra June-Aug., $3 extra for a site by the shore.) The relatively uncrowded **Potawatomi State Park,** 3740 Park Dr., is flanked by limestone cliffs just south of Sturgeon Bay off Rte. 42/57. (☎746-2890. 123 campsites, 19 open to walk-ins. 25 sites have electricity.) **Newport State Park,** 7 mi. from Ellison Bay off Rte. 42, is a wilderness preserve at the tip of the peninsula. Sites are accessible by hiking only. (☎854-2500. 16 sites, 3 open to walk-ins. No showers.) The untamed **Rock Island State Park** offers 40 remote sites off Washington Island's northern shore. (☎847-2235. Open late May to mid-Oct. Round-trip ferry ride $8, children 5-10 $4; with camping gear $1 extra.)

FOOD. Restaurants that stay open for dinner tend to be expensive, so savvy travelers might want to eat out early in the day and then stock up on groceries for an evening meal. The **Piggly Wiggly Super Market,** Country Walk Dr. in Sister Bay, is a good bet up north, while **Econo Foods,** 1250 N. 14th Ave., stocks larders in Sturgeon Bay. (Piggly Wiggly open M-Sa 9am-8pm, Su 9am-5pm. Econo Foods open 24hr.) Start off the day with lingonberry pancakes at **Al Johnson's Swedish Restaurant ❹,** 700-710 N. Bayshore Dr., in the middle of Sister Bay on Rte. 42. The restaurant is hard to miss; just look for the goats grazing atop the sod-covered roof. (☎854-2626. Dinner entrees $12-18. Open daily 6am-9pm; low-season 7am-8pm. AmEx/D/MC/V.) Farther south, at **Good Eggs ❶,** 9820 Brookside Ln., just off of Rte. 42 in Ephraim, you can gorge yourself on made-to-order omelets wrapped in flour tortillas at a table improvised from surfboards. (☎854-6621. Breakfast wraps from $4.25. Open mid-May to mid-Oct. daily 7am-1pm. Cash only.) Grab an afternoon snack on the east side of the peninsula at **Town Hall Bakery ❷,** 6225 Rte. 57, in Jacksonport. Watch the lace curtains wave in the breeze as you sip a cup of soup ($3.25), or sample a dish of the famous granola ($7) that is shipped nationwide. (☎823-2116. Live music in July F at 7:30pm. Cover $5-10. Open June-Aug. daily 7am-3pm; Sept. Th-Su 7am-3pm. Cash only.) Meatlovers sink their teeth into babyback ribs at the **Coyote Roadhouse ❸,** on County Rte. E, west of Baileys Harbor. (☎839-9192. Ribs $13.95. Open daily 11am-10pm. AmEx/D/MC/V.)

◙ ᴸ SIGHTS AND ENTERTAINMENT. At the base of the peninsula, the historic shipbuilding center of Sturgeon Bay houses the intriguing **Door County Maritime Museum,** 120 N. Madison St., downtown. The museum showcases artifacts from steamship gauges to old outboard motors and gives visitors a glimpse into a working periscope. (☎743-5958; www.dcmm.org. Open May-Oct. daily 9am-6pm; Nov.-Apr. daily 10am-5pm. $6.50, ages 5-17 $3.) The museum also operates an exhibit in the northern village of **Gill's Rock,** where visitors can explore a 1930s fishing boat. (☎854-1844. Open June to mid-Oct. daily 10am-5pm. $4.50, ages 5-17 $1.50.) Across the bridge from the Maritime Museum, the **Fairfield Center for Contemporary Art,** 242 Michigan St., has a permanent collection of sketches and sculptures by Henry Moore. Mixed-media work by glass sculptor Richard Jolley will be featured during the summer of 2006. (☎746-0001; www.fairfieldcenter.org. Open M-Sa 10am-5pm, Su 10am-3pm. $5, students $2.50.) Trade in the hurly-burly of Sturgeon Bay for the serene grounds of **Stone's Throw Winery,** at the intersection of Rte. A and E east of Egg Harbor. Stone's Throw grows its grapes in California and then ships them overnight to Wisconsin, yielding a strong crop of wines that visitors can sample to their heart's content. (☎839-9660. Wine tasting $3. Bottles from $9. Open daily 10am-5pm.) A laid-back crowd of college students and locals takes in live music every summer at ▓**Fishstock,** an excellent series of acoustic concerts entering its 6th season in a renovated dairy barn. (3127 Rte. F, east of Fish Creek. ☎839-2981; www.fishstockmusic.com. Live music July-Aug. Su 7pm. $10. Check website for a schedule of barn dances.) The **Skyway Drive-In,** on Rte. 42 between Fish Creek and Ephraim, screens double features the old-fashioned way. (☎854-9938. $6.50, ages 6-11 $3.50, under 5 free. Films start after sunset; call for schedule.) Just south of the Skyway, Peninsula State Park plays host to the outdoor **American Folklore Theatre,** where an increasingly high-profile troupe of actors performs original Wisconsin-themed shows. (☎854-6117; www.folkloretheatre.com. $14.50, ages 13-19 $7.50, ages 3-12 $4.50.)

⚑ OUTDOOR ACTIVITIES. Biking is the best way to take in the lighthouses, rocks, and white-sand beaches of Door's rugged eastern coastline. Village tourist offices have free bike maps. **Whitefish Dunes State Park,** off Rte. 57 south of Jacksonport, glimmers with extensive sand dunes, hiking/biking/skiing trails, and a well-kept wildlife preserve. (Open daily 8am-8pm. Vehicle permit required.) Just north of the Dunes off Rte. 57 on Cave Point Rd., **Cave Point County Park** offers unusual rock formations formed by freshwater erosion as well as a beautiful view of the lake. (Open daily 6am-9pm. Free.) **Ridges Sanctuary,** north of Baileys Harbor off Rte. Q, is home to more than 25 species of orchids and other endangered plants like the dwarf lake iris. Nature trails wind their way along crescent-shaped ridges formed by Lake Michigan, and travel across adjoining wetlands with wooden bridges. (☎839-2802. Nature center open late May to mid-Oct. daily 9am-4pm, although trails stay open after hours. Trail fee $3. Guided tours June-Aug. daily 9:30am and 1:30pm. $5, includes trail fee.) **Baileys Harbor Ridges Beach,** an uncrowded stretch of sand that allows for secluded swimming, is attached to the sanctuary on Ridges Rd. Water temperatures are chilly, even through the summer.

Accessed via Cana Island Rd. off Rte. Q, **Cana Island Lighthouse** extends into the lake, compelling visitors to cross the rocky path (at low tide) or wade through the frigid waters (at high tide) to reach its oft-photographed shores. The lighthouse is not normally open to visitors, although the Coast Guard decides on a year-by-year basis whether to offer tours on the third weekend in May. Call the Maritime Museum in Sturgeon Bay for more information. The keeper's house has a gift shop that is open throughout high season, and the island provides an expansive view of the bay. (Open May-Oct. daily 10am-5pm. $4, ages 5-17 $2.)

BOIL, FISH BOIL, TOIL, AND TROUBLE

Bring 5 gal. fresh water to a boil in a large metal cauldron over a hot fire. Throw in 25 lb. of small red potatoes, sliced but not peeled; 9min. later, add an equal quantity of small white onions, peeled. After 3min., lower freshly caught whitefish steaks into the cauldron using a heavy-duty colander, and add a generous shovelful of evaporated salt for seasoning. The fish oil will separate and condense on the surface of the water before starting to boil over and dribble into the fire. At this point, pour a coffee can's worth of fuel oil onto the fire and get out of the way! (Leave this step to a masterboiler.) The fish oil will, ignite and a fireball will kick up 8ft. into the air.

After the flames die down, lift the colander with heavy gloves and serve. The **Viking Grill**, on Rte. 42 in Ellison Bay, is the granddaddy of the Door County fish boil. Though the tablecloths are plasticky, the fish sure isn't: you can drag a fork through the tender, flaky meat and pull it away easily from the bones. Owner Dan Petersen still swears by the Wickman family's original recipe, and summer after summer the fish boil continues to raise eyebrows and fill bellies.

Viking Grill, on Rte. 42 (☎854-2998; www.thevikinggrill.com). Fish boils daily May-Oct. 4:30-7pm. $14, ages 12 and under $11. Cash only.

On the opposite coast, **Peninsula State Park** draws kayakers, anglers, and families on bicycles. More crowded than the beaches around Baileys Harbor, **Nicolet Beach** attracts sunbathers from all over the peninsula. (Open daily 6am-11pm. No lifeguards. Vehicle permit required.) One mile and 110 steps up from the beach, **Eagle Tower** offers the highest view of the shore and a chance to see beyond the waters of Green Bay on a clear day. Across from the Fish Creek entrance to Peninsula State Park, **Nor Door Sport and Cyclery**, 4007 Rte. 42, rents out bikes and winter equipment. (☎868-2275; www.nordoorsports.com. Bikes $5 per hr., $20 per day. Mountain bikes $7 per hr., $30 per day. Cross-country skis $10 per day. Open June-Oct. M-Sa 9am-6pm, Su 9am-5pm; Nov.-May M and F-Sa 10am-5pm, Su 10am-3pm.)

Six miles off the northern tip of the peninsula, **Washington Island** is separated from the mainland by **Death's Door**, a treacherous channel that brought about the demise of hundreds of seafaring vessels in the 19th century. Today, Coast Guard range lights and modern ferries have made the journey much safer, allowing daytrippers to pedal over 75 mi. of quiet country roads and grill up supper on **Gislason Public Beach**, across from Detroit Harbor. Two ferry companies, Washington Island Ferry (www.wisferry.com) and Island Clipper (www.islandclipper.com) depart from Gill's Rock 2-3 times per hr. in summer, less frequently in the low season. (Round-trip fare $10, ages 6-11 $5. Washington Island Ferry shuttles automobiles for $22 and bikes for $4; the Island Clipper does not carry cars, but bike transport is free. One-speed bikes can be rented at the island dock for $3.50 per hr.)

APOSTLE ISLANDS   ☎715

The National Lakeshore protects 22 breathtaking islands off the coast of northern Wisconsin, as well as a 12 mi. stretch of mainland shore. Bayfield, a tiny mainland town, serves as the access point to the islands. Tourism is primarily focused on the mainland and Madeline Island, where inns draw families looking for a back-to-nature weekend. Local adventure companies allow summer tourists of all levels of experience to enjoy kayaking, hiking, and camping among the sandstone bluffs.

◪ PRACTICAL INFORMATION. Most excursions begin in the sleepy mainland town of **Bayfield** (pop. 611), in northwest Wisconsin on the Lake Superior coast. The **Bay Area Rural Transit (BART),** 300 Industrial Park Rd., 21 mi. south on Rte. 13 in Ashland, offers a shuttle to Bayfield. (☎682-9664. 4 per day M-F 7am-

5pm. $2.10, students $1.75, seniors $1.35.) **Visitor Info: Bayfield Chamber of Commerce,** 42 S. Broad St. (☎779-3335 or 800-447-4094; www.bayfield.org. Open M-F 8:30am-5pm, Sa-Su 9am-3pm. Lobby with free local phone open 24hr.) **National Lakeshore Headquarters Visitors Center,** 415 Washington Ave., distributes hiking info and **camping permits** and screens a short film on the islands. (☎779-3398. Open mid-May to mid-Sept. daily 8am-4:30pm; mid-Sept. to mid-May M-F 8am-4:30pm. Permits for up to 14 consecutive days $15.) The **Bayfield Carnegie Library,** 37 N. Broad St., provides free **Internet** access in 30min. slots. (☎779-3953. Open M-Tu and Th 1-7:30pm, W and F 9:30am-5pm, Sa 9:30am-3pm.) For **short-term work** picking apples or raspberries, contact the **Bayfield Apple Company,** on County Rte. J, near Betzold Rd. (☎779-5700 or 800-363-4526. Raspberries in season mid- to late July; apples late Sept. to mid-Oct. Open daily 9am-6pm.) **Post Office:** 22 S. Broad St., in Bayfield. (☎779-5636. Open M-F 9am-4:30pm, Sa 9am-11am.) **Postal Code:** 54814. **Area Code:** 715.

⌂ ACCOMMODATIONS. In summer months, the budget pickings are slim for Bayfield; rooms should be booked weeks in advance for trips during July and August. For cheaper lodgings, check the motels along Lake Shore Dr. in Ashland, an easy 30min. drive south of Bayfield. Rooms start at $40, even in high season. The **Seagull Bay Motel ❸,** off Rte. 13 at S. 7th St., offers spacious, smoke-free rooms with cable TV and a hypnotic lake view. (☎779-5558; www.seagullbay.com. Mid-May to mid-Oct. $70-90; mid-Oct. to mid-May $45-75. MC/V.) **Greunke's Inn ❹,** 17 Rittenhouse Ave., has been accommodating guests for 140 years. Quaint country rooms and a homey atmosphere make this a great place to experience Bayfield hospitality. (☎779-5480 or 800-245-3072. Open May-Oct. Shared baths. No A/C. Rooms $55-130. AmEx/D/MC/V.) **Dalrymple Park ❶,** ¼ mi. north of town on Rte. 13, has 30 campsites and a sweeping view of Madeline Island. (Open mid-May to mid-Oct. No showers, self-regulated. No reservations. Sites $15.) **Apostle Islands Area Campground ❶,** ½ mi. south of Bayfield on Rte. J off Rte. 13, has 55 campsites buried deep in the woods of Bayfield. (☎779-5524. Open early May to early Oct. Reservations recommended 1 month in advance for July-Aug. Tent sites $17, with hookup $20, with full sewer and cable $27. Primitive cabins $40. Cash only.) Campers in the Bayfield area should come prepared to battle fierce mosquitoes.

▯ FOOD. The bright pink exterior is just the beginning at **Maggie's ❷,** 257 Manypenny Ave., where charbroiled burgers ($6-7) and zesty fajitas ($10) complement the deliciously kitschy flamingo decor. (☎779-5641; www.maggies-bayfield.com. Open M-F 11:30am-9pm, Sa-Su 11:30am-10pm. AmEx/D/MC/V.) One of the oldest establishments in Bayfield, **Greunke's Restaurant ❸,** 17 Rittenhouse Ave., at 1st St., has been feeding hungry fishermen for over a century. These days, Greunke's cooks up huge breakfasts by day ($6-7) and batter-dipped whitefish livers ($7) by night. Check out the shrine to the late John F. Kennedy, Jr., located next to the 1946 Wurlitzer jukebox. (☎779-5480. Fish boils W-Su 6:30-8pm. $11, children $6. Open M-Sa 6am-10pm, F-Su 7am-9:30pm. AmEx/D/DC/MC/V.) **Egg Toss Cafe ❷,** 41 Manypenny Ave., specializes in the first meal of the day, serving up Eggs Benedict with crab cakes ($9), and more traditional dishes for $6.50-9. (☎779-5181; www.eggtoss-bayfield.com. Open daily 6am-2pm. AmEx/D/MC/V.)

◨▥ SIGHTS AND OUTDOOR ACTIVITIES. The recently completed **Bayfield Heritage Center,** 30 N. Broad St., offers glimpses into the settlement's past as a lumber boomtown and fishing village. (☎779-5958; www.bayfieldheritage.org. Open mid-June to mid-Oct. Tu-Su 10am-5pm, mid-Oct. to mid-June M-F 10am-5pm. $5, under 18 free.) Spend an hour or two picking famously sweet strawberries up at the **James Erickson Orchard & Country Store,** 86600 Betzold Rd. (☎779-5438. U-pick

GREAT LAKES

strawberries $1.15 per lb. Strawberry season starts late June. Open late May to mid-Oct. M-Sa 10am-4pm, Su noon-4pm.) The best beach on the mainland is **Bayview Beach,** 6 mi. south of Bayfield along Rte. 13. Look for the green signs marking Bayview Park Rd., then turn down the dirt road to access Bayview's soft, red sands. Even after the summer hikers and beach bums head home for the season, Bayfield manages to attract a bumper crop of tourists with its annual **Apple Festival.** An incredible 50-80,000 visitors pour into town during the first full weekend of October, and the 2006 street fair in honor of Bayfield's 150th birthday promises to be more festive than ever. The slopeside **Big Top Chautauqua,** 3 mi. south of Bayfield off Hwy. 13 on Ski Hill Rd., draws folk and bluegrass headliners like Arlo Guthrie, in addition to staging their ever-popular "house shows," original musicals about life in northern Wisconsin. (☎373-5552 or 888-244-8386; www.bigtop.org. Open June-Sept. Call for showtimes. Tickets can be purchased at the Bayfield Branch Box Office, Rittenhouse Ave. and 1st St., next to Greunke's. Reserved seating for house shows $18, ages 12 and under $8; general admission $12/$4.)

While Madeline Island (see below) is the only one of the Apostle Islands with a year-round settlement, hikers and outdoors enthusiasts use Bayfield as their launchpad to a number of the other islands. Nearby **Stockton Island** and **Oak Island** are among the most popular for campers, although private sailboats dock out as far as **Rocky Island** and **York Island.** The lighthouses on **Raspberry** and **Michigan Islands** are open for tours in summer, while experienced kayakers can explore the breathtaking sea caves hollowed out of the cliffs on **Devil's Island.** The **Apostle Islands Cruise Service** runs a narrated 3hr. tour that provides newcomers with a brief look at the islands. For travelers hoping to do more than look out the window, the Cruise Service also drops campers off at Stockton and Oak Islands during July and August. (☎779-3925 or 800-323-7619. Tours depart the Bayfield City Dock mid-May to mid-Oct. daily 10am. $27, children $16. Reservations recommended. Round-trip shuttle to Stockton or Oak Island $30, children $17. Reservations required.) **Trek and Trail,** at 1st and Washington St. in Bayfield, rents bikes and kayaks. They also lead sea kayaking tours, ranging from a 2hr. intro to a 6-day odyssey through the caves and quarries of the outer islands. (☎800-354-8735. Bikes $5 per hr., $20 per day. 4hr. kayak rental from $20. All renters must complete a 3hr. kayaking safety course, offered daily 8:30am and 1pm. Safety course $50; reserve at least one day in advance. Tours start at $30. Open June-Oct.)

MADELINE ISLAND   ☎715

Funkier and more free-spirited than buttoned-up Bayfield, Madeline Island brings together a provocative combination of cigar-chomping millionaires and rakish artists with dreadlocks dangling in the wind. The year-round population assembles in February for an island-wide talent show and nine holes of golf on the ice. Rooms in the area fill during the summer; call ahead for reservations. The **Madeline Island Motel ❹,** on Col. Woods Ave. across from the ferry landing, has private patios with hanging plants attached to each of its rooms. (☎747-3000. TV, A/C, fridge, microwave. Continental breakfast included. Open Apr.-Nov. July to early Sept. doubles $95; Apr.-June and early Sept. to Nov. $70-80. D/MC/V.) **The Inn on Madeline Island ❺,** a 10min. walk south of the ferry landing, rents out lake houses and condos that are surprisingly affordable for travelers in groups. With 70+ rental properties to offer parties of four or more, The Inn can find lodgings with a variety of configurations and amenities. (☎747-6315 or 800-822-6315; www.madisland.com. Min. 2- to 3-night stay. Reserve well in advance. 50% of rental payment due with reservation. Rates from $150. MC/V.) Madeline Island has two campgrounds. **Big Bay Town Park ❶,** 6½ mi. from La Pointe off Big Bay Rd., sits next to tranquil Big Bay Lagoon. (☎747-6913. No reservations. Open mid-May to mid-Oct. Sites $15, with electricity

$20.) Across the lagoon, **Big Bay State Park ●** rents 60 rustic sites without electricity. (☎747-6425, reservations 888-947-2757; www.wiparks.net. Reservations $8.50. Sites $10-12. Daily vehicle permit $10, WI residents $5.) ▨**Tom's Burned Down Cafe,** 1 Middle Rd., is the nexus for all things hip, weird, and countercultural on Madeline Island. Burned to the ground in 1992, the bar and performance space rebuilt itself out of scrap metal, a huge tent, and a stubborn commitment to having a good time. (☎747-6100. Open mic Th; live music F-Sa. Cover $2-6. Open daily M-Th and Su 10am-2am, F-Sa 10am-2:30am.) **Ella's Island Cafe ❷,** to the left of the ferry landing, is a crowded breakfast joint in the morning and moonlights as a pie shop and bar some weekend nights in summer. (☎747-2400. Breakfast $3-9. Open W-Su 7:30am-noon, some weeks F-Sa 5-10pm. Cash only.)

With roughly five streets, downtown Madeline Island is easy to navigate. **Visitor Info: Madeline Island Chamber of Commerce,** on Main St. to the right of the ferry landing. (☎747-2801 or 888-475-3386; www.madelineisland.com. Open May-Oct. M-F 9am-5pm, Sa 9am-3pm; Nov.-Apr. M-F 10am-3pm.) For pamphlets about the island, visit the chamber's booth near the ferry landing in Bayfield. **Madeline Island Ferry Line** shuttles between Bayfield and La Pointe on Madeline Island. (☎747-2051; www.madferry.com. June-Aug. daily every 30min. 9:30am-6pm, every hr. 6:30-9:30am and 6-11pm. $4.75, ages 6-11 $2.50; bikes $2.50; cars $10.75. Mar.-May and Sept.-Dec. ferries run less frequently and prices drop.) In winter, the state highway department builds an ice road. During transition periods, the ferry service runs **windsleds** between the island and the mainland. **Motion to Go,** 102 Lake View Pl., on Middle Rd. about one block from the ferry, rents scooters and bikes. (☎747-6585. Mopeds $20 per hr.; mountain bikes $7 per hr., $26 per day. Open daily May to mid-June 9am-6pm; mid-June to July 8:30am-7pm; July-Aug. 8am-8pm; Sept. to mid-Oct. 9am-7pm.) Housed in an interconnected compound of 19th-century log buildings, the **Madeline Island Historical Museum** keeps the island's rich history alive with artifacts ranging from ice chisels and weasel traps to a Chippewa translation of the Protestant Bible. (☎747-2415. Open June to early Oct. daily 10am-5pm. $5.50, seniors $5, ages 5-12 $2.75.) The **Madeline Island Public Library,** on Library St. just off of Big Bay Rd., offers free **Internet** access. (☎747-3662. Open M and W 2-8pm; T and Th-F 10am-5pm; Sa 10am-noon.) The **Post Office** is just off the dock on Madeline Island in La Pointe. (☎747-3712. Open M-F 9am-noon and 12:30-4:20pm, Sa 9:30am-12:50pm.) **Postal Code:** 54850. **Area Code:** 715.

MINNESOTA

In the 19th century, floods of German and Scandinavian settlers edged native tribes out of the rich lands now known as Minnesota, a name derived from a Dakota word meaning "sky-tinted waters." Known as the Land of 10,000 Lakes, Minnesota's beauty stretches from the northern wilderness and Boundary Waters to the Twin Cities and the more settled south. From farmers to city-dwellers, Minnesotans persevere through harsh winters and cultivate warm, close-knit communities. Attempts to preserve the state's rugged northern frontier have helped raise awareness about Minnesota's natural resources and the culture of the Chippewa, the area's first inhabitants.

▨ PRACTICAL INFORMATION

Capital: St. Paul.

Visitor Info: Minnesota Office of Tourism, 100 Metro Sq., 121 7th Pl. E, St. Paul 55101 (☎651-296-5029 or 800-657-3700; www.exploreminnesota.com). Open M-F 8am-4:30pm.

Postal Abbreviation: MN. **Sales Tax:** 6.5%.

MINNEAPOLIS AND ST. PAUL ☎612

Native writer Garrison Keillor wrote that "the difference between St. Paul and Minneapolis is the difference between pumpernickel and Wonder bread." For years, St. Paul, viewed as a conservative, Irish-Catholic town, contrasted sharply with its young and metropolitan neighbor. Today, remnants of this distinction are evident in Minneapolis's big venues and bigger skyscrapers and St. Paul's traditional capitol and cathedrals, but it remains impossible to typecast the cities' diverse and cosmopolitan residents.

⌐ TRANSPORTATION

Airport: Minneapolis-St. Paul International (☎726-5555; www.mspairport.com), 20min. south of the cities on Rte. 5, off I-494 in Bloomington. From the airport, take the Hiawatha light rail line to Minneapolis or bus #54 to St. Paul. **Super Shuttle** (☎827-7777; www.supershuttle.com) goes to some hotels and both downtowns about every 30min. Desk open 8am-11pm. To **Minneapolis** ($13) and **St. Paul** ($11).

Trains: Amtrak, Midway Center, 730 Transfer Rd. (☎651-644-6012 or 800-872-7245; www.amtrak.com), off University Ave. SE and off I-94, between the Twin Cities. Bus #16 connects to both downtowns. Open daily 6:30am-11:30pm. The Empire Builder line runs once a day to **Chicago** (8hr., $46-100) and **Milwaukee** (6hr., $42-93).

Buses: Greyhound, 950 Hawthorne Ave. between 9th and 10th St. (☎371-3325; www.greyhound.com), in downtown Minneapolis. In St. Paul, 950 University Ave. at Rice St. (☎651-222-0507), 2 blocks west of the capitol. To **Chicago** (9-12hr., 5 per day, $61-68) and **Milwaukee** (7-9 hr., 4 per day, $50-55). $20 discount with 7-day advance purchase. Both routes depart from Minneapolis and St. Paul stations. Minneapolis station open daily 5:30am-1am; St. Paul station open daily 6:30am-8pm.

Public Transit: MetroTransit, 560 6th Ave. N (☎373-3333; www.metrotransit.org), serves both cities. Most major lines have no service 1-5am; some buses operate 24hr. Hiawatha light rail line runs 4am-1am from the Warehouse District through downtown to the airport and Mall of America. $1.50; seniors, ages 6-12, and disabled $0.50. Downtown zone $0.50. Peak fare (M-F 6-9am and 3-6:30pm) $2. Express lines $2.75, seniors, ages 6-12, and disabled $2. Transfers free. Of routes that connect the downtowns, bus #16 operates 24hr. (takes 30min.), bus # 94 (B, C, or D) takes 30min., and bus #50 runs limited rush hour service (36min.).

Taxi: Yellow Taxi, ☎824-4444 in Minneapolis, ☎651-222-4433 in St. Paul.

■ ⌐ ORIENTATION AND PRACTICAL INFORMATION

Public transit in the Twin Cities has improved with the Hiawatha light rail, but most people still rely on cars. Despite one-way streets and skewed numbered grids, the streets are not congested and driving in the city is manageable. Downtown Minneapolis lies about 10 mi. west of downtown St. Paul via **I-94. I-35** splits in the Twin Cities, with **I-35 W** serving Minneapolis and **I-35 E** serving St. Paul. **I-494** links I-35 W and E to the airport and the Mall of America, while **I-394** connects downtown Minneapolis to the western suburbs. **Hennepin Avenue** and the pedestrian **Nicollet Mall** are main roads in Minneapolis, dividing streets north-south and east-west, respectively; **Kellogg Avenue** and **7th Street** are main roads in St. Paul. For pedestrians, skyways are the main mode of movement in both downtowns, providing relief from the heat in the summer and protection from the long winters.

Visitor Info: Minneapolis Convention and Visitors Association, 250 Marquette Ave. (☎335-6000; www.minneapolis.org), in the Convention Center. Desk open M-Sa 8am-4:30pm, Su noon-5pm. **St. Paul Convention and Visitors Bureau,** 175 W. Kellogg Blvd., #502 (☎800-627-6101 or 265-4900; www.visitstpaul.com), in the River Centre. Open M-F 8am-4:30pm.

Hotlines: Crime Victim Center Crisis Line, ☎340-5400. **Rape/Sexual Assault Line,** ☎825-4357. Both 24hr. **Gay-Lesbian Helpline,** ☎822-8661. Operates M-F noon-midnight, Sa 4pm-midnight.

Internet Access: Minneapolis Public Library, 250 Marquette Ave. (☎630-6200; www.mplib.org); moving 1 block to 300 Nicollet Mall in spring 2006. The new library will offer wireless Internet. Open M, W, F 10am-5pm, Tu and Th 11am-6pm, Sa noon-5pm. **St. Paul Public Library,** 90 W. 4th St. between Washington and Market St. (☎651-266-7000; www.sppl.org). Open M 11:30am-8pm, Tu-W and F 9am-5:30pm, Th 9am-8pm, Sa 11am-4pm.

Post Office: In Minneapolis, 100 S. 1st St. at Marquette Ave. Open M-F 7am-8pm, Sa 9am-1pm. In St. Paul, 180 E. Kellogg Blvd. Open M-F 8:30am-5:30pm, Sa 9am-noon. (☎800-275-8777.) **Postal Codes:** Minneapolis 55401, St. Paul 55101. **Area Codes:** Minneapolis 612, St. Paul and eastern suburbs 651, southwestern suburbs 952, northwestern suburbs 763. In text, 612 unless otherwise noted.

ACCOMMODATIONS

The Twin Cities are filled with unpretentious, inexpensive accommodations. Minneapolis caters to a younger crowd and consequently has cheaper hotels; St. Paul offers classier establishments for those with fatter wallets. The **University of Minnesota Housing Office** (☎624-2994; www.umn.edu/housing/offcampus) keeps a list of local rooms ($15-60) for rent on a daily or weekly basis. The section of I-494 at Rte. 77, near the Mall of America, is lined with chain motels with rooms from $40. The nearest private campgrounds are about 15 mi. outside the city; the closest state park campgrounds include the **Three Rivers Park District** (Baker Park Reserve in Maple Plain, 21 mi. west), **Afton State Park** (20 mi. southeast), and the William O'Brian State Park (30 mi. east). Call **Minnesota State Parks** (☎651-296-6157 or 888-646-6367; www.stayatmnparks.com) or the **Minnesota Alliance of Campground Operators** (☎651-778-2400; www.hospitalitymn.com).

Minneapolis International Hostel (HI), 2400 Stevens Ave. S (☎522-5000; www.minneapolishostel.com), at 24th St. W, south of downtown by the Institute of Arts. Take bus #17 to 24th St. and walk 2 blocks east to Stevens. Visitors from around the world impart a strong community feel. Internet access and kitchen. Linen included. Reception daily 8am-midnight. Check-in 1pm. Check-out 11am. Reservations recommended. Dorms $20, with student ID or HI membership $19; private rooms $49. AmEx/MC/V. ●

Evelo's Bed and Breakfast, 2301 Bryant Ave. (☎374-9656), 2 blocks from Hennepin Ave. in Minneapolis. Take bus #17 to Bryant Ave. 3 lovingly tended, comfortable rooms in an exquisite 1897 Victorian home. Fresh flowers, continental breakfast, shared bathroom. Reservations and deposit required. Singles $65; doubles $85. MC/V. ●

Saloon Hotel (Hotel Amsterdam), 828 Hennepin Ave. (☎288-0459; www.gaympls.com), in downtown Minneapolis, between 8th and 9th St. Above the Saloon nightclub, this hotel has lodging and entertainment geared toward the GBLT community, but all are welcome. Lounge with TV and free Internet access. Private rooms with shared bathrooms. Reservations recommended. Singles $44; doubles $50-65. MC/V. ●

Exel Inn, 1739 Old Hudson Rd. (☎651-771-5566; www.exelinns.com), in St. Paul. Take a left off I-94E at Exit 245. Clean rooms, wireless Internet, cable, breakfast, laundry, A/C, and easy access to the Mall of America. Reservations recommended. Singles $45-55; doubles $60-65. AmEx/D/DC/MC/V. ❷

▐ FOOD

The Twin Cities' cosmopolitan vibe is reflected in its many culinary choices. **Uptown** Minneapolis, near the intersection of Lake St. and Hennepin Ave., offers funky restaurants and bars where the Twin Cities' young socialites meet after work. In downtown Minneapolis, the **Warehouse District,** on 1st Ave. N between 8th St. and Washington Ave., and **Nicollet Mall,** a 12-block pedestrian stretch of Nicollet Ave., attract locals and tourists with shops and simple food options ranging from burgers to Tex-Mex. South of downtown, Nicollet turns into **Eat Street,** a 17-block stretch of ethnic cuisine.

In St. Paul, the upscale **Grand Avenue,** between Lexington and Dale, is lined with laid-back restaurants and bars, while **Lowertown,** along Sibley St. near 6th St. downtown, is a popular nighttime hangout. Near the University of Minnesota (U of M) campus, **Dinkytown,** on the East Bank of the river, and the **Seven Corners** area of the West Bank, on Cedar Ave., cater to late-night student cravings. In the Twin Cities, many skip restaurants and go for area **cafes** (p. 572).

The **Minneapolis Farmers Market** off I-94W at E. Lyndale Ave. and 3rd Ave. N, offers an array of fruits, vegetables, and crafts. (☎333-1718; www.mplsfarmers-market.com. Free parking under I-94. Open late Apr. to Dec. daily 6am-1pm. Also located on Nicollet Mall May-Oct. Th 6am-6pm and Sa 8am-3pm.)

MINNEAPOLIS

Chino Latino, 2916 Hennepin Ave. (☎824-7878), at Lake St., Uptown. Trendy Latin-Asian cuisine that redefines "fusion." Indulge at the chic satay bar, sample the sushi, or rejuvenate after an evening at the Late Night Borracho Breakfast (10:30pm-close). "Hot Zone" dishes might require eating instructions from the waitstaff. Open M-Th and Su 4:30pm-1am, F-Sa 4:30pm-2am. Reservations recommended. AmEx/D/DC/MC/V. ❸

Bryant-Lake Bowl, 810 W. Lake St. (☎825-3737, show tickets ☎825-8949; www.bryantlakebowl.com), at Bryant St. near Uptown. This funky bowling alley/bar/cabaret serves food at friendly prices—ravioli and soups ensure that stylish bowlers throw strikes with full stomachs. Bowling $3.75. Entrees $8-15. Open daily 8am-2am. Kitchen open M-F 8am-midnight, Sa-Su 1pm-12:30am. AmEx/D/DC/MC/V. ❷

Loring Pasta Bar, 327 14th Ave. SE (☎378-4849; www.loringpastabar.com), in Dinkytown near the U of M campus. Whimsical and sophisticated, with a menu of flavors from around the globe. Here, saffron and cellophane noodles complement penne and linguine. Live music nightly, with salsa on Sa and tango DJ on Su. Sa cover $6. Open M-Sa 11:30am-1am, Su 5:30pm-1am; kitchen open until 11pm. AmEx/MC/V. ❸

Figlio, 3001 Hennepin Ave. (☎822-1688; www.figlio.com), at W. Lake St. in the Calhoun Square complex, Uptown. Boasts the "Best Late Night Dining" award for its scrumptious sandwiches (from $9) and delicious pastas and pizzas (from $11). You haven't lived until you've indulged in "Death By Chocolate" ($6). Open M-Th and Su 11:30am-1am, F-Sa 11:30am-2am. AmEx/D/DC/MC/V. ❸

Tacos Morelos, 14 26th St. W (☎870-5053), at Nicollet Ave. Practice your Spanish at one of the few authentic Mexican establishments in the Twin Cities. Try the "Enchiladas 3 Amigos" (3 enchiladas with different sauces; $12.50), or fill up on their famous tacos ($2.50 each). Entrees $9-16. Open daily 10am-10pm. AmEx/D/MC/V. ❸

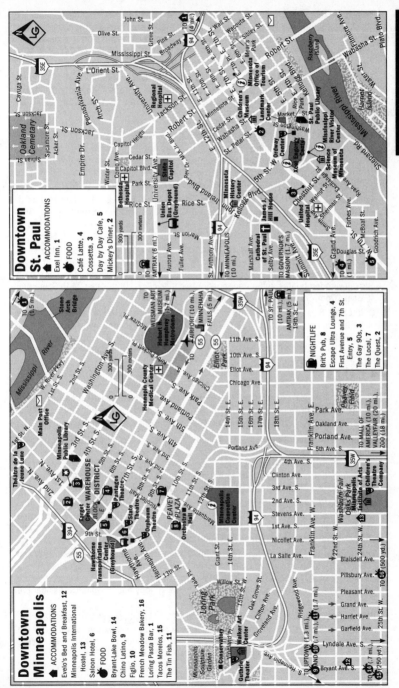

Downtown St. Paul

▲ ACCOMMODATIONS
Exel Inn, 1

🍴 FOOD
Café Latte, 4
Cossetta, 3
Day by Day Cafe, 5
Mickey's Diner, 2

Downtown Minneapolis

▲ ACCOMMODATIONS
Evelo's Bed and Breakfast, 12
Minneapolis International Hostel, 13
Saloon Hotel, 6

🍴 FOOD
Bryant-Lake Bowl, 14
Chino Latino, 9
Figlio, 10
French Meadow Bakery, 16
Loring Pasta Bar, 1
Tacos Morelos, 15
The Tin Fish, 11

🎵 NIGHTLIFE
Brit's Pub, 8
Escape Ultra Lounge, 4
First Avenue and 7th St. Entry, 5
The Gay 90s, 3
The Local, 7
The Quest, 2

French Meadow Bakery, 2610 Lyndale Ave. S (☎870-7855, www.organicbread.com), between 26th and 27th St., is the perfect place for a casual breakfast or lunch. Organic menu has vegan, vegetarian, and meat dishes served with fresh bread. For dessert, try the massive cinnamon rolls ($4). Breakfast and lunch $4-10. Dinner $8-24. Open M-Th and Su 6:30am-10pm, F-Sa 6:30am-11pm. AmEx/D/MC/V. ❷

The Tin Fish, 3000 Calhoun Pkwy. E (☎832-5840; www.thetinfish.com). A lakeside stand with the best fish in the area, the Tin Fish dishes up tasty fried and grilled tacos ($3-6) and platters ($12-15). Open early spring to late fall daily 11am-9pm. MC/V. ❷

ST. PAUL

▩**Mickey's Diner,** 36 W. 7th St. (☎651-222-5633), at St. Peter St. A 1937 diner on the National Register of Historic Places, Mickey's has not let the fame of magazine and movie appearances affect the amazing quality and quantity of its food. With classic chrome-and-vinyl decor, this place is the real deal. Steak and eggs from $7. Short stack of pancakes $4, full stack $4.50. Omelets $4.50-6. Open 24hr. MC/V. ❶

Cossetta, 211 W. 7th St. (☎651-222-3476). What began as an Italian market in 1911 now serves quality eat-in or take-out specialties. Try the veal parmigiana ($9), or Cossetta's famous pizza ($3-4 per slice). Open M-Sa 8:30am-9pm, Su 10am-9pm; in winter M-Th 11am-9pm, F-Sa 11am-10pm, Su 11am-8pm. MC/V. ❷

Day by Day Cafe, 477 W. 7th St. (☎227-0654; www.daybyday.com). Started in 1975 by an alcoholism treatment center, Day By Day now serves the community at large, with breakfast all day ($4.50-8), as well as lunch and dinner specials ($7.50-9), in its tall wooden booths and outdoor patio. Live music F 7-10pm. Open M-Th 6am-8pm, F 6am-10pm, Sa 6am-3pm, Su 7am-3pm. Cash only. ❷

Café Latte, 850 Grand Ave. (☎651-224-5687), at Victoria St. More substantial than a cafe and more gourmet than its prices would suggest, this food-and-wine bar is also famous for its heavenly desserts. Dishes like chicken-salsa chili ($5.50) delight hungry locals. Open M-W and Su 9am-10pm, Th 9am-11pm, F-Sa 9am-midnight. MC/V. ❷

▰ CAFES

Cafes are an integral part of the Twin Cities' nightlife. Particularly in Uptown Minneapolis, quirky coffeehouses caffeinate the masses and draw bar-sized crowds. Most complement their java with some of the cheapest food in town.

▩**Pandora's Cup and Gallery,** 2516 Hennepin Ave. (☎381-0700), at 25th St., Uptown. This vegan-friendly coffeehouse offers great coffee, organic sandwiches (portobello and Swiss; $5.50) and Internet access ($1 per 10min.). Hip patrons vie for spots on the retro furniture or outdoor patios to sip espresso ($1.50-2.50) and munch on peanut butter and jelly "sammiches" ($2.75). Open daily 8am-1am. D/MC/V.

Uncommon Grounds, 2809 Hennepin Ave. S (☎872-4811), at 28th St., Uptown. The "BMW of coffeeshops" uses secret ingredients to make the tastiest coffees ($2-5) and teas around. With velour booths and relaxing music, this coffeeshop lives up to its name. 1 drink per hr. min. Open M-F 5pm-1am, Sa-Su noon-1am. Cash or check only.

Vera's Cafe, 2901 Lyndale Ave. (☎822-3871; www.verascafe.com), between 29th and Lake St., Uptown, welcomes both gay and straight customers with its signature "White Zombie" ($4.40), free wireless Internet, and breakfast all day ($5-6). Regulars return daily for the great java and strong community feel. Happy hour 5-7pm. Occasional live music. Open daily 7am-midnight. MC/V.

Plan B Coffeehouse, 2717 Hennepin Ave. (☎872-1419), between 27th and 28th St., Uptown, is more subdued and intellectual, with serious readers and artwork. Try the "tripper's revenge" ($3.75) or frozen cheesecake on a stick ($2.50). Internet access $0.15 per min. Open M-Th and Su 9am-midnight, F-Sa 9am-1am. D/MC/V.

TIP **THE SCARLET LETTER.** Even Hester Prynne wouldn't feel quite so alone in Minneapolis's Uptown, where red "A"s cover residential and business windows. The "A" is for art (what else?) and is part of the local A Project (www.the-a-project.org) to raise awareness of and show support for public art. Keep an eye out for the very largest "A," at 2625 Bryant Ave. S.

The Tea Garden, 2601 Hennepin Ave. S (☎377-1700) at 26th St. and 1692 Grand Ave. (☎651-690-3495). Modern and unconventional in comparison to its coffeehouse neighbors, this cafe offers all manner of tea, including trendy bubble tea ($3-5) and free Internet to customers who buy a drink. Jazz, open mic, and other events M, F, Sa. Open M-Th and Su 9am-10pm, F-Sa 9am-1am. MC/V.

👁 SIGHTS

MINNEAPOLIS

LAKES AND RIVERS. In the land of 10,000 lakes, Minneapolis boasts many of its own: the city contains 22 lakes, along with 150 parks and 100 golf courses. **Lake Calhoun,** on the west end of Lake St., Uptown, is the largest of the bunch and is a recreational paradise. Scores of inline skaters, bicyclists, and runners loop the lake on all but the coldest days. Encircled by stately mansions, the serene **Lake of the Isles** has lovely views, but no public access to the water. Just southeast of Lake Calhoun on Sheridan St., **Lake Harriet** lures locals with tiny paddleboats and a bandshell with free concerts on summer nights. The city maintains 13 mi. of lakeside trails around the three lakes for strolling and biking. The **Twin Cities Biking Club** (www.biketcbc.org) offers rides led by experienced and trained volunteers ($2). For auto touring, the city has created the "Grand Rounds National Scenic Byway" (☎230-6446; www.byways.org), a 51 mi. ribbon of road connecting the lakes with the Minnesota River. **Calhoun Cycle Center,** one block east of Lake Calhoun, rents bikes for exploring the paths. *(1622 W. Lake St. ☎827-8231. Half-day $15-25, full day $25-40. Reservations a must; no same-day rental. Credit card and driver's license required. Open M-Th 10am-8pm, F-Su 9am-9pm.)* At the northeast corner of Lake Calhoun, **The Tin Fish** offers canoe and kayak rentals on the side of the restaurant pavilion. *(3000 E. Calhoun Pkwy. ☎823-5840; www.thetinfish.com. All boats $10 per hr. $20 deposit, driver's license, or credit card required. Open early spring to late fall daily, weather permitting, 10am, last boat out 6pm, last boat in 7pm.)* **Minnehaha Park** offers striking views of the impressive **Minnehaha Falls,** immortalized in Longfellow's *Song of Hiawatha. (Park is near the airport; take the light rail from 5th St. downtown. Falls are off Hiawatha Ave. at Minnehaha Pkwy.)*

MUSEUMS. Lakes are only the beginning of Minneapolis's appeal—locals and visitors have plenty to do during the (at least) six months of frigid winter. The **Minneapolis Institute of Arts,** south of downtown, showcases more than 100,000 art objects spanning 5000 years, including Rembrandt's *Lucretia* and the world-famous *Doryphoros,* Polykleitos's perfectly proportioned man. *(2400 3rd Ave. S. ☎870-3131 or 888-642-2787; www.artsmia.org. Open Tu-Sa 10am-5pm, Th until 9pm, Su 11am-5pm. Free.)* Southwest of downtown across from Loring Park, the recently expanded galleries of the world-renowned ◩**Walker Art Center** funnel visitors through contemporary art exhibits featuring film, photography, and other media. *(1750 Hennepin Ave. and 725 Vineland Pl. ☎375-7600; www.walkerart.org. Open Tu-W and Sa-Su 11am-5pm, Th-F 11am-9pm. $8, seniors $6, students $5, ages 12 and under free. Th 5-9pm and first Sa of each month free.)* Next to the Walker lies the **Minneapolis Sculpture Garden,** the largest urban sculpture garden in the US. Rotating exhibits join the iconic

Spoonbridge and Cherry sculpture. The adjacent **Cowles Conservatory** houses an array of plants and a Frank Gehry fish sculpture. (*Gardens open daily 6am-midnight; conservatory open Tu-Sa 10am-8pm, Su 10am-5pm. Both free.*) Gehry also holds the honor of having designed the cities' most unique structure: the U of M's **Weisman Art Museum,** on the East Bank of campus. The undulating pseudo-building was the rough draft for his famous Guggenheim Museum in Bilbao and hosts an inspired gallery of modern art with works by O'Keeffe, Warhol, and Kandinsky. (*333 E. River Rd.* ☎ *625-9494; www.weisman.umn.edu. Open Tu-W and F 10am-5pm, Th 10am-8pm, Sa-Su 11am-5pm. Free; suggested donation $3.*)

ST. PAUL

ARCHITECTURE. History and stately architecture define St. Paul. Mark Twain once said that the city "is put together in solid blocks of honest bricks and stone and has the air of intending to stay." Nowhere is this more evident than along ▨**Summit Avenue,** the nation's longest continuous stretch of Victorian houses, including the childhood home of novelist **F. Scott Fitzgerald** and the Minnesota **Governor's Mansion.** (*Fitzgerald: 593 Summit Ave. Currently a private residence. Governor's Mansion: 1006 Summit Ave.* ☎ *651-297-8177. Tours May-Oct. once a week 1-3pm. Call for more information. Reservations required. Free.*) Also on Summit, the magnificent home of railroad magnate **James J. Hill**—the largest and most expensive home in the state when it was completed in 1891—offers 1¼hr. tours. (*240 Summit Ave., 1 block from the Cathedral of St. Paul.* ☎ *651-297-2555; mnhs.org. Tours W-Sa 10am-3:30pm, Su 1-3:30pm. Reservations preferred. $8, seniors and students $6, ages 6-17 $4. Wheelchair accessible.*) The 1½hr. **Walking Tours of Summit Avenue** depart from the Hill House and explore the architectural and social history of the area. (☎ *651-297-2555. Sa 11am and 2pm, Su 2pm. $4-6. Reservations recommended.*) Golden horses top the ornate **State Capitol,** the world's largest unsupported marble dome. (*75 Rev. Dr. Martin Luther King, Jr. Blvd.* ☎ *651-296-2881; www.mnhs.org. Open M-F 9am-4pm, Sa 10am-3pm, Su 1-4pm. Tours every hr. M-F 9am-3pm, Sa 10am-2pm, Su 1-3pm. Free.*) The **Cathedral of St. Paul,** on a hill at the start of Summit Ave., faces the capitol. (*239 Selby Ave.* ☎ *651-228-1766; www.cathedralsaintpaul.org. Mass M-Th 7:30am and 5:15pm; F 7:30am; Sa 8am and 7pm; Su 8, 10am, noon, 5pm. Tours M, W, F 1pm. Open M-Th 7am-5:30pm, F 7am-4pm, Sa 7am-7pm, Su 7am-5pm.*)

HISTORY AND SCIENCE. The innovative ▨**Minnesota History Center** houses interactive, hands-on exhibits that entertain young and old alike. Learn how Minnesotans cope with their extreme seasons in "Weather Permitting," or practice the lindy in an old-fashioned diner setting. (*345 Kellogg Blvd. W. at John Ireland Blvd.* ☎ *651-296-6126 or 888-727-8386; www.mnhs.org. Open Memorial Day-Labor Day daily 10am-5pm; Sept.-May Tu 10am-8pm, W-Sa 10am-5pm, Su noon-5pm. $8, seniors and students $6, ages 6-17 $4. Wheelchair accessible.*) Downtown's **Landmark Center** is a grandly restored 1894 Federal Court building replete with towers and turrets, a collection of pianos, a concert hall, and four courtrooms. (*75 W. 5th St.* ☎ *651-292-3225; www.landmarkcenter.org. Open M-W and F 8am-5pm, Th 8am-8pm, Sa 10am-5pm, Su noon-5pm. Free tours Th 11am, Su 1pm.*) Out front, **Rice Park,** the oldest park in Minnesota, is an ideal place for a stroll or a picnic. The **Science Museum of Minnesota** includes a beautiful atrium, an exhibit on the human body, and an expanded paleontology hall. The "Virtual River Pilot" allows visitors to take a ride on the Mississippi River. (*120 W. Kellogg Blvd.* ☎ *651-221-9444; www.smm.org. Open mid-June to early Sept. M-Sa 9:30am-9pm, Su noon-5pm; low season M-W 9:30am-5pm, Th-Sa 9:30am-9pm, Su noon-5pm. $8.50, seniors and ages 4-12 $6.50; combo with omnitheater and 3D cinema $16/$12.50.*) For those with children, the **Children's Museum** is a big, interactive playground. In the summer, the roof becomes the Rooftop Artpark. (*10 W. 7th St.* ☎ *651-225-6000; www.mcm.org. Open Tu-Th and Sa-Su 9am-5pm, F 9am-8pm; in summer also M 9am-5pm. $8.*)

AMUSEMENTS. Located on 500 wooded acres out in Apple Valley, the **Minnesota Zoo** houses local and exotic animals in their natural habitats, including 50 endangered species, a Tiger Lair exhibit, and native beavers, lynx, and wolverines. *(13000 Zoo Blvd. Take Rte. 77 S to Zoo exit and follow signs. ☎ 952-431-9500 or 800-366-7811; www.mnzoo.org. Open June-Aug. daily 9am-6pm; Sept. and May M-F 9am-4pm, Sa-Su 9am-6pm; Oct.-Apr. daily 9am-4pm. $12, seniors $8.25, ages 3-12 $7. Parking $5.)* From St. Paul, escape to **Como Park,** off Lexington Pkwy., where you can visit the small zoo and an impressive conservatory with an award-winning collection of Bonsai trees and orchids. *(☎ 651-487-8200; www.comozooconservatory.org. Open daily Apr.-Sept. 10am-6pm; Oct.-Mar. 10am-4pm. Free; suggested donation $2.)* In Shakopee, even the most daring thrill-seekers will be satisfied at **Valleyfair,** an amusement park with five coasters and the heart-stopping Power Tower, which drops over 10 stories. *(1 Valleyfair Dr. Take I-35W south to Rte. 13 W. ☎ 800-386-7433; www.valleyfair.com. Open daily June-Aug.; May and Sept. select days. Opens daily 10am, call for closing times. $34, under 48 in. tall $18, under 2 free. Parking $8.)*

♫ ENTERTAINMENT

Second only to New York City in number of theater seats per capita, the Twin Cities are alive with drama and music. Most parks offer free concerts and shows on summer weekends, while theaters present classical and contemporary plays in winter. Music is also big here —the thriving alternative, pop, and classical music scenes fill out the wide range of options. For more info, read the free *City Pages* (www.citypages.com) and the *Pulse of the Twin Cities* (www.pulsetc.com).

THEATER
The renowned repertory ■**Guthrie Theater** draws praise for its mix of daring and classical productions. During the summer of 2006, the Guthrie will move from its location at 725 Vineland Pl. in Minneapolis to a new home on S. 2nd St. by the river. *(☎ 377-2224 or 877-447-8243; www.guthrietheater.org. Season Aug.-June. Box office open M-F 11am-8pm, Sa 10am-8pm, Su hours vary. $14-55, students and seniors $5 discount, ages 12-17 half-price with adult except Sa and opening nights. Rush tickets no later than 10min. before show $14; line starts 1-1½hr. before show.)* The historic **State Theatre,** 805 Hennepin Ave., the **Orpheum Theatre,** 910 Hennepin Ave. N, and the **Pantages Theatre,** 710 Hennepin Ave., comprise the Hennepin Theater District in downtown Minneapolis, with touring Broadway shows and musical events. *(Box office ☎ 339-7007; www.hennepintheaterdistrict.com. Located at the State Theatre. Open M-F 10am-6pm, Sa noon-3pm. Box offices at Orpheum and Pantages open 2hr. before each show. Tickets from $15.)* For family-oriented productions, the **Children's Theatre Company,** 2400 3rd Ave. S, next to the Minneapolis Institute of Arts, has first-rate plays. *(☎ 874-0400; www.childrenstheatre.org. Season runs late Aug. to early June. Box office open in season M-F 10am-5pm, Sa 9am-2pm, Su noon-5pm; in summer M-F 10am-4pm. $15-30; students, seniors, and children $9-24. Rush tickets 15min. before show $13.)* The ingenious **Théâtre de la Jeune Lune,** 105 1st St. N, stages critically acclaimed, off-the-beaten-path productions in an old warehouse. *(☎ 332-0048; www.jeunelune.org. Box office 333-6200. Open M-F 10am-6pm. Tickets $20-26.)* **Brave New Workshop,** 2605 Hennepin Ave. at 26th St., in Uptown, stages comedy shows and improv in an intimate club. *(☎ 332-6620; www.bravenewworkshop.com. Box office open M-Th 9:30am-5pm, F 9:30am-9pm, Sa 10am-11pm. Tickets $15-22.)*

MUSIC
The Twin Cities' vibrant music scene jams with everything from polka to hip-hop. **Sommerfest,** a month-long celebration of Viennese music put on in July by the **Minnesota Orchestra,** is the best of the cities' classical offerings. **Orchestra Hall,** 1111

Nicollet Mall, in downtown Minneapolis, hosts the event. (☎371-5656 or 800-292-4141; www.minnesotaorchestra.org. Box office open M-F 10am-5pm, Sa 10am-3pm, and 2hr. prior to performances. $15-65. Student rush tickets 30min. before show $10.) Nearby, **Peavey Plaza,** on Nicollet Mall, holds free nightly concerts and occasional film screenings. The **Saint Paul Chamber Orchestra,** the **Schubert Club,** and the **Minnesota Opera Company** all perform at St. Paul's glass-and-brick **Ordway Center for the Performing Arts,** 345 Washington St., which also hosts touring Broadway productions. (☎651-224-4222; www.ordway.org. Box office open M-F 10am-6pm, Sa 11am-3pm. Tickets $15-85). Bands gravitate to the artist Prince's studio complex, formerly and currently known as **Paisley Park,** in nearby Chanhassen.

SPORTS

The puffy **Hubert H. Humphrey Metrodome,** 900 S. 5th St., in downtown Minneapolis, houses the Twin Cities' most popular team, the NFL's **Minnesota Vikings** (☎338-4537; www.vikings.com), whose few single tickets sell out fast. Baseball's **Minnesota Twins** (☎375-7454; www.twinsbaseball.com) also play in the Metrodome, although a new venue may be in the works. The NBA's **Timberwolves** (☎673-1600; www.timberwolves.com) and the WNBA's **Lynx** (☎673-1600; www.wnba.com/lynx) howl at the **Target Center,** 601 1st Ave. (☎673-0900), between 6th and 7th St. in downtown Minneapolis. The NHL team the **Wild** (☎651-602-6000; www.wild.com) takes to the ice at St. Paul's **Xcel Energy Center,** 175 W. Kellogg Blvd. (☎651-265-4800; www.rivercentre.com). The soccer craze hits the Midwest with the minor-league **Thunder** (www.mnthunder.com) at the **National Sports Center** (☎763-785-5600; www.nscsports.com) in suburban Blaine.

FESTIVALS

The Twin Cities celebrate countless festivals, both to liven up the dreary winter days and to celebrate the coming of summer. In late January and early February, the **St. Paul Winter Carnival** (☎651-223-4700; www.winter-carnival.com), near the state capitol, cures cabin fever with ice fishing, skating, and an ice palace. Leading up to the 4th of July, St. Paul celebrates the **Taste of Minnesota** (☎651-772-9900; www.tasteofmn.org) with fireworks, concerts, and regional and ethnic cuisine from hordes of local vendors. The **Minneapolis Riverfront Fourth of July Celebration and Fireworks** is a family affair with trolley rides, concerts, food, and fireworks. On its coattails rides the 10-day **Minneapolis Aquatennial** (☎376-7669; www.aquatennial.org), with concerts and art exhibits glorifying the lakes. During the two weeks prior to Labor Day, everyone heads to the **Minnesota State Fair,** at Snelling and Como St. between Minneapolis and St. Paul. With cheese curds and walleye-on-a-stick, horse contests, and a variety of music, the fair provides a sampling of the area's flavor. (☎651-288-4400 or 651-642-2372; www.mnstatefair.org. $9, seniors and ages 5-12 $8, under 5 free. Advance tickets $7. Parking $9.)

◪ NIGHTLIFE

Minneapolis's vibrant youth culture feeds the Twin Cities' nightlife. Anchored by strong post-punk influences, the area's music scene remained localized until bands such as Soul Asylum, Hüsker Dü, and The Replacements made it big. A cross-section of the diverse nightlife options can be found in the downtown **Warehouse District** on Hennepin Ave., in **Dinkytown,** by U of M, and across the river on the **West Bank** (bounded on the west by I-35 W and to the south by I-94), especially on **Cedar Avenue.** The top floor of the **Mall of America** invites bar-hopping until the wee hours. All bars and clubs in both Minneapolis and St. Paul are smoke-free.

The Quest, 110 5th St. (☎338-3383; www.thequestclub.com), between 1st Ave. N and 2nd Ave. N in the Warehouse District. Once owned by Prince, this upper-class dance club pays homage to His Purple Highness with purple windows and lots of funk. Live salsa on W. Cover $10-15. Call ahead for age restrictions and hours.

Escape Ultra Lounge, 6000 Hennepin Ave. (☎333-8850; www.escapeultral-ounge.com), between 6th and 7th St. in the Warehouse District, casts itself as an "ultra lounge" where you should dress "to inspire." Changing themes and occasional live music draw new crowds each night. 21+, but call ahead for varying age restrictions. Cover $10-15. Open Tu-Su 9pm-2am.

Brit's Pub, 1110 Nicollet Mall (☎332-3908; www.britspub.com), between 11th and 12th St., allows patrons to go "lawn bowling" ($5 per person per hr.) on the rooftop garden. 18 beers ($5.50), the Stilton burger ($9), and fish and chips ($8-14) add to the British flavor. Open daily 11am-1am.

The Local, 931 Nicollet Mall (☎904-1005; www.the-local.com), at 10th St. in downtown Minneapolis. Irish pub that doubles as a restaurant ($10 weekday lunch specials) and bar. Outdoor patio and dark interior make for a mellow and intimate night out. Open M-Th 11am-11pm, F 11am-midnight, Sa 9am-midnight, Su 9am-11pm.

First Avenue and 7th St. Entry, 701 1st Ave. N (☎332-1775, box office ☎338-8388; www.first-avenue.com) in downtown Minneapolis. Rocks with the area's best live music. Tickets are a must for concerts, which feature the nation's hottest bands and music ranging from grunge to hip-hop to world beat. 21+ most nights. Cover $6-10, for concerts $30. Usually open M-Th 8pm-2am, F-Sa 9pm-3am, Su 7pm-2am.

The Gay 90s, 408 Hennepin Ave. (☎333-7755; www.gay90s.com), at 4th St., serves dinner and then lets loose for the night. Gigantic complex hosts thousands of gay and lesbian partiers in 6 bars and 3 dance floors, though the straight crowd is sizeable. Drag shows upstairs Tu-Su 9:30pm. M-Tu and F-Sa 21+, W-Th and Su 18+. Cover after 9pm $3-5. Open M-Sa 8am-2am, Su 10am-2am.

DULUTH ☎218

Originally an industrial town built upon timber and mining, Duluth today has tremendous appeal outside its role as a freshwater port harboring ships from over 60 different countries. The popularity of Canal Park and the Aerial Lift Bridge have enticed microbreweries, theaters, and museums to occupy the old factories down on the wharf, creating a sparkling haven on beautiful Lake Superior.

⌖ PRACTICAL INFORMATION. Greyhound, 4426 Grand Ave. (☎722-5591; www.greyhound.com; ticket office open daily 7am-5:45pm), stops 3 mi. west of downtown; take bus #1, 2, or 3. Buses run to Minneapolis (3hr., 2 per day, $25) and St. Ignace, MI (10½hr., 1 per day, $78). The **Duluth Transit Authority,** 2402 W. Michigan St., runs buses within the city. (☎722-7283; www.duluthtransit.com. Peak fare M-F 7-9am and 2:30-6pm $1, students $0.75; off-peak $0.50.) The **Port Town Trolley** takes tourists through downtown, Canal Park, and the Waterfront. (☎722-7283. Runs every 30min. June-Labor Day daily 11:30am-7pm. $0.25.) **Convention and Visitors Bureau:** 21 W. Superior St. at N. Lake Ave. (☎722-4011 or 800-438-5884; www.visitduluth.com. Open M-F 8:30am-5pm.) **Hotlines: Crisis Line,** ☎723-0099. Operates 24hr. **Internet Access: Duluth Public Library,** 520 W. Superior St. (☎723-3836; www.duluth.lib.mn.us. 1hr. free per day. Open M-Tu 10am-8:30pm, W-F 10am-5:30pm.) **Post Office:** 2800 W. Michigan St. (☎723-2526. Open M-F 8am-5pm, Sa 9am-1pm.) **Postal Code:** 55806. **Area Code:** 218.

GREAT LAKES

╔ **ACCOMMODATIONS.** Rates rise and rooms fill quickly during the summer months. **Voyageur Lakewalk Inn ❸**, 333 E. Superior St., off the Lakewalk, has comfortable rooms and continental breakfast. (☎722-3911. Office open daily 7am-11pm. Rooms in summer M-Th and Su $48, F-Sa $63; in winter $35/$45. AmEx/D/MC/V.) The **Chalet Motel ❸**, 1801 London Rd., 2 mi. west of downtown, offers well-decorated rooms with A/C near scenic Leif Erickson Park, which overlooks Lake Superior. (☎728-4238 or 800-235-2957. Singles M-Th and Su $45, F-Sa $55; doubles $58/$68. Prices lower in winter. D/MC/V.) A few miles south of town, the **Duluth Motel ❷**, 4415 Grand Ave., houses visitors in affordable, well-kept rooms across from the Greyhound station. (☎628-1008. Rooms in summer $35-50; in winter from $25. AmEx/D/MC/V.) For a decidedly less urban feel, the rocky **Jay Cooke State Park ❶**, 780 Hwy. 210 southwest of Duluth, draws in travelers with hiking, snowmobiling, cross-country skiing, and 83 campsites among the trees of the St. Louis River Valley. (☎384-4610 or 800-246-2267; www.stayatmnparks.com. Turn left at Exit 242 off I-35 and look for signs. Office open daily 9am-9pm. Reservations recommended; $8.50 reservation fee. Remote sites $11, with showers $15, with electricity $19. Vehicles $7 per day. MC/V.)

🍴🍷 **FOOD AND NIGHTLIFE. Fitger's Brewery Complex**, 600 E. Superior St., and the **Canal Park** region, south of downtown along Lake Ave., feature plenty of pleasant eateries. **The Brewhouse ❷**, located in Fitger's, has home-brewed beer like Big Boat Oatmeal Stout ($2), root beer on tap, and specialty burgers and sandwiches. (☎726-1392; www.brewhouse.net. Live entertainment nightly, live music F-Sa. Open M-W and Su 11am-1am, Th-Sa 11am-2am; kitchen closes M-F 10pm, Sa-Su 11pm. AmEx/D/DC/MC/V.) Located in an old pipe-fitting factory in Canal Park, **Grandma's Sports Garden ❷**, 425 S. Lake Ave., is a popular place in town, especially among the college crowd. Casual dining and original *bonottas* (rolled and stuffed pizzas) keep people coming over the river and through the woods to Grandma's. (☎722-4724. Entrees $8-14. DJs W and F-Sa. Happy hour M-F 3-6pm. Bar open daily 11am-2am. Restaurant open June-Aug. daily 11am-10pm; Sept.-May W-Th 5-10pm, F-Su 11:30am-10pm. AmEx/D/DC/MC/V.) In the basement of the DeWitt-Seitz Marketplace, **Amazing Grace Bakery & Cafe ❶**, 394 Lake Ave. S, serves fresh sandwiches in a funky atmosphere. (☎723-0075; www.amazinggracebakery.com. Live music usually F-Sa, $10 cover. Open mic M. Open daily 7am-11pm. AmEx/D/MC/V.) **Sara's Table ❸**, 1902 E. 8th St. at 19th Ave. E, cooks up delicious lunch dishes like the veggie burger with sweet potato fries ($7.25). Dinner is more expensive. (☎723-8569; www.taransmarketplace.com. Open in summer M-W 7am-9pm, Th 7am-10pm, F-Sa 7am-11pm, Su 8am-8pm; in winter M-Th 7am-9pm, F-Sa 7am-10pm, Su 8am-8pm. Kitchen closed 3:30-5pm. Free wireless Internet. MC/V.)

🎦🎵 **SIGHTS AND ENTERTAINMENT.** Duluth's proximity to majestic **Lake Superior** is its biggest draw. Nearly 400 mi. across, it is the largest body of fresh water in the world—indeed, it is so massive that when frozen, each person in the world could lay out his own 6 ft. by 6 ft. picnic blanket on its surface (it's true—we checked twice). Many visitors head down to **Canal Park** to watch the big ships go by at the ☒**Aerial Lift Bridge.** Accompanied by deafening horn blasts, this unique bridge climbs 138 ft. in one minute to allow vessels to pass. Traffic is generally heavier in the late afternoon, but check the **Boatwatcher's Hotline** (☎722-6489; www.lsmma.com) and the **Duluth Shipping News** (☎722-3119; www.duluthshipping-news.com), published daily and usually available by 3pm at the **Lake Superior Maritime Visitors Center**, by the Aerial Lift Bridge at Canal Park. The visitors center has displays on the history of commercial shipping on Lake Superior. (☎727-2497; www.lsmma.org. Open in summer daily 10am-9pm; spring and fall M-Th and Su

10am-4:30pm, F-Sa 10am-6pm; winter F-Su 10am-4:30pm.) Canal Park is also the beginning and end of the **Duluth Lakewalk,** a beautiful 3 mi. promenade. In an old train station in Canal Park, the **Midnight Sun Adventure Company,** 100 Lakeplace Dr., rents bikes and kayaks, and leads guided adventure tours. (☎727-1330; www.midnightsunsports.com. Bike rental: half-day $16, full day $30. Kayak rental $50/$95. Open M-Sa 10am-8pm, Su 10am-5pm.)

A 39-room neo-Jacobian mansion built on mining wealth, the **Historic Congden Estate,** 3300 London Rd., lies on the eastern outskirts of town and provides visitors with a glimpse of Duluth's most prosperous period. (☎726-8910 or 888-454-4536; www.glensheen.org. Open May-Oct. daily 9:30am-4pm; Nov.-Apr. F-Su 11am-2pm. $11, seniors $9, ages 6-12 $6, families $33.) Waterfront tours aboard the giant steamer **William A. Irvin** and the US Coast Guard Cutter *Sundew* reveal more of Duluth's shipping past. The *Irvin*, docked at Duluth's Downtown Waterfront, is longer than two football fields and was the "Queen of the Lakes" in her prime. (☎722-7876. Open Memorial Day-Labor Day M-Th and Su 9am-6pm, F-Sa 9am-8pm; May and Sept. to mid-Oct. M-Th and Su 10am-4pm, F-Sa 10am-6pm. 1hr. tours every 20min. $9, ages 3-12 $6.) Across the road from the *Irvin* is the **Duluth OMNI-MAX Theatre.** (☎727-0022. $7, students and seniors $6, 12 and under $5. Call for schedule.) Across the Aerial Lift Bridge, **Park Point** has excellent but cold swimming areas (Lake Superior's water averages 40°F), parks, and sandy beaches. The scenic **Willard Munger State Trail** links West Duluth to Jay Cooke State Park and continues on to Hinckley, providing 80 mi. of paved path perfect for bikes; the **Willard Munger Inn,** 7408 Grand Ave., takes care of rentals. (☎624-4814; www.mungerinn.com. $15 per 2hr.; $20 per 4hr.)

🔲**Great Lakes Aquarium,** 353 Harbor Dr., is America's first and only all-freshwater aquarium. Stop by to see spotted stingrays and bioluminescent fish. (☎740-3474; www.glaquarium.org. Open daily 10am-6pm. $13, seniors $10, ages 3-11 $7. Parking $3.) **The Depot,** 506 W. Michigan St., a former railroad station, contains four museums, including the **Lake Superior Railroad Museum** (www.lsrm.org), which allows visitors to enjoy the North Shore Scenic Railroad trip. (☎727-8025; www.duluthdepot.org. Open June-Aug. daily 9:30am-6pm; Sept.-May M-Sa 10am-5pm, Su 1-5pm. Depot $9, ages 3-13 $5. Railroad trip $11/$5. Combination tickets $17/$8.)

CHIPPEWA NATIONAL FOREST ☎218

Gleaming white strands of birch lace the pine forests of the Chippewa National Forest, home to the highest density of breeding bald eagles in the continental US. The national forest shares territory with the **Leech Lake Indian Reservation,** home to 3725 Chippewa tribespeople. The Chippewa, called Ojibwe in their native language, migrated from the Atlantic coast in the 18th century and, in the mid-19th century, were forced by the US government onto reservations such as Leech Lake.

The National Forest has plenty of affordable **camping ❶** options. The **Forest Office** (☎547-1044; www.fs.fed.us/r9/chippewa; open M-F 8am-4:30pm), just east of town on Rte. 200/371, has info on 23 campgrounds and more than 400 free primitive sites, as well as the **Stony Point National Forest Campground ❶,** in Stony Point. (☎877-444-6777; www.reserveusa.com. Self-regulated sites $20.)

For the northbound traveler, the town of **Walker,** in the southwest corner of the park, serves as an ideal gateway to the forest. Known as the "Fishing Capital of Minnesota," Walker draws thousands of tourists each summer. The **Leech Lake Area Chamber of Commerce** is north of Walker on Rte. 200/371, at 205 Minnesota Ave. (☎547-1313 or 800-833-1118; www.leech-lake.com. Open M-F 8:30am-4:30pm; May-Sept. also Sa 10am-2pm.) **Mike's Reel Repair and Video Rental,** in Hackensack, 10 mi. south of Walker on Rte. 371, has bike rentals for the Paul Bunyan Trail. (☎675-6976. Bikes $4 per hr., $20 per day. Open M-Th 9am-8pm, F-Sa 9am-9pm, Su

10am-3pm.) In **Cass Lake,** 20 mi. north of Walker, **Adventure Tours and Rentals,** 32326 Wolf Lake Rd. (☎800-635-8858), rents canoes and kayaks ($5 per hr., 2hr. min. Reservations only. Open 6am-dusk.) **Post Office:** 515 Michigan Ave. at 6th St. (☎547-1123. Open M-F 9am-4pm, Sa 9-11:30am.) **Postal Code:** 56484. **Area Code:** 218.

ITASCA STATE PARK   ☎218

One of Itasca State Park's claims to fame is the **Headwaters of the Mississippi,** which Henry Rowe Schoolcraft and his Native American guide Ozawinib discovered in 1832. Here people gather to cross over the Mississippi on the rock bridge where water flows both to the north and south. Thirty miles west of Chippewa National Forest on Rte. 200, Minnesota's popular state park is home to the oldest and largest tree in the state, representative of the large pine forests through which visitors can walk, bike, or drive. Seventeen incredible miles of paved trail and the 10 mi. Wilderness Road around the four park lakes keep visitors active and busy. A vacation spot in itself, the impeccable ⬛**Mississippi Headwaters Hostel (HI),** located in the park off Main Dr., stays open for weekends in the winter to facilitate access to the park's excellent cross-country skiing trails. (☎266-3415; www.himinnesota.org. Linen $4. Laundry and kitchen. Vehicle permit $7 per day. 2- to 3-night min. stay some weekends. Reservations recommended. Check-in M-Th and Su 5-10:30pm, F-Sa 5-11pm. Dorms $19-23, members $16-20. Private rooms July-Aug. and Jan.-Feb. $45-64, low season $27-38. Cash only.) Next door, **Itasca Sports Rental** rents bikes ($3.50 per hr.), motorized and non-motorized boats (from $4.50 per hr.), and fishing supplies. (☎218-266-2150, low season 657-2420; www.itascasports.com. Open daily in summer 7am-9pm; spring and fall daily 8am-6pm, but call for hours.) The **Itasca Park office,** through the north entrance down County Rd. 122, has camping info. (☎266-2100. Office open May to mid-Oct. M-F 8am-4:30pm, Sa-Su 8am-4pm; mid-Oct. to Apr. M-F 8am-4:30pm.)

IRON RANGE   ☎218

Lured initially by rumors of gold, the miners that rushed to join loggers and trappers in the Vermillion and Mesabi mountain ranges soon set their sights on iron instead. Today, the 120 mi. of wilderness and over 500 majestic lakes along the Iron Trail serve as a corridor to the Boundary Waters, the Mississippi Headwaters, and the north shores of Lake Superior. (☎800-777-8497; www.irontrail.org.) These days, the closest you can get to the mining techniques of old is a tour of the Soudan Underground Mine, but iron is still an important part of life here, as a matter of local pride and for the thriving automobile industry.

The town of Eveleth, 60 mi. north of Duluth on Rte. 53, has produced more elite hockey players than any other city of its size in the country. Not surprisingly, it is the home of the **US Hockey Hall of Fame,** 801 Hat Trick Ave., which honors American-born pucksters. (☎744-5167 or 800-443-7825; www.ushockeyhall.com. Open F-Sa 9am-5pm, Su 10am-3pm. $8, seniors and ages 13-17 $7, ages 6-12 $6, under 6 free.) Further proof that Eveleth takes hockey seriously is the new 110 ft., 10,000 lb. **World's Largest Hockey Stick,** which replaced the slightly less imposing 107 ft., 7,000 lb. stick built in 1995. Just follow the signs marked "Big Stick."

A deeper experience awaits in Soudan, 40 mi. northeast of Eveleth, which features an unforgettable journey a half-mile underground. The ⬛**Soudan Underground Mine State Park,** off Rte. 1, is the oldest, deepest, and purest iron ore mine in the state. In a fascinating 90min. tour, visitors experience the complete dark of the mine, the noise of the drills, and chilly 50°F temperatures while learning the history of ore workers in the Iron Range. (☎753-2245. Park open daily June-Sept. 9:30am-6pm; June-July tours every hr., Sept. every 2 hr. 10am-4pm. $9, ages 5-12 $6, 4 and under free; $7 state park vehicle permit required.) Two miles down the road, **McKinley Park Campground ❶**, on the shore of Lake Vermilion, has campsites with bathrooms, showers, laundry, bait and tackle, and a swimming beach. (☎753-5921, after hours 753-3806; www.mckinleypark.net. Open May-Sept. Office open M-Th and Su 8am-6pm, F-Sa 7am-9pm. 2-night min. stay on weekends, 3-night min. stay on holiday weekends. Sites $18, with electricity $25.)

The charming town of Ely serves as a launching pad into the **Boundary Waters Canoe Area Wilderness** (**BWCAW**; see **Boundary Waters,** p. 583), and thus supports an extensive range of wilderness outfitters who provide gear and guidance. The main attraction in town is the **International Wolf Center,** just north of downtown at 1396 Rte. 169, which houses eight gray wolves, issues BWCAW permits, and has displays on *canis lupus*. (☎365-4695 or 800-359-9653; www.wolf.org. Open July-Aug. daily 9am-7pm; mid-May to June and Sept. to mid-Oct. daily 9am-5pm; mid-Oct. to mid-May Sa-Su 10am-5pm. $7.50, seniors $6.50, ages 6-12 $4. Call for wolf presentation times. BWCAW permit office ☎365-7561. Open May-Sept. 6am-6pm.) If wolves aren't enough, a new **North American Bear Center** will be opening in June 2006 in Ely on Rte. 169. (365-7879; www.bear.org.) **Vince Shute Wildlife Sanctuary,** 70 mi. from Ely to the southwest of Orr, offers a guaranteed opportunity to see wild black bears who return every evening for feeding, a tradition started by a logger who used to put garbage out for the bears. (☎757-0172 or 800-357-9255; www.americanbear.org. Open June-Sept. Tu-Su 5pm-dusk, except during heavy rain. $5.) **The Brandenburg Gallery,** 11 E. Sheridan St., has a collection of works by Jim Brandenburg, a famous National Geographic photographer. (www.jimbrandenburg.com. Open M-Sa 10am-6pm, Su 10am-5pm.) **Stony Ridge Resort ❶**, 60 W. Lakeview Pl., off W. Shagawa Rd., has four cabins with fridge, cable, and a motor boat, as well as a few RV and tent sites. The owners also run a small cafe. (☎365-6757. RV and tent sites $15, $17 with showers; 1-bedroom cabins $80; 2-bedroom $95. Canoe rental $20 per day.) **Fall Lake Park ❶**, on County Road 182, offers 64 quiet RV and camping sites only 6 mi. from Ely with a boat launch, beach, canoe rentals, and direct access to BWCAW. (☎365-2963 or 877-444-6777; www.reserveusa.com. Office open M-W 9-11am and 3-7pm, F-Su 9-11am and 3-8pm. Sites $15; 30-amp hookup $18, 50-amp hookup $20.) The **Front Porch Coffee & Tea Co. ❶**, 343 E. Sheridan St., has pastries, wraps, and Internet access. (☎365-2326. Open M-Sa 6am-10pm, Su 6am-7pm. AmEx/D/MC/V.)

VOYAGEURS NATIONAL PARK ☎218

Named for the French-Canadian fur traders who once traversed the area, Voyageurs is one of Minnesota's best-kept secrets, providing an undeniably unique experience as a water-based park with fewer than 10 mi. of roads. The waterways that connect Minnesota's boundary with Ontario provide ample opportunities for fishing, camping, kayaking, canoeing, hiking, and birdwatching—all of which are accessible almost solely by boat. Today's voyagers are invited to leave the auto-dominated world and push off into the serene waters of the longest inland lake waterway on the continent. Summer visitors explore the hiking trails and camp on the islands, while winter visitors bundle up to cross-country ski and snowmobile. The dangers of undeveloped wilderness, however, still remain. Water should be boiled for at least 10min. and then treated; some fish contain mercury. Ticks carrying Lyme Disease have been found as well.

For hikers, the **Oberholtzer Trail** begins at the Rainy Lake Visitors Center and leads to two overlooks that showcase the range of flora found in the park. A wheelchair-accessible trail at Ash River yields a great view of Kabetogama Lake and serves as the starting point for the **Blind Ash Bay Trail.** The new 24 mi. **Kab-Ash Trail** has multiple entrances for extensive hiking and skiing but users should be cautious and bring a compass because markers are not always clear, and maintenance is spotty. The 9½ mi. **Cruiser Lake Trail system,** accessible by boat only from either Rainy Lake or Kabetogama Lake, offers hiking and canoeing and is known for great possibilities of seeing wildlife, though the only guaranteed moose sighting is the taxidermy at the Rainy Lake Visitors Center.

The reputable **Voyageurs Adventures ❷,** 10087 Gappa Road off Rte. 53. provides a wide variety of boat rentals (from $20), mandatory lessons ($10), guided trips (from $30), and cabins (from $45), as well as a water taxi and land shuttle service. (☎875-2037 or 877-465-2925; www.voyageursadventures.com. Open in summer daily 8am-8pm; call ahead for winter hours. MC/V.) **Woody's Fairly Reliable Guide Service ❹,** at Rainy Lake, features guided fishing, hunting, and snowmobiling daytrips from $275 for two people. Woody, the personable owner, also operates four spacious suites. (☎286-5001 or 866-410-5001; www.fairlyreliable.com. 2-person suites $655 per week, 4-person $1445 per week; $25 per extra person per night. D/MC/V.) The best way to experience the park is to camp at the free campsites accessible only by water. Private water taxis are available from several outfitters. There are several car-accessible sites as well, including the 61 beautiful, primitive sites at **Woodenfrog ❶,** about 4 mi. from Kabetogama Lake Visitors Center on Rte. 122, and the nine primitive sites at **Ash River ❶,** 3 mi. from the Ash River visitors center on Rte. 129. (☎753-2245. Sites $10.) Just south of International Falls, which inspired the fictional Frostbite Falls of *Rocky and Bullwinkle* fame, Rte. 53 is loaded with motels, including the darling **Hilltop Motel and Cabins ❸,** 2002 2nd Ave. W at Rte. 53, which offers immaculate rooms and friendly service. (☎283-2505 or 800-322-6671. Open mid-Apr. to mid-Oct. Singles $46; doubles $49. Reservations recommended. AmEx/D/MC/V.) **International Voyageurs RV Campground ❶,** 5min. south of town on Rte. 53 at City Rd. 24, has RV and tent sites with showers and laundry. (☎283-4679. Tent sites for 1-2 people $14, with hookup $18; additional person $2.) For home cooking at wallet-friendly prices, try **Grandma's Pantry ❶,** 2079 Spruce St. in Ranier off Rte. 11. (☎286-5484. Open M-F 6am-7pm, Sa 6am-10:30am. D/MC/V.)

On the way into Voyageurs from the south, visitors can stop at the **Voyageurs National Park and Orr Area Info Center,** 4429 Hwy. 53 in Orr, which has information on navigating Voyageurs. (☎757-3932 or 800-357-9255. Open June-Sept. daily 9am-6pm; Oct.-May Th-Sa 9am-4pm.) The **International Falls Area Chamber of Commerce,** 301 2nd Ave., downtown, hands out travel info on the area. (☎283-9400 or 800-325-5766; www.internationalfallsmn.us. Open M-F 8am-5pm.) Visitors can access the park through International Falls at the northern tip of Rte. 53, just below Ft. Frances, ON, or through **Crane Lake, Rainy Lake, Ash River,** or **Kabetogama Lake** (all east of Rte. 53). There are three **visitors centers** in the park: **Rainy Lake,** at the end of Rte. 11, 12 mi. east of International Falls (☎286-5258; www.rainylake.org. Open mid-May to Aug. daily 9am-5pm; May and Sept. W-Su 9am-5pm; Oct. to mid-May W-Su 10am-5pm), which has a large museum; **Ash River,** 8 mi. east of Rte. 53 on Rte. 129, then 3 mi. north (☎374-3221; www.ashriver.com. Open mid-May to Sept. Hours vary, call ahead); and **Kabetogama Lake,** 5 mi. east of Rte. 53 (☎875-2111; www.kabetogama.com. Open mid-May to Aug. daily 9am-5pm, Sept. W-Su 9am-5pm). *Rendezvous*, the visitors guide to the park, is available at visitors centers and provides information on outdoor recreation, outfitting, and lodging.

SCENIC DRIVE: NORTH SHORE DRIVE

The Lake Superior North Shore extends 646 mi. from Duluth to Sault Ste. Marie, ON, but Minnesota's **Route 61** glides through the trees from Duluth to Grand Portage and the Canadian border, offering a condensed 150 mi. version packed with beautiful shoreline and mesmerizing views of the vast lake. With jagged, glacier-carved edges and a seemingly limitless surface, the lake is a sharp contrast to the **Sawtooth Mountains,** which hover over the lake with stunning rock formations and tall, sweeping birch trees.

Though thriving fishing and logging industries once defined this area, tourism now plays a key role in the North Shore's vitality. Whether enjoying the serenity of the lake or hiking and camping on the **Superior Hiking Trail** (www.shta.org), visitors flock to the area year-round to enjoy its outdoor opportunities. Most of the small fishing towns along the shore maintain visitors centers; in picturesque **Two Harbors,** the knowledgeable staff at the **Lake County R.J. Houle Visitor Information Center,** 1330 Hwy. 61, 25 mi. from Duluth, offers stellar advice and personal anecdotes about each town on the Minnesota stretch of the North Shore. (☎834-4005 or 800-554-2116; www.lakecnty.com. Open daily 9am-1pm; varies in summer and winter.) On summer weekends, Rte. 61 is often congested with boat-towing pickup trucks and family-filled campers. Accommodations flanking the roadside fill up fast in summer; make reservations early. Bring warm clothes—temperatures can drop as low as 40°F, even during the summer.

While state parks along Rte. 61 boast striking views of the mirror-like lake, they also provide their own attractions. With 26 gorgeous stone structures created by the Civilian Conservation Corps, **Gooseberry Falls State Park ❶** is an lovely lodging option. (☎834-3855; www.dnr.state.mn.us/state_parks. Park open daily 8am-10pm. Visitors center open daily June-Sept. 9am-7pm; Oct.-May 9am-4pm. Sites with shower $15; vehicle permit $7 per day.) Gooseberry Falls offers 18 mi. of trails and five waterfalls, as well as a beautiful half-mile walk to the rocky shore. Three of the falls are located near the visitors center and are wheelchair accessible.

Eight miles down the road, the **Split Rock Lighthouse** hearkens back to the lake's industrial hey-day and has a spectacular view atop a 130 ft. cliff. Visitors can enter the lighthouse and light keeper's home, restored to look as they did during operation in the 1920s. (☎226-6372 or 888-727-8386; www.mnhs.org. Open mid-May to mid-Oct. daily 10am-6pm. 45min. tours every hr. $8, seniors and students $7, ages 6-17 $4.) Since Canada technically holds the upper half of a larger waterfall farther north, **Tettegouche State Park** can call itself home to the tallest waterfall in Minnesota. An easy three-quarter mi. hike leads to the 60 ft. High Falls. (☎226-6365. Park open daily 9am-8pm; visitors center open 9am-3pm.) Rte. 61 then winds its way through **Superior National Forest,** passing over countless winding rivers and creeks toward Tofte, where the 1526 ft. **Carlton Peak** dominates the landscape at Temperance State Park. In Tofte, outdoors enthusiasts can rent canoes ($24-42), kayaks ($28-42), and bikes ($22-42), plus join guided water trips at **Sawtooth Outfitters,** 7213 Hwy. 61. (☎663-7643; www.sawtoothoutfitters.com. Open mid-May to Aug. daily 7am-7pm; early May daily 8am-6pm; in winter M and Th-Su 8am-6pm.) The **Coho Cafe ❷,** in Tofte on Rte. 61, serves delicious pastries, pastas ($11-18), and pizzas (from $5), as well as strong coffee for the weary traveler. (☎663-8032. Open May-Oct. daily 7am-9pm. MC/V.) The pine-paneled **Cobblestone Cabins ❸,** off Rte. 61 two miles north of Tofte, has eight guest cabins and access to a cobblestone beach, canoes, a sauna on the beach, and kitchens. (☎633-7957. Open year-round; no running water in winter. Cabins $60-105. Cash or check only.)

GRAND MARAIS AND BOUNDARY WATERS ☎218

Near the north end of the 150 mi. scenic drive lies the fishing village and former artists' colony of Grand Marais (Ma-RAY), overlooking a large harbor with a lighthouse and marina. This popular tourist spot is a great place to sleep, eat, and enjoy the scenery. The family-owned **Nelson's Traveler's Rest ❷,** on Rte. 61, a half-mile west of town, has fully-equipped cabins with fireplaces, as well as a cabin split into two cheaper motel rooms. (☎387-1464 or 800-249-1285; www.travelersrest.com. Open mid-May to mid-Oct. Call far in advance for reservations. Min. stay 3 nights, max. stay 6 nights. Singles from $39; cabins from $54. D/MC/V.) **Grand Marais RV Park-Campground & Recreational Area ❶,** off Rte. 61 right before town on 8th Ave. W, has 300 wooded sites by the lake. (☎387-1712 or 800-998-0959. Office open daily 8am-8pm. Reservations recommended. Open May to mid-Oct. Sites $19.50; with water and electricity $23.50. July-Aug. $25/$29. $3 per additional adult. D/MC/V.)

Cheap and popular with locals and fishermen, **South of the Border Cafe ❶**, 4 W. Rte. 61, specializes in huge breakfasts and satisfying diner food. The bluefin herring sandwich is only $4. (☎387-1505. Breakfast under $7. Open daily 5am-2pm. Cash only.) Another favorite is the Friday night fish fry ($9) at the **Blue Water Cafe ❷**, at Wisconsin St. and 1st Ave. W. Every other night of the week, try their burgers, salads, and sandwiches. (☎387-1597; www.bluewatercafe.com. Open daily 6:30am-8pm. D/MC/V.) The consensus among locals is that the **Angry Trout Cafe ❸**, has the best food in town. At this organic and environmentally conscious eatery, you can top off your meal with a shot of pure maple syrup. (☎387-1265; www.angrytroutcafe.com. Lunch $9-11. Dinner $18-22. Open May-Oct., call for hours. MC/V.) **The Grand Marais Visitor Information Center,** 13 N. Broadway, is one block south of the town's one stoplight on Hwy. 61. (☎387-2524 or 888-922-5000; www.grandmarais.com. Hours vary by season; usually open M-Sa 10am-4pm.)

Grand Marais also serves as a gateway to the **Boundary Waters Canoe Area Wilderness (BWCAW),** a designated wilderness area of the Superior National Forest comprising 1.2 million acres of lakes, streams, and forests. The BWCAW is strict about when, where, and how many people it will allow to enter in order to preserve this pristine environment; phoning ahead is essential. Make reservations with the National Recreation Reservation Service. (☎877-444-6777 for camping, 877-550-6777 for BWCAW permits; www.reserveusa.com. Reservation fee $12. Self-issue permits at trailheads for day use free. Camping permits $10 per adult, children $5. Seasonal passes $40/$20.) More info is available at the Superior National Forest (☎218-626-4300). The **Gunflint Trail (County Road 12)** runs 57 mi. northwest from Grand Marais to Lake Saganaga, on the border of Canada. The road offers access to amazing trails and lakes and serves as the eastern entrance to the BWCAW. **The Gunflint Trail Association** has private hosts, lodges, and campgrounds spread throughout the trail. (☎800-338-6932.) One mile south of Grand Marais, the **Gunflint Ranger Station** distributes permits and has tourist information. (☎387-1750. Open May-Sept. daily 6am-6pm; Oct.-Apr. M-F 8am-4:30pm.) At Rte. 61 and Wisconsin St. is the **Gunflint Trail Information Center,** which provides information about the trail and the BWCAW, as well as help finding available sites among the private and Superior National Forest **campgrounds** (sites $12-17) on the trail. (☎387-3191. Open daily 9am-5pm.) A variety of outfitters are stationed along the Gunflint Trail. One of the best is the family-run **Bear Track Outfitting Company,** 2011 W. Hwy. 61, right across from the Ranger Station, whose knowledgeable staff supplies rentals and extended guided trips (4-person 6hr. guided trip $80), if requested a week in advance. Backpacking, fly-fishing, skiing, and snowshoeing gear is also available. (☎387-1162 or 800-795-8068; www.bear-track.com. Open in summer M-Sa 8am-6pm, Su 9am-5pm; call for winter hours.)

Many people believe that regional variation in the US is disappearing, thanks to the insidious and pervasive influence of television and mainstream American culture. There is hope for those of us who relish linguistic and cultural diversity, though: recent research by William Labov at the University of Pennsylvania and by Scott Golder and myself at Harvard University has found that regional variation is alive and well, and along some dimensions is even increasing between the major urban centers.

Consider, for instance, the preferred cover term for sweetened carbonated beverages. As can be seen in the map below, Southerners generally refer to them as coke, regardless of whether the beverages in question are actually made by the Coca-Cola Company; West and East coasters (including coastal Florida, which consists largely of transplanted New Yorkers) and individuals in Hawaii and the St. Louis, Milwaukee, and Green Bay spheres of influence predominantly employ soda. The remainder of the country prefers pop.

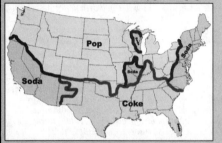

National television advertisements and shows generally employ soda, presumably due to the concentration of media outlets in soda areas New York City and California, but this has had no effect on the robust regional patterns. (The three primary terms do appear, however, to be undermining traditional local expressions such as tonic in Boston and cocola in the South.)

Another deeply entrenched, regionally conditioned food product is the long sandwich made with cold cuts. Its unmarked form in the US is submarine sandwich or just sub. Pennsylvanians (and New Jerseyites in the Philadelphia sphere of influence) call it a hoagie, New Yorkers call it a hero, western New Englanders call it a grinder, Mainers call it an Italian sandwich, and people in the New Orleans area call it a po' boy.

Confrontation between traditional regional terms and newer interlopers has created subtle variations in meaning in some areas. In the Boston sphere of influence, for instance, grinder is commonly relegated to hot subs, whereas sub is used for cold ones. Similarly, in stores in northern Vermont grinder refers to large (12 in.) subs, whereas hoagie is used for their small (6 in.) counterpart. Many in the Philadelphia area divide up the sub domain in the same manner as Boston, but hoagie is used for the cold version and steak sandwich for the hot one.

In other cases, the dialectal picture is so evenly distributed that there is no clear national standard, as with the terms for the machine out of which one drinks water in schools and other public spaces.

The preferred term in the southeastern half of the US is water fountain, whereas in the northwestern half it's drinking fountain. If you're in eastern Wisconsin or the Boston area, be sure to elicit bubbler from the locals.

These examples should suffice to show that regional variation is alive and well in the US. But where did these differences come from, and how have they resisted the influence of the American media juggernaut? The second question has a relatively straightforward answer: humans are generally unaware of the properties of their language, and normally assume that the way they behave and speak is the way everyone else does and should behave and speak. You, for example, were probably unaware before reading this that a large swathe of the US doesn't share your term for water fountains. Since humans are generally unaware of the idiosyncrasies of their own speech, it is to be expected that they would typically fail to notice that what is said on TV differs from their own forms.

The maps employed in this chapter were designed by Prof. Vaux on the basis of previously published materials (primarily William Labov's forthcoming *Atlas of North American English* and Frederick Cassidy's *Dictionary of American Regional English*) and his online survey of English dialects. Specific references are available on request by emailing the author at vaux@post.harvard.edu. Please note that all generalizations made here reflect statistical predominance, not absolute invariance. One can find individuals who say *soda* in the South, for example, but these are in the minority.

The examples adduced in this chapter are primarily lexical, due to the difficulty of conveying subtleties of pronunciation in a publication intended for non-linguists.

SETTLEMENT PATTERNS AND THE ORIGINS OF THE AMERICAN DIALECTS

The other question, involving the origins of linguistic variation, can be answered in part by considering the history of US settlement by speakers of English.

The continental US was settled by three main waves of English speakers: Walter Raleigh brought settlers primarily from the southwest of England to form the Chesapeake Bay Colony in 1607; Puritans from East Anglia came to the Massachusetts Bay Colony in 1620; and Scots-Irish, Northern English, and Germans came to America through Philadelphia in large numbers beginning in the 18th century. Settlers then moved horizontally westward across the country from these three hearths, giving rise to the three main dialect areas in the US: the South, the North, and the Midlands. The fourth area on the map, the West, contains a mixture of features imported from the other three.

The particular linguistic variables on which these dialect divisions are based in many cases can be connected to dialect differences in the areas of England from which the various settlers came. The original English-speaking settlers in New England, for example, came from East Anglia in the southeast of England. There, in the 17th century (and still today), "r"s were only pronounced before vowels, and "r"s were (and still are) inserted inside certain vowel sequences, as in draw[r]ing and John F. Kennedy's famous Cuba[r] and China[r]. The New England lengthening of "a" in words like aunt ("ahnt") and bath ("bahth") was also imported from the British dialect of East Anglia.

Other features cannot be connected to British antecedents so transparently, but nicely demonstrate the North/South/Midlands boundary. One of my favorite examples is the large wasplike critter that is usually seen when it stops by puddles to collect mud, which it then rolls into a ball and carries off to construct a nest. Northerners call this a mud wasp, midlanders and westerners call it a mud dauber, and southerners call it a dirt

dauber. Another such example is the small freshwater lobster-like critter, which is a crayfish in the North, a crawdad in the Midlands, and a crawfish or mudbug in the South.

The North breaks into two main areas, the Northeast and the Inland North. The Northeast and its crony, southeast coastal Florida, are roughly the home of sneakers; the rest of the country uses tennis shoes or gym shoes as the generic term for athletic shoes. The Inland North is most famous for pop and for the so-called "Rust Belt Vowel Shift." This is a change in the pronunciation of most of the American vowels that produces what is perceived by most Americans as "Midwestern," even though it is also found in eastern Rust Belt cities such as Rochester, Syracuse, and Utica, New York.

The Midlands region is home not only to mud dauber, but also to the oft-noted regionalisms warsh and the needs X-ed construction, as in the car needs warshed. The Midlands and the South together are home to catty-corner (diagonally across from), which in the North is normally kitty-corner. (My personal favorite expression for this concept is kitty wampus, which is used by a handful of individuals in the Upper Midwest.)

The South is home to the "pin-pen merger" ("i" and "e" are pronounced identically before "m," "n," and "ng"), preservation of the contrast in pronunciation between "w" and "wh" (as in witch and which respectively), use of y'all to address a group of individuals, multiple modal constructions (as in I might could do that), nekkid for "naked," and commode for "toilet."

The inland part of the South features gems such as rolling for the act of covering a house and/or its front yard in toilet paper. In the rest of country, this is generally called tp'ing or toilet papering. (It's wrapping in the Houston area.)

AMERICAN DIALECTS YOU HAVE TO HEAR

Since, as we have just seen, regional variation is alive and well in the US, where should one go to hear the most satisfying range of dialects? Here are some of my favorites, which also provide a representative sample of the main dialect groups in the country. (If you get to one of these locales and have trouble finding a really juicy local accent, try a police station, working-class bar, or farm.)

THE NORTHEAST

No linguistic tour of the Northeast would be complete without visiting the two main linguistic spheres of influence in the area, Boston and New York City. Though locals would probably die rather than admitting it, the two actually share a large number of linguistic features, such as pronouncing can (is able) differently than can (container), wearing sneakers and drinking soda, having no word for the roly poly/potato bug/sow bug/doodlebug (though the critter itself is just as rampant in the Northeast as anywhere else in the country), and pronouncing route to rhyme with moot and never with out.

Perhaps the most striking feature shared by these two areas is the behavior of "r": it disappears when not followed by a vowel (drawer is pronounced draw), and conversely gets inserted when between certain vowels (drawing comes out as drawring). Because these dialects don't allow "r" to follow a vowel within a syllable, they end up preserving vowel contrasts that were neutralized before "r" in other dialects. This is heard in the "3 Maries": Mary, marry, and merry are each pronounced differently, whereas in most of the country all three are homophonous. Similarly mirror and nearer have the same first vowel in most of the US, but not in Boston and New York City. Bostonians and New Yorkers pronounce words like hurry, Murray, furrow, and thorough with the vowel of hut, whereas most other Americans use the vowel in bird. And of course there's the first vowel in words like orange and horrible, which in most of the US is the same as in pore, but in Boston and New York City is closer to the vowel in dog.

New York City

Though New York City shares many important features with Boston and other parts of the Northeast, it is also in many ways a linguistic island, undergoing little influence from the rest of the country and—despite the ubiquity of New York accents on TV and in movies—propagating almost none of its peculiarities to the outside world. Its lack of linguistic influence can be connected to its stigmatization: two surveys in 1950 and the 1990s found that Americans considered New York City to have the worst speech in the country.

When you visit the New York City area (including neighboring parts of New Jersey and Long Island), be sure to listen for classic New Yorkisms. This includes the deletion of "h" before "u" (e.g. huge is pronounced yuge, and Houston becomes Youston), and the rounding of "a" to an "o"-like vowel before "l" in words like ball and call (the same vowel also shows up in words like water, talk, and dog). New Yorkers who don't have a thick local accent may not have these particular features, but they are sure to have other shibboleths like stoop (small front porch or steps in front of a house), on line instead of in line (e.g. We stood on line outside the movie theater for three hours), hero for sub, pie for pizza, and egg cream for a special soft drink made with seltzer water, chocolate syrup, and milk. You can also tell New Yorkers by their pronunciation of Manhattan and forward: they reduce the first vowel in the former (it comes out as Mn-hattan), and delete the first "r" in the latter (so it sounds like foe-ward). Believe it or not, it is also common in the New York City area to pronounce donkey to rhyme with monkey (which makes sense if you consider the spelling), even though they typically aren't aware that they are doing so.

New England

Moving up the coast to New England, we find that most people don't actually sound like John F. Kennedy, but they do all use cellar for basement (at least if it's unfinished), bulkhead for the external doors leading out of the cellar, and rotary for what others call a roundabout or traffic circle. New England itself is divided by the Connecticut River into two linguistically distinct areas, Eastern and Western.

Eastern New England: Boston

You can hear great Eastern New England speech almost anywhere in Maine, New Hampshire, Rhode Island, or Massachusetts, especially if you stay away from more affluent areas in the bigger cities, but I'll focus here on the Boston area. (Revere, South Boston, Somerville, and Dorchester are traditionally considered to harbor especially thick local accents.) Thanks to park your car in Harvard Yard and Nomar Garciaparra many Americans are familiar with the Boston pronunciation of -ar-, which generally comes out as something very similar to the Southern pronunciation of -ay- (Boston park sounds like Southern pike). The sequence -or- also has an interesting outcome in many words, being pronounced like the vowel in off. For instance, the Boston pop group LFO, in their 1999 song "Summer Girls," rhymed hornet with sonnet.

In the domain of vocabulary, be sure to get a frappe (or if you're in Rhode Island, a cabinet), a grinder, harlequin ice cream with jimmies or shots on it, and of course a tonic. (Frappes are milkshakes, harlequin is Neapolitan ice cream, and jimmies and shots are sprinkles.) You might also want to visit a package store (or packie for short) to buy some alcohol, or a spa to buy cigarettes and lottery tickets. There aren't many spas (small independent convenience stores, equivalent to party stores in Michigan, as used in the movie True Romance) left in the area at this point, but you can still find a few that haven't been replaced by 7-11 in Boston, Cambridge, Somerville, Allston, and Watertown.

The towns where you'll hear the best Boston accents (and classic local terms like wicked and pissa) also feature many triple deckers, three-family houses with three front porches stacked on top of one another. These seem to be less common in Connecticut, but if you happen to pass through that area, be sure to look out for tag sales (yard sales). Connecticut is also home to the term sleepy seed for the gunk that collects in the corner of your eye after you've been sleeping; not all Connecticutians have this expression, but your trip will have been worthwhile if you find someone who does.

Western New England: Vermont

West of the Connecticut River, I recommend you head up to the Northeast Kingdom in Vermont. Here you'll find the best Canadian features south of the border, thanks to the heavy French Canadian representation in the area, including toque ("tuke") for a woolen winter hat (known as a toboggan in some other parts of the country); poutin (put-SIN) for french fries coated with gravy and cheese curds, and sugar pie. This is also the land of the skidoo (snowmobile), the skidder (giant machine with jaws used to haul logs), and the camp (summer cabin, typically on a body of water). If you're wise enough to visit the Northeast Kingdom, be sure to check out how they pronounce the "a" and the "t" in the name of the local town Barton.

THE MIDLANDS

Pennsylvania

As you head out of the Northeast, you should try to stop through Pennsylvania, which is unique among the fifty states for having a significant number of dialect features peculiar to it. Some of these are due to the Pennsylvania Dutch presence in the region (redd up "clean up," gumband "rubber band" (cf. German Gummi "rubber"; now limited to parts of western Pennsylvania), toot "bag," rootch "scootch up (in a bed)"); the reasons for the restriction of other terms to Pennsylvania are less clear. To this category belongs hoagie, which as we already saw is limited to Pennsylvania plus the parts of New Jersey in Philadelphia's sphere of influence. Pennsylvania also shows extreme internal diversity: Philadelphia groups with the Northeastern dialects (e.g., in preferring soda), whereas Pittsburgh is tied to the Inland North (pop), the Midlands (many of my relatives there use the needs warshed construction), and the Appalachian region, of which it is the northernmost extremity.

Philadelphia and its satellites in southern New Jersey are perhaps best known for their pronunciation of water, which comes out as something like wooder. This conveniently shows up in the local term water ice, which refers to something between Italian ice and a snow cone. Residents of the Philly sphere of influence are also more likely than other Americans to bag school rather than skip school or play hooky. When you make your trip to Philly to hear these choice linguistic tidbits and you run short of money, be sure to ask where the MAC machine is, not the ATM or cash machine.

You should also make a special effort to visit the opposite end of the state, anchored by the beautiful city of Pittsburgh, which (unknown to most Americans) has its own distinctive dialect. Here the "aw" sound is replaced by something approaching "ah," as in dahntahn for downtown; "ay" similarly loses its "y" in certain situations, as in Pahrts for Pirates and Ahrn City for Iron City. The "o" in this region is very rounded in words like shot, and comes out sounding a lot like the New York vowel in ball. It is also popular to delete the "th-" at the beginning of unstressed words in certain collocations, such as up 'ere (for up there), like 'at, and 'n 'at (for and that), which western Pennsylvanians are fond of ending sentences with).

In terms of vocabulary, Pittsburgh and environs have some real whoppers, such as yins or you 'uns, used to address a group of two or more people; jagoff meaning "a jerk or loser" (shared with Chicagoland); jumbo "bologna sandwich"; and slippy "slippery."

These days many Pittsburgh residents don't have the traditional dialect, but you're sure to come across at least a few of the items just discussed. You'll have even better luck if you visit some of the unknown small towns in western Pennsylvania such as Franklin, Emlenton, and Oil City, which have satisfying variants of the Pittsburgh speech patterns and also happen to be unusually scenic.

Cincinnati

From Pittsburgh you're in striking distance of Cincinnati, one of the better representatives of the Midlands dialect region. Here, instead of inserting "r," as we saw in Boston and New York City, they insert "l": saw comes out as sawl, drawing as drawling, and so on. In the Cincinnati area one can also find drive-through liquor stores (and for some people, regular liquor stores) referred to as pony kegs. (Elsewhere in the US, on the other hand, pony keg usually refers to a small keg.)

THE RUST BELT

Milwaukee

Moving westward, the next interesting dialect zone is the Inland North or Rust Belt, within which I recommend Milwaukee, WI (not to be confused with Zilwaukee, MI.) Here, in the land so eloquently etymologized by Alice Cooper in *Wayne's World*, you will find—especially if you visit an area where there hasn't been much immigration, such as West Allis—not only the classic speech features identified with the Midwest (as canonized for example in the Da Bears skit on "Saturday Night Live"), but also features characteristic of areas other than the Midwest (freeway, otherwise associated with the West Coast; bubbler, most familiar from the Boston area; soda, otherwise characteristic of the West and East coasts). Milwaukeeans share some features with the rest of Wisconsin: they pronounce Milwaukee as Mwaukee and Wisconsin as W-scon-sin rather than Wis-con-sin; they refer to annoying Illinoisans as FIB's or fibbers (the full form of which is too saucy to explain here), and they eat frozen custard and butter burgers. They also share some features with the Upper Midwest, notably pronouncing bag as baig and using ramp or parking ramp for "parking garage" (the same forms surface in Minnesota and Buffalo). Milwaukee is also known for the cannibal sandwich, raw ground sirloin served on dark rye bread and covered with thin-sliced raw onions.

Milwaukee is only an hour and a half drive north of Chicago, yet it lacks many of the classic Chicagoisms, such as jagoff, gaper's block (a traffic jam caused by drivers slowing down to look at an accident or other diversion on the side of the road), black cow (root beer with vanilla ice cream, known elsewhere as a root beer float), expressway, and pop. It also differs from the more northern reaches of Wisconsin with respect to many of the classic Upper Midwestern features so cleverly reproduced in the movie Fargo, such as the monophthongal "e" and "o" in words like Minnesota and hey there. You can find the occasional inhabitant of Wisconsin's northern border with Minnesota who has Upper Midwest terms like pasties, whipping shitties (driving a car in tight circles, known elsewhere as doing donuts), hotdish (elsewhere called a casserole), and farmer matches (long wooden matches that light on any surface), but for the most part these are less commonly used than in Minnesota and the Dakotas (and the Upper Peninsula of Michigan in the case of pasties).

THE WEST

The San Fernando Valley

Moving ever westward, we come next to the West Coast. Here it is more difficult to find hardcore traditional dialects, largely because the West was settled relatively recently, and by individuals from a wide variety of different locales; one is hard-pressed to find any Californian (or other Westerner) whose family has been there for more than two generations. Perhaps the best place to start is the San Fernando Valley of California, home of the Valley Girl. Many of the Valley Girl quirks immortalized in Frank Zappa's 1982 song "Valley Girl" and the 1995 film Clueless are now profoundly out of favor, such as gnarly, barf out, grodie (to the max), gag me with a spoon, rad, for sure, as if, and bitchin'. Others are now ubiquitous throughout the US, such as totally, whatever, sooo X (as in, That's so like 5 years ago), and the use of like to report indirect speech or state of mind (as in, I was like, "No way!"). Others are still used in the area but have yet to infiltrate the rest of the country, such as flip a bitch or bust a bitch (make a U-turn) and bag on (make fun of, diss).

And if you're interested in figuring out whether someone's from northern or southern California, I recommend seeing if they use hella or hecka to mean "very" (e.g. that party was hella cool; characteristic of northern California), and if they refer to freeway numbers with or without "the" before them (Southern Californians refer to "the 5", "the 405", and so on, whereas northern Californians just use "5" and "405").

THE SOUTH

Looping back around the country we come to the South, which is perhaps the most linguistically distinct and coherent area in the US. This is not only home to obvious cases like y'all, initial stress on Thanksgiving, insurance, police, and cement, and the other features mentioned above, but also showcases feeder road (small road that runs parallel to a highway), wrapping (tp'ing), doodlebug (the crustacean that rolls into a ball when you touch it) in the Houston area, and party barns (drive-through liquor stores) in Texas (bootlegger, brew thru, and beer barn are also common terms for this in the South). The South as a whole differs from the rest of the country in pronouncing lawyer as law-yer, using tea to refer to cold sweet tea, and saying the devil's beating his wife when it rains while the sun is shining (elsewhere referred to as a sunshower, or by no name at all). The South is so different from the rest of the country that almost anywhere you go you will hear a range of great accents, but I especially recommend the Deep South (start with Mississippi or Alabama) and New Orleans.

New Orleans

Louisiana is famous for the Cajuns, a local group descended from the Acadians, French people who were exiled from Nova Scotia and settled in southern Louisiana in the 1760s. Some Cajuns still speak their own special creole, Cajun French, and this in turn has influenced the English dialect of the region. This can be seen in local expressions such as: by my house for "in/at my place" (e.g., he slept by my house last night), which is claimed to be based on the French expression chez moi; make dodo meaning "to sleep," based on Cajun French *fais do do;* make groceries meaning "do grocery shopping," cf. French *faire le marché;* and lagniappe, French for "a little something extra," e.g., when your butcher gives you a pound and two ounces of hot sausage but only charges you for a pound.

Some of the creole elements that have made their way into the local English dialect may be of African rather than French origin, such as where ya stay (at)? meaning "where do you live?", and gumbo, referring to a traditional southern soup-like dish, made with a rich roux (flour and butter) and usually including either sea food or sausage. The word gumbo is used in Gullah (an English-based creole spoken on the Sea Islands off the Carolina coast) to mean okra, and appears to have descended from a West African word meaning okra.

The New Orleans dialect of English also includes words drawn from other sources, such as yat (a typical neighborhood New Orleanian), neutral ground (the grassy or cement strip in the middle of the road), po' boy (basically a sub sandwich, though it can include fried oysters and other seafood and may be dressed, i.e., include lettuce, tomatoes, pickles, and mayonnaise), hickey (a knot or bump you get on your head when you bump or injure it), and alligator pear (an avocado).

HAWAII

Last but not least we come to Hawaii, which in many ways is the most interesting of the fifty states linguistically. Many Americans are aware of Hawaiian, the Austronesian language spoken by the indigenous residents of the Hawaiian Islands before the arrival of colonizers from Europe and Japan. Fewer, however, know of the English-based creole that has arisen since that time, known as Hawaiian Pidgin English, Hawaiian Creole English, or just Pidgin. This variety of English is spoken by a fairly large percentage of Hawaiians today, though they tend not to use it around haole (Caucasian) tourists.

Pidgin combines elements of all of the languages originally spoken by settlers, including Portuguese (cf. where you stay go? meaning "where are you going?", or I called you up and you weren't there already meaning "I called you up and you weren't there yet"), Hawaiian (haole, makapeapea "sleepy seed," lanai "porch," pau "finished"), Japanese (shoyu "soy sauce"), and even Californian/surfer (dude, sweet, awesome, freeway). They also have some English expressions all their own, such as shave ice (snowcone) and cockaroach (cockroach).

The syntax (word order) of Pidgin differs significantly from that of mainland English varieties, but resembles the English creoles of the Caribbean in important ways. This includes deletion of the verb be in certain contexts (e.g., if you one girl, no read dis meaning "if you're a girl, don't read this"), lack of inversion of the subject and finite verb in questions and subordinate clauses (e.g. doctah , you can pound my baby? Meaning "doctor, can you weigh my baby?", or how dey came up wid dat? meaning "how did they come up with that?"), null subjects (e.g. cannot! meaning "I can't!", or get shtrawberry? meaning "do you have strawberry [flavor]?"), and the use of "get" to express existential conditions ("there is," "there are"), as in get sharks? meaning "are there sharks [in there]?".

IN CONCLUSION

This tour only begins to scratch the surface of the range of English varieties to be found in the US, but it should provide enough fodder to keep you busy for a while on your travels, and with any luck will enable you to provide some entertainment for your hosts as well. And if the info I've provided here isn't enough to sate your thirst for American dialects, I urge you to visit the Sea Islands, where Gullah is still spoken, Tangier Island in Chesapeake Bay, and Ocracoke Island, off the coast of North Carolina. Each of these islands features a variety of English that will shock and titillate you; I'll leave the details for you to discover.

Professor Bert Vaux is a PhD in Linguistics and currently teaches at the University of Wisconsin-Milwaukee. He has written extensively on linguistics and dialects.

GREAT PLAINS

In 1803, the Louisiana Purchase doubled America's size, adding French territory west of the Mississippi at the bargain price of $0.03 per acre. Over time, the plains spawned legends of pioneers, cowboys, and Native Americans as they fought over land and struggled to learn the way of life that came to define the American West. The arrival of railroads and liberal land policies in the 19th century spurred an economic boom, until a drought during the Great Depression transformed the region into a dust bowl. Modern agriculture has reclaimed the soil, and the heartland of the US now thrives on farm products. The Plains are a vast land, where open sky and endless prairies stretch from horizon to horizon. While signs of humanity in the region are unmistakable—checkerboard farms, outlying Army posts, and railroad corridors—the region's most staggering sights are its works of nature, from the Badlands and the Black Hills to the mighty Missouri and Mississippi Rivers.

HIGHLIGHTS OF THE GREAT PLAINS

VENTURE into the depths of **Jewel Cave** and **Wind Cave** (p. 602) and the rugged wilderness of **Theodore Roosevelt National Park** (p. 595) and the **Badlands** (p. 598).

SLIDE down the famous "shoe chutes" at the **City Museum** in St. Louis (p. 628).

GAZE at the formidable **Mt. Rushmore** (p. 601) and **Crazy Horse Memorial** (p. 602).

UNBUCKLE your belt after feasting on the nation's best **beef** in Omaha, NE (p. 616).

MISBEHAVE like cowboys did when the West was wild in **Deadwood, SD** (p. 605).

NORTH DAKOTA

Vast open spaces usher visitors to North Dakota. An early visitor declared, "It's a beautiful land, but I doubt that human beings will ever live here." Posterity begs to differ. The stark, haunting lands that intimidated settlers eventually found willing tenants, and the territory became a state along with South Dakota on Nov. 2, 1889. One detail still muddles the event—President Benjamin Harrison concealed the order in which he signed the two bills, so both Dakotas claim to be the 39th state.

🛈 PRACTICAL INFORMATION

Capital: Bismarck.

Visitor Info: Tourism Department, 1600 E. Century Ave., Bismarck 58501 (☎800-435-5663; www.ndtourism.com). **Parks and Recreation Department,** 1600 E. Century Ave., Bismarck 58501 (☎328-5357; www.ndparks.com). **Game and Fish Department,** 100 N. Bismarck Expwy., Bismarck 58501 (☎328-6300). State offices open M-F 8am-5pm.

Postal Abbreviation: ND. **Sales Tax:** 5%.

BISMARCK   ☎701

In Bismarck, the people are friendly, the streets are clean, and the scenery is spectacular. Seas of yellow wildflowers, grids of green farmland, and fields of golden wheat blend with surprising harmony, creating breathtaking views along the Riv-

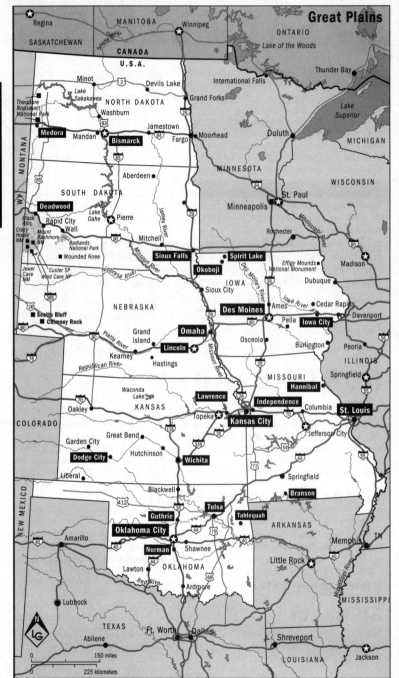

GREAT PLAINS

TIP

BUS' A MOVE. Greyhound has made significant schedule and route changes recently, decreasing the number of stops in the Great Plains area from 260 to 99. Many smaller bus lines have begun to pick up the slack, but travelers should plan ahead to account for higher prices and less convenient schedules. To get you from point A to point B faster, Amtrak still runs two daily lines through the region: the "Empire Builder," from Chicago to Seattle through North Dakota, and the "California Zephyr," from Chicago through southern Iowa and Nebraska.

erside Pkwy., a scenic stretch of road that is one of Bismarck's finest assets. Located at the center of the Lewis and Clark Trail, the city is an ideal place to learn about the state's rich pioneering and Native American history.

ORIENTATION AND PRACTICAL INFORMATION. Bismarck is on I-94, halfway between Fargo and Theodore Roosevelt National Park. The **Missouri River** separates Bismarck from Mandan, its neighbor to the west. **Washington Street, 7th Street** (one-way south) and **9th Street** (one-way north) are the main north-south thoroughfares and are intersected by **Divide Street, Main Street,** and the **Bismarck Expressway.** The **Bismarck Municipal Airport,** 2301 University Ave. (☎222-6502; www.bismarckairport.com), is two miles southeast of the city. Take the Bismarck Expwy. east from downtown and turn right on Airport Rd., then left onto University Ave. **Taxi: Taxi 9000,** ☎223-9000. **Capital Area Tansit (CAT)** buses depart from the **Bismarck-Mandan Transit Center,** 3750 E. Rosser Ave., and run throughout the city. (☎323-9228. Office open M-F 8am-5pm. $1; seniors, disabled, and children $0.50.) The **Bismarck-Mandan Convention and Visitors Bureau,** 1600 Burnt Boat Dr., at Exit 157 off I-94, distributes a visitor guide and coupons. (☎222-4308 or 800-767-3555; www.bismarkmandancvb.com. Open June-Oct. M-F 7:30am-7pm, Sa 8am-6pm, Su 10am-5pm; Nov.-May M-F 8am-5pm.) **Medical Services: St. Alexius Medical Center,** 900 E. Broadway Ave. (☎530-7000, Emergency and Trauma Center 530-7001). **Internet Access: Bismarck Public Library,** 515 N. 5th St. at B Ave. (☎222-6410; www.bismarcklibrary.org. Free wireless Internet; computer use $0.25 per 15min. Open M-Th 9am-9pm, F-Sa 9am-6pm, Su 1-6pm.) **Post Office:** 220 E. Rosser Ave. (☎221-6512. Open M-F 7:45am-5:30pm, Sa 9am-noon.) **Postal Code:** 58501. **Area Code:** 701.

ACCOMMODATIONS AND FOOD. Budget motels abound off I-94 at Exit 159 and on the Bismarck Expwy. The **Select Inn ❷,** 1505 Interchange Ave., left from Exit 159 off I-94, provides clean rooms, laundry access, breakfast, and wireless Internet. (☎223-8060 or 800-641-1000; www.selectinn.com. Singles $45; doubles $55. AAA discount. AmEx/D/DC/MC/V.) Located two blocks from the Capitol and much homier than a chain motel, the **White Lace B&B ❹,** 807 N. 6th St., boasts afternoon tea and comfy furnishings. (☎258-6877. Doubles $75. MC/V.) Three miles south of Bismarck, **General Sibley Campground ❶,** 5001 S. Washington St., has sites dotted with trees near the river. (☎222-1844; www.bisparks.org. Free showers and bikes for borrowing. Campground open May to mid-Oct. Office open daily 8am-9:30pm; park open daily 6am-10pm. $7; with electricity $17.) On the other side of the river, the beautiful **Fort Abraham Lincoln State Park ❶,** seven miles south of Mandan (see **Sights,** below) on Rte. 1806, has 95 sites on the Missouri River. (☎667-6340 or 800-807-4723. Reservations recommended. Primitive sites mid-May to Sept. $8, with electricity $14; Oct. to mid-May $5/$12. Vehicle fee $5.)

With an enormous Italian-inspired menu to complement its intimate atmosphere, **Walrus ❸,** 1136 N. 3rd St., in Arrowhead Plaza, is a local favorite. (☎250-0020. Pasta $10-15. Pizza $8-10. Sandwiches $5-10. Open M-Sa 10:30am-1am. D/DC/MC/V.) Housed in the old Northern Pacific train depot, **Fiesta Villa ❸,** 411 E. Main Ave., serves quesadillas with fresh guacamole ($7-9) and other Mexican and Tex-

I-94, ROAD OF CONCRETE WONDERS. Two gargantuan concrete monuments separated by 131 mi. of interstate symbolize North Dakota's past and present. Looming on the horizon in Jamestown, ND, at Exit 258, is the **world's largest buffalo**—a towering 24 ft. monument to the animals that once freely roamed the plains. Across the highway, a herd of real buffalo regards its concrete brother apathetically from behind a fence. In New Salem, ND, 33 mi. west of Bismarck, at Exit 127, Salem Sue, the **world's largest Holstein cow** (38 ft. tall and 50 ft. long), keeps an eye on the interstate and the spectacular patchwork fields of the plains. ($1 suggested donation.)

Mex fare. Margaritas shake up the atmosphere while rumbling trains shake the foundation below. (☎222-8075. Patio and bar 21+. Open M-Th 11am-10:30pm, F-Sa 11am-11pm; bar open until 1am on busy evenings. D/MC/V.) **Tropical Island ❸,** 1247 W. Divide Ave., is a southern escape with Caribbean fare. Try the "Extreme Burger" with jalapeño bacon ($8.50) or the Caribbean grilled chicken with pineapple mango salsa. (☎221-9858. Karaoke Th 9pm. Trivia F night. Open M-Sa 11am-11pm, Su 10am-10pm; bar open 1 hr. later. AmEx/MC/V.)

◙ **SIGHTS.** In the heart of downtown, the **North Dakota Heritage Center,** 612 E. Boulevard Ave., the official state history museum, has its own mastodon skeleton as well as other interesting exhibits. (☎328-2666. Open M-F 8am-5pm, Sa 8am-5pm, Su 11am-5pm. Free.) Visible from almost anywhere in the city, the **North Dakota State Capitol,** 600 E. Boulevard Ave, is a 19-story Art Deco building constructed between 1932 and 1934. The observation deck on the 18th floor is a perfect place to gaze at the prairie and the capitol's 130 acres of well-manicured grounds. (☎328-2480. Open M-F 7am-5:30pm. 30min. tours leave every hr. June-Aug. M-F 8-11am and 1-4pm, Sa 9-11am and 1-4pm, Su 1-4pm; Sept.-May M-F 8-11am and 1-4pm. Free.) The new **North Dakota Cowboy Hall of Fame,** 1110 College Dr., celebrates the colorful ranching and rodeo history of the West. (☎623-2000; www.northdakota-cowboy.com. Open May-Sept. daily 10am-8pm. $6.50, under 12 $3.50.) North Dakota's oldest state park, **Fort Abraham Lincoln State Park,** lies on Rte. 1806 in Mandan, along the Missouri River, in an area occupied by the Mandan Indians until they succumbed to smallpox in 1837. Lewis and Clark came through this area in 1804, and General George Armstrong Custer, commanding the 7th Cavalry, took up residence here several decades after that. Now, Fort Lincoln houses the **"On-a-Slant" Mandan Indian Village,** with several reconstructed earth lodges, as well as replicas of the cavalry post and Custer's well-kept Victorian home. (☎663-9571, low season 663-4758. Buildings open May-Oct. daily 9am-7pm; tours every half-hour 9am-6:30pm; park open daily 9am-9:30pm. Call for low-season hours. $5, students $3; vehicle fee $5.)

🎭🎶 **ENTERTAINMENT AND NIGHTLIFE.** The **Bismarck-Mandan Symphony Orchestra** plays in the magnificent **Belle Mehus Auditorium,** 201 N. 6th St. The symphony celebrates holidays in style—an estimated 8000 people turn up for their 4th of July concert on the steps of the Capitol building. (☎258-8345; www.bismarck-mandansymphony.org. Concert series Sept.-Apr. Tickets $10-35.) **Borrowed Buck's Roadhouse,** 118 S. 3rd St. at Front Ave., has a DJ and dancing every night. Rock music and themed nights fuel the old-fashioned fun; live bands take the stage once or twice a month. (☎224-1545. 21+. Open M-Sa 4pm-1am, Su noon-1am.) For a true country experience, try **Lonesome Dove,** 3929 Memorial Hwy. in Mandan, with live, toe-tappin' music Wednesday through Sunday. (☎663-2793. 21+. Cover $2. Open daily noon-1am.)

THEODORE ROOSEVELT NATIONAL PARK ☎701

After first visiting the Badlands to hunt buffalo, pre-White House Theodore
("Teddy") Roosevelt returned for spiritual renewal after the deaths of his mother
and wife. He was so influenced by its buttes and gorges, horseback riding, big-
game hunting, and cattle ranching, that he later claimed, "I never would have been
President if it weren't for my experiences in North Dakota." Roosevelt National
Park was created in 1947 as a monument to his conservation efforts, and its vast
open spaces and rugged outdoors opportunities preserve the spirit of the land that
inspired the rising president.

ORIENTATION AND PRACTICAL INFORMATION. The park is split into
the **North Unit** and **South Unit,** with the Little Missouri Grasslands in between. On
the radio, AM 1610 offers information about both parts of the park. The North Unit
is located 52 mi. north of I-94 off I-85. The entrance to the more developed South
Unit is at Exit 24 or 27 off I-94. The town of Medora serves as the gateway to the
South Unit. With a year-round population of less than 100, this revamped tourist
haven retains a local feel with old-fashioned ice-cream parlors and gift shops situated mere minutes from stunning natural scenery. The park **entrance fee** ($5 per
person, under 17 free; $10 max. per vehicle) covers 7-day admission to both the
North and South units. The **South Unit Visitors Center,** in Medora, maintains a mini-
museum displaying Roosevelt's guns, spurs, and old letters. (☎623-4466;
www.nps.gov/thro. Open late June to Sept. M-Th 8am-6pm, F-Su 8am-8pm; Sept. to
mid-June daily 8am-4:30pm.) The **North Unit Visitors Center** is located next to the
park entrance. (☎842-2333; www.nps.gov/thro. Open daily 9am-5:30pm. Call ahead
in winter.) **Dakota Cyclery,** 275 3rd Ave., rents bikes and leads bike tours of the Badlands by reservation. (☎623-4808 or 888-321-1218; www.dakotacyclery.com. Half-
day $20-30, full day $30-45. Tours $40-70. Open mid-May to early Oct. daily 8:30am-
6pm.) Off-road biking is not allowed in either unit of the park. Medora lacks a real
pharmacy and grocery store. However, both the **Ferris Store,** 251 Main St. (☎623-
4447; open daily 7am-10pm), and **Medora Convenience and Liquor,** on Pacific Ave. at
Main St. (☎623-4479; open daily 7am-11pm), sell basic pharmaceutical goods,
food, and cooking items. Medora Convenience and Liquor is also the town's only
gas station. There is a 24hr. **Wal-Mart** (☎225-8504; closed midnight Sa to noon Su)
in Dickinson, 30 mi. east on I-94. **South Unit Time Zone:** Mountain (2hr. behind Eastern). **North Unit Time Zone:** Central (1hr. behind Eastern). **Post Office:** 355 3rd Ave.,
in Medora. (☎623-4385. Open M-Sa 8am-7pm. Window service M-F 8am-11:45am
and 12:30-4:30pm, Sa 8:15-9:45am.) **Postal Code:** 58645. **Area Code:** 701.

ACCOMMODATIONS AND FOOD. Free backcountry camping permits are
available from the visitors centers. Both units have self-registration for campgrounds 5 mi. past the entrances by the river. **Cottonwood Campground ❶** lies 5 mi.
past the South Unit Visitors Center on Scenic Loop Dr., while the less-crowded
Juniper Campground ❶ is 5 mi. west of the North Unit Visitors Center. Be cautious:
the campgrounds are frequented by buffalo. Both campgrounds have toilets and
running water in the summer, but only pit toilets in the winter. (Check-out noon.
No hookups or showers. Sites $10; in winter $5.) Camping outside the park usually
yields more amenities and better food options. It's difficult to find cheap indoor or
low-season lodging in Medora, but Dickinson, 30 mi. east on I-94, contains several
affordable options year-round. The **Bunkhouse ❸,** 400 E. River Rd. S, has reasonable rates, A/C, cable TV, and a pool. (☎800-633-6721. Register at the Badlands
Motel at 500 Pacific Ave. Open late May to early Sept. Doubles $66; family units
$95. AmEx/D/MC/V.) For a bit more luxury, the historic **Rough Riders Hotel ❹,** 301

! The seclusion of Theodore Roosevelt National Park provides ample opportunity for wildlife contact, but be careful not to surprise the bison; you may wish to sing so they can hear you coming. Do not approach any animal, and beware of rattlesnakes and black widow spiders in prairie dog burrows. Even if you avoid the creepy-crawlies, watch out; prairie dogs have bites worse than their barks.

3rd Ave., has rooms with original furniture and an upscale restaurant. (☎800-633-6721. Restaurant open daily 7am-2pm and 5-9pm. In summer singles $85, doubles $100; weekends $10 more. Low season $45/$52. AmEx/D/MC/V.)

The **Iron Horse Saloon ❸**, 160 Pacific Ave., offers tons of burgers and greasy favorites, all served at the bar or on the patio. (☎623-9894. Breakfast, sandwiches, and burgers $4-9. Dinner entrees $10-20. Open daily June-Sept. 6am-1am; Oct.-May 10:30am-1am. AmEx/D/DC/MC/V.) Medora's **Fudge & Ice Cream Depot ❶**, on Pacific Ave., and **Marquis de Mores French Ice Cream ❶**, on 3rd Ave., offer sweet treats for the heat. (☎800-633-6721. One scoop $2. Both open June-Aug. daily 11am-7:30pm. Cash only.) **Cowboy Cafe ❷**, 215 4th St., is a popular spot for inexpensive specialties like french toast and ham and the Buffalo Burger dinner. (☎623-4343. Entrees $5-9. Open daily 6am-8pm; breakfast 6am-11am. Cash only.)

◙ ◻ **SIGHTS AND ENTERTAINMENT.** The popular **Medora Musical** is a song-and-dance extravaganza celebrating the glory of Teddy Roosevelt, North Dakota, and America. The patriotic show, held in the open-air **Burning Hills Amphitheatre** west of town, incorporates pyrotechnics, horses, and visiting comedians and performers. (Show runs early June to early Sept. daily 8:30-10:30pm. Tickets $24-28, students $13-15.) Before the show, at the nearby Tjaden Terrace, cast members serenade the audience as they feast at a rowdy Western **Pitchfork Steak Fondue,** where cooks put steaks on a pitchfork and dunk them into a vat of boiling oil. (Daily at 6pm. Reservations recommended. Steak $22, half steak $18.) Tickets for both the musical and the fondue are available in town at the **Harold Schafer Heritage Center,** 335 4th St. (☎800-633-6721; www.medora.com. Open daily 10am-6pm.)

◪ **OUTDOOR ACTIVITIES.** The South Unit is busier than the North Unit and includes the 36 mi. **Scenic Loop Drive,** from which all sights and trails are accessible. **Painted Canyon Overlook,** 7 mi. east of Medora off I-94, has its own visitors center with picnic tables, public phones, restrooms, and a breathtaking panoramic view of the Badlands. (☎575-4020. Open daily June-Aug. 8am-6pm; Apr.-May and Sept.-Oct. 8:30am-4:30pm.) The **Painted Canyon Trail** is a steep 1 mi. hiking loop that winds into the valley through shady wooded areas and scorching buttes. **Peaceful Valley Ranch,** 7 mi. into the South Unit, offers horseback excursions. (☎623-4568. Some age and height requirements. Open May-Sept. 6 trail rides (1½hr.) leave in summer daily 8:30am-2pm. Evening rides W, F, Sa in June; daily July-Aug. at 6pm. $25.) The **Ridgeline Trail** begins with a steep climb but is a relatively flat half-mile hiking trail. Signs along the way describe the ecology and geology of the terrain. For a more strenuous workout, try the **Coal Vein Trail,** 1 mi. off the main route on a dirt road. This three-quarter mile trail traces a seam of lignite coal that ignited and burned from 1951 to 1977; the searing heat of the blaze served as a natural kiln, baking the adjacent clay and sand. Constant winds morph the soft sands of **Wind Canyon,** while a short dirt path leading along the bluffs gives a closer look at the canyon walls and the river below. The third-largest **petrified forest** in the US is a day's hike into the park; expect to enter through a crawl space and walk about 1½ mi. to the first stumps. Free tours leave about every 30min. in the summer between 8:45am and 4:15pm from the South Unit Visitors Center for Teddy's Maltese Cross Cabin, built circa 1883. For more info on hiking, pick up *Frontier Frag-*

ments and the *Backcountry Guide* (both free) at one of the visitors centers. The guides at the state historic site **Chateau de Mores,** 3448 Chateau Rd., on the west side of town, detail Medora's history. (☎623-4355. Open May 16-Sept. 15 8:30am-6:30pm, last ticket sold at 5:50pm; in winter by appointment. $6, ages 6-15 $3, under 6 free.) The 96 mi. **Maah Daah Hey Trail** connects the North and South Units through the scenic Little Missouri Badlands. The popular trail was once a principal trade route for Native Americans in the area.

The North Unit is known for its more dramatic and varied scenery. Most of the land is designated wilderness, resulting in unlimited backcountry hiking possibilities. The North Unit's 14 mi. **Scenic Drive** is perfect for auto-touring, and connects the entrance to Oxbow Overlook. The 1 mi. **Little Mo Trail** weaves through woodlands and badlands near the Juniper Campground; the first half of the 1 mi. loop is paved and wheelchair accessible. The 4½ mi. loop **Caprock Coulee Trail** winds its way through a variety of habitats, climbing to an outlook over the Little Missouri River. The 11 mi. **Buckhorn Trail** is moderately strenuous and provides the only access to two prairie dog towns. Seasoned hikers delight in the challenging 18 mi. **Achenbach Trail,** which features vertical drops, uphill climbs, and two river crossings. Be sure to check trail conditions before attempting this hike.

SOUTH DAKOTA

With fewer than 10 people per square mile, South Dakota has the highest ratio of sights to people in all of the Great Plains. Colossal carvings such as Mt. Rushmore and the Crazy Horse Memorial, historical remnants like Deadwood, and stunning natural spectacles like the Black Hills and the Badlands draw summer crowds seeking scenic pictures and a taste of the West.

🔢 PRACTICAL INFORMATION

Capital: Pierre.

Visitor Info: Department of Tourism, 711 E. Wells Ave., Pierre 57501 (☎605-773-3301 or 800-952-3625; www.travelsd.com). Open M-F 8am-5pm. **US Forest Service,** 330 Mt. Rushmore Rd., Custer 57730 (☎605-673-4853). Open M-F 7:30am-4:30pm. **Game, Fish, and Parks Department,** 523 E. Capitol Ave., Foss Bldg., Pierre 57501 (☎605-773-3485, campground reservations 800-710-2267; www.campsd.com), has info on state parks and campgrounds. Open M-F 8am-5pm.

Postal Abbreviation: SD. **Sales Tax:** 4% (1-2% extra in some towns).

SIOUX FALLS   ☎605

As South Dakota's eastern gateway and largest city, Sioux Falls is a "family town": friendly, clean, and a little boring. Still, its small town feel makes it a refreshing stop en route to other destinations. Five miles west of Sioux Falls at Exit 390 off I-90, the ghost town of **Buffalo Ridge** has over 50 exhibits portraying life in the Old West. (☎528-3931. Open early Apr. to Oct. sunrise-sunset. $4, ages 5-12 $3.) The **Corn Palace,** 604 N. Main St. in Mitchell, 70 mi. west of Sioux Falls on I-90, was specifically designed to put the town on the map and now poses as a regal testament to the "a-maize-ing" power of corn. Dating back to 1892, the concrete structure is re-decorated each year using thousands of bushels of corn and grain. Come fall, it is the world's largest bird feeder. (☎866-273-2676; www.cornpalace.com. Open June-Aug. daily 8am-9pm; Apr.-May and Sept.-Oct. daily 8am-5pm; Nov.-Mar. M-F 8am-5pm. Annual festival around Labor Day. Free.) The **Pettigrew Home &**

Museum, 131 N. Duluth Ave. at 8th St., is the former home of a colorful South Dakotan senator who liked to collect things. (☎367-7097; www.siouxlandmuseaums.com. Open May-Sept. M-W and F-Sa 9am-5pm, Th 9am-9pm, Su noon-5pm; Oct.-Apr. daily noon-5pm. Tours every 30min. Free.) The **Sertoma Butterfly House,** 4320 S. Oxbow Ave., in Sertoma Park, is home to hundreds of butterflies from around the world (☎334-9466; www.sertomabutterflyhouse.org. Open in summer M-Sa 10am-6pm, Su 1-5pm; winter M-Sa 10am-4pm, Su 1-4pm. $6, ages 60+ $4.50, ages 4-18 $4, 3 and under free; families $18.)

Budget motels flank 41st St. at Exit 77 off I-29. The **Red Roof Inn ❷,** 3500 Gateway Blvd., is a good value with wireless Internet, large TVs, continental breakfast, and laundry facilities. (☎361-1864 or 800-733-7663. Singles $44; doubles $55. AAA discount. AmEx/D/DC/MC/V.) Of the many state parks near the city, **Split Rock City Park ❶,** 20 mi. northeast in Garretson, has the cheapest camping. From I-90 E, take Exit 406 to Rte. 11 N (Corson), and drive 10 mi. to Garretson; turn right at the sign for Devil's Gulch. (☎594-6721. Pit toilets and drinking water. Sites $6.) While in the area, visit **Devil's Gulch** and **Palisades State Park** for beautiful quartzite landscapes. **Phillips Avenue,** downtown between 9th and 12th St., is lined with coffeehouses and restaurants and leads to the city's namesake rapids in **Falls Park. Soda Falls ❶,** 209 S. Phillips Ave., at the back of Zandbroz Variety Store, has great sandwiches and sundaes. (☎331-5137. Open M-Sa 9am-8pm, Su noon-5pm. Cash only.) **Shalom Ethiopian Cafe ❸,** 1701 E. 10th St., is an oasis of flavor amidst bland strip malls, serving spicy dishes with *injera* bread. (☎339-2919. Entrees $6-12. Open daily 9am-10pm. AmEx/D/MC/V.) **Nitwits Comedy Club,** 431 N. Phillips Ave., showcases local talent and Hollywood imports. (☎274-9656 or 888-798-0277; www.nitwitscomedy.com. 21+. Cover $10. Box office opens W-F 6pm, Sa 3pm. Club office open Tu-F 10am-6pm. Reservations required. Shows W-Sa 7:30pm, F-Sa 10pm.)

Jefferson Lines, 610 E. 54th St. N. at W. 4th St., runs buses to Minneapolis (6hr., 2 per day, $52), Omaha (3½hr., 2 per day, $38), and Rapid City (6hr., 1 per day, $84). (☎336-0885 or 800-678-6543. Open M-Sa 8am-9pm, Su 8-11:30am and 2-9pm.) **Sioux Falls Transit** buses run throughout the city. (☎367-7183. Buses operate M-F 5:40am-6:50pm, Sa 8am-6:50pm. $1. Transfers free.) The **Sioux Falls Trolley** provides free rides around downtown. (☎367-7183. Runs Apr.-Sept. M-Sa 8am-10pm.) **Taxi: Yellow Cab,** ☎336-1616. **Visitor Info: Sioux Falls Convention and Visitors Bureau,** on Falls Park Dr. between Main Ave. and Weber Ave. (☎367-7430; www.siouxfallscvb.com. Open mid-Apr. to Sept. daily 9am-9pm; Oct. to mid-Apr. Sa-Su 9am-5pm; mid-Nov. to early Jan. also M-F 5-9pm, Sa-Su 9am-9pm for Christmas lights in the park.) **Medical Services: Avera McKennan Hospital and University Health Center,** 800 E. 21st St. (☎322-8000.) **Internet Access: Sioux Falls Public Library,** 201 N. Main Ave., at 8th St. (☎367-8740. 1½hr. limit per day. Open M-Th 9am-9pm, F 9am-6pm, Sa 9am-5pm; Sept.-May also Su 1-5pm.) **Post Office:** 320 S. 2nd Ave. (☎357-5001. Open M-F 8am-5:30pm, Sa 10am-1pm.) **Postal Code:** 57104. **Area Code:** 605.

BADLANDS NATIONAL PARK   ☎605

When faced with a mountainous wall of craggy rock formations looming over the prairie, early explorers were less than enthusiastic. The French called the hills *les mauvaises terres,* or "bad lands," and the name stuck. Still, not everyone feared the land—there is evidence that the Oglala Lakota named the lands *Paha ska,* or "white hills," and viewed them as sacred as the neighboring Black Hills. Spring and fall in the Badlands offer pleasant weather that is a relief from the extreme temperatures of summer and winter, but even at their worst, the Badlands are worth a visit. Mineral deposits lend layers of red, brown, and green to the rock formations, and the colorful moods of the Badlands change with the time and weather.

GREAT PLAINS

◼▧ ORIENTATION AND PRACTICAL INFORMATION. Badlands National Park consists of the **North Unit, Western Wilderness Area,** and **South Unit.** The most accessible, the North Unit, lies about 50 mi. east of Rapid City on I-90. The **entrance fee** ($10 per car, $5 per person on bike, foot, or motorcycle) comes with a free copy of *The Prairie Preamble* with trail map. The newly renovated **Ben Reifel Visitors Center,** 5 mi. inside the park's northeastern entrance, serves as the park headquarters. (☎433-5361. Open daily 9am-4pm.) A drive along **U.S. 240/Badlands Loop Road,** accessible from I-90, is an excellent introduction to the northern portion of the park. This scenic byway curves through rainbow-colored bluffs and has numerous turnoffs for views of the Badlands. Since the park was originally created to preserve its fossils, check some out at the awesome ◼**Pig Dig,** a functioning archaeological dig a quarter-mile south on Conata Road. (Open daily 9am-5pm.) The gravel **Sage Creek Rim Road,** west of U.S. 240, sees very few people and lots of animals. Highlights of the area include the Roberts Prairie Dog Town and the park's herds of bison and antelope. The more remote **White River Visitor Center** is located some 55 mi. to the southwest, off Rte. 27 in the park's less-traversed southern section. (☎455-2878. Open June-Aug. daily 9am-5pm.) Both visitors centers have potable water and restrooms. The **National Grasslands Visitors Center (Buffalo Gap),** 708 Main St., in Wall, has films and exhibits on the complex ecosystem of the surrounding area. (☎279-2125. Open daily June-Aug. 8am-5pm; Sept.-May 8am-4:30pm.) For more info, visit www.nps.gov/badl. **Area Code:** 605. **Time Zone:** Mountain (2hr. behind Eastern).

◖▮ FOOD AND ACCOMMODATIONS. In addition to the standard lodging and camping options, **backcountry camping ❶** (½ mi. from the road and out of sight) offers close contact with this austere landscape; be sure to pack plenty of water if pursuing this option. Contact one of the rangers at the Ben Reifel Visitor Center before heading out, and keep an eye out for bison, which are extremely dangerous. Within the park, the **Cedar Pass Lodge ❸,** next to the Ben Reifel Visitor Center, rents cabins with A/C and showers. (☎433-5460; www.cedarpasslodge.com. Open mid-Apr. to mid-Oct. Reservations recommended. 1-bedroom June-Aug. $65; May and Sept. $55. 2-bedroom $80/$70. Cottage $90. Check-in 2pm. Check-out 11am. AmEx/D/MC/V.) Owned by the same managers, the **Badlands Inn ❸,** a half-mile outside the park on U.S. 377, has rooms with A/C and decent views of the Badlands. (☎433-5401; www.badlandsinn.com. Check-in 2pm. Check-out 11am. Open mid-May to mid-Sept. Singles $65. AAA discount. AmEx/D/MC/V.) The **Badlands Budget Host Inn ❷,** right down the road, offers clean rooms, cabins with A/C, a campground, and an on-site restaurant. (☎433-5335 or 1-800-283-4678. Rooms $46-58. Cabins $30, linens not provided. Camping $12-15. D/MC/V.) If you'd rather sleep under the stars, the **Sage Creek Campground ❶,** 13 mi. from the Pinnacles entrance due south of Wall, is on a field with pit toilets and no water. (Take Sage Creek Rim Rd. off U.S. 240. Free.)

A true South Dakota experience, the **Cuny Table Cafe ❶,** 8 mi. west of the White River Visitor Center on Rte. 2, is marked only by an "Open" sign. Try the Indian tacos (fry bread piled with lettuce, tomato, beans, and beef) for $6. (☎455-2957. Open daily 5:30am-5:30pm. Cash only.) About 60 mi. north, by the Ben Reifel Visitor Center, the **Cedar Pass Lodge Restaurant ❷** has hearty breakfasts, buffalo burgers ($6), and pricier entrees after 5pm. (☎433-5460. Open daily mid-May to Aug. 7am-8:30pm; Apr.-May and Sept.-Oct. 8am-4pm. AmEx/D/MC/V.) In Interior, the **A&M Cafe ❷,** 2 mi. south of the Ben Reifel Visitors Center on Rte. 44, is a small but bustling cafe with generous breakfasts ($4-8) and ample sandwich platters for $4-7. (☎433-5340. Open daily 7am-8pm. D/MC/V.)

⚠ OUTDOOR ACTIVITIES. The 244,000-acre park protects large tracts of prairie and stark rock formations, and the Ben Reifel Visitors Center has plenty of info on camping and hiking. The handy *Prairie Preamble* has schedules of guided walks and talks, delivered by park rangers from June to August. **Hiking** is permitted throughout the entire park, but climbing on the formations and drifting from established trails can be dangerous. Backcountry adventures come easy in the western wilderness area, though well-marked trails are scarce. Hiking is discouraged in the wild and largely uncharted south unit, which has no paved roads or trails. For backcountry hiking, bring a compass, a map, and lots of water. Despite the burning heat in summer, long pants will help ward off poison ivy, cacti, ticks, and the venomous prairie rattlesnake. Four hiking trails begin off Loop Rd. near the Ben Reifel Visitor Center. The moderate **Cliff Shelf Nature Trail** (½ mi., 30min.) consists of stairs, a boardwalk, and unpaved paths and is the best bet for coming face-to-face with wildlife. The **Notch Trail** (1½ mi., 1-1½hr.) demands surefootedness through a canyon and a willingness to climb a shaky ladder at a 45° angle. Not for the faint of heart, the trail blazes around narrow ledges before making its way to the grand finale: a drop-off with an unbelievable view of the Cliff Shelf and White River Valley. **Door Trail** (¾ mi., 20min.) is wheelchair accessible for the first quarter-mile. The rest of the trail cuts through buttes and crevices for spectacular views of the surrounding countryside. **Window Trail** (¼ mi., 10min.) is more of a scenic overlook than an actual hike, with a wheelchair-accessible ramp and a splendid view. For horseback riding, check out **Badlands Trail Rides,** 1½ mi. south of the Ben Reifel Visitors Center on Rte. 377. (☎391-2028. Rides leave daily in summer 8am-7:30pm. 30min. ride $15; 1hr. ride $20.)

BLACK HILLS REGION

The Lakota called this region *Paha Sapa*, meaning "black hills," for the dark hue that the Ponderosa pines take on when seen from a distance. They considered the region so sacred that they would not settle there, only visit. The Treaty of 1868 gave the Black Hills and the rest of South Dakota west of the Missouri River to the tribe, but when gold was discovered in the 1870s, the US government snatched back 6000 sq. mi. Today, the area attracts millions of visitors annually with its collection of natural treasures, including Custer State Park, Wind Cave National Park, and Jewel Cave National Monument. Meanwhile, Mt. Rushmore and Crazy Horse are larger-than-life symbols of the cultural clash that defines the region's history.

BLACK HILLS NATIONAL FOREST   ☎605

The Black Hills region contains over 100 attractions, including a reptile farm and a Flintstones theme park, but the greatest sights are the natural ones. Most of the land in the Black Hills is part of the Black Hills National Forest and exercises the "multiple use" principle—mining, logging, ranching, and recreation all take place in close proximity. The forest itself provides opportunities for backcountry hiking, horseback riding, swimming, biking, and camping. In the national forest, the **visitors center**, on I-385 at Pactola Lake, offers a great view of the lake, wildlife exhibits, maps of the area, and details on backcountry camping. (☎343-8755. Open late May to early Sept. W-Su 9am-5pm.) In Rapid City, there is also the **Black Hills Visitor Information Center** at Exit 61 off I-90. (☎355-3700. Open daily June-Aug. 8am-8pm; Sept.-May 8am-5pm.) **Backcountry camping** in the national forest is free and allowed anywhere except around the three main lakes (see below), or within 200 ft. of roads, trails, or streams. Open fires are prohibited, but controlled fires in provided grates are allowed. Of the 31 **National Forest campgrounds ❶**, good ones include: **Pactola,** on the Pactola Reservoir just south of the junction of Rte. 44 and U.S. 385;

TIP **HOG HEAVEN.** Unless you've got a Harley underneath you, the Black Hills are best avoided during the first two weeks in August, when the **Sturgis Rally** takes over the area. Nearly 500,000 motorcyclists roar through the Hills, filling up campsites and motels and bringing traffic to a standstill.

Sheridan Lake, 5 mi. northeast of Hill City on U.S. 385 (north entrance for group sites, south entrance for individuals); and **Roubaix Lake,** 14 mi. south of Lead on U.S. 385. Sheridan and Roubaix have some sites open in the winter. Forest campgrounds are quiet and wooded with toilets and sometimes swimming. (Reservations ☎877-444-6777; www.reserveusa.com. No hookups. Sites at all 3 campgrounds $17-19.) The national forest extends into Wyoming, and the **Bearlodge Ranger Station** in Sundance directs visitors to the west. (☎307-283-1361. Open M-F 8am-4:30pm.) The Wyoming side of the forest draws fewer visitors and permits campfires. **I-90** skirts the northern border of the Black Hills from Spearfish in the west to Rapid City in the east. **U.S. 385** twists from Hot Springs in the south to Deadwood in the north. Speed-demons beware: beautiful winding routes hold drivers to half the speed of the interstate. Winter in the northern area of the Black Hills offers stellar skiing and snowmobiling. However, many attractions close or have limited hours, and most resorts and campgrounds are closed in winter.

MOUNT RUSHMORE
☎605

Mount Rushmore National Memorial boasts the faces that launched a thousand minivans. Though it's the most visited sight in the area, a pre-noon arrival should beat most of the crowds. Historian Doane Robinson originally conceived of this "shrine of democracy" in 1923 as a memorial for frontier heroes, carved among the spectacular Needles; sculptor Gutzon Borglum chose four presidents and a mountaintop instead. Borglum encountered all kinds of opposition to his work from those who felt that nature could not be improved, but he defended the scale of his masterpiece, finally completing the busts of Washington, Jefferson, Theodore Roosevelt, and Lincoln in 1941. The 465 ft. tall bodies were never completed—work ceased when US funds were diverted to WWII, shortly after Borglum's death. From the observation deck above the museum, the half-mile **Presidential Trail** loops closer to the Monument with various viewing spots. The trail also leads to Borglum's studio, where visitors can view Borglum's plaster model of the carving, as well as tools and designs for Mt. Rushmore. (☎666-4448; www.rushmoreborglum.com. Open daily June-Aug. 8am-7pm; May and Sept. 9am-6pm. Ranger talks every hr. on the ½hr.) During the summer, the **Mount Rushmore Memorial Amphitheater** hosts a nightly program with a patriotic speech and film. (☎574-2523; www.nps.gov/moru. May-Aug. 9pm, Sept. 8pm. All year long, light floods the monument from 9:30-10:30pm. Trail lights extinguished 11pm.) With presidential figures and historical scenes rendered in minute detail, the **National Presidential Wax Museum,** Hwy. 16A on the outskirts of Keystone, offers a glimpse of American history in a different medium. (☎666-4455; www.presidentialwaxmuseum.com. Open in the summer daily 9am-9pm; last admission 8pm. $10, seniors $8, ages 6-12 $7.)

Rapid City, less than an hour from Mt. Rushmore and other South Dakota attractions, has plenty of inexpensive motels. **Horsethief Lake Campground ❶** lies 2 mi. west of Mt. Rushmore on Rte. 244 and is operated by the Black Hills National Forest. Former President George Bush fished here in 1993; rumor has it the lake was stocked with fish to guarantee his success. (☎574-4402 or 877-444-6777; www.reserveusa.com. Water and flush toilets. Check-out 1pm. Reservations recommended on weekends. Sites $22. Wheelchair-accessible sites available.) The commercial **Mt. Rushmore KOA/Palmer Gulch Lodge ❷,** 7 mi. west of Mt. Rushmore on Palmer Gulch off Rte. 244, has campsites, cabins with showers, free wireless

Internet, two pools, laundry, horseback riding, a small strip mall, bike and car rentals, and free shuttle service to Mt. Rushmore and Crazy Horse. (☎574-2525 or 800-562-8503; www.palmergulch.com. Make reservations up to 2 months in advance for cabins. Open May-Sept. Sites June-Aug. $29, with water and electricity $37; cabins $55-63. May and Sept. $25/$33/$46-55. D/MC/V.)

Mount Rushmore National Monument is two miles from downtown Keystone. From Rapid City, take U.S. 16 and 16A to Keystone, and Rte. 244 up to the mountain. There is an $8 "annual parking permit" for the lot next to the entrance. The **Info Center** has maps, daily event schedules, and Ranger tours, which leave daily at 10:30am, 11:30am and every half-hour 1:30pm-4:30pm. Closer to the Monument, a state-of-the-art **museum** chronicles the monument's history in addition to showing a film that explains how the carving was accomplished—about 90% of the "sculpting" was done with dynamite. (Info center ☎574-3198, museum ☎574-3165. Both open daily in summer 8am-10pm; low-season 8am-5pm. Wheelchair accessible.)

CRAZY HORSE MEMORIAL   ☎605

In 1947, Lakota Chief Henry Standing Bear commissioned sculptor Korczak Ziolkowski to create a memorial to Crazy Horse as a reminder that Native Americans have their own heroes. A famed warrior who gained respect by refusing to sign treaties or live on government reservations, Crazy Horse was stabbed in the back by a treacherous white soldier in 1877. The Crazy Horse Memorial, which at its completion will be the world's largest sculpture, sits among the Black Hills, the Lakota tribe's sacred land, as a monumental tribute to the revered Native American leader. Construction of the monument began with a ground-breaking blast on June 3, 1948, and the completed face (all four of the Rushmore heads could fit inside it) was unveiled 50 years later. Believing that Crazy Horse should be a project funded by those who truly cared about the memorial, Ziolkowski twice refused offers of $10 million in federal funding. With admission prices covering most of the construction costs, Ziolkowski's wife Ruth and seven of their 10 children carry on his work, currently concentrating on the horse's head, which will be 219 ft. high. Eventually, Crazy Horse's entire torso and head, as well as part of his horse, will be carved into the mountain. The memorial, 4 mi. north of Custer on U.S. 385/U.S. 16, includes the **Indian Museum of North America,** the **Sculptor's Studio-Home,** and the **Native American Educational and Cultural Center,** which displays native crafts. During the first full weekend of June, visitors can trek 6¼ mi. up to the face in the annual **Volksmarch.** Otherwise, expect to pay $4 to take a bus to the foot of the statue. Admission includes access to a laser show detailing the history and future of the monument. (☎673-4681; www.crazyhorse.org. Open daily May-Sept. 7am-dark; Oct.-Apr. 8am-dark. Laser show May-Sept. 9:20pm. Monument lit nightly about 10min. after sunset for 1hr. $10, under 6 free; $24 per carload.)

WIND CAVE AND JEWEL CAVE   ☎605

In the cavern-riddled Black Hills, the subterranean scenery often rivals the above-ground sights. After the Black Hills formed from shifting plates of granite, water filled the cracked layers of limestone, creating the intricate and unusual structures that make up the area's prime underground real estate. **Wind Cave National Park** (☎745-4600; www.nps.gov/wica), adjacent to Custer State Park (p. 604) on Rte. 87 and U.S. 385, and **Jewel Cave National Monument** (☎673-2288; www.nps.gov/jeca), 13 mi. west of Custer off Rte. 16, are the area's treasured natural phenomena. When visiting, be sure to bring a sweater—Wind Cave hovers at 53°F, Jewel Cave is 49°F.

WIND CAVE. Wind Cave was discovered by Tom Bingham in 1881 when he heard the sound of air rushing out of the cave's only natural entrance. The wind was so strong that it knocked Tom's hat off, but when Tom returned to show his friends,

his hat got sucked in. This "breathing" of air force-
fully moving in and out of the cave results from
changes in outside pressure. Though Tom found the
entrance more than a century ago, scientists estimate
that only 5% of the volume of the cave has been
unearthed. Within the 115 mi. of the cave's depths
that have been explored, geologists have found a
lake over 200 ft. long. Instead of the typical crystal
formations of stalagmites and stalactites, Wind Cave
is known for housing over 95% of the world's "box-
work"—a honeycomb-like lattice of calcite covering
its walls. Five **tours** cover a spectrum of caving abilities. For detailed information, see the park's newsletter, *Passages*. (☎745-4600. Tours June-Aug. daily
8:40am-6pm; less frequently in low season. Parts of
some tours wheelchair accessible.) The **Garden of
Eden Tour** is the least strenuous. (1hr., ¼ mi., 4 per
day, 150 stairs. $7, ages 6-16 $3.50, under 6 free.) The
Natural Entrance Tour (1¼hr., ½ mi., 12-15 per day, 300
stairs) and the **Fairgrounds Tour** (1½hr., ½ mi., 8 per
day, 450 stairs) are both moderately strenuous, and
one of the two leaves about every 30min. ($9, ages 6-
16 $4.50, under 6 free.) Light your own way on the
more rigorous **Candlelight Tour.** (Limited to 10 people.
Min. age 8. 2hr. June-Aug. 10:30am and 1:30pm. $9,
ages 8-16 $4.50. Reservations recommended. "Non-
slip" soles on shoes required.) The difficult **Wild Cave
Tour,** an intro to basic caving, is limited to 10 people
ages 16+ who can fit through a 10 in. high passage-
way. (Parental consent required for under 18. 3-4hr.
tour daily 1pm. Reservations required. $23.) Tours
usually fill up an hour beforehand, so it's a good idea
to buy tickets in advance. **Wind Cave National Park Visitor Center** at RR1, P.O. Box 190, Hot Springs 57747,
can provide more info. (☎745-4600. Open June to
mid-Aug. daily 8am-7pm; winter hours vary.) The **Elk
Mountain Campground ❶,** 1 mi. north of the visitors
center, is an excellent spot in the woods that rarely
fills up and is protected from buffalo. (Potable water,
firewood, and restrooms. Self-registration. Sites mid-
May to mid-Sept. $12; mid-Sept. to mid-May $6.) **Backcountry camping** is allowed in the northwestern sector
of the park. Campers must have a permit, which is
free at the visitors center.

JEWEL CAVE. Distinguishing itself from nearby
Wind Cave, Jewel Cave is covered with many different calcite crystal formations. These walls enticed
the cave's discoverers to file a mining claim for the
"jewels," but they soon realized that giving tours
would be more profitable. Today the Park Service
continues this tradition. The **Scenic Tour** (1¼hr., ½
mi., 723 stairs) is a moderately strenuous walk that
highlights the chambers with the most interesting

crystal formations. (In summer every 20min. 8:20am-6pm; in winter call ahead. $8, ages 6-16 $4, under 6 free. Reservations recommended.) On the **Lantern Tour** (1¾hr.), you'll see roosting bats and walk, duck, and stoop by lantern. (In summer every hr. M-Sa 9am-5pm, Su 10, 11am, 1, 2, 4, 5pm; in winter call ahead. $8, ages 6-16 $4.) Pants, long sleeves, knee and elbow pads, gloves, hiking boots, and a willingness to get down and dirty are required for the 3-4hr. **Spelunking Tour,** limited to five people ages 16 and older. Don't wear your favorite clothes—manganese deposits will permanently stain them. (June-Aug. M-Th and Su at 12:30pm. $27. Reservations required, ☎673-2288 ext. 2. Must be able to fit through an 8½ in. by 2 ft. opening.) The **visitors center** has more info. (☎673-2288. Open daily June to mid-Aug. 8am-7:30pm; Oct. to mid-May 8am-4:30pm.) The **Mammoth Site,** 1800 W. U.S. 18 in Hot Springs, is a working archaeological site with fossils of mammoths and other creatures. (☎745-6017; www.mammothsite.com. Open mid-May to mid-Aug. daily 8am-8pm; early May and late Aug. daily 8am-6pm; Sept.-Oct. and Mar.-Apr. daily 8am-5pm; Nov.-Feb. M-Sa 9am-3:30pm, Su 11am-3:30pm. $6.75, seniors $6.25, ages 5-12 $4.75.)

CUSTER STATE PARK   ☎605

Peter Norbeck, governor of South Dakota in the late 1910s, loved to hike among the thin, towering rock formations that punctuate the prairie south of Sylvan Lake and Mt. Rushmore. In order to preserve the land, he created Custer State Park. The spectacular **Needles Highway (Route 87)** follows his favorite hiking route—Norbeck designed this road to be especially narrow and winding so that newcomers could experience the pleasures of discovery. (Road closed Nov.-Apr.) Norbeck's scenic drive continues outside the park on **Iron Mountain Road** (U.S. 16A), which runs from Mt. Rushmore to the east entrance. It takes drivers through a series of tunnels, "pigtail" curves, and switchbacks that yield stunning views of the national monument. Inside the park, the **Wildlife Loop Road** twists past a prairie dog town and through wilderness areas near prime hiking and camping territory. The park requires an **entrance fee** except for non-stop travel on U.S. 16A. (May-Oct. 7-day pass $5 per person, $12 per car; Nov.-Apr. $2.50/$6.) The **Peter Norbeck Visitor Center,** on U.S. 16A, half a mile west of the State Game Lodge, serves as the park's main info and program center. (☎255-4464; www.custerstatepark.info. Open daily June-Aug. 8am-8pm; Apr.-May and mid-Oct. to Nov. 9am-5pm; Sept. to mid.-Oct. 8am-6pm.) Aside from the visitors center, the best source for all the information on the park is found in *Tatanka*, the park's magazine guide, available at all entrances and most visitors centers in the area.

Both Trail 9 and Trail 4 will take you from Sylvan Lake to **Harney Peak,** (7242 ft.), the highest point east of the Rockies and west of the Pyrenees. Waiting at the top are amazing views of the Black Hills. The hike is a strenuous 6 mi. round-trip, so bring water and food, wear good shoes, and check the weather beforehand. The challenging 3 mi. **Sunday Gulch Trail** offers fun hiking, rock-scrambling, and some of the park's most amazing scenery. Visitors adore **Sylvan Lake,** on Needles Hwy., where you can swim, hike, fish, or boat. (☎575-2561. Boat rental $5 per 30min. Open daily 10am-7pm.) **Fishing** is allowed anywhere in the park, but a South Dakota fishing license is required. ($7 per day, non-residents $14. Available at Sylvan Lake.) The **Centennial Trail,** 111 mi. long, goes through Custer and is great for biking, horseback riding, and hiking. One-hour horse rides are available at **Blue Bell Lodge,** on Rte. 87 about a mile from the south entrance. (☎255-4571. Reservations recommended. $26, under 12 $20.) You can rent mountain bikes at the **Legion Lake Resort,** on U.S. 16A, 6 mi. west of the Norbeck Visitor Center. (☎255-4521. $10 per hr., $25 per half-day, $40 per day.) The majestic granite of the Needles makes for great rock climbing. For more info contact **Sylvan Rocks,** 208 Main St. in Hill City, 20 mi. north of Custer, which leads guided expeditions. (☎574-2425; www.sylvanrocks.com. Open in summer M-Tu and Th-Su 8am-11pm.)

Primitive camping is available for $2 per person per night in the **French Creek Natural Area ❶.** Self-register at each end of the area, accessible from the Blue Bell Lodge or near the Norbeck center. All eight of the park's **campgrounds ❶** have sites with showers and restrooms. No hookups are provided; only the Game Lodge Campground offers an RV dump station and two electric sites. (☎800-710-2267; www.campsd.com. Office open daily 6am-9pm. Most sites can be reserved; the entire park often fills in summer by 3pm. Sites $13-18. Non-resident reservation fee $5.) Slightly less touristy than Rapid City, the town of Custer is the most convenient base for exploring the Black Hills region. The sites and cabins at **Spokane Creek ❶,** 24631 Iron Mountain Rd., sit on a grassy bank near the east entrance to Custer State Park. Showers, a general store, and a cafe are available. (☎666-4609 or 800-261-9331. Sites $18; electric hookup $23-28; cabins from $35.) The charming **Shady Rest Motel ❸,** 238 Gordon Rd., sits on the hill overlooking Custer. It has homey cabins with kitchens, a hot tub, and friendly owners. (☎673-4478 or 800-567-8259. Closed in winter. Singles $60; doubles $65. D/MC/V.) **The Wrangler ❷,** 302 Mt. Rushmore Rd., is a local restaurant serving solid breakfasts ($3-6) and yummy buffalo burgers. (☎673-4271. Open M-Sa 5am-8pm, Su 6am-8pm. MC/V.) A culinary landmark in Custer, the purple-striped **Purple Pie Place ❶,** 19 Mt. Rushmore Rd., serves sandwiches, soup, and of course, the best pies for miles around. (☎673-4070. Free wireless Internet. Open daily 11am-10pm. MC/V.) The **Songbird Cafe ❶,** 440 Mt. Rushmore, provides welcome relief from buffalo burgers with tasty wraps and sandwiches. (☎673-5125. Free wireless Internet. Live music W-Sa. $7 cover Sa. Open M-Tu 9am-4pm, W-Th 9am-9pm, F-Sa 9am-10pm. MC/V.)

The **Custer Visitors Center,** 615 Washington St., helps visitors get situated in the area. (☎673-2244 or 800-992-9819; www.custersd.com. Open mid-May to Aug. M-F 8am-7pm, Sa-Su 9am-5pm; in winter M-F 8am-5pm.) **Custer County Public Library,** 447 Crook St. off U.S. 385, has wireless **Internet** access and computers. (☎673-8178. Open M-Tu and Th-F 11am-5:30pm, W 3-7pm, Sa 10am-3pm.)

DEADWOOD   ☎605

Gunslingers Wild Bill Hickok and Calamity Jane sauntered into Deadwood during the height of the Gold Rush in the summer of 1876. Bill stayed just long enough—three weeks—to spend eternity here. Jane and Bill now lie side-by-side in the **Mount Moriah Cemetery,** high on a hill south of downtown. (Office open May-Sept. daily 8am-8pm. $1, ages 5-12 $0.50. Tours anytime $3, ages 5-12 $1.50.) **Saloon #10,** 657 Main St., was forever immortalized by Wild Bill's murder. Hickok was shot holding black aces and eights, now known to poker players as a "dead man's hand." The shooting is reenacted on location daily in summer. (☎578-3346 or 800-952-9398; www.saloon10.com. Saloon open daily 8am-2am. Live music on weekends. Reenactments in summer daily at 1, 3, 5, 7pm.) Onlookers follow the scene as assassin Jack McCall is apprehended by authorities outside of Saloon #10 (in summer daily at 7:30pm) and tried at the Masonic Temple, 809 Main St. (in summer daily at 8pm). **Trolleys** ($0.50) circle downtown and provide a good overview of the sights Deadwood has to offer. Right outside Deadwood is Kevin Costner's museum, **Tatanka: Story of the Bison,** 1 mi. north on Rte. 85, an educational center with a spectacular outdoor sculpture of three riders pursuing bison over a cliff. The cafe serves bison meat dishes. (☎584-5678; www.storyofthebison.com. Open May-Sept. daily 9am-6pm. $7.50, ages 65+ $6.50, ages 6-12 $5.50.) Gambling takes center stage in this authentic western town—casinos line Main St., and many innocent-looking establishments have slot machines and poker tables waiting in the wings. There's live music outside the Stockade at the **Buffalo-Bodega Complex,** 658 Main St. (☎578-1300), which is packed with throngs of 24hr. gambling spots. For the fun of gambling without the high stakes, try your luck at the nickel slot machines. Deadwood offers several affordable accommodations, including the **Penny Motel ❷,** 818 Upper Main St., with standard, air-conditioned rooms. (☎578-1842 or 877-565-8140; www.pennymotel.com. Rooms $46-88; in fall $36-78; in winter $27-78. AmEx/D/MC/V.) The **Whistler Gulch Campground ❶,** in town off U.S. 85, has a pool, laundry facilities, and showers. (☎578-2092 or 800-704-7139; www.deadwood.com/whistler. Open May-Sept. Office open daily 9am-8pm. Check-out 11am. Sites $22, full hookup $35.) The **Deadwood History and Information Center,** 3 Siever St., behind Main Street's Silverado, can help with any questions. (☎578-2507 or 800-999-1876; www.deadwood.org. Open daily in summer 8am-7pm; in winter 9am-5pm.) **Post Office:** 68 Sherman St., in the Federal Building. (☎578-1505. Open M-F 8:15am-4:15pm, Sa 10am-noon.) **Postal Code:** 57732. **Area Code:** 605.

IOWA

Named for the Ioway Native Americans who lived along the state's riverbanks, Iowa contains one-fourth of all US Grade A farmland and prides itself on being the "heartland of the heartland." In this prototypical Midwestern state, agriculture and industry hold an elevated status. The land ripples with gentle hills between the two great rivers that sculpt its boundaries: the "Great Muddy" to the west and the "Mighty Miss" to the east. Despite its distinctly American landscape, Iowa's small towns and villages have managed to preserve their European cultural heritage.

▓ PRACTICAL INFORMATION

Capital: Des Moines.

Visitor Info: Iowa Tourism Office, 200 E. Grand Ave., Des Moines 50309 (☎515-242-4705 or 888-472-6035; www.traveliowa.com). Open M-F 8am-4:30pm.

Postal Abbreviation: IA. **Sales Tax:** 5%; most towns add an additional 1-2%.

DES MOINES   ☎515

Des Moines hums with the activity of its affable residents. The Skywalk, a maze of passageways connecting buildings downtown, is unparalleled in the Midwest. Beautiful parks traces the area's rivers and presents a welcome contrast to the now-bustling downtown area. From the "BarbeQlossal" at the World Pork Expo to world-class art, Des Moines's offerings run the gamut from kitsch to cosmopolitan.

▐ TRANSPORTATION

Airport: Des Moines International (DSM), 5800 Fleur Dr. (☎256-5100; www.dsmairport.com), 5 mi. southwest of downtown. M-F take bus #8 "Havens." Taxi $11-15.

Buses: Greyhound and Burlington Trailways, 1107 Keosauqua Way (☎243-1773 or 800-231-2222; www.greyhound.com; www.burlingtontrailways.com), at 12th St., just northwest of downtown; take bus #3, 5, or 6. To: **Chicago** (6-11hr., 6 per day, $40-45); **Iowa City** (2hr., 4 per day, $24-26); **Omaha** (2hr., 4 per day, $26-28); **St. Louis** (9-11hr., 4 per day, $73-78). Station open 4:45am-midnight.

Public Transit: Metropolitan Transit Authority (MTA), 1100 MTA Ln. (☎283-8100; www.dmmta.com), south of the 9th St. viaduct. Open M-F 8am-5pm. Buses run M-F usually 6am-11pm, Sa 6:45am-5:50pm. $1, ages 6-10 $0.75; seniors (except M-F 3-6pm) and disabled persons $0.50 with MTA ID card; transfers $0.10. Routes serve Clive, Des Moines, Urbandale, West Des Moines, and Windsor Heights. Maps are at the MTA office and website, the public library, and supermarkets.

Taxi: Yellow Cab, ☎243-1111.

Car Rental: Enterprise, 5601 Fleur Dr. (☎285-2525), just outside the airport, with speedy airport pickup. Open M-F 7:30am-6pm, Sa 9am-1pm.

⊞⊡ ORIENTATION AND PRACTICAL INFORMATION

I-80, Rte. 5 (the "Beltway"), and **U.S. 65** encircle Des Moines; **I-235** bisects the circle from east to west. Numbered streets run north-south, named streets east-west. Addresses begin with zero downtown at the **Des Moines River** and increase as you move east or west; **Grand Avenue** divides addresses north-south. Other east-west thoroughfares are **Locust Street, University Avenue** (home to Drake University), and **Hickman Road.** Note that numbered streets in Des Moines and West Des Moines are not the same; the renumbering starts with 63rd St. North-south streets change as they pass through different neighborhoods, so a map is helpful.

Visitor Info: Greater Des Moines Convention and Visitors Bureau, 400 Locust St., Ste. 265 (☎286-4960 or 800-451-2625; www.seedesmoines.com), in the Skywalk. Open M-F 8:30am-5pm. Up a few blocks are the **Greater Des Moines Partnership** and **Downtown Community Alliance,** 700 Locust St., Ste. 100 (☎286-4950 or 286-4953). Open M-F 8am-5pm; in summer closes at 4pm on F.

Medical Services: Mercy Medical Center, 1111 6th Ave. (☎247-3050), downtown.

Internet Access: Des Moines Public Library, 100 Locust St. (☎283-4152; www.desmoineslibrary.com) at 2nd Ave., will be moving to 1000 Grand Ave., at 10th St., in Apr. 2006. Open M-Th 9am-7pm, F 9am-6pm, Su 10am-5pm.

Post Office: 1165 2nd Ave. (☎283-7575), downtown just north of I-235. Open M-F 7:30am-5:30pm. **Postal Code:** 50318. **Area Code:** 515.

⊓ ACCOMMODATIONS

Downtown Des Moines is cluttered with high-end hotels. Cheap accommodations lie along Fleur Dr. by the airport, off I-80, and on Merle Hay Rd., 5 mi. northwest of downtown. Remember the 7% hotel tax, and be sure to make reservations a few months in advance for visits during the **Iowa State Fair** in August and at least one month in advance during the high school sports tournament season in March.

The Cottage, 1094 28th St. at Cottage Grove Ave. (☎277-7559), near Drake University. An elegant B&B in a 1920s-era home. 4 rooms with queen bed, private bath, and use of hot tub. Rooms M-Th $89, F-Su $99. Reservations required. AmEx/D/MC/V. ❹

Motel 6, 4817 Fleur Dr. (☎287-6364), 10min. south of downtown at the airport. Just what you'd expect—simple, secure rooms with free local calls and HBO. Laundry access. Must be 21 to rent room. Singles M-Th and Su $38, doubles $46; F-Sa $40/$48. AARP discount. 2 wheelchair-accessible rooms. AmEx/D/DC/MC/V. ❷

Iowa State Fair Campgrounds, (☎262-3111 ext. 203 or 800-545-3247; www.iowastatefair.org). Enter the main entrance of the fairgrounds at E. 30th St. and E. Grand Ave., follow E. Grand Ave., make a right on Hoover, then a left into the campground; or take

GREAT PLAINS

bus #1 "Fairgrounds" to the main gate and walk. 1800 campsites on 160 acres. No fires. Reservations accepted only during the State Fair in Aug. Open mid-Apr. to mid-Oct. Tent sites $15, water and electricity $18, full hookup $20. ●

FOOD

Restaurants flank **Court Avenue** downtown. Warm weather lures street vendors peddling gyros, hot dogs, and pizza to **Nollen Plaza**, on Locust St. between 3rd and 4th Ave. West Des Moines hosts budget eateries along Grand Ave. and in the antique-filled **Historic Valley Junction** at 5th St. and Railroad Ave. The **Downtown Farmers Market** (☎243-6625) sells fresh fruit and vegetables, baked goods, and ethnic food on Saturday mornings (mid-May to Oct. 7am-noon); Court Ave. between 1st and 4th St. is blocked off for the extravaganza. Surrounding neighborhoods hold evening (4-7pm) farmers markets of their own throughout the week. The **Skywalk** houses many places with cafeteria-style cuisine.

Cafe Su, 225 5th St. (☎274-5102), in West Des Moines, serves delicious Chinese food, with healthy options among the usual suspects ($8-14). Meals in the chic restaurant are topped off with chocolate-covered fortune cookies. Reservations recommended on weekends. Open Tu-Th 4:30-10pm, F-Sa 4:30-11pm, Su 4:30-9pm. ●

Raccoon River Brewing Co., 200 10th St. (☎362-5222), at Mulberry St. Enjoy a freshly brewed beer with barbecue chicken pizza ($10). Music on weekends. Open M-Th 11am-midnight, F-Sa 11am-2am; kitchen closes M-Th 10pm, F-Sa 11pm. AmEx/D/MC/V. ●

Bauder's Pharmacy and Fountain, 3802 Ingersoll Ave. (☎255-1124), at 38th St. A throwback to the good old days. Wax nostalgic while munching simple sandwiches ($2-4) at the lunch counter or shakes, floats, and malts from the soda fountain. Open M-F 8:30am-7pm, Sa 9am-4pm, Su 10am-2pm. D/MC/V. ●

Z'Mariks Noodle Cafe, 7450 Bridgewood Blvd. (☎558-6131), in West Des Moines, serves signature "bowlz" of noodles, rice, salad, and soup. Bowlz $5-8. Open daily 11am-9pm. AmEx/D/DC/MC/V. ●

SIGHTS

The **State Capitol,** E. 9th St. and Grand Ave., is regarded as one of the most beautiful capitol buildings in the US. Its impressive interior includes grand staircases and colorful glass mosaics. The gold-domed building also offers a clear view of the Des Moines skyline. (☎281-5591. Free tours every hr. except noon M-Sa 9:30am-3pm. Open M-F 8am-4:30pm, Sa 9am-4pm.) Nearby, the **State of Iowa Historical Building,** 600 E. Locust St., addresses the history of Iowa and Native American culture. In addition to the wonderful "A Few of Our Favorite Things," which showcases 100 inventions from the past century, the newest exhibit, "Witness To Change," traces the history of a mammoth skeleton. The building also houses the state historical library, archives, and a roof-top cafe. (☎281-5111; www.iowahistory.org. Open M-Sa 9am-4:30pm, Su noon-4:30pm. Free.)

The phenomenal ■**Des Moines Art Center,** 4700 Grand Ave. at 47th St., is composed of three contemporary buildings designed by world-renowned architects Eliel Saarinen, I.M. Pei, and Richard Meier. In addition to a collection of African tribal art, the museum contains modern masterpieces by Monet, Matisse, and Picasso, along with an expansive collection of pop, minimalist, and contemporary works by Andy Warhol, Eva Hesse, and Jeff Koons. (☎277-4405; www.desmoinesartcenter.org. Open Tu-W and F-Sa 11am-4pm, Th and 1st F of the month 11am-9pm, Su noon-4pm. Free.) Behind the Art Center lie the immaculately groomed **Rose Garden** and **Greenwood Pond,** a small lagoon where you can relax in

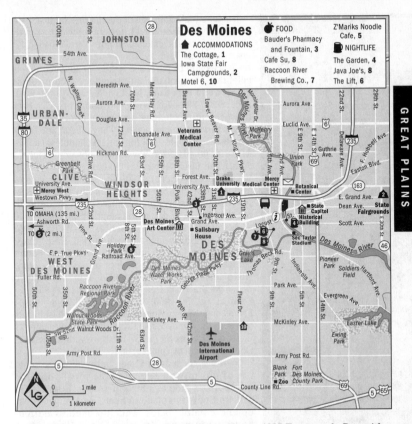

Des Moines

▲ ACCOMMODATIONS
The Cottage, **1**
Iowa State Fair
Campgrounds, **2**
Motel 6, **10**

🍎 FOOD
Bauder's Pharmacy
and Fountain, **3**
Cafe Su, **8**
Raccoon River
Brewing Co., **7**

Z'Mariks Noodle
Cafe, **5**

NIGHTLIFE
The Garden, **4**
Java Joe's, **8**
The Lift, **6**

the sun (or ice skate in the winter). **Salisbury House,** 4025 Tonawanda Dr., with entrances either at Grand Ave. or 42nd St., lets visitors explore an early 20th-century mansion in its original condition. With an incredible collection of art and rare books, this impressive 42-room home holds an eclectic collection of both oddball items and masterpieces. (☎274-1777; www.salisburyhouse.org. Open for tours June-Sept. M-F 11am, 1, 2pm and Su 1, 2, 3pm; May Tu-F 11am and 2pm; Mar.-Apr. and Oct.-Nov. Tu-Sa 11am and 2pm; Dec. Tu-F 2pm. $7, seniors $6, ages 6-12 $3.) East of the Des Moines River, the crystagon dome of the **Botanical Center,** 909 E. Robert D. Ray Dr. (E. 1st St.), is made of 665 triangular panels and fosters exotic flora and fauna. (☎323-6290. Open daily 10am-5pm. $4, seniors and ages 6-17 $2.)

🎵 🎭 ENTERTAINMENT AND NIGHTLIFE

On Wednesday, check out *Juice* (www.dmjuice.com), published by the Des Moines Register, for dining and entertainment reviews. On Thursdays, the Register's *Datebook* has listings of concerts, sporting events, and movies. Both are distributed throughout town. *Cityview*, a free local weekly, lists free events and is available at the Civic Center box office and most supermarkets.

LIKE A (STATE)HOUSE AFIRE

With its ornate staircases, hand-carved woodwork, and gorgeous chambers and libraries, the Iowa State Capitol building is a source of regional pride. But underneath the building's aesthetic beauty lies a deeper reason for why it symbolizes the solidarity and spirit of the state's residents.

In 1904, several decades after it was constructed, a fire sparked in one of the building's 106 chambers. In an effort to modernize the Capitol, a worker had been installing electric wires in the room, using a candle to illuminate his work. He accidentally left the candle burning in the attic room above the House of Representatives, and it didn't take long for passerby to realize that something other than fiery politics was heating up.

The fire brigade took an hour to arrive, only to discover that the water hoses were just a hair short of reaching the Capitol's doors. In the meantime, hundreds of locals flocked to the building and began helping. Those with brawn ran into the House chamber, dragging out furniture and other valuables from beneath the burning ceiling, while others constructed a human bucket chain so that they could try to stop the spreading blaze. To the surprise of the thwarted fire brigade, the locals were successful—only one room in the entire building was damaged.

The **Iowa State Fair,** one of the nation's largest, captivates Des Moines for 11 days in mid-August with prize cows, crafts, cakes, and corn. (☎800-545-3247; www.iowastatefair.org. Runs Aug. 10-20, 2006. Call for prices and to purchase tickets in advance.) Less celebrated but equally entertaining (for carnivores) is the **World Pork Expo,** held each June. (June 8-10, 2006; ☎847-838-6772; www.worldpork.org.) Tickets to watch minor league baseball's **Iowa Cubs,** Chicago's farm team, are a steal. They play at **Sec Taylor Stadium,** 1 Line Dr. Call for game schedules. (☎243-6111 or 800-464-2827; www.iowacubs.com. Tickets $4-8.) The **Civic Center,** 221 Walnut St. (☎246-2328; www.civiccenter.org), at 7th St., sponsors concerts and theater; call for info. **Jazz in July** (☎280-3222; www.metroarts.org) presents free concerts throughout the city every day of the month; grab a schedule at restaurants, the Civic Center, or Wells Fargo banks. On Fridays June through August, East Village (between the Capitol and river) hosts **Blues Before Sunset** on the southwest outdoor terrace of the State Historical Building. (☎281-4011. F 5-7pm.) **Music Under the Stars** has free concerts on the steps of the Capitol. (☎280-1350; June-July Su 6:30-8:30pm.) From June through August, **Nitefall on the River** brings music to the Simon Estes Riverfront Amphitheater at E. 1st and Locust St. (☎237-1386; www.dmparks.org. Concerts begin at 7pm. $8, under 12 free.)

Court Avenue and 4th Street, in the southeast corner of downtown, serves as the focal point for much of Des Moines's nightlife scene. **◙Java Joe's,** 214 4th St., is the place to hear Des Moines's best up-and-coming bands. This hip, mellow coffeehouse with Internet access ($1 per 10min., free wireless), sells exotic coffee blends and beer ($3). Vegetarians will delight in a creative array of sandwiches, all for $3-7. (☎288-5282; www.javajoescoffeehouse.com. Open M-W 7am-11pm, Th-Sa 7am-12:30am, Su 9am-11pm.) Inspired by its art-covered walls, **The Lift,** 222 4th St., serves so many kinds of creative martinis ($5-6), that you'll think you're at an ice cream parlor instead of a bar. (☎288-3777. Open M-Th and Su 5pm-2am, F 4:30pm-2am, Sa 7pm-2am.) **The Garden,** 112 SE 4th St., is a gay bar and nightclub with a video bar, dance floor, and performances every weekend. (☎243-3965; www.grdn.com. Open W-Su 8pm-2am.)

IOWA CITY ☎319

Home to the University of Iowa and its beloved Hawkeyes, Iowa City is full of collegiate flavor and youthful vitality. The downtown area has tons of cheap restaurants, trendy shops, and coffeehouses, while an active nightlife scene and college football fanaticism keep students happy. In summer, cultural activities in the city blossom.

■ ⁊ **ORIENTATION AND PRACTICAL INFORMATION.** Iowa City lies south of I-80, 114 mi. east of Des Moines. North-south **Madison** and **Johnson Street** and east-west **Market** and **Burlington Street** mark the boundaries of downtown. **Greyhound** and **Burlington Trailways,** both located at 170 E. Court St. (☎337-2127; www.greyhound.com; www.burlingtontrailways.com; station open M-F 9am-6pm, Sa-Su 9:30am-6pm) travel to: Chicago (4-6hr., 4 per day, $29-43); Des Moines (2hr., 4 per day, $20-22); Minneapolis (8-12hr., 2 per day, $39-64); St. Louis (8-11hr., 2 per day, $39-75). **Iowa City Transit** runs a free downtown shuttle M-F 7:30am-6:30pm when school is in session, in addition to its normal routes. (☎356-5151. Operates M-F 6:30am-10:30pm, Sa 6:30am-7pm. $0.75; ages 5-17 $0.50; seniors with pass $0.35 M-F 9am-3:30pm, after 6:30pm, and Sa.) The free **Cambus** runs daily on campus and downtown. (☎335-8633. Usually operates M-F 6:30am-midnight; winter also Sa-Su noon-midnight, summer also Sa-Su noon-6pm.) Taxi: **Old Capitol Cab,** ☎354-7662. The **Convention and Visitors Bureau,** 900 1st Ave., sits across the river in Coralville between U.S. 6 and I-80. (☎337-6592 or 800-283-6592; www.iowacitycoralville.com; open M-F 8am-5pm) and also runs an **information kiosk** at the Coral Ridge Mall (open M-Sa 10am-9pm, Su 11am-6pm). More info is available at the University of Iowa's **Campus Information Center,** in the Iowa Memorial Union at Madison and Jefferson St. (☎335-3055. Open Sept.-May M-F 8am-8pm, Sa noon-7pm, Su noon-4pm; June-Aug. M-F 8am-5pm.) **Medical Services: Mercy Iowa City,** on Market St. at Van Buren St. (☎358-2767 or 800-358-2767; www.mercyiowacity.org) is staffed daily 7am-midnight with registered nurses. **Internet Access: Iowa City Public Library,** 123 S. Linn St., has free wireless and two free 45min. sessions per day on their computers. (☎356-5200; www.icpl.org. Open M-Th 10am-9pm, F-Sa 10am-6pm, Su 1-5pm.) **Post Office:** 400 S. Clinton St. (☎354-1560. Open M-F 8:30am-5pm, Sa 9:30am-1pm.) **Postal Code:** 52240. **Area Code:** 319.

⁊⁊ **ACCOMMODATIONS AND FOOD.** One mile from Exit 244 off I-80 and eight blocks from downtown is the **Smiths' Bed and Breakfast ❸,** 314 Brown St., an 1890s home that has been modernized with three tastefully decorated guest rooms and A/C. (☎338-1316. Rooms $65; extended stays $50 per night. Cash or check only.) Cheap motels line U.S. 6 in **Coralville,** 2 mi. west of downtown, and **1st Avenue** at Exit 242 off I-80. One of the cheapest is the **Big Ten Inn ❷,** 707 1st Ave., which provides well-worn but comfortable rooms with HBO and A/C. (☎351-6131. Singles $33; doubles $45; prices increase significantly on football weekends. D/MC/V.) **Kent Park Campgrounds ❶,** 15 mi. west on U.S. 6, has 86 secluded sites near a lake with fishing, boating, and swimming. (☎645-2315. Free showers. Check-in before 10:30pm. Sites $10, with electricity $15.) The lively downtown centers around the open-air **Pedestrian Mall** on College and Dubuque St., where musicians serenade passersby and vendors man their food carts, sometimes until 3am. The **farmers market,** on the Chauncey Swan parking ramp between Washington and College St., has fresh produce, plants, cut flowers, and baked goods. (☎356-5110. Open May-Oct. W 5:30-7:30pm, Sa 7:30-11:30am.) The city's oldest family-owned restaurant, **Hamburg Inn #2 Inc. ❷,** 214 N. Linn St., affectionately called "The Burg," serves breakfast all day along with decadent pie shakes (milkshakes with a slice of pie blended in; $5) and chicken-fried steaks. (☎337-5512. Open daily 6am-11pm. D/MC/V.) **Masala ❷,** 9 S. Dubuque St., Iowa City's award-winning vegetarian Indian restaurant, may offer the best deals in town with its $6.65 lunch buffet and $6 Monday dinner special. (☎338-6199. Open daily 11am-2:30pm and 5-9:30pm. AmEx/D/

MC/V.) Next door, **Z'Mariks Noodle Cafe ❷**, 19 S. Dubuque St., is always packed. Customize "bowlz" of noodles or rice and wait for friendly servers to bring them to your table. (338-5500. Bowlz $5-8. Open daily 11am-9pm. AmEx/D/DC/MC/V.)

◪ SIGHTS. The University of Iowa's **Museum of Art,** 150 North Riverside Dr., has an impressive collection of European, African, and American art, including works by Iowan artists. (☎335-1727; www.uiowa.edu/uima. Open W and Sa-Su noon-5pm; Th-F noon-9pm. Free.) Also on campus, the **Museum of Natural History,** at Jefferson and Clinton St., details the ecology, geology, and Native American culture of Iowa with dioramas and a large collection of mounted mammals and birds. (☎335-0480; www.uiowa.edu/~nathist. Open Tu-F 10am-3pm, Sa 10am-5pm, Su 1-5pm. Free.) A short drive from downtown is **Plum Grove Historic Home,** 1030 Carroll St., off Kirkwood Ave., the 1844 home and garden of Robert Lucas, the first governor of the Iowa Territory. (☎351-5738; www.iowahistory.org. Open June-Oct. W-Su 1-5pm. Free.) In historic West Branch, 15min. northeast of the city (Exit 254 on I-80; follow signs), lies the **Herbert Hoover National Historic Site**. Take a walking tour of the cottage where the 31st President was born, a replica of his father's blacksmith shop, and the schoolhouse and Quaker meetinghouse he attended while growing up. The fascinating **Herbert Hoover Presidential Library-Museum** chronicles his entire life and presidency. (☎643-5301 or 643-2541; www.hooverassociation.org. Open daily 9am-5pm. $5, ages 62+ $2.50, under 17 free. Wheelchair accessible.)

◪◪ ENTERTAINMENT AND NIGHTLIFE. Each summer brings with it two exciting (and free!) festivals to Iowa City. The **Iowa Arts Festival** (☎337-7944; www.iowaartsfestival.com) is held in early June and gathers local artisans, music, and food. The **Iowa City Jazz Festival** (☎358-9346; www.iowacityjazzfestival.com) has drawn several big-name and national acts in recent years. With hordes of college students bar-hopping on the **Pedestrian Mall** ("Ped Mall") and loud music escaping from bars that double as dance clubs, Iowa City's weekends take up the better part of each week. For many students, the weekend begins with the "Thursday Night Special" (mug $5, unlimited refills $1.25) at **Brother's Bar and Grill,** 125 S. Dubuque St. in the Ped Mall, where loyal patrons return with their mugs week after week. (☎338-6373. Open M-Sa 11am-1:30am.) Local musicians play jazz and blues Th-Sa at 9:30pm (in summer, F-Sa only) at **The Sanctuary,** 405 S. Gilbert St., a casual restaurant and bar with 120 beers and cushy sofas. (☎351-5692; www.sanctuarypub.com. Cover usually $4-10. Bar open M-Sa 4pm-2am; restaurant open M-Th 4-11pm, F-Sa 4pm-midnight.) In summer, the **Friday Night Concert Series** offers everything from blues to salsa on the Ped Mall. (☎354-0863. 6:30-9:30pm.) The **Riverside Theatre,** 213 N. Gilbert St., puts on professional productions and holds a Shakespeare festival during the summer. (☎338-7672; www.riversidetheatre.org. Box Office open M-F noon-5pm. Tickets $19-22, under 18 $12.)

EFFIGY MOUNDS

Native Americans built the mysterious and striking Effigy Mounds nearly 1400 years ago. The enigmatic mounds are low-lying piles of earth formed into distinct geometric and animal shapes for spiritual purposes. Though they once covered much of the Midwest, farmers' plows have ensured that only some remain, mostly in western Wisconsin and eastern Iowa. One of the largest concentrations of intact mounds is the **Effigy Mounds National Monument,** 151 Hwy. 76, in Marquette, IA, 106 mi. west of Madison, WI along the Mississippi River. With striking views of the river from high, rocky bluffs, 11 mi. of winding trails provide access to the monument. North Unit features the popular Fire Point and South Unit includes the best-preserved collection of mounds, the Marching Bears. Take Rte. 18 W from Madison. (☎563-873-3491; www.nps.gov/efmo. Visitors center open June-early Sept.

daily 8am-6pm; closes earlier in fall and winter. Guided tours to Fire Point 11am and 2pm. Call ahead for other events. $3, max. per car $5, 16 and under free.) Seven miles south on Rte. 76 in McGregor is **Pike's Peak State Park ❶**. Follow Hwy. X56 from the south end of Main St. in McGregor up the twisty road 1½ mi. The park boasts amazing views, 24 mi. of trails, and 77 campsites. (☎563-873-2341. Park open daily 4am-10:30pm. Check-out 4pm. No reservations. Sites July-Aug. $11, with electricity $16; Sept.-June $8/$13.) **Wyalusing State Park ❶**, just across the Mississippi and 10 mi. south of Prairie du Chien in Wisconsin, offers more than 110 campsites overlooking the Wisconsin and Mississippi Rivers. (☎608-996-2261 or 888-947-2757; www.wyalusing.org. Vehicles $10. Campsites $12. Electricity $5.)

SPIRIT LAKE AND OKOBOJI ☎712

In an attempt to rival its neighbors, Iowa boasts its own "Great Lakes." **Spirit Lake, West Okoboji** (o-ka-bo-ja) **Lake**, and **East Okoboji Lake** are all popular vacation destinations. The 10,000-year-old, glacier-carved West Okoboji Lake ranks with Switzerland's Lake Geneva and Canada's Lake Louise as one of the most beautiful blue-water lakes in the world. It's hard to miss the amusement park in **Arnolds Park,** off Rte. 71, with its 1927 wooden roller coaster, kiddie rides, and ice cream shops. (☎332-2183 or 800-599-6995; www.arnoldspark.com. Open late May to mid-Sept. Usually opens at 11am; call for closing times. $17, children 3-4 ft. tall and seniors $13, under 3 ft. free. Individual ride tickets $0.75.) During summer, the park hosts concerts in the **Roof Garden** at 6pm on Thursdays and in the **Green Space** at 7:30pm or 8pm on Saturdays (call the park for info). The **Higgins Museum of Money,** 1507 Sanborne Ave., in Okoboji, has one of the most extensive collections of National Bank notes. Check out the invaluable error note, with $20 printed on one side and $10 on the other. (☎332-5859. Open mid-May to mid-Sept. Tu-Su 11am-5pm. Free.) **Lakes Art Center,** 2201 Hwy. 71, is a fun and funky space with an art gallery, tours, and a cool interactive "smart art" exhibit that experiments with drawing, color, and perspective. (☎332-7013; www.lakesart.org. Open Tu-F 10am-4pm, Sa-Su 1-4pm; June-Aug. M 10am-4pm.) Theater buffs can catch productions next door at the **Stephens College Okoboji Summer Theater.** (☎332-7773. Box office open M 10am-6pm, Tu-Sa 10am-9pm, Su 1-7pm. 9 shows June-Aug. Performances Tu-Sa at 8pm, Sa also 4:30pm, Su 6pm. $13, musicals $15; groups, students and seniors $11/$13, under 12 $6.50/$7.50.) For a dose of the outdoors, hike, skate, or bike **The Spine,** a

TOUR D'IOWA

Every year in early August, 10,000 Iowans learn to really love their flat homeland as they bike across the state on a week-long bicycle ride. **RAGBRAI,** the Des Moines Register's Annual Great Bicycle Ride Across Iowa, began in 1973 with two Des Moines Register columnists who challenged each other to the task. They invited the public along, and though only about 100 riders stuck with them, coverage of the event soon made it into an annual tradition. In 1974, 1700 riders made the entire seven-day trek, and numbers have continued to climb ever since.

The ride is mostly a camping event, with riders testing their outdoors abilities along with their athleticism. The route for the ride also changes every year, creating a flurry of one-night event planning along the line of small communities chosen as RAGBRAI pitstops. The starting city is traditionally the host to the kick-off RAGBRAI Expo, an annual bicycle trade show featuring the latest cycling technology and gear. The longest, largest, and oldest bike ride in the world, RAGBRAI has inspired more than 40 similar rides elsewhere. Any money left over from the race is donated to nonprofit organizations in Iowa.

Riders must apply for week or day passes to ride. $110 for week-long rider; $25 for day pass. Application due April 1. See www.ragbrai.org for more info.

moderate 14 mi. trail that is part of the network of Dickinson County Recreational Trails. Rent bikes at **Okoboji Expedition Co.,** 1021 Rte. 71 in Okoboji before the bridge. (☎332-9001; www.expeditionco.com. Open M-Sa 9am-6pm, Su 10am-4pm. Full-day bike rental $25-40.) Several beaches line the coast of Spirit Lake; consult the maps around town, or head to Sunset Beach by the "boardwalk" in Arnolds Park. Rent kayaks, boats, and jetskis at **Funtime Rentals** in Arnold's Park, south of the bridge on U.S. 71. (☎332-2540. Kayaks $25 per hr., $5 each additional hr. Boats $40-105 per hr. Jetskis $95 per hr. Open daily 9am-9pm. Credit card required.)

Budget accommodations in the immediate lake area are scarce. Cheap motels line U.S. 71 in Spencer, 15 mi. south of Okoboji. **The Northland Inn ❸,** 2059 Hwy. 9, at the junction of Rtes. 9 and 86, north of West Okoboji Lake, has a family atmosphere and rooms with fridges and microwaves. (☎336-1450. May-Sept. Singles $50, doubles $60; Oct.-Apr. usually $30/$40. AmEx/D/MC/V.) Pitch your tent year-round at tranquil **Marble Beach Campground ❶** (☎336-4437), in the state park on the shores of Spirit Lake. Other camping options include **Emerson Bay ❶** (☎337-3805) and **Gull's Point ❶** (☎337-3870), both off Rte. 86 on beautiful West Okoboji Lake. (Winter for all ☎337-3211. Sites at all 3 campgrounds $11; with electricity $16; cable only at Emerson Bay $18.) The **Koffee Kup Kafe ❶,** off U.S. 71 at Broadway in Arnolds Park, serves breakfast all day, with tasty pancakes for $1-3. (☎332-7657. Lunch $5-8. Open daily 6am-1pm. Cash only.) **Dagwoods ❶,** 1605 Hill Ave., in Spirit Lake, is popular with locals of all ages for its sandwiches, pizza, and shuffleboard. (☎336-3969. Sandwiches $4-5. Pizzas $10-16. Open daily 11am-9pm. AmEx/MC/V.) Dagwoods is also home to the **Funny Barn Comedy Club,** which has shows on summer evenings. (☎336-4888 for schedule and reservations; www.funnybarn.com.)

Visitors Center: Okoboji Spirit Center, 243 W. Broadway Ave., houses a brochure-packed welcome center and maritime museum that traces the history of the local lake industry. (☎800-270-2574; www.vacationokoboji.com. Open M-Sa 9am-7pm, Su 10am-5pm.) **Internet Access: Spirit Lake Public Library,** 702 16th St. off Hill Ave. (☎336-2667; www.spiritlakepubliclibrary.org. 30min. sessions. Computer lab closes 30min. before closing time. Wireless available. Open M-Th 11am-8pm, F-Sa 10am-5pm.) **Post Office:** 1513 Hill Ave., in Spirit Lake. (☎336-1683. Open M-F 8:30am-4:30pm, Sa 9-10am.) **Postal Code:** 51360. **Area Code:** 712.

NEBRASKA

Nebraska suffers from accusations of being boring, flat, and empty, but in reality, the landscape is the state's greatest attraction. Central Nebraska features the Sandhills, a region full of windblown, grassy dunes and tiny rural towns. The Panhandle has Western-style mountains and canyons, historical trails, and national monuments. For the more urbane traveler, Omaha and Lincoln feature quality sports, fine music, and some of America's best meat. While many might have the urge to speed through the Cornhusker State, patient travelers are rewarded with a surprisingly pleasant Great Plains experience.

◪ PRACTICAL INFORMATION

Capital: Lincoln.

Visitor Info: Nebraska Tourism Office, 301 Centennial Mall S, Lincoln 68509 (☎402-471-3796 or 877-632-7275; www.visitnebraska.org). Open M-F 8am-5pm. **Nebraska Game and Parks Commission,** 2200 N. 33rd St., Lincoln 68503 (☎402-471-0641 or 800-826-7275; www.outdoornebraska.org). Open M-F 8am-5pm. **State Soft Drink:** Kool-Aid.

Postal Abbreviation: NE. **Sales Tax:** 5.5%.

OMAHA
☎ 402

A city of seemingly endless sprawl, Omaha stretches over miles and miles of Nebraska's prairie. The heart of the city, however, is refreshingly compact, and Omaha's museums, world-renowned zoo, and sports complex are the envy of other cities. Downtown, the Old Market lures visitors with cafes, breweries, and nightclubs, while the Gene Leahy Mall boasts a popular and beautiful green path down to the banks of the Missouri River. The town has settled comfortably into its role as a gateway to the West, but is still constantly embracing new trends.

ORIENTATION AND PRACTICAL INFORMATION. Omaha is framed to the east by the **Missouri River,** to the west and north by **I-680,** and to the south by **I-80.** The city has numbered streets that run north-south and increase from the river; you can divide building numbers in addresses on named streets (east-west) by 100 to get the nearby numbered street. Inside the city, **Dodge Street** (Hwy. 6) is the main east-west thoroughfare while **I-480/Route 75** (Kennedy Expwy.) is the main north-south road. Downtown lies between the river and 24th St. and between Cuming and Leavenworth St. At night, avoid the north and south ends of 24th St., Ames Ave., and the area north of I-480. **Eppley Airfield,** 4501 Abbott Dr., only 4 mi. northeast of downtown, has domestic flights and is easily accessible from I-480/ Rte. 75, Pershing Dr., or Cuming Dr. (☎661-8017; www.eppleyairfield.com.) **Amtrak,** 1003 S. 9th St. (☎342-1501; www.amtrak.com; open 9:30pm-6:30am), at Pacific St., chugs to Chicago (10hr., 1 per day, $70-109) and Denver (10hr., 1 per day, $90-113). **Greyhound,** 2441 N. 11th St. (☎341-1906; www.greyhound.com; open 24hr.), runs to Des Moines (2-3hr., 3 per day, $26-28), Lincoln (1hr., 3 per day, $12), and St. Louis (9-10hr., 2 per day, $39-83). **Metro Area Transit (MAT),** 2222 Cumming St., handles local transportation. Get schedules of the system at 16th and Douglas St. near the library. (☎341-0800; www.metroareatransit.com. $1.25, ages 10-18 $1, ages 5-9 $0.50; transfers $0.05. Open M-F 8am-4:30pm.) **Taxi: Happy Cab,** ☎339-8294. **Visitor Info: Greater Omaha Convention and Visitors Bureau,** 1001 Farnam St., downtown. (☎444-4187 or 866-937-6624; www.visitomaha.com. Open M-Sa 9am-4:30pm; June-Aug. also Su 1-4:30pm.) The **Nebraska Travel Information Center,** 1212 Bob Gibson Blvd., is at Exit 454 off I-80 by the zoo. (☎595-3990. Open Apr.-Oct. daily 9am-5pm; Nov.-Mar. M-F 9am-5pm.) **Hotlines: Rape Crisis,** ☎345-7273 (24hr.), **First Call for Help,** ☎444-6666 (operates daily 7am-7pm). **Internet Access: Omaha Library,** 215 S. 15th St., between Douglas and Farnham. (☎444-4800; www.omahapubliclibrary.org. Open M-W 10am-8pm, Th-Sa 10am-6pm, Su 1-6pm; Su hours vary in summer.) **Post Office:** 1124 Pacific St. (☎348-2698. Open M-F 7:30am-6pm, Sa 7:30am-noon.) **Postal Code:** 68108. **Area Code:** 402.

ACCOMMODATIONS. Most budget-friendly lodgings are on the outskirts of downtown and midtown. The best deal downtown is the **Economy Inn ❸,** 2211 Douglas St., between 20th and 21st St., where rooms have A/C, cable, microwave, and fridge. (☎345-9565. Rooms $50-56. AmEx/D/MC/V.) The usual chains are located at I-80 Exits 445 and 449 (L St.) and near the airport. You won't miss the **Satellite Motel ❷,** 6006 L St., south of I-80 at Exit 450 (60th St.), with its round building and wedge-shaped rooms equipped with a fridge, microwave, and cable TV. (☎733-7373. Singles $45; doubles $51. MC/V.) **Relax Inn Motel & Suites ❸,** 4578 S. 60th St., just south of I-80 at Exit 450, has standard rooms with wireless Internet, and laundry facilities. (☎731-7300. Continental breakfast included. Singles $51; doubles $56. D/MC/V.) **Glen Cunningham Campground ❶,** on Rainwood Rd. north of I-680 Exit 9 (72nd St.), has lovely, shady sites next to Cunningham Lake. (☎444-4628. Showers. Open Apr. 15-Oct. 15. Tents $9; electricity $11; full hookup $15.)

GREAT PLAINS

◻ **FOOD.** It's no fun being a chicken, cow, or vegetarian in Omaha, where there is a fried chicken joint on every block and a steakhouse in every district. Once a warehouse area, the brick streets of the **Old Market,** on Jackson, Howard, and Harney St. between 10th and 13th, now feature popular shops, restaurants, and bars. The **farmers market** (☎345-5401; www.omahafarmersmarket.org) is located at 11th and Jackson St. on Saturday and 11th and Howard St. on Wednesday. (Open June-Sept. W 3-7pm, Sa 8am-12:30pm; May and Oct. Sa 8am-12:30pm.) For nothing less than the beefiest of beef, try **The Brass Grille ❹,** 1207 Harney St. in the Old Market. Omaha's specialty—tender, massive steaks—will run you $20-26, but cheaper options like pasta and salads are perfect for the frugal and/or vegetarian set. (☎342-4010; www.thebrassgrille.com. Open M 11am-2pm, Tu-Sa 11am-2pm and 5pm-late. AmEx/D/MC/V.) **M's Pub ❸,** 422 S. 11th St., in the Old Market, cooks up domestic and international delights (try the *lahvosh;* $7-11), while the trendy bar crowd sips beer in the industrial interior. (☎342-2550. Open M-Sa 11am-1am, Su 5-11pm; kitchen closes M-Sa at midnight. AmEx/D/DC/MC/V.) Omaha's starving vegetarians and vegans flock to **McFoster's Natural Kind Cafe ❷,** 302 S. 38th St. in midtown, which stocks soy and rice milk and has a selection of tempeh and free-range chicken dishes. (☎345-7477; www.mcfosters.com. Live music most nights. Open M-Th 11am-10pm, F-Sa 11am-11pm, Su 10am-3pm. MC/V.) When you get sick of the classic American food available everywhere in the city, head to Ahmed's **Persian Cuisine ❸,** 1006 Howard St. in the Old Market, which attracts worldly patrons with the smells of Mediterranean spices. (☎341-9616. Open Tu-Sa 11:30am-2pm and 5:30-10pm. AmEx/D/DC/MC/V.)

◼ **SIGHTS.** With the world's largest desert dome, indoor rainforest, and nocturnal exhibit, the ever-evolving ▧**Henry Doorly Zoo,** 3701 S. 10th St., has recently added the Orangutan Forest, whose residents swing wildly between the tree-tops, and the Hubbard Gorilla Valley, where great apes roam free and gawk at visitors. (☎733-8400; www.omahazoo.com. Take Exit 454 from I-80 and turn left at the sign for the stadium and zoo; continue until the road turns north onto 10th St. Open daily 9:30am-6pm, last entry 5pm. $10.25, ages 62+ $8.75, ages 5-11 $6.50.) About 30min. west on I-80, the **Wildlife Safari Park** lets visitors drive 4½ mi. through a nature preserve inhabited by elk, bison, sandhill cranes, wolves, and other beasts. (☎944-9453. Open Apr.-Oct. daily 9:30am-5pm. $5, seniors $4, ages 5-11 $3.)

The **Durham Western Heritage Museum,** 801 S. 10th St., occupies the former Union Train Station, an impressive Art Deco structure. Visitors can tour a Pullman car and explore several temporary exhibits before indulging in a malted milkshake at an authentic 1931 soda fountain. (☎444-5071; www.dwhm.org. Open Tu-Sa 10am-5pm, Su 1-5pm. $6, seniors $5, ages 3-12 $4.) Across the river in Council Bluffs, the **Union Pacific Railroad Museum,** 200 Pearl St., off Rte. 6, includes furniture from a train car intended for President Lincoln before his assassination, a locomotive simulator, and exhibits on the evolving technology of the railroad. (☎712-329-8307. Open Tu-Sa 10am-4pm. Free.) The **Joslyn Art Museum,** 2200 Dodge St., displays American and European art, including the original plaster cast of Degas's famous sculpture *Little Dancer* and colorful glasswork by Dale Chihuly. (☎342-3300; www.joslyn.org. "Jazz on the Green" July-Aug. Th 7-9pm. Free. Open Tu-Sa 10am-4pm, Su noon-4pm. $6, students and seniors $4, ages 5-17 $3.50; free Sa 10am-noon.) See the gargantuan remnants of US airpower from the past half-century in the enormous **Strategic Air and Space Museum,** at Exit 426 off I-80, in Ashland. The museum displays military aircraft, including a B-52 bomber and an SR-71—still the world's fastest plane. (☎827-3100 or 800-358-5029; www.strategicairandspace.com. Open daily 9am-5pm. $7, seniors and military $6, ages 5-12 $3. AAA discount.)

◨◧ ENTERTAINMENT AND NIGHTLIFE. The spanking new **Qwest Center Omaha,** 455 N. 10th St., hosts concerts and sporting events. (☎341-1500; www.omahameca.com. Box office open M-F 10am-6pm.) At **Rosenblatt Stadium,** across from the zoo on 13th St., you can watch the **Omaha Royals** round the bases from April to September. (☎738-5100; www.oroyals.com. Tickets $5-9. Wheelchair accessible.) The stadium also hosts the NCAA College Baseball World Series every June. From late June to early July, **Shakespeare on the Green** stages free performances in Elmwood Park, on 60th and Dodge St. (☎280-2391. Shows Th-Su 8pm.)

Punk and progressive folk have found a niche near several area universities; check the windows of the **Antiquarian Bookstore,** 1215 Harney St., and **Homers,** 114 Howard St., both in the Old Market, for the scoop on shows. Nearby, the subterranean **Dubliner,** 1205 Harney St., stages live Irish music on Friday and Saturday evenings. (☎342-5887; www.dublinerpubomaha.com. Cover $2-5. Most shows start 9pm. Open daily noon-1am.) The **13th Street Coffee Company,** 519 S. 13th St., brews three different varieties daily. (☎345-2883. Live blues and jazz most weekends. Open M-Th 6:30am-11pm, F 6:30am-midnight, Sa 8am-midnight, Su 9am-11pm.) A laptop-toting crew lounges on the comfy couches at the **Meeting Place,** 1123 Howard St., a trendy coffeehouse-bar hybrid. (☎884-0425. Open daily 8am-1am.) **The Max,** 1417 Jackson St., is one of the most popular gay bars in the state. With five bars, a dance floor, DJs, fountains, and a patio, The Max also attracts a straight crowd on Saturday nights. (☎346-4110; www.themaxomaha.com. Happy hour daily 4-9pm. 21+. Cover F $3, Sa $5, Su varies. Open daily 4pm-1am.)

LINCOLN ☎402

The spirit of Lincoln rises and falls with the success of its renowned college football team, the Nebraska Cornhuskers, though a recent drought of winning seasons has mellowed the city's famous football fervor. Off the field, Lincoln mixes stateliness with a distinctly collegiate atmosphere, hosting both the Nebraska state legislature and rows of bars heaving with frat-style hijinks.

◨▯ ORIENTATION AND PRACTICAL INFORMATION. Lincoln's grid makes sense—numbered streets increase as you go east, and lettered streets progress through the alphabet as you go north. **O Street** is the main east-west drag, becoming Hwy. 6 west of the city and Rte. 34 to the east. **R Street** runs along the south side of the **University of Nebraska-Lincoln (UNL).** Downtown lies between 7th and 16th St. and M and R St. There is plenty of parking, with metered, on-street, and garage parking available. **Lincoln Municipal Airport,** 2400 W. Adams St. at W. 12th St. (☎458-2480; www.lincolnairport.com), is located 5 mi. northwest of downtown off Cornhusker Hwy.; take Exit 399 off I-80. **Amtrak,** 201 N. 7th St. (☎476-1295; www.amtrak.com; open daily 11pm-6:30am), runs once daily to Denver (8hr., $89-111), Chicago (11hr., $94-117), and Omaha (1hr., $14-18). **Greyhound,** 940 P St. (☎474-1071; www.greyhound.com; ticket window open M-F 7:30am-6pm, Sa 9:30am-3pm), sends buses to: Chicago (12-13hr.; 3 per day; M-Th $49-88, F-Su $59-94); Denver (12hr., 1 per day, $49-89/$59-89); Kansas City (6-10hr., 2 per day, $42-50); Omaha (1hr., 3 per day, $12). **StarTran,** 710 J St., handles public transit. Schedules are available on buses, at the office on J St., and at many locations downtown. All downtown buses connect at 11th and O St., two blocks east of Historic Haymarket. (☎476-1234. Buses run M-F 5:15am-7:10pm, Sa 6am-7:10pm. $1, seniors $0.50.) **Taxi: Yellow Cab,** ☎477-4111. **Visitor Info: Lincoln Visitors Center,** 201 N. 7th St., at P St. in Lincoln Station. (☎434-5348 or 800-423-8212; www.lincoln.org. Open May-Sept. M-F 9am-8pm, Sa 8am-4pm, Su noon-4pm; Oct.-Apr. M-F 9am-6pm, Sa 10am-4pm, Su noon-4pm.) **Medical Services: Bryan LGH Medical Center East,** 1600 S. 48th St. (☎489-0200; www.bryanlgh.org.) **Internet Access: Lincoln Bennett Martin**

Public Library, 136 S. 14th St., at N St. (☎441-8500. Open M-Th 10am-9pm, F-Sa 10am-6pm, Su 1:30-5:30pm.) **Post Office:** 700 R St. (☎473-1728. Open M-F 7:30am-6pm, Sa 9am-1pm.) **Postal Code:** 68501. **Area Code:** 402.

⌂ ACCOMMODATIONS. There are a few inexpensive lodging options downtown. Cheaper places are on W. O St., near the airport, or east around the 5600 block of Cornhusker Hwy. (U.S. 6). The **Cornerstone Hostel (HI) ❶**, 640 N. 16th St., at U St. just south of Vine St. on frat row, is conveniently located in a church basement on the university's downtown campus. It rarely fills up and while there is no A/C, the organ music drifting from upstairs will take your mind off the heat. (☎476-0926. Linen included. Full kitchen, lounge, and laundry facilities. Internet access $2 per day. Curfew 11pm. Dorms $13, members $10.) **The Great Plains Budget Host Inn ❷**, 2732 O St., at 27th St., has large rooms with A/C and fridge. Take bus #9, the "O St. Shuttle." (☎476-3253 or 800-288-8499. Free parking and kitchenettes available. Singles $47; doubles $50. AAA discount 10%. AmEx/D/MC/V.) The elegant **Atwood House Bed and Breakfast ❸**, 740 S. 17th St., at G St., two blocks from the Capitol, is a gorgeous 1894 mansion that dazzles guests with antiques nestled in every corner and whirlpool baths in most suites. (☎438-4567 or 800-884-6554; www.atwoodhouse.com. Reservations required. Rooms $85-199. AmEx/D/MC/V.) To reach the convenient **Camp-A-Way ❶**, 200 Campers Cir. at 1st and Superior St., take Exit 401a from I-80, then Exit 1 from I-180/Rte. 34. Though next to a highway, the sites are peaceful and shaded. (☎476-2282 or 866-719-2267; www.camp-a-way.com. Showers, wireless Internet, laundry, heated pool. Reservations recommended in summer. Office open daily 8:30am-9pm. Sites $16, with water and electricity $24-26, full hookup $27-30. AAA discount. D/MC/V.)

⌷⌷ FOOD AND NIGHTLIFE. Historic Haymarket, 7th to 9th St. and O to R St., is a renovated warehouse district near the train tracks with restaurants, shops, and a **farmers market.** (☎435-7496. Open mid-May to mid-Oct. Sa 8am-noon.) **Maggie's Vegetarian Wraps ❶**, 311 N. 8th St., at Q St., sustains Lincoln's vegetarians and vegans with $1-2 pastries, huge $4-6 wraps, and the $5 free-range breakfast burrito, complemented by an intimate rainbow interior. (☎477-3959. Open M-F 8am-3pm. Cash only.) If you thought Nebraska was all meat-and-potatoes, stop by **La Mexicana ❸**, 1637 P St., in the back of a Mexican grocery, for huge, authentic dishes. (☎477-4845. Lunch specials $5-7. Entrees $13-14. Open daily 9am-9pm. D/MC/V.) **Lazlo's Brewery and Grill ❹**, 710 P St., prides itself on locally brewed beer ($4), fresh fish ($12-18), and steak ($16-24) served in a mellow, casual setting. (☎434-5636. Burgers, salads, and sandwiches $6-9. Open M-Th and Su 11am-10pm, F-Sa 11am-11pm. AmEx/D/MC/V.) The ivy-covered **Green Gateau Cafe ❹**, 330 10th St. at M St., draws people in for delicious and reasonably priced breakfast, brunch, and lunch dishes, like strawberry-stuffed French toast. (☎477-0330. Breakfast and brunch $5-10. Open M-Th 6:30am-9pm, F 6:30am-10pm, Sa 8am-10pm, Su 8am-9pm. MC/V.)

With as many as ten bars per block, Lincoln is obviously a college town. For Lincoln's live blues scene, try the suitably dark **Zoo Bar,** 136 N. 14th St., where Lincoln's sophisticated crowd congregates. (☎435-8754; www.zoobar.com. Live music Tu-Sa. Cover $5-15. Open M-F 3pm-1am, Sa 2pm-1am, Su 5-10pm.) **The Bricktop,** 1427 O St., caters to bumping, grinding, and all manner of shaking it with live music, DJ nights, and a hip, young crowd. (☎202-8780. 21+. Open M-Sa 5pm-1am, Su 8pm-1am.) **Duffy's Tavern,** 1412 O St., takes the college atmosphere and throws in a mix of live music, with local and bigger-name acts ranging from hard rock to country. (☎474-3543. Nightly drink specials. Open M-Sa 4pm-1am, Su 6pm-1am.)

◉ SIGHTS. Intricate mosaics and murals cover the walls, floor, and ceiling of the sophisticated "Tower on the Plains," the 400 ft. **Nebraska State Capitol,** at 15th and K St. Although outside renovations continue, the inside remains untouched and remarkable. A 19 ft. statue, *The Sower*, sits atop the building as a reminder of Nebraska's agricultural roots. (☎471-0448; www.capitol.org. Open M-F 8am-5pm, Sa 10am-5pm, Su 1-5pm. Free 45min. tours every hr. except 8am and noon.) On **Centennial Mall**, a renamed portion of 15th St., the **Museum of Nebraska History,** at P St., has a phenomenal collection of headdresses, moccasins, jewelry, and other artifacts from the Plains Indians, as well as a display on Nebraska's agricultural contributions to World War II. (☎471-4754. Open Tu-F 9am-4:30pm, Sa-Su 1-4:30pm. Suggested donation $2.) The **University of Nebraska State Museum,** at 14th and U St. in Morrill Hall, boasts a fossil collection that includes Archie, the largest mounted mammoth in any American museum. (☎472-2642; www.museum.unl.edu. Open M-Sa 9:30am-4:30pm, Su 1:30-4:30pm. $4, ages 5-18 $2, under 5 free; families $8.) Also on campus is the **Sheldon Memorial Art Gallery and Sculpture Garden,** at 12th and R St. With a focus on modern art, this is Lincoln's only (and therefore best) art museum. (☎472-2461. Open Tu-Th and Sa 10am-5pm, F 10am-8pm, Su noon-5pm. Free.) For a wheel-y good time, roll to the **National Museum of Roller Skating,** 4730 South St., at 48th St., located at the USA Roller Sports headquarters. (☎483-7551, ext. 16; www.rollerskatingmuseum.com. Open M-F 9am-5pm. Free.) At the end of August, the **Nebraska State Fair** entertains with live music, car races, tractor pulls, and more fried food than you'll ever want to eat. (☎474-5371; www.statefair.org. M-F $5, Sa-Su $7; ages 6-12 $2.) **Pioneers Park,** 3201 S. Coddington Ave., a quarter of a mile south of W. Van Dorn, is a perfect spot for a prairie picnic. In winter there is a sled run with lights open until 11pm. The **Pioneers Park Nature Center** has bison, elk, turtles, and snakes, and is the starting point for 8 mi. of trails. (☎441-7895. Park open dawn-dusk. Nature Center open June-Aug. M-Sa 8:30am-8:30pm, Su noon-8:30pm; Sept.-May M-Sa 8:30am-5pm, Su noon-5pm. Free. Wheelchair accessible.)

SCOTTS BLUFF AND CHIMNEY ROCK ☎308

Known to the Plains Indians as *Me-a-pa-te* ("hill that is hard to go around"), the imposing clay and sandstone highlands of **Scotts Bluff National Monument** were landmarks for people traveling the Oregon Trail in the 1800s. For some time the bluff was too dangerous to cross, but in the 1850s a single-file wagon trail was opened just south of the bluff through narrow **Mitchell's Pass,** where wagon wheels wore deep marks in the sandstone. Today, visitors can walk along a half-mile stretch of the original **Oregon Trail** at the pass, complete with a pair of covered wagons. The **Oregon Trail Museum,** at the **visitors center** and entrance on Rte. 92, relates the contradictory accounts of the mysterious death of Hiram Scott, the fur trader who gave the bluffs their name. (☎436-4340; www.nps.gov/scbl. Open daily in summer 8am-7pm; in winter 8am-5pm. $5 per carload, $3 per motorcycle.) To get to the top of the bluffs, hike the moderate **Saddle Rock Trail** (1½ mi. one-way) or motor up **Summit Drive.** (Shuttle available for hikers. Summit Dr. closes at 6:30pm.) At the top, you'll find two short **nature trails.** Guidebooks ($0.50) are available at the trailheads and the visitors center. The **North Overlook** is a half-mile paved walk with a view of the North Platte River Valley. The short and easy **South Overlook** (¼ mi.) provides a spectacular view of Scotts Bluff and the Oregon Trail route.

From U.S. 385, take U.S. 26 to Rte. 71 to Rte. 92; the monument is on Rte. 92 about 2 mi. west of **Gering** (not in the town of Scottsbluff). A 1¼ mi. bike trail links Gering with the visitors center at the base of the bluffs. Festive folk pack the towns near Gering each year for the carnival, concerts, and chili cook-off of the annual **Oregon Trail Days** festival. (☎436-4457; www.oregontraildays.com. July 13-16, 2006.) Twenty miles east on Rte. 92, south of Bayard, the 475 ft. spire of **Chimney Rock,** visible from miles away, served as another landmark for travelers on the Oregon Trail. There is no path up to the base of the rock due to the rough terrain and rattlesnakes. The Nebraska State Historical Society operates a **visitors center** on Chimney Rock Rd. off Rte. 92. (☎586-2581; www.nps.gov/chro. Open daily in summer 9am-5pm; in winter Tu-Su 9am-5pm. $3, under 18 free.) If you have time, continue down the road past the visitors center, take a right onto the gravel road, and follow it half a mile to the end. Here you will find a graveyard of Oregon Trail settlers and a closer view of the rock itself. **Area Code:** 308. **Time Zone:** Mountain.

SCENIC DRIVE: SANDHILLS SCENIC BYWAY

The **Sandhills Journey Scenic Byway** (Rte. 2) is 272 mi. in length from Grand Island to Alliance, and another 50 mi. takes the driver to the South Dakota border. The two-lane route parallels I-80 and is about the same length (allow 5hr.) but much more scenic, passing through endless rolling sand dunes covered in short prairie grass, interrupted only by bright blue lakes and the largest hand-planted forest in the US, the **Nebraska National Forest.** (Byway info: westbound ☎800-658-3178; eastbound ☎800-738-0648.) **Visitors centers** at Grand Island, Broken Bow, Thedford, and Alliance have brochures and maps. **Time Zone:** Mountain time (2hr. behind Eastern) west of Seneca, Central time (1hr. behind Eastern) east of Seneca.

Broken Bow is the most charming of the dozen or so towns along the byway; it has a grassy town square and some places to stop along the route. A good base for exploring central Nebraska, **Grand Island,** at the junction of Rte. 2, Hwy. 281, and U.S. 30, has several budget accommodations and a few attractions of its own. The beautiful, immaculate **Hall County Park Campground ❶** is perfect for a stop-over and offers shady, grassy sites with showers. (☎308-385-5087; www.hcgi.org. Open Apr. 15.-Oct. 15. 3-night max. stay. Sites $5, with hookup $10.) For a bite to eat in Grand Island, try the **Blue Moon ❶,** 313 W. 3rd St., which serves lunch, coffee, and delicious baked goods. (☎398-5214. Open M-Sa 7:30am-5pm. Cash or check only.) For an escape from the summer heat of the Great Plains, **Island Oasis Water Park** is a sure bet for fun in the sun at amazingly cheap prices. (☎385-5381; www.grand-island.com/oasis. Open June-Aug. usually noon-9pm. $5.50, seniors and ages 5-15 $4.50; families $19.)

A short detour 3 mi. north of Alliance on Hwy. 87 will bring you to **Carhenge,** a rough replica of Stonehenge made entirely out of stacked American cars from the 1950s and 60s. Jim Reinders created the structure in 1987 with Stonehenge in mind and continues to maintain the unique site. (www.carhenge.com. Open 24hr. Free.)

KANSAS

Kansas may be the most landlocked state (it contains the geographic center of the United States) but Kansans look on the bright side: they are equidistant from California and New York. Almost any non-interstate highway in this most rural of states makes for an ideal scenic drive, past undulating hills and fields of tallgrass prairie dotted with cows and picture-perfect towns. As the starting point of the Civil War, "Bleeding Kansas" provides myriad opportunities for the history buff. As highway signs remind travelers, this heartland has plenty of heart to go around.

◪ PRACTICAL INFORMATION

Capital: Topeka.

Visitor Info: Division of Travel and Tourism: 350 Speedway Blvd., Kansas City 66111 (☎800-252-6727; www.travelks.com). Open daily 9am-5pm.

Kansas Department of Wildlife and Parks, 512 SE 25th Ave., Pratt 67124 (☎620-672-5911; www.kdwp.state.ks.us). Open M-F 8am-5pm.

Postal Abbreviation: KS. **Sales Tax:** 5.3% or higher, depending on city.

WICHITA   ☎316

It may be the largest city in Kansas, but self-contained Wichita maintains a slow Midwestern pace. Always an agricultural hub for the Plains, since the early 20th century its economy has been increasingly shaped by aviation giants Boeing, Cessna, Learjet, and Beechcraft, all founded here. With a brick-and-gas-lantern Old Town District, and parks and museums along the grassy banks of the Arkansas River, Wichita is Kansas's cultural as well as economic center.

🔽 **ORIENTATION AND PRACTICAL INFORMATION.** Wichita lies on I-35, 170 mi. north of Oklahoma City and 200 mi. southwest of Kansas City. A small, quiet downtown makes for easy walking and parking. **Broadway Street** is the major north-south artery; **Douglas Avenue** is the major thoroughfare going east-west. Together, Broadway St. and Douglas Ave. divide the city into quadrants. **Kellogg Avenue (U.S. 54)** serves as an expressway through downtown and a main commercial strip. The closest **Amtrak** station, 414 N. Main St. (☎283-7533; www.amtrak.com; open M-F midnight-8am), 30 mi. north of Wichita in Newton, sends trains to Dodge City (2½hr., 1 per day, $26-51) and Kansas City (4½hr., 1 per day, $33-64). **Greyhound,** 308 S. Broadway St., at English St. (☎265-7711; www.greyhound.com; open daily 3am-6pm), runs to Kansas City and Oklahoma City (both 2¾hr., 2 per day, $33). **Wichita Transit** runs 18 bus routes in town, most of which begin at the Downtown Transit Center, 214 S. Topeka St., at William St. (☎265-7221. Transit center open M-F 6am-6pm, Sa 7am-5pm. Buses run M-F 5:45am-6:45pm, Sa 6:45am-5:45pm. $1, ages 6-17 $0.75, seniors and disabled $0.50; transfers $0.25.) **Visitor Info: Convention and Visitors Bureau,** 100 S. Main St., at Douglas Ave. (☎265-2800 or 800-288-9424; www.visitwichita.com. Open M-F 7:45am-5:15pm.) **Internet Access: Public Library,** 223 S. Main St. (☎261-8500. 1hr. use with ID. Open M-Th 10am-9pm, F-Sa 10am-5:30pm, Su 1-5pm.) **Post Office:** 330 W. 2nd St. N, at N. Waco St. (☎267-7710. Open M-F 7:30am-5pm, Sa 9am-noon.) **Postal Code:** 67202. **Area Code:** 316.

🛏🍴 **ACCOMMODATIONS AND FOOD.** Wichita offers a bounty of cheap, independently-run hotels about a mile north of downtown on N. Broadway St. Chains line **Kellogg Avenue,** 5-8 mi. west of downtown. The Victorian-era, three-bedroom **Renaissance 1887 Bed & Breakfast ❸,** 1018 N. Market St., features luxurious rooms and a free ride in a 1950s London taxicab. (☎519-4866; www.renaissance1887.com. Doubles M-Th and Su $55, F-Sa $80. Cash or check only). Only 10 blocks from downtown, the **Mark 8 Inn ❷,** 1130 N. Broadway St., has small, comfortable rooms with free local calls, cable TV, A/C, fridge, and laundry facilities. (☎265-4679 or 888-830-7268. Singles $30; doubles $34.) **All Seasons Campground ❶,** 15520 W. Maple, 9 mi. west of town, just past 151st St., has RV sites, a grassy tree-lined area for tents, bathrooms, and hot showers. (☎722-1154. Office open M-Sa 8am-noon and 3-8pm, Su 3-8pm. Tent sites $16. RV sites $21-23. AAA discount 10%. MC/V.) In the heart of Old Town in an old brick warehouse, the **River City Brewing Co.,** 150 N. Moseley St., has delicious home-brewed pints ($3.25) that complement sandwiches, burgers ($7-8), and pizza ($7-10). Try the homemade root beer with sassafras, licorice, and cinnamon. (☎263-2739. Open M-Th 11am-midnight, F-Sa 11am-2am, Su 11am-10pm. AmEx/D/MC/V.) The light Vietnamese cuisine at **Saigon ❷,** 1103 N. Broadway St., is a great alternative to barbecue. (☎262-8134. Soups $4.50-7. Noodle dishes $5.50-7. Open M-Th and Su 9am-9pm, F-Sa 10am-9pm. AmEx/D/

GREAT PLAINS

DC/MC/V.) **Hog Wild Pit Bar-B-Q ❶,** 1200 S. Rock Rd. (also at 233 S. West St. and 662 E. 47th St.), is a Wichita institution. The dinner platter (meat and two sides; $6.50) is lip-smackingly good. (☎618-7227. Open daily 11am-8pm. AmEx/MC/V.)

◙ **SIGHTS.** Most of Wichita's museums are situated along the Arkansas River for handy access and scenic vistas. Take the trolley or bus #12 to "Riverside." **Old Cowtown,** 1871 Sim Park Dr., is one of the best and largest re-created Western towns in the country, with dozens of living history interpreters. (☎264-6398; www.old-cowtown.org. Open Apr.-Oct. M-Sa 10am-5pm, Su noon-5pm. $7.25, seniors $6.50, AAA and ages 12-17 $5, ages 4-11 $4. MC/V.) The **Wichita Art Museum,** 1400 W. Museum Blvd., housed in an elegant, diamond-shaped building, has a handsome collection of 19th- and 20th-century works by the American masters, a strong focus on modernism, and several rotating exhibits of different media, with unusually progressive themes. (☎268-4921. Open Tu-Sa 10am-5pm, Su noon-5pm. $5, seniors and students with ID $4, ages 5-17 $2. Sa free.) **Botanica,** 701 N. Amindon St., is 10 acres of lovely gardens, with themes including the aquatic world, roses, Shakespeare, and butterflies. On Tuesday evenings, complimentary hors d'oeuvres and wine are served. (☎264-0448; www.botanica.org. Open M-Sa 9am-5pm, Su 1-5pm, Tu until 8pm. $6, seniors and AAA $5, ages 6-21 $3. MC/V.) The **Kansas Aviation Museum,** 3350 George Washington Blvd., next to the McConnell Air Force Base, south of town, includes several antique aircraft, from 1920s prop planes to 1980s private jets, both out on the tarmac and in the 1934 Art Deco terminal building itself. (☎683-9243. Open Tu-F 9am-4pm, Sa 1-5pm. $4, ages 6-12 $1.)

DODGE CITY   ☎620

In its heyday in the 1870s, Dodge City ("the wickedest little city in America") was a haven for gunfighters, prostitutes, and other lawless types. At one time, the main drag had one saloon for every 50 citizens, and today, downtown Dodge recreates the Old-West-style boardwalk with shops and watering holes along **Front Street.** Legendary lawmen Wyatt Earp and Bat Masterson earned their fame cleaning up the streets of Dodge. Disputes were settled man-to-man with a duel, and the slower draw ended up in **Boot Hill Cemetery,** so named for the boot-clad corpses buried there. The **Boot Hill Museum** on Front St. admits visitors to the old cemetery site with wooden grave markers based on real period newspaper articles and obituaries. It also has a "People of the Plains Exhibit" with a talking animatronic bison. (☎227-8188; www.boothill.org. Open June-Sept. daily 8am-8pm; low season M-Sa 9am-5pm, Su 1-5pm. $8, students and seniors $7.50, ages 6 and under free.) The town's most conspicuous residents, some 50,000 cows, reside on massive feedlots blanketing the hills. To see (and smell) them up close, take a short drive along the aptly named **Butter & Egg Rd.,** a mile east of town. Several historic homes dot the brick-lined streets of Boot Hill. One of the oldest and sturdiest, the 1881 **Home of Stone,** 112 E. Vine St., is open to the public and has guided tours. (☎800-653-9378. Open June-Aug. M-Sa 9am-5pm, Su 2-4pm. Free.) From a marked turnoff 9 mi. west of town on Hwy. 50, you can see wagon ruts where 19th-century pioneers on the **Santa Fe Trail** once traversed the rolling Kansas grasslands.

Cheap motels line Wyatt Earp Blvd. just west of town. One of the best places to hang your (cowboy) hat is the **Thunderbird Motel ❷,** 2300 W. Wyatt Earp Blvd., which offers very clean and well-furnished rooms with microfridges and HBO. (☎225-4143. Singles $33-35; doubles $38-42. AmEx/D/MC/V.) At **Water Sports Campground & RV Park ❶,** 500 E. Cherry St., campers can pitch their tents on grassy sites next to a lake that offers swimming, boating, and fishing. (☎225-8044. Laundry, hot showers. 2-person tent sites $17, with water and electricity $18, full hookup $22. Each additional person $2. Office open daily in summer 8am-8pm; in winter 8am-5pm. MC/V.) **Peppercorn's Bar & Grill ❸,** 1301 W. Wyatt Earp Blvd., is popular with locals and serves juicy steaks ($10-15) as well as cheaper burgers, salads, and sandwiches. (☎225-1396. Open M-Sa 11am-2am, Su 4pm-midnight. AmEx/D/MC/V.) Kansans take their pancakes seriously; see for yourself at **The Inn Pancake House,** 1610 W. Wyatt Earp, next to the Econolodge, where pancakes are served all day (3 for $3), along with burgers, sandwiches, and dinner platters. (☎225-6950. Entrees $6.50-7.25. Open daily 6am-10pm. AmEx/D/MC/V.)

Amtrak's unmanned station, at Central Ave. and Wyatt Earp Blvd. sends trains once daily to Albuquerque (11hr., $65-101) and Kansas City (7hr., $53-83). **Dodge City Convention and Visitors Bureau** is at 400 W. Wyatt Earp Blvd. (☎225-8186 or 800-653-9378; www.visitdodgecity.org. Open daily June-Sept. 8:30am-6:30pm; Oct.-May M-F 8:30am-5pm.) **Postal Code:** 67801. **Area Code:** 620.

LAWRENCE
☎785

Founded by Massachusetts abolitionists who were adamant that Kansas enter the union a free state, Lawrence was fiercely progressive from the get-go. Lawrence today seems to combine the best of New England and the Midwest, managing to be chic, cultural, and cosmopolitan while remaining at heart an old-fashioned, walkable town. The economy revolves around the ▨**University of Kansas's** campus (affectionately called KU to avoid confusion with the United Kingdom), situated atop Mt. Oread with commanding views of the prairie. The university, one of the oldest west of the Mississippi (founded 1866), is also one of the most beautiful in the country, with hilly streets and 150 years of architecture. The **KU Visitors Center,** 1502 Iowa St., is happy to offer guidance. (☎864-3911. Open M-F 8am-5pm.) Off campus, Lawrence has numerous first-rate artistic, architectural, and historical activities. The **Watkins Community Museum of History,** 1047 Massachusetts St., has exhibits on Lawrence history, from the important (the Civil War) to the very important (KU's world-famous basketball team), all in an 1888 bank. (☎841-4109; www.watkinsmuseum.org. Open Tu-W 10am-6pm, Th 10am-9pm, F 10am-5pm, Sa 10am-4pm. Suggested donation $3, children $2.) **Quantrill's Raid: The Lawrence Massacre,** a driving tour, traces the events leading to the murder of 200 men by pro-slavery vigilantes on August 21, 1863. **House Styles of Old West Lawrence,** a guide to Lawrence's Victorian homes, plots a route accessible on foot (45min.) or car.

Inexpensive motels are hard to find in Lawrence; look around Iowa and 6th St., just west of campus. Three blocks west of Massachusetts St. on 10th St., the **Halcyon House Bed and Breakfast ❸,** 1000 Ohio St., has comfy, affordable rooms in a convenient location. (☎841-0314. Rooms $49-149.) The **Westminster Inn and Suites ❸,** 2525 W. 6th St., is the least expensive motel in town, and provides standard rooms, a pool, and a full breakfast. (☎841-8410. Singles $45-50; doubles $55-60.) Campers can take their pick of the 400 grassy, shaded sites at **Clinton Lake State Park ❶,** 798 N. 1415 Rd., 6 mi. west of town on one of the largest reservoirs in Kansas. (☎842-8562. In summer sites $8, with water and electricity $15.50; in winter $7/$14.50. Park entry $6.50/$5.50. MC/V.) Massachusetts St. abounds with culinary delights of all persuasions, and most of them are affordable. **Wheatfields Bakery and Cafe ❷,** 904 Vermont St., is a New Age cafe with tasty sandwiches that range from Cuban roasted pork to a tempeh Reuben. Check out the huge cylindrical brick oven, used to bake their fresh artisan breads. (☎841-5553. Sandwiches $5-7. Coffee drinks $1-2.75. Open M-Sa 6:30am-8pm, Su 7:30am-4pm.) Cuisine at the popular **La Parilla ❷,** 814 Massachusetts St., is accented with Salvadoran, Costa Rican, Brazilian, and Mayan flavors. Try the Brazilian lemonade ($1.25), made with coconut milk and ginger. (☎841-1100. Open M and Su 11am-9pm, Tu-Th 11am-10pm, F-Sa 11am-3am.) For live music and a neighborhood bar feel, head to **Jazzhaus,** 926½ Massachusetts St., where local bands play five nights a week. (☎749-3320. Cover after 9pm $2-8; Tu $1, drinks $1.50. Open daily 4pm-2am; music begins at 10pm.)

Lawrence, just south of **I-70**, is considered part of greater Kansas City, but is separated from the suburbs of Kansas City, KS by about 10 mi. of farmland. There is an unstaffed **Amtrak** station at 413 E. 7th St.; trains chug to Chicago (9½hr., 1 per day, $56-88) and Kansas City, MO (1½hr., 1 per day, $9-12). **Greyhound,** 2447 W. 6th St. (☎843-5622; www.greyhound.com; ticket window open M-F 7:30am-4pm, Sa 7:30am-noon) runs buses to Dallas (13-15hr., 5 per day, $59-82), Denver (12-13hr., 3 per day, $74-79), and Kansas City, MO (1hr., 1 per day, $13). The **Lawrence Transit System (the "T"),** 930 E. 30th St., has schedules in local businesses, in the library, and on every bus. (☎832-3465. Open M-F 6am-8pm, Sa 7am-8pm. $0.50, seniors and disabled $0.25.) **Visitors Center:** 402 N. 2nd St., in the restored Union Pacific depot, has maps, brochures, and a 30min. film. (☎865-4499 or 888-529-5267. Open Apr.-Sept. M-Sa 8:30am-5:30pm, Su 1-5pm; Oct.-Mar. M-Sa 9am-5pm, Su 1-5pm.) **Internet Access: Public Library,** 707 Vermont Ave. (☎843-3833. Open M-F 9am-9pm, Sa 9am-6pm, Su 2-6pm.) **Post Office:** 645 Vermont St. (☎843-1681. Open M-F 8am-5:30pm, Sa 9am-noon.) **Postal Code:** 66044. **Area Code:** 785.

MISSOURI

Nestled in the middle of the country, Missouri serves as the gateway to the West while hugging the Midwest and South, blending the three identities into a state that defies regional stereotyping. Its large cities are defined by wide avenues, lazy rivers, humid summers, and blues and jazz wailing into the night. In the countryside, Bible factory outlets stand amid fireworks shacks and barbecue pits. Missouri's patchwork geography further complicates its characterization. In the north, near Iowa, amber waves of grain undulate. Along the Mississippi, towering bluffs inscribed with Native American pictographs evoke western canyonlands, while in Hannibal, cavers enjoy the limestone caverns that inspired Mark Twain.

▚ PRACTICAL INFORMATION

Capital: Jefferson City.

Visitor Info: Missouri Tourism Center, P.O. Box 1055, Jefferson City 65102 (☎573-751-4133 or 800-519-2100; www.missouritourism.org). Open M-F 8am-5pm; toll-free number 24hr. **Dept. of Natural Resources,** Division of State Parks, P.O. Box 176, Jefferson City 65102 (☎573-751-3443 or 800-361-4827). Open M-F 8am-5pm.

Postal Abbreviation: MO. **Sales Tax:** 5-7.5%, depending on county.

ST. LOUIS ☎314

Directly south of the junction of the Mississippi, Missouri, and Illinois rivers, St. Louis gained prominence in the 18th and 19th centuries as the US expanded west. The silvery Gateway Arch rises above the sprawling and diverse city, framing it against the mighty river that nurtured its growth. Combining Southern hospitality, Midwestern pragmatism, and Western optimism, St. Louis offers visitors both fast-paced urban life and lazy days spent floating on the Mississippi.

▛ TRANSPORTATION

Airport: Lambert-St. Louis International (☎426-8000; www.lambert-stlouis.com), 12 mi. northwest of the city on I-70. MetroLink and Bi-State bus #66 "Clayton Airport" provides easy access to downtown ($3). Taxi to downtown $30.

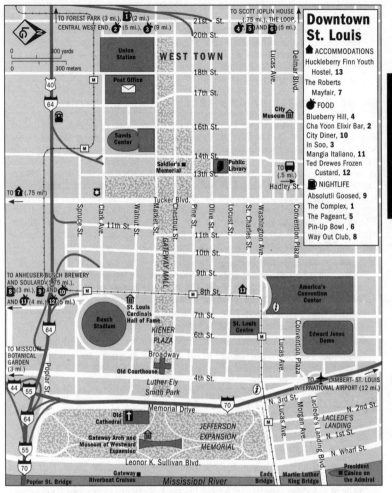

Trains: Amtrak, 550 S. 16th St. (☎621-5386; www.amtrak.com). Open daily 7am-11:30pm. To **Chicago** (5½hr., 4 per day, $22-62), **Kansas City** (5½hr., 2 per day, $25-32), and **Little Rock** (7½hr., 2 per day, $41-64).

Buses: Greyhound, 1450 N. 13th St. (☎231-4485; www.greyhound.com), at Cass Ave. From downtown, take Bi-State bus #30, less than 10min. away. Use caution in this area at night. Open 24hr. To **Chicago** (6-8hr., 9-10 per day, $39), **Kansas City** (4½-5hr., 4 per day, $33), and **Memphis** (4½-5½hr., 4 per day, $42).

Public Transit: Bi-State (☎231-2345; www.metrostlouis.org), also known as MetroBus, runs local buses. Info and schedules available at the **Metroride Service Center,** in the St. Louis Center. (☎982-1485. Open M-F 6am-8pm, Sa-Su 8am-5pm.) **MetroLink,** the light-rail system, runs from Lambert Airport through downtown and on to Shiloh, IL. Operates M-F 4:30am-12:15am, Sa-Su 5am-midnight. Travel for free in the "Ride Free

Zone" (from Laclede's Landing to Union Station) M-F 11:30am-1:30pm. Bi-State or MetroLink $1.50, seniors and ages 5-12 $0.75; transfers $0.25/$0.10. Day pass $4, available at MetroLink stations. **Shuttle Bugs** cruise around Forest Park and the Central West End. Operates M-F 6:45am-6pm, Sa-Su 10am-6pm. All-day pass $1. The **Shuttle Bee** buzzes around Forest Park, Clayton, Brentwood, and the Galleria. Operates M-F 5:40am-11:15pm, Sa-Su 7:30am-10:00pm.

Taxi: Yellow Cab, ☎361-2345.

ORIENTATION AND PRACTICAL INFORMATION

I-64 (U.S. 40) and **I-44** run east-west through the metropolitan area. Downtown is the area east of Tucker Blvd. between **Martin Luther King** and **Market Street,** which run north-south and divide the city. Numbered streets run parallel to the Mississippi, increasing to the west. The historic **Soulard** district borders the river south of downtown. **Forest Park** and the **University City Loop,** home to **Washington University** and old, stately homes, lie west of downtown; the Italian neighborhood called **The Hill** rests south of these neighborhoods. St. Louis is a driving town: metered street parking is plentiful, and private lots are often cheap (from $2 per day). While the safety situation in St. Louis has shown improvement of late, visitors are still well advised to be alert; areas in North County can be dangerous at night, and East St. Louis—across the river in Illinois—should be avoided.

Visitor Info: St. Louis Visitors Center, 308 Washington Ave. (☎241-1764). Open daily 9:30am-4:30pm. The *Official St. Louis Visitors Guide* and the monthly *Where: St. Louis,* contain helpful info and good maps. A second **info center** (☎342-5160) is inside America's Convention Center. Open M-F 9am-5pm, Sa 9am-2pm.

Hotlines: Rape Hotline, ☎531-2003. **Suicide Hotline,** ☎469-6644. Both operate 24hr. **Gay and Lesbian Hotline,** ☎367-0084. Operates M-Sa 6-10pm.

Medical Services: Barnes-Jewish Hospital, in the Central West End (☎747-3000).

Post Office: 1720 Market St. (☎436-4114). Open M-F 8am-8pm, Sa 8am-1pm. **Postal Code:** 63155. **Area Code:** 314 (in St. Louis), 636 (in St. Charles), 618 (in IL); in text, 314 unless noted otherwise.

ACCOMMODATIONS

Most budget lodging is far from downtown. For chain motels, try Lindbergh Blvd. (Rte. 67) near the airport, or the area north of the I-70/I-270 junction in Bridgeton, 5 mi. beyond the airport.

Huckleberry Finn Youth Hostel, 1908 S. 12th St. (☎241-0076), at Tucker Blvd. in the Soulard District. Take bus #73 "Carondelet." Weathered dorms could use a fresh coat of paint and shower sandals are a must, but great for meeting backpackers. Key deposit $5. Reception daily 8-10am and 6-10pm. Check-out 10am. Dorms $20. Cash only. ❶

The Roberts Mayfair, 806 St. Charles St. (☎421-2500). The custom of placing chocolates on a guest's pillow originated at this elegant Jazz Age hotel, which has played host to Cary Grant and Harry Truman. Standard rooms are spacious with marble-topped sinks and soft queen-sized beds. Rooms $79–169. AmEx/D/MC/V. ❹

Congress Airport Inn, 3433 N. Lindbergh Blvd. (☎739-5100), 1 mi. south of I-70, west of the airport. Clean accommodations just a 20min. drive from the Loop and close to the airport. Singles $45; doubles $52. AmEx/D/DC/MC/V. ❸

Dr. Edmund A. Babler Memorial State Park, 800 Guy Park (☎636-458-3813; www.mostateparks.com), in Wildwood. 10 mi. north of I-44 off Hwy. 109. Well-maintained facilities and hot showers nestled in a verdant setting. Tent sites Apr.-Oct. $8, Nov.-Mar. $7. RV sites with electric hookup $14/$12. ❶

🖸 FOOD

It's worth venturing well outside the downtown area to sample St. Louis cuisine at its best. The **Central West End** offers trendy cafes and upscale bars centered on **Euclid Avenue,** just north of Lindell Blvd.; take the MetroLink to "Central West End" and walk north, or catch the Shuttle Bug. St. Louis's historic Italian neighborhood, **The Hill,** southwest of downtown and just northwest of Tower Grove Park, produces plenty of inexpensive pasta; take bus #99 "Shaw-Russell." Ethnic restaurants, ranging from Vietnamese to Middle Eastern cuisine, spice up the **South Grand** area, at Grand Blvd. just south of Tower Grove Park; board bus #70 "Grand." Coffee shops and unique restaurants cluster on **University City Loop,** on Delmar Blvd. between Des Peres and Big Bend Blvd.

📑 Blueberry Hill, 6504 Delmar Blvd. (☎727-4444). Diners share the 9 rooms of this wacky St. Louis institution with Howdy Doody collectibles and giant baseball cards. Sandwiches ($5-7) and burgers (from $5.50) rule the roost at street level, while musical sets in the "Duck Room" have only added to the place's reputation. Music sets 21+. Cover $10-25. Open M-Sa 11am-1:30am, Su 11am-midnight. AmEx/D/DC/MC/V. ❷

In Soo, 8423 Olive Blvd. (☎997-7473), is home to some delectable Asian cuisine, including a formidable *moo-shu* ($16) and several authentically prepared Korean dishes. The chef's wife meticulously manages every aspect of the restaurant, personally wrapping the pancakes with tender loving care. Open M and W-F 11:30am-10pm, Sa 5-10pm, Su 11:30am-9pm. Cash or check only. ❸

Mangia Italiano, 3145 S. Grand Blvd. (☎664-8585), has earned its reputation with homemade pastas like *porcini tagliatelle* ($9). After hours, the place transforms into a smoky lair for lounge lizards. Lunch buffet $6 M-F 11am-2:30pm. Kitchen open M-Sa 11am-10pm, Su 5pm-10pm; bar open until 3am. AmEx/D/MC/V. ❸

Ted Drewes Frozen Custard, 4224 S. Grand Blvd. (☎352-7376), and 6726 Chippewa St. (☎481-2652), at Rte. 66. This roadside stand's signature blend of rich custard and candy is thick enough to be called a "concrete" ($2-4); each one undergoes a test for drips before serving. Grand Blvd. location open daily May-Aug. 11am-11pm; Chippewa St. location open year-round 11am-11pm. Cash only. ❶

Cha Yoon Elixir Bar, 4 N. Euclid Ave. (☎367-2209), is a chic sushi joint (6-piece roll $4-6) with an encyclopedic tea menu. Lounge on leather couches and sip tieguanyin oolong ($6 per pot), said to be hand-picked by monkeys who are trained to reach the most inaccessible tea trees. Open M-Th 11am-10pm, F-Sa 11am-11pm, Su 5-9pm; sushi bar closes 1hr. earlier. AmEx/D/MC/V. ❷

City Diner, 3139 S. Grand Blvd. (☎772-6100), has its retro shtick down to a science with Elvis posters and glittery booths. With everything on the menu available all day, you can tuck into an omelet (from $4.50) with the rowdy midnight crowd or pick at a platter of country-fried steak ($7.25) for an afternoon snack. Open M-Th 7am-11pm, F-Su 24hr. from 7am on F through 10pm Su. AmEx/D/DC/MC/V. ❷

🖸 SIGHTS

JEFFERSON EXPANSION MEMORIAL. At 630 ft., the **Gateway Arch**—the nation's tallest monument—towers gracefully over all of St. Louis and southern Illinois, serving as a testament to the city's historical role as the "Gateway to the West." Eero Saarinen's iconic design is impressive when viewed from the ground, and the ear-popping tram ride to the top allows visitors to see as far as 30 mi. on a clear day. Back on terra firma, the **Museum of Westward Expansion** recounts the settlement of the West through a series of photographs and artifacts that tell the white settlers' side of the story. (☎982-1410; www.gatewayarch.com. Museum and arch open daily in summer 8am-10pm; in winter 9am-6pm. Tram $10, ages 13-16 $7, ages 3-12 $3. Museum free.) Scope out the city from the water with **Gateway Riverboat Cruises;** tours leave from the docks in front of the arch. (☎877-982-1410. 1hr. riverboat tours daily; call for departure times. $10, ages 3-12 $4. Limited wheelchair access.) Across the street but still part of the Memorial, the magnificently ornate **Old Courthouse,** where the Dred Scott trial began, has been restored as a museum telling the story of the famous court case that pushed slave and free states closer to civil war. (11 N. 4th St. ☎655-1600. Open daily 8am-4:30pm. Call ahead for tour schedules. Free.)

DOWNTOWN AND WEST TOWN. Part eco-savvy installation art and part playground to end all playgrounds, the ▨**City Museum** is constructed from salvaged pieces of area buildings that were due to be demolished or discarded. The loading chutes of a former shoe factory get re-imagined as a twisting network of slides, while coils from an Anheuser-Busch cooling tank become a climbing ladder that wraps around itself like a cocoon. The recently opened World Aquarium is not worth the extra $5, but the five-story MonstroCity beckons with dizzying skywalks and lookout points like the cockpit of a passenger plane; there is no better spot for a creative date on weekend nights. (701 N. 15th St. ☎231-2489; www.citymuseum.org. Open June-Aug. M-Th 9am-5pm, F 9am-1am, Sa 10am-1am, Su 11am-5pm; Sept.-May closed M-Tu. $12, with admission to the World Aquarium $17; F-Sa after 5pm $8.) Several blocks north, the **Scott Joplin House** is an unassuming turn-of-the-century flat where the ragtime legend tickled the ivories until commercial success whisked him off to New York in 1907. The 45min. tour delves into Joplin's long-lasting influence on American music. (2658 Delmar Blvd. ☎340-5790. Open Mar.-Oct. M-Sa 10am-4pm, Su noon-4pm.; Nov.-Feb. Tu-Sa 10am-4pm. Tours leave on the hr.; last tour 3pm. $2.50, ages 6-12 $1.50. Wheelchair accessible.) Back downtown, the **St. Louis Cardinals Hall of Fame Museum** traces the history of the franchise from the glory days of Branch Rickey and Rogers Hornsby to the present day; the exhibit about the history of Busch Stadium has become particularly poignant since the old stadium shut its doors in 2005. An attached museum dedicated to the history of bowling should be skipped on any but the rainiest of days. (111 Stadium Plaza. ☎231-6340. Open Apr.-Sept. daily 9am-5pm, game days until 6:30pm; Oct.-Mar. Tu-Su 11am-4pm. $7.50, ages 66+ $7, under 16 $6. Wheelchair accessible.)

GRANT CENTER AND THE CENTRAL WEST END. In the early 1960s, the legendary nightspots and beatnik coffeehouses of **Gaslight Square** drew cultural icons like Lenny Bruce and Woody Allen to the corner of Olive St. and N. Boyle Ave. The Haight-Ashbury vibe lasted only a few years before the moneyed classes hit the suburbs; today, however, city leaders are working hard to incubate a new cultural district along N. Grand Blvd. One anchor of the new **Grant Center** area is the **Contemporary Art Museum St. Louis,** which has been tearing down and reassembling its galleries for new installations since it opened in 2003. (3750 Washington Blvd. ☎535-4660; www.contemporarystl.org. $5, seniors and students $3. Open Tu-W and F-Sa 10am-5pm, Th 10am-7pm, Su 10am-4pm. Free Tu. Museum closes for up to a month between shows; call ahead to confirm opening hours.) Just to the south, on the campus of St. Louis University, a former Jesuit chapel houses the ▨**Museum of Contemporary Religious Art (MOCRA),** which made waves in the mid-90s with a major exhibition on art and spirituality in the time of AIDS. In a more playful vein, MOCRA will present an installation of Andy Warhol's mylar-balloon piece "Silver Clouds" beginning in late August 2006. (221 N. Grand Blvd. ☎977-7170; http://mocra.slu.edu. Open Tu-Su 11am-4pm. Free. Museum closes for up to a month between shows; call ahead to confirm opening hours.) Deeper into the Central West End, the **Cathedral Basilica of St. Louis** traces the history of the Catholic faith through glittering mosaics that took more than half a century to complete. (4431 Lindell Blvd. MetroLink stop "Central West End" or bus #93 "Lindell" from downtown. ☎533-0544. Open daily 7am-5pm; tours M-F 10am-3pm. Free.)

GREAT PLAINS

FOREST PARK. Almost 500 acres larger than New York's Central Park, Forest Park attracted more than 19 million visitors to its statues and palaces in the 1904 World's Fair. Today, Forest Park upholds the City Beautiful vow to make high culture available for the masses; all of the major sights are free. *(Take MetroLink to Forest Park and catch the Shuttle Bug. All Forest Park sites are wheelchair accessible.)* It's easy to spend the better part of a day exploring the grounds of the **St. Louis Zoo,** from the field stations of the River's Edge exhibit to the chilly blast of the Penguin and Puffin Coast. *(☎ 781-0900; www.stlzoo.com. Open daily late May to early Sept. 8am-7pm; Sept.-May 9am-5pm. Free.)* The ground floor of the **St. Louis Art Museum** resembles a Who's Who of Renaissance and Impressionist art, although no visit is complete without a look at the Melanesian masks and carvings on the lower level. A major exhibition of contemporary abstract works will appear in summer 2006. *(☎ 721-0072; www.slam.org. Open Tu-Th and Sa-Su 10am-5pm, F 10am-9pm. Main museum free; special exhibits usually $10, seniors and students $8, ages 6-12 $6; F free. Free tours Tu-Su 1:30pm.)* The "Seeking St. Louis" exhibit at the **Missouri History Museum** presents vignettes from the city's past. Galleries extending off the main atrium are reserved for temporary exhibitions. *(At Lindell and DeBaliviere. ☎ 454-3150; www.mohistory.org. Open M and W-Su 10am-6pm, Tu 10am-8pm. Museum free. Special exhibits usually $5, seniors and students $4.)*

SOUTH OF DOWNTOWN. The historic neighborhood of **Soulard** is bounded by I-55 and 7th St. Its 19th-century brick townhouses made it one of the first districts to draw suburbanites back downtown in the 1970s, and today the ethnically and economically diverse area is known as one of the most tight-knit in the city. February brings one of the most raucous **Mardi Gras** celebrations outside New Orleans, while the **Soulard Farmers Market** sells fresh, inexpensive produce year-round. *(730 Carroll St. From downtown, travel south on Broadway or 7th St. to Lafayette. Take bus #40 "Soulard." ☎ 622-4180. Open W-F 8am-5:30pm, Sa 6am-5:30pm.)* At the end of 12th St., the **Anheuser-Busch Brewery,** the largest brewery in the world, pumps out 16.5 million 12 oz. servings of beer each day. The 1½hr. tour includes a glimpse of the famous Clydesdales and two beer samples. *(1127 Pestalozzi St. at 12th and Lynch St. Take bus #40 "Broadway" south from downtown. ☎ 557-2333; www.budweisertours.com. Tours June-Aug. M-Sa 9am-5pm, Su 11:30am-5pm; Mar.-May and Sept.-Oct. M-Sa 9am-4pm, Su 11:30am-4pm; Nov.-Feb. 10am-4pm, Su 11:30am-4pm. Wheelchair accessible.)* North of Tower Grove Park, the stunning ◙**Missouri Botanical Garden** is the oldest in the country, with the residential compound of founder Henry Shaw dating back to 1852. The 14-acre Japanese garden at the southwest corner of the garden dazzles with wooden footbridges and cascading cherry blossoms, although the shady English woodland garden and the rose gardens to the north have subtle charms of their own. *(4344 Shaw Blvd. From downtown, take I-44 west, or ride MetroLink to "Central West End" and take bus #13 "Union-Garden." ☎ 577-9400; www.mobot.org. Open daily 9am-5pm; June-Aug. W until 8pm. $7, seniors $5, under 12 free. Guided tours daily 1pm.)*

🎭 ENTERTAINMENT

Grand Center's **Powell Hall,** 718 N. Grand Blvd., is the acoustically distinguished and visually striking home of the renowned **St. Louis Symphony Orchestra.** (☎ 534-1700; www.slso.org. Performances late Sept. to early May F-Sa 8pm, Su 3pm. Box office open late May to mid-Aug. M-F 9am-5pm; mid-Aug. to late May M-Sa 9am-5pm. Tickets $12-99, students half-price for most shows.)

St. Louis offers theatergoers many choices. The outdoor **Municipal Opera,** known as the "Muny," presents hit musicals on summer nights in Forest Park. (☎ 361-1900; www.muny.com. Box office open June to mid-Aug. daily 9am-9pm. Tickets $8-58.) Other companies include the **St. Louis Black Repertory,** 634 N. Grand Blvd., Ste. 10F (☎ 534-3807; tickets $10-37) and the **Repertory Theatre of St. Louis,** 130 Edgar Rd.

THE HIDDEN DEAL

HOW SWEET THE SOUND

The St. Louis Symphony Orchestra (SLSO) rang in its 125th season on something of a sour note, with a contract dispute that left Powell Hall silent for 8 weeks during January and February 2005. Yet with a new contract in place and a new music director picking up the baton, the symphony is poised to continue its tradition of musical excellence. Music Director David Robinson is an enthusiastic proponent of 20th-and 21st-century orchestral works, and the SLSO's 2005-2006 season includes contemporary names like John Adams and George Benjamin as well as Brahms, Mahler, and Schumann.

Tickets for these concerts are priced as high as $105, but thanks to the SLSO's "50 Free" promotion, you can spend an evening at the symphony without paying a dime. Starting 90min. before every performance (except the Friday morning Coffee Concerts), the Powell Hall Symphony Box Office hands out 50 free tickets to thrifty music buffs who have gathered in the lobby. You'll need to fill out a membership card and present a photo ID, and there is a limit of 6 free tickets per patron per season. While lines do form by 6pm for some of the season's higher-profile concerts, there are plenty of other nights when tickets go unclaimed.

For more info, visit www.slso.org. or call ☎314-533-2500.

(☎968-4925), on the campus of Webster University. The **Fox Theatre,** 527 N. Grand Blvd., was an opulent "Temple to the Motion Picture" during the 1930s and is now at the heart of the Grand Center renaissance with its rock concerts and Broadway musicals. (☎534-1111; www.fabulousfox.com. Box office open M-Sa 10am-6pm, Su noon-4pm. Tours Tu, Th, Sa 10:30am. Tu $5, Th and Sa $8; under 12 $3.)

St. Louis ordinances permit gambling on the river for those over 21. The **President Casino on the Admiral** floats below the Arch on the Missouri side. (☎622-1111 or 800-772-3647; www.presidentcasino.com/stlouis. Open M-Th 8am-4am, F-Su 24hr. Entry tax $2.) On the Illinois side, the **Casino Queen** claims "the loosest slots in the Midwest." (☎800-777-0777; www.casinoqueen.com. Open daily 9am-7am.) Parking for both is free, and both are wheelchair accessible. **Six Flags St. Louis,** 30min. southwest of St. Louis on I-44 at Exit 261, rattles teeth with the mighty "Boss" wooden coaster and spins swimmers around a 60 ft. funnel at Hurricane Harbor Water Park. (☎636-938-4800; www.sixflags.com/stlouis. Open June to early Aug. M-F and Sa 10am-9pm, Su 10am-10pm; reduced hours Apr.-May and Sept.-Oct. $42, seniors and children under 48 in. $26.) The beloved **Cardinals** play baseball at **Busch Stadium.** (☎421-2400. Tickets $16-55.) Football's **Rams** hit the gridiron at the **Edward Jones Dome.** (☎425-8830. Tickets $44-85.) The **Blues** can cheer up as hockey returns to the **Savvis Center** at 14th St. and Clark Ave. (☎622-2500. Tickets $15-125.)

⚑ NIGHTLIFE

The *Riverfront Times* (free at many bars and clubs) and the "Get Out" section of the *Post-Dispatch* list weekly entertainment. On the riverfront, north of the Arch, **Laclede's Landing** gathers a string of bars and music venues into a pedestrian-friendly complex of historic buildings. Across the river, the wild and woolly dance clubs of **East St. Louis** stay open as late as 6am, while gay nightlife back on the Missouri side tends to cluster around **Manchester Road,** southeast of Forest Park.

▨ **Pin-Up Bowl,** 6191 Delmar Blvd. (☎727-5555; www.pinupbowl.com). Knock down pins while knocking back a cocktail ($7-8). 8 lanes available by the game ($3.50-5) or by the hour ($30-50). Shoes $3. 21+ after 9pm. Open M-Th 3pm-3am, F-Su noon-3am.

Way Out Club, 2525 S. Jefferson Ave. (☎664-7638; www.wayoutclub-stl.com), combines a laid-back bar for the hipster set and a performance space where local rock bands take the stage under the watchful eye of an imposing Jolly Green Giant statue. Cover for shows $3-6. 21+. Open M-Sa 8pm-1:30am.

The Complex, 3515 Chouteau Ave. (☎772-2645). Don't be put off by the dark, deserted area facing the street; circle around back to get into this popular gay club, featuring drag shows, a weekend martini lounge, and a huge Saturday turnout that includes many straight partygoers. Cover Tu and F-Su $5. 21+. Open Tu-Su 10pm-3am.

Absolutli Goosed, 3196 S. Grand Blvd. (☎772-0400), is the city's premier martini bar, serving up over 120 double-shot variations of the classic cocktail. Open W-Th and Su 4pm-midnight, F 4pm-1am, Sa 5pm-1am.

The Pageant, 6161 Delmar Blvd. (☎726-6161; www.thepageant.com). This Loop concert venue reels in national acts on the order of Elvis Costello and Bonnie Raitt, although tickets to the occasional new music showcase run just $5. Many shows are all-ages, but check website for ticket prices and 21+ restrictions. Doors usually open 7pm. The swanky **Halo Bar** (☎726-1414) is open daily 7pm-3am, but cracks its doors at 5pm on show nights and brings in DJs to spin F-Su nights.

HANNIBAL ☎573

Mark Twain's boyhood home sits on the Mississippi River, 100 mi. west of Springfield, Illinois, and 100 mi. northwest of St. Louis. Hannibal slept in obscurity until Twain (born Samuel Clemens) used it as the setting of *The Adventures of Tom Sawyer.* Tourists now flock to this small town to imagine Tom, Huck, and Becky romping around its old-fashioned streets. While this outpouring of interest has left many locals scratching their heads at the fuss, the friendly spirit of small-town Missouri still lingers in Hannibal amid the chain motels and souvenir shops.

The properties of the **Mark Twain Boyhood Home and Museum** line the northern half of Hannibal's Main St., with a recently completed **interpretive center,** 208 Hill St., selling tickets and presenting an illustrated timeline of the witty wordsmith's life. Glass dividers prevent visitors from getting close to the period furnishings in the cozy Clemens home, though the patent medicine bottles and draconian tooth hooks in **Grant's Drug Store** recall some of Tom Sawyer's most infamous run-ins with well-meaning adults. Farther down Main St., the **New Mark Twain Museum** features 15 illustrations done by Norman Rockwell for a reissue of Twain's classic novels. (☎221-9010; www.marktwainmuseum.org. Open June-Aug. daily 8am-6pm; Apr. and Sept.-Oct. daily 9am-5pm; May daily 8am-5pm; Nov.-Feb. M-Sa 10am-4pm, Su noon-4pm; Mar. M-Sa 9am-4pm, Su noon-4pm. Single ticket covers all sights; $8, seniors $6.50, ages 6-12 $3, under 5 free.) On the riverfront landing, the **Mark Twain Riverboat** steams down the Mississippi for a 1hr. sightseeing cruise that is part history, part folklore, and part advertisement for the land attractions. (☎221-3222; www.marktwainriverboat.com. Late May to early Sept. 3 per day; May and Sept.-Oct. 1 per day. $10, ages 5-12 $7.) The **Mark Twain Cave,** 1 mi. south of Hannibal on Rte. 79, winds through the complex series of caverns Twain explored as a boy. A 1hr. tour guides visitors to the author's favorite spots and details the myths and legends associated with the cave. Graffiti from as early as the 1830s, including Jesse James's signature, marks the walls. The cave tour includes the only section of the cave christened by Twain: **Aladdin's Castle,** the spot where Tom and Becky were "married." (☎221-1656; www.marktwaincave.com. Open June-Aug. daily 8am-8pm; Apr.-May and Sept.-Oct. daily 9am-6pm; Nov.-Mar. M-F 9am-4pm. $12, ages 5-12 $6.) Every 4th of July weekend, 100,000 fans converge on Hannibal for the fence-painting, frog-jumping fun of the **Tom Sawyer Days** festival.

Away from the river, Hannibal's historic district is dotted with beautiful 19th-century homes. The **Gilded Age Bed & Breakfast ❸**, 215 N. 6th St., is an 1871 mansion built by one of Twain's close friends and the site of an exorcism. A restored cupola offers riverfront views, but the home isn't haunted—at least not anymore. (☎248-1218; www.thegildedage.net. All rooms with A/C and private bath. Call ahead for reservations. Rooms $60-98. MC/V.) Wander down to the waterfront for an alligator sausage lunch basket ($6.75) at **Bubba's ❷**, 101 Church St., or stick around for dinner and devour a whole catfish ($10) rubbed with spicy seasonings. (☎221-5552. M-Sa 11am-9pm, Su 11am-3pm. D/MC/V.) The old-fashioned phosphates ($1.50) at **Main Street Soda Fountain ❶**, 207 S. Main St., are as tart and refreshing as they were back when the fountain was installed in 1906; hand-dipped ice cream cones ($1.50) are another good way to cool down on a summer afternoon. (☎248-1295. Open Tu-Su 11am-5pm. Cash only.)

The **Hannibal Convention and Visitors Bureau,** 505 N. 3rd St., offers free local calls and information. (☎221-2477; www.visithannibal.com. Open M-F 8am-6pm, Sa 9am-6pm, Su 9am-5pm.) **Post Office:** 801 Broadway. (☎221-0957. Open M-F 8:45am-4:45pm, Sa 9am-noon.) **Postal Code:** 63401. **Area Code:** 573.

KANSAS CITY   ☎816

With more miles of boulevard than Paris and more working fountains than Rome, Kansas City looks and acts more European than one might expect from the "Barbecue Capital of the World." Nonetheless, it maintains its big bad blues-and-jazz reputation in a city spanning two states: the highly suburbanized town in Kansas (KCKS) and the quicker-paced commercial metropolis in Missouri (KCMO).

⌐ TRANSPORTATION

Airport: Kansas City International (☎243-5237; www.flykci.com), 18 mi. northwest of KC off I-29. Take bus #129. **KCI Shuttle** (☎243-5000 or 800-243-6383) connects to downtown ($15) and Westport, Crown Center, and the Plaza ($16) in KCMO every 30min., and to Overland Park, Mission, and Lenexa in KCKS (up to $45) on demand. Operates daily 3:30am-midnight. Taxi to downtown $35.

Trains: Amtrak, 30 W. Pershing Rd. (☎421-3622; www.amtrak.com), in the newly renovated Union Station. Take bus #27. Open daily 6:30am-midnight. To **Chicago** (7-12hr., 2 per day, $38-100) and **St. Louis** (5-6hr., 2 per day, $25-58).

Buses: Greyhound, 1101 N. Troost St. (☎221-2835; www.greyhound.com). Use caution in this area at night. Open in summer 24hr.; in winter daily 5:30am-midnight. To **Chicago** (10-12hr., 7-8 per day, $57-61) and **St. Louis** (5hr., 6-7 per day, $35-38).

Public Transit: Kansas City Area Transportation Authority (Metro), 1200 E. 18th St. (☎221-0660; www.kcata.org), near Troost St. Most buses run 4:30am-midnight, though some have more limited schedules. $1, seniors and disabled $0.50; free transfers. $1.20 to Independence, MO.

Taxi: Yellow Cab, ☎471-5000.

✦ ❼ ORIENTATION AND PRACTICAL INFORMATION

The Kansas City metropolitan area is split between two states, Kansas and Missouri, and sprawls interminably, making travel difficult without a car. The Kansas side is almost entirely suburban; most sights worth visiting lie south or west of downtown on the Missouri side. All listings are for KCMO, unless otherwise indicated. **I-70** cuts east-west through the city, and **I-435** circles the two-state metro

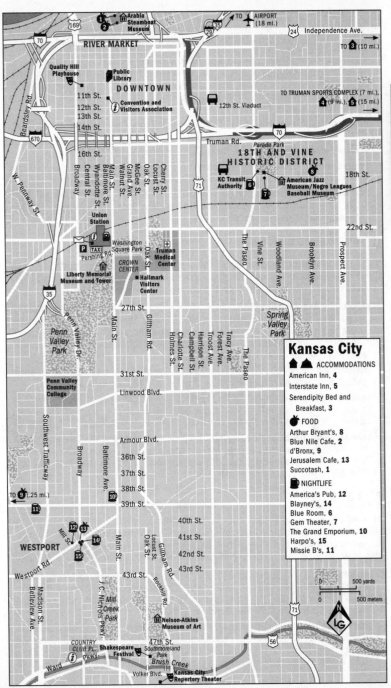

TO AIRPORT (18 mi.)

Independence Ave.

TO 3 (10 mi.)

169

70

RIVER MARKET

Quality Hill Playhouse

Public Library

DOWNTOWN

11th St.

Convention and Visitors Association

12th St. Viaduct

TO TRUMAN SPORTS COMPLEX (7 mi.),
4 (9 mi.) & 5 (15 mi.)

12th St.

13th St.

14th St.

Truman Rd.

Parade Park

70

16th St.

18TH AND VINE
HISTORIC DISTRICT

18th St.

KC Transit Authority 6

American Jazz Museum/Negro Leagues Baseball Museum

8

7

Main St.
Baltimore St.
Grand Ave.
Walnut St.

McGee St.
Locust St.

Cherry St.
Oak St.

71

22nd St.

Union Station

Washington Square Park

TAXI

Pershing Rd.

CROWN CENTER

Oak St.

Truman Medical Center

The Paseo

Vine St.

Woodland Ave.

Brooklyn Ave.

Prospect Ave.

Liberty Memorial Museum and Tower

35

Hallmark Visitors Center

27th St.

Spring Valley Park

Penn Valley Park

Gilham Rd.

Charlotte St.
Holmes St.

Campbell St.

Harrison St.

Troost Ave.
Forest Ave.
Tracy Ave.

The Paseo

Penn Valley Community College

31st St.

Linwood Blvd.

Main St.

Penn Valley Dr.

Broadway

Southwest Trafficway

Armour Blvd.

36th St.

37th St.

Baltimore Ave.

38th St.

39th St.

Locust St.
Oak St.

Gilham Rd.

40th St.

41st St.

42nd St.

43rd St.

TO 9 (.25 mi.)

11

12 13

14

WESTPORT

15

Mill St.

Westport Rd.

Madison St.
Belleview Ave.

Main St.

J.C. Nichols Pkwy.

Mill Creek Park

43rd St.

Rockhill Rd.

Nelson-Atkins Museum of Art

COUNTRY CLUB PL.

Shakespeare Festival

Ward Pkwy.

47th St.

Southmoreland Park

Brush Creek

Volker Blvd.

Kansas City Repertory Theater

56

0   500 yards
0   500 meters

N

Kansas City

⌂⌂ ACCOMMODATIONS

American Inn, 4
Interstate Inn, 5
Serendipity Bed and
  Breakfast, 3

🍅 FOOD

Arthur Bryant's, 8
Blue Nile Cafe, 2
d'Bronx, 9
Jerusalem Cafe, 13
Succotash, 1

▮ NIGHTLIFE

America's Pub, 12
Blayney's, 14
Blue Room, 6
Gem Theater, 7
The Grand Emporium, 10
Harpo's, 15
Missie B's, 11

Arabia Steamboat Museum

1

2

24

area. KCMO is laid out on a grid with numbered streets running east-west from the Missouri River well out into suburbs, and named streets running north-south. **Main Street** divides the city east-west. Metered parking is limited downtown.

Visitor Info: Convention and Visitors Association of Greater Kansas City, 1100 Main St., at 11th St. (☎221-5242 or 800-767-7700; www.visitkc.com), 22nd fl. of City Center Sq. Bldg. Open M-F 8:30am-5pm. Other locations at Country Club Plaza (☎691-3866; open M-Sa 10am-6pm, Su 11am-5pm) and Union Station (☎460-0220; open M-Sa 10am-10pm, Su noon-5pm).

Hotlines: Rape Crisis Line, ☎531-0233. **Synergy House Crisis Hotline,** ☎741-8700. Both 24hr.

Medical Services: Truman Medical Center, 2301 Holmes St. (☎404-1000).

Internet Access: Kansas City Public Library, 14 W. 10th St. (☎701-3400). 4hr. max. per day. Open M-W 9am-9pm, Th-F 9am-6pm, Sa 10am-5pm, Su 1-5pm.

Post Office: 30 W. Pershing Rd. (☎374-9101), inside Union Station. Open M-F 7am-7pm, Sa 8:30am-3:30pm. **Postal Code:** 64108. **Area Code:** 816 in Missouri, 913 in Kansas; in text 816 unless noted otherwise.

ACCOMMODATIONS

Accommodations in and around downtown KCMO tend to be overpriced—even the most meager motel room costs upwards of $60. To sleep for cheap, head 10-20 mi. east on I-70. The further you go, the cheaper the lodgings will be.

Serendipity Bed and Breakfast, 116 S. Pleasant St. (☎833-4719 or 800-203-4299), 10 mi. west of KCMO in Independence, MO. A 3-story 1887 brick home and carriage house within walking distance from downtown Independence. Music, bowls of candy, and Victorian-era novelties such as 19th-century Sears catalogues and stereoscopes fill each room. Rooms $45-70. D/MC/V. ❸

Interstate Inn (☎229-6311), off I-70 at Exit 18. Far from downtown, but the cheapest decent motel around. Singles from $29; doubles from $34. AmEx/D/MC/V. ❷

American Inn, 4141 S. Noland Rd. (☎373-8300), in Independence at Exit 12 off I-70, is a step up in the budget hotel food chain. Buildings in patriotic hues feature pleasant rooms with A/C and cable TV. Several pools. Singles from $40. AmEx/D/DC/MC/V. ❷

Lake Jacomo Campground (☎795-8200), 22 mi. southeast of KCMO. Take I-470 south to Colbern, then head east for 2 mi. Lots of water activities, 33 forested campsites, and a marina. Open year-round. Sites $10, with electricity $15, with water and electricity $18, full hookup $22. Cash only. ❶

FOOD

Although Kansas City is best known for its ubiquitous barbecue and unusually tangy ribs, there are a variety of dining options. The **Westport** area is home to eclectic restaurants and hip coffeehouses. Expensive chains have sprung up in **Country Club Plaza**, while ethnic fare can be found on **39th Street**, just east of the state line.

Succotash, 15 E. 3rd St. (☎421-2807), in the City Market building. Easter-egg-colored walls and highly creative food, with dishes like pear pecan pancakes with bacon ($6.50) and a cheddar, tart apple, and caramelized onion sandwich ($6). Open Tu-F 9am-2pm, Sa 8am-3pm, Su 9am-3pm. AmEx/MC/V. ❷

Blue Nile Cafe, 20 E. 5th St. (☎283-0990), in the City Market building. Delicious Ethiopian food. Intensely flavorful meat and vegetarian curries and stews ($8-13) eaten with spongy *injera* bread instead of utensils. Lunch special $6. Open M-Tu 11am-2:30pm, W-Th 11am-2:30pm and 5-8pm, F-Sa 11am-2:30 pm and 5-9pm. AmEx/DC/MC/V. ❸

Rheinland Restaurant, 208 N. Main St. (☎461-5383), in Independence. Authentic-tasting German goodies served by authentic-sounding waitresses. While dinner can be pricey, lunch prices are more reasonable. Sandwiches and wurst $7-9. Hefty pints $3.25. Open M and Su 11am-2:30pm, Tu-Sa 11am-9pm. ❷

Arthur Bryant's, 1727 Brooklyn Ave. (☎231-1123), 6 blocks east of 18th and Vine. Take the Brooklyn Exit off I-70 or bus #110 from downtown. The grand-daddy of KC barbecue and a perennial candidate for America's best barbecue. Bryant's "sandwiches" are a carnivore's delight—wimpy triangles of bread drowning in meaty perfection ($8). Open M-Th 10am-9:30pm, F-Sa 10am-10pm, Su 11am-8pm. AmEx/D/DC/MC/V. ❷

d'Bronx, 3904 Bell St. (☎531-0550), on the 39th St. restaurant row. A New York deli transplanted to Middle America, d'Bronx has over 35 kinds of subs (6 in. sub $4-6). Open M-W 10:30am-9pm, Th 10:30am-10pm, F-Sa 10:30am-11pm. AmEx/D/MC/V. ❷

Jerusalem Cafe, 431 Westport Rd. (☎756-2770). This casual, brick-walled Middle Eastern hangout is a great refuge for vegetarians in a bovine-centric city. Sandwiches $6-7. Kebabs $8-11. Open M-Sa 11am-10pm, Su noon-8pm. AmEx/D/DC/MC/V. ❷

◉ SIGHTS

18TH AND VINE. Jazz and blues once emanated from this neighborhood all night long. Today, the **18th and Vine Historic District,** still in the heart of KCMO's African-American community, offers a slightly more refined take on yesteryear with gussied-up buildings, museums, and performance venues (see **Nightlife,** p. 636). The ◩**Negro Leagues Baseball Museum** uses photographs, interactive exhibits, and thoughtful nostalgia to recall the era when African-Americans played a whole different ballgame. In the same building, the **American Jazz Museum** brings back the era with tributes to jazz greats and tons of memorabilia, like Louis Armstrong's lip salve. (1616 E. 18th St. Take bus #108 "Indiana." Baseball Museum: ☎221-1920; www.nlbm.com. Jazz Museum: ☎474-8463; www.americanjazzmuseum.com. Both open Tu-Sa 9am-6pm, Su noon-6pm. One museum $6, under 12 $2.50; both museums $8/$4.)

RIVER MARKET. Just south of the Missouri River, the Freeway separates downtown's monuments to capitalism from the city's hippest new neighborhood, where old brick warehouses are being converted into coffee shops, art studios, and loft units at an alarming rate. The neighborhood takes its name from the thrice-weekly farmers market, **City Market,** at 5th and Walnut St. (☎842-1271. W 9am-1pm, Sa 6:30am-2pm, Su 9am-3pm.) The area also offers plenty of opportunities for pleasant strolling and jogging via the paths along the Missouri River. Just next to City Market, the ◩**Arabia Steamboat Museum** is as unique as the treasures it houses. When the steamboat *Arabia* sank in 1854, its holds were full of commercial goods. When the Missouri River shifted a century later, excavations revealed that those goods had been perfectly preserved by layers of cold mud. Today, visitors can peek at a wealth of 19th-century treasures, and can take a behind-the-scenes look at the restoration process in working labs. (400 Grand Blvd. ☎471-1856; www.1856.com. Open M-Sa 10am-5pm, Su noon-5pm. $9.75, seniors $9.25, ages 4-12 $4.75.)

UNION STATION AND CROWN CENTER. The city likes to boast of its fountains and boulevards. The Bloch Fountain in front of ◩**Union Station,** 30 W. Pershing Rd., is one of the finest. This magnificent 1914 building, renovated in 1999 and now home to restaurants, shops, and a science museum in addition to Amtrak, is the largest train station in North America outside of New York. (Open daily 6am-midnight.) It is linked by a skywalk to **Crown Center,** 2405 Grand Ave., an upscale shopping center. Accessible from Hall's Department Store on the third floor of Crown Center is the **Hallmark Visitors Center,** where extensive family-friendly exhibits chronicle the history, design, and manufacturing process behind the famous greeting cards. (☎ *274-3613; www.hallmarkvisitorscenter.com. Open Tu-F 9am-5pm, Sa 9:30am-4:30pm. Free.)* Across from Union Station, the grassy slopes of **Penn Valley Park** rise to meet the base of the 217 ft. **Memorial Tower.** The tower is part of the **Liberty Memorial Museum,** 100 W. 26th St., the nation's only museum dedicated to World War I. All five allied commanders met together for the only time at the memorial's dedication in 1921. The museum is currently undergoing extensive renovations, but will re-open in fall 2006. *(☎ 784-1918. Call for hours and more information.)*

THE PLAZA. The most "European-influenced" section of Kansas City is undoubtedly **Country Club Plaza,** known as "the Plaza," the oldest and perhaps most picturesque shopping center in the US. Modeled after buildings in Sevilla, Spain, the Plaza boasts fountains, sculptures, hand-painted tiles, grinning gargoyles, luxury chain stores, and latte-sipping yuppies. The Plaza is also famous for its Christmas lights, lit annually on Thanksgiving Eve. *(4745 Central St. Take bus #39, 51, 56, 57, or 155. Plaza Customer Service Center: ☎ 753-0100. Free outdoor concerts June-Aug. Th 5pm-8pm, F-Sa 2pm-5pm.)* Three long blocks northeast of the Plaza, the world-class **Nelson-Atkins Museum of Art,** 4525 Oak St., contains one of the best East Asian art collections in the world, as well as European and American art from the Medieval to the Postmodern periods. The handsome grounds include a sculpture garden with 13 pieces by Henry Moore. The museum is under renovation until 2007; much of the museum is open, but call ahead to confirm which exhibits are open. *(Take bus #147, 155, 156, or 157. ☎ 561-4000; www.nelson-atkins.org. Open Tu-Th 10am-4pm, F 10am-9pm, Sa 10am-5pm, Su noon-5pm. Live jazz in the museum's Rozzelle Court Restaurant F 5:30-8:30pm. Suggested donation $5, seniors and students $4, under 18 $3. Admission is free during construction, except for special exhibits.)*

🎭 ENTERTAINMENT

From September to June, the **Kansas City Repertory Theatre,** 4949 Cherry St., southeast of the Plaza, stages classics ranging from Gilbert & Sullivan to Tennessee Williams. (☎ 235-2700; www.kcrep.org. Box office open M-F 10am-5pm. Tickets $22-45, students with ID $14-18; seniors $3 off.) **Quality Hill Playhouse,** 303 W. 10th St. downtown, produces off-Broadway plays and revues from September to June. (☎ 421-1700. Tickets available by phone or at the theater 1hr. before showtime. $23, students and seniors $21.) From late June to mid-July, the **Heart of America Shakespeare Festival** puts on free outdoor productions in Southmoreland Park at 47th and Oak St. (☎ 531-7728; www.kcshakes.org. Most nights 8pm.) Sports fans stampede to I-70 and Blue Ridge Cutoff (Exits 8-9), where the **Harry S. Truman Sports Complex** houses every professional team in the city. Inside the complex, **Arrowhead Stadium** is home to football's **Chiefs** (☎ 920-9400 or 800-676-5488; tickets $59-80) and soccer's **Wizards** (☎ 920-9300; tickets $14-23). Next door, the water-fountained **Kauffman Stadium** houses baseball's **Royals.** (☎ 921-8000 or 800-676-9257. Tickets $5-27. A stadium express bus runs from downtown and Country Club Plaza on game days for $5. Call ☎ 346-0348 for details.)

🎷 NIGHTLIFE

In the 1920s, jazz musician Count Basie and his "Kansas City Sound" reigned at the River City bars. Twenty years later, saxophonist Charlie "Bird" Parker took jazz in a new direction as he cultivated the sound of "bop," the forerunner to modern jazz. Today, the **Blue Room,** 1600 E. 18th St., connected to the American Jazz Museum (p. 635), continues KC's jazz tradition four nights a week with some of the smoothest acts in town. (☎ 474-2929. Cover F-Sa from $5. Bar open M 5pm-midnight, Th-F

5pm-1am, Sa 7pm-1am.) Across the street, the restored Art Deco **Gem Theater,** 1615 E. 18th St., stages top-tier regional and national blues and jazz acts. (☎474-6262. Tickets and info in the American Jazz Museum across the street.)

Harpo's, 4109 Pennsylvania Ave. (☎753-3434). A cornerstone of Westport's young nightlife. $0.25 beer on Tu attracts collegiates and other budget-conscious revelers to this woodwork-laden bar. Live music Sa. Cover Tu and Sa $3. Open daily 11am-3am.

The Grand Emporium, 3832 Main St. (☎531-1504), hosts live music from reggae to blues several nights a week. Order an obscure liquor so the bartender has to climb the ladder up the 20 ft. shelves. Cover and hours vary depending on act; call for details.

Blayney's, 415 Westport Rd. (☎561-3747). The Irish tavern upstairs is decent, but the earthy "blues cavern" downstairs is where the real action is. Try to make your own sense out of the bar's primary decoration: bras. Live music M-Sa: M Americana (folk/country/rockabilly) Tu-Sa blues. Cover $2-6. 21+. Open M-Sa 5pm-3am.

Missie B's, 805 W. 39th St. (☎561-0625). 2-story gay bar with DJs, dance floors, and drag shows M, W, F-Sa 11pm-2am. Cover F $3, Sa $5. 21+. Open M-Sa noon-3am.

America's Pub, 510 Westport Rd. (☎531-1313). A dark, popular Westport spot with a sunken dance floor, video screens, quieter spots to chill or play pool, and a young, lively crowd. Th $1 drinks. Cover $6. 21+. Open W-Sa 8pm-3am.

◤ DAYTRIP FROM KANSAS CITY

INDEPENDENCE, MO
Independence is 10 mi. east of Kansas City, off of U.S. 24. The Park Service runs a visitors center at Main and Truman St. (☎816-254-9929. Open daily 8:30am-5pm.)

The small town of Independence was once the last outpost of civilization for western-bound pioneers and (much later) the home of US President Harry S. Truman. Now enveloped by the sprawl of greater Kansas City, Independence still maintains an historic, small-town feel. The painstakingly preserved interior of the **Harry S. Truman Home,** 219 N. Delaware St., is furnished with artifacts from the family's elegant but unpretentious lifestyle. (☎254-9929. Purchase tickets at the visitors center, 5 blocks west in the square on Truman Rd. Tours M 9am-4:45pm, Tu-Su 8:30am-5pm; Sept.-May closed M. $4, ages 16 and under free.) The visitors center also has free maps of the **Truman Historic Walking Trail.** Among the 43 stops are the **Jackson County Courthouse,** 112 W. Lexington St., where Truman began his political life as a county judge, and **Clinton's Soda Fountain & Coffee Shop,** 100 W. Maple St., where he earned pocket change by sweeping floors. The candid ◧**Truman Presidential Museum and Library,** 500 W. Hwy. 24, recounts the life and administration of the man who became president just 82 days after taking the oath of office for the vice presidency. Exhibits focus on the Truman administration's often-controversial decisions, such as the bombing of Japan, and invite visitors to add their own opinions in interactive displays. (☎800-833-1225. Open M-W and F-Sa 9am-5pm, Th 9am-9pm, Su noon-5pm. $7, seniors $5, ages 6-10 $3.) Anyone who ever tried to get their oxen to ford the river in the computer game "The Oregon Trail" will appreciate the **National Frontier Trails Center,** 318 W. Pacific St., which lets visitors "follow" each of the three routes taken by wagon trains embarking from Independence: the Santa Fe Trail, the California Trail, and of course, the Oregon Trail. Interactive exhibits simulate the critical decisions facing pioneers along the way. (☎325-7575; www.frontiertrailscenter.org. Open M-Sa 9am-4:30pm, Su 12:30-4:30pm. $4, seniors $3.50, students 6-17 $2.50, under 5 free.)

BRANSON ☎417

Back in 1967, the Presley family had no idea the impact the tiny theater they opened on **West Route 76** would have. Now, over 30 years later, millions of tourists clog Branson's strip to visit the "live music show capital of the world." Billboards, motels, and giant showplaces call the masses to embrace all things plastic, franchised, and "wholesome." Branson boasts over 30 indoor theaters and a few outdoor ones as well, housing family variety shows, magic acts, comedians, plays, and music. Box office prices for most shows run $20-50, depending on who's playing. Never pay full price for a show or attraction in Branson—coupon books, including the *Sunny Day Guide* and the *Best Read Guide*, offer dozens of discounts.

To see a live battle between the North and the South, head to Dolly Parton's **Dixie Stampede,** 1525 W. Hwy. 76, where a friendly competition between Yankees and Rebs is staged on the backs of ostriches, horses, and other animals that lend themselves to trick riding. Ticket prices include a four-course "feast." (☎800-520-5101. Shows daily 5:30, also 8pm in Aug. and some weekends. $38, ages 4-11 $20. AAA discounts available.) Big-name country acts, such as Loretta Lynn and Billy Ray Cyrus, play the **Grand Palace,** 2700 W. Rte. 76. (☎334-7263 or 800-572-5223. Tickets vary by performance; call ahead for more info.) One of Branson's more unique shows is **The Shepherd of the Hills,** 5586 Rte. 76 W, an outdoor drama/dinner that tells the story of a preacher stranded in the Ozark mountains and his growing relationship with the people of the area. (☎334-4191 or 800-653-6288. Shows May Tu-W and F-Sa, June-Aug. M-Sa. Tickets $28, seniors $26, ages 4-16 $13.)

Motels along Rte. 76 generally start around $25, but prices often increase from July to September. Less tacky motels line Rte. 265, 4 mi. west of the strip, and Gretna Rd. at the west end of the strip. **Budget Inn ❶,** 325 N. Gretna Rd., has slightly dim but spacious rooms close to the action. (☎334-0292. A/C, free local calls, cable TV, and pool access. Rooms $29-48.) For a more colorful option, **JR's Motor Inn ❷,** 1944 W. 76 Country Blvd., has an on-site coffeeshop, free continental breakfast, and pool. (☎800-837-8531. Rates from $48-59.) For affordable eats, head downtown to the **Branson Cafe ❶,** 120 Main St. Burger and fries are only $4.45, and breakfast and lunch will set you back about $6. (☎334-3021. Open M-Sa 6am-8:00pm, Su 7am-3pm.) **Uncle Joe's Barbeque ❷,** 2819 W. Rte. 76, next to **Uncle Joe's Jazz,** serves barbecue sandwiches for $6 and tenderloin for $7. (☎334-4548. Jazz nightly in lounge. Open M-Su 11am-10pm. Lounge open Tu-Sa 5pm-1am.)

Branson is impossible without a car, but infuriating with one. Especially on weekends, endless traffic jams clog Hwy. 76, the two-lane road that runs by all the attractions in town. Avoid Branson at peak tourist times, like Saturday nights. **Gray Line Shuttle,** (☎339-2550), picks up from the Springfield airport and drops off in Branson area hotels. (Call to reserve. $36, 2-person minimum.) Branson's low-season runs from January to March, when many attractions close. Beware of fake "tourist information centers"—they are trying to sell you something. The real info center is the **Branson Chamber of Commerce and Convention and Visitors Bureau Welcome Center,** 269 Rte. 248, west of the Rte. 248/65 junction. (☎800-961-1221; www.explorebranson.com. Open M-Sa 8am-5pm, Su 10am-4pm; in summer M-Sa 8am-6pm.) **Area Code:** 417.

OKLAHOMA

An anomaly on the national map, the area that would become the state of Oklahoma was set aside well into the 19th century as "Indian Territory," a mixing pot where captured and subdued tribes from all over America were sent. But by the

1880s the frontier was considered closed and eager white settlers, known as "Sooners," saw Oklahoma as their last shot at free land. Today, Oklahoma is still home to the highest concentration of Native Americans in the country, though tribal names are more often associated with casinos and turnpikes than with anything else. Still, the state has plenty of culture and history, both cowboy and Native American, to go around.

◪ PRACTICAL INFORMATION

Capital: Oklahoma City.

Visitor Info: Oklahoma Tourism and Recreation Department, 120 N. Robinson Ave., 6th fl., Oklahoma City 73152 (☎230-8400 or 800-652-6552; www.travelok.com). Open M-F 8am-5pm.

Postal Abbreviation: OK. **Sales Tax:** 4.5%. **Tolls:** Oklahoma is fond of toll booths, so keep a wad of bills (and a roll of coins for unattended booths) handy.

TULSA   ☎918

First settled by Creek Native Americans arriving on the Trail of Tears, Tulsa's location on the Arkansas River made it a logical trading outpost. Contemporary Tulsa's Art Deco skyscrapers, French villas, Georgian mansions, and substantial Native American population reflect the varied heritage of the city locals call "T-Town."

▐▗ ◪ ORIENTATION AND PRACTICAL INFORMATION. Tulsa is divided into 1 sq. mi. quadrants. **Main Street** (north-south) and **Admiral Boulevard** (east-west) intersect downtown. Numbered streets run parallel to Admiral Blvd. Named streets run north-south in alphabetical order; those named after western cities are west of Main St., while eastern cities are east. **Tulsa International Airport** (☎838-5000; www.tulsaairports.com), just northeast of downtown, is accessible by I-244 or U.S. 169. A taxi to downtown costs $19. **Greyhound,** 317 S. Detroit Ave. (☎584-4428; www.greyhound.com; open 24hr.), goes to Dallas (6-7hr., 6 per day, $53), Oklahoma City (2hr., 6 per day, $21), and St. Louis (7-9hr., 5 per day, $76). **Metropolitan Tulsa Transit Authority,** 510 S. Rockford Ave., runs local buses. (☎582-2100. Buses start 5am-7am and finish 5:30pm-7:30pm; infrequent night service until 12:30am. $1.25, seniors and disabled $0.60, under 5 and 74+ free.) **Taxi: Yellow Checker Cab,** ☎582-6161. **Visitor Info: Tulsa Convention and Visitors Bureau,** Williams Center Tower Two, 2 W. 2nd St., #150. (☎585-1201 or 800-558-3311; www.visittulsa.com. Open M-F 8am-5pm.) **Medical Services: Hillcrest Medical Center,** 1120 S. Utica Ave. (☎579-1000). **Hotlines: Rape Crisis Hotline,** ☎744-7273. **Internet Access: Tulsa Public Library,** 400 Civic Center, at 4th and Denver. (☎596-7977. Open June-Aug. M-Th 9am-9pm, F-Sa 9am-5pm; Sept.-May. also Su 1-5pm. 90min. limit.) **Post Office:** 333 W. 4th St. (☎732-6651. Open M-F 7:30am-5pm.) **Postal Code:** 74103. **Area Code:** 918.

▐▗ ◖ ACCOMMODATIONS AND FOOD. Budget accommodations in Tulsa consist of freeway-side motels, with several near Exits 222C and 232 off I-44. **Georgetown Plaza Motel ❶,** 8502 E. 27th St., on the north side of I-44 right off Exit 232, has clean rooms, reasonable rates, and Georgian architecture. (☎622-6616. Rooms $26-35. AmEx/MC/V.) The **Gateway Motor Hotel ❷,** 5600 W. Skelly Dr., at Exit 222C, has standard rooms, plus DVD players and free Wi-Fi. (☎446-6611. Singles $29-37; additional person $4. AmEx/D/DC/MC/V.) Oklahoma institution **Cici's Pizza ❶,** 4949 S. Peoria St., just north of I-44, is an amazing deal: all-you-can-eat pizza, salad, and pasta for only $3.99. (☎744-8338. Open M-Th and Su 10am-10pm, F-Sa 10am-11pm. MC/V.) Located in a converted Art Deco movie theater, **The Brook Restaurant**

❷, 3401 S. Peoria, is a hip and sophisticated watering hole, with plenty of healthy options among the chicken and burgers, as well as martinis for $5-7. (☎748-9977. Open M-Sa 11am-1am, Su 11am-11pm. AmEx/D/MC/V.) Catering to the business crowd, the **Atlas Grill** ❶, 415 S. Boston Ave., in the historic Atlas Life Building, has daily specials like shrimp & mango soft tacos ($4.50-6) and creative sandwiches. (☎583-3111. Sandwiches $6. Open M-F 7am-3pm. AmEx/D/DC/MC/V.)

🆂 **SIGHTS.** In 1964, televangelist Oral Roberts dreamt that God commanded him to build a university. Today, 🔳**Oral Roberts University,** 7777 S. Lewis Ave., 6 mi. south of downtown, boasts one of the most whimsical, modern campuses in the country, abounding with unusual colors and forms, as well as the world's largest bronze statue—a pair of 60 ft. high praying hands. The **visitors center,** in the Prayer Tower, has superb views, an orientation video, and self-guided tours. (☎495-6807; www.oru.edu. Open Tu-Sa 10am-3:30pm, Su 1-3:30pm.) From its vantage point in the Osage foothills, 2 mi. northwest of downtown, the **Thomas Gilcrease Museum,** 1400 Gilcrease Museum Rd., contains the world's largest collection of Western American art, focusing on landscapes and life on the frontier. The museum also displays thousands of Native American artifacts, from jewelry to pipes to weapons. Take the "Gilcrease" exit off Rte. 412 or bus #114. (☎596-2700 or 888-655-2278; www.gilcrease.org. Open daily 10am-5pm. Suggested donation $3.) The **Philbrook Museum of Art,** 2727 S. Rockford Rd., has a little of everything, from Greek pottery to Indian basket weaving and French Impressionism, all housed in the Italian Renaissance-style villa of a 1920s oil tycoon. The 23 acres of exquisitely manicured gardens are perhaps the biggest draw. (☎749-7941 or 800-324-7941; www.philbrook.org. Take bus #105 "Peoria." Open Tu-Sa 10am-5pm, Th until 8pm. $7.50, students and seniors $5.50, under 13 free.)

🔳🔳 **ENTERTAINMENT AND NIGHTLIFE.** Tulsa thrives during the **International Mayfest** (☎582-6435; www.tulsamayfest.com), held May 18-21, 2006, which features live dance, music, and visual art exhibits. The **Greenwood Heritage Festival,** in the historic heart of Tulsa's African-American community, the 100 block of Greenwood Ave. just south of I-244, is held in mid-August, with jazz concerts, food, and more. Call the Greenwood Chamber of Commerce (☎585-2084) for details. The *Tulsa Pulse,* free at local restaurants, and "The Spot," in the Friday *Tulsa World,* both have entertainment info. The area known as **Brookside,** along the 3000 block of S. Peoria Ave. and 15th St. east of Peoria, is home to the city's chic-est nightlife. North of downtown in an old industrial building, the **Gypsy Coffee House,** 303 N. Cincinnati Ave., is a comfy hangout, with the standard gourmet coffee drinks and sandwiches. (☎295-2181. Coffee drinks $2-4. Sandwiches $4.50-6.25. Open Tu-Th 11am-2pm and 4pm-midnight, F 11am-2pm and 4pm-3am, Sa 2pm-3am, Su 2pm-midnight.) Sharing a corner with swanky clubs and wine bars, **Boston's,** 1738 Boston Ave., is more concerned with good music than the resumés of its clientele. Live music of every genre is played every night, with Oklahoman "Red Dirt" music on Wednesday nights. Bar and grill food is served until 10pm. (☎583-9520. Cover F-Sa $5, under 21 $7. Open M-F 4pm-2am, Sa 6pm-2am, Su 7pm-2am.)

🔳 **DAYTRIP FROM TULSA: TAHLEQUAH.** The Cherokee, having lost nearly one-quarter of their population along the Trail of Tears, began anew by placing their capital in Tahlequah, 66 mi. southeast of Tulsa on Rte. 51. In the center of town, on Cherokee Sq., stands the old **capitol building** of the Cherokee Nation, 101 S. Muskogee Ave. Built in 1870, it was the highest authority in Oklahoma until statehood. The town's **visitors center,** 123 E. Delaware St., has maps and info. (☎456-3742 or 800-456-4860. Open M-F 9am-5pm.) The **Cherokee Heritage Center,** 4 mi. south of town on Willis Rd., off Rte. 82, traces Cherokee history, from the Trail of Tears to self-government to the present day. Included in admission is a tour of **Ancient Village**, where Cherokee interpreters reenact 19th-century life. (☎ 456-6007 or 888-999-6007; www.cherokeeheritage.org. Center open Sept.-May M-Sa 10am-5pm, Su 1-5pm; June-Aug. M-W 10am-6pm, Th-Sa 10am-7pm, Su 1-5pm; closed Jan. $8.50, seniors and students $7.50, ages 5-18 $5. AAA discount 10%.)

OKLAHOMA CITY
☎ 405

For years, Oklahoma City was just a dusty stop for cattle drives and railroad trains. That all changed in the land run of 1889 when the city's population exploded from a few dozen people to 15,000 virtually overnight. But the city remained relatively quiet until the tragic bombing of the Federal Building in 1995 suddenly thrust this self-proclaimed "cowtown" into the modern age. As the site of the worst terrorist attack on US soil (until 9/11), Oklahoma City became a symbol of American patriotism and solidarity around the world.

■ 🔃 **ORIENTATION AND PRACTICAL INFORMATION.** Oklahoma City is laid out in a nearly perfect grid. **Santa Fe Avenue** divides the city from east to west, and **Reno Avenue** slices it north to south. Street parking is cheap and plentiful. Most sights lie downtown or a few miles north. **Will Rogers World Airport** (☎ 680-3200; www.flyokc.com) off Exit 116B on I-44, is southwest of downtown. **Amtrak** (www.amtrak.com) has an unattended station at 100 S. E.K. Gaylord Blvd., and runs to Fort Worth (4hr., 1 per day, $24-40). **Greyhound,** 427 W. Sheridan Ave. (☎ 235-4083; www.greyhound.com; open 24hr.), at Walker St., runs to Dallas (6hr., 4 per day, $45), Kansas City (6-10hr., 5 per day, $78), and Tulsa (2hr., 6 per day, $21). Most **Metro Transit** bus routes leave from the main terminal, 420 NW 5th St., which also has maps and info. (☎ 235-7433; www.gometro.org. Buses run M-F 5:30am-7:30pm, Sa 6:30am-5:30pm. $1.25, seniors and ages 6-17 $0.60.) Look for the **Oklahoma Spirit** trolley ($0.25, ages 60+ and disabled $0.10) downtown and in Bricktown. **Taxi: Yellow Cab,** ☎ 232-6161. The **Oklahoma City Convention and Visitors Bureau,** 189 W. Sheridan Ave., at Robinson St., has city info. (☎ 297-8912 or 800-225-5652; www.okccvb.org. Open M-F 8:30am-5pm.) **Internet Access: Oklahoma City Public Library,** 300 Park Ave. at Harvey. (☎ 231-8650. Open M-Th 9am-9pm, F 9am-6pm, Sa 9am-5pm, Su 1-6pm. 30min. max per day.) **Post Office:** 305 NW 5th St. (☎ 232-2198. Open M-F 7am-9pm, Sa 8am-5pm.) **Postal Code:** 73102. **Area Code:** 405.

🛏 **ACCOMMODATIONS.** Motels are along I-35 near downtown in both directions. The **Green Carpet Inn ❷,** 1629 S. I-35, has decent rooms and is very close to downtown. Take Exit 125D from I-35 after crossing the river and go to the south side of the freeway. (☎ 677-0551. Free donuts, coffee, pool, and HBO. Singles $26-30; doubles $34-45. AmEx/D/MC/V.) **Royal Inn ❷,** 2800 S. I-35, treats you to free local calls, HBO, and standard rooms. (☎ 672-0899. Singles $37; doubles $45. AmEx/D/MC/V.) Farther away but more scenic, **Lake Thunderbird State Park ❶** has campsites on swimmer-friendly Lake Thunderbird. Take I-40 16 mi. east to Exit 166, then go 10 mi. south on Choctaw Rd. until the road ends. The park is one mile to the east. (☎ 360-3572. Showers. Reception M-F 8am-5pm. Sites $8, with water and electricity $16-23; fully-equipped huts $45. Day use free.)

🍴🍸 **FOOD AND NIGHTLIFE.** Look for restaurants and bars in the **Paseo Arts District** (Dewey and 30th St.) and along **Western Avenue** (between 36th St. and Wilshire Blvd.). Several Asian restaurants cluster near **Classen Boulevard** and **28th Street.** In the Paseo Arts District, **Galileo Bar & Grill ❸,** 2009 Paseo, draws a crowd of teens, college kids, yuppies, and families. (☎ 415-7827. Gourmet pizzas $8. Entrees $7-20. Specialty martinis $5.50-7. Open Tu-Sa 11am-2am, Su 4pm-midnight.

GREAT PLAINS

AmEx/D/MC/V.) Drawing the barbecue faithful, **Leo's Original BBQ ❶**, 3631 N. Kelley St., is a hickory-smoking outfit in the northwest reaches of town. The strawberry banana cake ($2.50 per slice), served warm, is heavenly. (☎ 424-5367. Beef brisket sandwich and baked potato $4.35. Open M-Sa 11am-8pm. AmEx/D/MC/V.)

Bricktown, just east of downtown, is an old warehouse district turned yuppie entertainment district. It has a 1 mi. canal system inspired by San Antonio's Riverwalk. The **Bricktown Brewery,** 1 N. Oklahoma St., at Sheridan Ave., brews five beers daily ($3.25) in an appropriately brick building. (☎ 232-2739. Sandwiches and burgers $6.75. Upstairs 21+. Live music F-Sa; cover $5-15. Open M-Th 11am-midnight, F-Sa 11am-2am.) **City Walk,** 70 N. Oklahoma, houses seven clubs under one roof. Judge a bikini contest at Tequila Park, line dance inside City Limits, or sing along at Stooge's piano bar. (☎ 232-9255. 21+. Cover $5-8. Open F-Sa 8pm-2am.)

◳ ◱ SIGHTS AND ENTERTAINMENT. The ▧**Oklahoma City National Memorial,** at 5th and Harvey St., downtown, is a haunting testimonial to the victims of the 1995 bombing of the Murrah Federal Building. Outside lies the Field of Empty Chairs (one for each of the 169 victims), a stone gate, and a reflecting pool. The memorial is especially powerful at night, when each chair is lit. Indoors, the excellent museum traces the story of the bombing from the first few minutes to the immediate and long-term relief efforts and investigation using photographs, salvaged wreckage, teddy bears that miraculously survived the bombing, and media coverage from around the world. (☎ 235-3313; www.nps.gov/okci. Memorial: Open 24hr. Free. Museum: Open M-Sa 9am-6pm, Su 1-6pm. $7, seniors $6, students $5, under 6 free.) Old Cowtown is a shopping district designed for tourists, but at its heart is the real deal: the **Oklahoma City Stockyards,** 2500 Exchange Ave. (☎ 235-8675), the busiest in the world. Cattle auctions (M-W) begin at 8am and may last into the night. Visitors enter for free via a catwalk that soars over cattle herds from the parking lot northeast of the auction house. The **National Cowboy and Western Heritage Museum,** 1700 NE 63rd St., houses an extensive collection of Western art as well as exhibits on rodeos and Native Americans. In the entrance hall, James Earle Fraser's poignant sculpture *The End of the Trail* symbolizes the fate of Native Americans in the West. (☎ 478-2250; www.nationalcowboymuseum.org. Open daily 9am-5pm. $8.50, seniors $7, ages 6-12 $4. AAA discount $1.) An oasis in the city, the downtown **Myriad Gardens,** 301 W. Reno Ave., is a 17-acre botanical garden with flora ranging from desert to rainforest. Seventy feet in diameter, the cylindrical **Crystal Bridge** provides a unique setting for a tropical conservatory. (☎ 297-3995. Gardens: Open daily 7am-11pm. Free. Crystal Bridge: Open M-Sa 9am-6pm, Su noon-6pm. $6, students and seniors $5, ages 4-12 $3.) The **Oklahoma City Museum of Art,** 415 Couch Dr., has a standard collection of modern and classical art, but the dazzling and wildly inventive ▧**Dale Chihuly glass** pieces are alone worth the price of admission. (☎ 236-3100. Open Tu-W and F-Sa 10am-5pm, Th 10am-9pm, Su noon-5pm. $7; seniors, students, and children $5; under 4 free.) The **45th Infantry Division Museum,** 2145 NE 36th St., stocks artifacts from the Oklahoma-based 45th infantry division, covering the period from the Civil War to the Persian Gulf War. (☎ 424-5313. Open Tu-F 9am-4:15pm, Sa 10am-4:15pm, Su 1-4:15pm. Free.)

Oklahoma City hosts the **Red Earth Festival** (☎ 427-5228; June 2-4, 2006), the largest celebration of Native American culture. The **World Championship Quarter Horse Show** (www.aqha.com) is in the convention center each year in mid-November.

▰ DAYTRIPS FROM OKLAHOMA CITY. A college town with a charming Main Street, located 20 mi. south of Oklahoma City on I-35, **Norman** is home to the **University of Oklahoma (OU).** The **Fred Jones, Jr. Museum of Art** is a work of art in itself: nine "hut-like" galleries connected by glass hallways. (*555 Elm Ave. ☎ 325-3272. www.ou.edu/fjjma. Open Tu-Sa 10am-5pm, Su 1-5pm, Th until 9pm. $5, seniors $4, ages 6-17*

$3. Tu free.) The **Sam Noble Oklahoma Museum of Natural History,** at the southwest corner of the OU campus, has standard exhibits on prehistoric creatures and civilizations. Ride the "dinovator" 26 ft. up to stare down the world's largest Apatosaurus skeleton. *(2401 Chautauqua Ave. ☎325-4712; www.snomnh.ou.edu. Open Tu-Sa 10am-5pm, Su 1-5pm. $5, seniors $4, ages 6-17 $3.)*

As the location of the land grant office, **Guthrie** rose to prominence during the 1889 Land Run. The most cultured and elegant city in Oklahoma at the turn of the century, Guthrie even served as the state's first capital, though its reign only lasted three years. Nowadays, Guthrie boasts the largest contiguous national historic district in the country, with 400 blocks of outstanding Victorian architecture. Pick up maps and guides at the **visitors center.** *(212 W. Oklahoma Ave. ☎800-299-1889. Open M-F 9am-5pm.)* Guthrie is also home to the largest Masonic Temple in the world, the ▨**Scottish Rite Masonic Temple.** Guided 1¾hr. tours cover the exquisite architecture and furnishings of twelve period rooms and two auditoriums in this 6.5-acre masterpiece of a building. *(900 E. Oklahoma Ave. ☎282-1281. Tours M-F 10am and 2pm. $5, students and children free.)* The **Oklahoma Territorial Museum** tells the history surrounding the stampede-like land runs that were unique to this state. *(402 E. Oklahoma Ave. ☎282-1889. Open Tu-Sa 9am-5pm. Free; suggested donation $2.)*

GREAT PLAINS

TEXAS

The way Texans talk about their state, you'd think Texas was its own country—actually, it *was* its own country from 1836 to 1845. The fervently proud, independent citizens of the "Lone Star State" seem to prefer it that way, with their official road signs that proclaim "Don't Mess With Texas." After revolting against the Spanish in 1821 and splitting from Mexico in 1836, the Republic of Texas stood alone until 1845, when it entered the Union as the 28th state. The state's unofficial motto proclaims that "everything is bigger in Texas." This truth is evident in prolific wide-rimmed hats, boat-sized American autos, giant ranch spreads, countless steel skyscrapers, and oil refineries the size of small towns.

TEXAS

HIGHLIGHTS OF TEXAS

LICK your fingers after digging into some of the US's best barbecue at **Clark's Outpost**, near Dallas (p. 659).

REMEMBER the Alamo and wander the Riverwalk in **San Antonio** (below).

PULL on your cowboy boots and place your bid at the largest **livestock auction** in the country (p. 678).

◪ PRACTICAL INFORMATION

Capital: Austin.

Visitor Info: Texas Transportation Information Centers, ☎800-452-9292. For a free guidebook, call **Texas Tourism,** ☎800-888-8839; www.traveltex.com. **Texas Parks and Wildlife Department**, Austin Headquarters Complex, 4200 Smith School Rd., Austin, TX 78744 (☎800-792-1112).

Postal Abbreviation: TX. **Sales Tax:** 6-8.25%.

SAN ANTONIO   ☎210

Though best known as the home of the Alamo, the symbol of Texas's break from Mexico, San Antonio is better defined by its integration of Anglo and Hispanic cultures. The city proudly revels in its Mexican heritage, with missions, mariachis, and margaritas around every corner. San Antonio is definitely the biggest tourist destination in Texas, attracting eight million tourists each year to its easily walkable downtown, one-of-a-kind Riverwalk, and laidback atmosphere.

▛ TRANSPORTATION

Airport: San Antonio International Airport, 9800 Airport Blvd. (☎207-3411; www.sanantonio.gov/airport), 10 mi. north of town at I-410 and U.S. 281. Bus #2 runs downtown to Market and Alamo ($0.80). Taxi to downtown $18-20.

Trains: Amtrak, 350 Hoefgen St. (☎223-3226; www.amtrak.com), just north of the Alamodome and south of Commerce St. To: **Austin** (2½hr., 1 per day, $10-31); **Dallas** (5-7hr., 1 per day, $26-52); **El Paso** (12½hr., 1 per day, $52-82); and **Houston** (5hr., 1 per day, $67-105). Open daily midnight-8:15am and 9:30-11:59pm.

Buses: Greyhound, 500 N. Saint Mary's St. (☎270-5834; www.greyhound.com). To **Dallas** (5-6hr., 11 per day, $33) and **Houston** (3½hr., 8 per day $23). Open 24hr.

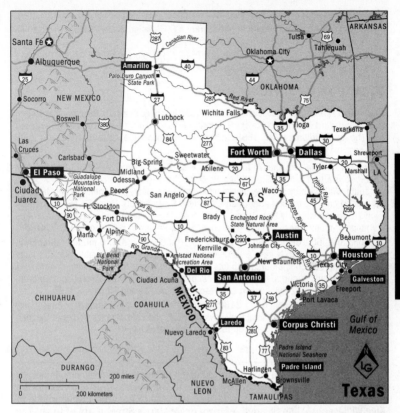

Texas

Public Transit: VIA Metropolitan Transit. Downtown information center at 260 E. Houston St. (☎475-9008. Open M-F 7am-6pm, Sa 9am-2pm.) Buses operate daily 5am-midnight; many routes stop at 6pm. Infrequent service to outlying areas. $0.80, transfers $0.15. 1-day pass $3. Also runs historic **streetcars** every 10min. on 4 color-coded routes to most attractions downtown. All four routes converge at the **Riverwalk Streetcar Station** on Alamo St. between Commerce and Market St.

Taxi: Yellow Checker Cab, ☎222-2222.

ORIENTATION AND PRACTICAL INFORMATION

The Alamo is the historic heart of San Antonio. The **Central Business District,** under which the Riverwalk runs, is just west of the Alamo. Major sights such as Market Square and HemisFair Park are within walking distance of the Alamo and are inside the inner loop formed by **I-35, I-37,** and **I-10.** Everything else worth seeing will be within the I-410 loop, which circles San Antonio with a 6 mi. radius.

Visitor Info: San Antonio Visitor Information Center, 317 Alamo Pl. (☎800-447-3372; www.sanantoniovisit.com), across from the Alamo. Open daily 9am-5pm.

Hotlines: Rape Crisis, ☎349-7273. Operates 24hr. **Supportive Services for the Elderly and Disabled,** ☎337-3550. Operates M-F 8am-noon and 1pm-5pm.

Medical Services: Metropolitan Methodist Hospital, 1310 McCullough Ave. (☎208-2200).

Internet Access: San Antonio Public Library, 600 Soledad St. (☎207-2500). Open M-Th 9am-9pm, F-Sa 9am-5pm, Su 11am-5pm.

Post Office: 615 E. Houston St. (☎800-275-8777), 1 block from the Alamo. Open M-F 9am-5pm. **Postal Code:** 78205. **Area Code:** 210.

ACCOMMODATIONS

For cheap motels, try **Roosevelt Avenue, Fredericksburg Road,** or **Broadway,** between downtown and Brackenridge Park. Frontage roads along **I-35** north of downtown and the **Austin Highway (Rte. 368)** are also dotted with cheaper and often safer lodgings several miles from downtown.

Bullis House Inn San Antonio International Hostel, 621 Pierce St. (☎223-9426). From Broadway, turn right on Grayson and go ¾ mi. The #20 bus runs on Carson St. 2 blocks south. With friendly management, a pool, and a rec room, San Antonio's only hostel is a good one. 42 beds in a ranch-style building. Breakfast $5. Linen $2.15. Key deposit $10. Reception daily 8am-10pm. Dorms $20. The main house is a B&B with a wide range of rooms, most with cable and queen bed. Rooms $55-99. AmEx/MC/V. ❶/❸

Alamo KOA, 602 Gembler Rd. (☎224-9296 or 800-562-7783), 6 mi. from downtown. Bus #24. From I-35 N, take SBC Center Pkwy. and turn left on Gembler Rd. This huge RV campground has an area with lots of grass and shade for tent campers. Amenities include a grill, showers, laundry facilities, pool, and free movies. Reception daily 8am-8:30pm. Sites $22, full hookup $32; each additional person $3. D/MC/V. ❶

Delux Inn, 3370 I-35 N (☎271-3160), off Exit 160, 5 mi. from downtown. Reasonably priced, clean rooms with fridge, microwave, HBO, and safe. Singles M-Th and Su $35, F-Sa $49; doubles $49/55. AAA discount. AmEx/D/MC/V. ❷

FOOD

Be prepared to pay dearly for dining along the **Riverwalk.** On weekends, hundreds of food booths crowd **Market Square.** Late in the day, prices drop and vendors are willing to negotiate. For quirky, eclectic food, head to the artsy neighborhood of **King William** on Alamo St. south of town or St. Mary's Street north of town. The Texas original diner **Pig Stand** has several locations around town, some of them even open 24hr.

Madhatters, 320 Beauregard St. (☎212-4832; www.madhatterstea.com), at S. Alamo St., on the Blue streetcar line. Madhatters brews the best tea this side of the rabbit hole. Quality breakfasts $4. Lunch $5. Free Wi-Fi. Full-out tea parties available ($18 for 2). Open M-F 7am-9pm, Sa 9am-9pm, Su 9am-6pm. AmEx/D/DC/MC/V. ❶

Liberty Bar, 328 E. Josephine St. (☎227-1187; www.liberty-bar.com), at Ave. A. Bus #7 or 8. Fresh produce and cuts of meat are used in Napa Valley-inspired cuisine, and almost nothing is above $12. Try the Karkade, an iced hibiscus and mint tea with fresh ginger and white grape juice ($2.50). Sandwiches $6-9. Open M-Sa 11:30am-10:30pm, Su 10:30am-10pm. Bar open until midnight or 1am. AmEx/D/MC/V. ❷

Josephine St. Steaks/Whiskey, 400 Josephine St. (☎224-6169), just west of Hwy. 281. Rough-hewn home cookin' is the daily special here. Take your arteries for a ride with the chicken-fried steak sandwich ($9) or the bacon-wrapped filet steak ($12). Lunch specials $6.50-8.50. Open M-Th 11am-10pm, F-Sa 11am-11pm. AmEx/D/DC/MC/V. ❸

Schilo's Delicatessen, 424 E. Commerce St. (☎223-6692), downtown between Presa and Losoya St. A German family-run deli since 1917, Schilo's (pronounced SHEE-lows) served cheap, filling lunches during the Great Depression. The tradition continues today with $5.10 lunch specials like corned beef and cabbage, beef stew, and the classic Reuben. Dinners $7-9. Open M-Sa 7am-8:30pm. AmEx/D/MC/V. ❷

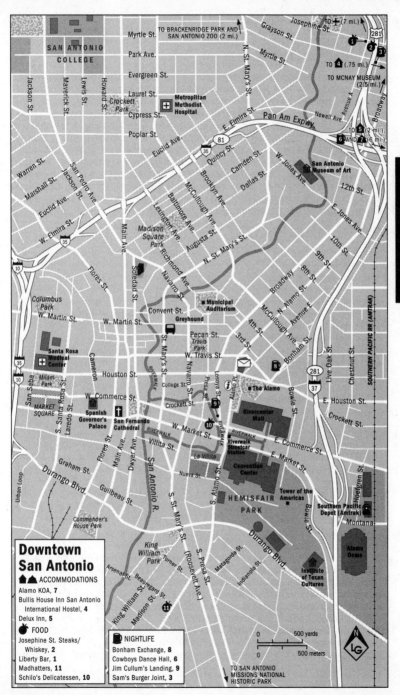

TEXAS

Downtown San Antonio

▲▲ ACCOMMODATIONS
Alamo KOA, 7
Bullis House Inn San Antonio
  International Hostel, 4
Delux Inn, 5

🍎 FOOD
Josephine St. Steaks/
  Whiskey, 2
Liberty Bar, 1
Madhatters, 11
Schilo's Delicatessen, 10

🍸 NIGHTLIFE
Bonham Exchange, 8
Cowboys Dance Hall, 6
Jim Cullum's Landing, 9
Sam's Burger Joint, 3

TO BRACKENRIDGE PARK AND
SAN ANTONIO ZOO (2 mi.)

TO ✚ (7 mi.)

TO ⓘ (.75 mi.)

TO MCNAY MUSEUM
(2/5 mi.)

TO ⑤ (2 mi.)
AND ⑦ (6 mi.)

San Antonio
Museum of Art

Metropolitan
Methodist
Hospital

San Antonio
College

Columbus
Park

Santa Rosa
Medical
Center

Madison
Square
Park

Municipal
Auditorium

Greyhound

Travis
Park

The Alamo

Rivercenter
Mall

Spanish
Governor's
Palace

San Fernando
Cathedral

Riverwalk
Streetcar
Studios

La Villita

Convention
Center

Tower of the
Americas

HEMISFAIR
PARK

King
William
Park

Commander's
House Park

Institute
of Texan
Cultures

Southern Pacific
Depot (Amtrak)

Alamo
Dome

0   500 yards
0   500 meters

TO SAN ANTONIO
MISSIONS NATIONAL
HISTORIC PARK

👁 SIGHTS

COLONIAL SAN ANTONIO

THE ALAMO. Built as a Spanish mission during the colonization of the New World, **The Alamo** has come to represent those who fought for Texas's independence and serves as a touchstone of Lone Star pride. For 12 days in 1836, a motley crew of Americans, Europeans, and Hispanic Tejanos defended the Alamo against the army of Mexican general Santa Ana, who was determined to reclaim the land for Mexico. On the 13th day, all 189 men were killed. The massacre united Texans behind the independence movement, and "Remember the Alamo!" became the rallying cry for Sam Houston's ultimately victorious forces. The site is presently under the stewardship of the Daughters of the Republic of Texas, who maintain museum exhibits, historic weapons including Jim Bowie's famous knife, and shrines to the fallen heroes. Historical talks are given every 30min. *(At the center of Alamo Pl. ☎ 225-1391; www.thealamo.org. Open M-Sa 9am-5:30pm, Su 10am-5:30pm. Free.)*

MISSIONS. Four missions built in the 1720s and 30s supplied San Antonio with agricultural products and newly converted Catholics. Today they make up the **San Antonio Missions National Historical Park.** Stretching 23 mi. south of the city along the San Antonio River, they are connected by the brown-signed Mission Trail road, which begins at the Alamo. Stopping at each mission takes a good half-day; some may wish to see only the first two. The missions are connected by biking and hiking trails, and the first two are served by Bus #42. The first is **Mission Concepción,** the oldest unrestored stone church in North America, where visitors can watch skilled craftsmen uncovering colorful frescoes on the walls. *(807 Mission Rd. ☎ 534-1540.)* **Mission San José,** the "Queen of the Missions," is the largest of the four and home to the park's visitors center. Most of the compound has been rebuilt and restored to its original grandeur. Catholic masses are held each Sunday at 7:30 (in Spanish), 9, and 10:30am—the noon "Mariachi Mass" is always packed. *(6701 San José Dr. ☎ 932-1001; www.nps.gov/saan.)* **Mission San Juan Capistrano** *(9101 Graf St.; ☎ 534-0749)* and **Mission San Francisco de la Espada** *(10040 Espada Rd.; ☎ 627-2021)* are smaller and simpler, but they surround the Espada Aqueduct, a remarkable engineering feat that allowed the river valley to be irrigated. Visitors can view the fully functional aqueduct as it carries water over the streams and valleys below.

SPANISH GOVERNOR'S PALACE. When San Antonio was the capitol of Texas, the seat of the government was the **Spanish Governor's Palace,** just east of Market Square. This museum is restored with period furniture, and the staff is happy to recount history. *(105 Plaza de Arms. ☎ 224-0601. Open M-Sa 9am-5pm, Su 10am-5pm. $1.50, ages 7-13 $0.75.)* Across the plaza is **San Fernando Cathedral,** the oldest cathedral in the United States. *(115 Main Plaza. ☎ 227-1297; www.sfcathedral.org.)*

DOWNTOWN SAN ANTONIO

RIVERWALK. After the Alamo, the most famous symbol of San Antonio is its 2½ mi. long **Riverwalk (Paseo del Río),** built in the 1930s by the WPA as a combination flood control and real estate project. Following the original course of the San Antonio River, it is a 3 ft. deep river lined on both sides with shaded pathways, picturesque gardens, shops, and cafes, all of which are below street level. The Riverwalk is touristy, but it is free and immensely pleasurable to simply walk along the riverbanks. **Río San Antonio Cruises** takes visitors on river rides. Tour boats leave from three locations: Rivercenter Mall, the Holiday Inn Riverwalk, and the Hilton Palacio Del Río. Dinner cruises are also available, and reservations should be made through one of the 20 participating restaurants on the Riverwalk. *(315 E. Commerce St. ☎ 244-5700 or 800-417-4139; www.sarivercruise.com. Open daily May-Aug. and Dec. 9am-10:30pm; Jan.-Apr. and Sept.-Nov. 10am-8pm. Narrated tours $6.50, seniors $4.50, ages 5 and under $1.50; shuttle service to any point on the Riverwalk $3.50.)* Along the southern arm of Riverwalk is **La Villita,** a Spanish-style artisan village where the public can watch artists work and purchase their creations. *(418 Villita. ☎ 207-8610. Shops open daily 10am-6pm.)* **Market Square** is a part-open-air, part-enclosed market where customers can haggle with vendors. Weekends feature the upbeat tunes of Tejano bands with a backbeat of buzzing frozen margarita machines. *(Between San Saba and Santa Rosa St. ☎ 207-8600. Shops open daily June to mid-Sept. 10am-8pm; mid-Sept. to May 10am-6pm.)* The **King William District** is a charming residential neighborhood along S. St. Mary's St., just south of downtown. Originally settled by German immigrants, the community's architecture makes for fine strolling and gallery-hopping.

HEMISFAIR PARK. Created for the 1968 World's Fair, **HemisFair Park,** on S. Alamo, contains an array of 60s era architecture, as well as the new convention center. The 750 ft. observation deck of the **Tower of the Americas** is temporarily closed and is scheduled to reopen in late 2006. At the southeast corner of the park, the **Institute of Texan Cultures** documents the histories and contributions of 20 different ethnic groups in Texas, from Czech to Chinese to Swedish. *(801 S Bowie St. ☎ 458-2300; www.the-museum.org. Open Tu-Sa 10am-6pm, Su noon-5pm. $7, seniors $4, ages 3-12 $4.)*

ST. PAUL SQUARE. South of Commerce St. and east of I-37, **St. Paul Square** is San Antonio's former red-light district. These alleys and cobblestone streets were the center of San Antonio's speakeasy scene during Prohibition and hosted some of the biggest names in jazz. In the 1960s, the largely black surrounding neighborhoods were razed to make room for HemisFair Park and, later, for the $187 million **Alamodome.** The 2005 NBA Champion San Antonio Spurs *(☎ 444-5000; www.spurs.com)* played here for just 10 years before moving to the SBC Center in 2002. The Alamodome now hosts soccer, gymnastics, and the circus. *(100 Montana St., at Hoefgen St. Yellow streetcar. ☎ 207-3663.)* Amtrak still stops in St. Paul Square, but the old Southern Pacific Depot now belongs to **Sunset Station,** a concert venue. Sunset Station invites the public to pick up a free self-guided tour of the beautifully restored 1902 depot as well as the surrounding neighborhood.

OUTSIDE THE CITY CENTER

MUSEUMS. The **San Antonio Museum of Art** is housed in the former Lone Star Brewery. In addition to Egyptian, Oceanic, and Asian art, in 1998 the museum established the **Nelson A. Rockefeller Center for Latin American Art,** the first of its kind in the US. Highlights include works by Diego Rivera. *(200 W. Jones Ave. Bus #7. ☎ 978-8100; www.samuseum.org. Open Tu 10am-8pm, W-Sa 10am-5pm, Su noon-6pm. $8, seniors $7, students $5, ages 4-11 $3; Tu 4-8pm free.)* Housed in the Spanish Mission-style McNay mansion in swanky Alamo Heights, the **McNay Art Museum** displays the collection of impressionist, post-impressionist, and expressionist masterpieces accumulated by Mrs. McNay, who stirred up controversy in the early 20th century as the first promoter of modern art in otherwise conservative Texas. The museum and 23-acre grounds are free to the public. *(6000 N. New Braunfels Ave., 3 mi. north off Broadway. ☎ 805-1756; www.mcnayart.org. Open Tu-F 10am-4pm, Th 10am-9pm, Sa 10am-5pm, Su noon-5pm. Grounds open daily 7am-7pm.)*

BRACKENRIDGE PARK. For diversion and greenery, head north to Brackenridge Park, whose 343 acres contain bike trails, a driving range, and a miniature train. *(Train runs daily 9:30am-6:30pm. $2.50, children $2.)* The Japanese-in-name-only Japanese tea garden will reopen in summer 2006. *(3910 N. Saint Mary's St. Open 5am-11pm.)* Just down St. Mary's St., the **San Antonio Zoo** boasts the nation's 3rd-largest animal collection, with 3800 animals and 750 species. *(3903 N. Saint Mary's St.* ☎ *734-7184; www.sa-zoo.org. Open daily late May to early Sept. 9am-6pm, grounds open until 8pm; early Sept. to late May 9am-5pm, grounds open until 6pm. $8, seniors and ages 3-11 $6.)*

🎵 🎭 ENTERTAINMENT AND NIGHTLIFE

The **Fiesta San Antonio** (☎ 227-5191; www.fiesta-sa.org; Apr. 21-30, 2006) ushers in spring with concerts, carnivals, and hoopla in honor of Texas's many heroes and cultures. The Battle of Flowers parade is a long-standing San Antonio tradition that began as a reenactment of the Battle of San Jacinto, using ammunition of a floral variety. In an event known as **First Fridays,** the art galleries in the King William District open their doors to the public on the first Friday of each month, also providing free food and drink. The **Theatre District,** just north of the Riverwalk, puts on concerts, operas, and plays in three restored 1950s movie houses. At night, the northern half of the Riverwalk transforms into a nightlife hub, albeit an expensive one. Clusters of funky, independent bars and clubs can be found in the artsy residential areas of King William, N. St. Mary's St. (around Woodlawn Ave.), and Josephine St. The *Friday Express* or weekly *Current* (available at the tourist office and many businesses in town) are guides to concerts and entertainment.

Sam's Burger Joint, 330 E. Grayson St. (☎ 223-2830), hosts the **Puro Poetry Slam** Tu 10pm ($3 cover) and free swing dancing lessons M 7pm. Singer-songwriter open mic night W (no cover). Local rock bands play Th-Sa ($5-10 cover). While enjoying the show, try the "Big Monster Burger," a pound of beef for $7. Call for hours.

Bonham Exchange, 411 Bonham St. (☎ 271-3811), around the corner from the Alamo. 1200-person capacity club is the place to be on weekend nights. Gay-friendly. Drink specials from $0.75. College night W. Cover up to $20; free before 10pm. Open W-Th 4pm-2:30am, F 4pm-3am, Sa 8pm-3am, Su 8pm-2:30am.

Jim Cullum's Landing, 123 Losoya St. (☎ 223-7266), on the Riverwalk. Old-time jazz by some old-timer musicians. Dixieland, bluegrass, jazz, swing, and standards. Cover $5; Su no cover. Open M-F 4pm-midnight, Sa-Su noon-1am; band plays at 8pm.

Cowboys Dance Hall, 3030 Rte. 410 NE (☎ 646-9378), plays 2 types of music—country and western. With a mechanical bull and 2 dance floors, you best bring your cowboy hat. Can't two-step? Don't worry: Th-Sa evenings begin with free dance lessons at 7pm. Th ladies free. Cover $3-20. 18+. Open W-Sa 8pm-3am.

AUSTIN   ☎ 512

Blending the trendiness of New York City's Soho and the mellowness of the West Coast, Austin is unlike any other place in Texas, making it an odd state capital. Refusing to turn into just another big city, Austin has maintained its soul, thanks in part to the "Keep Austin Weird" bumper sticker campaign. As the "Live Music Capital of the World" and home to 50,000 University of Texas (UT) students, liberal, alternative Austin is a lone star in the Lone Star State.

🚌 TRANSPORTATION

Airport: Austin Bergstrom International, 3600 Presidential Blvd. (☎ 530-2242; www.ci.austin.tx.us/austinairport). Take Hwy. 71 4½ mi. east from I-35 or take bus #100 (the Airport Flyer) or 350. Taxi to downtown $25.

Trains: Amtrak, 250 N. Lamar Blvd. (☎ 476-5684 or 800-872-7245; www.amtrak.com); take bus #38. Runs to **Dallas** (6hr., 1 per day, $22), **El Paso** (21hr., 3 per week, $131), and **San Antonio** (3½hr., 1 per day, $10).

AUSTIN FOR POCKET CHANGE. The live music center of the world. Texas's capital. The home of UT. Sound expensive? It doesn't have to be. Check into a **UT Co-op** (p. 653) and get a private room and three meals a day for just $20. If the co-op's meals aren't enough, you can snack on free samples at **Whole Foods Market** (p. 656) or head to the **UT campus** (p. 657) for $1.75 noodles from the food carts. You can work off the calories with a free early-morning or late-evening swim at **Barton Springs Pool** (p. 657). Stroll the free **Zilker Botanical Gardens** (p. 657) any time or, for a true spectacle, hang out on Congress Ave. and wait for the **bats** (p. 657). To get back to the co-op, borrow one of the town's free yellow **bicycles** (p. 651) and pedal your way home.

Buses: Greyhound, 916 E. Koenig Ln. (☎458-4463 or 800-231-2222; www.greyhound.com), 3 mi. north of downtown at Exit 238A off I-35. Station open 24hr. Runs to **Dallas** (3hr., 11 per day, $28), **Houston** (3½hr., 7 per day, $24), and **San Antonio** (2hr., 11 per day, $14). Buses #7 and 15 stop across the street.

Public Transit: Capitol Metro, 323 Congress Ave. (☎474-1200 or 800-474-1201; www.capmetro.org). Office has maps and schedules. Buses run 4am-midnight, but most start later and end earlier. Office open M-F 7:30am-5:30pm. $0.50; students $0.25; seniors, children, and disabled free. The **'Dillo Bus Service** runs downtown on Congress, Lavaca, San Jacinto, and 6th St. Most buses operate M-F every 10-15min.; off-peak service varies. Moonlight and Starlight 'Dillos 6pm-3am F and Sa. The 'Dillos, which look like trolleys, are always free. Free park 'n' ride lots at most 'Dillo terminals.

Taxi: American Yellow Checker Cab, ☎452-9999.

Bike Rental: Yellow bicycles are "free to ride but not to keep" as part of an effort to refurbish donated bikes for public use. Make sure to leave the bike in a conspicuous spot for the next person. **Waterloo Cycles,** 2815 Fruth St. (☎472-9253), rents bikes. Open M-W and F-Sa 10am-7pm, Th 10am-8pm, Su noon-5pm. Daily bike rental M-F $10-15, Sa-Su $15-20; includes helmet. Lock rental $5 ($1.50 each additional day).

✦🛈 ORIENTATION AND PRACTICAL INFORMATION

Downtown Austin sits on the north bank of the Colorado River, between **Mopac Expressway/Route 1** and **I-35,** two freeways that run north-south and parallel to one another. There are no cross-town freeways until **U.S. 290,** 3 mi. south of downtown. UT students converge on **Guadalupe Street ("The Drag"),** where music stores and cheap restaurants thrive. All downtown streets are oriented around the commanding **State Capitol,** with **Congress Avenue's** upscale eateries and classy shops leading directly toward the capitol. Funkier **South Congress (SoCo)** offers a mix of antique and thrift stores across the river, while downtown teems with nightlife, centered on **6th Street** and the **Warehouse District.** Austinites enjoy one of the largest greenbelt systems in the country with numerous trails and pools.

Visitor Info: Austin Convention and Visitors Bureau/Visitors Information Center, 209 E. 6th St. (☎478-0098 or 866-462-8784; www.austintexas.org). Open M-Th and Su 9am-6pm, F-Sa 9am-7pm. Sponsors free walking tours of the capitol, downtown, UT, and historic neighborhoods Mar.-Nov. Call ☎454-1545 for more info.

Medical Services: St. David's Medical Center, 919 E. 32nd St. (☎476-7111). Exit 136 off I-35, north of UT. Open 24hr.

Hotlines: Crisis Intervention Hotline, ☎472-4357. **SafePlace (Austin Rape Crisis Center Hotline),** ☎267-7233. Both operate 24hr. **Outyouth Gay/Lesbian Helpline,** ☎800-969-6884. Operates M-Sa 6:30-9pm.

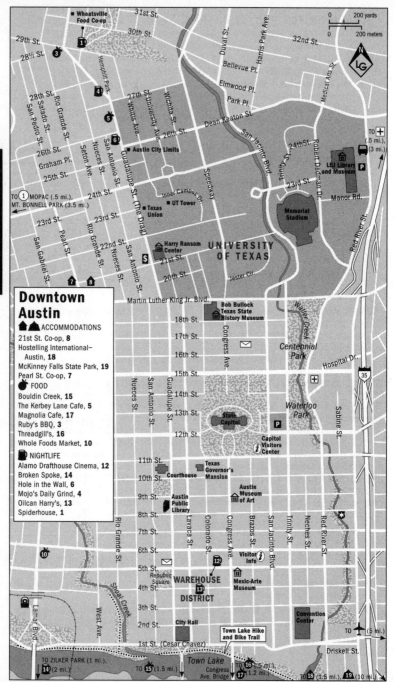

Downtown Austin

🏠🏠⛰ ACCOMMODATIONS
21st St. Co-op, 8
Hostelling International–
Austin, 18
McKinney Falls State Park, 19
Pearl St. Co-op, 7
🍴 FOOD
Bouldin Creek, 15
The Kerbey Lane Cafe, 5
Magnolia Cafe, 17
Ruby's BBQ, 3
Threadgill's, 16
Whole Foods Market, 10
🎭 NIGHTLIFE
Alamo Drafthouse Cinema, 12
Broken Spoke, 14
Hole in the Wall, 6
Mojo's Daily Grind, 4
Oilcan Harry's, 13
Spiderhouse, 1

Internet Access: Austin Public Library, 800 Guadalupe St. (☎974-7400). 2hr. max; ID required. Open M-Th 10am-9pm, F-Sa 10am-6pm, Su noon-6pm.

Post Office: 510 Guadalupe St. (☎494-2210), at 6th St. Open M-F 8:30am-6pm. **Postal Code:** 78701. **Area Code:** 512.

ACCOMMODATIONS

As befits its character, Austin offers some funky, alternative budget options in addition to the standard hostels and campgrounds. ▓**Co-ops** at UT peddle rooms with free meals to hostelers during the summer when school is out. (Call ☎476-5678, or check www.collegehouses.coop to find contact info for individual houses.) The **Austin Area Bed & Breakfast Association** (☎800-972-2333; www.austinareabandb.com.) coordinates several historic B&Bs, most of which start at $100 a night. Chain motels line I-35 running north and south of downtown.

21st St. Co-op, 707 W. 21st St. (☎476-5678). Take the red 'Dillo or bus #3. The spirit of the 60s lives on in this treehouse-style co-op. Colorful suites have private bedrooms. Kitchens and common rooms on each floor. Linen included. A/C. Single room and 3 meals per day $20. When you arrive, ask around for the membership coordinator who will get you set up with a room. Cash only. ❶

Pearl St. Co-op, 2000 Pearl St., one block west of 21st St. Co-op (☎476-5678). Pearl St. offers similar single rooms and the same amenities, meals, and prices as 21st St. but is slightly more orderly and less colorful. Pool and sundeck. Cash only. ❶

Hostelling International-Austin (HI), 2200 S. Lakeshore Blvd. (☎444-2294 or 800-725-2331), 3 mi. from downtown. Take bus #7 to Burton, then walk 3 blocks north. From I-35, take Exit 233, then take Riverside east to Lakeshore Blvd. On attractive Town Lake. Comfortable 24hr. common room. 4 single-sex dorms with 13 beds each. Communal showers. Rents bikes, kayaks, and canoes ($10). Linen included. Laundry and kitchen. No alcohol. Reception 8-11am and 5-10pm. Both wired and wireless Internet access $1 for entire stay. Dorms $20, members $17. AmEx/MC/V. ❶

McKinney Falls State Park, 5808 McKinney Falls Pkwy. (☎243-1643, reservations ☎389-8900), southeast of the city. Turn right on Burleson off Rte. 71 E, then right on McKinney Falls Pkwy. Campsites with ample shade and privacy near excellent swimming and 6 mi. of hiking trails. Gates open daily 8am-10pm. Primitive sites (accessible only by foot) $10, with water and electricity $14. Screen shelters sleep up to 8 for $32 (no cots or bedding provided). Day use $3 per person, under 13 free. ❶

FOOD

Cheap fast-food and take-out are abundant near the UT campus on **Guadalupe Street.** Patrons can often enjoy free or cheap appetizers with their drinks during happy hour in the **6th Street** clubs. South of the river, **Barton Springs Road** and **S. Congress Street** are home to a range of cuisines, including Mexican and barbecue joints. The **Warehouse District** has swankier options. **Wheatsville Food Co-op,** 3101 Guadalupe St., is the place to go for groceries. (☎478-2667. Open daily 9am-11pm.)

▓ **Magnolia Cafe,** 1920 S. Congress Ave. (☎445-0000); also at 2304 Lake Austin Blvd. (☎478-8645). Blending Tex-Mex, California cuisine, and diner fare, Magnolia serves exotic dishes at not-so-exotic prices. Try the tropical turkey tacos, with turkey, cheese, *pico de gallo*, and pineapple (2 for $6.75). Open 24hr. AmEx/D/MC/V. ❷

▓ **Bouldin Creek,** 1501 S. 1st St. (☎416-1601), at Elizabeth St. Cheap and delicious vegetarian and vegan food. Full coffee bar and bakery with salads, sandwiches, tacos, and omelettes all day. The portobello tacos ($5) are heavenly. Free Wi-Fi, books, and board games. Beer and wine. Open M-F 7am-midnight, Sa-Su 9am-midnight. MC/V. ❶

TEXAS

Parts of the **Texas Hill Country** are as country as they come. Longhorns graze on grassy plains between rolling hills, while rusty pickup trucks driven by big men in big hats dominate the roads. But the Hill Country is more than just ranches and cattle: the limestone-rich

TIME: 6hr.

DISTANCE: 190mi.

soil is well suited to wine-making and peach-growing. There is a noticeable German influence in the area, dating back to 1846 and the founding of **Fredericksburg.** The Hill Country Drive is not a time-saving route—to stop and appreciate each stop along the way would take at least two days—but there are plenty of campgrounds, B&Bs, and ranches along the way, making for ample resting points.

1 SCHLITTERBAHN. Schlitterbahn is a 65-acre waterpark extravaganza masquerading as a village in the Bavarian Alps. Schlitterbahn's endless water rides promise to entertain, but be prepared for long lines. Take I-35 to Exit 190B. (400 N. Liberty St. ☎830-625-2351. Call for hours; generally around 10am-8pm. Open May-Sept. Full-day $32, ages 3-11 $26.50; half-day $22.)

2 GUADALUPE RIVER TUBING Almost 2 million visitors per year come to the rivers around New Branfuels to spend a day drifting downstream in an inner tube. The Comal River is calm and ideal for families, while the Guadalupe River has more rapids, college students, and 30-packs of beer. **Dog Leg Hollow** rents tubes. (1137 River Terrace, off Loop 337 2mi. from I-35 exit 190B. ☎830-629-3009. Standard tube $14. Free parking.)

3 DRY COMAL CREEK VINEYARDS. Dry Comal Creek Vineyards, 1741 Herbelin Rd., 6 mi. west of New Braunfels on Rte. 46, is the only winery in the world to make wine from the Black Spanish grape, a Texas native created when 16th-century Spanish missionaries' grapes crossed with local grapes. (☎830-885-4121. Open W-Su noon-5pm. Tours $2. Tastings $2-5.)

4 GUADALUPE RIVER STATE PARK. Guadalupe River State Park, 25 mi. west of Dry Comal Creek on Rte. 46, offers camping, hiking, and swimming in the Guadalupe River. (☎830-438-2656, reservations 512-389-8900. Open M-F 8am-8pm, Sa 8am-10pm. Day fee $5 per person, under 12 free. Primitive sites $12; with water $13; with water and electricity $17.)

5 BOERNE. Antique shops and cutesy historical architecture line the main street of this town at the gateway to the Hill Country.

6 BANDERA. Bandera's wild west past has been preserved for today's tourists, who take snapshots of its "movie set" architecture. The **Frontier Times Museum,** 510 13th St., houses a collection of Old West memorabilia, artifacts, and odd knick-knacks. (☎830-796-3864. Open M-Sa 10am-4:30pm, Su 1-4:30pm. $2.)

7 MEDINA. Nestled among green hills on Rte. 16, 15 mi. west of Bandera, is Medina, the "apple capital of Texas." ■**Love Creek Orchards** (☎800-449-0882) pinpointed the only microclimate capable of growing apples in Texas. Keep the doctor away with free samples of their many varieties of fresh, organic apples. The 35 mi. of Rte. 16 north of Medina wind through some of the most breathtaking Texas country. *Be cautious of hairpin turns and steep inclines on this leg of the trip.*

8 KERRVILLE ARTS COMMUNITY. Kerrville and neighboring Ingram are home to a thriving art community. The **Kerrville Arts & Cultural Center,** 228 E. Garrett St. downtown, provides guides to nearby galleries and has an exhibit on iridescent rocks. (☎830-895-2911. Open Tu-Sa 10am-4pm, Su 1pm-4pm.) The **Museum of Western Art,** 1550 Bandera Hwy. (Rte. 173), south of Rte. 16, displays works by real cowboy artists. (☎830-896-2553. Open Tu-Sa 9am-5pm, Su 1-5pm. $5, seniors $3.50, ages 15-18 $2, ages 6-14 $1.)

9 FREDERICKSBURG. Twenty-five miles along Rte. 16 from Kerrville sits historic Fredericksburg, a German-rooted town of biergartens, wineries, and bratwurst. The **Fredericksburg Convention and Visitors Bureau,** 302 E. Austin St. behind the Nimitz Museum, has maps and information. (☎888-997-3600. Open M-F 8:30am-5pm, Sa-Su 9am-noon and 1-5pm.) The **National Museum of the Pacific War,** 340 E. Main St. downtown, honors hometown boy Admiral Nimitz, who was instrumental to the victory in the Pacific War. (☎830-997-4379. Open daily 10am-5pm. $5, students $2, under 11 free.)

SCENIC DRIVE

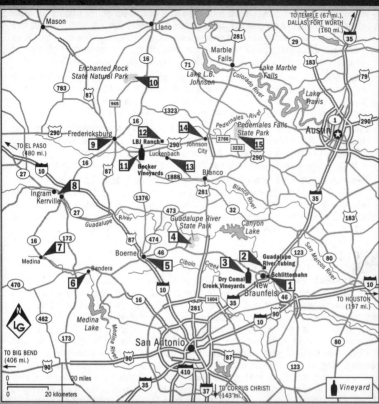

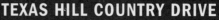

10 ENCHANTED ROCK STATE NATURAL PARK. The 440 ft. pink granite dome that rises from the dramatic landscape of ◼ **Enchanted Rock State Natural Park,** 18 mi. north of Fredericksburg on Rte. 965, is an awe-inspiring sight. The park has plenty more hiking and rock-climbing opportunities. (☎325-247-3903 or 800-792-1112. Open daily 8am-5pm. Entrance $5, under 12 free. Tent sites with shower, water, and grill $10; primitive sites $8. No RVs or trailers. Reservations strongly recommended.)

11 BECKER VINEYARDS. Ten miles east of Fredericksburg on U.S. 290, **Becker Vineyards,** on Jenschke Ln., offers free tastings as well as free tours of the winery. (☎830-644-2681. Open M-Th 10am-5pm, F-Sa 10am-6pm, Su noon-6pm.)

12 LBJ RANCH. LBJ National Historic Park consists of Johnson City and the Ranch. On the ranch, a **Living History Farm** shows visitors the rural beginnings of America's first cowboy president. (☎830-644-2252. Tours daily 10am-4pm; call for times. $6, ages 7-17 $3.) Named for LBJ's grandfather, Johnson City is the town where the 36th President grew up.

13 LUCKENBACH. Just off Rte. 1376, 4 mi. south of Fredericksburg, sits Luckenbach—really just an old general store and amphitheater, but to its seven residents, a "city." Crowds descend upon the town nightly to hear authentic folk and country music.

14 PEDERNALES FALLS STATE PARK. Nine miles east of Johnson City off Rte. 2766 is **Pedernales Falls State Park.** Waterfalls, hiking, tent sites, and tubing make the park a favorite getaway from Austin. (☎800-868-7304. Park open daily 8am-10pm; office open daily 8am-5pm. Entrance fee $4, under 12 free. Primitive sites $8; with water and electricity $18.)

SCENIC DRIVE

Whole Foods Market, 525 N. Lamar Blvd. (☎476-1206), at 6th St. The organic, all-natural chain was started in Austin, and this flagship store opened in 2005 with 80,000 square ft., a walk-in beer cooler, and in-house nut roasteries and fish smokeries. One third of the store is set aside for take-out and prepared foods. Outdoor patio, stream, and roof terrace. Free beer and wine tastings. Free Wi-Fi. Open daily 8am-10pm; coffeebar opens 6am. AmEx/D/MC/V. ❷

Ruby's BBQ, 512 W. 29th St. (☎477-1651), at Guadalupe St., uses naturally lean beef, farm-raised without hormones. Various succulent meats come as sandwiches, ribs, or fillets. Top it off with rosemary-infused homefries ($3) and blueberry cobbler ($4). Entrees $5-14. Open daily 11am-midnight. Cash or check only. ❷

The Kerbey Lane Cafe, 3704 Kerbey Ln. (☎451-1436). An Austin institution with other locations at 2700 Lamar Blvd., 2606 Guadalupe St., and 12602 Research Blvd. Their pancakes ($3.50-5) are renowned and come in buttermilk, gingerbread, or apple whole wheat. Vegetarian options include savory tomato pie. Open 24hr. AmEx/D/MC/V. ❷

Threadgill's, 301 W. Riverside Dr. (☎472-9304); also at 6416 N. Lamar Blvd. (☎451-5440). A legend in Austin since 1933, Threadgill's dishes up Southern barbecue, fried chicken ($9), and chicken-fried steak ($9) amidst antique beer signs. A variety of vegetarian and non-dairy side dishes. Live blues, rock, and country Th-Sa 7pm. Open M-Th 11am-10pm, F-Sa 11am-10:30pm, Su 10am-9:30pm. D/MC/V. ❷

◉ SIGHTS

GOVERNMENT. Proving that everything *is* bigger in Texas, Texans built their **State Capitol** seven ft. taller than its federal counterpart. It gets its pink hue from the Texas red granite that was used instead of the more traditional limestone. The capitol, its dome, the legislative chambers, and the underground extension are all open to the public. *(At Congress Ave. and 11th St. ☎463-0063. Open M-F 7am-10pm, Sa-Su 9am-8pm. Short tours every 15-30min. M-F 8:30am-4:30pm, Sa 9:30am-3:30pm, Su noon-3:30pm. Free.)* The **Capitol Visitors Center** has exhibits on the capitol's history and construction. *(112 E. 11th St. ☎305-8400. Open M-Sa 9am-5pm, Su noon-5pm. Free 2hr. parking at 12th and San Jacinto St. garage.)* Now that the White House is closed to visitors, get an up-close look at Dubya's old stomping grounds at the **Texas Governor's Mansion.** *(1010 Colorado St. ☎463-5516. Free tours M-Th every 20min. 10-11:40am.)*

MUSEUMS. Before the Bushes, there was another cowboy President from Texas. Lyndon B. Johnson forever improved life in the US with his "Great Society" policies, yet is remembered primarily for his errors in Vietnam. The **Lyndon B. Johnson Library and Museum** sets the public and personal life of the Texas native against the backdrop of a broader history of the American Presidency. A life-sized animatronic LBJ tells jokes and anecdotes on the second floor, while the 10th floor features a model of the Oval Office and an exhibit on Lady Bird Johnson, a great leader in her own right. *(2313 Red River St. Take bus #20. ☎721-0200; www.lbjlib.utexas.edu. Open daily 9am-5pm. Free.)* Texas has a history befitting its size, and it takes a three-story museum to tell it. The **Bob Bullock Texas State History Museum** traces Texas's nearly 500 years of Western settlement, with the usual hero-worship of Travis, Houston, and Austin tempered by balanced looks at the lives of minorities and the economy and culture of Texas over the years. *(1800 N. Congress Ave. ☎936-8746; www.thestoryoftexas.com. Open M-Sa 9am-6pm, Su noon-6pm. $5.50, seniors $4.50, ages 5-18 $3.)* The downtown **Austin Museum of Art** displays traveling exhibits of contemporary art, from photography to painting to mixed media. *(823 Congress Ave., at 9th St. ☎495-9224; www.amoa.org. Open Tu, W, F-Sa 10am- 6pm, Th 10am-8pm, Su noon-5pm. M and W-Su $5, seniors and students $4, under 12 free. Tu $1.)* A second branch, at 3809 W. 35th St., is housed in a Mediterranean-style villa in a beautiful country setting with an exquisite sculpture garden. *(Open daily 11am-4pm. Free.)*

The **Mexic-Arte Museum** features traveling exhibits by Mexican, Mexican-American, and Latino artists and seeks to promote cross-cultural learning and understanding. *(419 Congress Ave. ☎ 480-9373; www.mexic-artemuseum.org. Open M-Th 10am-6pm, F-Sa 10am-5pm, Su noon-5pm. $5, students and seniors $4, under 12 $1.)*

PARKS. Covert Park at Mount Bonnell offers a sweeping view of Lake Austin and Westlake Hills from the highest point in the city. *(3800 Mt. Bonnell Rd., off W. 35th St., 4 mi. NW of town.)* **Zilker Park,** just south of the Colorado River, has the standard recreational facilities plus several Austin-specific diversions. *(M-F free. Sa-Su parking $3.)* The **Botanical Gardens** contain a peaceful Japanese garden, a prehistoric garden that recreates the Cretaceous Period, and a garden that features plants native and well-adapted to Austin's climate. *(2100 Barton Springs Rd. Take bus #30. ☎ 477-8672. Open daily in summer 7am-7pm; low season 7am-5pm. Free.)* The **Umlauf Sculpture Garden** showcases the work of the late Charles Umlauf, longtime UT professor and prolific sculptor of wood, terra cotta, marble, and bronze. *(605 Robert E. Lee Rd., off Barton Springs Rd. ☎ 445-5582. Open W-F 10am-4:30pm, Sa-Su 1pm-4:30pm. $3.50, seniors $2.50, students $1.)* On hot days, Austinites flock to █**Barton Springs Pool,** a 1000 ft. long spring-fed swimming hole in Zilker Park. Flanked by walnut and pecan trees and with temperatures hovering around 68°F year-round, Barton Springs is a favorite destination of families by day and young people by night. *(☎ 974-6700. Open daily 5am-10pm; closed for cleaning Th 9am-7pm. $3, ages 12-17 $2, under 12 $1. Free daily 5-9am and 9-10pm.)*

The **Barton Springs Greenbelt** and several other creek trails around town offer good terrain for hiking and biking. Free spirits go *au naturel* in **Lake Travis** at **Hippie Hollow,** Texas's only public nude swimming and sunbathing haven, 15 mi. northeast of downtown. Take Mopac (Rte. 1) north to the F.M. 2222 exit. Follow 2222 west and turn left at I-620; Comanche Tr. will be on the right. *(7000 Comanche Tr. ☎ 854-7275. 18+. Open daily May-Sept. 8am-9pm; Sept. 10-Oct. and Mar.-Apr. 9am-7:30pm; Nov.-Feb. 9am-6pm; no entry after 8:30pm. Cars $10, pedestrians $5.)* In a longstanding Austin tradition, folks congregate at sunset at **The Oasis**, just up the road from Hippie Hollow. With its 45 decks, every one of the 2000 guests at this restaurant has an excellent view of the sunset over Lake Travis.

OTHER SIGHTS. In addition to its thriving nightlife, downtown Austin boasts some notable modern architecture. The new **City Hall** at 301 W. 2nd St., opened in 2004, is one of the most striking examples. The **University of Texas at Austin (UT)** is the wealthiest public university in the country, with an annual budget of over a billion dollars, and, with its over 50,000 students, the backbone of the city's cultural life. The **UT Tower**, a landmark in the center of campus, was the site of the infamous Charles Whitman sniper shootings in 1966. The **Harry Ransom Center,** in the southwest corner of campus, is the humanities research center, with collections including the Texas Declaration of Independence and a Gutenberg Bible, as well as rotating themed exhibits. *(☎ 471-8944. Open Tu-W and F 10am-5pm, Th 10am-7pm, Sa-Su noon-5pm. Free.)*

Just before dusk, head to the **Congress Avenue Bridge** and join thousands of others to watch the massive swarm of █**Mexican free-tail bats** emerge from their roosts to feed on the night's mosquitoes. When the bridge was reconstructed in 1980, the engineers unintentionally created crevices that formed ideal homes for the migrating bat colony. The city exterminated the night-flying creatures until **Bat Conservation International** moved to Austin to educate people about the benefits of their presence—the bats eat up to 3000 lb. of insects each night. Stand on the bridge itself to see the bats fly out from underneath, or on the southern riverbank under the bridge for a more panoramic view. *(www.batcon.org. For flight times, call the bat hotline at ☎ 416-5700, ext. 3636. Bats fly Mar.-Nov.)*

🎵 🎭 ENTERTAINMENT AND NIGHTLIFE

Beverly Sheffield Zilker Hillside Theater (☎479-9491; www.zilker.org), across from Barton Springs pool, hosts free outdoor , ballets, plays, musicals, and concerts most weekends from May to October. Entertainment industry giants and eager fans descend upon Austin for the 10-day **South by Southwest Music, Media, and Film Festival.** Nearly 1300 musical acts fill 50 stages, while movie screens show 180 films, making this festival the premier entertainment event in the Southwest. (☎467-7979; www.sxsw.com. Mar. 10-19, 2006.) The Austin Fine Arts Guild sponsors the **Fine Arts Festival,** April 1-2, 2006, attracting 200 national artists, local eateries, live music, and art activities. Austin's smaller events calendar is a mixed bag. Each spring, **Spamarama** (www.spamarama.com) gathers Spam fans from all walks of life to pay homage to the often misunderstood meat. A cookoff, samplings, sports, and live music at the Spam Jam are all in store.

Austin's title, "Live Music Capital of the World," is no exaggeration; on any given night, one can find literally any kind of music, from didgeridoo to jazz/rap fusion. Downtown, **6th St.** is lined with warehouse nightclubs and theme bars. Mellow night owls gather at the cocktail-lounges in the **4th St. Warehouse District.** Along **Red River St.,** bars and hard-rocking clubs have less of the glamour but all of the grit of 6th St. The long-running PBS series **Austin City Limits** (www.austincitylimits.com) tapes shows monthly at UT with big music stars. Tickets are free but shows aren't announced until the morning of, and people wait in line all day. If you aren't in the mood to face club crowds, try Austin's regionally unparalleled coffeehouse scene, which is concentrated both near UT and south of the river. The weekly *Austin Chronicle* (www.austinchronicle.com) and *XL-ent* provide details on current music performances, shows, and movies.

▓ Spiderhouse, 2968 Fruth St. (☎480-9562), off Guadalupe St. near the UT campus. Serves a wide variety of beer (pints $2.50-3.50), wine, and liquor. Large, shaded cobblestone patio with nightly movie screenings. Free Wi-Fi. Live music W-Su runs the gamut from techno to jazz. No cover. Open daily 8am-2am.

▓ Mojo's Daily Grind, 2714 Guadalupe St. (☎477-6656), fuels Austin's students, artists, hipsters, and other colorful constituents with coffee and beer, served under a cleverly altered Starbucks sign. Try the Iced Mojo ($2.75). Occasional DJ and open mic poetry. Open daily 9am-3am.

Alamo Drafthouse Cinema, 409B Colorado St. (☎476-1320; www.originalalamo.com), screens 2nd-runs, cult classics, and other offbeat films. See how great the *Karate Kid* is on the big screen or watch the Turkish *Wizard of Oz.* Full-service restaurant and bar allow for schmoozing before the movie and serve food and drinks inside the theater as well. Cover $5-10; M $1, W free at midnight. Website has movie schedules.

Hole in the Wall, 2538 Guadalupe St. (☎477-4747), at 26th St. Its self-effacing name belies the popularity of this renowned music spot. Daily live music spanning all genres, usually 9-10pm. Happy hour weekdays 1-10pm, weekends noon-7pm, all day M. 21+. No cover. Open M-F 1pm-2am, Sa-Su noon-2am.

Broken Spoke, 3201 S. Lamar Blvd. (☎442-6189; www.brokenspokeaustintx.com). One of the top honky-tonks in the land, complete with wagon wheel decor and Texan hospitality. The "tourist trap" room is full of country music memorabilia, dusty photographs, and LBJ's hat. Steaks from $8. All ages welcome for nightly music and dancing at 9pm. Cover $5-8, Tu free. Open Tu-Th 11am-midnight, F-Sa 11am-1am.

Oilcan Harry's, 211 W. 4th St. (☎320-8823). One of the biggest and best gay bars in Austin. 3 bars, pool table, and outdoor patio. Strippers perform Th and Sa-Su 10:30pm and midnight. Happy hour 2-10pm. 21+. No cover. Open daily 2pm-2am.

DALLAS ☎214

Denim and diamonds define the Dallas decor, skyline, and attitude. Rugged western virility coupled with cosmopolitan offerings create the city's truly Texan aura. Big Tex, an enormous cowboy float in Fair Park, welcomes visitors to one of the country's finest collections of Asian art and a slew of restaurants. While the intrigue surrounding the assassination of President John F. Kennedy haunts the city to this day, Dallas views itself as a city imbued with a maverick's spirit where, even though an urban landscape has replaced the sprawling plains, "the people still swagger and the frontier still calls."

▐ TRANSPORTATION

Airport: Dallas-Fort Worth International (☎972-574-8888; www.dfwairport.com) is halfway between Dallas and Fort Worth, accessible by Hwy. 183, Hwy. 114, and I-685. Catch the **Trinity Rail Express** (see below) to Dallas ($2.25) or Fort Worth ($1.25). For door-to-gate service, take the **Super Shuttle** (☎800-258-3826). 24hr. service. $16 per person to most metro locations. Taxi to downtown $40-45.

Trains: Amtrak, 400 S. Houston St. (☎653-1101; www.amtrak.com), in Union Station. Open daily 10am-5:30pm. 1 train per day to **Austin** (6½hr., $22-42) and **Little Rock** (7½hr., $47-91).

Buses: Greyhound, 205 S. Lamar St. (☎655-7727; www.greyhound.com), 3 blocks east of Union Station. Open 24hr. To **Austin** (3hr., 11 per day, $30) and **Houston** (4hr., 9 per day, $36).

Public Transit: Dallas Area Rapid Transit (DART), 1401 Pacific Ave. (☎979-1111; www.dart.org. Open M-F 6am-8pm, Sa-Su 8am-5pm.) Buses depart from 2 downtown transfer centers, East (Pacific and Pearl St.) and West (Pacific and Griffin St.). Most buses run downtown daily 5:30am-9:30pm, to suburbs until 8pm. Get a map at any tourist office or transit station. Local fare $1.25, all-day pass $2.50; express and longer trips $2.25/$4.50. **DART Light Rail** has 2 lines, Red and Blue, which converge downtown and branch out several miles north and south into the suburbs. Operates M-Sa 4am-midnight, Su 5am-midnight. Same fares as buses. The **M-Line Streetcar** is a free historic trolley that runs from the Downtown Arts District to Uptown along McKinney Ave. Runs M-F 7am-10pm, Sa 10am-10pm, Su 12:30-10pm. The **Trinity Rail Express (TRE)** is a commuter train service operating between Union Station and downtown Fort Worth (1hr.; M-F 22 per day, Sa 10 per day; $1.25-2.25).

Taxi: Yellow Cab Co., ☎426-6262.

✳ ⑦ ORIENTATION AND PRACTICAL INFORMATION

Downtown Dallas is bounded by **The Mixer,** a highway loop formed by the intersections of **I-30, I-35E, I-45, U.S. 175,** and **U.S. 75.** North of downtown are the ritzy residential and shopping districts of **Turtle Creek, Oaklawn, Highland Park,** and **University Park,** as well as the **Lower Greenville** entertainment district. East of downtown are **Deep Ellum, Fair Park,** and **White Rock Lake.** The **I-635** loop surrounds Dallas. The lateral highways **I-20, I-30,** and **Hwy. 183** run east to **Fort Worth.** Beware of ravenous parking meters, which demand feeding until 10pm.

Visitor Info: Dallas Convention and Visitors Bureau, 100 S. Houston St. (☎571-1300 or 800-232-5527; 24hr. events hotline 571-1301; www.visitdallas.com), in the Old Red Courthouse. Free Internet access. Open M-F 8am-5pm, Sa-Su 9am-5pm.

GLBT Resources: Dallas Gay and Lesbian Community Center, 2701 Reagan St. (☎528-0144). Open M-F 9am-9pm, Sa-Su 9am-6pm.

TEXAS

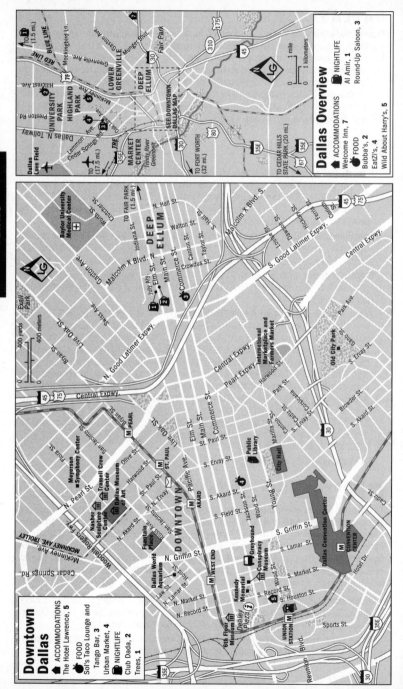

Dallas Overview

ACCOMMODATIONS
Welcome Inn, **7**

FOOD
Bubba's, **2**
EatZi's, **4**
Wild About Harry's, **5**

NIGHTLIFE
Al Amir, **1**
Round-Up Saloon, **3**

Downtown Dallas

ACCOMMODATIONS
The Hotel Lawrence, **5**

FOOD
Sol's Taco Lounge and
Tango Bar, **3**
Urban Market, **4**

NIGHTLIFE
Club Dada, **2**
Trees, **1**

Hotlines: Contact Counseling Crisis Line, ☎972-233-2233. 24hr.

Medical Services: Baylor University Medical Center, 3500 Gaston Ave. (☎820-0111).

Internet Access: Dallas Public Library, 1515 Young St. (☎670-1400), at Ervay St. Two 55min. sessions per day. Open M-Th 9am-9pm, F-Sa 9am-5pm, Su 1-5pm. Be careful around this area at night.

Post Office: 401 Dallas-Ft. Worth Tpk. (☎760-4545). Take Sylvan exit. Open 24hr. **General Delivery** mail should be addressed to the downtown branch, located at 400 N. Ervay St. Open M-F 8:30am-5pm. **Postal Code:** 75201; for General Delivery 75221. **Area Codes:** 214, 972, and 817. In text, 214 unless otherwise noted.

ACCOMMODATIONS

Cheap lodgings in Dallas are nearly impossible to come by; big events like college football's Cotton Bowl (Jan. 2, 2006) and the state fair in October exacerbate the problem. Look within 10 mi. of downtown along three of the major roads for inexpensive motels: north of downtown on **U.S. 75,** north along **I-35,** and east of **I-30.**

The Hotel Lawrence, 302 S. Houston St. (☎761-9090), conveniently located in the heart of downtown. A terrific value with stylish rooms, elegant ambiance, and quality service in a historic hotel. Free fitness center and computer room. Breakfast included. Singles and doubles $69-79; up to $109 during special events. AmEx/D/DC/MC/V. ❹

Welcome Inn, 3243 Merrifield Ave (☎826-3510). Exit at Dolphin Rd. (49A) off I-30, 3 mi. from downtown. Convenient location. HBO and free local calls. Singles and doubles $35. Weekly rate $120. AAA discount 10%. AmEx/D/DC/MC/V. ❷

Cedar Hill State Park (☎972-291-3900), 20min. from the city on Rte. 1382 off either U.S. 67 or I-20. 30 primitive walk-in sites and 320 sites with water and electricity nestled in a dense pine forest on a lake. Reserve at least 2 weeks in advance. Office open M-Th and Su 8am-5pm, F 8am-10pm, Sa 8am-7pm. 24hr. gate access with reservations. Primitive sites $7, with water and electricity $18. Park entry $5 per person. ❶

FOOD

Dallas boasts that it has more restaurants per capita than New York City. The city offers eclectic dining options, coupling urban delights with tried-and-true Texan fare. For the lowdown on dining options, pick up "Startime," in the Friday *Star-Telegram.* Stock up on produce at the **farmers market,** which occupies three blocks below Taylor St. downtown. (☎939-2808. Open daily 7am-6pm.)

EatZi's, 3403 Oaklawn Ave. (☎526-1515), at Lemmon Ave., 1 mi. east of Oaklawn exit from I-35 E. This grocery store, cafe, kitchen, and bakery is a culinary delight. Fabulous focaccia, sandwiches, and other delicacies. Fresh chef-prepared dinners ($5-10) 2-for-1 after 9pm. Sandwiches $6-9. Open daily 7am-10pm. AmEx/D/DC/MC/V. ❷

Urban Market, 1500 Jackson St. (☎741-3663). A market, cafe, and bar. Sandwiches $6. Entrees $8-11. Open M-F 6am-10pm, Sa-Su 8am-10pm. AmEx/D/MC/V. ❷

Sol's Taco Lounge and Tango Bar, 2626 Commerce St. (☎651-7657). Heaping Tex-Mex combo plates ($7-10) alongside 8 different kinds of fajitas ($11-20). M selected food half price. Happy hour M-F 4-7pm with $3 margaritas. Open M-Th and Su 8am-11pm, W 8am-midnight, F-Sa 8am-3am. AmEx/D/DC/MC/V. ❷

Bubba's, 6617 Hillcrest Dr. (☎373-6527), at Rosedale Ave., near SMU. For no-frills grub in the swankiest part of town, indulge in Bubba's famous fried chicken. Grab 2 huge pieces of chicken, 2 veggies, and a roll for $6-7. Banana pudding $2. Dine-in, drive-thru, or take-out. Open daily 6:30am-10pm. AmEx/D/DC/MC/V. ❷

Wild About Harry's, 3113 Knox St. (☎520-3113), in Highland Park. Gourmet hot dogs and frozen custard. Try a "Knox St. Dog," with Thousand Island dressing, sauerkraut, and swiss cheese (regular $3.45, jumbo $4.25). Single scoop of custard $2.25. Sundaes $3.75-5.25. Open M-Th and Su 11am-10pm, F-Sa 11am-11pm. Cash only. ❶

👁 SIGHTS

Attractions in Dallas tend to be overpriced; admission-weary travelers may wish to take to the streets. Downtown's monuments to capitalism span a century's worth of architecture, from Art Deco to I.M. Pei, and—thanks to fountains, plenty of shade, and the light rail—are surprisingly pedestrian-friendly.

JFK SIGHTS. John F. Kennedy's motorcade was passing through **Dealey Plaza** next to on Nov. 22, 1963 when bullets, most likely from the 6th floor of the Texas School Book Depository Building, mortally wounded the president. Today, in that same building, the **6th Floor Museum** traces the events of the assassination, and the subsequent investigations, theories, and conspiracies. *(411 Elm St. on Dealey Plaza. ☎ 747-6660; www.jfk.org. Open daily 9am-6pm. $10; seniors, students, and ages 6-18 $9. Audio guide $3.)* The **Kennedy Memorial,** a sculpture by Philip Johnson, looms nearby at Market and Main St. Conspiracy hounds have expounded upon the missing pieces of the puzzle for decades. Learn about their theories at the **Conspiracy Museum,** which delves into the mysteries of the accepted explanation of JFK's assassination with an *X-Files*-like paranoia. *(110 Market St., across from the Memorial. ☎ 741-3040. Open daily 10am-6pm. $10, students and seniors $6, children $3.)*

ART AND ARCHITECTURE. The architecture of the **Dallas Museum of Art** is as graceful and beautiful as its impressive collections of Egyptian, African, early American, Impressionist, Modern, and decorative art. *(1717 N. Harwood St. ☎922-1200; www.dm-art.org. Open Tu-Su 11am-5pm, Th until 9pm. $10, seniors and ages 12-17 $7, students with ID $5. Admission includes audio tour. Free Th 5-9pm and first Tu of each month. Jazz concerts Th 9pm in summer.)* The **Nasher Sculpture Center** displays modern works both indoors and in the garden. Life-sized human sculptures reach heights of 100 ft. in *Walking to the Sky*. *(2001 Flora St. ☎242-5100. Open Tu-Su 11am-5pm, Th until 9pm. $10, seniors $7, students $5, under 12 free.)* Just across Harwood St., the **Crow Collection of Asian Art** has Japanese prints, Chinese jade, and Indian ivory carvings, among other pieces. *(2010 Flora St., at Hardwood and Olive St. ☎979-6430. Open Tu-Su 10am-5pm, Th until 9pm. Free. Sculpture garden open 24hr.)* Architect **I.M. Pei** lists several Dallas landmarks among his many achievements. The **Wells Fargo Building,** at Ross Ave. and Field St., makes an indelible mark on the city's skyline. **Fountain Place,** in the building's plaza, consists of cascading pools, fountains, and water gardens. Pei also designed downtown's **Energy Plaza,** at Bryan and Ervay St., and **One Dallas Center,** at Bryan St. between St. Paul and Harwood St., but it is the striking **City Hall,** at Ervay St. and Young St., that marked his career breakthrough.

FISH, FLORA, AND FLIGHT. The **Dallas World Aquarium** fits an awful lot into one urban city block, including leopards, manatees, and a multi-tiered rainforest. *(1801 N. Griffin St. ☎720-2224; www.dwazoo.com. Open daily 10am-5pm. $16, seniors $14, ages 3-12 $9.)* At the **Dallas Arboretum,** 20 themed gardens occupy 66 tranquil acres near the shore of White Rock Lake. Try parking on a nearby residential street to avoid the parking fee. *(8617 Garland Rd. Bus #60. ☎515-6500. Open daily 9am-5pm. $8, seniors $7, ages 3-12 $5. Parking $5.)* The **American Airlines C. R. Smith Museum** traces the history of the world's largest airline. Exhibits give a behind-the-scenes look at airline operations on the ground and in the air using flight simulators and historic aircraft, and, for those who want a taste of the good life, the auditorium has first-class airplane seats. *(4601 Hwy. 360, at the FAA Rd. exit just south of the airport. ☎967-1560. Open Tu-Sa 10am-6pm. $4; students, seniors, and children $2.)*

FAIR PARK. Home to the **State Fair** since 1886, **Fair Park** has earned national landmark status for its collection of 1930s Art Deco architecture, the largest such collection in the country. The **Texas Star** ferris wheel dominates the park's skyline. *(Visit www.bigtex.com for info on the State Fair, held each October.)* The 277-acre park also hosts college football's **Cotton Bowl** *(Jan. 2, 2006).* **The Women's Museum: An Institute for the Future** has exhibits covering everything from Lucille Ball to birth control. Built in conjunction with the Smithsonian Institute, this new museum has a dramatic atrium as its centerpiece. *(3800 Parry Ave. ☎915-0860; www.thewomensmuseum.org. Open Tu-Su noon-5pm. $5, seniors and students $4, ages 5-12 $3.)*

HISTORIC DALLAS. Old City Park contains 35 restored 19th-century structures. There's a fee to tour the buildings, but the pleasant grounds are free. *(1717 Gano St., across I-30 from downtown. ☎421-5141; www.oldcitypark.org. Grounds open daily 5am-5pm. Exhibit buildings open Sept.-July Tu-Sa 10am-4pm, Su noon-4pm; Aug. Tu-Sa 10am-2pm, Su noon-2pm. $7, seniors $5, children $4.)* The **West End Historic District** is a brick-lined neighborhood of shops and restaurants a few blocks north of Dealey Plaza. Dallas's mansions are in the **Swiss Avenue Historic District** and along the ritzy streets of **Highland Park,** between Preston and Hillcrest Rd.

🎵 ENTERTAINMENT

The Observer is a free alternative weekly with unrivaled entertainment coverage. For the scoop on Dallas's gay scene, pick up copies of the *Dallas Voice* and *Texas Triangle* in Oaklawn shops and eateries.

The **Shakespeare in the Park** festival is held in Samuel-Grand Park, just northeast of Fair Park, from mid-June through July. (☎559-2778. Performances Tu-Su 8:15pm. Gates open 6:45pm; arrive early. Free tickets Tu-Th and Su.) At Fair Park, **Music Hall** hosts Broadway tours in the **Dallas Summer Musicals** series. (☎691-7200 for tickets; www.dallassummermusicals.org. Shows June-Oct. $11-74.) The **Dallas Symphony Orchestra** plays in the downtown **Meyerson Symphony Center,** 2301 Flora St. (☎692-0203; www.dallassymphony.com. Box office open M-Th 9am-6pm, F 10am-6pm. $12-100. Free tours available M and Th-Sa 1pm. Tours ☎670-3600.)

The **Mesquite Championship Rodeo,** 1818 Rodeo Dr., is one of the most competitive in the country. Take Exit 4 from I-635 S and stay on the service road. (☎972-285-8777; www.mesquiterodeo.com. Shows Apr. to late Sept. F-Sa 8pm. Gates open 6:30pm. $10, seniors and ages 3-12 $5. Barbecue dinner $11, children $7. Pony rides $3. Parking $3.)

DAMN, THAT'S SMOKIN'

While good barbecue is plentiful in Texas, truly great barbecue is harder to find. **Clark's Outpost,** in Tioga, TX, about 1½hr. north of Dallas, is one of the best, most authentic barbecue joints around.

The restaurant has catapulted Tioga, a town that used to be marked only as the birthplace of country-music legend Gene Autry, into the barbecue spotlight. Clark's food is ecstasy-inducing, with brisket treated with a delectably spicy rub and slow-cooked for 3½ days, giving it the smoky-sweet tang and tender, succulent texture that define great barbecue. The unique "French fried corn-on-the-cob" has been fried just long enough to make each kernel crispy and buttery. Barbecue sauce is served warm in old beer bottles, and black-and-white photos of Wild West heroes, wagons, cow skulls, and boots adorn the walls. Longing for a brewski to top off that meal? Well, Tioga is in a dry county, but it's possible to get around the law by becoming a "member." Pay a one-time $3 membership fee and drink to your heart's content (by law, no more than three drinks in an hour and one drink per subsequent hour).

Clark's Outpost, 101 Hwy. 277 at Gene Autry Dr., Tioga, TX. ☎904-437-2414 or 800-932-5051. Beef sandwich $4.50. Dinner with brisket, vegetables, and Texas toast $9. Open M-Th 11am-9pm, F-Sa 11am-9:30pm, Su 11am-8:30pm.

In Dallas, the moral order is God, Texas, country, and the **Cowboys.** See "The Boys" play football from September to January at **Texas Stadium,** at the junction of Rte. 12 and 183, west of Dallas in Irving. (☎972-785-5000. Ticket office open M-F 9am-5pm. Tickets $48-73.) **Ameriquest Field,** 1000 Ballpark Way, hosts the **Texas Rangers** from April to September. (☎817-273-5100. Ticket office open M-F 9am-6pm, Sa 10am-4pm, Su noon-4pm and 9am-9pm on game days. Tickets $5-75.) Experience the mystique of the game with a 1hr. tour of the locker room, dugout, and the press box on the **ballpark tour,** which also includes admission to **Legends of the Game Museum.** (☎817-273-5600. In-season non-game days tours every hr. M-Sa 9am-4pm, Su 11am-4pm; night-game days M-Sa 9am-2pm, Su 11am-2pm. Low-season Tu-Sa 10am-4pm. $10, students with ID and seniors $8, ages 4-18 $6.)

◨ NIGHTLIFE

Head east of downtown to **Deep Ellum,** a haven for blues legends in the 1920s, and for musicians of every type since the area was revived in the 1980s. The first Friday of every month is Deep Friday (www.deepfriday.com), when an $8 wrist band gets you into eight Deep Ellum clubs featuring local rock acts. Other nightlife centers include **Lower Greenville Avenue** and **Yale Boulevard,** near SMU's fraternity row. Gay nightlife centers on **Cedar Springs Road,** a bit north of downtown in **Oaklawn.**

Al Amir, 7402 Greenville Ave. (☎739-2647), at Pineland. Lebanese restaurant and multi-level club with hookah (W-Th $5 per table, F-Sa $15) and belly dancers (9:30, 11:30pm). Middle Eastern, Latin, and other international dance music. Bar and club 21+, restaurant all ages. Open W-Su 6pm-2am. F-Sa business casual dress. F-Sa $5 cover; free entry for females over 21 or parties with a food reservation on Sa.

Club Dada, 2720 Elm St. (☎744-3232). A diverse clientele, eclectic decor, and spacious outdoor patio. Live acts nightly at 8pm range from rock to classical to the occasional stand-up comic. Open mic Su. 21+. Cover W-Sa $5. Open W-Su 6pm-2am.

Trees, 2709 Elm St. (☎248-5902). A popular live music venue where grunge and swank coexist in a converted warehouse with a loft full of pool tables and tree trunks in the middle of the club. Bands play alternative rock music and everything else. 17+. Cover $2-25. open Th-Su 7pm-2am, sometimes M-W 7pm-2am.

Round-Up Saloon, 3912 Cedar Springs Rd. (☎522-9611), at Throckmorton St. Huge, country-western gay bar packs a large crowd on weekends. Free dance lessons M-Th 8:30pm. No cover. Open M-F 3pm-2am, Sa-Su noon-2am.

FORT WORTH   ☎817

If Dallas is the last Eastern city, Fort Worth is undoubtedly the first Western one. A mere 33 mi. west of Dallas on I-30, Fort Worth mixes raw Texan flair with cultural refinement. The city has three districts: the **Stockyards Historic District, Sundance Square,** and the **Cultural District.** Fort Worth's old stockyards, which were once the busiest in the country, have been turned into the city's largest tourist attraction. **Exchange Avenue** is the dusty main drag. Once lined with casinos and brothels catering to cowfolk with jingling pockets, its bars, restaurants, and shops now cater to the jingling pockets of tourists seeking what Fort Worth bills as a taste of the "authentic West." Catch the **cattle drive,** when cowboys and cowgirls rustle a team of longhorns down Exchange Ave. (www.fortworthstockyards.org.) The **White Elephant Saloon,** 106 Exchange Ave., a filming location in "Walker, Texas Ranger," has a ceiling plastered with celebrity cowboy hats. (☎624-8273. Cover M $2, F-Su $5-10. Open M-Th and Su noon-midnight, F-Sa noon-2am.) The **Cowtown Coliseum,** 121 Exchange Ave., hosts national-level **rodeos** and **Pawnee Bill's Wild West Show.** (Cowtown Coliseum: ☎625-1025 or 888-269-8696; www.cowtowncoliseum.com. Rodeos F-Sa 8pm. $9.50, seniors $7.50, ages 3-12 $6. Pawnee Bill's June-Aug. Sa-Su 2:30 and 4:30pm. Box office open F-Sa 6-8pm. $8, seniors $6.50, ages 3-12 $4.50.) The world's largest honky-tonk, **Billy Bob's Texas**, 2520 Rodeo Pl., draws crowds with country music's big names. The club has a restaurant, games, and 25 bar stations. (☎624-7117. Free dance lessons Th 7pm. Bull-riding F-Sa 9 and 10pm. Families welcome; under 18 must be with parent. Cover M-Th and Su before 8pm and F-Sa before 6pm $1. Open M-Sa 11am-2am, Su noon-2am.)

Sundance Square is the name given by promoters to what is essentially downtown Fort Worth. The 40-block brick-lined downtown is chock-full of trendy shops, museums, and restaurants. Parking lots are free after 5pm Monday through Friday and all day on weekends. The **Sid Richardson Collection of Western Art**, 309 Main St., is closed for renovation until summer 2006. (☎332-6554; www.sidrmuseum.org.) West of downtown along 7th St., Fort Worth boasts an astonishing array of high-caliber museums in the **Cultural District**. The █Modern Art Museum, 3200 Darnell, contains an excellent collection of art from the last half century, including sculpture, abstract art, and photography, all housed in a stunning structure surrounded by a reflecting pool. (☎866-824-5566; www.themodern.org. Open Tu-Sa 10am-5pm, Su 11am-5pm. $6, seniors and students $4, ages 12 and under free. W and 1st Su of month free.) The **National Cowgirl Museum and Hall of Fame**, 1720 Gendy St., argues that the cowgirl has long been a pioneer of women's rights. Exhibits examine cowgirls in pop culture, with their rhinestone-studded jackets, as well as real-life cowgirls. (☎336-4475; www.cowgirl.net. Open Tu-Sa 10am-5pm, Su noon-5pm; in summer also M 10am-5pm. $6, seniors $5, ages 3-12 $4.) The **Amon Carter Museum**, 3501 Camp Bowie Blvd., has a large collection of Western art and is renowned for its photographs of western landscapes. (☎738-1933; www.cartermuseum.org. Open Tu-Sa 10am-5pm, Th until 8pm, Su noon-5pm. Free.)

Next to Texas Christian University (TCU), the █Frog Theater Cafe, 3055 S. University Blvd., has created a novel dining environment: Not only has an old movie theater been converted into a cafe, but it continues to show movies (and cartoons) for free on the big screen. The projection booth is a coffee shop with leather sofas and free Internet access and Wi-Fi. (☎924-3764; www.frogtheater.org. Six-inch subs $2-4. Open M-Th 11am-9pm, F-Sa 11am-midnight. AmEx/D/MC/V.) A beautiful, old hacienda-turned-Mexican restaurant, **Joe T. Garcia's ❸**, 2201 N. Commerce St., just below the Stockyards, has a swimming pool on its patio and huge lunch fajita plates

THE LOCAL STORY

DESIGNER COWBOY BOOTS?

When you think of high fashion, certain places come to mind: Paris, Milan, New York, and...Dallas? Some might believe that the closest Dallas comes to a fashion show is the halftime performance by the Cowboys cheerleaders, but Dallas is, and has been for quite some time, a key player in the worldwide fashion industry.

The city's fashionable roots date back to the early 20th century. Dallas was strategically located between the cotton-producing Southern states, the wool-producing Midwestern states, and the consumer markets of Chicago, San Francisco, and the East Coast. The wives of rich Texas oil barons spent much of their time traveling in Europe. When they came home, they expected to find equally up-to-date looks. To address this niche, in 1907 Neiman Marcus opened its first store in, of all places, Dallas. Sears Roebuck and Montgomery Ward of Chicago soon incorporated Dallas designs into their products, which then spread across the country via mail-order catalogues. Dallas enlarged its role in the US clothing industry when J.C. Penney moved its headquarters there in 1988.

Today, Dallas's Highland Park has boutiques rivaling those of Paris and New York. With Market Center's FashionCenterDallas and Fashion Industry Gallery, Dallas's cowboys and their wives continue to go designer close to home.

($8.75). For dinner, Garcia's lets you choose only between fajitas and cheese enchiladas with two tacos. (☎626-8571. Dinner $9-12. Open M-Th 11am-2:30pm and 5-10pm, F-Sa 11am-11pm, Su 11am-10pm. Cash only.)

Trinity Railway Express (p. 659), **Amtrak,** and **city buses** share the **Intermodal Transportation Center,** at the corner of 9th and Jones St. (☎215-8600. Open M-F 5am-10pm, Sa 8am-10pm, Su 10:15am-5:30pm). **Visitor Info: Fort Worth Convention and Visitors Bureau,** 415 Throckmorton St., in Sundance Sq. (☎800-433-5747; www.fort-worth.com. Open M-F 8:30am-5pm, Sa 10am-4pm.) There are other branches in Stockyards, 130 E. Exchange Ave., and the Cultural District, 3401 W. Lancaster Ave. (All open M-F 9am-5pm, Sa 9am-6pm, Su 10am-6pm.) **Post Office:** 251 W. Lancaster Ave. (☎870-8104. Open M-F 8:30am-6pm.) **Postal Code:** 76102. **Area Code:** 817.

HOUSTON   ☎713

With the 4th-largest population of any US city, Houston can't hide its miles of seemingly endless strip malls and gridlocked traffic. Though known for sprawl and lack of planning, Houston has a revitalized downtown with a new light rail line, glorious modern architecture, stadiums, and state-of-the-art performing arts centers. Houston's prosperity, built on the wealth of its oil and maritime industries, shows in its immaculate streetscapes, parks, and public buildings. Yet beyond the skyscrapers, culture abounds in an impressive array of world-class restaurants, museums, and cultural organizations.

▐▀ TRANSPORTATION

Airport: George Bush Intercontinental Airport (☎281-230-3000; http://iah.houstonairportsystem.org), 25 mi. north of downtown. **Express Shuttle** (☎523-8888) runs vans to downtown (1hr., every 30min. 6:15am-11:15pm; $24, ages 5-12 $10, under 5 free) and locations in the suburbs (up to $35). **Metro bus 102** from Terminal C is cheaper (80min. to downtown; M-F every 10min., Sa-Su every 50min.; $1). **William P. Hobby Airport,** 7800 Airport Blvd. (☎640-3000; http://hou.houstonairportsystem.org), about 10 mi. south of downtown, is served by Southwest and other domestic airlines.

Trains: Amtrak, 902 Washington Ave. (☎800-872-7245; www.amtrak.com). Walk toward the ferris wheel to the well-lit theater district; at night, call a cab. To **New Orleans** (10 hr., 1 per day, $52-80) and **San Antonio** (5hr., 1 per day, $27-52). Open M 3pm-midnight; Tu, W, and F 4am-1:45pm and 3pm-midnight; Th and Su 4am-1:45pm.

Buses: Greyhound, 2121 Main St. (☎759-6565; www.greyhound.com), 1 block south of Downtown Transit Center METRORail station. Be careful at night in this area. To **Dallas** (4-6hr., 9 per day, $32), **San Antonio** (3½hr., 11 per day, $23), and **Santa Fe** (24hr., 3 per day, $119). Open 24hr.

Public Transit: Metropolitan Transit Authority (☎635-4000; www.ridemetro.org). Over 130 bus lines operate within a 25-30 mi. radius of downtown. Typically operates M-F 4:30am-1am. The new **METRORail** light rail, or Red Line, has 16 stops, running north-south from through Hermann Park, the Museum District, and downtown to University of Houston. Runs M-Th and Su until 12:45am, F-Sa until 2:45am. All transit $1, seniors $0.40, ages 5-11 $0.25; all-day pass $2. Free maps available at the **Houston Public Library** (see **Internet Access,** below) or at METRO stores. (720 Main or 1001 Travis St. Open M-F 7:30am-5:30pm.)

Taxi: United Cab, ☎699-0000.

Car Rental: Enterprise Rent-A-Car, 2101 Travis St. (☎651-7866). From $27 per day. $0.20 per mi. over 150 mi. 21+. Under-25 surcharge $10. Open M-F 7:30am-6pm, Sa 9am-3pm.

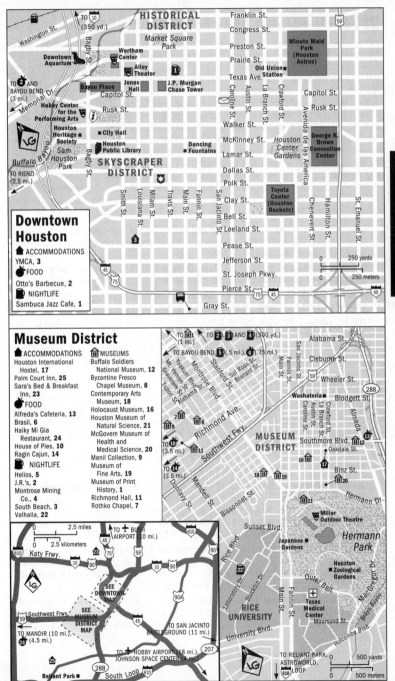

TEXAS

HISTORICAL DISTRICT

TO 10 (350 yd.)

Washington St.

Market Square Park

Franklin St.
Congress St.
Preston St.
Prairie St.
Texas Ave.

Minute Maid Park (Houston Astros)

Bagby St.

Downtown Aquarium

Wortham Center

Alley Theater

Old Union Station

59

TO 2 AND BAYOU BEND (3 mi.)

Bayou Place

Jones Hall

J.P. Morgan Chase Tower

Capitol St.

Caroline St.
Austin St.
La Branch St.
Crawford St.

Capitol St.
Rusk St.

Memorial Dr.

Hobby Center for the Performing Arts

Rusk St.

Houston Heritage Society

City Hall

Walker St.
McKinney St.

Avenida de las America

George R. Brown Convention Center

Buffalo Bayou

Sam Houston Park

Houston Public Library

Dancing Fountains

Lamar St.

Houston Center Gardens

Bagby St.

SKYSCRAPER DISTRICT

Dallas St.
Polk St.
Clay St.

TO RIENZI (2.5 mi.)

Smith St.
Louisiana St.
Milam St.
Travis St.
Main St.
Fannin St.
San Jacinto St.

Toyota Center (Houston Rockets)

Bell St.
Leeland St.

Chenevert St.
Hamilton St.
St. Emanuel St.

Pease St.
Jefferson St.
St. Joseph Pkwy.

0   250 yards

0   250 meters

Downtown Houston

🏠 ACCOMMODATIONS
YMCA, **3**

🍎 FOOD
Otto's Barbecue, **2**

🍸 NIGHTLIFE
Sambuca Jazz Cafe, **1**

45
75

St. Joseph Pkwy.
Pierce St.
Gray St.

45
45

Museum District

🏠 ACCOMMODATIONS
Houston International Hostel, **17**
Palm Court Inn, **25**
Sara's Bed & Breakfast Inn, **23**

🍎 FOOD
Alfreda's Cafeteria, **13**
Brasil, **6**
Haiky Mi Gia Restaurant, **24**
House of Pies, **10**
Ragin Cajun, **14**

🍸 NIGHTLIFE
Helios, **5**
J.R.'s, **2**
Montrose Mining Co., **4**
South Beach, **3**
Valhalla, **22**

🏛 MUSEUMS
Buffalo Soldiers National Museum, **12**
Byzantine Fresco Chapel Museum, **8**
Contemporary Arts Museum, **18**
Holocaust Museum, **16**
Houston Museum of Natural Science, **21**
McGovern Museum of Health and Medical Science, **20**
Menil Collection, **9**
Museum of Fine Arts, **19**
Museum of Print History, **1**
Richmond Hall, **11**
Rothko Chapel, **7**

TO 1 (1 mi.) TO 2, 3 AND 4 (300 yd.)

TO BAYOU BEND 5 (.5 mi.), 6 (.75 mi.)

Alabama St.
Cleburne St.

Mt. Vernon St.
Yoakum Blvd.
Graustark St.
Yupon St.
Alabama

Montrose Blvd.
Stanford St.
Sul Ross St.
Branard St.

San Jacinto St.
Fannin St.
Main St.

59

Wheeler St.

Richmond Ave.

288

Washateria

Blodgett St.

Crawford St.
La Branch St.
Austin St.
Caroline St.

9

8

MUSEUM DISTRICT

Almeda

Southwest Fwy.

TO 10 (3.5 mi.)

10

11

Southmore Blvd.

13

Oakdale St.

TO 14 (3.5 mi.)

14

Dunlavy St.
Mandell St.
Bissonnet St.

18

19

16

17

Binz St.

20

21

Miller Outdoor Theatre

Hermann Dr.

2.5 miles
2.5 kilometers

TO BUSH AIRPORT (20 mi.)

610

Katy Frwy.
Southwest Frwy.

610
45
75
59

23

90
610
90
90

10

90A

SEE DOWNTOWN MAP

SEE MUSEUM DISTRICT MAP

45

TO MANDIR (10 mi.) (4.5 mi.)

24

25

TO SAN JACINTO BATTLEGROUND (11 mi.)

207

TO HOBBY AIRPORT (18 mi.) JOHNSON SPACE CENTER (24 mi.)

Reliant Park

288

South Loop

610

Sunset Blvd.

Japanese Gardens

Hermann Park

Houston Zoological Gardens

Rice Blvd.

22

Laboratory Dr.
Stockton Dr.
Main St.
Fannin St.

Outer Belt

Texas Medical Center

MacGregor Dr.

RICE UNIVERSITY

University Blvd.

Moursund St.

Gray Bayou
Holcombe Blvd.

TO RELIANT PARK, ASTROWORLD, LOOP

610

0   500 yards
0   500 meters

✈ 🛈 ORIENTATION AND PRACTICAL INFORMATION

Houston covers 600 square mi., and that's just within the city limits. The Houston Metroplex is a vast agglomeration of suburbs, shopping malls, freeways, and mini-downtowns sprawling over thousands of square miles on the Gulf Plains. Downtown Houston, with its compact street grid, is the geographic and historic heart of the city. Much of downtown's foot traffic goes subterranean in the network of underground **tunnels** that connect most major buildings. The prime geographic indicators are freeways, and everything is either inside or outside **The Loop,** or **I-610.** Much of Houston's ritzy shopping is in the **Uptown District,** which runs along Westheimer Rd. from downtown to The Galleria, a complex of high-end chain stores. The **Museum District** lies south of downtown and is bordered on the south by Hermann Park, Rice University, and the Texas Medical Center. The **Katy Freeway,** or **I-10,** runs due west and is the axis of much of Houston's new development. Houston's vibrant gay community is concentrated in the trendy **Montrose District.** There is a small **Chinatown** just east of downtown, and a more suburban, sprawling Chinatown and **Little Vietnam,** or DiHo, along Bellaire Blvd. east of U.S. 59.

Visitor Info: Greater Houston Convention and Visitors Bureau, 901 Bagby St. (☎437-5200 or 800-446-8786; www.visithoustontexas.com), at the corner of Walker St. in City Hall. Open M-Sa 9am-4pm, Su 11am-4pm.

Hotlines: Crisis Center, ☎468-5463. **Rape Crisis,** ☎528-7273. **Women's Center,** ☎528-2121. **Gay and Lesbian Switchboard of Houston,** ☎529-3211. All 24hr.

Medical Services: St. Joseph Hospital Downtown, 1401 St. Joseph Pkwy. (☎757-1000). **Woman's Hospital of Texas,** 7600 Fannin St. (☎790-1234).

Internet Access: Houston Public Library, 500 McKinney St. (☎832-236-1313), at Bagby St. Open M-Th 9am-9pm, F-Sa 9am-6pm, Su 2-6pm. 30min. free Internet.

Post Office: 701 San Jacinto St. (☎800-275-8777). Open M-F 8am-5pm. **Postal Code:** 77052. **Area Codes:** 713, 281, and 832; in text, 713 unless indicated.

🏠 ACCOMMODATIONS

Cheap motels dot the city's major approaches, such as the **Katy Freeway (I-10W)** and the **Southwest Freeway (U.S. 59).** Some have rates in the $30 range, but they are often unsafe, dirty, and noisy. Motels along **South Main Street** are more convenient (on bus route #8). Most **campgrounds** in the Houston area lie a considerable distance from the city center: **Lake Houston State Park,** 30 mi. to the northeast, and **Brazos Bend,** 35 mi. to the southwest, are the nearest.

Houston International Hostel, 5302 Crawford St. (☎523-1009; www.houstonhostel.com), at Oakdale St., 3 blocks east and 5 blocks north of METRORail Museum District Station. 32 beds. Internet access and wireless ($10 unlimited access), kitchen, and common area. Reception 8-10am and 5-11pm. No dorm access 10am-5pm. Common area stays open all day. Single-sex dorms $15; private rooms $23. Cash only. ❶

Palm Court Inn, 8200 South Main St. (☎668-8000 or 800-255-8904; www.palmcourtinn.com), just below Kirby Dr. On bus route 18. Rooms overlook an attractive courtyard and pool with fountains and colored lights. Includes HBO and continental breakfast. Reception 24hr. Singles $41; doubles $49. AmEx/D/DC/MC/V. ❷

Sara's Bed & Breakfast Inn, 941 Heights Blvd. (☎868-1130; www.saras.com), between 9th and 10th Ave, in historic Houston Heights. On bus route 50. This family-run B&B occupies two Victorian homes, one dating back to 1909. All rooms are doubles furnished with antiques, and most have private bath. Airy dining room with full breakfast included. No official reception hours so call ahead. Check-in 3-7pm. Check-out noon. Rooms $70-145, most around $90. AAA discount 5%. AmEx/D/DC/MC/V. ❹

YMCA, 1600 Louisiana St. (☎758-9250; www.ymcahouston.org), between Pease and Bell St. Downtown location features singles with TVs and daily maid service. Women can only stay in rooms with private baths. Laundry and kitchen on each floor. Towel deposit $2.50. Key deposit $10. 24hr. reception. Check-in after 8am. Check-out noon. Singles $28, with private bath $33. Lower weekly and monthly rates. Another **branch** is located at 7903 South Loop E (☎643-2804), off the Broadway exit from I-610, near I-45. Take bus #50 to Broadway. AmEx/D/MC/V. ❶

■ FOOD

A city by the sea, Houston has harbored many immigrants, and Houston's food takes cues from their cultures and its neighbors, both domestic and foreign. Louisiana's Cajun influence blends seamlessly with soul food, Texas barbecue, and even Mexican food. With the newfound success of downtown have come pricier restaurants. Affordable, diverse options can be found throughout the city and on the commercial strips in the suburbs. Head to ethnic enclaves like the East End, Chinatown, or Little Vietnam for the best tacos or bubble tea.

■ Ragin Cajun, 4302 Richmond Ave. (☎623-6321), just past the railroad tracks. Scarf down buckets of crawfish on checkered picnic tables amidst walls chock-full of postcards and memorabilia while zydeco music plays cheerfully in the background. The Frozen Hurricane, New Orleans's favorite drink, packs quite a punch. Take-out and delivery available. Oyster bar and restaurant with table service in back. Entrees $4-11. Open M-Th 11am-10pm, F-Sa 11am-11pm, Su 11am-9pm. AmEx/D/DC/MC/V. ❷

■ Brasil, 2604 Dunlavy St. (☎528-1993). Take bus #82 down Westheimer. This hip coffeehouse also houses a bar, restaurant, and bakery. Munch California-style salads and pizzas with toppings such as goat cheese, spinach, eggplant, and basil between walls adorned by local artists' work, or head to the foliage-enclosed patio. Plenty of vegetarian options. Breakfast served. Pizza, salads, and sandwiches $6-8. Live music many nights. Draft beer $4-7. Open M-Sa 8am-2am, Su 8am-midnight. AmEx/D/MC/V. ❷

Haiky Mi Gia Restaurant, 10780 Bellaire Blvd. (☎281-933-1666), in the shopping center parking lots between Hwy. 8 and Hillcrest Dr. Take bus #2 down Bellaire. In the heart of Little Vietnam. Menu ranges from the tame and familiar, like rice plates and vermicelli, to exotic specialties, like coconut curry frog legs. The avocado smoothie ($3) is divine. Entrees $5-9. Open M-Th and Su 8am-1am, F-Sa 8am-3am. MC/V. ❷

Otto's Barbecue, 5502 Memorial Dr. (☎864-2573 or 864-8526), behind an old strip mall. A Houston institution since 1951, Otto's recreates a ranch house atmosphere with mouth-watering links and ribs. The Bush Plate is the favorite of a certain former President, who has been known to drop in. Open M-Sa 11am-9pm. AmEx/D/MC/V. ❷

Alfreda's Cafeteria, 5101 Almeda Rd. (☎523-6462), 3 blocks from Houston International Hostel, serves soul food for the penny-pincher. The special of the day ($5.50) includes meat, vegetables, and bread. Open daily 6:30am-7:30pm. AmEx/D/MC/V. ❶

House of Pies, 3112 Kirby Dr. (☎528-3816). Little has changed in this classic 60s diner, where 44 kinds of pies and cakes grace the formica countertops, drawing a diverse, sweet-toothed clientele. Try the Bayoo Goo pie, with pecans, cream cheese, vanilla custard, and whipped cream ($3.25). Breakfast (served all day), sandwiches, and entrees $5.50-7. Pies and cakes $2.50-3.50 per slice. Take-out available. Open 24hr. Also at 6142 Westheimer Rd. (☎782-1290). AmEx/D/DC/MC/V. ❶

TEXAS

TEXAS

🜨 SIGHTS

JOHNSON SPACE CENTER. The city's most popular attraction, **Space Center Houston,** is outside Houston city limits in Clear Lake, TX. Admission includes tours of the center's historic mission control, an abandoned prototype hangar, and the astronaut training facility, as well as educational film showings in Texas's largest Giant Screen theater. The complex also houses models of Gemini, Apollo, and Mercury crafts. No visit is complete without taking a moment to touch the moon rock on public display. *(1601 NASA Pkwy. 1. Take I-45 south to NASA Rd. (Exit 25) then head east 3 mi.; or take bus #246. ☎ 281-244-2100; www.spacecenter.org. Opens between 9-10am and closes between 5-7pm but hours vary, so call ahead. $18, seniors $17, ages 4-11 $14. Parking $4.)* The **Level 9 Tour** takes visitors to areas of the Space Center not usually open to tourists, including the New Mission Control Center, the Robotics Lab, the Space Environment Simulation Lab, and the Neutral Buoyancy Lab. For the wannabe rocketman (or woman), it's the only way to see the sights. *(☎ 244-2115. 1 4hr. tour per day M-F 11:50am. $63. Limited to 12 people, 16+ only; reservations recommended.)*

THE SAN JACINTO BATTLEGROUND STATE HISTORICAL SITE. The park commemorates Sam Houston's victory over Santa Ana's Mexican troops with a 570 ft. monument that, in true Texas fashion, is taller than the Washington Monument. The monument is closed temporarily for repairs; call ahead. In the monument's base is a small museum of Texas history told from a Texas point of view. The Battleship Texas, on the other side of the park, is the last remaining ship of the Dreadnought era and the only surviving battleship to have served in both World Wars. Visitors can explore the ship at will, even descending into the bowels of the engine room. *(Take Hwy. 225 E. to the Battleground Rd./Hwy. 134 exit and head north. Park open daily 9am-6pm. Free. Museum: ☎ 281-479-2421. Open daily 9am-6pm. Free. 35min. multimedia slide show daily every hr. 10am-5pm. $4.50, seniors $4, under 13 $3.50. Battleship: ☎ 281-479-2431. Open daily 10am-5pm. $7/$4/free.)*

HERMANN PARK. This 445-acre park provides respite from urban life as well as numerous opportunities for recreation. The grounds themselves are free and open all day long and include **McGovern Lake,** the reflecting pool, the Southern Pacific steam locomotive, and the **Miller Outdoor Theater.** The **Japanese Tea Garden** was designed by renowned landscape architect Ken Nakajima. Pleasure-seekers can rent a paddleboat on McGovern Lake *($7)* or ride the Kiddie Train *($2, weekends only).* Near the northern entrance of the park, the **Houston Museum of Natural Science** includes a planetarium, IMAX theater, and 60 ft.-high butterfly center, in addition to its permanent and traveling exhibits. Weiss Energy Hall covers a topic of local importance: oil, and the science associated with its production. The **Houston Zoological Gardens,** at the park's southern end, features over 700 species, including a special section for animals native to Texas. *(Museum of Natural Science: 1 Hermann Circle Dr. ☎ 639-4629; www.hmns.org. Exhibits open M-Sa 9am-6pm, Su 11am-6pm. Museum $6, seniors and under 12 $3.50; IMAX $7/$4.50; planetarium $5/$3.50; butterfly center $5/$3.50. Museum exhibits free 30min. before closing. Japanese tea garden: www.japanesegarden.org. Open daily 10am-6pm. Free. Zoo: 1513 N. MacGregor. ☎ 533-6500; www.houstonzoo.org. Open Mar.-Sept. 9am-6pm, Oct.-Feb. 9am-5pm. $7, seniors $5, ages 3-12 $3.)*

DOWNTOWN. Downtown Houston reads like a Who's Who of famous modern architects. Those who take the time to stroll Houston's streets at surface level (as opposed to retreating into the tunnels) will be rewarded by one of the richest samplings of business architecture in the United States, spanning over a century. At 70 floors, the **JP Morgan Chase Tower,** designed by I.M. Pei in 1981, is the tallest building in Houston. The public is welcome to take the elevator to the observation deck on the 60th floor to take in the 20 mi. vistas to the west. Outside the tower in the courtyard stands the largest freestanding sculpture by Juan Miró in the United States. *(600 Travis St. M-F 9am-5pm. Free.)* One block north on Travis St., the public can view the *Houston Chronicle's* **printing presses** in action through giant windows. Two blocks further up Travis St., **Market Square Park** is the historic center of Houston. Having declined into a parking lot in the mid-20th century, it is now restored as a handsome park square with tiles telling the history of Houston in black and white photos. Although there is much to see above ground, the **tunnels** should not be missed. A veritable underground city, 6.3 mi. of tunnel connect the buildings of downtown so that Houstonians can go from their cars to work to lunch to meet with a colleague in another building without ever stepping foot outside. The **Buffalo Bayou,** recently re-engineered and re-landscaped, forms the northwestern border of downtown. Just across the Bayou is the **Downtown Aquarium,** which is more of an entertainment complex than just a simple aquarium. *(410 Bagby St. ☎223-3474. Aquarium exhibits open M-Th and Su 10am-10pm, F-Sa 10am-11pm. $7.50, seniors $6.50, ages 2-12 $5.50. Restaurants and lounge operate on different hours—call to check.)*

ART ATTRACTIONS. At Houston's **Museum of Fine Arts,** the Caroline Weiss Law building showcases contemporary and modern collections, while the Audrey Jones Beck building displays everything from ancient European art to Impressionist pieces. Be sure to see Bouguereau's famous painting, "The Elder Sister," and the Glassell Collection of African Gold, considered one of the best of its kind in the world. *(1001 Bissonet. ☎639-7300; www.mfah.org. Open Tu-W 10am-5pm, Th 10am-9pm, F-Sa 10am-7pm, Su 12:15-7pm. $7, students and seniors $3.50. Audio tour $10/$5. Th free. Garden: 5101 Montrose Blvd. Open daily 9am-10pm. Free.)* Across the street, the **Contemporary Arts Museum** contains no permanent collections but rotates on a quarterly basis the works of well-known international artists in its dramatic, large rooms. *(5216 Montrose Blvd. ☎284-8258; www.camh.org. Open Tu-W and F-Sa 10am-5pm, Th 10am-9pm, Su noon-5pm. Free.)* The **Menil Collection** was founded in 1987 by the Menil family and consists of five buildings within a few blocks of each other in a peaceful residential neighborhood to the west of Montrose. Showcasing Surrealist paintings and sculptures, Byzantine and medieval artifacts, and other European, American, and African art, the Menil Collection also features touring installments. *(1515 Sul Ross. ☎525-9400; www.menil.org. Open W-Su 11am-7pm. Free.)* **Richmond Hall** contains nothing but the neon light sculptures of Dan Flavin. *(1500 Richmond Ave. Same hours as Menil.)* One block away from the Menil is the Rothko Chapel, housing 14 of abstract expressionist Mark Rothko's famous monochromatic paintings in a nondenominational sanctuary that also serves as a gathering place for local human rights activists. The Broken Obelisk sculpture out front provides a backdrop for area religious festivals staged on the chapel's grounds. *(1409 Sul Ross. Open daily 10am-6pm. Free.)* The **Byzantine Fresco Chapel Museum** displays the restored ornate dome and apse from a 13th-century Byzantine chapel in Cyprus that was rescued in 1983 from antiquity thieves. *(4011 Yupon. ☎521-3990. Open F-Su 11am-6pm. Free.)*

BAYOU BEND. Ima Hogg was once one of Houston's wealthiest women, and when she left her mansion and collections as the **Bayou Bend Collection and Gardens,** Houston gained one of the finest collections of American decorative art in the US. Hidden among the collection are portraits by John Singleton Copley and silver pieces by Paul Revere. Touring the gardens is a pleasant way to pass a couple of hours. *(1 Wescott St. ☎639-7750; www.mfah.org/bayoubend. Enter from Memorial Dr. and walk across the suspension bridge over the bayou. 90min. tours leave every 15min. Tu-Sa 10-11:30am and 1-2:45pm. On Sa afternoon, Su, and all month in Aug. visitors receive audio guidebooks in lieu of guides. $10, seniors and students $8.50, ages 10-18 $5, under 10 not permitted on tours. Gardens open Tu-Sa 10am-5pm, Su 1-5pm. 1hr. garden tours by reservation. $3,* *under 10 free.)* For the European counterpart to Bayou Bend, visit the Rienzi, located along the same ravine. **Rienzi Mansion** exhibits Georgian English decorative art including gilded footstools. *(1406 Kirby Dr. ☎ 639-7800. Open M and Th-Sa 10am-4pm, Su 1-5pm. $6, seniors $4. Viewing of the house is only available via tour; call ahead.)*

OTHER MUSEUMS. In the late 1800s, members of the all-black units in the American army were nicknamed "Buffalo Soldiers," both because of their naturally curly hair and as a sign of respect for their fighting spirit. The ▧**Buffalo Soldiers National Museum** contains artifacts, memorabilia, uniforms, and weapons illustrating the history of African-Americans in the armed forces. Though some of these artifacts rival the Smithsonian's collection, the museum's limited funds mean these objects aren't even protected by glass. *(1834 Southmore Blvd. ☎ 942-8920; www.buffalosoldiermuseum.com. Open M-F 10am-5pm, Sa 10am-4pm. Free.)* The ▧**Museum of Print History** is in a less convenient location than its counterparts in the Museum District, but its unique subject matter sets it apart. The collections contain hundreds of documents, maps, and facsimiles produced by antique printing presses, as well as dozens of the presses themselves. Visitors can watch artists-in-residence use a model of the Gutenburg press. *(1324 West Clay. ☎ 522-4652; www.printingmuseum.org. $5, seniors and students $2, Th free. Open Tu-Sa 10am-5pm.)* The cylindrical architecture of the **Holocaust Museum** is meant to evoke the smokestack of a concentration camp. The museum has a rotating art gallery and two films about the Holocaust. *(5401 Caroline St. ☎ 942-8000; www.hmh.org. Open M-F 9am-5pm, Sa-Su noon-5pm. Free.)* The **McGovern Museum of Health and Medical Science** uses games, interactive exhibits, and giant walk-through models of organs to teach children about physiology and the workings of the human body. *(1515 Hermann Dr. at Crawford. ☎ 521-1515; www.museumofhealth.org. Open Tu-Sa 9am-5pm, Su noon-5pm. $6, seniors and ages 4-17 $4, Th free.)* It looks like it belongs in 18th-century India, but **Mandir** is neither old nor a museum. Mandir is a brand-new temple of Swaminarayan Hinduism, made by thousands of pieces of marble that were carved in India. The Swaminarayans welcome the public, provided you remove your shoes and cover your shoulders and legs. The temperature inside the temple is 20 degrees cooler because of the marble, allowing the mind and body to relax. *(1150 Brand Lane. ☎ 281-499-7974; www.swaminarayan.org. Take U.S. 59 S to Kirkwood exit. Open daily 9am-8:45pm.)*

▐ ENTERTAINMENT

From March to October, symphony, opera, ballet companies, and various professional theaters stage free performances at the **Miller Outdoor Theatre** (☎ 284-8352), in Hermann Park. Pick up a schedule at the on-site concession stand, or visit www.milleroutdoortheatre.com. The annual **Shakespeare Festival** struts and frets upon the stage in August. The downtown **Alley Theatre,** 615 Texas Ave., puts on Broadway-caliber productions at moderate prices. (☎ 228-8421; www.alleytheatre.org. Tickets $37-54; student rush tickets 1hr. before the show $12 M-Th and Su, $20 F-Sa.) **Bayou Place,** 500 Texas Ave., contains the **Angelika Film Center,** which plays foreign as well as mainstream domestic films. (☎ 333-3456. $8, students $6.) Bayou Place also holds the Hard Rock Cafe and the **Verizon Wireless Theater** (☎ 230-1666), where big-name music tours often perform. The **Hobby Center for the Performing Arts,** 800 Bagby St. (☎ 315-2400; www.thehobbycenter.org), features a dome ceiling with a fiber optic display of the Texas night sky and hosts **Theatre Under the Stars,** America's largest nonprofit producer of musicals, as well as traveling Broadway productions in the **Broadway in Houston Series. Jones Hall,** 614 Louisiana St. (☎ 227-3974), stages more of Houston's highbrow entertainment. The **Houston Symphony Orchestra** performs in Jones Hall from September to May. (☎ 227-2787. Tickets $20-95.) Between October and May, the **Houston Grand Opera** produces eight operas in the nearby Wortham Center, 500 Texas Ave. (☎546-0200; www.houston-grandopera.org. Tickets $30-275; student rush tickets available day of show $15-30, call ahead to reserve.) Major League Baseball's **Houston Astros** (www.astros.com) play at Minute Maid Park (☎295-8000), located at the intersections of Texas, Crawford, and Congress St. near Union Station downtown. From February to mid-March, both the Reliant Center and Reliant Arena house the **Houston Livestock Show and Rodeo** (☎832-667-1000; www.hlsr.com). It's nothin' but net in the new downtown Toyota Center, at Polk and Crawford St., home of the NBA's **Houston Rockets** (www.rockets.com), while the NFL's **Houston Texans** (www.houstontexans.com) pass the pigskin at Reliant Stadium, 8400 Kirby Dr.

☒ NIGHTLIFE

Since the 2004 Super Bowl, downtown Houston has been reclaiming its stake in the city's nightlife. Most nightlife is concentrated along Main St., which is closed to traffic between Capitol and Congress St. from 4pm-2am on weekends to make way for partiers. METRORail heads right down Main St. and runs until 2am on weekends. Montrose is the center of the gay nightlife scene, and while its bars tend to be mostly gay, dance clubs in Montrose have a mixed crowd.

Sambuca Jazz Cafe, 909 Texas Ave. (☎ 224-5299). This wood-laden bar and restaurant hosts live jazz every night of the week. Performers range from blues to modern and free-form jazz to straight-ahead swing. Weekends tend to have more upbeat music for dancing. Cigar bar upstairs. Happy hour 4-7pm with $3 appetizers, $2 domestic beer, and $4 martinis. No cover. Open M-Th and Su 11am-midnight, F 11am-2am, Sa 5pm-2am.

Helios, 411 Westheimer Ave. (☎526-4648; www.heliosrising.org) at Taft St. Take bus #82. Set in an old Victorian home, this ragged mecca for artists, gays, and alternative minds is "so funky it's hip." Live music several nights a week spans reggae, hip-hop, punk, rock, and blues. Sometimes a $5-10 cover after 10pm, but mention *Let's Go* and get in free, or receive a drink special.

Valhalla, in Rice University's Keck Hall (☎348-3258). For "gods, heroes, mythical beings, and cheap beer," students, locals, and travelers alike descend to the depths of Keck Hall. Local microbrews from $0.85. Open M-F 4pm-2am, Su 7pm-2am.

J.R.'s, 808 Pacific St. (☎521-2519; www.jrsbarandgrill.com), **Montrose Mining Co.,** 807 Pacific St. (☎529-7488), and **South Beach,** 810 Pacific Ave. (☎529-7623; www.southbeachthenightclub.com). Take bus #82 down Westheimer to Crocker St., and walk 2 blocks north. 3 gay bars with 3 distinct atmospheres make for ideal bar-hopping. **J.R's** is the most laid-back and traditional bar. No cover. Open daily noon-2am. **Montrose Mining Co.** has more of a western feel, and patrons are more likely to be sporting leather. Open daily 4pm-2am. Swankier **South Beach,** with an iced martini bar and pulsing dance floor, attracts a mixed crowd, including plenty of hip, young straight people. Every hr., liquid nitrogen pours down from the ceiling, instantly chilling the bar by 20 degrees and plunging dancers into a sea of fog. Drink specials until 10pm. Cover up to $10. Open W-Su 9pm-5am.

GALVESTON ISLAND ☎409

Although only an hour from Houston, Galveston is a destination in its own right. It was once the largest and most powerful city in Texas, a claim to which over 6000 historic buildings stand testament. Things changed on in 1900, when a devastating hurricane ripped through the city and claimed 6000 lives, still the worst natural disaster in US history. By 1915 Houston had built its ship channel and Galveston lost its key role in the maritime industry. Today, the 32 mi. island is powered mainly by tourism, its cool sea breezes offering a much-needed respite from the Houston heat. Taking its name from the seawall that protects Galveston from hurricanes, **Seawall Boulevard** runs along the Gulf Coast and is full of cheap eats.

On the north side of the city, the historic commercial district, known as **The Strand,** boasts one of the largest collections of commercial Victorian buildings in the US. Trolleys clang along historic tracks that follow two routes, one to the University of Texas Medical School and one to Seawall Beach ($1). Free Wi-Fi hotspots are available at 23rd and Strand, 37th and Seawall, and 6th and Seawall. Of the numerous museums along the Strand, two of the best explore the industries that made this region great. The ▨**Galveston Railway Museum,** 123 Rosenburg St., at the west end of the Strand, housed in the restored Art Deco Union Station, pays homage to that history with displays, model trains, and, best of all, dozens of actual trains spanning an entire century. There has been no restoration; everything is in its original state, for better or for worse. With no off-limits areas, visitors are free to explore every corner of the trains, from the luxurious Pullman car parlors to the kitchen galleys to the locomotive cabs. (☎765-5700. Open daily 10am-4pm. $5, seniors $4.50, ages 4-12 $2.50. AAA discount $1.) The one-of-a-kind ▨**Ocean Star Offshore Energy Center,** Pier 19, Harborside Dr. at 20th St., demystifies the oil drilling rigs that dot the Gulf of Mexico horizon. The museum is located on a retired oil rig anchored just offshore and reached by a causeway. Explore the history, science, politics, and ecology of off-shore drilling, then head out to the deck of the rig to see the equipment up close. (☎766-7827. Open daily June-Aug. 10am-6pm; Sept.-May 10am-5pm. $6, seniors $5, ages 7-18 $4.)

In addition to The Strand, there are three other national historic districts in Galveston. Primarily residential, these districts are best explored on foot. Pick up a map at the visitors center to see the exact boundaries of the districts. Although most of the historic buildings are private homes, a few are open to public tours, including the elegant **Moody Mansion,** 2618 Broadway, at 26th St., former home of Galveston's leading family, which contains original furnishings and stunning stained glass. (☎762-7668. Open M-Sa 10am-4pm, Su noon-4pm. $6, seniors $5, ages 6-18 $3.) Three glass pyramids house a tropical rainforest, aquarium, science museum, and IMAX theater at **Moody Gardens,** 1 Hope Blvd., a tourist-oriented theme park. The grounds themselves are well-manicured and free. (From Seawall Blvd., take a right on 81st St. ☎683-4200 or 800-582-4673; www.moodygardens.com. Open daily in summer 10am-9pm; winter 9am-6pm.)

Let's face it: the real reason most people come to Galveston is for the beaches. The beach along Seawall Blvd. is free, and so is the street parking. For more amenities, head to one of the parks farther down the island, such as **#3 Beach Pocket Park,** which has restrooms, showers, playgrounds, and a concession stand. (Open daily 9am-6pm. $7 per car.) The only beach in Galveston that permits alcoholic beverages is **East Beach,** on the eastern edge of the island. Because of the booze, live music, and weekend bikini contests, it's more commonly known as "Party Beach." (www.eastbeachparty.com. $7; weekdays free after 5pm, weekends after 7:30pm.) For an even more raucous time, teenagers and college students take the free ferry to **Port Bolivar** and then drive to **Crystal Beach,** fondly dubbed "The Zoo" because it permits not only booze but firecrackers and bonfires. (Ferry operates 24hr. but the line is often over 1hr. long.) One of only four hostels in the state of Texas, **HI-Galveston ❶,** 201 Seawall Blvd., at the northern tip of town, is located inside the Sandpiper Motel and has direct beach access, free wireless Internet, coffee, laundry, kitchen, and a pool. The doors lock at 11pm but the 24hr. staff will let you in late. (☎765-9431; www.sandpipermotel.com. Dorms $19.50, members $18.50.) The oldest restaurant on the island, **The Original ❷,** 1401 Market St. dishes up tasty Tex-Mex, with enchilada plates starting at $5.50. (☎762-6001. Open M-Th 11am-9pm, F-Sa 8am-10pm, Su 8am-9:30pm.) Galveston is 51 mi. south of Houston on I-45.

CORPUS CHRISTI ☎361

Corpus Christi's shoreside location makes it a multifaceted money-maker. The warm waters from the Gulf of Mexico produce Corpus Christi's copious amounts of both tourists and crude oil. Summer vacationers are replaced in the cooler months by "winter Texans," a breed of northern mobile-home owners who head south to enjoy coastal warmth. Defined by its pricey knick-knacks, natural stretches of sand, and offshore oil derricks on the horizon, Corpus Christi is a unique Texas stopover.

▣ TRANSPORTATION. Greyhound, 702 N. Chaparral (☎882-9206; www.greyhound.com; open daily 7:30am-12:45am.), runs to Austin (6½hr., 3 per day, $31), Dallas (10-11hr., 8 per day, $49), and Houston (5hr., 7 per day, $24). **Regional Transit Authority** (☎289-2600), also known as the "B," operates a dozen bus routes within Corpus Christi. Get maps and schedules at the visitors center or at **The B Headquarters,** 1806 S. Alameda. (☎883-2287. Open M-F 8am-5pm.) City Hall, Port Ayers, Six Points, Padre Staples Mall, and the Staples St. stations are central transfer points. (Runs M-Sa 5:30am-9:30pm, Su 10am-7:30pm. Rush hour $0.50, off-peak $0.25; students, seniors, and children $0.25; transfers free.) The **Harbor Ferry** runs between the Art Museum, Aquarium, and downtown at People St. (Runs in summer daily 10:30am-6:30pm. All-day pass $3.) On the north side of Harbor Bridge, the free **Beach Shuttle** travels to the beach, aquarium, and other attractions. (Runs in summer daily 10:30am-6:30pm.) **Taxi: Yellow Cab,** ☎884-3211.

▰ PRACTICAL INFORMATION. Greater Corpus Christi lines the shores of Corpus Christi Bay. Downtown Corpus Christi is at the eastern edge of the bay, with residential districts stretching southward and the beaches of Padre Island rounding out the eastern shore of the bay. Most attractions, restaurants, and nightlife are in a walkable area either in downtown or on the island-like peninsula just north of Harbor Bridge. **Convention and Visitors Bureau,** 1823 N. Chaparral, six blocks north of I-37, has maps, brochures, and answers. (☎561-2000 or 800-766-2322; www.corpuschristicvb.org. Open daily 9am-5pm.) **Medical Services: Spohn Hospital Shoreline,** 600 Elizabeth St. (☎881-3000). **Hotlines: Battered Women and Rape Victims Shelter,** ☎881-8888. Operates 24hr. **Internet Access: Corpus Christi Public Library,** 805 Comanche, just west of the Central Business District. (☎880-7000. Open M-Th 9am-9pm, F-Sa 9am-6pm, Su 2-6pm. 30min. max.) **Post Office:** 809 Nueces Bay Blvd., just south of I-37 Exit 1E. (☎800-275-8777. Open M-F 8am-5:30pm, Sa 8am-1pm.) **Postal Code:** 78469. **Area Code:** 361.

▰ ACCOMMODATIONS. Posh hotels line the shoreline in downtown Corpus Christi. North of Harbor Bridge are several waterfront motels, but they are pricey as well. Cheap motels can be found along Leopard St. south of town or off of Exits 3-5 on I-37, a few miles north of town, with some even in the $25-35 range (though not all those are clean or safe). The **Railway Inn Suites ❸,** 4343 Ocean Dr., are located on the fashionable Ocean Drive, 4 mi. south of town on bus route #6. The railroad motif is carried out not just in memorabilia and artwork but also in a kiddie train that follows a ¼ mi. track around the hotel. The price and free continental breakfast make it a good choice for families. (☎729-7245; www.railwayinnsuites.com. M-F 2+ person suites from $60, Sa-Su from $70.) **Camping ❶** at Padre Island beaches starts at $10 (p. 676). **Labonte Park ❶,** right off I-37 at Exit 16, 18 mi. from downtown, allows free camping in a grassy area along the river. (☎241-1464. Toilets; no showers.) Pick up a permit from the **visitors center** next door. (Open daily 9am-5pm.)

TEXAS

⬛⬛ FOOD AND NIGHTLIFE. With the Gulf in its backyard, seafood dominates Corpus Christi's cuisine. **Pier 99 ❷,** 2822 N. Shoreline Dr., right next to the *USS Lexington,* serves it up fried, boiled, grilled, or blackened. (☎887-0764. Lunch specials $6-7. Po' boys $8. Live music F-Su. Open daily 11am-10pm.) **Akà Sushi ❸,** 415 N. Water St. at Lawrence St., prepares seafood in a slightly different style. The hearty Cajun Crawfish Roll and Corpus Tempura Roll blend the Japanese cuisine with Gulf influences. (☎882-8885. Lunch specials $7-10. Dinner $9-15. Open M-Th 11am-2:30pm and 5-10pm, F 11am-2:30pm and 5pm-11pm, Sa 5pm-11pm. MC/V.) Several bars and dance clubs line Chaparral in downtown, which is closed off for pedestrians Friday and Saturday nights. Groove to southern rhythm 'n' blues seven nights a week at **⬛Dr. Rockits Blues Bar,** 709 Chaparral, a classic bar with high ceilings, neon lights, and Jaegermeister on tap. (☎884-7634; www.drrockits-bluesbar.com. Cover $4-8. Open M-Th 4:30pm-2am, F-Sa 7pm-2am.) Boot-scoot to country at **Dead Eye Dick's,** then bump and grind to dance at **Stinger's,** both at 301 N. Chaparral St. (☎882-2192. 18+. Cover $3-8. Open Th-Sa 9pm-2am.)

◼ SIGHTS. Despite the ravenous gulls, Corpus Christi's **beaches** are without a doubt the city's top attraction. However, if it's beaches you're looking for, the best ones are actually located outside of the city on Padre Island, at least a 30min. drive away (p. 676). In-town swimming beaches are located next to the *USS Lexington* (metered parking) and at Magee Beach, just south of downtown (free parking). On the north side of Harbor Bridge, the **Texas State Aquarium,** 2710 N. Shoreline Blvd., focuses on animals native to the Gulf of Mexico. The state-of-the-art Dolphin Bay has above- and below-water viewing areas, with four shows a day. One exhibit features sharks and rays roaming, in true Texas fashion, beneath an oil platform. (☎881-1200 or 800-477-4853; www.texasstateaquarium.org. Open June-Aug. daily 9am-6pm; Sept.-May M-Sa 9am-5pm. $13, seniors $11, ages 4-12 $8. Parking $3.) Just next door floats the aircraft carrier **USS Lexington,** a WWII relic that made a cameo in the Hollywood blockbuster *Pearl Harbor.* The "Lex," as it is affectionately known, has completed secret missions in Formosa, Cuba, and Laos, served as a training vessel, and now welcomes tourists both below and above her decks, where 19 WWII planes sit on display. (☎888-4873 or 800-523-9539. Open daily June-Aug. 9am-6pm; Sept.-May 9am-5pm. $12, seniors $10, ages 4-12 $7.) Pick up $1-off coupons to the aquarium and ship at the visitors center. **Heritage Park,** 1581 Chaparral, near the visitors center, is a collection of historic homes representing different immigrant groups, laid out in an attractive park. (☎883-0639. Free.)

NORTH PADRE ISLAND ☎361

At over 100 mi., Padre Island is the longest stretch of undeveloped barrier island in the world. North Padre Island, east of Corpus Christi, is the more mellow cousin to South Padre Island and its hordes of drunken spring breakers, yet offers ample opportunities for adventure in windsurfing, swimming, and surf fishing. After reaching Padre Island by the JFK causeway from Corpus Christi, turn left for **Port Aransas** and **Mustang Island State Park,** or right for **Padre Balli County Park** and **Padre Island National Seashore (PINS).** There are also numbered beach access points that are not affiliated with any parks, but you'll need a sticker to park your car (year-long pass $6, available at Padre Balli). **Mustang Island State Park ❶** charges $3 for day use and an additional $7 for tent camping on the beach, with free use of the hot showers at the RV sites. **Padre Balli County Park ❶** offers less serenity but more activities. Campers choose from a narrow grass strip surrounded by asphalt, or the beach itself for $10 a night (no entrance fee; parking sticker required). Hot showers are available. **Bob Hall Pier,** the main fishing pier, is located right on the beach. (Open 24hr. Entrance fee $1. Pole rentals $25, $15 per half-day.)

Part of the National Park System, PINS has the cleanest and best-protected beaches, dunes, and grassland on the island. (Entrance $10 for 2 weeks, $20 for 1 year.) **Malaquite Visitors Center** is 5 mi. south of the Causeway and bridge to the island. (☎949-8068; www.nps.gov/pais. Open daily in summer 8:30am-6pm; winter 8:30am-4:30pm.) The **PINS Campground ❶**, 1 mi. north of the visitors center, has restrooms, free cold showers, and an asphalt area for RVs. (Sites $8.) Camping in unmarked sites farther down the beach is free, and campers still have 24hr. access to showers and bathrooms. A lucky few may spot an endangered Kemp's Ridley sea turtle and should report it to a ranger. Boat launching is possible from the **Grasslands Nature Trail**, a ¾ mi. paved loop through sand dunes and grasslands. Guide pamphlets are available at the trailhead. Entrance to **Bird Island Basin**, on the lagoon side of the island, is $10 for a yearly pass or $5 per day and can be purchased at the entrance station or Malaquite Visitors Center. Also on the lagoon side, **Worldwinds Windsurfing** rents a large range of windsurfing equipment as well as sea kayaks at one of the best windsurfing sites in the nation. (☎949-7472 or 800-793-7471. Beginner's rig and lesson $50. Single $20 per 2hr., $40 per day.) Two-wheel drive vehicles can drive on the first 5 mi. of beach below Malquite. Visitors with 4WD and a taste for solitude should make the 60 mi. trek to the **Mansfield Channel**, the most remote and untraveled area of the seashore, where shipwrecks still lie on the beach. Call the **PINS Headquarters** (☎949-8173), 3½ mi. south of the park entrance, for emergency assistance. **Area Code:** 361.

LAREDO   ☎956

Laredo is the busiest inland port on the entire United States border. One look at the steady procession of trains carrying finished automobiles into the US from Mexico makes this abundantly clear. Yet behind the bustle of trade lies the still-beating heart of an old town. Laredo was founded on San Agustín Plaza in 1755, and that plaza remains the center of life and activity in the town. You can pick up a free walking guide brochure at the **Convention and Visitors Bureau**, 501 San Agustín, and discover the fine architecture, spanning over two centuries, to be seen in downtown Laredo for yourself. (☎800-361-3360. Open M-F 8am-5pm, Sa 9am-5pm.) Laredo was the capital of the Republic of the Río Grande, a breakaway state from Mexico that existed for 10 months in 1840. The story of this unusual republic is told at the **Republic of the Río Grande Museum**, 1005 Zaragoza St. (☎727-0977. Open Tu-Sa 9am-4pm, Su 1pm-4pm. $1.) **Texas A&M International University (TAMIU)**, Bob Bullock Loop, just 2 mi. north of Lake Casa Blanca, attracts students from all over the world with its renowned Center for Western Hemispheric Trade and its elegant, symmetrical campus. If you take the short walk across International Bridge 2 ($0.80 to enter Mexico, $0.30 to re-enter the US), you'll find yourself instantly in Nuevo Laredo. Several finely landscaped squares and fountains await on the other side, but don't stray too far from the main boulevard, especially if visiting after dark. Cheap motels line San Bernardo St. **Lake Casa Blanca State Park ❶**, 5102 Bob Bullock Loop, has spacious campsites overlooking freshwater Lake Casa Blanca. (☎725-3826, reservations 512-389-8900. Sites $15 including $3 entrance fee.) Brush up on your Spanish and head to **Pancho Villa ❶**, 515 San Agustín, for $3 breakfast and $5 lunch plates. (☎729-9757. Open daily 7am-3pm.) **Greyhound**, 610 Salinas (☎723-4324; www.greyhound.com; open 24hr.), sends buses to Houston (6½hr., 6 per day, $30) and San Antonio (2¾hr., 11 per day, $20). The **Nuevo Laredo Tourist Bureau** is on the east side of Plaza Hidalgo. (☎867-712-7397. Open M-F 9am-2pm.) Free **Internet** access is available at the **Laredo Public Library**, 1120 E. Calton Rd. (☎795-2400. Open M and F-Sa 9am-6pm, Tu-Th 9am-8pm, Su 1pm-5pm.) **Post Office:** 1300 Matamoros. (☎800-275-8777. Open M-F 9am-5pm.) **Postal Code:** 78040. **Area Code:** 956.

TEXAS

WEST TEXAS

AMARILLO   ☎806

Named for the yellow clay of nearby Lake Meredith (*amarillo* is Spanish for "yellow"), Amarillo began as a railroad construction camp in 1887 and ultimately evolved into a Texas-size truck stop. After years of cattle and oil, Amarillo is now the prime overnight stop for motorists en route from Dallas, Houston, or Oklahoma City to Denver and other Western destinations. For travelers, it's little more than a one-day city, but what a grand, shiny stop it is.

◢◪ ORIENTATION AND PRACTICAL INFORMATION. Amarillo sits at the intersection of I-27, I-40, and U.S. 287/87. Chances are, you're arriving by car, and good thing, as this is definitely a city best explored behind the wheel. Rte. 335 (the Loop) encircles the city. The city's main street, **6th Avenue (Route 66)**, runs east-west through downtown. **Greyhound,** 700 S. Tyler (☎374-5371; www.greyhound.com; open 24hr.), runs to Dallas (8hr., 4 per day, $65-70) and Santa Fe (11hr., 3 per day, $59-64). **Amarillo City Transit,** 801 SE 23rd, operates eight bus routes departing from 3rd and Fillmore St. Maps are at the office. (☎378-3095. Buses run every 15-30min. M-Sa 6:30am-6:30pm. $0.75.) The **Amarillo Convention and Visitors Bureau,** 401 S. Buchanan St., has free maps and info. (☎374-8474 or 800-692-1338; www.amarillo-cvb.org. Open Apr.-Sept. M-F 9am-6pm, Sa-Su 10am-4pm.; Oct.-Mar. M-F 8:30am-5:30pm, Sa-Su noon-4pm.) **Internet Access: Public Library,** 413 E. 4th Ave., at Buchanan. (☎378-3054; Open M-Th 9am-9pm, Sa 9am-6pm, Su 2-6pm.) **Post Office:** 505 E. 9th Ave., at Buchanan St. (☎373-3192. Open M-F 8am-5pm.) **Postal Code:** 79105. **Area Code:** 806.

▐▐ ACCOMMODATIONS AND FOOD. Budget and chain motels crowd the sides of I-40, I-27, and U.S. 287/87 right near Amarillo, with room rates running in the $25-35 range. Try the **Big Texan Motel ❸,** 7701 I-40 E (take Exit 74), where each room is painted in its own color and style. There's a horse hotel out back in case you rode in on your trusty steed. (☎372-5000. Restaurant and swimming pool. Singles $45-50; doubles $60-65. AAA and AARP discount $5.) **Palo Duro Canyon** (p. 679), 23 mi. from town, has tent and RV sites for $10 and $15, respectively. **KOA Kampground ❶,** 1100 Folsom Rd., 10 mi. east of town, has friendly service and grassy, shaded tent sites. Take I-40 to Exit 75, go north to Rte. 60, then east 1 mi. (☎335-1792, 800-562-3431 for reservations. Pool in summer. Free Wi-Fi. Reception daily June-Aug. 8am-10pm; Sept.-May 8am-7pm. Tent sites $21, water and electricity $27-30, full hookup $28-31.) At I-40 and Georgia, north of the interstate, heaping portions and a friendly vibe make **Dyer's BBQ ❷** a favorite. The ribs plate includes three finger-lickin'-good ribs, potato salad, cole slaw, baked beans, apricots, and onion rings for $8. (☎358-7104. Open M-Sa 11am-10pm, Su 11am-9pm.) The bright yellow **Big Texan Steak Ranch ❸,** 7701 I-40 E, next to the Big Texan Motel, is a longtime Route 66 institution. Eat a 72 oz. steak in under an hour and receive the meal for free. Note, though, that an unfinished steak will set you back $50. If that's not your idea of fun, maybe the fried rattlesnake ($6.50) or Rocky Mountain "oysters" ($11) are. (☎372-6000. Free Wi-Fi. Open daily 7am-10:30pm. AmEx/D/DC/MC/V.) For Mexican eats, head to **Tacos García ❷,** 1100 S. Ross. Try the Laredo platter (3 roast beef *flautas* with rice, beans, and guacamole; $7.75), and delicious sopapillas for $3. (☎371-0411. Daily specials $5-6. Open M 10:30am-9:30pm, Tu-Sa 10:30am-10pm, Su 10:30am-3:30pm. AmEx/D/MC/V.)

⬛ **SIGHTS.** The ⬛**Amarillo Livestock Auction,** 100 Manhattan St., 1½ mi. east of town off 3rd Ave., is the largest livestock auction in the country. Visitors are welcome to sit alongside real-life cowboys as they bid on cows or to scale the catwalks and get a birds-eye view of the cattle pins who rustle the cattle up for auction. (☎373-7464. Auctions held Tu 10am until all the cows have been sold, usually around 4-5pm. Free.) The largest history museum in Texas, the **Panhandle-Plains Historical Museum,** 2401 4th Ave., 10 mi. south of Amarillo in nearby Canyon, covers the gamut of human history in the Panhandle, focusing on the commercial, agricultural, and industrial innovations that made life in this harsh environment possible. The museum features life-sized recreations of agricultural homesteads, oil derricks, and farm equipment in their natural settings. (On the West Texas A&M campus. ☎651-5235. Open Memorial Day to Labor Day M-Sa 9am-6pm, Su 1-6pm; low season M-Sa 9am-5pm, Su 1-6pm. $7, seniors $6, ages 4-13 $3.) The **American Quarter Horse Heritage Center and Museum,** 2601 I-40 E, at Exit 72A, tells of the history and achievements of the Quarter Horse, the first horse bred in the US and still the most popular horse in America. (☎376-5181; www.aqha.com. Open M-Sa 9am-5pm, Su noon-5pm. $4, seniors $3.50, ages 6-18 $2.50.) At the ⬛**Cadillac Ranch,** eccentric millionaire Stanley Marsh III planted 10 Cadillacs—model years 1948 to 1963—at the same angle as the Great Pyramids, and, as one local noted, "they didn't take root, neither." Take Hope Rd. (Exit 62) off I-40, 9 mi. west of Amarillo, and head ½ mi. west on the southern frontage road.

🔁 **DAYTRIP FROM AMARILLO: PALO DURO CANYON STATE PARK.** Twenty-three miles south of Amarillo, Palo Duro Canyon, the "Grand Canyon of Texas," covers 20,000 acres. Take I-27 to Exit 106 and head east on Rte. 217. The breathtaking 16 mi. **scenic drive** begins at the park headquarters, then drops down to the canyon floor and criss-crosses the Red River for 8 mi. Along this road are numerous trailheads and **campgrounds ❶.** There are 146 designated campsites (primitive sites $10, with water and electricity $15) and backcountry camping is allowed for $10. Be sure to be back at your site by 10pm, as that is when campgrounds staff lock the entrance gates. Hiking opportunities range from short, shady hikes along the river, such as the **Paseo del Río Trail** (2 mi.), to more challenging hikes involving elevation change, such as the **Lighthouse Trail** (5 mi.), which leads to a rock that was named "the lighthouse" for its uncanny resemblance. **Backcountry hiking** is permitted, but most visitors stick to the marked trails. Canyon temperatures often climb to 100°F; bring plenty of water. The **headquarters,** just inside the park, has trail maps and info on park activities. (☎488-2227. Open daily in summer 7am-10pm; winter 8am-5pm. Park open daily in summer 7am-10pm; winter 8am-10pm. $3, under 12 free.) A half-mile past the headquarters, the **visitors center** has exhibits on the canyon's history. (Open M-Sa 9am-5pm, Su 1-5pm.) **Old West Stables,** located inside the canyon, offers 1hr. and 4hr. guided horse tours through the canyon. (☎488-2180. Mar.-Nov. 10am, noon, 2, 4, 5:30pm; 1hr. rides $35, 4hr. $140. Wagon rides for groups of 10 or more $5 per person, children $3 per person. Reservations required for 4hr. rides.) The entertaining musical ⬛**Texas Legacies** is performed in the canyon's sprawling Pioneer Amphitheater. The play follows a Texas ranch family through joyous and turbulent times, but it is the production and natural setting that are truly spectacular. The canyon walls serve as the backdrop, and the sights and sounds of live horses and plenty of pyrotechnics reverberate through the 1700-seat outdoor amphitheater. (☎655-2181. Shows June-Aug. Tu-Sa 8:30pm. Tickets $11-27, under 12 $6-24. Pre-show barbecue 6:30pm. Barbecue $8.50, children $7.) **Area Code:** 806.

TEXAS

GUADALUPE MOUNTAINS NATIONAL PARK ☎915

Rising austerely above the parched West Texas desert, these peaks are the highest, most remote of the West Texas ranges. Mescalero Apaches hunted and camped on these lands until they were driven out by the US army. Today, Guadalupe Mountains National Park encompasses 86,000 acres of desert, caves, canyons, and highlands. From U.S. 62/180, drivers can see the park's most dramatic sights: **El Capitán,** a 2000 ft. limestone cliff, and **Guadalupe Peak,** which at 8749 ft. is the highest point in Texas. The mountains provide over 80 mi. of challenging desert trails. The major trailhead is at Pine Springs Campground. It's a strenuous full-day hike to the summit of the imposing Guadalupe Peak (8½ mi., 5-8hr.). A shorter trek (4¼ mi., 3-4hr.) traces the sheltered streambed of **Devil's Hall.** In **McKittrick Canyon,** sometimes called the most beautiful place in Texas, the landscape transitions from desert to woodland before your eyes. To get to the trail (4½-6¾ mi., 2-4hr.), take U.S. 62/180 6 mi. north from Pine Springs to the McKittrick turnoff, which goes another 4 mi. north to the trailhead (gate locked daily in summer 6pm-8am; winter 4:30pm-8am). The **El Capitán Trail** (11½ mi.) hugs the base of the cliff of the same name and offers a terrific view of the desert below.

The park's two campgrounds, **Pine Springs ❶,** just past park headquarters, and **Dog Canyon ❶,** south of the New Mexico border at the north end of the park, have water and restrooms but no hookups or showers. Pine Springs has 20 tent sites and 20 RV sites away from the road. (☎828-3251. No wood or charcoal fires. Reservations for groups only. Sites $8.) Dog Canyon is accessible by car via Rte. 137, 72 mi. from Carlsbad, NM and 110 mi. from Pine Springs, or by a full-day hike from Pine Springs. (☎828-3251. Open daily June-Aug. 8am-6pm; Sept.-May 8am-4:30pm. After hours, info is posted on the outside bulletin board.) Free **backcountry camping** is permitted in 10 designated areas; permits are available at the visitors center. The nearest food is at ✪**Nickel Creek Cafe ❶,** 5 mi. north of Pine Springs, where owner Jo is happy to cook hungry hikers cheap grub when not serving in her other official capacity as county judge. (☎828-3295. Burgers $3. Burritos $2. Usually open M-Sa 7am-2pm but call ahead. Cash only.)

Carlsbad, NM (p. 856), 55 mi. northeast, is a good base for visiting both Guadalupe Mountains and Carlsbad Caverns National Parks. The park's lack of development is attractive to backpackers, but it creates some inconveniences for motorists: the nearest gas is 35 mi. north in White's City, NM. **TNM&O Coaches** runs buses along U.S. 62/180 twice per day between Carlsbad and El Paso and will stop at the main visitors center if you call ahead. (☎915-532-3404 in El Paso, 806-765-6644 in Carlsbad. From Carlsbad 2½hr., $26; from El Paso 3hr., $22.) **Park Headquarters** are at Pine Springs, just off U.S. 62/180. Here, the main **visitors center** has maps, pamphlets, exhibits, and a theater. (☎828-3251; www.nps.gov/gumo. Open daily June-Aug. 8am-6pm; Sept.-May 8am-4:30pm.) Park entrance is free. Hiking and backcountry access is $3 per person, payable at trailheads. **Area Code:** 915.

EL PASO ☎915

El Paso, the largest US border town, boomed in the 17th century as a stopover on the east-west wagon route that followed the Río Grande through "the pass" (*el paso*) between the Rocky Mountains and the Sierra Madre. Today, the El Paso-Ciudad Juárez metropolitan area has nearly three million inhabitants. Nearly everyone speaks Spanish, and the majority are of Mexican descent. Downtown bustles during the day, but the action moves across the border after dark. Stay on El Paso St. if walking between San Antonio Ave. and the border late at night.

Historic **San Jacinto Plaza** has shaded benches and a fiberglass alligator sculpture honoring the three reptiles the city once kept there. For a view of El Paso, Juárez, and three states (Texas, New Mexico, and Chihuahua) take the **Wyler Aerial**

BORDER CROSSING. Traveling between the US and Mexico is generally an easy process, but security is still taken very seriously. Crossing can be as simple as a wave of the passport or as time-consuming as a full search of your car. To keep things moving along, make sure to have all necessary documents handy. It is illegal to cross the border anywhere except an open crossing station. See **Essentials**, p. 10, for more details on documents and procedures.

Tramway, at the end of McKinley Ave. on the east side of the Franklin Mountains, up to the 5632 ft. peak. (☎566-6622. Open in summer M and Th noon-5pm, F-Su noon-8pm; winter M, Th, and Su noon-5pm, F-Sa noon-7pm. $7, under 12 $4.) For somewhat less impressive vistas at a lower elevation, but for free, take Rim Rd./Scenic Dr. to **Murchison Park.** The **El Paso Museum of Art,** 1 Arts Festival Plaza, is one of the largest art museums in the Southwest, with over 5000 works. The collections of 19th- to 20th-century Southwestern art and 18th- to 19th-century Latin American colonial art are particularly extensive. (☎532-1707. Open Tu-Sa 9am-5pm, Su noon-5pm. Free.) The **El Paso Railroad and Transportation Museum,** 400 W. San Antonio Ave., recounts the history of this railway city, which marked the halfway point on the second Transcontinental Railroad and was the location of the first railroad from the US into Mexico. (☎422-3420. Open daily 9am-5pm. Free.) In the late 1800s, a drought altered the course of the Río Grande such that a tiny piece of the US remained across the new river channel. This set off a border dispute that wasn't resolved until the 1960s, when the river was re-routed a second time. **Chamizal National Memorial,** 800 S. San Marcial Dr., is located on the formerly contested site and tells the history of this geopolitical oddity. (☎532-7273. Open daily 10am-5pm. Free.) **Hueco Tanks State Historic Site,** 32 mi. east of town off U.S. 62, has rock climbing, bouldering, and hiking in cliffs adorned with ancient pictographs. Call ahead; only 70 people are allowed at once. (☎849-6684. Open Oct.-Apr. daily 8am-6pm; May-Sept. M-Th 8am-6pm, F-Su 7am-7pm. $4, under 13 free.)

The ⧄**Gardner Hotel ❶,** 311 E. Franklin between Stanton and Kansas, conveniently located downtown, is the oldest operating hotel in El Paso. Everything about the hotel is old-fashioned: elevators, light switches, ceiling fans, the service, and the prices. (☎532-3661; www.gardnerhotel.com. A/C and cable TV. Singles with shared bath $20-26; doubles with shared bath $28-35; larger rooms with private bath $35-43. MC/V.) The **El Paso International Hostel ❶** is part of the same hotel and has two bunk beds per room, kitchen, laundry, and Internet access. (☎532-3661; www.elpasohostel.com. Towels $0.50. Dorms $15. MC/V.) The nearest campsites are at **Hueco Tanks State Historic Site ❶,** 32 mi. east of town. (☎849-6684. Water and showers. Entrance $4. Sites $10, with water and electricity $12.) Downtown activity dies down around 5pm. Most of El Paso's restaurants are in strip malls throughout the suburbs. Along **Mesa Street,** near the University of Texas at El Paso (UTEP), are some particularly good options. Eat to your heart's delight at **Veggie Good ❶,** 3800 N. Mesa St. in University Hills Plaza, a buffet with an extensive salad bar, sandwiches, soups, fajitas, and five kinds of *aguas frescas*—all for only $6.50. (☎494-3068. Open M-F 11am-8pm, Sa 11:30am-7pm. AmEx/D/DC/MC/V.) At the **Tap Bar and Restaurant ❶,** 408 E. San Antonio, enjoy tasty $2-4 burritos or steak and shrimp ($11) with a mostly local crowd. (☎532-1848. Open M-Sa 9am-2am, Su noon-2am. Cash only.) **Jamocha Coffee and Fudge,** 2231 Mesa St., is a cheap local coffee shop where a white chocolate raspberry mocha costs only $2.50. With a patio, free Wi-Fi, and a cool vibe, this is the place to be. (☎838-7177. Sandwiches $5.50-7. Espresso $1.30. Open M-Sa 6am-midnight, Su 8am-midnight. Cash only.)

El Paso International Airport (☎780-4749; take Sun Metro bus #33 to the city center) has major airline service. **Amtrak** runs from **Union Train Depot,** 700 San Francisco St. (☎800-872-7245; www.amtrak.com; open M, W, F 6:15am-1:30pm, Tu, Th,

BORDER BLASTERS

In 1932, at a time when most US radio stations broadcast at no more than 50,000 watts, Dr. John Brinkley built a 500,000 watt station—the most powerful in the world—just across the border from Del Río, TX, in Ciudad Acuña, Mexico. Millions heard him sign on with his trademark, "And now from Del Río, Texas, the sunshine station between nations," which made Del Río a household name. Things, however, weren't easy for the doctor and his fellow "border blasters," a term given to US radio stations that broadcast at high power from Mexico. The village of Acuña tried several times to shut down Brinkley's station, so resentful were they of the constant buzz of electricity, the dead birds dropping out of the sky, and the barbed wire fences that had started giving electric shocks.

The station survived and by the late 1950s it had come under the ownership of Wolfman Jack, who began his own empire of million-watt border blasters in Del Río and Acuña. Jack would eventually buy multiple border blasters along the US-Mexico border, but it was from Acuña that many Americans, as well as people around the world, first heard the sounds of R&B. James Brown, Aretha Franklin, the Temptations, and Ray Charles all achieved mass popularity with white audiences thanks in part to their exposure through Jack's border blasters.

Sa 6:15am-9:30pm), to San Antonio (13hr., 3 per week, $67-131) and Tucson (6hr., 3 per week, $45-87). **Greyhound,** 200 W. San Antonio (☎532-2365; www.greyhound.com), near the Civic Center, runs to Albuquerque (5½hr., 3 per day, $38), Dallas (12-14hr., 8 per day, $56), and Tucson (6hr., 5 per day, $40). **El Paso-LA Bus Lines,** 720 Oregon St. (☎532-4061), at 6th Ave., offers cheap long-distance buses to Albuquerque (3 per day, $21), Denver (3 per day, $45), and Los Angeles (3 per day, $50). **Sun Metro** (☎533-3333) operates local buses ($1, students and under 18 $0.50) and downtown trolleys ($0.25). **Visitor Info: Visitors Center,** 1 Civic Center Plaza, at Santa Fe and San Francisco. (☎534-0601 or 800-351-6024; www.visitelpaso.com. Open M-F 8am-5pm.) **Post Office:** 219 Mills Ave. (☎532-8824. Open M-F 8am-5pm, Sa 8:30am-noon.) **Postal Code:** 79901. **Area Code:** 915.

DEL RIO   ☎830

Situated near the Chihuahuan Desert and alongside the Río Grande is a geological and cultural oasis called Del Río. A fine little American town in its own right, Del Río is also a model for internationalism. Del Río and its sister city in Mexico, Ciudad Acuña, might just be the friendliest pair of towns on the entire US border. Del Río's **Main Street** bustles with new life and restored storefronts without falling into the cutesy clichés that plague so many Main Streets. The **San Felipe Springs** are responsible for Del Río's lush tropical environment. Forty percent of the water in the Río Grande south of Del Río comes from these springs, by way of **San Felipe Creek.** A series of parks along the creek provide ideal swimming holes and excellent birdwatching. Kayaking is the most relaxing and practical way to access ▨**Parida Cave** and **Panther Cave,** where four 12,000-year-old Native American pictographs plaster the cave walls in brilliant colors. (From the Pecos River ramp. 50 mi. east of Del Río, Parida Cave is 3 mi. round-trip. Panther Cave takes all day.) Founded in 1883, long before Texas wine became the latest trend, **Val Verde Winery,** 100 Qualia Dr., off Hudson Ave., is the oldest continuously-operated winery in Texas—it stayed in business during prohibition by making grape juice. (☎775-9714; www.valverdewinery.com. Free tours and tastings. Open M-Sa 10am-5pm.) **Alamo Village,** 38 mi. east of Del Río off U.S. 90, is the largest outdoor movie set in the US. John Wayne built it for $12 million for his film *The Alamo,* and it has been used for everything from *Lonesome Dove* to Ken Burns's documentary *The West.* (☎563-2580; www.alamovillage.com. Amateur gunfight contests most Sa-Su. Open daily in summer 9am-6pm; in winter 9am-5pm. In summer $9.75, ages 6-11 $4.75; in winter $8.60/$4.30.)

In town, cheap motels line Veterans Blvd. **Amistad National Recreation Area ❶** has primitive lakeside campsites for $4. The **Governor's Landing ❶** sites have water hookup and cost $8. **Villa Del Río ❹**, 123 Hudson Dr., south of town, is a small family-run B&B in an 1887 Spanish-style home. The innkeepers serve border-influenced breakfasts every morning to guests. (☎768-1100. Rooms from $85. AmEx/MC/V.) The best food is across the border in visitor-friendly Ciudad Acuña. **La Cabañita 99 ❶**, 267 C. Galeana, in the heart of Acuña, lets you make your own tacos. The huge specialty platter features three meats, cilantro, sauces, onions, and corn tortillas (100 pesos/$10) is enough to feed four people. (☎877-772-1467. Cash only.) Back in the states, **Flamingo 50s Hamburgers ❶**, 1750 Veterans Blvd., has large $0.99 burgers and Hawaiian shaved ice. (☎775-4001. Open daily 9am-11pm. D/MC/V.)

Del Río International Airport, 1104 W. 10th St. (☎774-8538), serves Houston. **Amtrak,** 1 N. Main St. (800-872-7245; www.amtrak.com), runs to El Paso (8½hr., 3 per week, $51-99) and San Antonio (4hr., 3 per week, $25-48). **Kerrville Bus Lines,** at the Amtrak station, has daily service to San Antonio (3¼hr., 3 per day, $23). **Taxi: Del Río Taxi Service,** ☎775-4448. The border is 2 mi. south of Del Río. Park and walk across the ¾ mi. bridge (cars $2, pedestrians $0.25). The **visitors center,** 4121 Veterans Blvd., has information on swimming, water sports, and fishing. (☎775-7491. Open daily 8am-5pm.) The **Del Río Chamber of Commerce,** 1915 Veterans Blvd., has local info. (☎800-889-8149; www.drchamber.com. Open daily 8:30am-5pm.) **Hotlines: Amistad Family Violence and Rape Crisis Center** (☎775-9612) operates 24hr. **Medical Services: Val Verde Regional Medical Center,** 801 Bedell Ave. (☎703-1701). **Internet Access: Del Río Public Library,** 300 Spring St. (☎774-7595. Open M-Th 10am-7pm, F 10am-6pm, Sa-Su 1pm-5pm.) **Post Office:** 114 W. Broadway. (☎775-3388. Open M-F 9:30am-4:30pm.) **Postal Code:** 78840. **Area Code:** 830.

BIG BEND
NATIONAL PARK ☎432

The arid Chihuahuan Desert, lofty Chisos Mountains, and muddy Río Grande unite in a marriage of land, air, and water to form Big Bend National Park, one of Texas's most remote and wild natural areas. Roadrunners, coyotes, pig-like *javelinas*, mountain lions, and even a few black bears roam this 800,000-acre tract of land, where visitors can gaze over breathtaking desert vistas for miles on end and sleep under a clear, star-filled sky.

GIVING BACK

FREE PARKING

The Texas State Parks system is composed of some of the state's most beautiful, diverse terrain. While the parks represent untouched historic or natural wonders, human visitors have a tendency to make themselves at home, often threatening the natural beauty they came to enjoy. If you want to do your part to maintain the parks while you enjoy their splendor, the Texas Parks and Wildlife Department (TPWD) may have a job for you. TPWD welcomes people of all ages and levels of experience to become park volunteers in a variety of capacities. All volunteers receive free park entrance and a campsite in exchange for 25-30hr. of work per week.

Volunteer opportunities range from office and clerical duties to working in the great outdoors. Park hosts greet campers and provide them with information. Tour guides offer interpretation at historic sites. Trail volunteers make sure that trails stay adequately graded and pruned. Environmental restoration volunteers help to identify invasive plant species and replace them with native plants. Most park volunteers stay at least a month, but each park is open to negotiation.

For an application, write to the park of your choice, or contact Carolyn Gonzales, TPWD Volunteer Coordinator, 4200 Smith School Rd., Austin 78744 (☎512-389-4893).

▲▶ ORIENTATION AND PRACTICAL INFORMATION. There is no public transportation into or around the park. **Amtrak** stops in Alpine, 103 mi. north of the park entrance where **car rentals** are also available. Three roads lead south from U.S. 90 into the park: from Marfa, U.S. 67 to Rte. 170; from Alpine, Rte. 118; from Marathon, U.S. 385 (the fastest route). There are two **gas stations** within the park, one at **Panther Junction** (☎477-2294; open daily Sept.-Mar. 7am-7pm; Apr.-Aug. 8am-6pm; 24hr. credit card service), next to the park headquarters, and one at **Río Grande Village** (☎477-2293; open daily Mar.-May 9am-8pm; June-Feb. 9am-6pm). On Rte. 118, near the western park entrance, the **Study Butte Chevron** also sells gas. (Credit card access 24hr.) Park Headquarters are at **Panther Junction,** 26 mi. south of the northern park boundary. (☎477-2251, visitors center 477-1158; www.nps.gov/bibe. Open daily 8am-6pm. Vehicle pass $15 per week, pedestrians and bikers $5.) **Visitors centers** are located at **Persimmon Gap** (☎477-2393; open daily 8am-5pm), and **Chisos Basin** (☎477-2264; open daily 9am-4:30pm). The visitors centers at **Río Grande Village** (☎477-2271) and **Castalon** (☎477-2666) are only open from late May to August (both daily 9am-4:30pm). **Post Office:** The main office is in Panther Junction, next to Park Headquarters. (☎477-2238. Open M-F 8am-2:30pm.) Chisos Basin's post office is inside the grocery store. (Open M-Sa 9am-5pm.) **Postal Code:** 79834. **Area Code:** 432.

▮▮ ACCOMMODATIONS AND FOOD. The expensive **Chisos Mountains Lodge ❹,** in Chisos Basin, has both modern motel rooms and cottages built in the 1930s. Reservations are a must for the high season (winter)—the lodge is often booked a year in advance. (☎477-2291. Singles $86-105; doubles $97-117. Additional person $10. AmEx/D/MC/V.) The closest budget motel to the park, the **Chisos Mining Company Motel ❷,** on Rte. 170, ¾ mi. west of Rte. 118 in Terlingua, has clean rooms with A/C. (☎371-2254; www.cmcm.cc. Singles $45; doubles $56-66; 2- to 6-person cabins with kitchenettes $61-85. AmEx/D/MC/V.) The three developed campgrounds in the park don't take reservations and are first come, first served. During Thanksgiving, Christmas, March, and April the campgrounds fill early; call park headquarters to inquire about availability. (☎477-2251. All tent sites $10. No campfires.) **Chisos Basin Campground ❶,** at 5400 ft., has 65 sites, some with shade and privacy, all with running water and flush toilets. In the summer it is by far the best choice for tent campers. **Castalon Campground ❶,** at 2170 ft., and **Río Grande Village Campground ❶,** at 1850 ft., both feature grassy sites along the Río Grande with lots of shade. (Castalon: 35 sites; Río Grande: 100 sites. Sites at both $10.) Río Grande Village has showers ($1 for 5min.) at the **RV park ❶,** which has 25 full hookups. (Sites $18.50 for up to 2 people; $1 per additional person.) **Backcountry camping ❶** at any of dozens of sites is free but requires a permit from a visitors center.

Chisos Mountains Lodge contains the only **restaurant ❷** in the park, serving three meals a day. (Extensive breakfast buffet $8. Soup and salad bar $7. Dinner entrees $5-16. Open daily 7-10:30am, 11:30am-4pm, and 5-8pm; in winter also 8-9pm.) A small **grocery store** next to the lodge covers all food groups as well as beer at only $0.70 a can. (Open daily 9am-7pm.) Those willing to make the 25 mi. trip outside the park to **Terlingua,** or 5 mi. further west to **Terlingua Ghost Town,** will find a few additional dining and drinking establishments. At **Ms. Tracy's Cafe ❷,** 1001 Ghost Town Rd., Ms. Tracy herself chats with visitors while serving eggs ($4-7), hamburgers, burritos, and vegetarian dishes. (☎371-2888. Entrees $5-15. Open daily Sept.-May 7am-midnight; June-Aug. 7am-3pm.) Further down Ghost Town Rd., the lively **Starlight Theater Bar and Grill ❹** has steaks ($17-26), entrees like spicy chicken in avocado sauce ($12), and live music on weekends. (☎371-2326. Open daily 5-10pm; bar open M-F and Su 5pm-midnight, Sa 5pm-1am.)

⚠ OUTDOOR ACTIVITIES. Big Bend spans over 200 mi. of hiking trails, ranging from 30min. nature walks to multi-day backpacking trips. Always carry at least one gallon of water per person per day in the desert. For those short on time, the best sightseeing is along the ⬛**Ross Maxwell Scenic Drive,** a 30 mi. paved route from the western edge of the Chisos Mountains leading down to the Río Grande and Santa Eleña Canyon. Call ahead for road conditions.

Pick up hiking guides and maps at any of the visitors centers ($1-2). Some trails have free maps at the trailheads. The **Window Trail** (5¼ mi. round-trip, 2-3hr.) slopes downhill from the Chisos Basin parking lot or campground along the basin's drainage path to "The Window," where the mountains open up to the vast desert below in an impressive panorama. Departing from the same parking lot, the **Window View Trail** offers a view of The Window, as well as sunsets, from a distance. The **Lost Mine Trail** (4¾ mi. round-trip, 3-4hr.) starts at 5600 ft. and climbs an additional 1200 ft. for breathtaking views of the Chisos and the Sierra de Carmen in Mexico. Also in the Chisos, the **Emory Peak Trail** (9 mi. round-trip, 5-8hr.) is an intense climb to the highest peak in the park (7825 ft.). An easier walk ambles through the **Santa Eleña Canyon** (1.7 mi. round-trip, 1½hr.) along the Río Grande. If the line is too long for the showers, relax in the 104°F **hot springs** on the shores of the Río Grande.

Though damming has markedly decreased the river's flow, rafting on the Río Grande is still popular. Free permits and info are available at the visitors center. Several companies rent kayaks and offer river trips down the 118 mi. stretch of designated **Río Grande Wild and Scenic River.** In Terlingua on Hwy. 170, just west of Rte. 118, **Big Bend River Tours** rents canoes and rafts. Guided trips through canyons and rapids are available. (☎371-3033 or 800-545-4240; www.bigbendrivertours.com. Canoes $45 per day. Rafts $25 per day. Guided trips half-day $62, full day $130.) **Far-Flung Outdoor Center,** just past Big Bend River Tours, also runs canoe and rafting trips ranging from $63 for half-day all the way up to $1200 for 10-day adventures. It also offers Jeep rentals and themed tours. (☎371-2633 or 800-839-7238; www.ffoc.net. Jeep rentals $125 per day. Themed tours $40 per 2hr., $120 per day.) Both companies offer shuttle services to pick people up downriver.

TEXAS

ROCKY MOUNTAINS

Created by immense tectonic forces some 65 million years ago, the Rockies mark a vast wrinkle in the North American continent. Sculpted by eons of wind, water, and glaciers, their weathered peaks extend some 3000 mi. from northern Alberta (in Canada) down to New Mexico, soaring to altitudes exceeding two miles at some points. The highest peaks of the Rockies are accessible only to veteran mountain climbers and wildlife adapted for scant air and deep snow. Although the Rocky Mountain area supports less than 5% of the US population, each year millions flock to its spectacular parks, forests, and ski resorts, while extreme hikers follow the length of the Continental Divide. Nestled in valleys or springing from the surrounding plains, the region's mountain villages and cowboy towns welcome travelers year-round.

HIGHLIGHTS OF THE ROCKY MOUNTAINS

HIKE along the **Gunnison Route** through the Black Canyon (p. 712) or geyser-side paths in **Yellowstone National Park** (p. 723).

CRAWL through ancient Puebloan dwellings at **Mesa Verde National Park** (p. 720).

PEEK at marmots and majestic elk in **Rocky Mountain National Park** (p. 696).

CAREEN down the ski slopes in **Sawtooth** (p. 767), **Vail** (p. 703), or **Jackson** (p. 739).

CRUISE the unforgettable **Going-to-the-Sun Road** in Glacier National Park (p. 757) or Colorado's phenomenally high **San Juan Skyway** (p. 718).

COLORADO

In the high, thin air of Colorado, golf balls fly farther, eggs take longer to cook, and visitors get winded just getting out of bed. Hikers, skiers, and climbers worship Colorado's peaks and mountain enclaves. Denver, the country's highest capital, has long since shed its cow-town image and matured into the cultural center of the region. Colorado's extraordinary heights are matched only by its equally spectacular depths, like the Black Canyon of the Gunnison, etched over millions of years by the Gunnison River. Silver and gold attracted early settlers to Colorado, but it is Mother Nature's more rugged elements that appeal to modern-day adventurers.

⁊ PRACTICAL INFORMATION

Capital: Denver.

Visitor Info: Colorado Travel and Tourism Authority (CTTA), 1620 Broadway, Ste. 1700, Denver 80202 (☎303-893-3885, vacation guide 800-265-6723; www.colorado.com). **US Forest Service,** Rocky Mountain Region, 740 Sims St., Golden 80401, or P.O. Box 25127, Lakewood 80225 (☎303-275-5350). Open M-F 7:30am-4:30pm. **Ski Country USA,** 1507 Blake St., Denver 80202 (☎303-837-0793) provides info on all -area ski resorts.

Open M-F 9am-5pm. **Colorado State Parks,** 1313 Sherman St., #618, Denver 80203 (☎303-866-3437, state park reservations 800-678-2267). Open M-F 7am-4:45pm. $8 reservation fee for campsites; reserve at least 3 days in advance.

Postal Abbreviation: CO. **Sales Tax:** 7.4%.

DENVER ☎303

In 1858, the discovery of gold in the Rocky Mountains brought a rush of eager miners to northern Colorado. After an excruciating trek through the plains, the prospectors set up camp there before heading west into the "hills," and the frontier town of Denver was born. Modern-day Denver combines that true Western grit with urban sophistication. Boasting both the nation's largest park system and the largest amount of beer brewed in any US metropolitan area, there's always something to do in Denver.

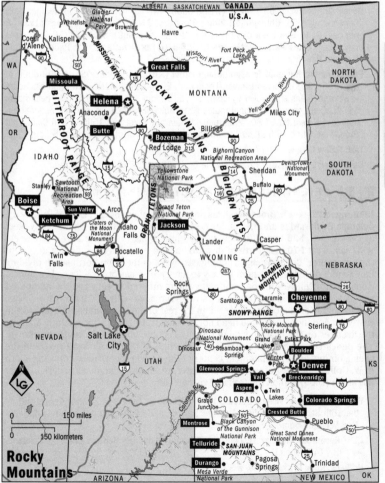

ROCKY MOUNTAINS

⌐ TRANSPORTATION

Airport: Denver International (☎342-2000; www.flydenver.com), 23 mi. northeast of downtown off I-70. Shuttles run from the airport to downtown and ski resorts. The **RTD Sky Ride** (☎299-6000) runs buses every hr. from the Market St. station to the airport. Office open M-F 6am-8pm, Sa-Su 9am-6pm. Buses operate daily 5am-10:30pm. $8, seniors and disabled $4, under 15 free. From the main terminal, **Supershuttle** (☎370-1300 or 800-525-3177) runs to downtown hotels (1hr., $19). Taxi downtown $50.

Trains: Amtrak, Union Station, 1701 Wynkoop St. (☎825-2583 or 800-872-7245; www.amtrak.com), at 17th St. Office open daily 5:30am-9pm. To **Chicago** (19hr., 1 per day, $82-161), **Salt Lake City** (15½hr., 1 per day, $57-111), and **San Francisco** (34hr., 1 per day, $83-163). **Winter Park Ski Train** (☎296-4754), leaves from the same building for **Winter Park.** Reservations required. Runs Jan.-Mar. Sa-Su; Aug. Sa only. Round-trip $49, ages 3-13 and 61+ $39.

Buses: Greyhound, 1055 19th St. (☎293-6555; www.greyhound.com). Office open daily 6am-midnight. To: **Chicago** (21-24hr., 6 per day, $105); **Colorado Springs** (1½hr., 8 per day, $14); **Salt Lake City** (9½-12hr., 2-4 per day, $59); **Santa Fe** (7½-9hr., 4 per day, $59). **Estes Park Shuttle** (☎970-586-5151) provides access to Rocky Mountain National Park from the airport and downtown ($39).

Public Transit: Regional Transportation District (RTD), 1600 Blake St. (☎299-6000 or 800-366-7433). Serves Denver, Longmont, Evergreen, Golden, and suburbs. Hours vary; many lines shut down by 9pm. $0.75, seniors and disabled $0.25; peak hours $1.25. Exact change. Regional routes go to Boulder, Nederland, and the national forests to the west for $3.50. Main terminals are at Market and 16th St. and Colfax and Broadway. A free 16th St. **mall shuttle** covers much of downtown. Runs daily 5am-1am.

Taxi: Yellow Cab, ☎777-7777.

Car Rental: Enterprise, 7720 Calawaba Ct. (☎800-720-7222), at the airport.

✦ ⚡ ORIENTATION AND PRACTICAL INFORMATION

Running north-south, **Broadway** slices downtown Denver in half. East of Broadway, **Colorado Boulevard** is another major north-south thoroughfare. Immediately west of Downtown, **I-25** winds its way north-south along the Platte River, intersects with east-west **I-70** just north of downtown, and provides the quickest access to the city center. **Colfax Avenue,** running east-west, is the main north-south dividing line. Gridded Denver is generally easy to navigate by car or bike. Travel complications most often result from confusing the numbered streets and the numbered avenues: both named and numbered streets run diagonally in the downtown area, at a 45-degree angle to the city's grid. In the rest of the city, numbered avenues run east-west and increase as you head north. Named streets run north-south. Many of the avenues on the eastern side of the city become numbered streets downtown. The pedestrian-only **16th Street Mall** is the hub of Denver's downtown, and the social, dining, and entertainment center of the city. At night, avoid traveling south of W. Colfax and west of Speer Blvd. Extra care should be taken after dark in **Lower Downtown (LoDo)** and on the Colfax Ave. corridor.

Visitor Info: Denver Visitors Bureau, 1600 California St. (☎892-1505; www.denver.org), in the 16th St. Mall. Open June-Aug. M-F 9am-6pm, Sa 9am-5pm, Su 11am-3pm; Sept.-May M-F 9am-5pm.

GLBT Resources: The Gay, Lesbian, and Bisexual Community Services Center of Colorado, ☎733-7743. Open M-F 9am-5pm.

Hotlines: Rape Crisis Hotline, ☎322-7273. 24hr.

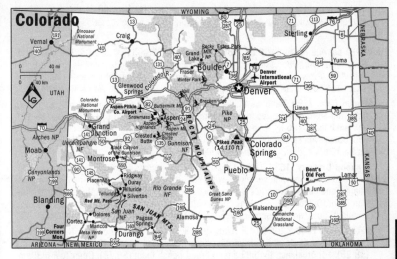

Internet Access: Public Library, 10 W. 14th Ave. (☎865-1351). Open M-Tu 10am-9pm, Th-Sa 10am-5:30pm, Su 1-5pm. Free.

Post Office: 951 20th St. (☎296-4744). Open M-F 7am-10:30pm, Sa 8:30am-10:30pm. **Postal Code:** 80202. **Area Code:** 303.

ACCOMMODATIONS

Inexpensive hotels line E. Colfax Ave., Broadway, and Colorado Blvd. Denver hotels tend to be business traveler-oriented, and have better rates on weekends.

Hostel of the Rocky Mountains (HI), 1717 Race St. (☎861-7777). A family atmosphere, in a pleasant residential area just east of downtown. Kitchen, basement lounge with comfy couches, library, and coin-op laundry. Breakfast included. Internet access $1 per 10min. Linen ($2). Key deposit $5. Reception 7-10am and 5-10pm. Reservations recommended. Dorms $17; private rooms $35. D/MC/V. ❶

Melbourne International Hotel & Hostel, 607 22nd St. (☎292-6386), at Welton. Wooden bunks, clean bathrooms, and large kitchen. Free Internet. Key deposit $10. Linen and towels $3. Reception 6am-9pm; call ahead for late arrivals. Dorms $16, students $13; private rooms $25. Cash only. ❶

Broadway Plaza Motel, 1111 Broadway (☎893-0303), 3 blocks south of the Capitol, is a well-preserved example of 1950s architecture. Spacious, clean rooms. Singles $45-55; doubles $55-65. AmEx/D/MC/V. ❸

Cherry Creek State Park, 4201 S. Parker Rd. (☎699-3860), in Aurora. Take I-25 to Exit 200, then north about 3 mi. on I-225 to the Parker Rd. exit. Pine trees provide limited shade. Boating, fishing, swimming, hiking, and horseback riding available. Arrive early. Open May-Dec. Sites $14, with electricity $22. Additional day-use fee $7. ❶

FOOD

Downtown Denver offers a full range of cuisines, from reasonably priced Greek and Ethiopian food on **East Colfax Avenue** to trendy new American in historic **LoDo.** You may wonder what sort of delicacies **"Rocky Mountain oysters"** are, especially given the city of Denver's distance from the ocean. Be warned: these salty-sweet bison testicles, sold at the **Buckhorn Exchange,** 1000 Osage St. (☎534-9505), do not hail from the sea.

🥘 **Wazee Lounge & Supper Club,** 1600 15th St. (☎623-9518), in LoDo. The black-and-white tiled floor, Depression-era wood paneling, and gas lights give this diner a bohemian feel. Pizza $6-8. Strombolis $8-9. Happy hour M-F 4-6pm. Kitchen open M-Sa 11am-1am, Su noon-11pm; bar closes M-Sa 2am, Su midnight. AmEx/MC/V. ❷

Mercury Cafe, 2199 California St. (☎294-9258), at 22nd St. Decorated with a new-age flair, "the Merc" specializes in homemade wheat bread, soups ($2-3), salads ($8-10), and enchiladas ($6-8). Live bands jam in the dining room, while the upstairs dance floor hosts evening swing (Tu, Th, Su) and tango (F) lessons. Open Tu-F 5:30-11pm, Sa-Su 9am-3pm and 5:30-11pm. Cash only. ❷

Wynkoop Brewery, 1634 18th St. (☎297-2700), across from Union Station in LoDo. Colorado's first brewpub serves its own beer (20 oz. $4), plus a menu including buffalo burgers and catfish tacos ($7-9). Improv comedy downstairs Th-Sa. Happy hour M-Th 3-6pm and 10-midnight, F 3-6pm, Su 9-midnight. Open M-Th 11am-11pm, F-Sa 11am-midnight, Su 11am-10pm; bar closes M-Sa 2am, Su midnight. AmEx/D/DC/MC/V. ❷

WaterCourse Foods, 206-214 E. 13th Ave. (☎832-7313), at Lincoln St. This innovative restaurant serves delicious vegetarian dishes, from tofu steaks ($12) to seitan fajitas ($8.25). For breakfast, try the banana bread french toast ($6.75). Open Tu-F 6:30am-10pm, Sa 8am-10pm, Su 8am-9pm. MC/V. ❷

Jerusalem Restaurant, 1890 E. Evans Ave. (☎777-8828), at High St. Falafel ($3.25), baba-ghanouj, and chicken shwarma (both $5), keep the Denver University crowd fed into the wee hours. Open M-Th and Su 9am-4am, F-Sa 9am-5am. AmEx/D/MC/V. ❶

⬡ SIGHTS

DOWNTOWN. Denver's **Civic Center Plaza** is the heart of downtown. At the east end, at E. Colfax Ave. and Grant St., the gold-domed **Capitol Building,** built of Colorado-mined granite, marble, and limestone, is a sensible place to begin your visit to the Mile High City. A small engraving on the 15th step up to the building's entrance marks 1 mi. above sea level; according to recent satellite measurements, the mile-high point is actually on the 13th step. (☎866-2604. *45min. tours every 30min. M-F 9am-3:30pm. Open M-F 7am-5pm. Wheelchair accessible.)* Near the Capitol is the **Denver Art Museum (DAM),** a "vertical" museum housing a world-class collection of Native American art and pre-Columbian artifacts and works by local artists. (*100 W. 14th Ave. ☎720-865-5000; www.denverartmuseum.org. Open Tu and Th-Sa 10am-5pm, W 10am-9pm, Su noon-5pm. Daily tours of special exhibits; call for times. $8; students and ages 13-18 and 65+ $6. Wheelchair accessible.)* **Grayline Tours** runs a 3hr. whirlwind introduction to Denver's major attractions with knowledgeable guides. (*☎289-2841. Departs daily at 8:30am and 1:30pm from the Cherry Creek Shopping Center. $30.)* Just north of the Pepsi Center, the **Denver Aquarium** offers spectacular exhibits on river systems and rainforests. The aquarium also houses over 15,000 marine creatures, including several species of sharks, otters, and the magnificent Napoleon wrasse. (*700 Water St. Exit 211 off I-25. RTD bus #10. ☎561-4450 or 888-561-4450; www.downtownaquarium.com. Open M-Th and Su 10am-10pm, F-Sa 10am-11pm. $13, after 6pm $10; ages 65+ $10/$8, ages 4-12 $8/$7.)*

CITY PARK AREA. The gigantic **Denver Museum of Nature and Science** hosts a multitude of captivating exhibits, including the Hall of Life, the Prehistoric Journey, and a superb exhibit on gems and minerals, including the largest gold nugget ever found in Colorado. Explore the skies in the museum's digital **Gates Planetarium.**

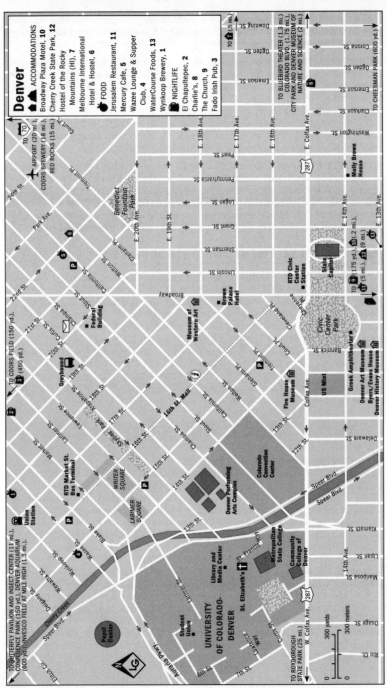

Denver

▲▲ ACCOMMODATIONS
Broadway Plaza Motel, **10**
Cherry Creek State Park, **12**
Hostel of the Rocky
  Mountains (HI), **7**
Melbourne International
  Hotel & Hostel, **6**

◆ FOOD
Jerusalem Restaurant, **11**
Mercury Cafe, **5**
Wazee Lounge & Supper
  Club, **4**
WaterCourse Foods, **13**
Wynkoop Brewery, **1**

🍸 NIGHTLIFE
El Chapultepec, **2**
Charlie's, **8**
The Church, **9**
Fado Irish Pub, **3**

TO 70 (5 mi.)

TO AIRPORT (20 mi.),
COORS BREWERY (18 mi.),
RED ROCKS (15 mi.)

TO BLUEBIRD THEATER (1.3 mi.),
COLORADO BLVD. (1.75 mi.),
CITY PARK AND DENVER MUSEUM OF
NATURE AND SCIENCE (2 mi.)

TO CHEESMAN PARK (600 yd.)

Molly Brown
House

Benedict
Fountain
Park

Museum of
Western Art

Brown
Palace
Hotel

TO 🚌 (5 mi.), 🚲 (9 mi.)

TO 9 (175 yd.), 🚲 (.2 mi.)

RTD Civic
Center
Station

State
Capitol

Civic
Center
Park

Fire House
Museum

US Mint

Greek Amphitheater
Denver Art Museum
Byers/Evans House
Denver History Museum

Federal
Building

Greyhound

TO COORS FIELD (150 yd.)

3 (450 yd.)

16th St. Mall

RTD Market St.
Bus Terminal

WRITER
SQUARE

LARIMER
SQUARE

Colorado
Convention
Center

Denver Performing
Arts Complex

Union
Station

Pepsi
Center

Library and
Media Center

St. Elizabeth's

St. Francis Way

Metropolitan
State College

Community
College of
Denver

UNIVERSITY
OF COLORADO–
DENVER

Student
Union

TO BUTTERFLY PAVILION AND INSECT CENTER (11 mi.),
CONFERENCE PARK (150 yd.), DENVER AQUARIUM
(600 yd.), INVESCO FIELD AT MILE HIGH (1.3 mi.)

TO ROXBOROUGH STATE PARK (25 mi.)

Cherry Creek

Speer Blvd.

W. Colfax Ave.

300 yards
300 meters

ROCKY MOUNTAINS

(2001 Colorado Blvd., at Montview Blvd. ☎322-7009 or 800-925-2250; www.dmns.org. Open daily 9am-5pm. $10, students and ages 3-18 and 60+ $6; IMAX and museum $15/$10; planetarium and museum $15/$10. Call for show times. Wheelchair accessible.)

COORS BREWERY. Located in nearby Golden, Coors is the largest one-site brewery in the world. It also has one of the nicest fitness centers in the corporate world, perhaps because its 3500 employees needs somewhere to work off the two free beers they receive after each shift. Free tours take visitors through the Coors brewing process and finish with free samples for those 21 and over. *(Take I-70 W to Exit 264; head west on 32nd Ave. for 4½ mi., then turn left on East St. and follow the signs. A shuttle bus runs from the parking lot to the brewery, after a very short historical tour of Golden. ☎277-5560. 40min. tours continuously M-Sa 10am-4pm.)*

BUTTERFLY PAVILION AND INSECT CENTER. Let exotic butterflies land on your shoulders at this unusual tropical conservatory, shielded from the Front Range's aridity by glass walls and misted water. In addition to the pavilion, a hands-on aquatic and insect center will bewitch young and old. *(6252 W. 104th Ave., in Westminster, just off U.S. 36 on the way to Boulder. ☎467-5441. Open in summer daily 9am-6pm; in winter daily 9am-5pm. $8, seniors $6, children 4-12 $5. Wheelchair accessible.)*

🎵 🎨 ENTERTAINMENT AND OUTDOOR ACTIVITIES

Life in Denver is never boring for sports fans. Major League Baseball's **Colorado Rockies** play at **Coors Field,** 2001 Blake St. (☎762-5437 or 800-388-7625. Tickets $4-45. $4 "Rockpile" bleacher tickets available 2hr. before gametime. 1¼hr. tours M-Sa at 10am, noon, and 2pm. $6, seniors and ages 3-12 $4.) As a reward for their back-to-back Super Bowl victories in the late 90s, football's **Denver Broncos** got a new and larger **Mile High Stadium** (officially renamed Invesco Field at Mile High), 1701 Bryant St. (☎720-258-3888. 1¼hr. tours every hr. Th-Sa 10am-2pm. $8, ages 3-12 and 65+ $6.) The stadium is also used by soccer's **Colorado Rapids** (☎299-1599). The NBA's **Denver Nuggets** and the NHL's **Colorado Avalanche** share the state-of-the-art **Pepsi Center,** 1000 Chopper Cir. (☎405-8556 for info on both teams. 1¼hr. tours M and W 10am, noon, 2pm; F 10:15am and 12:15pm. $5, children and seniors $4).

Denver has more public parks per square mile than any other city in the United States, providing visitors and locals alike plenty of prime space for bicycling, walking, or sun-bathing. **Cheesman Park,** 8th Ave. and Humboldt St., has picnic areas, manicured flower gardens, and a view of snow-capped peaks from endless green lawns. **Confluence Park,** at Cherry Creek and the South Platte River, lures bikers and runners with paved riverside paths and kayakers with rapids. One of the best parks for sporting events, **Washington Park,** at Louisiana Ave. and Downing St., hosts impromptu volleyball and soccer games almost every summer weekend. Paths for biking, jogging, and in-line skating encircle the park, and the two lakes in the middle are popular fishing spots. **Colorado State Parks** (see **Practical Information,** p. 686) has the lowdown on nearby state parks. At **Roxborough State Park** (☎973-3959), visitors can hike among rock formations in the **Dakota Hogback** ridge. Take U.S. 85 S, turn right on Titan Rd., and follow it 3½ mi. (Open dawn-dusk.) The mammoth 🏔**Red Rocks Amphitheater and Park** (☎697-4939), 12 mi. southwest of Denver, on I-70 at the Morrison exit, is carved into sandstone, and performers like R.E.M. and Motley Crue compete with the view. The park itself contains over 800 acres. (Park open daily 5am-11pm. Visitors center open daily mid-May to Sept. 8am-7pm; in winter 10am-4pm.) Forty miles west of Denver, the road to the top of **Mount Evans** (14,264 ft.) is the highest discontinuous paved road in North America. Take I-70 W to Rte. 103 in Idaho Springs. (☎567-2901. Open late May to early Sept. Daily vehicle fee $10.)

The **Denver Performing Arts Complex** (DPAC), at Speer Blvd. and Arapahoe St., is the largest arts complex in the nation and is home to the Denver Center for the Performing Arts, the Colorado Symphony, the Colorado Ballet, and Opera Colorado. (☎893-4100 or 800-641-1222. Box office open M-Sa 10am-6pm.) The **Denver Center Theater Company** performs new shows for free the Wednesday before the show opens. (☎893-4000. Tickets distributed beginning at 4pm the day of performance; call for schedule.) At the intimate **Geminal Stage Denver,** 2450 W. 44th Ave., every seat is a good one. Plays range from traditional to experimental. (☎455-7108. Shows F-Su $15-19.) **The Bluebird Theater,** 3317 E. Colfax Ave., hosts national and local musical acts. (☎322-2308. Live music W-Sa. Tickets free-$25.)

❀ FESTIVALS

Every January, Denver hosts the **National Western Stock Show & Rodeo,** 4655 Humboldt St., the nation's largest livestock show and one of the biggest rodeos. Good-looking cowboys compete for prize money while over 10,000 head of cattle, horses, sheep, and rabbits compete for "Best of Breed." Between big events, all sorts of oddball fun takes place, including western battle recreations, monkey sheep herders, and rodeo clowns. (☎295-1660; www.nationalwestern.com. Jan. 3-22, 2006. Tickets $10-20.) The whole area vibrates with ancient rhythms during the **Denver March Pow-Wow,** at the Denver Coliseum, 4600 Humboldt St., when over 1000 Native Americans from tribes all over North America dance together in full costume. (☎934-8045; www.denvermarchpowwow.org. Mid-March. 1-day pass $6, 3-day pass $12, under 6 and 60+ free.) The nation's most prestigious beer competition takes place every year at the end of September during the **Great American Beer Festival,** a celebration of almost 1500 beers from hundreds of breweries. Admission includes a tasting cup to capitalize on the free one-ounce samples. (☎447-0816; http://beertown.org/events/gabf/index.htm. Tickets $35-55.)

▣ NIGHTLIFE

Downtown Denver, especially the 16th St. Mall, is an attraction in itself, with ample shopping, dining, and people-watching opportunities. A copy of the free weekly *Westword* gives the lowdown on LoDo, where the action heads after dark.

The Church, 1160 Lincoln St. (☎832-3528), at 12th St. In a remodeled chapel complete with stained-glass windows, the Church boasts 4 full bars, 3 floors of dancing, a cigar lounge, and a weekend sushi bar. Th-F and Su 18+, Sa 21+. Cover Th $30, F-Sa after 9pm, Su after 10pm $5-10. Open Th and Su 9pm-2am, F-Sa 8pm-2am.

Fado Irish Pub, 1735 19th St. (☎297-0066), near Coors Field. Built in Ireland and brought to Denver piece by piece, Fado is authentic, from its perfect pints of Guinness to its intricate, wrought-iron bar. The place to be before and after Rockies games. Live Irish music W and Sa. Open daily 11:30am-2am; kitchen open until 10pm.

El Chapultepec, 1962 Market St. (☎295-9126), at 20th St., is a be-boppin' jazz holdover from Denver's 1950s Beat era. Live music nightly from 9pm. No cover. 1-drink min. per set. Open daily 8am-2am; kitchen open until 1am.

Charlie's, 900 E. Colfax Ave. (☎839-8890), at Emerson. A popular gay-friendly bar with 2 dance floors: 1 country-western, 1 Top 40. No cover. Open daily 11am-2am.

BOULDER   ☎303

The 1960s have been slow to fade in Boulder; the city is known to leftists as a little liberal haven in a vast conservative wasteland and to right-wingers as "The People's Republic of Boulder." Brimming with coffee shops, teahouses, and juice bars,

Boulder is also home to both the University of Colorado (CU) and Naropa University, the only accredited Buddhist university in the US. Seek spiritual enlightenment through meditation and healing workshops at Naropa, or pursue a physical awakening through Boulder's incredible outdoor activities, including biking, hiking, and rafting along Boulder Creek.

■ ⁊ ORIENTATION AND PRACTICAL INFORMATION. Boulder is a small city, easily accessible from Estes Park and Denver by **Highway 36.** The most developed area lies between **Broadway (Highway 7/93)** and **28th Street (Highway 36),** two busy north-south streets. Broadway, 28th St., **Arapahoe Avenue** and **Baseline Road** border the **University of Colorado (CU)** campus. The area immediately west of the school, across Broadway, is known as **the Hill** and features a number of restaurants, bars, and student-oriented shopping and entertainment. The pedestrian-only **Pearl Street Mall,** between 9th and 15th St., is lined with cafes, restaurants, and posh boutiques. Though **Greyhound** no longer serves Boulder, **RTD** runs buses from its station in Boulder, at 14th and Walnut St., to the Greyhound station in Denver. RTD also operates Boulder's extensive **public transit** system. (☎ 299-6000 or 800-366-7433. Station open M-F 6am-8pm, Sa-Su 9am-6pm. Local fare $1.25. Call for schedules.) **Taxi: Boulder Yellow Cab,** ☎ 777-7777. **Bike Rental: University Bicycles,** 839 Pearl St., downtown, rents mountain bikes. (☎ 444-4196. Bikes with helmet and lock $15 per 4hr., $25 per 24hr. Open in summer M-F 10am-7pm, Sa 10am-6pm, Su 10am-5pm; in winter M-Sa 10am-6pm, Su 10am-5pm.) **Visitor Info: Boulder Chamber of Commerce/ Visitors Service,** 2440 Pearl St., has info and free **Internet** access. (☎ 442-2911; www.bouldercoloradousa.com. Open M-Th 8:30am-5pm, F 8:30am-4pm.) A **summer visitors kiosk,** on the Pearl Street Mall between 13th and 14th, has literature and is occasionally staffed. **University of Colorado Information,** on the second floor of the University Memorial Center (UMC) student union, on the corner of Broadway and Euclid St., has free **Internet** access and local calls. (☎ 492-6161. Open in summer M-F 7am-10pm, Sa 9am-11pm, Su noon-10pm; Sept.-May M-Th 7am-midnight, F-Sa 7am-1am, Su 11am-midnight.) **Post Office:** 1905 15th St., at Walnut St. (☎ 938-3704. Open M-F 7:30am-5:30pm, Sa 10am-2pm.) **Postal Code:** 80302. **Area Code:** 303.

⁊ ACCOMMODATIONS. At the **Boulder International Hostel ❶,** 1107 12th St., at College Ave., youthful travelers fill the spacious downstairs lobby, surf the Internet ($2 per 30min.), and watch cable TV. The front door is locked after 11pm, but guests are given a code to enter after hours. (☎ 442-0522. Kitchen, laundry. Linen $5. Key deposit $10. 3-night max. stay in dorms during the summer. Reception 8am-11pm. Lockout 10am-5pm. Dorms in summer $19, in winter $17; singles $39/ $35; doubles $45/$39. AmEx/D/MC/V.) Located two miles west of Boulder off Canyon Blvd./Hwy. 119, **Boulder Mountain Lodge ❸,** 91 Four Mile Canyon Rd., treats guests to clean rooms, great rates, and a hot tub by Four Mile Creek. Campsites are also available on a first come, first served basis. (☎ 444-0882 or 800-458-0882. In summer singles $68, with full kitchen $88; in winter $53/$68. Sites $18.) The Victorian-era **Hotel Boulderado ❺,** 2115 13th St., is still one of the city's most popular hotels, in spite of (or perhaps because of) the rumored presence of a ghost on the fifth floor. (☎ 442-4344 or 800-433-4344. Standard queen in summer $175, in winter $135; with 2 queens $205/$155. AmEx/D/MC/V.) **Chautauqua Association ❸,** off Baseline Rd. at the foot of the Flatirons, has lodge rooms and private cottages. Turn at the Chautauqua Park sign and take Kinnikinic to Morning Glory Dr., or take RTD bus #203. (☎ 442-3282, ext. 11. Reception June to early Sept. M-F 8:30am-7pm, Sa-Su 9am-5pm; Sept.-May M-F 8:30am-noon and 1-5pm, Sa-Su 9am-3pm. Additional charge for stays fewer than 4 nights. Reserve months in advance. In summer lodge rooms $69-84, 1-bedroom suites $102-129; 2-bedroom cottages $127-224; 3-bedroom cottages $154-179. In winter, cottages $94-139. AmEx/MC/V.)

Camping info for **Arapahoe/Roosevelt National Forest ❶** is available from the **Boulder Ranger District,** 2140 Yarmouth Ave., north of town off Rte. 36. (☎541-2500, reservations 877-444-6777. Open mid-May to early Sept. M-Th 8am-4:30pm, F 8am-5:30pm, Sa 9am-3pm; Sept. to mid-May M-F 8am-4:30pm. Campsites open mid-May to Oct. Most sites have water; none have electricity. Sites $14.) **Kelly Dahl ❶,** 26 mi. southwest of Boulder on Hwy. 119, via Nederland, is the nearest National Forest campground. Though all of the campgrounds in this district fill very quickly, Kelly Dahl's 46 sites ($14), surrounded by pine trees and picnic tables, are usually available until much later in the day. For a quieter camping experience, **Rainbow Lakes ❶** lies 6½ mi. north of Nederland off Hwy. 72; turn at the Mountain Research Station (CR 116) and follow the gravel road for 5 mi. Drive slowly and carefully on the access road. The 16 primitive sites are first come, first served. (No water. Sites $8.)

◖ FOOD. The streets on the Hill, along the **Pearl Street Mall,** burst with eateries, natural food markets, and colorful bars. ▨**Half Fast Subs ❶,** 1215 13th St., makes over 90 oven-baked subs, all listed in colored chalk on the walls. Seven-inch subs of every imaginable variety are deliciously inexpensive—$5 or less. (☎449-0404. Happy hour with $4 subs and $4.50 pitchers M-F 5-7pm. Open M and Su 11am-10pm, Tu-Sa 11am-midnight. AmEx/D/MC/V.) Everything is "daily" at the **Walnut Cafe ❶,** 3073 Walnut Ave., where there's a new variety of quiche (with 2 sides $6.50) every day, in addition to a waffle, soup, grind (of coffee), and slab (of cake) du jour. Check out "pie day" on Tuesdays, when a slice of pie is just $2.25. (☎447-2315. Open daily 7am-4pm. AmEx/D/MC/V.) **Illegal Pete's ❶,** 1320 College Ave., on the Hill, and at 1447 Pearl St., on the Mall, constructs the burritos ($5-6) that sustain CU students. (Hill location: ☎444-3055. Open daily Sept.-May 11am-8pm; June-Aug. 11am-3:30pm. Pearl St. location: ☎440-3955. Open M-W and Su 7:30am-10:30pm, Th-Sa 7:30am-2:30am. AmEx/D/MC/V.) At **Moongate Asian Bistro ❷,** 1628 Pearl St., fill up on tasty noodle or rice bowls, salads, and sushi, all for under $9. (☎720-406-8888. Open M-Th and Su 11am-10pm, F-Sa 11am-11pm. AmEx/D/MC/V.) A Boulder classic, **The Sink ❷,** 1165 13th St., still awaits the return of its one-time janitor, Robert Redford, who quit his job and headed to Hollywood. The Sink serves surprisingly upscale cuisine amid wild graffiti, low ceilings, and hordes of students drinking into the wee hours. (☎444-7465. Burgers $6.50-9. Open M-Sa 11am-2am, Su noon-10pm; kitchen closes at 10pm.) Looking for something a little fresher? Twice a week, 13th St. shuts down between Canyon and Arapahoe for a **farmers market.** (Open Apr.-Oct. W 5-8pm, Sa 8am-2pm.)

◧ ◪ SIGHTS AND OUTDOOR ACTIVITIES. The ▨**Dushanbe Teahouse,** 1770 13th St., between Arapahoe and Canyon St., the only one of its kind in the Western hemisphere, was built by artists in Tajikistan, then piece-mailed from Boulder's sister city of Dushanbe. Today, a private restaurant leases the building and serves exotic dishes inside or on the patio. (☎442-4993. Tea $2-4. Lunch $7-9. Dinner $9-12. Open M-Th and Su 8am-9pm, F-Sa 8am-10pm. Tea time 3-5pm. Reservations recommended for tea.) The intimate **Leanin' Tree Museum,** 6055 Longbow Dr., presents an acclaimed collection of paintings and sculptures depicting Western themes from cattlemen to Native Americans. (☎530-1442, ext. 299; www.leanintreemuseum.com. Open M-F 8am-4:30pm, Sa-Su 10am-4pm. Free.) Minutes away, the **Celestial Seasonings Tea Company,** 4600 Sleepytime Dr., lures visitors with tea samples and free tours of the factory, including the sinus-busting Mint Room, featuring the "mind-clearing power" of peppermint and spearmint. (☎581-1202. Open M-Sa 9am-6pm, Su 11am-5pm. Tours every hr. M-Sa 10am-5pm, Su noon-4pm.)

Boulder is bursting with opportunities to get outdoors. Starting at **Scott Carpenter Park,** trails for biking, hiking, and roller blading follow the sometimes congested **Boulder Creek Path** to the foot of the mountains. **Chautauqua Park** has trails

ROCKY MOUNTAINS

varying in difficulty that climb up and around the **Flatirons.** Starting at the auditorium, the **Enchanted Mesa/McClintock Trail** is an easy two-mile loop through meadows and ponderosa pine forests. The challenging **Greg Canyon Trail** starts at the Baird Park parking lot and rises through pines above Saddle Rock, winding back down past Amphitheater Rocks. Before heading into the wilderness, grab a trail map at the entrance to Chautauqua Park. Road and mountain biking are both very popular; **University Bicycle** (see **Practical Information,** p. 694) rents both types of bike. One great area for smooth, shaded riding is the **Betasso Reserve** (closed W and Sa). A more technical area is **Walker Ranch,** an eight-mile loop of mostly single-track with a few challenging climbs and exciting descents thrown in. To get there, drive eight miles west on Baseline; trailhead will be on the left. To meet some new cycling friends, join the casual, weekly **cruiser ride** (starts Th 7pm at the Sports Garage, Spruce St.).

🎭🎶 **ENTERTAINMENT AND NIGHTLIFE.** An exciting street scene pounds through the Mall and the Hill; the university's kiosks have the lowdown on downtown happenings. The **University Memorial Center,** 1609 Euclid St. (☎492-6161; 16th St. becomes Euclid St. on campus), has info on events. From late June to mid-August, the **Colorado Shakespeare Festival** draws over 50,000 people to a red sandstone amphitheater on the CU campus. (☎492-0554; www.coloradoshakes.org. Tickets $10-50, previews $5-25. Student and senior discount $5.) The **Colorado Music Festival** hosts performances July through August in Chautauqua Park. (☎449-1397; www.coloradomusicfest.org. Tickets $12-45; lawn seats $5.) The local indie music scene is on display at the popular and retro-styled **Fox Theater and Cafe,** 1135 13th St. (☎443-3399; www.foxtheater.com).

The city of Boulder overflows with countless unique bars. For bluegrass, funk, and the best brews in Boulder (try the "Annapurna Amber"), head to the ▨**Mountain Sun Pub and Brewery,** 1535 Pearl St. (☎546-0886. Acoustic performances Su 10pm. Happy hour with $2 pints daily 4-6pm and 10pm-1am. Open M-Sa 11:30am-1am, Su noon-midnight; kitchen closes at 10pm.) Famous for serving the largest amount of Pabst Blue Ribbon within a four-state radius, the **Sundown Saloon,** 1136 Pearl St., has a large basement bar with pool tables, foosball, and a jukebox. (☎449-4987. Free pool until 10:30pm. Live bands some Th. Open daily noon-2am.) Completely transported from Ireland piece by piece, the bar at **Conor O'Neill's,** 1922 13th St., is a great place to have a Guinness. (☎449-1922. $3 Irish car bombs Su. Open M-F 11:30am-2am, Sa-Su 10am-2am; kitchen closes M-W and Su 10pm, Th-Sa 11pm.) **The West End Tavern,** 926 Pearl St., has a rooftop bar where views of the Flatirons, the cool night air, and regular film screenings make for an enchanting evening. (☎444-3535. Happy hour M-F 4-6pm. Drafts $3-4. 21+ after 10pm. Open M-Sa 11am-1am, Su 11:30am-1:30am; kitchen closes at 10pm.) For cheap drinks, locals go to **K's China,** 1325 Broadway, Unit 201, for $1.50 shots. (☎413-0000. Open daily 11:30am-2am.)

ROCKY MOUNTAIN NATIONAL PARK ☎970

Of all the national parks in the United States, Rocky Mountain National Park is the closest to heaven, with over 60 peaks surpassing 12,000 ft. Here among the clouds, the alpine tundra ecosystem supports bighorn sheep, dwarf wildflowers, and arctic shrubs in a landscape dotted with granite boulders and crystal lakes. The city of **Estes Park,** immediately east of the park, hosts the vast majority of would-be mountaineers. West of the park, the town of **Grand Lake,** on the edges of two glacial lakes, is a more tranquil base from which to explore the park's less touristed but equally stunning western side.

✦🛈 ORIENTATION AND PRACTICAL INFORMATION

The park is accessible from Boulder via **U.S. 36** or scenic **Route 7**. From the northeast, the park can be accessed from the Big Thompson Canyon via **U.S. 34,** but beware of flash floods. **Trail Ridge Road (Highway 34)** runs 48 mi. through the park.

Visitor Info: Park Headquarters and Visitor Center (☎586-1206), 2½ mi. west of Estes Park on Rte. 36, at the Beaver Meadows entrance to the park. Open daily mid-June to Aug. 8am-9pm; Sept. to mid-June 8am-4:30pm.

Kawuneeche Visitor Center (☎627-3471), just outside the park's western entrance, 1¼ mi. north of Grand Lake. Open daily mid-May to Aug. 8am-6pm; Sept. 8am-5pm; Oct. to mid-May 8am-4:30pm. Evening programs in summer Sa 7pm; call for winter programs.

Alpine Visitor Center, at the crest of Trail Ridge Rd., has a great view of the tundra. Open daily mid-June to late Aug. 9am-5pm; late May to mid-June and late Aug. to mid-Oct. 10am-4:30pm.

Lily Lake Visitor Center, 6 mi. south of Headquarters on Rte. 7. Open June-Oct. daily 9am-4:30pm.

Fall River Visitor Center, 5 mi. west of downtown Estes Park on Rte. 34 at the northern entrance to the park, is the newest center. Open May-Oct. daily 9am-5pm; in winter Sa-Su 9am-4pm.

Entrance Fee: $15 per car, $5 per motorcycle, bicyclist, or pedestrian; valid for 7 days.

Public Transit: A free **hiker's shuttle** runs two loops on the east side of the park in summer. See the park newspaper for a map of shuttle stops. From Bear Lake daily every 15min. 7am-7pm. From Moraine Park daily every 30min. 7:30am-7:30pm.

Weather Conditions: Park Weather and Road Conditions, ☎586-1333.

Medical Services: Estes Park Medical Center, ☎586-2317. **Park Emergency,** ☎586-1203.

Internet Access: Estes Park Public Library, 335 E. Elkhorn (☎586-8116). Open in summer M-Th 9am-9pm, F-Sa 9am-5pm, Su 1-5pm; in winter M-Th 10am-9pm, F-Sa 10am-5pm, Su 1-5pm.

Post Office: Grand Lake, 520 Center Dr. (☎627-3340). Open M-F 8:30am-5pm. **Postal Code:** 80447. **Estes Park,** 215 W. Riverside Dr. (☎586-0170). Open M-F 9am-5pm, Sa 10am-2:30pm. **Postal Code:** 80517. **Area Code:** 970.

♦ ACCOMMODATIONS

ESTES PARK
Estes Park has an abundance of expensive lodges. Travelers can find better deals on beds in the winter, when temperatures drop and crowds diminish.

YMCA of the Rockies, 2515 Tunnel Rd. (☎586-3341, ext. 1010), 2 mi. from the park entrance. Follow Rte. 36 to Rte. 66. Bright rooms with great views. Mini-golf, pool, horseback rides, fly-fishing. Call ahead; reservations for summer accepted starting Apr. 21. 4-person cabins $75, with kitchen and bath from $91; 5-person cabins $143; 7-person cabins $193. 1-day YMCA "guest membership" required: $3 per person. ❹

The Colorado Mountain School, 341 Moraine Ave. (☎586-5758 or 888-267-7783). Tidy, dorm-style accommodations are open to travelers unless booked by mountain-climbing students. 16 bunks with linen. Showers. Reservations recommended. Reception June-Sept. daily 8am-6pm; winter hours vary. Dorms $25. AmEx/D/MC/V. ❶

Saddle & Surrey Motel, 1341 S. Saint Vrain/Hwy. 7 (☎586-3326 or 800-204-6226; www.saddleandsurrey.com). Clean, comfy rooms. Outdoor pool and spa, microwave, fridge, A/C, breakfast, and cable TV. Singles $80; doubles $110. AmEx/D/MC/V. ❹

GRAND LAKE
Grand Lake is the snowmobile capital of Colorado and offers spectacular cross-country routes. Boating and fishing are popular summertime activities.

▧ **Shadowcliff Hostel (HI),** 405 Summerland Park Rd. (☎627-9220). From the western entrance, go left to Grand Lake, then turn left on W. Portal Rd. With excellent views of the lake, this hand-built pine lodge has more than comfortable beds: it also views itself as a spiritual retreat. Kitchen and showers. Internet $3 per 30min. Linen $2. 7-day min. stay for cabins. Open June-Sept. Dorms $20; private singles or doubles with shared bath $50, additional person $11. 6- to 8-person cabins $110-125. AmEx/D/MC/V. ❶

Sunset Motel, 505 Grand Ave. (☎627-3318). Cozy rooms with gas fireplaces, cable TV, large bathrooms, plus friendly owners and the only heated indoor pool in Grand Lake. In summer singles $65, doubles $80; in winter $50/$65. MC/V. ❸

Bluebird Motel, 30 River Dr. (☎627-9314), on Rte. 34 west of Grand Lake, overlooks Shadow Mountain Lake and the mountains. No phones; swimming pool access at the Sunset Motel. Singles $45; doubles $65. MC/V. ❷

▲ CAMPING

Visitors can camp a total of seven consecutive days within Rocky Mountain National Park. In the backcountry, the maximum stay increases to 14 days, but only from October to May. Campgrounds are open during the winter, though campers are responsible for clearing their own snow. All five **national park campgrounds** ❶ are $20 in the summer; winter sites are $14 unless otherwise noted. A backcountry camping **permit** ($20) is required in summer for stays in the park's 120 backcountry areas. Backcountry sites become less crowded the farther one hikes from the trailhead. **Sprague Lake** has a wheelchair-accessible backcountry site. On eastern slopes, permits ($20 in summer, free in winter) are available from the **Beaver Meadows Backcountry Office,** next to the park headquarters. (☎586-1242. Open daily mid-May to Oct. 7am-7pm; Nov. to mid-May 8am-5pm.) In the west, visit **Kawuneeche Visitors Center** (p. 697).

GRAND LAKE

The only national park campground on the western side of the park is the shaded and lovely **Timber Creek,** 10 mi. north of Grand Lake. Open year-round, Timber Creek offers 98 sites available on a first come, first served basis and is usually the last to fill. Campsites can also be found in the surrounding **Arapaho National Recreation Area** and the **Arapaho National Forest. Stillwater Campground** ❶, west of Grand Lake on the shores of Lake Granby, has 129 tranquil sites, a boat ramp, flush toilets, and wheelchair-accessible sites. (Open year-round; only the 11 sites in front of the gate are open in winter. Sites $17, with full hookup $22.) **Green Ridge Campground** ❶, on the south end of Shadow Mountain Lake, has 78 sites in close proximity to good fishing and hiking. (Open mid-May to mid-Nov. Sites $14.) Reservations are highly recommended for both campgrounds (☎877-444-6777; www.reserveusa.com).

EAST SIDE OF THE PARK

Moraine Park, 3 mi. west of Beaver Meadows Park Headquarters on Bear Lake Rd., is open year-round, though only some of its 247 sites are open in winter. In summer, **Glacier Basin,** 9 mi. from Estes Park, south of Moraine Park, provides 150 secluded sites near popular hiking trails; the Bear Lake shuttle buses also stop here. Both Moraine and Glacier Basin accept summer reservations. (☎800-365-2267; http://reservations.nps.gov.) **Aspenglen,** just west of the Fall River Visitor Center, usually fills quickly as well, with 54 first come, first served spots. **Longs Peak,** 8 mi. south on Hwy. 7, has 26 year-round tent sites.

⊙ FOOD

ESTES PARK

Sweet Basilico Cafe, 401 E. Elkhorn Ave. (☎586-3899). The intimate seating area over-flows with patrons enjoying delicious Italian cuisine. Sandwiches $6.25. Freshly made pastas $8-10. Open June-Sept. M-F 11am-10pm, Sa-Su 11:30am-10pm; Oct.-May Tu-F 11am-2:30pm and 4:30-9:30pm, Sa-Su 11:30am-9pm. AmEx/D/MC/V. ❷

The Notchtop Bakery & Cafe, 459 E. Wonderview, #44 (☎586-0272), in the upper Stan-ley Village Shopping Plaza, east of downtown off Rte. 34. Breads, pastries, and pies baked fresh every morning. Wireless Internet. Soups $4-5. Salads $5-8. Sandwiches and wraps $6-7. Open daily 7am-7pm. MC/V. ❷

Nepal's Cafe, 184 E. Elkhorn Ave. (☎577-7035), serves authentic Nepalese and Indian food. Daily curry buffet ($7.50) until 7:30pm. Open daily 11am-9pm. D/MC/V. ❷

GRAND LAKE

Chuck Hole Cafe, 1119 Grand Ave. (☎627-3509). A popular breakfast and lunch spot, this Grand Lake tradition has been doling out its homemade cinnamon rolls, Reubens ($7.50), and spicy chili since 1938. Open daily 7am-2pm. D/MC/V. ❷

Pancho and Lefty's, 1120 Grand Ave. (☎627-8773). With a patio overlooking Grand Lake and a bar large enough to fit most of the town's residents, Pancho and Lefty's is understandably cool. Try the *rellenos fritos* ($11.50) or crispy *chimichangas* ($11), and wash it down with a margarita ($3-7). Live music Th and Sa 8pm. Open daily June-Sept. 11am-11pm; Sept.-June 11am-9pm; kitchen closes at 9:30pm. D/MC/V. ❷

The Bear's Den, 612 Grand Ave. (☎627-3385). The best dinner deals in town. Mouth-watering chicken-fried steak $13. Open M-Sa 6am-10pm, Su 7am-9pm. D/MC/V. ❸

Grand Lake Brewing Company, 915 Grand Ave. (627-1711). A friendly microbrewery with delicious pizza, 8 homemade brews ($3-4), and fresh root beer. Open in summer M-Th 2-9pm, F-Sa 11am-11pm, Su 11am-6pm; winter hours vary. AmEx/D/MC/V. ❷

⚑ OUTDOOR ACTIVITIES

SCENIC DRIVES

The star of the park is **Trail Ridge Road** (U.S. 34), a 48 mi. stretch that rises 12,183 ft. above sea level into frigid tundra, where snow patches can be found through much of the summer. The round-trip drive takes roughly 3hr. by car in perfect condi-tions, but slow-moving tour buses and people stopping to ogle wildlife often slow traffic. The road is sometimes closed or inaccessible (especially from October to May) due to bad weather. Many sights within the park are accessible from Trail Ridge Rd. Heading west, steal an open view of the park from the boardwalk along the highway at **Many Parks Curve** (9,260 ft.). **Rainbow Curve** (10,829 ft.) and the **Forest Canyon Overlook** (11,716 ft.) offer impressive views of the vast tree-carpeted land-scape, formed by glacial action. At the **Rock Cut** pullout, the 30min. **Tundra Commu-nities Trail** is a rare opportunity to see fragile alpine tundra. Signposts along the paved trail explain local geology and wildlife. The **Lava Cliffs** attract crowds but are worth the hassle. After peaking at **Gore Range**, a mighty 12,183 ft. above sea level, Trail Ridge Rd. runs north to the **Alpine Visitors Center.** Entering the west side of the park past the Alpine Visitors Center, congestion lessens noticeably. **Wildlife viewing** along Trail Ridge Rd. is best in the early morning and evening. Elk usually congre-gate at higher elevations during the summer months and in open meadows off the

ROCKY MOUNTAINS

main road in fall. Natural mineral licks draw bighorn sheep to **Sheep Lakes.** Marmots and pica hang out at higher elevations, and winter visitors are treated to glimpses of ermine and snowshoe hares.

A wilder alternative to Trail Ridge Rd. is **Old Fall River Road.** Entering Rocky Mountain National Park from the east side on Rte. 34, you'll pass Sheep Lakes. Veer right toward the **Alluvial Fan** and Old Fall River Rd. Open only in the summer, Old Fall River Rd. starts at **Endovalley** picnic area and is a nine-mile, gravel, one-way, uphill road that features spectacular mountain views. (Sharp switchbacks. No trailers; max. vehicle length 25 ft.) The road intersects Trail Ridge Rd. behind the Alpine Visitors Center. **Bear Lake Road,** south of Trail Ridge Rd., leads to the most popular hiking trails within the park. **Moraine Park Museum,** off Bear Lake Rd. 1½ mi. from the Beaver Meadows entrance, has exhibits on the park's geology and ecosystem. (☎586-8842. Open in summer daily 9am-5pm.)

SCENIC HIKES

Numerous trailheads lie in the western half of the park, including the Continental Divide and its accompanying hiking trail. Trail Ridge Rd. ends in **Grand Lake,** a small town with ample outdoor opportunities. An overnight trek from Grand Lake into the scenic and remote **North** or **East Inlets** leaves the crowds behind. *Hiking Adventures in Rocky Mountain National Park* (available at the visitors center; $1) gives great details on the trails in the park.

Lake Nanita (11 mi., 5½hr.), rewards hikers who make the effort with a Kodak-moment view. Starts at North Inlet trailhead just north of Grand Lake. Don't let the easy and well-shaded first 6½ mi. fool you. After reaching **Cascade Falls** (3½ mi. from the trailhead), the trail ascends 2240 ft. through pristine wilderness to a fantastic view of the lake.

Lake Verna (7 mi., 3½hr.), starts at East Inlet trailhead at the far east end of Grand Lake. This strenuous hike gains a total of 1800 ft. in elevation as it passes **Adams Falls,** an easy quarter-mile from the trailhead, and **Lone Pine Lake** (5½ mi.), and rewards hikers with open views of **Mount Craig** before re-entering the forest. The culmination of the trail is an overlook of a lake edged by mountains and ponderosa pines.

Mill Creek (1½ mi., 40min.), beginning at Hollowell Park off Bear Lake Rd. This easy and pleasant trail (elevation gain 600 ft.) crosses an open meadow and then empties out into a serene field of aspen, providing a glimpse of beavers and soaring hawks.

Bear Lake Hikes. The park's most popular trails are all accessible from the Bear Lake Trailhead at the south end of Bear Lake Rd. The free hiker's shuttle (see **Practical Information,** p. 697) makes loop hiking very accessible.

Flattop Mountain (4½ mi., 3hr.), the most challenging and breathtaking of the Bear Lake hikes, climbs 2800 ft. to a vantage point along the Continental Divide. At the top, you can cross the tundra at the head of the Tyndall Glacier and follow the cairns 1 mi. to Hallet Peak (12,173 ft.).

Nymph (½ mi., 15min.); **Dream** (1 mi., 30min.); and **Emerald** (1¾ mi., 1hr.) lakes are a series of 3 glacial pools offering glimpses of the surrounding peaks. The first 2 legs of the hike are relatively easy, but the Emerald Lake portion is steep and rocky at points.

Lake Haiyaha (2¼ mi., 1¼hr.), forking left from the trail, has switchbacks through dense sub-alpine forests and superb views of the mountains. A scramble over the rocks at the end of the trail earns you a peek at the hidden (and sometimes difficult to find) Lake Haiyaha.

WINTER ACTIVITIES

Many people find that their favorite time to visit the park is in the winter, for **snowshoeing** and **cross-country skiing** in the Bear Lake Area, **sledding** and **tubing** in the Hidden Valley area (rentals all outside the park) and backcountry skiing throughout the park. Rocky Mountain continues to have ranger-led activities in the winter, including **snowshoe tours** (☎586-1223) and **guided cross-country skiing.** One exclusively winter activity is the popular **full moon walk,** available by reservation only

MUD SEASON. During mud season—typically May and October-November—many places close or shorten their hours, and lodging prices are generally lower. If you're traveling in the mountains during these months, be sure to call ahead.

Dec.-Mar. Call ahead for details (☎586-1206) as dates and locations change with the seasons. During the winter, Trail Ridge Rd. is closed from Many Parks Curve on the east side to the Colorado River trailhead on the west side, which makes the drive much longer (about 3½hr. one-way via I-70).

MOUNTAIN RESORTS ON I-70   ☎970

WINTER PARK AND THE FRASER VALLEY

Hwy. 40 connects Winter Park with Fraser just 2 mi. north, and together the towns thrive as a unique mountain community with genuine small-town charm. Nestled among mountain pines in the upper Fraser River Valley, the popular **Winter Park Resort** is the closest ski and summer resort to Denver, a mere 67 mi. from downtown. Named after a local lady of pleasure, the **Winter Park Mary Jane Ski Area** (☎726-5514 or 800-453-2525) is home to the first man-made ski trail in the western US; the trail was laid on land Mary Jane received for providing "favors" to local railroad workers and miners. The ski area boasts the most snow in Colorado, a 3060 ft. vertical drop, 22 lifts, and two mountains: Winter Park caters to families and beginners, while Mary Jane challenges experts with mogul-riddled trails. (1-day lift ticket $61, multi-day tickets $47-49 per day. Passes good at both mountains.) The resort also hosts a variety of summer activities, including a scenic chairlift, climbing walls, bungee jumps, and the longest alpine slide in Colorado. (Open mid-June to early Sept. daily 10am-5:30pm. Half-day park pass $38, full day $44.) **Fraser Tubing Hill,** half a mile off Hwy. 40 in Fraser, is another popular winter escape. (☎726-5954. Tube and lift $14 per hr., ages 7-15 $12 per hr. Open Tu-Th 2pm-9pm, F-Sa 10am-10pm, Su 10am-9pm.) Over 600 mi. of biking and hiking trails climb the mountains of the Continental Divide, and the **Zephyr Express** chairlift blows to the summit of Winter Park Mountain, allowing bikers and hikers to start at the top and then make their way down. (☎726-1564. Open mid-June to early Sept. daily 10am-5pm. Full-day chair pass $22, includes bike haul; single ride $16. Mountain bike rentals from $25 per half-day, $40 per day. 2hr. clinic $35; groups of 4 or more $25 per person.) **Viking Ski Shop,** on Hwy. 40, under the Viking Lodge, rents ski packages in winter and bikes in summer. (☎800-421-4013. Open daily June-Sept. 9am-5pm; Oct.-May 8am-9pm. Ski packages $14 per day for basic skis, $21 per day for performance skis; multi-day discounts available. Children rent skis free with adult rental. Bikes $18 per day for 2 road bikes, $24-36 for 2 mountain bikes. Helmets included.) **Mad Adventures,** on Hwy. 40 in Winter Park, is a popular whitewater rafting company that offers guided treks on wild Clear Creek and the Colorado River. Trips leave from Kremmling, about 45min. west of Winter Park on Hwy. 40. (☎726-5290 or 800-451-4844. Half-day $42.50, full day $62; ages 4-11 $35.50/$52.Open in summer daily 8am-5pm.) The **High Country Stampede Rodeo** bucks at the John Work Arena, west of Fraser on County Rd. 73, with competitions in calf roping, ladies' barrel racing, and bareback bronco and bull riding. (☎726-4118 or 800-903-7275. Open July-Aug. Sa nights. Western barbecue 4pm; $8, ages 6-13 $4. Rodeo 7:30pm; $10, ages 62+ $8, ages 6-13 $6.)

The glorious **🏔Rocky Mountain Inn and Hostel ❶,** on Hwy. 40, 2 mi. north of Winter Park in Fraser, has immaculate, newly renovated rooms with a Julia Child-caliber kitchen, as well as discounts on lift tickets, ski and mountain bike rentals, raft trips, and horseback rides. (☎726-8256 or 866-467-8351. Internet access $3 per hr.

ROCKY MOUNTAINS

Linen $3. Reception 8am-10pm. Dorms $19-22; private rooms from $79 in winter, $53 in summer. AmEx/D/MC/V.) The **Viking Lodge ❷**, on Hwy. 40 in Winter Park, next to the shuttle stop for the lifts, provides rooms with phones, TVs, access to the hot tub, sauna, and game room, and a 10% discount on rentals at the adjacent store. (☎ 726-8885 or 800-421-4013. Reception 8am-9pm. In winter singles $55-70, doubles $60-75; in summer $45/$50. AmEx/D/DC/MC/V.) The Fraser River Valley Lions Club maintains campgrounds in the Arapaho National Forest from mid-May to early September. The closest campground to town, **Idlewild ❶**, just 1½ mi. south of Winter Park on Hwy. 40, contains 24 sites along the Fraser River. (No hookups. 14-day max. stay. Sites with water $12.) Located on Hwy. 40 in downtown Fraser, **Crooked Creek Saloon and Eatery ❷**, 401 Zerex Ave., is a local landmark that dispenses wise advice: "Enjoy a few laughs, eat 'til it hurts, and drink 'til it feels better." Locals elbow up to the bar alongside mountain bikers and skiers year-round. (☎ 726-9250. Breakfast from $3. Burgers, pasta, and Mexican fare $6-9. Happy hour M-F 3-7pm; $2 domestic bottles, $0.25 hot wings. Open daily 7am-10pm; bar open until 1am. AmEx/D/DC/MC/V.) Deliciously healthy breakfasts ($3-10) and lunches ($4-10), including homemade bagels, are served on the patio at **Carver's Bakery Cafe ❷**, at the end of the Cooper Creek Mall off U.S. 40. (☎ 726-8202. Massive cinnamon rolls $2.25. Open M-Th and Sa-Su 7am-2pm. AmEx/MC/V.)

To reach Winter Park from Denver, take I-70 W to Hwy. 40. The **Lift Resort Shuttle** provides free bus service between Winter Park and Fraser. (☎ 726-4163. Runs July-Sept. Sa-Su and late Nov. to mid-Apr. daily 8am-5pm.) **Home James Transportation Services** runs door-to-door shuttles to and from Fraser, Winter Park, and the Denver airport. (☎ 726-5060 or 800-359-7536. Office open in winter daily 8am-6pm; call for summer hours. Reservations required. $46 to airport.) The **Ski Train** (☎ 303-296-4754; www.skitrain.com; Dec.-Mar. Sa-Su; Aug. Sa only) leaves Denver's Union Station for Winter Park. **Visitor Info: Winter Park-Fraser Valley Chamber of Commerce**, 78841 Hwy. 40. (☎ 726-4118 or 800-903-7275; www.playwinterpark.com. Open daily 8am-5pm.) **Snow Conditions:** ☎ 303-572-7669 or 800-729-5813. **Internet Access: Fraser Valley Library**, 421 Norgren Rd., (☎ 726-5689. Open M-W 10am-6pm, Th noon-8pm, F 10am-6pm, Sa 10am-4pm. Free.) **Post Office:** 520 Hwy. 40, in Fraser. (☎ 726-5578. Open M-F 8am-5pm, Sa 10am-noon.) **Postal Code:** 80442. **Area Code:** 970.

BRECKENRIDGE

Fashionable Breckenridge lies east of Vail on I-70, 9 mi. south of Frisco on Rte 9. One of the most popular ski resorts in the country, **Breckenridge** has a 3400 ft. vertical drop, 139 trails, 25 lifts, 2043 acres of skiable terrain, and the best halfpipe in North America. (☎ 453-5000 or 800-789-7669; www.breckenridge.com. Snow conditions ☎ 453-6118.) Most of the summer action takes place at the **Breckenridge Peak and Fun Park** on Peak 8, 3 mi. west of town on Ski Hill Rd., including a scenic chairlift ride (single ride $5), a superslide ($10, ages 7-12 and 65+ $8), Colorado's largest human maze ($6, ages 5-12 $5), and a climbing wall ($7 per climb; half-day $48, full day $60). The **Breckenridge Mountain Bike Park** at the same location offers a variety of biking trails. (Chairlift with bike haul $12, ages 7-12 $8. Bike rentals $19 for 2hr., half-day $29, full day $39.) "Super-passes" for unlimited use of the Fun Park and Mountain Bike Park are also available (half-day $48, all-day $60). In the summer, the **Breckenridge Music Festival** provides a wide selection of musical acts from classical and jazz to Broadway and blues. (☎ 453-9142; www.breckenridgemusicfestival.com. Early June to Aug. Box office open Tu-Su 10am-5pm. Many shows free, classical concerts $17-27, ages 18 and under $7.)

Despite the many expensive restaurants and stores in town, you can still find reasonably priced accommodations at the ⬛**Fireside Inn (HI) ❷**, 114 N. French St., two blocks east of Main St. on the corner of Wellington Rd. The indoor hot tub is great for *après*-ski and the "Afternoon Tea" presents a taste of British hospitality. (☎453-6456; www.firesideinn.com. Breakfast $4-8. Reception daily 8am-9:30pm. Check in 4-8pm. Dorms in winter $38; in summer $25. Private rooms $180/$65. MC/V.) A few miles north of town on Hwy. 9, next to the Breckenridge Golf Course, **Wayside Inn ❸**, 165 Tiger Rd., offers tidy rooms with a hot tub, a fireplace in the lounge, and an attractive price. (☎453-5540 or 800-927-7669. Jan. to mid-Apr. singles $88, doubles $98; mid-Apr. to late Nov. $45/$55; Dec. $65/$75. AmEx/D/MC/V.) Taste the difference of high-altitude slow-roasted coffee beans at **Clint's Bakery and Coffeehouse ❶**, 131 S. Main St., where you'll also find breakfast croissant sandwiches ($3.50), homemade quiche ($2.50), and soups made daily. The hot portobello mushroom and turkey pepperjack sandwich ($6) is a lunch favorite, as are the blackberry smoothies. (☎453-2990. Open daily 7am-8pm, sandwiches until 3pm. MC/V.) You know the burgers are going to be big at a place called **Fatty's ❷**, 106 S. Ridge St. With 10 TVs and $2 drafts during happy hour (daily 4-7pm), Fatty's knows how to keep the locals satisfied. (☎453-9802. Burgers $6-7. Open daily 11am-12:30am; kitchen closes at 10pm. AmEx/MC/V.) Spiced up with colorful murals and a straw-covered bar, **Rasta Pasta ❷**, 411 S. Main St., serves creative pasta entrees with Jamaican flair. (☎453-7467. Lunch entrees $4-7. Dinner $8-13. Open daily 11am-9pm. AmEx/D/MC/V.) The only young dance club in town, smoke-free **Cecilia's**, 500 S. Main St., also hosts open afterparties for ski events. (☎453-2243. Nightly drink specials. $1 beers W. Open daily 5pm-2am.)

   Free Ride Breckenridge shuttles skiers and bikers around town and to the mountains for free. (☎547-3140. Operates daily 6:30am-midnight.) **Summit Stage** provides free shuttle service from Breckenridge to surrounding areas in Summit County. (☎668-0999. Operates daily 6:30am-1:30am.) **Breckenridge Activities Center:** 137 S. Main St., at Washington St. (☎453-5579 or 877-864-0868. Open daily 9am-5pm.) **Ski Conditions and Weather:** ☎453-6118. **Breckenridge Medical Center:** 555 S. Park Ave. (☎453-1010.) **Internet Access: Summit County Library,** 504 Airport Rd. (☎453-6098. Open M-Th 9am-7pm, F 9am-5pm, Sa 1-5pm.) **Post Office:** 305 S. Ridge Rd. (☎453-5467. Open M-F 8am-5pm, Sa 10am-1pm.) **Postal Code:** 80424. **Area Code:** 970.

VAIL   ☎970

The largest one-mountain ski resort in all of North America, Vail has its fair share of ritzy hotels and boutiques, but it's the mountain that wows skiers with its prime powder and famed back bowls. With skiers and employees from around the world, the resort has an international feel unlike other Colorado ski towns. Discovered by Lord Gore in 1854, the Vail area was swarmed by prospectors during the 1870s gold rush. According to legend, the Ute tribe adored the area's rich supply of game, but became so upset with the white settlers that they set fire to the forest, creating the open terrain beloved by so many visitors today.

■🔊 **ORIENTATION AND PRACTICAL INFORMATION.** The communities of Vail consist of **East Vail, Vail Village, Lionshead Village, Cascade Village,** and **West Vail.** Vail Village and Lionshead Village, the centers of the action, are pedestrian-only; visitors must park in garages off **South Frontage Road.** Parking is free in summer, but $16 per day in winter. Free **Vail Buses** (☎477-3456) run a year-round loop within and around each of the villages. **ECOTransit** runs buses between Vail and the surrounding area, including Eagle, Edwards, and Beaver Creek. (☎328-3520. Office open daily in summer 7:30am-5:30pm; in winter 6am-10pm. $3.) **Greyhound,** in the Transportation Building next to the main visitors center (☎476-5137; ticket office open daily 7:30am-6pm), buses eager skiers to Denver (2hr., 4 per day, $22-24), Glenwood Springs (1½hr., 3 per day, $16-18), and Grand Junction (3½hr., 3 per day, $16-18). Vail's two **visitors centers** are both on S. Frontage Rd. The larger one is in Vail Village, at the **Vail Transportation Center** (☎479-1394 or 800-525-3875; open daily 9am-5pm); the smaller is at the parking lot in Lionshead Village (☎800-525-3875; open daily 9am-5pm). **Medical Services: Vail Valley Medical,** 181 W. Meadow Dr., Ste. 100 (☎486-2451). **Weather Conditions: Road report,** ☎476-2226. **Snow report,** ☎476-8888. **Internet Access: Vail Public Library,** 292 W. Meadow Dr. (☎479-2184. Open M-Th 10am-8pm, F-Su 11am-6pm.) **Post Office:** 1300 N. Frontage Rd. (☎476-5217. Open M-F 8:30am-5pm, Sa 8:30am-noon.) **Postal Code:** 81657. **Area Code:** 970.

⌂ ACCOMMODATIONS. The phrase "cheap lodging" is not part of Vail's vocabulary. Rooms in the resort town rarely dip below $175 per night in high season, but hotels and lodges offer big discounts during the slower seasons. The larger visitors center also has a 24hr. kiosk for surfing www.vailonsale.com, which lists last-minute lodging deals. The **Roost Lodge ❹,** 1783 N. Frontage Rd., right on the bus route in West Vail, has clean rooms with cable TV, fridge, microwave, and access to a jacuzzi, sauna, and indoor pool. (☎476-5451 or 800-873-3065. Continental breakfast in winter. Singles in winter $109-129; in summer from $59. AmEx/D/MC/V.) With cheaper rooms and easy access to the slopes, the small town of **Frisco,** located 2¼ mi. east of Vail and 9 mi. north of Breckenridge (p. 702), is a budget skier's delight. The home hostel **Just Bunks ❶,** 208 Teller St., in Frisco, has 4 comfy beds in a refurbished basement. (☎668-4757; www.justbunks.net. Beds in winter $30; in summer $25. Cash only.) The **Holy Cross Ranger District,** off I-70 at Exit 171, has info on the six summer campgrounds nearby. (☎827-5715. Open M-Sa 8am-5pm.) With 25 sites within hiking distance of the free East Vail Express bus, **Gore Creek ❶** is the closest campground to Vail. The first come, first served sites fill quickly on weekends. (Drinking water available. 10-day max. stay. Sites $14.)

◲◱ FOOD AND NIGHTLIFE. You'll never need to cook breakfast in Vail as long as the griddle is hot at ▓**DJ's Classic Diner ❶,** 616 W. Lionshead Plaza, on the west end of Lionshead Village. In winter, locals ski in around the clock to warm up with crepes ($4-6), omelets ($6-8), and pasta frittatas from $7.50. (☎476-2336. Open in winter 24hr.; in summer daily 7am-1pm. Cash only.) Right in the heart of Vail Village, **The Red Lion ❹,** 304 Bridge St. at Hanson Ranch Rd., was originally built as a hotel, but the owners had so many children that there were no rooms left for guests. Today it's renowned for succulent barbecue brisket ($13) and ribs. (☎476-7676. Open daily 11am-late. AmEx/D/DC/MC/V.) **Moe's Original BBQ ❷,** 616 W. Lionshead Plaza, offers Alabama-style barbecue with soul food specialties. The box lunches (meat and two sides; $9-10) might be the best deal in town. (☎479-7888. Open M-Sa 11am-sellout, usually about 3pm. Call ahead to have your food saved until 5pm. MC/V.) **La Cantina ❶,** in the Transportation Center, serves a fine selection of Mexican food ($3-6) at an even finer price. (☎476-7661. Open in summer M-Th and Su 11am-9pm, F-Sa 11am-10pm; call for winter hours. AmEx/MC/V.)

Both a sports bar and an upscale watering hole, **The Tap Room,** 333 Bridge St. in Vail Village, is consistently voted by locals Vail's best place to see and be seen. (☎479-0500, ext. 3. Open daily 10am-2am.) **Garfinkel's,** 536 E. Lionshead Cir., a hidden hangout accessible by foot in Vail's Lionshead Village (directly across from the gondola) calls out "Ski hard, party harder." (☎476-3789. Lunch $7-12. Dinner $11-20. Karaoke Sa. Open daily 11am-2am; kitchen closes at 10pm.) **The George,** 292 E. Meadow Dr., in the basement of the Mountain Haus Hotel in Vail Village, has an intense happy hour. (☎476-2656. Happy hour daily in winter 3pm-6pm; in summer 6pm-10pm. Open daily in winter 3pm-2am; in summer 6pm-2am.)

◪ SIGHTS. The history of Vail and the sports it loves best are extolled in the **Ski Hall of Fame,** in the **Colorado Ski and Snowboard Museum,** on the third level of the Vail Transportation Center. A fascinating exhibit focuses on the 10th Mountain

Division and its training in the Rockies for the rigors of fighting in the mountains of Italy during WWII. (☎476-1876 or 800-950-7410. Open June-Sept. and Nov.-Apr. Tu-Su 10am-5pm. Suggested donation $2.) In the summer, the **Gerald R. Ford Amphitheater,** at the east edge of Vail Village, presents a number of outdoor concerts, dance festivals, and theater productions. (☎476-2918. Box office open M-Sa 11am-5pm. Lawn seats $15-40; Tu free.) Next door in the lovely **Betty Ford Alpine Gardens,** stroll through the peaceful meditation and rock gardens. (☎476-0103. Guided tours M, Th, and Sa 10:30am. Open May-Sept. dawn-dusk. Free.) The **Vilar Center for the Arts,** in Beaver Creek, hosts performances of everything from Shakespeare to Sondheim. (☎845-8497 or 888-920-2787. Box office open M-Sa 11am-5pm.)

▲ OUTDOOR ACTIVITIES. Before hitting the slopes in Vail, the unequipped visit **Ski Base,** 610 W. Lionshead Cir. and 520 E. Lionshead Cir. The store transforms into the **Wheel Base Bike Shop** in the summer months. (☎476-5799. Skis, poles, and boots from $17 per day. Snowboard and boots from $22 per day. Path bikes $15 per 8hr.; mountain bikes from $31 per 8hr. Open daily in winter 8am-7pm; in summer 9am-6pm.) Vail caters to sun worshippers in the summer, when the ski runs turn into hiking and biking trails. The **Eagle Bahn Gondola** in Lionshead and the **Vista Bahn Chairlift,** part of the Vail Resort, whisk hikers, bikers, and sightseers to the top of the mountains for breathtaking views. (☎476-9090. Ticket office open daily 9:30am-4pm. Eagle Bahn open in summer M-W and Su 10am-4pm, Th-Sa 10am-9pm; in winter daily 8:30am-4pm. Vista Bahn open mid-July to early Sept. F-Su 10am-4pm. All-day pass on either Bahn $17, ages 5-12 and 65+ $10; with bike haul $29.) During the summer, visitors can bike the **Eagle Bahn Gondola Twilight Ride.** (Th-Sa 4-9pm. Free.) The Holy Cross Ranger District (p. 704) provides maps and information on the many snowmobile, cross-country skiing, and hiking routes clustered near Vail Pass. The **Gore Creek Fly Fisherman,** 193 Gore Creek Promenade, has free casting lessons daily at 10:30am. (☎476-3296. Rod rentals $15 per 24hr., with boots and waders $30.)

ASPEN ☎970

Aspen was founded in 1879 as a silver mining camp, but the silver ran out quickly and by 1940 the town was almost gone. Wealthy visionaries took one look at the location of the foundering village and transformed it into a lavish winter playground. Today, Aspen makes a point of keeping busy, and its skiing, scenery, and festivals are matched only by the pricetags in the exclusive boutiques scattered around downtown. To catch Aspen on the semi-cheap, stay in Glenwood Springs, 40 mi. north (p. 707).

☑ PRACTICAL INFORMATION. Aspen Shuttles and the **RFTA** provide year-round free transportation service around town, charging a small fare in the Roaring Fork Valley. Pick up route maps on the buses or at the **Rubey Park Transit Center,** on the corner of Mill and Durant St. (☎925-8484; www.rfta.com. Open daily 6:15am-2:15am; in low season closes earlier on Su. Fare $1-9.) **Visitors Centers:** 320 E. Hyman Ave., in the Wheeler Opera House (☎920-7148; open daily 10am-6pm); 425 Río Grand Pl. (☎925-1940 or 888-290-1324; open M-F 8am-5pm). The **Aspen Ranger District,** 806 W. Hallam, provides information on various hikes and camping within 15 mi. of Aspen. (☎925-3445. Open June-Aug. M-F 8am-5pm; Sept.-May M-F 8am-4:30pm. Topographic maps $6.) **Roads and Weather:** ☎877-315-7623. **Snow Report:** ☎925-1221 or 888-277-3676. **Internet Access: Pitkin County Library,** 120 N. Mill St. (☎925-4025. Open M-Th 10am-9pm, F-Sa 10am-6pm, Su noon-6pm.) **Post Office:** 235 Puppy Smith Rd. (☎925-7523. Open M-F 8:30am-5pm, Sa 9am-noon.) **Postal Code:** 81611. **Area Code:** 970.

ACCOMMODATIONS. Staying in Aspen means biting the bullet and reaching deep into your pockets. Nearby Glenwood Springs has more options and is easily accessible by car or RFTA. In downtown Aspen, the friendly and conveniently-located **Tyrolean Lodge ❸**, 200 W. Main St., prices rooms by floor: darker low-floor rooms are cheaper, while airy top-floor rooms are a bit more expensive. Whichever floor you choose, you'll get a full kitchenette and free shuttle rides to the ski areas. (☎925-4595 or 888-220-3809; www.tyroleanlodge.com. Office open 8:30am-1pm and 2pm-7pm.) Able to charm even the hardiest ski bum with continental breakfast, a pool, a steam room, and a hot tub, the **St. Moritz Lodge ❷**, 344 W. Hyman Ave., has more of a resort atmosphere. (☎925-3220 or 800-817-2069; www.stmoritzlodge.com. Reception hours 7am-7pm. Dorms $31-48, depending on season. Hotel rooms $83-207.) Wake up to a full breakfast prepared by professional chefs in the adorable **Little Red Ski Haus ❸**, 118 E. Cooper Ave., which has sparkling rooms and spacious bathrooms. (☎925-3333 or 866-630-6119; www.littleredskihaus.com. Dorm beds $60.) Unless more than 6 ft. of snow covers the ground, **camping ❶** is available in one of the nine National Forest campgrounds that lie within 10 mi. of Aspen. **Silver Bar, Silver Bell,** and **Silver Queen** campgrounds sit 5 mi. southwest of town on Maroon Creek Rd. and fill quickly. Four miles southeast on Rte. 82, **Difficult** campground usually has more openings. (☎877-444-6777. Reservations required. Water; no hookups. 5-day max. stay throughout the district. Open June to mid-Sept. Reservations recommended. Sites $15-16.) **The Red Brick,** 110 E. Hallam (☎920-5140), offers showers ($3.50) to campers and hikers.

FOOD. Always packed, the nationally-renowned **Hickory House ❸**, 730 W. Main St., smokes up award-winning barbecue favorites. (☎925-2313. Lunch specials $7-10. Dinner $10-20. Open daily 8am-2:30pm and 5-10pm. AmEx/D/DC/MC/V.) Try the famed beef stew at **Little Annie's Eating House ❸**, 517 E. Hyman Ave., a longtime Aspen staple. Every day, all day long, throw back a beer and a shot for just $2.75. (☎925-1098. Burgers $9. Veggie lasagna $11. Open daily 11:30am-1:30am; kitchen closes at 10pm. AmEx/D/MC/V.) With jukeboxes and TVs blaring, the **Cooper Street Pier ❷**, 508 E. Cooper St., is the local hot spot. Feast on the hamburger special (burger with fries and a soda or beer; $7.50) and $7.75 Coors pitchers during happy hour. (☎925-7758. Happy hour 3-6pm. Open daily 11am-2am; kitchen closes at 10pm. Cash only.) The **Main Street Bakery ❷**, 201 E. Main St., serves gourmet soups ($6), vegetarian sandwiches ($8-10), and fresh-squeezed juice ($2). Their patio offers *al fresco* dining and a prime people-watching spot. (☎925-6446. Open M-Sa 7am-9:30pm, Su 7am-4pm. AmEx/D/MC/V.) Fast, cheap, and easy, **The Big Wrap ❶**, 520 E. Durant Ave., rolls up gourmet wraps ($6.25), like the tasty "To Thai For." (☎544-1700. Fresh salads $5.20. Smoothies $4. Open M-Sa 10am-6pm. Cash only.) The only one of Aspen's famous mining saloons still open in its original locations, **The Red Onion,** 420 E. Cooper St., has daily lunch specials ($7) and microbrews ($3.75), as well as $3.50 margaritas at happy hour. (☎925-9043. Happy hour daily 4-6pm. Open daily 11am-10pm; bar open until 2am. AmEx/D/DC/MC/V.) For more cheap eats in Aspen, order smaller portions of regular dishes from "bar menus."

SKIING. Skiing is the main attraction in Aspen. The surrounding hills contain four ski areas: Aspen Mountain, Aspen Highlands, Buttermilk Mountain, and Snowmass, known collectively as **Aspen/Snowmass.** A free **Skier Shuttle Service** runs between the four mountains 8am-4:30pm. Interchangeable lift tickets enable the four areas to operate as a single extended resort; for the best deal, buy multi-day passes at least two weeks in advance. (☎923-1227 or 877-282-7736. Day passes from $72; college students 24 and under, ages 13-17, and ages 65-69 $64; ages 7-12 $43; ages 70+ and under 7 free. Prices vary by season.) **Incline Ski Shop,** 555 E. Durant (☎925-7748), one of the oldest and most experienced retailers around, rents boots and skis. Each of the mountains offers unique skiing opportunities of varying difficulty. **Buttermilk's** gentle slopes are perfect for beginners interested in lessons (and snowplowing down the mountain). The largest terrain park in North America, Buttermilk has won international acclaim and will host the **Winter X Games** until 2007. The **Highlands** now includes the steep cliffs of Highland Bowl and offers a diverse selection for advanced and expert skiers. **Aspen Mountain,** though smaller than the Highlands, also caters to experts; there are no easy trails. The granddaddy of the Aspen ski areas, **Snowmass** remains the most family-friendly. Its half-pipes and terrain parks are highly popular among snowboarders.

⚠ OUTDOOR ACTIVITIES. The **Silver Queen Gondola** heads to the 11,212 ft. summit of Aspen Mountain, providing an unparalleled panorama. (☎920-0719 or 800-525-6200. Open daily mid-June to early Sept. 10am-4pm; late Nov. to mid-April 9am-4pm. Day pass $18, ages 13-17 $15, ages 4-12 $10; week pass $35/$21/$28.) At Snowmass Mt., you can take a chairlift to the top and ride your mountain bike down. (Open in summer daily 9:30am-4pm. $8, children $4.) **Aspen Bike Rentals,** 555 E. Durant, at Hunter St., has great deals on mountain bike rentals. (☎925-8200. Front-suspension bike rental $30 per 4hr., $38 per 24hr.; full-suspension bike $34/$44. Open daily mid-June to Labor Day 8:30am-5:30pm; low season 9am-5pm.) Hikers can explore the magical **Maroon Bells,** two of Colorado's 54 14,000 ft. peaks, on the unforgettable 1½ mi. trek to Crater Lake, a high-altitude glacial lake. Maroon Creek Rd. is closed to traffic daily 9am-5pm in an effort to preserve the wilderness. RFTA tour buses to the Bells operate during these times and leave from Aspen Highlands Village every 20min. (☎925-8484. $5.50 per person.) If you're planning a hike outside these times, there is a $10 fee per car to drive into the area. The steep but short **Ute Trail** (2½ mi.) departs from Ute Ave. and weaves its way to the top of Aspen Mountain, a spectacular sunset-watching spot. The gentler **Río Grande Trail** wanders through town along the Roaring Fork and is popular for jogging and biking. Multi-day backpacking or mountain-biking treks throughout the White River Forest between Aspen, Vail, and Leadville can be complemented by night stays at the **10th Mountain Division Huts ❷,** built during WWII and carefully maintained ever since. The huts sleep 3-20 people and have heating stoves, propane burners, lighting, and mattresses. (☎925-5775; www.huts.org. Call for reservations. Open year-round. $25-39 per person.) For an adrenaline rush and a bird's-eye view of the region, **Aspen Paragliding,** 426 S. Spring St. (☎925-7625), does tandem jumps ($195), as well as ski and snowboard takeoffs in the winter. Though a fly-fishing trip requires pretty deep pockets, you can learn to cast for free with the experts in **Wagner Park** daily at noon during the summer (☎920-1128 for more info).

GLENWOOD SPRINGS ☎970

Next door to Aspen, Glenwood Springs allows budget travelers to stay near the famed slopes at refreshingly affordable prices. But Glenwood Springs is more than just Aspen's little brother. The hot springs are a popular year-round destination, and the spectacular Fairy Caves are considered one of the region's wonders. **Glenwood Hot Springs Lodge and Pool,** 401 N. River Rd., is a huge resort complex containing the world's largest outdoor mineral hot springs pool, a waterslide, and spas at various water temperatures. (☎945-6571 or 800-537-7946; www.hotspringspool.com. Open daily in summer 7:30am-10pm; in winter 9am-10pm. Day pass $14.25, after 9pm $9; ages 3-12 $9/$6.25; low season $12.) Sweat out the stress of travel in 112-117°F natural steam caves at **Yampah Spa and Vapor Caves,** 709 E. 6th St. (☎945-0667; www.yampahspa.com. Open daily 9am-9pm. $12, $6.75 with pass from Glenwood Springs Hostel.) While most skiers head to Aspen, Glenwood Spring's **Sunlight,** 10901 County Rd. 117, 10 mi. west of town., has relaxed family-style skiing. (☎945-7491 or 800-445-7931. $32 per day, ages 5-13 $21; hosteler discount.) Dubbed the 8th wonder of the world in 1896, the **Fairy Caves** were recently reopened to the public. **Glenwood Caverns,** 51000 Two Rivers Plaza Rd., explores the caves with both family-oriented and advanced tours, as well as amusement rides at the top of the tram. (☎945-4228 or 800-530-1635. www.glenwoodcaverns.com. Tram runs 8:30am-sunset; first Tu of every month begins at 11am. Call for winter hours. Tours 9am-9pm. Reservations required for 3hr. "wild" tour.)

Within walking distance of the springs and downtown, the ⓐ**Glenwood Springs Hostel (HI-AYH)** ❶, 1021 Grand Ave., consists of a spacious Victorian house and a newer building next door. The hostel offers a wide variety of trips and tours in the area, and offers discounts on skiing at Aspen. Amenities include two kitchens, the owner's amazing vinyl collection, a backyard patio, and a lounge with murals covering the walls. (☎945-8545 or 800-946-7835. Linen $2. Lockout 10am-4pm. Internet access. Max. stay 4 nights. Dorms $14, 4 nights $44; private singles $21; private doubles $29. AmEx/MC/V.) One of the least expensive motels in town, the **Frontier Lodge** ❸, 2834 Glen Ave. (Rte. 82), provides clean, spacious rooms with cable TV, A/C, fridge, microwave, and access to a hot tub. (☎945-5496 or 888-606-0602. June-Aug. singles $60-90, doubles $70-100; Sept.-May $30-50/$40-60. AAA discount.) Most other motels in the area are on the west side of the river on Rte. 82 or off Exit 116 from I-70. The **Daily Bread Cafe and Bakery** ❷, 729 Grand Ave., attracts locals with fresh, wholesome breakfasts and lunches. The quiche of the day (with salad or soup $6.75) is a favorite and usually sells out by early afternoon. (☎945-6253. Open M-F 7am-2pm, Sa 8am-2pm, Su 8am-noon. D/MC/V.) Shoot some pool as you digest a delicious burger ($6-8) at **Doc Holliday's Saloon** ❷, 724 Grand Ave. (☎945-9050. Open daily 10am-2am; kitchen 11am-11pm. MC/V.) The **Glenwood Farmer's Market** blooms downtown mid-June to mid-October on Tuesday evenings 4-8pm.

The **Roaring Fork Transit Agency** (**RFTA;** ☎925-8484; open M-F 9am-5pm) runs to Aspen (1½hr.; generally every 15min.; $6, ages 6-16 $5). The **White River National Forest Headquarters,** 9th and Grand Ave., has outdoor info. (☎945-2521. Open M-F 8am-5pm.) **Visitor Info: Glenwood Springs Chamber Resort Association,** 1102 Grand Ave. (☎945-6589. Open June-Aug. M-F 9am-5pm, Sa-Su 10am-5pm; Sept.-May M-F 9am-5pm, Sa-Su 10am-3pm. Brochure area open 24hr.) **Post Office:** 113 9th St. (☎945-5611. Open M-F 8am-6pm, Sa 9am-1pm.) **Postal Code:** 81601. **Area Code:** 970.

COLORADO SPRINGS   ☎719

Once a resort town frequented only by America's elite, Colorado Springs has grown to encompass neighboring Manitou Springs and Garden of the Gods; the metropolitan area is now the second-most visited in the state. Manitou Springs hosts the majority of the area's natural attractions, while the Garden of the Gods region takes its name from a Ute legend that its stunning red rocks were petrified bodies of enemies hurled down by the gods. Today, the formations remain a popular attraction, joined by the US Olympic Complex and the US Air Force Academy.

■ � **ORIENTATION AND PRACTICAL INFORMATION.** Colorado Springs is laid out in a grid of broad thoroughfares. **Nevada Avenue** is the main north-south strip through downtown, just east of **I-25,** though **Academy Boulevard** is generally faster. Starting at Nevada Ave., numbered streets ascend moving westward. **I-25** bisects downtown, separating Old Colorado City from the eastern, largely residential part of town. **Colorado Avenue** and **Pikes Peak Avenue** run east-west across the city. Just west of Old Colorado City lie Manitou Springs and the Pikes Peak Area. Colorado Ave. becomes **Manitou Avenue** as it extends into Manitou Springs. **Highway 24,** which comes from Limon to the east and heads into the Pike National Forest to the west, is the main thoroughfare to move from town to town. **Greyhound,** 120 S.

Weber St. (☎635-1505; www.greyhound.com; tickets sold daily 5:30am-10pm), runs buses to Albuquerque (8hr., 4 per day, $61), Denver (1½-2hr., 6 per day, $14), and Pueblo (1hr., 8 per day, $10). **Springs Transit,** 127 E. Kiowa St., at Nevada Ave., serves the local area, as well as Garden of the Gods, Manitou Springs, and Widefield. Pick up a schedule at the Kiowa bus terminal. (☎385-7433. $1.25, seniors and ages 6-11 $0.60, under 6 free. To Fountain $0.85 extra.) **Gray Line Tours,** 3704 W. Colorado Ave. (☎633-1181 or 800-345-8197; open M-F 8am-5pm), offers whitewater rafting trips on the Arkansas River (7hr.; $75, under 12 $40; includes lunch), as well as a combo tour of the US Air Force Academy and the Garden of the Gods (4hr.; $30, under 12 $15). **Taxi: Yellow Cab,** ☎634-5000. **Visitor Info: Visitors Bureau,** 515 S. Cascade Ave., at Cimarron. (☎635-7506 or 800-888-4748; www.coloradosprings-travel.com. Open M-F 8:30am-5pm, Sa-Su 9am-5pm.) **Internet Access: Penrose Public Library,** 20 N. Cascade Ave. (☎531-6333. Open M-Th 10am-9pm, F-Sa 10am-6pm, Su 1-5pm.) **Post Office:** 201 E. Pikes Peak Ave., at Nevada Ave. (☎570-5336. Open M-F 7:30am-5:30pm, Sa 8am-1pm.) **Postal Code:** 80903. **Area Code:** 719.

⌂ ACCOMMODATIONS. Motels can be found all along Nevada Ave. near downtown, although the best options are farther west in and around Manitou Springs. At the south entrance of the Garden of the Gods, **Beckers Lane Lodge ❷,** 115 Beckers Ln., supplies clean rooms with microwave, fridge, and cable TV, along with an outdoor swimming pool and laundry. (☎685-1866. Rooms $35-50. AmEx/MC/V.) In the heart of Manitou Springs, the full kitchens and spacious bathrooms of **Wheeler House ❸,** 36 Park Ave., provide a lovely home at the base of Pikes Peak. (☎685-4100 or 800-685-2399; www.wheelerhouse.com. Rooms from $62. D/MC/V.) Though many motels on the strip of Colorado Ave. between Old Colorado City and Manitou Springs are on the seedier side, the **Mountainscape Inn ❶,** 3445 West Colorado Ave, offers unbeatable prices accompanied by tidy rooms. (☎578-1773. Rooms from $27 in summer, $20 in winter. Call ahead for reservation details. AmEx/D/MC/V.) Several **Pike National Forest Campgrounds ❶** lie in the mountains flanking Pikes Peak, about 30min. from Colorado Springs. The **Pikes Peak Ranger District Office,** 601 S. Weber St. (☎636-1602; open M-F 8am-4:30pm), has maps. **Colorado, Painted Rocks,** and **South Meadows** campgrounds are near Manitou Park; others border U.S. 24 near the town of Lake George, 50 mi. west of the Springs. (Generally open late May to Sept. Sites $15.) Farther afield is the **Eleven Mile State Recreation Area ❶,** off County Rd. 90 from U.S. 24, about 1½ hr. from the Springs. (☎748-3401, reservations 800-678-2267. Showers, laundry. Reception M-Th and Su 7am-8pm, F-Sa 7am-9pm. Sites $12, with electricity $16; vehicle fee $5 per day.)

◖◗ FOOD AND NIGHTLIFE. Students and locals perch at outdoor tables in front of the cafes and restaurants lining **Tejon Avenue,** where a younger crowd fills the bars. More family establishments and fine eateries are in **Old Colorado City.** During the summer months, there are **farmers markets** throughout the city almost every day; the visitors center has a complete list. **Henri's ❷,** 2427 W. Colorado Ave., has served up chimichangas ($8) and a wide variety of *cerveza* for over 50 years. Drop in for a margarita during happy hour (M-F 4pm-6pm) or check out the strolling mariachi singers Friday and Saturday nights. (☎634-9031. Open Tu-Th and Su 11am-8am, F-Sa 11am-10pm. AmEx/D/MC/V.) Councilman Richard Skorman sells used books next door to his **Poor Richard's Restaurant ❷,** 324½ N. Tejon Ave., which attracts a diverse crowd seeking New York-style pizza. (☎632-7721. Cheese slices $3.50. Cheese pies $13. Sandwiches $7. Salads $5-7. Live folk music Tu. Bluegrass W. Celtic Th. Open M-Tu and Su 11am-9pm, W-Sa 11am-10pm.) Famous for their omelets ($5-7) and country-style skillets ($7-8), **The Olive Branch ❷,** 23 S. Tejon Ave., serves unbeatable breakfasts. (☎475-1199. Open daily 6:30am-9pm.)

Rum Bay Bourbon Street, 20 N. Tejon St., is a multilevel complex with six clubs included under one cover charge ($5). Besides the main Rum Bay club, the crowds swell into **Masquerade** (a disco club), **Copy Cats** (a karaoke bar), **Fat City** (a martini lounge with live blues), and **Sam's**—the world's smallest bar as noted in the *Guinness Book of World Records*. (☎ 634-3522. Specialty rum drinks $6-7. Ladies night W. 21+ after 8pm. Rum Bay open Tu-Sa 11am-2am; all other clubs open Th-Sa 6pm-2am.) For nightlife without N. Tejon's clubbing vibe, **Southside Johnny's,** 528 S. Tejon St., has cover-free music, a martini bar, and plenty of beers on tap. (☎ 444-8487. Beer $2.50-4. Live music W-Sa. 21+ F-Sa after 5pm. Open daily 11am-1:30am.)

◪ **SIGHTS.** Olympic hopefuls train with some of the world's most high-tech sports equipment at the **US Olympic Complex,** 1750 E. Boulder St., on the corner of Union St. The complex has free 1hr. tours. The best times to get a glimpse of athletes in training are typically 9:30am-noon and 3-5pm. (☎ 866-4618; www.usolympicteam.com. Hours vary; check the website for most current hours and tour times.) Tales of earlier quests for gold are recorded at the **Pioneers' Museum,** 215 S. Tejon Ave., which recounts the settling of Colorado Springs. Ride the birdcage elevator, walk through an old-time pharmacy, and sit in a restored courtroom. (☎ 385-5990. Open in summer Tu-Sa 10am-5pm, Su 1-5pm; in winter closed Su. Free.) The **World Figure Skating Museum and Hall of Fame,** 20 1st St., just north of Lake St., traces the history, art, and science of skating and boasts an extensive collection of rare medals and skating outfits. (☎ 635-5200; www.worldskatingmuseum.org. $3, ages 6-12 and 60+ $2. Open M-Sa 10am-4pm.) Chronicling the exploits of the rough-riding American cowboy, the **Pro Rodeo Hall of Fame and Museum,** Exit 147 immediately off I-25, is a monument to the rigors and triumphs of the quintessential Western lifestyle and its two centuries of history. (☎ 528-4764. Open daily 9am-5pm. $6, ages 6-12 $3.) Witness the spinning, casting, and etching process that has produced museum-quality pottery for decades at **Van Briggle Pottery,** Hwy. 24 and 21st St. (☎ 800-847-6341. Open M-Sa 8:30am-5pm, Su 1-5pm. Free tours M-Sa.)

◪ **OUTDOOR ACTIVITIES.** Between Rte. 24 (Colorado Ave.) and 30th St. in northwest Colorado Springs, the red rock towers and spires of the **Garden of the Gods Park** rise strikingly against a mountainous backdrop. (Open daily May-Oct. 5am-11pm; Nov.-Apr. 5am-9pm.) Climbers are lured by the large red rock faces and the 400 permanent routes. Climbers must register at the visitors center; $500 fines await those who climb without the free permit or proper gear. A number of exciting mountain biking trails cross the Garden as well. The park's hiking trails, including 2 mi. that are paved and wheelchair accessible, have great views of the rock formations and can easily be completed in one day. A map is available from the park's visitors center, 1805 N. 30th St., at Gateway Rd., which has a stellar 12min. movie, shown every 20min. in summer. (☎ 634-6666; http://gardenofgods.com. Open daily June-Aug. 8am-8pm; Sept.-May 9am-5pm. Walking tours daily 10am and 2pm; call for details on additional summer tours. Movie $2, children $1.)

The 14,110 ft. **Pikes Peak** is visible from almost any part of town. Ambitious hikers can ascend the peak along the strenuous, well-maintained **Barr Trail** (round-trip 26 mi.; 16hr.; 7500 ft. altitude gain). Overnight shelter is available at **Barr Camp** (7 mi. from the trailhead; also accessible by the Cog Railway) and the **Timberline Shelter** (8½ mi.). The trailhead is in Manitou Springs by the "Manitou Incline" sign on Ruxton Ave. Just down the street from the trailhead, visitors can hop on the **Pikes Peak Cog Railway,** 515 Ruxton Ave., which runs to the summit every 80min. From the summit, the Sangre de Cristo Mountains, the Continental Divide, and the state of Kansas unfold in front of you. (☎ 685-5401; www.cograilway.com. Open mid-Apr. to late Dec. 6-8 trips per day. Round-trip $28, ages 3-12 $15.50. Reservations recommended.) You can also drive up the gorgeous 10 mi. **Pikes Peak Highway**—it's worth every penny. (☎385-7325 or 800-318-9505. Open daily May to mid-Sept. 7am-7pm; mid-Sept. to Apr. 9am-3pm. $10, ages 6-15 $5; $35 max. per vehicle.)

For adventurous hiking, head to the contorted caverns of the **Cave of the Winds,** on Rte. 24, 6 mi. west of Exit 141 off I-25. Discovery and lantern tours go into the more untamed areas of the cave. (☎685-5444; www.caveofthewinds.com. Guided tours daily every 15min. late May to Aug. 9am-9pm; Sept. to late May 10am-5pm. 45min. guided tour $15, ages 6-15 $8. 1-1½hr. guided lantern tour $18/$9. Laser light show in summer daily 9pm $10/$5.) Just above Manitou Springs on Rte. 24, the **Cliff Dwellings Museum** contains replicas of ancestral Puebloan dwellings dating from AD 1100-1300 and actual ruins that serve as a backdrop for Santa Clara Puebloan dancers in colorful traditional dress performing from June to August. (☎685-5242 or 800-354-9971; www.cliffdwellingsmuseum.com. Open daily May-Sept. 9am-6pm; Oct.-Apr. 10am-5pm. $8.50, seniors $7.50, ages 7-12 $6.50.) The only waterfall in Colorado to make it onto *National Geographic's* list of the world's top waterfalls, **Seven Falls**, 10min. west of downtown on Cheyenne Blvd., cascades 181 ft. in seven distinct steps and is lit up on summer nights. The Mountain Elevator takes visitors who wish to skip the 184-step climb to a prime viewpoint. (☎632-0765; www.sevenfalls.com. Open daily in summer 8:30am-10:30pm, in winter 9am-4:15pm. Before 5pm $8.25, ages 6-15 $5.25; after 5pm $9.75/$6.25.

GREAT SAND DUNES   ☎719

In Great Sand Dunes National Park, billions of grains of sand make up dunes that have stood for almost a million years as landmarks for travelers, from ancient North American nomads to modern outdoors enthusiasts. Thousands of years of wind and water have made these 750 ft. dunes the tallest in North America. Within the park, the most popular hiking is on the sand dunes themselves. Since wind obliterates the footprints of yesterday's explorers, no designated trails exist on the dunes, and hiking up through the soft sand can be exhausting. The best times to hike the dunes are in the morning, when the sand is coolest and the risk of thunderstorms lowest, and in the evening, especially on full moon nights. At the base of the dunes is a large, flat sandy area where the seasonal **Medano Creek** has small waves, called "surge flow," from sand falling off the dunes, which makes the creek a popular spot for hiking, splashing, and sandcastle-building. The designated hiking trails elsewhere in the park often cross through multiple ecosystems in the Sangre de Cristo mountains. The half-mile **Montville Nature Trail** starts just north of the visitors center and is relatively flat. Off this trail, the more challenging **Mosca Pass Trail** (7 mi. round-trip) takes hikers into the high country through three different ecosystems. The worthwhile trek up **Zapata Falls,** just outside of the park (between Mi. 10 and 11 on Hwy. 150), leads hikers through a creek and narrow gorge to the base of a 30 ft. hidden waterfall.

Camping is the only option for lodging within the park. People often arrive at **Pinon Campground ❶** by 7:30am to secure one of the 88 campsites; the most coveted have views of the dunes. (☎378-6399. No showers or hookups. Open year-round. $12. No reservations. AmEx/MC/V.) Intrepid campers can pitch their tents on the dunes themselves or in one of the seven designated **backcountry camping** sites, though both of these options require hikes of at least an hour. Pick up **permits** ($10) and maps at the visitors center. Just outside the park, the private **Great Sand Dunes Oasis Campground and RV Park ❶**, 5400 Hwy 150 N., has showers, laundry, and hookups, but no views. (☎378-2222. Open May-Oct. Tent sites $14. Full hookups $23. AmEx/D/MC/V.) The cheapest and nicest indoor option in the area is the **Lodge Motel ❷**, 825 Hwy. 160 in Ft. Garland, which has clean rooms and new bathrooms. (☎379-2880. Singles $42; doubles $47. MC/V.) The only indoor option close to the park is the **Great Sand Dunes Lodge ❹**, 7900 Hwy 150 N., which has excellent views of the dunes and a heated indoor pool. (☎378-2900; www.gsd-lodge.com. Rooms $89. AmEx/MC/V.) For those camping in the park, Oasis Campground has a small **grocery** with limited sundries, as well as a **restaurant** that serves lunch and dinner. (☎378-2222. Lunch $5-8. Dinner $9-16. Open Memorial Day-Labor Day 8am-8pm.) Beyond the park, Alamosa offers a wide variety of restaurants. **Calvillo's ❷**, 400 Main St., in Alamosa, dishes up a generous Mexican buffet all day long. A la carte items, including the enchiladas ($6.50), are equally tasty. (☎587-5500. Open M-Th and Su 7am-9pm, F-Sa 7am-10pm. AmEx/MC/V.)

The Great Sand Dunes National Park lies on Rte. 160. The nearest towns are **Ft. Garland**, 29 mi. to the east, and **Alamosa**, 35 mi. to the west The **entrance fee** ($3, under 17 free) includes a copy of the park publication *Breezes* and a trail map. The **visitors center** is 3 mi. from the park entrance. (☎378-6399; www.nps.gov/grsa. Open Memorial Day-Labor Day 9am-6pm; call for winter hours.) **Medical Services: San Luis Valley Regional Medical Center,** in Alamosa (☎589-2511). **Post Office:** 505 3rd St., in Alamosa (☎519-4908). **Postal Code:** 81101. **Area Code:** 719.

SAN JUAN MOUNTAINS

Ask Coloradans for their favorite mountain retreats, and they're likely to name a peak, lake, stream, or town in the San Juan Range of southwestern Colorado. Four national forests—the **Uncompahgre** (un-cum-PAH-gray), the **Gunnison**, the **San Juan**, and the **Río Grande**—encircle this sprawling range. **Durango** is an ideal base camp for forays into these mountains. Northeast of Durango, the **Weminuche Wilderness** tempts the hardy backpacker with a vast expanse of rugged terrain. Get maps and hiking info from the **USFS headquarters** at 15 Burnett Ct., Durango. (☎247-4874. Open Apr. to mid-Dec. M-F 8am-5pm; mid-Dec. to Mar. M-F 8am-4:30pm.) The San Juan Mountains are easily accessible via U.S. 50, which is traveled by hundreds of thousands of tourists each summer. **Greyhound** serves the area, but very infrequently; traveling by car is the best option. The San Juans are loaded with campgrounds, making them one of the most economical places in Colorado to visit.

BLACK CANYON OF THE GUNNISON NATIONAL PARK ☎970

Native American parents used to tell their children that the light-colored strands of rock streaking through the walls of the Black Canyon were the hair of a blonde woman—and that if they got too close to the edge they would get tangled in it and fall. The edge of **Black Canyon of the Gunnison National Park** is a staggering place, literally—watch for those trembling knees. The Gunnison River slowly gouged out the 53 mi. long canyon, crafting a steep 2500 ft. gorge that is, in some places, deeper than it is wide. The Empire State Building, if placed at the bottom of the river, would reach barely halfway up the canyon walls.

Black Canyon lies 15 mi. east of the town of **Montrose**. The **South Rim** is easily accessible year-round via a 6 mi. drive off U.S. 50 ($8 per car, $4 walk-in or motorcycle); the wilder **North Rim** can only be reached by an 80 mi., 1-3 hr. detour around the canyon followed by a gravel road from Crawford off Rte. 92. The road is closed to cars in winter but open for cross-country skiing. Less than a mile past the South Rim entrance is the **visitors center** (see below), where the spectacular 6 mi. South Rim Drive begins. The route traces the edge of the canyon and boasts jaw-dropping vistas, including the spectacular **Chasm View,** where you can peer 2300 ft. down the highest cliff in Colorado at the Gunnison River and the "painted" south wall. Don't throw stones; you might kill a defenseless hiker in the canyon. On the South Rim, the moderate 2 mi. round-trip **Oak Flat Loop Trail** gives a good sense of the terrain below, while the North Rim's 7 mi. round-trip **North Vista Trail** provides a spectacular view. From the South Rim, you can scramble down the **Gunnison Route,** which drops 1800 ft. over a 1 mi. span, or tackle the incredibly difficult **Tomichi** or **Warner Routes,** which make good overnight hikes. Not surprisingly, the sheer walls of the Black Canyon are a climber's paradise; registration is required at the South Rim Visitors Center. Between the **Painted Wall** and **Cedar Point Overlooks,** a well-worn path leads to **Marmot Rocks,** which offer great bouldering for those not ready for the big walls. All inner-canyon use requires a free permit. On the South Rim, Chasm View, Sunset View, and Tomichi overlooks are all wheelchair accessible. Balanced Rock overlook, on the North Rim, is also wheelchair accessible.

At the canyon, the **South Rim Campground ❶** has 88 sites with pit toilets, charcoal grills, and limited water. Some sites are wheelchair accessible. (Sites $10, RV hookup $15.) The 13 sites at the **North Rim Campground ❶** are popular with climbers. (Sites with water and toilets $10.) The car-accessible route into the canyon leads to the pleasant **East Portal Campground ❶.** The steep 16% grade road, although paved, prohibits large vehicles, so the campground is free from RVs. (Sites with water and toilet $10). In Montrose, inexpensive motels line Main St./U.S. 50 east of downtown, including **Canyon Trails Inn ❷,** 1225 E. Main St. (☎249-3426. Hot tub, continental breakfast. Singles $48; doubles $62. AmEx/D/MC/V.) 🖾**Starvin' Arvin's ❸,** 1320 S. Townsend, is wildly popular with locals and visitors alike; it's been serving up cowboy-sized portions for as long as most can remember. Don't miss the 16 oz. steak and eggs breakfast for $14. (☎249-7787. Entrees $4-18. Open daily 6am-10pm. D/MC/V.) **Nay-Mex Tacos ❶,** 475 W. Main St., cooks up the best Mexican food around. (Tacos $1.50. Tostadas $2-3. Open M-F 11am-9pm, Sa-Su 9am-9pm. Cash only.) For tasty sandwiches ($6) and breakfasts ($7), head for the **Daily Bread Bakery and Cafe ❶,** 346 Main St. (☎249-8444. Open M-Sa 6am-3pm. Cash only.)

Greyhound, 1360 N. Townsend, just south of the Sun Valley truck stop, travels daily to Denver (7½hr., 2 per day, $45-59), Durango (3hr., 1 per day, $28-30), and Salt Lake City (8½ hr., 1 per day, $61-66), and less frequently to other destinations, such as Las Vegas and Dallas. (☎249-6673; www.greyhound.com. Open M-F 5:30am-1pm and 7:30-8pm, Sa 5:30-8:30am and 7:30-8pm, Su 11am-12:15pm and 7:30-8pm.) The bus also shuttles once a day between Montrose and the Gunnison station, 312 W. Hwy. 50 (☎641-0060), several blocks from the **Gunnison County Airport,** 711 Río Grande, and sometimes will make an extra stop upon request on U.S. 50, 6 mi. from the canyon ($17-18). A helpful **visitors center** sits on the canyon's South Rim. (☎249-1914, ext. 423; www.nps.gov/blca. Open daily May-Oct. 8am-6pm; Nov.-Apr. 8:30am-4pm.) **Post Office:** 321 S. 1st St., in Montrose (☎249-6654. Open M-F 8am-5pm, Sa 10am-noon.) **Postal Code:** 81401. **Area Code:** 970.

CRESTED BUTTE   ☎970

The compact town of Crested Butte, 27 mi. north of Gunnison on Rte. 135, was first settled by miners in the 1870s. The coal was exhausted in the 1950s, but a few years later the powder fields on the Butte began to attract skiers. Thanks to strict zoning rules, the downtown is a throwback to the early mining days. Just north of town, **Crested Butte Mountain Resort,** 12 Snowmass Rd., takes skiers to "the extreme limits," offering over 1075 acres of bowl skiing. With 15 lifts, a longest run of 2½ mi., and a drop of 3000 ft., the mountain aims to impress, and the views aren't bad either. (☎800-544-8448; www.skicb.com. Open mid-Nov. to mid-Apr. Prices vary. Day passes generally $69, ages 13-17 $52, ages 7-12 $35; ages 65-69 25% discount.) Crested Butte has several noteworthy summer festivals. Among these is the fun-loving **Fat Tire Bike Festival** (www.ftbw.com), four days of mountain biking, racing, and fraternizing at the end of June. Visitors and locals in hilarious costumes try to coast down the mountain as fast as possible without pedaling in the famous chainless race. In 1976, a group of cyclists rode from Crested Butte to

ROCKY MOUNTAINS

Aspen, starting the oldest mountain biking event in the world. Every September, bikers repeat the trek over the 12,705 ft. pass to Aspen and back during the **Pearl Pass Tour,** organized by the **Mountain Biking Hall of Fame,** 331 Elk Ave. (☎349-1880. Open Memorial Day-Labor Day daily 10am-8pm. $3; children free. MC/V.) Trail maps are available at bike shops like **The Alpineer,** 419 6th St. (☎349-5210. Open daily June to mid-Sept. and Dec. to mid-Apr. 9am-6pm; mid-Sept. to Nov. and mid-Apr. to May 10am-5pm. Front suspension bike $25 per day, $5 per hr.; full suspension bike $35/$8. Min. 3 hr. rental.) Once on wheels, all trails are accessible right from town or via the free shuttle (see below). Be sure to check snow conditions before heading out; some trails are closed into early July. Trails begin at the base of Mt. Crested Butte and extend into the Gothic area. **Trail 401** is a demanding and famous 24 mi. round-trip loop and the excellent downhill has great views of the valley and its wildflowers. For the same fun on a shorter ride, cut through on **Rustler's Gulch** trail. The short but beautiful **Strand Hill Trail** is an intermediate option. For those without wheels, the hike to **Green Lake** (3 mi.) is unbeatable.

Finding budget accommodations in the winter is about as easy as striking a vein of gold. Nonetheless, the ▧**Crested Butte International Hostel and Lodge (HI) ❶,** 615 Teocalli Ave., two blocks north of the four-way stop, treats travelers to gorgeous, modern facilities. Its huge kitchen and bright common area make it an ideal base for exploring the region. (☎349-0588 or 888-389-0588; www.crestedbuttehostel.com. Showers for non-guests $5. Laundry. 4- to 6-bed dorms $20-32; doubles $50-89. Spacious 3rd-fl. apartment sleeps up to 6; $125-210. Rates vary depending on season; call in advance for prices and reservations. Group discounts available. D/MC/V.) The US Forest Service operates a number of campgrounds in the area. **Cement Creek Campground ❶,** 10 mi. south of town off Hwy. 135, is near several hiking and motorbike trails and its namesake creek, in which the adventurous can find several hot springs. Contact **Gunnison National Forest Office,** 216 N. Colorado, 30 mi. south in Gunnison., for more info on area camping. (☎641-0471. Open M-F 7:30am-4:30pm.) **Pitas in Paradise ❶,** 214 Elk Ave., a self-proclaimed "Mediterranean Cafe with Soul," wows diners with its delicious gyros, salads, and smoothies. Watch your meal being made at the counter or sit down to wait for it in the backyard. (☎349-0897. Gyros $5.40. Salads $3.50-7. Open daily in summer daily 11am-10pm; in winter 11am-9pm. MC/V.) **The Secret Stash ❷,** 21 Elk Ave., at the west end of town, has one of the highest-altitude coffee roasters in the world and a menu that ranges from eclectic pizzas ($8-17) to wraps ($3.50-8) to grilled wings (10 for $7). Sip a soy latte in the garden or upstairs, where the cushy couches, mood lighting, and acoustic guitar recall a hippie's living room. (☎349-6245. Open M-Sa 5-10pm with additional lunch hours during summer and winter seasons. D/MC/V.) Serving delicious Indian and Thai dishes with plenty of vegetarian options, the **Ginger Cafe ❸,** 313 3rd Ave., also delivers in town and to the mountain. (349-7291. Entrees $8-13. Open daily 11am-10pm. MC/V.)

The **Crested Butte Chamber of Commerce** is at 601 Elk Ave. (☎800-545-4505; www.crestedbuttechamber.com. Open daily 9am-5pm.) A free shuttle to the mountain leaves from the chamber. (☎349-5616. Every 40min. 7:20-10:20am and 8pm-midnight, every 20min. 10:20am-8pm.) **Internet Access: The Old Rock Community Library,** 507 Maroon Ave. (☎349-6535. Open M, W, F 10am-6pm, Tu and Th 10am-7pm, Sa 10am-2pm.) **Post Office:** 217 Elk Ave. (☎349-5568. Open M-F 7:30am-4:30pm, Sa 10am-1pm.) **Postal Code:** 81224. **Area Code:** 970.

TELLURIDE ☎970

Site of the first bank Butch Cassidy ever robbed (the San Miguel), Telluride was very much a town of the Old West. Locals believe that their city's name derives from a contraction of "to hell you ride," likely a warning given to travelers. In the last few decades, outlaws have been replaced with film stars, and six-shooters with cinnamon buns. Skiers, hikers, and vacationers come to Telluride to pump gold and silver into the mountains, and the town also claims the most festivals per capita of any postal code in the US. Still, a small-town feeling prevails—rocking chairs sit outside brightly painted houses, and dogs lounge on storefront porches.

⚏ 🔊 ORIENTATION AND PRACTICAL INFORMATION. Telluride sits on Rte. 145, 125 mi. northwest of Durango in the San Juan Mountains. Most of the action lies on Colorado Ave./Rte. 145. The public bus line, **Galloping Goose,** runs through town on a regular basis. (☎728-5700. Every 20min. May-Oct. 7am-8pm; Nov. to mid-April 7am-midnight. Town loop free, outlying towns $1.) A free **gondola** runs continuously between downtown and Mountain Village, with spectacular views of the surrounding mountains. The station is at the corner of Oak St. and San Juan Ave. (☎728-8888. 15min. each way. Runs late May to early Apr. daily 7am-midnight.) **Taxi** service from **Mountain Limo** serves the western slope. (☎728-9606 or 888-546-6894. Airport fare $10.) The **visitors center,** 630 W. Colorado Ave., at Davis St. and W. Colorado Ave. near the entrance to town, has information on trails and festivals. (☎800-525-3455; www.visittelluride.com. Open in summer daily 9am-8pm; in winter daily 9am-6pm.) **Police:** ☎728-3818. **Hotlines: Rape Crisis,** ☎728-5660. **Medical Services: Telluride Medical Center,** 500 W. Pacific St. (☎728-3848). **Internet Access: Wilkinson Public Library,** 100 W. Pacific St. (☎728-4519. Open M-Th 10am-8pm, F-Sa 10am-6pm, Su noon-5pm.) **Post Office:** 150 S. Willow St. (☎728-3900. Open M-F 9am-5pm, Sa 10am-noon.) **Postal Code:** 81435. **Area Code:** 970.

⛏ ACCOMMODATIONS. If you're visiting Telluride during a festival, bring a sleeping bag; the cost of a bed is outrageous. Tucked behind the main downtown drag, the **Victorian Inn ❹,** 401 W. Pacific Ave., offers pleasant rooms with lace curtains. (☎728-6601 or 800-611-9893. Rooms from $75. AmEx/MC/V.) William Jennings Bryan delivered his "Cross of Gold" speech from the front balcony of the **New Sheridan Hotel ❹,** 231 W. Colorado Ave. If you can afford it, the luxurious rooms, full breakfast, and free Internet access justify the splurge. (☎728-4351 or 800-200-1891. Rooms with shared bath from $95.) 🏕**Sunshine Campground ❶,** 8 mi. south on Rte. 145, is situated among the aspens on a hillside with 360° views of all the surrounding peaks. (☎327-4261. No electricity or showers. No reservations. Open May-Sept. Sites $14.) The **Telluride Town Park Campground ❶,** east of down-

LIVIN' LA VETA LOCA

The small town of La Veta (pop. 924), nestled in the Spanish Peaks of Colorado, doesn't have world-renowned festivals like Telluride or an active skiing industry akin to Vail. What it does have is a vibrant culture disproportionate to its size. Locals, many of whom work via Internet or mail specialty products from their homes, often host both regional and national musical artists in their homes. Multiple art galleries also hide in the homes that dot La Veta's three paved streets.

The **Ryus Bakery** serves as a meeting spot for the aging hippies that have relocated to a town also home to ranchers and retired Ph.D.s. For travelers too caught up in La Veta's hip atmosphere to leave, the **1899 Inn** includes a full breakfast in the price of its lovely, early-American rooms. If you're looking for something to do before bed, head 15min. and 3,000 ft. up the mountain to the neighboring town of Cuchara. On summer nights, dogs will gather on the porch of the **Dog Bar** to enjoy the live music, even though they aren't allowed to join their owners for a drink inside.

Ryus Bakery, 129 W. Ryus (☎719-742-3830). Open Tu, Th, Sa 8am-1:30pm.

1899 Inn, 314 S. Main (☎719-742-3576). Rooms $55, with private bath $60; cottages $75.

Dog Bar, 34 Cuchara (☎719-742-3450). Open M-Th and Su 11am-midnight, F-Sa 11am-2am.

town, offers 29 nice, if closely spaced, sites along the San Miguel River. (☎728-2173. Water, full bathrooms, no hookups. 7-night max. stay. Office open mid-May to mid-Oct. M-W 8am-5pm, Th-F 8am-7pm, Sa-Su 8am-4pm. $15 per vehicle. Primitive sites $12.) During the Bluegrass Festival, ticket holders can lottery for spots in the campground. Hot showers ($3) are available at the high school.

◖ **FOOD. La Cocina de Luz ❷**, 123 E. Colorado Ave., serves authentic and affordable *taquería*-style Mexican cuisine. Featuring fresh handmade tortillas and fire-roasted chilis, La Cocina uses organic, local ingredients in their flavorful quesadillas, tamales ($6-10), and large selection of vegetarian options. (☎728-9355. Open M-Sa 9am-9pm. MC/V.) The popular **Honga's ❹**, 133 S. Oak, serves pan-Asian foods, including the delicious blackened tofu ($16), in an environmentally conscious setting. (☎728-5134. Dinner entrees $12-27. Open 5:30pm-late. Reservations recommended. AmEx/MC/V.) The wooden benches and long tables at **Fat Alley Barbeque ❸**, 122 S. Oak St., are reminiscent of the sawdust saloons of yore, but Telluride's miners never ate barbecue like this. (☎728-3985. Barbecue $7-18. Open daily 11:30am-10pm. AmEx/MC/V.) **Baked in Telluride ❷**, 127 S. Fir St., has enough rich coffee, pastries, pizza, and sandwiches to get you through a festival weekend, plus free Wi-Fi Internet access. The apple fritters ($2.50) and enormous calzones ($8-11) are justifiably popular. (☎728-4775. Open daily 5:30am-10pm.) Telluride also has a **farmers market,** 123 S. Oak St. (☎728-8701), on Friday afternoons.

◗◖ **ENTERTAINMENT AND NIGHTLIFE.** Given that only 2000 people live in Telluride, the sheer number of festivals in the town seems staggering. One weekend in July is actually designated the "Nothing Festival" to give locals a break from the onslaught of visitors and special events. For general festival info, contact the **Telluride Visitors Center** (☎800-525-3455). Gala events occur throughout the summer and fall, from the quirky **Mushroom Festival** (☎303-296-9359; www.shroomfestival.com; late Aug.) to the renowned **Bluegrass Festival.** (☎800-624-2422; www.planetbluegrass.com. 3rd weekend in June. $55 per day, 4-day pass $155.) The **Telluride International Film Festival** premiers some of the hippest independent flicks; *The Crying Game* and *The Piano* were both unveiled here. (☎728-4640; www.telluridefilmfestival.com. 1st weekend in Sept.) For most festivals (including the more expensive Bluegrass Festival and Jazz Celebration), volunteering to usher or perform other tasks can result in free admission. Call the contact number of the specific event for more info. Throughout the year, a number of performances go on at the **Sheridan Opera House,** 110 N. Oak St. (☎728-6363.) Advance tickets for these events can be purchased at **Telluride Ticket** (☎728-8199; www.tellurideticket.com).

Telluride may have a new-age air by day, but its bars still burst with old-fashioned fun by night. The lively **Last Dollar Saloon,** 100 E. Colorado Ave., affectionately referred to as "the Buck," is a favorite among locals. (☎728-4800. Beer $3-4.75. Open daily 11am-2am. Cash only.) Telluride's freshest musical talent jives at **Fly Me to the Moon Saloon,** 136 E. Colorado Ave., which thrills groovers with its spring-loaded dance floor. (☎728-6666. Cover $2-5. Open daily 3pm-late. Cash only.) The historic **New Sheridan Bar,** 231 W. Colorado Ave., inspires hubbub around town with $2 drinks during the Tuesday pool tournaments and Wednesday open poker nights. (☎728-9100. 21+ after 8pm. Open daily noon-2am.) For partiers out late, Telluride's free **"home safe" shuttle** will take you from the courthouse, 305 W. Colorado, to your front door. (Shuttle departs F-Sa 12:45 and 2:15am. Free.)

◪ **OUTDOOR ACTIVITIES.** Biking, hiking, and backpacking opportunities are endless; ghost towns and lakes are tucked behind almost every mountain crag. The tourist office has a list of suggestions for hikes in the area. The most popular trek (about 2hr.) is up the 4WD road to **Bridal Veil Falls,** the waterfall visible from almost anywhere in Telluride. The trailhead is at the end of Rte. 145. Continuing another 2½ mi. from the top of the falls will lead to **Silver Lake,** a steep but rewarding climb. Another popular hike is the **Bear Creek** trail, a gradual, easy 2 mi. hike to the Bear Creek waterfalls that starts on Pine St. From from the north end of Aspen St., the **Jud Wiebe Trail** takes you on a 2¾ mi. loop with panoramas of the entire valley. For more Rocky Mountain highs, ride the free gondola to St. Sophia station at the top of the mountain, where a number of hiking and biking trails run.

In winter, even avowed atheists can be spied praying before hitting the "Spiral Stairs" and the "Plunge," two of the Rockies' most gut-wrenching ski runs. For more info, contact the **Telluride Ski Resort,** P.O. Box 11155, Telluride 81435. (☎728-3856. Regular season lift tickets: full day $65; children $36; half-day $58/$28.) **Paragon Ski and Sport,** 213 W. Colorado Ave., rents bikes in summer and skis in winter. (☎728-4525. Bikes from $20 per half-day, $40 per day. Beginner ski package $19 per day. Open daily in ski season 8:30am-7pm; in summer 9am-7pm.)

SCENIC DRIVE: SAN JUAN SKYWAY

More a runway to the mountains and clouds than a terrestrial highway, the San Juan Skyway soars across the rooftop of the Rockies. Winding its way through San Juan and Uncompahgre National Forests, Old West mountain towns, and Native American ruins, the byway passes a remarkably wide range of southwestern Colorado's splendors. Reaching altitudes up to 11,000 ft., with breathtaking views of snowy peaks and verdant valleys, the San Juan Skyway is widely considered one of America's most beautiful drives. Travelers in this area inevitably drive at least parts of it as they head to destinations like Telluride, Durango, and Mesa Verde. Call the San Juan (☎970-247-4874) or Uncompahgre (☎970-874-6600) National Forests to check road conditions or to inquire about driving the skyway.

As a loop road consisting of Rtes. 550, 62, 145, and 160, the skyway can be started from anywhere along the loop. Beginning in Durango, the skyway heads north along **Route 550 N (Million Dollar Highway),** climbing into the San Juan Mountains parallel to the Animas River. Twenty-seven miles north of Durango, the road passes **Durango Mountain Resort** as it ascends. (☎800-979-9742. Annual snowfall 260 in. Open late Nov. to early Apr. 9am-4pm. Full-day lift ticket $55, under 12 $29.) At Mi. 64 on Rte. 550, the road reaches Molas Point, a whopping 10,910 ft. above sea level. Less than 1 mi. farther north, **Molas Lake Public Park Campground ❶** offers visitors an oasis with both tent and RV sites ($15) near a breathtaking little lake. (☎970-759-5557. Drinking water available, no hookups.)

Descending to a mere 9318 ft., the skyway passes through easygoing **Silverton.** A mining town until the early 1990s, Silverton is a subdued mountain village with a permanent population of just 500, but the town hosts over 250,000 visitors a year. One of the most exciting times to visit is the last weekend in June, when the **Silverton Jubilee** transforms the town into a three-day musical extravaganza featuring everything from bluegrass to funk. (☎800-752-4494; www.silvertonfestivals.org. 3-day pass $80, 2-day $65; if purchased before June 1 $70/$60.) The **visitors center** sits close to the entrance to town on Rte. 550. (☎387-5654 or 800-752-4494; www.silverton.org. Open daily June-Sept. 9am-6pm; Oct.-May 10am-4pm.) Hiking, mountain biking, and skiing at **Kendall Mountain** (lift tickets $7) await those who can still catch their breath. Nearby **Silverton Mountain** opened in 2005 for extreme skiing with a base altitude of 10,400 feet. Southeast of Silverton, 5 mi. up County Rd. 2, **Old Hundred Gold Mine** features tours 1600 ft. into the depths of one of the most interesting mines in Colorado. A chance to try your hand at panning gold is included. (☎970-387-5444; www.minetour.com. Tours depart daily early May to mid-Oct. every hr. on the hr., 10am-4pm. Arrive 20min. early. $15, ages 5-12 $8.)

From Silverton, the San Juan Skyway climbs higher until it reaches 11,018 ft. at Mi. 80 on Rte. 550. Known as **Red Mountain Pass,** this is the most dangerous part of the route in the winter; several snowplows (and their drivers) have gone off the steep cliffs here. Continuing north, the drive from Silverton to Ouray showcases stellar 14,000 ft. mountain peaks and defunct mines. In 1991, the Reclamation Act shut down most of the mines, leaving only remnants of the past. The skyway next arrives in **Ouray;** the **visitors center** is at the north end of town on Rte. 550. (☎325-4746 or 800-228-1876; www.ouraycolorado.com. Open in summer M-Sa 9am-6pm, Su 10am-4pm; in winter daily 10am-4pm.) With fabulous mountain views, well-preserved historic buildings, and hedonistic hot springs, this heavily Swiss-influenced town is a relaxing stop for the weary. Most hotels here have their own hot springs. Most notable is the unique vapor cave at the **Wiesbaden,** at 6th Ave. and 5th St., where visitors actually go inside the mountain. (☎970-325-4347. 3 hr. $12. Open 8am-9:45pm.) A clothing-optional experience awaits at **Orvis Hot Springs,** 1585 County Rd. 3, 1 mi. south of Ridgeway, a nude park with an several pools and places for lounging around, all with mineral-rich water. (☎970-626-5324. Open daily 9am-10pm. 1hr. $8; all-day $12.) Beyond Ouray, the skyway returns to Earth. Traversing mesas, Rte. 550 junctions with Rte. 62 in Ridgeway. Rte. 62 leads travelers to Placerville, where the skyway connects with Rte. 145.

Telluride (p. 714) awaits travelers next along Rte. 145. Past the Mountain Village, **Lizard Head Pass** offers a tranquil 6 mi. hike reaching over 12,000 ft. From the pass, the skyway glides down through the quiet towns of Rico and Dolores. Rte. 145 connects with Rte. 160 just east of Cortez and west of **Mesa Verde National Park** (p. 720), home of the cliff dwellings of the ancient Puebloan people. Moving east along Rte. 160, the skyway cuts through **Mancos** and finally returns to Durango.

DURANGO   ☎970

In its heyday, Durango was one of the main railroad junctions in the Southwest. Walking down the town's main thoroughfare, it's easy to see that Durango remains a crossroads. Today, this informal town attracts visitors with its mountain biking, skiing, and snowboarding. Dreadlocked, hemp-clad youths share the sidewalks with weathered ranchers in ten-gallon hats and stiff Wranglers; toned, brazen mountain bikers rub shoulders with camera-toting tourists in the bars.

⚎ 🖪 ORIENTATION AND PRACTICAL INFORMATION. Durango is at the intersection of U.S. 160 and 550. Streets run east-west and avenues run north-south, but everyone calls Main Ave., the principal road through town, "Main St." **Greyhound,** 275 E. 8th Ave. (☎259-2755; www.greyhound.com; open M-F 7:30am-1pm, Sa 7:30am-noon, Su and holidays 7:30-10am), runs once per day to Albuquerque (5hr., $47-53), Denver (11½hr., $61-72), and Grand Junction (5hr., $34-39). The **Durango Lift** provides trolley service in town. (☎259-5438. Runs Memorial Day-Labor Day M-F 6:30am-6:30pm, Sa 9:30am-6:30pm. $1, seniors $0.50.) **Taxi: Durango Transportation** ☎259-4818. The **Durango Area Tourism Office,** 111 S. Camino del Río, on the southeast side of town, has info on sights and hiking. (☎247-0312 or 800-525-8855; www.durango.org. Open in summer M-F 8am-6pm, Sa 8am-5pm, Su 10am-4pm; in winter M-F 8am-5pm.) **Road Conditions:** ☎264-5555. **Internet Access: Durango Public Library,** 1188 E. 2nd Ave. (☎375-3380. Open M-W 9am-9pm, Th-Su 9am-5:30pm; closed Su in summer.) **Post Office:** 222 W. 8th St. (☎247-3434. Open M-F 8am-5:30pm, Sa 9am-1pm.) **Postal Code:** 81301. **Area Code:** 970.

🖪 🖸 ACCOMMODATIONS AND FOOD. If you don't mind staying 25 mi. north of Durango, you'll be pampered at **Silverpick Lodge ❸,** 48475 U.S. 550, with luxurious rooms, goose-down comforters, hot tub, game room, laundry, and library. Call within 48hr. of check-in for their year-round "Last Second Special" and get any available room for only $48, about half the usual price. (☎259-6600. Rooms May-Sept. $79-99; call for low-season rates.) The reasonably priced **Budget Inn ❷**, 3077 Main Ave., offers clean rooms, a hot tub, an outdoor pool, and laundry facilities. (☎247-5222 or 800-257-5222; www.budgetinndurango.com. Cable TV, telephone; some rooms with microwave and fridge. Rooms June-Aug. $45-65; Sept.-Jan. $38-40; Jan.-May $34-37.) 17 mi. north of Durango, the **Haviland Lake Campground,** off Hwy. 550, tempts campers with 43 pleasant sites and new facilities. (☎247-4874. Sites $14; with water and electricity $18. No reservations.)

On Saturdays, locals in search of cheap, fresh produce flock to the **Durango Farmer's Market,** on 8th St. across from the post office. (☎375-6401. Open mid-June to mid-Oct. Sa 8am-noon.) Decked out with Texan and local paraphernalia, **Serious Texas BBQ ❶**, 3535 N. Main Ave., doles out generous ½ lb. portions of smoked meat ($6.50), Texas tacos ($4) and "cheezy potatoes" for $1.50. (☎247-2240. Open daily in summer 11am-9pm; in winter 11am-8pm. MC/V.) Durango has a disproportionate ratio of microbreweries to population. At **Carver's Restaurant and Brewpub ❷**, 1022 Main Ave., locals enjoy pitchers of home-brewed beer ($10) and bison bratwurst ($12) in hammocks on the outdoor patio. (☎259-2545. Breakfast $3-6. Open M-F 6:30am-10pm, Su 6:30am-1pm. AmEx/D/DC/MC/V.) **Steamworks Brewing Co. ❷**, 801 E. 2nd Ave, is a casual spot for a Cajun Boil (crab, shrimp, sausage, potatoes, and corn, all boiled in hot spices; $16.95) or a home-brewed beer. (☎259-9200. Pints $3.75. Open M-W and Su 11am-11pm, F-Sa 11am-midnight; bar open until 2am.) Right at the south end of town, **Kachina Kitchen ❶**, 325 S. Camino del Rio, in Centennial Center, just east of the junction of Hwys. 550 and 160, serves huge burrito and tamale platters ($5.15). Check out the over-stuffed sopapillas ($5.50) and hot Indian fry bread. (☎247-3536. Open M-Sa 10am-8pm. Cash only.)

◑◪ SIGHTS AND NIGHTLIFE. More a tourist attraction than a means of transportation, the **Durango and Silverton Narrow Gauge Train,** 479 Main St., runs up the Animas River Valley to the historic mining town of Silverton. In continuous operation since 1881, the old-fashioned, 100% coal-fed locomotives wheeze through the San Juans, making a 2hr. stop in Silverton before returning to Durango. The train also offers access to the Weminuche Wilderness, dropping off and picking up backpackers at various scenic points; call for more info. To shorten the trip, some people take a bus one way ($7, reservations required) or drive 20 min. north to Rockwood to pick up the train there. While waiting for the train, step into some of the very first iron horses at the **Railroad Museum** across the tracks. (☎247-2733; www.durangotrain.com. Office open daily June to mid-Aug. 7am-7:30pm; May and mid-Aug. to Oct. 7am-7pm; Nov.-Apr. 8am-5pm. Morning trains from Durango and afternoon trains from Silverton 9hr. including stop, layover day optional. Summer $62, ages 5-11 $32. Trains to Cascade Canyon late Nov. to early May $45/$22. Museum free with train fare.) The **Durango Pro Rodeo Series,** at the La Plata County Fairgrounds at 25th St. and Main Ave., moseys into town in summer. Saddling up on Friday and Saturday nights and sometimes Wednesday, the action starts at 7pm after a barbecue at 6pm. (☎602-237-6000; www.durangoprorodeo.com. Open mid-June to Aug. $12, under 12 $5; barbecue $7.) On U.S. 550, 7 mi. north of Durango, **Trimble Hot Springs** treats visitors to a community pool experience with better water; its mineral water fills three hot pools and a swimming pool. (☎247-0111; www.trimblehotsprings.com. Open in summer daily 8am-11pm; in winter M-Th and Su 9am-10pm, F-Sa 9am-11pm. $11, ages 3-12 $7.50; winter $9/$6.50.)

The ski-lodge atmosphere and frequent live music at **The Summit,** 600 Main Ave., near the train station, attract the college crowd as the main music venue in town, with pool ($0.75) and live acts W-Sa. (☎247-2324. Nightly drink specials. $2 pints W. 21+. Cover $3-10. Open M-Sa 7pm-2am.) **The Lost Dog,** 1150-B Main Ave., boasts a slightly swankier atmosphere, complete with lounge, dance floor, and tiki bar. (☎259-0430. Beer $3.50. Martinis $6. 80s Th. Club F. Hip-hop Sa. No cover. Open M and W-Su 4pm-2am; kitchen open until midnight.) The hysterical **Diamond Circle Melodrama,** in the Strater Hotel at 7th St. and Main Ave., delivers nightly dinner theater followed by vaudeville. (☎247-3400; www.diamondcirclemelodrama.com. Tickets $17-20. Student and senior discounts; call the box office for details.)

◪ **OUTDOOR ACTIVITIES.** In winter, **Durango Mountain Resort,** 27 mi. north on U.S. 550, hosts skiers and snowboarders of all levels (see **San Juan Skyway,** p. 718). Unlike most Colorado towns, however, Durango's busiest season is summer, when **mountain bikers** revel in the many desert and mountain trails, some of which connect to Moab, UT (p. 789) through the **San Juan Hut** system (☎626-3033; www.sanjuanhuts.com. Season pass $475, including food and maps.) Durango's trails are challenging, often involving very steep climbs and technical terrain for more expert cyclists. For easier day rides, head to **Horse Creek Gulch,** which offers mellow and smooth single-track riding after a steep half-mile climb. The extensive trail system here is well marked, with maps at every junction and both flat and mountainous trails, but the desert environment means very little shade. (Trailhead on 8th Ave., across from the bus station.) Many people head to the popular and more challenging **Hermosa Creek Trail;** the best way to travel this 21 mi. trail is to get dropped off near the top and ride south into Durango. Numerous other marked and unmarked trails exist in the Durango area; checking in bike shops for weather conditions and difficulty levels is highly recommended. One such shop is **Hassle Free Sports,** 2615 Main St. (☎259-3874 or 800-835-3800. www.hasslefreesports.com. Full suspension half-day $30, full day $40. Ski rental packages $23-32 per day. Open daily in summer 9:30am-6:30pm; in winter 8:30am-6pm.) **Southwest Adventures,** 1205 Camino del Río, offers mountain bikes, climbing and backpacking gear, and tours. (☎259-0370. Hard-tail bikes half-day $20, full day $35; hourly $8 per hr., 2hr. min. Tours $60-120. Open M-F 8am-6pm.) The Durango area is engulfed by the **San Juan National Forest.** Call the Forest Headquarters, 15 Burnett Ct., on Hwy. 160 ½ mi. west of Durango, for info on hiking and camping, especially if you're planning a trip into the massive Weminuche Wilderness, northeast of Durango. (☎247-4874. Open Apr. to mid-Dec. M-F 8am-5pm; mid-Dec. to Mar. M-F 8am-4:30pm.)

The **Animas River** offers rapids from placid Class II splashes to intense Class V battles. Keep in mind that the river is wilder and more powerful earlier in the summer, when runoff is strongest. **Durango Rivertrippers,** 720 Main Ave., leads whitewater rafting jaunts and rents inflatable kayaks. (☎259-0289 or 800-292-2885; www.durangorivertrippers.com. 2hr. rafting trip $25, children $17; half-day trip with lunch $35/$25. Kayaks $30 per 2hr. Open late May to mid-Aug. daily 8am-9pm.) The largest area outfitter is **Mild to Wild Rafting,** 701 Main Ave. (☎247-4789 or 800-567-6745. Half-day mild trips $41, children $32; full-day mild trips $65/$55; full-day intense trips $215, including wetsuit and narrow gauge train ticket to the jump-off point at Upper Animas River. Open Apr.-Sept. daily 9am-9pm.)

MESA VERDE NATIONAL PARK   ☎970

Native American tribes began to cultivate the valleys of southern Colorado about 1400 years ago. In the centuries that followed, the Ancestral Pueblo constructed a series of cliff dwellings beneath the overhanging sandstone shelves surrounding the mesa. Around AD 1275, the Pueblo people abruptly left behind their eerie and starkly beautiful dwellings, which weren't rediscovered until local ranchers stumbled upon the magnificent ruins of Cliff Palace in 1888. Established in 1906, Mesa Verde National Park is the only national park set aside exclusively to protect archaeological remains. Mesa Verde is not for the snap-a-shot-and-go tourist; the

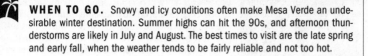

WHEN TO GO. Snowy and icy conditions often make Mesa Verde an undesirable winter destination. Summer highs can hit the 90s, and afternoon thunderstorms are likely in July and August. The best times to visit are the late spring and early fall, when the weather tends to be fairly reliable and not too hot.

best sites require a bit of physical effort to reach and are too extraordinary to let the camera do all the marveling. The park is going all out for its 2006 centennial; check www.mesaverde2006.org for an updated schedule of events.

⚡🔢 ORIENTATION AND PRACTICAL INFORMATION. The park's sole entrance lies at its north end, ½ mi. from a well-marked exit for the park off U.S. 160, 10 mi. east of **Cortez** and 8 mi. west of Mancos. The park's main road runs 21 mi. from the entrance station to Chapin Mesa and the park headquarters. 15 mi. into the park on the main road, a branch road heads out 12 mi. to Wetherill Mesa. An automobile is the best way to travel through the park, but no vehicles over 25 ft. in length are allowed on the road to Wetherill Mesa. There are two other options for intra-park transport. **Aramark Mesa Verde** runs daily bus tours. (☎529-4421 or 800-449-2288; www.visitmesaverde.com. Open mid-Apr. to mid-Oct. Half-day tours $32-34, under 12 $21-23; full day $53/$41.) A **tram** runs to Wetherill Mesa from the ranger kiosk in the parking lot (May-Sept., 30min. ride every 30min. 9:30am-4pm, free). Trailers and towed vehicles are prohibited past Morefield Campground; park in the lot before the entrance station. Much of the park is wheelchair accessible, though none of the tours are. There is **no gasoline** in the park; the closest is just across Hwy. 160, or in neighboring Cortez or Mancos.

The **Far View Visitors Center,** 15 mi. in on the main road, is the only place to buy tickets ($2.75) for guided tours. (☎529-5036. Open mid-Apr. to Oct. daily 8am-5pm.) When the visitors center is closed during the winter, head to the **Chapin Mesa Archaeological Museum.** (☎529-4631. Open June-Sept. daily 8am-6:30pm; Oct.-May 8am-5pm.) On summer evenings, the **Morefield Ranger Station** at Morefield Village offers advice and tour tickets for the following day. (☎564-6005. Open daily 5-8:30pm.) Information about the region is available at the **Colorado Welcome Center/ Cortez Chamber of Commerce,** 928 E. Main St., in Cortez. (☎565-4048. Open late May to early Sept. daily 8am-6pm; mid-Sept. to mid-May 8am-5pm.) Other services include: public **showers, laundry,** and **gas,** at Morefield Village (☎565-2407; open mid-Apr. to mid-Oct. 7am-9pm); **road and weather conditions** (☎529-4461); **general park information,** from park headquarters (☎529-4465); and **post office,** Chapin Mesa by the park headquarters and museum (☎529-4554; open M-F 9am-4:30pm, Sa 10am-1:45pm). **Postal code:** 81330. **Area Code:** 970.

🔢🔲 ACCOMMODATIONS AND FOOD. Lodging in the park is pricey. Rooms at Mesa Verde's only motel-style accommodation, the **Far View Lodge ❺,** are costly and not particularly interesting. (☎592-4422 or 800-449-2288. No TV. Open Apr.-Oct. June-Aug. rooms from $100; Apr.-May and Sept.-Oct. $80.) Options in neighboring Cortez are more plentiful. Spacious, affordable rooms make the **Sand Canyon Inn ❷,** 301 W. Main St., a popular choice for visitors. (☎565-8562. Reception 24hr. Check-out 11am. Singles $39; doubles $45.) Nearby, the **Ute Mountain Motel ❶,** 531 S. Broadway, has more basic rooms at a very attractive price. (☎565-8507. Reception 8am-11pm. Check-out 11am. Singles $30; doubles $38.) Mesa Verde's **Morefield Campground ❶,** 4 mi. into the park, is beautiful, and its 390 sites never fill, though you'll have to get there early to grab one of the 15 sites with full hookup. (☎565-2133 or 800-449-2288. Open Apr. to mid-Oct. Reception Memorial Day-Labor Day 7am-9pm; low-season 8am-8pm. Check-out 11am. Tent sites $20; RV hookup $25.) Basic camping supplies and groceries are available at the **Morefield Village**

ROCKY MOUNTAINS

MISS MESA VERDE

After their Puebloan inhabitants disappeared, the hidden cliff dwellings at Mesa Verde remained untouched for centuries. When the site was re-discovered in 1888, however, treasure-hunters began to remove ancient objects from the ruins. Some even had "digging picnics," sifting through the dwellings and often destroying them in the process. Though many people attempted to protect Mesa Verde, no one was particularly successful until Virginia McClurg took up the cause in 1893. Aggressive and determined, McClurg wrote articles and delivered speeches about the importance of preserving this piece of American history. She targeted her efforts at a circle of well-to-do women in need of what she called "an outlet for their suppressed zeal." In the 1890s, many upper-class women were taking on social activism outside the home, and McClurg's campaign to protect Mesa Verde became one of the most popular causes for women across the entire country.

McClurg organized nationwide fundraisers and petitions to show the government that people cared about the future of Mesa Verde. In 1906, the US Department of the Interior named Mesa Verde a national park. Though politicians and other benefactors made significant contributions, it was Virginia McClurg who jumpstarted the preservation of this archeological wonder.

General Store. (☎565-2133. Open daily Memorial Day-Labor Day 7am-9pm; low-season 8am-8pm.) Within the park's boundaries, two fairly similar cafeterias present standard buffet fare at slightly inflated prices. The **Far View Terrace Restaurant ❷**, near the main visitors center, has a better selection than the **Spruce Tree Terrace Restaurant ❷**, right near the museum. (Far View Terrace open in summer daily 6:30am-8pm. Spruce Tree Terrace open in summer daily 9am-6pm). At Morefield Campground, the **Knife Edge Restaurant ❶**, features a filling $7 all-you-can-eat pancake breakfast. (Open Memorial Day-Labor Day daily 7:30-10am.)

◪ ⚠ SIGHTS AND OUTDOOR ACTIVITIES. A good starting point, the **Far View Visitors Center** is a long 15 mi. drive from the entrance gate along Rte. 160. (☎529-4631. Open daily June-Sept. 8am-6:30pm; Oct.-May 8am-5pm.) After the visitors center, the park divides into **Chapin Mesa,** with the largest number of visible cliff dwellings, and the smaller and less-touristed **Wetherill Mesa.** The **Chapin Mesa Archaeological Museum,** along the first loop of the Chapin branch (before the dwellings), can give you an overview of the Ancestral Pueblo lifestyle and is a good place to start before exploring the mesa. Tours of the spectacular **Cliff Palace** explore the largest cliff dwelling in North America, with over 200 preserved rooms. (Open Apr.-Oct. daily 9am-6:30pm. 1hr. ranger-led tours depart every 30min.; $2.75.) The impressive **Balcony House** is a 40-room dwelling 600 ft. above the floor of Soda Canyon; entrance requires climbing several ladders and squeezing through a tunnel. (Open mid-May to mid-Oct. daily 9am-5:30pm. 1hr. ranger-led tours depart every 30min.; $2.75.) A few self-guided tours of sites are accessible from Chapin Mesa. **Spruce Tree House** is Mesa Verde's third-largest cliff dwelling and features a reconstructed *kiva* (ceremonial room) that you can explore. This is the only dwelling open in winter. (Trail ½ mi. Open daily 9am-6:30pm.) A more low-key approach to Chapin Mesa is the self-guided **Mesa Top Loop Road,** which passes a chronological progression of ruins. (6 mi. Open daily 8am-sunset.)

The long drive out to Wetherill Mesa illustrates the various stages of regeneration occurring in the forest, which has suffered many significant wildfires over the past century. From the ranger kiosk, 1½hr. tours of sprawling **Long House,** composed of 150 rooms and 21 *kivas,* include a tram ride that passes many such sites. (Open late May to early Sept. daily 10am-5pm. Tickets required for tour but not for tram; ticket holders seated first when space is tight.) **Step House,** also located on Wetherill Mesa, features a well-preserved set of prehistoric stairs as well as pictographs. (Open late May to early Sept. daily 10am-5pm.) On both mesas, early morning visits tend to be less crowded and cooler.

Mesa Verde also offers **hiking,** though none of the pleasant day hikes around the park would challenge an experienced hiker. Staying on established trails is critical to the preservation of Mesa Verde's archaeological remains. The visitors center has more information on the hikes. The **Petroglyph Point Trail** offers good views of the Spruce and Navajo Canyons as well as a few petroglyphs, and is the only trail to pass actual archeological sites along the way. (2.8 mi. Begins at the Spruce Tree House Trail.) **Spruce Canyon Trail** also begins from the Spruce Tree House Trail; this 2 mi. hike follows the bottom of Spruce Canyon before climbing to the mesa top, giving hikers the chance to experience the range of Mesa Verde environments.

WYOMING

The ninth-largest state in the Union, Wyoming is also the least populated. This is a place where men don cowboy hats and boots, and livestock outnumbers citizens. It is also a land of unique firsts: it was the first state to grant women the right to vote without later repealing it, and was the first to have a national monument (Devils Tower) and national park (Yellowstone) within its borders. Those expecting true cowboy culture will not be disappointed; Cheyenne's Frontier Days festival, held every July, is a celebration of all things Western.

PRACTICAL INFORMATION

Capital: Cheyenne.

Visitor Info: Wyoming Business Council Tourism Office, I-25 at College Dr., Cheyenne 82002 (☎307-777-7777 or 800-225-5996; www.wyomingtourism.org). Open daily 8am-5pm. **Dept. of Commerce, State Parks, and Historic Sites Division,** 122 W. 25th St., Herschler Bldg., 1st fl. E, Cheyenne 82002 (☎307-777-6323; http://wyo-parks.state.wy.us). Open M-F 8am-5pm. **Game and Fish Dept.,** 5400 Bishop Blvd., Cheyenne 82006 (☎307-777-4600; http://gf.state.wy.us). Open M-F 8am-5pm. **Wyoming Road Conditions:** 888-WYO-ROAD/996-7623.

Postal Abbreviation: WY. **Sales Tax:** 4%.

YELLOWSTONE NATIONAL PARK ☎307

Yellowstone National Park holds the dual distinction of being both the largest park in the contiguous United States as well as the first national park in the entire world. Though the roads are clogged with tourists eagerly snapping photos of geysers and wildlife, the park's incredible backcountry is so vast that you can go without seeing other people for days. Yellowstone also happens to be one of the largest active volcanoes in the world, with over 300 geysers and 10,000 geothermal features spewing steam and boiling water from beneath the earth's crust. Today, Yellowstone is still recovering from fires that burned over a third of the park in 1988. The destruction is especially evident in the western half of the park, where charred tree stumps line the roads. Despite the fires, Yellowstone retains its rugged beauty and sustains an incredible ecosystem. Following the reintroduction of wolves in 1995, the park once again became home to all of the animals that lived in the Yellowstone area before the arrival of Europeans, with the exception of the black-footed ferret.

YELLOWSTONE AT A GLANCE	
AREA: 2,219,791 acres.	**CLIMATE:** Extremely varied.
VISITORS: Almost 3 million annually.	**"ROUGHING" IT:** Embrace corporate behemoth Xanterra's camping options ($18), or arrive early for the Park Service's first come, first served sites.
HIGHLIGHTS: Wait for Old Faithful to erupt, faithfully, to an astonishing 140 ft.; walk the rim of the Grand Canyon of the Yellowstone; gaze at the morning wildlife in the Lamar Valley.	
	FEES: Entrance fee $20 per car, $10 per pedestrian. Backcountry permit free.

▐ TRANSPORTATION

The bulk of Yellowstone National Park lies in the northwest corner of Wyoming, with slivers in Montana and Idaho. There are five entrances to the park. **West Yellowstone, MT,** and **Gardiner, MT,** are the most developed entrance points. **Cooke City, MT,** the northeast entrance to the park, is a rustic town nestled in the mountains. East of Cooke City, the **Beartooth Highway (U.S. 212),** open only in summer, ascends the surrounding slopes for a breathtaking view of eastern Yellowstone. **Cody** lies 53 mi. east of the East Entrance to the park along U.S. 14/16/20. The southern entrance to the park is bordered by **Grand Teton National Park** (see p. 734). The only road in the park open year-round is the northern strip between the North Entrance and Cooke City. All other roads are open May-October. The park's **entrance fee** is good for 7 days at both Yellowstone and Grand Teton. (Cars $20, motorcycles $15, pedestrians $10.) Roll into **Yellowstone Bicycle and Video,** 132 Madison Ave., in West Yellowstone, for mountain bike rentals. (☎ 406-646-7815. Mountain bikes $4 per hr., $12.50 per 5hr., $19.50 per day. Open May-Oct. daily 8:30am-9pm; Nov.-Apr. 11am-7pm.)

▞ ORIENTATION

Yellowstone is huge; both the states of Rhode Island and Delaware could fit within the park's boundaries. The roadways within the park are designed in a figure-eight configuration, with side roads leading to the various park entrances and some of the lesser-known attractions. The most famous natural wonders (e.g., Old Faithful) are scattered along the Upper and Lower Loops. Construction and renovation of roads is always ongoing; call ahead (☎344-7381; www.nps.gov/yell) or consult the extremely helpful *Yellowstone Today,* available at the entrance, to find out which sections will be closed during your visit. Travel through the park can be arduously slow regardless of construction. The speed limit is 45 mph and is closely radar-patrolled; steep grades, tight curves, and frequent animal crossings can also cause driving delays.

❗ Yellowstone can be a dangerous place. While roadside wildlife may appear tame at first glance, these creatures are unpredictable and easily startled. Stay at least 75 ft. away from any animal, at least 300 ft. from bears. Both black bears and grizzly bears inhabit Yellowstone; consult a ranger about proper precautions before entering the backcountry. If you should see a bear, inform a ranger for the safety of others. Bison, regarded by many as mere overgrown cows, can actually travel at speeds of up to 30 mph; visitors are gored every year. Finally, watch for "widow makers"—dead trees that can fall over at any time, especially during high winds.

ROCKY MOUNTAINS

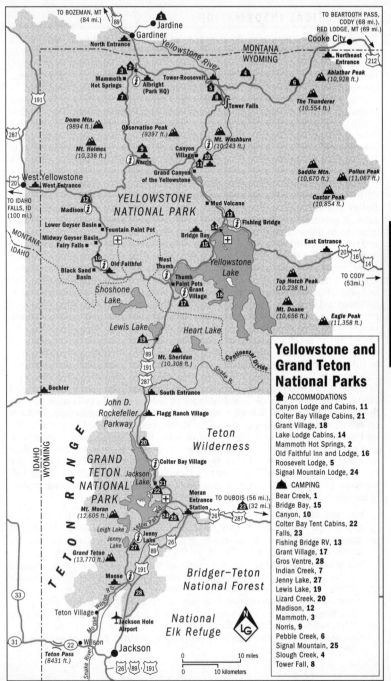

TO BOZEMAN, MT
(84 mi.)

TO BEARTOOTH PASS,
CODY (68 mi.),
RED LODGE, MT (69 mi.)

Jardine
Gardiner

North Entrance

Cooke City

MONTANA
WYOMING

Northeast
Entrance

Mammoth
Hot Springs

Tower-Roosevelt

Albright
(Park HQ)

Tower Falls

Ablathar Peak
(10,928 ft.)

The Thunderer
(10,554 ft.)

Dome Mtn.
(9894 ft.)

Observation Peak
(9397 ft.)

Mt. Washburn
(10,243 ft.)

Mt. Holmes
(10,336 ft.)

Canyon
Village

Norris

Saddle Mtn.
(10,670 ft.)

Pollux Peak
(11,067 ft.)

West Yellowstone

West Entrance

Grand Canyon
of the Yellowstone

Castor Peak
(10,854 ft.)

TO IDAHO
FALLS, ID
(100 mi.)

Madison

YELLOWSTONE
NATIONAL PARK

Mud Volcano

Fishing Bridge

MONTANA
IDAHO

Lower Geyser Basin

Fountain Paint Pot

Bridge Bay

East Entrance

Midway Geyser Basin
Fairy Falls

Old Faithful

West
Thumb

Yellowstone
Lake

TO CODY
(53mi.)

Black Sand
Basin

Thumb
Paint Pots
Grant
Village

Shoshone
Lake

Top Notch Peak
(10,238 ft.)

Lewis Lake

Heart Lake

Mt. Doane
(10,656 ft.)

Eagle Peak
(11,358 ft.)

Continental Divide

Mt. Sheridan
(10,308 ft.)

Snake R.

Bechler

South Entrance

Yellowstone and Grand Teton National Parks

John D.
Rockefeller
Parkway

Flagg Ranch Village

Teton
Wilderness

▲ ACCOMMODATIONS

Canyon Lodge and Cabins, 11
Colter Bay Village Cabins, 21
Grant Village, 18
Lake Lodge Cabins, 14
Mammoth Hot Springs, 2
Old Faithful Inn and Lodge, 16
Roosevelt Lodge, 5
Signal Mountain Lodge, 24

Colter Bay Village

GRAND
TETON
NATIONAL
PARK

Jackson
Lake

Moran
Entrance
Station

TO DUBOIS (56 mi.)
(32 mi.)

▲ CAMPING

Bear Creek, 1
Bridge Bay, 15
Canyon, 10
Colter Bay Tent Cabins, 22
Falls, 23
Fishing Bridge RV, 13
Grant Village, 17
Gros Ventre, 28
Indian Creek, 7
Jenny Lake, 27
Lewis Lake, 19
Lizard Creek, 20
Madison, 12
Mammoth, 3
Norris, 9
Pebble Creek, 6
Signal Mountain, 25
Slough Creek, 4
Tower Fall, 8

Mt. Moran
(12,605 ft.)

Leigh Lake

Jenny
Lake

Grand Teton
(13,770 ft.)

Moose

Bridger–Teton
National Forest

IDAHO
WYOMING

TETON RANGE

Teton Village

Jackson Hole
Airport

National
Elk Refuge

Wilson

Teton Pass
(8431 ft.)

Jackson

Snake River

Moose R.

Wilson R.

0   10 miles

0   10 kilometers

ROCKY MOUNTAINS

🖪 PRACTICAL INFORMATION

The park's high season extends roughly from mid-June to mid-September. If you visit during this period, expect large crowds, clogged roads, and filled-to-capacity motels and campsites. Most of the park shuts down from November to mid-April, then gradually reopens as the snow melts. Even in high season, Yellowstone's busiest time is mid-week—Tuesdays often draw larger crowds than weekends.

Over 95% of Yellowstone—almost 2 million acres—is backcountry. To venture overnight into the wilds of Yellowstone requires a **backcountry permit.** The permit is free if you reserve in person at any ranger station or visitors center no earlier than 48hr. in advance of the trip. There is almost always space available in the back-country, with over 300 designated sites, although the more popular areas fill up in July and August. In general, the deeper into the park you hike, the less likely it is that sites will be taken. For a $20 fee, you can reserve a permit ahead of time by writing to the **Central Backcountry Office,** P.O. Box 168, Yellowstone National Park 82190, and receive a **trip planning worksheet.** (☎344-2160. Open daily 8am-5pm.) Before heading into the backcountry, visitors must watch a short film outlining safety regulations. No firearms, pets, or mountain bikes are permitted in the back-country. In many backcountry areas campfires are not permitted; bring a stove and related cooking gear. Food, cooking utensils, and any items that might attract bears or wildlife should be stored 10 ft. off the ground and 4 ft. from the nearest tree. Camps are equipped with food poles between trees at this height: *use them.* Consult a ranger before embarking on a trail for tips on how to avoid bears, ice, and other natural hindrances, or check out the free *Backcountry Trip Planner.*

Fishing and **boating** are both allowed within the park, provided visitors follow a number of regulations. Permits, available at the Yellowstone General Store or any ranger station or visitors center, are required for fishing. Some areas may be closed due to feeding patterns of bears. The park's three native fish species are catch-and-release only, but if you catch the non-native lake trout, you are required to kill the fish. (Fishing permits $15 per 3 days, $20 per 7 days, $35 per year; ages 12-15 require a non-fee permit. Wyoming state licenses not valid in Yellowstone.) In addition to Yellowstone Lake, popular fishing spots include the Madison and Firehole rivers; the Firehole is available for fly-fishing only. To go boating or even floating on the lake, you'll need a **boating permit,** available at backcountry offices (check *Yellowstone Today*), Bridge Bay Marina, and the South, West, and North-east entrances to the park. (Motorized vessels $10 for 10-day pass, season pass $20; motor-free boats $5/$10.) **Xanterra** rents rowboats, outboards, and dockslips at Bridge Bay Marina. (☎344-7311. Open mid-June to early Sept. Rowboats $8 per hr., $36 per 8hr.; outboards $37 per hr.; dockslips $15-20 per night.) Parts of Yel-lowstone Lake and some other lakes are limited to non-motorized boating; inquire at the Lake Village or Grant Village ranger stations for more advice.

> **Visitor Info:** Most regions of the park have their own central visitors center. All centers offer general info and backcountry permits, but each has distinct hiking and camping regulations and features special regional exhibits. All stations are usually open late May to early Sept. daily 8am-7pm. Albright and Old Faithful are open year-round.
>
> **Albright Visitors Center** (☎344-2263), at Mammoth Hot Springs, features exhibits on the history of Yellowstone Park, along with stuffed examples of natural wildlife and a gallery of Thomas Moran's artwork. Open daily late May to early Sept. 8am-7pm; early Sept. to May 9am-5pm.
>
> **Canyon** (☎242-2550) features an exhibit on bison. Open late May to Aug. daily 8am-7pm.
>
> **Fishing Bridge** (☎242-2450). Exhibits describe local wildlife and Yellowstone Lake. Open daily late May to Aug. 8am-7pm; Sept. 9am-6pm.
>
> **Grant Village** (☎242-2650) has details on the 1988 fire and park wildlife. Open daily late May to Aug. 8am-7pm, Sept. 9am-6pm.

Madison (☎344-2821) has a bookstore. Open early June to Sept. daily 9am-5pm.

Norris (☎344-2812). Major exhibit depicts "Geothermic Features of the Park." Open late May to mid-Oct. daily 10am-5pm.

Old Faithful (☎545-2750). Learn about geysers and eruption predictions. Open daily late May to early Sept. 8am-7pm; early Sept. to May 9am-5pm. Info window open in summer until 8pm.

West Thumb (☎242-2652), on the southern edge of the lake, has a bookstore. Open late May to late Sept. daily 9am-5pm.

West Yellowstone Chamber of Commerce and Visitor Center, 30 Yellowstone Ave. (☎406-646-7701; www.westyellowstonechamber.com), West Yellowstone, MT, 2 blocks west of the park entrance. Offers information on all area public lands. Open late May to early Sept. daily 8am-8pm; early Sept. to early Nov. and mid-Apr. to late May M-F 8am-5pm.

General Park Information: ☎344-7381. **Weather:** ☎344-2113. **Road Report:** ☎344-2117. **Radio Information:** 1610AM.

Medical Services: Lake Clinic, Pharmacy, and Hospital (☎242-7241), across the road from the Lake Yellowstone Hotel. Clinic open late May to mid-Sept. daily 8:30am-8:30pm. Emergency room open May-Sept. 24hr. **Old Faithful Clinic** (☎545-7325), near the Old Faithful Inn. Open early May to mid-Sept. daily 7am-7pm. Emergency room open May-Sept. 24hr. **Mammoth Hot Springs Clinic** (☎344-7965). Open in summer daily 8:30am-5pm, Jan.-May and Sept.-Dec. M-Th 8:30am-5pm, F 8:30am-1pm.

Disabled Services: All entrances, visitors centers, and ranger stations offer the *Visitor Guide to Accessible Features.* Fishing Bridge RV Park, Madison, Bridge Bay, Canyon, and Grant campgrounds have accessible sites and restrooms; Lewis Lake and Slough Creek have accessible sites. Write the **Park Accessibility Coordinator,** P.O. Box 168, Yellowstone National Park, WY 82190. For more info visit www.nps.gov/yell.

Internet Access: West Yellowstone Public Library, 23 N. Dunraven St. (☎406-646-9017), West Yellowstone, MT. Open Tu and Th 10am-6pm, W 10am-8pm, F 10am-5pm, Sa 10am-3pm. Free.

Post Office: There are 5 post offices in the park: at **Lake, Old Faithful, Canyon, Grant,** and **Mammoth Hot Springs** (☎344-7764). All open M-F 8:30am-5pm. Specify which station when addressing mail. **Postal Code:** 82190. In **West Yellowstone, MT:** 209 Grizzly Ave. (☎406-646-7704). Open M-F 8:30am-5pm. **Postal Code:** 59758.

Area Codes: 307 (in the park), 406 (in West Yellowstone, Cooke City, and Gardiner, MT). In text, 307 unless noted otherwise.

ROCKY MOUNTAINS

ACCOMMODATIONS

Camping is cheap, but affordable indoor lodging can be found with some preparation. Lodging within the park can be hard to come by on short notice but can be a better deal than the motels situated on the parks's outskirts. During peak tourist months, motel room rates can skyrocket up to $100, but in-park lodging remains relatively inexpensive.

IN THE PARK

Xanterra (☎344-7311; www.travelyellowstone.com) controls all accommodations within the park, and employs a code to distinguish between cabins: "Roughrider" means no bath, no facilities; "Budget" includes a sink; "Pioneer" has a shower, toilet, and sink; "Frontier" is bigger and more plush; and "Western" is the very biggest. Even the swankiest cabins, however, aren't free-standing: most share a wall or two with a neighbor. Cabins without private bath have facilities nearby. All prices are based on two adults; Xanterra charges $10 for each additional adult. Reserve cabins well in advance of the June-to-September tourist season. Unless otherwise noted, all Xanterra accommodations accept all major credit cards.

■ **Old Faithful Inn and Lodge,** 30 mi. southeast of the West Yellowstone entrance, between Madison and Grant on the lower loop, is not only conveniently located in the heart of key attractions, it is also a masterpiece unto itself. The exterior of the lodge will be undergoing renovations until 2008, but you can still admire the cavernous 6-story central lobby and massive stone fireplace from numerous balconies and stairways, all built from solid tree trunks. Open mid-May to mid-Sept. Budget cabins $57; Frontier cabins $85; well-appointed hotel rooms from $81, with private bath $106-179. ❸

Roosevelt Lodge, in the northeast portion of the upper loop, 19 mi. north of Canyon Village. Cheap, scenic accommodations in a relatively isolated section of the park. Open June to early Sept. Roughrider cabins with wood-burning stoves $57; Frontier cabins $94. ❸

Canyon Lodge and Cabins, in Canyon Village at the middle of the figure-eight, overlooks the "Grand Canyon" of Yellowstone. Less rustic than Roosevelt Lodge, but centrally located and more popular among tourists. Open early June to mid-Sept. Budget cabins with bath $45; Pioneer cabins $61; Frontier cabins $83; Western cabins $121. ❸

Mammoth Hot Springs, on the northwest portion of the upper loop near the north entrance, is a good base for early-morning excursions in the Lamar Valley to the east, though it sits in a busy (albeit convenient) section of the park. Open early May to mid-Oct. Lattice-sided Budget cabins $65; Frontier cabins (some with porches) from $94; hotel rooms $74, with bath $99; hot tub cabins $164. ❸

Lake Lodge Cabins, 4 mi. south of Fishing Bridge, at the southeast corner of the lower loop, is a cluster of cabins from the 1920s and 50s, all just a stone's throw from Yellowstone Lake. Open mid-June to late Sept. Pioneer cabins $61; larger Western cabins $121. Next door, **Lake Yellowstone Hotel and Cabins** has yellow Frontier cabins with no lake view for $101. ❸/❹

Grant Village, at the southern part of the lower loop, has several new motel-style rooms situated right on Lake Yellowstone. Open late May through Sept. Motel rooms with bath $116. ❺

WEST YELLOWSTONE, ID

Guarding the west entrance of the park, West Yellowstone (pop. 1020) capitalizes on the hordes of tourists who pass through en route to the park. The closest of the border towns to popular park attractions, West Yellowstone has numerous budget motels. **West Yellowstone International Hostel** ❶, 139 Yellowstone Ave., provides the best indoor budget lodging around. (☎406-7745 or 800-838-7745. Internet access $5 per hr. Open late May to mid-Oct. Dorms $22; singles $29; doubles $39. AmEx/D/DC/MC/V.) **Lazy G Motel** ❸, 123 Hayden St., has 15 spacious 1970s-style rooms with queen beds, refrigerators, and cable TV. (☎406-646-7586. Open May-Mar. Singles $60; doubles $72. Reservations recommended. D/MC/V.)

GARDINER, MT

Near the park's north entrance, Gardiner presents a more limited and somewhat more expensive selection of accommodations options. **Hillcrest Cottages** ❸, on U.S. 89 across from the Exxon station, rents out tidy cabins with kitchenettes on a hillside overlooking town. (☎406-848-7353 or 800-970-7353. Open May to early Sept. Singles $70; doubles $80. 5-person rooms $98, $6 per additional adult, $2 per additional child. 8-person duplex $150. D/MC/V.) The compact rooms at **The Town Cafe and Motel** ❷, on Park St., across from the park's northern entrance, are among the best deals around. (☎406-848-7322. Cable TV. No phones. June-Sept. singles $45, doubles $55; Oct.-May $25/$30-35. MC/V.) **Bear Creek Camp** ❶, on Jardine Rd. 8 mi. northeast of Gardiner, has rugged backcountry sites deep in the midst of Gallatin National Forest. The unpaved gravel road leading to the sites offers stunning views of Mammoth's terraces, inside Yellowstone. (Pit toilets, no water. Free.)

COOKE CITY, MT

Lewis and Clark once deemed the area around Cooke City (pop. 90) impassable, and even now few people visit this rugged little town. Nonetheless, Cooke City is a great base for exploring Yellowstone's backcountry: it's conveniently situated between the park's northeast entrance and the junction of the **Chief Joseph Scenic Highway (Route 296)** and the **Beartooth Highway (Route 212).** The Beartooth Hwy. may be closed for construction in 2006 (☎888-285-4636 for updates). Built in 1936, the cabins at **Antler's Lodge ❸,** 311 Main St. E, have plenty of personality and a great mountain view. Hemingway spent several nights editing *For Whom the Bell Tolls* here. (☎406-838-2432; www.cookecityantlerslodge.com. Open in summer and fall. 2-person cabins $65-70, some with kitchenettes.) **Silver Gate and Pine Edge Cabins ❹,** on Hwy. 212 in Silver Gate, rents historic cabins, many with fully stocked kitchens, and five very basic motel rooms with private bath. (☎406-838-2371. Open year-round. 2-person cabins $59, 4-person $79, 6-person $102. Motel rooms in summer $72; in winter $55. MC/V.)

▓ CAMPING

Campsites fill quickly during the summer months; be prepared to make alternate arrangements. Call **Park Headquarters** (☎344-7381) for info on campsite vacancies or check at any of the visitors centers. The seven **National Park Service campgrounds ❶** are first come, first served. During the summer, these smaller campgrounds generally fill by 10am, and finding a site can be frustrating. Check-out time is 10am, and the best window for claiming a campsite is 8-10am. Their popularity arises from their often stunning locations; most are well worth the effort to secure a spot. Two of the most beautiful campgrounds are **Slough Creek Campground,** 10 mi. northeast of Tower Jct. (29 sites; vault toilets; open June-Oct.; $12) and **Pebble Creek Campground** (32 sites; vault toilets; no RVs; open early June to late Sept.; $12). Both are located in the northeast corner of the park, between Tower Fall and the Northeast Entrance in the Lamar Valley (generally the least congested area), and offer relatively isolated sites and good fishing. Travelers in the southern end of the park might try **Lewis Lake** (85 sites; vault toilets; open mid-June to early Nov.; $12), halfway between West Thumb and the South Entrance, a rugged campground with several walk-in tent sites that tend to fill up late in the day, if at all. **Tower Fall** (32 sites; vault toilets; open mid-May to late Sept.; $12) between the Northeast Entrance and Mammoth Hot Springs, has sites situated atop a hill, with fine views over mountain meadows. **Norris** (116 sites; water and flush toilets; open late May to late Sept.; $14); **Indian Creek,** between the Norris Geyser Basin and Mammoth Hot Springs (75 sites; vault toilets; open mid-June to mid-Sept.; $12); and **Mammoth** (85 sites; water and flush toilets; open year-round; $14; accessible sites available) are less scenic but still great places to camp. The lodges at Mammoth and Old Faithful have showers ($3), but no laundry.

Xanterra ❶, P.O. Box 165, Yellowstone National Park 82190, runs five of the 12 developed campgrounds (all $17, except Fishing Bridge RV) within the park: **Canyon,** with 272 spacious sites on forested hillsides, is the most pleasant, while **Madison,** with 277 sites on the banks of the Firehole River, has the advantage of being in the heart of the park's western attractions. **Grant Village** (425 sites) and **Bridge Bay** (432 sites), both near the shores of Yellowstone Lake, have little vegetation to provide privacy. Finally, **Fishing Bridge RV ❷** ($32; RVs only) provides closely-packed parking spots for larger motor homes and those desiring full hookups. All five sites have flush toilets, water, and dump stations. Canyon, Grant Village, and Fishing Bridge RV also have showers ($3, towel rental $0.75) and coin laundry facilities (open 7am-9pm). Campgrounds are usually open mid-May to early October, though Canyon has the shortest season: mid-June to mid-September Xanterra accepts advance and same-day reservations (☎344-7311). Reservations are accepted up to two years in advance. During peak summer months, on *any* day, it is best to make reservations at least a day ahead, especially for the more popular campgrounds listed first. The two largest Xanterra campgrounds, Grant Village and Bridge Bay, are the best bet for last-minute reservations.

FOOD

Buying food at the restaurants, snack bars, and cafeterias in the park can be expensive; stick to the **general stores** at each lodging location. The stores at Fishing Bridge, Lake, Grant Village, and Canyon sell lunch-counter-style food. (Open daily 7:30am-9pm, but times may vary.) Stock up at the **Food Round-Up Grocery Store,** 107 Dunraven St., in West Yellowstone. (☎406-646-7501. Open daily in summer 7am-10pm; in winter 7am-9pm.) At the original entrance to the park, Gardiner is less touristy than West Yellowstone; it is also moderately pricier. **Food Farm,** on U.S. 89 in Gardiner, has cheap food. (☎406-848-7524. Open M-Sa 7am-10pm, Su 8am-9pm.)

Running Bear Pancake House, 538 Madison Ave. (☎406-646-7703), in West Yellowstone, has inexpensive breakfasts and sandwiches in a friendly home-town atmosphere. Breakfast served all day; don't miss the special walnut and peach pancakes ($3-5). Burgers, salads, and sandwiches $5-7. Open daily 7am-2pm. D/MC/V. ❶

Helen's Corral Drive-In, on U.S. 89 in Gardiner (☎406-848-7627), rounds up half-pound buffalo burgers and pork chop sandwiches ($5-8) in a lively street-side setting. Open daily June-July 11am-11pm; Aug. 11am-1am. Cash only. ❷

Beartooth Cafe, 114 Main St. (☎406-838-2475), in Cooke City, serves gourmet food very unlike the usual park offerings. Breakfast $5-9. Sandwiches $6-7. Dinner entrees $15-20. Open late May to Sept. M-F 11am-10pm, Sa-Su 8am-10pm. MC/V. ❹

Grizzly Pad Grill and Cabins, 315 Main St. (☎406-838-2161), on Rte. 212 on the eastern side of Cooke City, serves the Grizzly Pad Special—a milkshake, fries, and large cheeseburger ($9). Alternatively, pick up a sack lunch ($7) or fried chicken (8 pc. $8) to go. Open daily late May to mid-Oct. 7am-9pm; Jan. to mid-Apr. hours vary. MC/V. ❷

Timberline Cafe, 135 Yellowstone Ave. (☎406-646-9349), in West Yellowstone, prepares travelers for a day in the park with a large salad bar and homemade pies. Burgers, sandwiches, and omelettes $6-8. Open daily 6:30am-10pm. AmEx/D/MC/V. ❷

K-Bar Restaurant (☎406-848-9995), on U.S. 89 just as it enters Gardiner, fixes up a fiery Mexican chipotle steak ($8) and meat-laden pizzas (8 in. $6.75). Don't let the rustic exterior fool you: this is one of the tastiest places to enjoy a pizza and beer after a trip in the park. Open daily 11am-10pm; full kitchen open M-F 11am-2pm. ❷

The Miner's Saloon (☎406-838-2214), 108 Main St., on Rte. 212 in downtown Cooke City, is the best place to go for a frosty Moose Drool beer ($3). Burgers and fish tacos $6-7. Poker night F-Sa. Open daily noon-10pm, bar until 2am. ❷

SIGHTS

Xanterra (☎344-7311) organizes tours, horseback rides, and chuckwagon dinners. These outdoor activities are expensive, however. A cheaper option is to explore the park's trails on your own. Visitors centers give out informative self-guided tour pamphlets with maps for each of the park's main attractions ($0.50). Trails to these sights are accessible from the road via walkways, usually extending ¼-1½ mi. into the various natural environments. Before you depart on a wilderness adventure, the **Yellowstone Historic Center,** on the corner of Canyon St. and Yellow-

ON THIN EARTH. Beware: the crust around many of Yellowstone's thermal basins, geysers, and hot springs is thin, and boiling, acidic water lies just beneath the surface. Stay on the marked paths and boardwalks at all times. In the backcountry, keep a good distance from hot springs and fumaroles.

stone Ave. in West Yellowstone, has extensive exhibits on park flora and fauna, earthquakes, fires, and historical development. (☎406-646-1100. Open mid-May to mid-Oct. daily 9am-9pm. $6, ages 62+ $5, students and ages 4-12 $4.)

Yellowstone is set apart from other national parks and forests in the Rockies by its **geothermal features**—the park protects the largest geothermal area in the world. The bulk of these geothermal wonders can be found on the western side of the park between Mammoth Hot Springs in the north and Old Faithful in the south. The most dramatic thermal fissures are the **geysers.** Hot liquid magma close to the surface of the earth superheats water from snow and rain until it boils and bubbles, eventually building up enough pressure to burst through the cracks with steamy force. The extremely volatile nature of this area means that attractions may change, appear, or disappear without warning.

While bison-jams and bear-gridlock may make wildlife seem more of a nuisance than an attraction, they afford a unique opportunity to see a number of native species co-existing in their natural environment. It is important wildlife-watching etiquette to pull off the road completely and kill the engine. The best times for viewing are early morning and just before dark, as most animals nap in the shade during the hot midday. The road between Tower-Roosevelt and the Northeast Entrance, in the untamed **Lamar River Valley,** often called the "Serengeti of Yellowstone," is one of the best places to see wolves, grizzlies, and herds of bison (among other species). Some species take to the higher elevations in the heat of summer, so travel earlier or later in the season (or hike to higher regions) to find the best viewing opportunities. Consult a ranger for more specific advice.

OLD FAITHFUL AREA

Yellowstone's trademark attraction, ▧**Old Faithful,** is the most predictable of the large geysers and has consistently pleased audiences since its discovery in 1870. Eruptions usually shoot 100-190 ft. in the air, typically occur every 45min.-2hr. (average 90min.), and last about 1½-5min. Predictions for the next eruption, accurate to within 10min., are posted at the Old Faithful Visitors Center. Old Faithful lies in the **Upper Geyser Basin,** 16 mi. south of the Madison area and 20 mi. west of Grant Village. This area has the largest concentration of geysers in the world and boardwalks connect them all. The spectacular rainbow spectrum of **Morning Glory Pool** is an easy 1½ mi. from Old Faithful, and provides up-close-and-personal views of hundreds of hydrothermal features along the way, including the tallest predictable geyser in the world, **Grand Geyser,** and the graceful **Riverside Geyser,** which spews at a 60° angle across the Firehole River. Between Old Faithful and Madison, along the Firehole River, lie the **Midway Geyser Basin** and the **Lower Geyser Basin.** Many of these geysers are visible from the side of the road, and stopping for a closer look is highly recommended. The **Excelsior Geyser Crater,** a large, steaming lake created by a powerful geyser blast, and the **Grand Prismatic Spring,** the largest hot spring in the park, located in the Midway Geyser Basin, sit about 5 mi. north of Old Faithful and are well worth the trip. Two miles north is the less developed but still thrilling **Firehole Lake Drive,** a 2 mi. side loop through hot lakes, springs, and dome geysers. Eight miles north of Old Faithful gurgles the **Fountain Paint Pot,** a bubbling pool of hot, milky white, brown, and grey mud. Four types of geothermal activity present in Yellowstone (geysers, mudpots, hot springs, and fumaroles) are found along the trails of the Firehole River. There is a strong temptation to wash

ROCKY MOUNTAINS

off the grime of camping in the hot water, but swimming in the hot springs is prohibited. You can swim in the **Firehole River,** near Firehole Canyon Dr., just south of
Madison Jct. Prepare for a chill; the name of the river is quite deceiving. Call park
info (☎344-7381) to make sure the river is open.

NORRIS GEYSER BASIN

Fourteen miles north of Madison and 21 mi. south of Mammoth, the colorful **Norris
Geyser Basin** is the oldest and hottest active thermal zone in the park. The geyser
has been erupting at temperatures of up to 459°F for over 115,000 years. The area
has a ½ mi. northern **Porcelain Basin** loop and a 1½ mi. southern **Back Basin** loop.
Echinus, in the Back Basin, is the largest known acid-water geyser, erupting 40-60
ft. every 1-4hr. Its neighbor, **Steamboat,** is the tallest active geyser in the world,
erupting over 300 ft. for 3 to 40min. Steamboat's eruptions, however, are unpredictable; major eruptions often occur months or even years apart.

MAMMOTH HOT SPRINGS

Shifting water sources, malleable travertine limestone deposits, and temperature-
sensitive, multicolored bacterial growth create the most rapidly changing natural
structure in the park. The hot spring terraces resemble huge wedding cakes at
Mammoth Hot Springs, 21 mi. north of the Norris Basin and 19 mi. west of Tower in
the northwest corner of the upper loop. The **Upper Terrace Drive,** 2 mi. south of
Mammoth Visitors Center, winds for 1½ mi. through colorful springs and rugged
travertine limestone ridges and terraces. When visiting, ask a local ranger where to
find the most active springs, as they vary in intensity from year to year. In recent
years, **Canary Spring,** on the south side of the main terrace, has been extremely
active as it expands into virgin forest, killing trees and bushes. Also ask about area
trails that provide some of the park's best wildlife viewing. Xanterra offers **horseback rides** just south of the hot springs. (☎344-7311; call at least 1 day ahead. Open
late May to mid-Aug. 5-7 trail rides per day 8:45am-6pm. $31 per hr., $50 per 2hr.)
Swimming is permitted in the **Boiling River,** 2½ mi. north. Park in the lot at the 49th
parallel sign and take the trail along the river back toward the park to the swimming area. Check with a ranger to make sure that this area is open.

GRAND CANYON

The east side's featured attraction, the ▣**Grand Canyon of the Yellowstone,** wears
rusty red and orange hues created by hot water acting on the rock. The canyon is
800-1200 ft. deep and 1500-4000 ft. wide. For a close-up view of the mighty **Lower
Falls** (308 ft.), hike down the short, steep **Uncle Tom's Trail** (over 300 steps). **Artist
Point,** on the southern rim, and **Lookout Point,** on the northern rim, offer broader
canyon vistas and are accessible from the road between Canyon and Fishing
Bridge. Keep an eye out for bighorn sheep along the canyon's rim. Xanterra also
runs **horseback rides** at Canyon and in the Tower-Roosevelt area 19 mi. north.
(☎344-7311; reservations required. Open June-Aug. 6-8 rides per day 7am-6pm. $31
per hr., $50 per 2hr.) **Stagecoach rides** ($8.75, ages 2-11 $7.25) along the canyon in
yellow wagons are available early June to early September at Roosevelt Lodge.

YELLOWSTONE LAKE AREA

In the southeast corner of the park, **Yellowstone Lake** is the largest high-altitude
lake in North America and serves as a protective area for the cutthroat trout. While
the surface of the lake may appear calm, geologists have found evidence of geothermal features at the bottom. **AmFac** offers lake cruises that leave from the
marina at Bridge Bay. (☎344-7311. 5-7 per day early June to mid-Sept. $9.75, ages 2-
11 $5.) Geysers and hot springs in **West Thumb** dump an average of 3100 gallons of
water into the lake per day. Notwithstanding this thermal boost, the temperature

of the lake remains quite cold, averaging 45°F during the summer. Visitors to the park once cooked freshly-caught trout in the boiling water of the **Fishing Cone** in the West Thumb central basin, but this is no longer permitted. Along this same loop on the west side of the lake, check out the **Thumb Paint Pots,** a field of puffing miniature mud volcanoes and chimneys. On the northern edge of the lake is **Fishing Bridge,** where fishing is now prohibited due to efforts to help the endangered trout population. The sulfurous odors of **Mud Volcano,** 6 mi. north of Fishing Bridge, can be distinguished from miles away, but the turbulent mudpots are worth the assault on your nose, caused by the creation of hydrogen sulfide gas by bacteria working on the naturally-occurring sulfur in the spring water. The unusual mudpots—with their rhythmic belching, acidic waters, and cavernous openings—have appropriate names such as **Dragon's Mouth, Sour Lake,** and **Black Dragon's Cauldron.**

OFF THE (EXTREMELY WELL) BEATEN PATH

Most visitors to Yellowstone never get out of their cars, and therefore miss out on over 1200 mi. of trails in the park. Options for exploring Yellowstone's more pristine areas range from short day-hikes to long backcountry trips. When planning a hike, pick up a topographical trail map ($9-10 at any visitors center) and ask a ranger to describe the network of trails. Some trails are poorly marked, so be sure of your skill with a map and compass before setting off on more obscure paths. Hiker should consult rangers to learn which areas were burned in the 1988 forest fires; burned areas have less shade, so hats, extra water, and sunscreen are musts.

In addition to the self-guided trails at major attractions, many worthwhile sights are only a few miles off the main road. The easy **Fairy Falls Trail** (5¼ mi. round-trip, 2½hr.), 3 mi. north of Old Faithful, provides a unique perspective on the Midway Geyser Basin and up-close views of 200 ft. high Fairy Falls. This easy round-trip trail begins in the parking lot marked "Fairy Falls" just south of Midway Geyser Basin. A more strenuous option is to follow the trail beyond the falls up Twin Buttes, a 650 ft. elevation gain, which turns this trail into a moderate, 4hr. round-trip hike. The trail to the top of **Mount Washburn** (5½ mi. round-trip, 4hr., 1380 ft. elevation gain) is enhanced by an enclosed observation area with sweeping views of the park's central environs, including the patchwork of old and new forests caused by the 1988 fires. This trail begins at the Chittenden Rd. parking area, 10 mi. north of Canyon Village, or Dunraven Pass, 6 mi. north of Canyon Village. A more challenging climb to the top of **Avalanche Peak** (4 mi., 4hr., final elevation 10,568 ft.) starts 8 mi. west of the East Entrance on East Entrance Rd. A steep ascent up several switchbacks opens to stunning panoramas out over Yellowstone Lake and the southern regions of the park, west to the Continental Divide and east to Shoshone National Forest. The trail along **Pebble Creek** (12 mi. one-way) makes a great trip though some of Yellowstone's most pristine backcountry. Beginning 1½ mi. west of the Northeast Entrance, the trail climbs steeply up a 1000 ft. ridge the first 1½ mi. before descending to the Pebble Creek Valley, following it mostly downhill for the remaining 10½ mi., exiting below Pebble Creek campground. Wildlife-viewing opportunities in this area are superb. This route is ideal with a second vehicle or bicycle, negating a return along the same route. There are dozens of extended backcountry trips in the park, including treks to the Black Canyon of the Yellowstone, in the north-central region, and to isolated Heart Lake in the south. Rangers can provide more detailed maps and information on these routes.

Nearly all of Yellowstone shuts down in winter. For those intrepid souls who wish to see the geothermal features at their most spectacular, in cold and snow, **Jackson Hole Snowmobile Tours,** 515 N. Cache St. in Jackson, leads the way, with guided treks to Old Faithful and the Grand Canyon. (☎ 733-6850 or 800-633-1733. $210-230 for snowmobile driver, $80 per adult passenger.)

SCENIC DRIVE: NORTH FORK DRIVE

Linking Yellowstone National Park with Cody, WY, the **Buffalo Bill Cody Scenic Byway (U.S. 14/16/20)** bridges the majestic peaks of the Absaroka Mountains (ab-SOR-ka) with the sagebrush lands of the Wyoming plains. This 52 mi. drive winds through the canyon created by the North Fork of the Shoshone River; the high granite walls and sedimentary formations of the **Shoshone Canyon** are noticeable from the road, as is the smell of sulfur from the DeMaris springs in the Shoshone River. Once the world's tallest dam, the **Buffalo Bill Dam Visitors Center and Reservoir,** 6 mi. west of Cody, was built between 1904 and 1910, and measures 350 ft. in height. (☎527-6076. Visitors center open daily June-Aug. 8am-8pm; May and Sept. 8am-6pm.) West of the dam, strange rock formations, created millions of years ago by volcanic eruptions in the Absarokas, dot the dusty hillsides. Continuing west to Yellowstone, sagebrush and small juniper trees gradually lead into the thick pine cover of the **Shoshone National Forest,** the country's first national forest. This area, known as the **Wapiti Valley,** is home to over 20 dude ranches. The **East Entrance** to Yellowstone National Park guards the west end of the scenic byway and is closed in winter. The **Chief Joseph Scenic Highway (Route 296)** connects Cooke City, MT, to Cody, WY, and passes through rugged mountains across **Dead Indian Summit.** The byway traces the route traveled by the Nez Percé as they evaded the US army in the summer of 1877. From Cody, follow the **Buffalo Bill Cody Scenic Byway** back into Yellowstone, completing a spectacular drive through western Wyoming.

GRAND TETON NATIONAL PARK ☎307

The Teton Range is the youngest in the entire Rocky Mountain system. Glaciers more than 2000 ft. thick sculpted the jagged peaks, carved U-shaped valleys, and gouged out Jenny, Leigh, and Phelps lakes. Though the Shoshone Indians called the range the "hoary-headed fathers," French trappers dubbed the three most prominent peaks—South Teton, Grand Teton, and Middle Teton—"Les trois tetons," meaning "the three breasts." Grand Teton National Park delights hikers with miles of both easy and strenuous trails as well as steep rock cliffs along the range's eastern face.

■✈? ORIENTATION AND PRACTICAL INFORMATION

Grand Teton's roads consist of a scenic loop through the park with approach roads coming from Jackson in the south, Dubois in the east, and Yellowstone in the north. There are three entrances to the park: Moose, Moran Jct., and near Teton Village. The east side of the main loop, **U.S. 89,** from Jackson to Yellowstone, offers excellent, free views of the Tetons. U.S. 89 in the park is open year-round. Those who enter the park must pay an **entrance fee.** ($20 per car, $15 per motorcycle, $10 per pedestrian or bicycle; annual pass $40. Passes good for 7 days in Grand Teton and Yellowstone.) Permits are required for all **backcountry camping** and are free if reserved in person within 24hr. of the trip. Reservations made more than 24hr. in advance require a $15 non-refundable fee. Requests are accepted by mail from January 1 to May 15; write to Grand Teton National Park, Permits Office, P.O. Drawer 170, Moose, WY 83012. (For more info, contact the **Moose Visitor Center,** ☎739-3309.) Advance reservations are recommended for sites in the popular mountain canyons or near lakes. After May 15, two-thirds of all backcountry spots are available first come, first served; the park staff can help plan routes and find campsites. Wood fires are only permitted in existing fire grates at designated areas. At high elevations, snow often remains into July, and the weather can become severe any time of the year, so severe weather gear is strongly advised.

CHEAP PARK-ING. Somewhere between the Grand Canyon and Grand Teton, the National Park Service's $10 and $20 entrance fees begin to add up. If you're going to be visiting three or more parks in a year, it's worth investing in a National Parks Pass ($50), which gets you into any national park in the US. The passes are available at any park's visitors center or at www.nps.gov.

Public Transit: Grand Teton Lodge Co. (☎800-628-9988) runs in summer from Colter Bay to Jackson Lake Lodge. (7 per day, round-trip $7.) Shuttles also run to **Jackson** (3 per day, $40) and the **Jackson Hole** airport (by reservation only, $30, round-trip $40).

Visitor Info: Visitors centers and campgrounds have free copies of the *Teewinot*, the park's newspaper, containing news and info on special programs, hiking, and camping. For general info and a visitor's packet, or to make backcountry camping reservations, contact **Park Headquarters** (☎739-3600; www.nps.gov/grte) or write Grand Teton National Park, P.O. Drawer 170, Moose WY 83012.

Moose Visitors Center and Park Headquarters (☎739-3399), Teton Park Rd., at the southern part of the park, ½ mi. west of Moose Jct. Open daily early June to early Sept. 8am-7pm; early Sept. to late May 8am-5pm.

Jenny Lake Visitors Center (☎739-3392), next to the Jenny Lake Campground at South Jenny Lake. Open daily early June to mid-Sept. 8am-7pm; late Sept. 8am-5pm.

Colter Bay Visitors Center (☎739-3594), on Jackson Lake in the northern part of the park. Houses the Indian Arts Museum. Open daily June to early Sept. 8am-7pm; May and Sept. 8am-5pm.

Info Lines: Weather, ☎739-3611. **Wyoming Highway Info Center,** ☎733-1731. **Wyoming Department of Transportation,** ☎888-996-7623. **Road Conditions,** ☎739-3682.

Emergency: Sheriff's Office, ☎733-2331. **Park Dispatch,** ☎739-3300.

Medical Services: Grand Teton Medical Clinic, Jackson Lake Lodge (☎543-2514, after hours 733-8002). Open daily late May to early Oct. 10am-6pm. **St. John's Medical Center,** 625 E. Broadway (☎733-3636), in Jackson.

Post Office: In Moose (☎733-3336), next to the Park Headquarters. Open M-F 9am-1pm and 1:30-5pm, Sa 10:30-11:30am. **Postal Code:** 83012. **Area Code:** 307.

ACCOMMODATIONS AND FOOD

The Grand Teton Lodge Company runs several accommodations in the park. (Reservations ☎800-628-9988; or write to the **Reservations Manager,** Grand Teton Lodge Co., P.O. Box 240, Moran, WY 83013. Deposit required.) Lodges are pricey, but there are two options for relatively affordable cabins at Colter Bay. **Signal Mountain Lodge ❹** (☎543-2831 or 800-672-6012) has scenic lodging on the shores of Jackson Lake. Options include rustic log cabins with private bath (doubles $99), lodge-style rooms (quads $132), and lakefront retreats with living areas and kitchenettes (6 people $199). **Colter Bay Village Cabins ❷** maintains 166 log cabins near Jackson Lake. A cabin with shared bath is one of the best deals in the area; book early. (☎800-628-9988. Open late May to late Sept. Reception 24hr. 2-person cabins with shared bath from $38. 1 room with private bath $75-112; 2 rooms with private bath $118-140.) **Colter Bay Tent Cabins ❷** offers primitive log and canvas shelters with wooden floors, wood-burning stoves, and bunks. Sleeping bags, cots, and blankets are available for rent. (☎800-628-9988. 66 cabins. Open early June to early Sept. Restrooms and $3.50 showers. 2-person tents $37; each additional person $5.)

The best way to eat in the Tetons is to bring your own food. Non-perishables are available at the **Trading Post Grocery,** in the Dornan's complex near the Moose VC, and the deli makes hefty subs for $5-6. (☎733-2415, ext. 201. Open daily May-Sept. 8am-8pm; Oct.-Apr. 8am-6pm; deli closes 1hr. earlier.) Jackson has an **Albertson's** supermarket, 105 Buffalo Way, at the intersection of W. Broadway and Rte. 22.

ROCKY MOUNTAINS

(☎733-5950. Open daily 6am-midnight.) Gather 'round pots of ribs, stew, and mashed potatoes at **Dornan's Chuckwagon ❷**, across from the Trading Post Grocery in Moose, for an authentic Old West dinner. (☎733-2415, ext. 203. Breakfast $5-7. Lunch $6-9. Chuckwagon dinner $14, ages 6-11 $7.) The **Trapper Grill ❸**, inside Signal Mountain Lodge, tops off a day of hiking with a heaping mound of nachos ($8-13), a meal unto itself. If you've still got room, the elk chili burgers ($8.50) are unbeatable. (☎543-2831. Breakfasts $7. Open early May to mid-Oct. 7am-10pm.) **John Colter Cafe Court ❷**, in Colter Bay, serves pizza, burgers, and sandwiches. (☎543-2811. Entrees $6-10. Open daily 11am-10pm.)

🏕 CAMPING

To stay in the Tetons without emptying your wallet, find a tent and pitch it. There are seven campgrounds in the park, five of which are operated on a first come, first served basis. (☎739-3603 for info. Sites generally open early May to late Sept.) All sites have restrooms, cold water, fire rings, and picnic tables; Signal Mountain, Gros Ventre, and Colter Bay have dump stations. The maximum stay is 14 days, except for Jenny Lake sites, where it is seven days. There is a maximum of six people and one vehicle per site; Colter Bay and Gros Ventre accept larger groups for $3 per person plus a $15 reservation fee.

Jenny Lake has 51 closely-spaced sites in the shadow of towering Mt. Teewinot, within walking distance of Jenny Lake. Sites usually fill by 8am, so get there early. No RVs. Open mid-May to late Sept. Vehicle sites $15, bicycle sites $5 per person. ❶

Signal Mountain, along the southeastern shore of Jackson Lake. The 80 sites, situated on a hillside overlooking the water, are more secluded than at Colter Bay and have the best views and lake access of any of the campgrounds. Usually full by 10am. Open early May to late Oct. Sites $15. ❶

Lizard Creek, closer to Yellowstone, has 63 spacious, secluded sites along the northern shore of Jackson Lake. Fills by 2pm. Open June to early Sept. Vehicle sites $15. ❶

Colter Bay, with 350 crowded sites, showers, a grocery store, laundromat, and two restaurants, is more suburb than wilderness. Sites fill by noon. Showers open 7:30am-9pm; $3. Open late May to late Sept. Vehicle sites $15, with full hookup $31. ❶

Gros Ventre, along the bank of the Gros Ventre River, close to Jackson. The biggest campground, with 360 sites and 5 group sites. The Tetons, however, are hidden from view by Blacktail Butte. The campground rarely fills and is the best bet for late arrivals. Open early May to mid-Oct. Sites $15. ❶

🏔 OUTDOOR ACTIVITIES

While Yellowstone captivates visitors with geysers and mudpots, the Tetons boast some of the most scenic mountains in the US, if not the world. Only 13 million years old, the Teton Range rises between 10,000 and 13,770 ft. in elevation. The absence of foothills creates spectacular mountain vistas that accentuate the range's steep rock faces. These dramatic rocks draw scores of climbers; hundreds of seasoned hikers also experience the beauty of the Teton backcountry.

HIKING

All visitors centers provide pamphlets about day hikes and sell guides and maps ($3-10). Rangers also lead informative hikes; check the *Teewinot* or the visitors centers for details. Before hitting the trail or planning extended hikes, be sure to check in either at a visitors center or at the ranger station; trails at higher elevations may still be snow-covered and thus require ice axes and experience with icy conditions. During years with heavy snowfall, prime hiking season does not begin until well into July. Getting a very early start in the day helps to avoid the crowds. In the past few years, bears have become more active in the park; be sure to educate yourself on bear safety and to carry bear spray (around $45) on all hikes.

The Cascade Canyon Trail to Lake Solitude (round-trip with boat ride 14½ mi., 8hr.; without boat ride 18½ mi., 10hr.) begins on the far side of tranquil Jenny Lake and follows Cascade Creek through a U-shaped valley carved by glaciers. The **Hidden Falls Waterfall** is located ½ mi. up; views of Teewinot, Mt. Owen, and Grand Teton are to the south. Hikers with more stamina can continue another ½ mi. upward toward **Inspiration Point** (elevation 7200 ft.), with stunning views eastward across Jackson Hole and the Gros Ventre Range. For some of the most spectacular hiking, trek 6¾ mi. farther to **Lake Solitude** (elevation 9024 ft.). Ranger-led trips to Inspiration Point depart from Jenny Lake Visitors Center every morning June-Aug. 8:30am. Hikers can reach the Cascade Canyon Trail by way of the 2 mi. trail around the south side of Jenny Lake or by taking one of the boat shuttles offered by **Jenny Lake Boating.** (☎734-9227. Boats leave Jenny Lake boat dock every 20min. daily 8am-6pm. $5, ages 5-12 $4; round-trip $7.50/$5.) Most hikers, including many families, choose one of these options. An alternative route begins at String Lake trailhead and traverses the isolated north side of Jenny Lake for 1¾ mi. Trail begins easy to moderate, but becomes more difficult.

Taggart Lake (3¼ mi. round-trip, 2hr., 277 ft. elevation gain) passes through the 1000-acre remains of the 1985 Beaver Creek fire, which conveniently removed most of the tree cover to allow an open view of the Tetons and Taggart lakeshore. This moderate trail also winds through a broad spectrum of plant and wildlife that has regrown since the fire; keep a lookout for marmots sunning themselves.

Bradley Lake (4 mi. round-trip, 3hr., 397 ft. elevation gain, moderate difficulty), beginning at Taggart Lake trailhead, proceeds up a glacial moraine to the more secluded Bradley Lake. For a longer trek, follow the trail another 1½ mi. along the eastern shore, over another moraine, and along a meadow for an elevation gain of 397 ft. before joining Amphitheater Lake Trail 1¾ mi. above the Lupine Meadows trailhead.

Surprise and Amphitheater Lakes (9¾ mi. round-trip, 8hr., 2958 ft. elevation gain), originating just south of Jenny Lake at the Lupine Meadows parking lot, is a strenuous trek with a significant elevation change along several switchbacks. 3 mi. into the trail, a fork directs hikers either to **Garnet Canyon** to the left or **Surprise Lake** and **Amphitheater Lake** to the right. Garnet Canyon is 1¼ mi. from the fork and provides access to several mountain-climbing routes up South, Middle, and Grand Teton. Camping at the trail's end requires a permit. Climbers should consult with park rangers for info on routes and conditions. The lakes are another 1¾ mi. from the fork; both are stunning examples of high alpine tarns gouged out by glaciers long since melted. Lupines, the purple flowers visible all along the roads in the park, bloom June-July along the trail.

Hermitage Point (8¾ mi. round-trip, 4hr., 100 ft. elevation gain, easy), beginning at Colter Bay, is a gentle hike along gently rolling meadows and streams and past Swan Lake and Heron Pond. The trail provides a unique perspective on Jackson Lake, which it approaches at several points, and is a prime spot for observing wildlife.

Static Peak Divide (15½ mi. round-trip, 10hr., 4020 ft. elevation gain, very challenging), one of the most difficult trails in the park, begins at the Death Canyon trailhead, 4½ mi. south of Moose Visitors Center on the Moose-Wilson road. The trail loops through whitebark pine forest and up numerous switchbacks over loose talus. With some of the best vistas in the park, the area is perfect for longer 2- to 3-day hikes (backcountry permit required). Prepare for ice in this area, even into August.

Cunningham Cabin Trail (¾ mi. round-trip, 1hr., 20 ft. elevation gain, easy) relives the history of early homesteading in the valley. Trailhead lies 6 mi. south of Moran Jct.

ROCKY MOUNTAINS

CLIMBING

Two companies offer more extreme backcountry adventures, including four-day packages that let beginners work their way up the famed Grand Teton. **Jackson Hole Mountain Guides and Climbing School,** 165 N. Glenwood St., in Jackson, has a one-day beginner course for $100 and a one-day guided climbing course for $125. More advanced programs are also available: one-day guided climbs that do not require training start at $175 and four-day Grand Teton ascents at $995. (☎733-4979 or 800-239-7642. Open daily 8:30am-5:30pm. Reservations required.) **Exum Mountain Guides** has similar classes and rates. (☎733-2297. 1-day beginner rock-climbing course $105. Guided 1- to 2-day climbs $110-385. Reservations required.)

BOATING, FISHING, AND BIKING

Getting out onto the water provides an entirely different perspective on the surrounding landscape. Non-motorized **boating** and hand-powered crafts are permitted on a number of lakes; motorboats are allowed only on Jackson, Jenny, and Phelps Lakes. Boating permits can be obtained at the Moose or Colter Bay Visitors Centers and are good in Yellowstone National Park as well. (Motorized boats weekly pass $10, annual pass $20; non-motorized craft $5/$10. Jetskis prohibited on all park waterways.) **Grand Teton Lodge Company** rents boats at Colter Bay and has scenic cruises of Jackson Lake leaving from Colter Bay Marina. (Colter Bay Marina ☎543-2811, Jenny Lake ☎733-2703. 1½hr. cruises $17, ages 3-11 $8. Canoes $10 per hr., motor boats $23 per hr.; 2hr. min. and $50 deposit. Rentals available daily May-Aug. 8am-4pm, depending on the water levels; call to check.) **Signal Mountain Lodge** rents boats and kayaks at Signal Mountain Marina on Jackson Lake. (☎543-2831. Large pontoon boats $62 per hr., motorboats $25 per hr., canoes $11.50 per hr., sea kayaks $11 per hr. Rentals available May-Aug.)

Fishing is permitted within the park with a Wyoming license, available at Moose Village Store, Signal Mountain Lodge, Colter Bay Marina, and Flagg Ranch Village. ($10 Wyoming Conservation stamp required with all annual fishing licenses. WY residents $3 per day; $18 per season, ages 14-18 $3 per season. Non-residents $10 per day; $75/$15 per season.) Women interested in learning how to fly-fish can learn with **Reel Women Fly Fishing Adventures,** an Idaho-based company developed to introduce women to this traditionally male-dominated sport. (☎208-787-2657. Full-day float trips $425, 2-day basic fly-fishing school $450. Reservations required.) **Jack Dennis Fishing Trips** also has float fishing trips on the Snake River and wading fishing trips in Grand Teton. (☎733-3270 or 800-570-3270. Both $375.) **Solitude Float Trips** sends raft floats down scenic Snake River. (☎733-2871. 10 mi. trip $42, ages 13 and under $27; 5 mi. trip $25/$18.)

Mountain biking is a popular activity on roads in the park, but is strictly forbidden on hiking trails. Outdoor equipment rentals are in the Dornan's complex. **Adventure Sports** rents bikes and provides advice on the best trails. (☎733-3307. Open May-Oct. daily 8am-8pm. Front suspension $8 per hr., $25 per day; full suspension $9/$28; kayaks and canoes $40 per 24hr. Credit card or deposit required.) **Snake River Angler** has fishing advice and rents rods. (☎733-3699. Open May-Oct. daily 8am-8pm. Rods $15-25 per day.) **Moosely Seconds** rents mountaineering and camping equipment. (☎739-1801. Open in summer daily 8am-8pm. Climbing shoes $5 per day, $25 per week; crampons $10/$50; ice axes $6/$30; trekking poles $4/$20.)

WINTER ACTIVITIES

In the winter, all hiking trails and the unplowed sections of Teton Park Rd. are open to **cross-country skiers** and **snowshoers.** Sign up for a free, ranger-led **snowshoe hike** at the Moose Visitor Center. (☎739-3399. 2hr. hikes depart Jan.-Mar. 2-4pm. Days vary; call for details.) **Snowmobiling** is only allowed on the Continental Divide Snowmobile Trail; pick up a $15 permit at the Moose Visitors Center and a map and guide at the Jackson Chamber of Commerce. **Grand Teton Park Snowmobile Rental,** in Moran Jct. at G.T.P. RV Resort, rents snowmobiles. (☎733-1980 or 800-563-6469. Half-day $89, full day $129; includes clothing, helmet, and boots. Snowmobile instruction included.) The Colter Bay and Moose parking lots are available for parking in the winter. All **campgrounds** close in winter, but **backcountry snow camping** (only for those who know what they're doing) is allowed with a permit obtained from the Moose Visitors Center. Before making plans, consider that temperatures regularly drop below -25°F. Be sure to carry extreme weather clothing and check with a ranger station for current weather and avalanche info.

SCENIC DRIVE: CENTENNIAL SCENIC DRIVE

Weaving through some of the most breathtaking expanses of uninhabited wilderness on earth, this all-day drive is a vacation unto itself. For 162 mi., the Centennial Scenic Byway passes by the high peaks, roaring whitewater rapids, and broad windswept plains of western Wyoming. The drive is open year-round but occasionally closes due to snow. The drive begins in the small frontier town of **Dubois,** home of the **National Bighorn Sheep Interpretive Center,** 907 W. Ramshorn St., a fascinating museum that educates visitors about the majestic creatures as they exist (many in endangered states) around the globe, from Alaska to Afghanistan. (☎455-3429 or 888-209-2795. Open daily late May to early Sept. 9am-8pm; in winter 9am-5pm. $2, under 12 $0.75; families $5. Wildlife tours start at 9am.) Leaving town on Rte. 26, the crumbly breccia of the volcanic Absaroka Mountains becomes visible to the north; the 11,920 ft. jagged pinnacles are those of **Ramshorn Peak.** Gently ascending through a conifer forest, the road eventually reaches **Togwotee Pass,** 30 mi. west of Dubois. Before the pass, 24 mi. west of Dubois, **Falls Camp ❶** is one of the region's best campgrounds, situated next to a massive waterfall concealed in the forest to the south of the highway. Even if you don't intend to enjoy this camp overnight, stop to be awed by the canyon. (Toilets, no water. Sites $8.)

As the road begins to descend, the famed panorama of the Teton mountain range becomes visible. The highest peak is Grand Teton (13,770 ft.); the exhibit at the **Teton Range Overlook** labels each visible peak in the skyline. After entering **Grand Teton National Park** (p. 734), the road winds through the flat plain of the **Buffalo Fork River.** This floodplain is the beginning of the wide, long valley known as Jackson Hole (early trappers referred to any high mountain valley as a hole). The road follows the **Snake River,** renowned for its whitewater rafting and kayaking. Nearing Jackson (p. 739), the 24,000-acre **National Elk Refuge,** winter home to thousands of elk, is visible to the east. To bypass Jackson, take U.S. 189/191 south. As the route turns east at Hoback Jct., one of the West's most popular whitewater rafting segments, the **Grand Canyon of the Snake,** is just downstream. The road winds through the deep and narrow Hoback Canyon. As the Tetons fade out of sight, the Wind River Range, home to several active glaciers, appears on the horizon, and soon the highest peak in Wyoming, **Gannet Peak** (13,804 ft.), rises majestically in the distance. The drive ends in the tiny, authentically Western town of Pinedale, where the **Museum of the Mountain Man,** 70 E. Hennick, chronicles the history of the Plains Indians, the fur trade, and the white settlement of western Wyoming. (☎877-686-6266. Open daily early May to late Sept. 9am-5pm; Oct. 9am-3pm; reservations required for other months. $5, ages 60+ $4, ages 6-12 $3.)

JACKSON ☎307

The southern gateway to Grand Teton and Yellowstone National Parks, Jackson (pop. 8000) teems with tourists in summer. But the area is equally renowned for its skiing—when in Jackson, you are also in Jackson Hole, the valley that separates the Teton and Gros Ventre mountain ranges. A playground for the rich and

ROCKY MOUNTAINS

famous, Jackson walks a fine line between staying chic enough for the *nouveau riche* and Western enough for the old-time cowboys. As a base for hiking, biking, rafting, fishing, and exploring the Tetons and Snake River, this town can't be beat.

■ ▐ ORIENTATION AND PRACTICAL INFORMATION. Downtown Jackson is centered around the intersection of **Broadway** (east-west) and **Cache Street** (north-south) and marked by **Town Square Park.** Most shops and restaurants are within a four-block radius of this intersection. South of town, at the intersection with Rte. 22, W. Broadway becomes U.S. 191/89/26. To get to **Teton Village,** take Rte. 22 to Rte. 390 (Teton Village Rd.) just before the town of Wilson. Winding backroads, unpaved at times, with close underbrush and frequent wildlife spottings, connect Teton Village to Moose and the southern entrance of the national park. North of Jackson, Cache St. turns into Rte. 89, leading directly into the park. **Jackson Hole Airport** is located between Moose and Jackson (☎733-7682). **Jackson Hole Express** (☎733-1719 or 800-652-9510) provides bus service to the Salt Lake City airport (5½hr., $66) and the Idaho Falls airport (2hr., $38). One bus to each location leaves daily at 6:30am. Reservations are required. **Jackson START** runs buses all around town and between Jackson and Teton Village. (☎733-4521. Runs daily mid-May to late Sept. 6am-10:30pm; early Dec. to early Apr. 6am-11pm; call for low-season schedule. In town free, on village roads $1, to Teton Village $3; under 9 free.) **Visitor Info:** The grass-covered roof of the **Jackson Hole and Greater Yellowstone Information Center,** 532 N. Cache St., hides an interior full of taxidermied elk, hands-on exhibits, and a wealth of information and reservations services. It also lists the times at which park campgrounds filled the previous day. (☎733-3316. Open early June to Sept. daily 8am-7pm; Oct. to early June M-F 8am-5pm.) **Internet Access: Jackson Library,** 125 Virginian Ln. (☎733-2164. Open M-Th 10am-9pm, F 10am-5:30pm, Sa 10am-5pm, Su 1-5pm.) **Post Office:** 1070 Maple Way, at Powderhorn Ln. (☎733-3650. Open M-F 8:30am-5pm, Sa 10am-1pm.) **Postal Code:** 83002. **Area Code:** 307.

▐ ACCOMMODATIONS. Jackson draws hordes of visitors year-round, making rooms outrageously expensive and hard to find without reservations. ◨**The Hostel X ❸,** 3315 McCollister Dr., 12 mi. northwest of Jackson in Teton Village, lets skiers and others stay close to the slopes for cheap. The hostel has free Internet access, a lounge with TVs, ping-pong and pool tables, and shelves of puzzles and games. Perks include laundry facilities, a ski-waxing room, and a convenient location just a close stumble from The Mangy Moose (see **Festivals and Nightlife,** below). All rooms are private with either four twin beds or one king-size bed. (☎733-3415. Open in summer and winter. Singles and doubles $55; triples and quads $68. MC/V.) Though the bunks at Jackson's own hostel, **The Bunkhouse ❶,** 215 N. Cache St., in the basement of the Anvil Motel, might not be the most appealing beds in town, they certainly are the cheapest. (☎733-3668. Showers, coin laundry, and ski storage. Showers for non-guests $6, including towel. Bunks $25. D/MC/V.) One of the few lodgings in Jackson with rooms under $100 during peak season, **Alpine Motel ❹,** 70 S. Jean, two blocks from the town square, provides basic rooms with cable TV, free local calls, and an outdoor pool. (☎739-3200. June-Sept. singles $80; doubles $88. Oct.-May from $60.) The primitive campgrounds in Grand Teton National Park and the 4.4 million acre **Bridger-Teton National Forest** offer the area's cheapest accommodations. **Gros Ventre** campground (p. 736) is only a 15min. drive north of Jackson on Rte. 89. There are 45 **developed campgrounds ❶** in the Bridger-Teton National Forest, including several along U.S. 26 east of Jackson. **Backcountry camping ❶** is free within the national forest; campers must stay at least 200 ft. from water and 100 ft. from trails. Consult with a ranger beforehand; some areas may be restricted. **Showers** ($6) are available at the Anvil Motel, 215 N. Cache St.

☐ FOOD. Jackson has dozens of restaurants, but few are suited to the budget traveler. Locals splurge at the **Rendezvous Bistro ❹**, 380 S. Broadway, savoring duck confit ($17) and escargot provençal ($6) in a bustling bistro setting. (☎739-1100. Open daily 5:30pm-late; closed Su in winter. AmEx/D/MC/V.) Locals rave about **Bubba's Bar-B-Que ❸**, 515 W. Broadway, a family restaurant that serves generous portions of ribs and sides. Most meals come with Bubba's famous biscuits. (☎733-2288. Lunch specials $7-9. 10 oz. sirloin $17. Open daily June-Aug. 6:30am-10pm; in winter 7am-9pm. AmEx/D/MC/V.) **The Bunnery ❷**, 130 N. Cache St., makes delicious breakfasts and baked goods, including omelets and the special O.S.M. (oats, sunflower, and millet) bread. (☎733-5474 or 800-349-0492. Breakfast $3-6. Omelets $8. Sandwiches $7-8. Pie slices $4. Open daily in summer 7am-9pm; in winter 7am-2pm. D/MC/V.) The low-key patio at **Pica's ❷**, 1160 Alpine Ln., is a great place to relax during happy hour (daily 4-6pm) or while gorging yourself on an inexpensive Mexican meal. (☎734-4457. Entrees $6-9. Open M-Sa 11am-10pm. AmEx/MC/V.) The aroma of authentic Thai cuisine lures diners to **Teton Thai ❷**, 135 N. Cache St., where the enormous daily lunch special is just $8. (☎733-0022. Entrees $10-12. Open M-F 11:30am-2:30pm and 5:30-9:30pm, Sa 5:30-9:30pm. Cash only.)

☰☰ FESTIVALS AND NIGHTLIFE. When the sun goes down on a long day of skiing, hiking, or rafting, Jackson has bars, concerts, and festivals to suit all tastes. Frontier justice is served at the **Town Square Shootout.** Live reenactments take place Monday through Saturday at 6:15pm during the summer in Jackson's town square. (☎733-3316. Free.) Catch cowboy fever at the **JH Rodeo**, held at the fairgrounds at Snow King Ave. and Flat Creek Dr. (☎733-2805. June to early Sept. W and Sa 8pm. $11, ages 4-12 $8; reserved tickets $14; families $35.) Over Memorial Day, tourists, locals, and nearby Native American tribes pour in for the dances and parades of **Old West Days;** for info, call the Chamber of Commerce (☎733-3316; www.jacksonholechamber.com). World-class musicians roll into Teton Village each summer during the **Grand Teton Music Festival** for shows like "Moosely Mozart and a Little Wolf." (☎733-3050, ticket office 733-1128; www.gtmf.org. Early July to late Aug. Festival orchestra concerts F-Sa 8pm $20-40. Spotlight concerts Th 8pm $15-60. Chamber music concerts Tu-W 8pm. $17, students and ages 6-18 $5. Half-price seats Th-F.) In mid-September, the **Jackson Hole Fall Arts Festival** (☎733-3316) showcases artists, musicians, and dancers in a week-long party that features everything from "Cowboy Jubilee Music" to a "Poetry Roundup."

For nighttime fun, head to **The Mangy Moose,** in Teton Village at the base of Jackson Hole Ski Resort, a quintessential ski bar. (☎733-4913, entertainment hotline 733-9779. Cover $5-15. Shows at 10pm. Open daily 11:30am-2am; kitchen open daily 5:30-10pm.) Slither on down to the **Snake River Brewery,** 265 S. Millward St., for the award-winning "Zonkers Stout." Pub favorite bratwursts are $6-9. (☎739-2337. Pints $3.50, pitchers $11. Open M-Th 11:30-midnight, F-Sa 11:30am-1am; food served until 11pm.) Live music and good beer (drafts $2.50) make the **Stagecoach Bar,** on Rte. 22 in Wilson, popular among locals, especially on Thursday's Disco Night. (☎733-4407. Live music M and Su. Open M-Sa 11am-2am, Su 11am-1am.)

☐ OUTDOOR ACTIVITIES. World-class skiing and climbing lie within minutes of Jackson, and **whitewater rafting** on the legendary Snake River is an adrenaline rush. Rafting is best in June, before the Jackson Dam flow is cut down in order to improve the fishing, which peaks in late July and August. **Barker-Ewing,** 45 W. Broadway, provides tours of varying lengths and difficulty levels, led by a highly experienced staff. (☎733-1000 or 800-448-4202. 8 mi. tour on a 14-person raft $44, ages 6-12 $34; on a more agile 8-person raft $50/$40. Gentle 13 mi. scenic trip $42/$27; overnight 16 mi. adventure $140/$110; 16 mi. tour with breakfast: 14-person

$76/$56, 8-person $72/$62.) **Leisure Sports,** 1075 Rte. 89, has boating and fishing equipment and the best deals on camping and backpacking rentals. (☎733-3040. Open daily in summer and winter 8am-6pm; in fall and spring 8am-5pm. 2-person tents $5 per day, 6-person tents $10 per day; sleeping bags $4 per day; backpacks $4 per day. Canoes and kayaks $35-45 per day; rafts $85-115 per day.) **Jackson Hole Mountain Resort,** 12 mi. north of Jackson in Teton Village, has some of the best runs in the US, including the jaw-droppingly steep Corbet's Couloir. (☎733-2292. Open early Dec. to Apr. Lift tickets $69, ages 15-21 $48, seniors and under age 14 $31.) Even after the snow melts, the **aerial tram** whisks tourists to the top of **Rendezvous Mountain** (elevation 10,450 ft.) for a view of the valley. (☎739-2753. Open late May to late Sept. daily 9am-6pm. $19, 65+ $15, ages 6-14 $8.) Located in the town of Jackson, **Snow King** presents a less expensive and less extreme skiing option. (☎733-5200. Open daily 10am-4pm, night skiing Th-Sa 4-8pm. Lift tickets: full day $35, half-day $25, 2hr. $17, night $15; ages 5-15 and 60+ $25/$15/$12/$10.) Snow King also has summer rides to the summit ($8 round-trip). Jackson Hole is a prime locale for **cross-country skiing. Skinny Skis,** 65 W. Delorney, in downtown Jackson, rents gear. (☎733-6094. Open daily June-Aug. and Dec.-Feb. 9am-8pm; low-season 9am-6pm. Rentals with skis, boots, and poles half-day $12; full day $18.)

CHEYENNE ☎307

"Cheyenne," the name of the Native American tribe that originally inhabited the region, was considered a prime candidate for the name of the whole Wyoming Territory. The moniker was struck down by notoriously priggish Senator Sherman, who pointed out that the pronunciation of Cheyenne closely resembled that of the French word *chienne*, meaning "bitch." Once one of the fastest-growing frontier towns, Cheyenne may have slowed down a bit, but its historical downtown area still exhibits rugged, traditional Western charm.

■■ **ORIENTATION AND PRACTICAL INFORMATION.** Located in the southeastern corner of Wyoming, Cheyenne is much closer to Colorado than it is to many of Wyoming's top tourist destinations—the city is an entire day's drive from Yellowstone. Two major interstates border Cheyenne: **I-25** runs north-south along the western edge of the city, while **I-80** runs east-west along the southern edge. The heart of downtown is the area just north of the historic train depot, at **Carey Avenue** and **W. Lincolnway,** also known as W. 16th St. Greyhound no longer serves the city, but **Powder River Transportation** (☎634-7744), 222 Deming Dr., at Warren Rd. off I-80, honors Greyhound passes and sends buses to Billings (10hr., 2 per day, $83-93), Denver (3½hr., 3 per day, $19-29), and Laramie (1hr., 1 per day, $13-23). For local travel, flag down one of the shuttle buses along the routes run by the **Cheyenne Transit Program.** (☎637-6253. Buses run M-F 6am-7pm, Sa 10am-6pm. $1, students $0.75. Daily 4-6pm all rides $0.50.) The **Cheyenne Street Railway Loop Tour** runs a trolley between major sights in the town. (Runs every 90min. M-F 10am-5:30pm. Maps and schedules available at the visitors center.) **Visitor Info: Cheyenne Area Convention and Visitors Bureau,** at 15th and Capitol Ave., in the Cheyenne Depot. (☎778-3133 or 800-426-5009; www.cheyenne.org. Open May-Sept. M-F 8am-7pm, Sa-Su 9am-5pm; Oct.-Apr. M-F 8am-5pm.) **Medical Services: United Medical Center,** 214 E. 23rd St. (☎634-2273). **Hotlines: Domestic Violence and Sexual Assault Line,** ☎637-7233. 24hr. **Internet Access: Laramie County Public Library,** 2800 Central Ave., has 30min. slots available. (☎634-3561. Open mid-May to mid-Sept. M-Th 10am-9pm, F-Sa 10am-6pm; mid-Sept. to mid-May also Su 1-5pm. Free.) **Post Office:** 4800 Converse Ave. (☎772-7080. Open M-F 7:30am-5:30pm, Sa 7am-1pm.) **Postal Code:** 82009. **Area Code:** 307.

ROCKY MOUNTAINS

ACCOMMODATIONS. As long as your visit doesn't coincide with Frontier Days (the last full week of July), it's easy to land a cheap room in Cheyenne. Budget motels line Lincolnway (16th St./U.S. 30) east and west of downtown. In addition to its prime downtown location, beautiful lobby, and posh bar, the historic **Plains Hotel ❸**, 1600 Central Ave., has comfy beds and airy rooms well worth the price. (☎638-3311. Singles and doubles from $99. AmEx/D/DC/MC/V.) Among the less-expensive motels, the renovated **Guest Ranch Motel ❷**, 1100 W. Lincolnway, stands out with clean rooms and new mattresses, plus cable TV, a microwave, and a fridge in every room. (☎634-2137. In summer singles $40, doubles $47; in winter $35/$40. AmEx/D/DC/MC/V.) Sleep among the bison, horses, and singing cowboys in the original bunkhouses at the **Terry Bison Ranch ❷**, 51 I-25 Service Rd. E, 5 mi. south of Cheyenne. The ranch offers a fishing lake, bison tours, horseback riding, and even stables to board your own horse. (☎634-4171. Private rooms with shared bath $40; cabins $80. Tent sites $15.) **Curt Gowdy State Park ❶**, 1319 Hynds Lodge Rd., 24 mi. west of Cheyenne on Happy Jack Rd. (Rte. 210), provides 150 camp-sites centered around two lakes. The park also allows horseback riding (bring your own horse) and archery. (☎632-7946, reservations 877-996-7275; www.wyo-park.com. Drinking water, dump station, boat dock. Sites $12, day use $4. Federal Bay and Sherman Hills areas are wheelchair accessible.)

FOOD. Cheyenne has only a smattering of reasonably-priced, non-chain res-taurants. The walls at the popular **Sanford's Grub and Pub ❷**, 115 E. 17th St., are blanketed with every type of kitsch imaginable, including hub caps and coyote skulls. The extensive menu includes everything from Cajun burgers topped with crab meat ($5-7) to gizzards ($6) and crawfish jambalaya ($13). Check out the game room downstairs. (☎634-3381. 55 beers on tap, 99 bottles of beer on the wall, and 132 different liquors. Open daily 11am-10pm. AmEx/D/MC/V.) A favorite with local politicians and businessmen, **The Albany ❹**, 1506 Capitol Ave., just across from the Depot, is the place to go for more upscale dining. The locally-raised prime rib ($17) and catfish ($12) are superb. (☎638-3507. Open daily 11am-9pm. AmEx/D/DC/MC/V.) For a dirt-cheap breakfast or lunch, the **Driftwood Cafe ❶**, 200 E. 18th St., at Warren St., complements its homestyle cooking with the feel of a quintessential mom-and-pop diner; it doesn't get more authentic than this. (☎634-5304. Burgers $3-6. Cinnamon rolls $1.50. Slice of pie $1.85. Open M-F 7am-3pm. Cash only.) Glitter glue quotations mark the pastel walls at **Zen's Bistro ❷**, 2606 E. Lincolnway, where you'll find a healthy selection of salads ($7) and sandwiches ($6.25), as well as a full espresso bar and Internet access. Sip your tea in the gar-den room, or take it to the back to see live music, poetry readings, and local art. (☎635-1889. Open M-F 7am-10pm, Sa 8am-10pm, Su 11am-4pm. AmEx/D/MC/V.)

SIGHTS. During the last week of July, make every effort to attend the one-of-a-kind **Cheyenne Frontier Days,** a 10-day festival of non-stop Western hoopla appropriately dubbed the "Daddy of 'Em All." The town's population triples in size to see the world's largest outdoor rodeo competition and partake of the free pan-cake breakfasts, parades, big-name country music performances, square dancing, steer wrestling, and chuckwagon racing. (☎778-7222 or 800-227-6336. July 21-30, 2006. Rodeo $11-23. Concerts $18-42.) During June and July, the **Cheyenne Gunsling-ers,** W. 16th and Carey, reenact Wild West gunfights. (☎653-1028. M-F 6pm, Sa high noon.) Take a free **S&V Carriage Ride** through historic downtown Cheyenne, board-ing in front of the Depot at W. 16th St. and Capitol Ave. (☎634-0167. Rides M and Th-Su noon-6pm.) The downtown area has a number of well-maintained historic buildings; pick up a free walking tour guide at the visitors center. The **Wyoming State Capitol,** at the base of Capitol Ave. on 24th St., has beautiful stained-glass

ROCKY MOUNTAINS

RIDE 'EM, COWBOY

Bobby Mote, a rodeo champion, travels across the country each year to compete in bareback riding events. Let's Go talked to Mote at Frontier Days about his life as a cowboy on the move.

LG: How did you get started in bareback riding?

A: I grew up riding horses. In high school my friends were all interested in bareback riding. If you had told me ten years ago I would be in the position I'm in now I would've had to pinch myself.

LG: So what's the most difficult part about what you do?

A: The traveling and keeping a positive attitude through all the ups and downs, because this is a sport filled with hills and valleys, and you have to keep the same attitude. You have to approach every day as another chance to win and do the best job you can.

LG: What should someone who's never seen a rodeo know?

A: A lot of people who haven't been around rodeo get caught up in all the stereotypes. They may have watched Urban Cowboy 20 years ago and think that's how cowboys are—hell-raisers, womanizers, you know. But we have families, we're married, this is how we pay the bills. This is what we do for a living, and we're professional athletes like any other, like NBA or NFL, only we don't have trainers and we don't have coaches. It's the only true individual sport out there.

windows and a gorgeous rotunda under the gold-leaf dome; self-guided tours are available. A giant stuffed bison on the first level is often all alone in the building: the Wyoming legislature meets only 30 days each year. (☎ 777-7220. Open M-F 8am-5pm. Free.) Across from the Capitol, the newly redone **Wyoming State Museum,** 2301 Central Ave., has 10 galleries that tackle all aspects of Wyoming, from public lands and wildlife to settlement and current issues. (☎ 777-7022. Open May-Oct. Tu-Sa 9am-4:30pm; Nov.-Apr. Tu-F 9am-4:30pm, Sa 10am-2pm. Free.) The **Old West Museum,** 4610 N. Carey Ave., in Frontier Park, houses a collection of Western memorabilia, including the third-largest carriage collection in the nation. (☎ 778-7290; www.oldwestmuseum.org. Open M-F 8:30am-5:30pm, Sa-Su 9am-5pm. $5, under 12 free.) To get to **Vedauwoo Recreation Area** (☎ 745-2300), 28 mi. west of Cheyenne, take Happy Jack Rd. (Rte. 210), then turn south on Vedauwoo Rd., or take Exit 329 north off I-80. Vedauwoo consists of a collection of oddly jumbled rocks eroded into seemingly impossible shapes by wind and weather. From the Arapaho word meaning "earthborn spirits," Vedauwoo was once considered a sacred place for vision quests; today, rock climbers worship the area's towering formations, which provide an excellent backdrop for hiking, picnics, and biking.

🎵 **NIGHTLIFE.** At the **Outlaw Saloon,** 3839 E. Lincolnway, live country music pours onto the dance floor and leaks out to the patio. (☎ 635-7552. Live music M-Sa 8:30pm-1:45am. Free dance lessons Th 7:30-8:30pm. Happy hour with free food M-F 5-7pm. Cover W-Sa $2. Open M-Sa 2pm-2am, Su noon-10pm.) The only brewery and only non-smoking bar in town, the **Snake River Pub & Grill,** 115 W. 15th St. in the Depot, attracts a young professional crowd with its microbrews. (☎ 634-7625. Nightly drink specials $2-3. Open M-Th 11am-11pm, F-Sa 11am-1am, Su 11am-8pm; kitchen closes M-Sa 11pm, Su 8pm.) Shoot pool upstairs at the **Crown Bar,** or descend below for hip-hop, Top 40, and alternative dance at the **Crown Underground,** 222 W. 16th St., at the corner of Carey St. (☎ 778-9202. Nightly drink specials from $1.75. Dancing Th-Sa 9pm-2am. Live music Sa 9pm-1:30am. Th ladies night and all drinks $1.75. Underground open W 9pm-midnight, F-Su 9pm-2am; bar open M-Sa 11am-2am, Su 11am-10pm; food served until 1am.) Hoof it with the locals at the only bar open past 10pm on Sundays, the **Cowboy Rockin' Rodeo,** 312 S. Greeley Hwy. The live music and large dance floor always draw a crowd. (☎ 637-3800. Live music Tu-Sa 9pm-1:30am. Open M-Sa 11am-2am, Su noon-2am.)

THE SNOWY RANGE ☎307

Local residents call the forested granite mountains to the east of the Platte Valley the Snowy Mountain Range. Snow falls nearly year-round on the higher peaks, and when the snow melts, quartzite outcroppings reflect the sun, creating the illusion of a snowy peak. The Snowy Range, 40 mi. west of Laramie, is part of **Medicine Bow National Forest.** Cross-country skiing is popular in the winter; campsites and trails usually don't open until May or June due to heavy snowfall. On the west side of the Snowy Range along Rte. 130, chase the cold away with the geothermal stylings of **Saratoga's hot springs,** running between 104° and 120°F, at the end of E. Walnut St. behind the public pool. (Free. Open 24hr.) Nearby, the **North Platte River** offers fishing and a chance to enjoy snowmelt mixed with the runoff of the hot springs. Fishing permits ($10) are available at **Hack's Tackle Outfitters,** 407 N. 1st St., which also sells hunting licenses and offers both fishing advice and guided trips. (☎326-9823. Scenic tours $40 per half-day, $90 per day. Fishing trips for 2 $235 per half-day, $350 per day. Canoes $35/$95; $100 per boat deposit required. Shuttles to any location on the river can be hired for a $25 flat fee, regardless of number of canoes or rafts onboard.) At **Snowy Range Ski and Recreation Area,** enjoy 25 moderately challenging downhill trails, cross-country trails, and a snowboard halfpipe. Take Exit 311 off I-80 to Rte. 130 W. (☎745-5750 or 800-462-7669. Open mid-Dec. to Easter. Full-day lift ticket $32, ages 6-12 and 60+ $18; half-day $25/$14.)

From late May to November, cars can drive 27 mi. through seas of pine and aspen trees, around treeless mountains and picture-perfect lakes at high elevations on the **Snowy Range Scenic Byway (Route 130).** To get there from the east, exit I-80 in Laramie; approaching from the west, exit at Walcott Jct., 22 mi. east of Rawlins. Early along the byway from the east, Barber Lake Rd. branches off along noisy Libby Creek, bypassing the entrance to the Snowy Range Ski Area before returning to Rte. 130. At the summit, the **Libby Flats Observation Point,** at the top of Snowy Range Pass (elevation 10,847 ft.), has a wildflower nature walk and an inspiring view of the surrounding alpine landscape. On bright days, delicate alpine sunflowers turn their faces to the sun. Before the road descends, don't miss the Silver Lake outlook, which features a gorgeous view of the waters and surrounding area. Keep an eye out for local fauna like bighorn sheep, pine martens, and yellow-bellied marmots. The challenging **Medicine Bow Trail** (4½ mi., 1600 ft. elevation change) has trailheads at both **Lake Marie** and **Lewis Lake** and climbs through rocky alpine terrain to **Medicine Bow Peak** (12,013 ft.), the highest point in the forest. All 16 of the park's developed **campgrounds ❶** are only open in summer and have toilets and water, but no hookups or showers. **Sugarloaf ❶** (16 sites) and **Brooklyn Lake ❶** (19 sites) are open July to September and are reservable through the National Recreation Reservation Service. (☎877-444-6777; www.reserveusa.com. Pit toilets, water provided. Max 14-night stay. Sites $10. Reservation fee $9.) A drive up **Kennaday Peak** (10,810 ft.), Rte. 130 to Rte. 100 and 215, at the end of Rte. 215, grants an impressive view.

Biking and driving are permitted only on designated trails in the high country and on trails below 10,000 ft. The 7 mi. **Corner Mountain Loop,** just west of Centennial Visitors Center, is a roller coaster ride through forests and meadows. In winter, the trails are used for cross-country skiing and snowmobiling. **Brush Creek Visitors Center,** at the west entrance, provides hiking, biking, camping, and bear safety info. (☎326-5562. Open daily mid-May to Oct. 8am-5pm.) **Centennial Visitors Center,** 1 mi. west of Centennial, is at the east entrance. (☎742-6023. Open daily 9am-4pm.) Get cross-country skiing equipment and trail info at the **Cross Country Connection,** 222 S. 2nd St., in Laramie. (☎721-2851. Open M-F 10am-6pm, Sa 9am-5pm, Su noon-4pm. $12 per day.) Downhill ski and snowboard rentals are available at **The Fine Edge,** 1660E N. 4th St. (☎745-4499. Open in winter M-Th 8am-6pm, F-Sa

7am-6:30pm, Su 7:30am-5pm; in summer M-Th 8am-6pm, F-Sa 8am-6:30pm, Su 10am-5pm. Skis $16 per full day, children $12. Snowboards $22/$17; boots $9. $300 credit card or check deposit required for snowboards.) **Area Code:** 307.

MONTANA

If anything dominates the Montana landscape more than the towering mountain peaks and shimmering glacial lakes, it's the sky—welcome to Big Sky country. With 25 million acres of national forest and public lands, Montana's grizzly bears, mountain lions, and pronghorn antelope outnumber the people. Nonetheless, small towns set against unadulterated mountain vistas have attracted new populations of artists and writers and support galleries and culture disproportionate to their populations. World-famous fishing rivers, 500 species of wildlife, thousands of ski trails, and endless miles of open road make Montana an American paradise.

⛰ PRACTICAL INFORMATION

Capital: Helena.

Visitor Info: Travel Montana, 301 S. Park, P.O. Box 200533, Helena 59620 (☎800-847-4868; www.visitmt.com). **National Forest Information,** Northern Region, Federal Bldg., 200 E. Broadway, Box 7669, Missoula 59807 (☎406-329-3511. Open M-F 8am-4:30pm). **Road Conditions:** ☎800-226-7623. Statewide.

Postal Abbreviation: MT. **Sales Tax:** None.

HELENA   ☎406

The appeal of the outdoors in Montana lures visitors to its capital city, where state politics and great hiking, biking, and fishing coexist happily. A product of the 1864 gold rush at Last Chance Gulch, Helena has transformed itself from a humble mining camp into a sophisticated city with an active art scene.

■⛰ **ORIENTATION AND PRACTICAL INFORMATION.** Helena sits west of I-15 on Hwy. 12. The main street has three names, starting off from the I-15 exit as **Cedar Street,** turning into **North Main Street** at Montana Ave., and becoming **Last Chance Gulch** downtown after crossing Lyndale Ave. These streets, along with **11th Avenue** and **Euclid Avenue (Highway 12),** are the major cross-town thoroughfares. There is no Greyhound service to Helena, but **Rimrock Stages,** 3100 E. Hwy. 12 (☎442-5860; www.rimrocktrailways.com) runs two buses per day: one heads north toward Glacier National Park, and one heads south, connecting to Billings (7hr., 1 per day, $40), Missoula (3½hr., 1 per day, $23), and Salt Lake City (13hr., 1 per day, $78). **Helena Area Transportation Service (HATS)** operates several bus routes around town. (☎447-1580. Every hr. M-F 6am-6pm. $1.50, seniors and disabled $0.85, under 5 free.) The HATS **trolley** runs in a loop to 10 downtown attractions. (☎447-1580. Every 30min. M-F 11am-6pm, Sa 11am-5pm. $0.50, day pass $1.50.) **Taxi: Capitol Taxi,** ☎449-5525. **Medical Services: Helena Urgent Care,** 33 Neill Ave. (☎443-5354. Open M-F 8am-8pm, Sa 8am-7pm, Su 10am-5pm.) **Visitor Info: Helena Chamber of Commerce,** 225 Cruse Ave. (☎442-4120 or 800-743-5362. Open M-F 8am-5pm.) **Internet Access: Lewis & Clark Library,** 120 S. Last Chance Gulch (☎446-1690. Open in summer M-Th 10am-8pm, F 10am-6pm, Sa 10am-5pm; in winter M-Th 10am-9pm, F 10am-6pm, Sa 10am-5pm, Su 1-5pm. Free.) **Post Office:** 2300 N. Harris St. (☎442-7946. Open M-F 8am-6pm, Sa 9am-noon.) **Postal Code:** 59601. **Area Code:** 406.

⌐ ACCOMMODATIONS. The nicest way to experience Helena is to camp in the surrounding recreation areas. If you'd rather stay in town, **Budget Inn Express ❷**, 524 N. Last Chance Gulch, has an attractive downtown location and large, tidy rooms. (☎442-0600 or 800-862-1334. Laundry, cable TV, and hot tub. In summer singles $40, doubles $50; in winter $37/$47. AmEx/D/MC/V.) The best deal in town for women, **Helena YWCA ❶**, 501 N. Park Ave., rents private singles with shared bath and use of a full kitchen and laundry facilities. (☎442-8774. Women only. Free Internet access. Key deposit $12. Singles $20.) Escape the heat at **Moose Creek Campground ❶**, 10 mi. west of Helena on U.S. 12, then 4 mi. southwest on Rimini Rd., which has pleasantly cool, forested camping alongside a stream. (Vault toilets, water. Open mid-May to mid-Sept. Sites $5.) Fifteen miles east of Helena, 13 public campgrounds line **Canyon Ferry Reservoir ❶**, popular for both fishing and boating; take either Canyon Ferry Rd. or Rte. 284 from U.S. 12. The campgrounds are open year-round, but can be prohibitively hot in summer. (7 campgrounds $8 per site. 6 campgrounds free.) The free **Fish Hawk Campground ❶**, on W. Shore Dr., has tent sites and toilets, but no drinking water. The **BOR Canyon Ferry Office**, 7700 Canyon Ferry Rd. (☎475-3310 or 475-3921), has more info.

◖▮ FOOD AND NIGHTLIFE. Local paintings and a forest of records dangle from a graffitied ceiling at the ▨**Staggering Ox ❷**, 400 Euclid Ave., in the Lundy Center. Their patented, award-winning bread is baked in a soup can and constructed into sandwiches with names like "Yo' Momma Osama" ($7) and "Headbanger's Hoagie" ($5). The very popular "bread guts" are sold with sauces such as "Camel Spit." (☎443-1729. Open M-Th 9am-8pm, Sa 10am-8pm, Su 11am-7pm. MC/V.) Enjoy an authentic taste of southern Europe at ▨**Mediterranean Grill ❹**, 42 S. Park Ave., enhanced by the friendly conversation of the Turkish-born chef and owner. Follow your appetizer of stuffed grape leaves ($6) with an eggplant dish ($12) or the salmon *amaretti* for $16. (☎495-1212. Open M-Sa 11am-9:30pm, Su 10am-2pm. AmEx/D/MC/V.) **Toi's Thai ❸**, 423 N. Last Chance Gulch, serves authentic Thai food, with fixed-price menus (soup, salad, main course and dessert; $18), family-style options, and a la carte (pad thai $11) in a cozy setting. (☎443-6656. Open Tu-Sa 5-9pm. MC/V.) All the meats, grains, and produce are organic and locally-grown at **No Sweat Cafe ❶**, 427 N. Last Chance Gulch, a popular hangout where whole-wheat pancakes ($4) and delightful egg dishes ($5-6) reign supreme. (☎442-6954. Open Tu-F 7am-2pm, Sa-Su 8am-2pm. Cash only.) Helena's weekly **farmers market** brings produce and crafts to Fuller Ave., downtown. (439-5576. May-Oct. Sa 9am-1pm.) **Miller's Crossing,** 52 S. Park Ave., has pool tables, a large dance floor, and live rock, folk, and blues some nights. A special $2.50 brew is always on tap. (☎442-3290. Cover $2-5. Open in summer M-F 11am-2am, Sa-Su 2pm-2am; in winter daily 11am-2am.) Dancing, gambling, and naked beer-sliding make **Hap's,** 1550 Railroad Ave., the place to join locals for cheap drinks. Before it gets too wild, folks play horseshoes in the backyard, shoot a game of pool, and try to "cut in line" on the Internet jukebox. (☎443-2804. Drafts $1-1.50. Mixed drinks from $2. Open daily 10am-2am.) **Bullwhacker's,** 22 N. Last Chance Gulch, in the Holiday Inn, has the wildest dance floor in town. The Texas Hold 'Em table heats up most nights at 8pm. (☎443-2200. Domestic beers $2, microbrews $3. Karaoke W and Su. Ladies' night Th. Open daily 6pm-2am.) Moving from location to location, **Alive at Five** tours the city on summer Wednesdays with live music and local food vendors. (☎447-1535. Festival runs mid-May to mid-Sept. W from 5pm.)

◪▮ SIGHTS AND OUTDOOR ACTIVITIES. A strategic point from which to begin an exploration of Helena, the **Montana Historical Society Museum,** 225 N. Roberts St., has chronological displays recounting the region's development through artifacts, maps, and clothing. Don't miss the stuffed rare white buffalo or the displays of military gear, including Nazi uniforms and medals brought back from WWII by returning American GIs. (☎444-2694 or 800-243-9900; www.montanahistoricalsociety.org. Open M-W and F-Sa 9am-5pm, Th 9am-8pm; Oct.-Apr. closed M. $5, ages 5-18 $1.) The historical society's popular 1hr. **Last Chance Tour Train** departs in front of the museum and features commentary on the city's historical buildings and sights. (☎442-1023. Tours M-Sa May and Sept. 3 per day; June 5 per day; July-Aug. 7 per day. $6.50, seniors $6, ages 4-12 $5.50.) The **State Capitol** building, 1301 6th Ave., at Montana Ave., has several pieces of notable artwork, including a giant mural by Charles M. Russell depicting the Salish Indians welcoming Lewis and Clark in 1804. At the top of the stairs is a statue of Jeannette Rankin, the first woman elected to Congress. (☎444-4789. Tours every hr. May-Sept.; self-guided tours available in winter. Open M-Sa 9am-3pm, Su noon-4pm; Oct.-Apr. Sa 10am-2pm. Free.) The towering spires of the **Cathedral of Saint Helena**, at Lawrence and Warren St., are visible throughout downtown. The marble, oak, and bronze furnishings and stained glass windows of this neo-Gothic structure emulate Vienna's Votive Church of the Sacred Heart. (☎442-5825. Open June-Aug. M-Sa 7am-9pm; Sept.-May M-Sa 7am-7pm. Guided tours available Tu-Th 1-3pm.) The small but lovely **Holter Museum**, 12 E. Lawrence Ave., displays paintings, photographs, and crafts. (☎442-6400; www.holtermuseum.org. Open in summer M-F 10am-6pm, Sa 10am-5pm, Su noon-5pm; in winter M-F 11am-6pm, Sa 11am-5pm, Su noon-5pm. Suggested donation $2, students and seniors $1; families $5.) The gold vanished from **Last Chance Gulch** long ago, but today this pedestrian mall offers restaurants, shops, and public artwork. The **Myrna Loy Center**, 15 S. Ewing St. (☎443-0287), presents foreign films, dance, music, and performance art in the historic former county jail. Artists-in-residence say there's really nowhere like "the Bray," speaking fondly of the **Archie Bray Foundation for the Ceramic Arts**, 2915 Country Club Ave. Take Euclid Ave./Hwy. 12 west, and make a right on Joslyn St. Visitors can view the incredible work in the gallery, tour the artists' studios, and take a self-guided walking tour of the grounds. (☎443-3502. Grounds open dawn-dusk; gallery open M-Sa 10am-5pm, Su 1-5pm. Free.)

Take in the entire city from the top of **Mount Helena** (5460 ft.); the trail begins at the Adams St. Trailhead, just west of Reeders Alley. Observe the Missouri River as Lewis and Clark did on a 2hr. boat tour of the **▧Gates of the Mountains**, 18 mi. north of Helena, off I-15 at Exit 209 (even though it says "no services"). Extensive commentary on local plants and birds makes for an educating journey. The boat stops near Mann Gulch, where a 1949 forest fire killed 13 smokejumpers. (☎458-5241. June-Sept. 2-7 tours per day; call for times. $10, seniors $9, ages 4-17 $6.)

▶ DAYTRIPS FROM HELENA

BUTTE ☎406

The slow-moving town of Butte was once the largest city in the Rockies; it was both wealthy, sitting atop an enormously rich mine, and progressive, with the first electric railroad. With a rich past, this second-largest historical district west of the Mississippi has hidden delights for any history buff. Buildings untouched for years are now open to visitors; **Old Butte Historical Adventures**, 117 N. Main St., and the **Rookwood Speakeasy Museum**, 24 N. Main St., both run entertaining and informative tours through abandoned speakeasies, business offices, and brothels, all replete with artifacts left behind by the original inhabitants. (☎498-3424. Open in summer daily 10am-4pm; in winter by appointment only. 1hr. tours depart every hr.; special 1½hr. tour daily 1pm. $7, ages 12-17 $1, under 12 free.) The wealth that supported more than 250 bars in 1917 had its roots in Butte's mineral deposits. Discover the workings of open-pit mining at the **Museum of Mining,** 155 Museum Way, located on an actual mine yard with much of the equipment left intact. (☎723-7211. Open daily in summer 9am-9pm. $7, ages 65+ $6, ages 13-18 $5, ages 5-12 $2.) Though it's not much to look at from the outside, the interior of the **Copper King Mansion,** 219 W. Granite St., reflects the opulence supported by the mine. Guided tours of this magnificently ornate house are available, but even better is staying in the beautiful rooms and waking up to a full breakfast. (☎782-7580. Tours June-Aug. daily 9am-4pm; May and Sept. daily 9am-4pm; Apr. Sa-Su 9am-4pm; Oct.-Mar. by appointment only. Rooms $60-95.) More information can be found at the **Butte Chamber of Commerce,** 1000 George St., which hands out maps, brochures, and advice. (☎723-3177. Open daily 8:30am-6:30pm.)

GREAT FALLS   ☎406

A city planned for the railroad rather than a boom-and-bust town like so many of its neighbors, easygoing Great Falls is also known as the "Electric City" for its early development of dams and hydroelectric power. The easy-to-navigate street system and ample city parks of today were not developed until the late 1880s; when Lewis and Clark arrived in June 1805 they had to spend quite some time on the 18 mi. portage around Great Falls's series of five waterfalls. Though the falls for which the city is named are less impressive nowadays due to the dam, two museums make a stop here worthwhile. The new **Lewis & Clark National Historic Trail Interpretive Center,** 4201 Giant Springs Rd., at Exit 280 off I-15, sits on the Missouri River and takes visitors through the expedition with detailed exhibits on the native peoples the explorers encountered and the flora and fauna they researched. Pelts, taxidermied birds, and preserved flowers from the expedition accompany interactive exhibits. The center also hosts special events daily; call for details. (☎727-8733. Open June-Sept. daily 9am-6pm; Oct.-May Tu-Sa 9am-5pm. $5, under 16 free. National Park Golden Eagle, Access, and Age Passports accepted.) Celebrated for capturing the spirit of the West in his paintings, sculptures, and letters, Charlie Russell fell in love with Montana after moving from Missouri. His vast array of work is housed in the **C.M. Russell Museum,** 400 13th St. N, next to his home and log cabin studio. (☎727-8787. Open in summer daily 9am-6pm; in winter Tu-Su 10am-5pm. Tours in summer M-F 10am and 2pm, Sa-Su 2pm. $8, seniors $6, students and ages 6-18 $3.)

BOZEMAN   ☎406

Busy Bozeman continues to grow as outdoor enthusiasts scramble to get in on the world-class fishing, ski areas, and endless hiking trails. After the sun sets, this boisterous town doesn't head to bed as quickly as many other places in Montana. Montana State University (MSU) students still don cowboy hats and drive pickup trucks, but the increasing diversity of the student body reflects the cultural vigor of this thriving community. The university is also home to the wonderful Museum of the Rockies, a base for paleontologists exploring the entire region.

■ ☑ ORIENTATION AND PRACTICAL INFORMATION. I-90 forms the northeast boundary of the city center. **Main Street** is the primary east-west road, intersecting I-90 at Exit 309. **Willson Avenue** and **19th Avenue** are the primary north-south routes, with the latter intersecting I-90 at Exit 305. Named streets run east-west; north-south avenues east of Willson Ave. are also named. North-south avenues west of Willson Ave. are numbered. **Greyhound** and **Rimrock Stages,** 1205 E. Main St. (☎587-3110; www.greyhound.com; open M-F 8am-5pm and 7-9pm, Sa 9am-5pm and 7-9pm, Su 3-5pm and 7-9pm), both send buses to Billings (3hr., 3 per day, $28),

Butte (2hr., 3 per day, $20), Helena (4hr., 1 per day, $20), and Missoula (5hr., 3 per day, $30). **Visitor Info: Bozeman Area Chamber of Commerce,** 2000 Commerce Way, at the corner of 19th Ave. and Baxter Ln. (☎586-5421 or 800-228-4224; www.bozemanchamber.com. Open M-F 8am-5pm.) **Summer Visitors Center,** 1003 N. 7th Ave. (Open Memorial Day-Labor Day daily 9am-6pm.) **Internet Access: Bozeman Public Library,** 220 E. Lamme St. (☎582-2400. Open M-Th 10am-8pm, F-Sa 10am-5pm, Su 1-5pm; in summer closed Su.) **Post Office:** 5711 E. Baxter Ln. (☎800-275-8777. Open M-F 8:30am-5pm, Sa 9am-1pm.) **Postal Code:** 59718. **Area Code:** 406.

ACCOMMODATIONS. Budget motels line Main St. and 7th Ave. north of Main. Only a 5min. walk from downtown, **Bozeman Backpacker's Hostel ❶,** 405 W. Olive St., has a kitchen, a welcoming porch, co-ed rooms, and the cheapest beds in town. (☎586-4659. Linens included. Laundry facilities. Dorms $16; private rooms with shared bath $35. Showers for non-guests $4. Cash only.) **The Imperial Inn ❸,** 122 W. Main, has clean rooms and particularly spacious singles in a prime downtown location. (☎586-3354. Singles $49; doubles $59. $10 cheaper in winter. AmEx/D/DC/MC/V.) **Langohr Campground ❶,** 11 mi. south of Bozeman on Hyalite Canyon Rd., has mostly sunny sites along Hyalite Creek. **Hood Creek ❶** and **Chisholm ❶** campgrounds, located 6 and 7 mi. farther up the canyon, respectively, are situated on the shores of the Hyalite Reservoir, beneath the forested peaks of the **Gallatin National Forest.** (Reservations ☎877-444-6777. Open mid-May to mid-Sept. Sites at all three campgrounds $10.) The private **Bear Canyon Campground ❶,** 4000 Bozeman Trail Rd., 4 mi. east of Bozeman at Exit 313 off I-90, has great views of the countryside from the heated outdoor pool. (☎587-1575 or 800-438-1575. Laundry and showers. Open May to mid-Oct. Sites $16, with water and electricity $21, full hookup $26. Each additional person $3.) The **Bozeman Ranger Station,** 3710 Fallon St., Ste. C (☎522-2520), has more info on camping in the Gallatin National Forest.

FOOD AND NIGHTLIFE. Inexpensive and chain eateries aimed at the college crowd line W. College Ave. near the university. **The Cateye Cafe ❷,** 23 N. Tracy Ave., is a downtown diner with a colorful paint job and a humorous menu, delighting in cats and all who love them. Banana bread french toast ($6.75), sandwiches on "fogatcha" bread ($7-8), and meatloaf and egg breakfasts ($7.75) satisfy any craving. (☎587-8844. Open M and W-F 7am-2:30pm, Sa-Su 7am-2pm.) **La Parrilla ❷,** 1533 W. Babcock Ave., wraps up just about everything in their giant 1 ft. tortillas, including homemade barbecue, fiery jambalaya, bison meat, and fresh seafood. (☎582-9511. Wraps $5-8. Open daily 11am-9pm. AmEx/D/DC/MC/V.) **Sweet Pea Bakery and Cafe ❷,** 19 S. Willson Ave., cooks healthy gourmet lunch and brunch with artistic flair. The mango chicken salad ($8.50) and quiche of the day ($9.50) are among Sweet Pea's most popular dishes. (☎586-8200. Open Tu 7am-3pm, W-Sa 7am-9pm. AmEx/D/MC/V.) The original in the popular Montana pizza chain, Bozeman's **MacKenzie River Pizza Co. ❸,** 232 E. Main St., is pure Montana, with rough-hewn tree-trunk pillars and murals of cattle herds. The selection of gourmet pizzas includes the "Sequoia," topped with basil pesto, sun-dried tomatoes, artichokes, and almonds. (☎587-0099. 12 in. pizzas $14-17. Open M-Th 11am-10pm, F-Sa 11am-11pm, Su noon-10pm. AmEx/D/MC/V.)

Get the lowdown on music and nightlife from the weekly *Tributary* or *The BoZone,* found at cafes, bars, and bookstores around town. Bozeman's summer concert series **Music on Main** (Th 7-8:30pm) is a popular way to kick off an evening downtown. The rooftop patio is always packed at **Crystal,** 123 E. Main St., where buckets of beer on ice await as partiers vie for a perch amidst the crowd. (☎587-2888. Open M-Sa 11am-11pm, Su 2-10pm.) Locals and travelers thirsty for good beer and great music head over to the **Zebra Cocktail Lounge,** in the basement at Rouse Ave. and Main St. The large selection of beers and hipster atmosphere draw

ROCKY MOUNTAINS

a young, cool crowd. (☎585-8851. W-Sa DJ or bands. Open daily 8pm-2am.) One of only two non-smoking bars in all of Bozeman, the **Rocking R Bar,** 211 E. Main St., lives up to its name with hot drink specials every night, all served in a classy setting. (☎587-9355. Free food W-F 5-9pm. Live music W and Sa. Karaoke Th. Open daily 11am-2am.) Sample some of Montana's best brews from the selection of more than 40 beers on tap at the **Montana Ale Works,** 611 E. Main St. This former train depot for the now-defunct Northern Pacific Railway Co. now houses six pool tables for serious sharks. (☎587-7700. Beer $3-5. Open M-Th and Su 4pm-11pm, F-Sa 4pm-midnight.)

◨ 🔏 SIGHTS AND OUTDOOR ACTIVITIES. Get up close and personal with dinosaurs at the ▧**Museum of the Rockies,** 600 West Kagy Blvd., near the university. Dr. Jack Horner (the inspiration for *Jurassic Park's* Alan Grant) and other paleontologists make this their base for excavating prehistoric remains throughout the West. Thoughtful curation, an outdoor challenge course featuring Lewis and Clark, and an incredible amount of fossils make this museum a must-see. (☎994-3466; www.museumoftherockies.org. Open in summer daily 8am-8pm; low season M-Sa 9am-5pm, Su 12:30-5pm. $9.50, ages 5-18 $6.50. AAA discount $1/$0.50.) In an old county jail, the **Gallatin Pioneer Museum,** 317 W. Main St., offers a look at gallows and jail cells as well as a reconstructed pioneer cabin. (☎522-8122; www.pioneermuseum.org. Open May-Sept. M-Sa 10am-4:30pm, Su 1-5pm; mid-Sept. to mid-May Tu-Sa 11am-4pm, Sa 1-4pm. $3, under 12 free.)

The **Bozeman Angler,** 23 E. Main St., leads trips with expert instruction in fly-fishing on the Yellowstone, Gallatin, Madison, and Missouri Rivers. (☎800-886-9111; www.bozemanangler.com. 3hr. group lesson $40 per person; full-day lesson $125 per person. 2-person float trip $350.) Surrounded by three renowned trout-fishing rivers—Yellowstone, Madison, and Gardiner—the small town of **Livingston,** about 25 mi. east of Bozeman off I-90, is an angler's heaven; the fly-fishing film *A River Runs Through It* was shot here. Livingston's Main St. features early 20th-century buildings, including bars, restaurants, fishing outfitters, small art galleries, and a few modern businesses. **Dan Bailey's,** 209 W. Park St., sells fishing licenses and rents gear. (☎222-1673 or 800-356-4052. 2-day fishing license $24.25, full-season $69.25. Rod and reel $20; waders and boots $15. Open in summer M-Sa 7am-7pm; in winter M-Sa 8am-6pm.)

The world-class ski area **Big Sky,** 45 mi. south of town on U.S. 191, has over 150 trails and short lift lines. For extreme skiers, the Lone Peak trams reach an altitude of 11,166 ft. (☎995-5000 or 800-548-4486. Open mid-Nov. to mid-Apr. Full-day ticket $59, students and ages 11-17 $47, seniors $30. Ski rentals $27-39, juniors $19. Snowboards $33.) In summer, scenic **lift rides** soar up Big Sky. (Open June to early Oct. daily 9:45am-5pm. $14, seniors $9, under 10 free.) Full suspension mountain bike rentals are also available at the top. ($23 per hr., $46 per 8hr.) Less crowded and less expensive than Big Sky, **Bridger Bowl Ski Area,** 15795 Bridger Canyon Rd., 16 mi. northeast of town on Hwy. 86, has trails for a variety of abilities. (☎587-2111 or 800-223-9609. Open early Dec. to early Apr. Full-day ticket $35, seniors $29, ages 6-12 $13. Ski rentals $20, juniors $10. Snowboards $30.)

Floating in the warm and shallow **Madison River** is a cheap and relaxing way to pass a long summer afternoon. Rent inner tubes ($4-8 per day) at **Big Boys Toys,** 28670 Norris Rd., west on Main St. 7 mi. from downtown. (☎587-4747. Open daily in summer 7:30am-6pm; in winter 8am-6pm. Canoes $25 per day; windgliders $25 per day. Cash or check deposit required.) **Yellowstone Raft Co.** shoots the rapids of the Gallatin River, 7 mi. north of the Big Sky area on U.S. 191. Trips meet at the office, between Mi. 55 and Mi. 56 on U.S. 191. (☎995-4613 or 800-348-4376. Half-day $42, children $32; full day $79/$63.)

LG: How did you start jumping?
A: I started working for the Helena National Forest as a summer job. Among other things like cleaning picnic tables, cutting brush, and patrolling, one of the things they train you to do is put out fires. So I started out as a young firefighter putting my way through college. The "problem" is that it gets in your blood and you become addicted to it. After 4 years of fire-fighting through college, I got a teaching degree and ended up continuing to fight fires in my summers off. I've been doing it for the past 27 years.

LG: What does smokejumper training involve?
A: You need recommendations and a minimum of 2 years firefighting experience. Many people apply and only a limited number get selected to go through rookie train-ing, which is over a month long. I would compare it to boot camp. They start their morning with calis-thenics, go through daily training, and have to pass physical fitness tests. People wash out at any time, and they need to make a minimum of 15 jumps before they're even allowed in a fire.

LG: What happens in a typical fire?
A: Smokejumpers are initial attack, so we get calls right when

MISSOULA ☎ 406

A liberal haven in a largely conservative state, Missoula attracts new residents every day with its revitalized downtown and bountiful outdoors opportunities. Missoula represents the cultural hub of the state to native Montanans, and the students at the University of Montana don't disagree. Downtown Missoula is lined with bars and coffeehouses spawned by the large student population. Twelve thousand years ago, the town was located at the bottom of a glacial lake; today, four different mountain ranges and five major rivers surround Missoula, supporting skiing during the winter and fly-fishing, hiking, and biking during the summer.

🛈 PRACTICAL INFORMATION. Flights stream into the **Missoula International Airport,** 5225 Hwy. 10 W (☎728-4381; www.msoairport.org), 6 mi. west of town. Follow Broadway, which turns into Hwy. 10/200. **Greyhound,** 1660 W. Broadway (☎549-2339; www.greyhound.com; ticket office open M-F 7am-12:30pm, 1:30-5pm, 7:45-8:30pm, Sa-Su 2:15-3:15pm and 7:45-8:45pm), sends buses to Bozeman (4½-5½hr., 3 per day, $30-40) and Spokane (4hr., 2 per day, $38-44). From the same terminal, **Rimrock Trailways** serves Whitefish via St. Ignatius and Kalispell (3½hr., 1 per day, $28-30) and Helena (5hr., 1 per day, $23-25). Catch a ride on **Mountain Line City Buses** from the Transfer Center, at Ryman and Pine St., or around town. (☎721-3333. Buses run M-F 6:45am-6:15pm, Sa 9:45am-5:15pm. $0.85, seniors $0.35, under 18 $0.25.) **Taxi: Yellow Cab** ☎543-6644. **Car Rental: Rent-A-Wreck,** 1905 W. Broadway. (☎721-3838 or 800-552-1138. 21+. $35-45 per day; 150 free mi., $0.25 each additional mi.) **Visitor Info: Missoula Chamber of Commerce,** 1121 E. Broadway, Ste. 103. (☎532-3250; www.missoulachamber.com. Open in summer M-F 8am-7pm, Sa-Su 10am-2pm; in winter M-F 8am-5pm.) **Medical Services:** St. Patrick Hospital, 500 W. Broadway (☎329-5635). **Internet Access: Missoula Public Library,** 301 E. Main St. (☎721-2665. Open M-Th 10am-9pm, F-Sa 10am-6pm.) **Post Office:** 1100 W. Kent St. (☎329-2248. Open M-F 8am-6pm, Sa 9am-1pm.) **Postal Code:** 59801. **Area Code:** 406.

🛏 ACCOMMODATIONS. There are no hostels in Missoula, but there are plenty of inexpensive alternatives along **Broadway,** both east and west of downtown. Rooms at the **City Center Motel ❷,** 338 E. Broadway, have cable TV, fridges, and microwaves. (☎543-3193. Singles $45; doubles $55. MC/V.) Downtown, but still in a quiet setting, the **Royal Motel ❷,** 338 Washington, has clean rooms with cable TV, fridges, and microwaves. (☎542-2184. June-Sept. singles $48; doubles $52. Oct.-May $40/$44. AmEx/D/MC/V.) The **Missoula/El-Mar KOA Kampground ❶**, 3450 Tina Ave., south of Broadway off Reserve St., has everything: a petting zoo, ice-cream socials, a pool, hot tub, mini-golf, and laundry facilities. Shaded tent sites are set apart from RVs. (☎549-0881 or 800-562-5366. 2-person sites $23, with water and electricity $25, full hookup $33. Cabins $40-48. Each additional person $3. AmEx/D/MC/V.) Though farther afield, many **National Forest campgrounds** line the highways spreading outward from Missoula. The closest is **Lolo Creek ❶**, 15 mi. west of Lolo and 22 mi. west of Missoula on Hwy. 12, which parallels the historic Lolo Trail used by the Nez Perce, Salish, and Kootenai tribes and also explored by Lewis and Clark. (☎329-3814. 17 sites with vault toilets and water. $10.)

⬛ FOOD. The culinary capital of Montana boasts a number of innovative, delicious, and thrifty eateries. Restaurants and coffeehouses line Higgins Ave., north of the Clark Fork River, downtown. Cozy red-leather "lovers" nooks upstairs at **The Bridge ❹**, 515 S. Higgins Ave. draw locals for special evenings out. Enjoy the stuffed eggplant ($17), wild salmon ($18), or the white or red sauce thin-crust pizzas. (☎542-0638. 12 in. pizzas $9-15. Open daily 5-10pm. AmEx/D/MC/V.) Boasting fine espresso and billiards, the hip **Raven Cafe ❷**, 130 E. Broadway, handles heavenly slices of quiche ($3) and black bird pizza pies (10 in. $7-8), as well as delicious breakfasts and decadent desserts. With free Internet access, a fresh jukebox, and plenty of books and magazines, the cafe keeps people sipping coffee for hours. (☎829-8188. Open M-Sa 8am-11pm, Su 8am-3pm. MC/V.) **Worden's ❶**, 451 N. Higgins Ave., serves sandwiches in three sizes: 4 in. roll ($4.50), 7 in. ($7.50), and 14 in. ($13.50); alternatively, chow down on the "frito pie" ($4). You can also pick up groceries while munching. (☎549-1293. Open M-Sa 7:30am-10pm, Su 9am-9pm.) **Tipu's ❷**, 115½ S. 4th St. W in the alley, is one of the only all-veggie establishments and the lone Indian restaurant in Montana, serving samosas and its own "curritos." (☎542-0622. Lunch buffet $7. Open daily 11:30am-9:30pm.) **Taco del Sol ❶**, 422 N. Higgins Ave., is the place for cheap eats; get $2 fish tacos or a hefty 14 in. Mission Burrito for under $4. (☎327-8929. Open M-Sa 11am-9pm, Su noon-9pm. Cash only.)

◪⬛ SIGHTS AND ENTERTAINMENT. Missoula's hottest sight is the **Aerial Fire Depot and Smokejumper Center,** 5756 W. Broadway, just past the airport, 7 mi. west of town. It's the nation's largest training base

the fire is detected and still fairly small. One of the great advantages smokejumpers have is that we are on an airplane above the fire with the door off. We take a good look at the terrain and see what the fire behavior is. People coming from the ground can only see smoke and don't know what they're getting into. Before we even jump out of the plane, we check for safety zones to see which ways we can approach the fire, pinpoint safe jump spots that are close to the fire but not endangering ourselves, and look for routes out of the fire. After we land in parachutes, we pack it up to put in a safe spot. The plane flies over and drops our cargo, which contains chainsaws, tools, water, freeze-dried food, everything we'll need to fight the fire and camp overnight.

LG: What is one of your most memorable smokejumping experiences?

A: This was about 21 years ago. I had just jumped a fire and we had it pretty well whipped. Smoke was coming off the last dying embers and the sun was coming up. As I was wiping the soot off my face, the dispatcher came on the radio and asked, "Is there a smokejumper there named Mark Wright?" I knew immediately what he was going to tell me. I started hooting and hollering as he announced, "Congratulations. You have a healthy baby girl."

for smokejumpers—aerial firefighters who parachute into remote forests and serve as an initial attack against wildfires. Displays and videos recount their heroism and skill. (☎329-4934. Open May-Sept. daily 8:30am-5pm. 45min.-1hr. tours daily at 10, 11am, 2, 3, 4pm. Free; donations accepted.) The **Carousel,** 101 Carousel Dr., in Caras Riverfront Park, is one of the oldest hand-carved carousels in America. (☎549-8382. Open daily June-Aug. 11am-7pm; Sept.-May 11am-5:30pm. $1.50, seniors and under 16 $0.50, disabled free.) Wondering what comes out at night in Montana? Learn about nocturnal animals and astronomy, as well as how naturalists do their job, at the newly opened **Montana Natural History Center,** 120 Hickory St. Call ahead for their Saturday discovery day events. (☎327-0405. Open Tu-F 10am-5pm, Sa hours vary. $1, ages 4-12 $0.50.)

Out to Lunch, also in Caras Riverfront Park, offers free performances in the summer months, along with plenty of food vendors; call the Missoula Downtown Association for more information on the annual event. (☎543-4238. June-Aug. W 11am-1:30pm.) If you miss "Out to Lunch," the food vendors return on Thursday nights for **Downtown Tonight,** which features live music, food, and a beer garden. (☎543-4238. June-Aug. Th 5:30-8:30pm.) Free concerts are also available on Wednesday nights courtesy of **Bonner Park Concerts,** in Bonner Park. (☎728-2400, ext. 7041. June-Aug. W 8pm.) Stock up on fresh local produce, flowers, and breads at the **farmers market** in Circle Sq. (☎543-4238. Mid-May to mid-Oct. Sa 8:30am-noon.) The **Clark Fork River Market** adds local meat and dairy products to the Saturday morning mix near the Millennium building by Caras Park. (542-0539. Mid-May to mid-Oct. Sa 8am-1pm.) The **Western Montana Fair and Rodeo,** held in August, has live music by big names like Brad Paisley and Chris LeDoux, plus a carnival, fireworks, a rodeo, and concession booths. (☎256-2422 or 800-366-8538; www.montanafair.com. Open 10am-10pm.)

■ **NIGHTLIFE.** College students swarm Missoula's downtown bar area—namely around Front St. and Higgins Ave.—throughout the school year. **The Iron Horse Brew Pub,** 501 N. Higgins Ave., always packs in a crowd on its large patios, and is popular with fraternity types. (☎728-8866. Drafts $3. Open daily 11am-2am.) Follow the advice of the "beer coaches" at **The Kettle House Brewing Co.,** 602 Myrtle, one block west of Higgins between 4th and 5th, and "support your local brewery." The Kettle House serves a delectable assortment of beers, including unusual hemp beer—called Bongwater Stout. (☎728-1660. Open M-Sa noon-9pm; no beer served after 8pm. 2 free samples; then $3-3.25 per pint.) Charlie B's, 420 N. Higgins Ave., draws bikers, farmers, students, and hippies alike. Framed photos of longtime regulars cover the walls. (☎549-3589. Drafts $2. Wells $2.50-3. Open daily 8am-2am.) The *Independent* and *Lively Times,* free at newsstands and cafes, have the lowdown on Missoula's music scene. The "Entertainer," in the Friday *Missoulian,* has event schedules.

■ **OUTDOOR ACTIVITIES.** Soak your weary feet at the **Lolo Hot Springs,** 35 mi. southwest of Missoula on Hwy 12. The 103-105°F springs were an ancient meeting place for local Native Americans and were frequented by Lewis and Clark in 1805. (☎273-2290 or 800-273-2290. Open daily June-Sept. 10am-10pm; Oct.-May 10am-8pm. $6.) Farther along Rte. 12 into Idaho over the difficult Lolo Pass are two free, clothing-optional natural hot springs, **Jerry Johnson** (35 mi. from Lolo Hot Springs, 1 mi. hike in) and **Weir** (45 mi. from Lolo, ½ mi. hike in). Indulge your sense of history at **Garnet Ghost Town,** Montana's most intact ghost town—well-preserved, but not commercialized. During mining's heyday at the turn of the century, the population reached several thousand. Today it is an eerie reminder of the transience of civilization. (☎329-3914. Take I-90 to Exit 109; follow Hwy. 200 to Mile 22, and turn right on Garnet Range Rd., mostly dirt and 25mph, for 11 miles. Open to most vehicular traffic mid-May to Sept. Snowmobiles are the only form of transportation Jan.-Apr. $3; ages 16 and under free.)

Parks, recreation areas, and nearby wilderness areas make Missoula an outdoor enthusiast's dream. The bicycle-friendly city is located along both the Trans-America and Great Parks bicycle routes, and all major streets have designated bike lanes. **Open Road Bicycles and Nordic Equipment,** 517 S. Orange St., has bike rentals. (☎549-2453. Front suspension $3.50 per hr., $18 per day; full suspension $7.50/$35. Open M-F 9am-6pm, Sa 10am-5pm, Su 11am-3pm.) **Adventure Cycling,** 150 E. Pine St., is the place to go for info about Trans-America and Great Parks routes. (☎721-1776 or 800-755-2453. Open M-F 8am-5pm.) The **Rattlesnake Wilderness National Recreation Area,** named after the shape of the river (there are no rattlers for miles), 11 mi. northeast of town off Exit 104 on I-90, and the **Pattee Canyon Recreation Area,** 3½ mi. east of Higgins on Pattee Canyon Dr., have excellent biking trails. Contact the **Missoula Ranger District,** Building 24-A at Fort Missoula, for trail info. Take Ft. Missoula Rd. from Reserve St. and make a left at the stop sign. (☎329-3814. Open M-F 7:30am-4pm.) **Missoulians on Bicycle** (www.missoulabike.org) hosts rides and events for cyclists in a fun collegiate atmosphere.

Alpine and Nordic skiing keep Missoulians busy during winter. To indulge the Nordic craving, **Pattee Canyon Recreation Area** has groomed trails close to town. **Marshall Mountain** is a great place to learn how to downhill ski, with 480 acres, night skiing, and free shuttles from downtown; take the East Missoula exit from I-90. (☎258-6000. $24 per day, ages 6-12 $19.) Experienced skiers should check out the **Montana Snowbowl,** 12 mi. northwest of Missoula, with a vertical drop of 2600 ft. and over 35 trails. Take the Reserve St. exit off I-90 and follow Grant Creek Rd., then turn left onto Snowbowl Rd. (☎549-9777. Open Nov.-Apr. daily 10am-4:30pm. Full day $31, seniors and students $18, ages 6-12 $14.)

Floating on rafts or inner tubes is a favorite local activity. The Blackfoot River, along Rte. 200 east of Bonner, makes a good afternoon float; take I-90 to Exit 109. Call the **Montana State Regional Parks and Wildlife Office,** 3201 Spurgin Rd., for more information about rafting locations. (☎542-5500. Open M-F 8am-5pm.) You can rent tubes or rafts from the **Army and Navy Economy Store,** 322 N. Higgins. (☎721-1315. Tubes $4 per day, $20 deposit required. Rafts $40 per day, credit card deposit required. Open M-F 9am-7:30pm, Sa 9am-5:30pm, Su 10am-5:30pm.) When tubing, it's useful to have two vehicles (dropping off a bike at the exit point works) since you'll float several miles downstream and away from your primary vehicle.

Hiking opportunities abound in the Missoula area. The relatively easy 30min. hike to the "M" (for the U of M, not Missoula) on Mount Sentinel has a tremendous view of Missoula and the surrounding peaks; continue another mile to the top of the mountain (elevation gain 620 ft.). The **Rattlesnake Wilderness National Recreation Area** makes for a great day of hiking; follow Van Buren St. and then Rattlesnake Dr. 4 mi. north from Missoula to the area entrance. Other popular areas include **Pattee Canyon** and **Blue Mountain,** south of town; for Blue Mountain, travel 2 mi. southwest on U.S. 93 and turn right on Blue Mountain Rd. For maps ($6) and hiking info, try the Missoula Ranger District (see above). For equipment rentals, stop by **The Trail Head,** 221 E. Front St. (☎543-6966. Open M-F 9:30am-8pm, Sa 9am-6pm, Su 11am-6pm. Tents $10-14 per day; backpacks $9; sleeping bags $5.)

Missoula is at the heart of Western Montana's **fly-fishing** country. The Bitterroot River is the place to catch brown trout, while the Blackfoot River is known for its bull trout. **Fishing licenses** are required and can be purchased from the **Department of Fish, Wildlife, and Parks,** 3201 Spurgin Rd., or from local sporting goods stores. (☎542-5500. One-time conservation fee $9.50. 2-day non-resident license $15, 10-day non-resident license $43.50.) **Kingfisher,** 926 E. Broadway, offers licenses and guided fishing trips. Their free fishing reports are published daily Mar. 1-Oct. 31 on their website. (☎721-6141 or 888-542-4911; www.kingfisherflyshop.com. 2-person full-day guided trip with rods, reels, and flies $365. Reservations recommended. Open daily June-Aug. 6am-8pm; Sept.-May 9am-5pm.)

FROM MISSOULA TO GLACIER

Beneath the towering peaks of Mission Mountain Range, **St. Ignatius Mission,** in St. Ignatius, is home to the first Jesuit mission in the Northwest, built in 1854 by Native Americans. The original log dormitories are still intact, as is the mission church. Inside, 58 bold murals by Joseph Carignano depict St. Ignatius Loyola, the mission's namesake. (☎745-2768. Open daily in summer 9am-8pm; in winter 9am-5pm. Free.) **RimRock Stages** (☎745-3501) buses stop a half-mile away in St. Ignatius, on Blaine St. The **National Bison Range** was established in 1908 in an effort to save the dwindling bison population from extinction. At one time 30-70 million of the creatures roamed the plains, but the population dropped to less than 1000 due to over-hunting. The 19,000-acre range is home to 350-500 bison as well as deer, elk, bighorn sheep, and mountain goats. The 2hr. **Red Sleep Mountain** self-guided tour is a 19 mi. drive on steep gravel roads and offers a spectacular view of the Flathead Valley and glimpses of wildlife, though binoculars are helpful. Not to be missed is the annual October roundup. To access the range from Missoula, take U.S. 93 north for 40 mi., then drive 5 mi. west on Rte. 200, and 5 mi. north on Rte. 212. (☎644-2211. Visitors center open M-F 8am-4:30pm. Red Sleep Mountain drive open mid-May to mid-Oct. daily 7am-7pm. $4 per vehicle.) With displays of old posters, uniforms, vintage cars, and motorcycles, the ▉**Miracle of America Museum,** on the frontage road to U.S. 93 (follow the signs), at the southern end of Polson, houses one of the country's greatest collections of Americana. A general store, saddlery, barber shop, soda fountain, and gas station sit among the memorabilia. (☎883-6804. Open June-Sept. daily 8am-8pm; Oct.-May M-Sa 8am-5pm, Su 2-6pm. $4, ages 3-12 $1.) Fresh fruit and fish stands line **Flathead Lake,** on U.S. 93 between Polson and Kalispell, the largest natural lake west of the Mississippi.

WATERTON-GLACIER PEACE PARK

Waterton-Glacier transcends international boundaries to encompass one of the most strikingly beautiful portions of the Rockies. The massive Rocky Mountain peaks span both parks, providing sanctuary for many endangered bears, bighorn sheep, moose, mountain goats, and gray wolves. Perched high in the northern Rockies, Glacier is sometimes called the "Crown of the Continent," and the high alpine lakes and glaciers shine like jewels.

▉ PRACTICAL INFORMATION

Technically one park, Waterton-Glacier is actually two distinct areas: the small **Waterton Lakes National Park** in Alberta, and the enormous **Glacier National Park** in Montana. There are several **border crossings** nearby: **Piegan/Carway,** at U.S. 89 (open daily 7am-11pm); **Roosville,** on U.S. 93 (open 24hr.); and **Chief Mountain,** at Rte. 17 (open daily June-Aug. 7am-10pm; mid- to late May and Sept. 9am-6pm). The fastest way to Waterton is to head north along the east side of Glacier, entering Canada through Chief Mountain. Since snow can be unpredictable, the parks are usually in full operation only from late May to early September—check conditions in advance. The *Waterton-Glacier Guide,* provided at any park entrance, has dates and times of trail, campground, and border crossing openings. To find out which park areas, hotels, and campsites will be open when you visit, contact the **Park Headquarters,** Waterton Lakes National Park, Waterton Park, AB T0K 2M0

(☎403-859-2224), or **Glacier National Park,** West Glacier, MT 59936 (☎406-888-7800). Mace and firewood are not allowed into Canada, and only bearspray with an EPA certification number, which you still must declare at customs.

GLACIER NATIONAL PARK ☎406

[⌐ TRANSPORTATION

Amtrak (☎226-4452; www.amtrak.com) traces a route along the southern edge of the park. The station in West Glacier is staffed mid-May to September, but the train still stops there in the winter. Trains chug daily to: East Glacier (1½hr., $15); Seattle (14hr., $120-160); Spokane (6hr., $61-79); Whitefish, MT (30min., $8-11). Amtrak also runs from East Glacier to Chicago (32hr., $204-265). **Rimrock Stages** (☎800-255-7655; www.rimrocktrailways.com), the only bus line that nears the park, stops in Kalispell at the Kalispell Bus Terminal, 3794 U.S. 2 E, and goes to Billings (8hr., 1 per day, $66) and Missoula (3hr., 1-2 per day, $23). A car is the most convenient mode of transport, particularly within the park. **Glacier Park, Inc.'s** (☎892-2525; www.glacierparkinc.com) red jammer buses run tours on Going-to-the-Sun Rd. (3hr. tours $28, 6½hr. $38; children $14/$19.) **Sun Tours** offers tours from East Glacier and St. Mary. (☎226-9220 or 800-786-9220. All-day tour from East Glacier $55, from St. Mary $40.) Shuttles for hikers ($8 per segment, under 12 $4) roam Going-to-the-Sun Rd. from early July to early September; schedules are available at visitors centers or at www.nps.gov/glac/shuttles.htm.

▟ ORIENTATION

There are few roads in Glacier, and the locals like it that way. Glacier's main thoroughfare is the **Going-to-the-Sun Road,** which connects the two primary points of entry, West Glacier and St. Mary. **U.S. 2** skirts the southern border of the park and is the fastest route from Browning and East Glacier to West Glacier. At the "Goat Lick," about halfway between East and West Glacier, mountain goats traverse steep cliffs to lap up the natural salt deposits. **Route 89** heads north along the eastern edge of the park past St. Mary. Those interested in visiting the northwestern section of the park can either take the unpaved **Outside North Fork Road** and enter through Polebridge or brave the rough, pothole-ridden **Inside North Fork Road,** which takes an hour longer. While most of Glacier is primitive backcountry, a number of villages provide lodging, gas, and food: St. Mary, Many Glacier, and Two Medicine in the east, and West Glacier, Apgar, and Polebridge in the west.

▐ PRACTICAL INFORMATION

The park's **admission fee** is $20 per car per week, $10 for pedestrians and cyclists; yearly passes $25. Each of the three **visitors centers** gives good advice on campsites, day-hikes, weather, flora, and fauna. The largest, **Saint Mary,** guards the east entrance of the park. (☎732-7750. Open daily July 9am-9pm; May-June and Sept. 8am-5pm.) **Apgar** is located at the west entrance. (☎888-7940. Open daily late June to Aug. 8am-7pm; May-June and Sept.-Oct. 9am-5pm.) A third visitors center graces **Logan Pass,** on the Going-to-the-Sun Rd. (Open daily July-Aug. 9am-7pm; Sept. 9am-4:30pm; June 9:30am-4:30pm.) The **Many Glacier** ranger station can also answer questions. (Open daily mid-May to mid-Sept. 8am-5pm.)

Visitors planning overnight backpacking trips must obtain the necessary **backcountry permit.** With the exception of the **Nyack/Coal Creek** camping zone, all backcountry camping must be at designated campsites equipped with pit toilets, tent sites, food preparation areas, and food hanging devices. (June-Sept. camping $4 per person per night, ages 9-16 $2; Oct.-May free. For an additional $20, reservations are accepted beginning in mid-Apr. for trips between June 15 and Oct. 31.) Reservations can be made in person at the Backcountry Permit Center at Apgar, St. Mary Visitors Center, Many Glacier Ranger Station, and Polebridge, or by writing to Backcountry Reservation Office, Glacier National Park, West Glacier, MT 59936. Pick up a free *Backcountry Camping Guide* from visitors centers or the **Backcountry Permit Center,** next to the visitors center in Apgar, which also has valuable info for those seeking to explore Glacier's less-traveled areas. (☎888-7857. Open daily July 7am-4pm; May-June and Sept. 8am-4pm.) **Medical Services: Kalispell Regional Medical Center,** 310 Sunny View Ln. (☎752-5111), north of Kalispell off Rte. 93. **North Valley Hospital,** 6575 Hwy. 93 in Whitefish (☎863-3500). **Post Office:** 110 Going-to-the-Sun Rd., in West Glacier. (☎888-5591. Open M-F 8:30am-12:30pm and 1:30-4:45pm.) **Postal Code:** 59936. **Area Code:** 406.

ACCOMMODATIONS

Staying indoors within Glacier National Park is expensive, but several affordable options lie just outside the park boundaries. On the west side of the park, the small, electricity-less town of ■**Polebridge** provides access to Glacier's remote and pristine northwest corner and is by far the best place in the area to see the park's two resident wolf camps. To get there from Apgar, take Camas Rd. north, then a right onto the poorly-marked gravel Outside North Fork Rd., just past a bridge over the North Fork of the Flathead River. (Avoid Inside North Fork Rd.—your car's shocks will surely thank you.) From Columbia Falls, take Rte. 486 N. To the east, inexpensive lodging is found just across the park border in **East Glacier. Glacier Park, Inc.** (☎756-2444; www.glacierparkinc.com) handles reservations for most in-park lodging.

■ **North Fork Hostel,** 80 Beaver Dr. (☎888-5241; www.nfhostel.com), in Polebridge; follow the signs through town. Wooden walls and kerosene lamps are reminiscent of a hunting retreat. Hot showers and fully-equipped kitchen, but no flush toilets. During the winter, wood-burning stoves warm frozen fingers after skiing or snowshoeing, and thick quilts keep guests warm at night. Call ahead for pickup from the West Glacier Amtrak station ($30-35). Canoes $20 per day; mountain bikes $15 per day; snowshoes $5 per day; nordic skis $5 per day. Showers $4 for non-guests. Linen $5. Check-in by 10pm. Check-out noon. Call ahead, especially in winter. Teepees $10 per person; dorms $15, $12 after 2 nights; cabins $30; log homes $65. AmEx/MC/V. ❶

Brownies Grocery (HI), 1020 Rte. 49 (☎226-4426), in East Glacier Park. Reception is in the grocery store; the hostel occupies the 2nd fl. Internet access $1.75 per 15min. Kitchen, showers, linens, laundry, and a stunning view. Key deposit $5. Check-in by 9pm; late arrivals call ahead. Check-out 10am. Reservations recommended; credit card required. Open May-Sept., weather permitting. Tent sites $10. Dorms $16, members $13; doubles $29/$26; room for 4-6 $41/$38. Extra bed $5. MC/V. ❶

Backpacker's Inn Hostel, 29 Dawson Ave. (☎226-9392), just east of the East Glacier Amtrak station and behind Serrano's Mexican Restaurant, Backpacker's Inn has 14 clean but narrow beds. Hot showers. Sleeping bags $1. Check-in by 10pm, at Serrano's. Open May-Sept. Dorms $10. Single room with queen-sized bed and full linen $20; double $30. ❶

Swiftcurrent Motor Inn (☎732-5531), 6 mi. from the entrance station in Many Glacier Valley, is one of the few budget motels in the area. Open early June to early Sept. 1-bedroom cabins $43; 2-bedroom cabins $53, with private bath $73. ❸

CAMPING

The Park Service runs 13 **campgrounds** ❶ in the park. All three visitors centers have updates on availability, though Logan Pass lags in accuracy due to a lack of electricity. The most popular campground on the east side is **Many Glacier,** whose amazing views cause it to fill by early afternoon; the 25 intimate sites at **Sprague Creek** are favorites on the west side (both $15). **Avalanche Creek,** conveniently located on the Going-to-the-Sun Rd., and **Two Medicine,** a more secluded campground in the eastern section of the park, have very pleasant sites and prime hiking access (both $15). The only reservable sites are at **Fish Creek** and **St. Mary,** two of Glacier's largest campgrounds. (Reservations ☎ 800-365-2267. Sites $17.)

FOOD

Polebridge Mercantile Store (☎ 888-5105), on Polebridge Loop Rd. ¼ mi. east of N. Fork Rd., has homemade pastries ($1-3) as splendid as the surrounding peaks. Gas, gifts, and groceries. Open daily June-Sept. 8am-9pm; Oct.-May 8am-6pm. MC/V. ❶

Northern Lights Saloon (☎ 888-5669), next to the Polebridge Mercantile. On Friday nights, locals and visitors flock to this friendly saloon for pizza ($10) and volleyball. On other nights, the saloon goes gourmet with dishes such as the "North Fork Pothole," a cacophony of rice, beans, and veggies ($7, with meat $9). The Montana-brewed pints ($3) are even tastier atop a tree-trunk bar stool. Open June-Sept. M-Th 4-9pm, F-Sa 5-9pm, Su 9am-noon and 4-9pm; bar open until midnight. Cash only. ❶

Two Sisters Cafe, (☎ 732-5535), 4 mi. north of St. Mary on Hwy. 89, near Babb. Locals rave about the sandwiches served with homemade potato chips ($7-9) at this personality-laden cafe. Try the St. Mary lake whitefish ($20), caught and processed locally. Open in summer daily 8am-9pm. MC/V. ❸

Whistle Stop Restaurant (☎ 226-9292), in East Glacier next to Brownies Grocery. Sample homemade delicacies at this restaurant best known for unbelievable deep-fried, huckleberry-injected french toast ($7). Open daily mid-May to mid-Sept. 7am-9pm; breakfast served until 11:30am. ❷

HIKING

Most of Glacier's spectacular scenery lies off the main roads and is accessible only by foot, though horses are also allowed on some trails. An extensive trail system has something for everyone, from short, easy day-hikes to rigorous backcountry expeditions. Stop by one of the visitors centers for maps with day-hikes. Beware of bears and mountain lions; ask the rangers about wildlife activity and specific safety precautions in the area in which you plan to hike.

Avalanche Lake (4 mi. round-trip, 3hr.) is a breathtaking trail and by far the most popular day-hike in the park. Starting north of Lake McDonald on Going-to-the-Sun Rd., this moderate hike climbs 500 ft. to picture-perfect panoramas.

Trail of the Cedars (¾ mi. loop, 20min.) begins at the same trailhead as Avalanche Lake and is an easy nature walk through the easternmost edge of the Pacific Rainforest. It also has a shorter, wheelchair-accessible section.

Numa Ridge Lookout (12 mi. round-trip, 9hr.) starts from the Bowman Lake Campground, northeast of Polebridge. After climbing 2930 ft., this challenging hike ends with sweeping vistas of Glacier's rugged northwest corner.

Grinnell Glacier Trail (11 mi. round-trip, 7hr.) passes within close proximity of several glaciers and follows along Grinnell Point and Mt. Grinnell, gaining a steady and moderate 1600 ft. Trailhead at the Many Glacier Picnic Area.

Hidden Lake Nature Trail (3 mi. round-trip, 2hr.), beginning at the Logan Pass Visitors Center, is a short and modest 460 ft. climb to a lookout of Hidden Lake and a chance to stretch your legs while winding along Going-to-the-Sun Rd.

◤ OUTDOOR ACTIVITIES

BIKING AND HORSEBACK RIDING

Opportunities for bicycling are limited and confined to designated bike paths; cycling on trails is prohibited. Although Going-to-the-Sun Rd. is a popular bike route, only experienced cyclists with legs of titanium should attempt this grueling ride; the sometimes nonexistent shoulder of the road can create hazardous situations. From mid-June to Labor Day, bike traffic is prohibited 11am-4pm from the Apgar campground to Sprague Creek and eastbound (uphill) from Logan Creek to Logan Pass. The Inside North Fork Rd., which runs from Kintla Lake to Fish Creek on the west side of the park, is good for mountain biking, as are the old logging roads in the Flathead National Forest. Ask at a visitors center for more details. **Glacier Cyclery** (☎862-6446), based in Whitefish, leads exciting "full moon" rides. Equestrians should check to make sure trails are open. Trail rides from **Mule Shoe Outfitters** (www.mule-shoe.com; open May to early Sept.; $47) are available at Many Glacier (☎732-4203) and Lake McDonald (☎888-5121).

BOATING

The **Glacier Park Boat Co.** (www.glacierparkboats.com) provides **boat tours** that explore all of Glacier's large lakes and surrounding peaks. Tours leave from: **Lake McDonald** (☎888-5727; 1hr., 5 per day, $10.50); **Many Glacier** (☎732-4480; 1¼hr., 7 per day, $13.50); **Rising Sun**, at St. Mary Lake (☎257-2426; 1-1½hr., 5 per day, $12-15); **Two Medicine** (☎226-4467; 45min., 5 per day, $10.50). Children ages 4-12 ride for half-price. The tours from Two Medicine, Rising Sun, and Many Glacier provide access to Glacier's backcountry. You can rent rowboats ($10 per hr.) at Lake McDonald, Many Glacier, Two Medicine, and Apgar; canoes ($10 per hr.) at Many Glacier, Two Medicine, and Apgar; kayaks ($10 per hr.) at Apgar and Many Glacier; and outboards ($17 per hr.) at Lake McDonald and Two Medicine. **Glacier Raft Co.,** in West Glacier, leads trips down the middle fork of the Flathead River. (☎888-5454 or 800-235-6781. Half-day $42, under 13 $32; full-day trip with lunch $73/$50.)

FISHING

The only permit required to fish in the park is the Montana state permit. Limits are generally high, but some areas are restricted, and certain species may be catch-and-release. Pick up *Fishing Regulations*, available at visitors centers. Lake Ellen Wilson, Gunsight Lake, and Elizabeth Lake are good places to sink a line. On Blackfeet tribal land, a special permit is needed.

WATERTON LAKES
NATIONAL PARK, ALBERTA ☎403

Canada's Waterton Lakes National Park, only a fraction of the size of its Montana neighbor, features spectacular scenery and activities without the summer crowds that plague Glacier. The tiny village of Waterton is a genuine alpine town, where the most complicated traffic jams are a result of wandering bighorn sheep.

BORDER CROSSING. Traveling between the US and Canada is generally an easy process, but security is still taken very seriously. Crossing can be as simple as a wave of the passport or as time-consuming as a full search of your car. To keep things moving along, make sure to have all necessary documents handy. It is illegal to cross the border anywhere except an open crossing station. See **Essentials** (p. 10) for more details on documents and procedures.

⚐ PRACTICAL INFORMATION. The one-day **entrance fee** is valid until 4pm the following day (CDN$6 per day, seniors CDN$5, ages 6-12 CDN$3; groups of up to seven people CDN$15). The only road from Waterton's entrance leads 5½ mi. south to **Waterton Park.** En route, stop at the **Waterton Lakes Visitors Center,** 5 mi. inside the park on Rte. 5, for a schedule of events and info about Waterton and the surrounding region. (☎859-5133. Open daily mid-May to Oct. 8am-7pm.) In winter, pick up info at **Park Administration,** 215 Mt. View Rd. (☎859-2224. Open M-F 8am-4pm.) Although businesses in the park accept US dollars, each has its own currency exchange rate. To get the most Canadian for the US dollar, exchange money at **Waterton Visitor Services,** 214 Mt. View Rd. in Tamarack Sq., which often has the best rate. (☎859-2378; www.watertonvisitorservices.com. Open daily July-Aug. 8am-6:30pm; May-June and Sept.-Oct. usually 8am-6pm.) **Pat's Gas and Cycle Rental,** 224 Mt. View Rd., Waterton, rents bikes. (☎859-2266. Path bikes CDN$8 for 1st hr., CDN$5 each additional hr., CDN$34 per day. Full suspension mountain bikes CDN$11/$45.) **Post Office:** In Waterton, on Windflower Ave. (☎859-2294. Open M, W, F 8:30am-4:30pm, Tu and Th 8:30am-4pm.) **Postal Code:** T0K 2M0. **Area Code:** 403

⌂ ACCOMMODATIONS AND FOOD. Camping in the park is very affordable. **Crandell ❶,** in a forest area on the road to Red Rock Canyon, has flush toilets and running water but no showers. (Open mid-May to late Sept. Sites CDN$19.) **Belly River ❶,** outside the park entrance on Chief Mountain Hwy. 3 mi. north of the border, has scenic, uncrowded primitive sites with pit toilets and water. (☎859-2224. Open mid-May to mid-Sept. Sites CDN$14.) Camp with 100 of your best RV pals at **Townsite ❶** in Waterton Park, which has showers and a lakeside vista, but no privacy. The walk-in sites are in a pleasant field totally separate from the RVs and are usually the last to fill. (Open mid-Apr. to late Oct. Walk-in sites CDN$21; sites CDN$24, full hookup CDN$33.) **Backcountry camping** requires a permit from the visitors center. Campsites are rarely full, and several, including **Crandell Lake ❶,** are less than an hour's hike from the trailhead. (☎859-5133. Permit CDN$9 per person per night. Reserve up to 90 days in advance for an additional CDN$12.) The **Waterton Alpine Hostel (HI) ❶,** in the Waterton Lakes Lodge, provides the cheapest indoor lodging. (☎859-2150 or 888-985-634. Discounted rate to fitness room and pool next door. Laundry and kitchen. CDN$35, members CDN$31. CDN$85 credit card deposit required. AmEx/MC/V.) It's simple to eat at **Pizza of Waterton ❷,** 103 Fountain Ave., where CDN$13 buys an 8in. pizza, a "make-your-own pasta," or a calzone. (859-2660. Open in summer daily noon-midnight; May to mid-June and mid-Sept. to mid-Nov. M-F 5-11pm, Sa-Su noon-midnight. MC/V.) The 9 in. subs at **The Big Scoop ❶,** on Waterton Ave., are a steal at CDN$6. (☎859-2346. Open May-Oct. M-Sa 10am-10pm, Su 1:30-10pm. AmEx/MC/V.)

EMERGENCY INFORMATION. Waterton Lakes does not have ☎911 service. In a park emergency, call the warden, ☎589-2636. For town emergencies, call the police, ☎859-2244. The nearest hospitals are in Cardston (☎653-4411) or Pincher Creek (☎627-3333).

⚞ OUTDOOR ACTIVITIES. Waterton Lakes has 120 mi. of trails of varying difficulty. A few of these trails link up with the trail network of Glacier National Park.
The **Hiker Shuttle** runs from Tamarack Village Sq., in town, to many trailheads.
(☎859-2378. Call the night before for reservations. CDN$10.) The moderately easy,
rolling **Waterton Lakeshore Trail** (8 mi., 4hr.) extends the length of the western shore
of Upper Waterton Lake, from Waterton townsite to Goat Haunt, MT, with great
views of the surrounding peaks. At the trail's end, the **Waterton Inter-Nation Shoreline Cruise Co.** will shuttle hikers back to Waterton (CDN$15). The cruise company
also ferries visitors to the trailhead for the popular **Crypt Lake Trail** (11 mi. round-
trip, 2297 ft. elevation gain, 6-7hr.), which trickles past waterfalls in a narrow canyon, through a 65 ft. natural tunnel, and onto a ridge that requires a cable for balance in the wind. After 5½ mi., it arrives at the icy Crypt Lake, which straddles the
international border. The Waterton Marina also runs a 2hr. **boat tour** of Upper
Waterton Lake. (☎859-2362. Crypt Lake water taxi: departs Waterton 9 and 10am;
returns from Crypt Landing 4 and 5:30pm. Round-trip CDN$14, ages 13-17 CDN$7,
ages 4-12 CDN$6.50. Tour: CDN$27, ages 13-17 CDN$14, ages 4-12 CDN$10. Open
mid-May to mid-Sept. Cash or traveler's checks only.) Taking a boat to Goat Haunt
is a wonderful way to start hiking deep in Glacier-Waterton's backcountry; a picture ID is necessary to go through customs at the ranger station. Horses are
allowed on many trails. **Alpine Stables,** ¾ mi. north of the village, conducts trail
rides. (☎859-2462. Open May-Sept. daily 9am-5pm. CDN$25.)

Fishing in Waterton requires a **license,** available from the visitors center (CDN$8
per day, CDN$25 per year). Popular fishing spots include the creeks that spill from
Cameron Lake, just east of the parking lot, and Crandell Lake, a 1 mi. hike. Rent
rowboats, paddleboats, kayaks, or canoes at **Cameron Lake Boat Rentals.** (☎859-
2396. CDN$22 first hr. for 2 people, CDN$17 each additional hr. Open daily June
15-Sept. 15 7:30am-7:30pm. Cash only.) Two popular scenic drives are **Cameron
Lake** and **Red Rock Canyon**, which has a 700m walk at the end as well as a 1km trail
to Blakiston Falls. The visitors center has more info.

IDAHO

The Rocky Mountains divide the state of Idaho into three distinct regions, each
with its own natural aesthetic. Northern Idaho possesses the greatest concentration of lakes in the western US, interspersed with lush, green valleys and rugged
mountain peaks. In central Idaho, ski slopes, hiking trails, and hot springs span
across the semi-arid landscape. To the southeast, world-famous potatoes are cultivated in valleys rich with volcanic sediment. Averaging just over 15 people per sq.
mi., much of the state is virtually untouched wilderness and national forest, making Idaho a mecca for outdoors enthusiasts. Idaho's towns and cities are also
worth exploring; the mountain outposts have an appeal all their own.

◪ PRACTICAL INFORMATION

Capital: Boise.

Visitor Info: Idaho Department of Commerce, 700 W. State St., P.O. Box 83720, Boise
83720 (☎208-334-2470 or 800-842-5858; www.visitid.org). **State Parks and Recreation
Dept.,** 5657 Warm Springs Ave., Boise 83716 (☎208334-4199). Open M-F 8am-5pm.
Idaho Outfitters and Guide Association, P.O. Box 95, Boise 83702 (☎800-494-3246;
www.ioga.org). Open in winter 8am-4:30pm; shorter hours in summer.

Postal Abbreviation: ID. **Sales Tax:** 6%. **Area Code:** 208.

ROCKY MOUNTAINS

BOISE ☎208

Built along the banks of the Boise River, Idaho's surprisingly cosmopolitan capital straddles the boundary between desert and mountains. A network of parks protects the natural landscape of the river banks, creating a greenbelt perfect for walking, biking, or in-line skating. Most of the city's sights cluster in the 10-block grid between the capitol and the river, making it easy to get around downtown.

◪◪ ORIENTATION AND PRACTICAL INFORMATION. The **Grove** is Boise's pedestrian-friendly town plaza, and its brick walkway extends along 8th St. between Main and Front St., the two main downtown thoroughfares. Front St. becomes I-184, sometimes called the Downtown Connector, at its west end. **Greyhound,** 1212 W. Bannock St., a few blocks west of downtown, runs to Portland (11hr., 2 per day, $55), Salt Lake City (7hr., 2 per day, $57), and Seattle (14hr., 3 per day, $53) daily. (☎343-3681; www.greyhound.com. Open M-Tu and F 6am-11:30pm, W-Th 6am-noon and 5-11:30pm, Sa-Su 6-11:30am and 7-11:30pm.) **Valley Ride** has several routes through the city. (☎336-1010. Buses operate M-F 5:15am-7:40pm, Sa 7:45am-6:45pm. $1, children $0.65, seniors/disabled $0.50. Maps available at the visitors center.) **McU Sports,** 822 W. Jefferson St., rents outdoor gear and offers hiking tips. (☎342-7734. Open M-Sa 9:30am-6pm, Su 11am-5pm. Mountain bikes $15 per half-day, $25 per day.) McU also has a ski shop, 2314 Bogus Basin Rd., at Bogus Basin, Boise's local ski area. (☎336-2300. Ski rental $17, children $15.) **Visitor Info: Downtown Boise Visitors Centre,** 245 8th St., at Boise Centre on the Grove. (☎344-5338. Open M-F 10am-4pm, Sa 10am-2pm.) **Internet Access: Boise Public Library,** 715 S. Capitol Blvd. (☎384-4076. Open M-Th 10am-9pm, F 10am-6pm, Sa 10am-5pm; Sept.-May also open Su noon-5pm.) **Post Office:** 750 W. Bannock St. (☎331-0037. Open M-F 8:30am-5pm.) **Postal Code:** 83702. **Area Code:** 208.

♖ ACCOMMODATIONS. Chain motels are concentrated around Exit 53 off I-84, near the airport. For those willing to drive 20min. to the nearby town of Nampa, **◪Hostel Boise (HI) ❶,** 17322 Can-Ada Rd., is a spectacular, inexpensive option with mountain views and evening campfires. Take Exit 38 off I-84 W and turn right onto Garrity Blvd., which turns into Can-Ada Rd. (☎467-6858. Airport pick-up or drop-off $10. Linen $1.50. Internet access $1 per 20min. 3-night max. stay. Check-in 5-10:30pm. Dorms $17, members $14; private room $31-35, $5 per additional person. MC/V.) **◪Bond Street Motel Apartments ❷,** 1680 N. Phillippi St., right off Fairview Ave. between Curtis and Orchard, rents beautiful, fully furnished studios and one-bedroom apartments with fully stocked kitchens. From I-184 take the Curtis St. exit. (☎322-4407 or 800-545-5345. Office open M-F 8am-5pm. Reservations recommended. Studio $49; 1 bedroom $55. Call for lower weekly rates. AmEx/D/MC/V.) The **University Inn ❸,** 2360 University Dr., next to Boise State University, has cable TV, continental breakfast, a free airport shuttle, and a pool and jacuzzi. (☎345-7170 or 800-345-7170. Singles $52-59; doubles $52-62. AmEx/D/DC/MC/V.) For those looking to stay downtown, the **Boise Centre Guest Lodge ❸,** 1314 Grove St., at the corner of 14th and Grove, offers simple rooms and an outdoor pool for reasonable rates. (☎342-9351. Rooms $41-55 during slow periods, higher at busier times. AmEx/D/DC/MC/V.) The **Boise National Forest/Bureau of Land Management Office,** 1387 S. Vinnell Way, near Exit 50a from I-84, provides info on RV-oriented **campgrounds ❶** and the campgrounds in the National Forest land surrounding Boise, which usually cost $10-12 per night. (☎373-4007. Open M-F 7:45am-4:30pm.)

◪◪ FOOD AND NIGHTLIFE. Boise offers much more than spuds for hungry budget travelers. The downtown area, centered around 8th and Main St., bustles with lunchtime delis, coffeeshops, ethnic cuisine, and several stylish bistros.

Moon's Kitchen ❶, 815 W. Bannock St., a vintage diner open since 1955, has blended malts ($4.50) and heaping chili burgers. (☎385-0472. Breakfast $4.50-7. Burgers $6.75-8.50. Open M-Sa 7:15am-7:30pm, Su 9am-2pm. AmEx/MC/V.) Locals throng to **Zeppole Baking Company ❶**, 217 N. 8th St., to enjoy gourmet sandwiches and fresh-baked bread at a steal. (☎345-2149. Lunch combos $4-5. Open M-Sa 7am-5pm, Su 8am-4pm. Cash only.) **Gernika Basque Pub & Eatery ❷**, 202 S. Capitol Blvd., is the place to experience unique Spanish cuisine. Try the sandwiches with pork loin, lamb, or chorizo, and finish off with rice pudding. (☎344-2175. Sandwiches $6-8. Open M 11am-11pm, Tu-Th 11am-midnight, F-Sa 11am-1am. AmEx/D/MC/V.) For fresh and creative vegetarian food, juice, and smoothies, try **Kulture Klatsch ❷**, 409 S. 8th St. (☎345-0452. Breakfast $4-7. Lunch $6-8. Dinner $7-10. Live jazz, folk, or rock Tu-Th 8-10pm, F-Sa 9-11pm, Su 11am-1pm. Open M 7am-3pm, Tu-Th 7am-10pm, F 7am-11pm, Sa 8am-11pm, Su 8am-3pm. MC/V.) Upstairs at **The Balcony Club,** 150 N. 8th St., #226, one block from the Grove, DJs spin nightly and 10 TVs surround the dance floor. All kinds of people gather at this gay-friendly bar to dance, relax on the outdoor terrace, and play pool. (☎336-1313. Cover F-Sa $3. Open daily 2pm-2am.) Cheap drinks and nightly live music draw locals to the **Blues Bouquet,** 1010 Main St. (☎345-6605. Drink specials every night $1-2. 21+. Cover M-Th and Su $1, F-Sa $3. Open M-Sa 5pm-2am, Su 8pm-2am.)

⑤ SIGHTS. The logical starting point for exploring Boise is **Julia Davis Park** (☎384-4240) at Myrtle St. and Capitol Blvd, with paddleboating, a bandshell featuring free summer entertainment, extensive rose gardens, and several of Boise's most popular museums. The **Boise Tour Train and River Float,** which covers about 75 city sights in 1¼hr., starts and ends in the park. Train tours can be followed by relaxing raft floats down the Boise River, with guides focusing on wildlife and plant lore. (☎342-4796. Tours Apr.-May Sa-Su 1, 2:30pm; late May-early Sept. M-Sa 10, 11:15am, 12:30, 1:45, 3pm; Su noon, 1:15, 2:30, 3:45pm; autumn W-Su noon, 1:30, 3pm. $7.50, with river float $30; ages 64+ $7/$27.50; ages 3-12 $5/$17.) Learn about Idaho and the Old West at the **Idaho Historical Museum,** 610 Julia Davis Dr., in the park, which showcases replicas of a 19th-century bar, high-class Idahoan parlors, and working-class homesteads, as well as Native American artifacts and displays on Idaho's Basque and Chinese populations. (☎334-2120. Open M-Sa 9am-5pm, in summer also Su 1-5pm. Adults $2, ages 6-18 $1, under 6 free.) Nearby, the **Boise Art Museum,** 670 Julia Davis Dr., displays works by artists from the northwest US. (☎345-8330; www.boiseartmuseum.org. Open M-W and F-Sa 10am-5pm, Th 10am-8pm, Su noon-5pm; Sept.-May closed M. $5, college students and ages 61+ $3, ages 6-18 $1. First Th of every month free.)

One of Boise's must-see attractions is the **Old Idaho State Penitentiary,** 2445 Old Penitentiary Rd. The penitentiary, in operation from 1870 to 1973, allows visitors to explore the 19th-century cells, death row, gallows, and solitary confinement areas. (☎334-2844. Open daily Memorial Day-Labor Day 10am-5pm; low season daily noon-5pm. $5, ages 6-18 $3.) On the grounds next to the penitentiary, the **Idaho Botanical Garden,** 2355 N. Penitentiary Rd., has extensive horticultural displays, including rose, herb, alpine, English, meditation, and water gardens. (☎343-8649 or 877-527-8233. Open M-F 9am-5pm, Sa-Su 10am-6pm. $4, 65+ $3, ages 6-18 $2.) A few miles south of Boise, the **World Center for Birds of Prey,** 566 W. Flying Hawk Ln., offers an up-close look at 10 rare and striking birds of prey, including California condors, harpy eagles, and bald eagles. From I-84, take Exit 50 and go south 6 mi. on S. Cole. (☎362-8687. Open daily Mar.-Oct. 9am-5pm; Nov.-Feb. 10am-4pm. $4, 61+ $3, ages 4-16 $2.) The fascinating **Basque Museum and Cultural Center,** 611 Grove St. at the corner of Grove St. and Capitol Blvd., offers an interpretive exhibit about Idaho's Basque population and its old-world heritage. (☎343-2671. Open Tu-F 10am-4pm, Sa 11am-3pm. Free.) The

Museum of Mining and Geology, 2455 N. Penitentiary Rd., has displays on mining, geology, gems, and fossils. (☎368-9876. Open Apr.-Oct. W-Su noon-5pm. Free.) For those looking for a bit of hiking, the parking lot for the Penitentiary offers access to a segment of Boise's **Ridge to Rivers trail network.** (☎368-9876; www.ridgetorivers.org. Open Apr.-Oct. W-Su noon-5pm. Free.)

🎭 **ENTERTAINMENT.** In the **Alive After Five** series, live music infuses the Grove from May to August, every Wednesday 5-8pm. On **First Thursday,** the first Thursday of each month from 5 to 9pm, stores throughout Boise host creative entertainment, ranging from free samples and giveaways to DJs and live music. (For both: ☎472-5200; www.downtownboise.org.) The **Capital City Public Market** takes over N. 8th St. between Main and Bannock St. from mid-April to October, every Saturday 9:30am-1:30pm, vending local produce and crafts. The **Boise River Greenbelt** provides over 20 miles of paved paths that extend along the Boise River. Fishing and tubing along the Greenbelt are popular summer pursuits. The ever-growing **Idaho Shakespeare Festival** hits town from June to September. (☎429-9908; www.idahoshakespeare.org. Tickets $18-26.) In late June, the **Spirit of Boise Balloon Classic** features hot-air balloons, a carnival, live music, and a scuba tank. (☎338-8887. Free.) Upcoming events are listed in Thursday's *Boise Weekly*.

KETCHUM AND SUN VALLEY ☎208

In 1935, Union Pacific chairman Averill Harriman sent Austrian Count Felix Schaffgotsch to scour the western US for a site to develop into a ski resort that would rival Europe's best. After traveling for months, the Count stumbled onto the small mining and sheep-herding town of Ketchum in Idaho's Wood River Valley and was awestruck. Harriman immediately purchased the land and built the world's first chairlift. Sun Valley was quickly recognized as a world-class ski resort, fulfilling Harriman's dream. The permanent population is only 5600, but traffic extends for miles in each direction in peak months. Skiing reigns supreme in winter, while biking, hiking, and fishing draw thrill-seekers in the summer.

🛈 **PRACTICAL INFORMATION.** The best times to visit Sun Valley are winter and summer. The town slows down in the low season (Oct.-Nov. and May-early June), but during these periods accommodations offer lower rates and the natural beauty remains unchanged. Most of the food and nightlife centers around Main St. (Rte. 75) in Ketchum. **Sun Valley Express** picks up door-to-door in the Sun Valley/ Ketchum area and runs daily to the Boise airport. (☎877-622-8267; www.sunvalleyexpress.com. 3hr. Leaves Sun Valley 8:30am; Dec.-Mar. also 6:30am and 12:30pm. Leaves Boise 2:45pm; Dec.-Mar. also 12:45 and 5:45pm. Closed late Oct. to late Nov. $59, under 12 $49; Dec.-Mar. and Aug. $69/$59. All vans TV/VCR equipped. Reservations required.) **KART,** Ketchum's bus service, has service in the city and the surrounding area. (☎726-7576. Runs daily 7:30am-midnight. Door-to-door service for disabled and elderly. Free.) **Visitor Info: Sun Valley/Ketchum Chamber & Visitors Bureau,** 251 Washington St. in Ketchum; follow signs from Main St. (☎725-2100 or 800-634-3347, ext. 2100; www.visitsunvalley.com. Open Nov.-Apr. and July-Sept. daily 9am-6pm; May-June and Oct. M-Sa 9am-5:30pm.) **Internet Access: Community Library,** 415 Spruce Ave. (☎726-3493. Open M and Sa 9am-6pm, Tu and Th noon-9pm, W 9am-9pm, F 1-6pm. Free.) **Post Office:** 151 W. 4th St. (☎726-5161. Open M-F 8am-5:30pm, Sa 11am-2pm.) **Postal Code:** 83340. **Area Code:** 208.

🏠 **ACCOMMODATIONS.** From early June to mid-October, camping is by far the best option for cheap sleep in the Sun Valley area. Check with the **Ketchum Ranger Station,** 206 Sun Valley Rd., just outside of Ketchum on the way to Sun Valley.

(☎622-5371. Open M-F 8:30am-5pm.) **Boundary Campground ❶**, 3 mi. northeast of town on Trail Creek Rd. past the Sun Valley resort, is closest to town and has eight wooded sites near a creek, as well as restrooms, water, and a picnic area. (7-night max. stay. Sites $10.) **Federal Gulch ❶** and **Sawmill Campground ❶**, both 15 mi. southeast of Ketchum on E. Fork Rd. off Hwy. 75, have three free sites amid groves of aspen trees with restrooms, grills, picnic areas, and a 3-day max. stay. Up Rte. 75 in the Sawtooth National Recreation Area (SNRA; p. 767) lie several scenic camping spots; **Murdock ❶** (11 sites with water; $10) and **Caribou ❶** (7 sites, no water; $8) are cheapest. They are, respectively, 2 and 3 mi. up the unpaved, but 2WD-suitable, N. Fork Rd., which begins as a paved road to the right of the visitors center. **North Fork ❶** (29 sites; $11) and **Wood River ❶** (30 sites; $11) are 8 and 10 mi. north of Ketchum, respectively, along Rte. 75, and are popular fishing spots along Big Wood River. Take the first campground road north of the SNRA headquarters. For comfortable rooms, refrigerators, an outdoor jacuzzi, and continental breakfast, try the **Lift Tower Lodge ❸**, 703 S. Main St. (☎726-5163 or 800-462-8646. Singles $66, each additional adult $10. AmEx/D/MC/V.) **Bald Mountain Lodge ❹**, 100 Picabo St., in the village at the base of the Warm Springs lift area, offers several expansive studios (as well as more expensive one-bedroom suites), complete with kitchenette. (☎726-4776. High-season studios $90, low-season $75. AmEx/D/MC/V.)

🍴 **FOOD AND NIGHTLIFE.** Ketchum's small confines bulge with over 90 restaurants, mostly catering to resort-goers' gourmet tastes, but relatively cheap food is available. **Strega Inc. ❸**, 360 1st Ave. N, is both an organic restaurant and a tea house (not to mention boutique), and offers three menus: the first with food, the second with tea, and the third with imported beers and wines. (☎726-6463. Salad and crepes $5-10. Gourmet pizza $12-14. Tea $2-8. Free wireless Internet. Open M-Th and Su 11am-10pm, F-Sa 11am-11pm. AmEx/MC/V.) Beer cans of all shapes and sizes grace the walls of **Grumpy's ❶**, 860 Warm Springs Rd., a flavorful hangout with a porch and views of the nearby resort. (Burgers $4.50-5.50. Goblet of beer $3.50. Open daily 11am-10pm.) Build your own burrito at **KB's Ketchum Burritos ❷**, on the corner of 6th and Washington St., or choose from their selection of "favorite" burritos ($8, vegetarian $6.25). Locals rave about the fish tacos and quesadillas. (☎726-2232. Open daily 11:30am-9pm. AmEx/D/DC/MC/V.) Chase back some stiff drinks at **Whiskey Jacques**, 251 N. Main St., which has nine televisions for sports junkies and $1 drink specials on Sunday and Tuesday. (☎726-5297. Live music most nights 9:30pm-2am. Happy hour daily 4-7pm. 21+ after 9pm. Cover $5. Open daily 4pm-2am. Kitchen open 5-9pm.) Head to the **Cellar Pub**, downstairs at 400 Sun Valley Rd., near Leadville Ave., for a young crowd, excellent burgers ($8-9), and inventive pints like the "straight jacket," Fog Horn beer and Jäger. (☎622-3832. 21+ after 10pm. Open daily 5pm-2am. Kitchen open until 10pm.)

🏔 **OUTDOOR ACTIVITIES.** The **Wood River and Sun Valley trail system** consists of over 20 mi. of paved trails for bikers, skiers, skaters, joggers, and horseback riders. The trail starts in Bellevue and parallels Hwy. 75 north through Ketchum and east around Dollar Mountain to Sun Valley, passing ski slopes and historic sites. The *Wood River Trails* pamphlet, available at the visitors center, has more info. Visible for miles, **Bald Mountain** is a beacon for serious skiers. Two plazas serve "Baldy"—River Run on the north side of town and Warm Springs on the south. Need some practice? The gentle slopes of **Dollar Mountain** are perfect for beginners. (☎622-6136, ski conditions 800-635-4150. Full-day lift ticket $67, 12 and under $38; half-day $50/$32. 2hr. beginner's lesson $45, beginner's package with lessons, rental, and lift ticket $85.) The **Nordic & Snowshoe Center**, behind Sun Valley Lodge, has 25 mi. of marked trails for cross-country skiing and snowshoe trekking. (☎800-786-8259. Full-day pass $13, ages 6-12 $7. Ski rental $16, snowshoe rental $15.

Group ski clinic $25.) If skiing isn't your thing, take a high-speed chairlift to the top of Bald Mountain and ride down on a mountain bike during the summer. (☎622-2231. Open in summer daily 9am-3:45pm. $15, day-pass $20; ages 3-12 $7/$10.) **The Elephant's Perch,** 280 East Ave., at Sun Valley Rd., has a complete stock of outdoor gear. (☎726-3497. Open M-Sa 9am-6pm, Su 10am-5pm. Bikes $15 per 4hr., $20 per day. Backpacks $15 per day. Tents $20 per day. Nordic ski packages $15-25 per day.) Inquire about biking trails at the visitors center or the SNRA Headquarters.

The **Sun Valley Summer Symphony,** behind the Sun Valley Lodge on the Esplanade, offers free open-air chamber and orchestral concerts in the first two weeks of August. (☎622-5607 for exact dates. Concerts 6:30-7:30pm.) **Rock, Latin,** and **bluegrass bands** gather at the public park on 1st St. and Washington Ave. every Wednesday in summer for a free show starting at 7:30pm. After a hard day on the trails, locals soak their weary legs in **hot springs** hidden in Ketchum's hills and canyons. Melting snow and rain can render the springs inaccessible in spring and early summer, but they are safe for swimming once the current subsides in July. The visitors center has suggestions on which pools are safe and accessible. One of the more accessible, non-commercial springs is **Warfield Hot Springs,** on largely unpaved Warm Springs Rd., 11 mi. west of Ketchum, which lingers right around 100°F. The commercial **Easley Hot Springs** is 12 mi. north of Ketchum on Rte. 75. (☎726-7522. Open in summer Tu and Th-Sa 11am-7pm, W 11am-5pm, Su noon-5pm; winter Sa 11am-5pm, Su noon-5pm. $6, under 15 $5, seniors $4.50.) For info on fishing, including equipment rentals, stop by **Silver Creek Outfitters,** 500 N. Main St. (☎726-5282 or 800 732-5687. Open M-Sa 9am-6pm, Su 9am-5pm; longer in high season.)

SAWTOOTH RECREATION AREA   ☎208

Established by Congress in 1972, the Sawtooth National Recreation Area (SNRA) sprawls over 756,000 acres—nearly the size of Rhode Island—including 217,000 acres of untouched wilderness. The park is home to four mountain ranges with more than 40 peaks over 10,000 ft.; the glacier-scoured Sawtooth and White Cloud Mountains tower above the surrounding landscape in the north, while the Smoky and Boulder Mountains dominate the southern horizon. Over 300 alpine lakes and the headwaters of four of Idaho's major rivers are situated in the park's dense forest. Needless to say, there is ample opportunity for world-class outdoor adventure.

◼️🔼 ORIENTATION AND PRACTICAL INFORMATION. The tiny, frontier-style town of **Stanley** (pop. 100), 60 mi. north of Ketchum on Hwy. 21, near the intersection with Hwy. 75, serves as a northern base for exploring Sawtooth. The main drag is located one block south of Rte. 21, along Ace of Diamonds St. **Lower Stanley** is a continuation of the business region and lies 1 mi. north of Stanley on Hwy. 75. The **Stanley Ranger Station,** 3 mi. south of Stanley on Rte. 75, has maps and SNRA passes. (☎774-3000. Open M-F 8:30am-noon and 1-4:30pm.) The **Redfish Lake Visitors Center** provides additional info, including free educational programs about wildlife and geology. The center also has a small museum about the Redfish Lake area. (☎774-3376. Open mid-June to early Sept. daily 9am-5pm; late May to mid-June Sa-Su 9am-5pm. Ranger programs nightly 9pm.) **Sawtooth National Recreation Area (SNRA) Headquarters,** 9 mi. north of Ketchum off Rte. 75, stocks detailed info on area forests, trails, and hot springs. (☎727-5013 or 800-260-5970. Open daily in summer 8:30am-5pm; winter 9am-3:30pm.) **Chamber of Commerce:** on Hwy. 21. (☎774-3411 or 800-878-7950; www.stanleycc.org. Open in summer daily 9am-5pm; reduced hours in winter.) **Internet Access: Stanley Community Library,** 33 Ace of Diamonds St. (☎774-2470. Open M noon-8pm, Tu-W and Sa noon-4pm, Th noon-6pm, F 8am-4pm. Unlimited use $3.) **Post Office:** 36 Ace of Diamonds St. (☎774-2230. Open M-F 8-11am and noon-5pm.) **Postal Code:** 83278. **Area Code:** 208.

ACCOMMODATIONS. For a real bed after a day in the wilderness, Stanley provides a few reasonably-priced options. Stay in motel rooms with a kitchenette or actual log cabins at **Jerry's Country Store: Salmon River Cabins and Motel ❸**, 19055 Hwy. 75 in Lower Stanley. (☎774-3566 or 800-972-4627. Rooms $75; cabins $60-70. AmEx/D/DC/MC/V.) **Redfish Lake Lodge ❸**, about 5 mi. south of Stanley on the shores of Redfish Lake, has comfy, historic lodge rooms and cabins come with refrigerators and kitchen areas. (☎774-3536. Rooms $62, cabins $120-170. AmEx/D/MC/V.) The SNRA also boasts 33 campgrounds throughout the park. (Reservations ☎877-444-6777; www.reserveusa.com.) **Alturas Lake ❶**, 21 mi. south of Stanley on Rte. 75 (the Alturas Lake Rd. turnoff is marked about 10 mi. north of Galena Pass), has three first come, first served campgrounds with fishing and swimming nearby. These 55 sites offer greater privacy and are more scenic than some other area campgrounds. (Vault toilets and water. $10.) The **Redfish Lake Campgrounds ❶**, 5 mi. south of Stanley off Rte. 75, are sometimes overcrowded but are close to Stanley and have a number of trailheads. (Sites $13 with 6- to 10-day max. stay.) East on Rte. 75, past Lower Stanley, the **Salmon River Corridor Campgrounds ❶** offer several camping options close to whitewater rafting, including **Salmon River, Casino Creek, Mormon Bend, and Upper and Lower O'Brian.** (Water available; no hookup. First come, first served. 10-day max. stay. Sites $11.) Showers are $2.50 at **Papa Brunee's Laundromat** on Ace of Diamonds St. in Stanley.

FOOD AND NIGHTLIFE. Dining options are somewhat limited in Stanley, but much of what's there is quite good. **Papa Brunee's Restaurant ❷**, on Ace of Diamonds St. downtown, serves deli sandwiches, meat-laden calzones, and pizzas with names like "The Bullfighter." (☎774-2536. 12 in. pizzas $8-10. Large calzone $6-8. Sandwiches $5.15. Open daily 11am-10pm. AmEx/D/MC/V.) The cozy **Stanley Baking Co. ❷**, 14 Wall St., offers wraps and sandwiches prepared on fresh bread. (☎774-6573. Breakfast $7.50-10.50. Lunch $8-10. Open daily 7am-2pm. MC/V.) For no-nonsense burgers and dogs, stop in at **Jimbo's Burg-R-Q ❶**, a stand along Hwy. 75 at the eastern edge of Lower Stanley. (Burgers from $4.75. Hot dogs $2.50. Open M-Tu and F-Sa 11am-8pm.) Stock up on food, gas, and fishing licenses at **Jerry's Country Store and Motel,** on Rte. 75 in Lower Stanley. (☎774-3566 or 800-972-4627. Open May-Sept. M-Sa 9am-9pm, Su 9am-5pm; winter hours vary.) Get your drinks at the **Kasino Club,** Ace of Diamonds St., complete with pool, foosball, and live music on the weekends. (☎774-3516. Open daily 6pm-midnight, longer hours on weekends).

OUTDOOR ACTIVITIES. The **Sawtooth Scenic Byway** (Rte. 75) spans 60 mi. of National Forest land between Ketchum and Stanley, following the Big Wood River and crossing Galena Pass at 8701 ft. Pause at **Galena Overlook,** 31 mi. north of Ketchum, which rises 2000 ft. above the plain below and provides one of the finest views in the Rockies. The SNRA's backcountry is perfect for hiking, boating, fishing, and mountain biking. Pick up a free map and inquire about trail conditions at SNRA Headquarters before heading into the park, particularly in early summer, when trails may be flooded. Much of the backcountry stays buried in snow well into the warm weather. Also watch out for black bears—ranger stations have info about necessary precautions. **Redfish Lake** is the source of many trails. Some popular, leisurely hikes include those to **Fishhook Creek** (4½ mi. round-trip, elevation gain 250 ft., excellent for children), **Bench Lakes** (8 mi. round-trip, elevation gain 1225 ft.), and the **Marshall Lake trail** (10 mi. round-trip, elevation gain 1500 ft.). Keep an eye out for native ospreys, Lincoln's sparrows, and ruby-crowned kinglets. The long, gentle loop around **Yellow Belly, Toxaway,** and **Petit Lakes** (16 mi. round-trip, elevation gain 1680 ft.) is a moderate overnight trip suitable for novice hikers. Starting at the **Inlet Trailhead** on the southern end of Redfish Lake, the challenging 10½ mi. round-trip trail to **Alpine Lake** (elevation gain 1800 ft.) rewards hikers with stunning views. Redfish Lake Lodge operates ferries to and from the south end of the lake to access the trailhead (one-way $6).

The Sawtooth Mountains have miles of mountain biking, but check a map: biking is prohibited in the Sawtooth Wilderness. **Riverwear,** on Rte. 21 in Stanley, rents bikes. (☎774-3592. Open daily 7am-10pm. Front suspension $22 per day, full suspension $32.) The 18 mi. **Fischer/Williams Creek Loop,** starting at the Williams Creek trailhead 10 mi. south of Stanley, is the most popular trail, ascending from 6800 ft. to an elevation of 8280 ft. Beginners will enjoy the dirt road that accesses the North Fork campgrounds from SNRA Headquarters. This passage parallels the North Fork of the Wood River for 5 mi. before branching off into narrow, steep trails for more experienced riders. The trails can be combined into loops; consult a trail map or a ranger. Advanced bikers can take on the challenging **Stanley Basin Trail** (20 mi. round-trip, elevation gain 2500 ft.), which ascends from the Stanley Creek turn-off. The steep **Boulder Basin Road,** 5 mi. from the SNRA Headquarters, leads to pristine Boulder Lake and an old mining camp.

Topographical maps ($6) and detailed trail books ($6-12) are available at **McCoy's Tackle and Gift Shop,** on Ace of Diamonds St., in addition to sporting goods, fishing tackle, and licenses. (☎774-3377. Licenses $11 for the first day, $4 each additional day. Open June-Sept. daily 8am-8pm; low-season hours vary.) **Sawtooth Adventure Company,** on Rte. 75 in Lower Stanley, rents kayaks and rafts and leads guided kayak, Class IV whitewater rafting, and fly-fishing trips along the Salmon River. (☎866-774-4644. Open daily May-Sept. 7am-9pm. Kayaks $25-50 per day. Rafts for 8 people $75 per day. Half-day kayak trips $30-65. Full-day fly-fishing trips $225.) For boat tours of the lake, head for **Redfish Lake Lodge Marina.** (☎774-3536. Open in summer daily 7am-8:30pm. 1hr. tours $10, ages 6-12 $5; 4-person min. Paddleboats $5 per 30min. Canoes $10 per hr., $32 per half-day, $50 per day. Single-person kayaks $7/$20/$35, doubles $10/$32/$50. Outboards $15/$50/$80. Aquacycles $15 per hr.) The least expensive way to enjoy the SNRA waters is to visit the hot springs just east of Stanley (info available at Chamber of Commerce; see **Practical Information** above). **Sunbeam Hot Springs,** 10 mi. northeast of Stanley on Rte. 75, triumphs over the rest at a scalding 150°F, though the water can be mixed with river water for a more pleasant soaking experience (river may be too high in late spring/early summer). The natural rock pools of **Kem Hot Springs,** 6 mi. northeast of Stanley on Rte. 75, in the Salmon River, are less commonly visited soaking spots. Both are free and open 24hr.

CRATERS OF THE MOON NATIONAL MONUMENT ☎208

A visitor to the other-worldly landscape of **Craters of the Moon National Monument** in the 1920s claimed it was "the strangest 75 square miles on the North American continent." The same geological hot spot responsible for the thermal activity in Yellowstone National Park created the monument's 750,000 acres of twisted lava formations; eruptions ended only 2000 years ago, and are expected to resume within the next 1000. Located 70 mi. southeast of Sun Valley at the junction of Rte. 20 and 26/93, Craters of the Moon promises visitors a fascinating mix of lava tube caves, molds of ancient trees, and long-hardened lava flows. (Entrance $5 per car, $3 per bike or pedestrian.) The **visitors center,** right before the entrance to the monument, has videos, displays, and inexpensive printed guides outlining the area's geological past. (☎527-3273. Open daily in summer 8am-6pm; low season 8am-4pm.) A 7 mi. **loop drive** winds through the major sights around the monument's northern end, while several shorter trails lead to intriguing rock formations and a variety of caves. The 2 mi. **Broken Top Loop,** starting at Tree Molds parking lot, goes through Buffalo Caves and is a quick but comprehensive survey of the

ROCKY MOUNTAINS

surrounding land; the short ■**Caves Trail,** further along the loop, leads to three large caves, each with a distinctive character. Don't forget sturdy shoes, water, sunscreen, and a hat, as the black rocks absorb heat and there are no trees for miles. If you plan to explore the caves, bring a flashlight.

There are 51 campsites scattered throughout the monument's single **campground ❶,** located just past the entrance station. (Open year-round. Water and restrooms available in summer only. Sites $10 in summer; lower in winter.) Wood fires are prohibited, but charcoal fires are permitted in the grills. Camping at unmarked sites in the dry lava wilderness of the park is possible with a free **backcountry permit,** available at the visitors center (see above). The inside of **Echo Crater,** reached via an easy 4 mi. hike from the Tree Molds parking lot, is a popular backcountry camping destination.The town of **Arco,** 18 mi. east of Craters of the Moon on Rte. 20, is the closest source of services and lodging. Arco claims to have been the first city in the world powered by atomic energy; on July 17, 1955, a local reactor fed energy to the town for two hours. Comfy, modern rooms with telephones and cable TV are available at the **D-K Motel ❷,** 316 S. Front St. (☎527-8282 or 800-231-0134. Laundry facilities. Singles $33; doubles $41-47.) With a big green rocking chair in front, **Pickle's Place ❶,** 440 S. Front St., is an easy diner to identify. Home of the atomic burger ($6-8) and the Black Russian sandwich ($6), Pickle's also dishes out breakfasts ($5-8) in plentiful portions. (☎527-9944. Dinner entrees $9-12. Open daily June-Aug. 6am-11pm; Sept.-May 6am-10pm.) The **Arco Deli Sandwich Shop ❷,** on Rte. 20/26/93, at Grand Ave. and Idaho St., serves fresh sandwiches. (☎527-3757. 6 in. sandwiches $4, 12 in. $7. Open M-F 8am-7pm, Sa 8am-6pm.)

The **Chamber of Commerce,** 159 N. Idaho St., has info on local attractions. (☎527-8977. Open M-Th 8am-5pm.) **Post Office:** 147 Lost River Ave. (☎527-3355. Open M-F 8:30am-5pm.) **Postal Code:** 83213. **Area Code:** 208.

THE SOUTHWEST

The Ancestral Puebloans of the 10th and 11th centuries were the first to discover that the Southwest's arid lands could support an agrarian civilization. Years later, in 1803, the US bought parts of the Southwest in the Louisiana Purchase, and claimed the rest of it in 1848 with the treaty that ended the US-Mexican War. The hope for a Western "empire of liberty," where Americans could live a virtuous farm life, motivated further expansion and inspired the region's individualist mentality. Today, the Southwest's vastness—from the dramatically colored canvas of Arizona's red rock and striking blue sky, to the breathtaking vistas of Utah's mountains—invites contemplation and awe, and the area's potential for outdoor adventures is as unparalleled as its kaleidoscopic mix of cultures. For more on the region, check out ◾*Let's Go: Southwest USA*.

HIGHLIGHTS OF THE SOUTHWEST

ACHIEVE nirvana (or at least a sense of vertigo) at the **Grand Canyon** (p. 803) and Utah's **"Fab Five"** National Parks (p. 791).

SOAK your cares away in the bubbling hot springs of **Truth or Consequences** (p. 851).

JINGLE the coins in your pocket one last time before offering them up to the shimmering slot machines of **Las Vegas** (p. 773).

SCRAMBLE past lush waterfalls to the mystical **Havasupai Reservation** (p. 810).

TITILLATE your taste buds with the chili-laden cuisine of **Albuquerque** (p. 845), **Santa Fe** (p. 836), and **Tucson** (p. 829).

NEVADA

Nevada's Great Basin stretches for hundreds of miles across land that rejects all but the hardiest forms of life. Three massive lakes—the man-made Lake Mead, the crystalline-blue Pyramid Lake, and the mountain-ringed Lake Tahoe—provide refreshing retreat from brutal desert heat. At the few outposts of human habitation, prostitution and gambling mark the state as a purveyor of loose, Wild West morality. Beyond patches of glaring lights, sin, and showtunes, Nevada is barren and dusty, but this hasn't kept it from becoming the fastest-growing state in the US. Nevada exemplifies America at its most excessive and contradictory.

ⓘ PRACTICAL INFORMATION

Capital: Carson City.

Visitor Info: Nevada Commission on Tourism, 401 N. Carson St., Carson City 89701 (☎800-638-2328. 24hr.). **Nevada Division of State Parks,** 1300 S. Curry St., Carson City 89703 (☎702-687-4384). Open M-F 8am-5pm.

Postal Abbreviation: NV. **Sales Tax:** 6.5-7.5%; 9% room tax in some counties.

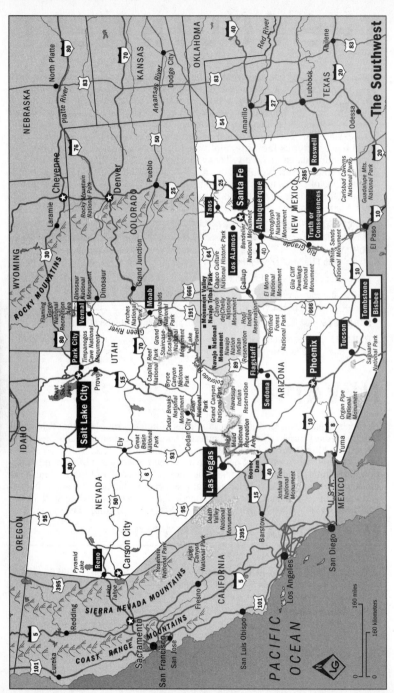

LAS VEGAS
☎702

Rising out of the Nevada desert, Las Vegas is a shimmering tribute to excess. Those who embrace it find vice, greed, and one very, very good time. Those not immediately enthralled by its frenetic pace may still find sleeping (and decision-making) nearly impossible with sparkling casinos, cheap gourmet food, free drinks, and spectacular attractions at every turn. Nowhere else do so many shed inhibitions and indulge with abandon. A word of caution: know thy tax bracket; walk in knowing what you want to spend and get out when you've spent it. In Las Vegas, there's a busted wallet and a broken heart for every garish neon light.

▐ TRANSPORTATION

Airport: McCarran International (☎261-5743), at the southwest end of the Strip. **Bell Trans** (☎739-5557) runs **shuttles** to the Strip ($4.75) and downtown ($6). Operates daily 4am-2am. Taxi to downtown $10-15; to the Strip $16-20.

Buses: Greyhound, 200 S. Main St. (☎384-9561 or 800-231-2222; www.greyhound.com), downtown at Carson Ave., near the Plaza Hotel/Casino. Runs to **L.A.** (5-7hr., 15 per day, $40) and **San Francisco** (14-16hr., 7 per day, $81).

Public Transportation: Citizens Area Transit (CAT; ☎228-7433). Bus #301 serves downtown and the Strip; #302 offers express service on the same route. Buses #108 and 109 serve the airport. Buses run daily 5:30am-1:30am (24hr. on the Strip). Strip routes $2, residential routes $1.25; seniors and ages 6-17 $1/$0.60. Day pass $5. Wheelchair accessible. **Downtown Transportation Center,** 300 N. Casino Center Blvd., at Stewart Ave. near the Fremont Street Experience, has schedules and maps (☎228-7433). **Las Vegas Strip Trolleys** (☎382-1404) cruise the Strip every 20min. daily 9:30am-1:30am. Trolley fare $1.75; day pass $5. Exact fare required. The **Monorail** (☎699-8299) runs along the Strip, connecting major casinos daily 7am-2am. $3; day pass $10.

Taxi: Yellow, Checker, and **Star,** ☎873-2000. **Ace,** ☎736-8383.

Car Rental: Sav-Mor Rent-A-Car, 5101 Rent-A-Car Rd. (☎736-1234 or 800-634-6779). **Dollar Rent-A-Car,** 2880 S. Las Vegas Blvd. (☎735-2922).

Limousine Rental: In case you want to live large, there's **Presidential Limousine** (☎731-5577). $35-80 per hr.

▄★ ▐ ORIENTATION AND PRACTICAL INFORMATION

Driving to Vegas from L.A. is a straight, 300 mi. shot on I-15 N (4½hr.). From Arizona, take I-40 W to Kingman and then U.S. 93 N. Las Vegas has two major casino areas. The **downtown** area, around 2nd and Fremont St., has been converted into a pedestrian promenade. The **Strip,** a collection of mammoth hotel-casinos, lies along **Las Vegas Boulevard.** Parallel to the east side of the Strip. In its shadow is **Paradise Road,** which is also strewn with casinos. Some areas of Las Vegas should be avoided, especially downtown areas far from the casino district. Despite its debauchery, Las Vegas has a **curfew.** Those under 18 aren't allowed in most public places late at night (M-Th and Su 10pm-5am, F-Sa midnight-5am), unless accompanied by an adult. Laws are even harsher on the Strip, where no one under 18 is allowed unaccompanied 9pm-5am—ever. **The drinking and gambling age is 21.**

Visitor Info: Las Vegas Convention and Visitors Authority, 3150 Paradise Rd. (☎892-0711 or 877-847-4858), at the corner of Paradise and Convention Center Dr., 4 blocks from the Strip in the big pink convention center by the Hilton. Helpful staff with up-to-date info on headliners, shows, hotel bargains, and buffets. Open M-F 8am-5pm.

Marriage: Marriage License Bureau, 200 S. 3rd St. (☎455-4415), in the courthouse. 18+ or parental consent. Licenses $55. Witness required. Open M-Th and Su 8am-midnight, F-Sa 24hr. Cash only. **Little White Wedding Chapel,** 1301 Las Vegas Blvd. (☎382-5943; www.alittlewhitechapel.com). Frank Sinatra, Michael Jordan, and Britney Spears have all been hitched here. Basic packages begin at $55 and end at the limits of imagination. All necessities included, like photographer, tux and gown, flowers, and, for honeymooners, a pink Caddy. Grab your marriage license first. Open 24hr.

Hotlines: Compulsive Gamblers Hotline, ☎800-567-8238. **Gamblers Anonymous,** ☎385-7732. **Rape Crisis Center Hotline,** ☎366-1640. **Suicide Prevention,** ☎731-2990 or 800-885-4673. All operate 24hr.

Post Office: 4975 Swenson St. (☎736-7649), near the Strip. Open M-F 8:30am-5pm. **Postal Code:** 89119. **Area Code:** 702.

⬛ ACCOMMODATIONS

Rates in Las Vegas fluctuate greatly; a room that normally costs $30 can cost hundreds during a convention weekend. **Vegas.com** (www.vegas.com) or **casino websites** often have the best prices. Free publications like *What's On in Las Vegas*, *Today in Las Vegas*, *24/7*, and *Vegas Visitor* list discounts, coupons, and event schedules. Hotels along the Strip are the center of the action and within walking distance of each other, but they sell out quickly and are much more expensive than comparable, off-Strip hotels. A number of motels concentrate around **Sahara Road** and **South Las Vegas Boulevard.** If you stay downtown, it is best to stay at one of the casinos near the **Fremont Street Experience** (p. 778). Budget motels also stretch along the southern end of the **Strip,** across from Mandalay Bay. In the rooms listed below, the **hotel taxes of 9%** (11% for downtown Fremont St.) are not included.

Excalibur, 3850 S. Las Vegas Blvd. (☎597-7777 or 800-937-7777), at Tropicana Ave. The best value of all the major resort casinos. Features a moat and drawbridge, 2 pools, a modern spa, and a monorail station with service to Luxor and Mandalay Bay. Rooms M-Th and Su $49-79, F-Sa $79-129. AmEx/D/DC/MC/V. ❸

USAHostels Las Vegas, 1322 Fremont St. (☎385-1150 or 800-550-8958; www.usahostels.com). Though it's far from the Strip's action, this hostel's staff keeps guests entertained. Nightly organized events like champagne limo tours of the Strip. Laundry. Breakfast included. Free wireless Internet. Passport, proof of international travel, or out-of-state college ID required. Dorms M-Th and Su $15-19, F-Sa $17-21; suites $40-42/$47-49. About $3 higher in the summer and peak times. ISIC discount. MC/V. ❷

Sin City Hostel, 1208 S. Las Vegas Blvd. (☎868-0222; www.sincityhostel.com). North of the heart of the Strip but south of Fremont St., this new hostel balances the excitement of the city with a restful atmosphere, allowing the young crowd to sleep it off in peace after partaking in wild clubbing tours. International passport or student ID required. Breakfast included. Dorms $20; private rooms with shared bath $40. AmEx/D/MC/V. ❷

🍴 FOOD

From swanky eateries run by celebrity chefs to gourmet buffets, culinary surprises abound in Las Vegas, usually at a great price.

Dishes, 3300 S. Las Vegas Blvd. (☎894-7111), in Treasure Island. A classy buffet with offerings ranging from sushi to made-to-order salads and filling pastas. The carving stations and scrumptious desserts are hard to beat. Breakfast $12. Lunch $15. Weekday dinner $20, weekend with steak and lobster $26. Open daily 7am-10:30pm. AmEx/D/DC/MC/V. ❸

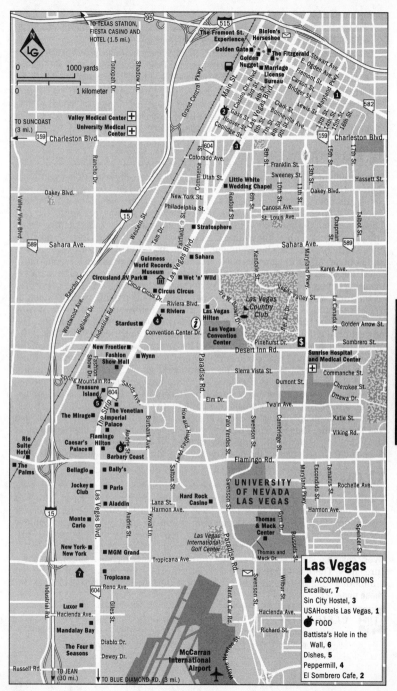

N
LG

0 _____ 1000 yards
0 _____ 1 kilometer

TO TEXAS STATION,
FIESTA CASINO AND
HOTEL (1.5 mi.)

TO SUNCOAST
(3 mi.)

The Fremont St.
Experience
Binion's
Horseshoe
Golden Gate
The Fitzgerald
Golden
Nugget
Marriage
License
Bureau

Valley Medical Center
University Medical
Center

Charleston Blvd.

Little White
Wedding Chapel

Stratosphere

Sahara Ave.

Guinness
World Records
Museum
Circusland RV Park
Sahara
Wet 'n' Wild
Circus Circus
Riviera
Riviera Blvd.
Stardust
Las Vegas
Hilton
Las Vegas
Convention
Center
Convention Center Dr.
Las Vegas
Country
Club

New Frontier
Fashion
Show Mall
Wynn
Treasure
Island
The Strip
The Mirage
The Venetian
Imperial
Palace
Flamingo
Hilton
Caesar's
Palace
Barbary Coast
Rio
Suite
Hotel
The
Palms
Bellagio
Bally's
Jockey
Club
Paris
Aladdin
Monte
Carlo
New York-
New York
MGM Grand
Hard Rock
Casino

Sunrise Hospital
and Medical Center

Desert Inn Rd.

UNIVERSITY
OF NEVADA
LAS VEGAS

Thomas
& Mack
Center
Thomas and
Meck Dr.

Las Vegas
International
Golf Center

Excalibur
Tropicana
Luxor
Mandalay Bay
The Four
Seasons

McCarran
International
Airport

TO JEAN
(30 mi.)
TO BLUE DIAMOND RD. (3 mi.)

THE SOUTHWEST

Las Vegas

🛏 ACCOMMODATIONS
Excalibur, 7
Sin City Hostel, 3
USAHostels Las Vegas, 1

🍴 FOOD
Battista's Hole in the
Wall, 6
Dishes, 5
Peppermill, 4
El Sombrero Cafe, 2

Peppermill, 2985 S. Las Vegas Blvd. (☎735-4177). A Vegas favorite for over 30 years, this Day-Glo purple restaurant serves up heaping plates of comfort food ($8-20) with an ambience straight from the 70s. Open 24hr. AmEx/MC/V. ❷

El Sombrero Cafe, 807 S. Main St. (☎382-9234). Where locals go for authentic Mexican food. Small room, huge portions, efficient service. Their combination plates ($9-11) offer a lot of food for a little money. Lunch $7. Open M-Sa 11am-9:30pm. AmEx/D/MC/V. ❷

Battista's Hole in the Wall, 4041 Audrie St. (☎732-1424), behind the Flamingo. 3 decades worth of celebrity photos, an accordion player, and the head of "Moosolini" (the Fascist moose) adorn the walls. Dinner ($19-35) includes all-you-can-drink wine. Open daily 5-10:30pm. Reservations recommended. AmEx/D/DC/MC/V. ❹

🎵 ENTERTAINMENT

Entertainment is Las Vegas's forte, and all hotels have city-wide ticket booths in their lobbies. Check out *What's On*, *Showbiz*, or *Today in Las Vegas* for shows, times, and prices. For a more opinionated perspective, try one of the independent weeklies—*Las Vegas Mercury*, *City Life*, *Las Vegas Weekly*, or "Neon," the *Las Vegas Review-Journal*'s weekly entertainment supplement. 🔳**Blue Man Group** stuns audiences with a stimulating blend of percussion, visual effects, and audience participation. The show's unique multimedia concept is wildly entertaining and popular, filling the group's custom theater at the Venetian on a regular basis ($63). **Cirque du Soleil's** artsy shows—*O*, *Mystère*, *Zumanity*, and *KÀ*—are awe-inspiring but bank-busting ($94-150). Performed at the Bellagio, **O** is easily the best of the four, with agile performers suspended above a moving pool. **Mystère,** at Treasure Island, is almost as impressive and often has $60 discount seats. At New York-New York, **Zumanity,** hosted by a drag queen, caters to an adult audience. The newest production, **KÀ,** explores duality through the experiences of twins at the MGM Grand. **Jubilee!,** at Bally's, and **Folies Bergere,** at the Tropicana, are two of the last remaining true Vegas-style revues with showgirls dancing about in rhinestones and feathers ($45-68). The **Tournament of Kings,** at Excalibur, is a (k)nightly dinner show where guests feast at a medieval banquet using only their hands, while rival kings joust and evil is vanquished ($55). Those looking for an illusionist will be thrilled by **David Copperfield** (appearing often at MGM; $80-100), while those who think the genre of magic needs a few new tricks will enjoy the irreverent **Penn and Teller** at the Río ($82). For a (relatively) cheap laugh, **Second City Scriptless,** at the Flamingo, is an improv show that inspired the television hit *Saturday Night Live* and features some of the country's best up-and-coming comedians ($32).

🏛 CASINOS

Casinos spend millions of dollars attracting big spenders to Las Vegas. Efforts to bring families to Sin City are evident everywhere, with arcades and thrill rides at every turn. Still, Vegas is no Disneyland. With the steamy nightclubs, topless revues, and scantily clad waitresses serving free liquor, it's clear that casinos' priorities center on the mature, moneyed crowd. Casinos are open 24hr. Almost every casino resort has a full casino, several restaurants, a club, a buffet, and a feature show. There is valuable art and architecture at every corner. Look for casino "funbooks" that feature deals on chips and entertainment. **Gambling is illegal for those under 21.**

CASINO TIPPING. To keep the luck flowing (and because it's nice), many players reward a good table dealer with a $1 tip next to their main bet. Casino etiquette also calls for a $1 tip per person for drink servers and buffet busers.

THE STRIP

The undisputed locus of Vegas's surging regeneration, the Strip is a neon fantasy-land teeming with people, casinos, restaurants, and sadly, inflated prices. The nation's 10 largest hotels line the legendary 3½ mi. stretch of Las Vegas Blvd.

Mandalay Bay, 3950 S. Las Vegas Blvd. (☎632-7777; www.mandalaybay.com). Undoubtedly Vegas's hippest casino, Mandalay Bay tries to convince New York and L.A. fashionistas they haven't left home. With swank restaurants and clubs, gambling seems an afterthought. Shark Reef has aquatic beasts from all over the globe, including 15 shark species ($16, children $10). House of Blues hosts some of Vegas's best music.

Bellagio, 3600 S. Las Vegas Blvd. (☎693-7444; www.bellagio.com). The world's largest 5-star hotel, made famous in the remake of *Ocean's Eleven.* Houses a gallery of fine art, the world's tallest chocolate fountain, and a floral conservatory that changes with the seasons. Check out the carefully choreographed dancing fountains in front of the casino and see the water leap several stories high to well-known classical pieces. (Free, every 30min. afternoons, every 15min. 7pm-midnight.)

Wynn, 3131 S. Las Vegas Blvd. (☎770-7000 or 888-320-7123; www.wynnlasvegas.com). This latest addition to the Strip more than competes with the Bellagio for classiest casino. The gambling floor is tastefully decorated, with flashing slot machine lights noticeably absent. Don't be put off by the subdued appearance; even if table limits are high, the dealers are friendly and the grounds are beautiful.

New York-New York, 3790 S. Las Vegas Blvd. (☎740-6969; www.nynyhotelcasino). An eye-catching, fun-filled casino brings a slice of the Big Apple to Sin City. Towers mimic the Manhattan skyline, the streets of a miniature Greenwich Village lead to an **ESPNZone,** and a walk under the Brooklyn Bridge brings you to the Manhattan Express (open daily 11am-11pm; $12), the wildest ride on the Strip.

Luxor, 3900 S. Las Vegas Blvd. (☎262-4000; www.luxor.com). This architectural marvel recreates the majestic pyramids of ancient Egypt in opaque glass and steel. Popular with young adults, but still family-friendly, Luxor has an IMAX theater, a full-scale replica of King Tut's Tomb, and numerous clubs.

Treasure Island (TI), 3300 S. Las Vegas Blvd. (☎894-7111; www.treasureisland.com). Catering to a younger crowd with raucous party clubs and chic lounges, the pirate's cove is the place to go for a big night out. See the *Sirens of TI* for a sea battle in one of Vegas's most scantily-clad shows, daily at 7, 8:30, 10pm, 1:30am.

Paris, 3655 S. Las Vegas Blvd. (☎946-7000; www.parislasvegas.com). From restaurants that resemble French cafes to replicas of the Arc de Triomphe, the French Opera House, and the Eiffel Tower, this resort adds a Parisian *je ne sais quoi* to Las Vegas.

Venetian, 3355 S. Las Vegas Blvd. (☎414-1000; www.venetian.com). Singing gondoliers serenade passengers on the chlorinated "canal" that runs through this palatial casino. Elaborate ceilings, the Guggenheim Hermitage Museum, and Madame Tussaud's wax museum evoke a little bit of old Europe, while the Blue Man Group adds some edge.

Caesar's Palace, 3570 S. Las Vegas Blvd. (☎731-7110; www.caesars.com). At Caesar's, busts abound; some are plaster and others are barely covered by the low-cut cocktail waitresses' outfits. The expensive Forum Shops provide numerous opportunities to leave your winnings in Vegas.

The Mirage, 3400 S. Las Vegas Blvd. (☎791-7111; www.mirage.com). This tropical oasis is home to a 20,000 gallon aquarium, a lush indoor rainforest, and several rare white tigers and lions. A volcano that puts science fair projects to shame erupts every 15min.

MGM Grand, 3799 S. Las Vegas Blvd. (☎891-1111; www.mgmgrand.com). A huge bronze lion guards Las Vegas's largest hotel (5000 rooms) as it glows like the Emerald City from *The Wizard of Oz.* Watch the big cats frolic in the tunnel overhead at the Lion Habitat. The MGM often hosts world-class sporting events and concerts.

Circus Circus, 2880 S. Las Vegas Blvd. (☎734-0410; www.circuscircus.com). Though far less glamorous than its younger neighbors, the free circus acts are reminiscent of the Strip's early, outlandish days. While parents run to card tables and slot machines, children flock to one of the world's largest indoor theme parks.

DOWNTOWN AND OFF-STRIP

Many of the Strip's theme park elements are absent in "old" downtown Vegas. **Glitter Gulch** has smaller hotels, cheaper alcohol and food, and table limits as low as $1. Years of decline were reversed with Las Vegas's rebound and the 1995 opening of the **Fremont Street Experience.** Now, a protective canopy of neon and construction of a pedestrian promenade have aided the area's renaissance, making it almost as entertaining and much more welcoming to the budget traveler.

Golden Gate, 1 Fremont St. (☎385-1906; www.goldengatecasino.com). Opened in 1906, Las Vegas's oldest hotel/casino now anchors the Fremont Street Experience and offers a thoroughly modern good time. Grab a famous 99-cent shrimp cocktail and sharpen your gambling skills in the laid-back atmosphere.

Golden Nugget, 129 Fremont St. (☎385-7111; www.goldennugget.com). An outpost of Strip-like class downtown, this 4-star hotel charms gamblers with marble floors, elegant chandeliers, and high-end gambling.

Palms, 4321 W. Flamingo Rd. (☎942-7777; www.palms.com). The ultimate venue to spot celebrities and party with the young and beautiful. The Skin Pool Lounge has swings and cabanas to enjoy before you hit the bars and clubs on the property.

▶ DAYTRIPS FROM LAS VEGAS

HOOVER DAM

From Las Vegas, take U.S. 93/95 26 mi. to Boulder City. From Boulder City, head east 5 mi. on U.S. 93. Parking on the Nevada side costs $5; parking is free on the Arizona side.

Built to subdue the flood-prone Colorado River and give vital water and energy to the Southwest, this ivory monolith took 5000 men five years to construct. By the time the dam was finished in 1935, 96 men had died. Their labor rendered a 726 ft. colossus that pumps more than four billion kilowatt-hours of power to Las Vegas and L.A. A lasting tribute to America's "think big" era, the dam is a spectacular engineering feat, weighing 6.6 million tons and measuring 660 ft. thick at its base and 1244 ft. across the canyon at its crest. Tours and an **interpretive center** explore the dam's history and future. (☎866-291-8687. Open daily 9am-5pm. Self-guided tours with short presentations $10, seniors $8, ages 7-16 $4.)

LAKE MEAD

From Las Vegas, take Lake Mead Blvd./Hwy. 147 off I-15 east 16 mi. to North-shore Rd.

The largest reservoir in the US, Lake Mead was created when Hoover Dam was constructed across the Colorado River in the 1930s. First-time visitors will benefit from a trip to the **Alan Bible Visitors Center,** 4 mi. east of Boulder City on Hwy. 93, where the helpful staff has brochures and maps. (☎702-293-8990; www.nps.gov/lame. Open daily 8:30am-4:30pm. 5-day entrance $3 per pedestrian, $5 per vehicle.) Falling water levels have left Lake Mead roughly half its usual depth, forcing boat ramps to close and exposing previously submerged hazards. Despite these conditions, Lake Mead is still a water recreation haven. Park service-approved outfitters rent boats and more on the shores; www.funonthelake.com has more info. Popular **Boulder Beach,** the departure point for many water-based activities is accessible from Lakeshore Dr. at the south end of the lake. (Restrooms, water. Sites $10.) Because of the oppressively hot summer temperatures, it may be a better idea to head for the higher (and cooler) elevations west of Las Vegas in July and August.

> **IT'S THE LAW.** The legal drinking and gambling age in Nevada is 21.

RENO
☎ **775**

Reno, with its decadent casinos cradled by snowcapped mountains, captures both the natural splendor and exciting prospects of the West. Acting as the hub of northern Nevada's tourist cluster, including nearby Lake Tahoe and Pyramid Lake, Reno is defined by a gritty glamour that falls short of the thrills of Las Vegas but still manages to supply gambling, entertainment, and dining in a few city blocks.

ORIENTATION AND PRACTICAL INFORMATION. Fifteen miles from the California border and 445 mi. north of Las Vegas, Reno sits at the intersection of **I-80,** which stretches between Chicago and San Francisco, and **Highway 395,** which traces the eastern slope of the Sierra Nevadas from Southern California to Washington. Many of the major casinos are in the **downtown** area between West and Center St. and between 2nd and 6th St. The neon-lit streets of downtown Reno are heavily patrolled, but avoid straying too far east of the city center at night. Relatively cheap accommodations can be found south of the Truckee River along **Virginia Street,** Reno's main drag. The #1 bus services Virginia St. from downtown Reno to Meadowood Mall. The *Reno/Tahoe Visitor Planner,* available at information kiosks throughout the city, contains a local map and is a helpful city guide. **Amtrak** is at 245 Evans Ave. (☎800-872-7245; www.amtrak.com. Open daily 7:30am-5pm.) **Greyhound,** 155 Stevenson St., sends buses to Las Vegas (15-22hr., 5 per day, $71), Salt Lake City (9½hr., 2 per day, $59), and San Francisco (5-7hr., 7 per day, $30). (☎322-2970; www.greyhound.com. Open 24hr.) **Visitor Info: Reno-Sparks Convention and Visitors Authority,** 4001 S. Virginia St. (☎800-367-7366; www.visitrenotahoe.com. Call ahead for hours.) **Post Office:** 50 S. Virginia St., at Mill St. (Open M-F 8:30am-5pm.) **Postal Code:** 89501. **Area Code:** 775.

ACCOMMODATIONS. Casino resort prices fluctuate daily, so be sure to call ahead. Inexpensive independent hotels also dot the casino area. Many offer clean, simple rooms perfect for the budget traveler, but in some cases, low rates may reflect a lack of wholesomeness, so inspecting your room is a wise move. Most hotels rent only to those 21 and older. The rates below don't include Reno's 13.5% hotel tax. The **Mizpah Hotel ❷,** 214 Lake St., at E. 2nd St., provides tidy rooms for affordable prices. Guests have access to the downstairs TV room and laundry facilities. (☎323-5194. Double bed with shared bath $26; queen bed with private bath and TV $33. $7 per additional person; max. 2 per room. 21+. Must have photo ID. AmEx/D/MC/V.) Off Hwy. 395 at the Glendale exit, the **Reno Hilton ❸,** 2500 E. 2nd St., is not in the casino district, but you won't miss a thing; the complex contains elegant rooms, a driving range, a bowling alley, a health club, a shopping mall, and a 115,000 sq. ft. casino floor. (☎800-648-5080. Rooms $35-149. AmEx/D/DC/MC/V.) The **Bonanza Inn ❷,** 214 W. 4th St. in downtown, is a solid option for people who want to be close to the action without spending a bundle. (☎322-8632 or 800-808-3303. King beds M-Th $35, F $55, Sa $65. AmEx/D/DC/MC/V.)

FOOD. Casinos offer a range of all-you-can-eat buffets, but you can escape the clutches of these giants to find inexpensive eateries with a more neighborhood feel. **The Pneumatic Diner ❷,** 501 W. 1st St., in Truckee River Terrace, is a funky, cramped diner that creates unique and tasty Italian, Mexican, French, and Middle Eastern concoctions. The delightfully irreverent menu provides a glossary of terms so you know what you're ordering. (☎786-8888, ext. 106. Open M-F 10am-11pm, Sa 9am-11pm, Su 8am-11pm. MC/V.) In a town filled with *taquerías,*

Miguel's ❷, 1415 S. Virginia St., is the best. (☎322-2722. Open Tu-Th 11am-9pm, F-Sa 11am-10pm, Su noon-8pm. D/MC/V.) Those who are tired of the prime rib that dominates the casino district will enjoy the award-winning Thai flavors of **Bangkok Cuisine ❷,** 55 Mt. Rose St. (☎322-0299. Open M-Sa 11am-10pm. AmEx/MC/V.)

🎭 **ENTERTAINMENT.** Almost all casinos offer live nighttime entertainment, but most shows are not worth the steep admission prices. At **Circus Circus,** 500 N. Sierra St., a small circus on the midway above the casino floor performs a variety of "big-top" shows approximately every 30min. (☎329-0711. Shows M-Th noon-11:45pm, F-Su 11:15am-11:45pm.) For entertainment listings and info on casino events, check out the free *This Week* or *Best Bets* magazines. *The Reno News & Review,* published every Thursday, provides an alternative look at weekly events. The **National Automobile Museum,** 10 S. Lake St. at Mill St., houses over 200 antique and one-of-a-kind vehicles, including Elvis's 1973 Cadillac and a gold-plated Delorean. (☎333-9300. Open M-Sa 9:30am-5:30pm, Su 10am-4pm. $8, seniors $7, ages 6-18 $3.) Jumpstart your adrenaline at the **Ultimate Rush Speed and Thrill Park,** 2500 E. 2nd St. by the Reno Hilton. The park offers the "Ultimate Rush," a combination sky-diving, bungee-jumping, and hang-gliding ride ($25), as well as go-karts ($6) and mini-golf ($5) for the less-daring. (☎786-7005. Opens daily at 11am.)

🚗 **DAYTRIP FROM RENO: PYRAMID LAKE.** Thirty miles north of Reno on Rte. 445, on the Paiute Indian Reservation, the deep turquoise Pyramid Lake is one of the most beautiful bodies of water in the US. The lake's pristine shores are a soothing respite from Reno's clanging slot machines and a fantastic spot for world-class trout fishing and boating. **Camping ❶** is allowed anywhere on the lake shore, but only designated areas have toilet facilities. Permits are required for day use ($6), camping ($9), and fishing ($7) and are available at the **Ranger Station** and **Marina,** housed in the same building, 2500 Lakeview Dr. (☎476-1156), in Sutcliffe. The **Pyramid Lake Museum and Visitors Center,** in Nixon, has interesting displays on the Paiute Tribe for those curious about more than just the lake's scenery. (☎574-1088. Open M-F 8am-4:30pm; summer also Sa 10am-4pm. Free.)

UTAH

In 1848, persecuted members of the Church of Jesus Christ of Latter-Day Saints (colloquially called Mormons) settled on the land that is now Utah, intending to establish their own theocratic state. Mormons eventually gave up their dreams of theocracy, and statehood was granted on January 4, 1896. Today the state's population is 70% Mormon—a religious presence that creates a haven for family values. Utah's citizens dwell primarily in the 100 mi. corridor along I-15, from Ogden to Provo. Outside this area, Utah's natural beauty dominates, intoxicating visitors in a way that Utah's watered-down 3.2% beer cannot.

🛈 PRACTICAL INFORMATION

Capital: Salt Lake City.

Visitor Info: Utah Travel Council, 300 N. State St., Salt Lake City 84114 (☎801-538-1030 or 800-200-1160; www.utah.com), across from the capitol building. Has the *Utah Vacation Planner*'s lists of motels, national parks, and campgrounds, and brochures on biking, rafting, and skiing. Open M-F 8am-5pm, Sa-Su 10am-5pm. **Utah Parks and Recreation,** 1594 W. North Temple, Ste. 116, Salt Lake City 84114 (☎801-538-7220). Info on camping, boating, and highways. Open M-F 8am-5pm.

THE SOUTHWEST

Controlled Substances: Mormons abstain from alcohol (also coffee and tea). State liquor stores are sparse, and grocery and convenience stores only sell beer. Restaurants serve wine, but licensing laws can split a room—you may have to move to the bar for a mixed drink. Places that sell hard alcohol must be "members only;" tourists can find a "sponsor"—i.e., an entering patron—or get a short-term membership, usually $5 for 2 weeks.

Postal Abbreviation: UT. **Sales Tax:** 5.75-7.75%.

SALT LAKE CITY ☎ 801

Tired from five months of travel across the plains, Brigham Young looked out across the Great Salt Lake and said: "This is the place." He believed that in this desolate valley his band of Mormon pioneers had finally found a haven where they could practice their religion freely. Though Mormons make up less than half of Salt Lake City's population today, Temple Square is still the focal point of downtown and the Church of Jesus Christ of Latter-Day Saints (LDS) continues to hold tremendous force over the city. The cultural mix engenders a city vibrant enough to have welcomed the world during the 2002 Winter Olympics. As the only American city with world-class skiing within 30min. of downtown, Salt Lake City also serves as home base for visitors to the seven surrounding ski meccas.

TRANSPORTATION

Airport: Salt Lake City International, 776 N. Terminal Dr. (☎575-2400), 6 mi. west of Temple Sq. UTA buses #50 and 150 run between the terminal and downtown ($1.25). Buses leave every hr. M-Sa 7am-11pm, Su 7am-6pm. Taxi to Temple Sq. about $15.

Trains: Amtrak, 340 S. 600 W. (☎322-3510; www.amtrak.com). Use caution in this area at night. To **Denver** (15hr., 1 per day, $75-112) and **San Francisco** (19hr., 1 per day, $77-115). Open daily 10:30pm-6am.

Buses: Greyhound Intermodal Hub, 600 W. 300 S. (☎355-9579; www.greyhound.com), next to the Amtrak station. To **Denver** (7-10hr., 5 per day, $54) and **Las Vegas** (12-13hr., 2 per day, $49). Open daily 6:30am-11:45pm; ticket window until 10:30pm.

Public Transit: Utah Transit Authority (UTA; ☎743-3882). Frequent service to University of Utah campus, buses to suburbs, airport, mountain canyons. The #11 express runs to Provo ($2.25). New TRAX light rail follows Main St. from downtown to Sandy and to the University of Utah. Buses every 20min.-1hr. M-Sa 6am-11pm. Fare $1-2, under 5 free. Maps available at libraries and the visitors center. UTA buses and TRAX trains traveling downtown near the major sites are free.

Taxi: Ute Cab, ☎359-7788. **Yellow Cab,** ☎521-2100. **City Cab,** ☎363-5550.

ORIENTATION AND PRACTICAL INFORMATION

Temple Square is the heart of downtown. Street names increase in increments of 100, indicating how many blocks east, west, north, or south they lie from Temple Sq.; the "0" points are **Main Street** (north-south) and **South Temple** (east-west). State St., West Temple, and North Temple are 100-level streets. Occasionally, streets are called 13th S. or 17th N., which are the same as 1300 S. or 1700 N. Local addresses often include cross streets. For example, a building on 13th S (1300 S) might be listed as 825 E. 1300 S., meaning the cross street is 800 E. (8th E.). Smaller streets and those that do not fit the grid pattern sometimes have non-numeric names.

Visitor Info: Salt Palace Convention Center and Salt Lake City Visitors Bureau, 90 S. West Temple (☎534-4902). Located in Salt Palace Convention Center. Open in summer M-F 8am-6pm, Sa-Su 9am-5pm; in winter daily 9am-5pm.

GLBT Resources: The **Little Lavender Book** (☎323-0727; www.lavenderbook.com), a directory of gay-friendly Salt Lake City services, is distributed twice yearly. The **Salt Lake Metro,** a free newspaper with articles on GLBT issues and events, is published bi-weekly.

Hotlines: Rape Crisis, ☎467-7273. **Suicide Prevention,** ☎483-5444. Both 24hr.

Internet Access: Salt Lake Public Library, 210 E 400 S (☎524-8200), a new high-tech facility. Open M-Th 9am-9pm, F-Sa 9am-6pm, Su 1-5pm.

Post Office: 230 W. 200 S. (☎532-5501), 1 block south and 1 block west of visitors center. Open M-F 8am-5pm, Sa 9am-2pm. **Postal Code:** 84101. **Area Code:** 801.

ACCOMMODATIONS

Affordable motels cluster at the southern end of downtown, around 200 W. and 600 S., and on North Temple. Prices rise during the Sundance Film Festival.

City Creek Inn, 230 W. North Temple (☎533-9100 or 866-533-4898), conveniently located by Temple Sq., has clean, ranch-style rooms. HBO, free local calls. Singles $53; doubles $63. In winter $48/$58. AAA discount. AmEx/D/MC/V. ❸

Ute Hostel (AAIH/Rucksackers), 21 E. Kelsey Ave. (☎595-1645 or 888-255-1192), near the intersection of 1300 S. and Main St., has cozy rooms and sparkling bathrooms. Free pickup from the airport, bus, and train stations. Check-in 24hr. Reservations recommended July-Sept. and Jan.-Mar. Dorms $15. Singles $30; doubles $35. Cash only. ❶

The Avenues Hostel (HI), 107 F St. (☎359-3855 or 800-467-8351). 15min. walk from Temple Sq. in a residential area. Free parking, a snazzy entertainment system, 2 kitchens, and mountain bike rentals ($10 per day, $100 deposit). Key deposit $5. Reception 7:30am-noon and 4-10:30pm. Reservations recommended July-Aug. and Jan.-Mar. Dorms $17, members $14. Private rooms with shared baths $31/$25. MC/V. ❶

Salt Lake City KOA, 1400 W. North Temple (☎328-0224), 14 blocks from Temple Square. In summer, camping here is a cheap way to stay near the city and on the bus line. Pool, hot tub, modem-friendly, RV hookups. Expect more RVs than tents. MC/V. ❶

FOOD

Good, cheap, and surprisingly varied restaurants pepper the city. For a quick bite, **ZCMI Mall** and **Crossroads Mall,** both across from Temple Sq., have food courts.

Ruth's Diner, 2100 Emigration Canyon Rd. (☎582-5807). Take Foothill Rd. to 8th/Sunnyside and follow into the canyon. The second-oldest restaurant in Utah and a Salt Lake City landmark for its huge portions. A full bar with live music at night. Omelets $6-8. For lunch, try the pan-seared salmon ($11). Open daily 8am-10pm. AmEx/D/MC/V. ❷

Red Iguana, 736 W. North Temple (☎322-1489). Famous for its *moles* ($12), this busy family-owned restaurant serves authentic Mexican in a festive atmosphere. Veggie nachos $6.25. Daily entree combo $11. Open M-Th 11am-10pm, F 11am-11pm, Sa 10am-11pm, Su 10am-9pm. AmEx/D/DC/MC/V. ❷

Sage's Cafe, 473 E. 300 S. (☎322-3790). This organic vegan cafe produces incredible meals, from the "Guac-N-Roll" sandwich ($8.50) to the "shiitake escargot" ($7). Sandwiches $6-9. Open W-Th 11:30am-2:30pm and 5-9:30pm, F 11:30am-2:30pm and 5-10pm, Sa 9am-10pm, Su 9am-9pm. AmEx/D/MC/V. ❷

Hires Big H, 425 S. 700 E. (☎364-4582). Drive in and flash your headlights to get a classic Big H burger ($3.35) and a "Frosty Mug" of root beer ($1.75) delivered carside. Inside seating available. Open in summer M-Th 10:30am-midnight, F-Sa 10:30am-12:30am; in winter M-Th 10:30am-11pm, F-Sa 10:30am-12:30am. AmEx/MC/V. ❶

THE SOUTHWEST

Salt Lake City

ACCOMMODATIONS
The Avenues Hostel (HI), **4**
City Creek Inn, **3**
Salt Lake City KOA, **5**
Ute Hostel, **13**

FOOD
Hires Big H, **11**
Orbit, **8**
Red Iguana, **2**
Ruth's Diner, **1**
Sage's Cafe, **9**

NIGHTLIFE
Bricks, **7**
Burt's Tiki Lounge, **14**
Port O'Call Social Club, **10**
Trapp Door, **6**
Vortex, **12**

Orbit, 540 W. 200 S. (☎322-3808), famed for its weekend brunch (smoked salmon Benedict and crabcakes Benedict), mixes Cajun, Mexican, and Asian flavors in a space-age interior. Wraps $8. Salads $6-11. Smoothie bar. Open M-Th 11am-10pm, F 11am-3am, Sa-Su 9am-3pm. All-day brunch Sa-Su. AmEx/D/MC/V. ❸

🅖 SIGHTS

LATTER-DAY SIGHTS. The center of the Mormon religion, **Temple Square** encloses the seat of the highest Mormon authority and the central temple. The square has two **visitors centers.** *(Both open daily 9am-9pm.)* Visitors can wander around the 35-acre square, but the temple is not open to the public. A visitor info line (☎800-537-9703) provides up-to-date hours and tour info. Guided 45min. tours leave from the flagpole every 10min. The beautiful **Joseph Smith Memorial Building** houses two restaurants with views of the city. (☎240-1266 *for tours. Open M-Sa 9am-9pm. Free.)* Temple Sq. is also home to the **Mormon Tabernacle** and its famed choir. Rehearsals and performances are free. *(Organ recitals M-Sa noon-12:30pm, Su 2-2:30pm; in summer also M-Sa 2-2:30pm. Choir rehearsals Th 8-9:30pm; choir broadcasts Su 9:30-10am, must be seated by 9:15am.)* In summer, free concerts play at **Assembly Hall** next door. (☎800-537-9703.)

THE SOUTHWEST

The **Church of Jesus Christ of Latter Day Saints Office Building** is the tallest building in town, and the elevator to the 26th floor grants a view of the Great Salt Lake. *(50 E. North Temple. ☎800-453-3860. Observation deck open M-F 9am-4:30pm, but accessible only by guided tour.)* The LDS church's collection of genealogical materials at the **Family Search Center,** 15 E. South Temple St., in the Joseph Smith Memorial Building. The actual collection is located in the **Family History Library.** *(35 N. West Temple. ☎240-2331. Search Center open M-F 9am-9pm, Sa 9am-5pm. Library open M 8am-5pm, Tu-Sa 8am-9pm. Free.)* Early Mormon history is recounted at the **Museum of Church History and Art,** 45 N. West Temple St., with an original 1830 Book of Mormon and Brigham Young's famous prayer bell. *(☎240-3310. Open M-F 9am-9pm, Sa-Su 10am-7pm.)*

MUSEUMS. Visiting exhibits and a permanent collection of international art wow enthusiasts at the guava-colored **Utah Museum of Fine Arts,** on the University of Utah campus, just off S. Campus Dr. *(☎581-7332. Open Tu and Th-F 10am-5pm, W 10am-8pm, Sa-Su 11am-5pm. $4; students and ages 6-18 and 65+ $2.)* Also on campus, the **Museum of Natural History** has displays on the history of the Wasatch Front, with an emphasis on anthropology, biology, and paleontology. *(☎581-6927. Open M-Sa 9:30am-5:30pm, Su noon-5pm. $6; ages 3-12, students, and seniors 62+ $3.50; under 3 free.)* The **Salt Lake Art Center** shows an impressive array of contemporary art and rotates exhibits every 2-3 months. *(20 S. West Temple. ☎328-4201. Open Tu-Th and Sa 10am-5pm, F 10am-9pm, Su 1-5pm. Suggested donation $2.)* Twenty-five miles southwest of downtown, the museum at the **▓Kennecott Utah Copper Bingham Canyon Mine,** 8362 W 10200 S, introduces visitors to the "Richest Hole on Earth." The mine itself, still fully functional, is the only man-made object besides the Great Wall of China that is visible from space. It's well worth the trip to see trucks hauling ore out of this massive copper mine. *(From downtown, take I-15 S to 7200 S. Exit west and proceed to 7800 S., which merges into the Bingham Hwy. Turn left (south) on Rte. 111 toward the entrance gate. ☎569-6287. Open daily Apr.-Oct. 8am-8pm, weather permitting. Cars $4; no motorcycles.)*

THE GREAT SALT LAKE. The Great Salt Lake, administered by Great Salt Lake State Marina, is a remnant of primordial Lake Bonneville and is so salty that only blue-green algae and brine shrimp can survive in it. The salt content varies 5-27%, providing the buoyancy credited with keeping the lake free of drownings. Decaying organic material on the shore gives the lake its pungent odor. **Antelope Island State Park,** in the middle of the lake, and separated from the city by Farmington Bay, is a great place to see free-roaming wildlife or go swimming. *(For the lake's south shore, take I-80 17 mi. west of Salt Lake City to Exit 104. To the island, take I-15 to Exit 335 and go 7 mi. west. ☎773-2941. Open daily in summer 7am-10pm; in winter dawn-dusk. Day use: vehicles $8, bicycles and pedestrians $4.)*

🎵 🎭 **ENTERTAINMENT AND NIGHTLIFE**

Salt Lake City's summer months are jammed with evening concerts. Every Tuesday and Friday at 8pm in June and July and 7:30pm in August, the **Temple Square Concert Series** presents a free outdoor concert in **Brigham Young Historic Park,** at the corner of State and North Temple, with music ranging from string quartets to acoustic guitar. *(☎240-2534; call for schedule.)* The **Utah Symphony Orchestra** performs in gold-leafed **Abravanel Hall,** 123 W. South Temple. *(☎533-6683. Office open M-F 10am-6pm, Sa 10am-2pm. Tickets Sept. to early May $15-40. Limited summer season with outdoor venues; call 1 week in advance.)* The University of Utah's **Red Butte Garden,** 300 Wakara Way *(☎587-9939; www.redbuttegarden.org),* has a summer concert series featuring national acts in an immaculate garden with stunning views of the entire Salt Lake basin.

The free *City Weekly* and *Salt Lake Metro* list events and are available at bars, clubs, and restaurants. Laws passed by early Mormon legislators make it illegal to serve alcohol in a public place. Hence, all liquor-serving institutions are "private clubs," serving only members and their "sponsored" guests. In order to get around this barrier, most bars and clubs charge a "temporary membership fee"—a cover. Despite all this, Salt Lake City has an active nightlife scene, centering on S. West Temple and the blocks near the railroad tracks.

Port O'Call Social Club, 72½ W. 400 S. (☎521-0589). An unassuming sports bar by day and dance club by night where it's not surprising to see fraternity brothers partying next to middle-aged couples. 80s night W. Live blues Th. Beer $3.50. Cover M-Th and Su $5, F $8, Sa $10. Open daily 11am-2am; during football season 10am-2am.

Burt's Tiki Lounge, 726 S. State St. (☎521-0572). A cozy watering hole with all the good services of a typical dive bar: live music and cheap drinks in an unpretentious environment. Karaoke Th. Draft beers $2. Cover $5. Open daily 5pm-2am.

Vortex, 404 S. West Temple (☎355-7746). A much younger crowd than most other SLC clubs. 4 levels of bumper-to-bumper grinding on shockwave dance floors occasionally spill out onto the patio deck by the pool. 18+. Cover $7. Open W-Sa 9pm-2am.

Bricks, 200 S. 600 W. (☎238-0255; www.bricksclub.com). The city's oldest and largest dance club, with arguably its best sound system. Separate 18+ and 21+ areas. Cover $5-7. Open daily 9:30pm-2am.

Trapp Door, 615 W. 100 S. (☎533-0173). A gay-friendly spot with a clubby dance floor where all ages get their groove on. Frequent drag shows—call for details. "Tongue 'n' Groove" F. Latin night Su. Drinks $3-8. Cover $5-10. Open Tu and Th-Su 9pm-2am.

🎿 SKIING

Utah sells itself with pictures of daring skiers on fresh powder, hailed by many (and many Utah license plates) as the greatest snow on earth. Seven major ski areas lie within 45min. of downtown Salt Lake, making Utah's capital a good base camp for the winter vacation paradise of the Wasatch Mountains. Call or check ski area websites for deals before purchasing lift tickets. Besides being fun, the Utah ski hills are also an excellent source of employment. If you are interested in working while you ski, check the employment section on each mountain's website or call Snowbird's **job hotline** (☎947-8240). Most slopes are open in the summer for hiking, mountain biking, and horseback riding. The area code for some resorts is ☎435. Unless noted, all other numbers share SLC's ☎801 area code.

Alta (☎359-1078; www.alta.com), 25 mi. southeast of Salt Lake City in Little Cottonwood Canyon. Cheap tickets and magnificent skiing. No-frills resort continues to eschew opulence and reject snowboarders. 500 in. of champagne powder annually. Open mid-Nov. to mid-Apr. daily 9:15am-4:30pm. Lift tickets: full day $47, half-day $37-42; day pass for beginner lifts $25; full-day joint ticket with nearby Snowbird $66.

Brighton (☎800-873-5512; www.skibrighton.com), in Big Cottonwood Canyon. Bargain skiing and snowboarding in a family-friendly atmosphere. Open early Nov. to late Apr. M-Sa 9am-9pm, Su 9am-4pm. Lift tickets: full day $41, half-day $35, night $25; ages 10 and under free. Rentals: ski or snowboard packages $26-32 per day, children $18.

Deer Valley (☎435-649-1000; www.deervalley.com), in Park City. Host of several 2002 Winter Olympics events. A world-class, if expensive, ski area. No snowboards. Open Dec.-Apr. daily 9am-4:15pm. Lift tickets: full day $69, half-day $48; seniors $48/$32; children $38/$30. Ski rentals: adult package $40-50 per day, children $30.

Solitude (☎800-748-4754; www.skisolitude.com), in Big Cottonwood Canyon 30min. south of Salt Lake. Uncrowded slopes and 6 mi. of nordic trails at Silver Lake. Open Nov. to late Apr. daily 9am-4pm. Lift tickets: full day $44, seniors $37, children $24, ages 70+ $10; half-day $37. Nordic Center full day $11, half-day $8. Rentals: $25 per day, snowboards $28, high-performance ski package $38.

The Canyons (☎435-649-5400; www.thecanyons.com), in Park City. Lodges, shops, and restaurants, and a ton of territory. 146 trails, 16 lifts. Open Nov.-Apr. M-F 9am-4pm, Sa-Su 8:30am-4pm. Lift tickets: full day $62, half-day $45; children and seniors $31/$24. Rentals: adult ski or board package $34-45 per day, child ski or board package $25. Free season pass in exchange for 1 day of work at the resort per week.

▶ DAYTRIPS FROM SALT LAKE CITY

PARK CITY
Park City is about 30 mi. east of Salt Lake City. From Salt Lake City, take I-80 east, then follow Rte. 40 south to Park City.

Host to many of the Olympic events in 2002, nearby **Park City** is the quintessential ski town. In the winter, Park City serves as the gateway to three ski areas; in warmer months, the mountains offer great hiking and mountain biking. Watch world-class athletes train at the **Utah Olympic Park,** 3000 Bear Hollow Dr. In Summer, ski-jumpers practice on special plastic and freestylers do multiple flips into a pool. Indoors is an interactive museum where you can simulate skiing like an Olympian. (☎435-658-4200 or 800-659-7275; www.olyparks.com. Open in summer daily 9am-6pm. $7, ages 3-17 and 65+ $5; with guided tour $9/$7; with admission to freestyle aerial shows Sa noon $12/$10.) Park City is also teeming with festivals and major athletic events, including the **NORBA (mountain-biking) nationals** in June and **free concerts** Wednesdays at Deer Valley. The **visitors center,** 1826 W. Olympic Pkwy., has more info. (☎658-4541. Open M-Sa 9am-6pm, Su 11am-4pm.)

Though prices soar during the high season, a few budget dining options still exist. A destination in its own right, the **Morning Ray/Evening Star Cafe ❷/❹,** 255 Main St., inside the Treasure Mountain Inn, is a local staple for breakfast and lunch, serving omelets like the "Powderhound" and "Backcountry" ($8.25). Though its alias changes to Evening Star at night, the cafe's fun hippie atmosphere remains the same. (☎435-649-5686. Breakfast and lunch entrees $6-10. Dinner entrees $12-18. Open daily 7am-2pm; W-Su also 5:30-9:30pm. AmEx/D/MC/V.) Cans line almost every inch of the walls at **Davanza's ❶,** 690 Park Ave., a pizzeria which also serves sandwiches and burgers. (☎649-2222. Burgers $5.50. AmEx/D/MC/V.) For a cold beer or a glimpse of famous skiiers, **Cisero's,** 306 Main St., is a good bet on any night. (☎649-6800. Live music F and Su. DJ W and Sa. Karaoke Th. $2.50 cocktails W. $1 drafts, $2 pizzas Su. Cover $5. Open daily 5pm-1am.)

TIMPANOGOS CAVE NATIONAL MONUMENT
Timpanogos Cave has just one entrance, via Rte. 92 (20 mi. south of Salt Lake City off I-15, Exit 287; Rte. 92 also connects with Rte. 189 northeast of Provo). The visitors center (☎801-756-5238; open mid-May to late Oct. daily 7am-5:30pm) has info on the cave.

Legend has it that a set of mountain lion tracks first led Martin Hansen to the cave that bears his name. **Hansen's Cave** is only one-third of the cave system of American Fork Canyon, collectively called **Timpanogos Cave.** In a rich alpine environment, Timpanogos lures speleologists (cave nuts) and tourists alike. Though early miners shipped boxcars of stalactites and other mineral wonders back east to sell to universities and museums, plenty remain to bedazzle guests along the 1hr. walk through the depths. The cave is open to visitors only through ranger-led tours;

tickets are sold at the visitors center. Reservations for summer weekends should be made far in advance. Bring water and warm layers: the rigorous hike to the cave climbs 1065 ft. over 1½ mi., but the temperature inside stays at 45°F. (☎801-756-5238. Open mid-May to late Oct. daily 7am-5:30pm. 3hr. hikes depart daily every 15min. 7am-4:15pm. $7, ages 6-15 $5, Golden Age Passport and ages 3-5 $3, ages 2 and under free.) An "Introduction to Caving" tour from the visitors center is a chance to get dirty and try spelunking for yourself (Reservations required; call ahead for times. $15.) The National Monument is dwarfed by the **Uinta National Forest,** which blankets the mountains of the Wasatch Range. The **Alpine Scenic Drive (Route 92)** provides great views of Mt. Timpanogos and other snowcapped peaks. The 20 mi. trip takes almost 1hr. one-way. (Open late May to late Oct.; not recommended for vehicles over 30 ft. long. 3-day Forest Service pass $3 per vehicle; 14-day pass $10; annual pass $25.) Two trails lead to the peak of **Mt. Timpanogos** (11,749 ft.). The **Timpooneke Trail** leaves from the Timpooneke Campground (18 mi.). The **Aspen Grove Trail,** which begins at the Aspen Grove Trailhead (6860 ft.), is shorter (16 mi.) but significantly steeper. Both trails meet at the summit at Emerald Lake. The **Pleasant Grove Ranger District** has info on area **campgrounds ❶.** (General info ☎801-785-3563; reservations 800-280-2267. Sites $11-13.) **Backcountry camping ❶** in the forest requires no permit or fee as long as you respect minimum-impact guidelines. While the National Park Service forbids camping within the national monument, **Little Mill Campground ❶,** on Rte. 92 past the monument, is a good jumping-off point. (Water, vault toilets. Open early May to late Sept. Sites $11.) **Timpanooke Campground ❶,** 2 mi. farther up the Alpine Loop, has more forested and private sites. (Water, vault toilets. Open mid-June to late Sept. Sites $10.)

DINOSAUR NATIONAL MONUMENT AND VERNAL ☎435

In 1908, paleontologist Earl Douglass lucked upon a river bank in eastern Utah brimming with fossilized dinosaur bones. Since then, some 350 million tons of dinosaur remains have been carted away from this Jurassic cemetery. Spectacular hiking and stark desert scenery surround the Monument and its remnants of prehistoric life. In summer, a shuttle whisks passengers from the western entrance to the **Dinosaur Quarry Visitors Center,** the only place in the park to see dinosaur bones. (☎781-7700. Open June-Aug. daily 9am-6pm, Sept.-May M-F 8am-4:30pm. Entrance fee $10 per car; $5 per cyclist, pedestrian, or tour-bus passenger.) The 4hr. **Journey Through Time** auto tour, available at Monument Headquarters (see below) is the only way to reach **Harper's Corner.** At the end of the road is an easy 2 mi. round-trip hike (1½-2hr.) leading to views of Echo Park and Whirlpool Canyon. Several hikes leave from the **Tour of the Tilted Rocks** auto tour (22 mi. round-trip), including the easy **Box Canyon** and **Hog Canyon** trails (each 1 mi. roundtrip). **Don Hatch River Expeditions,** 221 N. 400 E in Vernal, sends expeditions through the monument along Class II and III rapids. (☎789-4316 or 800-342-8243; www.hatchriver.com. Open M-F 8:30am-5pm, Sa-Su 8am-3pm. 1-day trip $66, ages 6-12 $56. Seniors 10% off.)

The most accessible camping spot, **Green River ❶,** along Cub Creek Rd. about 5 mi. from the entrance fee station, has 88 sites. (Flush toilets and water. Closed in winter. Sites $12.) Tall cottonwoods and sheer cliffs make **Echo Park ❶,** 13 mi. along Echo Park Rd. from Harper's Corner Dr. (4WD road; impassable when wet), the perfect location for an evening under the stars. (22 sites. Pit toilets and water in summer. Sites $8; free in winter when accessible. Tents only.) Free **backcountry camping ❶** permits are available from Monument Headquarters or the Quarry Visitors Center. Those less inclined to rough it should head to the **Sage Motel ❸,** 54 W. Main St., in Vernal, where each room has a different motif, ranging from "Wild West" to "Pink Panther." (☎789-1442 or 800-760-1442. A/C, satellite TV, and free local calls. In summer singles $55, doubles $72; in winter $46/$56. AmEx/D/MC/V.)

THE SOUTHWEST

Stockman's ❸, 1684 W. U.S. 40, in the Weston Hotel, lures hungry travelers with burgers ($6-8), all-you-can-eat sirloin steak ($13), and gargantuan desserts. (☎781-3030. Open M-F 10am-11pm, Sa 11:30am-11pm. AmEx/D/MC/V.) For homemade chili ($3) or a hefty ribeye ($15), head to the **7-11 Ranch Restaurant ❷**, 77 E. Main St. (☎789-1170. Open M-Sa 6am-10pm. MC/V.)

The monument's western entrance lies 20 mi. east of Vernal on Rte. 149, which splits from U.S. 40 southwest of the park in Jensen, UT. **Monument Headquarters,** 2 mi. east of Dinosaur, CO on U.S. 40, is the best point to begin exploring the Colorado side of the park. (☎970-374-3000. Open June-Aug. daily 8am-4:30pm, Sept.-May M-F 8am-4:30pm.) **Gas** is available in Vernal, Jensen, and Dinosaur, CO, but provisions and resources around the park are slim. The town of **Vernal,** 20 mi. west of Dinosaur Quarry on U.S. 40, is a popular base for exploring the monument. The **Northeast Utah Visitors Center,** 496 E. Main St., inside the Utah Field House of Natural History, has interactive exhibits, fossils, and an outdoor "dinosaur garden" with 16 full-size dinosaur replicas. (☎789-3799. Open daily in summer 8am-7pm; in winter 9am-5pm. $5, children and seniors $3.) The **Ashley National Forest Service Office,** 355 N. Vernal Ave., has info about outdoors activities in the Ashley and Uinta National Forests. (☎789-1181. Open M-F 8am-5pm.) **Post Office:** 67 N. 800 W (789-2393. Open M-F 9am-5pm, Sa 10am-1pm.) **Postal Code:** 84078. **Area Code:** 435.

FLAMING GORGE NATIONAL RECREATION AREA ☎435

Seen at sunset, the contrast between the red canyons and the Green River's aquamarine water makes the landscape glow. The centerpiece of the Flaming Gorge National Recreation Area, however, is the 91 mi. reservoir formed in 1963 by a dam in the Green River. Boats and fishermen descend into the gorge every summer to take advantage of its shimmering water and 350 mi. of scenic shoreline.

The Green River below the dam teems with trout, providing top-notch **fishing.** To fish, get a **permit,** available at Flaming Gorge Lodge (see below) and Flaming Gorge Recreation Services, at the Conoco in Dutch John. (☎885-3191. Open Mar.-Oct. M-F 7am-9pm, Sa-Su 7am-10pm; Nov.-Feb. daily 9am-5pm.) For more info, call the **Utah Division of Wildlife Resources,** 1594 W. North Temple, in Salt Lake City. (☎801-538-4700. Open M-F 7:30am-6pm.) **Cedar Springs Marina,** 2 mi. south of the dam, rents boats and offers guided fishing trips. (☎889-3795. Open Apr. 15-Oct. 15 daily 8am-6pm. 10-person pontoon boats from $120 per 3hr., $200 per day. 6-person fishing boats $50/$90.) **Spinner Fall Guide Service,** 18 South Blvd. in Dutch John, leads float trips through the gorge. (☎801-971-9553 or 877-811-3474. 2-person float trip with lunch and shuttle service $375.) Hikers and bikers will love the area's trails, some of which snake along dangerous cliff edges. All trails allow bikes. The flat **Canyon Rim Trail** (7 mi.) has access points at Red Canyon Visitors Center and several campgrounds, and features spectacular views of Flaming Gorge. From the dam, you can walk the **Little Hole** trail along the river, a scenic trail with plenty of chances to glimpse wildlife (7 mi. one-way). The strenuous **Elk Park Loop** (20 mi. round-trip) is perfect for mountain biking and departs from Rte. 44 at Deep Creek Rd., follows it to Forest Rd. 221 and Forest Rd. 105, skirts Browne Lake, and runs along **Old Carter and South Elk Park Trails.**

Camping is accessible with over 30 campgrounds around the lake. The campgrounds keep 50% of their sites open as first come, first served, so sites are generally easy to come by. (☎877-444-6777.) The **Flaming Gorge Ranger District** (☎784-3445) also has advice on sites. **Canyon Rim ❶**, on the road to Red Canyon Visitors Center, offers views of the red-walled gorge. (Vault toilets. Sites $14; late Oct. to late Apr. free.) The 19 sunny sites at **Dripping Springs ❶**, just past Dutch John on Rte. 191, are a prime fishing location. (Vault toilets. Reservations accepted. Sites $14.) The self-titled "civilized way to enjoy the great outdoors," the **Red Canyon**

Lodge ❸, 790 Red Canyon Rd., 2 mi. south of the visitors center on Rte. 44, 24 mi. south of Manila, is the nicest indoor lodging around, complete with luxury-resort activities, a private lake, and a restaurant. (☎889-3759. 2-person cabins with bath $95; 4-person $105; each additional adult $6, under 12 $2.)

From Vernal, follow U.S. 191 north to the recreation area on the **Flaming Gorge Scenic Byway**, which has 10 switchbacks and steep grades. The reservoir extends as far north as Green River, WY, and is also accessible from I-80 by way of Rte. 414 and Rte. 530 on the west side of the reservoir, as well as from U.S. 191, which continues along the eastern side. A recreation pass ($2 per day, $5 per 16 days, $20 per season) can be obtained at the **Flaming Gorge Visitors Center**, on U.S. 191 on the Flaming Gorge Dam. The visitors center also offers free tours of the dam. (☎885-3135. Open daily 8am-6pm; low season 10am-4pm.) A few miles off U.S. 191 and 3 mi. off Rte. 44 to Manila, the **Red Canyon Visitors Center** hangs 1360 ft. above the reservoir, offering staggering views into the canyon. (☎889-3713. Open late May to Aug. daily 10am-5pm.) **Post Office:** 4 South Blvd., in Dutch John. (☎885-3351. Open M-F 7:30am-3:30pm, Sa 8:30am-noon.) **Postal Code:** 84023. **Area Code:** 435.

MOAB   ☎435

Moab first flourished in the 1950s when uranium miners rushed to the area, transforming the town from a quiet hamlet into a gritty desert outpost. Today, mountain bikes and whitewater rafts have replaced the Geiger counter, and tourists flock to Moab, eager to bike the red slickrock, raft the rapids, and explore the surrounding Arches and Canyonlands National Parks. The town has adapted to its onslaught of visitors and adventure-seekers—guide companies, car repair shops, microbreweries, t-shirt shops, and organic cafes now fill the rooms of the old uranium mine headquarters on Main St. While driving around, check out the local radio station KZMU 89.7 for public radio by day and jazz by night.

⚌ 🛈 ORIENTATION AND PRACTICAL INFORMATION. Moab is 30 mi. south of I-70 on U.S. 191, just south of the junction with Rte. 128. The town center is 5 mi. south of the entrance to Arches National Park and 38 mi. north of the turnoff to the Needles section of Canyonlands National Park. U.S. 191 becomes Main St. for 5 mi. through downtown. The closest **Amtrak** (☎800-872-7245; www.amtrak.com) and **Greyhound** (☎800-454-2487; www.greyhound.com) stations are in Green River, 52 mi. northwest of town. Some hotels and hostels will pick guests up from the train or bus station for a fee. **Bighorn Express** (☎888-655-7433) runs daily to and from the Salt Lake City airport, stopping in Green River and Price. Shuttles leave from the Ramada Inn, 182 S. Main St. (4½hr.; departs Salt Lake City airport at 2pm, departs Moab at 7:30am; $54. Reservations recommended.) **Roadrunner Shuttle** (☎259-9402) and Coyote Shuttle (☎259-8656) take you where you want to go on or off the road in Moab. For a faster, more expensive option, **Salmon Air** offers shuttles between Salt Lake City airport and Moab. (For schedules and prices call ☎800-448-3413 or see www.salmonair.com.) The **Moab Information Center**, 3 Center St., at the intersection of Center and Main, has info on the city and surrounding parks. (☎259-8825 or 800-635-6622. Open daily May-Sept. 8am-9pm; Oct. 8am-8pm; Nov.-Apr. 8am-5pm.) **Internet Access:** Free at the **Grand County Library**, 100 E. 25 S. (☎259-5421. Open M-W 9am-9pm, Th-F 9am-7pm, Sa 9am-5pm.) **Post Office:** 50 E. 100 N. (☎259-7427. Open M-F 8am-5pm, Sa 9am-1pm.) **Postal Code:** 84532. **Area Code:** 435.

🏳 ACCOMMODATIONS. Chain motels line Main St., but Moab isn't cheap and rooms fill up fast from April to October. **🌄Lazy Lizard International Hostel ❶**, 1213 S. U.S. 191, is 1 mi. south of Moab on U.S. 191. The kitchen, lounge, outdoor patio,

THE SOUTHWEST

and hot tub draw a friendly mix of students, backpackers, and aging hippies to this comfortable hostel. (☎259-6057. Reception 8am-11pm, but late arrivals can be arranged. Check-out 11am. Reservations recommended for weekends in spring and fall. Tent sites $6; dorms $9. Private rooms $22-36; cabins $27-47. AmEx/D/MC/V.) The **Center Street Hotel ❷**, 96 E. Center St., a block off Main, is a mix between a high-class hostel and a bargain hotel. The hostel has shared bathrooms, common kitchen, and a lounge area. (☎259-7615 or 888-530-3134. Check-in at Kokopelli Lodge, 72 S. 100 E., 8:30am-9:30pm; check-out 11am. Rooms Nov.-Aug. $35; Sept.-Oct. $45. Each additional person $5. AmEx/D/MC/V.)

Hundreds of campsites blanket the greater Moab area, and camping is Moab's most convenient and affordable lodging option. **Goose Island, Hal Canyon, Oak Grove, Negro Bill, Drinks Canyon,** and **Big Bend Campgrounds ❶**, all on Rte. 128 (intersection at U.S. 191 and Rte. 128), sit right on the banks of the Colorado River, 3-9 mi. northeast of Moab. Signs for Negro Bill and Drinks Canyon are well hidden near the entrance to the other campgrounds. (☎259-2100. Fire pits. No drinking water, but toilets at all sites. Sites $5 at Negro Bill and Drinks Canyon, $10 at all the other campgrounds.)

◖ **FOOD.** The town of Moab is filled with bookstore cafes and quirky breakfast spots that open early for adventurers looking to get a head start on their day. ▪**EklectiCafé ❶**, 352 N. Main St., dishes out delicious pastries, coffee, and vegetarian dishes. You'll recognize it easily thanks to the giant mosaic of a coffee cup out front. (☎259-6896. Breakfast $3-7. Lunch $4-8. Open M-Sa 7:30am-2:30pm, Su 7:30am-1pm.) ▪**Mondo Café ❶**, 59 S. Main St., in McStiff's Plaza, proudly boasts that its coffee ($1) is "still legal in Utah." Laptop-toting customers can take advantage of their free wireless Internet or use the cafe's computer for $0.75 per 5min. (☎259-5551. Open daily 6:30am-9:30pm. MC/V.) **Milt's Stop & Eat ❶**, 356 Mill Creek Dr., grills up traditional 50s diner fare at low prices. Grab a stool at the counter or order a quick bite at the convenient walk-up window outside. (☎259-7424. Cheeseburgers $1.80. Malts $2. Open Tu-Sa 6am-8pm. Breakfast until 11:30am. Cash only.) **La Hacienda ❷**, 574 N. Main St., serves up Tex-Mex favorites. Enjoy Taco Tuesday (tacos $0.89) and Wenchilada Wednesday (enchiladdas $2) from 11am-2pm. (☎259-6319. AmEx/D/MC/V.)

◪ **OUTDOOR ACTIVITIES. Mountain biking** is the big draw in Moab and attracts thousands each year. The **Slickrock Trail** (10 mi.) is one of the most popular choices. Rolling up and down the slickrock outside Moab, the trail lacks big vertical gain, but is technically difficult. Novices may enjoy the Bar M Loop (7 mi.) or Gemini Bridges (14 mi.), while those looking for a challenge can check out the new, single-track Sovereign Trail. **Rim Cyclery**, 94 W. 100 N, rents road and mountain bikes, does repairs, and provides information on the trails. (☎259-5333 or 888-304-8219. Open daily 8am-6pm. Full suspension $38-58 per day.)

Countless rafting companies help outdoor enthusiasts explore the nearby Colorado and Green Rivers. ▪**Canyon Voyages Adventure Co.**, 211 N. Main St., has friendly, knowledgeable guides and will personalize their services to meet your specific skill level, whatever it may be. (☎800-733-6007. Half-day $36-49, ages 4-15 $26; full day $49/$39. Some tours include lunch with vegetarian options. Hiking tours also available.) Numerous outfitters can arrange horseback, motorboat, canoe, jeep, and helicopter rides for you. **Adrift Adventures** leads various rafting trips on the Colorado River and other adventure combinations, where the guides are known for their gourmet cuisine cooking skills. (☎800-874-4483. Rafting half-day $32, ages 4-15 $25, full day $43/$30.) **Camelot Adventure Lodge** offers unique 3hr. guided camel treks. (☎260-1783; www.camelotlodge.com. $125, meal included.)

UTAH'S NATURAL WONDERS

Arches, Canyonlands, Capitol Reef, Bryce Canyon, and Zion National Parks comprise Utah's Grand Circle of national parks, all connected by a series of scenic highways. In their midst lies the mammoth Grand Staircase-Escalante National Monument, sprawling south and east of Bryce Canyon and west of Capitol Reef. The spectacular arches, canyons, amphitheaters, plateaus, slickrock, and redrock of these public lands put them among the densest collection of geological and panoramic brilliance the nation has to offer.

From Moab, take U.S. 191 north 5 mi. to **Arches.** Continue 60 mi. north on U.S. 191 to Rte. 313 S and the Island in the Sky area of **Canyonlands.** To reach the Needles area of Canyonlands (87 mi.), take U.S. 191 south from Moab to Rte. 211 W. To get to **Capitol Reef,** continue south on U.S. 191, then take Rte. 95 northwest to Rte. 24. Continue west on Rte. 24, then move south onto Rte. 12 to reach **Grand Staircase-Escalante National Monument.** Scenic Rte. 12 runs south through Dixie National Forest and into **Bryce Canyon.** For **Zion,** follow Rte. 12 W to U.S. 89 S through Mt. Carmel Jct., and take Rte. 9 W. For those with a limited amount of time, a trip along Rts. 12 and 95 gives a great sense of the surrounding parks.

Southern Utah's two national forests are divided into districts, some of which lie near the national parks and serve as excellent places to stay on a cross-country jaunt. **Manti-La Sal National Forest** has two sections near Arches and the Needles area of Canyonlands. **Dixie National Forest** stretches from Capitol Reef through Bryce all the way to the western side of Zion. It may be 90°F in southern Utah, but you'll still see snow on the ground in these forests.

> **SD** **THE REAL DEAL.** If Utah's "Fab Five" national parks were to enter a beauty pageant, Bryce Canyon would take the tiara. The landscape's stark beauty is striking enough to stop even the most seasoned park-hopper in his tracks. Park rangers insist that if you're only going to see one US national park in a lifetime, Bryce should be that one—and they're right. —Lauren Sancken

ARCHES ☎ 435

Arches National Park draws travelers from around the world to explore its prehistoric grandeur, a geological miracle of balanced rocks and mammoth, human-like forms that sit among towers of red sandstone. Winding spires and hidden arches tower above the desert with a majesty that has emblazoned its image on Utah license plates and inspired its local nickname, "God's Country." Ironically, among the arches sits the "Fiery Furnace" and the "Devil's Garden." The dramatic beauty of Arches is a bit of heaven and hell mixed together in one.

■ ❼ **ORIENTATION AND PRACTICAL INFORMATION.** The park entrance is on U.S. 191, 5 mi. north of Moab. Although no public transit serves the park, shuttle bus companies go to both Arches and Moab from surrounding towns. Many visitors come in the summer, but 100°F temperatures make hiking difficult—be sure to bring plenty of water. The weather is best in the spring and fall, when temperate days and nights make for a comfortable stay. An entrance pass ($10 per car, $5 for pedestrians, bicycles, and motorcycles) covers admission for seven days and comes with a map of the park and the locations of the largest, best-known arches. If you are going to several National Parks, it makes sense to buy the $50 annual National Park Pass, good for entrance into all US National Parks up to a year from purchase. More detailed maps are available at the **visitors center** just inside the park entrance. (☎719-2299; www.nps.gov/arch. Open daily Oct.-Feb. 8am-4:30pm;

extended hours Mar.-Sept. 7:30am-6:30pm.) Check out the free ranger programs, nature walks, and evening lecture programs (daily 11am, 5, 9pm). For more info, go to the visitors center. Sign up early for guided walks into the Fiery Furnace; tours fill up fast and only experienced hikers can secure a permit. (Tours daily June-Sept. 9am; Oct-June 10am, 4pm. $8 tour/$2 permit.)

☂ CAMPING. The park's only campground, **Devil's Garden ❶,** has 52 excellent campsites amid piñons and giant sandstone formations. The campground is within walking distance of the Devil's Garden and Broken Arch trailheads, but is a winding 18 mi. from the visitors center. Reservations (www.reserveusa.com) are available for 30 of the sites between March 1 and October 31 for an additional $9. The remaining sites are available on a first come, first served basis at the visitors center beginning at 7:30am and can fill up very quickly in the high season. (☎719-2299. Bathrooms, water, no showers or wood-gathering. 1-week max. stay. Sites $10.) If the heat is too much at Arches, the **Manti-La Sal National Forest** offers a respite. Take Rte. 128 along the Colorado River and turn right at Castle Valley, or go south 6 mi. from Moab on U.S. 191 and turn left onto Loop Rd. Though a bit out of the way, the forest has many campgrounds, including the beautiful **Warner Lake ❶,** where sites sit 4000 ft. above Arches. ($10. Reserve at www.reserveusa.com.) Contact the Manti-La Sal National Forest (☎259-7155) for more info.

▨ HIKING. While the roads that snake through Arches offer exceptional scenery, the real points of interest are only accessible by foot. Those hiking in the summer will want to load up on water and sunscreen, and start early to avoid the midday heat. Stay on trails; the land may look barren, but the soil crust is home to microscopic life forms that footsteps can destroy. Pets are not allowed on trails.

The most popular hike in the park leads to the oft-photographed **Delicate Arch.** The trail (3 mi., 2½hr. round-trip) begins at the Wolfe Ranch parking area and climbs 480 ft. To view the spectacular arch without the arduous hike, take the wheelchair-accessible **Delicate Arch Viewpoint Trail** which begins in the Viewpoint parking area and takes around 15min. **Devil's Garden** (7¼ mi., 3-5hr. round-trip) is a challenging hike and requires some scrambling over rocks, but hardy travelers will be rewarded by the eight arches visible along the trail. The trek is not recommended in wet or snowy conditions. **Park Avenue** (1 mi., 30min.-1hr.) is a moderate hike that is gorgeous at sunset and the closest to the park entrance. **Fiery Furnace** runs through a labyrinth of narrow sandstone canyons, but there is no trail, so guides are strongly recommended for those who wish to explore this area. For an easier hike good for small children, try **Sand Dune Arch** (0.4 mi., 15-30min. round-trip) or **Broken Arch** (1.2 mi., 30min.-1hr.). Both can be accessed from the Sand Dune Arch parking area or Devil's Garden campground.

CANYONLANDS ☎435

Canyonlands is vast and rugged; each of its four sections has a personality all its own. The best views of the expansive red-rock canyon and the surrounding mountains are at the opposite ends of the park, in the Needles region and Island in the Sky. For the more adventurous, the Maze's 30 mi. labyrinth ranks as one of the most remote places on Earth, while the Rivers contains one of the most treacherous white-water runs in the US. The diversity of Canyonlands makes it a park to be photographed, explored, and, for the brave, to be reckoned with.

 Much of the park is composed of slickrock. Trails on or near slickrock are extremely treacherous in wet or icy conditions.

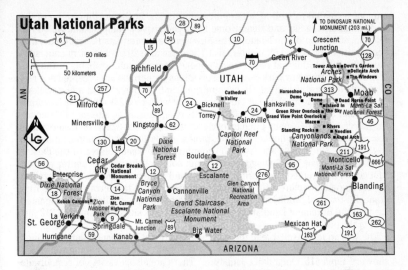

Utah National Parks

50 miles

50 kilometers

TO DINOSAUR NATIONAL
MONUMENT (203 mi.)

■ ⁊ ORIENTATION AND PRACTICAL INFORMATION. The four districts of Canyonlands are **Island in the Sky,** the **Needles,** the **Maze,** and the **Rivers.** The park also includes the detached **Horseshoe Canyon** district. Island in the Sky is the most popular and accessible region. Take U.S. 191 to Rte. 313, 10 mi. north of Moab and 22 mi. south of I-70. Follow Rte. 313 22 mi. southwest. The Needles, geared more toward backcountry adventure, is on Rte. 211, 40 mi. south of Moab and 14 mi. north of Monticello. To reach the Maze, from I-70, take Rte. 24 south for 29 mi. to a turnoff just past the entrance to Goblin Valley State Park. From there, a dirt road takes you 46 mi. to the southeast and to the ranger station. The Rivers, known for their first-class rapids, are best accessed through one of the rafting companies based in Moab. Horseshoe Canyon, home to prehistoric cultures and later a hideout of Butch Cassidy, is limited to day use and is 32 mi. east of Rte. 24 on a dirt road. None of the park districts are accessible by public transit, but the closest **Amtrak** (☎800-872-7245; www.amtrak.com) and **Greyhound** (☎800-454-2487; www.greyhound.com) stations are in Green River, 52 mi. northwest of Moab on I-70. **Coyote Shuttle** (☎259-8656) and **Roadrunner Shuttle** (☎259-9402), both based out of Moab, will take visitors to and from Canyonlands. Entrance fees vary according to district: Island in the Sky and Needles are $10 per car, but other parts of the park have no entrance fees. Island in the Sky, Needles, and the Maze each have a **visitors center.** (Island in the Sky Visitors Center: ☎259-4712. Needles Visitors Center: ☎259-4711. Maze Hans Flat Ranger Station: ☎259-2652. Horseshoe Canyon operates out of the Hans Flat Ranger Station. All open daily 8am-4:30pm; extended hours during high season.) Moab is the closest town to Island in the Sky, while both Monticello and Moab are close to the Needles. Green River and Hanksville (west of the park on Rte. 24) are closest to the Maze and each have several budget motels, restaurants, and cafes. All areas of the park can be contacted at www.nps.gov/cany. **Post Office:** 50 E. 100 N., in Moab. (☎259-7427. Open M-F 8am-5pm, Sa 9am-1pm.) **Postal Code:** 84532. **Area Code:** 435.

⁊⬗ ACCOMMODATIONS AND FOOD. Canyonlands does not have any indoor accommodations, so travelers who want rooms should stay in Moab, Monticello, Green River, or Hanksville, though Moab has the most options. Those who wish to camp are treated to well-maintained campgrounds. In the northern area of the park, Island in the Sky and Dead Horse Point each have a campground. **Willow Flat ❶,** 7 mi. southeast of the Island in the Sky Visitors Center, has 12 first come, first served sites. (Pit toilets. No water. $5.) There are also 20 backcountry campsites along the White Rim that require a $30 backcountry permit, available at the visitors center or from any park ranger; reservations for permits are accepted and recommended in spring and fall. Backcountry permits go quickly, but a few walk-up permits are usually available in the summer and winter. (☎259-4351.) Nearby **Dead Horse Point State Park ❶,** on Rte. 313, has 21 campsites. Nine sites are first come, first served and are usually filled by early afternoon. (☎800-322-3770. Reservations recommended. Water, hookups, picnic tables, and grills. $14, including admission to the park. Wheelchair accessible.) Camping in the Needles area of the park is available at **Squaw Flat Campground ❶,** 7 mi. south of the visitors center with 26 first come, first served sites, drinking water, and flush toilets ($10). The Maze has no developed campsites but **primitive campgrounds** dot the terrain and are first come, first served. Additionally, free primitive camping is available in designated areas of the Bureau of Land Management (BLM) lands situated along Rte. 313 just east of the park.

There is no food available in the park, so stock up at the **Needles Outpost,** which has gas, a pricey cafe, and groceries. (☎979-4007. Also has a campground and showers. Sites $15. Open daily 8am-4pm.) There are also a variety of restaurants located in Moab (p. 789), Monticello, Green River, and Hanksville.

🗺️⚠️ **SIGHTS AND OUTDOOR ACTIVITIES.** Each part of Canyonlands presents a unique view. Island in the Sky, a peninsula surrounded by deep canyons, is the best option for car touring. The **Grand View Point Overlook** and **Schafer Canyon Overlook,** both clearly marked, have awe-inspiring views of the mighty rivers that carved the canyons. Those wishing to stretch their legs can enjoy the easy **Mesa Arch Trail** (½ mi. round-trip) or the **Syncline Loop,** a challenging 8.3 mi. loop around the Upheaval Dome area with great viewpoints. For the most spectacular views of the Colorado River, ▨**Dead Horse Point State Park** is a few miles north of the Island entrance on Rte. 313. (☎259-2614 or 800-322-3770; write Box 609, Moab, UT 84532. Park open daily 6am-10pm; visitors center open daily 8am-5pm. Entrance fee $7.) On the way to the Needles district, the Canyon Rims Recreation Area is the gateway to the ▨**Needles Overlook** (22 mi. past the entrance), a stunning, panoramic view of Canyonlands, perfect for sunset picnics. The eerie spires of the wilder Needles district are best explored on foot. **Roadside Ruin** (¼ mi.), an easy trail to a Puebloan granary, is a quick introduction to the area's history. The **Slickrock Trail** (2½ mi. loop) is an intermediate hike with good views down into the canyons. The Maze contains only very challenging and technical backcountry hiking and climbing, and it is best to consult a guide. Horseshoe Canyon's **Great Gallery** (6½ mi.) displays looming rock art of 10 ft. human figures, estimated to have been drawn onto the cliffs sometime between 1000 and 2000 BC.

CAPITOL REEF   ☎435

Capitol Reef's feature attraction, the 100 mi. Waterpocket Fold, is a geologist's fantasy. With its impassible reefs, white-rock domes, hidden arches, and miles of twisting canyons, the 65-million-year-old fold bisects this "Land of the Sleeping Rainbow." Yet the cliffs and domes of this wrinkle in the earth's crust are not the park's only attraction. Ancient Native American petroglyphs and the orchards and buildings of early Mormon settlers make Capitol Reef a fascinating blend of both natural and cultural history.

▣▨ ORIENTATION AND PRACTICAL INFORMATION. The middle link in Utah's famous chain of five, Capitol Reef is on Rte. 24, flanked by the small towns of Hanksville to the east and Torrey to the west. The park is unreachable by major bus lines; the closest **Greyhound** (☎800-231-2222; www.greyhound.com) and **Amtrak** (☎800-872-7245; www.amtrak.com) stops are in Green River. Entrance to the park is free, though the scenic drive is $5 per vehicle. The **visitors center**, on Rte. 24, supplies travelers with free maps, trail brochures, and info on daily activities. (☎425-3791; www.nps.gov/care. Open daily June-Aug. 8am-6pm; Sept.-May 8am-4:30pm.) **Post Office:** 75 W. Main St., in Torrey. (☎425-3716. Open M-F 7:30am-1:30pm, Sa 7:30-11:00am.) **Postal Code:** 87175. **Area Code:** 435.

▨▣ ACCOMMODATIONS AND FOOD. The park's campgrounds offer sites on a first come, first served basis. The main campground, **Fruita ❶**, 1¼ mi. south of the visitors center off Rte. 24, sits among orchard fruit trees and has 71 sites with water and toilets. (Sites $10. Max. 8 people per site.) **Cedar Mesa Campground ❶**, on Notom-Bullfrog Rd., and **Cathedral Valley ❶**, in the north (accessible by 4WD or on foot), have five sites each; neither has water, but they're free. Both areas and all backcountry camping require a free **backcountry permit**, available at the visitors center. **Torrey**, a quaint, friendly town 11 mi. west of the visitors center on Rte. 24, has the closest lodging and restaurants. The ▨**Sandcreek RV Park, Campground, and Hostel ❶**, 540 W Main St., has an espresso bar, organic produce, local jewelry, and quiet lodgings, plus a spacious bathhouse and laundry room. The one dorm room houses eight beds, and there are also 12 tent sites and two rustic cabins that sleep up to four people. (☎425-3577 or 877-425-3578. Showers for non-guests $4. Linens $2. Laundry $5. Reception 7:30am-7pm. Check-out 11am. Open Apr. to mid-Oct. Dorms $10; tent sites $11, hookups $16-19; cabins $28-34. MC/V.) The **Capitol Reef Inn ❷**, 360 W Main St., is simple and comfortable with a Southwestern touch. (☎425-3271. Jacuzzi, minifridge. Reception 7am-10pm. Open Apr.-Oct. Rooms $44, each additional person $4. AmEx/D/MC/V.) For a delicious meal with a stunning view of Capitol Reef, dine at the ▨**Rim Rock Restaurant ❹**, 2523 E Highway 24. (☎425-3388. Open daily 5-9pm. AmEx/MC/V.) Though pricey, **Cafe Diablo ❺**, 599 W Main St., is worth the splurge for its unique approach to Southwestern cuisine. Rattlesnake ($9), pecan chicken ($18), and homemade ice cream with berries from the Capitol Reef orchard make dining an all-evening event. (☎425-3070. Open Apr. 15-Oct. 15 daily 5-10pm. MC/V.) More affordable food awaits at **Brink's Burgers ❶**, 163 E. Main St. Their basic burger, a quarter-pound of deliciousness, is only $2.60. (☎425-3710. Take-out available. Open daily 11am-9pm. Cash only.)

▣▨ SIGHTS AND OUTDOOR ACTIVITIES. You can see the Reef's towering and colorful landforms from your car on the 25 mi. **scenic drive**, a 1hr. round-trip that wiggles around the cliffs, washes, and canyon floors on paved and improved dirt roads. Along Rte. 24, you can view the bathroom-sized **Fruita Schoolhouse** built by Mormon settlers, 1000-year-old **petroglyphs** etched on stone walls, and **Panorama Point. Chimney Rock** and the **Castle** are two striking sandstone formations on the way. The ▨**Fruita orchards** line the roads throughout the park. You're welcome to eat as much free fruit as you want while in the park (usually cherries and apricots), but there is a nominal fee to take fruit out of the orchards. **Capitol Reef Back-county Outfitters**, 644 E. Rte. 24, is the umbrella organization for all the guides in the area. (☎425-2010; www.ridethereef.com. Guided tours: full day $135, half-day $80; fishing trips: $225/$135; horse rides: 1hr. $30, half-day $95, lunch included.) If you want to strike out on your own, most trailheads lie along Rte. 24 or the scenic drive. The easy **Capitol Gorge Trail** (2 mi. round-trip, 2-3hr.) runs off the scenic drive. The **Rim Overlook and Navajo Knobs Trail** (9 mi. round-trip, 4-8hr.), one of the

THE SOUTHWEST

more challenging routes in the park, departs from the Hickman Bridge parking area and climbs to the canyon rim above the river to breathtaking vistas. **Cassidy Arch** (3½ mi. round-trip), starting on Grand Wash Rd., is a steep, challenging climb that will take you above Butch Cassidy's famous arch, but it is a shorter alternative to other hikes if you're pressed for time. In the northern and southern sections of the park, all hikes are considered backcountry travel and overnight trips require a **free backcountry permit,** available at the visitors center or from any park ranger.

BRYCE CANYON   ☎435

A park that seems too fantastic to be real, Bryce Canyon is perhaps one of the only places in the US where you can hear "wow!" echoed in hundreds of languages as people look into the canyon of pines and hoodoos (columns of eccentrically-shaped rock) for the first time. As Ebenezer Bryce, a Mormon carpenter with a gift for understatement, once said, the canyon is "one hell of a place to lose a cow."

■ **ORIENTATION AND PRACTICAL INFORMATION.** Approaching from the west, Bryce lies 1½hr. east of Cedar City; take Rte. 14 or Rte. 20 to U.S. 89. From the east, take I-70 to U.S. 89, turn east on Rte. 12 at Bryce Jct. (7 mi. south of Panguitch), and drive 14 mi. to the Rte. 63 junction; head south 4 mi. to the park entrance. To limit park traffic, the Park Service has a free shuttle system that takes visitors to the visitors center, lodge, and scenic overlooks in air-conditioned comfort. (Shuttle runs daily every 12min. 9am-5pm.) Private vehicles can travel park roads, but the Park Service urges visitors to leave their cars outside the park. The entrance fee is $20 per car and $10 per pedestrian. The **visitors center** is just inside the park. (☎834-5322; www.nps.gov/brca. Open daily June-Aug. 8am-8pm; Apr.-May and Sept.-Oct. 8am-6pm; Nov.-Mar. 8am-4:30pm.) **Post Office:** in Ruby's Inn Store, just north of the park entrance. (☎834-8088. Open M-F 8:30am-noon and 12:30-4:30pm, Sa 8:30am-12:30pm.) **Postal Code:** 84717. **Area Code:** 435.

■ **ACCOMMODATIONS AND FOOD. North** and **Sunset Campgrounds** ❶, both within 3 mi. of the visitors center, have 209 campsites, toilets, picnic tables, and water. (North is open year-round. Reserve sites May 15-Oct. for an additional $9 at ☎877-444-6777. Sunset is open late spring to early fall and is first come, first served. Sites $10.) Two campgrounds lie west of Bryce on scenic Rte. 12, in Dixie National Forest. At 7400 ft., **Red Canyon Campground** ❶ has 36 sites amid red rocks. (Sites $11.) Obtain **backcountry camping permits** ($5) from the ranger at the visitors center. **King Creek Campground** ❶, 11 mi. from Bryce on Forest Service Road 087 off Rte. 12 (look for signs to Tropic Reservoir), features lakeside sites. (☎800-280-2267. Sites $10.) Sleeping inside the park requires either a tent and sleeping bag or a fat wallet, but good deals line Rte. 12 in Tropic or in Panguitch, which has over 15 inexpensive, independent motels. Winter rates are much lower, and during slow summers, look out for bargain walk-in rates. The **Country Inn Motel** ❷, 121 N. Main St. in Tropic, has newly-furnished rooms at good prices. (☎679-8600. Doubles $45, each additional adult $5; children free. AmEx/D/MC/V.)

> **TIP** **ON THE ROAD AGAIN.** Driving through southern Utah, roads near and through national parks can change from pavement to gravel or dirt without notice. Some roads may even become four-wheel drive (4WD) or all-terrain vehicle (ATV) only. Be sure to check with a local visitors center before zooming down non-highway roads in a vehicle that may not be up to the task.

Inside and immediately surrounding the national park, food options are scarce and require some driving. **Bryce Canyon Camper Store ❶** has pizza or prepackaged sandwiches ($2-3). For a sit-down lunch in the park, try the burgers and sandwiches ($7-8) at **Bryce Canyon Lodge Dining Room ❸**. Dinner is more expensive, and reservations are recommended. (☎834-5361. Dinner $15-22. Open Apr.-Oct. daily 6:30-10:30am, 11am-3:30pm, and 5:30-9:30pm. AmEx/D/MC/V.) All-you-can-eat golden pancakes ($3) beckon starving passersby at the **Hungry Coyote ❷**, 2 N. Main St. in Tropic. (☎679-8822. Dinner $10-15. Open daily Apr.-Oct. 6:30-10:30am and 5-10pm. AmEx/D/MC/V.) Several miles west of the park on Rte. 12, the **Bryce Pines Restaurant ❸** serves delicious meals. (☎834-5441. Sandwiches $5-8. Open daily in summer 6:30am-9:30pm. AmEx/D/MC/V.) In Panguitch, the **C-Stop Pizza and Deli ❶**, 561 E. Center St., practically gives away 10 in. pizzas with up to nine toppings for $5. (☎676-8366. Open M-Sa 10:30am-10pm. MC/V.) **Rock House Coffee**, 506 Main St. (☎676-2665), has espresso ($1.50), pastries ($1), and wireless Internet access.

◙ ⚑ SIGHTS AND OUTDOOR ACTIVITIES. Bryce's 18 mi. main road winds past spectacular lookouts, with Bryce and Inspiration Points providing quintessential postcard-worthy views of the canyon. One oft-missed viewpoint is **Fairyland Point,** at the north end of the park, 1 mi. off the main road, which has the best sights in the canyon. A range of hiking trails lure visitors from their cars. The **Rim Trail** can be accessed anywhere along the rim and has very little elevation change (11 mi., 4-6hr.). The moderate **Navajo/Queen's Garden Loop** (3 mi., 2-3hr.) is an excellent way to experience the canyon and see some of the park's most famous vistas. A less-traveled trail with great views of hoodoos and wildflowers in the summer is the **Tower Bridge Trail** (3½ mi., 2-3hr.). A more challenging option is the **Peek-A-Boo Loop** (3½ mi., 3-4hr.), which winds in and out of hoodoos. A word to the wise: the air is thin—if you start to feel short of breath, take a rest. Very sturdy shoes or hiking boots are a must for hiking into the canyon. **Canyon Trail Rides** arranges guided horseback rides. (☎679-8665. 2hr. rides $40, half-day $55.)

GRAND STAIRCASE-ESCALANTE NAT'L MONUMENT ☎435

Still one of the most unexplored and mysterious regions of the Southwest, Grand Staircase-Escalante is a relatively new monument, dedicated by President Bill Clinton in 1996. The last corner of American wilderness to be recorded by a cartographer, Grand Staircase-Escalante National Monument remains far more remote than its neighboring parks, and for this reason is secluded from much of the tourist bustle. With hidden slot canyons, dinosaur tracks, and reminders of ancient Native American civilizations, the 1.9 million acre area is a beautiful stretch of land, perfect for hiking and canyoneering.

The Staircase is big and wild, best suited to backcountry adventure. Only one developed trail, the moderate **Calf Creek Falls Trail,** exists in the entire monument, leading to a gorgeous 126 ft. waterfall. (6 mi. round-trip, 3-5hr. Accessible from Calf Creek Recreation Area 15 mi. east of Escalante on Rte. 12.) Though all other excursions are considered backcountry, don't be intimidated. **Hole-in-the-Rock Road,** heading south from Rte. 12 east of Escalante, is a primary access road (4WD) for the Canyon area and gives a chance to explore canyons and dinosaur tracks. The beautifully narrow slot canyons, **◙Spooky** and **Peek-A-Boo,** are well-traveled and geared toward experienced hikers with basic climbing ability. (3-4 mi., 3-5hr. 26 mi. down the Hole-in-the-Rock road, turn at sign for Dry Fork.) Dinosaur tracks, including a tail-drag, can be seen along the same road. **Death Hollow Wilderness,** a 30 mi. trek requiring technical climbing and stretches of swimming, is one of the most challenging routes. **◙Excursions of Escalante**, 125 E. Main in Escal-

THE BIG SPLURGE

CONQUER THE CANYONS

A canyoneering adventure through slot canyons and narrows might be paralled only by sky-diving for its sheer excitement value. Slipping sideways, nose against the rocks, sun and shadows gleaming through red canyons as you maneuver your body into acrobatic poses, canyoneering is the pinnacle of athletic and aesthetic rolled into one.

Canyoneering, broadly defined as the act of traveling through a canyon, is a sport unique to the Southwest and perfectly suited to Grand Staircase-Escalante's hidden canyons. You get a view into the Earth's layers that you can't see from the road and won't find hiking. Consider the hefty $100 per day cost as tuition for the most amazing geology lesson you'll ever take.

The best part, though, is the 100 ft. rappel at the end of certain canyons, a once-in-a-lifetime opportunity to become a human spider. Your heart may race, and you may get claustrophobic at times, but at the end of the tunnel, you'll definitely want to go back for more.

Excursions of Escalante (☎800-839-7567; www.excursions-escalante.com.) *leads guided canyoneering tours. Full-day canyoneering tour $100, meals and equipment included.*

ante, has award-winning and enthusiastic guides that will personalize backcountry outings, backpacking trips, and canyoneering through Escalante's slot canyons to your needs. (☎800-839-7567; www.excursions-escalante.com. Hiking trips $80 per day. Canyoneering $100 per day. Backpacking $200 per night. Prices include meals and equipment.) A **free backcountry permit** is required for all stays in the monument and can be obtained at any visitors center. Most routes require technical climbing or canyoneering skills, and the slot canyons and terrain are susceptible to extremely dangerous flash floods. Unless you are a seasoned backpacker and well prepared for your adventure, it may be a wise idea to hire a guide to show you these particular areas. It's always best to check in at the visitors center first.

The town of Escalante, located on Rte. 12, offers several motels, campgrounds, and cabin rentals. ◾**Escalante Outfitters ❷**, 320 W Main, is a gear store, espresso bar, and restaurant, with private cabins and tent sites. Wireless Internet is free inside the cafe. (☎826-4266; www.escalanteoutfitters.com. Tent sites $15; private cabins $30. AmEx/D/MC/V.) The 13 shaded sites at **Calf Creek Campground ❶**, 15 mi. east of Escalante, offer easy access to the Calf Creek Trail but fill up fast. (Toilets and water. Sites $7.) Two miles west of Escalante on Rte. 12, the **Escalante Petrified Forest State Park ❶** has 22 sites along the banks of the reservoir; swimming is allowed. (☎826-4466. Showers, restrooms. Sites $14.) ◾**Kiva Koffeehouse** is a pleasant surprise on Rte. 12, 12 mi. east of Escalante. (☎826-4550. Sandwiches $5. Open M and W-Su 8:30am-4:30pm. MC/V.) At **The Trailhead Cafe ❶,** you can relax on the patio with a smoothie after a day of canyoneering. In the summer, stick around in the evenings for pick-up volleyball games. (☎826-4714. Smoothies $4. Sandwiches and salads $8. Open Apr.-Nov. M, W-Sa, and Su 8am-6pm. Cash only.) For grill food and ice cream, head to the **Escalante Frosty Shop ❶**, 40 E. Main. (☎826-4488. Burgers $2-3. Ice cream $2. Open M-Sa 11:30am-8:30pm. Cash only.)

Stretching along Rte. 12 between Capitol Reef and Bryce Canyon, the enormity of the monument necessitates a visitors center in each of the gateway towns: Kanab, Big Water, Cannonville, Boulder, and Escalante. The best one is the **Escalante Interagency Visitors Center,** 755 W. Main St. in Escalante. (☎826-5499. Open daily Mar.-Oct. 7:30am-5:30pm; Nov.-Feb. 8am-4:30pm.) Hours vary by location, and Big Water, Cannonville, and Boulder are only open mid-Mar. to Oct. The monument headquarters is at **Kanab Field Office,** 190 E. Center St., in Kanab. (☎644-4300; www.ut.blm.gov/monument. Open daily late Mar. to mid-Nov. 7:30am-5:30pm.)

ZION NATIONAL PARK   ☎435

Zion is the most developed and popular national park in Utah, with 2.5 million visitors annually to attest to its beauty and reputation as a mystical place all its own. In the 1860s, Mormon settlers came to the area and enthusiastically proclaimed that they had found Zion, the promised land representing freedom from persecution. Brigham Young disagreed, however, and declared that the place was awfully nice, but "not Zion." The name "not Zion" stuck for years until a new wave of explorers dropped the "not," giving the park its present name. Zion may not be the promised land, but it's a park that will humble and redeem the most adventurous cliff-climbers, narrows-seekers, and hikers. With russet sandstone cliffs that are among the highest in the world and the Virgin River, one of the last free-flowing river systems on the Colorado Plateau, Zion is its own natural wonder.

■ ⁊ ORIENTATION AND PRACTICAL INFORMATION. Zion's main entrance is in **Springdale,** on Rte. 9, which borders the park to the south along the Virgin River, but the red-carpet entrance, guaranteed to build anticipation and awe, approaches Zion from the west. Take Rte. 9 from I-15 at Hurricane. From the east, pick up Rte. 9 from U.S. 89 at Mt. Carmel Jct. **Greyhound** (☎800-231-2222; www.greyhound.com), has service as far as Hurricane, while Zion Canyon Transportation (☎877-635-5993) has shuttle service from St. George to Zion (round-trip $27). The highway, campgrounds, visitors center, and museum are all accessible by car, but to enter the heart of the canyon, you'll need to park and take the **free shuttle bus,** which stops at all major trailheads and sites (every 6-10min.) and is an excellent way to get an overview of the park in just under 1½hr. Another free shuttle connects the park to food and lodgings in town. Organic architecture and an energy-efficient design make the **Zion Canyon Visitors Center** a sight in itself. Located just inside the south entrance, it has an info center, bookstore, and backcountry permit station. (☎772-7616; www.nps.gov/zion. Visitors center open daily late May to early Sept. 8am-7pm; mid-Apr. to late May and early Sept. to Oct. 8am-6pm; Oct. to mid-Apr. 8am-5pm. Permit station open daily Apr. 24-May 28 7am-5pm, May 29-Sept. 4 7am-7pm, and Sept. 5-Oct. 15 7am-6pm.) At the northwest entrance to the park, the **Kolob Canyon Visitors Center** has maps and info on the Kolob Canyon Scenic Drive and the surrounding trails. (☎586-9548. Open daily June-Aug. 8am-4:30pm; Apr.-May and Sept.-Oct. 7am-4:30pm.) The park's entrance fee is $10 for pedestrians and bikes and $20 per car. **Emergency:** ☎911 or 772-3322. **Post Office:** Stamps and mail drop in the visitors center; full-service in Springdale on Zion Park Blvd. **Postal Code:** 84767. **Area Code:** 435.

⎇ ACCOMMODATIONS. The cheapest indoor lodging is 30 mi. outside the park in Hurricane, where budget motels line I-15 and rooms run $35-50. In Springdale, the **El Río Lodge ❸,** 995 Zion Park Blvd., provides clean rooms, friendly service, and dazzling views. (☎772-3205 or 888-772-3205. Queen bed $49; two double beds $59. Winter rates slightly lower. AmEx/D/DC/MC/V.) Across the street, the **Terrace Brook Lodge ❸,** 990 Zion Park Blvd., has basic rooms. (☎800-342-6779. In summer singles $49, doubles $71; in winter $39/$61. AAA discount. D/MC/V.) The **Zion Canyon Campground ❶/RV Park ❶/Quality Inn ❸,** 479 Zion Park Blvd., in the same complex, provide some cheaper options with access to the Virgin River, a swimming pool, laundry, and showers. (☎772-3237. Tent sites $20. RV hookups $24. Hotel rooms $65. AmEx/D/MC/V.) More than 300 sites are available at the **South** and **Watchman Campgrounds ❶,** near the Zion Canyon visitors center. Campgrounds fill quickly in summer; arrive before noon to ensure a spot. Watchman Campground takes reservations, but South is first come, first served. (☎800-365-2267 for Watchman reservations. Drinking water and toilets. Sites $14.)

🖸 FOOD. The Zion Canyon Lodge houses the only in-park concessions. Inside, the **Castle Dome Cafe ❶** feeds hungry families and hikers. (☎772-3213. Burgers, salads, and subs $3-7. Open Apr.-Oct. daily 10am-7pm. Cash only.) Meanwhile, the **Red Rock Grill ❸** caters to a less rambunctious group. (☎772-3213. Entrees $15-22. Reservations recommended. Open daily 6-10am, 11:30am-2:30pm, and 6-10pm. AmEx/D/MC/V.) Just outside the park entrance, Springdale has a variety of hearty options. **🖾Oscar's Cafe ❸,** 948 Zion Park Blvd., happily fills hungry tummies with hints of spice and creative avocado use. Try their famous garlic burgers. (☎772-3232. Burgers $8-13. Sandwiches and burritos $7-8. Open daily 11am-10pm. AmEx/D/MC/V.) The **🖾Springdale Fruit Co. ❶,** 2491 Zion Park Blvd., 3 mi. south of Zion on Highway 9, sits in the midst of a breezy organic orchard and offers one of the best and cheapest picnic lunches around. The blueberry muffins are exceptional. (☎772-3222; www.springdalefruit.com. Sandwiches $5. Muffins $1. Open mid-Mar. to late Nov. daily 8am-8pm, but call ahead. MC/V.) Located in a former Mormon church with a beer garden out back, **Zion Pizza & Noodle Co. ❸,** 868 Zion Park Blvd. has a veggie lasagna that will make any carb-craver melt. (☎772-3815; www.zion-pizzanoodle.com. Pizza $9-14. Pasta $10. Open daily 4-10pm. Cash only.)

🖎 OUTDOOR ACTIVITIES. Zion accommodates casual scenery-seeking walkers as well as the more adventurous cliff-crawling crowd. While most of the park's trails won't have you praying for a stray mule, a few of the trails spiral around cliffs with narrow ledges and long drop-offs, so those with a fear of heights may want to choose their desired route carefully. The trails are serviced by a shuttle bus that delivers hikers to and from various trailheads (runs daily 5:45am-11pm). Shuttle maps are available at the visitors center. The **Riverside Walk** (2 mi., 1-2hr.), paved and wheelchair accessible, is Zion's easiest and most popular trail. It begins at the Temple of Sinawava at the north end of the shuttle route and runs along the Virgin River, leading to the Narrows. The **Emerald Pools Trail** (1-3 mi., 1-3hr.), the best way to see the park's waterfalls, is wheelchair accessible along the lower loop; however, the middle and upper loops are rather steep and fairly narrow. Although it may seem inviting, swimming is not allowed in the pools. The **Hidden Canyon Trail** (2 mi., 2-3hr.), is short but harrowing and grants visitors impressive valley views. The tough **Observation Point Trail** (8 mi., 5hr.) leads through **Echo Canyon,** a spectacular kaleidoscope of sandstone. **The Narrows** is one of the most popular areas in the entire park, and you can get a taste of it without a permit by continuing up the Riverside Walk (1-5hr.). Alternatively, you can obtain a backcountry permit and make the trip an overnight hike (requires a shuttle to the trailhead). The route, up to 16 mi. one-way, follows the riverbed through the neck of Zion Canyon above the end of the Riverwalk Trail. The trail is beautiful and remote, but be careful and always check in first at the visitors center—the canyon's high walls make flash floods here deadly. **Kolob Canyons,** the northwest region of the park, has its own impressive vistas and hiking trails. The **🖾Zion-Mt. Carmel Highway,** connecting the park's south and east entrances, winds through the canyon, offering excellent views of the valley and a ride through a 1¼ mi. long tunnel built in the 1920s. Though strenuous, the **Kolob Arch Trail** (14 mi., 8hr.) gives hikers a view of what is possibly the world's largest free-standing arch. Zion and the surrounding area also has a loyal **mountain biking** following. **Gooseberry Mesa,** about 15 mi. from Springdale, has great singletrack and novice trails, while the **J.E.M. Hurricane Trail** provides excellent views of Zion and the Pine Valley Mountains. For rentals, repairs, tours, advice, and showers, head to **Springdale Cycles,** 1458 Zion Park Blvd. (☎772-0575 or 800-776-2099; www.springdalecycles.com. Open daily 9am-7pm. Front suspension half-day $25, full day $35; full suspension $35/$45; children $7/$10.)

◙ **SIGHTS.** From May to August, visitors can enjoy music under the stars at the 2000-seat outdoor **Tanner Amphitheater**, 1 mi. from the park entrance, at the intersection of Lion Blvd. and Zion Park Blvd.; follow Lion Blvd. for 2 mi. to the theater. Concerts range from classical orchestral pieces to jazz to country, all surrounded by Zion's stunning cliffs. (☎652-7994; www.dixie.edu/tanner. Concerts begin at 8pm. Tickets $9, children under 18 $6.) Conveniently nestled in nearby Springdale is the █**Fatali Gallery**, 868 Zion Park Blvd. The gallery showcases Michael Fatali's illuminating photographs of desert canyons and is definitely worth a stop. (☎772-2422; www.fatali.com. Open daily 4-10pm.)

CEDAR BREAKS NATIONAL MONUMENT ☎435

Shaped like a gigantic amphitheater, the semicircle of canyons that compose Cedar Breaks National Monument measures more than 3 mi. in diameter and 2000 ft. in depth. The red, yellow, and even purple layers of sediment are emphasized by a gallery of spires, columns, and arches, all cut by the erosive powers of water, ice, and wind. To reach this geological marvel, take Rte. 14 east from Cedar City, then go north on Rte. 148 4 mi. to the entrance. (☎586-9451; www.nps.gov/cebr. Entrance $4 per person per week, ages 16 and under free.) A 28-site **campground ❶** on the edge of an alpine meadow (water, flush toilets; open mid-June to Sept.; sites $14; max. stay 7 nights) and the **visitors center** (☎586-0787; open daily June to mid-Oct. 8am-6pm) await at **Point Supreme.** Tourists travel to the Monument almost exclusively for the view, most easily seen by parking at the visitors center and walking to Point Supreme or by stopping at one of several vistas along the 5 mi. stretch of scenic Hwys. 148 and 143 within the monument. Cedar Breaks maintains two trails that provide a more detailed experience. Starting at the **Chessman Ridge Overlook** (10,467 ft., about 2 mi. from the visitors center), the 2 mi. round-trip **Alpine Pond Trail** follows the rim to a spring-fed alpine lake whose waters trickle into the breaks, incrementally eroding the landscape as they descend toward the Great Basin. The hike takes 1-2hr. and can be accompanied by a trail guide available at the visitors center or trailhead ($1). The 4 mi. round-trip **Ramparts Trail** departs from the visitors center at 10,300 ft. and traces the amphitheater's edge through a bristlecone grove to two breathtaking viewpoints. Though reaching the monument in the winter is difficult on snowy roads, winter recreationalists cherish the rolling meadows and serene winter scenery. There are no services inside the monument; the nearest gas, food, and lodging are in Cedar City and Brian Head.

LAKE POWELL AND GLEN CANYON 928

The decision to curb the Colorado River's steady flow to the Pacific was made in 1956, and 10 years and 10 million tons of concrete later, Glen Canyon Dam, the second-largest dam in the country, was completed. Backed into the once-remote Glen Canyon the mighty river created the expansive Lake Powell and spawned a vacation destination that draws visitors seeking the crown jewel of the US's national recreation areas. Both the **Rainbow Bridge National Monument** and **Antelope Canyon** attract countless tourists to revel in the artistry of water at work on sandstone canvas. Because the Rainbow Bridge remains sacred to area native cultures, visitors are asked not to approach, climb on, or pass through this breathtaking lesson in erosional art. Hiking to Rainbow Bridge on Navajo land requires a **hiking permit,** obtainable by writing Navajo Nation Parks and Recreation Department, Box 9000, Window Rock, AZ 86515. Antelope Canyon is divided by Rte. 98 into two parts: upper and lower. **Upper Antelope** is the more accessible; **Lower Antelope** involves climbing ladders and slipping through extremely narrow gaps. Lake Powell's 96 beautiful side canyons are extremely popular destinations, but to enjoy them, water transport is necessary. **Lake Powell Resorts and Marinas,** 100 Lake

Shore Rd. (☎800-528-6154), in Page, leads tours. **Twin Finn Diving**, 811 Vista Ave., in Page, AZ, rents kayaks. (☎928-645-3114. Kayaks $35-45 per day.)

The majority of indoor accommodations and restaurants are in Page, AZ, just southeast of the dam. Motels and unspectacular restaurants line Lake Powell Blvd., a U-shaped road connecting with **U.S. 89** both north and south of town. Named after the owner's affectionate Yorkie, **K.C.'s Motel ❷**, 126 S. 8th Ave., has spacious suites with cable TV. (☎645-2947. Rooms from $26. MC/V.) Visitors can camp nearly anywhere on the endless lakeshore, so long as they have a portable toilet and a permit. **Bullfrog Developed Campground ❶** has 78 first come, first served sites with bathrooms, picnic tables, water, and grills. (☎435-685-3000. Sites $18.) Dining options in Page are limited, barely escaping the hum-drum meat and potatoes or mediocre Mexican cuisine so pervasive in the area. If the meager choices have got you down, head to **Safeway**, 650 Elm St. (☎645-8155). Otherwise, try your luck with the eateries along Lake Powell Blvd. or N. Navajo Dr.

Four marinas operate along the perimeter of Lake Powell, offering gas, rentals, and groceries. The main access point from Arizona is **Wahweap Marina**, 6 mi. north of Page on Hwy. 89. The main access point from Utah is **Bullfrog Marina**, on Hwy. 267. The **Bullfrog Visitor Center** has exhibits on the area. (☎435-684-7400. Open Apr.-Oct. 8am-5pm.) The **Carl Hayden Visitor Center**, in Page, has info on the construction of the Dam. (☎928-608-6404. Open daily 8am-5pm, call for summer hours.) To get to Bullfrog, take Hwy. 24 S from I-70 to Hanksville, then Hwy. 95 to Hwy 276 to Bullfrog Basin. To get to Page, follow Hwy. 89 S through Utah, or take Hwy. 89 N from Arizona. **Postal Code:** 86040. **Area Code:** 928.

ARIZONA

The romantic backdrop for old Westerns and wandering cowboy spirits, Arizona is certainly dry and rugged, but this vibrant state defies any simple stereotype. Its borders contain the Grand Canyon, most of the Navajo Reservation, two bustling cities, and seven national forests, one of which is the world's largest ponderosa pine forest. The Sonoran desert's dry scrub, spotted with cacti and the occasional dusty town, makes for a stark but beautiful landscape, while Arizona's cities and mountain biking and hiking country provide enough variety for hours, days, or weeks of exploration. Populated primarily by Native Americans until the end of the 19th century, Arizona has been hit by waves of settlers: speculators and miners of the late 1800s, soldiers who returned after training here during World War II, and more recently, immigrants from Mexico. Traces of lost Native American civilizations remain prevalent, and the tribes' descendants occupy half of Arizona.

⚄ PRACTICAL INFORMATION

Capital: Phoenix.

Visitor Info: Arizona Tourism, 1110 W. Washington St., Ste. 155, Phoenix 85007 (☎602-364-3700 or 866-275-5816; www.arizonaguide.com). Open M-F 8am-5pm. **Arizona State Parks,** 1300 W. Washington St., Phoenix 85007 (☎602-542-4174; www.pr.state.az.us). Open M-F 8am-5pm.

Postal Abbreviation: AZ. **Sales Tax:** variable, around 5%.

Time Zone: Mountain Standard Time. With the exception of the Navajo Reservation, Arizona does not observe Daylight Saving Time.

GRAND CANYON

Each year, millions of people from across the globe are drawn to the magnificent Grand Canyon and crowd its rim with curiosity and high expectations. Skeptics often wonder if it deserves its grandiose reputation, but seeing one sunrise or sunset in the canyon is enough to make a believer out of the most reluctant visitor. First there's the space: 277 mi. long and over one mile deep, the enormous crevice overwhelms the human capacity for perception. Then there's the color: the shifts in hue translate to millions of years of geologic history and make the panoramic view even more awe-inspiring.

Grand Canyon National Park is divided into three sections: the popular South Rim, the more serene North Rim, and the canyon gorge itself, which begins at Lake Powell, AZ, and feeds into Lake Mead, NV. Between the National Park area and Lake Mead are the Hualapai and Havasupai Reservations, which offer separate entrances into the Canyon. Traveling between rims takes approximately 5½hr. via the long drive to the Lee's Ferry bridge or even longer via a grueling 13 mi. hike.

SOUTH RIM   ☎928

In the summer, everything on two legs or four wheels comes to this side of the Grand Canyon, primarily for the fantastic and easily accessed views from the rim. If you plan to visit at this time, be sure to make reservations for everything far in advance and prepare to battle crowds. A friendly Park Service staff, well-run facilities, and beautiful scenery generally make for enjoyable visits despite the high volume of people. Fewer tourists brave the canyon in the winter, so most hotels and facilities close during the low season.

⬛ TRANSPORTATION

There are two park entrances: the main **south entrance** is about 6 mi. from the visitors center, while the eastern **Desert View** entrance is 27 mi. away. Both are accessible via Rte. 64. From Las Vegas, the fastest route to the South Rim is U.S. 93 S to I-40 E, and then Rte. 64 N. From Flagstaff, head north on U.S. 180 to Rte. 64.

Trains: The **Grand Canyon Railway** (☎800-843-8724) runs a restored train, the same that serviced the park in 1901, from Williams, AZ, to the Grand Canyon (2¼hr.; leaves 10am, returns 3:30pm; $58, children $25). Guided train tours of the rim $29-39.

THE SOUTHWEST

Buses: Open Road Tours & Transportation (☎226-8060 or 877-226-8060) departs from Flagstaff (1 E. Rte. 66) daily at 8:30am, 3pm for the Grand Canyon. Return trips depart from Maswick Lodge at 11:45am, 5:45pm. (2hr.; $25, reservations recommended.)

Public Transit: Free shuttle buses run along the West Rim to Hermits Rest (1¼hr. round-trip; operates daily May-Sept. every 10-30min. 1hr. before sunrise to 1hr. after sunset) and the Village Loop (1hr. round-trip; operates daily every 10-30min. 1hr. before sunrise to 10pm). May-Sept., the Hermits Rest shuttle is the only way to access the West Rim area. A free **hiker's shuttle** runs between the info center and the South Kaibab Trailhead, on the East Rim near Yaki Point. Early buses run June-Aug. 4, 5, and 6am.

Taxi: Fred Harvey Transportation Company, ☎638-2822.

▪▪ ? ORIENTATION AND PRACTICAL INFORMATION

Posted maps and signs in the park make orientation easy. Lodges and services concentrate in **Grand Canyon Village,** at the west end of Park Entrance Rd. To the east lie the visitors center, campground, and general store, while most of the lodges and the **Bright Angel Trail** are in the west section. The **South Kaibab Trail** is off **Desert View Drive** east of the village. Free shuttle buses to eight rim overlooks run along **Hermit Road** in the west (closed to private vehicles in summer). Avoid walking on the drive; the rim trails are safer and more scenic. An **entrance pass** is $20 per car and $10 for travelers using other modes of transportation; the pass lasts one week. For most services in the park, call the main switchboard at ☎638-2631.

Visitor Info: The **Canyon View Information Plaza,** across from Mather Point by the park entrance, is the one-stop center for info, stocking the must-have *The Guide* ($12), pamphlets, and info on hiking. To get there, park at Mather Pt., then walk ½ mi. to the info plaza. (☎800-858-2808; www.grandcanyon.com, or www.nps.gov/grca.) The **transportation info desks** in the **Bright Angel Lodge** and the **Maswik Lodge** (☎638-2631) take reservations for mule rides, bus tours, plane tours, Phantom Ranch, taxis, and more. Open daily 6am-8pm.

Equipment Rental: At the gear counter in Canyon Village Marketplace in Market Plaza. Hiking boots and socks $8. Sleeping bags $9. 2-person tent $15, 4-person tent $16. Small day pack $4, large $6. Stoves $5. Deposit required. Open daily 7am-8pm.

Weather and Road Conditions: ☎638-7888.

Medical Services: Grand Canyon Clinic (☎638-2551). Turn left at the first stoplight after the South Rim entrance. Open M-F 7am-7pm, Sa 10am-4pm. 24hr. emergency aid.

Post Office: Grand Canyon Market Plaza (☎638-2512), next to the Marketplace. Open M-F 9am-4:30pm, Sa 11am-3pm. **Postal Code:** 86023. **Area Code:** 928.

▌ ACCOMMODATIONS

Indoor lodging within the park requires months of advance planning, but a few options exist just outside the park and even more within an hour's drive in neighboring Williams and Flagstaff. Summer rooms in the park should be reserved 11 months in advance (☎888-297-2757 or write Xanterra, 14001 E. Iliff, Ste. 600, Aurora, CO 80014). That said, there are frequent cancellations; if you arrive unprepared, check for vacancies or call the operator (☎638-2631) and ask to be connected with the proper lodge.

Bright Angel Lodge (☎638-2631), in Grand Canyon Village, sits in a historic building right on the rim. Very close to Bright Angel Trail and shuttle buses. Basic rooms $49; singles and doubles with shared bath $67, with private bath $71. "Historic" cabins, some with fireplaces, for 1 or 2 people $82. $7 per additional person. AmEx/D/DC/MC/V. ❸

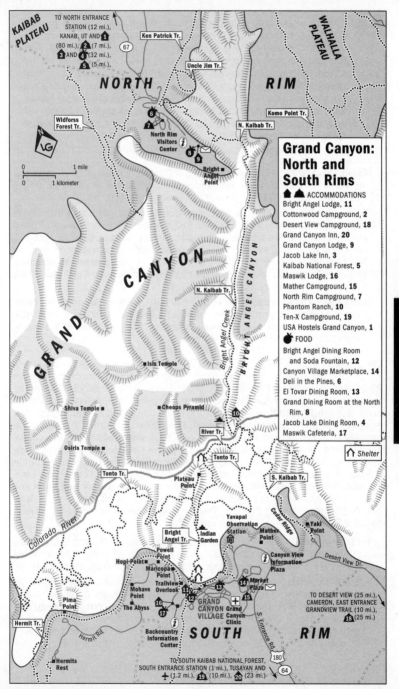

KAIBAB PLATEAU

TO NORTH ENTRANCE STATION (12 mi.), KANAB, UT AND **1** (80 mi.), **2** (7 mi.) **3** AND **4** (32 mi.), **5** (5 mi.)

Ken Patrick Tr.

67

Uncle Jim Tr.

N O R T H   R I M

WALHALLA PLATEAU

Widforss Forest Tr.

VG

0   1 mile
0   1 kilometer

6
7

North Rim Visitors Center

Komo Point Tr.

N. Kalbab Tr.

8
9

Bright Angel Point

Grand Canyon: North and South Rims

🏠🏕 **ACCOMMODATIONS**

Bright Angel Lodge, **11**
Cottonwood Campground, **2**
Desert View Campground, **18**
Grand Canyon Inn, **20**
Grand Canyon Lodge, **9**
Jacob Lake Inn, **3**
Kaibab National Forest, **5**
Maswik Lodge, **16**
Mather Campground, **15**
North Rim Campground, **7**
Phantom Ranch, **10**
Ten-X Campground, **19**
USA Hostels Grand Canyon, **1**

🍴 **FOOD**

Bright Angel Dining Room and Soda Fountain, **12**
Canyon Village Marketplace, **14**
Deli in the Pines, **6**
El Tovar Dining Room, **13**
Grand Dining Room at the North Rim, **8**
Jacob Lake Dining Room, **4**
Maswik Cafeteria, **17**

⌂ *Shelter*

G R A N D

C A N Y O N

■ Isis Temple

Shiva Temple ■

■ Cheops Pyramid

Osiris Temple ■

N. Kalbab Tr.

Bright Angel Creek

BRIGHT ANGEL CANYON

10

River Tr.

Tonto Tr.

Tonto Tr.

Plateau Point

S. Kalbab Tr.

Colorado River

Bright Angel Tr.

Powell Point

Hopi Point ■

Maricopa Point

Mohave Point ■

The Abyss

Pima Point ■

Hermit Tr.

Hermits Rest ■

Trailview Overlook

16
17
12
11
13
14
15

GRAND CANYON VILLAGE

Grand Canyon Clinic

Backcountry Information Center

Hermit Rd.

Indian Garden

Yavapai Observation Station

Mather Point

Yaki Point

Cedar Ridge

Canyon View Information Plaza

Market Plaza

Desert View Dr.

TO DESERT VIEW (25 mi.), CAMERON, EAST ENTRANCE GRANDVIEW TRAIL (10 mi.) **18** (25 mi.)

S O U T H   R I M

S. Entrance Rd.

180

TO SOUTH KAIBAB NATIONAL FOREST, SOUTH ENTRANCE STATION (1 mi.), TUSAYAN AND ✚ (1.2 mi.), **19** (10 mi.), **20** (23 mi.)

64

THE SOUTHWEST

> Seeing the canyon from the inside is harder than it looks. Even the young of body and heart should recall that there are no easy trails, and what starts as a downhill stroll can become a nightmarish 50° incline on the way back. Also, note that the lower you go, the hotter it gets; when it's 85°F on the rim, it's around 100°F at Indian Gardens and around 110°F at Phantom Ranch. Heat stroke, the greatest threat to a hiker, is marked by a monstrous headache and red, sweatless skin. **For a day-hike, take at least a gallon of water per person; drink at least a quart per hour hiking uphill under the hot sun.** Footwear with excellent tread is also necessary; the trails are steep, and every year careless hikers take what locals morbidly call "the 12-second tour." Parents should think twice about bringing children more than 1 mi. down any trail.

Maswik Lodge (☎ 638-2631), at the west end of Grand Canyon Village. Small, clean cabins with showers. Rooms with queen-sized beds and ceiling fans also available. Singles $76; doubles $120. $7-9 for each additional person. AmEx/D/DC/MC/V. ❹

Phantom Ranch (☎ 638-2631), on the canyon floor, a day's hike down the Kaibab Trail or Bright Angel Trail. Breakfast $17; box lunch $10; stew dinner $21; steak dinner $31; vegetarian option $21. Reservations are necessary and can be made up to 23 months in advance. If you're dying to sleep on the canyon floor but have no reservation, go to the Bright Angel transportation desk at 6am on the day prior to your planned stay and take a shot on the waiting list. Single-sex dorms $30; hard-to-get cabins for 1 or 2 people $80, $12 per additional person. AmEx/D/DC/MC/V. ❷

Grand Canyon Inn, (☎ 635-9203 or 800-635-9203; www.grand-canyon-inn.com). Located in Valle at the junction of Hwy. 180, 25min. from the park entrance. Clean, spacious rooms and a pool. 1-month advance reservations are recommended in summer. Singles $49; doubles $59. AmEX/D/MC/V. ❸

⚑ CAMPING

While lodgings in the park are usually filled before you've even decided to visit the Grand Canyon, camping is always a good second option. Some reservations can be made through **SPHERICS** (☎ 800-365-2267). If you do run out of options, you can camp for free in the **Kaibab National Forest,** along the south border of the park. No camping is allowed within a quarter-mile of U.S. 64. **Dispersed camping** sits conveniently along the oft-traveled N. Long Jim Loop Rd.—turn right about a mile south of the south entrance station. For quieter, more remote sites, follow signs for the Arizona Trail into the national forest between miles 252 and 253 on U.S. 64. Fires are heavily restricted or even banned in some areas; make sure you know the rules. Sleeping in cars is not permitted in the park, but it is allowed in the Kaibab Forest. For more info, contact the **Tusayan Ranger Station** (☎ 638-2443), Kaibab National Forest, P.O. Box 3088, Tusayan 86023.

Ten-X Campground (☎ 638-2443), in Kaibab National Forest, 10 mi. south of Grand Canyon Village off Rte. 64. Away from the highway, Ten-X offers 70 quality sites surrounded by pine trees. Toilets, water. First come, first served. Open May-Sept. Sites $10. ❶

Mather Campground (call SPHERICS, ☎ 800-365-2267), in Grand Canyon Village, 1 mi. south of the Canyon Village Marketplace; follow signs from Yavapai Lodge. 327 shady, relatively isolated sites. Those on foot or bike can snag a spot in a communal hiker/biker site (ban on cars is strictly enforced); they are usually available on a walk-up basis. 7-night max. stay. Individual sites $15. Communal hiker/biker sites $4 per person. For Apr.-Dec. reserve up to 5 months in advance; Jan.-Mar. first come, first served. ❶

Desert View Campground (☎ 638-7888), 25 mi. east of Grand Canyon Village. Far from the South Rim, but perfect for avoiding crowds. Just watch out for the tarantulas. Sites with toilets; no hookups, campfires, or reservations. Open mid-May to Oct. Sites $10. ❶

▌ FOOD

Fast food has yet to spawn in the South Rim (the closest McDonald's is 7 mi. south in Tusayan), but you can find slightly better-quality meals at fast-food prices. The **Canyon Village Marketplace ❶**, at Market Plaza, 1 mi. west of Mather Point on the main road, has a deli counter with the cheapest eats in the park, groceries, camping supplies, and enough Grand Canyon apparel to clothe your entire extended family. (☎ 638-2262. Sandwiches $2-4. Open daily 7am-8pm. AmEx/D/MC/V.) **Maswik Cafeteria ❶**, in Maswik Lodge, serves a variety of salads, soups, country favorites, and Mexican specialties. (☎ 638-2631. Hot entrees $6-7. Sandwiches $3-5. Open daily 6am-10pm. AmEx/D/DC/MC/V.) **Bright Angel Dining Room ❷**, in Bright Angel Lodge, is popular with families and serves breakfast, hot sandwiches, and Southwestern-style dinner entrees. (☎ 638-2631. Breakfast $6-7. Hot sandwiches $7-9. Dinner entrees $10-15. Open daily 6:30am-10pm. AmEx/D/DC/MC/V.) Just outside the dining room of the Bright Angel Lodge, the **Soda Fountain ❶** has the basics for those on the go, including eight flavors of ice cream, snack-bar sandwiches, soda, and candy. (Sandwiches $3-4. 1 scoop ice cream $2. Open seasonally, hours vary.) The classiest dining in the park can be found at the historic **El Tovar Dining Room ❹**, in the El Tovar Hotel in the Village. The grandly appointed dining room has a great view of the canyon and food that lives up to its surroundings. Try the lamb with rosemary demi-glace ($21). (☎ 638-2631, ext. 6432. Open daily 6:30am-10pm. Dinner reservations recommended. AmEx/D/DC/MC/V.)

▌ HIKING

Hikes in and around the Grand Canyon can be broken down into day-hikes and overnight hikes. Confusing an overnight hike for a day-hike can be a dangerous mistake, so heed the warnings of rangers and don't attempt to get down and back from the Colorado River in one day. All overnight trips require permits obtained from the Backcountry Office, located on the west side of Parking Lot E near Maswik Lodge ($10; camping fee $5). Permits often take up to four months to obtain, so request one as early as possible via the Internet (www.nps.gov/grca), mail (P.O. Box 129, Grand Canyon, AZ, 86023), or walk-up. For day-hikes into the canyon, be prepared to retrace every footstep uphill on the way back. An enjoyable hike usually means beginning before 7am or after 4pm; it's best to consult a ranger at the Canyon View Information Plaza before leaving. Park Service rangers also present a variety of guided hikes; times and details are listed in *The Guide*.

The **Rim, Bright Angel, South Kaibab**, and **River** trails are the only South Rim trails regularly maintained and patrolled by the Park Service. While other trails do exist, they are only for experienced hikers and may contain steep chutes and technical terrain. Consult a ranger and *The Guide* before heading out.

Rim Trail (12 mi. one way, 4-6hr.). With only a mild elevation change (about 200 ft.) and the security of the nearby shuttle, the Rim Trail is an excellent way to see the canyon from all different angles. The trail is handicapped accessible to Maricopa Point in the west and has 8 viewpoints along Hermit Rd. and 3 east of it. Convenience and easy access to viewpoints make this trail the most crowded, but toward the eastern and western ends, hikers have a bit more room. Hopi Point's panoramic canyon views make it a great place to watch the sun set; *The Guide* lists sunset and sunrise times.

Bright Angel Trail (up to 18 mi. round-trip, 1-2 days). Bright Angel's many switchbacks and water stations make it the into-the-canyon choice of moderate hikers. Depending on distance, the trail can be either a day or overnight hike. Departing from the Rim Trail near the western edge of the Grand Canyon Village, the first 1-2 mi. attract droves of day-hikers looking for a taste of canyon descent. Rest houses are strategically stationed 1½ and 3 mi. from the rim, each with water May-Sept. **Indian Gardens,** 4½ mi. down, offers restrooms, picnic tables, 15 backcountry campsites open year-round, and blessed shade. From rim to river, the trail drops 4460 ft. The round-trip is too strenuous for a day-hike—do not attempt to make it one. With a permit, overnighters can camp at Indian Gardens or on the canyon floor at Bright Angel Campground. Day-hikers are advised to go no farther than Indian Gardens (9¼ mi. round-trip) or Plateau Point (12¼ mi. round-trip). The **River Trail** (1¾ mi.) links the Bright Angel with South Kaibab at the base of the Canyon.

South Kaibab Trail (7 mi. to Phantom Ranch, 4-5hr.) is for those seeking a more challenging descent. Beginning at Yaki Pt. (7260 ft.), Kaibab is trickier, steeper, and lacks shade or water, but it rewards the intrepid with a better view of the canyon. The South Kaibab avoids the safety and obstructed views of a side-canyon route, as it winds directly down the ridge, offering panoramic views across the canyon. Day-hikes to Cedar Ridge (3 mi. round-trip) and Skeleton Point (6 mi. round-trip) are reasonable only for experienced hikers due to the trail's steep grade. Kaibab meets up with Bright Angel at the Colorado River. Fewer switchbacks and a more rapid descent make the South Kaibab Trail 1¾ mi. shorter than the Bright Angel to this point—guests staying at the Phantom Ranch or Bright Angel Campground can use either trail to reach the ranch.

◤ OUTDOOR ACTIVITIES

Beyond using your feet, there are other ways to explore the Canyon. **Mule trips** from the South Rim are an option, but they're expensive and often booked up to one year in advance. (☎303-297-2757. Daytrip to Plateau Point 6 mi. down the Bright Angel Trail $120, lunch included; overnight including lodging at Phantom Ranch and all meals $325.) Looking up at the Grand Canyon from a **whitewater raft** is another popular option but usually costs between $1500-3500 depending on trip length. Trips into the Grand Canyon vary from seven to 18 days and generally require one-year advanced booking. The *Trip Planner* (available by request at the info center or on-line) lists several guides licensed to offer trips in the canyon. Most guides run out of Flagstaff or Page, AZ. **Calmwater rafting** trips are also available for those not quite ready for a wet and wild time in the heart of the canyon. Drifting from Glen Canyon Dam to Lee's Ferry generally takes a half-day. **Aramark-Wilderness River Adventures** arranges such trips. (☎800-528-6154. $62, children $52.) If the views from the rim fail to dazzle or astound you, try the higher vantages provided by one of the park's many **flightseeing** companies, located at the Grand Canyon Airport outside of Tuyasan. **Grand Canyon Airlines** flies 45min. tours hourly in the summer. (☎866-235-9422; www.grandcanyonairlines.com. $99, children $69. Reservations recommended.) For a list of flight companies, visit the Grand Canyon Chamber of Commerce's website (www.grandcanyonchamber.org).

NORTH RIM   ☎928

If you're coming from Utah or Nevada or are looking to avoid the South Rim's crowds, the park's North Rim is rugged and serene, with a view almost as spectacular as that from the South Rim. Unfortunately, it's hard to reach by public transit and is a long drive by car. From October 15 to December 1, the North Rim is open for day use only, and from December 1 to May 15, it closes entirely. In summer, sunsets from the Grand Canyon Lodge are spectacular and worth the long trip.

✈ 🛈 ORIENTATION AND PRACTICAL INFORMATION

To reach the North Rim from the South Rim, take Rte. 64 E to U.S. 89 N, which runs into Alt. 89; from Alt. 89, follow Rte. 67 S to the edge. The drive is over 220 mi. From Utah, take Alt. 89 S from Fredonia. From Page, take U.S. 89 S to Alt. 89 to Rte. 67 S. Snow closes Rte. 67 from early December to mid-May, and park facilities (including the lodge) close mid-October through mid-May. The visitor parking lot, 12 mi. south of the park entrance, is near the end of Rte. 67, close to both the visitors center and North Rim Lodge. Trailhead parking is also available at the North Kaibab and Widforss trails and at scenic points along the road to Cape Royal.

Buses: Transcanyon, P.O. Box 348, Grand Canyon 86023 (☎638-2820). Buses run to the South Rim. (5hr.; late May to Oct. leaves 7am from North Rim Lodge, 1:30pm from Bright Angel Lodge at the South Rim; $65). Reservations required.

Public Transit: A **hikers' shuttle** runs from the North Rim Lodge to the North Kaibab Trailhead (departs late May to Oct. 6, 6:30am).

Visitor Info: North Rim Visitors Center (☎638-2611), on Rte. 67 just before the Lodge. Open May-Oct. daily 8am-6pm. **Kaibab Plateau Visitors Center** (☎643-7298), at Jacob Lake, next to the Inn. Issues backcountry permits and has displays on the creation of the canyon and its ecosystem. Open daily 8am-5pm, but hours may vary.

Weather Conditions: ☎638-7888. Updated daily 7am.

Post Office: Grand Canyon Lodge (☎638-2611). Open M-F 8-11am and 11:30am-4pm, Sa 8am-1pm. **Postal Code:** 86052. **Area Code:** 928.

▌ ACCOMMODATIONS

Staying inside on the North Rim is pricey and requires advance planning, but there are still many lodging options. If you can't get in-park lodging, many less-expensive accommodations can be found 80 mi. north in Kanab, UT.

▧ **USA Hostels Grand Canyon,** 143 E. 100 S. (☎435-644-5554 or 877-205-7136), in Kanab. USA features a laid-back and friendly atmosphere with funky-retro decor and an unbelievably well-stocked movie and book collection. The owners are happy to dispense canyon advice. Free all-you-can-eat pancake breakfast served every morning. Full kitchen, showers, laundry ($1.25), and free wireless Internet. Dorms $15. Private rooms $32. MC/V. ❶

Grand Canyon Lodge (☎638-2611, reservations 888-297-2757), on the edge of the rim. This swank but rustic lodge is the only indoor rim lodging in the park. The overlook near the reception area is open to all and a great place to relax in the comfort of leather sofas. Reception 24hr. Reserve as early as 6 months in advance, or 2 years in advance for 1 of the 4 rim-view cabins. Open mid-May to Oct. Cabins $92-121; motel rooms for up to 3 people $91. AmEx/D/DC/MC/V. ❺

North Rim Campground (call SPHERICS ☎800-365-2267), on Rte. 67 near the rim, is the only park campground on this side of the chasm, with spacious sites among the ponderosas. Reservations recommended in summer. Groceries, showers ($1.25 per 5min.), and laundry ($2) nearby. 7-night max. stay. Open mid-May to mid-Oct. Sites $15. ❶

Jacob Lake Inn (☎643-7232; www.jacoblake.com), 44 mi. north of the North Rim entrance at Jacob Lake. Lodge, gift shop, and cafe (see below). Reception daily 6am-9pm. Cabins for 2 $72-79; triples $119; motel units $91-99. AmEx/D/DC/MC/V. ❸

Kaibab National Forest runs from north of Jacob Lake to the park entrance. You can camp for free, as long as you're ¼ mi. from the road, water, or official campgrounds, and 1 mi. from any commercial facility. A strict fire ban is in effect. ❶

Cottonwood Campground, 7 mi. down the North Kaibab Trailhead, is a good resting place for those doing an overnight hike into the Canyon. Drinking water available May-Oct. Requires $5 camping permit from the Backcountry Office. ❶

🍴 FOOD

Grand Dining Room at the North Rim (☎ 638-2612, ext. 160). On the edge of the canyon, the North Rim Lodge's dining room treats guests to sweeping views. The breakfast buffet ($8) and lunch options (salads and burgers $6-10) are generic but affordable. Dinners (from $13) do justice to the grand atmosphere. Open daily 6:30-10am, 11:30am-2:30pm, 5-9:30pm. Reservations required for dinner. AmEx/D/DC/MC/V. ❸

Deli in the Pines, at the North Rim Lodge, specializes in no-frills dining on the go. Salads, sandwiches, and burgers $4-6; pizza by the slice $2.50. Open daily 7am-9pm. ❶

Jacob Lake Dining Room (☎ 643-7232; www.jacoblake.com), 30 mi. north of the park entrance, is a good alternative to North Rim establishments. The old-fashioned diner counter, full restaurant, and tempting bakery offer a variety of options. Pick up a gravity-defying milkshake ($4) to make the remaining drive more enjoyable. Breakfast $5-6. Dinner $12-15. AmEx/D/DC/MC/V. ❸

🥾 OUTDOORS

Hiking in the leafy North Rim seems like a trip to the mountains—the mountain just happens to be upside-down. While the temptation to plunge down into the canyon is strong, it would be an extraordinarily bad idea. The North Rim is at a surprisingly high elevation, so the air is very thin, and there are no easy trails down into the canyon. You should never attempt to hike to the river and back in a single day. Info on trails can be found in the North Rim's version of *The Guide.* Day-hikes of various lengths beckon the active North Rim visitor. The **Bright Angel Point Trail** (½ mi. round-trip, 30min.) departs from the lodge area, and the **Cape Royal Trail** (¾ mi. round-trip, 30min.; handicapped accessible) departs from the Cape Royal parking area. Both offer impressive views of the canyon with little effort. The **Wid-forss Trail** (up to 10 mi. round-trip, 6hr.) is a more challenging day-hike but offers views of both canyon and forest and can be tailored into a shorter hike. The **North Kaibab Trail** (28 mi. round-trip) is the only maintained trail into the canyon on the North Rim and is for only the most experienced hikers. Consult rangers before beginning this hike. Pick up the invaluable *Official Guide to Hiking the Grand Canyon* ($12), available in all visitors centers and gift shops. Overnight hikers must get permits from the **Backcountry Office** in the ranger station, just north of the campground entrance, 11½ mi. from the park entrance. ($10 permit plus $5 per person per night. Open daily 8am-noon and 1-5pm.) Park rangers run nature walks, lectures, and evening programs at the North Rim Campground and Lodge. The info desk or campground bulletin boards have schedules. One-hour ($30), half-day ($55), and full-day ($105) **mule trips** through **Canyon Trail Rides** circle the rim or descend into the canyon. (☎ 435-679-8665. In the lodge lobby. Open May-Oct. daily 8am-5pm. Cash only.) Reservations are recommended, but walk-ins can be accommodated more often than on the South Rim.

HAVASUPAI RESERVATION   ☎ 928

To the west of the bustle of the South Rim lies the beautiful Havasupai Reservation. Meaning "people of the blue-green water," the Havasupai live in a protected enclave at the base of the canyon, bordered by the national park. Ringed by dramatic sandstone faces, their village, Supai, rests on the shores of the Havasu River and is only accessible by a 10-mi. trail starting at the Hualapai Hilltop. Just beyond town, rushing crystal-clear water cascades over a series of spectacular falls. Such beauty attracts thousands each year. Camping permits are required for overnight hiking, so reservations should be made far in advance. For most, blistered feet or a saddle-sore rump make bathing in the cool waters even sweeter. Those traveling to Supai should make plans to stay in either Seligman, Peach Springs, or Flagstaff.

To reach the trailhead leading to **Supai,** take I-40 E to Rte. 66 at Seligman; follow Rte. 66 for 30 mi. until it meets Indian Rd. 18, which ends at the Hilltop after 60 mi. No roads lead to Supai, but mules and helicopters can be hired to carry bags or people. For mule reservations, contact **Havasupai Tourist Enterprise.** (☎448-2237. One-way $75, half of which is required as a deposit. Includes 4 pieces of luggage not exceeding 130 lb. total. Groups leave at 10am.) Another option is to take the helicopter service, **AirWest.** (☎623-516-2790. One way $85 plus baggage charge by weight; first come, first served.) The hike, a grueling, exposed 8 mi. to Supai and then an additional 2 mi. to the campground, is not to be underestimated. Do not hike down without a reservation—you may have to go right back to the trailhead. Reservations for the campground, lodge, and mules can be made by calling the Havasupai Tourist Enterprise. Visitors must check in at the **tourist office** in Supai before heading on to the campground. The village has a post office, general store, and cafe. Prices are high because everything must be brought in by mule or helicopter; bringing your own food is advised. All trash must be packed out. No **gas** or **water** is available past Rte. 66, so stock up beforehand.

The Havasupai tribe operates the ⬛**Havasupai Campground** and the Havasupai Lodge, both on the canyon floor. The campground, 2 mi. past Supai, lies between Havasu and Mooney Falls, bordering the Havasu River's blue-green water and swimmer-friendly lagoons. The tribe charges a one-time entry fee ($20 per visitor, $10 per night) at the campground. There are no showers or flush toilets. A spring provides fresh water, and the falls are close by. The **Havasupai Lodge ❹,** in Supai, offers basic accommodations. (☎448-2111. $125 for up to 4 people, plus the entrance fee.) The trail from Supai to the campground extends to **Mooney Falls** (1 mi. from campground), **Beaver Falls** (3 mi.), and the **Colorado** (8 mi.). The hike down to Mooney Falls is steep; extreme caution should be exercised—shoes with good tread are a must. Swimming and frolicking are both permitted and encouraged in the lush lagoons at the bottom of the falls.

FLAGSTAFF   ☎928

Born on the 4th of July, 1876, the city of Flagstaff began as a rest stop along the transcontinental railroad, its mountain springs providing precious aqueous refreshment on the long haul across the continent to the Pacific Ocean. Now Flagstaff's numerous outdoor shops point adventure-seekers to its incredible outdoor resources. Jaded travelers—backpackers and fannypackers alike—pass through on their way to the Grand Canyon, Sedona, and the Petrified Forest, all within daytrip distance by car or shuttle. The city's citizens welcome all to their unusual rock formations during the day and their hopping breweries at night; many of them wandered into town with camera in hand and ended up settling down themselves.

▐ TRANSPORTATION

Flagstaff sits 138 mi. north of Phoenix (take I-17), 26 mi. north of Sedona on U.S. 89A, and 81 mi. south of the Grand Canyon's south rim on U.S. 180.

Trains: Amtrak, 1 E. Rte. 66 (☎774-8679; www.amtrak.com), runs once per day to: **Albuquerque** (7hr., $63-110); **Chicago** (34hr., $177); **Kansas City** (26hr., $173); **Los Angeles** (12hr., $68-119). Station open daily 4:15am-11:45pm.

Buses: Two bus lines provide service to regional destinations. Check at the DuBeau and Grand Canyon International Hostels for their Grand Canyon and Sedona shuttles. (Grand Canyon $50; Sedona $25. Entrance fee and sack lunch included.)

Greyhound: 399 S. Malpais Ln. (☎774-4573), across from the Northern Arizona University (NAU) campus, 3 blocks southwest of the train station on U.S. 89A. Turn off 89A by Dairy Queen. To: **Albuquerque** (6½hr., 3 per day, $56); **Las Vegas** (5-6hr., 3 per day, $49); **Los Angeles** (10-12hr., 9 per day, $59); **Phoenix** (3hr., 6 per day, $25). Terminal open 24hr.

Open Road Tours & Transportation (☎226-8060 or 877-226-8060) offers daily trips to and from the Phoenix airport. (3hr., departs Flagstaff at 4:30, 7:30, 9:45am, 12:30, 3:30pm. $39. Departs Phoenix Sky Harbor Airport at 8:30, 11:30am, 2:30, 4:30, 7:30pm. $39.)

Public Transit: Mountain Line (☎779-6624). Routes cover most of town. Buses run every 30-60min. M-Sa. Route map and schedule available at visitors center in the Amtrak station. $1, seniors and children $0.50. Day pass $3/$1.50. Book of 20 passes $18/$9.

Taxi: Friendly Cab, ☎774-4444.

Car Rental: Enterprise Rent-A-Car, 100 N. Humphreys (☎774-9407).

■✳❷ ORIENTATION AND PRACTICAL INFORMATION

Downtown is between **Leroux Street** and **Aspen Street**, a block north of **Route 66** (formerly Santa Fe Ave.); the visitors center, bus station, hostels, and inexpensive restaurants and bars are all within a half-mile of this spot. **S. San Francisco Street,** a block east of Leroux St., has many outdoor shops. Split by Rte. 66, the more visited northern area is also the center of downtown. The area south of the tracks is less developed but has hostels and several eateries.

Visitor Info: Flagstaff Visitors Center, 1 E. Rte. 66 (☎774-9541 or 800-842-7293), in the Amtrak station, has brochures and maps. Open M-Sa 8am-5pm, Su 9am-4pm.

Police: 911 E. Sawmill Rd. (☎774-1414).

Medical Services: Flagstaff Medical Center, 1200 N. Beaver St. (☎779-3366). 24hr.

Internet Access: Free at NAU's **Cline Library** (☎523-2171). Take Riordan Rd. east from Rte. 66 and turn left on Knoles. Open May-Aug. M-Th 7:30am-10pm, F 7:30am-6pm, Sa 10:30am-5pm, Su noon-10pm; Sept.-Apr. M-Th 7:30am-11:30pm, F 7:30am-6pm, Sa 10:30am-6pm, Su 10:30am-11:30pm.

Post Office: 2400 N. Postal Blvd. (☎714-9302), on Rte. 66. Open M-F 9am-5pm, Sa 9am-noon. **Postal Code:** 86004. **Area Code:** 928.

▗ ACCOMMODATIONS

▨ **The DuBeau International Hostel,** 19 W. Phoenix Ave. (☎774-6731 or 800-398-7112; www.grandcanyonhostel.com). A block south of the train station, the DuBeau is the hotel of hostels. The common room, game room, and 2 sunny kitchens create a lively atmosphere. Breakfast and linen included. Internet $2 per 30min. Laundry $1.50. Grand Canyon and Sedona tours $50/$25. Reception 7am-midnight. Check-out 11am. June-Sept. dorms $18, Oct.-May $16. Private double $39/$35. MC/V. ❶

▨ **The Grand Canyon International Hostel,** 19 S. San Francisco St. (☎779-9421; www.grandcanyonhostel.com). Dubeau's sister hostel, just east of the DuBeau. Same great value and friendly atmosphere. Breakfast and linen included. Internet $2 per 30min. Laundry $1.50. Grand Canyon and Sedona tours $50/$25. Reception 7am-midnight. June-Sept. dorms $18, Oct.-May $16. Private double $41/$37. MC/V. ❶

The Weatherford Hotel, 23 N. Leroux St. (☎779-1919; www.weatherfordhotel.com), at Aspen and Leroux in downtown. Flagstaff's oldest hotel, dating to 1898. 8 spacious rooms with elegant furnishings. No TVs or in-room phones. Reservations recommended. Rooms M-F $60, Sa-Su $65; some rooms have shared baths. AmEx/D/DC/MC/V. ❸

⚑ CAMPING

Free **backcountry camping** is available in designated wilderness areas. Maps are available from the **Peaks Ranger Station**, 5075 N. 89A (☎526-0866). All backcountry sites must be at least 200 ft. from trails, waterways, and lakes. There is a 14-night max. stay in the **Coconino National Forest**; fire restrictions apply. For info on camping, call the **Coconino National Forest Line.** (☎527-3600. Open M-F 7:30am-4:30pm.) Lake Mary, a popular recreation site, is surrounded by campgrounds and backcountry spots. Campers should check with the **Mormon Lake Ranger District Station,** 4373 S. Lake Mary Rd., for information on specific trails and campsites. (☎774-1147. Open M-F 7:30am-4:30pm.) The following campgrounds are all just south of Flagstaff on Lake Mary Rd., which is accessible off of I-17 N, but must be reached by following Milton Rd. to Beulah Dr. when coming from the north.

Canyon Vista Campground, 6 mi. south on Mary Lake Rd. 10 basic but spacious sites with a few trees. Water, pit toilets. First come, first served. $12 per vehicle per night. ❶

Lakeview Campground, on the east side of Upper Lake Mary, 11½ mi. south on Lake Mary Rd., is surrounded by a pine forest with well-maintained sites. Water, pit toilets. First come, first served. Open May-Oct. $12 per vehicle per night. ❶

Pinegrove Campground (reservations ☎877-444-6777; www.reserveamerica.com), sits 5 mi. south of Lakeview at the other end of Upper Lake Mary. Close to the water under shady pine trees, Pinegrove is nothing short of picturesque. Drinking water, flush toilets, barbecues, fire pits. Showers $3. $15 per vehicle. ❶

🍴 FOOD

▨ **Macy's European Coffee House and Bakery,** 14 S. Beaver St. (☎774-2243), behind DuBeau hostel, has a European vintage flavor and a sunny interior. Gourmet hot chocolate and organic vegan pastries are baked to perfection, beckoning to everyone within smelling-distance. Try a mouthwatering sticky bun ($3) or the homemade granola ($4). Wireless Internet access. Open daily 6am-10pm; food served until 9pm. Cash only. ❶

Cafe Espress, 16 N. San Francisco St. (☎774-0541), is a local favorite for its healthy and creative cuisine. Breakfast includes delicious omelets and decadent strawberry crepes and champagne ($6). Breakfast $5-8. Lunch $5-10. Dinner $12-20. Espresso happy hour (50% off all drinks) M-F 3-5pm. Open daily 7am-5pm. AmEx/MC/V. ❸

Mountain Oasis Global Cuisine and Juice Bar, 11 E. Aspen St. (☎214-9270). This exotic downtown restaurant specializes in international cuisine with an emphasis on Mediterranean. Lunch $5-7. Dinner $8-16. Open M-Th and Su 11am-9pm, F-Sa 11am-10pm; may close early if business is slow. MC/V. ❸

The Black Bean, 12 E. Rte. 66 Gateway Plaza 104 (☎779-9905), serves hefty burritos ($4.75), hearty wraps ($5.50), and 7 varieties of homemade salsa. Open daily 11am-9pm, F-Sa until 11pm in summer. MC/V. ❷

📷 SIGHTS

In 1894, Percival Lowell chose Flagstaff as the site for an astronomical observatory and spent the rest of his life here. The **Lowell Observatory,** 1400 W. Mars Hill Rd., 1 mi. west of downtown, uphill off Rte. 66, is where he discovered Pluto and is still a functioning laboratory today. It also has a visitors center, astronomy exhibits, and daily tours (10am, 1, 3pm), as well as an excellent evening program about constellations that gives visitors a chance to look through the Alvan Clark refractor. (☎774-3358; www.lowell.edu. Open daily Mar.-Oct. 9am-5pm; Nov.-Feb. noon-5pm. Evening programs June-Aug. M-Sa 8pm; Mar.-May and Sept.-Oct. W and F-Sa 7:30pm; Nov.-Feb. F-Sa 7:30pm. $5, students and seniors $4, ages 5-17 $2.) The

THE SOUTHWEST

Museum of Northern Arizona, 3 mi. north of downtown on U.S. 180, details anything and everything about the land and peoples of the Colorado Plateau. The museum has a geology gallery but dedicates most of its space to the area's diverse cultures, traditions, and artistic works. It also hosts the annual Hopi (4th of July weekend), Navajo (first weekend in Aug.), and Hispanic (last weekend in Oct.) heritage marketplaces, celebrating each group's art and way of life. (☎774-5213; www.musnaz.org. Open daily 9am-5pm. $5, seniors $4, students $3, ages 7-17 $2.) **Riordan Mansion State Historic Park,** 409 W. Riordan Rd., off Milton Rd. next to Northern Arizona University, is the historic home of the Riordan family, the primary developers of the Arizona Lumber and Timber Co. The mansion, designed by Charles Whittlesey, has 40 furnished rooms for touring and is a wonderful example of Arts and Crafts style architecture. (☎779-4395. Open daily May-Oct. 8:30am-5pm; Nov.-Apr. 10:30am-5pm. Tours every hr. Tours $6, under 8 free.)

🎵 🎭 ENTERTAINMENT AND NIGHTLIFE

North of town by the museum, the **Coconino Center for the Arts,** 2300 Fort Valley Rd., contains exhibits, performances, and annual festivals. In summer, the **Native American Festival** is a must-see. Call for event details and weekend happenings. (☎779-2300; www.culturalpartners.org. July 1 to mid-Aug. Tu-Su 11am-5pm. Free.) The second weekend in June, the annual **Flagstaff Rodeo** brings barn dances, a carnival, and a cocktail waitress race. Events run from Friday to Sunday at the Coconino County Fair Grounds. (On U.S. 89A just south of town; the visitors center has details.) On Labor Day, the **Coconino County Fair** arrives with carnival rides, games, and animal competitions. **Theatrikos,** 11 W. Cherry Ave., a local theater company, performs new shows each month. (☎774-1662; www.theatrikos.com. Mainstage tickets $14. Opening night $17.50.) **The Orpheum Theatre,** 15 W. Aspen St., is the place to get your concert kicks with nightly performances by well-known musicians. (☎556-1580; www.orpheumpresents.com. Ticket prices vary. Most events are 21+, under 21 with parent.)

Two popular nightspots reside in the Hotel Weatherford, 23 N. Leroux St. **Charly's,** on the main floor, has nightly live music. **Zane Grey,** upstairs, has cheap drinks in a classy setting with comfy chairs. (☎779-1919. For both, happy hour daily 5-7pm, free taco bar F. Charly's open 11am-2am. Zane Grey open 5pm-2am.) **Joe's Place,** on the corner of S. San Francisco and Rte. 66, is a bit rowdier with indie bands on weekend nights and daily drink specials. (☎774-6281. Happy hour 4-7pm. Open daily 11am-2am.) If you feel the urge to two-step, the **Museum Club,** 3404 E. Rte. 66, a roadhouse dating back to Prohibition, is the spot for honky-tonk action. Dime beers on Wednesday 8pm-midnight bring in waves of college students. (☎526-9434. Cover $3-5. Open daily 11am-4am.)

🏔 OUTDOOR ACTIVITIES

With the northern **San Francisco Peaks** and the surrounding **Coconino National Forest,** Flagstaff has abundant skiing, hiking, and biking trails for both the rugged outdoorsman and those just interested in walking off last night's fun. Altitudes of over 7000 ft. make water a necessity for activity here, regardless of the season. In late spring and summer, national and state park rangers may close trails if the potential for fire is too high. **Backcountry camping ❶** is free. No permit is required, but it's wise to check in with a ranger station to alert them of your location.

SKIING AND HIKING

For both skiing and hiking, **The Arizona Snowbowl** is one of the best sites in Arizona. In winter, it maintains four chairlifts, a tow rope, and 32 trails, and the skiing takes place on **Agassiz Peak** (11,500 ft.). To reach the Snowbowl, take U.S. 180 about 7 mi. north to the Fairfield Snowbowl turnoff. (☎779-1951; www.arixonasnow-bowl.com. Open daily 9am-4pm. Lift tickets M-F half-day $27, full day $42; Sa-Su $34/$42; ages 8-12 $19/$24; under 7, ages 70+, and birthday people free.) **Equipment rental** is available on the mountain. (Half-day ski package $16, full day $22; extreme performance package $22/$32; snowboards $21/$29.)

Though snow might still be frosting the mountain top, summer hikers are eager to hit the trails. The most popular trail in the area is the strenuous hike to the majestic **Humphrey's Peak** (12,633 ft.), Arizona's highest mountain (4½ mi. one-way, 3hr.). The trail begins in the first parking lot at the Snowbowl ski area (7 mi. north of Flagstaff on U.S. 180) and climbs nearly 3400 ft. A more moderate hiking option is the **Kachina Trail** (5 mi. one-way, 2½hr.). Also leaving from the Snowbowl, it runs parallel to the road before winding through quiet aspen groves and lush ferns. Several other trails twist through the Coconino Forest. Detailed maps and trail advice are available at **Peaks Ranger Station**, 5075 N. 89A (☎526-0866). For the energetic hiker, the demanding **Elden Lookout Trail** (6 mi. round-trip, 5hr., 2400 ft.) is ideal for jaw-dropping mountaintop views. The trailhead is at the Peaks Ranger Station.

Those who don't want to work for the view can take the **Scenic Skyride**, at the base of the Snowbowl. This hour-long ride glides visitors up to 11,500 ft. for views of the Grand Canyon, downtown Flagstaff, and the surrounding mountains. (☎779-1951. Runs Memorial Day-Labor Day daily 10am-4pm; after Labor Day F-Su only).

MOUNTAIN BIKING

Schultz Creek Trailhead, on Schultz Pass Rd. off U.S. 180 N, is the starting point for many interconnected trails in the San Francisco Mountains, including the popular **Schultz Creek Trail.** The trail climbs north along the bottom of a ravine, and after almost 4 mi. splits into the difficult **Sunset Trail**, which heads south, and the eastbound **Little Elden Trail.** Sunset Trail climbs through the woods before cresting and descending along **Brookbank Trail**, down singletrack dropoffs and switchbacks. This 2 mi. stretch spits out riders onto Forest Service Road 557, which can be used to ride back to the trailhead or to access the more technical **Rocky Ridge Trail.** Bike rentals are available at **Flagstaff Adventure Sports**, 612 N. Humphreys. (☎877-572-2300. Bike rentals $25 per day, $35 overnight. Open M-Sa 10am-4pm.)

▶ DAYTRIPS FROM FLAGSTAFF

WALNUT CANYON NATIONAL MONUMENT

Walnut Canyon is 10 mi. east of Flagstaff. Take I-40 to Exit 204. Entrance to the monument costs $5 per person (free for children under 17).

Sprinkled with the ruins of 13th-century Sinaguan dwellings, Walnut Canyon National Monument is as interesting geologically as it is culturally. The shadier, north side of the Canyon is home to Ponderosa Pines and Douglas Firs while the southern side, exposed to full sun, is filled with desert juniper and yucca. A glassed-in observation deck in the **visitors center** overlooks the canyon. (☎526-3367. Open daily 8am-6pm; low season 8am-5pm) The steep **Island Trail** (1 mi. loop) snakes down into the canyon past 25 cliff dwellings. The **Rim Trail** (¾ mi., 20 min.) offers views of the canyon and passes rim-top sights. In summer, rangers lead 2 mi. hikes to remote cliff dwellings in Walnut Canyon. Reservations are required for these challenging 2½hr. hikes. (Tours from Memorial Day to Labor Day Sa 10am.)

SUNSET CRATER VOLCANO NATIONAL MONUMENT

Sunset Crater is 12 mi. north of Flagstaff on U.S. 89. The entrance fee ($5, under age 16 free) includes admission to Wupatki National Monument, below.

The 1000 ft. cinder cone of Sunset Crater Volcano National Monument is the result of nearly 200 years of periodic volcanic eruptions beginning in AD 1065. It's certainly not Pompeii, but it's still pretty cool. The easy **Lava Flow Nature Trail**, 1½ mi. east of the visitors center, meanders 1 mi. through the rocky black terrain that glows with tinges of yellow and red, inspiring the formation's name. Hiking up Sunset Crater itself is not allowed, but the **Lenox Crater Trail** is a tough ¼ mi. scramble up the loose cinders of a neighboring cone, followed by a quick slide back down. The **visitors center** explores the area's history. (☎526-0502. Open daily in summer 8am-6pm; in winter 8am-5pm.)

WUPATKI NATIONAL MONUMENT
Wupatki is 30 mi. northeast of Flagstaff (18 mi. northeast of Sunset Crater), off U.S. 89.

Wupatki has gorgeous views of the Painted Desert and fascinating Puebloan sights. The Sinagua people moved here after a Sunset Crater eruption forced them to evacuate in the 11th century, but archaeologists speculate that in less than 200 years, droughts, disease, and over-farming led the Sinagua to abandon these stone houses. The remnants of five pueblos form a loop off U.S. 89. The largest and most accessible, **Wupatki,** on a ½ mi. round-trip loop trail from the visitors center, is three stories high. The spectacular **Doney Mountain Trail** rises ½ mi. from the picnic area to the summit. Get info and trail guide brochures at the **visitors center.** Backcountry hiking is not permitted. (☎679-2365. Monument open daily 8am-5pm.)

SEDONA   ☎928

The Martians said to make frequent visits to Sedona may simply be mistaking its deep red rock towers for home. Dramatic copper-toned behemoths dotted with pines tower above, rising from the earth with such crowd appeal that they seem like manufactured tourist attractions—even though they aren't. Downtown may be overrun with pricey boutiques, but Sedona's sheer beauty and supernatural flair make the town impossible to skip.

⨻ PRACTICAL INFORMATION. Sedona is 120 mi. north of Phoenix (take I-17 north to Rte. 179) and 30 mi. south of Flagstaff (take I-17 south to Rte. 179). The **Sedona-Phoenix Shuttle** (☎282-2066) runs eight trips daily between Phoenix and Sedona ($40). The **Sedona Chamber of Commerce,** at Forest Rd. and U.S. 89A, has info on accommodations and local attractions. (☎282-7722. Open M-Sa 8:30am-5pm, Su 9am-3pm.) **Post Office:** 190 W. U.S. 89A. (☎282-3511. Open M-F 8:45am-5pm.) **Postal Code:** 86336. **Area Code:** 928.

⌂ ACCOMMODATIONS. Lodging in town is pricey, so it's not a bad idea to make Sedona a daytrip from Flagstaff or Cottonwood, 15 mi. south. The **White House Inn ❸,** 2986 W. U.S. 89A (☎282-6680), is the cheapest option, with basic singles and doubles from $47. Most campsites in the area cluster around U.S. 89A as it heads north to Flagstaff. There are plenty of private campgrounds, but most cater to the RV crowd rather than to backpackers. The **US Forest Service campsites ❶** along U.S. 89A are the best and cheapest option for tent-toters. North of Sedona, nine to 20 mi. from town, four separate campgrounds—**Manzanita, Bootlegger, Cave Springs, and Pine Flat (east and west) ❶**—maintain over 150 campsites along the canyon floor. The shady, creek-side locations make these sites popular in summer, so it's wise to arrive early. They all have similar facilities, with picnic tables and toilets, and all but Bootlegger have drinking water. Cave Springs and Pine Flat have a few reserveable sites, but the rest are first come, first served. (☎527-3600, reservations 877-444-6777. 7-night max. stay. Tent sites $18.) **Dead Horse Ranch State Park ❶,** just off U.S. 89 in Cottonwood and near Tuzigoot National Monument, has over 200 sites, many of which are surrounded by willows and cottonwoods. (☎634-5283. Restrooms, showers. First come, first served. Tent sites $12, with hookup $19.)

☐ FOOD. The Coffee Pot Restaurant ❷, 2050 W. U.S. 89A, a local favorite, serves 101 varieties of omelets ($4-9) all day and a Mexican and diner-style lunch. (☎282-6626. Lunch $5-9. Open daily 6am-2:30pm. MC/V.) **Mesquite Grille & BBQ ❷**, 250 Jordan Rd., has an Old West atmosphere and the lowest prices in town. (☎282-6533. Platters $7.50. Ribs $13. Open daily 11am-8pm. MC/V.) **Casa Rincón ❷**, 2620 W. U.S. 89A, attracts patrons with its daily happy hour (3-6pm; $3 margaritas), mouth-watering combos ($10-13), and live entertainment. (☎282-4849. Open daily 11:30am-9pm; cantina open until 1am. AmEx/MC/V.) For a post-hike reward with some divine homemade ice cream, head over to **The Black Cow Café ❶**, 229 N. U.S. 89. (☎203-9868. Waffle cones $3. Open daily 8am-9pm. MC/V.)

◨ SIGHTS. The best way to experience the area is to go to **Red Rock State Park,** 4050 Red Rock Loop Rd., which has several beautiful hiking trails, exhibits, and an interactive visitors center. Rangers lead nature hikes (10am and 2pm) into the formations and are happy to give trail advice. Quail, *javelinas*, and hummingbirds frequent the area, and bird walks are offered on Wednesday and Saturday at 7am. Call for a spot. (☎520-282-6907. $5 entrance fee. Park open daily Apr.-Sept. 8am-8pm; Oct.-Mar. 8am-5pm. Visitors center open daily 9am-5pm.) The **Chapel of the Holy Cross,** on Chapel Rd., lies at the base of a 1000 ft. rock wall and is wedged into the red sandstone. Visitors can go to church services or take in the gorgeous panoramic views with a walk around the outside. (☎282-4069. Open M-Sa 9am-5pm, Su 10am-5pm. Free.) A stretch of slippery creek bottom makes for a great natural waterpark at ▨**Slide Rock State Park.** Visitors can wade across colorful, smooth rocks or go down several natural water slides. The park also has a trail that leads through its apple orchards. (☎282-3034. Open daily in summer 8am-7pm; in winter 8am-5pm; in fall and spring 8am-6pm. Free.)

Tlaquepaque (Tlah-kee-PAH-kee), off U.S. 179, just southeast of the intersection with U.S. 89, is a resort village inside Sedona that functions as an upscale artisan and shopping plaza with restaurants and galleries. You may not have the cash to get one of the life-sized bronze wildlife statues (prices start at $5000 and soar to a bank-shattering $70,000), but you can stroll the gardens and admire the profusion of Spanish tile, artwork, and fountains scattered around

FROM THE ROAD

SPIRALING INTO THE VORTEX

Modern physics has long acknowledged the potential for the existence of other, unknown dimensions. Though unsettling to some, it is a cause for comfort to Sedona residents who believe in the supernatural.

Each year, Sedona attracts hundreds of visitors who hope to experience one of the area's vortex centers: swirling centers of energy that interact with anyone within a quarter-mile. Before entering Sedona, I had never heard of a vortex, so I didn't pay too much attention to the vortex-themed shops, mystic psychics, and bustling New Age scene. I happily set off for my first hike of the day along the Boynton Canyon Trail, distracted only by how unbearably hot it was. About halfway up the trail, though, I started to feel "funny." My stomach felt strange, ready to flip-flop, and my arms and chest were tingly, but strangely relaxed. I hypothesized dehydration bordering on insanity and aggressively gulped my water and finished the hike.

Back in Sedona, I happened to stop in an intriguing vortex shop and learned that I had been hiking on one of the four main vortex centers in Sedona. I'd like to think that I had a close encounter with the supernatural, but it could have just been the heat. Do vortexes actually exist? Perhaps. But then again, so do coincidences.

–Lauren Sancken

the plaza. Tlaquepaque is also home to **Shakespeare Sedona,** a theater troupe that presents two productions during the month of July. (☎203-9381 for info. Tickets $20, students $10.)

Montezuma Castle National Monument, 10 mi. south of Sedona on I-17, is a remarkable 45-room cliff dwelling built by the Sinagua in the 12th century. You can't get very close to the ruins, but the view from the path below is excellent. (☎567-3322. Open daily in summer 8am-6pm; in winter 8am-5pm. $3, under 17 free.) A limestone lake formed by the collapse of an underground cavern, **Montezuma Well,** off I-17, 11 mi. north of the castle, was once a source of water for the Sinagua. (Open daily 8am-6pm. Free.) Take U.S. 89A to Rte. 279 and continue through Cottonwood to reach **Tuzigoot National Monument,** 20 mi. from Sedona, which contains the remains of a Sinaguan village. (☎634-5564. Open daily 8am-6pm. $3, under 17 free.)

🅺 OUTDOOR ACTIVITIES. It's hard to go wrong with any of the well-maintained hiking trails in and around Sedona. Most trailheads are on the forest service roads that snake into hills and canyons. The US Forest Service publishes a free guide to recreation (available at any visitors center) that lists options for hiking, biking, and driving in "Red Rock Country." In Sedona, however, even the views and hikes aren't free and, in order to go on trails, your car has to sport a **Red Rock Pass,** a parking permit available from vending machines at most visitors centers and trailheads ($5 per day or $15 per week). Hiking highlights include the difficult **Wilson Mountain Loop** (5 mi.), which ascends Wilson Mountain, and the more moderate **Huckaby Trail** (6 mi.), which gives hot hikers a chance to swim in Oak Creek Canyon. For experimenting with the area's so-called vortex energy areas, **Boynton Canyon Trail** (5 mi.) is a moderate trail along the floor of Boynton Canyon. Others include **Cathedral Rock,** 4 mi. up Upper Red Rock Rd., and **Bell Rock,** 5 mi. on Hwy. 179. Biking offers similar wonders. Considered a rival to Moab by those in the mountain biking know-how, Sedona has over 100 mi. of interconnected trails. **Broken Arrow,** an intermediate trail of variable distance, is particularly popular. Tamer trails can be found along the **Bell Rock Pathway,** south of town. Bike rentals (from $7.50 per hr. or $25 per day) and trail information can be found at **Mountain Bike Heaven,** 1695 W. U.S. 89A. (☎282-1312. Open M-F 9am-6pm, Sa 8am-5pm, Su 9am-5pm.) Scenic drives are almost as plentiful as the rocks. The **Red Rock Loop** (20 mi., 1hr., off U.S. 89 west of town) is mostly paved, but provides some dirt road adventure and mind-blowing views of rock formations. The **Airport Mesa,** 1 mi. west on 89A, offers one of the best panoramic sunset views. For those hoping to see Sedona's wild side, many companies offer 4WD tours. **Adventure Company,** 336 Hwy. 179 at Tlaquepaque, has knowledgeable guides and great prices for some of Sedona's most famous 4x4 trails. (☎877-281-6622. Tours daily 8:30am-5:30pm. Call to reserve times at least 24hr. in advance. From $30, children from $15.)

NAVAJO RESERVATION

Today, the Navajo Nation is the largest reservation in the US, covering over 27,000 sq. mi. of northeastern Arizona, southeastern Utah, and northwestern New Mexico. Four sacred mountains watch over Navajo land—Mt. Blanca to the east, Mt. Taylor to the south, San Francisco Peak to the west, and Mt. Hesperus to the north. Anthropologists think the "Dineh" people, more commonly known as Navajo, are descended from groups of Athabascan people who migrated to the Southwest from Canada in the 14th and 15th centuries, but the Navajo see their existence as the culmination of a journey through three other worlds. In the second half of the 19th century, reservations evolved out of the US government's ad hoc attempts to end fighting between Native Americans and Anglos while facilitat-

Cultural sensitivity is very important on the reservation; despite the many state and interstate roads that traverse it, the land is both legally and culturally distinct. Driving or hiking off designated trails and established routes is considered trespassing unless you are with a guide. Possession and consumption of alcohol is prohibited on the reservation. The Navajo people have their own language and social norms. While many cultures find eye contact, firm handshakes, and cheerful conversation desirable, among the Navajo these behaviors are generally impolite. General photography is allowed unless otherwise stated, but photographing the Navajo people requires their permission (a gratuity is usually expected). As always, the best remedy for cultural friction is simple respect.

ing white settlement on native lands. The reservation system imposed a kind of wardship over Native Americans, which lasted for over a century, until Supreme Court decisions starting in the 1960s reasserted the tribes' standing as semi-sovereign nations. Today, most Navajo youth are fluent in both Navajo and English, and the importance of the native language continues to be emphasized throughout the Reservation. Often highlighted as cultural heroes are the Navajo Code Talkers, marines who disguised military transmissions using the Navajo language during World War II. Though the Navajo Nation continues to retain much of its ancestral way of life, many modern health problems threaten the Nation as a result of the radioactive contamination from 1950s uranium mines.

For a taste of the Navajo language and ritual songs, tune your radio to 660AM, "The Voice of the Navajo." Remember to advance your watch 1hr. during the summer; the Navajo Nation runs on **Mountain Daylight Time,** while the rest of Arizona, including the Hopi Reservation, does not observe daylight savings, operating on Pacific Standard Time in the summer and Mountain Standard Time in the winter. The reservation's **area code** is ☎928 in Arizona, 505 in New Mexico, 435 in Utah.

Monument Valley, Canyon de Chelly, Navajo National Monument, Rainbow Bridge, Antelope Canyon, and all their roads and trails are on Navajo land. Those planning to hike through Navajo territory need a backcountry permit at one of the **parks and recreation departments** or can mail a request with a money order or certified check to P.O. Box 9000, Window Rock, AZ 86515 ($5 per person). **Flagstaff, AZ** (p. 811) is a good gateway to the reservation, with car rental agencies, inexpensive accommodations, and Greyhound service on I-40. Budget travelers can camp at the National Monuments or Navajo campgrounds or stay in student-run motels in high schools around the reservation.

MONUMENT VALLEY   ☎435

The red sandstone mesas, buttes, and free-standing towers of Monument Valley Navajo Tribal Park have provided the rocky skyline for many Hollywood westerns, but long before John Wayne, the ancient Anasazi sustained small communities here. While you can see most of the formations from Hwy. 163, you can get closer by taking the park's 17 mi. scenic **Valley Drive,** which winds around 11 of the most spectacular formations, including the famous pair of **Mittens** and the slender **Totem Pole.** The gaping ditches, large rocks, and mudholes on this dirt road, however, can be jarring to both you and your car—observe the 15 mph speed limit and allow at least 1½hr. The valley can be viewed by foot as well by using the park's only self-guided trail, **Wildcat Trail** (3 mi., 2 hr.). Less-touristed parts of the valley can be reached only by 4WD vehicle, horse, or foot, usually with the assistance of a guide. The visitors center parking lot is crowded with booths selling jeep, horseback, and hiking tours. (1½hr. jeep tour about $35 per person, full day $100; horseback tours $40/$150. For more information, call **Black's Horseback Trailrides** ☎309-8834.) In

NOT ON OUR LAND

On April 25, 2005, Joe Shirley, Jr., the President of Navajo Nation, signed the first-ever Native American Tribal Law banning uranium mining in Navajo country. The legislation was a result of continued activism that began in the 1970s when Navajo miners tried to prove that their lung disease, cancer, and other health problems were directly linked to uranium mining in the 1940s-60s. In 1990, the US Congress passed legislation to compensate former miners and their families, but uranium remains a prevalent concern throughout the Navajo Nation.

Many mines in the area are still open, and several communities have yet to be surveyed to determine overall health impacts. Grassroots and community-based groups like the Eastern Navajo Dine Against Uranium Mining have helped to create the current legislation and block new proposals to mine in the area. What is most troubling is that despite the demonstrated dangers to health, uranium mining is still extremely appealing to local workers because Navajo Nation has few employment alternatives. Leroy Jackson, a former miner who now works as a tour guide, longs for the lucrative mining industry and its economic security. Even though he already has a chronic rash from uranium exposure, Jackson firmly states, "I would apply for a job again if I could."

winter, snow laces the rocky towers. Call the visitors center for road conditions. The park entrance is on U.S. 163 just south of the Utah border, 24 mi. north of **Kayenta**, at the intersection of U.S. 163 and U.S. 160. The **visitors center** has info, a gift shop, and restaurant. (☎727-3353. Park and visitors center open daily May-Sept. 6am-8pm; Oct.-Apr. 8am-5pm. $5, under 9 free; National Passes not accepted.) **Mitten View Campground ❶**, ¼ mi. from the visitors center and next to the parking lot, has a view and showers, but no hookups, little shade, and a lot of exposure to visitors and park staff. (Register at the visitors center; first come, first served. Sites $10; in winter $5.) Cheap motels can easily be found in **Mexican Hat, UT,** and **Bluff, UT.**

CANYON DE CHELLY   ☎928

The quiet and colorful Canyon de Chelly (da-SHAY), just north of Chinle on Navajo Rte. 7, contains the evidence of nearly 5000 years of human history. From the rim, you can gaze at the remains of ancient Puebloan homes still nestled into alcoves and perched precariously on ledges. Among these cliff dwellings and winding spires, Navajo farmers can still be seen working the land of the canyon floor using traditional agricultural practices. The canyon is best viewed from one of two scenic drives. The **North Rim Drive** (15¼ mi., 1½-2hr.) is a tour through four vistas of Canyon del Muerto, highlighted by petroglyphs, ancient Puebloan villages, and Massacre Cave, the site of an 1805 massacre by Spanish soldiers. The **South Rim Drive** (16 mi., 1½-2hr.) has seven views of the Canyon de Chelly which are more panoramic and include the 800-ft. Spider Rock sandstone spire. The **White House Trail,** 4 mi. from the visitors center along South Rim Dr., is a moderate hike (2½ mi. round-trip, 2hr.) that leads down to the canyon floor and the White House ruin. The drives and White House Trail are the only self-guided activities in the park; everything else must be under the supervision of an authorized Navajo guide.

The **visitors center** houses archaeological and cultural displays detailing the lives of the canyon's many inhabitants and has helpful advice (☎674-5500, Ex. 270. Open daily 8am-5pm. Free.) Visitors are cautioned to lock their doors and close windows at all overlooks, as thefts can occur. Jewelry and crafts are frequently sold at canyon overlooks and along the White House trail. Visitors must stay on established roads and trails—to deviate from them is considered trespassing. For guided hikes with authorized Navajo guides, visitors can sign up for one of two hikes in the visitors center. (9am, 1pm. $15. Arrive 30min. before hike time.)

Thunderbird Lodge ❹ is the park's only indoor accommodation. Behind the visitors center in a historic trading post, the Lodge provides modern, comfortable rooms. (☎674-5841. Showers, TV. Reservations recommended in summer. Rooms from $97. AmEx/D/DC/MC/V.) The same complex also contains a gift shop (open daily 8am-7pm), guide service (full-day tours $65, half-day $40), and a cafeteria (sandwiches $5, steaks $12-18; open daily 6:30am-8:30pm). Free camping is available in the 93 spacious, shady sites at **Cottonwood Campgrounds ❶,** just southwest of the visitors center. (Toilets, water, no showers. First come, first served. Free.) **Spider Rock Campground ❶,** 10 mi. from the visitors center, offers tent and RV sites and free guided day-hikes for guests. (☎1-877-910-CAMP. Firepits, primitive toilets, potable water. Tent sites $10; RV sites $15; hogan rentals $25-35.) For those who need an extra jolt before hitting the scenic drives, **Changing Woman Coffeehouse,** right before the turn for the South Rim Drive, is a small, outdoors operation with gourmet coffee and espresso ($2-3), picnic tables with out-of-print magazines, and Miles Davis wafting from a portable stereo.

NAVAJO NATIONAL MONUMENT   ☎520

Ancestors of today's Hopi occupied the cliffs of Tsegi Canyon from the late 1200s until hard times left the villages vacant twenty years later. The site contains three remarkable cliff dwellings. **Inscription House** has been closed to visitors since the 1960s due to its fragile condition, and the other two admit a very limited number of visitors. **Keet Seel,** one of the best-preserved ancestral Puebloan villages, can be reached only by a challenging 17 mi. round-trip hike (open late May to early Sept.). Hikers can stay overnight in a **free campground ❶** nearby (no facilities or drinking water). Reservations for free permits to visit Keet Seel can be made through the visitors center up to five months in advance. Only 20 people are allowed each day, so if you don't have a reservation, show up at the visitors center early. Ranger-led tours to **Betatakin,** a 135-room Puebloan complex, are limited to 25 people per tour. (5 mi. round-trip, 3-5hr. May to late Sept. 8:30, 11am; first come, first served.) The paved (but not wheelchair-accessible) 1 mi. round-trip **Sandal Trail** lets you gaze down on Betatakin from the top of the canyon. The **Aspen Forest Overlook Trail,** another 1 mi. hike, overlooks aspens and firs that are the remnants of an ancient forest. To get to the monument, take Rte. 564 from U.S. 160, 20 mi. southwest of Kayenta. The **visitors center** is 9 mi. down Rte. 564 and has local artisans demonstrating traditional crafts. (☎672-2700. Open daily in summer 8am-7pm; in winter 8am-5pm. Free, but donations accepted.) Two free campgrounds are located in the park. **Sunset View ❶** has 31 sites with water and toilets wedged among the pygmy conifer forest, and **Canyon View ❶** offers 11 primitive sites with great views.

HOPI RESERVATION   ☎928

The Hopi people, self-identified through closely-knit clan relationships, reside in twelve traditional villages in the desolate beauty of Black Mesa's arid valleys and prominent finger mesas. Landlocked by the Navajo Reservation, the Hopi Reservation is divided into three regions known, from east to west, as First, Second, and Third Mesas. Roadside stands brimming with Hopi pottery, baskets, and jewelry line the only paved highway, Hwy. 264, and though prices vary from stand to stand, visitors should feel free to browse or buy. Once off the reservation, however, visitors should be careful of imitation Hopi art and jewelry. **First Mesa** is the only region intended to accommodate visitors. To reach First Mesa, drive to Polacca and follow the signs to the **Ponsi Hall Community Center,** a general info center and starting point for guided tours. (☎737-2262. Open daily June-Aug. 9:30am-5pm, Sept.-May 10am-3pm. Tours last 1hr. and begin at opening time; the last tour departs 1hr. prior to closing. $8, children $5.) The villages on the **Second** and **Third**

Mesas are less developed for tourism. Photography and recording are strictly forbidden. On Second Mesa, though, the **Hopi Cultural Center,** 5 mi. west of the intersection of Rts. 264 and 87, serves as a visitors center and has the reservation's only museum, which focuses on the tribe's history and arts and crafts. (☎734-6650. Open M-F 9am-5pm, Sa-Su 9am-3pm. $3, under 14 $1.) The **Hopi Cultural Center Restaurant ❷** and the **Hopi Cultural Center Motel ❹,** one of the only accommodations on the reservation, are in the same complex. (☎734-2401. Restaurant: open daily Apr.-Sept. 6am-9pm; Oct.-Mar. 7am-8pm. Reservations recommended for motel rooms. Apr.-Sept. $90, Oct.-Mar. $60; $5 per additional person.) **Free camping ❶** is allowed at 10 primitive sites next to the Cultural Center.

Visitors can attend a few Hopi **village dances** during the year. Often announced only a few days in advance, these religious ceremonies usually occur on weekends and last from sunrise to sundown. The dances are formal; do not wear shorts, tank tops, or other casual wear. Photos, recordings, and sketches are strictly forbidden. Often several villages will hold dances on the same day, allowing tourists to village-hop. The **Harvest Dance,** in mid-September at Second Mesa, is spectacular, with tribes from all over the US. Nonetheless, each village has its own rules on visits during these ceremonial dances, so it is best to call in advance before making the trip. Ask at the cultural center or the **Hopi Cultural Preservation Office,** P.O. Box 123, Kykotsmovi 86039 (☎734-3613), for more info.

PETRIFIED FOREST NATIONAL PARK ☎520

Spreading over 60,000 acres, the Petrified Forest National Park looks something like the aftermath of a prehistoric Grateful Dead concert—a tie-dyed desert littered with rainbow-colored trees. Some 225 million years ago, when Arizona's desert was swampland, volcanic ash covered the logs, slowing their decay. Silica-infused water seeped through the wood, and the silica crystallized into quartz, combining with iron-rich minerals to produce rainbow hues. Colorful sediment was also laid down in this floodplain, creating the stunning colors that stripe the rock formations of the park's badlands. While these gem-like logs are sure to fascinate, the park itself lacks the grandeur and hiking trails of neighboring national parks, making it best as a daytrip. Most travelers opt to take the scenic 27 mi. park road from north to south. From the north, the **Painted Desert Rim Trail** (½ mi. one-way) skirts the mesa edge above the Lithodendron Wash and the Black Forest before ending at **Kachina Point,** one of the most popular viewpoints. The point provides access for travel into the **Painted Desert Wilderness,** the park's region for backcountry hiking and camping. Certainly worth a stop is the nearby **Painted Desert Inn,** 2 mi. from the north entrance. A former guest house built of petrified wood, the Inn is now a restored historic adobe structure that houses Native American cultural history exhibits. (☎928-524-6228. Open daily 8am-4:30pm.) The Petrified Forest part of the park begins after the road crosses I-40. Petroglyphs can be viewed by taking a short trail through the 100-room **Puerco Pueblo,** believed to have housed nearly 1200 people at once. Many more petroglyphs can be seen at **Newspaper Rock,** but only from a distance. At the fourth loop of the 3 mi. **Blue Mesa** drive, you can hike the **Blue Mesa Trail** (1 mi. round-trip, 45min.), a steep descent into the heart of the park's desolate and beautiful formations. The **Giant Logs Trail** (½ mi. loop) starts at the south visitors center and winds past the largest logs in the park. The **Long Logs Trail** (1¾ mi. loop) travels through the world's densest concentration of petrified wood. The **Agate House Trail** (2 mi. round-trip) leads to a partially restored pueblo of petrified wood. Although both trails start ¼ mi. to the east, the only parking is at the visitors center. Don't pick up the petrified wood—it's already scared enough. Also, taking fragments is illegal and traditionally unlucky.

The park can be split into two parts separated by I-40: the northern Painted Desert and the southern Petrified Forest. At each end of the 28 mi. road connecting the two is an entrance station and a **visitors center.** (Both open daily June-Aug. 7am-7pm; Sept.-May 8am-5pm, but hours vary in the spring and fall. Entrance $10 per vehicle, $5 per pedestrian or motorcycle.) With lookout points and trails along the road, driving from one end of the park to the other is a good way to take in the full spectrum of colors and landscapes. The park can be entered from either the north or the south, but the north entrance is best for orientation purposes. There is no public transit to the park. To reach the northern Painted Desert, take I-40 to Exit 311, 107 mi. east of Flagstaff and 65 mi. west of Gallup, NM. The **Painted Desert Visitors Center** shows a 20min. orientation video and has displays on the origins of the colorful desert. (☎524-6228. Open in summer daily 7am-7pm; call for low-season hours.) To reach the park's southern section, take U.S. 180 west 36 mi. from St. Johns, AZ, or east 19 mi. from Holbrook. Inside the south entrance, the **Rainbow Forest Museum and Visitors Center** gives a look at petrified logs and has info on local geology and paleontology. (☎524-6822. Open June-Aug. daily 7am-7pm, reduced hours in low season. Free.) Water, restrooms, and snack bars are located at both visitors center areas. The Painted Desert Visitors Center has gas and a convenience store. In case of **emergency,** call the ranger dispatch (☎524-9726). There are no campgrounds in the park, but **backcountry camping ❶** is allowed in the Painted Desert Wilderness with a free permit, available at either visitors center. Backpackers must park at Kachina Point and enter the wilderness via the 1 mi. access trail. No fires are allowed. Budget motels and diners line Rte. 66, but there are none right around the park. **Gallup** and **Holbrook** offer more lodging and eating options.

PHOENIX ☎602

The name Phoenix was chosen for this small farming community in the Sonoran Desert by settlers who thought their oasis had risen from ashes like the phoenix of Greek mythology. Today, the Sonoran Desert has become an increasingly popular winter destination for the sun-starved traveler, and the city's many arts and sports facilities have added dimension to what could otherwise be urban sprawl. An adolescent city (founded in 1881) with future growth in store, Phoenix has enough heat to fuel its growing creativity and suburbs and enough air-conditioning to keep it walking the cooler side of the fine line between "oasis" and "furnace."

▐ TRANSPORTATION

Airport: Sky Harbor International Airport (☎273-3300; www.phxskyharbor.com), just southeast of downtown. Take the Valley Metro red line bus into the city (3:15am-11:45pm, $1.25). **SuperShuttle** offers transportation to and from the airport; about $7 to downtown Phoenix (☎244-9000 or 800-258-3826).

Buses: Greyhound, 2115 E. Buckeye Rd. (☎389-4200; www.greyhound.com). Station open 24hr. To: **El Paso** (8hr., 8 per day, $40); **Los Angeles** (7hr., 11 per day, $40); **San Diego** (8hr., 5 per day, $54); **Tucson** (2hr., 13 per day, $20). There is no direct service to Phoenix, but **Amtrak** (☎800-872-7245; www.amtrak.com) operates connector buses to and from rail stations in Tucson and Flagstaff.

 CAN I HAVE YOUR DIGITS? Because of its explosive growth, the city has three area codes. 602 is limited to Phoenix proper, 623 is western greater Phoenix, and 480 is the East Valley (including Scottsdale, Tempe, and Mesa). Unless otherwise noted, all listings in the text are within the 602 area code.

THE SOUTHWEST

Public Transit: Downtown, **Valley Metro** (☎253-5000; www.valleymetro.org). Most bus lines run out of Central Station, at Central Ave. and Van Buren St. Most routes operate M-F 5am-8pm with reduced service Sa. $1.25; disabled, seniors, and children $0.60. All-day pass $3.60/$1.80, 10-ride pass $12/$6. Bus passes and system maps at the terminal or downtown visitors center. In Tempe, the **City of Tempe Transit Store,** 502 S. College Ave., Ste. 101, is the public transit headquarters. The red line runs to and from Phoenix, and the last few stops of the yellow line are in Tempe. The red line also services Mesa. Bus passes and system maps at the terminal. Loloma Station, just south of Indian School and Scottsdale Rd., is Scottsdale's main hub for local traffic. The green line runs along Thomas St. to Phoenix.

Taxi: Yellow Cab, ☎252-5252.

Car Rental: Enterprise Rent-A-Car, 1402 N. Central Ave. (☎257-4177; www.enterprise.com), with other offices throughout the city. Compact cars around $30 per day, with lower weekly and monthly rates. Valid credit card and driver's license required. N. Central St. office open M-F 8am-6pm, Sa 9am-noon; other offices' hours vary.

☀ 🛈 ORIENTATION AND PRACTICAL INFORMATION

The intersection of **Central Avenue** and **Washington Street** marks the heart of downtown. Central Ave. runs north-south, Washington St. east-west. Numbered avenues and streets both run north-south; avenues are numbered sequentially west from Central, while streets are numbered east. **Tempe,** east of Phoenix, is dominated by students from Arizona State University. **Mesa,** east of Tempe, is much larger with a large Mormon community and many suburban neighborhoods. **Scottsdale,** north of Tempe, is an upscale district with adobe-style mansions and shopping centers. These areas combine to form what is referred to as "The Valley."

Visitor Info: Phoenix and Valley of the Sun Convention and Visitors Center (☎254-6500 or 877-225-5749, info and calendar 252-5588; www.phoenixcvb.com). Downtown at S. 2nd St. and Adams St. Open M-F 8am-5pm. Free **Internet** access (15min. limit). Camping and outdoors info at the **Bureau of Land Management Office,** 222 N. Central Ave. (☎417-9200).

Hotlines: Crisis Hotline, ☎800-631-1314. 24hr. **Sexual Assault Hotline,** ☎254-9000. 24hr. **Suicide Prevention,** ☎480-784-1500. 24hr. **Gay Hotline,** ☎234-2752. Daily 10am-10pm.

Internet Access: The **Burton Barr Central Library,** 1221 N. Central Ave. (☎262-4636), offers free Internet access in 15min. slots. Open M-Th 10am-9pm, F-Sa 9am-6pm, Su noon-6pm.

Post Office: 522 N. Central Ave. (☎800-275-8777). Open M-F 8:30am-5pm. General delivery: 1441 E. Buckeye Rd. Open M-F 8:30am-5pm. **Postal Code:** 85034.

▟ ACCOMMODATIONS

Budget travelers should consider visiting Phoenix during July and August, when motels slash their prices by as much as 70%. In the winter, temperatures drop, the number of vacationers rises, vacancies are scarce, and prices go up; make reservations early. Although they are distant, the areas around Papago Fwy. and Black Canyon Hwy. are loaded with motels. **Mi Casa Su Casa/Old Pueblo Homestays Bed and Breakfast,** P.O. Box 950, Tempe 85280, arranges stays at B&Bs throughout Arizona, New Mexico, southern Utah, southern Nevada, and southern California. (☎800-456-0682. Open M-F 9am-5pm, Sa 9am-noon. Rooms from $45.) The reservationless should cruise the rows of motels on **Van Buren Street** east of downtown, toward the airport, but beware: parts of this area can be unsafe, and guests should examine a motel thoroughly before checking in.

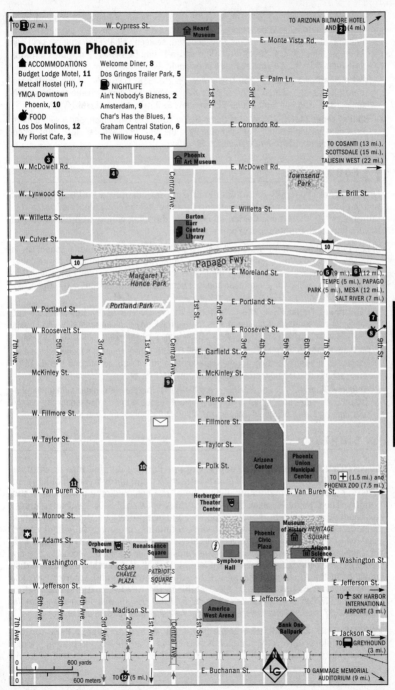

TO **11** (2 mi.)

W. Cypress St.

Heard Museum

TO ARIZONA BILTMORE HOTEL AND **2** (4 mi.)

E. Monte Vista Rd.

Downtown Phoenix

▲ ACCOMMODATIONS
Budget Lodge Motel, **11**
Metcalf Hostel (HI), **7**
YMCA Downtown Phoenix, **10**
🍎 FOOD
Los Dos Molinos, **12**
My Florist Cafe, **3**

Welcome Diner, **8**
Dos Gringos Trailer Park, **5**
🍸 NIGHTLIFE
Ain't Nobody's Bizness, **2**
Amsterdam, **9**
Char's Has the Blues, **1**
Graham Central Station, **6**
The Willow House, **4**

E. Palm Ln.

1st St.

3rd St.

7th St.

E. Coronado Rd.

TO COSANTI (13 mi.), SCOTTSDALE (15 mi.), TALIESIN WEST (22 mi.)

Phoenix Art Museum

W. McDowell Rd.

E. McDowell Rd.

Townsend Park

W. Lynwood St.

E. Brill St.

W. Willetta St.

E. Willetta St.

W. Culver St.

Burton Barr Central Library

10

Papago Fwy.

E. Moreland St.

TO **5** (9 mi.), **6** (12 mi.), TEMPE (5 mi.), PAPAGO PARK (5 mi.), MESA (12 mi.), SALT RIVER (7 mi.)

Margaret T. Hance Park

Portland Park

E. Portland St.

2nd St.

W. Portland St.

1st St.

E. Portland St.

7

W. Roosevelt St.

E. Roosevelt St.

8

7th Ave.

5th Ave.

3rd Ave.

1st Ave.

Central Ave.

E. Garfield St.

3rd St.

4th St.

5th St.

6th St.

7th St.

9th St.

McKinley St.

E. McKinley St.

9

E. Pierce St.

W. Fillmore St.

E. Fillmore St.

✉

W. Taylor St.

E. Taylor St.

E. Polk St.

Arizona Center

Phoenix Union Municipal Center

10

TO ✚ (1.5 mi.) and PHOENIX ZOO (7.5 mi.)

11

W. Van Buren St.

Herberger Theater Center

E. Van Buren St.

W. Monroe St.

Museum of History HERITAGE SQUARE

✡ W. Adams St.

Orpheum Theater

Renaissance Square

Phoenix Civic Plaza

Arizona Science Center E. Washington St.

W. Washington St.

CÉSAR CHÁVEZ PLAZA

PATRIOT'S SQUARE

ℹ

Symphony Hall

W. Jefferson St.

E. Jefferson St.

6th Ave.

5th Ave.

4th Ave.

3rd Ave.

2nd Ave.

1st Ave.

Central Ave.

1st St.

✉

Madison St.

America West Arena

E. Jefferson St.

TO ✚ SKY HARBOR INTERNATIONAL AIRPORT (3 mi.)

7th Ave.

Bank One Ballpark

E. Jackson St.

TO 🚌 GREYHOUND (3 mi.)

0   600 yards
0   600 meters

TO **12** (5 mi.)

LG

E. Buchanan St.

TO GAMMAGE MEMORIAL AUDITORIUM (9 mi.)

Metcalf Hostel (HI), 1026 N. 9th St. (☎254-9803), between Roosevelt and Portland a few blocks northeast of downtown. This hostel has the basics covered, but guests must pitch in with chores. Dorm rooms stay unlocked, so keep valuables in your car or in one of the hostel's lockers. Check-in 7-10am and 5-10pm. Dorms $17, members $15; private room $30-35. Cash or traveler's check only. ❶

YMCA Downtown Phoenix, 350 N. 1st Ave. (☎253-6181). Provides small, single-occupancy rooms and shared bathrooms for both women and men. Athletic facilities available. 18+. Reception 9am-10pm. $20 per day; $99 per week. AmEx/MC/V. ❶

Budget Lodge Motel, 402 W. Van Buren St. (☎254-7247), has nice rooms with a lobby entrance, making it one of the safer options in the area. Pool and free HBO. 24hr. reception. Rooms from $40. AmEx/D/MC/V. ❷

🔲 FOOD

Downtowners typically eat at small cafes under corporate buildings, most of which close on weekends. **McDowell** and **Camelback Road** have plenty of Asian restaurants, while the **Arizona Center,** an open-air shopping gallery at 3rd St. and Van Buren, has food, fountains, and palm trees.

▓ Los Dos Molinos, 8646 S. Central Ave. (☎243-9113), at 260 S. Alma School Dr. in Mesa. From downtown, go 8 mi. south on Central Ave. Lively, colorful, and with chiles hotter than hell, it's worth the trip. The food is authentic, and they "don't know mild," so be ready to swallow fire. No reservations. Enchiladas $3.50. Burritos $3-7. Open Tu-F 11am-2:30pm and 5-9pm, Sa 11am-9pm. AmEx/D/MC/V. ❷

Dos Gringos Trailer Park, 216 E. University Dr. (☎480-968-7879). Dos skirts the line between restaurant and nightspot with its laid-back day-drinking mentality and cheap, tasty Mexican dishes ($6). Open M-Sa 10am-1am, Su 11am-1am. AmEx/D/MC/V. ❷

My Florist Cafe, 530 W. McDowell Rd. (☎254-0333), serves gourmet sandwich and salad cuisine in a swanky setting. Try the asparagus salad with apricot-almond bread ($11). Live jazz nightly. Open daily 7am-midnight. AmEx/MC/V. ❷

Welcome Diner, 924 E. Roosevelt St. (☎495-1111). This cute little diner, with an emphasis on both "cute" and "little," is Norman Rockwell-esque with white-washed walls, cherry-red trim, and fresh bouquets. Burgers $6. Open M-Sa 7am-3pm. Cash only. ❶

👁 SIGHTS

DOWNTOWN. The center of Phoenix, Copper Park, is divided into downtown (south of I-10), with cultural and sports attractions, and uptown (north of I-10), an artistic quarter with many museums. One of the best regional museums in the country, The ▓**Heard Museum,** 2301 N. Central Ave. (☎252-8840), has Native American ancient and contemporary art, poetry, and sculpture. The Museum itself is a graceful adobe building with spanish tiles, fountains, and beautifully landscaped gardens. *(Open daily 9:30am-5pm. Free tours at noon, 1:30, 3pm. $10, seniors $9, ages 4-12 $6, students $5; Native Americans with status cards free. Free admission second Su of every month.)* Three blocks south, at Central and McDowell, the **Phoenix Art Museum** displays art of the American West and 19th-century European and American works. Look for the traveling photography exhibit in the newly-expanded building in 2006. *(1625 N. Central Ave., at McDowell Rd. ☎257-1880. Open Tu-W and F-Su 10am-5pm, Th 10am-9pm. $7, students and seniors $5, ages 6-17 $2. Free after 4:15pm and on Th.)*

PAPAGO PARK AND FARTHER EAST. Take bus #3 east to **Papago Park,** on the eastern outskirts of the city, for spectacular views of the desert and hiking, biking, and driving trails. In the park, the **Phoenix Zoo** has a formidable collection of tropical, African, and Southwestern critters. *(455 N. Galvin Pkwy. ☎273-1341. Open Sept.-May daily 9am-5pm; June-Aug. M-F 7am-1pm, Sa-Su 7am-4pm. $14, seniors $9, children $6.)* The ◼**Desert Botanical Garden** showcases colorful cacti, plants native to the Sonoran Desert, and rare breeds of succulents. *(1201 N. Galvin Pkwy. ☎941-1225. Guided tours daily Oct.-Apr. 11am and 1pm. Flashlight tours June-July Th and Sa at 7:30pm. Open daily May-Sept. 7am-8pm; Oct.-Apr. 8am-8pm. $9, seniors $8, students $5.)* Farther east of the city, in Mesa, flows the **Salt River,** one of the last remaining desert rivers in the US. **Salt River Tubing & Recreation** arranges tubing trips. *(☎480-984-3305; www.saltrivertubing.com. Open May-Sept. daily 9am-4pm. Tube rental $13 per day, includes shuttle service.)*

WRIGHT SIGHTS. Taliesin West was originally built as the winter camp of Frank Lloyd Wright's Taliesin architectural collective; in his later years he lived there full-time. It is now a campus for an architectural college run by his foundation. *(12621 Frank Lloyd Wright Blvd. Head east off the Cactus St. exit from Rte. 101. ☎480-860-2700; www.franklloydwright.org. Open Sept.-June daily 9am-4pm; July-Aug. M and Th-Su 9am-4pm. 1-1½hr. guided tours required. See website for specific tour info. In summer $14-16.50, in winter $18-22.50, students and seniors $12/$16; ages 4-12 $6.)* Wright also designed the impressive **Arizona Biltmore,** a palacial hotel with the largest interior of gold leafing in the US. Despite the hotel's posh atmosphere, viewing is free, and the Aztec Room and Ballroom are especially magnificent. *(24th St. and Missouri. ☎955-6600.)* One of the last buildings designed by Wright, the **Gammage Memorial Auditorium** is a stand-out with its unique rotunda shape and pink-and-beige earth tones. *(Mill Ave. and Apache Blvd., on the Arizona State University campus in Tempe. Take bus #60, or #22 on weekends. ☎965-3434. 20min. tours daily in winter.)* **Cosanti** is a working studio and bell foundry designed by Paolo Soleri, one of Wright's students. Visitors can watch artists work from the decorative terraces. *(6433 Doubletree Ranch Rd., in Scottsdale. ☎480-948-6145. Open M-Sa 9am-5pm, Su 11am-5pm. Suggested donation $1.)*

🎵 📷 ENTERTAINMENT AND NIGHTLIFE

Phoenix is stacked with stadiums, and the large facilities make it easy to get last-minute tickets. NBA basketball action heats up with the **Phoenix Suns** (☎379-7867) at the **America West Arena,** while the **Arizona Cardinals** (☎379-0101) will play NFL football in the new **Cardinals Stadium** starting in the 2006 season. The **Arizona Diamondbacks** (☎514-8400) use the fabulous **Bank One Ballpark** with a retractable roof, outfield swimming pool, and "beer gardens." (☎462-6799. Tickets from $7. $1 tickets available 2hr. before games; first come, first served. Tours of the stadium $6.)

The free *New Times Weekly,* available on magazine racks, lists schedules for Phoenix's after-hours scene. The *Cultural Calendar of Events* covers area entertainment in three-month intervals. The *Western Front* and *Echo,* both found in bars and clubs, cover GLBT nightlife. **The Willow House,** 149 W. McDowell Rd., is a self-proclaimed "artist's cove," combining a coffeehouse, deli, and musicians' hangout. (☎252-0272. No alcohol. 2-for-1 coffee happy hour M-F 4-7pm. Live music Sa 8pm. Open M-Th 7am-midnight, F 7am-1am, Sa 8am-1am, Su 8am-midnight.) **Char's Has the Blues,** 4631 N. 7th Ave., houses local blues acts. On Friday nights, come early for the barbecue. (☎230-0205; www.charshastheblues.com. 2-drink min. Open M-Th and Su 7:30pm-1am, F-Sa 7pm-1am. Cover F-Sa $7.) **Graham Central Station,** 7850 S. Priest Dr., in Tempe, has four venues under one roof. The smaller Top 40, retro, and karaoke venues supplement the good times of the Rockin' Rodeo, a western-themed club complete with mechanical bull. (☎480-496-0799. Open W-Su 6pm-2am. Cover up to $7.) ◼**Amsterdam,** 718 N. Central Ave., is a straight-friendly gay bar with plush leather sofas, antique mirrors, and 190 types of martinis. Recently voted "hottest bar of the year" by *Out* magazine, this is the first establishment in the US to have both a bar and salon license. (☎258-6122. M manicures and martinis $5. Open daily 4pm-2am.) A large, predominantly lesbian and gay bar, **Ain't Nobody's Bizness,** 3031 E. Indian School Rd. #7, has more space devoted to pool tables than to the dance floor, but dance and hip-hop music get people moving. (☎224-9977. Th $2 pitchers. Occasional cover. Open daily 4pm-2am.)

SCENIC DRIVE: APACHE TRAIL

A great daytrip from Phoenix, the **Apache Trail** wings from **Apache Junction,** a small mining town 40 mi. east of Phoenix, through the rugged, haunting **Superstition Mountains.** The trail, also known less creatively as **Route 88,** takes gazers through old ghost towns, along tranquil lakes, and finally to the Roosevelt Dam. It wasn't until the early 20th century that Rte. 88 was carved through the mountains to move supplies for the construction of the Dam. The road, loosely following ancestral Indian paths, became known as the Apache Trail to the early motorists who raced around the road's harrowing turns and along its 10% grades in their primitive cars, hoping for new records. Though the days of the Model T are gone, motorists still hug the turns as they climb the steep roadbed to one of the three beautiful man-made lakes along the Salt River or ogle the Superstition Mountain Wilderness's crags and canyons. Although the road is only about 50 mi. one-way, trips require at least 3hr. because of the partially unpaved, narrow roadbed. Info is available at the **Apache Junction Chamber of Commerce,** 112 E. 2nd Ave. (☎480-982-3141. Open M-F 8am-5pm, in summer 8am-4:30pm.) The car-less can drive with **Apache Trail Tours,** which offers on- and off-road Jeep tours. (☎480-982-7661. 2hr. all day tours from $70-165 per person, includes lunch. Reserve at least 1 day ahead.)

Sights along the drive include the **Superstition Mountain Museum,** 3½ mi. northeast of Apache Junction along the Apache Trail, where visitors can get info and check out an impressive collection of mining equipment and artifacts. (☎480-983-4888. $4, students $2. Open daily 9am-4pm.) **Goldfield Ghost Town,** on Rte. 88, 5 mi. north of the U.S. 60 junction, is a historically preserved 1890s mining town that functions as a touristy Old West caricature complete with fudge shop, saloons, and historical exhibits. (☎480-982-0276. Open daily 10am-5pm. $5.) **Goldfield Ghost Town Mining Tours** provides humorous and informative tours of the nearby mines. (☎480-983-0333. Open daily 10am-5pm. Mine tours $5, ages 6-12 $3). **Lost Dutchman State Park ❶,** 1 mi. farther north on Rte. 88, commemorates the legend of Jacob Waltz (i.e. the Dutchman), a prospector who allegedly hid a gold-mine in the Superstition Mountains. The park has nature trails, picnic sites, and campsites with showers. (☎480-982-4485. Entrance $5 per vehicle. Sites $12, with electricity $20.)

The first body of water on the trail, **Canyon Lake,** has no shortage of recreational activities for boaters and swimmers. Those without water transport can take the **Dolly Steamboat,** a 90min. narrated cruise on a vintage sternwheeler paddleboat. (☎480-827-9144; www.dollysteamboat.com. In summer departs Tu-Su noon; call for winter hours. $12, children $8.) Grab a saddle for a bar stool at **Tortilla Flat,** another refurbished ghost town 18 mi. farther north on Rte. 88. The town, once a stagecoach stop, keeps its spirits up and tourists fed with a restaurant, ice-cream shop, and saloon. Be sure to check out the walls in each shop, which are completely covered in money. According to legend, travelers taped money to the walls in case they were robbed along the trail. You can still tape named $1 bills to the walls for posterity, but so far no one has been back to claim their $1. (☎480-984-1776. Restaurant open M-F 9am-6pm, Sa-Su 8am-7pm.) **Tonto National Monument,** on Rte. 88, 5 mi. east of Lake Roosevelt, preserves 800-year-old masonry and Pueblo ruins. A short (½ mi.) but steep (350 ft.) trail leads from the visitors center up to the ruins. (☎928-467-2241. Open daily 8am-5pm, trail closes at 4pm. $4 per car.) **Tonto National Forest ❶** has nearby camping. (☎602-225-5200. Sites $4-11.) The trail ends at the **Theodore Roosevelt Dam** (finished in 1911), the last dam in the US built by hand. At the end of the trail, Rte. 60 is a scenic trip back to Phoenix.

TUCSON ☎ 520

A little bit country, a little bit south of the border, Tucson is a melting pot of culture, history, and often contradictory influences. Mexican property until 1854, the city retains much of its Mexican influence while also championing the rugged individualism of the American West. Home to the students of the University of Arizona, the soldiers of the Davis-Monthan Air Force Base, ranching cowboys, downtown artists, and suburban retirees, Tucson is the colorful fusion of a seemingly disparate variety of folk. Somehow though, amid the war machines and creative photography, honky tonk and Latin techno, irony gradually fades away into desert sunsets and half-empty margarita glasses.

▐ TRANSPORTATION

Airport: Tucson International Airport (☎573-8100; www.tucsonairport.org), on Valencia Rd., south of downtown. Bus #6 goes downtown from the terminal drop-off area. **Arizona Stagecoach** (☎881-4111; www.azstagecoach.com) goes downtown for $16-18.

Trains: Amtrak, 400 E. Toole Ave. (☎800-872-7245; www.amtrak.com), at 5th Ave. Open daily 10:15pm-5:30am. To **Albuquerque** (3 per week, $99) via **El Paso, Los Angeles** (10hr., 3 per week, $51), and **San Francisco** (18hr., 3 per week, $88) via **Los Angeles.** Book 2 weeks ahead or rates are substantially higher.

Buses: Greyhound, 2 S. 4th Ave. (☎792-3475; www.greyhound.com), between Congress St. and Broadway. Station open daily midnight-3am, 8:30am-11:59pm. To: **Albuquerque** (12-14hr., 6 per day, $87); **El Paso** (6hr., 6 per day, $40); **Los Angeles** (10-12hr., 13 per day, $48); **Phoenix** (2hr., 12 per day, $20).

Public Transit: Sun-Tran, (☎792-9222; www.suntran.com). Buses run from the Ronstadt terminal downtown at Congress and 6th Ave. $1; seniors and disabled $0.40, day pass $2. Most routes M-F 5:30am-10pm, Sa-Su 8am-7pm; times vary by route. Customer service center open M-F 6am-7pm, Sa-Su 8am-5pm.

Taxi: Yellow Cab, ☎624-6611.

Bike Rental: Fair Wheel Bikes, 1110 E. 6th St. (☎884-9018), at Fremont. $20-25 per day with $500 credit card deposit. Open M-F 9am-6pm, Sa 9am-5:30pm, Su noon-4pm.

✦ ▐ ORIENTATION AND PRACTICAL INFORMATION

Just east of I-10, Tucson's downtown area surrounds the intersection of **Broadway Boulevard** and **Stone Avenue,** two blocks from the train and bus terminals. The **University of Arizona** is 1 mi. northeast of downtown at the intersection of **North Park Avenue** and **Speedway Boulevard.** Avenues run north-south, streets east-west; because some of each are numbered, intersections like "6th and 6th" actually exist. Speedway Blvd., Broadway, and **Grant Road** are the quickest east-west routes through town. To go north-south, follow **Oracle Road** through the heart of the city, **Campbell Avenue** east of downtown, or **Swan Road** farther east.

Visitor Info: Tucson Convention and Visitors Bureau, 130 S. Scott Ave. (☎624-1817 or 800-638-8350), near Broadway. Open M-F 8am-5pm, Sa-Su 9am-4pm.

GLBT Resources: Gay, Lesbian, and Bisexual Community Center, 300 E. 6th St. (☎624-1779). Open M-F 10am-7pm, Sa 10am-5pm.

Hotlines: Rape Crisis, ☎624-7273. **Suicide Prevention,** ☎323-9373. Both 24hr.

Medical Services: University Medical Center, 1501 N. Campbell Ave. (☎694-0111).

Internet Access: University of Arizona Main Library, 1510 E. University Blvd. Open Sept.-May M-Th 7:30am-1am, F 7:30am-9pm, Sa 10am-9pm, Su 11am-1am; June-Aug. M-Th 7:30am-11pm, F 7:30am-6pm, Sa 9am-6pm, Su 11am-11pm. Free.

Post Office: 1501 S. Cherrybell Stra. (☎388-5129). Open M-F 8:30am-8pm, Sa 9am-1pm. **Postal Code:** 85726. **Area Code:** 520.

ACCOMMODATIONS

There's a direct correlation between the temperature in Tucson and the warmth of its lodging industry to budget travelers: expect the best deals in the scorching heat of summer. The **Tucson Gem and Mineral Show** is an added hazard for budget travelers, driving prices up during its two-week run at the end of January. In addition to the **backcountry camping ❶** available in **Saguaro National Park** and **Coronado State Forest,** there are a number of developed camping options. **Gilbert Ray Campground ❶** (☎883-4200), just outside Saguaro West, has 145 first come, first served campsites ($7) with toilets and drinking water. A variety of camping areas flank **Sky Island Scenic Byway** at Mt. Lemmon. All campgrounds charge an additional $5 road access fee. **Spencer Canyon ❶** (sites $12) and **Rose Canyon ❶** (sites $15) have water and toilets. Call the Santa Catalina Ranger District for more info (☎749-8700).

■ **Roadrunner Hostel,** 346 E. 12th St. (☎628-4709). An adobe home with artsy decor and a comfy living room. The owner is fond of dishing out homemade food and local info. Free Internet access, linens, and lockers. Laundry $1.75. Belgian waffle breakfast included. Dorms $18; private rooms with shared bath $38. Cash only. ❶

Hotel Congress and Hostel, 311 E. Congress St. (☎622-8848 or 800-722-8848). Across from the bus and train stations, this hotel-hostel has a distinct 1920s twist. Private rooms have a bath, phone, and vintage radio. Dorms $25. Private rooms in summer $79, in winter $90. 10% discount for students, military, and local artists. AmEx/D/MC/V. ❷

The Flamingo Hotel, 1300 N. Stone Ave. (☎770-1910 or 800-300-3533). Houses guests as well as Arizona's largest collection of Western movie posters. Dozens of themed rooms, from the Kevin Costner room to the Burt Lancaster suite, all with A/C, cable TV, and telephone. Laundry, breakfast, and pool. Rooms May-Aug. $40; Sept.-Nov. $45; Dec.-Apr. up to $85. AAA and AARP discounts. AmEx/D/MC. ❸

FOOD

Tucson brims with inexpensive and tasty eateries. Cheap Mexican definitely dominates the scene, but you can find pretty much every style of cooking imaginable.

■ **La Indita,** 622 N. 4th Ave. (☎792-0523). A family-run gem with hand-painted murals and mouthwatering Mexican dishes. The *carne seca*, a labor-intensive beef dish marinated in lime and green chiles and sun-dried for three days, is incredible. The food is still prepared by La Indita herself using unique family recipes. Open M-Th 11am-9pm, F 11am-6pm, Sa 6-9pm, Su 9am-9pm. MC/V. ❶

El Charro Cafe, 311 N. Court Ave. (☎ 620-1922), is the oldest family-operated Mexican restaurant in the US, and as rumor has it, is where the chimichanga was invented (accidentally). You may have to wait in line, but you'll be glad you did. Lunch $6-10. Dinner $10-15. Open M-Th and Su 11am-9pm, F-Sa 11am-10pm. AmEx/D/MC/V. ❸

Ha Long Bay, 6304 E. Broadway. (☎571-1338). When your tastebuds need a break from Mexican, this is the best Vietnamese for miles. Known locally for the hot and sour soup ($8) but has equally delicious stir-fry and vermicelli dishes ($6-8). MC/V. ❷

Bentley's House of Coffee and Tea, 1730 E. Speedway Blvd. (☎795-0338), is a warm, colorful cafe that covers all the meals and snacks in between. Linger for the free wireless Internet or for a big slice of homemade chocolate cake ($3). Two eggs and toast $4. Vegan tamales $5. Open M-Sa 7am-11pm, Su 8am-10pm. MC/V. ❶

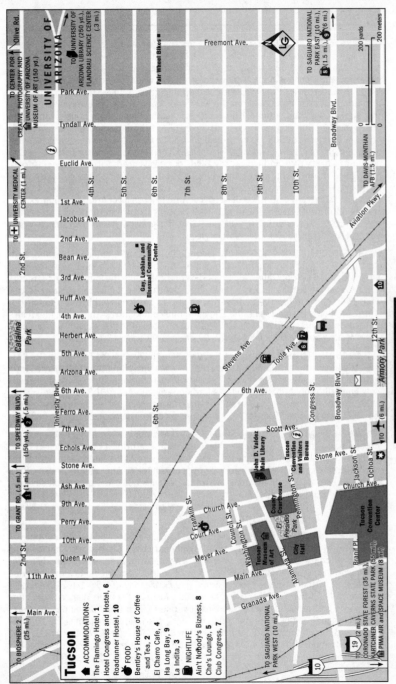

THE SOUTHWEST

Tucson

▲ ACCOMMODATIONS
The Flamingo Hotel, **1**
Hotel Congress and Hostel, **6**
Roadrunner Hostel, **10**

🍴 FOOD
Bentley's House of Coffee
and Tea, **2**
El Charro Cafe, **4**
Ha Long Bay, **9**
La Indita, **3**

🍸 NIGHTLIFE
Ain't Nobody's Bizness, **8**
Che's Lounge, **5**
Club Congress, **7**

UNIVERSITY OF ARIZONA

Catalina Park

TO BIOSPHERE 2 (25 mi.)
TO GRANT RD. (.5 mi.)
TO SPEEDWAY BLVD. (.5 mi.)

TO UNIVERSITY OF ARIZONA LIBRARY (250 yd.), FLANDRAU SCIENCE CENTER (.3 mi.)

TO CENTER FOR CREATIVE PHOTOGRAPHY AND UNIVERSITY OF ARIZONA MUSEUM OF ART (150 yd.)

TO UNIVERSITY MEDICAL CENTER (1 mi.)

Olive Rd.
Freemont Ave.
Park Ave.
Tyndall Ave.
Euclid Ave.
4th St.
5th St.
6th St.
7th St.
8th St.
9th St.
10th St.
1st Ave.
Jacobus Ave.
2nd Ave.
Bean Ave.
3rd Ave.
Huff Ave.
4th Ave.
Herbert Ave.
5th Ave.
Arizona Ave.
6th Ave.
Ferro Ave.
7th Ave.
Echols Ave.
Stone Ave.
Ash Ave.
9th Ave.
Perry Ave.
10th Ave.
Queen Ave.
11th Ave.
Main Ave.
2nd St.
University Blvd.
Stevens Ave.
6th St.
12th St.

Fair Wheel Bikes
Gay, Lesbian, and Bisexual Community Center
Broadway Blvd.
Toole Ave.
Congress St.
Scott Ave.
6th Ave.
John D. Valdez Main Library
Tucson Convention and Visitors Bureau
Stone Ave.
Ochoa St.
Jackson St.
Church Ave.
County Courthouse
El Presidio Park
Pennington St.
Franklin St.
Church Ave.
Court Ave.
Council St.
Washington St.
Meyer Ave.
Main Ave.
Alameda St.
City Hall
Tucson Museum of Art
Granada Ave.
Branif Pl.
Tucson Convention Center

Aviation Pkwy.
TO DAVIS-MONTHAN AFB (1.5 mi.)
TO SAGUARO NATIONAL PARK EAST (10 mi.)
Armory Park

TO SAGUARO NATIONAL PARK WEST (10 mi.)
TO CORONADO STATE FOREST (35 mi.), KARTCHNER CAVERNS STATE PARK (55 mi.), PIMA AIR and SPACE MUSEUM (8 mi.)

0   200 yards
0   200 meters

⊙ SIGHTS

UNIVERSITY OF ARIZONA. The campus is expansive and filled with parks, museums, and surrounding shops. The **visitors center** has details. *(845 E. University Blvd. ☎884-7516. Open M-F 9am-4pm.)* An alternative magnet lined with restaurants and galleries, **4th Avenue** is a great place to stroll. Between Speedway and Broadway Blvd., the street is a touristy historical shopping district. **University Boulevard** leads into the university grounds from the west and is edged with breweries and cafes that appeal to a young crowd. The **Center for Creative Photography** houses outstanding changing exhibits as well as the archives of Ansel Adams and Richard Avedon. *(1030 N. Olive. ☎621-7968. Open M-F 9am-5pm, Sa-Su noon-5pm. Archives available to the public through print-viewing appointments. Free.)* The **Flandrau Science Center,** on the corner of Cherry Ave. and University Blvd., dazzles visitors with a public observatory, laser show, and mineral museum. *(☎621-7827; www.flandrau.org. Open M-Tu 9am-5pm, W-Sa 9am-5pm and 7-9pm, Su noon-5pm. $3, under 14 $2. Shows $5/$4, seniors and students $4.50.)* The **University of Arizona Museum of Art** has an impressive collection of modern American and 18th-century Latin American art and sculpture. *(1031 N. Olive. ☎621-7567. Open mid-Sept. to mid-May M-F 9am-5pm, Su noon-4pm; May-Sept. M-F 10am-3:30pm, Su noon-4pm. Free.)*

EL PRESIDIO HISTORIC DISTRICT. Bounded by W. 6th, Alameda, N. Stone, and Granade Ave. in downtown, this 18th-century adobe neighborhood is now the artisan district of Tucson. Galleries, art studios and cafes line the surrounding streets, but the most interesting area can be explored by entering the **Tucson Museum of Art,** where you can wander the courtyards, sculpture gardens, and beautiful historic houses that now contain exhibits. The main museum features American, Mexican, and European art. *(140 N. Main Ave. ☎624-2333. Open M-Sa 10am-4pm, Su noon-4pm. Closed M late May to early Sept. $5, seniors $4, students $3, under 13 free. Su free.)*

OLD TUCSON STUDIOS. A taste of Hollywood in the desert, **Old Tucson Studios** has been the backdrop for numerous Western movies, including the 1938 movie *Arizona* and Will Smith's *Wild Wild West.* Now also a studio theme park, visitors can view gunfight reenactments and have barbecue at saloons. *(201 S. Kinney Rd. ☎883-0100; www.desertmuseum.org. Open early Sept. to late May daily 10am-6pm; late May to early Sept. M-F 10am-3pm, Sa 10am-4pm. Sometimes closed on M in winter. $13, ages 4-11 $8.)*

ARIZONA-SONORA DESERT MUSEUM. The ▨**Arizona-Sonora Desert Museum** is more of a zoo and nature preserve than a museum, featuring a range of desert habitats and over 300 animal species. The venomous reptile presentation is fantastic (daily 12:15pm), as is the raptor free flight program (Nov.-Apr., call for times). Visits should be made in the morning before the animals take their afternoon siestas. *(2021 N. Kinney Rd. Follow Speedway Blvd. west of the city as it becomes Gates Pass Rd., then Kinney Rd. ☎883-1083. Open daily Mar.-Sept. 7:30am-5pm, June-Sept. Sa until 10pm; Oct.-Feb. 8:30am-5pm. $9, ages 6-12 $4; Oct.-May. $12/$2.)*

PIMA AIR AND SPACE MUSEUM. Aerospace meets military history in an impressive museum with over 200 of the most significant aircraft in history. Visitors can stroll through different hangars on a tour ranging from President Kennedy's Air Force One to the SR-71 Blackbird Spyplane. The first hangar also has exhibits on female and African-American aviators. *(6000 E. Valencia Rd. ☎574-0462. Open daily 9am-4pm. $9.75, seniors $8.75, under 6 free.)* For a taste of the Cold War, visitors can buy passes to tour the **Titan Missile Museum,** one of 54 missile bases put on alert during 1954 and finally decommissioned in 1981. The main attraction is the Titan II rocket and the underground control room *(☎625-7736. Tours daily 9am-4pm).* Tours of the **Davis-Monthan Air Force Base** are also offered, but be prepared for rigorous security checks and possible cancellations. *(5 tours per day M-F. $6, ages 6-12 $3.)*

BIOSPHERE 2. Ninety-one feet high, with an area of more than three acres, Biosphere 2 is sealed off from Earth—"Biosphere 1"—by 500 tons of stainless steel. In 1991, eight research scientists locked themselves inside this giant greenhouse to monitor the behavior of five man-made ecosystems: savanna, rainforest, marsh, ocean, and desert. After two years, they began having oxygen problems and difficulty with food production. No one lives in Biosphere 2 now, but it is still used as a research facility and is open to the public by guided tour. *(30min. north of Tucson; follow Oracle Rd. north until it becomes Rte. 77 N. From Phoenix, take I-10 to Exit 185, follow Rte. 387 to Rte. 79 (Florence Hwy.), and proceed to Oracle Jct. and Rte. 77. ☎800-838-2462. Call for daily tour info. Open daily 8:30am-5:30pm, last admission 5pm. $20, ages 6-12 $13.)*

📞 NIGHTLIFE

The free *Tucson Weekly*, available in newsstands throughout the city, is the local authority on nightlife, while the weekend sections of *Star* or *Citizen* also provide good coverage. Bars and dance clubs line **University Boulevard, Speedway Boulevard,** and **North Oracle.** Downtown, **4th Avenue** supports a bustling night scene where most bars have live music, low cover charges, and a chill atmosphere.

    Club Congress, 311 E. Congress St. (☎622-8848), alternates DJs with live indie and rock concerts. The warehouse-like interior is always filled with hipster regulars. M 80s night with $0.80 vodkas. Cover $3-5. Open daily 9pm-1am.

    Che's Lounge, 350 4th Ave. (☎623-2088). A funky bar that houses an eclectic crowd with a flair for laughs and late-night conversations. Weekly $1 drafts and $2 wells. Show up early; there are lines early in the night on weekends and crowds during the week. Live music Sa. Open daily noon-1am.

    Ain't Nobody's Bizness, 2900 E. Broadway Blvd. (☎318-4838), is the big mama of the Tucson lesbian scene with a large bar, themed contests, and pool tournaments. "Biz" has some of the best dancing in Tucson. Open M-Tu 2pm-1am, W-Su 2pm-2am.

🏞 OUTDOOR ACTIVITIES

The best hiking nearby can be found at **Saguaro National Park,** which is split into two districts flanking Tucson to the west and east. The western half **(Tucson Mountain District)** is accessed by following Speedway Blvd. out of town and taking Kinney Rd. The **Red Hills Visitors Center** (☎733-5158) has exhibits on desert flora and fauna, as well as *The Saguaro Sentinel*, the park's free newspaper guide with all trail information. The **Bajada Loop Drive** runs only 6 mi. on a graded dirt road but passes through some of the most striking desert scenery the park has to offer. Trails include the wheelchair-accessible **Desert Discovery Nature Trail** (½ mi., 20min.) and the challenging **Hugh Norris Trail** (10 mi, 5-6hr.). The eastern portion of the park **(Rincón Mountain District),** accessed by going east on Speedway to Freeman Rd., is larger and has more trails, but the scenery is primarily the same. The **Rincón Visitors Center** (☎733-5153) offers natural history exhibits and guides to the park's activities. The **Cactus Forest Loop Drive** winds 8 mi. through impressive stands of saguaros, many of them well over 100 years old. Mountain biking is permitted only around the **Cactus Forest Loop Drive** and **Cactus Forest Trail,** at the western end of the park near the visitors center. (Both visitors centers open daily 9am-5pm. Park and auto loop open 7am-sunset. $10 entrance fee per vehicle.)

    The Tucson area offers a range of opportunities for cave enthusiasts. The caves of **Colossal Cave Mountain Park,** 16721 E. Old Spanish Trail, have been known to humans for over a thousand years, first by the Hohokam Indians and later by train robbers who used them for hideouts. In addition to 1hr. walking tours throughout the day, a special ladder tour through otherwise sealed-off tunnels, crawlspaces, and corridors can be arranged. (Exit 279 on I-10. ☎647-7275. Walking tours $8.50, ages 6-12 $5. Ladder tours M-F 11am or 2pm $15; Sa 6:15-9pm $35. Reservations required. Park open mid-Mar. to mid-Sept. M-Sa 8am-6pm, Su 8am-7pm; mid-Sept. to mid-Mar. M-Sa 9am-5pm, Su 9am-6pm. Park entrance fee $5 for vehicle, $1 for bike or walk-up.) **Kartchner Caverns State Park,** 1300 W. Washington, required engineering feats to make it accessible to visitors without disturbing its delicate environment. The result is a dimly-lit walkway with views of wet limestone spires, speleothems, ancient "soda-straws," and the largest cave column in Arizona. Two separate 1½hr. tours are offered in the cave: one exploring the Rotunda and Throne Rooms (year-round) and another through the Big Room (Sept.-Apr. or once the bats have finished breeding). Taking a tour is the only way to enter the cave, and only 500 people are allowed in the cave each day. Most tickets are reserved far in advance in winter, but approximately 100 tickets are held for walk-ups and dispensed at 7:30am. (Exit 302, 50 mi. from Tucson. ☎586-4100. Open daily 7:30am-6pm. Tours run every 30min. 8:30am-4:30pm. Entrance fee $5 per vehicle. Tours $19, ages 7-13 $10, in summer $8.50/$5. Reservations strongly recommended.)

TOMBSTONE ☎520

Two major fires, an earthquake, and enough duels to fill an entire cemetery have steeped Tombstone in legend, folklore, and unanswerable questions like, "Who really killed Johnny Ringo?" (the cowboys all claim responsibility). Today, the town "too tough to die" flaunts its lawless Western past as a tourist attraction. Cowboys swagger down Allen Street promising gunfight reenactments while dolled-up dames keep glasses full in the saloons. The popular **Shootout at the O.K. Corral** reenacts a gunfight daily at 2pm at the supposed fight site. Next door, in the **Tombstone Historama,** the voice of Vincent Price narrates the town's history. (☎457-3456. Shootout open daily 9am-5pm; arrive before 2pm reenactment. Historama shows daily every hr. 9am-4:30pm. Admission to both attractions $7.50.) The only original building in Tombstone, the **Bird Cage Theater** was named for the suspended cages that used to contain prostitutes. Now a museum, it was once home to the longest poker game in Western history (8 years, 5 months, and 3 days) and was the site of the fateful duel between Doc Holliday and the outlaw "King of the Cowboys," Johnny Ringo. Visitors can still see the bullet holes. (☎457-3421. Open daily 8am-6pm. Self-guided tour available. $6, seniors $5.50.) The tombstones of the town, largely the result of all that gunplay, stand in **Boothill Cemetery,** on Rte. 80 just north of town. (☎457-3421 or 800-457-3423. Open daily 7:30am-6pm. Free.)

If you want to stay in Tombstone, the **Trail Riders Inn ❷,** on the corner of 7th and Fremont, is one of the few options and has clean rooms with a homey feel. (☎457-3573. Singles from $30; doubles from $35. MC/V.) **Six Gun City Crazy Horse Saloon ❷,** at 5th and Toughnut, serves juicy burgers and $2 margaritas to visitors watching theatrical Wild West shows and staged gunfights. (☎457-3827. Shows at 11:30am, 1, 3pm. Open W-Su 11am-10pm. MC/V.) **Nellie Cashman's Restaurant ❶,** named after the "angel of the mining camps" who devoted her life to clean living and public service, is less Old West and a bit more down-home. Delicious half-pound burgers start at $5.50. (☎457-2212. Open daily 7:30am-9pm. AmEx/D/MC/V.) For "good whiskey and tolerable water," country music, and the remnants of dishonest underground activity, head to **Big Nose Kate's Saloon ❷,** on Allen St. (☎457-3107. Buffalo burgers $5-7. Open daily 10am-midnight. MC/V.)

Located some 80 mi. south of Tucson and roughly 20 mi. south of Benson, Tombstone makes a great daytrip. To get to Tombstone, take the Benson exit off I-10, then go south on Rte. 80. The nearest **Greyhound** station is in Benson. The **Tombstone Visitors Center,** on 4th St. and Allen, provides brochures and maps, although Tombstone is so small that nothing is hard to find. (☎457-3929. Open daily 9am-5pm.) **Internet** access is available at **Gitt Wired,** at 5th and Fremont. (☎457-3250. Open 7am-5pm. $0.15 per min.) **Post office:** 100 N. Haskell Ave. **Postal Code:** 85638. **Area Code:** 520.

BISBEE   ☎520

Located 100 mi. southeast of Tucson and 20 mi. south of Tombstone, Bisbee, a former mining town, is now a cliff-side artistic haven full of painters and hat-makers with a contagious zest for life. The small galleries and tiny cafes that line the streets give Bisbee a European air, but the open pit mine on the edge of town is a reminder of its Old West roots. **Queen Mines,** on the Rte. 80 interchange entering Old Bisbee, stopped operating in 1943 but now gives 1¼hr. subterranean tours. (☎432-2071. Tours at 9, 10:30am, noon, 2, 3:30pm. $12, ages 4-15 $5.) The Smithsonian-affiliated **Mining and Historical Museum,** 5 Copper Queen, highlights the discovery of Bisbee's copper surplus and the lives of the fortune-seekers who extracted it. (☎432-7071. Open daily 10am-4pm. $4, seniors $3.50, under 3 free.) About 18 mi. west of Bisbee on Rte. 92, along Mexico's border, **Coronado National Memorial** marks the place where Francisco Coronado and his expedition first entered American territory. **Coronado Cave,** a small dry cave, is three-quarters of a mile from the **visitors center** along a short, steep path. A free permit is required to explore the cave, and can be picked up at the visitors center; each caver must have two flashlights. (☎366-5515. Park open daily dawn-dusk. Visitors center open daily 8am-5pm.) **Ramsey Canyon Preserve,** 5 mi. farther down the road, attracts nearly as many bird-watchers as birds. The preserve is in the middle of major migratory routes, and thousands of hummingbirds throng here in summer. (Open daily 8am-5pm. $5, under 16 free. 1st Sa of every month free.)

The **Shady Dell RV and Vintage Trailerpark ❷,** 1 Old Douglas Rd. rents vintage aluminum trailers with original decor; some even have phonographs. (☎432-3567. Laundry, phones, and showers on site. RV sites available. Trailers from $40.) Just outside of town, the **Double Adobe Campground and Recreational Ranch ❶,** 5057 W. Double Adobe Rd., has tent sites inside a wildlife habitat. (☎364-4000. Tent sites $12, RV hookups $17.) For a brighten-your-day breakfast in a sunny brick building, head to the ⬛**Bisbee Breakfast Club (B.B.C.) ❷,** 75 Erie St., just outside historic Bisbee. (☎432-5885. Open M and Th-Su 7am-3pm. MC/V.) **Prickly Pear Cafe ❶,** 105 Tombstone Canyon, prepares wholesome sandwiches and salads. (☎432-7337. Open M-Th 11am-8pm, F-Sa 8am-9pm, Su 8am-4pm. Cash only.)

LOCAL LEGEND

HAUNTED HOTEL

Ghosts are a dime a dozen in historic Bisbee. In fact, haunted hearsay is one of the main reasons people come to stay at the Copper Queen Hotel. Visitors jot down ghost sightings and strange occurrences nearly every day in the voluminous Ghost Registries in the hotel lobby. Most entries follow one of four storylines, giving the hotel staff good reason to believe that four ghosts, with four different haunting personalities, are still walking the Copper Queen's long halls and winding staircases.

Rose, a rarely sighted ghost, is fond of rousing guests in the middle of the night with the haunting aroma of chocolate cake. Another ghost, wearing a cape and top hat, is trailed by the pungent scent of a good cigar. While sleeping, men in the hotel have reported hearing the soft whisper of Julia Lowell, a young prostitute who committed suicide in the hotel. The youngest and most mischievous ghost of the bunch is a child who moves objects around and giggles loudly. Even if you're not adventurous enough to spend the night with these friendly spirits, the Ghost Registries are still worth skimming. After all, these local "residents" are one of Bisbee's greatest attractions.

Copper Queen Hotel ❹, 11 Howell Ave. (☎ 432-2216). Rooms from $85-115.

The **Bisbee Visitor Center,** 2 Copper Queen Plaza, has an eager-to-please staff and plenty of maps. (☎432-5421. Open M-F 9am-5pm, Sa 10am-4pm, Su 11am-4pm.) The **post office,** 6 Main St., is one block south of Exit 80. (☎432-2052. Open M-F 8:30am-4:30pm.) **Postal Code:** 85603. **Area Code:** 520.

NEW MEXICO

In New Mexico, nature's eccentricities provide outdoor enthusiasts with the landscape they need to explore the limits of their abilities and interests. Still, even the wildest outdoor adventurers get distracted by the galleries of Santa Fe, the nightclubs of Albuquerque, and the pueblos of northern New Mexico. With a rich cultural mosaic of Mexican, Native American, and European influence, historical and archaeological discovery is a never-ending process in New Mexico, and travelers would be remiss not to tap into its rich past. After all is said and done, save some time to wander across white sand dunes or relax in the bubbly warmth of natural hot springs. They don't call it the "Land of Enchantment" for nothing.

◪ PRACTICAL INFORMATION

Capital: Santa Fe.

Visitor Info: New Mexico Dept. of Tourism, 491 Old Santa Fe Trail, Santa Fe 87501 (☎800-545-2040; www.newmexico.org). Open M-F 8am-5pm. **Park and Recreation Division,** 2040 S. Pacheco, Santa Fe 87505 (☎505-827-7173). Open M-F 8am-5pm. **US Forest Service,** 517 Gold Ave. SW, Albuquerque 87102 (☎505-842-3292). Open M-F 8am-4:30pm.

Postal Abbreviation: NM. **Sales Tax:** 7%.

SANTA FE ☎ 505

Nestled between dramatic red mesas and forests of piñon trees, Santa Fe is the artistic soul of the Southwest's pueblo country. Even as it evokes a primitive sense of earth, sky, and mountain, the city remains a renowned cosmopolitan center of food and culture, with plentiful museums, ground-breaking galleries, and distinctive Northern New Mexican cuisine. If the city's artistic and culinary accomplishments don't captivate you, the inspiring natural environment, perfumed with smoky hatch chiles and piñons, certainly will.

◧ TRANSPORTATION

Trains: Amtrak's nearest station is in Lamy (☎466-4511; www.amtrak.com), 18 mi. south on U.S. 285. 1 train per day to: **Albuquerque** (1½hr., $25); **Flagstaff** (7½hr., $80); **Kansas City** (17hr., $165); **Los Angeles** (19hr., $112). Call ☎982-8829 for a shuttle to Santa Fe ($18). Open M-Th and Sa-Su 9am-5pm, F 10:30am-2:30pm.

Buses: Greyhound, 858 St. Michael's Dr. (☎471-0008; www.greyhound.com), goes to **Albuquerque** (1¼hr., 4 per day, $10.50), **Denver** (8-9hr., 4 per day, $59), and **Taos** (1½hr., 2 per day, $16). Open M-F 7am-5:30pm and 7:30-9:35pm, Sa-Su 7-9am, 12:30-1:30pm, 3:30-5pm, and 7:30-9:35pm.

Public Transit: Santa Fe Trails, 2931 Rufina St. (☎955-2001). Schedules at the visitors center or the public transit office. Runs 9 downtown bus routes M-F 6am-11pm, Sa 8am-8pm, Su (routes 1, 2, 4, and M only) 10am-7pm. Most routes start at the downtown Sheridan Transit Center, 1 block from the plaza between Marcy St. and Palace Ave. Buses

#21 and 24 go down Cerrillos Rd., the M goes to the museums on Camino Lejo, and 5 passes the Greyhound station between St. Vincent Hospital and the W. Alameda Commons. $1; students, seniors, and under 17 $0.50; day pass $2.

Sandía Shuttle Express (☎474-5696 or 888-775-5696) runs from downtown hotels to the Albuquerque airport (the main airport that services Santa Fe) every hr. 5am-5pm. From Albuquerque to Santa Fe hourly 8:45am-6:45pm ($23, round-trip $43). Reserve at least 4 days in advance. Open M-F 6am-6pm, Sa-Su 6am-5pm.

Car Rental: Enterprise Rent-a-Car, 2641 Cerrillos Rd. (☎473-3600). Must be 21+ with driver's license and major credit card. Open M-F 8am-6pm, Sa 9am-noon.

⚡ ORIENTATION

Abutting the **Sangre de Cristo Mountains,** Sante Fe stands at an elevation of 7000 ft., 58 mi. northeast of Albuquerque on I-25. The streets of downtown Santa Fe seem to wind without rhyme or reason; locals say the roads were built on old burro paths. It may be helpful to think of the city as a wagon wheel, with the **Plaza** in the center and roads leading outward like spokes. **Paseo de Peralta** forms a loop around the downtown area, and the main roads leading out toward I-25 are **Cerrillos Road, St. Francis Drive,** and **Old Santa Fe Trail.** Except for the museums southeast of the city center, most upscale restaurants and sights in Santa Fe cluster within a few blocks of the downtown Plaza, inside the loop formed by the Paseo de Peralta. Narrow streets make driving troublesome; park your car and pound the pavement. Several public **parking lots** are within walking distance of the plaza, charging $8-14 for a full day. The municipal parking lot is the most convenient, one block south of the plaza on Water St. between Don Gaspar Ave. and Shelby St. Though you'll be a slave to the bus schedule, look into the free parking at Museum Hill or the Villa Linda Mall and ride the bus to and from downtown.

⚡ PRACTICAL INFORMATION

Visitor Info: Visitors Information Center, 491 Old Santa Fe Trail (☎875-7400 or 800-545-2040). Open daily 8am-6:30pm; low season 8am-5pm. **Santa Fe Convention and Visitors Bureau,** 201 W. Marcy St. (☎800-777-2489 or 955-6200). Open M-F 8am-5pm. **Info booth** at the northwest corner of the plaza, next to the First National Bank. Open mid-May to Aug. daily 9:30am-4:30pm.

Hotlines: Rape Crisis, ☎986-9111. **Gay and Lesbian Information Line,** ☎891-3647. Both operate 24hr.

Medical Services: St. Vincent Hospital, 455 St. Michael's Dr. (☎983-3361).

Internet Access: Santa Fe Public Library, 145 Washington Ave. (☎955-6781), 1 block northeast of the Plaza. Open M-Th 10am-9pm, F-Sa 10am-6pm, Su 1-5pm.

Post Office: 120 S. Federal Pl. (☎988-6351), next to the courthouse. Open M-F 7:30am-5:45pm, Sa 9am-1pm. **Postal Code:** 87501. **Area Code:** 505.

⚡ ACCOMMODATIONS

Hotels in Santa Fe are definitely on the expensive side. As early as May, start booking ahead for the **Indian Market** (third week in Aug.) and **Fiesta de Santa Fe** (mid-Sept.). In general, the motels along **Cerrillos Road** have the best prices, but even these places run $50-70 per night. For budget travelers, nearby camping is pleasant during the summer, not to mention easier on the wallet. Two popular sites for **free primitive camping** are **Big Tesuque ❶** and **Ski Basin Campgrounds ❶,** on national forest land. Both are off Rte. 475 toward the Ski Basin and have pit toilets.

▨ **Pueblo Bonito Bed and Breakfast,** 138 W. Manhattan Ave. (☎984-8001), at Galisteo St. This quiet, century-old adobe compound houses 18 cozy private rooms less than a 5min. walk from the downtown plaza. Luxury perks include a fireplace in each room, hot tub, lavish breakfast buffet, and afternoon tea. Reception 8am-10pm. Rooms May-Oct. $130-165, Mar.-Apr. and Nov.-Dec. $95-125, Jan.-Feb. $85-115. AmEx/D/MC/V. ❺

Santa Fe International Hostel, 1412 Cerrillos Rd. (☎988-1153). Conveniently located and the only cheap option for indoor accommodations, this hostel provides a large kitchen, free linens, parking, and occasionally food. Laundry $2.25. Dorms $15; private rooms from $35. Cash only. ❷

Silver Saddle Motel, 2810 Cerrillos Rd. (☎471-7663). Comfortable adobe rooms decorated with cowboy paraphernalia have A/C and cable TV. Reception 7am-11:30pm. In summer singles $59; doubles $65. In winter $40/$45. AmEx/D/MC/V. ❸

Hyde State Park Campground (☎983-7175), 8 mi. from Santa Fe on Rte. 475. Over 50 sites in a quiet forest with water, pit toilets, and shelters. Sites $10, hookup $14. ❶

🍴 FOOD

The **Santa Fe Farmers Market,** near the intersection of Guadalupe St. and Paseo de Peralta, has fresh fruits and vegetables. (☎983-4098. Open late Apr. to early Nov. Tu and Sa 7am-noon. Call for indoor winter location and hours.)

▨ **Upper Crust Pizza,** 329 Old Santa Fe Trail (☎982-0000). The fresh and wholesome ingredients (try the whole wheat crust), unpretentious outdoor patio, and solidly delicious pizza make this spot one of Santa Fe's best. Pizza $11-17. Calzones $6.75. Open daily in summer 11am-11pm; in winter 11am-10pm. AmEx/D/MC/V. ❷

▨ **Cloud Cliff,** 1805 2nd St. (☎983-6254). This bakery and cafe might be the most mouthwatering place in Sante Fe. The cookies ($1.50) are heavenly, and the all organic breakfast menu is unbeatable. Try the bread basket ($4) for a sampler. Sandwiches $6. Open M-F 7am-5pm, Sa-Su 8am-3pm. MC/V. ❷

Cafe Pasqual's, 121 Don Gaspar Ave. (☎983-9340). Named for the patron saint of cooking, this restaurant dishes up deliciously inventive Southwestern cuisine. Lines stretch out the door for the fantastic omelets ($10) and salmon, black bean, and blue cheese burritos ($16). Dinner reservations recommended. Open M-Sa 7am-3pm and 5:30-10:30pm, Su 8am-2pm and 5:30-10:30pm. AmEx/MC/V. ❹

Tia Sophia's, 210 W. San Francisco St. (☎983-9880). This unassuming diner near the plaza serves traditional New Mexican favorites with little pretense and plenty of taste. The most popular item is the Atrisco plate (chile stew, cheese enchilada, beans, posole, and a sopapilla; $7). Open M-Sa 7am-2pm. MC/V. ❷

👁 🎵 SIGHTS AND ENTERTAINMENT

The grassy **Plaza de Santa Fe** is a good starting point for exploring the city's museums, sanctuaries, and galleries. Since 1609, the plaza has been the site of religious ceremonies, military gatherings, markets, cockfights, and public punishments. Today, it shelters ritzy shops, Native American artisan stalls, and packs of loitering tourists. Historic **walking tours** leave from the blue doors of the Palace of the Governors on Lincoln Ave. (Apr.-Oct. M-Sa 10:15am. $10, under 17 free with adult.)

MNM MUSEUMS. Sante Fe is home to world-class museums. Five are run by the Museum of New Mexico; the visitors center on Museum Hill, 706 Camino Lejo, has info. (☎476-1249. Open Tu-Su 10am-4pm.) A 4-day pass includes admission to all five museums and can be bought at any of them. (☎827-6463; www.museumofnewmexico.org. Open Tu-Su 10am-5pm. $7, under 16 free. The 2 downtown

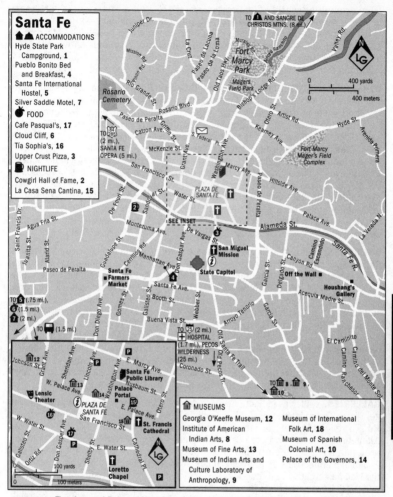

Santa Fe

▲■ ACCOMMODATIONS
Hyde State Park
  Campground, **1**
Pueblo Bonito Bed
  and Breakfast, **4**
Santa Fe International
  Hostel, **5**
Silver Saddle Motel, **7**
🍖 FOOD
Cafe Pasqual's, **17**
Cloud Cliff, **6**
Tía Sophia's, **16**
Upper Crust Pizza, **3**
🍷 NIGHTLIFE
Cowgirl Hall of Fame, **2**
La Casa Sena Cantina, **15**

🏛 MUSEUMS
Georgia O'Keeffe Museum, **12**
Institute of American
  Indian Arts, **8**
Museum of Fine Arts, **13**
Museum of Indian Arts and
  Culture Laboratory of
  Anthropology, **9**
Museum of International
  Folk Art, **18**
Museum of Spanish
  Colonial Art, **10**
Palace of the Governors, **14**

museums—Fine Arts and Palace of the Governors—are both free F 5-8pm. *4-day pass $15.*) In a
large adobe building on the northwest corner of the plaza, the **Museum of Fine
Arts** dazzles visitors with the works of major Southwestern artists, a beautiful
courtyard, and galleries for special exhibitions. *(107 W. Palace Ave. ☎476-5041.)*
The **Palace of the Governors,** on the north side of the plaza, is the oldest public
building in the US and was the seat of seven successive governments after its
construction in 1610. The *hacienda*-style palace is now a museum with exhibits on 400 years of Southwestern history. Outside, sellers of Native art line the
Palace Portal, an active marketplace since the early 19th century. *(107 W. Palace
Ave. ☎476-5100.)* The most distinctive museums in town are 2 mi. south of the
Plaza on Old Santa Fe Trail at Museum Hill. The fascinating **🖼Museum of International Folk Art** explores the beauty of everyday objects through its vibrant
collection of small handmade toys, furniture, clothing, costumes, and jewelry

from around the world. *(706 Camino Lejo. ☎476-1200.)* Next door, the **Museum of Indian Arts and Culture Laboratory of Anthropology** displays Native American artwork, photos, and artifacts. *(710 Camino Lejo. ☎476-1250.)* The **Museum of Spanish Colonial Art** houses an extensive collection of artifacts showcasing the artistic traditions of territories that were once part of the Spanish Empire, spanning four continents and 500 years. *(750 Camino Lejo. ☎982-2226.)*

OTHER PLAZA MUSEUMS. The popular 🖼**Georgia O'Keeffe Museum** pays tribute to the famous New Mexican artist with up-close views of her famous flower paintings and some of her more abstract works. In 2006, the museum will emphasize her works on paper, emphasizing her versatility. *(217 Johnson St. ☎946-1017. Open daily 10am-5pm. $8, under 17 and students with ID free. F 5-8pm free. Audio tour $5.)* Downtown's **Institute of American Indian Arts Museum** houses a large collection of contemporary Indian art that reflects many of the cross-cultural and historical influences in Native art. *(108 Cathedral Pl. ☎983-8900. Open June-Sept. M-Sa 9am-5pm, Su 10am-5pm; Oct.-May M-Sa 10am-5pm, Su noon-5pm. $4, students and seniors $2, under 16 free.)* The **New Mexico State Capitol** was built in 1966 in the form of the Zia sun symbol. The House and Senate galleries are open to the public, and the building also contains an impressive art collection. *(☎986-4589. 5 blocks south of the Plaza on Old Santa Fe Trail. Open M-F 7am-7pm; June-Aug. also Sa 8am-5pm. Free tours M-F 10am and 2pm.)*

CHURCHES. Santa Fe's Catholic roots are evident in the Romanesque **St. Francis Cathedral,** built from 1869 to 1886 under the direction of Archbishop Lamy to help convert westerners to Catholicism. *(213 Cathedral Pl. 1 block east of the Plaza on San Francisco St. ☎982-5619. Open daily 7:30am-5:30pm.)* The **Loretto Chapel** was the first Gothic building west of the Mississippi River. The church is famous for its spiral staircase—both its builder and the details of its construction are a mystery. *(207 Old Santa Fe Trail. 2 blocks south of the cathedral. ☎982-0092. Open M-Sa 9am-4:45pm, Su 10:30am-5pm. $2.50, seniors and children $2, under 7 free.)* About five blocks southeast of the plaza lies the **San Miguel Mission,** the oldest functioning church in the US with the oldest bell in the country, made in Spain in 1356. The Mission was built in 1610 by the Tlaxcalan Indians. *(At DeVargas St. and Old Santa Fe Trail. ☎988-9504. Open M-Sa 9am-5pm, Su 10am-4pm; may close earlier in winter. Mass Su 5pm. $1.)*

GALLERIES. Galleries in Santa Fe are a dime a dozen; there are so many, you can get dizzy. The most successful local artists live and sell their work along Canyon Rd. To reach the galleries, leave the Plaza on San Francisco Dr., take a left on Alameda St., a right on Paseo de Peralta, and a left on Canyon Rd. Most galleries are open from 10am until 5pm and contain interesting and often fantastically expensive collections, from western landscapes to mammoth bronze statues. **Off the Wall** has creative and functional art and a small cafe and patio. *(616 Canyon Rd. ☎983-8337. Open daily 10am-5pm.)* **Houshang's Gallery** is filled with local paintings while eclectic steel sculptures line the exterior. Though expensive, it's a well worth a look. *(713 Canyon Rd. ☎800-756-3322. Open 10am-5pm daily.)*

🌸 🎵 FESTIVALS AND ENTERTAINMENT

The **Santa Fe Jazz and International Music Festival** runs through the month of July, showcasing the talent of some of the world's finest musicians. *(☎988-1234; www.santafejazzfestival.com. Tickets $20-40 per show, 7-show pass $119-238. 2 free shows take place at noon in the Plaza in mid-July. All other shows at Lensic Theater, 7:30pm.)* The Santa Fe Plaza is home to three of the US's largest festivals. The **Spanish Market,** a combination celebration and sale of Hispanic-influenced artwork, comes to town the third week in July. In the third week of August, **Indian Market,** the nation's largest and most impressive showcase of Native American culture and art, floods the plaza. The **Southwestern Association for Indian Arts** (☎983-5220) has more info. Don Diego de Vargas's reconquest of New Mexico in 1692 marked the end of the 12-year Pueblo Rebellion, now celebrated during the three-day **Fiesta de Santa Fe** (☎988-7575; www.santafefiesta.org). Held in mid-September, festivities begin with the burning of the Zozobra (a 50 ft. marionette) and include street dancing, processions, and political satires. The New Mexican publishes a guide and a schedule of the fiesta's events.

Poetic verse and distinguished acting invade the city each summer when **Shakespeare in Santa Fe** raises its curtain. The shows play in an open-air theater on the St. John's College campus from late June to late August. (Shows run F-Su 7:30pm. Call to check schedule. Reserved seating tickets $15-32; lawn seating free, but suggested donation $5. Tickets available at show or call ☎982-2910.) The **Santa Fe Opera,** on Opera Dr., performs outdoors against a mountain backdrop. Nights are cool; bring a blanket. The 2006 season includes *Carmen, The Magic Flute, Salome,* and *The Tempest.* (7 mi. north of Santa Fe on Rte. 84/285. ☎800-280-4654 or 986-5900; www.santafeopera.org. July W and F-Sa at 9pm; Aug. M-Sa at 8 or 8:30pm. Tickets $20-130, rush standing-room tickets $8-15; 50% student discount on same-day reserved seats. Box office is at opera house; call or drop by the day of the show for prices and availability.) The **Santa Fe Chamber Music Festival** celebrates the works of Baroque, Classical, Romantic, and 20th-century composers in the **St. Francis Auditorium of the Museum of Fine Arts** and the **Lensic Theater.** (☎983-2075, tickets 982-1890; www.sfcmf.org. Mid-July to mid-Aug. $16-40, students $10.)

🎷 NIGHTLIFE

The diverse citizens of Santa Fe—from retired Wall Street investment bankers to world-famous (or starving) artists—ensure varied nightlife. The town's laid-back demeanor, however, doesn't disappear when the sun goes down. The talented waitstaff at **La Casa Sena Cantina,** 125 E. Palace Ave., serenades its middle-aged regulars with jazz standards and Broadway showtunes. The rustic, classy interior is a relaxing place to sip a drink, sample a wildly decadent dessert, and enjoy the show. (☎988-9232. Open M-Th and Su 5:30-10pm, F-Sa 5:30-11pm.) The **Cowgirl Hall of Fame,** 319 S. Guadalupe St., has live music hoe-downs that range from bluegrass to rock 9pm-1am each night. Barbecue, Mexican food, and burgers ($7) are served all evening, with midnight food specials and 12 microbrews on tap. (☎982-2565. Cowgirl margaritas $5. Sa-Su ranch breakfast. Happy hour 4-6pm with $2 drink specials. 21+ after midnight. Cover varies but is rarely more than $3. Open M-F 11am-2am, Sa 8:30am-2am, Su 8:30am-midnight.)

🏔 OUTDOOR ACTIVITIES

The nearby **Sangre de Cristo Mountains** reach heights of over 12,000 ft. and offer countless opportunities for hikers, bikers, and skiers. The **Pecos** and **Río Grande** rivers make great playgrounds for kayakers and rafters. Before heading into the wilderness, stop by the **Public Lands Information Center,** 1474 Rodeo Rd., near the intersection of St. Francis Rd. and I-25, to pick up maps and advice. (☎438-7542 or 877-276-9404; www.publiclands.org. Open M-F 8:30am-4:30pm.)

The closest **hiking** trails to Santa Fe are along Rte. 475 on the way to the Santa Fe Ski Area. On this road, 10 mi. northeast of town, the easy **Tesuque Creek Trail** (2hr., 4 mi.) leads through the forest to a flowing stream. Near the end of Rte. 475 and the Santa Fe Ski Area, trailheads venture into the 223,000 acre **Pecos Wilderness,** making them cool summer options for escaping the heat of the day. The swath of virgin forest is perfect for extended backpacking trips. For a rewarding day-hike

14 mi. northeast of Santa Fe on Rte. 475, the strenuous climb to the top of 12,622 ft. **Santa Fe Baldy** (8-9hr., 14 mi.) has an amazing view of the Pecos Wilderness. Forty miles southwest of Santa Fe, **Kasha-Katuwe Tent Rocks National Monument** provides a surreal landscape with its sinewy, gray rocks. The national monument has beautiful hiking trails but is largely undeveloped. (☎761-8704. Take I-25 S from Santa Fe, take Exit 259, and follow the signs. Open daily Apr.-Oct. 7am-7pm; Nov.-Mar. 8am-5pm; day use only. $5 per vehicle.)

The best skiing is 16 mi. northeast of downtown, at **Ski Santa Fe.** Located in the Sangre de Cristo Mountains on Rte. 475, the ski area has six lifts (4 chairs and 2 surface lifts) servicing 43 trails (20% beginner, 40% intermediate, 40% advanced) on 600 acres with a 1650 ft. vertical drop. (☎982-4429; www.skisantafe.com. Open late Nov. to early Apr. daily 9am-4pm. Lift tickets: full day $47, teens $38, children and seniors $34; half-day $34. Rental packages start at $18.)

▶ DAYTRIPS FROM SANTA FE

BANDELIER NATIONAL MONUMENT

Bandelier is 40 mi. northwest of Santa Fe. Take U.S. 285 to 502 W, then follow the signs to the monument. The park entrance fee is $10 per vehicle and $5 per pedestrian; National Park passes are accepted.

Bandelier National Monument features the remnants of over 2400 cliff dwellings and pueblos amid 50 sq. mi. of mesas and rugged canyons. The park centers around Frijoles Canyon, the site of many natural caves and settlements along the canyon floor that were occupied for roughly 500 years. The **visitors center,** 3 mi. into the park at the bottom of Frijoles Canyon, has a free archaeological museum and shows a short video. There are few placards along the pathways, but trail guides for the most popular hikes are available for $1. (☎672-3861, ext. 517. Open daily June-Aug. 8am-6pm; Sept. to late Oct. 9am-5:30pm; late Oct. to late Mar. 8am-4:30pm; late Mar. to May 9am-5:30pm.) The 1½ mi. **Main Loop Trail** begins at the back porch of the visitors center and passes the ruins of **Tyuonyi Pueblo** and the aptly named **Long House,** an 800 ft. section of adjoining, multi-storied stone homes. The trail is wheelchair accessible along a paved path, but caves can only be viewed up close by climbing the ladders. Those with more time should go half a mile farther to **Alcove House,** a *kiva* carved into a natural alcove, high above the canyon floor and accessible only by climbing four ladders. For a longer hike, the **Falls Trail** (5 mi.) heads to the Río Grande River, passing waterfalls along the way. Free permits are required for backcountry hiking and camping and can be obtained at the visitors center. Just past the main entrance, **Juniper Campground ❶** offers the only developed camping in the park, with water and toilets (sites $12).

LOS ALAMOS

Los Alamos is located 35 mi. northwest of Santa Fe. Take U.S. 285 to 502 W.

Known only as the mysterious P.O. Box 1663 during the heyday of the Manhattan Project, Los Alamos is no longer the nation's biggest secret. Overlooking the Río Grande Valley, Los Alamos hovers above the Pueblo and Bayo Canyons on thin finger-like mesas, 35 mi. northeast of Santa Fe. The birthplace of the atomic bomb, Los Alamos attracts visitors with its natural beauty, outdoor activities, and the allure of its secret past. In town, the **Bradbury Science Museum,** at 15th St. and Central, explains the history of the Los Alamos National Laboratory and its endeavors with short documentaries and hands-on exhibits. (☎667-4444. Open M and Sa-Su 1-5pm, Tu-F 9am-5pm. Free.) The **⬛Black Hole,** 4015 Arkansas Ave., is a quirky gem of an atomic junkyard that sells all the junk the laboratory doesn't want anymore, including 50-year-old calculators, fiber-optic cables, flow gauges, time-mark generators, optical comparators, and other technological flotsam. Hear stories from the nuclear-resistant owner and watch a 10min. video about nuclear history in the area. Leave with your very own $2 atomic bomb detonator cable. (☎662-5053. Open M-Sa 10am-5pm.) Nearby, the **Santa Fe National Forest** has countless trails for hiking and biking in and along the town's many canyons. Fifteen miles west on Rte. 4, the 89,000 acres of the **Valles Caldera**, a lush volcanic crater, is now a quiet National Preserve with miles of hiking trails and incredible canyon views. Trails only accommodate a limited number of visitors each day for hiking, fishing, and horse-drawn wagon or van tours, so make reservations in advance. (☎877-851-8946; www.vallescaldera.gov. Permits $10, ages 15 and under $5; other fees apply for fishing licenses and touring.) **Los Alamos Visitors Center** is at 109 Central Park Sq., at Central Ave. just west of 15th St., and has information and brochures on the area. (☎661-4815. Open M-F 9am-5pm, Sa 9am-4pm, Su 10am-3pm.)

TAOS ☎505

Before 1955, Taos was a remote artists' colony in the Sangre de Cristo Mountains. When the ski valley opened and the thrill-seekers trickled in, they soon realized that the area also boasted the best whitewater rafting in New Mexico, as well as excellent hiking, mountain biking, and rock climbing. By the 1970s, Taos had become a paradise for outdoor adventurers, extreme athletes, and contemporary artists, and the deluge of tourists wasn't far behind. Today, Taos maintains an unlikely balance of ski resort culture and bohemian spirit.

⚎🛈 ORIENTATION AND PRACTICAL INFORMATION. Taos is 79 mi. north of Santa Fe (p. 836), between the dramatic Río Grande Gorge and Wheeler Peak. **Paseo del Pueblo** (Rte. 68) is the town's main north-south thoroughfare, called **Paseo del Pueblo Norte** north of Kit Carson Rd. and **Paseo del Pueblo Sur** to the south. Traffic on Paseo del Pueblo can move in inches during the summer and ski season—use Rte. 240 and Upper Ranchitos Rd. as a bypass if possible. Drivers should park at the metered **Camino de la Placita**, a block west of the plaza, in any of the free municipal parking lots, or at meters on side streets. The **Taos Chamber of Commerce and Visitors Bureau**, 1139 Paseo del Pueblo Sur, 2 mi. south of town at the junction of Rte. 68 and Paseo del Cañón, has maps and info on accommodations. (☎758-3873. Open in summer daily 9am-5pm, in winter closed Su.) The **Carson National Forest Office**, 208 Cruz Alta Rd., has info on camping and hiking. (☎758-6200. Open M-F 8am-4:30pm.) **Internet Access: Public Library,** 402 Camino de la Placita. (☎758-3063. Open M noon-6pm, Tu-F 10am-6pm, Sa 10am-5pm. $1 per 30min.) **Post Office:** 318 Paseo del Pueblo Norte. (☎758-2081. Open M-F 8:30am-5pm.) **Postal Code:** 87571. **Area Code:** 505.

🛏 ACCOMMODATIONS. The **Abominable Snowmansion Hostel (HI) ❶,** 9 mi. north of Taos in the village of Arroyo Seco, has spacious dorms, a huge kitchen, and a comfy living room. A hostel by summer and ski lodge by winter, the Snowmansion is only 9 mi. west of the ski valley. Teepees and camping are also available in the warmer months. (☎776-8298. Reception 8am-noon and 4-10pm. Reservations recommended. Dec. to mid-Apr. dorms, tent sites, and dorm teepees $22, mid-Apr. to Nov. $19; private rooms $40-54/$32-44. MC/V.) The **Budget Host Motel ❷,** 1798 Paseo del Pueblo Sur, 3¼ mi. south of the plaza, has clean rooms with basic amenities and continental breakfast. (☎758-2524 or 800-323-6009. Singles $44-50; doubles $49-61. AAA discount 10%. MC/V.)

Camping around Taos is easy with a car, and considering the area's natural beauty, sleeping under the stars is an appealing option. The **Orilla Verde Recreation Area ❶,** 15 mi. south of Taos on Rte. 68, has five campgrounds in the scenic **Río**

Grande Gorge. (☎751-4899 or 758-8851. Water and toilets. Sites $7.) The **Carson National Forest** has four campgrounds to the east of Taos. Tent sites sit along a stream and are surrounded by tall pines and piñon forest. The closest two, **El Nogal ❶** and **Las Petacas ❶**, are 2 and 4 mi. east of Taos, respectively, and have vault toilets but no drinking water. For more info, contact the **Carson National Forest Office** in Taos (☎758-6200). Campgrounds on the road to Taos Ski Valley are free, but have no facilities. **Backcountry camping ❶** doesn't require a permit. Dispersed camping is popular along Rte. 518 south of Taos and Forest Rd. 437; park on the side of the road and pitch your tent a few hundred feet inside.

❑ FOOD. Restaurants cluster around Taos Plaza and Bent St. but cheaper options can be found north of town along Paseo del Pueblo. ▨**Taos Pizza Out Back ❷**, 712 Paseo del Pueblo Norte, serves gourmet pizza made with local organic vegetables, meats, and cheeses. Entertain yourself by helping to cover the restaurant's exterior with crayon graffiti, and when your food comes, be ready to dip your pizza in the sweet basil-pesto sauce. (☎758-3112. Large pizza $16-20. Slice $4-7. Open daily 11am-10pm. MC/V.) **Michael's Kitchen ❷**, 304 Paseo del Pueblo Norte, specializes in hearty family-style dining, with traditional Mexican dishes, fresh baked goods, and the best breakfast in town available all day long. (☎758-4178. Open daily 7am-8:30pm. AmEx/MC/V.) **Abe's Cantina y Cocina ❶**, 6 mi. north of Taos on the road to Taos Ski Valley in the village of Arroyo Seco, has cheap, homestyle New Mexican food and some basic grocery items. (☎776-8516. Open M-F 7am-5:30pm, Sa 7am-1:30pm, bar open until around 10pm. AmEx/D/MC/V.) **Taos Wrappers ❶**, 616 Paseo del Pueblo Sur, caters to the lighter side of luncheon dining with delicious wraps, inventive soups, and lots of veggie options. (☎751-9727. Open in summer M-F 11am-4pm, Sa-Su 8am-4pm; in winter M-F 11am-1pm, Sa 11am-2pm. Cash or check only.) **Eske's Pub and Eatery ❷**, 106 Des Georges Ln., is the place to go for late-night food and entertainment. Try the Fatty (tortilla filled with mashed potatoes and feta cheese; $9.50) or one of the burgers ($7.50). Live music every weekend night and seven beers on tap make this one of the livelier hangouts in Taos. (☎758-1517. Open daily 11am-10:30pm. MC/V.)

◙ SIGHTS. For a small town, Taos has a surprising number of high-quality art museums. The ▨**Taos Art Museum** at Fechin House, 227 Paseo del Pueblo Norte, exhibits the oil paintings, watercolors, and sketches of the Taos Society of Artists, originally formed in 1915. The collection is housed inside the Spanish Mission-style home of Russian immigrant, Taos resident, and portrait painter Nicolai Fechin. (☎758-2690. Open June-Sept. Tu-Su 10am-5pm; Oct.-May W-Su 10am-4pm. $6, students $5, children $3.) The **Millicent Rogers Museum,** 1504 Millicent Rogers Rd., 4 mi. north of the plaza on Rte. 64, has an extravagant collection of Indian jewelry, Navajo textiles, Pueblo pottery, and Apache baskets that belonged to Millicent Rogers, a fashion maven and New York socialite. There is also a gallery dedicated to the ceramic works of the María Martínez family, known for their innovative black-on-black pottery. (☎758-2462. Open Apr.-Oct. daily 10am-5pm; Nov.-Mar. Tu-Su 10am-5pm. $7, students and seniors $6, under 16 $2.) The **Harwood Museum,** 238 Ledoux St., houses a large collection of Hispanic art, works by 20th-century local artists, and a gallery of Agnes Martin, a minimalist painter. (☎758-9826. Parking on Ranchitos Rd. Open Tu-Sa 10am-5pm, Su noon-5pm. $7, seniors $6, children under 7 free.) The **Martínez Hacienda,** 2 mi. southwest of the plaza on Ranchitos Rd., is one of the few surviving Spanish Colonial mansions in the US. Built in 1804, this fortress-like structure housed the prosperous Martínez family and the headquarters of their farming and trading operation. The restored 21-room *hacienda* has exhibits on life in the northern reaches of the Spanish Empire. (☎758-1000. Open daily May-Oct. 9am-5pm; Nov.-Apr. 10am-4pm. $6, ages 6-15 $3.)

The five-story adobe homes of the █Taos Pueblo are between 700 and 1000 years old, making the pueblo the oldest continuously inhabited settlement in the US. Taos Pueblo was named a UNESCO World Heritage Site in 1992, and is the only pueblo in Northern New Mexico where the inhabitants still live traditionally. The pueblo includes the **St. Jerome Church,** built in 1850, ruins of the old church and cemetery, adobe houses, and *kivas.* (☎758-1028. Guided tours daily May-Sept.; self-guided tours available. Open daily May-Sept. 8am-4:30pm; Oct.-Apr. 8am-4pm. $10, students $5, 12 and under free. Camera permit $5.)

█ OUTDOOR ACTIVITIES. Known by most winter enthusiasts as one of the best ski resorts in the country, **Taos Ski Valley,** about 15 mi. northeast of town on Rte. 150, has 72 trails and 12 lifts. Ski Valley boasts over 2500 ft. of vertical drop and over 300 in. of annual snowfall. (☎776-2291, lodging info 800-992-7669, ski conditions 776-2916. Lift tickets $31-51.) Reserve a room in advance if you plan to come in the winter holiday season. There are also two smaller, family-oriented ski areas near Taos: **Angel Fire** (☎377-6401; lift tickets $48, ages 7-12 $31) and **Red River** (☎800-494-9117; lift tickets $49, teens $43, ages 4-12 and seniors $34). Multi-day passes are available for use at all three resorts (from $36 per day). In summer, the nearly deserted ski valley and the nearby **Wheeler Peak Wilderness** become a hiker's paradise (most trails begin off Rte. 150). The ascent of **Wheeler Peak,** the highest point in New Mexico at 13,161 ft., is a strenuous 16 mi. round-trip trek that begins at the Twining Campground in Taos Ski Valley. Due to the town's location near New Mexico's wild Río Grande, **river rafting** is very popular in Taos. **Los Ríos River Runners** (☎776-8854 or 800-544-1181), **Far Flung Adventures** (☎758-2628 or 800-359-2627), and **Native Sons Adventures** (☎758-9342 or 800-753-7559) all offer a range of guided half-day ($46-55) and full day ($89-109) rafting trips. The best trail for mountain biking in the area is the South Boundary Trail, a 27 mi. loop that moves from an altitude of 7000-11,000 feet, featuring three ecosystem changes. For bike rentals, visit **Gearing Up Bicycle Shop,** 129 Paseo del Pueblo Sur. (☎751-0365. Open daily 9:30am-6pm. Bikes $35 per day. Basic tune-up $35. Ride to the trailhead $70.)

ALBUQUERQUE ☎505

Located at the crossroads of the Southwest, Albuquerque buzzes with history and culture, nurturing ethnic restaurants, offbeat galleries, quirky cafes, and raging nightclubs. Rte. 66 (now Central Ave.) may no longer appear on maps, but it's alive and kicking here. The mythic highway radiates a palpable energy that gives shops, restaurants, and bars on the thoroughfare a distinctive spirit found nowhere else in the state. Downtown Albuquerque may lack East Coast elegance, but it has a cosmopolitan feel of its own, deriving from its unique combination of students, cowboys, bankers, and government employees.

▐ TRANSPORTATION

Airport: Albuquerque International, 2200 Sunport Blvd. SE (☎244-7700), south of downtown. Take bus #50 from 5th St. and Central Ave., or pick it up along Yale Blvd. **Airport Shuttle** (☎765-1234) runs to the city ($12, additional person $5).

Trains: Amtrak, 214 1st St. SW (☎842-9650; www.amtrak.com). 1 train per day to: **Flagstaff** (4hr., $73); **Kansas City** (17hr., $110); **Los Angeles** (16hr., $83); **Santa Fe** (1hr. to Lamy and 20min. shuttle; $36). Reservations required. Station open daily 10am-6pm.

Buses: Greyhound (☎243-4435; www.greyhound.com) and **TNM&O Coaches** (☎806-763-5389), at 300 2nd St. Both run buses from 3 blocks south of Central Ave. To **Denver** (10hr., 4 per day, $64), **Los Angeles** (18hr., 6 per day, $78), and **Santa Fe** (1½hr., 4 per day, $10). Station open 24hr.

Public Transit: Sun-Tran Transit, 601 Yale Blvd. SE (☎843-9200). Open M-F 8am-6pm, Sa 8am-noon. Maps at visitors centers, the transit office, and the main library. Most buses run M-Sa 6:30am-8:30pm and leave from Central Ave. and 5th St. Bus #66 runs down Central Ave. $1, seniors and ages 5-18 $0.25. Request free transfers from driver.

Taxi: Albuquerque Cab, ☎883-4888.

ORIENTATION AND PRACTICAL INFORMATION

Central Avenue (Route 66), is still Albuquerque's main thoroughfare, running through all the city's major neighborhoods. **Central Avenue** (east-west) and **I-25** (north-south) divide Albuquerque into four quadrants. All downtown addresses come with a quadrant designation: NE, NW, SE, or SW. The adobe campus of the **University of New Mexico (UNM)** spreads along Central Ave. from University Ave. to Carlisle St. **Nob Hill,** the area of Central Ave. around Carlisle St., features bookstores, coffee shops, and art galleries. The revitalized **downtown** lies on Central Ave. between 10th St. and Broadway. Historic **Old Town Plaza** sits between San Felipe, North Plaza, South Plaza, and Romero, a block north of Central Ave.

Visitor Info: Old Town Visitors Center, 303 Romero St. NW (☎800-733-9918), in the shopping plaza west of the church. Open daily Apr.-Oct. 9am-5pm; Nov.-Mar. 9:30am-4:30pm. Airport **info booth** open M-F and Su 9:30am-8pm, Sa 9:30am-4:30pm.

Hotlines: Rape Crisis Center, ☎266-7711. **Gay and Lesbian Information Line,** ☎891-3647. Both operate 24hr.

Medical Services: Presbyterian Hospital, 1100 Central Ave. SE (☎841-1234).

Internet Access: Albuquerque Main Public Library, 501 Copper Ave. NW (☎768-5141). Open M and Th-Sa 10am-6pm, Tu-W 10am-7pm. Free.

Post Office: 1135 Broadway Blvd. NE (☎346-8044). Open M-F 8am-5:30pm. **Postal Code:** 87101. **Area Code:** 505.

ACCOMMODATIONS

Cheap motels line **Central Avenue,** but be sure to evaluate the quality of your room before paying. Most chain motels and hotels drop their prices in summer. During the balloon festival (p. 849), rooms are scarce; call ahead for reservations.

Sandía Mountain Hostel, 12234 Rte. 14 N (☎281-4117), in nearby Cedar Crest. Take I-40 E to Exit 175 and go 4 mi. north on Rte. 14. Call ahead for pickup in Albuquerque. Only 10 mi. from the Sandía Ski Area, this ski chateau has high ceilings and handcrafted furniture. Fireplace, spacious dorm rooms, and a family of donkeys out back. Linen $1. Coin-op laundry. Dorms $14; private rooms $32. Tent sites $10. MC/V. ❶

Route 66 Youth Hostel, 1012 Central Ave. SW (☎247-1813), between downtown and Old Town. Get your kicks at this inviting hostel with simple but clean rooms. Chores required. Linen $1. Key deposit $5. Reception daily 7:30-10:30am and 4-11pm. Check-out 10:30am. Dorms $17; private rooms with shared bath $22-33. Cash or check only. ❶

Coronado Campground (☎980-8256). About 15 mi. north of Albuquerque. Take I-25 to Exit 242, and follow the signs. On the banks of the Río Grande. Adobe shelters offer respite from the heat. Toilets, showers, and water. Open M and W-Su 8:30am-5pm. Tent sites $8, with shelters and picnic tables $11, with full hookup $18-20. ❶

FOOD

A diverse ethnic community, hordes of hungry interstate travelers, and a lot of green chiles make Albuquerque a surprisingly tasty destination. The area around the University of New Mexico is the best bet for visitors seeking inexpensive eat-

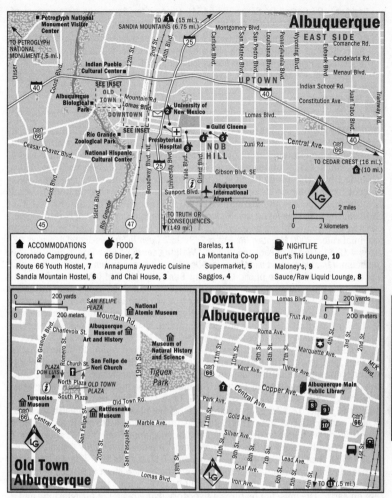

Albuquerque

EAST SIDE

TO PETROGLYPH NATIONAL MONUMENT (.5 mi.)

Petroglyph National Monument Visitor Center

TO 1 (15 mi.), SANDIA MOUNTAINS (6.75 mi.)

Indian Pueblo Cultural Center

Albuquerque Biological Park

OLD TOWN

SEE INSET

DOWNTOWN

SEE INSET

Río Grande Zoological Park

National Hispanic Cultural Center

University of New Mexico

Presbyterian Hospital

Guild Cinema

NOB HILL

TO CEDAR CREST (16 mi.), 6 (10 mi.)

Albuquerque International Airport

TO TRUTH OR CONSEQUENCES (149 mi.)

0   2 miles
0   2 kilometers

▲ ACCOMMODATIONS	🍎 FOOD		🍸 NIGHTLIFE
Coronado Campground, 1	66 Diner, 2	Barelas, 11	Burt's Tiki Lounge, 10
Route 66 Youth Hostel, 7	Annapurna Ayuvedic Cuisine	La Montanita Co-op	Maloney's, 9
Sandía Mountain Hostel, 6	and Chai House, 3	Supermarket, 5	Sauce/Raw Liquid Lounge, 8
		Saggios, 4	

Old Town Albuquerque

0   200 yards
0   200 meters

SAN FELIPE PLAZA

National Atomic Museum

Mountain Rd.

Charlevoix St.

Albuquerque Museum of Art and History

Museum of Natural History and Science

San Felipe de Neri Church

PLAZA DON LUIS

North Plaza OLD TOWN PLAZA

South Plaza

Tiguex Park

Turquoise Museum

Rattlesnake Museum

Downtown Albuquerque

0   200 yards
0   200 meters

Lomas Blvd.

Fruit Ave.

Roma Ave.

Marquette Ave.

Tijeras Ave.

Kent Ave.

Copper Ave.

Albuquerque Main Public Library

Central Ave.

Park Ave.

Gold Ave.

Silver Ave.

Lead Ave.

Coal Ave.

Iron Ave.

TO 11 (.5 mi.)

THE SOUTHWEST

eries. Farther east, **Nob Hill** is a yuppie feeding frenzy. Groceries are available at **La Montanita Co-op Supermarket**, 3500 Central Ave SE (☎265-4631; open M-Sa 7am-10pm, Su 8am-10pm).

🍴 **Barelas**, 1502 4th St. (☎843-7577), can be identified by the long line out the door. This local favorite has the best *huevos rancheros* around ($5) and small, medium, and large New Mexican plates. The *Carne Adovado* is fantastic. Open M-F 7:30am-3pm, Sa 7:30am-2:30pm. D/MC/V. ●

🍴 **Annapurna Ayurvedic Cuisine & Chai House**, 513 San Mateo Blvd. NE (☎262-2424), on the corner of Silver and Yale St. Vegetarian Indian cuisine that is guaranteed to leave you feeling happier, healthier, and infinitely more relaxed. The baked bananas in wheat-free crepes ($5.50) are particularly toothsome. Free wireless Internet access. Chai happy hour M-F 3-5pm. Open M-Sa 7am-8pm, Su 10am-2pm. MC/V. ●

Saggios, 107 Cornell Dr. SE (☎255-5454). Over-the-top Italian with huge portions of pasta and pizza. Open M-Th and Su 11am-10pm, F-Sa 11am-11pm. AmEx/MC/V. ❷

66 Diner, 1405 Central Ave. NE (☎247-1421). The best milkshakes and diner fare in town. Cozy up inside one of the pink-and-green booths for grilled cheese ($4), their trademark "Pile Up" ($7), or a homemade Route 66 rootbeer ($2.50). Open M-Th 11am-11pm, F 11am-midnight, Sa 8am-midnight, Su 8am-10pm. AmEx/D/MC/V. ❶

👁 SIGHTS

OLD TOWN. When the railroad cut through Albuquerque in the 19th century, it missed Old Town by almost 2 mi. As downtown grew around the railroad, Old Town remained untouched until the 1950s, when the city realized that it had a tourist magnet right under its nose. Just north of Central Ave. and east of Río Grande Blvd., the adobe plaza still looks much like it did over 100 years ago, except for the ubiquitous restaurants, gift shops, and jewelry vendors. Several wonderful museums and attractions surround the plaza. To the northeast, the ▨**Albuquerque Museum of Art and History** showcases four centuries of New Mexican art and history, including an excellent exhibit on the Conquistadors and Spanish colonial rule. *(2000 Mountain Rd. NW. ☎243-7255. Open Tu-Su 9am-5pm. $4, seniors $2, ages 4-12 $1. First W of each month free.)* **Walking tours** of Old Town meet at the museum. *(1hr. tours depart mid-Mar. to mid-Dec. Tu-Su 11am. Free with museum admission.)* On the north side of the plaza, the quaint **San Felipe de Neri Church** is a Spanish-style adobe church dating to 1706. The church is by far Old Town's most beautiful building. *(Open daily 9am-5pm; accompanying museum open M-Sa 10am-4pm. Su mass in English 7 and 10:15am; in Spanish 8:30am.)* Nearby, the **National Atomic Museum** has enthralling exhibits on nuclear physics, the social history of the Cold War, and the Manhattan Project. *(1905 Mountain Rd. NW. ☎245-2137. Open daily 9am-5pm. $5, ages 6-17 and 60+ $4.)* No visit to Old Town is complete without seeing the ▨**Rattlesnake Museum,** just south of the plaza. Earn a "Certificate of Bravery" by visiting the largest collection of live rattlesnakes in the world, with over 30 species ranging from the deadly Mojave to the tiny Pygmy. The museum also includes several species of tarantulas. *(202 San Felipe NW. ☎242-6569. Open M-Sa 10am-6pm, Su 1-5pm. $3.50, seniors $3, under 18 $2.50.)* Just one block off the plaza is the **Turquoise Museum,** which highlights the mineralogy, geology, and mining history of the precious stone, along with how to distinguish genuine turquoise from the imitation. Don't be fooled by the exterior: this is a true "gem" of a museum. *(2107 Central Ave. NW. ☎247-8650. Open M-Sa 10am-4pm. $4; seniors, ages 7-17, and AAA $3.)* Spike and Alberta, two statuesque dinosaurs, greet tourists outside the **New Mexico Museum of Natural History and Science,** where interactive exhibits take visitors through the history of life on earth. The museum features a five-story dyna-theater, a planetarium, and a simulated ride through the world of the dinosaurs. *(1801 Mountain Rd. NW. ☎841-2802. Open daily 9am-5pm, closed M in Sept and Jan. $6, ages 60+ $5, ages 3-12 $3; admission and theater ticket $11/$9/$5.)*

ALBUQUERQUE BIOLOGICAL PARK. A top-notch zoo, aquarium, and botanical garden in one complex make for a wild afternoon in the city. The **Albuquerque Aquarium** has a 285,000 gallon mini-ocean, complete with sharks and a coral reef. Connected to the aquarium is the **Río Grande Botanic Garden,** lined with desert plants. A couple of blocks away, the **Río Grande Zoological Park** is one of the top zoos in the nation. Visitors can see over 250 animal species and watch caretakers feed seals and sea lions. *(Aquarium and garden: 2601 Central Ave. NW. Zoo: 903 10th St. SW. ☎248-8500. Open daily 9am-5pm. Feedings daily 10:30am and 3:30pm. Admission to zoo or aquarium and botanic gardens $7, seniors and ages 3-12 $3. All 3 parks $10/$5.)*

CULTURAL ATTRACTIONS. The mammoth ⬛**National Hispanic Cultural Center** has an excellent art museum that explores folk art and representations of Hispanic social and cultural life in America. The 2006 season features an exhibit on Latin American posters and mass politics. *(1701 4th St. SW, on the corner of Bridge St. ☎246-2261. Open Tu-Su 10am-5pm. $3, seniors $2, under 16 free. Su $1.)* The **Indian Pueblo Cultural Center** has a commercial edge but still provides a good introduction to the history, culture, and art of the 19 American Indian pueblos of New Mexico. You're welcome to wander the museum at your leisure, but it's much better with a guided tour. The center also contains a museum and restaurant. *(2401 12th St. NW. ☎843-7270. Take bus #36 from downtown. Museum open daily 9am-5pm. Art demonstrations Sa-Su 10am-3pm, Native American dances Sa-Su 11am and 2pm. $6, seniors $5, students $3.)*

🌺📻 FESTIVALS AND NIGHTLIFE

If you're looking for a change from honky-tonk, Albuquerque is an oasis of interesting bars, jamming nightclubs, and art film houses. Check flyers posted around the university area for live music shows or pick up a copy of *Alibi*, the free local weekly. During the first week of October, hundreds of aeronauts take flight in the in the **Albuquerque International Balloon Fiesta.** Even the most grounded of souls will enjoy the week's barbecues, musical events, and the sky full of colorful hot air balloons. (☎888-422-7277; www.balloonfiesta.com. Admission $6.) Most nightlife huddles on Central Ave., downtown, and near the university. Nob Hill establishments tend to be the most gay-friendly.

Sauce/Raw Liquid Lounge, 405 Central Ave. NW (☎242-5839), is a magnet for trendy twentysomethings looking for a place to drink and dance the night away. A shadow dancer sets a semi-scandalous mood in Sauce's dim interior, while the adjoining Raw pumps hip-hop. Latin/salsa W. Open Tu-Su 4pm-2am.

Maloney's, 325 Central Ave. NE (☎242-7422), packs college kids and yuppies into its comfortable brewpub interior and popular outdoor patio. Pub fare ($8-9) is available throughout the evening, but the focus shifts to the 15 beers on tap ($4) as the night wears on. Open M-Sa 11am-2am, Su 11am-midnight.

Burt's Tiki Lounge, 313 Gold Ave. SW (☎247-2878). Situated a block south of Central Ave. Surf and tiki paraphernalia line the walls and ceiling, while anything from funk to punk to hip-hop takes the stage. Tropical drinks $6 and beer $4. Live music Tu-Sa and occasionally M. Open M-Sa 8pm-2am.

🏔 OUTDOOR ACTIVITIES

The name of the **Sandía Mountains,** from the Spanish word for "watermelon," is a nod to the sunset-pink hue of their crest, which rises a mile above Albuquerque and has countless hiking trails and picnic areas. One of the most popular and rewarding trails in New Mexico, the **La Luz Trail** (7½ mi.) begins at Juan Tabo Picnic Area and climbs to the top of the Sandía Crest. In summer, it's best to get an early start to avoid afternoon storms. From Exit 167 on I-40, drive north on Tramway Blvd. 10 mi. to Forest Rd. 333. Follow Trail 137 for 7 mi., and then take Trail 84 to the top. To get to the top without a lot of effort, visitors can ride the longest tramway in the world, the **Sandía Peak Tramway,** 10 Tramway Loop NE. (☎856-7325. Runs every 20min. daily 9am-9pm. $15, ages 62+ $13, ages 5-12 $10.) The Sandía Mountains have excellent biking trails. Try the moderate **Foothills Trail** (7 mi.), which starts at the Elena Gallegos Picnic Area, off Tramway Blvd., and skirts the bottom of the mountains. The most popular place for biking is the **Sandía Peak Ski Area,** 6 mi. up Rte. 536 on the way to Sandía Crest. Bikers can take their bikes up

THE SOUTHWEST

the chairlift and then ride down on 35 mi. of mountain trails and rollers. (☎242-9133. Chairlifts run June-Sept. Th-Su 10am-4pm. $8, full-day lift ticket $14. Bike rentals at the summit $38 per day. Helmets required.)

Sandía Peak Ski Area, only 30min. from downtown, is a convenient ski area for those who can't escape to Taos or Ruidoso. Six lifts service 25 short trails (35% beginner; 55% intermediate; 10% advanced) on 200 skiable acres. The summit (10,378 ft.) tops a vertical drop of 1700 ft. (☎242-9133. Open mid-Dec. to mid-Mar. M-F 9am-4pm, Sa-Su 8:30am-4pm. Full day $40, half-day $29; ages 13-20 $33/$25, seniors and ages 13 and under $30/$22.) There are also excellent cross-country skiing trails in the **Cibola National Forest,** particularly the North Crest and 10-K trails.

▶ DAYTRIP FROM ALBUQUERQUE

PETROGLYPH NATIONAL MONUMENT. Located on Albuquerque's west side, this national monument features more than 20,000 images etched into lava rocks between 1300 and 1680 AD by Pueblo Indians and Spanish settlers. The petroglyphs range from mysterious images to more recognizable animals, peoples, and crosses. The park encompasses much of the 17 mi. West Mesa, a ridge of black basalt boulders that formed as a result of volcanic activity 130,000 years ago. The most accessible petroglyphs can be found via three short, easy trails (5-30min.) at **Boca Negra Canyon,** 2 mi. north of the visitors center. For those interested in extended hiking, the **Rinconada Canyon Trail** (2½ mi.), 1 mi. south of the visitors center, is an easy desert hike to intricate rock art along the base of the West Mesa. Due to recent thefts, park rangers advise all hikers not to leave any valuables in their cars at the trailhead. To see the nearby volcanoes, take Exit 149 off I-40 and follow Paseo del Volcán to a dirt road. The volcanoes are 4¼ mi. north of the exit. *(To reach the Petroglyph National Monument, take I-40 to Unser Blvd. (Exit 154) and follow signs to the park. ☎899-0205. Park open daily 8am-5pm. Admission to Boca Negra Canyon M-F $1, Sa-Su $2; National Parks Passport accepted. Rinconada Canyon and volcanoes free.)*

CHACO CULTURE NATIONAL HISTORICAL PARK   ☎505

Sun-scorched Chaco Canyon served as the first great settlement of the Ancestral Puebloans and the center of a complex civilization that began around 800 AD and lasted nearly 400 years. The nine Great Houses, massive and intricate multi-story dwellings, date from the ninth century and are among the most well preserved ruins in the Southwest. The most celebrated of these ancient works is Pueblo Bonito, a massive D-shaped structure with many interior *kivas* and two plazas. The historical and cultural sacredness of Chaco Canyon was officially recognized in 1987, when it was designated a World Heritage site. Today Chaco is revered by all visitors who venture into the desert, as well as by the Hopi, Navajo, and Puebloan people who consider the mystical canyon part of their sacred homeland.

The **Chaco Visitors Center,** at the east end of the park, has a free museum with Ancestral Puebloan art and films that detail the known and unknown aspects of the ruins. The free Chaco Night Sky Program—an astronomy program and solar observation—is held Tuesday, Friday, and Saturday at 9pm. All the ruins have explanatory brochures ($0.50-0.75), and, during the summer, rangers lead guided tours of Pueblo Bonito (daily 10am and 2pm) and Hungo Pavi (daily 4pm) from the respective Great House parking lots. (☎786-7014. Open daily 8am-5pm. $8 per vehicle.) The largest sites, including **Pueblo Bonito** and **Chetro Ketl,** are accessible by paths from the main road, but **backcountry hiking trails** lead to many others; get a free **backcountry permit** from the visitors center before leaving. One of the best backcountry hikes is the moderately strenuous ▓**Pueblo Alto Trail** (5½ mi. round-trip, 3-4hr.). After a scramble to the mesa top along a Chacoan path, the trail loops around the mesa and canyon rims, providing access to Pueblo Alto and New Alto, as well as impressive views of Pueblo Bonito, Chetro Ketl, and the San Juan Basin.

An inexpensive lodging option nearby is the █**Circle A Ranch ❶**, just northwest of Cuba, a two-story adobe *hacienda* on a spacious mountain ranch. The comfy living room and shady terrace make it a peaceful place to relax, aided by the massages from the on-site therapists ($35 per 30min). The ranch is 5 mi. east of U.S. 550 on Los Piños Rd. Turn at the cattle guard and follow the signs along Los Piños. (☎289-3350. Reservations recommended. Dorms $20; private rooms $45, with bath $55; tent sites $20. D/MC/V.) **The Gallo Campground ❶**, 1 mi. from the visitors center, offers serene desert camping for $10 per site; register at the campground. The 48 tent and RV sites are near a small ruin and have access to tables and toilets. Since there is no food in the park, **Presciliano's Cafe ❷**, 6478 Hwy. 550 in Cuba, is a good place to silence your growling stomach. The giant cinnamon rolls ($2) and breakfast menu are incredible. (☎289-3177. Burgers $6. Mexican entrees $6-8. Open daily in summer 8:30am-10pm; in winter 8:30am-9pm.)

Chaco Canyon is 92 mi. northeast of Gallup, NM. From the north, take U.S. 550 (formerly Rte. 44) to County Rd. 7900 (3 mi. east of Nageezi and 50 mi. west of Cuba), follow the road for 21 mi., then take the 16 mi. County Rd. 7950 into the park. From the south, take Rte. 9 from Crownpoint (home of the nearest ATM and grocery store) 36 mi. east to the park turnoff in Pueblo Pintado; turn north onto unpaved Rte. 57 for 20 mi. There is no gas in the park, and gas stations en route are few and far between, but there is one at the intersection of Rte. 550 and County Road 7900. Call the park (☎988-6727) to ask about road conditions, which may deteriorate in bad weather, necessitating 4WD or leading to road closures.

EL MORRO NATIONAL MONUMENT ☎505

Limited in terms of size and outdoor opportunities, El Morro National Monument's centerpiece is **Inscription Rock,** showcasing the signatures of Spanish and English explorers and settlers dating back to 1605. The monument has two hiking options. The half-mile, wheelchair-accessible **Inscription Trail** winds past the rock, providing excellent views of the signatures, neighboring petroglyphs, and a rainwater pool. The **Mesa Top Trail** (2 mi., 1hr.) climbs 200 ft. to the top of the rock before skirting the edge of an ancient pueblo. This trail is well-marked and has impressive panoramas of the region. A trail guide that details the most famous engravings and provides translations of those in foreign script is available at the visitors center ($1). The trails close 1hr. before the visitors center. The monument is located west of the Continental Divide on Rte. 53, 125 mi. west of Albuquerque, 42 mi. west of the I-40 exit at Grants, and 56 mi. southeast of Gallup. The **visitors center** includes a small museum and warnings against adding your own graffiti. (☎783-4226. Open daily Memorial Day-Labor Day 8am-7pm; spring and fall 9am-6pm; winter 9am-5pm. Call ahead. $3, under 17 free.) The small **El Morro Campground ❶** rarely fills and has running water and primitive toilets (9 first come, first served sites $5).

TRUTH OR CONSEQUENCES ☎505

In 1950, the popular radio game show *Truth or Consequences* celebrated its 10th anniversary by seeking a town to rename in its honor. Cities from all over the US volunteered, and Hot Springs, NM, was selected. Renamed Truth or Consequences on national television, this dusty town became the center of public attention. Today, the odd name still draws inquisitive tourists, but the majority of visitors come for the hot springs along the Río Grande. The baths in "T or C" (pronounced tee-er-see) definitely take the meaning of relaxation to a whole new level.

THE SOUTHWEST

⚓ 🏃 ORIENTATION AND PRACTICAL INFORMATION. T or C sits about 150 mi. south of Albuquerque on I-25. **Greyhound,** 8 Date St. (☎894-3649), runs to Albuquerque (3hr., 1 per day, $30-40). The **visitors center,** 211 Main St., has free maps and excellent brochures about area accommodations, events, and attractions. (☎894-1968. Open M-F 9am-4:30pm, Sa 9am-1pm.) **Internet Access: Public Library,** 325 Library Ln. (☎894-3027. Open daily 9am-7pm). **Post Office:** 300 Main St. Open M-F 9am-3pm. **Postal Code:** 87901. **Area Code:** 505.

🌀 🍴 ACCOMMODATIONS AND FOOD. Riverbend Hot Springs Hostel ❶, 100 Austin St., has the nicest outdoor mineral baths in the area and is conveniently located along the Río Grande. Because most of the staff's energy is put into maintaining the baths, the hostel itself can be grubby, but the laid-back atmosphere more than makes up for it. (☎894-6183; www.nmhotsprings.com. Reception 8am-10pm; call ahead for late-night arrivals. Linen included. Kitchen and laundry. Key deposit $5. Dorms $20; private rooms $36-55. Tent sites $17. AmEx/D/MC/V.) Budget hotels line N. Date St., just off I-25 at Exit 70. Most offer standard lodging for around $25, but you'll have to go elsewhere for hot springs. Downtown, the **Charles Motel and Spa ❷,** 601 Broadway, has large, cozy rooms with indoor mineral baths and roof-top jacuzzis. (☎894-7154 or 800-317-4518; www.charlesspa.com. Singles $39; doubles $45. AmEx/D/MC/V.) Campers at the nearby **Elephant Butte Lake State Park ❶** have access to restrooms and cold showers. (Primitive sites $8; developed sites with showers $10, with electricity $14.)

Nearly all of the restaurants in Truth or Consequences are as easy on the wallet as the area's baths are on the body. For gourmet food at budget prices, try the **Pacific Grille ❷,** 304 S. Pershing St. With its eclectic menu of various Asian and seafood specialties, this is one of the best eateries in all of Truth or Consequences. (☎894-7687. Entrees $6-10. Open M-Sa 11am-2pm, 5pm-8pm. AmEx/D/MC/V.) **Bar-B-Que on Broadway ❷,** 308 Broadway, dishes up plentiful breakfast specials that start at $2.50 and hearty barbecue lunches running $5-8. (☎894-7047. Open M-Sa 7am-4pm. MC/V.) The **Happy Belly Deli ❶,** 313 Broadway, lives up to its name with satisfying food, a beautiful garden patio, and low prices. (☎894-3354. Open Tu-F 7am-4pm, Sa 8am-4pm. MC/V.)

🌅 🏔 SIGHTS AND OUTDOOR ACTIVITIES. The town's main attractions are its **mineral baths;** Apache legend and local testament claim the baths will heal virtually any ailment. The only outdoor tubs are located at the **Riverbend Hot Springs Hostel** (see above), where there are four alongside the Río Grande. You can even head for the chilly river if you want some refreshment after cleansing your pores in the hot water. Access to the baths is $10 per hr. for the public, but complimentary for hostel guests. (Open daily 7-10am and 7-10pm.)

Five miles north of T or C, **Elephant Butte Lake State Park** features New Mexico's largest lake (take Date St. north to a sign for Elephant Butte; turn right onto Hwy. 181 and follow the signs). A public works project dammed up the Río Grande in 1916 after the resolution of a major water rights dispute between the US and Mexico. The resulting lake is named after the elephantine rock formation at its southern end. The park has sandy beaches and a marina (day use $5). **Marina del Sur,** just inside the park, rents all kinds of boats. (☎744-5567. Must be 21+ to rent. Jet skis $135 per 3hr. Kayaks $20 per 3hr.) **Sports Adventure,** on the lake at the end of Long Point Rd. and also at Rock Canyon Rd., both north of the town of Elephant Butte, rents jet skis. (☎744-5557 or 888-736-8420. Rentals front $49 per hr.) There is a **visitors center** at the entrance to the park with a small, free museum on the area's natural history. (☎877-664-7787. Open M-F 7:30am-4pm, Sa-Su 7:30am-10pm.) An easy 1½ mi. trail begins in the parking lot just past the visitors center.

GILA CLIFF DWELLINGS NATIONAL MONUMENT ☎ 505

The mysterious Gila Cliff Dwellings National Monument is set distantly into the **Gila National Forest** amid acres of mountains and pine forest. The monument contains more than 40 stone and timber rooms carved into the cliff's caves by the Mogollon tribe during the 13th century. About a dozen families lived here for 20 years, farming on the mesa top and along the river. During the early 14th century, however, the Mogollon abandoned their homes, leaving the ruins as their only trace. Today, visitors have the unique opportunity to explore inside the ruins using traditional ladders. The one mile round-trip hike to the dwellings begins with a steep ascent up the canyon walls, but the rest of the hike is fairly easy. A trail guide ($0.50) can be purchased at the trailhead or at the visitors center. Those who want more info about the ruins can go on one of the free, ranger-guided tours (11am and 2pm) that meet at the first overhang. (Dwellings open daily late May to early Sept. 8am-6pm; late Sept. to early May 9am-4pm. $3, under 12 free.) Visitors can also check out several natural hot springs in the forest. Ask at the visitors center for specific trail information. **Jordan Hot Spring** can be reached via Little Bear Canyon Trail (6 mi.) or Middle Fork Trail (8 mi.), while the closer, more popular **Light-feather Hot Spring** is only half a mile behind the visitors center.

The park has two campgrounds: **Upper** and **Lower Scorpion ❶.** Both are located along the road on the way to the trailhead. Water and pit toilets are available in the summer. Both are free. The nearest indoor accommodations can be found at the comfy **Grey Feathers Bed & Breakfast ❸,** 20 mi. south at the intersection of Forest Rd. 15 and Rte. 35. Not only does this remote lodge have a wedding chapel and barbershop, but it also draws as many as 4000 hummingbirds on some summer weekends, making it a quirky and quiet place to relax and bird-watch. (☎ 536-3206. Singles $40-45; doubles $45-50; suites $65-75. AmEx/D/MC/V.) The adjoining **cafe ❶** offers sandwiches, great homemade cookies, and ice cream. (Sandwiches $3-7. Ice cream $1.25 per scoop. Open M and W-Su 8am-4pm. AmEx/D/MC/V.) The only options for dinner near Gila are in Silver City, so plan ahead or go into town to the locally adored **Jalisco Cafe ❷,** 103 S. Bullard St., for Mexican dishes ($6-10) and hibiscus iced tea. (☎ 388-2060. Open M-Sa 11am-8:30pm. MC/V.)

Gila Cliff Dwellings National Monument is 44 mi. north of Silver City on Rte. 15. The road is narrow, winding, and requires about 2hr. Road conditions can be impassable in winter, so pay attention to the weather and road conditions. The **visitors center,** at the end of Rte. 15, shows a film and sells maps of the Gila National Forest. (☎ 536-9461. Open daily in summer 8am-5pm; in winter 8am-4:30pm.)

WHITE SANDS NAT'L MONUMENT ☎ 505

Putting the red rocks and cacti of other monuments to shame, White Sands National Monument is arguably the black sheep of the Southwest but the white wonder of the world. The dune field formed as rainwater flushed the minerals from the nearby peaks into Lake Lucero. As the lake evaporated in the desert heat, the gypsum crystals were left behind and now form the 275 mi. of blindingly white sand dunes. These drifts of fine sand create the look of arctic tundra, but don't be fooled: the midday sun assaults the shadeless dunes with practically unbearable light and heat—be prepared with protective clothing and eyewear, heavy-duty sunscreen, and plenty of water. Trekking or rolling through the dunes can provide hours of mindless fun or mindful soul-searching, especially at sunset.

■ ⚏ **ORIENTATION AND PRACTICAL INFORMATION.** White Sands is on Rte. 70, 15 mi. southwest of Alamogordo and 52 mi. northeast of Las Cruces. The **visitors center** itself has a small museum with an introductory video and a gift shop.

(☎479-6124. Park open daily June-Aug. 7am-10pm, last entrance 9pm; Sept.-May 7am-sunset. Visitors center open daily June-Aug. 8am-7pm; Sept.-May 8am-5pm. The entrance booth distributes a park map. Park admission $3, under 16 free.) Rte. 70 is prone to closures because of the nearby military base, and delays can run up to 1hr.; call the visitors center to check the road status. The nearest **ATM, food, grocery store, hospital, Internet** access, and **post office** are in Alamogordo. No public transit serves the park. For more info, visit www.nps.gov/whsa.

⌐ ACCOMMODATIONS. The only way to sleep in the park is to camp at one of the **backcountry campsites ❶.** Ten daily permits for the sites ($3 per person plus the park entry fee) are first come, first served. The sites have no water or toilets, and are not accessible by road, requiring up to a 2 mi. hike through the dunes. Campers must register in person at the visitors center and be at their sites before dark. Campfires are prohibited, but stoves are allowed. Sleeping amid the white dunes is extraordinary, but plan ahead because sites fill up early on full-moon nights. Occasionally, the sites are closed due to missile range launches. For indoor lodging, the only options are in Alamogordo. **Classic Inn ❷,** 710 N. White Sands Blvd., has comfortable and clean rooms. (☎437-0210. Singles $27; doubles $34. AmEx/MC/V.)

◙⃠ SIGHTS AND OUTDOOR ACTIVITIES. The 8 mi. **Dunes Drive** is a good way see White Sands. However, really experiencing the monument means getting out and walking the dunes. Off-trail hiking is allowed anywhere in the eastern section of the park. Anyone considering a backcountry hike should bring a compass and map—it's easy to get lost. The only wheelchair-accessible trail in the park is the **Interdune Boardwalk,** expected to be renovated by 2006, an easy quarter-mile walk above the sand. The best hike is the **Alkali Flat Trail** (4½ mi.), a moderately strenuous loop through the heart of the dunes to the parched, salty lakebed of Lake Otero, but it isn't necessary to hike the whole thing in order to see spectacular vistas. The trail is marked by white posts with orange reflective tape, but do not attempt this hike in strong winds, when blowing sand makes it easy to lose the trail. Bring lots of water and protect yourself from the sun. There is a free, guided **sunset stroll** every evening at 7pm (call ahead to the visitors center), and on summer nights, park rangers give evening talks on various topics (June-Aug. 8:30pm). On full-moon nights in the summer, the park stays open late (until 11pm, last entrance 10pm), and a guest speaker presents a program on a topic relating to the Southwest at 8:30pm. A **star talk** takes place most Fridays during the summer at 8:30pm. During the **Perseid Meteor Shower** (around the second week of August), the park stays open until midnight. Once a month, a ranger-guided expedition heads for the dry crystal bed of **Lake Lucero.** (Tours 3hr., 1½ mi. Reservations required. $3.) Twenty miles north of White Sands off U.S. 70, the **White Sands Missile Range Museum,** the birthplace of U.S. space and missile activity, has an extensive collection of missiles, not to mention the original Darth Vader mask used in Star Wars. (☎678-8824; www.wsmr-history.org. Open M-F 8am-4pm, Sa-Su 10am-3pm. Free.)

ROSWELL ☎505

Roswell was an otherwise small town known only for its dairy industry when life was unexpectedly shaken up by extraterrestials. The fascination began in July 1947, when an alien spacecraft reportedly crashed on a ranch. The official press release reported that the military had recovered pieces of a "flying saucer," but a retraction followed the next day—the wreckage, the government claimed, was actually a weather balloon. The incident was the birth of alien-curiosity in Roswell and the beginning of multiple government conspiracy theories. Today, traveling skeptics and alien enthusiasts have made tourism a far more lucrative industry than dairy cows, and most leave Roswell entertained, if not enlightened. During the first week of July, the **UFO Festival** celebrates the anniversary of the encounter, attracting thousands for the music, costume contest, and 5km "Alien Chase" race. With a plastic flying saucer above its storefront, the popular ⊠**International UFO Museum and Research Center,** 114 N. Main St., recounts the events near Roswell in 1947. Exhibits contain numerous testimonials and newspaper clippings about the incident and several letters from convinced presidents and senators (what do Jimmy Carter and Ronald Reagan have in common?). The research library, full of government reports and UFO documentation, is the only one of its kind in the country. (☎625-9495. Open daily 9am-5pm. Free. Audio tour $1.)

Cheap motels and hotels line Main St., but the **Frontier Motel ❷,** 3010 N. Main St., is the best, with clean, large rooms, a pool, and wireless Internet. (☎622-1400. Breakfast included. Singles from $32; doubles from $36. AmEx/D/DC/MC/V.) Fast-food restaurants are as prevalent in Roswell as allusions to alien life, and they are concentrated along N. Main St. and W. 2nd St. Side streets are home to less-commercial budget eateries. **Nuthin' Fancy Cafe ❶,** 2103 N. Main St., takes pride in its simple, well-prepared, and delicious meals, promising guests "home cooking without the mess." (☎623-4098. Chicken entrees $8. Slice of homemade pie $2. Open daily 6am-9pm. MC/V.) **Tía Juana's ❹,** 3601 N. Main St., is the kind of funky Tex-Mex restaurant that the big chains try to imitate. Try the chile-rubbed ribeye for $15, or refresh yourself with something from the huge margarita menu. (☎624-6113. Margaritas $5-8. Dining room open M-Th 11am-9:30pm, F-Sa 11am-10pm, Su 11am-9pm; bar open daily 11am-10pm. AmEx/D/MC/V.)

Aside from its extraterrestrial peculiarities, Roswell is a relatively normal town. The intersection of **2nd Street** (Rte. 70/380) and **Main Street** (Rte. 285) is the center of the Roswell galaxy. To reach Roswell from Albuquerque, head 89 mi. south on I-25 to San Antonio, then 153 mi. east on U.S. 380. **Greyhound,** 1100 N. Virginia Ave. (☎622-2510; www.greyhound.com), in conjunction with TNM&O Coaches, runs buses to Albuquerque (4hr., 1-2 per day, $36-38) and El Paso (4½hr., 3 per day, $41-44). **Pecos Trails Transit,** 515 N. Main St., runs buses all over town. (☎624-6766. Open M-F 6am-10:30pm, Sa 7:10am-10pm, Su 10:30am-7pm. $0.75, students $0.50, seniors $0.35.) The **visitors center** is at 426 N. Main St. (☎624-0889 or 623-5695. Open M-F 8:30am-5:30pm, Sa-Su 10am-3pm.) Free **Internet** access is available at the **Roswell Public Library,** 301 N. Pennsylvania Ave.

LOCAL LEGEND

ROSWELL RAKEOVER?

Something crashed onto Mac Brazel's ranch on July 4, 1947, but what it was is still up for debate. Most Roswell residents believe it was a flying saucer and have piles of evidence, even a museum, to prove it. Others, guffawing at the extraterrestrial hype, theorize it was a weather balloon or a physics experiment gone awry. Either way, the series of events that took place just after the crash are worthy of note.

The perplexed Brazel took a sackful of the debris to Fort Worth and US Army Intelligence. Brazel was told to step out of the room, and claims that, when he returned, the original debris had been replaced with pieces of weather balloon wreckage. Later, Roswell undertaker Glenn Davis received a strange call from the Army air field, asking how many child-sized caskets he had in stock and how to preserve bodies that had been exposed to the weather. A nurse was brought in to examine several bodies. She was transferred to England the next day, but before leaving, gave Davis hand-drawn pictures of the alien forms she had examined.

The mysterious case has been closed for many years, and dozens of senators and even former presidents have been denied access to any information. So, do aliens exist? And did they crash at Roswell? No one really knows, but some people seem pretty convinced.

(☎622-7101. Open M-Tu 9am-9pm, W-Sa 9am-6pm, Su 2-6pm.) **Post Office:** 415 N. Pennsylvania Ave. (☎623-7232. Open M-F 7:30am-5:30pm, Sa 8am-noon.) **Postal Code:** 88202. **Area Code:** 505.

CARLSBAD CAVERNS NATIONAL PARK   ☎505

Filled with enormous and haunting cave chambers, the world's deepest limestone cave, and six-story speleothems, Carlsbad Caverns can prompt even the most jaded caver to do a double-take. Though Native Americans have inhabited the Carlsbad area for centuries, the caves were not documented until the turn of the 20th century, when explorers noticed the hundreds of thousands of Mexican free-tailed bats swirling around the seemingly normal hillside at sunset. The aptly-named **Big Room** is the park's central and most accessible attraction. To call this cave spectacular would be an understatement; if you are pressed for time, this is the park's must-see. A 1¼ mi. self-guided tour circumscribes the 14-acre chamber, highlighting subterranean wonders like the Hall of Giants, the Rock of Ages, and the Bottomless Pit. (Natural entrance open daily June to mid-Aug. 8:30am-3:30pm; mid-Aug. to May 8:30am-2pm. Elevators open daily June to mid-Aug. 8:30am-5pm; mid-Aug. to May 8:30am-3:30pm. $6, ages 6-15 $3. Audio tour $3. Segments of trail wheelchair accessible.) The **King's Palace Tour,** guided by a ranger, goes through four of the cave's lowest rooms. (May-Aug. 1½hr. tours every hr. 10-11am and 1-3pm; Sept.-Apr. 10am and 2pm only. $8, Golden Age Passport holders and ages 6-15 $4. Reservations recommended.) Other guided tours in the Big Room include a tour though the **Left Hand Tunnel** lit only by lanterns. (2hr., daily 9am, $7), and a moderately strenuous tour of the **Lower Cave** that descends 50 ft. on ladders. (3hr., M-F 1pm, $20. Bring gloves and 4 AA batteries.) Plan your visit for late afternoon to catch the **bat flight.** The ritual, during which hungry bats storm out of the cave at a rate of 6000 per min., is preceded by a ranger talk. (May-Oct. daily just before sunset. Call ahead for specific times.) **Wild caves** can be explored with a backcountry cave permit (free, but applications must be sent to the visitors center at least one month in advance; call ☎785-2232, ext. 3104). **Backcountry hiking** is permitted above ground, but a free permit (available at the visitors center) is required and a map and at least a gallon of water per person per day are recommended. The **Caverns Visitors Center** has trail maps and tour info. (☎785-2232. Open daily June to late Aug. 8am-7pm; late Aug. to May 8am-5:30pm.) Make reservations through the Guided Tour Reservation Hotline (☎800-967-2283) or at http://reservations.nps.gov.

Tours of the undeveloped **Slaughter Canyon Cave** are a rugged caving experience. A car is required to get there; there's no public transit, and the parking lot is 23 mi. down unpaved Rte. 418, several miles south of the main entrance to the park on U.S. 62/180. The cave entrance is a steep, strenuous half-mile from the lot. Ranger-led tours (bring a flashlight) traverse difficult and slippery terrain; there are no paved trails or handrails. (2hr. tours June-Aug. Sa-Su 10am and 1pm, Sept.-May 10am only. $15, Golden Age Passport holders and ages 6-15 $7.50. Call the visitors center at least 2 days ahead for reservations.) Tours of the **Hall of the White Giant** and **Spider Cave** require crawling and climbing through tight passages. (☎800-967-2283. Tours 4hr., 1 per week. $20. Call at least a month in advance for reservations.)

A slew of budget motels line U.S. 62/180 south of downtown Carlsbad. The **Stage Coach Inn ❷**, 1819 S. Canal St., offers the best value of the lot with an outdoor pool, indoor jacuzzi, and laundry. Rooms have A/C, cable, and refrigerators. (☎887-1148. Singles $34-40; doubles $36-47. AAA and AARP discount 15%. D/MC/V.) The **Carlsbad RV Park and Campground ❶**, 4301 National Parks Hwy. 4 mi. south of town, has two wooden cabins with a full-size bed, two bunk beds, A/C, cable, microwave, and refrigerator. Tent camping is also available. All guests have access to showers, swimming pool, and game room. (☎885-6333. Breakfast included Sa-Su. Cabin $32;

linen not provided. Tent sites $14.50. MC/V.) Fuel up for the caverns with fresh-baked pastries and coffee at the ⬛Blue House Bakery and Cafe ❶, 609 N. Canyon. This converted (blue) house has sandwiches, smoothies, and a relaxing garden patio. (☎628-0555. Open M-F 6am-2pm, Sa 7am-noon. Cash only.) For lunch or dinner, everyone loves Lucy's Mexicali Restaurant and Entertainment Club ❷, 701 S. Canal St. Lucy's serves the best tamales ($2) around. (☎887-7714. Live music and karaoke Sa-Su. Open M-Th 11am-8pm, F-Sa 11am-11pm. AmEx/MC/V.)

The closest town to the park, though a bit of a tourist pit stop, is White's City, on U.S. 62/180, 20 mi. southwest of the larger Carlsbad and 6 mi. from the visitors center. Flash floods occasionally close the roads; call the park for road conditions. El Paso, TX (p. 680) is the nearest big city, 150 mi. west past Guadalupe Mountains National Park (p. 680). Greyhound, with TNM&O Coaches, runs three buses per day between El Paso and Carlsbad (3hr., $38.50) and will stop at White's City. Post Office: 23 Carlsbad Caverns Hwy. (☎785-2220. Open M-F 8am-noon and 12:30-4:30pm, Sa 8am-noon.) Postal Code: 88268. Area Code: 505.

THE SOUTHWEST

CALIFORNIA

California, and its iconic Hwy. 1, offer a wild ride—exhilaration doesn't begin to describe the feeling of being poised upon the very western edge of the country, with better times and wilder sights in the cliff-hugging turns ahead, and the past receding in your rearview mirror. Glaring movie spotlights, clanging San Francisco cable cars, vanilla-scented Jeffrey pines, alpine lakes, and ghostly desert landscapes all thrive in California. Indeed, there's so much going on you'd need a whole book (like ▧*Let's Go: California*) to describe it.

HIGHLIGHTS OF CALIFORNIA

GAWK at the hardbodies on Venice Beach, stroll down the Walk of Fame, or (window-) shop along Rodeo Drive, all while eating an IN-N-OUT burger, in **Los Angeles** (p. 896).

CRUISE the rugged, spectacular cliffs of the **Central Coast** (p. 891).

MARVEL at the tallest waterfall in North America at **Yosemite National Park** (p. 935).

GULP glass after glass of free wine at the countless vineyards of **Napa Valley** (p. 882).

PEER past the towers of San Francisco's **Golden Gate Bridge** and watch the sun fade into the Pacific Ocean (p. 858).

▧ PRACTICAL INFORMATION

Capital: Sacramento.

Visitor Info: California Office of Tourism, P.O. Box 1499, Sacramento 95812 (☎800-862-2543; www.visitcalifornia.com). **California State Parks Department,** P.O. Box 942896, Sacramento 94296 (☎800-777-0369; www.parks.ca.gov).

Postal Abbreviation: CA. **Sales Tax:** 7-8%, depending on county.

SAN FRANCISCO ☎415

If California is a state of mind, San Francisco is euphoria. This city will take you to new highs, leaving your mind spinning, your taste buds tingling, and your calves aching. Though it's smaller than most "big" cities, the City by the Bay more than compensates for its size with personality that simply won't quit. The dazzling views, daunting hills, one-of-a-kind neighborhoods, and laidback citizens have a unique charisma. The city packs an incredible amount of vitality into its 47 sq. mi. of thriving art communities, bustling shops, and diverse nightlife. For more coverage of San Francisco, see ▧*Let's Go: San Francisco.*

✈ INTERCITY TRANSPORTATION

San Francisco is 403 mi. north of Los Angeles and 390 mi. south of Oregon. The city lies at the northern tip of the peninsula that separates the San Francisco Bay from the Pacific Ocean. San Francisco is 6hr. from L.A. via I-5, 8hr. via U.S. 101, or 9½hr. via Hwy. 1. From inland California, **I-5** approaches the city from the north and south via **I-580** and **I-80,** which runs across the **Bay Bridge.** From the north, U.S. 101 and Hwy. 1 come over the **Golden Gate Bridge.**

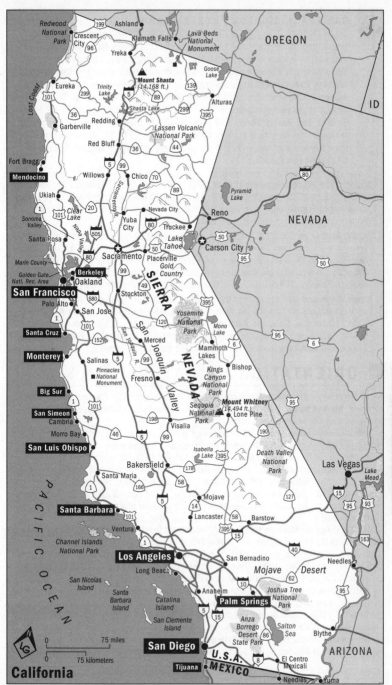

California

SAN FRANCISCO FOR POCKET CHANGE. Life in the City by the Bay isn't cheap by any means, but you don't have to leave penniless. Drop your bag at one of the city's many hostels, or camp at **Marin Headlands** (p. 881) and hike into town across the Golden Gate Bridge. To get acquainted, stroll through the city's diverse neighborhoods and attractions with a free **City Guides Walking Tour** (www.sfcityguides.org). Test your bartering skills at the **produce stands** in Chinatown (p. 868) or along 24th St. in the **Mission** (p. 869), and pick up the makings of a fine meal for next to nothing. Got a spare dollar? Stop at **Dick Lee Pastry Shop,** 777 Jackson St., in Chinatown, for six delicious steamed pork buns for $1.10, or **La Victoria,** 2937 24th St., in the Mission, for the city's best *pan dulce* ($1). If you've still got energy, the **Legion of Honor** (p. 872) is free on Tuesdays.

Airport: San Francisco International (SFO; ☎650-821-8211; ground transportation info 650-821-2732; www.flysfo.com), 15 mi. south of downtown via U.S. 101. **Bay Area Rapid Transit** (BART; ☎989-2278; www.bart.gov), runs M-F 4am-midnight, Sa 6am-midnight, Su 8am-midnight. $5 to downtown.

Trains: Amtrak (☎800-872-7245; www.amtrak.com). Connects from both Oakland and Emeryville to downtown SF ($4-7). To **Los Angeles** (8-12hr., 5 per day, $50). **Caltrain** (☎800-660-4287; www.caltrain.org), at 4th and King St. in SoMa (operates M-F 5am-midnight, Sa-Su unreliable due to construction), is a regional commuter train that runs south to Palo Alto ($4.50, seniors and under 12 $2.25) and San Jose ($5.25/$2.50).

Buses: Greyhound runs buses from the **Transbay Terminal,** 425 Mission St. (☎495-1569; www.greyhound.com), between Fremont and 1st St. downtown. To **Los Angeles** (8-13hr., 16 per day, $43) and **Portland** (15-17hr., 5 per day, $65). **Golden Gate Transit** (Marin County, ☎923-2000; www.goldengate.org), **AC Transit** (East Bay, ☎510-817-1717), and **SamTrans** (San Mateo County) also stop at the terminal.

◪ ORIENTATION

San Francisco's diverse neighborhoods are loosely organized along a few central arteries. **Market Street** runs on a diagonal from the Ferry Building, through downtown, and all the way to the Castro.

Retail-heavy **Union Square,** the center of downtown, is just north of Market St. North of Union Square, **North Beach,** a historically Italian area, overflows with restaurants and cafes, while **Chinatown** is the largest Chinese community outside of Asia. The skyscrapers of the **Financial District** crowd east toward the **Embarcadero** and west to the high-culture **Civic Center,** which lines Market St. and is bounded on the west by Van Ness Ave. Between Union Sq. and Civic Center is the **Tenderloin,** where drugs, crime, and homelessness prevail despite attempts at urban renewal. Northwest of Union Sq., old money presides over ritzy **Nob Hill,** newer money walks its dogs on **Russian Hill,** and Fillmore St. leads north to the Victorians of **Pacific Heights,** as well as the few *udon*-filled blocks of **Japantown.**

South of Market St. to the east, the **South of Market Area (SoMa)** plays host to museums near 3rd St. and thumping clubs scattered among industrial buildings down to 14th St. To the southwest of SoMa, the trendy **Mission,** largely populated by Latino residents during the day and hip barhoppers by night, takes over south of 14th St., merging into the diners and cafes of the **Castro,** a legendary gay neighborhood. To the south, **Bernal Heights** and **Noe Valley** are largely residential.

Vast **Golden Gate Park** dominates the western half of the peninsula, surrounded by the former hippie haven of the **Haight** to the east and the residential and largely Asian **Richmond District** to the north. **Lincoln Park** reaches westward to the ocean, connecting to Ocean Beach at the foot of Golden Gate Park. The majestic **Golden Gate Bridge** stretches over the bay from the **Presidio** in San Francisco's northwest corner. Heading east from the bridge, the posh stucco of the **Marina,** cultural **Fort Mason,** and touristy **Fisherman's Wharf** line the north shore of the peninsula. **Alcatraz** sits isolated in the bay.

▣ LOCAL TRANSPORTATION

San Francisco Municipal Railway (MUNI; ☎673-6864; www.sfmuni.com) is a system of buses, cable cars, subways, and streetcars and is the most efficient way to get around the city. Runs daily 6am-1am. $1.25, seniors and ages 5-17 $0.35. **MUNI passports** are valid on all MUNI vehicles (1-day $9, 3-day $15, 7-day $20). Weekly pass ($12) is valid for a single work week but requires an additional $1 to ride the cable cars. Wheelchair access varies among routes; all below-ground stations, but not all above-ground sites, are accessible.

Cable cars: Operated by MUNI (see above). Noisy, slow, and usually crammed full, but charming relics. To avoid mobs, ride in the early morning. The **Powell-Mason (PM)** line, which runs to the wharf, is the most popular. The **California (C)** line, from the Financial District up through Nob Hill, is usually the least crowded, but the **Powell-Hyde (PH)** line, with the steepest hills and the sharpest turns, may be the most fun. $3, under 6 free; $1 before 7am and after 9pm. No transfers.

Bay Area Rapid Transit (BART; ☎989-2278; www.bart.org) operates trains along 5 lines connecting San Francisco with **East Bay** cities, including Berkeley. All stations provide maps and schedules. There are 8 BART stops in San Francisco proper. Runs M-F 4am-midnight, Sa 6am-midnight, Su 8am-midnight. $1.25-5. Wheelchair accessible.

Car Rental: City, 1748 Folsom St. (☎877-861-1312; www.cityrentacar.com), between Duboce and 14th St. $32-40 per day, $170 per week. 21+; under-25 surcharge $8 per day. Open M-F 7:30am-6pm, Sa 9am-4pm. Also at 1433 Bush St. (☎866-359-1331) and 41 San Bruno Ave., near SFO (☎866-630-6769).

Taxi: National Cab, ☎648-4444. **Yellow Cab,** ☎626-2345.

☞TIP **PREVENT RUNAWAYS.** San Francisco's hilly terrain makes parking a challenge. When parking facing uphill, turn the front wheels away from the curb, and, if driving a standard transmission, leave the car in first gear. If your car starts to roll, it will stop (hopefully) when the tires hit the curb. When facing downhill, turn the wheels toward the curb and, if driving a standard transmission, leave the car in reverse. Always set the emergency brake.

☑ PRACTICAL INFORMATION

Visitor Info: Visitor Information Center (☎391-2000, 24hr. info 391-2001; www.sfvisitor.org), in Hallidie Plaza. Open M-F 9am-5pm, Sa-Su 9am-3pm; Nov.-June closed Su.

Hotlines: AIDS Hotline, ☎863-2437. **Crisis Line for the Handicapped,** ☎800-426-4263. **Drug Crisis Line,** ☎362-3400. **Rape Crisis Center,** ☎647-7273.

Internet Access: San Francisco Public Library Main Branch, 100 Larkin St. (☎557-4400; http://sfpl.lib.ca.us), at Grove St. Open M and Sa 10am-6pm, Tu-Th 9am-8pm, F noon-6pm, Su noon-5pm. Free. Check www.cheesebikini.com for area wireless locations.

Post Office: Pine Station, 1400 Pine St. (☎351-2435), at Larkin. Open M-F 8am-5:30pm, Sa 8am-3pm. Also at **Macy's Station,** 170 O'Farrell St. in Macy's, near Union Square. Open M-Sa 10am-5:30pm, Su 11am-5pm. **Postal Code:** 94109.

Area Code: ☎415, unless otherwise noted.

Downtown San Francisco

▐ ACCOMMODATIONS

For those who don't mind sharing a room with strangers, many San Francisco hostels are homier and cheaper than most budget hotels. B&Bs are often the most comfortable and friendly, albeit expensive, option. A wide selection of budget and more luxurious accommodations can be found throughout the city.

HOSTELS

▨ San Francisco International Guesthouse, 2976 23rd St. (☎641-1411), in the Mission. No sign; look for the blue Victorian with yellow trim near the corner of Harrison and 23rd St. Hardwood floors and relaxing common areas make this an excellent lodging option in the city . Passport required. TV area, kitchens, and phones. Free linens, Internet, and coffee. 5-night min. stay. No reservations; call a few days ahead for availability. Dorms $16; doubles $32. Cash only. ❶

▨ Adelaide Hostel and Hotel, 5 Isadora Duncan Ln. (☎359-1915 or 877-359-1915; www.adelaidehostel.com), at the end of an alley off Taylor St. between Geary and Post St. in Union Sq. Classy decor and chic furniture entice an international crowd. TV and wash basin in each room. Breakfast included. Free linens, Internet, and safe deposit. Towels $1. Laundry (wash $1.50, dry $1.50). Key deposit $10. 4-night max. stay. Dorms $20-24; private rooms $55-70. AmEx/D/DC/MC/V. ❶

Green Tortoise Hostel, 494 Broadway (☎834-1000; www.greentortoise.com), off Columbus Ave. in North Beach. Fun-seeking travelers love the spacious common room and helpful staff. Continental breakfast (daily) and dinner (M, W, F) included. Free sauna, linens, towels, Internet, and storage. Laundry (wash $1.25, dry $0.75). Key deposit $20. 10-night max. stay. Check-in noon. Check-out 11am. Reserve 1 week in advance in summer. Dorms $20-24; private rooms $52-60. MC/V. ❶

Interclub Globe Hostel, 10 Hallam Pl. (☎431-0540), off Folsom between 7th and 8th St. in SoMa. A cool hostel primarily for young international travelers. Happening common room has pool table, TV, microwave, and fridge. Linen $2.50. Passport or out-of-state ID required. Mostly first come, first served but reservations sometimes possible. Key deposit $10. 14-day max. stay. Dorms $18-20; private rooms $50-80. Cash only. ❶

Fisherman's Wharf (HI), Bldg. #240 (☎771-7277), in Fort Mason. Once you enter the complex at the corner of Bay and Franklin St., the hostel is at the corner of Funston and Pope St. past the administrative buildings. Looks and feels like summer camp. Huge kitchen and cafe with vegetarian dinner. Quiet hours from 11pm. No smoking or alcohol. Bike storage, lockers, and parking. Laundry (wash $1, dry $1). Check-in 2:30pm. Reserve well in advance. Dorms $28. HI hostels also near Union Square at 685 Ellis St. (☎474-5721) and 312 Mason St. (☎788-5604). AmEx/D/MC/V. ❶

Pacific Tradewinds, 680 Sacramento St. (☎800-486-7975), near Union Sq. Squeaky-clean kitchen, comfortable dorms, TV lounge, and roomy dining area. Free linens, Internet, and lockers. Key deposit $20. Check-in 8am-11:30pm. Dorms $17-24. MC/V. ❶

HOTELS

San Remo Hotel, 2237 Mason St. (☎776-8688; www.sanremohotel.com), between Chestnut and Francisco St. in Russian Hill. Rooms furnished with elegant antiques. The penthouse offers a private garden and an amazing view of the city. Laundry (wash $1.50, dry $1). Check-in 2pm. Check-out 11am. Reservations recommended. Singles and doubles $55-75. Penthouse $155; reserve 2-3 months ahead. AmEx/DC/MC/V. ❸

San Francisco Zen Center, 300 Page St. (☎863-3136; www.sfzc.org), near Laguna St. in the Lower Haight. The Zen Center offers 6 breezy, unadorned rooms whose courtyard views instill a meditative peace of mind, at least until the 5am wake-up alarm. Breakfast included in daily rates; all meals included in the discounted weekly (10% off) or monthly (25% off) rates. Singles and doubles $66-120. AmEx/D/MC/V. ❸

Phoenix Hotel, 601 Eddy St. (☎776-1380 or 800-248-9466; www.jdvhospitality.com), at Larkin St. in the Tenderloin. Delightful cabanas-by-the-pool setup, with breezy courtyard. Brightly-painted and furnished 70s retro rooms. Parking included. Singles and doubles from $99, in low season from $89. Suites $179-265. AmEx/D/DC/MC/V. ❺

BED & BREAKFASTS

Hayes Valley Inn, 417 Gough St. (☎431-9131, reservations 800-930-7999; www.hayesvalleyinn.com), just north of Hayes St. in Hayes Valley. European-style B&B with tastefully furnished rooms, shared baths, and Victorian parlor. Rooms have cable TV, phone, and private sink. Some smoking rooms. Check-in 3pm. Check-out 11am. Reservations recommended. Singles $49; doubles $53-75. MC/V. ❷

Red Victorian Bed, Breakfast, and Art, 1665 Haight St. (☎864-1978; www.red-vic.com), west of Belvedere St. Themed rooms and a mini meditation room. Reception 9am-9pm. Check-in 3-6pm or by appointment. Reservations recommended. Rooms $86-200. Discounts for stays longer than 3 days. AmEx/D/DC/MC/V. ❹

The Parker Guest House, 520 Church St. (☎621-3222 or 888-520-7275; www.parker-guesthouse.com), near 17th St. in the Castro. Extravagant, stylish, and regularly voted best GLBT B&B in the city. Spa and steam room. Breakfast overlooking rose gardens and complimentary wine social each afternoon. Parking $15 per day. 2-night min. stay on weekends; 4-night min. stay some holiday weekends. Check-in 3pm. Reservations recommended. Rooms from $119, with private bath from $149. AmEx/D/MC/V. ❺

Ansonia Abbey Bed & Breakfast, 711 Post St. (☎673-2670), near Union Sq. A budget-conscious, conveniently located B&B catering to a young, international crowd. TV and phone. Free breakfast, dinner, and wireless Internet. Double bed with shared bath $56; queen bed with private bath $79; family-sized suites $89. AmEx/MC/V. ❸

◘ FOOD

UNION SQUARE

Cafe Mason, 320 Mason St. (☎544-0320). The sparkly vinyl booths and curving red-and-yellow ceiling are clear indications that this diner is more than just a greasy spoon. Cafe Mason functions as a diner, cafe, bistro, or watering hole, depending on the time of day, and draws a diverse clientele to match. Burgers $8. Veggie omelets $8. Pumpkin crepes $11. Open 24hr. AmEx/MC/V. ❷

King of Thai Noodle House, 184 O'Farrell St. (☎677-9991), at Powell St. Other locations around SF. Considered one of the city's best Thai restaurants, the King quickly serves up more-than-generous portions of authentic noodle dishes, soups, and curries for next to nothing. The flavorful roast duck noodle soup ($6) and vegetarian egg rolls ($4.50) are outstanding. Open daily 11:30am-1:30am. Cash only. ❶

Café Bean, 800 Sutter St. (☎346-9527). A crazy cosmopolitan atmosphere and the restorative powers of Dutch pancakes ($4-7) offer jet-setting diners much-needed respite. Parisian posters, maps of Amsterdam, and German road signs hang above makeshift couches. Creative sandwiches $5-8. Internet $3 per 20min. Open M-Sa 6am-7pm, Su 6am-5pm; kitchen closes earlier, usually around 3pm. Cash only. ❷

NORTH BEACH AND CHINATOWN

▨ **Chef Jia,** 925 Kearny St. (☎398-1626), at Pacific St. Chef Jia's insanely cheap and delicious food consistently draws a local crowd. Known for lunch and dinner specials ($5), and the celebrated signature dishes, such as the rolling lettuce chicken with pine nuts ($9). Entrees $6-10. Open M-Th 11:30am-10pm, F 11:30am-11pm, Sa-Su 5-10:30pm. Cash only. ❷

L'Osteria del Forno, 519 Columbus Ave. (☎982-1124), between Green and Union St. in North Beach. The lively staff at this casual Italian eatery serves terrific thin-crust pizzas (slices $3-5, whole pizzas $11-19) and filling focaccia sandwiches ($5-7). Salads and antipasti $5-9. Entrees $9-15. Open M, W-Th, Su 11:30am-10pm, F-Sa 11:30am-10:30pm. Cash only. ❸

House of Nanking, 919 Kearny St. (☎421-1429), near Columbus Ave. Heaping portions of excellent Chinese food are served at this famous, tourist-laden Chinatown institution. Entrees $8-12. Open M-F 11am-10pm, Sa noon-10pm, Su noon-9:30pm. MC/V. ❸

CIVIC CENTER AND THE TENDERLOIN

The California Culinary Academy, 625 Polk St. (☎216-4329), between Turk and Eddy St. Academy students cook behind a viewing window. The Tu-W *prix-fixe* 3-course meal—available for lunch ($16) or dinner ($24)—indulges patrons with ambitious culinary combinations. Wine pairings with each course are a steal at $5. Grand buffet lunch ($22) and dinner ($38) Th-F; reserve 1 week ahead. Open Tu-F 11:30am-1pm and 6-8pm. AmEx/D/MC/V. ❺

Lalita Thai Restaurant and Bar, 96 McAllister St. (☎552-5744), at Leavenworth St. Mood lighting, an elaborate mural, and a touch of plastic foliage set the scene. The $20 4-course *prix-fixe* dinner special (available before 9pm) is a favorite. Intricately seasoned lunch specials $8. Dinner entrees around $11. Open M-F 11am-10pm, Sa 4:30-10pm. Dinner reservations recommended, especially on weekends. AmEx/MC/V. ❸

CALIFORNIA

SOMA, THE MISSION, AND THE CASTRO

■ **The Butler and the Chef Cafe,** 155A S. Park St. (☎896-2075; www.thebutlerandth-echef.com), between Bryant, Brannan, 2nd, and 3rd St. This stellar reproduction of a Parisian street cafe overlooks a historic park. Whether you choose the amazing *Croque Mademoiselle* ($9) or the quiche-of-the-day ($10), you get a complimentary home-made chocolate truffle. Open daily 8am-4pm. AmEx/D/MC/V. ❷

Taquería Cancún, 2288 Mission St. (☎252-9560), at 19th St. Also at 3211 Mission St. (☎550-1414), at Cesar Chavez Ave., and 1003 Market St. (☎864-6773), at 6th St. Delicious burritos (with veggie or meat; $4) and egg dishes served with chips and salsa, tortillas, and choice of sausage, ham, or salsa ($5). Open M-Th and Su 9am-1:45am, F-Sa 9am-2:45am. Cash only. ❶

Bissap Baobab, 2323 Mission St. (☎826-9287), at 19th St. Dine on the unique, well-seasoned cuisine of West Africa. The *Dibi* chicken ($8) is marinated and served with a deliciously tangy onion sauce and plantains, while the *Mafe* vegetables ($7) come covered in a spicy peanut sauce. Open Tu-Su 6-10:30pm. MC/V. ❷

Welcome Home, 464 Castro St. (☎626-3600), near the Castro Theatre. Whether placing a doily under your milkshake ($4) or playfully reminding you that shakes and burgers ($8-9) were made for each other, Welcome Home's friendly waitstaff and comfort food live up to their name. Open M-F 8am-3pm, Sa-Su 8am-4pm. Cash only. ❸

THE HAIGHT AND THE RICHMOND DISTRICT

■ **Rigolo,** 3465 California St. (☎876-7777), near Locust St. in Laurel Heights. Outstanding French-inspired pastas, sandwiches (pulled pork on olive bread $8), and thin-crust piz-zas. The real draws are the incredible breads and baked goods. Lasagna $10. Pizzas $10. Brioche $2.25. Open M-Sa 8am-9pm, Su 8am-8pm. MC/V. ❷

Pork Store Cafe, 1451 Haight St. (☎864-6981), between Masonic Ave. and Ashbury St. in the Upper Haight. 2 delicious healthy options ("Tim's Healthy Thursdays" and "Mike's Low Carb Special"; each $7) pack in enough spinach, avocado, and salsa to hold their own against the Piggy Special ($7). The biscuits and gravy deserve especially high praise. Open M-F 8am-10pm, Sa-Su 8am-11pm. AmEx/D/DC/MC/V. ❷

Q, 225 Clement St. (☎752-2298), at 3rd Ave. in Inner Richmond. The funky decor doesn't quite match up with the amazing comfort food, but with macaroni and cheese with tater tots on top, who's complaining? Draws a local crowd so you may have to wait in the bar and sample the marvelous beer selection. Entrees $8-13. Open M-F 11am-3pm and 5-10pm, Sa 10am-11pm, Su 10am-10pm. MC/V. ❷

PACIFIC HEIGHTS AND THE MARINA

La Boulangerie, 2325 Pine St. (☎440-0356; www.baybread.com), at Fillmore St. Homesick Friendly management serves Parisian-style *macarons,* richly textured *can-nelés,* and the most delicious almond croissants this side of the Seine. Breads $2-7. Pastries $1-3. Small selection of savory tarts and sandwiches $4.25. Check the website for additional SF locations. Open Tu-Sa 8am-6pm, Su 8am-4pm. MC/V. ❶

Home Plate, 2274 Lombard St. (☎922-4663), off Pierce St. in the Marina. This inven-tive breakfast and lunch joint serves apple buckwheat pancakes ($5.50) and home-made apricot-pistachio granola ($4.25). Complimentary scones with homemade mango or mixed fruit jam. Open daily 7am-4pm. MC/V. ❶

La Méditerranée, 2210 Fillmore St. (☎921-2956; www.cafelamed.com), between Sac-ramento and Clay St. Also at 288 Noe St. (☎431-7210), at 16th and Market St. in the Castro and 2936 College Ave. (☎510-540-7773) in Berkeley. Harkens back to modest

Greek and Lebanese traditions but adds a chic twist. Lunch specials (served until 5pm; $7.25) and entrees are light and Mediterranean-inspired. Entrees $8-10. Open M-Th and Su 11am-10pm, F-Sa 11am-11pm. AmEx/MC/V.

◉ SIGHTS

UNION SQUARE

Union Square, a recently redesigned public plaza with grassy terraces perfect for street performers and people-watching, anchors this commercial and cultural district. Clothing stores, hotels, restaurants, galleries, and theaters jam the surrounding streets, but the area hasn't always been so tourist-friendly. Around 1900, murders on Union Square's Morton Alley averaged one per week and prostitutes waved to their favorite customers from second-story windows. After the 1906 earthquake and fires destroyed most of the brothels, merchants moved in and renamed the alley **Maiden Lane** in hopes of changing the street's image. Today, the pedestrian-only street that extends two blocks from Union Square's eastern side is lined with the understated facades of big-name designer shops. Architecture enthusiasts will love the artful swirling brick and spiral interior of **Xanadu Gallery,** 140 Maiden Ln., the only Frank Lloyd Wright building in SF. (☎392-9999; www.xanadugallery.us. Open M-Sa 10am-6pm.)

NORTH BEACH

▨**CITY LIGHTS BOOKSTORE.** Beat writers came to national attention when Lawrence Ferlinghetti's City Lights Bookstore (est. 1953) published Allen Ginsberg's *Howl*, which was banned in 1956 and then subjected to an extended trial at the end of which a judge found the poem "not obscene." A glance around the store confirms the obvious radical leanings of a bookstore rooted in the subversive potential of intellectual countermovements. City Lights has expanded since its Beat days and now stocks a selection of fiction, poetry, and non-fiction, but remains committed to publishing young writers and providing readers with as many viewpoints as possible. *(2261 Columbus Ave. ☎362-8193. Open daily 10am-midnight.)*

WASHINGTON SQUARE. North Beach's piazza, a pretty, tree-lined lawn, fills every morning with practitioners of *tai chi.* By noon, sunbathers and picnickers take over. This was the site of Joe DiMaggio's wedding to his first wife, Dorothy Arnold (and not, as you may hear, to his second wife, Marilyn Monroe). The **St. Peter and St. Paul Catholic Church** invites tired sightseers to take refuge in its dark wooden nave or to get a crick in the neck as they stare up at its double spires. *(666 Filbert St.)* Turn-of-the-century San Francisco philanthropist Lillie Hitchcock Coit donated the **Volunteer Firemen Memorial** after being rescued from a fire as a young girl. *(Washington Sq. is bordered by Union, Filbert, Stockton, and Powell St.)*

COIT TOWER. Coit Tower (est. 1933) stands 210 ft. high and commands a spectacular view of the city and the bay on a clear day. During the Depression, the Works Progress Administration employed artists to decorate the interior with murals that depict laborers at work. The murals are open to the public and are all located in the tower lobby (free). The top of the tower can only be accessed via elevator. *(MUNI bus #39. By car, follow Lombard St. to the top, where there is free 30min. parking daily 10am-6:30pm. Tower: ☎362-0808. Open daily 10am-6:30pm. Free guided tour of the murals Sa 11am. Elevator $3.75, seniors $2.50, ages 6-12 $1.50, under 6 free.)*

CALIFORNIA

CHINATOWN

WAVERLY PLACE. This little alley offers offbeat architecture without the garishness of Grant Ave. Near the intersection with Sacramento St., the fire escapes are painted in pinks and greens and held together by railings made of intricate Chinese patterns. Closer to Washington St., the alley is also home to **Tien Hou Temple,** the oldest Chinese temple in the US. *(Between Sacramento and Washington St. and between Stockton St. and Grant Ave. Tien Hou Temple at 125 Waverly Pl.)*

ROSS ALLEY. Ross Alley was once lined with brothels and gambling houses; today, it epitomizes the cramped look of old Chinatown. The alley has starred in such films as *Big Trouble in Little China, Karate Kid II,* and *Indiana Jones and the Temple of Doom. (Ross Alley is located off Washington St., between Stockton and Grant St.)* Squeeze into a tiny doorway to watch fortune cookies being shaped by hand at the **Golden Gate Cookie Factory.** All cookies that don't meet the baker's high standards are put in big tins for free taste-testing. *(56 Ross Alley.* ☎ *781-3956. Open daily 9am-8pm. Bag of cookies $1-3, with "funny," "sexy," or "lucky" fortunes $5.)*

CIVIC CENTER

The palatial **San Francisco City Hall,** modeled after Rome's St. Peter's Basilica, is the centerpiece of the largest gathering of Beaux Arts architecture in the US. *(1 Dr. Carlton B. Goodlett Pl., at Van Ness Ave.* ☎ *554-4000. Open M-F 8am-8pm.)* **United Nations Plaza** hosts the city's **farmers market.** *(Just off Market St. Market open in summer W and Su 7am-3pm.)* The seating in the glass-and-brass **Louise M. Davies Symphony Hall** was designed to give most audience members a close-up view of performers. Visually, the building is a smashing success, as is the **San Francisco Symphony.** *(201 Van Ness Ave.* ☎ *552-8000.)* The **San Francisco Opera Company** and **San Francisco Ballet** perform at the **War Memorial Opera House.** *(301 Van Ness Ave., between Grove and McAllister St.)*

NOB HILL AND RUSSIAN HILL

THE CROOKEDEST STREET IN THE WORLD. The famous curves of **Lombard Street** were installed in the 1920s so that horse-drawn carriages could negotiate the extremely steep hill. From the top, both pedestrians and passengers enjoy the view of the city and harbor. *(Between Hyde and Leavenworth St., running down Russian Hill.)*

GRACE CATHEDRAL AND HUNTINGTON PARK. The largest Gothic edifice west of the Mississippi, **Grace Cathedral** is Nob Hill's stained-glass crown. The castings of its portals are such exact imitations of the Baptistry in Florence that they were used to restore the originals. Inside, murals mix San Franciscan and national history with saintly scenes. The altar of the AIDS Interfaith Memorial Chapel celebrates the church's "inclusive community." *(1100 California St., between Jones and Taylor St.* ☎ *749-6300; www.gracecathedral.org. Open M-F and Su 7am-6pm, Sa 8am-6pm. Services: M-F 7:30, 9am, 12:10pm; Sa 9am and 3pm; Su 7:30, 8:15, 11am, 6pm. Additional services Th 5:15pm and mid-Sept. to mid-June Su 3pm. Tours M-F 1-3pm, Sa 11:30am-1:30pm, Su 12:30-2pm. Self-guided tours available anytime. Suggested donation $5.)* Outside, the turf and trees of **Huntington Park** are equipped with a playground and sunbathers.

PACIFIC HEIGHTS AND JAPANTOWN

Between Union and Sacramento St., Pacific Heights has the greatest number of Victorian buildings in the city. The streets surrounding Alta Plaza Park and Lafayette Park have an abundance of grand homes. The public library offers free tours of Pacific Heights mansions. *(www.sfcityguides.com. Tours meet in Alta Plaza atop the stairs at Pierce and Clay St. every Sa and 3rd Tu at 11am.)* **St. Dominic's Cathedral** wows visitors with its towering altar—featuring an elaborate sculpture of Jesus and the 12 apostles—and its imposing gray stone and Gothic-style facade. *(2390 Bush St., at Steiner St. Open M-Sa 6:30am-5:30pm, Su 7:30am-9pm. Mass M-F 6:30, 8am, 5:30pm; Sa 8am and 5:30pm; Su 7:30am quiet mass, 9:30am family mass, 11:30am solemn choral, 1:30pm Spanish, 5:30pm contemporary music, 9pm candlelight service.)*

THE MISSION

The Mission is slowly outgrowing its reputation as one of the most underappreciated neighborhoods in the city. The intersection of Mission and **16th Street** and the length of 24th St. are perhaps the most pulsing, personality-filled areas in all of San Francisco, where shops cater to vegetarian diets, political radicals, and literary dissenters, and produce is sold on the sidewalks. Founded in 1776 in the old heart of San Francisco, the **Mission Dolores** is thought to be the city's oldest building. Due to its proximity to the Laguna de Nuestra Señora de los Dolores (Lagoon of Our Lady of Sorrows), the Mission became universally known as *Misión de los Dolores*. Bougainvillea, poppies, and birds of paradise bloom in its cemetery, featured in Alfred Hitchcock's 1958 film *Vertigo*. *(3321 16th St., at Dolores St. ☎621-8203. Open May-Oct. M-F and Su 9am-4:30pm; Nov.-Apr. daily 9am-4pm. $3, ages 5-12 $2. Mass in English M-F 7:30 and 9am, Sa 5pm, Su 8 and 10am; in Spanish Su noon.)* The magnificent **murals** scattered throughout the mission certainly warrant straying from the main thoroughfare. Standouts include the political murals of **Balmy Alley** off 24th St. between Harrison and Folsom St., the face of **St. Peter's Church** at 24th and Florida St., and the latest addition to the mural scene, **Mona Caron's mural** at 300 Church St., at the corner of 15th St. one block south of Market St.

THE CASTRO

The concept, as well as the reality, of an all-queer neighborhood draws GLBT tourists and their friends to the Castro. Beyond the glitz of shimmering bodies and the gyms where they are sculpted, the Castro harbors a more playful side. A slew of kitschy stores and a contingent of rebellious youth add flair to the picture-perfect streets, where couples make a full-time job out of seeing and being seen. For architecture without the walk, head to the **Castro Theatre,** an Art Deco appropriation of a Mexican cathedral design with a lavishly refurbished interior. *(429 Castro St.)*

TWIN PEAKS

Tourist hub by day, lovebird locale by night—the lookout-turned-make out point atop Twin Peaks offers the best views of the city. From Alcatraz to the Transamerica Pyramid to a big rainbow flag at the foot of Market St. in the Castro, all major landmarks are on display. Scramble up the other peak for a view to the west. *(The peaks are located between Portola Dr., Clarendon Ave., and Upper Market St. From Noe Valley, take MUNI bus #48 to Diamond Heights. From elsewhere in the city, take MUNI bus K, L, or M to Forest Hills, then MUNI bus #36.)* For a scenic route by car, bike, or foot, take 17th St. to Clayton St. to Clarendon Ave. and head up Twin Peaks Blvd. to the top.

THE HAIGHT

All around Haight and Ashbury St., vestiges of the 1960s remain in inexpensive bars and ethnic restaurants. Action-packed street life, anarchist literature, and shops selling pipes for, um, tobacco carry on the legacy of the free-love era. The former homes of several countercultural legends continue to attract visitors. From the corner of Haight and Ashbury St., walk up Ashbury St. to #710, just south of Waller St., to see the house occupied by the **Grateful Dead.** Look across the street for the **Hell's Angels'** house. If you walk back to Haight St., go right three blocks and make a left on Lyon St. to check out **Janis Joplin's** old abode. *(122 Lyon St., between Page and Oak St.)* Cross the Panhandle, continue three blocks to Fulton St., turn right, and wander seven blocks toward the park to see where the Manson "family" planned murder and mayhem at the **Charles Manson** mansion. *(2400 Fulton St., at Willard St.)* **Buena Vista Park,** which runs along Haight St. between Central and Baker St. and continues south, resembles a jungle complete with a dense canopy but should be avoided at night. Across **Alamo Square's** grassy slope, a string of brightly colored Victorian homes known as the **Painted Ladies** glow against the skyline.

GOLDEN GATE PARK

In-line skaters, neo-flower children, and sunbathers converge in this lush city oasis. The park has a municipal golf course, equestrian center, sports fields, tennis courts, and stadium. On Sundays, traffic is banned from park roads, and bicycles and in-line skates come out in full force. The **visitors center** is located in the Beach Chalet on the western edge of the park. (☎751-2766. Open daily 9am-5pm.)

GARDENS. The soil of Golden Gate Park is rich enough to support a wealth of flowers. The **Strybing Arboretum and Botanical Gardens** are home to over 7000 varieties of plants, including collections from Chile, New Zealand, and the tropical, high-altitude New World Cloud Forests. Within its grounds, the **Garden of Fragrance** is designed for the visually impaired; all labels are in Braille and the plants are chosen for their textures and scents. Near the Music Concourse off South Dr., the **Shakespeare Garden** contains almost every flower and plant ever mentioned by the Bard. Plaques with the relevant quotations are displayed, and maps help you find your favorite hyacinths and rue. *(Open daily dawn-dusk.)* The **Japanese Cherry Orchard,** at Lincoln Way and South Dr., blooms the first week in April. Created for the 1894 Mid-Winter Exposition, the elegant **Japanese Tea Garden** is a serene collection of wooden buildings, small pools, graceful footbridges, and carefully pruned trees. (☎752-4227. Open daily in summer 8:30am-6pm; in winter 8:30am-5pm. $3.50, seniors and ages 6-12 $1.25. Free in summer 8:30-9:30am and 5-6pm; in winter 8:30-9:30am and 4-5pm.)

LINCOLN PARK AND OCEAN BEACH

At the northwest end of San Francisco, **Lincoln Park** has spectacular views of the Pacific and the Golden Gate Bridge. The meandering paths and historical sights are ideal for an afternoon hike or summertime picnic. **Ocean Beach,** the largest and most popular of San Francisco's beaches, begins south of Point Lobos and extends down the northwestern edge of the city's coastline. The strong undertow along the point is very dangerous, but die-hard surfers still brave the treacherous currents, gnarly waves, and the ice-cold water.

GOLDEN GATE BRIDGE AND THE PRESIDIO

When John Fremont coined the term "Golden Gate" in 1846, he meant to name the harbor entrance to the San Francisco Bay. In 1937, however, the colorful name became permanently associated with Joseph Strauss's engineering masterpiece—the **Golden Gate Bridge.** Built for only $35 million, the bridge stretches across 1¼ mi. of ocean, its towers looming 65 stories above the bay. It can sway up to 27 ft. in each direction during high winds. The views from the bridge are amazing, especially from the Vista Point at the Marin end. To see the bridge in its entirety, it's best to get a bit farther away. Fort Point and Fort Baker in the Presidio, Land's End in Lincoln Park, Mt. Livermore on Angel Island, and Hawk Hill off Conzelman Rd. in the Marin Headlands all offer spectacular views on clear days. *(MUNI #28 and 29 buses take passengers to the bridge. By car, take Lincoln Blvd.)*

When Spanish settlers forged up the San Francisco peninsula from Baja California in 1769, they established *presidios*, or military outposts, as they went. San Francisco's **Presidio,** the northernmost point of Spanish territory in North America, was dedicated in 1776. It was passed to the US as part of the 1848 Treaty of Guadalupe Hidalgo. It is now part of the **Golden Gate National Recreation Area (GGNRA)**, run by the National Park Service, but don't go expecting to see any major sights.

MARINA AND FORT MASON

PALACE OF FINE ARTS. With its massive open-air rotunda and curving colonnades, the **Palace of Fine Arts** is one of the most impressive structures in the city and its surrounding parklands are a popular picnic spot. It was originally built to commemorate the opening of the Panama Canal and testify to San Francisco's recovery from the 1906 earthquake. Shakespeare's plays are often performed here during the summer. *(On Baker St., between Jefferson and Bay St. next to the Exploratorium. Open daily 6am-9pm. Free.)* The **Palace of Fine Arts Theater,** located behind the rotunda, also hosts various dance and theater performances and film festivals. *(☎ 563-6504; www.palaceoffinearts.org. Call for showtimes and ticket prices.)*

FORT MASON. A decommissioned military post, Fort Mason is now home to many nonprofit and arts-promoting organizations. Most have very little to offer the casual visitor, and consequently the area remains unknown to most travelers, making it a quiet waterfront counterpart to the tourist blitz of Fisherman's Wharf. A seashore pathway connects Fort Mason to the Wharf area. The grounds are also the headquarters of the Golden Gate National Recreation Area. *(The park is at the eastern portion of Fort Mason, near Gashouse Cove. ☎ 441-3400, ext. 3; www.fortmason.org.)*

FISHERMAN'S WHARF AND THE BAY

Piers 39 through 45 on the waterfront provide access to San Francisco's most famous and touristy attractions. Easily visible from boats and the waterfront is Alcatraz Island.

ALCATRAZ. In its 29 years as a maximum-security federal penitentiary, **Alcatraz** harbored a menacing cast of characters, including Al "Scarface" Capone, George "Machine Gun" Kelly, and Robert "The Birdman" Stroud. There were 14 separate escape attempts—some desperate, defiant bolts for freedom, others carefully calculated and innovative. Only one man is known to have survived crossing the bay—he was later recaptured. On "the Rock," the cell-block audio tour takes you back to the infamous days of Alcatraz. Ranger-guided tours leave throughout the day and explore the island's 200 years of occupation, from a hunting and fishing ground for Native Americans to a Civil War outpost to a military prison, a fed-

HOOFIN' IT

San Francisco's amazingly unique neighborhoods, with varied backgrounds, ethnic makeups, and architectural styles, beg for exploration. Before you resign yourself to paying for another touristy trolley ride, lace up your walking shoes and go on a **San Francisco City Guides'** free walking tour. City Guides is a non-profit organization affiliated with the SF Public Library whose volunteers lead visitors all around the city.

You can pick from over 30 tours, depending on your interests. One of the most popular tours is of the Coit Tower murals, where the group gets to see some murals not generally available to the public. Larger groups also gather to visit the landmark Victorian homes, Nob Hill, and Chinatown. Other tours cater to the more offbeat. "Bawdy & Naughty" retraces the old stomping grounds of the Gold Rush's "professional women," while an evening tour explores former beatnik watering holes.

Most of these fun, informal, but highly informative tours last 1½-2hr. There are plenty of stories to be told and places to be explored, and the local guides ensure that by the end of the journey, you know SF and its neighborhoods a little better. Sore calves, however, are unavoidable.

No reservations necessary. See www.sfcityguides.org, call ☎ 557-4266, or pick up a brochure at visitors centers for schedules.

eral prison, and finally a birthplace of the Native American civil rights movement. Now part of the Golden Gate National Recreation Area, Alcatraz is home to diverse plants and tons of tourists. *(The Blue and Gold Fleet runs to Alcatraz. ☎705-8200, tickets 705-5555; www.blueandgoldfleet.com. 14 per day. $11 round-trip, with audio tour $16; ages 62+ $9.75/$15; ages 5-11 $8.25/$11. Often sells out in summer. Reserve in advance.)*

GHIRARDELLI SQUARE. A true chocolate-lovers' heaven, Ghirardelli Sq. houses a mall in what was once a traditional chocolate factory. Here, everyone's got a golden ticket to the **Ghirardelli Chocolate Manufactory,** with its vast selection of chocolatey goodies, as well as the **Ghirardelli Chocolate Shop and Caffe,** which sells a smaller selection of chocolates. Both hand out **free samples** of chocolate, but the Caffe is less crowded. *(Mall: 900 N. Point St. ☎775-5500; www.ghirardellisq.com. Stores open in summer M-Sa 10am-9pm, Su 10am-6pm. Manufactory: Open M-Th and Su 10am-11pm, F-Sa 10am-midnight. Chocolate Shop and Caffe: ☎474-1414. Open M-Th and Su 9am-11pm, F-Sa 9am-midnight.)*

🏛 MUSEUMS

■ **SAN FRANCISCO MUSEUM OF MODERN ART (SFMOMA).** This black-and-white cylindrical museum houses 5 spacious floors of photography, painting, media, and sculpture, with an emphasis on architecture and design. It houses the largest selection of 20th-century American and European art this side of New York City. *(151 3rd St., between Mission and Howard St. ☎357-4000; www.sfmoma.org. 4 free gallery tours per day. Open Memorial Day-Labor Day M-Tu and F-Su 10am-6pm, Th 10am-9pm; Labor Day-Memorial Day M-Tu and F-Su 11am-6pm, Th 11am-9pm. $12.50, seniors $8, students $7, under 13 free. Th 6-9pm half-price. 1st Tu of each month free.)*

EXPLORATORIUM. This museum features over 650 interactive displays—including mini-tornadoes, computer planet-managing, and giant bubble-makers—that explain the world's wonders. The Tactile Dome, a dark maze of tunnels, slides, and crevices, refines your sense of touch. *(3601 Lyon St., in the Marina. ☎563-7337 or 561-0360; www.exploratorium.edu. Open Tu-Su 10am-5pm. $12; students, seniors, disabled, and ages 13-17 $9.50; ages 12-17 $8. Free 1st W of each month. Tactile Dome $15, includes museum admission; reservations recommended.)*

CALIFORNIA PALACE OF THE LEGION OF HONOR. Outside the museum, a copy of Rodin's *Thinker* beckons visitors into the courtyard, where a glass pyramid recalls the Louvre. A thorough catalogue of great masters, from the medieval to the modern, hangs inside and extensive statuary and decorative art collections are spread throughout. Other draws include a 4500-pipe organ, played in free recitals *(Sa-Su 4pm)*. Outside the Palace lies the **Holocaust memorial.** *(In Lincoln Park. ☎863-3330; www.legionofhonor.org. Open Tu-Su 9:30am-5pm. $10, seniors $7, under 17 $6, under 12 free. $2 discount with MUNI transfer; Tu free.)*

CALIFORNIA ACADEMY OF SCIENCES. This is the temporary location (until 2008) of the Golden Gate Park museums. The Steinhart Aquarium, home to over 600 aquatic species, is more lively than the Natural History Museum. *(875 Howard St., between 4th and 5th St. in SoMa. ☎750-7145; www.calacademy.org. Open daily 10am-5pm. $7; seniors, students, and ages 12-17 $4.50; ages 4-11 $2. Free 1st W of each month.)*

YERBA BUENA CENTER FOR THE ARTS. The Yerba Buena Center includes both theater and gallery space, with programs emphasizing the creative process, performance, film, viewer involvement, and local multicultural work. It is surrounded by the Yerba Buena Rooftop Gardens, a vast, popular expanse of granite terraces, waterfalls, fountains, and foliage. Also on the grounds is a restored 1906 carousel.

(701 Mission St. ☎978-2787; www.yerbabuenaarts.org. Open Tu-W and F-Su noon-5pm, Th noon-8pm. Free tours 1st Th of each month 6pm. $6, seniors and students $3. Free 1st Tu of each month. Gardens open daily 6am-10pm. Free. Carousel runs daily 11am-6pm; 2 rides $2.)

MUSEUM OF CRAFT AND FOLK ART. The MOCFA brings together a fascinating collection of crafts and functional art (clothing, furniture, and jewelry) from past and present, near and far, showcasing anything that makes daily life beautiful. *(51 Yerba Buena Ln., between 2nd and 3rd St. in SoMa. ☎775-0991; www.mocfa.org. Open Tu-Su 11am-5pm, Sa 10am-5pm. $4, seniors and ages 12-17 $3, under 12 free.)*

SAN FRANCISCO ART INSTITUTE. The oldest art school west of the Mississippi, the Institute is lodged in a converted mission and has produced several American greats, including Mark Rothko, Ansel Adams, Imogen Cunningham, Dorothea Lange, and James Weeks. To the left as you enter is the Diego Rivera Gallery, one wall of which is covered by a huge 1931 Rivera mural. *(800 Chestnut St., in North Beach. ☎771-7020 or 800-345-7324; www.sfai.edu. Weekly student exhibits with receptions Tu 5-7pm. Open daily June-Aug. 9am-8pm; Sept.-May 9am-9pm. Professional exhibits are housed in the Walter and McBean Galleries. Open Tu-Sa 11am-6pm.)*

🎭 ENTERTAINMENT

MUSIC

Look for the latest live music listings in *S.F. Weekly* and *The Guardian*. Hardcore audiophiles should snag a copy of *Bay Area Music (BAM)*.

▓ **Bottom of the Hill,** 1233 17th St. (☎626-4455, 24hr. info 621-4455; www.bottomofthe-hill.com), between Missouri and Texas St., in Potrero Hill. This intimate club is the best place to see up-and-comers playing everything from alternative to pop, with a focus on rock. The White Stripes, Incubus, and Kid Rock all passed through here. Most Su afternoons in summer feature local bands and all-you-can-eat barbecue for $5 (from 4pm). Usually 21+, with occasional all-ages shows. Cover $5-20. Reservations recommended. Happy hour W-F 4-7pm, otherwise doors open at 8:30pm.

The Independent, 628 Divisadero St. (☎771-1421), at Hayes St., in the Lower Haight. Voted SF's best small live music venue with diverse listings of hip-hop and everything from indie rock and punk to funk, jazz, and reggae. Cover $10-30. Box office open M-F 11am-6pm and 1hr. before the show. Most shows 8pm.

Boom Boom Room, 1601 Fillmore St. (☎673-8000, bar 673-8040; www.boomboom-blues.com), at Geary St., near Japantown. Boom Boom is known as the city's home of "blues, boogie, soul, groove, and funk." The dim interior features live music, often big-name acts, nightly at 9:20pm. Beer $2.50. Mixed drinks $4. Happy hour 4-7:30pm. Cover $5-15, usually free on Su. Open M-F 4pm-2am, Sa-Su 3pm-2am.

Biscuits & Blues, 401 Mason St. (☎292-2583; www.biscuitsandbluessf.com), at Geary St., in Union Sq. Serves Southern fare like spicy jambalaya ($14), but nightly live blues really makes things simmer. Entrees $11-16. Drinks $3-7. Happy hour until 7:30pm with $2 drafts, $4 specialty drinks. All ages. Call for tickets $5-20. Dinner served M-W and Su 6pm-midnight, Th-Sa 6pm-11:30pm. Open M-Sa 6pm-1am, Su 5-10pm.

THEATER

Downtown, **Mason Street** and **Geary Street** constitute **"Theater Row,"** the city's prime place for theatrical entertainment. **TIX Bay Area,** located in a kiosk in Union Sq. on the corner of Geary and Powell St., is a Ticketmaster outlet with tickets for almost all shows and concerts in the city. Buy a seat in advance, or try for cash-only, half-price tickets on the day of the show. *(☎433-7827; www.theatrebayarea.org. Open Tu-Th 11am-6pm, F-Sa 11am-7pm, Su 10am-3pm.)*

Theatre Rhinoceros, 2926 16th St. (☎861-5079; www.therhino.org), at S. Van Ness Ave., in the Mission. From the drag queen starlet to the audacious onstage lesbian lovers, the mural in the foyer says it all: queer, fabulous, diverse. The oldest queer theater in the world. Tickets $15-30; $15 for students and seniors for Su and Th performances. Box office open W-Su 1-6pm. Call in advance for wheelchair access.

Geary Theater, 405 Geary St. (☎749-2228; www.act-sfbay.org), at Mason St., in Union Sq. Home to the renowned American Conservatory Theater, the jewel in SF's theatrical crown. The elegant theater is a show-stealer in its own right. Tickets $12-73 (cheaper for previews and on weekdays). Half-price student, teacher, and senior tickets available 2hr. before showtime. Box office open M and Su noon-6pm, Tu-Sa noon-8pm.

The Orpheum, 1192 Market St. (☎512-7770; www.bestofbroadway-sf.com), at Hyde St., near the Civic Center. Hosts the big Broadway shows. The Orpheum box office also serves 2 sister theaters in the area: **Golden Gate Theatre,** 1 Taylor St., at Market St.; and **Curran Theatre,** 445 Geary St. Box office open M 10am-6pm, Tu-Sa 10am-8:30pm; on show days also Su 11am-7pm.

Magic Theatre, Bldg. D, 3rd fl. (☎441-8822; www.magictheatre.org), in Fort Mason. Stages both international and American premieres. Tickets Tu-Th $25-33; F-Su $30-38; previews $20-25. Senior and student rush tickets available 30min. before the show ($10). Shows at 8 or 8:30pm. Box office open Tu-Sa noon-5pm.

DANCE

▨**Alonzo King's Lines Contemporary Ballet,** 26 7th St. (☎863-3040; www.linesballet.org), at Market St., in Civic Center. One of San Francisco's premier dance companies, specializing in modern and contemporary ballet. Dancers combine elegant classical moves with athletic flair to the music of great living jazz and world music composers. Tours extensively but 2-week fall season and 1-week spring season are performed at the Yerba Buena Center for the Arts. Tickets $20-50.

San Francisco Ballet (☎865-2000; www.sfballet.org), in the Opera House in Civic Center. One of the largest US ballet companies. Season runs late Jan. to early May. Tickets from $30; available online or by phone M-F noon-4pm. Box office opens at noon on performance days. Student, senior, and military tickets $10-20 for same-day performance.

SPORTS

The **San Francisco Giants** (☎800-734-4268, tickets 510-762-2277; www.sfgiants.com) play at "the best address in baseball," ▨**SBC Park** (formerly Pac Bell Park) in SoMa, on the water off Townsend St. Barry Bonds, the single-season record holder for home runs, has hit several famous bombs into McCovey Cove, a portion of San Francisco Bay just beyond right field where ball-hungry boaters congregate. Most games sell out before the season starts, except for 500 seats reserved for day-of-game sale. Those not wanting to pay or unable to get tickets can watch the action for free through a fence below the right field bleachers. (Tickets $10-45. Tours of the park at 10:30am and 12:30pm daily, except game days; ☎972-2400. $10.) The NFL's **49ers** (☎468-2249; www.49ers.com) still play at the windy **Candlestick Park** (☎467-1994). Now officially called **Monster Park,** the stadium is 8 mi. south of the city with its own exit off U.S. 101. MUNI offers express round-trip service to the park via the 9x, 28x, and 47x buses (www.sfmuni.com or call 511 for transit info).

▧ FESTIVALS

Musical, cultural, ethnic, and queer festivals take place year-round in San Francisco. The High Holy Day of the queer calendar, ▨**Pride Day** celebrates with a parade and events downtown starting at 10:30am. (☎864-3733; www.sfpride.org.

Last week of June.) The leather-and-chains gang lets it all hang out at the **Folsom Street Fair,** Pride Day's ruder, raunchier little brother. (On Folsom St. between 7th and 11th St. ☎861-3247; www.folsomstreetfair.com. Last week of Sept.) In fall, the **San Francisco Fringe Festival** (☎931-1094; www.sffringe.org), beginning the first Thursday after Labor Day, is experimental theater at its finest, with over 60 international companies presenting short shows, all for less than $8. **Ghirardelli Square Chocolate Festival** (☎775-5500; www.ghirardellisq.com), in Ghirardelli Sq., makes the beginning of September a chocolate paradise. Follow the drummers and dancing skeletons to **Día de los Muertos** (Day of the Dead; ☎821-1155), the festive Mexican celebration of the dead. The party starts on the evening of November 2 at the Mission Cultural Center, 2868 Mission St. at 25th St.

◪ NIGHTLIFE

Nightlife in San Francisco is as varied as the city's personal ads. Everyone from the shy first-timer to the bearded strap daddy can find places to go on a Saturday (or Tuesday) night. The spots listed below are divided into bars and clubs, but the lines get pretty blurred in SF after dark, and even cafes hop at night. For additional information, check out the nightlife listings in the *S.F. Weekly, S.F. Bay Guardian,* and *Metropolitan.* **All clubs listed are 21+.**

BARS AND LOUNGES

▧ **Noc Noc,** 5574 Haight St. (☎861-5811), between Steiner and Fillmore St., in the Lower Haight. The only place in the Haight that gets happening before 10pm. Neo-hippies and other inheritors of the Haight-Ashbury aesthetic mingle at high-backed bar stools, relax cross-legged on the padded floor cushions, or otherwise ensconce themselves in the bar's dimly lit nooks and crannies. Happy hour daily 5-7pm; pints $2.50. Open daily 5pm-2am.

111 Minna St. (☎974-1719; www.111minnagallery.com), at 2nd St., in SoMa. A funky gallery by day and hipster groove-spot by night. The bar turns club W 5-10pm for a crowded night of progressive house music. Check for openings and receptions. Cocktails and beer $4. Cover usually $5-10. Gallery open M-F noon-5pm. Bar hours vary widely; call or check website for calendar and hours.

Lush Lounge, 1092 Post St. (☎771-2022; www.thelushlounge.com), at Polk St., in Nob Hill. Dim lighting, Hollywood throwback decor, and frozen margaritas ($3). Nostalgia tunes stream through the speakers. Open daily 4pm-2am; in summer M-Tu from 5pm.

Swig, 561 Geary St. (☎931-7292; www.swig-bar.com), between Taylor and Jones St., in Union Sq. Outfitted with an intimate back room and an upstairs smoking lounge, this chic morning cafe, trendy power lunch site, and hopping nightclub has already entertained Eminem and the Wallflowers. Open daily 6am-2am.

CLUBS

El Río, 3158 Mission St. (☎282-3325), between César Chavez and Valencia St., in the Mission. El Río sprawls in all directions with a chill lounge and expansive dance floor. The patio is center stage for young, stylin' urbanites who while away the hours playing cards and smoking cigars. Diverse international crowd. M $1 drinks. Tu $2 margaritas, free pool. "Arabian Nights" Th. World music F. Live salsa Su. Cover M $2, Th after 10pm $5, Su $7. Open M-Th 5pm-2am, F-Su 3pm-2am.

Pink, 2925 16th St. (☎431-8889), at S. Van Ness Ave., in the Mission. Pink satin and gossamer draperies lend a chic lounge feel during the week, but expect clubbers F-Sa. A mix of world music, soulful house, Cuban jazz, and Afro beats blasts on the speakers. Cover $5, F-Sa $10. Open Tu-Th and Su 9:30pm-2am, F-Sa 9:30pm-3am.

The EndUp, 401 6th St. (☎646-0999; www.theendup.com), at Harrison St. in SoMa. A wide range of people, many of them beautiful, inevitably end up here for after-hours fun. DJs spin progressive house for a very energetic, mostly straight crowd. "Otherwhirled" party Sa 6am-noon. Infamous "T" Dance (27 years strong) Su 6am-8pm. Cover $10-15. Open Th 10:30pm-4am, F 10pm-6am, Sa 6am-noon and 10pm-4am, Su 6am-8pm.

GLBT NIGHTLIFE

■ **Divas,** 1081 Post St. (☎928-6006; www.divassf.com), at Polk St., in the Tenderloin. This full-time transgender nightclub is simply fabulous and gets even better after 11:30pm. 1st level bar, 2nd level dance floor, 3rd level TV lounge. Tu Talent (singing, comedy, lip synching); $50 prize. Pole dancers W-Th. Midnight drag show F-Sa. Happy hour M-F 5-7pm with $3 well drinks, wine, domestic beer. Drinks normally $4-8. Cover W-Th $7, F-Sa $10. Ladies free before 11pm. Open daily 6am-2am.

The Bar on Castro, 456 Castro St. (☎626-7220), between Market and 18th St. Padded walls and dark plush couches perfect for eyeing the stylish young crowd, scoping the techno-raging dance floor, or watching *Queer as Folk* on Su. Happy hour M-F 3-8pm; beer $2.25. Su beer $1.75. Open M-F 4pm-2am, Sa-Su noon-2am.

Wild Side West, 424 Cortland Ave. (☎647-3099), at Wool St., in Bernal Heights. The oldest lesbian bar in SF is a friendly neighborhood favorite for women and men alike. The hidden highlight is a backyard jungle with benches, fountains, and scrap-art statues contributed by patrons. Open daily 1pm-2am.

THE BAY AREA

BERKELEY   ☎510

Berkeley implanted itself in the nation's consciousness as a haven for progressive iconoclasts in 1964, when activist Mario Savio led the UC Berkeley student body in a series of highly visible protests. While the town remains staunchly liberal, true radicals may chuckle at the irony of today's yuppified Berkeley, where polished storefronts sell organic goods to a niche market of Marxists with bourgeois incomes. Catering to its stylish students and hippies, Berkeley's restaurants range from high California cuisine to family-run Asian takeout, and its bookstores provide the perfect material for an afternoon spent sunning in the park, making the city an ideal trip from San Francisco.

■ ■ **ORIENTATION AND PRACTICAL INFORMATION.** Berkeley lies across the Bay Bridge northeast of San Francisco, just north of Oakland. If you're driving from SF, cross the Bay Bridge on **I-80** and take one of the four Berkeley exits. The **University Avenue Exit** leads most directly to UC Berkeley and downtown. **Shattuck Avenue** is west of campus and is Berkeley's main north-south route. The heart of town, **Telegraph Avenue,** runs south from the UC Berkeley Student Union. **Bay Area Rapid Transit (BART)** has three Berkeley stops. The Downtown Berkeley station, 2160 Shattuck Ave., at Center St., is close to the western edge of campus, while the North Berkeley station, at Delaware and Sacramento St., lies four blocks north of University Ave. The Ashby stop, at Ashby and Adeline St., provides access to South Berkeley. (☎465-2278; www.bart.gov. 20-30min. to downtown SF, $2.90-3.10.) **Alameda County Transit** city buses #15, 40, 43, and 51 run from the Berkeley BART station to downtown Oakland on Martin Luther King, Jr. Way, Telegraph Ave., Shattuck Ave., and Broadway, respectively ($1.50; seniors, disabled, and ages 5-12 $0.75; under 5 free; transfers $0.25). **Visitor Info: Berkeley Convention and Visitor Bureau,** 2015 Center St., at Milvia St., has area maps and tons of brochures.

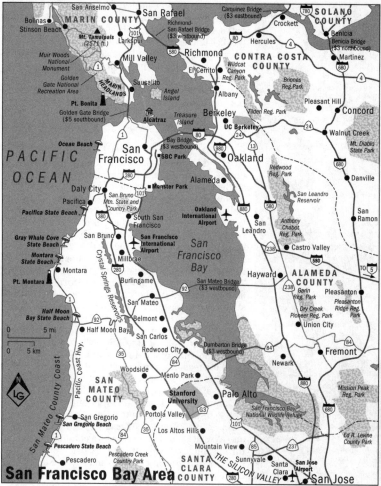

San Francisco Bay Area

(☎549-8710. Open M-F 9am-1pm and 2-5pm.) **UC Berkeley Visitors Center,** 101 University Hall, at the corner of University Ave. and Oxford St., offers maps, campus info, and tours. (☎642-5215; www.berkeley.edu. Open M-F 8:30am-4:30pm.) **Internet Access: Berkeley Public Library,** 2090 Kittredge St. (☎981-6100. Open M-Tu noon-8pm, W-Sa 10am-6pm. Free.) **Post Office:** 2000 Allston Way, at Milvia St. (☎649-3155. Open M-F 9am-5pm, Sa 9am-3pm.) **Postal Code:** 94704. **Area Code:** 510.

ⅿ ACCOMMODATIONS. Though the naive visitor might expect to find Berkeley overrun with communes and hostels, there are surprisingly few cheap accommodations in Berkeley. The **Berkeley-Oakland Bed and Breakfast Network** (☎547-6380; www.bbonline.com/ca/berkeley-oakland) coordinates some great East Bay B&Bs with a range of rates (singles $85-175). No-frills motels line University Ave. between Shattuck and Sacramento St.; ritzier places reside downtown, especially

MUSIC TO MY EARS

From its 1990 founding on Tele-graph Ave., Amoeba Music has been called a "shoppers' para-dise" and the "world's greatest record store." The store was cre-ated by music lovers (all staff are either musicians, music junkies, or both) to cater to smaller, niche markets and to allow their cus-tomers to create the best music collections possible.

As the world's largest indepen-dent record store, they stock thousands of titles criss-crossing all genres and media. You'll find Gwen Stefani and Coldplay next to Ella Fitzgerald on vinyl and New Kids on the Block on cassette. On top of that, there is a selection of imported music and a massive video and DVD collection.

Most appealing to the budget traveler, the racks of used music and movies are dirt-cheap, with CDs you'd actually want to listen to going for as little as $2. The only thing Amoeba lacks is the all-too-common record store music snobbery. As an added bonus, the friendly staff members may transform into in-house DJs in the San Francisco or Hollywood stores during the evening. At Amoeba, it's all about the music.

Amoeba Music, 2455 Telegraph Ave. (☎510-549-1125). Open M-Sa 10am-10:30pm, Su 11am-9pm. Other locations in San Francisco and Hollywood.

on Durant Ave. **UC Berkeley Summer Visitor Housing ❸** has simple college dorms, a great location, shared baths, and free linens, towels, and Internet access. (☎642-4108. Open June to mid-Aug. Check-in 3-6pm or call ahead. Singles and doubles $55 per night, $330 per week. D/MC/V.) The **YMCA ❷,** 2001 Allston Way, features such amenities as a communal kitchen, shared bath, computer room, and TV lounge. Use of the pool and fitness facilities is included. (☎848-6800. 10-night max. stay. Reception 7am-9:30pm. 18+. Sin-gles $39-46; doubles $50-60.)

◘ **FOOD.** Berkeley's **Gourmet Ghetto,** at Shattuck Ave. and Cedar St., is where "California Cuisine" began. The north end of **Telegraph Avenue** caters to student appetites and wallets, with late-night offer-ings of all varieties along **Durant Avenue.** If you'd rather talk to a cow than eat one, you're in luck; Ber-keley does greens like nowhere else. A growing num-ber of international eateries are helping to diversify the area. **Solano Avenue** to the north is great for Asian cuisine and budget grub, while **4th Street** to the west is home to trendy upscale eats. ▧**Chez Panisse ❺,** 1517 Shattuck Ave., epitomizes California Cuisine, and was opened by chef Alice Waters in 1971. Alice still prepares the nightly fixed menu (4 courses; $50-75) in the cozy downstairs restaurant. Upstairs, the more casual cafe serves similar, but less expensive, fare. (☎548-5525, cafe 548-5049; www.chezpa-nisse.com. Starters $7-13. Entrees $15-20. Reserva-tions for restaurant or cafe strongly recommended; available up to 1 month in advance. Restaurant open M-Sa 6-9:30pm. Cafe open M-Th 11:30am-3pm and 5-10:30pm, F-Sa 11:30am-3:30pm and 5-11:30pm.) Voted the best pizza in the Bay Area by the *San Francisco Chronicle,* ▧**Zachary's Pizza ❸,** 1853 Sol-ano Ave., at Colusa Ave., attracts a cult-like following for its Chicago-style stuffed pies. The spinach and mushroom is Zachary's "Pride and Joy." (☎525-5950. Large pies $19-28. Open M-Th and Su 11am-9:30pm, F-Sa 11am-10:30pm. Cash only.) **Café Intermezzo ❶,** 2442 Telegraph Ave., at Haste St., serves heaping sal-ads ($3.50-7), huge sandwiches on freshly baked bread, and hot soups. (☎849-4592. Sandwiches $5. Open daily 10am-10pm. Cash only.)

▨ **SIGHTS.** In 1868, the private College of Califor-nia and the public Agricultural, Mining, and Mechani-cal Arts College united as the **University of California.** The 178-acre university in Berkeley was the first of nine University of California campuses, so by senior-ity it has sole right to the nickname "Cal." The cam-pus is bounded on the south by Bancroft Way, on the west by Oxford St., on the north by Hearst Ave., and on the east by Tilden Park. From Telegraph Ave., enter through **Sather Gate** into **Sproul Plaza,** both sites of celebrated student sit-ins and bloody confrontations with police. Free 90min. tours explore the campus each day. (Tours M-Sa 10am, Su 1pm. Weekday tours depart from 101 University Hall; weekend tours depart from the Campanile.) **Sather Tower** is the official name of the Campanile, the tallest building on campus; you can ride to its observation level for a great view of the San Francisco Bay. (Open M-F 10am-4pm, $2; tip-top is not wheelchair accessible.) The ▓**Berkeley Art Museum (BAM),** 2626 Bancroft Way, is most respected for its collection of 20th-century American and Asian art. BAM will be celebrating its centennial in 2006 with an exhibition of visual and historical treasures from the original Bancroft collection, the only library to have survived the 1906 earthquake and fire. The **Pacific Film Archive** is a branch of BAM and has over 500 public screenings each year; check online for details. (☎642-0808; www.bampfa.berkeley.edu. Open W and F-Su 11am-5pm, Th 11am-7pm. $8; students, seniors, disabled, and ages 12-17 $5. First Th of each month free.) You haven't really visited Berkeley until you've been on **Telegraph Avenue,** lined with a motley assortment of cafes, bookstores, and used clothing and record stores, plus a few sidewalk stands from which the mutterings of ex-hippies provide a soundtrack for window shopping. In the forested hills in the eastern part of the city lies beautiful **Tilden Regional Park.** By car or bike, take Spruce St. to Grizzly Peak Blvd. to Canon Ave. Hiking, biking, running, and riding trails criss-cross the park and provide impressive views of the Bay Area. (☎562-7275. Open daily 8am-10pm. Free.) Inside the park, the small beach at **Lake Anza** is a popular swimming spot on the hottest summer days. (☎843-2137. Open in summer daily 11am-10pm. $3.50, seniors and children $2.50.)

▓ **NIGHTLIFE.** ▓**Jupiter,** 2181 Shattuck Ave., near the BART station, houses a huge beer garden and offers live music and terrific wood-fired pizza for $8. (☎843-8277. Open M-Th 11:30am-1am, F 11:30am-2am, Sa noon-2am, Su noon-midnight.) **Blakes,** 2367 Telegraph Ave., near Durant Ave., is a jam-packed and unabashed meat market. (☎848-0886. Local bands W-Sa. Power hour M-F 2-6pm; $0.75 off pints and cocktails. Drink specials 9pm-midnight; W $1 PBR, Th $2.75 well drinks. Cover $2-12. Open M-F 11:30am-2am, Sa noon-2am, Su noon-1am.) The boisterous and friendly **Triple Rock Brewery,** 1920 Shattuck Ave., north of Berkeley Way, was the first of Berkeley's many brewpubs. (☎843-2739. Award-winning Red Rock Ale $3.75. Open M-W and Su 11:30am-midnight, Th-Sa 11:30am-1am; rooftop garden closes 10pm; kitchen closes M-W and Su 10pm, Th-Sa 11:30pm.)

MARIN COUNTY ☎415

Just across the Golden Gate Bridge, Marin (muh-RIN) County is strikingly beautiful, politically liberal, and visibly wealthy. Suburbia rules in the east part of the county, but on the west side, the cathedral-like stillness of ancient redwoods, sharp scent of eucalyptus (though not a native species), brilliant wildflowers, high, windy bluffs, and crashing surf converge along Hwy. 1.

▐ TRANSPORTATION

Buses: Golden Gate Transit (☎455-2000, in SF 923-2000; www.goldengate.org), provides bus service between San Francisco and Marin County via the Golden Gate Bridge, as well as local service in Marin ($3.25). **West Marin Stagecoach** (☎526-3239; www.marin-stagecoach.org) provides weekday service connecting West Marin communities to the rest of the county. Stops include: Muir Beach, Pt. Reyes Station, Samuel P. Taylor Park, San Anselmo, and Stinson Beach. Call for schedules and routes. $1.50.

CALIFORNIA

Ferries: Golden Gate Ferry (☎455-2000) runs from San Francisco to the Sausalito terminal at the end of Market St. and to the Larkspur terminal ($6.45, under 18 $4.85, seniors and disabled $3.20). **Blue and Gold Fleet** (☎773-1188) runs ferries from Pier 41 at Fisherman's Wharf to Sausalito and Tiburon ($7.50, ages 5-12 $4.25, under 5 free). Offices open M-F 6am-8pm, Sa-Su 7am-8pm.

Taxi: Belaire Cab Co. ☎388-1234.

Bike Rental: Cycle Analysis (☎663-9164; www.cyclepointreyes.com), a trailer in the empty, grassy lot at 4th and Main St. off Hwy. 1 in Point Reyes Station. Rents unsuspended bikes ($10 per hr., $32 per day), front-suspension mountain bikes ($12/$35), and child trailers ($30 per day). Emergency repairs and advice for self-guided tours. Open M-Th by appointment, F-Su 10am-5pm.

■ 🔢 ORIENTATION AND PRACTICAL INFORMATION

The Marin peninsula lies at the northern end of the San Francisco Bay and is connected to the city by **U.S. 101** via the **Golden Gate Bridge.** U.S. 101 extends north inland to Santa Rosa and Sonoma County, while **Route 1** winds north along the Pacific coast. The **Richmond-San Rafael Bridge** connects Marin to the East Bay via I-**580.** Gas is scarce and expensive in West Marin, so fill up in town before you head out for the coast. Drivers should exercise caution in West Marin, where roads are narrow, sinuous, and perched on the edges of cliffs.

Visitor Information: There are several visitors centers throughout the county; one for Marin County itself and several for its parks and outdoors attractions.

Marin County Visitors Bureau, 1013 Larkspur Landing Cr. (☎925-2060; www.marincvb.org), near the Sir Francis Drake Blvd. exit off U.S. 101, by the ferry terminal. Open M-F 9am-5pm.

Point Reyes National Seashore Headquarters (also referred to as Bear Valley Visitor Center; ☎464-5100; www.nps.gov/pore), on Bear Valley Rd., ½ mi. west of Olema. Open M-F 9am-5pm, Sa-Su and holidays 8am-5pm.

Pan Toll Ranger's Station, 801 Panoramic Hwy. (☎388-2070), in Mt. Tamalpais State Park, about 2½ mi. inland from Stinson Beach. Bus #63 stops on weekends (about 5 per day). Open daily June-Aug. 9am-6pm; Sept.-May intermittently.

Muir Woods National Monument Visitors Center (☎388-2596; www.nps.gov/muwo), near the entrance to Muir Woods. Muir Woods trail map $2 (free download on website). Open daily Sept.-May 9am-6pm; June-Aug. 8am-8pm.

Marin Headlands Visitors Center, Bldg. 948, Fort Barry (☎331-1540), at Bunker and Field Rd. The center is also a museum. Open daily 9:30am-4:30pm. Wheelchair accessible.

Post Office: 15 Calle del Mar (☎868-1504), at Shoreline Hwy. in Stinson Beach. Open M-F 8:30am-5pm. **Postal Code:** 94970. **Area Code:** 415.

🏠 ACCOMMODATIONS

▓ **West Point Inn** (☎388-9955, reservations 646-0702), on Mt. Tamalpais, 2 mi. up Old Stage Rd. Park at the Pan Toll Ranger Station ($6, seniors $5) and hike or bike up. Not the lap of luxury, but one hell of an experience. Propane-generated heat, light, and refrigeration; no electricity. Bring sleeping bag, food, and flashlight. 7 private rooms, 5 private cabins, and a well-equipped kitchen. Chore required. Reservations required. Sa vacancies are rare. Closed M and Su nights. $35, under 18 $18, under 5 free. ❷

Marin Headlands Hostel (HI), at Fort Berry (☎331-2777; www.norcalhostels.org). Take the Alexander Ave. exit and follow the signs at Fort Berry. A converted century-old house with an international collection of backpackers. Office open 7:30am-11:30pm. Linens $1. Towels $0.50. Alcohol prohibited. Dorms $18-22. ❶

Point Reyes Hostel (HI), just off Limoatour Rd., (☎663-8811; norcalhostels.org), 2 mi. from Limatour beach in the Point Reyes National Seashore. Miles from civilization, this unique hostel provides shelter and solace in the wilderness. Linen $1; sleeping bags encouraged. Towels $1. Chore required. Check-in 4:30-9:30pm. Check-out 10am. Lock-out 10am-4:30pm. Dorms $18, under 17 $10. ❶

The Headlands (☎331-1540; www.nps.gov/goga/camping/index.htm) offers 3 walk-in campgrounds with 11 primitive campsites for individual backpackers and small groups. No water. No fires or pets allowed. Showers and kitchen ($2 each) at Headlands Hostel. Free cold showers at Rodeo Beach. 3-day max. stay per site; 9-day max. stay per year. Reserve up to 90 days in advance. All individual sites free with a permit from the Marin Headlands Visitors Center (see above). ❶

FOOD

Marinites take their fruit juices, tofu, and double-shot cappuccinos very seriously; restaurateurs know this, and raise their alfalfa sprouts and prices accordingly.

Venice Gourmet Delicatessen, 625 Bridgeway (☎332-3544), in Sausalito. Serves a wide variety of sandwiches ($3.75-6.50) and side dishes ($1.50-5) in a Mediterranean-style marketplace. A few outdoor tables have a stunning view of the San Francisco sky-line, but the sandwiches are perfect for a picnic at the beach. Open daily 9am-6pm; summer weekends until 7pm. ❷

Avatar's Punjabi Burrito, 15 Madrona St. (☎381-8293), in Mill Valley. Take chickpeas, rice, chutney, yogurt, and spice; add tofu and meats; and wrap in yummy Indian flat-bread for an inspired and filling meal. Burritos $5.50-8.50. Open M-Sa 11am-8pm. ❷

Bubba's Diner, 566 San Anselmo Ave. (☎459-6862), in San Anselmo. A local favorite with all the essentials. All-day breakfast, including "chocoholic" pancakes ($8), pre-pared next to the old-fashioned counter. Open M and W-F 9am-9pm, Sa-Su 8am-9pm. ❸

SIGHTS

Marin's proximity to San Francisco makes it a popular daytrip destination. Almost everything worth seeing or doing in Marin is outdoors. An efficient visitor can hop between parks and enjoy several short hikes along the coast and through the red-wood forests in the same day, topping it off with dinner in one of the small cities, but the roads are winding and the RVs ahead of you will probably slow you down.

MARIN HEADLANDS. Fog-shrouded hills just west of the Golden Gate Bridge con-stitute the Marin Headlands. These windswept ridges, precipitous cliffs, and hid-den sandy beaches offer superb hiking and biking within minutes of downtown SF. For instant gratification, drive up to any of the several look-out spots and pose for your own postcard-perfect shot of the Golden Gate Bridge and the city skyline.

POINT REYES NATIONAL SEASHORE. Surrounded by nearly 100 mi. of isolated coastline, Point Reyes National Seashore is a wilderness of pine forests, chaparral ridges, and grassy foothills. *(Hwy. 1 provides direct access to the park from the north or south; Sir Francis Drake Blvd. comes west from U.S. 101 at San Rafael.)* The **Point Reyes Light-house** is at the very tip of the dramatic, windswept point. From December to Feb-ruary, migrating gray whales can be spotted from the overlook. *(Follow Sir Francis Drake Blvd. to its end, 20 mi. from the visitors center. Lighthouse Visitors Center ☎669-1534. Access to lighthouse via 300 stairs. Open M and Th-Su 10am-4:30pm.)*

MOUNT TAMALPAIS AND MUIR WOODS. Between the towns of eastern Marin and the rocky bluffs of western Marin rests beautiful **Mount Tamalpais State Park** (Mt. Tam). The park has miles of challenging trails on and around Mt. Tam (2571

CALIFORNIA

ft.). The bubbling waterfall on Cataract Trail *(off Hwy. 1, follow signs)* and the Gardner Lookout on the east peak are worthy destinations. *(☎388-2070. Free. Parking $6, seniors $5.)* Visit the Pan Toll Ranger Station, on Panoramic Hwy., for trail suggestions and biking restrictions. On weekends and holidays, bus #63 stops at the ranger station between the Golden Gate Bridge and Stinson Beach. At the center of the state park is **Muir Woods National Monument,** a 560-acre grove of ancient redwoods. Spared from logging by the steep sides of Redwood Canyon, these massive redwoods tower over the rest of the silent forest. Go in the evening to avoid crowds. *(5 mi. west of U.S. 101 on Hwy. 1. ☎388-2595. Open 8am-dusk. $3, under 17 free.)*

BEACHES. Sheltered **Muir Beach** is scenic and popular with families. The crowds thin out significantly after a 5min. climb on the shore rocks to the left. *(Open dawn-9pm.)* Six miles to the north, ▓**Stinson Beach** attracts a younger, rowdier surfer crowd, although cold and windy conditions often leave them languishing on dry land. *(Bus #63 runs from Sausalito to Stinson Beach on weekends and holidays. Open 9am-1hr. after sunset.)* The Bard visits Stinson Beach from July to October during **Shakespeare at Stinson.** *(☎868-1115; www.shakespeareatstinson.org.)* Between Muir and Stinson Beaches lies Red Rocks Beach, where many beachgoers do without their swimsuits. The beach is a secluded spot reached by a steep hike from a parking area 1 mi. south of Stinson Beach.

WINE COUNTRY

NAPA VALLEY   ☎707

Napa catapulted American wine into the big leagues in 1976, when a bottle of red from the area's Stag's Leap Vineyards beat a bottle of critically acclaimed (and unfailingly French) Château Lafitte-Rothschild in a blind taste test in Paris. Napa Valley is certainly the best-known of America's wine-growing regions. Its grape-dotted hills, natural hot springs, and consistently gorgeous weather attract everyone from the well-to-do urbanite staying in a high-priced B&B to the group of tourists cruising in a rental limousine. Expect insufferable traffic congestion, especially at the south end of Napa where all the major highways meet. Napa's dense collection of vineyards promises winery after winery of intoxicating pleasure and vistas that are equally disarming.

◢ ⃗ ORIENTATION AND PRACTICAL INFORMATION

Scenic **Route 29 (Saint Helena Highway)** runs north from **Napa** through Napa Valley and the well-groomed villages of **Yountville** and **Saint Helena** (where it's called Main St.) to **Calistoga's** soothing spas. The relatively short distances between wineries may seem unpleasantly long on weekends when the roads crawl with visitors. The **Silverado Trail,** parallel to Rte. 29, is much less crowded and accesses many wineries, but watch out for cyclists. Napa is 14 mi. east of Sonoma on **Route 12.** From San Francisco, take U.S. 101 over the Golden Gate Bridge, then follow Rte. 37 east to catch Rte. 29, which runs north to Napa.

Public Transit: Valley Intercity Neighborhood Express (VINE), 1151 Pearl St. (☎800-696-6443, TDD 226-9722; www.napavalleyvine.net), has a few bus services that cover the entire stretch of Napa Valley from Vallejo to Calistoga. Schedules vary, generally M-Sa 6:30am-7pm. $1-2.50, students $0.75-1.80, seniors $0.50-1.25. Ask for free transfers. The nearest **Greyhound** station is in Vallejo at 1500 Lemon St. (☎643-7661 or 800-231-2222; www.greyhound.com).

Bike Rental: **St. Helena Cyclery,** 1156 Main St. (☎963-7736; www.sthelenacyclery.com). Hybrid bikes $10 per hr., $30 per day; road bikes $50 per day; tandem bikes $70 per day. All bikes come with maps, helmet, and lock. Reservations recommended. Open M-Sa 9:30am-5:30pm, Su 10am-5pm.

Visitor Info: Napa Valley Conference & Visitors Bureau, 1310 Town Ctr. (☎226-7459; www.napavalley.org). Provides free maps, helpful info, and the useful *Napa Valley Guidebook* ($6). Ask about any specials from local businesses. Open daily 9am-5pm. **St. Helena Chamber of Commerce,** 1010A Main St. (☎963-4456; www.sthelena.com). Eager to help. Open M-F 10am-5pm, Sa 11am-3pm. **Calistoga Chamber of Commerce,** 1458 Lincoln Ave. (☎942-6333; www.calistogafun.com). Open M-F 10am-5pm, Sa 10am-4pm, Su 11am-3pm.

Winery Tours: Napa Valley Wine Train, 1275 McKinstry St. (☎253-2111 or 800-427-4124; www.winetrain.com), offers dining and drinking on board, traveling from Napa to St. Helena and back. Train ride 3hr. M-F 11am and 6pm; Sa-Su 8:30am, 12:10, 5:30pm. Ticket and meal plans $35-90. Advance reservations and payments required.

Police: 1539 1st St. (☎253-4451), in Napa; 1234 Washington St. (☎942-2810), in Calistoga.

Medical Services: Queen of the Valley Hospital, 1000 Trancas St. (☎252-4411), in Napa.

Post Office: 1625 Trancas St. (☎255-0190), in Napa. Open M-F 9am-5pm. **Postal Code:** 94558. **Area Code:** 707.

ACCOMMODATIONS

Rooms in Napa Valley go quickly despite high prices; reserve ahead. Though Napa is close to the Bay Area, smaller towns prove more wallet-friendly. Although certainly not cheap, Calistoga is a good first choice; the quaint town is a short drive from many wineries and is close to Old Faithful Geyser, Petrified Forest, and Bothe-Napa State Park. It is also home to natural hot-spring spas. Campers will save a bundle, but should be prepared for intense summer heat.

Golden Haven Hot Springs Spa and Resort, 1713 Lake St. (☎942-6793; www.goldenhaven.com), a few blocks from Lincoln Ave., in Calistoga. Large and tastefully decorated rooms. TV, fridge, and private bath, but no phones. Mineral swimming pool and hot tub access. No children under 16 F-Sa. 2-night min. stay on weekends. Room with queen-sized bed $79-95, with private sauna $129-149; king-sized bed $85-99, with kitchenette $119-149, with jacuzzi $155-199. ❹

WATERING THE WINE

California's sunny climate produces more than just a nice tan; it also yields the world's most alcoholic wines. The mild weather encourages grapes to develop higher sugar concentrations, resulting in the full-bodied wines for which the state is known. In the past, most California wines contained 12-13% alcohol, but over the last decade growers have begun ripening grapes on the vine for a longer period of time in order to develop a more complex flavor. This practice also allows for the development of more sugar, and, once all of that extra sugar ferments, higher alcohol content. Today, the majority of California wines have between 14% and 18% alcohol. It may seem like a small difference, but a 15% bottle of wine has 25% more alcohol than a 12% bottle.

Some critics say the boost in alcohol alters the wine drinker's experience, because the alcohol overpowers the wine's unique flavor. Rather than destroy the balance of their wines, some vintners have taken to adding water during the fermentation process to dilute the potent wine. Purists condemn the practice as fraudulent, while proponents maintain "watering back" results in a better, more elegant wine. Consumers don't appear to have noticed the debate, and continue to support California's wineries, which exported $15 billion worth of wine last year.

Calistoga Inn and Brewery, 1250 Lincoln Ave. (☎942-4101; www.calistogainn.com), at the corner of Rte. 29, in Calistoga. 18 simple, country rooms that barely fit a queen-sized bed. Shared bathrooms. Microbrewery and restaurant downstairs. Rooms May-Oct. M-Th and Su $75, F $100, Sa $125; low season M-F and Su $65, Sa $100. ❹

Bothe-Napa Valley State Park, 3801 Rte. 29 (☎942-4575, reservations 800-444-7275; www.napanet.net/~bothe), north of St. Helena. 50 rustic sites near Ritchey Creek Canyon. Toilets, fire pits, and picnic tables at each site. Pool $3, under 17 $1. Hot showers $0.25 per 3min. Check-in 2pm. Park open daily 8am-dusk. Sites for up to 8 people and 1 vehicle $25. Picnic area day use $8. ❶

🍴 FOOD

Extremely cheap eats aren't an option in Wine Country. Picnics are a potentially inexpensive alternative—many wineries have picnic grounds, but most require patronage. The **Napa Farmers Market,** 500 1st St., at Soscol Ave., offers a sampling of the valley's produce. (☎252-7142. Open Tu and Sa 7:30am-noon.) **Cal Mart,** 1491 Lincoln Ave. (☎942-6271), in Calistoga, provides reasonably priced groceries.

Taylor's Automatic Refresher, 933 Main St. (☎963-3486), on Rte. 29, in St. Helena. Roadside stand with burgers, sandwiches, fries, and the obligatory wine selection. The Texas Burger (pepper jack cheese, guacamole, salsa, and jalapenos; $8) pairs well with a thick milkshake ($5). Outdoor seating. Open daily 10:30am-9pm. ❷

First Squeeze Cafe and Juice Bar, 1126 1st St. (☎224-6762), in Napa. A friendly staff serves up healthy favorites like the Vanessa (grilled tofu with avocado on nut bread), huevos rancheros ($8), and fruit smoothies ($4). Beer and wine $2.50-3.50. Breakfast served until 2pm. Open M-F 7am-3pm, Sa-Su 8am-3pm. AmEx/D/DC/MC/V. ❷

Checkers, 1414 Lincoln Ave. (☎942-9300), in Calistoga. A nice but casual bistro, Checkers specializes in mouthwatering pizzas (sun-dried tomato and artichoke $17) and pastas (spinach and mozzarella ravioli $12). Carnivores should come at lunch for thick sandwiches like roasted leg of lamb on focaccia ($9). Open 11:30am-9:30pm, lunch sandwiches served until 3pm. ❸

🍷 WINERIES

There are over 250 wineries in Napa County, nearly two-thirds of which line Rte. 29 and the Silverado Trail in Napa Valley. Some wineries have free tastings, some have free tours, and some charge for both; all have large selections of bottled wine available for purchase at prices cheaper than in stores. A good way to begin your Napa Valley experience is with a tour such as the ones offered at **Domaine Carneros,** or a free tastings class, like the one on Saturday mornings at **Goosecross Cellars,** 1119 State Ln. (☎944-1986; open daily 11am-4pm; classes Sa 11am-12:30pm), in Yountville. **◼V. Sattui,** named "Best Winery in California" at the 2004 California State Fair, is one of the few wineries in the valley that only sells at its winery, which means great prices. The family-owned operation also has a gourmet cheese counter, meat shop, and bakery. (1111 White Ln., at Rte. 29, in St. Helena. ☎963-7774 or 800-799-2337; www.vsattui.com. Picnic area for customers. Very popular and crowded free tastings. Open daily Mar.-Oct. 9am-6pm; Nov.-Feb. 9am-5pm.) **◼Mumm Napa** produces only sparkling wines, but has a variety of them designed to fit any palette. A free tour illuminates the sparkling winemaking process and tastings are done in a seated, restaurant-like atmosphere. The winery also houses a magnificent photography gallery. (8445 Silverado Trail, in Rutherford. ☎967-7700; www.mummnapa.com. Tours hourly 10am-3pm, no reservation needed. Open daily 10am-5pm.) **◼Kirkland Ranch** is a family-operated winery with windows overlooking the production facilities. True to its country-western style, the winery's log walls are adorned with family pictures of cattle-herding cowboys, and the very drinkable wines are surprisingly affordable. (1 Kirkland Ranch Rd., south of Napa off Rte. 29. ☎254-9100; www.kirklandranchwinery.com. Tours by appointment. Tastings $5 for 4 selections. Open daily 10am-4pm.) **Robert Mondavi Winery** is massive and touristy, with a beautiful mission-style visitors complex, three tasting rooms selling by the glass ($4-15), and the atmosphere of a luxury resort. (7801 Rte. 29, 8 mi. north of Napa. ☎963-9611 or 888-766-6328; www.robertmondaviwinery.com. Vineyard and winery tour daily every hr. 10am-4pm $15; includes 3 tastes and hors d'oeuvres. Reserve 1hr. in advance. Open daily 9am-5pm.) **Niebaum-Coppola Estate Winery** was purchased by famed director Francis Ford Coppola and his wife in 1975. Restoring the historic 1880 Inglenook Chateau and Niebaum vineyards to production capacity, Coppola also added a free family history museum upstairs that contains film memorabilia, including the desk from *The Godfather* and his Oscar and Golden Globe statues. (1991 St. Helena Hwy. ☎968-1100, tours 968-1161. 4 tastes and commemorative glass $12-30. Vineyard tours daily 11am; historical tours 10:30am, 12:30, 2:30pm; $20. Open daily 10am-5pm.)

👁 🥾 SIGHTS AND OUTDOOR ACTIVITIES

Napa's gentle terrain makes for an excellent bike tour. The area is fairly flat, although small bike lanes, speeding cars, and blistering heat can make routes more challenging, especially after a few samples of wine. The 26 mi. **Silverado Trail** has a wider bike path than Rte. 29. To soothe your weary quads and hamstrings, visit Calistoga, which is known as the "Hot Springs of the West." Its odiferous mud baths, luxuriant massages, and refreshing mineral showers will feel even more welcome after a hard day of wine-tasting. Be sure to hydrate beforehand; alcohol-thinned blood and heat don't mix. A basic package with a mud bath, mineral bath, eucalyptus steam, and blanket wrap costs around $50. Salt scrubs and facials are each about $50. **The Calistoga Village Inn and Spa** boasts friendly service and heavenly treatments. (☎942-0991. Mud bath $60. 50min. massage $85. Body wrap $95.) **Golden Haven** also offers full spa services. (☎942-6793; www.goldenhaven.com. Mud bath $74. 30min. massage $48. 30min. facial $48. Prices lower in winter.)

SONOMA VALLEY ☎707

A carefully crafted charm prevails in sprawling Sonoma Valley, providing a quieter alternative to Napa. Many wineries are on winding side roads rather than a freeway strip, dispersing traffic and creating a more intimate wine-tasting experience. Sonoma Plaza is surrounded by art galleries, novelty shops, clothing stores, and restaurants. Petaluma, west of the Sonoma Valley, has more budget-friendly lodgings than the expensive wine country.

▐ TRANSPORTATION

From San Francisco, take **U.S. 101 N** over the Golden Gate Bridge; then follow Rte. 37 E to Rte. 116 N, which turns into Rte. 121 N and crosses Rte. 12 N to Sonoma. Alternatively, follow U.S. 101 N to Petaluma and cross over to Sonoma by Rte. 116. Driving time from San Francisco is about 1-1½hr. **Route 12** traverses the length of Sonoma Valley, from **Sonoma** through **Glen Ellen** to **Kenwood** in the north. The center of downtown Sonoma is **Sonoma Plaza,** which contains City Hall and the visitors center. **Broadway** dead-ends at Napa St. in front of City Hall. Numbered streets run north-south. **Petaluma** lies to the west and is connected to Sonoma by **Route 116,** which becomes **Lakeville Street** in Petaluma.

CALIFORNIA

Buses: Sonoma County Transit (☎576-7433 or 800-345-7433; www.sctransit.com) serves the entire county. Bus #30 runs from **Sonoma** to **Santa Rosa** (daily every 1-1½hr. weekdays 6am-9:30pm, weekends 7am-7pm; $2.50, students $2.15, seniors and disabled $1.25, under 6 free); #44 and 48 go from **Santa Rosa** to **Petaluma** (daily; $2.10, students $1.80, seniors and disabled $1.05). Within Sonoma, county buses must be flagged down at bus stops (daily 8am-4:25pm; $1.10/0.90/0.55). **Golden Gate Transit** (from Sonoma County ☎541-2000, from SF 415-923-2000) runs buses frequently between **San Francisco** and **Santa Rosa.**

Bike Rental: Sonoma Valley Cyclery, 20093 Broadway (☎935-3377). $6 per hr., $20 per day; includes helmet, lock, and bags. Open M-Sa 10am-6pm, Su 10am-4pm.

▐ PRACTICAL INFORMATION

Visitor Info: Sonoma Valley Visitors Bureau, 453 1st St. E (☎996-1090; www.sonomavalley.com), in Sonoma Plaza. Maps available. Open daily 9am-5pm. **Petaluma Visitors Program,** 800 Baywood Dr. (☎762-2785), at Lakeville St. The free visitor's guide has listings of restaurants and activities. Open daily 9am-5pm.

Police: In Sonoma ☎996-3602. In Petaluma ☎778-4372.

Medical Services: Petaluma Valley Hospital, 400 N. McDowell Blvd. (☎778-1111).

Post Office: Sonoma, 617 Broadway (☎996-9311), at Patten St. Open M-F 8:30am-5pm. Postal Code: 95476. Petaluma, 120 4th St. (☎800-275-8777). Open M-F 8:30am-5pm, Sa 10am-2pm. **Postal Code:** 94952. **Area Code:** 707

▐ ACCOMMODATIONS

Pickings are pretty slim for lodging; rooms are scarce even on weekdays and generally start at $90. Less-expensive motels cluster along **U.S. 101** in Santa Rosa and Petaluma. Campers with cars should try the **Russian River Valley** to the west.

▨ **Sonoma Creek Inn,** 239 Boyes Blvd. (☎939-9463 or 888-712-1289), west off Hwy. 12, in Sonoma. Just 10min. from the Sonoma Plaza. Cheaper than most places in the area, but just as nice. Bold and colorful rooms with fridge, cable TV, and full bath; most with adobe patio. Rooms M-Th and Su $89, with patio $99; F-Sa $149/$159. ❹

Redwood Inn, 1670 Santa Rosa Ave. (☎545-0474), in Santa Rosa. At least a 30min. drive from Sonoma. Comfortable, motel-style rooms with cable TV, phone, and bath; some with kitchenette. Rooms with 1 bed $60-75, 2 beds $70-85; $5 less in winter. ❸

Sugarloaf Ridge State Park, 2605 Adobe Canyon Rd. (☎833-5712, reservations 800-444-7275; www.reserveamerica.com), off Rte. 12, north of Kenwood in the Mayacamas mountains. 49 sites with tables and fire rings. Arranged around a central meadow with flush toilets and running water (but no showers). In summer and fall, take advantage of Ferguson Observatory inside the park; see www.rfo.org for details. Sites $15-20. ❶

▐ FOOD

Seasonal produce is available directly from area farms or at roadside stands and farmers markets. Those in the area toward the end of the summer should ask about the ambrosial **crane melon,** a tasty hybrid of fruits grown only on the Crane Farm north of Petaluma. The **Sonoma Market,** 520 W. Napa St., in the Sonoma Valley Center, is an old-fashioned grocery store with deli sandwiches ($5-7) and produce. (☎996-0563. Open daily 6am-9pm.) The **Fruit Basket,** 18474 Sonoma Hwy., sells inexpensive fruit. (☎996-7433. Open daily 7am-7pm.) A deli-style boulangerie, the **Basque Cafe ❷,** 460 1st St. E, specializes in fresh breads, pastries, and delicious sandwiches. Their breakfast ($1.25-4.50) is a great way to start the day, and the prosciutto and brie sandwich ($8) will keep it going. (☎ 935-7686. Open daily 7am-6pm.) In Sonoma, even the pubs are classy, as is showcased at **Murphy's Irish Pub** ❸, 464 1st St. E, with a warm wood interior and a good-natured staff that welcomes newcomers with a perfectly pulled pint. Favorites include the fish and chips ($12), and any of the beers, ales, or whiskeys. (☎935-0660; www.sonoma-pub.com. Trivia night 2nd and 4th W of each month. Live music Th 7:30pm, F-Sa 8pm, Su 6pm. Open M-Th and Su 11am-11pm, F-Sa 11am-midnight.)

☷ WINERIES

Sonoma Valley's wineries, near Sonoma and Kenwood, are less touristy but just as elegant as Napa's. As an added bonus, there are more complimentary tastings of current vintages. ▨**Benziger,** certified as biodynamic, is a family-owned and operated winery that brings a great deal of care to the winemaking process in order to preserve the natural character of its grapes. (1883 London Ranch Rd. ☎888-490-2739 or 935-4014; www.benziger.com. Comprehensive 45min. tram ride tour through the vineyards runs in summer daily every 30min. 11am-3:30pm and includes reserve tasting and 20% off purchases; $10, under 21 $5. Self-guided tours lead from the parking lot through the vineyards and peacock aviary. Tastings of current vintage $5, estate and reserves $10. Open daily 10am-5pm.) ▨**Gundlach-Bundschu,** established in 1858, is the second-oldest winery in Sonoma and the oldest family-owned and run winery in the country. A quiet, refined tasting room and high-quality wines draw people from across the country. (2000 Denmark St., off 8th St. E. ☎938-5277; www.gunbun.com. Free wine storage cave tours Sa-Su every 30min. noon-3:30pm. Tastings $5 for 4-6 samples. Open daily 11am-4:30pm.) **Buena Vista** is the oldest premium winery in the valley. Famous stone buildings are preserved just as Mr. Haraszthy built them in 1857 when he founded the California wine industry. Its park-like grounds are a great stop for learning a little bit about the history of American winemaking. (18000 Old Winery Rd.; take E. Napa St. from Sonoma Plaza and turn left on Old Winery Rd. ☎938-1266; www.buenavistawinery.com. Historical presentation and guided tour daily 11am and 2pm; $15. Tastings $5; includes glass. Open daily 10am-5pm.) **Ledson Winery and Vineyards,** a relatively new Merlot estate, does not market its wines. The stunning French-Normandy "castle" houses a lavish parlor and an equally impressive gourmet marketplace featuring fine cheeses, sauces, and exclusive fruit spreads. (7335 Sonoma Hwy. ☎833-2330; www.ledson.com. Monthly events themed around holidays. Tastings $5-10. Open daily 10am-5pm.)

☷ SIGHTS

SONOMA STATE HISTORIC PARK. A series of structures surround the town plaza and are known collectively as the historic park. At the northeast corner of the square, an adobe church stands on the site of the **Mission San Francisco-Solano,** the northernmost and last of the 21 Franciscan missions. Built in 1826 by Padre Jose Altimira, the mission contains a fragment of the original California Republic flag, the rest of which was burned in the 1906 San Francisco earthquake fires. Other attractions include Gold Rush era hotels, army barracks, and the Victorian home of General Vallejo. (*E. Spain and 1st St. ☎938-1519. Open daily 10am-5pm. $2, children under 17 free. Includes admission to all sites.*)

JACK LONDON STATE PARK. Around the turn of the 20th century, hard-drinking and hard-living Jack London, author of *The Call of the Wild* and *White Fang,* bought 1400 acres here, determined to create his dream home. London's hopes were frustrated when the estate's main building, **Wolf House,** was destroyed by arsonists in 1913. London died three years after the fire and is buried in the park, his grave marked by a volcanic boulder intended for the construction of his house. The remains of Wolf House are accessed by a half-mile trail. The nearby **House of Happy Walls,** built by London's widow in his honor, is now a two-story museum devoted to the writer. Scenic trails cross the property, allowing visitors access to what London called "Beauty Ranch." *(Take Hwy. 12 4 mi. north from Sonoma to Arnold Ln. and follow signs.* ☎ *938-5216. Park open daily 10am-dusk. Museum open daily 10am-5pm.)*

THE CENTRAL COAST

The 400 mi. stretch of coastline between L.A. and San Francisco embodies all things Californian—rolling surf, a seaside highway built for cruising, dramatic bluffs topped by weathered pines, self-actualizing New-Age adherents, and always a hint of the offbeat. This is the solitary magnificence that inspired John Steinbeck's novels and Jack Kerouac's musings. The landmarks along the way—Hearst Castle, the Monterey Bay Aquarium, the historic missions—are well worth visiting, but the real highlight of the Central Coast is the journey itself.

SANTA CRUZ   ☎ 831

Negotiating the liminal space between NorCal and SoCal, Santa Cruz (pop. 56,000) embraces sculpted surfers, aging hippies, free-thinking students, and same-sex couples. The atmosphere here is fun-loving but far from hedonistic, intellectual but nowhere near stuffy. This small city exudes fun, whether you find it gobbling cotton candy on the Boardwalk or sipping wheatgrass at poetry readings.

■◪ **ORIENTATION AND PRACTICAL INFORMATION.** Santa Cruz is on the northern tip of Monterey Bay, 65 mi. south of San Francisco. Through west Santa Cruz, Hwy. 1 becomes **Mission Street.** The **University of California at Santa Cruz (UCSC)** blankets the hills inland from Mission St. Southeast of Mission St. lies the waterfront, where **Beach Street** and **West Cliff Drive** run roughly east-west along the coastline. The many shops, restaurants, and clubs of downtown straddle **Pacific Avenue.** Many lots around downtown offer 3hr. free **parking,** and day-long free parking can be found west of town along W. Cliff Dr., about a 10min. walk from the beach. **Greyhound,** 425 Front St. (☎ 423-1800; www.greyhound.com; open daily 6-6:30am, 8:30am-12:30pm, 2:30-7:15pm, 9:30-10pm), runs to L.A. (8-10hr., 8 per day, $43), San Francisco (2½-3hr., 5 per day, $11), and San Jose (1hr., 4 per day, $6). **Santa Cruz Metropolitan Transit District (SCMTD),** 920 Pacific Ave., handles local transportation. (☎ 425-8600; www.scmtd.com. Open M-F 8am-4pm. Buses run daily 6am-11pm. $1.50, seniors and disabled $0.75, under 46 in. free; day pass $4.50/$2.25/free.) Pick up the *Santa Cruz County Traveler's Guide* at **Santa Cruz County Conference and Visitor Council,** 1211 Ocean St. (☎ 425-1234 or 800-833-3494; www.santacruzca.org. Open M-Sa 9am-5pm, Su 10am-4pm.) **Post Office:** 850 Front St. (☎ 426-8184. Open M-F 9am-5pm.) **Postal Code:** 95060. **Area Code:** 831.

▐▐ **ACCOMMODATIONS AND FOOD.** Santa Cruz gets jam-packed in summer, especially on weekends; room rates skyrocket and vacancies plummet. Always make reservations. **Carmelita Cottage Santa Cruz Hostel (HI) ❶,** 321 Main St., is a collection of small Victorian cottages that function as a 40-bed hostel. (☎ 423-8304. Chores requested. Towels $0.50. Overnight parking free, day permits $1.25. July-Aug. 3-night max. stay. Reception 8-10am and 5-10pm. Lockout 10am-5pm. Strict curfew 11pm. No alcohol. Dorms $21, members $18, ages 12-17 $14, ages 4-11 $10, under 4 free.) The **Harbor Inn ❸**, 645 7th Ave., is a beautiful, historic 19-room hotel east of the harbor and well off the main drag. In late June, pick plums from the trees out back. (☎479-9731. Free parking. Fridges, microwaves, and cable TV. Office open M-Sa 10am-7pm, Su noon-5pm. Rooms $49-79, with private bath $69-129.) Camping may be the best budget option. Twenty-five miles northwest of Santa Cruz, ▨**Big Basin Redwoods State Park ❶**, California's oldest state park and home to 18,000 acres of old growth and recovering redwood forest, has great sites and breezy trails. (☎338-8860; www.bigbasin.org. Sites $25.)

A few eateries can be found along the beachfront, but downtown is home to the most reasonably priced restaurants, pizza joints, and coffee shops. Fresh produce and ready-to-eat goodies are sold at the **farmers market** (W 2:30-6:30pm) at Lincoln and Cedar St. downtown. **Zoccoli's ❷**, 1534 Pacific Ave., downtown, is a tasty Italian deli that uses only the freshest ingredients and has all of the makings for a semi-gourmet beachside picnic. (☎423-1711. Sandwiches $5-6. Open in summer M-Sa 9am-7pm, Su 10am-6pm; low season daily 9am-6pm.) After a day at the beach, grab a generously-sized burrito ($2) with the locals at **Las Palmas Taco Bar ❶**, 55 Front St., by the wharf. Tasty tacos are a mere $1.50 and combo plates with rice, beans, and excellent tortillas run $4.50-7. (☎429-1220. Open M-Th and Su 10am-9pm, F-Sa 10am-10pm.)

◪ **SIGHTS.** Santa Cruz has a great beach, but the water is frigid—it requires courage (and sometimes a wetsuit) to take full advantage of the waves. Many casual beachgoers catch their thrills on the **Santa Cruz Beach Boardwalk.** First opened in 1907, the boardwalk is now a three-block strip of rides, guess-your-weight booths, shooting galleries, arcade games, and corn-dog vendors. It's a gloriously tacky throwback to 50s-era beach culture. The traditional favorite is the **Giant Dipper,** the 1924 wooden roller coaster where Dirty Harry met his enemy in 1983's *Sudden Impact.* (Boardwalk open daily Memorial Day-Labor Day, plus many low-season weekends and holidays; arcade open year-round. Rides require 4-6 tickets apiece. 60 tickets $33, all-day pass $27. Mini-golf $5. Look for flyers with special deals.) The **Santa Cruz Wharf,** off Beach St., is the longest car-accessible pier on the West Coast. Seafood restaurants and souvenir shops will try to distract you from expansive views of the ocean. Munch on a caramel apple from local favorite **Marini's,** at the wharf's end, and watch the sea lions on the rocks below. (☎423-7258. Open M-Th and Su 10am-9:30pm, F-Sa 10am-11pm.)

◪◪ **BEACHES AND OUTDOOR ACTIVITIES.** The **Santa Cruz Beach (Cowell Beach)** is broad, reasonably clean, and packed with volleyball players. Novice surfers and families may prefer semi-sheltered **Cowell Cove,** just west of the wharf, and the more secluded beaches that line Hwy. 1. The best vantage points for watching surfers are along W. Cliff Dr. To learn more about surfing, stop in at the small **surfing museum** in the lighthouse overlooking **Steamer Lane** at Lighthouse Point, the deep water where Hawaiian "Duke" Kahanamoku kick-started California's surf culture a century ago. For surfing lessons, contact the **Richard Schmidt Surf School** or ask around for him at the beach. (☎423-0928; www.richardschmidt.com. 1hr. private lesson $80, 2hr. group lesson $80. Lessons include equipment.)

Around the point at the end of W. Cliff Dr. is **Natural Bridges State Beach.** Only one natural bridge remains standing, but the unblemished beach still has fascinating tidepools, and tours during **monarch butterfly** season (Oct.-Mar.). In November and December, thousands of the stunning *lepidoptera* swarm the beach and cover the nearby eucalyptus groves with their orange wings. (☎423-4609. Open daily 8am-dusk. Parking $6, seniors $5, disabled $3.) **Kayak Connection,** 413 Lake Ave., offers tours of Elkhorn Slough and Santa Cruz Harbor ($40-45), and rents ocean-

CALIFORNIA

The freedom and rural beauty of California's wild Central Coast can be shocking given the major cities of northern and southern California, but the rolling rangelands, exposed seacliffs, overgrown forests, and clear blue waters unfurling along **Highway 1** are truly magnificent. This awe-inspiring scenic drive connects two portions of the legendary Hwy. 1—the **San Luis Obispo North Coast Byway** and the **Big Sur Coast Highway**—in an unforgettable journey through some of the West's most rugged and majestic terrain.

1 SAN LUIS OBISPO (SLO). A once-sleepy little city kept young only by the students of **Cal Poly State University,** SLO has seen tremendous growth in recent years, fueled by Angelenos fleeing the city and tourists searching for the rolling wine country featured in the film *Sideways.* Wine-lovers, and all travelers planning to scope out the coast, should drop by the SLO **visitors center** to pick up maps and collect advice. (1039 Chorro St. ☎805-781-2777. Open M 10am-5pm, Tu-W 8am-5pm, Th 8am-8pm, F 8am-7pm, Sa 10am-7pm, Su 11am-5pm.) Before leaving town, swing by the **Bubble Gum Alley,** where people have been sticking their gum since 1960 (off Higuera St., between Broad and Garden St.), the outlandish **Madonna Inn** (just south of town) to marvel at the gaudy pink interior, and, of course, the **Mission San Luis Obispo de Tolosa,** founded in 1772 and now the center of downtown. For a good night's sleep before heading out in the morning, the **Hostel Obispo (HI)** offers cozy digs. (1617 Santa Rosa St. ☎805-544-4679.) **House of Bread,** 858 Higuera St., has fresh-baked, gooey cinnamon rolls, perfect for breakfast on the go. (☎805-542-0255. Open M-Sa 7am-7pm, Su 9am-5pm.)

2 MORRO BAY. The isolated beauty of **Montana de Oro State Park** is a sneak peek of the untamed coastline and is popular with hikers and mountain bikers. In town, stroll along the **Embarcadero** (Front St.) and watch peregrine falcons soar above massive **Morro Rock,** the 576-ft.-tall evidence of a 23 million-year-old volcano, which stands just offshore. Fishermen sell the day's catch along the docks near where **Giovanni's,** 1001 Front St., serves up great fish and chips ($8) and chowder in a bread bowl ($6). Hone your chess skills at **Centennial Park's** giant chessboard, with its 16 sq. ft. board and 20 lb. redwood pieces. (☎805-772-6278 for reservations.)

3 CAYUCOS. A small beach town just beginning to succumb to tourist trappings, **Cayucos** (ky-YOO-cuss) is nestled right along the water. The wood-fronted antique shops and restaurants on Ocean Ave. are cheesy Old West, but watching surfers wipe out as they ride waves by the pier is totally tubular.

TIME: 5-7hr.

DISTANCE: 129 mi.

4 CAMBRIA. The shops, cafes, and galleries of Cambria's Main St. can blur together in a haze of cutesiness, but this little village is a relaxing, welcoming place. Beautiful **Moonstone Beach** has a rugged yet accessible coast, tide pools, a new boardwalk, and a beach freckled with smooth pebbles. To see a less conventional side of Cambria, take a tour of **Nitt Witt Ridge,** a three-story home built entirely of trash. (881 Hillcrest Dr. ☎805-927-2690.) Spend the night in the homey comfort of the outstanding **⬛Bridge Street Inn ❷,** 4314 Bridge St. (☎805-927-7653; www.bridgestreetinncambria.com. Dorms $19; private rooms $40-70.)

5 HEARST SAN SIMEON STATE HISTORIC PARK. Also known as **Hearst Castle,** this park is sprawled across a mountaintop 8 mi. up from Cambria. The opulent vacation home of media magnate William Randolph Hearst was constructed over 28 years and possesses a commanding view of the Pacific Ocean and the Santa Lucia Range. The European-inspired complex, designed by Hearst and architect Julia Morgan, hosted countless movie stars during the 1920s and 30s. Daily tours lead you through parts of the 165-room "casa grande," three accompanying guesthouses, and 127 acres of gardens, pools, and walkways. (☎805-927-2010 for info, 800-444-4445 for reservations, 866-712-2286 for wheelchair-accessible reservations; www.hearstcastle.com. Visitors center open daily 8am-6pm. Reserve tours in advance. Each tour climbs 150-370 stairs. 1¾hr. tours $24, ages 6-12 $12, under 6 free.)

6 PIEDRAS BLANCAS. Located two "vista point" turnouts north of San Simeon, charming **Piedras Blancas Lighthouse** protrudes from the white rocks that give the area its name. Look closely at the beach to see sunning **elephant seals.** Expectant mothers and big-eyed newborn pups rule in January and February, with the bulls arriving shortly thereafter for breeding season, but the blubbery beasts can be spotted most any time of the year.

7 RAGGED POINT. This remote outpost, 8 mi. north, is the coast at its wildest. The curves of the road become sharper, the cliffs higher, and the vegetation more tangled, so turn up the music and roll down the windows, but keep your eyes on the road. The combination motel, restaurant, grocery store, espresso bar, and inflated-price gas station is the only identifier of the area. There is a marked 15-20min. trail down the bluff to the ocean.

8 BIG SUR. Big Sur is a region rather than a precise destination and covers everything from redwood forests to rocky shores with crashing surf and golden beaches. **Pfeiffer Big Sur State Park** (entrance $8) offers redwood groves, easy hiking (Pfeiffer Falls is a good choice), birdwatching opportunities (look for California condors), and swimming holes along the Big Sur River. Big Sur's most fiercely guarded treasure is **Pfeiffer Beach** (entrance $5), a quarter-mile south of Big Sur Station on an unmarked, unpaved, narrow westbound road. An offshore rock formation protects sea caves and seagulls from the pounding ocean waves and frames breathtaking sunsets. Although it lacks beach access, **Julia Pfeiffer Burns State Park,** 11 mi. south of Big Sur Station, has some of the area's best hiking trails. The Ewoldsen Trail winds through the towering Redwoods and along McWay Creek on a moderately strenuous climb to a sweeping ocean view (4½ mi. round-trip). Easily accessible via a quarter-mile semi-paved path is McWay Cove, home of sea otters and an 80 ft. waterfall where McWay Creek flows into the ocean. The spectacular scenery and well-kept facilities in the area make **camping ❶** a popular option. Reserve state park campsites ($25) at least a month in advance by calling Reserve America (☎800-444-7275; $7.50 reservation fee), or take your chances with the 24 first come, first served primitive hike-in sites at **Andrew Molera State Park.** (Sites $10. Sites generally fill by early afternoon.) A cushier lodging option is the **Fernwood Resort ❶/❹.** (☎831-667-2422; www.fernwoodbigsur.com. Shaded sites $27; motel rooms $89-119.) Ten miles north of Big Sur, the **Bixby Bridge** attracts hordes of photographers eager to snap pictures of the 1932 concrete arch, one of the 10 highest single-span bridges in the world.

going **kayaks** at decent rates. (☎479-1121. Closed-deck singles $33 per 4hr., $40 per day; plastic doubles $45/$55. Paddle, life jacket, brief instruction, and wetsuit included. Open M-F 10am-5pm, Sa-Su 9am-6pm.)

🔲 **NIGHTLIFE.** There are comprehensive events listings in the free *Metro Santa Cruz*, and in "Spotlight" in Friday's *Sentinel*. The Boardwalk bandstand offers free summertime Friday concerts around 6:30 and 8:30pm. Make it onto the Wall of Fame at ▓**99 Bottles Restaurant and Pub,** 110 Walnut Ave., in the heart of downtown, by making it through all 99 beers—though hopefully not in one sitting. (☎459-9999. Beers $4, pitchers $9. Happy hour M and F 4-6pm, Tu and W 10pm-close, and Th all day. Trivia night W. Live music Th. 21+ after 10pm. Open M-Th 11:30am-1:30am, F-Sa 11:30am-2am, Su 11:30am-midnight; kitchen closes daily 10pm.) The mega-popular club **Blue Lagoon,** 923 Pacific Ave., has won many awards, including "best place you can't take your parents." (☎423-7117. Stronger-than-the-bouncer drinks $3-4. Happy hour daily 4-9pm; $2.75 drinks. Cover $1-3 after 10pm. Open daily 4pm-2am.)

MONTEREY ☎831

Monterey (pop. 33,000) is rightfully proud to be considered the cradle of Californian history. The bay was claimed by the Spanish in the 16th century and briefly served as the first capital of California. After lapsing into obscurity in the mid-19th century, Monterey was revived as a resort town by vacationers eager to experience its natural beauty. Luxury hotels and tourist shops are plentiful nowadays, and though the Cannery Row of Steinbeck fame has all but vanished, red-tiled roofs and a bustling waterfront stand as testimony to the city's colorful past.

🔢 **PRACTICAL INFORMATION.** Monterey-Salinas Transit (MST; ☎888-678-2871; www.mst.org) is the convenient public transit system. A free MST trolley serves major tourist sights during the summer. The free *Rider's Guide*, available on buses, at motels, and at the visitors center, has complete route info. ($1.75; exact change only. Day pass $3.50, with service to Big Sur $7.) **Visitor Info: Monterey Peninsula Visitor and Convention Bureau,** 150 Olivier St. (☎657-6400 or 888-221-1010; www.montereyinfo.org. Open M-F 9am-5pm.) **Post Office:** 565 Hartnell St. (☎372-3021. Open M-F 8:30am-5pm, Sa 10am-2pm.) **Postal Code:** 93940. **Area Code:** 831.

🔢🔲 **ACCOMMODATIONS AND FOOD.** Inexpensive hotels line the 2000 block of **Fremont Street** in Monterey (bus #9 or 10). Others cluster along **Munras Avenue** between downtown Monterey and Hwy. 1. The **Monterey Hostel (HI) ❷,** 778 Hawthorne St., one block west of Lighthouse Ave., is a clean, modern, 45-bed hostel with a gigantic common room. (☎649-0375. Free linens and parking. Towels $0.50. Check-in 5-8pm. Curfew 1am. Reservations essential June-Sept. Dorms $25, members $22, ages 7-17 $17; private rooms for 2-5 people $60-74. MC/V.) **Del Monte Beach Inn ❹,** 1110 Del Monte Blvd., near downtown and across from the beach, is a Victorian-style inn with pleasant rooms. (☎649-4410. Check-in 2-6pm. Reservations recommended. Rooms $66; with private bath $77-88.) Call the **Monterey Parks** line (☎755-4895 or 888-588-2267) for camping info.

Once a hub for the canned sardine industry, Monterey Bay now yields crab, red snapper, and salmon. Seafood is bountiful but expensive—early-bird specials (usually 4-6:30pm) are easiest on the wallet. **Fisherman's Wharf** has stalls with smoked salmon sandwiches ($7) and free chowder samples. Get free samples of fruit, cheese, and seafood at the **Old Monterey Market Place,** on Alvarado St. (☎655-2607. Open Tu 4-8pm.) 🔲**First Awakenings ❷,** 125 Oceanview Blvd., in the outlet mall near the Aquarium, specializes in big portions of healthy, homemade brunch favorites. A single plate-sized signature pancake is a meal ($3.75), and a full stack ($6.75) is food for a day. Try them with wheatgerm for a satisfying crunch, or order up an overstuffed omelet ($7) or towering Reuben ($7.50) to enjoy by the firepit. (☎372-1125. Open M-F 7am-2pm, Sa-Su 7am-2:30pm.) **Turtle Bay Taqueria ❶**, 431 Tyler St., at Bonifacio in downtown, combines fresh local produce and seafood to create flavorful and filling Mexican-inspired dishes. Top a charbroiled snapper taco ($2.50) or tilapia Cancun burrito ($6) with the zesty mango salsa. (☎333-1500. Open M-Th 11am-9pm, F-Sa 11am-9:30pm, Su 11:30am-9pm.)

◙ **SIGHTS.** The extraordinary ▨**Monterey Bay Aquarium,** 886 Cannery Row, with nearly 200 outstanding exhibits and galleries, has been voted the nation's best. Gaze through the world's largest window at an enormous marine habitat with sea turtles, giant sunfish, large sharks, and yellow- and blue-fin tuna, or marvel at the three-story kelp forest. Special exhibits relate jellyfish to various art forms and explore the myths and mysteries of sharks. The thrice-daily feeding of the sea otters is a crowd-pleaser; for a literal feeding frenzy, check out **Outer Bay** (Tu, Th, Sa-Su 11am). The lines are unbelievable; pick up tickets the day before and save 20-40min. (☎648-4888 or 800-756-3737; www.montereybayaquarium.org. Open daily June to early Sept. and holidays 9:30am-6pm; early Sept. to May 10am-6pm. $22, ages 65+ $20, students and ages 13-17 $18, disabled and ages 3-12 $11.) **Cannery Row** was once a dilapidated street of languishing sardine-packing plants, but restaurants and t-shirt shops have begun to take over. The **Great Cannery Row Mural** covers 400 ft. of a construction-site barrier on the 700 block with depictions of 1930s and 40s Monterey. The best time to go **whale-watching** is during gray whale migration season (Nov.-Apr.), but humpbacks and blue whales can be spotted on a hit-or-miss basis year-round. **Chris' Whale Watching,** 48 Fisherman's Wharf, offers tours and charters. (☎375-5951. 3hr. tours May-Nov. $25, under 13 $15. 2hr. gray whale migration tours Dec.-Apr. $18/$12.) In nearby Carmel, the amazing 550-acre, state-run wildlife sanctuary of ▨**Point Lobos Reserve** is popular with skindivers and day-hikers. From the cliffs, watch otters, sea lions, seals, brown pelicans, and gulls. There are also tidepools, scuba access, and marvelous vantage points for watching the winter whale migration. (☎624-4909. Open daily Apr.-Oct. 9am-7pm; Nov.-Mar. 9am-5pm. $9 per car, or park on the highway and walk or bike in for free. Required diving reservations ☎624-8413. Dive fee $7.)

SANTA BARBARA ☎805

Santa Barbara (pop. 92,500) epitomizes worry-free living, and with mountains to one side and the ocean to the other, there's no reason to complain. Spanish Revival architecture dominates State St., a pedestrian-friendly, palm-lined promenade of cafes, thrift stores, boutiques, and galleries. The city's golden beaches, scenic drives, and leisurely pace make it a frequent weekend escape for the wealthy and an attractive destination for surfers, artists, and backpackers.

▮ **TRANSPORTATION**

Many downtown parking lots and streets offer 1¼hr. of **free parking;** try the underground lots at Paseo Nuevo, accessible on the 700 block of Chapala St. All parking is free on Sundays. **Biking** is a nice alternative to driving. The **Cabrillo Bikeway** runs east-west along the beach from the Bird Refuge to the City College campus.

Trains: Amtrak, 209 State St. (☎963-1015 or 800-872-7245; www.amtrak.com). Be careful around the station after dark. Open daily 5:45am-10pm. To **L.A.** (3hr., 7 per day, $21) and **San Francisco** (10hr., 3 per day, $59-67).

Buses: Greyhound, 34 W. Carrillo St. (☎965-7551; www.greyhound.com), at Chapala St. Open daily 5am-8:15pm and 11pm-midnight. To **L.A.** (2-3hr., 8 per day, $12) and **San Francisco** (8-10hr., 6 per day, $33). **Santa Barbara Metropolitan Transit District (MTD),** 1020 Chapala St. (☎683-3702), at Cabrillo Blvd. behind the Greyhound station, provides bus schedules and serves as a transfer point. Open M-F 6am-7pm, Sa 8am-6pm, Su 9am-6pm. The MTD runs a purple **crosstown shuttle** from Franklin Center on Montecito St. to Mountain and Valerio. $1.25, seniors and disabled $0.60, under 45 in. free; 10-ride pass $10; transfers free. Runs M-F 7am-6pm. The **downtown-waterfront shuttle** ($0.25) along State St. and Cabrillo Blvd. runs every 15min. M-Th and Su 10am-6pm, F-Sa 10am-10pm. Stops marked by circular blue signs.

■ ? ORIENTATION AND PRACTICAL INFORMATION

Santa Barbara is 92 mi. northwest of L.A. and 27 mi. from Ventura on **U.S. 101.** Since the town is built along an irregular stretch of shoreline, its street grid is slightly skewed. The beach lies at the south end of the city, and **State Street,** the main drag, runs northwest from the waterfront. All streets are designated east and west from State St. The major east-west artery is **U.S. 101,** and **Cabrillo Boulevard** runs along the coastline.

Visitor Info: Tourist Office, 1 Garden St. (☎965-3021 or 800-676-1266), at Cabrillo Blvd. across from the beach. Open July-Aug. M-Sa 9am-6pm, Su 10am-5pm; Sept.-Nov. and Feb.-June M-Sa 9am-5pm, Su 10am-5pm; Dec.-Jan. M-Sa 9am-4pm, Su 10am-4pm. 24hr. computer with info on dining, shopping, hotels, and entertainment.

Medical Services: Cottage Hospital, Pueblo St. (☎682-7111), at Bath St.

Internet Access: Santa Barbara Public Library, 40 E. Anapamu St. (☎962-7653). Free wireless Internet. Open M-Th 10am-9pm, F-Sa 10am-5:30pm, Su 1-5pm.

Post Office: 836 Anacapa St. (☎564-2226), 1 block east of State St. Open M-F 8am-6pm, Sa 9am-5pm. **Postal Code:** 93102.

■ ACCOMMODATIONS

A 10min. drive north or south on U.S. 101 will lead you to cheaper lodging than that in Santa Barbara proper. **Motel 6 ❸** is always an option—the chain originated in Santa Barbara and has several locations in town. It may have cramped dorms, but the **Santa Barbara Tourist Hostel ❶,** 134 Chapala St., is also a block west of bustling State St., mere blocks from the beach, and next to the train station, making it a convenient place to stay. (☎963-0154. Free linens, towels, wireless Internet, and parking. Discounted bike and boogie-board rentals. Laundry. Key deposit $10. Dorms $21-23. Doubles July-Aug. $59-65; May-June and Sept. $55-59; Oct.-Apr. $49-55.) Welcoming and meticulously clean, the European-style ▧**Hotel State Street ❹,** 121 State St., is two blocks from the beach and near the train station. (☎966-6586. Reservations recommended. Rooms with sinks and cable TV July-Aug. $95-145; Sept.-June $59-105.) **Carpinteria State Park ❶,** 12 mi. south of Santa Barbara, has beachfront camping. (☎800-444-7275. Reservations recommended. Sites $25.)

▢ FOOD

Hip State St. is lined with fashionable cafes while cheap taquerías lie four blocks west, along Milpas St. The reproduction of the Sistine Chapel ceiling at **Palazzio ❹,** 1026 State St., is nearly as impressive as the enormous pasta dishes ($17-20, half-portion $12-15), amazing garlic rolls, and serve-yourself wine. (☎564-1985. Lunch $7.75-10. Open M-Th and Su 11:30am-3pm and 5:30-11pm, F-Sa 11:30am-3pm and 5:30pm-midnight.) Bourbon St. spice meets Santa Barbara class at **The Palace Grill**

❺, 8 E. Cota St., a Cajun-Creole-Caribbean restaurant worth the splurge. (☎963-5000. Fish and grill selections $14-26. Booze-y bread pudding souffle $5. Open M-Th and Su 11:30am-3pm and 5:30-10pm, F-Sa 11:30am-3pm and 5:30-11pm.) Hungry Santa Barbarans rave about the authentic French cuisine at **Pacific Crepes ❷**, 705 Anacapa St. (☎882-1123. Open Tu-Sa 10am-3pm and 5:30-9pm, Su 9am-3pm.)

🔍 SIGHTS

SANTA BARBARA ZOOLOGICAL GARDENS. This delightfully leafy habitat has such an open feel that the animals seem kept in captivity only by sheer lethargy. A mini-train provides a tour of the exhibits, including a miniaturized African plain where giraffes stroll lazily, silhouetted against the Pacific. Make sure to see the zoo's magnificent pair of endangered snow leopards. (*500 Niños Dr., off Cabrillo Blvd. from U.S. 101. Take bus #14 or the downtown-waterfront shuttle. ☎962-5339. Open daily 10am-5pm. $9, seniors and ages 2-12 $7, under 2 free. Train $1.50, children $1. Parking $3.*)

BEACHES AND ACTIVITIES. Santa Barbara's beaches are breathtaking, lined on one side by flourishing palm trees and on the other by sailboats around the harbor. The powdery sand and happy sunbathers at **East** and **Leadbetter Beaches** flank the wharf on either side. **Wheel Fun Rentals** will rent beachgoers a ▓retro surrey: a covered (often with fringe on top), Flintstone-esque bicycle seating up to nine. (*22 State St. ☎966-2282. Surreys $24-44 per 2hr., depending on number of riders. Normal bikes $7 per hr. Open daily 8am-8:30pm.*) **Beach House** rents surfboards and bodyboards. (*10 State St. ☎963-1281. Surfboards $7 per hr., $10 per half-day. Bodyboards $4/$10. Wetsuits $4/$10. Credit card required. Open M-Th and Su 9am-7pm, F-Sa 9am-8pm.*)

STATE STREET. State St., Santa Barbara's red-tiled tribute to its Hispanic roots, runs a straight, tree-lined 2 mi. through the center of the city. Among the shops, restaurants, and clubs are cultural and historical landmarks, not to mention countless opportunities for people-watching. The **Red Tile Tour,** a free walking-tour guide and map available at the visitors center, leads pedestrians to some of Santa Barbara's finest Spanish-style architecture. Farther down State St., the **Santa Barbara Museum of Art** owns an impressive collection of classical Greek, Asian, and European works, mostly donated by wealthy local residents. (*1130 State St. ☎963-4364. Open Tu-Su 11am-5pm. $9, seniors $7, students ages 6-17 $5, under 6 free. Free Su.*)

MISSION SANTA BARBARA. Praised as the "Queen of Missions" when built in 1786, the mission was restored after the 1812 earthquake and assumed its present incarnation in 1820. Towers with Moorish windows stand around a Greco-Roman temple and facade, while a cheerful fountain bubbles outside. (*At the end of Los Olivos St. Take bus #22. ☎682-4149. Open daily 9am-5pm. Self-guided museum tour starts at the gift shop. Mass M-F 7:30am, Sa 4pm, Su 7:30, 9, 10:30am, noon. $4, under 12 free.*)

HIKING. Very popular **Inspiration Point** is a 3½ mi. round-trip hike that climbs 800 ft. Half of the hike is an easy walk on a paved road; the other half consists of a series of mountainside switchbacks. The reward on a clear day is an extensive view of the city, the ocean, and the Channel Islands. Following the creek upstream will lead to **Seven Falls.** (*From Mission Santa Barbara, drive toward the mountains and turn right onto Foothill Rd. Turn left onto Mission Canyon Rd. and continue 1 mi. Bear left onto Tunnel Rd. and drive 1¼ mi. to its end.*) **Rattlesnake Canyon Trail** (3½ mi. round-trip, 1000 ft. elevation gain) is a moderate hike up-canyon to the Tunnel Trail junction. It starts along a shady, secluded creek, then climbs through chaparral to a high desert meadow. (*From Mission Santa Barbara, drive toward the mountains and turn right onto Foothill Rd. Turn left onto Mission Canyon Rd. and continue for ½ mi. Make a sharp right onto Las Conas Rd. and travel 1 mi. Look for a large sign on the left side of the road.*)

UNIVERSITY OF CALIFORNIA AT SANTA BARBARA (UCSB). This beautiful outpost of the UC system is actually in Goleta, an unremarkable suburb of Santa Barbara, but the beachside dorms and gorgeous student body more than make up for the peripheral location. UCSB's excellent **art museum** houses the Sedgwick Collection of 15th- to 17th-century European paintings. *(From Santa Barbara, take U.S. 101 7 mi. north to the UCSB exit, or take bus #11. ☎893-7564. Open W-Su noon-5pm. Free.)* From November to February, hordes of **monarch butterflies** cling to the eucalyptus trees in Ellwood Grove, just west of UCSB, and at the end of Coronado St. off Hollister Ave.; take the Glen Annie/Storke Rd. exit off U.S. 101.

▣ NIGHTLIFE

Every night, the clubs on **State Street,** particularly the stretch of street between Haley and Cañon Perdido St., are packed. Consult the *Independent* to see who's playing on a given night. ◪**Sharkeez,** 416 State St., is a wild college hangout, with live mermaids swimming in the tank behind the bar Thursday to Saturday from 11pm on. (☎963-9680; www.sharkeez.net. Happy hour M-F 3-6:30pm with 2-for-1 beers, shots, cocktails, pitchers, and yes, buckets. 2-for-1 margaritas or mai tais Tu. College night with domestic draft beers, shots, and cocktails $1.50 Th. $2 martinis F. Open M-F 11am-2am, Sa-Su 10am-2am; kitchen closes 10pm.) **Q's Sushi A-Go-Go,** 409 State St., is classy but fun, boasting a three-level bar and eight pool tables. (☎966-9177. No jeans, tanks, or sandals. Sushi $3-14. Sake $3-5. Happy hour M-F 4-7pm; 20% off sushi rolls, 50% off drinks and selected appetizers. International night M. 80s night Tu. Karaoke W. College night Th. Cover Sa after 9pm $5. Open M-Sa 4pm-2am.)

LOS ANGELES

There's a reason 17 million people choose to live in the sprawling collection of neighborhoods and freeways known as the City of Angels. Yes, the traffic is terrible, the smog is worse, the socio-economic divisions are tense, and the plastic surgery rate is high. However, many find L.A.'s ever-changing scene enthralling, and battle to seek out the trendiest beaches, freshest clubs, hottest artists, and best ethnic food, all as the sun shines through their car windows. In this movie-obsessed town, everyone either works in the industry, wants to work in the industry, or is related to someone who does.

✈ INTERCITY TRANSPORTATION

Three major freeways connect Los Angeles to the rest of the state of California. **I-5,** which travels the length of California, bisects L.A. on a north-south axis; it continues north to Sacramento and south to San Diego. **U.S. 101** links L.A. to other coastal cities, heading west from Pasadena before turning north toward San Francisco and running parallel to I-5. **I-10** stretches west from L.A., providing access to Las Vegas and Arizona.

Airport: Los Angeles International Airport (LAX) is in Westchester, about 15 mi. southwest of downtown. LAX information (☎310-646-5252) aids Spanish and English speakers. Airport police (☎310-646-7911) patrol 24hr. Travelers Aid, a service for airport info, transportation, accommodations, and major transit emergencies, is in all terminals. (☎310-646-2270. Open M-F 9am-5pm.)

Trains: Amtrak, Union Station, 800 N. Alameda St. (☎213-683-6729 or 800-872-7245; www.amtrak.com), at the northeastern edge of downtown. Open 24hr.

Buses: Greyhound (☎800-231-2222 or 213-629-8401; www.greyhound.com). The most convenient service is found at the **Hollywood Terminal,** 1715 N. Cahuenga Blvd. (☎323-466-6381. Open daily 6:30am-9:30pm.) From there, buses run to: **Las Vegas** (5-8hr., 10 per day, $40); **San Diego** (2½-4hr., 14 per day, $17); **San Francisco** (7-12hr., 10 per day, $43); **Santa Barbara** (2½hr., 7 per day, $12); **Downtown Tijuana** (3½-5hr., 6 per day, $21). The downtown station, 1716 E. 7th St. (☎213-629-8536), at Alameda St., is in an extremely rough neighborhood. If you must get off in downtown, be very careful near 7th and Alameda St., one block southwest of the station, where you can catch MTA bus #60 traveling north to Union Station.

✈ ORIENTATION

I-5 (Golden State Freeway), I-405 (San Diego Freeway), I-110 (Harbor Freeway), U.S. 101 (Hollywood Freeway), and the **Pacific Coast Highway (PCH or Highway 1)** all run north-south. **I-10 (Santa Monica Freeway)** runs east-west, connecting Santa Monica to downtown and beyond. I-5 intersects I-10 east of downtown and is one of the two major north-south thruways. I-405, which stretches from Orange County in the south all the way through L.A., parallels I-5 closer to the coast, separating Santa Monica and Malibu from the inland Westside, and is often gridlocked. The best way to orient yourself is by learning a couple of important freeways and remaining aware of L.A.'s natural landmarks; the ocean is west and the mountains are east.

THE COAST. Santa Monica reigns over the coast with high-end shopping and lavish houses. **Malibu,** its wealthier neighbor to the north, is purely focused on the beach, and its seaside cliffs are home to many incognito celebrities. **Venice** and **Marina del Rey** extend south along Santa Monica's ocean beach path and into crazier territory. Drum circles and in-line skaters populate Venice, while Marina del Rey caters to the yachting set. The beaches of South Bay are relaxed and fun.

THE WESTSIDE. East of I-405, the Westside sits comfortably along Santa Monica Blvd. This is the cleanest, most happening part of the city. UCLA brings students to **Westwood** and **West L.A.,** while the neighboring hills of **Bel Air, Brentwood,** and **Pacific Palisades** accommodate stellar homes and the impressive Getty Center. **Beverly Hills** is, as always, the land of luxury shopping and gaudy mansions. Still on the Westside, but inching toward eastern messiness, predominantly gay **West Hollywood** is the center of much of the city's best nightlife and shopping.

HOLLYWOOD. Hollywood, in its faded glamour and neon excitement, lies just up Sunset Blvd. from West Hollywood. It's ideal for late-night eats and celebrity stalking, and holds many of the city's most famous landmarks. Lodging is among the cheapest available. South of Hollywood, the **Wilshire District** houses Miracle Mile.

EAST OF HOLLYWOOD. East of Hollywood are the bohemian neighborhoods **Los Feliz** and **Silver Lake,** and the greenery of Griffith Park. Southeast, **downtown L.A.** *does* exist and is undergoing a minor rejuvenation with the recent construction of Frank Gehry's Walt Disney Concert Hall. Farther east, at the foot of the San Gabriel Mountains, **Pasadena** has old-time charm and hosts the Rose Bowl. Movies are made and theme parks reign in the **San Fernando Valley,** north of downtown on I-5.

☎ LOCAL TRANSPORTATION

Whether they're driving pimped-out low-riders, road-hugging sports cars, or sparkling luxury sedans, Angelenos love their cars with a fervor that comes from constant contact with the road. L.A.'s roadways are often jammed; heavy traffic moves toward downtown from 7 to 10am on weekdays and streams outbound from 4 to

AREA CODES. L.A. is big. Really big. **213** covers Downtown L.A. **323** covers Hollywood, Huntington Park, Montebello, and West Hollywood. **310** covers Beverly Hills, Santa Monica, and the Westside. **562** covers Long Beach and the South Bay. **626** covers Pasadena. **818** covers Burbank, Glendale, and the San Fernando Valley. **909** covers San Bernardino and Riverside.

7pm. However, since L.A. has a huge population that doesn't work 9 to 5, traffic can be as bad at 1pm as it is at 6pm. No matter how crowded the freeway is, it's almost always quicker and safer than taking surface streets to your destination. The **Automobile Club of Southern California,** 2601 S. Figueroa St., at Adams Blvd., has additional driving info and maps. Club privileges are free for AAA members and cost $2-3 for nonmembers. (☎213-741-3686, emergency assistance 800-400-4222. Open M-F 9am-5pm.) Anyone needing non-emergency roadside assistance can dial #399 on their cellphone to be connected with the appropriate aid.

As a result of this obsession with driving, public transportation systems are limited and inconvenient. Though renting a car is expensive, your own set of wheels is the best way to navigate the sprawling city. If you must forgo the rental, use the subway and the bus to get around. Walking or biking around the city is simply not feasible—distances are just too great. However, some colorful areas such as Melrose, the Third St. Promenade in Santa Monica, Venice Beach, Hollywood, and Old Town Pasadena, are best explored by foot. At night, those on foot, especially outside the Westside, should exercise caution. *If you hitchhike, you will probably die.* It is exceptionally dangerous, not to mention illegal. Don't even consider it.

Local Buses: Metropolitan Transit Authority (MTA) Metro Customer Center, Gateway Transit Center, Union Station E. Portal (open M-F 6am-6:30pm) in downtown. Bus fare $1.25 (transfer $0.25), seniors and disabled $0.45 (transfer $0.10); exact change required. The Metro Day Pass ($3) allows for unlimited rail and bus rides and can be purchased on any metro bus or rail station. Transfers can be made between MTA lines or to other transit authorities. Unless otherwise noted, all route numbers are MTA; BBBus stands for **Big Blue Bus** and indicates Santa Monica buses. (☎800-266-6883; www.mta.net. Open M-F 6am-8:30pm, Sa-Su 8am-6pm.) The local **DASH shuttle** (☎213-808-2273; www.ladottransit.com), designed for short neighborhood hops, serves many major tourist destinations. Fare $0.25.

Subway: The **Blue Line** runs north-south between Long Beach and Los Angeles. The **Green Line** goes east-west from Norwalk to Redondo Beach, with shuttle service to LAX at Aviation/I-105. The **Red Line** runs from Union Station and downtown through Hollywood to the San Fernando Valley. The new **Gold Line** (Pasadena line) connects to the Red Line at Union Station and then runs northeast to Pasadena. $1.25, bus and rail transfers $0.35; seniors and disabled $0.45/$0.10. All lines run daily 5am-12:30am.

Taxi: Independent, ☎323-666-0050 or 800-521-8294. **L.A. Taxi/Yellow Cab Co.,** ☎310-808-1000 or 800-200-1085. **Bell Cab,** ☎888-235-5222.

Car Rental: Universal Rent-A-Car, 920 S. La Brea Ave. (☎323-954-1186). Cars from $20 per day with 150 mi. free, $140 per week with 1050 mi. free. No under-25 surcharge. Open M-F 8am-6pm, Sa-Su 9am-5pm.

◪ PRACTICAL INFORMATION

Visitor Info: L.A. Convention and Visitor Bureau, 685 S. Figueroa St. (☎213-689-8822; www.visitlanow.com), between Wilshire Blvd. and 7th St. in the Financial District. Staff speaks English, French, German, and Japanese. Detailed bus map of L.A. available, along with tourist and entertainment info. Open M-F 8:30am-5pm.

Hotline: Rape Crisis, ☎310-392-8381.

Los Angeles and Vicinity
SEE COLOR INSERTS FOR MORE LOS ANGELES AREA MAPS

Medical Services: Cedars-Sinai Medical Center, 8700 Beverly Blvd. (☎310-423-3277, emergency 423-8605). **Good Samaritan Hospital,** 1225 Wilshire Blvd. (☎213-977-2121, emergency 977-2420). **UCLA Medical Center,** 10833 Le Conte Ave. (☎310-825-9111, emergency 825-2111).

Post Office: Central branch at 7001 S. Central Ave. (☎800-275-8777). Open M-F 7am-7pm, Sa 7am-3pm. Hollywood branch at 6457 Santa Monica Blvd. Open M-F 8:30am-7pm, Sa 8:30am-5pm. **Postal Code:** 90052.

▓ ACCOMMODATIONS

In choosing where to stay, the first consideration should be location. Those visiting for beach culture should choose lodgings in Venice or Santa Monica. Avid sightseers will be better off in Hollywood or the more expensive (but cleaner and nicer) Westside. One campground fairly close to Los Angeles is **Leo Carrillo State Beach ❶** (☎805-488-5223), on Hwy. 1 about 20 mi. north of Malibu. It has 135 sites equipped with flush toilets and showers (sites $13). Listed prices do not include L.A.'s 14% hotel tax.

THE COAST

Los Angeles Surf City Hostel, 26 Pier Ave. (☎798-2323), in Pier Plaza in Hermosa Beach, the center of the local scene. A young, mostly international clientele enjoys the beach by day and the clubs by night. Helpful staff dispenses advice and maps and coordinates tours. Free breakfast, linens, and towels. Passport or driver's license required. Key deposit $10. 28-night max. stay; 3-day max. stay for US citizens. Reservations recommended. Dorms $19-21; private rooms $50. MC/V. ❶

Seaview Motel, 1760 Ocean Ave. (☎310-393-6711), in Santa Monica. Tastefully decorated rooms, a patio ideal for sunbathing, and a path straight to the beach. Prime location at a reasonable price. Singles to quads $65-75. MC/V. ❸

Venice Beach Cotel, 25 Windward Ave. (☎310-399-7649; www.venicebeachcotel.com). Situated right off the Venice Beach Boardwalk and easily identifiable by its row of international flags on display. International staff and guests. Tennis rackets, table tennis, and boogie boards ($20 deposit). Passport required. Key deposit $5. Reservations recommended. Dorms with ocean view and bath $15-19; doubles $36-52; triples with bath $66. MC/V. ❶

THE WESTSIDE

Orbit Hotel and Hostel, 7950 Melrose Ave. (☎323-655-1510 or 877-672-4887; www.orbithotel.com), a block west of Fairfax Ave., in West Hollywood. Central location and retro-chic decor. TV and game room, courtyard, and late-night party room with bright furniture. Small cafe with breakfast and dinner for around $5. Dorms accept only international students with passport. Free linens, towels, and parking. Internet access. Dorms $18-24; private rooms for up to 4 $70-90. MC/V. ❶

Hotel Claremont, 1044 Tiverton Ave. (☎310-208-5957 or 800-266-5957), near UCLA in Westwood Village. The Claremont is a house-like hotel in a beautiful area, still owned by the same family that built it over 60 years ago. All rooms are equipped with ceiling fans and small private baths. Fridge and microwave next to a Victorian-style TV lounge. Free newspapers and wireless Internet. Reservations recommended. Singles $60; doubles $70-79. AmEx/D/MC/V. ❸

HOLLYWOOD

USA Hostels Hollywood, 1624 Schrader Blvd. (☎323-462-3777 or 800-524-6783; www.usahostels.com), south of Hollywood Blvd., west of Cahuenga Blvd. Buzzing with young travelers and filled with energy. Nice kitchen and big-screen TV lounge. Special events nightly. Free beach shuttles run Tu, Th, Sa. Free pancake breakfast, linens, and wireless Internet. Parking $6 per day. Dorms $22-28; private rooms for 2-4 people $57-69. International passport or out-of-state student ID required. MC/V. ❶

Orange Drive Manor, 1764 N. Orange Dr. (☎323-850-0350). A converted 1920s minimansion in a residential neighborhood just a block off Hollywood Blvd. Grandeur (and lack of sign) disguise this rambling hostel. Cable TV lounge. Lockers $0.75. Internet $1 per 10min. Key deposit $20. Parking $5. Reservations recommended. Dorms $22-26; private rooms $48-64. ISIC discount $2. Cash or traveler's check only. ❷

Hollywood International Hostel, 6820 Hollywood Blvd. (☎800-750-6561), across the street from Hollywood and Highland. Lounge, kitchen, shared baths. Free breakfast and linens. International passport required. Roomy dorms $18. Cash only. ❶

◨ FOOD

From celebrity eateries to taco wagons, there's no shortage of great food in L.A. The city's diversity is reflected in its exotic cuisine. If you like to cook, **Trader Joe's** specializes in cheap gourmet food. There are 74 locations in SoCal; call ☎800-746-7857 to find one. (Most open daily 9am-9pm.) L.A.'s ◧**farmers market,** 6333 W. 3rd St., at Fairfax Ave., draws 3 million people every year with produce stalls, international food booths, handicraft shops, and a phenomenal juice bar. A cheaper and less touristy source of produce is the **Grand Central Public Market,** 317 S. Broadway, between 3rd and 4th St. downtown. Entrances are on both Broadway and Hill St. between 3rd and 4th St. (☎213-624-2378. Open daily 9am-6pm.)

THE COAST

◧ **Rose Cafe and Market,** 220 Rose Ave. (☎310-399-0711), at Main St., in Venice. Cafe features local art, industrial architecture, and healthy deli specials, including sandwiches ($6-8) and a wide variety of salads ($6-8) available from 11:30am. Limited menu after 3pm. Open M-F 7am-5:30pm, Sa 8am-6pm, Su 8am-5pm. AmEx/MC/V. ❷

Fritto Misto, 601 Colorado Ave. (☎310-458-2829), at 6th St., in Santa Monica. This "Neighborhood Italian Cafe" lets you create your own pasta (from $6). Weekend lunch special of all-you-can-eat calamari and salad $12. Vegetarian entrees $8-12. Open M-Th 11:30am-10pm, F-Sa 11:30am-10:30pm, Su 11:30am-9:30pm. AmEx/D/MC/V. ❸

Neptune's Net Seafood, 42505 Hwy. 1 (☎310-457-3095), in Malibu. Known for some of the best, most affordable seafood in Malibu. Refuel after a day on the beach with a deliciously deep-fried calamari, fish, and chips combo basket ($11). Seafood entrees $4-10. Open M-Th 10:30am-8pm, F 10:30am-9pm, Sa-Su 10am-8:30pm. D/MC/V. ❸

The Spot, 110 2nd St. (☎310-376-2355; www.worldfamousspot.com), in Hermosa Beach. The oldest vegetarian restaurant in L.A. and a favorite with local hippies. "Inflation Buster" combos like the "Dear George" include veggies on pasta or rice with tofu ($6-8). Homemade bread and desserts $3.50. Open daily 11am-10pm. Cash only. ❷

THE WESTSIDE

◧ **The Apple Pan,** 10801 W. Pico Blvd. (☎310-475-3585), 1 block east of Westwood Blvd. across from the Westside Pavilion, in West L.A. Not much has changed since the diner opened in 1947. No tables, no frills,

---

THE HIDDEN DEAL

DOLLAR DIDDIE

A dollar doesn't buy much these days, especially around L.A., but anyone passing through Westwood Village can use a single greenback to get a piece of handheld goodness in the form of a freshly made ice cream sandwich from **Diddie Reese Cookies.**

A line of patrons stretching down the block from the small storefront ensures that cookies ranging from your standard chocolate chip (which tastes anything but standard) to the more exotic white chocolate macadamia nut are baked fresh throughout the day to meet demand. Each customer steps up to the counter, picks out two cookies and one of twelve ice cream flavors, and the clerks quickly put together a generous, neatly wrapped ice cream sandwich. You're free to mix-and-match, leading to mouthwatering combos like white chocolate cookie with espresso ice cream or one chocolate chip and one double chocolate cookie with mint chip ice cream. Then hand the clerk your dollar and dig in.

If you want to try Diddie Reese's baked goods but aren't ready for a full-on sugar coma, you can pick out three cookies or brownies for $1. A buck also gets you two cookies and milk, juice, or coffee. Talk about your dollar going a long way.

Diddie Reese Cookies, 926 Broxton Ave. (☎310-208-0448), in Westwood Village. Open M-Th 10am-midnight, F 10am-1am, Sa noon-1am, Su noon-midnight.

just a white linoleum counter where you can enjoy juicy hickory burgers ($7), crispy fries ($3), and humongous slices of fresh-baked apple pie ($5). Open Tu-Th and Su 11am-midnight, F-Sa 11am-1am. Cash only. ❷

Sak's Teriyaki, 1121 Glendon Ave. (☎310-208-2002), in Westwood. UCLA students pack this teriyaki joint, ordering the not-so-authentic but oh-so-tender skewers of meat and veggies (with rice, gyoza, and salad; $4-9). Open daily 11am-10pm. Cash only. ❶

Barney's Beanery, 8447 Santa Monica Blvd. (☎310-656-5777), brings back L.A.'s good ol' days with nostalgic furnishings and a menu that lists the famous celebrities that have enjoyed the house specialty chili ($5). Barney's proudly boasts "if we don't have it, you don't need it" and with over 1000 menu items and 125 bottled beers, they're probably right. Specialty pizzas $8-24. Potato skins with any toppings you can think of $6-9. Open daily 11am-1am. AmEx/MC/V. ❸

Bossa Nova, 685 N. Robertson Blvd. (☎310-657-5070), in West Hollywood. At lunchtime, the patio of this laid-back Brazilian/Italian restaurant fills up with stars in shades who come for the incredible plantains. By the end of the night, everyone's here. Entrees $10-18. Open daily 11am-4am. Reservations recommended. AmEx/MC/V. ❹

HOLLYWOOD

▨**Canter's,** 419 N. Fairfax Ave. (☎323-651-2030), north of Beverly Blvd. An L.A. institution and the heart and soul of historically Jewish Fairfax since 1931. Baseball-sized matzoh balls in chicken broth ($4.50) and giant pastrami or corned beef sandwiches ($9) are wildly popular. Beer $2.50. Lounge with nightly free rock, blues, jazz, and cabaret-pop (from 10pm). Open 24hr. AmEx/D/MC/V. ❷

Roscoe's House of Chicken and Waffles, 1514 Gower St. (☎323-466-7453), at Sunset Blvd. Also at 5006 W. Pico Blvd, in West L.A. The down-home feel and comfort food menu make this place popular. "1 succulent chicken breast and 1 delicious waffle" $8. Open M-Th and Su 8:30am-midnight, F-Sa 8:30am-4am. AmEx/MC/V. ❷

Pink's Hot Dog Stand, 709 N. La Brea Ave. (☎323-931-4223; www.pinksholly-wood.com), at Melrose Ave. Pink's serves up chili-slathered goodness in a bun, attracting droves of tourists and Angelenos alike. Try the special "Ozzy Osbourne Spicy Dog" for $5. Standard chili dogs run $2.40. Open M-Th and Su 9:30am-2am, F-Sa 9:30am-3am. Cash only. ❶

EAST OF HOLLYWOOD

▨**Philippe, The Original,** 1001 N. Alameda St. (☎213-628-3781; www.philippes.com), 2 blocks north of Union Station, downtown. Philippe invented the French Dip sandwich here back in 1918, when he dropped a roll into a pan filled with sizzling hot oil. Choose from pork, beef, ham, turkey, or lamb filling ($5). Free parking. Open daily 6am-10pm. Cash only. ❶

Fair Oaks Pharmacy and Soda Fountain, 1526 Mission St. (☎626-799-1414), at Fair Oaks Ave. in South Pasadena. From Colorado Blvd., go south 1 mi. on Fair Oaks Ave. to Mission St. Open since 1915, this old-fashioned soda fountain serves huge triple-decker club sandwiches ($7.50) and their famous phosphates made with soda water and flavored syrup ($2). Shakes and malts $5. Soda fountain open M-Th 9am-8pm, F-Sa 9am-9pm, Su 11am-8pm. Lunch served until 5pm daily. AmEx/D/MC/V. ❶

The Pantry, 877 S. Figueroa St. (☎213-972-9279), in downtown. Since 1924, it hasn't closed once—not for the earthquakes, not for the 1992 riots (when it served as a National Guard outpost), and not even when a taxicab drove through the front wall. This diner is known for its large portions, free cole slaw, and fresh sourdough bread. Giant breakfast specials $6. Lunch sandwiches $8. Open 24hr. Cash only. ❷

◎ SIGHTS

SANTA MONICA

Santa Monica is known more for its lively shoreside scene than for its surf, and the area on and around the carnival pier is filled with hawkers and local tourist activity. The fun spills over onto the pedestrian-only Third St. Promenade, where street performers and a farmers market add a bit of spice to the outdoor mall-ish ambience. Farther inland, along Main St. and beyond, a smattering of galleries, design shops, and museums testify to the city's love for art and culture.

SANTA MONICA PIER, PACIFIC PARK, AND THE BEACH. The famed pier is the heart of Santa Monica Beach and home to the roller coasters, arcades, and Ferris wheels of Pacific Park. Look for the small aquarium and free TV show tickets near the north entrance to the pier. *(Off Hwy. 1 on the way to Venice Beach from Santa Monica Beach. ☎ 458-8900; www.santamonicapier.org. Pier free and open 24hr. Park open in summer M-Th and Su 11am-11pm, F-Sa 11am-12:30am; winter hours vary. Ticket window closes 30min. before the park closes. Tickets $2 each; most rides 2-3 tickets. Day pass $20, children under 42 in. $11.)* The paved **Ocean Front Walk** is a palm-lined mini-freeway of cyclists, skaters, and runners, stretching 20¼ mi. along the beach between Santa Monica and Torrance. Immediately south of the pier on Ocean Front Walk, skilled players match wits at the public chess tables at the **International Chess Park.** Opposite the chess masters is the original location of **Muscle Beach** (now in Venice Beach), where bodybuilders and athletes lifted impossibly heavy weights and posed in briefs in the 1930s-50s.

THIRD STREET PROMENADE. Angelenos claim that nobody walks in L.A., but if shopping is involved, all rules go out the car window. The Third Street Promenade, an ultra-popular pedestrianized three blocks of mosaic art tiles, fountains, and patio restaurants, is home to trendy shopping ranging from overpriced bikini shops to some of L.A.'s best bookstores. On Wednesday and Saturday mornings, the area transforms into a popular **farmers market** selling fresh California flowers and produce, with Saturdays featuring exclusively organic products. *(Between Broadway and Wilshire in downtown Santa Monica. 4th St. exit from I-10. Open 8:30am-1:30pm.)*

MALIBU, VENICE, AND SOUTH BAY

North of Santa Monica along the Pacific Coast Highway (PCH), the cityscape gives way to appealing stretches of sandy, sewage-free shoreline. **Malibu's** beaches are clean, relatively uncrowded, and easily the best in L.A. County for surfers, sunbathers, and swimmers alike. Along the 30000 block of PCH, 30min. west of Santa Monica, stretches ▨**Zuma Beach,** L.A. County's northernmost, largest, and most popular sandbox. **Zuma Westward,** located at Point Dume State Beach, just south of Zuma Beach, is less crowded and more relaxing. You can jet through the wave tubes at **Surfrider Beach,** a section of Malibu Lagoon State Beach north of the pier at 23000 PCH. Walk there via the Zonker Harris Access Way at 22700 PCH.

Venice is a carnivalesque beach town where guitar-toting, wild-eyed, tie-dyed residents sculpt masterpieces in sand, compose them in graffiti, or just talk gibberish. Grab a corn dog and head to **Ocean Front Walk,** where street people converge on clusters of benches, evangelists drown out off-color comedians, panhandlers solicit donations, and bodybuilders of both sexes pump iron in skimpy spandex outfits at **Muscle Beach,** 1800 Ocean Front Walk, closest to 18th St. and Pacific Ave. About 20 mi. southwest of downtown L.A. are the South Bay beaches of **Manhattan Beach, Hermosa Beach,** and **Redondo Beach.** Manhattan Beach is favored for surfing; Hermosa Beach, L.A. County's most popular urban beach, is also one of the cleanest. Both host elite beach volleyball and surf competitions (☎ 426-8000;

www.avp.com or www.surffestival.org). Most visit Redondo Beach for its harbor, pier, and seafood-rich boardwalk. **The Strand** is a concrete bike path that runs from Santa Monica (where it's called Ocean Front Walk) to Hermosa Beach.

WESTWOOD

Westwood, an area east of I-405 and north of Wilshire Blvd., is home to the **University of California at Los Angeles (UCLA),** a prototypical California university, with grassy open spaces, dazzling sunshine, massive brick buildings, and deeply tanned bodies on 400 acres in the foothills of the Santa Monica Mountains. Once voted the #1 jock school in the country by *Sports Illustrated*, UCLA also boasts an illustrious film school whose graduates include James Dean, Jim Morrison, Oliver Stone, Francis Ford Coppola, and Tim Robbins. Just south of campus, the **Hammer Art Museum,** 10899 Wilshire Blvd., houses the world's largest collection of works by 19th-century French satirist Honoré Daumier, as well as Van Gogh's *Hospital at Saint-Rémy*. (☎310-443-7000; www.hammer.ucla.edu. Open Tu-W and F-Sa 11am-7pm, Th 11am-9pm, Su 11am-5pm. $5, seniors $3, students and under 17 free. Th free.) UCLA's art collection continues outdoors with the **Murphy Sculpture Garden,** in the northeast corner of campus, which contains over 70 pieces by major artists like Auguste Rodin and Henri Matisse scattered under the trees. Over 5000 plant species flourish in the UCLA **Botanical Gardens,** in the eastern part of campus, at the intersection of Le Conte and Hilgard Ave. Stop at an information booth inside each entrance to get a parking day pass ($7). Just south of UCLA, **Westwood Village** is a walkable area with trendy stores and affordable restaurants.

BEVERLY HILLS

Beverly Hills glows in the mystique of expensive hotels, ritzy boutiques, and movie stars galore. You can live it up here simply by throwing on your trendiest jeans, slipping on some shades, and making clerks work for the money they think you have. Pick up a star map, available all over town for around $5, to drive by the houses of celebrities. The heart of designer shopping pulses along **Rodeo Drive** and throughout the **Golden Triangle,** a wedge formed by Beverly Dr., Wilshire Blvd., and Santa Monica Blvd. Stroll past the stone-fronted stores, breathe in the sweet smell of money, and check out your hot self in the smoked glass windows of **Armani,** 436 N. Rodeo Dr. The divine triple-whammy of **Cartier** (370 N. Rodeo Dr.), **Gucci** (347 N. Rodeo Dr.), and **Chanel** (400 N. Rodeo Dr.) sits on prime real estate, where rents approach $40,000 per month. At the south end of Rodeo Dr. (the end closest to Wilshire Blvd.) is pedestrian-only **2 Rodeo Drive,** a.k.a. **Via Rodeo,** which houses Dior, Tiffany, and numerous salons frequented by the stars. Across the way is the venerable **Regent Beverly Wilshire Hotel,** 9500 Wilshire Blvd., where Julia Roberts went from Hollywood hooker to Richard Gere's queen in *Pretty Woman.* A ludicrously extravagant retreat as famous as the starlets who romanced here, the salmon-colored **Beverly Hills Hotel,** 9641 Sunset Blvd. (☎276-2251), sits among 12 acres of tropical gardens and pools. Marilyn Monroe reportedly had trysts with both JFK and RFK in one of the 22 "bungalows." In case you were wondering, rooms run $395-455, bungalows $450-3400, and suites $835-5200.

WEST HOLLYWOOD

Bring your walking shoes and spend a day on the 3 mi. strip of **Melrose Avenue** from Highland Ave. west to the intersection of Doheny Dr. and Santa Monica Blvd. This strip began to develop its funky flair in the late 1980s when art galleries, designer stores, lounge-like coffee shops, used clothing and music stores, and restaurants began to take over. Now the hippest stretch lies between La Brea and Fairfax Ave. North of the mammoth **Beverly Center Mall,** 8500 Beverly Blvd. (☎310-854-0071;

open M-F 10am-9pm, Sa 10am-8pm, Su 11am-6pm), is the **Pacific Design Center,** 8687 Melrose Ave. (☎310-657-0800; www.pacificdesigncenter.com), a sea-green glass complex nicknamed the Blue Whale and constructed in the shape of a wave.

HOLLYWOOD

Exploring the Hollywood area takes a pair of sunglasses, a camera, some cash, and a high tolerance for crowds. **Hollywood Boulevard** is the center of tourist madness, home to the Walk of Fame, famous theaters, and ubiquitous souvenir shops.

HOLLYWOOD SIGN. Those 50 ft. high, 30 ft. wide, slightly crooked letters perched on Mt. Lee in Griffith Park stand as a universal symbol of the city. The original 1923 sign read "HOLLYWOODLAND" as an advertisement for a new subdivision in the Hollywood Hills. The sign has been a target of many college pranks, which have made it read everything from "Hollyweird" to "Ollywood" (after the infamous Lt. Col. Oliver North). A fence keeps you 40 ft. away and views are sometimes obscured by smog. *(Getting close requires a strenuous 2½ mi. hike. Take plenty of water. From Franklin Ave., go north on Canyon Dr. to its end, where parking is free. Walk up beyond the gates; Brush Canyon Trail starts where Canyon Dr. becomes unpaved. At the top of the hill, follow the road to your left; the sign looms just below. For those satisfied with driving, go east on Franklin Ave. and then north on Beachwood, and drive up until you are forced to drive down.)*

GRAUMAN'S CHINESE THEATRE. Loosely modeled on a Chinese temple, this monumental, eye-catching theater is a Hollywood icon and frequently rolls out the red carpet for movie premieres. The exterior columns were imported from China, where they once supported a Ming Dynasty temple. The theatre houses a collection of celebrity footprints as well as other star trademarks—Whoopi Goldberg's dreadlocks, R2D2's wheels, and George Burns's cigar. *(6925 Hollywood Blvd., between Highland and Orange St. ☎323-463-9576. 4-5 tours per day; call ahead. $8, under 6 free.)*

WALK OF FAME. Pedestrian traffic along Hollywood Blvd. mimics L.A.'s congested freeways, as tourists stop mid-stride to gawk at the sidewalk's over 2000 bronze-inlaid stars, which are inscribed with the names of the famous, the infamous, and the downright obscure. Stars are awarded for achievements in movies, radio, television, recording, or live performance; only Gene Autry has a star in all five categories. The stars have no particular order, so don't try to find a method to the madness. New inductees to the Walk of Fame include Matthew Broderick and TV legal eagle Judge Judy. To catch today's (or yesterday's) stars in person, call the Chamber of Commerce for info on star-unveiling ceremonies. *(☎323-469-8311; www.hollywoodchamber.net. Free.)*

HOLLYWOOD AND HIGHLAND. The sprawling **Hollywood and Highland Center** contains brand-name stores, high-profile restaurants, nightlife, a 640-room hotel, and the $94 million **Kodak Theater,** built specifically for the Academy Awards and also home to the finals of American Idol. *(☎323-960-2331. Center open M-Sa 10am-10pm, Su 10am-7pm with various restaurants, theaters, and clubs open later. Parking $2 per 4hr. with validation. Kodak box office ☎323-308-6363. Open daily 10am-6pm; on performance days until 9pm. Tours in summer every 30min. 10:30am-4pm; in winter 10:30am-2:30pm. $15, seniors and under 12 $10.)*

CAPITOL RECORDS TOWER. The **Capitol Records Tower** was designed to look like a stack of records with a needle on top blinking H-O-L-L-Y-W-O-O-D in Morse code. A faded, yet still impressive mural of jazz legends occupies the building's southern face, and the tower becomes Hollywood's tallest Christmas tree each December. *(1750 Vine St., at the famous address of Hollywood and Vine.)*

GRIFFITH PARK AREA

GRIFFITH PARK. For a breath of fresh air and a respite from city life, take to the rugged slopes of Griffith Park, the nation's largest municipal park, nestled in the hills between U.S. 101, I-5, and Rte. 134. A stark contrast to the concrete heights of downtown and the star-studded streets of Hollywood, the park's dry grass foothills and scrub-forested valleys are the site of many outdoor diversions. Some 52 mi. of hiking trails, three golf courses, a planetarium, a zoo, museums, and the 6000-seat Greek Theatre are all found within its rolling 4107 acres. *(Visitors center and ranger headquarters: 4730 Crystal Spring Dr. ☎323-913-4688, emergency 913-7390. Park open daily 5am-10:30pm.)* The park has numerous equestrian trails and places to saddle up, such as **J.P. Stables.** *(914 S. Mariposa St., in Burbank. ☎818-843-9890. Open daily 7:30am-6pm. 1st hr. $20, each additional hr. $12. Cash only.)*

AUTRY MUSEUM OF THE AMERICAN WEST. City slickers and lone rangers may discover that the American West is not what they thought—this museum insists that the real is not the reel, drawing the line between Old West fact and fiction. The main level focuses on myth and imagination in the creation of the American West, and visitors can gawk at items like Annie Oakley's pistols and Hopalong Cassidy's costume alongside the sketches and paintings of 19th-century American artists. The lower level explores the West with Indian artifacts, a trading post replica, and a tribute to cowboys of the past and present. *(4700 Western Heritage Way. ☎323-667-2000. Open Tu-W and F-Su 10am-5pm, Th 10am-8pm. $7.50, students and seniors $5, ages 2-12 $3. Free Th after 4pm and on the 2nd Tu of each month.)*

PLANETARIUM AND OBSERVATORY. The world-famous white stucco and copper domes of the mountaintop observatory would be visible from nearly any point in L.A. were it not for the smog. The observatory parking lot lends a terrific view of the Hollywood sign. You may remember the planetarium from the James Dean film *Rebel Without A Cause.* The observatory and planetarium are closed until mid-May 2006 for renovation. In the meantime, visitors can check out the modest displays and mini-planetarium at the **Griffith Observatory Satellite** in the northern corner of Griffith Park. *(Drive to the top of Mt. Hollywood on Vermont Ave. or Hillhurst St. from Los Feliz Blvd., or take MTA #180 or 181 from Hollywood Blvd. ☎323-664-1181 or 664-1191; www.griffithobs.org. Open Tu-F 1-10pm, Sa-Su 10am-10pm.)*

L.A. ZOO. Much of the park is undergoing renovations, but rare animals from the around the world are still on display through the 113 well-kept acres. The zoo's five sea lions are a big hit, as are the red apes and chimps. *(5333 Zoo Dr. From Los Feliz Blvd., take Crystal Springs Dr. into the park; the zoo will be on your left. ☎644-4200; www.lazoo.org. Open daily July-Aug. 10am-6pm; Sept.-June 10am-5pm. Animals are tucked into bed for the night starting 1hr. before closing. $10, seniors $7, ages 2-12 $5.)*

FOREST LAWN CEMETERY. A rather twisted sense of celebrity sightseeing may lead some to Glendale, where you can gaze upon stars who can't run away when pestered. Among the illustrious dead are Clark Gable, George Burns, and Jimmy Stewart. The cemetery has a 30 ft. by 15 ft. stained glass reproduction of Leonardo da Vinci's *The Last Supper* (presented every 30min. 9:30am-4pm). If you're still obsessed with oversized art, swing by the Forest Lawn in Hollywood Hills (only a 10min. drive) to see "Birth of Liberty," America's largest historical mosaic. *(1712 S. Glendale Ave. ☎800-204-3131. Open daily 8am-6pm. Mausoleum open 9am-4:30pm.)*

DOWNTOWN

The **DASH Shuttle** runs six lines downtown that cover most of the major tourist destinations. ($0.25; ask for a free transfer.) Due to expensive short-term lot parking ($3 per 20min.) and exorbitant meter prices ($0.25 per 10min.), it's best to park in a public lot ($5-10 per day) and hit the pavement on foot. The **L.A. Visitors Center,** 685 S. Figueroa St., between Wilshire and 7th St., has pamphlets and answers to your travel queries. (☎213-689-8822. Open M-F 8am-4pm, Sa 8:30am-5pm.)

EL PUEBLO HISTORIC PARK. The historic birthplace of L.A. is now known as El Pueblo de Los Angeles Historical Monument, bordered by Cesar Chávez Ave., Alameda St., Hollywood Fwy., and Spring St. (DASH B). Established in 1825, the Plaza is the center of El Pueblo, and hosts several festivals including the Mexican Independence celebration (Sept. 16), **Día de los Muertos** celebrations (Nov. 1-2), and **Cinco de Mayo** (May 5). As you wander through the area, check out the plaques found on the walls and sidewalks for all sorts of fun historical facts about the area and its former inhabitants. **Olvera Street** resembles a colorful Mexican marketplace, selling all sorts of things you don't really need. Feel free to bargain at *puestos* (vendor stalls) for everything from Mexican handicrafts and food to personalized t-shirts. The **Avila Adobe** (ca. 1818), 10 E. Olvera St., is the "oldest" house in the city, and the **Sepulveda House,** 12 Olvera St., contains a small museum and visitors center, providing information and a short film outlining the history of Los Angeles. *(Avila Adobe open daily 9am-3pm. Sepulveda House open M-Sa 10am-3pm.)*

MUSIC CENTER. The Music Center is an enormous, beautiful complex most easily identified by the sweeping silver curves of the Frank Gehry-designed ◪**Walt Disney Concert Hall.** This gleaming 2265-seat structure is the brand-new home of the L.A. Philharmonic and the L.A. Master Chorale. *(151 S. Grand Ave. ☎213-972-7211; www.disneyhall.org. Audio tours available 10am-3pm daily. $10, seniors and students $8.)* The musical fun continues next door with the **Dorothy Chandler Pavilion,** home of the L.A. Opera *(☎213-972-8001; www.laopera.org)* and former site of the Academy Awards. Also part of the Music Center are the **Mark Taper Forum** and the **Ahmanson Theatre,** known for their world-class shows. *(☎213-628-2772; www.taperahmanson.com. Tours of the center M-F 11:30am, 12:30, 1:30pm as performances permit. Go to the information booth in the large outdoor courtyard between the theaters.)*

MUSEUM OF CONTEMPORARY ART (MOCA). MOCA features an extensive and varied collection of American and European art dating from 1940, including abstract expressionism, pop art, and photography. The Frank Gehry-renovated **MOCA at the Geffen Contemporary** was once the garage for the LAPD fleet. The "Temporary Contemporary" and its highly-acclaimed art exhibitions eventually became permanent, to the delight of its adoring public. *(250 S. Grand Ave. ☎213-626-6222; www.moca.org.)* Additional visual arts displays can be found at the **Pacific Design Center** complex. *(8687 Melrose Ave. Free. All locations open M and F 11am-5pm, Th 11am-8pm, Sa-Su 11am-6pm. $8, students and seniors $5, under 12 free. Free Th 5-8pm. Admission good for both MOCA locations. Shuttle between the 2 locations available.)*

OTHER SIGHTS. One of the best-known buildings in SoCal, **City Hall** "has starred in more movies than most actors." *(200 N. Spring St.)* Bargain hounds can haggle to their hearts' delight in the **Fashion District,** which is bordered by 6th and 9th St. along Los Angeles St. At 1017 ft., the tallest building between Chicago and Hong Kong, the **US Bank Tower,** punctuates the L.A. skyline with its glass crown and is brilliantly lit at night. *(633 W. 5th St.)* The **Westin Bonaventure Hotel** is composed of five sleek cylinders sheathed in black glass, and has appeared in *Rain Man, In the Line of Fire,* and *Heat. (404 S. Figueroa St.)* Slightly southeast of the Bonaventure is the historic **Millenium Biltmore Hotel,** designed by Schultze and Weaver, best known for New York's Waldorf-Astoria. *(506 S. Grand Ave.)* After trekking around downtown, visit the soothing **James Irvine Garden,** better known as *Seiryu-en* or "Garden of the Pure Stream." *(244 S. San Pedro St. by the Japanese American Cultural and Community Center in Little Tokyo. ☎213-628-2725; www.jaccc.org. Garden open daily 9am-*

5pm.) North of Exposition Park, the **University of Southern California (USC)** brings a youthful character to the streets of downtown. (☎ *213-740-2311; www.usc.edu. Campus tours offered M-F every hr. 10am-3pm; call ☎ 213-740-6605 to confirm availability.*)

PASADENA AREA

Though just 15min. northeast of downtown Los Angeles, Pasadena cultivates a very different atmosphere, managing to feel like a small town while still offering the shopping, entertainment, and attractions of the big city. **Old Town,** the area surrounding the intersection of Fair Oaks Blvd. and Colorado Blvd., and **Paseo Colorado,** just east along Colorado Blvd., are vibrant shopping and dining districts located at the heart of the reinvigorated historical city.

■ **NORTON SIMON MUSEUM OF ART.** West of Old Town, the **Simon Museum** houses a world-class, well-curated collection of Western and Southeast Asian art spanning seven centuries. Paintings by Van Gogh, Monet, and Picasso are featured. The bronzes by Degas and the 79,000 sq. ft. sculpture garden surrounding a Monet-inspired lily pool are particularly impressive. (*411 W. Colorado Blvd. ☎ 626-449-6840. Open M, W-Th, and Sa-Su noon-6pm, F noon-9pm. $6, seniors $3, students and under 18 free. Free parking.*)

■ **HUNTINGTON LIBRARY, ART GALLERY, AND BOTANICAL GARDENS.** South of Pasadena in San Marino, the Huntington's 150 stunning acres of gardens are broken into 15 thematic areas including the Rose Garden, the Desert Garden, and the Japanese Garden. As tempting as the grounds may be, picnicking and sunbathing among the greens are strictly forbidden. The library holds one of the most important collections of rare books and British and American manuscripts in the world, including a Gutenberg Bible, Benjamin Franklin's handwritten autobiography, a 1410 manuscript of Chaucer's *Canterbury Tales*, and a number of Shakespeare's first folios. The art gallery is known for its 18th- and 19th-century British and French paintings. No visit here is complete without taking tea in the Rose Garden Tea Room. (*1151 Oxford Rd., between Huntington Dr. and California Blvd. ☎ 405-2100; www.huntington.org. Open Memorial Day-Labor Day Tu-Su 10:30am-4:30pm; Labor Day-Memorial Day Tu-F noon-4:30pm, Sa-Su 10:30am-4:30pm. $15, seniors $12, students $10, ages 5-11 $6, under 5 free. Free 1st Th of each month. Rose Garden set tea Tu-Su $15; reservations required, call ☎ 405-2125.*)

ROSE BOWL. Pasadena's most famous landmark, the Rose Bowl is a sand-colored, 90,000-seat stadium that is home to the college football clash between the champions of the Big Ten and Pac 10 conferences each New Year's Day. (*1001 Rose Bowl Dr., west of town. ☎ 577-3100; www.rosebowlstadium.com.*) The Bowl also hosts a huge flea market with upwards of 2000 vendors. (*☎ 323-560-7469. 2nd Su of each month 9am-4:30pm. Admission 5-7am $20, 7-8am $15, 8-9am $10, 9am-3pm $7.*)

CALTECH. Some of the world's greatest scientific minds do their work at the sunny, stone-and-tile campus of the California Institute of Technology (Caltech), southeast of Old Town between Del Mar Blvd. and California Blvd. Founded in 1891, Caltech has amassed a faculty that includes several Nobel laureates and a student body that prides itself both on its staggering collective intellect and its loony practical jokes, which range from unscrewing all the chairs in a lecture hall and bolting them in backwards to reworking the Hollywood sign to read "Caltech." (*1201 E. California Blvd., about 2½ mi. southeast of Old Town. ☎ 626-395-6327. Self-guided tour brochures available at the Visitors Center, 315 S. Hill Ave., between Colorado Blvd. and Del Mar Blvd. Tours M-F 2pm.*) NASA's **Jet Propulsion Laboratory,** about 5 mi. north of Old Town, executed the journey of the Mars Pathfinder. Ask to see pictures of the face of Mars. (*4800 Oak Grove Dr. ☎ 818-354-9314. Free tours by appointment.*)

DESCANSO GARDENS. Often overshadowed by the larger Huntington, the lush 165-acre gardens are the surprisingly impressive home of North America's largest camellia forest, with more than 34,000 plants, many of them over 20 ft. tall. To see plants in full bloom, visit between late autumn and early spring. The gardens also include lilac gardens and the sprawling International Rosarium rose collection. *(1418 Descanso Dr., by the intersection of Fwy. 2 and Fwy. 210, west of Pasadena. ☎818-949-4200; www.descansogardens.org. Open daily 9am-5pm. $7, students and seniors $5, ages 5-12 $2. Tram tours $3 Tu-Su 1, 2, 3pm, also 11am on weekends. Free parking.)*

SAN FERNANDO VALLEY

The Valley can't seem to shake the infamy it gained for breeding the Valley Girl, who started a worldwide trend in the 1980s with her huge hair, and, ohmigod, like, totally far-out mall adventures. But the Valley deserves some respect; all of the major movie studios (and many pornographers) make their blockbusters here. Passing Burbank on Rte. 134, you may catch glimpses of the Valley's most lucrative studios: **Universal, Warner Bros., NBC,** and **Disney.** To best experience the industry, attend a **free TV show taping** or take a studio tour.

■ **UNIVERSAL STUDIOS.** A movie and television studio that happens to have the world's first and largest movie-themed amusement park attached, Universal Studios Hollywood is the most popular tourist spot in Tinseltown. The signature Studio Tour tram brings riders face-to-face with King Kong and Jaws, rattles through a massive earthquake, and wanders past blockbuster sets including *War of the Worlds*, *Apollo 13*, *Jurassic Park*, *Psycho*, and many more. But for some, the 45min. tour plays second fiddle to the park's interactive attractions. While the movie may have bombed, the live stunts and pyrotechnics at *Waterworld* are impressive, and you can test your mettle by participating in *Fear Factor Live*, an extreme audience participation show. *(Take U.S. 101 to the Universal Center Dr. exit. By MTA rail: exit North Hollywood Red Line at Universal Station. ☎800-864-8377; www.universalstudios.com. Hours vary, check online; generally open July-Aug. M-Th 9am-8pm, F-Su 9am-9pm; Sept.-June M-F 10am-6pm, Sa-Su 10am-7pm. $53, under 48 in. $43, under 3 free. Parking $10.)*

■ **J. PAUL GETTY CENTER & MUSEUM.** Wedding classical materials with modernist form, renowned architect Richard Meier designed the stunning $1 billion complex known as "The Getty." The museum consists of five pavilions containing the Getty's manuscripts, drawings, photographs, decorative arts, sculptures, and paintings spanning seven centuries. The pavilions surround the Robert Irwin-designed Central Garden, a living work of art that changes with the seasons. *(1200 Getty Center Dr. Take the Getty Center Dr. exit off I-405. ☎310-440-7300; www.getty.edu. Open Tu-Th and Su 10am-6pm, F-Sa 10am-9pm. Free. Audio guides $3. Parking $7.)*

UNIVERSAL CITY WALK. This neon strip of shopping, dining, movie theaters, and nightlife is the Valley's more colorful, less charming answer to Santa Monica's Third St. Promenade. You can find everything from a mammoth green guitar outside the Hard Rock Cafe to trendy clothing or mechanical bulls at Saddle Ranch restaurant-nightclub. *(At Universal Studios. ☎818-622-4455; www.citywalkhollywood.com. City Walk parking $10; rebate with purchase of 2 or more movie tickets.)*

MAGIC MOUNTAIN. At the opposite end of the Valley, 40min. north of L.A. in Valencia, is thrill-ride heaven **Six Flags Magic Mountain,** boasting the most roller coasters in the world. Its newest addition, **Scream!,** is Southern California's first floorless mega-coaster where your feet dangle in the air as you scream through 4000 ft. of twists, plunges, and loops. **X** boasts of being the world's only 4-D roller coaster with front and back flips. It also happens to have mammoth lines, so go early in the day. Next door, Six Flags's waterpark **Hurricane Harbor** features the

CALIFORNIA

world's tallest enclosed speed slide. *(Take U.S. 101 N to U.S. 170 N to I-5 N to Magic Mountain Pkwy. ☎661-255-4100; www.sixflags.com. Open Apr.-Aug. daily; Sept.-Mar. weekends and holidays. Hours vary; check the website. $48, seniors and under 48 in. tall $30, under 2 free. Parking $8. Hurricane Harbor: ☎661-255-4527. Open May-Sept.; hours vary. $23, seniors and under 48 in. $17, under 2 free. Admission to both parks $58.)*

MIRACLE MILE

Museums are found all over the greater Los Angeles area, but a district known as the **Miracle Mile,** on Wilshire Blvd. between La Brea and Fairfax, is home to many of the most impressive.

LOS ANGELES COUNTY MUSEUM OF ART (LACMA). Opened in 1965, LACMA is the largest museum on the West Coast. The Steve Martin Gallery, in the Anderson Building, holds the famed comedian's collection of Dadaist and Surrealist works. *(5905 Wilshire Blvd. in the Wilshire District. ☎323-857-6000; www.lacma.org. Open M-Tu and Th noon-8pm, F noon-9pm, Sa-Su 11am-8pm. $9, students and seniors $5, under 18 free. Free 2nd Tu of each month and daily after 5pm. Free jazz F 5:30-8:30pm, chamber music Su 6-7pm. Film tickets $8, seniors and students $6. Parking $5, free after 7pm.)*

PETERSEN AUTOMOTIVE MUSEUM (PAM). The PAM showcases one of L.A.'s enduring symbols—the automobile. PAM is the world's largest car museum, with over 150 classic cars, hot rods, motorcycles, and celebrity cars on display at any given time. A joint exhibition with Fender Guitars pairs rock stars with their cars and guitars. Special exhibits on alternative power cars, the origin of the convertible, and Ferraris are slated to appear throughout 2006. *(6060 Wilshire Blvd. at Fairfax Ave., in the Wilshire District. ☎323-930-2277; www.petersen.org. Open Tu-Su 10am-6pm; Discovery Center closes 4pm. $10, students and seniors $5, ages 5-12 $3, under 5 free. Parking $6.)*

GEORGE C. PAGE MUSEUM OF LA BREA DISCOVERIES. The smelly La Brea Tar Pits fill the area with an acrid petroleum stench and provide bones for this natural history museum. The skeletons of thirsty prehistoric animals who became stuck and perished in these oozing tar pools are on display. You can feel what it's like to be trapped in tar and play with the sabertooth cat skull. A viewing station, where archaeologists work in the summer, is at Pit 91. *(5801 Wilshire Blvd. ☎323-934-7243. Museum open M-F 9:30am-5pm, Sa-Su 10am-5pm. Museum tours W-Su 2:15pm. $7, students and seniors $4.50, ages 5-12 $2. Free 1st Tu of each month. Parking $6 with validation.)*

♫ ENTERTAINMENT

FILM AND TELEVISION STUDIOS

A visit to the world's entertainment capital isn't complete without some exposure to the business of making a movie or TV show. Fortunately, most production companies oblige. **Paramount** (☎323-956-5000), **NBC** (☎818-840-3537), and **Warner Bros.** (☎818-954-1744) offer 2hr. guided tours that take you onto sets and through backlots. The best way to get a feel for the industry is to land yourself tickets to a taping. Tickets are free, but studios tend to overbook, so holding a ticket does not always guarantee you'll get in; show up early. **NBC,** 3000 W. Alameda Ave., at W. Olive Ave. in Burbank, is your best bet. Arrive at the ticket office on a weekday before 8am for passes to Jay Leno's **Tonight Show,** filmed at 4:30pm the same day (2 tickets per person, must be 16+). Studio tours run on the hour. (☎818-840-3537. Tours M-F 9am-3pm. $7.50, ages 5-12 $4.) Many of NBC's "Must-See TV" shows are taped at **Warner Bros.,** 4000 Warner Blvd. (☎818-954-6000), in Burbank—call the studio at least five business days in advance to secure tickets.

A **CBS box office,** 7800 Beverly Blvd., next to the farmers market (p. 903) in West Hollywood, hands out free tickets to Bob Barker's game-show masterpiece *The Price is Right* (taped M-Th) up to one week in advance. Tickets can be difficult to obtain. (☎323-575-2458. 18+. Open M-F 9am-5pm.) You can request up to ten tickets on a specific date by sending a self-addressed, stamped envelope to *The Price is Right* Tickets, 7800 Beverly Blvd., Los Angeles, CA 90036, about four to six weeks in advance. If all else fails, **Audiences Unlimited, Inc.,** 100 Universal City Plaza, Building 4250, Universal City, CA 91608 (☎818-506-0067; www.tvtickets.com), is a great resource. Most sitcoms do not film in the late spring to early summer months, but resume in late July or early August.

MOVIES

L.A.'s movie palaces show films the way they were meant to be seen—on a big screen, in plush seats, and with top-quality sound. The huge theaters at **Universal City,** as well as those in **Westwood Village** near UCLA, are incredibly popular, especially on weekends; expect long lines. **Santa Monica** has 22 screens within the three blocks between Santa Monica Pl. and Wilshire Blvd. along Third St. Promenade.

To ogle the stars as they walk the red carpet into the theater for a premiere, check the four main premiere venues: **Grauman's Chinese** (about 2 per month), **El Capitán** (Disney films only), and **Mann's Village** and **Bruin,** in Westwood. For info on what's playing, call ☎323-777-3456 or read the daily Calendar section of the *L.A. Times.* Devotees of second-run, foreign-language, and experimental films are rewarded by the Santa Monica theaters away from the Promenade. Foreign films play consistently at the eight **Laemmle Theaters** in Beverly Hills (☎310-274-6869), West Hollywood (☎323-848-3500), Santa Monica (☎310-394-9741), Pasadena (☎626-844-6500), and downtown (☎213-617-0268).

LIVE THEATER AND MUSIC

L.A.'s live theater scene does not hold the weight of New York's Broadway, but its 115 "equity waiver theaters" (under 100 seats) offer dizzying, eclectic choices for theatergoers, who can also view small productions in art galleries, universities, parks, and even garages. Browse listings in the *L.A. Weekly* to find out what's hot.

L.A.'s music venues range from small clubs to massive amphitheaters. The **Wiltern** (☎213-380-5005) shows alterna-rock/folk acts. The **Hollywood Palladium** (☎323-962-7600) is of comparable size with 3500 seats. Midsized acts head for the **Universal Amphitheater** (☎818-622-4440). Huge indoor sports arenas, such as the **Great Western Forum** (☎310-330-7300) and the newer **Staples Center** (☎213-742-7100), double as concert halls for big acts. Few dare to play at the 100,000-seat **Los Angeles Memorial Coliseum and Sports Arena;** only U2, Depeche Mode, Guns 'n' Roses, and the Warped Tour have filled the stands in recent years. Call Ticketmaster (☎213-480-3232) to purchase tickets for any of these venues.

🌊 **Hollywood Bowl,** 2301 N. Highland Ave. (☎323-850-2000), in Hollywood. L.A.'s premier outdoor music venue hosts a music festival from early July to mid-Sept. Free rehearsals by the Philharmonic and visiting performers usually Tu and Th 10:30am. Parking ($11-12) at the Bowl is limited. Other lots at 10601 and 10801 Ventura Blvd., near Universal City; at the Kodak Theatre at 6801 Hollywood Blvd.; and at the L.A. Zoo, 5333 Zoo Dr. (parking $5, shuttle $2.50; departs every 10-20min. starting 1½hr. before showtime). Call Ticketmaster (☎213-480-3232) to purchase tickets.

Geffen Playhouse, 11301 Wilshire Blvd. (☎310-208-5454), at Brentwood Theater, in Westwood. Fresh from renovation, it's home to Off-Broadway and Tony Award-winning shows. Tickets $34-46; $10 student rush tickets available 1hr. before the show.

Pasadena Playhouse, 39 S. El Molino Ave. (☎626-356-7529 or 800-233-3123; www.pasadenaplayhouse.org), in Pasadena. California's premier theater and historical landmark has spawned Broadway careers and productions. Tickets $35-60. Call for rush tickets. Shows Tu-F 8pm, Sa 5 and 9pm, Su 2 and 7pm.

SPORTS

Exposition Park and the often dangerous city of **Inglewood,** southwest of the park, are home to many sports teams. The **USC Trojans** play football at the **L.A. Memorial Coliseum,** 3911 S. Figueroa St. (☎213-740-4672), which seats over 100,000 spectators. The NBA's **L.A. Clippers** (☎213-742-7500) seek a revival while the **L.A. Lakers** (☎310-426-6000) cope with the post-dynasty blues at the new **Staples Center,** 1111 S. Figueroa St. (☎213-742-7100, box office 213-742-7340), along with the **L.A. Kings** hockey team (☎888-546-4752) and the WNBA's **L.A. Sparks** (☎310-330-3939). Call Ticketmaster (☎213-480-3232) for tickets. About 3 mi. northeast of downtown, **Elysian Park** curves around the northern portion of Chávez Ravine, home of **Dodger Stadium** and the popular **L.A. Dodgers** baseball team. Single-game tickets ($6-21) are a hot commodity during the April to October season, especially if the Dodgers are playing well. (Call ☎323-224-1448 for info and advance tickets.)

⬛ NIGHTLIFE

L.A.'s nightlife scene is constantly shifting. Pick up a copy of *L.A. Weekly* or the *L.A. Times*'s Calendar section for the latest news. Given the extremely short shelf life and unpredictability of the L.A. club scene, late-night restaurants have become the reliable fallback option, popular with underage club kids and celebs in rehab. Many coffeehouses stay open late and have open-mic nights or live music. Though it's hard to barhop when the best places are a 30min. drive from each other (don't forget your designated driver), L.A.'s **bars** run the gamut from casual beach hangouts to swanky hotel lounges. With the highest number of bands per capita in the world, L.A. is famous for its club scene, much of which focuses around the Sunset Strip and comes with a hefty price tag. To enter the club scene, it's best to be at least 21 (it also helps to be a beautiful woman). If you're over 18, you can still find a space to dance, though it may mean a hefty cover charge in a less desirable venue. **All bars and clubs are 21+ unless otherwise noted.**

THE COAST

The waterfront areas are packed with brewpubs, dance clubs, and surfer hangouts. ◪**The Kettle,** 1138 N. Highland Ave., at the corner of Manhattan Beach Blvd. in Manhattan Beach, is filled with surfers feasting on heaping platefuls of homestyle cooking. After sipping beer or wine (served until midnight), prepare for the morning with the "Hangover" omelet ($7), containing green chilis and jack cheese. (☎562-545-8511. Salads and sandwiches $7-9. Open 24hr.) The dark red glow of "eastern" decor and the cool live music give **Temple Bar,** 1026 Wilshire Blvd., in Santa Monica, its smooth vibe. The food and drink, like house favorites coconut-crusted red snapper ($10) and mojitos ($8), complete the bar's eclectic mix. (☎310-393-6611. Live music nightly. Open daily 8pm-2am.)

THE WESTSIDE

The Sunset Strip and West Hollywood contain the city's densest concentration of nightlife. Chic lounges, grungy clubs, and happy group hangouts can all be found.

▨ **Standard Lounge,** 8300 Sunset Blvd. (☎323-822-3111), in the Standard Hotel. No dress code, no cover, no guest list, but you'd never know it. Insanely chic—Carrie Bradshaw drank in the mirrored, jewel-toned interior in the "Sex and Another City" episode of *Sex and the City.* Drinks $9. DJ nightly. Open daily 10pm-2am.

Jerry's Famous Deli, 8701 Beverly Blvd. (☎310-289-1811), at San Vicente Ave. Also at 10925 Weyburn Ave. (☎310-208-3354), in Westwood, and 12655 Ventura Blvd. (☎818-980-4245), in Studio City in the Valley. The valet should be your first indication that this is no regular deli. The sleek red leather and sky-high prices should be your second. That said, the atmosphere is inviting, and the food is perfect for your 4am snack. Jumbo triple-deckers $13-14. Salads served in a pizza crust $10-13. Open 24hr.

Miyagi's, 8225 Sunset Blvd. (☎323-650-3524). With 3 levels, 7 sushi bars (rolls $6-8), 6 liquor bars, and indoor waterfalls, this Japanese-themed restaurant, bar, lounge, and hip-hop dance club is a Strip hot spot. Sake bomb $4.50. Open daily 5:30pm-2am.

The Rainbow Bar and Grill, 9015 Sunset Blvd. (☎310-278-4232; www.rainbowbarand-grill.com). Dark red vinyl booths, dim lighting, loud music, and colorful characters set the scene. Marilyn Monroe met Joe DiMaggio here. Brooklyn-quality pizza $15. Homemade lasagna $13. Open M-F 11am-2am, Sa-Su 5pm-2am.

HOLLYWOOD AND POINTS EAST

Hollywood and its immediately neighboring areas are up-and-comers in the Los Angeles nightlife world. Known for being more laidback than the uber-ritzy clubs of the Sunset Strip, these distinctive nightspots have managed to gather a strong following and can be just as fashionable as any on the Strip.

▨ **Highland Grounds,** 742 N. Highland Ave. (466-1507; www.highlandgrounds.com). Intimate, laid-back coffeehouse, restaurant, and live music venue. A diverse crowd gathers for hearty brunch (served until 4pm; $5-9). The hip come out at night for live music, fire pit conversations, and a late-night veggie-friendly menu ($7-9). Beer and wine $0.50-6.50. Open M 9am-5pm, Tu-Th 9am-midnight, F-Sa 9am-1am, Su 9am-4pm.

3 of Clubs, 1123 N. Vine St. (☎323-462-6441), at Santa Monica Blvd., in Hollywood, in a strip mall. Look for the small "cocktails" sign. Simple, classy, and spacious hardwood bar famous for its starring role in the movie *Swingers.* A local watering hole early during the week, then a happening dance club on the weekend. Live bands Th. DJ F-Sa. Open daily 6pm-2am.

Lucky Strike Lanes, 6801 Hollywood Blvd. (☎323-467-7776; www.bowlluck-ystrike.com), in the Hollywood & Higland Complex. You're more likely to be bowling next to a celebrity than your Uncle Joe and his buddies. With 12 lanes, plush seating, state-of-the-art video screens, a pumping audio system, DJs, and a full bar, Lucky Strike is an upscale, hip version of any bowling alley you've been to. Open daily 11am-2am. 21+ after 7pm. Bowling $5-8, shoes $4. Call to make lane reservations.

The Derby, 4500 Los Feliz Blvd. (☎323-663-8979; www.the-derby.com), at Hillhurst Ave., in Los Feliz. Ladies, grab your pearls and Marilyn Monroe-tribute dress; many dress the 40s part. Full bar. Free swing lessons Su 6:30pm. Cover F-Sa $5-12. Open daily 7:30pm-2am; back bar (no cover) open daily 5pm-2am.

Beauty Bar, 1638 Cahuenga Blvd. (☎323-464-7676), in Hollywood. Get a manicure while sipping a cocktail in a time warp of a 1960s beauty parlor. Martinis are so much headier when sitting under an old-school hair dryer. Beautify while boozing on drinks like the "Perm" or the "Platinum Blonde" ($8, with manicure $10). DJ nightly 10pm. Open M-W and Su 9pm-2am, Th-Sa 6pm-2am.

CALIFORNIA

COMEDY CLUBS

L.A.'s comedy clubs are among the best in the world. You can catch new comedians or watch skilled veterans hone new material. The **Comedy Store,** 8433 Sunset Blvd., in West Hollywood, has three rooms, each featuring a different type of comedy. The Main Room and Original Room host headliner comedians, while the Belly Room provides a testing ground for up-and-comers. (☎323-650-6268. Drinks $5-9; 2-drink min. 21+. Main Room and Original Room cover M-F $15, Sa-Su $20. Belly Room no cover. Showtimes vary; call a week ahead to reserve tickets. Open daily until 2am; Main Room only open Sa.) The **Groundling Theater,** 7307 Melrose Ave., in Hollywood, is one of the most popular improv and comedy clubs in town. Illustrious alums of the club include Pee Wee Herman and many current and former *Saturday Night Live* regulars, including Will Ferrell and Chris Kattan. (☎323-934-4747; www.groundlings.com. Shows W-Th 8pm, F-Sa 8 and 10pm, Su 7:30pm. Tickets $13-20.)

GLBT NIGHTLIFE

The slice of Santa Monica Blvd. in West Hollywood is the Sunset Strip of GLBT nightlife. All of the clubs listed below are in West Hollywood. In addition to clubs in that area, many "straight" clubs have gay nights; check *L.A. Weekly* or contact the Gay and Lesbian Community Services Center for more information. The free weekly magazine *fab!* lists happenings in the GLBT community. **All clubs are 21+ unless otherwise noted.**

▨ **The Abbey,** 692 N. Robertson Blvd. (☎310-289-8410), at Santa Monica Blvd. 6 candlelit rooms, 2 huge bars, a large outdoor patio, and a hall of private booths make this beautiful lounge and dance club the best gay nightspot in town. The comfy couches cry out for some lovin', but get there early or wait outside. Open daily 8am-2am.

Micky's, 8857 Santa Monica Blvd. (☎310-657-1176). On Sa night when bars close, head to Micky's for another 2hr. of grooving. Music is mostly electronica and techno, although hip-hop is sometimes sprinkled into the mix. Tu college night. Happy hour M-F 5-9pm. Cover $3-10. Open Th-F 4pm-2am, Sa 11pm-4am, Su 11pm-2am.

Here, 696 N. Robertson St. (☎310-360-8455), at the corner of Santa Monica Blvd. Known for Su nights when the bartenders dress up in scandalous surfer shorts, this sleek gay bar and dance club caters to the well-dressed and trendy. DJs spin a mix of house and hip-hop. Don't miss the frozen cosmopolitans ($8). Th lesbian night. Happy hour daily 4-8pm; drinks $2-3 off. Open daily 4pm-2am.

Trunks, 8809 Santa Monica Blvd. (☎310-652-1015), a friendly and popular neighborhood gay and lesbian bar. Open daily 1pm-2am.

ORANGE COUNTY ☎714/949

Directly south of L.A. County lies Orange County. Composed of 34 cities, it is a microcosm of Southern California: dazzling sandy shoreline, bronzed beach bums, oversized shopping malls, homogenous suburban neighborhoods, and frustrating traffic snarls. As one of California's staunchest Republican enclaves, Orange County (and no, they don't actually call it "The O.C.") supports big business and has the multimillion-dollar hillside mansions oozing luxury cars and disaffected teens to prove it. Disneyland, the stronghold of the Walt Disney Company's ever-expanding empire, is the premier inland attraction. The coast runs the gamut from the budget- and party-friendly surf burg of Huntington Beach to the opulent excess of Newport Beach and the artistic vibe of Laguna. Farther south lies the quiet mission of San Juan Capistrano, set amid rolling hills that spill onto the laid-back beaches of Dana Point and San Clemente.

🛈 PRACTICAL INFORMATION

Airport: John Wayne Airport, 18601 Airport Way (☎949-252-5200), in Santa Ana. 20min. from Anaheim. Domestic flights only.

Trains: Amtrak (☎800-872-7245; www.amtrak.com) stations, from north to south: **Fullerton,** 120 E. Santa Fe Ave. (☎714-992-0530); **Santa Ana,** 1000 E. Santa Ana Blvd. (☎714-547-8389); **Irvine,** 15215 Barranca Pkwy. (☎949-753-9713); **San Juan Capistrano,** 26701 Verdugo St. (☎949-240-2972).

Buses: Greyhound (☎800-231-2222; www.greyhound.com) has 3 stations in the area. **Anaheim,** 100 W. Winston Rd. (☎714-999-1256), 3 blocks south of Disneyland. Open daily 6:30am-12:45pm and 2:40-9:15pm. **Santa Ana,** 1000 E. Santa Ana Blvd. (☎714-542-2215). Open daily 6:15am-8:30pm. **San Clemente,** 2421 S. El Camino Real (☎949-366-2646). Open daily 7am-9pm.

Public Transit: Orange County Transportation Authority (OCTA; ☎714-636-7433; www.octa.net), 550 S. Main St., in Orange. Useful for getting from Santa Ana and Fullerton Amtrak stations to Disneyland and for beach-hopping along the coast. Long Beach, in L.A. County, serves as the terminus for several OCTA lines. Bus #1 travels the coast from Long Beach to San Clemente (every hr. until 8pm); #25, 33, and 35 travel from Fullerton to Huntington Beach; #91 goes from Laguna Hills to San Clemente. ($1.25, day pass $3.) **Info center** open M-F 6am-8pm, Sa-Su 8am-5pm. **MTA Info** (☎213-626-4455 or 800-266-6883) available by phone daily 5am-10:45pm. MTA buses run from L.A. to Disneyland and Knott's Berry Farm.

Visitor Info: Anaheim Area Visitors and Convention Bureau, 800 W. Katella Ave. (☎714-765-8888; www.anaheimoc.org), in Anaheim Convention Ctr. Open M-F 8am-5pm. **Newport Visitors Bureau,** 110 Newport Center Dr., #120 (☎949-719-6100 or 800-942-6278), in Newport Beach. Eager-to-help staff, maps of area attractions, and events brochures. Open M-F 8am-5pm. **Laguna Beach Visitors Bureau,** 252 Broadway (☎949-497-9229). Open M-F 9am-5pm, Sa 10am-4pm, Su noon-4pm.

Police: Anaheim, 425 S. Harbor Blvd. (☎714-765-1900). **Huntington Beach,** 2000 Main St. (☎714-960-8811).

Hotlines: Sexual Assault Hotline, ☎714-957-2737. **Orange County Referral Hotline,** ☎714-894-4242. **Surf and Weather Conditions,** ☎213-554-1212.

Medical Services: St. Jude Medical Center, 101 E. Valencia Mesa Dr. (☎714-871-3280), in Fullerton. **Lestonnac Free Clinic,** 1215 E. Chapman Ave. (☎714-633-4600). Hours vary; call for an appointment.

Post Office: 701 N. Loara St. (☎714-520-2639 or 800-275-8777), 1 block north of Anaheim Plaza, in Anaheim. Open M-F 8:30am-5pm, Sa 9am-3pm. **Postal Code:** 92803. **Area Codes:** 714 (Anaheim, Santa Ana, Orange, Garden Grove), 949 (Newport, Laguna, Irvine, Mission Viejo, San Juan Capistrano).

🏠 ACCOMMODATIONS

Countless budget chain motels and garden-variety rooms flank Disneyland on all sides. Keep watch for family and group rates posted on marquees, and seek out establishments offering the **3-for-2 passport** (3 days of Disney for the price of 2).

▓ **Huntington Beach Hostel,** 421 8th St. (☎714-536-3315), 4 blocks inland from PCH, at Pecan Ave. in Huntington Beach. Take OCTA #29 (which also goes to Knott's Berry Farm) or #50. A laidback base for beach activity. Breakfast and linen included. Common bath, kitchen, TV room, coin-op laundry, Internet access, and deck. Surfboards, boogie boards, and bikes to borrow. Key deposit $5. Check-in 8am-11pm. Reserve a month in advance for summer weekends. Dorms $21; doubles $50. MC/V. ❶

CALIFORNIA

Fullerton Hostel (HI), 1700 N. Harbor Blvd. (☎714-738-3721), in Fullerton, 10min. north of Disneyland. Shuttle from L.A. Airport $21. OCTA bus #43 runs along Harbor Blvd. to Disneyland. In the woods and away from the themed craziness of nearby Anaheim, this hostel has a homey, suburban feel and a diverse crowd. The enthusiastic staff invites questions but forbids drinking. Kitchen, relaxing living room, communal bathrooms. Laundry $1.50. 7-night max. stay. Check-in 8am-11pm. Reservations recommended. Open June-Sept. Dorms $22, members $19. MC/V. ❶

Hotel Laguna, 425 S. Coast Hwy. (949-494-1151), on the sand in Laguna Beach. This posh place was Laguna's first hotel. The modern interior has handsomely furnished rooms, many with outstanding ocean and garden views. Continental breakfast included. Rooms May-Sept. from $130; Sept.-May from $100. AmEx/D/DC/MC/V. ❺

◨ FOOD

With wealthy residents and a location on the coast, Orange County thrives on light California cuisine and exquisitely fresh seafood.

▨ **Rutabegorz,** 211 N. Pomona Blvd. (☎714-738-9339; www.rutabegorz.com), 1 block east of Harbor Blvd. in Fullerton. Also at 264 N. Glassell St. (☎714-633-3260), in Orange; and 158 W. Main St. (☎731-9807), in Tustin. This hippie-cum-hipster joint has a 20-page recycled newsprint menu. Crepes, curries, quesadillas, and club sandwiches are all fresh and veggie-heavy (all $7-9). Smoothies, veggie juices, and coffee drinks $2-4. Open M-Th 11am-10pm, F-Sa 11am-11pm, Su 4-9pm. AmEx/D/MC/V. ❷

Michele's Sugar Shack Cafe, 213½ Main St. (☎714-536-0355), in Huntington Beach. Big omelets, crispy hashbrowns and blue plate lunch specials (each $5-6). Open M-Tu and Th 6am-4pm, W 6am-8pm, F-Su 6am-5pm. AmEx/D/MC/V. ❷

C'est la Vie Restaurant and Bakery, 373 S. Coast Hwy. (☎949-497-5100), just south of Broadway in Laguna Beach. Enjoy rich quiches, light salads and lunch specials, and designer martinis on the patio. Most dishes $7-14. Martinis $8.50. Open M-Th 9:30am-10:30pm, F-Sa 8:30am-11:30pm, Su 8:30am-10:30pm. AmEx/D/MC/V. ❸

◉ ◨ SIGHTS AND BEACHES

DISNEYLAND. Disneyland calls itself the "Happiest Place on Earth," and the child in everyone agrees. After a full day there, your feet and your precious wallet may not. Weekday and low-season visitors will undoubtedly be the happiest, but the clever can wait for parades and gigantic Disney characters to distract shrieking children, utilize the line-busting FastPass program, or come at night to avoid the worst of the crowds. Recently, Disneyland introduced its new kid brother, "California Adventure," to the theme park family. The park features ambitious attractions divided into four districts. **Sunshine Plaza,** the gateway to the park, is anchored by a 50 ft. tall sun enlivened by a flood of red, orange, and yellow lights at night. **Golden State** offers an eight-acre mini-wilderness, a citrus grove, a winery, and even a replica of San Francisco. **Paradise Pier** is dedicated to the so-called "Golden Age" of amusement parks, with rollercoasters like **California Screamin'** and the stomach-dropping **Tower of Terror.** Finally, the **Hollywood Pictures Backlot** realizes your aspirations of stardom without any embarrassing before-you-were-famous photos. *(Main entrance on Harbor Blvd. and a smaller one on Katella Ave. ☎714-781-4565; www.disneyland.com. Disneyland open daily 8am-midnight; hours may vary. California Adventure open daily 8am-10pm. Disneyland passport or California Adventure passport $56, ages 3-9 $46, under 3 free; allows repeated single-day entrance. 2- and 3-day passes also available. Combination ticket $76, ages 3-9 $66. Parking $8.)*

(K)NOT(T) DISNEYLAND. Knott's Berry Farm has more intense rides and is slightly easier on the wallet than Disney, although this means less size and diversity. The park's highlights include **Camp Snoopy** for the kids and roller coasters like **Boomerang** and **Ghostrider,** the largest wooden roller coaster in the West, for the brave. The latest addition, **Xcelerator,** goes from 0 to 80 mph in 2.3 seconds. *(8039 Beach Blvd., at La Palma Ave., 5 mi. northeast of Disneyland. Recorded info ☎ 714-220-5200. Open M-Th and Su 10am-10pm, F-Sa 10am-11pm; hours may vary. $45, ages 3-11 $15, under 3 free; after 4pm all tickets half-price. Parking under 3hr. free, each additional hr. $2; all-day parking $8.)* **Soak City USA,** themed like a 1950s beach town, is Knott's effort to make a splash in the already-drenched water park scene. *(Next to Knott's. ☎ 220-5200. Open M-Th and Su 10am-6pm, F-Sa 10am-7pm; hours may vary. $26, ages 3-11 $15, under 3 free.)*

SPORTS. For more evidence of Disney's world domination, catch a game by one of the teams they own. The major league Anaheim Angels play baseball from early April to October at Edison Field. *(☎ 940-2000 or 800-626-4357. General tickets $9-44.)* The NHL's Mighty Ducks play at Arrowhead Pond *(☎ 714-704-2400).*

ORANGE COUNTY BEACH COMMUNITIES. Orange County's beach communities have cleaner sand, better surf, and less madness than their L.A. counterparts; it is here that L.A. residents seek refuge. **Huntington Beach** is a perfect beach bum playground with a large beach, volleyball nets, and waves. This town has surf lore galore, and the proof is on the **Surfing Walk of Fame** and in the **International Surfing Museum.** *(Walk of Fame: the sidewalk along PCH at Main St. Museum: 411 Olive St. ☎ 714-960-3483. Open daily noon-5pm; in spring and summer Sa-Su open 9am-6pm. $2, students $1.)* Multimillion-dollar homes, the world's largest leisure-craft harbor, and Balboa Peninsula are all packed closely enough on the **Newport Beach** oceanfront to make even New Yorkers feel claustrophobic. Surfing, beach volleyball, shopping, and looking hot are all popular activities. Punctuated by rocky cliffs, shady coves, and lush hillside vegetation, lovely, artsy **Laguna Beach's** character is decidedly Mediterranean. **Ocean Avenue,** at the Pacific Coast Hwy., and **Main Beach** are the prime parading areas. The **Laguna Art Museum** showcases local and state art, including some excellent early 20th-century Impressionist works. *(307 Cliff Dr. ☎ 949-494-8971; www.lagunaartmuseum.com. Open daily 11am-5pm. Tours daily 2pm. $9, students and seniors $7, under 12 free.)* The evocative **Mission San Juan Capistrano,** 30min. south of Anaheim on I-5, was established by Father Junípero Serra and is considered the jewel of the missions. *(On the corner of Ortega Hwy. and Camino Capistrano. ☎ 949-234-1300; www.missionsjc.com. Open daily 8:30am-5pm. $6, ages 60+ $5, ages 4-11 $4, under 3 free.)*

BIG BEAR ☎ 909

Big Bear is easily Southern California's most popular mountain and lake resort. Los Angelenos hit the slopes in the winter, and in the summer, the central lake provides ample opportunities for fishing, sailing, and watersports, while the nearby mountains and forest offer enjoyable hikes and well-preserved campgrounds.

Hiking the trails in the surrounding mountains is a superb way to explore the San Bernardino wilderness. Head to the **Big Bear Discovery Center (BBDC),** on Hwy. 38, for maps, trail descriptions, and the *Visitor's Guide to the San Bernardino National Forest.* (Open daily mid-May to mid-Oct. 8am-6pm; mid-Oct. to mid-May 9am-4:30pm.) The 3½ mi. **Alpine Pedal Path** follows a paved course from the Stanfield Cutoff to the BBDC along the lake's north shore. The moderately difficult 2½ mi. **Castle Rock Trail,** starting 1 mi. east of the dam on Hwy. 18, is a steep haul to stupendous views of Big Bear Lake. In summer, **mountain biking** takes over the Big Bear area. Grab a *Ride and Trail Guide* at the BBDC or at **Snow Summit,** 1 mi. west of Big Bear Lake, which runs lifts in summer, providing access to the surrounding Forest Service lands. If you aren't ready to grind down the mountain, a

CALIFORNIA

THE INS-N-OUTS OF IN-N-OUT

From its simple beginning in 1948 as a burger stand in Baldwin Park, just east of Los Angeles, **IN-N-OUT Burger** has come a long way. Its distinctive yellow-and-red sign is now ubiquitous across California, Nevada, and Arizona. Many first-time visitors are surprised to see a menu with just five choices (hamburger, cheeseburger, double-double, fries, and shake), but IN-N-OUT offers far more. The restaurant also has a "secret menu" from which many more items can be ordered simply by knowing what to ask for. Next time you place your order, keep these other options in mind. They aren't on the menu, but they're available at all locations.

Animal Style: The burger of your choice grilled in mustard with lettuce, tomato, pickles, grilled onions, and IN-N-OUT's special sandwich spread.

Protein Style: Burger of your choice wrapped in a lettuce leaf instead of a bun.

Double Meat: Two beef patties, no cheese.

Flying Dutchman: Two beef patties, two slices of cheese, nothing else.

Wish Burger: No meat.

3x3: Three beef patties, three slices of cheese, lettuce, tomato, and spread on a bun. (Also available in the monster 4x4.)

Fries Animal Style: Fries with cheese, special spread, onions.

scenic round-trip ride can be picked up for the same price. (☎866-5766. Open M-F and Su 9am-4pm, Sa 8am-5pm. One-way with bicycle $10, ages 7-12 $5. Helmet required.) **Team Big Bear,** 476 Concklin Rd., operating out of the Mountain Bike Shop at the base of Snow Summit, rents bikes and sponsors organized bike races each summer. (☎866-4565. $9 per hr., $27 for 4hr., $50 per day; helmet included.) Big Bear Lake is well-stocked with rainbow trout and catfish. State **fishing** licenses are available at sporting goods stores (day $10, season $28). Boats can be rented at **Holloway's Marina,** 398 Edgemor Rd., on the south shore. (☎866-5706 or 800-448-5335; www.bigbearboating.com. $80-185 per day.)

When snow conditions are favorable, ski areas quickly run out of lift tickets, which may be purchased through Ticketmaster (☎714-740-2000). **Big Bear Mountain Resorts** (www.bigbearmountainresorts.com) splits 55 runs between two ski resorts. The huge vertical drops and adventure skiing terrain at **Bear Mountain,** 43101 Goldmine Dr., are geared toward freestyle skiing and snowboarding. (☎585-2519; www.bearmtn.com.) **Snow Summit,** 880 Summit Blvd., is a more family-oriented resort with snowmaking, night skiing, and a well-rounded assortment of beginner runs. (☎866-5766; www.snowsummit.com. Lift tickets are interchangeable, and a shuttle runs between the 2 parks. Lift tickets $49, ages 13-21 $39, ages 7-12 $19; holidays $59/$49/$25. Skis $27 per day; snowboards $30 per day. Deposit required for rentals.) **Snow Valley,** 35100 Hwy. 18, near Running Springs, is the most family-oriented resort in Big Bear and even has a "snow play" area if you want to frolic in the fluffy white stuff without strapping skis on. (☎867-2751; www.snow-valley.com. Lift tickets $44, ages 6-12 $17. Ski rental $17; snowboard $30.) **Renting** ski equipment from the ski stores along Big Bear Blvd. can save you up to half the price of renting at the mountains. **Cross-country skiing** is very popular in Big Bear. The **Rim Nordic Ski Area,** across from Snow Valley, is a network of cross-country ski trails. An Adventure Passport ($5) is required.

As Big Bear is a year-round destination, rooms below $50 a night are often only found down the mountain in San Bernardino. **Big Bear Boulevard** is lined with lodging possibilities. **Robinhood Inn ❹,** 40797 Lakeview Dr., has a courtyard complete with spa and barbecue, and many rooms have fireplaces and kitchenettes. (☎866-4643. Singles and doubles in summer from $64; suites for up to 6 people under $100. Winter rates much higher. AmEx/D/MC/V.) **Serrano ❶,** 40650 N. Shore Ln., off Hwy. 38, in Fawnskin, is the most popular campground in Big Bear, with flat, roomy sites, many of which are located right along the highway. (☎866-8021, reservations 877-444-6777. Flush toilets and showers. Sites $24, with hookup $34.) Food can get pricey, so those with kitchens should buy groceries at **Stater Bros.**, 42171 Big Bear Blvd. (☎866-5211. Open daily 7am-11pm.) Cutesy cafes and roadside burger stands circle the lake, providing ample opportunity to satisfy your stomach. For a more relaxing meal, the **Peppercorn Grille ❷**, 553 Pine Knot Ave., in the Village, has $9 lunch specials of mainly American and California cuisine. (☎866-5405. Open daily 11am-3pm and 5-9pm.)

To reach Big Bear, take **I-10** to **Route 30** in San Bernardino and follow Rte. 30 north to **Route 330** (Mountain Rd.), which turns into **Route 18,** a winding 30-45min. ascent. Rte. 18 hits the west end of Big Bear Lake and forks—Rte. 18 goes along the south shore to Big Bear Lake City and **Route 38** goes along the north shore to the BBDC. Driving time from L.A. is about 2½hr., barring serious weekend traffic or road closures. Driving to Big Bear should not be attempted during the winter without checking road conditions with **CalTrans** (☎427-7623; www.dot.ca.gov). **Mountain Area Regional Transit Authority (MARTA)** runs two **buses** per day (M-Sa) from the Greyhound station in San Bernardino to Big Bear. (☎878-5200. $5.) The **Big Bear Chamber of Commerce**, 630 Bartlett Rd., in Big Bear Village, has a treasure trove of maps and brochures. (☎866-4608; www.bigbearchamber.com. Open M-F 8am-5pm, Sa-Su 9am-5pm.) **Post Office:** 472 Pine Knot Blvd. (☎866-7481; open M-F 8:30am-5pm, Sa 10am-noon). **Postal Code:** 92315. **Area Code:** 909.

SAN DIEGO   ☎619

The locals call it "America's Finest City," and visitors pulling into this picturesque port will soon understand why. In a state where every town stakes a claim on paradise, San Diego may be Southern California's best return on the promises of a golden state, offering perfectly sunny weather almost every day of the year and a vibrant, varied city that is simultaneously cosmopolitan and chill.

▐ TRANSPORTATION

San Diego is in the southwest corner of California, 127 mi. south of L.A. and 15 mi. north of the Mexican border. **I-5** runs south from L.A. through the cities of Oceanside and Carlsbad, skirting the eastern edge of downtown on its way to the Mexican border; **I-15** runs northeast through the desert to Las Vegas; and **I-8** runs east-west along downtown's northern boundary, connecting the desert with Ocean Beach.

Airport: San Diego International (Lindbergh Field), at the northwest edge of downtown. Call **Airport Ambassadors** (☎231-7361 or 231-5230) for info. Open daily 8am-11pm. Bus #992 goes downtown ($2.25), as do cabs ($8-10). **Cloud 9 Shuttle** (☎800-974-8853) offers affordable shared van transportation throughout the region.

Trains: Amtrak, 1050 Kettner Blvd. (☎800-872-7245; www.amtrak.com), just north of Broadway in the Santa Fe Depot. Station has info on bus, trolley, car, and boat transportation. Ticket office open daily 5:15am-10:15pm. To **L.A.** (10 per day, 3 hr., $30).

Buses: Greyhound, 120 W. Broadway (☎239-8082 or 800-231-2222; www.greyhound.com), at 1st St. Ticket office open 24hr. To **L.A.** (24 per day, $16) and **Tijuana, Mex.** (8 per day, $6).

Public Transit: San Diego Metropolitan Transit System (MTS). 24hr. info line, **Info Express** (☎685-4900), has info on San Diego transit ($1.25-3 depending on distance). The **Transit Store** at 1st Ave. and Broadway also has info. Get a 1- to 4-day **Day Tripper Pass** if you plan to use public transit more than once. Open M-F 8:30am-5:30pm, Sa-Su noon-4pm. 1-day pass $5, 2-day $9, 3-day $12, 4-day $15.

CALIFORNIA

Car Rental: Atwest Rent A Car, 3045 Rosecrans St., #215 (☎619-223-2343; www.atwestrentacar.com), near the airport. Cars from $30 per day. Under-25 surcharge $5-15 per day. Insurance $17 per day if driving to Mexico. Open daily 8am-11pm.

✴ 🔁 ORIENTATION AND PRACTICAL INFORMATION

The epicenter of inland San Diego tourism is historic **Balboa Park.** Northwest of the park is the stylish **Hillcrest** neighborhood, the city's gay enclave and home to plenty of great shopping and restaurants. **Downtown** attractions are centered in the corridor that includes the area's business and **waterfront** districts. The downtown core is laid out in a grid, with many one-way streets. The **Gaslamp Quarter,** the nexus of San Diego nightlife, sits in the southern section of downtown between 4th and 6th St. and contains many of San Diego's signature theaters, clubs, and restaurants. Farther north and near the water, **Little Italy** is its own tiny international epicenter of food and entertainment. Just north of downtown in the southeast corner of the I-5 and I-8 junction lies a little slice of old Mexico known as **Old Town.** Along the **coast,** San Diego Bay opens up south of downtown, bounded by classy **Coronado Island.** Northwest of town sits the collection of shiny beaches and man-made inlets known as **Mission Bay,** home to several laidback, sun-soaked communities including **Ocean, Mission,** and **Pacific Beaches.** A jaunt up the coast leads to the tourist haven of **La Jolla.**

Visitor Info: San Diego Convention and Visitors Bureau, W. Broadway and Harbor Dr., near the Cruise Ship Terminal. (☎236-1212; www.sandiego.org. Open June-Aug. daily 9am-5pm, Sept.-May M-Tu and Th-Su 9am-4pm.)

Library: San Diego Public Library, 820 E St. (☎236-5800), offers **Internet** access and Wi-Fi. Open M and W noon-8pm, Tu and Th-Sa 9:30am-5:30pm, Su 1-5pm.

Police: ☎531-2000.

Hotlines: GLBT Crisis Line, ☎800-479-3339. **Rape Hotline,** ☎233-3088.

Post Office: Hillcrest Station, 3911 Cleveland Ave. (☎295-5091). Open M-F 7:30am-6pm, Sa 8:30am-4pm. **Postal Code:** 92103.

Area Code: Most of San Diego, including downtown, Coronado, and Ocean Beach: 619. Northern San Diego area codes (including Del Mar, La Jolla, parts of North County, and Pacific Beach): 858 and 760. In text, 619 unless otherwise noted.

🏠 ACCOMMODATIONS

Beyond the hostel and residential hotel scene, San Diego is littered with generic chain motels, which are generally clean and safe. There is a popular cluster known as **Hotel Circle** (2-3 mi. east of I-5 along I-8), where summer prices begin at $65 for a single and $75 for a double during the week ($75 and $85, respectively, on weekends). If you're willing to drive a bit to save on your hotel bills, better deals can often be found in the surrounding area of Chula Vista, to the south. Several beaches in North County, as well as one on Coronado, are state parks and allow camping, but you'll want to reserve early, especially on weekends.

🏨 **USA Hostels San Diego,** 726 5th Ave. (☎232-3100 or 800-438-8622; www.usahostels.com), between F and G St. in the Gaslamp Quarter. Right in the middle of a popular clubbing street. Hosts parties and organizes Tijuana tours and Gaslamp pub crawls. Free breakfast, linen, and lockers. Coin-op laundry. Internet $2 per 20min. Reserve private rooms in advance. International passport or out-of-state student ID required. Dorms $22; private rooms $54. ISIC, VIP, and BUNAC discount $2. MC/V. ❶

Downtown San Diego

♠ **ACCOMMODATIONS**
Old Town Inn, **1**
San Diego Downtown Hostel (HI), **21**
USA Hostels San Diego, **19**

♥ **FOOD**
Casa Guadalajara, **2**
The Corvette Diner, **5**
Cotijas, **3**
Kansas City Barbecue, **20**
Kono's Surf Club, **4**

■ **NIGHTLIFE**
The Bitter End, **18**
Bourbon Street, **7**
The Casbah, **8**
Croce's, **17**
The Flame, **6**

🏛 MUSEUM
Aerospace Museum, **14**
Automotive Museum, **13**
Maritime Museum, **15**
Museum of Art, **10**
Museum of
  Contemporary Art, **16**
Museum of Man, **9**
Museum of Natural History, **11**
Museum of
  Photographic Arts, **12**

San Diego Downtown Hostel (HI), 521 Market St. (☎525-1531 or 800-909-4776, ext. 156; www.sandiegohostels.org), at 5th Ave., in the heart of the Gaslamp Quarter. The same amenities as the hostel above, just with a slightly calmer atmosphere. Its clean and colorful interior and many common areas draw an international crowd. No alcohol. Breakfast, linens, and towels included. Discounted bike rentals and tours. Lockers (bring a lock) and laundry available. Internet $4 per hr. Reception 6:30am-12:30am. 4- to 10-bed dorms $22-27, members $19-24; private rooms $47-62. MC/V. ❶

Old Town Inn, 4444 Pacific Hwy. (☎800-643-3025), near I-5 and I-8, a 10min. walk from Old Town. Clean rooms with standard amenities. Across the street from the trolley station; perfect for those without cars. Some rooms have kitchenettes. Pool access. Large continental breakfast included. Standard rooms from $70. AmEx/D/MC/V. ❸

◘ FOOD

With its large Hispanic population and proximity to Mexico, San Diego is renowned for exemplary Mexican cuisine. The culinary scene is truly dominated, however, by the opposing forces of trendy, upscale restaurants in the Gaslamp Quarter and Hillcrest and the cheap, deliciously filling beachfront eateries.

■ **Casa Guadalajara,** 4105 Taylor St. (☎299-5111), in Old Town, just north of Plaza del Pasado. With its brightly painted tiles, heavy wooden furniture, and lush, shady patio you'll feel like you're in a pristine version of Mexico. Big combination platters ($9-13) and heaping plates of delectable *carnitas* with guacamole and fresh tortillas ($11) are overshadowed only by the intoxicating selection of margaritas ($5-12). Open M-Th and Su 7am-10pm, F-Sa 7am-midnight. AmEx/D/DC/MC/V. ❸

The Corvette Diner, 3946 5th Ave. (☎542-1001), in Hillcrest. This 50s-style diner has more chrome than Detroit and more neon than Las Vegas. Greasy-spoon classics and a number of unique creations like the Rory Burger (peanut butter and bacon burger; $7). Open M-Th and Su 11am-10pm, F-Sa 11am-midnight. AmEx/D/DC/MC/V. ❷

Kono's Surf Club, 704 Garnet Ave. (☎483-1669), across from the Crystal Pier in Pacific Beach, serves up legendary burritos, but the long lines send locals to **Cotijas,** 1092 Garnet Ave. (☎273-5753). The 2 are unaffiliated, but both serve up huge burritos with a wide variety of fillings ($2-5). Open M-F 7am-3pm, Sa-Su 7am-4pm. D/MC/V. ❶

Kansas City Barbecue, 610 W. Market St. (☎231-9680), near Seaport Village. The setting for *Top Gun*'s "Great Balls of Fire" scene. While the wooden piano remains, all that's left of Goose, Maverick, and Charlie is an abundance of autographed posters and neon signs. Vegetarians will find themselves in the Danger Zone in this barbecue-slathered meatfest. Entrees $9-16. Open daily 11am-1am. D/MC/V. ❸

◙ SIGHTS

San Diego's world-famous attractions are varied enough to keep any traveler engaged. Pick up the free weekly *Reader* for local event listings. The **San Diego 3-for-1 Pass** ($99, ages 3-9 $75) offers unlimited admission for five consecutive days at a discounted price to three of the city's premier sights: Sea World, the San Diego Zoo, and the San Diego Wild Animal Park. Visit www.sandiegozoo.org or the websites of the other two parks for information and online ticketing.

■ **SAN DIEGO ZOO.** With over 100 acres of exquisite habitats, this zoo well deserves its reputation as one of the finest in the world. At the legendary **panda** exhibit you can get close enough to see the bamboo stuck between their teeth, but go before noon to avoid long lines. The educational 40min. **double-decker bus tour** covers about 75% of the zoo. The express bus will take you to any of five stops throughout the park anytime during the day. The **Skyfari Aerial Tramway** rises 170 ft. above the park and can save on walking time. Don't expect to see anything but the tops of trees and the skyline. *(One-way $2.)* If the bus and tramway appeal to you, purchase your tickets when you buy zoo admission. *(2920 Zoo Dr., Balboa Park. ☎234-3153; www.sandiegozoo.org. Open daily late June to early Sept. 9am-10pm; early Sept. to late June 9am-dusk. $21, ages 3-11 $14; with unlimited use of narrated bus tour, express bus, and aerial train $32/$20. Military in uniform free. Free on Founder's Day, the 1st M in Oct.)*

DOWNTOWN. Petco Park, the new home of the **San Diego Padres,** offers excellent views from almost every seat. *(Games Mar.-Oct. Check www.padres.com for schedule and tickets.)* The **Gaslamp Quarter** contains antique shops, Victorian buildings, trendy restaurants, and nightclubs (see **Entertainment and Nightlife,** p. 925). The steel-and-glass structure of the **San Diego Museum of Contemporary Art** is a small gallery whose two floors display frequently changing exhibits. *(1001 Kettner Blvd. ☎234-1001. Open M-Tu and Th-Su 11am-5pm. Free.)* Housed within some of San Diego's oldest ships, the **San Diego Maritime Museum** showcases San Diego's rich maritime history and maintains three ships. *(1492 N. Harbor Dr. ☎234-9153; www.sdmaritime.org. Open daily 9am-8pm. $10; seniors, military, and ages 13-17 $8; ages 6-12 $7. With 30min. boat excursion $11/$9/$8.)* The Embarcadero has boardwalk shops and museums that face moored windjammers, cruise ships, and the occasional naval destroyer. *(Most afternoon tours of naval craft free.)* The jewel of San Diego's redevelopment efforts is Horton Plaza, at Broadway and 4th, a pastel, open-air, multi-level shopping center.

BALBOA PARK AND THE EL PRADO MUSEUMS. Constructed and painstakingly landscaped for the 1915 Panama-California and the 1935 California Pacific International Expositions, Balboa is America's largest urban cultural park. It is a central feature of San Diego, containing 15 museums, several performing arts venues, and eight gardens within its 1200 beautiful acres. Most of the museums reside within the Spanish-Renaissance buildings that line **El Prado Street,** which runs east-west through the park's central **Plaza de Panama.** The Passport to Balboa Park provides admission to (and is available for purchase at) all park museums. It's a great way for adults to see all of the museums, but those eligible for student and senior discounts should make sure the passport benefits them. The Best of Balboa Park passport also includes admission to all ticketed options at the zoo. The **Balboa Visitors Center,** in the Plaza de Panama, sells park maps and the Passport to Balboa Park. *(1549 El Prado St. ☎239-0512. www.balboapark.org. Open daily late June to early Sept. 9:30am-5pm; low season 9:30am-4:30pm. Passport to Balboa Park $30. Best of Balboa Park passport $55. Park maps $0.50.)* Creationists beware: the **Museum of Man** dedicates an entire floor to the 98.4% of DNA we share with chimpanzees. Another hall displays mummies from around the world. *(On the west end of the park. ☎239-2001; www.museumofman.org. Open daily 10am-4:30pm. $6, seniors $5, ages 6-17 $3; free 3rd Tu of each month.)* The small, ultra-modern **Museum of Photographic Arts (MOPA)** features classic and contemporary photography. Its film program ranges from cult classic film festivals to technical examination of more serious cinematic works. *(☎238-7559; www.mopa.org. Open M-W and F-Su 10am-5pm, Th 10am-9pm. $6; students, seniors, and military $4. Free 2nd Tu of each month. Films $10.)* The **Reuben H. Fleet Space Theater and Science Center** has interactive exhibits sure to delight your inner nerd, plus the world's first hemispheric Omnimax theater. *(1875 El Prado Way. ☎238-1233; www.rhfleet.org. Open daily 9:30am-8pm. $6.75, with Omnimax show $12; seniors $6/$9.75; ages 3-12 $5.50/$8.75. Free 1st Tu of each month.)* The **San Diego Museum of Art** has a collection ranging from ancient Asian and European masterpieces to contemporary Californian works. At the adjoining outdoor **Sculpture Garden Court,** a sensuous Henry Moore piece presides over other large abstract blocks. *(☎232-7931; www.sdmart.org. Open Tu-W and F-Su 10am-6pm, Th 10am-9pm. $9; seniors, students, and ages 18-24 $7; ages 6-17 $4. Special exhibits $2-20.)* The **Aerospace Museum** displays 24 full-scale replicas and 44 original planes, as well as exhibits on aviation history and the International Space Station project. *(2001 Pan American Plaza. ☎234-8291; www.aerospacemuseum.org. Open daily 10am-4:30pm; extended summer hours. $9, students and seniors $7, ages 6-17 $4, military and under age 6 free. Free 4th Tu of each month.)* The fragrant **Botanical Building** may look like a giant wooden cage, but it's filled with plants, not birds. The orchid collection, set among murmuring fountains, is particularly striking. *(2200 Park Blvd. ☎235-1100. Botanical Building open M-W and F-Su 10am-4pm. Free.)* At the east side of the park, the **Desert Garden** and **Rose Garden** prove a salient floral contrast. The surprisingly lush Desert Garden is in full bloom from January to March, while the roses are best admired between April and December.

OLD TOWN. In 1769, Father Serra, supported by a brigade of Spanish infantry, established the first of 21 missions that would eventually line the California coast in the area now known as **Old Town.** The remnants of this early settlement have become one of San Diego's tourist mainstays. The most popular of the area's attractions is **Plaza del Pasado,** containing museums, shops, and restaurants in the State Park's early 19th-century buildings. Visitors are free to wander the grounds and explore the many museums and living history displays as they learn about California's early days. Guided tours are also available M-F 11am, Sa-Su 11am and 2pm, leaving from the Robinson-Rose House, which functions as a **visitors center.** *(Open daily 10am-5pm.)* Daytime tours of the **Whaley House,** which stands on the site of San Diego's first gallows, are little more than a walk through an old house. Nighttime tours are said to be much more interesting, as it is one of two official haunted houses recognized by the State of California. *(2482 San Diego Ave. ☎ 298-2482, tours 293-0117. Open daily 10am-10pm. $5, seniors $4, ages 3-12 $2. After 7pm $10/$8/$4.)* The stout adobe walls of the **Serra Museum** were raised at the site of the original fort and mission in 1929 and now present displays on the history of California. *(2727 Presidio Dr., in Presidio Park. ☎ 297-3258. Open F-Su 10am-4:30pm. $5; seniors, students, and military $4; ages 6-17 $2.)*

CORONADO ISLAND. A slender 7 mi. strip of hauled sand known as the "Silver Strand" tethers lovely Coronado "Island" to the mainland near Imperial Beach. Coronado's most famed sight is its Victorian-style **Hotel Del Coronado,** one of America's largest wooden buildings. *(1500 Orange Ave. ☎ 435-6611.)* Coronado also has a huge military presence, and its entire northern chunk comprises the **North Island Naval Air Station,** the birthplace of American naval aviation. In fact, it was Navy men who carted sand to connect the island to the rest of Coronado in 1947.

OCEAN, MISSION, AND PACIFIC BEACHES. Much of San Diego's younger population flocks to these communities for the surf and hopping nightlife; not surprisingly, noisy bars and grills crowd these shores (see **Food,** p. 922, and **Entertainment and Nightlife,** p. 925). The three beaches line up consecutively, but each has its own flavor. **Ocean Beach (O.B.)** cultivates a homegrown, earthy atmosphere. With local hippies lounging in the gentle surf, O.B. is the most laid-back of the beaches and the best place to learn the art of wave-riding. Farther north, **Mission Beach,** at the corner of W. Mission Bay Dr. and Mission Blvd., is a people-watcher's paradise. **Belmont Park,** a combination amusement park and shopping center, draws a large, family-friendly crowd. **Pacific Beach** caters to the good-looking, beer-drinking college crowds, and its boisterous **Garnet Avenue** is home to the best nightlife. **Ocean Front Walk** is packed with joggers, cyclists, and beachfront shops.

SEA WORLD. With its occasionally oppressive crowds and often long lines, you may forget why you're there, but Seaworld remains a staple San Diego attraction. Each year millions flock to the park to see Shamu, the park's famous killer whale, soak his audience with his signature bellyflop splash. There are many other goofy and surprisingly charming animal shows. The dolphin show, featuring highly trained and intelligent Atlantic bottlenose dolphins, including the high-jumping Dolly the Dolphin, is a crowd favorite. Those looking to cool down without a face full of saltwater should head to the free **Budweiser's Beer School and brewery.** The 30min. class, **free beer,** and general merriment come courtesy of Anheuser-Busch, the proud owners of Sea World. *(☎ 800-380-3203; www.seaworld.com. Open in summer daily 9am-11pm. The park opens at 10am in winter, but closing hours vary. $51, ages 3-9 $41; special deals sometimes available online. Parking $8, RVs $10.)*

LA JOLLA. This affluent seaside neighborhood has few budget options, but offers some of the finest public beaches in the San Diego area. **La Jolla Cove,** a small beach lined with sandstone cliffs near the commercial district, is popular with photographers, picnickers, snorkelers, and brilliantly colored Garibaldi goldfish. Wander south along the cliffs to a striking semi-circular inlet known as **The Children's Pool** or **Casa**, home to a thriving sea lion community. Some of the best breakers in the county are in La Jolla at **Tourmaline Beach** and **Wind 'n' Sea Beach**. However, these are notoriously territorial spots, so outsiders may be advised to surf elsewhere. **La Jolla Shores** has gentle swells ideal for new surfers and boogie boarders. **Black's Beach** is not officially a nude beach, but that doesn't seem to stop sunbathers from going *au naturel*. The beach is accessible only via a precarious 1 mi. path from Torrey Pines State Beach, so use caution getting there, but then catch some rays and look out for hangliders on the cliffs above.

Overlooking La Jolla Shores, the **Birch Aquarium at the Scripps Institute of Oceanography** has great educational exhibits including a tank of oozing jellyfish, a large collection of seahorses, and a 70,000-gallon kelp and shark tank. *(2300 Expedition Way, off Torrey Pines. ☎858-534-3474; www.aquarium.ucsd.edu. Open daily 9am-5pm. $10, seniors $8.50, students $7, ages 3-17 $6.50.)* The **San Diego Museum of Contemporary Art**, bigger and better than the downtown branch, houses parts of the permanent collection of pop, minimalist, and conceptualist art from the 1950s onward, as well as rotating exhibitions. The museum is as visually stunning as the art it contains, with gorgeous ocean views, high ceilings, and light-filled spaces. *(700 Prospect St. ☎858-454-3541; www.mcasd.org. Open M-Tu and F-Su 11am-5pm, Th 11am-7pm. $6; students, seniors, military, and ages 12-18 $2. 3rd Tu and 1st Su of every month free.)* Be sure to check out the glass terraces and buttresses of **Geisel Library** at the **University of California San Diego (UCSD)**, a space-age structure endowed by La Jolla resident Theodore Geisel, better known as Dr. Seuss, the late children's author. *(☎858-534-2208.)*

🎵 🎷 ENTERTAINMENT AND NIGHTLIFE

Nightlife in San Diego is concentrated in several distinct pockets. Posh locals and party-seeking tourists flock to the **Gaslamp Quarter**, where numerous restaurants and bars feature live music. The **Hillcrest** area, next to Balboa Park, draws a young, largely gay crowd to its clubs and dining spots. Away from downtown, the **beach areas** (especially Garnet Ave. in Pacific Beach) are loaded with clubs, bars, and cheap eateries that attract college-age revelers. The city's definitive source of entertainment info is the free *Reader*, available in coffeehouses and visitors centers. Listings can also be found in the Thursday *San Diego Union-Tribune*. If boozin' isn't your idea of nightlife, you can spend a more sedate evening at one of San Diego's excellent theaters, such as the **Balboa Theatre**, 225 Broadway Ave. (☎544-1000), or the **Horton Grand Theatre**, 444 4th Ave. (☎234-9583), both downtown. The **La Jolla Playhouse**, 2910 La Jolla Village Dr., presents shows on the UCSD campus. (☎858-550-1010; www.lajollaplayhouse.com.)

Croce's Top Hat Bar and Grille and **Croce's Jazz Bar**, 802 5th Ave. (☎233-4355), at F St. in the Gaslamp Quarter. A warm, classy combo rock/blues bar and jazz bar opened by Ingrid Croce, widow of singer Jim Croce. Live music nightly from 8:30pm. Cover $5-$10. Top Hat open F-Sa 7pm-1:30am. Jazz Bar open daily 5:30pm-12:30am.

The Bitter End, 770 5th Ave. (☎338-9300), in the Gaslamp Quarter. This 3-level dance club is always packed with those dressed to impress, so leave the torn Levi's and sandals at home. The main floor is a popular watering hole, while upstairs is a swanky lounge. DJs spin everything from hip-hop to Top 40 to trance downstairs. Happy hour Th-F 3-7pm. 21+. Cover $10 after 9pm. Open daily 5pm-2am.

Bourbon Street, 4612 Park Blvd. (☎291-0173), in University Heights. A perennially popular gay bar with nightly entertainment. Watch the game in the front pub area, then move to the covered patio and dance floor for some more serious mixin' and minglin'. Karaoke Tu 9pm. $3 martinis Th 4-7pm. 21+. No cover. Open daily 4pm-2am.

The Casbah, 2501 Kettner Blvd. (☎232-4355), at Laurel St., near the airport. Eddie Vedder of Pearl Jam owns this intimate spot, one of the best live music venues in the city. Cover varies. 21+. Hours vary; usually 5pm-2am.

The Flame, 3780 Park Blvd. (☎295-4163), in Hillcrest. One of the most popular lesbian dance clubs in the nation. Come early to find parking. 21+. Open daily 5pm-2am.

TIJUANA, MEXICO   ☎664

Just minutes from San Diego lies the most notorious specimen of border subculture: Tijuana. Often referred to as "TJ," the city's cheap booze, haggling vendors, and kitschy, unapologetic hedonism attract 30 million US visitors each year. But Tijuana is more than just another Sin City. As one of Mexico's wealthiest cities, it teems with megastores, museums, and monstrous industrial activity. However, most travelers stick to Revolución, the city's main strip, which reverberates with mariachi bands, thumping dance beats from the packed nightclubs, and the sounds of eager tourists unloading wads of cash on everything from *jai alai* gambling to slimy strip shows. As an introduction to Mexican culture, flashy, trashy TJ is about as unrepresentative and unrepentant as they come.

■■ ☎ **ORIENTATION AND PRACTICAL INFORMATION.** For the vast majority of visitors, Tijuana simply is **Avenida Revolución,** in the middle of **Zona Centro,** the tourist hot spot. *Calles* run east-west and are named and numbered; *avenidas* run parallel to Revolución and perpendicular to the *calles*. The **tourist office** is located in the small booth on the corner of Revolución and Calle 3. English-speaking staff offer good maps and advice. (☎685-2210. Open M-Th 10am-4pm, F-Su 10am-7pm. Other, less-dependable branches at the Mexicoach station and at the border crossing.) The **Customs Office** is at the border on the Mexican side after crossing the San Ysidro bridge. (☎683-1390. Open 24hr.) **Consulates: Canada,** Germán Gedovius 10411-101, in the Zona Río. (☎684-0461, after-hours emergency 800-706-2900. Open M-F 9am-1pm.) **UK,** Salinas 1500, in Col. Aviación, La Mesa. (☎681-5320. Open M-F 9am-2pm.) **US,** Tapachula Sur 96, in Col. Hipódromo, next to the racetrack southeast of town. (☎622-7400. Open M-F 8am-4pm.) In an **emergency,** call the San Diego office at ☎619-692-2154 and leave a message; an officer will respond. Banks along Constitución **exchange money.** Banamex, Constitución at Calle 4 (☎688-0021; open M-F 8:30am-4:30pm), has shorter lines than the more central **HSBC,** Revolución 129, at Calle 2 (☎688-1914; open M-F 8am-7pm, Sa 8am-3pm). Both have 24hr. **ATMs.** *Casas de cambio* offer better rates but may charge commission and refuse to exchange traveler's checks. **Police:** ☎685-6557, tourist assistance 688-0555. Constitución at Calle 8. English spoken. **Medical Services: Hospital General,** Centenario 10851 (☎684-0237 or 684-0922), in the Zona Río. **Post Office:** on Negrete at Calle 1. (☎684-7950. Open M-F 8am-5pm, Sa 9am-1pm.) **Postal Code:** 22000. **Area Code:** 664.

☎☎ **ACCOMMODATIONS AND FOOD.** As a general rule, hotels in Tijuana become less reputable the farther north you go. Avoid any in the area downhill from Calle 1 (the Zona Norte). Rooms at some motels may not fit the standards of cleanliness expected by US travelers; however, hoteliers are generally very open

BORDER CROSSING. Traveling between the US and Mexico is generally an easy process, but security is still taken very seriously. Crossing can be as simple as a wave of the passport or as time-consuming as a full search of your car. To keep things moving along, make sure to have all necessary documents handy. It is illegal to cross the border anywhere except an open crossing station. See **Essentials,** p. 10, for more details on documents and procedures.

about showing you a room before you check in. Just make sure you get the room you inspect. **Hotel La Villa de Zaragoza ❷**, Madero 1120, between Calle 7 and 8, will impress all but the snobbiest of travelers with spacious rooms, cable TV, phone, and king-size beds. (☎685-1832. Laundry, room service, and 24hr. security. Singles from 437 pesos; doubles 517 pesos. Reservations accepted. MC/V.) If budget is your bottom line, **Hotel Colonial ❶**, Calle 6 1812, between Constitución and Niños Héroes, has clean rooms with A/C and private baths in a quieter, residential neighborhood. (☎688-1720. Singles and doubles 260 pesos. Cash only.)

As with most things in Tijuana, in-your-face promoters try to herd tourists into the overpriced restaurants lining **Revolución**. For cheap food, **taco stands ❶** all over the *centro* sell several tacos or a *torta* for 10-15 pesos. **Restaurante Ricardo's Tortas ❶**, at Madero and Calle 7, serves the best *tortas* in town (25-40 pesos). Try the *super especial*, with ham, *carne asada*, cheese, avocado, tomato, and mayo. (☎685-4031. Open 24hr.) **La Cantina de los Remedios ❷**, Diego Rivera 19, in the Zona Río, is a colorful place with competing *mariachis*, lots of tequila, and a big crowd. Mexican cuisine starts at 80 pesos and extends well beyond the usual options. (☎634-3065. Open M-Th 1pm-midnight, F-Sa 1pm-2am, Su 1-10pm.)

◪ SIGHTS AND FIGHTS. Many of the most entertaining sights in town are on Revolución, with clubs, streetside stores, and painted *burros* ready to pose for tourists' pictures (for a nominal fee) on every street corner. While the so-called "attractions" of the main drag tend to be touristy, Tijuana's cultural assets and parks counter this. The huge plaza of Tijuana's cultural center, **Centro Cultural Tijuana (CECUT)**, is the most visually striking feature of Paseo de los Héroes. In the building behind the sphere, the superb ◪**Museo de las Californias** traces the history of the peninsula from its earliest inhabitants to the 21st century. (☎687-9633. Museum open Tu-Su 10am-7pm. 20 pesos, students and children 12 pesos.) Those with a sense of adventure can make their way to the sprawling state-run park of **Parque Morelos**, Blvd. de los Insurgentes 26000, to enjoy the small zoo or take a pleasant walk. (Take an orange-and-grey communal cab for 8 pesos on Calle 5 and Madero. ☎625-2469. Open Tu-Su 9am-5pm. 5 pesos, children 2 pesos; parking 10 pesos.) If you're in town on the right Sunday, you can watch the graceful yet savage battle of *toreador* versus bull in one of Tijuana's two bullrings. **El Toreo de Tijuana**, southeast of town just off Agua Caliente, hosts the first round of fights. (Catch a bus on Calle 2a west of Revolución. May-Aug. every other Su at 4pm.) The seaside **Plaza Monumental** hosts the second round (Aug.-Oct.). Mexicoach sends buses (round-trip US$4) to Plaza Monumental on fight days. Alternatively, take the blue-and-white local buses (5 pesos) on Calle 3 at Constitución all the way down Calle 2. Tickets to both rings go on sale at the gate (☎688-2100 or 681-7084) or at the Mexicoach office (☎685-1470) on Revolución between Calle 6 and 7 the Wednesday before a fight. (Tickets 50-350 pesos.)

◪ NIGHTLIFE. In the 1920s, Prohibition drove US citizens south of the border to revel in the forbidden, fermented nectars of cacti, grapes, and hops. Tijuana, with a legal drinking age of 18, is still a favorite imbibing destination for Americans. Stroll down Revolución after dusk and you'll be bombarded with thumping music, neon lights, and abrasive club promoters hawking "three-for-one" margaritas and buckets of beer at bargain prices. Those who prefer laid-back nights of good conversation, or simply the ability to hear their friends, are in the wrong place. **Animale**, Revolución at Calle 3, is the biggest, glitziest, and loudest hedonistic haven in Tijuana. (Open daily 10am-4am.) A sublimely wacky world of life-sized plaster clowns and an authentic yellow school bus can be found at **Iguanas-Ranas**, Revolución at Calle 3a. (☎685-1422. Open M-Th 10am-2am, F-Su 10am-5am.) At **People's**, Revolución and Calle 2, fluorescent constellations and

THE HIDDEN DEAL

IN HOT WATER

In a town that caters to the rich with swanky restaurants, exclusive golf clubs, and posh spas, the Spa Resort Casino's "Taking of the Waters" treatment is a rare opportunity to live the good life without a celebrity budget.

Built on the site of Palm Springs' primary mineral springs, Spa Resort Casino is operated by the Agua Caliente band of the Cahuilla Indians, who have lived in the Palm Springs area for over a thousand years. It is the only spa facility in the US with individual tubs fed by natural hot springs. The Taking of the Water is the spa's signature treatment and is designed for total relaxation and rejuvenation. Guests are escorted to steam, sauna, and aromatherapy rooms, followed by a soak in a private tub filled with the famed mineral waters. The treatment ends with a visit to the Tranquility Room, where a comfy cot and sheets ease the transition back into the real world.

As an added bonus, guests are invited to repeat various steps of treatment and receive all-day access to the spa's fitness center and beautifully landscaped swimming pools. With a full range of massage and body treatments designed to fit a full range of wallet sizes, how much can this hour of unadulterated bliss and pampering cost? A mere $35.

For more info, call the Spa Resort Casino at ☎888-293-0180.

crudely painted sportsmen decorate the terrace, and revelers guzzle beers to American rock music. (☎688-2706. Open M-Th 10am-2am, F-Su 10am-4am.)

THE CALIFORNIA DESERT

California's desert is one of the most beautiful places in the world; it's also one of the loneliest. Deserted roads cut through endless expanses of barren earth and landscapes that seem completely untouched by civilization. Exploration turns up elusive treasures: diverse flora and fauna, staggering topographical variation, and scattered relics of the American frontier. Throughout the year, the desert switches from a pleasantly warm refuge to an unbearable wasteland and back again.

PALM SPRINGS   ☎760

From its first known inhabitants, the Cahuilla, to today's fun-loving geriatrics, the restorative oasis of Palm Springs has attracted an odd menagerie of old and young. With warm winter temperatures, celebrity residents, and a casino, this city is a sunny break from everyday life.

Mt. San Jacinto State Park, Palm Springs's primary landmark, offers outdoor recreation like hiking and cross-country skiing. If the 10,804 ft. peak seems too strenuous, the world-famous **Palm Springs Aerial Tramway** can whisk you to the top in 10min. and even rotates to ensure you get a full view of the valley floor. After 3pm, the Ride & Dine option includes dinner at the cafeteria-style Top of the Tram restaurant. (☎325-1449 or 888-515-8726. Trams run at least every 30min. M-F 10am-10:30pm, Sa-Su 8am-10:30pm. Round-trip $21, ages 60+ $19, ages 3-12 $14. Ride & Dine $30, children $19.) Experience Palm Springs's heralded golf scene by hitting the links at **Tahquitz Creek Golf Resort,** 1885 Golf Club Dr., a club managed by Arnold Palmer. (☎328-1005 or 800-743-2211. Green fees $110 in high season, but with sharp summer discounts.)

Despite Palm Springs's reputation as a luxury getaway, affordable lodgings do exist; check out the north and south edges of the downtown area just off Palm Canyon Dr. or look online for deals before you go. The **Royal Sun Inn ❸,** 1700 S. Palm Canyon Dr., has large, well-furnished rooms for more-than-reasonable rates. Many have views of the nearby San Jacinto Mountains. (☎327-1504. King bed from $39 in summer to $79 in winter. Breakfast included. AmEx/D/DC/MC/V.) Palm Springs offers an array of culinary treats, from standard burger joints to ultra-trendy fusion cuisine. Satisfying and inexpensive Thai cuisine is served at ⊠**Thai Smile ❷**, 651 N. Palm Canyon Dr. Don't miss the $6 lunch specials. (☎320-5503. Open daily 11:30am-10pm. AmEx/D/MC/V.) The shaded patio of the **Rock Garden Cafe ❷**, 777 S. Palm Canyon Dr., is the perfect place to enjoy one of their many omelets, burgers, or cocktails. (☎327-8840. Burgers $8. Omelets $7. Cocktails $5. Open daily 7am-midnight. AmEx/D/DC/MC/V.) To experience Palm Springs's heralded nightlife, head to **Village Pub**, 266 S. Palm Canyon Dr., to relive your college days by swilling beer and grooving to folksy rock with a diverse international crowd. (☎323-3265. Open daily 11am-2am. AmEx/D/MC/V.)

Greyhound, 311 N. Indian Canyon Dr. (☎325-2053; www.greyhound.com), runs buses to L.A. (3-4hr., 6 per day, $26), Las Vegas (6-9hr., 5 per day, $64), and San Diego (4-11hr., 5 per day, $30). **SunBus** covers Coachella Valley cities. (☎343-3451. $1.25.) With plenty of brochures and info, the **Visitor Center**, 2781 N. Palm Canyon Dr. (☎778-8415 or 800-347-7746; www.palm-springs.org), is a good stop for first-time visitors. **Post Office**: 333 E. Amado Rd. (☎322-4111. Open M-F 8am-5pm, Sa 9am-3pm.) **Postal Code**: 92262. **Area Code**: 760.

JOSHUA TREE NATIONAL PARK ☎760

When devout Mormon pioneers crossed this faith-testing desert in the 19th century, they named the enigmatic tree they encountered after the Biblical prophet Joshua. The tree's crooked limbs resembled the Hebrew general, and, with arms upraised, seemed to beckon these Latter-Day pioneers to the Promised Land. The Joshua tree forests still inspire reverent awe, but the park, centered around the intersection of the Colorado and Mojave deserts, is also home to some of the most popular climbing rocks in the US.

▣ ? **ORIENTATION AND PRACTICAL INFORMATION.** The park is bordered by three highways: **I-10** to the south, **Route 62 (Twentynine Palms Highway)** to the west and north, and **Route 177** to the east. The north entrances are off Rte. 62 at the towns of **Joshua Tree** and **Twentynine Palms**. The south entrance is at **Cottonwood Spring**, off I-10 at Rte. 195, southeast of Palm Springs. The park entrance fee, valid for a week, is $5 per person, $10 per car. **Visitor Info: Headquarters and Oasis Visitor Center**, 74485 National Park Dr. (☎367-5500; www.nps.gov/jotr. Open daily 8am-5pm.) **Post Office**: 73839 Gorgonio Dr., in Twentynine Palms. (☎800-275-8777. Open M-F 8:30am-5pm, Sa 9am-noon.) **Postal Code**: 92277. **Area Code**: 760.

▲ ACCOMMODATIONS. Most park campgrounds don't accept reservations, but reservations can be made at Black Rock, Indian Cove, and all group sites (☎800-365-2267). ⊠**Jumbo Rocks ❶**, 4400 ft., near Skull Rock Trail on the eastern edge of Queen Valley, is the highest and coolest campground, with sites amongst granite formations. (Pit toilets, no water. Sites $5.) **Indian Cove ❶**, 3200 ft., on the north edge of Wonderland of Rocks, is popular among climbers. (Sites $10; group sites $20-35.) **Cottonwood**, in the south, and **Black Rock**, near Yucca Valley, offer water and flush toilets (both $10). Experienced campers can register for a **backcountry permit** at the visitors center or at self-service boards throughout the park. Those who can't stomach desert campgrounds will find inexpensive motels in Twentynine Palms. The **29 Palms Inn ❹**, 73950 Inn Dr., is an attraction in its own right: in addition to 23 bungalows and rooms facing the Mora Oasis, Robert Plant composed "29 Palms" here. (☎367-3505; www.29palmsinn.com. Continental breakfast. Pool. Reservations required Feb.-Apr. Doubles Oct.-May M-Th and Su $60-95, F-Sa $85-135; June-Sept. $50-75/$75-115. AmEx/D/DC/MC/V.)

⚐ OUTDOOR ACTIVITIES. Over 80% of Joshua Tree is designated wilderness, safeguarding it against development and paved roads. Even so, many of the densest stands of Joshua Trees and more curious rock formations are to be found along the roadways in the western portion of the park, making a **driving tour** an easy way to explore. All roads are well marked, and signs labeled "Exhibit Ahead" lead to unique floral and geological formations. One of these tours, a 34 mi. stretch winding through the park on **Park Boulevard,** provides access to the park's most outstanding sights and hikes. An especially spectacular detour is **Keys View,** 5185 ft., 6 mi. off Park Blvd. and just west of Ryan Campground. On a clear day, you can see Palm Springs and Mexico, and the sunrise from here is always spectacular. Toward Cottonwood, on Pinto Basin Rd., the **Cholla Cactus Garden** is home to many "teddy bear" cacti but is mostly known as a transition zone between the ecosystems of the Colorado Desert and the higher, slightly cooler Mojave Desert. Those with **4WD** vehicles have even more options for exploration, including the 18 mi. **Geology Tour Road,** west of Jumbo Rocks off Park Blvd., which climbs through striking rock formations and ends in the Little San Bernardino Mountains.

Hiking is the best way to see Joshua Tree, but those eager to explore should pack plenty of water and be alert to changing weather and possible flash flood conditions. Anticipate slow progress even on short walks; the oppressive heat and the scarcity of shade can strain even the hardiest hikers. The easy **Hidden Valley Trail** leads you between boulders and into a tucked-away hollow that was once the secret hideaway of cattle rustlers (1 mi. loop with interpretive signs). The summit of **Ryan Mountain** provides a 360° panorama of the surrounding country, but those with less time will want to forgo the sunbaked, 3 mi. round-trip climb in favor of scrambling up the bluff at Keys View. Visitors centers have info on the park's other hikes, which range from a 15min. wheelchair accessible stroll leading to the **Oasis of Mara** to a three-day trek along the 35 mi. **California Riding and Hiking Trail.**

The crack-split granite of Joshua Tree provides some of the best rock climbing and bouldering in the world for experts and novices alike. The renowned boulders at **Wonderland of Rocks** and **Hidden Valley** are always swarming with hard-bodied climbers, making Joshua Tree the most climbed area in America. Adventurous beginners will find thrills at the **Skull Rock Interpretive Walk,** which runs between Jumbo Rocks and Skull Rock. The walk offers info on local plants and animals, and exciting yet non-technical scrambles to the tops of monstrous boulders.

DEATH VALLEY NATIONAL PARK ☎ 760

The devil owns a lot of real estate in Death Valley's 3.3 million acres: he grows crops at Devil's Cornfield and hits the links at Devil's Golf Course, and the park is home to Hell's Gate itself. Indeed, the area's extreme heat and surreal landscape make it inhospitable enough to belong to the dark side. Winter temperatures dip well below freezing in the mountains, and summer readings in the valley average 115°F. The second-highest temperature ever recorded in the world (134°F in the shade) was measured at the valley's Furnace Creek Ranch on July 10, 1913.

⛾ TRANSPORTATION. Cars are the only way to get to and around Death Valley, but conditions are notoriously hard on vehicles. **Radiator water** (*not* for drinking) is available at critical points on Rte. 178 and 190 and Nevada Rte. 374. There are only four **gas stations** in the park (Furnace Creek, Scotty's Castle, Stovepipe Wells, Panamint Springs), and though prices are hefty, be sure to keep the tank at least half full at all times. Always travel with two gallons of water per person per day. In the case of a breakdown, stay in the shade of your vehicle. Of the seven **park entrances,** most visitors choose Rte. 190 from the east. The road is well maintained, and the visitors center is relatively close. However, since most of the major sights adjoin

Badwater Road, the north-south road, the daytripper can see more of the park by entering from the southeast (Rte. 178 W from Rte. 127 at Shoshone) or the north (direct to Scotty's Castle via Nevada Rte. 267). Unskilled mountain drivers in passenger cars should not attempt to enter on the smaller Titus Canyon or Emigrant Canyon Dr. While it may look convenient to enter the park's north end near Big Pine, the road is not maintained and its use is not advisable at most times of year. No regular public transportation runs in the Valley. Attempting to hitchhike through Death Valley is akin to suicide.

⑦ PRACTICAL INFORMATION. Visitor Info: Furnace Creek Visitors Center, on Rte. 190 in the Valley's east-central section. (☎786-3244; www.nps.gov/deva. Open daily Mar.-Jan. 8am-6pm, Dec.-Feb. 8am-5pm.) Contact stations are at **Grapevine** (☎786-2313), at Rte. 190 and 267 near Scotty's Castle, **Shoshone** (☎832-4308), at Rte. 127 and 178 outside the Valley's southeast border, and **Beatty, NV** (☎702-553-2200), on Nevada Rte. 374. Pick up a copy of the *Death Valley Visitor's Guide* newspaper at any ranger station. Fill up on gas outside Death Valley at Lone Pine, Olancha, Shoshone, or Beatty, NV. **Post Office: Furnace Creek Ranch** (☎800-275-8777). Open M-F 8:30am-5pm. **Postal Code:** 92328. **Area Code:** 760.

⌂ ACCOMMODATIONS. Motel rooms in surrounding towns are cheaper than those in Death Valley but can be over an hour away from top sights. Never assume that rooms will be available, but your chances (and the prices) will be better in the summer. In winter, camping with a stock of groceries saves money and driving time. In summer, camping can get quite uncomfortable. **Furnace Creek Ranch ❹,** in Furnace Creek, has a supremely convenient location next to the visitors center. You can also tee up on the world's lowest golf course. (☎786-2345; www.furnacecreekresort.com. Singles and doubles in summer from $105; in winter from $125. AmEx/D/DC/MC/V.) The National Park Service maintains nine **campgrounds ❶** in Death Valley. All have toilets but no showers, and stays are limited to 30 days (except Furnace Creek, with a 14 day limit). **Backcountry camping** is free and legal. You must check in at the visitors center and pitch tents at least 2 mi. from your car and any road and a quarter mile from any backcountry water source.

◎ SIGHTS. With the blooming of desert plants, springtime brings special beauty to Death Valley. Year-round, the area's slanted mountains melt into canyons colored by trace minerals, making for surprisingly pretty hiking. **Golden Canyon Trail** is an easy trail winding through one such colorful draw (1 mi. one-way from Golden Canyon trailhead, 2 mi. south of Hwy. 190 on Badwater Rd.). There are countless other trails to occupy the gentlest wanderer and hardiest adventurer. Visitors should keep in mind that Death Valley can be a very dangerous place to hike. Not only is it hot and shadeless, but distances can be very deceiving; mountains that appear to be quite close to the road can actually be several miles away. No matter what your plans are, carry at least a gallon of water per person and start drinking before you are thirsty to prevent dehydration. Ironically, flash floods are a real danger, so be aware of the weather at all times. Camera-toters should keep in mind that the best photo opportunities are at sunrise and sunset. Rangers often set up telescopes at **Zabriskie Point** to capitalize on the Valley's clear skies. Many of the park's most spectacular sights are accessible from the air-conditioned comfort of your car. One of the best views is at **Dante's View,** reached by a 13 mi. paved road from Rte. 190. **Badwater,** a briny pool four times saltier than the ocean, is at the lowest point (282 ft. below sea level) in the Western Hemisphere. **Artist's Drive,** 10 mi. south of the visitors center, is a one-way loop that contorts its way through brightly colored rock formations. The loop's early ochres and burnt siennas give

CALIFORNIA

way at **Artist's Palette** to vivid green, yellow, periwinkle, and pink mineral deposits in the hillside. About 5 mi. south is **Devil's Golf Course,** a vast expanse of gnarled salt pillars formed by flooding and evaporation; jagged crystalline deposits, some quite delicate and beautiful, stretch as far as the eye can see.

THE SIERRA NEVADA

The Sierra Nevada Mountain Range is known as California's backbone, stretching 450 mi. from stifling Death Valley in the south to near the Oregon border in the north. Its magnificent, jagged peaks—including Mt. Whitney, the tallest mountain in the continental US—are a tribute to the area's active geological past. Breathtaking U-shaped valleys testify to the more recent tempering influence of granite-smoothing glaciation. The Sierra Nevada, whose name fittingly translates as "snowy range," also contains Lake Tahoe's crystalline waters, Sequoia National Park's towering redwoods, and Yosemite's incredible waterfalls.

LAKE TAHOE   ☎530

Shimmering blue water, pristine beaches, immense mountains, and an unobtrusive but ubiquitous commercial presence make Tahoe an ideal destination for boating, fishing, skiing, hiking, and spending money. Each season brings wonders of its own to Tahoe; accordingly, tourist season is year long.

▐ TRANSPORTATION

Trains: Amtrak, 10000 E. River St. (☎800-872-7245; www.amtrak.com), in Truckee, CA. 1 train daily to **Oakland/San Francisco** (6½hr., $45-93), **Reno** (1hr., $10-21), and **Sacramento** (4½hr., $22-40). Open daily 9am-5pm.

Buses: Greyhound (☎800-231-2222; www.greyhound.com), in Truckee, is the closest station. Buses roll to **Reno** (1hr., 2 per day, $11), **Sacramento** (3hr., 3 per day, $21), and **San Francisco** (5½hr., 3 per day, $30).

Tahoe Area Regional Transport (TART; ☎550-1212 or 800-736-6365; www.laketahoetransit.com). Connects the western and northern shores from Incline Village to Meeks Bay, where it joins with South Lake Tahoe (BlueGO) buses in the summer at a transfer station. Stops daily every 30-60min., depending on the route. Buses also run from Tahoe City to Truckee and Squaw Valley and back (5 per day 7:30am-4:45pm). $1.25. Day pass $3. Exact fare required.

BlueGO (☎541-7149; www.bluego.org). Operates routes along the South Shore, including from Stateline, NV to the Hwy. 89/50 transit center. Runs approximately 6:40am-12:40am. $1.75. Day pass $3. 10 ride pass $15. Also, seasonal service to Heavenly ski resort.

BlueGO Door to Door (☎541-7149) runs door-to-door service within city limits (24hr., $3) and within El Dorado County (7am-7pm, $5).

◆ ▐ ORIENTATION AND PRACTICAL INFORMATION

Located in the northern Sierra Nevada on the California-Nevada border, Lake Tahoe is 3hr. from San Francisco. The lake sits 100 mi. northeast of Sacramento (via **Highway 50**) and 35 mi. southwest of Reno (via **Highway 395** and **431**). Lake Tahoe is divided into two main regions, **North Shore** and **South Shore**. The North Shore includes **Tahoe City** in California and **Incline Village** in Nevada; the South Shore includes **South Lake Tahoe** in California and **Stateline** in Nevada.

Visitor Info: N. Lake Tahoe Visitors Bureau, 380 N. Lake Blvd. (☎583-3494; www.mytahoevacation.com). A helpful office with tons of info on the area. Open M-F 8:30am-5pm, Sa-Su 8:30am-5pm. **Taylor Creek Visitors Center** (USFS; ☎543-2674;

www.fs.fed.us/r5/ltbmu), 3 mi. north of S. Lake Tahoe on Hwy. 89. Permits for Desolation Wilderness. Camping fee $5 per person per night, $10 per person for 2 or more nights, yearly pass $20; under 12 free. Reservations (☎644-6048; $5) are available for overnight permits mid-June to Sept. 6. Open daily mid-June to Sept. 8am-5:30pm; May 31 to mid-June and Oct. 8am-4pm.

Medical Services: Incline Village Community Hospital, 880 Alder Ave. (☎775-833-4100), off Hwy. 28 in Incline Village. **Barton Memorial Hospital,** 2170 South Ave. (☎541-3420), at 3rd St. and South Ave. off Lake Tahoe Blvd. in South Lake.

Post Office: Tahoe City, 950 N. Lake Blvd. (☎800-275-8777). Open M-F 8:30am-5pm. **Postal Code:** 96145. **South Lake Tahoe,** 1046 Al Tahoe Blvd. (☎800-275-8777). Open M-F 8:30am-5pm, Sa noon-2pm. **Postal Code:** 96150. **Area Code:** 530 in CA, 775 in NV; in text, 530 unless otherwise noted.

ACCOMMODATIONS

The South Shore hosts many of the cheapest motels, which usually have basic amenities. Accommodations on the North Shore, while pricier and fewer in number, are generally more refined. In Tahoe City and Incline Village, the priciest lodgings tend to be booked solid for weekends and holidays; reserve well in advance. Fall and spring are the cheapest times to visit Tahoe. Whatever your budget, the area's campgrounds are great options in warmer months.

Tahoe Valley Lodge, 2214 Lake Tahoe Blvd. (☎800-669-7544 or 541-0353; www.tahoevalleylodge.com), in South Lake. Enjoy exquisite comfort in rooms decorated with a log-cabin theme. All rooms come equipped with a queen-size bed, cable TV, and coffeemaker; many have microwave, refrigerator, and jacuzzi. Queen beds M-Th and Su $95, F-Sa $125. AmEx/DC/MC/V. ❹

Elizabeth Lodge, 3918 Pioneer Trail (☎544-2417), in South Lake, 1 block off Lake Tahoe Blvd. Serviceable rooms with perhaps the lowest prices in town. Queen bed with TV and phone M-Th and Su $28, F $39, Sa $49. AmEx/D/MC/V. ❷

Tahoe State Recreation Area (☎583-3074), on the eastern edge of Tahoe City off Hwy. 28. In these 39 compact sites within walking distance of downtown Tahoe City (and adjacent to a shopping center), you may not feel like you're camping. Water, flush toilets, and showers ($0.50). Open May-Nov. Sites $15; $4 per additional vehicle. ❶

FOOD

In the south, casinos offer low-priced buffets while posh dining clubs line the lakefront, but grills and burger joints promise delicious food at reasonable prices.

Sprouts Natural Foods Cafe, 3123 Harrison Ave. (☎541-6969), at the intersection of Lake Tahoe Blvd. and Alameda Ave. in South Lake. Creative natural foods for a health-conscious crowd. Try a breakfast burrito with avocados ($5), a fresh smoothie ($3-3.75), or a shot of wheatgrass ($2). Open daily 8am-9pm. Cash or check only. ❶

The Red Hut Cafe, 2749 Lake Tahoe Blvd. (☎541-9024), in South Lake, and another location at 227 Kingsbury Grade (☎588-7488). A Tahoe original since 1959. Friendly staff serves homestyle cooking and outstanding daily specials. Whipped cream and fruit piled atop a waffle $6.25. Avocado burgers $7.50. Open daily 6am-2pm. Cash only. ❶

Bridgetender Tavern and Grill, 65 W. Lake Blvd. (☎583-3342), in Tahoe City. A local favorite known for juicy ½ lb. burgers ($8). The service can be a bit slow, but both the rustic interior or the scenic outdoor patio overlooking the Truckee River are great for recovering from a busy day on the lake. Open M-Th and Su 11am-11pm, F-Sa 11am-midnight. MC/V. ❸

CALIFORNIA

⚠ OUTDOOR ACTIVITIES

BEACHES

Many beaches dot Lake Tahoe, providing the perfect setting for sun-bathing and people-watching. Parking costs $3-8; bargain hunters should park in turn-outs on the main road and walk. On the North Shore, **Sand Harbor Beach,** 2 mi. south of Incline Village on Hwy. 28, has granite boulders and clear waters that attract swimmers, snorkelers, and boaters. **Baldwin Beach,** on the South Shore, and neighboring **Pope Beach,** near the southernmost point of the lake off Hwy. 89, are popular, shaded expanses of shoreline. Quiet spots on both can be found on the edges. **Nevada Beach,** on the east shore, 3 mi. north of South Lake Tahoe off Hwy. 50, is close to casinos but offers sanctuary from slot machines. Recently renovated **Zephyr Cove Beach,** 5 mi. north of S. Lake Tahoe, hosts a youthful party crowd keen on beer and bikinis. The West Shore offers **Meeks Bay,** 12 mi. south of Tahoe City, a family-oriented beach with picnic tables and volleyball courts. **D.L. Bliss State Park,** 17 mi. south of Tahoe City on Hwy. 89, is home to **Lester** and **Calawee Cove Beaches** on striking Rubicon Bay and is a trailhead for the Rubicon Trail.

HIKING

The 165 mi. **Tahoe Rim Trail** was decades in the making and now encircles the lake, following the ridge tops of the basin, and welcomes hikers, equestrians, and, in most areas, mountain bikers. On the western shore, the route is part of the Pacific Crest Trail. In the north, **Mount Rose,** at 10,778 ft., is one of the tallest mountains in the region as well as one of the best climbs. The panoramic view from the summit includes views of the lake, Reno, and the surrounding Sierra Nevada. Take Hwy. 431 north from Incline Village to the trailhead (6+ mi., strenuous 2200 ft. climb). The rugged trails and mountain streams of **Granite Chief Wilderness,** west of Squaw Valley, wind through forests in 5000 ft. valleys up to the summits of 9000 ft. peaks. The **Alpine Meadows Trailhead,** at the end of Alpine Meadows Rd. off Hwy. 89 between Truckee and Tahoe City, and the **Pacific Crest Trailhead,** at the end of Barker Pass Rd. (Blackwood Canyon Rd.), provide convenient access into the wilderness. The picturesque ⚑**Emerald Bay,** on Hwy. 89 between S. Lake Tahoe and Tahoe City, is breathtaking from the road but is best explored on foot. Waterfalls cascade down the mountains above this partially enclosed bay, which contains Lake Tahoe's only island, Fannette. The **Rubicon Trail,** accessible from **Emerald Bay State Park, D.L. Bliss State Park,** or **Vikingsholm,** winds along the beach and granite cliffs (6 mi.). The various trailheads allow you to customize the length and difficulty of your hike, but stunning vistas are found all along the way.

ROCK CLIMBING

Alpenglow Sports, 415 N. Lake Blvd., in Tahoe City, provides climbing literature and know-how. (☎583-6917. Shoe rental $8 per day. Open M-F 10am-5pm, Sa-Su 9am-6pm.) Pleasant climbs abound in Lake Tahoe, but safety precautions are a must. The inexperienced can try bouldering in **D.L. Bliss State Park.** The South Shore has many popular climbing spots, including the celebrated **Ninety-Foot Wall** at Emerald Bay, Twin Crags at Tahoe City, and Big Chief near Squaw Valley. **Lover's Leap,** in S. Lake Tahoe, is an incredible, albeit crowded, route spanning two giant cliffs.

SKIING

With world-class slopes, 15 ski resorts, knee-deep powder, and California sun, Tahoe is the stuff of skiers' dreams. Conditions range from winter storms to t-shirt weather; snow covers the slopes into early summer. Rates listed are for peak season. ⚑**Squaw Valley,** 5 mi. north of Tahoe City off Hwy. 89, site of the 1960 Winter

Olympics, has 4000 acres of terrain across six Sierra peaks. The 33 ski lifts, including the 110-passenger cable car and high-speed gondola, access runs for all levels. (☎583-5585 or 888-766-9321; www.squaw.com. Open late Nov. to May. Full-day lift ticket $62. Half-day $45, ages 13-15 and 65-75 $31, under 12 $5, ages 76+. Night skiing mid-Dec. to mid-Apr. daily 4-9pm; $20.) The largest and most popular resort is **Heavenly,** on Ski Run Blvd. off S. Lake Tahoe Blvd., with over 4800 acres and 91 runs. Its vertical drop is 3500 ft., Tahoe's biggest. (☎775-586-7000; www.skiheavenly.com. Full-day lift ticket $57, ages 13-18 $47, seniors and ages 6-12 $29.)

A great way to enjoy Tahoe's snow-covered forests is to **cross-country ski** along the thick braid of trails around the lake. **Spooner Lake,** at the junction of Hwy. 50 and 28, offers 57 mi. of machine-groomed trails and incredible views. (☎775-749-5349; www.spoonerlake.com. M, W-F, Su $16.50, Tu $10, Sa $21; ages 13-18 $9.) **Tahoe X-C,** 2 mi. northeast of Tahoe City on Dollar Hill off Hwy. 28, maintains 40 mi. of trails for all abilities. (☎583-5475. Adult all-day $20, after 12:30pm $15, after 3pm $10. $5 discount for ages 10-17 and 60+.) Snowshoeing is often easier to pick up. Follow hiking or cross-country trails, or trudge off into the woods. Equipment rentals are available at local sporting goods stores for about $15 per day.

YOSEMITE NATIONAL PARK ☎209

Yosemite became a national park over 100 years ago, but the geological history of the park began eons before that. About 50 million years ago, the flat floor and granite walls of Yosemite Valley, the park's most spectacular and popular area, were no more than a slow-moving river and rolling hills. Then the Sierra Nevada rose, the Merced River slowly etched deeper into the valley floor, and glaciers carved out the valley's trademark "U" shape. Today, Yosemite is the most famous of the national parks and for good reason; world-class sightseeing, outdoor activities, an unimaginable geologic history, and incredible biodiversity are just a few of its offerings. Yosemite Valley, the bustling, awe-inspiring heart of the park, still lives up to its old name: "The Incomparable Valley."

▐ **TRANSPORTATION. Yosemite VIA** runs buses from the Merced bus station at 16th and N St. (☎888-727-5287. 4 trips per day, $10.) VIA also meets Amtrak trains at the Merced train station. Tickets can be purchased from the driver. (☎800-842-5463. Operates M-F 8am-5pm. Fares include park entry.) **Yosemite Area Regional Transportation System (YARTS)** provides four daily trips to Yosemite from Merced, making convenient stops along the way, and sends one bus a day along Rte. 120 and 395, hitting Mammoth and June Lakes, Lee Vining, and Tuolumne Meadows. (☎388-9589 or 877-989-2787. Buses depart Merced 7, 8:45, 10:30am, 5:25pm. Round-trip $20. Fares include park entry.) **Amtrak** (☎800-872-7245;

CALIFORNIA

AT A GLANCE	
AREA: 1189 sq. mi.	**CAMPING:** Reservations necessary. 7-night max. stay in the valley and Wawona; 14-night max. stay elsewhere. Free wilderness permit is required for backcountry camping in the high country; backcountry camping is not permitted in Yosemite Valley.
CLIMATE: Temperate forest.	
FEATURES: Tuolumne (tuh-WALL-um-ee) Meadows, Mariposa Grove, Hetch Hetchy Reservoir, Yosemite Valley.	
HIGHLIGHTS: Swimming in Tenaya Lake, climbing El Capitán, getting sprayed at Vernal Falls.	**FEES AND RESERVATIONS:** Entrance fee $20 per car; $10 per pedestrian, cyclist, or bus passenger. Valid for 7 days. Annual pass $40.
GATEWAYS: Fresno, Merced, Manteca, and Lee Vining.	

www.amtrak.com) runs **trains** from Los Angeles (6hr, 5 per day, $33-36) and San Francisco (3hr., 4 per day, $33) to Merced and then a bus from Merced to Yosemite (4 per day, $24). Despite traffic and congestion, the best way to see Yosemite is by **car.** Be sure to fill the tank before heading out, as there is no gas in Yosemite Valley except for emergency gas at the Village Garage ($15 for 5 gallons). There are pricey 24hr. gas stations at Crane Flat, Tuolumne Meadows, and Wawona. (☎372-8320. Open daily 8am-noon and 1-5pm. 24hr. towing service. Emergency gasoline available. AAA and National Auto Club accepted.) Rent **bikes** from **Yosemite Lodge** (☎372-1208) or **Curry Village.** (☎372-8319. Bikes $7.50 per hr., $24.50 per day. Driver's license or credit card required as deposit. Both open in summer daily 8:30am-7pm, weather permitting; open on a limited basis after Sept. 6.)

■■ **ORIENTATION AND PRACTICAL INFORMATION.** Yosemite covers 1170 sq. mi. of terrain, 95% of which is designated as wilderness. The park has four main entrances: Hwy. 120 in the west (Big Oak Flat), Hwy. 120 in the east (Tioga Pass), Hwy. 140 in the west (Arch Rock), and Hwy. 41 in the south (Wawona). Hwys. 120 and 140 lead to the center of activity, **Yosemite Valley,** which contains the area's most enduring monuments, including **El Capitán, Half Dome,** and **Yosemite Falls. Yosemite Village,** the Valley's service and info center, is the least natural and most crowded part of the park, with most of the park's dining and accommodations. **Tuolumne Meadows,** a rock-strewn alpine meadow in the northeast, is the heart of Yosemite's high country and the park's backpacking base camp. **Wawona,** in the south, is a historic, upscale development that features museums and a golf course. **Mariposa Grove,** near Wawona, is the park's largest stand of giant sequoia trees. In the northwest corner, **Hetch Hetchy Reservoir,** created by the damming of the Tuolumne River to provide water for San Francisco, is the park's quietest area, yet still offers much of the same natural beauty. Yosemite has a phone number and website for **General Park Information** (☎372-0200; www.yosemite.org). For other park info, visit the **Yosemite Valley Visitors Center** in Yosemite Village. (☎372-0299. Open daily in summer 8am-6pm; winter 9am-5pm. The **Wilderness Center** in Yosemite Village takes wilderness permit reservations up to 24 weeks in advance (☎372-0740; www.nps.gov/yose/wilderness. $5 per person per reservation. Open M-F 8:30am-4:30pm). **Tuolumne Meadows Visitors Center,** near the campground of the same name, is the high-country headquarters. (☎372-0263. Open in summer daily 9am-7pm.) **Yosemite Mountaineering School,** in Tuolumne Meadows and Curry Village, teaches rock climbing classes and rents sleeping bags ($10.50 per day) and backpacks ($8.50; 3rd day half-price), with a driver's license or credit card required as deposit. (☎372-8344. Open daily 8:30am-noon and 1-5pm.) Yosemite operates a 24hr. number for **Weather and Road Conditions.** (☎372-0200.) For medical services, head to the **Yosemite Medical Clinic,** in Yosemite Valley. (☎372-4637. 24hr. emergency room. Open M-Sa 8am-5pm.) **Post Office: Yosemite Village,** next to the visitors center. Open M-F 8:30am-5pm, Sa 10am-noon. **Postal Code:** 95389. **Area Code:** 209.

⌂ ACCOMMODATIONS. When American Transcendentalist Ralph Waldo Emerson visited Yosemite in 1884, the park's accommodations were so simple that he was awakened in the morning by the clucking of a hen climbing over his bed. These days, Yosemite's lodgings have become much more comfortable. Reservations are necessary and can be made up to one year in advance (☎559-252-4848; www.yosemitepark.com). All park lodgings provide access to dining, laundry, showers, and supplies. **Curry Village ❹,** 2 mi. southeast of Yosemite Village, has a wide range of dining options, a comfortable lounge, a pool, an outdoor amphitheater, a store, and an ice rink from November to February. It is the most convenient lodging in the park, but the area is always crowded. (☎252-4848. Canvas tent cabins $69; cabins $85, with bath $108; standard motel rooms $112. AmEx/D/MC/V.)

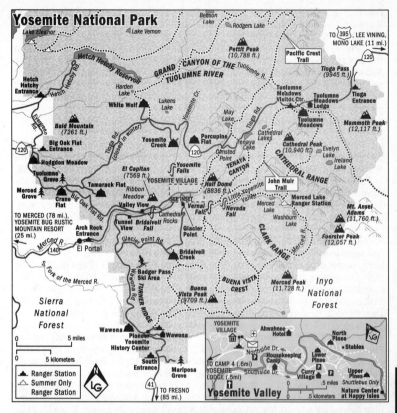

Yosemite National Park

The army barracks-style **Housekeeping Camp ❸** is a less developed and more adventurous option. "Camping shelters" for up to four include two bunk beds, a double bed, a picnic table, and a fire pit. (☎372-8338. Camping equipment rental. Shelters for 1-4 people $75. AmEx/D/MC/V.) **Tuolumne Meadows Lodge ❸**, on Tioga Pass Rd., in the park's northeastern corner, has rustic accommodations. (☎372-8413. Canvas-sided cabins, wood stoves, no electricity $75; additional adult $9, child $4. AmEx/D/MC/V.) Outside the park, the ❊**Yosemite Bug Rustic Mountain Resort (HI) ❷**, on Rte. 140 in Midpines, 25 mi. west of the park, is a woodsy, spirited hostel where backpackers lounge in the cafe and on the porches. (☎966-6666; www.yosemitebug.com. Swimming hole. Free wireless Internet. Dorms $18, members $15; tent cabins $30-50; private rooms $40-70, with bath $55-115. D/MC/V.)

🏕 **CAMPING.** One of the first views of Yosemite a visitor gets during the summer may be of the endless "tent cities" in the valley. Make reservations as far in advance as possible, especially in summer. (☎800-436-7275; http://reservations.nps.gov. Reserve by phone or online daily 7am-7pm.) All Valley campgrounds fill completely every summer night. No matter how pretty it looks, all natural stream water must be boiled, filtered, or treated. **Backcountry camping** is prohibited in the Valley but encouraged outside it. Information and permits can be obtained at the Wilderness Centers at Yosemite Village, Wawona, or Big Oak Flat.

Catering to seasoned climbers, **Camp 4 ❶**, 4000 ft., at the western end of the valley, past Yosemite Lodge, has 35 walk-in sites that fill up before 9am. Meet new friends; every site is filled with six random people. (Water, flush toilets, and tables. First come, first served. Limited parking. Sites $5 per person.) Escape the RVs in the 25 sites saved for walk-in hikers at **Tuolumne Meadows ❶**, 8600 ft., on Rte. 120, 55 mi. east of the Valley. (152 sites require advance reservations, 152 saved for same-day reservations. Open July-Sept., depending on snow. Drive-in sites $18; backpacker sites $3 per person.) Very crowded but convenient, the **Pines Campgrounds ❶** (Upper, Lower, and North) are all located in the Valley and provide 379 sites among the pines for tents or RVs. (Reservations required. All sites $18.)

🍴 **FOOD.** Even with its inflated prices, the wide selection at the **Village Store** is your best bet for groceries. (Open daily June-Sept. 8am-10pm; Oct.-May 8am-9pm.) With views of Yosemite Falls from nearly every seat, **Mountain Room Restaurant ❺**, in Yosemite Lodge, is ideal for a post-hike dinner. (☎372-1274. Hearty fare $17-29. Casual dress. Open daily 5:30-10pm. AmEx/D/MC/V.) **Degnan's Delicatessen ❷**, in Yosemite Village, draws a crowd for its great sandwiches and inexpensive convenience store. (☎372-8454. Sandwiches $6. Open daily 7am-5pm. AmEx/D/MC/V.)

🏞 **OUTDOOR ACTIVITIES.** Although the view is better outside of the car, you can see a lot of Yosemite from the bucket seat, and if you only have one day in the park, **scenic drives** are the way to see the sights. **Highway 120 (Tioga Road)** is the highest highway strip in America. The road is only open during the summer, and travelers are treated to spectacular panoramas and beautiful glades from Crane Flat in the west to Tuolumne Meadows in the east. Tioga Rd. then crests Tioga Pass (9945 ft.) before descending to the lunar landscape of Mono Lake outside the park's eastern boundary. No less incredible are the views afforded by the southern approach to Yosemite, **Route 41.** Most recognizable is the **Wawona Tunnel Turn-out** (also known as Inspiration Point), which gives outstanding panoramic views that many visitors will recognize from Ansel Adams photographs. From here, Yosemite Valley unfurls its humbling beauty. **El Capitán,** the largest granite monolith in the world (3593 ft. base to summit), looms over awestruck crowds. Opposite El Capitán, **Bridalveil Falls** drops 620 ft. (the equivalent of a 62-story building). A drive into the valley's heart leads to the staggering Upper and Lower **Yosemite Falls** (combined, the highest waterfall in North America at 2425 ft.). Incredible views of the falls are available at many parking lots and turn-outs, but completely avoiding the traffic jams and shoulder-to-shoulder tourists photographing the sight may be difficult. In the valley's eastern end stands **Half Dome** (8842 ft.), a distinctive, rounded rock formation that can be seen from virtually everywhere in the valley.

Glacier Point Road, off Hwy. 41 in the southern part of the park, meanders past lush meadows and rounded domes. At its end, **Glacier Point** gives a bird's-eye view of the Valley floor, considered one of the most spectacular views on earth. If you can maneuver around the other awestruck tourists, you'll be treated to a view of Half Dome presiding over the Valley's east side and riotous Nevada Falls seemingly reduced to a tranquil silver ribbon. Arrive at sunset and watch the fiery colors fade over the valley as the stars and moon appear. When the moon is full, this is an extraordinary (and even more popular) place to visit.

With two or more days in Yosemite, it's worthwhile to explore some of its trails. World-class hiking abounds for anyone willing to lace up a pair of boots, though sneakers will suffice for a few trails. Daytrip trails are well populated—at nearly any point in the day, you may find yourself stuck behind groups of other tourists. Set your alarm clock, because hiking just after sunrise is the best and sometimes the only way to beat the crowds, but even then, trails like Half Dome are busy. The visitors center has leaflets listing day-hikes for all hiking levels and maps of all regions of the park. The exceptional **Mist Trail** (6 mi.) starts at Happy Isles trail-head (shuttle bus stop #16) at the valley's eastern end. The trail runs parallel to the Merced River to the base of Vernal Falls. From there, steep and slippery steps carved out of the granite put you next to the falls, which sprinkles, sprays, or drenches hikers with its mist, depending on the time of year. The trail ends at the top of the falls, but those with buns of steel can continue to the top of Nevada Falls and then circle back down to the trailhead along the John Muir Trail. The strenu-ous hike to the top of **Half Dome** is another popular option. This hike, also starting at the Happy Isles trailhead, yields the thrill of conquering Yosemite's most recog-nizable monument. The 16 mi. hike is only recommended for those in good condi-tion and comfortable with heights. Half Dome attracts lightning and mid-summer thunderstorms; early-morning departures are best.

The **Mirror Lake Loop** is a flat 3 mi. walk past Mirror Lake (½ mi.), up Tenaya Creek, and back. The **Lower Yosemite Falls Trail** is a favorite, starting across from Yosemite Lodge. On moonlit nights, mysterious moonbows (nighttime rainbows) can often be spotted above the water. **Upper Yosemite Falls Trail,** a backbreaking 3½ mi. trek to the summit, climbs 2700 ft. but rewards the intrepid hiker with an over-view of the vertiginous 2425 ft. drop. Those with energy to spare can trudge on to **Yosemite Point** or **Eagle Peak,** where views of the Valley below rival those from Gla-cier Point. The trail begins with an extremely steep, unshaded ascent. Leaving the marked trail is not wise—a sign warns, "If you go over the waterfall, you will die." The steep **Four Mile Trail** (actually 4½ mi. long) is a switchbacked climb from the Valley to Glacier Point. The strenuous hike through white fir and sugar pine for-ests has sporadic Valley views, giving a sense of the Valley's soaring heights.

WINTER

In Yosemite's quietest season, the landscape undergoes a facelift as the waterfalls freeze and the meadows frost over. Unlike much of the park, Yosemite Valley remains accessible year-round. **Route 140** from Merced, an all-weather entrance, is usually open and clear. Although Tioga Pass and Glacier Point Rd. close at the first sign of snow, **Route 41** and **Route 120** typically remain traversable. Verify road con-ditions before traveling (☎372-0200) and carry tire chains.

Well-marked trails for **cross-country skiing** and **snowshoeing** cut into the back-country of the Valley's South Rim at Badger Pass and Crane Flat. Rangers host snowshoe walks from mid-December to March, but the serene forests are perhaps best explored without guidance. Guided cross-country skiing trips to Glacier Point (☎327-8444) with meals and hut lodgings are available. The state's oldest ski resort, **Badger Pass Ski Area,** on Glacier Point Rd. south of Yosemite Valley, is the park's only downhill ski area, and has a family atmosphere. **Ice skating** at Curry Village is beautiful, with Half Dome towering above a groomed outdoor rink encircled by snow-covered pines. (☎372-8341. Open in winter daily 3:30-6pm and 7-9:30pm; also 8:30-11am and noon-2:30pm on weekends. $6.50, children $5. Skate rental $3.25.)

MAMMOTH LAKES   ☎760

Home to one of the most popular ski resorts in the U.S., the town of Mammoth Lakes (pop. 5305) is a giant year-round playground. The snowfall averages over 350 in. per year, creating 3500 acres of skiable terrain. When the snow melts, mountain bikers invade to take on Mammoth Mountain, skateboarders come to test their skills in competitions, and fisherfolk come to the magma-warmed creeks. A **free shuttle bus (MAS)** transports skiers between lifts and the ski lodge.

Devil's Postpile National Monument is a stunning 60 ft. wall made of eerily uniform hexagonal rock columns. Pristine wilderness surrounds the Postpile, with brilliant **Rainbow Falls** accessible via a moderate 2½ mi. one-way hike. (Open in summer daily 7am-7:30pm.) The **Inyo Craters** are curious open pits 600 ft. across with blue-

CALIFORNIA

green water at the bottom formed by volcanic activity within the last 2000 years. The ¼ mi. path to the craters can be reached from Mammoth Scenic Loop Rd. The climbing wall at **Mammoth Mountain Adventure Center,** at Mammoth Mountain base camp, is a fun diversion for novices and experienced climbers. (☎924-5683. Open daily 10am-5pm. $7 per climb, $19 per hr.) The **Mammoth Mountain Gondola** affords mile-high views. (☎934-2571. Open daily 9am-4:30pm. Round-trip $16, children $8; day pass $25.) Exit the gondola at the top to tackle more than 80 mi. of twisted trails in **Mammoth Mountain Bike Park;** the ride starts at 11,053 ft. and heads straight down on rocky ski trails. (☎934-0706. Open 9am-4:30pm. Day pass $32, children $16. Unlimited day pass and bike rental $65/$33. Helmets required.) The high altitude and piles of snow often allow **Mammoth Mountain,** a favorite for southern California's Tahoe-less skiers, to stay open into June. (☎800-626-6684 or 934-0745. Open in winter daily 8:30am-4pm. $63, ages 13-18 $47).

As in most ski resort towns, lodging is much more expensive in winter. Condo rentals are good for groups of three or more and start at $100 per night. **Mammoth Reservation Bureau** (☎800-462-5571; www.mammothvacations.com) can make arrangements. For lone travelers, dorm-style motels are cheapest. Reservations are highly recommended. **Davison St. Guest House ❶,** 19 Davison Rd., at Lake Mary Rd., is the best value in town, offering guests small yet comfortable rooms and an inviting common room with views of the surrounding mountains. (☎924-2188. Dorms $25; private rooms $55, with bath $75. AmEx/D/MC/V.) There are nearly 20 Inyo Forest public **campgrounds ❶** (sites $14-16) in the area. All sites have piped water and most are near fishing and hiking. Contact the **Mammoth Ranger District** (☎924-5500) for info or drop by the visitors center, just east of town (open daily 8am-5pm). **Paul Schat's Bakery and Cafe ❶,** 3305 Main St., has the best sandwiches in town. (☎934-6055. Open M-Th and Su 5:30am-6pm, F-Sa 5:30am-8pm. Deli 9am-3pm daily. MC/V.) **Angel's ❶,** 3516 Main St., serves homestyle cooking, excellent barbecue, and a variety of beers that will hit the spot after a long day on the mountain. (☎934-7427. Open daily 11:30am-9pm. AmEx/D/MC/V.)

THE NORTH COAST

Windswept and larger than life, the North Coast winds from the San Francisco Bay Area to the Oregon border. Redwoods tower over black-sand beaches deserted save for the sea lions, otters frolic next to jutting rock formations, and U.S. 101 snakes along cliffs between pounding surf and humbling redwoods. The North Coast's untouched wilderness is simply stunning.

MENDOCINO   ☎707

Teetering on bluffs over the ocean, isolated Mendocino (pop. 1107) is a coastal community of art galleries, craft shops, bakeries, and B&Bs. Just west of the village, the earth falls into the Pacific at the impressive ▨**Mendocino Headlands.** A meadow of tall grass and wildflowers separates the town from the rocky shore. Poor drainage and thin, acidic soil have created stunted vegetation at the **Pygmy Forest** in Van Damme State Park. To get to the forest, drive 3 mi. south of town, past the main park entrance, then turn left on Little River Airport Rd. and drive 3 mi.

Jughandle Creek Farm ❶, about 3 mi. north of Mendocino off Hwy. 1, across the street from the Jug Handle State Reserve, is a beautiful 39-acre complex of gardens, forest, campsites, small rustic cabins, and a century-old Victorian home with private and dorm rooms. Trails on the property lead to the coast. (☎964-4630. Reservations recommended in summer. Rooms $27, students $21. Cabins $35 per person. Sites $11. $5 off for 1hr. of chores.) Inside the main entrance of Van

Damme State Park, three **campgrounds ❶**—one traditional, one hike and bike, and one environmental—provide a wide range of options. (☎937-5397. Traditional has running water and toilets; others are primitive. Sites $15-20.) The four campgrounds at **MacKerricher State Park ❶,** 2½ mi. north of Fort Bragg, total 184 campsites scattered between 9 mi. of beaches and the shores of Lake Cleon. The sites have excellent views of tide pool life, passing seals, sea lions, and migratory whales. (☎937-5804. Showers, flush toilets, bathrooms, and drinkable water. Sites $20.) For picnic supplies head to **Mendosa's Market,** 10501 Lansing St., which stocks all the basics, plus some organic produce and breads. (☎937-5879. Open daily 8am-9pm.) Mendocino restaurants are often pricey, but the food is excellent. The **Bay View Cafe ❸,** 45040 Main St., lives up to its name with big picture windows overlooking the headlands, making it a great place to enjoy the decadent hot crab sandwich ($14) or peppery clam chowder. (☎937-4197. Open daily 11am-8pm.)

Tiny Mendocino sits on **Highway 1,** right on the Pacific coast, 30 mi. west of U.S. 101 and 12 mi. south of Fort Bragg. Like all northern coast areas, Mendocino can be very chilly, even in summer. Travelers should prepare for 40-70°F temperatures. The nearest **Greyhound** station (☎800-231-2222; www.greyhound.com) is two hours away in Ukiah. **Mendocino Transit Authority,** 241 Plant Rd. (☎800-696-4682), in Ukiah, makes one round-trip daily between Mendocino and Santa Rosa ($16), stopping at Willits ($2.75) and Ukiah ($4.25) on the way. The bus leaves from the Cookie Company, at Lansing and Ukiah St. **Visitor Info: Fort Bragg-Mendocino Coast Chamber of Commerce,** 332 N. Main St., in Fort Bragg. (☎961-6300 or 800-726-2780. Open M-F 9am-noon and 12:30-5pm, Sa 9am-3pm.) **Park Info:** ☎937-5804, or the **Ford House Mendocino Headlands Visitors Center** on Main St. in Mendocino. (☎937-5804. Open M-F 11am-4pm.) **Internet Access: Fort Bragg Library,** 499 Laurel St., in Fort Bragg. (☎964-2020. Open Tu and Th 10am-6pm, W noon-8pm, F-Sa 10am-5pm. Free.) **Medical Services: Mendocino Coast District Hospital,** 700 River Dr. (☎961-1234), in Fort Bragg. **Post Office:** 10500 Ford St., in Mendocino. (☎937-5282. Open M-F 7:30am-4:30pm.) **Postal Code:** 95460. **Area Code:** 707.

AVENUE OF THE GIANTS   ☎707

About 10 mi. north of Garberville on U.S. 101 in Humboldt Redwoods State Park, the Avenue of the Giants splits off the highway and winds its way through 32 mi. of redwoods, the world's largest living organisms above ground level. The roads can be narrow enough for you to worry about the fate of your side mirrors, but that's part of the fun. The staff at **Humboldt Redwoods State Park Visitors Center** can highlight the area's groves, facilities, trails, and bike routes. (☎946-2263. Open daily Apr.-Oct. 9am-5pm; Nov.-Mar. 10am-4pm.) Sleep under the massive trees at the park's many **campsites ❶,** which have coin showers, flush toilets, and fire rings. (☎946-2409. Sites $20.) For some up-close giant viewing, try the half-mile loop at **Founder's Grove,** featuring the 1300- to 1500-year-old **Founder's Tree** and the former tallest tree in Humboldt Redwoods State Park, the fallen 362 ft. **Dyerville Giant,** whose massive, three-story root-ball looks like a mythic entanglement of evil. Uncrowded trails wind through **Rockefeller Forest** in the park's northern section, which contains the largest grove of continuous old-growth redwoods in the world.

REDWOOD NAT'L AND STATE PARKS   ☎707

The redwoods are the last remaining stretch of the old-growth forest that used to blanket two million acres of northern California and Oregon. Within the parks, the world's tallest trees continue to grow in quiet splendor while black bears and mountain lions roam the backwoods and elk graze the meadows.

CALIFORNIA

🛈 PRACTICAL INFORMATION

Redwood National and State Parks is an umbrella term for four contiguous parks. From south to north, they are: **Redwood National Park, Prairie Creek Redwoods State Park, Del Norte Coast Redwoods State Park,** and **Jedediah Smith Redwoods State Park.**

Fees: Fees vary by park and are different for camping, parking, and hiking. There is usually no entrance fee. Day-use fees ($4 per car) for parking and picnic areas are typical.

Auto Repairs: AAA Emergency Road Service (☎800-222-4357; www.aaa.com). 24hr.

Visitor Info: Redwood National Park Headquarters and Information Center, 1111 2nd St. (☎464-6101, ext. 5826), in Crescent City. Headquarters of the entire park, but 3 other visitors centers are also well informed. Open daily 9am-5pm.

Medical Services: Sutter Coast Hospital, 800 E. Washington Blvd. (☎464-8511; www.suttercoast.org), in Crescent City.

Internet Access: Del Norte County Library, 190 Price Mall (☎464-9793), at 2nd St. and I St., in Crescent City. $1 per 30min. Open M and W-Th 10am-6pm, Tu noon-8pm.

Post Office: 751 2nd St. (☎464-2151), at H St., in Crescent City. Open M-F 8:30am-5pm, Sa noon-2pm. **Postal Code:** 95531. **Area Code:** 707.

🛏 ACCOMMODATIONS

🏚 **Redwood Hostel (HI),** 14480 U.S. 101 (☎482-8265 or 800-295-1905; www.redwood-hostel.com), at Wilson Creek Rd., 7 mi. north of Klamath. A prime beach location and great sunset views. Free Internet. Check-in 5-10pm. Check-out 10am. Reservations recommended in summer. Dorms $16-20; under age 17 half-price; doubles $49. MC/V. ❶

Historic Requa Inn, 451 Requa Rd. (☎482-1425 or 866-800-8777; www.requainn.com), west off U.S. 101. This B&B has thoughtfully decorated suites. Elegant dinner M-Sa (entrees $12-22). Reservations recommended June-Sept. Rooms May-Sept. $85-135, Oct.-Apr. $79-120. AmEx/D/MC/V. ❹

Jedediah Smith Redwoods State Park, (☎464-6101, ext. 5112), 9 mi. east of Crescent City off U.S. 199. 106 RV and tent sites in old-growth redwood forest. Picnic tables, water, restrooms, and showers. Campfire programs and nature walks offered during the summer. Sites $20; day-use $5. ❶

Mill Creek Campground, (☎800-444-7275), 6 mi. south of Crescent City off U.S. 101, in Del Norte Coast Redwoods SP. 145 RV and tent sites in second-growth redwood forest. Restrooms, showers, bearproof lockers. Open June-Aug. Sites $20; day-use $5. ❶

🍴 FOOD

There are more picnic tables than restaurants in the area, so the best option for food is probably the supermarket. In Crescent City, head to the 24hr. **Safeway,** 475 M St. (☎465-3353), on U.S. 101 between 2nd and 5th St. The **Klamath Market,** 166 Klamath Blvd., has an ATM. (☎482-0211. Open M-Sa 8am-9pm, Su 9am-5pm.) The mom-and-pop **Palm Cafe ❷,** on U.S. 101, is one of the few places to eat in Orick; the homemade pies are wonderful. (☎488-3381. Pie slices $3. Open daily 5am-8pm. MC/V.) **Glen's Bakery and Restaurant ❶,** at 3rd and G St., in Crescent City, opened in 1947 and has always been a family affair. Dedicated regulars love the plate-sized pancakes. (☎464-2914. Breakfast served all day. Sandwiches $5.50-8. Pancakes $4. Open Tu-F 5am-6:30pm, Sa 5am-2pm. MC/V.)

♨ OUTDOOR ACTIVITIES

All plants and animals in the park are protected—even feathers dropped by birds of prey are off-limits. California **fishing licenses** (1 day $10) are required for fresh and saltwater fishing off any natural formation, but fishing is free from any man-made structure. There are minimum-weight and maximum-catch requirements specific to both fresh and saltwater fishing. Contact the **Fish and Game Department** (☎ 445-6493; www.dfg.ca.gov) for more information.

The **Orick Area** covers the southernmost section of Redwood National and State Parks. The **Kuchel Visitors Center** lies on U.S. 101, 1 mi. south of Orick (☎ 464-6101, ext. 5265). A popular sight is the **Tall Trees Grove,** a 3 mi. trail down to a grove of some of the world's tallest trees. The grove is accessible by car to those with permits (free from the visitors center in Crescent City) when the road is open. Allow at least 3-4hr. for the trip. The 70 mi. of criss-crossing trails in the **Prairie Creek Area** can be confusing. Be sure to pick up a trail map ($1) at the **Prairie Creek Visitor Center,** off U.S. 101 in Prairie Creek Redwoods State Park (☎ 464-6101, ext. 5300; open daily Memorial Day-Labor Day 9am-5pm). The **James Irvine Trail** (4½ mi.) snakes through a prehistoric garden of towering old-growth redwoods. The less ambitious can cruise part of the **Foothill Trail** (¾ mi.) to a 1500-year-old behemoth, the 306 ft. **Big Tree.** The northern **Klamath Area** connects Prairie Creek with Del Norte State Park; the main attraction is the spectacular coastline. The **Klamath Overlook,** where Requa Rd. meets the steep **Coastal Trail** (42 mi.), is an excellent whale-watching site. Crescent City is the nearest substantial city and an outstanding base for exploring the parks. The **Battery Point Lighthouse** is on a causeway jutting out from Front St. and houses a museum open only during low tide. (☎ 464-3089. Open Apr.-Sept. W-Su 10am-4pm, tide permitting; Nov.-Mar. F-Sa at low tide. $3, children $1.) From June to August, **tidepool walks** leave from Enderts Beach. (At the turnoff 4 mi. south of Crescent City; call ☎ 464-6101, ext. 5064, for schedules.)

CALIFORNIA

PACIFIC NORTHWEST

The Pacific Northwest became the center of national attention when gold rushes and the Oregon Trail ushered hordes of settlers into the region. In the 1840s, Senator Stephen Douglas argued that the Cascade Range would make a good natural border between Oregon and Washington, but the Columbia River, perpendicular to the Cascades, became the border instead. Yet even today, the range and not the river is the region's most important cultural divide: in the wet, lush land west of the Cascades lie the two microchip, mocha, and music meccas of Portland and Seattle; to the east sprawls farmland and an arid plateau. For more info on the region, see ▨*Let's Go: Pacific Northwest Adventure Guide*.

HIGHLIGHTS OF THE PACIFIC NORTHWEST

SIP java while strolling through the offbeat neighborhoods, spectacular museums, and quirky cafes of **Seattle** (p. 957).

EXPLORE the remains of a volcano at **Crater Lake National Park** (p. 955) or the icy peaks of the dormant **Mt. Rainier** (p. 978).

MEDITATE upon the mossy grandeur of **Olympic National Park** (p. 973).

SKIM through hundreds of dusty volumes at **Powell's City of Books** (p. 949).

REVEL in the low prices and natural beauty of **Vancouver, British Columbia** (p. 982).

OREGON

Lured by plentiful forests and promises of gold and riches, entire families liquidated their possessions, sank their life savings into covered wagons, corn meal, and oxen, and high-tailed it to Oregon (OR-uh-gun) in search of prosperity and a new way of life. The resulting population of outdoors-enthusiasts and fledgling townspeople joined the Union in 1859, and has since become an eclectic mix of treehuggers and suave big-city types. Today, Oregon remains as popular destination as ever for backpackers, cyclists, anglers, beach crawlers, and families alike. With everything from excellent microbrews to untouched wilderness, Oregon is still a great reason to cross the Continental Divide.

▨ PRACTICAL INFORMATION

Capital: Salem.

Visitor Info: Oregon Tourism Commission, 775 Summer St. NE, Salem 97310 (☎800-547-7842; www.traveloregon.com). **Oregon State Parks and Recreation Dept.,** 725 Summer St. NE, Ste. C, Salem 97301 (☎800-551-6949; www.prd.state.or.us).

Postal Abbreviation: OR. **Sales Tax:** None.

PORTLAND ☎503

An award-winning transit system and pedestrian-friendly streets make Portland feel more like a pleasantly overgrown town than a crowded metropolis. With over 250 parks, the pristine Willamette River, and snow-capped Mt. Hood in the hori-

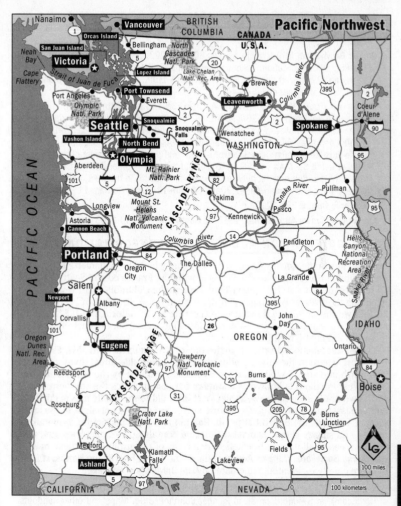

Pacific Northwest

zon, the City of Roses basks in the natural beauty surrounding it. In the rainy season, Portlanders flood pubs and clubs to sip java while musicians strum and sing. In the summer, music from outdoor performances fills the air from Pioneer Courthouse Square to the lawn of the Oregon Zoo in Washington Park. And throughout it all, the best beer pours from the taps in the microbrewery capital of the US.

TRANSPORTATION

Airport: Portland International Airport (PDX) (☎ 460-4234; www.flypdx.com) is well-served by almost every major airline. The airport is connected to the city center of Portland by **MAX Red Line,** an efficient light rail system (38min.; runs every 15min. 5am-11:30pm; $1.70).

Trains: Amtrak, 800 NW 6th Ave., (☎800-872-7245; www.amtrak.com), in Union Station, at Hoyt St. Open daily 7:45am-9pm. To **Eugene** (2½hr., 5 per day, $19-32) and **Seattle** (4hr., 4 per day, $25-40).

Buses: Greyhound, 550 NW 6th Ave. (☎800-231-2222; www.greyhound.com), at NW Glisan St. by Union Station. Ticket counter open daily 6-11:15am and 12:05-12:45pm. To **Eugene** (2½-4hr., 9 per day, $17), **Seattle** (3-4½hr., 8 per day, $22-24), and **Spokane** (7½-11hr., 4 per day, $41-44).

Public Transit: Tri-Met, 701 SW 6th Ave. (☎238-7433; www.trimet.org), in Pioneer Courthouse Sq. Open M-F 8:30am-5:30pm. Buses generally run as early as 5am and as late as 1:30am on weekdays, 12:30am on weekends. $1.40-1.70; ages 7-18 $1.10; disabled and ages 65+ $0.65; day pass $3.50. All of the city's public transit is free in the **No-Fare Zone ("Fareless Square"):** north and east of I-405, west of the river and south of Irving St. **MAX** (☎228-7246), based at the Customer Service Center, is Tri-Met's light rail train running between downtown, Hillsboro in the west, and Gresham in the east. Runs M-F around 4am-1:30am, Sa 5am-12:30am, Su 5am-11:30pm.

Taxi: Radio Cab, ☎227-1212.

Car Rental: Crown Auto Rental, 1315 NE Sandy Blvd. (☎230-1103).

✦ ⁊ ORIENTATION AND PRACTICAL INFORMATION

Portland lies in the northwest corner of Oregon, where the Willamette River joins the Columbia River. **I-5** connects Portland with San Francisco and Seattle, while **I-84** follows the path of the Oregon Trail through the Columbia River Gorge, heading along the Oregon-Washington border toward Boise, ID. West of Portland, **U.S. 30** follows the Columbia downstream (northwest) to Astoria, but **U.S. 26** is the most direct path to the coast. **I-405** runs in a loop west from I-5, encircling downtown and linking I-5 with U.S. 26 and 30.

Every street name in Portland carries one of five prefixes: **N, NE, NW, SE,** or **SW,** indicating where in the city the address is found. **Burnside Street** divides the city into north and south, while east and west are separated by the **Willamette River.** Southwest Portland is known as **downtown** but also includes the southern end of Old Town and a slice of the wealthier **West Hills. Old Town,** mostly in NW Portland, encompasses most of the city's historic sector. Be cautious at night in the areas around W. Burnside St. To the north, **Nob Hill** and **Pearl District** hold revitalized homes and snazzy shops. **Southeast** Portland contains parks, factories, and residential areas of all income brackets; a rich array of restaurants and theaters lines **Hawthorne Boulevard. Williams Avenue** frames "the North." **North** and **Northeast** Portland are chiefly residential, punctuated by the **University of Portland.**

Visitor Info: Visitors Association (POVA), 701 SW 6th Ave. (☎275-9750; www.travelportland.com), at SW Morrison St. in Pioneer Courthouse Sq. Maps and other handouts. Open M-F 8:30am-5:30pm, Sa 10am-4pm.

Internet Access: Found at the elegant **Central Library,** 801 SW 10th Ave. (☎988-5123; www.multcolib.org), between Yamhill and Taylor. 1hr. free with a guest pass from customer service. Open M and Th-Sa 10am-8pm, Tu-W 10am-6pm, Su noon-5pm.

Post Office: 715 NW Hoyt St. (☎800-275-8777). Open M-F 7am-6:30pm, Sa 8:30am-5pm. **Postal Code:** 97208. **Area Code:** 503.

⌂ ACCOMMODATIONS

Although chain hotels dominate downtown and smaller motels steadily raise prices, Portland still welcomes the budget traveler. Prices drop as you leave the city center, and inexpensive motels can be found on SE Powell Blvd. and the southern end of SW 4th Ave. Accommodations in Portland fill up during the summer months, especially during the Rose Festival, so make your reservations early.

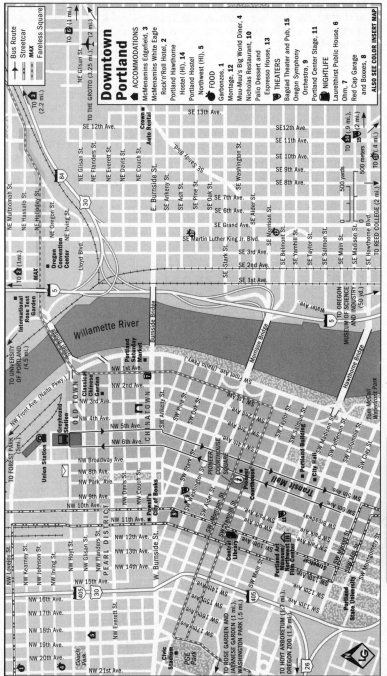

Downtown Portland

♦ ACCOMMODATIONS
McMenamins Edgefield, **3**
McMenamins White Eagle
Rock'n'Roll Hotel, **2**
Portland Hawthorne
Hostel (HI), **14**
Portland Hostel
Northwest (HI), **5**

⬥ FOOD
Garbonzos, **1**
Montage, **12**
Muu-Muu's Big World Diner, **4**
Nicholas Restaurant, **10**
Palio Dessert and
Espresso House, **13**

▼ THEATERS
Bagdad Theater and Pub, **15**
Oregon Symphony
Orchestra, **9**
Portland Center Stage, **11**

▬ NIGHTLIFE
Laurelthirst Public House, **6**
Ohm, **7**
Red Cap Garage
and Boxes, **8**

ALSO SEE COLOR INSERT MAP

**PACIFIC
NORTHWEST**

🏚 **H.I. Portland Hawthorne Hostel,** 3031 SE Hawthorne Blvd. (☎236-3380). Take bus #14 to SE 30th Ave. A laid-back hostel with a lively common space and a huge porch. $1 pancakes. Linen included. Internet access $1 per 16min. Reception 8am-10pm. Check-out 11am. Dorms June-Sept. $22, members $19; Oct.-May $19/$16. Private rooms June-Sept. $47/$44; Nov.-Feb. $38/$35; Mar.-May $41/$38. AmEx/D/MC/V. ●

H.I. Portland Hostel Northwest, 1818 NW Glisan St. (☎241-2783), at 18th Ave., between Nob Hill and the Pearl District. This snug Victorian building has a kitchen, Internet access ($1 for 16min.), lockers, laundry, and an espresso bar. Linen $1. Reception 8am-11pm. Reservations recommended. Dorms June-Sept. $22, members $19; Oct.-May $19/$16. Private doubles June-Sept. from $49; Oct.-May from $36. V/DC/MC. ●

McMenamins Edgefield, 2126 SW Halsey St. (☎669-8610; www.mcmenamins.com), in Troutdale. Take MAX east to the Gateway Station, then Tri-Met bus #24 east to the main entrance. This 38-acre former farm is a posh escape that keeps 2 single-sex hostel rooms with 12 beds each. On-site brewery, vineyards, and 18-hole golf course. Lockers included. Reception 24hr. No reservations for the hostel. Dorms $30; European-style rooms $50-90; with private bath $95-115. AmEx/D/DC/MC/V. ❷/❹

McMenamins White Eagle Rock'n'Roll Hotel, 836 N. Russell St. (☎282-6810; www.mcmenamins.com), near the northern I-5/I-405 interchange, in North Portland. 11 simple but welcoming rooms. Cafe and saloon on the first level. Bunk room $30; full $40; queen $50. AmEx/D/DC/MC/V. ●

🍴 FOOD

Downtown can be expensive, but the quirky restaurants and cafes in the NW and SE quadrants have reasonable prices. The lunch trucks dispersed throughout the city generally have tasty authentic food for cheap.

🍴 **Montage,** 301 SE Morrison St. (☎234-1324). Take bus #15 to the east end of the Morrison Bridge and walk under it. Straight-laced, mainstream Portlanders enter a surreal land of Cajun dining while seated Last-Supper-style underneath a macaroni-framed mural. Oyster shooters $1.75. Gator jambalaya $14.75. Open M-Th and Su 11:30am-2pm and 6pm-2am, F-Sa 11:30am-2pm and 6pm-4am. MC/V. ❷

🍴 **Nicholas Restaurant,** 318 SE Grand Ave. (☎235-5123), between Oak and Pine. Phenomenal Lebanese and Middle Eastern food in a relaxed atmosphere. The *mezzas* ($8) are fantastic. Sandwiches $5-6. Open M-Sa 11am-9pm, Su noon-9pm. Cash only. ❷

Muu-Muu's Big World Diner, 612 NW 21st Ave. (☎223-8169), at Hoyt St. Bus #17. Gourmet dishes served with artful goofiness amidst red velvet curtains and gold upholstery. Brutus salad, "the one that kills a Caesar," $6.50. 'Shroom-wich $8. Open M-F 11:30am-1am, Sa-Su 10am-1am. AmEx/D/DC/MC/V. ❷

Garbonzos, 922 NW 21st Ave. (☎227-4196), at Hoyt St. Bus #17. A quiet eatery with delicious Mediterranean food. The falafel plate, 6 balls and 6 sides ($7), gives a scrumptious sample of the menu's variety. Open daily 11am-11pm. AmEx/D/MC/V. ❷

Palio Dessert and Espresso House, 1996 SE Ladd St. (☎232-9214). Bus #10. A tranquil cafe with Mexican mochas ($3), *cafe miel* ($3), and sandwiches ($5.75). Free wireless Internet access. Open M-F 7am-11pm, Sa-Su 8am-11pm. MC/V. ●

👁 SIGHTS

PARKS AND GARDENS. Less than 2 miles west of downtown, in the middle of the posh neighborhoods of **West Hills,** mammoth **Washington Park** has miles of beautiful trails and serene gardens. If possible, schedule in a day to enjoy the park to its fullest. The pride of the City of Roses, the 🌹**International Rose Test Garden** is the most spectacular of Washington Park's attractions, boasting over 500 varieties of roses. The 4½ acres of crimson, pink, and yellow blooms are more than just a beautiful garden for people to gawk at; they're a testing ground for new breeds of roses. *(400 SW Kingston St. ☎823-3636. Open daily 7:30am-9pm. Free.)* Just across from the Rose Garden, the fabulous **Japanese Garden** completes the one-two punch of the park. *(611 SW Kingston Ave. ☎223-1321; www.japanesegarden.com. Open Apr.-Sept. M noon-7pm, Tu-Su 10am-7pm; Oct.-Mar. M noon-4pm, Tu-Su 10am-4pm. Tours daily mid-Apr. to Oct. 10:45am, 1, 2:30pm. $6.75, seniors and college students with ID $5, students $4, under 6 free.)* Forming the wooded backdrop for the rest of Washington Park's sights, the **Hoyt Arboretum** features 183 acres of trees and 12 mi. of trails. *(44000 SW Fairview Blvd. ☎823-8733. Visitors center open M-F 9am-4pm, Sa 9am-3pm. Free guided tours leave from the visitors center the first Sa of each month at 10am.)* **Forest Park,** 5000 acres of undeveloped wilderness stretching north from Washington Park, provides an idea of what the area was like before the arrival of Lewis and Clark. A web of trails leads into abundant forests, past scenic overviews, and through idyllic picnic areas. The largest Ming-style garden outside of China, the **Classical Chinese Garden** occupies an entire city block. *(NW 3rd and Everett. ☎228-8131; www.portlandchinesegarden.org. Open daily Apr.-Oct. 9am-6pm; Nov.-Mar. 10am-5pm. Ticket office closes ½hr. before closing. Free guided tours at noon and 1pm daily. $7, seniors $6, students $5.50, under 6 free.)*

MUSEUMS. The **Portland Art Museum (PAM)** sets itself apart from the rest of Portland's burgeoning arts scene on the strength of its collections, especially in Asian and Native American art. *(1219 SW Park, at Jefferson St. on the west side of S. Block Park. Bus #6, 58, 63. ☎226-2811; www.portlandartmuseum.org. Open Tu-W and Sa 10am-5pm, Th-F 10am-8pm, Su noon-5pm. Th-F closes at 5pm in winter. $10; $12 during some exhibitions; students and seniors $9, ages 5-19 $6, under 5 free.)* The ◙**Oregon Museum of Science and Industry (OMSI)** keeps visitors mesmerized with exhibits like an earthquake simulator chamber, an Omnimax theater, and the Kendall Planetarium. *(1945 SE Water Ave., 2 blocks south of Hawthorne Blvd., next to the river. Bus #63. ☎797-4000; www.omsi.edu. Open early June to early Sept. daily 9:30am-7pm; early Sept. to early June Tu-Su 9:30am-5:30pm. Museum and Omnimax admission $8.50, seniors and ages 3-13 $6.50, under 3 free. Omnimax ☎797-4640. Shows on the hr. M-Tu and Su 10am-7pm, F-Sa 11am-9pm. Planetarium ☎797-4646. Shows daily every 30min. 11am-4:30pm. $5.50. Combo ticket for museum, Omnimax, and either the planetarium or the submarine $19, seniors or ages 3-13 $15.)*

OTHER SIGHTS. The still-operational **Pioneer Courthouse,** at 5th Ave. and Morrison St., is the centerpiece of the **Pioneer Courthouse Square.** Tourists and urbanites of every ilk hang out in the brick quadrangle known as "Portland's Living Room." *(701 SW 6th Ave. ☎223-1613. Music Tu, Th noon-1pm.)* On the edge of the NW district, ◙**Powell's City of Books** is a must-see for anyone who gets excited about the written word. Nine color-coded rooms and 68,000 square ft. of floor space contain almost a million new and used volumes. If you like to dawdle in bookstores, be sure to bring a sleeping bag and rations. *(1005 W. Burnside St. Bus #20. ☎228-4651 or 800-878-7323; www.powells.com. Open daily 9am-11pm.)* **The Grotto,** a 62-acre Catholic sanctuary, has magnificent religious sculptures and shrines. *(Sandy Blvd. at NE 85th. ☎254-7371; www.thegrotto.org. Open daily late May to early Sept. 9am-7:30pm; early Sept. to late Nov. and Feb. to late May 9am-5:30pm; late Nov. to Jan. 9am-4pm.)* The **Oregon Zoo** has gained fame for its successful efforts at ◙**elephant breeding.** Exhibits include a goat habitat and a marine pool. *(4001 SW Canyon Rd. ☎226-1561; www.oregonzoo.com. Open daily Apr.-Sept. 9am-7pm; Oct.-Mar. 9am-4pm. $9.50, ages 65+ $8, ages 3-11 $6.50, under 3 free; $2 admission on the 2nd Tu of each month.)* **Portland Saturday Market,** under the Burnside Bridge between SW 1st Ave. and SW Naito Parkway, hosts all types of artisans selling their crafts and an international food court. *(☎222-6072; www.saturdaymarket.org. Open Mar.-Dec. Sa 10am-5pm and Su 11am-4:30pm.)*

THE LOCAL STORY

HAIR OF THE DOG

Hidden among factories and behind one of the least pretentious facades of any brewery around, ◪ *Hair of the Dog Brewing Company produces what might just be the best beer in a city known for its quality microbreweries. Let's Go took a tour of the small-scale brewery from co-owner Alan Sprints and got the skinny on the brewing process. These brews are superlative, and the experience is an essential notch on any microbrewery fan's belt. (4509 SE 23rd Ave. ☎232-6585; www.hairofthedog.com. Tours by appointment weekdays only. 12 oz. bottles $3, 1.5L "magnums" $10.)*

LG: Do your beers ferment in bottles?
A: They do ferment in the bottles, but it's a very small refermentation, just enough to get bubbles... if you do any more than that the bottles will explode.

LG: But they mature like wine?
A: Yeah.

LG: What's the reason for that?
A: Higher alcohol content, more hops, and the bottle conditioning process...it's like champagne, where the product is naturally fermented. That's a better environment for the product to age.

LG: Does that help to prevent contamination?
A: Refermentation scavenges oxygen out of the liquid, and that helps stop failing and off-flavors that might occur in beer if it ages.

♫ ENTERTAINMENT

Portland's daily newspaper, the *Oregonian*, lists upcoming events in its Friday edition (www.oregonlive.com/oregonian), and the free cultural reader, the Wednesday *Willamette Week*, is a reliable guide to local music, plays, and art (www.wweek.com). The **Oregon Symphony Orchestra,** 923 SW Washington St., plays classical and pop concerts from September to June. On Sundays and Mondays, students can buy $5 tickets one week before showtime. (☎228-1353 or 800-228-7343; www.orsymphony.org. Box office open M-F 9am-5pm, in **Symphony Season** also Sa 9am-5pm. $17-76; "Symphony Sunday" afternoon concerts $10-15.) **High Noon Tunes,** at Pioneer Courthouse Sq., hosts rock, jazz, folk, and world music. (☎223-1613. July-Aug. Tu and Th noon-1pm.)

Portland Center Stage, in the Newmark Theater at SW Broadway and SW Main St., will perform *The Fantasticks, Crowns,* and the world premier of *Celebrity Row* in its 2006 season. (☎274-6588; www.pcs.org. Open late Sept. to Apr. $27-55. $15 tickets available for ages 30 and under except on F and Sa nights and Su matinees.) The **Bagdad Theater and Pub,** 3702 SE Hawthorne Blvd., is housed in a former vaudeville theater, with a separate pub in front. The theater plays second-run films, while the pub offers 200+ ales. (☎236-9234; www.mcmenamins.com. Some shows 21+. Open M-Sa 11am-1am, Su noon-midnight.) The **Portland Trail Blazers** play at the **Rose Garden Arena,** 1 Center Ct. (☎321-321; www.nba.com/blazers).

The **Northwest Film Center,** 1219 SW Park Ave., shows classics, documentaries, and off-beat flicks almost everyday. The Center also hosts the **Portland International Film Festival** in the last two weeks of February, with a constantly growing number of films from around the world. (☎221-1156; www.nwfilm.com. Box office opens 30min. before each show. $7, students and seniors $6.) Portland's premier summer event is the **Rose Festival** (☎227-2681; www.rosefestival.org), during the first three weeks of June. In early July, the outrageously fun three-day ◪**Waterfront Blues Festival** draws some of the world's finest blues artists. (☎800-973-3378; www.waterfrontbluesfest.com. Admission $5 and 2 cans of food to benefit the Oregon Food Bank.) The **Oregon Brewers Festival,** on the last full weekend in July, is the continent's largest gathering of independent brewers at an incredible party at Waterfront Park. (☎297-3150; www.oregonbrewfest.com. Mug $4 (required to taste); tastings $1 each, $4 to fill. Under 21 must be accompanied by parent.)

◾ NIGHTLIFE

Once a rowdy frontier town, always a rowdy frontier town. Portland's clubs cater to everyone from the college athlete to the neo-goth aesthete.

◾ **Laurelthirst Public House,** 2958 NE Glisan St. (☎232-1504), at 30th Ave. Bus #19. Local talent makes a name for itself in 2 intimate rooms of groovin', boozin', and schmoozin'. Veggie burgers and sandwiches $5-8. Free pool before 5pm daily, $1 off microbrews M-F before 5pm. Cover $3-6 after 9pm. Open daily 9am-1am.

Ohm, 31 NW 1st Ave. (☎796-0909), just off Couch St. near the underpass below the Burnside Bridge. Dance in the cool brick interior or mingle with the trendy crowd outside. F-Sa often up-and-coming live bands 21+. Cover $5-10. Open Tu-Sa 9pm-2am.

Red Cap Garage and Boxxes, 341 SW 10th Ave. (☎221-7262; www.boxxes.com), are two gay bars that become one around 10pm. Magic happens at the 23-screen video and karaoke bar in Boxxes, while Red Cap fills an upscale niche. Cover $2-5 after 10pm Th, F, Sa. Open Tu-Su 3pm-2:30am.

CANNON BEACH   ☎503

Cannon Beach has come a long way since a rusty cannon from a shipwrecked schooner washed ashore, giving the area its name. Today, Cannon Beach is home to an impressive array of boutiques, bakeries, and galleries, making it a more refined alternative to the commercialism and miles of strip-malls that have developed in many Oregon coastal towns. **Ecola State Park** ($3), at the north end of town, attracts picnickers, hikers, and surfers alike with its view of the dramatic volcanic coastline. Ecola Point's view of hulking **Haystack Rock,** covered with seagulls, barnacles, and the occasional sea lion, is stunning. **Indian Beach,** accessible off U.S. 101 north of Cannon Beach, is a gorgeous surfing destination where surfers can catch waves between volcanic rock walls and then rinse off the salt in the nearby freshwater stream. **Sandcastle Day** transforms Cannon Beach's shores into a fantastic architectural menagerie on one Saturday in the middle of June.

Pleasant but pricey motels line Hemlock St. ◾**Seaside International Hostel (HI) ❶,** 930 N Holladay Dr., in Seaside, has nightly movies, a full kitchen, and an espresso bar. (☎738-7911. Internet access. Dorms $22, members $19; private rooms $59/$48. $2 off for touring cyclists. Canoe rental $10 per 2hr. Single kayak $12 per 2hr. D/MC/V.) The stunning ◾**Oswald West State Park ❶,** 10 mi. south of Cannon Beach, is a

LG: Are you more interested in product consistency, or do you prefer experimenting with different brews?
A: I enjoy when people like using our beer for celebrating special events and special occasions...it makes me feel good. If it wasn't for people that enjoyed drinking the beer, brewing it wouldn't be so much fun.

LG: What about the name of the brewery, Hair of the Dog?
A: Originally, the term literally referred to using the hair of a dog that bit you to help heal the bite. They'd chase a dog down, cut off some of its hair, [then] wrap it around the wound. And that helped chase away the evil spirit.

LG: And that's also for a hangover?
A: Yes, the term later became used in reference to curing a hangover—drinking some of the "hair of the dog" you had the night before (like more beer).

LG: Do these beers, having a higher alcohol content, give drinkers a stronger hangover the next morning?
A: All I know is we've generated quite a few hangovers.

LG: Oh yeah...? *[Feels forehead and eyes the empty glass warily.]*
A: Whether the hangovers are worse or not, I don't know. It depends on what you are used to drinking. We only use quality ingredients, so you should have a quality hangover.

tiny headland rainforest with 30 campsites accessible by a ¼ mi. trail off U.S. 101. The park provides wheelbarrows for transporting gear from the parking lot. (☎800-551-6949. Open Mar.-Oct. First come, first served. Sites May-Sept. $14; Oct.-Apr. $10.) Most of the dining deals in Cannon Beach are down Hemlock St. in midtown. **Lazy Susan Grill & Scoop ❷**, 156 N. Hemlock St., has a woodsy interior and serves excellent homemade scones. (☎436-9551. Open daily 8am-9pm. MC/V.) **Bill's Tavern ❷**, 188 N. Hemlock St., is a local spot for down-to-earth eatin' and drinkin'. (☎436-2202. Burgers $6-8. Pints $3.25. Open M-Tu and Th-Su 11:30am-midnight, W 4:30pm-midnight. Kitchen closes around 9:30pm. D/MC/V.)

Cannon Beach lies 8 mi. south of Seaside, 42 mi. north of Tillamook on U.S. 101 and 79 mi. from Portland via U.S. 26. The four exits into town from U.S. 101 all lead to Hemlock St., lined with galleries and restaurants. **Cannon Beach Shuttle** ($0.75) traverses the downtown area daily. Visitor info is at the **Cannon Beach Chamber of Commerce Visitor Center,** 207 Spruce St. (☎436-2623; www.cannonbeach.org. Open M-Sa 10am-5pm, Su 11am-4pm.) **Mike's Bike Shop,** 248 N. Spruce St., rents mountain bikes. (☎436-1266 or 800-492-1266; www.mikesbike.com. Open daily 10am-6pm. $9 per hr., $30 per day; beach tricycle $10 per 90min.) **Post Office:** 163 N. Hemlock St. (☎436-2822; open M-F 9am-5pm). **Postal Code:** 97110. **Area Code:** 503.

NEWPORT ☎541

After the miles of malls along U.S. 101, Newport's renovated waterfront area of pleasantly kitschy restaurants and shops is a delight. Newport's claim to fame, however, is the **Oregon Coast Aquarium,** 2820 SE Ferry Slip Rd., at the south end of the bridge. This world-class aquarium housed Keiko, the much-loved orca star of the movie *Free Willy*, before he returned to his childhood waters near Iceland. (☎867-3474; www.aquarium.org. Open daily Memorial Day to Labor Day 9am-6pm; Labor Day to Memorial Day 10am-5pm. $12, seniors $10, ages 3-12 $7.) The ■**Mark O. Hatfield Marine Science Center** is the hub of Oregon State University's coastal research. The live octopus is off-limits, but sea anemones, slippery slugs, and bottom-dwelling fish await your curiosity in the touch tanks. (At the south end of the bridge on Marine Science Dr. ☎867-0100; www.hmsc.oregonstate.edu. Open daily Memorial Day to Labor Day 10am-5pm; Labor Day to Memorial Day M and Th-Su 10am-4pm. Donations of $4 per person or $10 per family requested.) In town, the wide, sandy **Nye Beach** is perfect for relaxing along the coast. Three miles to the north, you can watch for grey whales from the **Yaquina Head Outstanding Natural Area.**

The ■**Sylvia Beach Hotel ❸**, 267 NW Cliff St., has a variety of rooms devoted to literary themes in addition to dorms. Try the Edgar Allen Poe room if you dare. (☎265-5428 or 888-795-8422; www.sylviabeachhotel.com. Breakfast included. Dorms $26; private rooms $68-178. AmEx/MC/V.) The **Money Saver Motel ❷**, 861 SW Coast Hwy. 101, just north of the Bay Bridge, offers clean rooms. (☎265-2277 or 888-4613969. Singles from $40; doubles from $45.) One mile south of the Bay Bridge, **South Beach State Park ❶** has camping near the quiet beach. (☎867-4715, reservations 800-452-5687. Campsites $4; RV sites $22.) The granddaddy of all Newport establishments, ■**Mo's Restaurant ❷,** 622 Bay Blvd., is famous for its clam chowder. If "Old Mo's" is packed, head across the street to **Mo's Annex ❷**, at 657 Bay Blvd., which dishes up the same food in a less historic atmosphere. (Mo's Restaurant: ☎265-2979. Open daily 11am-10pm. Annex: ☎265-7512. Open M-W and F-Su 11am-9pm, Th 11am-10pm. AmEx/D/DC/MC/V.) **April's at Nye Beach ❹,** 749 3rd St. NW, has excellent Italian and Mediterranean fare. (☎265-6855. Dinner $15-21. Reservations recommended. Open W-Su 5-9pm. AmEx/MC/V.)

Newport is bordered on the west by the foggy Pacific Ocean and on the south by Yaquina Bay. U.S. 101, known as the **Coast Highway,** divides east and west Newport. U.S. 20, known as **Olive Street,** bisects the north and south sides of town. **Grey-**

hound, 956 10th St. SW (☎265-2253; www.greyhound.com), at Bailey St., runs to Portland (3½-5 hr., 3 per day, $21), San Francisco (17-23hr., 3 per day, $95), Seattle (7-9hr., 3 per day, $51). The **Newport Chamber of Commerce,** 555 Coast Hwy. SW, provides tourist info. (☎265-8801; www.newportchamber.org. Open M-F 8:30am-5pm; in summer also Sa-Su 10am-4pm). **Post Office:** 310 2nd St. SW (☎800-275-8777; open M-F 8:30am-5pm, Sa 10am-noon). **Postal Code:** 97365.

EUGENE   ☎541

Epicenter of the organic foods movement and a haven for hippies, Eugene has a well-deserved liberal reputation. Home to the University of Oregon, the city is packed with college students during the school year but mellows out considerably in summer. Eugene's Saturday market, nearby outdoor activities, and overall sunny disposition make Oregon's second-largest city one of its most attractive.

■◪ ORIENTATION AND PRACTICAL INFORMATION. Eugene lies 111 mi. south of Portland on I-5. The main north-south arteries are, from west to east, **Willamette Street, Oak Street,** and **Pearl Street. High Street Highway 99** also runs east-west and splits in town—**6th Avenue** goes west, and **7th Avenue** goes east. The numbered avenues run east-west and increase toward the south. Eugene's main student drag, **13th Avenue,** leads to the **University of Oregon (U of O)** in the southeast of town. The Whitaker area, around Blair Blvd. near 6th Ave., can be unsafe at night. **Amtrak,** 433 Willamette St. (☎687-1383; www.amtrak.com; open daily 5:15am-9pm), at 4th Ave., runs to Portland (2½-3hr., 5 per day, $19-32) and Seattle (6-8hr., 3 per day, $38-65). Avoid the 12:44pm train—it tends to be 1-7hr. late. **Greyhound,** 987 Pearl St. (☎344-6265; www.greyhound.com; open M-F 6am-9:30pm, Sa-Su 6:15-10:45am and 12:30-9:30pm), at 10th Ave., runs to Portland (2-4hr., 8 per day, $18.50) and Seattle (6-9hr., 6 per day, $35). **Lane Transit District (LTD)** handles public transit. Map and timetables are at the LTD Service Center, in Eugene Station at 11th Ave. and Willamette St. (☎687-5555; www.ltd.org. Runs M-F 6am-10:40pm, Sa 7:30am-10:40pm, Su 8:30am-7:30pm. $1.25, seniors and under 18 $0.60. Day pass $2.50/$1.25.) **Visitor Info: Lane County Convention and Visitors Association,** 754 Olive St., just off 10th Ave. (☎484-5307 or 800-547-5445; www.visitlanecounty.org. Courtesy phone. Free maps. Open late May to early Sept. M-F 8am-5pm, Sa-Su 10am-4pm; closed Su early Sept. to late May.) The **Ranger Station,** about 60 mi. east of Eugene on Rte. 126, sells maps and $3-per-day parking passes for the National Forest. (☎822-3381. Open late May to mid-Oct. daily 8am-4:30pm; closed Sa-Su mid-Oct. to late May.) There's free **Internet** access at the **Eugene Public Library,** 100 W. 10th Ave. (☎682-5450. Open M-Th 10am-6pm, F-Sa 10am-8pm.) Free Internet is also available at the **Lane County Convention and Visitors Association** (see above). **Post Office:** 520 Willamette St., at 5th Ave. (☎800-275-8777. Open M-F 8:30am-5:30pm, Sa 10am-2pm.) **Postal Code:** 97401. **Area Code:** 541.

◪◲ ACCOMMODATIONS AND FOOD. The cheapest motels are on E. Broadway and W. 7th Ave. Make reservations early; motels are packed on big football weekends. The ◪**Eugene Hummingbird Hostel ❶,** 2352 Willamette St., is a graceful neighborhood home and a wonderful escape from the city, with a book-lined living room, (vegetarian) kitchen, and mellow atmosphere. (☎349-0589. Check-in 5-10pm. Lockout 11am-5pm. Dorms $19, members $16; private rooms from $30.) East on Rte. 58 and 126, the immense **Willamette National Forest ❶** is full of campsites ($6-18). Eugene's downtown area specializes in gourmet food. The University hangout zone at 13th Ave. and Kincaid St. has grab-and-go joints, and natural food stores are everywhere. ◪**Keystone Cafe ❶,** 395 W. 5th St., serves creative breakfast and lunch concoctions to vegans, vegetarians, and omnivores alike. (☎342-2075.

Pancakes $4. Open Tu-Th 7am-2pm, F-Sa 7am-3pm.) **Cozmic Pizza ❶**, 199 W. 8th Ave., has delicious vegetarian pizzas with gourmet toppings. (☎338-9333; www.cozmicpizza.com. Wireless Internet access. Open M-Th 11am-11pm, F 11am-midnight, Sa 4pm-midnight, Su 4pm-11pm.)

◙ **SIGHTS.** Every Saturday the area around 8th Ave. and Willamette St. fills for the ▓**Saturday Market,** with artisans hawking everything from hemp shopping bags to tarot readings. Next to the shopping stalls is the **farmers market,** where you can buy organic produce. (☎686-8885; www.eugenesaturdaymarket.org. Open Apr. to mid-Nov. Sa 9am-5pm; June-Oct. also Tu 10am-3pm.) Take time to see the ivy-covered halls that set the scene for National Lampoon's *Animal House* at the **University of Oregon.** (At E. 13th Ave. and Agate St. ☎346-3014; www.uoregon.edu. Tours M-F 10am and 2pm, Sa 10am.) The **Museum of Natural and Cultural History,** 1680 E. 15th Ave., at Agate St., showcases relics from indigenous cultures, including one of the world's oldest pairs of shoes. (☎346-3024; http://natural-history.uoregon. edu. Open W-Su noon-5pm. Adults $3, seniors and under 9 $2.)

The *Eugene Weekly* (www.eugeneweekly.com) lists concerts and local events. During the **Oregon Bach Festival** for sixteen days in June and July, Baroque authority Helmut Rilling conducts performances of Bach's concertos. (☎346-5666 or 800-457-1486; www.oregonbachfestival.com. Concert and lecture series $19, students and seniors $12; main events $22-49.) The vast ▓**Oregon Country Fair,** the most exciting event of the summer, takes place in **Veneta,** 13 mi. west of town on Rte. 126. Started in 1969 as a fundraiser for a local school, the fair has become a magical annual gathering of hippies, musicians, misfits, and activists. During the festival, 50,000 people enjoy 10 stages worth of shows and 300 booths of art, clothing, herbal remedies, furniture, food, and free hugs. Most people park for free at Civic Stadium, at 19th and Willamette in Eugene. From there, free wheelchair-accessible buses run every 10-15min. 10am-7pm. (☎343-4298; www.oregoncountryfair.org. Every year on the weekend after the 4th of July. Tickets F and Su $13, Sa $16.)

▜ **OUTDOOR ACTIVITIES.** Within a 1½hr. drive from Eugene, the McKenzie River has several stretches of class II-III whitewater, best enjoyed in June, when warm weather and high water conspire for a thrilling but comfortable ride. The Upper McKenzie is continuous for 14 mi. and can be paddled in 2-2½hr. **High Country Expeditions** (☎888-461-7238; www.highcountryexpeditions.com), on Belknap Springs Road about 5 mi. east of McKenzie Bridge, is one of the few rafting companies to float the Upper McKenzie. (Half-day $55, full day $85. Student and senior discounts.) The large, popular Cougar Lake features the Terwilliger Hot Springs, known by all as **Cougar Hot Springs.** Drive through the town of Blue River, 60 mi. east of Eugene on Rte. 126, and then turn right onto Aufderheide Dr. (Forest Service Rd. 19), and follow the road 7¼ mi. as it winds on the right side of Cougar Reservoir. (Open dawn-dusk. Clothing optional. $3 parking fee.)

East of Eugene, Rte. 126 runs adjacent to the beautiful McKenzie River, and on a clear day, the Three Sisters of the Cascades are visible. Just east of the town of McKenzie Bridge, about 70 mi. east of Eugene, the road splits into a scenic byway loop; Rte. 242 climbs east to the lava fields of McKenzie Pass, while Rte. 126 turns north over Santiam Pass and meets back with Rte. 242 in Sisters. Often blocked by snow until July, Rte. 242 tunnels between **Mount Washington** and the **Three Sisters Wilderness** before rising to McKenzie Pass. The 26 mi. **McKenzie River Trail** starts 1½ mi. west of the ranger station and leads through mossy forests to two of Oregon's most spectacular waterfalls—**Koosah Falls** and **Sahalie Falls.** Ambitious hikers can sign up for overnight permits at the ranger station and head for the high country, where hiking opportunities are endless.

■ NIGHTLIFE. Come nightfall, bearded hippies mingle with pierced anarchists and muscle-bound frat boys in Eugene's eclectic nightlife scene. In the *Animal House* tradition, the row by the university along 13th Ave. is often dominated by fraternity-style beer bashes. **■Sam Bond's Garage,** 407 Blair Blvd., is a laid-back hangout in the Whitaker neighborhood. Live music every night complements an always-evolving selection of local microbrews ($3.50 per pint). Take bus #50 or 52. (☎431-6603; www.sambonds.com. 21+ after 8:30pm. Open daily 4pm-2:30am.) **John Henry's,** 77 W. Broadway, is Eugene's prime site for punk, reggae, and virtually any other kind of live music. Call or check the website for schedule and covers. (☎342-3358; www.johnhenrysclub.com. Open daily 9pm-2:30am.) **The Downtown Lounge/ Diablo's,** 959 Pearl St., is a casual scene with pool tables upstairs and a hip crowd shaking their thangs downstairs. (☎343-2346; www.diablosdowntown.com. Cover $2-3. Open M-F 11am-2:30pm, Sa-Su 3pm-2:30am.)

CRATER LAKE NATIONAL PARK ☎541

The deepest lake in the US, the seventh deepest in the world, and one of the most beautiful anywhere, Crater Lake is one of Oregon's signature attractions. Formed about 7700 years ago in a cataclysmic eruption of Mt. Mazama, the lake began as a deep caldera and gradually filled with centuries worth of snowmelt. The circular lake plunges from its shores to a depth of 1943 ft., enchanting tourists with its impossibly blue waters. It is only a 300 ft. walk from the **Rim Village Visitors Center** (☎594-3090; open June-Sept. daily 9:30am-5pm) to the **Sinnott Memorial Overlook,** the park's most panoramic and accessible view. Above the lake, **Rim Drive,** which does not open entirely until mid-July, is a 33 mi. loop around the rim of the caldera. Trails to **Watchman Peak** (¾ mi., 1hr.), on the lake's west side, are the most spectacular. The strenuous 2½ mi. hike up **Mount Scott,** the park's highest peak (almost 9000 ft.), starts at the lake's eastern edge. The steep **Cleetwood Cove Trail** (2¼ mi., 2hr.) leaves from the north edge of the lake and is the only route down to the lake's edge. All trails provide breathtaking views of **Wizard Island,** a cinder cone rising 760 ft. above the western portion of the lake, and **Phantom Ship Rock,** a spooky rock formation in the southeast edge. In addition to trails around the lake, the park has over 140 mi. of wilderness trails. Picnics, fishing (with artificial lures only), and swimming are allowed, but water temperatures only reach about 50°F. Park rangers lead free tours periodically in the summer and winter. (Tour info ☎594-3000.)

A convenient base for forays to Crater Lake, **Klamath Falls** has several affordable hotels. The **Townhouse Motel ❶,** 5323 6th St., 3 mi. south of Main St., has very tidy rooms. (☎882-0924. Cable TV, A/C. Singles $32; doubles $38. MC/V.) There are multiple campgrounds near the lake. **Williamson River Campground ❶,** run by the National Forest Service, is 30 mi. north of Klamath Falls on U.S. 97 N and offers secluded modern tent sites along the river ($6). Near the park's south entrance off Hwy. 62, the huge **Mazama Village Campground ❶** provides first come, first served tent sites, plus a gas station and general store. (☎594-2255, ext. 3703. Showers $0.75 per 4min. Laundry $1.75. Open early June to mid-Oct. Sites $18, with electricity $23; RV sites $20.) While eating cheap isn't easy in Crater Lake, Klamath Falls has some affordable dining and a **Safeway,** 2740 S. 6th St. (☎273-3510). Where's **Waldo's Mongolian Grill and Tavern ❷**? It's at 610 Main St. and grills your choice of veggies and meat. (☎884-6863. Bowls $7-11. Open daily 11:30am-9pm. MC/V.)

Crater Lake averages over 44 ft. of snow per year, and snowbound roads can keep the northern entrance closed until July (call ☎594-3000 for road closures). The park's southern entrance is open year-round. The **entrance fee** is $10 for cars, and $5 for hikers and cyclists. **Amtrak,** 1600 Oak St. (☎884-2822; www.amtrak.com; open daily 7:30-11am and 8:30-10:15pm), and **Greyhound,** 435 S. Spring St. (☎883-2609; www.greyhound.com; open M-F 9am-5pm, Sa-Su 9-11am), are both in Klamath Falls. One train per day runs to Redding, CA (4½hr., $32), and one bus per day rolls to Eugene (6½hr., $39) and then on to Portland ($46-50). **Visitor Info: Chamber of Commerce,** 706 Main St. (☎884-5193 or 877-552-6284; www.klamath.org. Open M-F 8am-5pm.) The **William G. Steel Center** issues free backcountry camping permits. (☎594-3000; www.nps.gov/crla. Open daily 9am-4pm.) **Post Office:** 317 S. 7th St. in Klamath Falls. (☎800-275-8777. Open M-F 7:30am-5:30pm, Sa 9am-noon.) **Postal Code:** 97604. **Area Code:** 541.

ASHLAND   ☎541

Situated near the California border, Ashland mixes hip youth culture with a certain dead British man, setting an unlikely but intriguing stage for the world-famous █**Oregon Shakespeare Festival** (☎482-4331; www.osfashland.org). From mid-February to October, drama devotees can choose from 11 Shakespearean and contemporary works performed in Ashland's three elegant theaters: the outdoor **Elizabethan Stage,** the **Angus Bowmer Theater,** and the **New Theater.** The 2006 schedule includes *The Winter's Tale, The Merry Wives of Windsor,* and Oscar Wilde's *The Importance of Being Earnest.* Purchase tickets six months in advance. (In summer $29-55; in spring and fall $23-44. Children under 6 not admitted. Discounts for those under 18.) At 9:30am, the **box office,** 15 S. Pioneer St., releases any unsold tickets for the day's performances and sells 20 standing room tickets ($13) for sold-out shows on the Elizabethan Stage. Half-price rush tickets are sometimes available 1hr. before performances. **Backstage tours** provide a wonderful glimpse of the festival from behind the curtain. (Tours Tu-Sa 10am. $11, ages 6-17 $8.25.)

In winter, Ashland is a budget paradise; in summer, hotel and B&B rates double while the hostel bulges. Only rogues and peasant slaves arrive without reservations. █**Ashland Hostel ❶,** 150 N. Main St., is well-kept and cheery, making it an ideal place to sleep, perchance to dream. (☎482-9217. Linen $2. Free Internet access. Check-in 5-10pm. Lockout 10am-5pm. Dorms $21; private rooms $50. Cash only.) The historic **Columbia Hotel ❹,** 262½ E. Main St., oozes with 1920s charm. (☎482-3726 or 800-718-2530; www.columbiahotel.com. June-Oct. rooms from $69; low season from $49. MC/V.) Campers should check out the free **Mount Ashland Campground ❶,** 20 mi. south of Ashland off I-5 at Exit 6. Follow signs for Mt. Ashland Ski Area through the parking lot. (7 sites with pit toilets. No drinking water.)

The incredible food selection on N. and E. Main St. has earned the plaza a strong culinary reputation. **The Ashland Food Cooperative,** 237 1st St., stocks cheap and organic groceries. (☎482-2237; www.asfs.org. Open M-Sa 8am-9pm, Su 9am-9pm.) If you're sick of the Man keeping you down, fight back at **Evo's Java House and Revolutionary Cafe ❶,** 376 E. Main St., where the politics are as radical as the $5 veggie burritos and sandwiches. (☎482-2261. Open daily 7am-6pm. AmEx/D/MC/V.) Nobody doth protest too much at the food at **Morning Glory ❸,** 1149 Siskiyou Blvd. (☎488-8636; www.morninggloryrestaurant.com. Open daily 7am-2pm. AmEx/D/MC/V.) Ashland's nightlife concentrates around N. and E. Main St. Try the excellent microbrews at **Siskiyou Brew Pub,** 31 Water St., just off N. Main St. (☎482-7718. Occasional live music. 21+ after 9pm. Open M-Th 4-11pm, F-Su 3-11pm.)

Ashland is in the foothills of the Siskiyou and Cascade Ranges, 285 mi. south of Portland and 15 mi. north of the California border, near the junction of **I-5** and **Route 66. Route 99** cuts through the middle of town on a northwest-southeast axis and becomes **North Main Street** as it enters town from the west, and then splits briefly into **East Main Street** and **Lithia Way. Visitor Info: Chamber of Commerce,** 110 E. Main St. (☎482-3486; www.ashlandchamber.com. Open M-F 9am-5pm.) **Ashland District Ranger Station,** 645 Washington St., off Rte. 66 by Exit 14 on I-5, has info on hiking, biking, and the Pacific Crest Trail. (☎482-3333; www.fs.fed.us/r6/rogue. Open M-F 8am-1pm and 2-4:30pm.) **Post Office:** 120 N. 1st St., at Lithia Way. (☎800-275-8777. Open M-F 9am-5pm.) **Postal Code:** 97520. **Area Code:** 541.

WASHINGTON

On Washington's western shores, Pacific storms feed one of the world's only temperate rainforests in Olympic National Park. Just east, clouds linger over Seattle through much of the year, hiding the Emerald City. Visitors to Puget Sound can experience everything from isolation in the San Juan Islands to cosmopolitan entertainment on the mainland. Past the Cascades, the state's eastern half spreads out into fertile farmlands and grassy plains.

⋒ PRACTICAL INFORMATION

Capital: Olympia.

Visitor Info: Washington State Tourism, Dept. of Community, Trade, and Economic Development, P.O. Box 42500, Olympia 98504 (☎800-544-1800; www.experiencewashington.com). **Washington State Parks and Recreation Commission,** P.O. Box 42650, Olympia 98504 (☎360-902-8844 or 888-226-7688; www.parks.wa.gov).

Postal Abbreviation: WA. **Sales Tax:** 7-9%, depending on the county.

SEATTLE   ☎206

Seattle's mix of mountain views, clean streets, espresso stands, and rainy weather was the magic formula of the 90s, attracting transplants from across the US. The droves of newcomers provide an interesting contrast to the older residents who remember Seattle as a city-town, not a thriving metropolis bubbling over with young millionaires. Software and dot-com money have helped drive rent sky-high in some areas, but the grungy, punk-loving street culture still prevails in others. The city is shrouded in cloud cover 200 days a year, but when the skies clear, Seattleites rejoice that "the mountain is out" and head for the country.

▄ TRANSPORTATION

Airport: Seattle-Tacoma International (Sea-Tac; ☎433-5388; www.portseattle.org), on Federal Way, 15 mi. south of Seattle, exit right off I-5 to Rte. 518 (follow signs).

Trains: Amtrak, King St. Station, 303 S. Jackson St. (☎382-4125, reservations 800-872-7245; www.amtrak.com), 1 block east of Pioneer Sq. Ticket office open daily 6:15am-8pm. To: **Portland** (3½hr., 4 per day, $25-40); **Spokane** (8hr., 1 per day, $37-81); **Tacoma** (45min., 4 per day, $6-16); **Vancouver** (3½hr., 1 per day, $25-39). Amtrak also offers 4 buses per day to Vancouver for $25 from King St. Station.

Buses: Greyhound (☎628-5526 or 800-231-2222; www.greyhound.com), at 8th Ave. and Stewart St. The station can get seedy after dark. Ticket office and station open daily 6:30am-1am. To: **Portland** (6hr., 8 per day, $22-24); **Spokane** (7hr., 5 per day, $30-32); **Tacoma** (1½hr., 6 per day, $6); **Vancouver** (6½hr., 6 per day, $26-28).

Ferries: Washington State Ferries (☎464-6400 or 888-808-7977; www.wsdot.wa.gov/ferries) has 2 terminals in Seattle. The main terminal is downtown, at Colman Dock, Pier 52. Service to **Bainbridge Island** (35min.; $6.10, with car $13.30); **Bremerton** on the Kitsap Peninsula (60min.; $6.10, with car $13.30), and **Vashon Island** (30min., passengers only, $8.10). Ferries for Bremerton and Bainbridge depart frequently 6am-1am from Pier 52; ferries for Vashon run 6am-8pm from Pier 50. The **Victoria Clipper** (☎800-888-2535, reservations 448-5000; www.victoriaclipper.com) goes to **Victoria** from Pier 69. (3hr.; 6 per day mid-May to early Sept., 2 per day mid-Sept. to Apr.; $66-81, under 12 half-price; bikes $10, no cars.)

Public Transit: Metro Transit, Customer Service Offices, King St. Center, 201 S. Jackson St., at 2nd Ave. S, and the Transit Tunnel in Westlake Station, downtown. (☎553-3000, or 800-542-7876; http://transit.metrokc.gov.) King St. Center open M-F 8am-5pm; Westlake Station open M-F 9am-5pm. Fares are based on a 2-zone system. **Zone 1** is everything within the city limits (peak hours $1.50, off-peak $1.25). **Zone 2** is everything else (peak $2, off-peak $1.25). Ages 5-17 always $0.50. **Peak hours** in both zones are M-F 6-9am and 3-6pm. Weekend day passes $2.50. Ride free daily 6am-7pm in the downtown **ride free area,** bordered by S. Jackson St. to the south, 6th Ave. and I-5 to the east, Blanchard St. on the north, and the waterfront to the west. Outside ride free area, pay-as-you-board buses head toward downtown and pay-as-you-leave buses head away from downtown. Transfers free.

Taxi: Farwest Taxi, ☎622-1717. **Orange Cab Co.,** ☎522-8800.

Car Rental: Enterprise, 11342 Lake City Way NE (☎364-3127).

⚓ ORIENTATION

Seattle stretches from north to south on an isthmus between **Puget Sound** to the west and **Lake Washington** to the east. The city is easily accessible by car via **I-5,** which runs north-south through the city, and by **I-90** from the east, which ends at I-5 southeast of downtown. Get to **downtown** (including **Pioneer Square, Pike Place Market,** and the **waterfront**) from I-5 by taking any of the exits between James and Stewart St. Take the Mercer St./Fairview Ave. exit to the **Seattle Center;** follow signs from there. The Denny Way exit leads to **Capitol Hill,** and, farther north, the 45th St. exit heads toward the **University District.** The less crowded **Route 99,** also called Aurora, runs parallel to I-5 and skirts the western side of downtown.

🛈 PRACTICAL INFORMATION

Tourist Information: Seattle's **Citywide Concierge Center** is housed inside the **Convention and Visitors Bureau** (☎461-5840; www.seeseattle.org), at 7th and Pike St., on the 1st fl. of the convention center. Helpful staff doles out maps, brochures, newspapers, and Metro schedules, and can help visitors find lodging. Open late May to early Sept. M-F 9am-6pm, Sa-Su 10am-4pm; early Sept. to late May M-F 9am-5pm.

Outdoor Information: Seattle Parks and Recreation Department, 100 Dexter Ave. N (☎684-4075; www.ci.seattle.wa.us/parks). Open M-F 8am-5pm. **Outdoor Recreation Information Center,** 222 Yale Ave. (☎470-4060; www.nps.gov/ccso/oric.htm), in REI. Does not sell permits. Free brochures on hiking trails. Open M-F and Su 10:30am-8pm, Sa 10am-8pm. Closed M late Sept. to late spring.

Medical Services: International District Emergency Center, 720 8th Ave. S, Ste. 100 (☎461-3235). Medics with multilingual assistance available. Clinic open M-F 9am-6pm, Sa 9am-4:30pm; phone 24hr. **Swedish Medical Center, Providence Campus,** 500 16th Ave. (☎320-2111), for urgent care and cardiac. 24hr.

Internet Access: Seattle Central Library, 1000 4th Ave. (☎386-4636; www.spl.org), at Madison. 15min. free Internet with photo ID.; free unlimited wireless Internet. Open M-W 10am-8pm, Th-Sa 10am-6pm, Su 1-5pm.

Post Office: 301 Union St. (☎748-5417 or 800-275-8777), at 3rd Ave. downtown. Open M-F 7:30am-5:30pm. **Postal Code:** 98101. **Area Code:** 206.

🏠 ACCOMMODATIONS

Pacific Reservation Service (☎800-684-2932) can arrange B&B singles for $50-65. For motels far from downtown, drive north on Aurora Ave. or take bus #26 to Fremont.

SEATTLE FOR POCKET CHANGE. Don't be discouraged by Seattle's software money and expensive espresso; you can experience the best of Seattle even if you're no Bill Gates. The vibrant **Pike Place Market** (p. 963) is well worth exploring for people-watching and some first-rate fish-hurling, all available free of charge. Take a wallet-friendly stroll on the trails of the lush **UW Arboretum** (p. 964) or along the **waterfront** of Union Bay, and then settle down for a picnic on the lawn at the **Seattle Center** (p. 964). The otherworldly exterior of the **Experience Music Project** (p. 964) is as impressive, if not more so, as the various collections and exhibits housed inside. And, in the summertime, free concerts take place midday Monday through Friday, thanks to the **Out to Lunch** series (p. 965).

HI-Seattle, 84 Union St. (☎622-5443 or 888-622-5443; www.hiseattle.org), at Western Ave. by the waterfront. Take Union St. from downtown; follow signs down the stairs under the Pike Pub & Brewery. Continental breakfast. Laundry. Internet $0.08 per min. 7-night max. stay in summer. Reception 24hr. Reservations recommended. Dorms $27, members $24. 2- to 4-person rooms $69/$99. AmEx/MC/V. ❶

Green Tortoise Backpacker's Hostel, 1525 2nd Ave. (☎340-1222; www.greentortoise.net), between Pike and Pine St. on the #174 or 194 bus route, is known for throwing parties from time to time. Breakfast included. Free Internet access. Open mic W. Key deposit $20 cash only. Reception 24hr. Dorms $23; private rooms $52. Small additional charge for credit cards. MC/V. ❶

Moore Hotel, 1926 2nd Ave. (☎448-4851 or 800-421-5508; www.moorehotel.com), 1 block east of Pike Place Market. Built in 1907, the Moore Hotel has a swanky lobby and cavernous hallways. "European-style" (with smaller beds and shared bathrooms) singles from $45; doubles $55. Standard singles $62; doubles $79. Large suites $95-150. MC/V. ❷

The College Inn, 4000 University Way NE (☎633-4441; www.collegeinnseattle.com), across the street from the University of Washington campus. This historic landmark offers charming European-style rooms. Continental breakfast. Free Internet access. Reservations recommended. Singles from $45; doubles from $55. MC/V/D. ❸

◖ FOOD

Though known primarily for their coffee-loving ways, Seattleites are big into healthy cuisine, especially seafood. **Puget Sound Consumer Coops (PCCs),** are local health-food markets with locations across the city. (In Green Lake: ☎525-3586; 7504 Aurora Ave. N.) Capitol Hill, the U District, and Fremont close main streets on summer Saturdays for **farmers markets.**

PIKE PLACE MARKET AND DOWNTOWN

In 1907, angry citizens got fed up with the middle-man, and local farmers began selling produce directly to locals by the waterfront, creating the Pike Place Market. Today tourists mob the marketplace for fresh produce, a laid-back Seattle vibe, and the flying fish that are hurled from shelves to scales in the Main Arcade. (Open M-Sa 9am-6pm, Su 11am-5pm. Produce and fish open earlier; restaurants and lounges close later.)

Piroshky, Piroshky, 1908 Pike Pl. (☎441-6068), between Virginia and Stewart St. The Russian piroshky is a croissant-like dough baked and stuffed with sausages, mushrooms, cheeses, salmon, or apples doused in cinnamon ($3-4). The $5.95 soup and piroshky combo is a steal. Open daily 8am-6pm. MC/V. ❶

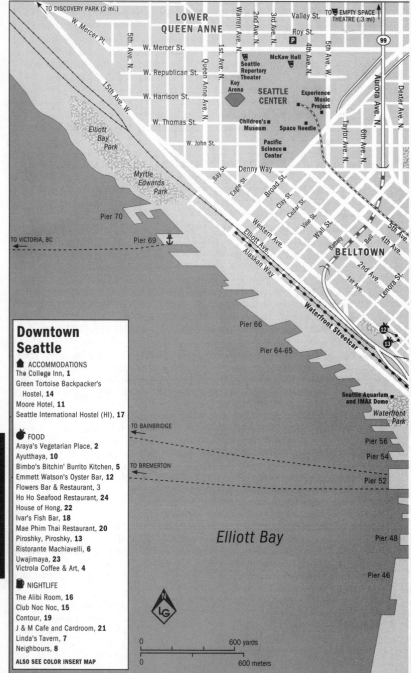

TO DISCOVERY PARK (2 mi.)

W. Mercer Pl.

LOWER QUEEN ANNE

Valley St.

TO EMPTY SPACE THEATRE (.3 mi)

W. Mercer St.

Roy St.

W. Republican St.

McKaw Hall

Seattle Repertory Theater

W. Harrison St.

Key Arena

SEATTLE CENTER

Experience Music Project

W. Thomas St.

Children's Museum

Space Needle

W. John St.

Pacific Science Center

Elliott Bay Park

Denny Way

Myrtle Edwards Park

Bay St.

Broad St.

Eagle St.

Clay St.

Pier 70

Cedar St.

Vine St.

Western Ave.

Wall St.

TO VICTORIA, BC

Pier 69

Elliott Ave.

Battery

Bell

BELLTOWN

Alaskan Way

Pier 66

Waterfront Streetcar

Pier 64-65

Downtown Seattle

🛏 ACCOMMODATIONS
The College Inn, **1**
Green Tortoise Backpacker's Hostel, **14**
Moore Hotel, **11**
Seattle International Hostel (HI), **17**

🍴 FOOD
Araya's Vegetarian Place, **2**
Ayutthaya, **10**
Bimbo's Bitchin' Burrito Kitchen, **5**
Emmett Watson's Oyster Bar, **12**
Flowers Bar & Restaurant, **3**
Ho Ho Seafood Restaurant, **24**
House of Hong, **22**
Ivar's Fish Bar, **18**
Mae Phim Thai Restaurant, **20**
Piroshky, Piroshky, **13**
Ristorante Machiavelli, **6**
Uwajimaya, **23**
Victrola Coffee & Art, **4**

🌙 NIGHTLIFE
The Alibi Room, **16**
Club Noc Noc, **15**
Contour, **19**
J & M Cafe and Cardroom, **21**
Linda's Tavern, **7**
Neighbours, **8**
ALSO SEE COLOR INSERT MAP

TO BAINBRIDGE

Seattle Aquarium and IMAX Dome

Waterfront Park

Pier 56

Pier 54

TO BREMERTON

Pier 52

Elliott Bay

Pier 48

Pier 46

0   600 yards
0   600 meters

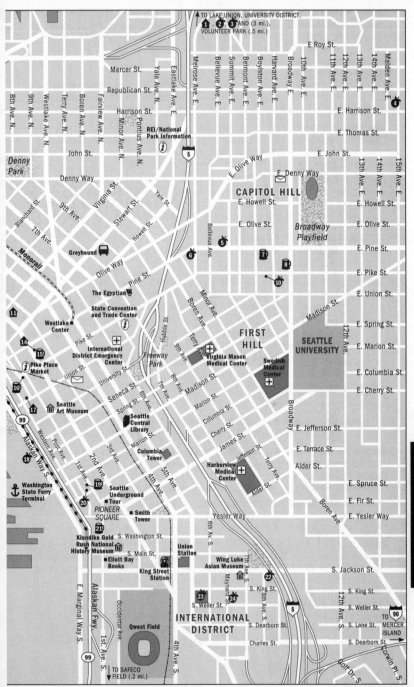

TO LAKE UNION, UNIVERSITY DISTRICT,
1 . **2** . **3** AND (3 mi.),
VOLUNTEER PARK (.5 mi.)

E Roy St.

Mercer St.
Republican St.
Harrison St.

E. Harrison St.

E. Thomas St.

REI/National
Park Information

John St.

E. John St.

Denny
Park

Denny Way

E. Olive Way

E. Denny Way

CAPITOL HILL
E. Howell St.

E. Howell St.

E. Olive St.

*Broadway
Playfield*

E. Olive St.

E. Pine St.

Blanchard St.

Virginia St.

Stewart St.

Howell St.

Greyhound

Olive Way

Pine St.

E. Pine St.

E. Pike St.

The Egyptian

State Convention
and Trade Center

E. Union St.

**FIRST
HILL**

E. Spring St.

**SEATTLE
UNIVERSITY**

E. Marion St.

Westlake
Center

Pike St.

International
District Emergency
Center

*Freeway
Park*

Virginia Mason
Medical Center

Swedish
Medical
Center

E. Columbia St.

Pike Place
Market

Seneca St.

Madison St.

Marion St.

E. Cherry St.

Seattle
Art Museum

Spring St.

Columbia St.

E. Jefferson St.

Seattle
Central
Library

Cherry St.

James St.

E. Terrace St.

Columbia
Tower

Harborview
Medical Center

Alder St.

E. Spruce St.

Washington
State Ferry
Terminal

Seattle
Underground
Tour

*PIONEER
SQUARE*

Smith
Tower

Yesler Way

E. Fir St.

E. Yesler Way

Klondike Gold
Rush National
History Museum

S. Washington St.

S. Main St.

Union
Station

Eliott Bay
Books

King Street
Station

Wing Luke
Asian Museum

S. Jackson St.

S. King St.

S. King St.

Qwest Field

S. Weller St.

S. Weller St.

**INTERNATIONAL
DISTRICT**

S. Dearborn St.

S. Lane St.

TO
MERCER
ISLAND

Charles St.

S. Dearborn St.

TO SAFECO
FIELD (.2 mi.)

Emmett Watson's Oyster Bar, 1916 Pike Pl. (☎448-7721), inside the building between Virginia and Stewart St., serves seafood in blue-checkered booths. Try the Oyster Bar Special—2 oysters, 3 shrimp, and a heaping bowl of chowder ($7.75). Open M-Th 11:30am-7pm, F-Sa 11:30am-8pm, Su 11:30am-6pm. MC/V. ❷

THE WATERFRONT

Budget eaters, steer clear of Pioneer Sq. Instead, take a picnic to **Waterfall Gardens,** on the corner of S. Main St. and 2nd Ave. S. The garden sports tables and chairs and a man-made waterfall that masks traffic outside. (Open daily dawn-dusk.)

▨ **Mae Phim Thai Restaurant,** 94 Columbia St. (☎624-2979), a few blocks north of the waterfront between 1st and Post Ave. Delicious, inexpensive Thai cuisine served quickly in a no frills hole-in-the-wall location. For lovers of pad-thai, this spot is hard to beat. All dishes $6. Open M-F 11am-7pm, Sa noon-7pm. Cash only. ❷

Ivar's Fish Bar, Pier 54 (☎467-8063). A fast-food window that serves all kinds of sea-food—from clam chowder ($2.50) to clams and chips ($5.30). Open M-Th and Su 11am-midnight, F-Sa 11am-2am. MC/V. For a more upscale meal, try **Ivar's Restaurant** next door (Open M-Th and Su 11am-10pm, F-Sa 11am-11pm. MC/V). ❶/❸

INTERNATIONAL DISTRICT

Along King and Jackson St., between 5th and 8th Ave. east of Qwest Field, Seattle's International District is packed with great eateries.

▨ **Uwajimaya,** 600 5th Ave. S (☎624-6248). The Uwajimaya Village is a city block of Asian groceries and gifts; it's the largest Japanese department store in the region. Don't miss the food court's panorama of delicacies. Open M-Sa 9am-10pm, Su 9am- 9pm. ❷

House of Hong, 409 8th Ave. S (☎622-7997), at S. Jackson St. Dim sum daily 10am-5pm at this upscale restaurant. Standard Chinese cuisine $8-13. Open M-F 10am-midnight, Sa 9:30am-midnight, Su 9:30am-10pm. AmEx/MC/V. ❸

Ho Ho Seafood Restaurant, 653 S. Weller St. (☎382-9671). Generous portions of Cantonese-prepared seafood, including steamed rock cod ($8.25). Lunch $5-7 (until 4pm). Dinner $7-12. Open M-Th and Su 11am-1am, F-Sa 11am-3am. MC/V. ❷

CAPITOL HILL

With bronze dance-steps on the sidewalks and neon storefronts, Broadway Ave. is home to numerous espresso houses, imaginative cafes, and funky nightclubs.

▨ **Bimbo's Bitchin' Burrito Kitchen,** 506 E. Pine St. (☎329-9978). The name explains it, and the decorations prove it. Walk right through the door to the bar, **Cha Cha,** for $3.50 tequila shots. Spicy Bimbo's burrito $4.25. Tacos $2.50. Happy hour daily 4-7pm; bar open until 2am. Open M-Th noon-11pm, F-Sa noon-2am, Su 2-10pm. MC/V. ❶

Ristorante Machiavelli, 1215 Pine St. (☎621-7941). A small, bustling Italian place with simple decor and hearty food. The gnocchi is widely considered the best in town. Pasta $8-10. Open M-Sa 5-11pm; bar open until 2am. MC/V. ❸

Ayutthaya, 727 E. Pike St. (☎324-8833). Thai food infused with Caribbean spices in a quiet mint-green nook. Generous lunch entrees $5.75-6.50; go for those with spice if you can handle the kick, but be sure to save room for the deep-fried banana dessert ($2.50). Open M-Sa 11am-2:30pm and 5-9pm. AmEx/D/DC/MC/V. ❷

UNIVERSITY DISTRICT

The neighborhood around the immense **University of Washington** ("U-Dub"), north of downtown between Union and Portage Bay, supports funky shops, international restaurants, and coffeehouses. The best of each lies within a few blocks of University Way, known as "the Ave."

■ **Araya's Vegetarian Place,** 1121 NE 45th St. (☎524-4332). One of the top vegan restaurants in Seattle, Araya's lunch buffet has all the classics—curries and pad thai—plus some unconventional offerings ($6.95). Buffet 11:30am-3:30pm. Open M-Th 11:30am-9pm, F-Sa 11:30am-9:30pm, Su 5-9pm. AmEx/D/MC/V. ❷

Flowers Bar & Restaurant, 4247 University Way NE (☎633-1903). This 1920s landmark was a flower shop; now, the mirrored ceiling reflects an all-you-can-eat Mediterranean buffet ($7.99). Daily drink specials. Open M-Sa 11am-2am, Su 11am-midnight; bar open Th-Sa 6pm-2am. AmEx/D/MC/V. ❷

▐ CAFES

The coffee bean is Seattle's first love; you can't walk a single block without passing an institution of caffeination. The city's obsession with Italian-style espresso drinks even has gas stations pumping out thick, dark, soupy java.

■ **Victrola Coffee & Art,** 411 15th Ave. E (☎325-6520; www.victrolacoffee.com). On mellow 15th Ave., this cafe possesses atmosphere in abundance, balancing private sitting space with inviting sofas. Signature espresso roasts ($1.95 for a double shot), sandwiches ($4.95-5.75), and top-notch pastries ($2). Open daily 5:30am-11pm.

Cafe Besalu, 5909 24th Ave. NW (☎789-1463). The coffee is good, but the real draw is Cafe Besalu's delectable pastries—from artisan bread to croissants and brioches ($0.95-3.25)—baked fresh in the open kitchen. Open W-Su 7am-3pm.

◉ SIGHTS

Most of the city's major sights are within walking distance or in the Metro's ride free zone. Seattle has unparalleled public art installations downtown (self-guided tours begin at the visitors center) and plentiful galleries. While dot-com success drove Seattle's collective worth up and some of the local artists out, the money has begun to pay off; the investments of Seattle-based millionaires have brought new architecture in the Experience Music Project (EMP), the new Seattle Central Library, and the upcoming Olympic Sculpture Park. Just outside cosmopolitan downtown, Seattle boasts over 300 areas of well-watered greenery.

DOWNTOWN AND THE WATERFRONT

Designed by Rem Koolhaus, the transparent, ultra-modern ■**Seattle Central Library,** 1000 4th Ave., at Madison St., hovers above the downtown street with jagged angles and floating floors. (☎386-4636; www.spl.org. Free 1hr. general tours M-W 12:30, 2:30, 4:30pm; Th-Sa 10:30am, 12:30, 2:30, 4:30pm; Su 2 and 4pm. Free 1hr. architectural tours M-W 5:30 and 6:45pm, Sa-Su 1:30 and 3:30pm. Open M-W 10am-8pm, Th-Sa 10am-6pm, Su 1-5pm.) The ■**Pike Place Market,** 1531 Western Ave., is definitely worth a look, even if food is not on your mind. Tours start at the Market Heritage Center. (☎682-7453; www.pikeplacemarket.com. $7, under 18 and 60+ $5. Open W-Su 11am and 2pm.) The **Pike Place Hillclimb** descends from the south end of Pike Place Market to Alaskan Way and the waterfront. The **Seattle Art Museum (SAM),** 100 University St., at 1st Ave., boasts the region's largest collection of African, Native American, and Asian art. Just up the hill is the museum's **Rental/Sales Gallery,** with local art for perusal or purchase. (☎654-3100; www.seattleartmuseum.org. Open Tu-W and F-Su 10am-5pm, Th 10am-9pm. $7; students, ages 62+ and 12-17 $5; under 12 free; first Sa of the month free. Special exhibits $5-15. Rental/Sales Gallery: 1220 3rd Ave. ☎343-1101; www.seattleartmuseum.org/artrentals. Open M-Sa 11am-5pm.) The **Seattle Underground Tour,** 608 1st Ave. in Pioneer Sq., offers an entertaining glimpse into Seattle's clumsy beginnings, including exploring subterranean Pioneer Square buildings that were ground level a century ago. Tours are guided by a knowledgeable, funny staff. (☎ 682-4646; www.undergroundtour.com. 3-9 1½hr. tours daily 10am-6pm, but call ahead.)

THE SEATTLE CENTER

The 1962 World's Fair demanded a Seattle Center to herald the city of the future. Now the Center houses everything from carnival rides to ballet performances. It is bordered by Denny Way, W. Mercer St., 1st Ave., and 5th Ave., and has eight gates, each with a map of its facilities. It is also accessible by a short **monorail** which runs from downtown's **Westlake Center.** (400 Pine St. ☎ 625-0280; www.seattlemonorail.com. Monorail every 10min. M-F 7:30am-11pm, Sa-Su 9am-11pm. $1.50, seniors $0.75, ages 5-12 $0.50.) The Center's anchor point is the **Center House,** which holds a food court and info desk. The **International Fountain** squirts water 20 ft. in the air from all angles off its silver, hemispherical base. (Info desk open daily 11am-6pm. For info about special events, call ☎ 684-7200; www.seattlecenter.com.)

The ◙**Experience Music Project (EMP),** 325 5th Ave., at the Seattle Center, is a must-see for any visitor to Seattle, whether musician or not. The brainchild of Seattle billionaire and Microsoft co-founder Paul Allen, EMP was initially intended as a shrine to Allen's music idol, Jimi Hendrix. The project eventually ballooned to include a $350 million budget, sophisticated technology, dozens of ethnomusicologists and multimedia specialists, a collection of over 80,000 musical artifacts, and the world-renowned architect Frank Gehry. The result? The rock 'n' roll museum of the future. Even if you don't go inside, the building alone—sheet metal molded into abstract curves and acid-dyed gold, silver, purple, light blue, and red—is spectacular. Inside, check out the guitar Hendrix smashed on a London stage, the Sound Lab's hands-on, state-of-the-art computer teaching devices that let you try your own hand at music making, a collection of guitars covering the past two centuries, and On Stage, a first-class karaoke stage gone haywire. (☎ 367-5483 or 877-367-5483; www.emplive.com. Open late May to early Sept. daily 10am-8pm; early Sept. to late May M-Th and Su 10am-6pm, F-Sa 10am-8pm. $20; military with ID, seniors, and ages 13-17 $16; ages 7-12 $15. Free live entertainment Tu-Su in the lounge.)

The **Space Needle** was built in 1962 for the World's Fair. When this 607-ft. rotating building was constructed, it was hailed as futuristic and daring. Today, the Space Needle is the symbol of Seattle. It has a great view and is an invaluable landmark for the disoriented. The needle houses an observation tower and a high-end rotating restaurant. (400 Broad St. ☎ 905-2100; www.spaceneedle.com. Open daily 9am-midnight. $13, seniors $11, ages 4-13 $6.)

THE INTERNATIONAL DISTRICT/CHINATOWN

What do you do when you have too much good art to exhibit all at once? Open a second museum, which is what SAM did, creating the ◙**Seattle Asian Art Museum (SAAM),** 1400 E. Prospect St., in Volunteer Park, just past the water tower. The collection is particularly strong in Chinese art, but the museum also has exhibits on Buddhist art and daily life in Japan. (☎ 654-3100; www.seattleartmuseum.org. Open Tu-W and F-Su 10am-5pm, Th 10am-9pm. Suggested donation $3, under 12 free; free with SAM ticket from the previous 7 days; SAAM ticket good for $3 discount at SAM. First Th and Sa of every month free.) The ◙**Wing Luke Asian Museum,** 407 7th Ave. S, gives a description of life in an Asian-American community, showing work by local Asian artists. One permanent exhibit is Camp Harmony, a replica of barracks from a Japanese internment camp during WWII. (☎ 623-5124; www.wingluke.org. Open Tu-F 11am-4:30pm, Sa-Su noon-4pm. $4, students and seniors $3, ages 5-12 $2. First Th of every month free.) The **University of Washington Arboretum,** 10 blocks east of Volunteer Park, has excellent trails amongst over 4000 species of trees and flowers. Take bus #11, 43, or 48 from downtown. Explore the carefully crafted gardens, including a serene Japanese Garden, Rhododendron Glen, and Azalea Way. Tours depart the Graham Visitor Center, at the southern end of the arboretum on Lake Washington Blvd. (☎543-8800; http://depts.washington.edu/wpa. Open daily dawn-dusk, visitors center 10am-4pm. Free tours 1pm on the first Su of each month or by appointment. Japanese Garden open Apr.-Nov. 10am-dusk. $2.50, students and ages 60+ $1.50.)

🎵 ENTERTAINMENT

Seattle has a world-renowned underground music scene and a bustling theater community. For concerts and other listings, check out Seattle's free weekly publication, the *Seattle Weekly* (www.seattleweekly.com). One regular occurrence in the city is the free **Out to Lunch** series (☎623-0340; schedules at www.downtownseattle.com), which brings everything from reggae to folk dancing to parks, squares, and buildings. (June-Sept. M-F noon-1:30pm.)

MUSIC

The **Seattle Opera** performs from October to August in **McCaw Hall.** The culmination of a 10-year renovation project, the Opera House reopened in 2003, with a glass facade, decked-out lobbies, and a modernized auditorium. Opera buffs should reserve in advance, but rush tickets are sometimes available. (☎389-7676 or 800-426-1619; www.seattleopera.com. Ticket office at 1020 John St., below the 13 Coins Restaurant parking lot. Students and seniors can get half-price tickets 1½hr. before performances at the ticket office. Open M-F 9am-5pm. Tickets from $35.) The **Seattle Symphony** performs in the beautiful **Benaroya Hall,** 200 University St., at 3rd Ave., from September to June. Free organ concerts attract crowds on the first Monday of every month at 12:30pm. (☎212-4700, tickets 215-4747; www.seattlesymphony.org. Ticket office open M-F 10am-6pm, Sa 1-6pm. Ticket prices vary by concert, but most nights have a limited amount of $15 seats; most tickets $25-39; seniors and students $10 day of show when available.)

THEATER AND CINEMA

Seattle has many plays and alternative works, particularly by talented amateur groups. Rush tickets are often available at half-price on the day of the show from **Ticket/Ticket.** (☎324-2744. Locations in Capitol Hill and Pike Place. Cash only.) **The Empty Space Theatre,** 3509 Fremont Ave. N, 1½ blocks north of the Fremont Bridge, presents comedies from October to early July. (☎547-7500. Tickets $20-40. Half-price tickets 30min. before curtain.) **Seattle Repertory Theater,** 155 Mercer St., at the Bagley Wright Theater in the Seattle Center, has winter productions. (☎443-2222; www.seattlerep.org. Tickets $15-45, ages 65+ $32, under 25 $10. Rush tickets 30min. before curtain. Ticket office open M-F 10am-6pm.)

Seattle is a cinephile's paradise. Most of the theaters screening non-Hollywood films are on Capitol Hill and in the University District. On summer Saturdays (mid-June to late August), **Fremont Outdoor Movies** begins at dusk at the corner of 35th Ave. and Finney Ave. N. in Fremont, in the U-Park lot. (☎781-4230. Entrance 7pm; live music 8pm. $5.) **The Egyptian,** 801 E. Pine St., at Harvard Ave. on Capitol Hill, hosts the **Seattle International Film Festival** (☎324-9997; www.seattlefilm.com) at the end of May and the first week of June. (☎781-5755. $9, seniors $6.)

SPORTS

The Mariners, or "M's," play baseball in the half-billion-dollar, hangar-like **Safeco Field,** at 1st Ave. S and Royal Brougham Way S, under a giant retractable roof. (☎622-4487; www.mariners.org. Tickets from $7.) The NHL **Seahawks** play in the newly and recently dubbed **Qwest Field,** one of the most modern football fields in the world. (☎628-0888; www.seahawks.com. Tickets from $33.) On the other side of town, **Key Arena,** in the Seattle Center, hosts Seattle's NBA basketball team, the **Supersonics.** (☎628-0888; www.supersonics.com. Tickets from $9.)

❄ FESTIVALS

Pick up the visitors center's *Calendar of Events* (www.seeseattle.org/events) for coupons and listings. The first Thursday of each month, the art community sponsors **First Thursday,** a free gallery walk where galleries and art cafes open to the city. The **Fremont Fair** (☎694-6706; www.fremontfair.com), in honor of the summer solstice, is in mid-June, with the **Fremont Solstice Parade,** led by dozens of bicyclists wearing only body paint. The International District holds an annual two-day bash in mid-July, with arts and crafts, East Asian and Pacific food booths, and presentations by groups from the Radical Women/Freedom Socialist Party to cultural dancers. Call **Chinatown Discovery** for info (☎382-1197; www.seattlechinatowntour.com). **Bumbershoot,** a giant four-day festival, caps off Labor Day weekend with major rock bands, street musicians, and a young, exuberant crowd. (☎281-7788; www.bumbershoot.org. 4 days $55 in advance, up to $85 day of; 2 days $30-45; 1 day $18-28. Some events require additional tickets.)

Puget Sound's yachting season starts in May. **Maritime Week,** in the third week of May, and the **Shilshole Boats Afloat Show** (☎634-0911; www.boatsafloatshow.com), in mid-September, let boaters show off their craft. Over the 4th of July weekend, the Center for Wooden Boats sponsors the free **Wooden Boat Festival and Classic Speedboat Show** (☎382-2628; www.cwb.org) on Lake Union, which includes a demonstration of boat-building skills. The finale is the **Quick and Daring Boatbuilding Contest,** in which competitors sail wooden boats of their own design that they built in the previous 24hr. using limited tools and materials.

◀ NIGHTLIFE

DOWNTOWN

▨ **The Alibi Room,** 85 Pike St. (☎623-3180; www.alibiroom.com), across from Market Theater, in Post Alley in Pike Place. A friendly indie filmmaker-type hangout, with a bookshelf of scripts at the entrance. Bar with music. Downstairs dance floor open F-Sa. Mediterranean-style cuisine; brunch Sa-Su. Open daily 11am-2am.

Club Noc Noc, 1516 2nd Ave., between Pike and Pine (☎223-1333; www.clubnocnoc.com). Casual and spacious, with exposed brick walls, lots of red lighting, and a dance floor, Club Noc Noc embraces everyone from goths to frat boys. Drink specials feature Pabst Blue Ribbon (M $0.50, Su $0.25) and an outstanding 5-9pm happy hour ($2 for drinks). Cover $5 after 9pm. Open daily 5pm-2am.

PIONEER SQUARE

Pioneer Square is a hot spot, hopping with twentysomethings and cover bands.

J & M Cafe and Cardroom, 201 1st Ave. (☎292-0663), is in the center of Pioneer Sq. A member of the "Club Stamp," which gives patrons access to a total of nine participating Pioneer Sq. bars for a single cover charge (M-Th and Su $5, F-Sa $10).

Contour, 807 1st Ave. (☎447-7704; www.clubcontour.com). Intimate and elegant, the paintings, windows, and swanky statues make for a decadent dance spot. Happy hour M-F 3-8pm, Sa-Su 2-8pm, with $2 food, $2 beer, and $3.50 cocktails. Cover up to $12. Open M 3pm-2am, Tu-Th 11:30am-2am, F 11:30am-5am, Sa 2pm-5am, Su 2pm-2am.

CAPITOL HILL

East off Broadway, Pine St. is a lively, funky low-rise neighborhood with numerous clubs and bars.

▨ **Linda's Tavern,** 707 E. Pine St. (☎325-1220). A quirky post-gig local scene with pool tables and comfort food ($4-10). On Tu DJ spins jazz, alternative, and rock. Happy hour 7-9pm. Open daily 4pm-2am.

Neighbours, 1509 Broadway (☎324-5358; www.neighboursonline.com). Enter from the alley off Pike. A fixture in Seattle's gay scene, Neighbours is a techno-slick dance club. Frequent drag nights. Open Tu-W and Su 4pm-2am, Th 4pm-3am, F-Sa 4pm-4am.

⚔ OUTDOOR ACTIVITIES

Biking is very popular in Seattle: the city prides itself on 30 mi. of bike-pedestrian trails, 90 mi. of signed bike routes, and 16 mi. of bike lanes on city streets. Each year up to 8000 cyclists participate in the 190 mi. **Seattle to Portland Classic (STP)** in late June or early July. Call the **Cascade Bicycle Club** (☎522-2453; www.cascade.org) for info. On **Bicycle Saturdays/Sundays** from May to September, Lake Washington Blvd. is open only to cyclists 10am-6pm (usually on the second Saturday and third Sunday of each month). Contact the **Seattle Parks and Recreation Activities Office** (☎684-4075; www.cityofseattle.net/parks) for info. For hiking opportunities outside the city, see **North Bend and Snoqualmie** (p. 967).

▶ DAYTRIP FROM SEATTLE

VASHON ISLAND

Vashon Island stretches between Seattle and Tacoma on its east side and between South-worth and Gig Harbor in the west. Washington State Ferries (☎464-6400 or 800-843-3779; www.wsdot.wa.gov/ferries) runs a passenger-only ferry to Vashon Island from Seattle (see Transportation, p. 957). Car-accessible ferries to Vashon Island depart frequently from West Seattle (20min. from Fauntleroy). Visit www.wsdot.wa.gov/ferries/for more info. To reach the town of Vashon, 4½ mi. south from the ferry terminal, take either bus #118 or 119 (fares same as Seattle).

Only a 25min. ferry ride from Seattle, Vashon Island is like the San Juan Islands without the tourists. Most of the island is covered in Douglas fir, rolling cherry orchards, wildflowers, and strawberry fields, and all roads lead to rocky beaches. **Point Robinson Park** is a gorgeous spot for a picnic; free tours (☎217-6123) of the 1885 **Coast Guard lighthouse** are available. **Vashon Island Kayak Co.**, at Burton Acres Park, Jensen Point Boat Launch, runs guided tours and rents sea kayaks. (☎463-9257. Open F-Su 10am-5pm. Singles $18 per hr., $58 per day; doubles $28/$80.) Over 500 acres of woods in the middle of the island are interlaced with hiking and mountain biking trails. The **Vashon Park District** has more info. (☎463-9602; www.vashonparkdistrict.org. Open daily 8am-4pm.) The ▨**Vashon Island AYH Ranch Hostel (HI)** ❶, at 12119 SW Cove Rd., west of Vashon Hwy., is a rural haven with a laid-back vibe. "The ranch" offers bunks, Sioux teepees, and even covered wagons. (☎463-2592; www.vashonhostel.com. Free pancake breakfast and 1-speed bikes. Mountain bikes $6 per day. Office open 9am-10pm; later check-in can be arranged. Full hostel open May-Oct.; private double open year-round. Dorms $19, members $16. Private double $45/$55; $10 per extra person; children half-price. Shuttle to morning ferry $2. MC/V.) The **Chamber of Commerce**, 17232 SW Vashon Hwy., has maps and a friendly staff willing to point visitors in the right direction. (☎463-6217; www.vashonchamber.com. Open Tu-Sa 10am-3pm.)

NORTH BEND AND SNOQUALMIE   ☎425

Though only 30 mi. outside Seattle, the towns of North Bend and Snoqualmie feel like distant mountain outposts. The area—called the **Snoqualmie Valley**—is a gateway between the Cascades and the lowlands surrounding Puget Sound. Just downstream of Snoqualmie and a few steps from the road, **Snoqualmie Falls** plummets a spectacular 270 ft. onto the rocks below. One hundred feet taller than Niagara Falls, Snoqualmie Falls is Washington's second-most popular natural attraction, following Mount Rainier. View the falls from the vista spot above or via the steep, short hike down to the base. The view from the bottom is stunning; just be prepared for a substantial trek back. (Take the Snoqualmie Parkway exit from I-90.) Looming over North Bend in nearby **Tiger Mountain State Forest** is craggy **Mount Si,** home to one of the region's most popular trails (the **Mount Si Trail**). With approximately 3700 ft. of elevation gain over 4 mi., the hike is a training ground for local distance runners. The trail ends at **Haystack Basin,** a false summit; do not proceed higher without the appropriate rock-climbing equipment. (Take I-90 E to SE Mt. Si Rd., 2 mi. from Middle Fork.) The more mild **Twin Falls Trail** (2½ mi. round-trip) in **Olallie State Park,** just east of North Bend, passes by giant moss-covered trees, one of the twin waterfalls, and a 125 ft. wide gorge. (Take Exit 34 off I-90, turn right, and follow signs.) The area also offers ample opportunities for biking, kayaking, and fishing. The **Snoqualmie Valley Chamber of Commerce** has more info (see below).

Those looking to spend the night in the area can find camping nearby at **Tinkham Campground ❶,** 12 mi. east of North Bend (take Exit 42 off I-90, turn right onto Tinkham Rd. 55; the campground is on the left). The bulk of the sites can be reserved (☎877-444-6777; reserveusa.com), though a handful are first come, first served sites (all sites $16). If staying in town better suits your fancy, the **Sunset Motel ❷** at 227 W. North Bend Way in North Bend provides basic rooms. (☎888-0381. Singles $50-65, doubles $65. AmEx/D/MC/V.) North Bend has no shortage of inexpensive food options. ◪**George's Bakery and Deli ❷,** 127 North Bend Way, is a cozy spot serving delectable pastries, quiche, and sandwiches. (☎888-0632. Open Tu-F 6:30am-5pm, Sa 7:30am-5:30pm, Su 7:30am-5pm. MC/V.) For the some of the best burgers in the Northwest with a side of unpretentious, old-fashioned character, stop in at **Scott's Dairy Freeze ❶,** 234 E. North Bend Way. (☎888-2301. Burgers $3-5. Shakes $2-3. Open daily 10am-9pm. MC/V.)

The **Snoqualmie Valley Chamber of Commerce:** P.O. Box 357, North Bend, WA, 98045 (☎888-4440; www.snovalley.org. Take Exit 31 off I-90 E to North Bend). **Internet Access: North Bend Library,** 115 E. 4th St. (☎888-0554. Open M-Th 10:30am-8:30pm, F 10:30am-6pm, Sa 10:30am-5pm, Su 1-5pm.) **Post Office:** 451 E North Bend Way in North Bend (☎800-275-8777. Open M-F 9am-5pm, Sa 10am-2pm); 8264 Olmstead Ln. SE in Snoqualmie (☎800-275-8777. M-F 9am-4:30pm). **Postal Code:** 98045 (North Bend); 98065 (Snoqualmie). **Area Code:** 425.

OLYMPIA   ☎360

From musicians and artists to state politicians, an undeniably diverse crowd occupies Washington's capital city. Evergreen State College lies a few miles from the city center, throwing a liberal, tree-hugging student body into the mix. Located at the southern end of Puget Sound, Olympia is a gateway to the Olympic Peninsula and only a short hop from Mt. Rainier and the rest of the Cascade range. With a population just over 40,000, the city has a pleasant daytime town feel that transforms into a remarkably active bar scene at night.

◪ **PRACTICAL INFORMATION.** Settled at the junction of **I-5** and **U.S. 101** between **Tumwater** (to the south, I-5 Exit 102) and **Lacey** (to the east, I-5 Exit 108), Olympia makes a convenient stop on any north-south journey. **Amtrak,** 6600 Yelm Hwy. (☎923-4602; www.amtrak.com; open daily 8:15am-noon, 1:45-3:30pm, and 5:30-8:30pm), runs to Portland (2-2½hr., 4 per day, $18-23) and Seattle (1¾hr., 4 per day, $13-16). **Greyhound,** 107 7th Ave. SE (☎357-5541; www.greyhound.com), at Capitol Way, goes to Portland (2¾hr., 5 per day, $22-24) and Seattle (1¾hr., 5-6 per day, $9-10). **Intercity Transit (IT)** runs almost everywhere in Thurston County. (☎786-1881 or 800-287-6348; www.intercitytransit.com. $0.75; day pass $1.50.) **Visitor Info: Washington State Capitol Visitors Center,** 103 14th Ave. SW; follow the signs from I-5. (☎586-3460; www.ga.wa.gov/visitor. Open M-F 8am-5pm; May-Sept. also Sa-Su 9am-4pm.) The **Olympic National Forest Headquarters,** 1835 Black Lake Blvd. SW, has info on trails and camping. (☎956-2400; www.fs.fed.us/r6/olympic. Open M-F 8am-4:30pm.) **Post Office:** 900 Jefferson St. SE (☎357-2289. Open M-F 7:30am-6pm, Sa 9am-4pm.) **Postal Code:** 98501. **Area Code:** 360.

ACCOMMODATIONS AND FOOD. Motels in Olympia and their $60-80 rooms generally cater to policy-makers; chains in nearby Tumwater are more affordable. Try **Motel 6 ②,** 400 W. Lee St. (☎754-7320. Singles from $40; doubles from $46). **Millersylvania State Park ❶,** 12245 Tilly Rd. S, 10 mi. south of Olympia, has 168 sites. Take Exit 95 off I-5, turn onto Rte. 121 N, and follow signs. (☎753-1519, reservations 888-226-7688. Showers $0.25 per 3min. Hiker or biker sites $10; drive-in sites $16, with hookup $22.) Diners, veggie eateries, and Asian quickstops line 4th Ave. east of Columbia. The **⛽Olympia Farmers Market,** 700 N. Capitol Way, sells baked goods and other fantastic fare. (☎352-9096; www.farmers-market.org. Open Apr.-Oct. Th-Su 10am-3pm; Nov.-Dec. Sa-Su 10am-3pm.) **The Spar Cafe & Bar ❸,** 114 E. 4th Ave., has been an icon for beer, burgers, and cigars for decades. (☎357-6444. Live jazz Sa. Cafe open M-Th 6am-9pm, F-Sa 6am-10pm, Su 6am-8pm; bar open M-Th 11am-midnight, F-Sa 11am-2am. AmEx/D/DC/MC/V.)

SIGHTS. Olympia's crowning glory is the **State Capitol,** 416 14th Ave. SW, a complex of government buildings, fountains, manicured gardens, veterans' monuments, and the phenomenal, recently remodeled Legislative Building, styled after St. Peter's Basilica in Rome. Tours depart from just inside the front steps, at 4th and Capitol. (☎902-8880. Tours every hr. daily. 10am-3pm. Building open M-F 8am-5pm, Sa-Su 10am-4pm.) **Wolf Haven International,** 3111 Offut Lake Rd., 10 mi. south of the capital, is a permanent home for captive-born gray wolves reclaimed from zoos and illegal owners. Tours offer an up-close look at this beautiful, oft-vilified species. (☎264-4695 or 800-448-9653; www.wolfhaven.org. Open May-Sept. M and W-Su 10am-5pm; Oct.-Apr. M and W-Su 10am-4pm. 45min. tours every hr., last tour leaves 1hr. before closing. $7, seniors $6, ages 3-12 $5.) The **Nisqually National Wildlife Refuge** shelters 500 species of plants and animals by protecting the Nisqually River's estuary and its diverse mix of tidal mudflats, marshes, grasslands, and forest ecosystems, all laced with miles of trails. Visitors come to walk and to birdwatch, as both bald eagles and Northern spotted owls nest in the area. The visitors center loans out free binoculars and info packets—just leave behind some form of ID. Take Exit 114 off I-5 between Olympia and Tacoma. (☎753-9467; www.nisqually.fws.gov. Visitors center office open W-Su 9am-4pm. Park office open M-F 7:30am-4pm. Park open dawn-dusk. Trails closed to cyclists, joggers, and pets. $3 per car.)

NIGHTLIFE. Olympia's thriving nightlife seems to have outgrown its daylife. The *Olympian* (www.theolympian.com) lists live music events. **⛽Fishbowl Brewpub,** 515 Jefferson St. SE, reflects Olympia's love for the sea and beer: the British ales served here are named after fish. (☎943-3650; www.fishbrewing.com. Ales $3.50. Happy hour M-Th 10-11pm. Open M-Sa 11am-midnight, Su noon-10pm.) At **Eastside Club and Tavern,** 410 E. 4th St., old and young come to dance, play pool, and sip microbrews. (☎357-9985; www.olywa.net/dwight/eastsideclub. Pints $2.75, M $1.75, Th $2. Happy hour with $2.25 pints daily 4-7pm. Open M-F noon-2am, Sa-Su 3pm-2am.) Townsfolk gather for "slabs" of pizza, seafood baskets, and

26 regional microbrews at **4th Avenue Alehouse & Eatery,** 210 4th Ave. E. (☎786-1444; www.the4thave.com. Pizza $5.25. Pints $3. Happy hour daily 5-7pm. Live music Th-Sa 9pm. Cover $3-10. Open M-F 11:30am-2am, F-Sa noon-2am.)

SAN JUAN ISLANDS ☎360

Made up of hundreds of tiny islands and forested parks, the San Juan Islands are an explorer's dream, enjoying nearly perfect weather. From May to September, the sun shines almost every day, and only a few inches of rain fall each summer month in this "rain shadow" of the Olympic Mountains. Tourists storm the islands in July and August; early June and September tend to be slightly less packed.

▐ INTER-ISLAND TRANSPORTATION

Washington State Ferries, has frequent daily service to Lopez (50min.), Orcas (1½hr.), San Juan Island (1½hr.), and Shaw (1¼hr.) from Anacortes. Travel time to the islands depends on the number of stops. To save on fares, travel directly to the westernmost island on your itinerary, then return: eastbound traffic travels for free. The ferries are packed in the summer so arrive at least 1hr. (2hr. on weekends) before departure. (☎206-464-6400 or 800-843-3779; www.wsdot.wa.gov/ferries. May to mid-Oct. $12, vehicles $33, bikes $4; mid-Oct. to May $10/$25/$2. Cash only outside Anacortes. Eastbound traffic free. Westbound inter-island: passengers free, vehicles $17.40.) The **Bellingham Airporter** (☎380-8800 or 866-235-5247; www.airporter.com) shuttles between Sea-Tac and Anacortes (12 per day to Anacortes, 10 per day continue to ferries; $31). **Island Commuter** (☎738-8099 or 800-443-4552; www.islandcommuter.com) departs Bellingham for Friday Harbor (2½hr., 1 per day) and islands on the way ($39, round-trip $49; ages 6-12 $25/$20; under 6 free). **Victoria Clipper** (☎800-888-2535; www.victoriaclipper.com) departs Seattle's Pier 69 daily for San Juan Island, arriving at Spring St. landing in Friday Harbor (2½hr.; 2 per day; round-trip $110/$133, ages 11 and under $33-40).

SAN JUAN ISLAND
The biggest and most popular of the islands, San Juan is easy to explore because the ferry docks right in town, the roads are good for cyclists, and a shuttle bus services the island. The **West Side Road** traverses gorgeous scenery and provides the best chance for seeing orcas. Mullis Rd. merges with Cattle Point Rd. and goes straight into **American Camp,** on the south side of the island, one of two parts of the **San Juan National Historical Park. English Camp,** the second half of the park, lies on West Valley Rd. in **Garrison Bay.** (Buildings open June-Aug. daily 9am-5pm.) On Saturday afternoons in June and July, the two camps alternate performing re-enactments of daily life from the time of the Pig War, a mid-19th-century squabble between the US and Britain over control of the islands. (☎378-2240. Open June-Aug. daily dawn-11pm; Sept.-May Th-Su dawn-11pm. Visitors centers open June-Aug. daily 8:30am-5pm; Sept.-May Th-Su 8:30am-4:30pm. Guided walks June-Sept. Sa 11:30am. Re-enactments Sa 12:30-3:30.) **Lime Kiln Point State Park,** along West Side Rd., is the best whale-watching spot in the area.

📖**Wayfarer's Rest ❶,** 35 Malcolm St., is a 10min. walk from the ferry onto Argyle St.; turn left at the church. This house-turned-hostel has driftwood bunks, a patio, a full kitchen, and laundry. (☎378-6428; www.rockisland.com/~wayfarersrest. Linens included. Bike rental $15 per day. Check-in 2-9pm. May-Sept. dorms $25; private rooms and cabins from $60. Oct.-April $22/$55. MC/V.) **San Juan County Park ❶,** 50 San Juan Park Rd., 10 mi. west of Friday Harbor, has 20 sites perched on a bluff with a fantastic sunset view. (☎378-1842; www.co.san-juan.wa.us/parks. Reservations strongly recommended in summer; in winter, all sites are first come, first served. Reservation fee $7. Sites $6; vehicle sites $25.) **Hungry Clam Fish and Chips ❷**, 130 1st St., serves fresh beer-battered seafood. (☎378-3474. Open daily late May to early Sept. 11am-9pm; early Sept. to late May 11am-7pm. MC/V.)

San Juan Transit (☎378-8887 or 800-887-8387; www.sanjuantransit.com) travels from Friday Harbor to Roche Harbor on the hour. ($5; day pass $10. Tours depart Friday Harbor at 11am and 1:30pm. $17.) **Island Bicycles,** 380 Argyle Ave. rents bikes. (☎378-4941; www.islandbicycles.com. $7 per hr., $35 per day. Open daily 9am-6pm.) The **Chamber of Commerce,** 1 Front St. 2A, is at Front and Spring St. (☎378-5240 or 888-468-3701; www.sanjuanisland.org or www.guidetosanjuans.com. Open Apr.-Nov. M-F 10am-4pm. Call for low-season hours.)

ORCAS ISLAND

A small population of retirees, artists, and farmers dwells here in understated homes surrounded by red madrona trees. **Moran State Park** is unquestionably Orcas' star attraction. Over 30 mi. of hiking trails range from a 1hr. jaunt around **Mountain Lake** to a day-long trek up the south face of **Mount Constitution** (2407 ft.), the highest peak on the islands. The peak also offers one of the best 360° marine viewpoints in North America. Partway down, **Cascade Falls** is spectacular in the spring and early summer. South of Moran, the trail to **Obstruction Pass Beach** is the best way to clamber down to the rocky shores. **Shearwater Adventures** runs sea kayak tours exploring various parts of the island. (☎376-4699; shearwaterkayaks.com. 3hr. tour with 30min. of dry-land training $49 per person.) **Crescent Beach Kayak,** on the highway 1 mi. east of Eastsound, rents kayaks for use around Crescent Beach. (☎376-2464. $18 per hr., $50 per half-day. Open daily 9am-7pm.)

Doe Bay Resort ❶, on Pt. Lawrence Rd., off Olga Rd., is a relaxing former commune complete with a clothing-optional hot tub and yoga classes. (☎376-2291; www.doebay.com. Sauna $10 per day. 1½hr. yoga classes $10. Reception 11am-9pm. Dorms M-Th and Su $20, F-Sa $25; camping $30/$35; private rooms from $50/$55; yurts $70/$75. MC/V.) The resort also houses a **cafe ❷**, which serves organic dishes. (☎376-8059. Open daily 8am-2pm; W-Su also 5-9pm. MC/V.) **Moran State Park ❶**, on Horseshoe Hwy. (Olga Rd.), is 15 mi. from the ferry landing. Follow Horseshoe Hwy. into the park, 14 mi. from the ferry on the east side of the island. The 151 campgrounds spread out along **Cascade Lake are** the islands' most popular camping. (☎902-8844, reservations 888-226-7688. 12 primitive sites open year-round. Showers $0.50 per 3min. Standard sites $16; primitive sites $10.)

THE BIG SPLURGE

TAKE THE PLUNGE

Don't come to the San Juan Islands—or anywhere in the Pacific Northwest, for that matter—expecting to spend much time in the ocean. With water temperatures in the San Juans hovering at 48-52°F year-round, swimming isn't much of an option. As a result, visitors to the San Juans choose between two options: kayaking or a whale-watching tour. Whale-watching cruises cover a lot of distance and offer a chance to see orcas, but feel like a ferry ride; kayaking gets you up close to the water, but you can't cover a lot of distance.

Eagle's Eye Tours, owned and operated by Captain Nan Simpson, offers the best of both worlds for those willing to pay a little extra. Passengers don weatherproof mustang suits and explore the waterways of the San Juans in Nan's 21 ft. Bullfrog boat. The boat is small enough to maneuver close to shore, right at water level, and moves much faster than any sloth-like whale-cruiser. You'll also get a highly personal tour for your money: there are no more than six passengers at a time, and Nan stops the boat to recount local history and point out bald eagles.

Eagle's Eye Tours (☎472-0296; www.eagleseyetours.com). 2hr. trips $75; 10% discount for seniors, military, students, teachers, and nurses. Charter trips for up to 6 people $350. No children under 12.

The ferry lands on the southwest tip of Orcas; the main town of Eastsound is 9 mi. northeast. Olga and Doe Bay are an additional 8 and 11 mi., respectively, down the island's eastern side. **Orcas Island Shuttle** (☎376-7433; www.orcasislandshuttle.com) runs public buses through most of the island ($5; day pass $10; bikes $1 extra per ride). **Dolphin Bay Bicycles,** at the ferry landing, rents bikes for $30 per day. (☎376-4157; www.rockisland.com/~dolphin. Reservations recommended.)

LOPEZ ISLAND

Smaller than either Orcas or San Juan, Lopez lacks some of the tourist facilities of the larger islands. Still, the island is a blessing for those looking for solitary beaches, bicycling without car traffic, and a small-town atmosphere. On the southwest end of the island, the small **Shark Reef County Park** has well-maintained hiking trails leading to a rocky beach. The even smaller **Agate Beach Country Park** is home to a calm, deserted beach. **Lopez Village** is a tiny town 4½ mi. from the ferry dock off Fisherman Bay Rd. Roads on the island are ideal for biking. To rent a bike, go to **Lopez Bicycle Works** (☎468-2847; www.lopezbicycleworks.com. Open Apr.-Oct. daily 10am-5pm. Bikes $7 per hr., $30 per day.) **Spencer Spit State Park ❶,** on the northeast corner of the island about 3½ mi. from the ferry terminal, has seven beach sites and 30 wooded sites. (☎468-2251, reservations 888-226-7688. Park open Apr.-Oct. dawn-10pm. Sites $16. Reservations required.) Find delicious breads ($3-5) and pastries ($3) at **◼Holly B's Bakery ❶,** Lopez Plaza in Lopez Village. The ham and gruyère croissant ($3) is a favorite. (☎468-2133. Open early Apr. to late Nov. M and W-Sa 7am-5pm, Su 7am-4pm; winter hours vary. Cash only.)

OLYMPIC PENINSULA

Due west of Seattle and its busy Puget Sound neighbors, the Olympic Peninsula is a backpacking paradise. Olympic National Park dominates much of the peninsula, preserving its glacier-capped mountains and temperate rainforests. To the west, the Pacific Ocean stretches from rugged beaches to a distant horizon; to the north, the Strait of Juan de Fuca separates the Olympic Peninsula from Vancouver Island; and to the east, Hood Canal and the Kitsap Peninsula isolate this sparsely inhabited wilderness from Seattle's urban sprawl.

PORT TOWNSEND   ☎360

When rumors circulated in the late 1800s that the railroad would connect Port Townsend to the east, wealthy families flocked to the overlooking bluffs, constructing elaborate Victorian homes and stately public buildings. The railroad actually bypassed Port Townsend, but the neglected town was rediscovered in the 1970s and turned into a vibrant and creative community. Now, in addition to cafes, galleries, and bookstores, Port Townsend takes advantage of its 19th-century flavor to entice those heading to the park onto Rte. 20 into town. The **Ann Starrett Mansion,** 744 Clay St., has nationally renowned Victorian architecture, frescoed ceilings, and a three-tiered spiral staircase. (☎385-3205 or 800-321-0644; www.starrettmansion.com. Tours daily noon-3pm. $3.) **Point Hudson,** where Admiralty Inlet and Port Townsend Bay meet, is the hub of a small shipbuilding area. Check out boatbuilders crafting sea kayaks and sailboats. North of Point Hudson are several miles of beach and the beautiful **Chetzemoka Park,** at Garfield and Jackson St., with an ocean view and endless manicured flowerbeds.

The **◼Olympic Hostel (HI) ❶,** 272 Battery Way, in Fort Worden State Park, 1½ mi. from town, is a converted WWII barracks and one of the best hostels in the Pacific Northwest with its immaculate rooms and beautiful setting. (☎385-0655; www.olympichostel.org. Make-your-own pancake breakfast $2-3. Linen $2.

Check-in 5-10pm. Check-out 9:30am. Reservations recommended. Dorms $17, members $14. MC/V.) To reach the small, homey **Marrowstone Island Hostel (HI) ❶**, 10621 Flagler Rd., in Fort Flagler State Park on Marrowstone Island and 20 mi. from Port Townsend, go south on Rte. 19, which connects to Rte. 116 E and leads into the park. (☎385-1288. Check-in 5-10pm. Lockout 10am-5pm. Reservations recommended. Open June-Sept. Dorms $17, members $14. MC/V.) Camp close to the beach or in the nearby forest at the 116-site **Fort Flagler State Park ❶**. (☎385-1259. Check-in 2:30pm. Check-out 1pm. Quiet hours 10pm-6:30am. Open for camping Mar.-Oct. Reservations recommended. Hiker or biker sites $10; car $16; RV $22.) Dine on delicious organic cuisine at the cheery **Sweet Laurette & Cyndee's Cafe and Patisserie ❷**, 1029 Lawrence St., uptown. The lemon ricotta pancakes are particularly tasty. (☎385-4880. Breakfast $5-9. Lunch $7-12. Open M-F 7am-5pm, Sa 8am-5pm, Su 8am-3pm. MC/V.) **El Sarape ❷**, 628 Water St., serves a variety of Mexican dishes with a full bar to boot. (☎379-9343. Burritos $5-7. Dinner $7-11. Open in summer M-Th and Su 11am-9pm, F-Sa 11am-10pm; in winter M-Th and Su 11am-8pm, F-Sa 11am-9pm. AmEx/D/MC/V.)

Port Townsend sits at the terminus of **Route 20** on the northeastern corner of the Olympic Peninsula. It can be reached by **U.S. 101**, or from the Kitsap Peninsula across the Hood Canal Bridge. From Poulsbo, **Jefferson County Transit** runs to Port Townsend. (☎385-4777; www.jeffersontransit.com. M-F 4 per day, Sa-Su 2 per day. $1.25.) **Washington State Ferries** (☎206-464-6400; www.wsdot.wa.gov/ferries) go between Port Townsend and Keystone on Whidby Island (30min.; $2.35, car and driver $8.20-10.30). **P.T. Cyclery**, 232 Tyler St., rents mountain bikes. (☎385-6470; www.olympus.net/ptcyclery. $7 per hr., $25 per day. Open M-Sa 9am-6pm.) **Visitor Info: Port Townsend Chamber of Commerce**, 2437 E. Sims Way, southwest of town on Rte. 20. (☎385-2722 or 888-365-6978; www.ptchamber.org. Open M-F 9am-5pm, Sa 10am-4pm, Su 11am-4pm.) **Post Office:** 1322 Washington St. (☎385-1600. Open M-F 9am-5pm, Sa 10am-2pm.) **Postal Code:** 98368. **Area Code:** 360.

OLYMPIC NATIONAL PARK ☎360

Olympic National Park (ONP) is certainly the centerpiece of the Olympic Peninsula, sheltering one of the most diverse landscapes of any region in the world. The towering peaks, covered in snow from the water-laden winds and drastically carved by ancient glaciers, form the most dramatic feature of the park. Roads lead to many corners of Olympic National Park, but with over 90% of the park roadless, they only hint at the depths of its wilderness. A foray into the backcountry leaves summer tourists behind and reveals the park's richness and diversity.

▉✴ ❼ ORIENTATION AND PRACTICAL INFORMATION

Each side of the park has one major settlement—**Port Townsend** to the east, **Port Angeles** to the north, and **Forks** to the west. U.S. 101 forms an upside-down "U," passing through almost every small town. The park's eastern rim runs up to Port Townsend, from which the heavily-touristed northern rim extends westward. Along a winding detour on Rte. 112, off U.S. 101 going west, the tiny town of **Neah Bay** and stunning **Cape Flattery** perch at the tip of the peninsula. Temperate rainforests lie on the west side of ONP and in the **Hoh, Queets,** and **Quinalt River valleys,** where low valleys claim the ocean moisture before it slides up the mountains' sides. July, August, and September are the best months for visiting Olympic National Park, as roads and trails become saturated in early fall, though visitors can enjoy beach walks throughout spring and fall. **Entrance passes** are available at ranger stations and park entrances ($10 per car, $5 per hiker or biker; good for 1 week). **Olympic National Park Visitors Center**, 3002 Mt. Angeles Rd., is off Race St. in

Port Angeles. (☎565-3130; www.nps.gov/olym/home.htm. Open daily May to early Sept. 9am-4:30pm; late Sept. to Apr. 10am-4pm.) The staff at the **Olympic National Park Wilderness Information Center** (☎565-3100; www.nps.gov/olym/wic), just behind the visitors center, helps design trips within the park.

ACCOMMODATIONS

The closest budget accommodations are at the ▨**Rainforest Hostel ❶**, 169312 U.S. 101, 20 mi. south of Forks. Follow the signs from U.S. 101. The hostel boasts a large co-ed dorm, two rooms for couples, and a family room. (☎374-2270; www.rainforesthostel.com. Chore required. Internet $0.10 per min. for first 15min., $0.05 per additional min. Laundry $2. Sites $4.50. Dorms $8.50; couples rooms $18. Cash or traveler's checks only.) Olympic National Park maintains many **campgrounds ❶**, some of which can be reserved (☎800-280-2267; www.reserveusa.com), but most camping is first come, first served. **Backcountry camping ❶** in the park costs $2 per person per night, and there is a $5 registration fee per group. The Washington Department of Natural Resources allows free backcountry camping 300 ft. from any state road on DNR land, mostly accessible via the western shore along the Hoh and Clearwater Rivers. From July to September, most spaces are taken by 2pm, while very popular sites fill by noon.

OUTDOOR ACTIVITIES

EASTERN RIM

The eastern rim stuns visitors with its canals and grandiose views of the peninsula and Puget Sound. Steep trails lead up **Mt. Ellinor**, 5 mi. past Staircase on Rte. 119. Hikers can choose the 3 mi. path or an equally steep but shorter journey to the summit; look for signs to the Upper Trailhead along Forest Rd. #2419-04. Adventurers who hit the mountain before late July should bring snow clothes to "mach" (as in Mach 1) down a ¼ mi. snow chute. In the nearby National Forest, a 3¼ mi. hike goes to **Lena Lake**, 14 mi. north of Hoodsport off U.S. 101; follow Forest Service Rd. 25 off U.S. 101 for 8 mi. to the trailhead. The Forest Service charges $3 per trailhead pass. The **West Forks Dosewallip Trail**, a 10½ mi. trek to **Mount Anderson Glacier**, is the shortest route to any glacier in the park. The road to **Mount Walker Viewpoint**, 5 mi. south of Quilcene on U.S. 101, has sheer dropoffs and shouldn't be attempted in bad weather or a temperamental car. A view of Hood Canal, Puget Sound, Mt. Rainier, and Seattle awaits travelers at the top.

NORTHERN RIM

The most developed section of Olympic National Park lies along its northern rim, near the Port Angeles settlement, where glaciers, rainforests, and sunsets over the Pacific are only a short drive away. Farthest east off U.S. 101 lies **Deer Park**, where trails tend to be uncrowded. Past Deer Park, the **Royal Basin Trail** meanders 6¼ mi. to the **Royal Basin Waterfall**. The road up **Hurricane Ridge** is a curvy drive, so be cautious. Before July, walking on the ridge usually involves some snow-stepping. Clear days provide splendid views of Mt. Olympus and Vancouver Island set against a foreground of snow and indigo lupine. From here, the uphill **High Ridge Trail** is a short walk from Sunset Point. On weekends from late December to late March, the Park Service organizes snowshoe walks on the ridge. The **Sol Duc trailhead** is a starting point for those heading up, but crowds thin dramatically above **Sol Duc Falls**. The **Eagle Ranger Station** has information. (☎327-3534. Open in summer daily 8am-4:30pm.)

NEAH BAY AND CAPE FLATTERY

At the westernmost point on the Juan de Fuca Strait and north of the park's western rim is **Neah Bay,** known as the "Pompeii of the Pacific." The only town in the **Makah Reservation,** Neah Bay is a 500-year-old village that was buried in a landslide at Cape Alava. The Makah Nation, whose recorded history goes back 2000 years, still lives here. Just inside the reservation, the **Makah Cultural and Research Center,** in Neah Bay on Rte. 112, has artifacts from the archæological site. (☎645-2711; www.makah.com/mcrchome.htm. Open June to mid-Sept. daily 10am-5pm; mid-Sept. to May W-Su 10am-5pm. Free tours W-Su noon-4pm. $5, students and seniors $4.) For over 80 years, Native Americans from around the region have come for canoe races, dances, and bone games during **Makah Days,** a festival held the last weekend of August. (☎645-2711; www.makah.com/makahdays.htm. $7 permit required per car.) ▓**Cape Flattery,** the northwesternmost point in the contiguous US, lies just outside Neah Bay. Take the road through town until it turns to dirt, then past the "Marine Viewing Area" sign to a parking area where a half-mile trail leads to the breathtaking cape. **Clallam Transit System** runs bus #14 from Oak St. in Port Angeles to Sappho, then #16 to Neah Bay. (☎452-4511; www.clallamtransit.com. $0.75, ages 6-19 $0.50, seniors $0.25; day pass $2.) You can also reach Neah Bay and Cape Flattery by detour from U.S. 101. From Port Angeles, Rte. 112 leads west to Neah Bay; Rte. 113 runs north from Sappho to Rte. 112.

COASTAL ZONE

Pristine coastline traces the park's far western region for 57 mi., separated from the rest of ONP by U.S. 101 and non-park timber land. Eerie fields of driftwood, sculptured arches, and dripping caves frame flaming sunsets, while the waves are punctuated by rugged sea stacks. Between the Quinault and Hoh Reservations, U.S. 101 hugs the coast for 15 mi., with parking lots a short walk from the sand. North of where the highway meets the coast, **Beach #4** has abundant tide pools plastered with sea stars. **Beach #6,** 3 mi. north at Mi. 160, is a favorite whale-watching spot. Near Mi. 165, sea otters and eagles hang amid tide pools and sea stacks at **Ruby Beach.** Beach camping is permitted north of the Hoh Reservation between **Oil City** and **Third Beach** and north of the Quileute Reservation between **Hole-In-the-Wall** and **Shi-Shi Beach.** Day hikers and backpackers adore the 9 mi. loop that begins at **Ozette Lake.** The trail has two 3 mi. legs leading along boardwalks through the rainforest. One heads toward sea stacks at **Cape Alava,** and the other goes to a beach at **Sand Point.** A 3 mi. hike down the coast links the two legs, passing ancient petroglyphs. The **Ozette Ranger Station** has more info (☎963-2725). Campers should be sure to reserve permits (☎565-3100) in advance.

WESTERN RIM

In the rainforests of ONP's western rim, ferns, mosses, and giant old-growth trees blanket the earth. The drive along the **Hoh River Valley,** actively logged land, is alternately overgrown and barren. **Hoh Rainforest Visitors Center** is a 45min. drive from U.S. 101 on the western rim. (☎374-6925; www.nps.gov/olym. Open mid-June to early Sept. daily 9am-4pm; in winter F-Su only.) From the visitors center, take the ¾ mi. **Hall of Mosses Trail** for a tour of the rainforest. With a smattering of educational panels explaining natural quirks, the **Spruce Nature Trail** leads 1¼ mi. through the forest and along the Hoh River. The **Hoh Rainforest Trail** is the area's most heavily traveled path, starting at the visitors center and edging the Hoh River for 18 mi. before reaching **Blue Glacier** on the shoulder of Mt. Olympus. The 4 mi. **Quinault Lake Loop** and ½ mi. **Maple Glade Trail** leave from the **Quinault Ranger Station,** 353 S. Shore Rd. (☎288-2525. Open May-Sept. M-F 8am-4:30pm, Sa-Su 9am-4pm; Oct.-Apr. M-F 9am-4:30pm.) Snow-seekers go to **Three Lakes Point,** which is snowy until July. **Quinault Lake** lures anglers, rowers, and canoers. The **Lake Quinault Lodge,** by the ranger station, rents boats. (☎ 288-2900 or 800-562-6672; www.visitlakequinault.com. Rentals from $11 per hr.)

CASCADE RANGE

Intercepting the moist Pacific air, the Cascades divide Washington into the lush, wet green of the west and the dry plains of the east. The Cascades are most accessible from July to September; many of the mountain passes are snowed in during the rest of the year, making access extremely difficult. Mt. Baker, Vernon, Glacier, Adams, and the stunning Mt. Rainier and Mt. St. Helens are accessible by four major roads. The North Cascades Hwy. (Rte. 20) is the most breathtaking and runs to North Cascades National Park. Scenic U.S. 2 leaves Everett for Stevens Pass and descends along the Wenatchee River. U.S. 12 approaches Mt. Rainier through White Pass and reaches Mt. St. Helens from the north. I-90 sends four lanes from Seattle past the ski resorts of Snoqualmie Pass and eastward towards Spokane.

MOUNT SAINT HELENS   ☎ 360

In one cataclysmic blast on May 18, 1980, Mt. St. Helens erupted, transforming what had been a perfect cone into a crater. The force of the ash-filled blast reduced the mountain's height by 1300 ft. and razed forests, strewing trees like matchsticks. Ash from the crater rocketed 17 mi. upward, blackening the sky. The explosion was 27,000 times the force of the atomic bomb dropped on Hiroshima. Today, Mt. St. Helens is comprised of part of the **Gifford Pinchot National Forest,** as well as **Mount Saint Helens National Volcanic Monument.** Mt. St. Helens is still an active volcano and began to belch smoke and ash once more in September 2004.

■■ ■ **ORIENTATION AND PRACTICAL INFORMATION.** To take the most popular and worthwhile approach into town, take Exit 49 off **I-5** and use **Route 504,** otherwise known as the **Spirit Lake Memorial Highway.** The 52 mi. road has astounding views of the crater and includes the Mt. St. Helens Visitor Center, the Coldwater Ridge Visitor Center, and the Johnston Ridge Observatory. **Route 503** skirts the south side of the volcano until it becomes **Forest Service Road 90.** From there, **Forest Service Road 83** leads to lava caves and the Climber's Bivouac, a launching pad for treks up the mountain. Views from this side don't highlight the destruction from the 1980 eruption, but the green glens and remnants of age-old lava and mud flows make up for it with great camping and hiking. For a northern approach, take **U.S. 12** east from I-5 (Exit 68). The towns of **Mossyrock, Morton,** and **Randle** along U.S. 12 offer the closest major services. Vigorous winter rains often spoil access roads; check at a ranger station for road closures before heading out.

The monument charges entrance fees at almost every visitors center, viewpoint, and cave. (1-day all-access $6, ages 15 and under free. Individual monument fees $3/$1.) With interactive exhibits, **Mount Saint Helens Visitors Center,** across from Seaquest State Park on Rte. 504, is most visitors' first stop. A detailed exhibit looks at the events leading up to the 1980 eruption in increments of years, months, days, and finally, seconds. (☎ 274-0962. Open daily Apr. to late Oct. 9am-5pm; late Oct. to Mar. 9am-4pm.) **Coldwater Ridge Visitors Center,** 38 mi. farther on Rte. 504, has a superb view of the crater along with trails leading to Coldwater Lake. (☎ 274-2214. Open in summer daily 10am-6pm; call for winter hours.) Overlooking the crater, **Johnston Ridge Observatory,** at the end of Rte. 504, focuses on geological exhibits and offers the best roadside view of the crater. A fantastic 16min. film features a digital recreation of the blast that fills in the space between the famous stills depicting the eruption. (☎274-2143. Open May-Oct. daily 10am-6pm.) **Pine Creek Information Station,** 17 mi. east of Cougar on Rd. 90, shows a film of the eruption. This station is the only place in the south of the park with free water. (☎449-7800. Open mid-June to Sept. daily 9am-6pm.) **Apes Headquarters,** at Ape Cave on Rd. 8303 on the south side of the volcano, is 3 mi. north of the Rd. 83/ Rd. 90 junction. Rangers guide lantern walks into a 1900-year-old lava tube. (Open late May to Sept. daily 10am-5:30pm. Guided walks on the half-hour daily 10:30am-4:30pm.)

▐▐▌ CAMPING AND FOOD. Although the monument itself has no camp-grounds, a number are scattered throughout the surrounding national forest. Free dispersed camping is allowed within the monument, but finding a site takes luck. **Iron Creek Campground ❶** is the closest campsite to Mt. St. Helens, situated in a moss- and fern-filled forest with good hiking nearby. All 97 sites can fill up on busy weekends. (☎877-444-6777. Reservations strongly recommended in summer. Sites $16-18.) **Swift Campground ❶,** 30min. east of Cougar on Rd. 90, just west of the Pine Creek Information Station, has spacious sites on Swift Reservoir and is one of the most popular campgrounds in the area. Sites ($14) go on a first come, first served basis. Along Yale Lake are **Cougar Campground ❶** and **Beaver Bay ❶,** two and four miles east of Cougar, respectively. Cougar Lake has 60 sites that are more spread out and private than Beaver Bay's 78 sites; both first come, first served. (☎503-813-6666. Sites $14-26.) **Jack's Restaurant and Country Store ❷,** 13411 Louis River Rd., five miles west of Cougar (I-5 Exit 21) on Rte. 503, serves standard American fare. (☎231-4276. Breakfast $4-8. Lunch $6-9. Dinner $6-10. M pizza $2, beer $1. Tu all-you-can-eat shrimp. F all-you-can eat fish. Open M-Th and Su 6am-9pm, F-Sa 6am-10pm. AmEx/D/MC/V.) The only food on the eastern side of the monument is at **Cascade Peaks Restaurant ❶,** at Mi. 10 on Rd. 99, which serves basic, cafeteria-style food. (Burgers $4.50. Open daily 10am-6pm. MC/V.)

▐▌ OUTDOOR ACTIVITIES. Along each approach, short trails loop into the land-scape. The 1hr. drive from the Mt. St. Helens Visitors Center to Johnston Ridge offers spectacular views of the crater and its resurgence of life. Another 10 mi. east, the hike along **Johnston Ridge,** where geologist David Johnston died studying the eruption, offers unbeatable views of the crater. On the way west along Rd. 99, **Bear Meadow** provides the first stop, an excellent view of Mt. St. Helens, and the last restrooms before Rd. 99 ends at **Windy Ridge.** The monument begins just west of Bear Meadow, where Rd. 26 and 99 meet. Rangers lead ½ mi. walks around emerald **Meta Lake;** meet at Miner's Car at the junction of Rd. 26 and 99. (Tours 12:45 and 3pm daily late June to Sept.) Farther west on Rd. 99, **Independence Pass Trail #227** is a difficult 3½ mi. hike overlooking Spirit Lake, with views of the crater and dome. For a serious hike, continue along this trail to its intersection with the spectacular **Norway Pass Trail,** which runs 8 mi. through the blast zone to the newly reopened **Mt. Margaret peak.** Farther west, the 2 mi. **Harmony Trail #224** provides the only shore access to Spirit Lake. From Windy Ridge, a steep ash hill called the "sand ladder" grants a magnificent view of the crater from 3½ mi. away. Due to the recent activity, the mountain itself is closed indefinitely to hikers. Cavers should head to **Ape Cave,** 5 mi. east of Cougar just off Rd. 83. The cave is a broken 2½ mi. lava tube formed by an ancient eruption. When exploring the cave, wear a jacket and sturdy shoes, and take at least two flashlights or lanterns. Rangers lead 10 free guided cave explorations per day (p. 976).

PACIFIC NORTHWEST

MOUNT RAINIER NATIONAL PARK ☎360

At 14,411 ft., Mt. Rainier (ray-NEER) presides regally over the Cascade Range as the giant among giants. The Klickitat native people called it Tahoma, or "Mountain of God," but Rainier is simply "the Mountain" to most Washington residents. Perpetually snowcapped, this dormant volcano draws thousands of visitors from around the globe. Clouds mask the mountain at least 200 days each year, frustrating visitors who come solely to see its distinctive summit. Its sharp ridges, steep gullies, and glaciers make Rainier inhospitable to the thousands of climbers who attempt its summit each year. Non-alpinists can explore over 305 mi. of trails that weave through old-growth forests, alpine meadows, and bubbling hot springs.

■🛂 **ORIENTATION AND PRACTICAL INFORMATION.** To reach Mt. Rainier from the northwest, take **I-5** to Tacoma, then go east on **Route 512,** south on **Route 7,** and east on **Route 706.** Rte. 706, open year-round, runs through the town of Ashford and into the park by the **Nisqually** entrance, leading to the visitors centers of **Longmire** and **Paradise.** Snow usually closes all other park roads from November to May. **Stevens Canyon Road** connects the southeast corner of the national park with Paradise, Longmire, and the Nisqually entrance, unfolding superb vistas of Rainier and the Tatoosh Range along the way. Mt. Rainier is 65 mi. from Tacoma and 90 mi. from Seattle; call a ranger station for road updates.

The best place to plan a backcountry trip is at the **Longmire Wilderness Information Center** (☎569-4453; open late May to early Oct. daily 7:30am-5pm), east of the Nisqually entrance; or the **White River Wilderness Information Center** (☎569-6030; open late May to Sept. M-W and Su 7:30am-4:30 pm, Th-F 7:30am-8pm, Sa 7am-5pm), off Rte. 410 on the park's east side. Both distribute free **backcountry permits,** good for seven days. An **entrance fee** is required. ($10 per car, $5 per hiker. Gates open 24hr.) **Rainier Mountaineering, Inc. (RMI),** in the Rainier Base Camp complex on S.R. 706 E in Ashford, rents gear and leads summit climbs. (☎888-892-5462; www.rmiguides.com. Open May-Sept. daily 7am-8pm; Oct.-Apr. M-F 9am-5pm.) All kinds of equipment are available to rent or buy at **Summit Haus,** 30027 S.R. 706 E, in Ashford. (☎800-238-5756. Sleeping bag $30 per day; $50 per 5 days. Ice axe $15 per day; $30 per 5 days. Open daily in summer 7am-8pm; call for low-season hours.) **Post Office:** Inside National Park Inn, in Longmire. (Open M-F 8:30am-5pm, Sa 8:30am-noon.) **Postal Code:** 98397. **Area Code:** 360.

▐▐ **ACCOMMODATIONS AND FOOD. Hotel Packwood ❷,** 104 Main St., in Packwood, was established as a Historic Landmark in 1912. (☎494-5431; www.packwoodwa.com. Singles $29; doubles from $35. D/MC/V.) Originally a logger and mill worker's bunkhouse, **Whittaker's Bunkhouse ❶,** 6 mi. west of the Nisqually entrance, offers homey rooms loosely reminiscent of an alpine lodge, with a hot tub and espresso bar, but no kitchen or linens. (☎569-2439; whittakers-bunkhouse.com. Reservations strongly recommended. Bunks $30; private rooms $80-130. AmEx/MC/V.) **Camping ❶** in the park is first come, first served from mid-June to late September. (Low-season reservations ☎800-365-2267; http://reservations.nps.gov. Prices range from free to $15.) National park campgrounds all have wheelchair-accessible facilities, but no hookups or showers. Coin-operated showers are available at Jackson Memorial Visitors Center, in Paradise. **Sunshine Point ❶** (18 sites, $10), near the Nisqually entrance, and **Cougar Rock ❶** (200 sites, $15), 2¼ mi. north of Longmire, are in the southwest. The serene high canopy of **Ohanapecosh ❶** (205 sites, $15) is 11 mi. north of Packwood on Rte. 123, in the southeast. **White River ❶** (112 sites, $10) is 5 mi. west of White River on the way to Sunrise, in the northeast. **Backcountry camping** requires a **permit,** free from ranger stations and visitors centers. Fires are prohibited in the backcountry. Hikers with a valid permit can camp at trailside, alpine, and snowfield sites (most with toilets and water). **Blanton's Market,** 13040 U.S. 12, in Packwood, is the closest decent supermarket and has an ATM. (☎494-6101. Open M-F 7am-9pm, Sa-Su 7am-10pm.) **Wild Berry Restaurant ❷,** 37718 S.R. 706 E, 1 mi. outside the Nisqually entrance, serves home-style meals with several vegetarian options and fresh pies. Sack lunches are also available. (☎569-2379. Sandwiches $7. Dinner $8-9. Open daily 7am-9pm. D/MC/V.)

🏔 **OUTDOOR ACTIVITIES.** There are far too many hiking trails to list—Mt. Rainier National Park is Washington's most versatile area, with room for summer tourists, rugged winter explorers, and all those in between. One option is a **ranger-led interpretive hike,** which can cover anything from area history to local wildflowers. Each visitors center conducts its own hikes, and most campgrounds have evening talks. The most interesting and inevitably full are those at Paradise.

Mt. Adams and Mt. St. Helens can be seen from mountain trails like **Paradise** (1½ mi.), **Pinnacle Peak** (2½ mi.), **Eagle Peak** (7 mi.), and **Van Trump Park** (5½ mi.). One of the oldest stands of trees in Washington, the **Grove of Patriarchs** grows near the Ohanapecosh Visitors Center. An easy 1½ mi. walk leads to these 500- to 1000-year-old Douglas firs, cedars, and hemlocks. The **Summerland** and **Indian Bar Trails** are excellent for serious backpacking—this is where rangers go on their days off. **Carbon River Valley,** in the park's northwest corner, is one of the only inland rainforests in the US and provides access to the Wonderland Trail. Winter storms keep the road beyond the Carbon River entrance in constant disrepair. The hike to 🏔**Camp Muir** (9 mi. round-trip), the most popular staging ground for summit attempts, is also a challenging day hike, beginning on **Skyline Trail,** a scenic 6 mi. loop reaching its peak at the 7000 ft. Panorama Point. The latter half of the hike to Muir is covered in snow throughout the year; only those skilled in snow travel with the proper equipment should attempt it. A segment of the **Pacific Crest Trail,** which runs from Mexico to the Canadian border, dodges in and out of the park's southeast corner. The undeniable behemoth of all the park's routes is the infamous 🏔**Wonderland Trail,** 94 mi. of challenging terrain that circumnavigates the whole mountain. Arguably more difficult than the mountain ascent, the route passes through every type of scenery imaginable: dark forest, bright snowfields, rushing rivers, and rocky moraines. A full hike of the route requires experience and careful planning; be sure to spend plenty of time at a ranger station before setting out. A trip to the summit requires substantial preparation and expense. The ascent involves a vertical rise of more than 9000 ft. over a distance of 9 mi., usually taking two days and an overnight stay at Camp Muir on the south side (10,000 ft.) or Camp Schurman on the east side (9500 ft.). Permits for summit climbs are $30.

LEAVENWORTH ☎509

After Leavenworth's logging industry collapsed in the 1960s, desperate officials undertook a daring experiment in tourism and transformed the town into a German village. Now Leavenworth is thriving, complete with Bavarian-style buildings, free-flowing beer, and polka music. Visitors to "Washington's Little Bavaria" can almost always be guaranteed a celebration of some sort, though there are some that stand out. **Icefest,** in mid-January, is a winter festival with sleigh rides and a dogsled competition, while mid-May brings **Maifest,** with a parade and live music. (☎548-5807; www.leavenworth.com.) Still, no Bavarian town—contrived or otherwise—would be complete without its own **Oktoberfest,** held during the first two weekends in October. (☎548-7021; www.oktoberfestleavenworth.com.) Leavenworth's main outdoor attraction is the **Alpine Lakes Wilderness,** also home to Icicle Valley. Icicle Creek Canyon, with **Icicle Ridge** to the north and **Mount Stuart** to the south, stretches into the eastern core of the Wilderness and contains some of the best-loved trails in Washington backcountry. The moderate **Icicle Ridge Trail** (26 mi. one-way), off Icicle Rd. on the south end of U.S. 2, follows the ridge all the way to Steven Pass and connects the trails on the northern side. East of Mt. Stuart, the mystical **Enchantment Basin,** a chain of backcountry lakes framed by rock peaks, attracts backpackers willing to trudge up to the 7000 ft. basin and climbers anxious to try their hand at its jagged spires, called the Cashmere Crags.

Leavenworth's booming tourist industry has generated a niche for dozens of expensive faux-Bavarian lodgings. The centrally located **Linderhof Motor Inn ❹,** 690 Hwy. 2, has cozy rooms with handcrafted furniture, an outdoor hot tub and pool, and continental breakfast. (☎548-5283 or 800-828-5680; www.linderhof.com. Rooms $71-113. AmEx/D/MC/V.) Camping is available at several different sites on Icicle Creek Rd., which heads southwest out of town on Hwy. 2. The closest sites, **Eightmile ❶,** are—surprise—8 mi. out, at a National Forest campground (sites $13). The other sites range from 9½ mi. to 19 mi. out, and all have fewer than 20 sites, with the exception of **Johnny Creek ❶,** 12½ mi. up the road, with 65 sites ($11). For more info, contact the Leavenworth Ranger District (see below). Predictably, Leavenworth's food mimics German cuisine; surprisingly, it often succeeds. Nibble on the delectable cinnamon rolls ($2), cookies ($1), and bread ($3) at ◪**Homefires Bakery ❶,** 13013 Bayne Rd. (☎548-7362. Open M and Th-Su 9am-5pm. AmEx/D/MC/V.) There are more pubs serving up goulash and wieners than you can imagine; one worth trying is **Andreas Keller Restaurant ❷,** 829 Front St., if only for its $8 Bratwurst Reuben. (☎548-6000; www.andreaskellerrestaurant.com. Open M-W and Su 11am-9pm; Th-Sa 11am-11pm. Live Bavarian music Jan.-June M and F-Su 6pm-closing; June-Jan. nightly 6pm-closing. MC/V.) **The Cheesemonger's Shop ❶,** 633 Front St., has savory cheeses to tempt any palate. Prices start at $6 and go up and up. (☎877-888-7389; www.cheesemongersshop.com. Open M-Th and Su 10am-5pm, F-Sa 10am-6pm. AmEx/D/MC/V.)

Leavenworth is near Washington's geographic center, on the eastern slope of the Cascades. From Seattle, follow I-5 north to Exit 194, then U.S. 2 east for 126 mi. **Visitor Info: Chamber of Commerce,** 940 Hwy. 2, has brochures. (☎548-5807; www.leavenworth.org. Open M-Th 8am-5pm, F-Sa 8am-6pm, Su 10am-4pm; winter M-Sa 8am-5pm.) The **Leavenworth Ranger District,** 600 Sherborne St., has extensive information on trails and permits. (☎548-6977. Open daily 7:45am-4:30pm.) **Internet Access: North Central Regional Library System,** 201 E. Harrison Ave. (☎769-2315. Open M-Th 10am-8pm, F-Sa 10am-6pm, Su noon-6pm.) **Post Office:** 960 Hwy. 2 (☎548-7212. Open M-F 9am-5pm, Sa 9-11am.) **Postal Code:** 98826. **Area Code:** 509.

SPOKANE   ☎509

Spokane (spoe-KAN) may have peaked when the 1974 World's Fair came to town; parks, department stores, and skyways sprang up in preparation for a promising future that never quite arrived. Today, cafes catering to the college crowd from Gonzaga and nearby Eastern Washington Universities along with 50s-style burger joints make for a suburban atmosphere, but the surrounding wilderness provides plenty of opportunities to enjoy the dry climate and diverse terrain.

🄵 **PRACTICAL INFORMATION.** Spokane is 280 mi. east of Seattle on I-90, between Exits 279 and 282. **Spokane International Airport** (☎624-3218; www.spokaneairports.net) is off I-90, 8 mi. southwest of town. **Amtrak,** 221 W. 1st Ave. (☎624-5144 or 800-872-7245; www.amtrak.com; station open 24hr.), at Bernard St., runs to Portland (7hr., 2 per day, $45) and Seattle (7½ hr., 1 per day, $48). **Greyhound,** 221 W 1st Ave. (☎624-5251 or 800-231-2222; www.greyhound.com), is in the same building as Amtrak. Buses to: Portland (7-10hr., 3 per day, $40) and Seattle (6hr., 5 per day, $30). Station open 24hr. **Spokane Transit Authority,** 701 W. Riverside St., serves the greater Spokane area. (☎328-7433; www.spokanetransit.com. STA plaza bus shop open M-F 6:30am-6pm, Sa noon-5pm. $1, seniors $0.50.) **Visitor Info: Spokane Regional Convention and Visitors Bureau,** 201 W. Main Ave; take Exit 281 off I-90. (☎624-1341 or 888-776-5263; www.visitspokane.com. Open M-F 8:30am-5pm, Sa 9am-5pm.) **Internet Access: Spokane Public Library,** 906 W. Main Ave. (☎444-5300; www.spokanelibrary.org.) Free Internet access in 15min. slots. Open Tu-W 10am-8pm, Th-Sa 10am-6pm. **Post Office:** 904 W. Riverside Ave. (☎800-275-8777). Open M-F 8am-5pm. **Postal Code:** 99210. **Area Code:** 509.

⚠️🏠 ACCOMMODATIONS AND FOOD. Numerous motels are sprinkled in the outskirts of downtown, especially along I-90, Rte. 2, and Division Ave. The **Ramada Limited City Center ❸,** 123 S. Post St., has basic rooms in a convenient location. (☎838-8504 or 800-210-8465. Breakfast included. Shuttle to the airport $5. Singles from $40; doubles from $50. AmEx/D/MC/V.) **Boulevard Inn ❷,** 2905 W. Sunset Blvd., 2 mi. west of town on Rte. 2., rents rooms so clean you could eat off the floor. (☎747-1060. *Let's Go* does not recommend eating off the floor. Singles $33; doubles $49. AmEx/MC/V.) **Riverside State Park ❷** is 6 mi. from downtown on Rifle Club Rd., off Rte. 291 (Nine Mile Rd.), and has 16 standard sites and 15 utility hookup sites near the beautiful Spokane River. (☎465-5064; www.riverside-statepark.org. Showers $0.25 per 3min. Standard sites $16. Utility hookup sites $22.) **❇️High Nooner Gourmet Sandwiches ❷,** 237 W. Riverside Ave., offers sandwiches loaded with fresh ingredients. The "Unforgettable Nooner," with turkey, bacon, avocado, tomato, and cream cheese ($6), is definitely unforgettable. (☎838-5288. Open M-F 10am-3pm. AmEx/MC/V.) **Frank's Diner ❷,** 1516 W 2nd Ave., at Walnut St., speedily serves breakfast food all day long in a 1906 observation railroad car. (☎747-8798. Breakfast $4-8. Open daily 6am-8pm. D/DC/MC/V.) At **Dick's Hamburgers ❶,** 10 E. 3rd Ave., at Division St., customers eat in parked cars and pay 50s-era prices. (☎747-2481. Burgers $0.75. Shakes $1. Open daily 8am-1am daily. Cash only.) **Trick Shot Dixie's Outlaw Saloon and BBQ,** 321 W. Sprague Ave., has tangy barbecue and bottle-tossing bartenders. (☎624-4549. Live music most nights. Happy hour Tu-F 5-8pm. Open Tu-Sa 11am-2am.)

📷🏞️ SIGHTS AND OUTDOOR ACTIVITIES. One of the most beautiful spots in Spokane, **❇️Manito Park** boasts six distinct areas of lovingly-maintained flower-beds. Make sure to frolic among the scent of 150 varieties of blooming roses on Rosehill in late June. *(4 W. 21st Ave. From downtown, go south on Bernard St. and turn left on 21st Ave. Park open summer 4am-11pm; winter 5am-10pm; buildings open 8am-dusk. Free.)* Developed for the 1974 World's Fair, the **Riverfront Park** is Spokane's civic center and the perfect place for a pleasant stroll. Riverfront's **IMAX Theater** houses a five-story movie screen and a small amusement park. On the park's edge lies the historic **Carousel,** hand carved by Charles Loof of Coney Island carousel fame. *(507 N. Howard St. ☎456-4386; www.spokaneriverfrontpark.com. IMAX: ☎626-6686. Open daily 11am-9pm. $9.50, ages 13-17 $8.50, ages 3-12 $7.50. Carousel: Open M-Th and Su 10am-8pm, F-Sa 10am-10pm. $2, ages 3-12 and seniors $1. A 1-day pass $15.)* The **Northwest Museum of Arts and Culture,** or the Mac, as it is fondly known, is the crown jewel of Spokane's attractions, with five galleries focusing on local artists. *(2316 W. 1st Ave. ☎456-3931; www.northwestmuseum.org. Open Tu-Sa 11am-5pm. $7, students and ages 62+ $5, children ages 5 and under free. First F of the month admission by donation.)*

Only 30 miles northeast of the city, **Mount Spokane State Park** provides 14,000 acres of outdoor options, including 100 mi. of hiking trails and the massive **Ski and Snowboard Park** with a 2065 ft. vertical drop (☎238-2220; www.mtspokane.com). Try the 1½ mi. **Entrance Loop Trail** for a brief stroll, the easy 5 mi. **Day Mountain Loop** to see rocky meadows, or the 4½ **Hay Ridge Loop** for scenic stream-crossings. *(At the end of State Rd. 206, 15 mi. east of Rte. 2. ☎238-4258. Camping available in summer at the Bald Knob Campground.*

12 sites with fire grates $15. Parking permit $5. Park open summer 6:30am-dusk, winter 8am-10pm.) In **Riverside State Park,** the scenic **Centennial Trail** runs 37 mi. from Nine Mile Dam all the way to the Idaho border and is paved for the benefit of hikers, bikers, skiers, and sledders alike. (9711 W. Charles Rd. ☎624-7188; www.spokanecentennialtrail.org.)

BRITISH COLUMBIA

British Columbia (BC) is Canada's westernmost province, with over 900,000km² bordering four US states (Washington, Idaho, Montana, and Alaska), two territories (the Yukon and Northwest), and a province (Alberta). Residents swear backwards and forwards that BC is the most beautiful place on earth, and most visitors come to agree with them. Small, developed communities surround vibrant metropolitan areas like Vancouver and Victoria, and breathtaking wilderness is never more than a short drive away.

BORDER CROSSING. Traveling between the US and Canada is generally an easy process, but security is still taken very seriously. Crossing can be as simple as a wave of the passport or as time-consuming as a full search of your car. To keep things moving along, make sure to have all necessary documents handy. It is illegal to cross the border anywhere except an open crossing station. See **Essentials,** p. 10, for more details on documents and procedures.

▐ PRACTICAL INFORMATION

Capital: Victoria.

Visitor Info: Tourism British Columbia, 1166 Alberni St., Vancouver V6E 3Z3 (☎800-435-5622; www.hellobc.com). **British Columbia Parks Headquarters,** www.bcparks.ca.

Postal Abbreviation: BC. **Sales Tax:** 7% PST, plus 7% GST. **Drinking Age:** 19.

VANCOUVER   ☎604

Even more so than most cities in North America, Vancouver boasts a thriving multicultural populace; the Cantonese influence is so strong that it is commonly joked that Chinese will soon become Canada's third national language. You'll find Asian flavor in everything from peaceful manicured gardens to raucous annual festivals to the cuisine in one of the largest Chinatowns in North America. It may sound like an overwhelming metropolis but, surrounded on three sides by water and closely hemmed in by the Coast Mountain Range, Vancouver can never stray too far from its humble logging-town roots. From the hip neighborhood of Gastown to the therapeutic walks of Stanley Park, Vancouver's diversity, location, and worldly yet laid-back atmosphere keeps its residents friendly and the tourist influx constant.

▐ TRANSPORTATION

Airport: Vancouver International Airport (☎207-7077; www.yvr.ca), on Sea Island, 23km south of the city center. **Visitors center** (☎207-1598) open daily 8:30am-11:30pm. For downtown, take bus #424 and transfer to the 98 B-line. An **Airporter** bus (☎946-8866 or 800-668-3141) goes to downtown hotels and the bus station. 4 per hr.; runs 6:30am-11pm; CDN$12, seniors CDN$9, ages 5-12 CDN$5.

Trains: VIA Rail, 1150 Station St. (☎888-842-7245; www.viarail.com), runs eastbound trains. Station open M, W-Th, Sa 8:30am-6pm; Tu, F, Su 9am-7pm. 3 trains per week to **Edmonton, AB** (23hr., CDN$268) and **Jasper, AB** (17hr., CDN$200). **Amtrak,** 1150 Station St. (☎800-872-7245; www.amtrak.com), goes to **Seattle, WA** (3¾hr., 1 per day, CDN$25-39). Amtrak also runs 4 buses per day to Seattle (CDN$25).

Buses: Greyhound USA, 1150 Station St. (☎800-229-9424; www.greyhound.com), runs buses to **Seattle, WA** (5hr., 6 per day, CDN$26-28.) **Pacific Coach Lines,** 1150 Station St. (☎604-662-8074; www.pacificcoach.com), runs to **Victoria, BC** nearly every time a ferry sails (3½hr.; CDN$32-33.50 includes ferry). **Quick Shuttle** (☎940-4428 or 800-665-2122; www.quickcoach.com) makes 8 trips per day from the Holiday Inn on 1110 Howe St. via the airport to: **Bellingham, WA** (2½hr.; CDN$22, students CDN$17); **Seattle, WA** (4hr.; CDN$33, students CDN$22); **Sea-Tac (Seattle-Tacoma) Airport** (4½hr.; CDN$41, students CDN$29).

Ferries: BC Ferries (☎888-223-3779; www.bcferries.com) connects Vancouver to the **Gulf Islands,** the **Sechelt Peninsula,** and **Vancouver Island.** Ferries to **Victoria** (1½hr.; 8-16 per day; CDN$10.50; bikes CDN$2.50, cars CDN$35-37) and other Vancouver Island destinations leave from the **Tsawwassen Terminal,** 25km south of the city center (take Hwy. 99 to Hwy. 17). To reach downtown from Tsawwassen by bus (1hr.), take #640 "Scott Rd. Station," or take #404 "Airport" to the Ladner Exchange, and then transfer to bus #601.

Public Transit: Translink (☎953-3333; www.translink.bc.ca) covers most of the city and suburbs, with easy access to the airport and the ferry terminals. The city is divided into 3 fare zones. Riding in the **central zone,** which encompasses most of Vancouver, or any one zone, costs CDN$2.25. During peak hours (M-F before 6:30pm), it costs CDN$3.25 to travel between 2 zones and CDN$4.50 for 3 zones. During off-peak hours, all zones are CDN$2.25. Ask for a **free transfer** (good for 1½hr.) on buses. **Day passes** CDN$8.

Taxi: Vancouver Taxi, ☎871-1111. **Black Top Cabs,** ☎731-1111. 24hr.

ORIENTATION AND PRACTICAL INFORMATION

Vancouver is in the southwestern corner of mainland British Columbia. South of the city flows the **Fraser River.** The **Georgia Strait,** to the west, separates the mainland from Vancouver Island. **Downtown** is on a peninsula that juts into the Burrard Inlet; **Stanley Park** occupies the northern chunk of the peninsula. The **Lions Gate Bridge** over Burrard Inlet links Stanley Park with North and West Vancouver, known as "West Van." The two are collectively known as the **North Shore.** The bridges over False Creek south of downtown link it with **Kitsilano ("Kits")** and the rest of the city. West of Burrard St. is the **West Side** or **West End. Gastown** and **Chinatown** are east of downtown. The **University of British Columbia (UBC)** lies on the west end of Kits on Point Grey. The **Trans-Canada Highway (Hwy. 1)** enters town from the east, and **Highway 99** runs north-south.

Visitor Info: 200 Burrard St., plaza level (☎683-2000; www.tourismvancouver.com). BC-wide info on hotels and activities. Open daily 8:30am-7pm.

GLBT Resources: The Centre, 1170 Bute St. (☎684-5307; www.lgtbcentrevancouver.com), has info and counseling M-F 9am-7pm. *Xtra West* (www.xtra.ca) is the gay/lesbian biweekly, available here and around Davie St. in the West End.

Hotlines: Crisis Center ☎872-3311. Operates 24hr.

Medical Services: Vancouver General Hospital, 855 W. 12th Ave. (☎875-4111). **UBC Hospital,** 2211 Westbrook Mall (☎822-7121), on the UBC campus.

Internet Access: Free at the **Vancouver Public Library,** 350 W. Georgia St. (☎331-3600; www.vpl.vancouver.bc.ca). Open M-Th 10am-9pm, F-Sa 10am-6pm, Su 1-5pm.

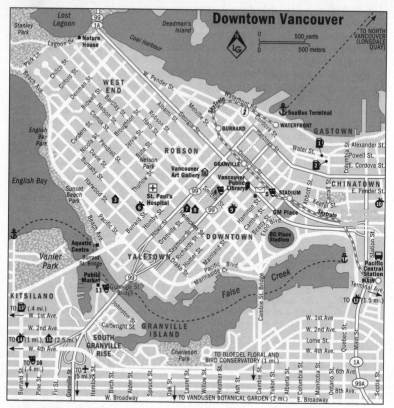

Downtown Vancouver

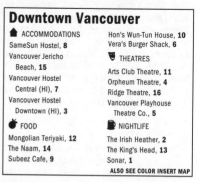

Post Office: 349 W. Georgia St. (☎662-5725). Open M-F 8am-5:30pm. **Postal Code:** V6B 3P7. **Area Code:** 604.

⚑ ACCOMMODATIONS

▨ **Vancouver Hostel Central (HI),** 1025 Granville St. (☎685-5335 or 888-203-8333). A posh hostel located in the heart of downtown. 41 spacious dorms and 36 private rooms. Breakfast and linen included. Free Internet access. Reception 24hr. Check-in noon. Check-out 11am. Reservations recommended. Dorms June-Sept. CDN$32, members CDN$28; Oct.-May CDN$24/CDN$20. Private rooms June-Sept. CDN$66/CDN$58; Oct.-May CDN$76/CDN$68. MC/V. ❶

▨ **SameSun Hostel,** 1018 Granville St. (☎682-8226 or 888-844-7875; www.samesun.com), on the corner of Nelson St. A technicolor hangout in a neighborhood with great nightlife. CDN$5 refunds on taxis from the train station. Laundry CDN$2. Internet CDN$6 per hr. Dorms CDN$28; private doubles CDN$56, with bath CDN$61. MC/V. ❶

Downtown Vancouver

⚑ ACCOMMODATIONS
SameSun Hostel, **8**
Vancouver Jericho
 Beach, **15**
Vancouver Hostel
 Central (HI), **7**
Vancouver Hostel
 Downtown (HI), **3**

🍎 FOOD
Mongolian Teriyaki, **12**
The Naam, **14**
Subeez Cafe, **9**

Hon's Wun-Tun House, **10**
Vera's Burger Shack, **6**

🎭 THEATRES
Arts Club Theatre, **11**
Orpheum Theatre, **4**
Ridge Theatre, **16**
Vancouver Playhouse
 Theatre Co., **5**

🎵 NIGHTLIFE
The Irish Heather, **2**
The King's Head, **13**
Sonar, **1**

ALSO SEE COLOR INSERT MAP

PACIFIC NORTHWEST

Vancouver Hostel Downtown (HI), 1114 Burnaby St. (☎684-4565 or 888-203-4302), in the West End. A sleek 225-bed facility. Full kitchen. Linen included. Internet CDN$4 per hr. Reception 24hr. Check-in 24hr. Check-out 11am. Reservations recommended. Dorms June-Sept. CDN$32, members CDN$28; Oct.-May CDN$29/CDN$25. Private rooms June-Sept. CDN$70/CDN$62; Oct.-May CDN$76/CDN$68. MC/V. ❶

Vancouver Jericho Beach (HI), 1515 Discovery St. (☎224-3208 or 888-203-4303), in serene Jericho Beach Park. Follow 4th Ave. west past Alma, go right at the fork, and follow signs. Bus #4 from Granville St. Full kitchen. Cafe serving breakfast (CDN$6) and dinner (CDN$7-8). Linen included. Laundry facilities. Check-in 24hr. Check-out 11am. Open May-Sept. CDN$24, members CDN$20. MC/V. ❶

🍴 FOOD

🦐 **The Naam,** 2724 W. 4th Ave. (☎738-7151; www.thenaam.com), a half-block east of MacDonald St. Bus #4 or 7 from Granville Mall. Diverse vegetarian menu with a welcoming, homey atmosphere. Crying Tiger Thai stir-fry CDN$9.25; dairy-free ice cream CDN$4. Live music nightly 7-10pm. Open 24hr. AmEx/DC/MC/V. ❷

Subeez Cafe, 891 Homer St. (☎687-6107), at Robson St., downtown. A cavernous cafe populated with hipster youth. An eclectic menu complements a hefty wine list and home-spun beats (DJs Th-Su 10pm-1am). Entrees CDN$10-20. Open M-F 11:30am-1am, Sa 11am-1am, Su 11am-midnight. MC/V. ❸

Hon's Wun-Tun House, 268 Keefer St., #108 (☎688-0871). With over 300 options on the menu at this bustling Cantonese noodle house, choosing a meal could take longer than eating it. Entrees CDN$4-10. Open M-Th 9am-9pm, F-Su 9am-11pm. Cash only. ❶

Mongolian Teriyaki, 1918 Commercial Dr. (☎253-5607). Chef's fry up your choice of meats, veggies, sauces, and noodles and serve it with miso soup, rice and salad for CDN$5.75 (large bowl CDN$6.75). Open daily 11am-9:30pm. AmEx/D/DC/MC/V. ❷

Vera's Burger Shack, 1030 Davie St. (☎893-8372; www.verasburgershack.com), in the heart of the West End. Though Vera's burgers (CDN$5-9) are considered by many to be the best in Vancouver, this fun burger joint also offers sandwiches (CDN$5-8) and salads (CDN$6). Open M-W and Su 11am-11pm, Th-Sa 11am-2pm. V. ❷

👁 SIGHTS

🖼 **VANCOUVER ART GALLERY.** This gallery is host to fantastic temporary exhibitions and a varied collection of contemporary art and design from the West Coast. *(750 Hornby St., in Robson Sq. ☎662-4700; www.vanartgallery.bc.ca. Open Apr.-Oct. M-W and F-Su 10am-5:30pm, Th 10am-9pm; call for hours Nov.-Mar. CDN$15, seniors CDN$11, students CDN$10, under 12 free; Th 5-9pm suggested CDN$5 donation. 2-for-1 HI discount.)*

GARDENS. The city's temperate climate and ample rain allows flora to flourish. Locals take great pride in private gardens and public parks filled with plant life. Some 55 acres of former golf course have been converted into the immense 🌿 **VanDusen Botanical Garden,** which showcases 7500 kinds of plants from six continents, an international sculpture collection, and over 60 species of birds interspersed in the Fragrance Garden and Bonsai House. *(5251 Oak St., at W. 37th. Take #17 "Oak" bus to W. 37th and Oak. ☎878-9274. Free parking. Open daily June-Aug. 10am-9pm; Sept. and Apr. 10am-6pm; Oct.-Mar. 10am-4pm; Apr. 10am-6pm. Apr.-Sept. CDN$7.75, ages 65+ CDN$5.50, ages 13-18 CDN$5.75 , ages 6-12 CDN$4; families CDN$12. Sept.-Mar. rates are about CDN$2 less for each age range. Wheelchair accessible.)* Journey to the tropics inside the **Bloedel Floral and Bird Conservatory,** a triodetic geodesic dome made of plexiglass and aluminum tubing. The conservatory, a constant 18°C (65°F), is home to 500 types of plants and 150 types of birds and provides great views of downtown. *(Center of Queen Elizabeth Park on Cambie and 37th Ave., a few blocks east of VanDusen. ☎ 257-8570. Open Apr.-Sept. M-F 9am-8pm, Sa-Su 10am-9pm; Feb.-Mar. daily 10am-5:30pm; Nov.-Jan. daily 10am-5pm; Feb.-Mar. daily 10am-5:30pm. CDN$4.25, seniors CDN$3, ages 13-18 CDN$3.20, ages 6-12 CDN$2, under 6 free.)*

UNIVERSITY OF BRITISH COLUMBIA (UBC). One of the best places to visit at UBC is the breathtaking ■**Museum of Anthropology.** The high-ceilinged building contains totems and other carvings made by the region's indigenous peoples. *(6393 NW Marine Dr. Bus #4 or 10 from Granville St. Museum. ☎ 822-5087; www.moa.ubc.ca. Open June-Sept. M and W-Su 10am-5pm, Tu 10am-9pm. CDN$9, students and ages 65+ CDN$7, under 6 free; Tu after 5pm free.)* Just down the road, a single gardener tends the **Nitobe Memorial Garden,** the finest classical Shinto garden outside of Japan. During a visit the garden, the current Emperor of Japan allegedly said, "I am in Japan." *(☎ 822-6038; www.nitobe.org. Open daily mid-Mar. to mid.-Oct. 10am-6pm; mid-Oct. to mid-Mar. 10am-2:30pm. Mid-Mar. to mid-Oct. CDN$4, ages 65+ CDN$3, students CDN$2.50; mid-Oct. to mid-Mar. free.)* The **Botanical Gardens** encompass eight magnificent gardens in the central campus. *(6804 SW Marine Dr. ☎ 822-9666; www.ubcbotanical-garden.org. Same hours as Nitobe Garden. CDN$6, ages 65+ CDN$4, students CDN$3. Dual ticket for both Nitobe and the Botanical Gardens CDN$8.)*

STANLEY PARK. Established in 1889 at the tip of the downtown peninsula of Vancouver, the sprawling 1000-acre **Stanley Park** is a testament to the foresight of Vancouver's urban planners. The thickly wooded park is laced with nuermous cycling and hiking trails and surrounded by a popular 10km **seawall promenade.** *(☎ 257-8400. To get to the park, take the #19 bus. A free shuttle runs throughout the park on the half-hr., late June to Sept. 10am-6:30pm.)* The ■**Vancouver Aquarium** features exotic aquatic animals, a shark tank with weekly feedings, and, in the summer months, up to 8000 Costa Rican butterflies. Dolphins, beluga whales, sea otters, and sea lions perform in shows daily. *(☎ 659-3474. Open daily July-Aug. 9:30am-7pm; Sept.-June 10am-5:30pm. CDN$17.50; students, seniors, and ages 13-18 CDN$13; ages 4-12 CDN$10; under 3 free.)* Nature walks start from the **Nature House,** underneath the Lost Lagoon bus loop. *(☎ 257-8544. 2hr. nature walks Su 1-3pm. CDN$5, under 12 free. Nature House open June-Aug. F-Su 11am-7pm.)* The park's edges boast a few restaurants, tennis courts, a cinder running track, beaches, and an outdoor theater, the **Malkin Bowl** *(☎ 687-0174).*

🎵 🎭 ENTERTAINMENT AND NIGHTLIFE

The **Vancouver Symphony Orchestra** (☎ 876-3434; www.vancouversymphony.ca) plays from October to early June in the **Orpheum Theatre,** at the corner of Smithe and Seymour St. The **Vancouver Playhouse Theatre Co.** (☎ 873-3311), on Dunsmuir and Georgia St., and the **Arts Club Theatre** (☎ 687-1644), on Granville Island, stage various low-key shows throughout the year. The **Ridge Theatre,** 3131 Arbutus, shows foreign and vintage double-features. (☎ 738-6311; www.ridgetheatre.com. CDN$6, W matinee CDN$5.)

■ **The Irish Heather,** 217 Carrall St. (☎ 688-9779; irishheather.com). This 2nd-highest seller of Guinness in BC serves 20 oz. drafts (CDN$6.20), as well as bangers and mash (CDN$14). Live music Th. Open daily noon-midnight. In the back find its sister establishment, the **Shebeen Whiskey House,** which boasts innumerable varieties of whiskey (CDN$5 and up...way up). Open Th-Sa 5pm-midnight.

Sonar, 66 Water St. (☎683-6695; www.sonar.bc.ca). A beat factory popular with the college and 20-something crowd. 4 bars. Specials nightly (CDN$3.50-4.50); draft specials Tu only. Themes usually sanctuary Su, house W, techno F, hip-hop Sa; M and Tu vary. Open Su, Tu-W, and some M and Th 9pm-2am, F-Sa 9pm-3am.

The King's Head, 1618 Yew St. (☎738-6966), just downhill from 1st St., in Kitsilano. Cheap drinks, cheap food, and a fun location near the beach. Daily specials. CDN$3.75 pints. Bands play acoustic sets W-Sa. Open M-Sa 8am-1am, Su 8am-midnight.

VICTORIA   ☎250

Clean, polite, and tourist-friendly, Victoria is a homier alternative to cosmopolitan Vancouver. Many tourist operations would have you believe that Victoria fell off Great Britain in a neat little chunk complete with perfectly groomed gardens and afternoon tea, but in fact, Victoria's British flavor was created in the 1950s to attract tourists. Today, double-decker buses motor past indigenous art galleries, New Age bookstores, and countless English pubs. Victoria also lies within easy distance of the rest of Vancouver Island's outdoor paradise.

▌ PRACTICAL INFORMATION. Victoria surrounds the **Inner Harbour;** the main north-south streets are **Government Street** and **Douglas Street.** To the north, Douglas St. becomes Hwy. 1, which runs to Nanaimo. **Blanshard Street,** one block to the east, becomes Hwy. 17. **BC Ferries** (☎888-223-3779; www.bcferries.com) departs Swartz Bay to Vancouver's Tsawwassen terminal (1½hr.; 8-16 per day; CDN$10.50; bikes CDN$2.50, cars CDN$34-37), and to the Gulf Islands. **Victoria Clipper** (☎800-888-2535; www.victoriaclipper.com) ferries travel to Seattle. (2-3hr. May-Sept. 3 per day, Oct.-Apr. 1 per day. CDN$66-81. Reservations recommended.) **Victoria Taxi** (☎383-7111; www.victoriataxi.com) serves the city. **Tourism Victoria,** 812 Wharf St., at Government St, has info. (☎953-2033. Open daily July-Aug. 8:30am-6:30pm; Sept.-June 9am-5pm.) **Post office:** 706 Yates St. (☎267-1177. Open M-F 8am-5pm.) **Postal Code:** V8W 2L9. **Area Code:** 250.

▐ ACCOMMODATIONS. The colorful **█Ocean Island Backpackers Inn ❶,** 791 Pandora St., downtown, boasts a better lounge than most clubs, tastier food than most restaurants, and accommodations comparable to many hotels; this is undoubtedly one of the finest hostels in Canada. (☎385-1788 or 888-888-4180; www.oceanisland.com. Linen and locker included. Internet access CDN$1 for 15 min. Parking CDN$5. Reception 24hr. Dorms CDN$18-24, students and HI members CDN$18-22; private rooms CDN$25-59. MC/V.) **Victoria International Hostel (HI) ❶,** 516 Yates St., offers barracks-style dorms and private rooms in a central but relatively quiet spot. (☎385-4511. Laundry CDN$3.50. Dorms CDN$21-24, members CDN$17-20; private rooms CDN$44-48/CDN$40-44. MC/V.) **Goldstream Provincial Park ❶,** 2930 Trans-Canada Hwy., 16 km northwest of Victoria, offers tent sites in a forested riverside area with great hiking trails and swimming in the Goldstream River. (☎391-2300 or 800-689-9025. Toilets and showers. Sites CDN$22.)

▐▌ FOOD AND NIGHTLIFE. Diverse food options exist in Victoria, if you know where to go. **Chinatown** extends from Fisgard and Government St. to the northwest. **Cook St. Village,** between McKenzie and Park St., has an eclectic mix of creative restaurants. **█John's Place ❷,** 723 Pandora St., dishes up fare with Mediterranean flair and a Thai twist. (☎389-0711; www.johnsplace.ca. Lunch CDN$6-10. Dinner CDN$10-15. Open M-Th 7am-9pm, F 7am-10pm, Sa 8am-4pm and 5-10pm, Su 8am-4pm and 5-9pm. AmEx/MC/V.) A trip to Victoria is not complete without a spot of tea. The Saturday and Sunday High Tea (CDN$14.50) at the **James Bay Tea Room & Restaurant ❷,** 332 Menzies St., at Superior St. behind the Parliament Buildings, is delightful and significantly less expensive than the famous High Tea at the Empress Hotel. (☎382-8282. Open M-Sa 7am-5pm, Su 8am-5pm. AmEx/ MC/V.) English pubs, watering holes, and clubs abound throughout town. Live music is available practically every night, and the free weekly *Monday Magazine* (www.mondaymag.com) will keep you updated on who's playing when and where. **Steamers Public House,** 570 Yates St., attracts a college-age dancing crowd and serves everything from burgers (CDN$9-10) to flatbread (CDN$9-10). It's the best Sunday entertainment in town. (☎381-4340; www.steamerspub.ca. Open stage M, jazz night Tu. Live music nightly. Open daily 11:30am-2am. AmEx/MC/V.)

SIGHTS AND OUTDOOR ACTIVITIES. For excellent exhibits on the province's geological and cultural history, check out the **Royal British Columbia Museum,** 675 Belleville St. (☎356-7226; www.royalbcmuseum.bc.ca. Open daily 9am-5pm. CDN$12.50; students, ages 6-18 and 65+ CDN$8.70, under 6 free. IMAX 10am-9pm. With museum entrance CDN$21, students CDN$18.20, ages 6-18 and 65+ CDN$17, under 6 CDN$5.) Unwind with a liver-educating tour of the **Vancouver Island Brewery,** 2330 Government St. (☎361-0007; www.vanislandbrewery.com. 1hr. tours M and Th 1pm, F 1 and 3pm, and Sa 3pm. CDN$6 admission, four 4-oz. samples and souvenir pint glass. 19+ to taste.) The world-famous **Butchart Gardens** includes 55 acres of gardens, fountains, and wheelchair accessible paths. Outstanding fireworks on Saturday evenings in July and August draw out the locals. (☎652-4422; www.butchartgardens.com. Bus #75 "Central Saanich" runs from downtown. Open daily mid-June to Aug. 9am-10:30pm; shorter hours in winter. CDN$21, ages 13-17 CDN$11, ages 5-12 CDN$2, under 5 free.) The **Gray Line** offers a package from downtown that includes round-trip transportation and admission to the gardens. (☎388-6539. CDN$47, youth CDN$35, children CDN$14.75.) Mountain bikers can tackle the **Galloping Goose,** a 100km trail beginning downtown and continuing to the west coast of the island through towns, rainforests, and canyons. **Ocean River Sports,** 1824 Store St., offers kayak rentals, tours, and lessons. (☎381-4233 or 800-909-4233; www.oceanriver.com. Open M-Th 9:30am-6pm, F 9:30am-8pm, Sa 9:30am-5:30pm, Su 11am-5pm. Single kayak CDN$40 per day; double kayak CDN$60.)

DISTANCES (MI.) AND TRAVEL TIMES (BY BUS)

	Atlanta	Boston	Chic.	Dallas	D.C.	Denver	L.A.	Miami	N. Orl.	NYC	Phila.	Phnx.	St. Lou.	Sa. Fran.	Seattle	Trnto.	Vanc.	Mont.
Atlanta		1108	717	783	632	1406	2366	653	474	886	778	1863	560	2492	2699	959	2825	1240
Boston	22hr.		996	1794	442	1990	3017	1533	1542	194	333	2697	1190	3111	3105	555	3242	326
Chicago	14hr.	20hr.		937	715	1023	2047	1237	928	807	767	1791	302	2145	2108	537	2245	537
Dallas	15hr.	35hr.	18hr.		1326	794	1450	1322	507	1576	1459	906	629	1740	2112	1457	2255	1763
D.C.	12hr.	8hr.	14hr.	24hr.		1700	2689	1043	1085	225	139	2350	845	2840	2788	526	3292	665
Denver	27hr.	38hr.	20hr.	15hr.	29hr.		1026	2046	1341	1785	1759	790	860	1267	1313	1508	1458	1864
L.A.	45hr.	57hr.	39hr.	28hr.	55hr.	20hr.		2780	2005	2787	2723	371	1837	384	1141	2404	1285	2888
Miami	13hr.	30hr.	24hr.	26hr.	20hr.	39hr.	53hr.		856	1346	1214	2368	1197	3086	3368	1564	3505	1676
New O.	9hr.	31hr.	18hr.	10hr.	21hr.	26hr.	38hr.	17hr.		1332	1247	1535	677	2331	2639	1320	2561	1654
NYC	18hr.	4hr.	16hr.	31hr.	5hr.	35hr.	53hr.	26hr.	27hr.		104	2592	999	2923	2912	496	3085	386
Phila.	18hr.	6hr.	16hr.	19hr.	3hr.	33hr.	50hr.	23hr.	23hr.	2hr.		2511	904	2883	2872	503	3009	465
Phoenix	40hr.	49hr.	39hr.	19hr.	43hr.	17hr.	8hr.	47hr.	30hr.	45hr.	44hr.		1503	753	1510	2069	1654	2638
St. Louis	11hr.	23hr.	6hr.	13hr.	15hr.	17hr.	35hr.	23hr.	13hr.	19hr.	16hr.	32hr.		2113	2139	810	2276	1128
San Fran.	47hr.	60hr.	41hr.	47hr.	60hr.	33hr.	7hr.	59hr.	43hr.	56hr.	54hr.	15hr.	45hr.		807	2630	951	2985
Seattle	52hr.	59hr.	40hr.	40hr.	54hr.	25hr.	22hr.	65hr.	50hr.	55hr.	54hr.	28hr.	36hr.	16hr.		2623	146	2964
Toronto	21hr.	11hr.	10hr.	26hr.	11hr.	26hr.	48hr.	29hr.	13hr.	11hr.	13hr.	48hr.	14hr.	49hr.	48hr.		4563	655
Vancr.	54hr.	61hr.	42hr.	43hr.	60hr.	27hr.	24hr.	67hr.	54hr.	57hr.	56hr.	30hr.	38hr.	18hr.	2hr.	53hr.		4861
Montreal	23hr.	6hr.	17hr.	28hr.	12hr.	39hr.	53hr.	32hr.	31hr.	7hr.	9hr.	53hr.	23hr.	56hr.	55hr.	7hr.	55hr.	

DISTANCES

INDEX

INDEX